RANGE ROVER
1995/2001 MY
Workshop Manual

LRL 0326ENG BB

Which includes the following publications:
LRL 0326ENG - Workshop Manual
LRL 0004ENG (3rd Edition) – 4.0 & 4.6 Litre V8 Engine Overhaul Manual
LRL 0003ENG (3rd Edition) – R380 Manual Gearbox Overhaul Manual
LRL 0090ENG – Borg Warner 44-62 Transfer Gearbox Overhaul Manual

Publication part No. LRL 0326ENG BB (which incorporates the copyright publications above)

This Workshop Manual - LRL 0326ENG - covers all Range Rover models powered by 4.0 & 4.6 V8 Petrol Engines & BMW 2.5 Diesel Engines from 1995 up to the end of the 2001 model year.

Supplementary publications in this edition:
LRL 0326ENG BB
include the following overhaul manuals:

LRL 0004ENG (3rd Edition) – 4.0 & 4.6 V8 Litre V8 Engine Overhaul Manual
LRL 0003ENG (3rd Edition) – R380 Manual Gearbox Overhaul Manual
LRL 0090 – Borg Warner 44-62 Transfer Gearbox Overhaul Manual

Workshop manual
RANGE ROVER

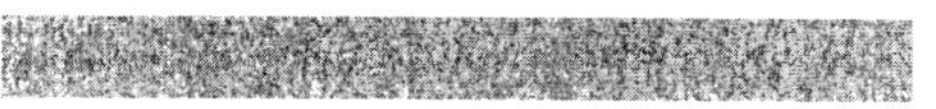

This manual covers vehicles from 1995 to 2001 MY

This manual supersedes:
Workshop manual VDR100370
Body Repair Manual LRL0085

Published by Rover Technical Communication

Publication part no. LRL0326ENG

01
04
05
07
09

10

12

17
19

26

30

33

37

41
44
47

51
54

57

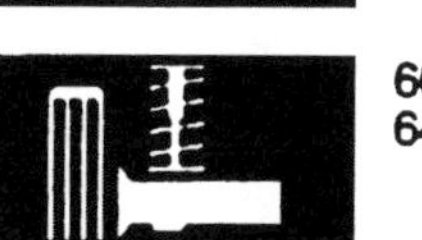
60
64

70

75
76
78

80
82

CONTENTS

Page

INFORMATION

INTRODUCTION

This workshop manual covers the New Range Rover vehicle from introduction in 1995, and is designed to be used in conjunction with Electrical Troubleshooting Manual LRL0329 and Electrical Circuit Diagrams YVB101590 (2nd Edition). Amendments and additional pages will be issued to ensure that the manual covers latest models. Amendments and additions will be identified by the addition of a dated footer at the bottom of the page.

This Workshop Manual is designed to assist skilled technicians in the efficient repair and maintenance of Range Rover vehicles.

Individuals who undertake their own repairs should have some skill and training, and limit repairs to components which could not affect the safety of the vehicle or its passengers. Any repairs required to safety critical items such as steering, brakes, suspension or supplementary restraint system should be carried out by a Range Rover Dealer. Repairs to such items should NEVER be attempted by untrained individuals.

WARNINGS, CAUTIONS and **NOTES** are given throughout this Manual in the following form:

WARNING: Procedures which must be followed precisely to avoid the possibility of personal injury.

CAUTION: This calls attention to procedures which must be followed to avoid damage to components.

NOTE: This calls attention to methods which make a job easier or gives helpful information.

DIMENSIONS

The dimensions quoted are to design engineering specification. Alternative unit equivalents, shown in brackets following the dimensions, have been converted from the original specification.

REFERENCES

References to the left or right hand side in the manual are made when viewing the vehicle from the rear. With the engine and gearbox assembly removed, the water pump end of the engine is referred to as the front.

To reduce repetition, some operations covered in this Manual do not include reference to testing the vehicle after repair.

It is essential that work is inspected and tested after completion and if necessary a road test of the vehicle is carried out particularly where safety related items are concerned.

REPAIRS AND REPLACEMENTS

When replacement parts are required it is essential that Range Rover parts are used.
Attention is particularly drawn to the following points concerning repairs and the fitting of replacement parts and accessories: Safety features embodied in the vehicle may be impaired if other than Range Rover parts are fitted. In certain territories, legislation prohibits the fitting of parts not to the vehicle manufacturer's specification. Torque spanner values given in the Workshop Manual must be strictly adhered to. Locking devices, where specified, must be fitted. If the efficiency of a locking device is impaired during removal it must be replaced with a new one. Certain fasteners must not be re-used. These fasteners are specified in the Workshop Manual.

POISONOUS SUBSTANCES

Many liquids and other substances used are toxic and should not be consumed under any circumstances, and should be kept away from open wounds. These substances amongst others include anti-freeze, brake fluid, fuel, oil, windscreen washer additives, air conditioning refrigerant, lubricants and various adhesives.

FUEL HANDLING PRECAUTIONS

The following information provides basic precautions which must be observed if fuel is to be handled safely. It also outlines other potential risks which must not be ignored.

This information is issued for basic guidance only; in any case of doubt, seek advice from your local Fire Officer or Fire Department.

Fuel vapour is highly flammable and in confined spaces is also very explosive and toxic.

When fuel evaporates it produces 150 times its own volume in vapour, which when diluted with air becomes a readily ignitable mixture. The vapour is heavier than air and will always fall to the lowest level. It can readily be distributed throughout a workshop by air currents, consequently, even a small spillage of fuel is very dangerous.

Always have a fire extinguisher containing **FOAM CO_2 GAS**, or **POWDER** close at hand when handling fuel, or when dismantling fuel systems and in areas where fuel containers are stored.

WARNING: It is imperative that the battery is not disconnected during fuel system repairs as arcing at the battery terminal could ignite fuel vapour in the atmosphere. Always disconnect the vehicle battery BEFORE carrying out work on the fuel system.

Whenever fuel is being handled, transferred or stored, or when fuel systems are being dismantled, all forms of ignition must be extinguished or removed, any leadlamps used must be flame proof and kept clear of spillage.

No one should be permitted to repair components associated with fuel without first having had fuel system training.

Hot fuel handling precautions

WARNING: Before commencing any operation requiring fuel to be drained from the fuel tank, the following procedure must be adhered to:

1. Allow sufficient time for the fuel to cool, thus avoiding contact with hot fuels.
2. Vent the system by removing the fuel filler cap in a well ventilated area. Refit the filler cap until the commencement of fuel drainage.

Fuel transfer

WARNING: Fuel must not be extracted or drained from any vehicle while it is standing over a pit.

The transfer of fuel from the vehicle fuel tank must be carried out in a well ventilated area. An approved transfer tank must be used according to the transfer tank manufacturer's instructions and local regulations, including attention to grounding of tanks.

Fuel tank removal

A **FUEL VAPOUR** warning label must be attached to the fuel tank upon removal from the vehicle.

Fuel tank repair

Under no circumstances should a repair to any tank be attempted.

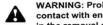

SYNTHETIC RUBBER

Many 'O' ring seals, flexible pipes and other similar items which appear to be natural rubber are made of synthetic materials called Fluoroelastomers. Under normal operating conditions this material is safe, and does not present a health hazard. However, if the material is damaged by fire or excessive heat, it can break down and produce highly corrosive Hydrofluoric acid which can cause serious burns on contact with skin. Should the material be in a burnt or overheated condition, handle only with seamless industrial gloves. Decontaminate and dispose of the gloves immediately after use.

If skin contact does occur, remove any contaminated clothing immediately and obtain medical assistance without delay. In the meantime, wash the affected area with copious amounts of cold water or limewater for fifteen to sixty minutes.

RECOMMENDED SEALANTS

A number of branded products are recommended in this manual for use during maintenance and repair work.
These items include:
HYLOMAR GASKET AND JOINTING COMPOUND
and
HYLOSIL RTV SILICON COMPOUND.

They should be available locally from garage equipment suppliers. If there is any problem obtaining supplies, contact the following company for advice and the address of the nearest supplier.

MacDERMID LUBRICANTS LTD.
Hylo House,
Cale lane,
New Springs,
Wigan
WN2 1JR
United Kingdom

Tel: 01942 824242
Fax: 01942 501110

USED ENGINE OIL

WARNING: Prolonged and repeated contact with engine or motor oil will result in the removal of natural fats from the skin, leading to dryness, irritation and dermatitis.

Used engine oil contains potentially harmful contaminants which may cause skin cancer. Adequate means of skin protection and washing facilities should be provided.

Handling precautions

1. Avoid prolonged and repeated contact with oils, particularly used engine oils.
2. Wear protective clothing, including impervious gloves where applicable.
3. Do not put oily rags in pockets.
4. Avoid contaminating clothes, particularly underwear, with oil.
5. Overalls must be cleaned regularly. Discard unwashable clothing and oil impregnated footwear.
6. First aid treatment must be obtained immediately for open cuts and wounds.
7. Use barrier creams, before each work period, to help the removal of oil from the skin.
8. Wash with soap and water to ensure all oil is removed (skin cleansers and nail brushes will help). Preparations containing lanolin replace the natural skin oils which have been removed.
9. Do not use gasoline, kerosene, diesel fuel, petrol, thinners or solvents for washing the skin.
10. If skin disorders develop, obtain medical advice.
11. Where practicable, degrease components prior to handling.
12. Where there is a risk of eye contact, eye protection should be worn, for example, goggles or face shields; in addition an eye wash facility should be provided.

Disposing of used oils

Environmental protection precaution

It is illegal to pour used oil onto the ground, down sewers or drains, or into waterways.

Dispose of used oil through authorised waste disposal contractors. If in doubt, contact your Local Authority for advice on disposal facilities.

ACCESSORIES AND CONVERSIONS

DO NOT FIT unapproved accessories or conversions, as they could affect the safety of the vehicle.
Land Rover will not accept liability for death, personal injury, or damage to property which may occur as a direct result of the fitment of non-approved conversions to the Range Rover.

WHEELS AND TYRES

WARNING: DO NOT replace the road wheels with any type other than genuine Range Rover wheels which are designed for multi-purpose on and off road use and have very important relationships with the proper operation of the suspension system and vehicle handling. Replacement tyres must be of the make and sizes recommended for the vehicle, and all tyres must be the same make, ply rating and tread pattern.

CAUTION: When refitting a road wheel, apply a suitable anti-seize compound such as Raworth 33/04, to the spigot bore of the wheel. This will prevent possible seizure of the wheel to the hub spigot. Ensure that no compound comes into contact with the braking components.

STEAM CLEANING

To prevent consequential rusting, any steam cleaning within the engine bay **MUST** be followed by careful re-waxing of the metallic components affected.
Particular attention must be given to the steering column, engine water pipes, hose clips and ignition coil clamp.

SPECIFICATION

The specification details and instructions set out in this Manual apply only to a range of vehicles and not to any particular one. For the specification of a particular vehicle, purchasers should consult their Dealer.
The Manufacturers reserve the right to vary their specifications with or without notice, and at such times and in such manner as they think fit. Major as well as minor changes may be involved in accordance with the Manufacturer's policy of constant product improvement.

While every effort is made to ensure the accuracy of the particulars contained in this Manual, neither the Manufacturer nor Dealer, by whom this Manual is supplied, shall in any circumstances be held liable for any inaccuracy or the consequences thereof.

SPECIAL SERVICE TOOLS

The use of approved special service tools is important. They are essential if service operations are to be carried out efficiently, and safely. Where special tools are specified, **only these tools should be used to avoid the possibility of personal injury or damage to the components.** Also the amount of time which they save can be considerable.

Every special tool is designed with the close co-operation of Land Rover, and no tool is put into production which has not been tested and approved by us. New tools are only introduced where an operation cannot be satisfactorily carried out using existing tools or standard equipment. The user is therefore assured that the tool is necessary and that it will perform accurately, efficiently and safely.

Special tools bulletins will be issued periodically giving details of new tools as they are introduced.

All orders and enquiries from the United Kingdom should be sent direct to V. L. Churchill. Overseas orders should be placed with the local V. L. Churchill distributor, where one exists. Countries where there is no distributor may order direct from:

V. L. Churchill Limited,
PO Box 3,
Daventry, Northants,
England, NN11 4NF.

The tools recommended in this Workshop Manual are listed in a multi-language illustrated catalogue, publication number **LPA ST ML 95**, which is obtainable from V. L. Churchill Limited at the above address.

COPYRIGHT

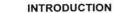

JACKING

The following instructions must be carried out before raising the vehicle off the ground.

1. Use a solid level ground surface.
2. Apply parking brake.
3. Select 'P' or 1st gear in main gearbox.
4. Select Low range in transfer gearbox.

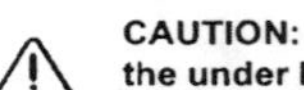

CAUTION: To avoid damage occurring to the under body components of the vehicle the following jacking procedures must be adhered to.

DO NOT POSITION JACKS OR AXLE STANDS UNDER THE FOLLOWING COMPONENTS.

Body structure	**Air suspension pipes**
Bumpers	**Fuel lines**
Brake lines	**Front radius arms**
Panhard rod	**Steering linkage**
Rear Trailing links	**Fuel tank**
Engine sump	**Gearbox bell housing**

CAUTION: If supporting vehicle by the front crossmember, the safety stands must be positioned carefully to avoid damage to air suspension pipes.

Vehicle jack

The jack provided with the vehicle is only intended to be used in an emergency, for changing a wheel. Do **NOT** use the jack for any other purpose. Refer to Owner's Manual for vehicle jack location points and procedure. Never work under a vehicle supported by the vehicle jack.

Hydraulic jack

A hydraulic jack with a minimum 1500 kg, 3,300 lbs load capacity must be used.

CAUTION: Do not commence work on the underside of the vehicle until suitable axle stands have been positioned under the axle.

Raise the front of the vehicle

1. Position cup of hydraulic arm under differential casing.

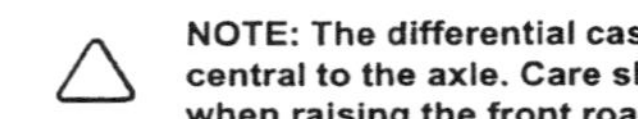

NOTE: The differential casing is not central to the axle. Care should be taken when raising the front road wheels off the ground as the rear axle has less sway stiffness.

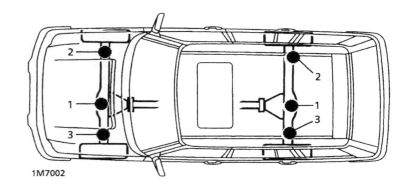

1M7002

2. Raise front road wheels to enable an axle stand to be installed under left hand axle tube.
3. Position an axle stand under right hand axle tube, carefully lower jack until axle sits securely on both axle stands, remove trolley jack.
4. Before commencing work on underside of vehicle re-check security of vehicle on stands.
5. Reverse procedure when removing vehicle from stands.

Raise rear of vehicle

1. Position cup of hydraulic arm under differential casing.
2. Raise vehicle to enable axle stands to be installed under left and right hand axle tubes.
3. Lower jack until axle sits securely on axle stands, remove trolley jack.
4. Before commencing work on underside of vehicle re-check security of vehicle on stands.
5. Reverse procedure when removing vehicle from stands.

HYDRAULIC VEHICLE RAMP (FOUR POST)

Use only a 'drive on' type ramp which supports vehicle by its own road wheels. If a 'wheel-free' condition is required, use a 'drive on' ramp incorporating a 'wheel-free' system that supports under axle casings. Alternatively, place vehicle on a firm, flat floor and support on axle stands.

TWO POST VEHICLE RAMPS

The manufacturer of RANGE ROVER VEHICLES DOES NOT recommend using 'Two Post' ramps that employ four adjustable support arms. These are NOT considered safe for Range Rover vehicles.
If a vehicle is installed on a Two Post ramp, responsibility for safety of the vehicle and personnel performing service operations is attributable to the Service Provider.

DYNAMOMETER TESTING - VEHICLES WITH ANTI-LOCK BRAKES (ABS)

WARNING: Do not attempt to test ABS function on a dynamometer

Four wheel dynamometers

NOTE: Before testing a vehicle on a four wheel dynamometer disconnect the valve relay. ***See Electrical Trouble Shooting Manual.***
The ABS function will not work, the ABS warning light will illuminate. Normal braking will be available.

Provided that front and rear rollers are rotating at identical speeds and that normal workshop safety standards are applied, there is no speed restriction during testing except any that may apply to the tyres.

Two wheel dynamometers

IMPORTANT: Use a four wheel dynamometer for brake testing if possible.

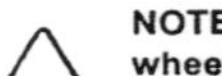

NOTE: ABS will not function on a two wheel dynamometer. The ABS light will illuminate during testing. Normal braking will be available.

If brake testing on a single rig is necessary it must be carried out with propeller shaft to the rear axle removed, AND neutral selected in BOTH main and transfer boxes.

If checking engine performance, the transfer box must be in high range and drive shaft to stationary axle removed.

WARNING: Vehicles from 99 MY are fitted with 4 wheel traction control, which must be disabled prior to testing on a single axle dynamometer.

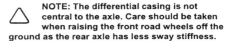

JUMP STARTING

WARNING: Hydrogen and oxygen gases are produced during normal battery operation. This gas mixture can explode if flames, sparks or lighted tobacco are brought near battery. When charging or using a battery in an enclosed space, always provide ventilation and shield your eyes.

Keep out of reach of children. Batteries contain sulphuric acid. Avoid contact with skin, eyes, or clothing. Also, shield eyes when working near battery to protect against possible splashing of acid solution. In case of acid contact with skin, eyes, or clothing, flush immediately with water for a minimum of fifteen minutes. If acid is swallowed, drink large quantities of milk or water, followed by milk of magnesia, a beaten egg, or vegetable oil. SEEK MEDICAL AID IMMEDIATELY.

To Jump Start - Negative Ground Battery

WARNING: To avoid any possibility of injury use particular care when connecting a booster battery to a discharged battery.

1. Position vehicles so that jump leads will reach, ensuring that vehicles **DO NOT TOUCH,** alternatively a fully charged slave battery may be positioned on floor adjacent to vehicle.
2. Ensure that ignition and all electrical accessories are switched off; the parking brake must be applied and neutral selected on a manual gearbox; for an automatic gearbox select neutral (N) or park (P). Connect the jump leads as follows;

A. Connect one end of first jumper cable to positive (+) terminal of booster battery.
B. Connect other end of first jumper cable to positive (+) terminal of discharged battery.
C. Connect one end of second jumper cable to negative terminal of booster battery.
D. Connect other end of second jumper cable to a good earth point on the engine, **NOT TO NEGATIVE TERMINAL OF DISCHARGED BATTERY.** Keep jumper lead away from moving parts, pulleys, drive belts and fan blade assembly.

WARNING: Making final cable connection could cause an electrical arc which if made near battery could cause an explosion.

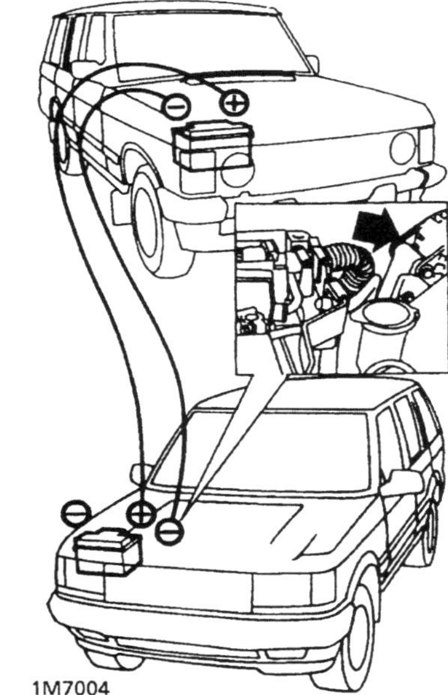

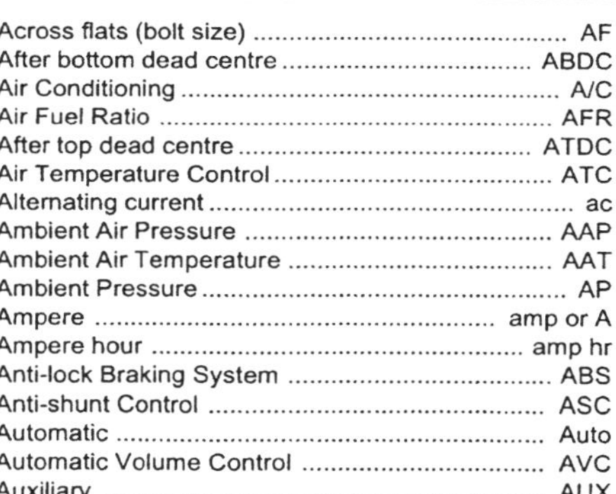

1M7004

3. If booster battery is installed in another vehicle, start engine and allow to idle.
4. Start engine of vehicle with discharged battery, following starting procedure in Owners' Manual.

CAUTION: If vehicle fails to start within a maximum time of 12 seconds, switch ignition off and investigate cause. Failing to follow this instruction could result in irrepairable damage to catalysts.

5. Remove negative (-) jumper cable from the engine and then terminal of booster battery.
6. Remove positive (+) jumper cable from positive terminals of booster battery and discharged battery.

ABBREVIATIONS AND SYMBOLS USED IN THIS MANUAL

Across flats (bolt size) .... AF
After bottom dead centre .... ABDC
Air Conditioning .... A/C
Air Fuel Ratio .... AFR
After top dead centre .... ATDC
Air Temperature Control .... ATC
Alternating current .... ac
Ambient Air Pressure .... AAP
Ambient Air Temperature .... AAT
Ambient Pressure .... AP
Ampere .... amp or A
Ampere hour .... amp hr
Anti-lock Braking System .... ABS
Anti-shunt Control .... ASC
Automatic .... Auto
Automatic Volume Control .... AVC
Auxiliary .... AUX

Battery Backed-Up Sounder .... BBUS
Before bottom dead centre .... BBDC
Before top dead centre .... BTDC
Body Electrical Control Module .... BeCM
Boost Pressure .... BP
Bottom dead centre .... BDC
Brake horse power .... bhp
Brake Pedal Positions .... BPP
British Standards .... BS

Camshaft Position .... CMP
Calculated Load Value CLV
Canister Vent Solenoid .... CVS
Carbon Dioxide .... CO_2
Carbon monoxide .... CO
Celsius C
Centimetre .... cm
Central Door Locking .... CDL
Centre Differential Control .... CDC
Centre High Mounted Stop Lamp .... CHMSL
Chlorofluorocarbon .... CFC
Clutch Pedal Position .... CPP
Compact Disc .... CD
Compact Disc - Read Only Memory .... CD-ROM
Controller Area Network .... CAN
Crankshaft Position .... CKP
Cubic centimetre .... cm^3
Cubic feet per minute .... ft^3/min
Cubic inch .... in^3

dB .... Decibels
Degree (angle) .... deg or °
Degree (temperature) .... deg or °
Diagnostic Control Unit .... DCU
Dial Test Indicator .... DTI
Diameter .... dia.

Digital Diesel Electronics .... DDE
Digital Signal Processing .... DSP
Digital Versatile Disc .... DVD
Direct current .... dc
Direct Ignition System .... DIS
Direct Injection .... DI
Directional Control Valve .... DCV
Double Overhead Camshaft .... DOHC
Dual Mass Flywheel .... DMF

Electronic Air Control Valve .... EACV
Electronic Air Suspension .... EAS
Electronic Automatic Transmission .... EAT
Electronic Brake pressure Distribution .... EBD
Electronic Control Unit .... ECU
Electronic Diesel Control .... EDC
Electronic Erasable Programmable Read Only Memory .... EEPROM
Electronic Fuel Injection .... EFI
Electronic Traction Control .... ETC
Electronic Unit Injector .... EUI
Electronic Vacuum Regulator .... EVR
Electrical Reference Library .... ERL
Emergency Key Access .... EKA
Emergency Locking Retractor .... ELR
Engine Control Module .... ECM
Engine Coolant Temperature .... ECT
Engine Fuel Temperature .... EFT
Engine Management System .... EMS
Enhanced Other Network .... EON
European Community Directive .... ECD
European Norm .... EN
European Economic Community .... EEC
European On Board Diagnostics .... EOBD
Evaporative Emission .... EVAP
Exhaust Gas Recirculation .... EGR

Fahrenheit .... F
Fast Throttle Control .... FTC
Feet .... ft
Feet per minute .... ft/min
Field Effect Transistor .... FET
Fifth 5th
First 1st
Fluid ounce .... fl oz
Foot pounds (torque) .... lbf.ft
Fourth 4th
Fuel Burning Heater .... FBH
Fuel Injection Pump .... FIP

Gallons .... gal
Gallons (US) .... US gal
Gramme (force) .... gf
Gramme (mass) .... g
Greenwich Mean Time .... GMT
Global Positioning System .... GPS
Gravity .... g

Heated Front Screen ... HFS
Heated oxygen sensor ... HO_2S
Heated Rear Window ... HRW
Height Dilation Of Precision ... HDOP
High ... HI
High compression ... hc
High Density Polyethylene ... HDPE
High Molecular Weight ... HMW
High Strength Low Alloy ... HSLA
High tension (electrical) ... HT or ht
Hill Descent Control ... HDC
Hour ... h
Hydrocarbons ... HC
Hydrofluorocarbon ... HFC

Idle Air Control Valve ... IACV
In Car Entertainment ... ICE
Inches of mercury ... in. Hg
Inches ... in
Inertia-fuel Shut Off ... IFS
Injector Pulse Width ... IPW
Inlet Throttle ... ILT
Intake Air Temperature ... IAT
Intermediate Frequency ... IF
Internal diameter ... I.D. or i.dia.
International Organisation for Standardisation ... ISO

Kilogramme (force) ... kgf
Kilogramme (mass.) ... kg
Kilogramme centimetre (torque) ... kgf.cm
Kilogrammes per hour ... kg/h
Kilogramme per square millimetre ... kgf/mm^2
Kilogramme per square centimetre ... kgf/cm^2
Kilogramme metres (torque) ... kgf.m
Kilometres ... km
Kilometres per hour ... km/h
KiloPascal ... kPa
Kilowatts ... kW
Kilovolts ... kV
Knock Sensor ... KS

Left-hand ... LH
Left-hand Drive ... LHD
Left-hand thread ... LHThd
Light Emitting Diode ... LED
Litres ... l
Liquid Crystal Display ... LCD
Liquid Vapour Separator ... LVS
Low ... LO
Low compression ... lc
Low Emission Vehicle ... LEV
Low tension ... l.t.

Malfunction Indicator Light ... MIL
Manifold Absolute Pressure ... MAP
Mass Air Flow ... MAF
Maximum ... max.
MegaPascal ... MPa
Metal Oxide Semiconductor Field Effect Transistor ... MOSFET

Metre ... m
Millilitre ... ml
Millimetre ... mm
Miles per gallon ... mpg
Miles per hour ... mph
Minus (of tolerance) ... -
Minimum ... min.
Minute (angle) ... '
Model Year ... MY
Modular Engine Management System ... MEMS
Motorised Valve ... MV
Multi-Function Logic ... MFL
Multi-Function Unit ... MFU
Multi-Point injection ... MPi
Multiport Fuel Injection ... MFI

Negative (electrical) ... -ve
Negative Temperature Coefficient ... NTC
Newton metres (torque) ... Nm
Nitrogen Dioxide ... NO_2
Non-Return Valve ... NRV
North American Specification ... NAS
Number ... No.

Off-road Mode ... ORM
Ohms ... ohm
On Board Diagnostics ... OBD
On Board Monitoring ... OBM
Organic Acid Technology ... OAT
Ounces (force) ... ozf
Ounces (mass) ... oz
Ounce inch (torque) ... ozf.in.
Outside diameter ... O.D. or o.dia.
Overhead Cam ... OHC
Oxides of Nitrogen ... NOx

Part number ... Part No.
Percentage ... %
Pints ... pt
Pints (US) ... US pt
Plus or Minus ... ±
Plus (tolerance) ... +
Polytetrafluorethylene ... PTFE
Position Dilation Of Position ... PDOP
Positive (electrical) ... +ve
Positive Crankcase Ventilation ... PCV
Positive Temperature Coefficient ... PTC
Pound (force) ... lbf
Pounds force feet ... lbf.ft
Pounds inch (torque) ... lbf.in
Pound (mass) ... lb(s)
Pounds per square inch ... psi
Pounds per square inch ... lbf/in^2
Power Assisted Steering ... PAS
Pressure Conscious Reducing Valve ... PCRV
Printed Circuit Board ... PCB
Programme Information ... PI
Pulses Per Second ... PPS
Pulse Width Modulation ... PWM

Radio Data Service ... RDS
Radio Frequency ... RF
Radius ... r
Ratio ... :
Read Only Memory ... ROM
Red/Green/Blue ... RGB
Reference ... ref.
Regionalisation ... REG
Research Octane Number ... RON
Rest Of World ... ROW
Revolution per minute ... rev/min
Right-hand ... RH
Right-hand Drive ... RHD
Roll Over Valve ... ROV
Rover Engineering Standards ... RES

Second (angle) ... "
Second (numerical order) ... 2nd
Secondary Air Injection ... SAI
Self Levelling and Anti-Lock Brake System ... SLABS
Self Levelling Suspension ... SLS
Single Overhead Camshaft ... SOHC
Single Point Entry ... SPE
Society of Automotive Engineers ... SAE
Specific gravity ... sp.gr.
Square centimetres ... cm^2
Square inches ... in^2
Standard ... std.
Standard wire gauge ... s.w.g.
Supplementary Restraint System ... SRS
Synchroniser/Synchromesh ... synchro.

Temperature, Manifold Absolute Pressure ... TMAP
Third ... 3rd
Thermostsatic Expansion Valve ... TXV
Three Way Catalyst ... TWC
Throttle Position ... TP
Top Dead Centre ... TDC
Torsional Vibration ... TV
Traffic Announcement ... TA
Traffic Management Control ... TMC

United Kingdom ... UK
United States ... US
US gallons per hour ... US galls/h

Variable ... Var.
Variable Intake System ... VIS
Variable Reluctance Sensor ... VRS
Vehicle Identification Number ... VIN
Vehicle Information Communications System ... VICS
Vehicle Speed Sensor ... VSS
Velocity Dilation Of Precision ... VDOP
Volts ... V

Watts ... W
Wide Open Throttle ... WOT

SCREW THREADS
American Standard Taper Pipe ... NPTF
British Standard Pipe ... BSP
Unified Coarse ... UNC
Unified Fine ... UNF

VEHICLE IDENTIFICATION NUMBER (VIN)

An adhesive label containing the Vehicle Identification Number and the recommended maximum vehicle weights is located on the left hand side of the bonnet locking platform.
The number is also stamped on the outside of the chassis in the front RH wheel arch to the rear of the anti-roll bar link.

NOTE: It may be necessary to remove underseal in order to locate the number; ensure underseal is restored on completion.

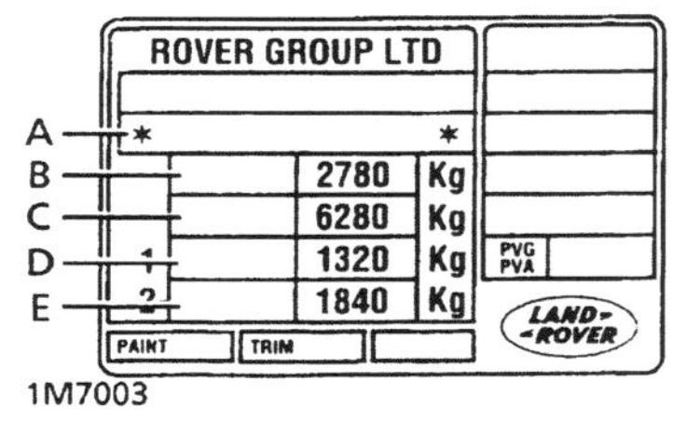

1M7003

Key to Vehicle Identification Number Plate

A. VIN (17 digits)
B. Maximum permitted laden weight for vehicle
C. Maximum vehicle and trailer weight
D. Maximum road weight-front axle
E. Maximum road weight-rear axle

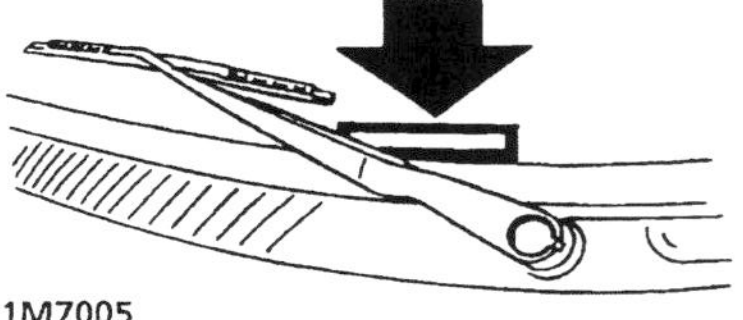
1M7005

In addition, the VIN is stamped on a plate which is visible through the left side of the windscreen.

Federal (USA) vehicle identification number

An adhesive label containing the Vehicle Identification Number, date of manufacture and gross axle weight ratings is fixed to the lock face of the front left hand door. The information includes wheel and tyre sizes and tyre pressures at gross axle weight ratings.

LOCATION OF IDENTIFICATION NUMBERS

Engine serial number - V8 engine

Stamped on a cast pad on the cylinder block, between numbers 3 and 5 cylinders.

NOTE: The engine compression ratio is stamped above the serial number.

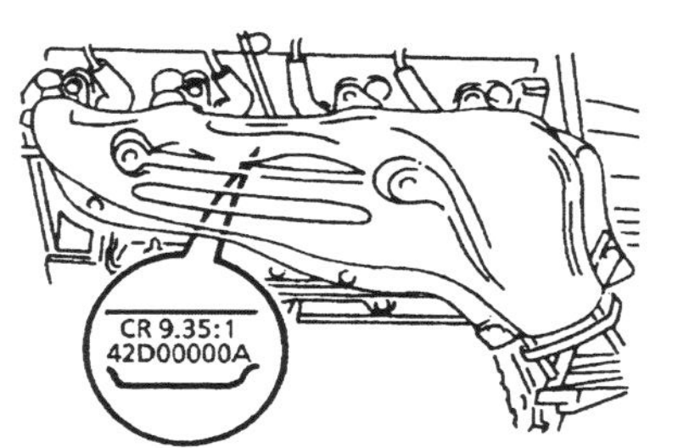

1M7006

Engine serial number - BMW Diesel engine

Stamped on the LH side of the cylinder block above the sump.

Main gearbox R380 - 5 speed

Stamped on a cast pad on the bottom right hand side of the gearbox.

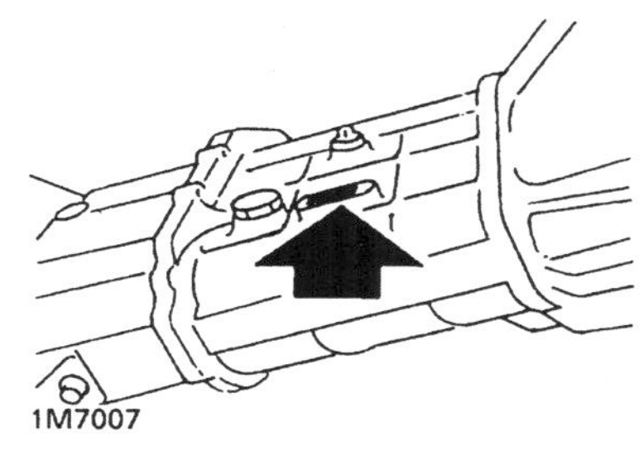
1M7007

Automatic gearbox ZF4HP22/ZF4HP24

Stamped on a plate riveted to the bottom left hand side of the gearbox casing.

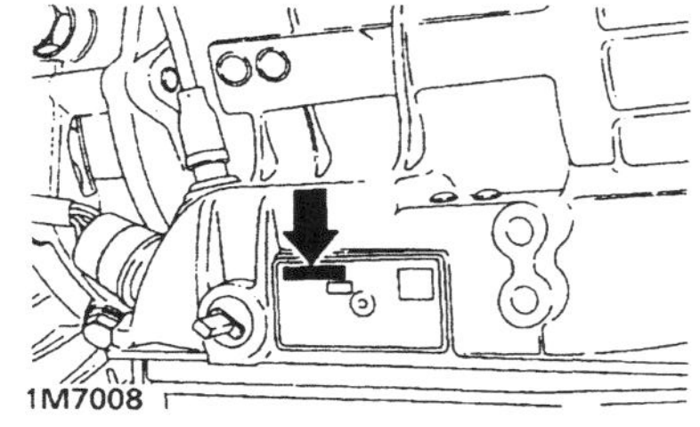
1M7008

Transfer gearbox-Borg Warner

Stamped on a plate attached to the gearbox casing, between filler/level and drain plug.

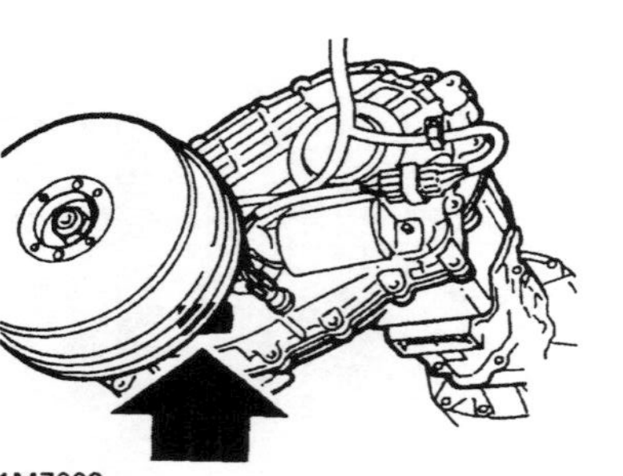

1M7009

Front and rear axle

Stamped on the left hand axle tubes.

Vehicle identification number (VIN)

Made up of 17 digits, these numbers are used to identify manufacturer, model range, specification, body type, engine, transmission/steering, model year, plant and build sequence number and serve to identify the vehicle.

This example shows the sequence:

European code

S AL LP A M J 7 M A

- S Europe
- AL UK
- LP Range Rover
- A European Spec.
- M 4 Door Station Wagon
- J 4.6 Litre Fuel Injection
- 7 Manual right steering
- M 1995 Model Year
- A Solihull

Federal (USA) code

S AL P V 1 2 4 2 S A

- S Europe
- AL UK
- P Range Rover
- V North America Spec.
- 1 4 Door Station Wagon
- 2 4.0 Litre fuel injection
- 4 Automatic, Left Hand Steering
- 2 Check Digit
- S 1995 Model Year
- A Solihull

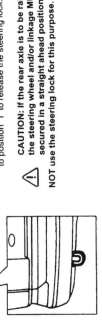

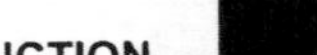

EMERGENCY TOWING

CAUTION: The New Range Rover has permanent four-wheel drive. The following instructions must be adhered to when towing:-

Towing the vehicle on four wheels

If it is necessary to recover the vehicle by towing on all four wheels, 'Transfer neutral' **MUST** be selected.

1. With the starter key removed, insert a fuse of 5 amps or more in fuse position '11' in the RH seat fuse box.
2. Turn the starter switch to position '2'; the transfer box will now automatically select neutral.
3. Wait until the message centre displays 'TRANSFER NEUTRAL' and then turn the starter switch off, position '0'.
4. Turn the starter switch to position '1' to unlock the steering and leave in this position while the vehicle is being towed.

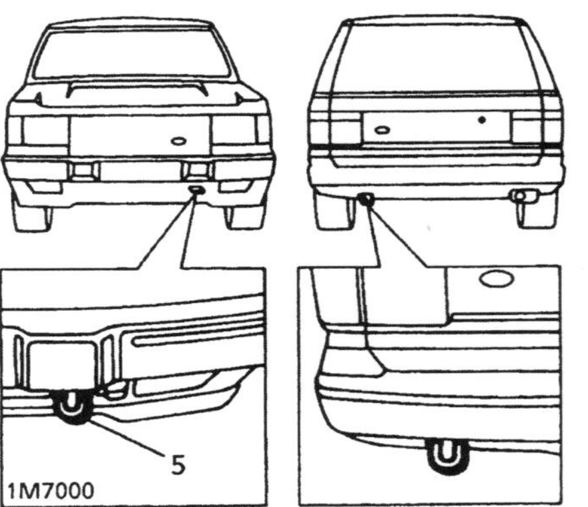

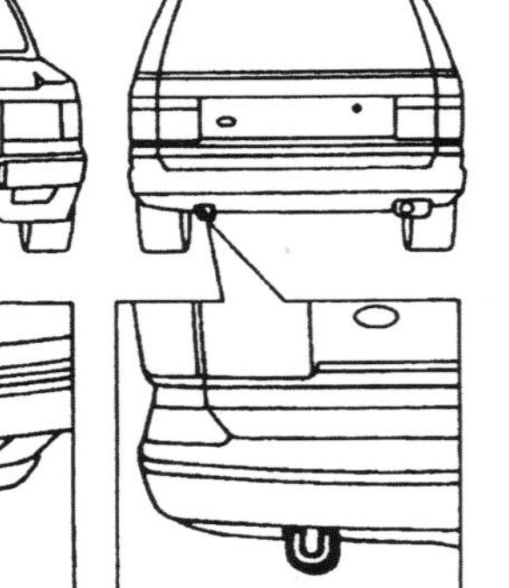

1M7000

5. Secure tow rope to the front towing eye.
6. Release the parking brake.

CAUTION: Power assistance for braking and steering systems will not be provided without the engine running. Greater pedal pressure will be required to apply the brakes, the steering wheel will require greater effort to turn the front wheels.
The vehicle tow connection should be used only in normal road conditions.

CAUTION: DO NOT remove the starter key or turn the switch to position '0' when the vehicle is in motion.

7. To reactivate the transfer box after towing, turn the starter switch off to position '0' and remove the fuse from position '11'. On automatic vehicles the transfer box will automatically engage the Low or High gear range.
8. On manual vehicles, first press the range change switch. The transfer box will then engage the Low or High gear range.

Suspended tow by breakdown vehicle

CAUTION: To prevent vehicle damage, front or rear propeller shaft MUST be removed, dependant upon which axle is being trailed.

9. To facilitate reassembly, first mark the propeller shaft drive flanges at transfer box and axle.
10. Remove propeller shaft fixings and lift shaft from vehicle.
11. If the front axle is to be trailed, turn ignition key to position '1' to release the steering lock.

CAUTION: If the rear axle is to be raised, the steering wheel and/or linkage MUST be secured in a straight ahead position. DO NOT use the steering lock for this purpose.

TRANSPORTING THE VEHICLE BY TRAILER

If the vehicle should require transporting on a trailer or the back of a lorry, the air suspension must be set to 'ACCESS' before being lashed. ***See FRONT SUSPENSION, Description and operation.***

Lashing eyes are provided on the front and rear chassis cross members to facilitate the securing of the vehicle, as shown.

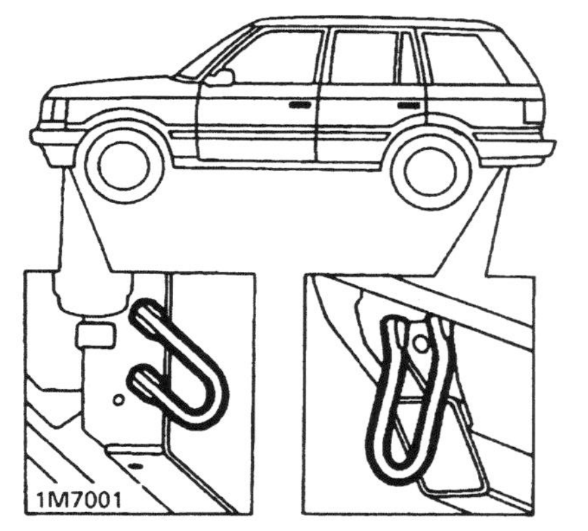

CAUTION: DO NOT secure lashing hooks or trailer fixings to any other part of the vehicle.

CAUTION: If the air suspension cannot be set to the 'ACCESS' position, then the vehicle must be lashed by its wheels and not the lashing eyes.

Install vehicle on the trailer and apply park brake. Select neutral in main gearbox; this will prevent damage to the parking pawl of the automatic gearbox.

Notes

04 - GENERAL SPECIFICATION DATA

CONTENTS

ENGINE - 4.0 V8

Type	4.0 litre V8	
Number of cylinders	Eight, two banks of four	
Bore	94.00 - 94.04 mm	3.7008 - 3.7024 in
Stroke	71.04 - 71.20 mm	2.7966 - 2.8031 in
Capacity	3950 cm³	241 cu in
Valve operation	Overhead by push-rod	
Compression ratio	**High Compression**	**Low Compression**
Up to 99MY	9.35:1	8.2:1
From 99MY	9.38:1	8.23:1
Maximum power (at 4750 rev/min)		
Up to 99MY	140 kW	132 kW
From 99MY		
All except NAS	136 kW	132 kW
NAS only	140 kW	-

Crankshaft

Main journal diameter	63.500 - 63.487 mm	2.50 - 2.4995 in
Crankpin journal diameter	55.513 - 55.500 mm	2.1856 - 2.1850 in
Crankshaft end thrust/end float	Taken on thrust washers of centre main bearing	
	0.10 - 0.20 mm	0.004 - 0.008 in

Main bearings

Number and type		
Up to 99MY	5, Vandervell shells	
From 99MY	5, Glacier Vandervell / AS15	
Material	Lead bronze with lead-indium overlay	
Diametrical clearance	0.010 - 0.048 mm	0.0004 - 0.002 in

Connecting rods

Type	Horizontally split big-end, plain small-end	
Length between centres	155.12 - 155.22 mm	6.1071 - 6.1110 in

Big-end bearings

Type and material		
Up to 99MY	Vandervell VP Lead bronze with lead-indium overlay	
From 99MY	Glacier Vandervell GPL2120 / AS124A	
Diametrical clearance	0.015 - 0.055 mm	0.0006 - 0.002 in

Piston pins

Length	60.00 - 60.50 mm	2.3622 - 2.3819 in
Diameter	23.995 - 24.000 mm	0.9447 - 0.9449 in
Fit-in connecting rod	Press fit	
Clearance in piston	0.015 - 0.006 mm	0.00059 - 0.00024 in

Pistons

Clearance in bore, measured 10 mm from base of skirt at right angles to piston pin		
Up to 99MY	0.020 - 0.050 mm	0.0008 - 0.0020 in
From 99MY	0.022 - 0.067 mm	0.0009 - 0.0026 in

Piston rings

Number of compression rings	2	
Number of oil control rings	1	
No 1 compression ring	Nitrided steel barrel faced	
No 2 compression ring	Tapered spherical barrel marked 'TOP'	
Width of compression rings		
Bottom	1.478 - 1.49 mm	0.0582 - 0.0587 in
Top		
Up to 99MY	1.21 - 1.23 mm	0.0476 - 0.0484 in
From 99MY	1.17 - 1.19 mm	0.0461 - 0.0479 in
Compression ring gap		
Bottom	0.40 - 0.65 mm	0.0157 - 0.0256 in
Top	0.3 - 0.5 mm	0.0118 - 0.0197 in
Oil control ring type		
Up to 99MY	Aclonoform	
From 99MY	3 Piece Aeconoform	
Oil control ring width	3.0 mm	0.1181 in
Oil control ring rail gap	0.38-1.40 mm	0.0150 - 0.0551 in

Camshaft

Location	Central	
Bearings	Non serviceable	
Number of bearings	5	
Drive	Chain 9.52 mm pitch x 54 pitches.	
Camshaft end float		
Up to 99MY	0.076 - 0.355 mm	0.003 - 0.014 in
From 99MY	0.075 - 0.350 mm	0.002 - 0.013 in

Tappets .... Hydraulic self-adjusting

Valves

Length		
Inlet	116.59 - 117.35 mm	4.590 - 4.620 in
Exhaust	116.59 - 117.35 mm	4.590 - 4.620 in
Seat angle	**Up to 99MY**	**From 99MY**
Inlet	46° - 46° 25'	45° - 45° 30'
Exhaust	46° - 46° 25'	45° - 45° 30'
Head diameter		
Inlet	39.75 - 40.00 mm	1.565 - 1.575 in
Exhaust	34.227 - 34.48 mm	1.3475 - 1.3575 in
Stem diameter		
Inlet	8.664 - 8.679 mm	0.3411 - 0.3417 in
Exhaust	8.651 - 8.666 mm	0.3406 - 0.3412 in
Stem to guide clearance		
Inlet	0.025 - 0.066 mm	0.0010 - 0.0026 in
Exhaust	0.038 - 0.078 mm	0.0015 - 0.0031 in
Valve lift (inlet and exhaust)	9.94 mm	0.3913 in
Valve spring length fitted		
Up to 99MY	40.40 mm (1.59 in) at pressure of 29.5 kg (65 lb)	
From 99MY	40.93 mm (1.61 in) at pressure of 29.5 kg (65 lb)	

Lubrication

System type	Wet sump, pressure fed
Oil pump type	Crank driven rotor
Oil pressure	
Up to 99MY	2.06 to 2.7 bar (30 to 40 lbf/in²) at 2400 rev/min with engine warm
From 99MY	3.45 bar (50 lbf/in²) at 2000 rev/min with engine warm
Oil filter-internal	Wire screen, pump intake filter in sump
Oil filter-external	Full flow, self-contained cartridge

ENGINE - 4.6 V8

Type	4.6 litre V8	
Number of cylinders	Eight, two banks of four	
Bore	94.00 - 94.04 mm	3.7008 - 3.7024 in
Stroke	81.92 - 82.08 mm	3.2252 - 3.2315 in
Capacity	4554 cm³	278 cu in
Valve operation	Overhead by push-rod	
Compression ratio	**High Compression**	**Low Compression**
Up to 99MY	9.35:1	8.36:1
From 99MY	9.37:1	8.37:1
Maximum power (at 4750 rev/min)		
Up to 99MY	165.5 kW	157 kW
From 99MY		
All except NAS	160 kW	150 kW
NAS only	165.5 kW	

Crankshaft

Main journal diameter	63.500 - 63.487 mm	2.50 - 2.4995 in
Crankpin journal diameter	55.513 - 55.500 mm	2.21 - 2.20 in
Crankshaft end thrust/end float	Taken on thrust washers of centre main bearing	
	0.10 - 0.20 mm	0.004 - 0.008 in

Main bearings

Number and type		
Up to 99MY	5, Vandervell shells	
From 99MY	5, Glacier Vandervell / AS15	
Material	Lead bronze with lead-indium overlay	
Diametrical clearance	0.010 - 0.048 mm	0.0004 - 0.002 in

Connecting rods

Type	Horizontally split big-end, plain small-end	
Length between centres	149.68 - 149.78 mm	5.893 - 5.897 in

Big-end bearings

Type and material		
Up to 99MY	Vandervell VP Lead bronze with lead-indium overlay	
From 99MY	Glacier Vandervell GPL2120/AS124A	
Diametrical clearance	0.015 - 0.055 mm	0.0006 - 0.002 in

Piston pins

Length	60.00 - 60.50 mm	2.3622 - 2.3819 in
Diameter	23.995 - 24.000 mm	0.9447 - 0.9449 in
Fit-in connecting rod	Press fit	
Clearance in piston	0.015 - 0.006 mm	0.0006 - 0.0002 in

Pistons

Clearance in bore, measured at bottom of skirt at right angles to piston pin		
Up to 99MY	0.020 - 0.050 mm	0.0008 - 0.0020 in
From 99MY	0.022 - 0.067 mm	0.0009 - 0.0026 in

Piston rings

Number of compression rings	2	
Number of oil control rings	1	
No 1 compression ring	Nitrided steel barrel faced	
No 2 compression ring	Tapered spherical barrel marked 'TOP'	
Width of compression rings		
Bottom	1.478 - 1.49 mm	0.0582 - 0.0587 in
Top		
Up to 99MY	1.21 - 1.23 mm	0.0476 - 0.0484 in
From 99MY	1.17 - 1.19 mm	0.0461 - 0.0479 in
Compression ring gap		
Bottom	0.40 - 0.65 mm	0.0157 - 0.0256 in
Top	0.3 - 0.5 mm	0.0118 - 0.0197 in
Oil control ring type		
Up to 99MY	Aclonoform	
From 99MY	3 Piece Aeconoform	
Oil control ring width	3.0 mm	0.1181 in
Oil control ring rail gap	0.38-1.40 mm	0.0150 - 0.0551 in

Camshaft

Location	Central	
Bearings	Non serviceable	
Number of bearings	5	
Drive	Chain 9.52 mm pitch x 54 pitches.	
Camshaft end float		
Up to 99MY	0.076 - 0.355 mm	0.003 - 0.014 in
From 99MY	0.075 - 0.350 mm	0.002 - 0.013 in

Tappets	Hydraulic self-adjusting	

Valves

Length		
Inlet	116.59 - 117.35 mm	4.590 - 4.620 in
Exhaust	116.59 - 117.35 mm	4.590 - 4.620 in
Seat angle	**Up to 99MY**	**From 99MY**
Inlet	46° - 46° 25'	45° - 45° 30'
Exhaust	46° - 46° 25'	45° - 45° 30'
Head diameter		
Inlet	39.75 - 40.00 mm	1.565 - 1.575 in
Exhaust	34.227 - 34.48 mm	1.3475 - 1.3575 in
Stem diameter		
Inlet	8.664 - 8.679 mm	0.3411 - 0.3417 in
Exhaust	8.651 - 8.666 mm	0.3406 - 0.3412 in
Stem to guide clearance		
Inlet	0.025 - 0.066 mm	0.0010 - 0.0026 in
Exhaust	0.038 - 0.078 mm	0.0015 - 0.0031 in
Valve lift (inlet and exhaust)	9.94 mm	0.3913 in
Valve spring length fitted		
Up to 99MY	40.40 mm (1.59 in) at pressure of 29.5 kg (65 lb)	
From 99MY	40.93 mm (1.61 in) at pressure of 29.5 kg (65 lb)	

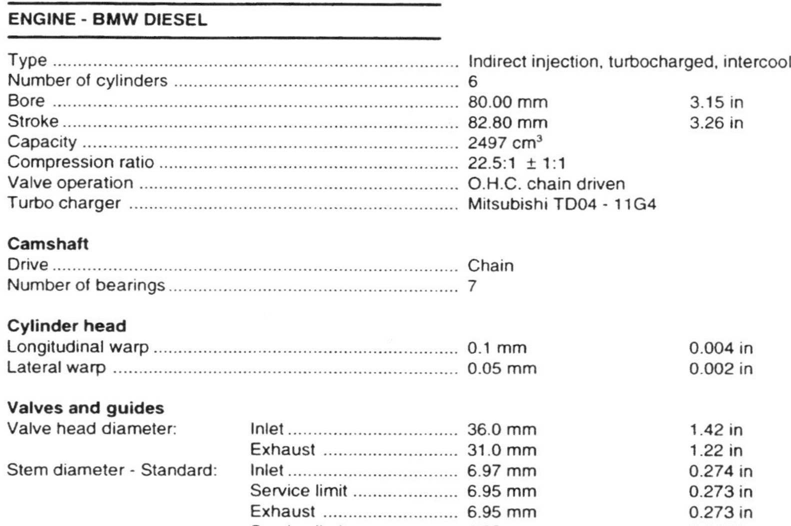

Lubrication

System type	Wet sump, pressure fed
Oil pump type	Crank driven rotor
Oil pressure	
Up to 99MY	2.06 to 2.7 bar (30 to 40 lbf/in^2) at 2400 rev/min with engine warm
From 99MY	3.45 bar (50 lbf/in^2) at 2000 rev/min with engine warm
Oil filter-internal	Wire screen, pump intake filter in sump
Oil filter-external	Full flow, self-contained cartridge

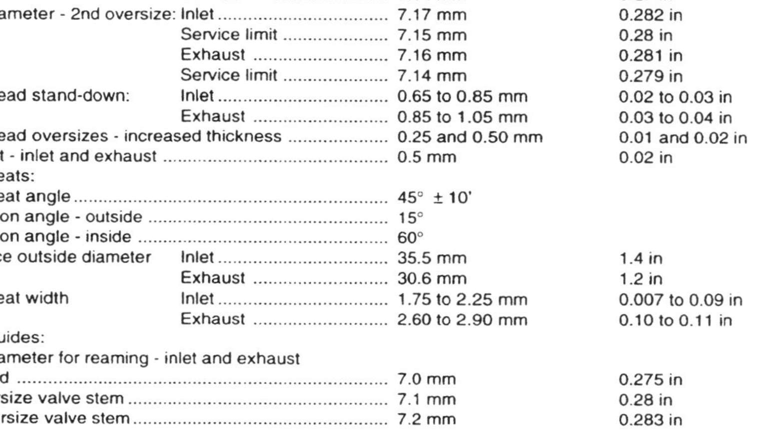

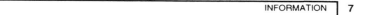

ENGINE - BMW DIESEL

Type		Indirect injection, turbocharged, intercooled	
Number of cylinders		6	
Bore		80.00 mm	3.15 in
Stroke		82.80 mm	3.26 in
Capacity		2497 cm^3	
Compression ratio		22.5:1 ± 1:1	
Valve operation		O.H.C. chain driven	
Turbo charger		Mitsubishi TD04 - 11G4	
Camshaft			
Drive		Chain	
Number of bearings		7	
Cylinder head			
Longitudinal warp		0.1 mm	0.004 in
Lateral warp		0.05 mm	0.002 in
Valves and guides			
Valve head diameter:	Inlet	36.0 mm	1.42 in
	Exhaust	31.0 mm	1.22 in
Stem diameter - Standard:	Inlet	6.97 mm	0.274 in
	Service limit	6.95 mm	0.273 in
	Exhaust	6.95 mm	0.273 in
	Service limit	6.93 mm	0.272 in
Stem diameter - 1st oversize:	Inlet	7.07 mm	0.28 in
	Service limit	7.05 mm	0.277 in
	Exhaust	7.06 mm	0.278 in
	Service limit	7.04 mm	0.27 in
Stem diameter - 2nd oversize:	Inlet	7.17 mm	0.282 in
	Service limit	7.15 mm	0.28 in
	Exhaust	7.16 mm	0.281 in
	Service limit	7.14 mm	0.279 in
Valve head stand-down:	Inlet	0.65 to 0.85 mm	0.02 to 0.03 in
	Exhaust	0.85 to 1.05 mm	0.03 to 0.04 in
Valve head oversizes - increased thickness		0.25 and 0.50 mm	0.01 and 0.02 in
Valve tilt - inlet and exhaust		0.5 mm	0.02 in
Valve seats:			
Valve seat angle		45° ± 10'	
Correction angle - outside		15°	
Correction angle - inside		60°	
Seat face outside diameter	Inlet	35.5 mm	1.4 in
	Exhaust	30.6 mm	1.2 in
Valve seat width	Inlet	1.75 to 2.25 mm	0.007 to 0.09 in
	Exhaust	2.60 to 2.90 mm	0.10 to 0.11 in
Valve guides:			
Inner diameter for reaming - inlet and exhaust			
Standard		7.0 mm	0.275 in
1st oversize valve stem		7.1 mm	0.28 in
2nd oversize valve stem		7.2 mm	0.283 in

Crankshaft

Main bearing bearing journal diameter		
Yellow	59.984 to 59.990 mm	2.3616 to 2.3618 in
Green	59.977 to 59.983 mm	2.3612 to 2.3615 in
White	59.971 to 59.976 mm	2.3610 to 2.3611 in
Oversize bearings	0.25 and 0.50 mm	0.01 and 0.02 in
Big-end journal diameter:		
Standard	44.975 to 45.00 mm	1.770 to 1.771 in
1st undersize - Size 1 - 0.25 mm (0.01 in)	44.725 to 44.75 mm	1.761 to 1.762 in
2nd undersize - Size 2 - 0.50 mm (0.02 in)	44.475 to 44.50 mm	1.751 to 1.752 in
Oversize bearings	0.25 and 0.50 mm	0.01 and 0.02 in
Crankshaft end float	0.080 to 0.163 mm	0.003 to 0.006 in

Main bearings

Number and type	7 halved shells with oil grooves	
Diametrical clearance	0.020 to 0.058 mm	0.001 to 0.002 in

Connecting rods

Diametrical clearance (big-end bearings)	0.010 to 0.055 mm	0.0004 to 0.002 in
Gudgeon pin bush bore	28.995 to 29.021 mm	1.142 to 1.143 in
Maximum deviation of connecting rod parallelism	0.05 mm	0.002 in
Maximum distortion	0.5 mm	0.02 in

Pistons

Type	Aluminium alloy, combustion chamber in crown	
Piston diameter measured 7 mm (0.27 in) from lower edge and at right angles to gudgeon pin	79.96 mm ± 0.009	3.14 ± 0.004 in
Intermediate size	80.04 mm ± 0.009	3.15 ± 0.004 in
Oversize 1	80.21 ± 0.009	3.16 ± 0.004 in
Piston running clearance	0.031 to 0.63 mm	0.0012 to 0.002 in

Piston rings

Type:		
Top	Double keystone	
Second	Taper faced	
Oil control	Bevelled ring with spring	
Gap in bore:		
All	0.2 to 0.4 mm	0.008 to 0.020 in
Clearance in piston grooves:		
Top	Not measured	
Second	0.040 to 0.072 mm	0.002 to 0.004 in
Oil control	0.030 to 0.065 mm	0.001 to 0.003 in

Cylinder bores

Standard	80.00 to 80.04 mm	3.150 to 3.151 in
Intermediate	80.08 to 80.12 mm	3.153 to 3.154 in
1st oversize	80.25 to 80.29 mm	3.20 to 3.21 in
Maximum ovality	0.04 mm	0.002 in
Maximum taper	0.04 mm	0.002 in

Lubrication

System	Wet sump, pressure fed	
Oil pressure, at idle	2.0 bar	29.0 lbf/in²
Regulated pressure	3.8 bar	55.0 lbf/in²
Oil pump:		
Type	Internal gear type pump, mounted on front of engine	
Drive	Direct from crankshaft	
Radial clearance:		
Inner rotor/bearing sleeve	0.065 mm	0.003 in max.
Outer rotor/pump body	0.4 mm	0.02 in max.
Axial clearance:		
Inner rotor/pump body	0.065 mm	0.003 in
Outer rotor/pump body	0.070 mm	0.004 in
Oil pressure relief valve	piston operated, non-adjustable	
Relief valve spring:		
Length relaxed	84.10 mm	3.3 in
Oil filter	Disposable cartridge	
Engine oil cooler	Mounted on front of coolant radiator	

ENGINE MANAGEMENT SYSTEM (EMS) V8 ENGINE

Type
- Up to 99MY .... Sagem - Lucas Gems 8 hot wire system, electronically controlled
- From 99MY .... Bosch Motronic M5.2.1, electronically controlled

Fuel pump .... High pressure electrical, immersed in the fuel tank

Fuel pump delivery pressure
- Up to 99MY .... 2.4-2.6 bar   34-37 lbf/in^2
- From 99MY .... 3.5 bar   50.75 lbf/in^2

Fuel filter .... Bosch in-line filter 'canister' type

Mass airflow sensor
Make and type
- Up to 99MY .... Lucas 'Hot Wire' 20AM
- From 99MY .... Bosch EH1174 (includes air intake temperature sensor)

Injectors
Make and type
- Up to 99MY .... Lucas D1000
- From 99MY .... Bosch EV6C

Electronic Control Module
Make and type
- Up to 99MY .... Lucas GEMS 8.2
- From 99MY .... Bosch M5.2.1

Fuel pressure regulator
Make and type
- Up to 99MY .... Lucas 8RV
- From 99MY .... Rochester (part of fuel pump)

Coolant temperature sensor
Make and type .... Lucas 8TT

Bypass air valve (Stepper motor)
Make and type
- Up to 99MY .... Lucas 3ACM
- From 99MY .... Bosch

Throttle position sensor
Make and type
- Up to 99MY .... Lucas 3TP
- From 99MY .... Bosch DKG1

Heated oxygen sensor - catalyst vehicles
Make and type
- Up to 99MY .... Lucas 4LS
- From 99MY .... Bosch LSH

Camshaft position sensor
Make and Land Rover part no.
- Up to 99MY .... Honeywell ERR2261
- From 99MY .... Lucas ERR6170

Crankshaft position sensor
Make and type
- Up to 99MY .... Lucas 4CS
- From 99MY .... Bosch DG6

Knock sensor
Make and type
- Up to 99MY .... Lucas 2KS
- From 99MY .... Bosch KS1S

Intake air temperature sensor
Make and type
- Up to 99MY .... Lucas 10TT
- From 99MY .... Not applicable (combined with MAF sensor)

Ignition coils
Make and type
- Up to 99MY .... Lucas 2DIS2
- From 99MY .... Bosch 0 221 503 407

Fuel temperature sensor
Make and type
- Up to 99MY .... Lucas 6TT
- From 99MY .... Not applicable

FUEL SYSTEM - BMW DIESEL ENGINE

Injection pump type	Bosch rotary R515
Injection pump timing	0.95 mm ± 0.02 lift at T.D.C
Injectors	***See ENGINE TUNING DATA, Information.***
Heater plugs	***See ENGINE TUNING DATA, Information.***
Fuel lift pump type	Electric in tank fuel pump
Fuel filter	Paper element type
Air cleaner	Paper element type
Turbocharger	Mitsubishi TD04 11G4

COOLING SYSTEM - V8 ENGINE

System type	Pressurized, spill return, thermostatically controlled water and anti freeze mixture. Vertical flow radiator with remote header tank and pump assisted.	
Cooling fan	9 blade axial flow. Viscous coupling.	
Pump type	Centrifugal, impeller, belt driven.	
Thermostat opening		
Up to 99MY	88 °C	190 °F
From 99MY	85 ± 5 °C	185 ± 9 °F
Expansion tank cap pressure (system pressure)	1.0 bar	15 lbf/in²

COOLING SYSTEM - BMW DIESEL ENGINE

System type	Pressurized, spill return, thermostatically controlled water and anti freeze mixture. Pump assisted thermo syphon. Coolant radiator combined with oil cooler and turbo intercooler.	
Cooling fan	11 blade axial flow 433 mm diameter. 1.44:1 drive ratio. Viscous coupling.	
Pump type	Centrifugal, impeller, belt driven.	
Thermostat opening	80 °C	176 °F
Expansion tank cap pressure (system pressure)	1.0 bar	15 lbf/in²

MANUAL TRANSMISSION

Clutch

Make and type - V8 engine	AP Borg and Beck, diaphragm spring
Clutch plate diameter	265 mm (10,43 in.)
Make and type - Diesel engine	Valeo, diaphragm spring
Clutch plate diameter	242 mm (9.53 in.)

Transfer gearbox

Borg Warner	Two speed reduction on main gearbox output, front and rear drive permanently engaged via a centre differential controlled by a Viscous unit giving a 50/50 nominal front and rear torque split.

Transfer gearbox ratios

High	1.216:1
Low	3.271:1

Manual gearbox

Type R380	5 speed, single helical constant mesh with synchromesh on all gears

Manual gearbox ratios:

5th	0.731:1
4th	1.000:1
3rd	1.397:1
2nd	2.132:1
1st	3.321:1
Reverse	3.429:1
Diesel models low first gear	3.692:1

Overall ratio (final drive):	**High transfer**	**Low transfer**
5th	3.15:1	8.46:1
4th	4.30:1	11.58:1
3rd	6.01:1	16.18:1
2nd	9.18:1	24.69:1
1st	14.29:1	38.45:1
Reverse	14.76:1	39.70:1
Diesel models low 1st gear	15.89:1	42.75:1

Propeller shafts

Type:	
Front	Tubular 51mm diameter
Rear	Tubular 51mm diameter
Universal joints	Open type Hooks O3EHD

Rear axle

Type	Spiral bevel
Ratio	3.54:1

Front axle

Type	Spiral bevel
Ratio	3.54:1

AUTOMATIC TRANSMISSION

Automatic gearbox

Model	
Up to 99MY	ZF4HP22
From 99MY	ZF4HP24
Type	Four speed and reverse epicyclic gears with fluid torque converter and lock up.

Transfer gearbox

Borg Warner	Two speed reduction on main gearbox output, front and rear drive permanently engaged via a centre differential controlled by a Viscous unit giving a 50/50 nominal front and rear torque split.

Transfer gearbox ratios

High	1.216:1
Low	3.271:1

Automatic gearbox ratios

4th	0.728:1
3rd	1.000:1
2nd	1.480:1
1st	2.480:1
Reverse	2.086:1

Overall ratio (final drive):	**High transfer**	**Low transfer**
4th	3.13:1	8.43:1
3rd	4.30:1	11.58:1
2nd	6.37:1	17.14:1
1st	10.67:1	28.72:1
Reverse	8.98:1	24.15:1

Propeller shafts

Type:	
Front	Tubular 51mm diameter
Rear	Tubular 51mm diameter
Universal joints	Open type Hooks O3EHD

Rear axle

Type	Spiral bevel
Ratio	3.54:1

Front axle

Type	Spiral bevel
Ratio	3.54:1

STEERING

Power steering box

Make/type	ZF type 8055, recirculating ball steering gear
Steering wheel turns, lock-to-lock	3.2

Steering pump

Make/type:	
V8 engine	ZF type 7691, vane type
Diesel engine	ZF type7681, vane type

Steering geometry

Steering wheel diameter	406.4mm (16 in.)	
Toe-out measurement	0.6 to 1.80mm (0.02 - 0.07 in.)	
Toe-out included angle	0°5' to 0°15'	
Camber angle	0°	**NOTE:**
Castor angle	4°	**Check at**
Swivel pin inclination static	8°	**kerbweight**

SUSPENSION

Type:	
Air suspension	Variable rate air springs controlled by an ECU giving 5 height profiles. Automatic self levelling. Automatic standard and low profiles. Driver selected access, low and high profiles. Lateral location of axle by Panhard rod.
Front	Fore and aft location by two radius arms. Lateral location of axle by a Panhard rod.
Rear	Fore and aft movement controlled by two trailing arms. Lateral location of axle by a Panhard rod.

SHOCK ABSORBERS

Type	Telescopic, double-acting non-adjustable

AIR CONDITIONING

System	CFC free expansion valve system
Compressor	
V8 up to 99MY	Sanden TRS105N
V8 from 99MY and diesel	Nippon Denso 10PA17

BRAKES

Front service brake
Caliper .... Lucas Colette, single sided, two piston
Operation .... Power hydraulic, self-adjusting
Disc .... Reverse ventilated, outboard
Disc diameter .... 297.2 mm (11.7 in.)
Disc thickness .... 25 mm (1 in.)
Wear limit .... 22.0 mm (0.87 in.)
Disc run out maximum .... 0.15 mm (0.006 in)
Pad area .... 64.9 cm^2 (10 in^2) per pad
Total swept area .... 844 cm^2 (130.8 in^2) per disc
Pad minimum thickness .... 2 mm (0.08 in.)

Rear service brake
Caliper .... Lucas Colette,single sided, single piston
Operation .... Power hydraulic, self-adjusting
Disc .... Solid, outboard
Disc diameter .... 304.0 mm (12 in.)
Disc thickness .... 12.6 mm (0.5 in.)
Wear limit .... 11.7 mm (0.46 in.)
Disc run out maximum .... 0.15 mm (0.006 in)
Pad area .... 34.4 cm^2 (5.33 in^2) per pad
Total swept area .... 798 cm^2 (123.7 in^2) per disc
Pad minimum thickness .... 2 mm (0.08 in.)

Parking brake
Type .... Mechanical-cable operated drum brake on the rear of the transfer gearbox output shaft
Drum internal diameter .... 254mm (10 in.)
Width .... 70mm (2.75 in)

Anti-lock brake system
Manufacturer/type .... Wabco/power hydraulic - 4 channel, 4 wheel sensed integrated anti-lock brake system.
ABS control .... Microprocessor based ECU
System split .... Front/rear
Power source .... Electrically driven pump
Power storage .... Hydraulic accumulator
Maximum boost pressure .... 180 bar
Reservoir .... Built in low fluid warning. Supplies clutch hydraulic system

Electronic traction control
Type .... Integrated with ABS system
ETC control .... Integrated with ABS ECU

ELECTRICAL

System .... 12 volt, negative ground

Battery
Make: .... Land Rover Parts and Equipment maintenance free
Type:
V8 .... 072, 72 amp/hr
Diesel .... 664, 107 amp/hr

Alternator
Make and type
V8 up to 99MY and diesel .... Magnetti Marelli A133, 100A, 105A or 120A
V8 from 99MY .... Bosch NC90/150, 150A

Fuses
Type .... Autofuse (blade type) blow ratings to suit individual circuits

Horns
Make/type .... Klamix (Mixo) TR99

Starter motor
Make and type:
V8 Engine .... Bosch 331.303.006.808 pre-engaged
Diesel Engine .... Bosch 0.001.362.092 pre-engaged

REPLACEMENT BULBS

BULB LOCATION	TYPE
Exterior:	
Dip/main headlamps	12V - 60/55W (Halogen)
Inboard main beam headlamps	12V - 55W (Halogen)
Front fog lamps	12V - 55W H3 (Halogen)
Sidelamps	12V - 5W capless
Tail lamps	12V - 5W capless
Rear fog lamps	12V - 21W bayonet
Reverse lamps	12V - 21W bayonet
Stop lamps	12V - 21W bayonet
Direction indicator lamps	12V - 21W bayonet
Side repeater lamps	12V - 5W capless
Number plate lamps	12V - 5W capless
Interior:	
Front interior roof lamps	12V - 10W 'Festoon'
Map reading lamp	12V - 5W capless
Rear interior roof lamps	12V - 5W 'Festoon'
Map reading lamp	12V - 5W capless
Puddle lamps	12V - 3W capless
Glovebox lamp	12V - 5W 'Festoon'
Vanity mirror lamp	12V - 1.2W 'Festoon'
Rear footwell lamp	12V - 5W 'Festoon'
Load space lamp	12V - 10W 'Festoon'
Clock illumination	12V - 2W bayonet
Cigar lighter illumination	12V - 1.2W capless
Auxiliary switch illumination	12V - 0.2W capless
Auxiliary switch warning lamp	12V - 0.2W capless
Heater/air conditioning graphics illumination	12V - 1.2W capless
Instrument panel:	
Instrument panel illumination	14V - 3.4W T10 bulb/holder unit
Warning lamps	14V - 1.4W T5 bulb/holder unit
LCD background	14V - 1.4W T5 bulb/holder unit

NOTE: The correct specification Toshiba bulbs must be used in the instrument panel to ensure the correct level of illumination.

CAUTION: The fitting of new bulbs with wattages in excess of those specified will result in damage to vehicle wiring and switches.

VEHICLE WEIGHTS AND PAYLOAD

When loading a vehicle to its maximum (Gross Vehicle Weight), consideration must be taken of the vehicle kerb weight and the distribution of the payload to ensure that axle loadings do not exceed the permitted maximum values. It is the customer's responsibility to limit the vehicle's payload in an appropriate manner such that neither maximum axle loads nor Gross Vehicle Weight are exceeded.

GROSS VEHICLE WEIGHT

	Petrol Models	Diesel Models
Front Axle	1320 kg (2910 lb)	1320 kg (2910 lb)
Rear Axle	1840 kg (4056 lb)	1840 kg (4056 lb)
Total	2780 kg (6129 lb)	2780 kg (6129 lb)
Maximum Payload	603 kg (1329 lb)	596 kg (1314 lb)

EEC KERB WEIGHT AND DISTRIBUTION

	4.0 Litre Manual	4.0 Litre Automatic	4.6 Litre Automatic
EEC Kerb Weight	2090 kg (4607 lb)	2100 kg (4629 lb)	2220 kg (4894 lb)
Front Axle	1095 kg (2414 lb)	1100 kg (2425 lb)	1165 kg (2568 lb)
Rear Axle	995 kg (2193 lb)	1000 kg (2204 lb)	1055 kg (2325 lb)

	2.5 Diesel Manual	2.5 Diesel Automatic
EEC Kerb Weight	2115 kg (4662 lb)	2130 kg (4695 lb)
Front Axle	1110 kg (2447 lb)	1120 kg (2469 lb)
Rear Axle	1005 kg (2215 lb)	1010 kg (2226 lb)

NOTE: EEC KERB WEIGHT is the minimum vehicle specification plus full fuel tank and 75 kg (165lb) driver.

NOTE: GROSS VEHICLE WEIGHT is the maximum all-up weight of the vehicle including driver, passengers, and equipment. This figure is liable to vary according to legal requirements in certain countries.

NOTE: MAXIMUM ROOF RACK LOAD (including weight of rack) 75 kg (165 lb) must be included in total vehicle weight.

VEHICLE DIMENSIONS

	mm	inches
Overall length	4713	185.6
Width excluding door mirrors	1853	73.0
Width including door mirrors	2228	87.7
Overall height at standard profile	1817.5	71.6
Wheelbase	2745	108.1
Track:		
Front	1540	60.6
Rear	1530	60.2

Turning circle between kerbs .... 11.9 m (39 ft)

TYRE PRESSURES

Normal on and off-road use. All speeds and loads

	Front	Rear
bar	1.9	2.6
lbf/in^2	28	38
kgf/cm^2	2.0	2.7

NOTE: Check pressures with tyres cold

WARNING: After any off-road driving, tyres and wheels should be inspected for damage, particularly if high cruising speeds are subsequently to be used.

WHEELS AND TYRES

Wheel type and size .... Alloy 7.00J X 16 (use with 235/70 tyres)
Alloy 8.00J X 16 (use with 255/65 tyres)
Alloy 8.00J X 18 (use with 255/55 tyres)

WARNING: All vehicles are fitted with tubeless alloy road wheels as original equipment. Note that these wheels DO NOT accept inner tubes and tubed tyres MUST NOT be fitted.

Notes

05 - ENGINE TUNING DATA

CONTENTS

Page

INFORMATION

ENGINE - 4.0 V8

Type ..... 4.0 Litre V8

Firing order 1-8-4-3-6-5-7-2

Cylinder Numbers
Left bank 1-3-5-7
Right bank 2-4-6-8

No 1 Cylinder location ..... Pulley end of left bank

Spark plugs
Make and type
Up to 99MY ..... Champion RN11YCC
From 99MY ..... Champion RC11PYB4
Gap
Up to 99MY ..... 0.90 - 1.00 mm 0.035 - 0.040 in
From 99MY ..... 1.00 mm 0.040 in

Valve timing	Inlet	Exhaust
Opens	28°BTDC	66°BBDC
Closes	77°ABDC	39°ATDC

Idle speed - controlled by Engine Management System
Up to 99MY ..... 700 ± 20 rev/min
From 99MY ..... 660 rev/min

Base idle setting ..... Not adjustable (idle air control valve position checked via TestBook)

CO at idle (vehicles without heated oxygen sensors)
Up to 99MY ..... 1.0 - 2.0 %
From 99MY ..... 0.5 - 1.0 %

Calculated Load Value (CLV) - Engine fully warm, in neutral gear, with all loads off
At Idle ..... 2.8 to 3.8%
At 2500 rev/min ..... 10% ± 1%

Air mass flow at sea level - Engine fully warm, in neutral gear, with all loads off
At Idle ..... 20 kg/hr ± 3 kg\hr
At 2500 rev/min ..... 60 kg\hr ± 3 kg\hr

ENGINE - 4.6 V8

Type .... 4.6 Litre V8

Firing order 1-8-4-3-6-5-7-2

Cylinder Numbers
Left bank 1-3-5-7
Right bank 2-4-6-8

No 1 Cylinder location .... Pulley end of left bank

Spark plugs
Make and type
Up to 99MY .... Champion RN11YCC
From 99MY .... Champion RC11PYB4
Gap
Up to 99MY .... 0.90 - 1.00 mm 0.035 - 0.040 in
From 99MY .... 1.00 mm 0.040 in

Valve Timing	**Inlet**	**Exhaust**
Up to 99MY		
Opens	14°BTDC	64°BBDC
Closes	70°ABDC	20°ATDC
From 99MY		
Opens	28°BTDC	72°BBDC
Closes	64°ABDC	20°ATDC

Idle speed - controlled by Engine Management System
Up to 99MY .... 700 ± 20 rev/min
From 99MY .... 660 rev/min

Base idle setting .... Not adjustable (idle air control valve position checked via TestBook)

CO at idle (vehicles without heated oxygen sensors)
Up to 99MY .... 1.0 - 2.0 %
From 99MY .... 0.5 - 1.0 %

Calculated Load Value (CLV) - Engine fully warm, in neutral gear, with all loads off
At Idle .... 2.8 to 3.8%
At 2500 rev/min .... 10% ± 1%

Air mass flow at sea level - Engine fully warm, in neutral gear, with all loads off
At Idle .... 20 kg/hr ± 3 kg\hr
At 2500 rev/min .... 61 kg\hr ± 3 kg\hr

ENGINE - BMW DIESEL

ENGINE

Type .... 2.5 Litre turbocharged diesel, indirect injection engine with intercooler
Firing order 1-5-3-6-2-4
Injection timing at TDC, No.1 cylinder .... 0.95 ± 0.02 mm lift 0.04 ± 0.0008 in lift

Timing marks:
Valve timing .... Slot for pin in flywheel

Injection timing .... Dial gauge inserted into pump

Maximum governed speeds:
Full load (speed cut-off starts) .... 4400 rev/min
No load (flight speed) .... 4950 ± 150 rev/min
Idle speed .... 750 ± 50 rev/min

INJECTION PUMP

Make/type:
Digital Diesel Electronic Control - DDE .... Bosch rotary R515 type with electronic control of fuel and timing. Constant pressure delivery valves.

Direction of rotation .... Clockwise, viewed from drive end

INJECTORS

Make/type
Standard .... Bosch KCA 21 S 71
Nozzle type .... DN O SD 300
Opening (injection) pressure
Minimum pressure .... 140 bar 2030 lbf/in²
Maximum pressure .... 160 bar 2320 lbf/in²
Maximum pressure deviation .... 10 bar 145 lbf/in²
Needle lift sensor in no.4 injector .... Bosch KCA 21 S 76

HEATER PLUGS

Make/type .... Beru, probe type, 12 volts
Temperature after 5 seconds of operation .... 800°C
Resistance at 20 °C .... 0.4 - 0.6 Ohms

TURBOCHARGER

Make/type .... Mitsubishi/TD04 - 11G4

06 - TORQUE VALUES

CONTENTS

Description	Nm	lbf.ft
10 - MAINTENANCE		
Road wheels	108	80
Spark plugs	20	15
Air suspension air reservoir drain plug	70	52
Sump drain plug - BMW diesel		
- M12	25	18
- M22	60	44
Sump drain plug - V8 petrol up to 99MY	45	33
Sump drain plug - V8 petrol from 99MY	32	24
Manual gearbox oil drain plug	30	22
Manual gearbox oil filler/level plug	30	22
Transfer gearbox oil drain plug	30	22
Transfer gearbox oil filler/level plug	30	22
12 - ENGINE - BMW DIESEL		
Adaptor DA 102-85 to No. 1 glow plug location	20	15
Glow plug to cylinder head	20	15
Feed wires to glow plugs	4	3
* Camshaft cover bolts	15	11
+ Crankshaft pulley hub bolt:		
- Stage 1	100	74
- Stage 2 - Tighten further	60°	60°
- Stage 3 - Tighten further	60°	60°
- Stage 4 - Tighten further	30°	30°
Damper and pulley to hub bolts	23	17
Pulley to water pump bolts	10	7
Crankshaft rear oil seal to cylinder block:		
- M6 bolts	10	7
- M8 bolts	22	16
Manual gearbox harness bracket bolt	6	4
+ Propeller shaft flanges nuts and bolts	48	35
Engine mounting nuts	45	33
Manual gear lever bolts	25	18
Pipes to air conditioning compressor bolts	23	17
Pipes to air conditioning condenser	15	11
Feed hose to PAS pump union	30	22
Pipes to gearbox oil cooler	30	22
+ Flywheel to crankshaft bolts - manual gearbox	105	77
+ Drive plate to crankshaft bolts - automatic gearbox	120	88
Front cover to cylinder block bolts	10	7
Steering pump bracket to front cover / cylinder block bolts	22	16

Item	Nm	lbf.ft
+ * Cylinder head bolts:		
- Stage 1 - Tighten to	80	59
- Stage 2 - Slacken	180°	180°
- Stage 3 - Tighten to	50	37
- Stage 4 - Tighten further	90°	90°
- Stage 5 - Tighten further	90°	90°
- Stage 6 - Run engine	25 mins	25 mins
- Stage 7 - Allow to cool	-	-
- Stage 8 - Tighten further	90°	90°
Cylinder head to timing cover nut and bolts:		
- M6	10	7
- M7	15	11
- M8	20	15
Camshaft cover blanking plate bolts	22	16
Drive belt tensioner plug	20	15
+ Camshaft sprocket bolt:		
- Stage 1 - Tighten to	20	15
- Stage 2 - Tighten further	35°	35°
Turbocharger to exhaust manifold bolts	45	33
Pipes to engine oil cooler	30	22
Oil filter bolt	33	24
Oil filter head to cylinder block bolts	22	16
Oil pump bolts	22	16
Oil pick-up strainer bolts	10	7
Oil pressure switch	40	30
Oil sump to cylinder block bolts:		
- M6 8.8	10	7
- M6 10.9	12	9
- M8	20	15
Oil pump cover screws	20	15
Oil sump drain plug:		
- M12	25	18
- M22	60	44
Fuel injection pump sprocket nut	50	37
Timing chain tensioner access plug	40	30
Camshaft bearing cap nuts:		
- M6	10	7
- M7	15	11
- M8	20	15
+*Main bearing cap bolts:		
- Stage 1	20	15
- Stage 2 - Tighten further	50°	50°
Oil cooling jets	12	9
+ Reinforcing plate bolts:		
- M8	22	16
- M10	43	32

Item	Nm	lbf.ft
Cylinder block coolant drain plug	25	18
+*Big-end bearing cap bolts:		
- Stage 1	5	4
- Stage 2	20	15
- Stage 3 - Tighten further	70°	70°

+ New nuts/bolts must be fitted
* Tighten in sequence

12 - ENGINE - V8 PETROL

Item	Nm	lbf.ft
Alternator mounting bracket to engine bolts	40	30
Camshaft drive gear bolt	50	37
Coolant rail to inlet manifold bolt	22	16
Crankshaft pulley bolt	270	200
Water pump pulley bolts	22	16
Hub aligner to crankshaft Allen screws		
- automatic gearbox	85	63
Drive plate clamp ring bolts - automatic gearbox	45	33
Flywheel to crankshaft bolts - manual gearbox	80	59
Manual gearbox harness bracket bolt	6	4
+ Propeller shaft flanges nuts and bolts	48	35
Engine mounting nuts	45	33
Manual gear lever bolts	25	18
Pipes to air conditioning compressor bolts	23	17
Pipes to air conditioning condenser	15	11
Feed hose to PAS pump union	16	12
Pipes to engine oil cooler	30	22
Gearbox cooler pipes to LH engine mounting bracket bolt	18	13
Pipes to gearbox oil cooler	30	22
Fuel pipe to fuel rail union	16	12
Camshaft position sensor to timing cover bolt	8	6
Oil pressure switch to timing cover	15	11
Water pump to timing cover bolts	22	16
* Timing cover bolts	22	16
Camshaft position sensor multiplug bracket bolts	22	16
* Cylinder head bolts:		
- Stage 1	20	15
- Stage 2 - Tighten further	90°	90°
- Stage 3 - Tighten further	90°	90°
Oil cooler pipes to front cover	15	11
Auxiliary drive belt tensioner bolt - up to 99MY	50	37
Auxiliary drive belt tensioner bolt - from 99MY	45	33
Auxiliary drive belt idler pulley bolt	50	37
Auxiliary drive belt cover bolts	18	13
Oil filter head adaptor	13	9
Oil pick-up strainer bolts	8	6
Oil pick-up strainer to main bearing cap nut	25	18
+ Engine mounting flange nuts	45	33
Engine rear mounting to gearbox bolts	45	33

Crossmember to chassis	45	33
+ Gearbox mounting to crossmember nuts/bolts	45	33
Rear engine mounting to gearbox bolts	45	33
Rocker cover to cylinder head bolts - up to 99MY:		
Stage 1	4	3
Stage 2	8	6
Stage 3 - re-torque to:	8	6
+ Rocker cover to cylinder head bolts - from 99MY:		
Stage 1	3	2.2
Stage 2	7	5.2
* Rocker shaft to cylinder head bolts	38	28
* Oil sump to cylinder block nuts/bolts	23	17
Oil sump to bell housing bolts	45	33
Oil sump drain plug - up to 99MY	45	33
Oil sump drain plug - from 99MY	32	24

+ New nuts/bolts must be fitted
* Tighten in sequence

17 - EMISSION CONTROL

SAI control valve to engine manifold bracket bolts	10	7
Vacuum reservoir to mounting bracket bolt	10	7
SAI pump rubber mountings	10	7
SAI pump to mounting bracket nuts	10	7
SAI air injection pipe unions	25	18

19 - FUEL SYSTEM - BMW DIESEL

Fuel injection pump flange nuts	22	16
Rear support bolt	22	16
Fuel injection pump access hole bolt	25	18
High pressure pipes to fuel injection pump unions	20	15
High pressure pipes to injectors unions	20	15
Air suspension drier to air cleaner bolt	8	6
Engine coolant temperature sensor	18	13
Crankshaft position sensor to bracket bolt	8	6
Fuel feed pipe to fuel injection pump and filter union	14	10
Glow plugs to cylinder head	20	15
Feed wires to glow plugs nuts	4	3
+ Sprocket to fuel injection pump nut	50	37
Fuel return pipe to fuel injection pump	25	18
Adaptor to fuel filter	10	7
Fuel filter hollow bolt	14	10
Fuel injectors to cylinder head	65	48
Air intake sensor to inlet manifold	14	10
Throttle position sensor bolts	5	4
Turbocharger to exhaust manifold bolts	45	33
Oil feed pipe to turbocharger banjo bolt	25	18
Fuel feed and return pipes to tank unit	16	12

+ New nut must be fitted

19 - FUEL SYSTEM - V8 PETROL

Intake air temperature sensor to air cleaner	8	6
Air suspension drier to air cleaner bolts	8	6
Camshaft position sensor to timing cover bolt	8	6
Engine coolant temperature sensor to manifold	20	15
Crankshaft position sensor to cylinder block adaptor plate bolts	6	4
Fuel pressure regulator to fuel rail bolts	10	7
Ignition coil bracket to inlet manifold nuts	8	6
Fuel feed pipe to fuel rail union	16	12
Ram housing to inlet manifold bolts	24	18
Fuel temperature sensor to fuel rail	17	13
Heated oxygen sensor	20	15
Spark plugs to cylinder head	20	15
Fuel rail/ignition coil bracket to manifold nuts	8	6
Throttle position sensor clamp plate bolts	2	1.5
RH knock sensor to cylinder block	16	12
Fuel pressure regulator bolts	10	7
Stepper motor bolts	2	1.5
Idle air control bolts	2.3	2
Water jacket to plenum chamber bolts	13	10
Throttle linkage bracket to plenum chamber bolts	8	6
Plenum chamber to ram pipe housing bolts	24	18
Throttle potentiometer to stepper motor bolts	2	1.5
Fuel hoses to filter	20	15
Fuel feed and return pipes to tank unit	16	12
Fuel spill return pipe to tank	16	12
Fuel feed pipe to filter	20	15

26 - COOLING SYSTEM - BMW DIESEL

Radiator drain plug	6	4
Oil cooler pipes to radiator - manual gearbox	30	22
Water pump bolts	10	7
Pulley to water pump bolts	10	7
Fan to coupling bolts	10	7
Viscous coupling to water pump	40	30
Thermostat housing to front cover bolts	10	7
Coolant connecting pipe to front cover bolt	10	7

26 - COOLING SYSTEM - V8 PETROL

Radiator drain plug	6	4
Fan to coupling bolts	24	18
Fan assembly to water pump	56	41
Water pump bolts	22	16
Pulley to water pump bolts	22	16

30 - MANIFOLD AND EXHAUST SYSTEM - BMW DIESEL

* Exhaust manifold to cylinder head nuts	22	16
Turbocharger to manifold bolts	45	33
Coolant connecting pipe to front cover bolt	10	7
Front pipe to turbocharger nuts:		
- Stage 1	14	10
- Stage 2 - Slacken 2.5 turns	-	-
* Inlet manifold to cylinder head nuts	22	16
Intermediate exhaust pipe flange nuts	25	18
97MY on:		
Tail pipe flange to intermediate pipe flange nuts	25	18

* Tighten progressively working from centre outwards

30 - MANIFOLD AND EXHAUST SYSTEM - V8 PETROL

* Exhaust manifold to cylinder head bolts	55	40
Outer heat shield bolts	8	6
RH shock absorber top mounting bolt	85	63
Front exhaust pipe to manifold nuts - up to 99MY	50	37
Front exhaust pipe to manifold nuts - from 99MY	30	22
Front exhaust pipe to intermediate pipe nuts	25	18
+ Gearbox cross member to chassis nuts and bolts	45	33
+ Gearbox mounting to cross member flange nuts	45	33
* Inlet manifold to cylinder head bolts:		
Ignition coil bracket to inlet manifold nuts	8	6
Fuel feed pipe to fuel rail union	16	12
Inlet manifold to cylinder head bolts:		
- Stage 1 - Tighten gasket clamp bolts	0.7	0.5
- Stage 2 - Tighten manifold bolts	10	7
- Stage 3 - Tighten manifold bolts	50	37
- Stage 4 - Tighten gasket clamp bolts	17	12
97 MY on:		
Heated oxygen sensor to front pipe	20	15
LH to RH tail pipe clamps	65	48
Tail pipe flange to intermediate pipe flange nuts	25	18
RH tail pipe to LH tail pipe nut	65	48

+ New nuts/bolts must be fitted
* Tighten in sequence

33 - CLUTCH - BMW DIESEL

Cover to flywheel bolts:		
- M8 8.8	24	18
- M8 10.9	34	25
Clutch housing bolts:		
- M8	27	20
- M10	51	38
- M12	86	63
Slave cylinder to clutch housing bolts	45	33

33 - CLUTCH - V8 PETROL

Cover to flywheel bolts	40	30
Clutch housing bolts	40	30
Slave cylinder to clutch housing bolts	45	33

37 - MANUAL GEARBOX - R380

Bell housing extension to gearbox bolts	45	33
Clutch release bearing spigot bolts	18	13
Transfer gearbox to gearbox bolts	45	33
Gearbox to bell housing bolts	45	33
+ Propeller shafts to transfer box drive flanges nuts	48	35
Gear lever bolts	25	18
Selector remote housing to gearbox bolts	25	18
Pipes to oil cooler unions	30	22

+ New nuts must be fitted

41 - TRANSFER GEARBOX

Ratio motor to transfer gearbox bolts	10	7
+ Front and rear output shaft flanges Nyloc nut	148	109
+ Propeller shaft flanges nuts	48	35
Transfer gearbox to gearbox bolts	45	33
Gear lever bolts	25	18

+ New nuts must be fitted

44 - AUTOMATIC GEARBOX - ZF

Oil drain plug	15	11
Oil filler / level plug	30	22
Extension housing bolts	25	18
Parking pawl guide Torx screw	10	7
Breather pipes to gearbox bolts	15	11
Intermediate plate Allen plugs (M14)	40	30
Intermediate plate Allen plugs (M20)	50	37
Fluid pump to intermediate plate bolts	10	7
Oil cooler adaptors	42	30
Valve block to gearbox bolts	8	6
Lock-up solenoid valve, retaining fork Torx screw	8	6
Lock-up solenoid valve assembly to valve body Torx screws	8	6
Pressure regulator to valve body Torx screws	8	6
Fluid filter to valve block bolts	8	6
Oil pick-up tube bolt	8	6
Fluid pan to gearbox bolts	8	6
Oil filler tube to fluid pan (up to 99MY)	70	52
Snubber bar to crossmember (from 99MY)	45	33
Transfer gearbox to gearbox bolts	45	33
Gearbox to engine bolts	45	33
Fluid cooler pipe unions	22	16
Gearbox mounting assembly bolts	45	33
+ Propeller shafts to transfer box output flanges nuts	48	35
Torque converter to drive plate bolts - from 99MY	50	37

+ New nuts must be fitted

47 - PROPELLER SHAFTS

+ Front propeller shaft nuts	48	35
+ Rear propeller shaft to differential drive flange nuts	48	35
Rear propeller shaft to brake drum nuts	48	35

+ New nuts must be fitted

51 - REAR AXLE AND FINAL DRIVE

Axle to trailing arms:		
- M12 nuts and bolts	125	92
- M16 nuts and bolts - 8.8 Grade	160	118
- M16 nuts and bolts - 10.9 Grade	240	177
Trailing arms to chassis bolts	160	118
Shock absorbers to axle nuts	45	33
Panhard rod to axle bolt	200	148
+ Propeller shaft to rear axle nuts	48	35
Differential to axle case nuts	40	30
Differential drive flange:		
- Nut (to 1997.5 MY)	135	100
- Bolt (1997.5 MY onwards)	100	74
Mass damper to rear axle bolts	45	33

+ New nuts must be fitted

54 - FRONT AXLE AND FINAL DRIVE

Differential to axle case nuts	40	30
+ Propeller shaft to differential nuts	48	35
Radius arms to axle nuts and bolts	125	92
Radius arms to chassis nuts	160	118
Shock absorbers to axle nuts	45	33
Air spring securing pin retaining bolts	20	15
+ Propeller shaft to front axle nuts	48	35
Track rods to steering knuckles nuts	50	37
Panhard rod to axle bolt	200	148
Drag link to steering knuckle nut	50	37
Brake calipers to steering knuckles bolts	220	162
Mass damper to front axle bolts	45	33

+ New nuts must be fitted

57 - STEERING

Fluid pipes to PAS pump:		
- M14	30	22
- M16	50	37
Feed hose to PAS pump union:		
- BMW diesel	30	22
- V8 petrol	16	12
Track rod adjuster clamps nuts and bolts:		
- 8 mm	22	16
- 10 mm	47	35
Steering column to bulkhead bolts	25	18
Steering column to pedal box nuts and bolts	25	18
Steering column universal joints bolts	25	18
Drag link clamps nuts and bolts:		
- 8 mm	22	16
- 10 mm	47	35
Drag link to drop arm and swivel hubs nuts and bolts	50	37
Damper to drag link nut and bolt:		
- 95 & 96 MY	125	92
- 97 MY on	50	37
Damper to chassis fixing	125	92
Feed hose to steering box banjo bolt	30	22
Return hose to steering box banjo bolt	50	37
Bleed screw	4	3
Steering box to chassis nuts and bolts	125	92
Drag link to drop arm nut	50	37
PAS pump to bracket bolts	22	16
PAS pulley to pump bolts	22	16

	Nm	lbf.ft
V8 petrol:		
- PAS pump and compressor mounting bracket to engine bolts	40	30
- PAS pump to mounting bracket bolts - up to 99MY	18	13
- PAS pump to mounting bracket bolts - from 99MY	22	16
- Pulley to PAS pump bolts	25	18
Steering wheel bolt	33	24
Pad to steering wheel bolts	8	6
Track rods to steering knuckles nuts	80	59
Road wheel nuts	108	80
Composite link to axle nuts:		
- M12	125	92
- M16	160	118
Composite link to chassis nut	160	118
PAS reservoir to radiator bracket bolt	10	7
PAS pipes to steering box nut	25	18

60 - FRONT SUSPENSION

Air hose to compressor union	7	5
Compressor to air supply unit nuts	2	1.5
Air reservoir to air bracket bolts	25	18
Anti-roll bar rubber bush clamp bolts	125	92
Anti-roll bar link nuts	125	92
Compressor air inlet filter	1	0.75
Air drier to bracket	12	9
Height sensor retaining bolts:		
- 95 & 96 MY	12	9
- 97 MY on	6	4
Height sensor link to radius arm nut	8	6
Heat shield bracket/height sensor bolts	6	4
Heat shield to bracket bolts	6	4
Hub and drive shaft assembly bolts	135	100
Drive shaft nut	260	192
Panhard rod to chassis nut and bolt	200	148
Panhard rod to axle bolt	200	148
Panhard rod to axle securing bolt locking plate screw	20	15
Radius arm to chassis	160	118
Radius arm to axle nut and bolt	125	92
Shock absorber upper retaining bolt	125	92
Shock absorber lower retaining bolt	45	33
Road wheel nuts	108	80
Swivel hub upper joint to axle nut	110	81
Swivel hub lower joint to axle nut	160	118
Track and drag links to swivel hub nuts	80	59
Pressure switch to valve block	23	17
Solenoid coil to valve block screws	1.5	1
Front air spring to axle bolt	20	15
Air distribution box to body bolt	6	4
Air drier to air cleaner bolt	3	2

64 - REAR SUSPENSION

Height sensor to chassis bolts:		
- 95 & 96 MY	12	9
- 97 MY on	6	4
Hub to axle case bolts	65	48
Drive shaft nut	260	192
Panhard rod to chassis nut and bolt	200	148
Panhard rod to axle bolt	200	148
Panhard rod to axle locking plate screw	20	15
Shock absorber top mounting bolt	125	92
Shock absorber lower mounting nut	45	33
Road wheel nuts	108	80
Trailing arm to chassis nuts and bolts:		
- M12	125	92
- M16	160	118

70 - BRAKES

Parking brake shoe adjusting bolt	25	18
High pressure hose to pump banjo bolt	24	18
Pump/motor to mounting nuts	8	6
High pressure hose to booster unit banjo bolt	24	18
Booster unit to pedal box bolts	45	33
Brake pipes to booster unit unions	14	10
Front caliper to hub bolts	165	122
Flexible hose to front caliper banjo bolt	32	24
Rear caliper to hub bolts	100	74
Flexible hose to rear caliper banjo bolt	32	24
ECU to bracket bolts	6	4
Front brake disc shield bolts	8	6
Brake disc screw	25	18
Rear brake disc shield strap bolts	8	6
Rear brake disc shield bolts	8	6
Rear brake disc screw	25	18
Rear caliper bolts	100	74
Front brake pads guide pin bolt	30	22
Road wheel nuts	108	80
Rear brake pads guide pin bolts	30	22
Propeller shaft to parking brake drum bolts	48	35
PCRV valve to valance bolts	8	6
Pipes to PCRV unions	14	10
Pump motor to valance nuts	8	6
High pressure hose to pump banjo bolt	24	18
Reservoir bracket bolt	10	7

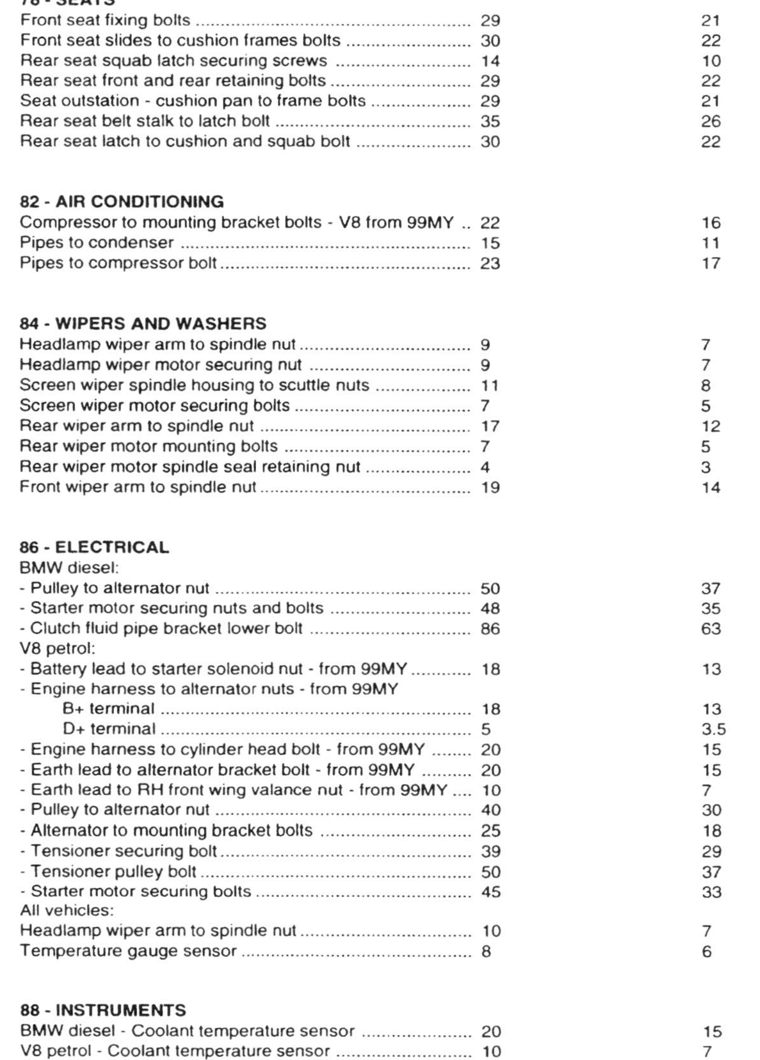

75 - SUPPLEMENTARY RESTRAINT SYSTEM

Crash sensor bolts	9	7
DCU bolts	9	7
Driver's air bag module to steering wheel bolts	9	7
Passenger's air bag module to fascia Torx screws	9	7
Side impact airbag nuts	5.5	4

76 - CHASSIS AND BODY

Front door hinge bolts	30	22
Striker bolts	22	16
Rear door hinge bolts	25	18
Chassis crossmember to chassis nuts and bolts	45	33
Gearbox mounting to crossmember nuts	45	33
Front bumper valance bolts	70	52
Rear bumper and support bracket bolts	29	22
Rear bumper valance mounting bolts	70	52
Road wheel nuts	108	80
Pedal box to fascia bolt	25	18
Fascia to base of 'A' post nuts	25	18
Fascia to scuttle panel bolts	25	18
Fascia to tunnel brackets nuts	25	18
Gear lever to gearbox remote bolts	25	18
Air conditioning pipes to TXV clamp bolt	6	4
Seat belt top mountings - 'B' and 'D' posts bolts	25	18
Front seat belt stalk bolt	35	26
Front seat belt reel bolts - up to 99MY	35	26
Front seat belt reel bolts - from 99MY	32	24
Front seat belt upper anchorage bolt - up to 99MY	25	18
Front seat belt upper anchorage bolt - from 99MY	22	16
Front seat belt to seat mounting bolt - from 99MY	32	24
Seat belt adjustable mounting to 'B' post bolts	25	18
Seat belt adjustable mounting to 'D' post bolts	25	18
Rear seat belt to seat pan bolt	35	26
Rear seat stalk to squab hinge bolt	35	26
Rear seat belt to upper anchorage point nut	25	18
Rear seat belt reel bolt	35	26
Rear seat squab to cushion bolts	45	33
Tailgate hinge bolts	25	18
Tailgate support stays to body bolt	22	16
Tailgate striker bolts	8	6
Wind deflector Torx screws	2	1.5
Sunroof guide assembly screws:		
Front	3	2.2
Rear	1.5	1.1
Sunroof motor screws	2	1.5
Sunroof cable locator screws	3	2.2
Sunroof to body bolts	6	4.5
Sunroof tilt mechanism screws	5	4
Sunroof panel nuts	5	4

78 - SEATS

Front seat fixing bolts	29	21
Front seat slides to cushion frames bolts	30	22
Rear seat squab latch securing screws	14	10
Rear seat front and rear retaining bolts	29	22
Seat outstation - cushion pan to frame bolts	29	21
Rear seat belt stalk to latch bolt	35	26
Rear seat latch to cushion and squab bolt	30	22

82 - AIR CONDITIONING

Compressor to mounting bracket bolts - V8 from 99MY	22	16
Pipes to condenser	15	11
Pipes to compressor bolt	23	17

84 - WIPERS AND WASHERS

Headlamp wiper arm to spindle nut	9	7
Headlamp wiper motor securing nut	9	7
Screen wiper spindle housing to scuttle nuts	11	8
Screen wiper motor securing bolts	7	5
Rear wiper arm to spindle nut	17	12
Rear wiper motor mounting bolts	7	5
Rear wiper motor spindle seal retaining nut	4	3
Front wiper arm to spindle nut	19	14

86 - ELECTRICAL

BMW diesel:		
- Pulley to alternator nut	50	37
- Starter motor securing nuts and bolts	48	35
- Clutch fluid pipe bracket lower bolt	86	63
V8 petrol:		
- Battery lead to starter solenoid nut - from 99MY	18	13
- Engine harness to alternator nuts - from 99MY		
B+ terminal	18	13
D+ terminal	5	3.5
- Engine harness to cylinder head bolt - from 99MY	20	15
- Earth lead to alternator bracket bolt - from 99MY	20	15
- Earth lead to RH front wing valance nut - from 99MY	10	7
- Pulley to alternator nut	40	30
- Alternator to mounting bracket bolts	25	18
- Tensioner securing bolt	39	29
- Tensioner pulley bolt	50	37
- Starter motor securing bolts	45	33
All vehicles:		
Headlamp wiper arm to spindle nut	10	7
Temperature gauge sensor	8	6

88 - INSTRUMENTS

BMW diesel - Coolant temperature sensor	20	15
V8 petrol - Coolant temperature sensor	10	7

NOTE: Torque values given below are for all screws and bolts not listed.

METRIC	**Nm**	**lbf.ft**
M5	6	4
M6	10	7
M8	25	18
M10	45	33
M12	90	66
M14	105	77
M16	180	132

UNC/UNF		
1/4	10	7
5/16	24	18
3/8	39	29
7/16	78	58
1/2	90	66
5/8	136	100

Notes

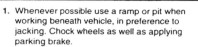

07 - GENERAL FITTING REMINDERS

CONTENTS

Page

INFORMATION

GENERAL FITTING REMINDERS

WORKSHOP SAFETY IS YOUR RESPONSIBILITY!

The suggestions, cautions and warnings in the section are intended to serve as reminders for trained and experienced mechanics. This manual is not a course in automotive mechanics or workshop safety.

Shop equipment, shop environment, and the use and disposal of solvents, fluids, and chemicals are subject to government regulations which are intended to provide a level of safety. It is your responsibility to know and comply with such regulations.

PRECAUTIONS AGAINST DAMAGE

1. Always fit covers to protect wings before commencing work in engine compartment.
2. Cover seats and carpets, wear clean overalls and wash hands or wear gloves before working inside vehicle.
3. Avoid spilling hydraulic fluid or battery acid on paint work. Wash off with water immediately if this occurs. Use Polythene sheets to protect carpets and seats.
4. Always use a recommended Service Tool, or a satisfactory equivalent, where specified.
5. Protect temporarily exposed screw threads by replacing nuts or fitting plastic caps.

SAFETY PRECAUTIONS

1. Whenever possible use a ramp or pit when working beneath vehicle, in preference to jacking. Chock wheels as well as applying parking brake.

WARNING: Do not use a pit when removing fuel system components.

2. Never rely on a jack alone to support vehicle. Use axle stands carefully placed at jacking points to provide rigid support.
3. Ensure that a suitable form of fire extinguisher is conveniently located.
4. Check that any lifting equipment used has adequate capacity and is fully serviceable.
5. Disconnect negative (grounded) terminal of vehicle battery.

WARNING: Do not disconnect any pipes in air conditioning refrigeration system, unless trained and instructed to do so. A refrigerant is used which can cause blindness if allowed to contact eyes.

6. Ensure that adequate ventilation is provided when volatile degreasing agents are being used.
7. Do not apply heat in an attempt to free stiff nuts or fittings; as well as causing damage to protective coatings, there is a risk of damage to electronic equipment and brake linings from stray heat.

PREPARATION

1. Before removing a component, clean it and its surrounding areas as thoroughly as possible.
2. Blank off any openings exposed by component removal, using greaseproof paper and masking tape.
3. Immediately seal fuel, oil or hydraulic lines when separated, using plastic caps or plugs, to prevent loss of fluid and entry of dirt.
4. Close open ends of oilways, exposed by component removal, with tapered hardwood plugs or readily visible plastic plugs.
5. Immediately a component is removed, place it in a suitable container; use a separate container for each component and its associated parts.
6. Before dismantling a component, clean it thoroughly with a recommended cleaning agent; check that agent is suitable for all materials of component.
7. Clean bench and provide marking materials, labels, containers and locking wire before dismantling a component.

DISMANTLING

1. Observe scrupulous cleanliness when dismantling components, particularly when brake, fuel or hydraulic system parts are being worked on. A particle of dirt or a cloth fragment could cause a dangerous malfunction if trapped in these systems.
2. Blow out all tapped holes, crevices, oilways and fluid passages with an air line. Ensure that any O-rings used for sealing are correctly replaced or renewed, if disturbed.
3. Use marking ink to identify mating parts, to ensure correct reassembly. If a centre punch or scriber is used they may initiate cracks or distortion of components.
4. Wire together mating parts where necessary to prevent accidental interchange (e.g. roller bearing components).
5. Wire labels on to all parts which are to be renewed, and to parts requiring further inspection before being passed for reassembly; place these parts in separate containers from those containing parts for rebuild.
6. Do not discard a part due for renewal until after comparing it with a new part, to ensure that its correct replacement has been obtained.

INSPECTION-GENERAL

1. Never inspect a component for wear or dimensional check unless it is absolutely clean; a slight smear of grease can conceal an incipient failure.
2. When a component is to be checked dimensionally against figures quoted for it, use correct equipment (surface plates, micrometers, dial gauges, etc.) in serviceable condition. Makeshift checking equipment can be dangerous.
3. Reject a component if its dimensions are outside limits quoted, or if damage is apparent. A part may, however, be refitted if its critical dimension is exactly limit size, and is otherwise satisfactory.
4. Use 'Plastigauge' 12 Type PG-1 for checking bearing surface clearances. Directions for its use, and a scale giving bearing clearances in 0,0025 mm steps are provided with it.

BALL AND ROLLER BEARINGS

CAUTION: Never refit a ball or roller bearing without first ensuring that it is in a fully serviceable condition.

1. Remove all traces of lubricant from bearing under inspection by washing in a suitable degreaser; maintain absolute cleanliness throughout operations.
2. Inspect visually for markings of any form on rolling elements, raceways, outer surface of outer rings or inner surface of inner rings. Reject any bearings found to be marked, since any marking in these areas indicates onset of wear.
3. Holding inner race between finger and thumb of one hand, spin outer race and check that it revolves absolutely smoothly. Repeat, holding outer race and spinning inner race.
4. Rotate outer ring gently with a reciprocating motion, while holding inner ring; feel for any check or obstruction to rotation, and reject bearing if action is not perfectly smooth.
5. Lubricate bearing generously with lubricant appropriate to installation.
6. Inspect shaft and bearing housing for discoloration or other marking suggesting that movement has taken place between bearing and seatings. (This is particularly to be expected if related markings were found in operation 2).
7. Ensure that shaft and housing are clean and free from burrs before fitting bearing.
8. If one bearing assembly of a pair shows an imperfection it is generally advisable to replace both with new bearings; an exception could be made if the faulty bearing had covered a low mileage, and it could be established that damage was confined to it only.
9. When fitting bearing to shaft, apply force only to inner ring of bearing, and only to outer ring when fitting into housing. (Refer to ST1042M).

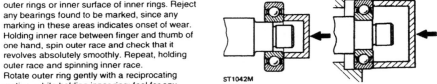

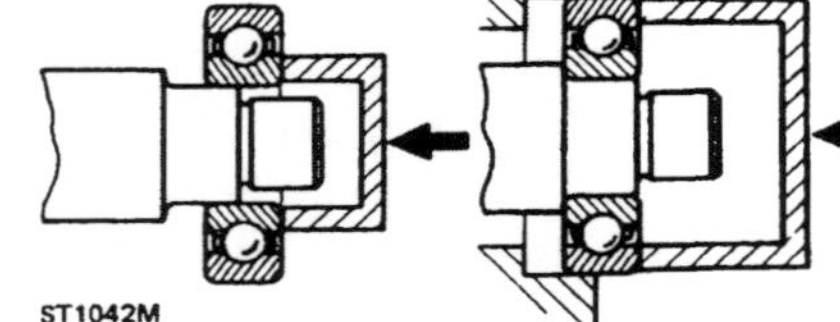
ST1042M

10. In the case of grease lubricated bearings (e.g. hub bearings) fill space between bearing and outer seal with recommended grade of grease before fitting seal.
11. Always mark components of separable bearings (e.g. taper roller bearings) when dismantling, to ensure correct reassembly. Never fit new rollers in a used outer ring, always fit a complete new bearing assembly.

OIL SEALS

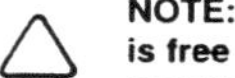

NOTE: Ensure that the seal running track is free from pits, scores, corrosion and general damage prior to fitting replacement seal.

1. Always fit new oil seals when rebuilding an assembly.
2. Carefully examine seal before fitting to ensure that it is clean and undamaged.
3. Coat the sealing lips with clean grease; pack dust excluder seals with grease, and heavily grease duplex seals in cavity between sealing lips.
4. Ensure that seal spring, if provided, is correctly fitted.
5. Place lip of seal towards fluid to be sealed and slide into position on shaft, using fitting sleeve when possible to protect sealing lip from damage by sharp corners, threads or splines. If fitting sleeve is not available, use plastic tube or tape to prevent damage to sealing lip.

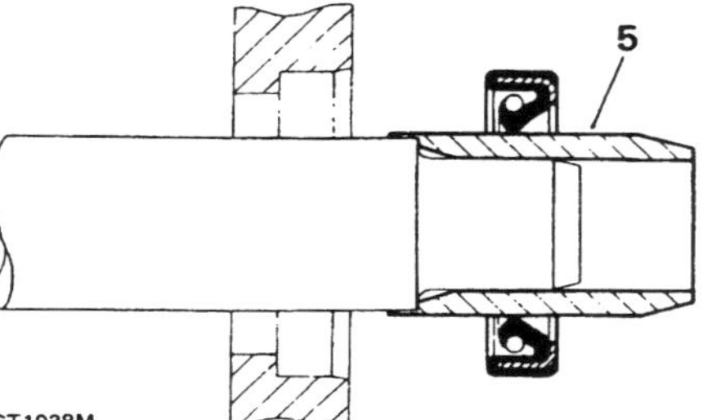

ST1038M

6. Grease outside diameter of seal, place square to housing recess and press into position, using great care and if possible a 'bell piece' to ensure that seal is not tilted. (In some cases it may be preferable to fit seal to housing before fitting to shaft). Never let weight of unsupported shaft rest in seal.

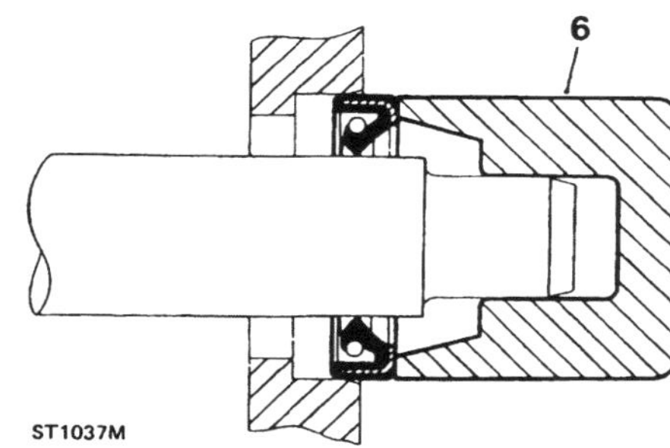

ST1037M

7. If correct service tool is not available, use a suitable drift approximately 0.4mm (0.015 in) smaller than outside diameter of seal. Use a hammer **VERY GENTLY** on drift if a suitable press is not available.
8. Press or drift seal in to depth of housing if housing is shouldered, or flush with face of housing where no shoulder is provided. Ensure that the seal does not enter the housing in a tilted position.

NOTE: Most cases of failure or leakage of oil seals are due to careless fitting, and resulting damage to both seals and sealing surfaces. Care in fitting is essential if good results are to be obtained. NEVER use a seal which has been improperly stored or handled, such as hung on a hook or nail.

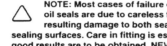

JOINTS AND JOINT FACES

1. Always use correct gaskets where they are specified.
2. Use jointing compound only when recommended. Otherwise fit joints dry.
3. When jointing compound is used, apply in a thin uniform film to metal surfaces; take great care to prevent it from entering oilways, pipes or blind tapped holes.
4. Remove all traces of old jointing materials prior to reassembly. Do not use a tool which could damage joint faces.
5. Inspect joint faces for scratches or burrs and remove with a fine file or oil stone; do not allow removed material or dirt to enter tapped holes or enclosed parts.
6. Blow out any pipes, channels or crevices with compressed air, fit new 'O' rings or seals displaced by air blast.

FLEXIBLE HYDRAULIC PIPES, HOSES

1. Before removing any brake or power steering hose, clean end fittings and area surrounding them as thoroughly as possible.
2. Obtain appropriate plugs or caps before detaching hose end fittings, so that ports can be immediately covered to exclude dirt.
3. Clean hose externally and blow through with airline. Examine carefully for cracks, separation of plies, security of end fittings and external damage. Reject any hose found faulty.
4. When refitting hose, ensure that no unnecessary bends are introduced, and that hose is not twisted before or during tightening of union nuts.
5. Containers for hydraulic fluid must be kept absolutely clean.
6. Do not store brake fluid in an unsealed container. It will absorb water, and fluid in this condition would be dangerous to use due to a lowering of its boiling point.
7. Do not allow brake fluid to be contaminated with mineral oil, or use a container which has previously contained mineral oil.
8. Do not re-use brake fluid bled from system.
9. Always use clean brake fluid to clean hydraulic components.
10. Fit a cap to seal a hydraulic union and a plug to its socket after removal to prevent ingress of dirt.
11. Absolute cleanliness must be observed with hydraulic components at all times.
12. After any work on hydraulic systems, inspect carefully for leaks underneath the vehicle while a second operator applies maximum pressure to the brakes (engine running) and operates the steering.

FUEL SYSTEM HOSES

CAUTION: All fuel hoses are made up of two laminations, an armoured rubber outer sleeve and an inner viton core. If any of the fuel system hoses have been disconnected, it is imperative that the internal bore is inspected to ensure that the viton lining has not become separated from the amoured outer sleeve. A new hose must be fitted if separation is evident.

RR2302M

COOLING SYSTEM HOSES

CAUTION: The following precautions MUST be followed to ensure that integrity of cooling hoses and their connections to system components are maintained.

Hose orientation and connection

1. Correct orientation of cooling hoses is important in ensuring that the hose does not become fatigued or damaged through contact with adjacent components.
2. Where 'timing' marks are provided on the hose and corresponding connection, these must be used to ensure correct orientation.
3. Hoses must be pushed fully onto their connection points. Usually, a moulded form on the stub pipe provides a positive indicator.

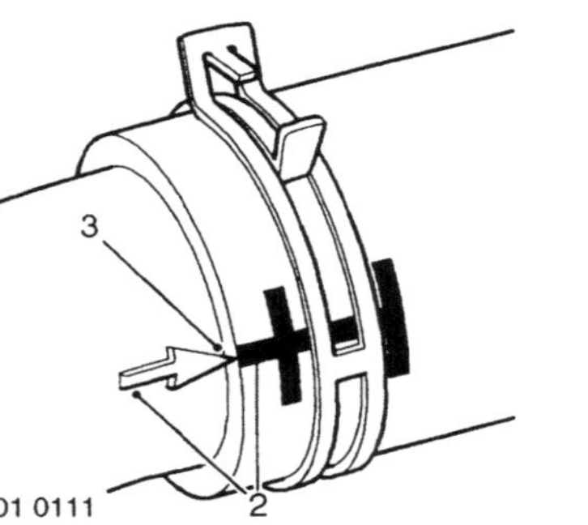

M01 0111

Hose clips

4. Markings are usually provided on the hose to indicate the the correct clip position. If no markings are provided, position the clip directly behind the retaining lip at the end of the stub as shown.
5. Worm drive clips should be oriented with the crimped side of the drive housing facing towards the end of the hose, or the hose may become pinched between the clip and the stub pipe retaining lip.

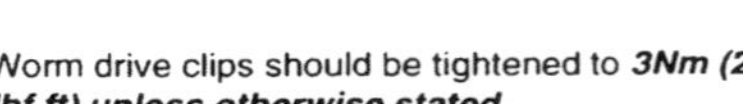

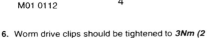

M01 0112

6. Worm drive clips should be tightened to ***3Nm (2 lbf.ft) unless otherwise stated.***

CAUTION: Ensure that hose clips do not foul adjacent components.

Heat protection

7. Always ensure that heatshields and protective sheathing are in good condition. Replace if damage is evident.
8. Particular care must be taken when routing hoses close to hot engine components, such as the exhaust manifold and the Exhaust Gas Recirculation (EGR) pipe.

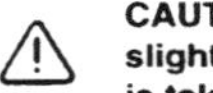

CAUTION: Hoses will relax and deflect slightly when hot; ensure this movement is taken into account when routing and securing hoses.

METRIC BOLT IDENTIFICATION

1. An ISO metric bolt or screw, made of steel and larger than 6 mm in diameter can be identified by either of the symbols ISO M or M embossed or indented on top of the head.
2. In addition to marks to identify the manufacture, the head is also marked with symbols to indicate the strength grade, e.g. 8.8, 12.9 or 14.9, where the first figure gives the minimum tensile strength of the bolt material in tens of kgf/mm^2.
3. Zinc plated ISO metric bolts and nuts are chromate passivated, a gold-bronze colour.

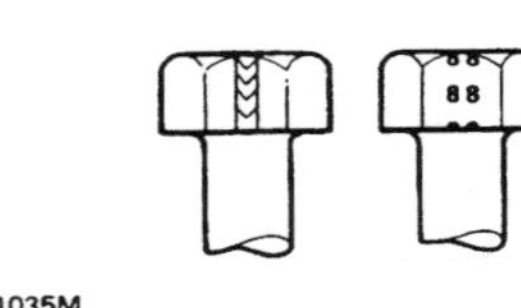

ST1035M

METRIC NUT IDENTIFICATION

1. A nut with an ISO metric thread is marked on one face or on one of the flats of the hexagon with the strength grade symbol 8, 12 or 14. Some nuts with a strength 4, 5 or 6 are also marked and some have the metric symbol M on the flat opposite the strength grade marking.
2. A clock face system is used as an alternative method of indicating the strength grade. The external chamfers or a face of the nut is marked in a position relative to the appropriate hour mark on a clock face to indicate the strength grade.
3. A dot is used to locate the 12 o'clock position and a dash to indicate the strength grade. If the grade is above 12, two dots identify the 12 o'clock position.

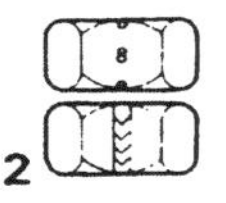
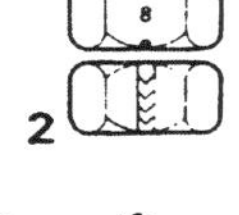

ST1036M

KEYS AND KEYWAYS

1. Remove burrs from edges of keyways with a fine file and clean thoroughly before attempting to refit key.
2. Clean and inspect key closely; keys are suitable for refitting only if indistinguishable from new, as any indentation may indicate the onset of wear.

TAB WASHERS

1. Fit new washers in all places where they are used. Always fit a new tab washer.
2. Ensure that the new tab washer is of the same design as that replaced.

SPLIT PINS

1. Fit new split pins throughout when replacing any unit.
2. Always fit split pins where cotter pins were originally used. Do not substitute spring washers: there is always a good reason for the use of a split pin.
3. All split pins should be fitted as shown unless otherwise stated.

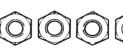

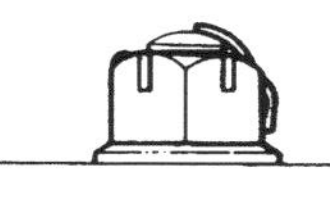

ST1030M

NUTS

1. When tightening a slotted or castellated nut never loosen it back to insert split pin or locking wire except in those recommended cases where this forms part of an adjustment. If difficulty is experienced, alternative washers or nuts should be selected, or washer thickness reduced.
2. Where self-locking nuts have been removed it is advisable to replace them with new ones of the same type.

NOTE: Where bearing pre-load is involved nuts should be tightened in accordance with special instructions.

LOCKING WIRE

1. Fit new locking wire of the correct type for all assemblies incorporating it.
2. Arrange wire so that its tension tends to tighten the bolt heads, or nuts, to which it is fitted.

SCREW THREADS

1. Both UNF and Metric threads to ISO standards are used. See below for thread identification.
2. Damaged threads must always be discarded. Cleaning up threads with a die or tap impairs the strength and closeness of fit of the threads and is not recommended.
3. Always ensure that replacement bolts are at least equal in strength to those replaced.
4. Do not allow oil, grease or jointing compound to enter blind threaded holes. The hydraulic action on screwing in the bolt or stud could split the housing.
5. Always tighten a nut or bolt to the recommended torque value. Damaged or corroded threads can affect the torque reading.
6. To check or re-tighten a bolt or screw to a specified torque value first loosen a quarter of a turn, then re-tighten to the correct value.
7. Oil thread lightly before tightening to ensure a free running thread, except in the case of threads treated with sealant/lubricant, and self-locking nuts.

UNIFIED THREAD IDENTIFICATION

1. **Bolts**
   A circular recess is stamped in the upper surface of the bolt head.
2. **Nuts**
   A continuous line of circles is indented on one of the flats of the hexagon, parallel to the axis of the nut.
3. **Studs, Brake Rods, etc.**
   The component is reduced to the core diameter for a short length at its extremity.

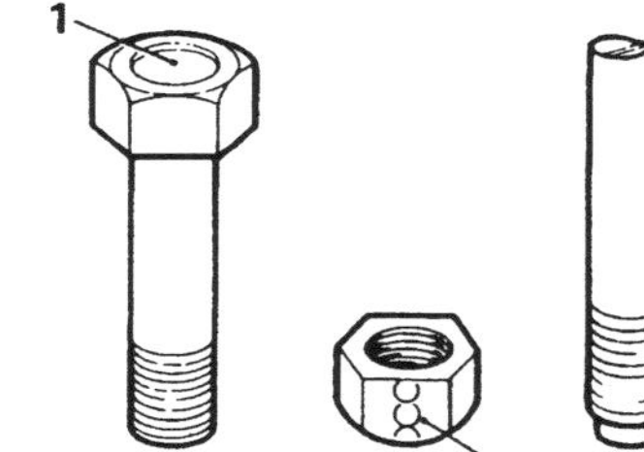

ST1039M

09 - LUBRICANTS, FLUIDS AND CAPACITIES

CONTENTS

Page

INFORMATION

RECOMMENDED LUBRICANTS AND FLUIDS - NAS VEHICLES

AMBIENT TEMPERATURE °C: -30 -20 -10 0 10 20 30 40 50

COMPONENT	SPECIFICATION	VISCOSITY
Engine	Use oils to API service level SG, SH or SJ or ILSAC GF2 or ACEA A2:96	5W/20
		5W/30
		5W/40
		5W/50
		10W/30
		10W/40 10W/50 10W/60
		15W/40 15W/50
		20W/40 20W/50
Final drive units	Texaco Multigear	75W 90R
Main Gearbox Automatic	ATF Dexron III	
Main Gearbox Manual	Texaco MTF 94	
Transfer box	ATF Dexron III	
Power steering	ATF Dexron III or Texamatic 9226	

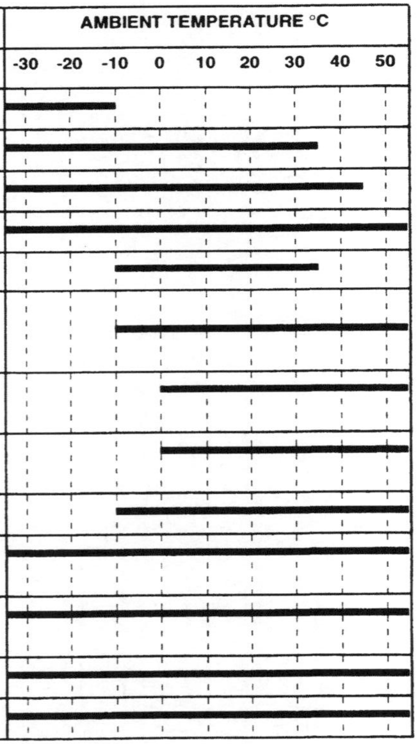

See page 3 for remaining vehicle fluids

RECOMMENDED LUBRICANTS AND FLUIDS - ALL EXCEPT NAS VEHICLES

All climates and conditions

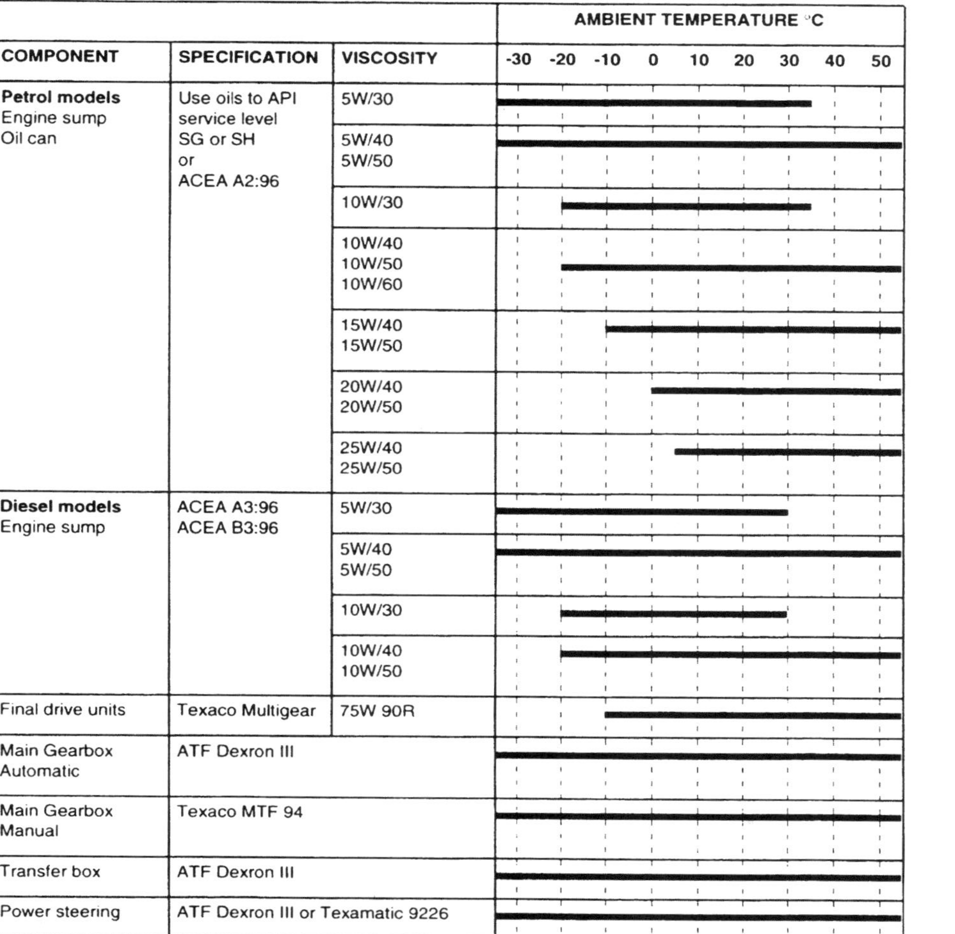

COMPONENT	SPECIFICATION	VISCOSITY	AMBIENT TEMPERATURE °C (-30 -20 -10 0 10 20 30 40 50)
Petrol models Engine sump Oil can	Use oils to API service level SG or SH or ACEA A2:96	5W/30	-30 to approx. 35
		5W/40 5W/50	-30 to 50
		10W/30	-20 to approx. 35
		10W/40 10W/50 10W/60	-20 to 50
		15W/40 15W/50	-10 to 50
		20W/40 20W/50	0 to 50
		25W/40 25W/50	approx. 5 to 50
Diesel models Engine sump	ACEA A3:96 ACEA B3:96	5W/30	-30 to 30
		5W/40 5W/50	-30 to 50
		10W/30	-20 to 30
		10W/40 10W/50	-20 to 50
Final drive units	Texaco Multigear	75W 90R	-10 to 50
Main Gearbox Automatic	ATF Dexron III		-30 to 50
Main Gearbox Manual	Texaco MTF 94		-30 to 50
Transfer box	ATF Dexron III		-30 to 50
Power steering	ATF Dexron III or Texamatic 9226		-30 to 50

Propeller shaft Front and Rear Lubrication nipples .... NLGI - 2 Multi-purpose Lithium based GREASE

Door check straps .... Rocol SM500 molygrease

Door locks .... Fuchs Renocal FN745

Brake and clutch reservoirs .... Brake fluids having a minimum boiling point of 260°C (500 °F) and complying with FMVSS 116 DOT4

Engine cooling system .... Use an ethylene glycol based anti-freeze (containing no methanol) with non-phosphate corrosion inhibitors suitable for use in aluminium engines to ensure the protection of the cooling system against frost and corrosion in all seasons.

Battery lugs, earthing surfaces where paint has been removed .... Petroleum jelly.
NOTE: Do not use Silicone Grease

Air conditioning system refrigerant .... Refrigerant R134a
CAUTION: DO NOT use any other type of refrigerant.

Air conditioning compressor oil
- V8 up to 99MY .... Sanden SP10
- V8 from 99MY and diesel .... Nippon Denso ND-OIL 8

ABS sensor bush .... Silicone grease: Staborags NBU - Wabco 830 502,0634
Wacker chemie 704 - Wabco 830 502,0164
Kluber GL301

LUBRICATION PRACTICE

Use a high quality oil of the correct viscosity range and service classification in the engine during maintenance and when topping up. The use of oil not to the correct specification can lead to high oil and fuel consumption and ultimately to damaged components.

Oil to the correct specification contains additives which disperse the corrosive acids formed by combustion and prevent the formation of sludge which can block the oilways. Additional oil additives should not be used. Always adhere to the recommended servicing intervals.

WARNING: Many liquids and other substances used in motor vehicles are poisonous. They must not be consumed and must be kept away from open wounds. These substances, among others, include anti-freeze windscreen washer additives, lubricants and various adhesives.

CAPACITIES

The following capacity figures are approximate and provided as a guide only. Refer to Section 10 for correct checking procedure for powertrain oil levels.

Engine sump and filter - Petrol		
From dry	6.6 litres	14.0 US pints
Refill	5.8 litres	12.3 US pints
Engine sump and filter - Diesel		
From dry	9.5 litres	20 US pints
Refill	8.7 litres	18.4 US pints
Manual gearbox		
From dry	2.7 litres	5.7 US pints
Refill	2.2 litres	4.6 US pints
Automatic gearbox		
4.6 V8 up to '99MY	11 litres	23.2 US pints
4.0 V8 (& 4.6 V8 from '99MY)	9.7 litres	20.5 US pints
Diesel	9.7 litres	20.5 US pints
Transfer box		
From dry	2.4 litres	5.0 US pints
Refill	2.0 litres	4.2 US pints
Front axle		
From dry	1.7 litres	3.6 US pints
Refill	1.6 litres	3.4 US pints
Rear axle		
From dry	1.7 litres	3.6 US pints
Refill	1.6 litres	3.4 US pints
Power steering box and reservoir	1.7 litres	3.6 US pints
Cooling system	11.3 litres	24 US pints
Fuel tank		
Petrol	100 litres	26.4 US gallons
Diesel	90 litres	24 US gallons
Air conditioning system		
Refrigerant charge weight		
V8 up to 99MY	1250 grammes	44 oz
V8 from 99MY	1380 ± 25 grammes	49 ± 1 oz
Diesel	1100 grammes	39 oz
Refrigerant oil in system		
V8 up to 99MY	150 cm^3	0.32 US pint
V8 from 99MY	180 cm^3	0.38 US pint
Diesel	140 cm^3	0.30 US pint

ANTI-FREEZE

ENGINE TYPE	MIXTURE STRENGTH	PERCENTAGE CONCENTRATION	PROTECTION LOWER TEMPERATURE LIMIT
V8 Engine Diesel Engine	One part anti-freeze One part water	50%	
Complete protection Vehicle may be driven away immediately from cold			- 33°F - 36°C
Safe limit protection Coolant in mushy state. Engine may be started and driven away after warm-up period			- 41°C - 42°F
Lower protection Prevents frost damage to cylinder head, block and radiator. Thaw out before starting engine			- 47°C - 53°F

CAUTION: Anti-freeze content must never be allowed to fall below 25% otherwise damage to the engine is liable to occur. Also, anti-freeze content should not exceed 60% as this will greatly reduce the cooling effect of the coolant.

FUEL REQUIREMENTS

Catalyst vehicles

Vehicles equipped with catalytic converter are designed to use ONLY unleaded fuel. Unleaded fuel must be used for the emission control system to operate properly. Its use will also reduce spark plug fouling, exhaust system corrosion and engine oil deterioration.

Using fuel that contains lead will result in damage to the emission control system and could result in loss of warranty coverage. The effectiveness of the catalysts in the catalytic converters will be seriously impaired if leaded fuel is used. The vehicle is equipped with an electronic fuel injection system, which includes two oxygen sensors (4 oxygen sensors on NAS vehicles). Leaded fuel will damage the sensors, and will deteriorate the emission control system.

Regulations require that pumps delivering unleaded fuel be labelled **UNLEADED.** Only these pumps have nozzles which fit the filler neck of the vehicle fuel tank.

RECOMMENDED FUEL

Petrol engines

Use petrol conforming to European standard EN228

Low compression engines
With catalytic converter .... 91 RON minimum unleaded
Without catalytic converter
4.0 litre .... 91 RON minimum unleaded or 91 RON minimum leaded
4.6 litre .... 91 RON minimum unleaded or 91 RON minimum leaded
High compression engines .... 95 RON minimum unleaded

NOTE: It is possible to use unleaded fuel with a 91 RON minimum octane rating for high compression engines, but performance will be adversely affected.

Using fuel with an octane rating lower than stated above could seriously impair vehicle performance.

Diesel engines .... Diesel fuel to European standard EN 590; minimum Cetane No. 45

In the interests of optimum vehicle performance, the use of oxygenated fuels such as blends of methanol/gasoline or ethanol/gasoline (e.g. 'Gasohol') is not recommended. If oxygenated fuels are to be used, be aware of the following maximum limits for the percentage of fuel additive that is allowed in the relevant markets:

NAS specification:
Methyl Tertiary Butyl Ether (MTBE) 15%
Ethyl Tertiary Butyl Ether (ETBE) 15%
Ethanol (Ethyl or grain alcohol) 10%

CAUTION: Wherever possible, avoid using fuel containing Methanol

European specification (EN 228):
Methyl Tertiary Butyl Ether (MTBE) 15%
Ethyl Tertiary Butyl Ether (ETBE) 15%
Ethanol (Ethanol (Ethyl or grain alcohol) 5%
Methanol with co-solvents 3%

CAUTION: Take care not to spill fuel during refuelling.

10 - MAINTENANCE

CONTENTS

Page

MAINTENANCE

SERVICE SCHEDULE

The following section describes the items detailed in the vehicle Service Schedule. Where required, instructions are given for carrying out the service procedure, or a cross reference is given to where the procedure may be found in the manual.

Service schedule sheets are published separately to reflect the needs and intervals for each vehicle variant. Procedures given in the workshop manual must be used in conjunction with the service schedule sheets.

Service schedule sheets are available in pads from:

Land Rover Merchandising
PO Box 534
Erdington
Birmingham B24 0QS
England

VEHICLE INTERIOR

CHECK CONDITION AND SECURITY OF SEATS, SEAT BELT MOUNTINGS AND BELTS, BUCKLES AND OPERATION OF INERTIA SEAT BELTS.

CHECK CONDITION/OPERATION OF FRONT/REAR/HEADLAMP WASHERS AND WIPER BLADES.

CHECK OPERATION OF PARK BRAKE, ADJUST IF NECESSARY.

The park brake should be fully operational on third notch of ratchet. If adjustment is required. ***See BRAKES, Adjustment.***

VEHICLE EXTERIOR

CHECK/ADJUST HEADLAMP AND AUXILIARY LAMP ALIGNMENT.

REMOVE ROAD WHEELS. CHECK TYRES.

Check tyres (including spare) for compliance with manufacturers' specification. Check visually for cuts, lumps, bulges, uneven tread wear and tread depth. Check tyre pressures.

INSPECT BRAKE PADS FOR WEAR, CALIPERS FOR LEAKS AND DISCS FOR CONDITION

Fit new pads if minimum thickness is less than 3.0 mm. (1/8 in.)

For front brake pad renewal. ***See BRAKES, Repair.***

For rear brake pad renewal. ***See BRAKES, Repair.***

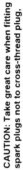

WARNING: When renewing brake pads, it is essential that only genuine components with correct grade of lining are used. Always fit new pads in axle sets, NEVER individually or as a single wheel set. Serious consequences could result from out of balance braking due to mixing of linings.

REFIT ROAD WHEELS

Fit road wheels in original hub position. Secure in position with wheel nuts, do not fully tighten wheel nuts at this stage, lower vehicle and finally tighten wheel nuts. Tighten to ***108 Nm. (80 lbf.ft)***

CAUTION: When refitting a road wheel, apply a suitable anti-seize compound such as Raworth 33/04, to the spigot bore of the wheel. This will prevent possible seizure of the wheel to the hub spigot. Ensure that no compound comes into contact with the braking components.

CHECK FRONT WHEEL ALIGNMENT

Use recognised wheel alignment equipment to perform this check. ***See STEERING, Adjustment.***

LUBRICATE DOOR LOCKS, CHECK STRAPS, BONNET CATCHES AND FUEL FLAP.

UNDER BONNET MAINTENANCE

CHECK COOLING, INTERCOOLER AND HEATER SYSTEMS FOR LEAKS, HOSES FOR SECURITY AND CONDITION. TOP UP AS NECESSARY.

CAUTION: Cooling system hoses should be changed at first signs of deterioration.

RENEW SPARK PLUGS

CAUTION: Take great care when fitting spark plugs not to cross-thread plug, otherwise costly damage to cylinder head will result. It is essential that correct type of spark plugs is fitted. Incorrect grade of plugs may lead to piston overheating and engine failure. Only use approved spark plugs, use of unapproved spark plugs may cause the misfire detection system to malfunction.

Remove

1. Disconnect battery negative lead.
2. Remove H.T. leads from spark plugs.

NOTE: Note lead connections to ensure correct re-assembly.

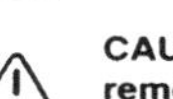

CAUTION: To avoid damage to H.T. leads, remove them by pulling the rubber boot NOT the lead.

3. Remove plugs and washers.
4. Ensure plugs are set to correct gap: 0.89 - 1.01mm (0.035 - 0.040in). ***See FUEL SYSTEM, Repair.***

NOTE: Do not attempt to clean or adjust gaps on spark plugs fitted after 99MY. If a spark plug problem exists, try substituting the defective spark plug with a new one.

5. Fit new spark plugs and washers. Tighten to ***20 Nm (15 lbf ft)***
6. Ensure H.T. leads are correctly refitted. ***See FUEL SYSTEM, Repair.***
7. Reconnect battery negative lead.

RENEW FUEL FILTER ELEMENT (DIESEL)

Renew fuel filter. ***See FUEL SYSTEM, Repair.***

DRAIN WATER FROM FUEL FILTER (DIESEL)

RENEW AIR FILTER ELEMENT AND CLEAN DRAIN HOLE (DIESEL)

RENEW AIR FILTER ELEMENT AND CLEAN DRAIN HOLE (V8)

1. Release 4 clips, lift air cleaner cover.
2. Remove air filter element.
3. Fit new element ensuring it locates correctly in air cleaner body.

RENEW POLLEN FILTERS

Renew pollen filters. ***See HEATING AND VENTILATION, Repair.***

RENEW CHARCOAL CANISTER, CHECK EVAPORATIVE LOSS SYSTEM AND FILLER CAP SEAL (V8)

Renew charcoal canister. ***See EMISSION CONTROL, Repair.***

CHECK CONDITION OF ANCILLARY DRIVE BELT/S (poly V)

Renew drive belts if damaged.

RENEW ANCILLARY DRIVE BELT (POLY V)

Alternator Drive Belt - Renew. ***See ELECTRICAL, Repair.***

CHECK/TOP UP AUTOMATIC TRANSMISSION FLUID - up to 99MY

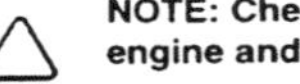

CAUTION: When replacing the dipstick, ensure that the handle lugs fully engage with tube.

NOTE: Check the fluid level only when the engine and gearbox are cold.

1. Ensure vehicle is level, then select 'P' (park) and start the engine.
2. With the engine running at idle speed and both footbrake and hand brake applied, move the selector lever to position '1' and then back to position 'P'.
3. Still with the engine running remove dipstick, wipe using lint free cloth.
4. Reinsert the dipstick fully and withdraw again to check the level.

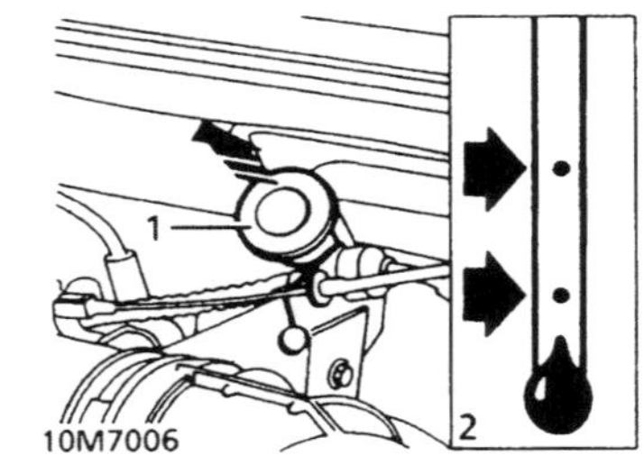

5. Check fluid level registers between MAX and MIN marking on dipstick. For fluid recommendations. ***See LUBRICANTS, FLUIDS AND CAPACITIES, Information.***

CHECK/TOP UP AUTOMATIC TRANSMISSION FLUID - from 99MY

1. Refer to gearbox drain and refil procedure. ***See AUTOMATIC GEARBOX, Repair.***

CHECK/TOP UP POWER STEERING FLUID RESERVOIR

NOTE: Power steering fluid level is checked when fluid is cold with engine switched off.

1. Clean filler cap.
2. Remove dipstick, wipe using lint free cloth.

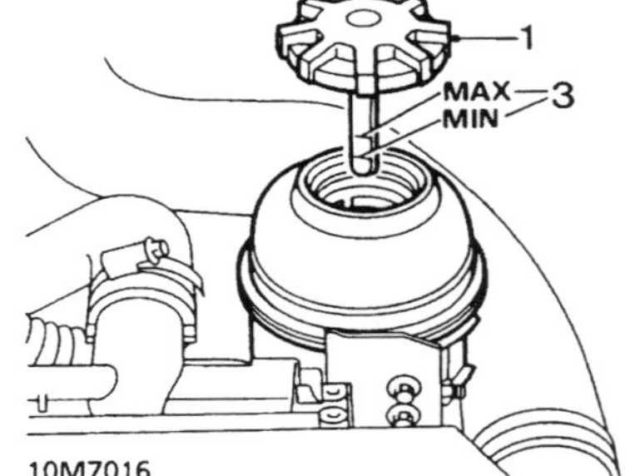

3. Fit cap fully, remove cap, check fluid level registers between the two markings on the dipstick. For fluid recommendations. ***See LUBRICANTS, FLUIDS AND CAPACITIES, Information.***

CHECK/TOP UP BRAKE/CLUTCH FLUID RESERVOIR

WARNING: Clean reservoir body and filler cap before removing cap. Use only fluid from a sealed container.

NOTE: Clutch master cylinder is supplied by the brake fluid reservoir. Use following procedure if topping up is required.

1. Turn ignition ON, to activate hydraulic pump. If pump does not activate, depress brake pedal several times until it is heard to operate.
2. When pump stops, check that level is between 'MIN' and 'MAX' marks.
3. If level is below 'MIN' mark on reservoir, top up, using correct fluid. ***See LUBRICANTS, FLUIDS AND CAPACITIES, Information.***

CHECK/TOP UP WASHER RESERVOIR

Top up washer reservoir to within 25 mm of bottom of filler neck. Use the correct quantity of screen washer additive to assist removing mud, flies and road film and protect against freezing.

LUBRICATE ACCELERATOR AND CRUISE CONTROL LINKAGES

REMOVE BATTERY CONNECTIONS

Clean, coat with petroleum jelly and refit terminals.

The exterior of the battery should be wiped clean to remove any dirt or grease.

NOTE: From '96 MY, the alarm sounder may be fitted with a back-up battery, the purpose of which is to power the anti-theft alarm if the main battery is disconnected. On these vehicles it is essential to adopt the following procedure before disconnecting the terminals in order to prevent the alarm from sounding:

1. Turn starter switch 'on' and then 'off'.
2. Disconnect the battery WITHIN 17 SECONDS (if the battery is not disconnected within 17 seconds, the alarm will sound).

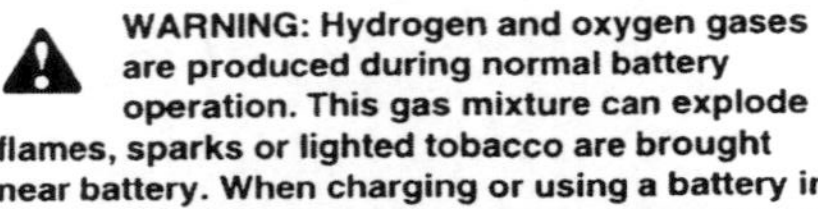

WARNING: Hydrogen and oxygen gases are produced during normal battery operation. This gas mixture can explode if flames, sparks or lighted tobacco are brought near battery. When charging or using a battery in an enclosed space, always provide ventilation and shield your eyes.

Batteries contain sulphuric acid. Avoid contact with skin, eyes, or clothing. Also, shield your eyes when working near battery to protect against possible splashing of acid solution. In case of acid contact with skin, eyes, or clothing, flush immediately with water for a minimum of fifteen minutes. If acid is swallowed, drink large quantities of milk or water, followed by milk of magnesia, a beaten egg, or vegetable oil. SEEK MEDICAL AID IMMEDIATELY.

A low maintenance battery is installed in the vehicle. Dependent upon climate conditions electrolyte levels should be checked as follows:

Temperate climates every three years.

Hot climates every year.

CHECK INTERCOOLER/RADIATOR FOR EXTERNAL OBSTRUCTIONS

FLUSH DIESEL INTERCOOLER ELEMENT

Remove intercooler. ***See FUEL SYSTEM, Repair.***

Flush the intercooler using ICI GENKLENE following the manufacturer's instructions. Dry the intercooler completely and check for damage or deterioration. Fit a new intercooler if necessary.

CHECK CONDITION OF STEERING INTERMEDIATE SHAFT

The intermediate shaft has a red indicator clip fitted which must be inspected at service, or after the vehicle has been subjected to an impact. If the clip is not present, or is not fully seated against the clamp plate, a new intermediate shaft must be fitted. ***See STEERING, Repair.***

DEPRESSURISE ELECTRONIC AIR SUSPENSION.

Depressurise air suspension system using TestBook.

RENEW ELECTRONIC AIR SUSPENSION COMPRESSOR INTAKE AND EXHAUST FILTERS.

Compressor inlet filter. ***See FRONT SUSPENSION, Repair.***

REMOVE/REFIT AIR RESERVOIR DRAIN PLUG.

1. Clean area around reservoir drain plug.
2. Partially open drain plug, allow residual air to escape.

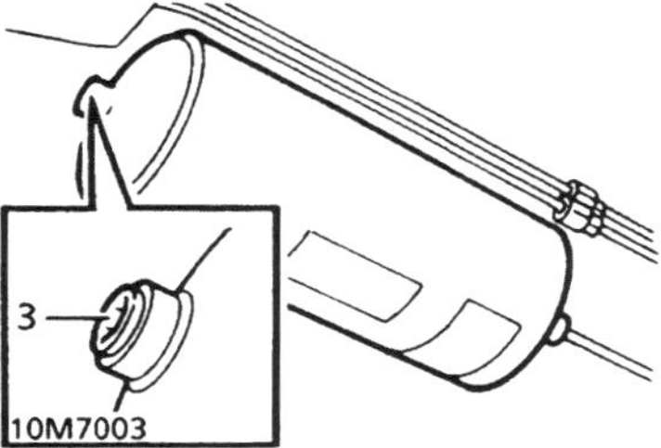
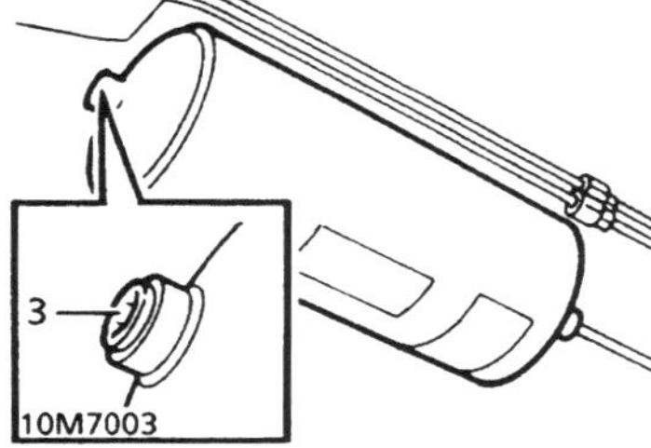

10M7003

3. Remove drain plug.
4. Renew air dryer if there is evidence of water in the system. ***See FRONT SUSPENSION, Repair.***
5. Fit drain plug. Tighten to ***70 Nm. (52 lbf.ft)***

REPRESSURISE AIR SUSPENSION SYSTEM.

UNDER VEHICLE MAINTENANCE

This section covers renewal of lubricating oils for vehicle major units and other components requiring lubrication, as detailed in the Sevice Schedule. For lubricant recommendations. ***See LUBRICANTS, FLUIDS AND CAPACITIES, Information.***
If possible drain oil when it is warm. Always clean drain and filler/level plugs before removing.
Disconnect vehicle battery to prevent engine being started and vehicle moved inadvertently, while oil changing is taking place.
Allow oil to drain completely, except where blown sand or dirt can enter drain holes. In these conditions clean and refit drain plugs immediately main bulk of oil has drained.
Always refill with oil of correct make and specification recommended in lubrication charts and from sealed containers.

RENEW ENGINE OIL AND FILTER - DIESEL

1. Ensure vehicle is level.
2. Run engine to warm oil, switch off ignition.
3. Disconnect battery negative lead.
4. Place a suitable drain tray under drain plug.

5

10M7008

5. Remove drain plug from sump. Allow oil to drain completely.
6. Fit new sealing washer, fit plug and tighten to:-
M12 plug - ***25 Nm (18 lbf.ft)***
M22 plug - ***60 Nm (44 lbf.ft)***
7. Fit new oil filter. ***See ENGINE, Repair.***
8. Fill engine with correct quantity of new oil, check level.
9. Reconnect battery negative lead.
10. Start engine and run at 2500 rpm until oil warning lamp extinguishes (approximately 5 seconds).
11. Stop engine, check for oil leaks, check oil level. Top-up if necessary.

RENEW ENGINE OIL AND FILTER - V8

1. Ensure vehicle is level.
2. Run engine to warm oil, switch off ignition.
3. Disconnect battery negative lead.
4. Place suitable drain tray under drain plug.

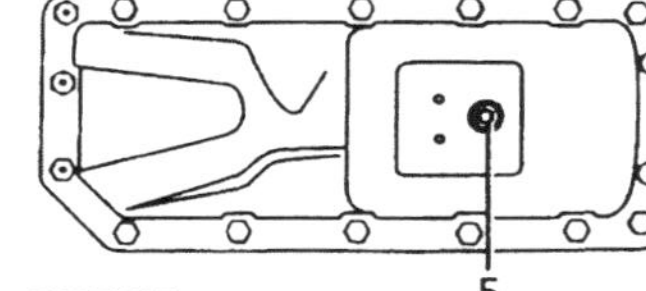

10M7007

5. Remove drain plug from sump. Allow oil to drain completely.
6. Fit new copper washer and refit plug. Tighten to:
Up to 99MY - ***45 Nm (33 lbf.ft).***
From 99MY - ***32 Nm (24 lbf.ft).***
7. Place drain tray under oil filter.

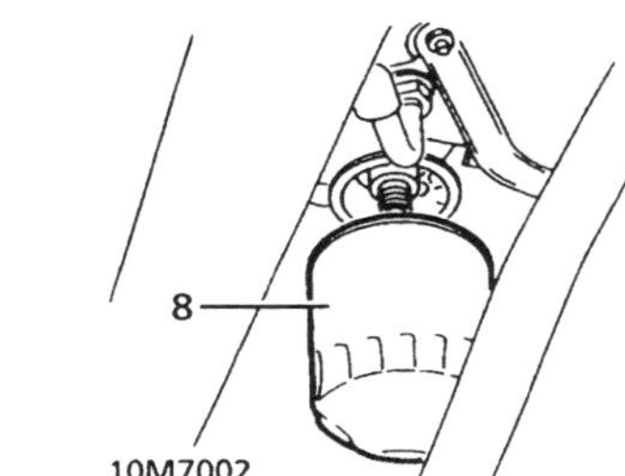

10M7002

8. Unscrew filter anti-clockwise.
9. Clean oil cooler adaptor mating face. Coat rubber washer of new filter with clean engine oil. Screw filter on clockwise until rubber sealing ring touches machined face, tighten a further half turn by hand only. **DO NOT** overtighten.
10. Clean outside of oil filler cap, remove from filler neck. Clean inside cap.
11. Pour in correct quantity of new oil of correct grade from a sealed container to high mark on dipstick and firmly replace filler cap. **DO NOT FILL ABOVE 'HIGH' MARK.**
12. Reconnect battery negative lead.
13. Run engine and check for leaks from filter. Stop engine, allow oil to run back into sump for a few minutes, check oil level again and top up if necessary.

NOTE: When checking oil level, ensure that the oil can symbol on dipstick is correct way up when viewed from left hand side of vehicle.

RENEW MANUAL GEARBOX OIL.

1. Ensure vehicle is level. Place a suitable drain tray under gearbox.
2. Disconnect battery negative lead.
3. Clean area around filler/level and drain plugs. Remove both plugs. Allow oil to drain completely.

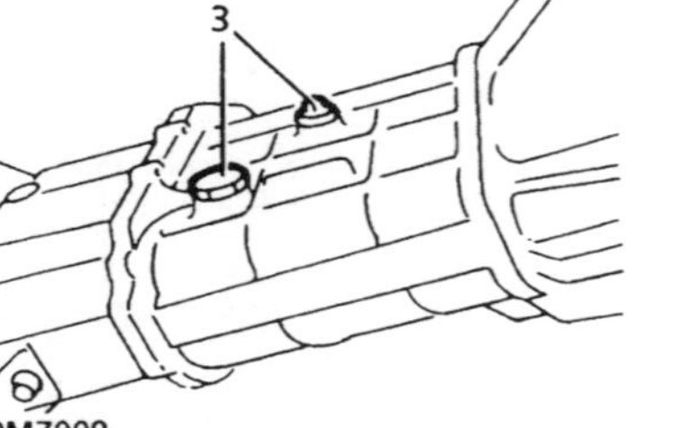

10M7009

4. Fit and tighten drain plug to ***30 Nm. (22 lbf.ft)***
5. Inject new oil into the gearbox until it runs out of filler hole. Fit and tighten plug to ***30 Nm. (22 lbf.ft)***
6. Reconnect battery negative lead.

CHECK/TOP UP GEARBOX OIL

1. Ensure vehicle is level.
2. Remove oil filler level plug. If necessary, inject new oil into the gearbox until it runs out of filler hole. Fit and tighten plug to ***30 Nm. (22 lbf.ft)***

RENEW AUTOMATIC GEARBOX FLUID AND FILTER

For procedure. ***See AUTOMATIC GEARBOX, Repair.***

RENEW TRANSFER BOX OIL

1. Ensure vehicle is level. Place a suitable drain tray under gearbox. Disconnect battery negative lead.
2. Clean area around filler/level plug. Remove filler/level plug.
3. Clean area around drain plug. Remove drain plug. Allow oil to drain completely.

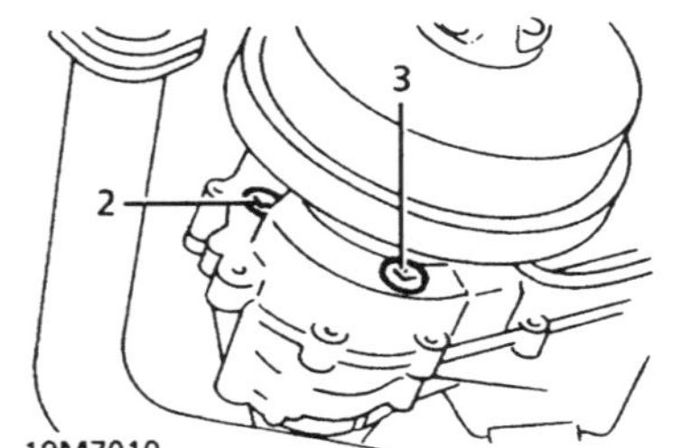

10M7010

4. Thoroughly clean drain plug threads, apply Hylomar sealant. Fit drain plug. Tighten to ***30 Nm. (22 lbf.ft)***
5. Inject new oil into the gearbox until it runs out of filler hole.
6. Thoroughly clean filler/level plug threads, apply Hylomar sealant. Fit plug. Tighten to ***30 Nm. (22 lbf.ft)***
7. Reconnect battery negative lead.

CHECK TRANSFER BOX OIL LEVEL

1. Ensure vehicle is level. Place a suitable drain tray under gearbox.
2. Disconnect battery negative lead.
3. Clean area around filler/level plug.
4. Remove plug. If required, inject new oil into the gearbox until it runs out of filler hole.
5. Thoroughly clean filler/level plug threads, apply Hylomar sealant. Fit plug to ***30 Nm. (22 lbf.ft)***
6. Reconnect battery negative lead.

RENEW FRONT AND REAR AXLE OIL

NOTE: To ensure correct oil level the vehicle must be in 'STANDARD' ride height when checking/topping up axle oil.

1. Ensure vehicle is level. Place a suitable drain tray under axle to be drained.
2. Clean area around filler/level and drain plugs. Remove both plugs. Allow oil to drain completely.

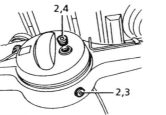

10M7011

3. Clean and fit drain plug. Inject new oil into the axle until it runs out of filler hole.
4. Clean and fit filler/level plug. Wipe away surplus oil.

CHECK FRONT AND REAR AXLE OIL LEVEL

NOTE: To ensure correct oil level the vehicle must be in 'STANDARD' ride height when checking/topping up axle oil.

1. Place vehicle on lift or level ground.
2. Clean area around filler plug. Remove filler plug.
3. If necessary, inject new oil into the axle until it runs out of filler hole.
4. Clean and fit filler/level plug. Wipe away surplus oil.

LUBRICATE PROPELLER SHAFT SLIDING AND UNIVERSAL JOINTS

1. Clean all grease nipples on front and rear propeller shafts.
2. Using a low pressure hand grease gun, apply recommended grease to grease nipples on propeller shaft universal and sliding joints.

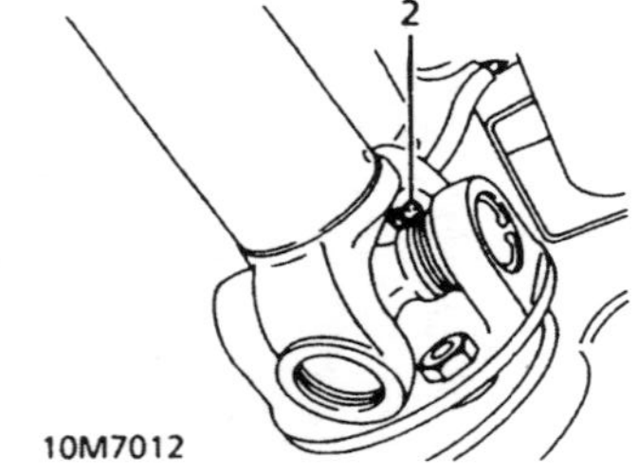

10M7012

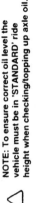

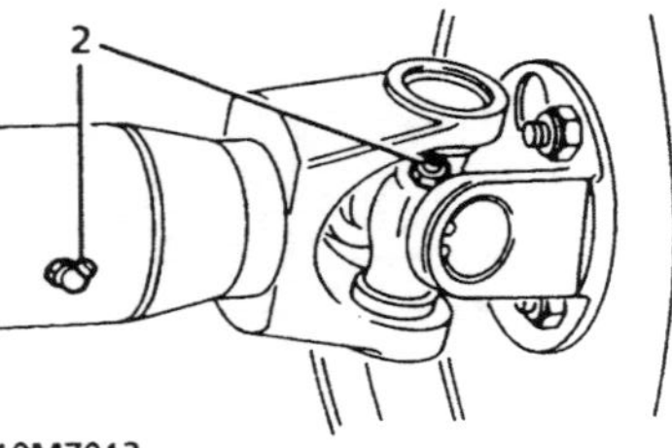

10M7013

REPLACE FUEL FILTER (V8)

To renew fuel filter. ***See FUEL SYSTEM, Repair.***

CHECK VISUALLY HEATSHIELDS, BRAKE, FUEL, CLUTCH PIPES/UNIONS FOR CHAFING, LEAKS AND CORROSION. INVESTIGATE IF NECESSARY.

CHECK EXHAUST SYSTEM FOR LEAKS, SECURITY AND DAMAGE.

RENEW HEATED OXYGEN SENSORS (HO_2S) (CATALYST VEHICLES).

To renew oxygen sensors. ***See FUEL SYSTEM, Repair.***

RENEW CATALYTIC CONVERTERS (V8)

To renew catalytic converters. ***See MANIFOLD AND EXHAUST SYSTEM, Repair.***

CHECK FOR CHAFING, CORROSION AND FLUID LEAKS FROM STEERING AND SUSPENSION SYSTEMS, HYDRAULIC PIPES AND UNIONS.

CHECK/TIGHTEN SUSPENSION, STEERING UNIT AND STEERING ROD BALL JOINT FIXINGS, CHECK CONDITION OF BALL JOINTS AND DUST COVERS.

Ball joints are lubricated for their normal life during manufacture and require no further lubrication. Joints should be checked at specified intervals but more frequently if the vehicle is used continuously under arduous conditions. Any ball joints exhibiting wear or dislodged/damaged dust covers will require the entire joint to be replaced.

CHECK AIR SUSPENSION PIPES AND SPRINGS FOR SECURITY AND DAMAGE.

CHECK SHOCK ABSORBERS/HEIGHT SENSORS AND HARNESS ASSEMBLY FOR LEAKAGE AND DAMAGE.

CHECK ROAD WHEEL SPEED SENSOR HARNESS FOR DAMAGE.

CARRY OUT ROAD TEST, CHECK FOR CORRECT FUNCTION OF ALL VEHICLE SYSTEMS.

ENDORSE THE SERVICE RECORD.

REPORT ANY UNUSUAL FEATURES OF VEHICLE CONDITION AND ADDITIONAL WORK REQUIRED.

IMPORTANT

Antifreeze

At three yearly intervals, or at the onset of the third winter, the cooling system must be drained, flushed and refilled with the correct water and antifreeze solution

Air bags

The front air bags on SRS vehicles must be renewed every 10 years. The side air bags must be renewed every 15 years.

IT IS RECOMMENDED THAT:

At 20,000 km (12,000 miles) intervals, clean sunroof drain tubes and channels, lubricate guide rails and slides.

At 60,000 km (36,000 miles) intervals or every 3 years, whichever is the earlier, the hydraulic brake fluid should be completely renewed.

At 120,000 km (72,000 miles) intervals or 6 years, whichever is earlier, all hydraulic brake fluid seals and flexible brake hoses should be renewed. All working surfaces of the caliper cylinders should be examined and components renewed where necessary.

Vehicles used extensively in arduous/off road operating conditions will require the road wheel speed sensors, brake pads, calipers, hoses and pipes to be checked at 1600 km (1000 mile) intervals.

Vehicles used extensively in arduous/off road operating conditions will require the air suspension compressor inlet and exhaust filters to be replaced at more frequent intervals.

Every 3 years the vehicle locking handset batteries should be renewed.

When the vehicle is used in dusty or field conditions or deep wading, frequent attention to the air cleaner may be required.

WARNING: Two wheel roller tests must not be carried out. Four wheel roller tests must be restricted to 5 km/h (3 mph).

Notes

12 - ENGINE

CONTENTS

DESCRIPTION

The diesel engine fitted to New Range Rover is a 2.5 litre, liquid cooled, 6 cylinder, in-line unit. It has an electronically regulated fuel injection system and is turbocharged. Power output is increased by the turbocharger which delivers compressed air to the combustion chambers via an intercooler.

The engine develops 100 kW (134 hp) at 4400 RPM.

Engine performance is managed by a Digital Diesel Electronics (DDE) system. This system monitors and controls all engine functions such as the injection timing, delivery volume and charge-air intercooling. For full description of the DDE system, ***See FUEL SYSTEM, Description and operation.***

The flywheel is a dual-mass unit and is hydraulically damped to prevent transmission rattle in all operating conditions. Attached to the flywheel, around its circumference at 60 degree intervals, are six position pins. These are used by the DDE system to determine engine speed and crankshaft position.

The engine comprises the following main systems and components:

Crankcase
Cylinder head
Air intake system
Forced aspiration system
Injection system - ***See FUEL SYSTEM, Description and operation.***
Lubrication system
Cooling system - ***See COOLING SYSTEM, Description and operation.***
Auxiliary driven assemblies

Crankcase

The cast steel crankcase, which incorporates a cooling water jacket, is machined and bored to form a cylinder block (cylinder bore 80 mm) and a crankshaft housing. These contain the pistons, connecting rods and the crankshaft. Bolted to the underside of the crankcase is an aluminium reinforcement plate with an integrated oil deflector. The reinforcement plate increases crankcase stability and prevents oil foaming and ventilation losses.

Pistons

Each piston is manufactured from aluminium and has three grooves to accommodate piston rings. The top ring is a 15°keystone ring, the centre ring is a tapered compression ring and the lower ring is spring-loaded oil ring. The piston skirt is phosphated and graphited while the piston crown has a V-patterned groove machined into it. The V-patterned groove forms part of the combustion chamber, which is designed on a swirl chamber principle. This reduces fuel consumption, exhaust emission and smoke produced at full load. Piston cooling is by oil which is directed to the underside of each piston through crankcase-mounted spray jets; drillings in the piston allow oil to circulate thoroughly.

Pistons have a stroke of 82.8 mm and are attached to the connecting rods by 27 mm diameter gudgeon pins

Connecting rods

Power is transmitted to the crankshaft through the forged steel connecting rods.

Crankshaft

The crankshaft is forged from high-tensile steel and has seven main bearing journals. Journals are supported in bearing shells fitted to the crankcase; dynamic balancing of the crankshaft is achieved by the use of 12 balance weights. An axially decoupled torsional vibration damper suppresses longitudinal vibration of the crankshaft to reduce noise.

Crankshafts are available in three sizes which have different journal sizes - standard size, undersize 1 and undersize 2. A colour code, yellow, green or white denotes the actual size of the journals.

At its front end, the crankshaft drives a close coupled oil pump for the engine lubrication system and the fuel injection pump timing chain. The timing chain connects the crankshaft mounted sprocket and injector pump drive sprocket. A second timing chain takes drive from the injector pump sprocket to the overhead camshaft in the cylinder head.

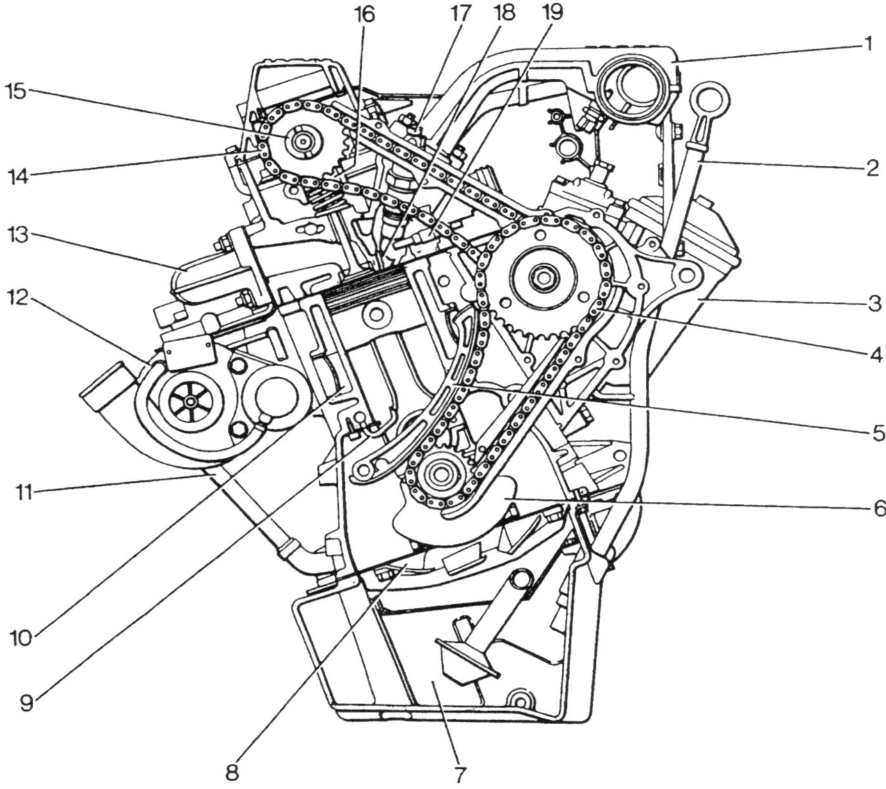

12M7135

1. Charge air collector
2. Oil dipstick
3. Oil filter
4. Fuel injection pump chain drive
5. Tensioner rail - chain drive
6. Crankshaft
7. Oil sump
8. Reinforcement plate
9. Piston cooling jet
10. Cooling water jacket
11. Oil return from turbocharger
12. Turbocharger
13. Exhaust manifold
14. Camshaft drive chain
15. Camshaft
16. Hydraulic tappet
17. Fuel injector
18. Swirl chamber
19. Glow plug

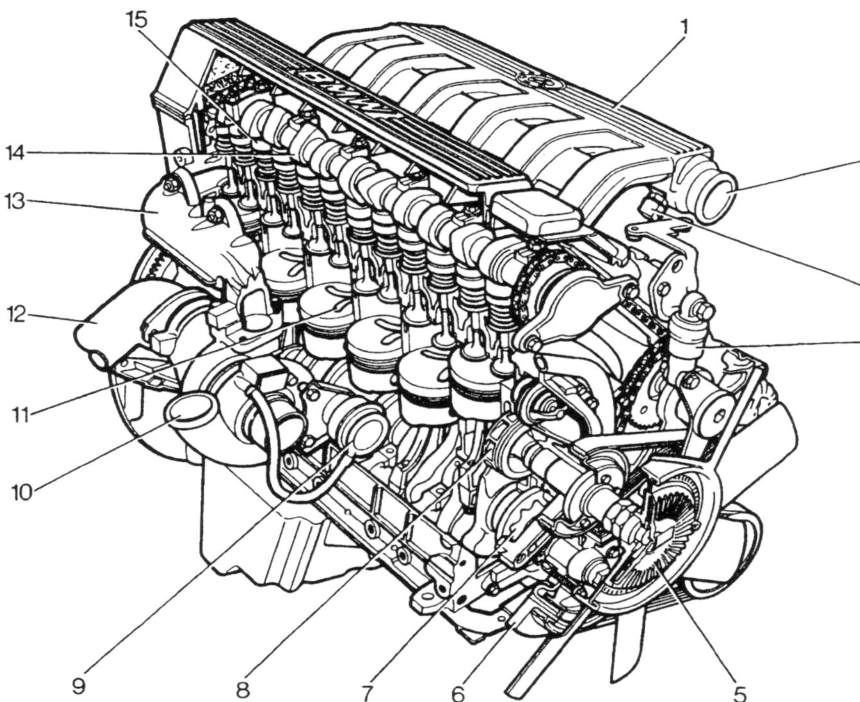

12M7136

1. Charge air collector
2. Connection from intercooler
3. Intake air temperature sensor groove
4. Hydraulic damper - tensioner roller
5. Radiator fan and viscous coupling
6. Torsional vibration damper
7. Oil pump
8. Water pump
9. Vacuum cell for turbocharger
10. Turbocharger air intake
11. Piston crown, V-pattern
12. Exhaust pipe from turbocharger
13. Exhaust manifold
14. Overhead camshaft
15. Hydraulic tappet

Cylinder head

The aluminium cylinder head houses the chain driven overhead camshaft, the valve gear and fuel injectors.

Coolant enters the cylinder head from the crankcase. The coolant flow is across the cylinder head and out to the heater matrix and radiator.

An oil separator with wire mesh filter is installed in the camshaft cover.

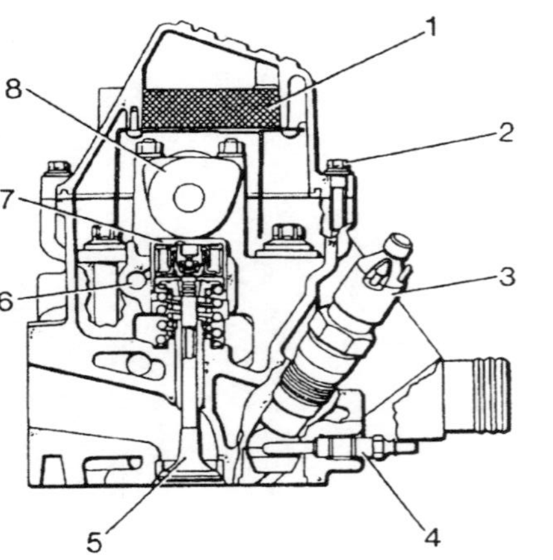

1. Oil separator
2. Camshaft cover bolts
3. Fuel injector
4. Glow plug
5. Outlet valve
6. Oil supply duct
7. Hydraulic tappet
8. Camshaft

Camshaft

Seven bearings support the camshaft in the cylinder head. The camshaft is chain driven from the fuel injection pump drive sprocket, which itself is chain driven from the crankshaft. Both the injection pump timing chain and the camshaft timing chain run within guide rails and are tensioned automatically by tension rails and a chain adjuster mechanism.

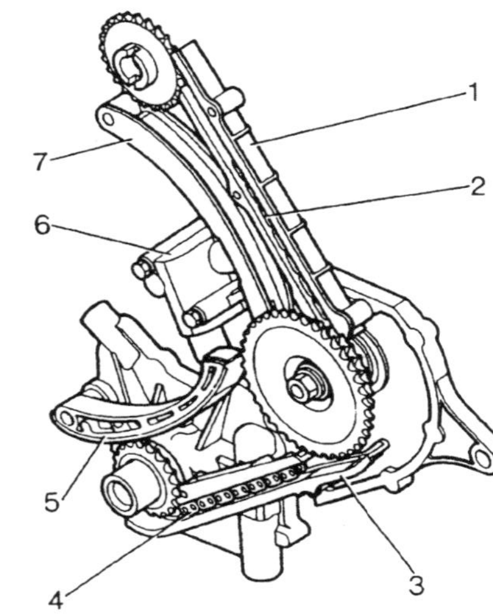

1. Guide rail
2. Camshaft drive chain
3. Guide rail
4. Injection pump drive chain
5. Tension rail
6. Chain adjuster
7. Tension rail

Valve gear

The camshaft operates the inlet and exhaust valves through bucket-type tappets with hydraulic valve clearance adjustment. The hydraulic tappets are leakproof, eliminating rattle during the first few revolutions of the engine. Valves are available in standard size or oversize and are identified by a number stamped on the stem. Valves are coated during manufacture and DO NOT need to be lapped when they are renewed.

Fuel injectors

Fuel is delivered to each cylinder through fuel injector nozzles. An injector is screwed into a pre-combustion chamber (swirl chamber) at each cylinder position.

The precombustion chambers are also fitted with glow plugs. Each injector comprises a nozzle holder and contains a spring-loaded needle valve; the nozzle holder of cylinder No 4 incorporates a sender which senses the time of fuel ejection by recognising needle movement. This information is utilised by the DDE system - ***See ENGINE MANAGEMENT, Description.***

12M7139

1. Fuel injector
2. Glow plug
3. Pre-combustion chamber
4. Piston crown, V-patterned groove

Air intake

Fresh air is drawn in through an air cleaner assembly secured to the left hand inner wing of the vehicle. The air cleaner assembly comprises a housing which contains a paper filter element. The rectangular, two-part housing is constructed from moulded plastic and incorporates an air inlet and an air outlet.

The air cleaner delivers filtered air to the turbocharger.

Forced aspiration system

Forced aspiration is by an exhaust driven turbocharger. Compressed air, from the turbocharger, passes through an intercooler to the charge air collector mounted on the cylinder head.

Turbocharger

The turbocharger consists of a compressor housing and a turbine housing bolted to the exhaust manifold. The compressor housing has an ambient air inlet and a compressed air outlet. The turbine housing has an exhaust gas inlet and an exhaust gas outlet. Both compressor and turbine housings are bolted to a central bearing housing. The bearing housing contains two pressure lubricated bearings which provide support for the rotor shaft. An exhaust-gas driven turbine mounted at one end of the rotor shaft, drives a centrifugal compressor mounted at the other.

To regulate charge air pressure, a by-pass plate is installed on the exhaust side of the turbocharger. The by-pass plate is connected to a pneumatic pressure actuator.

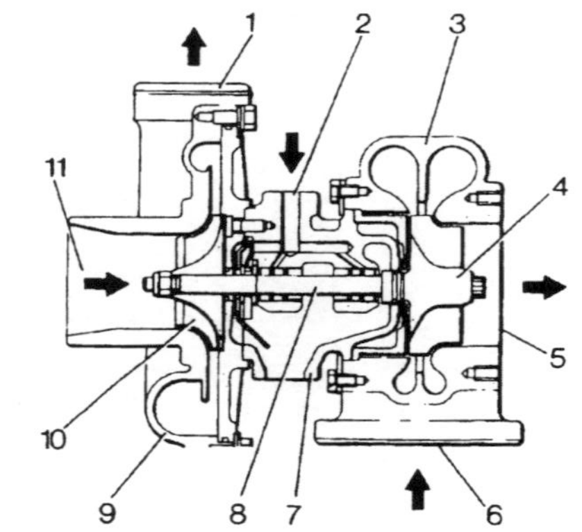

1. Charge air outlet
2. Pressurised oil from engine
3. Turbine housing
4. Turbine
5. Exhaust gas outlet
6. Exhaust gas inlet
7. Bearing housing
8. Rotor shaft
9. Compressor housing
10. Compressor
11. Air intake

Intercooler

To lower the temperature of the charge air, and therefore increase its density, an intercooler is fitted between the turbocharger and the charge air collector.

Charge air collector

The charge air collector is bolted to the cylinder head and consists of a manifold having a single inlet and six individual outlets, one to each cylinder. Intake charge air pressure and charge air temperature sensors mounted on the collector are linked to the control unit of the DDE system. The air temperature sensor has a black connector and is fitted at the front of the air collector. The pressure sensor is a small, black plastic sensor mounted on the fuel filter bracket. It is connected to the air collector through a tube.

Operation

When the engine is running, exhaust gas impinges on the turbine vanes of the turbocharger causing the turbine to rotate. The rotor shaft transmits drive from the turbine to the inlet centrifugal compressor. Air is drawn into the compressor from the air cleaner and compressed air is discharged to the charge air collector via the intercooler.

Charge air pressure is regulated by operation of the by-pass plate.

12M7141

1. By-pass plate actuator
2. Charge air pressure sensor
3. Intake air (charge air) temperature sensor
4. DDE system control unit

Lubrication system

The lubrication system comprises the sump, pump, oil filter and oil ducts.

Sump

This is a one-piece, rigid, aluminium, die-cast unit bolted to underside of the crankcase. An oil deflector plate is attached to the crankcase reinforcing shell above the sump. The sump incorporates a drain plug and a dip-stick guide pipe.

Oil pump

An internal gear-type pump is mounted on the front end of the crankshaft. It is directly driven by the crankshaft. The pump consists of a body which houses a driven rotor and a stator. Pump pressure is regulated by a piston operated pressure relief valve housed within the body of the pump.

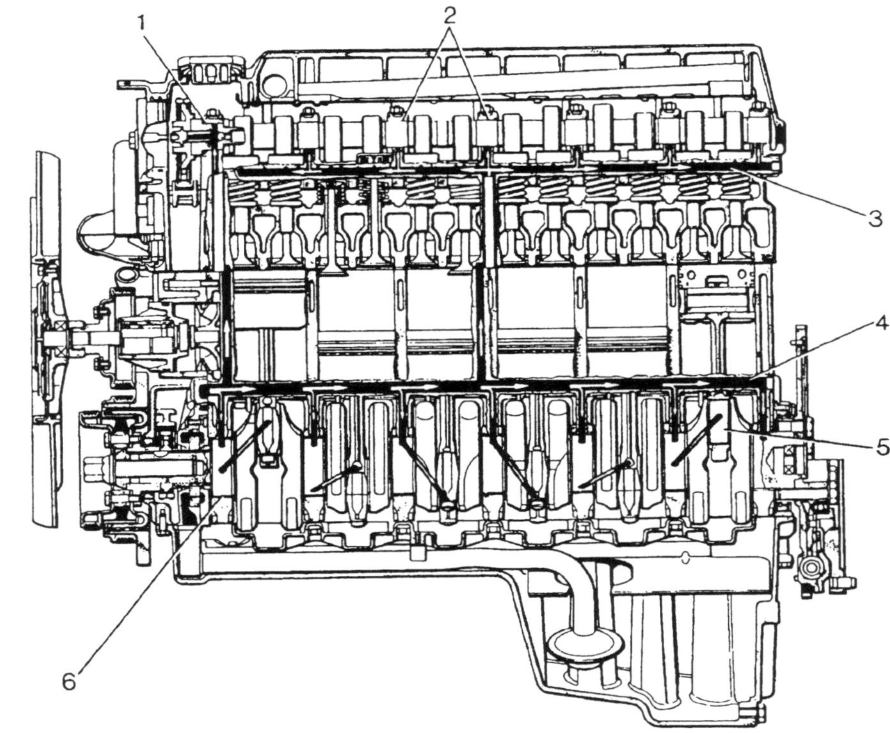

1. Camshaft bearing
2. Camshaft bearings
3. Oil duct
4. Main oil duct
5. Big end bearing
6. Main crankshaft bearing

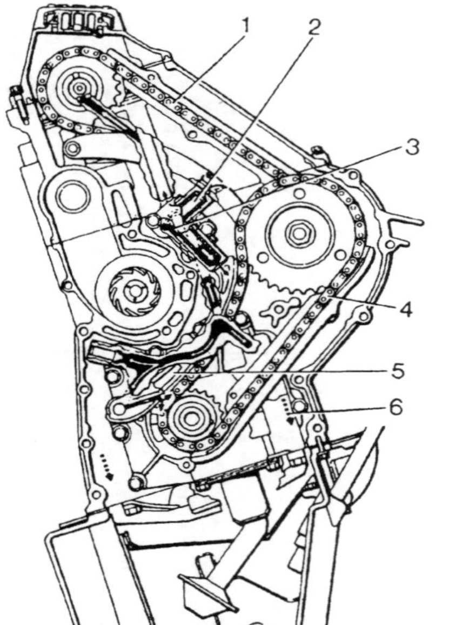

12M7143

1. Camshaft timing chain drive
2. Upper tension rail
3. Chain adjuster
4. Injection timing
5. Lower tension rail
6. Oil return

Oil filter

The oil filter is vertically-mounted below the charge air collector. It consists of a filter element contained within a housing which is screwed to a filter head. A filter by-pass valve is installed in the housing, while the filter head holds a thermostat. The thermostat promotes quick warm up of the engine by preventing oil circulating through the oil cooler when the oil temperature is low. The thermostat operates at 80°C.

Oil ducts

Oil circulates around the engine, and is delivered to the turbocharger bearings, through ducts and oilways. A longitudinal main oil duct allows oil to be delivered to the crankshaft bearings. Vertical ducts from the main duct allow oil to the piston cooling jets and to the camshaft bearings.

Operation

Refer to the lubrication system circuit diagrams for lubrication system operating details.

Auxiliary driven assemblies

The auxiliary driven assemblies consist of the following:

Water pump
Power steering pump
Alternator

The water pump, alternator and power steering pump are driven from the crankshaft by means of a decoupled pulley and a 5-rib, automatically tensioned, V-belt.

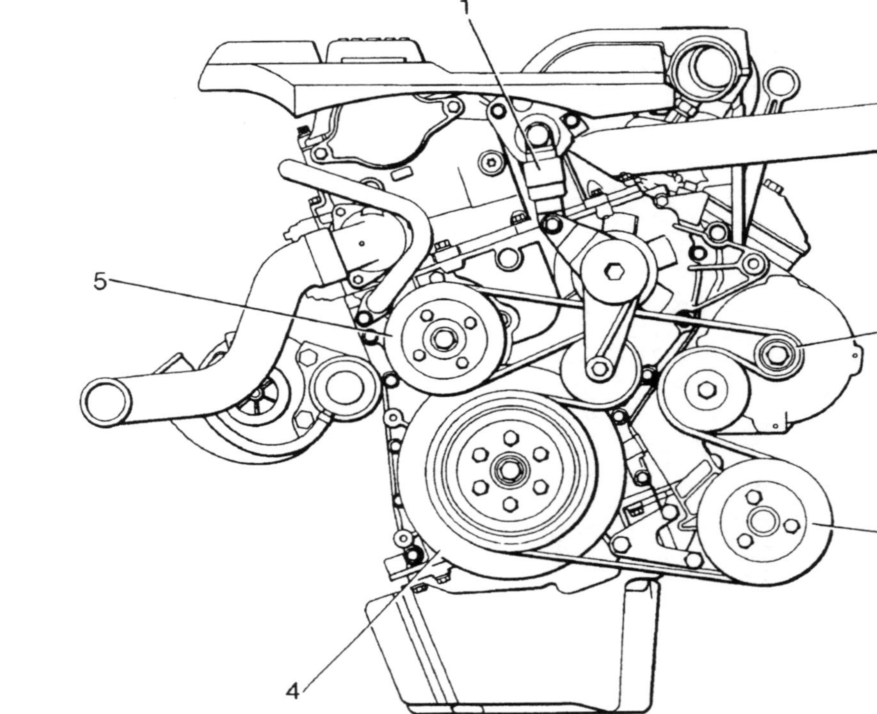

12M7144

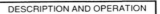

1. Belt tensioning element
2. Alternator drive
3. Power steering pump drive
4. Torsional vibration damper with decoupled pulley
5. Water pump drive

Notes

CYLINDER PRESSURE CHECK - DIESEL

Service repair no - 19.60.31

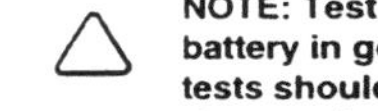

NOTE: Test must only be carried out with battery in good condition. Compression tests should not be used as the sole means of assessing the state of an engine. They must only be used to support other symptoms or the results of other tests.

1. Disconnect battery negative lead.
2. Remove glow plugs. ***See FUEL SYSTEM, Repair.***
3. Release cover and disconnect lead from stop solenoid.
4. Remove 2 screws securing harness trunking to cylinder block and position trunking aside.
5. Reconnect battery negative lead.
6. Using kit LRT-19-007 fit adaptor DA 102-85 to number 1 glow plug location. Tighten to ***20Nm (15 lbf.ft).***
7. Connect gauge to adaptor and tighten securely.

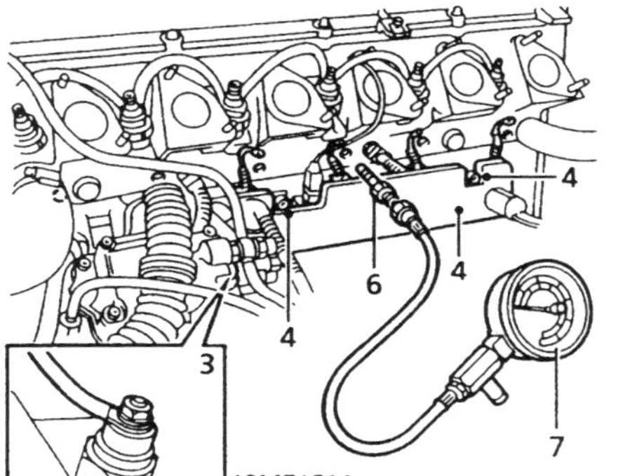

8. Operate the starter motor until the gauge needle reaches its highest reading and mark with the pointer.
9. Repeat operations 6 to 8 on remaining cylinders.
10. All readings should be at least 20 bar and within approximately 3 bar of each other.
11. If any reading is low, inject 4 shots of clean engine oil into glowplug hole and repeat test. Low readings on both wet and dry tests indicate a badly seating valve or leaking cylinder head gasket. Low readings on a dry test and satisfactory wet test results indicate piston ring and/or cylinder bore problems.
12. Disconnect battery negative lead.
13. Remove test equipment.
14. Connect stop solenoid.
15. Align harness trunking and secure with screws.
16. Fit glow plugs, ***See FUEL SYSTEM, Repair.***
17. Reconnect battery negative lead.

CAMSHAFT COVER GASKET - NON EGR

Service repair no - 12.29.40

Remove

1. Disconnect battery negative lead.
2. Remove 4 screws securing injector covers. Remove covers.

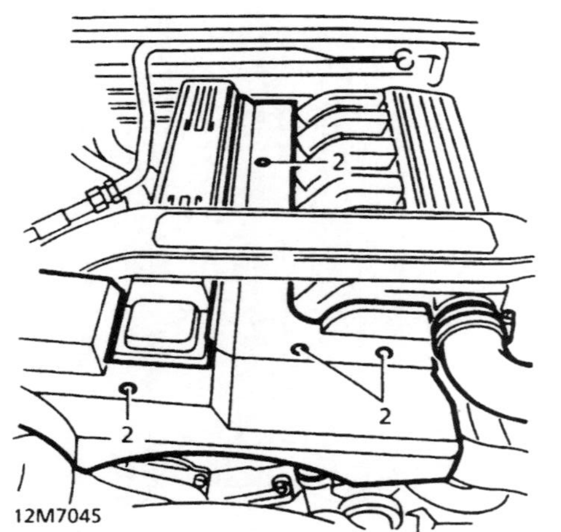

12M7045

3. Release intake hose from ducting.
4. Release turbocharger intake hose from ducting.

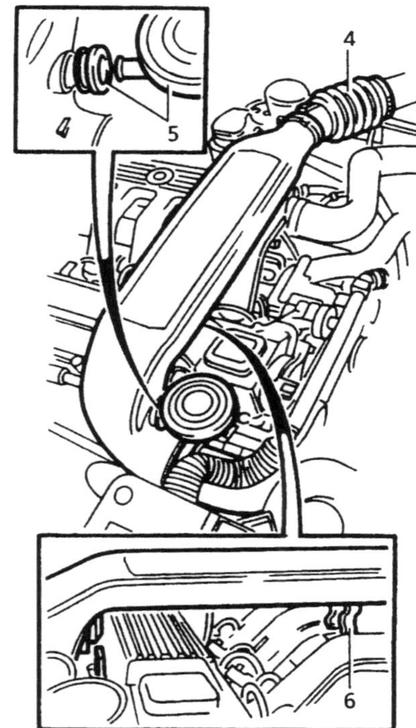

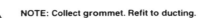

12M7046

5. Release breather valve from intake ducting grommet.

NOTE: Collect grommet. Refit to ducting.

6. Disengage 2 clips. Remove intake ducting.
7. Remove 3 bolts securing intake ducting bracket and exhaust manifold heat shield to camshaft cover. Collect bracket.

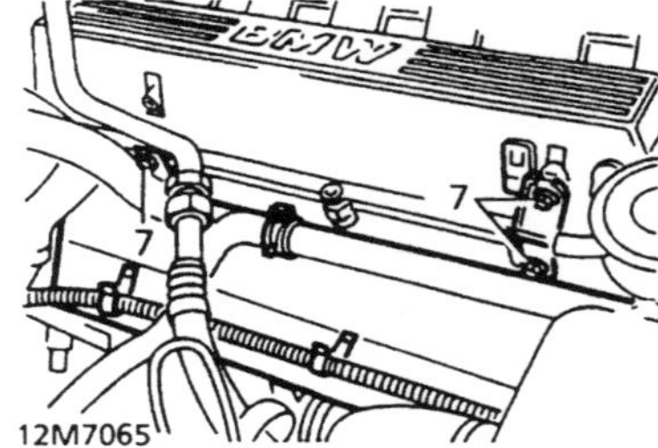

12M7065

8. Remove 10 bolts securing camshaft cover to cylinder head.
9. Remove camshaft cover. Collect gasket and discard.

Refit

10. Ensure mating faces are clean.
11. Fit gasket to camshaft cover.
12. Position camshaft cover on cylinder head. Ensure gasket is correctly seated.

NOTE: Protrusion on rear of gasket can snag on bearing cap during positioning of cover.

13. Fit camshaft cover bolts. Tighten in diagonal sequence, working from centre outwards to ***15 Nm. (11 lbf.ft)***
14. Align exhaust manifold heat shield. Position intake ducting bracket.
15. Secure ducting bracket and heat shield with bolts.
16. Position intake ducting. Engage clips.
17. Engage breather valve into ducting grommet.
18. Connect ducting to turbocharger intake hose. Secure clip.
19. Connect intake hose to ducting. Secure clip.
20. Fit injector covers. Secure with screws.
21. Reconnect battery negative lead.

CAMSHAFT COVER GASKET - WITH EGR

Service repair no - 12.29.40

Remove

1. Disconnect battery negative terminal.
2. Remove air intake ducting. ***See FUEL SYSTEM, Repair.***
3. Remove 2 bolts securing harness trunking and position trunking aside.
4. Remove 3 bolts securing intake ducting bracket and exhaust manifold heat shield to camshaft cover. Collect bracket.
5. Remove 10 bolts securing camshaft cover to cylinder head.
6. Collect sealing washers.
7. Remove camshaft cover. Collect gasket and discard.

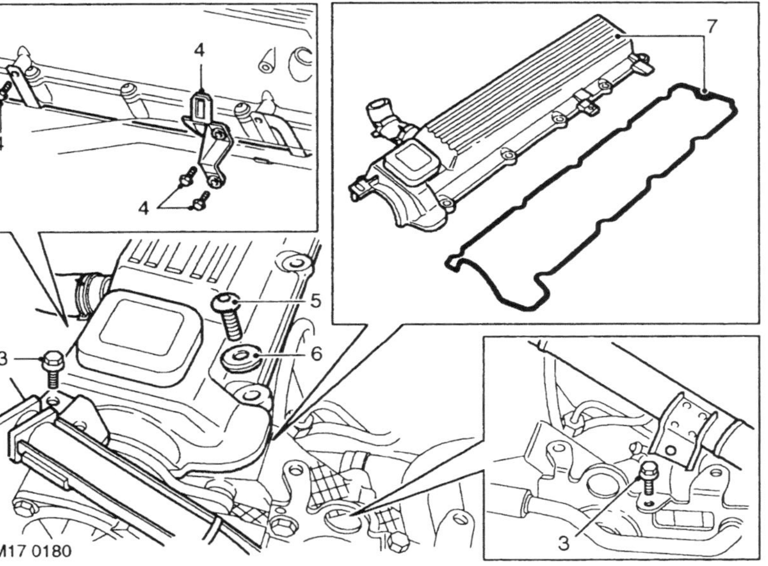

M17 0180

Refit

8. Inspect sealing washers, renew as necessary.
9. Ensure mating faces are clean.
10. Fit gasket to camshaft cover.
11. Position camshaft cover on cylinder head. Ensure gasket is correctly seated.

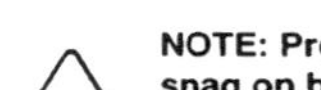

NOTE: Protrusion on rear of gasket can snag on bearing cap during positioning of cover.

12. Fit camshaft cover bolts. Tighten in diagonal sequence, working from centre outwards to ***15 Nm (11 lbf.ft).***
13. Align exhaust manifold heat shield. Position intake ducting bracket.
14. Secure ducting bracket and heat shield with bolts.
15. Fit air intake ducting. ***See FUEL SYSTEM, Repair.***
16. Connect battery negative terminal.

CRANKSHAFT PULLEY AND FRONT COVER OIL SEAL

Service repair no - 12.21.01 - Crankshaft Pulley
Service repair no - 12.65.05 - Timing Gear Cover Oil Seal

Remove

1. Disconnect battery negative lead.
2. Remove radiator. ***See COOLING SYSTEM, Repair.***
3. Remove cover from air conditioning drive belt tensioner.
4. Release drive belt tension. Remove drive belt.
5. Slacken 4 water pump pulley bolts.

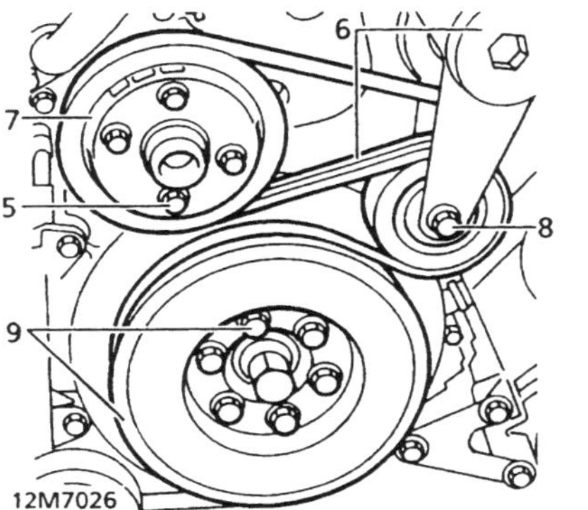

12M7026

6. Release auxiliary drive belt tension. Remove belt.
7. Remove water pump pulley bolts. Remove pulley.
8. Remove bolt from auxilary drive belt tensioner pulley. Remove pulley.
9. Remove 6 bolts securing vibration damper and air conditioning pulley to vibration damper hub. Remove damper and pulley.

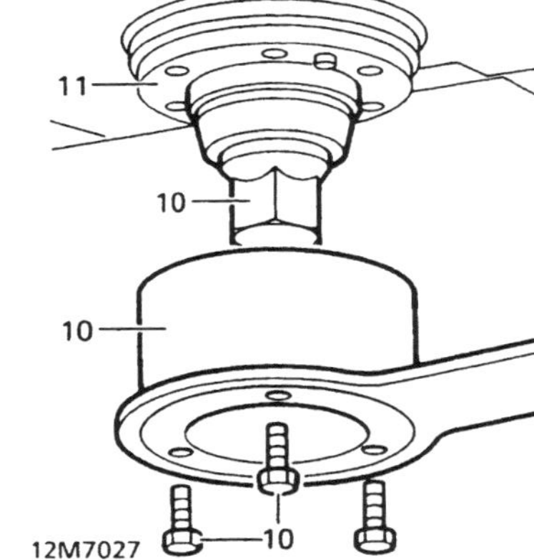

12M7027

10. Secure LRT-12-105 to hub with 3 bolts. Remove and discard hub retaining bolt.
11. Note orientation of shouldered washer. Remove hub and tool.
12. Remove seal from front cover.

Refit

13. Ensure mating faces are clean.
14. Lubricate outer face of seal.
15. Locate seal in timing cover.
16. Using LRT-12-111, push seal home until flush with face of timing cover.
17. Lubricate lip of oil seal. Fit crankshaft pulley hub.
18. Hold hub using LRT-12-105. Secure with new bolt and tighten to ***100 Nm (74 lbf.ft) plus 150 ° torque angle.***
19. Fit damper and pulley to hub. Secure with bolts. Tighten to ***23 Nm. (17 lbf.ft)***
20. Fit auxilary belt tensioner pulley. Secure with bolt.
21. Fit pulley to water pump. Secure with bolts. Tighten to ***10 Nm. (7 lbf.ft)***
22. Rotate auxilary drive belt tensioner. Fit drive belt.
23. Fit and tension air conditioning drive belt. ***See AIR CONDITIONING, Repair.***
24. Fit radiator. ***See COOLING SYSTEM, Repair.***
25. Reconnect battery negative lead.

CRANKSHAFT REAR OIL SEAL

Service repair no - 12.21.20

NOTE: Seal and carrier are supplied as an assembly.

Remove

1. Disconnect battery negative lead.
2. Remove flywheel. ***See this section.***
3. Remove sump. ***See this section.***
4. Remove 6 bolts securing seal carrier to cylinder block.

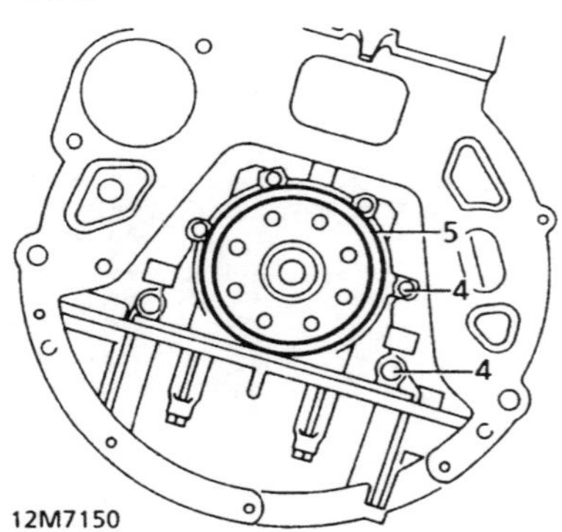

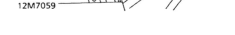

12M7150

5. Remove seal carrier from location dowels.
6. Collect gasket and discard.

Refit

7. Ensure mating faces are clean.
8. Position new gasket.
9. Lubricate seal guide LRT-12-107 with engine oil. Position over crankshaft boss.
10. Lubricate oil seal lip. Position seal carrier squarely over guide. Locate carrier onto dowels.
11. Remove guide.
12. Secure carrier with bolts.
    M6, Tighten to ***10 Nm. (7 lbf.ft)***
    M8, Tighten to ***22 Nm. (16 lbf.ft)***
13. Fit sump. ***See this section.***
14. Fit flywheel. ***See this section.***
15. Reconnect battery negative lead.

ENGINE AND GEARBOX

Service repair no - 12.37.01.99

Remove

1. Position vehicle on four post lift.
2. Remove battery. ***See ELECTRICAL, Repair.***
3. With assistance, release bonnet struts from body locations. Retain bonnet in vertical position using stay clips.

WARNING: Only open the bonnet to the vertical position with the vehicle on a horizontal surface in the workshop. This position is not intended to be used outdoors where the bonnet could be affected by winds.

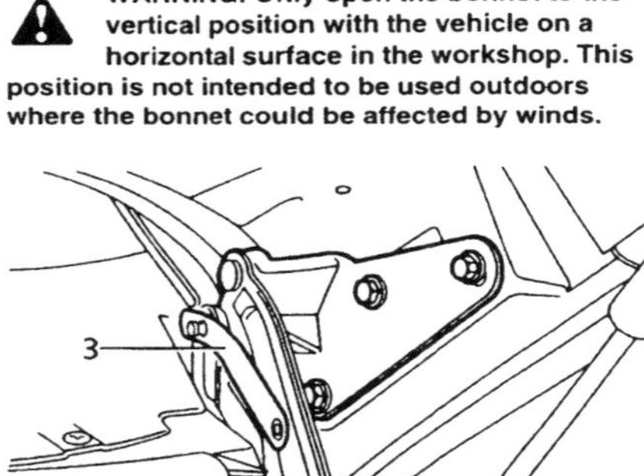

12M7059

4. Remove inlet manifold. ***See MANIFOLD AND EXHAUST SYSTEM, Repair.***
5. Remove ECM. ***See FUEL SYSTEM, Repair.***
6. Remove 2 screws securing engine harness clamp to battery tray. Collect harness clamp.

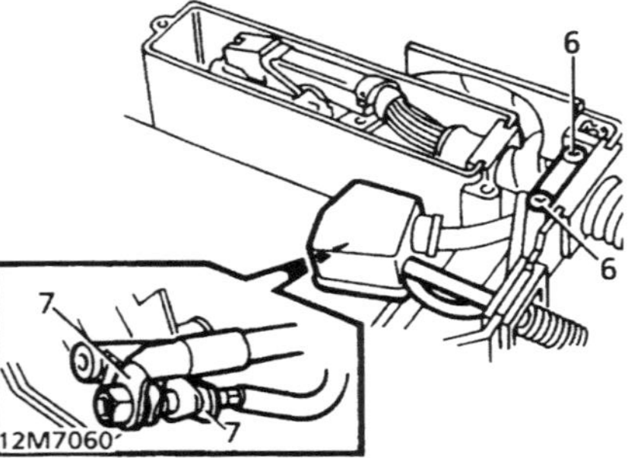

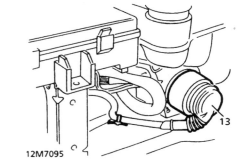

12M7060

7. Release starter feed wire and glow plug relay feed from battery terminal clamp.
8. Remove 4 bolts securing battery tray. Remove battery tray.

12M7061

9. Release earth lead from shock absorber turret.

12M7062

10. Remove 3 bolts securing fuse box. Lift fuse box for access.

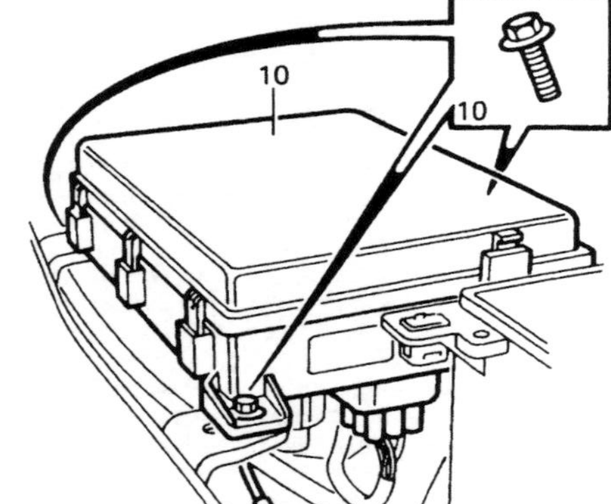

12M7063

11. Disconnect engine harness multiplug from base of fuse box.
12. Release earth wire from valance stud.
13. Disconnect engine harness multiplug from main harness.

12M7095

14. Release engine harness clip from valance. Tie harness aside over engine.
15. Disconnect fuel feed line from fuel heater/filter head. Remove 'O' rings and discard.

12M7064

16. Release clip. Disconnect fuel return hose from Fuel Injection Pump (FIP).
17. Disconnect multiplugs from fuel heater and turbo boost sensor.
18. Position harness aside over engine.
19. Drain cooling system. ***See COOLING SYSTEM, Repair.***
20. Discharge air conditioning system. ***See AIR CONDITIONING, Adjustment.***
21. Remove cooling fan. ***See COOLING SYSTEM, Repair.***
22. Remove engine oil cooler. ***See this section.***

23. Disconnect gearbox oil cooler. Remove 'O' rings and discard. Tie pipes aside on engine.

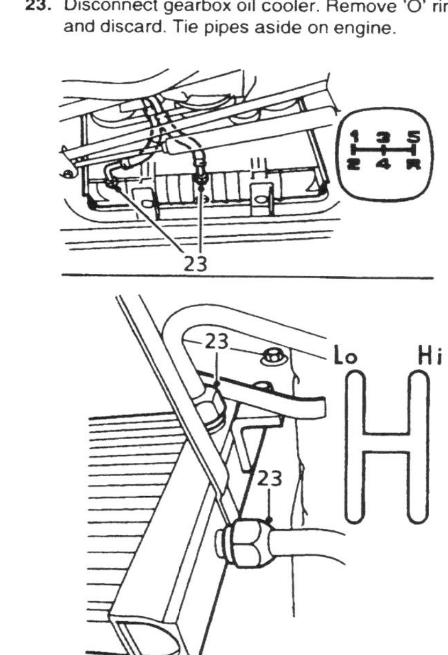

12M7154

CAUTION: Where pipes are disconnected, plug pipes and ports to prevent ingress of dirt.

24. Disconnect bottom hose from radiator.

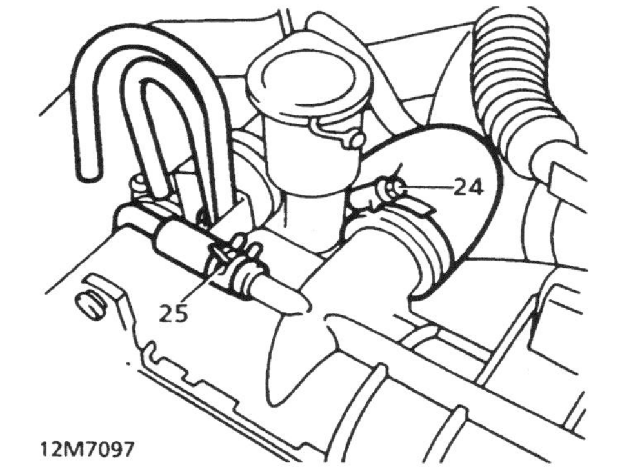

12M7097

25. Disconnect coolant bleed hose from radiator.

26. Release 2 fog lamp breather hoses from clips on either side of radiator.
27. Disconnect 2 heater hoses from engine coolant pipes.

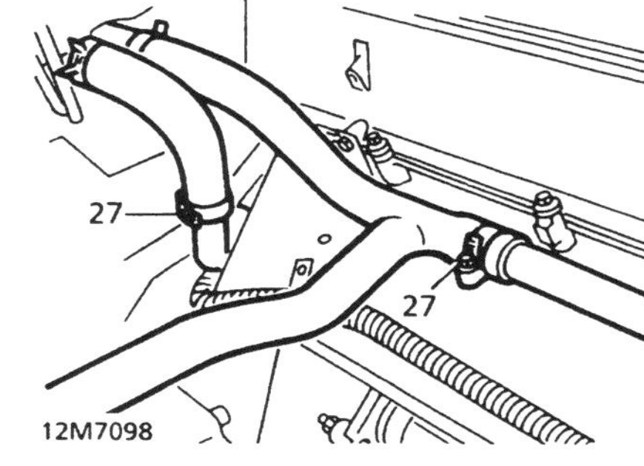

12M7098

28. Position container beneath power steering reservoir to catch spillage.
29. Disconnect return pipe from reservoir. Tie reservoir aside to engine.

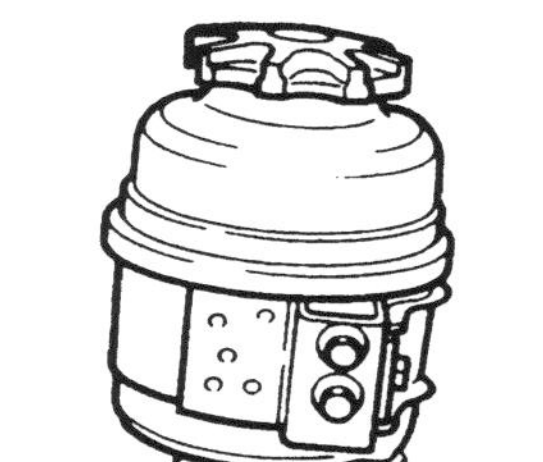

12M7099

30. Disconnect feed pipe from power steering pump. Remove sealing washers and discard. Tie pipe aside to chassis.

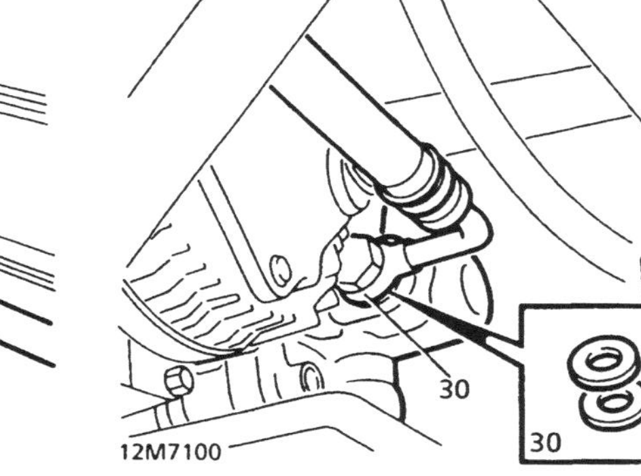

12M7100

31. Remove bolt and screw securing washer bottle filler neck. Remove filler neck.

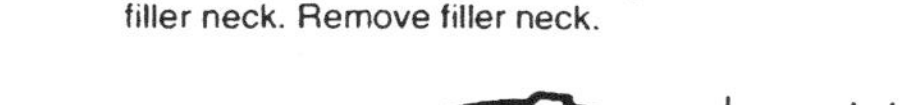

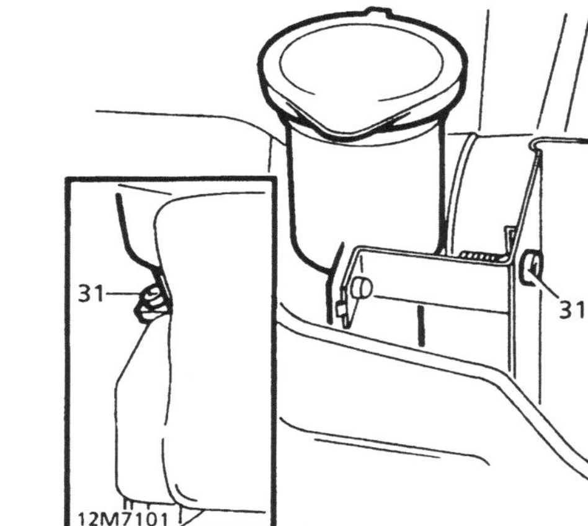

12M7101

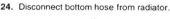

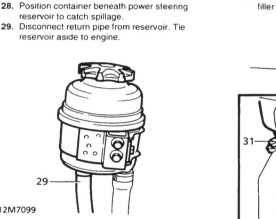

32. Disconnect 2 pipes from air conditioning condenser. Remove 'O' rings and discard.

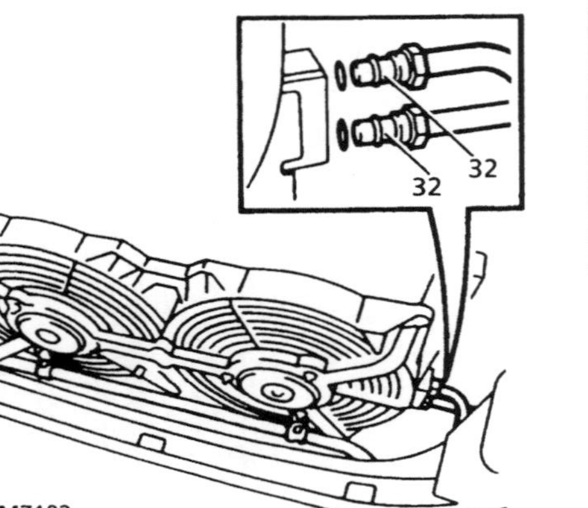

12M7102

33. Disconnect 2 pipes from air conditioning compressor. Remove 'O' rings and discard. Place pipes aside.

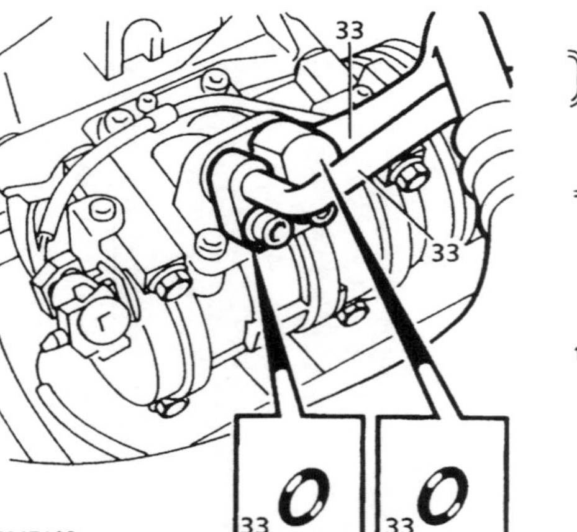

12M7103

34. Remove 2 nuts and bolts securing radiator mountings to chassis.

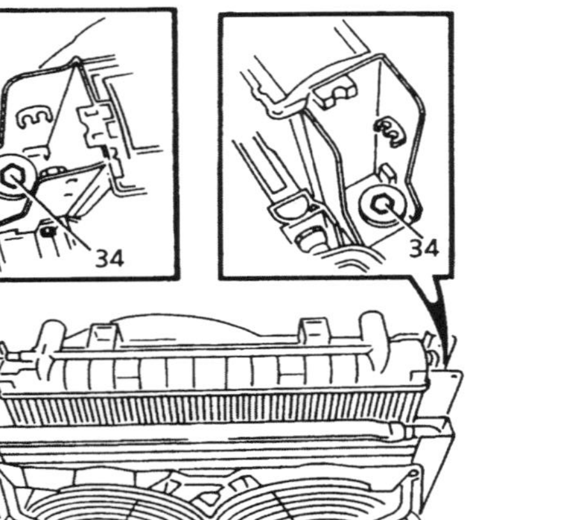

12M7104

35. Disconnect 2 condenser cooling fan multiplugs.

12M7105

36. Remove 2 nuts securing air conditioning pipe to condenser fans. Release pipe.

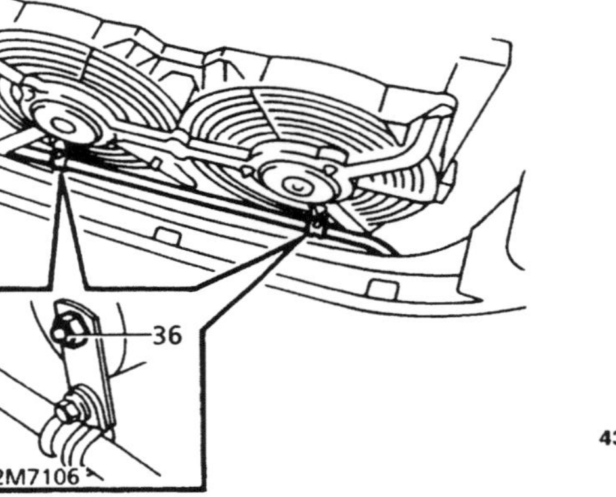

12M7106

37. With assistance, remove radiator/condenser assembly.

Manual Vehicles:

38. Clamp clutch flexible hose using approved brake hose clamp.

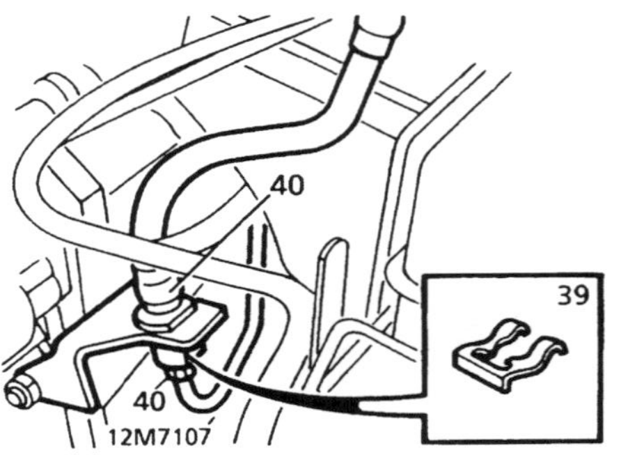

12M7107

39. Remove clip securing flexible hose to gearbox bracket.
40. Disconnect clutch flexible hose at gearbox pipe. Position hose aside.
41. Remove centre console. ***See CHASSIS AND BODY, Repair.***
42. Remove 6 nuts securing gaiter ring. Remove ring and gaiter.

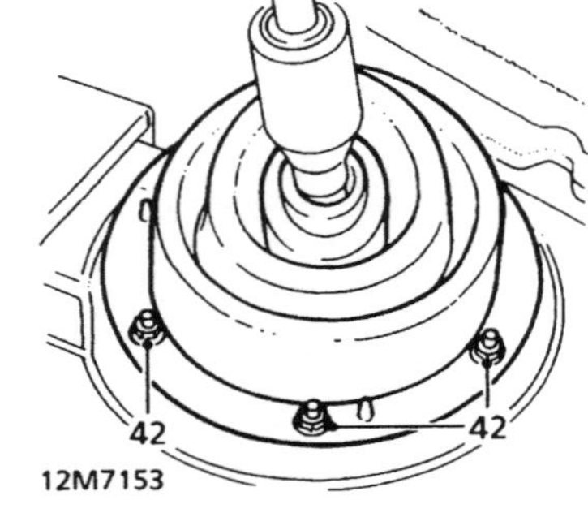

12M7153

43. Remove 2 bolts securing gear lever. Remove lever.

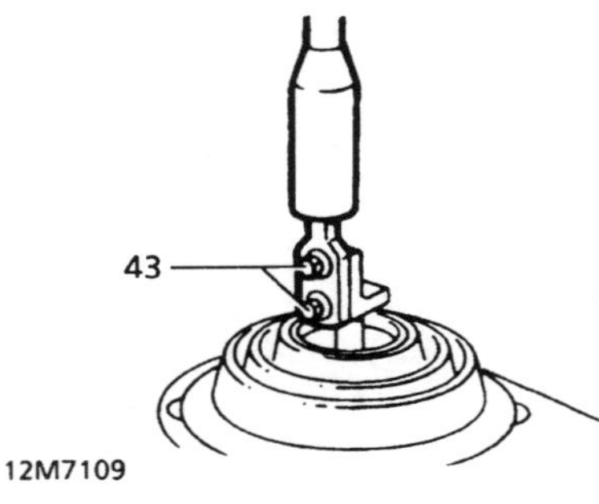

12M7109

Automatic Vehicles:

44. Remove window switch pack. ***See ELECTRICAL, Repair.***

All Vehicles:

45. Release handbrake. Remove handbrake cable clevis pin.

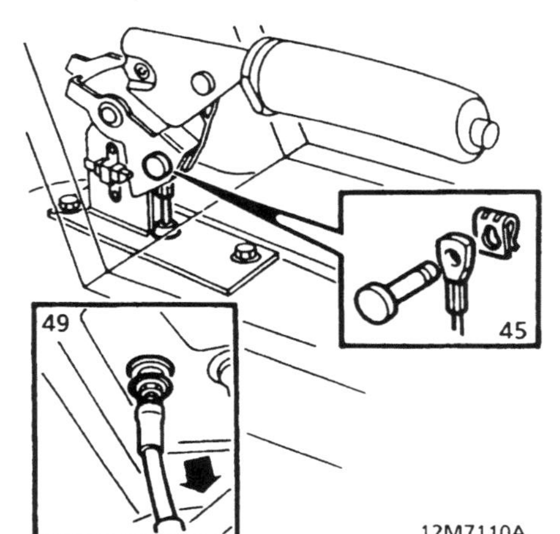

12M7110A

46. Raise lift. Drain gearbox, transfer box and engine fluids. ***See SECTION 10, Maintenance.***
47. Using a transmission jack, support transmission under brake drum.
48. Remove chassis cross member. ***See CHASSIS AND BODY, Repair.***
Remove exhaust front pipe. ***See MANIFOLD AND EXHAUST SYSTEM, Repair.***
49. Release hand brake cable from grommet in tunnel.
50. Remove 4 bolts securing rear propeller shaft guard. Remove guard.

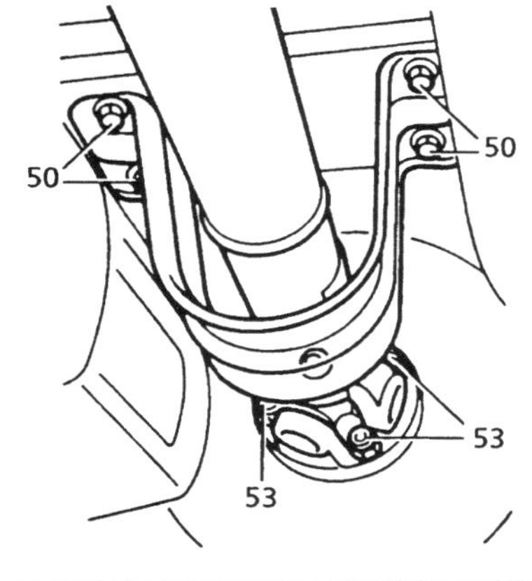

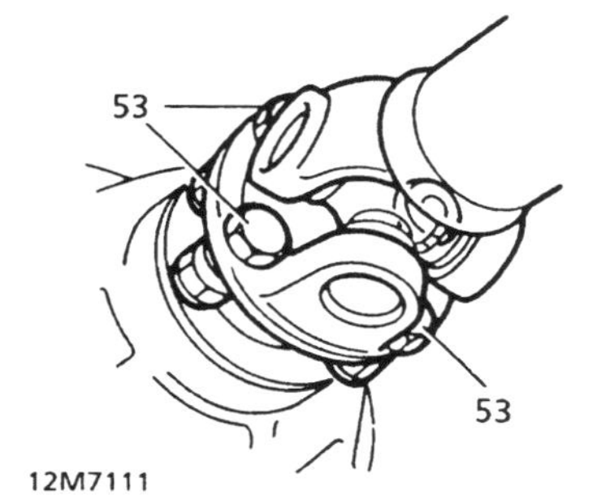

12M7111

51. Mark positions of propeller shafts and transfer box flanges to aid reassembly.
52. Raise one wheel on each axle to allow rotation of propeller shafts.
53. Remove 4 nuts from rear flange and 4 nuts and bolts from front flange. Disconnect propeller shafts. Tie aside.
54. Lower gearbox for access.

Automatic Vehicles:

55. Disconnect gear selector cable trunnion from gearbox lever. Remove 2 bolts securing selector cable abutment bracket to gearbox.
56. Place selector cable aside.

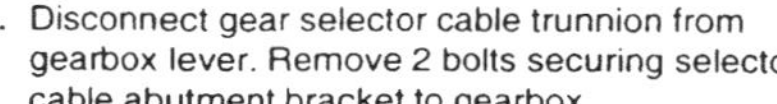

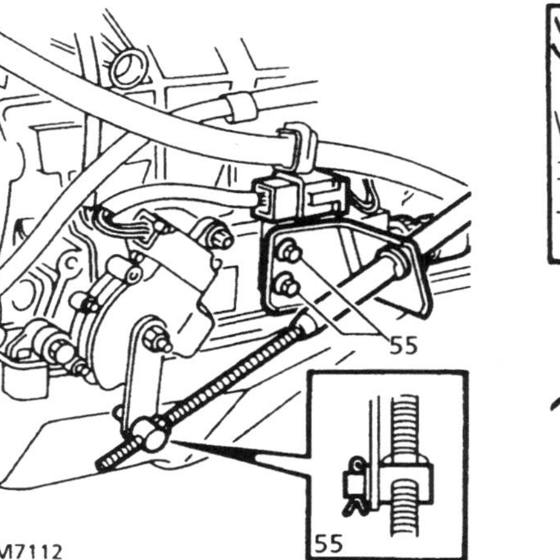

12M7112

57. Disconnect multiplugs from gear selection positon switch and gearbox speed sensor.

All Vehicles:

58. Disconnect 2 Lucars from transfer box fluid temperature sensor.

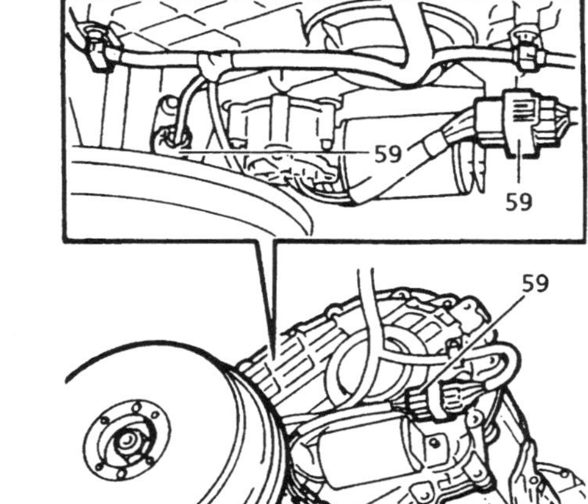

12M7113A

59. Disconnect multiplugs from High/Low motor and output shaft speed sensor.

Manual Vehicles:

60. Disconnect multiplugs from reverse and neutral switches. Remove bolt securing harness bracket to gearbox. Release harness from clips on gearbox brackets.

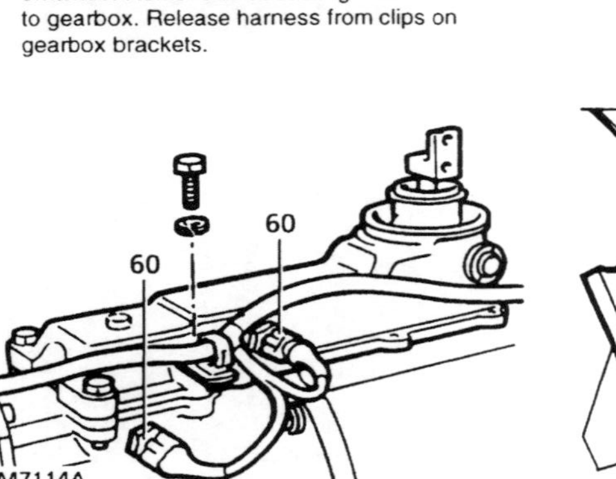

12M7114A

All Vehicles:

61. Disconnect engine harness to gearbox harness multiplug. Position harness aside.

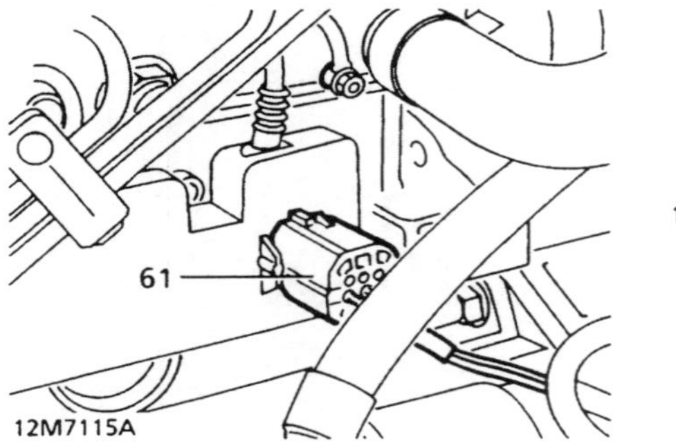

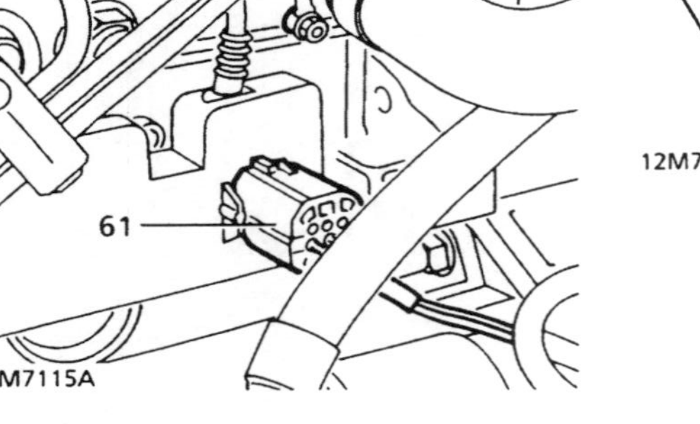

12M7115A

62. Remove 4 nuts securing each engine mount to engine bracket.

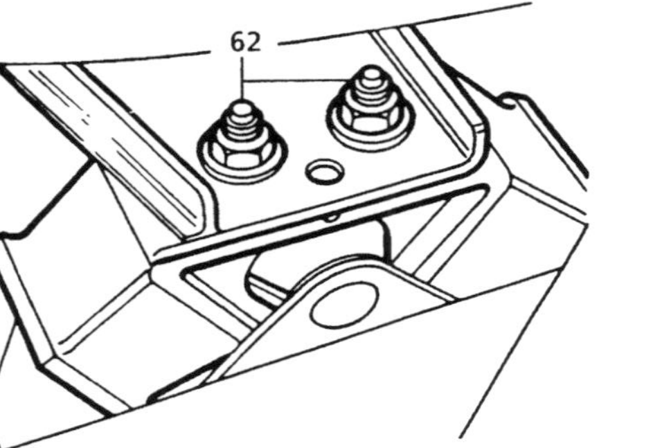

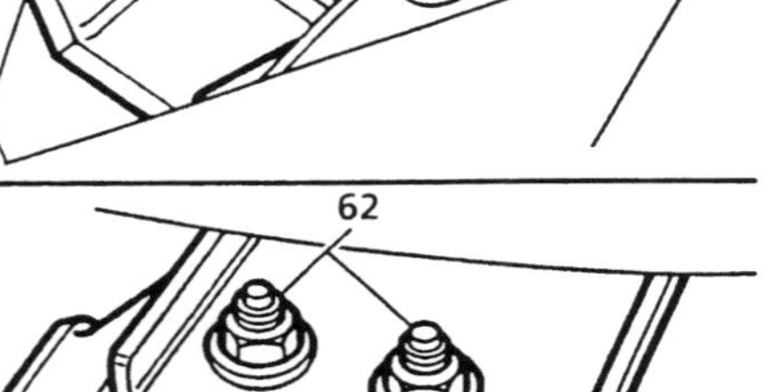

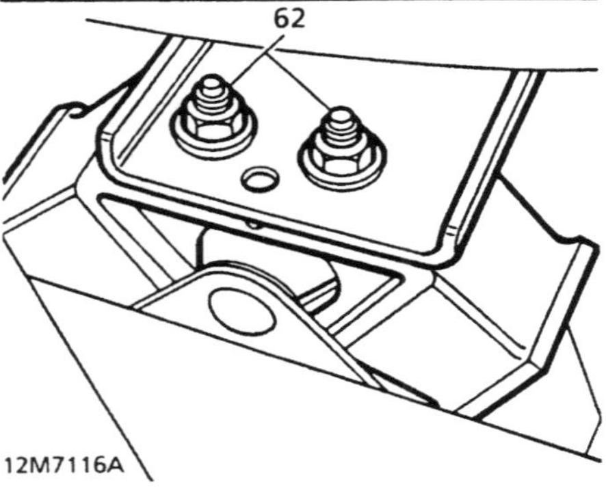

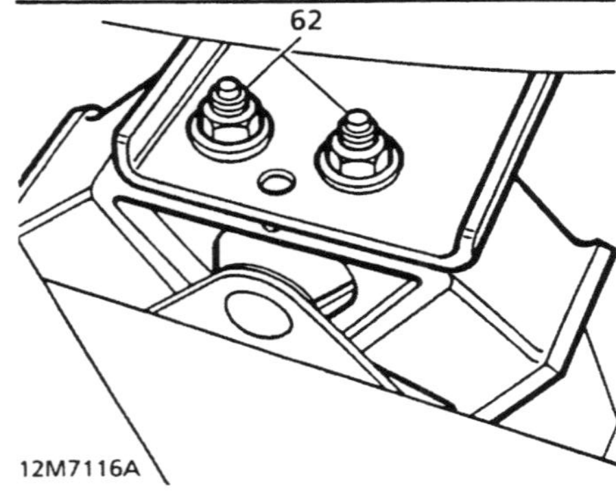

12M7116A

63. Remove 4 nuts securing each engine mount to chassis. Discard nuts.

63

63

12M7117A

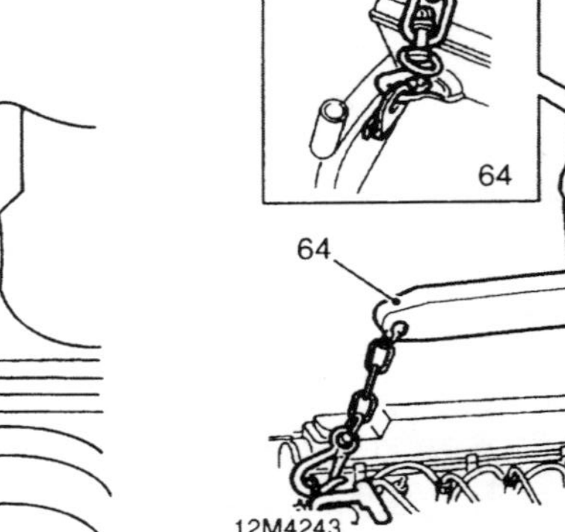

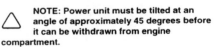

12M4243

64. Fit lifting bracket to engine lifting eyes. Attach suitable hoist.

65. Raise engine slightly. Ensure that lifting bracket does not foul bulkhead. Remove both engine mountings.

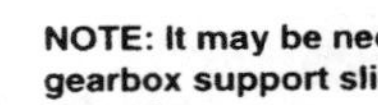

NOTE: It may be necessary to lower gearbox support slightly during above operation.

66. Raise power unit and draw forward.

67. Lower support from transmission.

NOTE: Power unit must be tilted at an angle of approximately 45 degrees before it can be withdrawn from engine compartment.

68. Remove engine/transmission assembly.

Refit

69. Raise power unit. Guide into engine bay.
70. Position transmission jack beneath transmission brake drum.
71. With assistance, raise transmission and lower engine until engine mountings can be fitted.
72. Attach mountings to chassis with new flange nuts. Do not tighten at this stage.

CAUTION: Engine mountings must be fitted with centre bolt head facing outboard as shown.

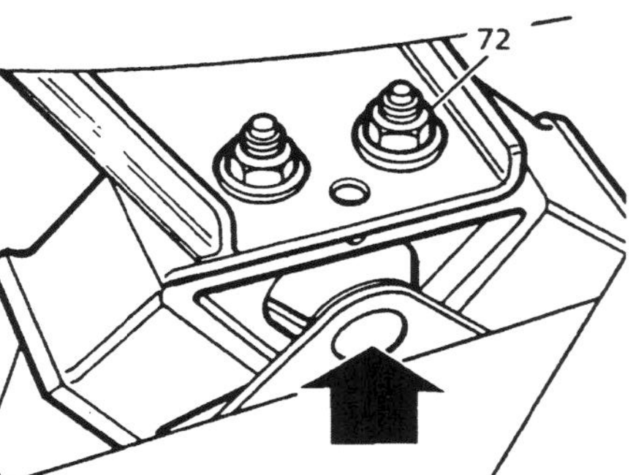

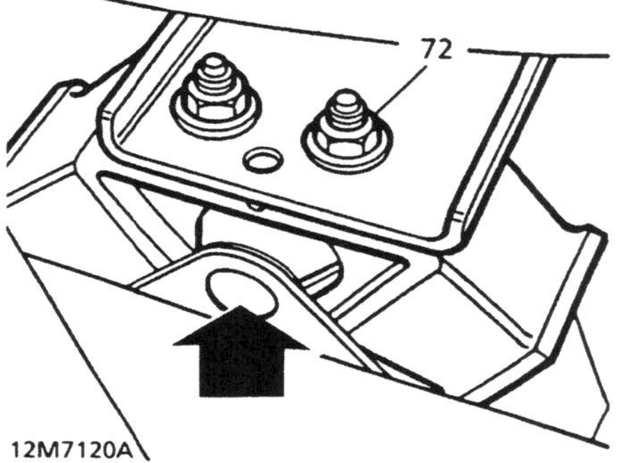

73. Lower and guide engine onto mounting studs.
74. Attach engine to mountings with new flange nuts. Do not tighten at this stage.
75. Release lifting bracket from engine lifting eyes. Remove hoist.
76. Route gearbox harness. Secure with clips.
77. Connect multiplug to engine harness
78. Connect multiplugs to High/Low motor and output shaft speed sensor.

Manual Vehicles:

79. Secure gearbox harness bracket with bolt. Tighten to ***6 Nm. (4 lbf.ft).***
80. Connect multiplugs to reverse and neutral switches.
81. Secure harness to gearbox bracket with clips.
82. Connect Lucars to transfer box fluid temperature sensor.
83. Raise transmission on jack.
84. Align harness bracket to gearbox.

Automatic Vehicles:

85. Connect multiplugs to gear selection position switch and gearbox speed sensor.
86. Position selector cable abutment bracket to gearbox. Secure with bolts.
87. Adjust gear selector cable. ***See AUTOMATIC GEARBOX, Adjustment.***

All Vehicles:

88. Raise one wheel on each axle to allow rotation of propeller shafts.
89. Position shafts to transfer box flanges. Align marks.
90. Secure propeller shaft flanges with nuts and bolts. Tighten to ***48 Nm. (35 lbf.ft)***
91. Fit propeller shaft guard. Tighten bolts.
92. Guide hand brake cable through grommet in transmission tunnel.
93. Fit exhaust front pipe. ***See MANIFOLD AND EXHAUST SYSTEM, Repair.***
94. Fit chassis cross member. ***See CHASSIS AND BODY, Repair.***
95. Remove support from under transmission.
96. Tighten engine mounting nuts to ***45 Nm. (33 lbf.ft)***
97. Lower lift.
98. Connect handbrake cable to lever, secure with clevis pin and clip.

Manual Vehicles:

99. Fit seal around gearbox remote housing to transmission tunnel aperture.
100. Fit gear lever bolts. Tighten to ***25 Nm. (18 lbf.ft)***
101. Fit gaiter and ring. Secure with nuts.
102. Fit centre console. ***See CHASSIS AND BODY, Repair.***

Automatic Vehicles:

103. Fit window switch pack. ***See ELECTRICAL, Repair.***

Manual Vehicles:

104. Connect clutch flexible hose. Remove hose clamp.
105. Secure flexible hose union to gearbox bracket with clip.
106. Bleed clutch hydraulic system. ***See CLUTCH, Repair.***

All Vehicles:

107. With assistance, position radiator/condenser assembly.
108. Connect multiplugs to condenser cooling fans.
109. Engage radiator in lower mounting rubbers. Secure with nuts and bolts.
110. Align air conditioning pipe to condenser fans. Secure with nuts.
111. Remove plugs from air conditioning compressor and pipes.
112. Fit new 'O' rings to compressor pipes. Lubricate 'O' rings with compressor oil. Connect to compressor.
113. Fit compressor connection bolts. Tighten to ***23 Nm. (17 lbs.ft)***
114. Remove plugs from air conditioning condenser and pipes.
115. Fit new 'O' rings to condenser pipes. Lubricate 'O' rings with compressor oil. Secure pipes to condenser. Tighten to ***15 Nm. (11 lbf.ft)***
116. Fit washer bottle filler neck. Secure with bolt and screw.
117. Remove plugs from power steering pump and pipes.
118. Using new sealing washers, secure feed pipe to power steering pump. Tighten to ***30 Nm. (22 lbf.ft)***
119. Untie power steering reservoir from engine. Remove plugs. Connect return pipe. Secure return pipe to reservoir with clip.
120. Secure fog lamp breather hoses to clips on either side of radiator.
121. Connect heater hoses to engine coolant pipes. Secure with clips.
122. Connect coolant bleed hose to radiator. Secure with clip.
123. Connect bottom hose to radiator. Secure with clip.
124. Remove plugs from transmission oil cooler and pipes.
125. Lubricate pipes with transmission fluid, fit new 'O' rings. Connect to oil cooler. Tighten to ***30 Nm. (22 lbf.ft)***
126. Replenish transmission fluids. ***See LUBRICANTS, FLUIDS AND CAPACITIES, Information.***
127. Fit engine oil cooler. ***See this section.***
128. Fit cooling fan. ***See COOLING SYSTEM, Repair.***
129. Evacuate and recharge air conditioning system. ***See AIR CONDITIONING, Adjustment.***
130. Refill cooling system. ***See COOLING SYSTEM, Repair.***
131. Refill engine oil. ***See LUBRICANTS, FLUIDS AND CAPACITIES, Information.***
132. Connect multiplugs to fuel heater and turbo boost sensor.
133. Connect fuel return hose to FIP. Secure with clip.
134. Using new 'O' rings, connect fuel feed hose to fuel heater/filter head.
135. Route engine harness along valance. Secure clip.
136. Connect engine harness multiplug to main harness. Secure earth terminal to valance stud.
137. Connect engine harness multiplug to base of fuse box.
138. Position fuse box. Secure with bolts.
139. Position earth lead to shock absorber turret. Secure with bolt.
140. Fit battery tray. Secure with bolts.
141. Fit starter feed wire to battery positive terminal clamp. Secure with nut.
142. Position engine harness to battery tray. Secure harness grommets.
143. Secure harness clamp to battery tray with screws.

144. Fit ECM. ***See FUEL SYSTEM, Repair.***
145. Fit inlet manifold. ***See MANIFOLD AND EXHAUST SYSTEM, Repair.***
146. Refit battery. ***See ELECTRICAL, Repair.***
147. With assistance, release bonnet stay clips. Engage bonnet struts.

CAUTION: Ensure bonnet stay clips are returned to their original positions as shown.

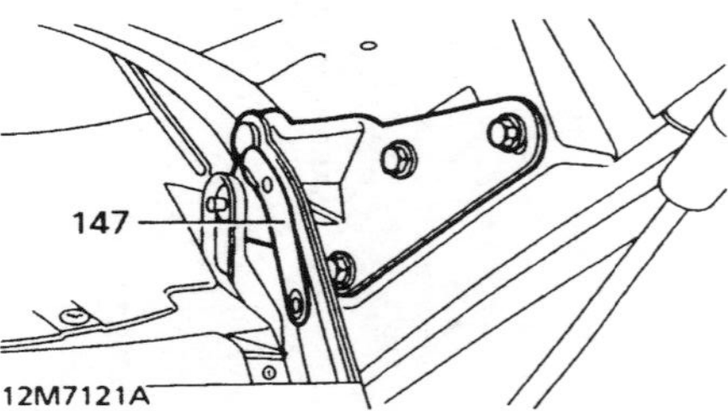

148. Start engine. Check for fuel, coolant and oil leaks.

FLYWHEEL/DRIVE PLATE

Service repair no - 12.53.07

Remove

1. Disconnect battery negative lead.
2. *Manual gearbox:* Remove clutch assembly. ***See CLUTCH, Repair.***
3. *Automatic gearbox:* Remove gearbox. ***See AUTOMATIC GEARBOX, Repair.***
4. Lock flywheel/drive plate using LRT-12-106.
5. Remove and discard 8 bolts securing flywheel/drive plate.
6. Remove flywheel/drive plate.

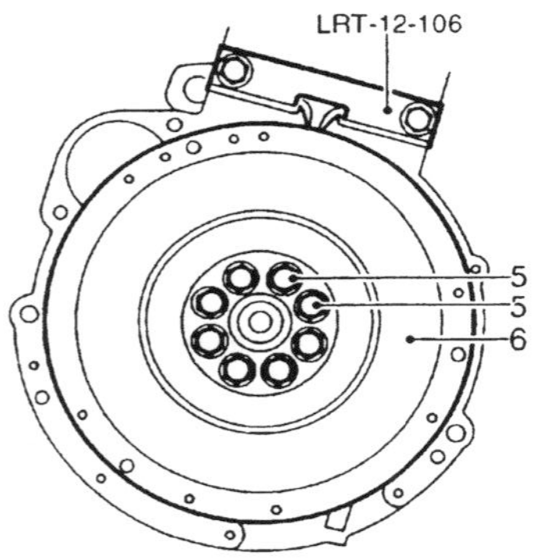

NOTE: Flywheel illustrated

Inspection

7. Inspect flywheel clutch face/drive plate for cracks, scores or overheating.
8. Inspect ring gear for worn, chipped or broken teeth.
9. Replace defective parts as necessary.

Refit

10. Ensure mating faces, dowel and dowel locations are clean.
11. Position flywheel/drive plate to crankshaft, locate dowel.
12. Secure flywheel/drive plate with new bolts. Tighten bolts to:
    Flywheel - ***105 Nm. (77 lbf.ft)***
    Drive plate - ***120 Nm (88 lbf.ft)***
13. Manual gearbox: Fit clutch assembly. ***See CLUTCH, Repair.***
14. *Automatic gearbox:* Fit gearbox. ***See AUTOMATIC GEARBOX, Repair.***
15. Reconnect battery negative lead.

FRONT COVER GASKET

Service repair no - 12.65.04

Remove

1. Disconnect battery negative lead.
2. Remove cylinder head gasket. ***See this section.***
3. Remove sump. ***See this section.***
4. Remove alternator. ***See ELECTRICAL, Repair.***
5. Remove crankshaft pulley. ***See this section.***

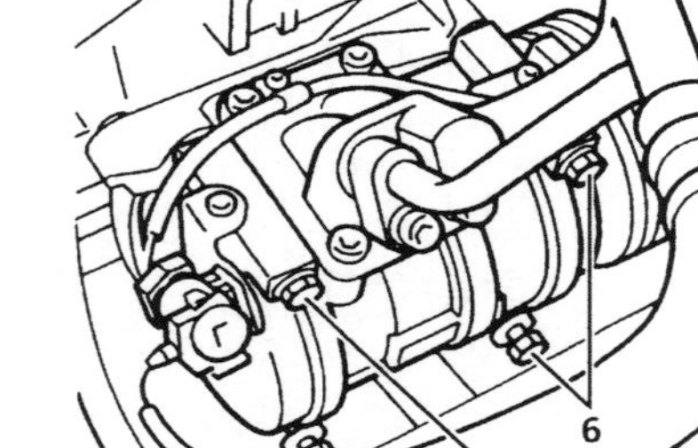

6. Remove 4 bolts securing air conditioning compressor to bracket. Tie compressor aside.

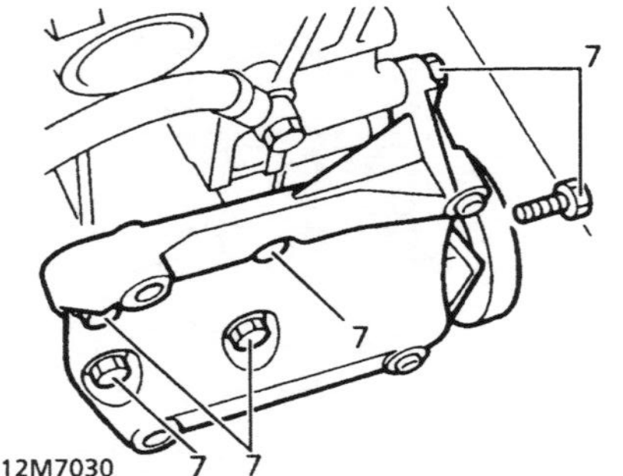

7. Remove 6 bolts securing compressor bracket to cylinder block and front cover. Remove compressor bracket.

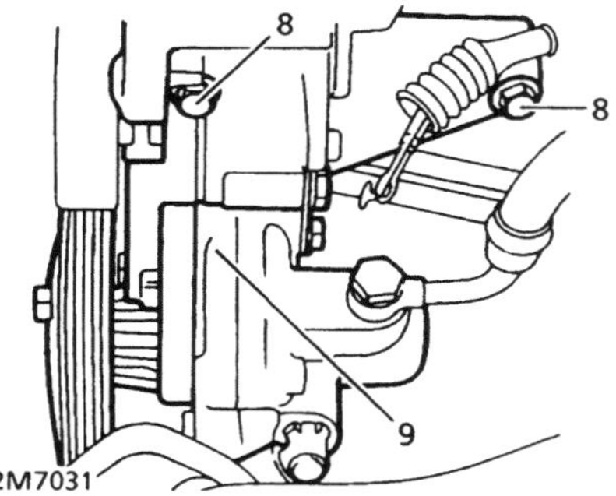

12M7031

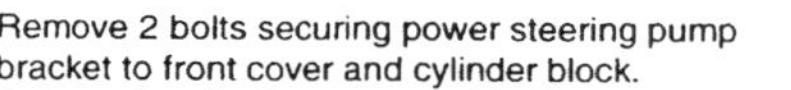

8. Remove 2 bolts securing power steering pump bracket to front cover and cylinder block.
9. Release bracket/pump assembly. Tie aside.

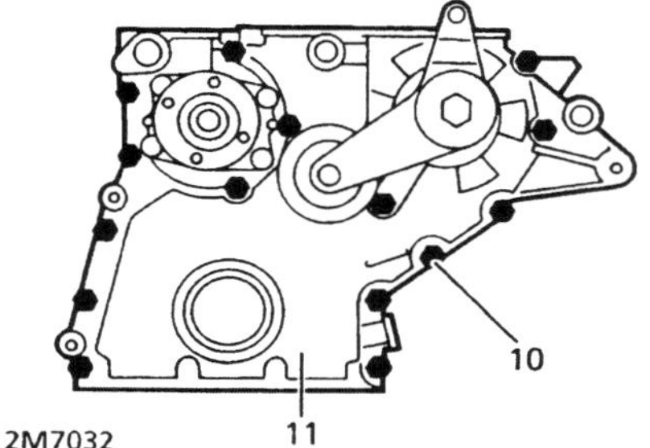

12M7032

10. Remove 15 bolts securing front cover to cylinder block.
11. Remove front cover from 2 cylinder block ring dowels.

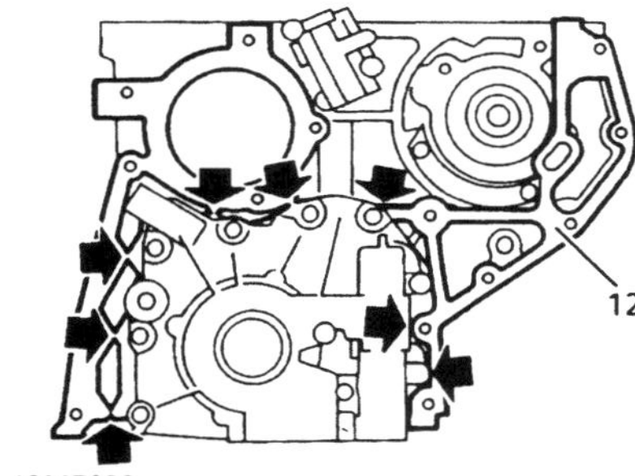

12M7033

12. Remove and discard gasket.

NOTE: Front cover gasket is integral with oil pump gasket. When removing front cover only, separate gaskets by cutting at points shown.

Refit

13. Ensure mating faces are clean.
14. Position new gasket on cylinder block.
15. Align front cover to cylinder block dowels. Secure with bolts. Tighten to ***10 Nm. (7 lbf.ft)***
16. Position power steering pump on cylinder block dowel.
17. Secure steering pump bracket to front cover and cylinder block with bolts. Tighten to ***22 Nm. (16 lbf.ft)***
18. Position air conditioning compressor bracket to cylinder block. Secure with bolts.
19. Position compressor on mounting bracket ring dowels. Secure with bolts.
20. Fit crankshaft pulley. ***See this section.***
21. Fit alternator. ***See ELECTRICAL, Repair.***
22. Fit sump. ***See this section.***
23. Fit cylinder head gasket. ***See this section.***
24. Reconnect battery negative lead.

CAMSHAFT

Service repair no - 12.13.02

Remove

1. Remove camshaft cover. ***See this section.*** *Vehicles with EGR:* Remove EGR vacuum pump. ***See EMISSION CONTROL, Repair.***

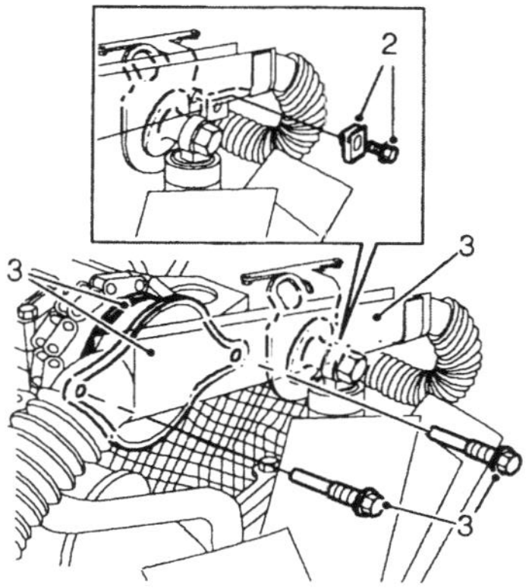

12M4175A

2. Remove bolt securing harness trunking, recover nut plate.
3. *Vehicles without EGR:* Remove 2 bolts securing camshaft front cover plate, remove cover plate; remove and discard 'O' ring. Lay harness trunking aside.

4. Remove plastic plug from flywheel/drive plate timing pin access hole.

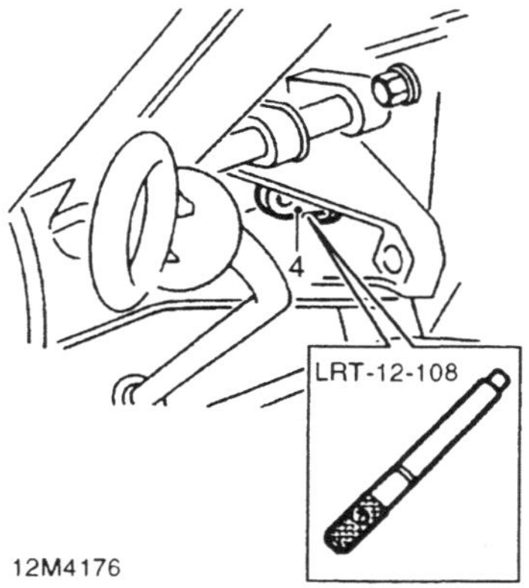

12M4176

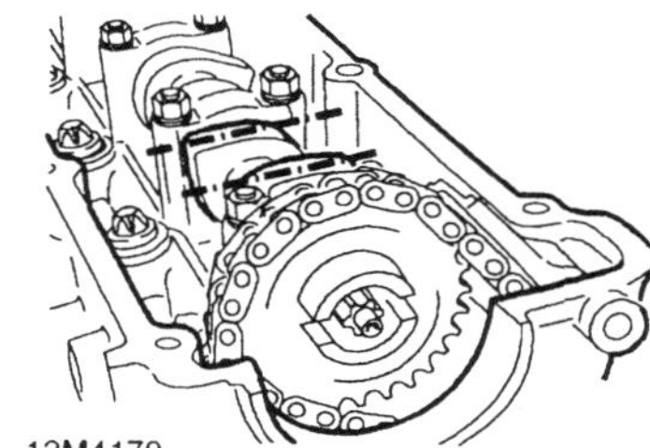

12M4179

5. Rotate crankshaft clockwise until No.1 piston is at top dead centre (TDC) on its compression stroke. Insert timing pin LRT-12-108 into hole in flywheel/drive plate.

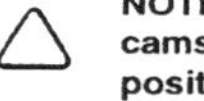

NOTE: TDC No. 1 is indicated when camshaft lobes of No. 1 cylinder are positioned as shown.

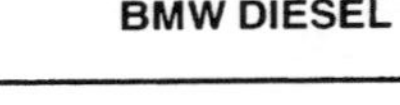

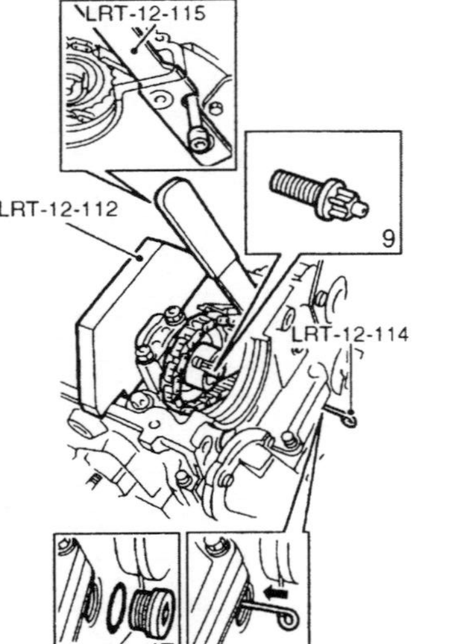

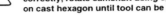

12M4177

6. Fit camshaft holding tool LRT-12-112.
7. Remove timing chain tensioner access plug, remove and discard sealing washer.
8. Using tool LRT-12-115, retract timing chain tensioner and insert tensioner pin LRT-12-114 to retain tensioner plunger.

CAUTION: Ensure eye of tensioner pin LRT-12-114 is vertical not horizontal.

9. Remove bolt securing camshaft sprocket, remove sprocket.

NOTE: Do not discard bolt at this stage.

10. Remove camshaft holding tool LRT-12-112.

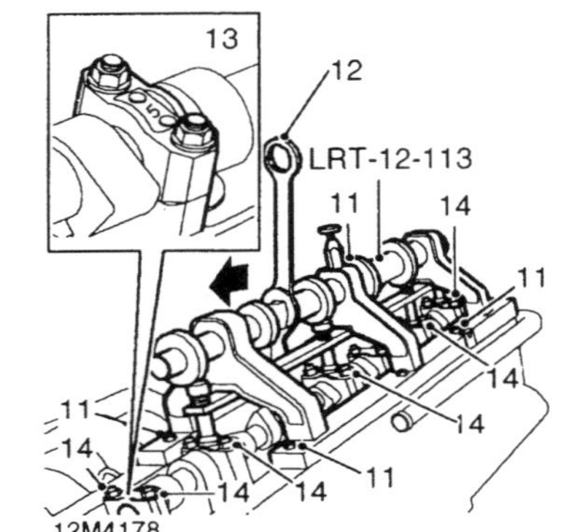

12M4178

11. Locate tool LRT-12-113 on cylinder head, secure with tool with camshaft cover bolts.
12. Rotate shaft of tool LRT-12-113 to load camshaft bearing caps.
13. Ensure camshaft bearing caps are suitably identified to their fitted positions.

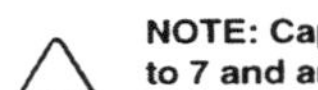
NOTE: Caps should be numbered from 1 to 7 and are read from the front of the engine.

14. Remove nuts securing camshaft bearing caps.
15. Rotate shaft of tool LRT-12-113 until loading is removed from camshaft bearing caps, remove tool.
16. Remove camshaft bearing caps.
17. Remove camshaft.

Inspection

18. Clean camshaft, bearing caps and journals in cylinder head.
19. Check cam lobes for signs of wear, pitting or scoring.
20. Check journals on camshaft, bearing caps and cylinder head for signs of wear, overheating and scoring.
21. Lubricate cam followers, camshaft bearing caps and journals with engine oil.
22. Clean sealant from threads of front cover plate bolt and bolt hole.

CAUTION: Do not use a tap.

Refit

23. Remove timing pin LRT-12-108 from flywheel/drive plate.
24. Rotate crankshaft **anti-clockwise** approximately 30°

12M4180

25. Fit camshaft with lobes of No.1 cylinder facing upwards.
26. Fit camshaft bearing caps ensuring No.1 cap is at front of engine and cap identification marks are on exhaust manifold side.
27. Locate tool LRT-12-113 on cylinder head, secure tool with camshaft cover bolts.
28. Rotate shaft of tool LRT-12-113 to load camshaft bearing caps.
29. Fit camshaft bearing cap nuts and tighten to:
M6 - ***10 Nm (7 lbf.ft)***
M7 - ***15 Nm (11 lbf/ft)***
M8 - ***20 Nm (15 lbf/ft)***
30. Rotate shaft of tool LRT-12-113 until loading is removed from camshaft bearing caps, remove tool.

CAUTION: The tappets expand when camshaft is removed. To avoid pistons contacting valves, observe the following wait times before rotating pistons back to top dead centre (TDC).
Above 20° C - 4 minutes
10° C to 20° C - 11 minutes
0° C to 10° C - 30 minutes
Below 0° C - 75 minutes

31. Rotate crankshaft clockwise until No.1 piston is at top dead centre (TDC) and timing pin LRT-12-108 can be inserted in flywheel/drive plate; fit camshaft holding tool LRT-12-112.

NOTE: If camshaft is not positioned correctly, rotate camshaft using spanner on cast hexagon until tool can be fitted.

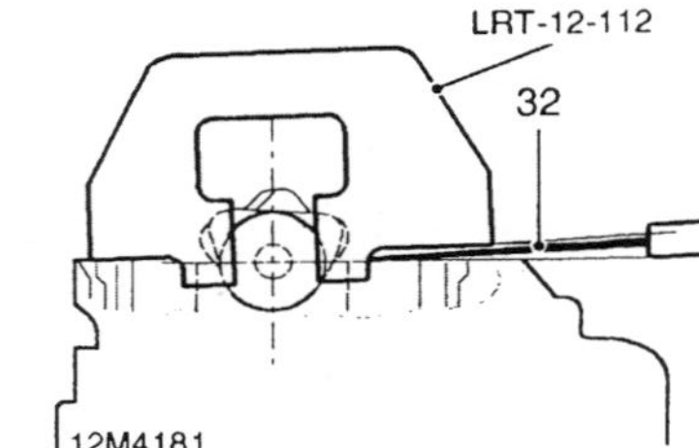

12M4181

32. *Engines with recorded mileage in excess of 20,000 km (12,500 miles):* Insert a 4.61 mm (0.18 in) thickness of feeler gauges between camshaft holding tool LRT-12-112 and inlet manifold side of cylinder head.
33. *All engines:* Fit camshaft sprocket.
34. Fit new camshaft sprocket bolt and tighten to:
Stage 1 - ***20 Nm (15 lbf.ft).***
Stage 2 - Further 35°

NOTE: Use angular torque wrench.

35. Using tool LRT-12-115, retract timing chain tensioner rail slightly and remove tensioner pin LRT-12-114.
36. Fit new sealing washer to timing chain tensioner access plug, fit plug and tighten to ***20 Nm (15 lbf.ft)*** .
37. Remove timing pin LRT-12-108 from flywheel/drive plate.
38. Fit plastic plug in timing pin access hole.

39. Apply STC 3373 sealant to camshaft front cover plate dowel bolt.
40. Lubricate new 'O' ring with engine oil.
41. Position harness trunking.
42. *Vehicles without EGR:* Fit 'O' ring and camshaft front cover plate, fit bolts and tighten to ***22 Nm (16 lbf.ft)***.

CAUTION: Ensure dowel bolt passes through timing chain guide rail.

43. Position nut plate to bracket, fit and tighten harness trunking bolt.
44. Fit camshaft cover. ***See this section.***
45. *Vehicles with EGR:* Fit EGR vacuum pump. ***See EMISSION CONTROL, Repair.***

CYLINDER HEAD GASKET

Service repair no - 12.29.02

Remove

1. Disconnect battery negative lead.
2. Remove fan cowl. ***See COOLING SYSTEM, Repair.***
3. Remove high pressure fuel pipe assembly. ***See FUEL SYSTEM, Repair.***
4. Remove camshaft cover. ***See this section.***
5. *Vehicles with EGR:* Remove EGR vacuum pump. ***See EMISSION CONTROL, Repair.***
6. Remove exhaust manifold heat shield. ***See MANIFOLD AND EXHAUST SYSTEM, Repair.***
7. Remove 3 bolts securing turbocharger to exhaust manifold. Collect gasket and discard.

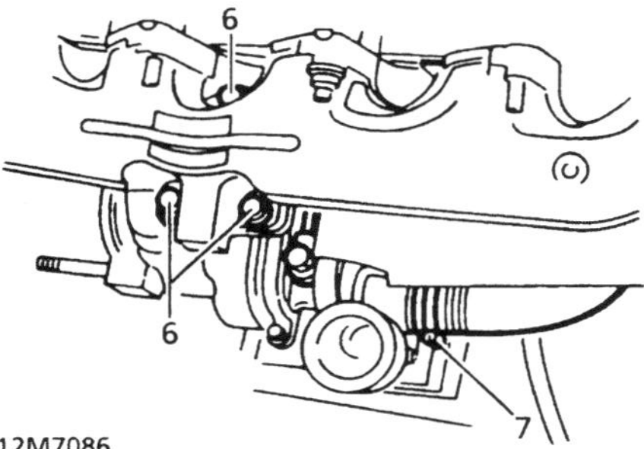

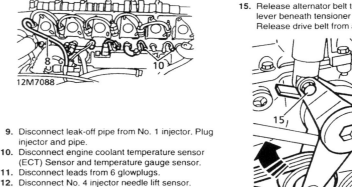

12M7086

8. Remove turbocharger intake hose. Plug turbocharger intake.

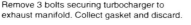

12M7088

9. Disconnect leak-off pipe from No. 1 injector. Plug injector and pipe.
10. Disconnect engine coolant temperature sensor (ECT) Sensor and temperature gauge sensor.
11. Disconnect leads from 6 glowplugs.
12. Disconnect No. 4 injector needle lift sensor.

Vehicles without EGR

13. Remove 2 bolts securing harness trunking to cylinder head. Tie trunking aside.

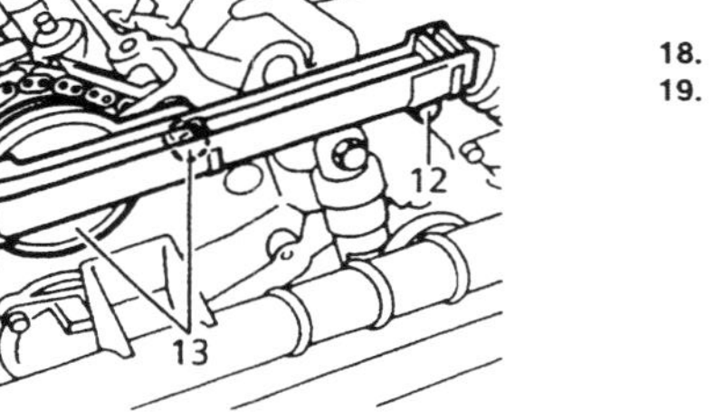

12M7147

14. Remove remaining bolt securing camshaft end cover. Remove cover. Discard 'O' ring.

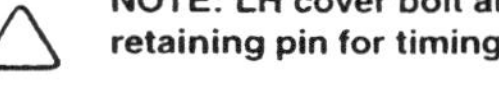

NOTE: LH cover bolt also serves as retaining pin for timing chain guide rail.

All vehicles

15. Release alternator belt tension using a suitable lever beneath tensioner damper as shown. Release drive belt from alternator pulley.

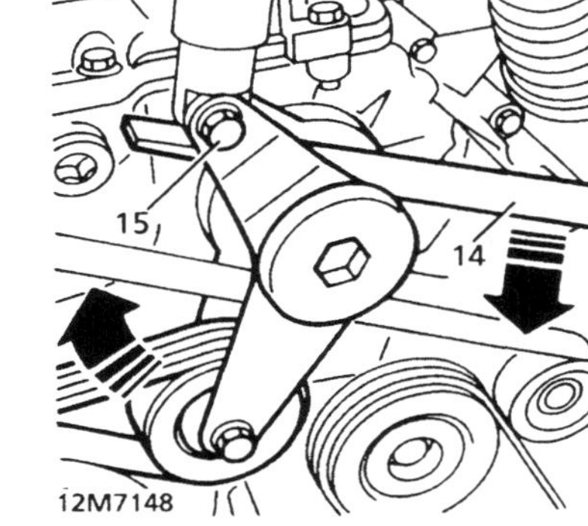

12M7148

16. Remove bolt securing damper to drive belt tensioner.
17. Release hoses from thermostat housing and cylinder head.
18. Disconnect heater hose from cylinder head.
19. Remove plastic plug from flywheel timing pin access hole. Insert timing pin LRT-12-108.

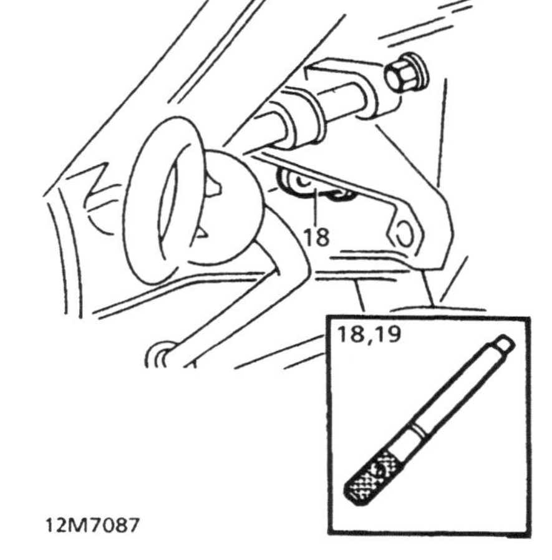

12M7087

20. Turn crankshaft clockwise until No. 1 piston is at Top Dead Centre (TDC) on its compression stroke. Locate timing pin into flywheel.

NOTE: TDC No. 1 indicated by camshaft lobes of No. 1 cylinder pointing upwards.

21. Fit camshaft holding tool LRT-12-112.
22. Remove timing chain tensioner access plug. Collect sealing washer and discard.
23. Using tool LRT-12-115, lever timing chain tensioner rail to slack position. Insert tool LRT-12-114 to retain tensioner plunger.

12M7089

24. Remove bolt securing camshaft sprocket. Remove sprocket.

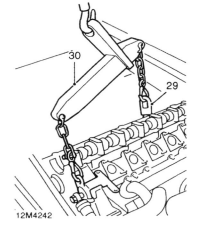

12M7090

25. Remove timing chain tensioner and guide rail pins. Remove 'O' rings and discard.
26. Remove timing chain tensioner rail.
27. Remove 5 bolts and 1 nut securing cylinder head to timing cover.
28. Remove camshaft holding tool.

CAUTION: Do not rotate camshaft.

29. Using sequence shown, progressively slacken and remove 14 cylinder head bolts. Discard bolts.

NOTE: LH rear bolt cannot be removed due to proximity of bulkhead.

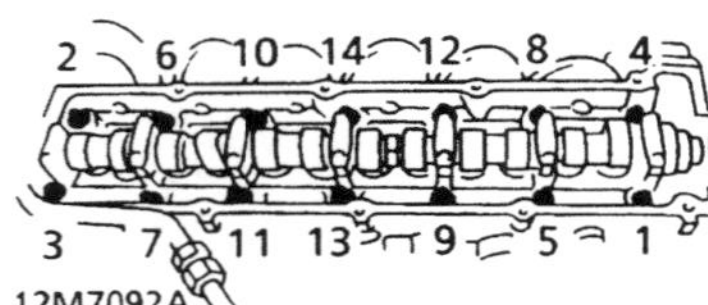

12M7092A

30. Attach suitable lifting eye to upper rear inlet manifold stud.

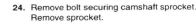

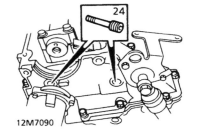

12M4242

31. Attach hoist to lifting eyes. Remove cylinder head, remove and discard LH rear cylinder head bolt.

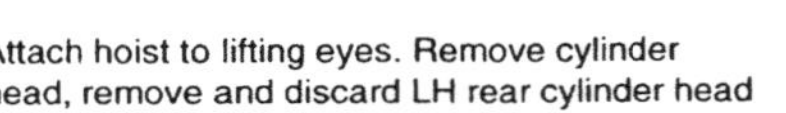

NOTE: 2 ring dowels locate cylinder head to block.

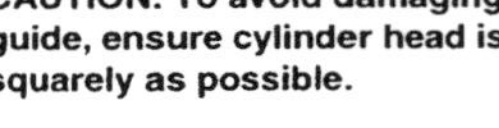
CAUTION: To avoid damaging timing chain guide, ensure cylinder head is lifted as squarely as possible.

32. Remove cylinder head gasket.
33. Check number of thickness identification holes before discarding gasket.

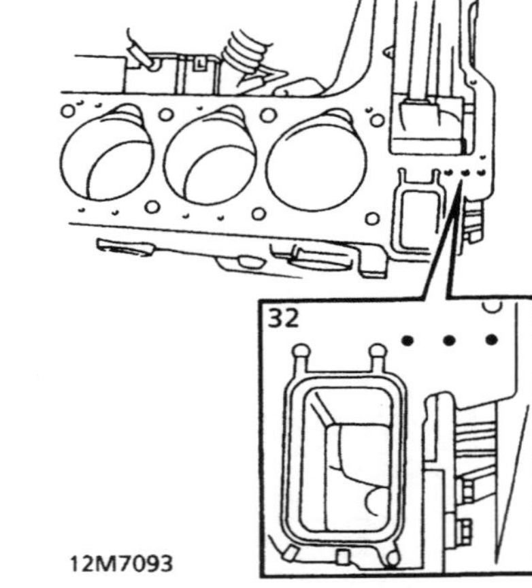

12M7093

CAUTION: Check cylinder head for warping, see Cylinder head warp check. If crankshaft, pistons or connecting rods have been renewed, new cylinder head gasket thickness must be determined using the following Piston Protrusion Check procedure. If above items have not been disturbed, continue at Refit using gasket with same thickness identification as original.

Piston Protrusion - Check

34. Ensure cylinder block face and piston crowns are clean.
35. Position a dial gauge with suitable base to cylinder block.

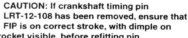

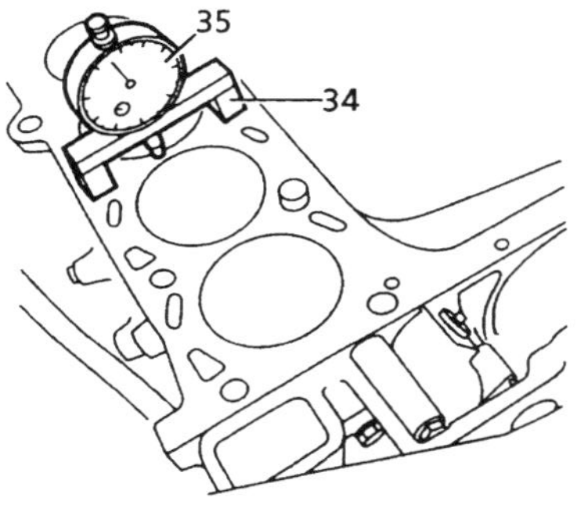

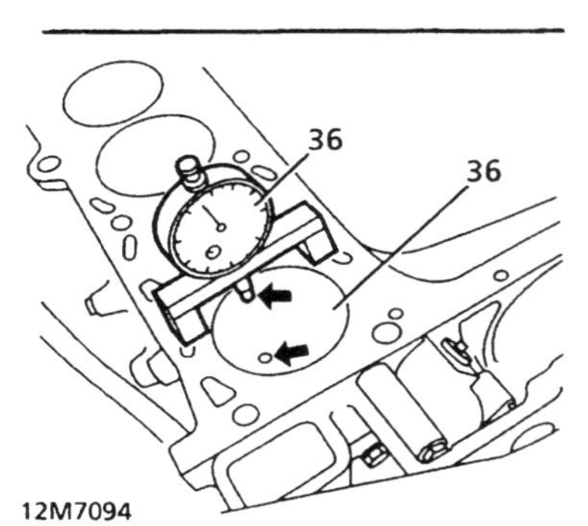

12M7094

36. Preload and zero gauge on cylinder block face.
37. Move gauge onto piston crown. Measure protrusion of No. 1 piston in two positions as shown. Take average of readings. Record results.
38. Repeat protrusion check on piston No. 6.
39. Remove timing pin LRT-12-108 from flywheel.
40. Record protrusion of remaining pistons. Ensure that readings are taken at **exactly** TDC.

NOTE: Top Dead Centre must be located using dial gauge.

41. Calculate average piston protrusion to determine required gasket thickness:
Up to 0.76mm = 2 identification holes
Over 0.76mm = 3 identification holes

NOTE: If any piston protrudes more then 0.81mm, a gasket with 3 identification holes must be fitted.

Cylinder head warp - check

42. Remove all traces of carbon and gasket material from cylinder head.

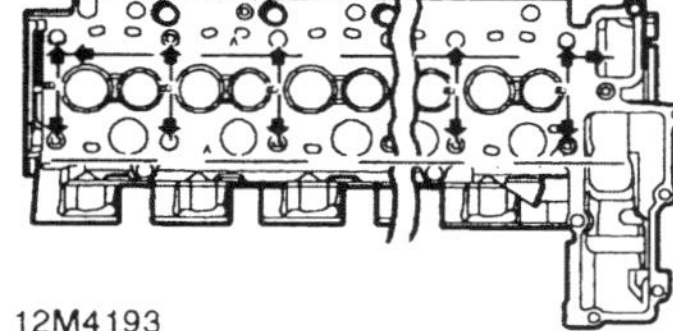

12M4193

43. Using a straight edge and feeler gauges, check cylinder head for distortion along lines shown in illustration and compare with figures given:
Longitudinal warp **A** = 0.1 mm (0.004 in)
Lateral warp **B** = 0.05 mm (0.002 in)
44. Replace cylinder head if figures obtained exceed those given.

NOTE: Cylinder heads may not be refaced.

Refit

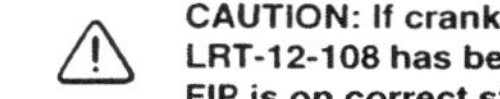

CAUTION: If crankshaft timing pin LRT-12-108 has been removed, ensure that FIP is on correct stroke, with dimple on FIP sprocket visible, before refitting pin.

45. Ensure all mating faces are clean.
46. Check cylinder block ring dowels for condition and correct location.
47. Apply 1.5mm bead of Unipart sealant STC 3373 to joint lines of cylinder block and timing cover.
48. Fit cylinder head gasket of correct thickness.
49. Fit tool LRT-12-112 to ensure camshaft is in correct position. If necessary, turn camshaft using spanner on cast hexagon.

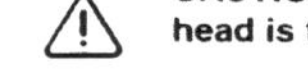

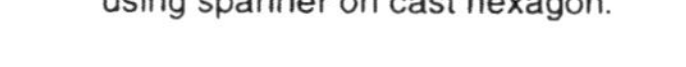

CAUTION: Do not turn camshaft if cylinder head is fitted to cylinder block.

NOTE: Fit a lightly oiled, new cylinder head bolt in LH rear location.

50. Position cylinder head on cylinder block. Ensure timing chain guide is not fouled and rear LH bolt enters bolt hole in cylinder block. Locate cylinder head on ring dowels.
51. Disconnect lifting chains. Remove lifting eye.
52. Lightly lubricate new cylinder head bolts. Fit bolts. Tighten, in sequence shown, in the following stages.
Stage 1 = 80 Nm (59 lbf.ft)
Stage 2 = Loosen by 180°
Stage 3 = 50 Nm (37 lbf.ft)
Stage 4 = Tighten 90°
Stage 5 = Tighten 90°
Stage 6 = Run engine for 25 minutes
Stage 7 = Stop engine, allow to cool
Stage 8 = Tighten 90°

NOTE: Tighten using angular torque wrench.

13 9 5 1 3 7 11
12 8 4 2 6 10 14

12M7092

53. Secure cylinder head to timing cover with bolts and nut.
M7 - ***15 Nm. (11 lbf.ft)***
M8 - ***20 Nm. (15 lbf.ft)***
54. Fit camshaft timing chain tensioner rail.
55. Using new 'O' rings, fit tensioner and guide rail pins.
56. Engage timing chain with camshaft sprocket. Position sprocket on camshaft.
57. Fit NEW camshaft sprocket bolt.

NOTE: Important; if engine has covered more than 20,000 km (12,500 miles), insert a feeler gauge of 4.61 mm (0.18 in) thickness between cylinder head face and inlet manifold side of LRT-12-112 prior to tightening bolt.

58. With LRT-12-112 fitted to camshaft, tighten camshaft sprocket bolt to ***20 Nm. (15 lbf.ft).***
59. Using a suitable torque angle gauge, further tighten bolt by 35°.
60. Remove LRT-12-112.
61. Using tool LRT-12-115, lever tensioner rail to slack position. Remove LRT-12-114 from tensioner plunger.
62. Using a new sealing washer, refit access plug.

63. Remove LRT-12-108 from flywheel. Fit plastic plug.
64. Connect cooling hoses. Secure with clips.
65. Align damper to tensioner. Secure with bolt.
66. Lever tensioner to slack position. Engage drive belt over alternator pulley.

Vehicles without EGR

67. Using a new 'O' ring, fit camshaft end cover.

NOTE: Apply Loctite 577 sealant to threads of LH camshaft end cover bolt.

68. Align harness trunking to cylinder head. Secure camshaft end cover and harness trunking with bolts.

All Vehicles

69. Connect No. 4 injector needle lift sensor.
70. Connect leads to glowplugs.
71. Connect ECT sensor and temperature gauge sensor.
72. Remove plugs. Connect leak-off pipe to No. 1 injector.
73. Remove plug, fit intake hose to turbocharger. Secure with clip.
74. Position new gasket on exhaust manifold. Fit turbocharger.
75. Secure with bolts. ***45 Nm. (33 lbf.ft)***
76. Fit exhaust manifold heat shield. ***See MANIFOLD AND EXHAUST SYSTEM, Repair.***
77. Fit camshaft cover. ***See this section.***
78. *Vehicles with EGR:* Fit EGR vacuum pump. ***See EMISSION CONTROL, Repair.***
79. Fit high pressure fuel pipes. ***See FUEL SYSTEM, Repair.***
80. Fit fan cowl. ***See COOLING SYSTEM, Repair.***
81. Reconnect battery negative lead.

VALVES AND TAPPETS

Service repair no - 12.29.59

Remove

1. Remove camshaft. ***See this section.***
2. Remove inlet manifold. ***See MANIFOLD AND EXHAUST SYSTEM, Repair.***
3. Remove exhaust manifold. ***See MANIFOLD AND EXHAUST SYSTEM, Repair.***
4. Remove injectors. ***See FUEL SYSTEM, Repair.***
5. Remove glow plugs. ***See FUEL SYSTEM, Repair.***
6. Remove cylinder head. ***See this section.***
7. Remove tappets and store in their fitted order.

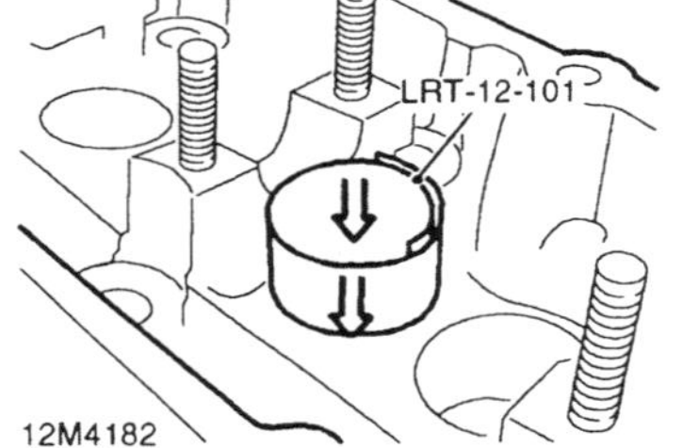
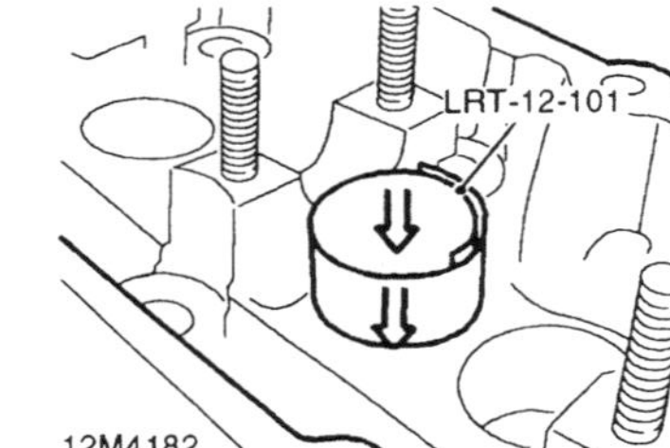

12M4182

8. Insert protective sleeve LRT-12-101 in tappet bore.

12M4183A

9. Position tool LRT-12-034 on valve.
10. Compress valve spring.
11. Remove 2 collets using a stick magnet.
12. Release tool LRT-12-034, collect valve spring cup, valve spring and spring seat, discard valve spring.

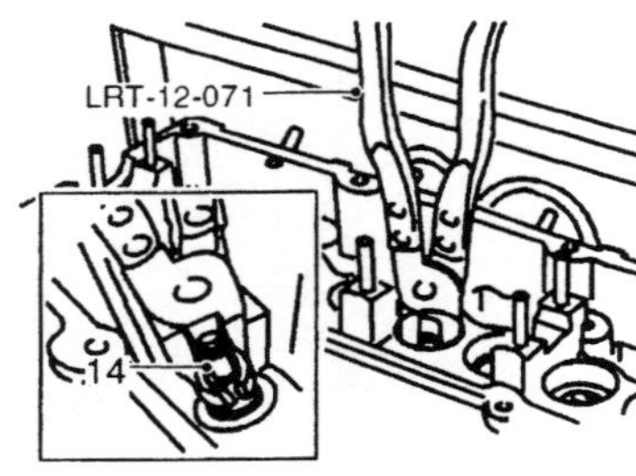

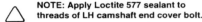

12M4184

13. Remove valve stem oil seal using LRT-12-071, discard seal.
14. Remove valve.

CAUTION: Store valve components in their fitted order.

15. Repeat above procedures for remaining valves.
16. Clean all components.

Inspection

Valves

17. Remove carbon from valves, valve guides and seats.
18. Check valves for signs of burning, cracking and pitting of valve seats.
19. Check head diameter of each valve:
    Inlet = 36.0 mm (1.42 in)
    Exhaust = 31.0 mm (1.22 in)
20. Check stem diameter of each valve, half-way along stem and compare diameters with dimensions given to determine stem sizes of valves fitted and valve stem wear.
    Standard:
    Inlet = 6.97 mm (0.274 in)
    Service limit = 6.95 mm (0.273 in)
    Exhaust = 6.95 mm (0.273 in)
    Service limit = 6.93 mm (0.272 in)

    1st oversize:
    Inlet = 7.07 mm (0.28 in)
    Service limit = 7.05 mm (0.277 in)
    Exhaust = 7.06 mm (0.278 in)
    Service limit = 7.04 mm (0.27 in)

    2nd oversize:
    Inlet = 7.17 mm (0.282 in)
    Service limit = 7.15 mm (0.28 in)
    Exhaust = 7.16 mm (0.281 in)
    Service limit = 7.14 mm (0.279 in)
21. If valve stems are worn in excess of service limits, valves with next oversize stems must be fitted and valve guides reamed to correct size.

Valve guides

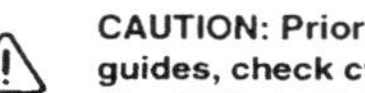
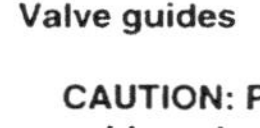

CAUTION: Prior to checking/reaming valve guides, check cylinder head for warping. ***See Cylinder head gasket.***

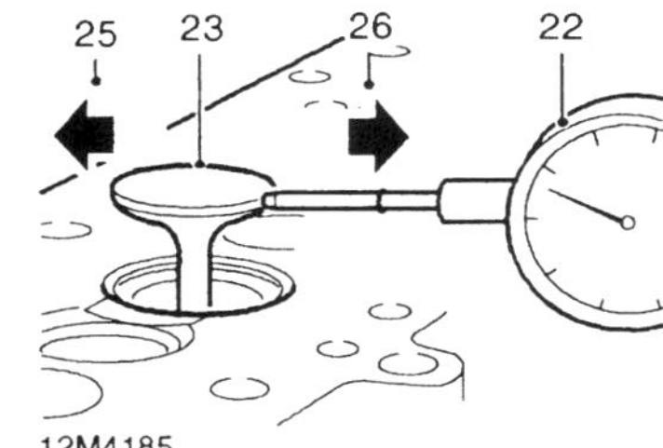
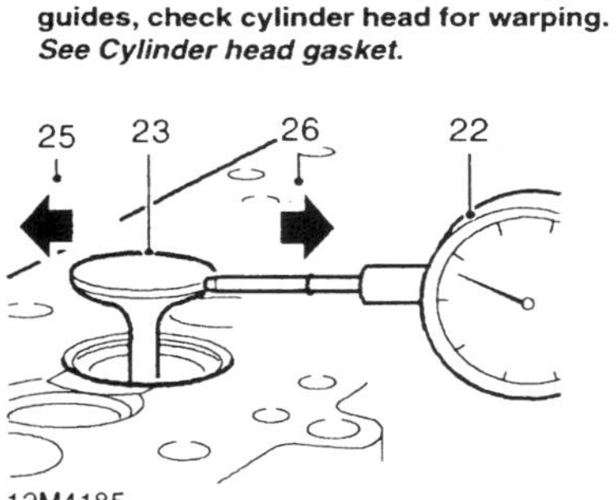

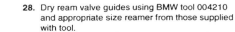

12M4185

22. Position a suitable DTI to cylinder head adjacent to No.1 valve seat.
23. Insert a new valve with same stem diameter as the original in the valve guide.
24. Position end of valve stem flush with spring end of guide.
25. Move valve away from DTI, pre-load gauge and note pre-load reading.
26. Move valve towards DTI, note gauge reading and subtract pre-load from this figure. Compare final figure obtained with tilt figure:
    Valve tilt - inlet and exhaust = 0.5 mm (0.02 in).
27. If tilt figure exceeds above dimension, original valve must be replaced with next oversize valve and valve guide reamed to next oversize.
    Valve guide inside diameter - inlet and exhaust:
    Standard = 7.0 mm (0.275 in)
    For 1st oversize valve stem = 7.1 mm (0.28 in)
    For 2nd oversize valve stem = 7.2 mm (0.283 in)

NOTE: Valve guides may not be replaced.

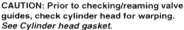

12M4186

28. Dry ream valve guides using BMW tool 004210 and appropriate size reamer from those supplied with tool.
29. Ream valve guide from combustion chamber side, rotate tool once only in a downwards direction; remove all traces of swarf on completion.

Check valve head stand-down

30. *Original valves:* Lap valves to their seats, remove all traces of grinding paste on completion.
31. *Replacement valves:* Do not lap valves to their seats.
32. Insert No.1 valve into its guide.

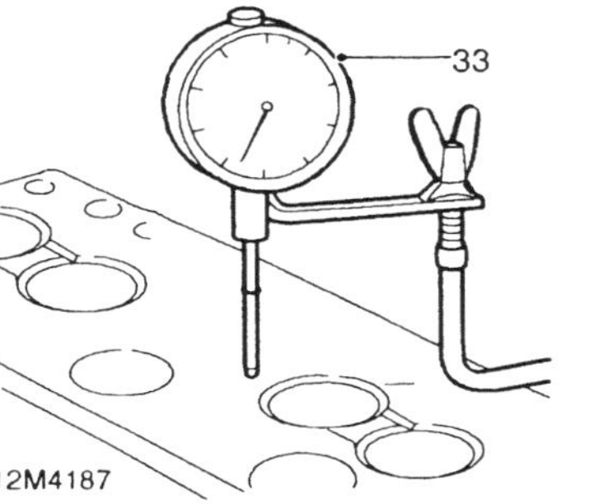

12M4187

33. Position suitable DTI to cylinder head, pre-load then zero gauge.

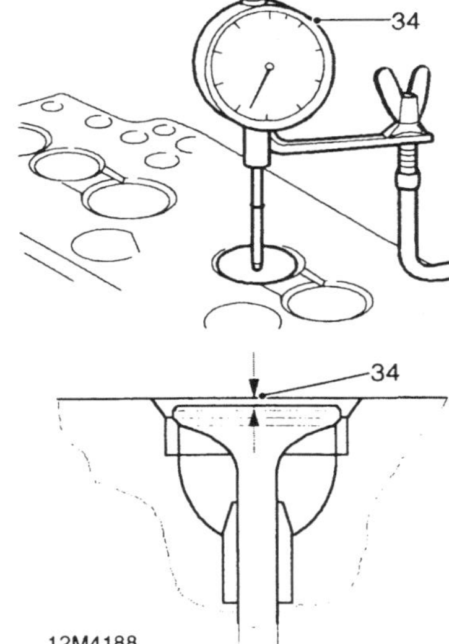

12M4188

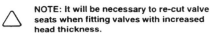

34. Position DTI to centre of valve, measure valve head stand-down and compare with figures given:
    Inlet = 0.65 to 0.85 mm (0.02 to 0.03 in)
    Exhaust = 0.85 to 1.05 mm (0.03 to 0.04 in)
35. Replace any valve having stand-down in excess of figures given with a valve having an increased head thickness.
36. Refer to the following to determine thickness of valve head required ensuring that valves with correct size stem diameter are obtained.

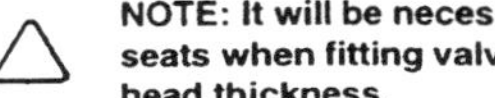

NOTE: It will be necessary to re-cut valve seats when fitting valves with increased head thickness.

Standard valve stem diameter:
Head thickness increase - 0.25 mm (0.01 in)
Identification marks - RO

1st oversize valve stem:
Head thickness increase - 0.25 mm (0.01 in)
Identification marks - R1
Head thickness increase - 0.50 mm (0.02 in)
Identification marks - R2

2nd oversize stem:
Head thickness increase - 0.50 mm (0.02 in)
Identification marks - R3

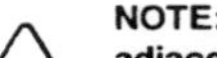

NOTE: Identification marks will be found adjacent to cotter grooves.

Valve seat - recut

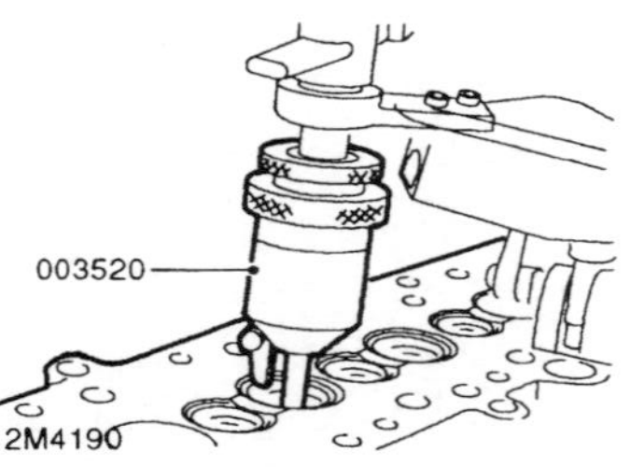

37. Recut valve seats using BMW tool 003520.
Head thickness:
0.25 mm (0.01 in) - Increase depth by 0.25 mm (0.01 in)
0.50 mm (0.02 in) - Increase depth by 0.50 mm (0.02 in)

D B E A C

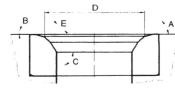

12M4191

38. Use BMW tool 003580 to obtain specified valve seat dimensions:
Valve seat angle **A** = 45° ± 10'
Correction angle - outside **B** = 15°
Correction angle - inside **C** = 60°
Seat face outside diameter **D**:
Inlet valve = 35.5 mm (1.4 in)
Exhaust valve = 30.6 mm (1.2 in)
Valve seat width **E**:
Inlet valve = 1.75 to 2.25 mm (0.07 to 0.09 in)
Exhaust valve = 2.60 to 2.90 mm (0.10 to 0.11 in)
39. Remove all traces of swarf on completion.

CAUTION: Do not lap replacement valves to their seats.

Refit

40. Lubricate all components including valve guides and new valve stem oil seals with engine oil.
41. Insert protective sleeve LRT-12-101 in tappet bore.

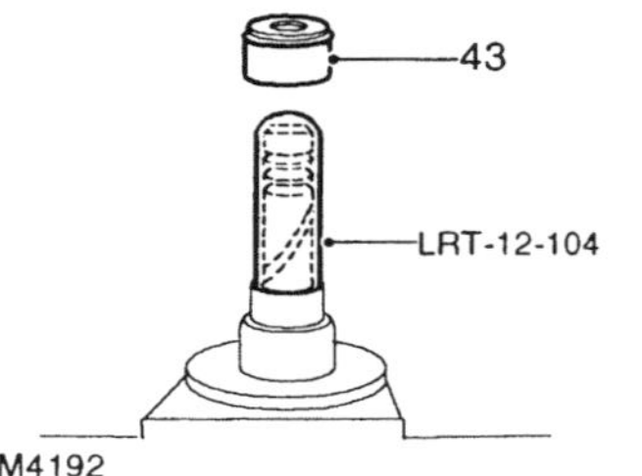

12M4192

42. Fit protection sleeve LRT-12-104 on valve stem.
43. Fit new valve stem oil seal.

NOTE: Inlet valve stem oil seals are coloured RED whilst exhaust valve stem oil seals are coloured GREEN.

44. Press valve stem oil seal into position using tool LRT-12-071, remove protection sleeve LRT-12-104.
45. Fit valve spring seat, new valve spring and spring cup.
46. Compress valve spring using tool LRT-12-034, fit 2 collets.
47. Remove protection sleeve LRT-12-101.
48. Repeat procedures for remaining valves.
49. Lubricate tappet bores and tappets with engine oil, fit tappets to their original locations.
50. Fit cylinder head. ***See this section.***
51. Fit exhaust manifolds. ***See MANIFOLD AND EXHAUST SYSTEM, Repair.***
52. Fit glow plugs. ***See FUEL SYSTEM, Repair.***
53. Fit injectors. ***See FUEL SYSTEM, Repair.***
54. Fit inlet manifolds. ***See MANIFOLD AND EXHAUST SYSTEM, Repair.***
55. Fit camshaft. ***See this section.***

OIL COOLER

Service repair no - 12.60.68

Remove

1. Remove intercooler. ***See FUEL SYSTEM, Repair.***
2. Remove 2 trim fixing studs securing LH deflector panel. Remove panel.

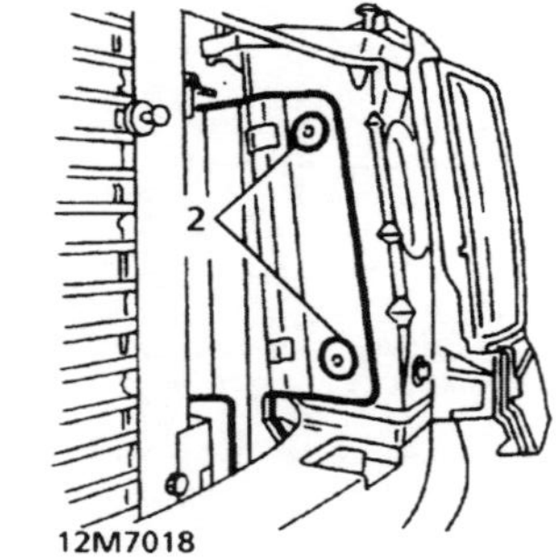

12M7018

3. Position container to catch oil spillage.
4. Disconnect oil cooler upper hose. Remove 'O' ring and discard.

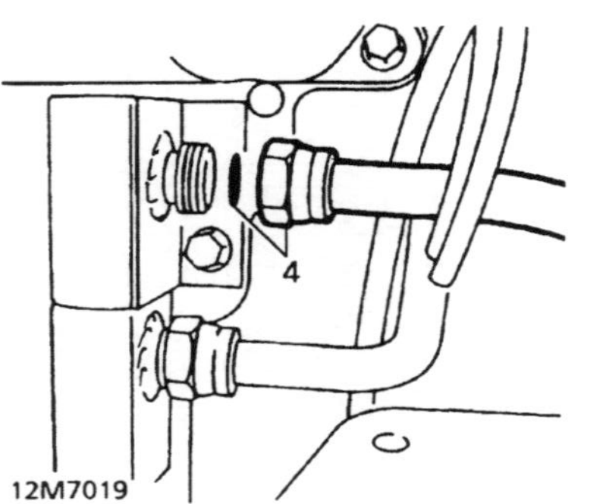

12M7019

5. Plug hose and cooler.
6. Release left hand fog lamp breather tubes from radiator bracket clips.

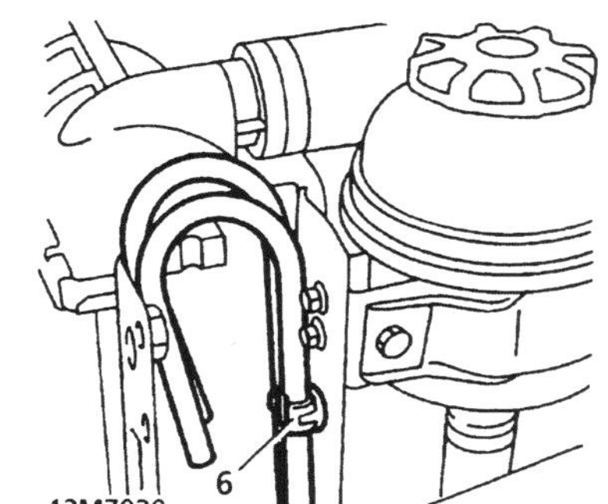

12M7020

7. Remove 2 bolts securing oil cooler to radiator bracket.

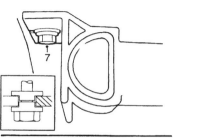

12M3904

⚠ **CAUTION: The RH side of the oil cooler has a sliding mount which allows the cooler to expand and contact with changes in temperature. Incorrect tightening torque of the RH fixing will lead to cooler damage.**

8. Raise oil cooler for access.
9. Disconnect lower hose. Remove 'O' ring and discard.

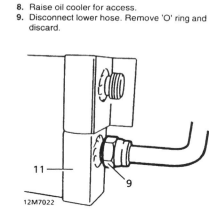

12M7022

10. Plug hose and cooler.
11. Remove oil cooler.

Refit

12. Position oil cooler. Remove plugs.
13. Using new 'O' ring, connect lower hose to oil cooler. Tighten to ***30 Nm. (22 lbf.ft).***
14. Lower cooler to radiator bracket.
15. Apply Loctite 270 Stud Lock to threads of RH fixing.
16. Assemble spacers to fixing and secure fixing to radiator bracket, finger tight.
17. Engage slot in RH side of cooler to spacers.
18. RH fixing Tighten to ***5 Nm (4 lbf.ft).***
    LH fixing Tighten to ***25 Nm (19 lbf.ft).***
19. Using new 'O' ring, connect upper pipe to oil cooler. Tighten to ***30 Nm. (22 lbf.ft)***
20. Remove container.
21. Secure fog lamp breather tubes to radiator bracket clips.
22. Fit deflector panel. Secure with studs.
23. Fit intercooler. ***See FUEL SYSTEM, Repair.***
24. Check engine oil level. Top-up if necessary.

OIL FILTER - UP TO 1998MY

Service repair no - 12.60.02

Remove

1. Drain engine oil. ***See SECTION 10, Maintenance.***
2. Position cloth beneath oil filter casing to catch spillage.
3. Remove bolt securing cover to filter casing. Collect 'O' ring and discard .
4. Remove cap. Collect 'O' ring and discard.
5. Remove filter element and discard.

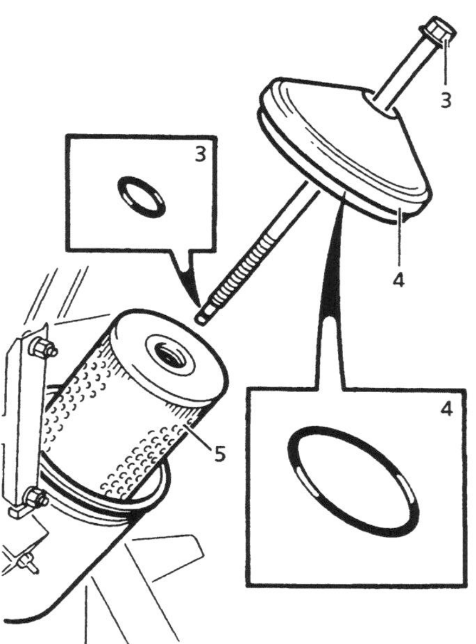

12M7034

NOTE: Oil in filter casing will run back into sump once cover is removed.

Refit

6. Clean filter casing and cap.
7. Fit filter element.
8. Using new 'O' rings, position cap. Secure with bolt. Tighten to ***33 Nm. (24 lbf.ft)***
9. Replenish engine oil. ***See LUBRICANTS, FLUIDS AND CAPACITIES, Information.***
10. Start engine. Run at 2500 rev/min until oil pressure warning light extinguishes.

NOTE: Oil pressure warning light will extinguish after approximately 5 seconds.

11. Stop engine. Recheck oil level.

OIL FILTER 1998MY ONWARDS

Service repair no - 12.60.02

Remove

1. Drain engine oil. ***See SECTION 10, Maintenance.***
2. Position cloth beneath oil filter casing to catch spillage.
3. Using a socket wrench, carefully loosen cap and allow oil to drain back into sump.
4. Remove cap and collect 3 'O' ring seals. Discard seals.
5. Remove filter element and discard.

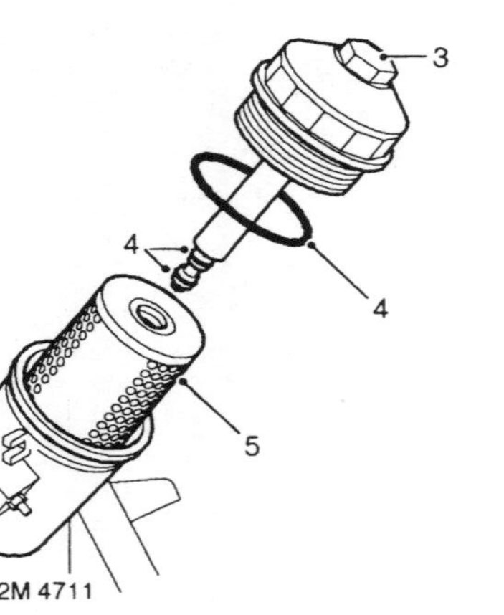

12M 4711

Refit

6. Clean filter casing and cap.
7. Fit filter element.
8. Lubricate new 'O' ring seals using engine oil.
9. Fit cap and tighten to ***25 Nm. (18 lbf.ft)***
10. Replenish engine oil. ***See LUBRICANTS, FLUIDS AND CAPACITIES, Information.***
11. Start engine. Run at 2500 rev/min until oil pressure warning light extinguishes.

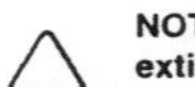

NOTE: Oil pressure warning light will extinguish after approximately 5 seconds.

12. Stop engine. Recheck oil level.

OIL PUMP

Service repair no - 12.60.26

Remove

1. Remove timing chains and sprockets. ***See this section.***
2. Remove sump. ***See this section.***
3. Remove 3 bolts securing oil pick-up strainer to oil pump and deflector plate.

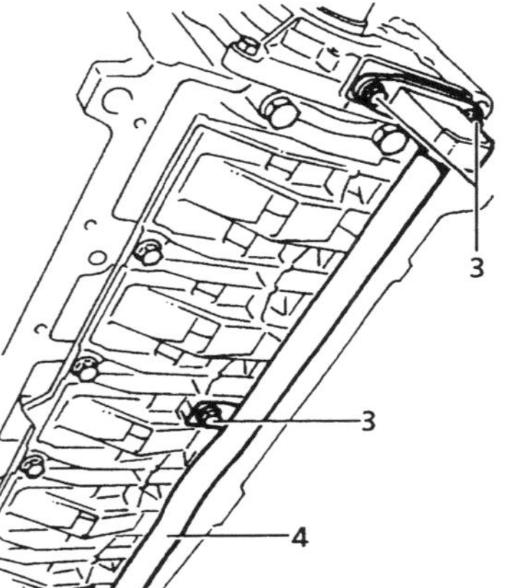

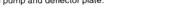

12M7051

4. Remove pick-up strainer. Collect gasket.
5. Remove lower chain guide.
6. Remove woodruff key from crankshaft.

12M7052

7. Remove 8 bolts securing oil pump to cylinder block.
8. Remove pump. Collect gasket.

Refit

9. Ensure mating faces are clean.
10. Position new oil pump/front cover gasket to cylinder block.
11. Refit oil pump. Fit bolts, finger tight.
12. Fit tool LRT-12-116 over crankshaft. Tighten centre screw by hand to centralise oil pump.

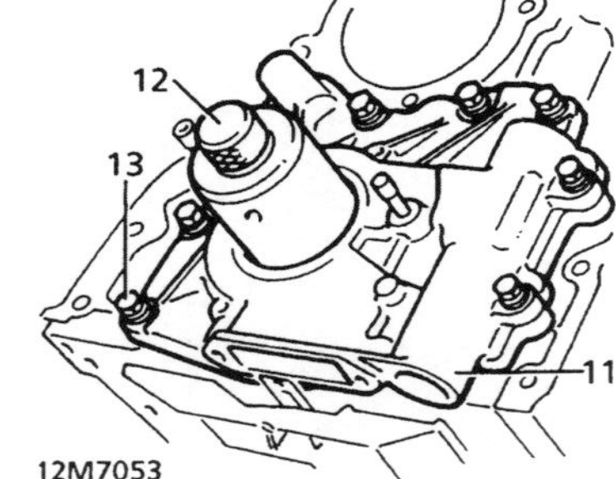

12M7053

13. Tighten oil pump bolts to ***22 Nm. (16 lbf.ft)***
14. Remove tool from crankshaft.
15. Fit woodruff key to crankshaft.
16. Fit lower chain guide.
17. Using a new gasket, position oil pick-up strainer. Secure with bolts. Tighten to ***10 Nm. (7 lbf.ft)***
18. Fit timing chains and sprockets. ***See this section.***
19. Reconnect battery negative lead.

OIL PUMP AND OIL PRESSURE RELIEF VALVE - OVERHAUL

Service repair no - 12.60.32

1. Remove oil pump. ***See this section.***

Oil pump

NOTE: Oil pump is only supplied as an assembly but the following dimensional checks checks may be carried out to determine serviceability.

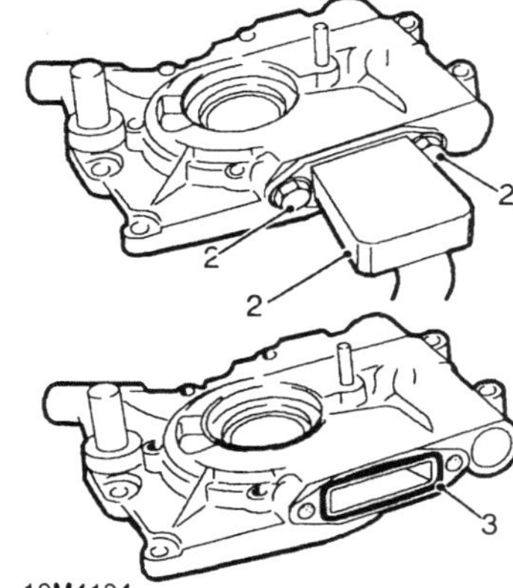

12M4194

2. *If fitted* : Remove 2 bolts securing oil pick-up pipe, remove pipe.
3. Remove and discard seal.

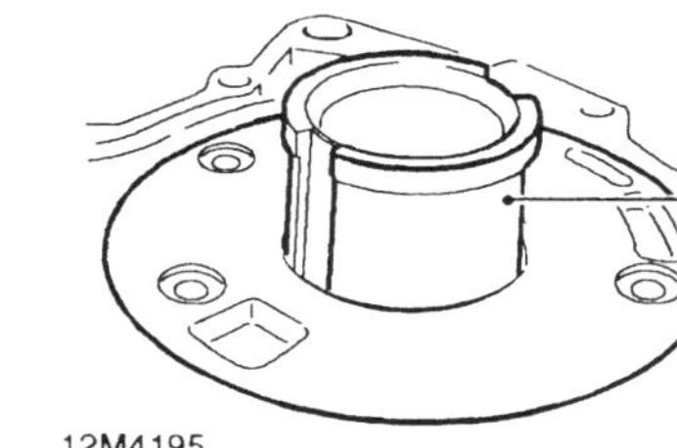

12M4195

4. Press flanged bush out from front of oil pump.

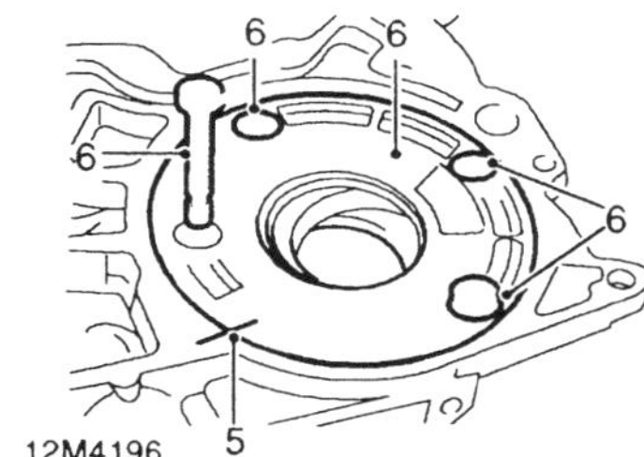

12M4196

5. Make suitable alignment marks between cover plate and pump housing.
6. Noting fitted position of special screw, remove 4 screws securing cover plate, remove plate.

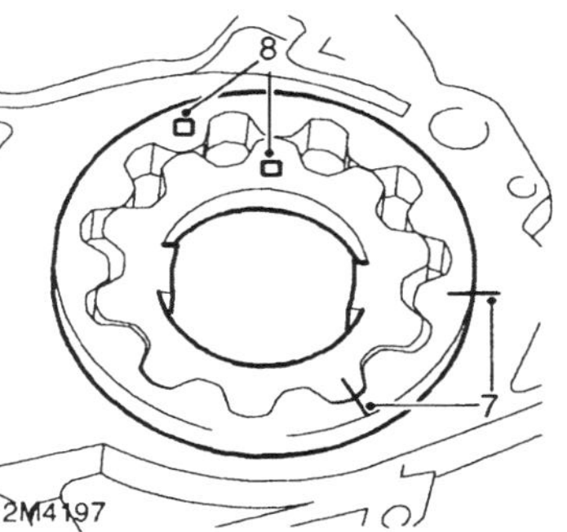

12M4197

7. Make suitable alignment marks between inner and outer rotors and pump housing.
8. Clean rotors and recess in pump housing, fit rotors ensuring square identification marks face towards cover plate and reference marks are aligned.

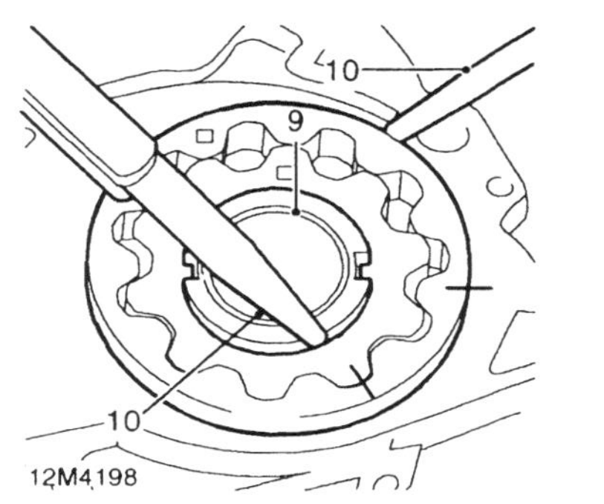

12M4198

9. Insert flanged bush into inner rotor with flange on rotor side of pump.
10. Using feeler gauges, check clearance between outer rotor to pump body and inner rotor to flanged bush and compare with figures given:
Outer rotor to pump housing = 0.4 mm (0.02 in) - maximum
Inner rotor to flanged bush = 0.065 mm (0.003 in) - maximum

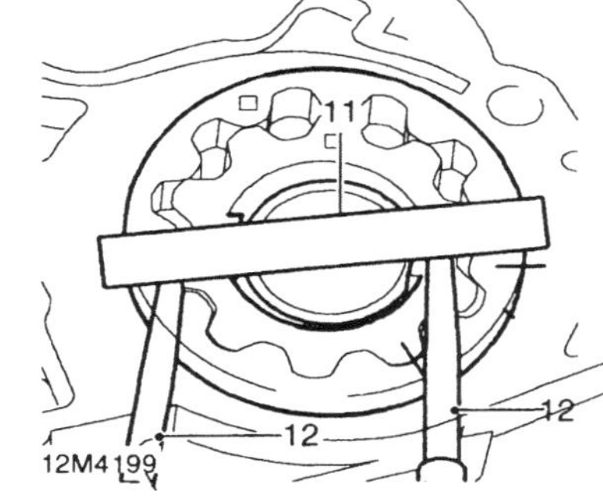

12M4199

11. Remove flanged bush, position a straight edge across both rotors and the pump body.
12. Using feeler gauges inserted between straight edge and on each side of inner and outer rotors, measure axial clearance between rotors and pump body and compare with figures given:
Outer rotor to pump body axial clearance = 0.070 mm (0.004 in) - maximum
Inner rotor to pump body axial clearance = 0.065 mm (0.003 in) - maximum
13. If any of the clearances obtained exceed figures given, pump assembly must be replaced.

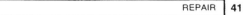

Oil pressure relief valve

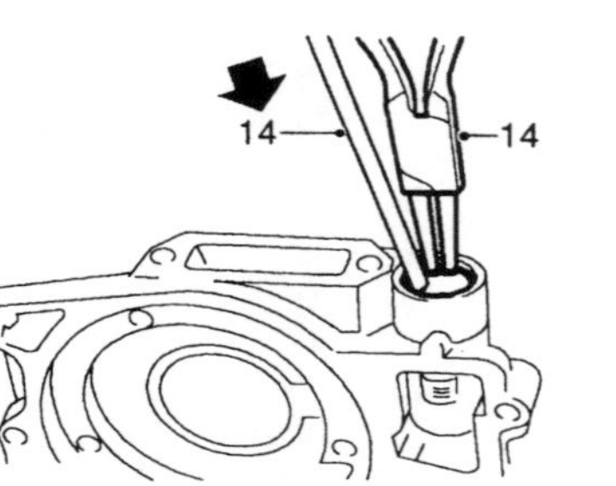

12M4200

14. Using a suitable mandrel, depress sleeve and remove circlip.

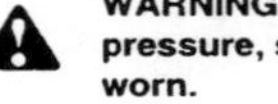

WARNING: Sleeve is under strong spring pressure, suitable eye protection must Lbe worn.

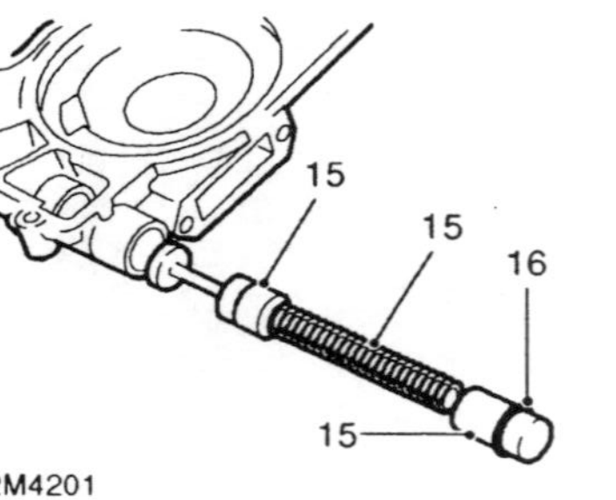

12M4201

15. Gradually release spring pressure, remove sleeve, spring and piston.
16. Remove and discard 'O' ring.
17. Clean all components, check piston, sleeve and relief valve bore for damage, scoring and signs of wear.
18. Check relief valve spring free length:
    Free length = 84.1 mm (3.3 in)
19. Renew relief valve as an assembly.

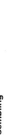

Oil pump and oil pressure relief valve - assembling

20. Lubricate all components with engine oil.
21. Fit a new 'O' ring to sleeve.
22. Insert piston, spring and sleeve into relief valve bore, depress sleeve and fit circlip.

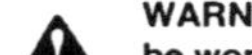

WARNING: Suitable eye protection must be worn.

23. Check that circlip is correctly seated in groove.
24. Insert rotors into pump ensuring that square identification marks are toward cover.
25. Fit cover plate ensuring reference marks are aligned.
26. Fit 4 screws ensuring special screw is in its original location, tighten screws to ***20 Nm (15 lbf.ft).***
27. Fit flanged bush ensuring that flange is on cover plate side of pump.
28. Position new seal to oil pick-up pipe, fit pipe.
29. Fit 2 bolts and tighten to ***10 Nm (7 lbf.ft).***
30. Fit oil pump. ***See this section.***

OIL PRESSURE SWITCH

Service repair no - 12.60.50

Remove

1. Disconnect switch multiplug.
2. Remove switch. Collect sealing washer and discard.

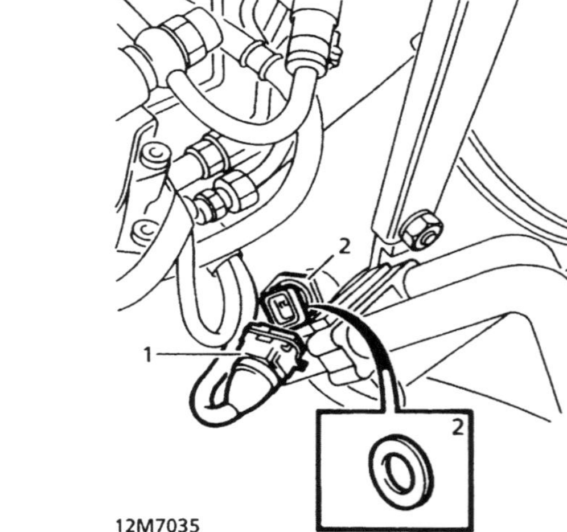

12M7035

Refit

3. Ensure mating faces are clean.
4. Fit a new sealing washer, oil threads of switch and fit switch. Tighten to ***40 Nm. (30 lbf.ft)***
5. Connect multiplug.

SUMP

Service repair no - 12.60.44

Remove

1. Raise vehicle on four post lift.
2. Disconnect battery negative lead.
3. Remove nut and bolt securing dipstick tube. Remove tube. Remove and discard 'O' ring.

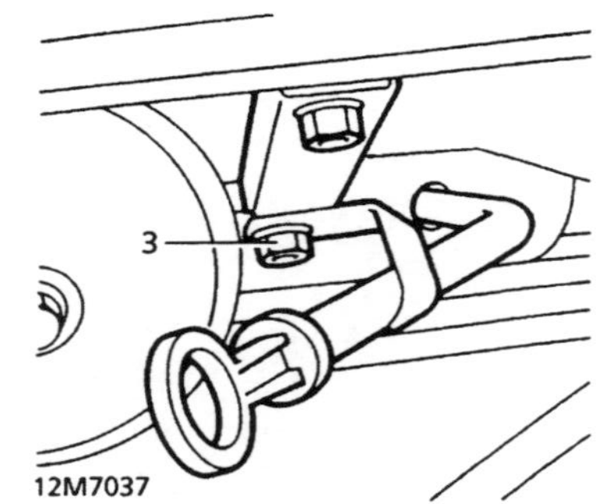

12M7037

4. Raise lift.
5. Position support under chassis front cross member.

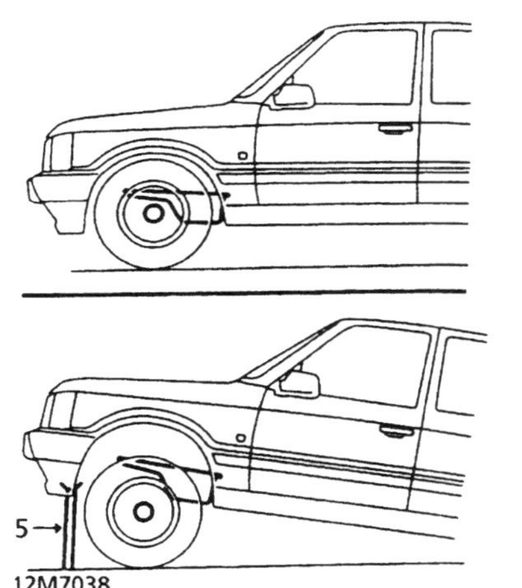

12M7038

6. Lower lift to give clearance between front axle and sump.

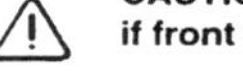

CAUTION: Do not lower axle from chassis if front shock absorbers are disconnected.

7. Drain oil from sump. Refit sump plug.
8. Remove bolt securing power steering pump bracket to sump.

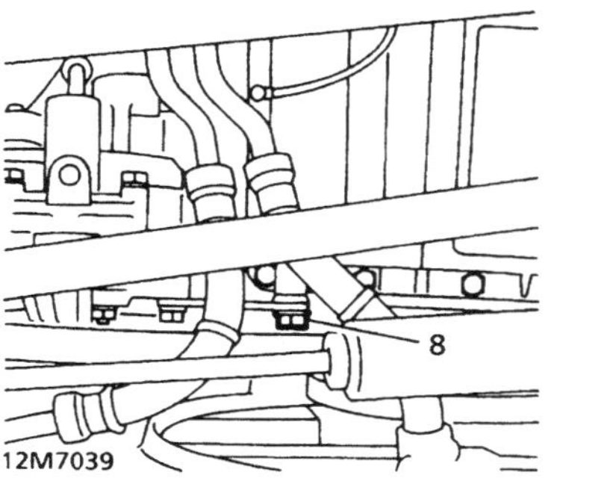

12M7039

9. Remove 29 bolts securing sump. Remove sump and gasket.

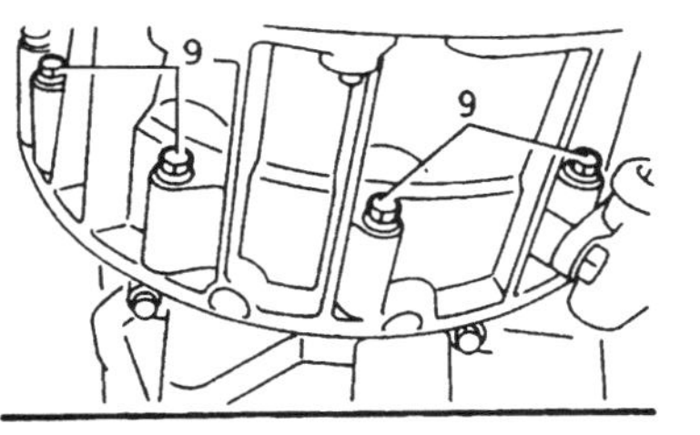

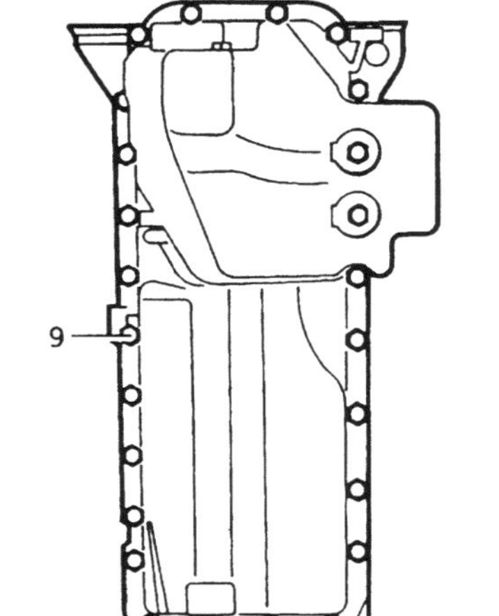

12M7040

Refit

10. Ensure mating faces are clean.
11. Clean sump.
12. Fit gasket to sump. Fill front and rear openings in gasket with STC 3373 sealant.
13. Position sump to cylinder block.
14. Secure sump with bolts.
    M6 - ***10 Nm. (7 lbf.ft)***
    M6 - ***12 Nm (9 lbf.ft)***
    M8 - ***20 Nm. (15 lbf.ft)***
15. Tighten sump plug to:-
    M12 - ***25 Nm (18 lbf.ft)***
    M22 - ***60 Nm (44 lbf.ft)***
16. Position power steering pump bracket on sump. Secure with bolt.
17. Raise lift. Remove chassis support.
18. Lower lift.
19. Lubricate new dipstick tube 'O' ring with clean engine oil.
20. Fit 'O' ring to dipstick tube. Fit tube. Secure with nut and bolt.
21. Refill engine oil. ***See LUBRICANTS, FLUIDS AND CAPACITIES, Information.***
22. Reconnect battery negative lead.

BIG-END BEARINGS

Service repair no - 12.17.16

Remove

1. Remove sump. ***See this section.***

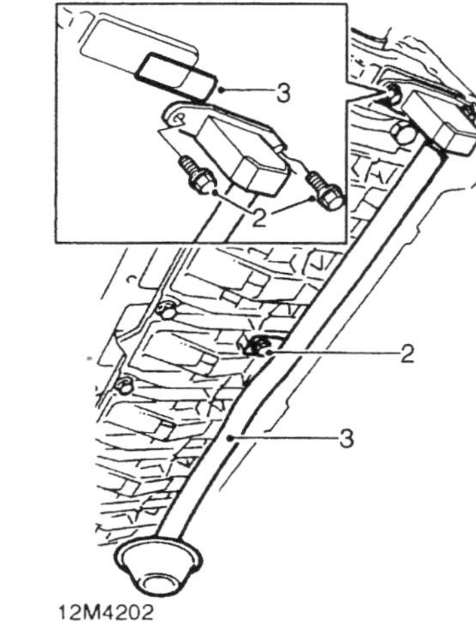

12M4202

2. Remove 3 bolts securing oil pick-up pipe.
3. Remove oil pick-up pipe, remove and discard seal.

12M4203

4. Progressively slacken then remove and discard 10 bolts securing reinforcing plate,
5. Remove reinforcing plate.
6. Carefully rotate crankshaft to gain access to connecting rod bolts.

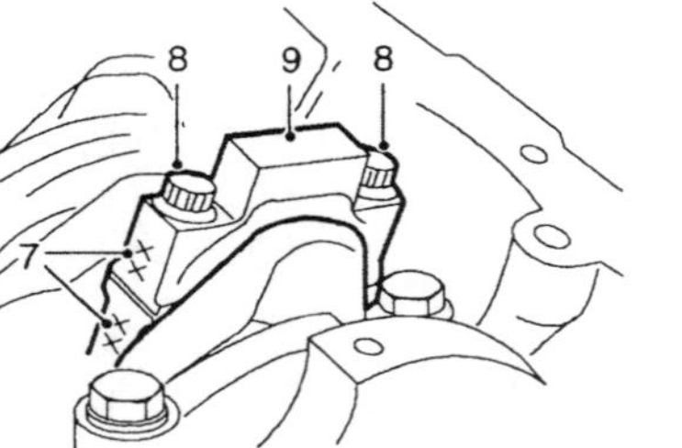

12M4204

7. Ensure that connecting rods and big-end bearing caps are suitably identified to each other.
8. Remove big-end bearing cap bolts.

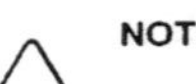

NOTE: Do not discard bolts at this stage.

9. Remove big-end bearing caps, remove and discard big-end bearing shells.

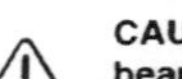

CAUTION: Dowel located, do not tap bearing caps sideways.

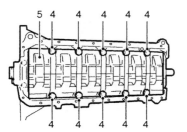

10. Remove and discard big-end bearing shells from connecting rods.

CAUTION: Take care when carrying out above operation that piston does not contact valves. Keep big-end bearing caps and bolts in their fitted order.

Inspection

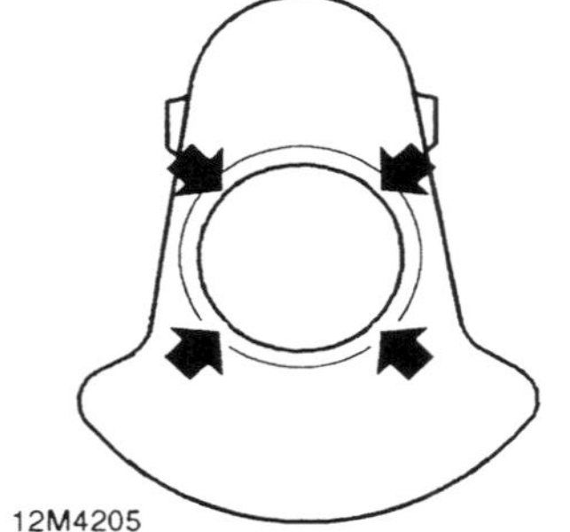

12M4205

11. Measure and record crankshaft big-end journal diameter, take 4 measurements at 90° intervals.

NOTE: There are 3 sizes of crankshaft big-end journals, Standard, Size 1 and Size 2. Crankshafts with either Standard or Size 1 journals may be ground to the next undersize and the appropriate oversize big-end bearing shells fitted.
Standard = 44.975 to 45.00mm (1.770 to 1.771 in)
Size 1 - 0.25 (0.01 in) undersize = 44.725 to 44.75mm (1.761 to 1.762 in)
Size 2 - 0.50mm (0.02 in) undersize = 44.475 to 44.50 mm (1.751 to 1.752 in)

12. Repeat above procedures for remaining big-end journals.

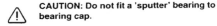

Check big-end bearing clearances

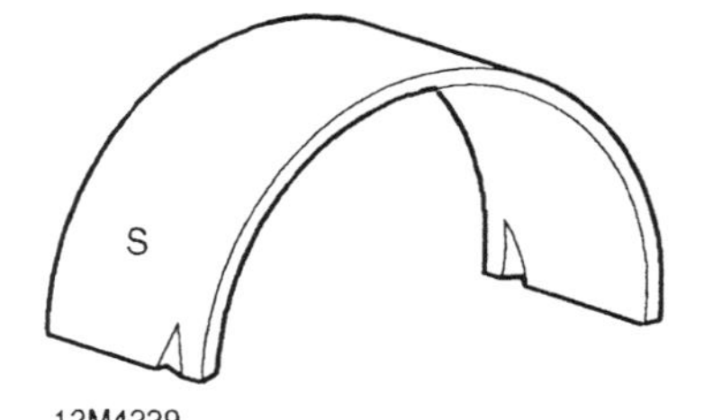

12M4229

NOTE: Big-end bearing shells are available in 3 sizes - Standard, 0.25 (0.01 in) and 0.50 (0.02 in) oversize and are colour coded RED or BLUE. Additionally, the connecting rod bearing shell is of the 'sputter' type and can be identified by a letter S or a series of XXX on the outside of the shell. Sputter bearings must be fitted to the connecting rod.

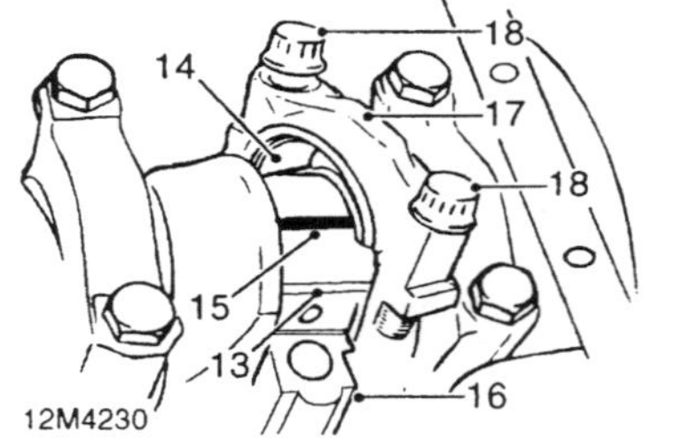

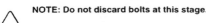

12M4230

13. Fit a new RED colour coded big-end bearing shell of the appropriate size in connecting rod.

CAUTION: Ensure bearing shell is of the 'sputter' type.

14. Fit a new BLUE colour coded big-end bearing shell of the appropriate size in the big-end bearing cap.

CAUTION: Do not fit a 'sputter' bearing to bearing cap.

15. Place a strip of Plastigage across crankshaft big-end journal.
16. Pull connecting rod on to journal.
17. Fit big-end bearing cap ensuring reference marks on connecting rod and cap are aligned.
18. Fit original big-end bearing cap bolts and tighten to:
Stage 1 - ***5 Nm (4 lbf.ft)***
Stage 2 - ***20 Nm (15 lbf.ft)***
Stage 3 - Use angular torque wrench and tighten further 70°

CAUTION: Do not rotate crankshaft.

19. Remove big-end bearing cap.

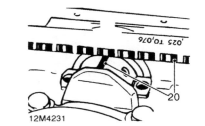

12M4231

20. Using scale provided, measure width of Plastigage on bearing journal and compare with bearing clearance:
Big-end bearing clearance = 0.010 to 0.055 mm (0.0004 to 0.002 in)
21. If correct clearance cannot be obtained with bearing shells available, crankshaft journals must be ground to next undersize and the appropriate oversize big-end bearing shells fitted.

22. Retain selected bearing shell with connecting rod and bearing cap.
23. Remove all traces of Plastigage using an oily rag.
24. Repeat above procedures for remaining big-end bearings.
25. Discard original big-end bearing cap bolts.

Refit

26. Lubricate crankshaft journals and selected big-end bearing shells with engine oil.
27. Fit selected big-end bearing shells to connecting rod and big-end bearing cap ensuring that 'sputter' bearing is fitted to connecting rod.

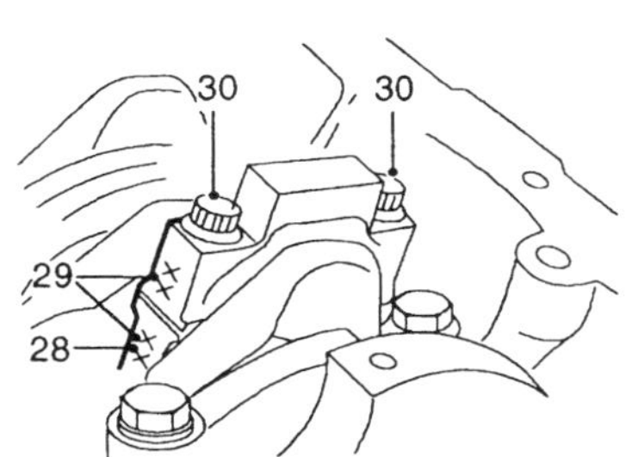

12M4232

28. Pull connecting rod down on to crankshaft journal.
29. Fit big-end bearing cap ensuring that reference marks on cap and rod are aligned.
30. Fit new big-end bearing cap bolts and tighten to:
Stage 1 - ***5 Nm (4 lbf.ft)***
Stage 2 - ***20 Nm (15 lbf.ft)***
Stage 3 - Use angular torque wrench and tighten further 70°.

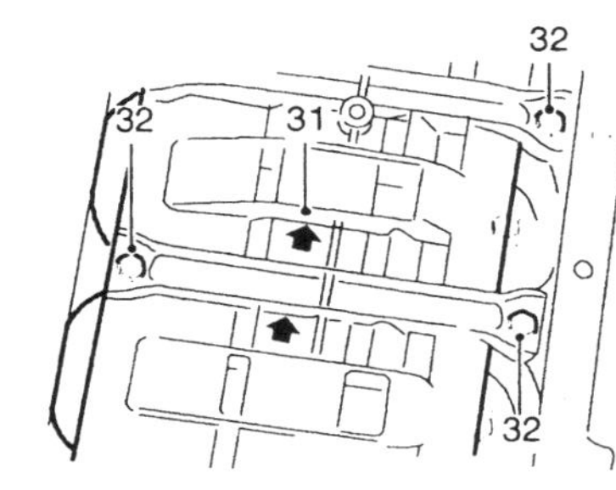

12M4233

31. Position reinforcing plate to crankcase ensuring that arrows on plate are pointing towards front of engine.
32. Fit 10 new bolts and tighten from centre outwards to :
M4 - ***22 Nm (16 lbf.ft)***
M10 - ***43 Nm (32 lbf.ft)***

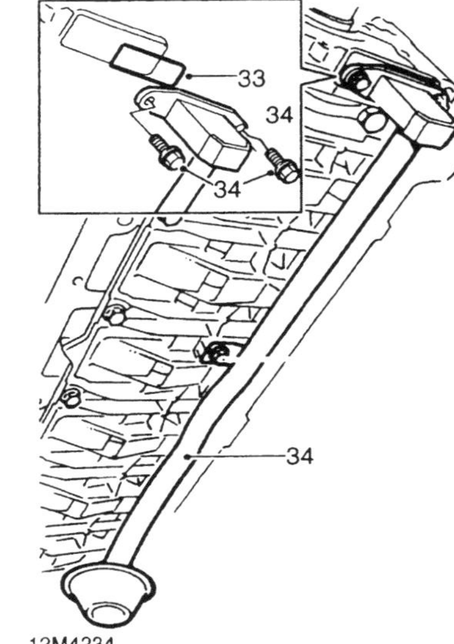

12M4234

33. Position new seal to oil pump.
34. Fit oil pick-up pipe, fit 3 bolts and tighten to ***10 Nm (7 lbf.ft)***
35. Fit sump. ***See this section.***

PISTONS, CONNECTING RODS AND CYLINDER BORES

Service repair no - 12.17.03

Remove

1. Remove cylinder head. ***See this section.***
2. Remove big-end bearings. ***See this section.***
3. Push piston and connecting rod to top of cylinder bore, remove piston and connecting rod.
4. Suitably identify piston and connecting rod to its cylinder bore.
5. Repeat above procedure for remaining pistons and connectimng rods.

Pistons and connecting rods - dismantling

6. Remove and discard piston rings.

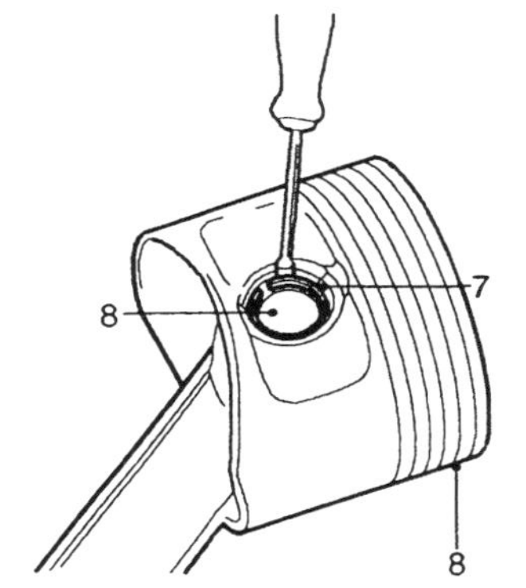

12M4207

7. Remove and discard snap rings retaining gudgeon pin.
8. Remove gudgeon pin, remove piston from connecting rod.

CAUTION: Keep each piston, gudgeon pin and connecting rod together as a set.

9. Remove carbon from piston crowns, and piston ring grooves.

CAUTION: Do not attempt to remove carbon or deposits from piston skirts as graphite coating will be destroyed.

Pistons - inspection

10. Check piston for signs of burning and skirt for scoring or damage.

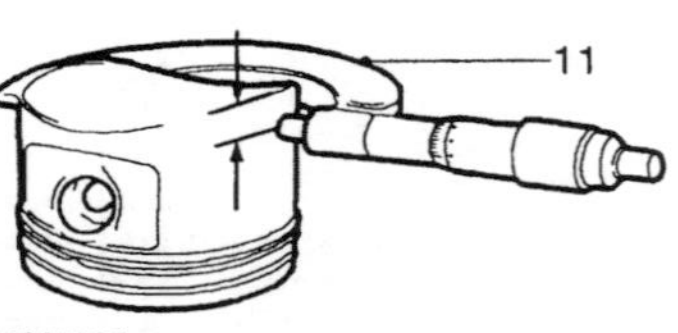

12M4208

11. Measure and record piston diameter at a point 7.0 mm (0.27 in) from bottom of skirt and at right angles to gudgeon pin holes.

NOTE: Three sizes of piston may be fitted: Standard = 79.96 ± 0.009 mm (3.14 ± 0.0004 in)
Intermediate = 80.04 ± 0.009 mm (3.15 ± 0.0004 in)
1st oversize = 80.21 ± 0.009 mm (3.16 ± 0.0004 in)

12. Check gudgeon pin holes in piston for signs of ovality.
13. Repeat above procedures for remaining pistons.

Connecting rods - inspection

14. Check that oil feed passages are clear.
15. Check dowels in connecting rods and big-end bearing caps for security, replace as necessary.
16. Check gudgeon pin bush in connecting rod for wear:
Gudgeon pin bush bore = 28.995 to 29.021 mm (1.142 to 1.143 in)
17. Replace worn bushes as necessary.

CAUTION: When fitting new bushes, ensure oil holes in bush and connecting rod are aligned.

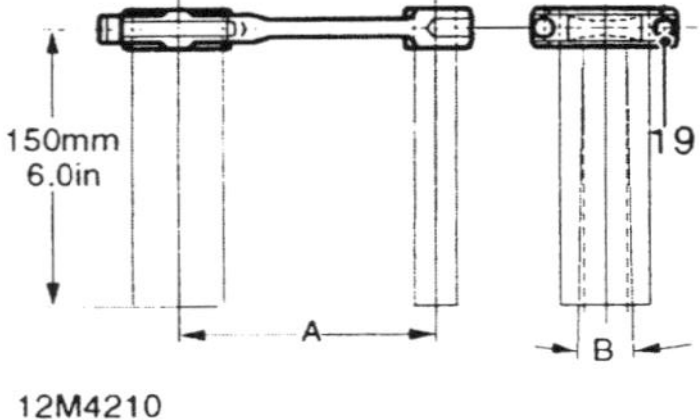

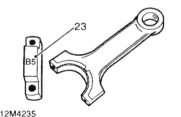

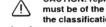

12M4210

18. Check connecting rods for distortion, fit a new BLUE colour coded 'sputter' big-end bearing shell to the connecting rod and a new RED colour coded shell to the big-end bearing cap.
19. Fit original big-end bearing cap bolts and tighten to ***5 Nm (4 lbf.ft).***
20. Check parallelism of connecting rods on both sides of rod.
Maximum deviation **A** = 0.05 mm (0.002 in)

NOTE: Measurement must be taken approximately 150 mm (6.0 in) from centre line of rod:

21. Check for distortion on both sides of connecting rod:
Maximum distortion **B** = 0.5 mm (0.02 in)
22. Repeat above procedures for remaining connecting rods.

12M4235

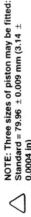

23. Replace connecting rods as necessary, do not attempt to straighten distorted rods.

CAUTION: replacement connecting rods must be of the same weight classification, the classification is embossed on the main bearing caps.

Cylinder bores - inspection

24. De-glaze cylinder bores, check bores for scoring.
25. Remove all traces of cylinder head gasket and carbon deposits from cylinder block.

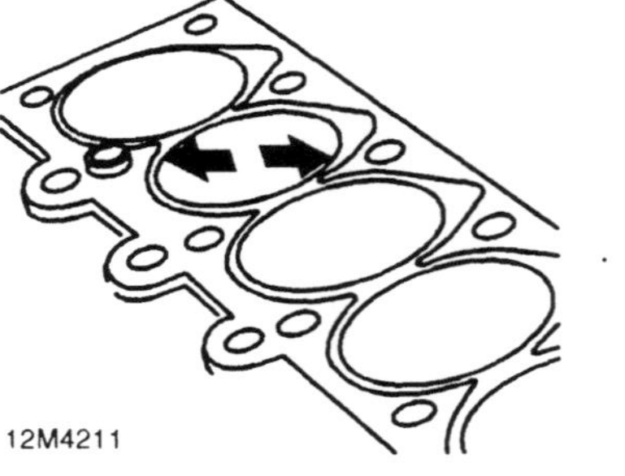
12M4211

26. Check and record cylinder bore diameter at bottom, centre and top of bore ensuring that measurements are taken at the angle shown.
27. Compare figures obtained with the following and determine cylinder bore size:
Standard = 80.00 to 80.04 mm (3.150 to 3.151 in)
Intermediate = 80.08 to 80.12 mm (3.153 to 3.154 in)
1st oversize = 80.25 to 80.29 mm (3.20 to 3.21 in)

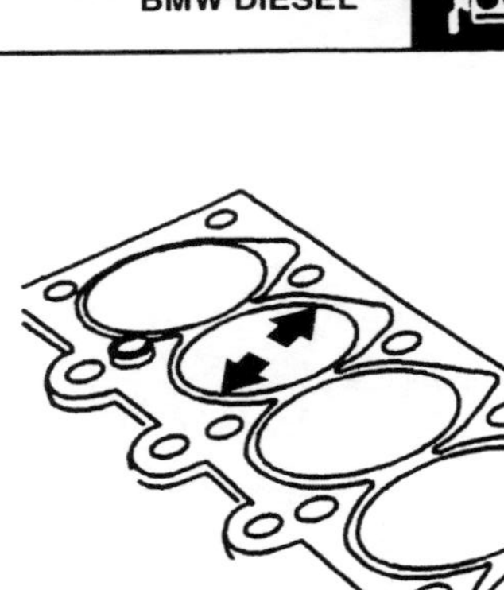
12M4212

28. Repeat procedure at angle shown and from the 2 sets of measurements obtained, calculate cylinder bore ovality and taper:
Maximum ovality = 0.04 mm (0.002 in)
Maximum taper = 0.04 mm (0.002 in)
29. Compare piston diameter with cylinder bore size and determine piston to bore clearance:
Piston to bore clearance = 0.031 to 0.063 mm (0.0012 to 0.002 in)

NOTE: For engines which have been 'run in,' the above clearance may be increased to 0.213 mm (0.008 in).

30. Standard and intermediate size cylinder bores which are worn in excess of limits given may be rebored to next oversize and the appropriate oversize pistons fitted.

Piston rings - check

CAUTION: Ensure that replacement piston rings are the correct size for the pistons to be fitted.

31. Lubricate cylinder bores and new piston rings with engine oil.

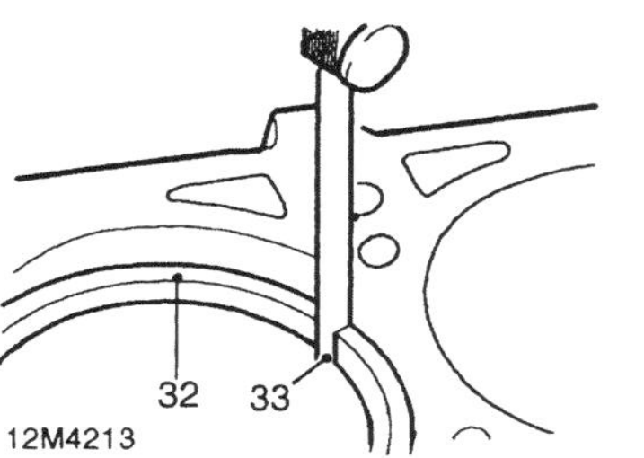

12M4213

32. Insert 1 set of piston rings in turn into No. 1 cylinder bore.
33. Check piston ring gaps using feeler gauges: Piston ring gap - 1st, 2nd and oil control rings = 0.2 to 0.4 mm (0.008 to 0.020 in)

CAUTION: If ring gaps are too wide, it will be necessary to rebore cylinder(s) to next size and fit appropriate size pistons and rings.

34. Suitably identify the piston rings with No.1 cylinder and retain with the piston and connecting rod for that cylinder.
35. Repeat above procedures for remaining cylinders.
36. Lubricate pistons and ring grooves with engine oil.

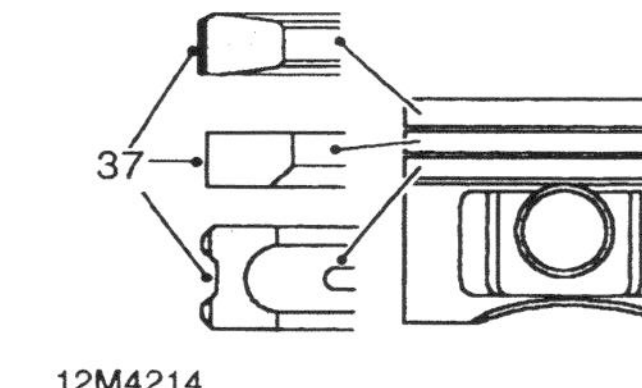

12M4214

37. Fit oil control, 2nd and 1st compression rings to piston.

NOTE: 1st and 2nd rings are marked TOP.

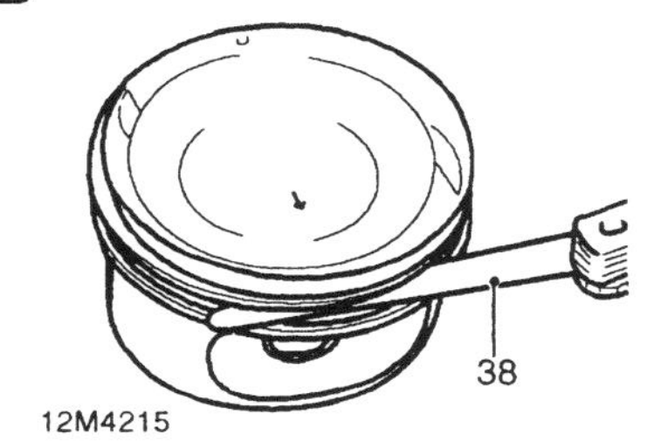

12M4215

38. Using feeler gauges, measure clearance between piston ring groove and 2nd compression and oil control rings.
Ring to groove clearance:
1st compression - not checked
2nd compression = 0.040 to 0.072 mm (0.002 to0.004 in)
Oil control = 0.030 to 0.065 mm (0.001 to 0.003 in)
39. Check that 1st compression ring is free to move in groove.
40. Repeat above procedures for remaining pistons and rings.

Pistons and connecting rods - assembling

12M4216

41. Assemble each piston to its connecting rod ensuring that the number on the rod is positioned relative to the arrow on the piston crown as shown.

12M4217

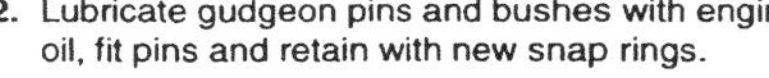

42. Lubricate gudgeon pins and bushes with engine oil, fit pins and retain with new snap rings.

NOTE: Position snap ring gaps opposite recess in piston.

Pistons and connecting rods - refit

43. Lubricate pistons, rings and cylinder bores with engine oil.
44. Position piston ring gaps at 120° to each other ensuring that they are not over gudgeon pin.

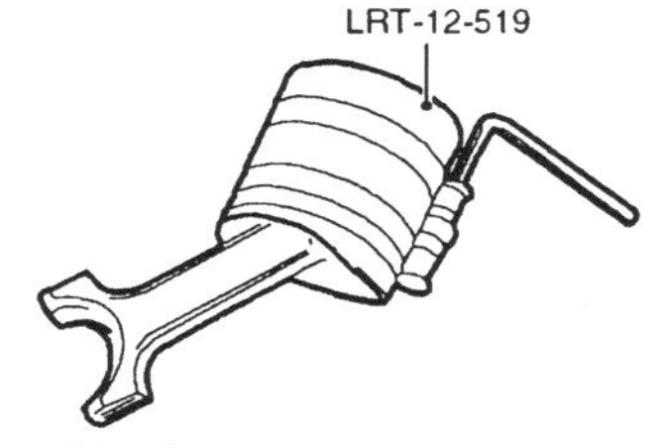

12M4218

45. Compress piston rings using LRT-12-519.

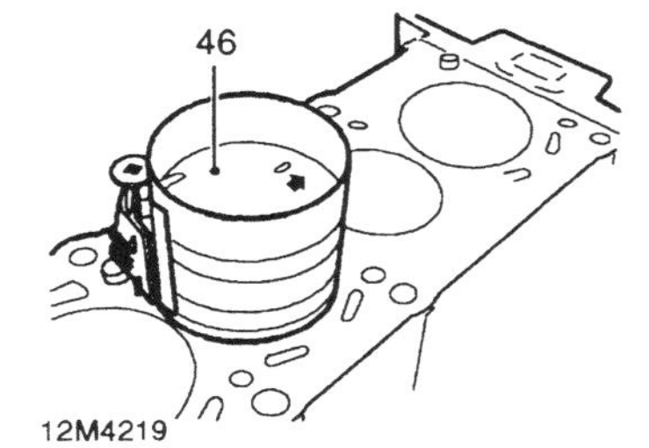

12M4219

46. Fit each piston and connecting rod to its respective cylinder in turn ensuring that arrow on piston crown is pointing towards front of engine.

CAUTION: Fit pistons using hand pressure only.

47. Fit big-end bearings. ***See this section.***
48. Fit cylinder head. ***See this section.***

CRANKSHAFT AND MAIN BEARINGS

Service repair no - 12.21.33/01

Remove

1. Remove engine and gearbox. ***See this section.***
2. Remove oil pump. ***See this section.***
3. Remove crankshaft rear oil seal. ***See this section.***
4. Remove pistons and connecting rods. ***See this section.***

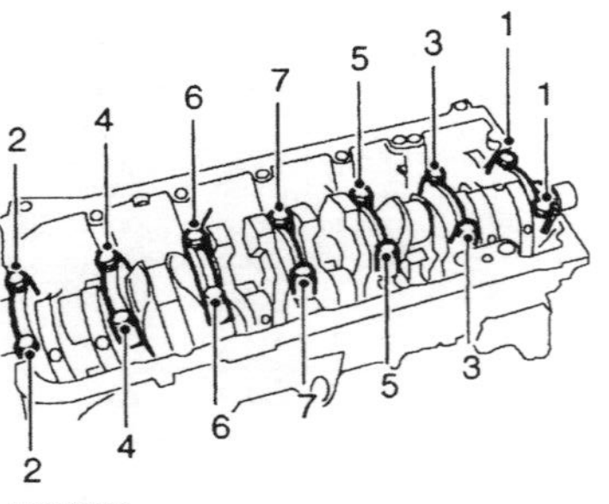

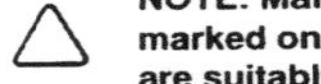

12M4220

5. Using sequence shown, progressively slacken then remove main bearing cap bolts.

NOTE: Do not discard bolts at this stage.

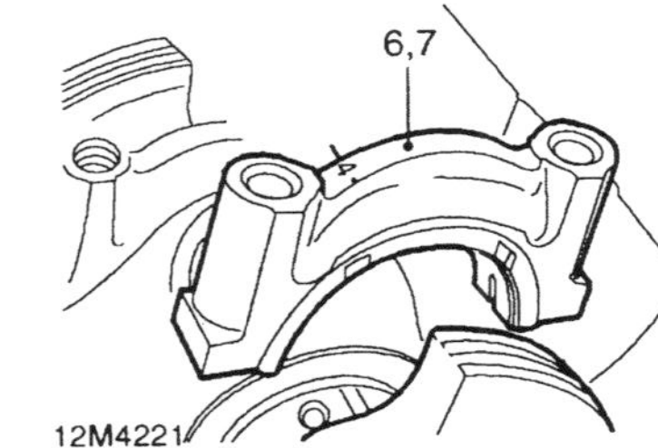

12M4221

6. Ensure that main bearing caps 1 to 5 are suitably identified on the exhaust manifold side of the engine.

NOTE: Main bearing caps 6 and 7 are not marked on production, ensure that they are suitably identified to their fitted positions. Bearing cap 6 carries the integral thrust/main bearing shell.

7. Remove main bearing caps.
8. Remove and discard main bearing shells from caps.
9. Lift out crankshaft.
10. Remove and discard main bearing shells from cylinder block.
11. Clean crankshaft, ensure all oilways are clear.
12. Clean main bearing caps and bearing shell locations in cylinder block; ensure bearing cap bolt holes are clean and dry.
13. Clean original bearing cap bolts and lightly oil threads.

Inspection

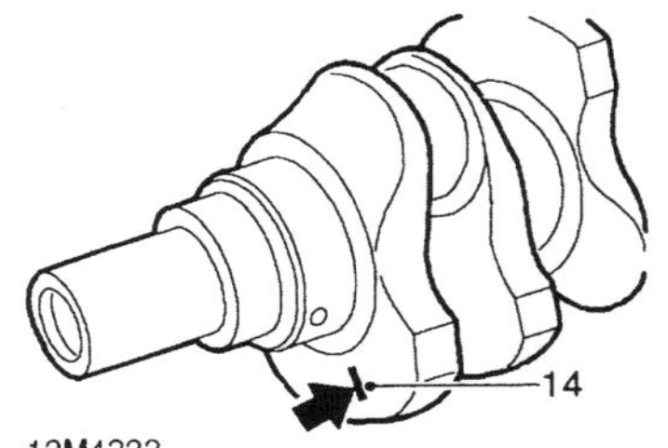

12M4222

14. Check front web of crankshaft to determine if main bearing journals have been ground undersize.
No paint mark - Standard journals
1 paint mark - Journals are 0.25 mm (0.01 in) undersize
2 paint marks - Journals are 0.50 mm (0.02 in) undersize

NOTE: Each of the three main journal sizes has a triple colour classification which corresponds to the colour code of the main bearing cap shells, a colour code on the edge of the balance webs will indicate the actual size.

15. Measure and record main journal diameters and compare with the sizes given below. Take 4 measurements of each journal at 90° intervals to check for appropriate specified size and ovality.
Standard:
Yellow = 59.984 to 59.990 mm (2.3616 to 2.3618 in)
Green = 59.977 to 59.983 mm (2.3612 to 2.3615 in)
White = 59.971 to 59.976 mm (2.3610 to 2.3611 in)

Undersize 1 - 0.25 mm (0.01 in):
Yellow = 59.734 to 59.740 mm (3.3522 to 2.3526 in)
Green = 59.727 to 59.733 mm (2.3514 to 2.3520 in)
White = 59.721 to 50.726 mm (2.3512 to 2.3514 in)

Undersize 2 - 0.50 mm (0.02 in):
Yellow = 59.484 to 59.490 mm (2.3418 to 2.3420 in)
Green = 59.477 to 59.483 mm (2.3414 to 2.3417 in)
White = 59.471 to 59.476 mm (2.3413 to 2.3415 in)

16. If standard or undersize 1 journals are found to be oval, the crankshaft may be ground to the next undersize.
17. If journals are worn below the original colour code size but ovality is within limits, then the next size main bearing shells should be fitted in the main bearing caps and cylinder block when carrying out the Plastigage check.

NOTE: If journals are worn below the lowest colour size for standard or undersize 1 journals, crankshaft may be ground to the next undersize. Ensure that paint stripe(s) to denote that grinding has been carried out are marked on the crankshaft front web.

Check crankshaft main bearing clearances

18. Fit new, appropriate size yellow main bearing shells in cylinder block at positions 1 to 5 and 7.
19. Fit new, appropriate yellow thrust/main bearing shell in cylinder block at position 6.

⚠ **NOTE: Thrust portion of bearing shells fitted in cylinder block and main bearing cap should be the thinnest of the range available -** ***See crankshaft end-float - check.***

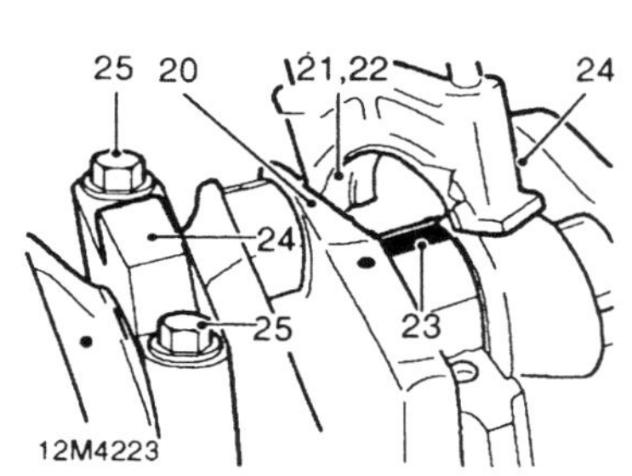

12M4223

20. Position crankshaft in cylinder block.
21. Check colour coding on crankshaft webs and fit new, appropriate size main bearing shells of the same colour coding in main bearing caps numbers 1 to 5 and 7.
22. Fit new, appropriate size thrust/main bearing shell of the same colour coding in number 6 main bearing cap.
23. Place a strip of Plastigage across each main bearing journal.
24. Fit main bearing caps ensuring that identification marks are on exhaust manifold side of engine.
25. Fit original main bearing cap bolts.
26. Align main bearing caps to crankcase.

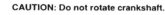

12M4224

27. Using sequence shown, tighten main bearing cap bolts to ***20 Nm (15 lbf.ft).***
28. Using a suitable angular torque wrench, tighten bolts in sequence a further 50°

⚠ **CAUTION: Do not rotate crankshaft.**

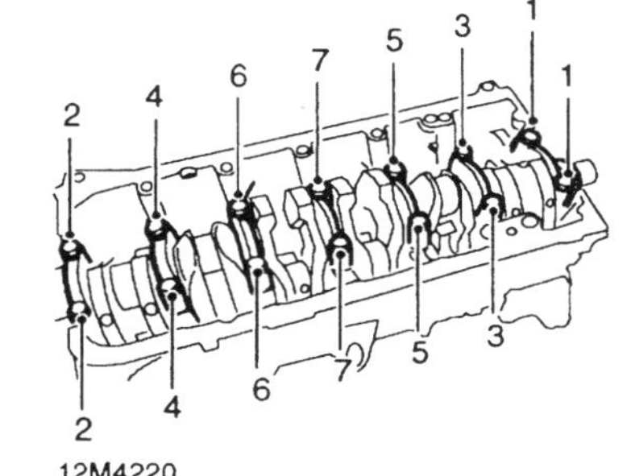

12M4220

29. Using sequence shown, progressively slacken then remove main bearing cap bolts.
30. Remove main bearing caps and shells.

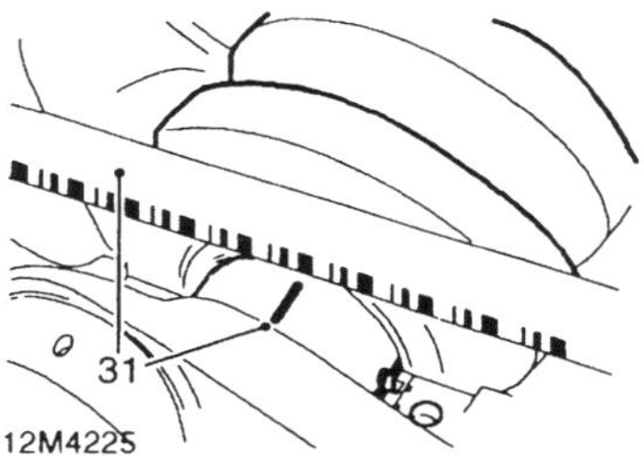

12M4225

31. Using scale provided, measure width of Plastigage on each main bearing journal and compare with specified bearing clearances: Main bearing clearance = 0.020 to 0.058 mm (0.001 to 0.002 in)
32. If clearances are incorrect, select alternative main bearing cap shell(s) from the range available and repeat check.

⚠ **NOTE: If colour coding of selected bearing shell(s) differs from colour marked on adlacent crankshaft web, ensure correct colour is marked on web on completion.**

33. Remove all traces of Plastigage using an oily rag.
34. Fit selected main bearing shells to main bearing caps.
35. Remove crankshaft, lubricate journals and main bearing shells with engine oil.

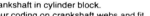

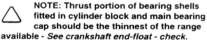

Crankshaft end float - check

36. Fit crankshaft, fit main bearing caps ensuring that reference marks are on exhaust manifold side of engine.
37. Align main bearing caps to crankcase.

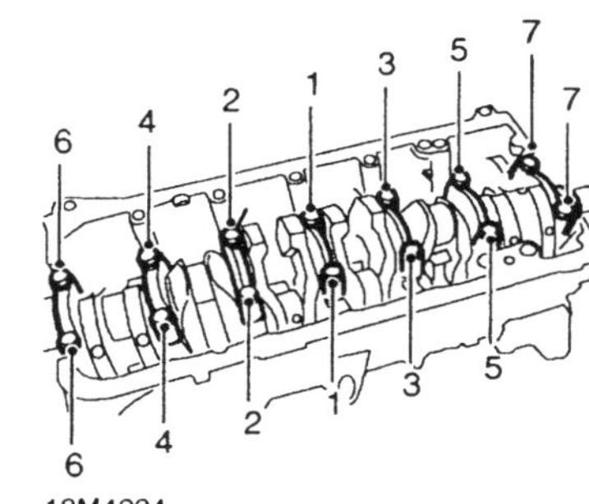

12M4224

38. Fit original main bearing cap bolts and tighten in sequence shown to ***20 Nm (15 lbf.ft)*** then using an angular torque wrench, tighten in sequence a further 50° .

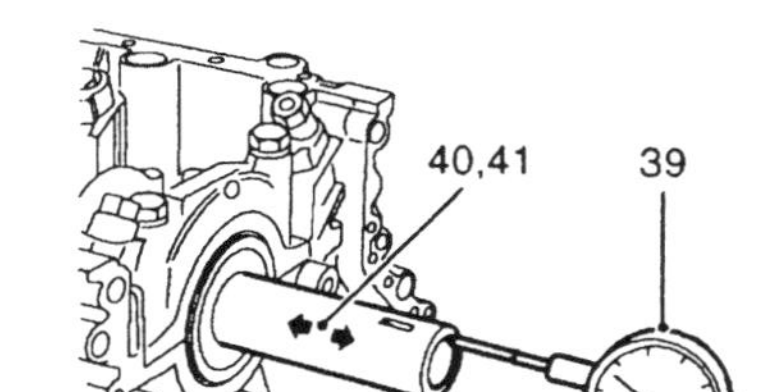

12M4226

39. Position a suitable DTI to front of crankshaft.
40. Move crankshaft fully rearwards and zero gauge.
41. Move crankshaft fully forwards and note end-float reading on gauge.
Crankshaft end-float = 0.080 to 0.163 mm (0.003 to 0.006 in)

Crankshaft end-float incorrect:

42. Remove crankshaft.
43. Select combined thrust/main bearing shells from the range available to give correct end-float ensuring that correct colour coding/size of bearing shell is maintained.

NOTE: Each of the thrust/main bearing shell sizes has three widths of shell available:
Standard = 25.0 mm (0.94 in)
Size 1 = 25.2 mm (0.992 in)
Size 2 = 25.4 mm (1.00 in)

44. Fit selected thrust/main bearing shells in cylinder block and main bearing caps.
45. Fit crankshaft and main bearing caps ensuring that identification marks are on exhaust manifold side of engine and repeat check as necessary until end-float is correct.
46. Discard original main bearing cap bolts on completion.

Crankshaft end-float correct:

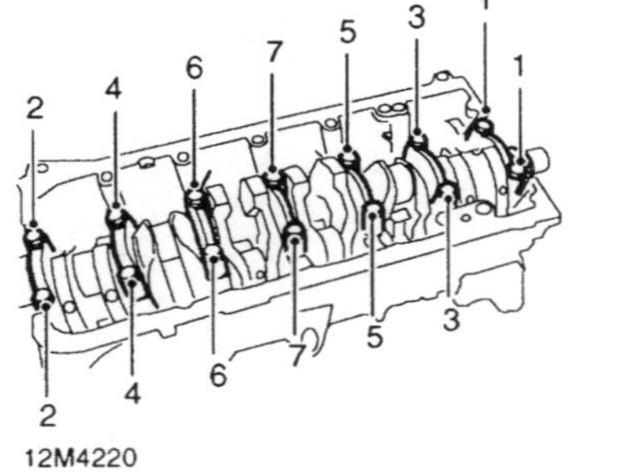

12M4220

47. Using sequence shown, progressively slacken then remove main bearing cap bolts; discard bolts.

Refit

48. Lightly oil threads of new main bearing cap bolts.
49. Fit main bearing cap bolts, align main bearing caps to crankcase.

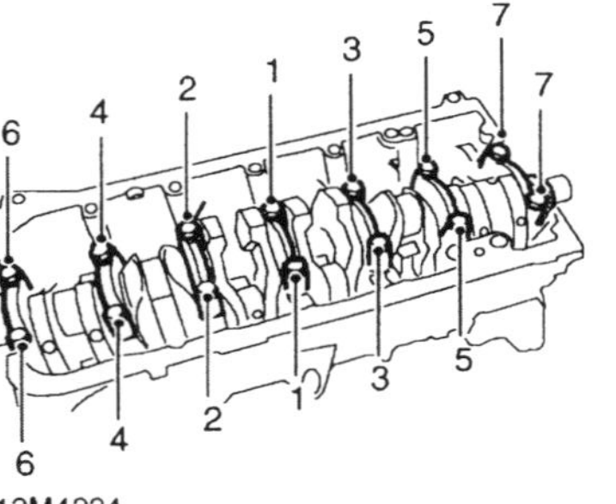

12M4224

50. Tighten main bearing cap bolts in sequence shown using the following procedure:
Stage 1 - Tighten in sequence shown to ***20 Nm (15 lbf.ft).***
Stage 2 - Slacken bolts on number 6 main bearing cap.
Stage 3 - Using a hide mallet, strike each end of crankshaft to centralise thrust/main bearing shells.
Stage 4 - Tighten number 6 main bearing cap bolts to ***20 Nm (15 lbf.ft)***
Stage 5 - Using an angular torque wrench, tighten all main bearing cap bolts in sequence a further 50°.
51. Fit pistons and connecting rods. ***See this section.***
52. Fit crankshaft rear oil seal. ***See this section.***
53. Fit oil pump. ***See this section.***
54. Fit engine and gearbox. ***See this section.***

CRANKSHAFT SPIGOT BEARING

Service repair no - 12.21.45/01

Remove

1. Remove flywheel/drive plate. ***See this section.***

LRT-12-109

12M4227

2. Remove spigot bearing using LRT-12-109, discard bearing.

Refit

3. Clean spigot bearing recess in crankshaft.

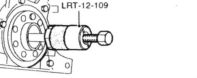

LRT-12-110
4

12M4228

4. Position new spigot bearing to crankshaft.
5. Drift bearing fully into crankshaft using LRT-12-110.
6. Fit flywheel/drive plate. ***See this section.***

TIMING CHAINS AND SPROCKETS

Service repair no - 12.65.12

Remove

1. Disconnect battery negative lead.
2. Remove front cover. ***See this section.***
3. Remove upper timing chain guide rail.

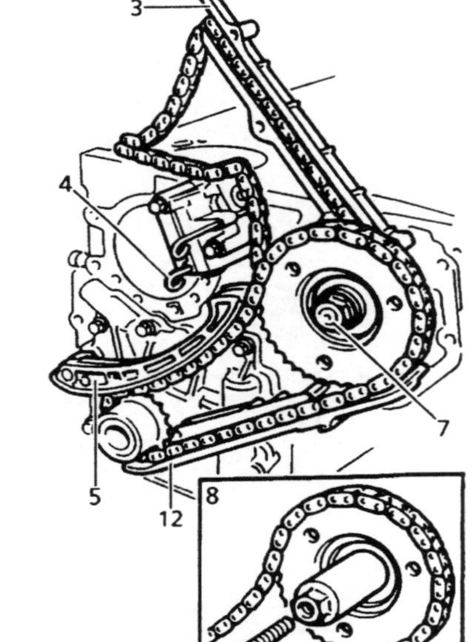

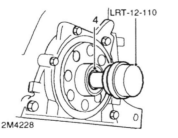

12M7054

4. Using a suitable lever, retract lower chain tensioner plunger. Insert retaining pin LRT-12-114.
5. Remove lower timing chain tensioner rail.
6. Ensure timing pin LRT-12-108 is still located in flywheel.

7. Remove nut from Fuel Injection Pump (FIP) sprocket.
8. Remove centre bolt from tool LRT-12-119. Screw body of tool onto FIP sprocket.
9. Fit centre bolt to tool. Pull sprocket from FIP.
10. Withdraw sprockets and chains as an assembly.
11. Remove tool from FIP sprocket.
12. Remove lower timing chain guide rail.

Refit

13. Ensure mating faces are clean.
14. Lubricate timing chains with clean engine oil.
15. Fit lower chain guide.
16. Assemble sprockets to lower timing chain. Ensure dimples on sprockets align with chain 'bright' links.

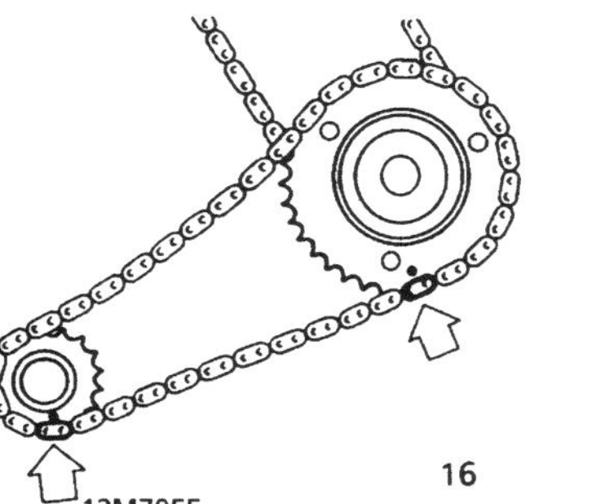

17. Engage upper timing chain over rear sprocket.
18. Engage sprockets over crankshaft and FIP shaft. Ensure sprockets/bright links remain aligned.

NOTE: Align FIP shaft to sprocket keyways using tool LRT-12-118 prior to fully engaging sprockets.

19. Secure FIP sprocket with nut. Tighten to ***50 Nm. (37 lbf.ft)***
20. Fit lower timing chain tensioner rail.
21. Depress tensioner plunger using a suitable lever. Remove retaining pin LRT-12-114.
22. Fit upper timing chain guide rail.
23. Refit front cover. ***See this section.***
24. Check and adjust fuel injection pump timing. ***See FUEL SYSTEM, Adjustment.***
25. Reconnect battery negative lead.

Notes

12 - ENGINE

CONTENTS

Page

LAND ROVER V8

DESCRIPTION AND OPERATION

REPAIR

V8 ENGINE - from 99MY

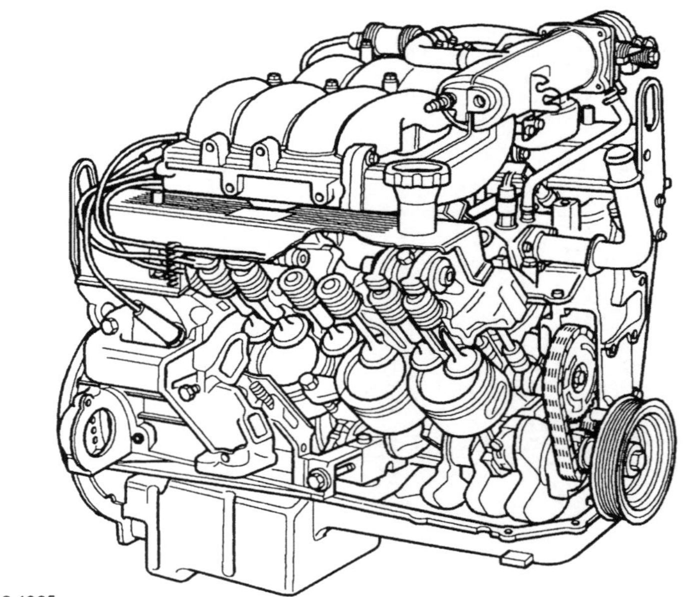

M12 4965

CYLINDER HEAD COMPONENTS - from 99MY

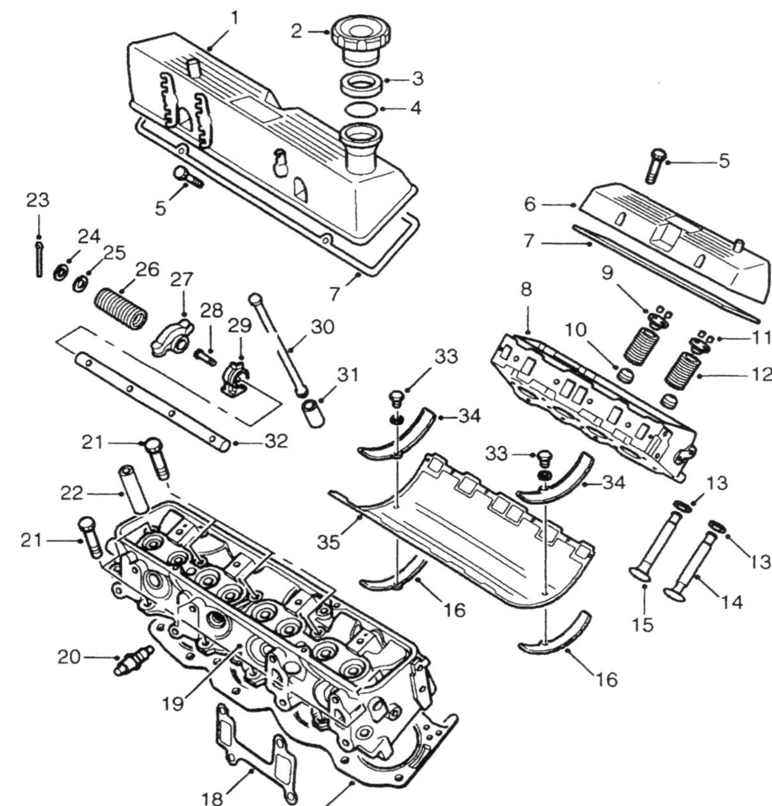

1. Rocker cover - right hand
2. Engine oil filler cap
3. Oil filler dust cap seal
4. 'O' ring - oil filler cap
5. Bolt - rocker cover (4 off; 2 x short, 2 x long)
6. Rocker cover - left hand
7. Gasket - rocker cover
8. Cylinder head - left hand
9. Valve spring cap (16 off)
10. Valve stem oil seals (16 off)
11. Collets (16 pairs)
12. Valve spring (16 off)
13. Valve seat insert (16 off)
14. Exhaust valve (8 off)
15. Inlet valve (8 off)
16. Seal - inlet manifold gasket (2 off)
17. Gasket - cylinder head (2 off)
18. Gasket - exhaust manifold
19. Cylinder head - right hand
20. Spark plug (8 off)
21. Bolt - cylinder head (3 x long & 7 x short per cylinder head)
22. Valve guide (16 off)
23. Split pin (4 off)
24. Washers - plain (4 off)
25. Washers - spring (4 off)
26. Spring - rocker shaft (6 off)
27. Rocker arm
28. Pedestal bolt
29. Pedestal
30. Push rod
31. Hydraulic tappet
32. Rocker shaft
33. Screw/washer - inlet manifold gasket clamp (2 off)
34. Clamp - inlet manifold gasket (2 off)
35. Gasket - inlet manifold

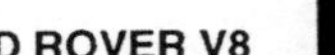

CYLINDER BLOCK COMPONENTS - from 99MY

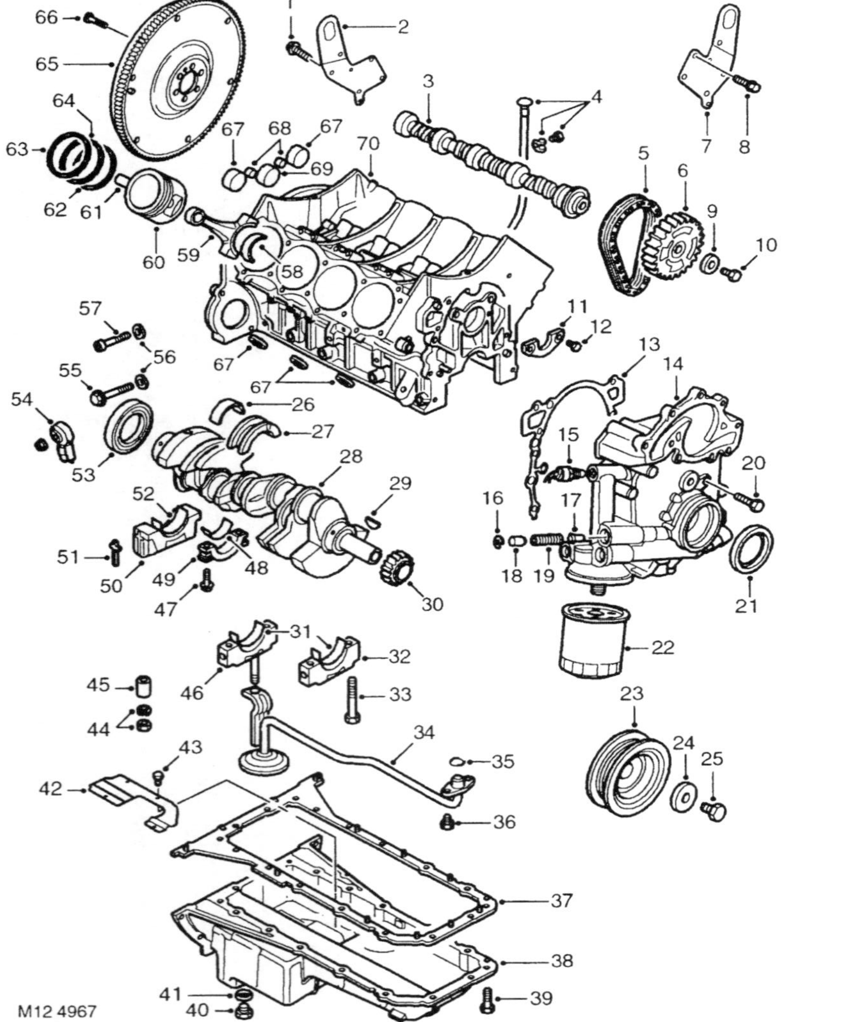

1. Bolt - Rear lifting eye (2 off)
2. Rear lifting eye
3. Camshaft
4. Dipstick, dipstick tube, clamp and bolt
5. Timing chain
6. Camshaft sprocket
7. Front lifting eye
8. Bolt - Front lifting eye (2 off)
9. Washer
10. Bolt - camshaft timing gear
11. Thrust plate - camshaft end-float
12. Bolt - camshaft thrust plate
13. Gasket - front cover
14. Front cover
15. Oil pressure switch
16. Circlip
17. Plunger - oil pressure relief valve
18. Plug - oil pressure relief valve
19. Spring - oil pressure relief valve
20. Bolt
21. Crankshaft front oil seal
22. Oil filter element
23. Crankshaft front pulley
24. Washer
25. Bolt - crankshaft front pulley
26. Upper main bearing seal
27. Upper centre main bearing shell and thrust washer
28. Crankshaft
29. Woodruff key
30. Crankshaft timing gear
31. Lower main bearing shells
32. Numbers 1, 2 and 3 main bearings
33. Bolt - main bearing caps
34. Oil pick-up pipe and strainer
35. 'O' ring
36. Screw - oil pick-up pipe (2 off)
37. Gasket - sump
38. Sump
39. Bolt - sump
40. Oil sump drain plug
41. Sealing washer
42. Baffle plate - oil sump
43. Screws - baffle plate (4 off)
44. Stiffener and nut - oil pick-up pipe to main bearing cap
45. Spacer - oil pick-up pipe to main bearing cap
46. Number 4 main bearing cap
47. Bolt - connecting rod big-end bearing cap
48. Connecting rod big-end bearing shell - lower
49. Connecting rod big-end bearing cap
50. Number 5 - rear main bearing cap
51. Cruciform seal - rear main bearing cap
52. Number 5 - rear main bearing seal
53. Crankshaft rear oil seal
54. Crankshaft knock sensor
55. Side bolt - main bearing cap
56. Dowty washers
57. Side Allen bolt - main bearing cap
58. Connecting rod big-end bearing shell - upper
59. Connecting rod
60. Piston
61. Gudgeon pin
62. Oil control ring
63. Top compression ring
64. 2nd compression ring
65. Flywheel / drive plate and starter ring gear
66. Bolt - flywheel / drive plate
67. Core plugs
68. Tappet oil gallery plugs (2 off)
69. Plug - Camshaft rear bore
70. Cylinder block

DESCRIPTION - up to 99MY

For description and operation of V8 engine before 99MY, refer to 4.0/4.6 V8 Engine Overhaul Manual.

DESCRIPTION - from 99MY

General

The V8 petrol engine is an eight cylinder, water cooled unit having two banks of four cylinders positioned at 90 degrees to each other. The engine comprises five main castings - two cylinder heads, cylinder block, front cover and the oil sump, all of which are manufactured from aluminium alloy. The engine is available in 4.0 litre and 4.6 litre versions and each type can be supplied as high compression or low compression variants, dependent on market requirements.

Cylinder heads

The cylinder heads are fitted with replaceable valve guides and valve seat inserts with the combustion chambers formed in the head. Each cylinder head is sealed to the cylinder block with a multi-layer gasket. The exhaust manifolds are bolted to the outside of each cylinder head whilst the inlet manifolds are located in the centre of the 'Vee' and are bolted to the inside face of each head. Inlet and exhaust manifolds are sealed to the cylinder heads by means of gaskets.

Each cylinder has a single inlet and exhaust valve. The exhaust valves are of the 'carbon break' type, a recess on the valve stem prevents a build-up of carbon in the valve guide by dislodging particles of carbon as the valve stem moves up and down the guide. Inlet and exhaust valve stem oil seals are fitted at the top of each valve guide. Valve operation is by means of rocker arms, push rods and hydraulic tappets. Each of the rocker arms is located on a rocker shaft which is supported by means of pedestals bolted to the cylinder heads. A spring, positioned on either side of each rocker arm, maintains the correct relative position of the arm to its valve stem. The rocker arms are operated directly by the push rods which pass through drillings in the cylinder heads and cylinder block. The bottom end of each push rod locates in a hydraulic tappet operated by the single, chain driven camshaft.

The rocker covers are bolted to the cylinder heads and are sealed to the heads by a rubber gasket. Stub pipes for crankcase ventilation hose connections are fitted to each rocker cover, the pipe in the right hand rocker cover incorporates an oil separator. The engine oil filler cap is situated in the right hand cover.

Cylinder block and camshaft

The cylinder block is fitted with cast iron cylinder liners which are shrink-fitted and locate on stops in the block. The camshaft is positioned in the centre of the cylinder block and runs in one-piece bearing shells which are line bored after fitting. Camshaft end-float is controlled by a thrust plate bolted to the front of the cylinder block. A timing gear, chain driven by the crankshaft timing gear is bolted to the front of the camshaft.

Crankshaft and main bearings

The crankshaft is carried in five main bearings. The upper main bearing shell locations are an integral part of the cylinder block casting. The lower main bearing caps are bolted to the cylinder block on either side of the upper bearing shell locations with an additional bolt being inserted into each cap from either side of the cylinder block. The rear main bearing cap carries the crankshaft rear oil seal and is sealed to the cylinder block by means of cruciform shaped seals in each side of the cap. Number four main bearing cap carries the stud fixing for the oil pick-up pipe. Lower main bearing shells are plain whilst the upper shells have an oil feed hole and are grooved. Crankshaft end-float is controlled by the thrust faces of the upper centre shell. The crankshaft timing gear is located on the front of the crankshaft by means of a Woodruff key which is also used to drive the gear type oil pump. The drive plate incorporates the crankshaft position sensor reluctor ring, and the assembly is dowel located and bolted to the crankshaft.

Front cover

The front cover is bolted to the front of the cylinder block and is sealed to the block with a gasket. The disposable, full-flow oil filter canister is screwed to the front cover, which also carries the oil pressure switch, oil pressure relief valve and crankshaft front oil seal. The gear type oil pump is integral with the front cover which also has an internal oilway to direct oil from the oil cooler to the filter.

Oil sump

The oil sump is bolted to the bottom of the cylinder block and the front cover and is sealed to both components with a one-piece gasket. A removable baffle to prevent oil surge is fitted in the sump. The oil pick-up pipe and strainer assembly is positioned within the sump. The assembly is attached at the pick-up end to a stud screwed into number four main bearing cap and at the delivery end to the oil pump. The oil drain plug is located in the bottom of the sump and is sealed with a washer.

Pistons and connecting rods

Each of the aluminium alloy pistons has two compression rings and an oil control ring. The pistons are secured to the connecting rods by semi-floating gudgeon pins. Each gudgeon pin is offset by 0.5 mm (0.02 in). The top of each piston is recessed, the depth of recess determining the compression ratio of the engine. Plain big-end bearing shells are fitted to each connecting rod and cap.

Lubrication

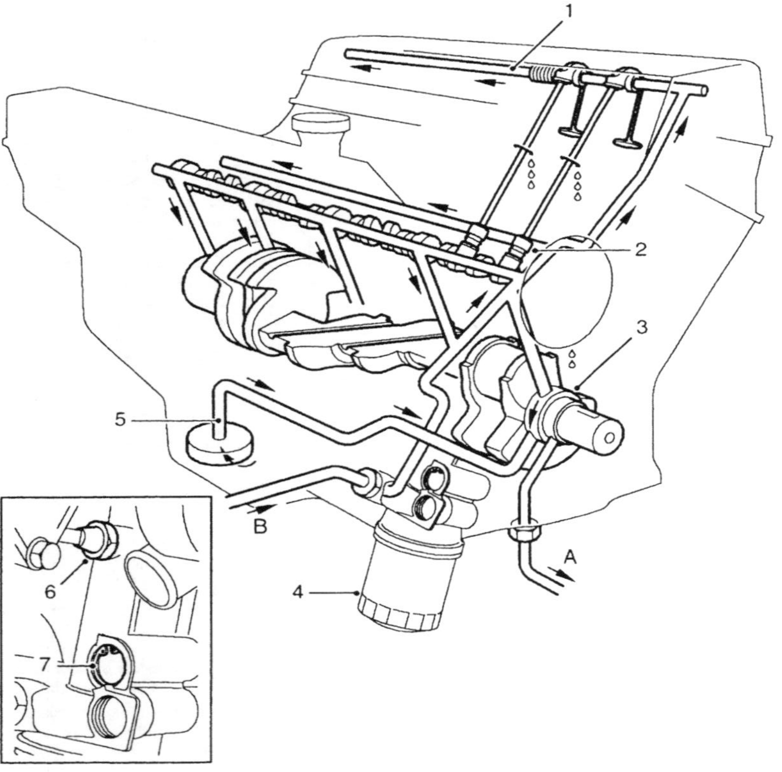

M12 4968

1. Rocker shaft assembly
2. Hydraulic tappet
3. Oil pump
4. Oil filter element
5. Oil pick-up pipe and strainer
6. Oil pressure switch
7. Oil pressure relief valve

A. - to oil cooler
B. - from oil cooler

Oil is drawn from the sump through a strainer and into the oil pump via the oil pick-up pipe. Pressurised oil from the pump passes through the oil cooler mounted in front of the radiator and returns to the full-flow oil filter element. Oil from the filter passes into the main oil gallery and through internal drillings to the crankshaft where it is directed to each main bearing and to the big-end bearings via numbers 1, 3 and 5 main bearings. Excess oil pressure is relieved by the oil pressure relief valve. An internal drilling in the cylinder block directs oil to the camshaft where it passes through further internal drillings to the hydraulic tappets, camshaft bearing journals and rocker shafts. Lubrication to the pistons, small ends and cylinder bores is by oil grooves machined in the connecting rods and by splash.

Oil pressure switch

The oil pressure warning light switch registers low oil pressure in the main oil gallery on the outflow side of the filter. Whilst the engine is running and oil pressure is correct, the switch is open. When the ignition is switched on or if oil pressure drops below the pressure setting of the switch, the switch closes and the low oil pressure warning lamp located in the instrument pack will illuminate.

Hydraulic tappets

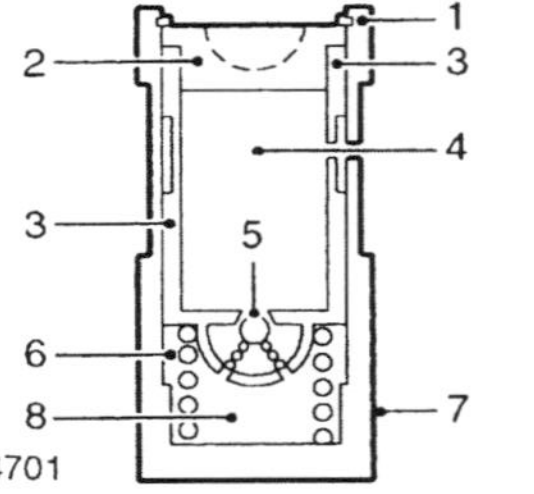

M12 4701

1. Clip
2. Pushrod seat
3. Inner sleeve
4. Upper chamber
5. Non-return ball valve
6. Spring
7. Outer sleeve
8. Lower chamber

The hydraulic tappet provides maintenance free, quiet operation of the valves. This is achieved by utilizing engine oil pressure to eliminate the clearance between the rocker arms and valve stems. When the valve is closed, engine oil pressure present in the upper chamber, passes through the non-return ball valve and into the lower chamber. When the cam begins to lift the outer sleeve, the resistance of the valve spring, felt through the push rod and seat, causes the tappet inner sleeve to move downwards inside the outer sleeve. This downwards movement closes the non-return ball valve and increases the pressure in the lower chamber sufficiently to ensure that the valve is fully opened by the push rod. As the tappet moves off the peak of the cam, the non-return ball valve opens thereby allowing the pressure in both chambers to equalize. This ensures that the valve will be fully closed when the tappet is on the back of the cam.

Crankcase ventilation

A positive crankcase ventilation system is used to vent crankcase gases to the air induction system. Gases are drawn from the left hand rocker cover to a tapping in the throttle body. An oil separator is incorporated in the hose connection stub pipe in the right hand rocker cover, gases from this connection are drawn to a tapping in the inlet manifold.

Notes

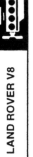

CRANKSHAFT PULLEY AND FRONT COVER OIL SEAL - up to 99MY

Service repair no - 12.21.01 - Crankshaft Pulley
Service repair no - 12.21.14 - Front Cover Oil Seal

Remove

1. Disconnect battery negative lead.
2. Remove cooling fan. ***See COOLING SYSTEM, Repair.***

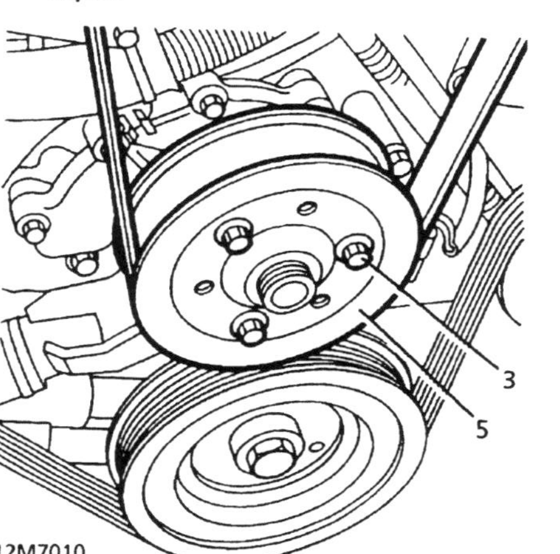

12M7010

3. Slacken 3 water pump pulley securing bolts.
4. Remove alternator drive belt.
5. Remove water pump pulley bolts. Remove pulley.
6. Raise vehicle on four post lift.Remove acoustic cover if applicable. ***See CHASSIS AND BODY, Repair.***
7. Secure LRT-12-080 to crankshaft pulley with 4 bolts.

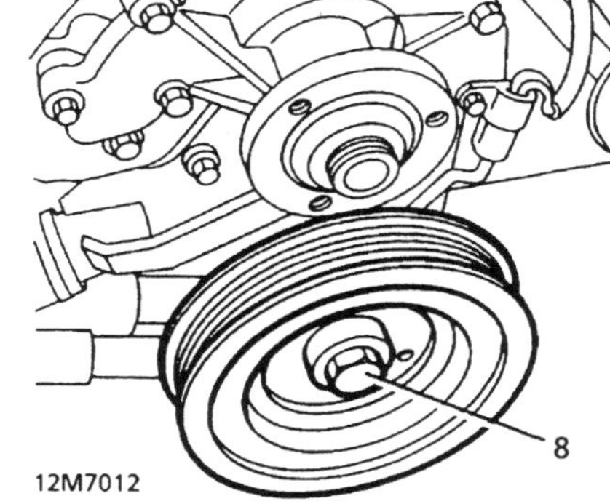

12M7012

8. Remove crankshaft pulley bolt. Collect pulley and tool.

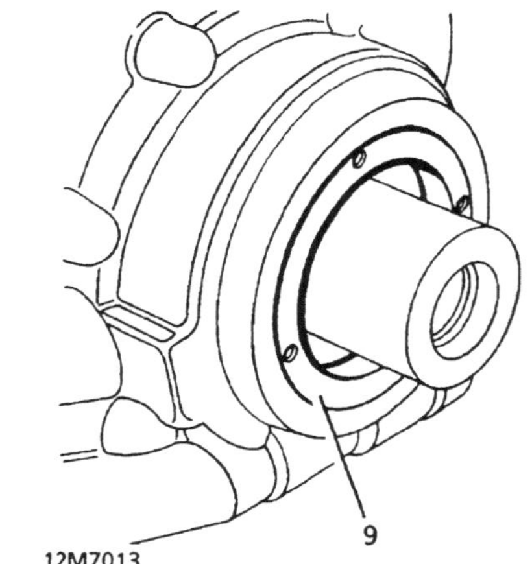

12M7013

9. Using LRT-12-088, remove oil seal from front cover.

CAUTION: Do not damage front cover.

Refit

10. Clean seal register and crankshaft pulley.
11. Lubricate outer face of seal.
12. Using LRT-12-089, fit seal to cover.
13. Lubricate oil seal lip. Fit crankshaft pulley.
14. Refit crankshaft pulley bolt. Tighten to ***270 Nm. (200 lbf.ft)***
15. Ensure mating faces between flywheel access cover and gearbox are clean.
16. Lower vehicle.
17. Ensure mating faces between water pump pulley and pump are clean.
18. Refit water pump pulley. Tighten to ***22 Nm. (16 lbf.ft)***
19. Refit alternator drive belt.
20. Refit cooling fan. ***See COOLING SYSTEM, Repair.***
21. Reconnect battery negative lead.

CRANKSHAFT PULLEY AND FRONT COVER OIL SEAL - from 99MY

Service repair no - 12.21.01 Crankshaft pulley
Service repair no - 12.21.14 Front cover oil seal

Remove

1. Remove auxiliary drive belt. ***See ELECTRICAL, Repair.***

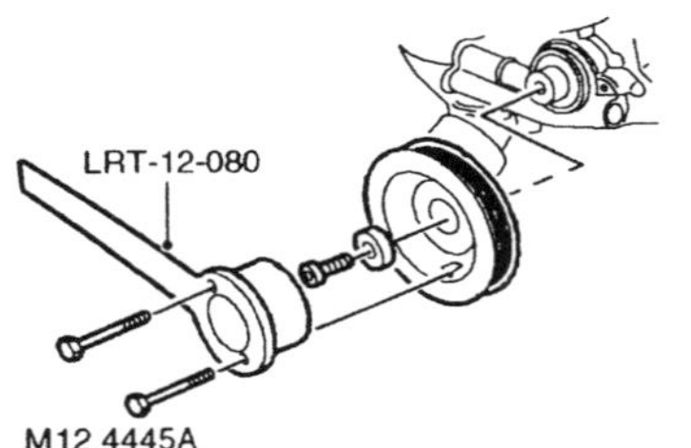

M12 4445A

2. Secure LRT-12-080 to crankshaft pulley with 2 bolts.
3. Remove crankshaft pulley bolt.
4. Remove crankshaft pulley.

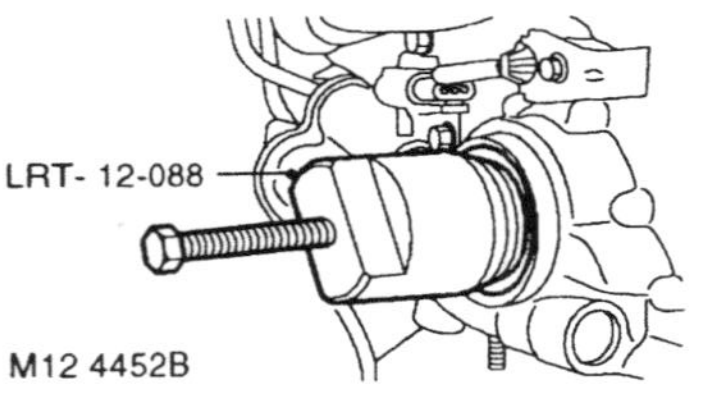

M12 4452B

5. Using LRT-12-088, remove oil seal from front cover.

Refit

6. Clean seal register in front cover and crankshaft pulley.

LRT- 12-089

M12 4732A

7. Lubricate outer face of seal and fit seal to front cover using LRT-12-089
8. Fit crankshaft pulley and tighten bolt to ***270 Nm (200 lbf.ft.).***
9. Remove LRT-12-080 from crankshaft pulley.
10. Fit auxiliary drive belt. ***See ELECTRICAL, Repair.***

CRANKSHAFT REAR OIL SEAL

Service repair no - 12.21.20

Remove

1. **Manual Vehicles:** Remove flywheel. ***See this section.***
2. **Automatic Vehicles:** Remove drive plate. ***See this section.***

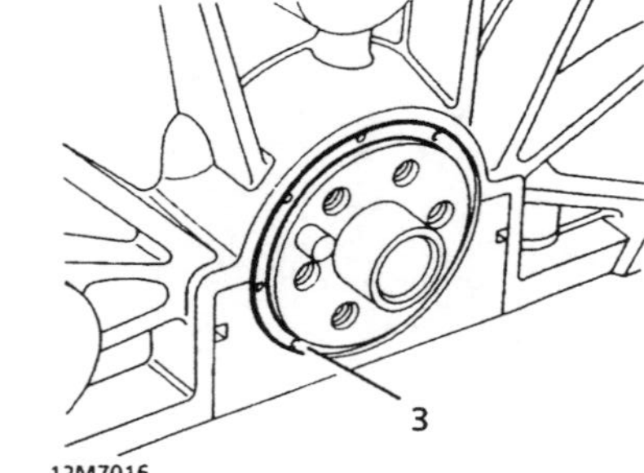

12M7016

3. Remove oil seal from location.

CAUTION: Do not damage seal location or running surface on crankshaft.

Refit

4. Ensure both seal location and running surface on crankshaft are clean.
5. Ensure mating faces of flywheel and crankshaft are clean.
6. Lubricate seal guide LRT-12-095 with clean engine oil. Position over crankshaft boss.

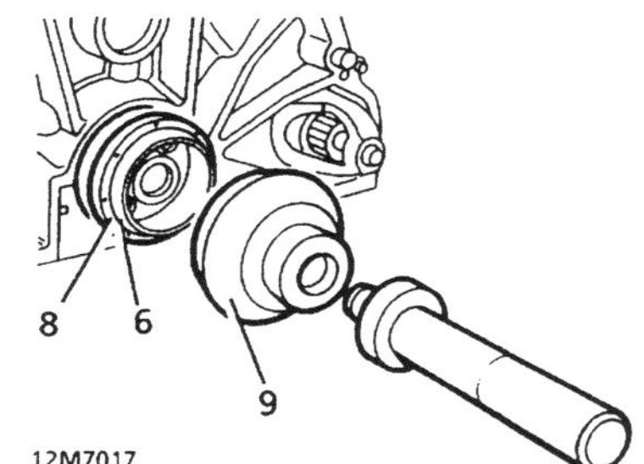

12M7017

7. Lubricate oil seal lip.
8. Position seal squarely. Remove guide.
9. Drift seal into location using LRT-12-091.
10. **Manual Vehicles:** Fit flywheel. ***See this section.***
11. **Automatic Vehicles:** Fit drive plate. ***See this section.***

DRIVE PLATE - AUTOMATIC - up to 99MY

Service repair no - 12.53.13

Remove

1. Remove automatic gearbox and torque converter. ***See AUTOMATIC GEARBOX, Repair.***

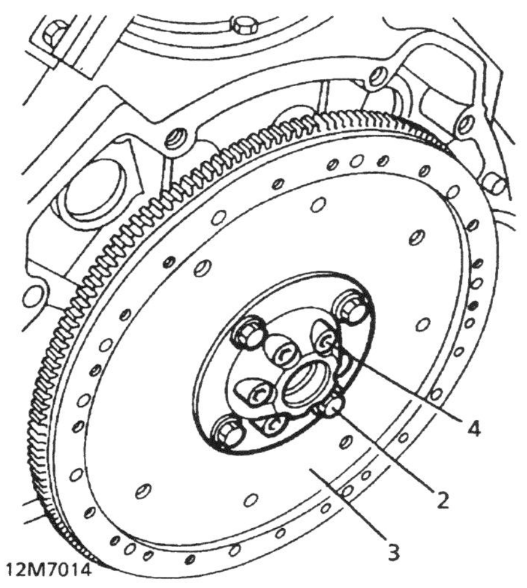

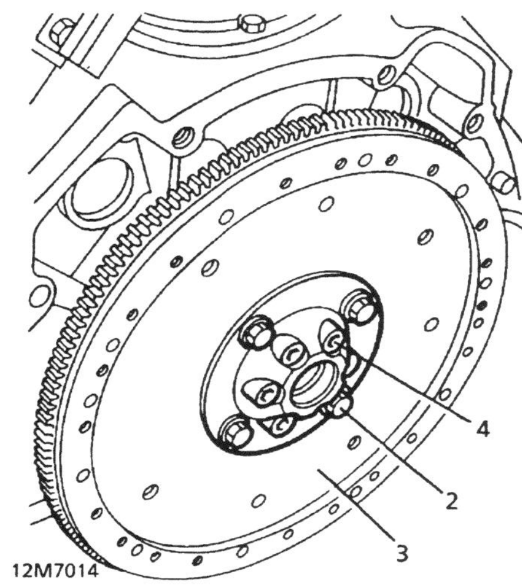

12M7014

2. Remove 4 clamp ring bolts. Collect clamp ring.
3. Remove flexible drive plate/starter ring gear assembly from hub aligner.
4. Remove 6 screws from hub aligner. Remove hub aligner from crankshaft. Collect spacer.
5. Check drive plate for dis'ortion or cracks. Check starter ring gear for chipped or broken teeth. If either component shows signs of damage, fit a new assembly.

Refit

6. Ensure all mating surfaces are clean.
7. Fit spacer and hub aligner to crankshaft.
8. Fit hub aligner screws. Tighten to ***85 Nm. (63 lbf.ft)***
9. Fit drive plate and clamp ring.
10. Fit clamp ring bolts. Tighten to ***45 Nm. (33 lbf.ft)***
11. Fit automatic gearbox and converter assembly. ***See AUTOMATIC GEARBOX, Repair.***

DRIVE PLATE - AUTOMATIC - from 99MY

Service repair no - 12.53.13

Remove

1. Remove gearbox. ***See AUTOMATIC GEARBOX, Repair.***
2. Remove CKP sensor. ***See FUEL SYSTEM, Repair.***

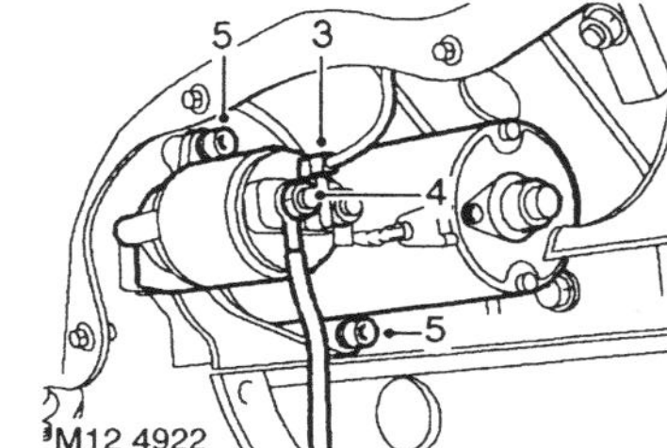

M12 4922

3. Remove Lucar from starter solenoid.
4. Remove nut securing battery lead to starter solenoid and disconnect lead.
5. Remove 2 Allen screws securing starter motor and remove starter motor.

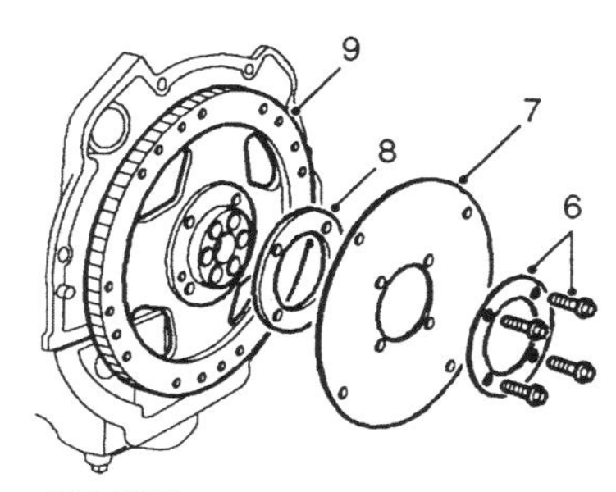

M12 4923

6. Remove 4 bolts securing drive plate clamp ring and remove ring.
7. Remove drive plate from hub.
8. Remove spacer.
9. Remove starter ring gear.

Refit

10. Clean starter ring gear and hub, clean dowel and dowel hole.
11. Fit starter ring gear to hub.
12. Clean spacer, clamp ring and mating face on hub.
13. Clean drive plate and check for cracks and distortion.
14. Fit spacer to hub, fit drive plate and clamp ring. Tighten bolts to ***45 Nm (33 lbf.ft).***
15. Clean starter motor and mating face.
16. Fit starter motor and tighten Allen screws to ***45 Nm (33 lbf.ft).***
17. Connect battery lead to starter solenoid and secure with nut.
18. Connect lucar to starter solenoid.
19. Fit CKP sensor. ***See FUEL SYSTEM, Repair.***
20. Fit gearbox. ***See AUTOMATIC GEARBOX, Repair.***

ENGINE AND GEARBOX - up to 99MY

Service repair no - 12.37.01/99

Remove

1. Position vehicle on four post lift.
2. Remove battery. ***See ELECTRICAL, Repair.***
3. Remove ECM. ***See FUEL SYSTEM, Repair.***
4. Remove 2 screws securing engine harness clamp to battery tray. Collect clamp.
5. Release starter feed wire from battery terminal clamp.
6. Release earth lead from alternator bracket.
7. Release fuel return hose clip. Release fuel return hose from regulator connecting pipe.
8. Release fuel feed pipe from fuel rail.
9. Disconnect multiplug from purge valve.
10. Release purge hose from ram pipe housing.
11. Remove purge valve securing bolt from shock absorber turret. Place valve aside.
12. Disconnect multiplug from air flow meter.
13. Release harness from intake hose.
14. Slacken clip securing intake hose to plenum chamber.
15. Remove intake hose/air flow meter assembly.
16. Position harness across engine.
17. Disconnect throttle and cruise control cables from throttle linkage.
18. Release cables from abutment bracket.
19. Disconnect top hose from inlet manifold.
20. Disconnect heater hose from inlet manifold. Release hose from clip. Place hose aside.
21. Disconnect coolant hose from plenum chamber water jacket. Release hose from 2 clips. Place hose aside on valance.
22. Remove 4 bolts securing battery tray. Remove battery tray.

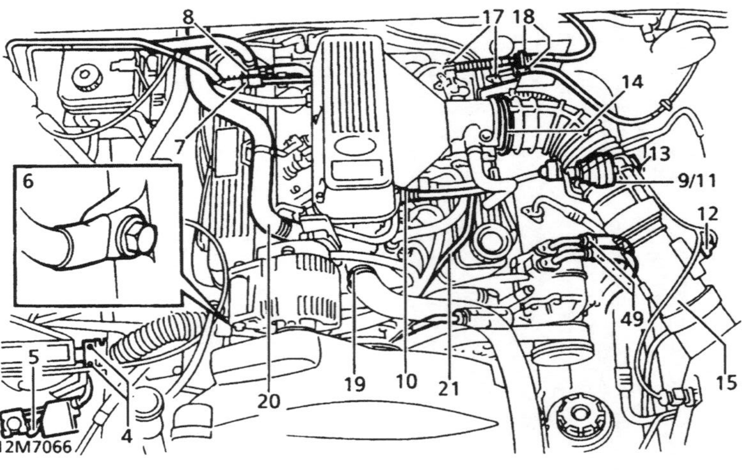

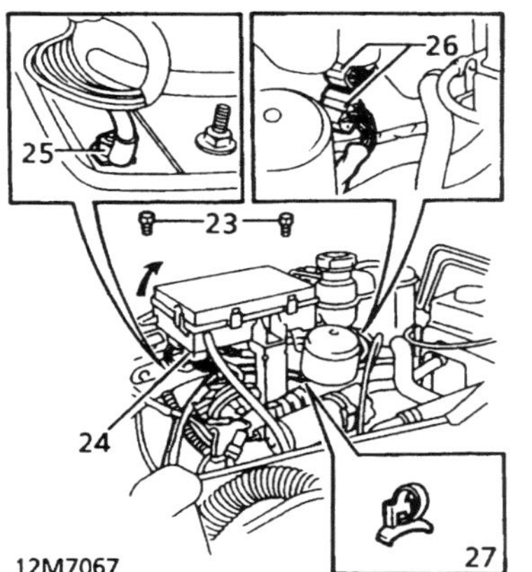

12M7067

23. Remove 2 bolts securing fuse box. Pivot fuse box for access.
24. Disconnect engine harness multiplug from base of fuse box.
25. Release earth wire from valance stud.
26. Disconnect 2 engine harness multiplugs from main harness.
27. Release engine harness clip from valance. Tie harness aside over engine.
28. With assistance, release bonnet struts from body locations. Retain bonnet in vertical position using stay clips.

WARNING: Only open the bonnet to the vertical position with the vehicle on a horizontal surface in the workshop. This position is not intended to be used outdoors where the bonnet could be affected by winds.

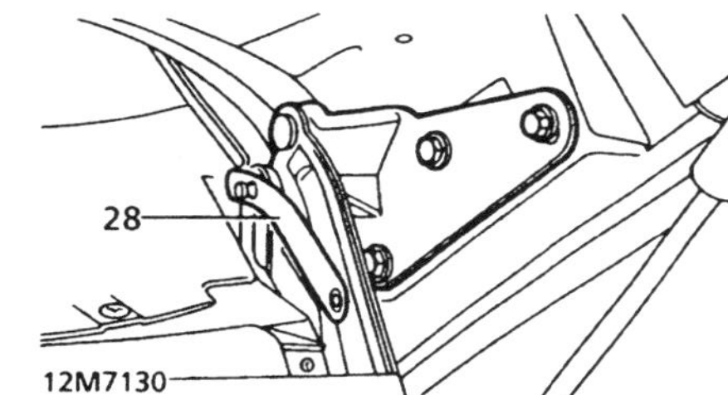

12M7130

29. Depressurise fuel system. ***See FUEL SYSTEM, Repair.***
30. Remove air cleaner. ***See FUEL SYSTEM, Repair.***
31. Drain cooling system. ***See COOLING SYSTEM, Repair.***
32. Discharge air conditioning system. ***See AIR CONDITIONING, Adjustment.***
33. Remove cooling fan and viscous coupling. ***See COOLING SYSTEM, Repair.***
34. Remove front grille. ***See CHASSIS AND BODY, Repair.***
35. Remove 4 bolts securing bonnet platform.

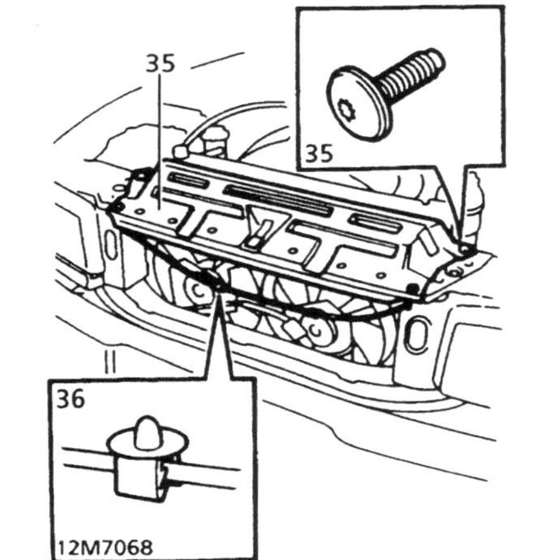

12M7068

36. Release straps securing bonnet release cable to platform. Remove platform.
37. Remove 2 studs securing each radiator air deflector. Remove both deflectors.

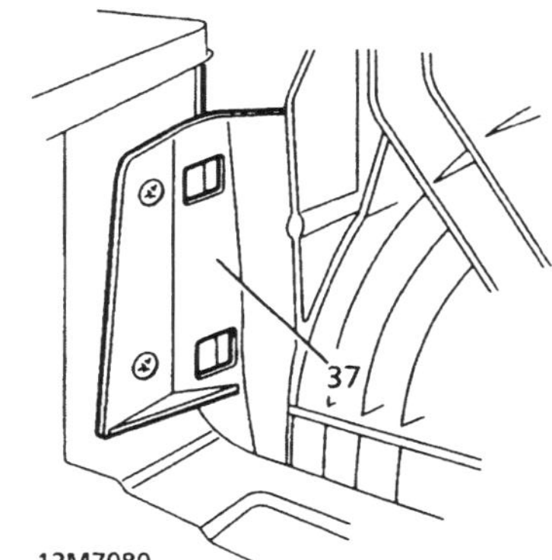

12M7080

38. Remove bolt and screw securing washer bottle filler neck. Remove filler neck.

CAUTION: Where pipes are disconnected, plug pipes and ports to prevent ingress of dirt.

39. Disconnect engine and gearbox oil coolers. Remove 'O' rings and discard. Tie pipes aside on engine.

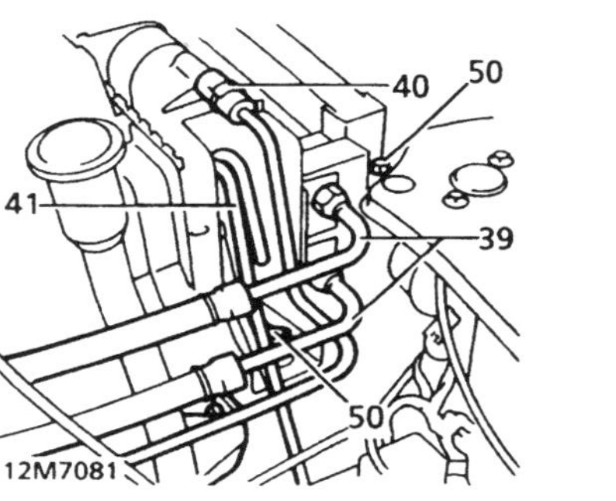

12M7081

40. Disconnect coolant bleed hose from radiator.

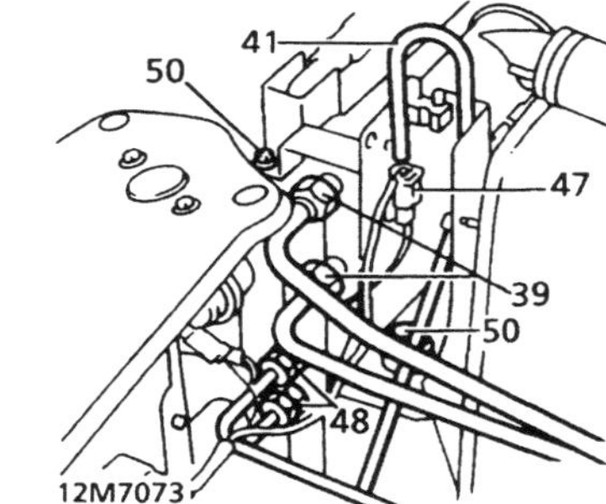

12M7073

41. Release 2 fog lamp breather hoses from clips on either side of radiator.
42. Disconnect 3 coolant hoses from thermostat housing.
43. Remove 2 bolts securing power steering fluid reservoir to radiator.

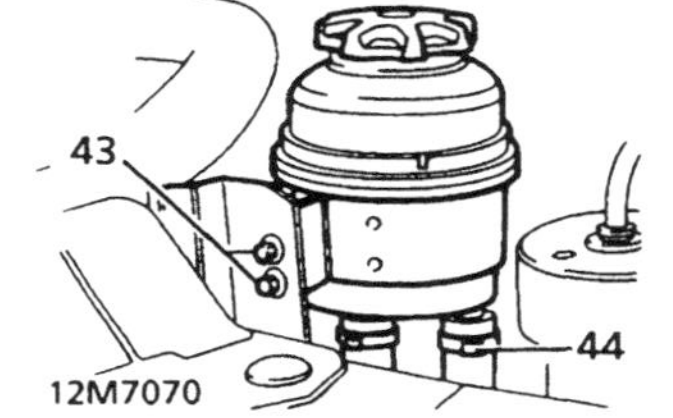

12M7070

NOTE: Position container beneath power steering reservoir to catch spillage.

44. Disconnect return pipe from reservoir. Tie reservoir aside to engine.
45. Disconnect feed pipe from power steering pump. Remove 'O' rings and discard.

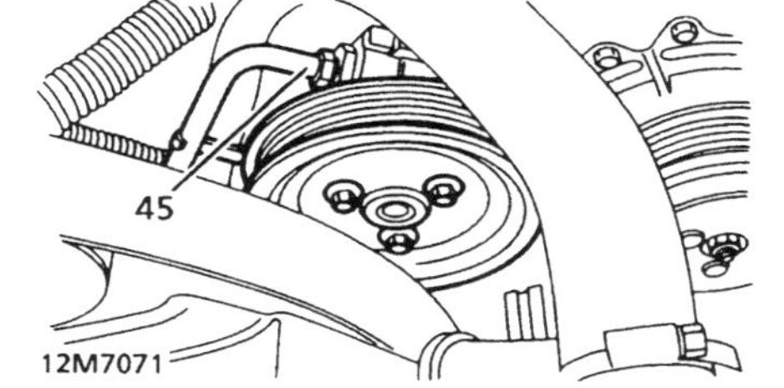

12M7071

46. Release feed pipe clip from bracket. Place pipe aside.
47. Disconnect multiplug from gearbox oil temperature sensor.
48. Disconnect 2 pipes from air conditioning condenser. Remove 'O' rings and discard.
49. Disconnect 2 pipes from air conditioning compressor. Remove 'O' rings and discard. Place pipes aside.
50. Remove 2 nuts and bolts securing radiator mountings to chassis.
51. With assistance, raise radiator assembly for access to condenser cooling fan connections.

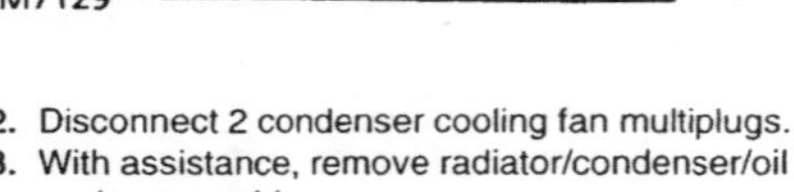

52. Disconnect 2 condenser cooling fan multiplugs.
53. With assistance, remove radiator/condenser/oil cooler assembly.

Manual Vehicles:

54. Clamp clutch flexible hose using an approved brake hose clamp.
55. Remove clip securing flexible hose to gearbox bracket.
56. Disconnect clutch flexible hose at gearbox pipe. Position hose aside.

Automatic Vehicles:

57. Remove window switch pack. ***See ELECTRICAL, Repair.***

Manual Vehicles:

58. Remove centre console. ***See CHASSIS AND BODY, Repair.***
59. Remove 6 nuts securing gaiter ring. Remove ring and gaiter.

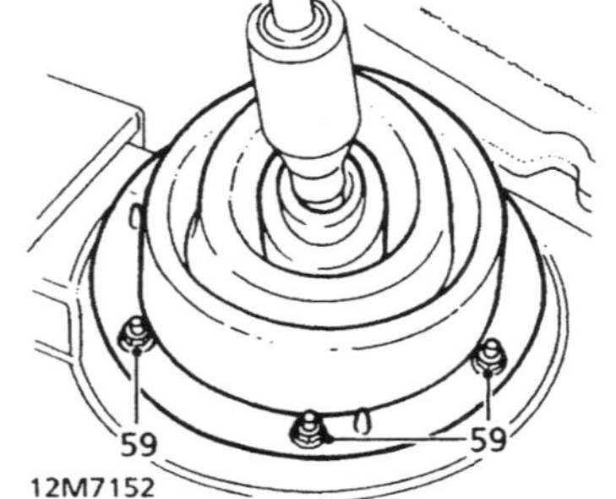

60. Remove 2 bolts securing gear lever. Remove lever.

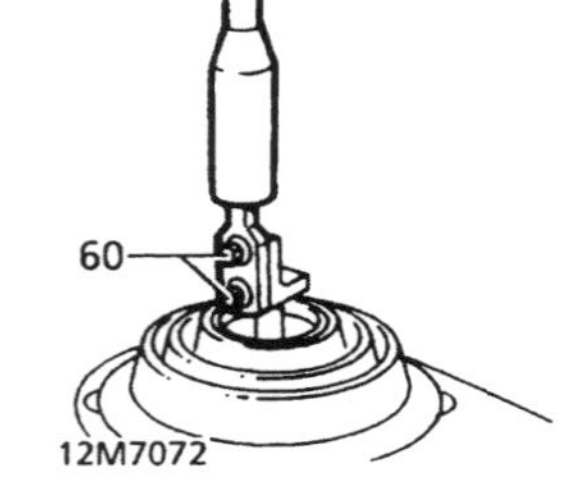

All Vehicles:

61. Release handbrake. Release handbrake cable clevis pin.

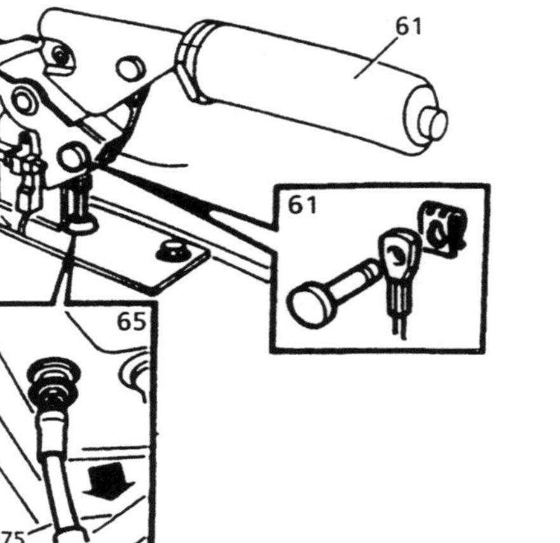

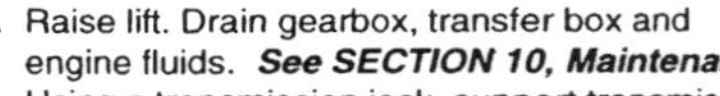

62. Raise lift. Drain gearbox, transfer box and engine fluids. ***See SECTION 10, Maintenance.***
63. Using a transmission jack, support transmission under brake drum.
64. Remove exhaust front pipe. ***See MANIFOLD AND EXHAUST SYSTEM, Repair.***
65. Release hand brake cable from grommet in tunnel.
66. Remove 4 bolts securing rear propeller shaft guard. Remove guard.

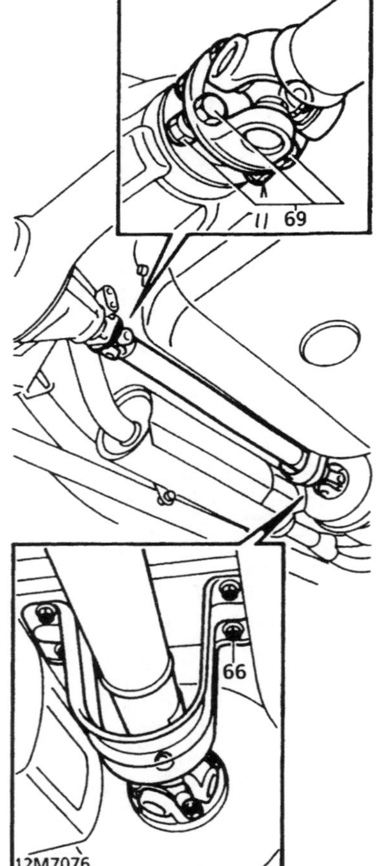

67. Mark transfer box and propeller shaft flanges to aid reassembly.
68. Raise one wheel on each axle to allow rotation of propeller shafts.
69. Remove 4 nuts and bolts from each flange. Disconnect propeller shafts. Tie aside.
70. **Automatic Vehicles:** Disconnect gear selector cable trunnion from gearbox lever. Remove 2 bolts securing selector cable abutment bracket to gearbox. Place selector cable aside.

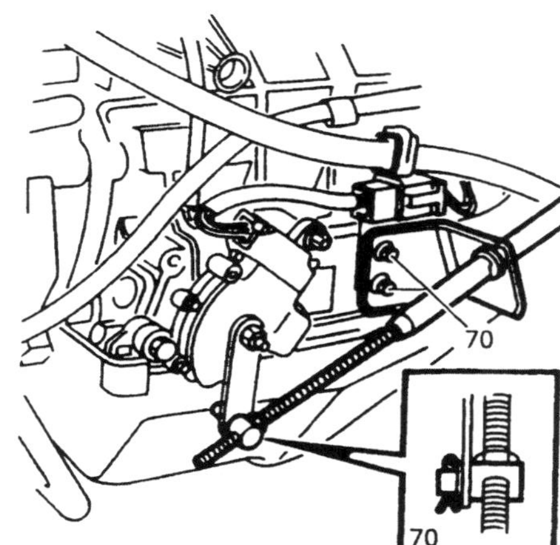

12M7077

71. Lower gearbox for access.
72. Disconnect 2 Lucars from transfer box fluid temperature sensor.

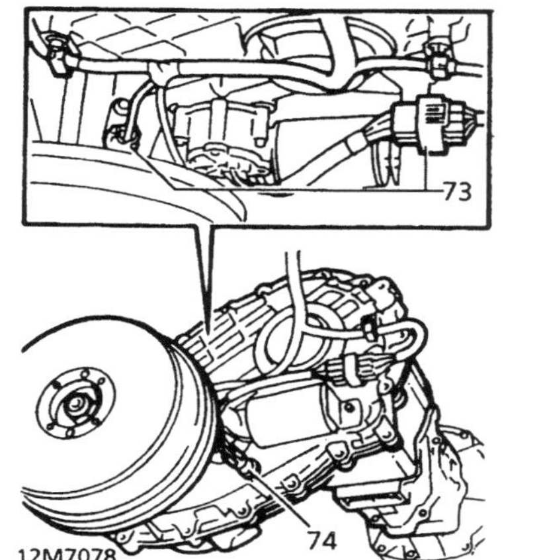

12M7078

73. Disconnect multiplugs from High/Low motor and output shaft speed sensor.
74. **Automatic Vehicles:** Disconnect multiplugs from gear selection position switch and gearbox speed sensor.

75. **Manual Vehicles:** Disconnect multiplugs from reverse and neutral switches. Remove bolt securing harness bracket to gearbox. Release harness from clips on gearbox brackets.

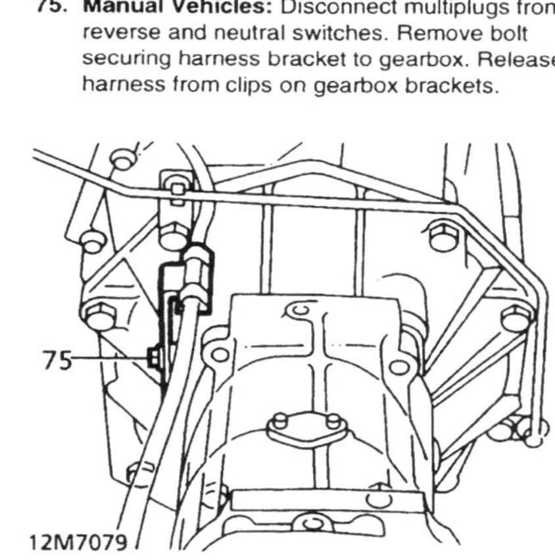

12M7079

76. Disconnect engine harness to gearbox harness multiplug. Position harness aside.
77. Remove 4 nuts securing each engine mount to chassis and engine brackets. Discard nuts.

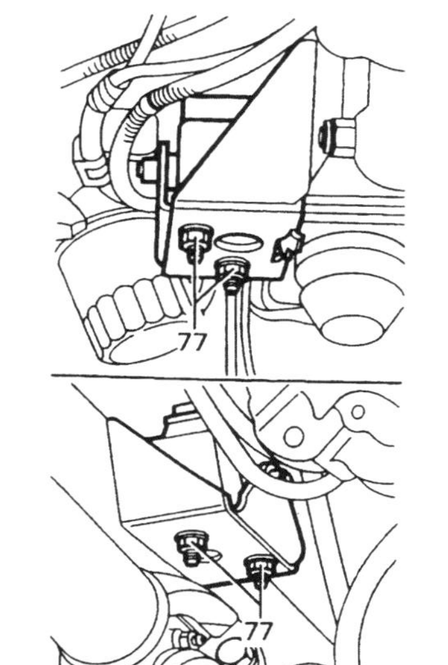
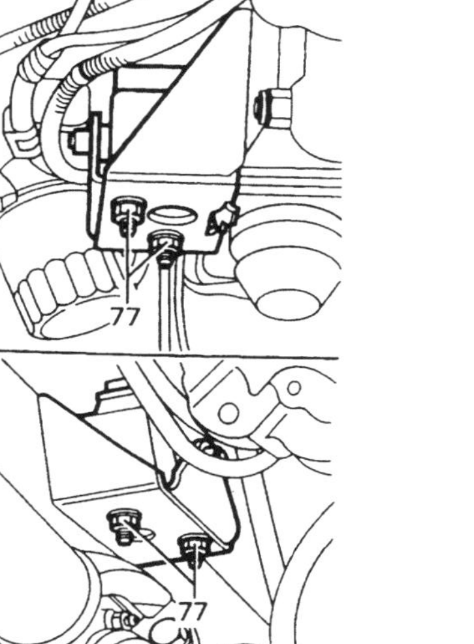

12M7082

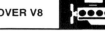

78. Remove oil filler cap.
79. Place cloth over plenum chamber to protect from damage during lifting.
80. Shorten front chain of lifting bracket to 2 links as shown.

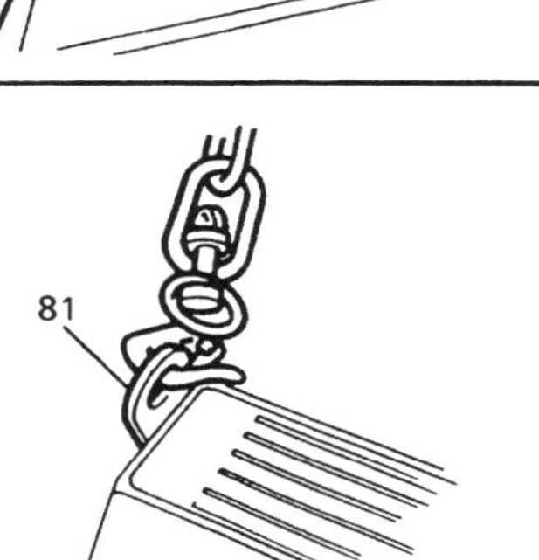

12M7131

81. Fit lifting bracket to engine lifting eyes. Attach suitable hoist.
82. Raise engine slightly. Ensure that lifting bracket does not foul bulkhead. Remove both engine mountings.

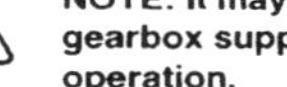
NOTE: It may be necessary to lower gearbox support slightly during above operation.

83. Raise power unit and draw forward. Lower support from transmission.

NOTE: Power unit must be tilted at an angle of approximately 45 degrees before it can be withdrawn from engine compartment.

84. Remove engine/transmission assembly.

Refit

85. Raise power unit. Guide into engine bay.
86. Position transmission jack beneath transmission brake drum.
87. With assistance, raise transmission and lower engine until engine mountings can be fitted.

CAUTION: Ensure all under body wax is removed from mating surfaces of fixings before fitting.

88. Attach mountings to chassis with new flange nuts. Do not tighten at this stage.

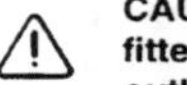

CAUTION: Engine mountings must be fitted with centre bolt head facing outboard as shown.

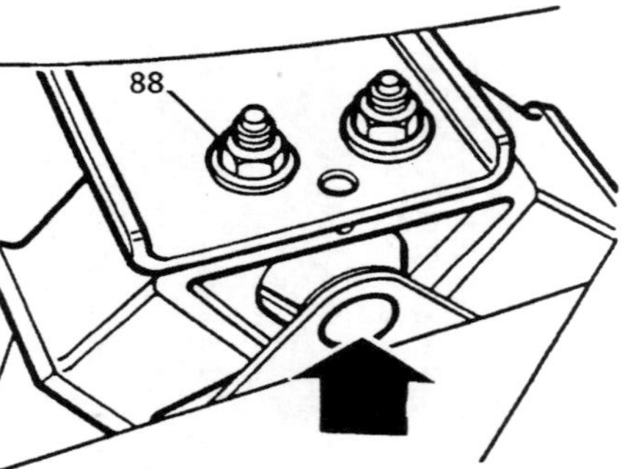

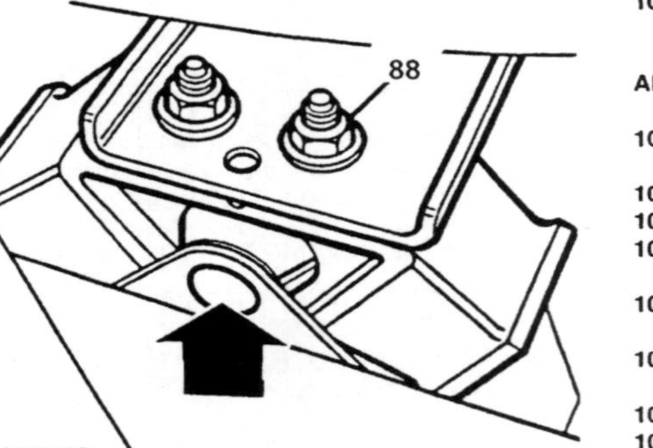

12M7133

89. Lower and guide engine onto mounting studs.
90. Attach engine to mountings with new flange nuts. Do not tighten at this stage.
91. Release lifting bracket from engine lifting eyes. Remove hoist.
92. Route gearbox harness. Secure with clips.
93. Connect multiplug to engine harness.
94. Connect multiplugs to High/Low motor and output shaft speed sensor.

Manual Vehicles:

95. Secure gearbox harness bracket with bolt. Tighten to ***6 Nm. (4 lbf.ft).***
96. Connect multiplugs to reverse and neutral switches.
97. Secure harness to gearbox bracket with clips.

Automatic Vehicles:

98. Connect multiplugs to gear selection position switch and gearbox speed sensor.
99. Position selector cable abutment bracket to gearbox. Secure with bolts.
100. Adjust gear selector cable. ***See AUTOMATIC GEARBOX, Adjustment.***

All Vehicles:

101. Connect Lucars to transfer box fluid temperature sensor.
102. Raise gearbox on transmission jack.
103. Align harness bracket to gearbox.
104. Raise one wheel on each axle to allow rotation of propeller shafts.
105. Position shafts to transfer box flanges. Align marks.
106. Secure propeller shaft flanges with nuts and bolts. Tighten to ***48 Nm. (35 lbf.ft)***
107. Fit propeller shaft guard. Tighten bolts.
108. Guide hand brake cable through grommet in transmission tunnel.
109. Fit exhaust front pipe and chassis cross member. ***See MANIFOLD AND EXHAUST SYSTEM, Repair.***
110. Remove support from under transmission.
111. Tighten engine mounting nuts to ***45 Nm. (33 lbf.ft)***

112. Lower lift.
113. Connect handbrake cable to lever, secure with clevis pin and clip.

Manual Vehicles:

114. Fit seal around gearbox remote housing to transmission tunnel aperture.
115. Position gear lever. Secure with bolts. Tighten to ***25 Nm. (18 lbf.ft)***
116. Fit gaiter and ring. Secure with bolts.
117. Fit centre console. ***See CHASSIS AND BODY, Repair.***
118. Connect clutch flexible hose. Remove hose clamp.
119. Secure flexible hose union to gearbox bracket with clip.
120. Bleed clutch hydraulic system. ***See CLUTCH, Repair.***

Automatic Vehicles:

121. Fit window switch pack. ***See ELECTRICAL, Repair.***

All Vehicles:

122. With assistance, position radiator/condenser/oil cooler assembly.
123. Connect multiplugs to condenser cooling fans.
124. Engage radiator in lower mounting rubbers. Secure with nuts and bolts.
125. Remove plugs from air conditioning compressor and pipes.
126. Fit new 'O' rings to compressor pipes. Lubricate 'O' rings with compressor oil. Connect to compressor.
127. Fit compressor connection bolts. Tighten to ***23 Nm. (17 lbf.ft)***
128. Remove plugs from air conditioning condenser and pipes.
129. Fit new 'O' rings to condenser pipes. Lubricate 'O' rings with compressor oil. Secure pipes to condenser. Tighten to ***15 Nm. (11 lbf.ft)***
130. Connect gearbox oil temperature multiplug.
131. Remove plugs from power steering pump and pipes.
132. Fit new 'O' rings to power steering pipes. Lubricate 'O' rings with power steering fluid. Secure to power steering pump. Tighten to ***16 Nm. (12 lbf.ft)***
133. Untie power steering reservoir from engine. Remove plugs. Connect return pipe. Secure return pipe to reservoir with clip.
134. Position reservoir to radiator. Secure with bolts.
135. Secure fog lamp breather hoses to clips on either side of radiator.
136. Route plenum chamber hose along front of engine. Secure in clips.
137. Connect hose to plenum chamber water jacket. Secure with clip.
138. Connect coolant hoses to radiator, thermostat housing and inlet manifold. Secure hoses with clips.
139. Remove plugs from oil coolers and pipes.
140. Lubricate pipes with clean fluid. Fit new 'O' rings. Connect to oil coolers. Tighten to ***30 Nm. (22 lbf.ft)***
141. Fit washer bottle filler neck. Secure with bolt and screw.
142. Fit radiator deflector panels. Secure with studs.
143. Position bonnet platform. Secure bonnet release cable to platform with clips.
144. Secure bonnet platform with bolts.
145. Fit front grille. ***See CHASSIS AND BODY, Repair.***
146. Fit cooling fan and viscous coupling. ***See COOLING SYSTEM, Repair.***
147. Evacuate and recharge air conditioning system. ***See AIR CONDITIONING, Adjustment.***
148. Refill cooling system. ***See COOLING SYSTEM, Repair.***
149. Replenish transmission fluids. ***See LUBRICANTS, FLUIDS AND CAPACITIES, Information.***
150. Replenish engine oil. ***See LUBRICANTS, FLUIDS AND CAPACITIES, Information.***
151. Fit oil filler cap.
152. Route engine harness along valance. Secure clip.
153. Connect engine harness multiplugs to main harness. Secure earth terminal to valance stud.
154. Connect engine harness multiplug to base of fuse box.
155. Position fuse box. Secure with bolts.
156. Position earth lead to alternator bracket. Secure with bolt.
157. Fit battery tray. Secure with bolts.
158. Fit starter feed wire to battery positive terminal clamp. Secure with nut.
159. Position engine harness to battery tray. Secure harness grommets.
160. Secure harness clamp to battery tray with screws.

161. Fit ECM. ***See FUEL SYSTEM, Repair.***
162. Fit throttle and cruise control cables to abutment bracket. Secure cruise control cable with 'C' clip.
163. Position cable trunnions to throttle linkage. Secure with clevis and split pins.
164. Adjust throttle cable free-play. ***See FUEL SYSTEM, Adjustment.***
165. Adjust cruise control cable. ***See CRUISE CONTROL, Adjustment.***
166. Fit intake hose and air flow meter assembly to plenum chamber. Secure with clip. Connect multiplug to air flow meter.
167. Connect multiplug to purge valve.
168. Position purge valve on shock absorber turret. Secure with bolt.
169. Connect purge hose to ram pipe housing.
170. Secure harness to clip on intake hose.
171. Fit air cleaner. ***See FUEL SYSTEM, Repair.***
172. Remove plugs from fuel hoses and fuel rail connections.
173. Connect fuel feed pipe to fuel rail. Tighten to ***16 Nm. (12 lbf.ft)***
174. Connect return hose to pressure regulator pipe. Secure with clip.
175. Refit battery. ***See ELECTRICAL, Repair.***
176. With assistance, release bonnet stay clips. Engage bonnet struts.

CAUTION: Ensure bonnet stay clips are returned to their original positions as shown.

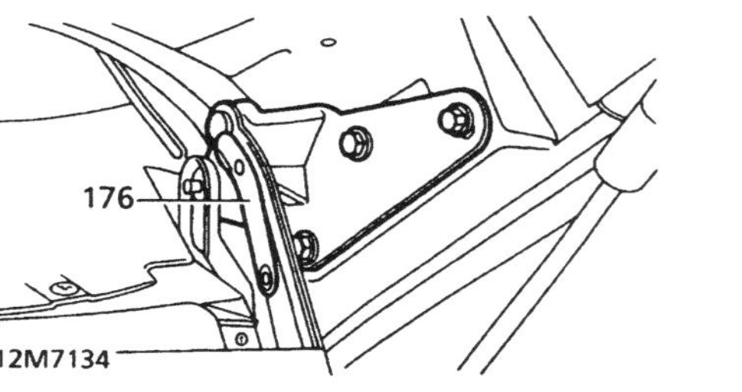

177. Start engine. Check for fuel, coolant and oil leaks.

ENGINE AND ANCILLIARIES - from 99MY

Service repair no - 12.41.01.99

Remove

1. Drain engine oil and remove oil filter.
2. Remove radiator. ***See COOLING SYSTEM, Repair.***
3. Remove ignition coils. ***See FUEL SYSTEM, Repair.***

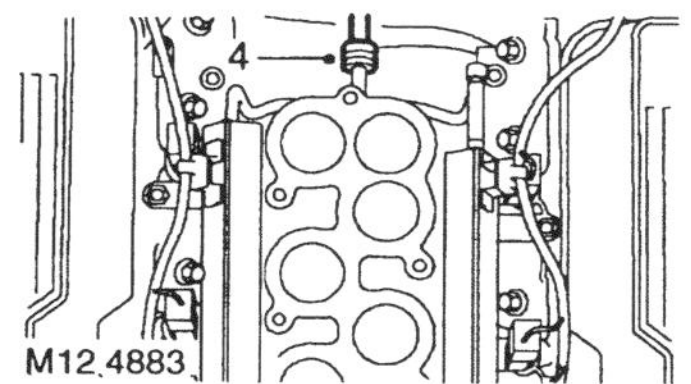

4. Position absorbent material to catch any fuel spillage and disconnect fuel pipe from rail.

CAUTION: Plug the connections.

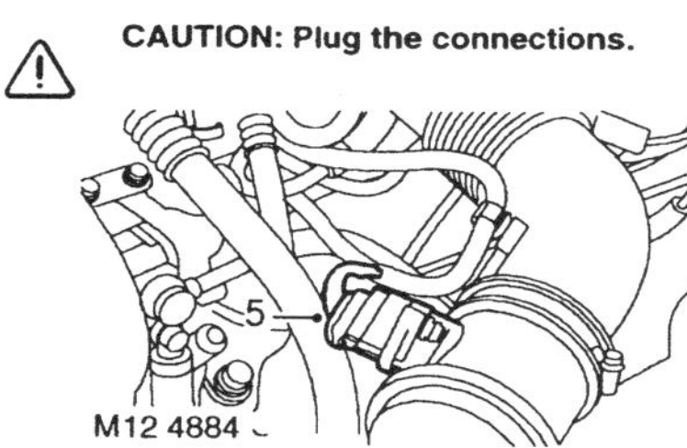

5. Disconnect MAF sensor multiplug.

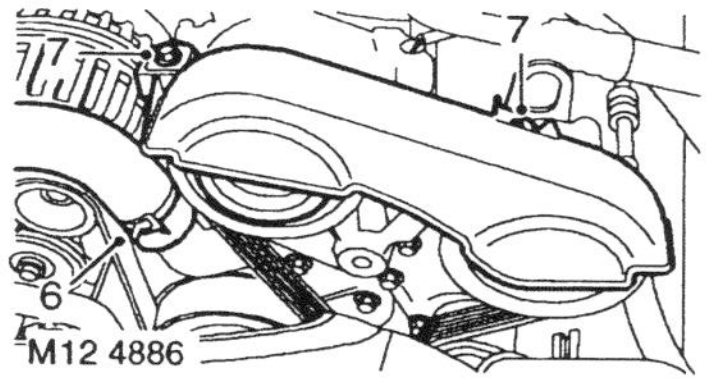

7
6
M12 4886

6. Release clip and remove top hose from adaptor on inlet manifold.
7. Remove 2 bolts securing auxilliary drive belt cover, remove cover and collect spacers.

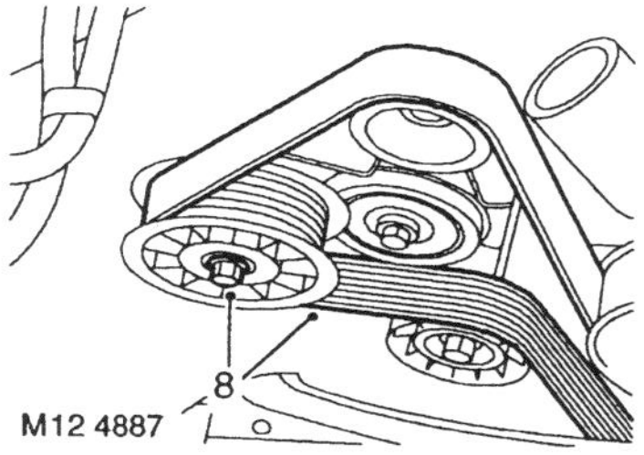

8
M12 4887

8. Using a 15 mm spanner, release auxiliary drive belt tension and remove drive belt.

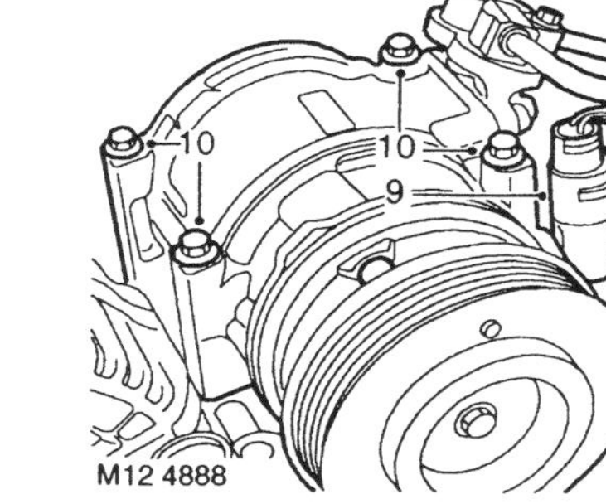

9. Disconnect A/C compressor multiplug.
10. Remove 4 bolts securing A/C compressor, release compressor and tie aside.

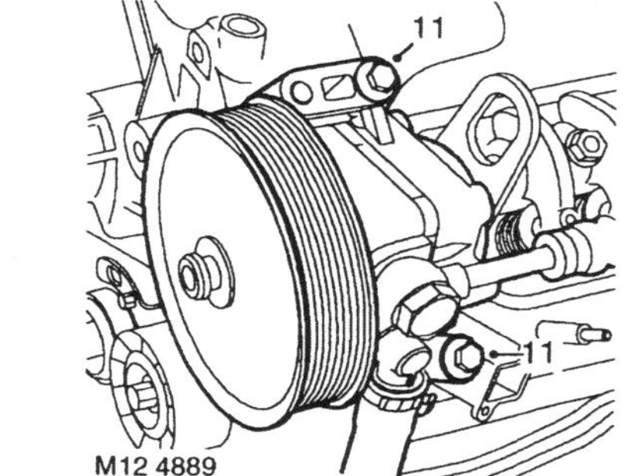

11. Remove 2 bolts securing PAS pump to mounting bracket, release pump and tie pump aside.

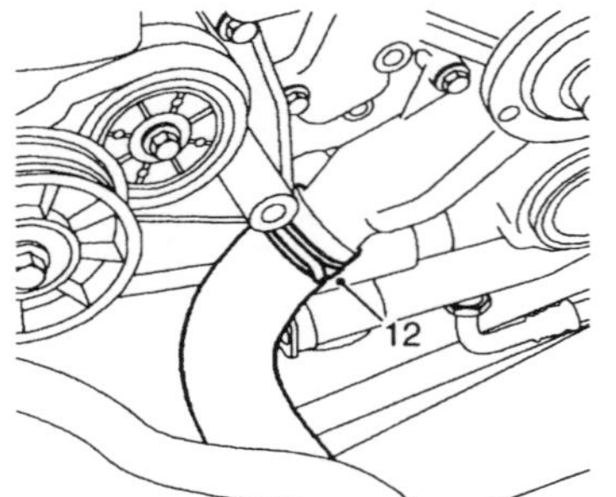

M12 4890

12. Release clip and disconnect coolant hose from water pump.

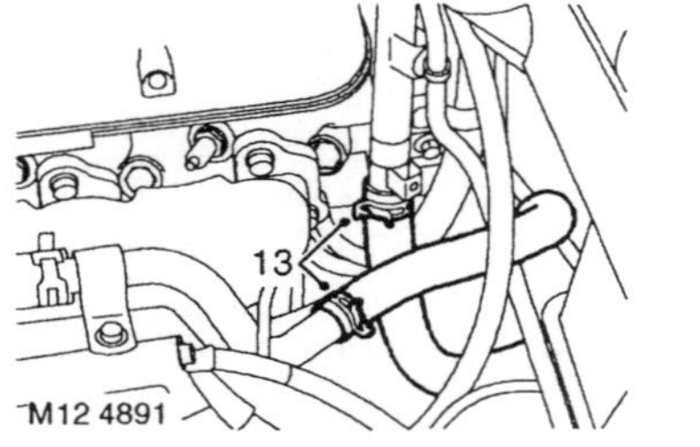

M12 4891

13. Release 2 clips securing coolant hoses to coolant rails, release hoses and remove hoses and thermostat housing.

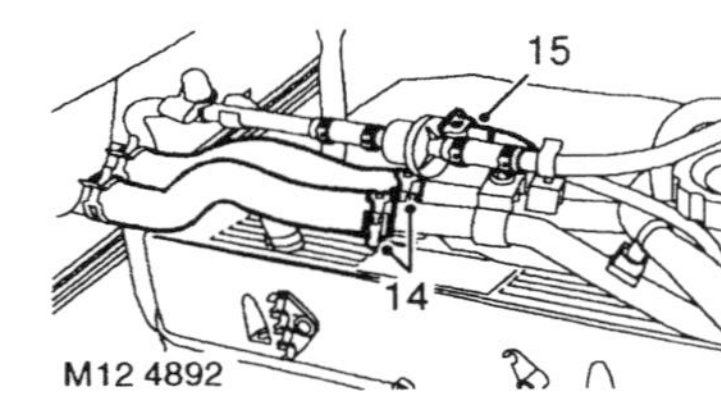

M12 4892

14. Release 2 clips securing heater hoses to coolant rails and disconnect hoses from rails.
15. Disconnect multiplug from purge valve and position EVAP pipe aside.

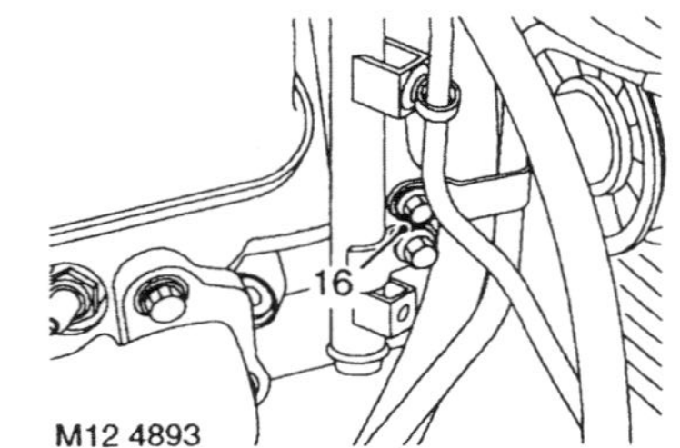

M12 4893

16. Remove bolt securing engine oil cooler return pipe to alternator mounting bracket.

M12 4894

17. Loosen engine oil cooler feed and return pipe unions from oil pump.
18. Release feed and return pipes, remove and discard 'O' rings.

CAUTION: Plug the connections.

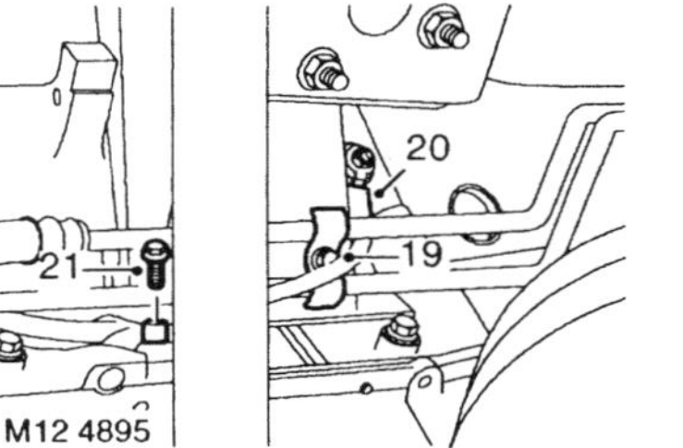

M12 4895

19. Remove bolt securing gearbox fluid cooler pipes clamp to engine LH mounting bracket and remove clamp and spacer.
20. Disconnect multiplug from LH KS.
21. Remove bolt securing harness 'P' clip to cylinder block.

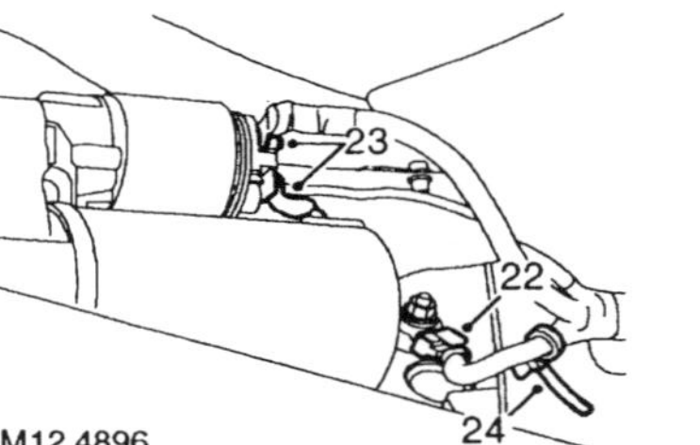

M12 4896

22. Disconnect multiplug from RH KS.
23. Remove nut securing battery lead to starter solenoid, release lead and disconnect lucar from solenoid.
24. Release clip securing harness to engine RH mounting bracket.

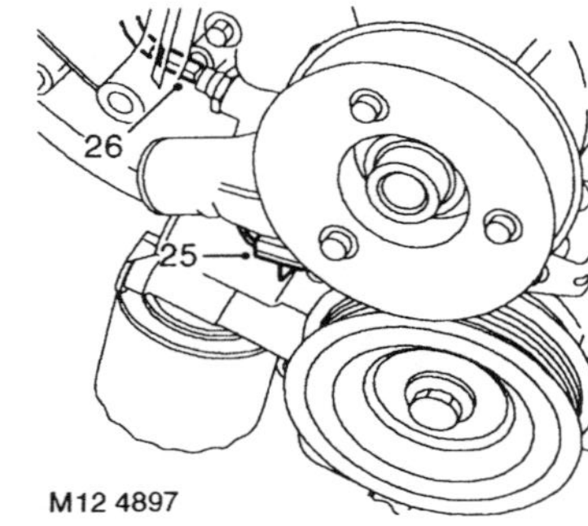

M12 4897

25. Disconnect multiplug from CMP sensor.
26. Disconnect Lucar from oil pressure switch.

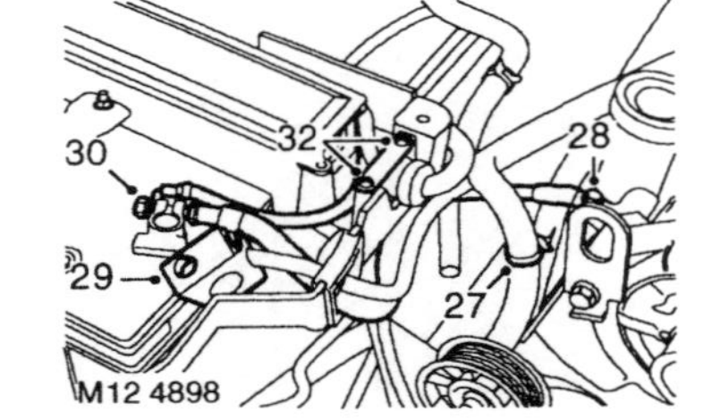

M12 4898

27. Release clip securing harness to coolant rail.
28. Remove bolt securing engine earth lead and position lead aside.
29. Release cover from battery positive terminal.
30. Remove nut securing positive lead to battery terminal, release fuse box feed lead, and disconnect positive lead from battery terminal.
31. Release positive lead from battery carrier.
32. Remove 2 screws and remove harness clamp from battery carrier.

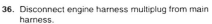

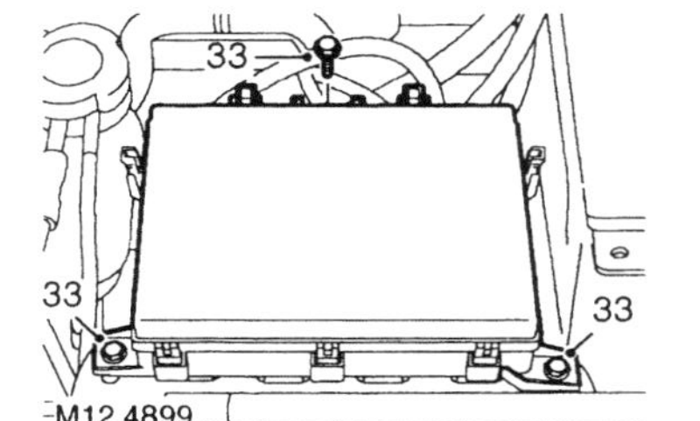

33. Remove 3 bolts securing under bonnet fuse box.

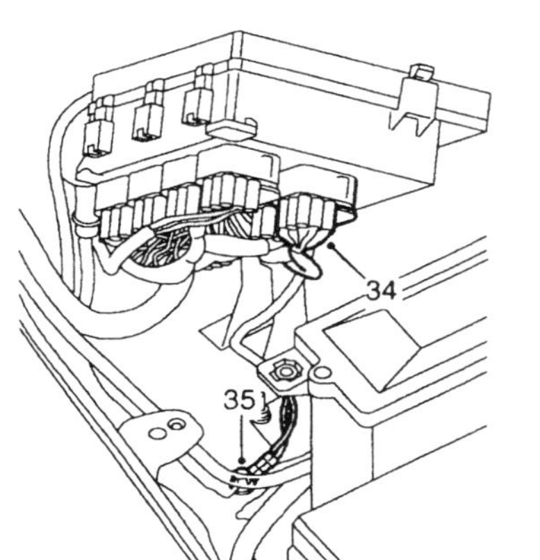

34. Disconnect engine harness multiplug from fuse box.
35. Remove nut and disconnect 2 earth leads from RH wing valance.

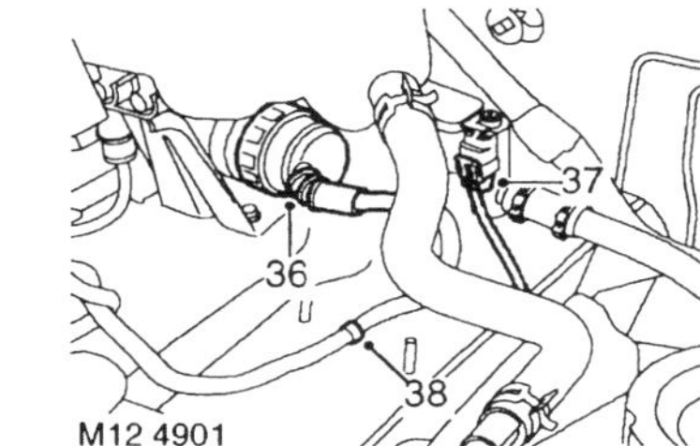

36. Disconnect engine harness multiplug from main harness.
37. Disconnect multiplug from Canister Vent Solenoid (CVS) unit.
38. Release clip securing harness to RH wing valance.

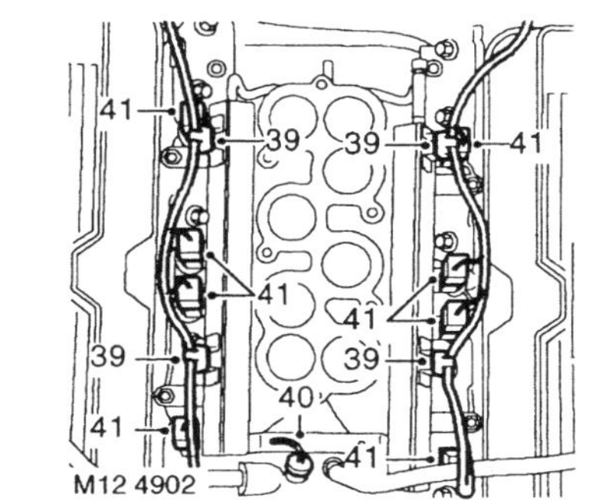

39. Release harness clips from fuel rail and heater coolant pipe.
40. Disconnect multiplug from ECT sensor.
41. Disconnect multiplugs from fuel injectors.

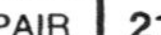

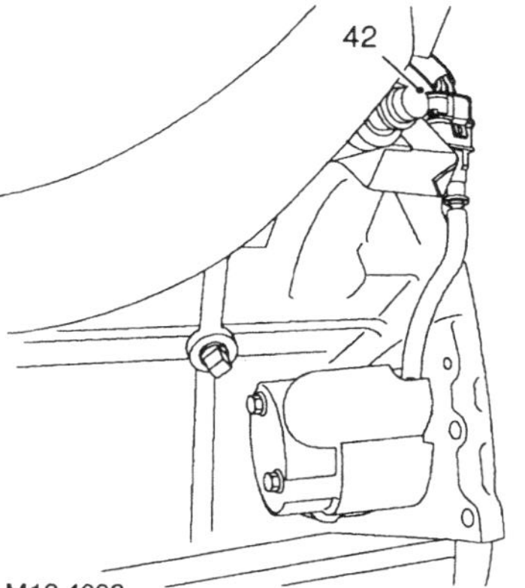

42. Disconnect multiplug from CKP sensor.

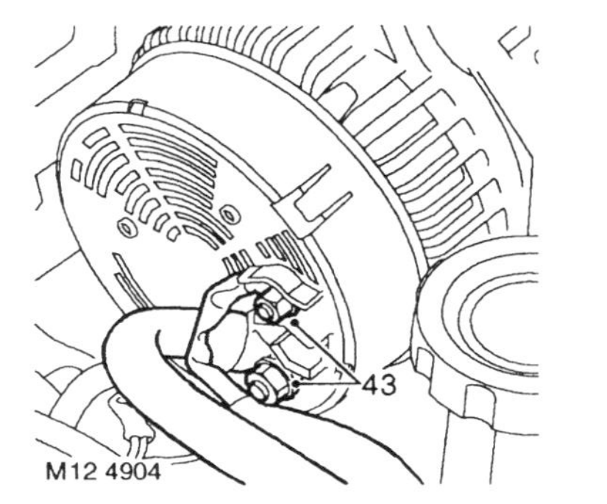

43. Remove 2 nuts securing engine harness to alternator.

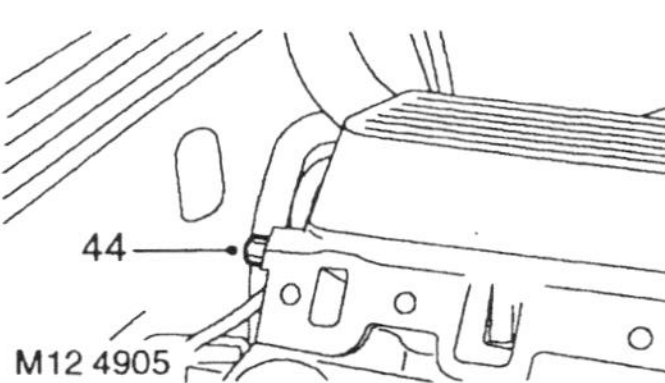

44. Remove bolt securing engine harness 'P' clip to rear of LH cylinder head.

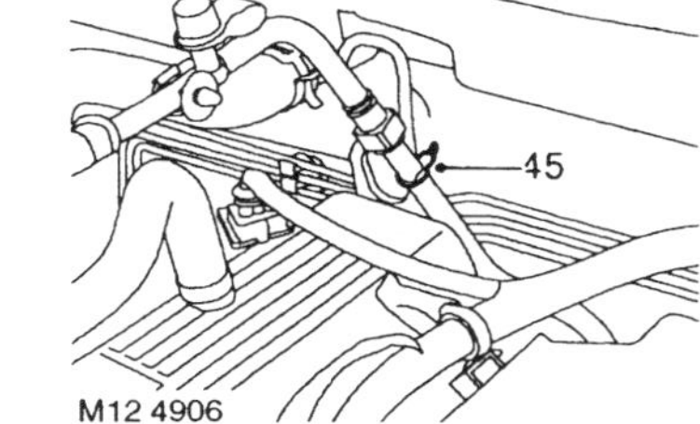

45. Remove cable tie securing purge pipe to engine rear lifting eye.
46. Move harness clear of engine.
47. Raise vehicle on ramp.

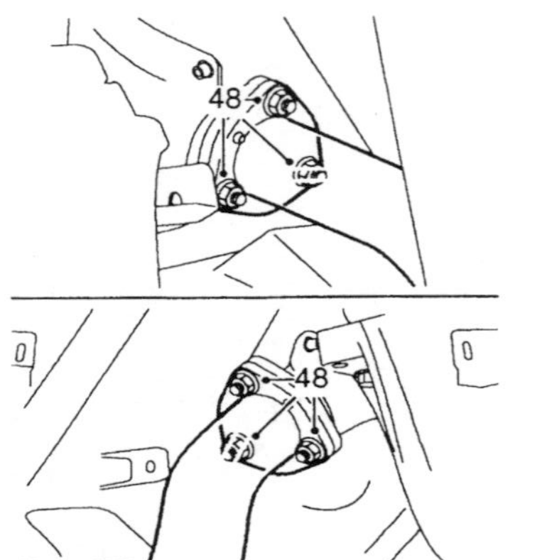

M12 4907

48. Remove 6 nuts securing exhaust front pipes to exhaust manifolds and collect gaskets.

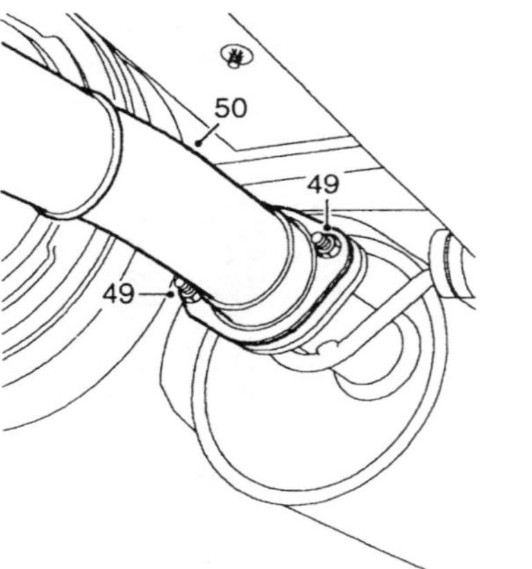

49. Remove 2 nuts securing exhaust front pipe to intermediate pipe.
50. Release exhaust front pipe from intermediate pipe.

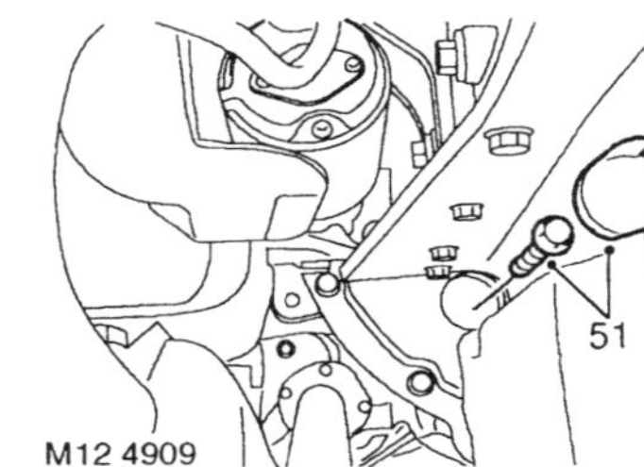

M12 4909

51. Remove access plug and remove 4 bolts securing torque converter to drive plate.

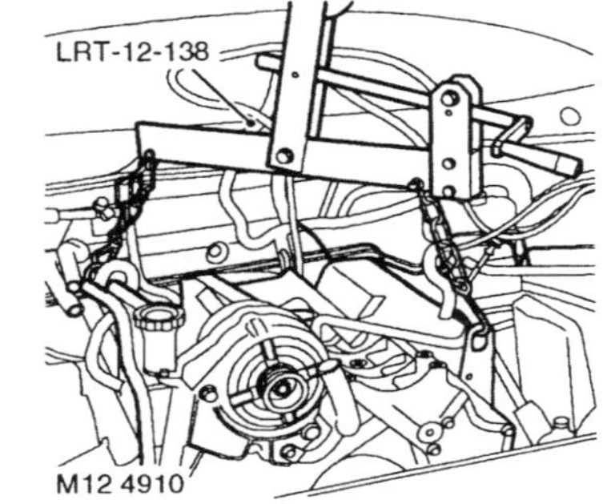

M12 4910

52. Using hoist and LRT-12-138 connected to engine lifting eyes provided, support engine weight.

M12 4911

53. Remove 8 nuts securing engine mountings, raise engine and remove engine mountings.

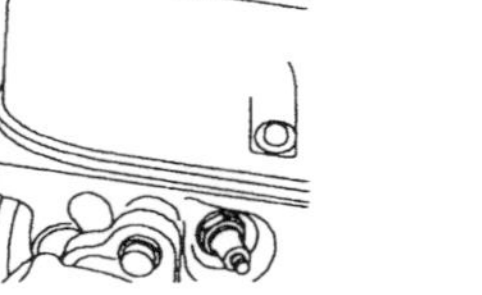

M12 4912

54. Remove bolt securing earth strap to RH cylinder head.
55. Release 3 breather hoses from RH lifting eye.

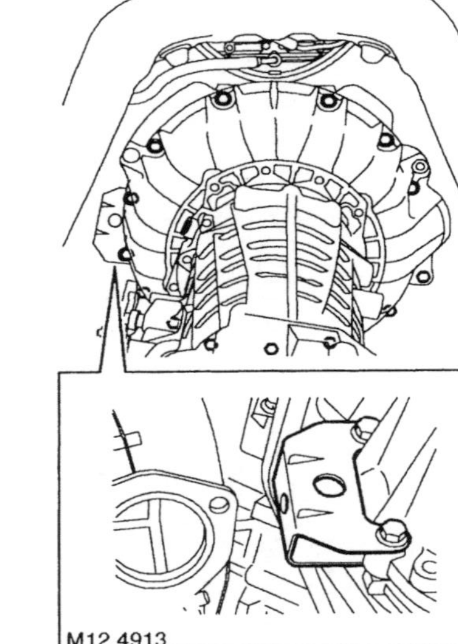
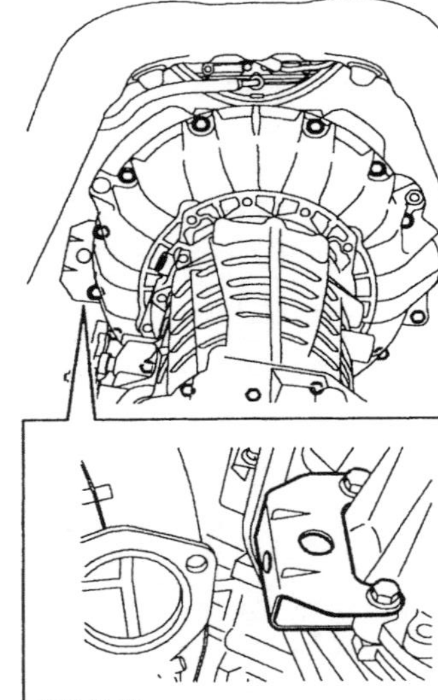
M12 4913

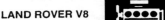

56. Remove 12 bolts securing engine to gearbox and remove crash bracket.
57. Support gearbox on a jack.
58. Remove 2 remaining bolts securing engine to gearbox and with assistance, remove engine from gearbox dowels and remove engine from engine bay.
59. Care must be taken when releasing engine from dowels to ensure torque convertor remains fully engaged with gearbox.

Refit

60. Clean mating faces of engine and gearbox, dowel and dowel holes.
61. Ensure drive plate and convertor mating faces are clean.

62. With assistance position engine in engine bay, align to gearbox and locate on dowels.
63. Fit crash bracket to gearbox flange and fit and tighten engine to gearbox bolts to ***45 Nm (33 lbf.ft).***
64. Lower and remove support from gearbox.
65. Fit breather hoses to clip on engine RH lifting eye.
66. Position earth strap to RH cylinder head and secure with bolt.
67. Fit engine mountings, lower engine onto mountings and tighten nuts to ***45 Nm (33 lbf.ft).***
68. Lower lifting equipment and remove from engine.
69. Align torque converter and drive plate. Fit bolts and tighten to ***50 Nm (37 lbf.ft).***
70. Fit access plug.
71. Ensure mating face of exhaust front pipe , intermediate pipe and exhaust manifolds are clean.
72. Use new gaskets, fit front pipe to exhaust manifolds and tighten nuts to ***30 Nm (22 lbf.ft).***
73. Fit intermediate pipe to front pipe, align clamp and tighten nuts to ***25 Nm (18 lbf.ft).***
74. Secure purge pipe to rear engine lift eye with cable tie.
75. Fit bolt to secure harness 'P' clip to LH cylinder head.
76. Connect harness to alternator and tighten B + terminal nut to ***18 Nm (13 lbf.ft)*** *and D + terminal nut to* ***5 Nm (3.5 lbf.ft).***
77. Connect multiplug to CKP sensor.
78. Connect multiplugs to fuel injectors and ECT sensor.
79. Fit harness clips to fuel rail and heater coolant pipe.
80. Connect multiplug to Canister Vent Solenoid (CVS) unit.
81. Connect engine harness multiplug to main harness.
82. Connect earth leads to stud on RH wing valance and tighten nut to ***10 Nm (7 lbf.ft).***
83. Connect engine harness multiplug to fuse box.
84. Secure harness clip to RH wing valance.
85. Fit bolts to secure fuse box.
86. Fit harness clamp to battery carrier and secure with screws.
87. Fit battery positive lead to battery carrier and connect cable to battery terminal. Connect fuse box positive feed to terminal clamp bolt and secure with nut. Fit terminal cover.
88. Fit engine earth lead to alternator bracket and tighten bolt to ***20 Nm (15 lbf.ft).***
89. Secure harness to coolant rail.
90. Connect Lucar to oil pressure switch.
91. Connect multiplug to CMP sensor.
92. Connect battery lead to starter solenoid and tighten nut to ***18 Nm (13 lbf.ft).***
93. Connect Lucar to starter solenoid.
94. Connect multiplug to RH KS and secure harness clip to engine RH mounting bracket.
95. Connect multiplug to LH KS, align harness 'P' clip to cylinder block and tighten bolt to ***20 Nm (15 lbf.ft).***
96. Align gearbox oil cooler pipes, fit spacer and clamp and tighten bolt to ***18 Nm (13 lbf.ft).***
97. Ensure engine oil cooler pipe unions are clean. Fit new 'O' rings, connect pipes to oil pump and tighten unions to ***15 Nm (11 lbf.ft).***
98. Align engine oil cooler return pipe to alternator mounting bracket and secure with bolt.
99. Align EVAP pipe and connect multiplug to purge valve.
100. Connect and secure heater hoses to coolant rails.
101. Fit thermostat housing and hose assembly. Connect and secure hoses to coolant rails.
102. Connect and secure coolant hose to water pump.
103. Ensure PAS pump and mating face is clean . Fit PAS pump to mounting bracket and tighten bolts to ***22 Nm (16 lbf.ft).***
104. Ensure compressor and mating face is clean. Fit compressor to mounting bracket and tighten bolts to ***22 Nm (16 lbf.ft).***
105. Connect multiplug to compressor.
106. Ensure auxiliary drive belt pulley grooves are clean and free from damage.
107. Fit new drive belt to pulleys, and ensure belt is correctly aligned in pulley grooves.
108. With assistance, hold tensioner fully clockwise and fit drive belt to remaining pulley.
109. Fit auxiliary drive belt cover and spacers and tighten bolts to ***18 Nm (13 lbf.ft).***
110. Connect and secure coolant top hose to adaptor on inlet manifold.
111. Connect multiplug to MAF sensor.
112. Ensure connection is clean and connect fuel pipe to fuel rail.
113. Fit ignition coils. ***See FUEL SYSTEM, Repair.***
114. Fit radiator. ***See COOLING SYSTEM, Repair.***
115. Fit engine oil filter and fill engine with engine oil. ***See LUBRICANTS, FLUIDS AND CAPACITIES, Information.***
116. Check and if necessary top up gearbox oil.

FLYWHEEL

Service repair no - 12.53.07

Remove

1. Remove clutch assembly. ***See CLUTCH, Repair.***
2. Rotate flywheel until location dowel is opposite starter motor.
3. Remove 6 flywheel securing bolts. Remove flywheel.

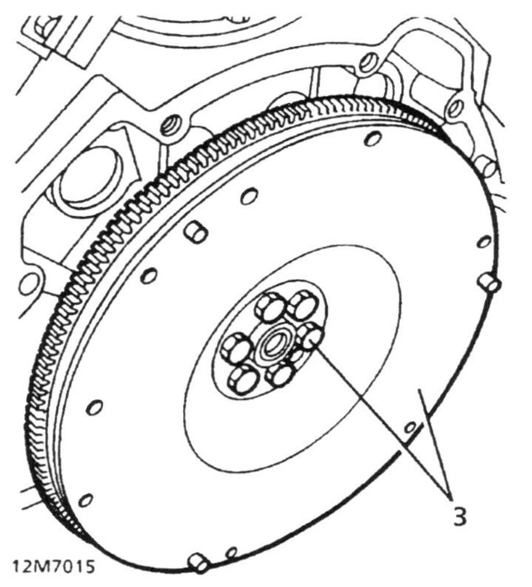

4. Inspect flywheel clutch face for cracks, scores or overheating.
5. Inspect ring gear for worn, chipped or broken teeth.

Refit

6. Ensure mating surfaces, dowel and dowel locations in both flywheel and crankshaft are clean.
7. Offer flywheel up to crankshaft. Locate on dowel.
8. Refit flywheel bolts. Tighten to ***80 Nm. (59 lbf.ft)***
9. Refit clutch assembly. ***See CLUTCH, Repair.***

FRONT COVER GASKET AND OIL PUMP - up to 99MY

Service repair no - 12.65.04 - Front Cover Gasket
Service repair no - 12.60.26 - Oil Pump

Remove

1. Raise vehicle on four post lift.
2. Disconnect battery negative lead.
3. Raise lift.
4. Drain cooling system. ***See COOLING SYSTEM, Repair.***
5. Remove oil sump. ***See this section.***
6. Remove 2 bolts and nut securing oil pick up strainer.

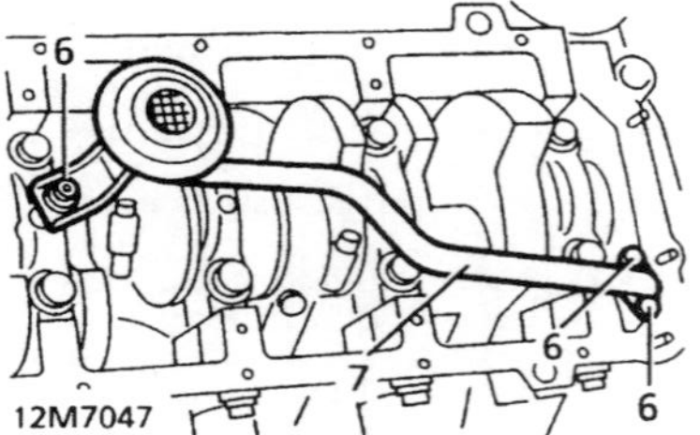

12M7047

7. Remove strainer and 'O' ring.
8. Remove oil filter. ***See SECTION 10, Maintenance.***
9. Remove stand from under front cross member. Lower vehicle.
10. Remove crankshaft pulley. ***See this section.***
11. Remove auxiliary drive belt tensioner.
12. Slacken bottom hose clip. Remove hose from water pump.

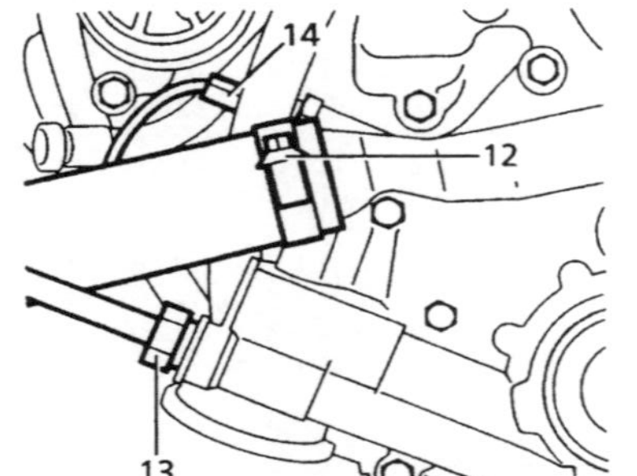

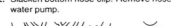

12M7048

13. Disconnect oil cooler hoses from front cover. Plug hoses and connections.
14. Disconnect Lucar from oil pressure switch.
15. Disconnect multiplug from camshaft sensor.

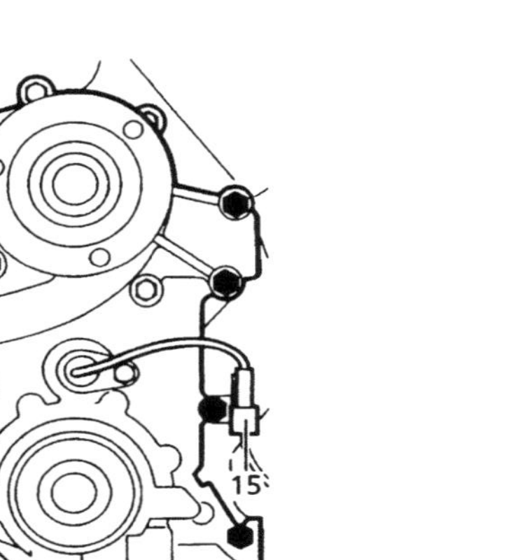

12M7049

16. Remove 9 bolts securing front cover.
17. Release cover from 2 dowels. Remove cover.
18. Remove gasket.
19. Remove seal from cover.

Do not carry out further dismantling if component is removed for access only.

20. Remove 6 remaining bolts securing water pump to cover. Remove water pump and gasket.

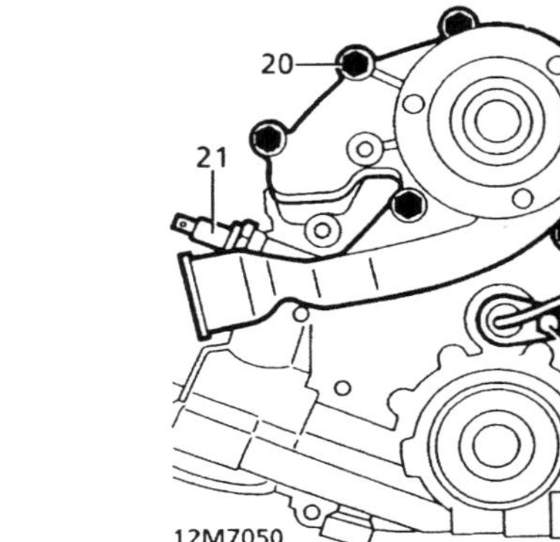

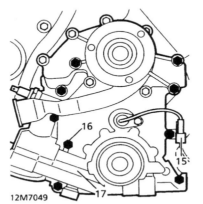

12M7050

21. Remove oil pressure switch.
22. Remove bolt securing camshaft sensor. Remove sensor from front cover.
23. Ensure mating faces of camshaft sensor and front cover are clean.
24. Refit sensor.
25. Refit sensor bolt. Tighten to ***8 Nm. (6 lbf.ft)***
26. Ensure thread of oil pressure switch is clean.
27. Refit switch to front cover. Tighten to ***15 Nm. (11 lbf.ft)***
28. Ensure water pump, its mating face, dowel and dowel hole are clean.
29. Refit water pump and new gasket.
30. Refit water pump bolts. Tighten to ***22 Nm. (16 lbf.ft)***

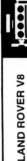

Refit

31. Ensure cover, its mating face, dowels and dowel holes are clean.
32. Ensure crankshaft and oil pump mating faces are clean.
33. Ensure oil seal register in cover is clean.

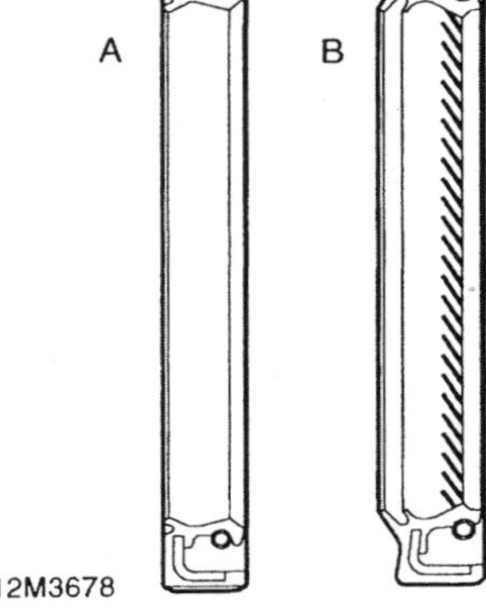

12M3678

A- Early type seal
B- Later type seal - use as replacement for all covers

34. Lubricate new front cover oil seal with Shell Retinax LX grease ensuring that space between seal lips is filled with grease.

CAUTION: Do not use any other type of grease.

35. Using LRT-12-089, fit seal to cover.

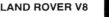

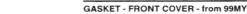

12M7085

36. Fit alignment tool LRT-12-090 to end of crankshaft.
37. Position front cover gasket on engine.
38. Position front cover on engine, align pump drive gear with key in crankshaft. Fit cover onto dowels.

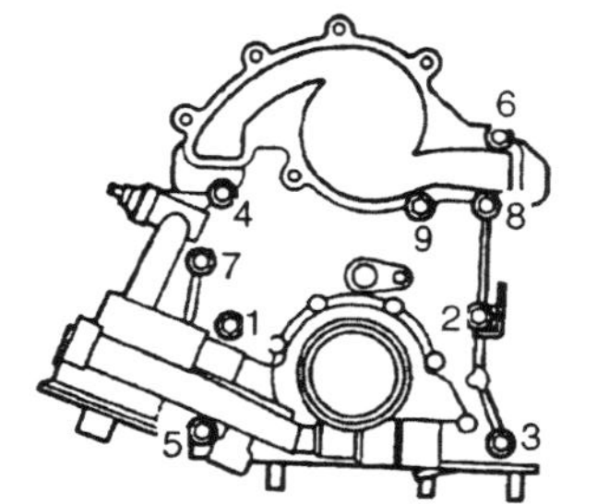

12M1398

39. Refit front cover bolts, tighten in sequence shown to ***22 Nm. (16 lbf.ft).***
40. Align camshaft sensor multiplug bracket. Refit bolts. Tighten to ***22 Nm. (16 lbf.ft)***
41. Connect camshaft sensor multiplug. Connect Lucar to oil pressure switch terminal.
42. Remove plugs from oil cooler hoses and cover.

⚠ **CAUTION: Over tightening of oil cooler hose unions can crack front cover.**

43. Fit new 'O' ring seals, reconnect hoses to cover. Tighten to ***15 Nm. (11 lbf.ft)***
44. Reposition engine harness under auxiliary drive belt tensioner.
45. Refit tensioner and bolt. Tighten to ***50 Nm. (37 lbf.ft)***
46. Refit bottom hose to water pump. Tighten clip.
47. Fit engine oil filter. ***See SECTION 10, Maintenance.***
48. Refit crankshaft pulley. ***See this section.***
49. Ensure oil pick up strainer is clean.
50. Refit strainer and new 'O' ring to engine.
51. Refit strainer bolts. Tighten to ***8 Nm. (6 lbf.ft)***
52. Refit strainer nut to main bearing cap. Tighten to ***25 Nm. (18 lbf.ft)***
53. Refit sump. ***See this section.***
54. Refill cooling system. ***See COOLING SYSTEM, Repair.***
55. Reconnect battery negative lead.

GASKET - FRONT COVER - from 99MY

Service repair no - 12.65.04

Remove

1. Remove oil pick-up strainer. ***See this section.***
2. Remove front cover oil seal. ***See this section.***
3. Drain cooling system. ***See COOLING SYSTEM, Repair.***

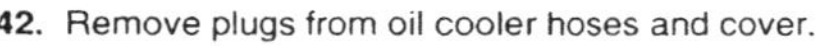
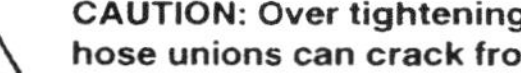
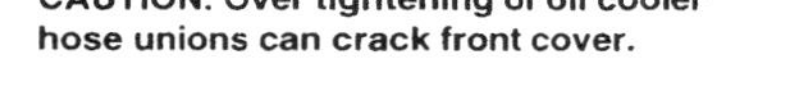

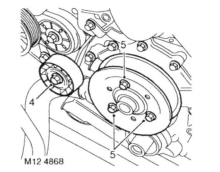

M12 4868

4. Remove bolt securing auxiliary belt jockey pulley and remove pulley.
5. Remove 3 bolts securing water pump pulley and remove pulley.

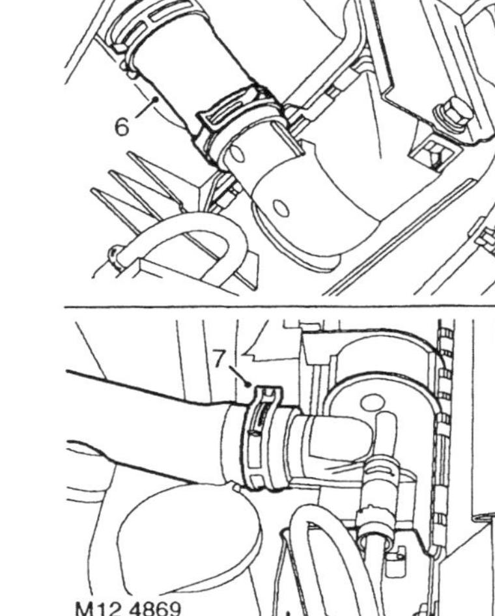

M12 4869

6. Release clip and disconnect bottom hose from radiator.
7. Release clip and disconnect top hose from radiator.

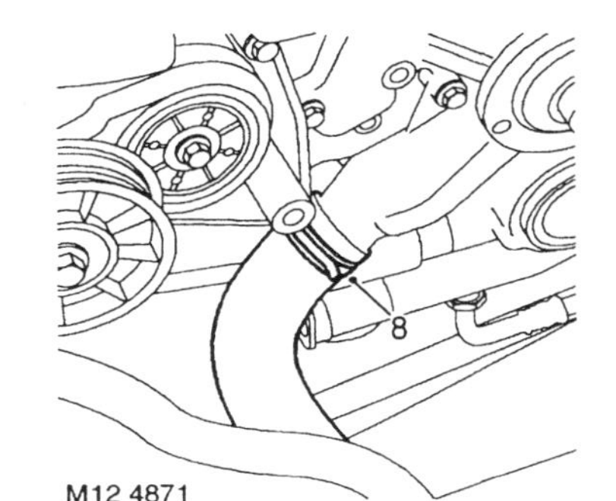

M12 4871

8. Release clip and disconnect coolant hose from water pump.
9. Release thermostat housing from radiator cowl and move hoses clear of front cover.

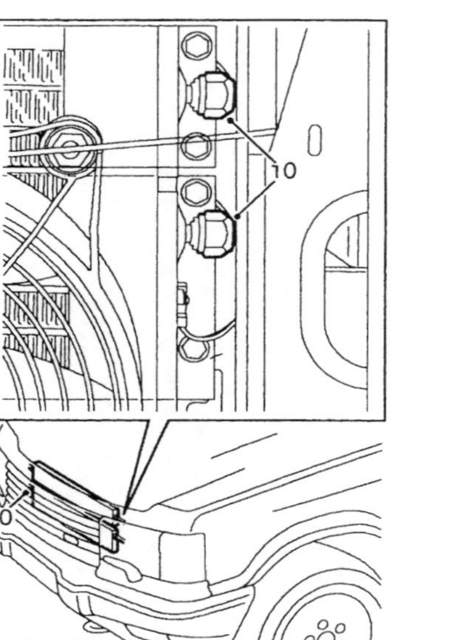

10. Position cloth to collect spillage and loosen both gearbox fluid cooler pipe unions and engine oil cooler inlet pipe union.

11. Remove 2 clips securing radiator cowl and remove cowl.

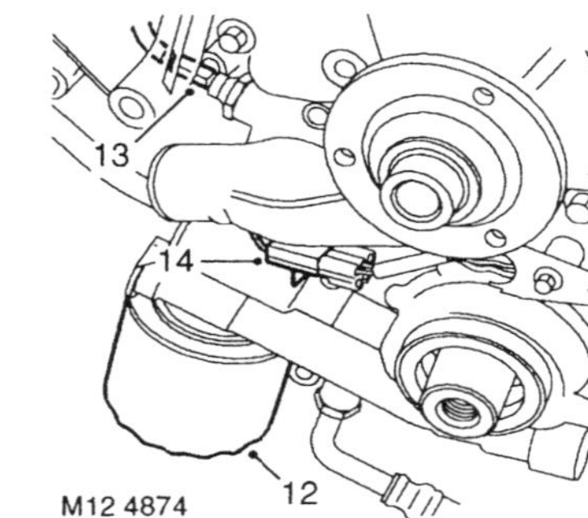

12. Remove engine oil filter.
13. Disconnect Lucar from oil pressure switch.
14. Disconnect multiplug from CMP sensor.

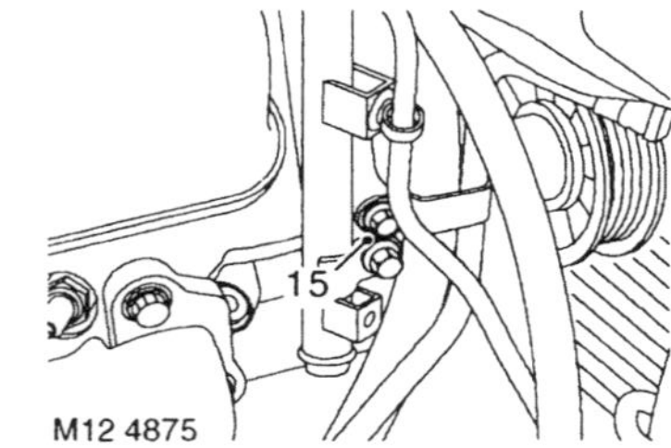

15. Remove bolt securing engine oil cooler return pipe to alternator bracket.

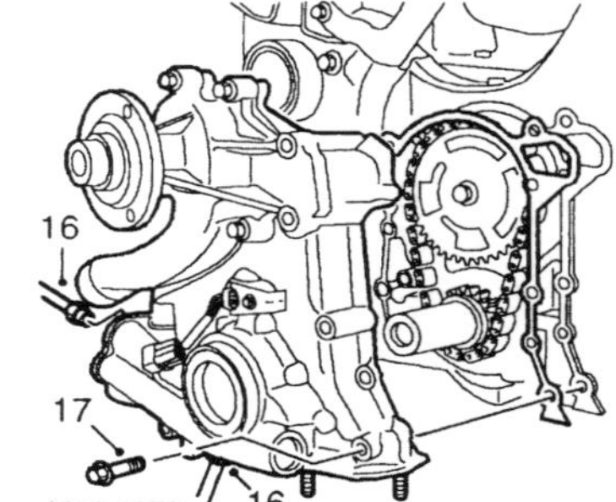

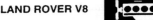

16. Loosen unions and disconnect oil cooler feed and return pipes from front cover , remove and discard 'O' rings.

CAUTION: Plug the connections.

17. Remove 9 bolts securing front gear cover and remove cover. Remove and discard gasket.

Refit

18. Clean mating faces of front cover and cylinder block. Clean dowels and dowel holes.
19. Fit new gasket onto dowels in cylinder block.

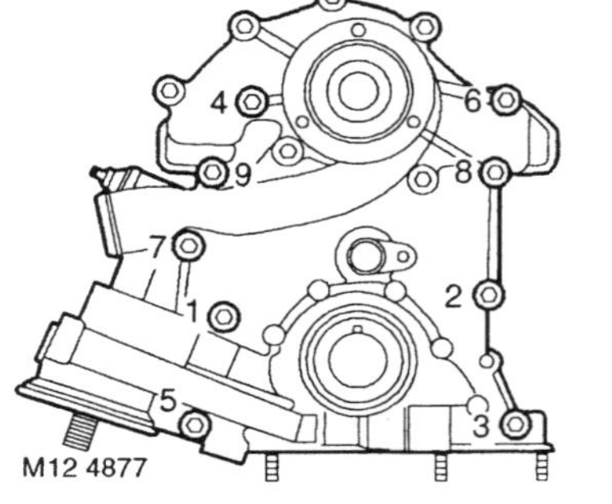
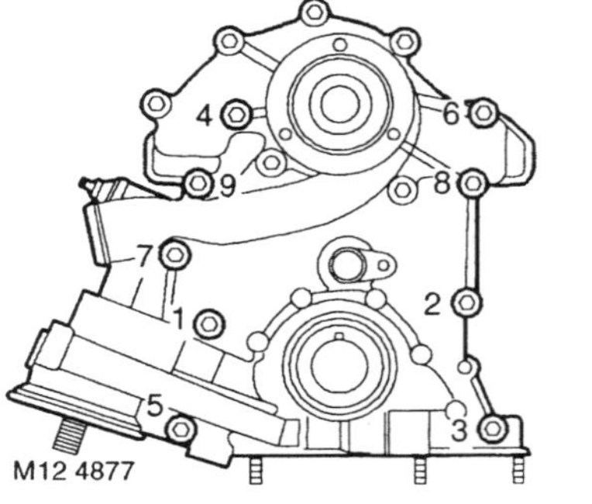

20. Fit front cover to cylinder block and tighten bolts in sequence shown to ***22 Nm (16 lbf.ft).*** *Ensure CMP sensor multiplug bracket is secured by bolt.*
21. Fit new 'O' rings to oil cooler pipes, connect pipes to front cover and tighten unions to ***15 Nm (11 lbf.ft).***
22. Fit bolt securing oil cooler return pipe to alternator mounting bracket.
23. Connect Lucar to oil pressure switch.
24. Connect multiplug to CMP sensor.
25. Ensure oil filter seal and mating face on front cover is clean.
26. Lubricate seal with clean engine oil and fit engine oil filter.
27. Fit radiator cowl and secure with clips.
28. Fit oil cooler pipes into recesses in radiator cowl and tighten pipe unions to ***30 Nm (22 lbf.ft).***
29. Fit thermostat housing to radiator cowl.
30. Connect bottom coolant hose to radiator and secure with clip.
31. Connect hose to water pump and secure with clip.
32. Connect top hose to radiator and secure with clip.
33. Ensure mating faces of water pump pulley and drive flange are clean, fit pulley and tighten bolts to ***22 Nm (16 lbf.ft).***
34. Fit auxiliary belt jockey pulley and tighten bolt to ***50 Nm (37 lbf.ft).***
35. Fit front cover oil seal. ***See this section.***
36. Fit oil pick-up strainer. ***See this section.***
37. Refill cooling system. ***See COOLING SYSTEM, Repair.***

FRONT COVER AND OIL PUMP ASSEMBLY

Service repair no - 12.60.26

Remove

1. Remove front cover gasket *See this section.*

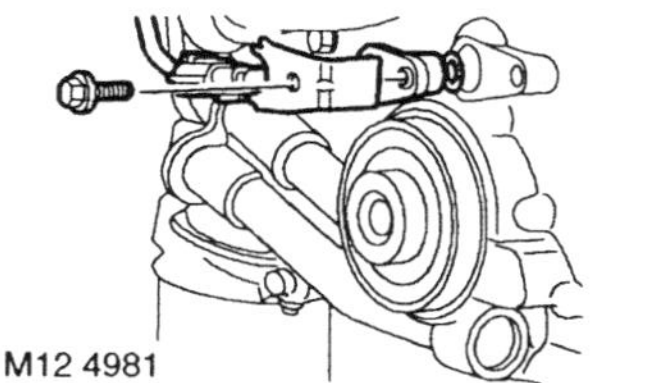

M12 4981

2. Remove bolt securing CMP sensor, remove clamp and sensor. Discard 'O' ring.

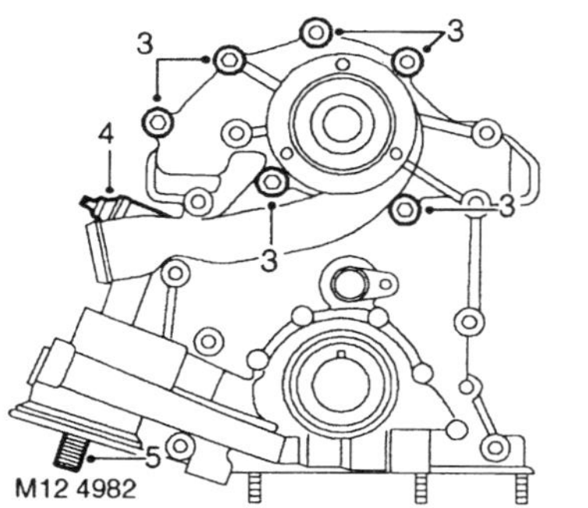

M12 4982

3. Remove 6 bolts securing water pump, remove pump and discard gasket.
4. Remove oil pressure switch and discard 'O' ring.
5. Remove oil filter cartridge. *See this section.*

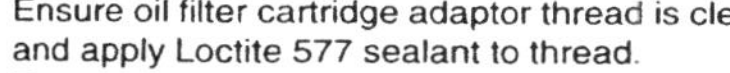

Refit

6. Ensure oil filter cartridge adaptor thread is clean and apply Loctite 577 sealant to thread.
7. Ensure oil pressure switch and mating face is clean.
8. Fit new 'O' ring and tighten switch to ***15 Nm (11 lbf.ft).***
9. Clean water pump and mating face.
10. Use a new gasket and fit water pump. Tighten bolts securing water pump to ***22 Nm (16 lbf.ft).***
11. Ensure CMP sensor is clean, fit new 'O' ring and fit sensor to cover.
12. Fit clamp to CMP sensor and tighten bolt to ***8 Nm (6 lbf.ft).***
13. Fit front cover gasket. *See this section.*

ENGINE MOUNTINGS - up to 99MY

Service repair no - 12.45.01 - LH
Service repair no - 12.45.02 - RH

Remove

1. Disconnect battery negative lead.
2. With assistance, release bonnet struts from body locations. Retain bonnet in vertical position using stay clips.

WARNING: Only open the bonnet to the vertical position with the vehicle on a horizontal surface in the workshop. This position is not intended to be used outdoors where the bonnet could be affected by winds.

3. **Right Hand Mounting Only:** Fit lifting eye to alternator bracket.
4. **RHD - Right Hand Mounting Only:** Remove steering column intermediate shaft. ***See STEERING, Repair.***
5. **Left Hand Mounting Only:** To prevent strain on cruise control cable, disconnect from abutment and actuator diaphragm.

12M7056

6. Raise vehicle on four post lift.

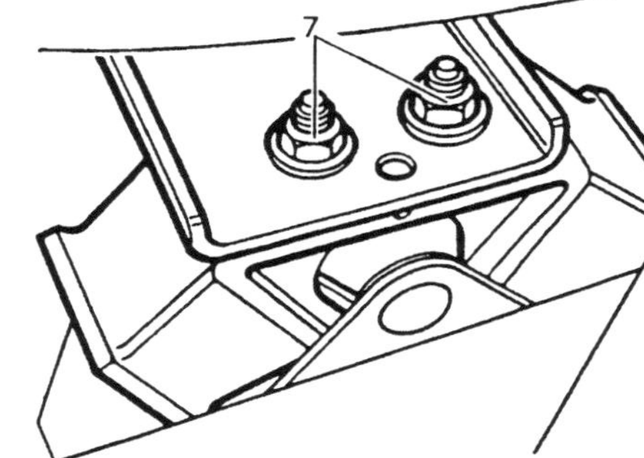

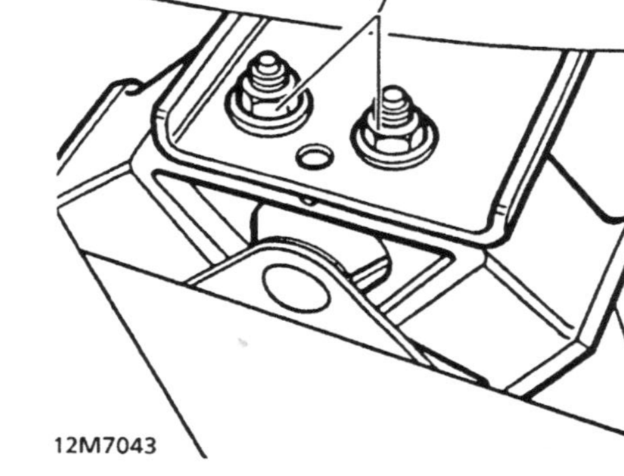

12M7043

7. Remove 4 nuts securing mounting to chassis and engine. Discard nuts.

12M7044

8. Connect hoist to lifting eye. Raise relevant side of engine.

CAUTION: Raise engine by minimum necessary to remove mounting. Ensure ignition coils do not foul bulkhead.

9. Remove engine mounting.

Refit

10. Fit engine mounting. Ensure domed head of centre bolt faces toward chassis.
11. Align mounting studs. Lower engine. Disconnect hoist.
12. Fit new engine mounting flange nuts. Tighten to ***45 Nm. (33 lbf.ft)***
13. Lower vehicle.
14. **Left Hand Mounting Only:** Connect cruise control cable to abutment bracket and actuator diaphragm.
15. Adjust cable free-play if necessary. ***See CRUISE CONTROL, Adjustment.***
16. **RHD - Right Hand Mounting Only:** Fit steering column intermediate shaft. ***See STEERING, Repair.***
17. **Right Hand Mounting Only:** Remove lifting eye from alternator bracket.
18. With assistance, release bonnet stay clips. Engage bonnet struts.

CAUTION: Ensure bonnet stay clips are returned to their original positions as shown.

19. Reconnect battery negative lead.

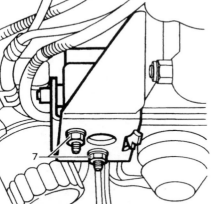

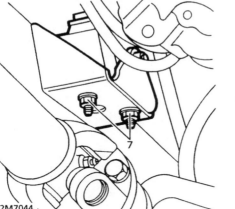

ENGINE MOUNTINGS - from 99MY

Service repair no - 12.45.11 - LH
Service repair no - 12.45.12 - RH

Remove

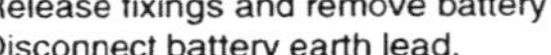

1. With assistance, release bonnet struts and retain bonnet in vertical position with stay clips.
2. Release fixings and remove battery cover.
3. Disconnect battery earth lead.

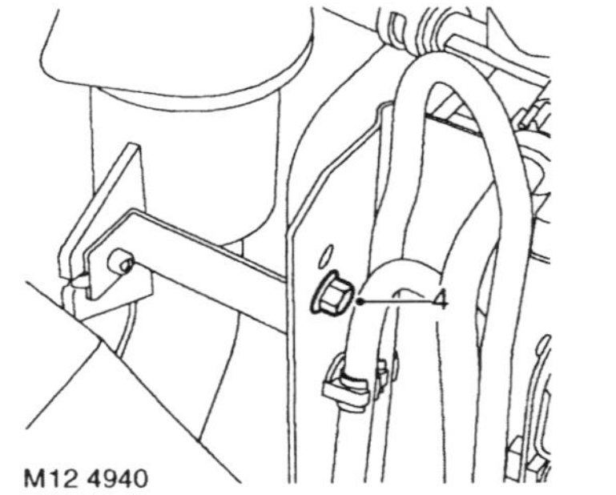

M12 4940

4. Remove bolt securing screen washer filler tube.

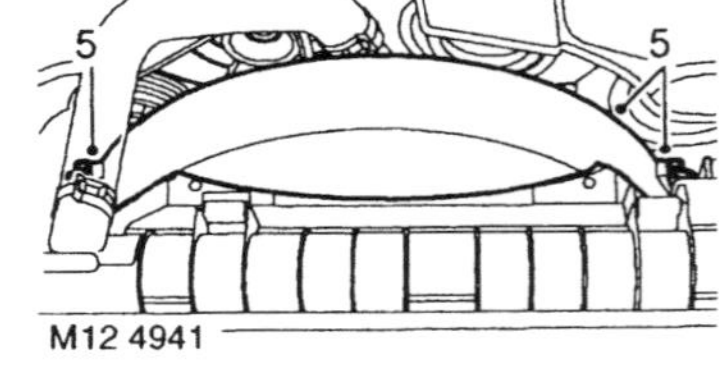

M12 4941

5. Release 2 clips and remove cooling fan cowl.

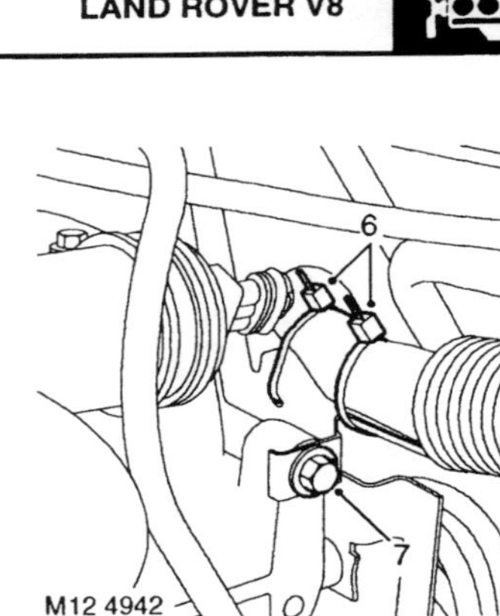

M12 4942

6. Remove ties securing harness to support bracket at rear of engine and move harness clear of bracket.
7. Remove bolt securing harness support bracket and remove bracket.
8. **Right hand engine mounting:** Fit suitable lifting eye to alternator fixing bolt.
9. **RHD - Right hand engine mounting:** Remove steering column intermediate shaft. ***See STEERING, Repair.***
10. Raise vehicle on 4 post ramp.

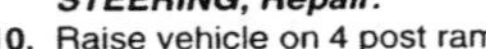

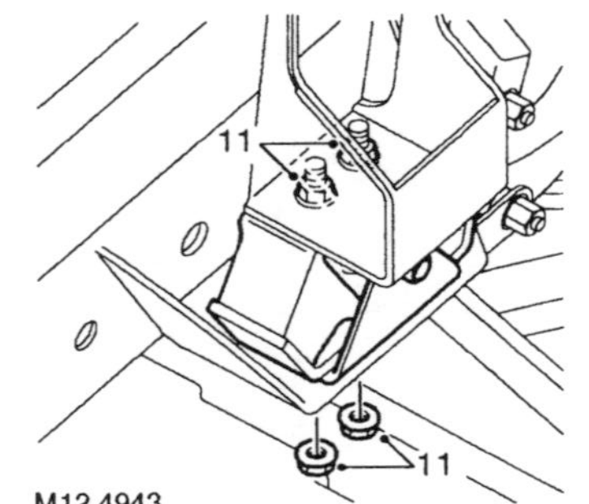

M12 4943

11. Remove and discard 4 nuts securing engine mounting.
12. Connect hoist to lifting eye and raise relevant side of engine.
13. Remove engine mounting.

Refit

14. Fit engine mounting. Ensure domed head of centre bolt faces towards chassis.
15. Carefully lower engine onto mounting and disconnect hoist.
16. Fit new engine mounting nuts and tighten to ***45 Nm (33 lbf.ft).***
17. Lower vehicle.
18. **RHD - Right hand engine mounting:** Fit steering column intermediate shaft ***See STEERING, Repair.***
19. **Right hand mounting:** Remove lifting eye from alternator fixing bolt.
20. Fit harness support bracket and secure with bolt.
21. Lay harness onto bracket and secure with cable ties.
22. Fit cooling fan cowl and secure with clips.
23. Fit bolt to secure screen washer reservoir filler tube.
24. Connect battery earth lead.
25. Fit battery cover and secure with fixings.
26. With assistance, release bonnet stay clips and engage bonnet struts.

REAR ENGINE MOUNTING

Service repair no - 12.45.08

Remove

1. Raise vehicle on 4 post ramp.
2. Support transmission using a suitable stand.

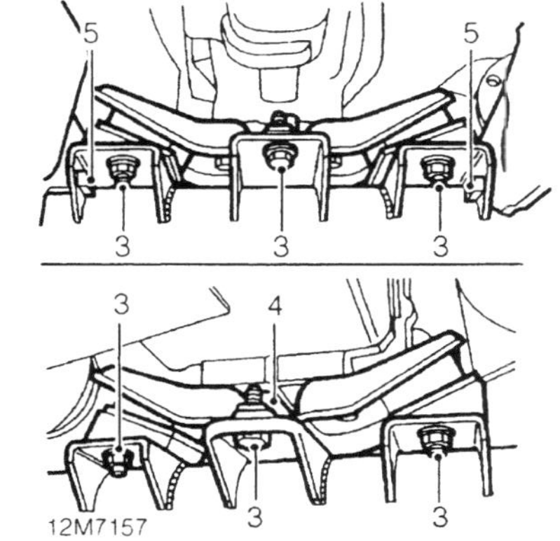

12M7157

3. Remove 4 nuts and 2 bolts securing mounting to crossmember and discard nuts.
4. Remove transmission snubber bar.
5. If applicable, remove 2 bolts securing rear of gearbox side acoustic covers to crossmember.

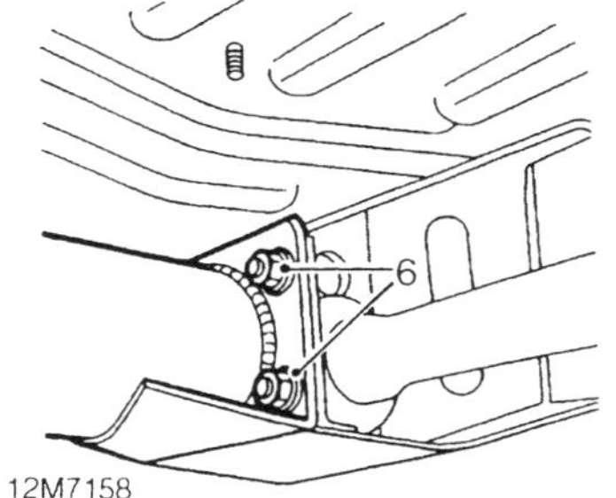

12M7158

6. Remove 3 of 4 nuts and bolts securing each side of crossmember to chassis.
7. With assistance, remove remaining bolt securing crossmember and remove crossmember.

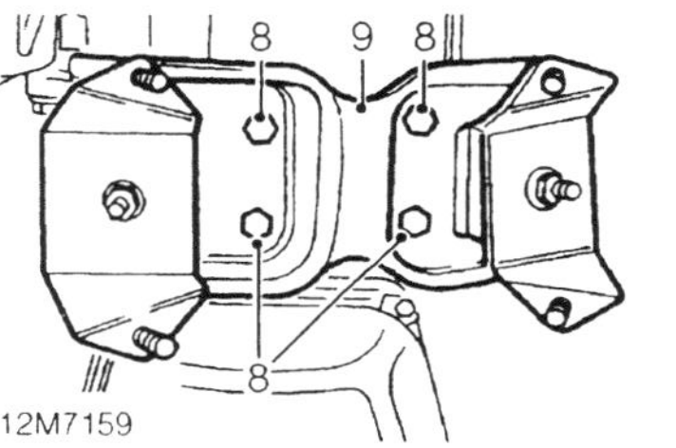

12M7159

8. Remove 4 bolts securing mounting to gearbox.
9. Remove mounting assembly.

Refit

CAUTION: Ensure all under body wax is removed from mating surfaces of fixings before fitting.

10. Fit mounting to gearbox, fit bolts and tighten to ***45 Nm. (33 lbf.ft)***
11. Using assistance, fit crossmember to chassis.
12. Fit nuts and bolts and tighten to ***45 Nm. (33 lbf.ft)***
13. Fit transmission snubber bar.
14. Fit NEW flange nuts and bolts securing transmission mount to crossmember and tighten to ***45 Nm. (33 lbf.ft)***
15. Remove transmission stand.
16. If applicable, align rear of side acoustic covers to crossmember and secure with bolts.

OIL FILTER

Service repair no - 12.60.04

Remove

1. Raise front of vehicle.

WARNING: Support on safety stands.

2. Remove engine acoustic cover (if applicable). ***See CHASSIS AND BODY, Repair.***
3. Position drain tray to catch spillage.

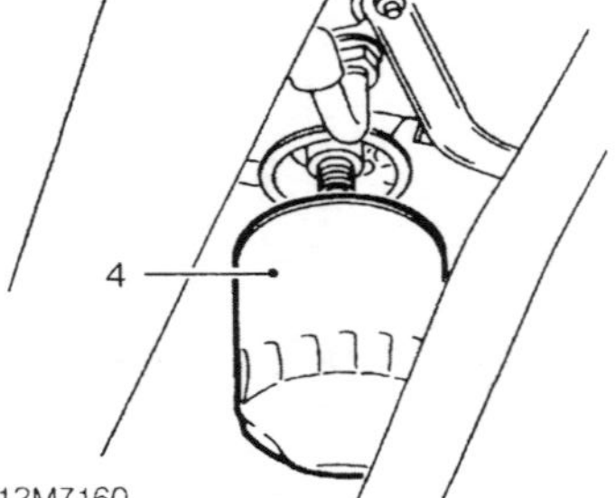

12M7160

4. Remove oil filter cartridge.

Refit

5. Clean mating face of oil pump.
6. Lubricate oil filter seal with clean engine oil.
7. Fit oil filter and tighten until rubber seal contacts machined face. Tighten a further half turn by hand.

CAUTION: DO NOT overtighten oil filter.

8. Run engine to allow oil to fill filter.
9. Stop engine, check and top up oil level. ***See LUBRICANTS, FLUIDS AND CAPACITIES, Information.***
10. Fit engine acoustic cover (if applicable). ***See CHASSIS AND BODY, Repair.***
11. Remove stand(s) and lower vehicle.

OIL COOLER

Service repair no - 12.60.68

Remove

1. Disconnect battery negative lead.
2. Raise the vehicle.

WARNING: Support on safety stands.

3. Remove front grille. ***See CHASSIS AND BODY, Repair.***
4. Release 2 clips securing bonnet release cable to bonnet platform.

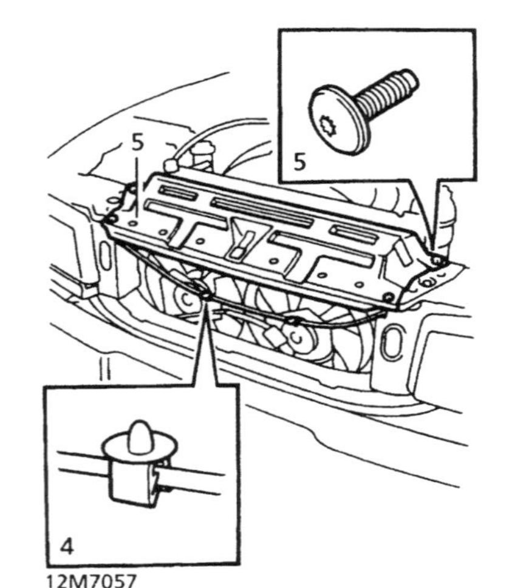

12M7057

5. Remove 4 bolts securing bonnet platform. Remove platform.
6. Remove 4 bolts from condenser mounting brackets. Collect 2 brackets.

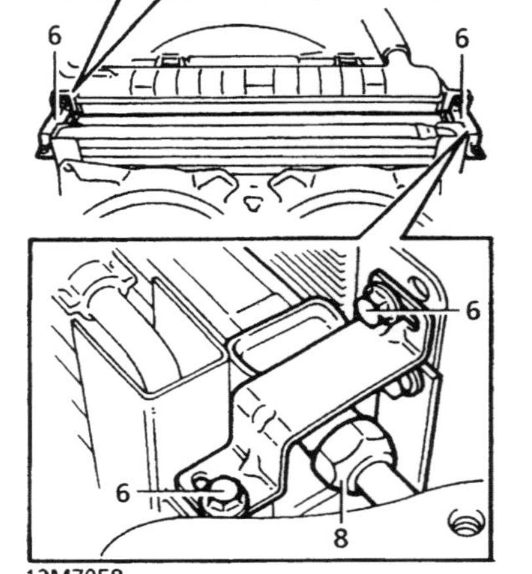

12M7058

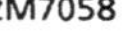

7. Position container to catch oil spillage.
8. Disconnect pipes from oil cooler. Remove 'O' rings and discard.
9. Remove 2 bolts securing oil cooler to radiator bracket.
10. Remove oil cooler.

Refit

11. Position oil cooler to radiator bracket. Secure with bolts.
12. Using new 'O' rings, connect pipes to oil cooler. Tighten unions to ***30 Nm. (22 lbf.ft)***
13. Remove container.
14. Position condenser brackets. Secure with bolts.
15. Fit bonnet platform. Secure with bolts.
16. Secure release cable to bonnet platform with clips.
17. Fit front grille. ***See CHASSIS AND BODY, Repair.***
18. Remove safety stands. Lower vehicle.
19. Reconnect battery negative lead.
20. Check engine oil level. Top-up if necessary.

OIL PRESSURE SWITCH - up to 99MY

Service repair no - 12.60.50

Remove

1. Disconnect battery negative lead.
   Remove cooling fan. ***See COOLING SYSTEM, Repair.***
2. Remove alternator drive belt tensioner. ***See ELECTRICAL, Repair.***
3. Disconnect Lucar from oil pressure switch.
4. Remove switch and discard 'O' ring.

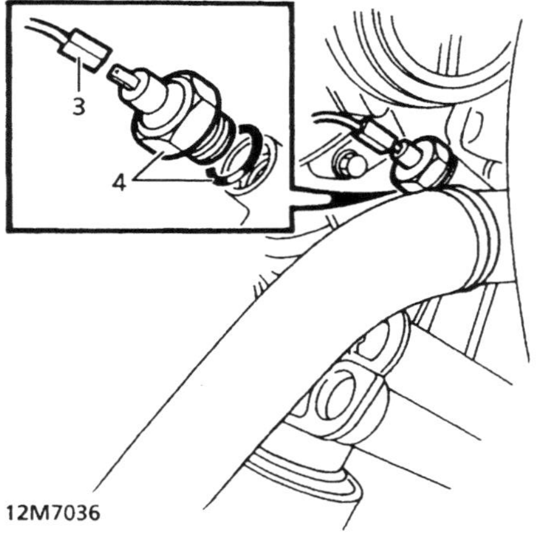

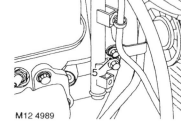

12M7036

Refit

5. Ensure switch thread and seating in front cover are clean.
6. Lubricate new 'O' ring with clean engine oil. Fit to switch.
7. Fit switch. Tighten to ***15 Nm. (11 lbf.ft)***
8. Refit alternator drive belt tensioner. ***See ELECTRICAL, Repair.***
9. Fit cooling fan. ***See COOLING SYSTEM, Repair.***
10. Reconnect battery negative lead.

OIL PRESSURE SWITCH - from 99MY

Service repair no - 12.60.50

Remove

1. Release fixings and remove battery cover.
2. Disconnect battery earth lead.
3. Raise vehicle on 4 post ramp.
4. Remove oil filter. ***See this section.***

M12 4989

5. Remove bolt securing engine oil cooler return pipe to alternator support bracket.

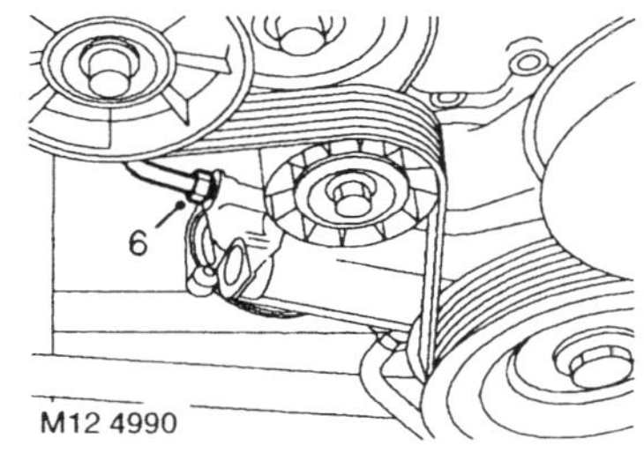

M12 4990

6. Loosen union and remove oil cooler return pipe.

M12 4984

7. Disconnect Lucar from oil pressure switch.
8. Position container below switch to catch oil spillage.
9. Remove oil pressure switch and discard 'O' ring.

Refit

10. Clean oil pressure switch threads.
11. Fit new 'O' ring to switch.
12. Fit oil pressure switch and tighten to ***15 Nm (11 lbf.ft).***
13. Connect Lucar.
14. Ensure oil cooler return pipe union is clean and fit new 'O' ring to pipe.
15. Align oil cooler return pipe to alternator support bracket and fit but do not tighten bolt at this stage.
16. Tighten oil cooler return pipe union to ***15 Nm (11 lbf.ft).***
17. Tighten bolt securing oil cooler return pipe to alternator support bracket.
18. Fit oil filter. ***See this section.***
19. Connect battery earth lead.
20. Fit battery cover and secure with fixings.
21. Top up engine oil.

STRAINER - OIL PICK-UP

Service repair no - 12.60.20

Remove

1. Remove sump gasket. ***See this section.***

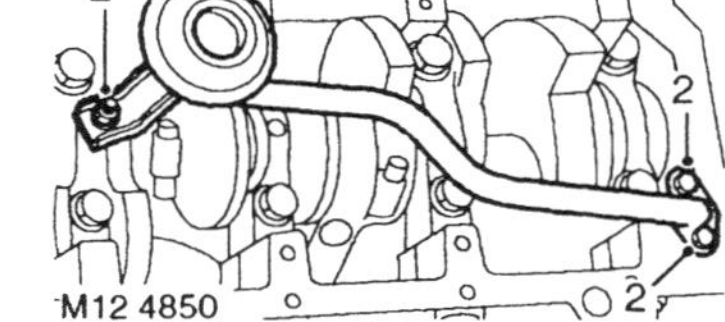

M12 4850

2. Remove 2 bolts and 1 nut securing oil pick-up strainer.
3. Remove oil pick-up strainer.
4. Collect spacer from stud.
5. Remove and discard 'O'ring.

Refit

6. Clean oil pick-up strainer and 'O' ring recess.
7. Lubricate and fit new 'O' ring.
8. Locate spacer on stud.
9. Position oil pick-up strainer, fit and tighten, bolts to ***10 Nm (7 lbf.ft)*** *and, nut to* ***22 Nm (17 lbf.ft).***
10. Fit new sump gasket. ***See this section.***

ROCKER COVER GASKET - up to 99MY

Service repair no - 12.29.39 - Gaskets - Pair
Service repair no - 12.29.40 - LH Cover Gasket
Service repair no - 12.29.41 - RH Cover Gasket

Remove

1. Disconnect battery negative lead.
2. Disconnect crankcase breather hose from cover.

NOTE: Instructions 3,4,5 & 6 apply to *RH Cover Only.*

3. Depressurise fuel system. ***See FUEL SYSTEM, Repair.***
4. Remove fuel feed pipe from fuel rail.
5. Release fuel pressure regulator return pipe from clip.
6. Release heater hose from clip on inlet manifold.

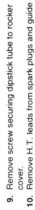

NOTE: Instructions 7,8 & 9 apply to *LH Cover Only.*

7. Release plenum chamber. Place aside for access. ***See FUEL SYSTEM, Repair.***
8. Release purge hose from ram pipe housing. Place hose aside.

12M7000

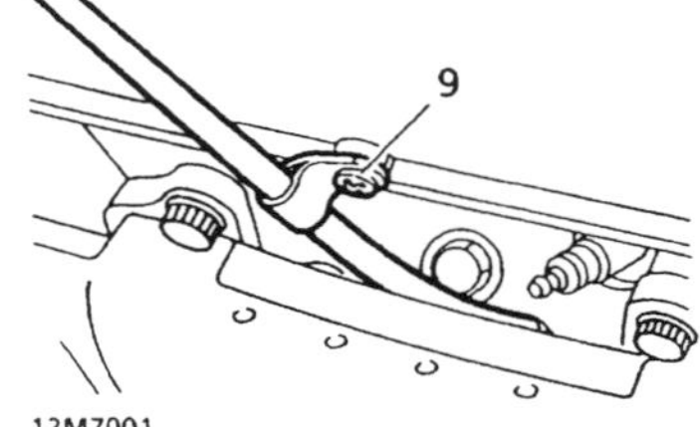

12M7001

9. Remove screw securing dipstick tube to rocker cover.
10. Remove H.T. leads from spark plugs and guide clips on rocker covers.

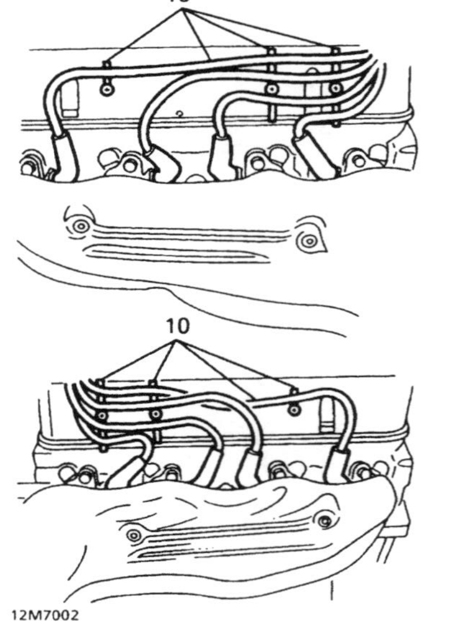

12M7002

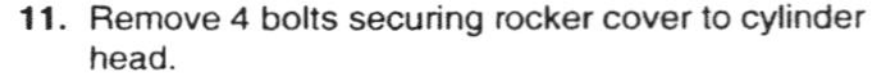

11. Remove 4 bolts securing rocker cover to cylinder head.

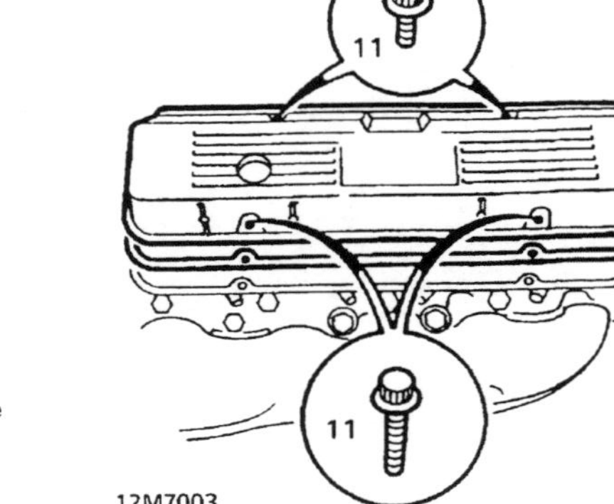

12M7003

12. Remove rocker cover.
13. Remove and discard rocker cover gasket.

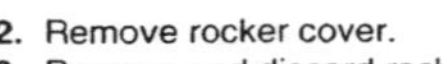

Refit

14. Clean mating faces between rocker cover and cylinder head.
15. Refit rocker cover to cylinder head using a new gasket.
16. Fit rocker cover bolts and tighten by diagonal selection to :
    Stage 1 - ***4 Nm (3 lbf.ft)***
    Stage 2 - ***8 Nm (6 lbf.ft)***
    Stage 3 - Re-torque to ***8 Nm (6 lbf.ft)***
17. Refit H.T. leads to spark plugs. Secure leads to rocker cover clips.
18. Align dipstick tube. Secure to rocker cover with screw.
19. Reconnect purge hose to ram pipe housing.
20. Refit plenum chamber. ***See FUEL SYSTEM, Repair.***
21. Secure heater hose to clip on inlet manifold.
22. Secure fuel pressure regulator return pipe in clip.
23. Reconnect fuel feed pipe to fuel rail.
24. Reconnect breather hose to rocker cover.
25. Reconnect battery negative lead.

ROCKER COVER GASKET (LH) - from 99MY

Service repair no - 12.29.40

Remove

1. Remove upper inlet manifold gasket ***See MANIFOLD AND EXHAUST SYSTEM, Repair.***

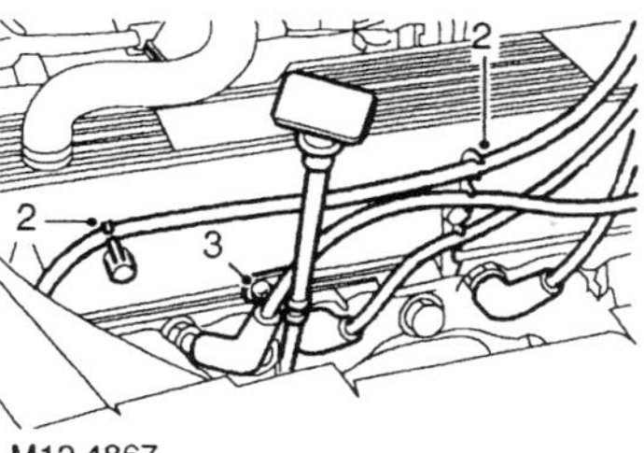

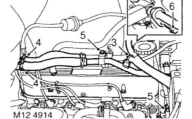

M12 4867

2. Release HT leads from clips on rocker cover.
3. Remove screw securing dip stick tube.

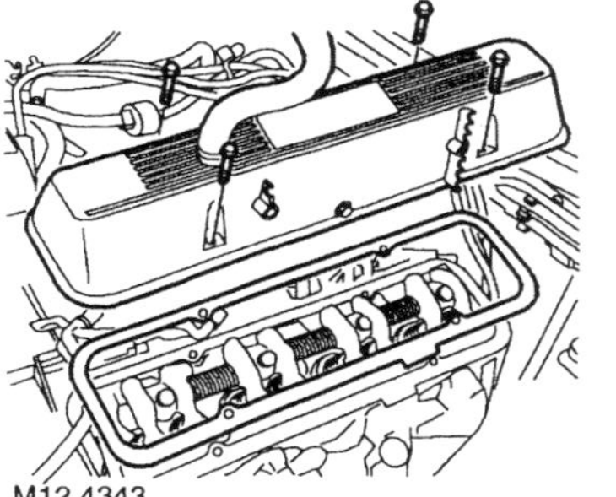
M12 4343

4. Remove and discard 4 bolts securing rocker cover.
5. Remove rocker cover and gasket.

Refit

6. Clean mating faces of rocker cover and cylinder head.
7. Position new gasket on cylinder head.
8. Locate rocker cover on gasket and install securing bolts.
9. Ensure gasket outer rim is correctly located around periphery of rocker cover, then tighten bolts in diagonally opposite sequence to:
Stage 1 - ***3 Nm (2.2 lbf.ft).***
Stage 2 - ***7 Nm (5.2 lbf.ft).***
10. Fit and tighten screw securing dip stick tube.
11. Fit plug leads to clips on rocker cover.
12. Fit upper inlet manifold gasket. ***See MANIFOLD AND EXHAUST SYSTEM, Repair.***

ROCKER COVER GASKET (RH) - from 99MY

Service repair no - 12.29.41

Remove

1. Drain cooling system. ***See COOLING SYSTEM, Repair.***
2. Remove upper inlet manifold gasket. ***See MANIFOLD AND EXHAUST SYSTEM, Repair.***

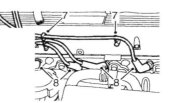

M12 4914

3. Release engine harness clip from coolant rail and move harness clear of rocker cover.
4. Release clips and disconnect coolant hoses from heater.
5. Remove 2 bolts securing coolant rails and move outer rail clear of rocker cover.
6. Remove bolt securing inner coolant rail to inlet manifold, remove rail and discard 'O' ring.
7. Release HT leads from clips on rocker cover.

8. Disconnect HT leads from spark plugs and move clear of rocker cover.

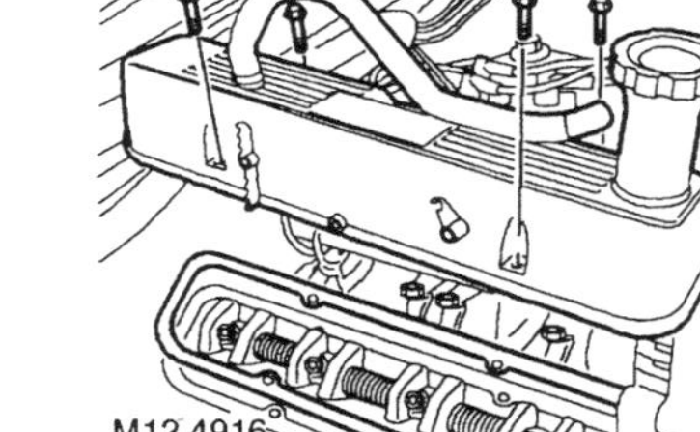
M12 4916

9. Remove and discard 4 bolts securing rocker cover.
10. Remove rocker cover and gasket.

Refit

11. Clean mating faces of rocker cover and cylinder head.
12. Position new gasket on cylinder head.
13. Locate rocker cover on gasket and install securing bolts.
14. Ensure gasket outer rim is correctly located around periphery of rocker cover, then tighten bolts in diagonally opposite sequence to:
Stage 1 - ***3 Nm (2.2 lbf.ft).***
Stage 2 - ***7 Nm (5.2 lbf.ft).***
15. Connect HT leads to spark plugs and fit leads to clips on rocker cover.
16. Clean coolant rail 'O' ring recess.
17. Lubricate and fit new 'O' ring to coolant rail, fit rail to inlet manifold and tighten bolt to ***22 Nm (16 lbf.ft).***
18. Align outer coolant rail and fit and tighten bolts.
19. Connect coolant hoses to heater and secure with clips.
20. Reposition engine harness and secure with clip to coolant rail.
21. Fit upper inlet manifold gasket. ***See MANIFOLD AND EXHAUST SYSTEM, Repair.***
22. Refill cooling system. ***See COOLING SYSTEM, Repair.***

ROCKER SHAFT - OVERHAUL

Service repair no - 12.29.49 - LH Shaft
Service repair no - 12.29.50 - RH Shaft
Service repair no - 12.29.55 - Both Shafts

Remove

1. Disconnect battery negative lead.
2. Remove relevant rocker cover. ***See this section.***

NOTE: If both shafts are to be removed, identify each assembly to ensure refitment on original cylinder bank.

3. Remove 4 bolts securing rocker shaft assembly.

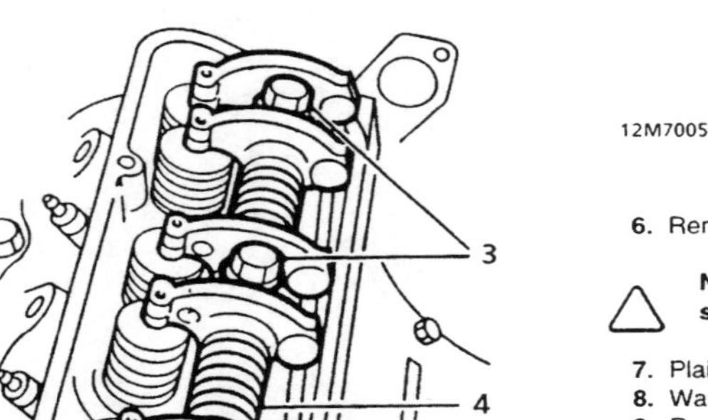

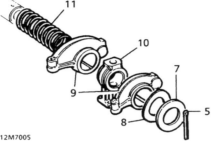

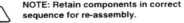

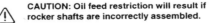

12M7004

4. Remove rocker shaft assembly. Ensure pushrods remain seated in tappets.
Do not carry out further dismantling if component is removed for access only.
5. Remove and discard split pin from one end of rocker shaft.

12M7005

6. Remove the following components:

NOTE: Retain components in correct sequence for re-assembly.

7. Plain washer.
8. Wave washer.
9. Rocker arms.
10. Rocker pillars.
11. Springs.
12. Clean all components.
13. Inspect all components for wear.
14. Inspect rocker shaft and bores in rocker arms. If excessively worn or scored, fit new components.
15. Replace all weak or broken springs.
16. Lubricate all moving parts with clean engine oil.
17. Re-assemble rocker shafts. Ensure that components are returned to their original positions, use new split pins to retain components.
18. Ensure shaft identification groove is positioned at one o'clock, with pushrod locations of rocker arms to the right.

CAUTION: Oil feed restriction will result if rocker shafts are incorrectly assembled.

Refit

19. Refit rocker shaft to original cylinder bank.
20. Engage push-rods in rocker arm locations.
21. Refit rocker shaft securing bolts. Tighten working from centre outwards to ***38 Nm (28 lbf.ft).***
22. Refit rocker cover. ***See this section.***
23. Reconnect battery negative lead.

SUMP - up to 99MY

Service repair no - 12.60.44

Remove

1. Disconnect battery earth lead.

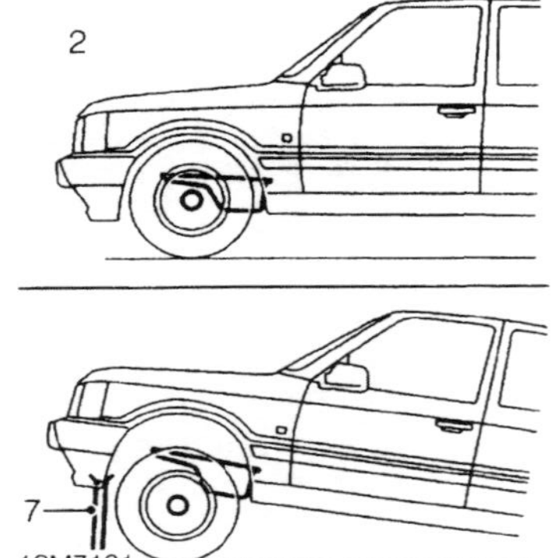

12M7161

2. Raise vehicle on 4 post ramp.
3. Remove engine acoustic cover (if applicable). ***See CHASSIS AND BODY, Repair.***
4. Remove gearbox acoustic cover (if applicable). ***See CHASSIS AND BODY, Repair.***
5. Remove engine oil dip stick.
6. Drain engine oil from sump. Refit sump plug.
7. Position support under chassis front crossmember.
8. Lower ramp to give clearance between front axle and sump.

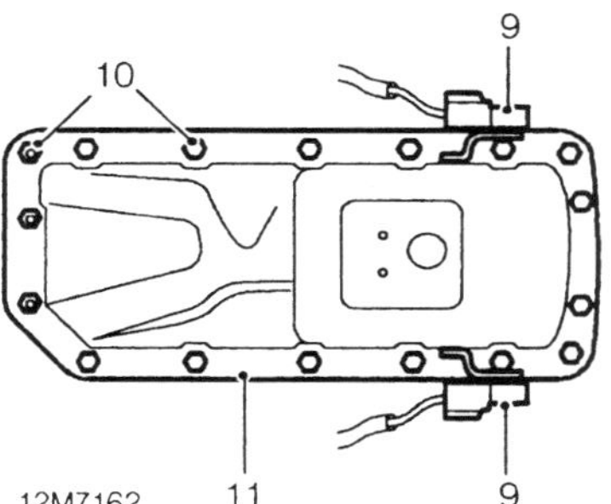

12M7162

9. Release 2 heated oxygen sensor multiplugs from sump brackets.
10. Remove 3 nuts and 14 bolts securing sump to cylinder block.
11. Remove sump.

Refit

12. Clean sealant from mating faces of sump and cylinder block.

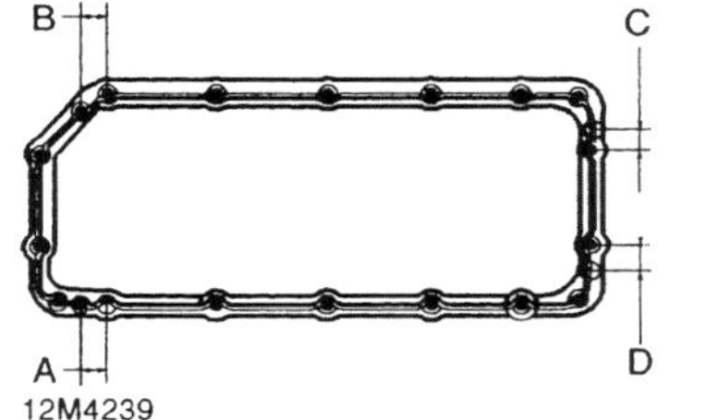

12M4239

13. Apply a bead of Hylosil type 101 or 106 sealant to joint face of sump as shown.
Bead width - areas A, B, C and D = 12 mm (0.5 in)
Bead width - remaining areas = 5 mm (0.20 in)
Bead length - areas A and B = 32 mm (1.23 in)
Bead length - remaining areas = 19 mm (0.75 in)

CAUTION: Do not spread sealant bead. Sump must be fitted immediately after applying sealant bead.

14. Position sump to cylinder block taking care not to disturb sealant bead.

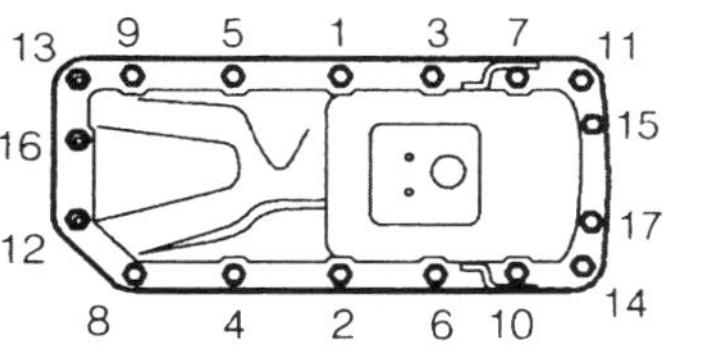

12M7163

15. Fit nuts and bolts securing sump to cylinder block and tighten in the sequence shown to ***23 Nm (17 lbf.ft)***.
16. Fit sump plug and tighten to ***45 Nm (33 lbf.ft).***
17. Engage oxygen sensor multiplugs to sump brackets.
18. Fit engine acoustic cover (if applicable). ***See CHASSIS AND BODY, Repair.***
19. Fit gearbox acoustic cover (if applicable). ***See CHASSIS AND BODY, Repair.***
20. Raise ramp and remove support.
21. Lower vehicle.
22. Fill engine oil. ***See LUBRICANTS, FLUIDS AND CAPACITIES, Information.***
23. Fit dip stick.

SUMP GASKET - from 99MY

Service repair no - 12.60.38

Remove

1. Release fixings and remove battery cover.
2. Disconnect battery earth lead.
3. Remove dipstick.
4. Raise vehicle on ramp
5. Drain engine oil. ***See LUBRICANTS, FLUIDS AND CAPACITIES, Information.***
6. Raise front of vehicle under body to increase clearance between engine and front axle.

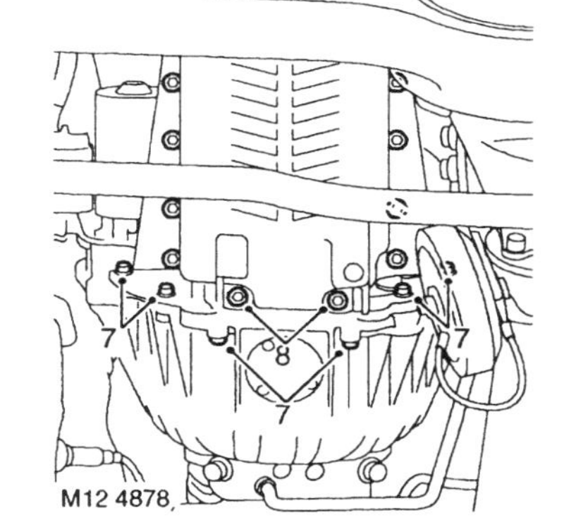

M12 4878

7. Remove 2 forward facing and 4 rearward facing bolts securing sump to bell housing.
8. Remove 2 bolts in sump recess.
9. Remove 3 nuts securing front of sump.
0. Remove 12 bolts securing sump flange to engine.
1. Manoeuvre sump over front axle and remove sump.
2. Discard sump gasket.

Refit

13. Clean all traces of RTV sealant from sump and sump mating faces using a wide, flat-bladed implement or solvent

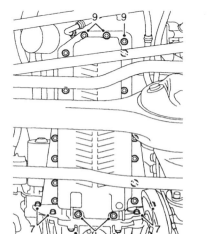

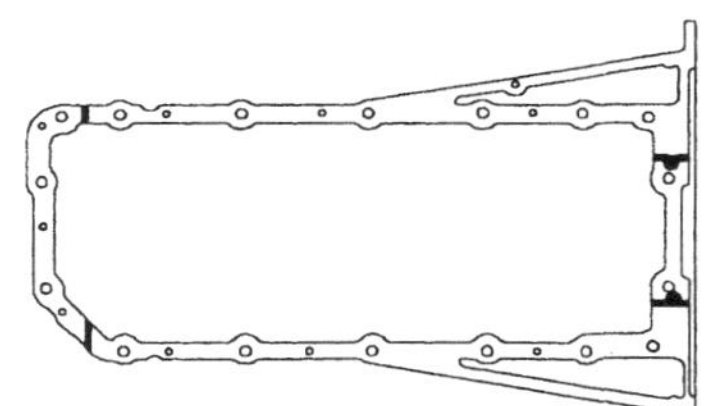
M12 4669

14. Apply a bead of RTV sealant 5mm wide across the cylinder block to front cover joint and across the cylinder block to rear main bearing joint. Apply a globule of RTV to cover end of cruciform seal, (see illustration).
15. Fit new gasket to sump, ensuring that locating tags are correctly positioned.

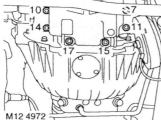

M12 4972

16. Fit sump and tighten sump bolts and nuts in sequence illustrated to ***23 Nm (17 lbf.ft).***
17. Fit and tighten bolts securing sump to bell housing to ***45 Nm (33 lbf.ft).***
18. Lower vehicle.
19. Refill engine oil and fit dip stick.
20. Connect battery earth lead.
21. Fit battery cover and secure with fixings.

TAPPETS - ENGINE SET

Service repair no - 12.29.57

Remove

1. Disconnect battery negative lead.
2. Remove inlet manifold gasket. ***See MANIFOLD AND EXHAUST SYSTEM, Repair.***
3. Remove both rocker shaft assemblies. ***See this section.***

NOTE: Identify each rocker shaft assembly to ensure refitment on original cylinder bank.

4. Remove pushrods, retain in fitted order.
5. Remove tappets.

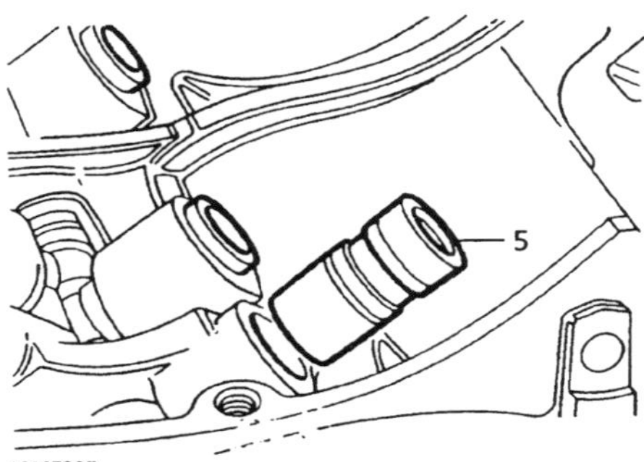

12M7007

NOTE: If tappets are to be refitted, retain with respective pushrods.

6. Clean tappets.
7. Check for even, circular wear patterns on camshaft contact area.

NOTE: If contact area is pitted, or square wear patterns have developed, renew tappets. Inspect camshaft lobes for excessive wear.

8. Inspect tappet body for excessive wear or scoring.

NOTE: If scoring or deep wear patterns extend up to oil feed area, replace tappet.

9. Inspect pushrod seats in tappets. If surface is rough or pitted, replace tappet.
10. Clean and inspect tappet bores in engine block.
11. Ensure that tappets rotate freely in their respective bores.
12. Inspect pushrods for straightness.
13. Inspect pushrod contact surfaces. If surfaces are rough or pitted, replace pushrod.
14. Inspect pushrod seats in valve rocker arms. If surfaces are rough or pitted, replace rocker arm.

Refit

15. Immerse tappets in clean engine oil.
16. Lubricate tappet bores with clean engine oil.
17. Refit tappets in removed order.
18. Refit pushrods in removed order.
19. Refit rocker shaft assemblies. ***See this section.***
20. Refit inlet manifold gasket. ***See MANIFOLD AND EXHAUST SYSTEM, Repair.***
21. Reconnect battery negative lead.

CYLINDER HEAD GASKET (LH) - from 99MY

Service repair no - 12.29.02

Remove

1. Remove inlet manifold gasket ***See MANIFOLD AND EXHAUST SYSTEM, Repair.***
2. Remove exhaust manifold gasket ***See MANIFOLD AND EXHAUST SYSTEM, Repair.***

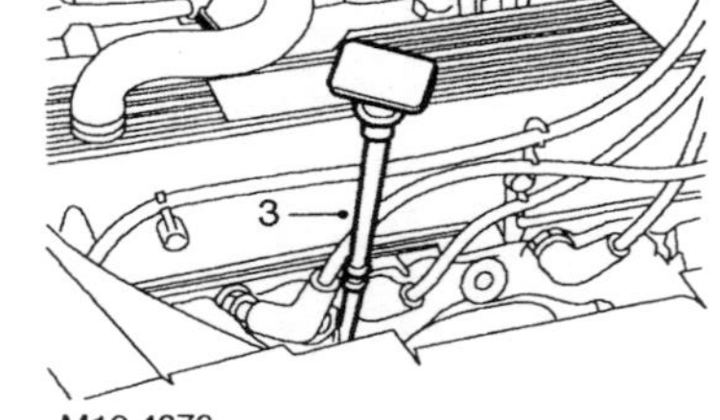

M12 4879

3. Remove dipstick and dipstick tube. Remove four screws securing rocker cover and remove rocker cover.

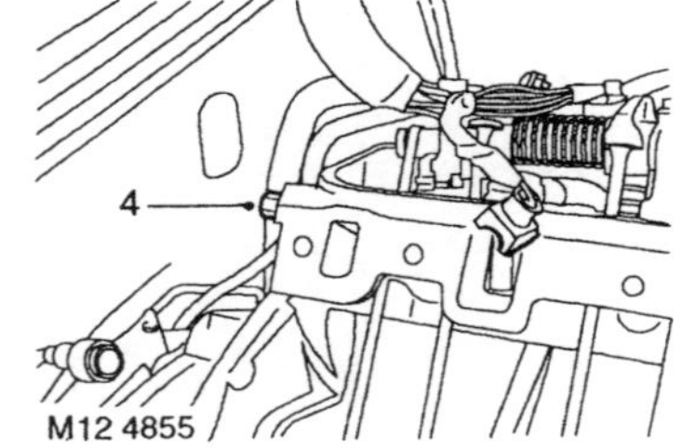

M12 4855

4. Remove bolt securing engine harness to rear of cylinder head.

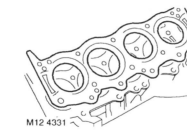

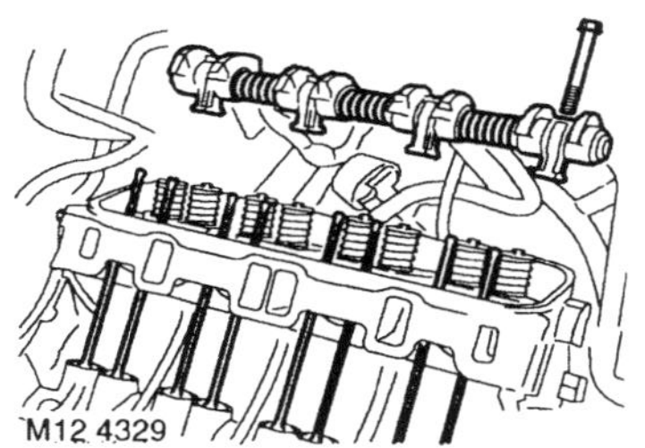
M12 4329

M12 4331

5. Progressively remove 4 bolts securing rocker shaft and remove rocker shaft.
6. Remove push rods.

NOTE: Store push rods in their fitted order.

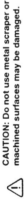

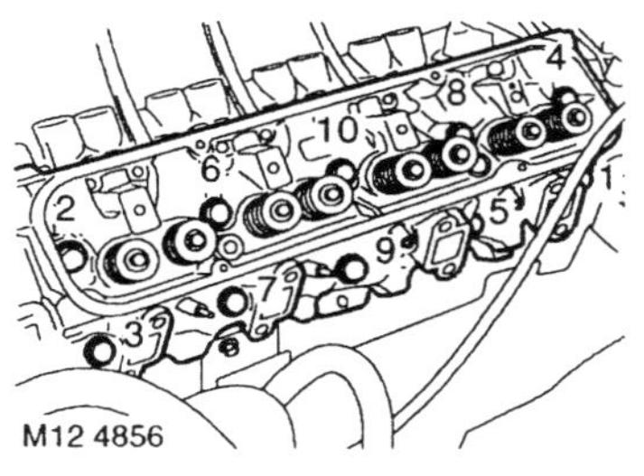

M12 4856

7. In the sequence shown remove 10 bolts securing the cylinder head to block.
8. Remove cylinder head.

9. Remove cylinder head gasket.

Refit

10. Clean mating faces of cylinder block and head using suitable gasket removal spray and a plastic scraper, ensure that bolt holes in block are clean and dry.

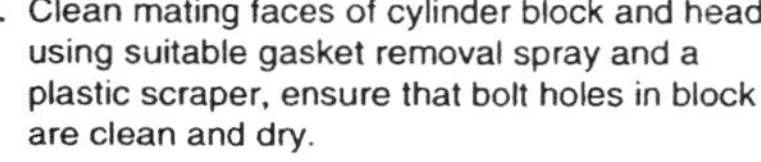

CAUTION: Do not use metal scraper or machined surfaces may be damaged.

11. Check head and block faces for warping and pitting.
12. Fit cylinder head gasket with the word TOP uppermost.

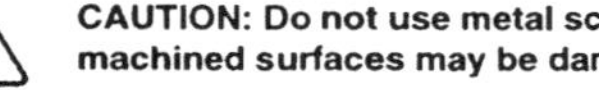

NOTE: Gasket must be fitted dry.

13. Carefully fit cylinder head and locate on dowels.
14. Lightly lubricate new cylinder head bolt threads with clean engine oil.

NOTE: Long bolts: 1, 3, 5.

M12 4857

15. Fit bolts and tighten in the sequence shown to ***20 Nm (15 lbf.ft)*** *then* ***90*** *°, then a further* ***90*** *°*
16. Clean push rods.
17. Lubricate ends of push rods with clean engine oil.
18. Fit push rods in their removed order.
19. Clean base of rocker pillars and mating faces on cylinder head.
20. Clean contact suface on rockers, valves and push rods.
21. Lubricate contact surfaces and rocker shaft with clean engine oil.
22. Fit rocker shaft assembly and engage push rods.
23. Tighten rocker shaft securing bolts progressively to ***38 Nm (28 lbf.ft).***
24. Fit and tighten engine harness bolt to ***20 Nm (15 lbf.ft).***
25. Refit rocker cover.
26. Ensure dipstick tube and mating face on cylinder block is clean.
27. Apply Loctite 638 to end of dipstick tube and fit tube and dipstick to cylinder block.
28. Fit exhaust manifold. ***See MANIFOLD AND EXHAUST SYSTEM, Repair.***
29. Fit inlet manifold gasket. ***See MANIFOLD AND EXHAUST SYSTEM, Repair.***

CYLINDER HEAD GASKET (RH) - from 99MY

Service repair no - 12.29.03

Remove

1. Remove inlet manifold gasket. ***See MANIFOLD AND EXHAUST SYSTEM, Repair.***
2. Remove RH exhaust manifold gasket. ***See MANIFOLD AND EXHAUST SYSTEM, Repair.***

NOTE: RHD models: Exhaust manifold will remain captive in engine bay but clear of cylinder head.

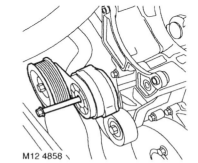

M12 4858

3. Remove bolt securing auxiliary drive belt tensioner and remove tensioner.

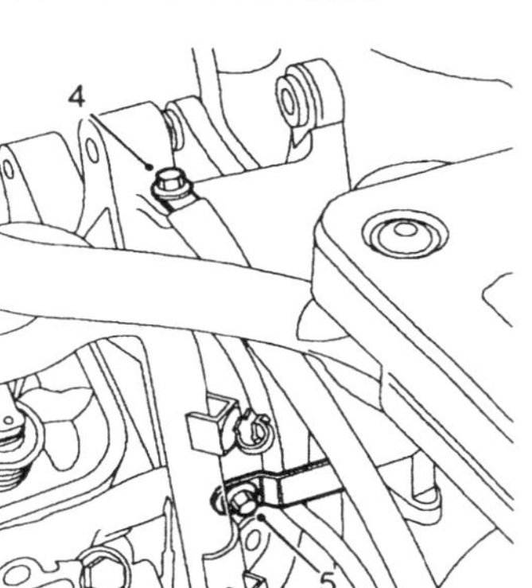

M12 4859

4. Remove bolt securing engine earth lead.
5. Remove bolt securing engine oil cooler pipe to alternator mounting bracket.

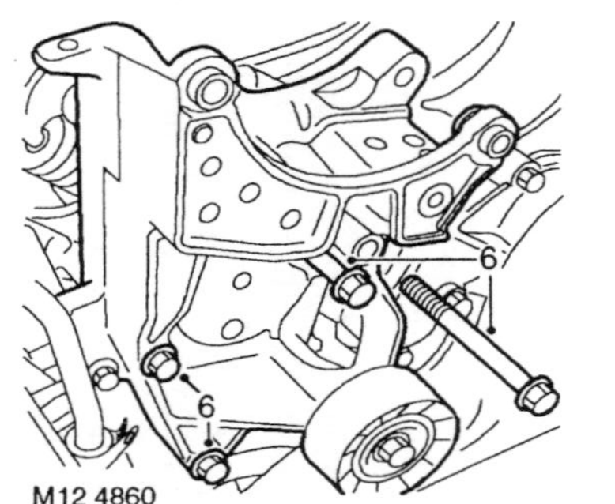

M12 4860

6. Remove 4 bolts securing alternator mounting bracket and remove bracket.

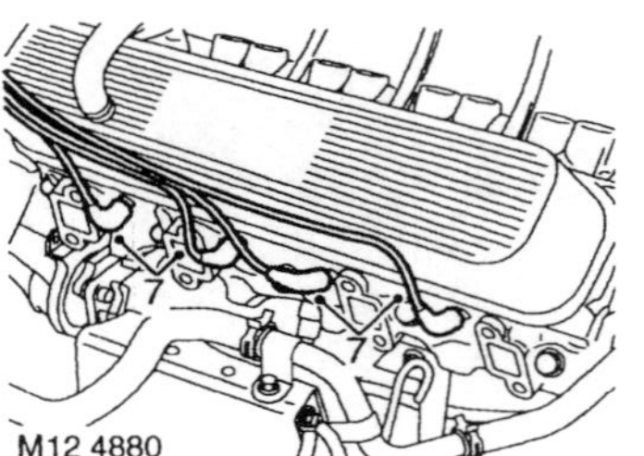

M12 4880

7. Disconnect HT leads from spark plugs.
8. Remove rocker cover.

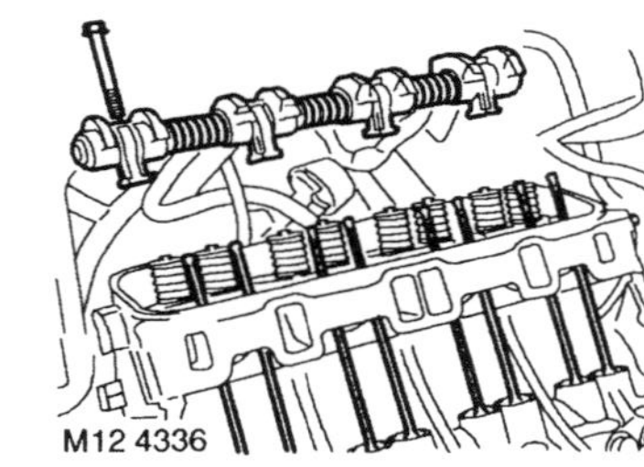
M12 4336

9. Progressively remove 4 bolts securing the rocker shaft and remove rocker shaft assembly.
10. Remove push rods.

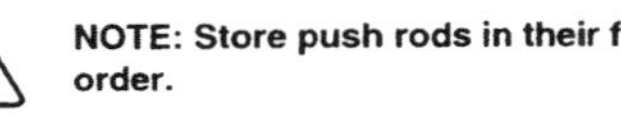
NOTE: Store push rods in their fitted order.

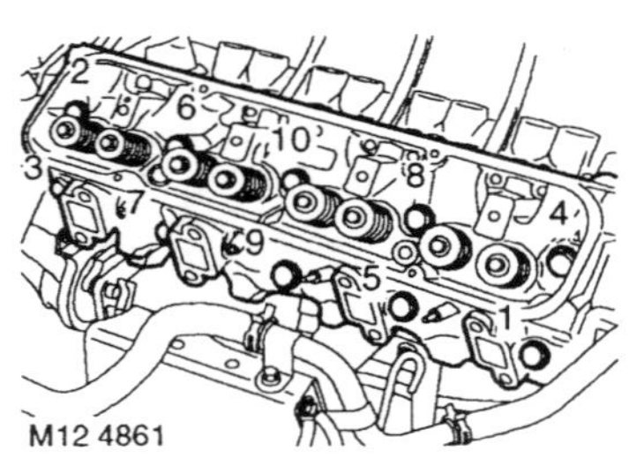

M12 4861

11. In the sequence shown remove 10 bolts securing the cylinder head.
12. Remove cylinder head.

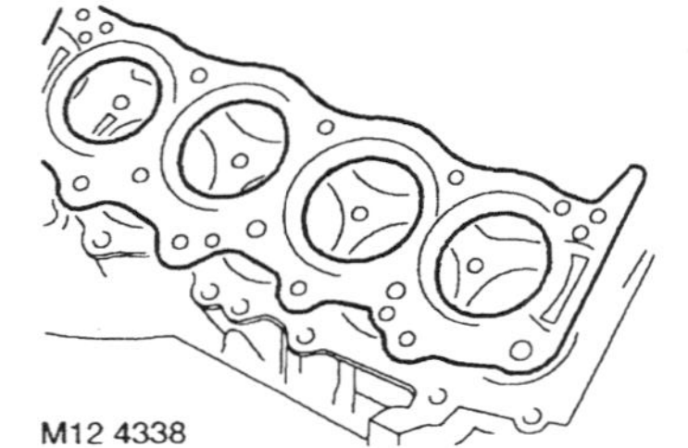
M12 4338

13. Remove cylinder head gasket.

Refit

14. Use a suitable gasket removal spray and plastic scraper to clean cylinder head and cylinder block mating faces. Ensure bolt holes are left clean and dry.

CAUTION: Do not use metal scraper or machined surfaces may be damaged.

15. Check head and block faces for warping and pitting.
16. Fit cylinder head gasket with the word TOP uppermost.

NOTE: Gasket must be fitted dry.

17. Carefully fit cylinder head and locate on dowels.
18. Lightly lubricate new cylinder head bolt threads with clean engine oil.

NOTE: Long bolts: 1, 3, 5. short bolts: 2, 4, 6, 7, 8, 9, 10.

19. Fit bolts and tighten in the sequence shown to ***20 Nm (15 lbf.ft)*** *then* ***90*** *°, then a further* ***90*** *°.*
20. Clean push rods.
21. Lubricate ends of push rods with clean engine oil.
22. Fit push rods in their removed order.
23. Clean base of rocker pillars and mating face on cylinder head.
24. Clean contact surface on rockers, valves and push rods.
25. Lubricate contact surface and rocker shaft with clean engine oil.
26. Fit rocker shaft assembly and engage push rods. Tighten bolts progressively to ***38 Nm (28 lbf.ft).***
27. Fit rocker cover.
28. Position alternator mounting bracket, fit and tighten bolts to ***40 Nm (30 lbf.ft).***
29. Position engine harness, align oil cooler pipe and secure with bolt.
30. Position auxiliary drive belt tensioner, fit bolt and tighten to ***45 Nm (33 lbf.ft).***
31. Position engine earth lead, fit bolt and tighten to ***22 Nm (16 lbf.ft).***
32. Connect HT leads to spark plugs.
33. Fit exhaust manifold gasket. ***See MANIFOLD AND EXHAUST SYSTEM, Repair.***
34. Fit inlet manifold gasket. ***See MANIFOLD AND EXHAUST SYSTEM, Repair.***
35. Remove stand(s) and lower vehicle.

TIMING CHAIN AND GEARS - from 99MY

Service repair no - 12.65.12

Remove

1. Remove front cover gasket. ***See this section.***

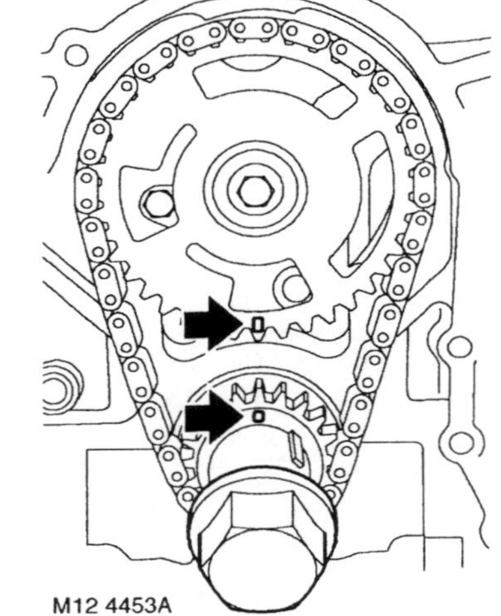
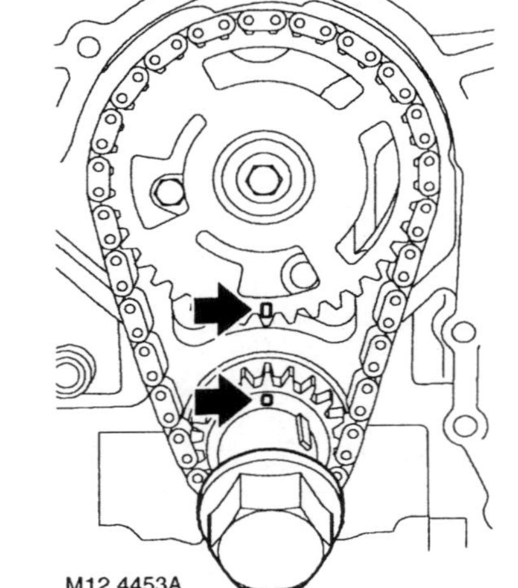
M12 4453A

2. Fit crankshaft pulley bolt and rotate engine to align timing marks. Remove crankshaft pulley bolt.

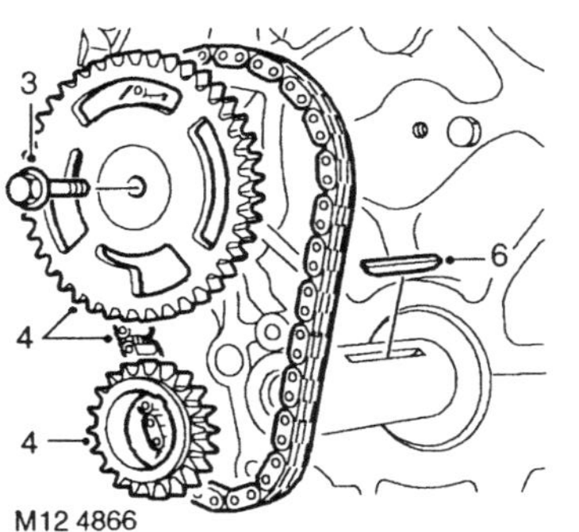

M12 4866

3. Restrain camshaft gear and remove gear retaining bolt.
4. Remove camshaft drive chain and gears as an assembly.
5. Remove gears from chain.
6. If necessary remove key from crankshaft.

Refit

7. Clean timing chain, gears and gear locations.
8. Fit key to crankshaft.
9. Temporarily fit gears to camshaft and crankshaft. If necessary, rotate shafts to align timing marks.

NOTE: When aligned correctly, the timing marks will face each other: the crankshaft gear with its timing mark at twelve 0'clock position and the camshaft with its timing mark at six 0'clock position.

10. Remove gears from shafts and fit to timing chain.
11. With timing marks aligned, fit timing chain and gears as an assembly.
12. Restrain the camshaft gear and tighten retaining bolt to ***50 Nm (37 lbf.ft)***.
13. Fit front cover gasket ***See this section.***
14. Reconnect battery negative lead.

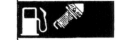

CONTENTS

Page

17 - EMISSION CONTROL

CONTENTS

EMISSION CONTROL - BMW DIESEL

Crankcase Ventilation Control

The purpose of the crankcase ventilation system is to ensure that any gases entering the inside of the engine are redirected into the air intake and do not accumulate in the engine.

Vehicles without EGR

The camshaft cover is connected via a pipe to the air intake duct to the turbocharger. When the engine is running, gases are drawn from the crankcase and the camshaft cover into the air intake duct due to the pressure difference between the air induction into the turbocharger and the inside of the engine.

As the gases are drawn into the camshaft cover, they pass through a wire mesh filter which separates oil from the gases. A Mann Hummel type valve is located in the pipe to the intake duct. The valve allows crankcase ventilation at low engine speeds but closes at high engine speeds to prevent excessive crankcase depression.

Vehicles with EGR

The Mann Hummel type valve is no longer used and the camshaft cover is fitted with a pressure regulating valve. The valve is located in the front of the cover and is connected by a pipe to the air intake duct. The purpose of the regulating valve is to maintain a constant vacuum of 20 mbar inside the engine crankcase, improving crankcase ventilation under all operating conditions.

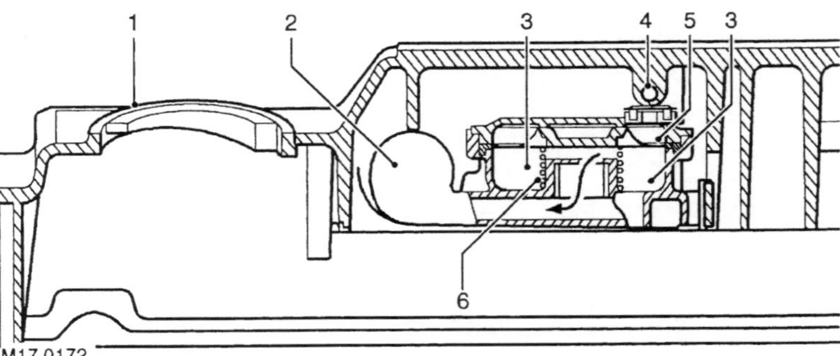

1. Camshaft cover
2. Blow-by pipe
3. Internal engine pressure
4. Atmospheric vent
5. Membrane
6. Spring

The pressure regulating valve comprises a membrane held in the open position by a spring. The membrane and spring are subject to engine crankcase pressure and intake manifold depression on one side and atmospheric pressure on the other side. When crankcase pressure rises, gases are drawn from the engine past the open membrane and into the air intake manifold by the intake manifold depression.

When the intake manifold depression exceeds the crankcase pressure, the membrane moves against the spring pressure and engine crankcase pressure. This causes the membrane to lower and cover the port, preventing excessive depression in the crankcase.

Exhaust Gas Recirculation (EGR)

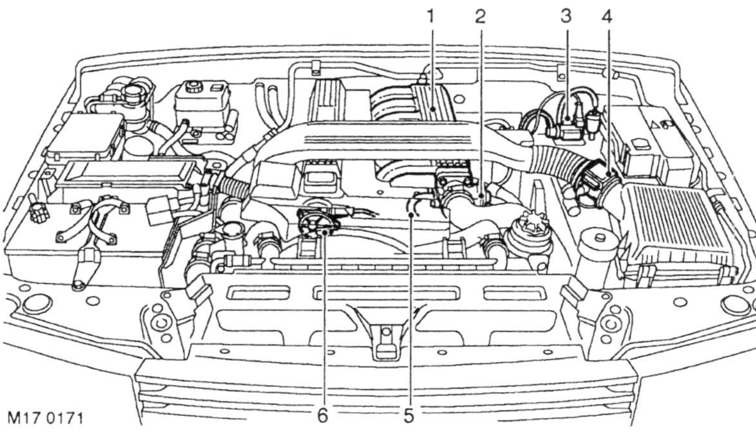

M17 0171

Component location

1. Intake Manifold
2. EGR Valve
3. EGR Modulator Valve
4. Mass Air Flow (MAF) Sensor
5. Pipe - Exhaust Manifold to EGR Valve
6. Vacuum Pump - EGR System

During certain running conditions, the EGR system directs exhaust gases into the intake manifold to be used in the combustion process. The principal affect of this is to reduce combustion temperatures by reducing the amount of oxygen fed into the combustion chamber, which in turn reduces Oxides of Nitrogen (NO_x) emissions. Up to 50% of the intake air can be replaced by exhaust gas.

Recirculating too much exhaust gas can result in higher emissions of soot, HC and CO due to insufficient air. The precise quantity of recirculated gas is controlled by the ECM to ensure that optimum conditions are maintained.

The ECM controls an EGR modulator valve mounted on the LH inner wing. This valve, when modulated, opens an EGR valve on the inlet manifold and directs exhaust gases into the inlet manifold. The EGR modulator valve controls the supply of vacuum from a vacuum pump located at the front of the cylinder head.

Exhaust gases are fed from a metal pipe on the exhaust manifold to the EGR valve on the inlet manifold. The pipe is secured at each end by a flanged connection secured by two bolts.

In operation, the ECM monitors engine conditions and signals the EGR modulator to supply a vacuum to the EGR valve.

The EGR valve opens allowing exhaust gases to be drawn into the air intake manifold. The exhaust gas replaces a proportion of the air drawn into the intake manifold. Less air flows through the MAF sensor which consequently requires a lower electrical current to maintain its temperature. The change of current is read by the ECM which calculates the amount of exhaust gas being recirculated.

The mapping in the ECM monitors the MAF sensor current changes and alters the signal current supplied to the EGR modulator, varying the vacuum to operate the EGR valve. In this way, the ECM controls the amount of exhaust gas recirculated to maintain the engine at its optimum operating parameters.

The EGR system does not operate when starting the engine, at engine overrun or when the engine is at full load. The ECM may also prevent EGR system operation if the electrical signal from the MAF sensor is insufficient or if a given speed or injection volume is exceeded.

Vacuum pump

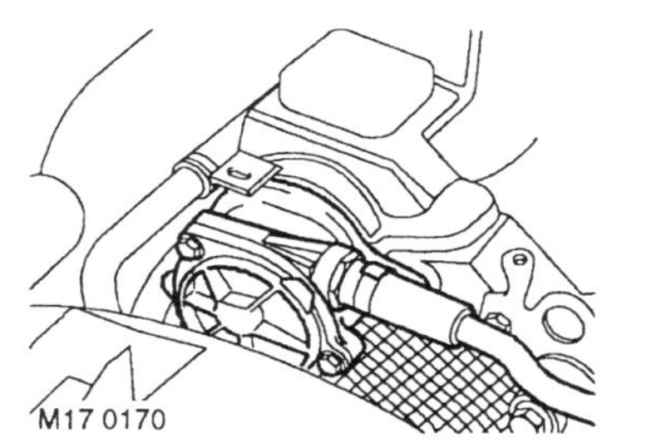
M17 0170

The vacuum pump is located at the front of the engine on the cylinder head. The pump is sealed to the cylinder head with a sealing ring and secured with two bolts.

The pump is driven from the camshaft via two drive dogs which engage with corresponding slots in the end of the camshaft. Engine oil is supplied through a nozzle in the end of the camshaft gear to lubricate the vacuum pump. The pump is connected to the EGR modulator valve via a pipe and hose.

EGR Valve

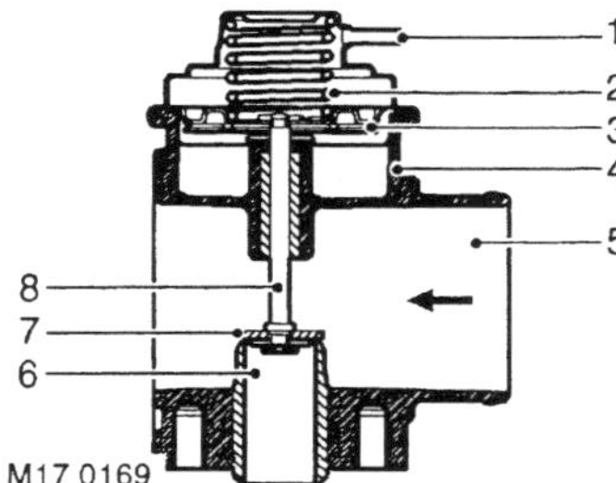

M17 0169

1. Vacuum connection
2. Spring
3. Diaphragm
4. Housing
5. Air inlet connection
6. EGR pipe connection
7. Seal
8. Rod

The EGR valve is located on the forward end of the intake manifold. The valve is sealed to the manifold with an O-ring and secured with four bolts. The EGR valve comprises a diaphragm, housing and valve.

The EGR valve is mounted on an aluminium housing which also provides for the connection of the air intake hose from the intercooler. The valve is positioned opposite the exhaust gas pipe intake connection. The valve is connected to the diaphragm by a rod and is held in the closed position by a spring.

Vacuum supplied by the EGR modulator valve acts on the diaphragm, overcoming the spring pressure and pulling the valve open up to 2.5 mm (0.1 in.). This exposes the exhaust gas pipe connection and allows gases to be drawn into the intake manifold. When the vacuum is removed the diaphragm moves under spring pressure, closing the valve and sealing the EGR pipe inlet with a seal on the valve. The extent to which the valve opens is controlled by the vacuum level supplied from the EGR modulator, which in turn is controlled by the ECM.

EGR Modulator valve

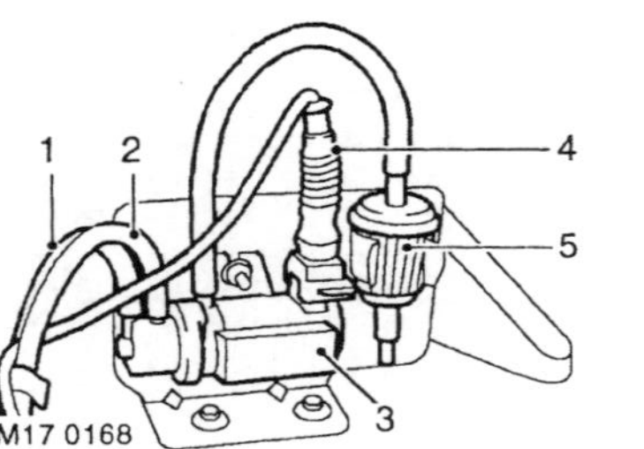

1. Vacuum pipe to EGR valve
2. Vacuum pipe from vacuum pump
3. Modulator valve
4. Electrical connector
5. Air filter

The EGR modulator valve is located in the engine compartment on the left inner wing near the bulkhead.

The EGR modulator is vacuum operated through a solenoid valve. When the ECM determines that EGR should take place, the solenoid valve is modulated and vacuum, supplied from the vacuum pump, opens the EGR valve. When EGR is not required, the ECM switches the control solenoid to close the vacuum to the EGR valve.

The modulator valve receives full vacuum from the pump and is also subjected to atmospheric pressure supplied from an air filter attached to the side of the EGR modulator valve. The vacuum and atmospheric pressure are mixed inside the modulator valve by electrical actuation of the solenoid creating a controlled vacuum.

Failure of the EGR modulator valve may result in a reduction of engine performance and the EGR may shut down or operate at full EGR.

Mass Air Flow (MAF) Sensor

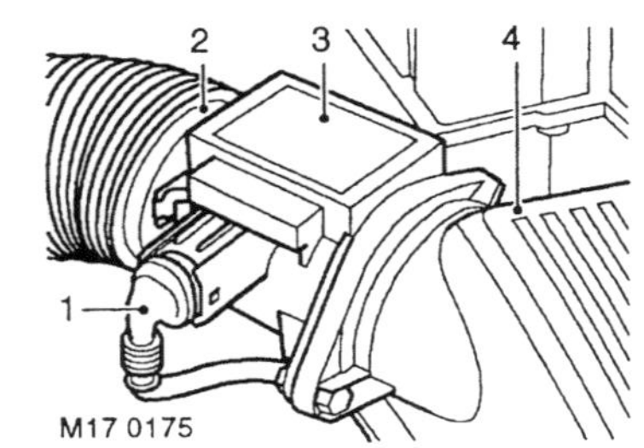

1. Electrical connector
2. Air cleaner outlet pipe
3. MAF sensor
4. Air cleaner housing

The MAF sensor, located in the air cleaner outlet pipe, monitors the amount of air being drawn into the intake manifold. This data is used by the ECM to calculate the injected fuel volume, the intake air temperature and the rate of EGR.

The MAF sensor is a hot film sensor which has a heated surface maintained by an electrical current at a constant temperature. With cool air flowing past the sensor, the volume of air drawn into the intake manifold is measured by the electrical current required to keep the temperature of the hot film sensor constant.

EMISSION CONTROL - LAND ROVER V8

Engine design has evolved in order to minimise the emission of harmful by-products. Emission control systems are fitted to Land Rover vehicles which are designed to maintain the emission levels within the legal limits pertaining for the specified market.

Despite the utilisation of specialised emission control equipment, it is still necessary to ensure that the engine is correctly maintained and is in good mechanical order so that it operates at its optimal condition. In particular, ignition timing has an effect on the production of HC and NO_x emissions, with the harmful emissions rising as the ignition timing is advanced.

CAUTION: In many countries it is against the law for a vehicle owner or an unauthorised dealer to modify or tamper with emission control equipment. In some cases, the vehicle owner and/or the dealer may even be liable for prosecution.

The engine management ECM is fundamental for controlling the emission control systems. In addition to controlling normal operation, the system complies with On Board Diagnostic (OBD) system strategies. The system monitors and reports on faults detected with ignition, fuelling and exhaust systems which cause an excessive increase in tailpipe emissions. This includes component failures, engine misfires, catalyst damage, catalyst efficiency, fuel evaporative loss and exhaust leaks.

When an emission relevant fault is determined, the fault condition is stored in the ECM memory. For NAS vehicles, the MIL warning lamp on the instrument pack will be illuminated when the fault is confirmed. Confirmation of a fault condition occurs if the fault is found to be present during the driving cycle subsequent to the one when the fault was first detected. ***See FUEL SYSTEM, Description and operation.***

The following types of supplementary control system are used to reduce harmful emissions released into the atmosphere from the vehicle:

- **Crankcase emission control -** also known as blow-by gas emissions from the engine crankcase.
- **Exhaust emission control -** to limit the undesirable by-products of combustion.
- **Fuel vapour evaporative loss control -** to restrict the emission of fuel through evaporation from the fuel system.
- **Fuel leak detection system (NAS only) -** an on board diagnostic (OBD) test to check the evaporative emission system for the presence of fuel evaporation leaks from the fuel tank to the purge valve.
- **Secondary air injection system (NAS only) -** to reduce emissions experienced during cold starting of the engine.

Crankcase ventilation system

The concentration of hydrocarbons in the crankcase of an engine is much greater than that in the vehicle's exhaust system. In order to prevent the emission of these hydrocarbons into the atmosphere, crankcase emission control systems are employed and are a standard legal requirement.

The crankcase ventilation system is an integral part of the air supply to the engine combustion chambers and it is often overlooked when diagnosing problems associated with engine performance. A blocked ventilation pipe, filter or excessive air leak into the inlet system through a damaged pipe or leaking gasket can affect the air:fuel mixture, performance and economy of the engine. Periodically check the ventilation hoses are not cracked and that they are securely fitted to form airtight connections at their relevant ports.

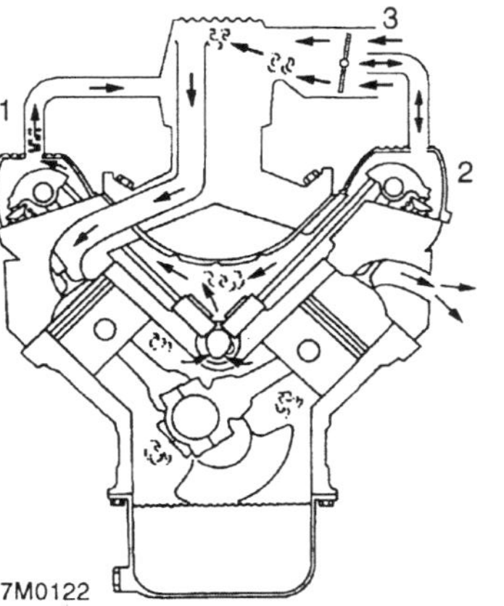

17M0122

The purpose of the crankcase ventilation system is to ensure that any noxious gas generated in the engine crankcase is rendered harmless by burning them in the combustion chambers. Burning the crankcase vapours in a controlled manner decreases the HC pollutants that could be emitted and helps to prevent the development of sludge in the engine oil as well as increasing fuel economy.

When the engine is running in cruise conditions, or at idle, manifold pressure is low and the majority of gasses are drawn into the inlet manifold through an oil/vapour separator (1), located in the RH rocker cover. At the same time, filtered air is drawn from the throttle body (3) into the engine via the LH rocker cover (2). The oil/vapour separator serves to prevent oil mist being drawn into the engine.

During periods of driving at Wide Open Throttle (WOT), pressure at either side of the throttle disc equalizes (manifold depression collapses). The larger ventilation opening (3), positioned in the fast moving stream of intake air, now offers more 'pull' than the small opening (1) in the RH rocker cover, and the flow of ventilation reverses. Gases are drawn from the LH rocker cover into the throttle body (3).

Crankcase ventilation system - from 99MY

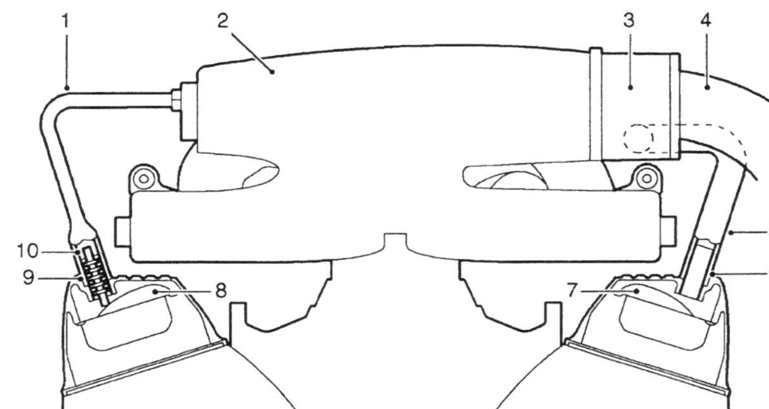

M17 0160

1. Hose - RH rocker cover to inlet manifold
2. Inlet manifold
3. Throttle body
4. Air intake
5. Hose - LH rocker cover to inlet manifold
6. LH rocker cover breather tube (without oil separator)
7. LH rocker cover baffle
8. RH rocker cover baffle
9. RH rocker cover breather tube
10. Oil separator (integral with breather tube)

A spiral oil separator is located in the stub pipe to the ventilation hose on the right hand cylinder rocker cover, where oil is separated and returned to the cylinder head. The rubber ventilation hose from the right hand rocker cover is routed to a port on the right hand side of the inlet manifold plenum chamber, where the returned gases mix with the fresh inlet air passing through the throttle butterfly valve. The stub pipe on the left hand rocker cover does not contain an oil separator, and the ventilation hose is routed to the throttle body housing at the air inlet side of the butterfly valve. The ventilation hoses are attached to the stub pipe by metal band clamps.

Oil laden noxious gas in the engine crankcase is drawn through the spiral oil separator. The mass of fresh air which is drawn in from the atmospheric side of the throttle butterfly to mix with the returned crankcase gas depends on the throttle position and the engine speed.

Exhaust emission control.

The fuel injection system provides accurately metered quantities of fuel to the combustion chambers to ensure the most efficient air to fuel ratio under all operating conditions. A further improvement to combustion is made by measuring the oxygen content of the exhaust gases to enable the quantity of fuel injected to be varied in accordance with the prevailing engine operation and ambient conditions; any unsatisfactory composition of the exhaust gas is then corrected by adjustments made to the fuelling by the ECM.

The main components of the exhaust emission system are two catalytic converters which are an integral part of the front exhaust pipe assembly. The catalytic converters are included in the system to reduce the emission, to atmosphere, of carbon monoxide (CO), oxides of nitrogen (NO_x), and hydrocarbons (HC). The active constituents of the converters are platinum (Pt), palladium (PD) and rhodium (Rh). **Catalytic converters for NAS low emission vehicles (LEVs) from 2000MY have active constituents of palladium and rhodium only).** The correct functioning of the converters is dependent upon close control of the oxygen concentration in the exhaust gas entering the catalysts.

The basic control loop comprises the engine (controlled system), the heated oxygen sensors (measuring elements), the engine management ECM (control) and the injectors and ignition (actuators). Other factors also influence the calculations of the ECM, such as air flow, air intake temperature and throttle position. Additionally, special driving conditions are compensated for such as starting, acceleration, deceleration, overrun and full load. ***See FUEL SYSTEM, Description and operation.***

The reliability of the ignition system is critical for efficient catalytic converter operation, since misfiring will lead to irreparable damage of the catalytic converter due to the overheating that occurs when unburned combustion gases are burnt inside it.

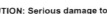

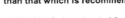

CAUTION: If the engine is misfiring, it should be shut down immediately and the cause rectified. Failure to do so will result in irreparable damage to the catalytic converter.

CAUTION: Ensure the exhaust system is free from leaks. Exhaust leaks upstream of the catalytic converter could cause internal damage to the catalytic converter.

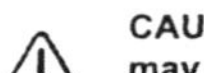

CAUTION: Serious damage to the engine may occur if a lower octane number fuel than that which is recommended is used.

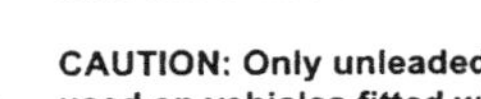

CAUTION: Only unleaded fuel must be used on vehicles fitted with catalytic converters; serious damage to the catalytic converter and oxygen sensors will occur if leaded fuel is used. A reminder label is adhered to the inside of the fuel filler flap. As a further safeguard, the filler neck is designed to accommodate only unleaded fuel pump nozzles.

The oxygen content of the exhaust gas is signalled to the Engine Control Module (ECM) by two Heated Oxygen Sensors (HO2S) located in the exhaust front pipes, upstream of each catalytic converter. The ECM can then make an appropriate adjustment to the fuel supply to correct the composition of the exhaust gases.

North American Specification (NAS) vehicles have additional Heated Oxygen Sensors, positioned downstream of each catalytic converter. The ECM uses the signals from these sensors to determine whether the catalysts are working efficiently.

HO_2S sensors and exhaust system - up to 99MY

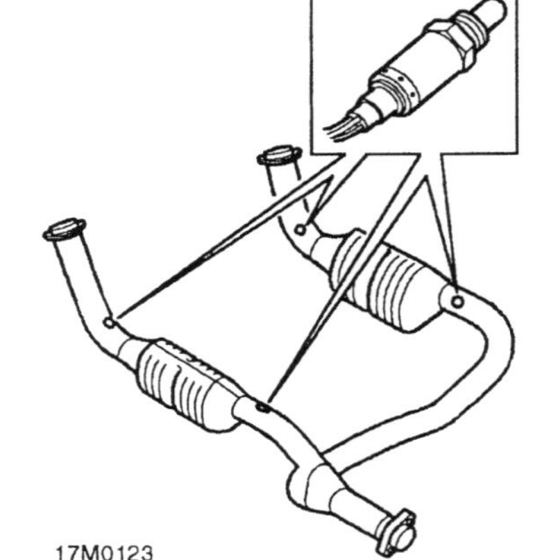

17M0123

Detail of front pipe showing location of oxygen sensors. Only NAS vehicles have four sensors, Rest of World vehicles have two sensors, one mounted upstream (towards the exhaust manifold) of each catalytic converter.

HO_2S sensors and exhaust system - from 99MY

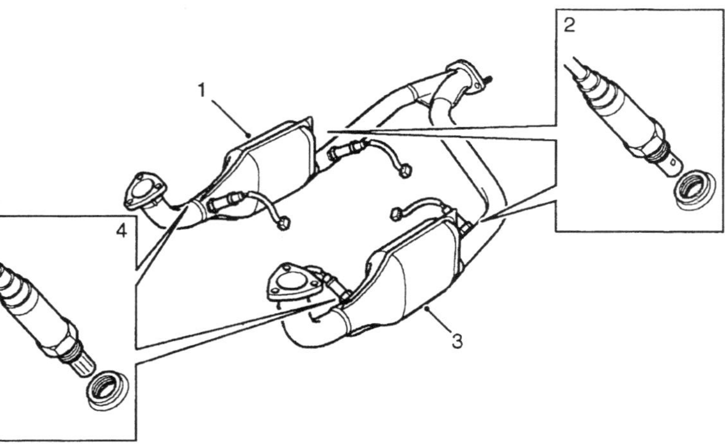

M17 0187

1. RH catalytic converter
2. Heated oxygen (HO_2S) sensors - post-catalytic converter (2 off - NAS only).
3. LH catalytic converter
4. Heated oxygen (HO_2S) sensors - pre-catalytic converter (2 off).

The oxygen content of the exhaust gas is monitored by heated oxygen (HO_2S) sensors using either a four sensor (NAS only) or two sensor setup, dependent on market destination and legislative requirements. Signals from the HO_2S sensors are input to the engine management ECM, which correspond to the level of oxygen detected in the exhaust gas. From ECM analysis of the data, necessary changes to the air:fuel mixture and ignition timing can be made to bring the emission levels back within acceptable limits under all operating conditions.

Changes to the air:fuel ratio are needed when the engine is operating under particular conditions such as cold starting, idle, cruise, full throttle or high altitude. In order to maintain an optimum air:fuel ratio for differing conditions, the engine management control system uses sensors to determine data which enable it to select the ideal ratio by increasing or decreasing the air to fuel ratio.

NOTE: Some markets do not legislate for closed loop fuelling control and in this instance no heated oxygen sensors will be fitted to the exhaust system.

On open loop systems, improved fuel economy can be arranged by increasing the quantity of air to fuel to create a lean mixture during part-throttle conditions. On closed loop systems, lean running conditions are not implemented as the system automatically optimises the air:fuel ratio to the stoichiometric ideal.

A higher proportion of fuel can be supplied to create a rich mixture during idle and full-throttle operation. Rich running at wide open throttle (WOT) is used for improved performance and high load to keep the exhaust temperature down and protect the catalysts and exhaust valves.

The voltage of the HO_2S sensors at the stoichiometric point is 450 to 500mV. The voltage decreases to between 100 and 500 mV if there is an increase in oxygen content(i.e. lean mixture). The voltage increases to between 500 and 1000mV if there is a decrease in oxygen content, signifying a rich mixture.

The HO_2S sensor needs to operate at high temperatures in order to function correctly (350°C (662°F)). To achieve this, the sensors have integral heater elements, controlled by a pulse width modulated (PWM) signal from the ECM. The heater element warms the sensor's ceramic layer from the inside so that the sensor is hot enough for operation. The heater elements are supplied with current immediately following engine start and are ready for closed loop control within 20 to 30 seconds (longer at cold ambient temperatures less than 0°C (32°F)). Heating is also necessary during low load conditions when the temperature of the exhaust gases is insufficient to maintain the required sensor temperatures. The maximum tip temperature is 930°C (1706°F).

A non-functioning heater element will delay the sensor's readiness for closed loop control and influences emissions. A diagnostic routine is utilised to measure both sensor heater current and the heater supply voltage so its resistance can be calculated. The function is active once per drive cycle, as long as the heater has been switched on for a pre-defined period and the current has stabilised. The PWM duty cycle is carefully controlled to prevent thermal shock to cold sensors.

The heated oxygen sensors age with mileage, causing an increase in the response time to switch from rich to lean and lean to rich. This increase in response time influences the closed loop control and leads to progressively increased emissions. The response time of the pre-catalytic converter sensors are monitored by measuring the period of rich to lean and lean to rich switching. The ECM monitors the switching time, and if the threshold period is exceeded, the fault will be detected and stored in the ECM as a fault code (the MIL light will be illuminated on NAS vehicles). NAS vehicle engine calibration uses downstream sensors to compensate for aged upstream sensors, thereby maintaining low emissions.

Diagnosis of electrical faults is continuously monitored for both the pre-catalytic converter sensors and the post-catalytic converter sensors (NAS only). This is achieved by checking the signal against maximum and minimum thresholds for open and short circuit conditions. For NAS vehicles, if the pre- and post-catalytic sensors are inadvertently transposed, the lambda signals will go to maximum but opposite extremes and the system will automatically revert to open loop fuelling. The additional sensors for NAS vehicles provide mandatory monitoring of catalyst conversion efficiency and long term fuelling adaptations.

Failure of the closed loop control of the exhaust emission system may be attributable to one of the failure modes indicated below:

- Mechanical fitting and integrity of the sensor.
- Sensor open circuit / disconnected.
- Short circuit to vehicle supply or ground.
- Lambda ratio outside operating band.
- Crossed sensors.
- Contamination from leaded fuel or other sources.
- Change in sensor characteristic.
- Harness damage.
- Air leak into exhaust system (cracked pipe / weld or loose fixings).

System failure will be indicated by the following symptoms:

- MIL light on (NAS only).
- Default to open-loop fuelling for the defective cylinder bank.
- If sensors are crossed, engine will run normally after initial start and then become progressively unstable with one bank going to its maximum rich clamp and the other bank going to its maximum lean clamp - the system will then revert to open-loop fuelling.
- High CO reading.
- Strong smell of H_2S (rotten eggs).
- Excessive emissions.

See FUEL SYSTEM, Description and operation.

SECONDARY AIR INJECTION SYSTEM - COMPONENT LOCATION

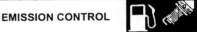

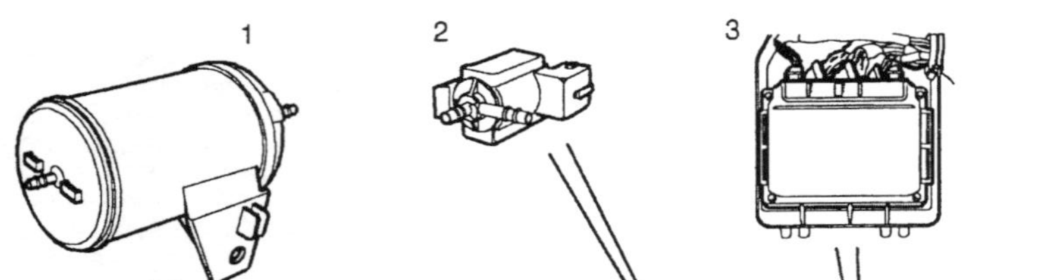

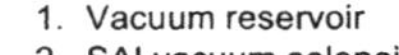

1. Vacuum reservoir
2. SAI vacuum solenoid valve
3. Engine Control Module (ECM)
4. Fuse 26 - Engine Compartment Fusebox
5. Main relay - Engine Compartment Fusebox
6. SAI pump relay - Engine Compartment Fusebox
7. Fuselink 2 - Engine Compartment Fusebox
8. Secondary Air Injection (SAI) pump
9. SAI control valves (2 off)

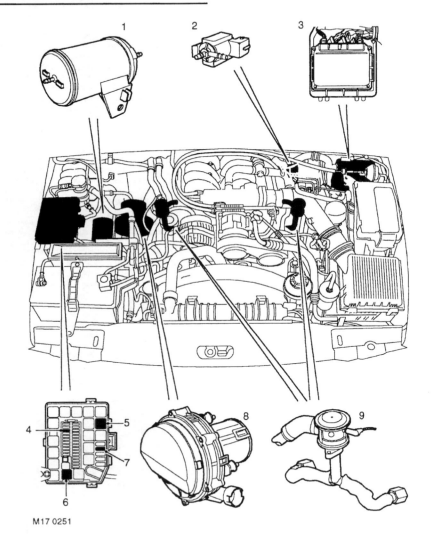

Secondary air injection system - description

The secondary air injection (SAI) system comprises the following components:

- Secondary air injection pump
- SAI vacuum solenoid valve
- SAI control valves (2 off, 1 for each bank of cylinders)
- SAI pump relay
- Vacuum reservoir
- Vacuum harness and pipes

The SAI system is used to limit the emission of carbon monoxide (CO) and hydrocarbons (HCs) that are prevalent in the exhaust during cold starting of a spark ignition engine.

The concentration of hydrocarbons experienced during cold starting at low temperatures are particularly high until the engine and catalytic converter reach normal operating temperature. The lower the cold start temperature, the greater the prevalence of hydrocarbons emitted from the engine.

There are several reasons for the increase of HC emissions at low cold start temperatures, including the tendancy for fuel to be deposited on the cylinder walls, which is then displaced during the piston cycle and expunged during the exhaust stroke. As the engine warms up through operation, the cylinder walls no longer retain a film of fuel and most of the hydrocarbons will be burnt off during the combustion process.

The SAI pump is used to provide a supply of air into the exhaust ports in the cylinder head, onto the back of the exhaust valves, during the cold start period. The hot unburnt fuel particles leaving the combustion chamber mix with the air injected into the exhaust ports and immediately combust. This subsequent combustion of the unburnt and partially burnt CO and HC particles help to reduce the emission of these pollutants from the exhaust system. The additional heat generated in the exhaust manifold also provides rapid heating of the exhaust system catalytic converters. The additional oxygen which is delivered to the catalytic converters also generate an exothermic reaction which causes the catalytic converters to 'light off' quickly.

The catalytic converters only start to provide effective treatment of emission pollutants when they reach an operating temperature of approximately 250°C (482°F) and need to be between temperatures of 400°C (752°F) and 800°C (1472°F) for optimum efficiency. Consequently, the heat produced by the secondary air injection "afterburning", reduces the time delay before the catalysts reach an efficient operating temperature.

The engine control module (ECM) checks the engine coolant temperature when the engine is started, and if it is below 55°C (131°F), the SAI pump is started. Secondary air injection will remain operational for a period controlled by the ECM and is dependent on the starting temperature of the engine. This varies from approximately 95 seconds for a start temperature of 8°C (46°F) to 30 seconds for a start temperature of 55°C (131°F). The SAI pump operation can be cut short due to excessive engine speed or load.

Air from the SAI pump is supplied to the SAI control valves via pipework and an intermediate T-piece which splits the air flow evenly to each bank.

At the same time the SAI pump is started, the ECM operates a SAI vacuum solenoid valve, which opens to allow vacuum from the vacuum reservoir to be applied to the vacuum operated SAI control valves on each side of the engine. When the vacuum is applied to the SAI control valves, they open simultaneously to allow the air from the SAI pump through to the exhaust ports. Secondary air is injected into the inner most exhaust ports on each bank.

When the ECM breaks the ground circuit to de-energise the SAI vacuum solenoid valve, the vacuum supply to the SAI control valves is cut off and the valves close to prevent further air being injected into the exhaust manifold. At the same time as the SAI vacuum solenoid valve is closed, the ECM opens the ground circuit to the SAI pump relay, to stop the SAI pump.

A vacuum reservoir is included in the vacuum line between the intake manifold and the SAI vacuum solenoid valve. This prevents changes in vacuum pressure from the intake manifold being passed on to cause fluctuations of the SAI vacuum solenoid valve. The vacuum reservoir contains a one way valve and ensures a constant vacuum is available for the SAI solenoid valve operation. This is particularly important when the vehicle is at high altitude.

Secondary air injection system - operation

When the engine is started, the engine control module (ECM) checks the engine coolant temperature and if it is below 55°C (131°F), the ECM grounds the electrical connection to the coil of the SAI pump relay.

The Main and Secondary Air Injection (SAI) pump relays are located in the engine compartment fusebox. A 12V battery supply is fed to the contacts of the SAI pump relay via fuselink 2. When the ECM completes the earth path, the coil energises and closes the contacts of the SAI pump relay to supply 12V to the SAI pump. The SAI pump starts to operate, and will continue to do so until the ECM switches off the earth connection to the coil of the SAI pump relay.

An earth connection from the Main relay coil is connected to the ECM. When the ECM completes the earth path, the coil energises and closes the contacts of the Main relay. When the contacts of the Main relay are closed, a 12V battery supply is fed to the SAI vacuum solenoid valve via fuse 26 in the engine compartment fusebox. The ECM grounds the electrical connection to the SAI vacuum solenoid valve at the same time as it switches on the SAI pump motor.

The SAI pump remains operational for a period determined by the ECM and depends on the starting temperature of the engine, or for a maximum operation period determined by the ECM if the target engine coolant temperature has not been reached in the usual time.

When the SAI vacuum solenoid valve is energised, a vacuum is provided to the operation control ports on both of the vacuum operated SAI control valves at the exhaust manifolds. The control vacuum is sourced from the intake manifold depression and routed to the SAI control valves via a vacuum reservoir and the SAI vacuum solenoid valve.

The vacuum reservoir is included in the vacuum supply circuit to prevent vacuum fluctuations caused by changes in the intake manifold depression affecting the smooth operation of the SAI control valves.

When a vacuum is applied to the control ports of the SAI control valves, the valves open to allow pressurised air from the SAI pump to pass through to the exhaust ports in the cylinder heads for combustion.

When the ECM has determined that the SAI pump has operated for the desired duration, it switches off the earth paths to the SAI pump relay and the SAI vacuum solenoid valve. With the SAI vacuum solenoid valve de-energised, the valve closes, cutting off the vacuum supply to the SAI control valves. The SAI control valves close immediately and completely to prevent any further pressurised air from the SAI pump entering the exhaust manifolds.

The engine coolant temperature sensor incurs a time lag in respect of detecting a change in temperature and the SAI pump automatically enters a 'soak period' between operations to prevent the SAI pump overheating. The ECM also compares the switch off and start up temperatures, to determine whether it is necessary to operate the SAI pump. This prevents the pump running repeatedly and overheating on repeat starts.

Other factors which may prevent or stop SAI pump operation include the prevailing engine speed/load conditions.

Evaporative emission control system - pre advanced EVAPS.

The system is designed to prevent harmful fuel vapour escaping to the atmosphere. The system comprises a vapour separator (C) and a two way valve (D), both located on the fuel filler neck (A), an Evaporative Emissions (EVAP) canister and an EVAP canister purge valve.

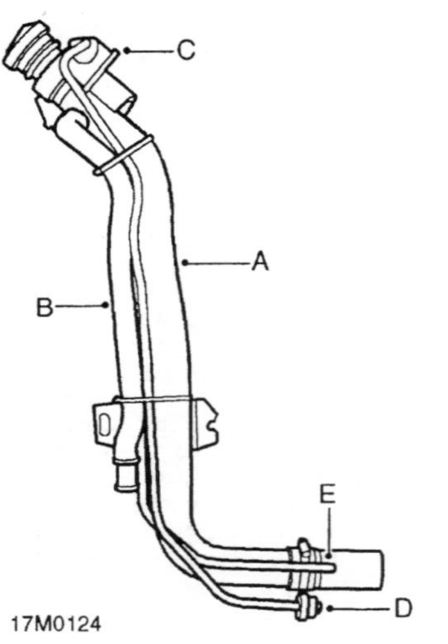

17M0124

A Fuel filler neck
B External fill breather pipe
C Fuel/vapour separator
D Two way valve - fuel vapour to EVAP canister
E Fuel vapour from fuel tank

During conditions of high ambient temperatures, fuel in the tank vapourises, and pressure rises. Fuel vapour enters the vapour separator and any liquid fuel runs back to the tank. Three roll over valves (ROVs) are fitted in the fuel tank vapour lines. These valves prevent liquid fuel entering the vapour separator if the vehicle rolls over. When pressure rises above 5 to 7 kPa (0.7 to 1.0 lbf/in^2), the two way valve opens and allows fuel vapour to flow to the EVAP canister where it is stored in the canister's activated charcoal element. When the correct engine operating conditions are met, the Engine Control Module (ECM) opens the EVAP canister purge valve and vapour is drawn from the canister, into the plenum chamber to be burned in the engine. Fresh air is drawn into the canister through a vent to take up the volume of displaced vapour. If the two way valve should fail, or the main vapour line becomes blocked, excess pressure is vented to atmosphere through a valve in the fuel filler cap. Similarly, the cap vent valve will open to prevent the tank collapsing if excessive vacuum is present.

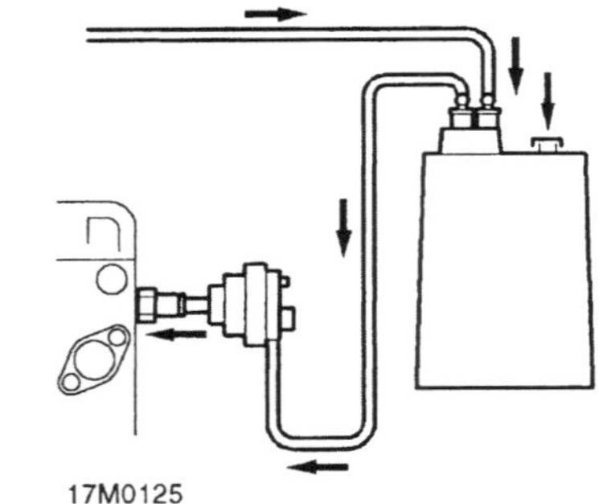

17M0125

When the temperature of fuel in the tank reduces, pressure also reduces and vapour must be drawn back into the tank. When tank pressure drops into vacuum, the two way valve opens, allowing fuel vapour to be drawn out of the EVAP canister into the fuel tank. Again, fresh air is drawn into the canister to take up the displaced volume.

EVAPORATIVE CONTROL SYSTEM - PRE ADVANCED EVAPS

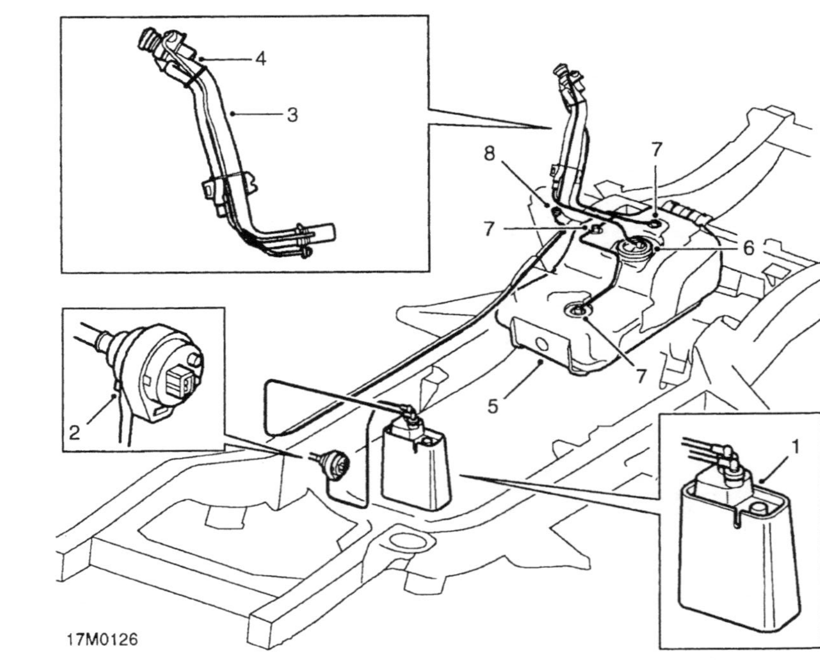

17M0126

1. EVAP canister
2. EVAP canister purge valve
3. Fuel filler neck assembly
4. Fuel/vapour separator
5. Fuel tank
6. Fuel pump and gauge sender unit
7. Roll over valves
8. Two way valve

EVAPORATIVE EMISSION CONTROL SYSTEM - ADVANCED EVAPS (up to 99MY)

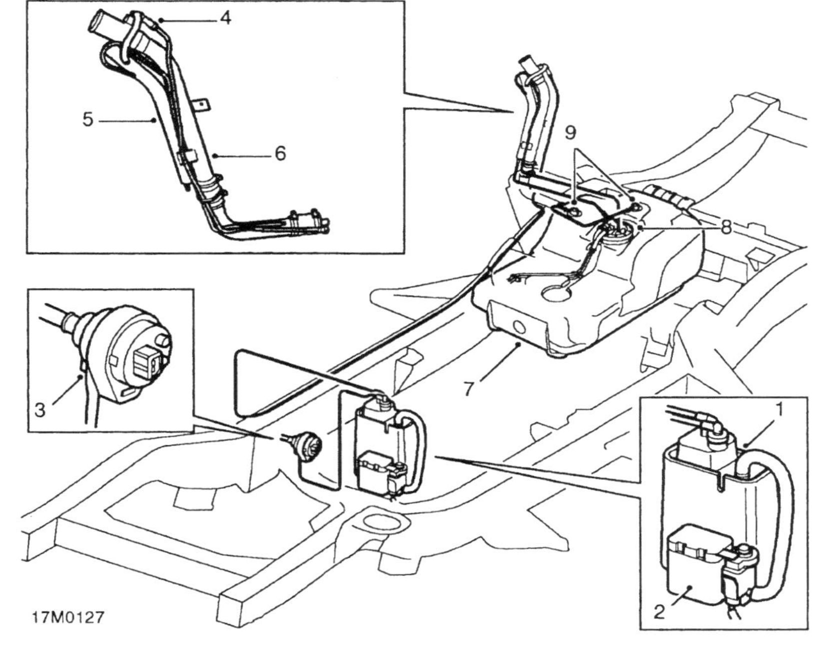

Component location

1. EVAP canister
2. EVAP canister vent solenoid (ECVS)
3. EVAP canister purge valve
4. Anti-trickle fill valve
5. Liquid/vapour separator
6. Fuel filler neck assembly
7. Fuel tank
8. Fuel pump and gauge sender unit, incorporating fuel tank pressure sensor
9. Roll over valves

EVAPORATIVE EMISSION CONTROL SYSTEM - ADVANCED EVAPS (from 99MY)

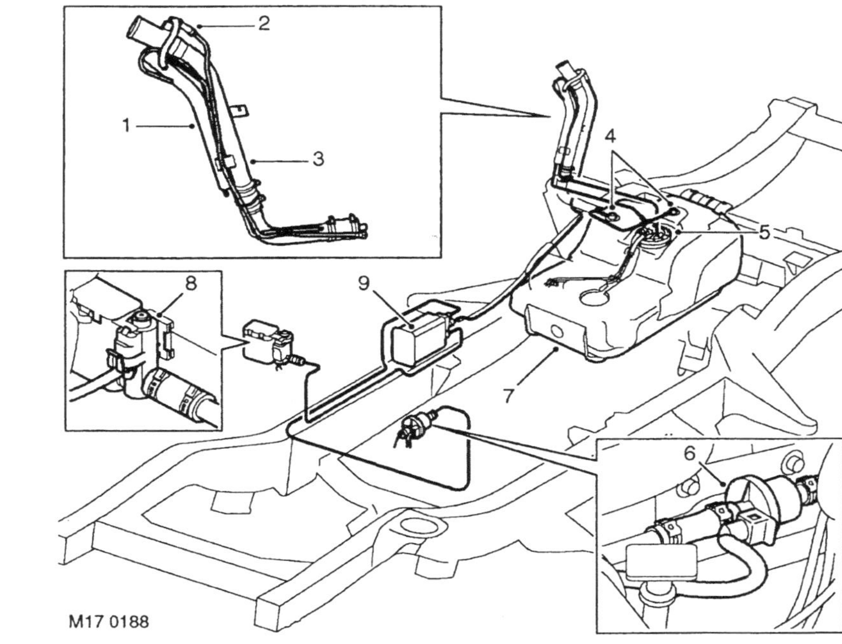

Component location

1. Liquid/vapour separator
2. Anti-trickle fill valve
3. Fuel filler neck assembly
4. Roll over valves
5. Fuel pump and gauge sender unit, incorporating fuel tank pressure sensor (NAS only)
6. EVAP canister purge valve
7. Fuel tank
8. Canister vent solenoid (CVS) unit
9. EVAP canister

99MY component location continued:

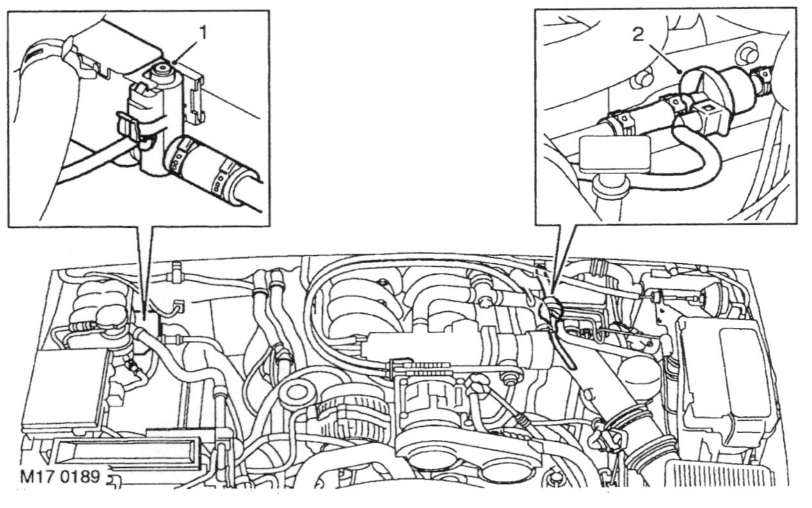

1. Canister Vent Solenoid (CVS) unit - (NAS only)
2. Purge valve

Identification

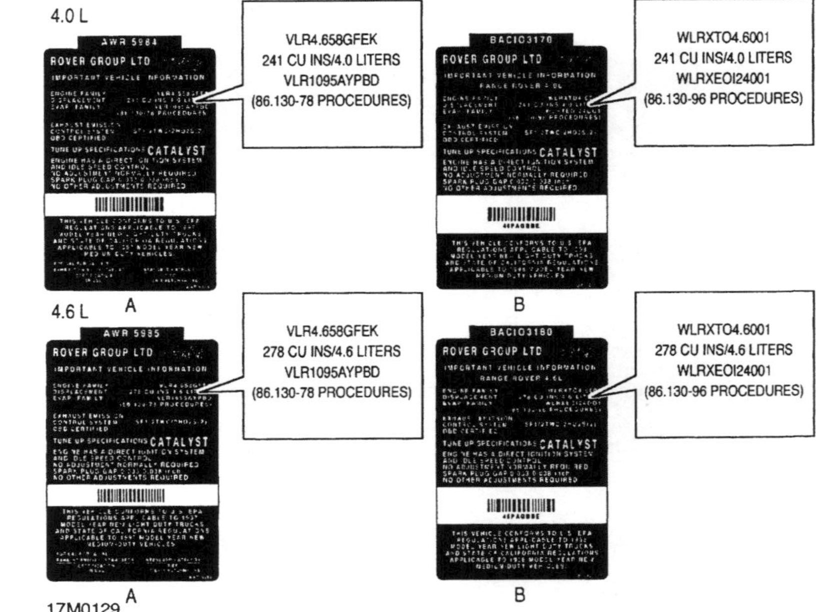

The system was introduced on all North American specification vehicles from 1998 Model Year. Advanced EVAP vehicles can be recognised by the information contained in the **EVAP. FAMILY** entry on the underbonnet Emission label (mounted on the bonnet lock platform).

A - Vehicles without advanced EVAPS
VLR1095AYPBD

B - Vehicles with advanced EVAPS
WLRXEO124001

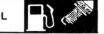

Evaporative emission control system - Advanced EVAPS.

The evaporation emission control system is used to reduce the level of hydrocarbons emitted into the atmosphere from the fuel system. The system comprises a vapour separator (B) and an anti-trickle valve (A), both located on the fuel filler neck (F), an Evaporative Emissions (EVAP) canister and an EVAP canister purge valve. A Canister vent solenoid (CVS) unit is mounted in front of the EVAP canister on vehicles up to 99MY. On vehicles from 99MY the CVS unit is mounted near the bulkhead on the RHS of the engine bay. The CVS unit is used by the ECM to control fresh air supply to the canister.

On NAS vehicles, the fuel pump and gauge sender unit incorporates a pressure sensor which is used by the ECM, in conjunction with the CVS unit, to determine the presence of leaks which may cause vapour to escape. This system is added for compliance with OBD measures.

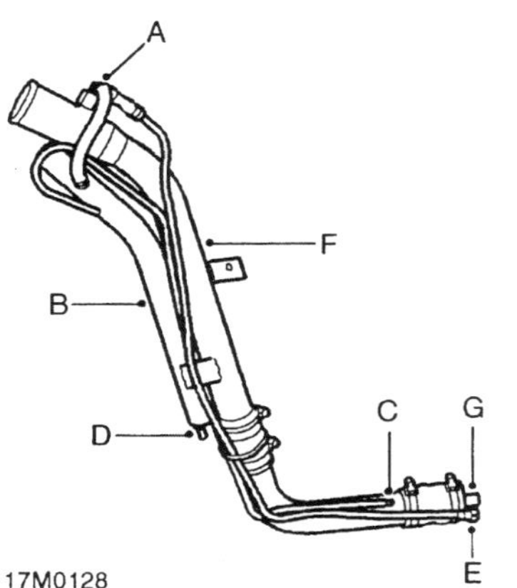

17M0128

A Anti-trickle fill valve
B Liquid/Vapour Separator
C Vent line to pressure sensor
D From fuel tank to liquid/vapour separator
E From EVAP canister to anti-trickle fill valve
F Fuel filler neck assembly
G Internal fill breather hose

During conditions of high ambient temperatures, fuel in the tank vapourises, and pressure rises. Fuel vapour enters the vapour separator and any liquid fuel runs back to the tank. Two roll over valves are fitted in the fuel tank vapour lines. These valves prevent liquid fuel entering the vapour separator if the vehicle rolls over. The advanced EVAPS system has no two way valve, so vapour is free to flow to the EVAP canister, where it is stored in the canister's activated charcoal element. When the correct engine operating conditions are met, the Engine Control Module (ECM) opens the EVAP canister purge valve and vapour is drawn from the canister, into the plenum chamber to be burned in the engine. Fresh air is drawn into the canister through the EVAP canister vent solenoid to take up the volume of displaced vapour. During normal operating conditions, and when the engine is switched off, the vent solenoid remains open and the fuel tank is free to breath through the EVAP canister. If the vent solenoid should fail, or the main vapour line becomes blocked, excess pressure is vented to atmosphere through a valve in the fuel filler cap. Similarly, the cap vent valve will open to prevent the tank collapsing if excessive vacuum is present.

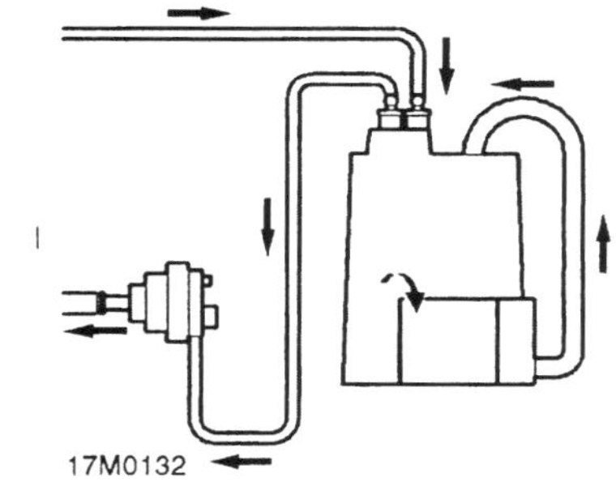
17M0132

When the temperature of fuel in the tank reduces, pressure also reduces and vapour must be drawn back into the tank. Fresh air is drawn into the canister, through the open vent solenoid, to take up the displaced volume.

An anti-trickle fill valve is fitted to the filler neck in the line between the tank and EVAP canister. The function of this valve is to prevent the user overfilling the tank by trickling fuel into the neck, thereby preserving the vapour space in the tank to allow for fuel expansion during hot weather.

The valve creates a blockage in the vent line during the fuel filling process. The valve is operated by the action of inserting the fuel filler gun. With the valve in the closed position, air displaced during filling exits the tank only through the internal fill breather. When the fuel level reaches the level of the fill breather, the filler neck fills with fuel, shutting off the filler gun.

The breather ports from the EVAP canister are located high up in the engine bay (CVS unit on NAS vehicles, snorkel tubes on ROW vehicles), to prevent water ingress during vehicle wading.

The advanced evaporative loss control system used on NAS vehicles is similar to the standard system, but also includes a CVS unit and an in-tank pressure sensor to monitor the pressure build-up for determining whether leaks are present.

The function of the CVS unit is to block the atmospheric vent side of the EVAP canister to enable the ECM to carry out the EVAP system leak check. The leak check is only carried out when the vehicle is stationary and the engine is running at idle speed. The test uses the natural rate of fuel evaporation and engine manifold depression. Failure of the leak check will result in illumination of the Malfunction Indicator Lamp (MIL).

The fuel evaporation leak detection is included as part of the On-Board Diagnostics (OBD) strategy and checks for leaks greater than 1mm (0.04 in.) in diameter. During checking, the vent and purge lines are closed for a reference check on system pressure to be determined. Then the purge valve is opened, exposing the fuel tank and vent lines to engine vacuum. The ECM then checks the signal from the fuel tank pressure sensor for any pressure increase (i.e loss of vacuum) which would indicate a leakage.

Any fuel evaporation system leaks which occur between the output of the purge valve and the connection to the inlet manifold cannot be determined using this test, but this type of fault will be detected through the fuelling adaption diagnostics.

EXHAUST EMISSION CONTROL COMPONENTS - (from 99MY)

Catalytic converters

The catalytic converters are located in each of the front pipes from the exhaust manifolds. The catalytic converter's housings are fabricated from stainless steel and are fully welded at all joints. Each catalytic converter contains two elements of an extruded ceramic substrate which is formed into a honeycomb of small cells with a density of 62 cells / cm^2. The ceramic element is coated with a special surface treatment called 'washcoat' which increases the surface area of the catalyst element by approximately 7000 times. A coating is applied to the washcoat which contains the precious elements Platinum (Pt), Palladium (PD) and Rhodium(Rh) in the following relative concentrations: **1 Pt : 21.6 PD : 1 Rh.**

The metallic coating of platinum and palladium oxidize the carbon monoxide and hydrocarbons and convert them into water (H_2O) and carbon dioxide (CO_2). The coating of rhodium removes the oxygen from nitrogen oxide (NO_x) and converts it into nitrogen (N_2).

NOTE: Catalytic converters for NAS low emission vehicles (LEVS) from 2000MY have active constituents of Palladium and Rhodium only. The proportion of active constituents are 14 PD: 1 Rh, and the Palladium coating is used to oxidise the carbon monoxide and hydrocarbons in the exhaust gas.

CAUTION: Catalytic converters contain ceramic material which is very fragile. Avoid heavy impacts on the converter casing.

CAUTION: Serious damage to the catalytic converter will occur if leaded fuel or a lower octane number fuel than recommended is used. The fuel tank filler neck is designed to accomodate only unleaded fuel pump nozzles.

WARNING: To prevent personal injury from a hot exhaust system, do not attempt to disconnect any components until the exhaust system has cooled down.

Heated oxygen (HO_2S) sensors

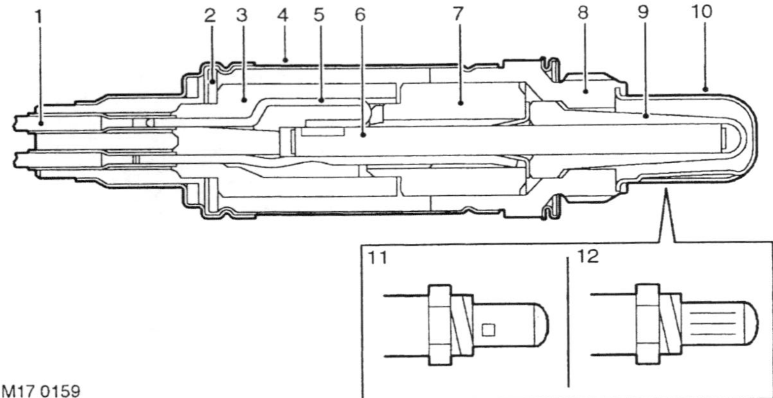

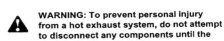

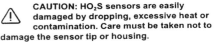

M17 0159

1. Connection cable
2. Disc spring
3. Ceramic support tube
4. Protective sleeve
5. Clamp connection for heating element
6. Heating element
7. Contact element
8. Sensor housing
9. Active sensor ceramic
10. Protective tube
11. Post-catalytic converter sensor (NAS spec. only)
12. Pre-catalytic converter sensor

The heated oxygen sensor is an integral part of the exhaust emission control system and is used in conjunction with the catalytic converters and the engine management control ECM to ensure that the air:fuel mixture ratio stays around the stoichiometric ideal, where the catalytic converters are most effective. Combinations of four (NAS only) or two heated oxygen sensors are used in the exhaust system, dependent on market legislation.

The heated oxygen sensors are screwed into threaded mountings welded into the front exhaust pipes at suitable locations. They are used to detect the level of residual oxygen in the exhaust gas to provide an instantaneous indication of whether combustion is complete. By positioning sensors in the stream of exhaust gases from each separate bank of the exhaust manifold, the engine management system is better able to control the fuelling requirements on each bank independently of the other. This facilitates much closer control of the air:fuel ratio and optimises catalytic converter efficiency.

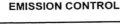

CAUTION: HO_2S sensors are easily damaged by dropping, excessive heat or contamination. Care must be taken not to damage the sensor tip or housing.

The HO_2S sensors consist of a ceramic body (Galvanic cell) which is practically a pure oxygen-ion conductor made from a mixed oxide of zirconium and yttrium. The ceramic is then coated with gas-permeable platinum, which when heated to a sufficiently high temperature (above 350°C) generates a voltage which is proportional to the oxygen content in the exhaust gas stream.

The sensor is protected by an outer tube with a restricted flow opening to prevent the sensor's ceramic from being cooled by low temperature gases at start up. The pre-catalytic sensors are identified by three slots in the protective tube, whereas the post-catalytic sensors have four square indentations and a hole in the end of the protective tube (NAS only). The post-catalytic sensors have improved signal quality, but a slower response rate. **It is important not to confuse the sensor signal pins; the signal pins are gold plated, whilst the heater supply pins are tinned, mixing them up will cause contamination and adversely affect system performance.**

The HO_2S sensors should be treated with extreme care, since the ceramic material within them can be easily cracked if they are dropped, banged or over-torqued. The sensors should be torqued to the recommended values indicated in the repair procedures. Apply anti-seize compound to the sensor's threads when refitting.

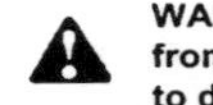

WARNING: Some types of anti-seize compound used in service are a potential health hazard. Avoid skin contact.

WARNING: To prevent personal injury from a hot exhaust system, do not attempt to disconnect any components until the exhaust system has cooled down.

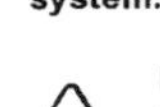

CAUTION: Do not allow anti-seize compound to come into contact with the tip of the sensor or enter the exhaust system.

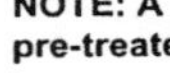

NOTE: A new HO_2S sensor is supplied with pre-treated anti-seize compound.

SECONDARY AIR INJECTION SYSTEM COMPONENTS

Secondary air injection (SAI) pump

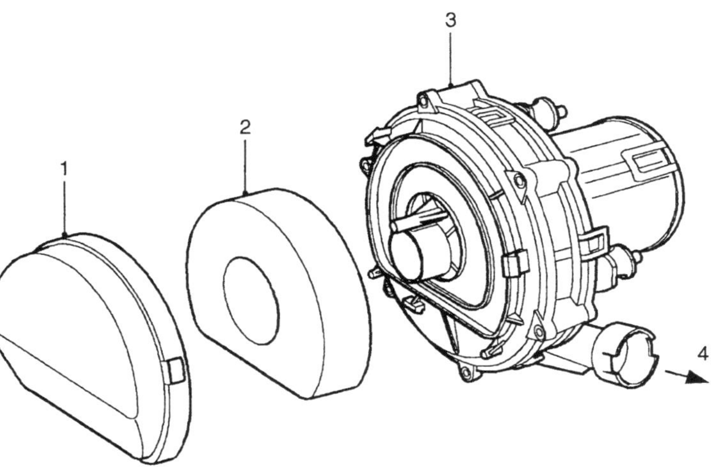

M17 0214

1. SAI pump cover
2. Foam filter
3. SAI pump
4. Pressurised air to exhaust manifolds

The SAI pump is attached to a bracket at the RH side of the engine compartment. The pump is electrically powered from a 12V battery supply via a dedicated relay and supplies approximately 35 kg/hr of air when the vehicle is at idle in Neutral / Park on a start from 20°C (68°F).

Air is drawn into the pump through vents in its front cover and is then passed through a foam filter to remove particulates before air injection. The air is delivered to the exhaust manifold on each side of the engine through a combination of plastic and metal pipes.

The air delivery pipe is a flexible plastic type, and is connected to the air pump outlet via a plastic quick-fit connector. The other end of the flexible plastic pipe connects to the fixed metal pipework via a short rubber hose. The metal delivery pipe has a fabricated T-piece included where the air is split for delivery to each exhaust manifold via the vacuum operated SAI control valves.

The pipes from the T-piece to each of the SAI control valves are approximately the same length, so that the pressure and mass of the air delivered to each bank will be equal. The ends of the pipes are connected to the inlet port of each SAI control valve through short rubber hose connections.

The T-piece is mounted at the rear of the engine (by the ignition coils) and features a welded mounting bracket which is fixed to the engine by two studs and nuts.

The foam filter in the air intake of the SAI pump provides noise reduction and protects the pump from damage due to particulate contamination. In addition, the pump is fitted on rubber mountings to help prevent noise generated by pump operation from being transmitted through the vehicle body into the passenger compartment.

The SAI pump has an integral thermal cut-out switch, to stop pump operation when the pump overheats. The pump automatically enters a 'soak period' between operations, to allow the pump motor a cooling off period.

Secondary air injection (SAI) pump relay

The secondary air injection pump relay is located in the engine compartment fusebox. The engine control module (ECM) is used to control the operation of the SAI pump via the SAI pump relay. Power to the SAI relay contacts is via fuselink 2 which is located in the engine compartment fusebox.

Secondary air injection (SAI) vacuum solenoid valve

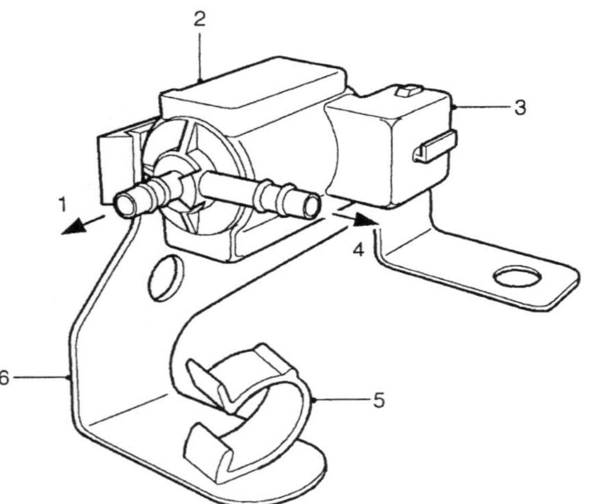

M17 0215

1. Vacuum port to intake manifold (via vacuum reservoir)
2. SAI vacuum solenoid valve
3. Electrical connector
4. Vacuum port to vacuum operated SAI control valves
5. Purge valve clip
6. Mounting bracket

The SAI vacuum solenoid valve is located at the rear LH side of the engine, mounted on a bracket with the EVAP system purge valve and electrically controlled by the ECM.

Vacuum to the SAI vacuum solenoid valve is provided from the intake manifold depression via a vacuum reservoir. A small bore vacuum hose with rubber elbow connections at each end provides the vacuum route between the vacuum reservoir and SAI vacuum solenoid valve. A similar hose with a larger size elbow connector, connects the SAI vacuum solenoid valve to the SAI control valves on each side of the engine via an intermediate connection. The SAI vacuum solenoid valve port to the SAI control valves is located at a right angle to the port to the vacuum reservoir.

The intermediate connection in the vacuum supply line splits the vacuum equally between the two SAI control valves and is located midpoint in front of the inlet manifold. All vacuum hose lines are protected by flexible plastic sleeving.

Electrical connection to the SAI vacuum solenoid valve is via a 2-pin connector. A 12V electrical power supply to the valve is provided via the Main relay and Fuse 26 in the engine compartment fusebox. The ground connection is via the ECM which controls the SAI vacuum solenoid valve operation. **Note that the harness connector to the SAI solenoid valve is grey, and must not be confused with the harness connector to the EVAP system purge valve which is black.**

The ECM switches on the SAI vacuum solenoid valve at the same time as initiating SAI pump operation. When the SAI vacuum solenoid valve is open, a steady vacuum supply is allowed through to open the two vacuum operated SAI control valves. When the ECM breaks the earth path to the SAI vacuum solenoid valve, the valve closes and immediately shuts off the vacuum supply to the two SAI control valves at the same time as SAI pump operation is terminated.

SAI control valves

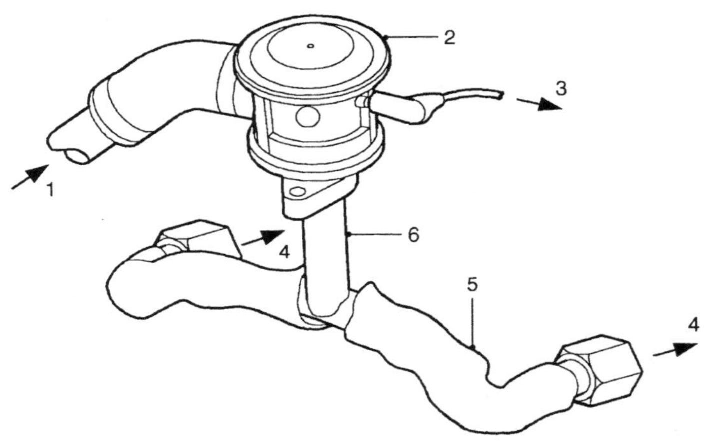

M17 0216

1. Pressurised air from SAI pump
2. Vacuum operated SAI control valve
3. Vacuum hose from SAI vacuum solenoid valve
4. Pressurised air to exhaust manifold
5. Protective heat sleeving
6. Air delivery pipe to exhaust manifold

The SAI control valves are located on brackets at each side of the engine.

The air injection supply pipes connect to a large bore port on the side of each SAI control valve via a short rubber connection hose. A small bore vacuum port is located on each SAI control valve at the opposite side to the air injection supply port. The vacuum supply to each vacuum operated SAI control valve is through small bore nylon hoses from the SAI vacuum solenoid valve. An intermediate connector is included in the vacuum supply line to split the vacuum applied to each SAI control valve, so that both valves open and close simultaneously.

When a vacuum is applied to the SAI control valves, the valve opens to allow the pressurised air from the SAI pump through to the exhaust manifolds. The injection air is output from each SAI control valve through a port in the bottom of each unit. A metal pipe connects between the output port of each SAI control valve and each exhaust manifold via an intermediate T-piece. The T-piece splits the pressurised air delivered to ports at the outer side of the two centre exhaust ports on each cylinder head. The pipes between the T-piece and the exhaust manifold are enclosed in thermal sleeving to protect the surrounding components from the very high heat of the exhaust gas, particularly at high engine speeds and loads.

When the SAI vacuum solenoid valve is de-energised, the vacuum supply line opens to atmosphere, this causes the vacuum operated valves to close automatically and completely to prevent further air injection.

Vacuum reservoir

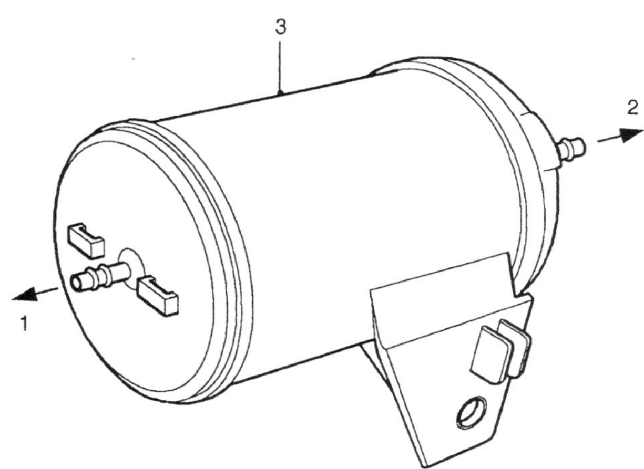

M17 0218

1. Vacuum port to SAI vacuum solenoid valve
2. Vacuum port to intake manifold (one-way valve end)
3. Vacuum reservoir

A vacuum reservoir is included in the vacuum supply line between the intake manifold and the SAI vacuum solenoid valve. The vacuum reservoir contains a one-way valve, to stop depression leaking back towards the intake manifold side. The reservoir holds a constant vacuum so that the SAI control valves open instantaneously as soon as the SAI vacuum solenoid valve is energised.

The vacuum reservoir is a plastic canister construction located on the SAI pump bracket at the RH side of the engine compartment. It is important to ensure the reservoir is fitted in the correct orientation, and the correct vacuum hoses are attached to their corresponding ports. The one-way valve end of the reservoir is the cap end which connects to the inlet manifold.

A small bore nylon hose is used to connect the one-way valve end of the vacuum reservoir to a port on the RH side of the inlet manifold. A further small bore nylon hose connects between the other port on the vacuum reservoir and a port on the front of the SAI vacuum solenoid valve.

EVAPORATIVE EMISSION SYSTEM CONTROL COMPONENTS - (from 99MY)

Purge valve

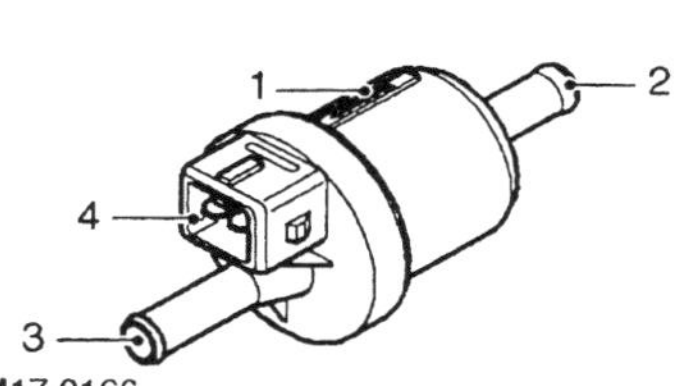

M17 0166

1. Direction of flow indicator
2. Inlet port - from EVAP canister
3. Outlet port - to inlet manifold
4. Harness connector

The EVAP canister purge valve is located in the engine bay at the LH side of the engine intake manifold. On NAS vehicles with secondary air injection, the purge valve is fixed to a metal bracket together with the SAI vacuum solenoid valve; the purge valve is fixed to the bracket by two plastic clips.

The outlet side of the purge valve is connected to a stub pipe on the back of the inlet manifold plenum chamber (through a combination of rubber and nylon pipes). The connector to the plenum chamber stub pipe is a quick-release type, plastic 90°female elbow. A short hose/pipe is connected between the inlet side of the purge valve and a service port.

The purge valve has a plastic housing, and a directional arrow is moulded onto the side of the casing to indicate the direction of flow. The head of the arrow points to the outlet side of the valve which connects to the plenum chamber.

A service port is connected in line between the EVAP canister and the inlet side of the purge valve and is rated at 1 psi maximum regulated pressure. The service port must be mounted horizontally and is located close to the bulkhead at the rear left hand side of the engine bay.

The service port is used for pressure testing using specialist nitrogen test equipment for localising the source of leaks. A pipe/hose from the inlet side of the service port connects to a quick-fit connector that mates to the purge pipe leading to the EVAP canister beneath the vehicle.

Purge valve operation is controlled by the engine control module (ECM). The purge valve has a two-pin electrical connector which links to the ECM via the engine harness. **Note that the harness connector to the SAI solenoid valve is grey, and must not be confused with the harness connector to the EVAP system purge valve which is black.**

One pin of the connector is the power supply source and the other is the switched earth from the ECM (pulse width modulated (PWM) signal) which is used to control the purge valve operation time.

When the purge valve is earthed by the ECM, the valve opens to allow hydrocarbons stored in the EVAP canister to be purged to the engine inlet manifold for combustion.

If the purge valve breaks or becomes stuck in the open or closed position, the EVAP system will cease to function and there are no default measures available. The ECM will store the fault in memory and illuminate the MIL warning lamp. If the purge valve is stuck in the open position, a rich air:fuel mixture is likely to result at the intake manifold, this could cause the engine to misfire and fuelling adaptions will change. The following failure modes are possible:

- Sticking valve
- Valve blocked
- Connector or harness wiring fault (open or short circuit)
- Valve stuck open

Canister Vent Solenoid (CVS) unit - (NAS only)

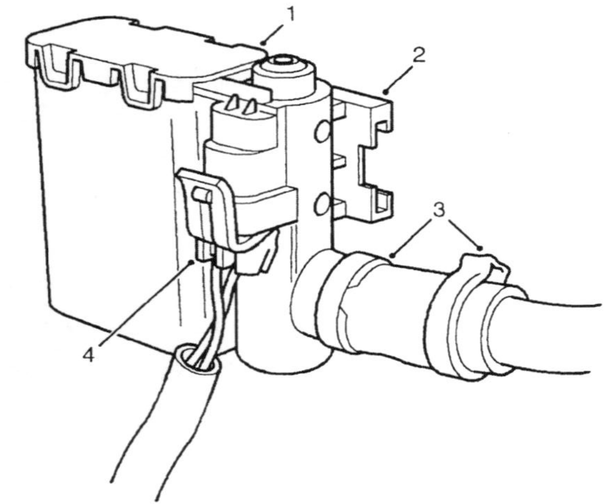

M17 0165

1. CVS unit
2. Mounting bracket
3. Spring clips to pipe from EVAP canister
4. Harness connector

The CVS unit is mounted at the rear right hand side of the engine bay on a slide-on bracket. The vent pipe from the EVAP canister is connected to a stub pipe on the CVS unit via a short rubber hose. The rubber hose is connected to the CVS unit and plastic pipe by two metal band clips. A two-pin connector links to the engine management ECM via the engine harness for solenoid control. One wire is for the voltage feed, the other is the valve drive line to the ECM. The solenoid is operated when the ECM grounds the circuit.

The valve is normally open, allowing any build up of air pressure within the evaporation system to escape, whilst retaining the environmentally harmful hydrocarbons in the EVAP canister.

When the ECM is required to run a fuel evaporation system test, the CVS valve is energised and closes to seal the system. The ECM is then able to measure the pressure in the EVAP system using the fuel tank pressure sensor. The ECM performs electrical integrity checks on the CVS valve to determine wiring or power supply faults. The ECM can also detect a valve blockage if the signal from the fuel tank pressure sensor indicates a depressurising fuel tank while the CVS valve should be open to atmosphere. The following failure modes are possible:

- Connector or wiring harness fault (open or short circuit)
- Valve stuck open or shut
- Valve blocked

EVAP canister

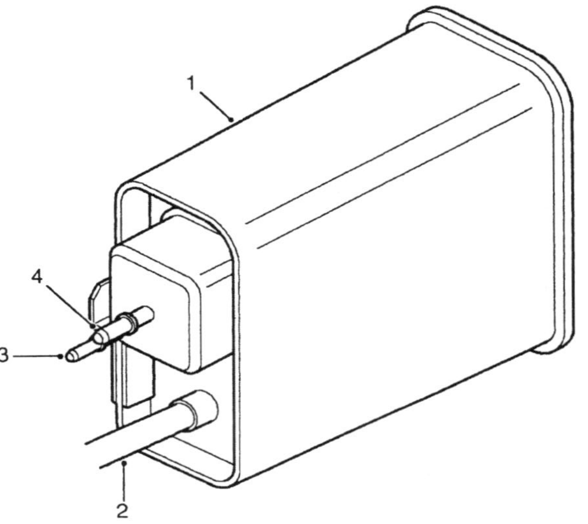

M17 0164

1. EVAP canister
2. Port to breather tube (CVS unit on NAS vehicles)
3. Port - vent line from fuel tank
4. Port - purge line

The EVAP canister is mounted on a bracket which is fitted beneath the vehicle on the RH side of the chassis. The ports of the EVAP canister face towards the rear of the vehicle. Each EVAP canister port has a moulded inscription next to it for identification of the 'purge', 'tank' and 'air' connections.

The NAS and ROW EVAP canisters are of similar appearance, but use charcoal of different consistency. The ROW vehicles use granular charcoal of 11 bwc (butane working capacity) and NAS vehicles use pelletised charcoal with a higher absorption capacity of 15 bwc. All canisters are of rectangular shape and have purge foam retention.

The vent line from the fuel tank to the EVAP canister connects to the vent port on the canister by means of a straight quick-fit connector. The vent line terminates in a quick-fit connector at the fuel filler.

The nylon pipe to atmosphere connects to a port on the EVAP canister via a short rubber hose secured with metal band clips. The atmosphere end of the pipe terminates in a quick-fit connector to the pipe leading to the CVS unit on NAS vehicles and a snorkel tube situated behind the engine at the bulkhead on ROW vehicles. The bore of the nylon breather pipe used on NAS vehicles is larger than that used on ROW vehicles.

The purge line from the EVAP canister is connected to the inlet manifold plenum after the throttle body via a purge valve and service port. The pipe between the EVAP canister and the purge valve is routed over the transmission and into the LH side of the engine bay. The pipe clips to the purge port on the EVAP canister by means of an elbowed quick-fit connector and the connection is covered by a rubber seal which is held in position on the port stub pipe.

The pipes are clipped at various points along the pipe runs and tied together with tie straps at suitable points along the runs.

Fuel tank pressure sensor - (NAS only)

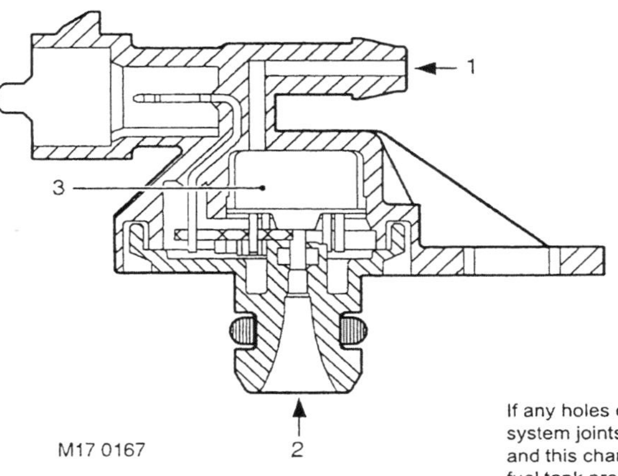

1. Ambient pressure
2. Tank pressure
3. Sensor cell

A fuel tank pressure sensor is fitted to NAS vehicles with advanced EVAPS, it is used by the ECM during an EVAP system leak test, in accordance with the on board diagnostics (OBD) strategy.

The fuel tank pressure sensor is located in the top flange of the fuel tank sender/ fuel pump module and is a non-serviceable item (i.e. if the sensor becomes defective, the entire fuel tank sender unit must be replaced). The fuel tank pressure sensor connector is accessible through the fuel pump access hatch in the rear floor of the vehicle.

The pressure sensor is basically a piezo-resistive sensor element with associated circuitry for signal amplification and temperature compensation. The active surface is exposed to ambient pressure by an opening in the cap and by the reference port. It is protected from humidity by a silicon gel. The tank pressure is fed up to a pressure port at the rear side of the diaphragm.

Fuel evaporation leaks are diagnosed by the ECM monitoring the sensor for a drop in vacuum pressure during test conditions. The EVAP system is sealed by the CVS valve and purge valve after a vacuum has been set up in the system from the intake manifold while the purge valve is open and the CVS valve is closed.

If any holes or leaks are present at the evaporation system joints, the vacuum pressure will gradually drop and this change in pressure will be detected by the fuel tank pressure sensor. The system is sensitive enough to detect leaks down to 1mm (0.04 in.) in diameter.

The fuel tank pressure sensor is part of the NAS OBD system, a component failure will not be noticed by the driver, but if the ECM detects a fault, it will be stored in the diagnostic memory and the MIL light will be illuminated on the instrument pack. Possible failures are listed below:

- Damaged or blocked sensor
- Harness/connector faulty
- Sensor earthing problem
- Open circuit
- Short circuit to battery voltage
- Short circuit to ground
- ECM fault

Fuel vapour separator

The fuel vapour separator is located under the right rear wheel arch next to the filler neck and protected by the wheel arch lining. The connections to the separator unit are quick release devices at the end of the flexible hoses which connect the fuel tank to the inlet side of the separator and the outlet of the separator to the evaporation vent line.

TESTING EVAPORATIVE EMISSION CONTROL - PRE ADVANCED EVAPS

The following pressure test procedure is intended to provide a method for ensuring that the system does not leak excessively and will effectively control evaporative emissions.

Equipment required.

Nitrogen cylinder (compressed air may be used to pressure the system when there has NEVER been fuel present in the fuel or evaporative control systems).

Water manometer 0 - 100 cm (0 - 30" H2O or more).

Pipework and a "T" piece.

Method.

1. Ensure that there is at least two gallons of fuel in the petrol tank unless there has never been any fuel in the system.
2. Disconnect, at the EVAP canister, the pipe to the fuel tank vapour separator.
3. Connect this pipe to the nitrogen cylinder and the water manometer using the "T" piece.
4. Pressurize the system to between 67.3 and 70.0 cm (26.5 and 27.5 inches) of water, allow the reading to stabilize, then turn off the nitrogen supply.
5. Measure the pressure drop within a period of 2 minutes 30 seconds. If the drop is greater than 6.3 cm (2.5 inches) of water the system has failed the test. Note that a fully sealed system will show a slight increase in pressure.
6. Should the system fail the test, maintain the pressure in the system and apply a soap solution round all the joints and connections until bubbles appear to reveal the source of the leak.
7. Repeat the test and if successful, dismantle the test equipment and reconnect the pipe to the EVAP canister.

LEAK DETECTION PROCEDURE - ADVANCED EVAPS

1. Connect TestBook to the vehicle and confirm that the fault code(s) displayed relate to an EVAP system fault.
2. Examine components in fuel and EVAP system for damage or poorly connected joints.
3. Repair or replace components to rectify any faults found, then reset the Malfunction Indicator Lamp (MIL) using TestBook.
4. Carry out Drive Cycle, ***See this section.***
5. Using TestBook confirm that the Evaporative Loss Control (ELC) Inspection and Maintenance (IM) flag has cleared. This procedure should confirm that the ELC test was carried out during the drive cycle and that the fault was cured.
6. If the IM flag is still shown, use TestBook to interrogate the engine management system to ascertain which of the following situations exists:

- If a fault code is shown, then further investigation is required, proceed to the next step.
- If the IM flag is still shown, but no faults are indicated the conditions for the ELC check have not been met and the drive cycle must be repeated.

7. Connect the EVAP Diagnostic Station to the service port and carry out the procedures given in the operating instructions supplied with the equipment.

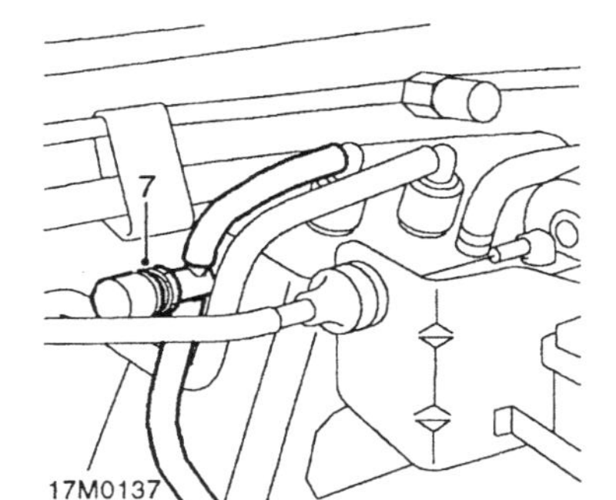

8. Rectify faults indicated by the EVAP Diagnostic Station and return to step 4.

DRIVE CYCLES - up to 99MY

1. Switch on ignition for 30 seconds.
2. Ensure that coolant temperature is less than 30 °C (86 °F).
3. Start engine and allow to idle for 2 minutes.
4. Perform 2 light accelerations 0 to 35 mph (0 to 56 km/h) with light pedal pressure.
5. Perform 2 medium accelerations 0 to 45 mph (0 to 72 km/h) with moderate pedal pressure.
6. Perform 2 hard accelerations 0 to 55 mph (0 to 88 km/h) with heavy pedal pressure.
7. Cruise at 60 mph (96 km/h) for 5 minutes.
8. Cruise at 50 mph (80 km/h) for 5 minutes.
9. Cruise at 35 mph (56 km/h) for 5 minutes.
10. Allow engine to idle for 2 minutes.
11. Connect TestBook and check for fault codes.

DRIVE CYCLES - from 99MY

The following are the Testbook drive cycles

Drive cycle A:

1. Switch on the ignition for 30 seconds.
2. Ensure engine coolant temperature is less than 60°C (140°F).
3. Start the engine and allow to idle for 2 minutes.
4. Connect Testbook and check for fault codes.

Drive cycle B:

1. Switch ignition on for 30 seconds.
2. Ensure engine coolant temperature is less than 60°C (140°F).
3. Start the engine and allow to idle for 2 minutes.
4. Perform two light accelerations (0 to 35 mph) (0 to 60 km/h) with light pedal pressure).
5. Perform two medium accelerations (0 to 45 mph) (0 to 70 km/h) with moderate pedal pressure).
6. Perform two hard accelerations (0 to 55 mph) (0 to 90 km/h) with heavy pedal pressure).
7. Allow engine to idle for two minutes.
8. Connect Testbook and check for fault codes.

Drive cycle C1 (vehicles without advanced EVAPS):

1. Switch ignition on for 30 seconds.
2. Ensure engine coolant temperature is less than 60°C (140°F).
3. Start the engine and allow to idle for 2 minutes.
4. Perform two light accelerations (0 to 35 mph) (0 to 60 km/h) with light pedal pressure).
5. Perform two medium accelerations (0 to 45 mph) (0 to 70 km/h) with moderate pedal pressure).
6. Perform two hard accelerations (0 to 55 mph) (0 to 90 km/h) with heavy pedal pressure).
7. Cruise at 60 mph (100 km/h) for 5 minutes.
8. Cruise at 50 mph (80 km/h) for 5 minutes.
9. Allow engine to idle for 2 minutes.
10. Connect Testbook and check for fault codes.

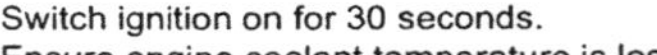

Drive cycle C2 (vehicles with advanced EVAPS):

1. Switch ignition on for 30 seconds.
2. Ensure engine coolant temperature is less than 60°C (140°F).
3. Start the engine and allow to idle for 2 minutes.
4. Perform two light accelerations (0 to 35 mph) (0 to 60 km/h) with light pedal pressure).
5. Perform two medium accelerations (0 to 45 mph) (0 to 70 km/h) with moderate pedal pressure).
6. Perform two hard accelerations (0 to 55 mph) (0 to 90 km/h) with heavy pedal pressure).
7. Cruise at 60 mph (100 km/h) for 8 minutes.
8. Cruise at 50 mph (80 km/h) for 3 minutes.
9. Allow engine to idle for 3 minutes.
10. Connect Testbook and check for fault codes.

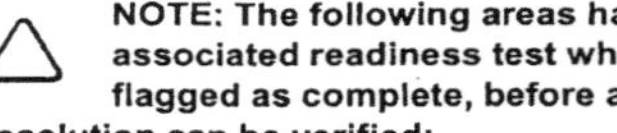

NOTE: The following areas have an associated readiness test which must be flagged as complete, before a problem resolution can be verified:

- *Catalytic converter fault;*
- *Evaporative loss system fault;*
- *HO_2S sensor fault;*
- *HO_2S sensor heater fault.*

When carrying out a drive cycle C to determine a fault in the above areas, select the readiness test icon to verify that the test has been flagged as complete.

Drive cycle D:

1. Switch ignition on for 30 seconds.
2. Ensure engine coolant temperature is less than 35°C (95°F).
3. Start the engine and allow to idle for 2 minutes.
4. Perform two light accelerations (0 to 35 mph) (0 to 60 km/h) with light pedal pressure).
5. Perform two medium accelerations (0 to 45 mph) (0 to 70 km/h) with moderate pedal pressure).
6. Perform two hard accelerations (0 to 55 mph) (0 to 90 km/h) with heavy pedal pressure).
7. Cruise at 60 mph (100 km/h) for 5 minutes.
8. Cruise at 50 mph (80 km/h) for 5 minutes.
9. Cruise at 35 mph (60 km/h) for 5 minutes.
10. Allow engine to idle for 2 minutes.
11. Connect Testbook and check for fault codes.

Drive cycle E:

1. Ensure the fuel tank is more than a quarter full.
2. Carry out drive cycle A.
3. Switch off ignition.
4. Leave vehicle undisturbed for 20 minutes.
5. Switch on ignition.
6. Connect Testbook and check for fault codes.

CATALYST HEAT SHIELDS

Service repair no - 17.50.05

Remove

1. Remove exhaust front pipe. ***See MANIFOLD AND EXHAUST SYSTEM, Repair.***
2. Remove 5 retaining washers securing heat shield to floor pan studs.

17M7002

3. Remove heat shield. Discard retaining washers.

Refit

4. Reverse removal procedure.

EVAP CANISTER - PRE-ADVANCED EVAPS

Service repair no - 17.15.13

Remove

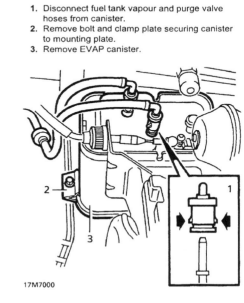

1. Disconnect fuel tank vapour and purge valve hoses from canister.
2. Remove bolt and clamp plate securing canister to mounting plate.
3. Remove EVAP canister.

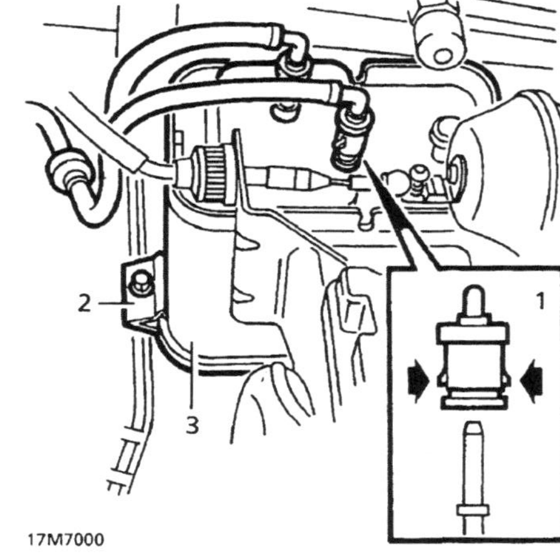

17M7000

Refit

4. Reverse removal procedure.

EVAP CANISTER - ADVANCED EVAPS (up to 99MY)

Service repair no - 17.15.13

Remove

1. Disconnect battery earth lead.

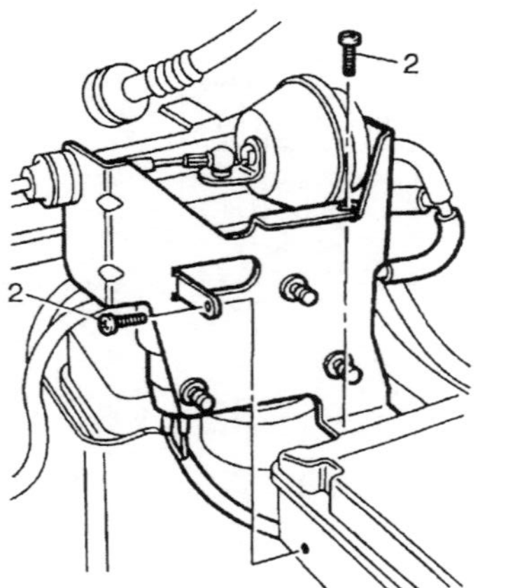

17M0120

2. Remove 2 screws securing cruise control actuator bracket to suspension control box.
3. Position cruise control actuator assembly aside.

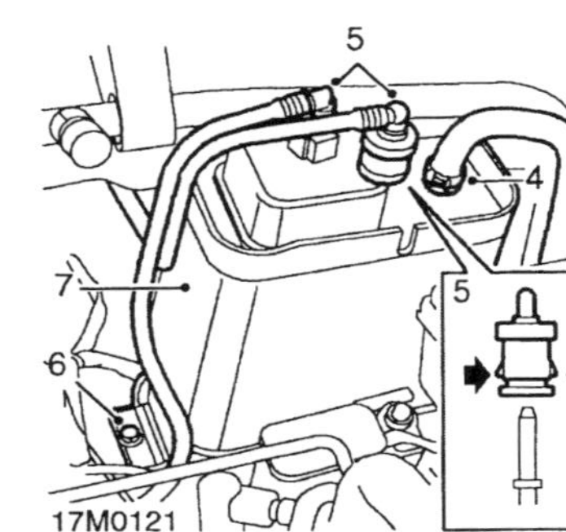

17M0121

4. Release clip securing vent solenoid hose to cannister and disconnect hose.
5. Release vent and purge quickfit connectors from canister.
6. Remove bolt securing canister to mounting bracket and collect clamp plate.
7. Remove canister.

Refit

8. Position canister to mounting bracket.
9. Position clamp plate and secure canister to bracket with bolt.
10. Connect purge and vent hoses to cannister, ensuring that quickfit connectors correctly engage.
11. Connect vent solenoid hose to canister and secure clip.
12. Align cruise control actuator bracket to suspension control box and secure with screws.
13. Connect battery earth lead.

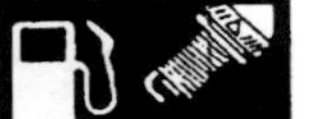

EVAP CANISTER - from 99MY

Service repair no - 17.15.13

Remove

1. Release fixings and remove battery cover.
2. Disconnect battery earth lead.
3. Raise vehicle on lift.

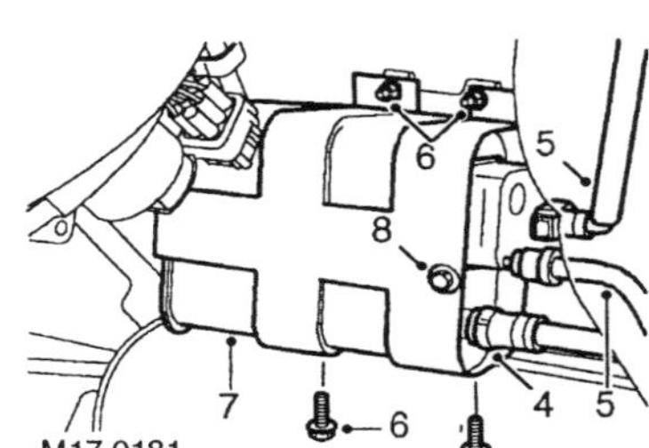

M17 0181

4. Release clip and disconnect air hose from canister.
5. Release and remove purge and tank pipes from canister.
6. Remove 2 nuts and 2 bolts securing EVAP canister to chassis.
7. Remove EVAP canister.
8. Remove bolt securing bracket to canister and remove canister.

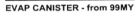

CAUTION: Plug the connections.

Refit

9. Fit bracket to canister and secure with bolt.
10. Fit canister to chassis and secure with nuts and bolts.
11. Ensure all connections are clean.
12. Connect purge and tank pipes to canister.
13. Connect air hose to canister and secure hose with clip.
14. Lower vehicle.
15. Connect battery earth lead.
16. Fit battery cover and secure with fixings.

EVAP CANISTER - LEVS

Service repair no - 17.15.13

Remove

1. Raise vehicle on 4 post ramp.

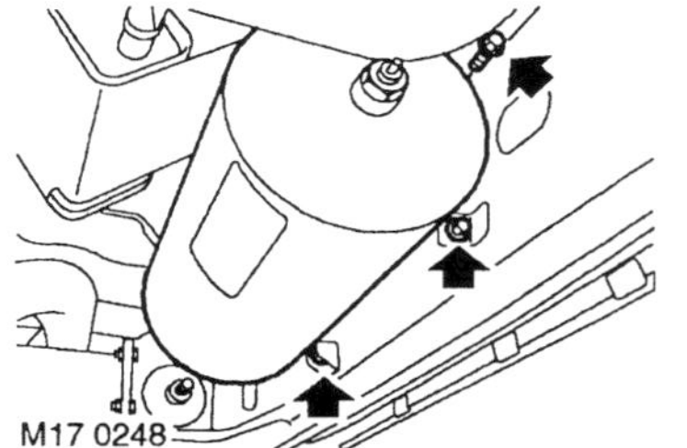

M17 0248

2. Remove 3 bolts securing air suspension reservoir to mounting brackets.
3. Release air suspension reservoir and carefully move aside.

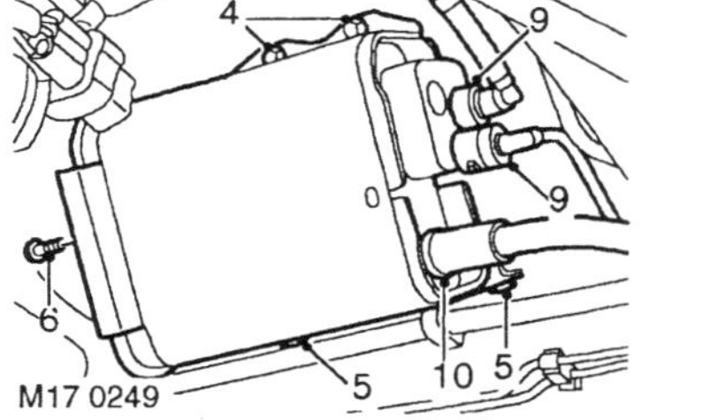

M17 0249

4. Remove 2 bolts securing EVAP canister mounting bracket to body.
5. Remove 2 nuts securing EVAP canister mounting bracket to body.
6. Remove bolt securing EVAP canister to mounting bracket. Collect nut and mounting bracket.
7. Remove mounting bracket.
8. Position cloth to absorb any fuel spillage.
9. Release purge and tank vent pipes from EVAP canister.
10. Remove clip securing CVS valve pipe to EVAP canister.
11. Release pipe from EVAP canister and remove canister.

CAUTION: Plug the connections.

Refit

12. Remove plugs and ensure all connections are clean.
13. Connect CVS valve pipe to EVAP canister and secure with clip.
14. Connect purge and tank vent pipes to EVAP canister.
15. Position mounting bracket to EVAP canister and secure with bolt.
16. Position mounting bracket to body and secure with nuts.
17. Fit and tighten bolts securing mounting bracket to body.
18. Lower vehicle.

PURGE VALVE - up to 97MY

Service repair no - 17.15.39

Remove

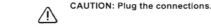

1. Disconnect multiplug from purge valve.
2. Disconnect hoses from EVAP canister and ram pipe housing.
3. Remove bolt securing valve to shock absorber turret. Remove purge valve.

17M7001

Refit

4. Reverse removal procedure.

PURGE VALVE - 97MY to 99MY

Service repair no - 17.15.39

Remove

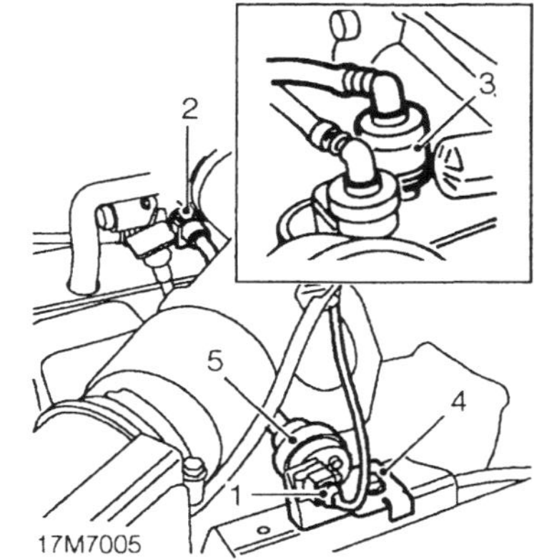

17M7005

1. Disconnect multiplug from purge valve.
2. Depress quick release connector tabs and disconnect hose from throttle housing.
3. Depress quick release connector tabs and disconnect hose from EVAP canister.
4. Remove bolt securing purge valve to shock absorber turret.
5. Remove purge valve.

Refit

6. Position purge valve to shock absorber turret.
7. Fit and tighten bolt securing purge valve to shock absorber turret.
8. Clean hose connections.
9. Connect hoses to EVAP canister and throttle housing.

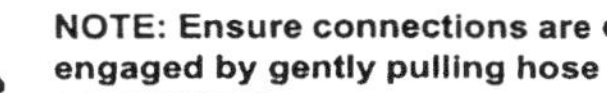

NOTE: Ensure connections are correctly engaged by gently pulling hose connections.

10. Connect multiplug to purge valve.

PURGE VALVE - from 99MY

Service repair no - 17.15.39

Remove

1. Release fixings and remove battery cover.
2. Disconnect battery earth lead.

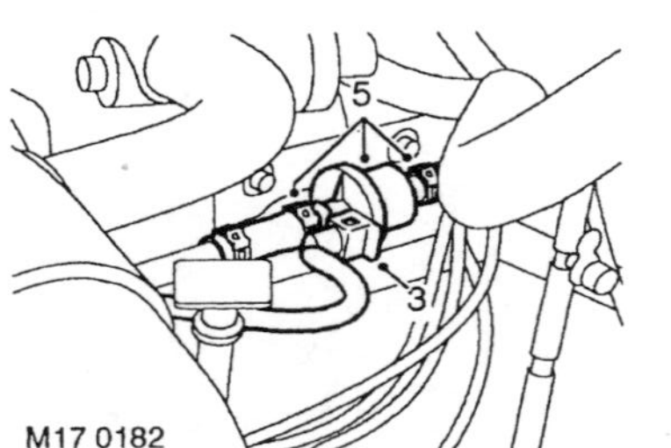

M17 0182

3. Disconnect multiplug from purge control valve.
4. Release purge control valve and hoses from clips.
5. Disconnect hoses from purge control valve and remove valve.

CAUTION: Plug the connections.

Refit

6. Position purge control valve, connect hoses and secure with clips.
7. Fit purge control valve and hoses to clips.
8. Connect multiplug to purge control valve.
9. Connect battery earth lead.
10. Fit battery cover and secure with fixings.

EVAP CANISTER VENT SOLENOID - up to 99MY

Service repair no - 17.15.47

Remove

1. Disconnect battery earth lead.

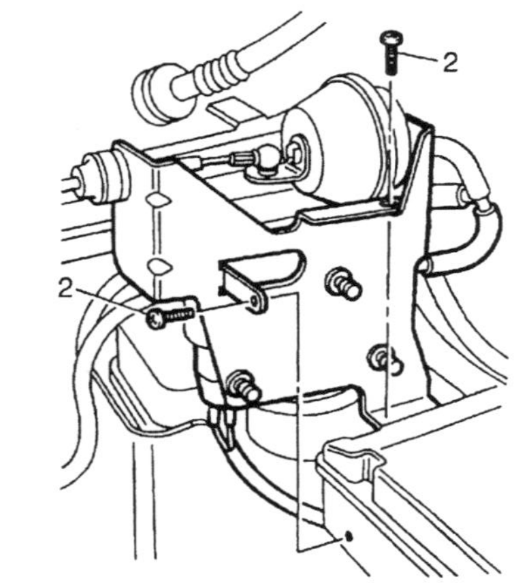

17M0120

2. Remove 2 screws securing cruise control actuator bracket to suspension control box.
3. Position cruise control actuator assembly aside.

17M0119

4. Release vent solenoid from EVAP canister bracket for access to hose clip and connector.
5. Disconnect multiplug from vent solenoid.
6. Release clip and remove vent solenoid from hose.

Refit

7. Fit vent solenoid to hose and secure hose clip.
8. Connect multiplug to vent solenoid.
9. Position vent solenoid to bracket and engage clip.
10. Align cruise control actuator bracket to suspension control box and secure with screws.
11. Connect battery earth lead.

EVAP CANISTER VENT SOLENOID - from 99MY

Service repair no - 17.15.47

Remove

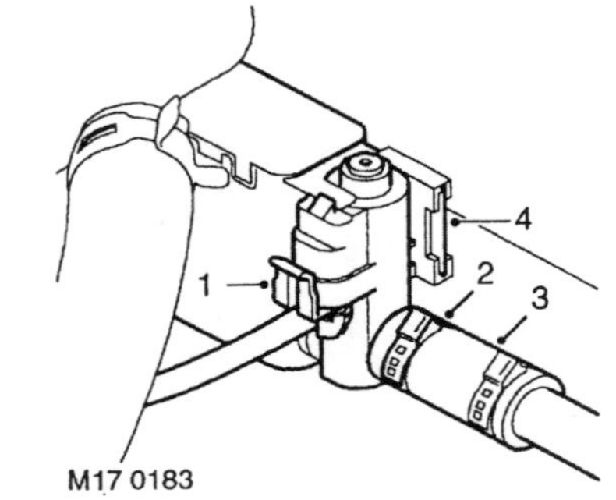

M17 0183

1. Disconnect multiplug from vent solenoid.
2. Remove clip securing hose to vent solenoid.
3. Disconnect hose from vent solenoid.

CAUTION: Plug the connections.

4. Release clip and remove vent solenoid from bracket.

Refit

5. Fit vent solenoid to bracket.
6. Connect hose to vent solenoid.
7. Fit clip to secure hose to vent solenoid.
8. Connect multiplug to vent solenoid.

EXHAUST GAS RECIRCULATION (EGR) VALVE - DIESEL

Service repair no - 17.45.01

Remove

1. Disconnect battery negative terminal.
2. Disconnect vacuum hose from EGR valve.
3. Slacken clip and disconnect intercooler hose from EGR valve.
4. Remove 2 bolts securing EGR pipe to EGR valve.
5. Remove 4 bolts securing EGR valve to intake manifold.
6. Remove EGR valve and collect seal from intake manifold.

CAUTION: Care must be taken when extracting seal to ensure recess in intake manifold is not damaged.

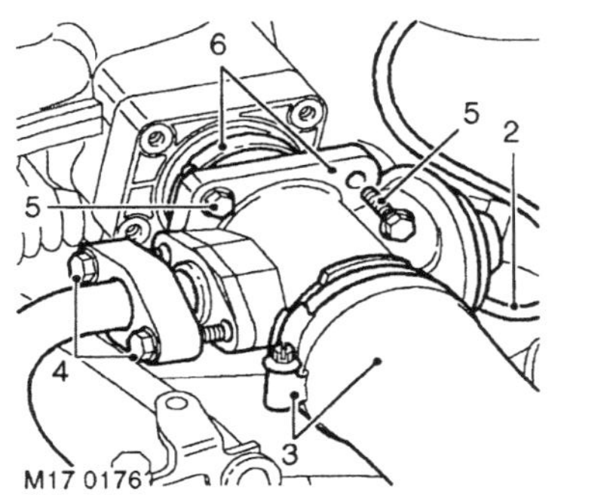

7. Clean sealing faces of manifold, EGR valve and EGR pipe.

Refit

8. Fit new seal to intake manifold recess.
9. Position EGR valve to intake manifold and secure with bolts. Tighten bolts to ***10 Nm (7 lbf.in).***
10. Engage EGR pipe to valve, align flange and secure with bolts. Tighten bolts to ***22 Nm (16 lbf.in).***
11. Connect intercooler hose to EGR valve and secure with clip.
12. Connect vacuum hose to EGR valve.
13. Connect battery negative terminal.

MODULATOR VALVE - EGR

Service repair no - 17.45.04

Remove

1. Disconnect vent hose from solenoid valve.

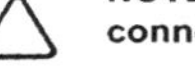

NOTE: Record hose positions to aid connection.

2. Disconnect EGR valve and vacuum pump hoses from solenoid valve.

CAUTION: Plug the connections.

3. Disconnect multiplug from solenoid valve.
4. Remove 2 nuts securing solenoid valve to mounting and remove valve.

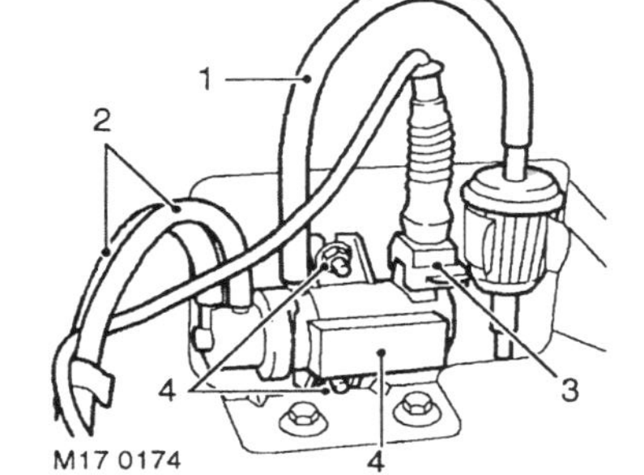

Refit

5. Fit solenoid valve to mounting and secure with nuts.
6. Connect multiplug to valve.
7. Connect vent hose and vacuum hoses to solenoid valve.

VACUUM PUMP - EGR SYSTEM

Service repair no - 17.45.30

Remove

1. Disconnect battery negative terminal.
2. Remove camshaft cover. ***See ENGINE, Repair.***
3. Position harness trunking aside.
4. Release clip and disconnect pipe from vacuum pump.
5. Remove 2 bolts securing vacuum pump.

NOTE: Dowel bolt is used to secure inlet manifold side of vacuum pump.

6. Remove vacuum pump and discard 'O' ring seal.

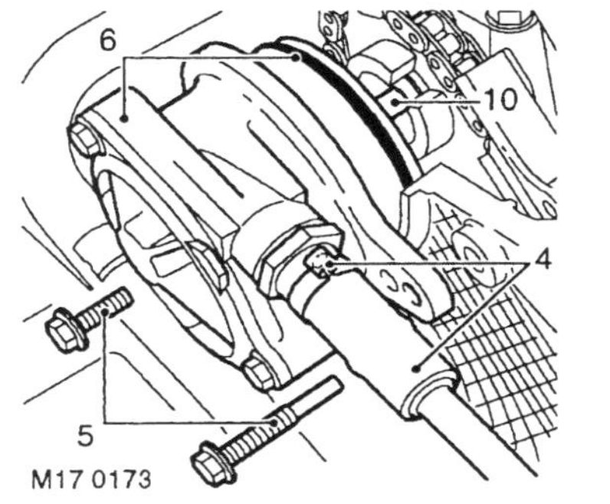

7. Clean sealing faces of vacuum pump and cylinder head.

Refit

8. Fit new 'O' ring seal to vacuum pump.
9. Apply STC 3373 to threads of dowel bolt.
10. Position vacuum pump and engage drive dog with camshaft slot.
11. Secure vacuum pump with bolts. Tighten to ***22 Nm (16 lbf.ft).***

CAUTION: Ensure that dowel bolt passes through timing chain guide rail bolt.

12. Connect pipe to vacuum pump and secure with clip.
13. Align harness trunking.
14. Fit camshaft cover. ***See ENGINE, Repair.***
15. Connect battery negative terminal.

SOLENOID - EVAP CANNISTER VENT VALVE (CVS)

Service repair no - 17.15.47

Remove

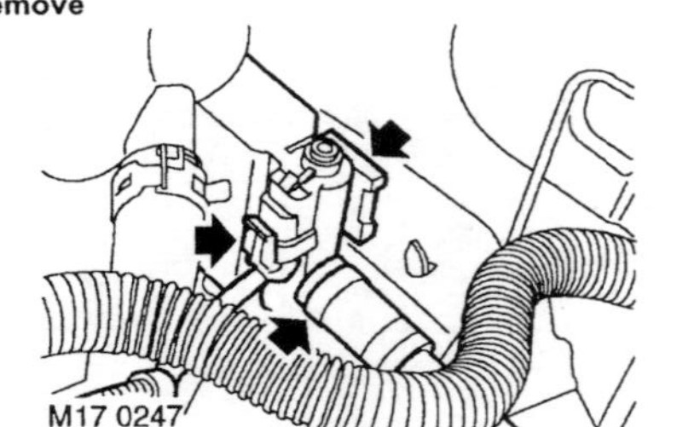
M17 0247

1. Disconnect multiplug from CVS unit.
2. Remove clip securing hose to CVS unit.
3. Disconnect hose from CVS unit.

CAUTION: Plug the connections.

4. Remove CVS unit from bracket.

Refit

5. Fit CVS unit to bracket.
6. Connect hose to CVS unit.
7. Fit clip to secure hose to CVS unit.
8. Connect multiplug to CVS unit.

CONTROL VALVE - SECONDARY AIR INJECTION (SAI)

Service repair no - 17.25.02

Remove

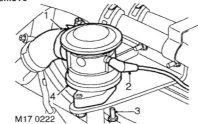

M17 0222

1. Release clip and disconnect air hose from valve.
2. Disconnect vacuum hose from valve.
3. Remove 2 bolts securing valve to air manifold.
4. Remove valve and discard gasket.

Refit

5. Clean air valve and mating face on manifold.
6. Fit new gasket and fit valve. Tighten bolts to ***10 Nm (7 lbf.ft)*** .
7. Connect vacuum hose.
8. Connect air hose and secure with clip.

RESERVOIR - VACUUM - SECONDARY AIR INJECTION (SAI)

Service repair no - 17.25.04

Remove

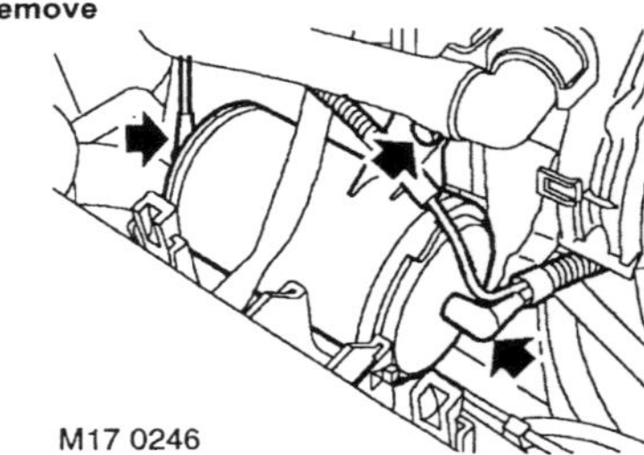
M17 0246

1. Disconnect 2 vacuum hoses from reservoir.
2. Remove bolt securing reservoir to mounting bracket and collect reservoir.

Refit

3. Position reservoir to mounting bracket and tighten bolt to ***10 Nm (7 lbf.ft)*** .
4. Connect vacuum hoses to reservoir.

PUMP - SECONDARY AIR INJECTION (SAI)

Service repair no - 17.25.07

Remove

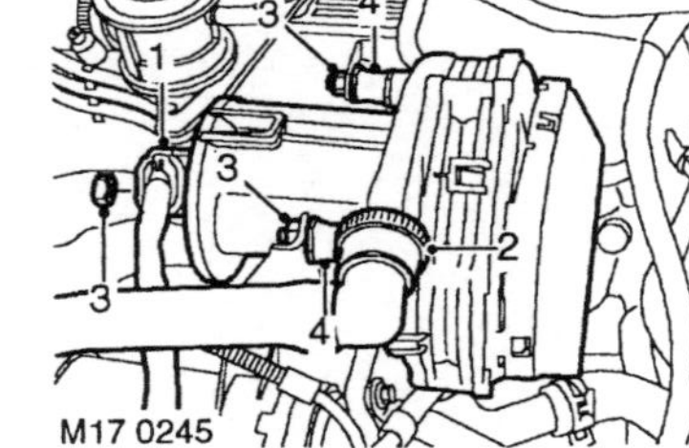

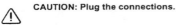

M17 0245

1. Disconnect multiplug from air pump.
2. Release clip and disconnect air hose from air pump.
3. Remove 3 nuts securing air pump to mounting bracket and remove pump.
4. Remove 3 mountings from air pump.

Refit

5. Fit mountings to air pump and tighten to ***10 Nm (7 lbf.ft)*** .
6. Fit air pump to mounting bracket and tighten nuts to ***10 Nm (7 lbf.ft)*** .
7. Connect air hose and secure with clip.
8. Connect multiplug to air pump.

AIR MANIFOLD - LH - SECONDARY AIR INJECTION (SAI)

Service repair no - 17.25.17

Remove

1. Remove SAI control valve. ***See this section.***

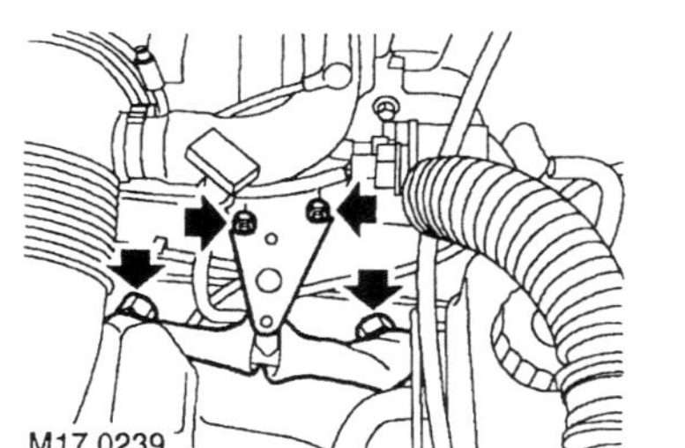

2. Loosen 2 union nuts securing air manifold to cylinder head adaptors.
3. Remove 2 nuts securing air manifold bracket to inlet manifold.
4. Remove air manifold.

Refit

5. Clean air manifold and cylinder head adaptors.
6. Fit air manifold and start union nuts.
7. Fit nuts securing air manifold to inlet manifold.
8. Tighten air manifold unions to ***25 Nm (18 lbf.ft)***.
9. Fit SAI control valve. ***See this section.***

AIR MANIFOLD - RH - SECONDARY AIR INJECTION (SAI)

Service repair no - 17.25.18

Remove

1. Remove SAI control valve. ***See this section.***
2. Remove heater feed and return pipes. ***See HEATING AND VENTILATION, Repair.***

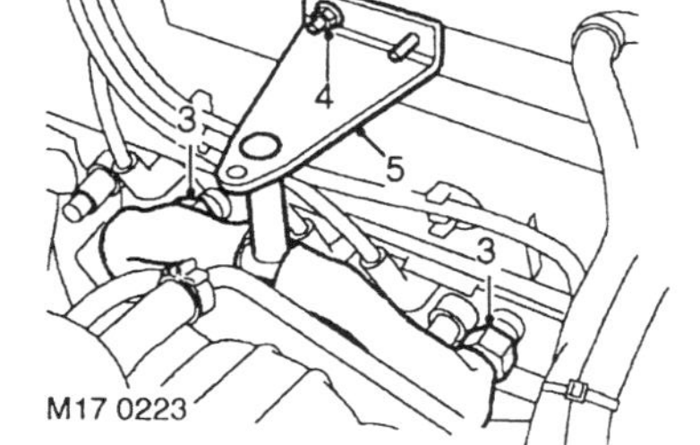

3. Loosen 2 union nuts securing air manifold to cylinder head adaptors.
4. Remove nut securing air manifold bracket to inlet manifold.
5. Remove air manifold.

Refit

6. Clean air manifold and cylinder head adaptors.
7. Fit air manifold and start union nuts.
8. Fit nut securing air manifold to inlet manifold.
9. Tighten air manifold unions to ***25 Nm***.
10. Fit heater return and feed pipes. ***See HEATING AND VENTILATION, Repair.***
11. Fit SAI control valve. ***See this section.***

SOLENOID - VACUUM - SECONDARY AIR INJECTION (SAI)

Service repair no - 17.25.47

Remove

2
1
3
2
M17 0244

1. Release multiplug from solenoid.
2. Disconnect 2 vacuum hoses from solenoid.
3. Release solenoid from mounting bracket and remove.

Refit

4. Secure solenoid to mounting bracket.
5. Connect vacuum hoses and multiplug to solenoid.

PIPE - SECONDARY AIR INJECTION (SAI)

Service repair no - 17.25.59

Remove

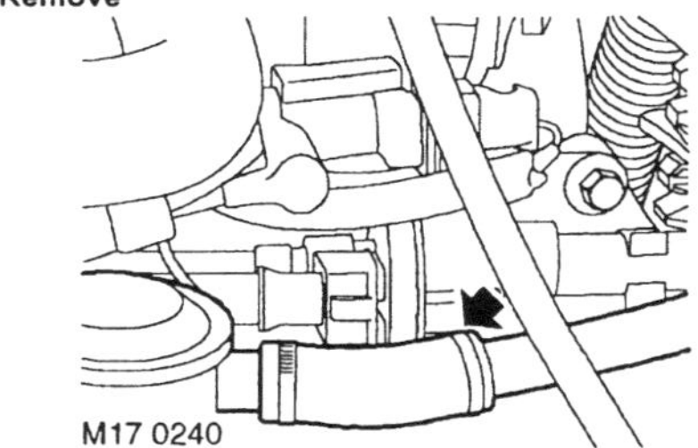

1. Loosen clip securing RH SAI control valve hose to air injection pipe.
2. Release hose from air injection pipe.

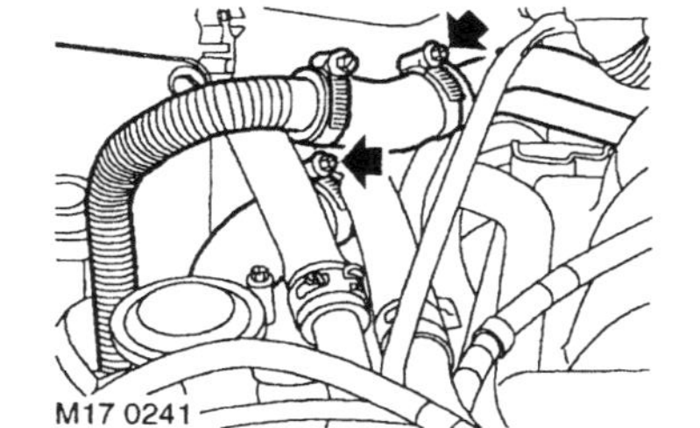

3. Loosen clip securing SAI pump hose to air injection pipe.
4. Release hose from air injection pipe.
5. Loosen clip securing LH SAI control valve hose to air injection pipe.
6. Release hose from air injection pipe.

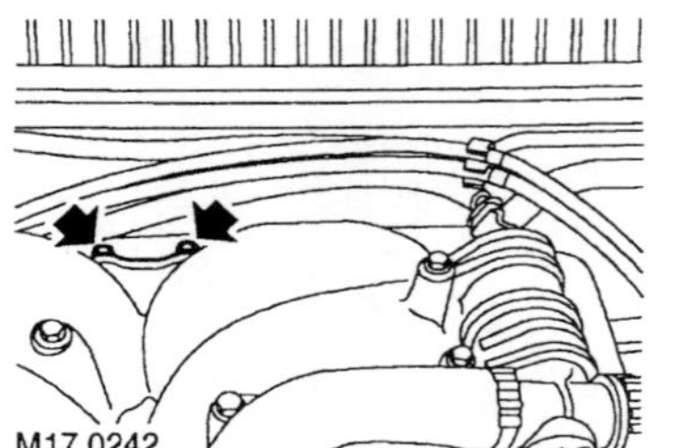

7. Remove 2 nuts securing air injection pipe to air intake plenum.

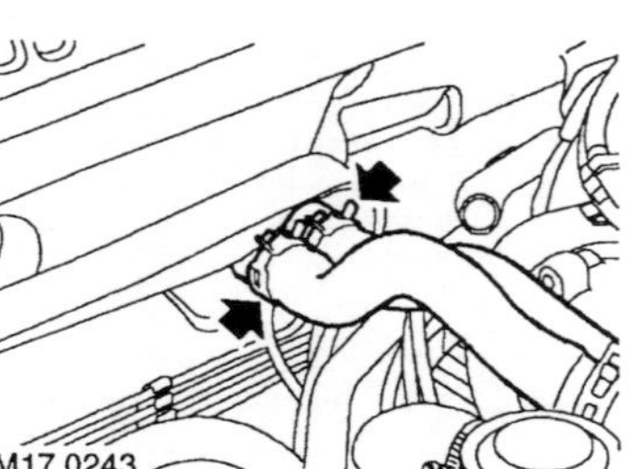

8. Position drain tin to collect any coolant spillage.
9. Release clips securing heater hoses to heater.
10. Release hoses from heater.
11. Remove air injection pipe.

Refit

12. Fit air injection pipe to rear of air intake plenum and tighten nuts.
13. Connect heater hoses to heater and secure with clips.
14. Connect SAI pump hose to air injection pipe and secure with clip.
15. Connect LH and RH SAI control valve hoses to air injection pipe and secure with clips.
16. Remove drain tin.
17. Top up engine coolant.

Notes

19 - FUEL SYSTEM

CONTENTS

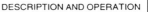

DESCRIPTION

Operation of the engine is monitored and controlled by a Digital Diesel Electronics (DDE) system. The DDE system electronically regulates injection timing and fuel delivery rate under all operating conditions.

The system comprises:

- An engine control module
- Output devices
- Input devices
- An injection pump

Engine Control Module (ECM)

The 55-pin engine control module (ECM) is located under the bonnet, in a compartment of the battery tray. It consists of an input section, two microprocessors, No. 1 and No. 2, and an output section. The microprocessors receive input signals from the various input devices and calculate the necessary response to the output devices. Calculations are based on fixed, pre-programmed data. Data is manipulated within function blocks:

Microprocessor function blocks

The following function blocks are provided in microprocessor 1:

- Injection timing (start of injection) control
- Output of self-diagnosis results

The following function blocks are provided in microprocessor 2:

- Injection quantity control with special start quantity control and full load quantity limitation
- Engine speed control
- Running stability control and vibration damping
- Exhaust emission limitation and overheating protection
- Cruise control

Fault diagnosis

Operating faults are registered by the ECM and held within a defect code memory. TestBook connected into the diagnostic socket beneath the fascia, can be used to interrogate the ECM for stored faults and perform diagnostic routines. The ECM is also connected to a warning lamp on the instrument panel.

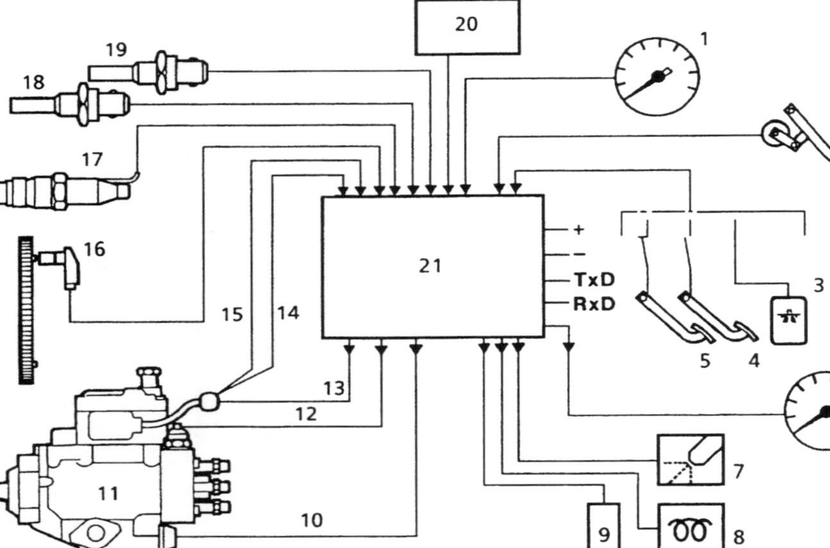

18M7013A

Fuel system inputs/outputs - Vehicles without EGR

1. Vehicle speed signal
2. Throttle position sensor - linked to accelerator pedal
3. Cruise control selector (optional)
4. Brake switch
5. Clutch switch
6. Engine speed signal
7. Diagnostic lamp
8. Glow plug lamp
9. Heater time relay
10. Injection timing device
11. Fuel injection pump
12. Stop solenoid
13. Quantity servo control unit
14. Quantity servo control unit potentiometer
15. Fuel temperature sensor
16. Crankshaft position sensor
17. Start of injection sensor
18. Coolant temperature sensor
19. Intake air temperature sensor
20. Manifold absolute pressure sensor
21. Engine Control Module (ECM)

M18 0286

Fuel system inputs/outputs - Vehicles with EGR

1. Vehicle speed signal
2. Throttle position sensor - linked to accelerator pedal
3. Cruise control selector (optional)
4. Brake switch
5. Clutch switch
6. Engine speed signal
7. Diagnostic lamp
8. Glow plug lamp
9. Heater time relay
10. Injection timing device
11. Fuel injection pump
12. Stop solenoid
13. Quantity servo control unit
14. Quantity servo control unit potentiometer
15. Fuel temperature sensor
16. Crankshaft position sensor
17. Start of injection sensor
18. Coolant temperature sensor
19. Manifold Absolute Pressure (MAP) sensor
20. Mass Air Flow (MAF) sensor
21. EGR Modulator valve
22. Engine Control Module (ECM)

Input devices

Input devices of the DDE system comprise the following:

Crankshaft position sensor
Start of injection sensor
Fuel temperature sensor
Coolant temperature sensor
Intake air temperature sensor
Manifold absolute pressure sensor
Vehicle speed signal
Throttle position sensor
Servo unit potentiometer (drive potentiometer) on quantity servo control unit
Clutch switch
Brake switches
Cruise control selector (if fitted)

Crankshaft position sensor (CKP sensor)

Attached to the flywheel of the engine are six position pins. These are equally spaced around the crankshaft circumference at 60 degree intervals.

To determine engine speed and crankshaft position, an inductive CKP sensor is mounted on the crankcase adjacent to the flywheel. The CKP sensor consists of a body containing a coil and a permanent magnet which provides a magnetic field. The CKP sensor is situated so that an air gap exists between it and the position pins. Air gap distance is critical for correct operation.

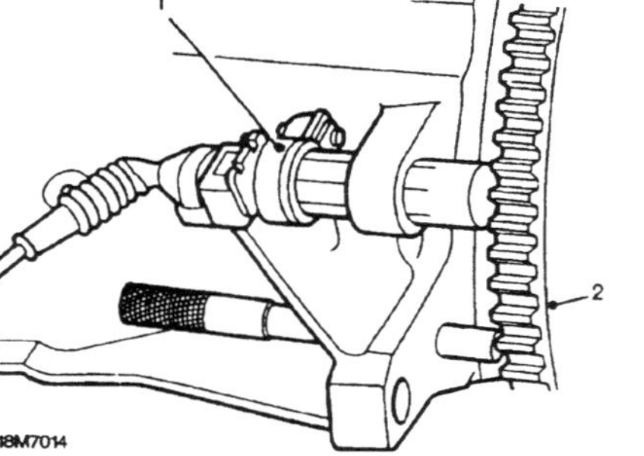

1. Sensor
2. Flywheel

As the flywheel rotates, position pins pass the CKP sensor and disturb the magnetic field, inducing voltage pulses in the coil. The pulses are transmitted to the ECM.
When the flywheel rotates one complete revolution, six pulses are transmitted to the ECM. The ECM determines engine speed by calculating how many pulses occur within a given time. The output from the CKP sensor is also used, in conjunction with the start of injection sensor, to determine and control ignition timing.

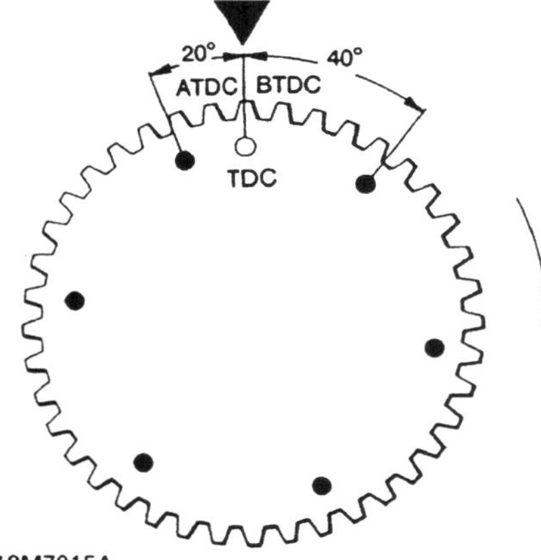

18M7015A

The flywheel position pins are spaced so that at TDC, one pin is 40 degrees before TDC while the other is 20 degrees after TDC as shown. To determine which pulse represents 40 degrees before, or 20 degrees after TDC, the control unit requires additional information from the start of injection sensor.

Start of injection sensor

The start of fuel injection is registered by this sensor which is incorporated in No 4 injector.

The sensor consists of a coil which surrounds the shaft of an extended injection needle. The coil is fed a DC supply from the ECM which produces a magnetic field.

When the needle is moved under the influence of fuel pressure, the magnetic field is disturbed which induces an AC voltage in the coil. The induced voltage is registered in the ECM as a reference point for the start of injection.

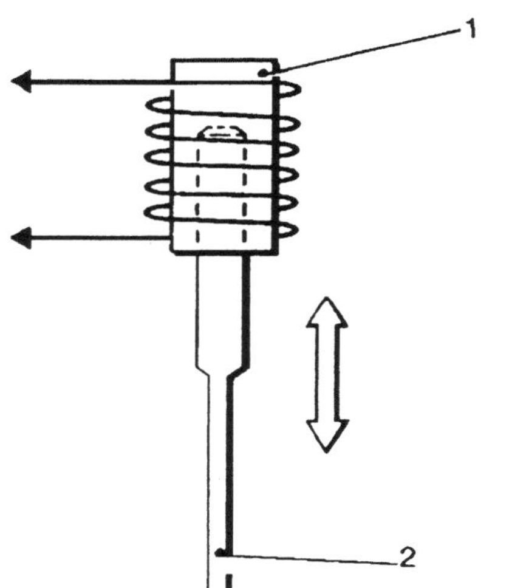

1. Coil
2. Injector needle

The ECM uses the input signals from the start of injection sensor, together with signals from the crankshaft position sensor, to detect the actual start of injection angle. The detected actual value is adjusted by the ECM to a nominal value via the injection timing solenoid.

Fuel temperature sensor

Fuel temperature is monitored by a sensor located in the fuel injection pump. This sensor is of the negative temperature coefficient (NTC) type, designed to reduce its resistance with increasing temperature.

When the system is operating, the ECM regularly checks the sensor resistance. As fuel density varies with temperature, the information received is used to calculate the correct quantity of fuel to inject.

Engine coolant temperature sensor (ECT sensor)

The temperature of the engine coolant is monitored by a ECT sensor located on the cylinder head.

The ECT sensor is of the NTC type and is similar in operation to the fuel temperature sensor previously described.

The ECM uses this information to adjust the basic injection timing and quantity values for all operating conditions.

Intake air temperature sensor (IAT sensor) - Vehicles without EGR

Intake air temperature is monitored by a IAT sensor in the intake manifold. The IAT sensor is of the NTC type and is similar in operation to the fuel temperature sensor previously described.

The ECM uses the information received from the IAT sensor, in conjunction with the manifold absolute pressure sensor, to determine the volume of air being be drawn in to the engine.

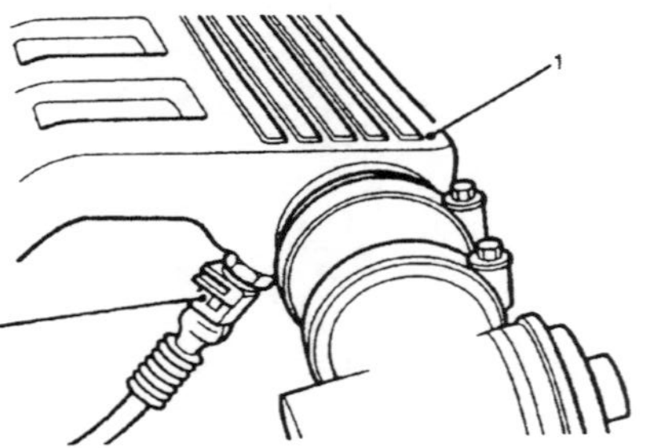

18M7017

1. Intake manifold
2. IAT sensor

EGR Modulator valve - Vehicles with EGR

The EGR modulator valve is located in the engine compartment on the left inner wing near the bulkhead. The EGR modulator valve is used to control the EGR valve and is controlled by the ECM. ***See EMISSION CONTROL, Description and operation.***

Manifold absolute pressure sensor (MAP sensor)

Inlet air pressure is monitored by a silicon diaphram type sensor mounted on top of the fuel filter and connected, via a pressure tube to the intake manifold. The MAP sensor is connected electrically to the ECM.

When inlet air pressure changes, pressure in the detection chamber causes the diaphragms to deflect. This alters the length of each resistor, changing their resistance value. The change is detected by electronics within the MAP sensor which varies the output voltage. This is converted to a pressure reading in the ECM.

Manifold absolute pressure, when linked to inlet air temperature, gives an accurate measurement of the charge volume. The ECM adjusts fuelling as necessary.

Mass air flow sensor (MAF sensor) - Vehicles with EGR

The MAF sensor is located in the air inlet pipe from the air cleaner and is connected electrically to the ECM. The sensor replaces the Air Intake Temperature (IAT) sensor previously used on Pre-EGR vehicles.

The MAF sensor comprises a hot film sensor which has a heated surface maintained by an electrical current at a constant temperature. With cool air flowing past the sensor, the volume of air drawn into the intake manifold is measured by the electrical current required to keep the temperature of the hot film sensor constant.

The MAF sensor records the amount of incoming air being drawn into the engine. The ECM uses this information to control the Exhaust Gas Recirculation (EGR) process. ***See EMISSION CONTROL, Description and operation.***

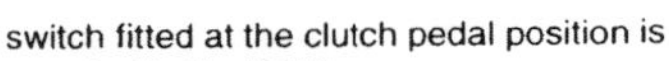

Vehicle speed signal

Vehicle speed is monitored by the ECM from the ABS ECU.

The ECM uses vehicle speed data when adjusting idle stabilisation, cruise control and fuel delivery.

Throttle position sensor (TP sensor)

The position, selected by the driver, of the accelerator pedal is signalled to the ECM by the TP sensor. This is linked, mechanically to the pedal and electrically to the ECM.

The sender consists of a thick film TP sensor together with a sender switch (9 degree switch). With the accelerator pedal at rest the switch is open. When the pedal is moved past the 9 degree position the switch closes.

When the ignition is switched ON, pedal position is signalled to the ECM. Pedal movement causes voltage through the TP sensor to vary and the ECM uses this to measure:

- Required engine speed
- Rate of acceleration
- Rate of deceleration

The ECM calculates the rate of change of the voltage signal in a positive (accelerate) or negative (decelerate) direction. From this, acceleration enrichment, deceleration fuel metering or overrun fuel cut-off can be carried out by the system.

The sender switch is used together with the voltage from the TP sensor to check the operation of the circuit. When the pedal is moved, the switch signals a logic input to the ECM. The ECM then checks the voltage signal from the TP sensor. This voltage is compared with a pre-programmed value to check that the TP sensor is working correctly.

Servo unit potentiometer (drive potentiometer) on quantity servo control unit

This potentiometer signals a voltage to the ECM. The voltage value is used to calculate the position of the control spool in the injection pump quantity servo control unit - See description of this item.

Clutch switch

A switch fitted at the clutch pedal position is connected to the ECM.

The switch detects when the clutch is depressed. This input is used to deactivate the cruise control and various driveability strategies.

Brake switch

The brake pedal is fitted with a twin contact switch which provides two outputs. Both outputs send signals to the ECM. Both signals are used by the system to test the operation of the brake circuit, and to deactivate the cruise control.

Output devices

Output devices of the DDE system comprise the following:

Quantity servo control unit
Stop solenoid
Injection timing device
Heater time relay
Diagnosis and preheater lamps
Fuel consumption indicator in instrument pack

Quantity servo control unit

The servo is used to accurately control the amount of fuel delivered to the injectors. It is housed within the fuel injection pump. ***See Injection pump.***

The unit consists of a rotary magnet mounted on an eccentric shaft; the shaft engages with the control spool of the pump. The rotary magnet is fitted with a return spring and moves under the influence of a control coil. The magnet rotates through an arc of about 60 degrees which moves the control spool from zero to maximum fuel delivery position. The eccentric shaft engages with the control spool at one end, while the opposite end operates a rotary potentiometer.

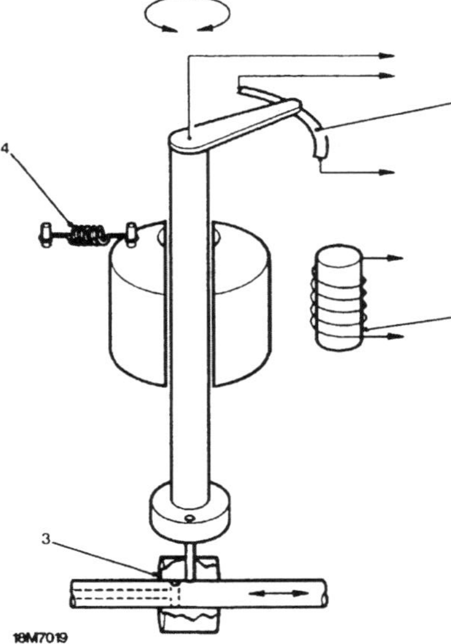

1. Rotary potentiometer
2. Control coil
3. Control spool
4. Return spring

When the control coil is energised the rotary magnet and eccentric shaft move against spring pressure. Rotary movement of the eccentric shaft is converted into linear movement of the control spool. This allows more fuel to be delivered to the injectors.

When the control coil is de-energised the return spring causes the rotary magnet and eccentric shaft to resume their original position. The control spool is moved to the zero position.

The control unit accurately controls the position of the control spool to achieve the desired engine performance.

Stop solenoid

This is a solenoid operated valve located on the high pressure section of the injection pump. When the ignition is switched ON it receives voltage supply and the valve opens allowing fuel to flow.

When the ignition is switched OFF the valve closes and the fuel supply is cut.

Injection timing device

This injection timing device is housed within the fuel injection pump. It consists of a spring-loaded plunger and a solenoid. The spring loaded plunger moves under the influence of pump working pressure. The solenoid is controlled by a pulsed frequency signal from the control unit.

When the pump is operating the solenoid regulates the speed dependent, internal pump pressure into working pressure. This moves the plunger against spring tension.

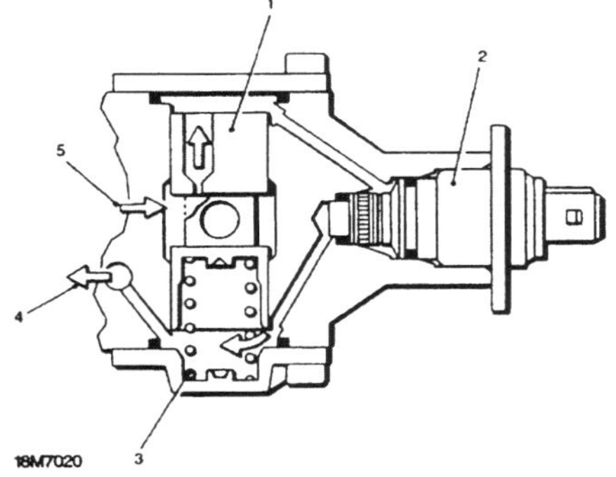

1. Plunger
2. Solenoid
3. Spring
4. Pump feed pressure
5. Pump internal pressure

Injection is retarded with an energised solenoid and the resultant pressure drop. The beginning of injection is advanced with a de-energised solenoid and the resultant pressure rise.

Heater time relay

Glow plug preheating time is regulated by the heater timer relay in the heating time control unit. This connects to the glow plugs in the cylinder head and to the ECM.

The control unit monitors and operates the glow plugs; operating time for the glow plugs is dependent on engine temperature.

Fuel injection pump (FIP)

The FIP is of the vane-type and is chain driven from the front end of the crankshaft. Fuel delivery from the FIP to the injectors is regulated by the movement of a control spool. Movement of the control spool increases or decreases the fuel delivery rate to meet engine operating requirements.

The FIP houses the following items that either send signals to the ECM, or responds to signals sent from the ECM:

Fuel quantity servo unit

Moves the control spool to regulate the amount of fuel delivered to injectors.

Servo unit potentiometer

Used by the control unit to calculate the position of the control spool.

Injection timing device

Regulates pump speed dependent on internal pump pressure.

Fuel temperature sensor

Monitors fuel temperature.

Stop solenoid

Cuts fuel delivery to the injectors when de-energised.

These items have been previously described in this section - ***See Input devices or Output devices*** as applicable.

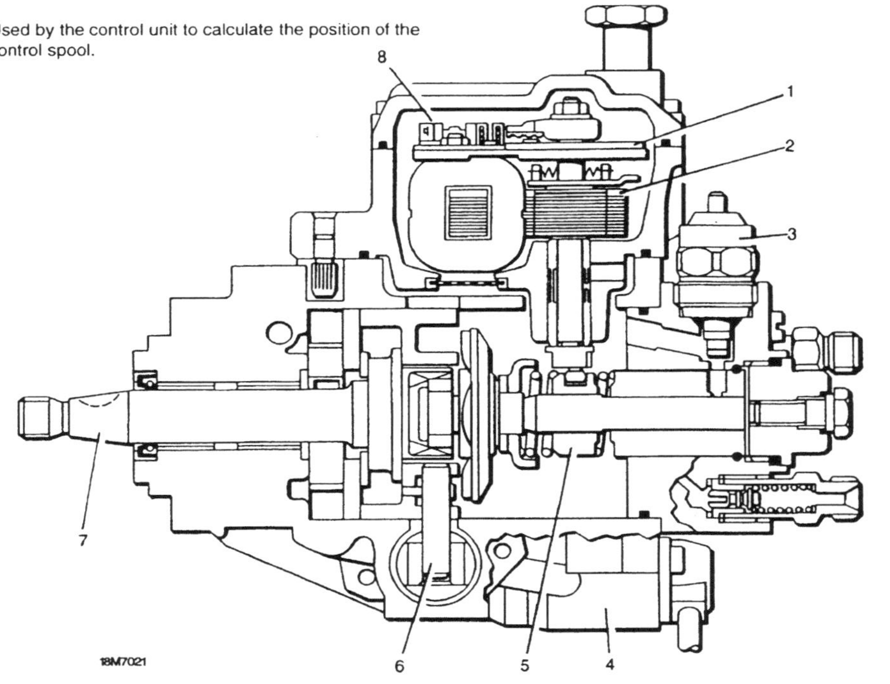

1. Rotary potentiometer
2. Quantity control servo unit
3. Stop solenoid
4. Injection timing device solenoid valve
5. Control spool
6. Timing device plunger
7. Drive shaft
8. Fuel temperature sensor

OPERATION

General

The digital diesel electronics system (DDE) facilitates exact control of injection quantity and injection timing under all operating conditions. As a result, fuel consumption and exhaust emissions are kept to a minimum.

Malfunctions

If a fault occurs in any of the following circuits: manifold absolute pressure sensor, fuel temperature sensor or coolant temperature sensor, the ECM will provide substitute values. In the case of a faulty throttle position sensor, start of injection sensor or injection timing device, the engine will run at a reduced performance level.

If the servo unit potentiometer or servo unit fails, the injection system is deactivated. The engine shuts down as a result.

Injection timing (Start of Injection) control

The start of injection is controlled by the injection timing device in the injection pump. A solenoid valve modulates the internal pump pressure on one side of the system so that a defined start of injection is set. When no power is applied, the solenoid valve is closed, resulting in advanced injection timing (start of injection).

Injection quantity control

Injection quantity control is achieved by the quantity servo control unit in the injection pump. The servo acts on the pump control spool to vary the effective stroke of the pump piston (injection quantity). The position of the control spool is signalled back via the servo potentiometer to the ECM. The ECM compares the actual value with the nominal value and, if necessary, adjustment is carried out until the nominal injection quantity value is achieved. The servo control unit is set to zero delivery when no power is applied.

Start control

To determine the quantity of fuel to inject during starting, the ECM uses signals from the coolant temperature sensor, fuel temperature sensor, crankshaft position sensor and throttle position sensor.

Engine speed control

After starting, an idle speed control function cuts in after a certain engine speed threshold has been exceeded. This is calculated by the ECM dependent on the coolant temperature and the active loads. The idle speed can be adjusted by means of TestBook.

The maximum engine speed is limited by the ECM by reducing the injection quantity.

Running stability control and jolt damping

The running stability control system is used for engine speed stabilization when idling. Controlled injection quantity correction counteracts the irregularities which occur in the individual cylinders as the result of dispersion of the injected fuel quantity.

In the case of spontaneous change in the position of the accelerator pedal or a sudden change in the driving resistance, vibrations occur which, in conjunction with the control frequency of the injection hydraulics, can result in jolts and jerks.

On the basis of segment-by-segment angle evaluation in the input sequence, the engine speed signals provide the information which is used for corrective control (rotation irregularities) in the quantity servo control unit. The prerequisite for this function is the input of the vehicle speed signal.

Exhaust emission limitation and overheating protection

At high ambient air temperatures and at increasing altitude, the full load quantity is reduced in order to limit exhaust emission. The full load fuel quantity is also reduced when the permissible water temperature is exceeded in the high speed range.

Cruise control

The required driving statuses: acceleration or resume driving speed can be set or selected using the steering wheel switches. These functions are active with a vehicle speed of more than 40 km/h (25 mph).

Air conditioning compressor cut-out

The ECM switches off the air conditioning compressor during driving conditions demanding high torque requirements (starting off, accelerating). The compressor is also cut-out at high water temperatures (more than 110°C) in order to protect the engine.

Self-diagnosis

The task of the self-diagnosis function is to detect malfunctions in the DDE system and to make available substitute values and emergency programs. The ECM stores a record of faults, including intermittent faults which can be interrogated using TestBook.

Notes

FUEL INJECTION PUMP TIMING - CHECK AND ADJUST

Service repair no - 19.30.01

Check

1. Disconnect battery negative lead.
2. Remove intake manifold. ***See MANIFOLD AND EXHAUST SYSTEM, Repair.***
3. Remove cooling fan cowl. ***See COOLING SYSTEM, Repair.***

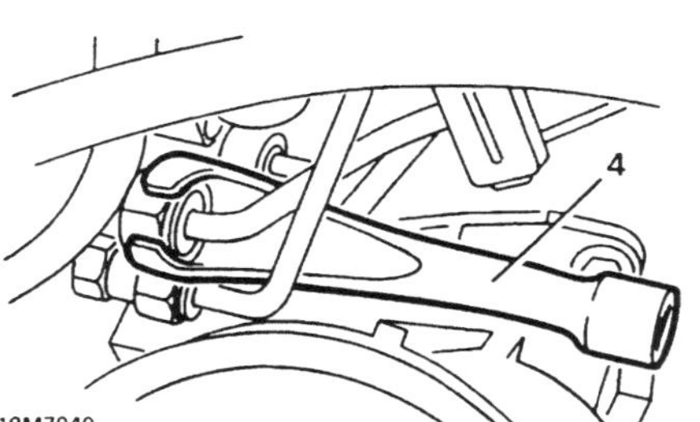

19M7040

4. Loosen high pressure pipe unions at injectors and Fuel Injection Pump (FIP) using LRT-12-117.

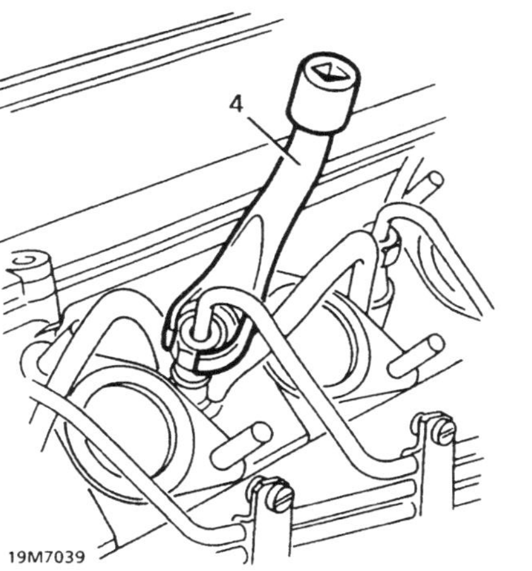

19M7039

CAUTION: Hold delivery valves against rotation as pipe unions are loosened.

5. Remove oil filler cap.
6. Observe No. 1 camshaft lobe. Turn engine clockwise until lobe points vertically upwards.

19M7041

NOTE: This indicates that the engine is approximately 90° Before Top Dead Centre (BTDC) with No. 1 cylinder on its compression stroke.

7. Remove bolt from timing access hole in FIP. Collect sealing washer.

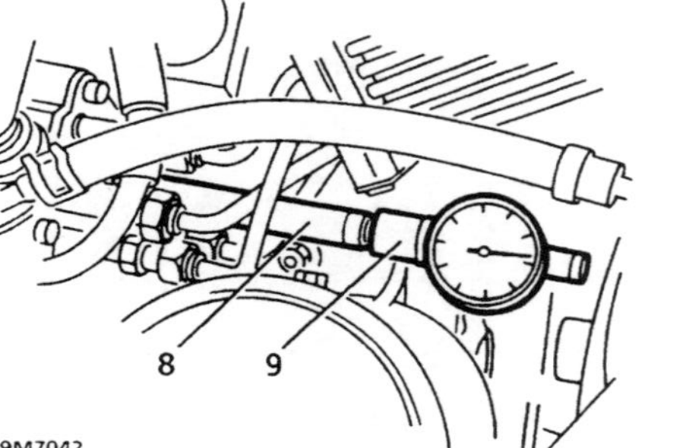

19M7042

8. Fit injection pump timing gauge holder LRT-12-121 into access hole.
9. Fit dial gauge and preload by approximately 2mm. Secure dial gauge in holder.

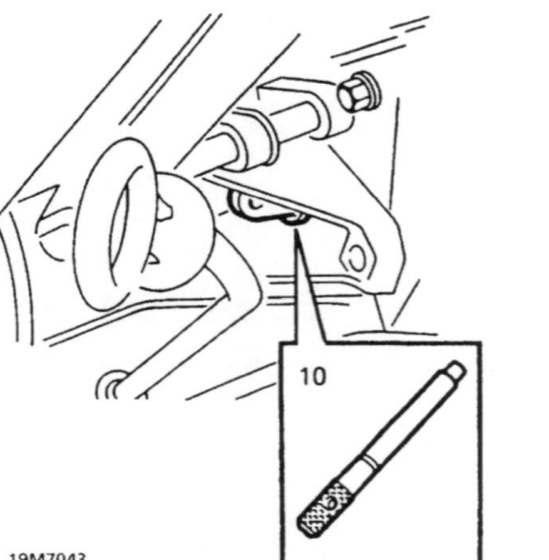

19M7043

10. Remove plastic plug from flywheel timing pin access hole. Insert timing pin LRT-12-108.

11. Rotate engine slowly clockwise until dial gauge needle reaches its lowest point. Zero gauge.
12. Continue turning crankshaft in a clockwise direction until timing pin locates into flywheel.

Check reading:
Engines with less than
20,000km = 0.95mm ± 0.02mm (0.4 ± 0.001 in)
Engines with more than
20,000km = 0.90mm ± 0.02mm (0.035 ± 0.001 in)

If in tolerance, continue at **Assemble.**
If out of tolerance, carry out adjustment as follows:

Adjust

13. Slacken 2 flange nuts and 1 support bolt securing FIP.

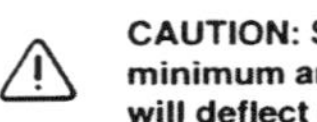

CAUTION: Slacken flange nuts by minimum amount. Timing chain tension will deflect pump if bolts are over loose, leading to false readings.

14. Rotate pump on mounting until correct reading is achieved.

NOTE: Ensure final movement of pump head is made towards the engine.

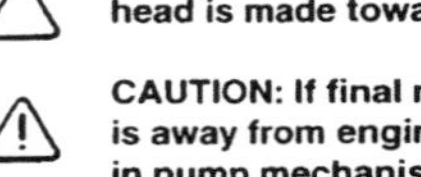

CAUTION: If final movement of pump head is away from engine, backlash will be left in pump mechanism, leading to false readings.

15. Tighten pump flange nuts to ***22 Nm. (16 lbf.ft)***
16. Remove flywheel timing pin.
17. Repeat from operation 6 to verify timing.
18. Refit plastic plug to flywheel timing pin hole.
19. Tighten rear support bolt to ***22 Nm. (16 lbf.ft)***

Assemble

20. Remove dial gauge and holder.
21. Fit bolt to FIP timing access hole, use a new sealing washer if necessary. Tighten to ***25 Nm. (18 lbf.ft)***
22. Using LRT-12-117, tighten high pressure pipe unions on injection pump to ***20 Nm. (15 lbf.ft). Do not tighten pipes at injectors.***

CAUTION: Hold delivery valves against rotation as pipe unions are tightened.

23. Fit oil filler cap.
24. Fit cooling fan cowl. ***See COOLING SYSTEM, Repair.***
25. Fit intake manifold. ***See MANIFOLD AND EXHAUST SYSTEM, Repair.***
26. Reconnect battery negative lead.
27. With assistance, crank engine. As fuel emerges at injector connections, secure each pipe union using tool LRT-12-117. Tighten to ***20 Nm (15 lbf.ft)***

WARNING: Engine will start during high pressure pipe bleeding procedure.

Notes

GLOW PLUG CONTROL UNIT

Service repair no - 19.60.33

Remove

1. Disconnect battery negative lead.
2. Remove 2 screws securing ECM housing cover. Remove cover.

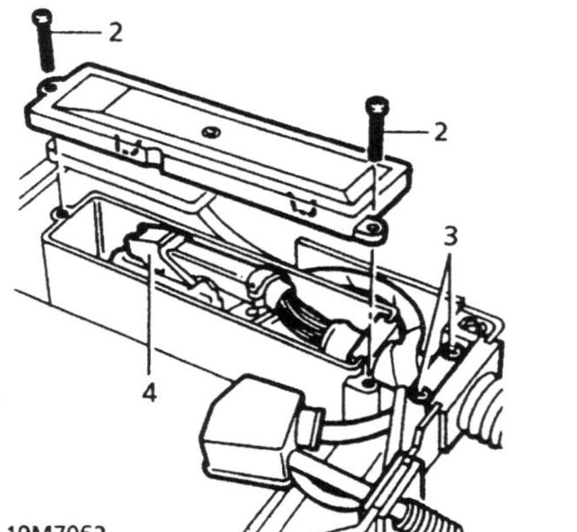

19M7062

3. Remove 2 harness clamp screws. Remove harness clamp.
4. Lift ECM and control unit from housing.
5. Remove nut securing battery cable to control unit. Release cable.

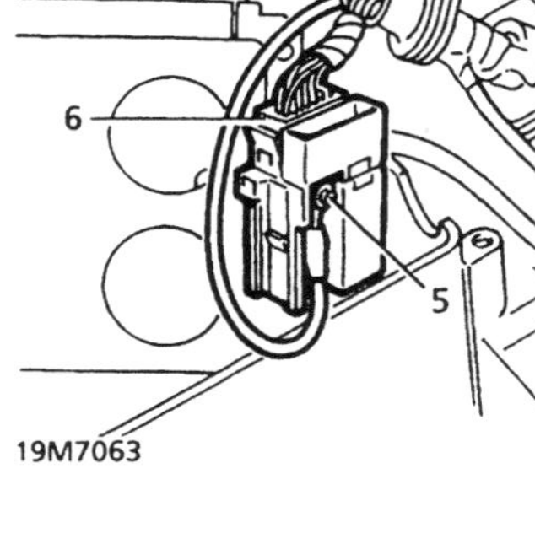

19M7063

6. Disconnect multiplug. Remove control unit.

Refit

7. Reverse removal procedure.

AIR CLEANER ASSEMBLY

Service repair no - 19.10.01

Remove

1. Release intake hose from air cleaner.

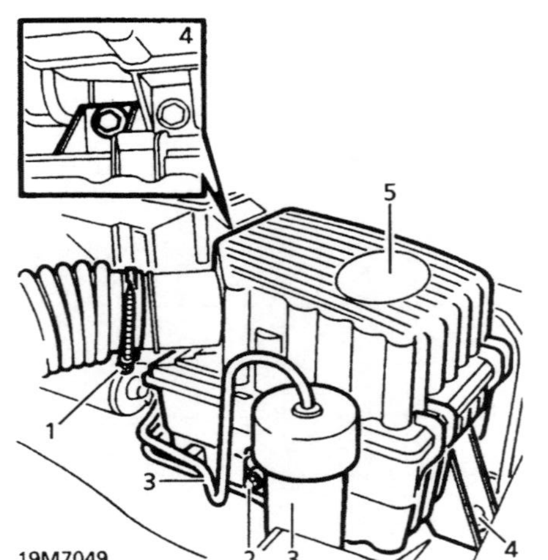

19M7049

2. Remove bolt securing air suspension dryer to air cleaner.
3. Release dryer pipes from air cleaner. Position dryer aside.
4. Remove 2 bolts securing air cleaner to valance.
5. Release air cleaner lug from valance grommet. Remove air cleaner.
6. If necessary, remove seal.

Refit

7. If removed, refit seal to air cleaner.
8. Position air cleaner assembly. Engage lug to valance grommet. Secure with bolts.
9. Position air suspension dryer to air cleaner. Secure with bolt. Tighten to ***8 Nm. (6 lbf.ft)***
10. Engage dryer pipes to clips.
11. Connect intake hose to air cleaner. Secure with clip.

ENGINE COOLANT TEMPERATURE SENSOR (ECT SENSOR)

Service repair no - 18.30.10

Remove

1. Partially drain cooling system. ***See COOLING SYSTEM, Repair.***
2. Disconnect ECT sensor multiplug.
3. Remove ECT sensor. Collect sealing washer and discard.

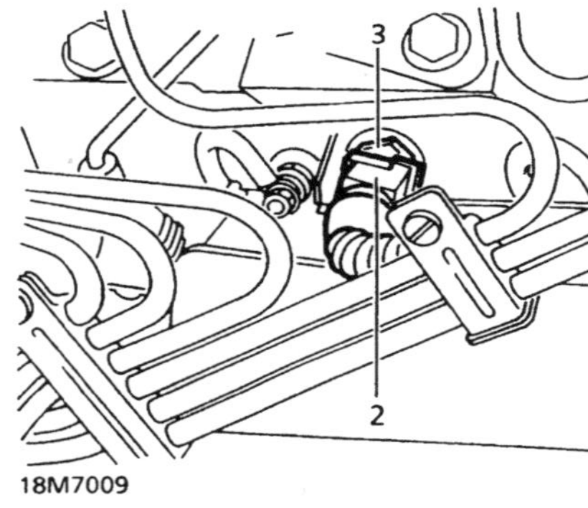

18M7009

Refit

4. Ensure mating faces are clean.
5. Using a new sealing washer, fit ECT sensor. Tighten to ***18 Nm. (13 lbf.ft)***
6. Connect multiplug to ECT sensor.
7. Refill cooling system. ***See COOLING SYSTEM, Repair.***
8. Run engine to normal operating temperature. Check for leaks around ECT sensor.

CRANKSHAFT POSITION SENSOR (CKP SENSOR)

Service repair no - 18.30.12

Remove

1. Disconnect battery negative lead.
2. Remove cooling fan cowl. ***See COOLING SYSTEM, Repair.***

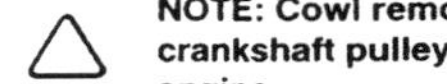

NOTE: Cowl removed to give access to crankshaft pulley for manual cranking of engine.

3. Disconnect CKP sensor multiplug.

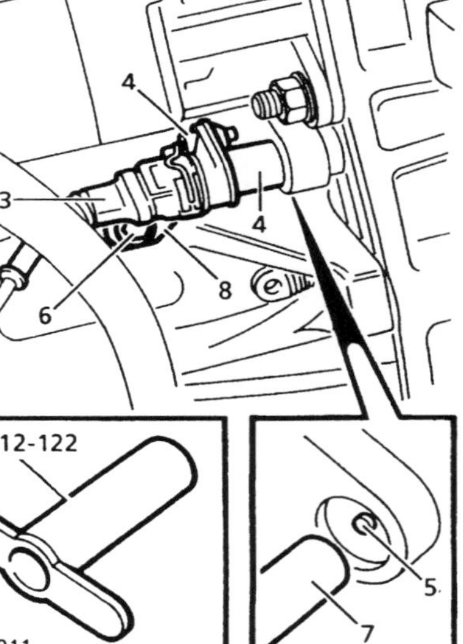

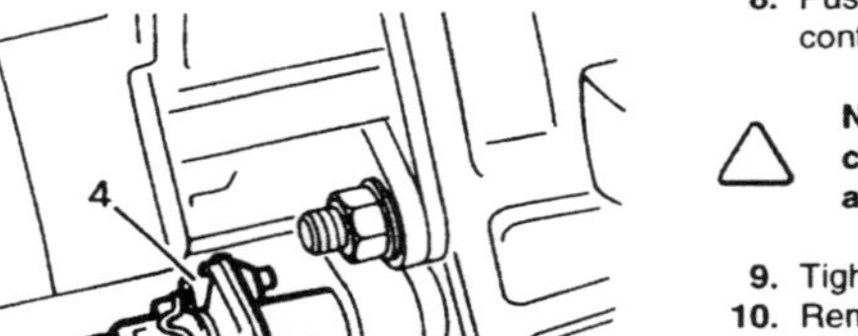
18M7011

4. Remove bolt securing CKP sensor to bracket. Remove CKP sensor.

CKP Sensor Bracket - Adjust

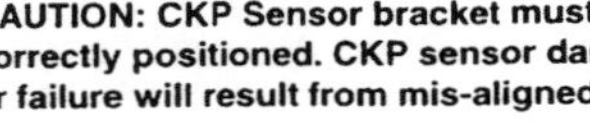

CAUTION: CKP Sensor bracket must be correctly positioned. CKP sensor damage or failure will result from mis-aligned bracket.

5. Rotate crankshaft until flywheel TDC pole is central to CKP sensor aperture.

NOTE: Use mirror and lamp to view flywheel poles.

6. Slacken bolt securing CKP sensor bracket to cylinder block.
7. Position LRT-12-122 to CKP sensor bracket. Secure with bolt.
8. Push CKP sensor bracket rearwards until tool contacts flywheel pole.

NOTE: Tool positions bracket allowing for correct air gap between CKP sensor nose and flywheel poles.

9. Tighten bolt securing bracket to cylinder block.
10. Remove bolt securing tool to bracket. Remove tool.

Refit

11. Fit CKP sensor to bracket. Secure with bolt. Tighten to ***Max 8 Nm. (6 lbf.ft)***
12. Connect CKP sensor multiplug.
13. Fit cooling fan cowl. ***See COOLING SYSTEM, Repair.***
14. Reconnect battery negative lead.

ENGINE CONTROL MODULE (ECM)

Service repair no - 18.30.03

Remove

1. Disconnect battery negative lead.
2. Remove 2 screws securing ECM housing cover. Remove cover

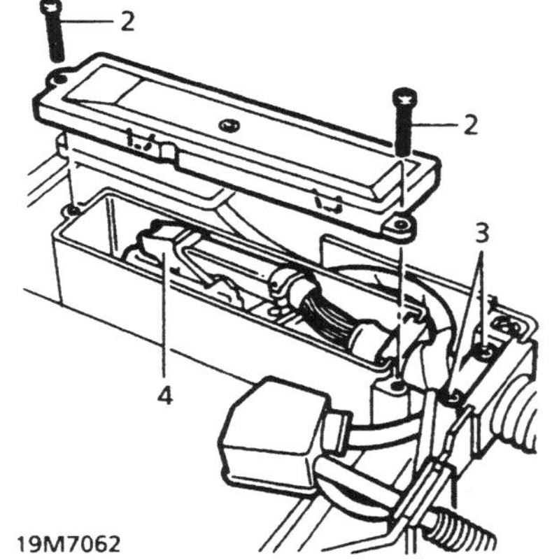

19M7062

3. Slacken 2 harness clamp screws.
4. Lift ECM slightly for access. Disconnect multiplug.
5. Remove ECM from housing.
6. Remove carrier plate from ECM.

Refit

7. Reverse removal procedure.

FUEL FILTER

Service repair no - 19.25.07

Remove

1. Disconnect battery negative lead.
2. Position container beneath fuel filter to catch spillage.

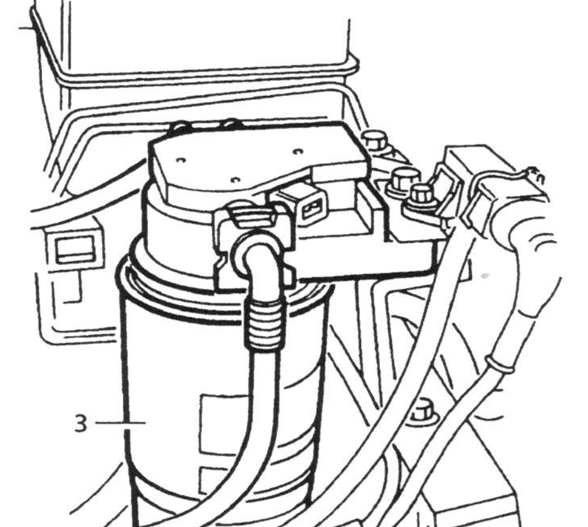

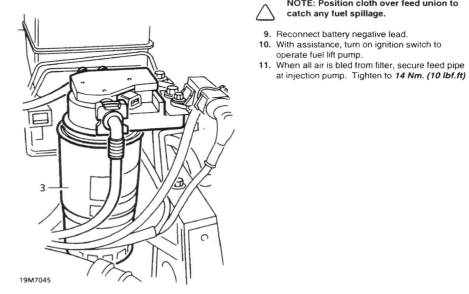

19M7045

3. Remove filter using strap wrench.

Refit

4. Ensure mating faces are clean.
5. Lubricate seal on new filter with clean diesel fuel.
6. Fit filter to filter head. Tighten securely by hand.
7. Remove container.
8. Slacken fuel feed union at fuel injection pump using LRT-12-117.

NOTE: Position cloth over feed union to catch any fuel spillage.

9. Reconnect battery negative lead.
10. With assistance, turn on ignition switch to operate fuel lift pump.
11. When all air is bled from filter, secure feed pipe at injection pump. Tighten to ***14 Nm. (10 lbf.ft)***

FUEL HEATER/FILTER HEAD

Service repair no - 19.25.20

Remove

1. Disconnect battery negative lead.
2. Remove fuel filter. ***See this section.***

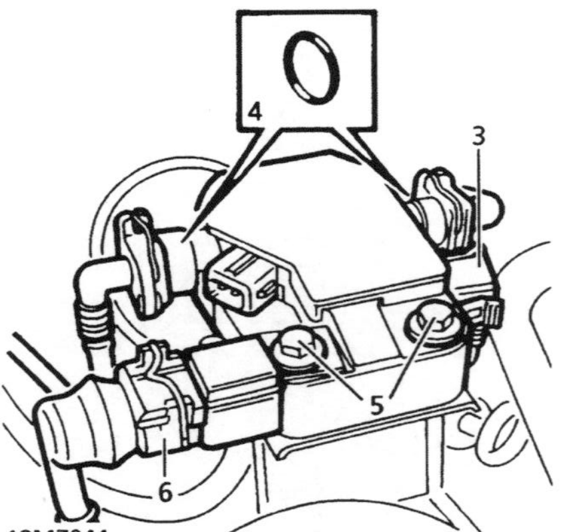

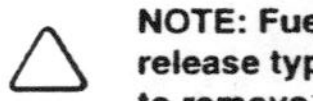

19M7044

3. Disconnect multiplug from fuel heater.
4. Disconnect fuel lines from filter head. Remove 2 'O' rings from each connection and discard.

> **NOTE: Fuel line connections are of quick release type. Press retainer, pull fuel line to remove.**

5. Remove 2 bolts securing fuel heater to bracket.
6. Position Manifold Absolute Pressure (MAP) sensor aside. Remove fuel heater.

Refit

7. Align fuel heater to bracket. Position MAP sensor.
8. Secure fuel heater and MAP sensor to bracket with bolts.
9. Fit new 'O' rings to fuel connections. Lubricate with diesel fuel.
10. Connect fuel lines and multiplug to fuel heater.
11. Fit fuel filter. ***See this section.***
12. Reconnect battery negative lead.

GLOW PLUGS

Service repair no - 19.60.31

Remove

1. Disconnect battery negative lead.
2. Remove injector high pressure pipe assembly. ***See this section.***
3. Remove nuts and disconnect feed wires from glow plugs.
4. Using a deep 12mm socket, remove glow plugs.

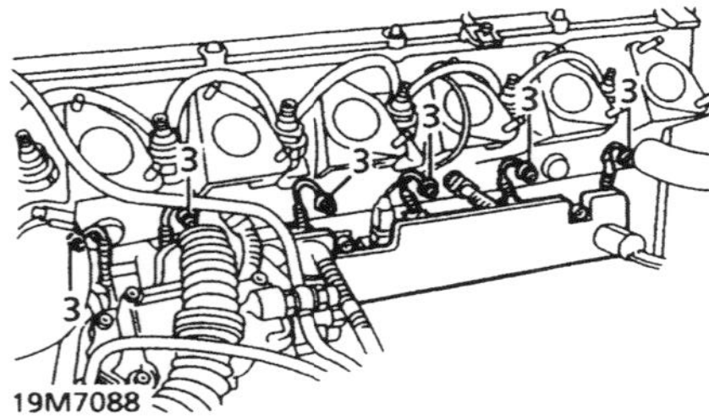

19M7088

Refit

5. Ensure glow plug threads and locations in cylinder head are clean.
6. Fit glow plugs. Tighten to ***20Nm (15lbf.ft).***
7. Connect feed wires and tighten nuts to ***4Nm (3lbf.ft).***
8. Fit injector pipe assembly. ***See this section.***
9. Reconnect battery negative lead.

FUEL INJECTION PUMP (FIP)

Service repair no - 19.30.07

Remove

1. Disconnect battery negative lead.
2. Remove high pressure pipes. ***See this section.***
3. Remove cooling fan cowl. ***See COOLING SYSTEM, Repair.***
4. Disconnect lead from stop solenoid terminal.

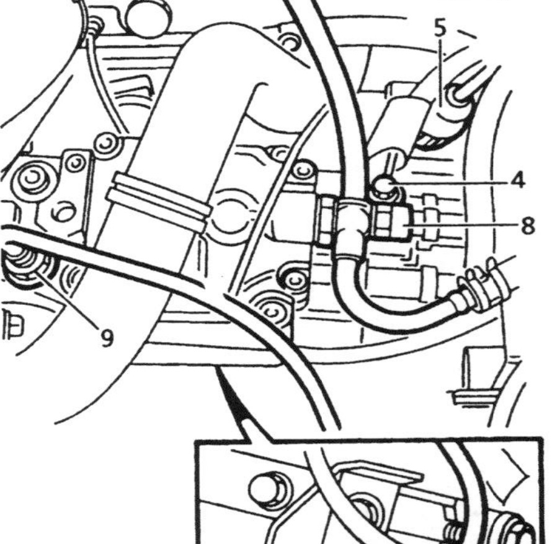

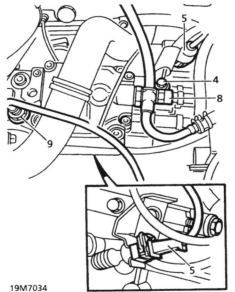

19M7034

5. Disconnect FIP harness multiplug.
6. Disconnect oil pressure switch.
7. Disconnect FIP cycle valve multiplug.

> **NOTE: Position cloth beneath FIP to catch fuel spillage.**

8. Disconnect fuel return pipe. Collect sealing washers.
9. Using tool LRT-12-117, disconnect fuel feed pipe at FIP.
10. Plug pipes and connections.
11. Remove plastic plug from flywheel timing pin access hole.

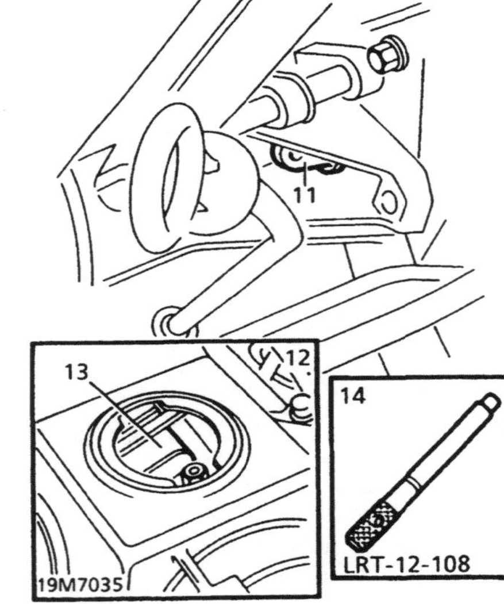

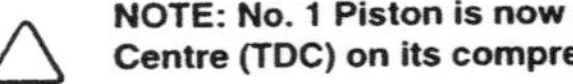

12. Remove oil filler cap. Observe No. 1 camshaft lobe.
13. Rotate crankshaft clockwise until camshaft lobe points towards inlet side of engine.
14. Insert timing pin LRT-12-108 into access hole. Locate into flywheel timing hole.

> **NOTE: No. 1 Piston is now at Top Dead Centre (TDC) on its compression stroke.**

15. Remove end cap from auxiliary belt tensioner fulcrum. Collect 'O' ring and discard.

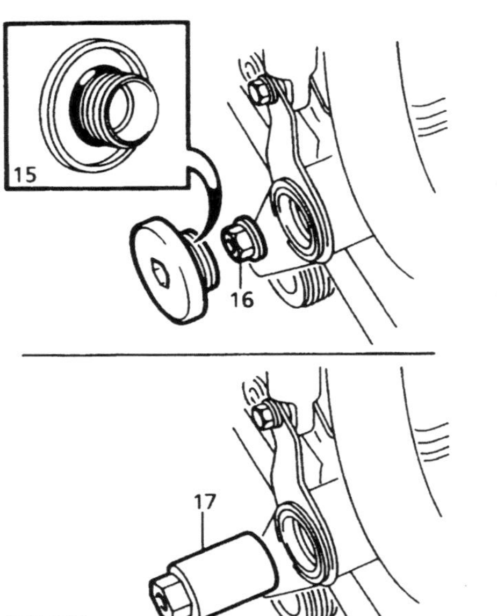

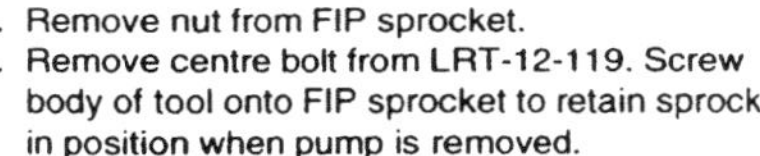

19M7036

16. Remove nut from FIP sprocket.
17. Remove centre bolt from LRT-12-119. Screw body of tool onto FIP sprocket to retain sprocket in position when pump is removed.
18. Remove 2 flange nuts and 1 support bolt securing FIP to timing case.

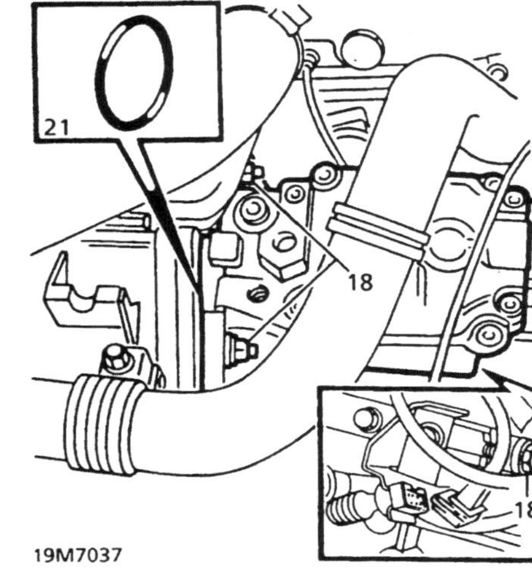

19M7037

19. Fit centre bolt to LRT-12-119. Press FIP from sprocket.

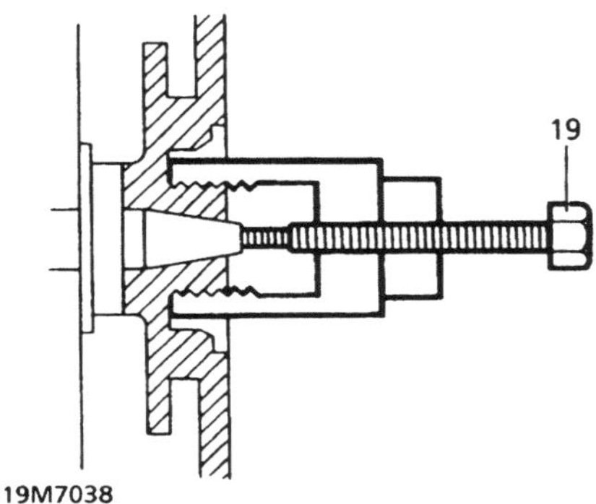

19M7038

20. Remove FIP from timing case.
21. Remove FIP. Collect 'O' ring and discard.
22. Remove centre bolt from LRT-12-119.

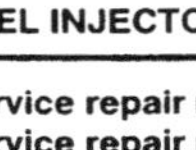

CAUTION: If body of tool is removed, FIP sprocket will drop into timing case.

Refit

23. Ensure mating faces are clean.
24. Ensure woodruff key on FIP drive shaft aligns with sprocket keyway. If necessary, turn pump shaft using tool LRT-12-118.
25. Fit new 'O' ring. Position pump to timing case.
26. Secure pump to timing case with nuts and bolts. Do not tighten at this stage.
27. Remove body of LRT-12-119 from injection pump sprocket.
28. Fit nut to injection pump shaft. Tighten to ***50 Nm. (37 lbf.ft)***
29. Using a new 'O' ring, fit end cap to auxiliary belt tensioner fulcrum.
30. Adjust injection timing. ***See Adjustment.***
31. Remove plugs from FIP connections and pipes.
32. Connect fuel feed pipe to FIP using LRT-12-117. Tighten to ***14 Nm. (10 lbf.ft)***
33. Using new sealing washers, connect fuel return pipe. Tighten to ***25 Nm. (18 lbf.ft)***
34. Connect FIP harness and cycle valve multiplugs.
35. Connect oil pressure switch.
36. Connect lead to stop solenoid terminal.
37. Fit cooling fan cowl. ***See COOLING SYSTEM, Repair.***
38. Fit high pressure pipes. ***See this section.***
39. Reconnect battery negative lead.

FUEL INJECTORS

Service repair no - 19.60.10 - Injectors - each
Service repair no - 19.60.12 - Injectors - set

Remove

1. Disconnect battery negative lead.
2. Remove high pressure pipes. ***See this section.***
3. Disconnect leak-off pipes from injector. Plug connections.

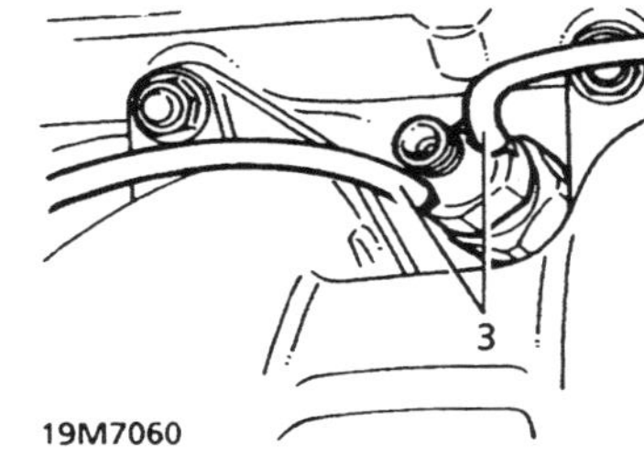

19M7060

4. **No. 4 injector only:** Disconnect needle lift sensor multiplug.

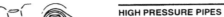

19M7061

5. Remove injector using tool LRT-12-120.

NOTE: Special tool has cut-out for needle lift sensor multiplug. Thread flylead through tool. Ensure lead and connector are not damaged during injector removal or refitting.

6. Collect sealing washer and discard.

Refit

7. Ensure injector nozzle and cylinder head bore are clean.
8. Apply anti-seize compound to injector threads.
9. Position injector with new sealing washer to cylinder head. Using LRT-12-120. Tighten to ***65 Nm. (48 lbf.ft)***
10. **No. 4 injector only:** Connect needle lift sensor multiplug.
11. Remove plugs. Connect leak-off pipes.
12. Fit high pressure pipe assembly. ***See this section.***
13. Reconnect battery negative lead.

HIGH PRESSURE PIPES

Service repair no - 19.60.14

Remove

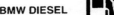

1. Disconnect battery negative lead.
2. Remove inlet manifold. ***See MANIFOLD AND EXHAUST SYSTEM, Repair.***
3. Using LRT-12-117, disconnect high pressure pipes at Fuel Injection Pump (FIP) and injectors.

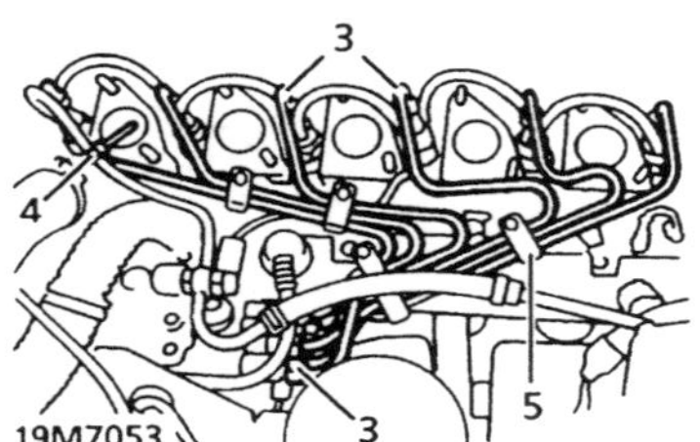

19M7053

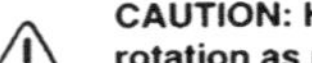

CAUTION: Hold delivery valves against rotation as pipe unions are loosened.

4. Remove clip securing leak-off pipe to No. 1 high pressure pipe.
5. Remove high pressure pipe assembly.
6. Plug high pressure pipes and connections.

Refit

7. Ensure all pipes and connections are clean,
8. Remove plugs. Position pipe assembly.
9. Using LRT-12-117, secure high pressure pipes to injection pump. Tighten to ***22 Nm. (16 lbf.ft)***

CAUTION: Hold delivery valves against rotation as pipe unions are tightened.

10. Connect pipes to injectors. Do not tighten.
11. Secure leak-off pipe to No. 1 high pressure pipe with clip.
12. Fit inlet manifold. ***See MANIFOLD AND EXHAUST SYSTEM, Repair.***
13. Reconnect battery negative lead.
14. With assistance, crank engine. As fuel emerges at injector connections, secure each pipe union using tool LRT-12-117. Tighten to ***22 Nm. (16 lbf.ft)***

CAUTION: Engine will start during high pressure pipe bleeding procedure.

INTAKE AIR TEMPERATURE SENSOR (IAT SENSOR) - VEHICLES WITHOUT EGR

Service repair no - 18.30.09

Remove

1. Disconnect multiplug.
2. Remove sensor from intake manifold. Discard sealing washer.

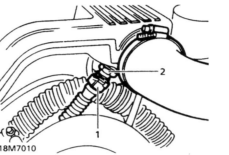

18M7010

Refit

3. Ensure mating faces are clean.
4. Using a new sealing washer, fit sensor to intake manifold. Tighten to ***14 Nm. (10 lbf.ft)***
5. Connect multiplug.

MANIFOLD ABSOLUTE PRESSURE (MAP) SENSOR

Service repair no - 19.42.34

Remove

1. Disconnect multiplug from sensor.
2. Remove nut and bolt. Release sensor from bracket.
3. Release clip. Remove sensor from hose.

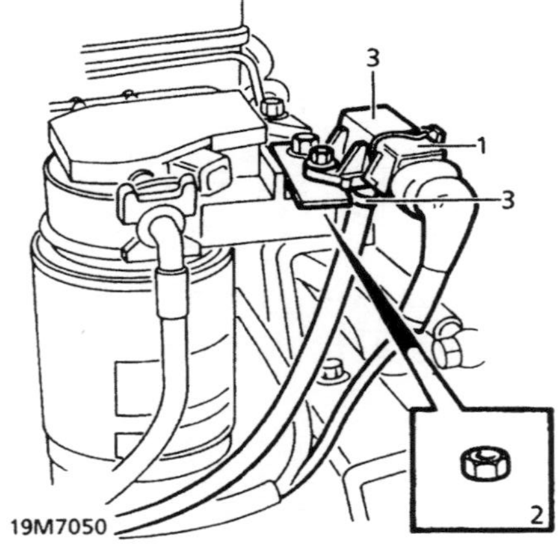

19M7050

Refit

4. Reverse removal procedure.

THROTTLE POSITION SENSOR (TP SENSOR)

Service repair no - 19.22.49

Remove

1. Disconnect battery negative lead.
2. Remove drivers side fascia closing panel. ***See CHASSIS AND BODY, Repair.***
3. Remove 3 scrivet fasteners securing lower closing panel. Release panel to gain access to blower motor ducting.

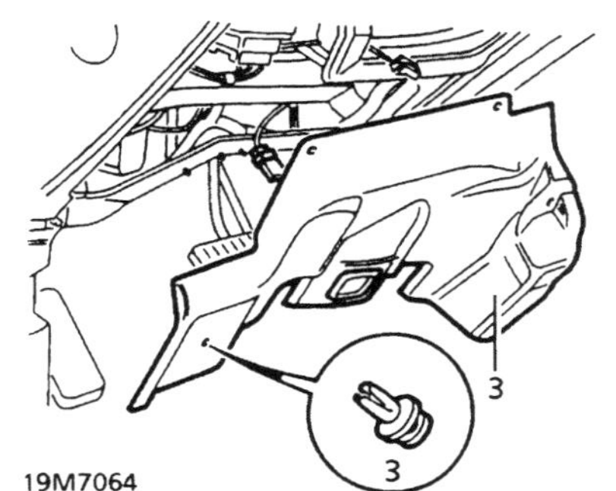

19M7064

4. Release ducting from blower motor housing and heater. Remove blower motor ducting.
5. Release linkage from ball joint on TP sensor lever.

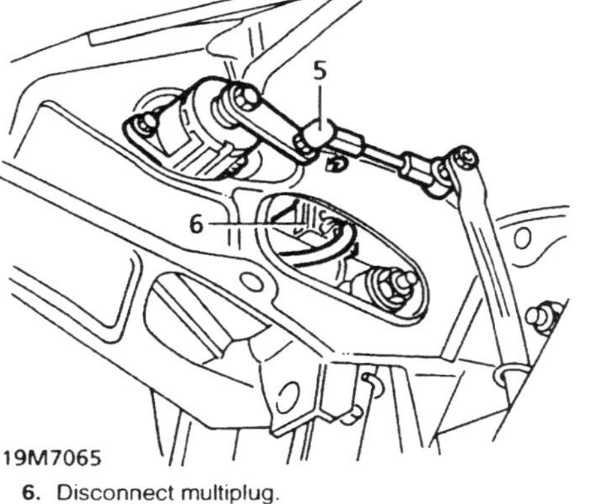

19M7065

6. Disconnect multiplug.
7. Remove 2 bolts securing TP sensor to pedal box.
8. Release TP sensor harness from pedal box. Remove TP sensor.

Refit

9. Position TP sensor. Route harness correctly over pedal box.
10. Secure TP sensor with bolts. Tighten to ***5 Nm. (4 lbf.ft)***
11. Connect linkage to TP sensor lever ball joint.
12. Connect multiplug.
13. Fit blower ducting. Engage to heater and blower motor housing.
14. Align lower closing panel. Secure with scrivet fasteners.
15. Fit drivers side fascia closing panel. ***See CHASSIS AND BODY, Repair.***
16. Reconnect battery negative lead.

TURBOCHARGER

Service repair no - 19.42.01

Remove

1. Disconnect battery negative lead.
2. Raise the vehicle.

WARNING: Support on safety stands.

3. Remove exhaust system front pipe. ***See MANIFOLD AND EXHAUST SYSTEM, Repair.***
4. Remove heat shield. ***See MANIFOLD AND EXHAUST SYSTEM, Repair.***
5. Disconnect intake hose from turbocharger.

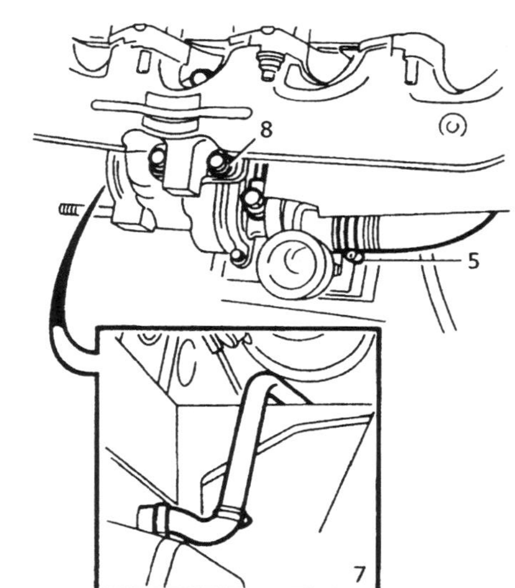

19M7046

6. Disconnect oil feed pipe from turbocharger. Collect sealing washers and discard.
7. Disconnect oil drain hose from turbocharger.
8. Remove 3 bolts securing turbocharger to exhaust manifold.
9. Remove turbocharger. Collect gasket and discard.

NOTE: Plug all connections to prevent ingress of dirt.

Refit

10. Ensure all mating faces are clean.
11. Remove plugs. Position new gasket on manifold. Position turbocharger.
12. Secure turbocharger with bolts. Tighten to ***45 Nm. (33 lbf.ft)***
13. Connect oil drain hose to turbocharger. Secure with clip.
14. Position oil feed pipe with new washers. Secure with banjo bolt. Tighten to ***25 Nm. (18 lbf.ft)***
15. Connect intake hose to turbocharger. Secure with clip.
16. Fit exhaust system front pipe. ***See MANIFOLD AND EXHAUST SYSTEM, Repair.***
17. Fit heat shield. ***See MANIFOLD AND EXHAUST SYSTEM, Repair.***
18. Remove safety stands. Lower vehicle.
19. Reconnect battery negative lead.

INTERCOOLER

Service repair no - 19.42.15

Remove

1. Remove battery. *See **ELECTRICAL, Repair.***

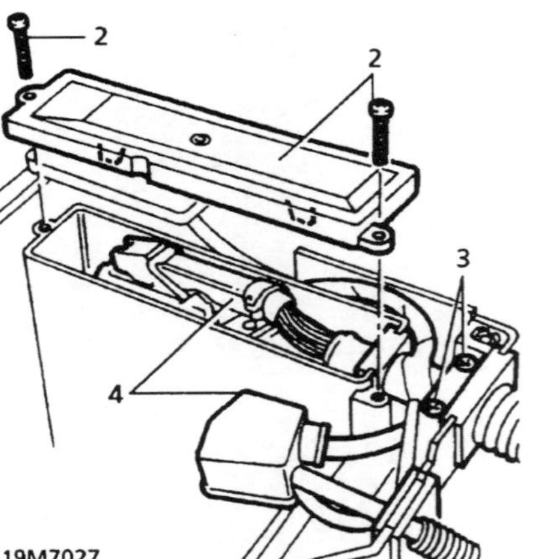

19M7027

2. Remove 2 screws securing fuel ECM cover. Remove cover.
3. Remove 2 screws securing ECM harness clamp. Remove clamp.
4. Remove ECM from battery box. Position ECM and battery harness aside.

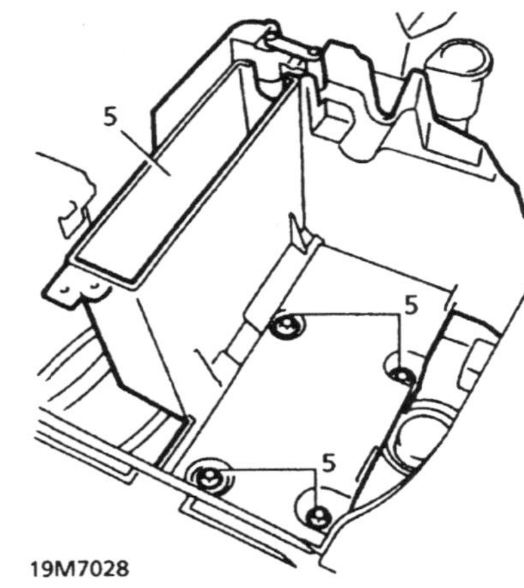

19M7028

5. Remove 4 bolts securing battery box. Remove battery box.
6. Remove front grille. ***See CHASSIS AND BODY, Repair.***
7. Remove 4 bolts securing bonnet platform.

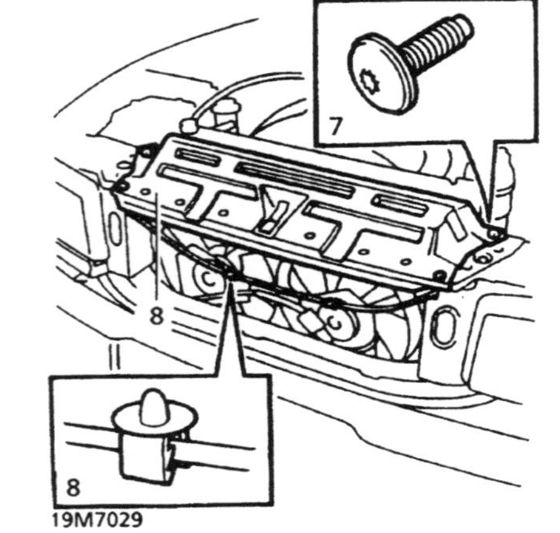

19M7029

8. Release bonnet release cable clips from platform. Remove platform.

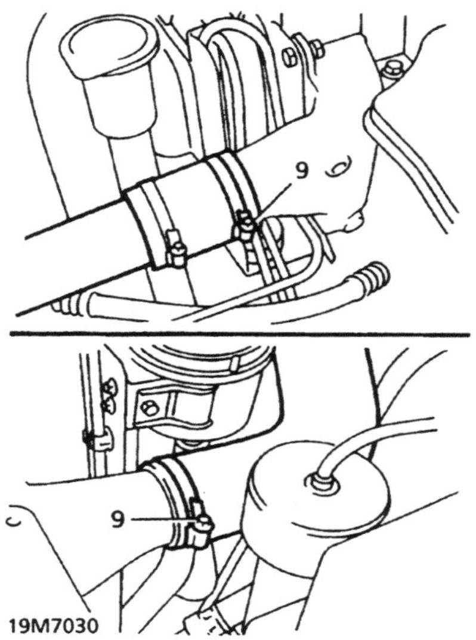

19M7030

9. Disconnect hoses from intercooler.

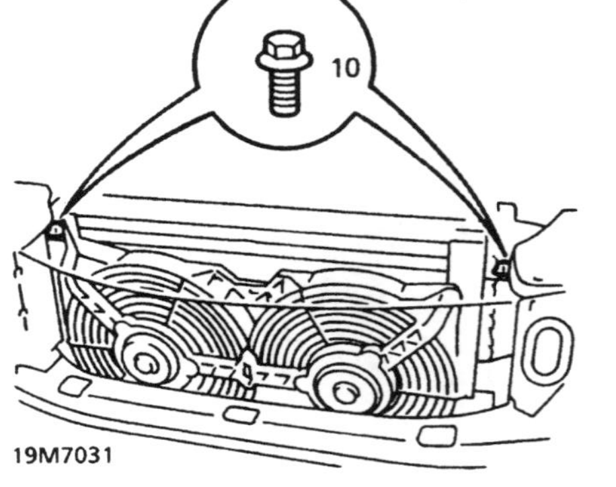

19M7031

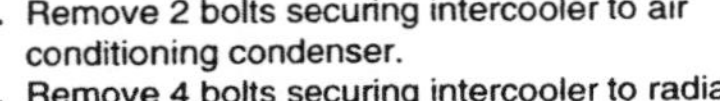

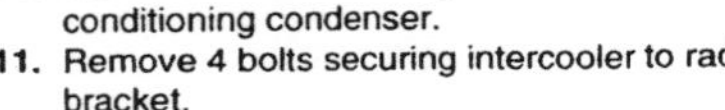

10. Remove 2 bolts securing intercooler to air conditioning condenser.
11. Remove 4 bolts securing intercooler to radiator bracket.

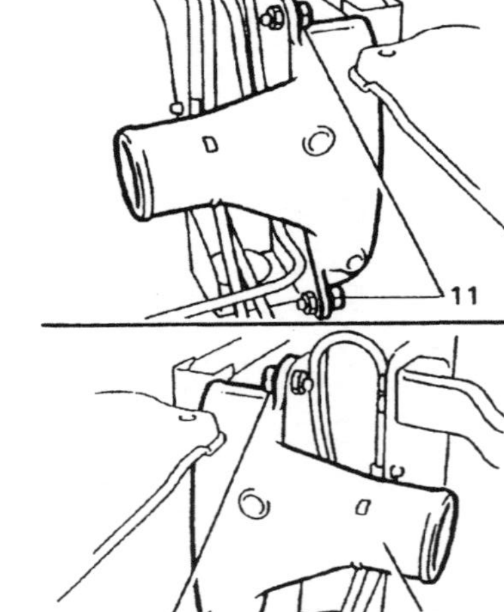

19M7032

12. Remove intercooler.

Refit

13. Reverse removal procedure.

FILLER NECK ASSEMBLY

Service repair no - 19.55.07

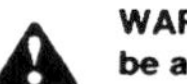

WARNING: If fuel tank is full, fuel level will be above filler neck aperture in the tank. If gauge indicates over 75%, drain a minimum 10 litres of fuel from tank.

Remove

1. Disconnect battery negative lead.
2. Remove rear wheel arch liner. ***See CHASSIS AND BODY, Repair.***
3. Remove fuel filler cap.
4. Slacken clips securing hoses to filler neck.

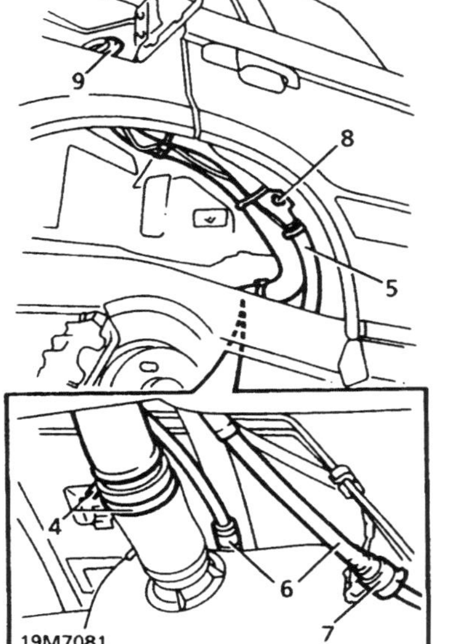

19M7081

5. Release fill breather hose from filler neck.
6. **Petrol Models Only:** Disconnect fuel tank and charcoal canister hoses from vapour separator.
7. **Diesel Models Only:** Release cap from quick release connector. Disconnect breather hose.
8. Remove nut securing filler neck to wheel arch.
9. Release filler neck from fuel tank hose and grommet in body aperture.
10. Remove filler neck assembly.

Refit

11. Apply liquid soap to grommet and mating surface of filler neck.
12. Reverse removal procedure.

FUEL TANK, PUMP AND GAUGE SENDER UNIT

Service repair no - 19.55.01 - Fuel Tank
Service repair no - 19.45.08 - Fuel Pump
Service repair no - 88.25.32 - Fuel gauge Tank Unit

Remove

1. Disconnect battery negative lead.
2. **Petrol Models Only:** Depressurise fuel system. ***See this section.***
3. Remove contents of fuel tank into an approved closed container.
4. Remove fuel filler neck. ***See this section.***
5. Raise vehicle on four post lift.
6. Position container beneath fuel filter to catch spillage.
7. **Petrol Models Only:** Disconnect feed pipe from fuel filter.
8. **Diesel Models Only:** Disconnect feed pipe at connection, forward of fuel tank.

7
9
19M7076

9. Disconnect return pipe, forward of tank.
10. Plug pipes and connections.
11. Support tank with jack.
12. Remove 3 nuts and 2 bolts securing tank cradle to floor pan.

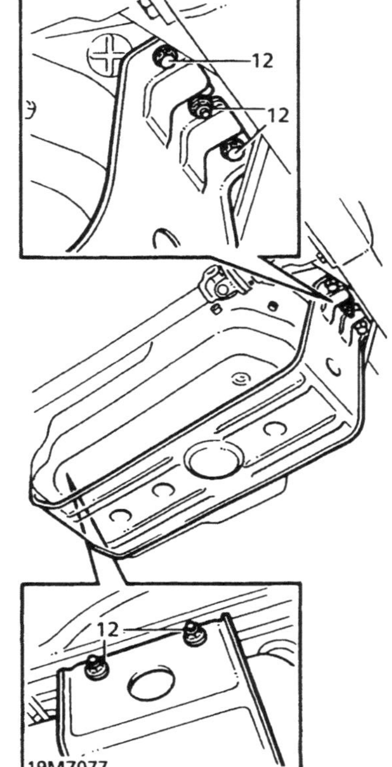

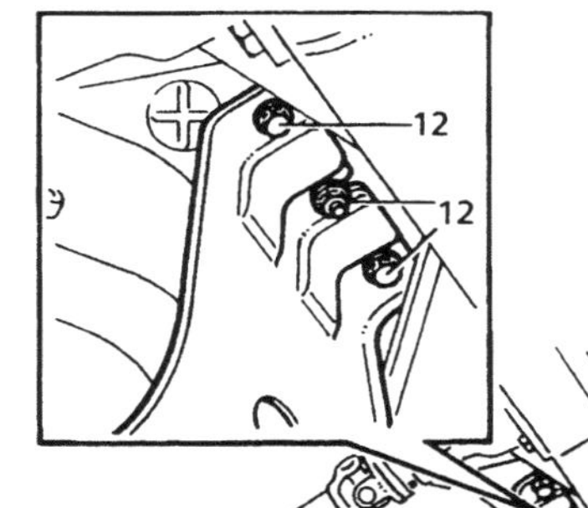

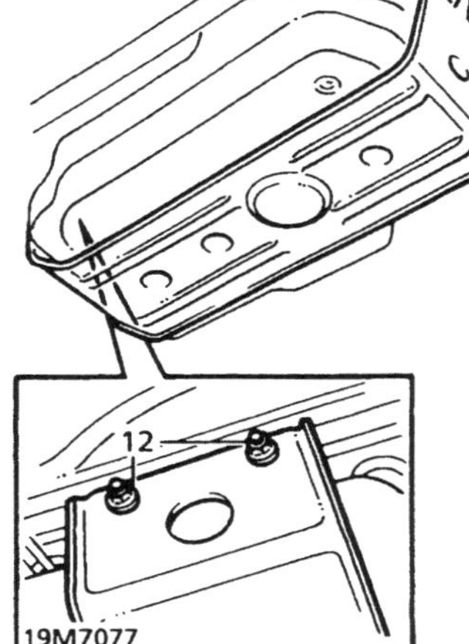

19M7077

13. Lower tank by 150mm. Disconnect multiplug from fuel tank unit.

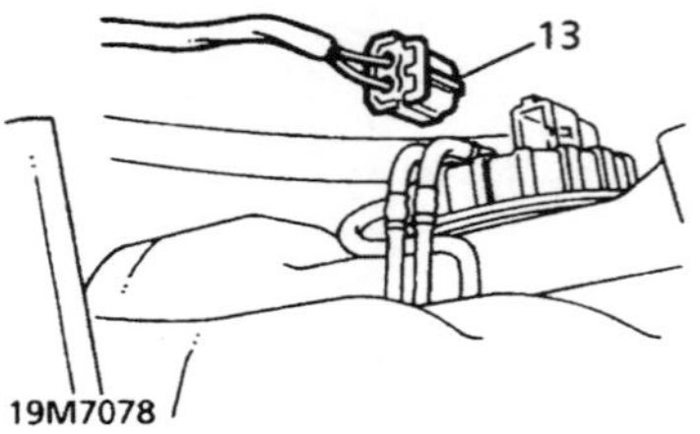

14. Lower tank assembly. Remove from jack. ***Do not carry out further dismantling if component is removed for access only.***

Disassemble

15. Remove tank from cradle.
16. Slacken clip. Remove fill breather pipe from tank unit.

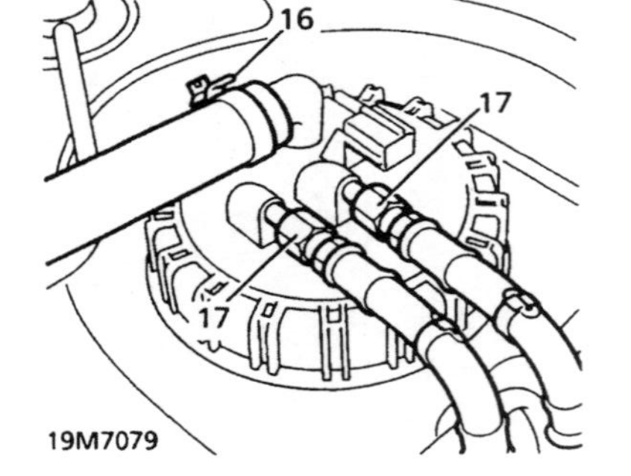

17. Disconnect feed and return pipes from tank unit. Remove each pipe from 2 fuel tank clips.
18. Remove tank unit retaining ring using LRT-19-001. Remove assembly from tank.

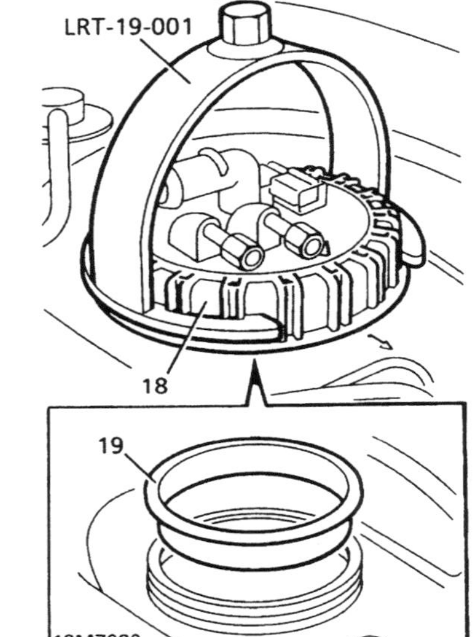

WARNING: A quantity of fuel will be retained in the unit, care must be taken to avoid excessive spillage during removal.

19. Remove tank unit sealing rubber and discard.

Reassemble

20. Fit new sealing rubber.
21. Fit tank unit. Align location marks.
22. Fit retaining ring using LRT-19-001.
23. Connect fuel feed and return pipes to tank unit. Tighten to ***16 Nm. (12 lbf.ft)***
24. Secure pipes to fuel tank clips.
25. Position fill breather pipe to tank unit. Secure with clip.
26. Position tank in cradle.

Refit

27. Raise fuel tank assembly on jack until multiplug can be connected to tank unit.
28. Raise tank. Align cradle mounting points. Secure with nuts and bolts.
29. Remove plugs from pipes and connections.
30. **Petrol Models Only:** Using new 'O' ring, connect fuel spill return pipe. Tighten to ***16 Nm. (12 lbf.ft)***
31. **Petrol Models Only:** Using new 'O' ring, connect fuel feed pipe to filter. Tighten to ***20 Nm. (15 lbf.ft)***
32. **Diesel Models Only:** Connect fuel feed and return pipes.
33. Lower vehicle.
34. Refit fuel filler neck. ***See this section.***
35. Refill fuel tank.
36. Reconnect battery negative lead.

MASS AIR FLOW (MAF) SENSOR - DIESEL WITH EGR

Service repair no - 19.22.25

Remove

1. Disconnect multiplug from MAF sensor.
2. Slacken clip and disconnect intake hose from MAF sensor.
3. Remove 2 bolts securing MAF sensor to air cleaner.
4. Remove MAF sensor and collect 'O' ring seal.

NOTE: Discard 'O' ring seal.

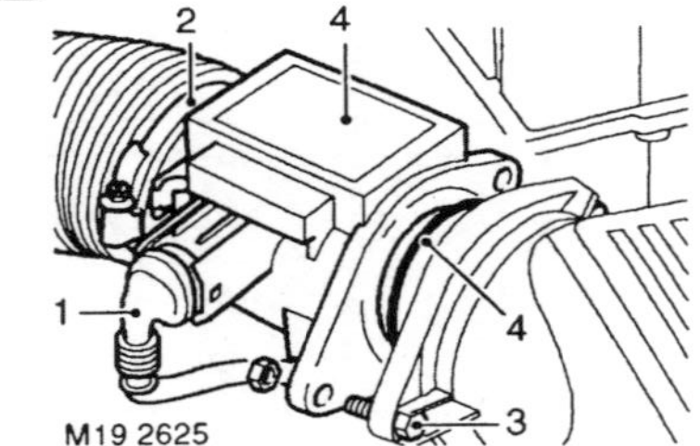

Refit

5. Position new 'O' ring seal to MAF sensor.
6. Engage MAF sensor to air cleaner and secure with bolts. Tighten bolts to 10Nm (7 lbf.in).
7. Connect intake hose and secure with clip.
8. Connect multiplug to MAF sensor.

DUCTING - AIR INTAKE - DIESEL WITH EGR

Service repair no - 19.10.27

Remove

1. Disconnect battery negative terminal.
2. Remove 4 bolts securing injector cover and remove cover.
3. Slacken clip securing intake hose to intake ducting and disconnect hose.
4. Release clip securing breather hose to intake ducting.
5. Slacken clip securing intake duct to turbo duct.
6. Carefully release intake duct from clips on intake manifold and camshaft cover.

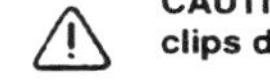

CAUTION: Care must be taken to ensure clips do not become damaged.

7. Disengage duct from breather hose and turbo duct. Remove intake duct assembly.

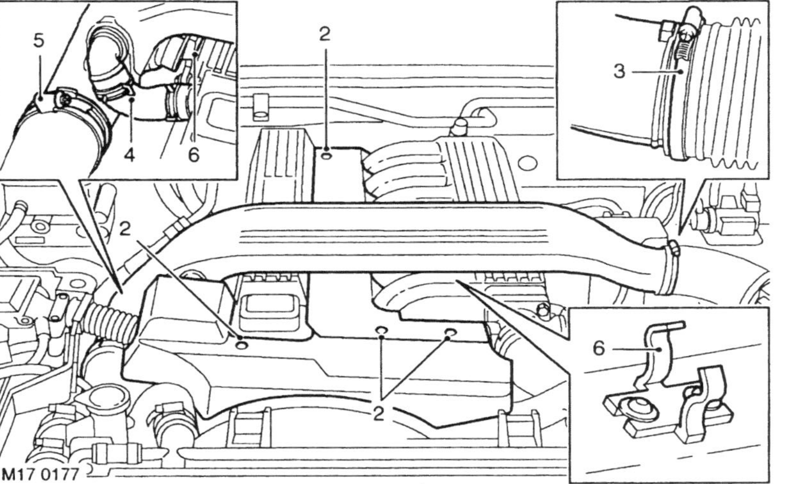

Refit

8. Position intake duct. Engage turbo duct and breather hose.
9. Carefully engage intake duct clips to camshaft cover and inlet manifold locations.

CAUTION: Ensure that manifold clips are correctly engaged before pushing duct downwards or clips may be damaged.

10. Connect intake hose to intake duct.
11. Secure clips on intake turbo duct, intake hose and breather hose.
12. Position injector cover and secure with bolts. Tighten bolts to Tighten to ***10 Nm (7 lbf.in).***
13. Connect battery negative terminal.

CONTENTS

Page

LAND ROVER V8

DESCRIPTION AND OPERATION

ADJUSTMENT

REPAIR

19 - FUEL SYSTEM

CONTENTS

ENGINE MANAGEMENT SYSTEM - up to 99MY

Description

The V8 engine for models prior to 99MY is controlled by a Sagem GEMS engine management system. The ECM uses sensors to determine ambient conditions and operating data and uses this data and the information stored in an internal memory map to control the electronic ignition and fuel injection. The system features idle speed control, fault monitoring, security immobilisation and engine load management functions. GEMS can be interrogated via the diagnostic socket to access fault codes and other diagnostic information using Testbook.

The engine management system (EMS) maintains optimum engine performance over the entire operating range. The correct amount of fuel is metered into each cylinder inlet tract and the ignition timing is adjusted at each spark plug.

The system is controlled by the engine control module (ECM) which receives data from sensors located on and around the engine. From this information it provides the correct fuel requirements and ignition timing at all engine loads and speeds.

The fuel injection system uses a hot wire mass air flow (MAF) sensor to calculate the quantity of air flowing into the engine.

The ignition system does not use a distributor. It is a direct ignition system (DIS), using four double ended coils. The circuit to each coil is completed by switching inside the ECM.

The on-board diagnostic system detects any faults which may occur within the EMS. Fault diagnosis includes failure of any EMS sensors and actuators, emissions related items, fuel supply and exhaust systems.

The system incorporates certain default strategies to enable the vehicle to be driven in case of sensor failure. This may mean that a fault is not detected by the driver. The fault is indicated by illumination of the malfunction indicator light (MIL) on North American specification vehicles.

A further feature of the system is 'robust immobilisation', fitted to European specification vehicles. Upon arming the alarm, the EMS ECM disables the injectors and the Body electrical Control Module (BeCM) inhibits the crank relay (the vehicle cannot be started until the alarm is disarmed).

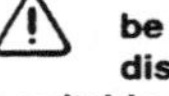

CAUTION: System sensor connectors can be contaminated by oil or coolant when disconnected during repair or testing. Use a suitable cap to prevent dirt or fluid ingress.

ENGINE MANAGEMENT SYSTEM COMPONENT LOCATION - up to 99MY

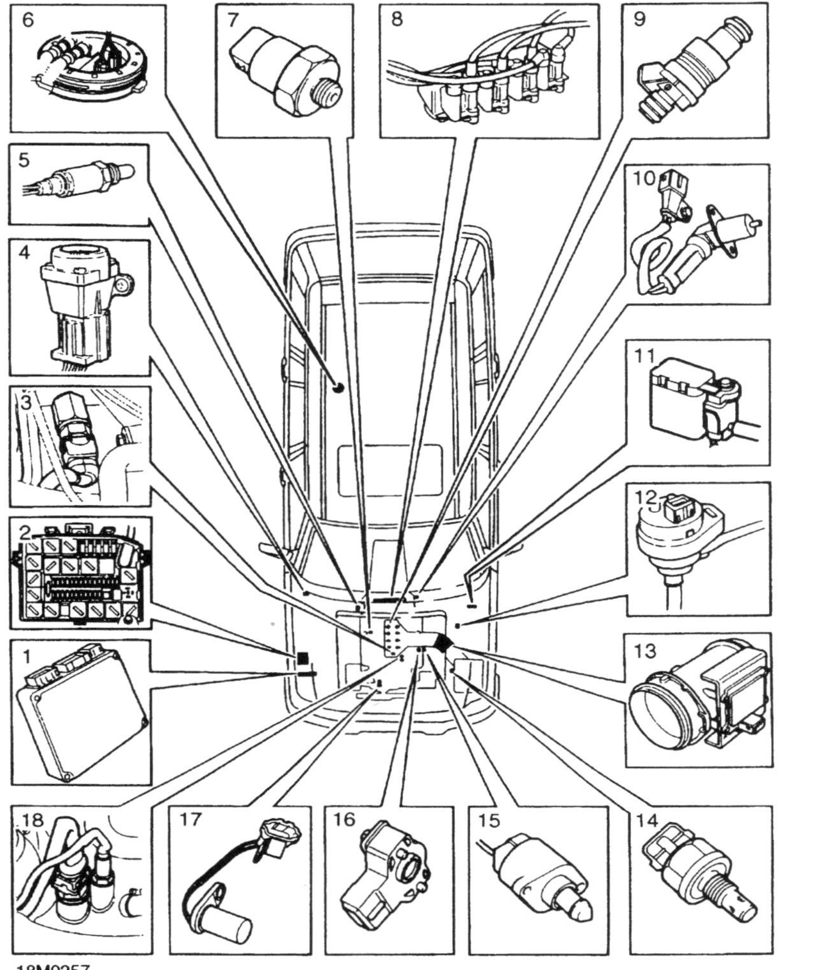

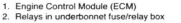

18M0257

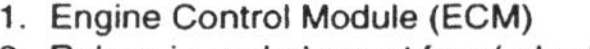

1. Engine Control Module (ECM)
2. Relays in underbonnet fuse/relay box
   - Main relay
   - Ignition relay
   - Starter motor relay
   - Fuel pump relay

3. Engine Fuel Temperature (EFT) sensor
4. Inertia Fuel Shut-off (IFS) switch
5. Heated Oxygen Sensor (HO_2S)
6. Fuel pump and gauge sensor (Advanced EVAPS unit also incorporates tank pressure sensor)
7. Knock Sensors (KS) (2 off)
8. Ignition coils
9. Fuel injectors
10. Crankshaft position (CKP) sensor (early type shown)
11. EVAP Canister Vent Solenoid (ECVS) - Advanced EVAPS only
12. EVAP canister purge valve
13. Mass air flow (MAF) sensor
14. Intake Air Temperature (IAT) sensor
15. Idle Air Control (IAC) Valve
16. Throttle Position (TP) sensor
17. Camshaft Position (CMP) sensor
18. Engine coolant temperature (ECT) sensor

ENGINE MANAGEMENT SYSTEM SCHEMATIC - up to 99MY

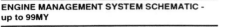

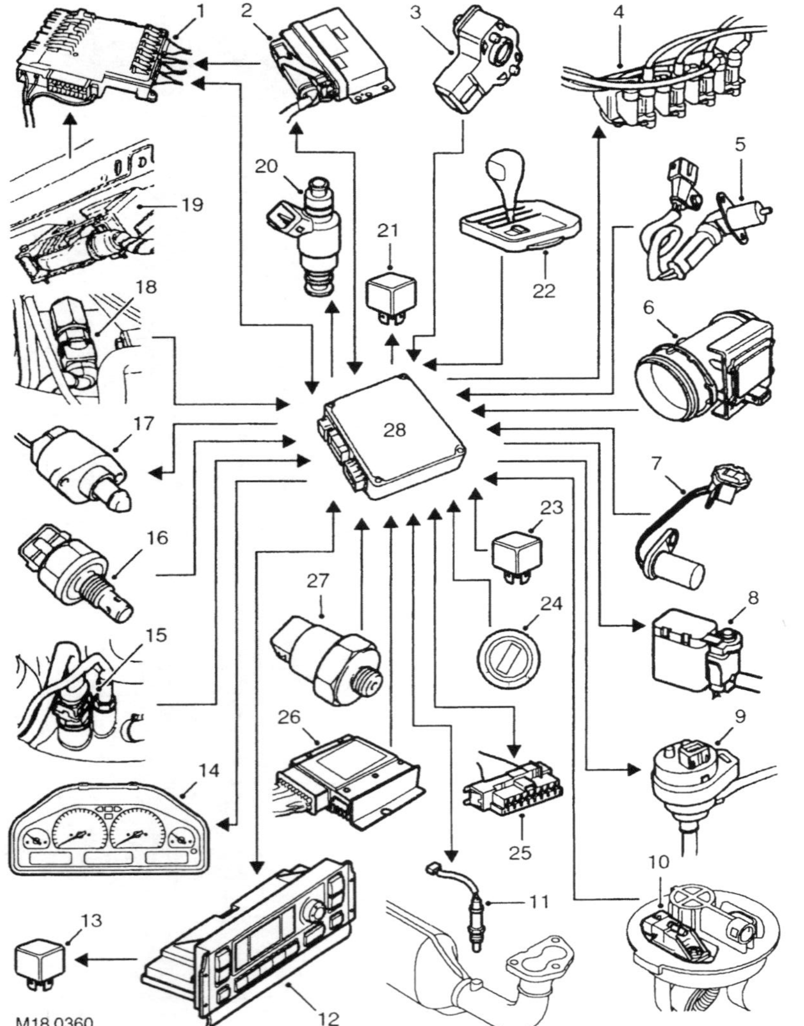

1. Body electrical Control Module (BeCM)- (Inputs and Outputs)
   - Engine speed signal - (Output)
   - Engine immobilisation security signal - (Input)
   - Road speed signal - (Input from ABS ECU via BeCM)
   - Check engine / Service engine soon (NAS) warning lamp - (Output)
   - Fuel level signal - (Input)
2. Electronic Automatic Transmission (EAT) ECU - (Inputs and Outputs)
   - Engine torque signal - (Output)
   - Throttle angle signal - (Output)
   - Ignition retard - (Input)
   - Engine speed signal - (Output via BeCM)
3. Throttle Position (TP) sensor - (Input)
4. Ignition coils (4 off) - (Output)
5. Crankshaft speed and position (CKP) sensor - (Input)
6. Mass air flow (MAF) sensor - (Input)
7. Camshaft position (CMP) sensor - (Input)
8. Canister vent solenoid (CVS) unit - (Output- NAS Advanced EVAPs system only)
9. Purge valve - (Output)
10. Fuel tank pressure sensor - (Input - NAS Advanced EVAPs system only)
11. HO_2S sensors (0, 2 or 4 off dependent on market legislation)
   - (Input signal and HO_2S sensor heater supply output)
12. HEVAC unit - (Inputs and Outputs)
   - Air Con Request - (Output)
   - Air Con Grant - (Output)
   - Condenser Fan Request - (Input)
   - Heated Front Screen - (Input via BeCM for idle speed compensation)
13. Condenser Fan Relay - (Output)
14. Instrument pack - (Fuel used signal output)
15. Engine coolant temperature (ECT) sensor - (Input)
16. Intake air temperature (IAT) sensor - (Input)
17. Idle Air Control Valve (IACV) - (Output)
18. Fuel temperature sensor - (Input)
19. ABS ECU (Rough road signal) - (Input via BeCM)
20. Fuel injectors (8 off) - (Output)
21. Fuel pump relay - (Output)
22. Park / Neutral Switch - (Input)
23. Main power relay - (Input)
24. Ignition supply (Ignition sense) - (Input)
25. Diagnostic connector - (bi-directional)
26. Transfer box ECU - (MIL request input)
27. Knock (KS) sensors (2 off) - (Input)

This page is intentionally left blank

ENGINE MANAGEMENT SYSTEM - from 99MY

Description

The V8 engine for models from 99MY is controlled by a Bosch Motronic 5.2.1 engine management system. The ECM uses sensors to determine ambient conditions and operating data and uses this data and the information stored in an internal memory map to control the electronic ignition and fuel injection. The system features:

- Idle speed control (ISC)
- Adherance to regulatory emissions standards
- Adherance to OBDII legislation for NAS vehicles
- Security immobilisation
- Fuelling quantity
- Exhaust emission control using HO_2S sensors and closed loop fuelling
- Knock control
- Ignition timing
- Interfaces with other electronic systems including Electronic Automatic Transmission (EAT) ECU, Transfer Box ECU, ABS ECU, BeCM and instrument pack.

The engine management system controls the engine fuelling by providing full sequential injection to all cylinders. Ignition is controlled by a direct ignition system which is provided by four double ended ignition coils operating on the wasted spark principle.

Sensors used in the engine management system include:

- Mass air flow sensor - to determine the mass of air entering the engine
- Throttle position sensor - to detect the current throttle angle
- Coolant temperature sensor - to detect current engine coolant temperature
- Exhaust gas sensors (HO_2S) sensors - to determine the exhaust emission levels

The ECM software program processes these signals and determines what actions to implement based on these signals and the internal mapped data settings.

The on-board diagnostic system detects any faults which may occur within the EMS. The system monitors and reports on any ignition, fuelling or exhaust faults which cause an excessive increase in emissions. Fault diagnosis includes failure of any EMS sensors and actuators, as well as misfire, catalyst damage, catalyst efficiency, fuel evaporative loss control and exhaust leaks.

The system incorporates certain default strategies to enable the vehicle to be driven in case of sensor failure. This may mean that a fault is not detected by the driver. The fault is indicated by illumination of the malfunction indicator lamp (MIL) on North American specification vehicles.

The ECM also communicates with the EAT ECU using a CAN data link for the transmission of OBD information.

A further feature of the system is 'robust immobilisation', (fitted to vehicles in most markets). Upon arming the alarm, the EMS ECM disables the injectors and the Body electrical Control Module (BeCM) inhibits the crank relay (the vehicle cannot be started until the alarm is disarmed).

CAUTION: System sensor connectors can be contaminated by oil or coolant when disconnected during repair or testing. Use a suitable cap to prevent dirt or fluid ingress.

ENGINE MANAGEMENT SYSTEM COMPONENT LOCATION - from 99MY

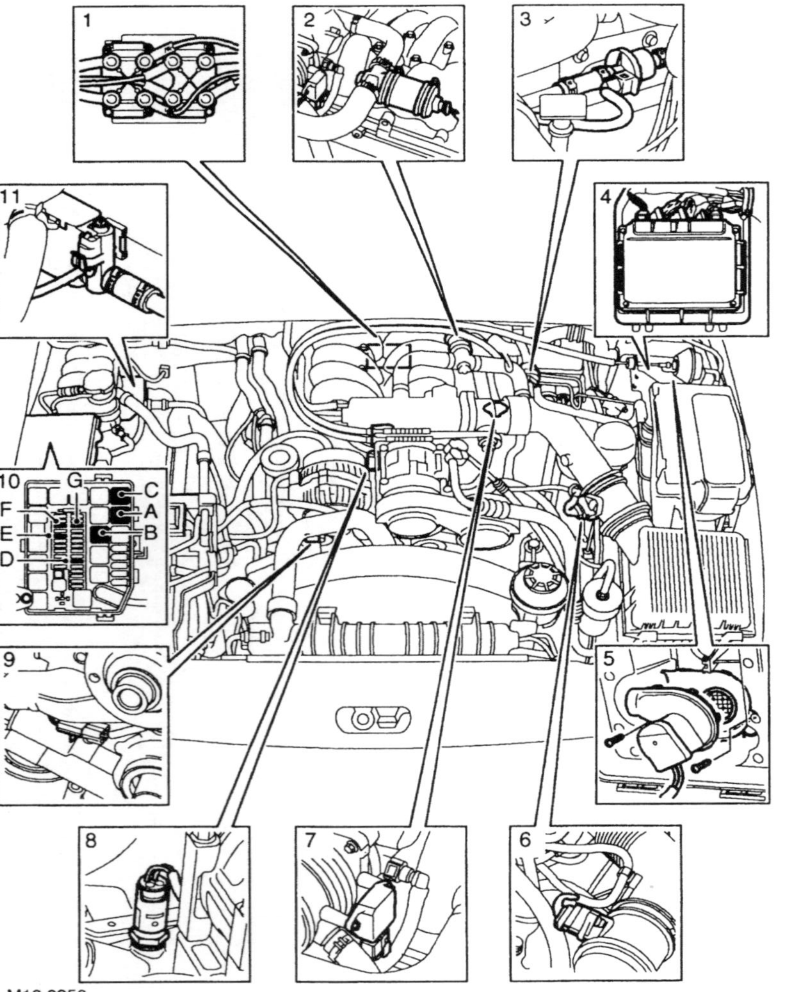

M18 0358

1. Ignition coils
2. Idle Air Control Valve (IACV)
3. Purge valve
4. Engine Control Module (ECM)
5. "E-box" cooling fan
6. MAF Sensor & IAT Sensor
7. Throttle Position Sensor
8. Engine Coolant Temperature (ECT) Sensor
9. Camshaft Position (CMP) Sensor
10. Engine Compartment Relay and Fusebox
    - A - Main Relay
    - B - Ignition Relay
    - C - Air Conditioning On/Off Relay
    - D - Battery supply fuse (30A)
    - E - Ignition relay supply fuse (30A)
    - F - Main relay output fuse (20A)
    - G - Main relay output fuse (30A)
11. Canister Vent Solenoid (CVS) Valve

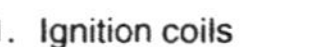

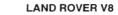

ENGINE MANAGEMENT SYSTEM COMPONENT LOCATION - from 99MY (Continued)

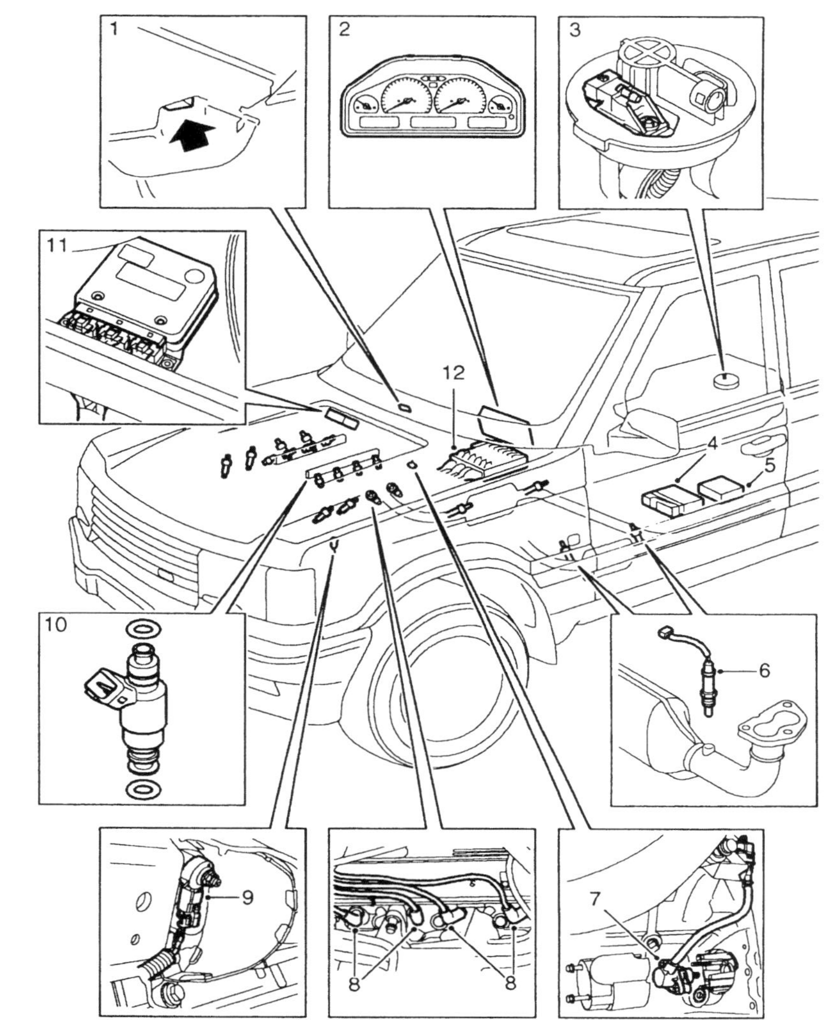

M18 0359

1. Diagnostic connector
2. Instrument pack
   - Check engine / Service engine soon (NAS only) warning lamp
   - Tachometer
   - Fuel used
3. Fuel tank pressure sensor
4. Electronic Automatic Transmission (EAT) ECU
5. Transfer Box ECU
6. HO_2S sensors
7. Crankshaft position sensor
8. Spark plugs and HT leads
9. Knock sensor
10. Fuel injectors
11. ABS ECU
12. Body electronic Control Module (BeCM)

ENGINE MANAGEMENT SYSTEM SCHEMATIC - from 99MY

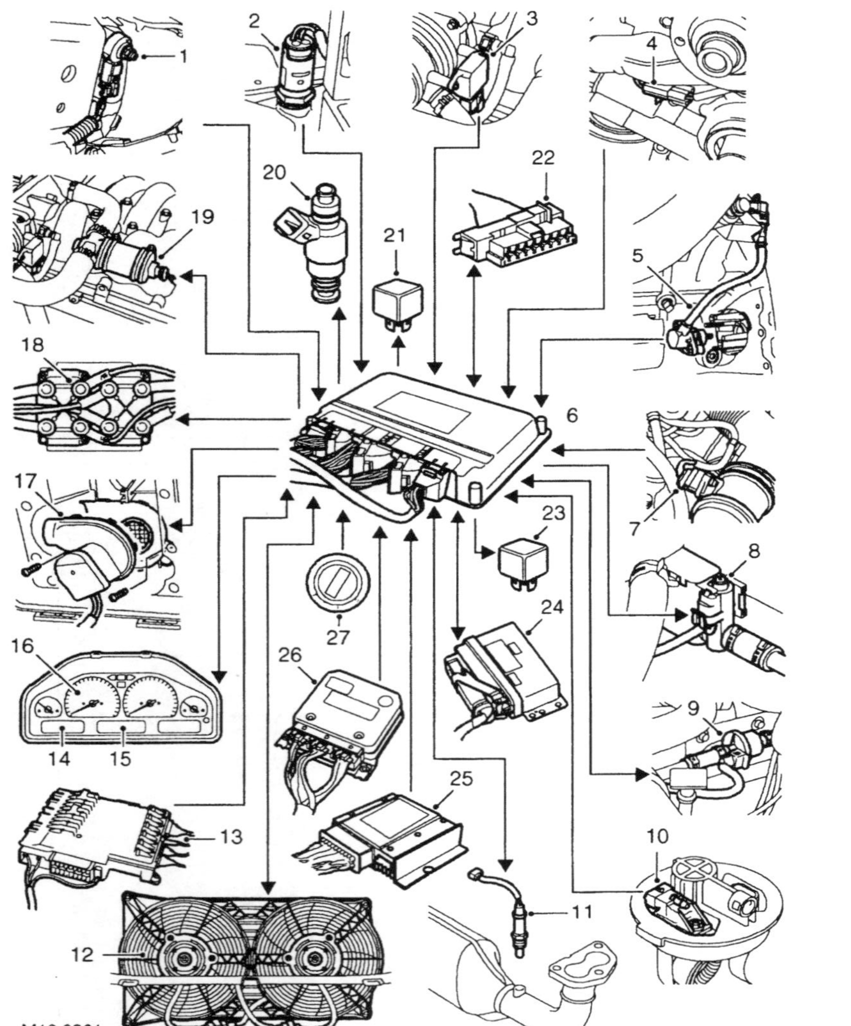

ECM engine interface inputs:

1. Knock sensor (2 off)
2. Engine coolant temperature (ECT) sensor
3. Throttle position (TP) sensor
4. Camshaft position (CMP) sensor
5. Crankshaft speed and position sensor
6. Engine control module (ECM)
7. Mass air flow (MAF) / Inlet air temperature (IAT) sensor

Fuel system:

8. Canister vent solenoid (CVS) valve (output)
9. Purge valve (output)
10. Fuel tank pressure sensor (input)

Emissions:

11. Heated oxygen sensors (0, 2 or 4 dependent on market destination)
    - HO_2S sensor signal inputs
    - HO_2S sensor heater supply outputs

Air Conditioning System:

12. - Air conditioning compressor (output)
    - Air conditioning condenser fan relay (output)
    - Air conditioning request (input)
    - Condenser fan request (input)

BeCM:

13. BeCM
    - Immobilisation signal (input)
    - Fuel tank level signal (input)

Instrument pack:

14. Check Engine / Service Engine Soon (NAS) warning lamp (output)
15. Fuel used signal - display (output)
16. Tachometer (output)

E-box:

17. E-box cooling fan control (output)

ECM engine interface outputs:

18. Ignition coils (4 off)
19. Idle air control (IAC) actuator
20. Fuel injectors (8 off)
21. Fuel pump relay

Diagnostics:

22. Diagnostic connector (bi-directional)

Power supply:

23. Main relay (input)

Electronic Control Unit interfaces:

24. Electronic Automatic Transmission (EAT) ECU (via bi-directional CAN link)
25. Transfer Box ECU (MIL request)
26. ABS ECU (Rough road signal)

Ignition switched power supply:

27. Ignition switch - position II (input)

COMPONENT DESCRIPTIONS - up to 99MY

Engine Control Module (ECM) - (up to 99MY)

The engine control module (ECM) prior to 99MY is a GEMS (Generic Engine Management System), it is located in a plastic moulded box behind the battery in the engine compartment.

The ECM has various sensors fitted to the engine to allow it to monitor engine condition. The ECM processes these signals and decides what actions to carry out to maintain driveability, after comparing the information from these signals to mapped data within its memory.

The black plastic case which houses the ECM protects it from sources of contamination including heat. The ECM itself is contained in a cast aluminium case. The ECM has 3 independent connectors totalling 90 pins, of which up to 66 are used, dependent on market variations.

Input / Output

M18 0364

C509:18-pin black connector
C507:36-pin red connector
C505:36-pin black connector

18-pin black connector (C509):

This connector is used primarily for ECM power and earth connections.

NOTE: Voltages and other measurements given are approximations only. Actual values will depend on particular specification and will be effected by accuracy and calibration of the measurement tool used and impedances caused by harness wiring etc.

ECM pin details for Connector C509:

Pin No.	Description	Input/Output	Voltage
1	Coil driver - Cylinders 5 & 8	Output	0 - 12V
2	Not used	-	-
3	Not used	-	-
4	Throttle Position Sensor	Output	5V supply
5	ECM to chassis ground	Ground	0V
6	Not used	-	-
7	Main relay supply	Input	0 - 12V
8	Ignition sense	Input	0 - 12V
9	ECM to chassis ground	Ground	0V
10	ECM to chassis ground	Ground	0V
11	Crankshaft (CKP) sensor -ve	Ground	0V
12	Crankshaft (CKP) sensor +ve	Analogue input	18V (average) at 480Hz
13	Coil driver - Cylinders 2 & 3	Output	0 - 12V
14	Coil driver - Cylinders 1 & 6	Output	0 - 12V
15	Coil driver - Cylinders 4 & 7	Output	0 - 12V
16	ECM to chassis ground	Ground	0V
17	Main relay control	Output	switched to ground
18	Not used	-	-

36-pin red connector (C507):

This connector is used primarily for sensor inputs to the ECM.

NOTE: Voltages and other measurements given are approximations only. Actual values will depend on particular specification and will be effected by accuracy and calibration of the measurement tool used and impedances caused by harness wiring etc.

ECM pin details for Connector C507:

Pin No.	Description	Input/Output	Voltage
1	Rough road detected	Input	0 -12V
2	Camshaft position (CMP) sensor	Input (2 pulses per engine revolution)	12V (average)
3	Not used	-	-
4	Transfer box (Low range detected)	Input	0 - 12V
5	Not used	-	-
6	Not used	-	-
7	Fuel level	Input (out of range and validity check only)	0 - 12V
8	HO_2S Bank B Upstream	Input	0V (Rich) - 5V (Lean)
9	Not used	-	-
10	Knock sensor ground	Ground	0V
11	Knock sensor A	Input	Voltage signal proportional to level of knock detected
12	Knock sensor B	Input	Voltage signal proportional to level of knock detected
13	Air temperature sensor	Input	1 k-ohm to 1.3 k-ohm at 40°C (140°F)
14	Coolant temperature sensor	Input	4.7V at -30°C (-22°F) to 0.25V at 130°C (266°F); 2.0V at 40°C (104°F)
15	Throttle position sensor	Input	0 to 5V (0.6V at idle; 4.5V typical max.)
16	Mass air flow (MAF) Sensor	Analogue input	0 to 5V (1.4V at idle)
17	HO_2S sensor Bank A Downstream	Input	0V (Rich) - 5V (Lean)

ECM pin details for Connector C507 continued:

Pin No.	Description	Input/Output	Units
18	Park / Neutral Switch	Input	0V (Park/Neutral) - 12V (Drive)
19	Not used	-	-
20	Diagnostic 'L' Line	Bi-directional	Serial 0 - 12V
21	Heated front windshield	Output	0V or 12V
22	Not used	-	-
23	Diagnostic 'K' Line	Bi-directional	Serial 0 - 12V
24	Not used	-	-
25	Not used	-	-
26	Immobilization	Input	Serial 0 - 12V (366 baud)
27	Vehicle speed	Input	PWM 0 - 12V (8000 pulses / mile)
28	A/C request	Output	0V or 12V
29	Condenser cooling fan request	Input	0V or 12V
30	Fuel Pressure sensor (from 97.5 MY)	Input	1 k-ohm to 1.3 k-ohm at 40°C (140°F)
31	Ignition Retard Request (EAT ECU)	Input	12V PWM
32	HO_2S sensor	Ground	0V
33	HO_2S sensor Bank B Downstream	Input	0V (Rich) - 5V (Lean)
34	HO_2S sensor Bank A Upstream	Input	0V (Rich) - 5V (Lean)
35	Fuel temperature sensor	Input	1 k-ohm to 1.3 k-ohm at 40°C (140°F)
36	Sensor ground	Ground	0V

36-pin black connector (C505):

This connector is used primarily for outputs to actuators and sensors driven by the ECM.

NOTE: Voltages and other measurements given are approximations only. Actual values will depend on particular specification and will be effected by accuracy and calibration of the measurement tool used and impedances caused by harness wiring etc.

ECM pin details for Connector C505:

Pin No.	Description	Input/Output	Units
1	A/C grant	Output	0V or 12V
2	Fuel used	Output	Serial 0 - 12V (12000 pulses per litre)
3	Condenser cooling fan	Output drive	Switch to ground
4	Not used	-	-
5	Not used	-	-
6	Canister vent solenoid (from 97.5 MY)	Output	0 - 12V
7	Not used	-	-
8	Not used	-	-
9	Not used	-	-
10	Not used	-	-
11	Injector - Cylinder 3	Output	0 - 12V
12	Not used	-	-
13	Injector - Cylinder 1	Output	0 - 12V
14	Not used	-	-
15	IACV-D Stepper motor	Output	stepped by sequentially changing voltage polarity
16	IACV-B Stepper motor	Output	stepped by sequentially changing voltage polarity
17	Injector - Cylinder 6	Output	0 - 12V
18	Injector - Cylinder 8	Output	0 - 12V
19	Purge valve	Output	0 - 12V (100 Hz)
20	Not used	-	-

ECM pin details for Connector C505 continued:

Pin No.	Description	Input/Output	Voltage
21	HO_2S sensor Upstream - Heater supply	Output	Heater resistance = 5.7 ohms
22	Malfunction Indicator Lamp (MIL)	Output drive	Switch to ground
23	Engine speed output	Output	12V square wave (4 pulses per revolution)
24	Fuel pump relay	Output drive	Switch to ground
25	Not used	-	-
26	Not used	-	-
27	Throttle position	Analogue input	0 - 5V (1.4V at idle)
28	HO_2S sensor Upstream - Heater supply	Output	Heater resistance = 5.7 ohms
29	Engine torque	Output	12V PWM
30	Injector - Cylinder 4	Output	0 - 12V
31	Not used	-	-
32	Injector - Cylinder 7	Output	0 - 12V
33	Injector - Cylinder 5	Output	0 - 12V
34	IACV-C Stepper motor	Output	stepped by sequentially changing voltage polarity
35	IACV-A Stepper motor	Output	stepped by sequentially changing voltage polarity
36	Injector - Cylinder 2	Output	0 - 12V

Crankshaft position (CKP) sensor - (up to 99MY)

The crankshaft position sensor is the most important sensor on the engine. It is located in the left hand side of the flywheel housing and uses a different thickness of spacer for manual and automatic gearboxes. The signal it produces informs the ECM:
- the engine is turning
- how fast the engine is turning
- which stage the engine is at in the cycle

As there is no default strategy, failure of the CKP sensor will result in the engine failing to start. The fault is indicated by illumination of the malfunction indicator light (MIL) on North American specification vehicles.

The output signal from the CKP sensor is obtained from the magnetic path being made and broken as the reluctor ring teeth pass the sensor tip. The reluctor ring has 35 teeth and one missing tooth spaced at 10°intervals. The missing tooth is positioned at 20°after TDC.

Fault codes:

- **P0335** -Crankshaft sensor circuit fault - no signal
- **P0336** -Crankshaft sensor generating poor quality signal

Camshaft position (CMP) sensor - (up to 99MY)

The camshaft sensor is located in the engine front cover, between the belt pulleys. It is a Hall Effect device which produces four pulses for every two revolutions of the engine. The signal is used for two purposes, injector timing corrections for fully sequential fuelling and active knock control. The CMP sensor signal pulses are generated from four gaps on the cam wheel, one gap is smaller than the other three, consequently one of the pulses is longer than the others.

If the camshaft sensor fails, default operation is to continue normal ignition timing. The fuel injectors will be actuated sequentially, timing the injection with respect to top dead centre. Injection will either be correct or one revolution out of synchronisation. The fault is not easily detected by the driver. The fault is indicated by illumination of the malfunction indicator light (MIL) on North American specification vehicles.

Fault codes:

- **P0340 -** Camshaft sensor circuit fault or signal timing different from crankshaft sensor signal.

NOTE: It is physically possible to interchange the camshaft gear wheel fitted to pre-99MY and post-99MY vehicles. However, because the GEMS and Motronic systems are incompatible, an incorrect camshaft signal will be received by the ECM and a P0340 fault code will result.

Mass air flow (MAF) sensor - (up to 99MY)

The 'hot wire' type mass air flow sensor is mounted rigidly to the air filter and is connected by flexible hose to the plenum chamber inlet. The MAF sensor is a hot wire anenometer. The main sensing element of the sensor is a heated wire, positioned in the stream of intake air. Changes in intake air flow changes the temperature, and hence resistance, of the wire. The ECM measures this change in resistance and calculates the amount of air flowing into the engine.

As there is no default strategy, failure will result in the engine starting, and dying when it reaches 550 rev/min, when the ECM detects no MAF sensor signal. The fault is indicated by illumination of the malfunction indicator light (MIL) on North American specification vehicles.

Intake Air Temperature (IAT) sensor - (up to 99MY)

The IAT sensor is another resistive sensor, located in the body of the air cleaner. The sensor resistance varies with changes in air temperature. The signal from the IAT sensor is used to retard the ignition timing if the air temperature rises above 55°C. If the sensor is disconnected or failure occurs a default value will be used by the system. The default value selected will represent nominal operating conditions. The fault may not be evident to the driver, there may be slight power loss in high ambient temperatures. The fault is indicated by illumination of the malfunction indicator light (MIL) on North American specification vehicles.

Throttle Position (TP) sensor - (up to 99MY)

The throttle position sensor is mounted on the throttle body in line with the throttle plate shaft. The sensor is a variable resistor, the signal from which (0 - 5V) informs the ECM of the actual position of the throttle disc and the rate of change of throttle position. This information is used by the ECM for regulation of acceleration enrichment fuelling. Sensor failure will adversely affect the acceleration performance. The closed throttle voltage is continuously monitored and updated when engine conditions indicate that the throttle is closed.

The GEMS ECM performs a throttle potentiometer range check by cross checking with the measured air flow. If the two values do not correlate and fuelling feedback indicates that fuelling and therefore airflow is correct, the potentiometer is assumed to have failed. In the event that a fault is detected, GEMS supplies a default value dependent on air flow.

The throttle angle is also supplied to the gearbox ECM, the loss of this signal will result in poor gear change quality and loss of kickdown.

WARNING: If the throttle potentiometer is changed, it is necessary to reset the closed throttle voltage.

Fault codes:

- **P0121 -** Throttle potentiometer signal inconsistent with MAF, IACV, air temperature and engine rpm.
- **P0122 -** Throttle potentiometer circuit low input
- **P0123 -** Throttle potentiometer circuit high input

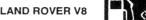

Engine Coolant Temperature (ECT) sensor - (up to 99MY)

The sensor is located at the top front of the engine, to the right of the alternator and in front of the plenum chamber.

The sensor comprises a temperature dependant resistive metal strip. The resistance of the strip varies considerably with coolant temperature, i.e. from 28K ohms at - 30°C to 90 ohms at 130°C. At 85°C the resistance is 300 ohms. The ECT sensor signal is vital to engine running, as the correct fuelling is dependant upon engine temperature i.e. richer mixture at low temperatures.

If the sensor is disconnected or failure occurs, a default value will be supplied to the system. The initial default value selected will be based on the value of the air intake temperature. This will increase to a nominal warmed up value over a given time, programmed for each default value. The fault may not be evident to the driver, there may be a hot restart problem. The fault is indicated by illumination of the malfunction indicator light (MIL) on North American specification vehicles.

Fault codes:

- **P0116 -** Coolant temperature sensor - falling temperature fault
- **P0117 -** Coolant temperature sensor circuit low range fault
- **P0118 -** Coolant temperature sensor circuit high range fault
- **P0125 -** Coolant temperature sensor - no warm-up fault

Engine Fuel Temperature (EFT) sensor - (up to 99MY)

The EFT sensor is located on the fuel rail by cylinders 3 and 5. The sensor measures the temperature of the rail rather than the fuel. The resistance varies with changes in temperature. The signal is used to increase the injection pulse time when undergoing hot restarts. When the fuel is hot, vapourisation can occur in the fuel rail and bubbles form in the injectors. Increasing the pulse time helps flush the fuel vapour away. An EFT sensor fault may not be evident to the driver, there may be a hot restart problem. The fault is indicated by illumination of the malfunction indicator light (MIL) on North American specification vehicles.

Fault codes:

- **P0181 -** Fuel temperature sensor fault - reading invalid compared with water temperature
- **P0182 -** Fuel temperature sensor circuit low range fault
- **P0183 -** Fuel temperature sensor circuit high range fault

Knock Sensors (KS) - up to 99MY

The knock sensor produces an output voltage which is proportional to mechanical vibration caused by the engine. A sensor is located in each cylinder bank between 2/4 and 3/5 cylinders. The ECM calculates if the engine is knocking by taking camshaft and crankshaft sensor signals to determine the position of the engine in the combustion cycle.

The ECM can also work out exactly which cylinder is knocking and progressively retards the ignition on that particular cylinder until the knock disappears. It then advances the ignition to find the optimum ignition timing for that cylinder.

The ECM can simutaneously adjust the timing of each cylinder for knock. It is possible that all eight cylinders could have different advance angles at the same time. If the camshaft sensor fails, the knock control will be disabled.

Fault codes:

- **P0331 -** Continuous knock on bank B
- **P0332 -** Knock background noise low, bank B
- **P0333 -** Knock background noise high, bank B
- **P0326 -** Continuous knock on bank A
- **P0327 -** Knock background noise low, bank A
- **P0328 -** Knock background noise high, bank A

Ignition coils - up to 99MY

The electronic ignition system uses four double ended coils. The ignition coils are mounted on a bracket fitted to the rear of the engine. The circuit to each coil is completed by switching within the ECM, allowing each coil to charge. When the ECM determines the correct ignition point, it switches off current supply to the coil which in turn causes the magnetic field around the coil's primary winding to collapse, inducing ht voltage in the secondary winding and in the iron core of the coil. High tension voltage, of different polarities, is produced at either end of the coil's core and is transmitted to two cylinders simultaneously, one on compression stroke, the other on exhaust stroke. This is called the wasted spark principle.

Note that coil 1 feeds cylinders 1 and 6, coil 2 feeds cylinders 5 and 8, coil 3 feeds cylinders 4 and 7, and coil 4 feeds cylinders 2 and 3. The resistance of the spark plug in the compression cylinder is higher than that in the exhaust cylinder and hence more spark energy is dissipated in the compression cylinder. Coil failure will result in a lack of ignition, resulting in a misfire in the related cylinders. The fault is indicated by illumination of the malfunction indicator light (MIL) on North American specification vehicles.

Fuel injectors - (up to 99MY)

A multiport Sequential Fuel Injection (SFI) system is used which utilises one injector per cylinder. Each injector comprises a small solenoid which is activated by the ECM to allow a metered quantity of fuel to pass into the combustion chamber. Due to the pressure in the fuel rail and the shape of the injector orifice, the fuel is injected into the cylinder in a fine spray which aids combustion. In the unlikely event of total injector failure or leakage which will cause a rich mixture, a misfire will occur in the affected cylinder. The fault is indicated by illumination of the malfunction indicator light (MIL) on North American specification vehicles.

Fault codes:

- **P0201** - Injector circuit fault, cylinder 1
- **P0202** - Injector circuit fault, cylinder 2
- **P0203** - Injector circuit fault, cylinder 3
- **P0204** - Injector circuit fault, cylinder 4
- **P0205** - Injector circuit fault, cylinder 5
- **P0206** - Injector circuit fault, cylinder 6
- **P0207** - Injector circuit fault, cylinder 7
- **P0208** - Injector circuit fault, cylinder 8
- **P1201** - Injector circuit open or ground short, cylinder 1
- **P1202** - Injector circuit open or ground short, cylinder 2
- **P1203** - Injector circuit open or ground short, cylinder 3
- **P1204** - Injector circuit open or ground short, cylinder 4
- **P1205** - Injector circuit open or ground short, cylinder 5
- **P1206** - Injector circuit open or ground short, cylinder 6
- **P1207** - Injector circuit open or ground short, cylinder 7
- **P1208** - Injector circuit open or ground short, cylinder 8

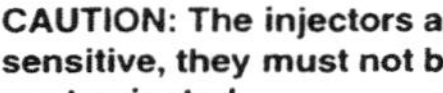

CAUTION: The injectors are extremely sensitive, they must not be dropped or contaminated.

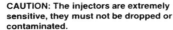

CAUTION: When assembling the injector to the fuel rail, only use clean engine oil to aid assembly. DO NOT use petroleum jelly or other forms of grease, as this will contaminate the injector.

The injectors can be checked using a multimeter to test the resistance values:

- Injector resistance at 20°C = 16.2 ohms ± 0.5 ohms

Idle Air Control (IAC) valve - up to 99MY

The idle speed control stepper motor is located on the side of the inlet manifold. Idle speed is controlled by the stepper motor, which comprises two coils, mounted to the throttle housing. When energised in the correct sequence, the coils move a plunger which opens or closes the throttle bypass valve controlling the quantity of idle air. The stepper motor controls idle speed by moving the plunger a set distance called a step. Fully open is 200 steps (180 steps for vehicles up to 97MY) and fully closed 0 steps. Failure of the stepper motor will result in low or high idle speed, poor idle, engine stall or non start. If the number of recorded steps changes beyond a set threshold (opening or closing) without a corresponding change in airflow, then a fault code will be stored. The GEMS diagnostics also check for short circuit conditions during normal stepper operation and open circuit during power down. Detected faults are indicated by illumination of the malfunction indicator light (MIL) on North American specification vehicles.

The stepper motor coil resistance is 53 ohms ± 2 ohms.

CAUTION: The pintle must not be moved by force.

Fault codes:

- **P0506** - Low idle speed
- **P0507** - High idle speed
- **P1508** - IACV stepper motor open circuit
- **P1509** - IACV stepper motor short circuit

Heated Oxygen Sensor (HO_2S) - up to 99MY

The heated oxygen sensors consist of a titanium metal sensor surrounded by a gas permeable ceramic coating. Oxygen in the exhaust gas diffuses through the ceramic coating on the sensor, and reacts with the titanium wire altering the resistance of the wire. From this resistance change the ECM calculates the amount of oxygen in the exhaust gas. The injected fuel quantity is then adjusted to achieve the correct air:fuel ratio, thus reducing the emissions of carbon monoxide (CO), hydrocarbons (HC), and oxides of nitrogen (NO_x). Two HO_2S sensors are fitted, one in each exhaust front pipe and positioned in front of the catalytic convertor. On North American specification vehicles, an additional HO_2S sensor is fitted behind each catalytic converter. These additional sensors are used to monitor the operating eficiency of the catalysts. Note that if the wiring to these sensors is crossed, the vehicle will start and idle correctly until the sensors reach operating temperature. Then the ECM will read the signals from them and send one bank of cylinders very rich and the other very weak. The engine will misfire, have a rough idle and emit black smoke, with possible catalyst damage.

The oxygen sensors are heated to ensure rapid warm up and continued operation when the exhaust temperature may be below the working temperature of the sensor. Both the upstream sensor heaters and the downstream sensor heaters are connected in parallel. The heaters are directly driven from the GEMS ECM by a pulse width modulated (PWM) signal to enable temperature control of the heater to be achieved. When the sensor is powered up, the duty ratio of the PWM signal to the heater is started low and then increased over a period of approximately 30 seconds. This is to ensure the sensor is not heated up too quickly, which might cause the ceramic interior of the sensor to crack. The duty ratio of the heater signal may be altered during normal operation to maintain sensor temperature.

In the event of sensor failure, the system will default to 'open loop' operation. Fuelling will be calculated using signals from the remaining ECM inputs.

On North American Specification vehicles, a fault with any of the HO_2S sensors is indicated by illumination of the malfunction indicator light (MIL). ECM diagnostics also use the Heated Oxygen Sensors to detect catalyst damage, misfire and fuel system faults.

CAUTION: Although robust within the vehicle environment, Heated Oxygen Sensors are easily damaged by dropping, excessive heat and contamination. Care must be exercised when working on the exhaust system not to damage the sensor housing or tip.

Fault codes:

- **P0130 -** Oxygen sensor circuit slow response, upstream sensor bank A
- **P0136 -** Oxygen sensor circuit slow response, upstream sensor bank A
- **P0150 -** Oxygen sensor circuit slow response, upstream sensor bank B
- **P0156 -** Oxygen sensor circuit slow response, upstream sensor bank B
- **P0131 -** Oxygen sensor circuit low voltage, upstream sensor bank A
- **P0151 -** Oxygen sensor circuit low voltage, upstream sensor bank B
- **P0137 -** Oxygen sensor circuit low voltage, downstream sensor bank A
- **P0157 -** Oxygen sensor circuit low voltage, downstream sensor bank B
- **P0132 -** Oxygen sensor circuit high voltage, upstream sensor bank A
- **P0152 -** Oxygen sensor circuit high voltage, upstream sensor bank B
- **P0138 -** Oxygen sensor circuit high voltage, downstream sensor bank A
- **P0158 -** Oxygen sensor circuit high voltage, downstream sensor bank B
- **P0133 -** Oxygen sensor circuit slow response, upstream sensor bank A
- **P0153 -** Oxygen sensor circuit slow response, upstream sensor bank B
- **P0139 -** Oxygen sensor circuit slow response, downstream sensor bank A
- **P0159 -** Oxygen sensor circuit slow response, downstream sensor bank B
- **P1138 -** Oxygen sensor problem with switching lean, sensor(s) for bank A
- **P1158 -** Oxygen sensor problem with switching lean, sensor(s) for bank B
- **P1137 -** Oxygen sensor problem with switching rich, sensor(s) for bank A
- **P1157 -** Oxygen sensor problem with switching rich, sensor(s) for bank B
- **P1139 -** Oxygen sensor circuit switching period too long bank A
- **P1159 -** Oxygen sensor circuit switching period too long bank B
- **P1171 -** System too lean bank A and bank B
- **P1172 -** System too rich bank A and bank B
- **P0171 -** System too lean bank A
- **P0174 -** System too lean bank B
- **P0172 -** System too rich bank A
- **P0175 -** System too rich bank B
- **P1185 -** Oxygen sensor heater circuit open circuit, upstream sensors
- **P1186 -** Oxygen sensor heater circuit short circuit, upstream sensors
- **P1187 -** Oxygen sensor heater circuit inferred open circuit, upstream sensors
- **P1188 -** Oxygen sensor heater circuit high resistance, upstream sensors
- **P1189 -** Oxygen sensor heater circuit inferred low resistance, upstream sensors
- **P1190 -** Oxygen sensor heater circuit low resistance, upstream sensors

- **P1191 -** Oxygen sensor heater circuit open circuit, downstream sensors
- **P1192 -** Oxygen sensor heater circuit short circuit, downstream sensors
- **P1193 -** Oxygen sensor heater circuit inferred open circuit, downstream sensors
- **P1194 -** Oxygen sensor heater circuit high resistance, downstream sensors
- **P1195 -** Oxygen sensor heater circuit inferred low resistance, downstream sensors
- **P1196 -** Oxygen sensor heater circuit low resistance, downstream sensors
- **P0420 -** Catalyst efficiency is low, bank A
- **P0430 -** Catalyst efficiency is low, bank B

Fuel pressure regulator - (up to 99MY only)

The fuel pressure regulator is a mechanical device controlled by manifold depression and is mounted at the rear of the engine in the fuel rail. The regulator ensures that fuel pressure is maintained at a constant pressure difference to that in the inlet manifold. As manifold depression increases, the regulated fuel pressure is reduced in direct proportion. When pressure exceeds the regulator setting, excess fuel is spill returned to the fuel tank swirl pot which contains the fuel pick up strainer.

Failure of the regulator will result in a rich mixture at idle but normal at full load, or a rich mixture resulting in engine flooding, or a weak mixture. Although the fault will not illuminate the MIL, faults caused by the failure may be indicated.

Accumulator - (up to 99MY only)

Certain derivatives have an accumulator fitted into the feed line connection at the fuel rail. The purpose of this device is to damp out pulsations in the fuel system caused by the normal opening and closing of the injectors. These pulsations, called injector knock, may otherwise be detected inside the vehicle.

Relays - (up to 99MY)

The engine management system employs four relays, which are all located in the main under bonnet fusebox.

Main Relay:

The main relay supplies the power feed to the ECM to feed the fuel injectors (8 amps)and air flow meter (4 amps). This relay is controlled by the GEMS ECM which has a second power feed. This enables the ECM to remain powered up after ignition is switched off. During this 'ECM power down routine' the ECM records all temperature readings and powers the stepper motor to the cold start position. Failure of this relay will result in the engine management ECM not being powered up, resulting in engine not starting due to absence of fuel and ignition.

Starter Motor Relay:

The starter motor relay is ignition key controlled and activated with the key in position 3 only. Releasing the key after cranking cuts supply to the relay and switches off the starter motor. Failure of this relay will result in the starter motor not working.

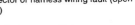

Ignition Relay:

The ignition relay supplies the power feed to the coils (6.5 amps), purge valve (1 amp, non-continuous) and heating elements of the HO^2S sensors (8 amps, non-continuous). The relay is ignition key controlled, when the key is turned off, supply to the coils is immediately cut. Failure of this relay will result in no ignition.

Ignition switch sense:

This is used to initiate the power up and power down routines within GEMS. The input is supplied from the ignition relay. When the ignition is turned on, the ignition relay is energised and the GEMS ECM starts its power up routines and turns on the ECM main relay, the main power to GEMS and its associated system components. When the ignition is turned off, GEMS will usually maintain its powered up state for several seconds (up to 20 minutes in extreme cases when cooling fans are required) while it inititiates its power down routine. On completion of the power down routine, the ECM main relay is turned off.

Fuel Pump Relay:

The fuel pump relay is fed from the ignition relay and controlled by the ECM. The relay is activated in ignition key position 2 to prime the fuel system for a period of time controlled by the ECM. Failure of this relay will result in no fuel pressure.

Advanced Evaporative Emissions System - 98MY to 99MY (NAS only)

The Advanced evaporative emissions system is included on NAS vehicles from 98MY in compliance with OBD strategies. The system has the capability of detecting holes in the fuel system down to 1 mm (0.04 in.). The leak tests are performed by the ECM, allowing the tank to be depressurised and measuring the pressure over a period of time.

See EMISSION CONTROL, Description and operation.

Fault codes:

- **P1440 -** Purge valve stuck open.
- **P0442 -** Evaporative loss control system - small leak
- **P0448 -** Evaporative loss control system - major leak
- **P0496 -** Evaporative loss control system - major leak
- **P0446 -** Purge canister closure valve information
- **P1447 -** Purge canister closure valve - poor performance

Fuel Tank Pressure Sensor

This sensor is used on NAS vehicles with advanced evaporative emissions systems. The sensor is located in the fuel tank sender unit and is not a serviceable item. The GEMS ECM checks for any fuel system leaks through joints and holes, by measuring the pressure drop after the vent seal valve is shut. The diagnostic system performs out of range and validity checks.

The following failure modes are possible:

- Connector or harness open circuit
- Sensor earthing problem
- Blocked sensor

Certain failure modes may cause the 5V supply voltage which is shared with the throttle position sensor to be reduced to less than 1V.

Fault codes:

- **P0451 -** Fuel tank pressure sensor poor performance fault
- **P0452 -** Fuel tank pressure sensor low range fault
- **P0453 -** Fuel tank pressure sensor high range fault

See EMISSION CONTROL, Description and operation.

EVAP Canister Purge Valve

The purge valve is controlled by the GEMS ECM and allows hydrocarbons stored in the EVAP canister to be purged to the engine inlet manifold for burning. Electrical circuit integrity and system flow checks are performed.

If a purge valve breaks or becomes stuck, the purge system will cease to function, and there is no default operation measures. GEMS will store the fault if the correct monitoring conditions have been achieved (45 seconds after 15 minutes running). If a valve is stuck open, the engine may misfire and the fuelling adaptions will change.

The following failure modes are possible:

- Sticking valve
- Valve blocked
- Connector or harness wiring fault (open or short circuit)
- Valve stuck open

Fault codes:

- **P0441 -** Purge valve flow fault
- **P0443 -** Purge valve open or short circuit

See EMISSION CONTROL, Description and operation.

EVAP Canister Vent Solenoid (CVS) Valve

The CVS unit is located at the left hand side of the engine bay. The vent seal valve is normally open. When the GEMS ECM is required to run a fuel system test, the vent valve is closed to seal the system. The ECM is then able to measure the pressure in the fuel system using the fuel tank pressure sensor. Electrical integrity checks are performed on the CVS valve and a valve blockage can be determined from a depressurising fuel tank.

The following failure modes are possible:

- Connector or harness wiring fault (open or short circuit)
- Valve stuck open or shut
- Valve blocked

See EMISSION CONTROL, Description and operation.

Inertia Fuel Shut-off (IFS) Switch

The inertia switch isolates the power supply to the fuel pump in the event of sudden deceleration, as encountered during an accident. The inertia switch is located in the right hand side footwell behind an access flap. It is reset by depressing the central plunger at the top of the switch.

Electronic Automatic Gearbox Interface - up to 99MY

Engine Torque Signal

The engine torque signal is calculated by the GEMS ECM and output to the gearbox ECU in a 12 volt PWM signal format. Warm up status of GEMS is passed on start-up for OBDII purposes.

Throttle Angle Signal

The throttle signal is output by the GEMS ECM to the gearbox ECU in a 12 volt PWM signal format. The signal is used to calculate when a gear change is necessary. If a fault occurs with this signal, then the gearbox ECU assumes a default throttle angle. The signal is also used to indicate engine temperature at starting.

Ignition Retard (Torque Reduction)

The gearbox ECU calculates the optimum shift point and in order to produce a smooth gear change, sends a torque reduction signal to the GEMS ECM which retards the ignition so reducing the engine torque to allow a smooth shift.

Engine Speed Signal

The engine speed signal is output to the gearbox ECU via the Body electronic control module (BeCM). The signal comprises a 12 volt square wave with 4 pulses for every engine revolution.

The following fault modes are possible:

- Harness wiring or connector faulty
- Power up problems
- Faulty gearbox ECU

Fault codes:

- **P1775 -** Gearbox has signalled a fault condition to the ECM
- **P1776 -** Gearbox ignition retard request duration fault
- **P1777 -** Gearbox ignition retard request line fault

See AUTOMATIC GEARBOX, Description and operation.

COMPONENT DESCRIPTIONS - from 99MY

Engine Control Module (ECM) - (from 99MY)

From 99MY the Engine Control Module (ECM) is a Bosch Motronic 5.2.1. which is mounted in a plastic "E-box" located on the LH side of the engine bay bulkhead. The ECM is cooled by a dedicated fan, which supplies cabin air into the plastic E-box to provide a suitable temperature environment for the ECM. The working temperature of the ECM is monitored by an internal temperature sensor.

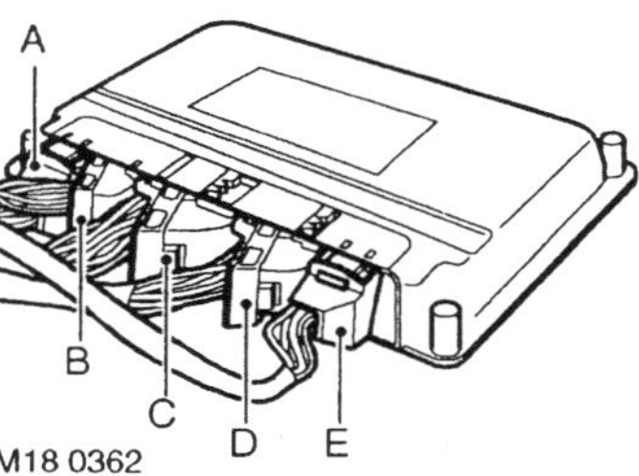

M18 0362

A. 9-pin connector (C0634)
B. 24-pin connector (C0635)
C. 52-pin connector (C0636)
D. 40-pin connector (C0637)
E. 9-pin connector (C0638)

The E-box is a moulded black plastic case which houses the ECM and protects it from sources of contamination. The ECM itself is contained in a cast aluminium case. The ECM has 5 independent connectors totalling 134 pins, of which up to 74 are used, dependent on market variations. The ECM and connectors can be accessed by positioning the cruise control pneumatic actuator and pump assembly aside, lifting the two plastic clips at the top of the e-box and pulling the E-box lid upwards and out. The ECM is held in position in the lid of the box by two plastic brackets. The ECM connectors have to be disengaged sequentially to release them from the unit. Similarly, when the connectors are reconnected to the ECM, the correct sequence must be observed.

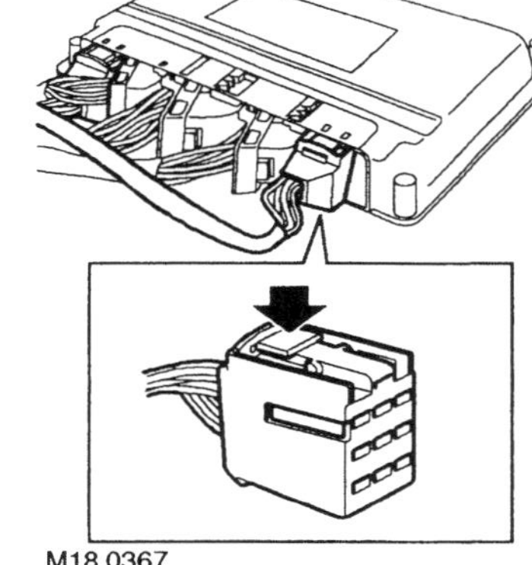
M18 0367

Connectors C0634 and C0638 are square type and have release buttons on their front face which have to be pressed to enable them to be removed.

M18 0366

The ECM memorises the positions of the crankshaft and the camshaft when the engine has stopped via the CKP and CMP sensors. This allows immediate sequential fuel injection and ignition timing during cranking. This information is lost if battery voltage is too low (i.e. flat battery). So the facility will be disabled for the first engine start after battery reconnection.

The ECM has various sensors fitted to the engine to allow it to monitor engine condition. The ECM processes these signals and decides what actions to carry out to maintain driveability, after comparing the information from these signals to mapped data within its memory.

CAUTION: Do not connect test probes connected to battery positive supply to any ground pins on the ECM. THIS MAY DESTROY THE ECM.

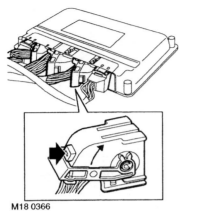

Connectors C0635, C0636 and C0637 are angled and have release buttons located on the top face. The release buttons have to be pressed and the locking levers pulled back to enable the connectors to be disconnected from the ECM. Each of the connectors have two integral blocks, one grey and one black, which can be removed from the connector housing to enable access to the back of the plugs. Block removal is achieved by pressing the locking tags and sliding the connector blocks outwards.

The E-box lid has two location tags on the bottom edge which have to be aligned with the corresponding holes in the E-box case before clipping the top of the lid into position. Care should be taken not to trap any wires when closing the E-box lid.

The ECM uses a 'flash' electronic erasable programmable read only memory (EEPROM). This enables the ECM to be externally configured, to ensure that the ECM can be updated with any new information; this also allows the ECM to be configured as many times as is necessary to meet changing specifications and legislation.

Input / Output

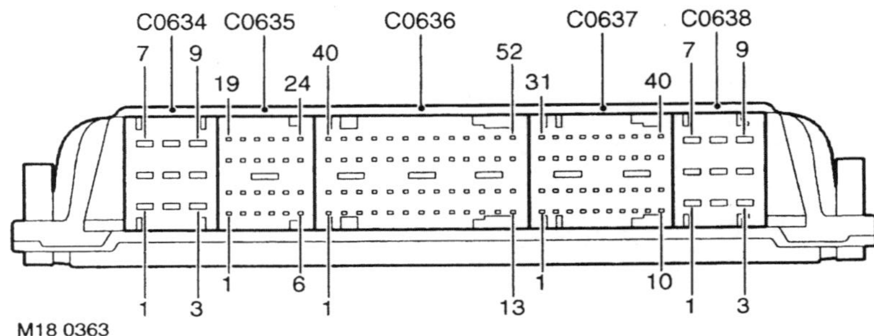

M18 0363

C0634: 9-pin connector
C0635: 24-pin connector
C0636: 52-pin connector
C0637: 40-pin connector
C0638: 9-pin connector

Connector 1 (C0634):

This connector contains 9 pins and is used primarily for ECM power input and earth. The ECM requires a permanent battery supply, if this permanent feed is lost i.e. the battery discharges or is disconnected, the ECM will lose its adapted values and its Diagnostic Trouble Codes (DTC). These adapted values are a vital part of the engine management's rolling adaptive strategy. Without an adaptive strategy, driveability, performance, emission control and fuel consumption are adversely affected. The ECM can be affected by high voltage inputs, so care must be taken when removing and replacing the ECM.

ECM pin details for Connector C0634:

Pin No.	Description	Input/Output	Voltage
1	Ignition position "II"	Input	12V
2	Not used	-	-
3	Not used	-	-
4	Chassis ground	Ground	0V
5	Fuel injector ground	Ground	0V
6	Power stage ground	Ground	0V
7	Battery supply	Input	12V
8	Main relay switched supply	Input switched	0 - 12V
9	Not used	-	-

Connector 2 (C0635):

This connector contains 24 pins and is primarily used for the Heated Oxygen (HO_2S) Sensor's control and earth. An output to a heater circuit in each HO_2S sensor is also required; this is to assist in heating the tip of the sensors to enable closed loop fuelling to be implemented quickly after cold starting.

ECM pin details for Connector C0635:

Pin No.	Description	Input/Output	Voltage
1	HO_2S sensor heater RH bank - downstream	Output drive	PWM 12 - 0V
2	Not used	-	-
3	Not used	-	-
4	Not used	-	-
5	Not used	-	-
6	Not used	-	-
7	HO_2S sensor heater LH bank - downstream	Output drive	PWM 12 - 0V
8	HO_2S sensor RH bank - downstream	Ground signal	0V
9	HO_2S sensor LH bank - upstream	Ground signal	0V
10	HO_2S sensor RH bank - upstream	Ground signal	0V
11	HO_2S sensor LH bank - downstream	Ground signal	0V
12	Not used	-	-
13	HO_2S sensor heater RH bank - upstream	Output drive	PWM 12 - 0V
14	HO_2S sensor RH bank - downstream	Input signal	Analogue 0 - 5V
15	HO_2S sensor LH bank - upstream	Input signal	Analogue 0 - 5V
16	HO_2S sensor RH bank - upstream	Input signal	Analogue 0 - 5V
17	HO_2S sensor LH bank - downstream	Input signal	Analogue 0 - 5V
18	Fuel pump relay	Output drive	Switch to ground
19	HO_2S sensor heater LH bank - upstream	Output drive	PWM 12 - 0V
20	Not used	-	-
21	Not used	-	-
22	Not used	-	-
23	Main relay output	Output drive	Switch to ground
24	Not used	-	-

Connector 3 (C0636):

This connector contains 52 pins and is used for most sensor and actuator inputs and outputs. Sensor and actuator control is vital to ensure that the ECM maintains adaptive strategy.

ECM pin details for Connector C0636:

Pin No.	Description	Input/Output	Voltage
1	Fuel injector cylinder number 2	Output drive	Switch to ground
2	Fuel injector cylinder number 5	Output drive	Switch to ground
3	Purge valve drive	Output signal	PWM 12 - 0V
4	SAI vacuum solenoid valve (NAS vehicles from 2000MY only)	Output drive	Switch to ground
5	Not used	-	-
6	Fuel tank pressure sensor (NAS vehicles with Advanced EVAPS only)	Ground	0V
7	MAF sensor 5V supply	Output, reference	5V
8	Not used	-	-
9	MAF sensor earth	Ground	0V
10	Throttle pot sensor 5V supply	Output reference	5V
11	Not used	-	-
12	Not used	-	-
13	Not used	-	-
14	Fuel injector cylinder number 7	Output drive	Switch to ground
15	Fuel injector cylinder number 6	Output drive	Switch to ground
16	SAI pump relay (NAS vehicles from 2000MY only)	Output drive	Switch to ground
17	Camshaft (CMP) sensor screen	Ground	0V
18	Not used	-	-
19	Not used	-	-
20	Camshaft (CMP) sensor signal	Input signal	Digital switch 0 - 12V
21	Coolant temperature (ECT) sensor	Ground	0V
22	Coolant temperature (ECT) sensor signal	Input signal	Analogue 0 - 5V
23	MAF sensor signal	Input signal	Analogue 0 - 5V
24	Throttle potentiometer signal	Input signal	Analogue 0 - 5V

ECM pin details for Connector C0636 continued:

Pin No.	Description	Input/Output	Voltage
25	Throttle potentiometer	Ground	0V
26	Not used	-	-
27	Fuel injector cylinder number 3	Output drive	Switch to ground
28	Fuel injector cylinder number 8	Output drive	Switch to ground
29	Not used	-	-
30	Canister vent solenoid (CVS) shut-off valve (NAS vehicles with Advanced EVAPs only)	Output drive	Switch to ground
31	Air conditioner condenser fan drive	Output drive	Switch to ground
32	Crankshaft (CKP) sensor signal	Input signal	Analogue 0 - 300V pk.
33	Not used	-	-
34	Intake air temperature (IAT) sensor	Input signal	Analogue 0 - 5V
35	Knock sensor RH bank	Ground	0V
36	Knock sensor RH bank	Input signal	Analogue 0V
37	Not used	-	-
38	Not used	-	-
39	Not used	-	-
40	Fuel injector cylinder number 4	Output drive	Switch to ground
41	Fuel injector cylinder number 1	Output drive	Switch to ground
42	Idle speed actuator open	Output signal	PWM 12 - 0V
43	Idle speed actuator close	Output signal	PWM 12 - 0V
44	Instrument Pack - Coolant sensor output	Output signal	PWM 0 - 12V
45	Crankshaft position (CKP) sensor screen ground	Ground	0V
46	Crankshaft position (CKP) sensor reference ground	Ground	0V
47	Not used	-	-
48	Knock sensor LH bank	Ground	0V

ECM pin details for Connector C0636 continued:

Pin No.	Description	Input/Output	Voltage
49	Knock sensor LH bank	Input signal	Analogue 0V
50	Not used	-	-
51	Not used	-	-
52	Not used	-	-

Connector 4 (C0637):

This connector contains 40 pins and facilitates the use of Testbook via the Diagnostic connector. Also contained in this connector is the Malfunction Indicator Lamp (MIL), this instrument panel lamp informs the driver of concerns within the engine management system.

ECM pin details for Connector C0637:

Pin No.	Description	Input/Output	Voltage
1	Not used	-	-
2	Not used	-	-
3	Not used	-	-
4	Not used	-	-
5	Not used	-	-
6	Not used	-	-
7	Not used	-	-
8	Low fuel level	Input signal	Active high
9	Fuel tank pressure sensor (NAS vehicles with Advanced EVAPs only)	Output reference	5V
10	ECM E-box cooling fan	Output drive	Switch to ground
11	Not used	-	-
12	BeCM Low fuel level signal	Ground	12V - 0V (when fuel level low)
13	Not used	-	-
14	Fuel tank pressure sensor (NAS vehicles with Advanced EVAPs only)	Input signal	Analogue 0 - 5V
15	Not used	-	-
16	Air conditioning compressor	Input signal	Active low
17	Engine speed output	Output signal	PWM 0 - 5V
18	Not used	-	-

ECM pin details for Connector C0637 continued:

Pin No.	Description	Input/Output	Voltage
19	Not used	-	-
20	MIL "ON"	Output drive	Switch to ground
21	Not used	-	-
22	Road speed sensor	Input signal	PWM 0 - 12V
23	Not used	-	-
24	Not used	-	-
25	Not used	-	-
26	Not used	-	-
27	Not used	-	-
28	Not used	-	-
29	Air con compressor relay	Output drive	Switch to ground
30	Not used	-	-
31	Not used	-	-
32	Diagnostic K-line	Bi-directional	Serial 0 - 12V
33	Immobiliser serial W link	Input signal	Serial 0 - 12V
34	Rough road signal	Input signal	PWM 0 -12V
35	Not used	-	-
36	CAN bus 'high line'	Bi-directional	5 - 2.5V
37	CAN bus 'low-line'	Bi-directional	0 - 2.5V
38	Air conditioning stand by relay	Input signal	Active low
39	Not used	-	-
40	Not used	-	-

Connector 5 (C0638):

This connector contains 9 pins and is used to control the ignition system. The ignition coils are supplied with power and a switching earth completes the circuit.

ECM pin details for Connector C0638:

Pin No.	Description	Input/Output	Voltage
1	Not used	-	-
2	Ignition coil cylinders 2+3	Output drive	Switch to ground
3	Not used	-	-
4	Not used	-	-
5	Ignition screen	Ground	0V
6	Ignition coil cylinders 4 + 7	Output drive	Switch to ground
7	Ignition coil cylinders 1 + 6	Output drive	Switch to ground
8	Ignition coil cylinders 5 + 8	Output drive	Switch to ground
9	Not used	-	-

Crankshaft speed and position (CKP) sensor - (from 99MY)

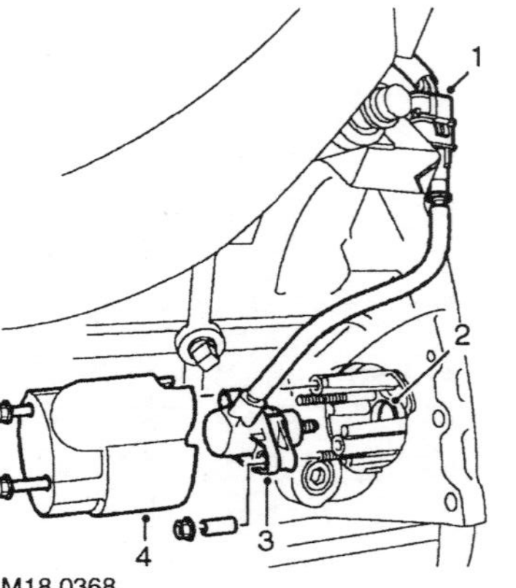

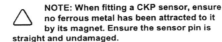

M18 0368

1. Multiplug
2. Aperture to reluctor ring
3. CKP sensor
4. Heatshield

The CKP sensor is located at the lower, rear LH side of the engine below cylinder number 7. The CKP sensor is protected by a heatshield which is attached to the rear flange of the engine block by two M5 bolts. The CKP sensor itself is located on two studs and fixed in position by two M5 nuts and 18mm spacers. The sensor has a flying lead which terminates in a 3-pin multiplug that connects to the engine harness and is mounted to a bracket to the rear of the left hand cylinder head.

The tip of the CKP sensor protrudes through an aperture in the engine block rear flange, adjacent to the outer circumference of the flywheel. A 60-tooth reluctor ring is included on the flywheel which provides the reference signal to the crankshaft position sensor.

The ECM uses the signal produced at the CKP sensor to determine the position of the crankshaft to enable accurate ignition and fuel injection timing. The ECM also determines the engine speed at any particular instance through analysis of the frequency of fluctuations induced in the CKP sensor as the teeth of the reluctor ring pass by the sensor tip.

The CKP sensor is a variable reluctance sensor, and contains a permanent magnet and soft iron core surrounded by a copper winding. As the reluctor ring passes by the sensor tip it causes a voltage to be induced in the sensor, consequently the CKP sensor does not need a power supply for operation. The signal wires of the CKP sensor are surrounded by a grounded screen to prevent noise being induced in the signal wires and causing a spurious interference signal being passed to the ECM.

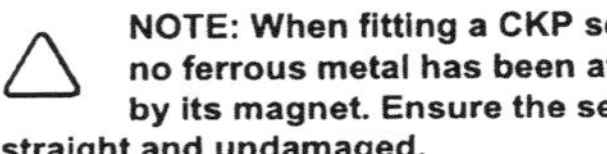
NOTE: When fitting a CKP sensor, ensure no ferrous metal has been attracted to it by its magnet. Ensure the sensor pin is straight and undamaged.

The reluctor ring teeth are spaced at 6° intervals and are 3° wide. Two of the reluctor ring teeth are removed, to provide a reference mark which indicates when the crankshaft is at 60°BTDC for number 1 cylinder. The remaining 58 teeth cause an AC voltage to be induced in the sensor pick-up, with the amplitude of the signal increasing with rising engine speed. The voltage generated is an analogue signal capable of peak amplitude voltages of up to 300V.

The distance of the tip from the top of the reluctor ring teeth is important as the amplitude of the detected signal will be reduced in proportion to an increase in the gap between the sensor tip and the top of the reluctor ring teeth. If the air gap becomes too wide, the CKP signal could become too weak and possible misfires could occur. Spacers are included in the CKP sensor kit which are used to ensure the correct gap between the sensor tip and reluctor ring teeth.

The ECM uses the falling edge of the signal waveform as its reference for each reluctor ring tooth. Consequently, if the input signal wire and reference ground wire are inadvertently reversed, the ECM will react by providing a 3° advance in ignition timing.

If the crankshaft sensor fails, the engine will stop and fail to restart. There is no back-up strategy or limp home facility programmed into the ECM. If a fault occurs whilst the engine is running, the engine will stall and a fault code will be stored in ECM memory. If the fault develops while the engine is not running, the engine may not be capable of starting and no fault code will be available. In this case, the MIL light will still be illuminated.

In the event of a CKP sensor signal failure, the following symptoms may be observed:

- Engine cranks but fails to start
- MIL remains on at all times
- Engine misfires (CKP incorrectly fitted)
- Engine runs roughly or stalls (CKP incorrectly fitted)
- Tachometer fails to work
- Flywheel adaption reset -- ferrous contamination

Possible causes of CKP sensor failure include the following:

- CKP sensor not fitted correctly (or assembly loose)
- Incorrect length spacers fitted
- Sensor/wiring open or short circuit
- Sensor bent or damaged by reluctor ring
- Water ingress at sensor connector
- ECM unable to detect the software reference point.
- Ferrous contamination of crank sensor pin/reluctor.

Whenever a new CKP sensor is fitted or the flywheel is removed, the adaptive values have to be reset using Testbook.

Should a malfunction of the component occur, the following fault codes may be evident and can be retrieved by Testbook:

- **P0335 -** (reference mark is outside search window with engine speed above 500 rev/min for more than 2 revolutions.
- **P0336 -** (incorrect number of teeth detected ± 1 tooth between reference marks with engine speed above 500 rev/min.

In addition to crankshaft position, the ECM also uses the CKP sensor signal to determine engine speed. The ECM shares the engine speed information with the electronic automatic transmission (EAT) ECU by transmitting the data via the CAN link. Engine speed output is also provided to the instrument pack (tachometer), for which the output signal is scaled down to 4 pulses per crankshaft revolution.

The ECM also has a quick start facility, where the position of the crankshaft and camshaft are memorised when the engine is stopped. This stored information is used to facilitate immediate sequential fuelling during cranking.

Camshaft Position (CMP) sensor - (from 99MY)

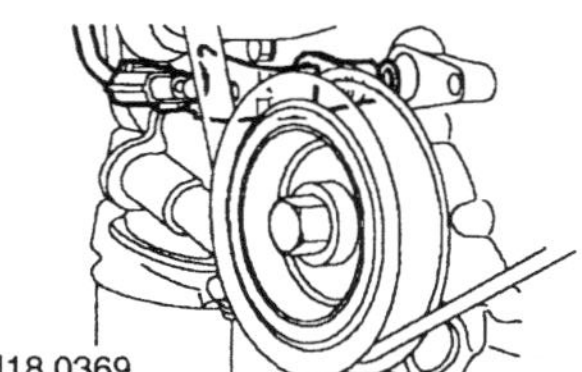

M18 0369

The CMP sensor is located at the front of the engine block, above and behind the crankshaft pulley. The sensor is clamped into position by means of a single bolt. An 'O'ring is used to seal the interface between the sensor and the aperture in the engine front cover.

The sensor has three wires which terminate in a multiplug secured to a bracket on the left of the crankshaft pulley. A short link lead is used to connect the sensor to the engine harness. The wires to the sensor have the following functions:

- Power supply from engine compartment fusebox
- Camshaft input signal to ECM
- Screen to chassis ground connection

The CMP sensor is a Hall effect sensor which produces four pulses for every two engine revolutions. The sensing element is positioned less than 2mm from the side of the camshaft gear wheel. The camshaft gear wheel has four slots machined at 90°intervals which allows the identification of four cylinder positions every camshaft revolution. Cylinder recognition is used to enable sequential fuel injection and knock control and is also used for diagnostic purposes. The slots in the camshaft gear wheel are shaped to provide unequal timing pulses for determining TDC on No.1 cylinder. The camshaft and crankshaft drives must also be correctly aligned, since the ECM uses the crankshaft "missing teeth" marker to determine crankshaft and camshaft position and provide a reference mark which is 60°BTDC on No.1 cylinder.

The CMP sensor uses the Hall effect to act as a magnetic switch for switching battery voltage on or off depending on the position of the camshaft gear wheel in relationship to the sensor. This results in a square wave input between 0 and 12V at the ECM input pin.

Symptoms of a CMP sensor failure include the following:

- Ignition timing reverts to default values from ECM memory with loss of cylinder correction.
- Loss of active knock control and diagnostics.
- Loss of cylinder identification for misfire diagnostics.
- Loss of quick synchronisation of crankshaft and camshaft for cranking/start up.
- Fuel injection could be 360°out of phase at engine restart.
- Front HO_2S sensor ageing period diagnostic could become disabled (NAS only).

The cause of CMP sensor failure may be attributable to one of the following conditions:

- Sensor open circuit.
- Sensor signal line short circuit to vehicle battery supply.
- Sensor signal line or voltage supply line short circuit to vehicle ground.
- Incorrect fitting of the sensor.
- Excessive camshaft gear wheel tolerance.
- Excessive camshaft endfloat.
- Camshaft and crankshaft misalignment.
- Speed signal correlation with CKP sensor signal.
- Cam wheel magnetised / residual magnetism.

Should a malfunction of the component occur the following fault codes may be evident and can be retrieved by Testbook:

- **P0340 -** (Signal open & short circuit to vehicle supply or ground).

The fault condition has to be detected for more than 100 cam pulses (25 revolutions) when the engine speed is greater than 500 rev/min.

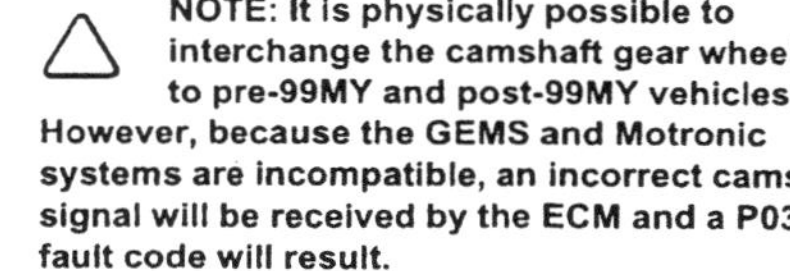

NOTE: It is physically possible to interchange the camshaft gear wheel fitted to pre-99MY and post-99MY vehicles. However, because the GEMS and Motronic systems are incompatible, an incorrect camshaft signal will be received by the ECM and a P0340 fault code will result.

Mass Air Flow (MAF) and Intake Air Temperature (IAT) sensor - (from 99MY)

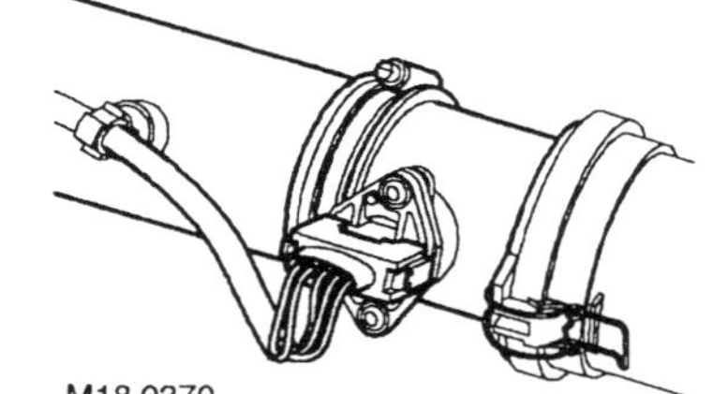

M18 0370

The MAF/IAT sensor is located at the RHS of the engine compartment, in the air intake duct between the air filter housing and the inlet manifold. The complete assembly forms part of the air intake tube, but the sensor itself is attached by two torx screws and can be removed from the intake tube if necessary.

The upper section of the intake tube containing the MAF/IAT sensor is embossed with an arrow indicating the direction of air flow, always ensure the unit is fitted in the correct orientation.

CAUTION: Take care handling the sensor unit, it should not be dropped or roughly handled, ensure that the unit remains free of contamination.

The sensor has a five pin connector which connects to the ECM via the engine harness. The connector has silver plated terminals for low current signals and corrosion protection. The harness is clipped to prevent vibration of the terminals.

MAF SENSOR

The Mass Air Flow sensor utilises a "hot film" element contained in the air intake tube to monitor the mass flow of the air stream being drawn into the engine. The MAF sensor contains two sensing elements, one element is controlled at ambient temperature (e.g. 25°C (77°F), while the other is heated to 200°C (360°F) above the ambient temperature (e.g. 225°C (437°F)).

When the intake air passes the heated element, it cools it down, so lowering the resistance of the hot film element. In order to maintain the same temperature, the circuit to the heated element has to supply more current. The change in current causes a corresponding change in potential difference to be detected in the monitoring circuit. This change is supplied to the ECM as a voltage between 0 and 5V, where it is processed by the ECM's internal mapping to interpret the data as a measure of the mass of air flow.

The measured air mass flow is used by the ECM to determine the fuel quantity to be injected in order to maintain the stoichiometric air:fuel mixture for optimum engine performance and low emissions.

The MAF sensor receives a power supply via the engine compartment fusebox, and a 5V reference signal from the ECM. The MAF sensor and the IAT sensor share a common ground connection and each provide a separate signal input to the ECM.

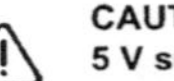

CAUTION: Do not apply 12 V directly to the 5 V supply terminal, this will destroy the internal circuitry. The connector terminals are silver plated - avoid probing with multimeter test leads.

If the MAF sensor fails, the ECM implements a backup strategy which is based on throttle angle, air temperature and engine speed. A MAF sensor failure may result in the following symptoms being experienced:

- The engine rpm may relapse slightly during driving and then recover.
- Difficulty in starting and/or frequent stalling of engine.
- Poor throttle response
- Degraded engine performance.
- Emissions control and idle speed control inoperative.
- MAF sensor signal offset.

A MAF sensor failure is likely to occur for the following reasons:

- Sensor open circuit of voltage supply, signal or ground lines.
- Short circuit of signal line to vehicle supply or ground.
- Contaminated / damaged sensor element.
- Air leak after the MAF sensor.
- Inlet air restriction.
- Poor connection or resistance in wiring harness causing signal offset.

If the MAF sensor should fail, the following fault codes will be generated by the ECM diagnostics, which can be retrieved by Testbook:

- **P0102 -** (MAF signal less than the speed dependent minimum threshold).
- **P0103 -** (MAF signal greater than the speed dependent maximum threshold).

Intake-air density varies with temperature, the ECM needs to be aware of these changes so that corrective calculations can be incorporated into the ECM's fuelling and ignition timing strategies. The intake air temperature value is also used by the ECM as a reference when implementing compensation for an ECT failure.

IAT SENSOR

The intake air temperature sensor utilises a thermistor with a negative temperature co-efficient (as temperature rises, thermistor resistance decreases). The change in resistance causes a change in input voltage at the ECM. The ECM converts the voltage value it receives to provide an indication of the temperature of the inlet air.

If the IAT sensor fails, the ECM substitutes a default value for air temperature of 45°C (113°F). An IAT sensor failure may result in the following symptoms being experienced:

- Catalyst monitoring affected due to exhaust temperature model.
- Warm-up ignition angle affected.
- ISC speed adaption disabled
- ISC actuator blocked test disabled
- Fuelling adaptions disabled.
- Condenser fan hot restart inhibited

An IAT sensor failure is likely to occur for the following reasons:

- Sensor open circuit.
- Sensor signal line short circuit to vehicle 12V supply or ground.
- Damaged sensor element
- Bad connection or increased resistance in wiring harness.

If the IAT sensor should fail, the following fault codes will be generated by the ECM diagnostics, which can be retrieved by Testbook:

- **P0112 -** (air temperature signal is less than the minimum threshold - after a sufficient time (more than three minutes) for exhaust warm-up has been allowed).
- **P0113 -** (air temperature signal greater than the maximum threshold).

Throttle Position (TP) sensor - (from 99MY)

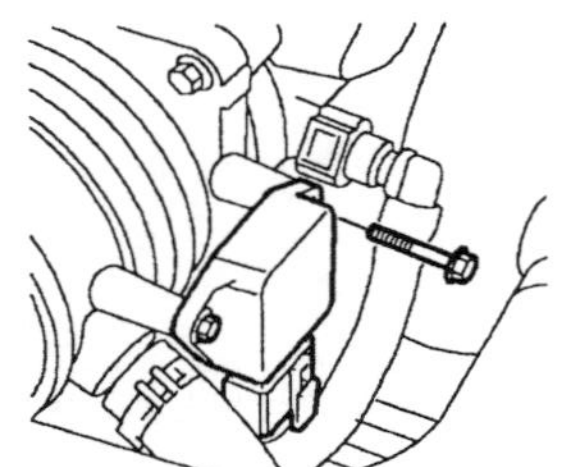

M18 0371

The TP sensor is located on the rear of the throttle body assembly in the engine compartment and fixed to its mounting studs by two screws.

The TP sensor is a potentiometer having a resistance track that is connected to a stabilized 5V supply at one end of its track and ground at the other end of the track. The potentiometer wiper arm is connected to the throttle plate assembly and provides a signal to the ECM which is an analogue voltage between 0.3V (closed throttle) and 4.5V (wide open throttle), corresponding to the throttle valve angle. The TP sensor connector terminals are gold plated for good conductivity and corrosion resistance; care should be exercised if it is necessary to probe the connector and sensor terminals.

The TP sensor enables the ECM to determine the throttle valve's position and angular velocity. The ECM uses the data from the throttle valve position for determining intake-air volume, which it uses for calculating the necessary fuel injection duration under various operating conditions. The data from the throttle valve's angular velocity is used mainly for acceleration/deceleration compensation. The ECM also uses closed throttle position for idle speed control in conjunction with road speed.

The TP sensor also supplies the ECM with information to enable the overrun fuel shut off strategy to be implemented. When the ECM receives closed throttle information from the TP sensor, it closes the injectors for the duration of the closed throttle time.

A software strategy within the ECM enables the closed throttle position to be learnt, so that the sensor can be fitted without the need for adjustment.

The throttle position signal is also supplied to the EAT ECU from the ECM using the CAN communication link. The EAT ECU uses the throttle position data to determine the correct point for gear shifts and acceleration kickdown.

If the TP sensor signal fails, the ECM uses a default value derived from engine load and speed. A TP sensor failure may result in the following symptoms being experienced:

- Poor throttle response and degraded engine performance
- Emission control failure.
- Closed loop idle speed control inoperative.
- Automatic gearbox kickdown inoperative.
- Incorrect altitude adaption
- MIL illuminated (NAS only)

A TP sensor failure is likely to occur for the following reasons:

- Sensor open circuit
- Short circuit of signal line to vehicle supply, 5V supply or ground.
- Bad connection or increased resistance in wiring harness causing signal offset.
- Blocked air filter (load monitoring, ratio of the TP sensor to air flow).
- Restricted air inlet (load monitoring, ratio of the TP sensor to air flow).

If the TP sensor should fail, the following fault codes will be generated by the ECM diagnostics, which can be retrieved by Testbook:

- **P0101 -** (load monitoring, the ratio of throttle position to air flow).
- **P0122 -** (signal less than the minimum threshold).
- **P0123 -** (signal greater than the maximum threshold).

Engine Coolant Temperature (ECT) sensor - (from 99MY)

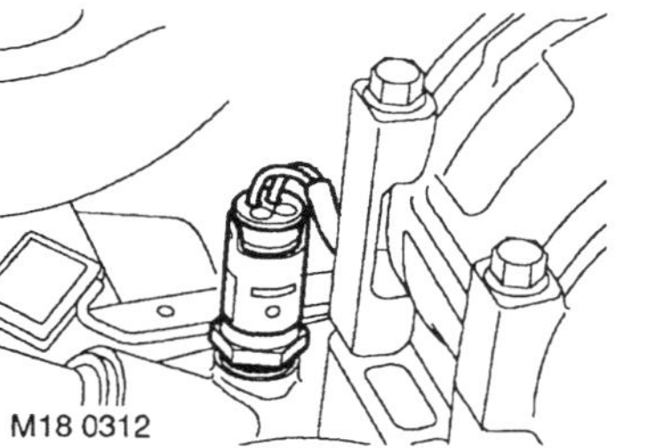

The ECT sensor is located at the top front of the engine, adjacent to the coolant outlet pipe. The sensor screws into a thread in the inlet manifold and incorporates a sealing ring between the faces of the sensor and manifold.

The ECT sensor multiplug has four wires; two are the signal and ground connections used by the ECM, the other two are used by the body control module (BeCM) for control of the temperature warning lamp operation on the instrument pack.

The sensor contains two thermistors with negative temperature co-efficients; as temperature increases, the thermistor's resistance decreases. The ECM receives a corresponding analogue input voltage between 0 and 5V.

NOTE: The temperature / resistance characteristics of the two thermistors differ, and so it is important to maintain the correct pin-outs.

The ECM uses the information received from the ECT sensor to make adjustments to the engine operating conditions. The ECM ensures a richer air:fuel mixture is available at lower block temperatures for good quality starts and smooth running. The mixture is then made leaner as the engine temperature rises to maintain low emissions and good performance.

For NAS vehicles with secondary air injection, the signal from the ECT sensor is monitored at engine start, to determine whether the conditions are cold enough to warrant secondary air injection to be employed. The ECT sensor is then monitored to switch off the secondary air injection when the required engine coolant temperature has been attained.

If the sensor fails, the ECM uses a substitute software routine that changes default value during warm up, based on the signal from the inlet air temperature sensor. When the software model reaches a coolant temperature of 60°C (140°F) the ECM implements a fixed default value of 85°C (185°F). The ECM coolant model also forms part of the diagnostics that is performed for detecting a temperature sensor fault, as well as open and short circuit tests.

Temperature	Voltage
-50°C	5V
-20°C	4.8V
10°C	4.2V
40°C	2.8V
70°C	1.4V
100°C	0.6V
130°C	0.2V

NOTE: All voltages listed are approximate.

A coolant temperature circuit failure may result in the following symptoms:

- Poor cold and warm/hot starting and driveability.
- Instrument pack temperature warning lamp will illuminate.
- MIL will be illuminated.
- Temperature gauge reads excessively hot or cold.
- Cooling fan will not run
- SAI pump will operate at engine start up even when engine is hot (NAS with secondary air injection system only).

The ECT sensor can fail in the following ways, or supply an incorrect signal:

- Sensor open circuit.
- Short circuit to vehicle supply.
- Short circuit to earth.
- Incorrect mechanical fitting.
- Signal fixed above 40°C (140°F) will not be detected.
- Signal fixed below 40°C (140°F) not detected.

Should a malfunction of the component occur, the following fault codes may be evident and can be retrieved by Testbook:

- **P0116 -** (Signal differs too much from temperature model for longer than 2.54s)
- **P0117 -** (Open circuit or short circuit to battery supply)
- **P0118 -** (Short circuit to ground)

Knock Sensors (KS) - from 99MY

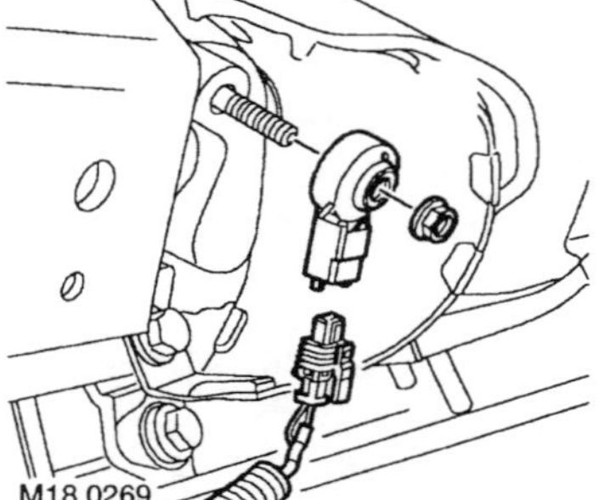
M18 0269

The ECM utilises active knock control, which serves to prevent engine damage through pre-ignition or detonation. Knock control is effective under all operating conditions, enabling the engine to operate without additional safety margins.

Two knock sensors are used, one mounted each side of the cylinder block between the two centre cylinders of each bank. Each sensor has two wires; a signal wire providing input to the ECM and a ground (screen). Each of the sensors monitor the 'knock' from four cylinders (Cylinder No's: 1, 3, 5 & 7 and Cylinder No's: 2, 4, 6 & 8).

CAUTION: The connector and sensor terminals are gold plated to provide good conductivity and resistance to corrosion and high temperatures. Be careful not to damage terminals if probing with test equipment.

The knock sensors consist of piezo-ceramic crystals that oscillate to create a voltage signal. During pre-ignition, the frequency of crystal oscillation increases which alters the signal output to the ECM.

The signal is processed by comparing it to signal profiles contained in memory which indicate a pre-ignition condition. If pre-ignition conditions are evident, the ECM retards the ignition on that cylinder for a number of cycles. The ignition timing gradually reverts to its original setting.

The ignition system is calibrated to run on 95 RON Premium fuel for optimum fuel economy and performance characteristics. The system can also function satisfactorily with 91 RON Regular fuel. If the vehicle is refuelled with a lower grade of fuel some audible detonation may be heard until the system adaptions are complete for the new fuel grade.

If a knock sensor should fail, the following symptoms may be observed:

- Possible rough running
- Reduction in engine performance

A knock sensor failure is likely to occur for the following reasons:

- Sensor open circuit
- Short circuit to vehicle supply or ground
- Faulty component
- Loose sensor - incorrectly torqued

If knock control is disabled, a default "safe ignition map" is used.

If a knock sensor should fail, the following fault codes will be generated by the ECM diagnostics, which can be retrieved by Testbook:

- **P0327 -** (LH bank signal less than the threshold value determined from the ECM model above 2200 rpm)
- **P0328 -** (LH bank signal greater than the threshold value determined from the ECM model above 2200 rpm)
- **P0332 -** (RH bank signal less than the threshold value determined from the ECM model above 2200 rpm)
- **P0333 -** (RH bank signal greater than the threshold value determined from the ECM model above 2200 rpm)

Noise induced on the battery supply line could be misinterpreted as a knock signal and cause a maximum knock fault. A maximum fault could be caused by a short circuit to the battery supply or in the case of extreme mechanical engine noise / piston slap. A minimum fault is usually due to an open circuit.

Ignition coils

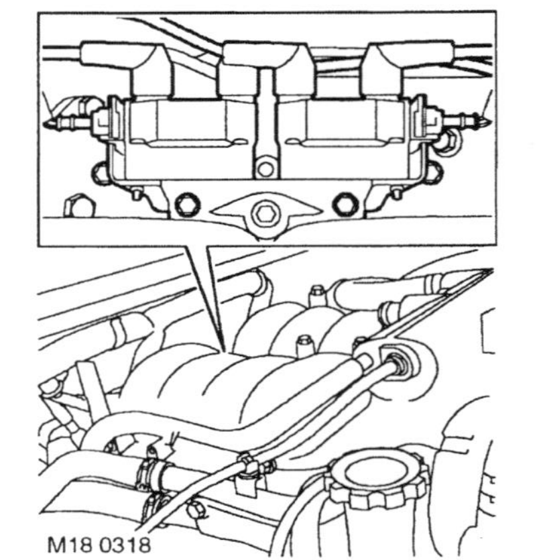
M18 0318

The electronic ignition system is fitted with two quad coils which are directly driven by the ECM. The ignition coils are mounted on a bracket fitted to the rear of the engine. The circuit to each coil is completed by switching within the ECM, allowing each coil to charge. When the ECM determines the correct ignition point, it switches off current supply to the coil which in turn causes the magnetic field around the coil's primary winding to collapse, inducing ht voltage in the secondary winding and in the iron core of the coil. High tension voltage, of different polarities, is produced at either end of the coil's core and is transmitted to two cylinders simultaneously, one on compression stroke, the other on exhaust stroke. This is called the wasted spark principle.

Note that coil 1 feeds cylinders 1 and 6, coil 2 feeds cylinders 5 and 8, coil 3 feeds cylinders 4 and 7, and coil 4 feeds cylinders 2 and 3. The resistance of the spark plug in the compression cylinder is higher than that in the exhaust cylinder and hence more spark energy is dissipated in the compression cylinder. Coil failure will result in a lack of ignition, resulting in a misfire in the related cylinders. The fault is indicated by illumination of the malfunction indicator light (MIL) on North American specification vehicles.

The positive supply to the coils is fed via a common fuse and ignition relay located in the engine compartment fusebox. Each coil supply feed has an RFI suppression capacitor fitted adjacent to the coil mounting bracket. The ignition primary wires are screened to suppress the emission of radio frequency interference, with the screens being grounded at a connection on the ECM.

WARNING: The ignition coils operate at very high voltages, do not attempt repair operations and procedures on the ignition high tension / secondary system when the engine is running.

The ECM calculates the dwell timing from battery voltage and engine speed data to ensure sufficient secondary (spark) energy is always available without excessive primary current flow, thus avoiding overheating or damage to the ignition coils.

The spark timing for each individual cylinder is calculated by the ECM using an internal memory map under consideration of the following inputs:

- Engine speed
- Engine load
- Engine temperature
- Knock control
- Automatic gearbox shift control
- Idle speed control

The nominal value for a warm engine at idle is 12°BTDC

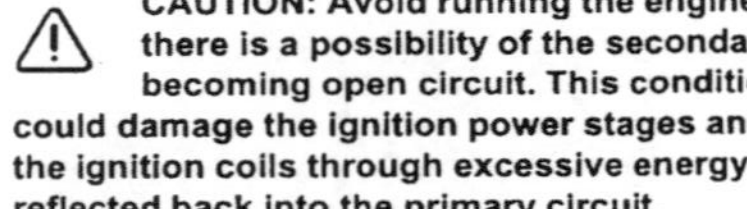

CAUTION: Avoid running the engine if there is a possibility of the secondary (ht) becoming open circuit. This condition could damage the ignition power stages and / or the ignition coils through excessive energy being reflected back into the primary circuit.

NOTE: Testbook is not able to perform diagnostics to the primary power stage coils. Ignition related faults are monitored indirectly via the misfire detection system and its fault codes (NAS vehicles only).

Resistance measurements of the primary and secondary sides of the ignition coils can be performed using a suitable multimeter. Default values are:

- Nominal primary coil resistance (up to 99MY) = 0.8 ohms
- Nominal primary coil resistance (from 99MY) = 0.5 ohms ± 0.05 ohms at 20°C (68°F)
- Nominal secondary coil resistance = 13.3 k-ohms ± 1.3 k-ohms at 20°C (68°F)

If an ignition coil should fail, the following symptoms may be observed:

- Engine will not start - loss of spark
- Engine misfire on specific cylinders

An ignition coil failure is likely to occur for the following reasons:

- Connector or harness fault
- Coil open circuit
- Short circuit to vehicle battery supply or ground
- Faulty component

Fuel injectors - from 99MY

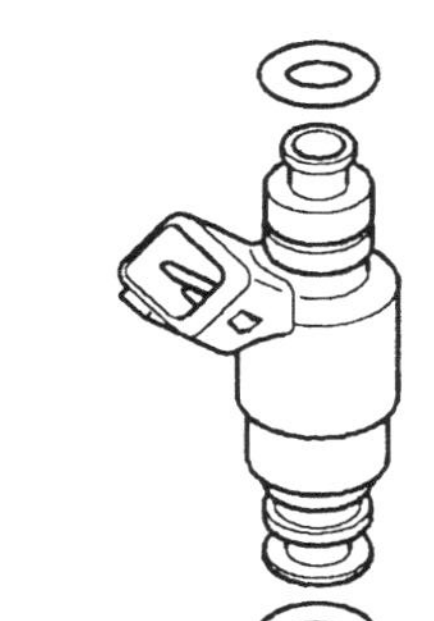

M17 0191

The fuel injectors are located beneath the air inlet manifold. They utilise an electrical solenoid which lifts an injector needle off its seat to allow fuel injection to take place. The fuel injectors provide excellent fuel atomisation in the lower portion of the inlet manifold, the air:fuel mixture is then drawn into the cylinders to provide optimum combustion characteristics and excellent driveability.

A fuel pressure test point is provided by means of a Schrader valve positioned between the rear of the engine and the bulkhead, above the coil packs.

There are eight fuel injectors, one per cylinder which the ECM operates sequentially. All the injectors are fed from a common fuel rail as part of the returnless fuel system. Fuel pressure is maintained at a constant 3.5 bar (52 $lbf.in^2$) by a regulator that is integral with the fuel pump.

CAUTION: The injectors are extremely sensitive, they must not be dropped or contaminated.

CAUTION: When assembling the injector to the fuel rail, only use clean engine oil to aid assembly. DO NOT use petroleum jelly or other forms of grease, as this will contaminate the injector.

The injectors can be checked using a multimeter to test the resistance values:

- Injector resistance at 20°C = 14.5 ohms ± 0.7 ohms

If an injector should fail, the following symptoms may be observed:

- Rough running
- Difficult starting
- Engine misfire
- Possible catalyst damage
- High emissions
- Fuelling and idle speed control adaptations disabled

A fuel injector failure is likely to occur for the following reasons:

- Actuator open circuit
- Short circuit to vehicle 12V supply or ground
- Blocked or restricted injector
- Low fuel pressure

If a fuel injector should fail, the following fault codes will be generated by the ECM diagnostics, which can be retrieved by Testbook:

Injector 1

- **P0201 -** Open circuit
- **P0261 -** Short circuit to ground
- **P0262 -** Short circuit to battery supply

Injector 2

- **P0202 -** Open circuit
- **P0264 -** Short circuit to ground
- **P0265 -** Short circuit to battery supply

Injector 3

- **P0203 -** Open circuit
- **P0267 -** Short circuit to ground
- **P0268 -** Short circuit to battery supply

Injector 4

- **P0204 -** Open circuit
- **P0270 -** Short circuit to ground
- **P0271 -** Short circuit to battery supply

Injector 5

- **P0205 -** Open circuit
- **P0273 -** Short circuit to ground
- **P0274 -** Short circuit to battery supply

Injector 6

- **P0206 -** Open circuit
- **P0276 -** Short circuit to ground
- **P0277 -** Short circuit to battery supply

Injector 7

- **P0207 -** Open circuit
- **P0279 -** Short circuit to ground
- **P0280 -** Short circuit to battery supply

Injector 8

- **P0208 -** Open circuit
- **P0282 -** Short circuit to ground
- **P0283 -** Short circuit to battery supply

All injectors

- **P0170 -** High leak rate detection
- **P0300 to P0308 -** Misfire detected excess emissions - blocked or restricted injector
- **P0300 to P0308 -** Misfire detected catalyst damage - blocked or restricted injector

Specific P-code number depends on which cylinder(s) is experiencing the fault.

Idle Air Control Valve (IACV) - from 99MY

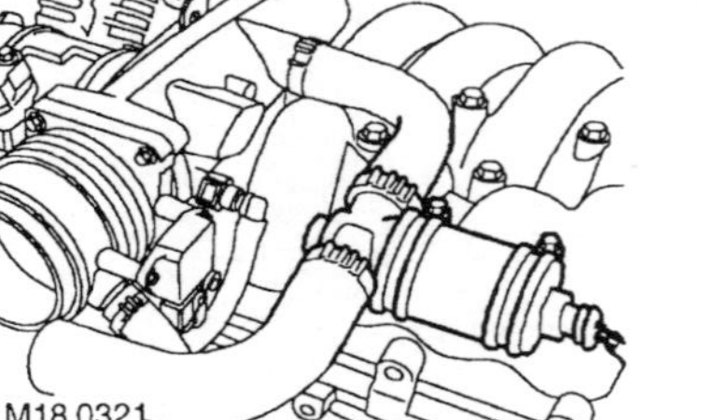

M18 0321

The idle air control valve is positioned at the top rear of the engine, on the side of the air inlet pipe. The unit is clamped to the inlet manifold by two bolts passing through 'P' clips.

A grey three-pin connector is provided at the back of the unit. One wire supplies the voltage feed from the engine compartment fusebox, while the other two wires carry the valve positioning control signals.

The IACV is used to make adjustments to optimise the engine idle speed under all operating conditions. Engine load at idle will vary in reaction to a combination of conditions and influences such as engine friction, water pump , air conditioning, altitude etc. The IACV utilises closed loop control to compensate for the changing conditions by regulating the air flow into the engine.

The IACV utilises two electromagnetic coils which use opposing PWM signals to control the positioning of a rotary valve. The rotary valve position determines how much air is allowed to flow through the bypass route.

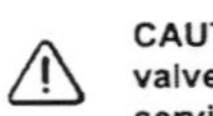

CAUTION: Do not try to forcibly set the valve position, the actuator cannot be serviced. In the event of failure the IACV must be replaced as a unit.

If one of the electrical circuits supplying the PWM signals fails, the ECM switches off the other circuit to prevent the valve from biasing towards a maximum or minimum setting. Under these conditions, a default position for the valve is provided by a permanent magnet, which sets the valve position to maintain the idle speed at a fixed value of approximately 1200 rpm with no load applied.

During cold start conditions, the idle speed is held at 1200 rpm in neutral for 20 seconds. Ignition timing is retarded as a catalyst heating strategy.

If the IACV should fail, the following symptoms may be observed:

- Either low or high idle speed
- Engine stalls
- Difficult starting
- Raised idle speed in default condition.

An IACV failure is likely to occur for the following reasons:

- Rotary valve seized
- Faulty actuator
- Connector or harness fault
- Intake system air leak
- Actuator port or hoses blocked, restricted or crimped

If the IACV should fail, the following fault codes will be generated by the ECM diagnostics, which can be retrieved by Testbook:

- **P0505 -** Blocked IACV valve - rpm error high or low
- **P1510 -** Short circuit to battery supply - opening winding
- **P1513 -** Short circuit to ground - opening winding
- **P1514 -** Open circuit - opening winding
- **P1553 -** Short circuit to battery supply - closing windings
- **P1552 -** Short circuit to ground - closing winding
- **P1551 -** Open circuit - closing winding

Heated Oxygen Sensors (HO_2S) - from 99MY

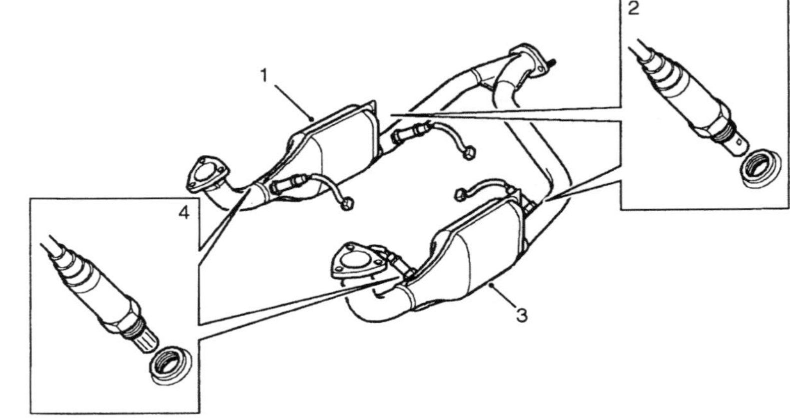

M17 0187

1. RH catalytic converter
2. Heated oxygen sensors - post-catalytic converters (2 off - NAS only)
3. LH catalytic converter
4. Heated oxygen sensors - pre-catalytic converters (2 off)

The number of heated oxygen (HO_2S) sensors fitted to a vehicle is dependent on the particular market requirements:

- 4 - HO_2S sensors (NAS vehicles)
- 2 - HO_2S (UK, European, Australia & Japan vehicles)
- 0 - HO_2S (Gulf & ROW vehicles)

The HO_2S sensors monitor the level of oxygen in the exhaust gases and the resulting data is used by the ECM to control the air:fuel mixture to provide the most efficient mix under all operating conditions. By positioning a sensor in the stream of exhaust gases from each bank of cylinders of the V8 engine enables the ECM to control the fuelling on each bank independently. This allows the ECM to provide more accurate control of the air:fuel ratio and monitor catalytic converter efficiency.

Two upstream sensors are utilised in markets where closed loop fuelling is the only mandatory requirement. For markets where closed loop fuelling control is not mandatory, HO_2S sensors are not included.

NAS vehicles utilise four HO_2S sensors, one upstream of each catalyst and one downstream of each catalyst. This arrangement is used to monitor catalytic converter efficiency and so determine when a catalyst is no longer working effectively. Obtaining catalytic converter efficiency data is a mandatory requirement of the ECM OBD strategy. The downstream sensors also provide for long term fuelling adaptions.

The basic closed control loop comprises the engine (controlled system), the heated oxygen sensors (measuring elements) and the engine management ECM (control) and the injectors and ignition (actuators). Although other factors also influence the calculations of the ECM, such as air flow, air intake temperature and throttle position. Additionally, special driving conditions are compensated for such as starting, acceleration and full load.

From cold start the ECM runs an open loop strategy, which is kept in place until the sensor's working temperature has been reached.

The heated oxygen sensors age with mileage, which will cause an increase in their response time for switching from rich to lean and lean to rich. The increase in response time influences the closed loop control and leads to progressively increased emissions. If the response rate is diagnosed to be exceeding a preset threshold, an error code will be stored in the ECM and the MIL warning lamp will be illuminated (NAS only).

The heated oxygen sensor is protected by an outer tube with a restricted flow opening to prevent the sensor's ceramics from being cooled by low temperature exhaust gases at start up. The pre-catalytic sensors are identified by three slots in the protective tube, whereas the post-catalytic sensors have four square indentations and a hole in the end of the protective tube (NAS only).

NOTE: The maximum working temperature of the tip of the HO_2S sensor is 930 °C (1706°F); temperatures higher than this will damage the sensor.

The heater elements are controlled by a PWM signal from the ECM. The heater elements are operated immediately following engine start and also during low load conditions when the temperature of the exhaust gases is insufficient to maintain the required sensor temperatures. The heater element warms the sensor's ceramic layer from the inside so that the sensor is hot enough for operation. After start up, the sensors are ready for closed loop control within about 20 to 30 seconds.

If the heater element fails, the ECM will not allow closed loop fuelling to be implemented until the sensor has achieved the required temperature. A diagnostic routine is utilised to measure both sensor heater current and the heater supply voltage, so its resistance can be calculated. The function is active once per drive cycle, as long as the heater has been switched on for a pre-defined period and the current has stabilised. The PWM duty cycle is carefully controlled to prevent thermal shock to cold sensors.

The pre-catalytic and post-catalytic converters are not interchangeable, and although it is possible to mount them in transposed positions, their harness connections are of different gender and colour:

- Upstream sensors have orange connectors.
- Downstream sensors have grey connectors.

It is important not to confuse the sensor signal pins; the signal pins are gold plated, whilst the heater supply pins are tinned, mixing them up will cause contamination and effect system performance with time.

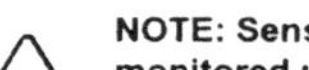

NOTE: Sensor voltage is most easily monitored using "Testbook".

If a heated oxygen sensor should fail, the following symptoms may be observed:

- Default to open loop fuelling on the catalyst bank with the failed sensor.
- If sensor get crossed, the engine will run normally after the initial start, but then become progressively unstable. One bank will clamp at the maximum rich level, and the other bank will clamp at maximum lean. The system will then revert to open loop fuelling.
- High CO reading
- Excess emissions
- Strong smell of hydrogen sulphide (H_2S) until the ECM defaults to open loop fuelling
- MIL lamp illuminated (NAS only)

A heated oxygen sensor failure is likely to occur for the following reasons:

- Damaged or incorrectly fitted sensor
- Sensor open circuit or disconnected
- Short circuit to vehicle supply or ground
- Stoichiometric ratio outside the correct operating band
- Contamination from leaded fuel or other sources
- Change in sensor characteristics - Chemical Shift Down (CSD)
- Sensors from LH and RH banks crossed
- Air leak into exhaust system (cracked pipe / weld or loose fixings)

Diagnosis of electrical faults is continually monitored by the ECM in both the upstream sensors and downstream sensors (NAS only). The sensor signal is checked against stored minimum and maximum threshold values equating to short and open circuit conditions.

If an HO_2S sensor should fail, the following fault codes will be generated by the ECM diagnostics, which can be retrieved by Testbook:

- **P1129** - Front heated oxygen sensors transposed

Upstream sensor LH bank - electrical (NAS only)

- **P0130** - Stoichiometric ratio outside operating band
- **P0132** - Short circuit to battery supply
- **P0134** - Open circuit

Downstream sensor LH bank - electrical

- **P0136** - Stoichiometric ratio outside operating band
- **P0137** - Short circuit to battery supply
- **P0138** - Short circuit to ground or chemical shift down
- **P0140** - Open circuit

Upstream sensor RH bank - electrical (NAS only)

- **P0150** - Stoichiometric ratio outside operating band
- **P0152** - Short circuit to battery supply
- **P0154** - Open circuit

Downstream sensor RH bank - electrical

- **P0156** - Stoichiometric ratio outside operating band
- **P0157** - Short circuit to ground
- **P0158** - Short circuit to battery voltage
- **P0160** - Open circuit

Upstream sensors aged (NAS only)

- **P0133** - Upstream sensor aged - Period time too short LH bank
- **P0133** - Upstream sensor aged - Period time too long LH bank
- **P0153** - Upstream sensor aged - Period time too short RH bank
- **P0153** - Upstream sensor aged - Period time too long RH bank
- **P1170** - Upstream sensor aged - ATV adaption too lean LH bank
- **P1170** - Upstream sensor aged - ATV adaption too rich LH bank
- **P1173** - Upstream sensor aged - ATV adaption too lean RH bank
- **P1173** - Upstream sensor aged - ATV adaption too rich RH bank

Sensor Heater faults

- **P0135** - Upstream heater LH bank - Short circuit (NAS only)
- **P0135** - Upstream heater LH bank - Open circuit (NAS only)
- **P0141** - Downstream heater LH bank - Short circuit
- **P0141** - Downstream heater LH bank - Open circuit
- **P0155** - Upstream heater RH bank - Short circuit (NAS only)
- **P0155** - Upstream heater RH bank - Open circuit (NAS only)
- **P0161** - Downstream heater LH bank - Short circuit
- **P0161** - Downstream heater LH bank - Open circuit

A diagnostic routine is used to measure both sensor heater current and the heater supply voltage so its resistance can be calculated. The function is active once per drive cycle as long as the heater has been switched on for a pre-defined period and the current has stabilised. The PWM duty cycle is carefully controlled to prevent thermal shock to cold sensors.

On NAS vehicles, the catalysts are monitored to determine emission pollutant conversion efficiency; the following fault codes will be generated by the ECM diagnostics, which can be retrieved by Testbook:

- **P0420** - Catalyst efficiency deteriorated LH bank
- **P0430** - Catalyst efficiency deteriorated RH bank

See EMISSION CONTROL, Description and operation.

Fuel pump relay - from 99MY

The fuel pump relay is fitted in the engine compartment fusebox which is situated at the front right hand side of the engine compartment. The relay is a four-pin normally open type, encapsulated in a yellow plastic housing.

The fuel supplied to the injectors from the in-tank fuel pump is controlled by the ECM via the fuel pump relay. During engine cranking, the fuel pump relay is activated by the ECM allowing the fuel system to be pressurised to 3.5 bar (52 $lbf.in^2$). The pump relay is then deactivated until engine start has been achieved.

Battery voltage is supplied via the engine compartment fusebox and relay activation is achieved by ground path switching through the ECM.

If the fuel pump relay should fail, the following symptoms may be observed:

- Engine stalls or will not start
- No fuel pressure at the fuel injectors

A fuel pump relay failure is likely to occur for the following reasons:

- Relay drive open circuit
- Short circuit to vehicle supply or ground
- Component failure

If the fuel pump relay should fail, the following fault codes will be generated by the ECM diagnostics, which can be retrieved by Testbook:

- **P1230** - Fuel pump relay open circuit - not the fuel pump itself
- **P1231** - Fuel pump relay short circuit to battery supply - not the fuel pump itself
- **P1232** - Fuel pump relay short circuit to ground - not the fuel pump itself

Advanced Evaporative Emissions System - from 99MY (NAS only)

The Bosch Motronic 5.2.1 ECM includes control for the evaporative emissions system components, its purpose is to minimise the evaporative loss of fuel vapour from the fuel system to the atmosphere. This is achieved by venting the system through an EVAP canister filled with vapour absorbing charcoal. The charcoal acts like a sponge and stores the vapour until the canister is purged under the control of the ECM.

Fuel vapour is stored in the activated charcoal canister for retention when the vehicle is not operating. When the vehicle is operating, fuel vapour is drawn from the canister into the engine via a purge control valve. The vapour is then delivered to the intake plenum chamber to be supplied to the engine cylinders where it is burned in the combustion process.

See EMISSION CONTROL, Description and operation.

Fuel Filling

During fuel filling, the fuel vapour displaced from the fuel tank is allowed to escape to atmosphere; valves within the fuel filler prevent any vapour escaping through the EVAP canister as this can adversely effect the fuel cut-off height. Only fuel vapour generated whilst driving is prevented from escaping to atmosphere by absorption into the EVAP canister. The fuel filler shuts off to leave the tank approximately 10% empty to ensure the roll over valves (ROVs) are always above the fuel level and so vapour can escape to the EVAP canister and the tank can breathe. The back pressures normally generated during fuel filling are too low to open the pressure relief valve, but vapour pressures accumulated during driving are higher and can open the pressure relief valve. Should the vehicle be overturned, the ROVs shut off to prevent any fuel spillage.

Fuel Tank Venting

Fuel vapour generated from within the fuel tank as the fuel heats up is stored in the tank until the pressure exceeds the operating pressure of the two-way valve. When the two-way valve opens, the fuel vapour passes along the vent line from the fuel tank via the fuel tank vapour separator to the evaporation inlet port of the EVAP canister.

Liquid fuel must not be allowed to contaminate the charcoal in the EVAP canister. To prevent this, the fuel vapour separator fitted to the fuel filler neck allows fuel to drain back into the tank. As the fuel vapour cools, it condenses and is allowed to flow back into the fuel tank from the vent line by way of the two-way valve.

The EVAP canister contains charcoal pellets which absorbs and stores the fuel vapour from the fuel tank while the engine is not running. When the canister is not being purged, the fuel vapour remains in the canister and clean air exits the canister via the air inlet port.

ECM Purge Control

The engine management ECM controls the output signals to the purge valve and the canister vent solenoid (CVS) valve, and receives an input from the fuel tank pressure sensor. The system will not work properly if there is a leakage or clogging within the system, or if the purge valve cannot be controlled.

When the engine is running, the ECM decides when conditions are correct for the vapour to be purged from the canister and opens the canister purge valve. This connects a manifold vacuum line to the canister and fuel vapour containing the hydrocarbons is drawn from the canister's charcoal element to be burned in the engine. Clean air is drawn into the canister through the air inlet port to fill the displaced volume of vapour.

The purge valve remains closed below preset coolant and engine speed values to protect the engine tune and catalytic converter performance. If the EVAP canister was purged during cold running or at idling speed the additional enrichment in the fuel mixture would delay the catalytic converter light off time and cause erratic idle. When the purge valve is opened, fuel vapour from the EVAP canister is drawn into the plenum chamber downside of the throttle housing, to be delivered to the combustion chambers for burning.

The purge valve is opened and closed in accordance with a PWM signal supplied from the ECM. Possible failure modes associated with the purge valve failure are listed below:

- Valve drive open circuit
- Short circuit to vehicle supply or ground
- Purge valve or pipework blocked or restricted
- Purge valve stuck open
- Pipework joints leaking or disconnected.

Possible symptoms associated with purge valve or associated pipework failure is listed below:

- Engine may stall on return to idle if purge valve is stuck open
- Poor idling quality if the purge valve is stuck open
- Fuelling adaptions forced excessively lean if the EVAP canister is clear and the purge valve is stuck open.
- Fuelling adaptions forced excessively rich if the EVAP canister is saturated and the purge valve is stuck open.
- Saturation of the EVAP canister if the purge valve is stuck closed.

To maintain driveability and effective emission control, purging control must be closely controlled by the ECM, as a 1% concentration of fuel vapour from the EVAP canister in the air intake may shift the air:fuel ratio by as much as 20%. The ECM must purge the fuel vapour from the EVAP canister at regular intervals as its storage capacity is limited and an excessive build-up of fuel pressure in the system could increase the likelihood of vapour leaks. Canister purging is cycled with the fuelling adaption as both cannot be active at the same time. The ECM alters the PWM signal to the purge valve to control the rate of purging of the canister to maintain the optimum stoichiometric air:fuel mixture for the engine.

See EMISSION CONTROL, Description and operation.

Leak Test

The evaporative emission system used on NAS vehicles includes a fuel pressure sensor and a canister vent solenoid (CVS) valve. The system is capable of detecting holes in the fuel system down to 1 mm (0.04 in.).

The test is carried out in three parts:

First the purge valve and the CVS valve closes off the storage system and the vent pressure increases due to the fuel vapour pressure level in the tank. If the pressure level is greater than the acceptable limit, the test will abort because a false leak test response will result. In part two of the test, the purge valve is opened (preferably with the engine idling) and the fuel tank pressure will decrease due to purge operation. In part three of the test, the leak measurement test is performed. The pressure response of the tests determines the level of the leak, and if greater than the limit on two consecutive tests, the ECM stores the fault in diagnostic memory and the MIL light on the instrument pack is illuminated. The test is only carried out at idle with the vehicle stationary. Following the test, the system returns to normal purge operation after the CVS valve opens. The in-tank pressure sensor monitors the pressure build-up to determine whether leaks are present.

Possible reasons for a test failure are listed below:

- Fuel filler not tightened or cap missing
- Sensor or actuator open circuit
- Short circuit to vehicle supply or ground
- Either purge or CVS valve stuck open
- Either purge or CVS valve stuck closed or blocked pipe
- Piping broken or not connected
- Loose or leaking connection

If the piping is broken forward of the purge valve or is not connected, the engine may run rough and fuelling adaptions will drift. The fault will not be detected by the test, but by the engine management ECM detecting that the fuelling adaption is suspended. The evaluation of the leakage is dependent on the differential pressure between the fuel tank and the ambient atmospheric pressure. The diagnostic test is disabled at altitudes above 2,800 metres (9,500 ft).

The fuel tank pressure sensor is included as part of the OBD system. A failure of the fuel tank pressure sensor will not be noticed by the driver, but if the ECM detects a fault, it will be stored in the diagnostic memory and the MIL warning lamp will be illuminated on the instrument pack

Possible fuel tank pressure sensor failures are listed below:

- Damaged sensor
- Harness wiring or connector faulty
- Open circuit
- Short circuit to battery voltage or ground
- ECM fault

Possible symptoms of a fuel tank pressure sensor failure are listed below:

- Fuel tank pressure sensor poor performance
- Fuel tank pressure sensor low range fault
- Fuel tank pressure sensor high range fault

Fault codes associated with the evaporative emission control system are listed below:

- **P0171 -** Multiplication fuelling adaption (Max.) exceeded lean limit - LH bank
- **P0172 -** Multiplication fuelling adaption (Min.) exceeded lean limit - LH bank
- **P0174 -** Multiplication fuelling adaption (Max.) exceeded lean limit - RH bank
- **P0175 -** Multiplication fuelling adaption (Min.) exceeded lean limit - RH bank
- **P0171 -** Additive fuelling adaption (Max.) exceeded lean limit - LH bank
- **P0172 -** Additive fuelling adaption (Min.) exceeded lean limit - LH bank
- **P0174 -** Additive fuelling adaption (Max.) exceeded lean limit - RH bank
- **P0175 -** Additive fuelling adaption (Min.) exceeded lean limit - RH bank
- **P0440 -** Purge valve not sealing
- **P0442 -** Small leak within system
- **P0443 -** Purge valve power stage short circuit to battery voltage
- **P0444 -** Purge valve power stage open circuit
- **P0445 -** Purge valve power stage short circuit to ground
- **P0445 -** Large leak within system
- **P0446 -** CVS valve / filter / pipe blocked
- **P0447 -** CVS valve open circuit
- **P0448 -** CVS valve short circuit to ground
- **P0449 -** CVS valve short circuit to battery voltage
- **P0451 -** Fuel tank pressure signal stuck high within range
- **P0452 -** Fuel tank pressure signal short circuit to battery voltage (out of range - high)
- **P0453 -** Fuel tank pressure sensor signal short circuit to ground or open circuit (out of range - low)

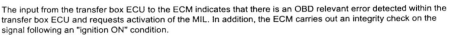

Secondary air injection system (NAS only from 2000MY)

Refer to EMISSION CONTROL section for description of the secondary air injection system components.

Inertia Fuel Shut-off (IFS) Switch

The inertia switch isolates the power supply to the fuel pump in the event of sudden deceleration, as encountered during an accident. The inertia switch is located in the right hand side footwell behind an access flap. It is reset by depressing the central plunger at the top of the switch.

E-box Cooling Fan control - from 99MY only

The cooling fan is utilised to provide a cool temperature environment for the Bosch Motronic 5.2.1 ECM in the under bonnet mounted E-box. The fan provides cabin air into the E-box and operation is controlled by the ECM. The ECM contains an internal temperature sensor which it uses to determine when cooling fan operation is necessary.

Spark plugs - from 99MY

The spark plugs are platinum tipped on both centre and earth electrodes to provide a long maintenance free life and exceptional cold starting performance.

CAUTION: Do not clean the spark plugs or attempt to reset the spark plug gap.

CAUTION: If the wrong specification spark plugs are used, the misfire detection system is likely to malfunction and corresponding error codes will be stored in the ECM diagnostic memory. Only use the recommended spark plugs.

In the event of a spark plug failure, a misfire on a specific cylinder may be observed.

A spark plug failure may occur for the following reasons:

- Connector or wiring fault
- Faulty plug (e.g. wrong gap, damaged electrodes etc.)
- Incorrect spark plugs fitted
- Breakdown of high tension lead causing tracking to chassis earth

High tension (ht) leads

The ht leads are routed from the ignition coils at the back of the engine to four spark plugs on each bank of the engine block.

An ht lead failure will result in a misfire condition on a specific cylinder.

An ht lead failure may occur for the following reasons:

- Connector / wiring fault
- Faulty lead causing spark tracking to chassis earth
- Damage to ht lead during gearbox removal

Electronic Automatic Gearbox Interface - from 99MY

The ECM communicates with the EAT ECU via a Controller Area Network (CAN). This is used for the gearshift torque interface and as a means for transmitting OBD information between the two control units. The EAT ECU passes OBD data and requests to the ECM which controls the storage of diagnostics data and MIL activation. Unlike the GEMS ECM, the Bosch M5.2.1 does not store gearbox faults. The MIL activation request can be checked with Testbook.

The CAN network is a high speed serial interface operating at 500 k-baud. The system is a differential bus using a twisted pair. If either or both wires of the twisted pair CAN bus is open or short circuited, a CAN time out fault will occur and the EAT ECU defaults to third gear.

See AUTOMATIC GEARBOX, Description and operation.

Transfer Box ECU (MIL input) - from 99MY (NAS only)

The input from the transfer box ECU to the ECM indicates that there is an OBD relevant error detected within the transfer box ECU and requests activation of the MIL. In addition, the ECM carries out an integrity check on the signal following an "ignition ON" condition.

See TRANSFER BOX, Description and operation.

Engine Speed Output - from 99MY

The ECM supplies engine speed information to various vehicle systems (instrument pack etc.). The system uses an output frequency of 4 pulses per engine revolution.

HeVAC system interface - from 99MY

The diagnostics for the condenser fans and A/C grant signal is disabled and so it is not possible to detect open and short circuit conditions on these lines.

The condenser fans can be switched on by either the HeVAC ECU or the engine management ECM (to assist engine cooling) or by the fan control logic.

See HEATING AND VENTILATION, Description and operation.

See AIR CONDITIONING, Description and operation.

Fuel used signal - from 99MY

This output is required to provide fuel consumption information to the trip computer.

Fuel level input - from 99MY

This input is required by the ECM as part of the misfire detection strategy, in order to record a "low fuel" situation was present when misfire was detected and logged as a fault. The signal is received as an analogue signal from the fuel tank sender unit.

Fuel Level State	Sender Resistance	Fuel Level Signal Voltage
Full	19 ohm	1.00 V
Empty	270 ohm	3.16 V
Low Fuel Lamp ON threshold	above 175 ohm	2.77 V
Low Fuel Lamp OFF threshold	less than 117 ohm	2.40 V

Notes

FUEL TANK - DRAIN

Service repair no - 19.55.02

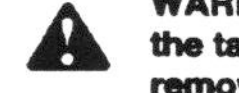

WARNING: Fuel must be drained through the tank fill stub, with the filler neck removed. In some circumstances, the fuel level could be above the level of the stub. If the fuel gauge indicates more than 75% full prior to draining, a minimum of 10 litres of fuel must first be removed through the fuel return line as detailed below.

WARNING: The fuel tank must be completely drained before it is removed.

WARNING: Petrol/gasoline vapour is highly flammable and in confined spaces is also explosive and toxic. Always have a fire extinguisher containing FOAM, CO_2 GAS or POWDER close to hand when handling or draining fuel. See 01 Introduction.

CAUTION: Before disconnecting any part of the fuel system, it is imperative that all dust, dirt and debris is removed from around components to prevent ingress of foreign matter into the fuel system.

WARNING: Follow manufacturer's instructions for connection and safe use of equipment.

NOTE: Assuming the fuel tank is FULL, drain the following quantities:

Renew fuel pump = COMPLETE DRAIN

Renew fuel filler neck = 10 litres (2.6 US Gallons)

Renew Fuel Tank = COMPLETE DRAIN

1. Depressurise fuel system. ***See Repair.***
2. Disconnect battery earth lead.

Fuel gauge indicated over 75% full:

3. Using a bowser, with a suitable hose connection into the fuel return line, either at the fuel rail, or at the under floor connection, forward of the fuel tank, drain a minimum 10 litres (2.6 US Gallons) from fuel tank.

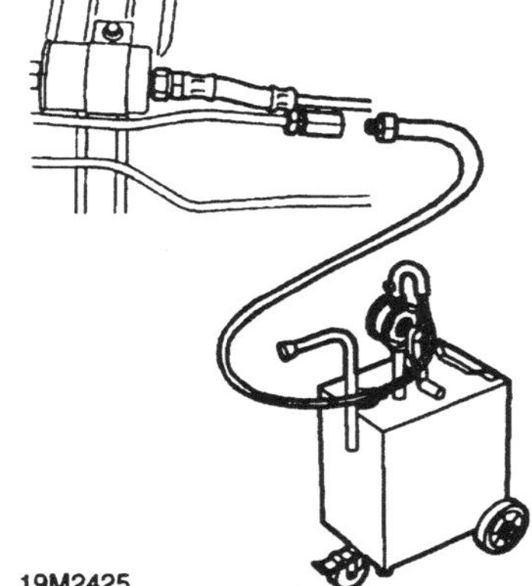

19M2425

Fuel level at least 10 litres (2.6 US gallons) from full:

4. Remove fuel filler neck. ***See Repair.***
5. Using a suitable length of plastic tube, inserted through the fuel tank fill stub, drain contents of tank into a closed container.

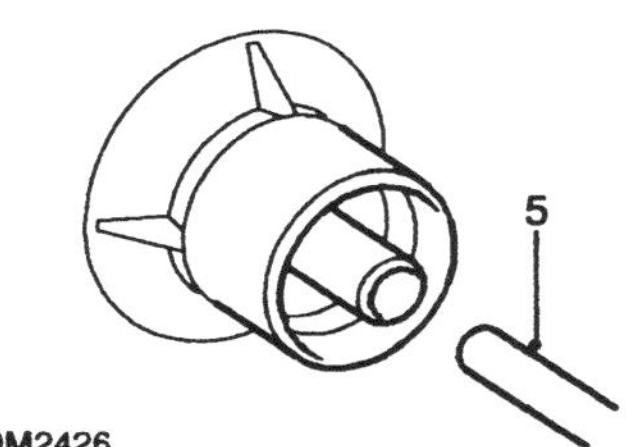

19M2426

6. Fit filler neck. ***See Repair.***
7. Connect battery earth lead.

THROTTLE CABLE - up to 99MY

Service repair no - 19.20.05

Adjust

NOTE: Accurate setting of this cable is critical to correct operation of automatic transmission.

1. Ensure throttle lever is against stop in closed position.

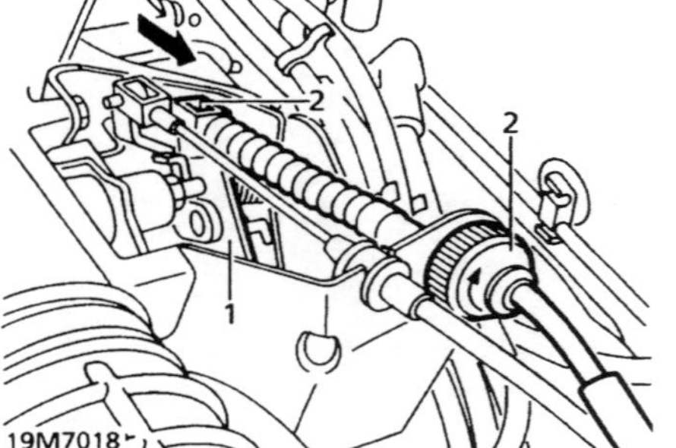

19M7018

2. Rotate thumb-wheel clockwise until all slack is removed from cable. (Throttle lever is about to lift from stop)
3. Back off thumb-wheel anti-clockwise by one quarter of a turn.
4. Check cruise control cable adjustment.
5. If necessary, adjust cruise control cable. ***See CRUISE CONTROL, Adjustment.***

THROTTLE CABLE - from 99MY

Service repair no - 19.20.05

Adjust

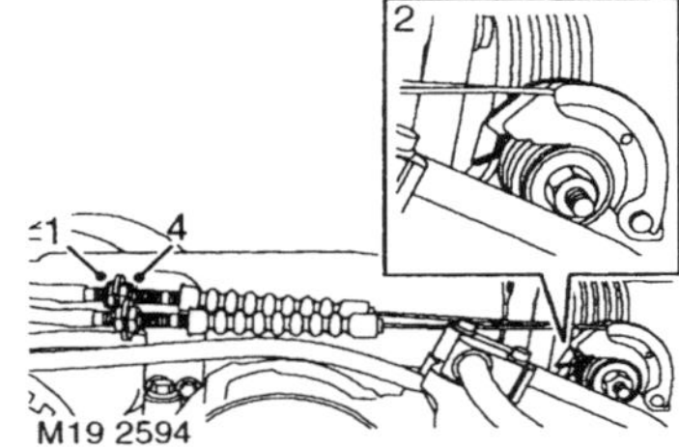

M19 2594

1. Loosen outer cable locknuts.
2. Adjust the rear locknut until it is in contact with the back of the abutment bracket and the throttle lever is in contact with the inner driven lever.
3. Ensure that the driven lever remains in contact with the throttle stop screw, (throttle closed).
4. Tighten cable front nut to lock cable to abutment bracket and tighten lock nut.

ENGINE TUNING - up to 99MY

Service repair no - 19.22.13

The position of the Idle Air Control (IAC) valve can be checked using TestBook and adjusted if necessary through the by-pass screw in the plenum chamber. The bypass screw is covered by a tamper proof plug which can be extracted using a self tapping screw.

Vehicles in certain markets are not fitted with oxygen sensors or active catalytic converters. Certain specification vehicles may have active catalytic converters fitted, but do not use oxygen sensors. This is referred to as an open loop catalyst system. All vehicles without oxygen sensors must have the exhaust CO content checked periodically using an approved CO meter and adjusted if necessary using TestBook.

On vehicles with open loop catalyst systems, exhaust CO content must be checked upstream of the catalyst, **NOT at the tailpipe**.

Preliminary Checks

1. Ensure that air filter and fuel filter elements are in a serviceable condition.
2. Check air intake system, including vacuum pipes and hoses for correct routing and freedom from leaks and restriction.
3. Electrical connections must be secure and leads correctly routed.
4. Check ignition system integrity using an approved Engine Analyser.

Procedure

Vehicles without oxygen sensors:

5. Ensure exhaust gas analyser is warmed and calibrated ready for use.
6. **Non catalyst vehicles:** Connect exhaust gas analyser to tailpipe.
7. Disconnect purge valve pipe at charcoal canister.

CAUTION: Do not disconnect purge valve electrical multiplug.

19M7087

Open loop catalyst vehicles:

8. Remove blanking plug from RH exhaust front pipe, forward of the catalyst.
9. Fit sampling pipe and tighten securely.

CAUTION: Air leaks at the sampling pipe will cause incorrect readings.

10. Connect exhaust gas analyser to sampling pipe.

NOTE: When refitting the blanking plug apply nickel based grease to the thread.

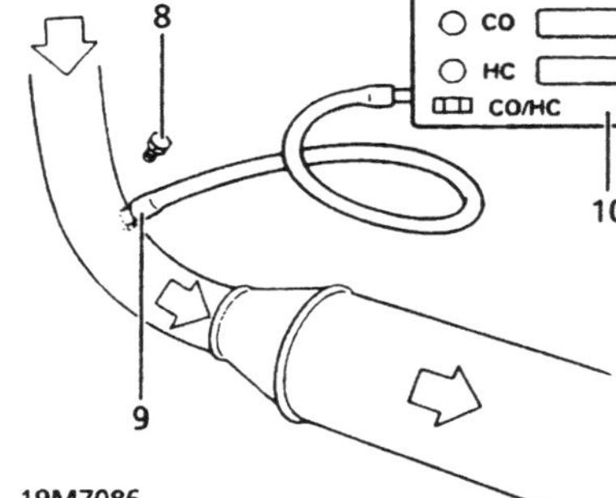

19M7086

All vehicles:

11. Ensure air conditioning and all electical loads are off. Vehicle must be in neutral or park with air suspension in kneel and disabled.
12. Carry out tuning or base idle setting procedure as applicable using TestBook.

AIR CLEANER ASSEMBLY - up to 97MY

Service repair no - 19.10.01

Remove

1. Release 2 clips securing air flow meter to air cleaner.
2. Release air flow meter. Remove 'O' ring and discard.
3. Disconnect intake air temperature sensor.

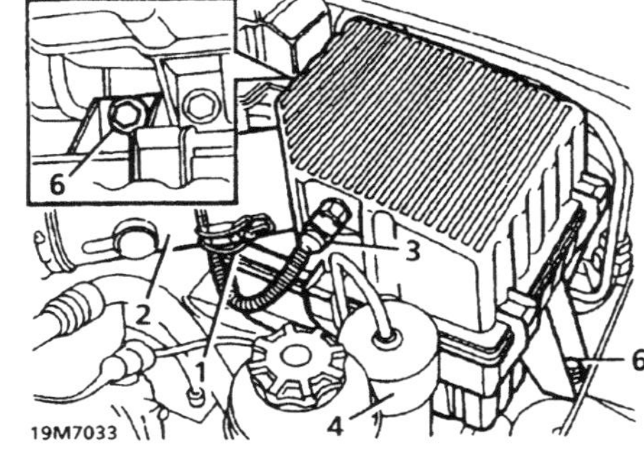

19M7033

4. Remove bolt securing air suspension dryer to air cleaner.
5. Release dryer pipes from 2 clips. Position dryer aside.
6. Remove 2 bolts securing air cleaner to valance.
7. Release air cleaner lug from valance grommet. Remove air cleaner.
8. If necessary, remove intake air temperature sensor.
9. Remove seal.

Refit

10. If removed, refit intake air temperature sensor with seal to air cleaner. Tighten to ***8 Nm. (6 lbf.ft)***
11. Position air cleaner assembly. Engage lug to valance grommet. Secure with bolts.
12. Position air suspension dryer to air cleaner. Secure with bolt. Tighten to ***8 Nm. (6 lbf.ft)***
13. Engage dryer pipes to clips.
14. Connect multiplug to intake air temperature sensor.
15. Fit new 'O' ring to air flow meter.
16. Secure air flow meter to air cleaner with clips.

AIR CLEANER ASSEMBLY - from 97MY

Service repair no - 19.10.01

Remove

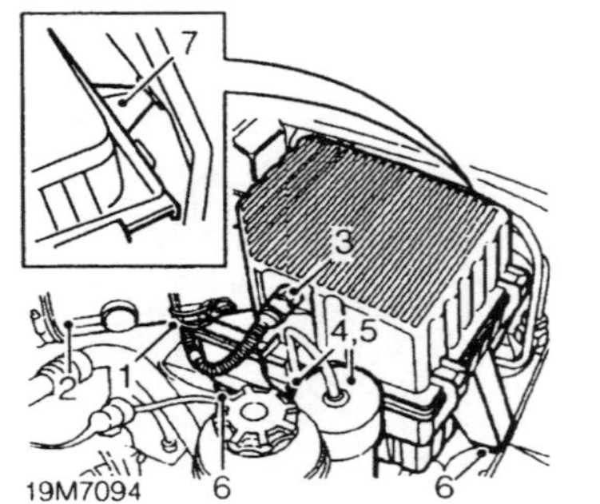

19M7094

1. Release 2 clips securing mass air flow (MAF) meter to air cleaner.
2. Release MAF meter from air cleaner. Remove and discard 'O' ring from MAF sensor.
3. Disconnect multiplug from air temperature sensor.
4. Remove bolt securing air suspension air dryer to air cleaner.
5. Release air dryer from air cleaner and position aside.
6. Release air cleaner from 2 valance grommets.
7. Remove air cleaner from inner wing grommet. ***Do not carry out further dismantling if component is removed for access only.***

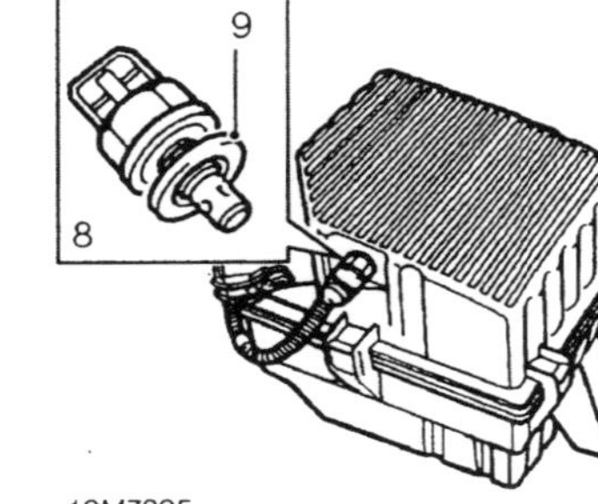

19M7095

8. Remove air temperature sensor from air cleaner.
9. Remove and discard air temperature sensor seal.
10. Fit new seal to air cleaner.
11. Fit air temperature sensor to air cleaner and tighten to ***8 Nm. (6 lbf.ft)***

Refit

12. Fit air cleaner lugs to inner wing and valance grommets. Ensure lugs are fully engaged to grommets.
13. Position air dryer to air cleaner, fit bolt and tighten to ***8 Nm. (6 lbf.ft)***
14. Connect multiplug to air temperature sensor.
15. Fit new 'O' ring seal to MAF meter.
16. Engage MAF meter to air cleaner and secure with clips.

ELEMENT - AIR CLEANER - from 99MY

Service repair no - 19.10.10

Remove

1. Release 3 fixings and remove battery cover.
2. Disconnect battery earth lead.

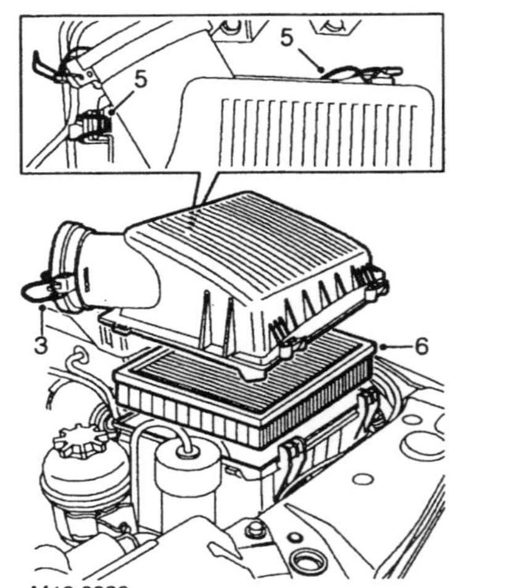

M19 2633

3. Release 2 clips securing air flow meter to air cleaner assembly.
4. Release air flow meter and position aside.
5. Release 2 clips securing air cleaner top cover and remove cover.
6. Remove air cleaner element.

Refit

7. Clean inside of air cleaner case and cover.
8. Fit new air cleaner element.
9. Fit air cleaner cover and secure with clips.
10. Connect air flow meter to air cleaner assembly and secure with clips.
11. Connect battery earth lead.
12. Fit battery cover and secure with fixings.

AIR INTAKE HOSE - up to 99MY

Service repair no - 19.10.17

Remove

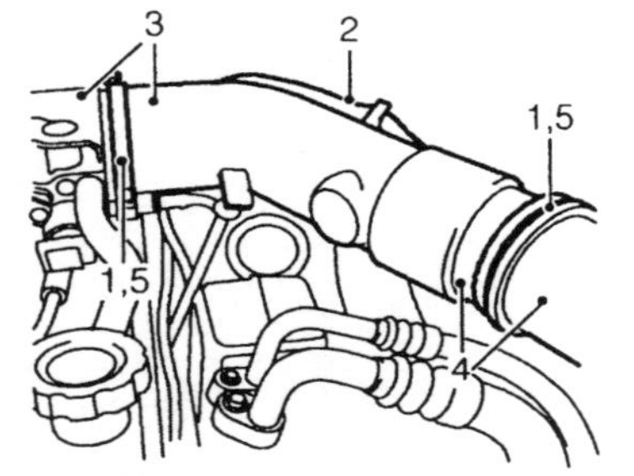

19M7089

1. Loosen 2 clips securing intake hose to plenum chamber and mass air flow sensor.
2. Release harness from intake hose clip.
3. Release intake hose from plenum chamber.
4. Remove intake hose from mass air flow sensor.
5. Remove 2 clips from intake hose.

Refit

6. Fit clips to intake hose.
7. Fit intake hose to mass air flow sensor.
8. Connect intake hose to plenum chamber.
9. Tighten clips securing intake hose to plenum and MAF sensor.
10. Engage harness to intake hose clip.

CAMSHAFT POSITION (CMP) SENSOR - up to 99MY

Service repair no - 18.30.24

Remove

1. Disconnect battery negative lead.
2. Release 2 clips securing upper fan cowl. Remove cowl.

19M7056

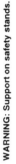

3. Release tension from auxiliary belt. Remove belt from crankshaft pulley.

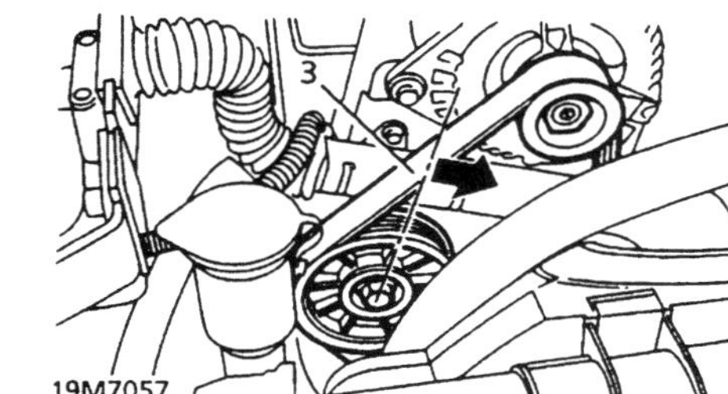

19M7057

4. Release CMP sensor connector from bracket. Disconnect multiplug.

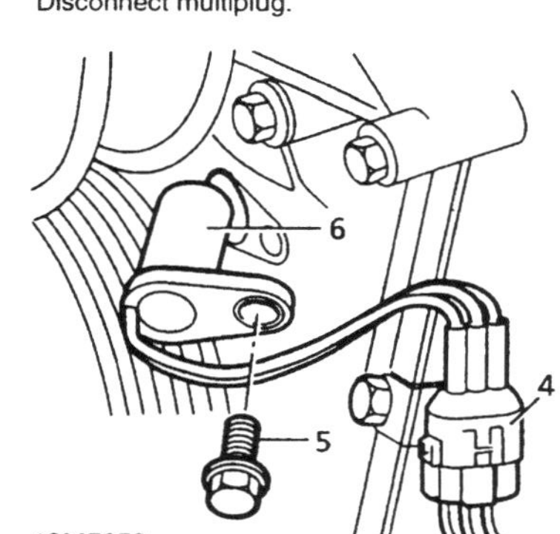

19M7058

5. Remove bolt securing CMP sensor to front cover.
6. Remove CMP sensor.

Refit

7. Ensure mating surfaces are clean.
8. Engage CMP sensor in front cover location. Secure with bolt. Tighten to ***8 Nm. (6 lbf.ft)***
9. Secure CMP sensor connector to bracket. Connect multiplug.
10. Turn auxiliary belt tensioner. Refit belt to crankshaft pulley.
11. Fit upper fan cowl. Secure with clips.
12. Reconnect battery negative lead.

CAMSHAFT POSITION (CMP) SENSOR - from 99MY

Service repair no - 18.30.24

Remove

1. Release fixings and remove battery cover.
2. Disconnect battery earth lead.
3. Raise front of vehicle.

WARNING: Support on safety stands.

4. Disconnect engine harness from CMP sensor.

M18 0334

5. Disconnect CMP sensor multiplug from bracket.
6. Remove bolt from clamp securing CMP sensor to front cover.
7. Remove clamp and sensor. Discard 'O' ring from CMP sensor.

Refit

8. Ensure CMP sensor is clean, fit new 'O' ring and sensor to cover.
9. Fit clamp to CMP sensor and tighten bolt to ***8 Nm (6 lbf.ft).***
10. Fit sensor multiplug to bracket and connect engine harness to multiplug.
11. Lower vehicle.
12. Connect battery earth lead.
13. Fit battery cover and secure with fixings.

ENGINE COOLANT TEMPERATURE (ECT) SENSOR - up to 99MY

Service repair no - 18.30.10

Remove

1. Partially drain cooling system. ***See COOLING SYSTEM, Repair.***
2. Disconnect ECT sensor multiplug.
3. Position rag around ECT sensor to catch spillage.
4. Remove ECT sensor. Collect and discard copper washer.

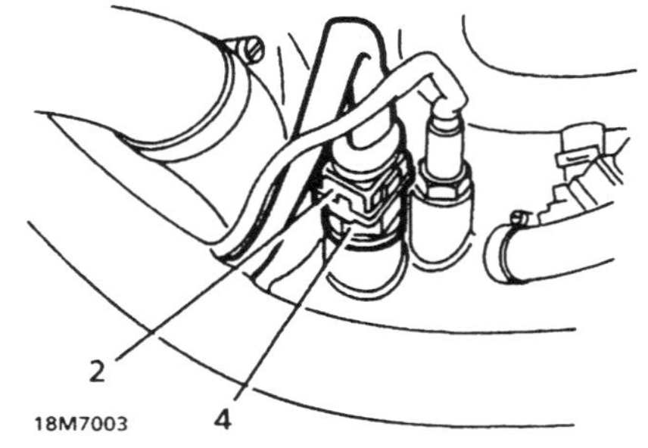

18M7003

Refit

5. Ensure ECT sensor seat in manifold is clean.
6. Coat sensor threads with Loctite 577 and fit a new copper washer.
7. Fit ECT sensor. Tighten to ***20 Nm. (15 lbf.ft).***
8. Connect multiplug to ECT sensor.
9. Refill cooling system. ***See COOLING SYSTEM, Repair.***
10. Run engine to normal operating temperature. Check for leaks around ECT sensor.

ENGINE COOLANT TEMPERATURE (ECT) SENSOR - from 99MY

Service repair no - 18.30.10

Remove

1. Release fixings and remove battery cover.
2. Disconnect battery earth lead.
3. Drain sufficient coolant to ensure no spillage during removal of ECT sensor. ***See COOLING SYSTEM, Repair.***
4. Remove alternator drive belt. ***See ELECTRICAL, Repair.***

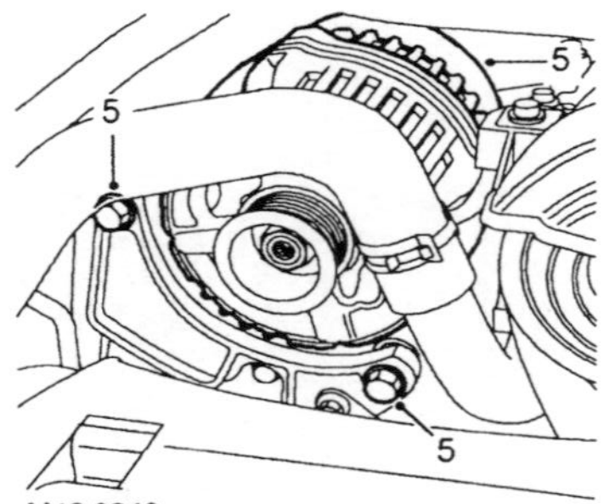

M18 0340

5. Remove 2 bolts securing alternator, release alternator from support bracket and position aside.

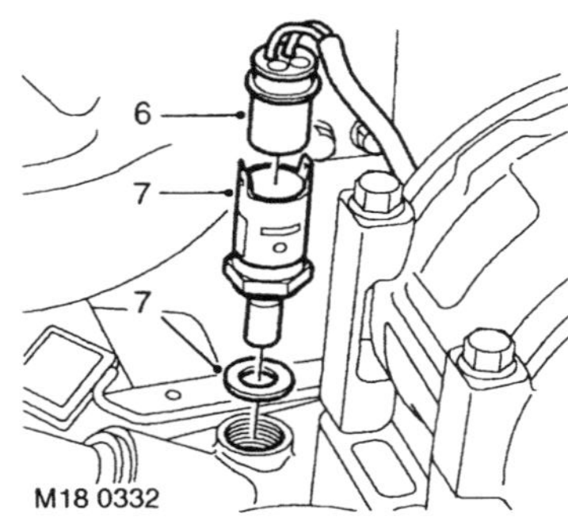

M18 0332

6. Disconnect multiplug from ECT sensor.
7. Remove sensor from inlet manifold and discard sealing washer.

Refit

8. Clean sealant from threads in manifold.
9. Apply Loctite 577 to sensor threads.
10. Fit new sealing washer to coolant sensor and tighten sensor to ***10 Nm (8 lbf. ft).*** Connect multiplug.
11. Position alternator, fit bolts and tighten to ***45 Nm (33 lbf.ft).***
12. Fit alternator drive belt. ***See ELECTRICAL, Repair.***
13. Top up cooling system. ***See COOLING SYSTEM, Repair.***
14. Connect battery earth lead.
15. Fit battery cover and secure with fixings.

CRANKSHAFT POSITION (CKP) SENSOR - up to 97MY

Service repair no - 18.30.12

Remove

CAUTION: 4.6 litre automatic vehicles have a spacer fitted to the engine speed sensor.

1. Disconnect battery negative lead.
2. Disconnect multiplug from CKP sensor fly-lead.
3. Remove bolt securing CKP sensor connector to bracket.

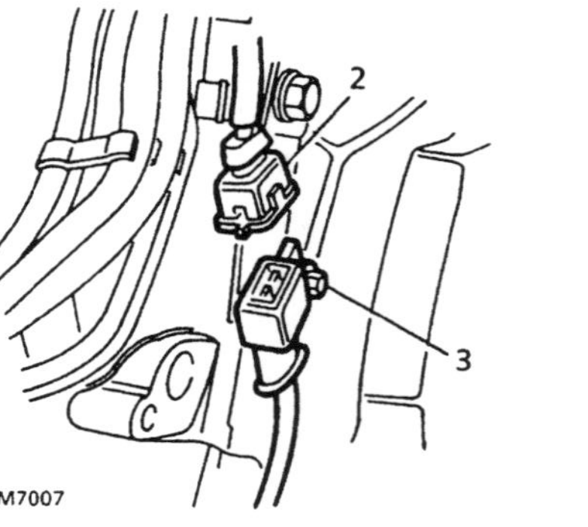

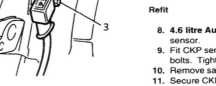

18M7007

4. Raise the vehicle.

WARNING: Support on safety stands.

5. Remove 2 bolts securing CKP sensor to cylinder block adaptor plate.

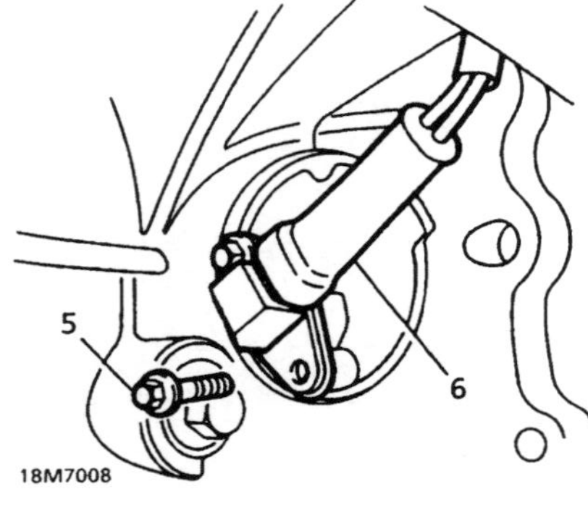

18M7008

6. Remove CKP sensor.
7. **4.6 litre Automatic Only:** Collect spacer from sensor.

Refit

8. **4.6 litre Automatic Only:** Fit spacer to CKP sensor.
9. Fit CKP sensor to adaptor plate. Secure with bolts. Tighten to ***6 Nm. (4 lbf.ft)***
10. Remove safety stands. Lower vehicle.
11. Secure CKP sensor connector to bracket with bolt.
12. Connect CKP sensor multiplug.
13. Reconnect battery negative lead.

CRANKSHAFT POSITION (CKP) SENSOR - 97MY to 99MY

Service repair no - 18.30.12

CAUTION: System sensor connectors can be contaminated by oil or coolant when disconnected during repair or testing. Use a suitable cap to prevent dirt or fluid ingress.

Remove

1. Disconnect battery earth lead.
2. Raise front of vehicle.

WARNING: Support on safety stands.

3. Remove gearbox LH acoustic cover. ***See CHASSIS AND BODY, Repair.***

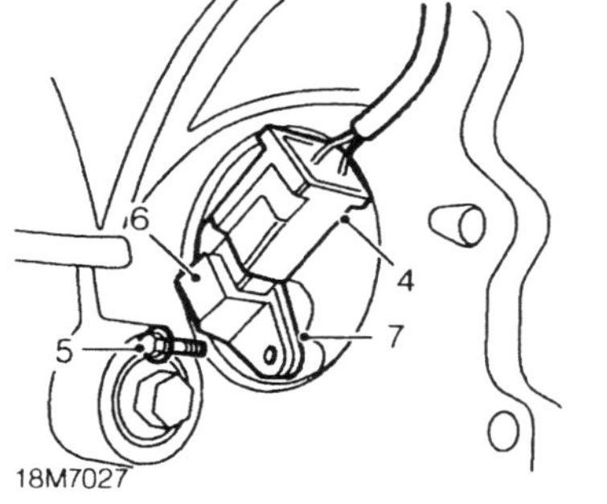

4. Disconnect multiplug from CKP sensor.
5. Remove bolt securing CKP sensor to cylinder block adaptor plate.
6. Remove CKP sensor.
7. Collect spacer from sensor.

Refit

8. Fit spacer to CKP sensor.
9. Fit CKP sensor to adaptor plate.
10. Fit bolt securing sensor to adaptor plate and tighten to ***6 Nm. (4 lbf.ft)***
11. Connect multiplug to CKP sensor.
12. Fit gearbox LH acoustic cover. ***See CHASSIS AND BODY, Repair.***
13. Remove stand(s) and lower vehicle.

CRANKSHAFT POSITION (CKP) SENSOR - from 99MY

Service repair no - 18.30.12

Remove

1. Release fixings and remove battery cover.
2. Disconnect battery earth lead.
3. Raise front of vehicle.

WARNING: Support on safety stands.

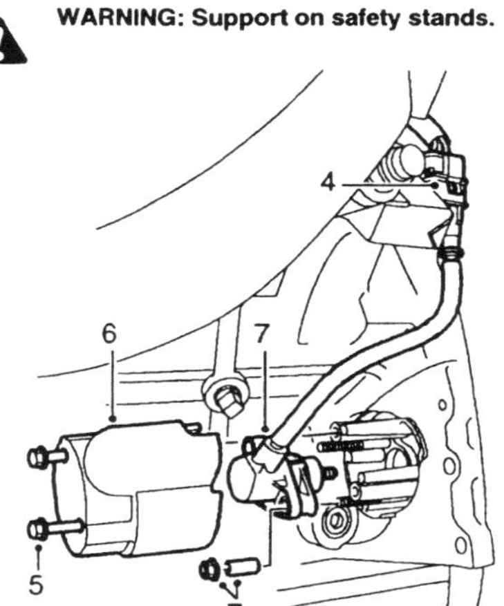

4. Release CKP sensor multiplug from bracket and disconnect multiplug from engine harness.
5. Remove 2 bolts securing CKP sensor heat shield.
6. Remove heat shield.
7. Remove 2 nuts securing CKP sensor, remove 2 spacers, sensor and sensor mounting.

Refit

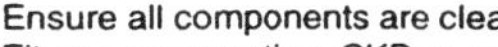

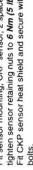

8. Ensure all components are clean.
9. Fit sensor mounting, CKP sensor, 2 spacers and tighten sensor retaining nuts to ***6 Nm (5 lbf.ft).***
10. Fit CKP sensor heat shield and secure with bolts.
11. Connect sensor multiplug to engine harness and fit multiplug to bracket.
12. Remove stand(s) and lower vehicle.
13. Connect battery earth lead.
14. Fit and secure battery cover.

FUEL SYSTEM - DEPRESSURISE

WARNING: Fuel pressure of up to 2.5 bar will be present in the system, even if the engine has not been run for some time. Always depressurise the system before disconnecting any components in the fuel feed line (between fuel pump and pressure regulator). The spilling of fuel is unavoidable during this operation. Ensure that all necessary precautions are taken to prevent fire and explosion.

NOTE: Fuel pressure can be relieved at fuel rail feed union or fuel filter unions.

1. Position cloth around relevant union to protect against fuel spray.
2. Carefully slacken union.
3. Tighten union to correct torque once pressure has relieved.

ENGINE CONTROL MODULE (ECM) - up to 99MY

Service repair no - 18.30.01

Remove

1. Disconnect battery negative lead.

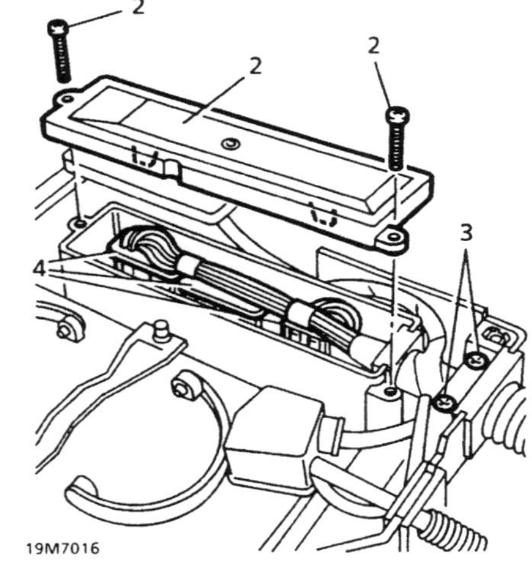

19M7016

2. Remove 2 screws securing ECM housing cover. Remove cover
3. Slacken 2 harness clamp screws.
4. Lift ECM slightly for access. Disconnect 3 multiplugs.
5. Remove ECM from housing.
6. Remove carrier plate from ECM.

Refit

7. Reverse removal procedure.

ENGINE CONTROL MODULE (ECM) - from 99MY

Service repair no - 18.30.01

Remove

1. Release fixings and remove battery cover.
2. Disconnect battery earth lead.

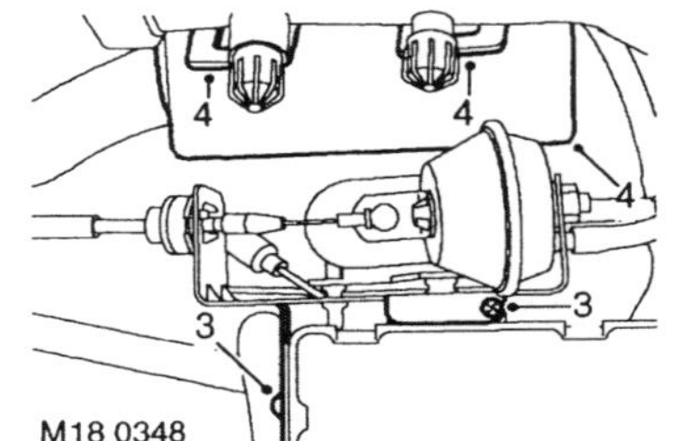

M18 0348

3. Remove 2 screws securing cruise control assembly to EAS housing cover and position aside.
4. Release 2 fixings securing ECM housing cover and release cover.

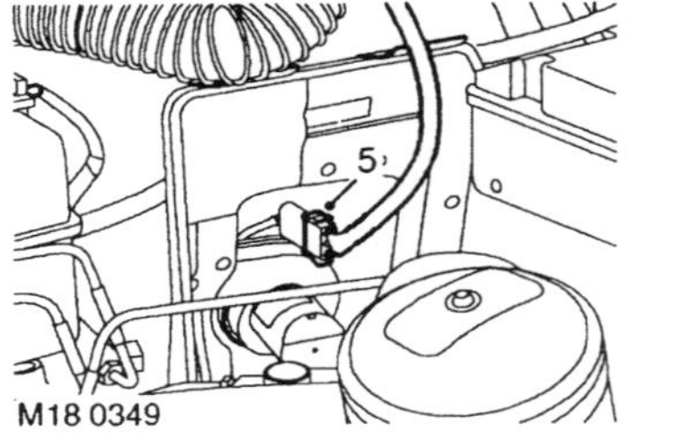

M18 0349

5. Disconnect ECM cooling fan multiplug.

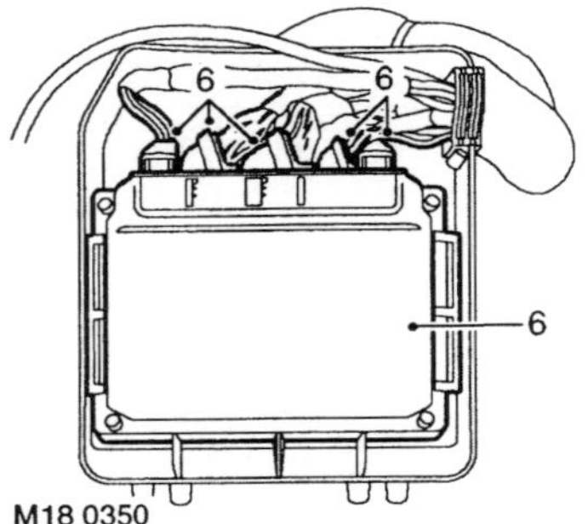

M18 0350

6. Release ECM from housing cover, disconnect multiplugs and remove ECM.

Refit

7. Position ECM and connect multiplugs.
8. Fit ECM to housing cover and connect ECM cooling fan multiplug.
9. Fit ECM housing cover to main housing and secure with fixings.
10. Position cruise control assembly to EAS housing cover and secure with screws.
11. Connect battery earth lead.
12. Fit battery cover and secure with fixings.

ENGINE MANAGEMENT SYSTEM SCHEMATIC - from 99MY

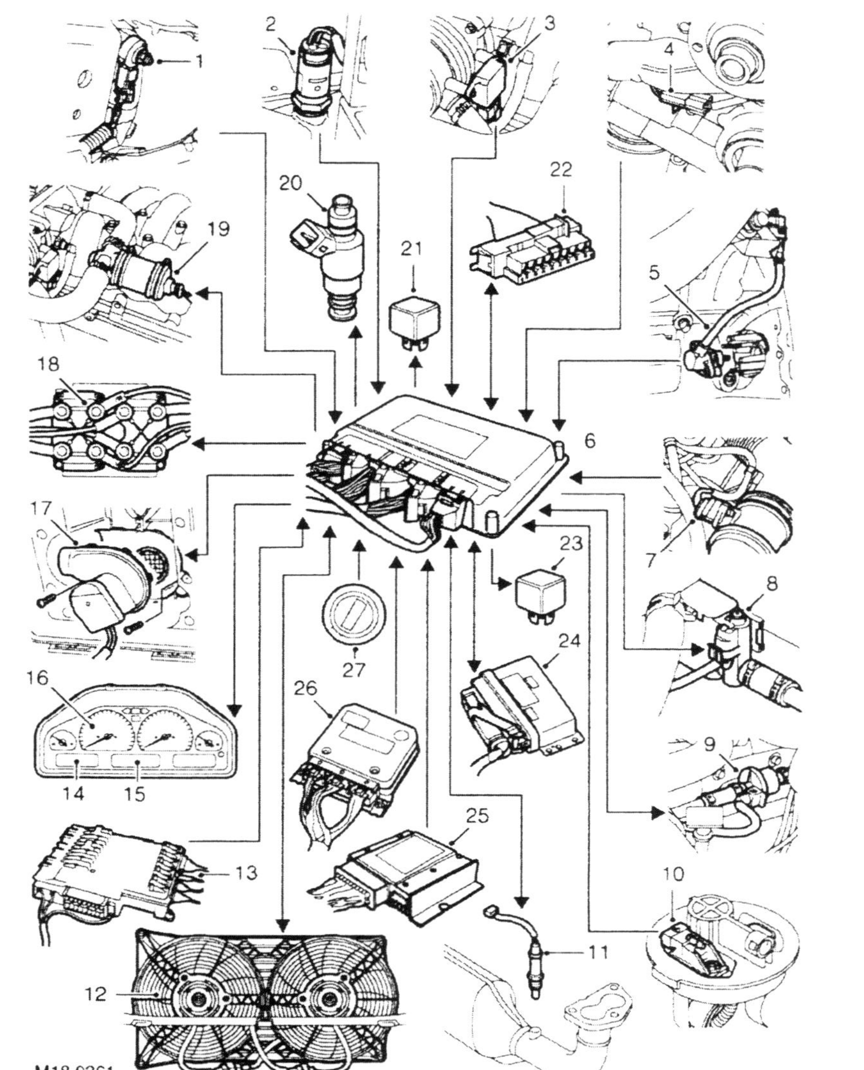

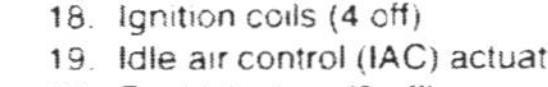

ECM engine interface inputs:

1. Knock sensor (2 off)
2. Engine coolant temperature (ECT) sensor
3. Throttle position (TP) sensor
4. Camshaft position (CMP) sensor
5. Crankshaft speed and position sensor
6. Engine control module (ECM)
7. Mass air flow (MAF) / Inlet air temperature (IAT) sensor

Fuel system:

8. Canister vent solenoid (CVS) valve (output)
9. Purge valve (output)
10. Fuel tank pressure sensor (input)

Emissions:

11. Heated oxygen sensors (0, 2 or 4 dependent on market destination)
   - HO_2S sensor signal inputs
   - HO_2S sensor heater supply outputs

Air Conditioning System:

12. - Air conditioning compressor (output)
   - Air conditioning condenser fan relay (output)
   - Air conditioning request (input)
   - Condenser fan request (input)

BeCM:

13. BeCM
   - Immobilisation signal (input)
   - Fuel tank level signal (input)

Instrument pack:

14. Check Engine / Service Engine Soon (NAS) warning lamp (output)
15. Fuel used signal - display (output)
16. Tachometer (output)

E-box:

17. E-box cooling fan control (output)

ECM engine interface outputs:

18. Ignition coils (4 off)
19. Idle air control (IAC) actuator
20. Fuel injectors (8 off)
21. Fuel pump relay

Diagnostics:

22. Diagnostic connector (bi-directional)

Power supply:

23. Main relay (input)

Electronic Control Unit interfaces:

24. Electronic Automatic Transmission (EAT) ECU (via bi-directional CAN link)
25. Transfer Box ECU (MIL request)
26. ABS ECU (Rough road signal)

Ignition switched power supply:

27. Ignition switch - position II (input)

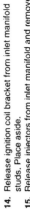

FUEL RAIL AND INJECTORS - up to 99MY

Service repair no - 19.60.04 - Fuel Rail
Service repair no - 19.60.12 - Injectors

Remove

1. Disconnect battery negative lead.
2. Depressurise fuel system. ***See this section.***
3. Release plenum chamber and place aside. ***See this section.***
4. Release purge hose, crankcase breather hose and pressure regulator vacuum hose from ram housing.

19M7000

5. Remove 6 bolts securing ram housing to inlet manifold.
6. Place small packing block on inlet manifold. Lever between packing block and ram pipe housing to break seal.

CAUTION: Do not lever against fuel rail.

7. Remove ram housing from 2 dowels.
8. Place cloth over inlet manifold to prevent ingress of debris.

9. Disconnect 8 injector multiplugs.

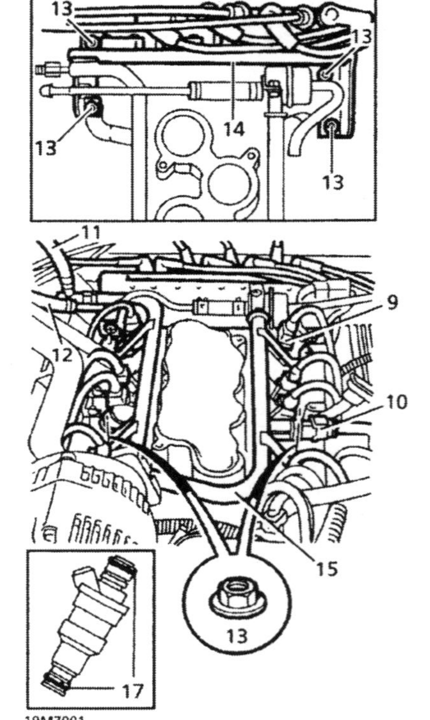

19M7001

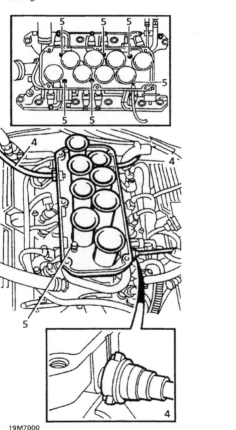

10. Disconnect fuel temperature sensor multiplug.
11. Disconnect fuel feed hose from fuel rail.
12. Disconnect fuel return hose from pressure regulator pipe.

NOTE: Advanced EVAPS vehicles have a threaded connection to the return hose.

13. Remove 6 nuts securing fuel rail and ignition coil bracket to inlet manifold.
14. Release ignition coil bracket from inlet manifold studs. Place aside.
15. Release injectors from inlet manifold and remove fuel rail assembly.
Do not carry out further dismantling if component is removed for access only.
16. Remove 8 clips securing injectors to fuel rail. Remove injectors.

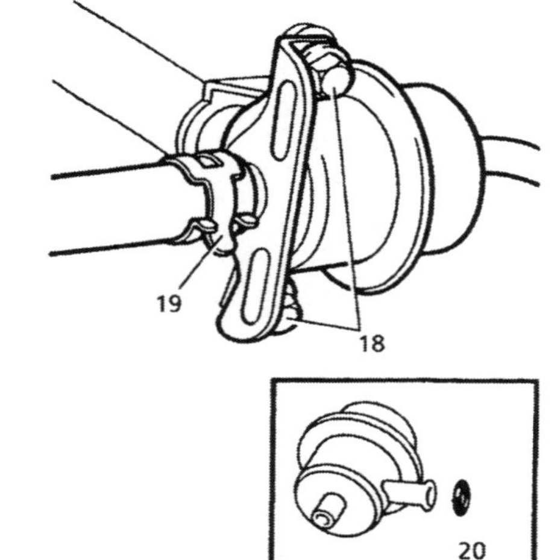

19M7002

17. Remove 2 'O' rings from each injector and discard.
18. Remove 2 screws securing fuel pressure regulator to fuel rail.
19. Release return pipe from clip. Remove pressure regulator assembly.
20. Remove 'O' ring from fuel pressure regulator and discard.

Refit

21. Ensure mating surfaces between inlet manifold and ram pipe housing are clean.
22. Ensure all locations in fuel rail and inlet manifold are clean.
23. Fit new 'O' rings to injectors and fuel pressure regulator.
24. Lubricate 'O' rings with silicone grease.
25. Fit fuel pressure regulator to fuel rail. Secure with bolts. Tighten to ***10 Nm. (7 lbf.ft)***
26. Engage regulator return pipe in clip.
27. Fit injectors to fuel rail. Secure with clips.
28. Position fuel rail to inlet manifold. Engage injectors, one bank at a time.
29. Position ignition coil bracket on inlet manifold studs.
30. Secure ignition coil bracket and fuel rail to inlet manifold with nuts. Tighten to ***8 Nm. (6 lbf.ft)***
31. Connect return hose to pressure regulator pipe. Secure with clip.
32. Connect fuel feed pipe to fuel rail. Tighten union to ***16 Nm. (12 lbf.ft)***
33. Connect multiplugs to fuel injectors and fuel temperature sensor.
34. Remove cloth from inlet manifold.
35. Apply a thin, uniform coating of Loctite 577 sealant to mating face of inlet manifold.
36. Fit ram pipe housing to inlet manifold. Secure with bolts. Tighten to ***24 Nm. (18 lbf.ft)***
37. Connect purge hose, crankcase breather hose and pressure regulator vacuum hose to ram pipe housing.
38. Fit plenum chamber. ***See this section.***
39. Reconnect battery negative lead.
40. Start engine. Check for leaks around fuel rail and injectors.

FUEL RAIL AND INJECTORS - from 99MY

Service repair no - 19.60.04 - Fuel Rail
Service repair no - 19.60.12 - Injectors

Remove

1. Remove upper inlet manifold gasket. ***See MANIFOLD AND EXHAUST SYSTEM, Repair.***
2. Release HT leads from clips on rocker covers and from spark plugs.

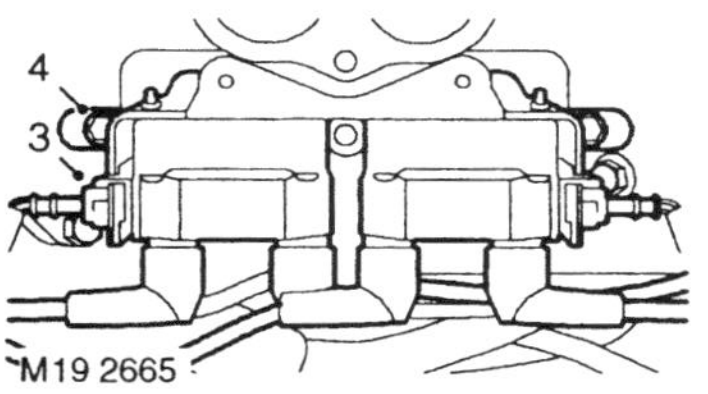

M19 2665

3. Disconnect multiplugs from coils.
4. Remove 2 lower coil fixing bolts and remove coil assembly.
5. Position absorbent cloth beneath fuel pipe to catch spillage.

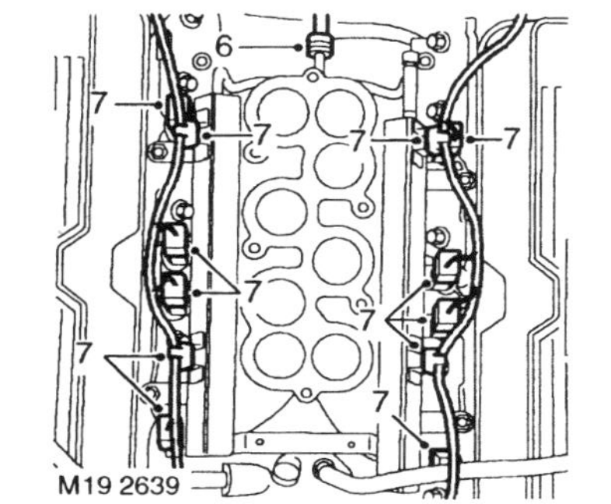

M19 2639

6. Disconnect fuel feed hose from fuel rail

CAUTION: Plug the connections.

7. Release injector harness clips from fuel rail and disconnect injector multiplugs.

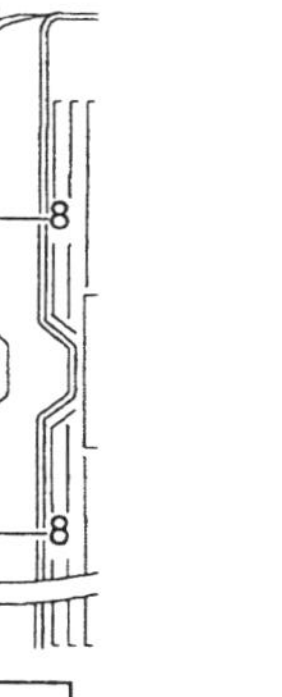

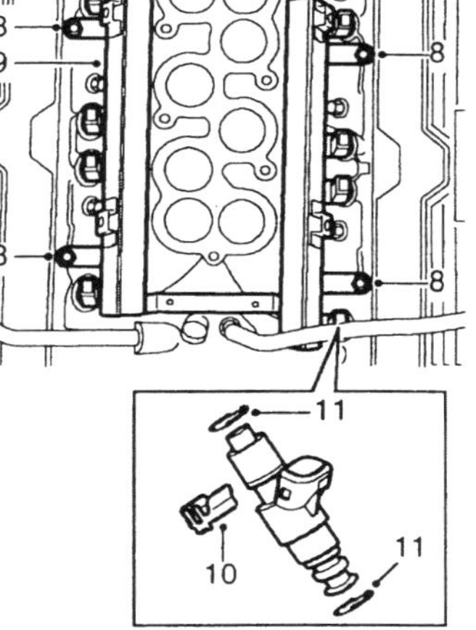

M19 2641

8. Remove 4 bolts securing fuel rail to inlet manifold.
9. Release injectors from inlet manifold and remove fuel rail and injectors.
10. Release spring clips securing injectors to fuel rail and remove fuel injectors.
11. Remove and discard 2 'O' rings from each injector.
12. Fit protective caps to each end of injectors.

Refit

13. Clean injectors and recesses in fuel rail and inlet manifold.
14. Lubricate new 'O' rings with silicone grease and fit to each end of injectors.
15. Fit injectors to fuel rail.
16. Secure injectors to fuel rail with spring clips.
17. Position fuel rail assembly and push-fit each injector into inlet manifold.
18. Fit bolts securing fuel rail to inlet manifold and tighten to ***9 Nm (6 lbf.ft).***
19. Connect fuel feed hose to fuel rail.
20. Connect injector harness multiplugs and secure to fuel rail.
21. Carefully position coil assembly, fit 2 lower fixing bolts but do not tighten at this stage.
22. Connect multiplugs to coils.
23. Fit HT leads to spark plugs and clips on rocker covers.
24. Fit upper inlet manifold gasket. ***See MANIFOLD AND EXHAUST SYSTEM, Repair.***

ENGINE FUEL TEMPERATURE (EFT) SENSOR

Service repair no - 19.22.08

Remove

NOTE: Because fuel leakage will not occur when sensor is removed, it is not necessary to depressurise the fuel system for this operation.

1. Disconnect battery negative lead.
2. Disconnect multiplug from fuel temperature sensor.
3. Remove sensor from fuel rail.

19M7003

Refit

4. Ensure sensor and location in fuel rail are clean.
5. Fit sensor. Tighten to ***17 Nm. (13 lbf.ft)***
6. Connect multiplug.
7. Reconnect battery negative lead.

HEATED OXYGEN SENSOR (HO_2S)- FRONT (up to 99MY) AND REAR

Service repair no - 19.22.16 - Front
Service repair no - 19.22.17 - Rear (NAS Spec. only)

Remove

1. Raise the vehicle.

WARNING: Support on safety stands.

2. Remove clip securing HO_2S lead.

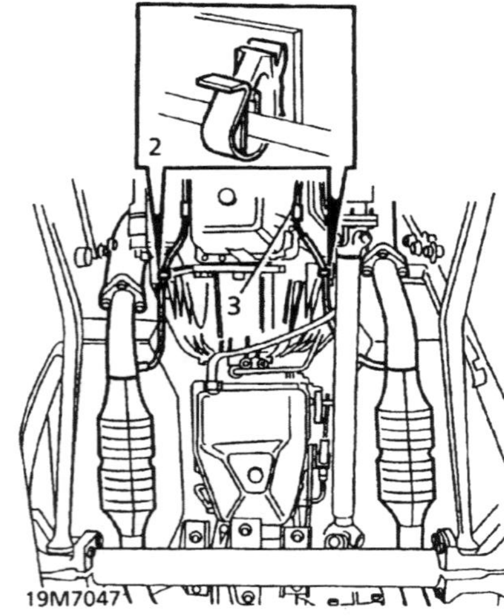
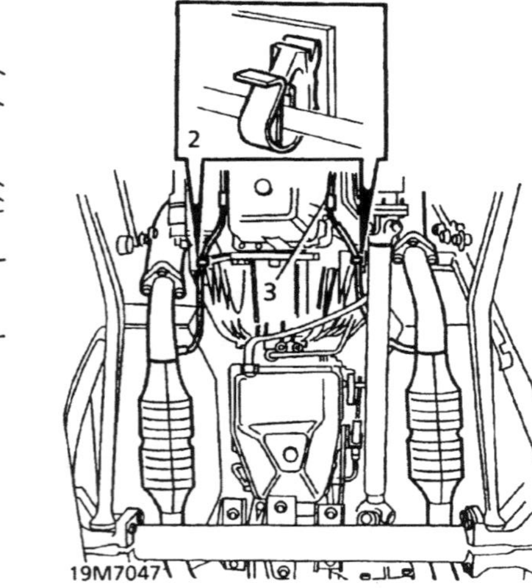

19M7047

3. Release HO_2S multiplug from bracket on sump or transfer gearbox. Disconnect multiplug from engine harness.

19M7048

CAUTION: Although robust within the vehicle environment, HO_2S sensors are easily damaged by dropping, excessive heat and contamination. Care must be exercised when working on the exhaust system not to damage the sensor housing or tip.

4. Remove sensor from exhaust front pipe. Remove sealing washer and discard.

Refit

5. Ensure mating faces are clean.

NOTE: New HO_2S is supplied pre-treated with anti-seize compound.

6. If refitting existing HO_2S, coat threads with anti-seize compound.

CAUTION: Do not allow anti-seize compound to come into contact with HO_2S nose or enter exhaust system.

7. Position HO_2S with new sealing washer on exhaust pipe. Tighten to ***20 Nm. (15 lbf.ft)***
8. Connect multiplug to engine harness. Secure to bracket.
9. Secure lead in clip.
10. Remove stands. Lower vehicle.

HEATED OXYGEN SENSOR (HO2S) - FRONT - from 99MY

Service repair no - 19.22.16

Remove

1. Raise vehicle on ramp.

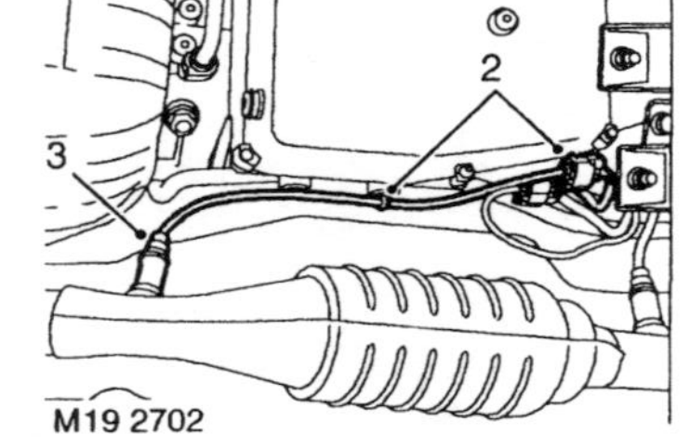

M19 2702

2. Release HO_2S harness from clip if fitted, and disconnect HO_2S multiplug.
3. Remove HO_2S from exhaust front pipe.

Refit

4. If refitting existing HO_2S apply anti-seize compound to threads.
5. Fit new sealing washer to HO_2S.
6. Fit HO2S and tighten to ***45 Nm (33 lbf.ft).***
7. Connect HO_2S multiplug and secure harness to clip.
8. Lower vehicle.

SPARK PLUGS

Service repair no - 18.20.02

Remove

1. Remove air intake hose. ***See this section.***

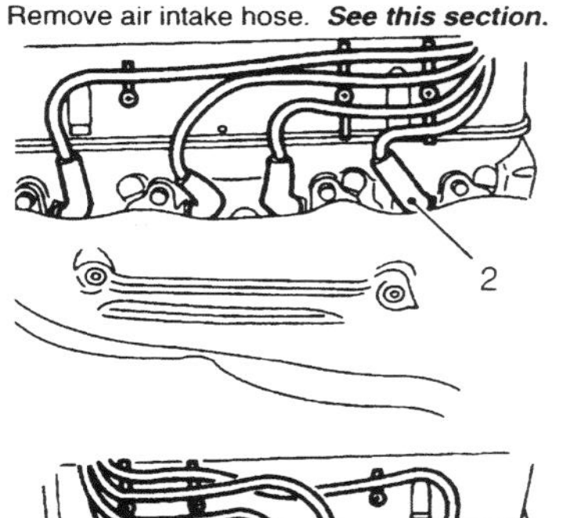

18M7025

2. Disconnect 8 h.t. leads from spark plugs.

CAUTION: To avoid damage to h.t. leads, disconnect them by pulling the rubber boot NOT the lead.

3. Remove 8 spark plugs and washers from cylinder heads.

Refit

CAUTION: Take care not to cross-thread spark plugs when fitting as costly damage to the cylinder head will result. It is essential that correct type of spark plug is fitted. Incorrect grade of spark plugs may lead to piston overheating and engine failure.

4. Ensure spark plug gaps are between 0.89 - 1.01 mm and set gap if necessary.
5. Fit spark plugs to cylinder heads and tighten to ***20 Nm. (15 lbf.ft)***
6. Connect h.t. leads to spark plugs.
7. Fit air intake hose. ***See this section.***

H.T. LEADS

Service repair no - 18.20.11

Remove

1. Remove air intake hose. ***See this section.***

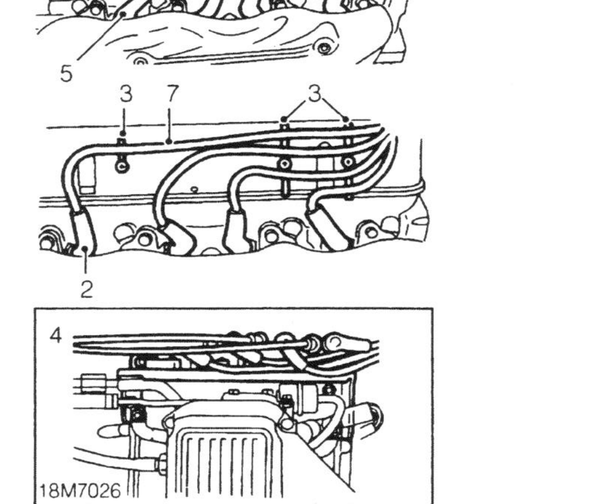

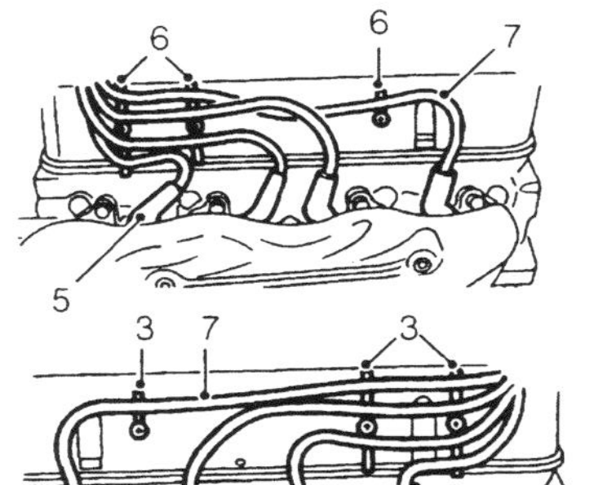

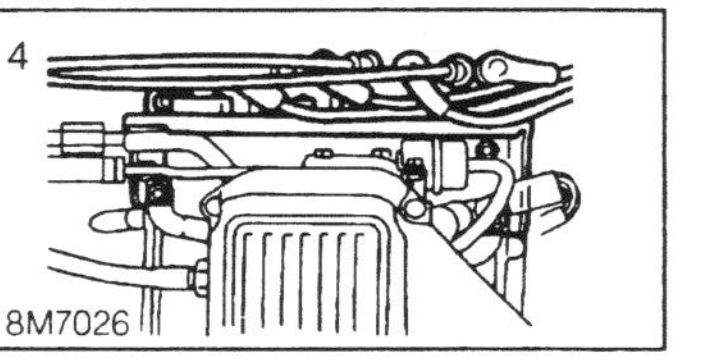

18M7026

2. Disconnect 4 h.t. leads from LH cylinder head spark plugs.

CAUTION: To avoid damage to h.t. leads, disconnect them by pulling on the rubber boot, NOT the lead.

3. Release h.t. leads from 8 camshaft cover clips.
4. Disconnect 8 h.t. leads from ignition coils.
5. Disconnect 4 h.t. leads from RH cylinder head spark plugs.
6. Release h.t. leads from 8 camshaft cover clips.
7. Remove 8 h.t. leads
8. Remove 4 clips securing h.t. leads to each other.

Refit

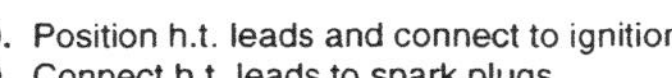

9. Position h.t. leads and connect to ignition coils.
10. Connect h.t. leads to spark plugs.
11. Engage h.t. leads to camshaft cover clips.
12. Fit clips securing h.t. leads to each other.

IGNITION COILS - up to 99MY

Service repair no - 18.20.45 - Set
Service repair no - 18.20.43 - Each
Service repair no - 18.20.44 - Extra - Each

Remove

1. Disconnect battery negative lead.
2. Disconnect H.T. leads from ignition coils. Note positions of leads.
3. Place H.T. leads aside.

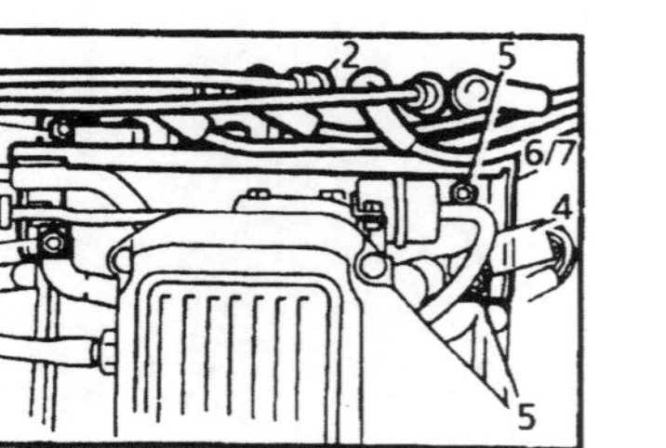

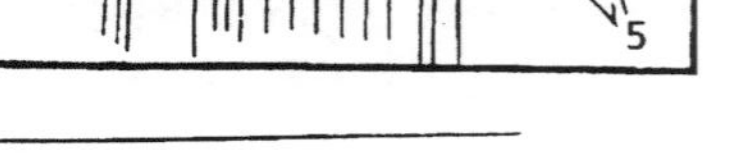

18M7000

4. Disconnect ignition coil multiplug.
5. Remove 6 nuts securing fuel rail and ignition coil bracket to inlet manifold.
6. Lift fuel rail slightly for access. Release ignition coil bracket from inlet manifold studs.

⚠ **CAUTION: Do not completely withdraw injectors from fitted locations.**

7. Remove ignition coils assembly.
8. Remove terminal cover.

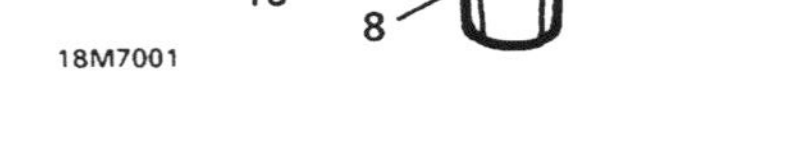

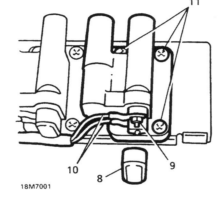

18M7001

9. Remove 2 nuts securing wires to coil terminals.
10. Remove wires from terminals. Note wire positions.
11. Remove 3 screws securing ignition coil to bracket. Remove coil.

Refit

12. Fit ignition coil to bracket. Secure with screws.
13. Connect wires to terminals. Secure with nuts.
14. Fit terminal cover.
15. Position ignition coil bracket on inlet manifold studs.
16. Secure fuel rail and ignition coil bracket with nuts. Tighten to ***8 Nm. (6 lbf.ft)***
17. Connect multiplug.
18. Connect H.T. leads to respective coil towers.
19. Reconnect battery negative lead.

IGNITION COILS - from 99MY

Service repair no - 18.20.45

Remove

1. Remove upper inlet manifold gasket. ***See MANIFOLD AND EXHAUST SYSTEM, Repair.***

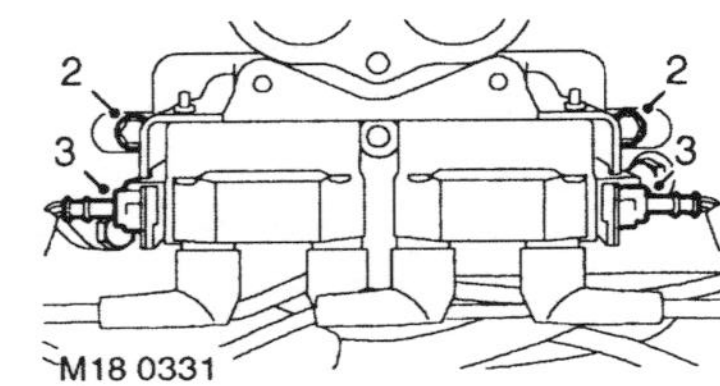

M18 0331

2. Remove 2 lower coil fixing bolts.
3. Disconnect multiplugs from coils.

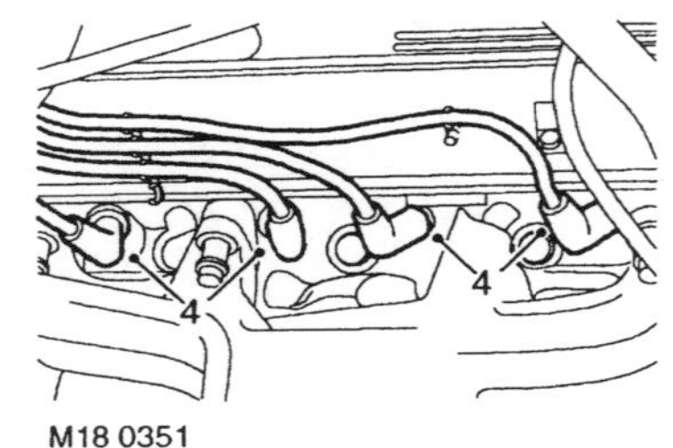

M18 0351

4. Release HT leads from rocker covers and disconnect HT leads from plugs.
5. Carefully manoeuvre coil assembly from between engine and bulkhead.

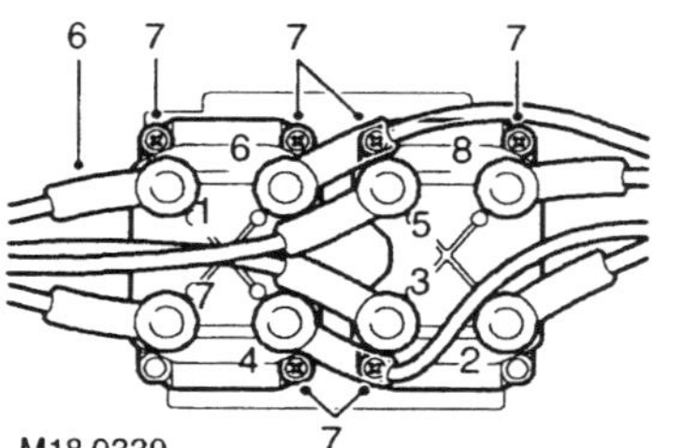

M18 0339

6. Noting their fitted position disconnect HT leads from coils.
7. Remove 6 screws securing coils to support bracket and remove coils.

Refit

8. Position coils to support bracket, fit and tighten screws.
9. Connect HT leads to coils ensuring they are in the correct position.
10. Carefully position coil assembly between engine and bulkhead.
11. Connect HT leads to plugs and secure HT leads to rocker covers.
12. Connect multiplugs to coils.
13. Fit 2 lower coil fixing bolts but do not tighten at this stage.
14. Fit upper inlet manifold gasket. ***See MANIFOLD AND EXHAUST SYSTEM, Repair.***

INERTIA FUEL SHUT OFF (IFS) SWITCH

Service repair no - 19.22.09

Remove

1. Release 300mm of door seal from base of RH 'A' post.

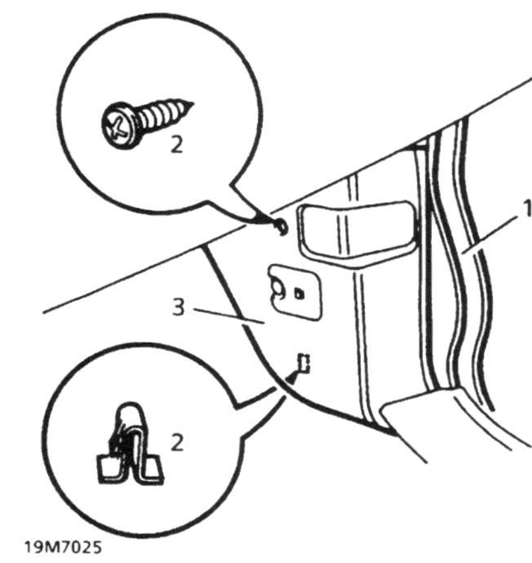

19M7025

2. Remove 'A' post lower finisher securing screw. Remove finisher from sprag clip.
3. Remove RH lower 'A' post finisher.

4. Disconnect multiplug. Remove 2 screws securing IFS switch to 'A' post.
5. Remove IFS switch.

19M7026

Refit

6. Reverse removal procedure.

INTAKE AIR TEMPERATURE (IAT) SENSOR

Service repair no - 18.30.09

Remove

1. Disconnect multiplug from IAT sensor.
2. Remove IAT sensor from air cleaner.

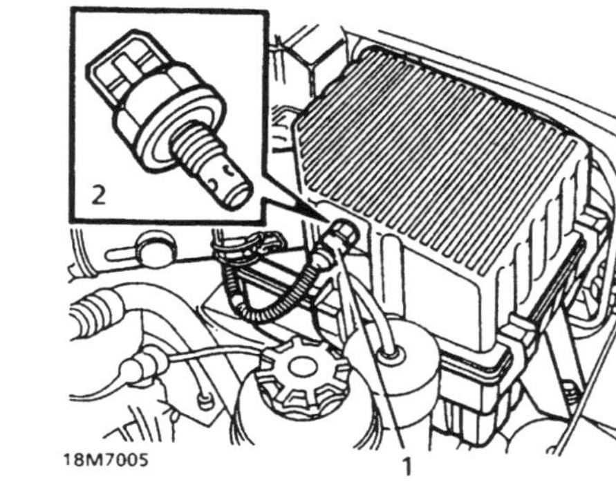

18M7005

Refit

3. Fit IAT sensor. Tighten to ***8 Nm. (6 lbf.ft)***
4. Connect multiplug.

THROTTLE POSITION (TP) SENSOR - up to 99MY

Service repair no - 19.22.49

Remove

1. Disconnect multiplug from TP sensor.
2. Remove 2 bolts securing TP sensor. Collect clamp plate.
3. Remove TP sensor.

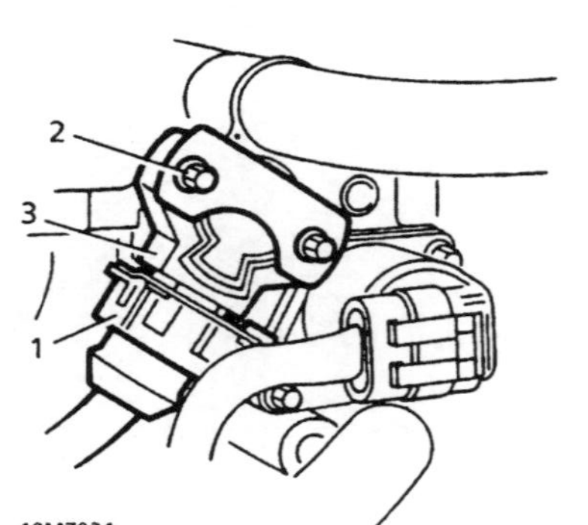

19M7024

Refit

4. Fit TP sensor. Ensure drive engages correctly with throttle spindle.
5. Position clamp plate. Secure TP sensor with bolts. Tighten to ***2 Nm. (1.5 lbf.ft)***
6. Connect multiplug.

THROTTLE POSITION (TP) SENSOR - from 99MY

Service repair no - 19.22.49

Remove

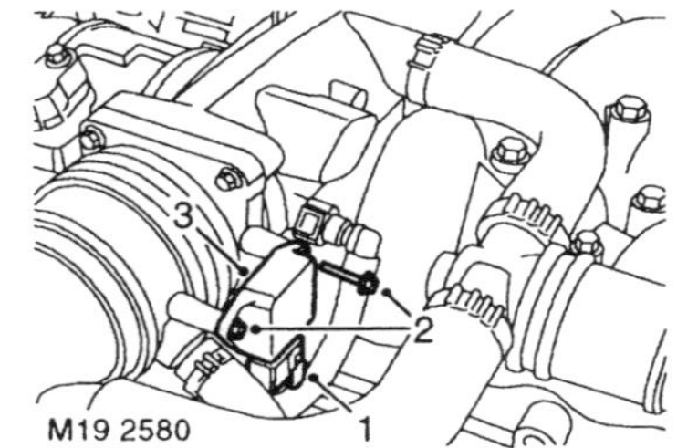

M19 2580

1. Disconnect TP sensor multiplug.
2. Remove 2 bolts securing TP sensor to throttle body.
3. Remove TP sensor and discard 'O' ring.

Refit

4. Clean TP sensor and throttle body mating faces.
5. Using a new 'O' ring, position TP sensor, fit bolts and tighten to ***2.2 Nm (1.5 lbf.ft).***
6. Connect TP sensor multiplug.
7. If fitting new TP sensor, connect Testbook to check for correct operation.

KNOCK SENSOR (KS) - up to 99MY

Service repair no - 18.30.28 - Sensor - LH
Service repair no - 18.30.30 - Sensor - RH

CAUTION: Due to the sensitivity of the sensors, do not apply tape or sealant to sensor threads.

Remove

1. Raise the vehicle.

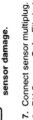

WARNING: Support on safety stands.

2. **RH Sensor Only:** Remove starter motor. ***See ELECTRICAL, Repair.***
3. Disconnect sensor multiplug.
4. Remove sensor from cylinder block.

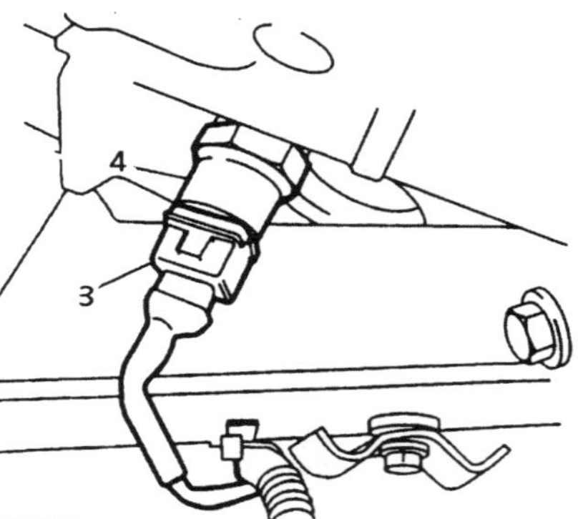

18M7006

Refit

5. Ensure sensor location in cylinder block is clean.
6. Fit sensor. Tighten to ***16 Nm. (12 lbf.ft)***

CAUTION: Failure to tighten sensor to correct torque will result in malfunction or sensor damage.

7. Connect sensor multiplug.
8. **RH Sensor Only:** Fit starter motor. ***See ELECTRICAL, Repair.***
9. Remove safety stands. Lower vehicle.

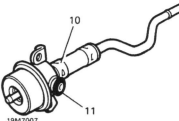

KNOCK (KS) SENSOR - from 99MY

Service repair no - 18.30.28 - Sensor - LH
Service repair no - 18.30.30 - Sensor - RH

Remove

1. Release fixings and remove battery cover.
2. Disconnect battery earth lead.
3. Raise front of vehicle.

WARNING: Support on safety stands.

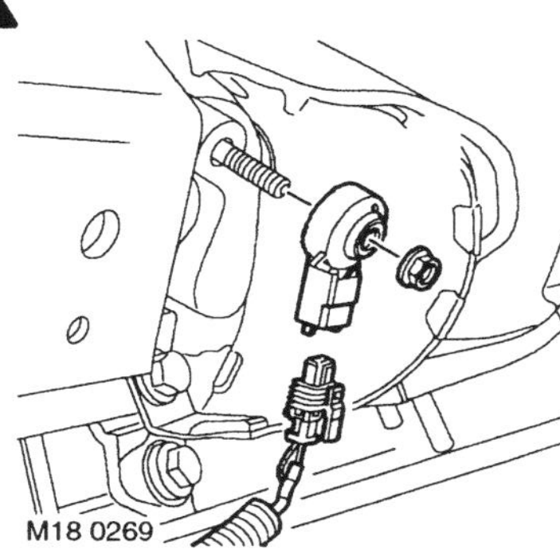

4. Disconnect multiplug from KS.
5. Remove nut securing KS to cylinder block and remove KS.

Refit

6. Clean mating faces of KS and block.
7. Fit KS to block and tighten nut to ***22 Nm (17 lbf.ft).***
8. Connect multiplug to KS.
9. Remove stand(s) and lower vehicle.
10. Connect battery earth lead.
11. Fit and secure battery cover.

FUEL PRESSURE REGULATOR

Service repair no - 19.45.06

Remove

1. Disconnect battery negative lead.
2. Depressurise fuel system. ***See this section.***
3. Release fuel return pipe clip. Remove fuel return pipe from regulator connecting pipe.

NOTE: Advanced EVAPS vehicles have a threaded connection to the return hose.

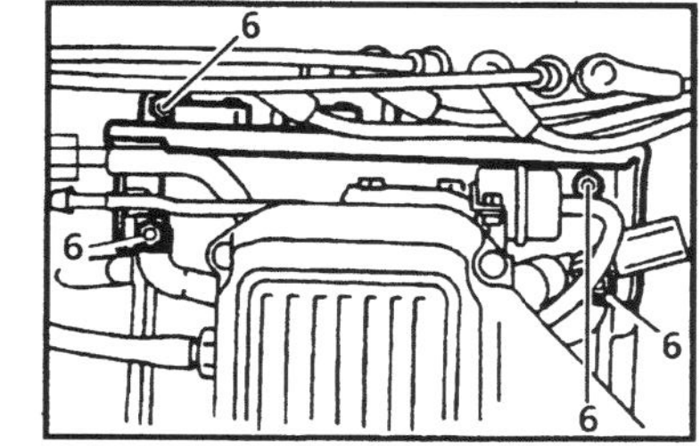

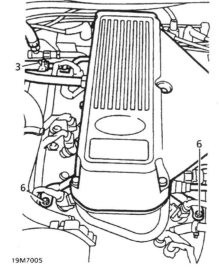

4. Release regulator connecting pipe from clip.
5. Disconnect vacuum hose from fuel pressure regulator.

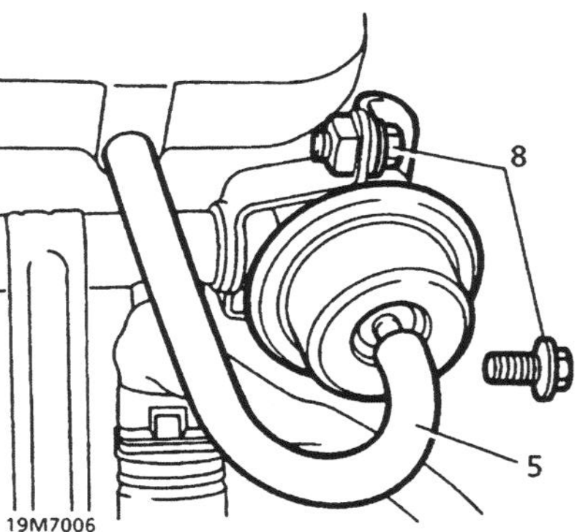

6. Remove 6 nuts securing fuel rail and ignition coil bracket to inlet manifold.
7. Lift fuel rail slightly for access. Release ignition coil bracket from inlet manifold studs. Place aside.

CAUTION: Do not completely withdraw injectors from fitted locations.

8. Remove bolts securing fuel pressure regulator to fuel rail.
9. Remove fuel pressure regulator assembly.
10. Release connecting pipe and hose assembly from regulator.

10
11
19M7007

11. Remove 'O' ring and spacer ring from fuel pressure regulator. Discard 'O' ring.

Refit

12. Ensure locations on fuel pressure regulator and fuel rail are clean.
13. Fit new spacer ring and 'O' ring to fuel pressure regulator. Lubricate 'O' ring with silicone grease.
14. Fit connecting pipe assembly to fuel pressure regulator. Secure clip.
15. Fit pressure regulator assembly to fuel rail. Secure with bolts. Tighten to ***10 Nm. (7 lbf.ft)***
16. Secure regulator connecting pipe in clip.
17. Align ignition coil bracket to inlet manifold studs.
18. Secure ignition coil bracket and fuel rail to inlet manifold with nuts. Tighten to ***8 Nm. (6 lbf.ft)***
19. Connect return pipe to regulator connecting pipe. Secure with clip.

NOTE: Advanced EVAPS vehicles have a threaded connection to the return hose.

20. Connect vacuum hose to fuel pressure regulator.
21. Reconnect battery negative lead.
22. Start engine. Check for leaks around fuel pressure regulator, fuel feed and fuel return unions.

IDLE AIR CONTROL (IAC) VALVE - up to 99MY

Service repair no - 19.22.54

Remove

1. Disconnect battery negative lead.
2. Disconnect IAC multiplug.
3. Remove 2 bolts, remove IAC. Discard gasket.

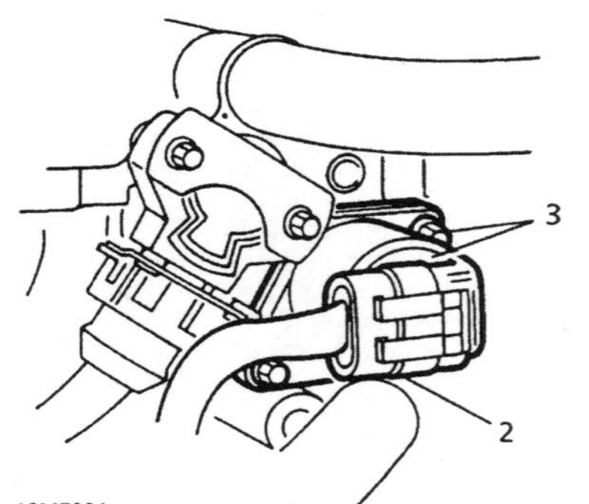

18M7004

Refit

4. Ensure all mating faces are clean.
5. Using a new gasket, fit IAC. Secure with bolts. Tightened to ***2.3 Nm. (2 lbf.ft)***
6. Connect multiplug.
7. Reconnect battery negative lead.

IDLE AIR CONTROL (IAC) VALVE - from 99MY

Service repair no - 19.22.54

Remove

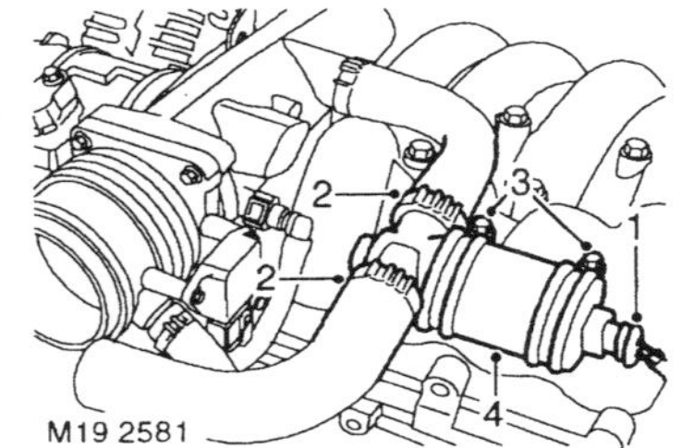

M19 2581

1. Disconnect IAC valve multiplug.
2. Release and remove 2 clips securing air hoses and release hoses.
3. Remove 2 screws securing IAC valve to inlet manifold.
4. Collect IAC valve clamps and remove IAC valve.

Refit

5. Position IAC valve, locate clamps, fit screws and tighten to ***8.5 Nm (6 lbf.ft).***
6. Position air hoses and secure clips.
7. Connect IAC valve multiplug.
8. Connect Testbook to clear any fault codes.

PLENUM CHAMBER - up to 97MY

Service repair no - 19.22.46

Remove

1. Disconnect battery negative lead.
2. Slacken clip securing intake hose to plenum chamber. Release hose.
3. Remove throttle and cruise control cables from throttle linkage.
4. Remove throttle and cruise control cable from abutment bracket.
5. Release harness clip from throttle linkage bracket.
6. Disconnect breather hose from plenum chamber.
7. Disconnect multiplugs from idle air control (IAC) and throttle position sensor (TP Sensor).
8. Remove 6 bolts securing plenum chamber. Remove plenum chamber from ram pipe housing.
9. Place cloth over ram pipes to prevent ingress of foreign matter.

Do not carry out further dismantling if component is removed for access only.

10. Clamp coolant hoses with an approved hose clamp.
11. Disconnect coolant hoses from water jacket. Remove plenum chamber.
12. Remove 4 bolts securing water jacket to plenum chamber. Remove water jacket. Remove gasket and discard.

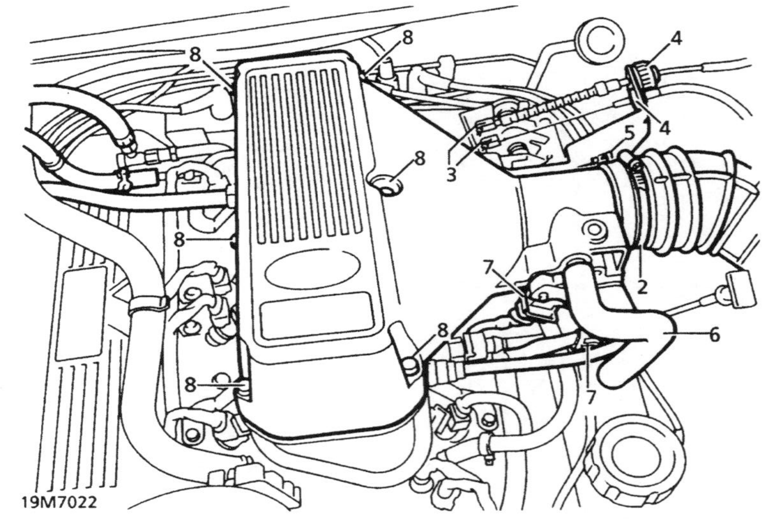

19M7022

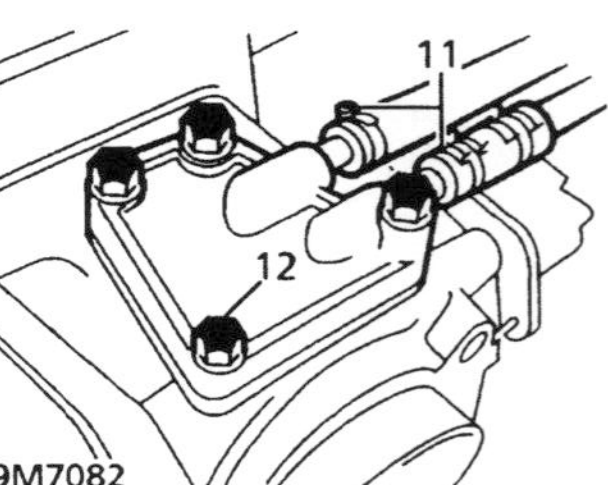

19M7082

13. Remove 3 bolts securing throttle linkage bracket to plenum chamber. Remove bracket. Collect return spring.

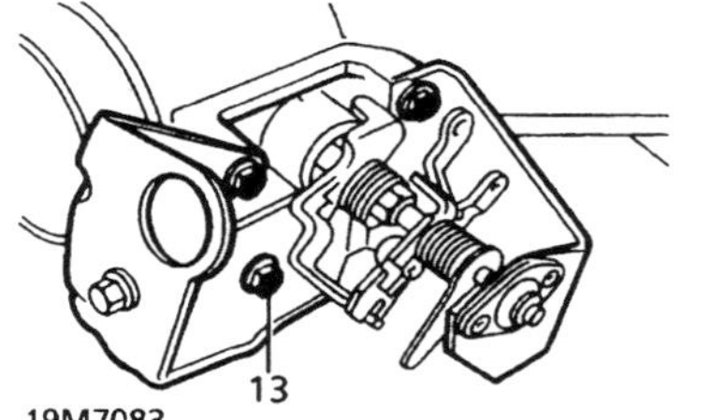

19M7083

14. Remove 2 bolts securing TP sensor. Collect clamp plate. Remove TP sensor.

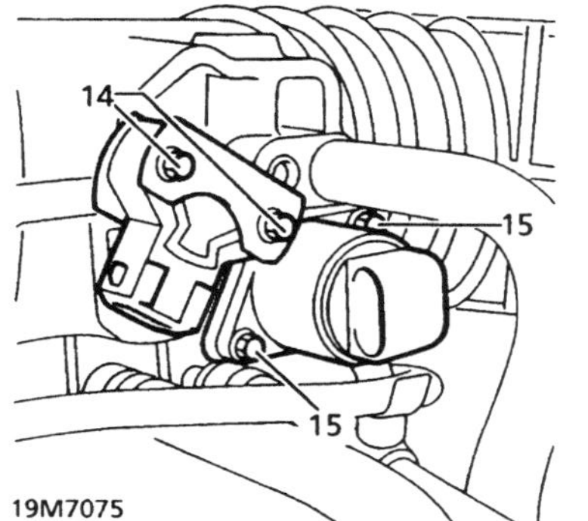

19M7075

15. Remove 2 bolts securing IAC. Remove motor. Remove gasket and discard.

Refit

16. Ensure all mating surfaces are clean.
17. Fit TP sensor. Ensure drive engages correctly with throttle spindle.
18. Position clamp plate. Secure TP sensor with bolts. Tighten to ***2 Nm. (2 lbf.ft)***
19. Using a new gasket, fit IAC. Secure with bolts. Tighten to ***2.3 Nm. (1.8 lbf.ft)***
20. Ensure mating faces of water jacket and plenum chamber are clean.
21. Using a new gasket, fit water jacket. Secure with bolts. Tighten to ***13 Nm. (10 lbf.ft)***
22. Position throttle linkage bracket, fit and engage return spring.
23. Secure linkage bracket to plenum chamber with bolts. Tighten to ***8 Nm. (6 lbf.ft)***
24. Ensure mating faces of plenum chamber and ram pipe housing are clean.
25. Position plenum chamber. Connect coolant hoses to water jacket. Secure with clips.
26. Remove clamp from coolant pipes.
27. Apply a thin, uniform coating of Loctite 577 sealant to sealing face of plenum chamber.
28. Fit plenum chamber.
29. Fit plenum chamber bolts. Tighten to ***24 Nm. (18 lbf.ft)***
30. Connect multiplugs to TP sensor and IAC.
31. Connect breather hose to plenum chamber.
32. Secure harness clip to throttle linkage bracket.
33. Engage throttle cable and cruise control cable to abutment. Secure cruise control cable with 'C' clip.
34. Align cables to throttle linkage. Fit clevis pins. Secure clevis pins with split pins.
35. Adjust throttle cable. ***See Adjustment.***
36. Connect intake hose. Secure with clip.
37. Reconnect battery negative lead.
38. Top up cooling system.
39. Check base idle speed. Adjust if necessary.

If 4.6 ***See ENGINE TUNING DATA, Information.***
If 4.0 ***See ENGINE TUNING DATA, Information.***

PLENUM CHAMBER - 97MY to 99MY

Service repair no - 19.22.46

Remove

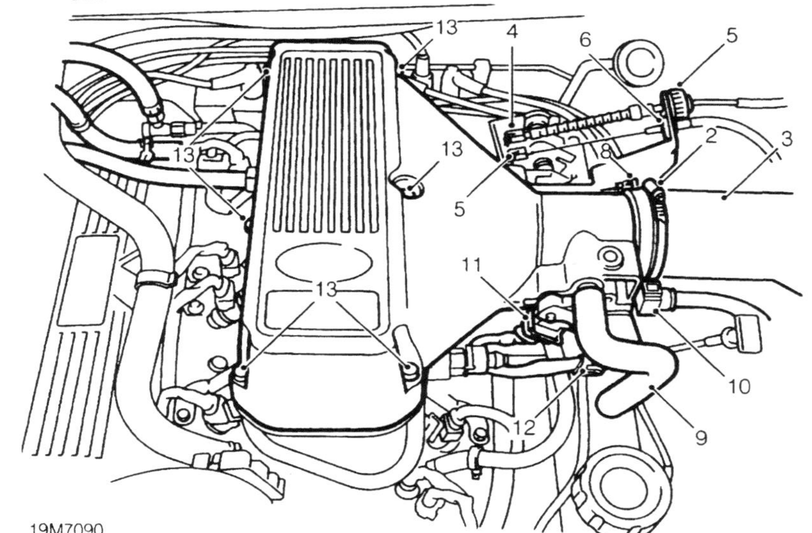

19M7090

1. Remove battery cover and disconnect battery.
2. Loosen clip securing air intake hose to plenum chamber.
3. Disconnect air intake hose from plenum chamber.
4. Remove split pin and clevis pin securing throttle cable to throttle linkage.
5. Remove split pin and clevis pin securing cruise control cable to throttle linkage and release cable adjuster from abutment bracket.
6. Remove 'C' clip securing cruise control cable abutment to bracket and position cable aside.
7. Release clip securing throttle cable abutment to bracket and position cable aside.
8. Release clip securing harness to cable abutment bracket and position aside.
9. Disconnect breather hose from plenum chamber.
10. Release clip and disconnect purge hose from plenum chamber.
11. Disconnect multiplug from throttle potentiometer.
12. Disconnect multiplug from stepper motor.
13. Remove 6 bolts securing plenum chamber to ram housing.
14. Release plenum chamber from ram housing.
15. Fit hose clamp to 2 plenum chamber coolant hoses.
16. Position cloth to catch spillage.

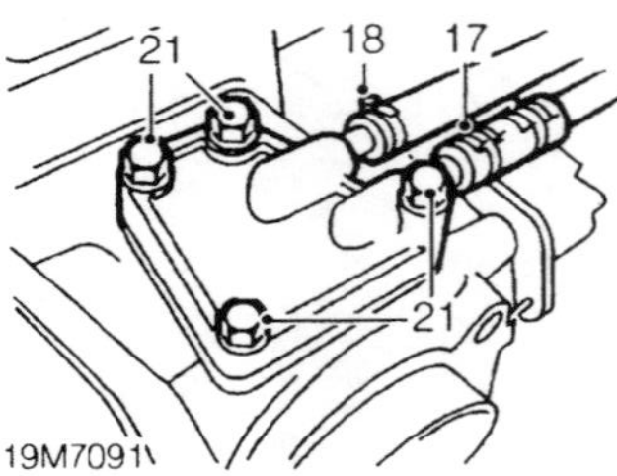

17. Release clip securing coolant hose to plenum water jacket and disconnect hose.
18. Loosen clip securing coolant hose to plenum water jacket and disconnect hose.
19. Remove plenum chamber assembly.
20. Place clean cloth over intake pipes to prevent dirt ingress.

Do not carry out further dismantling if component is removed for access only.

21. Remove 4 bolts securing water jacket to plenum chamber.
22. Remove water jacket and sealing gasket.
23. Position throttle linkage to gain access to bolt.

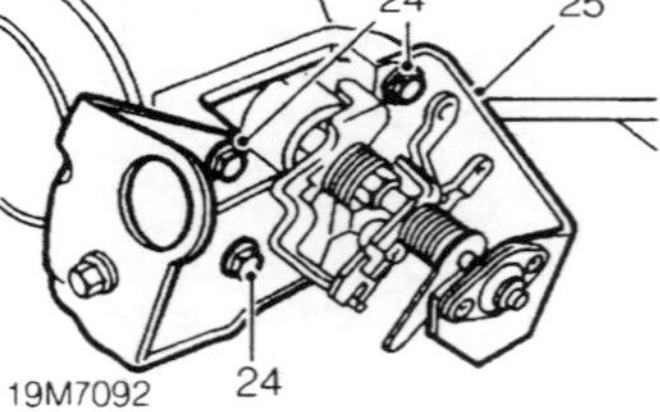

24. Remove 3 bolts securing throttle linkage to plenum chamber.
25. Remove throttle linkage and bracket.
26. Collect spring.

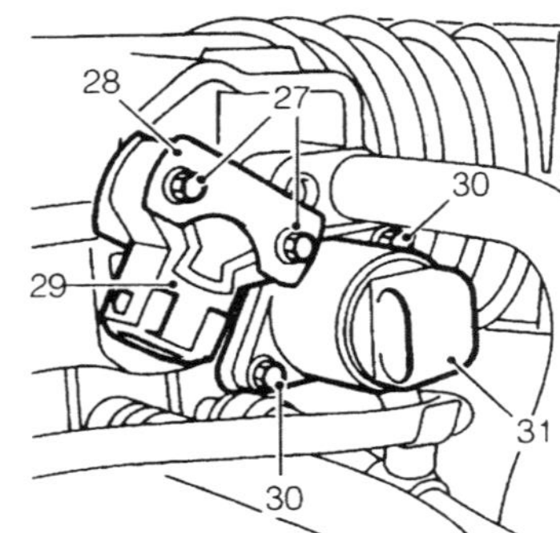

27. Remove 2 bolts securing throttle potentiometer to plenum chamber.
28. Collect clamp plate.
29. Remove throttle potentiometer.
30. Remove 2 bolts securing stepper motor to plenum chamber.
31. Remove stepper motor and collect gasket.
32. Position throttle linkage bracket and spring to plenum chamber.
33. Engage spring to linkage.
34. Fit bolts securing throttle linkage to plenum and tighten to ***8 Nm. (6 lbf.ft)***
35. Clean mating faces of throttle potentiometer and stepper motor.
36. Fit throttle potentiometer, ensuring spindle is correctly engaged.
37. Fit retaining plate and bolts and tighten to ***2 Nm. (1.5 lbf.ft)***
38. Fit NEW stepper motor gasket to plenum chamber.
39. Fit stepper motor.
40. Fit bolts securing stepper motor to plenum chamber and tighten to ***2 Nm. (1.5 lbf.ft)***
41. Clean mating faces of water jacket and plenum chamber.
42. Fit NEW water jacket gasket to plenum chamber.
43. Fit water jacket to plenum chamber.
44. Fit bolts securing water jacket to plenum chamber and tighten to ***13 Nm. (10 lbf.ft)***

Refit

45. Clean mating faces of plenum chamber and ram housing.
46. Connect coolant hose to water jacket and secure with clip.
47. Connect second coolant hose to water jacket and secure with clip.
48. Remove hose clamps.
49. Apply a thin, uniform coating of Loctite 577 sealant to mating face of plenum chamber.
50. Fit plenum chamber to ram housing.
51. Fit bolts securing plenum chamber to ram housing and tighten to ***24 Nm. (18 lbf.ft)***
52. Connect multiplugs to stepper motor and throttle potentiometer.
53. Connect purge hose to plenum chamber. Ensure connector is securely mated.
54. Connect breather hose to plenum chamber.
55. Position harness to throttle linkage bracket and secure clip.
56. Engage throttle cable abutment clip to bracket.
57. Align throttle cable to throttle linkage, fit clevis pin and split pin.
58. Position cruise control cable abutment to bracket and secure with 'C' clip.
59. Align cruise control cable to throttle linkage, fit clevis pin and split pin.
60. Adjust throttle cable. ***See Adjustment.***
61. Connect air intake hose to plenum chamber and secure with clip.
62. Connect battery and fit cover.
63. Top up cooling system.
64. Check base idle speed. Adjust if necessary.

If 4.6 ***See ENGINE TUNING DATA, Information.***
If 4.0 ***See ENGINE TUNING DATA, Information.***

PLENUM CHAMBER - from 99MY

Service repair no - 19.22.46

Remove

1. Remove upper inlet manifold gasket. ***See MANIFOLD AND EXHAUST SYSTEM, Repair.***

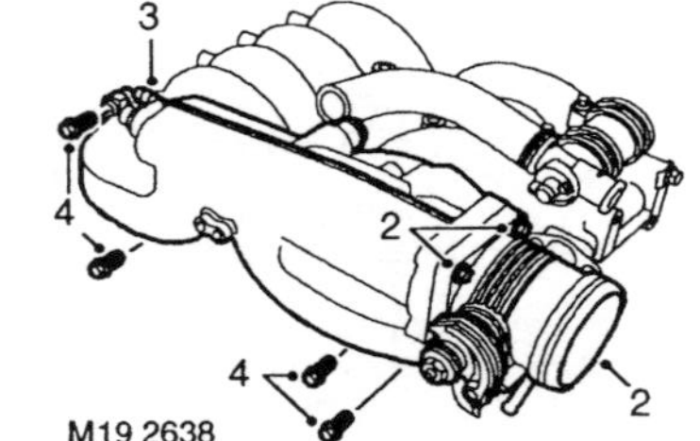

2. Remove 4 bolts securing throttle body to plenum chamber, remove throttle body and collect gasket.
3. Remove breather hose adaptor.
4. Remove 4 bolts securing plenum chamber to upper manifold and remove plenum chamber.
5. Collect plenum chamber gaskets.

Refit

6. Clean plenum chamber and upper manifold mating faces.
7. Using new gaskets, position plenum chamber, fit bolts and tighten to ***22 Nm (16 lbf.ft).***
8. Fit and tighten breather adaptor to ***6 Nm (4.5 lbf.ft).***
9. Clean plenum chamber and throttle body mating faces.
10. Using a new gasket, position throttle body, fit bolts and tighten to ***9 Nm (6 lbf.ft).***
11. Fit upper inlet manifold gasket. ***See MANIFOLD AND EXHAUST SYSTEM, Repair.***

FUEL FILTER

Service repair no - 19.25.02

Remove

1. Disconnect battery negative lead.
2. Depressurise fuel system. ***See this section.***
3. Raise the vehicle.

WARNING: Support on safety stands.

4. Position container beneath fuel filter to catch spillage.
5. Disconnect fuel hoses from filter.

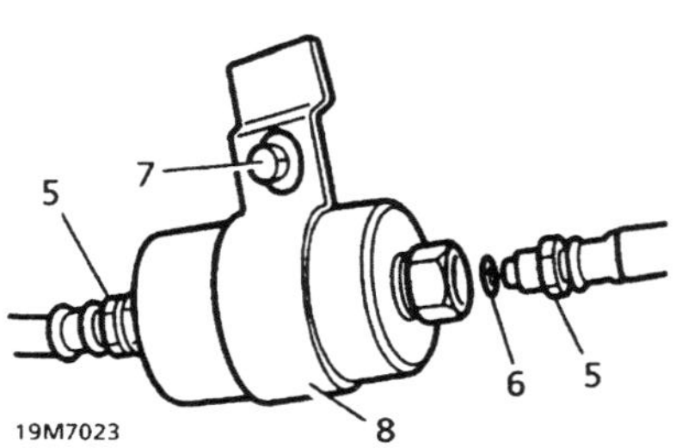

19M7023

6. Remove 'O' rings and discard.
7. Remove bolt securing filter and strap assembly. Remove assembly.

Refit

8. Transfer strap to new fuel filter.
9. Position filter and strap assembly to floor pan. Ensure that flow arrow points toward front of vehicle.
10. Secure filter strap with bolt.
11. Using new 'O' rings, connect fuel hoses to filter. Tighten to ***20 Nm. (15 lbf.ft)***
12. Remove container beneath filter.
13. Remove safety stands. Lower vehicle.
14. Reconnect battery negative lead.

THROTTLE CABLE - up to 99MY

Service repair no - 19.20.06

Remove

1. Remove split pin and clevis pin securing cable to throttle linkage.

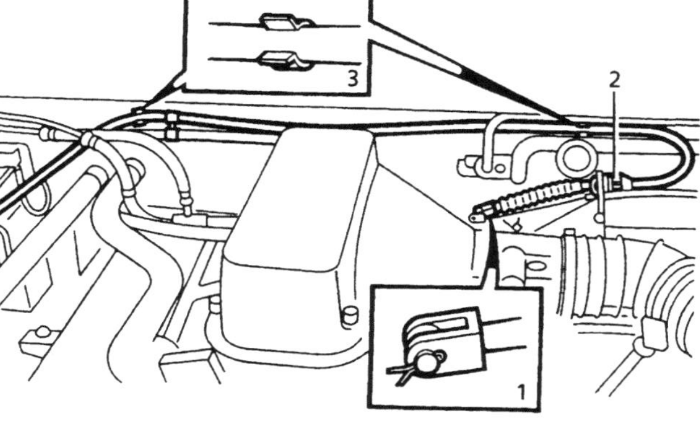

19M7009

2. Release cable adjuster from abutment bracket.
3. Release cable from 3 clips along bulkhead and single clip on brake booster bracket.
4. Remove driver's side fascia closing panel. ***See CHASSIS AND BODY, Repair.***
5. Remove 3 scrivet fasteners securing lower closing panel.
6. Release panel for access to blower motor ducting.

19M7010

7. Release ducting from blower motor housing and heater. Remove blower motor ducting.
8. Release cable from throttle pedal.
9. Release cable outer from bulkhead location. Remove throttle cable assembly.

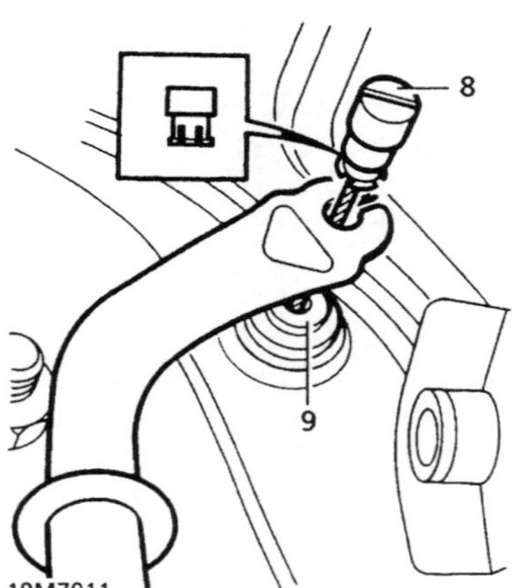

Refit

10. Lubricate bulkhead end of outer cable with liquid soap to aid fitment.
11. Fully engage cable outer into bulkhead location. Connect cable to throttle pedal.
12. Position blower ducting. Engage onto heater and blower motor housing locations.
13. Position lower closing panel. Secure with scrivet fasteners.
14. Fit driver's side fascia closing panel. ***See CHASSIS AND BODY, Repair.***
15. Route cable along bulkhead. Secure to clips
16. Engage cable adjuster to abutment bracket.
17. Align cable trunnion to throttle linkage. Secure with clevis pin and split pin.
18. Check and adjust throttle cable free-play. ***See Adjustment.***

THROTTLE CABLE - from 99MY

Service repair no - 19.20.06

1. Remove closing panel from fascia. ***See CHASSIS AND BODY, Repair.***

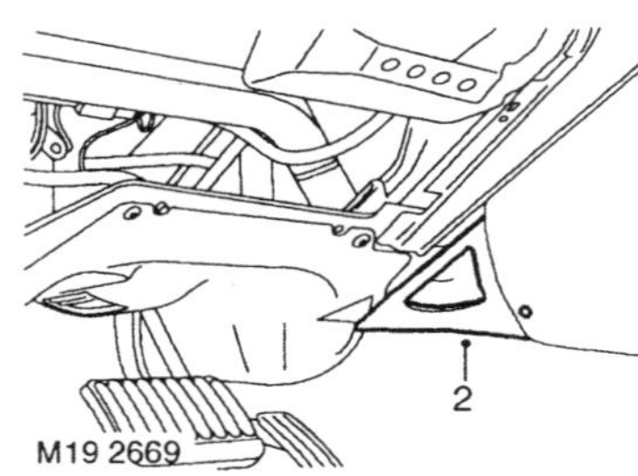

2. Remove screw and remove heater outlet duct.

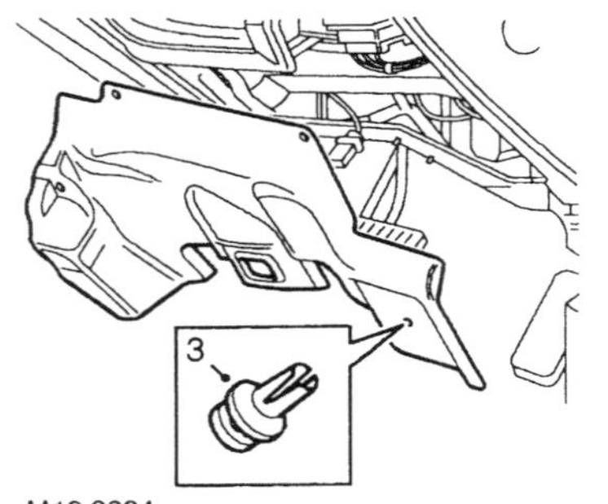

3. Remove 4 scrivets and remove access panel from fascia.
4. Release and remove heater air duct for access to throttle pedal lever.

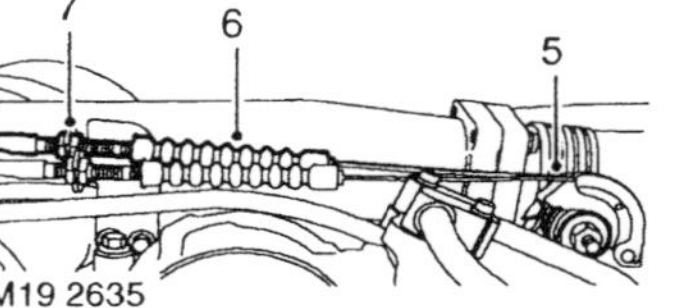
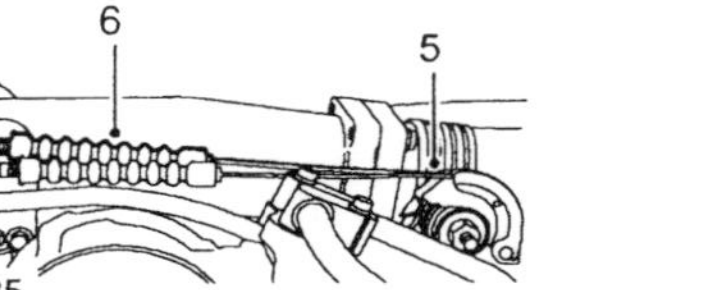
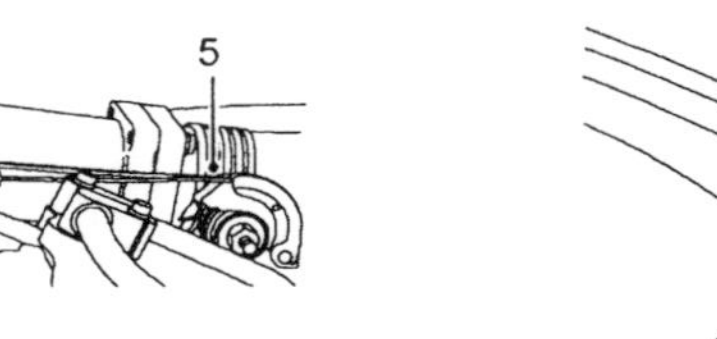
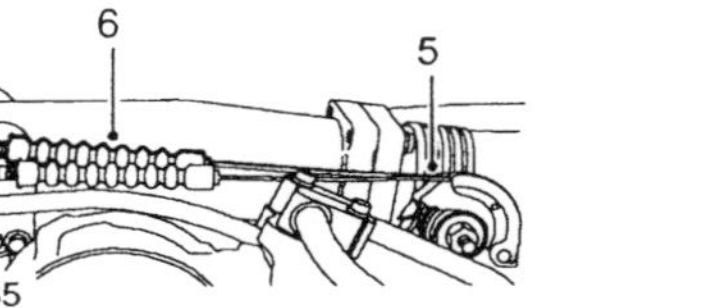
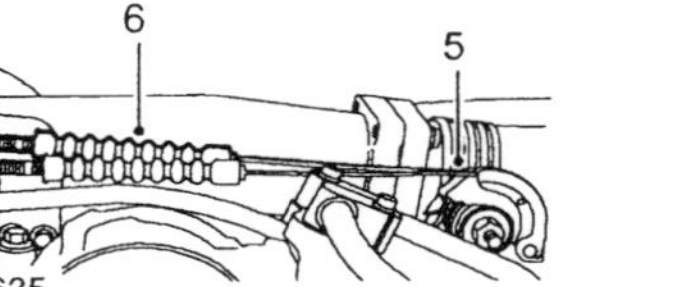

5. Disconnect inner cable from throttle cam.
6. Release cable gaiter.
7. Loosen locknuts and disconnect throttle cable from abutment bracket.

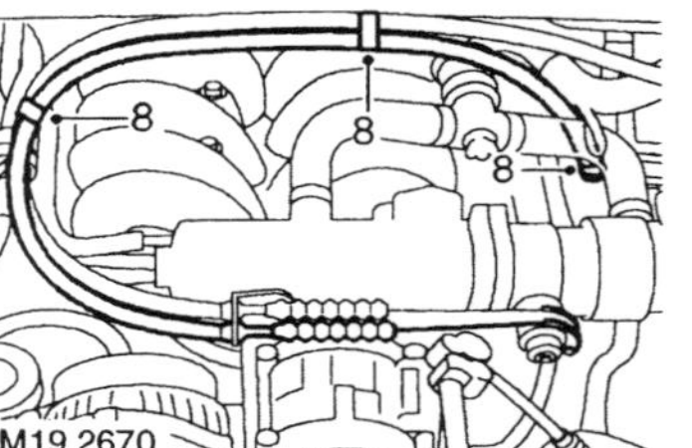

8. Release throttle cable from 3 clips.

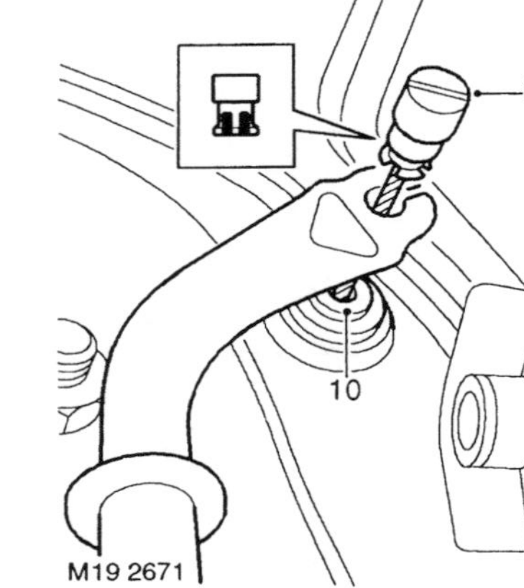

9. Release and disconnect inner cable from throttle lever.
10. Release throttle cable from bulkhead and remove from vehicle.

Refit

11. Apply liquid soap to bulkhead end of outer cable.
12. Fit throttle cable to bulkhead, connect and secure inner cable to pedal lever.
13. Fit throttle cable to abutment bracket and connect inner cable to throttle cam.
14. Fit throttle cable to clips.
15. Adjust throttle cable. ***See Adjustment.***
16. Secure gaiter to outer cable.
17. Refit heater air duct.
18. Fit closing panel and secure with scrivets.
19. Fit heater outlet duct and secure with screw.
20. Fit closing panel to fascia. ***See CHASSIS AND BODY, Repair.***

FILLER NECK ASSEMBLY - PRE-ADVANCED EVAPS

Service repair no - 19.55.07

WARNING: If fuel tank is full, fuel level will be above filler neck aperture in the tank. If gauge indicates over 75%, drain a minimum of 10 litres of fuel from tank.

Remove

1. Disconnect battery negative lead.
2. Remove rear wheel arch liner. ***See CHASSIS AND BODY, Repair.***
3. Remove fuel filler cap.
4. Slacken clips securing hoses to filler neck.

19M7081

5. Release fill breather hose from filler neck.
6. **Petrol Models Only:** Disconnect fuel tank and charcoal canister hoses from vapour separator.
7. **Diesel Models Only:** Release cap from quick release connector. Disconnect breather hose.
8. Remove nut securing filler neck to wheel arch.
9. Release filler neck from fuel tank hose and grommet in body aperture.
10. Remove filler neck assembly.

Refit

11. Apply liquid soap to grommet and mating surface of filler neck.
12. Reverse removal procedure.

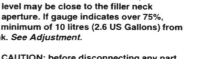

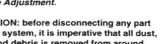

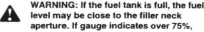

FUEL FILLER NECK - ADVANCED EVAPS

Service repair no - 19.55.07

Remove

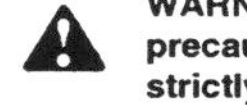

WARNING: Ensure that fuel handling precautions given in 01 - Introduction are strictly adhered to when carrying out following instructions.

WARNING: If the fuel tank is full, the fuel level may be close to the filler neck aperture. If gauge indicates over 75%, drain a minimum of 10 litres (2.6 US Gallons) from fuel tank. *See Adjustment.*

CAUTION: before disconnecting any part of the system, it is imperative that all dust, dirt and debris is removed from around components to prevent ingress of foreign matter into fuel system.

Remove

1. Open fuel filler flap and remove filler cap.
2. Disconnect battery earth lead.
3. Remove RH rear wheel arch liner. ***See CHASSIS AND BODY, Repair.***
4. Remove nut securing filler neck bracket to stud.
5. Disconnect vent line quickfit connectors at fuel/vapour separator and under body connection.
6. Disconnect pressure sensor breather pipe connection.

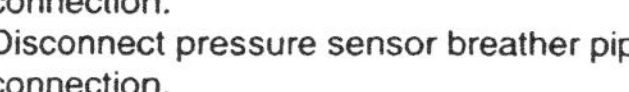

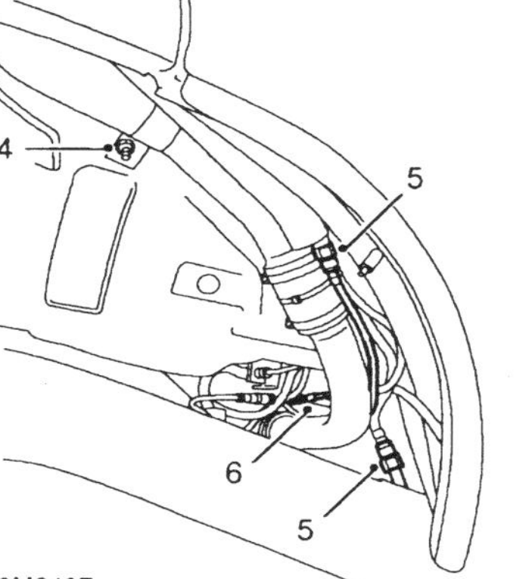

19M2427

7. Remove shear cap from clip securing neck assembly to tank.
8. Slacken clip securing neck assembly to tank.
9. Release filler neck bracket from body stud. Push filler neck down then forwards to release from aperture grommet.
10. Remove filler neck assembly.

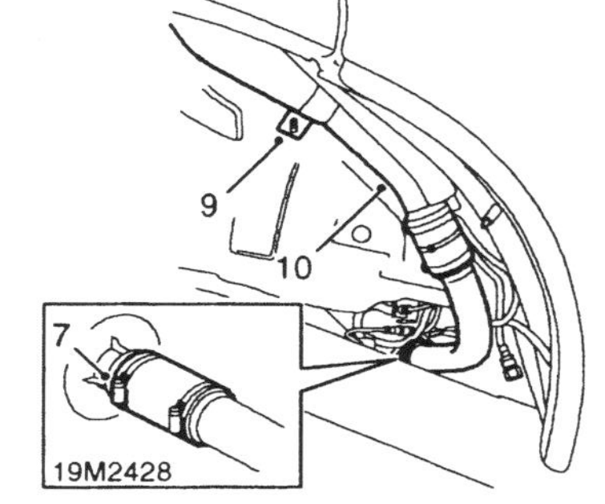

19M2428

Refit

CAUTION: Hose clips used on the filler neck of advanced EVAPS vehicles have a special 'shear' cap to ensure the correct tightening torque is achieved. Always use NEW clips of the correct type.

11. Loosely position new clip to filler neck hose.
12. Position filler neck assembly to fuel tank stub, rotated anti-clockwise as shown.
13. Engage internal breather hose to fuel tank inner stub.

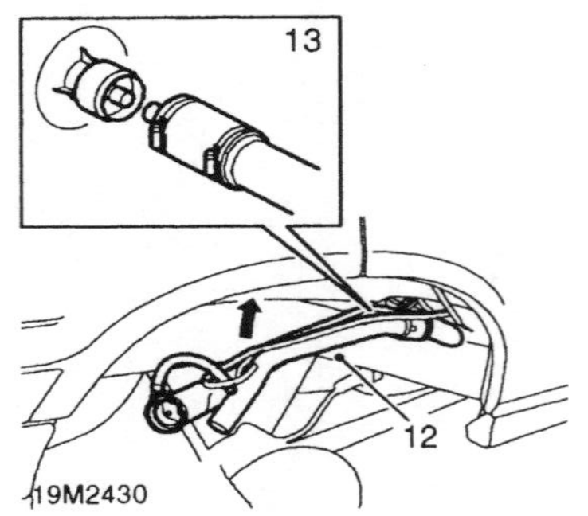

14. Engage filler neck hose with fuel tank stub.
15. Manoeuvre filler neck into position and engage with grommet.
16. Engage filler neck bracket with body stud and secure with nut.
17. Tighten clip securing hose to fuel tank stub until cap shears off.
18. Connect vent lines to fuel/vapour separator and under floor connection, ensuring that quickfit connections fully engage.
19. Connect pressure sensor breather line.
20. Replenish fuel if necessary.
21. Fit filler cap and tighten in accordance with instructions.
22. Close filler flap.
23. Connect battery earth lead.

ANTI-TRICKLE FILL VALVE - ADVANCED EVAPS

Service repair no - 19.55.31

Remove

1. Remove the fuel filler neck. ***See this section.***

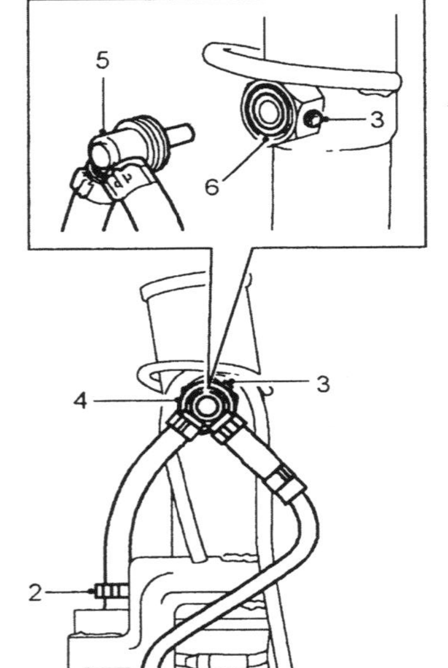

2. Release the cobra clip securing the hose to the liquid/vapour separator and disconnect the hose.
3. Loosen the grub screw on the valve nut, two complete turns.
4. Loosen the valve nut completely.

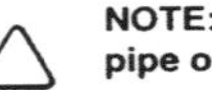

NOTE: The nut is held captive by the stub pipe on the filler neck.

5. Carefully remove the valve and hose assembly from the filler neck

Refit

6. Fit a new 'O' ring to the recess in the stub pipe.
7. Fit the valve and hose assembly to the filler neck stub pipe, ensuring that the 'O' ring is fitted around the body of the valve as it is pushed into the filler neck stub pipe.
8. Hand tighten the nut, then tighten to ***3 Nm.***
9. Tighten the grub screw to ***2 Nm.***
10. Connect the hose to the liquid/vapour separator and secure with the cobra clip.
11. Fit the fuel filler neck. ***See this section.***

FUEL TANK, PUMP AND GAUGE SENDER UNIT - PRE-ADVANCED EVAPS

Service repair no - 19.55.01 - Fuel Tank
Service repair no - 19.45.08 - Fuel Pump
Service repair no - 88.25.32 - Fuel gauge Tank Unit

Remove

1. Disconnect battery negative lead.
2. **Petrol Models Only:** Depressurise fuel system. ***See this section.***
3. Remove contents of fuel tank into an approved closed container.
4. Remove fuel filler neck. ***See this section.***
5. Raise vehicle on four post lift.
6. Position container beneath fuel filter to catch spillage.
7. **Petrol Models Only:** Disconnect feed pipe from fuel filter.
8. **Diesel Models Only:** Disconnect feed pipe at connection, forward of fuel tank.

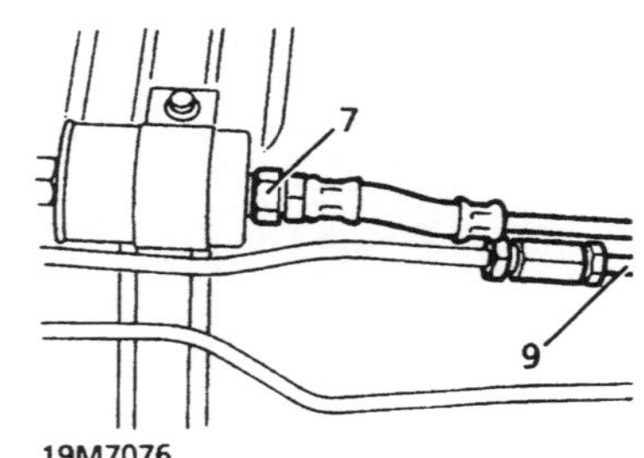

9. Disconnect return pipe, forward of tank.
10. Plug pipes and connections.
11. Support tank with jack.
12. Remove 3 nuts and 2 bolts securing tank cradle to floor pan.

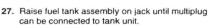

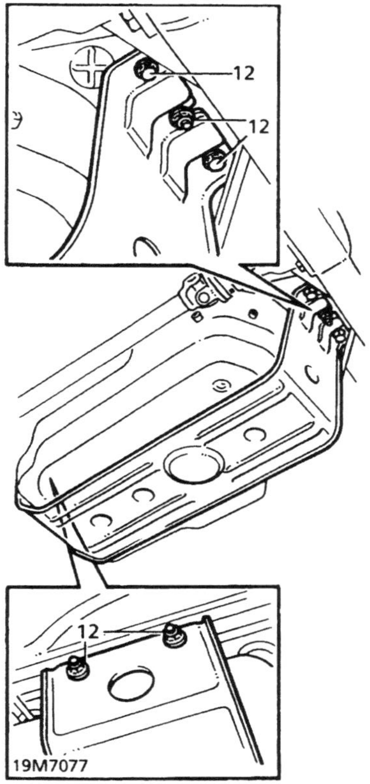

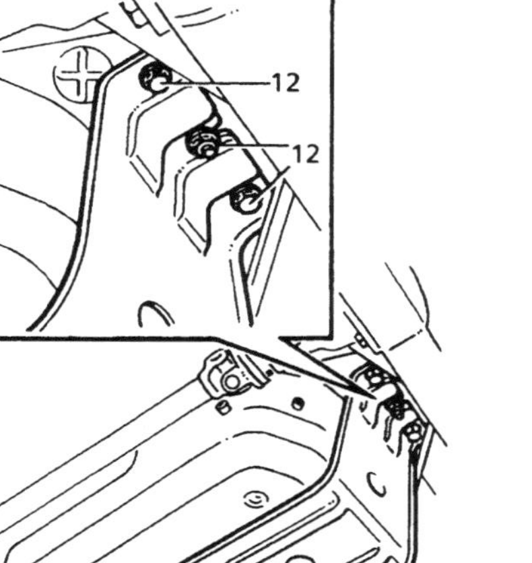

13. Lower tank by 150mm. Disconnect multiplug from fuel tank unit.

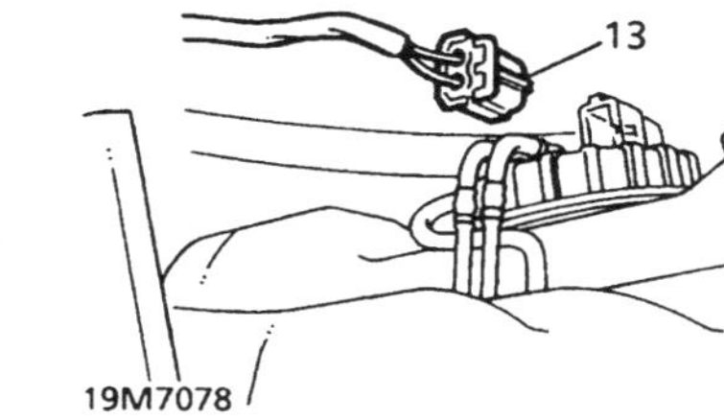

14. Lower tank assembly. Remove from jack. ***Do not carry out further dismantling if component is removed for access only.***

Disassemble

15. Remove tank from cradle.
16. Slacken clip. Remove fill breather pipe from tank unit.

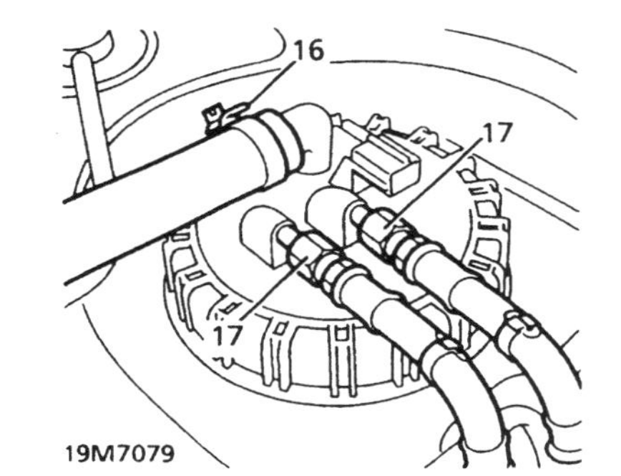

17. Disconnect feed and return pipes from tank unit. Remove each pipe from 2 fuel tank clips.
18. Remove tank unit retaining ring using LRT-19-001. Remove assembly from tank.

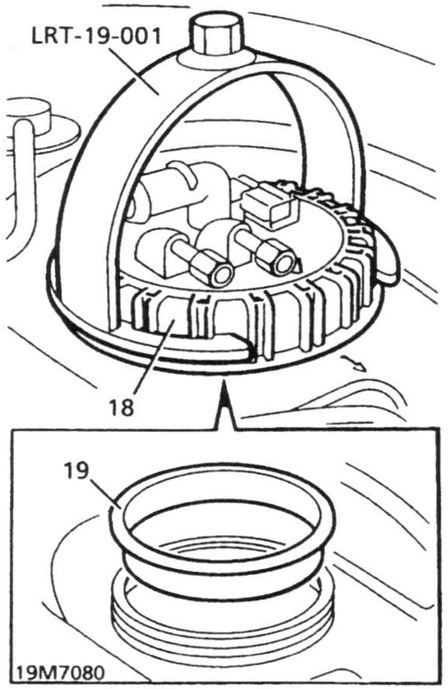

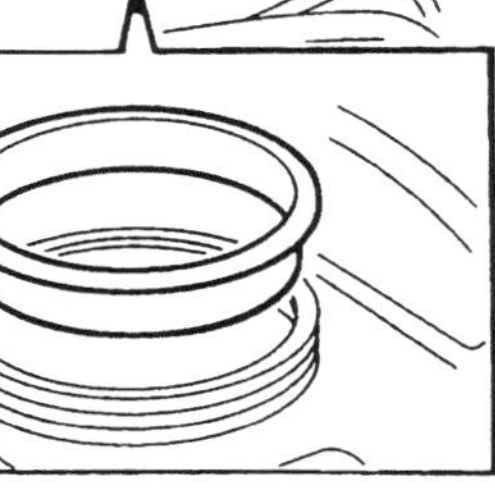

WARNING: A quantity of fuel will be retained in the unit, care must be taken to avoid excessive spillage during removal.

19. Remove tank unit sealing rubber and discard.

Reassemble

20. Fit new sealing rubber.
21. Fit tank unit. Align location marks.
22. Fit retaining ring using LRT-19-001.
23. Connect fuel feed and return pipes to tank unit. Tighten to ***16 Nm. (12 lbf.ft)***
24. Secure pipes to fuel tank clips.
25. Position fill breather pipe to tank unit. Secure with clip.
26. Position tank in cradle.

Refit

27. Raise fuel tank assembly on jack until multiplug can be connected to tank unit.
28. Raise tank. Align cradle mounting points. Secure with nuts and bolts.
29. Remove plugs from pipes and connections.
30. **Petrol Models Only:** Using new 'O' ring, connect fuel spill return pipe. Tighten to ***16 Nm. (12 lbf.ft)***
31. **Petrol Models Only:** Using new 'O' ring, connect fuel feed pipe to filter. Tighten to ***20 Nm. (15 lbf.ft)***
32. **Diesel Models Only:** Connect fuel feed and return pipes.
33. Lower vehicle.
34. Refit fuel filler neck. ***See this section.***
35. Refill fuel tank.
36. Reconnect battery negative lead.

FUEL TANK, PUMP AND GAUGE SENDER UNIT - ADVANCED EVAPS

Service repair no - 19.55.01 - Fuel Tank
Service repair no - 19.45.08 - Fuel Pump
Service repair no - 88.25.32 - Fuel Gauge Tank Unit

Remove

WARNING: Ensure that fuel handling precautions given in 01 - Introduction are strictly adhered to when carrying out following instructions.

CAUTION: before disconnecting any part of the system, it is imperative that all dust, dirt and debris is removed from around components to prevent ingress of foreign matter into fuel system.

Remove

1. Raise vehicle on 4 post ramp.
2. Disconnect battery earth lead.
3. Depressurise fuel system. ***See this section.***
4. Drain fuel tank completely. ***See this section.***

NOTE: Fuel tank draining includes removal of fuel filler neck.

5. Position container beneath fuel filter to catch spillage.
6. Disconnect fuel feed pipe at rear of filter.
7. Disconnect fuel return pipe.

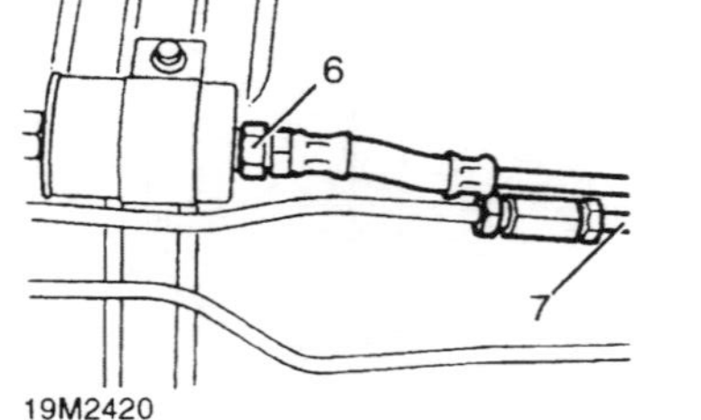

19M2420

8. Remove and discard 'O' rings. Plug all pipes and connections.
9. Support tank with jack.
10. Remove 3 nuts and 2 bolts securing tank cradle to floor pan.

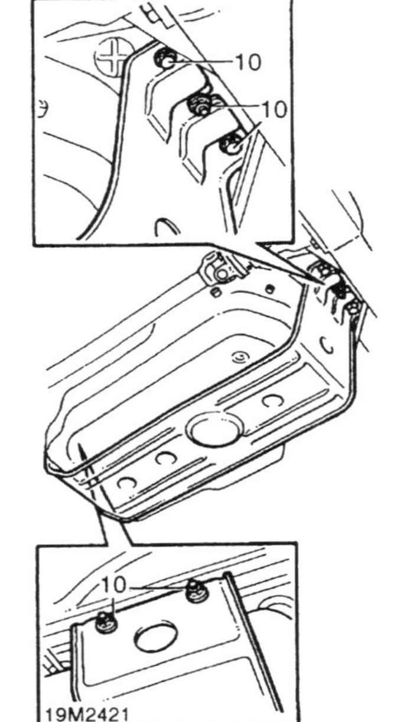

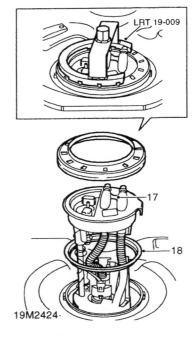

19M2421

11. Lower tank by 150mm (6in) and disconnect 2 multiplugs from tank unit.

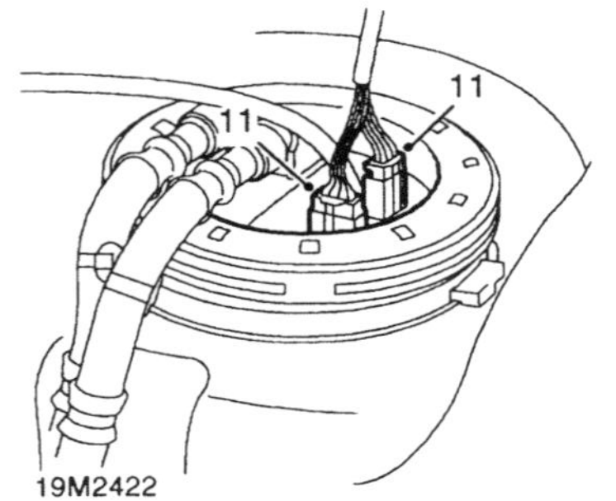

19M2422

12. Lower tank assembly and remove from jack.

Disassemble

13. Remove tank from cradle.
14. Disconnect and remove breather hose from pressure sensor.
15. Disconnect feed and return pipes at tank unit and remove pipes.

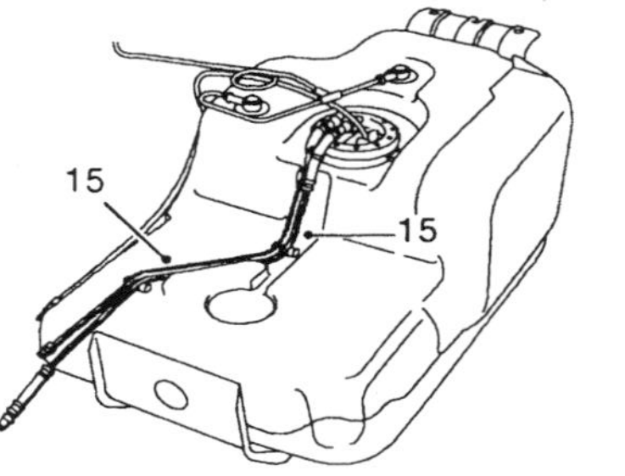

19M2423

16. Remove tank unit locking ring using LRT-19-009.

WARNING: A quantity of fuel will be retained in the unit. Care must be taken to avoid excessive spillage during removal.

17. Remove tank unit using the lifting eye provided.

CAUTION: Do not lift the unit using the feed and return stubs as this may damage the stubs.

18. Remove tank unit sealing rubber and discard.

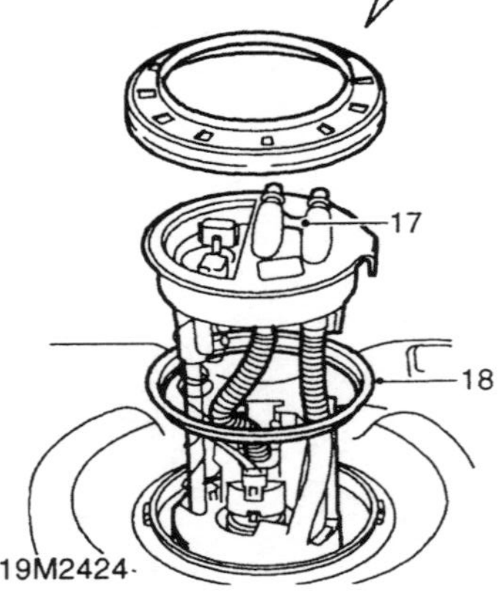

19M2424

Reassemble

19. Fit new sealing rubber to tank unit.
20. Carefully fit tank unit and align aperture tab.
21. Tighten retaining ring to ***35Nm (26lbf.ft)*** using tool LRT-19-009.
22. Fit fuel pipes and engage to tank clips.
23. Fit breather hose to pressure sensor.
24. Position tank in cradle.
25. Position tank assembly to jack.

Refit

26. Raise fuel tank assembly on jack until multiplugs can be connected.
27. Connect multiplugs to tank unit.
28. Raise tank and align to mountings. Secure tank with nuts and bolts.
29. Remove plugs from pipes and connections.
30. Connect and tighten fuel feed and return unions using new 'O' rings.
31. Lower vehicle.
32. Fit fuel filler neck. ***See this section.***
33. Refill fuel tank.
34. Connect battery earth lead.

FUEL TANK FILLER CAP - ADVANCED EVAPS

Service repair no - 19.55.08

Remove

1. Open filler flap.
2. Remove nut securing retaining strap to body.

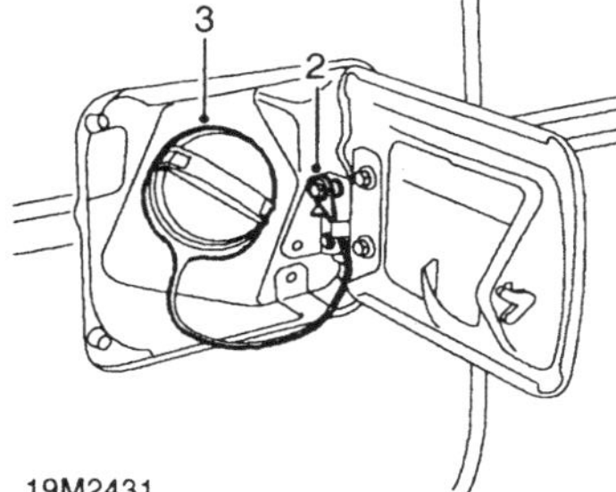

3. Remove cap.

Refit

4. Fit cap, ensuring that it is tightened in accordance with instruction label.
5. Position cap retaining strap to stud and secure with nut.
6. Close fuel filler flap.

THROTTLE BODY - from 99MY

Service repair no - 19.22.45

Remove

1. Drain sufficient coolant to allow for removal of throttle body.

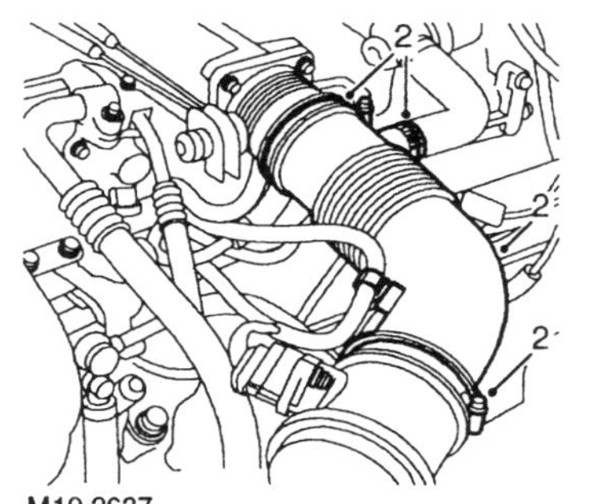

2. Loosen 3 clips securing air intake hose, release air intake hose and position aside.

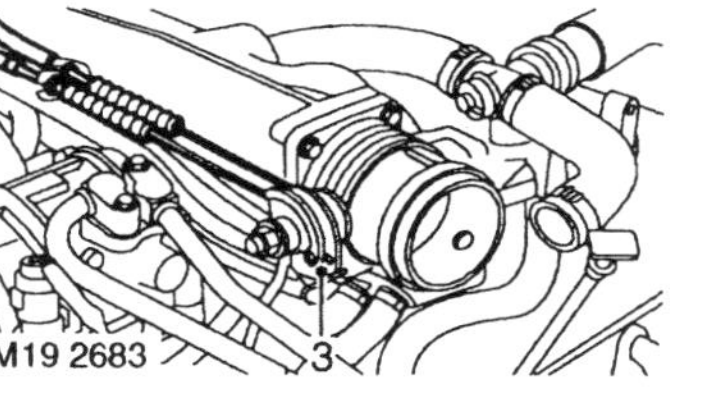

3. Disconnect throttle and cruise control cables from throttle body cams.

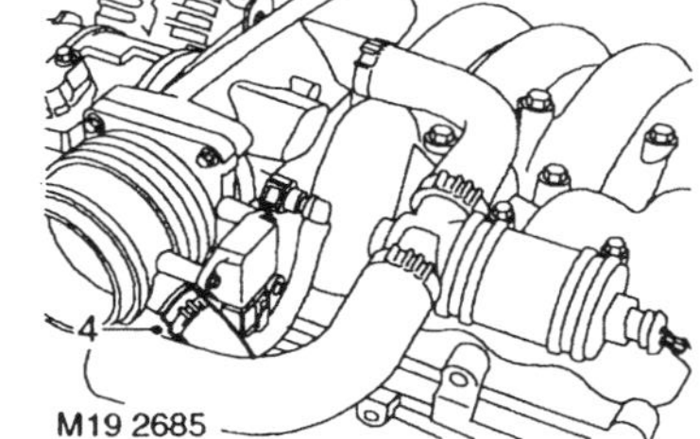

4. Loosen clip securing breather hose and release hose.
5. Remove TP sensor. ***See this section.***

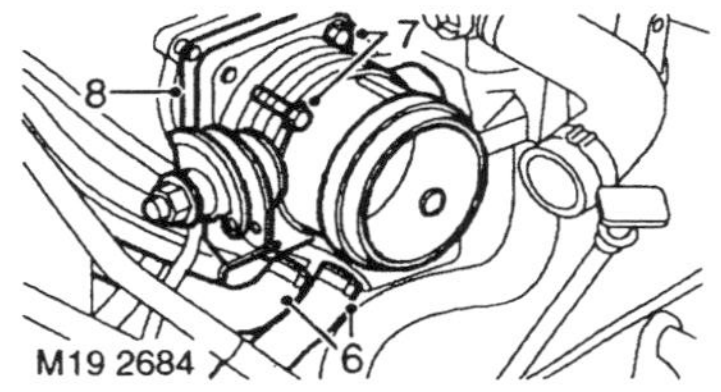

6. Release 2 clips securing coolant hoses to throttle body and release hoses.
7. Remove 4 bolts securing throttle body to plenum chamber and remove throttle body.
8. Remove and discard gasket.

Refit

9. Clean plenum chamber and throttle body mating faces.
10. Using a new gasket, position throttle body, fit bolts and tighten to ***9 Nm (7 lbf.ft).***
11. Fit coolant hoses and secure clips.
12. Fit breather hose and secure clip.
13. Fit TP sensor. ***See this section.***
14. Connect throttle and cruise control cables.
15. Position air intake hose and secure clips.
16. Refill cooling system.

CONTENTS

DESCRIPTION - V8

The cruise control system consists of electro-mechanical devices and comprises of the following components.

Electronic Control Unit (ECU)

The microprocessor based ECU evaluates the signals received from the driver controls, BeCM (vehicle speed signal), brake pedal switch and clutch pedal switch on manual vehicles. The ECU activates a vacuum pump as required. The ECU has a memory function to store desired cruise speed. The memory is cleared when power to the cruise ECU is cut, i.e. when the main cruise control switch is turned off.

Driver operated switches

The driver controls cruise operation from 3 switches. The main cruise control switch is located on the centre switch pack and activates the cruise control system. 2 further switches are located in the steering wheel. 'Set/+' informs the ECU of the required cruise speed. 'Res' temporarily switches cruise control off but retains the previously set cruise speed. Pressing 'Res' a second time resumes the previously selected cruise speed.

Vehicle speed signal

The cruise control ECU receives a road speed signal from the BeCM, which in turn receives the signal from the ABS ECU. The cruise control ECU compares the road speed signal with the required cruise speed and adjusts the output to the vacuum pump as necessary. Cruise control will not operate below the low speed threshold of 28 mph or above the high speed threshold of 125 mph.

Brake pedal switch

The vehicle utilised 2 brake pedal switchs, mounted on the pedal box. One switch is normally closed with the brake pedal released while the other is normally open. The normally closed switch also incorporates a vent valve to rapidly deplete actuator vacuum when cruise control is disengaged. When the brake pedal is pressed, the signal from each brake switch is monitored by the cruise control ECU which switches the vacuum pump off.

Clutch pedal switch

The clutch pedal switch is located on the pedal box and is identical to the previously described brake pedal switch with vent valve.

Vacuum pump

When cruise control is active and cruise ECU inputs are acceptable, the ECU energises the vacuum pump motor. The vacuum pump creates a vacuum in the actuator which operates the throttle linkage. When the required speed has been achieved, the ECU switches off the vacuum pump. The ECU also controls a dump valve which allows system vacuum to vent to atmosphere.

Actuator

The actuator provides the servo mechanical link between the cruise control system and the throttle linkage.

Neutral lock-out - automatic vehicles

Cruise control is disengaged when neutral or park is selected in the main gearbox. The cruise control ECU receives a signal from the BeCM.

Engine overspeed - manual vehicles

Cruise control is disengaged if the engine speed exceeds 5000 rpm. The cruise control ECU receives the engine speed signal from the BeCM.

DESCRIPTION - DIESEL

Diesel vehicles utilise the electronic diesel control (EDC) system for cruise control. As the EDC has complete control of the fuelling system, the only additional inputs required for cruise control are, driver controls, vehicle speed, brake and clutch signals. The individual components are as previously described by V8 vehicles.

CABLE - CRUISE CONTROL - ADJUST - UP TO 99MY

Service repair no - 19.75.09

1. Ensure throttle cable is adjusted correctly. ***See this section.***
2. Using light finger pressure only, push cruise control lever towards plenum chamber to remove all free play from cruise control cable.

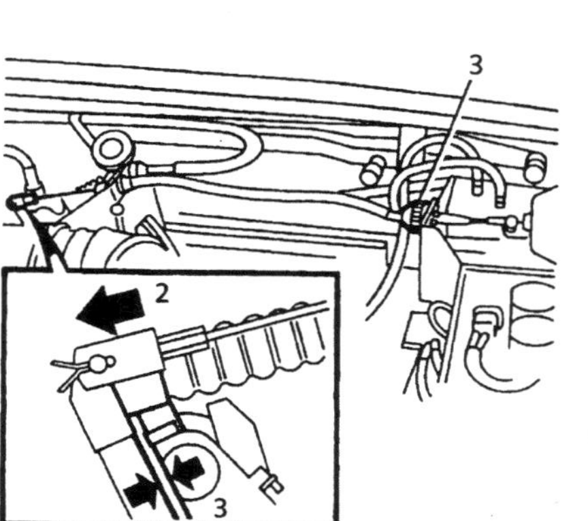

19M7014

3. Adjust cable outer length by turning plastic thumb screw to achieve a clearance of between 0.5 mm and 1.5 mm.

CABLE - CRUISE CONTROL - ADJUST - FROM 99MY

Service repair no - 19.75.11

Check

1. Ensure that the throttle cable is correctly adjusted. ***See this section.***

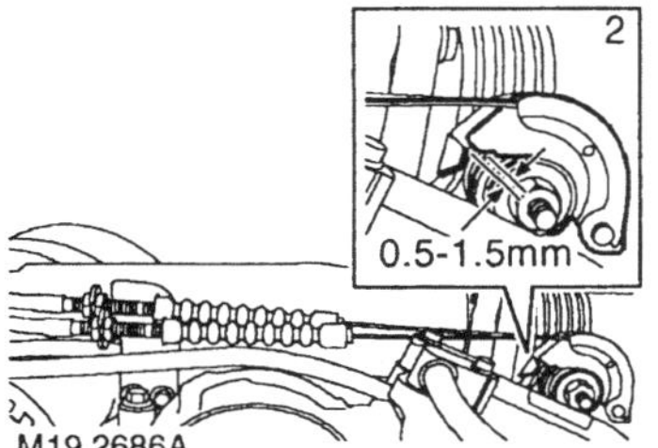

M19 2686A

2. Check for a 0.5 - 1.5mm gap between cruise control cable cam and throttle cable driven lever.

Adjust

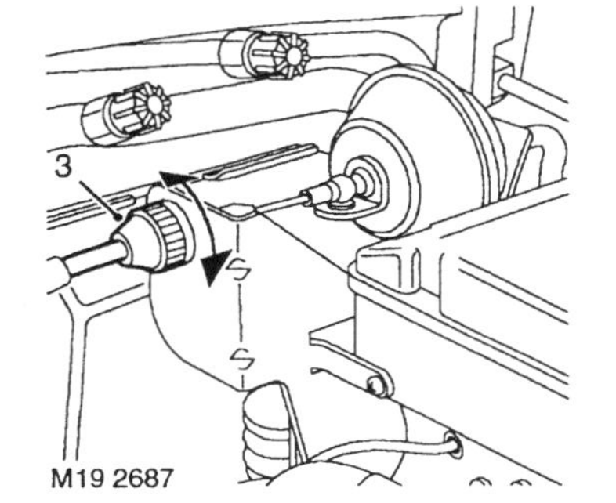

M19 2687

3. Rotate cruise control cable adjusting nut to give a 0.5 - 1.5mm gap between the cruise control cable cam and throttle cable driven lever.

CRUISE CONTROL ECU

Service repair no - 19.75.49

Remove

1. Remove fascia closing panel. ***See CHASSIS AND BODY, Repair.***
2. Remove 2 bolts securing ECU bracket to fascia. Release bracket to gain access to fixings.
3. Disconnect multiplug from ECU.
4. Remove 2 bolts securing ECU. Remove ECU.

19M7015

Refit

5. Reverse removal procedure.

CRUISE CONTROL ACTUATOR

Service repair no - 19.75.05

Remove

1. Disconnect vacuum hose from actuator.
2. Disconnect control cable from ball joint on actuator diaphragm.
3. Remove nut securing actuator to bracket. Remove actuator.

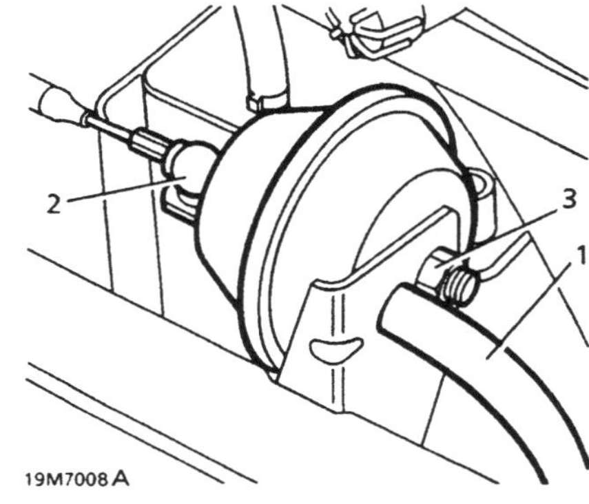

19M7008A

Refit

4. Position actuator to bracket. Secure with nut.
5. Connect vacuum hose. Secure cable to actuator ball joint.
6. Adjust cruise control cable. ***See CRUISE CONTROL, Adjustment.***

SET AND RESUME SWITCHES - CRUISE CONTROL

Service repair no - 19.75.36 - Set Switch
Service repair no - 19.75.37 - Resume Switch

Remove

1. Remove steering wheel switch pack assembly. ***See ELECTRICAL, Repair.***

Refit

2. Reverse removal procedure.

CRUISE CONTROL - VACUUM CONTROL UNIT

Service repair no - 19.75.06

Remove

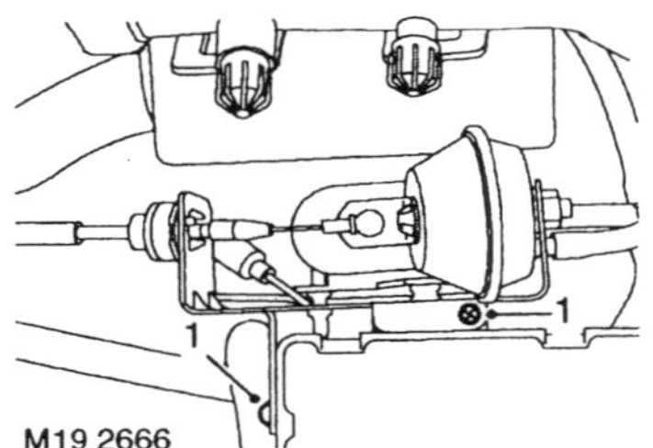

M19 2666

1. Remove 2 screws securing actuator bracket.

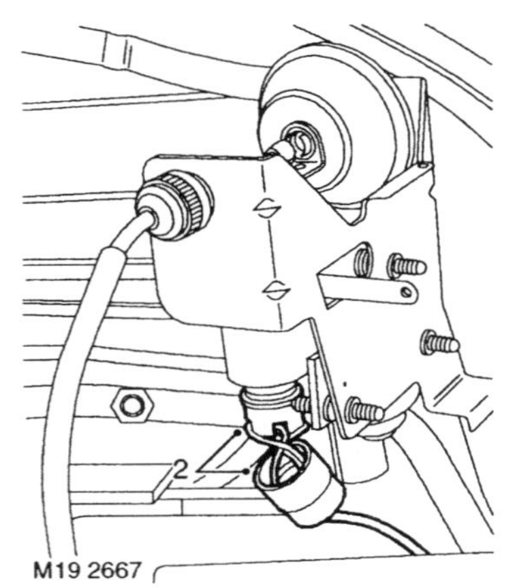

M19 2667

2. Release cover and disconnect multiplug from vacuum control unit.

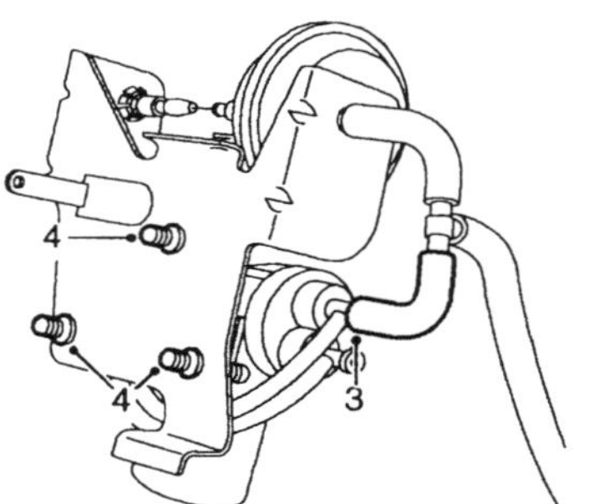

M19 2668

3. Remove vacuum hose from control unit.
4. Release 3 rubber mountings and remove control unit.
5. Remove 3 rubber mountings from control unit.

Refit

6. Fit rubber mountings to control unit.
7. Position control unit and secure mountings.
8. Connect vacuum hose to control unit.
9. Connect multiplug and fit cover.
10. Position actuator bracket and secure with screws.

BRAKE AND CLUTCH PEDAL SWITCHES/VENT VALVES - CRUISE CONTROL

Service repair no - 19.75.34 - Clutch Switch
Service repair no - 19.75.35 - Brake Switch (not fitted to diesel variants)

Remove

1. Remove drivers side fascia closing panel. ***See CHASSIS AND BODY, Repair.***
2. Remove 3 scrivet fasteners securing lower closing panel. Release panel to gain access to blower motor ducting.

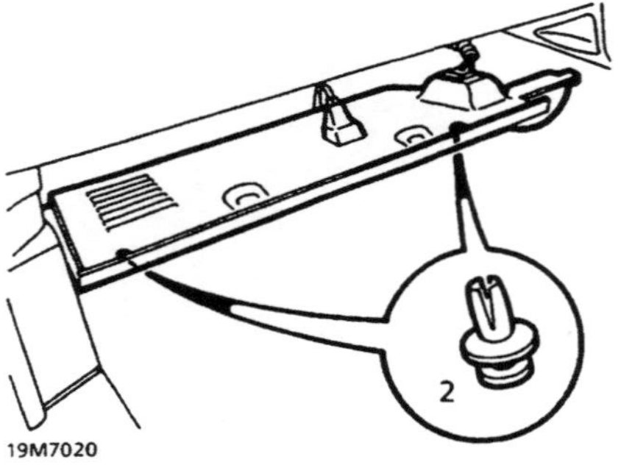

19M7020

3. Release ducting from blower motor housing and heater. Remove blower motor ducting.
4. Release switch/vent valve from pedal bracket.

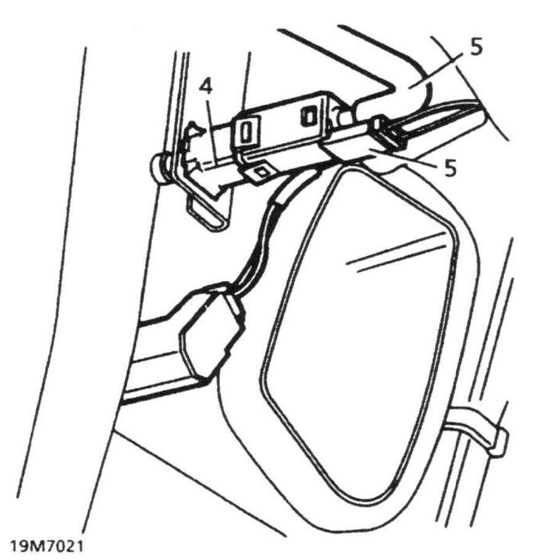

19M7021

5. Disconnect vacuum hose and multiplug from switch.

NOTE: Vacuum hose fitted to petrol variants only.

6. Remove switch/vent valve.

Refit

7. Reverse removal procedure.

NOTE: The switch/vent valve is factory set and does not require adjustment in service.

CRUISE CONTROL - SWITCH INVERTER/CONVERTER

Service repair no - 19.75.22

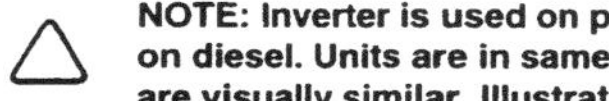

NOTE: Inverter is used on petrol, converter on diesel. Units are in same position and are visually similar. Illustration 19M7054 shows petrol condition, diesel vehicles do not have the cruise control ECU.

Remove

1. Remove fascia closing panel. ***See CHASSIS AND BODY, Repair.***
2. Release inverter/converter multiplug from bracket.

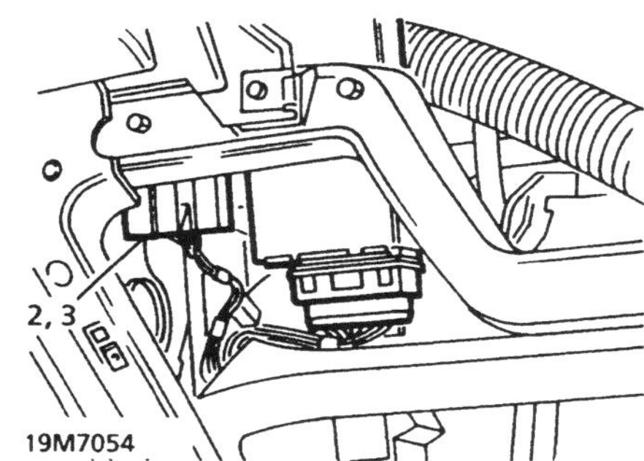

19M7054

3. Remove inverter/converter from multiplug.

Refit

4. Reverse removal procedure.

CABLE - CRUISE CONTROL - UP TO 99MY

Service repair no - 19.75.10

Remove

1. Release cable from actuator. Disengage adjuster from actuator abutment bracket.
2. Remove split pin and clevis pin from cable trunnion.
3. Remove 'C' clip securing cable to abutment bracket. Remove cable.

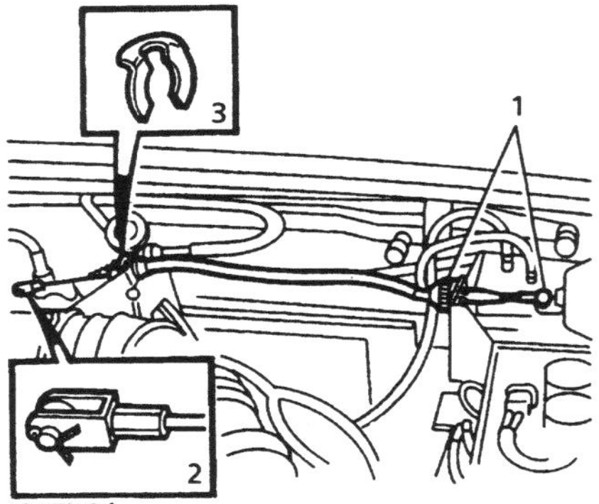

19M7013A

Refit

4. Position cable through abutment bracket. Secure with 'C' clip.
5. Position cable trunnion to throttle linkage. Secure with clevis pin and split pin.
6. Engage cable adjuster to actuator abutment bracket. Connect cable to actuator diaphragm.
7. Adjust cruise control cable. ***See CRUISE CONTROL, Adjustment.***

CABLE - CRUISE CONTROL - FROM 99MY

Service repair no - 19.75.10

Remove

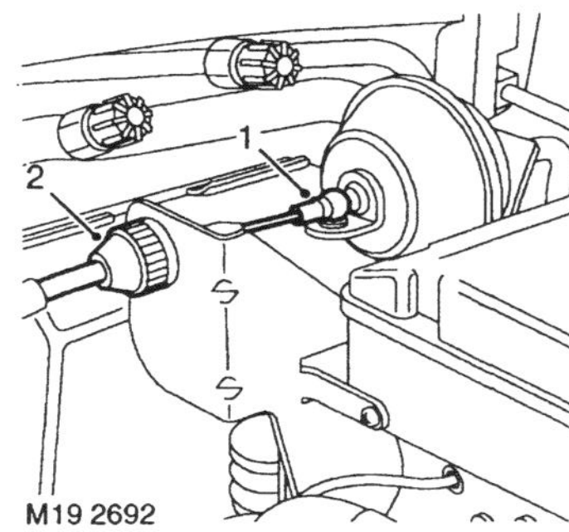

M19 2692

1. Disconnect inner cable from actuator.
2. Release cable from actuator mounting bracket.

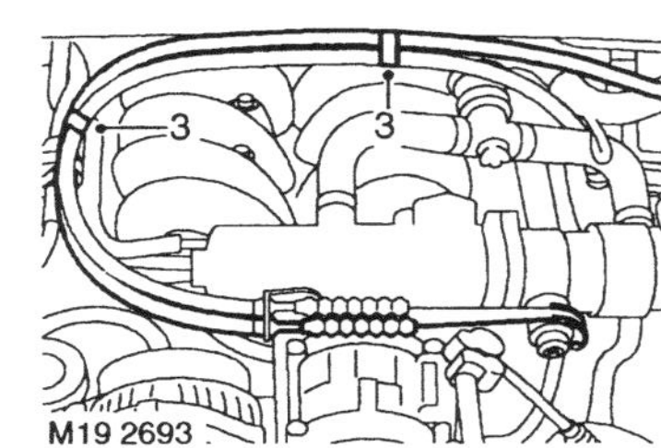

M19 2693

3. Release cable from 2 support clips.

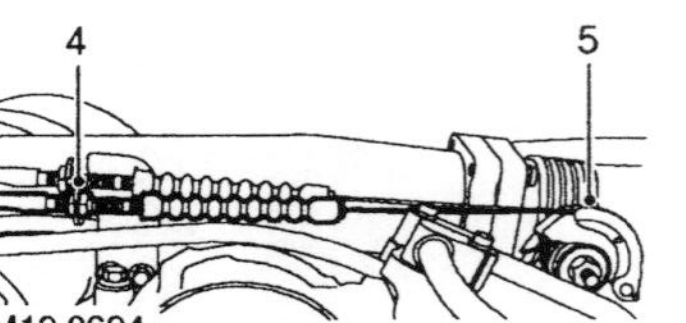

4. Loosen cable locknuts, release cable from abutment bracket.
5. Release inner cable from operating lever and remove cable.

Refit

6. Position cable and connect to operating lever.
7. Position cable to abutment bracket.
8. Fit cable to support clips.
9. Fit cable to actuator mounting bracket and connect inner cable to actuator.
10. Adjust cruise control cable. ***See Adjustment.***

Notes

CONTENTS

Page

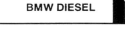

BMW DIESEL

DESCRIPTION AND OPERATION

FAULT DIAGNOSIS

REPAIR

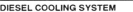

DIESEL COOLING SYSTEM

The complete cooling system installed in vehicles with diesel engines incorporates four independent cooling functions:- Engine (coolant) cooling; Turbo (charge air) intercooling; Engine oil cooling; Gearbox oil cooling.

Both intercooler and engine oil cooler are mounted in front of the radiator while the gearbox oil cooler on manual vehicles is an integral part of the radiator. Pre-formed pipes/hoses are used to link the components within the separate systems, as shown in 26M7029.

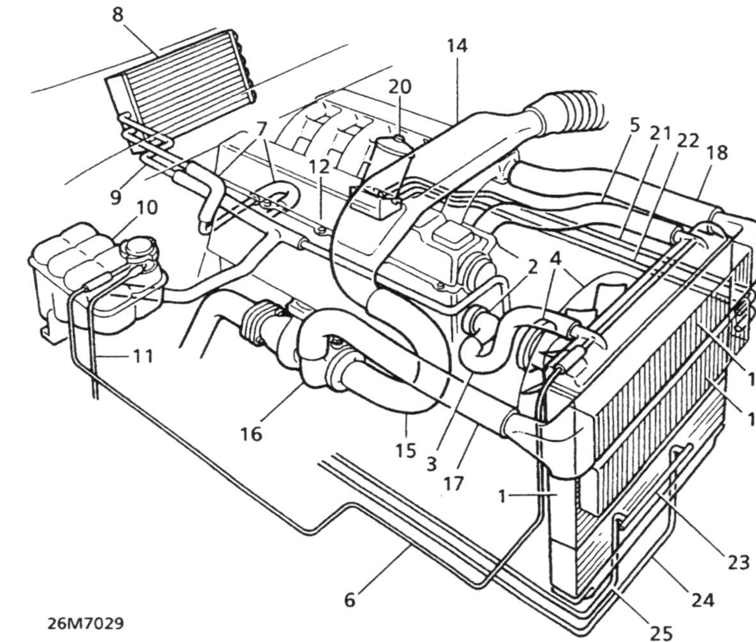

26M7029

Engine cooling system

1. Radiator
2. Thermostat housing
3. Radiator return hose
4. Viscous fan and water pump
5. Radiator top hose
6. Radiator bleed pipe
7. Heater feed pipe
8. Heater matrix
9. Heater return pipe
10. Expansion tank
11. Overflow/breather pipe
12. Crankcase
13. Intercooler
14. Cross-over duct
15. Link hose
16. Turbocharger
17. Inlet pipe
18. Feed hose
19. Engine oil cooler
20. Oil filter
21. Feed pipe, engine oil cooler
22. Return pipe, engine oil cooler
23. Gearbox oil cooler (manual gearbox, oil cooler shown)
24. Feed pipe, gearbox oil cooler
25. Return pipe, gearbox oil cooler

ENGINE COOLING

Description

The 2.5 litre diesel engine uses a pressurized cooling system and a vertical flow, two row matrix radiator. An expansion tank, mounted on the RH side of the engine compartment, provides a fluid reservoir for the coolant system.

A belt driven centrifugal water pump, complete with viscous fan, is fitted to the engine front timing cover and pumps coolant to the engine crankcase and cylinder head. The thermostat housing, located at the front of the crankcase, see 26M7030, is fitted with a separate vent valve.

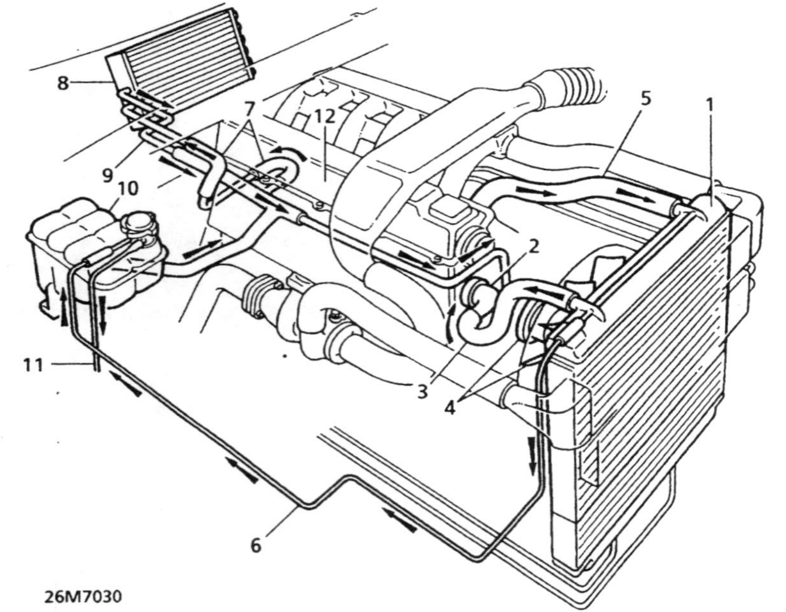

Engine cooling system

1. Radiator
2. Thermostat/housing
3. Radiator return hose
4. Viscous fan and water pump
5. Radiator top hose
6. Radiator bleed pipe
7. Heater feed pipe
8. Heater matrix
9. Heater return pipe
10. Expansion tank
11. Overflow/breather pipe
12. Crankcase

COOLANT CIRCULATION

Operation

When the engine is started from cold, the thermostat, integral in the housing (2), prevents any coolant circulation through the radiator by closing off the supply from the radiator. During the engine warm up, the water pump (4) pumps coolant around the cylinders in the crankcase (12) and through separate galleries to the cylinder head. At the rear LH side of the cylinder head, a proportion of the flow is diverted through a heater feed pipe (7). The heater feed pipe is connected to the heater matrix (8), which is housed in the distribution unit of the heating and ventilation system. This coolant is then carried, via the heater return pipe (9) back to the water pump. The remaining coolant flows through a bypass port at the front of the cylinder head back to the water pump to complete the cycle.

When normal engine running temperature is reached, the thermostat opens and a secondary valve closes the bypass port. With the thermostat open, coolant is circulated through the top hose (5) to the radiator. Coolant is drawn from the base of the radiator by the water pump. Coolant circulation through the crankcase and cylinder head to the heater matrix remains the same.

An integral bleed pipe (6), connects the top of the radiator to the expansion tank and aids bleeding of air from the coolant system. The expansion tank cap contains a pressure valve which allows excessive pressure and coolant to vent to the overflow pipe (11) if the system has been overfilled.

VISCOUS FAN

The viscous drive unit for the cooling fan on diesel engines work on the same principal as that fitted on V8 engines but is of slightly different size. ***See this section.***

INTERCOOLER

Description

The intercooler (1) is an aluminium heat exchanger, with integral side tanks, comprising a single row matrix incorporating fifteen internal cooling tubes. A cross-over duct (2) directs air from the air cleaner, through a link hose (3) to the turbocharger (4). Air is directed under pressure from the turbocharger to the intercooler via the pre-formed inlet pipe (5). The cooled air is fed to the inlet manifold through the feed hose (6), see 26M 7031.

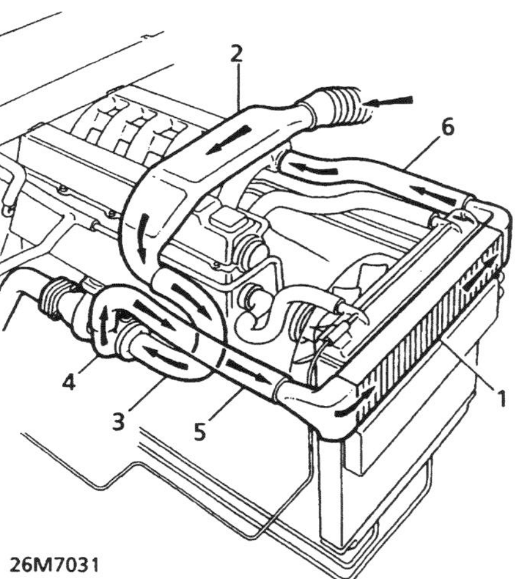

26M7031

Intercooler

1. Intercooler
2. Cross-over duct
3. Link hose
4. Turbocharger
5. Inlet pipe
6. Feed hose

Operation

The 2.5 litre diesel has a high power output and is subject to high running temperatures. Compression in the turbocharger heats the air considerably, so that it expands. As a result the air charge mass per cylinder is reduced, having a negative effect on power output. The charge-air intercooler cools the air before it reaches the cylinders, thus increasing its density. This increases power output through increased mass of oxygen in the combustion process as well as maximising engine durability through maintaining lower piston and head temperatures.

ENGINE OIL COOLER

Description

The engine oil cooler is located in front of the radiator, below the intercooler, and comprises a two pass, single row matrix with twelve internal cooling tubes. Pre-formed feed and return pipes/hoses are used to link the oil filter housing and oil cooler, as shown in 26M7032.

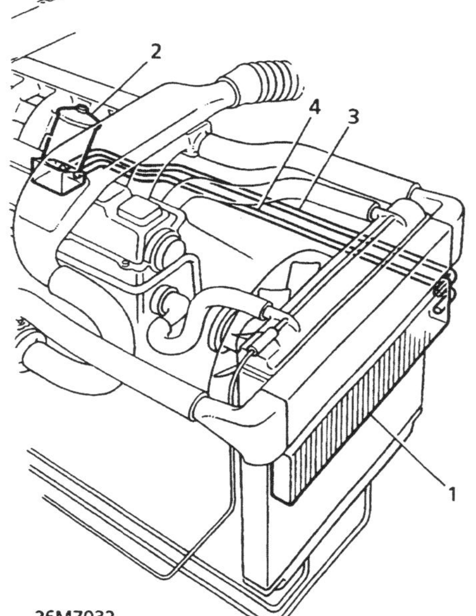

26M7032

Engine oil cooler

1. Engine oil cooler
2. Oil filter
3. Feed pipe
4. Return pipe

Operation

When the engine reaches its normal operating temperature, oil, drawn through a steel strainer in the sump, is pumped under pressure from the filter housing (2) to the oil cooler (1) via the feed pipe (3). Ambient air, forced through the front grille of the vehicle and assisted by the pull of the viscous fan, is dispersed across the oil cooler. The cooled oil then passes through a return pipe (4) to the filter housing before being distributed by the oil pump to the various internal engine components.

GEARBOX OIL COOLER - MANUAL

Description

The gearbox oil cooler on manual vehicles is an integral part of the radiator and is a brass concentric tube type. The cooler is immersed in a separate water tank at the base of the radiator. The inner core, which has its own water jacket within the cooling tube, carries the transmission oil via feed and return pipes, see 26M7033.

Operation

Oil is pumped under pressure from the gearbox through the feed pipe (3) into the tube (2) of the oil cooler tank. With a combination of water and ram air cooling, through the front grille of the vehicle and assisted by the pull of the viscous fan, the cooled transmission oil is routed back to the gearbox via the return pipe (4), to repeat the cycle.

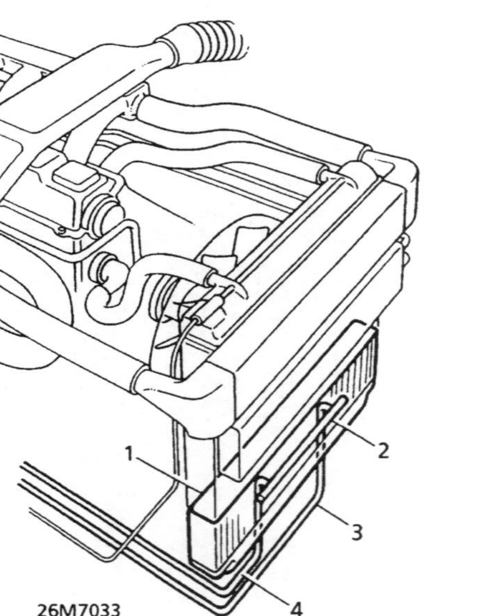

Gearbox oil cooler, manual transmission

1. Gearbox oil cooler tank
2. Coolant tube
3. Feed pipe, oil cooler
4. Return pipe, oil cooler

GEARBOX OIL COOLER - AUTOMATIC

Description

On diesel models with automatic transmission an independent oil cooler is used and is mounted on the LH side of the vehicle behind the front bumper. The oil cooler comprises a cast aluminium radiator, two pass, single row matrix with sixteen internal cooling tubes. Pre-formed feed and return pipes/hoses are used to link the automatic transmission and oil cooler.

Operation

On automatic vehicles the coolant process relies on ram air only through an aperture in the LH side of the bumper moulding. Air is dispersed over the oil cooler, the cooled oil then being fed back,via the return pipe (3), to run parallel with the feed pipe to the LH side of the transmission.

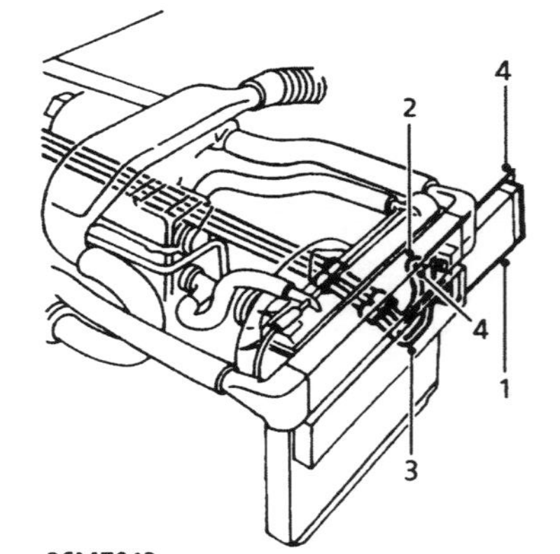

Gearbox oil cooler, automatic transmission

1. Gearbox oil cooler
2. Feed pipe, oil cooler
3. Return pipe, oil cooler
4. Mounting brackets

Notes

COOLING SYSTEM FAULTS

This section covers mechanical faults that could occur in the complete cooling system :- 1 Engine (coolant) cooling; 2 Turbo intercooling; 3. Engine oil cooling; 4. Gearbox oil cooling.

Before conducting any visual checks within the separate systems and undertaking detailed diagnosis procedures. ***See Description and operation.***

1. ENGINE (COOLANT) COOLING SYSTEM

Symptom - Engine Overheating

POSSIBLE CAUSE	REMEDY
1. Engine coolant low.	1. Allow engine to cool. Top up expansion tank to correct level, with engine running at idle. Check cooling system for leaks and rectify if necessary.
2. Loose drive belt.	2. Check/renew drive belt tensioner or renew drive belt. ***See ELECTRICAL, Repair.***
3. Coolant in radiator frozen.	3. Slowly thaw and drain cooling system. ***See Repair.***
4. Air flow through radiator restricted or blocked.	4. Apply air pressure to engine side of radiator to clear obstruction. If mud or dirt is evident, carefully use a hose.
5. External leaks from water pump, engine gaskets, thermostat housing or pipe/hoses.	5. Check for visual causes and rectify.
6. Viscous fan not operating correctly or inoperative.	6. Renew viscous fan unit. ***See Repair.***
7. Thermostat seized in closed position.	7. Check radiator bottom hose for coolant flow through radiator. If cold a faulty thermostat is confirmed. Renew thermostat. ***See Repair.***

Symptom - Engine Overheating Continued

POSSIBLE CAUSE	REMEDY
8. Air in cooling system.	8. Check coolant level. Run engine at fast idle (approximately 2,000 rpm) with expansion tank cap off. Top up coolant level with engine at idle and refit expansion tank cap.
9. Air conditioning condenser fans not operating correctly or inoperative.	9. ***See AIR CONDITIONING, Fault diagnosis.***
10. Temperature gauge or sender unit giving inaccurate readings.	10. Refer to **TestBook** .
11. Coolant leakage across cylinder head gasket.	11. Carry out cylinder pressure test to determine if pressure is leaking into cooling system, causing over pressurising and loss of coolant. Renew cylinder head gasket.
12. Engine oil contamination of cooling system due to leaking.	12. Renew cylinder head gasket. ***See ENGINE, Repair.***
13. Coolant contamination of lubrication system.	13. Renew inlet manifold or front cover gaskets. ***See MANIFOLD AND EXHAUST SYSTEM, Repair.*** or ***See ENGINE, Repair.***

Symptom - Engine Runs Cold

POSSIBLE CAUSE	REMEDY
1. Thermostat seized in open or partially open position.	1. Remove thermostat housing and check operation of thermostat. Renew, if necessary. ***See Repair.***
2. Temperature gauge or sender unit giving inaccurate readings.	2. Refer to **TestBook** .
3. Viscous fan not operating correctly.	3. Renew viscous fan unit. ***See Repair.***
4. Air conditioning condenser fans operating continuosly.	4. Refer to **TestBook** .

2. TURBO INTERCOOLING SYSTEM

Symptom - Loss of Performance

POSSIBLE CAUSE	REMEDY
1. Cooling air flow through intercooler matrix restricted or blocked.	1. Apply air pressure to engine side of radiator to clear obsruction. If mud or dirt is evident, carefully use a hose.
2. Charge-air flow through intercooler matrix restricted.	2. Check for blocked air cleaner element and renew, if necessary. ***See SECTION 10, Maintenance.***
3. Blocked air cleaner.	3. Renew air cleaner element. ***See SECTION 10, Maintenance.***
4. Pipe/hose leaks in intercooler system.	4. Tighten all joint connections or renew components as necessary.
5. Turbocharger not operating correctly or inoperative.	5. Substitute parts and recheck. ***See FUEL SYSTEM, Repair.***
6. Customer fitted grille blind restricting cooling air flow.	6. Remove blind or advise accordingly.

3. ENGINE OIL COOLING SYSTEM

Symptom - Engine Oil Overheating

POSSIBLE CAUSE	REMEDY
1. Air flow through oil cooler matrix restricted or blocked.	1. Apply air pressure to engine side of radiator to clear obstruction. If mud or dirt is evident carefully use a hose.
2. Blocked or damaged oil cooler or pipe/hoses, restricting engine oil flow.	2. Check for visual damage and renew components where necessary.
3. Oil cooler relief valve seized in closed position.	3. Remove and check relief valve. Renew if necessary.

4. GEARBOX OIL COOLING SYSTEM

Symptom - Gearbox Oil Overheating

POSSIBLE CAUSE	REMEDY
1. Blocked or damaged oil cooler or pipe/hoses restricting gearbox oil flow.	1. Check for visual damage and renew components where necessary.
2. Leaking coolant from oil cooler water tank.	2. Remove radiator, inspect for source of leak and repair. ***See Repair.***
3. Vehicle being driven in wrong gear.	3. Advise owner/driver accordingly.

NOTE: Critical warning messages relating to the complete cooling system are displayed on the message centre of the instrument pack, should a fault occur in any of the separate systems.

COOLANT - DRAIN AND REFILL

Service repair no - 26.10.01

Drain

WARNING: Do not remove expansion tank filler cap when engine is hot. The cooling system is pressurised. Personal scalding could result.

1. Raise the vehicle.

WARNING: Support on safety stands.

2. Remove expansion tank filler cap to assist draining.

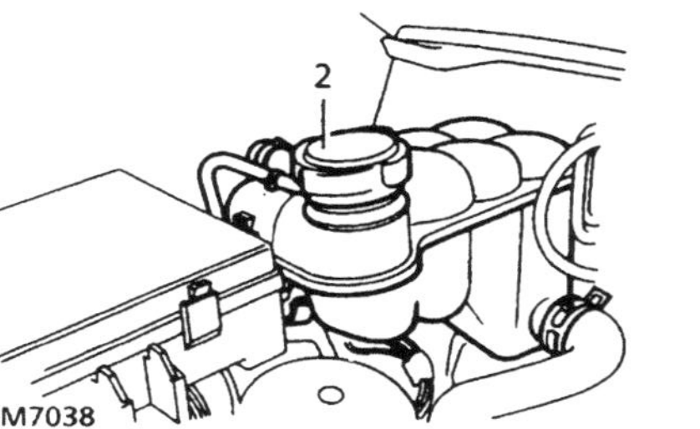

26M7038

3. Position container beneath radiator.
4. Remove plug from base of radiator. Allow coolant to drain.

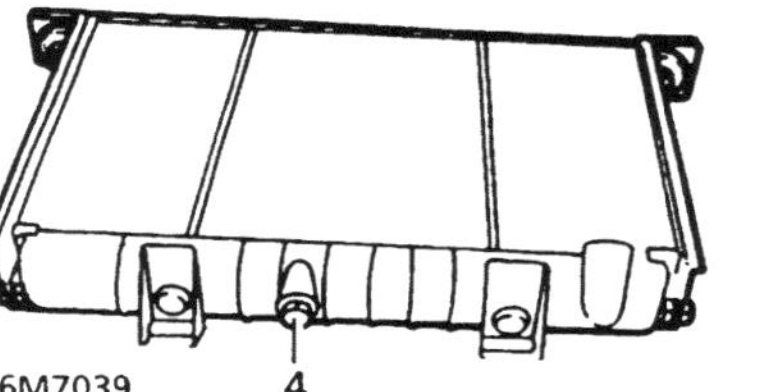

26M7039

5. If system is only being partially drained, contin at **Refill.**
6. Reposition container. Remove cylinder block drain plug. Allow coolant to drain.

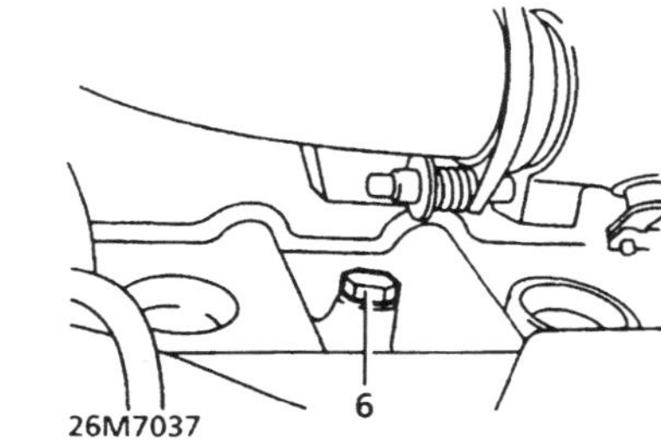

26M7037

7. Clean drain plug threads. Apply a coating of 'Loctite 577'. Refit plug to block. Tighten securely.

Refill

8. Ensure sufficient coolant solution is available. ***See LUBRICANTS, FLUIDS AND CAPACITIES, Information.***
9. Inspect radiator drain plug 'O' ring, renew if required.
10. Fit drain plug to radiator. Tighten to ***Max 6 Nm. (4 lbf.ft)***
11. Remove safety stands. Lower vehicle.
12. Disconnect radiator bleed hose at the radiator.
13. Blow through hose to clear any residual coolant. Reconnect hose.
14. Fill expansion tank until coolant is level with base of neck.
15. Start engine, continue filling at expansion tank until coolant level stabilises at the 'COLD LEVEL' marking.
16. Run the engine until the thermostat opens (top hose becomes warm).
17. Stop engine, allow to cool.
18. Check coolant level, top-up as necessary.
19. Refit expansion tank filler cap.

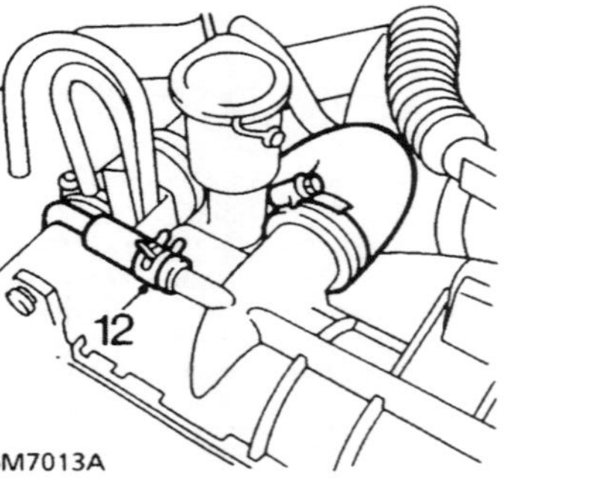

26M7013A

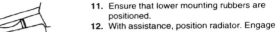

RADIATOR

Service repair no - 26.40.04

Remove

1. Disconnect battery negative lead.
2. Raise the vehicle.

WARNING: Support on safety stands.

3. Drain cooling system. ***See this section.***
4. Remove viscous coupling. ***See this section.***
5. Release bottom hose from radiator.
6. Release expansion tank hose from radiator.

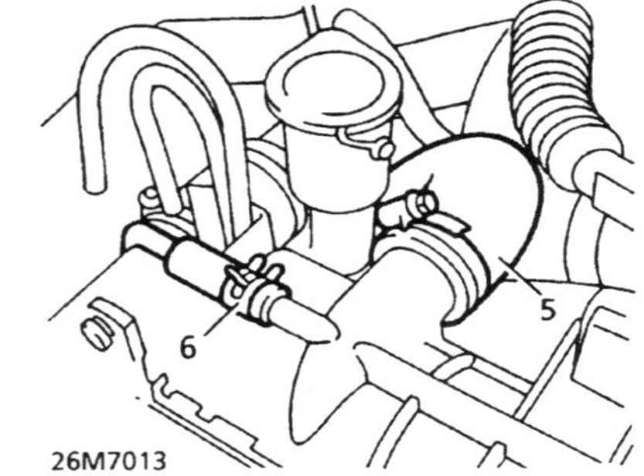

26M7013

7. **ManualVehicles:**Disconnect gearbox oil cooler pipes from radiator. Remove 'O' rings and discard.
8. **Manual Vehicles:**Plug oil cooler pipes and connections.
9. Remove 2 bolts securing radiator to bracket. Remove radiator assembly.

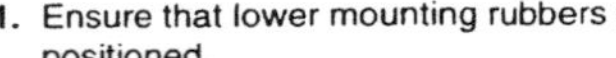

26M7014

10. If necessary, remove 2 clips securing cowl to radiator. Remove cowl.

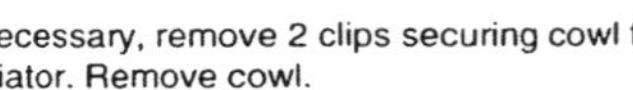
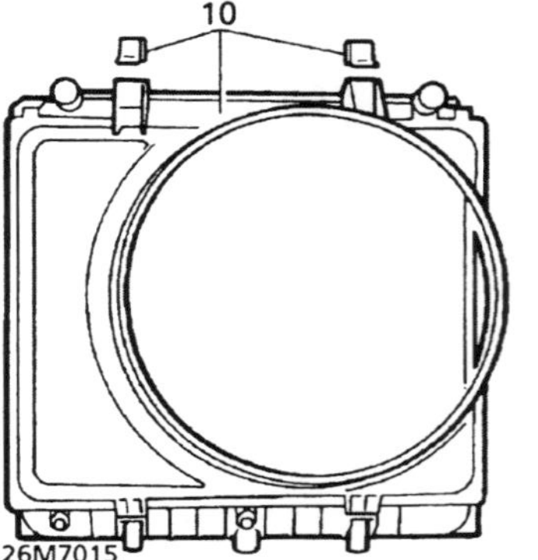

26M7015

Refit

11. Ensure that lower mounting rubbers are positioned.
12. With assistance, position radiator. Engage mountings. Secure with bolts.
13. **Manual Vehicles:**Remove plugs from oil cooler pipes and connections.
14. **Manual Vehicles:**Using new 'O' rings, connect gearbox oil cooler pipes. Tighten to ***30 Nm. (22 lbf.ft)***
15. Fit viscous coupling. ***See this section.***
16. Connect cooling hoses to radiator. Secure with clips.
17. Refill cooling system. ***See this section.***
18. Remove safety stands. Lower vehicle.
19. Reconnect battery negative lead.
20. **Manual Vehicles:**Top-up gearbox fluid. ***See SECTION 10, Maintenance.***

WATER PUMP

Service repair no - 26.50.01

Remove

1. Remove radiator assembly. ***See this section.***
2. Slacken 4 water pump pulley bolts.

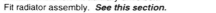

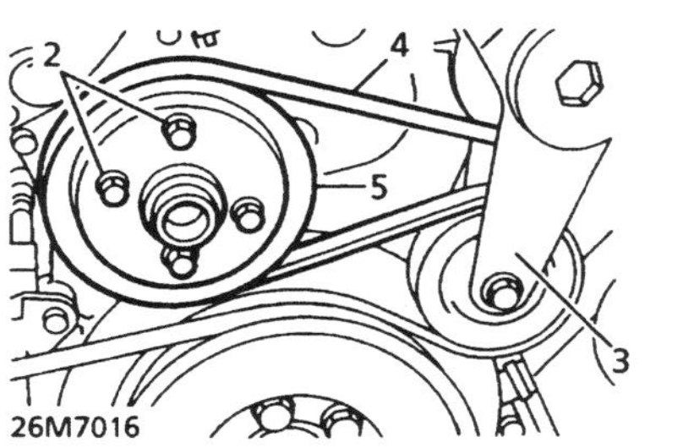

26M7016

3. Release tension from auxilary drive belt.
4. Release belt from water pump pulley.
5. Remove pulley bolts. Remove pulley.
6. Remove 4 bolts securing water pump.

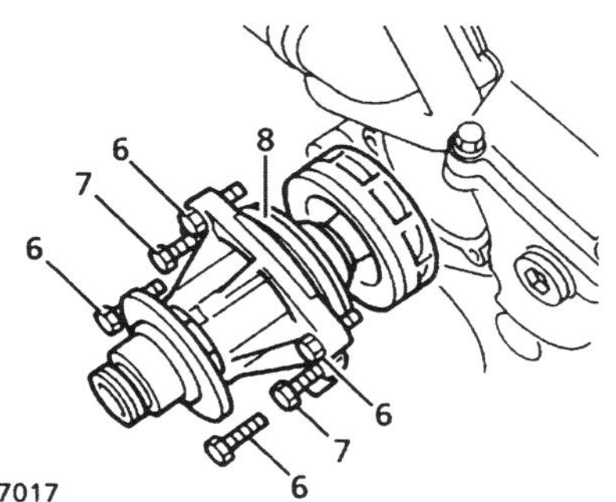

26M7017

7. Fit 2 M6 bolts into tapped holes of water pump. Extract pump.
8. Remove 'O' ring and extraction bolts.

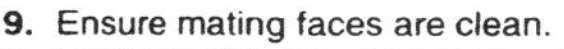

Refit

9. Ensure mating faces are clean.
10. Lubricate 'O' ring with petroleum jelly. Fit to water pump.
11. Fit water pump. Secure with bolts. Tighten to ***10 Nm. (7 lbf.ft)***
12. Fit water pump pulley. Secure with bolts. Tighten to ***10 Nm. (7 lbf.ft)***
13. Rotate tensioner. Fit auxilary drive belt.
14. Fit radiator assembly. ***See this section.***

VISCOUS COUPLING AND FAN ASSEMBLY

Service repair no - 26.25.19

Remove

1. Disconnect battery negative lead.
2. Raise the vehicle.

WARNING: Support on safety stands.

3. Drain cooling system. ***See this section.***
4. Remove 3 bolts securing upper fan cowl. Remove cowl.

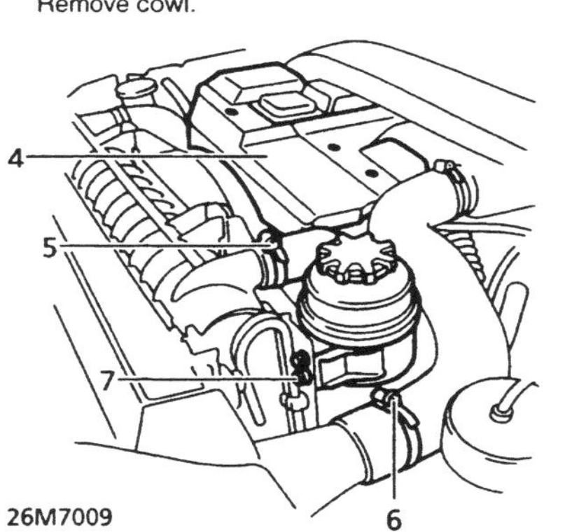

26M7009

5. Release top hose from radiator. Position hose aside.
6. Release outlet hose from intercooler. Position hose aside.
7. Remove 2 bolts securing power steering reservoir to radiator bracket. Position reservoir aside.
8. Using special tools LRT-12-093 and LRT-12-094 unscrew viscous coupling.

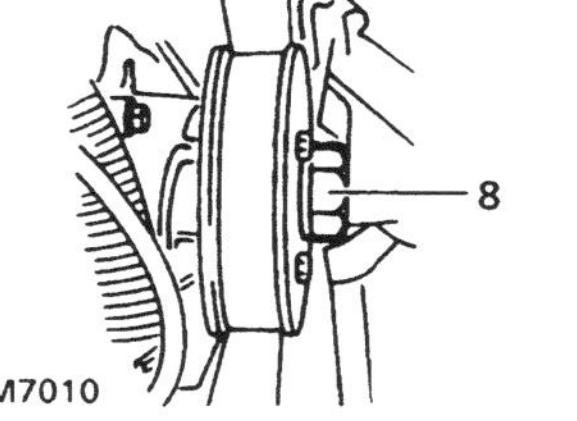

26M7010

NOTE: Viscous coupling is fitted with a LH thread.

9. Remove viscous coupling assembly from LH side of radiator.
10. ***Do not carry out further dismantling if component is removed for access only.***
11. Remove 4 bolts securing fan to coupling. Remove coupling.

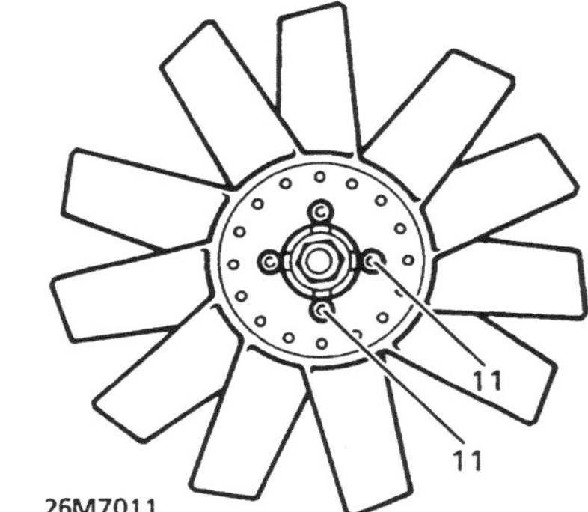

26M7011

Refit

12. Ensure mating faces are clean.
13. Fit fan to coupling. Secure with bolts. Tighten to ***10 Nm. (7 lbf.ft)***
14. Position viscous coupling assembly.
15. Engage to pump. Using special tools LRT-12-093 and LRT-12-094. Tighten to ***40 Nm. (29 lbf.ft)***
16. Connect hoses to intercooler and radiator. Secure with clips.
17. Position power steering fluid reservoir to radiator bracket. Secure with bolts.
18. Position upper fan cowl. Secure with bolts.
19. Refill cooling system. ***See this section.***
20. Remove safety stands. Lower vehicle.
21. Reconnect battery negative lead.

THERMOSTAT

Service repair no - 26.45.01

Remove

1. Disconnect battery negative lead.
2. Raise the vehicle.

WARNING: Support on safety stands.

3. Remove cooling fan cowl. ***See this section.***
4. Release intake hose from ducting.

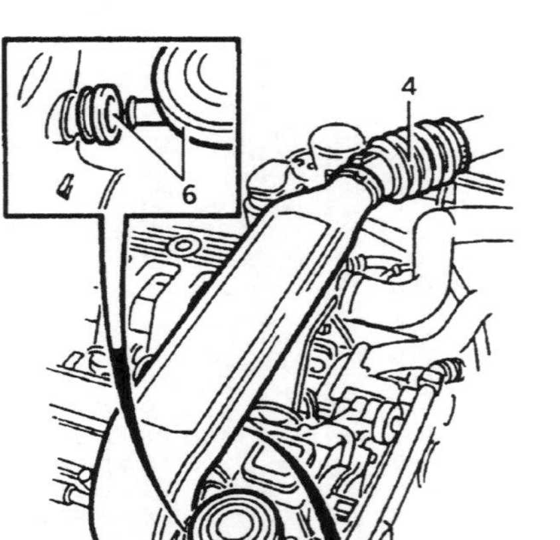

26M7018

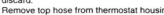

5. Release turbocharger intake hose from ducting.
6. Release breather valve from intake ducting grommet.

NOTE: Collect grommet. Refit to ducting.

7. Disengage 2 clips securing intake ducting. Remove ducting.
8. Remove 3 bolts securing intake ducting bracket and exhaust manifold heat shield to camshaft cover. Collect bracket.

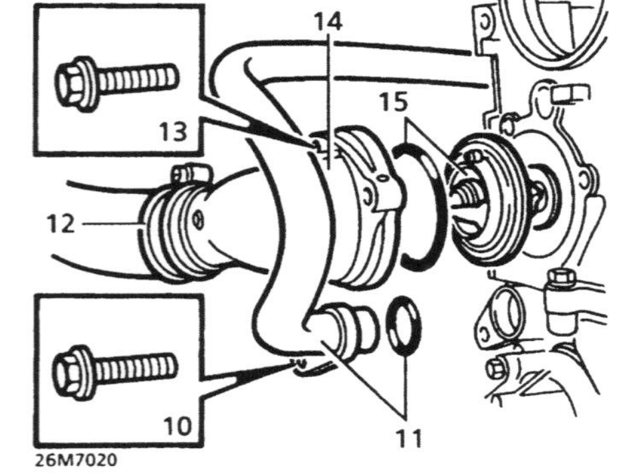

26M7019

9. Disconnect heater hose from coolant connecting pipe.
10. Remove bolt securing coolant connecting pipe to engine front cover.

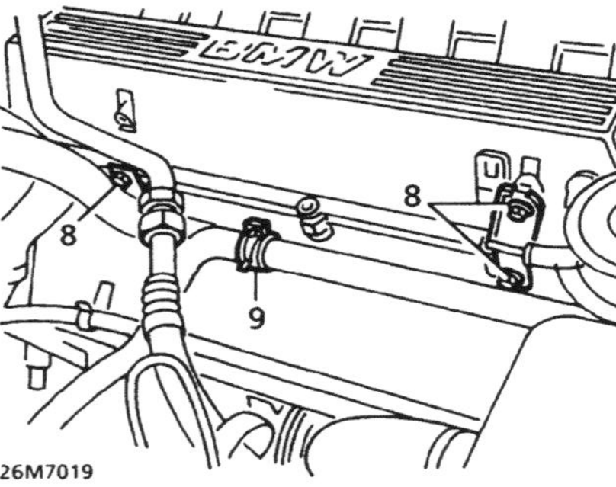

26M7020

11. Remove coolant pipe. Remove 'O' ring and discard.
12. Remove top hose from thermostat housing.
13. Remove 3 bolts securing thermostat housing to engine front cover.
14. Remove thermostat housing.
15. Collect thermostat. Remove 'O' ring and discard.

Refit

16. Lubricate new 'O' ring with clean coolant solution. Fit to thermostat.
17. Locate thermostat in housing.

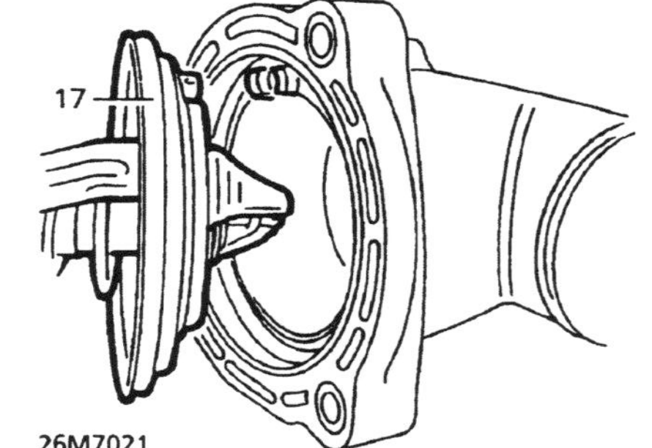

26M7021

CAUTION: Ensure that ball valve is correctly located.

18. Position thermostat and housing assembly. Secure with bolts. Tighten to ***10 Nm. (7 lbf.ft)***
19. Fit top hose to thermostat. Secure with clip.
20. Using a new 'O' ring, position coolant pipe. Engage to engine front cover.
21. Secure connecting pipe to front cover with bolt. Tighten to ***10 Nm. (7 lbf.ft)***
22. Connect heater hose. Secure with clip.
23. Align exhaust manifold heat shield. Position intake ducting bracket.
24. Secure ducting bracket and heat shield with bolts.
25. Position intake ducting. Engage clips.
26. Engage breather valve into ducting grommet.
27. Connect ducting to turbocharger intake hose. Secure with clip.
28. Connect intake hose to ducting. Secure with clip.
29. Fit cooling fan cowl. ***See this section.***
30. Remove safety stands. Lower vehicle.
31. Reconnect battery negative lead.

COOLING FAN COWL

Service repair no - 26.25.11

Remove

1. Disconnect battery negative lead.
2. Raise the vehicle.

WARNING: Support on safety stands.

3. Remove viscous coupling and fan assembly. ***See this section.***
4. Disconnect bottom hose from radiator.
5. Remove 2 clips securing cowl to radiator.
6. Remove cooling fan cowl from radiator.

Refit

7. Reverse removal procedure.

CONTENTS

Page

LAND ROVER V8

DESCRIPTION AND OPERATION

FAULT DIAGNOSIS

REPAIR

V8 cooling system component layout - up to 99MY

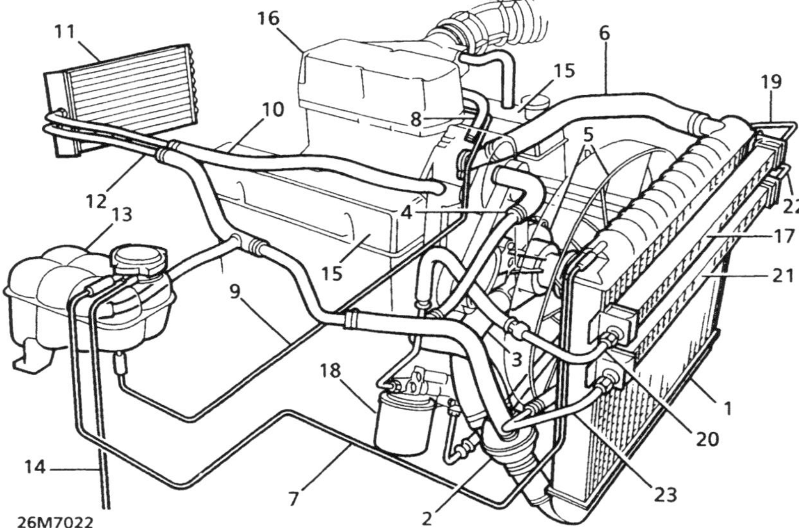

1. Radiator
2. Thermostat housing
3. Bottom hose
4. Bypass hose
5. Viscous fan and water pump
6. Radiator top hose
7. Radiator bleed pipe
8. Plenum chamber feed pipe
9. Plenum chamber bleed pipe
10. Heater feed hose
11. Heater matrix
12. Heater return hose
13. Expansion tank
14. Overflow/Breather pipe
15. Cylinder banks
16. Plenum chamber
17. Engine oil cooler
18. Engine oil filter
19. Feed pipe, engine oil cooler
20. Return pipe, engine oil cooler
21. Gearbox oil cooler
22. Feed pipe, gearbox oil cooler
23. Return pipe, gearbox oil cooler

V8 cooling system component layout - from 99MY

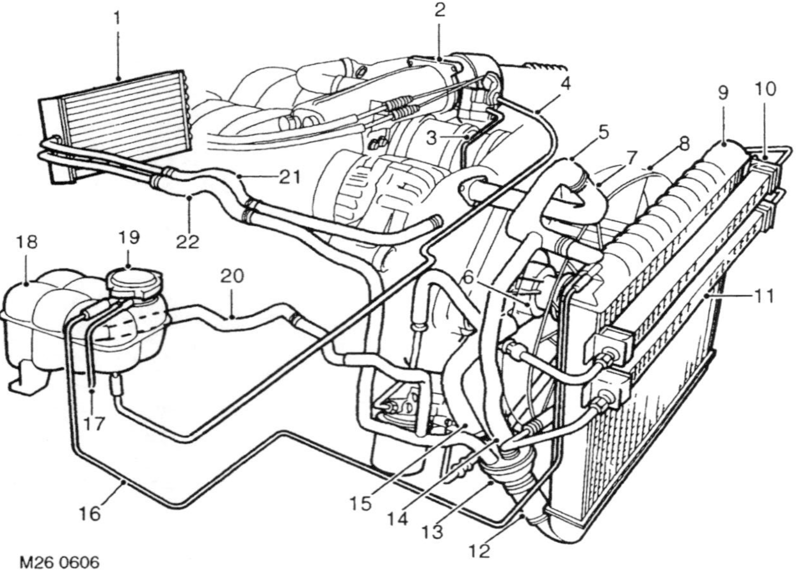

1. Heater matrix
2. Throttle housing
3. Throttle housing inlet hose
4. Throttle housing return pipe
5. Radiator top hose
6. Coolant pump
7. Manifold outlet pipe
8. Viscous fan
9. Radiator
10. Engine oil cooler
11. Gearbox oil cooler
12. Radiator bottom hose
13. Thermostat housing
14. By-pass hose
15. Coolant pump feed hose
16. Radiator bleed pipe
17. Overflow/breather pipe
18. Expansion tank
19. Pressure cap
20. Expansion hose
21. Heater inlet hose/pipe
22. Heater return hose/pipe

ENGINE COOLING - DESCRIPTION

General

The complete cooling system installed in vehicles with V8 engines incorporates three independent functions:- Engine (coolant) cooling; Engine oil cooling; Gearbox oil cooling.

Engine and gearbox oil coolers are mounted in front of the radiator and linked to their separate systems by pre-formed pipes and hoses.

The cooling system used on the V8 engine is a pressurised, by-pass type system which allows coolant to circulate around the engine block and heater matrix when the thermostat is closed. With coolant not passing through the radiator, faster heater warm-up is promoted which in turn improves passenger comfort.

A coolant pump is located in a housing at the front of the engine and is driven by a drive belt. The water pump is connected into the coolant passages cast into the cylinder block and pumps coolant from the radiator through the cylinder block and heater circuit.

A viscous fan is attached to the water pump drive pulley. The fan is secured by a left hand threaded nut to the pulley spindle. The fan draws air through the radiator to assist in cooling when the vehicle is stationary. The fan rotational speed is controlled relative to the running temperature of the engine by a thermostatic valve regulated by a bi-metallic coil.

The cooling system uses a 50/50 mix of anti-freeze and water.

Thermostat housing

A 'four way' thermostat housing, located at the bottom of the fan cowling behind the radiator, is used to link the main components within the engine cooling system. The four connections locate the radiator bottom hose, top hose, by-pass hose and coolant pump feed hose.

The plastic housing contains a wax element thermostat. The thermostat and housing are a sealed unit and cannot be replaced individually. The thermostat is used to maintain the coolant at the optimum temperature for efficient combustion and to aid engine warm-up.

The thermostat is closed at temperatures below approximately 80 °C (176 °F). When the coolant temperature reaches between 80 to 84 °C (176 to 183 °F) the thermostat starts to open and is fully open at approximately 96 °C (204 °F). In this condition the full flow of coolant is directed through the radiator.

Inlet manifold cooling connections

With the thermostat open, coolant leaves the cylinder block via an outlet pipe and top hose attached to the front of the inlet manifold. The top hose is connected to the top of the radiator.

Hot coolant from the cylinder block is also directed from the inlet manifold via pipes and hoses to the heater matrix. Coolant is circulated through the heater matrix at all times when the engine is running.

Plenum chamber - up to 99MY

The plenum chamber is heated with a supply of coolant from a supply pipe from the inlet manifold to a plate on the underside of the throttle on the plenum. The hot coolant prevents the air intake and throttle linkage from icing. A bleed pipe returns coolant from the plenum chamber to the expansion tank.

Throttle housing - from 99MY

A tapping from the inlet manifold supplies coolant to the throttle housing via a hose. The coolant circulates through a plate attached to the bottom of the throttle housing and is returned through a plastic bleed pipe to the expansion tank. The hot coolant heats the throttle housing preventing ice from forming.

ECT sensor and temperature gauge sender unit - up to 99MY

An Engine Coolant Temperature (ECT) sensor and a temperature gauge sender unit are located on the inlet manifold adjacent to the outlet pipe. The ECT sensor monitors coolant temperature emerging from the engine and sends signals relating to coolant temperature to the ECM for engine management. The temperature gauge sender unit operates the warning lamp and temperature gauge in the instrument pack. ***See FUEL SYSTEM - Engine Management, Description and operation.***

ECT sensor - from 99MY

An Engine Coolant Temperature (ECT) sensor is located on the inlet manifold adjacent to the outlet pipe. The ECT sensor monitors coolant temperature emerging from the engine and sends signals relating to coolant temperature to the ECM for engine management and to the instrument pack for temperature gauge operation. ***See FUEL SYSTEM - Engine Management, Description and operation.***

Expansion tank

The expansion tank is located in the engine compartment and attached to the right hand inner wing. The tank is made from moulded plastic and has a maximum coolant level when cold mark moulded on the side.

Excess coolant created by heat expansion is returned to the expansion tank from the bleed pipe at the top of the radiator. An outlet pipe is connected into the thermostat housing and replaces coolant displaced by heat expansion into the system when the engine is cool.

The tank is fitted with a sealed pressure cap. The cap contains a pressure relief valve which opens to allow excessive pressure and coolant to vent through the overflow pipe. The relief valve opens at a pressure of 1.4 bar (20 lbf.in) and above.

Heater matrix

The heater matrix is fitted in the distribution unit of the heating and ventilation system inside the passenger compartment. Two pipes pass through the bulkhead and provide coolant flow to and from the matrix.

The matrix is constructed from aluminium with two end tanks interconnected with tubes. Aluminium fins are located between the tubes and conduct heat away from the hot coolant flowing through the tubes. Air from the heater assembly is warmed as it passes through the matrix fins. The warm air is then distributed into the passenger compartment as required. ***See HEATING AND VENTILATION, Description and operation.***

Radiator

The radiator is located at the front of the vehicle. The vertical flow radiator is manufactured from aluminium with moulded plastic tanks at the top and bottom, interconnected with tubes. Aluminium fins are located between the tubes and conduct heat from the hot coolant flowing through the tubes, reducing the coolant temperature as it passes through the radiator. Air intake from the front of the vehicle when moving carries heat away from the fins. When the vehicle is stationary, the viscous fan draws air through the fins to prevent the engine from overheating.

Two connections at the top of the radiator provide for the attachment of the top hose and bleed pipe. A connection at the bottom of the radiator allows for the attachment of the bottom hose to the thermostat housing.

Two coolers are located in front of the cooling radiator. The upper cooler provides cooling of the engine oil and the lower cooler provides cooling for the gearbox oil.
See MANUAL GEARBOX, Description and operation.
See AUTOMATIC GEARBOX, Description and operation.
See ENGINE, Description and operation.

Pipes and hoses

The coolant circuit comprises flexible hoses and metal formed pipes which direct coolant into and out of the engine, radiator and heater matrix. Plastic pipes are used for the bleed and overflow pipes to the expansion tank.

A drain plug is fitted to each cylinder bank in the cylinder block. These are used to drain the block of coolant.

Coolant pump

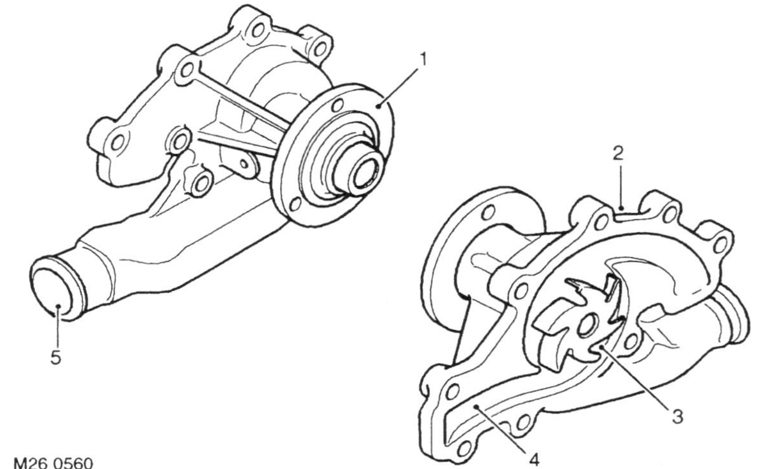

1. Pulley flange
2. Body
3. Impeller
4. Gallery
5. Inlet connection

The coolant pump is attached to the front of the cylinder block with nine bolts and sealed between the pump housing and the cylinder block with a gasket. The pump comprises a shaft which passes through an alloy housing.

The outer end of the shaft has a flange which allows for the attachment of the pump drive pulley which is secured with three bolts. The drive pulley is driven by the grooved auxiliary drive belt and rotates at the same speed as the crankshaft. The inner end of the shaft is fitted with an impeller which draws coolant from the thermostat housing and circulates it through galleries in the cylinder block and through the heater matrix.

The shaft is supported on bearings in the housing which are packed with grease and sealed for life. A seal is positioned in the housing to further protect the bearings from the ingress of coolant. The seal is manufactured from a synthetic material which will allow for the expansion of the casing when hot coolant is present.

The cast alloy housing has a hose connection which provides the attachment for the coolant pump feed hose. The housing connects with galleries in the cylinder block and distributes coolant from the pump impeller into the galleries and water jackets.

Viscous fan

The viscous drive unit for the engine cooling fan provides a means of controlling the speed of the fan relative to the temperature of the engine. The viscous fan unit is a type of fluid coupling, which drives the fan blades by means of 'silicon fluid'.

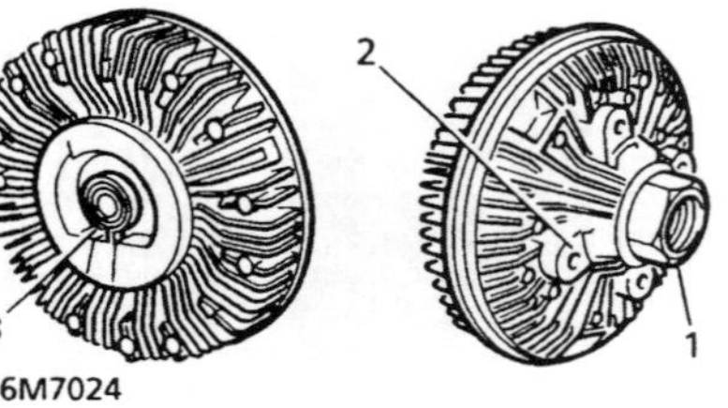

26M7024

1. Input (drive) member
2. Output (driven) member
3. Sensing mechanism (bi-metal coil)

Cooling system coolant flow - up to 99MY

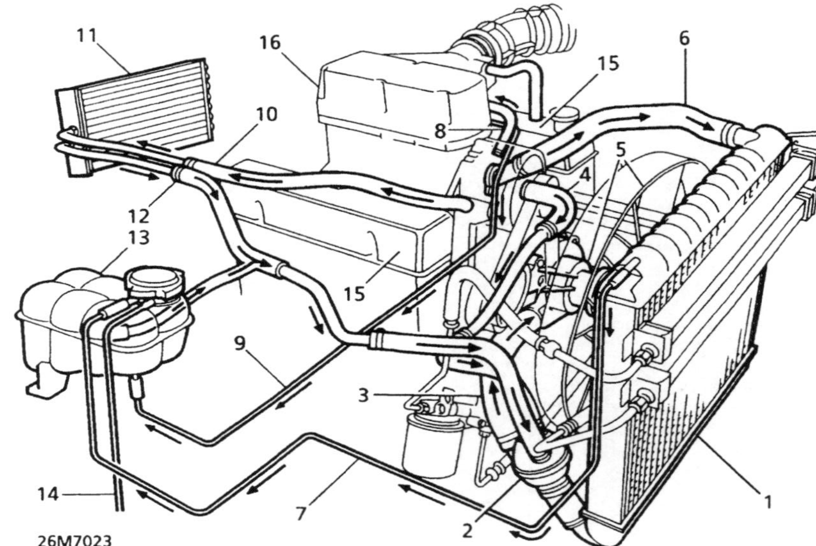

26M7023

1. Radiator
2. Thermostat housing
3. Bottom hose
4. Bypass hose
5. Viscous fan and water pump
6. Radiator top hose
7. Radiator bleed pipe
8. Plenum chamber feed pipe
9. Plenum chamber bleed pipe
10. Heater feed hose
11. Heater matrix
12. Heater return hose
13. Expansion tank
14. Overflow/breather pipe
15. Cylinder banks
16. Plenum chamber

Cooling system coolant flow - from 99MY

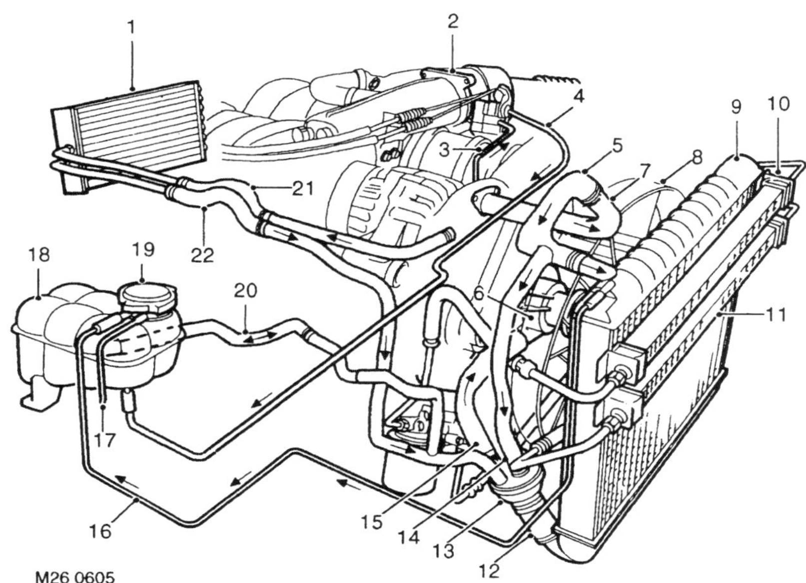

1. Heater matrix
2. Throttle housing
3. Throttle housing inlet hose
4. Throttle housing return pipe
5. Radiator top hose
6. Coolant pump
7. Manifold outlet pipe
8. Viscous fan
9. Radiator
10. Engine oil cooler
11. Gearbox oil cooler
12. Radiator bottom hose
13. Thermostat housing
14. By-pass hose
15. Coolant pump feed hose
16. Radiator bleed pipe
17. Overflow/breather pipe
18. Expansion tank
19. Pressure cap
20. Expansion hose
21. Heater inlet hose/pipe
22. Heater return hose/pipe

ENGINE COOLING - OPERATION

Coolant flow

Engine warm up - up to 99MY

When the engine is started from cold, the thermostat, integral in the housing, prevents any coolant circulation through the radiator by closing off the supply from the radiator bottom hose.

During engine warm up, the water pump moves coolant around the cylinders to the rear of the engine block and along the galleries in both cylinder banks. At the rear of the cylinder block the coolant rises through a large port in both cylinder head/block joint faces to the inlet manifold.

From the manifold, the coolant flow is divided between the by-pass hose, the heater feed hose and the plenum chamber feed pipe. The heater feed hose supplies the heater matrix, located within the distribution unit of the heating and ventilation system. The coolant is then carried, via the heater return hose, back to the thermostat housing to complete the cycle.

The heater matrix acts as a heat exchanger reducing coolant temperature as it passes through the matrix. With the thermostat closed and coolant flowing around the by-pass circuit, the cooling system is operating at maximum heater performance.

The plenum chamber is heated by a flow of coolant through the feed pipe from the inlet manifold. A bleed pipe returns the coolant from the plenum chamber across the engine to the expansion tank.

Engine hot - up to 99MY

When normal engine running temperature is reached, the main valve of the thermostat opens and a secondary valve closes the bypass port. With the thermostat open, coolant is circulated through the top hose to the radiator.

The air flowing between the tubes cools the coolant as it passes through the radiator. A controlled flow of the lower temperature coolant is drawn from the base of the radiator, through the bottom hose, by the water pump and blended with hot coolant returning from the heater matrix. Coolant circulation through cylinder block and cylinder heads to the heater matrix and plenum chamber remains the same.

Coolant is drawn from the base of the radiator, through the bottom hose, by the water pump. Coolant circulation through the cylinder block and cylinder heads to the heater matrix and plenum chamber remains the same.

An integral bleed pipe connects the top of the radiator to the expansion tank and aids bleeding of air from the coolant system. The expansion tank cap contains a pressure valve which allows excessive pressure and coolant to vent to the overflow pipe if the system has been overfilled.

Engine warm up - from 99MY

When the engine is started from cold, the thermostat, integral in the housing, prevents any coolant circulation through the radiator by closing off the supply from the radiator bottom hose.

During engine warm up, the water pump moves coolant around the cylinders to the rear of the engine block and along the galleries in both cylinder banks. At the rear of the cylinder block the coolant rises through a large port in both cylinder head/block joint faces to the inlet manifold.

From the manifold, the coolant flow is divided between the outlet pipe and the top hose by-pass connection to the thermostat housing, the heater inlet pipe and hose and the throttle housing inlet hose.

The heater inlet pipe and hose supply the heater matrix, located within the distribution unit of the heating and ventilation system. The coolant is then carried, via the heater return hose and pipe, back to the thermostat housing to complete the cycle.

The heater matrix acts as a heat exchanger reducing coolant temperature as it passes through the matrix. With the thermostat closed and coolant flowing around the by-pass circuit, the cooling system is operating at maximum heater performance.

The throttle housing inlet hose allows coolant to flow from the inlet manifold to the plate attached to the bottom of the throttle housing. A return pipe directs coolant flow from the throttle housing to the expansion tank.

Engine hot - from 99MY

When normal engine running temperature is reached, the main valve of the thermostat opens and a secondary valve closes the bypass port from the top hose. With the thermostat open, coolant is circulated through the top hose to the radiator.

The air flowing between the tubes cools the coolant as it passes through the radiator. A controlled flow of the lower temperature coolant is drawn from the base of the radiator, through the bottom hose, by the water pump and blended with hot coolant returning from the heater matrix. Coolant circulation through the cylinder block and cylinder heads to the heater matrix and throttle housing remains the same.

A bleed pipe connects the top of the radiator to the expansion tank and aids bleeding of air from the coolant system. The expansion tank cap contains a pressure valve which allows excessive pressure and coolant to vent to the overflow pipe if the system has been overfilled.

Viscous fan

There are two main components of the viscous fan drive : An input (drive) member consisting of a threaded shaft passing through a bearing into the clutch plate and secured to the water pump. An output (driven) member comprises the main body to which the fan attaches, with the temperature sensing mechanism (bi-metal coil) and pump plates.

The fan drive only has to be engaged periodically, between 5% and 10% of the time during normal driving conditions, because usually the vehicle is cooled by ram air.

A bi-metal coil senses air temperature behind the radiator. When a pre-determined temperature is reached, the coil opens a valve which allows fluid to enter the drive area. Centrifugal force circulates the fluid to the annular drive area. There are two sets of annular grooves, one in the drive clutch and the other in the drive body, a specific clearance being provided between the two sets of grooves. When this clearance is filled with viscous fluid a shearing action, caused by the speed differential between the two drive components, transmits torque to the fan. The fluid is thrown to the outside of the unit by centrifugal force from where it is then re-circulated to the reservoir via the pump plate adjacent to the drive member.

If the engine speed is increased, the amount of slip will also increase to limit the maximum fan speed.

Viscous unit disengaged (engine at normal operating temperature)

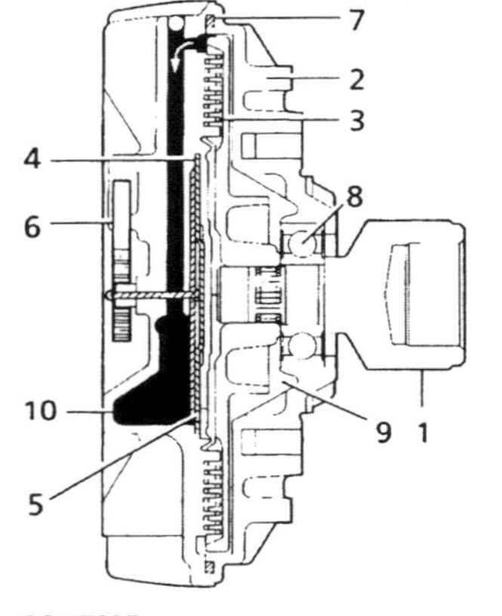

26M7025

1. Input (drive) member
2. Output (driven) member
3. Running clearance
4. Pump plate
5. Valve (closed)
6. Sensing mechanism (bi-metal coil)
7. Fluid seal
8. Bearing,input member
9. Fluid chamber
10. Fluid reservoir

Viscous unit engaged (hot running temperature)

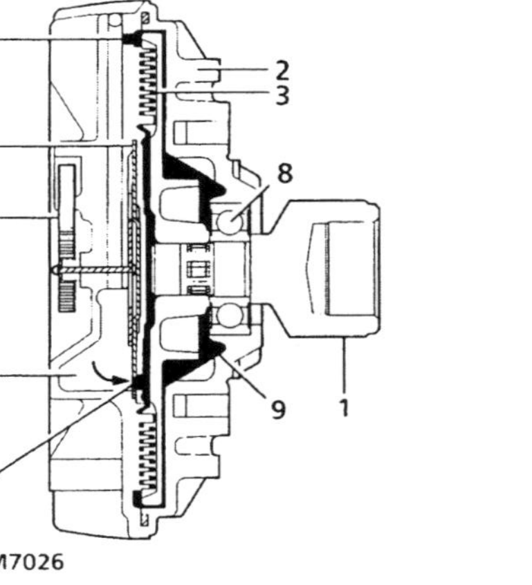

26M7026

Bi-metal coil expanded, valve open.

When the air temperature from the radiator drops sufficiently, the bi-metal coil closes the valve and prevents fluid entering the drive area, see 26M7026. The fluid that is in the drive area will gradually pump out into the reservoir and the fan will return to an idle condition.

Engine oil cooler

The engine oil cooler is located in front of the radiator above the gearbox oil cooler and comprises a single row matrix; on 4.0 litre models three internal cooling tubes are used; 4.6 litre models use a larger matrix incorporating six cooling tubes. Pre-formed feed and return pipes/hoses are used to link the cylinder block, oil filter and oil cooler. The oil cooler is mounted above the gearbox oil cooler, fixed to the radiator side frame.

Oil drawn through a steel gauze strainer in the sump, is pumped under pressure through the feed pipe into the oil cooler. Ambient air, forced through the front grille of the vehicle and assisted by the pull of the viscous fan, is dispersed across the oil cooler. The cooled oil then passes through the return pipe to the filter, before being distributed from the cylinder block to the various internal engine components.

Engine oil cooler - up to 99MY shown

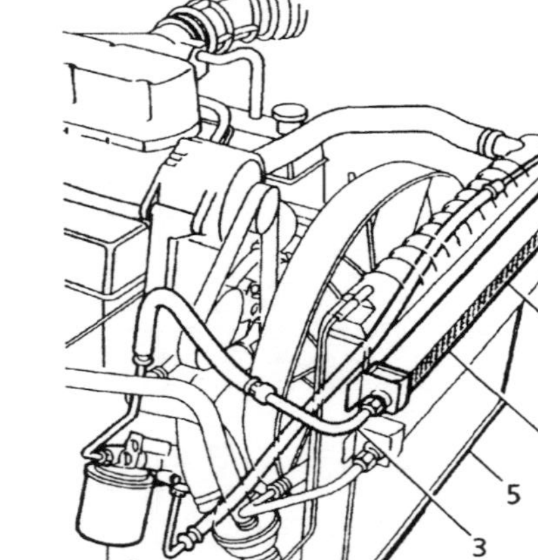
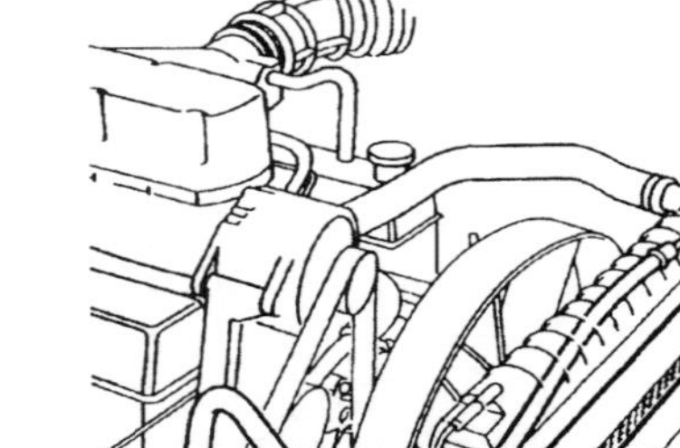

26M7027

1. Engine oil cooler
2. Feed pipe
3. Return pipe
4. Oil filter
5. Radiator
6. Gearbox oil cooler

Gearbox oil cooler

The gearbox oil cooler is located below the engine oil cooler in front of the radiator and comprises a single row matrix. On vehicles fitted with manual gearboxes three internal cooling tubes are used, on vehicles with automatic transmission a larger matrix, incorporating twelve coolant tubes is fitted. Pre-formed feed and return pipes/hoses are used to link the gearbox and oil cooler.

Oil is pumped under pressure from the gearbox through the feed pipe into the oil cooler. Ambient air, forced through the front grille of the vehicle and assisted by the pull of the viscous fan, is dispersed over the oil cooler. The cooled oil then passes through the return pipe, which is routed under the engine to run parallel with the feed pipe back to the LH side of the gearbox.

Gearbox oil cooler - up to 99MY shown

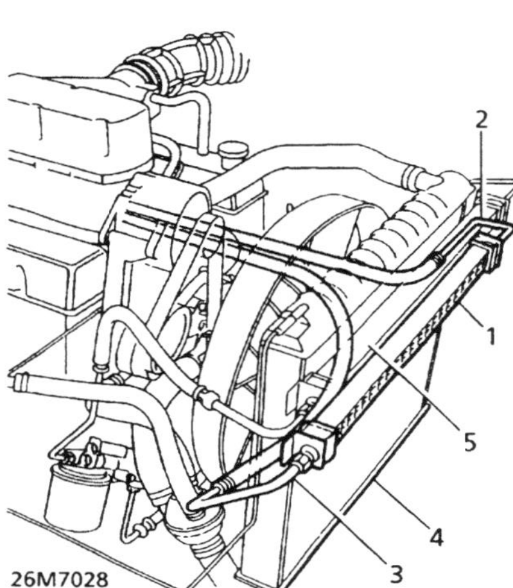

1. Gearbox oil cooler
2. Feed pipe
3. Return pipe
4. Radiator
5. Engine oil cooler

COOLING SYSTEM FAULTS

This section covers mechanical faults that could occur in the complete cooling system :

1. Engine (coolant) cooling;
2. Engine oil cooling;
3. Gearbox oil cooling.

Before conducting any visual checks within the separate systems and undertaking detailed diagnosis procedures. ***See Description and operation.***

1. ENGINE (COOLANT) COOLING SYSTEM

Symptom - Engine Overheating

POSSIBLE CAUSE	REMEDY
1. Engine coolant low.	1. Allow engine to cool. Top up expansion tank to correct level, with engine running at idle. Check cooling system for leaks and rectify, if necessary.
2. Loose drive belt.	2. Check/renew drive belt tensioner or renew drive belt. ***See ELECTRICAL, Repair.***
3. Coolant in radiator frozen.	3. Slowly thaw and drain cooling system. ***See Repair.***
4. Air flow through radiator restricted or blocked.	4. Apply air pressure to engine side of radiator to clear obstruction. If mud or dirt is evident, carefully use a hose.
5. External leaks from water pump, engine gaskets, thermostat housing or pipe/hoses.	5. Check for visual causes and rectify.
6. Viscous fan not operating correctly or inoperative.	6. Renew viscous fan unit. ***See Repair.***
7. Thermostat seized in closed position.	7. Check radiator bottom hose for coolant flow through radiator. If cold a faulty thermostat is confirmed. Renew thermostat housing assembly. ***See Repair.***

Symptom - Engine Overheating, continued

POSSIBLE CAUSE	REMEDY
8. Air in cooling system.	8. Check coolant level. Run engine at fast idle (approximately 2,000 rpm) with expansion tank cap off. Top up coolant level with engine at idle and refit expansion tank cap.
9. Air conditioning condenser fans not operating correctly or inoperative.	9. ***See AIR CONDITIONING, Fault diagnosis.***
10. Temperature gauge or sender unit giving inaccurate readings.	10. Substitute parts and compare new readings.
11. Coolant leakage across cylinder head gasket.	11. Carry out cylinder pressure test to determine if pressure is leaking into cooling system, causing over pressurising and loss of coolant. Renew cylinder head gasket.
12. Engine oil contamination of cooling system due to leaking.	12. Renew cylinder head gasket. ***See ENGINE, Repair.***
13. Coolant contamination of lubrication system.	13. Renew inlet manifold or front cover gaskets. ***See MANIFOLD AND EXHAUST SYSTEM, Repair.*** or ***See ENGINE, Repair.***

Symptom - Engine Runs Cold

POSSIBLE CAUSE	REMEDY
1. Thermostat seized in open or partially open position.	1. Remove thermostat housing and check operation of thermostat. Renew, if necessary. ***See Repair.***
2. Temperature gauge or sender unit giving inaccurate readings.	2. Substitute parts and compare new readings.
3. Viscous fan not operating correctly.	3. Renew viscous fan unit. ***See Repair.***
4. Air conditioning condenser fans operating continuously.	4. Refer to **TestBook** .

2. ENGINE OIL COOLING SYSTEM

Symptom - Engine Oil Overheating

POSSIBLE CAUSE	REMEDY
1. Air flow through oil cooler matrix restricted or blocked.	1. Apply air pressure to engine side of radiator to clear obstruction. If mud or dirt is evident, carefully use a hose.
2. Blocked or damaged oil cooler or pipe/hoses restricting engine oil flow.	2. Check for visual damage and renew components where necessary.
3. Oil cooler relief valve seized in closed position.	3. Remove and check relief valve. Renew, if necessary.

3. GEARBOX OIL COOLING SYSTEM

SYMPTOM - Gearbox Oil Overheating

POSSIBLE CAUSE	REMEDY
1. Air flow through oil cooler matrix restricted or blocked.	1. Apply air pressure to engine side of radiator to clear obstruction. If mud or dirt is evident, carefully use a hose.
2. Damaged oil cooler or pipe/hoses restricting gearbox oil flow.	2. Check for visual damage and renew components where necessary.
3. Vehicle being driven in wrong gear.	3. Advise owner/driver accordingly.

NOTE: Critical warning messages relating to the complete cooling system are displayed on the message centre in the lower section of the instrument pack, should a fault occur in any of the separate systems.

Notes

COOLANT - DRAIN AND REFILL

Service repair no - 26.10.01

Drain

WARNING: Do not remove expansion tank filler cap when engine is hot. The cooling system is pressurised. Personal scalding could result.

1. Raise the vehicle.

WARNING: Support on safety stands.

2. Remove expansion tank filler cap to assist draining.

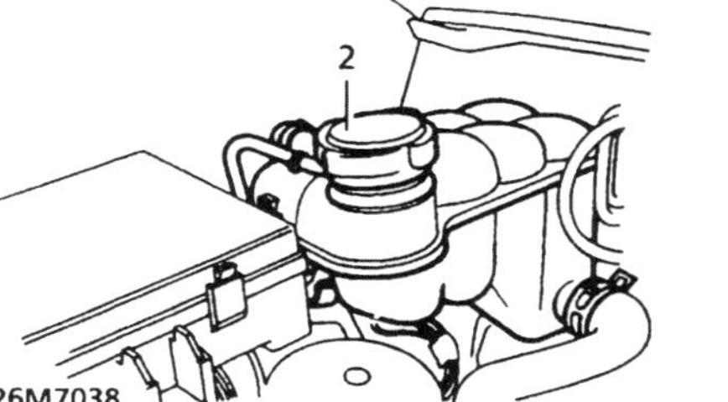

26M7038

3. Position container beneath radiator.
4. Remove plug from base of radiator. Allow coolant to drain.

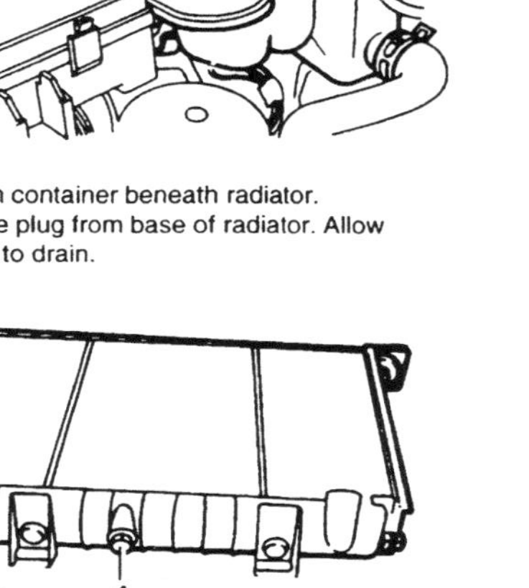

26M7039

5. If system is only being partially drained, continue at **Refill.**
6. Reposition container. Remove LH cylinder block drain plug. Allow coolant to drain.

26M7040

NOTE: Do not remove RH cylinder block drain plug.

7. Clean drain plug threads. Apply a coating of 'Loctite 577'. Refit plug to block. Tighten securely.

Refill

8. Ensure sufficient coolant solution is available. ***See LUBRICANTS, FLUIDS AND CAPACITIES, Information.***
9. Inspect radiator drain plug 'O' ring, renew if required.
10. Fit drain plug to radiator. Tighten to ***Max 6 Nm. (4 lbf.ft)***
11. Remove safety stands. Lower vehicle.
12. Disconnect radiator bleed hose at the radiator.
13. Blow through hose to clear any residual coolant. Reconnect hose.

CAUTION: If radiator bleed hose is not cleared of coolant, air may become trapped at top of radiator during refill, leading to subsequent engine overheating.

14. Fill expansion tank until coolant is level with base of neck.
15. Start engine, continue filling at expansion tank until coolant level stabilises at the 'COLD LEVEL' marking.
16. Run the engine until the thermostat opens (top hose becomes warm).
17. Stop engine, allow to cool.
18. Check coolant level, top-up as necessary.
19. Refit expansion tank filler cap.

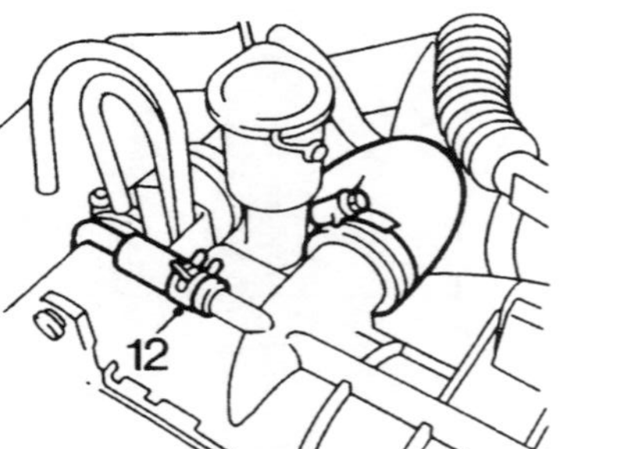

26M7013A

RADIATOR

Service repair no - 26.40.04

Remove

1. Disconnect battery negative lead.
2. Raise the vehicle.

WARNING: Support on safety stands.

3. Drain cooling system. ***See this section.***
4. Release clips securing upper cooling fan cowl. Remove cowl.

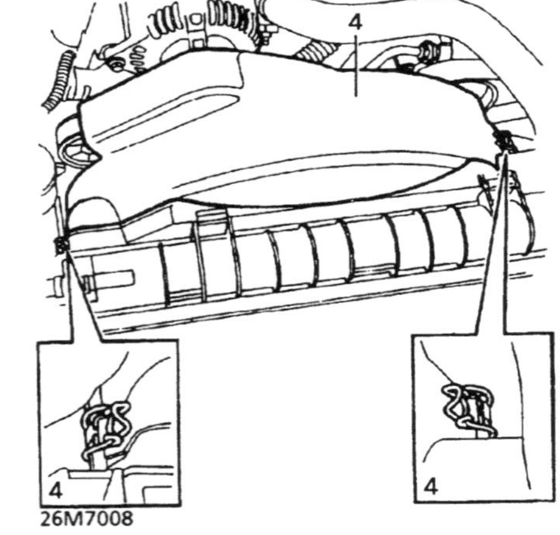

26M7008

5. Release top hose from radiator.
6. Release expansion tank hose from radiator.

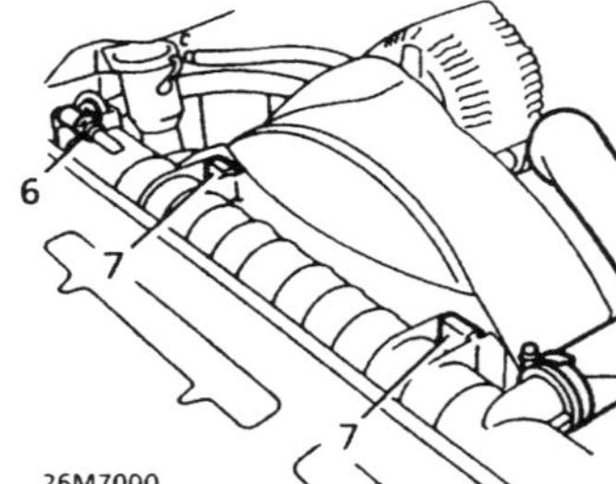

26M7000

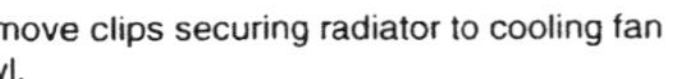

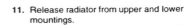

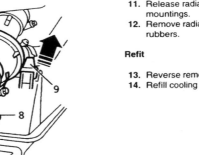

7. Remove clips securing radiator to cooling fan cowl.

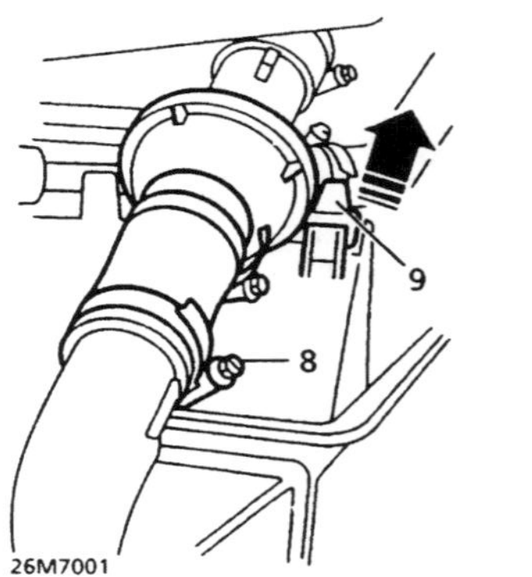

26M7001

8. Slacken bottom hose clips at radiator and thermostat housing.
9. Release thermostat housing from fan cowl. Remove bottom hose.
10. Remove 2 bolts securing radiator to mounting bracket.

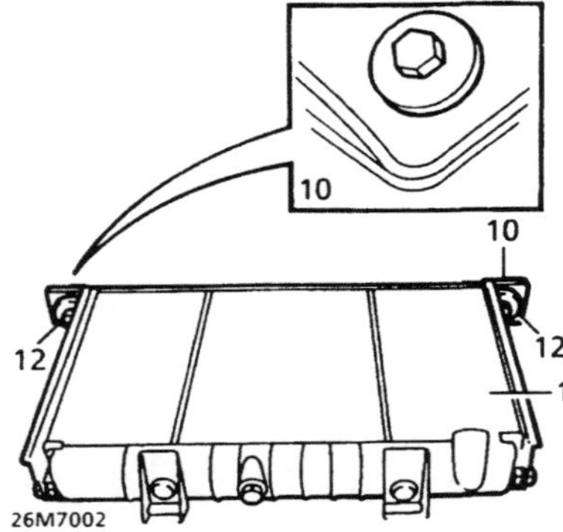

26M7002

11. Release radiator from upper and lower mountings.
12. Remove radiator. Collect lower mounting rubbers.

Refit

13. Reverse removal procedure.
14. Refill cooling system. ***See this section.***

VISCOUS COUPLING AND FAN ASSEMBLY - UP TO 99MY

Service repair no - 26.25.19

Special tools:
LRT-12-093
LRT-12-094 - Viscous coupling removal

Remove

1. Disconnect battery negative lead.

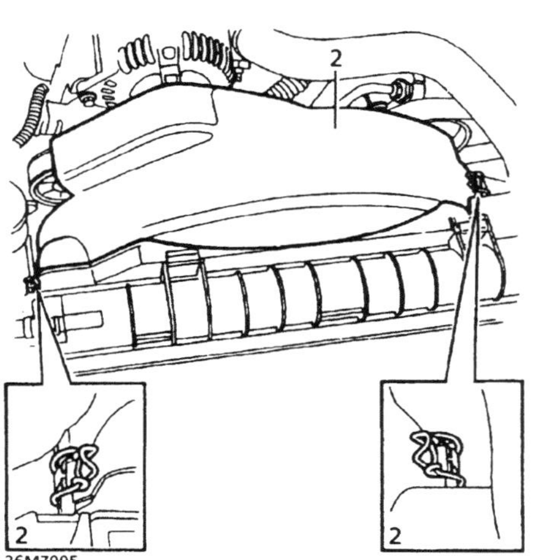

26M7005

2. Release 2 clips securing cooling fan upper cowl. Remove cowl.

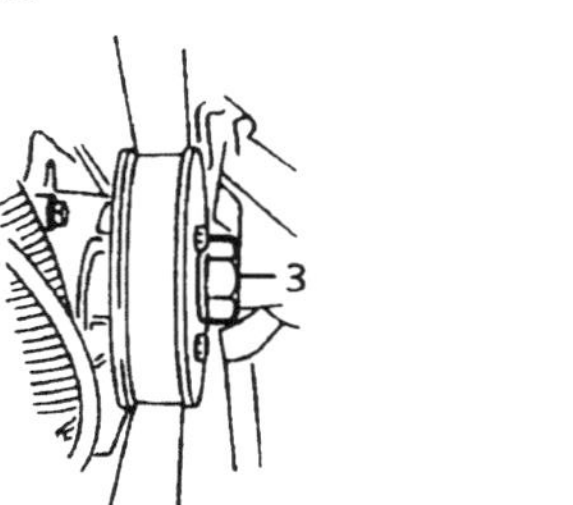

26M7006

3. Using LRT-12-093 and LRT-12-094 unscrew viscous coupling from water pump.

NOTE: Viscous coupling is secured with a RH thread.

4. Remove fan and coupling assembly.

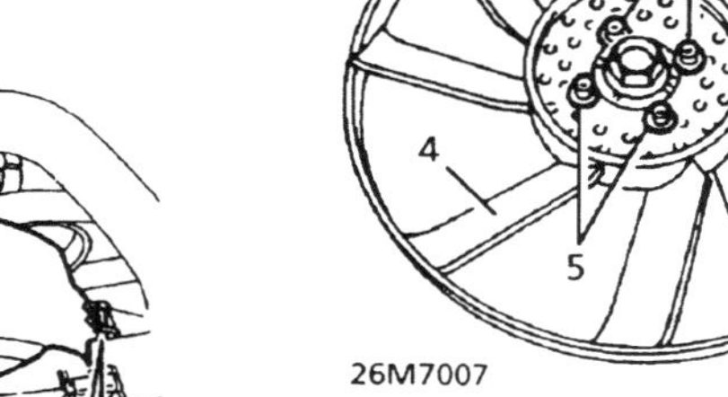

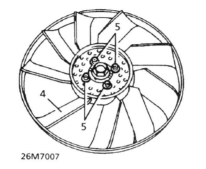

26M7007

Do not carry out further dismantling if component is removed for access only.

5. Remove 4 bolts securing coupling to fan. Remove coupling.

Refit

6. Ensure mating faces are clean.
7. Fit fan to coupling. Secure with bolts. Tighten to ***24 Nm. (18 lbf.ft)***
8. Using LRT-12-093 and LRT-12-094, fit fan assembly to pump. Tighten to ***56 Nm. (41 lbf.ft.)***
9. Fit cooling fan upper cowl. Secure with clips.
10. Reconnect battery negative lead.

VISCOUS COUPLING AND FAN ASSEMBLY - FROM 99MY

Service repair no - 26.25.19

Remove

1. Release fixings and remove battery cover.
2. Disconnect battery earth lead.

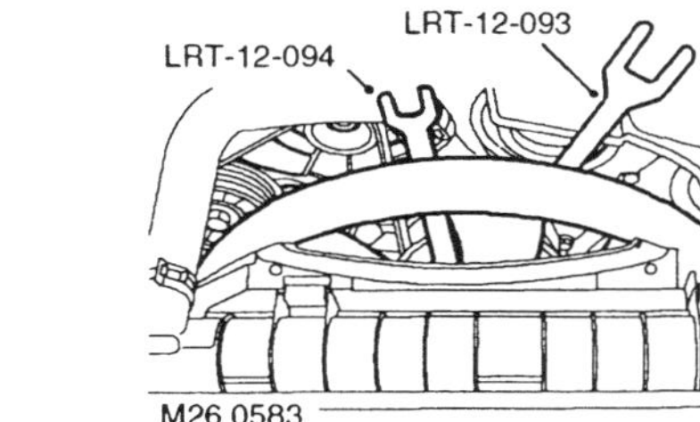

M26 0581

3. Remove bolt securing washer reservoir filler tube support bracket to radiator bracket.

M26 0582

4. Release 2 clips securing fan cowl and remove fan cowl.

M26 0583

5. Remove cooling fan using LRT-12-093 andLRT-12-094.

Refit

6. Position cooling fan and tighten using LRT-12-093 andLRT-12-094.
7. Fit fan cowl and secure with clips.
8. Align washer reservoir filler tube bracket and secure with bolt.
9. Connect battery earth lead.
10. Fit battery cover and secure with fixings.

WATER PUMP - UP TO 99MY

Service repair no - 26.50.01

Remove

1. Drain cooling system. ***See this section.***
2. Remove cooling fan. ***See this section.***
3. Slacken water pump pulley bolts.

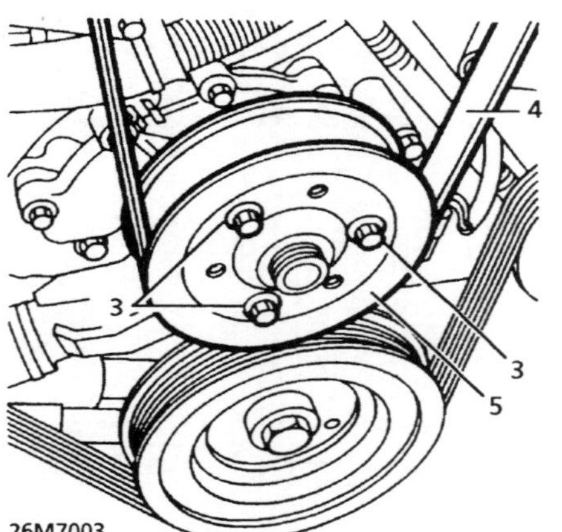

26M7003

4. Release tension from water pump drive belt. Remove belt.
5. Remove water pump pulley.

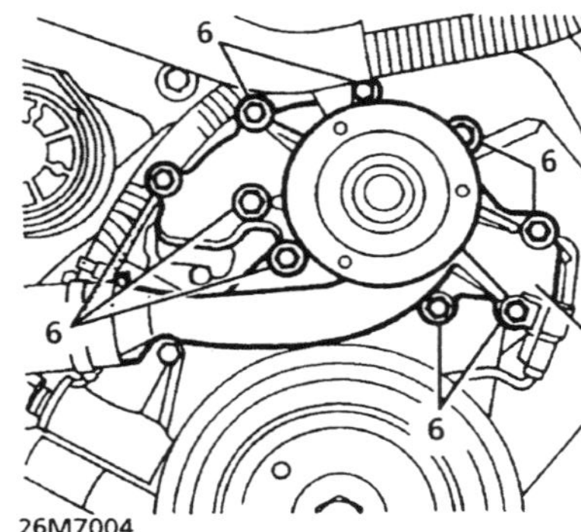

26M7004

6. Remove 9 bolts securing water pump.
7. Remove water pump and gasket.

Refit

8. Ensure mating faces are clean.
9. Fit water pump with new gasket.
10. Position water pump. Secure with bolts. Tighten to ***22 Nm. (16 lbf.ft)***
11. Fit water pump pulley. Secure with bolts. Tighten to ***22 Nm. (16 lbf.ft)***
12. Fit water pump drive belt.
13. Fit cooling fan. ***See this section.***
14. Fill cooling system. ***See this section.***

WATER PUMP - FROM 99MY

Service repair no - 26.50.01

Remove

1. Drain cooling system. ***See this section.***

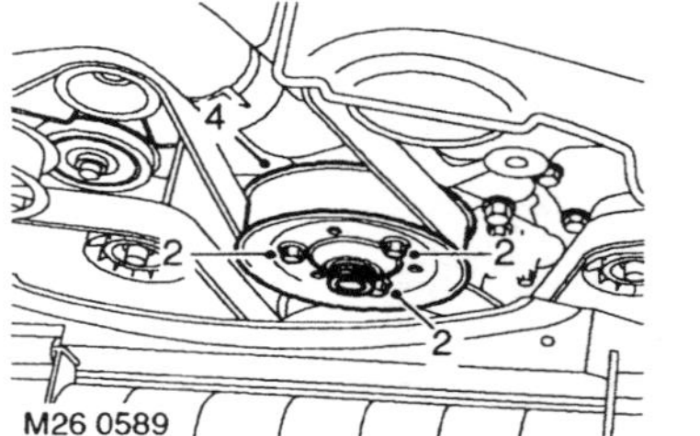

M26 0589

2. Loosen 3 bolts securing water pump pulley to water pump.
3. Remove auxiliary drive belt. ***See ELECTRICAL, Repair.***
4. Remove 3 bolts securing pulley to water pump and remove pulley.

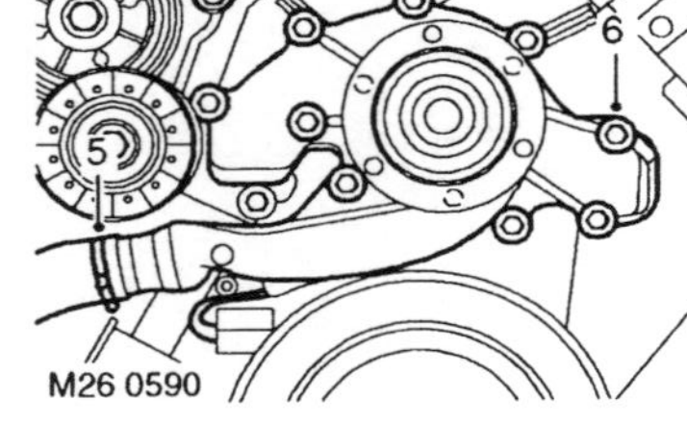

M26 0590

5. Release clip and disconnect coolant hose from water pump.
6. Remove 9 bolts securing water pump, remove water pump and discard gasket.

Refit

7. Clean water pump and mating face.
8. Fit new gasket and water pump, tighten bolts to ***24 Nm (18 lbf.ft).***
9. Connect coolant hose to water pump and secure with clip.
10. Ensure mating faces of water pump pulley and flange are clean, fit pulley and tighten bolts to ***22 Nm (17 lbf.ft).***
11. Fit auxiliary drive belt. ***See ELECTRICAL, Repair.***
12. Refill cooling system. ***See this section.***

THERMOSTAT - UP TO 99MY

Service repair no - 26.45.01

Remove

1. Disconnect battery earth lead.
2. Raise vehicle on 4 post ramp.
3. Remove engine acoustic cover (if applicable). ***See CHASSIS AND BODY, Repair.***
4. Drain cooling system. ***See this section.***

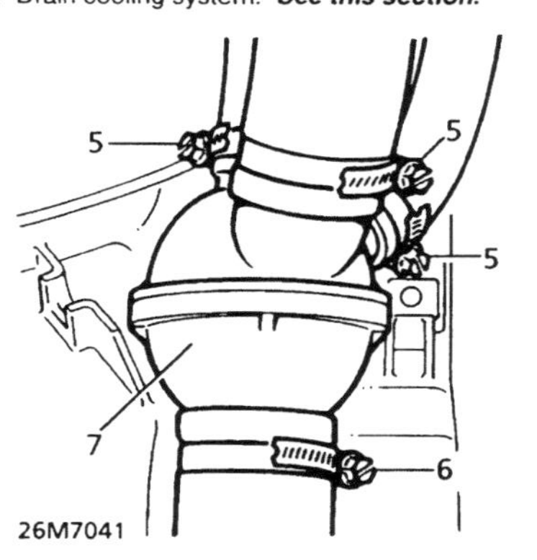

26M7041

5. Loosen 3 upper hose clips and disconnect 3 hoses from top of thermostat housing.
6. Loosen lower hose clip and disconnect hose from bottom of thermostat housing.
7. Release 2 clips securing thermostat to housing radiator cowl and remove thermostat housing.

Refit

8. Position thermostat housing and connect to radiator hose.
9. Connect hoses to top of thermostat housing.
10. Tighten clips securing hoses to thermostat housing.
11. Engage thermostat housing to radiator cowl clips.
12. Fill coolant system. ***See this section.***
13. Fit engine acoustic cover (if applicable). ***See CHASSIS AND BODY, Repair.***

THERMOSTAT - FROM 99MY

Service repair no - 26.45.09

Remove

1. Drain cooling system. ***See this section.***
2. Remove cooling fan. ***See this section.***

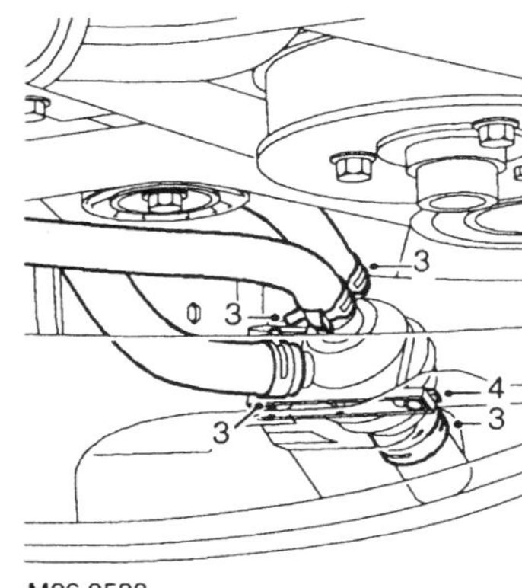

M26 0588

3. Release 3 clips and disconnect coolant hoses from thermostat.
4. Release clip securing thermostat to fan cowl and remove thermostat.

Refit

5. Position thermostat and secure to cowl.
6. Fit hoses to thermostat and secure with clips.
7. Fit cooling fan. ***See this section.***
8. Fill cooling system. ***See this section.***

EXPANSION TANK

Service repair no - 26.15.01

NOTE: This operation covers all models

Remove

1. Position container to collect coolant spillage.
2. Disconnect heater hose and radiator bleed hose from expansion tank.

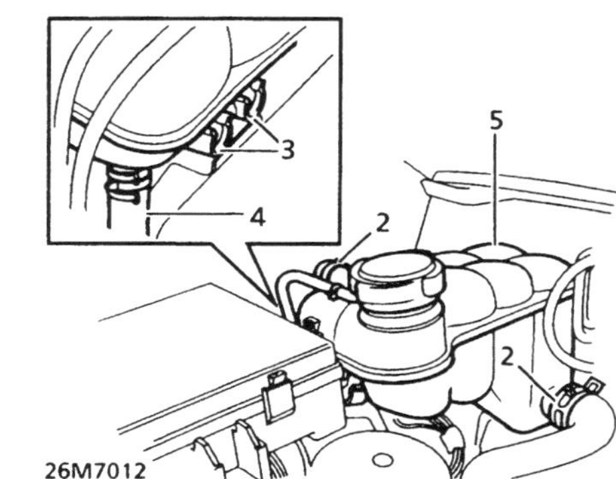

26M7012

3. Release expansion tank from clips.
4. **Petrol only:** Disconnect throttle housing coolant bleed hose from expansion tank.
5. Remove expansion tank.

Refit

6. Reverse removal procedure.
7. Check and top up cooling system.

CONTENTS

EXHAUST MANIFOLD GASKETS - V8 - UP TO 99MY

Service repair no - 30.15.16 - Right Hand
Service repair no - 30.15.17 - Left Hand

1. Disconnect battery negative lead.
2. Raise vehicle on four post lift.
3. Remove 3 nuts securing each front pipe flange to exhaust manifold.

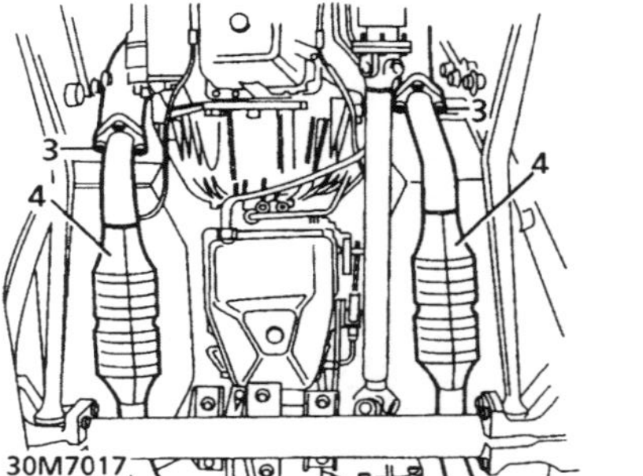

4. Release front pipe from exhaust manifolds. Collect gaskets.
5. Lower lift.

NOTE: Instructions 6 to 11 apply to *Left Hand Manifold Only*

6. Release intake hose from plenum chamber.

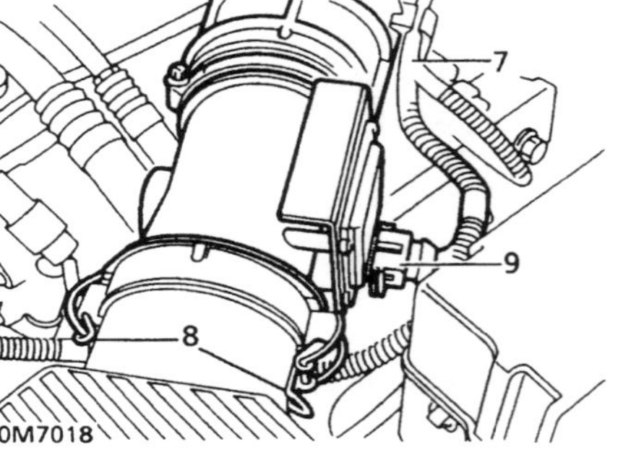

7. Release harness from intake hose clip.
8. Release 2 clips securing air flow meter to air cleaner. Release meter. Collect 'O' ring.
9. Disconnect multiplug from air flow meter. Remove meter.
10. Release purge hose from ram pipe housing.
11. Remove purge valve securing bolt from shock absorber turret. Place valve aside.

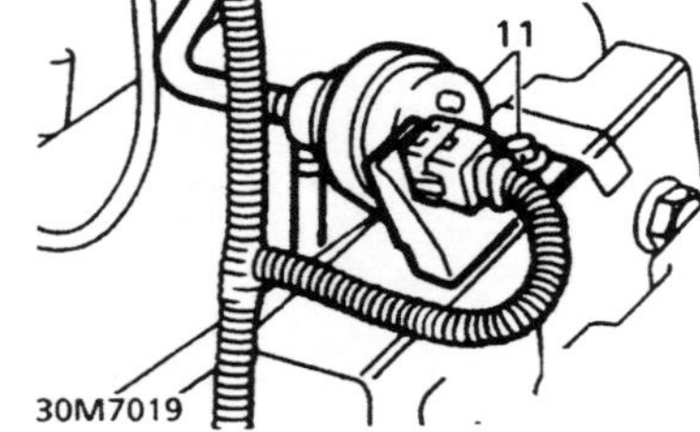

NOTE: Instructions 12,13 & 14 apply to *Right Hand Manifold Only.*

12. Release spark plug caps. Release H.T. leads from clips on rocker cover. Place leads aside.

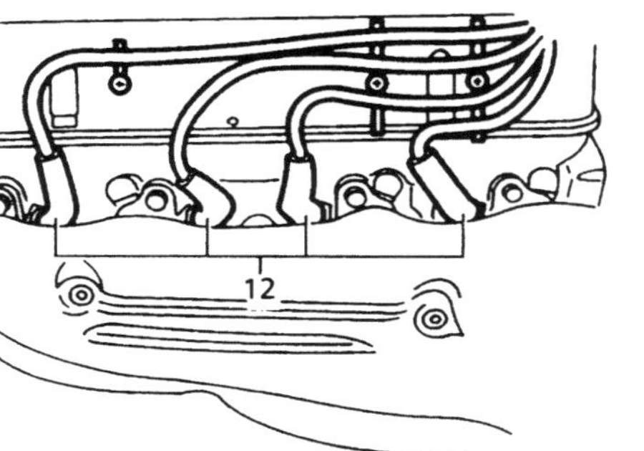

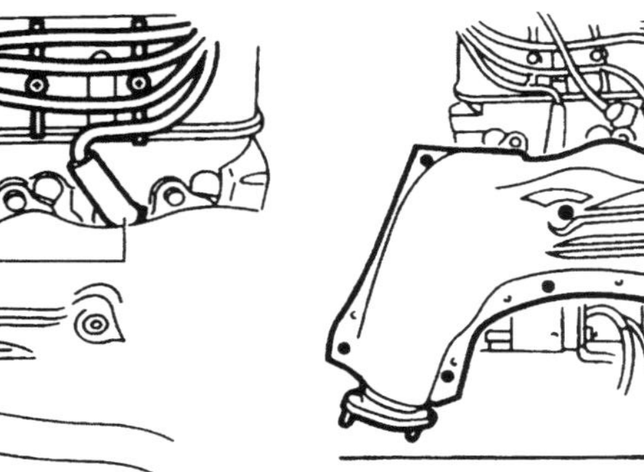

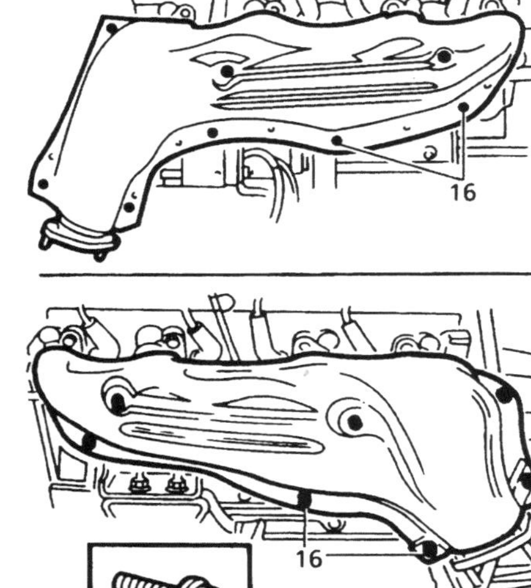

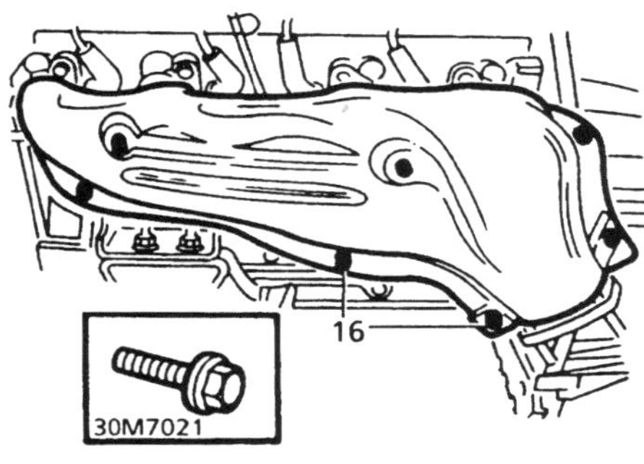

30M7020

13. Remove screw securing H.T. lead clip to rocker cover. Remove clip.
14. Unscrew RH shock absorber top mounting bolt to provide additional clearance for heat shield removal.

NOTE: Do not remove bolt.

15. Right Hand Drive - Right Hand Manifold Only. Remove intermediate steering shaft. ***See STEERING, Repair.***
16. Remove 8 bolts (RH manifold) or 7 bolts (LH manifold) securing outer heat shield to manifold. Remove heat shield.

17. Remove 8 bolts securing exhaust manifold to cylinder head. Remove manifold. Collect gaskets.

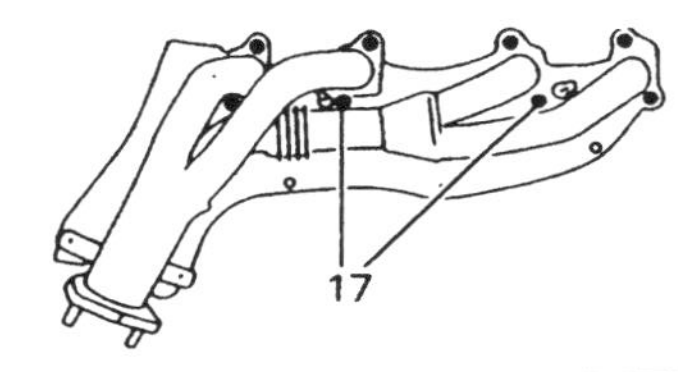

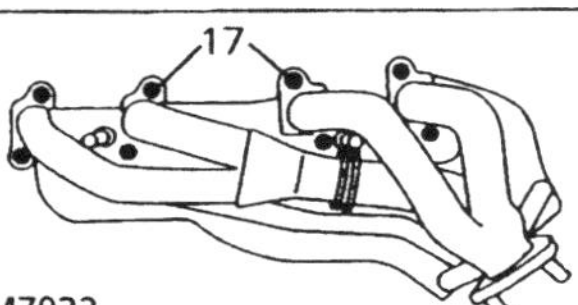

30M7022

Refit

18. Ensure mating faces are clean.
19. Position manifold on cylinder head. Align new gaskets.
20. Secure manifold with bolts. Tighten to ***55 Nm. (40 lbf.ft)*** in sequence shown.

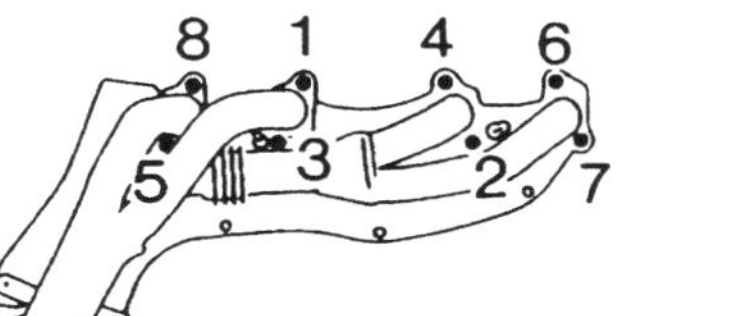

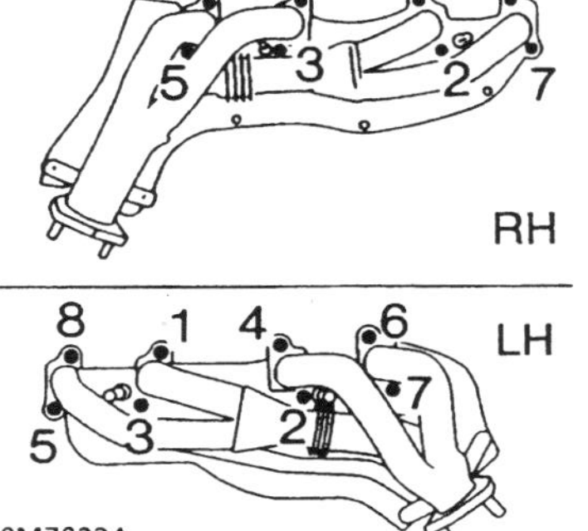

30M7022A

21. Fit outer heat shield. Secure with bolts. Tighten to ***8 Nm. (6 lbf.ft)***
22. Position purge valve on shock absorber turret. Secure with bolt.
23. Connect purge hose to ram pipe housing.
24. Fit air flow meter/hose assembly to plenum chamber. Secure with clip.
25. Connect multiplug to air flow meter.
26. Fit 'O' ring to air flow meter. Secure meter to air cleaner with clips.
27. Engage harness in intake hose clip.
28. Tighten RH shock absorber top mounting bolt to ***85 Nm. (63 lbf.ft)***
29. Position H.T. lead clip on rocker cover. Secure with screw.
30. Route H.T. leads. Secure in clips. Connect plug caps.
31. If removed, fit intermediate steering shaft. ***See STEERING, Repair.***
32. Raise lift.
33. Fit new gasket to front pipe. Position pipe to exhaust manifold. Secure with nuts. Tighten to ***50 Nm. (37 lbf.ft)***
34. Reconnect battery negative lead.

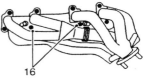

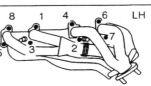

EXHAUST MANIFOLD GASKETS - V8 - FROM 99MY

Service repair no - 30.15.16 - Right Hand
Service repair no - 30.15.17 - Left Hand

1. Release 3 fixings and remove battery cover.
2. Disconnect battery negative lead.
3. Raise vehicle on four post lift.

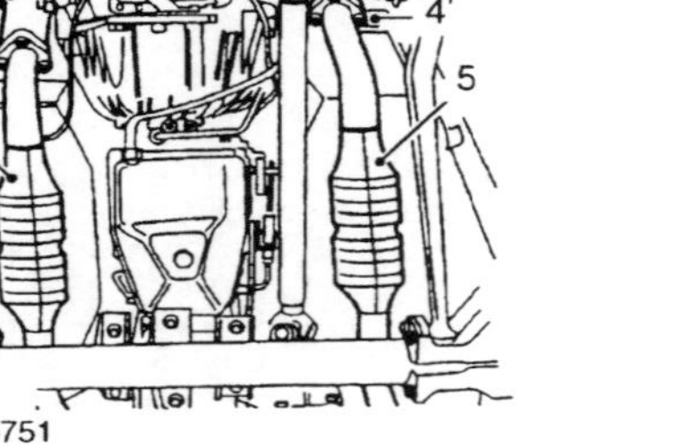

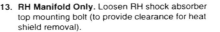

M30 0751

4. Remove 3 nuts securing each front pipe flange to exhaust manifold.
5. Release front pipe from exhaust manifold. Collect gaskets.
6. Lower lift.

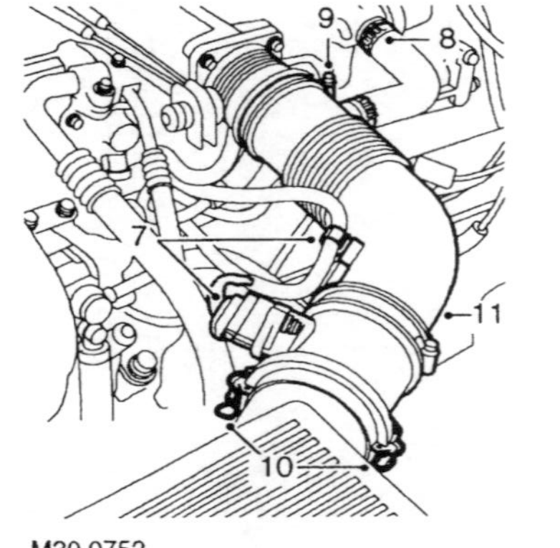

M30 0752

7. Disconnect multiplug from MAF sensor and release harness from clip on air intake hose.
8. Release clip and disconnect hose from IAC valve.
9. Loosen clip and disconnect air intake hose from throttle body.
10. Release two clips securing MAF sensor to air cleaner.
11. Remove MAF sensor and hose assembly. Collect 'O' ring.

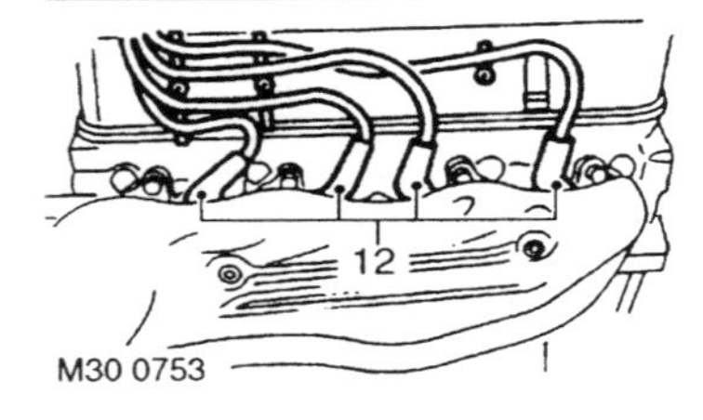

M30 0753

12. Release spark plug caps. Release H.T. leads from clips on rocker cover. Place leads aside.

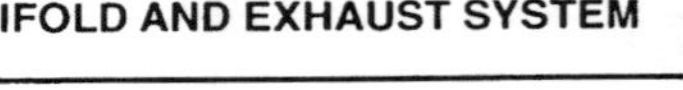

13. **RH Manifold Only.** Loosen RH shock absorber top mounting bolt (to provide clearance for heat shield removal).

NOTE: Do not remove bolt.

14. **RHD, RH Manifold Only.** Remove steering column intermediate shaft. ***See STEERING, Repair.***

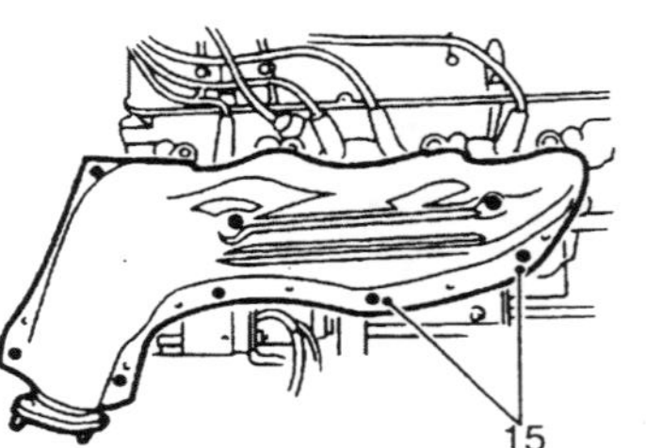

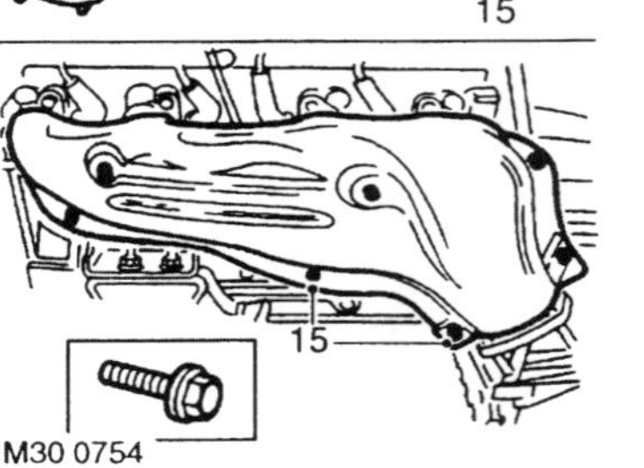

M30 0754

15. Remove 8 (RH exhaust manifold) or 7 (LH exhaust manifold) bolts securing outer heat shield to manifold. Remove heat shield.

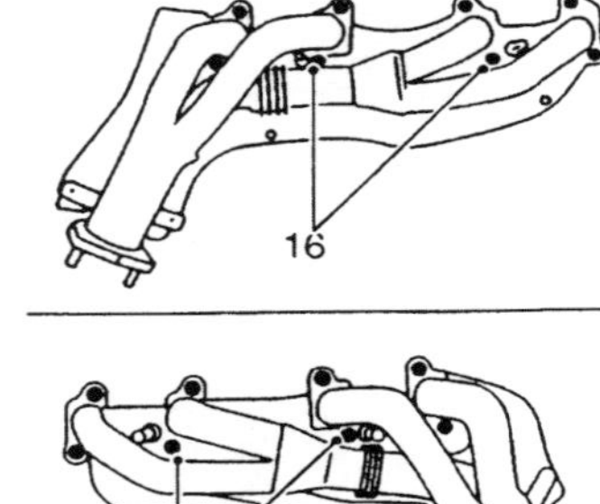

M30 0755

16. Remove 8 bolts securing exhaust manifold to cylinder head. Remove exhaust manifold and collect gaskets.

Refit

17. Ensure mating faces are clean.
18. Position manifold on cylinder head. Align new gaskets.

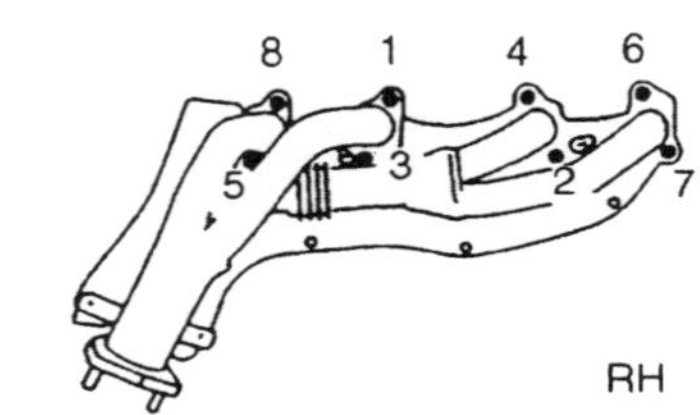

M30 0756

19. Secure manifold with bolts. Tighten to ***55 Nm (40 lbf.ft)*** in sequence shown.

20. Fit outer heat shield. Secure with bolts. Tighten to ***8 Nm (6 lbf.ft).***
21. Fit MAF sensor and hose assembly to throttle body. Secure with clip.
22. Fit 'O' ring to MAF sensor. Secure MAF sensor to air cleaner with clips.
23. Connect multiplug to MAF sensor. Engage harness in clip on air intake hose.
24. **RH Manifold Only.** Tighten RH shock absorber top mounting bolt to ***85 Nm (63 lbf.ft).***
25. Route H.T. leads. Secure in clips. Connect plug caps.
26. **RHD, RH Manifold Only.** Fit steering column intermediate shaft. ***See STEERING, Repair.***
27. Raise lift.
28. Fit new gasket to front pipe. Position pipe to exhaust manifold. Secure with nuts. Tighten to ***50 Nm (37 lbf.ft).***
29. Reconnect battery negative lead.
30. Fit battery cover and secure with fixings.

EXHAUST MANIFOLD GASKETS - DIESEL

Service repair no - 30.15.12

Remove

1. Disconnect battery negative lead.
2. Raise the vehicle.

WARNING: Support on safety stands.

3. Remove heat shield. ***See this section.***
4. Remove 3 bolts securing turbocharger to exhaust manifold. Collect gasket and discard.

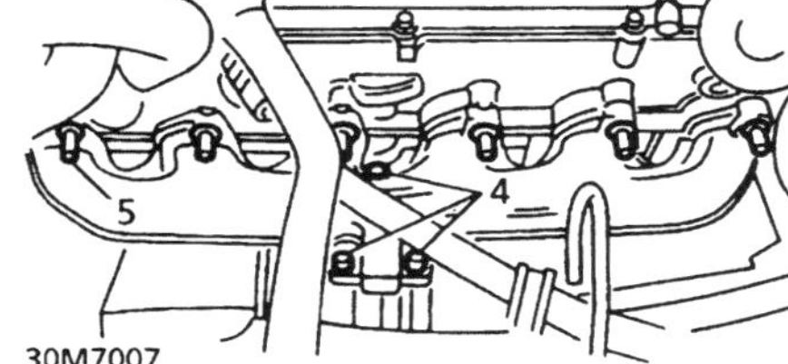

30M7007

5. Remove 12 nuts and flat washers securing exhaust manifold to cylinder head. *Vehicles with EGR:* Remove 2 bolts securing EGR pipe flange to manifold. Position pipe aside.
6. Remove exhaust manifold. Collect gaskets and discard.

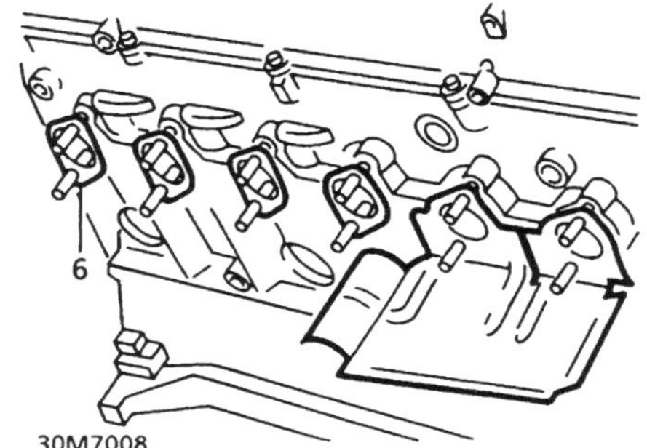

30M7008

NOTE: The gasket fitted to No. 1 & 2 exhaust ports acts as a turbocharger heat shield.

Refit

7. Ensure mating faces are clean.
8. Position new gaskets and turbocharger heat shield to cylinder head studs. Ensure tabs face outwards.
9. Position exhaust manifold. Secure with nuts and flat washers. Working from centre outwards, progressively tighten to ***22 Nm. (16 lbf.ft).***
10. *Vehicles with EGR:* Secure EGR pipe flange to manifold with bolts. Tighten to ***22 Nm. (16 lbf.ft).***
11. Position turbocharger with new gasket to exhaust manifold. Secure with bolts. Tighten to ***45 Nm. (33 lbf.ft).***
12. Fit heat shield. ***See this section.***
13. Remove safety stands. Lower vehicle.
14. Reconnect battery negative lead.

EXHAUST MANIFOLD HEAT SHIELD - DIESEL

Service repair no - 30.15.09

Remove

1. Disconnect battery negative lead.
2. Raise the vehicle.

WARNING: Support on safety stands.

3. Remove cooling fan cowl. ***See COOLING SYSTEM, Repair.***
4. Release intake hose from ducting.
5. Release turbocharger intake hose from ducting.
6. Release breather valve from intake ducting grommet.

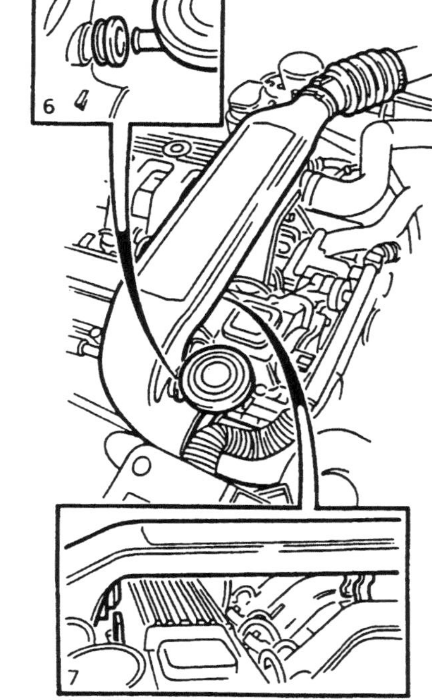

30M7009

NOTE: Collect grommet. Refit to ducting.

7. Disengage 2 clips securing intake ducting. Remove ducting.
8. Remove 3 bolts securing intake ducting bracket and exhaust manifold heat shield to camshaft cover. Collect bracket.

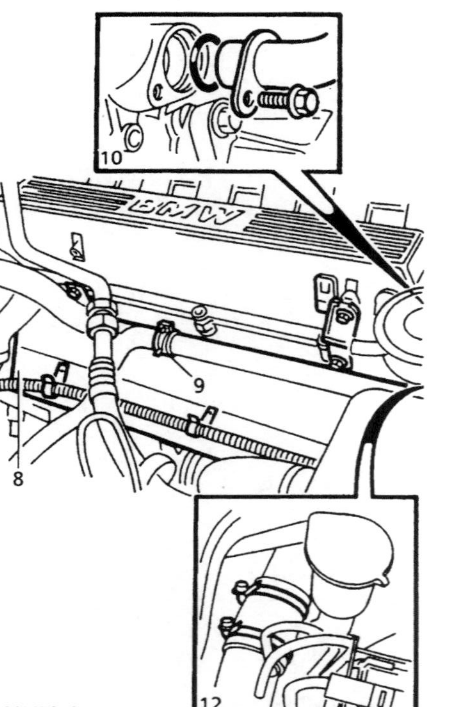

30M7010

9. Disconnect heater hose from coolant connecting pipe.
10. Remove bolt securing coolant connecting pipe to engine front cover.
11. Remove coolant pipe. Remove 'O' ring and discard.
12. Slacken clips securing turbocharger oulet hose to turbocharger and intercooler.
13. Remove turbocharger outlet hose assembly.
14. Release harness from 2 heat shield clips.
15. Remove heat shield.

Refit

16. Position heat shield.
17. Secure harness to heat shield clips.
18. Position outlet hose to turbocharger and intercooler. Secure with clips.
19. Using a new 'O' ring, position coolant pipe. Engage to engine front cover.
20. Secure connecting pipe to front cover with bolt. Tighten to ***10 Nm. (7 lbf.ft)***
21. Connect heater hose. Secure with clip.
22. Align exhaust manifold heat shield. Position intake ducting bracket.
23. Secure ducting bracket and heat shield with bolts.
24. Position intake ducting. Engage clips.
25. Engage breather valve into ducting grommet.
26. Connect ducting to turbocharger intake hose. Secure with clip.
27. Connect intake hose to ducting. Secure with clip.
28. Fit cooling fan cowl. ***See COOLING SYSTEM, Repair.***
29. Remove safety stands. Lower vehicle.
30. Reconnect battery negative lead.

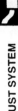

EXHAUST FRONT PIPE - V8

Service repair no - 30.10.09

Remove

1. Raise vehicle on four post lift.
2. Support transmission with a suitable stand.

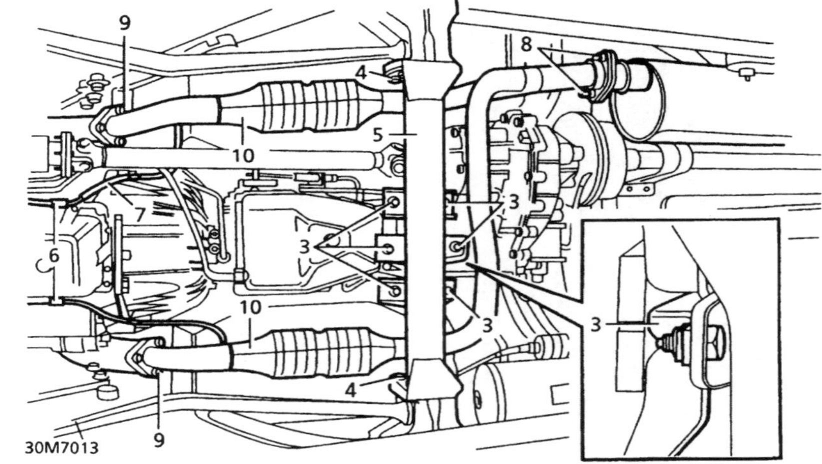

30M7013

3. Remove 6 nuts securing transmission mount to crossmember. Remove snubber bar. Discard nuts.
4. Remove 3 of 4 nuts and bolts securing each side of crossmember to chassis.
5. With assistance, remove remaining bolt securing crossmember. Remove crossmember.
6. Disconnect heated oxygen sensor (HO2S) harnesses. Release multiplugs from sump brackets.
7. Remove cable tie securing L.H. HO2S harness to gearbox bracket.
8. Remove 2 nuts securing front pipe to intermediate pipe flanges.
9. Remove 6 nuts securing front pipe to exhaust manifold flanges.
10. Remove front pipe. Collect front pipe to manifold gaskets.
11. If necessary, remove HO2S. ***See FUEL SYSTEM, Repair.***

Refit

12. Ensure mating faces are clean.
13. If removed, fit HO2S. ***See FUEL SYSTEM, Repair.***
14. Position front pipe assembly with gaskets to manifolds. Secure with nuts. Tighten to ***50 Nm. (37 lbf.ft)***
15. Secure front pipe to intermediate pipe flange with nuts. Tighten to ***25 Nm. (18 lbf.ft)***
16. Secure LH HO2S harness to gearbox bracket with cable tie.
17. Connect HO2S harnesses. Secure multiplugs to sump brackets.
18. With assistance, position transmission crossmember on chassis. Secure with nuts and bolts. Tighten to ***45 Nm. (33 lbf.ft)***
19. Fit snubber bar. Secure transmission mount to crossmember with new flange nuts. Tighten to ***45 Nm. (33 lbf.ft)***
20. Remove support from transmission.
21. Lower vehicle.

EXHAUST FRONT PIPE - V8 - FROM 97MY UP TO 99MY

Service repair no - 30.10.09

Remove

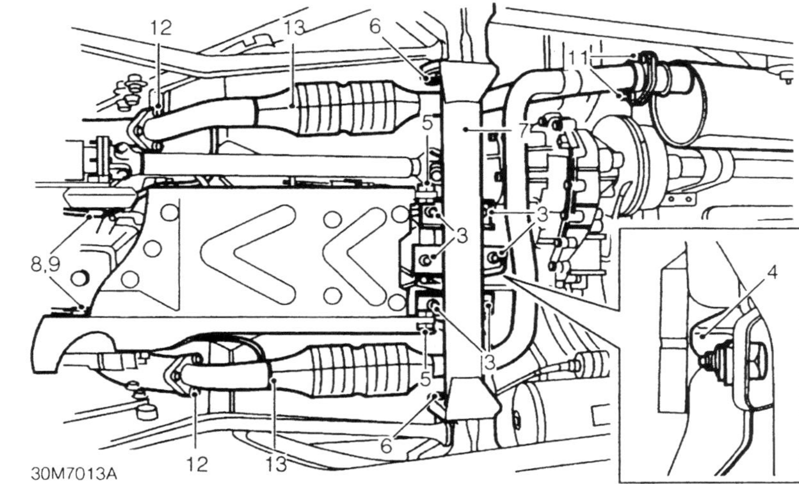

1. Raise vehicle on 4 post ramp.
2. Support transmission using a suitable stand.
3. Remove 4 nuts and 2 bolts securing transmission mount to crossmember and discard nuts.
4. Remove transmission snubber bar.
5. Remove 2 bolts securing rear of side acoustic covers to crossmember.
6. Remove 3 of 4 nuts and bolts securing each side of crossmember to chassis.
7. With assistance, remove remaining bolt securing crossmember and remove crossmember.
8. Disconnect 2 oxygen sensor harness multiplugs from oxygen sensor flylead.
9. Release 2 oxygen sensor flylead multiplugs from brackets.
10. Release flyleads from 2 clips.
11. Remove 2 nuts securing front pipe to intermediate pipe flange.
12. Remove 6 nuts securing front pipe to exhaust manifold down pipe flanges
13. Using assistance, remove front pipe and collect 2 front pipe to manifold gaskets.

Do not carry out further dismantling if component is removed for access only.

14. Remove 2 heated oxygen sensors from front pipe and discard sealing washers.
15. Fit NEW sealing washers to heated oxygen sensors.
16. Fit heated oxygen sensors to front pipe and tighten to ***20 Nm. (15 lbf.ft)***

Refit

17. Ensure all mating faces are clean.
18. Using assistance, position front pipe and NEW gaskets to manifold.
19. Fit but do not tighten nuts securing front pipe to manifolds.
20. Align front pipe to intermediate pipe, fit nuts and tighten to ***25 Nm. (18 lbf.ft)***
21. Tighten front pipe to manifold nuts to ***50 Nm. (37 lbf.ft)***
22. Connect heated oxygen sensor multiplugs to brackets.
23. Connect oxygen sensor multiplugs.
24. Connect oxygen sensor fly leads to clips.
25. Using assistance, fit crossmember to chassis.
26. Fit nuts and bolts and tighten to ***45 Nm. (33 lbf.ft)***
27. Fit transmission snubber bar.
28. Fit bolts and NEW flange nuts securing transmission mount to crossmember and tighten to ***45 Nm. (33 lbf.ft)***
29. Remove transmission stand.
30. Align rear of side acoustic covers to crossmember and secure with threaded fasteners.

EXHAUST FRONT PIPE - V8 - FROM 99MY

Service repair no - 30.10.09

Remove

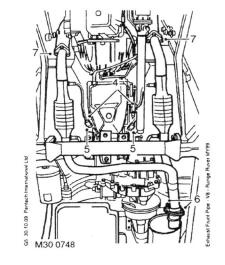

1. Release fixings and remove battery cover.
2. Disconnect battery earth lead.
3. Remove chassis crossmember. *See **CHASSIS AND BODY, Repair.***

GS 30.10.09 Pentech International Ltd

M30 0748

Exhaust Front Pipe - V8 - Range Rover MY99

4. Disconnect 2 front HO2S multiplugs and release RH HO2S harness from clip on sump.
5. Release 2 rear HO2S multiplugs from brackets, disconnect from harness and release harness from 2 clips.
6. Remove 2 nuts securing exhaust front pipe to intermediate flange.
7. Remove 6 nuts securing front exhaust pipe to exhaust manifold down pipe flanges.

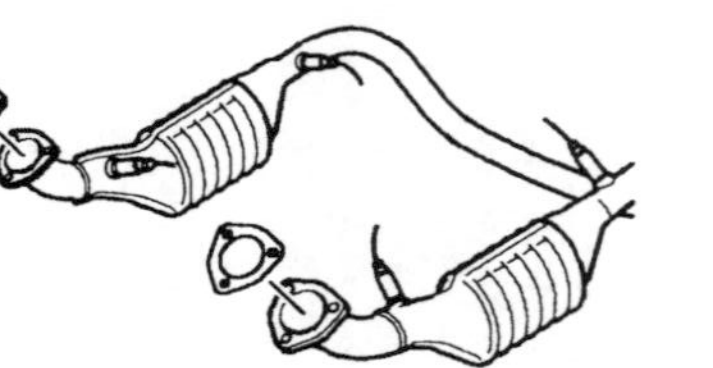

M30 0749

8. With assistance, remove exhaust front pipe and collect 2 front pipe to manifold gaskets.
9. Remove 4 HO2S from exhaust manifold and discard sealing washers.

Refit

10. Clean mating faces of exhaust front pipe, manifolds and intermediate pipe.
11. Use new sealing washers and fit and tighten HO2S to ***20 Nm (15 lbf.ft).***
12. Use new flange gaskets and with assistance, fit exhaust front pipe to manifolds. Fit nuts but do not tighten at this stage.
13. Align intermediate pipe to front pipe and tighten clamp nuts to ***25 Nm (18 lbf.ft)***
14. Tighten front pipe to manifold nuts to ***50 Nm (37 lbf.ft).***
15. Connect HO2S multiplugs to harness and secure multiplugs to brackets.
16. Secure RH front and rear HO2S harness to clips.
17. Fit chassis crossmember. ***See CHASSIS AND BODY, Repair.***
18. Connect battery earth lead.
19. Fit battery cover and secure with fixings.

EXHAUST FRONT PIPE - DIESEL

Service repair no - 30.10.09

Remove

1. Raise vehicle on four post lift.
2. Remove 2 nuts and bolts securing front pipe to intermediate pipe flange.

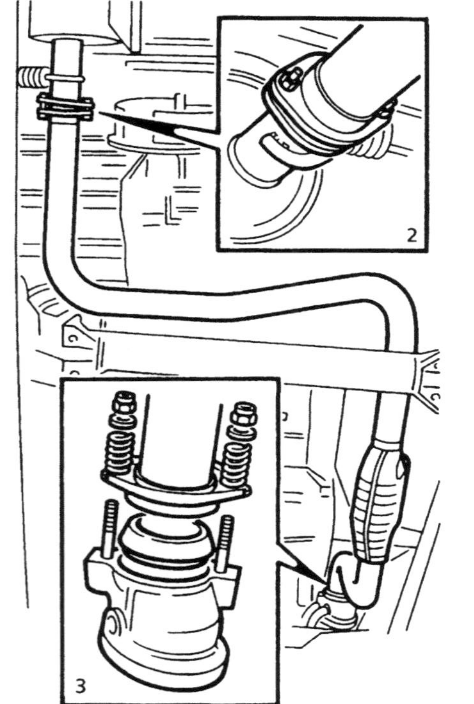

30M7011

3. Remove 2 nuts securing front pipe flange to turbocharger oulet. Collect springs and flat washers.

4. With assistance, manoeuvre front pipe rearwards over chassis crossmember.
5. Remove front pipe.
6. Collect olive.

Refit

7. Ensure mating faces are clean.
8. With assistance, manoeuvre pipe forwards over chassis crossmember into position.
9. Position olive. Fit front pipe flange over turbocharger studs. Secure with nuts, springs and washers.
10. Tighten nuts to ***14 Nm. (10 lbf.ft).*** Back off by 2.5 turns.
11. Position rear flange to intermediate pipe. Secure with nuts. Tighten to ***25 Nm. (18 lbf.ft)***
12. Lower lift.

INLET MANIFOLD GASKET - V8 - UP TO 99MY

Service repair no - 30.15.08

Remove

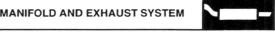

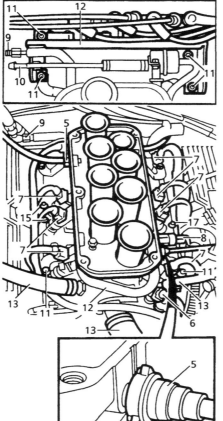

1. Depressurise fuel system. ***See FUEL SYSTEM, Repair.***
2. Drain cooling system. ***See COOLING SYSTEM, Repair.***
3. Remove alternator. ***See ELECTRICAL, Repair.***
4. Remove plenum chamber. ***See FUEL SYSTEM, Repair.***
5. Release purge and crankcase breather hoses from ram pipe housing.
6. Disconnect coolant temperature and temperature gauge sensors.
7. Disconnect 8 injector multiplugs.
8. Disconnect fuel temperature sensor multiplug.
9. Disconnect fuel feed hose from fuel rail.
10. Disconnect fuel return hose from pressure regulator pipe.
11. Remove 6 nuts securing fuel rail and ignition coil bracket to inlet manifold.
12. Lift fuel rail slightly for access. Release ignition coil bracket from inlet manifold studs. Place aside.
13. Disconnect coolant hoses from inlet manifold
14. Disconnect plenum chamber coolant hose from inlet manifold.
15. Remove 2 bolts securing harness to RH side of inlet manifold.
16. Place harness and heater hose aside.
17. Remove bolt securing harness to LH side of inlet manifold.

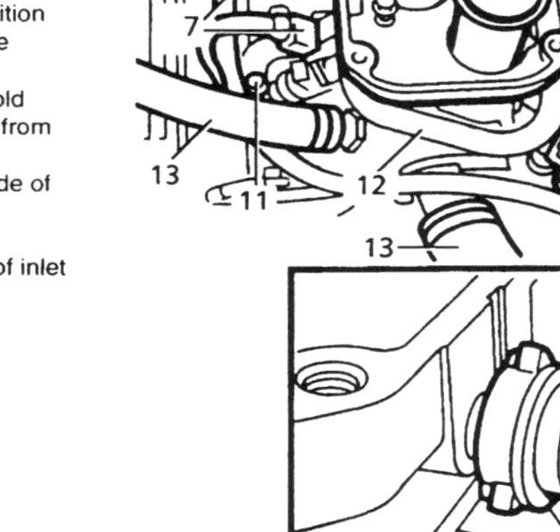

30M7015

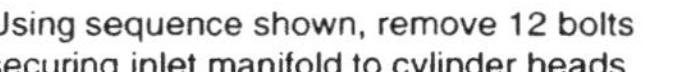

18. Using sequence shown, remove 12 bolts securing inlet manifold to cylinder heads

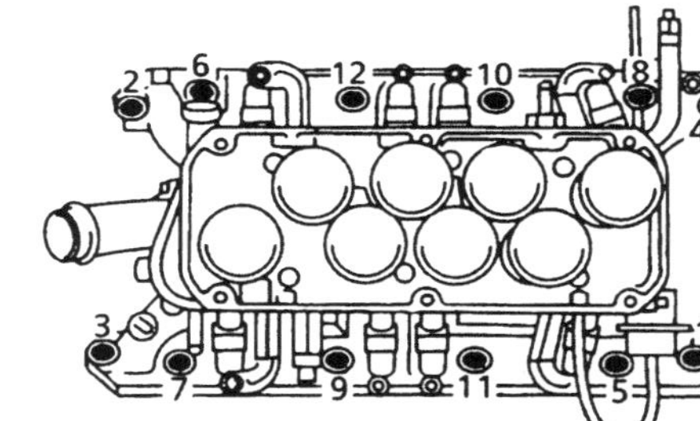

30M7016

19. Remove inlet manifold assembly.
20. Remove bolts and clamps securing manifold gasket to cylinder block.
21. Remove inlet manifold gasket and discard.
22. Remove gasket seals and discard.

Refit

23. Ensure mating faces are clean.
24. Apply a thin bead of Loctite Superflex (black) sealant to 4 notches between cylinder head and block.
25. Position new gasket seals. Ensure ends engage correctly in notches.
26. Fit new inlet manifold gasket.
27. Position manifold gasket clamps. Fit bolts and tighten to ***0.7 Nm (0.5 lbf.ft)*** .
28. With assistance to hold harness and ignition coils aside, position inlet manifold assembly.

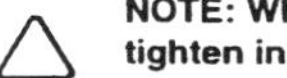

NOTE: When fitting inlet manifold bolts, tighten in reverse of removal sequence.

29. Fit inlet manifold bolts. Initially tighten to ***10 Nm. (7 lbf.ft)***
30. Finally tighten bolts to ***50 Nm. (37 lbf.ft).***
31. Tighten gasket clamp bolts to ***17 Nm. (13 lbf.ft).***
32. Position RH injector harness and heater hose bracket on inlet manifold. Secure with bolts.
33. Fit plenum chamber coolant hose to inlet manifold. Secure with clip.
34. Connect 3 cooling hoses to inlet manifold. Secure with clips.
35. Position ignition coil bracket on inlet manifold studs. Secure with nuts. Tighten to ***8 Nm. (6 lbf.ft).***
36. Connect fuel feed pipe to fuel rail. Tighten to ***16 Nm. (12 lbf.ft).***
37. Connect return hose to pressure regulator pipe. Secure with clip.
38. Connect multiplugs to fuel injectors and fuel temperature sensor.
39. Connect coolant temperature sensor and temperature gauge sensor.
40. Connect purge and crankcase breather hose to ram pipe housing.
41. Fit plenum chamber. ***See FUEL SYSTEM, Repair.***
42. Refill cooling system. ***See COOLING SYSTEM, Repair.***
43. Fit alternator. ***See ELECTRICAL, Repair.***
44. Start engine. Check for leaks around fuel rail and injectors.

GASKET - INLET MANIFOLD - LOWER- FROM 99MY

Service repair no - 30.15.08

Remove

1. Remove RH and LH rocker cover gaskets. ***See ENGINE, Repair.***

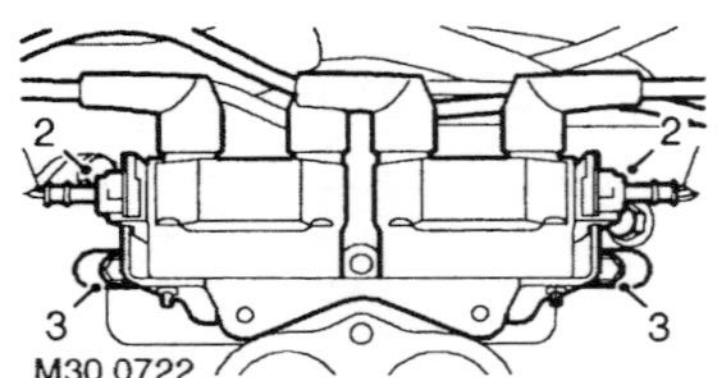

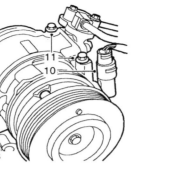

M30 0722

2. Disconnect multiplugs from coils.
3. Remove 2 bolts securing coils and remove coils.

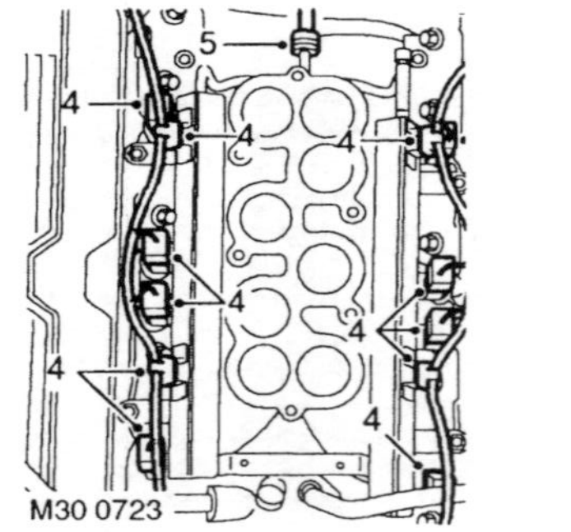

M30 0723

4. Release leads from fuel rails and disconnect LH and RH injector multiplugs.
5. Position absorbent cloth to catch any fuel spillage and disconnect fuel pipe.

CAUTION: Plug the connections.

6. Remove auxiliary drive belt. ***See ELECTRICAL, Repair.***

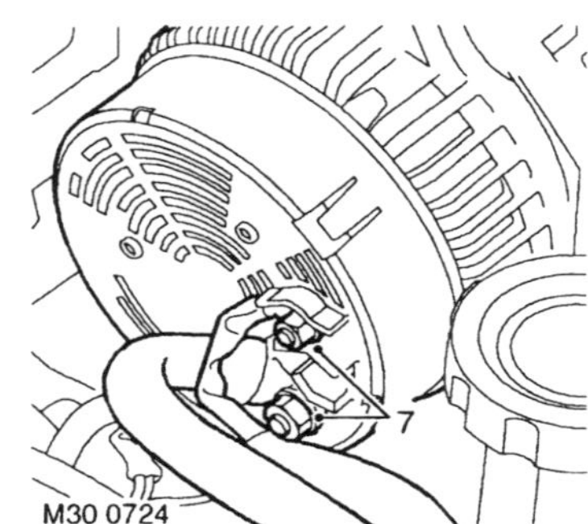

M30 0724

7. Remove 2 nuts securing leads to alternator and release leads.

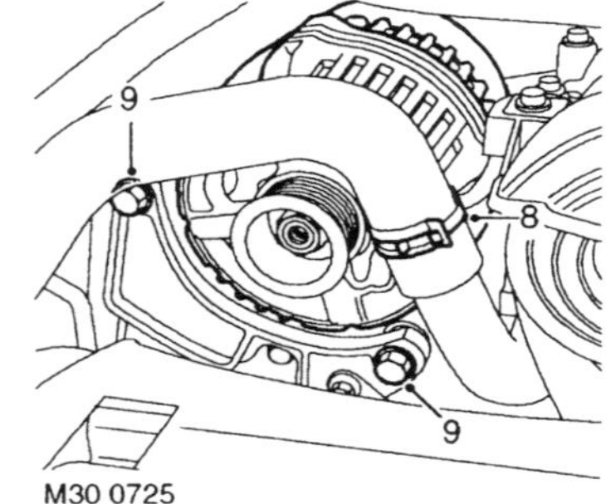

M30 0725

8. Release clip securing top hose to outlet pipe and release hose.
9. Remove 2 bolts securing alternator and remove alternator.

M30 0726

10. Disconnect multiplug from compressor.
11. Remove 4 bolts securing compressor to mounting bracket and position compressor aside.

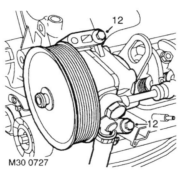

M30 0727

12. Remove 2 bolts securing PAS pump to mounting bracket and position aside.

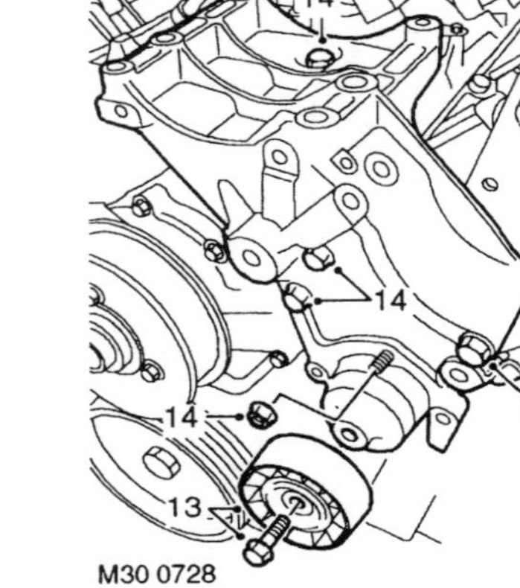

M30 0728

13. Remove bolt securing jockey pulley to mounting bracket and remove pulley.
14. Remove 4 bolts and one nut securing mounting bracket and remove mounting bracket .

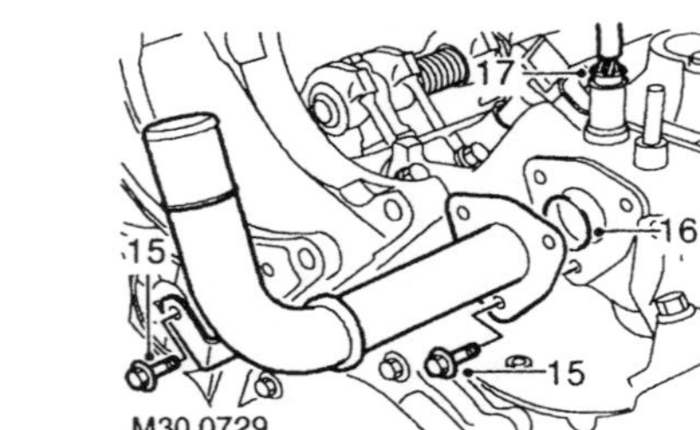

M30 0729

15. Remove 4 bolts securing top hose outlet pipe and remove outlet pipe.
16. Remove and discard 'O' ring.
17. Disconnect ECT sensor multiplug.

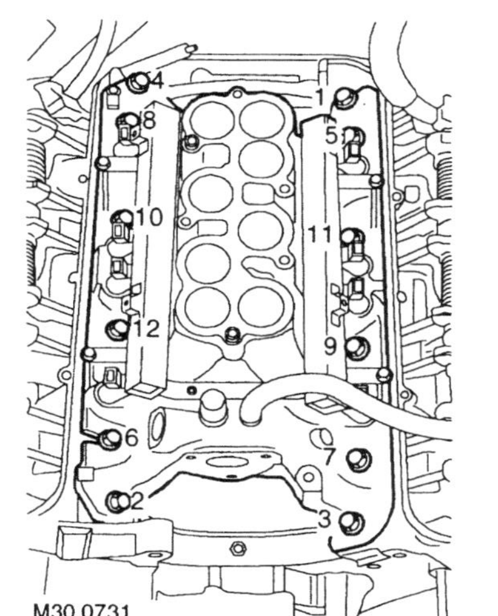

M30 0731

18. Using the sequence shown, remove 12 bolts securing inlet manifold.
19. Remove inlet manifold assembly.

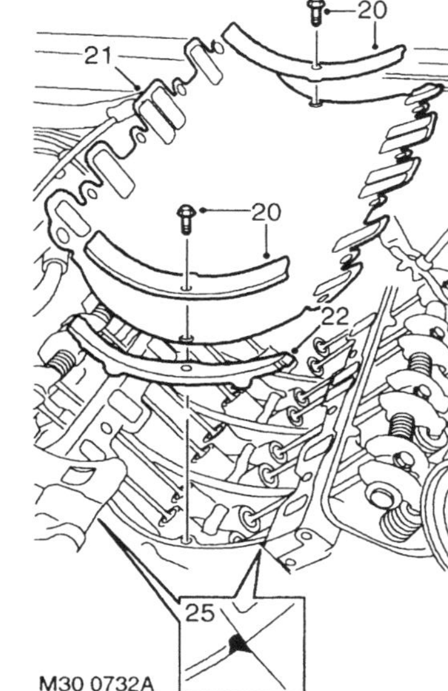

M30 0732A

20. Remove 2 bolts securing manifold gasket clamps and collect gasket clamps.
21. Remove inlet manifold gasket.
22. Remove gasket seals.

Refit

23. Clean RTV from head and block notches.
24. Clean mating faces of block, head and manifold.
25. Apply RTV silicone sealant in the four 'V' shaped notches between the ends of the cylinder head and the cylinder block joint.
26. Fit new gasket seals, ensure ends engage correctly in notches.
27. Fit new manifold gasket.
28. Position gasket clamps, fit bolts but do not tighten at this stage.
29. Position inlet manifold assembly.

△ **NOTE: When fitting inlet manifold bolts, tighten in reverse of removal sequence.**

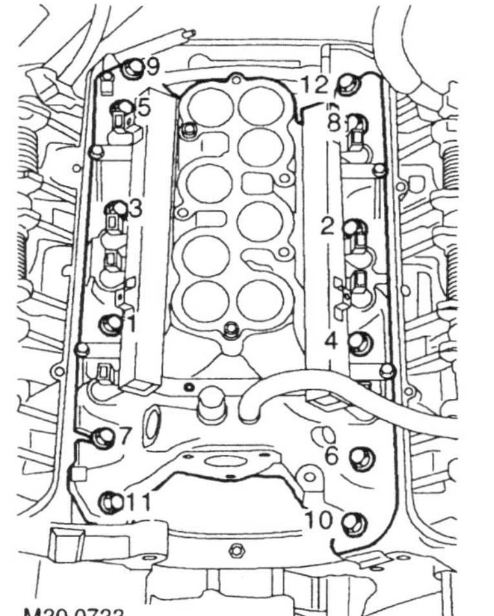

M30 0733

30. Fit manifold bolts and in the sequence shown tighten bolts initially to ***10 Nm (8 lbf.ft)***, then tighten to ***51 Nm (38 lbf.ft).***
31. Tighten gasket clamp bolts to ***18 Nm (14 lbf.ft).***
32. Connect fuel pipe.
33. Connect multiplug to ECT sensor.
34. Clean top hose outlet pipe mating faces.
35. Lubricate and fit new 'O' ring to outlet pipe.
36. Position outlet pipe, fit and tighten bolts to ***22 Nm (16 lbf.ft).***
37. Position mounting bracket, fit and tighten, bolts to***40 Nm (30 lbf.ft)***, and nut to ***10 Nm (7 lbf.ft).***
38. Fit jockey pulley and tighten bolt to ***50 Nm (37 lbf.ft).***
39. Clean PAS pump dowels and dowel holes.
40. Position PAS pump to mounting bracket, locate on dowels and fit and tighten bolts to ***40 Nm (30 lbf.ft).***
41. Clean compressor dowels and dowel holes.
42. Position compressor, locate on dowels and fit and tighten bolts to ***25 Nm (18 lbf.ft).***
43. Connect multiplug to compressor.
44. Position alternator, fit and tighten bolts to ***45 Nm (34 lbf.ft).***
45. Position top hose and secure clip.
46. Connect alternator cables, fit nuts and tighten B+ nut to ***18 Nm (13 lbf.ft)*** max and D+ nut to ***5 Nm (3.5 lbf.ft)*** max. B+ and D+ are marked on the rear of the alternator, adjacent ot each cable connector. Fit leads to alternator and tighten nuts.
47. Fit auxiliary drive belt. ***See ELECTRICAL, Repair.***
48. Connect injector multiplugs and secure leads to fuel rail.
49. Position coils and fit bolts but do not tighten at this stage.
50. Connect multiplugs to coils.
51. Fit rocker cover gaskets. ***See ENGINE, Repair.***

GASKET - INLET MANIFOLD - UPPER - FROM 99MY

Service repair no - 30.15.24

Remove

1. Release 3 fixings and remove battery cover.
2. Disconnect battery earth lead.
3. Remove gas struts from bonnet.
4. With assistance support bonnet on hinge extension arms.

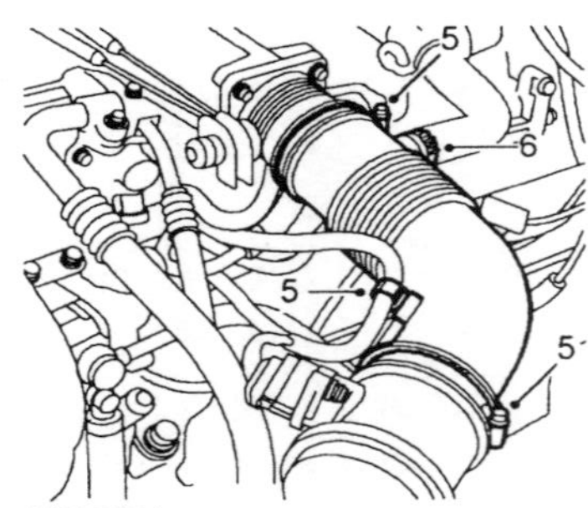

5. Loosen 2 clips securing air intake hose, release air intake hose and disconnect harness from clip on hose.
6. Release clip securing IAC hose to air intake hose and remove air intake hose.

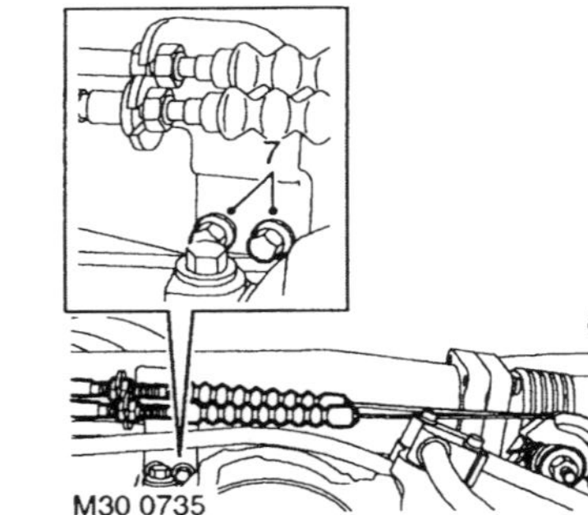

7. Remove 2 bolts securing abutment bracket to plenum chamber and position aside.
8. Release throttle and cruise control cables from clips and throttle cams and position aside.

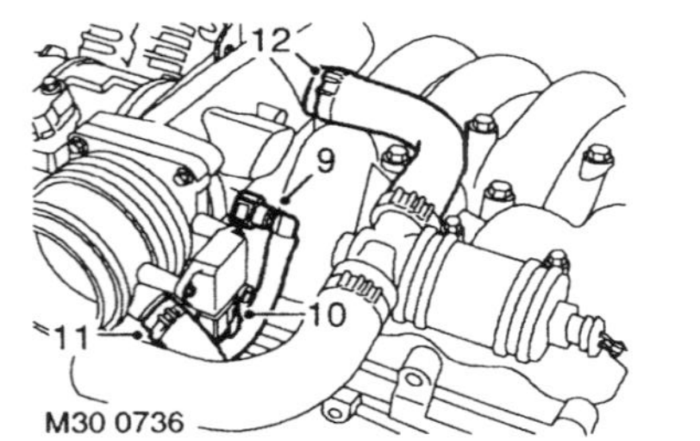

9. Disconnect EVAP pipe from plenum chamber and clip on upper manifold.
10. Disconnect multiplug from TP sensor.
11. Release clip securing breather hose to throttle body and release breather hose.
12. Release clip and disconnect IAC hose from plenum chamber.

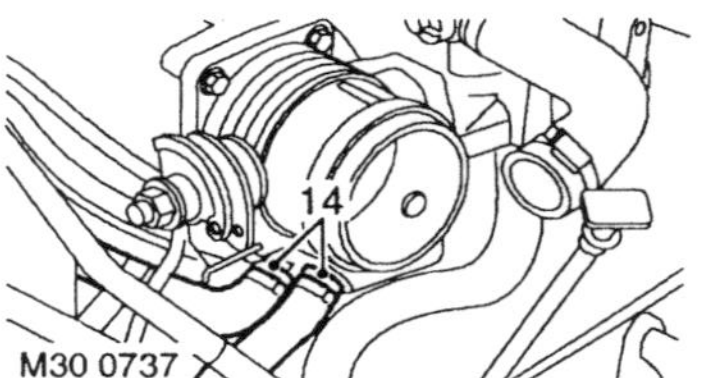

13. Position a container below throttle body to collect coolant.
14. Release clips securing coolant hoses to throttle body and release hoses.

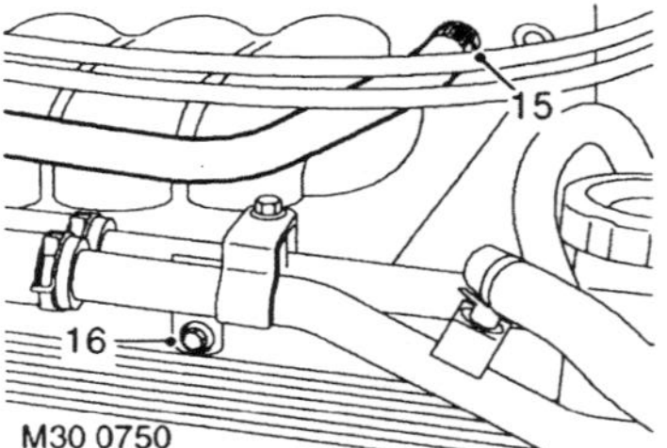

15. Release clip and disconnect engine breather hose from plenum chamber.
16. Remove bolt securing coolant rails.

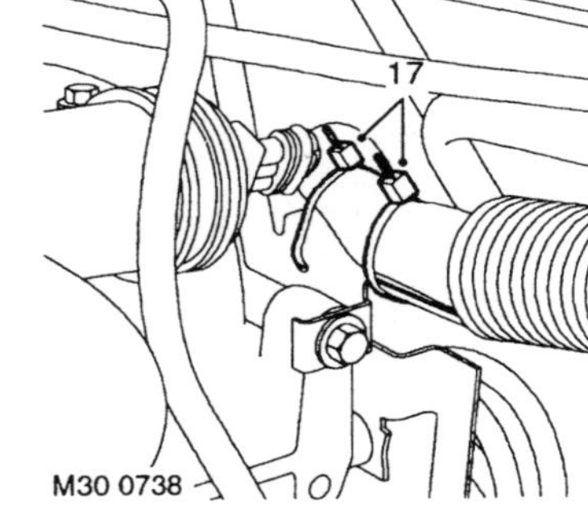

17. Remove 2 cable ties securing engine harness to clip on upper manifold.

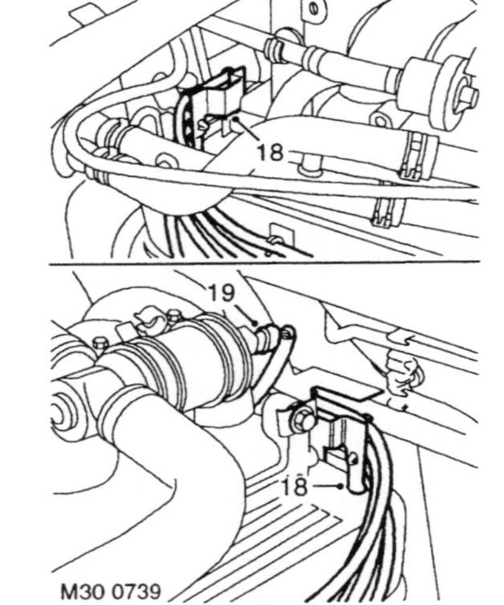

18. Release HT leads from clips on upper inlet manifold.
19. Disconnect multiplug from IAC valve.

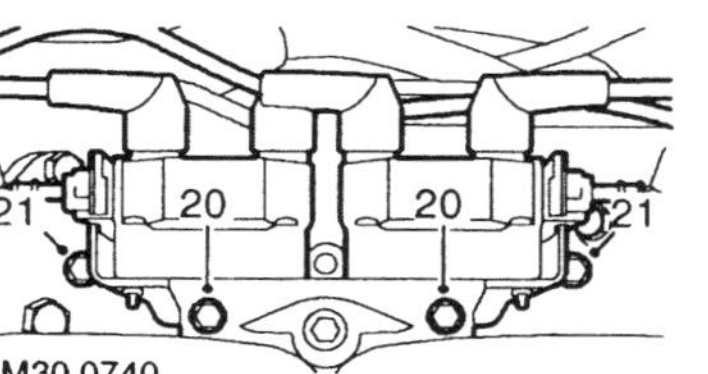

M30 0740

20. Remove 2 bolts securing top of coils.
21. Loosen 2 bolts securing bottom of coils to block but do not remove bolts.

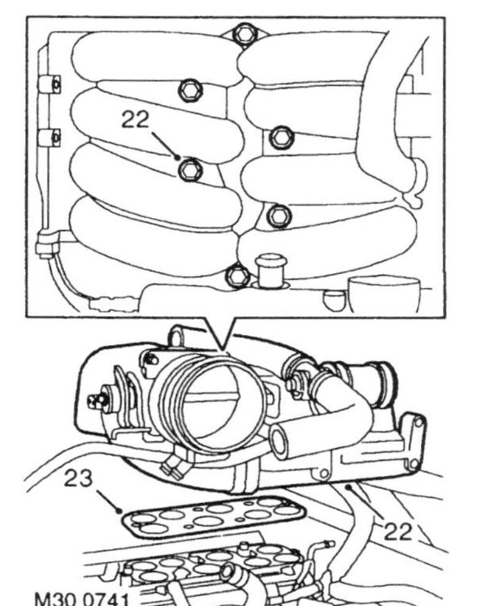

M30 0741

22. Remove 6 bolts securing upper manifold and remove upper manifold.
23. Collect upper manifold gasket.

Refit

24. Clean inlet manifold and upper manifold mating faces, dowels and dowel holes.
25. Using a new gasket, position upper manifold. Fit bolts, and working in a diagonal sequence, tighten to ***22 Nm (16 lbf.ft).***
26. Fit 2 top bolts securing coils to manifold and tighten all coil fixing bolts to ***8 Nm (6 lbf.ft).***
27. Connect IAC valve multiplug.
28. Secure HT leads to upper manifold clips.
29. Connect multiplug to TP sensor.
30. Position engine harness in manifold clip and secure with new cable ties.
31. Fit and tighten coolant rail bolt to ***22 Nm (16 lbf.ft).***
32. Connect breather hose to plenum and secure with clip.
33. Connect IAC hose to plenum chamber and secure with clip.
34. Position coolant hoses to throttle body and secure hose clips.
35. Fit breather hose to throttle body and secure clip.
36. Connect multiplug to TP sensor.
37. Connect EVAP pipe to plenum chamber and clip on upper manifold.
38. Connect throttle and cruise control cables to clips and secure in throttle body cams.
39. Position abutment bracket to upper manifold, fit and tighten bolts.
40. Fit air intake hose, tighten 2 clips and connect harness to clip on hose.
41. Connect IAC hose to air intake hose and secure with clip.
42. Top-up cooling system.
43. Lower bonnet and connect gas struts.
44. Connect battery earth lead.
45. Fit battery cover and secure fixings.

INLET MANIFOLD GASKETS - DIESEL - VEHICLES WITHOUT EGR

Service repair no - 30.15.08

Remove

1. Disconnect battery negative lead.

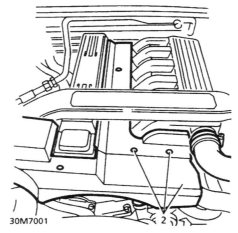

30M7001

2. Remove 4 screws securing injector covers. Remove covers.

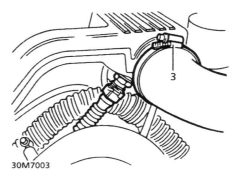

30M7003

3. Release intake hose from ducting.
4. Release turbocharger intake hose from ducting.
5. Release breather valve from grommet in intake ducting.

30M7002

NOTE: Collect grommet. Refit to ducting.

6. Disengage 2 clips. Remove intake ducting.
7. Disconnect intake hose from manifold.
8. Disconnect multiplug from intake temperature sensor.
9. Release fuel return hose from inlet manifold clip.

10. Remove 2 nuts and bolts securing stays to inlet manifold.

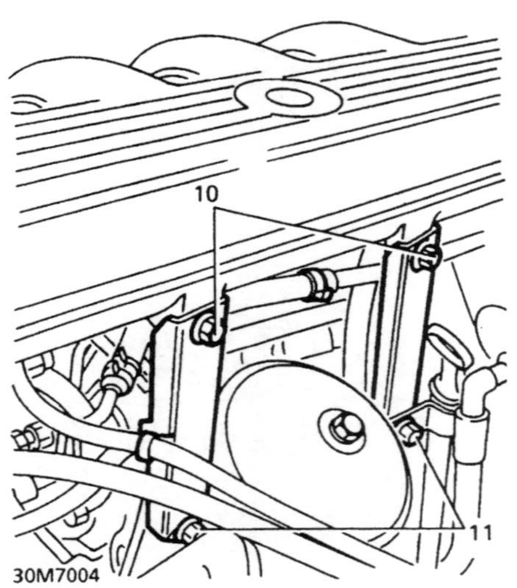

30M7004

11. Slacken 2 nuts securing manifold stays to oil filter casing.
12. Release clip securing manifold pressure sensing pipe to stay.

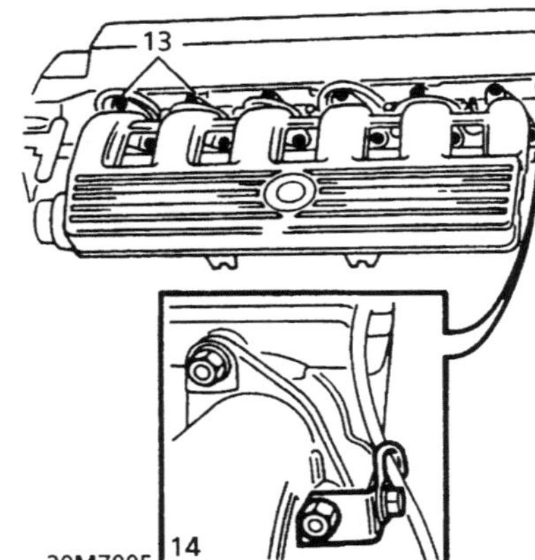

30M7005

13. Remove 12 nuts securing intake manifold to cylinder head.
14. Release gearbox breather hose bracket from rearmost manifold stud.
15. Release manifold from studs. Ensure that injector leak off pipes do not foul on manifold flanges.
16. Place manifold aside. Do not strain manifold pressure sensing hose.

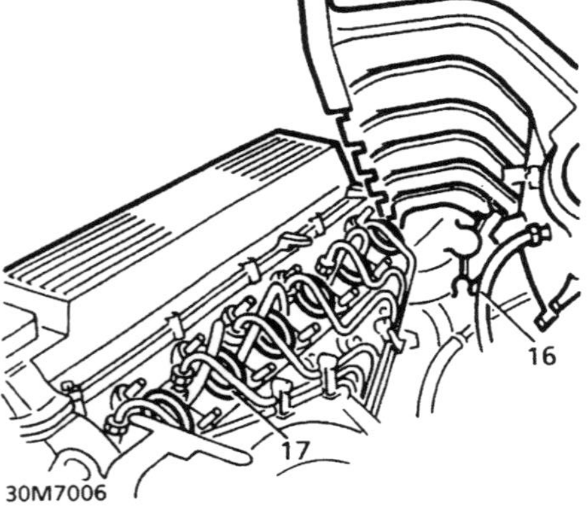

30M7006

17. Collect 6 inlet manifold gaskets.
18. Position cloth over inlet ports to prevent dirt ingress.

Refit

19. Ensure mating faces are clean.
20. Position intake manifold with gaskets on studs. Ensure injector leak off pipes are not fouled.
21. Position gearbox breather hose bracket on rearmost manifold stud.
22. Secure manifold with nuts. Progressively tighten to ***22 Nm. (16 lbf.ft)***
23. Position manifold stays. Secure with nuts and bolts.
24. Secure manifold pressure sensing hose to stay with clip.
25. Connect multiplug to intake temperature sensor.
26. Engage fuel return hose into inlet manifold clip.
27. Connect intake hose. Secure with clip.
28. Position intake ducting. Engage clips.
29. Engage breather valve into ducting grommet.
30. Connect ducting to turbocharger intake hose. Secure with clip.
31. Connect intake hose to ducting. Secure with clip.
32. Fit injector covers. Secure with screws.
33. Reconnect battery negative lead.

INTAKE MANIFOLD GASKETS - DIESEL WITH EGR

Service repair no - 30.15.08

Remove

1. Disconnect battery negative terminal.
2. Remove air intake ducting. ***See this section.***
3. Disconnect vacuum hose from EGR valve.
4. Slacken clip and disconnect intercooler hose from EGR valve.
5. Remove 2 bolts securing EGR pipe to EGR valve.

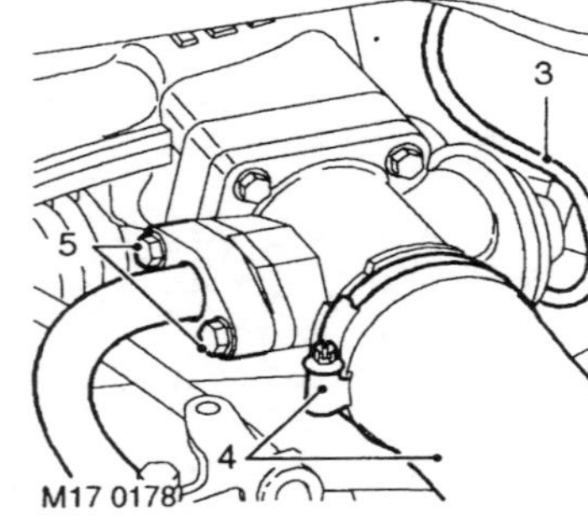

M17 0178

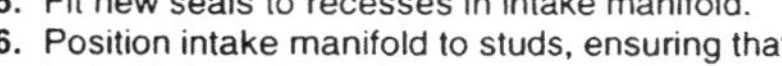

6. Disengage clip on underside of intake manifold. Release wiring harness and vacuum hoses.
7. Release fuel return hose and EGR vacuum pipe from clips on underside of manifold.
8. Remove 12 nuts securing intake manifold to cylinder head.
9. Release gearbox breather hoses from rearmost manifold stud.
10. Release manifold from from studs. Ensure that injector leak off pipes do not foul on manifold flanges.
11. Position manifold aside.

CAUTION: Ensure manifold pressure sensing hose is not strained.

12. Remove 6 seals from intake manifold ports.

CAUTION: Care must be taken when extracting seals to ensure recesses in intake manifold are not damaged.

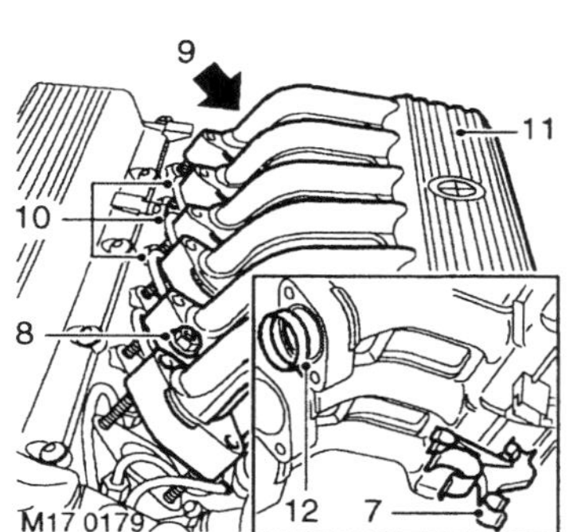

13. Clean mating faces of intake manifold and cylinder head.
14. Position cloth over inlet ports to prevent dirt ingress.

Refit

15. Fit new seals to recesses in intake manifold.
16. Position intake manifold to studs, ensuring that leak off pipes do not become trapped beneath flanges.
17. Position gearbox breather hose bracket to rearmost stud.
18. Secure manifold with nuts and progressively tighten to ***22Nm (16 lbf.in).***
19. Position and secure fuel return hose, harnesses and vacuum hoses to clips on underside of manifold.
20. Engage EGR pipe to valve, align flange and secure with bolts. Tighten bolts to ***22 Nm (16 lbf.in).***
21. Connect intercooler hose to EGR valve and secure with clip.
22. Connect vacuum hose to EGR valve.
23. Fit air intake ducting. ***See this section.***
24. Connect battery negative terminal.

INTERMEDIATE AND REAR PIPES

Service repair no - 30.10.11 - Intermediate Pipe
Service repair no - 30.10.22 - Rear Pipe

Remove

1. Raise vehicle on four post lift.
2. Remove 4 nuts securing intermediate pipe flanges to front and rear pipes.

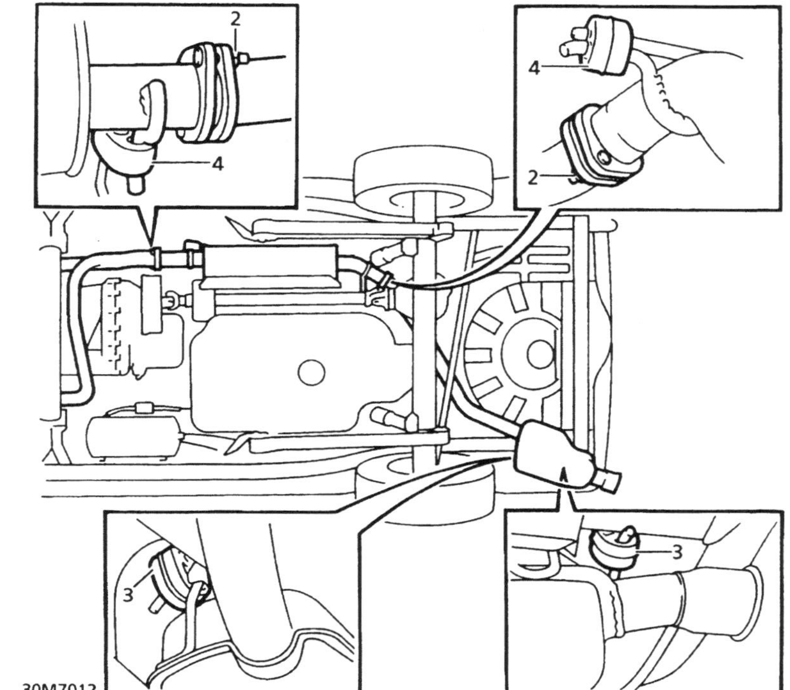

3. Release 2 mounting rubbers. Remove rear pipe.
4. With assistance, release 2 mounting rubbers. Remove intermediate pipe.

Refit

5. Ensure mating faces are clean.
6. With assistance, position intermediate pipe. Secure with mounting rubbers.
7. Position rear pipe. Secure with mounting rubbers.
8. Position intermediate pipe flanges. Secure with nuts. Tighten to ***25 Nm. (18 lbf.ft).***

TAIL PIPE - LH - FROM 97MY

Service repair no - 30.10.22

Remove

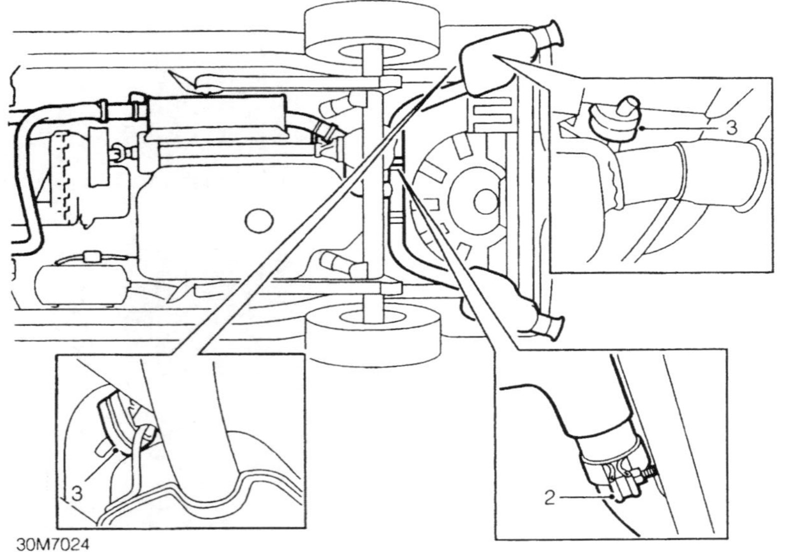

30M7024

1. Raise vehicle on 4 post ramp.
2. Loosen clamp securing LH tail pipe to RH tail pipe.
3. Release LH tail pipe from 2 mounting rubbers.
4. Release LH tail pipe from RH tail pipe and remove tail pipe.

Refit

5. Clean tail pipe mating faces.
6. Position LH tail pipe to vehicle and fit to mounting rubbers.
7. Engage LH tail pipe to RH tail pipe and tighten clamp to ***65 Nm. (48 lbf.ft)***

TAIL PIPE - RH - FROM 97MY

Service repair no - 30.10.52

Remove

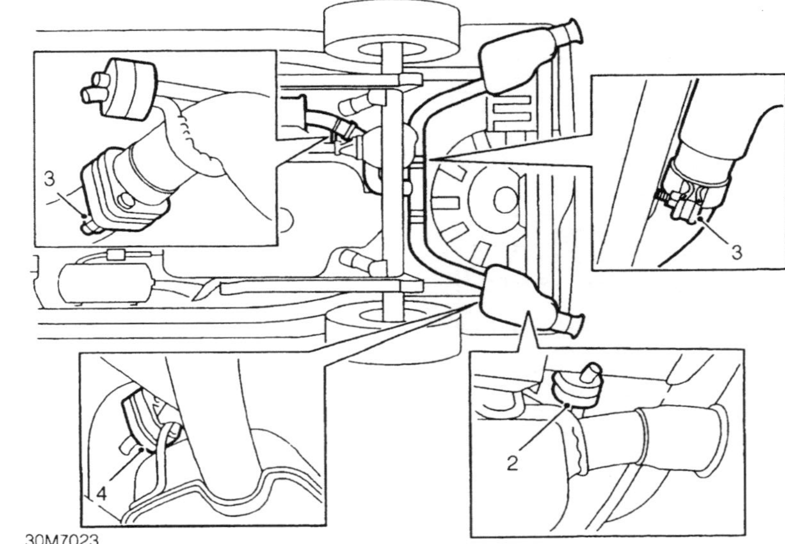

30M7023

1. Raise vehicle on 4 post ramp.
2. Loosen clamp securing LH tail pipe to RH tail pipe.
3. Remove 2 nuts securing tail pipe flange to intermediate pipe flange.
4. Release RH tail pipe from 2 mounting rubbers.
5. With assistance, release RH tail pipe from LH tail pipe and remove tail pipe.

Refit

6. Clean tail pipe mating faces.
7. With assistance, position RH tail pipe to vehicle and fit to mounting rubbers.
8. Engage RH tail pipe to LH tail pipe.
9. Align tail pipe flange to intermediate pipe flange and fit nuts. Tighten nuts to ***25 Nm. (18 lbf.ft)***
10. Tighten nut securing RH tail pipe to LH tail pipe to ***65 Nm. (48 lbf.ft)*** .

33 - CLUTCH

CONTENTS

Page

REPAIR

HYDRAULIC SYSTEM BLEED

Service repair no - 33.15.01

1. Top-up clutch master cylinder. ***See LUBRICANTS, FLUIDS AND CAPACITIES, Information.***

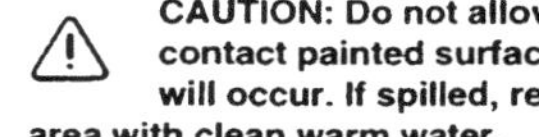

CAUTION: Do not allow brake fluid to contact painted surfaces. Paint damage will occur. If spilled, remove fluid. Wash area with clean warm water.

2. Clean area around slave cylinder bleed screw.
3. Connect bleed tube to bleed screw. Immerse free end of tube into container of brake fluid.

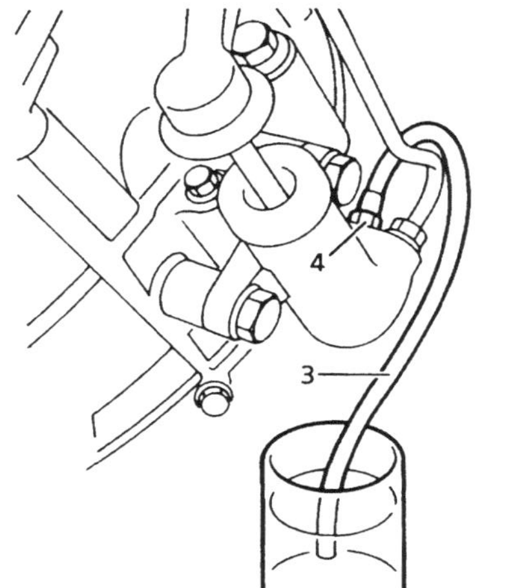

33M7014

4. Hold clutch pedal down. Slacken bleed screw.
5. Release clutch pedal, allow it to return unassisted. Depress pedal again.

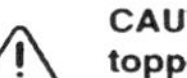

CAUTION: Ensure master cylinder is topped up at frequent intervals. Use only fresh fluid.

6. Repeat procedure until fluid issuing from bleed tube is free from air bubbles.
7. Tighten bleed screw. Remove bleed tube.
8. Top-up master cylinder.

CLUTCH ASSEMBLY - V8

Service repair no - 33.10.07

Remove

1. Remove gearbox assembly. ***See MANUAL GEARBOX, Repair.***
2. Release push rod gaiter from clutch lever.
3. Remove 2 bolts securing clutch slave cylinder. Tie cylinder aside.

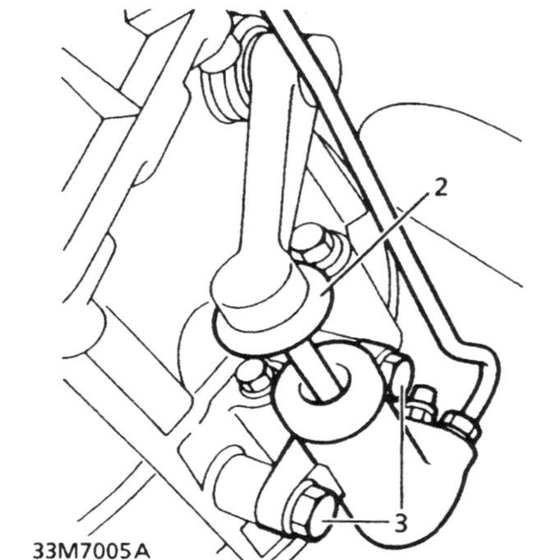

33M7005A

4. Remove 9 bolts securing flywheel access cover to clutch housing. Remove cover.

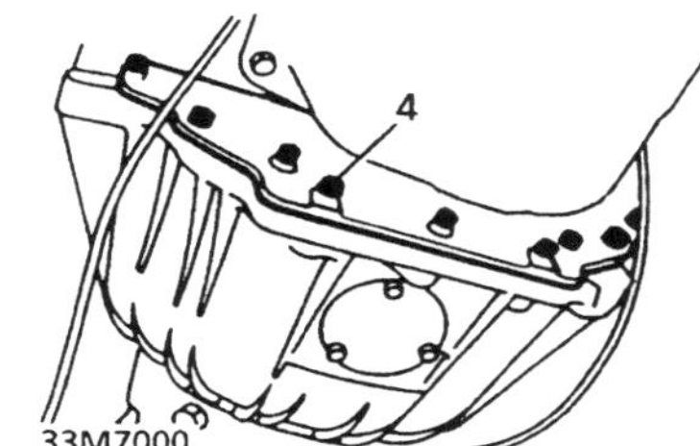

33M7000

5. Remove 8 bolts securing clutch housing. Disengage release lever from release bearing. Remove clutch housing.

33M7001

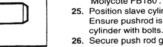

6. If clutch cover is to be refitted, mark cover and flywheel to aid re-assembly.
7. Restrain flywheel.
8. Working diagonally, sequentially slacken 6 bolts securing clutch cover to flywheel. Remove bolts.

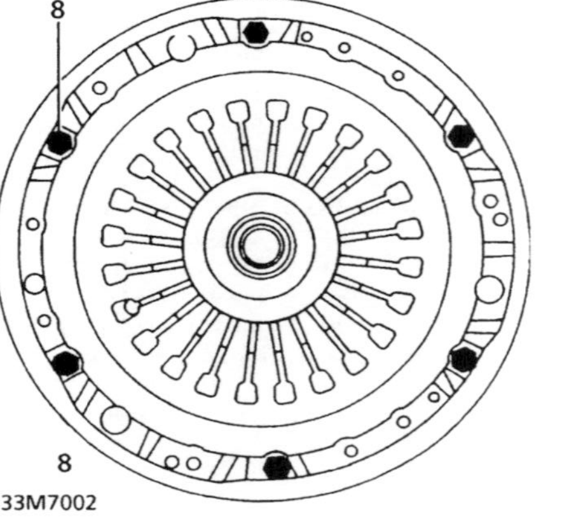

33M7002

9. Remove cover assembly. Collect friction plate.

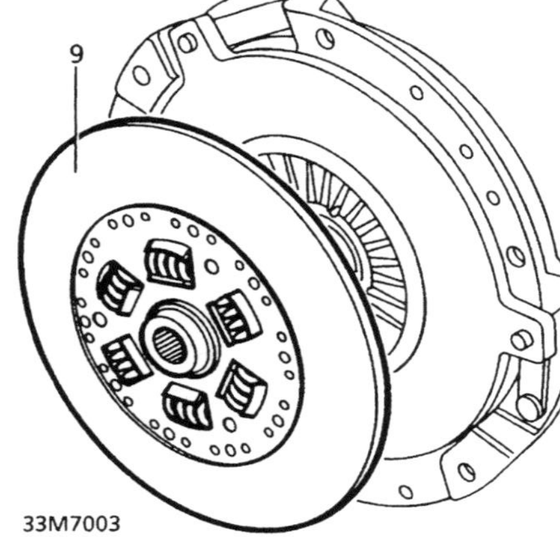

33M7003

Check

10. Check linings of friction plate for excessive or uneven wear, burning or contamination.
11. Check splines of friction plate for excessive wear.
12. Check friction surface of cover for burning distortion or scoring.
13. Check fingers of cover for cracks and distortion.
14. Check release bearing for smooth operation.
15. Renew components as necessary.

CAUTION: Bearing is packed with grease, do not wash in solvent.

Refit

16. Ensure mating faces are clean.

NOTE: New friction plates are supplied with splines pre-greased.

17. If refitting existing friction plate, smear splines with 'Molycote FB180'.
18. Position friction plate on flywheel. Fit LRT-12-001 to align plate.

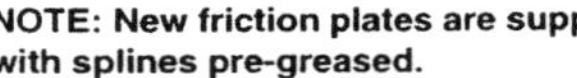

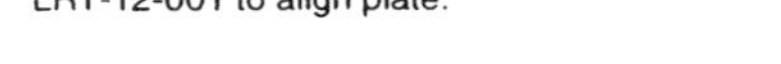
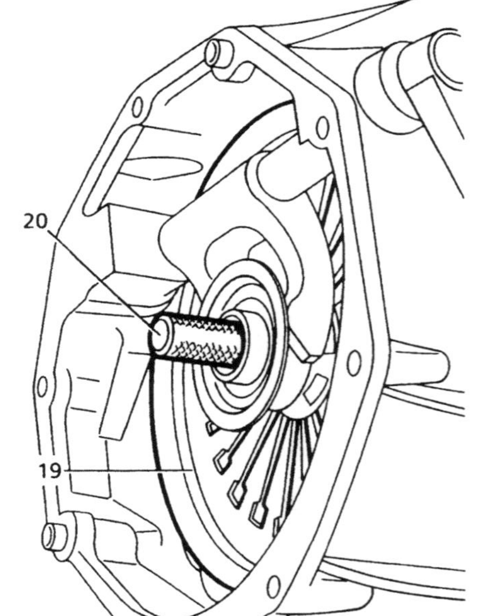

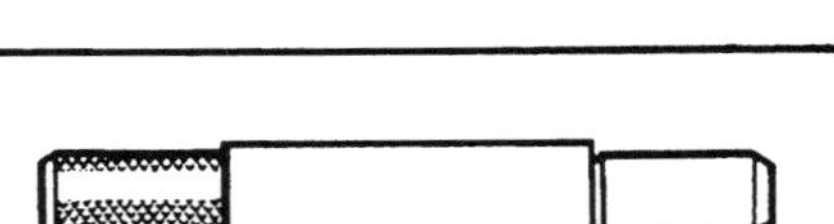
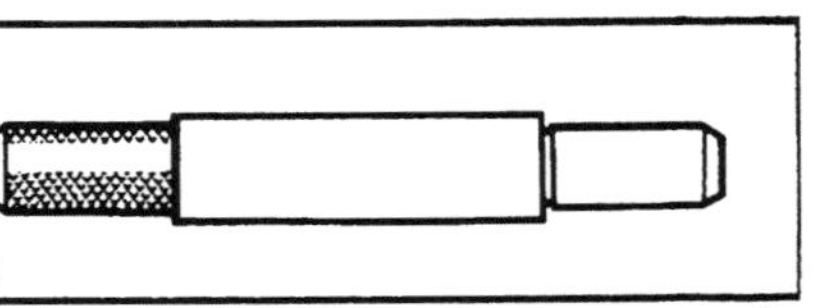
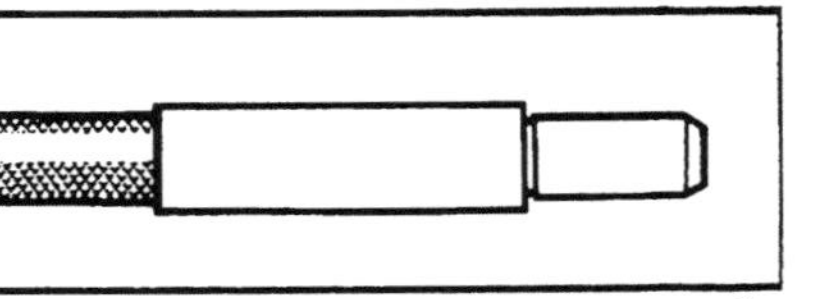
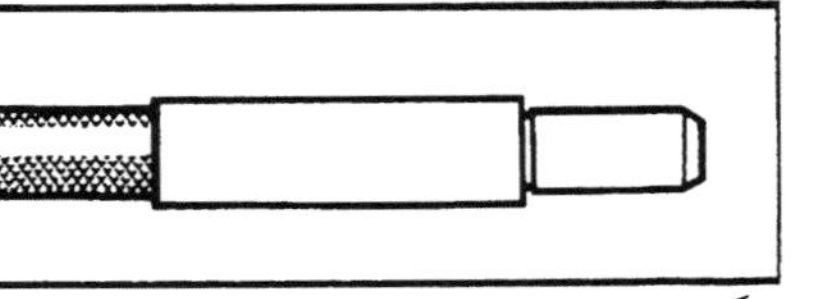
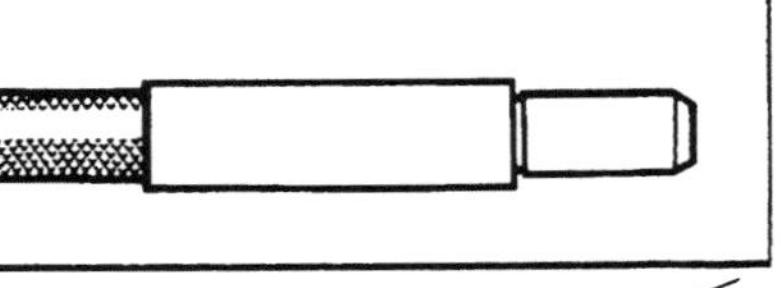
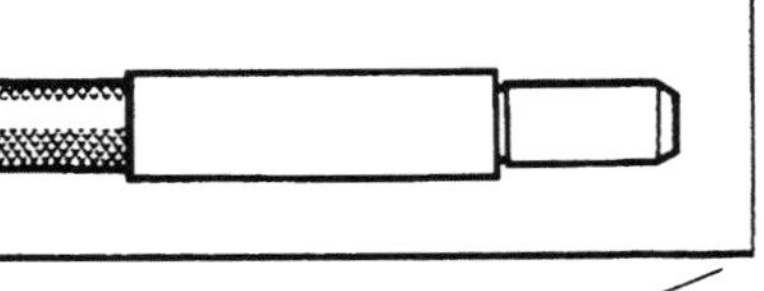
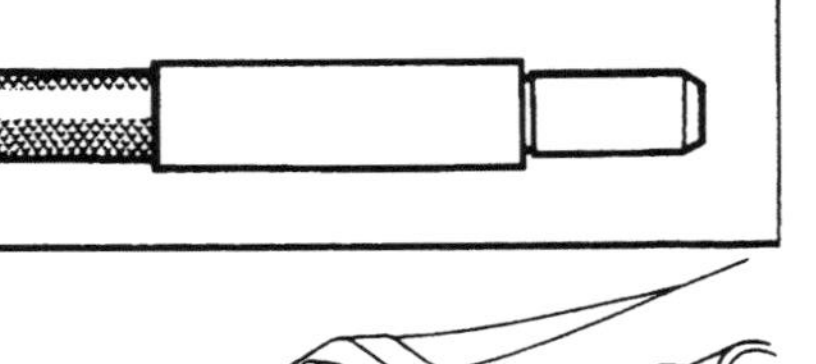
33M7004

19. Position cover. Locate on dowels.

NOTE: If original cover is refitted, align marks.

20. Secure cover with bolts. Tighten progressively, in a diagonal sequence to ***40 Nm. (30 lbf.ft).*** Remove LRT-12-001.
21. Position clutch housing onto dowels. Ensure release fork engages with release bearing.
22. Secure clutch housing with bolts. Tighten to ***40 Nm. (30 lbf.ft)***
23. Position flywheel access cover. Secure with bolts.
24. Smear release lever push rod socket with 'Molycote FB180'.
25. Position slave cylinder on clutch housing. Ensure pushrod is engaged with lever. Secure cylinder with bolts. Tighten to ***45 Nm. (33 lbf.ft)***
26. Secure push rod gaiter to clutch lever.
27. Fit gearbox assembly. ***See MANUAL GEARBOX, Repair.***

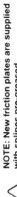

CLUTCH ASSEMBLY - DIESEL

Service repair no - 33.10.07

Remove

1. Remove gearbox assembly. ***See MANUAL GEARBOX, Repair.***
2. Remove starter motor. ***See ELECTRICAL, Repair.***
3. Release push rod gaiter from clutch lever.

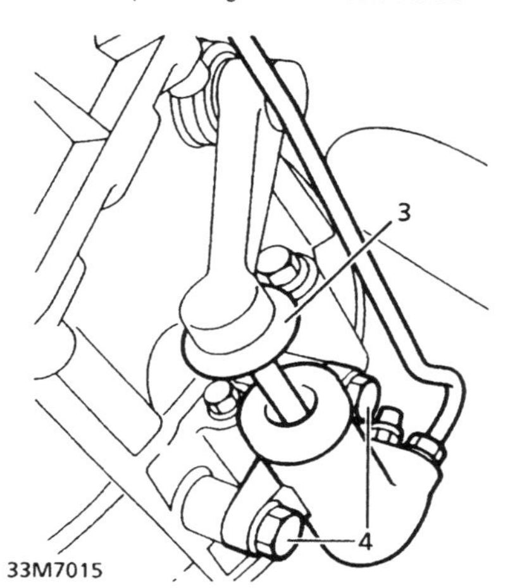

33M7015

4. Remove 2 bolts securing clutch slave cylinder. Tie cylinder aside.
5. Release clutch fluid pipe from clips. Move pipe bracket clear of clutch housing.
6. Remove 7 remaining bolts securing clutch housing. Disengage release lever from release bearing. Remove clutch housing.

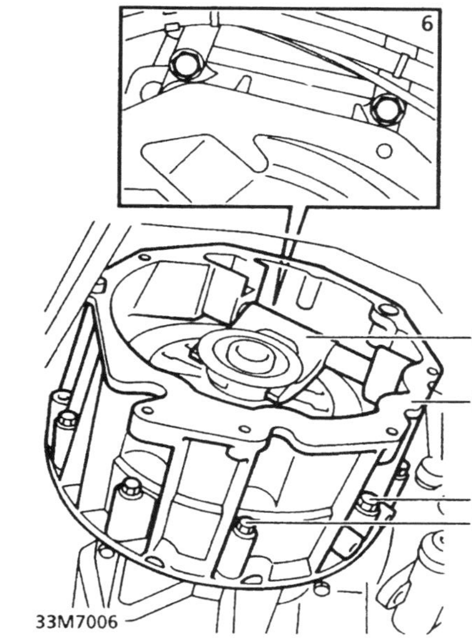

33M7006

NOTE: Spacer plate may become detached from dowels but remain captive behind flywheel.

7. If clutch cover is to be refitted, mark cover and flywheel to aid re-assembly.
8. Fit LRT-12-106 to flywheel. Secure tool to cylinder block with bolts.

33M7007

9. Working diagonally, sequentially slacken 6 bolts securing clutch cover to flywheel. Remove bolts.
10. Remove cover assembly. Collect friction plate.

Check

11. Check linings of friction plate for excessive or uneaven wear, burning or contamination.
12. Check splines of friction plate for excessive wear.
13. Check friction surface of cover for burning, distortion or scoring.
14. Check fingers of cover for cracks and distortion.
15. Check release bearing for smooth operation.
16. Renew components as necessary.

CAUTION: Release bearing is packed with grease, do not wash in solvent.

Refit

17. Ensure mating faces are clean.

NOTE: New friction plates are supplied with splines pre-greased.

18. Smear friction plate splines with 'Molycote BR2'.
19. Position friction plate on flywheel. Fit LRT-12-123 to align plate.
20. Position cover, locate on dowels.

NOTE: If original cover is refitted, align marks.

21. Secure cover with bolts. Tighten progressively, in a diagonal sequence, to:
    M8 8.8 - ***24 Nm (18 lbf.ft)***
    M8 10.9 - ***34 Nm (25 lbf.ft)***
22. Remove LRT-12-123 and LRT-12-106.
23. Position spacer plate onto dowels.
24. Position clutch housing onto dowels. Ensure release fork engages with release bearing.
25. Align clutch fluid pipe bracket and coolant pipe with clutch housing.
26. Secure clutch housing with bolts.
    M8 - Tighten to ***27 Nm. (20 lbf .ft)***
    M10 - Tighten to ***51 Nm. (38 lbf.ft)***
    M12 - Tighten to ***86 Nm. (63 lbf.ft)***
27. Smear push rod socket of release lever with 'Molycote FB180'.
28. Position slave cylinder on clutch housing. Ensure push rod has engaged with lever. Secure cylinder with bolts. Tighten to ***45 Nm. (33 lbf.ft)***
29. Secure push rod gaiter to clutch lever.
30. Secure fluid pipe to clips.
31. Fit starter motor. ***See ELECTRICAL, Repair.***
32. Fit gearbox assembly. ***See MANUAL GEARBOX, Repair.***

MASTER CYLINDER

Service repair no - 33.20.01

Remove

1. Remove fascia closing panel. ***See CHASSIS AND BODY, Repair.***
2. Remove 4 scrivets securing lower closing panel. Disconnect multiplug from footwell lamp. Remove panel.

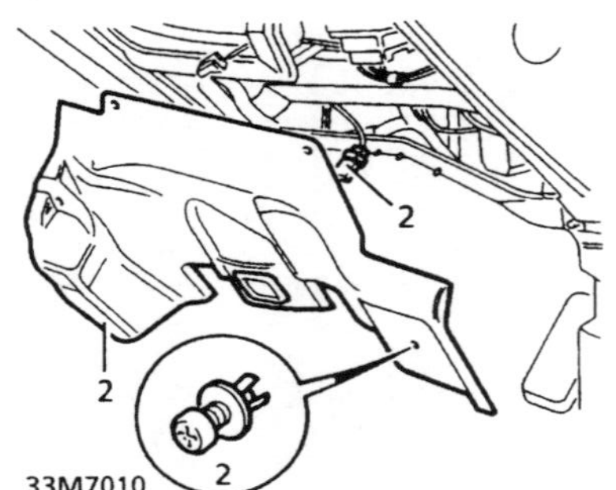

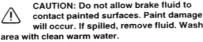

33M7010

3. Remove spring clip and clevis pin from master cylinder push rod.

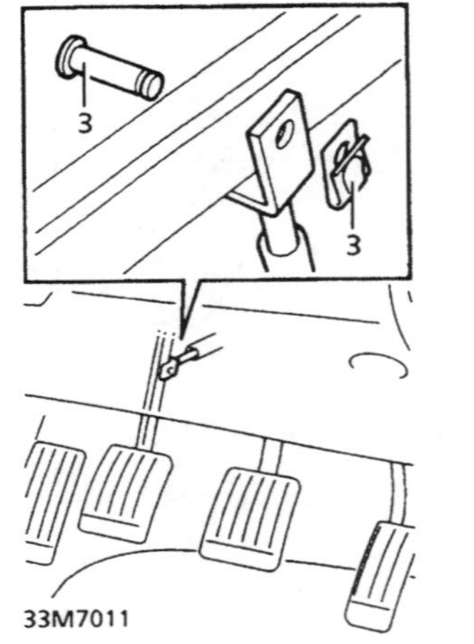

33M7011

4. Position cloth beneath master cylinder to absorb fluid spillage.

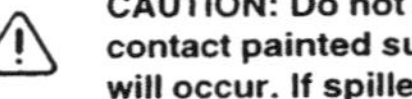

CAUTION: Do not allow brake fluid to contact painted surfaces. Paint damage will occur. If spilled, remove fluid. Wash area with clean warm water.

5. Disconnect reservoir hose from master cylinder. Plug hose and connection.

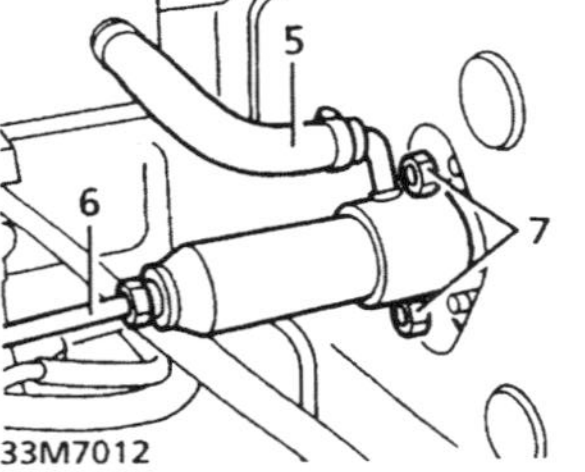

33M7012

6. Disconnect pressure pipe from master cylinder. Plug pipe and connection.
7. Remove 2 nuts securing master cylinder to bulkhead. Remove master cylinder.

Refit

8. Ensure mating faces are clean.
9. Reverse removal procedure.
10. Bleed clutch system. ***See this section.***

SLAVE CYLINDER

Service repair no - 33.35.01

Remove

1. Raise the vehicle.

WARNING: Support on safety stands.

2. Position container to collect fluid spillage.

CAUTION: Do not allow brake fluid to contact painted surfaces. Paint damage will occur. If spilled, remove fluid. Wash area with clean warm water.

3. Disconnect fluid pipe. Release pipe from clip. Plug pipe and connection.

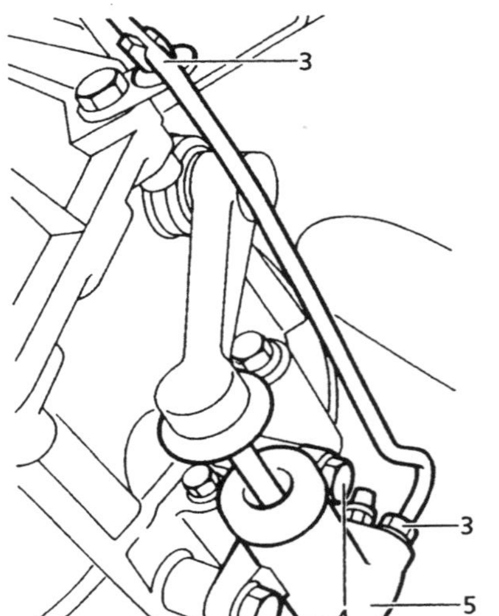

33M7013

4. Remove 2 bolts securing cylinder.
5. Remove cylinder from clutch housing and push rod.

Refit

6. Ensure mating faces are clean.
7. Position cylinder to clutch housing and push rod. Secure with bolts. Tighten to ***45 Nm. (33 lbf.ft)***
8. Remove plugs from pipe and cylinder. Connect pipe to cylinder. Tighten union.
9. Secure pipe to clip.
10. Bleed hydraulic system. ***See this section.***
11. Remove safety stands. Lower vehicle.

SLAVE CYLINDER - FROM 97MY

Service repair no - 33.35.01

Remove

1. Raise front of vehicle.

WARNING: Support on safety stands.

2. Remove gearbox RH acoustic cover. ***See CHASSIS AND BODY, Repair.***
3. Position container to collect fluid spillage.

CAUTION: Do not allow brake fluid to contact painted surfaces. Paint damage will occur. Thoroughly clean spillages with clean, warm water.

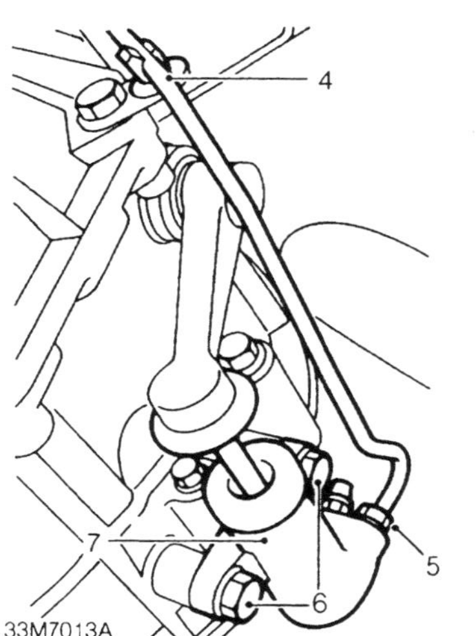

4. Release pipe from clip.
5. Remove pipe union from slave cylinder.

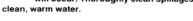

CAUTION: Plug the connections.

6. Remove 2 bolts securing slave cylinder to clutch housing.
7. Remove slave cylinder from push rod.

Refit

8. Ensure mating surfaces of slave cylinder and clutch housing are clean.
9. Clean pushrod.
10. Fit slave cylinder to push rod and align to clutch housing.
11. Fit bolts securing slave cylinder to clutch housing and tighten to ***25 Nm. (18lbf.ft)***
12. Remove plugs from slave cylinder and pipe union.
13. Clean pipe union and slave cylinder.
14. Connect and tighten pipe union to slave cylinder.
15. Secure pipe to clip.
16. Bleed clutch system. ***See this section.***
17. Fit gearbox RH acoustic cover. ***See CHASSIS AND BODY, Repair.***

Notes

37 - MANUAL GEARBOX

CONTENTS

Page

R380 GEARBOX

REPAIR

GEARBOX

Service repair no - 37.20.02 - Gearbox Renew
Service repair no - 37.20.02/99 - Gearbox Remove for Access

Remove

1. Raise vehicle on four post lift.
2. Disconnect battery negative lead.
3. **Petrol Vehicles:** Release 2 clips securing cooling fan cowling to radiator. Remove cowl.
4. Remove centre console. ***See CHASSIS AND BODY, Repair.***

5. Remove 6 nuts securing gaiter ring. Remove ring and gaiter

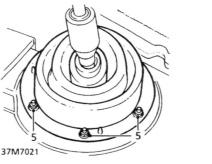

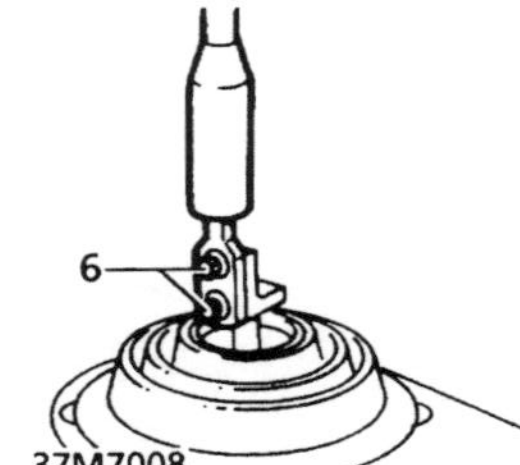

6. Remove 2 bolts securing gear lever. Remove lever.
7. Remove handbrake cable clevis pin.
8. Release handbrake cable from grommet in tunnel. Refit cable grommet to tunnel.

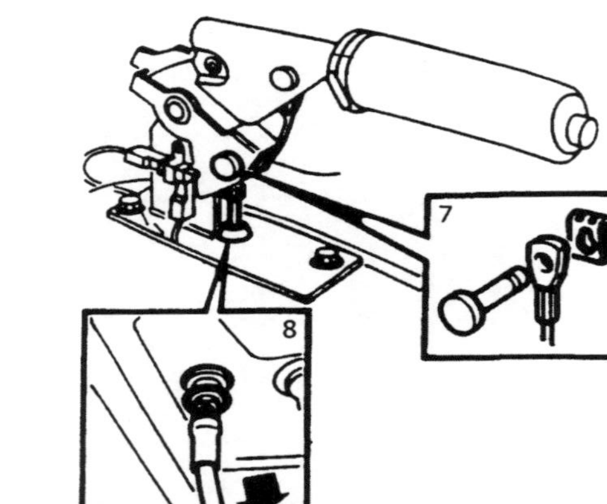

9. Raise lift. Drain gearbox and transfer box oil. ***See SECTION 10, Maintenance.***
10. Remove exhaust front pipe. ***See MANIFOLD AND EXHAUST SYSTEM, Repair.***
11. **Diesel Vehicles:** Remove chassis crossmember. ***See CHASSIS AND BODY, Repair.***
12. Remove 4 bolts securing rear propeller shaft guard. Remove guard.

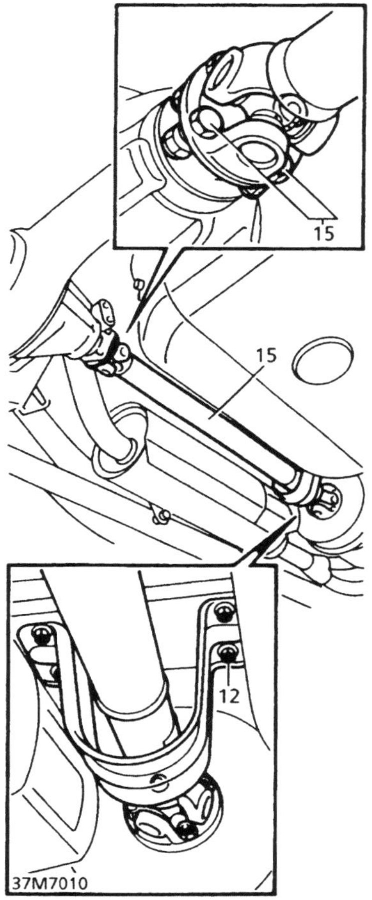

37M7010

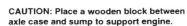

13. Mark transfer box and propeller shaft flanges to aid re-assembly.
14. Raise one wheel on each axle to allow rotation of propeller shafts.
15. Remove 4 nuts and bolts from each flange. Disconnect propeller shafts. Tie aside.

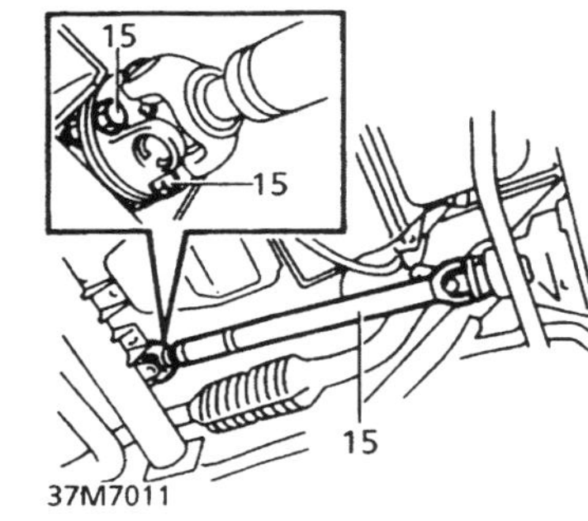
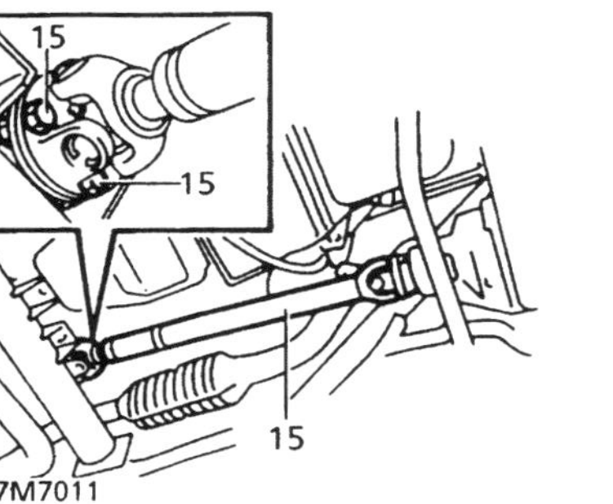

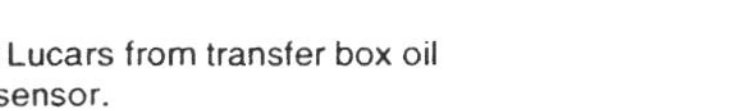

37M7011

16. Disconnect 2 Lucars from transfer box oil temperature sensor.

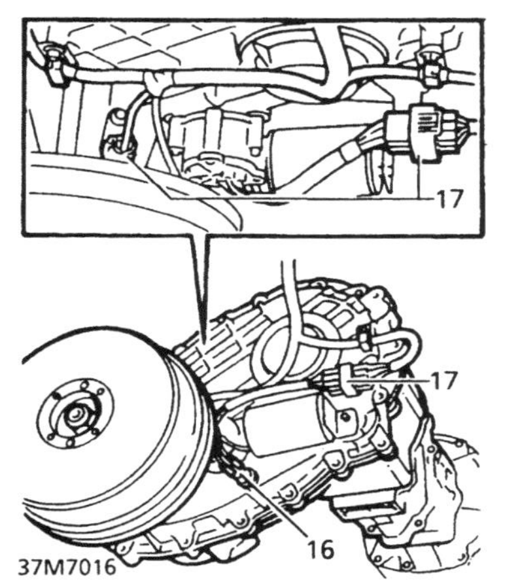

37M7016

17. Disconnect multiplugs from high/low motor and output shaft speed sensor.

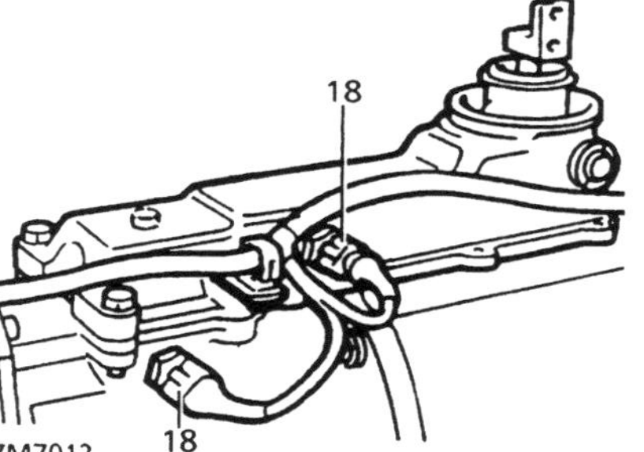

37M7012

18. Disconnect multiplugs from reverse and neutral switches.
19. Release harness from clips.
20. Remove 3 bolts securing oil cooler pipe adaptor to gearbox.
21. Release adaptor, collect 2 'O' rings and discard. Plug connections.

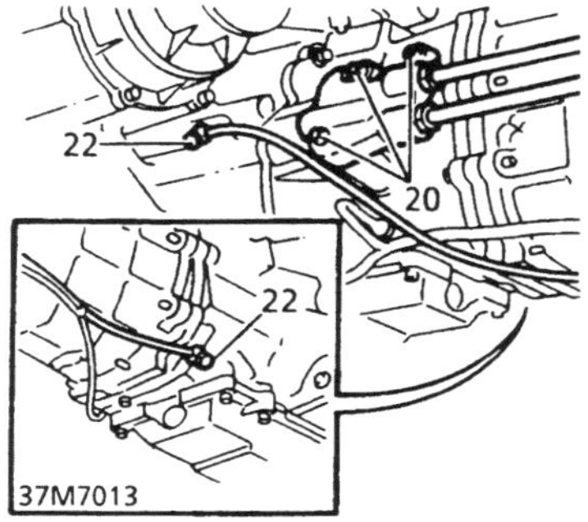

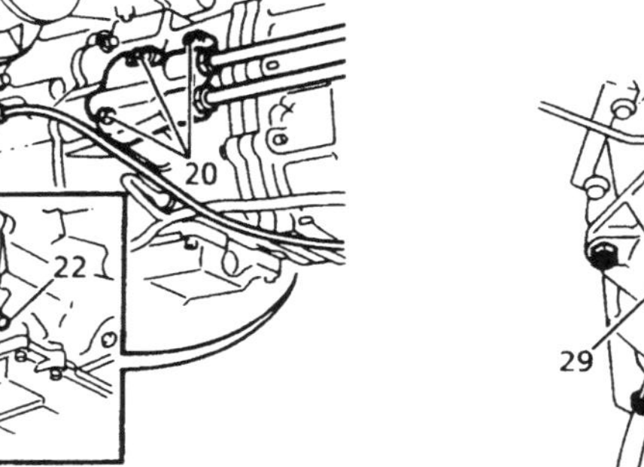

37M7013

22. Remove banjo bolts securing breather pipes to gearbox and transfer box.
23. Collect 2 sealing washers from each union and discard. Plug pipes and connections.
24. Tie breather and oil cooler pipes aside.
25. Position adaptor plate to transmission lift. Secure with bolts.

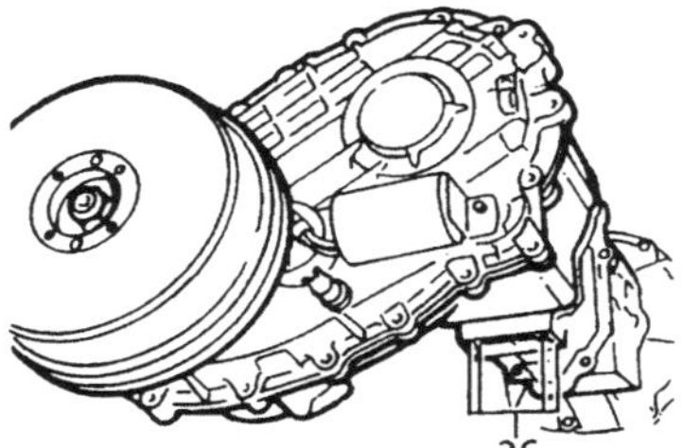

37M7014

26. Raise transmission lift into position. Secure adaptor plate to gearbox mounting bracket holes with 4 bolts.
27. Remove transmission stand.
28. Lower transmission for access.

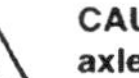

CAUTION: Place a wooden block between axle case and sump to support engine.

29. Remove bolt securing harness bracket to gearbox.

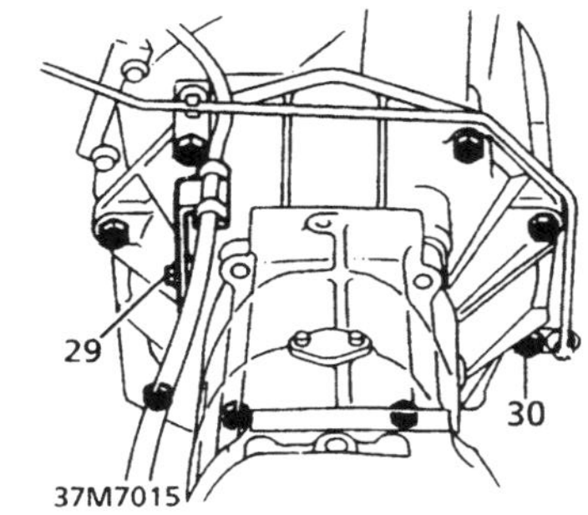

37M7015

30. Remove 8 bolts securing gearbox to bell housing.

CAUTION: Do not allow the weight of the gearbox to be supported by the clutch.

31. With assistance, release gearbox from clutch plate splines.
32. Lower transmission assembly away from vehicle.
33. ***Do not carry out further dismantling if component is removed for access only.***
34. Attach lifting eyes to transmission.
35. Attach hoist to lifting eyes. Take weight of transmission.
36. Remove lift adaptor. Hoist transmission assembly onto bench.
37. Fit lifting eye to transmission brake drum. Raise gearbox on end.

CAUTION: Position packers beneath bell housing extension to provide clearance for input shaft.

38. Remove 6 bolts securing transfer box to gearbox. Release from 2 ring dowels. Remove transfer box.

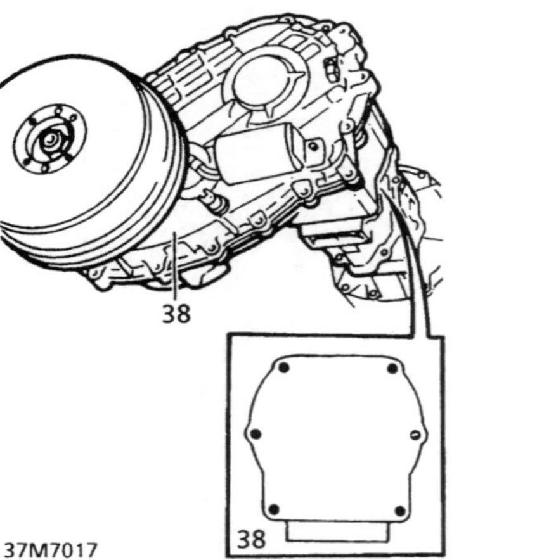

37M7017

39. Remove 2 bolts securing clutch release bearing spigot. Remove spigot.

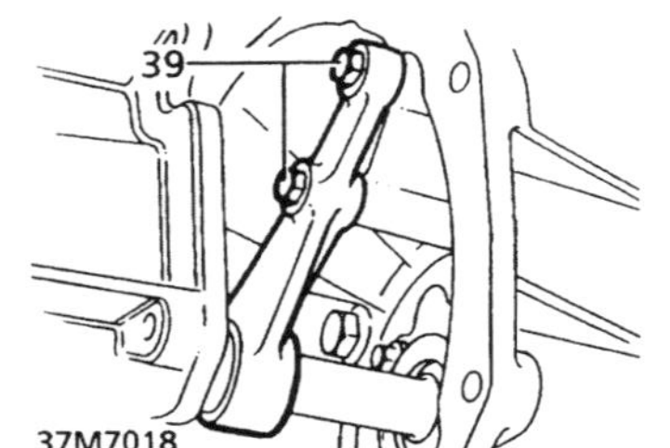

37M7018

40. Lay gearbox on side. Position bell housing extension over edge of bench.
41. Remove 6 bolts securing bell housing extension. Release from 2 ring dowels. Remove from gearbox.

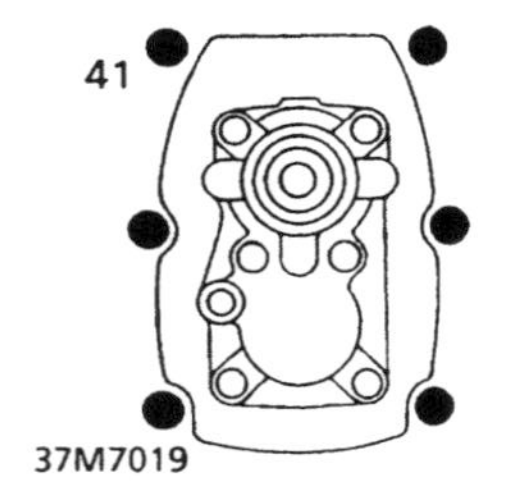

37M7019

42. Ensure mating faces are clean.
43. Clean release bearing spigot. Lightly coat running surface with grease. ***See LUBRICANTS, FLUIDS AND CAPACITIES, Information.***
44. Position bell housing extension to gearbox. Engage ring dowels. Secure with bolts. Tighten to ***45 Nm. (33 lbf.ft)***
45. Position clutch release bearing spigot. Secure with bolts. Tighten to ***18 Nm. (13 lbf.ft)***

46. Place gearbox on end. Position transfer box.
47. Engage transfer box to ring dowels. Secure to gearbox with bolts. Tighten to ***45 Nm. (33 lbf.ft)***
48. Place transmission on side. Fit lifting eyes.
49. Raise transmission to lift adaptor. Secure to adaptor plate with bolts.
50. Detach hoist. Remove lifting eyes.

Refit

51. With assistance, depress clutch pedal. Align clutch friction plate with either:
    LRT-12-001 **Petrol models** or
    LRT-12-123 **Diesel models.**
52. Release clutch pedal. Remove aligning tool.
53. Select gear to aid input shaft alignment.
54. Position transmission to engine. Engage input shaft to friction plate splines.

CAUTION: Do not allow the weight of the gearbox to be supported by the clutch.

55. Engage bell housing ring dowels. Secure gearbox to bell housing with bolts. Tighten to ***45 Nm. (33 lbf.ft)***
56. Select neutral.
57. Raise transmission. Support under brake drum with transmission jack.
58. Remove transmission lift adaptor. Remove lift.
59. Untie breather and oil cooler pipes.
60. Remove plugs from pipes pipes and connections.
61. Fit new 'O' rings to oil cooler pipe adaptor. Position adaptor to gearbox. Secure with bolts.
62. Fit new sealing washers to breather pipes. Position pipes. Secure with banjo bolts.
63. Position harness bracket to gearbox and secure with bolt.
64. Secure harness to clips.
65. Connect multiplugs to reverse and neutral switches.
66. Connect multiplugs to high/low motor and output shaft speed sensor.
67. Connect Lucar terminals to transfer box oil temperature sensor.
68. Raise one wheel on each axle to allow rotation of propeller shafts.
69. Position propeller shafts to transfer box flanges. Align marks.
70. Secure shafts with nuts and bolts. Tighten to ***48 Nm. (35 lbf.ft)***
71. Fit rear propeller shaft guard. Secure with bolts.
72. Route handbrake cable through grommet in transmission tunnel.
73. **Diesel Vehicles.** Fit chassis cross member. ***See CHASSIS AND BODY, Repair.***
74. Fit exhaust front pipe. ***See MANIFOLD AND EXHAUST SYSTEM, Repair.***
75. Refill gearbox and transfer box fluids. ***See LUBRICANTS, FLUIDS AND CAPACITIES, Information.***
76. Fit seal around gearbox remote housing to transmission tunnel aperture.
77. Connect handbrake cable to lever. Secure with clevis pin and clip.
78. Position gear lever. Secure with bolts. Tighten to ***25 Nm. (18 lbf.ft)***
79. Fit gaiter and ring. secure with nuts.
80. Fit centre console. ***See CHASSIS AND BODY, Repair.***
81. **Petrol Vehicles.** Position radiator cooling fan cowling. Secure with clips.
82. Reconnect battery negative lead.

OUTPUT SHAFT SEAL

Service repair no - 37.23.01

Remove

1. Disconnect battery negative lead.
2. Remove transfer box. ***See TRANSFER BOX, Repair.***
3. Lever seal from extension housing.

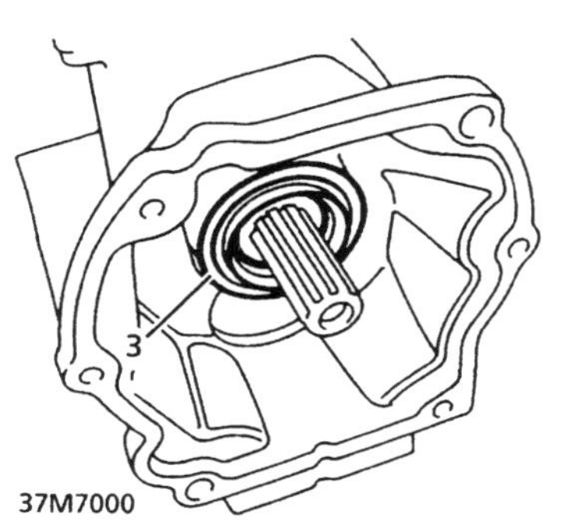

37M7000

⚠ **CAUTION: Ensure seal location does not become damaged.**

Refit

4. Ensure mating faces are clean.
5. Lubricate seal lip with transmission oil.
6. Using LRT-37-014, fit seal to extension housing.
7. Fit transfer box. ***See TRANSFER BOX, Repair.***
8. Reconnect battery negative lead.

SELECTOR REMOTE HOUSING

Service repair no - 37.16.29

Remove

1. Raise vehicle on four post lift.
2. Disconnect battery negative lead.
3. Remove centre console. ***See CHASSIS AND BODY, Repair.***
4. Remove 6 nuts securing gaiter ring. Remove ring and gaiter.

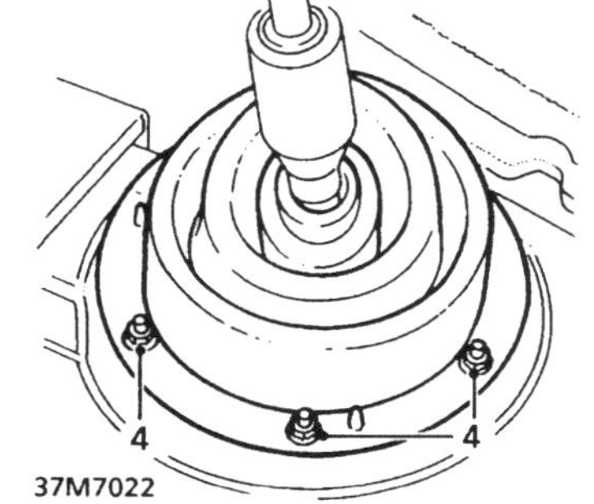

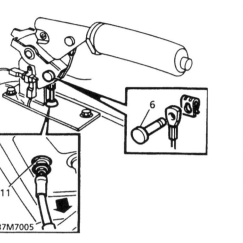

37M7022

5. Remove 2 bolts securing gear lever. Remove lever.

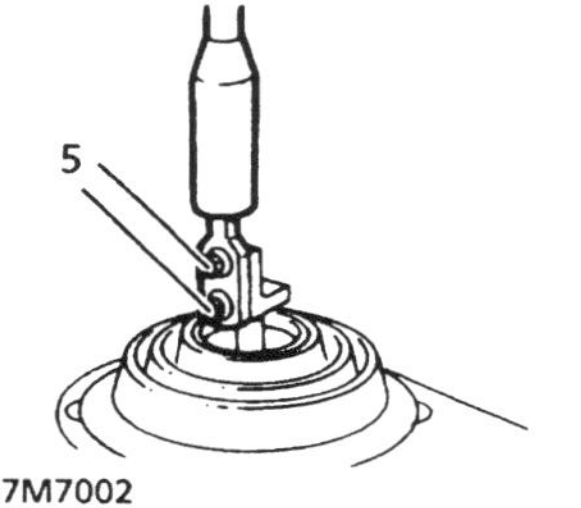

37M7002

6. Remove handbrake cable clevis pin.

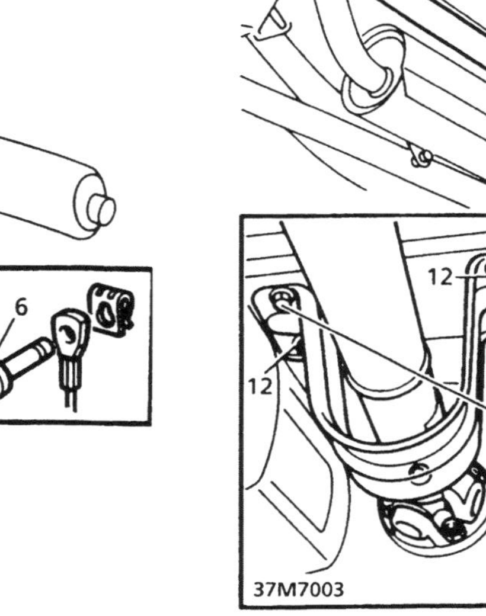

37M7005

37M7003

7. Raise lift.
8. Support gearbox using transmission jack.
9. Remove exhaust front pipe. ***See MANIFOLD AND EXHAUST SYSTEM, Repair.***
10. **Diesel Vehicles.** Remove chassis cross member. ***See CHASSIS AND BODY, Repair.***
11. Release hand brake cable from grommet in tunnel. Refit grommet to tunnel.
12. Remove 4 bolts securing propeller shaft guard. Remove guard.

13. Disconnect 2 Lucars from transfer box oil temperature sensor.

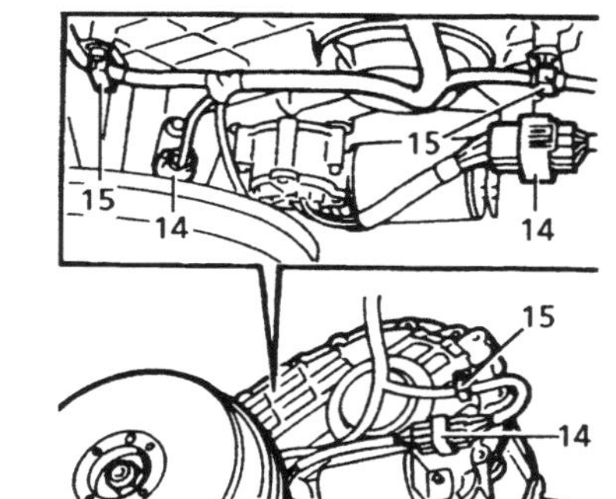

37M7006

14. Disconnect multiplugs from High/Low motor and output shaft speed sensor.
15. Release harness from 2 clips on transfer gearbox brackets.
16. Lower gearbox for access.

CAUTION: Ensure engine does not foul bulkhead.

17. Disconnect neutral switch multiplug.

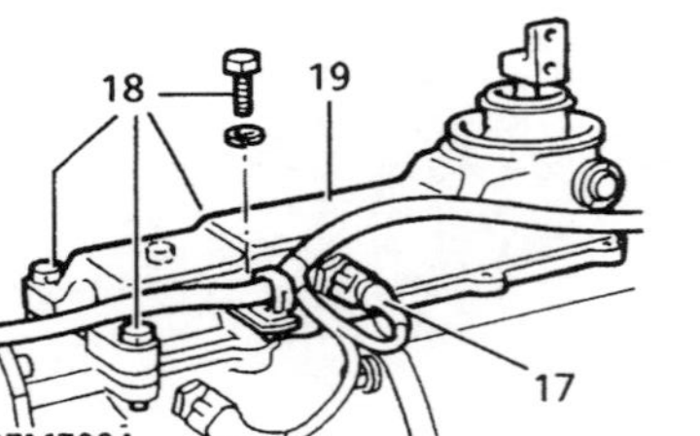

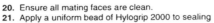

37M7004

18. Remove 4 bolts securing remote housing to gearbox. Position harness bracket aside.
19. Remove selector remote housing from 2 location dowels.

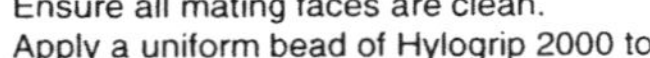

Refit

20. Ensure all mating faces are clean.
21. Apply a uniform bead of Hylogrip 2000 to sealing face of remote housing as shown.
22. Position remote housing. Engage remote spigot into selector yoke.
23. Engage housing to location dowels. Align harness bracket.
24. Secure remote housing with bolts. Tighten to ***25 Nm. (18 lbf.ft)***
25. Connect neutral switch multiplug.
26. Connect multiplugs to High/Low motor and output shaft speed sensor.
27. Connect Lucars to transfer box fluid temperature sensor.
28. Secure harness in clips.
29. Position propeller shaft guard. Secure with bolts.
30. Route hand brake cable through grommet in transmission tunnel.
31. Fit exhaust front pipe. ***See MANIFOLD AND EXHAUST SYSTEM, Repair.***
32. **Diesel Vehicles.** Fit chassis cross member. ***See CHASSIS AND BODY, Repair.***
33. Remove jack. Lower lift.
34. Connect handbrake cable to lever. Secure with clevis pin and clip.
35. Fit seal around gearbox remote housing to transmission tunnel aperture.
36. Position gear lever. Secure with bolts. Tighten to ***25 Nm. (18 lbf.ft)***
37. Fit gaiter and ring. Secure with nuts.
38. Fit centre console. ***See CHASSIS AND BODY, Repair.***
39. Reconnect battery negative lead.

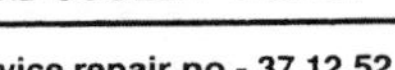

FLUID COOLER - PETROL

Service repair no - 37.12.52

Remove

1. Disconnect battery negative lead.
2. Remove engine oil cooler. ***See ENGINE, Repair.***
3. Remove 4 trim studs securing air deflectors. Remove deflectors.
4. Position container to collect fluid spillage.
5. Unscrew fluid pipe union nuts. Collect 'O' rings and discard.

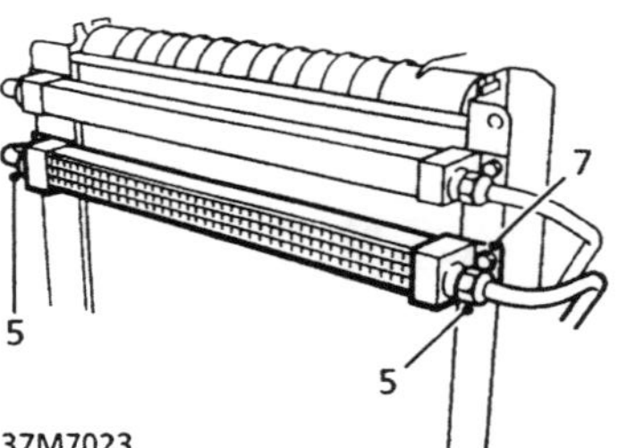

37M7023

6. Plug pipes and connections.
7. Remove 4 bolts securing cooler to radiator bracket.
8. Remove cooler.

Refit

9. Fit cooler.
10. Fit and tighten 4 bolts securing cooler to mounting bracket.
11. Remove plugs from cooler and pipes.
12. Ensure pipe unions are clean.
13. Lubricate new 'O' rings seals with clean fluid. Fit seals to pipes.
14. Connect pipes to cooler. Tighten to ***30 Nm. (22 lbf.ft)***
15. Remove container.
16. Fit air deflectors and secure with studs.
17. Fit engine oil cooler. ***See ENGINE, Repair.***
18. Reconnect battery negative lead.
19. Top up gearbox fluid. ***See SECTION 10, Maintenance.***

FLUID COOLER - DIESEL

Service repair no - 37.12.52

Remove

1. Remove radiator. ***See COOLING SYSTEM, Repair.***

Refit

2. Reverse removal procedure.

41 - TRANSFER BOX

CONTENTS

Page

DESCRIPTION AND OPERATION

REPAIR

Transfer box component layout

M41 7643

1. High/low switch (Manual vehicles only)
2. BeCM
3. Selector lever assembly (Automatic transmission vehicles only)
4. EAT ECU (Automatic transmission vehicles only)
5. Transfer box ECU
6. Transfer box
7. Gearbox (Automatic transmission shown)

Transfer box control schematic

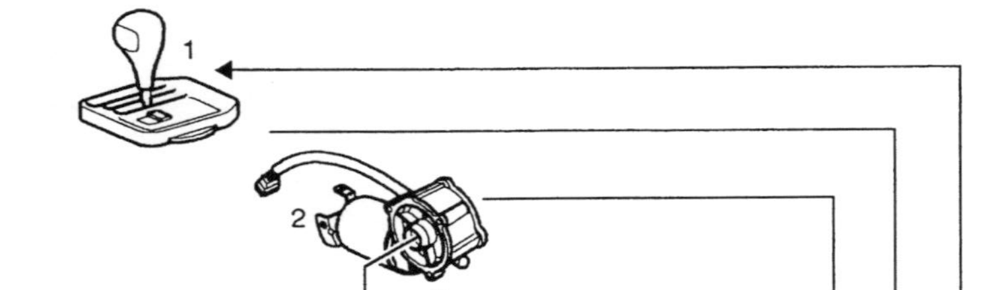

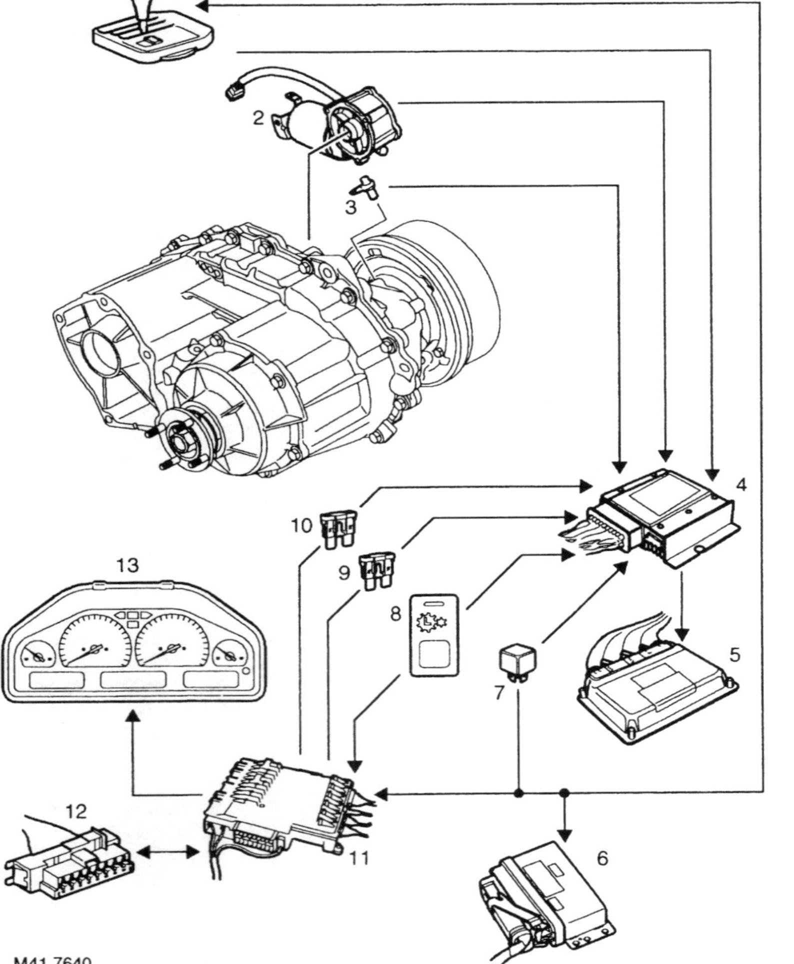

M41 7640

1. Automatic transmission and transfer box selector
2. Speed sensor
3. Ratio control motor
4. Transfer Box ECU
5. ECM (NAS vehicles only)
6. EAT ECU (Automatic transmission only)
7. Neutral switch (Manual transmission only)
8. High/Low fascia switch (Manual transmission only)
9. BeCM Fuse 4 Battery supply to Transfer Box ECU and ratio control motor
10. BeCM Fuse 6 Ignition supply to Transfer Box ECU
11. BeCM
12. Diagnostic socket
13. Instrument pack

TRANSFER BOX - DESCRIPTION

General

All models are fitted with a Borg Warner transfer box. The transfer box is a four wheel drive, two speed ratio reducing gearbox with high and low range outputs selected electrically by the driver.

A differential is fitted between the front and rear output shafts to allow the propeller shafts to rotate at different speeds when the vehicle is cornering. Drive to the front propeller shaft is through a viscous coupling, which eliminates the requirement for a differential lock.

The high and low ranges are selected by the driver. On manual transmission vehicles a switch is located on the fascia and when pressed selects low range. On automatic transmission vehicles high and low ranges are selected by moving the auto transmission selector lever across the H-gate to the required position.

On all vehicles, when the transfer box has changed to high range, 'HIGH' is displayed momentarily in the instrument pack message centre. On automatic transmission vehicles, if low range is selected, the message centre momentarily displays 'LOW' and then permanently displays 'L'. On manual transmission vehicles the message centre permanently displays 'LOW'.

The high and low range selection is performed by a ratio control motor located on the transfer box. The motor is controlled by a Transfer Box ECU located below the LH front seat. The ECU is connected electrically to other ECU's to ensure that all conditions for a successful range change are correct. The transfer box ECU receives inputs and provides outputs to/from the following ECU's:

- Body electrical Control Module (BeCM)
- Electronic Automatic Transmission (EAT) ECU
- Engine Control Module (ECM) (NAS only).

High/low range selection - Automatic transmission vehicles

On automatic transmission vehicles, high and low range selection is performed using the transmission selector lever. The selector lever assembly consists of a lever and a cover attached to a cast base. The base is located on a gasket and secured to the transmission tunnel.

The base has an 'H' pattern for the lever to move in. The lever is hinged to the base and is moved across the 'H' pattern to select HI or LO range operating a microswitch located in the base. The driver's side of the 'H' pattern is the high range selection in all markets.

The cover incorporates LED lever position indicators for high and low range gear selection. Operation of the LED indicators are controlled by the BeCM. The selected range is displayed by the LED's being illuminated brightly, with the unused range LED's dimmed. An electrical connector at the rear of the cover connects the selector lever assembly to the vehicle wiring.

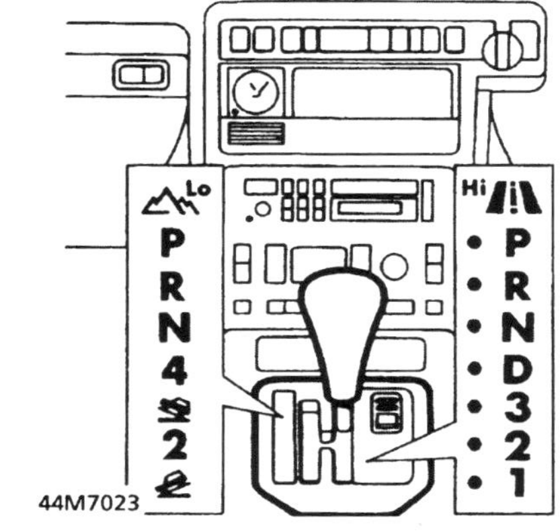

High/low range selection - Manual transmission vehicles

On manual transmission vehicles, high and low range selection is performed using a latching pushbutton switch on the fascia. The switch has an indicator lamp which flashes when the transfer box is changing range and is permanently illuminated in low range.

Transfer Box

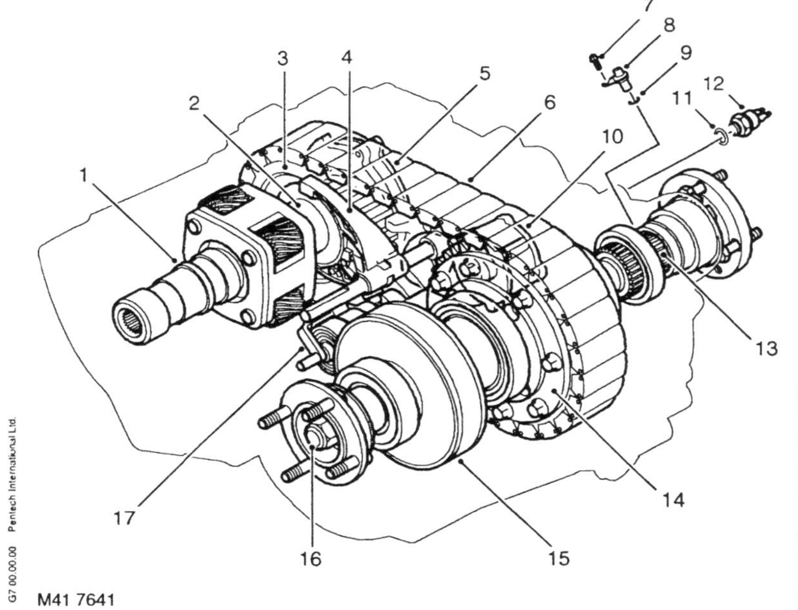

1. Epicyclic gear set
2. Reduction hub
3. Drive gear
4. Selector fork
5. Oil pump
6. Morse chain
7. Bolt
8. Speed sensor
9. 'O' ring
10. Ratio control motor
11. Temperature sensor
12. Sealing washer
13. Rear output shaft
14. Differential unit
15. Viscous coupling unit
16. Front output shaft
17. Selector spool

NOTE: For a detailed description of the transfer gearbox refer to the Borg Warner Overhaul Manual.

The transfer box comprises:
- a front and rear casing
- an epicyclic gear set
- a viscous coupling
- a differential unit
- a ratio control motor
- a lubrication pump.

The epicyclic gear set is located in the front casing and comprises a sun gear and four planet gears. The sun gear receives the drive from the gearbox output shaft and transfers the drive directly to a reduction hub. The reduction hub is located on a splined intermediate shaft which rotates at the same speed.

The reduction hub is moved along the intermediate shaft by the selector spool and the ratio control motor to one of three positions; high, low and neutral.

In the high position, the reduction hub is driven directly from the sun gear and rotates the intermediate shaft at the same speed as the gearbox output shaft.

In the low position, the reduction hub is engaged with the planet carrier and rotates at a lower speed than the gearbox output shaft.

In the neutral position, the reduction hub is not engaged with either the sun gear or the planet carrier and no drive is passed from the gearbox output shaft to the intermediate shaft.

Differential unit

Drive from the intermediate shaft is transferred by a morse chain to the differential unit. The differential unit comprises sun and planet gears. The rear output passes through the differential unit sun gear shaft and engages with the planet carrier. The splined forward end of the rear output shaft provides location for the viscous coupling unit inner spline. The outer diameter of the sun gear shaft engages with the outer splines of the viscous coupling unit.

Viscous coupling unit

The viscous coupling operates in conjunction with the differential unit to control the proportion of drive torque transferred to the front and rear drive shafts. The viscous coupling is a sealed unit filled with a silicon jelly which surrounds discs within the unit. The silicon jelly has properties which increase its viscosity and resistance to flow when agitated and heated.

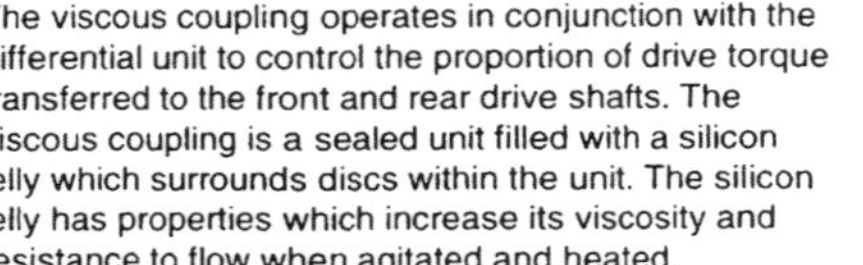

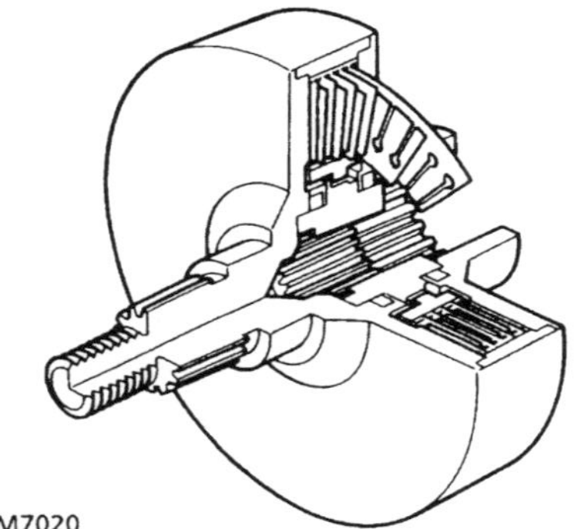

41M7020

During normal driving conditions, slight variations in the relative speed of each drive shaft is insufficient to increase the viscosity of the silicon jelly. Therefore the resistance within the viscous coupling is low.

In off-road conditions, when the wheels lose grip on loose or muddy surfaces, a greater difference in the rotational speeds of the front and rear drive shafts exists. The slippage, due to the difference in rotational speeds of the drive shafts, within the viscous coupling agitates the silicon jelly causing heat which increases the viscosity. The increased viscosity increases the drag between the discs forcing both sets of discs to rotate at similar speeds, reducing axle slippage and increasing traction. The viscous coupling removes the need for a manually controlled differential lock.

Selector mechanism

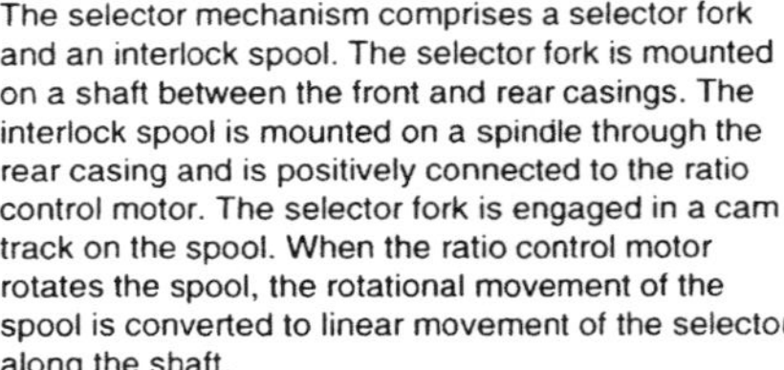

The selector mechanism comprises a selector fork and an interlock spool. The selector fork is mounted on a shaft between the front and rear casings. The interlock spool is mounted on a spindle through the rear casing and is positively connected to the ratio control motor. The selector fork is engaged in a cam track on the spool. When the ratio control motor rotates the spool, the rotational movement of the spool is converted to linear movement of the selector along the shaft.

The selector is engaged with the reduction hub. The linear movement of the selector moves the reduction hub in the epicyclic gear set changing the ratio between high, low or neutral.

Lubrication

Lubrication is provided by a low geroter plunger type oil pump which is driven from the epicyclic gear set. The oil pump passes oil through oil ways in the components to lubricate the epicyclic gear set. The differential unit and morse chain are partially immersed in oil and are lubricated as the components rotate.

Transfer Box Electrical Components

Ratio control motor

The ratio control motor is located on the rear casing of the transfer box and secured with four bolts. The motor comprises a conventional single speed permanent magnet type motor. The motor spindle has a worm which engages with a worm wheel in a housing at the end of the motor. The worm wheel is attached to the spindle of the selector interlock spool inside the transfer box.

The worm wheel also drives a motor encoder which comprises four position switches. The transfer box ECU provides a 5 V signal to each switch and interprets the transfer box range by monitoring the condition of each switch.

The transfer box ECU reads the motor position in the form of a binary code with each switch either open or closed circuit. The ECU measures between the switches and an encoder ground on connector pin 19.

By using the combinations of the switches, the transfer box ECU can calculate the transfer box position and how the motor should operate to select the desired range. If the transfer box should move to a position outside the normal condition, i.e. left of high range, the ECU can move the motor to the correct position.

The table below shows the motor switch states and the corresponding motor position for each state.

Switch 1	Switch 2	Switch 3	Switch 4	Motor position
Pin 17	Pin 32	Pin 31	Pin 7	
Open	Open	Open	Closed	Left stop
Open	Closed	Open	Closed	Left of high
Closed	Closed	Open	Closed	High range
Closed	Closed	Closed	Closed	Right of high
Open	Closed	Closed	Closed	Zone 1
Open	Closed	Closed	Open	Neutral
Closed	Closed	Closed	Open	Zone 2
Closed	Open	Closed	Open	Low range
Closed	Open	Closed	Closed	Right stop

Speed sensor

The speed sensor is located in the rear casing and secured with a screw. A toothed reluctor ring is integrated on the rear output shaft. The inductive speed sensor senses the reluctor ring and produces a sine wave, impulse type signal as each tooth on the reluctor ring passes the sensor.

The transfer box ECU processes the signal from the speed sensor and compares this to a stored speed value in the memory to determine if a range change is allowed.

NOTE: The speed sensor is dedicated to the transfer box ECU to determine if a range change can be permitted.

Temperature sensor

The temperature sensor is screwed into the rear casing. The sensor has two Lucar connectors. One connector is attached to an earth eyelet connector, the other is connected to the BeCM.

When the transfer box oil reaches a temperature of between 140 and 150 °C (284 and 302 °F), contacts in the switch close, completing an earth path to the BeCM. The BeCM uses the completed earth path as a signal to generate a 'TRANSFER OVRHEAT' message in the message centre. The 'TRANSFER OVRHEAT' message is displayed alternately with a 'REFER HANDBOOK' message. When the transfer box oil cools to between 126 and 134 °C (258 and 273 °F), the switch contacts open and the 'TRANSFER OVRHEAT' message is extinguished.

Transfer box ECU

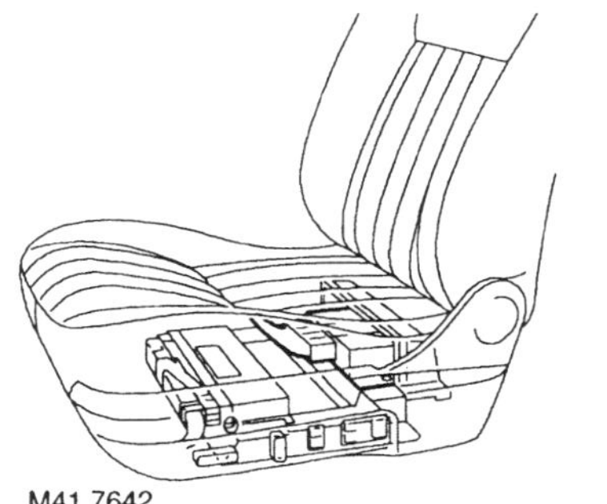

M41 7642

Transfer box ECU

The transfer box ECU is located below the front LH seat and is identified from the other ECU's located under the seat by its single 36 pin harness connector. The connector supplies power, earth, signal and sensor information to/from the ECU and other ECU's for transmission operation.

The BeCM, located below the right hand front seat, contains its own integral fusebox. The transfer box ECU receives a battery power supply from the BeCM via fuse number 4. An ignition on signal is also supplied from the BeCM via fuse 6. The ignition on signal is supplied to different ECU connector pins for manual and automatic transmission vehicles.

On NAS only vehicles, if a fault occurs which prevents the transfer box moving from low to high range, the transfer box ECU outputs a signal to the ECM which is interpreted as an OBDII fault flag.

The transfer box ECU provides feed and return paths to the ratio control motor to operate the motor in the required direction. Two pins are used to supply power to the motor in each direction. The feed is supplied from two pins to avoid overload and heat generation which would occur if one pin was used. A 5 V signal current is supplied to the four motor encoder switches which are used by the ratio control motor to determine motor position.

Speed signals from the transfer box speed sensor are received as an input to the transfer box ECU which calculates whether the speed is below the threshold to allow a range change.

Range change request signals are received from the H-gate selector switch on automatic transmission vehicles or the high/low switch on manual vehicles.

On automatic transmission vehicles, a park/neutral signal is transmitted from the BeCM to the transfer box ECU. On manual transmission vehicles, a neutral switch located in the transmission provides an earth signal which is used by the ECU and BeCM to determine that the transmission is in neutral. The park/neutral and neutral signal are used by the ECU to allow a range change only when the transmission is in neutral.

Outputs are provided by the transfer box ECU to the BeCM for high and low range status. The BeCM uses the signals for instrument pack message centre display of range status.

Transfer box ECU connector face view

Transfer box ECU connector pin details

Pin No.	Description	Input/Output
1	Motor drive - Counter clockwise	Output
2	Motor drive - Counter clockwise	Output
3	Not used	-
4	Ignition - Manual vehicles only	Input
5	Power earth	Input
6	Not used	-
7	Motor position switch 4	Input
8 to 12	Not used	-
13	Vehicle speed signal	Input
14	Low range status	Output
15	Transfer box neutral select	Input
16	Not used	-
17	Motor position switch 1	Input
18	Not used	-
19	Motor encoder earth	Output
20	Not used	-
21	Ignition - Automatic vehicles only	Input
22	Not used	-
23	Battery supply	Input
24	Battery supply	Input
25	Motor drive - Clockwise	Output

Pin No.	Description	Input/Output
26	Motor drive - Clockwise	Output
27	Not used	-
28	Transfer box OBDII link	Output
29	Power earth	Input
30	Vehicle speed signal earth	Input
31	Motor position switch 3	Input
32	Motor switch position 2	Input
33	High/Low range select	Input
34	Park/Neutral (Auto) Neutral (Manual) Signal	Input
35	High range status line	Output
36	Neutral range status line	Output

TRANSFER BOX - OPERATION

Transfer Box

Drive is transmitted to the transfer box from the gearbox output shaft which is permanently engaged in the sun gear of the epicyclic gear set. In high range the sun gear transmits drive directly to the selector sleeve. In low range, when the selector spool has moved the selector sleeve, the sun gear transmits drive through the planet carrier.

The rotation of the selector sleeve is transferred to the intermediate shaft. A gear attached to the intermediate shaft carries the morse chain which transfers the drive to the differential unit.

The rear output shaft passes through the differential unit and rotates at the same speed. The viscous coupling passes drive from the rear output shaft to the front output shaft. When the silicon fluid in the viscous coupling becomes warm its resistance to shear increases passing more drive to the front drive shaft increasing traction.

Electrical Operation

Range change

NOTE: Range changes should be performed with the vehicle stationary and although range changes are possible at very low speeds, this practice is not recommended.

Automatic transmission

To change range the vehicle speed must be reduced to below 5 mph (8 km/h). Move the gear selector to neutral and then across the H-gate into the neutral position in the selected range. The appropriate LED illuminations on the selected range side of the selector cover will flash and an audible warning will sound. The flashing LED's and the audible warning will continue while the ratio control motor is moving the transfer box to the selected range.

When the ratio control motor has moved the transfer box into the selected range the LED's will stop flashing, the audible warning will stop and a message is displayed in the message centre. The desired gear can be selected and the vehicle can be driven as required.

If the vehicle is moving above 5 mph (8 km/h) or the selector lever is moved into gear before the range change is complete, the change will not occur and a 'SLOW DOWN' or 'SELECT NEUTRAL' message will be displayed in the message centre.

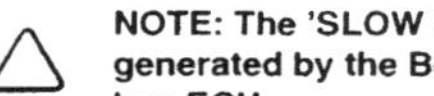

NOTE: The 'SLOW DOWN' message is generated by the BeCM, not the transfer box ECU.

The transfer box can be placed in the 'Neutral' position by moving the selector lever into the 'PARK' position. Insert a spare fuse (minimum 5 Amp) into fuse position 11 on the BeCM. After 5 seconds the transfer box moves to the neutral position, an audible warning will sound, a 'TRANSFER NEUTRAL' message is displayed in the message centre and the high and low LED illumination on the selector cover will extinguish.

Manual transmission

To change from high to low the vehicle speed must be below 5 mph (8 km/h) or from low to high the vehicle speed must be below 15 mph (24 Km/h).

Select neutral with the gear lever and press the high/low switch on the fascia. The indicator lamp on the switch will flash as the range change takes place. If the change is from high to low the lamp will continuously illuminate when the change is successfully completed. If the change is from low to high the lamp will extinguish when the change is complete. The message centre displays the selected range.

If a range change is requested and the vehicle is moving too fast or neutral has not been selected, the indicator lamp on the switch will flash and a 'SLOW DOWN' or 'SELECT NEUTRAL' message will appear in the message centre.

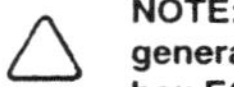

NOTE: The 'SLOW DOWN' message is generated by the BeCM, not the transfer box ECU.

The transfer box can be placed in the 'Neutral' position by placing the gear lever in neutral and inserting a spare fuse (minimum 5 Amp) into fuse position 11 on the BeCM. After 5 seconds the transfer box moves to neutral, an audible warning will sound and a 'TRANSFER NEUTRAL' message is displayed in the message centre.

Range information - Automatic transmission

High range

When the transfer box is in high range the message centre only displays the selected gear and the high range side of the selector lever cover is illuminated in green.

High to low range

When a change from high to low range is requested:

- The low range selector cover LED's flash in orange
- The high range selector cover LED's remain illuminated in green
- The transfer box amber warning lamp in the instrument pack flashes while the range change is taking place.

When the range change is complete:

- The low range selector cover LED's are continuously illuminated in orange
- The high range selector cover green LED illumination goes off
- The transfer box warning lamp goes off
- The message centre displays 'LOW' and after several seconds displays 'L' in front of the selected gear.

Low to high range

When a change from low to high range is requested:

- The high range selector cover LED's flash in green
- The low range selector cover LED's remain illuminated in orange
- The transfer box warning lamp in the instrument pack flashes while the range change is taking place.

When the range change is complete:

- The high range selector cover LED's are continuously illuminated in green
- The low range selector cover orange LED illumination goes off
- The transfer box warning lamp goes off
- The message centre displays 'HIGH' for several seconds, then 'HIGH' is removed and only the selected gear is displayed.

Range selection parameters incorrect

If a range change is requested and the vehicle speed is too high:

- The LED illumination on the selected side of the cover will flash
- A 'SLOW DOWN' message is displayed in the message centre
- The transfer box warning lamp in the instrument pack flashes.

If a range change is requested and the selector lever is moved before the range change is complete:

- The LED illumination on the selected side of the cover will flash
- A 'SELECT NEUTRAL' message is displayed in the message centre
- The BeCM will initiate an audible warning
- The transfer box warning lamp in the instrument pack flashes.

Transfer box to neutral

When a spare fuse (5 Amp minimum) is inserted in BeCM fuse position 11 to select transfer box neutral:

- A five second delay is initiated before the transfer box moves to neutral
- The BeCM initiates an audible warning
- A 'TRANSFER NEUTRAL' message is displayed in the message centre.

Range information - Manual transmission

High range

When the transfer box is in high range, the message centre does not display any transmission information and the high/low request switch indicator lamp is off.

High to low range

When a change from high to low is requested:

- The high/low switch indicator lamp flashes
- The transfer box warning lamp in the instrument pack flashes.

When the range change is complete:

- The high/low switch indicator lamp is illuminated continuously
- The transfer box warning lamp goes off
- A 'LOW' message is continuously displayed in the message centre.

Low to high range

When a change from low to high range is requested:

- The high/low switch indicator lamp flashes
- The transfer box warning lamp in the instrument pack flashes.

When the range change is complete:

- The high/low switch indicator lamp goes off
- The transfer box warning lamp goes off
- The message centre displays 'HIGH' for several seconds.

Range selection parameters incorrect

If a range change is requested and the vehicle speed is too high:

- The high/low switch indicator lamp will flash
- The transfer box warning lamp in the instrument pack will flash
- A 'SLOW DOWN' message is displayed in the message centre.

If a range change is requested and the transmission is in gear or a gear selected before range change is complete:

- The high/low switch indicator lamp will flash
- The transfer box warning lamp in the instrument pack will flash
- A 'SELECT NEUTRAL' message is displayed in the message centre for several seconds. If the vehicle remains in gear the message will not be repeated.

Transfer box to neutral

When a spare fuse (5 Amp minimum) is inserted in BeCM fuse position 11 to select transfer box neutral:

- A five second delay is initiated before the transfer box moves to neutral
- The BeCM initiates an audible warning
- A 'TRANSFER NEUTRAL' message is displayed in the message centre.

ELECTRONIC CONTROL UNIT

Service repair no - 41.30.01

Remove

1. Position left hand front seat fully up and forward.
2. Disconnect battery negative lead.
3. Remove 2 screws securing heater air duct. Remove duct.

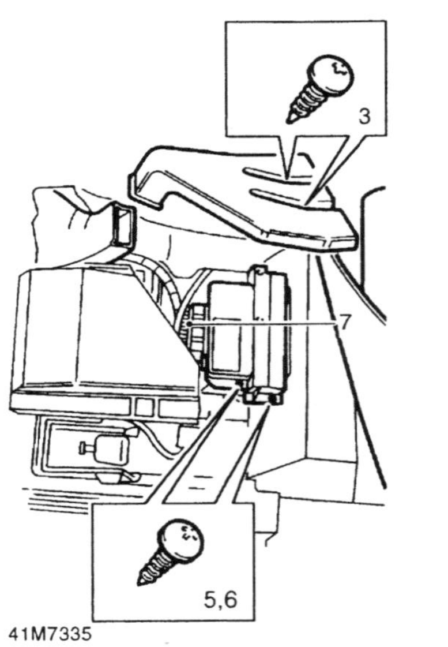

4. Raise carpet and underlay for access.
5. Remove 2 screws securing heater duct mounting. Remove mounting.
6. Remove 2 screws securing ECU.
7. Disconnect multiplug. Remove ECU.

Refit

8. Position ECU. Connect multiplug. Secure with screws.
9. Position heater duct mounting. Secure with screws.
10. Position underlay and carpet.
11. Position heater air duct. Secure with screws.
12. Reposition front seat.
13. Reconnect battery negative lead.

RATIO CONTROL MOTOR

Service repair no - 41.30.03

Remove

1. Raise vehicle on four post lift.
2. Disconnect battery negative lead.
3. Disconnect temperature sensor.
4. Disconnect motor multiplug.
5. Remove 4 bolts securing motor to transfer gearbox.
6. Remove motor.

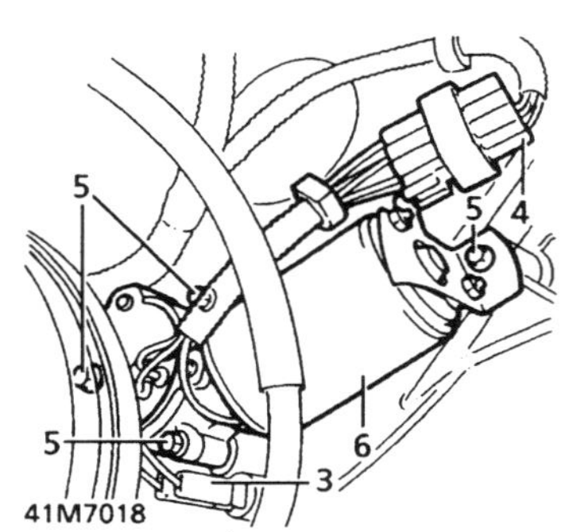

Refit

7. Fit motor and engage to drive spindle.
8. Tighten bolts to ***10Nm (7 lbf.ft).***
9. Connect motor and temperature sensor.
10. Reconnect battery negative lead.
11. Lower vehicle.

INPUT SHAFT OIL SEAL

Service repair no - 41.20.50

1. Disconnect battery negative lead.
2. Remove transfer box. ***See this section.***
3. Lever seal from location in transfer box.

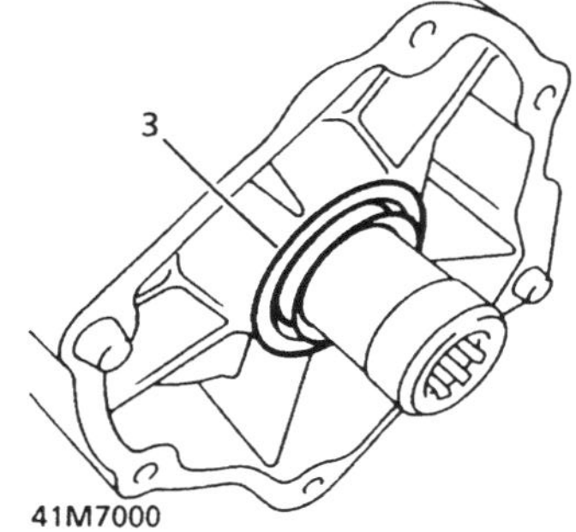

CAUTION: Ensure seal location does not become damaged.

Refit

4. Ensure mating faces are clean.
5. Lubricate seal lip with transmission fluid.
6. Using LRT-41-011, fit seal to transfer box.
7. Fit transfer box. ***See this section.***
8. Reconnect battery negative lead.

OUTPUT SHAFT OIL SEAL - FRONT

Service repair no - 41.20.51

Remove

1. Remove chassis cross member. ***See CHASSIS AND BODY, Repair.***
2. Mark propeller shaft and transfer gearbox flanges to aid assembly.
3. Remove 4 nuts and bolts securing propeller shaft flange. Tie shaft aside.

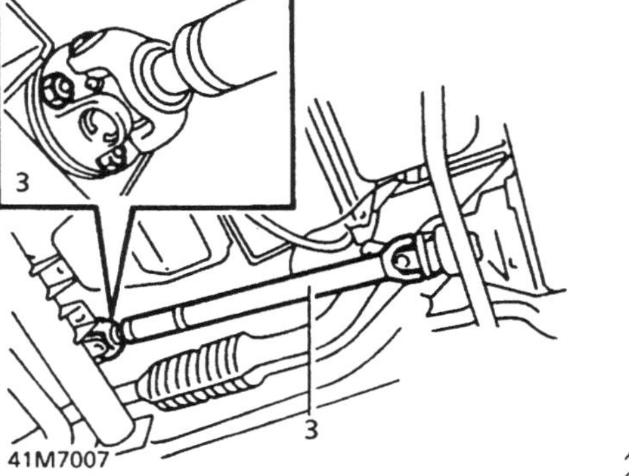

4. Use LRT-51-003 to restrain transfer box drive flange. Remove nut and discard. Collect washer.

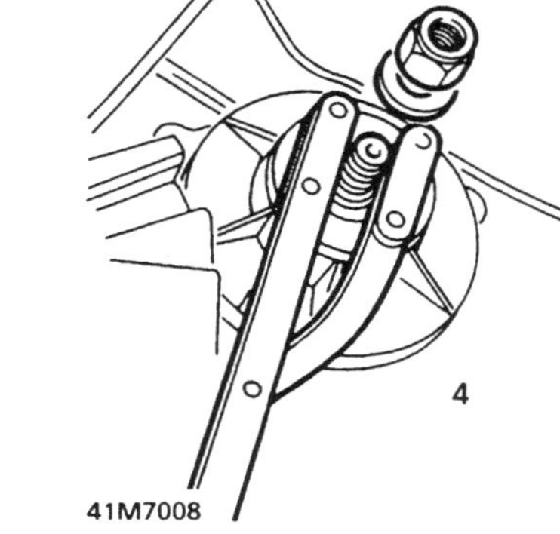

5. Using LRT-99-500 if necessary, withdraw flange from transfer box. Collect sealing washer.

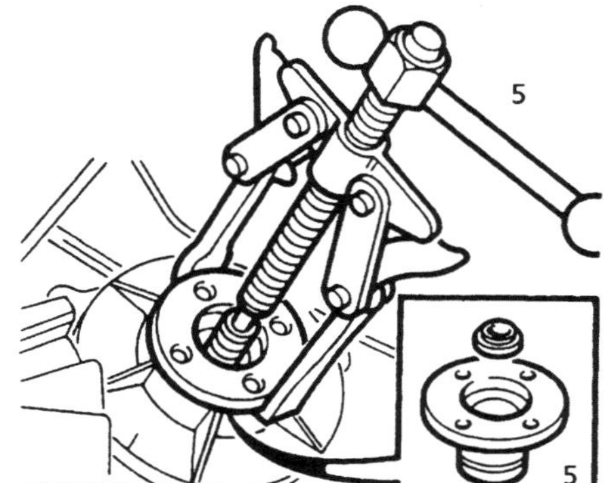

6. Lever seal from location in transfer box.

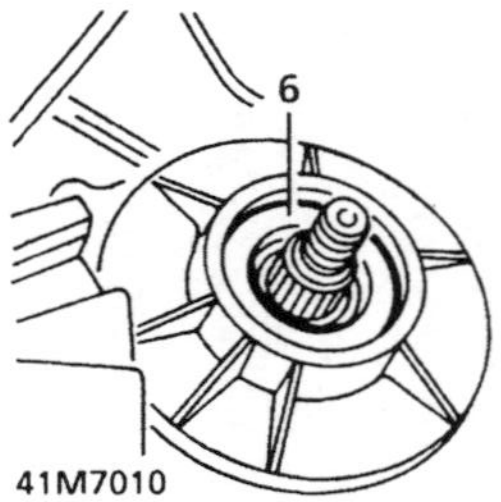

6

41M7010

⚠ **CAUTION: Ensure seal location does not become damaged.**

Refit

7. Ensure mating faces are clean.
8. Lubricate seal lip with transmission fluid.
9. Fit seal using LRT-41-011.

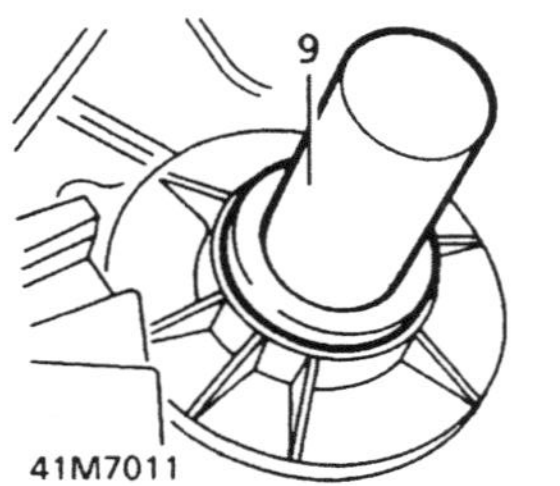

41M7011

10. Position flange. Fit sealing washer.
11. Use LRT-51-003 to restrain flange.
12. Secure flange with washer and new Nyloc nut. Tighten to ***148 Nm. (109 lbf.ft)***
13. Position propeller shaft to output flange. Align marks.
14. Secure propeller shaft with nuts and bolts. Tighten to ***48 Nm. (35 lbf.ft)***
15. Fit chassis cross member. ***See CHASSIS AND BODY, Repair.***
16. Replenish transfer box oil. ***See LUBRICANTS, FLUIDS AND CAPACITIES, Information.***

OUTPUT SHAFT OIL SEAL - REAR

Service repair no - 41.20.54

Remove

1. Raise vehicle on four post lift.
2. Disconnect battery negative lead.
3. Release handbrake.
4. Raise lift.
5. Remove 4 bolts securing propeller shaft guard to floor pan. Remove guard.

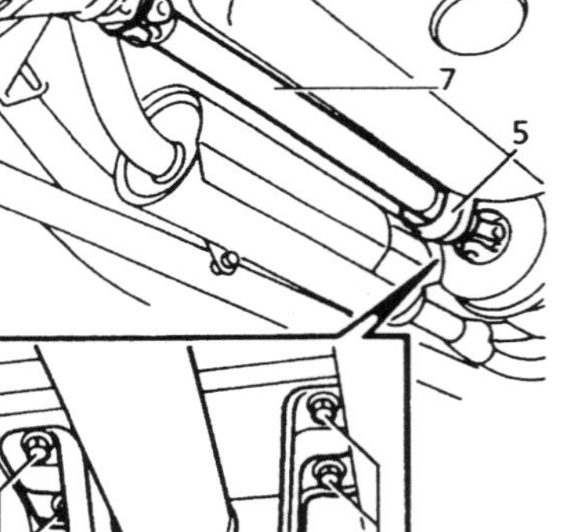
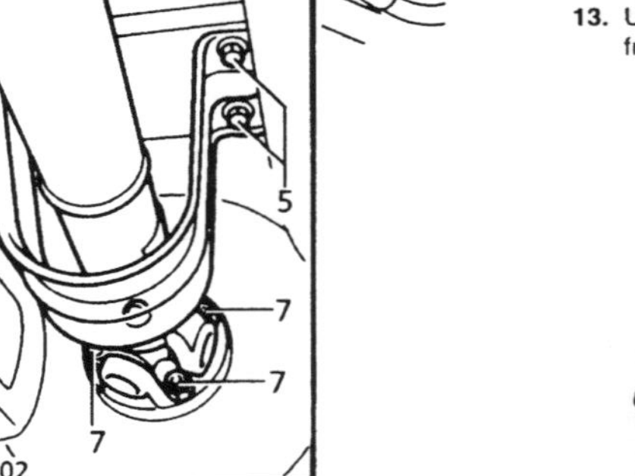

41M7002

6. Mark propeller shaft flange and brake drum to aid assembly.
7. Remove 4 nuts securing propeller shaft flange to brake drum. Release shaft. Tie aside.

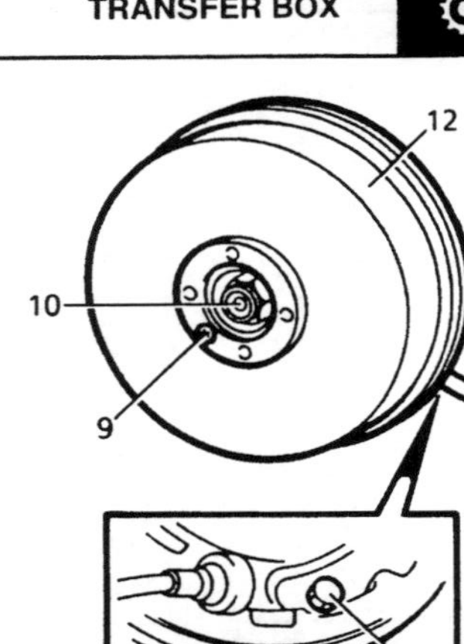

41M7005

8. Apply handbrake.
9. Remove screw securing brake drum to flange.
10. Remove nut and washer securing flange to output shaft, discard nut.
11. Release handbrake. Slacken park brake drum adjusting screw.
12. Remove park brake drum.
13. Using LRT-99-500 if necessary, withdraw flange from transfer box. Collect sealing washer.

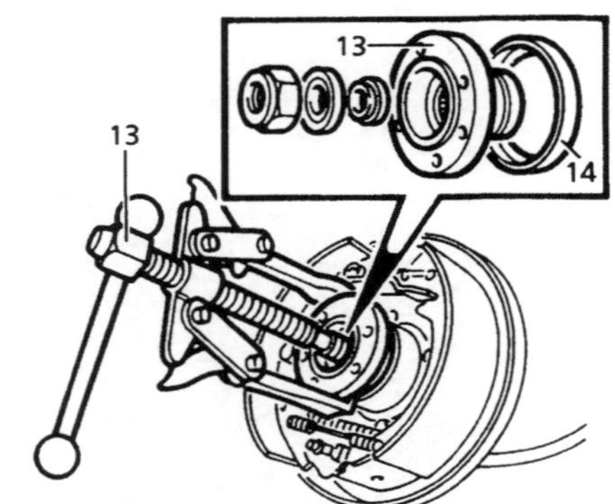
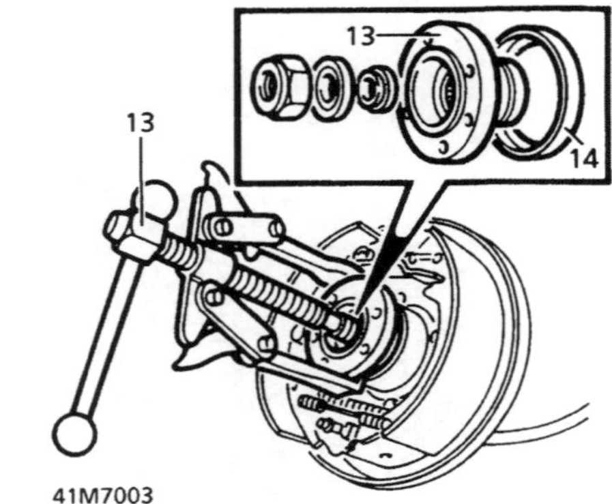

41M7003

14. Remove dust shield.
15. Lever seal from location in casing.

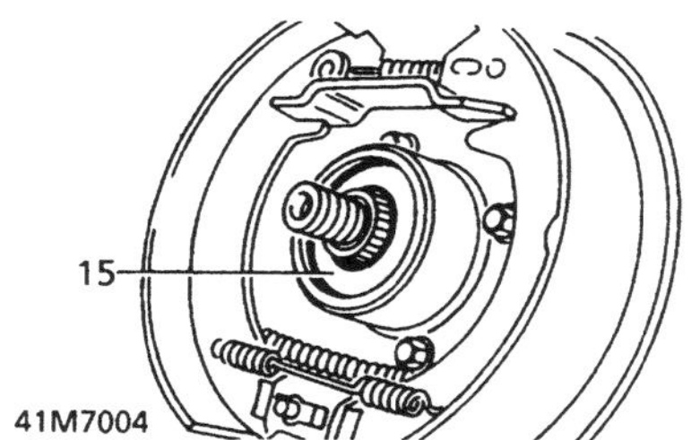

41M7004

⚠ **CAUTION: Ensure seal location does not become damaged.**

Refit

16. Ensure mating faces are clean.
17. Lubricate seal lip with transmission fluid.
18. Fit seal using LRT-41-011.

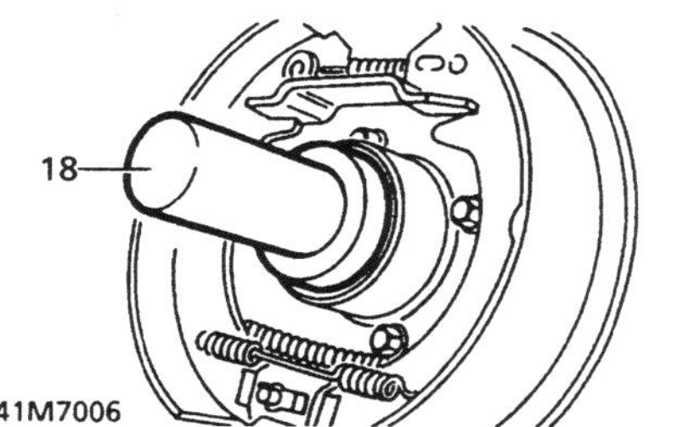

41M7006

19. Position dust shield.
20. Position flange. Fit sealing washer.
21. Fit flat washer and new Nyloc nut, finger tight.
22. Position brake drum. Secure to flange with screw.
23. Adjust park brake shoes. ***See BRAKES, Adjustment.***
24. Apply handbrake.
25. Tighten flange nut to ***148 Nm. (109 lbf.ft)***
26. Position propeller shaft flange on brake drum. Align marks.
27. Secure propeller shaft with bolts. Tighten to ***48 Nm. (35 lbf.ft)***
28. Fit propeller shaft guard. Secure with bolts.
29. Replenish transfer box oil. ***See LUBRICANTS, FLUIDS AND CAPACITIES, Information.***
30. Lower lift.
31. Reconnect battery negative lead.

TRANSFER BOX - UP TO 99MY

Service repair no - 41.20.25

Remove

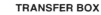

1. Position vehicle on four post lift.
2. Disconnect battery negative lead.
3. **Automatic Vehicles.**Remove window switch pack. ***See ELECTRICAL, Repair.***

Manual Vehicles:

4. Remove centre console. ***See CHASSIS AND BODY, Repair.***
5. Remove 6 nuts securing gaiter ring. Remove ring and gaiter.

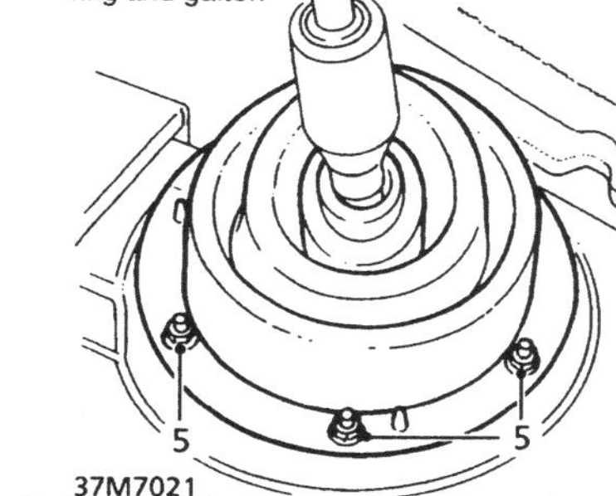

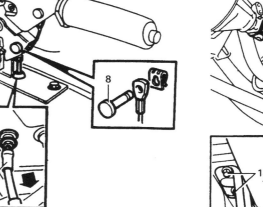

37M7021

6. Remove 2 bolts securing gear lever. Remove lever.

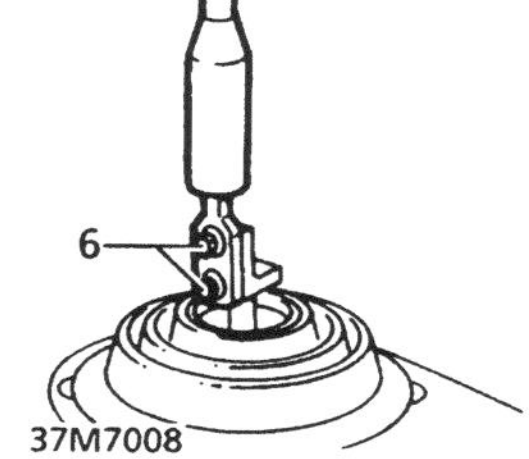

37M7008

All Vehicles:

7. Release handbrake.
8. Remove handbrake cable clevis pin.

8
13
41M7014

9. Raise lift. Drain gearbox and transfer box oil. ***See SECTION 10, Maintenance.***
10. Support transmission with cross beam.
11. Remove exhaust front pipe. ***See MANIFOLD AND EXHAUST SYSTEM, Repair.***
12. **Diesel Vehicles.** Remove chassis cross member. ***See CHASSIS AND BODY, Repair.***
13. Release hand brake cable from grommet in tunnel.
14. Remove 4 bolts securing rear propeller shaft guard. Remove guard.

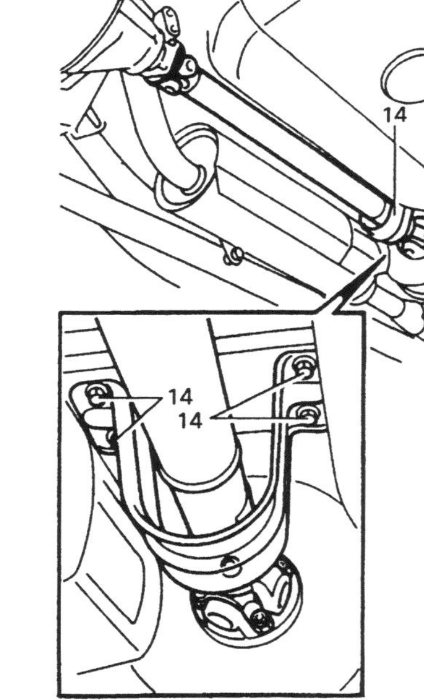

41M7015

15. Mark flanges on propeller shafts and transfer box to aid reassembly.
16. Raise one wheel on each axle to allow rotation of propeller shafts.
17. Remove fixings securing shafts to transfer box. Release shafts. Tie aside.
18. **Automatic Vehicles.**Disconnect gear selector cable trunnion from gearbox lever. Remove 2 bolts securing selector cable abutment bracket to gearbox. Place selector cable aside.

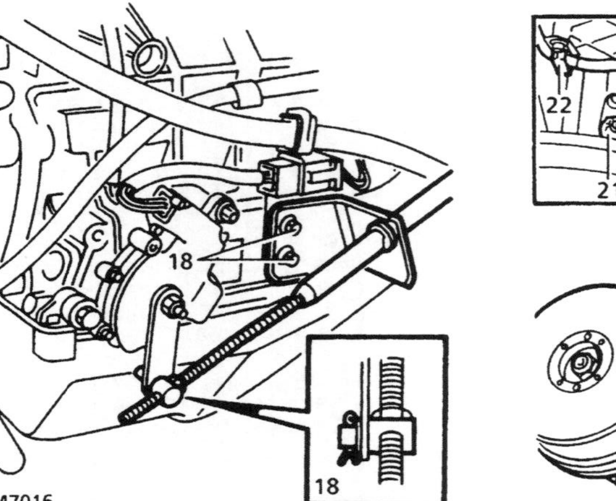

41M7016

19. Lower gearbox for access.
20. Disconnect 2 Lucars from transfer box fluid temperature sensor.

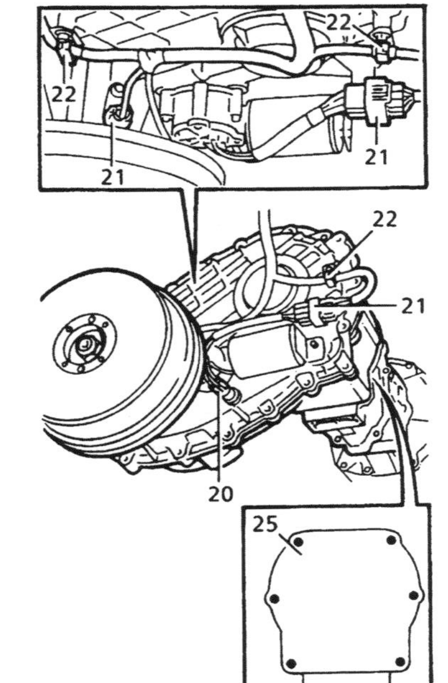

41M7017

21. Disconnect multiplugs from High/Low motor and output shaft speed sensor.
22. Release harness from 2 clips on transfer box brackets.
23. Position adaptor plate LRT-99-012 to transmission lift. Secure with bolts.
24. Raise transmission lift. Secure adaptor plate to transfer gearbox.
25. Remove 6 bolts securing transfer box.
26. Adjusting tilt as necessary, release transfer box from gearbox. Lower transmission lift.

Refit

27. **Manual Vehicles:** Renew gearbox output shaft seal. ***See MANUAL GEARBOX, Repair.***
28. **Automatic Vehicles:** Renew gearbox output shaft seal. ***See AUTOMATIC GEARBOX, Repair.***
29. Ensure mating faces are clean.
30. Lubricate input shaft with transmission fluid.
31. Raise transfer box on lift. Adjust tilt as necessary to align shafts.
32. Engage shafts. Locate transfer box dowels to gearbox.
33. Secure transfer box to gearbox with bolts. Tighten to ***45 Nm. (33 lbf.ft)***
34. Remove transmission lift.
35. Connect multiplugs to High/Low motor and output shaft speed sensor.
36. Connect Lucars to transfer box fluid temperature sensor.
37. Secure harness in clips.
38. Raise gearbox on cross beam.
39. **Automatic vehicles.** Position selector cable abutment bracket to gearbox. Secure with bolts.
40. Raise one wheel on each axle to allow rotation of propeller shafts.
41. Position propeller shafts to transfer box flanges. Align marks.
42. Secure shafts with nuts and bolts. Tighten to ***48 Nm. (35 lbf.ft)***
43. Fit propeller shaft guard. Tighten bolts.
44. Guide hand brake cable through grommet in transmission tunnel.
45. Fit exhaust front pipe. ***See MANIFOLD AND EXHAUST SYSTEM, Repair.***
46. **Diesel Vehicles.** Fit chassis cross member. ***See CHASSIS AND BODY, Repair.***
47. **Automatic Vehicles:** Adjust gear selector cable. ***See AUTOMATIC GEARBOX, Adjustment.***
48. Replenish gearbox and transfer box fluids. ***See LUBRICANTS, FLUIDS AND CAPACITIES, Information.***
49. Lower lift.
50. Connect handbrake cable to lever, secure with clevis pin and clip.

Manual Vehicles:

51. Fit seal around gearbox remote housing to transmission tunnel aperture.
52. Position gear lever. Secure with bolts. Tighten to ***25 Nm. (18 lbf.ft)***
53. Fit gaiter and ring. Secure with nuts.
54. Fit centre console. ***See CHASSIS AND BODY, Repair.***
55. **Automatic Vehicles:**Fit window switch pack. ***See ELECTRICAL, Repair.***
56. Reconnect battery negative lead.

TRANSFER BOX - FROM 99MY

Service repair no - 41.20.25.

Remove

1. Position vehicle on a four post lift.
2. Release fixings and remove battery cover.
3. Disconnect battery earth lead.

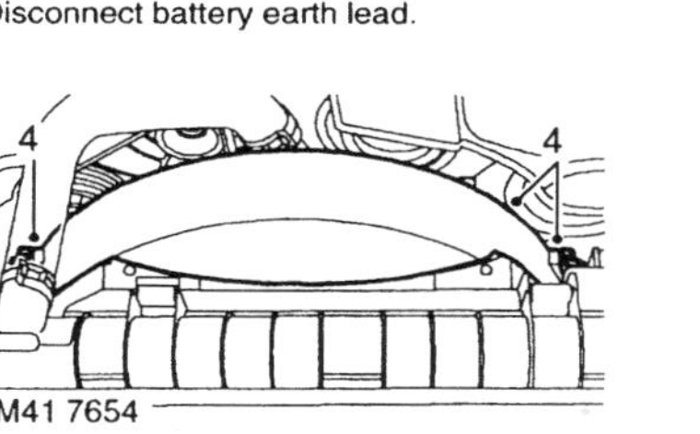

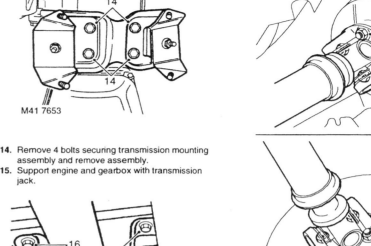

M41 7654

4. Release clips securing cooling fan cowl and remove cowl.
5. **Automatic models:** Remove window switch pack. ***See ELECTRICAL, Repair.***
6. **Manual models:** Remove centre console. ***See CHASSIS AND BODY, Repair.***

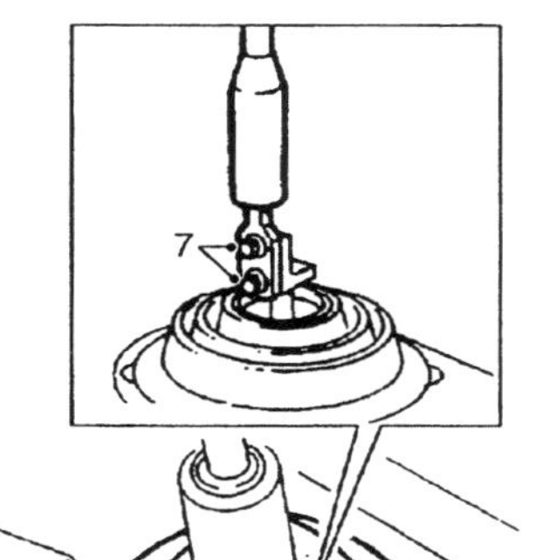

M41 7631

7. **Manual models:** Remove 6 nuts securing gaiter ring and remove gaiter ring and gaiter. Remove 2 bolts securing gear lever and remove lever.

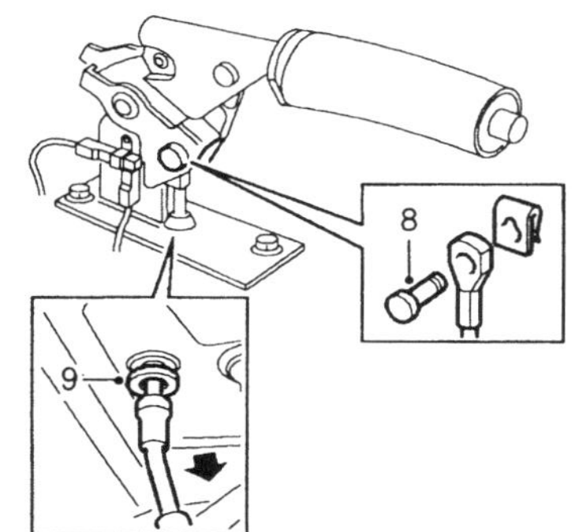

M41 7632

8. With the handbrake released, remove clip and clevis pin securing handbrake cable to handbrake.
9. Raise vehicle and release handbrake cable and grommet from tunnel.
10. Drain gearbox fluid. ***See AUTOMATIC GEARBOX, Repair.***
11. Drain transfer box oil. ***See SECTION 10, Maintenance. See LUBRICANTS, FLUIDS AND CAPACITIES, Information.***
12. **Petrol models:** Remove exhaust front pipe. ***See MANIFOLD AND EXHAUST SYSTEM, Repair.***
13. **Diesel models:** Remove chassis crossmember. ***See CHASSIS AND BODY, Repair.***

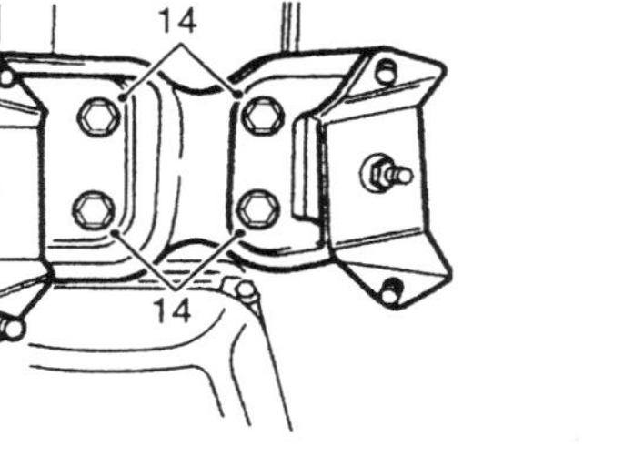

M41 7653

14. Remove 4 bolts securing transmission mounting assembly and remove assembly.
15. Support engine and gearbox with transmission jack.

M41 7633

16. Remove 4 bolts securing rear propeller shaft guard and remove guard.
17. Mark transfer box and propeller shaft flanges to aid re-assembly.
18. Raise one wheel on each axle to allow rotation of propeller shafts.

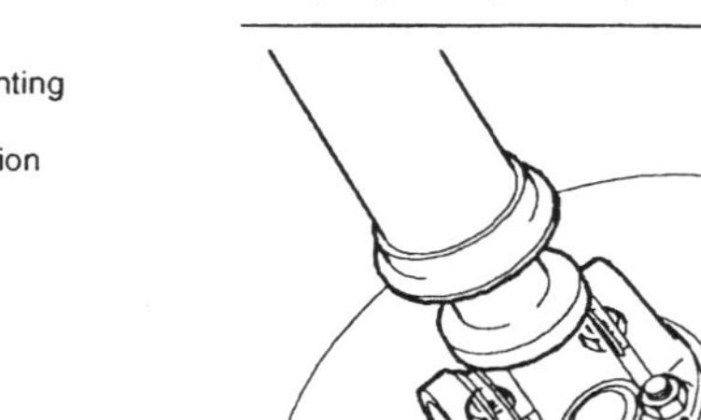

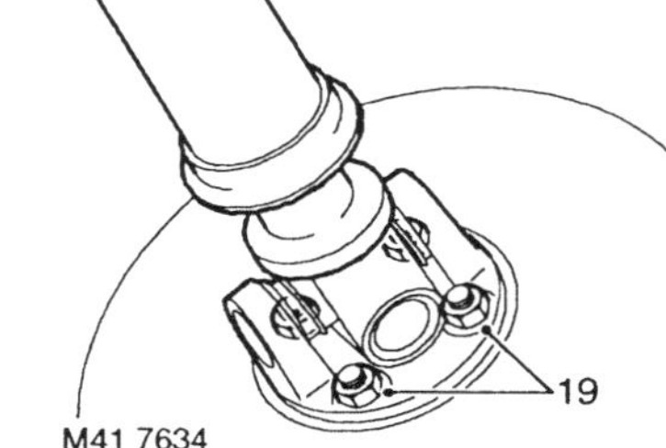

M41 7634

19. Remove 4 nuts from each propeller shaft flange.
20. Release propeller shafts and tie aside.
21. Lower transmission for access.

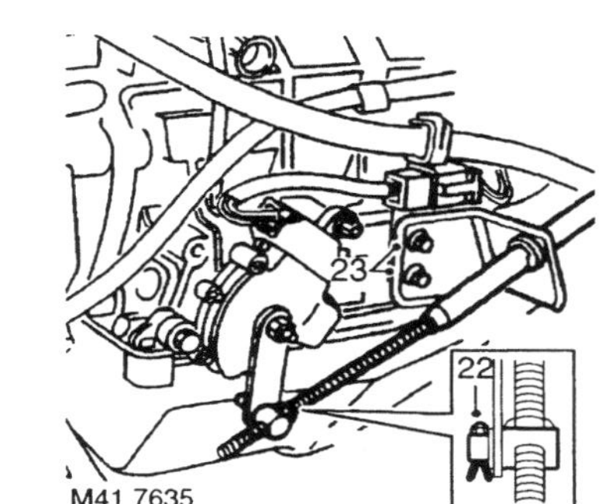

M41 7635

22. **Automatic models:** Remove split pin securing gear selector cable trunnion to gearbox lever and release trunnion.

23. Remove 2 bolts securing gear selector cable abutment bracket and harness support bracket to gearbox, and position selector cable and brackets aside.

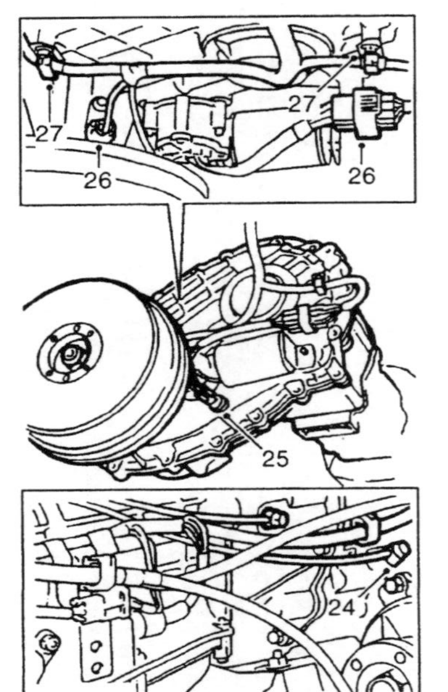

M41 7636

24. Remove banjo bolt securing breather pipe to transfer box, remove and discard sealing washer.

CAUTION: Plug the connections.

25. Disconnect 2 Lucars from transfer box oil temperature sensor.
26. Disconnect multiplugs from High/Low motor and output shaft speed sensor.
27. Release harness from 2 clips.

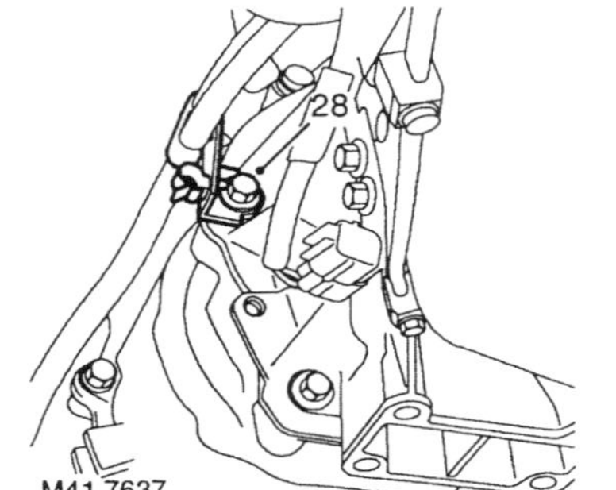

M41 7637

28. Remove bolt securing fuel pipe and purge pipe retaining bracket to transfer box and release bracket.

M41 7638

29. Position adaptor plate LRT-99-012 to transmission lift and secure with nuts and bolts.
30. Raise and adjust transmission lift so that LRT-99-012 is correctly located to transfer box.

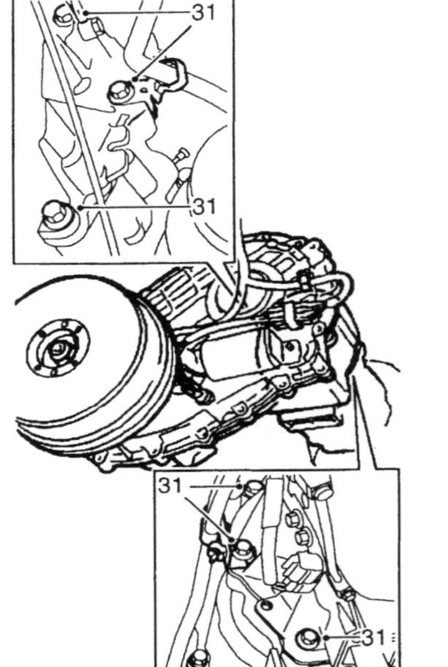

M41 7639

31. Remove 6 bolts securing transfer box to gearbox and release 2 harness clip mounting brackets.
32. Adjust transmission lift as necessary, release and remove transfer box.
33. Remove seal from transfer box casing using a suitable lever.

CAUTION: Ensure seal location does not become damaged as seal is levered from casing.

34. Remove seal from gearbox casing using a suitable lever.

Refit

35. Ensure seal location faces on gearbox are clean.
36. Lubricate oil seal lip with transmission fluid
37. **Automatic models:** Using LRT-44-001 fit seal to gearbox casing.
38. **Manual models:** Using LRT-37-014 fit seal to extension housing.
39. Ensure seal location faces on transfer box are clean.
40. Lubricate oil seal lip with transfer box oil.
41. Using LRT-41-011 fit seal to transfer box.
42. Clean transfer and gearbox mating faces and dowel and dowel holes.
43. Lubricate transfer box input shaft with transmission fluid.
44. Raise transfer box on lift and adjust angle of lift as necessary to align shafts.
45. Engage shafts and locate transfer box dowels to gearbox.
46. Fit bolts securing transfer box to gearbox and tighten to ***45 Nm (33 lbf.ft).*** Ensure that the 2 harness clip mounting brackets are correctly fitted when fitting bolts.
47. Secure harness to clips.
48. Align bracket securing fuel pipe and purge pipe to transfer box and secure with bolt.
49. Connect multiplugs to High/Low motor and output shaft speed sensor.
50. Connect 2 Lucars to transfer box fluid temperature sensor.
51. Clean breather pipe bolt and banjo, fit new sealing washers and tighten bolt to ***15 Nm (11 lbf.ft).***
52. Align harness support bracket and gear selector cable abutment bracket to gear box, and secure with bolts.
53. **Automatic models:** Connect gear selector cable trunnion to gearbox lever and secure with split pin.

54. Adjust gear selector cable. ***See AUTOMATIC GEARBOX, Repair.***
55. Raise transmission.
56. Clean propeller shaft and transfer box flanges.
57. Fit propeller shafts to transfer box flanges and align marks.
58. Fit nuts to propeller shafts and tighten to ***48 Nm (35 lbf.ft).***
59. Fit rear propeller shaft guard and secure with bolts.
60. Fit and engage handbrake cable grommet into transmission tunnel.
61. Fit transmission mounting assembly and tighten bolts to ***44 Nm (33 lbf.ft).***
62. Support transmission under brake drum.
63. Lower lift and remove adaptor plate LRT-99-012 from lift.
64. **Petrol models:** Fit exhaust front pipe. ***See MANIFOLD AND EXHAUST SYSTEM, Repair.***
65. **Diesel models:** Fit chassis crossmember. ***See CHASSIS AND BODY, Repair.***
66. Connect handbrake cable to lever, fit clevis pin and secure pin with clip.
67. **Manual models:** Position gear lever and tighten bolts to ***25 Nm (18 lbf.ft).*** Fit gaiter and gaiter ring and secure with nuts.
68. **Manual models:** Fit centre console. ***See CHASSIS AND BODY, Repair.***
69. **Automatic models:** Fit window switch pack. ***See ELECTRICAL, Repair.***
70. Position fan cowl and secure with clips.
71. Connect battery earth lead.
72. Fit battery cover and secure with fixings.
73. Fill transfer box with oil. ***See SECTION 10, Maintenance. See LUBRICANTS, FLUIDS AND CAPACITIES, Information.***
74. Fill gearbox with fluid. ***See AUTOMATIC GEARBOX, Repair.***

Notes

44 - AUTOMATIC GEARBOX

CONTENTS

Page

ZF AUTO

DESCRIPTION AND OPERATION

ADJUSTMENT

REPAIR

Electronic Automatic Transmission component layout

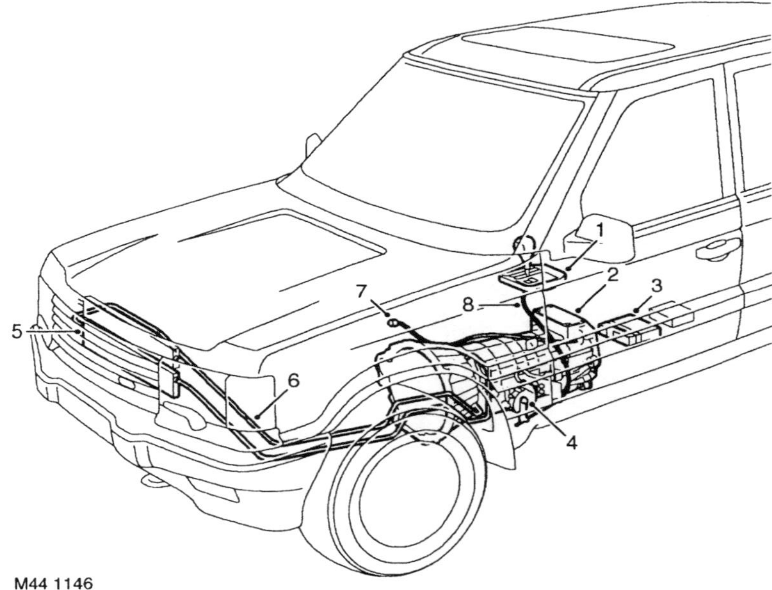

M44 1146

1. Selector lever assembly
2. Gearbox
3. Electronic Automatic Transmission (EAT) ECU
4. Selector position switch
5. Oil cooler
6. Fluid lines
7. Breather tube
8. Selector cable

Electronic Automatic Transmission control schematic

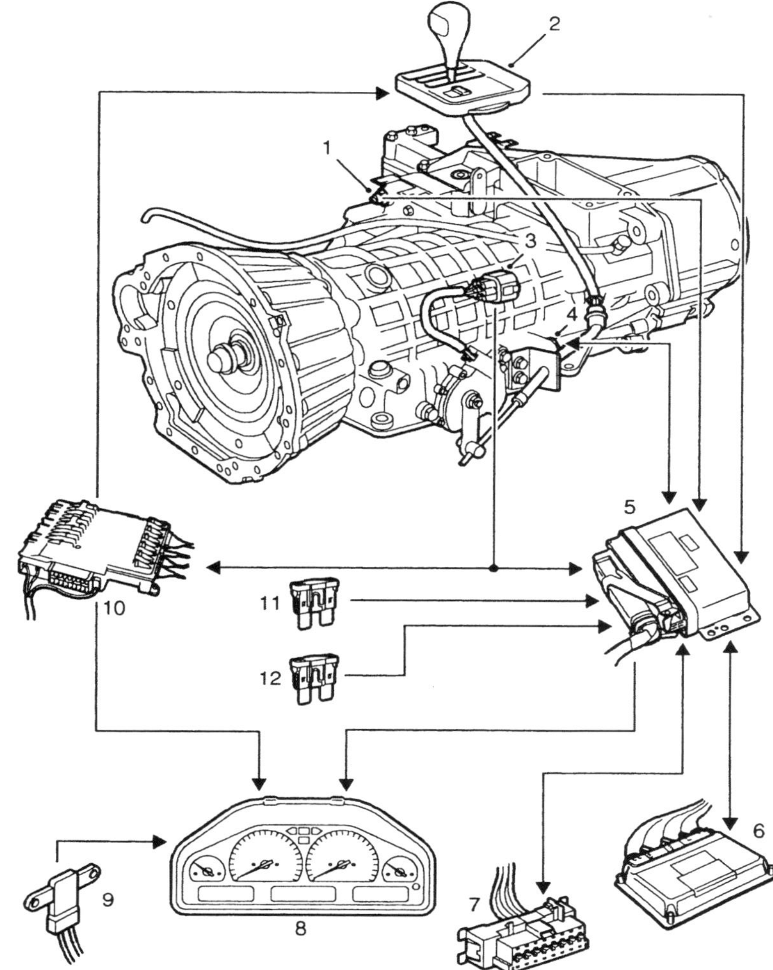

1. Transmission high/low switch
2. Mode switch
3. Gear position switch connector
4. Solenoid valve/speed sensor connector
5. Electronic Automatic Transmission (EAT) ECU
6. Engine Control Module (ECM)
7. Diagnostic socket
8. Instrument pack
9. Transmission fluid temperature sensor
10. Body electrical Control Module (BeCM)
11. Battery power supply
12. Ignition power supply

AUTOMATIC TRANSMISSION - DESCRIPTION

General

The ZF4HP22 transmission is used on 2.5 litre Diesel and 4.0 litre petrol models. 4.6 litre petrol models use the ZF4HP24 transmission unit to accomodate the increased power output of the larger engine. Both units are of similar construction with the ZF4HP24 unit being slightly longer with an increased oil capacity. The operation of both units is the same.

Automatic transmission vehicles are fitted with an 'H-gate' selector mechanism. The selector mechanism combines the operation of the transmission selector lever and the transfer box high/low gear gear range selection. Selections on the selector lever assembly are transmitted by a selector cable to a gear position switch.

The gear position switch on the transmission passes gear selection signals to an Electronic Automatic Transmission (EAT) ECU located below the LH front seat, which outputs the appropriate control signals to an electro-hydraulic valve block in the transmission. A mode switch enables the driver to change the control mode of the EAT ECU between manual, economy and sport. The EAT ECU provides signals to the message centre in the instrument pack to indicate the control mode and system status.

The gearbox features a pressure lubrication system and is cooled by pumping the lubricant through an oil cooler located in front of the engine cooling radiator.

From 99MY onwards, petrol models feature a revised EAT ECU with Controller Area Network (CAN) digital communications between the EAT ECU and the ECM.

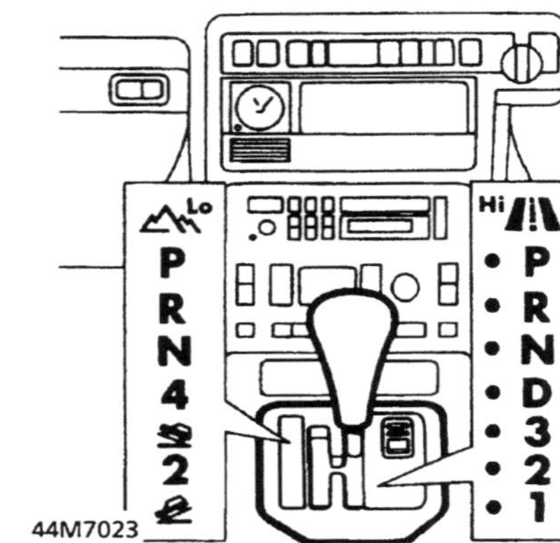

44M7023

H-gate selector lever assembly

The selector lever assembly consists of a lever and a cover attached to a cast base. The base is located on a gasket and secured to the transmission tunnel and has an 'H' pattern for the lever to move in. The lever is hinged to the base and a latch in the lever engages with detents in the base to provide positive location for the lever positions. The latch is disengaged by pressing a release button on the lever knob as shown in the lever illustration below.

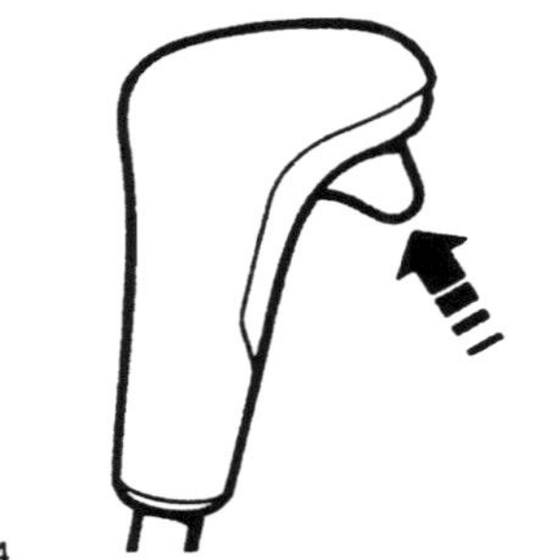
44M7024

Except for lever movement between positions D and 3 (high range) and 4 and 3 (low range), the button must be pressed before the lever can be moved. In some markets, vehicles incorporate an interlock solenoid at the bottom of the lever, which prevents the lever being moved from P unless the ignition switch is in position II and the foot brake is applied.

The cover incorporates LED lever position indicators and the mode switch. The lever position indicators illuminate to show the position of the selector lever. The driver's side of the H-gate is labelled 'Hi' and is used to select the high range gears. The passenger side of the H-gate is labelled 'Lo' and is used to select the low range gears. Movement of the selector lever across the H-gate selects high and low transfer box gear ranges.

The LED indicators are controlled by the Body electrical Control Module (BeCM). A mode switch is located on the driver's side of the cover. The mode switch is used by the driver to select sport mode used in the high range gears and manual mode used in the low range gears. The mode switch is a non-latching hinged switch that, when pressed, connects an earth to the EAT ECU to request a change of mode. Sport and Manual indicator lamps on the cover illuminate to show the mode selected. The message centre in the instrument pack also displays 'S' for sport mode and 'LM' for manual mode along with the selected gear.

An electrical connector at the rear of the cover connects the selector lever assembly to the vehicle wiring.

Selector cable

The selector cable is a Bowden type cable that connects the selector lever assembly to a selector lever on the gearbox. 'C' clips secure the ends of the outer cable to brackets on the selector lever assembly and the selector lever. The inner cable is adjustable at the connection of the inner cable with the gearbox selector lever.

Gearbox

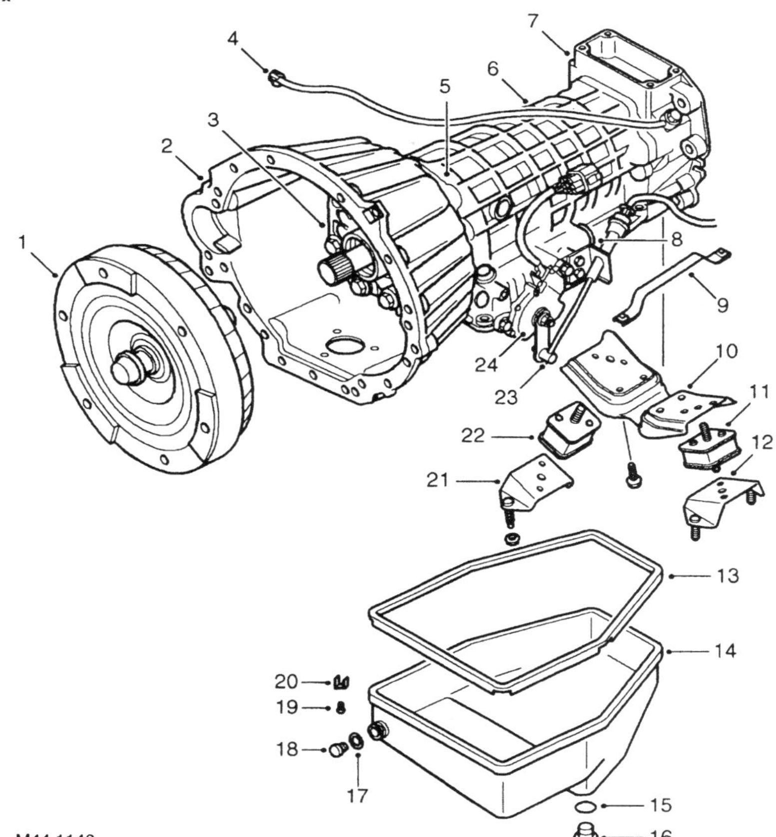

M44 1148

Gearbox

1. Torque converter
2. Torque converter housing
3. Fluid pump
4. Breather tube
5. Intermediate plate
6. Gearbox housing
7. Rear extension housing
8. Electrical connector
9. Snubbing bar
10. Upper mounting bracket
11. Mounting rubber
12. Lower mounting bracket
13. Gasket
14. Sump
15. 'O' ring
16. Drain plug
17. 'O' ring
18. Filler/level plug
19. Bolt
20. Clamp
21. Lower mounting bracket
22. Mounting rubber
23. Selector lever
24. Gear position switch

The gearbox consists of a torque converter housing, an intermediate plate, a gearbox housing and a rear extension housing, bolted together in series. The rear of the gearbox is supported by a rubber mounting installed between a mounting bracket on the gearbox and the LH chassis rail. A heat shield is installed on the mounting to protect it from the exhaust.

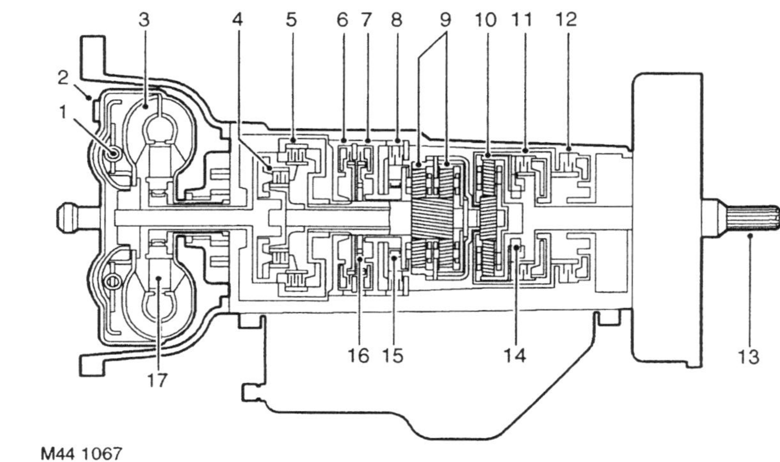

M44 1067

Sectioned view of gearbox

1. Lock-up clutch
2. Impeller
3. Turbine
4. Forward drive clutch
5. Reverse drive clutch
6. Brake clutch
7. Brake clutch
8. Brake clutch
9. Epicyclic gear set
10. Epicyclic gear set
11. Clutch
12. Brake clutch
13. Output shaft
14. Freewheel (one way clutch)
15. Freewheel (one way clutch)
16. Freewheel (one way clutch)
17. Stator and one way clutch

Valve block

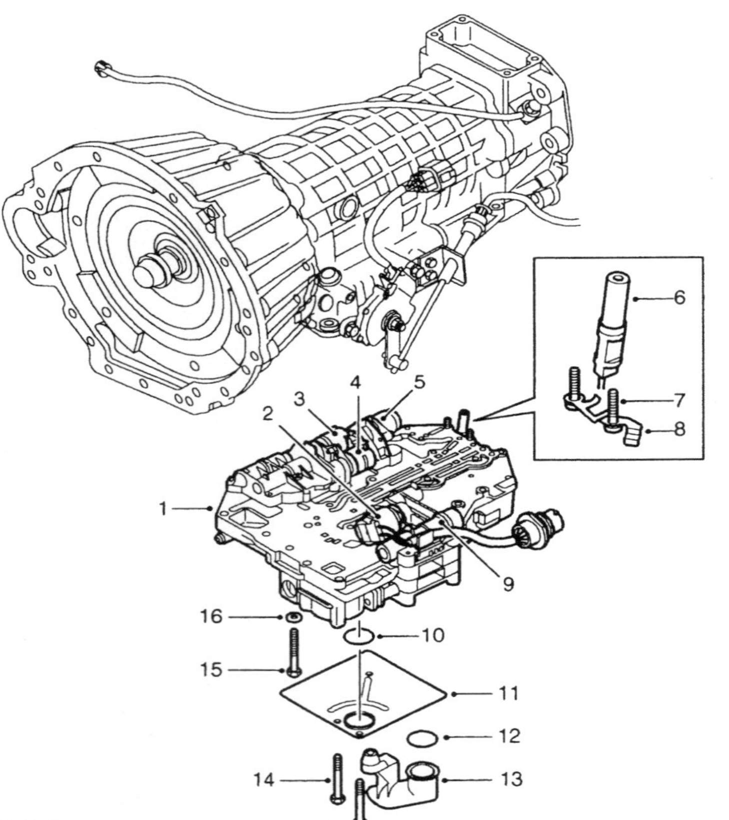

Valve block

1. Valve block
2. Pressure regulating solenoid valve (MV 4)
3. Shift control solenoid valve (MV 2)
4. Shift control solenoid valve (MV 1)
5. Lock-up solenoid valve (MV 3)
6. Output shaft speed sensor
7. Bolt
8. Sensor retaining clip
9. Manual valve
10. 'O' ring
11. Filter
12. 'O' ring
13. Suction pipe
14. Bolt
15. Bolt
16. Washer

Torque converter housing

On 2.5 litre Diesel models a 260 mm (10.2 in) diameter torque converter is used. On 4.0 and 4.6 litre petrol models a 280 mm (11 in) diameter torque converter is used. On 4.6 litre petrol models up to 99MY the torque converter is longer than the torque converter used on 4.0 litre petrol models. From 99MY, both the 4.0 and 4.6 litre petrol models use the shorter torque converter previously used on up to 99MY 4.0 litre models.

The torque converter housing attaches the gearbox to the engine and contains the torque converter. The torque converter is connected to the engine drive plate and transmits the drive from the engine to the gearbox input shaft. When engaged, a hydraulic lock-up clutch in the torque converter prevents slippage, to give a direct drive from the engine to the gearbox for improved efficiency.

Intermediate plate

The intermediate plate supports the gearbox input shaft and provides the interface between the transmission fluid pump and the lubrication circuit. The pump attaches to the front of the intermediate plate and is driven by an impeller in the torque converter. The pump pressurises transmission fluid drawn from the sump on the gearbox housing. The pressurised fluid then circulates through the torque converter and gearbox housing components for cooling, lubrication and gear shift purposes. Ports around the outer periphery of the intermediate plate provide the inlet and outlet connections to the fluid cooler and a pressure take-off point for servicing.

On ZF4HP24 gearboxes, the intermediate plate is 15 mm (0.6 in) thicker than fitted to the ZF4HP22 gearbox to accomodate a larger fluid pump unit. To compensate for the increased length of the intermediate plate, the rear extension housing is 15 mm (0.6 in) shorter than that fitted to the ZF4HP22 gearbox.

Gearbox housing

The gearbox housing contains two epicyclic gear sets on input and output shafts. Hydraulic clutches on the shafts control which elements of the gear sets are engaged, and their direction of rotation, to produce the P and N selections, four forward gear ratios and one reverse gear ratio.

Gear ratios

Gear	Ratio
1st	2.480:1
2nd	1.480:1
3rd	1.000:1
4th	0.728:1
Reverse	2.086:1

The lock-up and brake clutches are operated by pressurised transmission fluid from the valve block in the sump. A manual valve and four solenoid valves, also known as Motorised Valves (MV), control the supply of pressurised transmission fluid from the valve block:

- The manual valve controls the fluid supply for P, R, N and D selector positions. The four solenoid valves operate accordingly to operate shift control, lock-up and shift quality.
- Solenoid valves MV 1 and MV 2 control the supplies that operate the brake clutches for shift control. They are also used to prevent accidental engagement of reverse when moving forwards and a forward gear when moving backwards.
- Solenoid valve MV 3 controls the supply that operates the lock-up clutch.
- Solenoid valve MV 4 modulates the pressure of the supplies to the brake clutches, to control shift quality.

Operation of the manual valve is controlled by the selector lever assembly. In the gearbox, a selector shaft engages with the manual valve. The selector shaft is connected to the selector lever assembly via the selector cable and a selector lever on the left side of the gearbox. The selector shaft also operates a mechanism that locks the output shaft when P is selected.

Operation of the solenoid valves is controlled by the EAT ECU.

An output shaft speed sensor in the gearbox housing outputs a signal to the EAT ECU. The EAT ECU compares output shaft speed with engine speed to determine the engaged gear and output shaft speed with vehicle speed to confirm the range selected on the transfer box. The speed sensor signal is a diagnostic function and not essential for correct gearbox operation.

A bayonet lock electrical connector in the gearbox casing, to the rear of the selector lever, connects the solenoid valves and the output shaft speed sensor to the vehicle wiring.

A pressed steel sump encloses the valve block and collects transmission fluid draining from the gearbox housing. A suction pipe and filter on the underside of the valve block connect to the inlet side of the fluid pump. A magnet is installed in the sump to collect any magnetic particles that may be present. A level plug and a drain plug are installed in the sump for servicing.

Rear extension housing

The rear extension housing provides the interface between the gearbox housing and the transfer box. A splined output shaft transmits the drive from the gearbox to the transfer box. A seal in the rear of the housing prevents leakage past the extension shaft. A breather pipe, attached to the left side of the rear extension housing, ventilates the interior of the gearbox and rear extension housings to atmosphere. The open end of the breather pipe is located in the engine compartment at the right rear corner of the engine, against the bulkhead. On 99MY V8 vehicles, the breather pipe is also located against the bulkhead, but the the open end is routed down the bulkhead and located below the converter housing.

Gearbox power flows

The following Figures show the power flow through the gearbox for each forward gear when D is selected, and for reverse. The key to the Item numbers on the Figures, and in parenthesis in the accompanying text, can be found on the 'Sectioned view of gearbox' Figure.

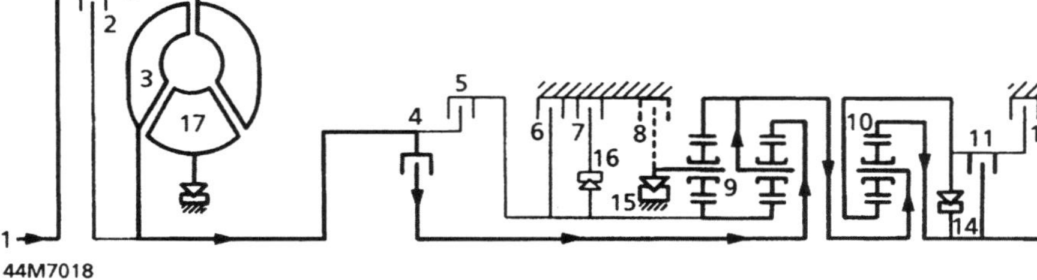

44M7018

1st Gear (D selected)

Clutches (4) and (11) are engaged. The front planet gear carrier of gear set (9) locks against the gearbox housing through freewheel (15) when the engine powers the vehicle, and freewheels when the vehicle is coasting. Gear set (10) rotates as a solid unit with the front planet gear carrier.

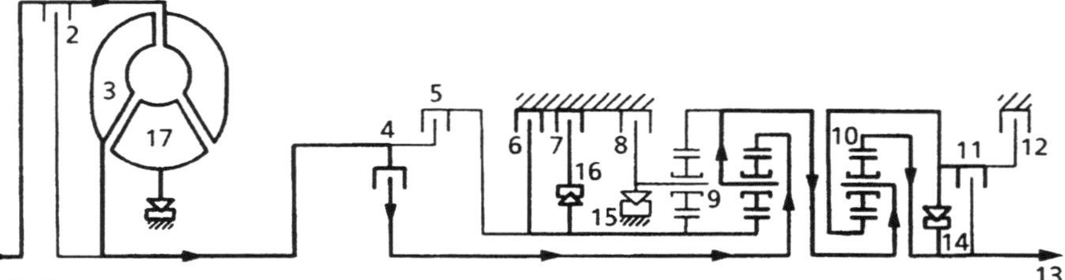

44M7019

2nd Gear (D selected)

Clutches (4), (6), (7) and (11) are engaged. Freewheel (15) overruns. The hollow shaft with the sun wheel of gear set (9) is locked. Gear set (10) also rotates as a solid unit.

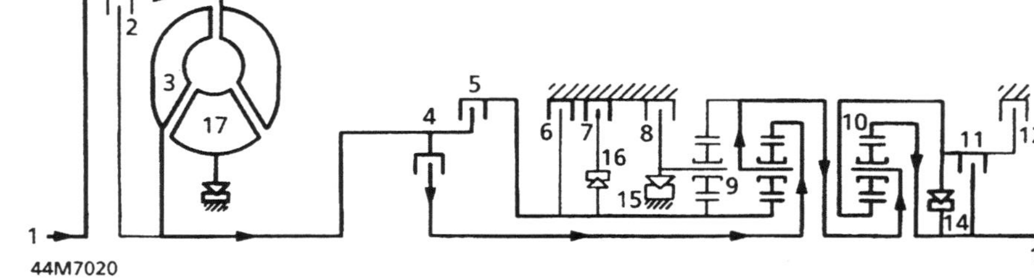

44M7020

3rd Gear (D selected)

Clutches (4), (5), (7) and (11) are engaged. Freewheels (15) and (16) are overrun. Gear sets (9) and (10) rotate as a solid unit.

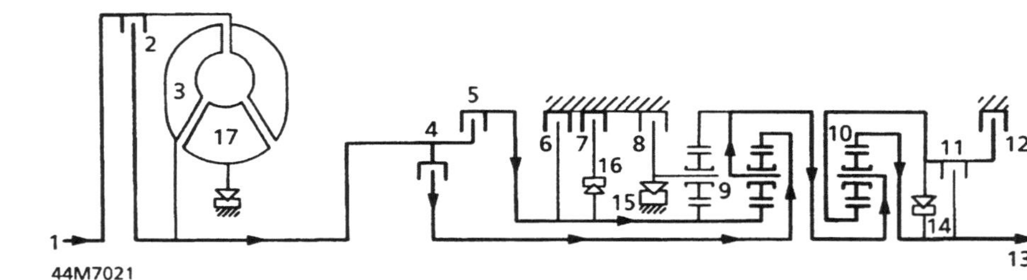

44M7021

4th Gear (D selected)

Clutches (4), (5), (7) and (12) are engaged. Freewheels (14), (15) and (16) are overrun. Gear set (9) rotates as a solid unit. The hollow shaft with the sun wheel of gear set (10) is locked.

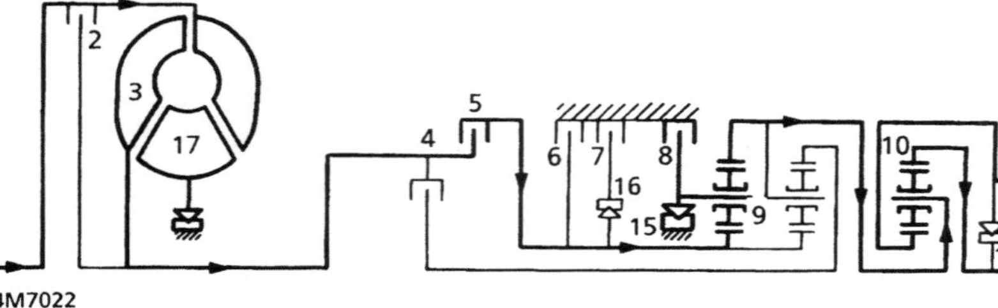

44M7022

Reverse gear

Clutches (5), (8) and (11) are engaged. The front planet gear carrier of gear set (9) is locked. Gear set (10) also rotates as a solid block.

Gear position switch

The gear position switch outputs signals that are related to the position of the selector lever assembly. The switch is installed on the selector shaft on the left side of the gearbox. Slotted mounting holes allow the switch to be turned relative to the shaft for adjustment. A fly lead connects the switch to the vehicle wiring.

Movement of the selector lever assembly turns the selector shaft, which connects with three sliding contacts in the switch. The contacts are identified as the X, Y and Z. When closed:

- The X, Y and Z contacts output a combination of earth signals to the EAT ECU as shown in the table below.
- The outputs of the X, Y and Z contacts are monitored by the EAT ECU, ECM and the BeCM to determine the position of the selector lever assembly.

The signals are interpreted by the EAT ECU for the correct gear selection. The ECM uses the signals to control for example engine idle speed etc. The BeCM uses the signals to illuminate the gear selection display on the selector cover, operate the reverse lamps, wiper reverse operation and message centre display etc.

Gear position switch X, Y, Z outputs

Position switch	ECU pin	P	R	N	D	3	2	1
Line 1 (X)	36	0V	0V	-	-	0V	0V	0V
Line 2 (Y)	8	-	0V	0V	0V	0V	-	-
Line 3 (Z)	37	-	-	-	0V	0V	0V	-

Fluid Cooler

M44 1150

1. Outlet connection
2. Fixing bracket
3. Inlet connection
4. Fixing bracket
5. Temperature sensor

Transmission fluid from the gearbox is circulated through a cooler located at the front of the radiator. Fluid lines from the transmission are connected to each end tank of the fluid cooler. A temperature sensor on the LH end tank provides the instrument pack with an input of transmission fluid temperature. If the temperature exceeds between 120 and 130 °C, the instrument pack message centre displays 'GEARBOX OVRHEAT'. The message remains displayed until the temperature of the fluid returns to between 82 and 88 °C.

EAT ECU

The EAT ECU operates the solenoid valves in the gearbox to provide automatic control of gear shifts and torque converter lock-up. The EAT ECU is attached to a bracket which is secured to the cabin floor below the LH front seat.

Diesel vehicles from 95MY and petrol vehicles up to 99MY

A 55 pin connector links the EAT ECU to the vehicle wiring. Software in the ECU monitors hard wired inputs and exchanges information via hard wired connections with the ECM, BeCM and instrument pack.

Petrol vehicles from 99MY

A 75 pin connector links the EAT ECU to the vehicle wiring. Software in the EAT ECU monitors hard wired inputs and exchanges information with the ECM on a Controller Area Network (CAN) bus to determine gear shift and torque converter lock-up requirements. Resultant control signals are then output to the gearbox solenoid valves.

The CAN bus, introduced on 99MY petrol vehicles, provides the communication link between the ECM and the EAT ECU. Inputs and outputs to and from each control unit are transmitted via two twisted wire connections, CAN high and CAN low.

The CAN bus allows more engine data to be passed to the EAT ECU which, on earlier vehicles, would require a number of additional hardwired connections.

The additional engine data is used by the EAT ECU to give improved transmission quality and allows the EAT ECU to operate in a greater number of default modes in the event of sensor failure. Inputs and outputs on the CAN communication bus are listed in the table that follows.

CAN communications between EAT ECU and ECM - Petrol vehicles from 99MY

Inputs from ECM	Outputs to ECM
CAN version identifier	Calculated gear
Emissions (OBDII) control	Diagnostic information
Engine air intake temperature	Emission (OBDII) fault status
Engine speed	Engine torque reduction request
Engine speed fault flag	Gear position switch information
Engine temperature	Output shaft speed
Engine torque	Mode information
Engine torque fault flag	Shift information
Friction torque	Torque converter lock-up solenoid
Maximum engine torque	
Reduced engine torque	
Road speed	
Status of engine speed torque reduction	
Throttle position	

EAT ECU connector - Diesel vehicles from 95MY and petrol vehicles up to 99MY

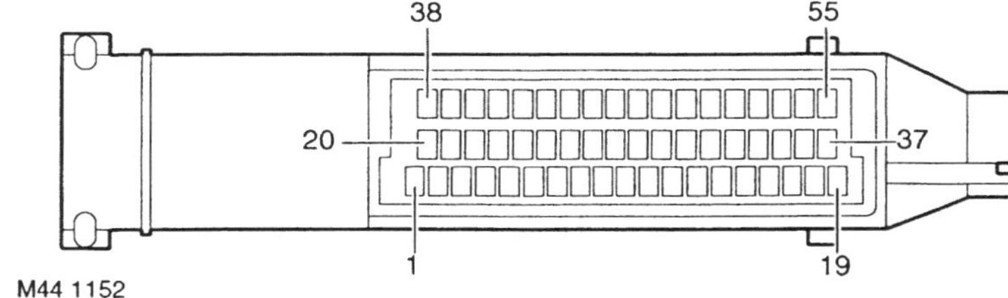

M44 1152

EAT ECU connector pin details - Diesel vehicles from 95MY and petrol vehicles up to 99MY

Pin No.	Description	Input/Output
1	Ignition supply	Input
2	Vehicle speed sensor (positive)	Input
3	Engine speed	Input
4	Not used	-
5	Shift control solenoid valve (MV1)	Output
6	Pressure regulator solenoid valve (MV4)	-
7	Electronics earth	-
8 to 13	Not used	-
14	Gear position switch, Y contacts	Input
15	Diagnostics, L line	Input/Output
16	MES 1 - message centre display	Output
17/18	Not used	-
19	Solenoid valves power supply	Output
20	Earth (screen)	
21	Engine torque PWM	Input
22/23	Not used	-
24	Shift control solenoid valve (MV2)	Output
25	Not used	-

EAT ECU connector pin details - Diesel vehicles from 95MY and petrol vehicles up to 99MY (continued)

Pin No.	Description	Input/Output
26	Power earth	-
27/28	Not used	-
29	Mode switch	Input
31	MES 2 - message centre display	Output
30	Not used	-
32	Torque reduction request	Output
33	Gear position switch, Z contacts	Input
34 to 37	Not used	-
38	Vehicle speed sensor (negative)	Input
39	Battery supply	Input
40/41	Not used	-
42	Torque converter solenoid (MV3)	Output
43 to 45	Not used	-
46	Transmission high/low switch	Input
47	Throttle position PWM	Input
48/49	Not used	-
50	Gear position switch, X contacts	Input
51	Diagnostics, K line	Input/Output
51 to 55	Not used	-

EAT ECU connector - Petrol vehicles from 99MY

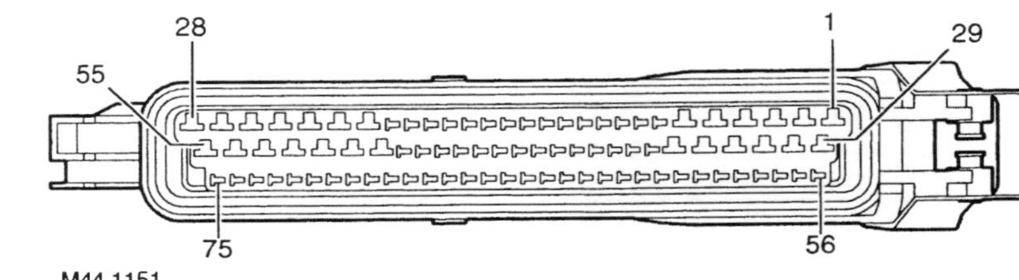

M44 1151

EAT ECU connector pin details - Petrol vehicles from 99MY

Pin No.	Description	Input/Output
1 to 4	Not used	-
5	Pressure regulator solenoid valve (MV 4)	Output
6	Power earth	-
7	Not used	-
8	Gear position switch, Y contacts	Input
9 to 12	Not used	-
13	Transmission high/low switch	Input
14	Gearbox output shaft speed sensor, negative	Input
15	Gearbox output shaft speed sensor, cable screen	-
16	CAN high	Input/Output
17 to 24	Not used	-
25	MES 1 - message centre display	Output
26	Battery supply	Input
27	Not used	-
28	Electronics earth	-
29	Not used	-
30	Shift control solenoid valve (MV 1)	Output

EAT ECU connector pin details - From 99MY (continued)

Pin No.	Description	Input/Output
31	Diagnostics, K line	Input/Output
32	Converter lock-up solenoid valve (MV 3)	Output
33	Shift control solenoid valve (MV 2)	Output
34/35	Not used	-
36	Gear position switch, X contacts	Input
37	Gear position switch, Z contacts	Input
38 to 41	Not used	-
42	Gearbox output shaft speed sensor, positive	Input
43	Not used	-
44	CAN low	Input/Output
45	Mode switch	Input
46 to 50	Not used	-
51	MES 2 - message centre display	Output
52	Not used	-
53	Solenoid valves power supply	Output
54	Ignition power supply	Input
55 to 75	Not used	-

OPERATION

General

The gear position switch outputs are monitored by the BeCM and the EAT ECU. The BeCM outputs gear position signals to illuminate the position indicators each side of the gear selector lever and on the message centre in the instrument pack.

In D, 3, 2, and 1, the EAT ECU outputs control signals to the gearbox to select the required gear.

In D, all forward gears are available for selection by the EAT ECU. In 3, 2 and 1, a corresponding limit is imposed on the highest gear available for selection. When R is selected, reverse gear only engages if the vehicle is stationary or moving at 5 mph (8 km/h) or less.

Selector Lever Interlock (where fitted)

The interlock solenoid on the selector lever is de-energised unless the foot brake is applied while the ignition is on. While de-energised, the interlock solenoid allows the selector lever to move through the range unless P is selected.

On entering the P position, the interlock solenoid engages a latch which locks the selector lever. When the ignition is on and the foot brake is applied, the BeCM energises the interlock solenoid, which disengages the latch and allows the selector lever to be moved out of P.

Economy, Sport and Manual Modes

During the power-up procedure after the ignition is switched on, the EAT ECU defaults to an economy mode. Pressing the mode switch causes the EAT ECU to change between the economy mode and the sport or the manual mode, depending on the range selected on the transfer box:

- If the transfer box is in high range, the EAT ECU changes to the sport mode and illuminates the sport mode lamp on the selector cover and displays 'S' in the instrument pack message centre. In the sport mode the gearbox is more responsive to accelerator pedal movement. Downshifts occur earlier and upshifts occur later.
- If the transfer box is in low range, the EAT ECU changes to the manual mode and illuminates the manual mode lamp on the selector cover and displays 'LM' in the instrument pack message centre. Kickdown is disabled and the EAT ECU maintains the gearbox in the gear selected on the selector lever (D = 4th gear) to give improved off road performance. Downshifts occur only to prevent the engine stalling.

  From a standing start, the vehicle pulls away in 1st gear and, if a higher gear is selected, upshifts almost immediately to the selected gear (shifts of more than one gear can occur).
- After a second press of the mode switch the EAT ECU reverts to the economy mode, for the range selected on the transfer box, and extinguishes the related mode lamp on the selector cover and removes the 'S' or 'LM' display in the instrument pack message centre.
- When the vehicle is in the default mode (i.e. high range and economy) and towing or driving up steep gradients, the EAT ECU will select a shift pattern appropriate to the driving conditions. If a heavy trailer is being towed or a steep gradient is encountered, the transmission will hold in the gears longer than in normal operation.

Shift Control

To provide the different driving characteristics for each mode of operation, the EAT ECU incorporates different shift maps of throttle position/road speed. Base shift points are derived from the appropriate shift map. When a shift is required, the EAT ECU sends a request to the ECM for a reduction in engine torque, in order to produce a smoother shift. The percentage of torque reduction requested varies according to the operating conditions at the time of the request.

When the EAT ECU receives confirmation of the torque reduction from the ECM, it then signals the shift solenoid valves in the gearbox to produce the shift. To further improve shift quality, the EAT ECU also signals the pressure regulating solenoid valve to modulate the hydraulic pressure and so control the rate of engagement and disengagement of the brake clutches.

With time, the components in a gearbox wear and the duration of the gear shifts tends to increase, which has an adverse effect on the brake clutches. To counteract this, the EAT ECU applies a pressure adaptation to each shift. To calculate the adaptations, the EAT ECU monitors the pressure modulation used, and time taken, for each shift. If a subsequent shift of the same type, in terms of throttle position and engine speed, has a longer duration, the EAT ECU stores an adaptation for that type of shift in a volatile memory. The adaptation is then included in future pressure calculations for that type of shift, to restore shift duration to the nominal.

Kickdown

The EAT ECU monitors the input of the throttle position sensor to determine when kickdown is required and select a gear to give the best available acceleration. When it detects a kickdown situation, the EAT ECU immediately initiates a down shift of one or two gears or will maintain the current gear to avoid engine overspeed.

Torque Converter Lock-Up

The EAT ECU energises the lock-up solenoid valve to engage the lock-up clutch. Lock-up clutch operation is dependent on throttle position, engine speed, operating mode and the range selected on the transfer box.

High Range

Unique lock-up maps, similar to the shift maps, are incorporated in the economy and sport modes for all forward gears. Engagement and disengagement of the lock-up clutch is dependent on throttle position and engine speed.

Low Range

To enhance off road control, particularly when manoeuvering at low speeds, torque converter lock-up does not occur when there is any degree of throttle opening. When the throttle is closed above a preset engine speed, the lock-up clutch engages to provide maximum engine braking.

Increased Load/Reduced Torque Compensation

To aid performance and driveability in the high range economy mode, the EAT ECU has three adaptive shift and lock-up maps. These maps delay upshifts and torque converter lock-up similar to the sport mode if the inputs from the engine indicate:

- A sustained high load on the engine, such as occurs when the vehicle is ascending a steep gradient or towing a trailer.
- The EAT ECU monitors the engine inputs and selects the most appropriate adaptive map for the prevailing conditions.
- On vehicles from 99MY, a lower than normal engine torque, such as occurs at altitude or high ambient temperatures.

Diagnostics

While the ignition is on, the EAT ECU diagnoses the system for faults. The extent of the diagnostic capability at any particular time depends on the prevailing operating conditions, e.g. it is not possible to check torque converter lock-up while the vehicle is stationary, or to check for a short circuit to earth if the circuit concerned is already at a low potential.

If a fault is detected, the EAT ECU immediately stores a fault code and the values of three operating parameters associated with the fault. Depending on the fault, there are four possible effects:

- The fault has little effect on gearbox operation or vehicle emissions. The driver will probably not notice any change and the warning lamps remain extinguished.
- All gears are available but kickdown does not function. 'GEARBOX FAULT' will be displayed on the instrument pack message centre. The MIL remains extinguished.
- Limp home mode is selected and vehicle performance is greatly reduced. 'GEARBOX FAULT' will be displayed on the instrument pack message centre. If the fault is detected on a second consecutive drive cycle, the MIL illuminates.

Fault effects and warning indications - Diesel vehicles from 95MY and petrol vehicles up to 99MY

Fault code	Fault description	Effect	MIL Warning lamp	'GEARBOX FAULT' message
1	* Solenoid supply malfunction	Limp home mode in third if stationary, fourth if moving.	On	Yes
2	* EAT ECU data corrupted (ROM and checksum values disagree)	Limp home mode in third if stationary, fourth if moving.	On †	Yes
5	* Throttle angle malfunction	Substitute throttle angle of 30% used.	On	Yes
6	* Shift solenoid MV1 malfunction	Limp home mode in third if stationary, fourth if moving.	On	Yes
6	* Shift solenoid MV1 short	Limp home mode in third if stationary, fourth if moving.	On	Yes
7	* Shift solenoid MV2 malfunction	Limp home mode in third if stationary, fourth if moving.	On	Yes
7	* Shift solenoid MV2 short	Limp home mode in third if stationary, fourth if moving.	On	Yes
9	* MES 1 fault	No default condition. BeCM recognises sport mode as a fault, economy as low range manual and manual as economy.	No	No
10	* MES 2 fault	No default condition. BeCM recognises sport mode as a fault, economy as low range manual and manual as economy.	No	No
12	* Throttle angle electrical short	Substitute throttle angle of 30% used.	On	Yes
13	* EAT ECU circuit output state does not match command state	Limp home mode in third if stationary, fourth if moving.	On	Yes
20	* Solenoid supply malfunction	Limp home mode in third if stationary, fourth if moving.	On †	Yes
21	* Engine speed signal out of range	Limp home mode in third if stationary, fourth if moving.	On †	Yes
21	* Engine speed, no signal	Limp home mode in third if stationary, fourth if moving.	On †	Yes
22	* Pressure control regulator malfunction	Limp home mode in third if stationary, fourth if moving.	On	Yes

*= Emissions (OBDII) relevant

†= MIL illuminates immediately (in all other faults, MIL on illuminates in the 2nd consecutive drive cycle if the fault is still present)

Fault effects and warning indications - Diesel vehicles from 95MY and petrol vehicles up to 99MY (continued)

Fault code	Fault description	Effect	MIL Warning lamp	'GEARBOX FAULT' message
22	* Pressure control regulator electrical short	Limp home mode in third if stationary, fourth if moving.	On	Yes
23	* Engine torque reduction	Shift pressure to maximum, no shift ignition retard, harsh gear shifts/engagement.	On	Yes
24	* Output speed sensor signal out of range	Limp home mode in third if stationary, fourth if moving.	On	Yes
26	* Engine torque signal out of range	Shift pressure to maximum, harsh, erratic or elongated shifts can occur.	On	Yes
27	* Output speed sensor, no signal	Limp home mode in third if stationary, fourth if moving.	On	Yes
28	* EAT ECU data corrupted (ROM and EEPROM values disagree)	Limp home mode in third if stationary, fourth if moving.	On †	Yes
30	* Gear position switch status inaccurate with engine running	Limp home mode in third if stationary, fourth if moving.	On	Yes
31	* Gear position switch status inaccurate when starting engine	Limp home mode in third if stationary, fourth if moving.	On	Yes

The following fault codes apply to Diesel vehicles from 97MY onwards and petrol vehicles up to 99MY only

40	* First gear ratio incorrect	Limp home mode in third if stationary, fourth if moving.	On	Yes
41	* Second gear ratio incorrect	Limp home mode in third if stationary, fourth if moving.	On	Yes
42	* Third gear ratio incorrect	Limp home mode in third if stationary, fourth if moving.	On	Yes
43	* Fourth gear ratio incorrect	Limp home mode in third if stationary, fourth if moving.	On	Yes
44	* Torque converter lock-up gear ratio incorrect	Limp home mode in third if stationary, fourth if moving.	On	Yes

*= Emissions (OBDII) relevant

†= MIL illuminates immediately (in all other faults, MIL on illuminates in the 2nd consecutive drive cycle if the fault is still present)

Fault effects and warning indications - Petrol vehicles from 99MY

Fault code OBDII (TestBook)	Fault description	Effect	MIL Warning lamp	'GEARBOX FAULT' message
P0705 (14, 23)	* Gear position switch, incorrect outputs	Maintains current gear in low range, limp home mode in high range. Shift pressure to maximum, harsh gear shifts/engagement.	On	Yes
P7021 (21)	* Downshift safety monitor prevented downshift which would have caused engine overspeed	Maintains current gear in low range, limp home mode in high range. Shift pressure to maximum, harsh gear shifts/engagement.	On	Yes
P0722 (22)	* Torque converter slipping	Maintains current gear in low range, limp home mode in high range. Shift pressure to maximum, harsh gear shifts/engagement.	On	Yes
P0731 (29)	* Ratio monitoring, implausable 1st gear ratio	No apparent effect.	On	No
P0732 (30)	* Ratio monitoring, implausable 2nd gear ratio	No apparent effect.	On	No
P0733 (31)	* Ratio monitoring, implausable 3rd gear ratio	No apparent effect.	On	No
P0734 (32)	* Ratio monitoring, implausable 4th gear ratio	No apparent effect.	On	No
P0741 (5)	* Torque converter lock-up clutch fault	May effect driveability.	On	No
P0743 (7, 25)	* Torque converter lock-up solenoid (MV 3), open or short circuit	Limp home mode in low and high ranges. Shift pressure to maximum, harsh gear shifts/engagement.	On	Yes
P0748 (10, 28)	* Pressure regulating solenoid (MV 4), open or short circuit	Limp home mode in low and high ranges. Shift pressure to maximum, harsh gear shifts/engagement.	On	Yes
P0753 (8, 26)	* Shift solenoid (MV 1), open or short circuit	Limp home mode in low and high ranges. Shift pressure to maximum, harsh gear shifts/engagement.	On	Yes

*= Emissions (OBDII) relevant

†= MIL illuminates immediately (in all other faults, MIL on illuminates in the 2nd consecutive drive cycle if the fault is still present)

Fault effects and warning indicators - Petrol vehicles from 99MY (continued)

Fault code OBDII (TestBook)	Fault description	Effect	MIL Warning lamp	'GEARBOX FAULT' message
P0758 (9, 27)	* Shift solenoid (MV 2), open or short circuit	Limp home mode in low and high ranges. Shift pressure to maximum, harsh gear shifts/engagement.	On	Yes
P1562 (24)	* Battery supply below 9 V while engine running	Maintains current gear in low range, limp home mode in high range. Shift pressure to maximum, harsh gear shifts/engagement.	Off	Yes
P1601 (4)	* ECU, EEPROM checksum	Limp home mode in low and high ranges. Shift pressure to maximum, harsh gear shifts/engagement.	On	On
P1602 (36)	* Transmission calibration selection incorrect or invalid	Default to 4.0 litre calibration.	On	Yes
P1606 (3)	* ECU fault, EEPROM communication	No apparent effect.	On †	No
P1606 (6)	* Watchdog check, ECU fault	Limp home mode in low and high ranges. Shift pressure to maximum, harsh gear shifts/engagement.	On	Yes
P1612 (2)	* Solenoid valves power supply relay, sticking closed or open circuit	Limp home mode in low and high ranges. Shift pressure to maximum, harsh gear shifts/engagement.	On	Yes
P1613 (1)	* Solenoid valves power supply relay, sticking open or short circuit	Limp home mode in low and high ranges. Shift pressure to maximum, harsh gear shifts/engagement.	On	Yes
P1705 (39)	Transmission high/low range, implausable input	No apparent effect.	On	No
P1810 (12, 13)	BeCM to message centre circuit fault	Message centre does not display 'S' or 'LM'. No effect on gearbox operation.	On	No
P1841 (16)	* CAN bus fault	Maintains current gear in low range, limp home mode in high range. Shift pressure to maximum, harsh gear shifts/engagement.	On	Yes
P1842 (15)	* CAN level monitoring	Maintains current gear in low range, limp home mode in high range. Shift pressure to maximum, harsh gear shifts/engagement.	On	Yes

*= Emissions (OBDII) relevant

†= MIL illuminates immediately (in all other faults, MIL on illuminates in the 2nd consecutive drive cycle if the fault is still present)

Fault effects and warning indicators - Petrol vehicles from 99MY (continued)

Fault code OBDII (TestBook)	Fault description	Effect	MIL Warning lamp	'GEARBOX FAULT' message
P1843 (17)	* CAN time-out monitoring	Maintains current gear in low range, limp home mode in high range. Shift pressure to maximum, harsh gear shifts/engagement.	On	Yes
P1884 (11)	* CAN message: Engine friction invalid	No apparent effect.	On	No
P1884 (18)	* CAN message: Throttle position invalid	Substitute throttle angle of 50% adopted. No kickdown. Operates in Economy mode only.	On	Yes
P1884 (19)	CAN message: Engine temperature invalid	Substitute engine temperature derived from other inputs. No apparent effect.	On	No
P1884 (20)	CAN message: Road speed invalid	No apparent effect.	On	No
P1884 (33, 34)	CAN message: Engine torque invalid	Substitute engine torque derived from other inputs. May affect shift quality.	On	No
P1884 (35)	CAN message: Engine speed invalid	Maintains current gear in low range, limp home mode in high range. Shift pressure to maximum, harsh gear shifts/engagement.	On	Yes
P1884 (37)	CAN message: Engine air intake temperature invalid	No apparent effect	On	No
P1884 (38)	Altitude shift control invalid	No reduced torque compensation, possible reduction in performance/driveability at altitude or high ambient temperatures.	On	No

*= Emissions (OBDII) relevant

†= MIL illuminates immediately (in all other faults, MIL on illuminates in the 2nd consecutive drive cycle if the fault is still present)

The fault codes can be accessed using TestBook. On vehicles up to 99MY the automatic transmission fault codes are a numeric code recognised by TestBook. On V8 vehicles from 99MY the automatic transmission fault codes are both numeric and OBDII 'P' codes recognised by TestBook and other suitable scantools.

After the detection of a fault, the effects remain active for the remainder of the drive cycle. In subsequent drive cycles, as soon as the EAT ECU diagnoses the fault is no longer present, it resumes normal control of the gearbox. The conditions required to diagnose that the fault is no longer present depend on the fault. Some faults require the engine to be started, others require only that the ignition is switched on.

After a fault has not recurred for forty warm-up cycles, the fault is deleted from the EAT ECU memory. Only five different faults can be stored in the memory at any one time. If a further fault occurs, the fault with the lowest priority will be replaced by the new fault.

Mechanical Limp Home

In the mechanical limp home mode in high range, gear engagement is controlled by the manual valve. The gearbox is fixed in 4th gear if the fault occurs while the vehicle is moving, or 3rd gear if the fault occurs while the vehicle is stationary. 3rd gear is also engaged if a vehicle is brought to a stop and the selector lever is moved out of, and back into, D.

Neutral and reverse gear are also available.

In the mechnaical limp home mode in low range, depending on the severity of the fault, the engaged gear is held until the vehicle is brought to a stop. The gearbox then selects and holds 3rd gear.

Calibration Selection

EAT ECU's differ between NAS, UK/Europe and ROW markets and are identified by differentiation between the part numbers.

On V8 vehicles from 99MY, the ECU contains two calibrations for 4.0 and 4.6 litre engines. When a replacement ECU is fitted, the correct ECU calibration must be selected or the ECU will store a gearbox fault and 'GEARBOX FAULT' will be displayed in the message centre. The vehicle can still be driven and is not in 'limp home mode'.

Removed EAT ECU's remember their calibration setting and if re-fitted to the same vehicle will not require calibration. A new EAT ECU will require calibration using TestBook.

If an ECU is fitted from another vehicle, the message centre will not display the 'GEARBOX FAULT' message. The correct calibration level must be selected or premature gearbox failure will occur.

USING THE H-GATE

To make a change from high to low or vice versa, the vehicle must be stationary.

- Apply the brakes and select 'N'
- Move the selector lever into the cross-piece of the 'H-gate'and select the new gear range, the panel illumination will flash before becoming constant and an audible warning will sound.
- When the illumination is constant select the gear required.

CAUTION: If a gear is selected before the gear transfer is complete, a 'clunk' or grinding sound will be heard because the electric shift motor has not completed the operation.
If this occurs and the panel illumination continues to flash, reselect neutral and try again when the illumination becomes constant.
If the vehicle is moving when a transfer gear change is attempted, the message centre will display 'SLOW DOWN'.
If an attempt is made to change the gear range with the gear selector out of neutral, 'SELECT NEUTRAL' will be displayed.

High Range Gears

Use the high range for all normal road driving and off-road driving across dry, level terrain. An audible warning will sound, the selector lever illumination will flash and the transfer box warning lamp will flash while the range change is taking place. The message centre will momentarily display 'HIGH' as soon as high range is selected, and then display the gear selected.

Selector lever positions:

'P' Park

In this position the wheels are locked to prevent the vehicle from moving. Select **only** with the vehicle stationary.

'R' Reverse

Select **only** when the vehicle is stationary.

'N' Neutral

Use this position when the vehicle is stationary and the engine is to idle for a short period.

'D' Drive

Select 'D' for all normal driving on good road surfaces. Fully automatic gear changing occurs on all forward gears according to vehicle speed and accelerator position.

'3'

Automatic gear changing is limited to first, second and third gears only. Use in congested traffic conditions and for town driving.

'2'

Automatic gear changing is limited to first and second gear ratios only. Use when driving up steep gradients and for negotiating very narrow, twisting roads. This position also provides moderate engine braking for descending slopes.

'1'

First gear only is engaged and should be used on very severe gradients, especially when towing or when maximum engine braking is required.

NOTE: If position '2' or '1' is selected from 'D' or '3' while the vehicle is travelling at high speed, then third gear will immediately engage. Progressive deceleration will then cause downshifts into second and then first gear when appropriately low road speeds are reached.

'Sport' Mode

In 'Sport' mode gear changing is delayed to make optimum use of the engine's power when increased acceleration is required or when negotiating long inclines or twisting roads. Press the mode switch, see 44M7025, with the gearbox in high range, to select 'Sport' mode. The message centre will momentarily display 'SPORT' and then 'S' along with the selected gear. Pressing the switch a second time returns the gearbox to its normal operation within the high range.

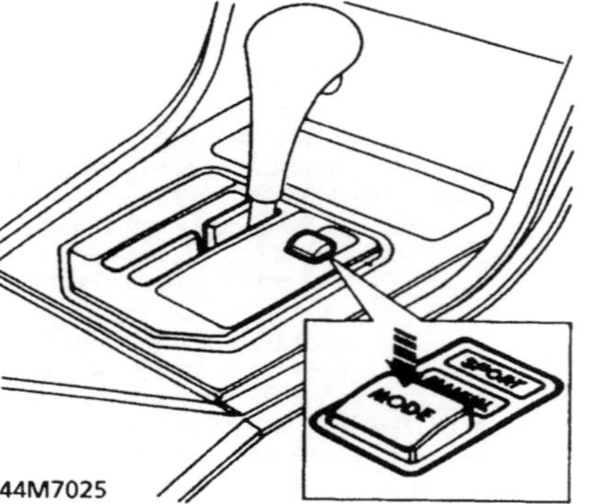

44M7025

Low Range Gears

Use low range gears in any situation where low speed manouvering is necessary, such as reversing a trailer or negotiating a boulder strewn river bed; also use low range for extreme off-road conditions. An audible warning will sound, the selector lever illumination will flash and the transfer box warning lamp will flash while the range change is taking place. The message centre will momentarily display 'LOW' when the low range is selected, and then 'L' along with the relevant gear selected.

Selector lever positions:

'P' Park

As high range.

'R' Reverse

As high range

'N' Neutral

As high range

'4'

Select '4' to optimize vehicle performance for good off-road conditions; fully automatic gear changing occurs on all forward gears according to vehicle speed and accelerator position.

'3'

Automatic gear changing is limited to first, second and third gears only and should be used for reasonable off-road conditions and ascending gradients.

'2'

Automatic gear changing is limited to first and second ratios only when maximum engine performance is required to ascend steep gradients. This position also provides moderate engine braking for descending slopes.

'1'

Select '1' on very severe gradients, particularly when towing, when maximum engine performance and engine braking is required.

'Manual' Mode

This mode enables the transmission to function as a manual gearbox in low range, providing maximum vehicle control and engine braking - ideal for use in severe off-road conditions. Press the mode switch, see 44M7025, to select 'Manual' mode; the message centre momentarily displays 'LOW' and then 'LM' along with the selected gear. Pressing the switch a second time returns the gearbox to its normal function within the low range.

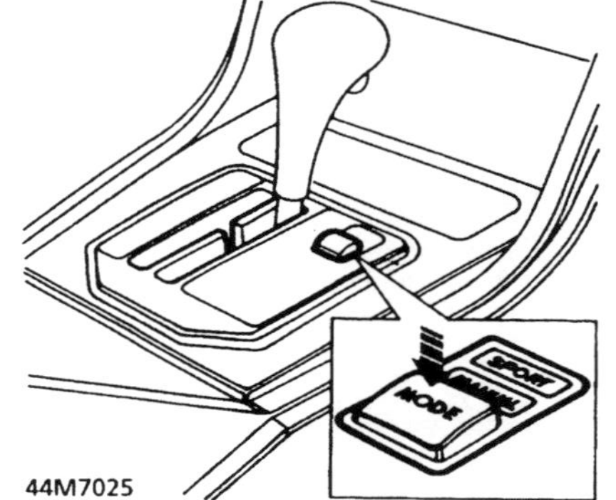

44M7025

'Transfer Neutral'

If it is necessary for the vehicle to be towed on all four wheels, 'Transfer neutral' **MUST** be selected. For full details. ***See INTRODUCTION, Information.***

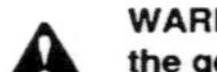

WARNING: Always leave the vehicle with the gear selector in 'P' (Park) position when parked, even when the starter key is not removed. Failure to do so will result in the battery discharging.

GENERAL PRECAUTIONS

The refrigerant used in the air conditioning system is HFC (Hydrofluorocarbon) R134a.

WARNING: R134a is a hazardous liquid and when handled incorrectly can cause serious injury. Suitable protective clothing must be worn when carrying out servicing operations on the air conditioning system.

WARNING: R134a is odourless and colourless. Do not handle or discharge in an enclosed area, or in any area where the vapour or liquid can come in contact with naked flame or hot metal. R134a is not flammable but can form a highly toxic gas.

WARNING: Do not smoke or weld in areas where R134a is in use. Inhalation of concentrations of the vapour can cause dizziness, disorientation. uncoordination, narcosis, nausea or vomiting.

WARNING: Do not allow fluids other than R134a or compressor lubricant to enter the air conditioning system. Spontaneous combustion may occur.

WARNING: R134a splashed on any part of the body will cause immediate freezing of that area. Also refrigerant cylinders and replenishment trolleys when discharging will freeze skin to them if contact is made.

WARNING: The refrigerant used in an air conditioning system must be reclaimed in accordance with the recommendations given with a Refrigerant Recovery Recycling Recharging Station.

NOTE: Suitable protective clothing comprises: Wrap around safety glasses or helmet, heatproof gloves, rubber apron or waterproof overalls and rubber boots.

REMEDIAL ACTIONS

1. If liquid R134a strikes the eye, do not rub it. Gently run large quantities of eyewash over the eye to raise the temperature. If eyewash is not available cool, clean water may be used. Cover eye with clean pad and seek immediate medical attention.
2. If liquid R134a is splashed on the skin run large quantities of water over the area as soon as possible to raise the temperature. Carry out the same actions if skin comes into contact with discharging cylinders. Wrap affected parts in blankets or similar material and seek immediate medical attention.
3. If suspected of being overcome by inhalation of R134a vapour seek fresh air. If unconscious remove to fresh air. Apply artificial respiration and/or oxygen and seek immediate medical attention.

NOTE: Due to its low evaporating temperature of -30°C, R134a should be handled with care.

WARNING: Do not allow a refrigerant container to be heated by a direct flame or to be placed near any heating appliance. A refrigerant container must not be heated above 50°C.

WARNING: Do not leave a container of refrigerant without its cap fitted. Do not transport a container of refrigerant that is unrestrained, especially in the boot of a car.

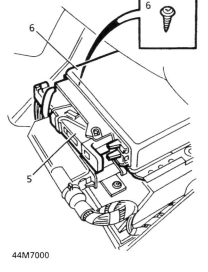

ELECTRONIC CONTROL UNIT

Service repair no - 44.15.46

Remove

1. Move left hand front seat fully rearwards. Raise cushion for access.

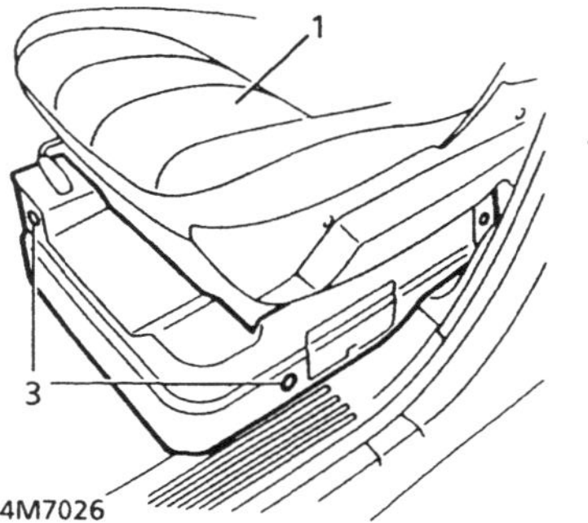

44M7026

2. Disconnect battery negative lead.
3. Remove 3 fixings securing trim to seat base. Remove trim.
4. Remove 2 screws securing cover to ECU. Remove cover.

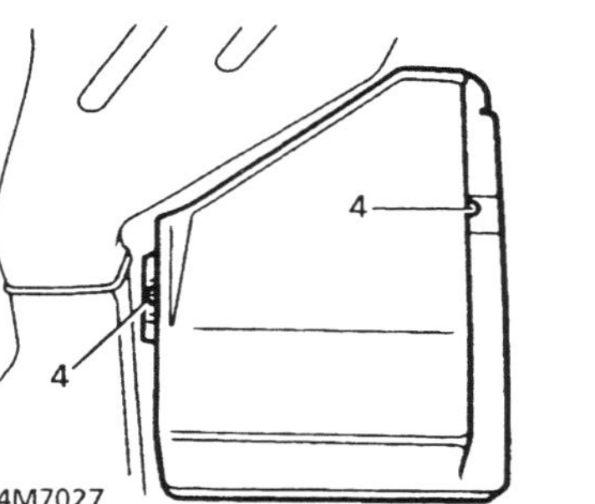

44M7027

5. Release multiplug from ECU.

44M7000

6. Remove screw securing ECU. Remove ECU.

Refit

7. Reverse removal procedure.

FLUID PAN AND FILTER

Service repair no - 44.24.04 - Fluid Pan
Service repair no - 44.24.05 - Gasket
Service repair no - 44.24.07 - Fluid Filter

Remove

1. Raise vehicle on four post lift.
2. Drain transmission fluid.

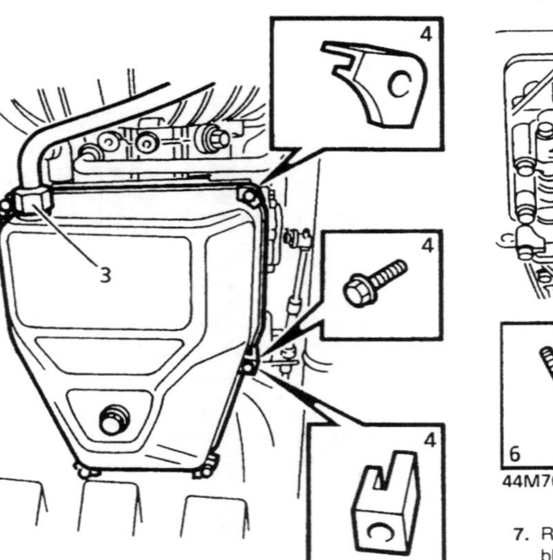

44M7001

3. **Up to 99MY:** Release fluid filler tube from pan.

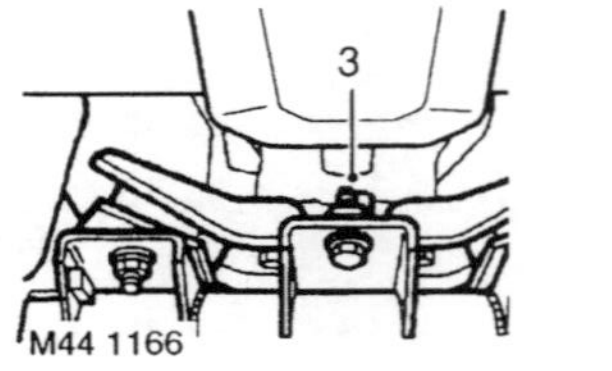

M44 1166

From 99MY: Loosen forward bolt securing snubber bar to cross member.

4. Remove 6 bolts securing fluid pan to transmission. Remove fluid pan. Collect retaining plates.
5. Remove gasket and discard.

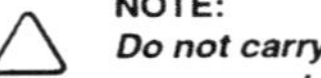

NOTE:
Do not carry out further dismantling if component is removed for access only.

6. Remove bolt securing oil pick-up tube. Remove pick-up tube. Collect spacer.

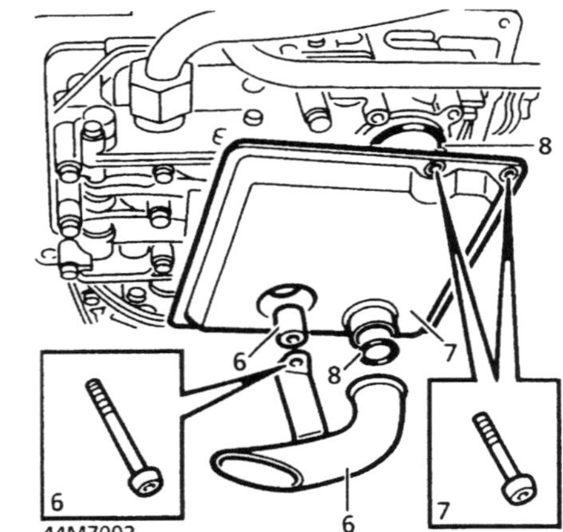

44M7002

7. Remove remaining 2 bolts securing filter to valve block. Remove filter.
8. Remove 'O' rings and discard.

Refit

9. Ensure mating faces are clean.
10. Fit new 'O' rings to fluid filter. Lubricate with clean transmission fluid.
11. Position fluid filter. Secure with bolts. Tighten to ***8 Nm (6 lbf.ft).***
12. Position oil pick-up tube and spacer. Secure with bolt. Tighten to ***8 Nm (6 lbf.ft).***
13. Fit new gasket to fluid pan. Position pan on gearbox. Secure with bolts and retaining plates. Tighten to ***8 Nm (6 lbf.ft).***
14. **Up to 99MY:** Fit oil filler tube. Tighten to ***70 Nm (52 lbf.ft).***
    From 99MY: Tighten forward bolt securing snubber bar to cross member to ***45 Nm (33 lbf.ft).***
15. Lower vehicle.
16. Refill transmission fluid. ***See LUBRICANTS, FLUIDS AND CAPACITIES, Information.***

TORQUE CONVERTER OIL SEAL

Service repair no - 44.17.07 Torque Convertor
Service repair no - 44.17.11 Oil Seal

Remove

1. Remove gearbox. ***See this section.***

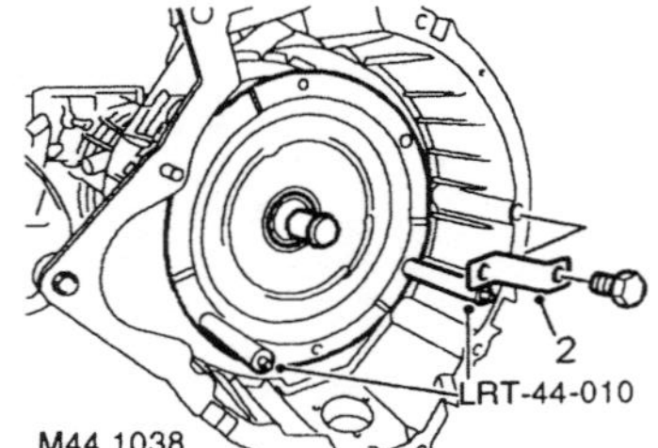

M44 1038

2. Remove retaining strap.
3. Fit LRT-44-010 to torque converter and remove torque converter from gearbox. Remove LRT-44-010 from torque converter.

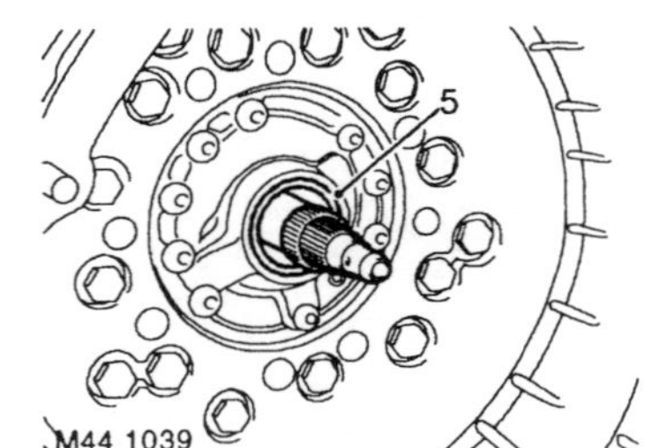

M44 1039

4. Position container beneath toque converter housing to catch fluid spillage.
5. Remove oil seal from torque converter housing.

Refit

6. Clean oil seal running surfaces.
7. Lubricate oil seal with transmission fluid.
8. Fit new seal using LRT-44-001 into converter housing.
9. Fit LRT-44-010 to torque converter.
10. Align oil pump drive and fit torque converter to gearbox.
11. Remove LRT-44-010 from torque converter.
12. Fit torque converter retaining strap.
13. Fit gearbox. ***See this section.***

AUTOMATIC GEARBOX - UP TO 99MY

Service repair no - 44.20.02/99

Remove

1. Position vehicle on four post lift.
2. Disconnect battery negative lead.
3. **Petrol Vehicles:** Release clips securing cooling fan cowling. Remove cowling.

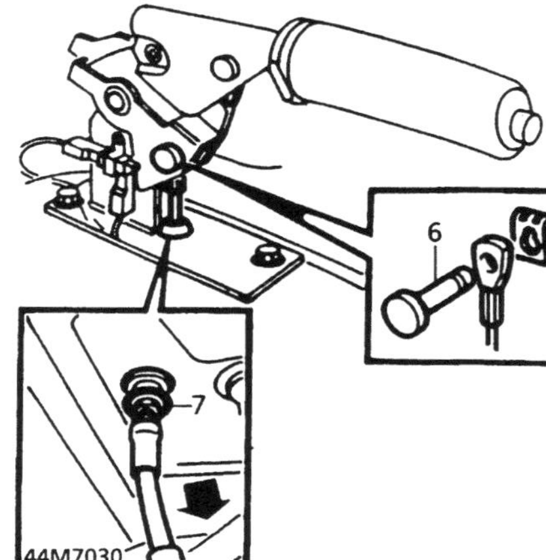

4. Remove bolt securing gearbox filler tube to engine.

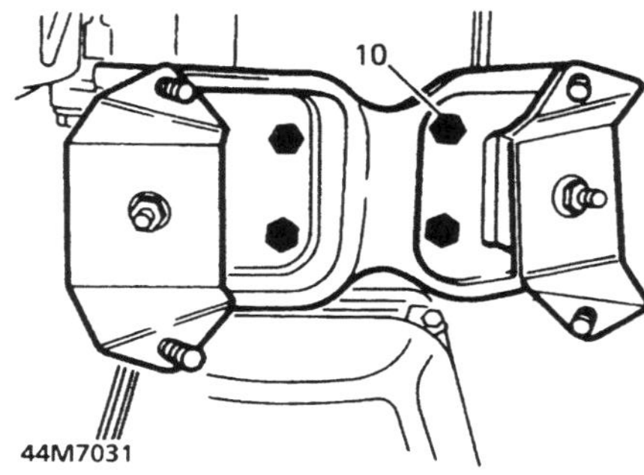

5. Remove window switch pack. ***See ELECTRICAL, Repair.***
6. Release handbrake. Remove handbrake cable clevis pin.

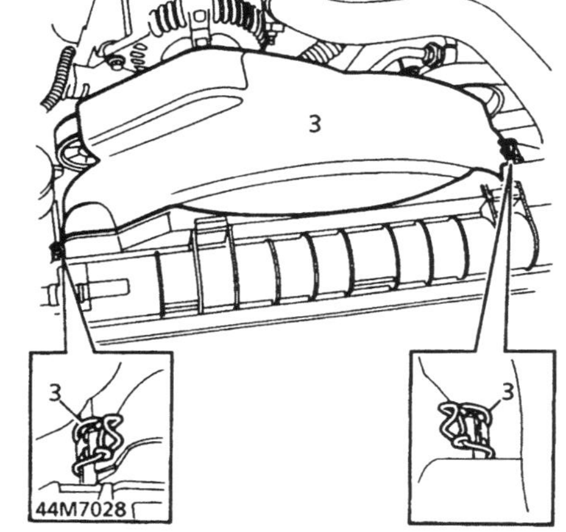

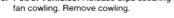

7. Release hand brake cable from grommet in tunnel.
8. Raise lift. Drain gearbox and transfer box fluids. ***See SECTION 10, Maintenance.***
9. Remove exhaust front pipe. ***See MANIFOLD AND EXHAUST SYSTEM, Repair.*** ***Diesel Vehicles:****Remove chassis cross member.* ***See CHASSIS AND BODY, Repair.***
10. Remove 4 bolts securing transmission mounting assembly. Remove assembly.

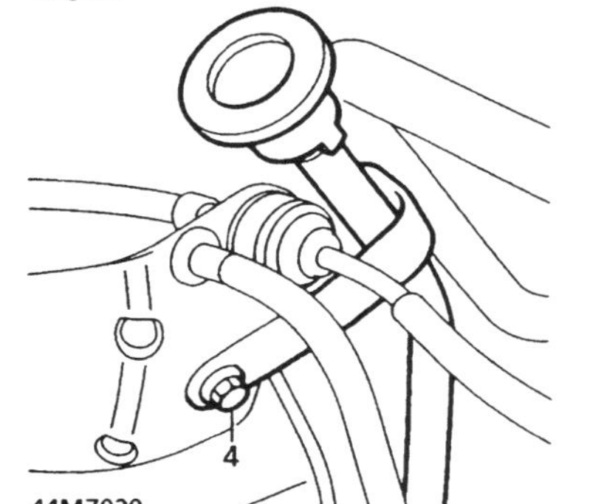

11. Position transmission lift adaptor LRT-99-007. Secure to transmission mounting bracket location with bolts. Remove transmission jack from under brake drum.

12. Remove 4 bolts securing rear propeller shaft guard. Remove guard.

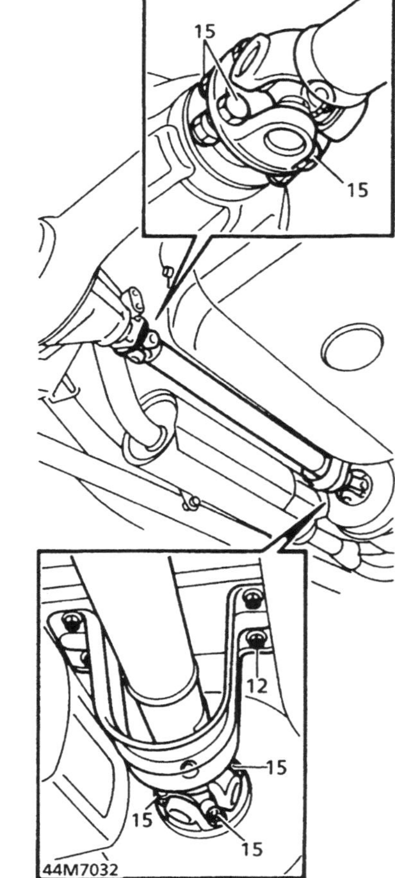

13. Mark transfer box and propeller shaft flanges to aid re-assembly.
14. Raise one wheel on each axle to allow rotation of propeller shafts.
15. Remove 4 bolts from each flange. Disconnect propeller shafts. Tie aside.

44M7033

16. Lower gearbox for access.

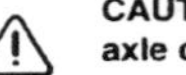

CAUTION: Place wooden block between axle case and sump to support engine.

17. Disconnect gear selector cable trunnion from gearbox lever. Remove 2 bolts securing selector cable abutment bracket to gearbox. Place selector cable aside.

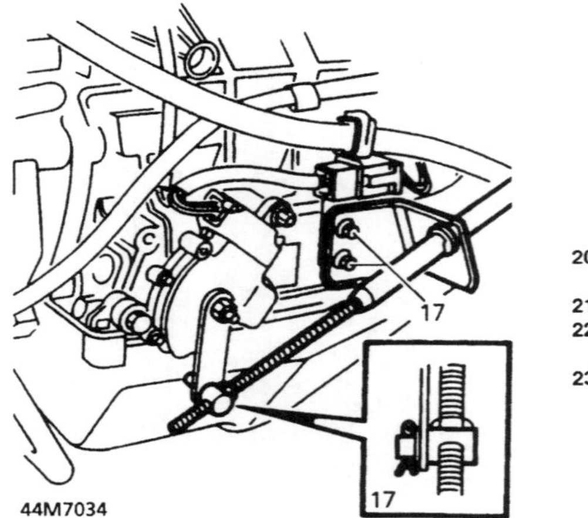

44M7034

18. Disconnect 2 Lucars from transfer box fluid temperature sensor.

19. Disconnect multiplugs from High/Low motor and output shaft speed sensor.

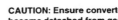

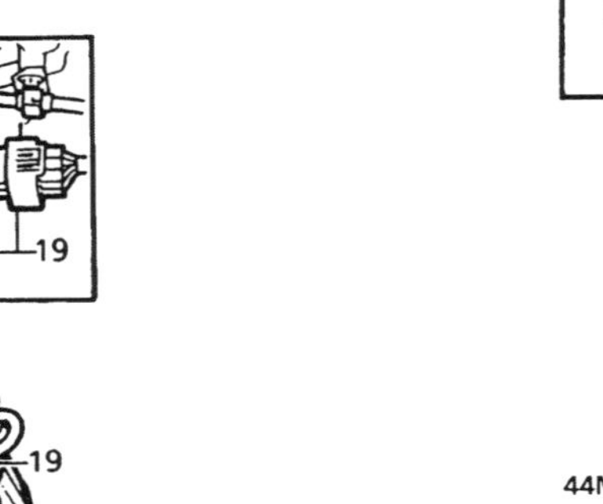

44M7035

20. Disconnect multiplugs from gear selection position switch and gearbox speed sensor.
21. Release harness from clips.
22. Remove bolt from clamp securing gearbox cooler pipes to engine.
23. Disconnect transmission cooler pipes. Remove 'O' rings and discard. Plug pipes and connections.

44M7036

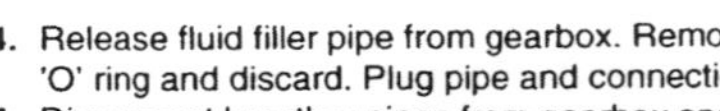

24. Release fluid filler pipe from gearbox. Remove 'O' ring and discard. Plug pipe and connection.
25. Disconnect breather pipes from gearbox and transfer box. Plug Pipes and connections.
26. Remove 3 bolts securing converter housing lower access cover. Remove cover. Collect gasket.
27. Remove 9 bolts securing converter drive plate access cover. Remove cover.

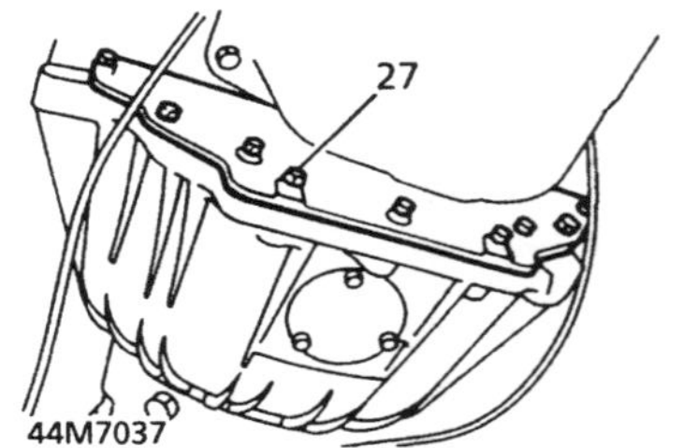

44M7037

28. Mark drive plate and converter to aid re-assembly.
29. Remove 4 bolts securing drive plate to converter.

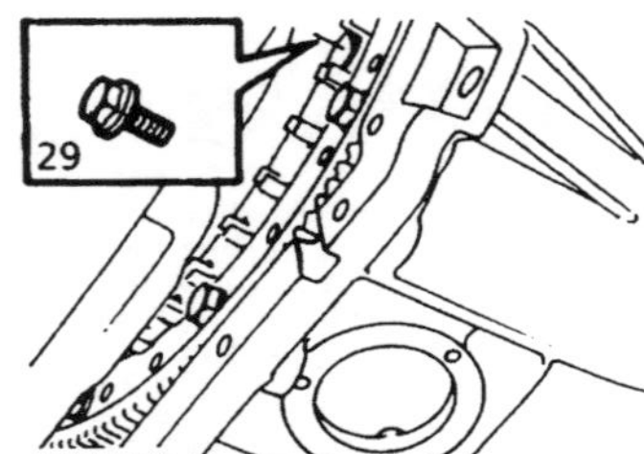

44M7038

30. Remove 8 bolts securing converter housing to engine.

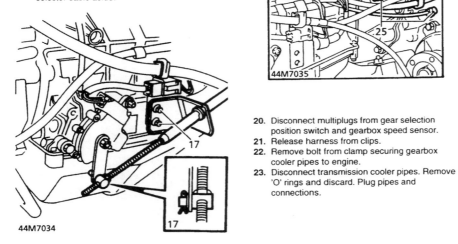

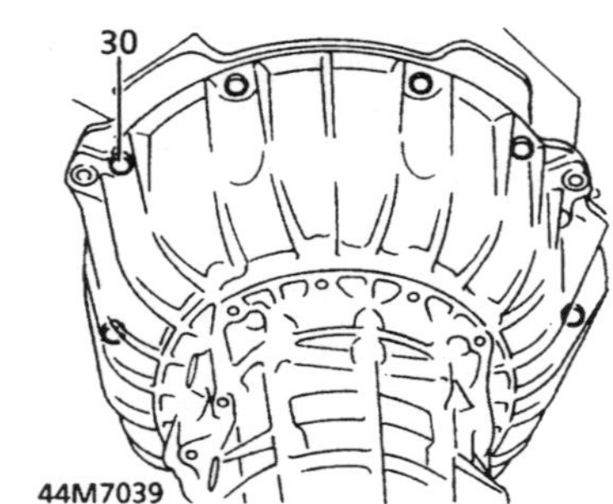

44M7039

31. Remove transmission assembly.

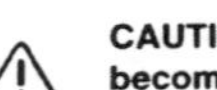

CAUTION: Ensure converter does not become detached from gearbox.

32. Fit retaining strap to converter. Secure with 2 nuts and bolts.

Do not carry out further dismantling if component is removed for access only.

33. Lower transmission assembly from vehicle.
34. Attach lifting eyes to transmission.

35. Attach hoist to lifting eyes. Take weight of transmission.
36. Remove lift adaptor. Hoist transmission assembly onto bench.
37. Fit lifting eye to transmission brake drum. Raise gearbox on end.

CAUTION: Position packers beneath bell housing extension to provide clearance for input shaft.

38. Remove 6 bolts securing transfer box to gearbox. Release from 2 ring dowels. Remove transfer box.

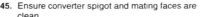

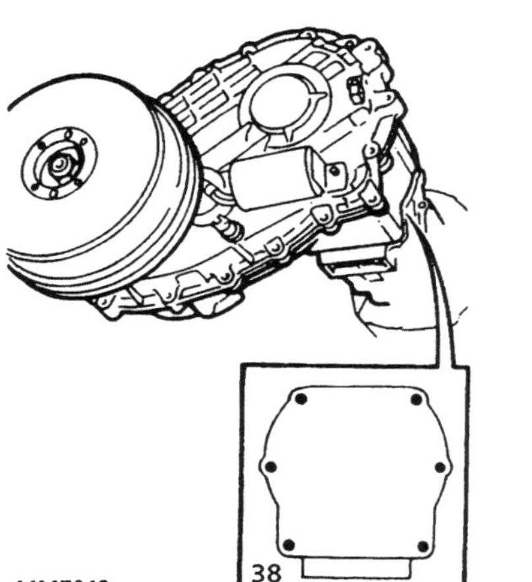

44M7042

39. Ensure mating faces are clean.
40. Place gearbox on end. Position transfer box.
41. Engage transfer box to ring dowels. Secure to gearbox with bolts. Tighten to ***45 Nm. (33 lbf.ft)***
42. Place transmission on side. Fit lifting eyes.
43. Attach transmission to lift adaptor. Secure with bolts.
44. Detach hoist. Remove lifting eyes.

Refit

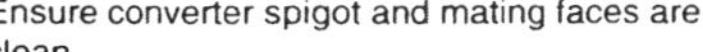

45. Ensure converter spigot and mating faces are clean.
46. Remove converter retaining strap.
47. Position transmission to engine. Secure with bolts. Tighten to ***42 Nm. (31 lbf.ft)***
48. Position drive plate to converter. Align marks. Secure with bolts. Tighten to ***45 Nm. (33 lbf.ft)***
49. Position converter access panels. Use a new gasket with lower panel. Secure panels with bolts.
50. Remove plugs from breather pipes and connections.
51. Using new sealing washers, secure breather pipes to gearbox and transfer box with banjo bolts.
52. Fit new seals to fluid filler and cooler pipes. Connect pipes to transmission. Tighten to ***30 Nm. (22 lbf.ft)***
53. Fit clamp to cooler pipes. Secure to engine with bolt.
54. Route gearbox harness. Secure with clips.
55. Connect multiplugs to High/Low motor and output shaft speed sensor.
56. Connect multiplugs to gear selection position switch and gearbox speed sensor.
57. Connect Lucars to transfer box fluid temperature sensor.
58. Align harness bracket to gearbox.
59. Position selector cable abutment bracket to gearbox. Secure with bolts.
60. Raise transmission. Support under brake drum with transmission jack.
61. Remove transmission lift adaptor. Remove lift.
62. Position transmission mounting assembly. Secure with bolts. Tighten to ***45 Nm. (33 lbf.ft)***
63. Adjust gear selector cable. ***See Adjustment.***

64. Raise one wheel on each axle to allow rotation of propeller shafts.
65. Position shafts to transfer box flanges. Align marks.
66. Secure shafts with nuts and bolts. Tighten to ***48 Nm. (35 lbf.ft)***
67. Fit propeller shaft guard. Secure with bolts.
68. Guide hand brake cable through grommet in transmission tunnel.
69. **Diesel Vehicles:**Fit chassis cross member. ***See CHASSIS AND BODY, Repair.***
70. Fit exhaust front pipe. ***See MANIFOLD AND EXHAUST SYSTEM, Repair.***
71. Fill transfer box with oil. ***See LUBRICANTS, FLUIDS AND CAPACITIES, Information.***
72. Lower Vehicle
73. Connect handbrake cable to lever.
74. Fit window switch pack. ***See ELECTRICAL, Repair.***
75. Position gearbox filler tube to engine. Secure with bolt.
76. **Petrol Engines:**Position cooling fan cowl. Secure with clips.
77. Fill gearbox with fluid. ***See LUBRICANTS, FLUIDS AND CAPACITIES, Information.***
78. Reconnect battery negative lead.

AUTOMATIC GEARBOX - FROM 99MY

Service repair no - 44.20.04.99

Remove

1. Position vehicle on a four post lift.
2. Release fixings from battery cover and remove cover.
3. Disconnect battery earth lead.

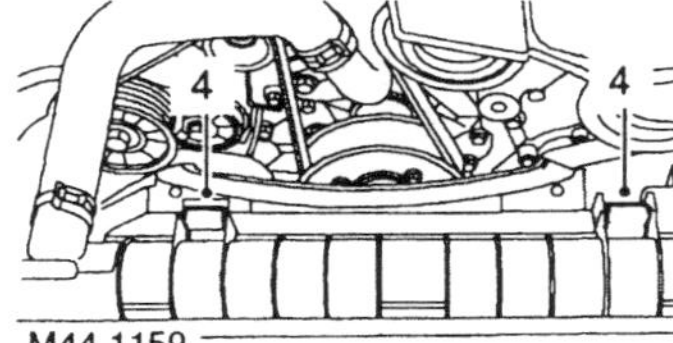

M44 1159

4. **Petrol models:** Release clips securing cooling fan cowl and remove cowl.

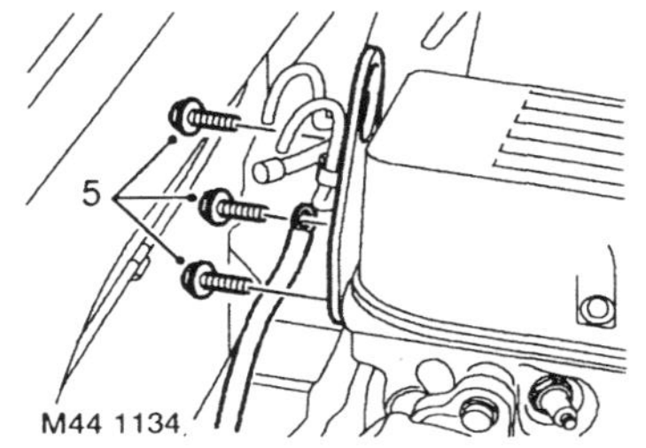

M44 1134

5. **Petrol models:** Remove 3 bolts securing engine RH lifting eye to cylinder head and position earth strap and lifting eye aside.
6. **Diesel Models:** Remove starter motor. ***See ELECTRICAL, Repair.***
7. Remove window switch pack. ***See ELECTRICAL, Repair.***

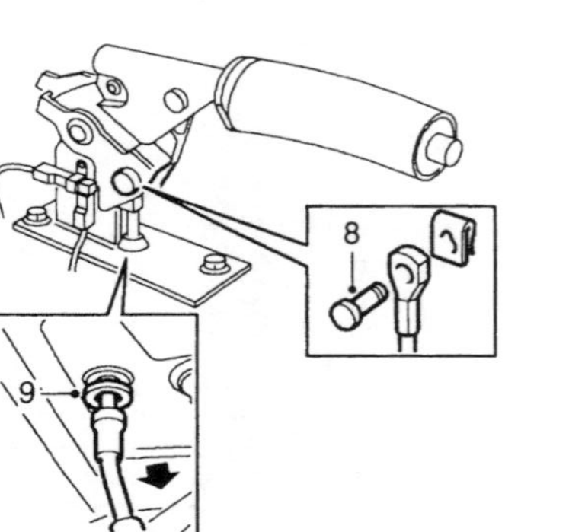

M44 1135

8. With the handbrake released, remove clip and clevis pin securing handbrake cable to handbrake.
9. Raise vehicle and release handbrake cable and grommet from tunnel.
10. Drain gearbox ***See this section. See LUBRICANTS, FLUIDS AND CAPACITIES, Information.***
11. Drain transfer gearbox fluid. ***See SECTION 10, Maintenance. See LUBRICANTS, FLUIDS AND CAPACITIES, Information.***
12. **Petrol models:** Remove exhaust front pipe. ***See MANIFOLD AND EXHAUST SYSTEM, Repair.***
13. **Diesel models:** Remove chassis crossmember. ***See CHASSIS AND BODY, Repair.***

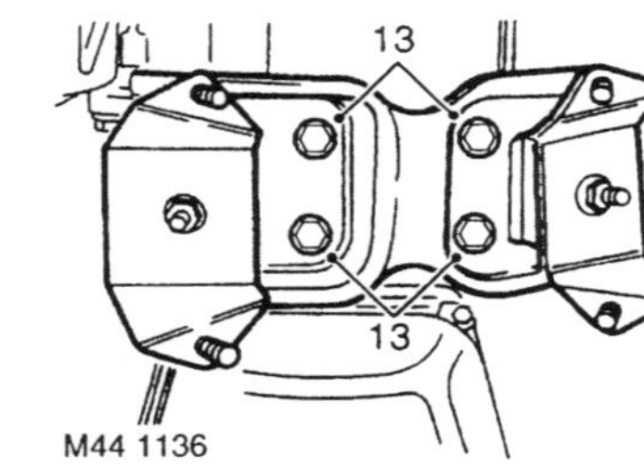

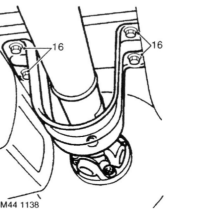

M44 1136

14. Remove 4 bolts securing transmission mounting assembly and remove assembly.

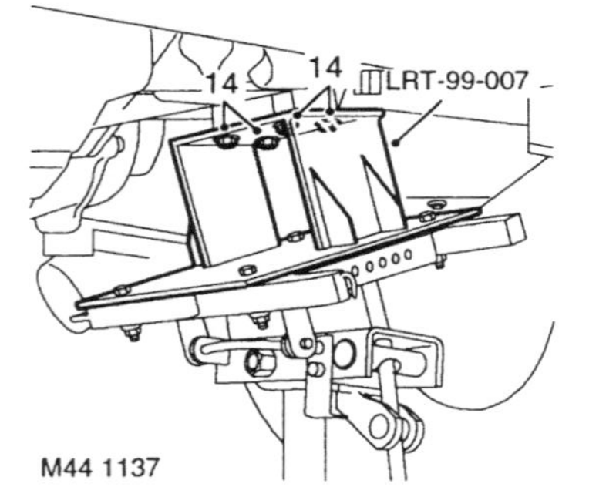

M44 1137

15. Fit LRT-99-007, to transmission jack and secure to transmission mounting bracket location holes with bolts.
16. Remove transmission jack from under brake drum.

M44 1138

17. Remove 4 bolts securing rear propeller shaft guard and remove guard.
18. Raise one wheel on each axle to allow rotation of propeller shafts.
19. Mark transfer box and propeller shaft flanges to aid re-assembly.

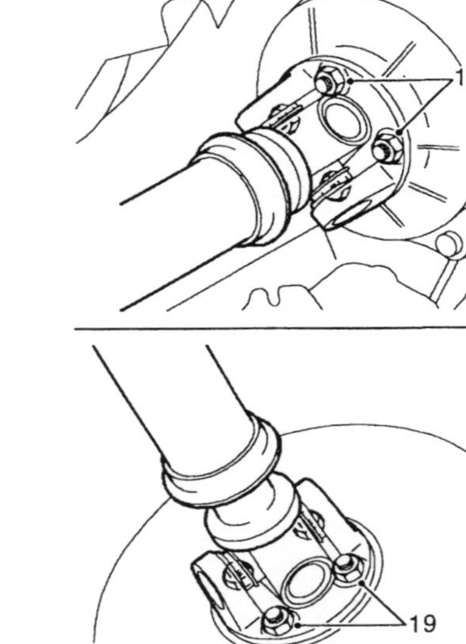

M44 1139

20. Remove 4 nuts from each propeller shaft flange.
21. Release propeller shafts and tie aside.
22. Lower gearbox for access.

CAUTION: Position jack and wooden block under sump to support engine.

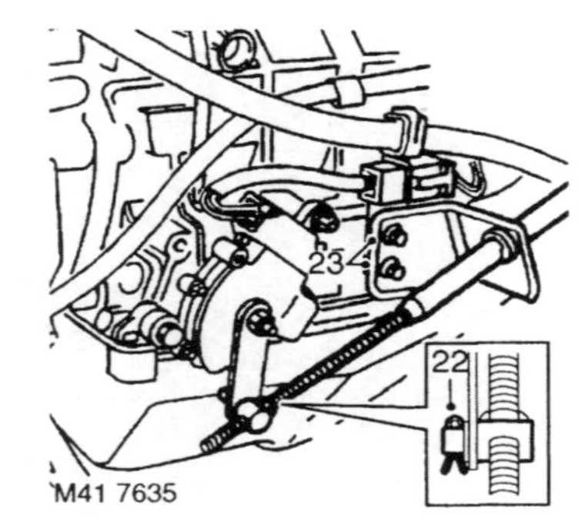

M41 7635

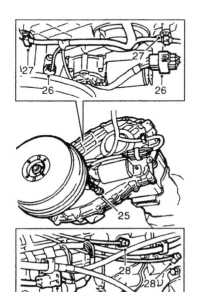

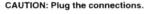

23. Remove split pin securing gear selector cable trunnion to gearbox lever and release trunnion.
24. Remove 2 bolts securing gear selector cable abutment bracket and harness support bracket to gearbox, and position selector cable and brackets aside.

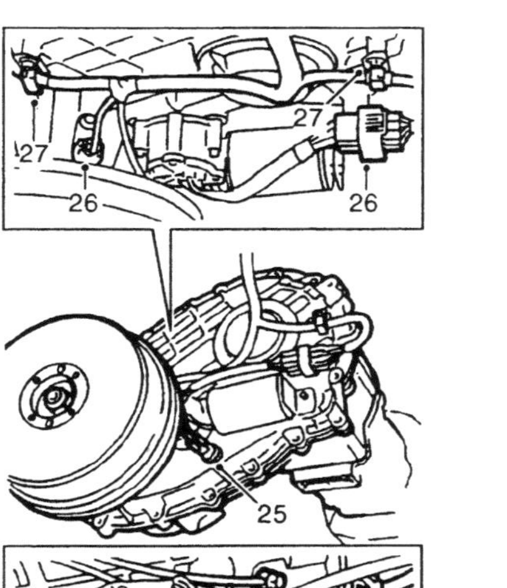

M44 1141

25. Disconnect multiplugs from gear selection position switch and gearbox speed sensor.
26. Disconnect 2 Lucars from transfer box fluid temperature sensor.
27. Disconnect multiplugs from High/Low motor and output shaft speed sensor.
28. Release harness from 3 clips.
29. Remove 2 banjo bolts securing breather pipes to gearbox and transfer box, remove and discard sealing washers.

CAUTION: Plug the connections.

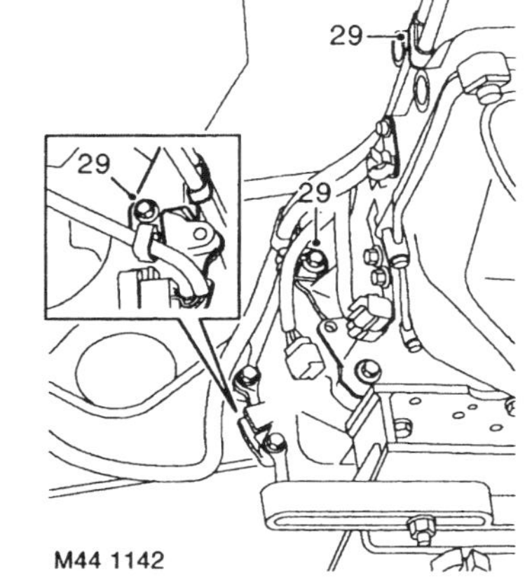

M44 1142

30. Remove 2 bolts and release 1 clip securing fuel and purge pipe retaining brackets to gearbox and transfer box.

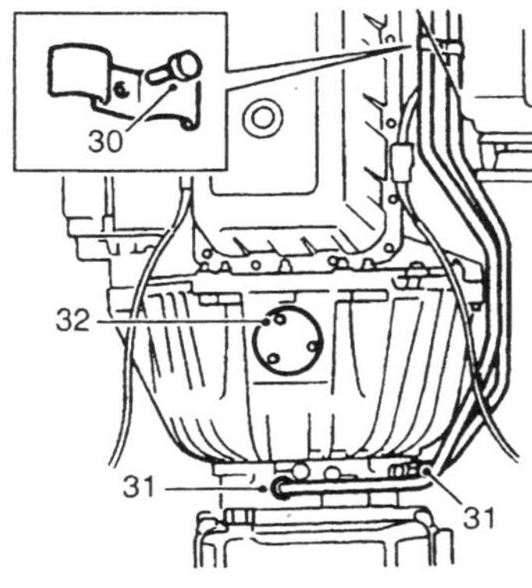

M44 1143

31. Remove bolt from clamp securing gearbox fluid cooler pipes to engine.
32. Loosen unions and release gearbox oil cooler pipes, discard 'O' rings.

CAUTION: Plug the connections.

33. Remove 3 bolts securing converter housing lower access cover, remove cover and discard gasket.

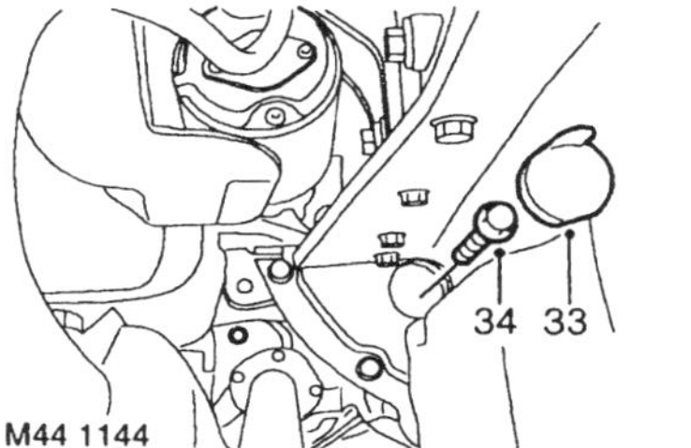

M44 1144

34. Remove access plug and mark drive plate and torque convertor to aid re-assembly.
35. Rotate engine to gain access and remove 4 bolts securing drive plate to convertor.

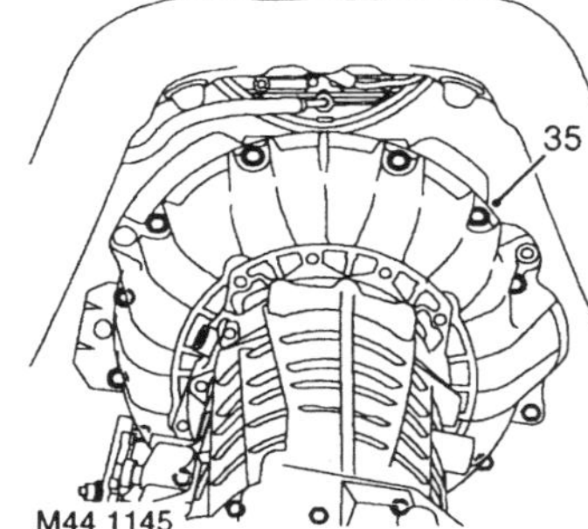

M44 1145

36. Remove 14 bolts securing gearbox to engine and collect crash bracket.
37. With assistance remove transmission assembly.

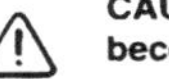
CAUTION: Ensure converter does not become detached from gearbox.

38. Fit retaining strap to converter and secure with 2 nuts and bolts.

Refit

39. Clean mating faces of engine and gearbox, dowel and dowel holes.
40. Ensure drive plate and convertor mating faces are clean.
41. Remove 2 nuts and bolts and remove convertor retaining strap.
42. With assistance, fit transmission assembly to engine.
43. Fit crash bracket to gearbox flange and fit and tighten engine to gearbox bolts to ***46 Nm (34 lbf.ft).***
44. Align drive plate to convertor and tighten bolts to ***50 Nm (37 lbf.ft).***
45. Fit access plug.
46. Fit new gasket and lower access cover. Secure cover with bolts.
47. Clean gearbox fluid cooler pipe unions, fit new 'O' rings and tighten union nuts to ***30 Nm (22 lbf.ft).***
48. Clean breather pipe bolts and banjos, fit new sealing washers and tighten bolts to ***15 Nm (11 lbf.ft).***
49. Fit gearbox fluid cooler pipe clamp and secure with bolt.
50. Align fuel and purge pipe brackets to gearbox and transfer box and secure with 2 bolts and 1 clip.
51. Connect multiplugs to output shaft speed sensor and High/Low motor.
52. Connect Lucars to transfer box temperature sensor.
53. Connect multiplugs to gearbox selection position switch and gearbox speed sensor.
54. Secure harness to clips.
55. Align harness support bracket and gear selector cable abutment bracket to gearbox and secure with bolts.
56. Connect gear selector cable trunnion to lever and fit split pin.
57. Adjust gear selector cable. ***See this section.***
58. Raise gearbox on transmission jack.
59. Fit and engage handbrake cable grommet in transmission tunnel.
60. Clean propeller shaft and transfer box flanges.
61. Fit shafts to transfer box flanges, align marks and tighten nuts to ***48 Nm (35 lbf.ft).***
62. Fit rear propeller shaft guard and secure with bolts.
63. Position transmission jack under brake drum.
64. Remove 4 bolts securing LRT-99-007 to transmission and remove support.
65. Fit transmission mounting assembly and tighten bolts to ***44 Nm (33 lbf.ft).***
66. **Diesel models:** Fit chassis crossmember. ***See CHASSIS AND BODY, Repair.***
67. **Petrol models:** Fit exhaust front pipe. ***See MANIFOLD AND EXHAUST SYSTEM, Repair.***
68. Connect handbrake cable to lever, fit clevis pin and secure pin with clip.
69. Fit window switch pack. ***See ELECTRICAL, Repair.***
70. **Diesel models:** Fit starter motor. ***See ELECTRICAL, Repair.***
71. **Petrol models:** Fit engine RH lifting eye, align earth strap and secure with bolts.
72. **Petrol models:** Fit cooling fan cowl and secure with clips.
73. Connect battery earth lead.
74. Fit and secure battery cover.
75. Fill transfer box with oil. ***See SECTION 10, Maintenance. See LUBRICANTS, FLUIDS AND CAPACITIES, Information.***
76. Fill gearbox with fluid. ***See this section.***

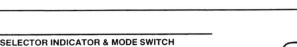

SELECTOR INDICATOR & MODE SWITCH

Service repair no - 44.15.10 - Selector Indicator

NOTE: The E.A.T. Mode switch is integral with the selector indicator assembly and cannot be serviced separately.

Remove

1. Remove electric window switch pack. ***See ELECTRICAL, Repair.***
2. Remove screw at rear of gear lever applique. Raise rear of applique. Disengage 2 spring clips at forward end.

44M7014

3. Disconnect cigar lighter multiplug. Release cigar lighter bulb. Remove selector lever applique.
4. Remove screw securing selector knob. Remove knob.

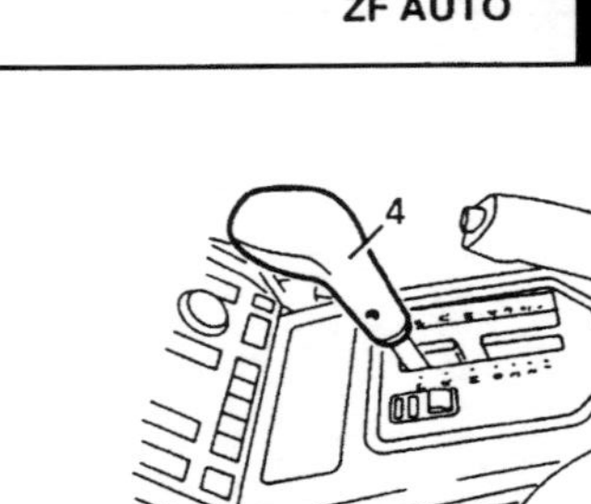

44M7015

5. Remove 3 screws securing selector indicator.

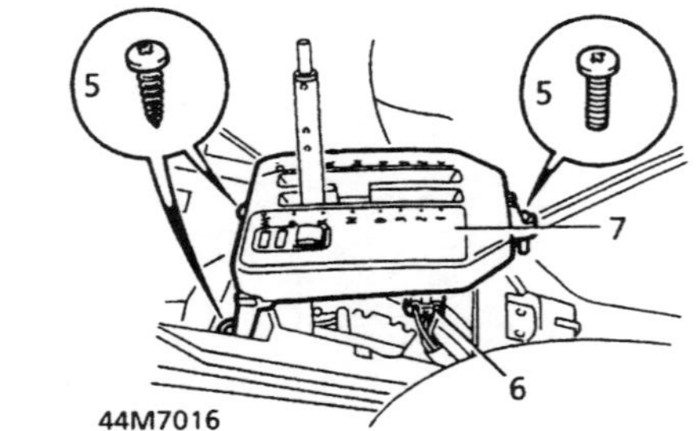

44M7016

6. Raise selector indicator. Disconnect multiplug.
7. Remove selector indicator.

Refit

8. Reverse removal procedure.

SELECTOR LEVER ASSEMBLY

Service repair no - 44.15.04

Remove

1. Select 'P'. Remove ignition key.

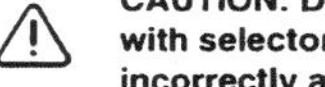

CAUTION: Do not attempt to start vehicle with selector cable disconnected, incorrectly adjusted, or selector interlock solenoid overridden.

2. Remove centre console. ***See CHASSIS AND BODY, Repair.***
3. Remove sound deadener pad.

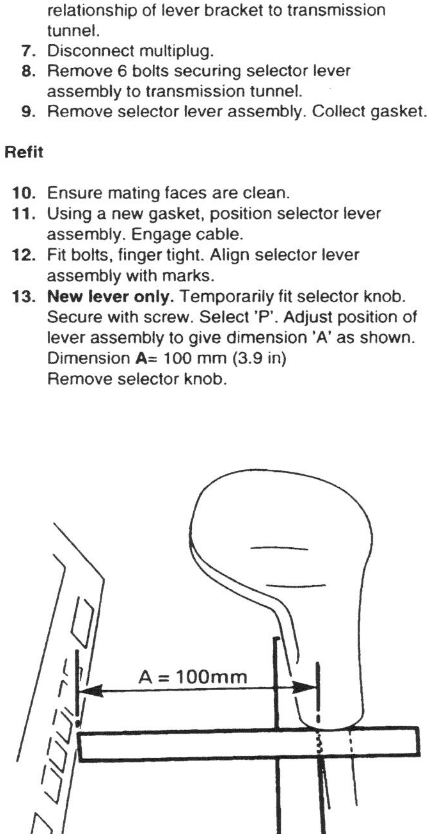

44M7004

4. Select '1'. Disconnect selector cable from lever.

NOTE: North American and Japanese vehicles are fitted with a gear selector interlock mechanism. To move selector lever from 'P', activate interlock solenoid manually with 3mm screwdriver as shown.

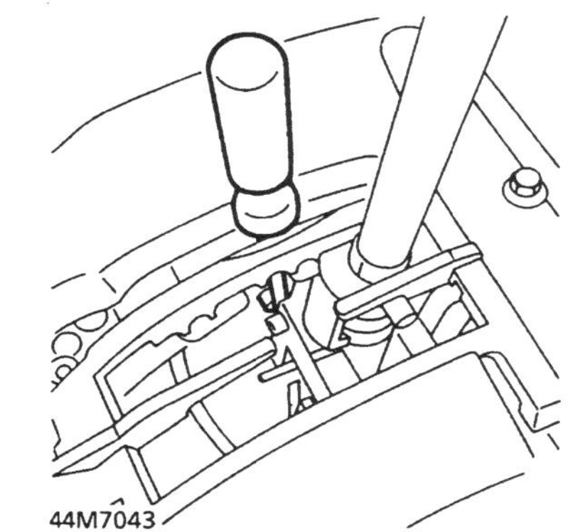

44M7043

5. Remove 'C' clip securing cable outer to selector lever bracket.

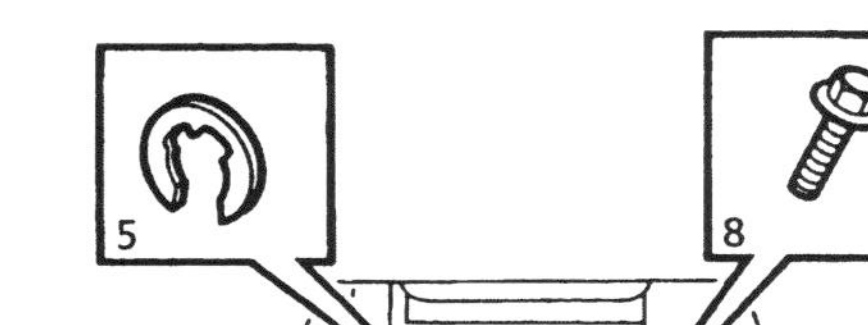
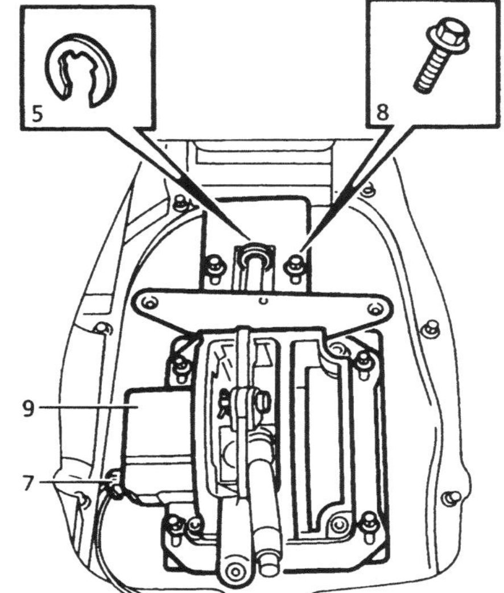

44M7005

6. If selector lever assembly is to be refitted, mark relationship of lever bracket to transmission tunnel.
7. Disconnect multiplug.
8. Remove 6 bolts securing selector lever assembly to transmission tunnel.
9. Remove selector lever assembly. Collect gasket.

Refit

10. Ensure mating faces are clean.
11. Using a new gasket, position selector lever assembly. Engage cable.
12. Fit bolts, finger tight. Align selector lever assembly with marks.
13. **New lever only.** Temporarily fit selector knob. Secure with screw. Select 'P'. Adjust position of lever assembly to give dimension 'A' as shown. Dimension **A**= 100 mm (3.9 in) Remove selector knob.

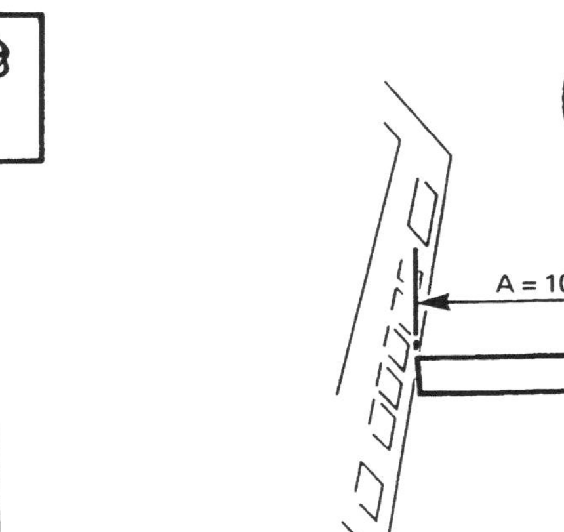

44M7013A

14. Tighten selector lever assembly fixings.
15. Connect multiplug.
16. Secure cable lever bracket with 'C' clip.
17. Align cable to lever. Secure with clevis and split pins.
18. Fit sound deadener pad.
19. Fit centre console. ***See CHASSIS AND BODY, Repair.***
20. Engage cable in gearbox abutment bracket. Secure with 'C' clip.
21. Adjust selector cable. ***See this section.***

SEAL - SELECTOR SHAFT

Service repair no - 44.15.34

Remove

1. Position vehicle on a four post lift.
2. Release fixings from battery cover and remove cover.
3. Disconnect battery earth lead.

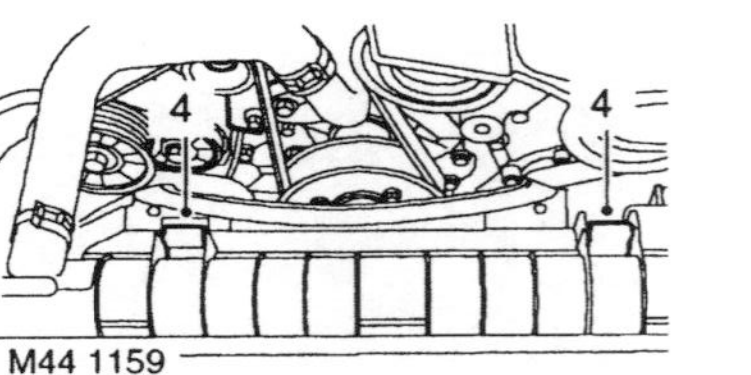

M44 1159

4. **Petrol models:** Release clips securing cooling fan cowl and remove cowl.

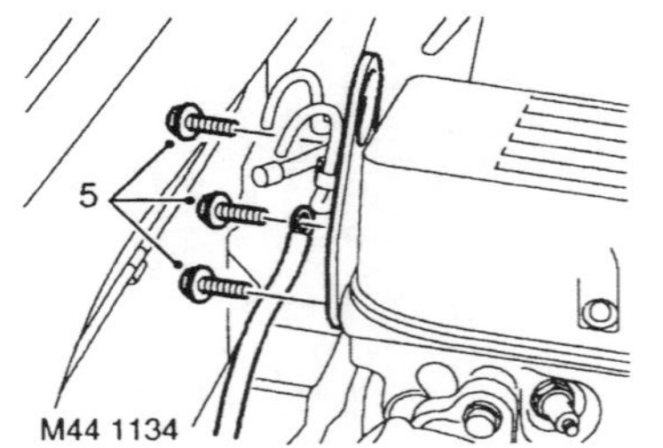

M44 1134

5. **Petrol models:** Remove 3 bolts securing engine RH lifting eye to cylinder head and position earth strap and lifting eye aside.
6. Remove window switch pack. ***See ELECTRICAL, Repair.***

M44 1169

7. With the handbrake released, remove clip and clevis pin securing handbrake cable to handbrake.
8. Raise vehicle and release handbrake cable and grommet from tunnel.
9. **Petrol models:** Remove exhaust front pipe. ***See MANIFOLD AND EXHAUST SYSTEM, Repair.***
10. **Diesel models:** Remove chassis crossmember. ***See CHASSIS AND BODY, Repair.***

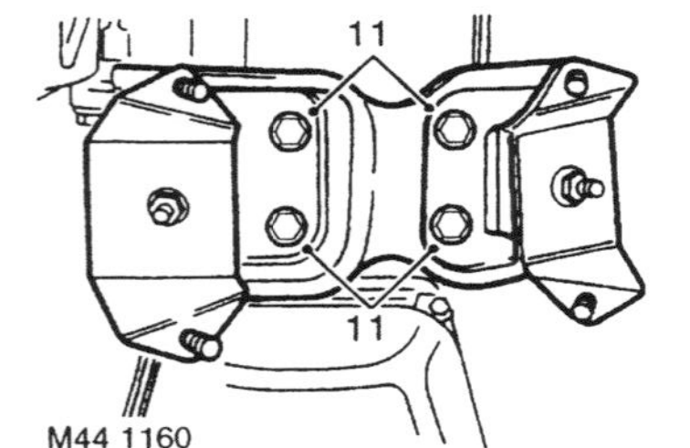

M44 1160

11. Remove 4 bolts securing transmission mounting assembly and remove assembly.

M44 1161

12. Remove 4 bolts securing rear propeller shaft guard and remove guard.
13. Raise one wheel on each axle to allow rotation of propeller shafts.
14. Mark transfer box and propeller shaft flanges to aid re-assembly.

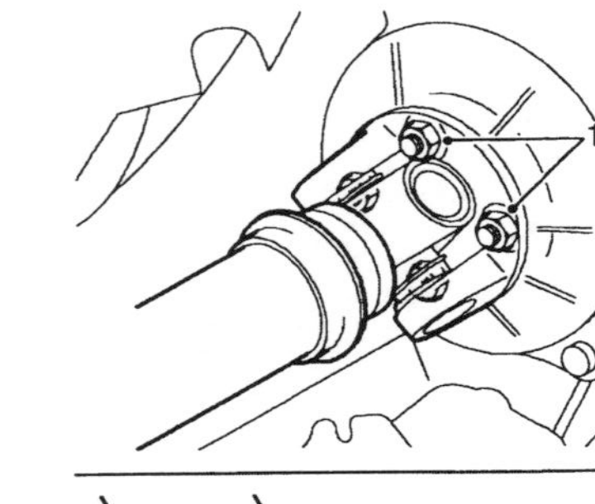

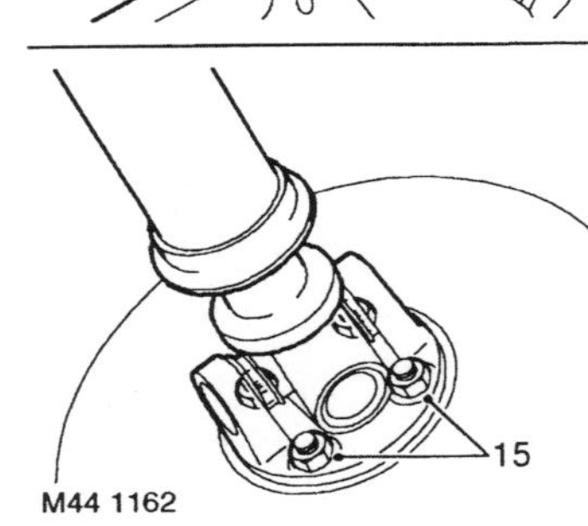

M44 1162

15. Remove 4 bolts from each propeller shaft flange.
16. Release propeller shafts and tie aside.
17. Lower gearbox for access.

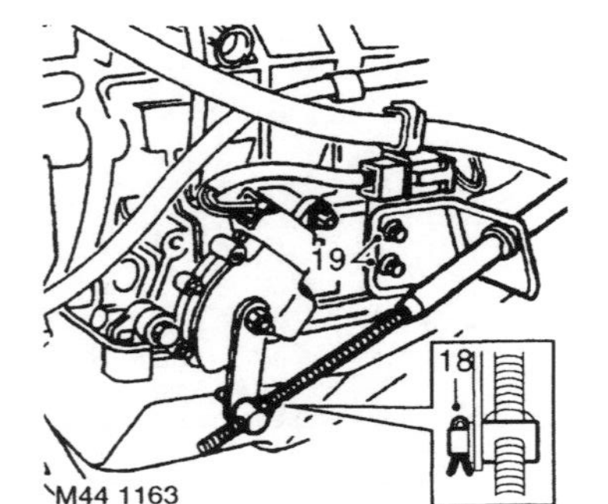

M44 1163

18. Remove split pin securing gear selector cable trunnion to gear selector lever and release trunnion.
19. Remove 2 bolts securing gear selector cable abutment bracket and harness support bracket to gearbox.

20. Position selector cable and bracket aside.
21. Lower gearbox support to gain access to selector shaft.
22. Remove valve block. ***See this section.***

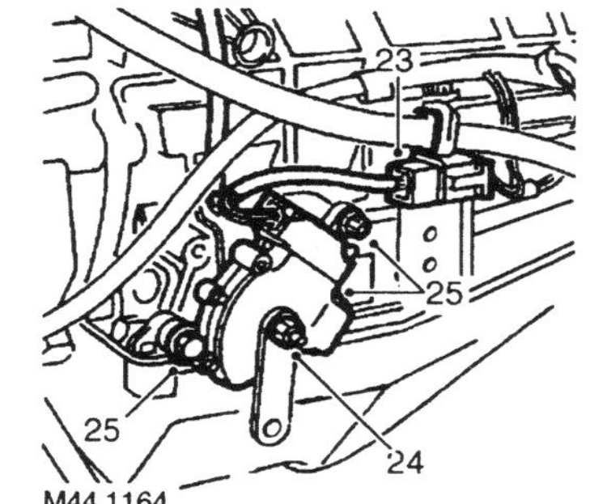

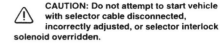

M44 1164

23. Disconnect harness from gear selector switch multiplug and release multiplug from bracket.
24. Remove nut securing selector shaft lever and release lever from shaft.
25. Remove bolt and nut securing gear selector switch to gearbox and remove switch.

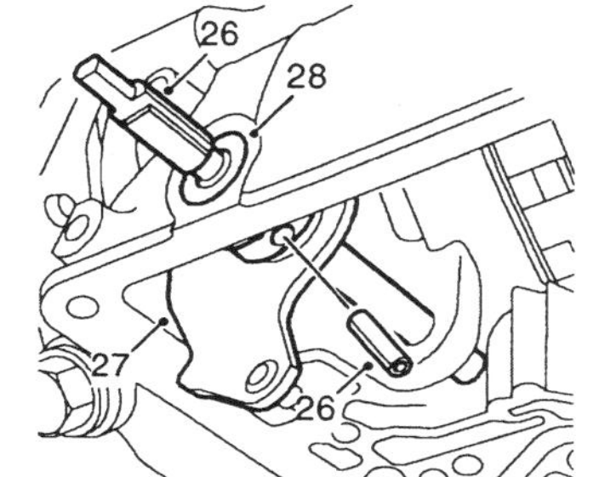

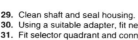

M44 1165

26. Drift out and discard selector quadrant roll pin. Remove selector shaft.
27. Remove selector quadrant and connecting rod.
28. Remove oil seal taking care not to damage seal housing.

Refit

29. Clean shaft and seal housing.
30. Using a suitable adapter, fit new seal.
31. Fit selector quadrant and connecting rod.
32. Fit selector shaft and secure to quadrant using new roll pin.
33. Fit valve block. ***See this section.***
34. Position selector switch and tighten nut and bolt.
35. Position selector shaft lever and tighten nut.
36. Fit selector switch multiplug to bracket and connect harness to multiplug.
37. Align harness support bracket and gear selector cable abutment bracket to gearbox and secure with bolts.
38. Connect gear selector cable trunion to lever and fit split pin.
39. Adjust gear selector cable. ***See this section.***
40. Raise gearbox on transmission jack.
41. Fit handbrake cable through transmission tunnel.
42. Clean propeller shaft and transfer box flanges.
43. Fit shafts to transfer box flanges, align marks and tighten nuts and bolts to ***48 Nm (35 lbf.ft).***
44. Fit rear propeller shaft guard and secure with bolts.
45. Fit transmission mounting assembly and tighten bolts to ***44 Nm (33 lbf.ft).***
46. **Diesel models:** Fit chassis crossmember. ***See CHASSIS AND BODY, Repair.***
47. **Petrol models:** Fit exhaust front pipe. ***See MANIFOLD AND EXHAUST SYSTEM, Repair.***
48. Connect handbrake cable to lever and fit clevis pin and clip.
49. Fit window switch pack. ***See ELECTRICAL, Repair.***
50. **Petrol models:** Fit engine RH lifting eye, align earth strap and secure with bolts.
51. **Petrol models:** Fit cooling fan cowl and secure with clips.
52. Connect battery earth lead.
53. Fit and secure battery cover.

OUTPUT SHAFT SEAL

Service repair no - 44.20.18

Remove

1. Disconnect battery negative lead.
2. Remove transfer box. ***See TRANSFER BOX, Repair.***
3. Drain fluid from gearbox. ***See SECTION 10, Maintenance.***
4. Remove seal from gearbox casing using a suitable lever.

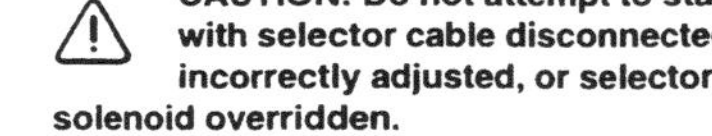

CAUTION: Ensure location does not become damaged as seal is levered from casing.

44M7041

Refit

5. Clean seal location and running surface on transfer gearbox input shaft.
6. Lubricate seal lip with clean transmission fluid.
7. Fit seal to gearbox casing using LRT-44-001
8. Fit transfer box. ***See TRANSFER BOX, Repair.***
9. Reconnect battery negative lead.
10. Replenish transmission fluids. ***See LUBRICANTS, FLUIDS AND CAPACITIES, Information.***

SELECTOR CABLE

Service repair no - 44.15.08

Remove

1. Select 'P'. Remove ignition key.

CAUTION: Do not attempt to start vehicle with selector cable disconnected, incorrectly adjusted, or selector interlock solenoid overridden.

2. Raise the vehicle.

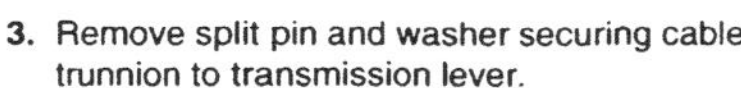

WARNING: Support on safety stands.

3. Remove split pin and washer securing cable trunnion to transmission lever.

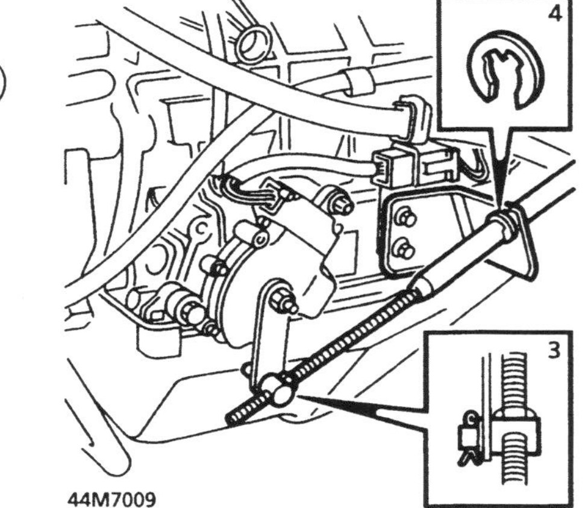

44M7009

4. Remove 'C' clip securing cable to transmission abutment bracket. Remove cable.
5. Remove centre console. ***See CHASSIS AND BODY, Repair.***
6. Remove sound deadener pad.

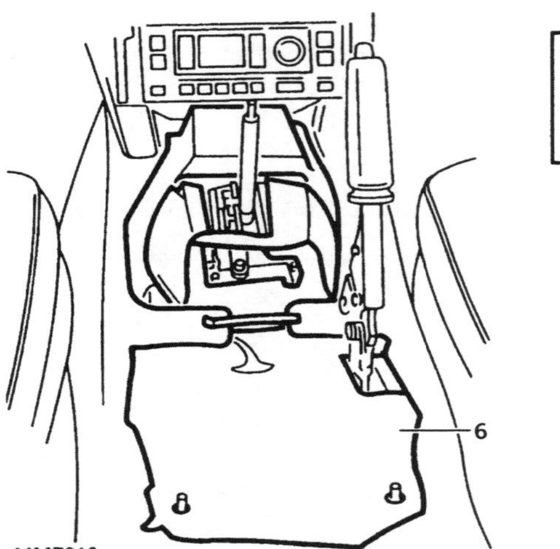

44M7010

7. Select '1'. Disconnect selector cable to lever.

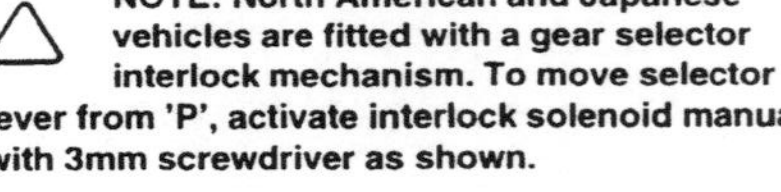

NOTE: North American and Japanese vehicles are fitted with a gear selector interlock mechanism. To move selector lever from 'P', activate interlock solenoid manually with 3mm screwdriver as shown.

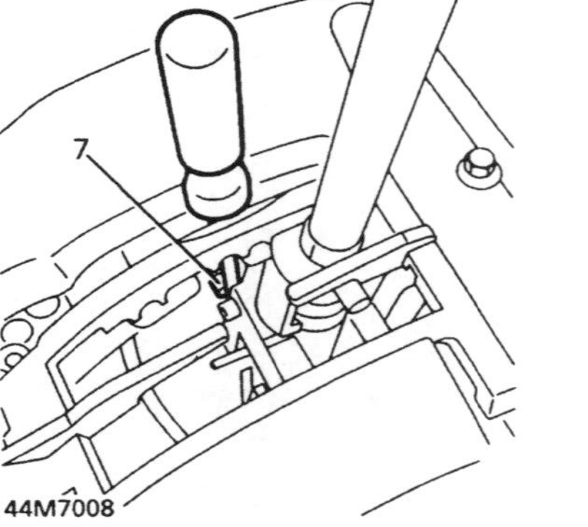

44M7008

8. Remove 'C' clip securing cable to underside of vehicle. Remove cable.

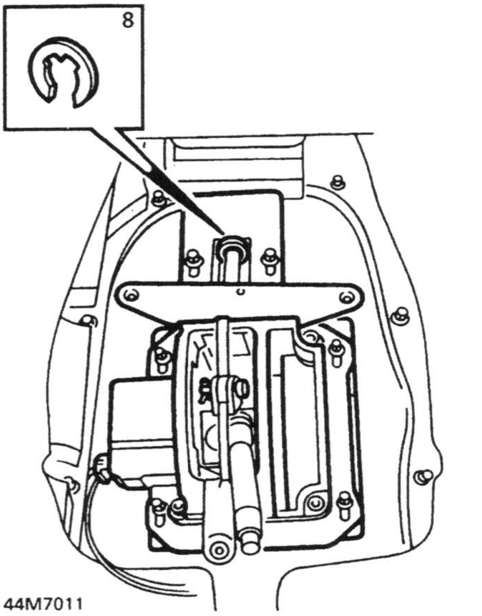

44M7011

Refit

9. Reverse removal procedure.
10. Adjust selector cable. ***See Adjustment.***

SELECTOR POSITION SWITCH

Service repair no - 44.15.19

Remove

1. Raise vehicle on four post lift.Select 'P'. Raise lift.
2. Remove nut securing selector lever to selector shaft. Release lever.

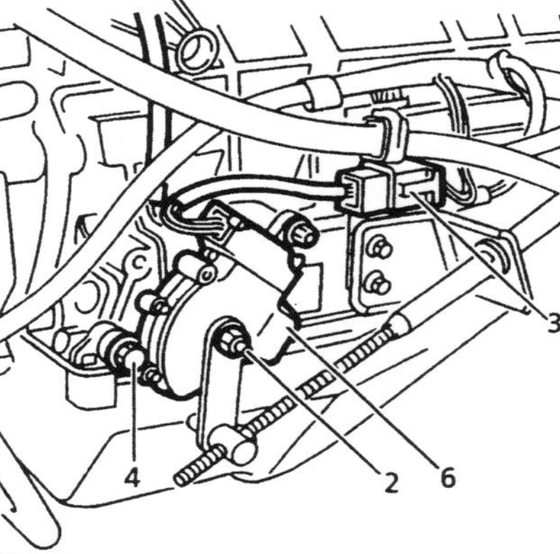

44M7012

3. Release switch multiplug from bracket. Disconnect from vehicle harness.
4. Remove nut and bolt securing position switch.
5. Release switch from selector shaft. Remove breather hose.
6. Remove switch.

Refit

7. Ensure 'P' is selected by rotating selector shaft fully clockwise.
8. Engage 'N' by rotating selector shaft anti-clockwise by 2 detents.
9. Connect breather hose to switch. Connect multiplug to vehicle harness. Secure to bracket.
10. Engage switch on selector shaft. Fit nut to stud, fit bolt. Do not tighten.
11. Fit setting tool LRT-44-011 to shaft.
12. Insert setting pin into tool. Rotate switch until setting pin engages with hole in switch as shown.

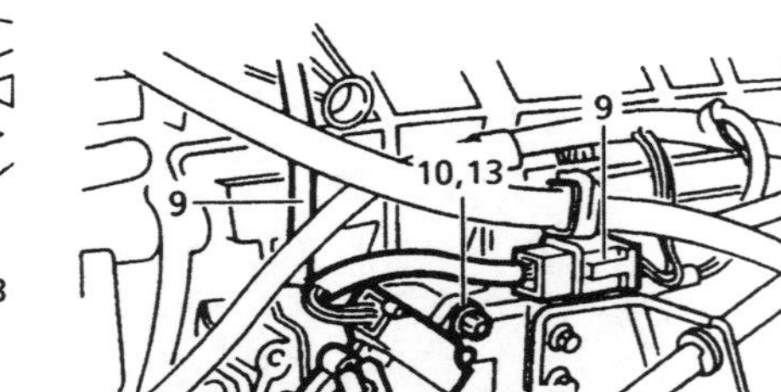

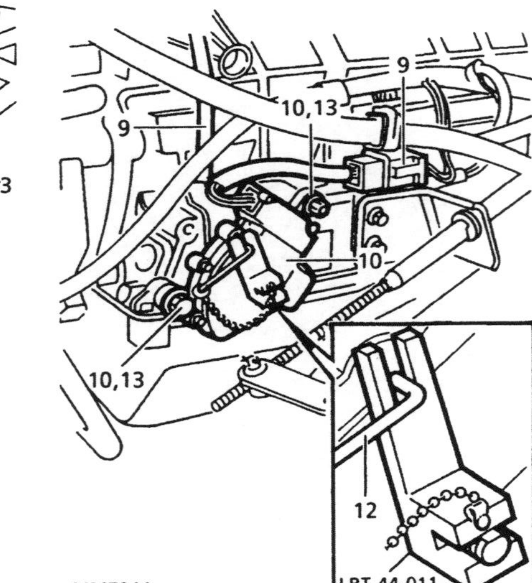

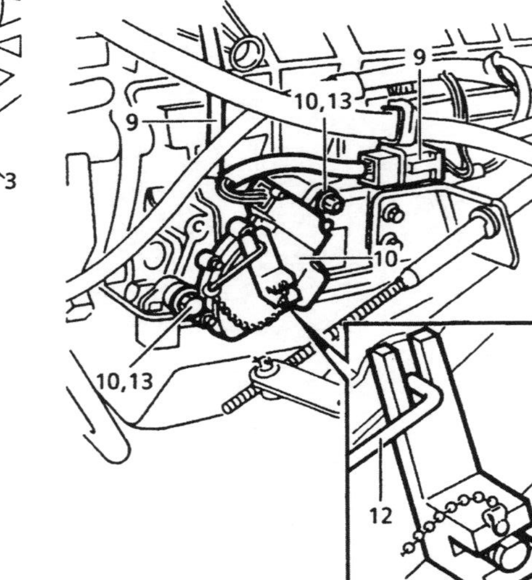

44M7044

13. Tighten nut and bolt. Remove setting tool.
14. Fit selector lever to shaft. Secure with nut.
15. Lower vehicle.

FLUID COOLER - V8 - UP TO 99MY

Service repair no - 44.24.10

Remove

1. Disconnect battery negative lead.
2. Remove engine oil cooler. ***See ENGINE, Repair.***
3. Remove 4 trim studs securing air deflectors. Remove deflectors.
4. Position container to collect fluid spillage.
5. Unscrew fluid cooler pipe union nuts and discard 'O' rings.

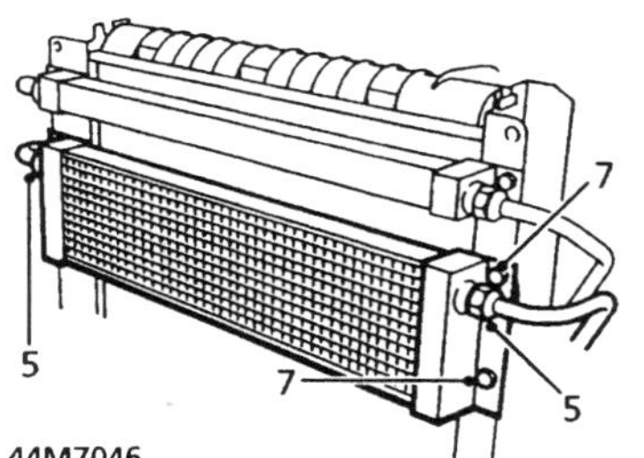

6. Plug cooler and pipes.
7. Remove 4 bolts securing fluid cooler to radiator mounting bracket.
8. Remove fluid cooler.

Refit

9. Fit fluid cooler.
10. Fit and tighten 4 bolts securing cooler to mounting bracket.
11. Remove plugs from cooler and pipes.
12. Ensure pipe unions are clean.
13. Lubricate new 'O'rings with clean fluid and fit to pipes.
14. Connect pipes to cooler. Tighten union nuts to ***30 Nm. (22 lbf.ft)***
15. Remove container.
16. Fit air deflectors and secure with studs.
17. Fit engine oil cooler. ***See ENGINE, Repair.***
18. Reconnect battery negative lead.
19. Top up gearbox fluid. ***See SECTION 10, Maintenance.***

FLUID COOLER - V8 - FROM 99MY

Service repair no - 44.24.10

Remove

1. Remove engine oil cooler. ***See ENGINE, Repair.***
2. Position absorbent cloth under each gearbox cooler pipe connection to collect spillage.

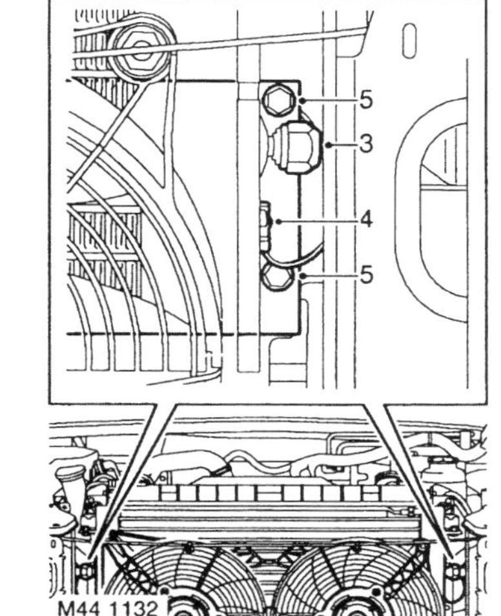

3. Loosen unions and release pipes from cooler, discard 'O' rings.

CAUTION: Plug the connections.

4. Remove 2 screws securing fluid temperature sensor to cooler.
5. Remove 4 bolts securing fluid cooler to radiator mounting brackets and remove cooler.

Refit

6. Clean fluid cooler and pipe connections.
7. Fit new fluid cooler to radiator, engage in locations, fit and tighten bolts.
8. Position fluid temperature sensor and secure with screws.
9. Using new 'O' rings connect pipes to cooler and tighten unions to ***30 Nm (22 lbf.ft).***
10. Top up gearbox fluid.
11. Fit engine oil cooler. ***See ENGINE, Repair.***

FLUID COOLER - DIESEL

Service repair no - 44.24.10

Remove

1. Disconnect battery negative lead.
2. Raise vehicle on four post lift.
3. Positon container to collect fluid spillage.
4. Unscrew fluid pipe union nuts and discard 'O' rings.

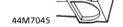

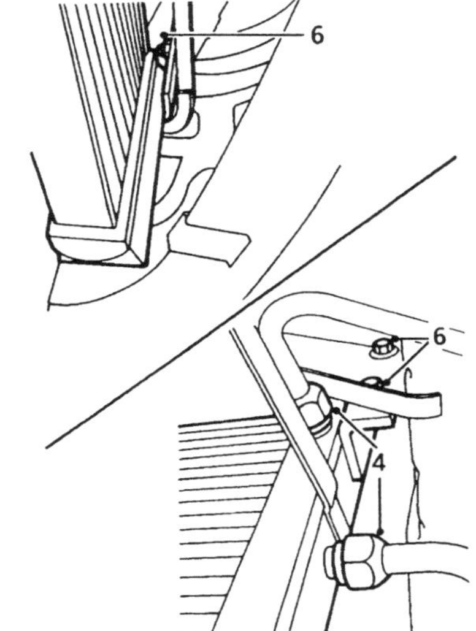

5. Plug cooler and pipes.
6. Remove 3 bolts securing fluid cooler to chassis bracket.
7. Remove fluid cooler.

Refit

8. Fit fluid cooler.
9. Fit and tighten 3 bolts securing cooler to chassis bracket.
10. Remove plugs from cooler and pipes.
11. Ensure pipe unions are clean.
12. Lubricate new 'O' rings with clean fluid and fit to pipes.
13. Connect pipes to cooler. Tighten union nuts to ***30 Nm. (22 lb.ft).***
14. Remove container.
15. Lower vehicle.
16. Reconnect battery negative lead.
17. Top up gearbox fluid, ***See SECTION 10, Maintenance.***

SEAL - VALVE BLOCK - SET

Service repair no - 44.20.13

Remove

1. Remove valve body assembly. ***See this section.***

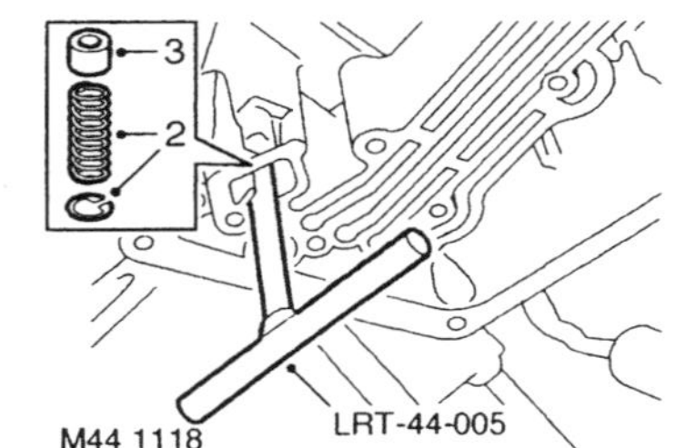

M44 1118

2. Remove circlips and springs from gearbox casing noting location of long and short springs.
3. Remove and discard seals using LRT-44-005 from gearbox casing.

Refit

4. Clean gearbox casing, springs and circlips.

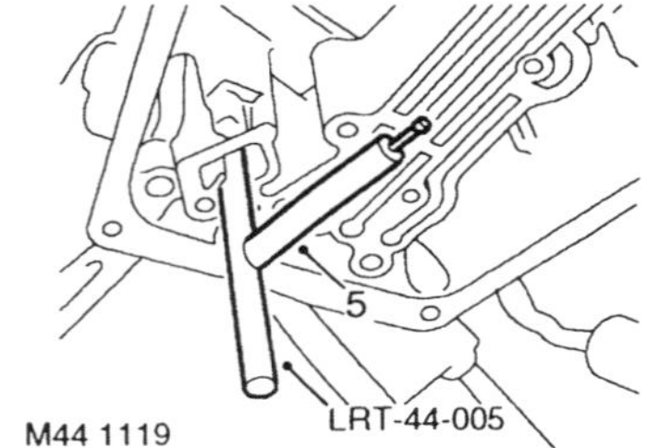

M44 1119

5. Fit new seals using LRT-44-005, ensure seals are fully seated.

M44 1120

6. Position springs in their correct locations and secure with circlips.
7. Fit valve body assembly. ***See this section.***

SEAL - REAR EXTENSION HOUSING

Service repair no - 44.20.18

Remove

1. Remove transfer gearbox. ***See TRANSFER BOX, Repair.***

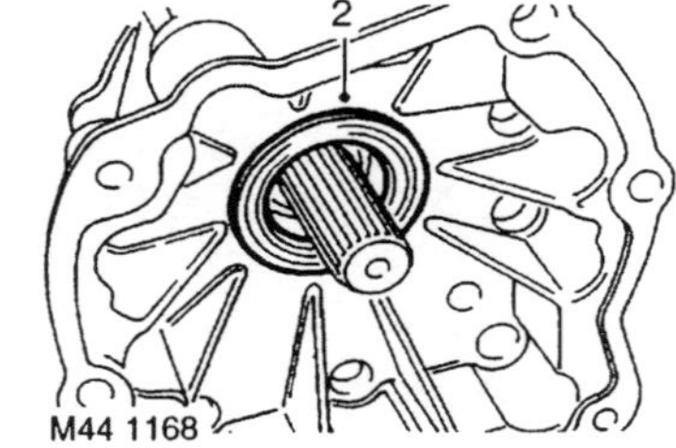

M44 1168

2. Remove rear extension housing oil seal from gearbox.

Refit

3. Clean oil seal recess in gearbox and running surface on input shaft.
4. Lubricate oil seal running surface with transmission fluid.
5. Using LRT-44-001 fit oil seal to extension housing.
6. Fit transfer gearbox. ***See TRANSFER BOX, Repair.***

GASKET - REAR EXTENSION HOUSING

Service repair no - 44.20.19

Remove

1. Remove transfer gearbox. ***See TRANSFER BOX, Repair.***

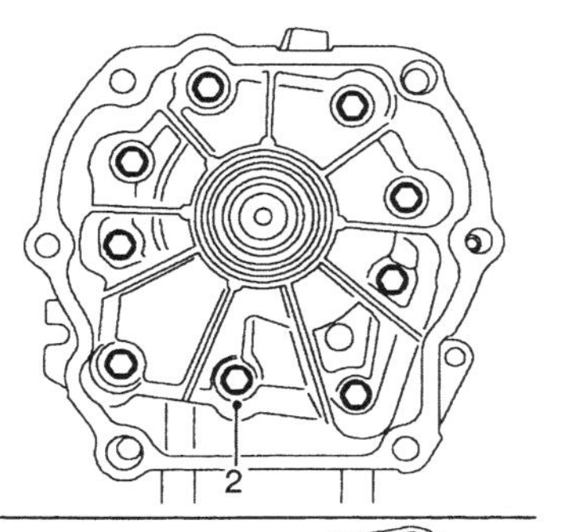

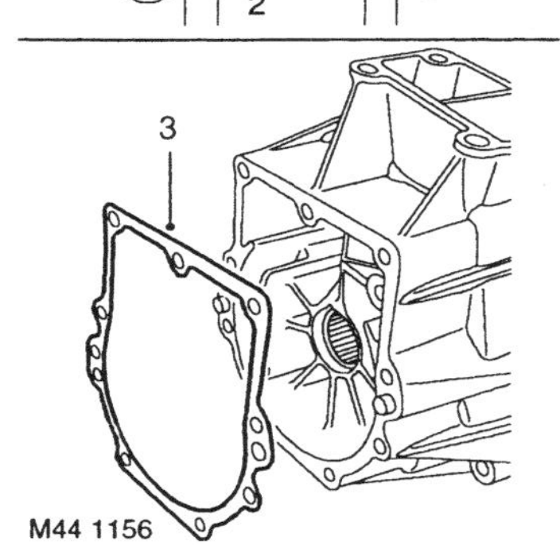

M44 1156

2. Remove 9 bolts securing rear extension housing to gearbox case and remove housing.
3. Remove and discard gasket.

Refit

4. Clean rear extension and mating face, dowel and dowel holes.
5. Fit new gasket to gearbox case.
6. Fit rear extension housing and tighten bolts to 23 Nm (16 lbf.ft).
7. Fit transfer gearbox. ***See TRANSFER BOX, Repair.***

GEARBOX - DRAIN AND REFILL - FROM 99MY

Service repair no - 44.24.02

Drain

1. Position vehicle on ramp.
2. Apply handbrake and position chocks under front and rear wheels.
3. Position container under gearbox.
4. Remove gearbox drain plug and discard sealing washer.

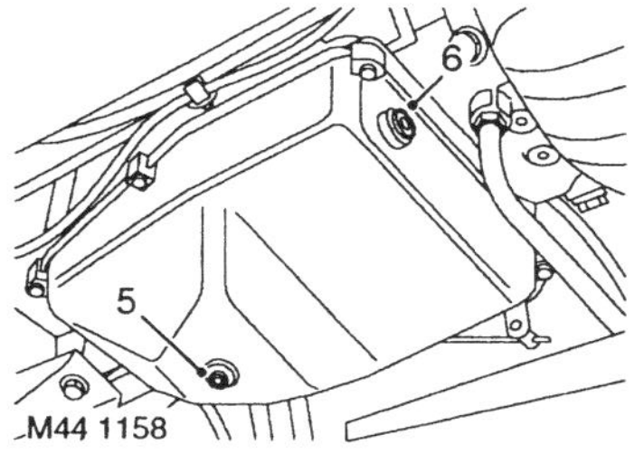

M44 1158

5. Refit drain plug using new sealing washer and tighten to ***15 Nm (11 lbf.ft).***
6. Remove filler/level plug and discard sealing washer.

Refill

7. Refill gearbox to bottom of filler/level plug hole with correct grade of fluid.
8. Ensure gear lever in the 'P' position, start engine and move selector lever through all gear positions and back to 'P' position.
9. With the engine idling, continue filling gearbox until a small thread of fluid runs from filler/level orifice.
10. Refit filler/level plug using a new sealing washer and tighten to ***30 Nm (22 lbf.ft).***
11. Lower vehicle.

PARKING PAWL ASSEMBLY

Service repair no - 44.28.07

Remove

1. Remove rear extension housing gasket. ***See this section.***

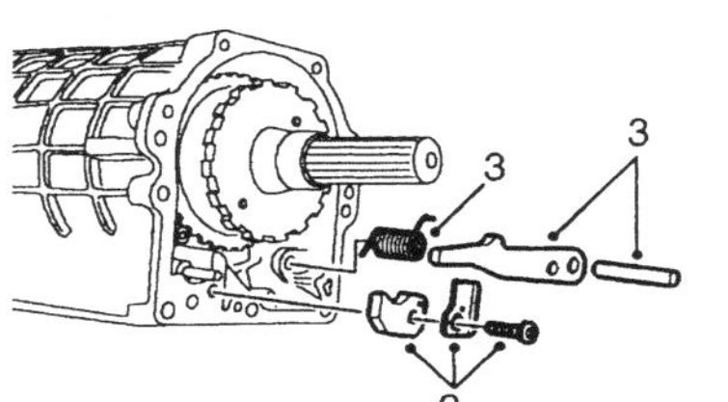

M44 1153

2. Remove Torx screw and discard, lift off parking pawl guide and guide plate.
3. Remove ratchet, spring and pivot pin.

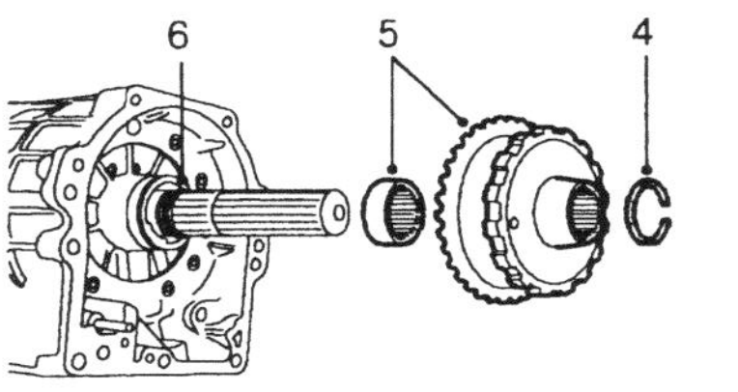

M44 1154

4. Remove and discard circlip from output shaft.
5. Remove bearing track and park lock gear.
6. Remove and discard 'O' ring from output shaft.

Refit

7. Clean park lock components.
8. Lubricate and fit new 'O' ring to output shaft.
9. Position park lock gear, bearing track and secure with new circlip.
10. Position pivot pin, spring and ratchet.
11. Position parking pawl guide and guide plate, tighten Torx screw to ***10 Nm (7 lbf.ft).***
12. Clean extension housing and gearbox case.
13. Position new gasket to gearbox case.
14. Position extension housing and tighten bolts to ***23 Nm (17 lbf.ft).***
15. Fit rear extension housing gasket. ***See this section.***

VALVE BODY ASSEMBLY

Service repair no - 44.40.01

Remove

1. Remove gearbox fluid filter. ***See this section.***
2. Remove 2 bolts securing speed sensor harness bracket to valve block.

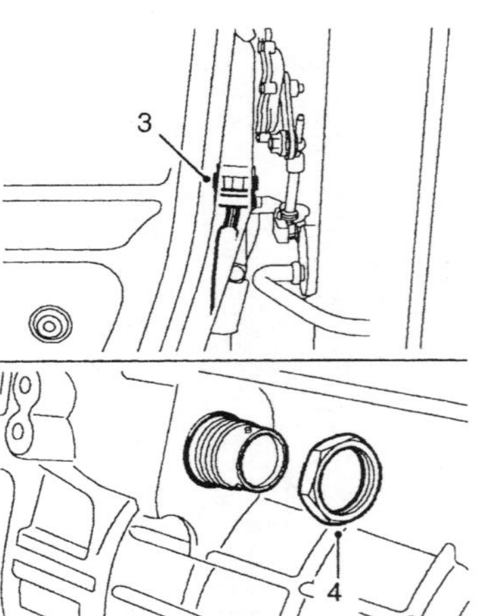

3. Disconnect multiplug from gearbox housing.
4. Using a 30 mm socket, remove nut securing multiplug connector block from gearbox housing.
5. Remove 6 long bolts securing valve block to gearbox.
6. Remove 5 short bolts securing valve block to gearbox.
7. Release speed sensor and remove valve block.
8. Remove and discard 'O' ring from multiplug connector.

Refit

9. Clean valve block and mating faces.
10. Fit new 'O' ring to multiplug connector block.
11. With assistance, position multiplug to gearbox housing and tighten nut.
12. Align valve block to gearbox, ensure manual valve is correctly located. Position speed sensor retaining bracket, and tighten screws to ***8 Nm (6 lbf.ft).***
13. Connect multiplug to gearbox connector.
14. Fit gearbox fluid filter. ***See this section.***

47 - PROPELLER SHAFTS

CONTENTS

Page

REPAIR

PROPELLER SHAFT - FRONT

Service repair no - 47.15.02

Remove

1. Raise vehicle on four post lift.
2. Mark propeller shaft and drive flanges for reassembly.
3. With assistance, remove 4 nuts and bolts securing each propeller shaft flange.

NOTE: Raise 1 front road wheel and rotate propeller shaft as necessary to gain access to all fixings.

CAUTION: Assistance is necessary to support propeller shaft when fixings are removed.

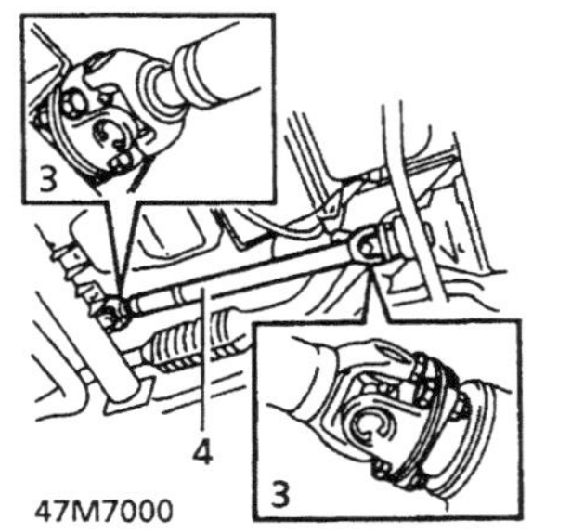

47M7000

4. Remove propeller shaft.

Refit

5. Clean mating faces of flanges.
6. Position propeller shaft. Align flange markings.
7. Fit bolts and new Nyloc nuts. Tighten to ***48 Nm (35 lbf.ft)***

NOTE: Fit bolts with heads toward transfer box and away from differential.

8. Lower vehicle.

PROPELLER SHAFT - REAR

Service repair no - 47.15.03

Remove

1. Raise vehicle on four post lift.

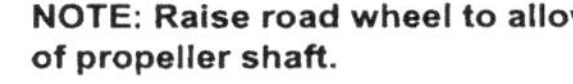

NOTE: Raise road wheel to allow rotation of propeller shaft.

2. Mark propeller shaft and drive flanges to aid re-assembly.
3. Remove 4 bolts securing propeller shaft guard to floor pan. Remove guard.
4. Remove 4 nuts securing propeller shaft to brake drum.
5. With assistance, remove 4 nuts and bolts securing propeller shaft to differential drive flange. Remove shaft.

Refit

6. Ensure mating faces are clean.
7. Position shaft to differential drive flange. Align marks.
8. Secure with bolts new Nyloc nuts. Tighten to ***48 Nm. (35 lbf.ft)***

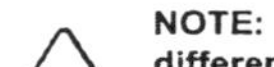

NOTE: Bolts fitted with heads away from differential.

9. Position shaft to brake drum. Align marks. Secure with nuts. Tighten to ***48 Nm. (35 lbf.ft)***
10. Position propeller shaft guard. Secure with bolts.
11. Lower lift.

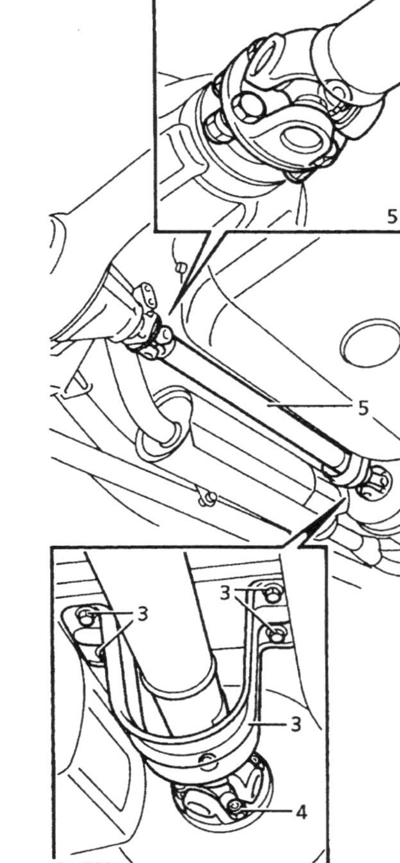

47M7001A

51 - REAR AXLE AND FINAL DRIVE

CONTENTS

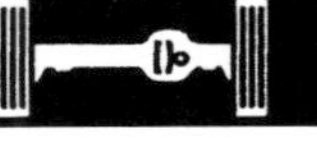

REAR AXLE

Service repair no - 51.25.01

Remove

WARNING: When lowering or repositioning axle, an additional two persons are required.

WARNING: Before commencing work, depressurise air suspension. ***See FRONT SUSPENSION, Repair.***

1. Raise the vehicle.

WARNING: Support on safety stands.

2. Support axle with hydraulic jack.
3. Remove rear road wheels.
4. Mark differential and propeller shaft flanges to aid reassembly.
5. Remove 4 nuts and bolts securing propeller shaft to differential. Release shaft and tie aside; discard nuts.

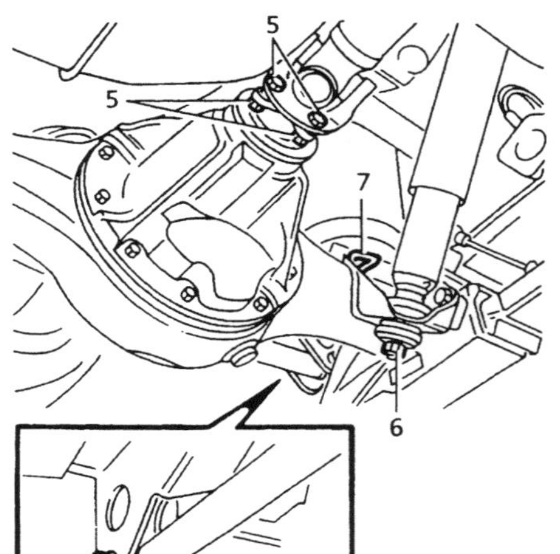

51M7000

6. Remove 2 nuts securing shock absorbers to axle.
7. Remove 'R' clips retaining air springs to axle.
8. Remove bolt securing panhard rod to axle. Release rod. Tie aside.

Up to 97MY:

9. Release ABS sensor multiplug from body bracket. Disconnect multiplug. Release lead from body clips.

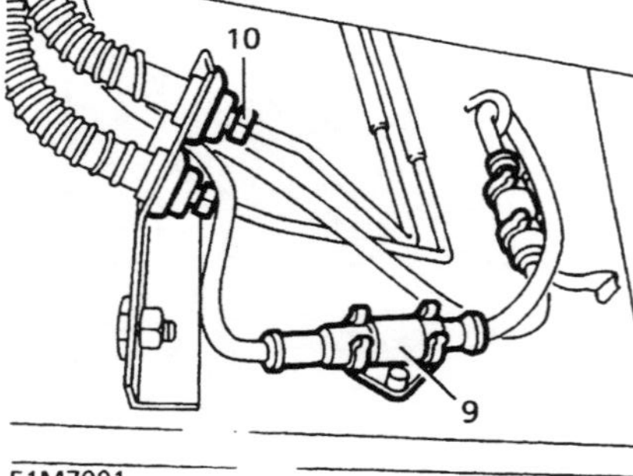

51M7001

10. Disconnect brake pipes from body bracket. Plug pipes and connections.
11. Remove 2 clips securing brake pipes to body bracket.

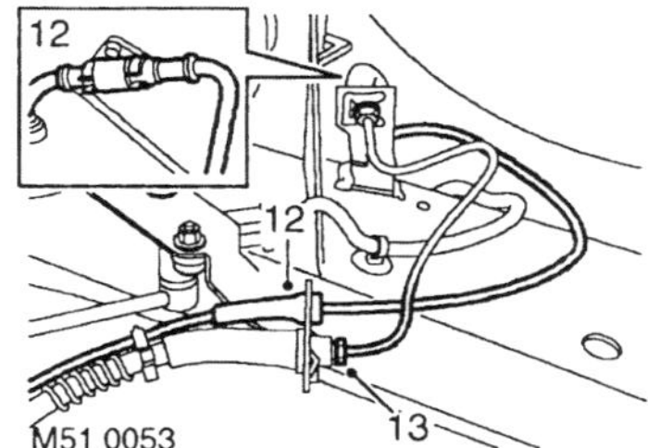

M51 0053

From 97MY:

12. At LH and RH ends of axle, release ABS sensor multiplug from chassis rail upper bracket. Disconnect multiplug and release ABS sensor lead from chassis rail lower bracket.
13. At LH and RH ends of axle, disconnect brake pipe from brake hose at chassis rail lower bracket. Remove clip and release brake hose from chassis rail lower bracket. Plug open connections.

All models:

14. Remove banjo bolt and strap securing breather hose to axle. Plug hose and connection.
15. Release height sensors from trailing arms.

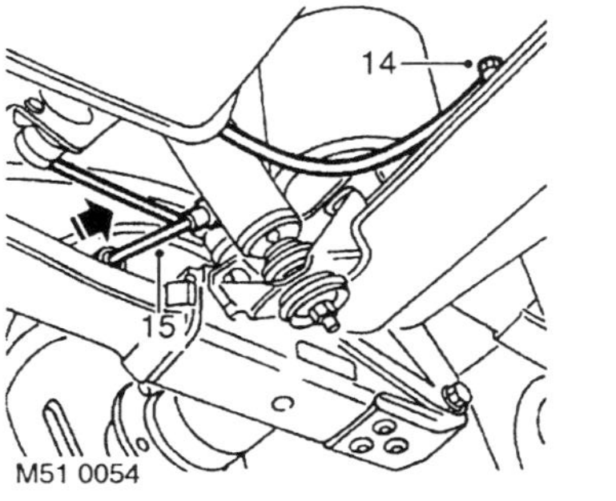

M51 0054

16. Slacken 2 nuts and bolts securing trailing arms to chassis.

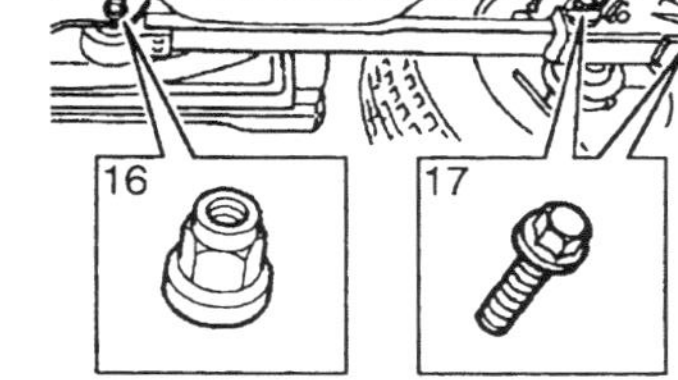

M51 0055

17. Remove 4 nuts and bolts securing trailing arms to axle.
18. With assistance lower axle. Release suspension units.
19. Remove axle from vehicle.

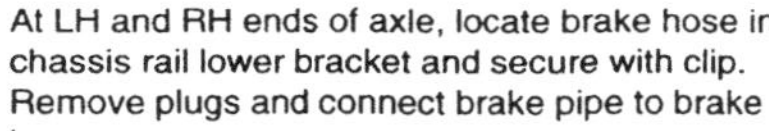

Refit

20. With assistance, position axle and align suspension units.
21. Raise axle up to trailing arms.
22. Secure axle to trailing arms with nuts and bolts. M16 with 8.8 strength grade - Tighten to ***160 Nm. (118 lbf.ft),*** M16 with 10.9 strength grade - Tighten to ***240 Nm. (177 lbf.ft),*** M12 - Tighten to ***125 Nm. (92 lbf.ft)***
23. Remove safety stands. Lower vehicle.
24. Tighten bolts securing trailing arms to chassis. Tighten to ***160 Nm. (118 lbf.ft)***
25. Retain air springs with 'R' clips.
26. Secure height sensors to trailing arms.
27. Position shock absorbers on axle. Secure with nuts. Tighten to ***45 Nm. (33 lbf.ft)***
28. Ensure all pipes and connections are clean.
29. Using new sealing washers, connect breather hose to axle with banjo bolt.
30. Secure hose to axle with strap.

Up to 97MY:

31. Position brake pipes to body bracket. Remove plugs. Connect pipes.
32. Secure pipes with clips.
33. Connect ABS sensor multiplug. Secure multiplug to body bracket. Secure lead to body clips.

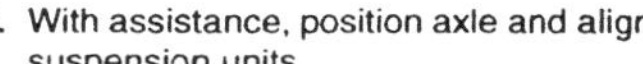

From 97MY:

34. At LH and RH ends of axle, locate brake hose in chassis rail lower bracket and secure with clip. Remove plugs and connect brake pipe to brake hose.
35. At LH and RH ends of axle, connect ABS sensor multiplug and secure to chassis rail upper bracket. Secure ABS sensor lead to chassis rail lower bracket. Ensure ABS sensor lead is retained in clips on brake hose.

All models:

36. Position panhard rod to axle. Secure with bolt. Tighten to ***200 Nm. (148 lbf.ft)***
37. Position propeller shaft. Align marks on flanges.
38. Secure shaft with bolts and new nuts. Tighten to ***48 Nm. (35 lbf.ft)***
39. Replenish axle oil. ***See LUBRICANTS, FLUIDS AND CAPACITIES, Information.***
40. Bleed brakes. ***See BRAKES, Repair.***

DIFFERENTIAL ASSEMBLY

Service repair no - 51.15.01

Remove

1. Remove hubs and half shafts. ***See REAR SUSPENSION, Repair.***
2. Drain axle oil.
3. Mark differential and propeller shaft flanges to aid reassembly.
4. Remove 4 nuts and bolts securing propeller shaft to differential. Release shaft and tie aside; discard nuts.

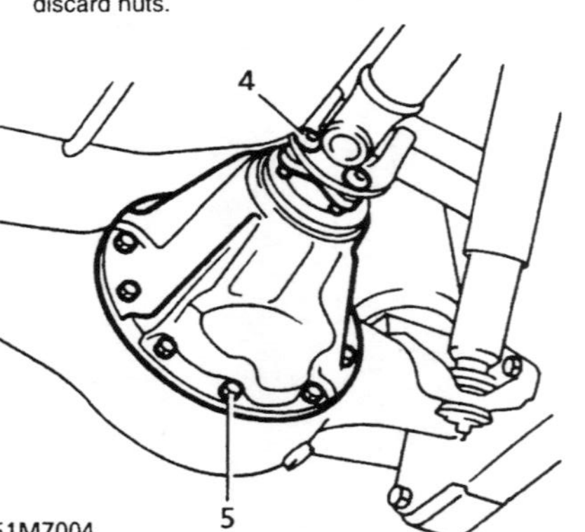
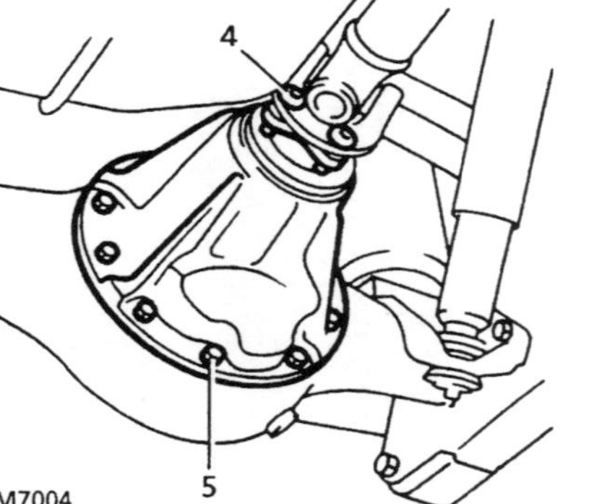

51M7004

5. Remove 10 nuts securing differential to axle case.
6. Remove differential.

Refit

7. Ensure mating faces are clean.
8. Apply a bead of RTV sealant to axle case.
9. Position differential. Secure with nuts. Tighten to ***40 Nm. (30 lbf.ft)***
10. Position propeller shaft. Align marks on flanges.
11. Secure shaft with bolts and new nuts. Tighten to ***48 Nm. (35 lbf.ft)***
12. Refit hubs and half shafts. ***See REAR SUSPENSION, Repair.***
13. Replenish axle oil. ***See LUBRICANTS, FLUIDS AND CAPACITIES, Information.***

OIL SEAL - PINION

Service repair no - 51.20.01

Remove

1. Raise the vehicle.

WARNING: Support on safety stands.

2. Mark propeller shaft and differential flanges to aid reassembly.
3. Remove 4 nuts and bolts securing propeller shaft to differential. Release shaft and tie aside; discard nuts.

3

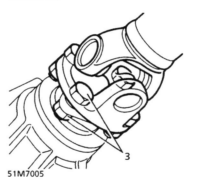

51M7005

4. Hold differential flange with LRT-51-003. Remove nut or bolt securing drive flange to differential pinion.

CAUTION: Vehicles up to 1997.5 Model Year have pinion flanges secured with a nut. Later vehicles use a flange bolt. It is important that each fixing type is tightened to the correct torque.

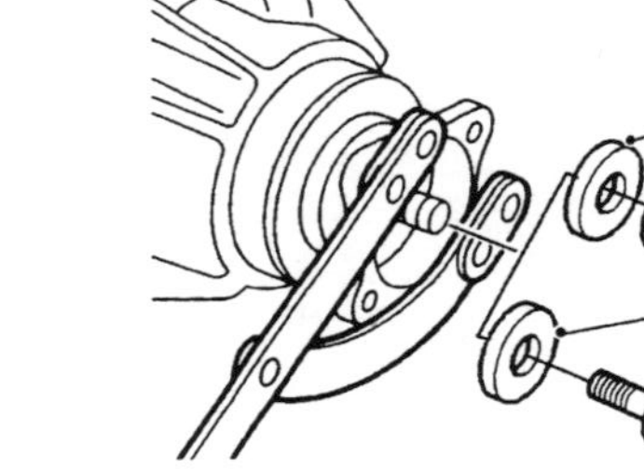

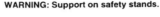

51M7006B

5. Remove flange. Remove oil seal.

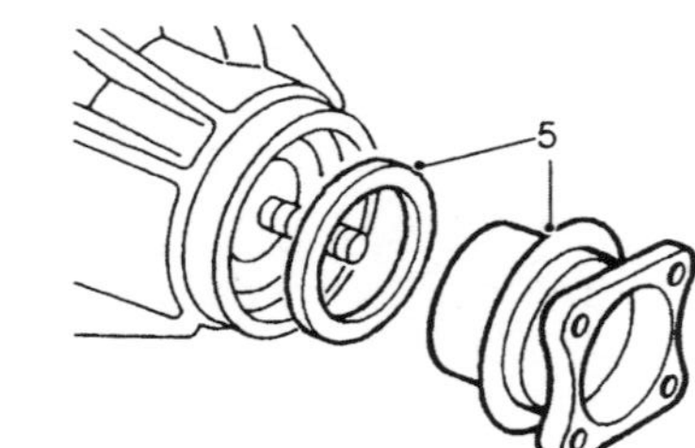
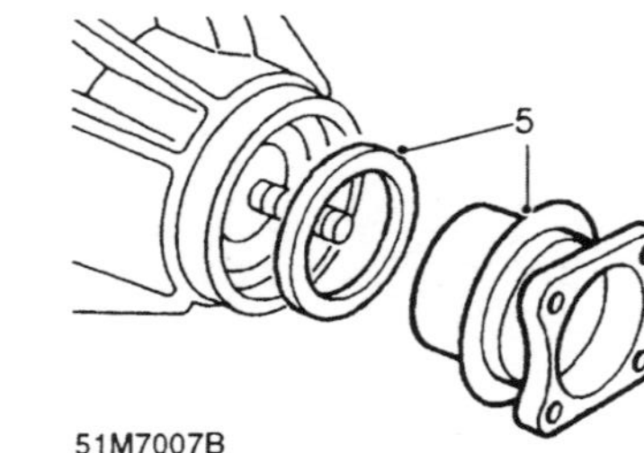

51M7007B

Refit

6. Ensure mating surfaces are clean.
7. Lubricate oil seal lips with axle oil.
8. Using LRT-51-009, fit seal to differential.
9. Position flange. Hold with LRT-51-003. Tighten nut to ***135 Nm. (100 lbf.ft).*** Tighten bolt to ***100 Nm. (74 lbf.ft).***
10. Position propeller shaft. Align marks on flanges.
11. Secure shaft with bolts and new nuts. Tighten to ***48 Nm. (35 lbf.ft)***
12. Replenish axle oil. ***See LUBRICANTS, FLUIDS AND CAPACITIES, Information.***
13. Remove safety stands. Lower vehicle.

MASS DAMPER

Service repair no - 51.25.10

Remove

1. Raise rear of vehicle.

WARNING: Support on safety stands.

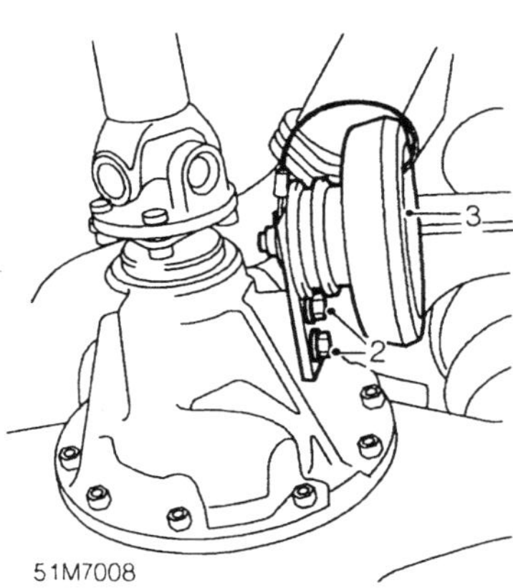

51M7008

2. Remove 2 bolts securing mass damper to rear axle.
3. Remove rear mass damper.

Refit

4. Position mass damper to rear axle, fit bolts and tighten to ***45 Nm. (33 lbf.ft)***
5. Remove stand(s) and lower vehicle.

Notes

54 - FRONT AXLE AND FINAL DRIVE

CONTENTS

Page

REPAIR

DIFFERENTIAL ASSEMBLY

Service repair no - 54.10.01

Remove

1. Remove track rod. ***See STEERING, Repair.***
2. Drain axle oil.
3. Remove hub assemblies. ***See FRONT SUSPENSION, Repair.***
4. Mark differential and propeller shaft flanges to aid reassembly.
5. Remove 4 nuts and bolts securing propeller shaft to differential; discard nuts. Release shaft, tie aside.

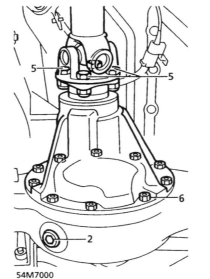

54M7000

6. Remove 10 nuts securing differential to axle case. Remove differential.

Refit

7. Ensure mating faces are clean.
8. Apply a bead of RTV sealant to axle case.
9. Position differential. Secure with nuts. Tighten to ***40 Nm. (30 lbf.ft)***
10. Position propeller shaft. Align marks on flanges.
11. Secure shaft with bolts and new nuts. Tighten to ***48 Nm. (35 lbf.ft)***
12. Refit hub assemblies. ***See FRONT SUSPENSION, Repair.***
13. Refit track rod. ***See STEERING, Repair.***
14. Replenish axle oil. ***See LUBRICANTS, FLUIDS AND CAPACITIES, Information.***

FRONT AXLE

Service repair no - 54.15.01

Remove

WARNING: When lowering or repositioning axle, an additional two persons are required.

WARNING: Before commencing work, depressurise air suspension. ***See FRONT SUSPENSION, Repair.***

1. Remove brake pads. ***See BRAKES, Repair.***
2. Remove 2 bolts securing each brake caliper assembly to steering knuckles. Release caliper. Tie aside.

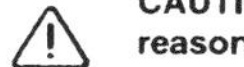

CAUTION: If a sensor is removed for any reason, a NEW sensor bush must be fitted.

3. Remove ABS sensors and brake hoses from steering knuckles.
4. Remove nut securing drag link to steering knuckle. Release taper joint.

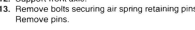

54M7002

5. Remove bolt securing panhard rod to axle. Release panhard rod. Tie aside.
6. Remove anti roll bar. ***See FRONT SUSPENSION, Repair.***
7. Remove 2 nuts securing track rod ball joints to steering knuckles. Release taper joints. Remove track rod.
8. Mark differential and propeller shaft flanges to aid reassembly.
9. Remove 4 nuts and bolts securing propeller shaft to differential; discard nuts. Release shaft and tie aside.

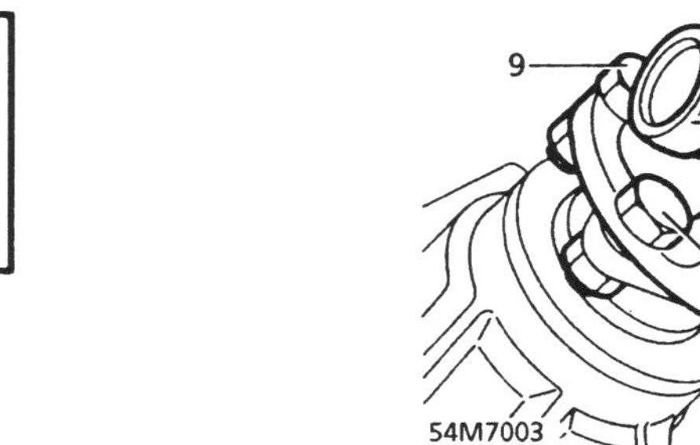

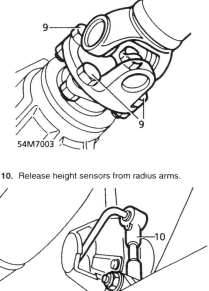

54M7003

10. Release height sensors from radius arms.

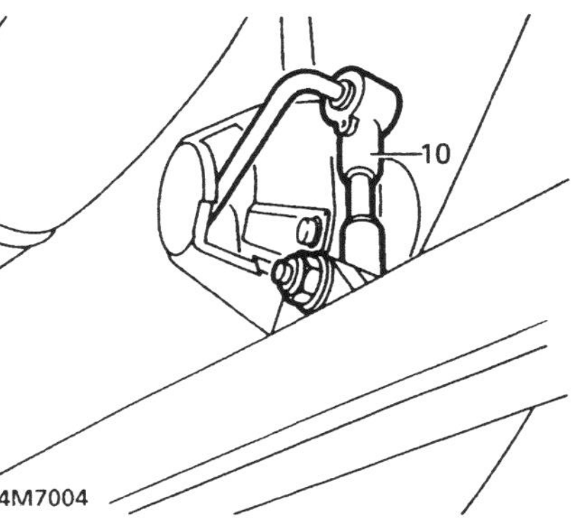

54M7004

11. Remove banjo bolt securing breather hose to axle case. Collect sealing washers. Plug hose and connection.

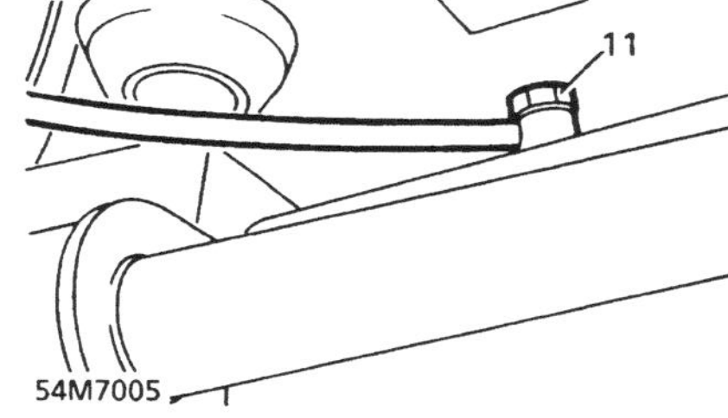

54M7005

12. Support front axle.
13. Remove bolts securing air spring retaining pins. Remove pins.

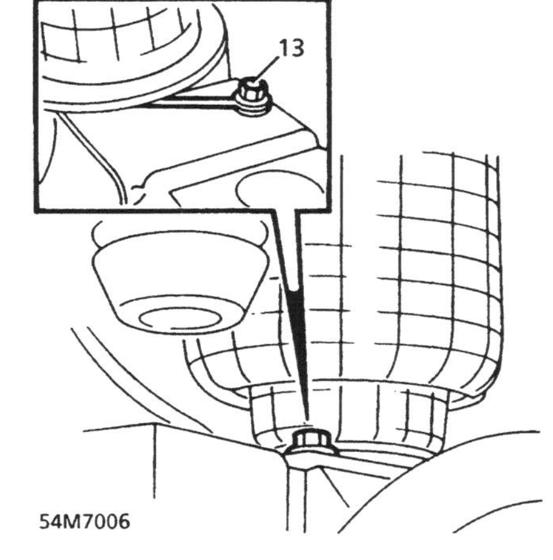

54M7006

14. Release air springs from axle.
15. Remove 2 nuts securing shock absorbers to axle. Release shock absorbers. Collect mounting rubbers.

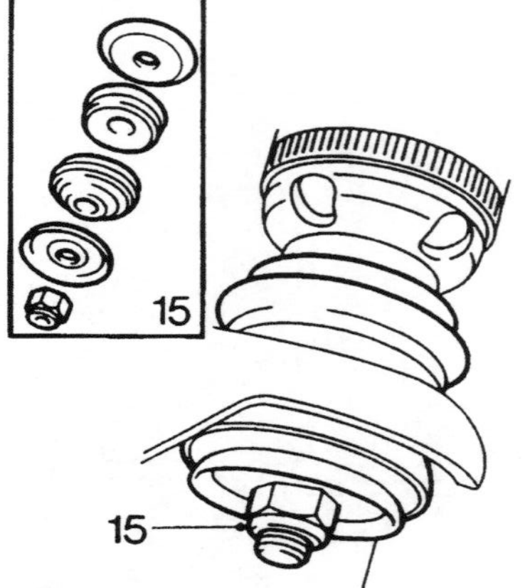

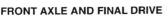

54M7007A

16. Remove 2 nuts securing radius arms to chassis brackets.

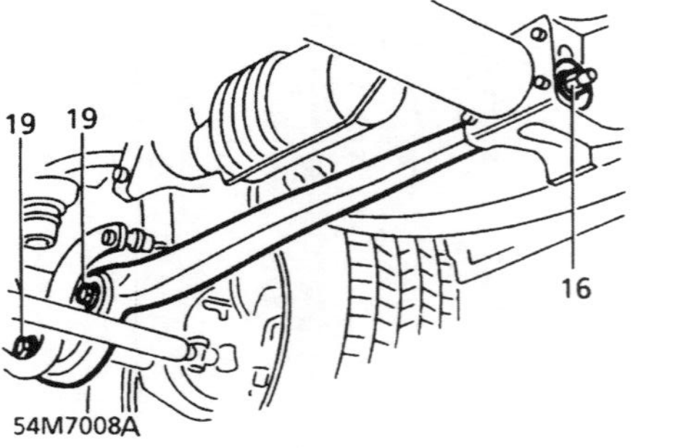

54M7008A

17. With assistance, lower and move axle forward. Release radius arms from chassis brackets. Collect rubber bushes.
18. Remove axle from vehicle.
19. Remove 2 nuts and bolts securing each radius arm. Remove radius arms.

Refit

20. Ensure mating faces are clean.
21. Position radius arms to axle. Secure with nuts and bolts. Tighten to ***125 Nm. (92 lbf.ft)***
22. Position axle under vehicle.
23. With assistance, raise axle, locating radius arms and rubber bushes into chassis locations.
24. Secure radius arms with nuts. Tighten to ***160 Nm. (118 lbf.ft)***
25. Position shock absorbers with mounting rubbers to axle. Secure with nuts. Tighten to ***45 Nm. (33 lbf.ft)***
26. Align air springs. Fit securing pins. Fit pin retaining bolts. Tighten to ***20 Nm. (15 lbf.ft)***
27. Remove plugs from breather hose and connections. Secure to axle with banjo bolt and new sealing washers.
28. Connect height sensor links to radius arms.
29. Position propeller shaft to differential flange. Align marks.
30. Secure propeller shaft with bolts and new nuts. Tighten to ***48 Nm. (35 lbf.ft)***
31. Position track rod to steering knuckles. Secure with nuts. Tighten to ***80 Nm. (59 lbf.ft)***
32. Fit anti roll bar. ***See FRONT SUSPENSION, Repair.***
33. Position panhard rod. Secure with bolt. Tighten to ***200 Nm. (148 lbf.ft)***
34. Position drag link on steering knuckle. Secure with nut. Tighten to ***80 Nm.(59 lbf.ft)***
35. Lightly coat ABS sensors with silicone grease. ***See LUBRICANTS, FLUIDS AND CAPACITIES, Information.***
36. Fit ABS sensors, new bushes and brake hoses to steering knuckles.
37. Position caliper assemblies to steering knuckles. Secure with bolts. Tighten to ***220 Nm. (162 lbf.ft)***
38. Fit brake pads. ***See BRAKES, Repair.***
39. Replenish axle oil. ***See LUBRICANTS, FLUIDS AND CAPACITIES, Information.***

MASS DAMPER

Service repair no - 54.15.10

Remove

1. Raise front of vehicle.

WARNING: Support on safety stands.

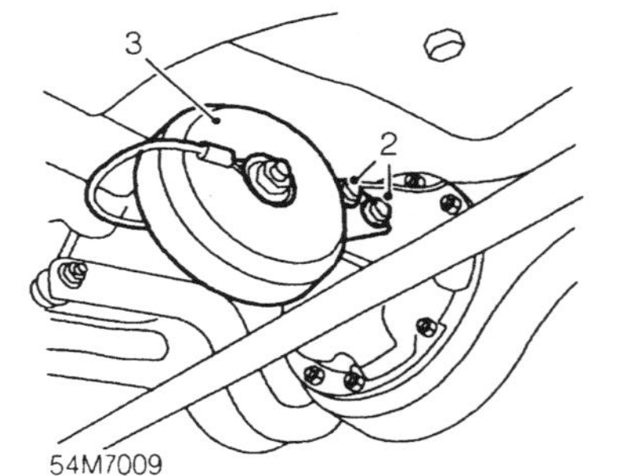

54M7009

2. Remove 2 bolts securing mass damper to front axle.
3. Remove front mass damper.

Refit

4. Position mass damper to front axle, fit bolts and tighten to ***45 Nm. (33 lbf.ft)***
5. Remove stand(s) and lower vehicle.

FRONT AXLE CASE OIL SEAL

Service repair no - 54.15.04

Remove

As front hub. ***See FRONT SUSPENSION, Repair.***

57 - STEERING

CONTENTS

STEERING SYSTEM

Description

The steering system incorporates a safety steering column, designed to collapse on impact. The tilt and axial position of the column are adjustable, operated by a single column mounted control. The range of tilt and axial adjustment available depends on Model Year and market.

The design of the intermediate steering shaft prevents a frontal impact moving the upper column towards the driver. The intermediate shaft has a red indicator clip fitted which must be inspected at service, and after the vehicle has been subjected to an impact. If the clip is not present, or is not fully seated against the clamp plate, a new assembly must be fitted. The steering box is connected to the road wheels by the drag link and track rod. A hydraulic steering damper connected between the drag link and chassis absorbs shocks in the steering caused by road wheel deflections when operating on rough terrain.

Steering column adjustment range

Model year	Market	Tilt positions	Axial movement, mm (in)
Up to 97.5	All except Japan and NAS	5	64 (2.5)
	Japan	3	64 (2.5)
	NAS	3	64 (2.5)
From 97.5	All except Japan and NAS	5	64 (2.5)
	Japan	5	64 (2.5)
	NAS	8	34 (1.3)

Power steering

The power steering system consists of an hydraulic pump, a power steering box and a fluid reservoir. The fluid reservoir supplies fluid to the hydraulic pump. This vane type pump is belt driven from the front of the engine. Pressurised fluid flows via a pressure and flow limiting valve to the power steering box. In the steering box, valve spools operated by movement of the steering wheel direct fluid pressure to the appropriate side of the piston to provide power assistance.

Power steering system

1. Steering column
2. Steering column intermediate shaft
3. Steering box
4. Hydraulic pump (pump for V8 up to 99MY shown - other pumps similar)
5. Oil reservoir
6. Drop arm
7. Hydraulic pipes

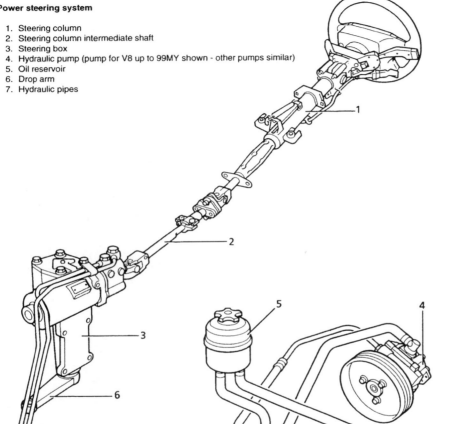

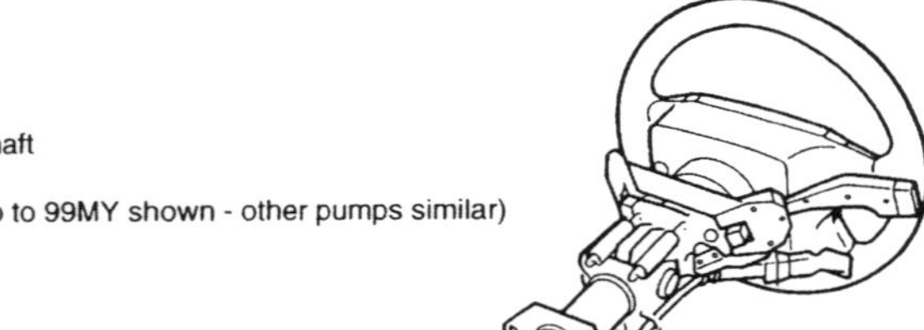
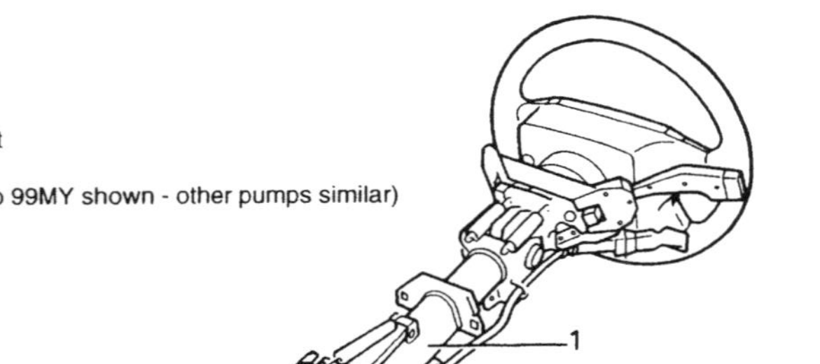

57M7035

POWER STEERING SYSTEM OPERATION

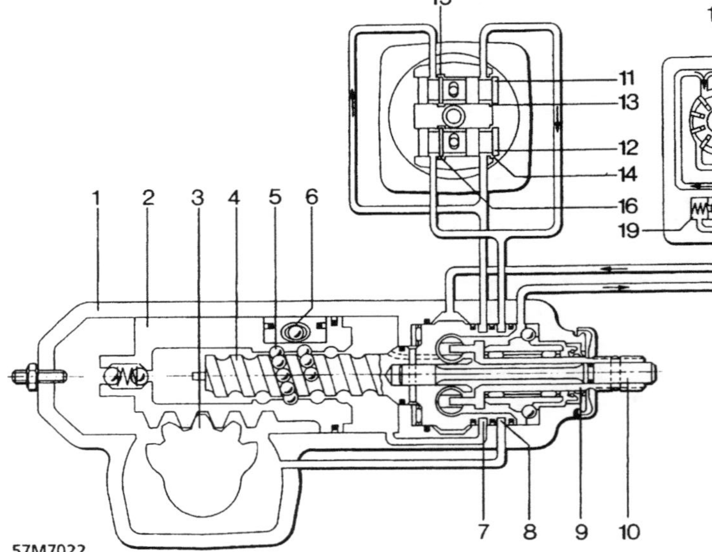

57M7022

ZF recirculating ball power steering gear with ZF vane type pump

1. Steering housing
2. Piston
3. Sector shaft
4. Worm
5. Recirculating balls
6. Recirculating tube
7. Radial groove
8. Radial groove
9. Input shaft
10. Torsion bar
11. Valve spool
12. Valve spool
13. Inlet grooves
14. Inlet grooves
15. Return grooves
16. Return grooves
17. Fluid reservoir
18. Hydraulic pump
19. Pressure and flow limiting valve

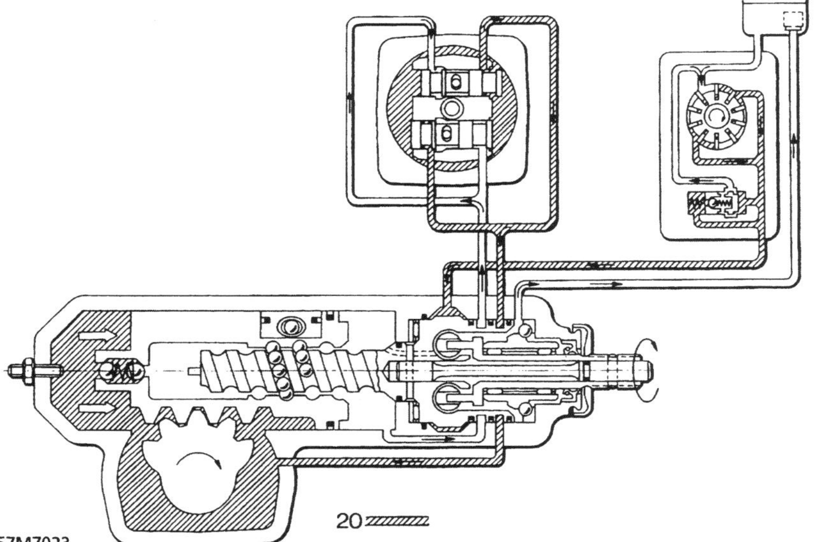

20. Hydraulic flow steering wheel turned clockwise

NOTE: The illustrations show a sectional view of the steering box with a section through the valve spools directly above to demonstrate valve spool movement and fluid flow.

Illustration 57M7022 shows steering wheel in the straight ahead position, valve spools in the neutral position.

Illustration 57M7023 shows hydraulic flow when steering wheel is turned clockwise.

The steering housing (1) contains a complete mechanical steering gear box and the steering control valve. It also forms the power cylinder.

Steering wheel rotation is converted into axial movement of the piston (2) by a chain of balls (5) running in the worm (4). When the worm is rotated, the balls enter the recirculating tube (6) and pass to the other end to form an endless chain. The sector shaft (3), which is at right angles to the piston axis, is rotated by meshing teeth. The steering drop arm, fitted to the sector shaft, transmits steering movement via the steering linkage to the road wheels.

The worm is connected to the input shaft (9) by the torsion bar (10). The worm head contains two valve spools (11 and 12), which are at right angles to the axis of the worm. Two pins on the input shaft engage, without play, in the valve spools. When the steering wheel is turned, there is relative rotation between the input shaft and the worm which is made possible by the torsion bar. The valve spools follow the movement of the steering column, when the torsion bar twists the pistons are moved from the neutral position into their working position. When the steering wheel is released, the torsion bar and the valve pistons return to the neutral position. The force required at the steering wheel to overcome the torsion bar and therefore move the valves from the neutral position provides the driver with good steering feel.

Hydraulic fluid flow

Fluid from the hydraulic pump (18) flows into an annular chamber and surrounds the part of the valve body which houses the two valve spools. When the valve is in the neutral position, see illustration 57M7022, the fluid flows through the inlet grooves (13) and (14) to the radial grooves (7) and (8). The radial grooves are connected via oilways to the right and left hand cylinder chambers. Fluid also flows back to the fluid reservoir (17) through the open return grooves (15) and (16). When the steering wheel is turned clockwise, see illustration 57M7023, the piston (2) moves to the right in the power cylinder. At the same time the valve spools are moved into their working position. Valve spool (11) moves to the right, inlet groove (13) is opened. Valve spool (12) moves to the left, closing inlet groove (14). Pressure fluid now flows via radial groove (8) to the left hand side of the cylinder, assisting movement of the steering wheel. The fluid in the right hand cylinder is pushed out by the piston, and flows back to the fluid reservoir via radial groove (7) and return groove (15). When the steering wheel is turned anti-clockwise the valve operation is reversed, pressure fluid flowing to the right hand side of the cylinder.

The quantity of fluid required for the system is adjusted by the pressure and flow limiting valve (19) in the PAS pump. The flow limiting valve ensures that maximum demand for pressure fluid is met regardless of engine speed.

Steering limit valve

A steering limit valve is incorporated in the piston head (2) as a safeguard against overloading the steering linkage, lock stops and hydraulic pump. This ball valve is always shut by pressure in the left or right hand cylinder. However shortly before the piston reaches full travel in either direction, the valve is opened by a pin, resulting in pressure drop. Hydraulic assistance is greatly reduced, and full lock can only be achieved with increased manual effort by the driver.

Adjustment

The shape of the sector shaft gearing makes axial adjustment of the shaft possible. This allows any play between the two gears, which might occur after a long period in service, to be eliminated using the sector shaft adjuster screw.

Notes

....

STEERING SYSTEM FAULTS

This section covers possible mechanical and hydraulic faults that could occur in the steering system components. Visual checks of components within the system should be carried out before undertaking detailed fault diagnosis procedures.

Symptom - Insufficient Power Steering Assistance.

POSSIBLE CAUSE	REMEDY
1. Low fluid level in oil reservoir.	1. Top up reservoir to correct level.
2. Leaking oil from steering system caused by loose pipe/hose connections or worn/damaged steering components.	2. Tighten all relevant connections or check for visual/damage etc and renew if necessary.
3. Loose drive belt.	3. Check/renew drive belt tensioner or renew drive belt. Refer to Drive belt tensioner. ***See ELECTRICAL, Repair.*** or Refer to Alternator drive belt. ***See ELECTRICAL, Repair.***
4. Faulty PAS pump or steering box.	4. Carry out PAS Test to check hydraulic pressures. If necessary, renew steering box or pump. Refer to Power steering box. ***See Repair.*** or Refer to Power steering pump. ***See Repair.***
5. Engine idle speed too low.	5. Refer to **TestBook** .

Symptom - Excessive Kick Back Through Steering Wheel - When Driven On Rough Terrain.

POSSIBLE CAUSE	REMEDY
1. Worn/damaged steering damper.	1. Renew steering damper. ***See Repair.***
2. Free play in steering ball joints and linkage.	2. Check components for wear and renew as necessary. ***See Repair.***
3. Free play in front hub assembly.	3. Check components for wear and renew as necessary. ***See FRONT SUSPENSION, Repair.***
4. Worn front suspension component bushes.	4. Check component bushes for wear and renew as necessary. ***See FRONT SUSPENSION, Repair.***

Symptom - Heavy Steering

POSSIBLE CAUSE	REMEDY
1. Insufficient power assistance	1. Carry out PAS Test to check cause and rectify as necessary.
2. Front tyres under inflated.	2. Inflate tyres to correct pressures. ***See GENERAL SPECIFICATION DATA, Information.***
3. Incorrect tyres fitted.	3. Fit tyres of correct specification. ***See GENERAL SPECIFICATION DATA, Information.***
4. Seized steering ball joints and linkage.	4. Check components for wear and renew as necessary. ***See Repair.***
5. Seized front hub assembly components.	5. Check components for wear and renew as necessary. ***See FRONT SUSPENSION, Repair.***
6. Seized or worn steering box internal components.	6. Check components and renew as necessary. ***See Repair.***
7. Steering column intermediate shaft universal joint stiff or seized.	7. Inspect universal joints and lubricate if joints are okay. Renew intermediate shaft if universal joint is badly seized. ***See Repair.***
8. Steering column bearings and/or universal joint stiff or seized.	8. Inspect universal joint and lubricate if joint is okay. If universal joint is okay this would indicate seized column bearings. Renew steering column. ***See Repair.***

Symptom - Light Steering or Free Play At Steering Wheel.

POSSIBLE CAUSE	REMEDY
1. Front tyres over inflated.	1. Inflate tyres to correct pressure. ***See GENERAL SPECIFICATION DATA, Information.***
2. Incorrect tyres fitted.	2. Fit tyres of correct specification. ***See GENERAL SPECIFICATION DATA, Information.***
3. Worn front suspension component bushes.	3. Check component bushes for wear and renew as necessary. ***See FRONT SUSPENSION, Repair.***
4. Excessive free play in steering linkage.	4. Check steering linkage components and adjust or renew as necessary ***See Repair.***
5. Excessive free play in swivel pin.	5. Check swivel pin components and adjust or renew as necessary.
6. Steering box alignment incorrect causing excessive back lash. 7. Excessive free play in steering column intermediate shaft universal joint.	6. Centralize steering box. ***See Repair.*** 7. Check and renew intermediate shaft. ***See Repair.***
8. Excessive free play in steering column bearings or universal joint.	8. Renew steering column. ***See Repair.***

Symptom - Steering Vibration, Road Wheel Shimmy - Wobble.

POSSIBLE CAUSE	REMEDY
1. Road wheel/s out of balance.	1. Rebalance road wheel/s.
2. Worn/damaged steering damper.	2. Renew steering damper. ***See Repair.***
3. Worn PAS components, mountings and fixings.	3. Check and renew steering components, mountings and fixings as necessary. ***See Repair.***
4. Worn front suspension components, mountings and fixings.	4. Check and renew suspension components, mountings and fixings. ***See FRONT SUSPENSION, Repair.***
5. Incorrect steering geometry.	5. Carry out full steering geometry check. ***See Adjustment.***

Symptom - Steering Stablity and Veer Under Braking.

POSSIBLE CAUSE	REMEDY
1. Unbalanced front tyre pressures, side to side.	1. Ensure that front tyres are inflated to correct pressure. ***See GENERAL SPECIFICATION DATA, Information.***
2. Oil contamination of brake discs and pads.	2. Thoroughly clean brake discs and renew brake pads, in axle sets. ***See BRAKES, Repair.*** Check cause of contamination and rectify as necessary.
3. Seized front brake caliper pistons or damaged brake discs.	3. Renew brake caliper. Refer to Front caliper. ***See BRAKES, Repair.*** or Refer to Brake disc and shield. ***See BRAKES, Repair.***

Symptom - Steering Veer - General

POSSIBLE CAUSE	REMEDY
1. Front tyre construction different, side to side	1. Swap front tyres side to side. If vehicle now veers in other direction, fit new tyres. ***See GENERAL SPECIFICATION DATA, Information.***
2. Steering box set off centre.	2. Centralize steering box. ***See Adjustment.***

Symptom - Poor Directional Stability

POSSIBLE CAUSE	REMEDY
1. Worn/damaged steering damper.	1. Renew steering damper. ***See Repair.***
2. Road wheel/s out of balance.	2. Rebalance road wheels.
3. Front or/and rear tyres inflated to different pressures.	3. Ensure that all tyres are inflated to specified pressures. ***See GENERAL SPECIFICATION DATA, Information.***
4. Faulty component/s in front suspension system.	4. Check front suspension components. ***See FRONT SUSPENSION, Fault diagnosis.***
5. Faulty component/s in rear suspension system.	5. Check rear suspension components. ***See REAR SUSPENSION, Fault diagnosis.***

Symptom - Power Steering System - Excessive Noise.

POSSIBLE CAUSE	REMEDY
1. Incorrect fluid level in oil reservoir.	1. Top up or drain fluid to correct level and bleed PAS system. ***See Repair.***
2. High pressure hose from steering pump to box in foul condition with chassis or body.	2. Check that hose is correctly routed and secured.
3. Excessive lock angle, giving loud 'hiss'.	3. Adjust steering lock to correct position. ***See Adjustment.***
4. Insufficient lock angle, giving squeal on full lock.	4. Adjust steering lock to correct position. ***See Adjustment.***
5. Air in the PAS system, giving a continuous moan.	5. Bleed the PAS system. ***See Repair.***
6. Seized steering pump bearings.	6. Renew pump. ***See Repair.***
7. Start up noise from PAS in excessive cold climate.	7. Use optional Cold Climate PAS Fluid.

POWER STEERING SYSTEM - TEST

Service repair no - 57.90.10/01

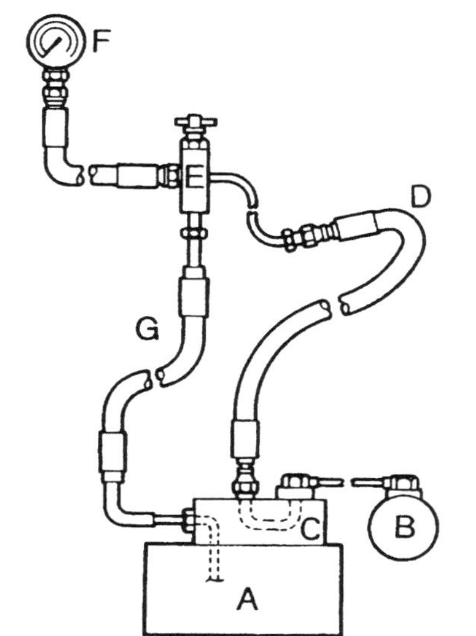

57M7036

- **A** Steering box
- **B** Steering pump
- **C** Adaptor block LRT-57-031
- **D** Hose LRT-57-031
- **E** Test valve LRT-57-001
- **F** Pressure gauge LRT-57-005
- **G** Hose LRT-57-030

Test Equipment - Assembly

1. Remove nut securing existing high and low pressure pipes to steering box **A**.
2. Remove both banjo bolts from steering box. Collect sealing washers.
3. Release existing pipes beneath radiator to allow manipulation at steering box.
4. Connect existing low pressure pipe to steering box. Secure with banjo bolt.
5. Fit hose **D** to adaptor block **C**. Fit assembly to high pressure port of steering box. Secure with banjo bolt.
6. Connect existing high pressure pipe to adaptor block. Secure with banjo bolt.

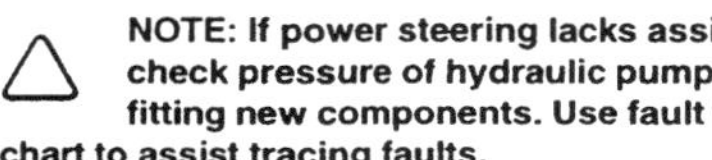

NOTE: The high pressure pipe and hose D, could be transposed depending on hand of drive.

7. Fit hose **G** to adaptor block **C**.
8. Connect pressure guage **F** to test valve **E**. Connect hoses **D** and **G** to test valve **E**.
9. Ensure steering system is free from leaks. Maintain maximum fluid level during test.

Test Procedure

NOTE: If power steering lacks assistance, check pressure of hydraulic pump before fitting new components. Use fault finding chart to assist tracing faults.

1. A hydraulic pressure guage and adaptor is used to test the power steering system.
2. When testing the system, turn the steering wheel gradually while reading the pressure guage.
3. With the test valve open start the engine.
4. With the engine at 1500 rev/min, turn the steering wheel. Hold on full lock.
5. Repeat pressure check in opposite lock.
6. The test pressure should be between 35 and 75 bar (507 and 1090 lbf/in^2), depending on the road surface. Pressure will drop back to between 32 and 48 bar (464 and 696 lbf/in^2), when held in full lock.
7. With the engine idling, release the steering wheel. Pressure should read below 7 bar (102 lbf/in^2).
8. Pressures outside the above tolerances indicate a fault.
9. To determine if the fault is in the steering box or steering pump. Close the test valve, for a maximum of five seconds.

CAUTION: Pump damage will occur if test valve is closed for longer periods.

10. If the gauge does not register between 100 and 110 bar (1450 and 1595 lnf/in^2) (maximum pump pressure), the pump is faulty.
11. If maximum pump pressure is correct, suspect the steering box.
12. On completion, remove the test equipment and, using new sealing washers, connect pipes to pump with banjo bolts.

M16 bolts: Tighten to *50 Nm. (37 lbf.ft).*
M14 bolts: Tighten to *30 Nm. (22 lbf.ft).*

13. Check fluid level. ***See LUBRICANTS, FLUIDS AND CAPACITIES, Information.***
14. Bleed power steering system. ***See Repair.***

FRONT WHEEL ALIGNMENT

Service repair no - 57.65.01

1. Ensure tyre pressures are correct, vehicle is at kerbside weight and on a level surface.
2. Release handbrake.
3. Roll vehicle backwards and forwards to relieve stresses in steering/front suspension.

NOTE: Ensure that alignment equipment is properly calibrated. Take an average of three readings. Use recommended equipment only.

4. Check that front wheel alignment is within tolerance. ***See GENERAL SPECIFICATION DATA, Information.***

Adjust

5. Slacken track rod adjuster clamping nuts and bolts.

6
5

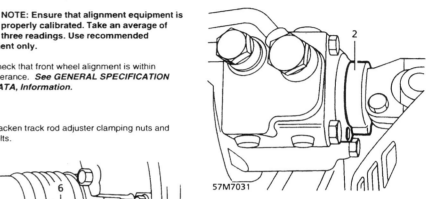

57M7030

6. Rotate adjuster to give correct alignment.
7. Roll vehicle backwards and forwards to relieve stresses in steering/front suspension.
8. Recheck front wheel alignment, taking average of three readings.
9. Repeat procedure as necessary to obtain correct alignment.

CAUTION: Ensure that adjuster clamping nuts and bolts are positioned as shown or wheel rim foul will result.

10. Tighten track rod adjuster fixings to ***8mm, 22Nm. (16 lbf.ft), 10mm, 47Nm, (35 lbf.ft).***

STEERING BOX CENTRALISATION

Check

NOTE: Markings on steering box and pinion indicate when steering box is centralised.

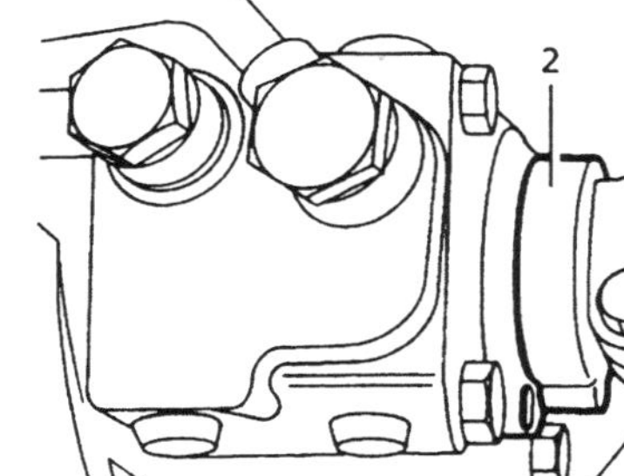

57M7031

1. Move backward then forward by at least 2 vehicle lengths to ensure that road wheels are pointing straight ahead.
2. Check for correct alignment of steering box markings.

Adjust

3. Slacken drag link adjuster clamp nuts and bolts.
4. Rotate adjuster to align steering box.

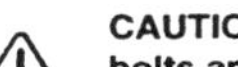

CAUTION: Ensure adjuster clamp nuts and bolts are positioned clear of drop arm.

57M7032

5. Recheck steering box alignment.
6. Tighten adjuster clamps to ***8mm, 22 Nm. (16 lbf.ft), 10mm, 47 Nm, (35 lbf.ft).***
7. Check steering wheel for correct alignment. If necessary, remove wheel and centralise. ***See Repair.***

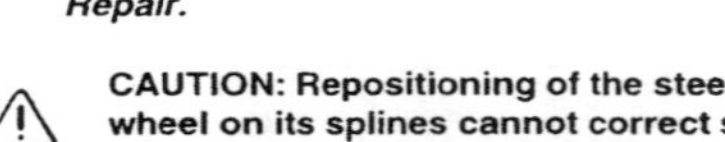

CAUTION: Repositioning of the steering wheel on its splines cannot correct small (less than 5 °) errors in steering wheel alignment. Always rectify small errors in alignment by adjusting the drag link as detailed above, ensuring that steering box centralisation is maintained.

Road Test

8. Carry out a short road test over an even surface. Check for correct alignment of steering wheel. Ensure that vehicle follows a straight track.

LOCK STOP ADJUST

Service repair no - 57.65.03

Adjust

1. Raise the vehicle.

WARNING: Support on safety stands.

2. Slacken LH lock stop locknut. Screw stop bolt clockwise, fully into hub.

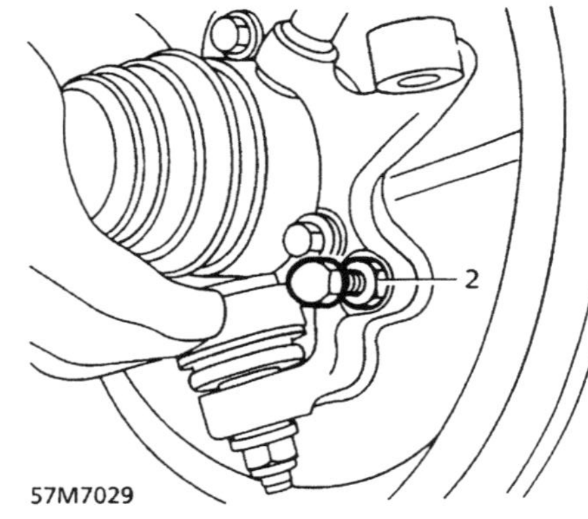

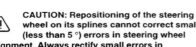

57M7029

3. With assistance, start the engine, turn steering onto right hand lock until resistance is felt.

NOTE: Resistance is created by hydraulic limiter inside steering box.

4. With the steering held, unscrew anti-clockwise, stop bolt until it contacts the axle. Screw bolt back in clockwise, by 3 flats.
5. Tighten locknut.
6. Return steering to centre. Turn back to full right hand lock to check adjustment.

NOTE: Resistance should be felt prior to lock stop operation.

7. Repeat for RH lock stop.
8. Stop engine.
9. Remove safety stands. Lower vehicle.

STEERING COLUMN

Service repair no - 57.40.01

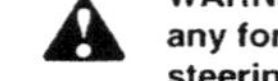

WARNING: Under no circumstances must any form of lubricant be applied to the steering column. If noise or harshness is present in the column a new unit must be fitted

Remove

1. Disconnect battery negative lead.

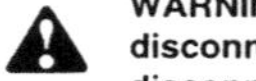

WARNING: If vehicle is fitted with SRS, disconnect both battery terminals. Always disconnect negative terminal first.

2. Remove intermediate steering shaft. ***See this section.***
3. Remove 4 scrivet fasteners securing closing panel beneath steering column.

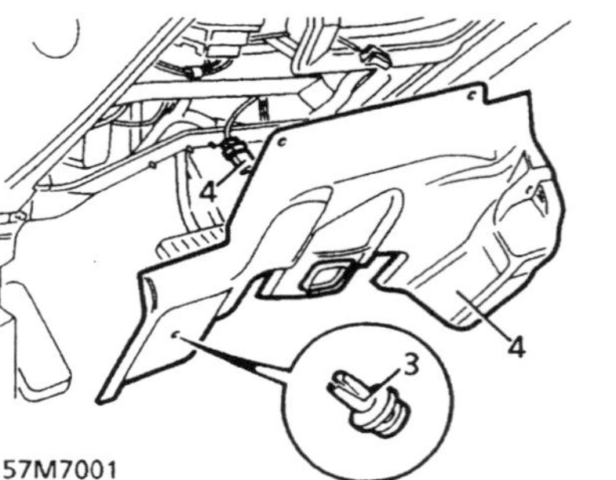

57M7001

4. Release closing panel from fascia. Disconnect footwell lamp multiplug, remove panel.
5. Remove steering column nacelle. ***See this section.***
6. Remove screws securing indicator switch stalk to column. Release stalk, remove from multiplug.

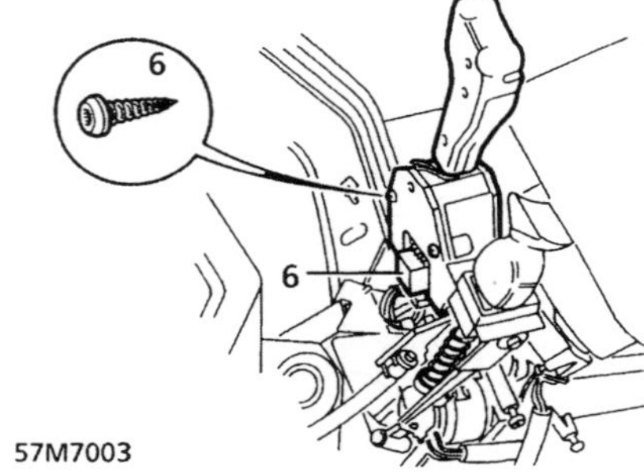

57M7003

7. Remove screws securing wiper switch stalk to column. Release stalk, remove from multiplug.

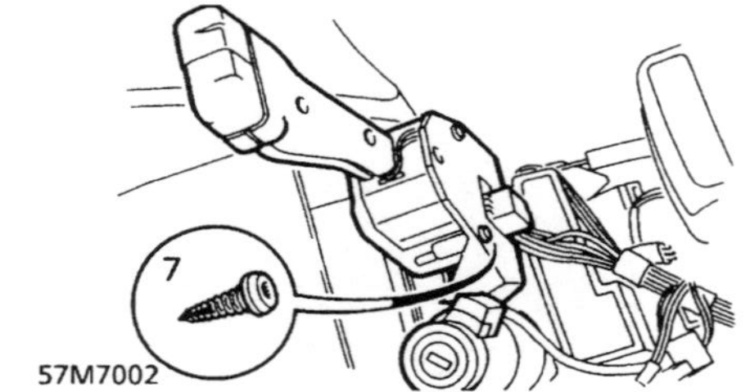

57M7002

8. Disconnect ignition switch, 'key in' sensor, rotary coupler and SRS system multiplugs.

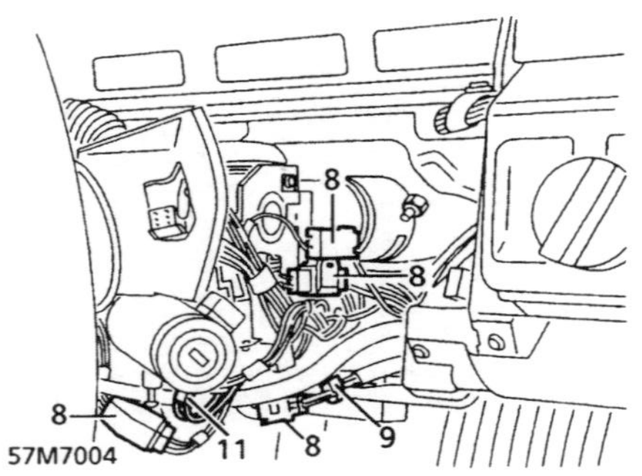

57M7004

WARNING: The SRS connector beneath the steering column must be disconnected prior to removal of the air bag module.

9. Remove 2 clips securing SRS harness to steering column harness.
10. Release clip securing harness to column.
11. Release illumination bulb from lock barrel. Release bulb harness from clip.
12. Disconnect multiplug from key inhibit solenoid (shift interlock).
13. Release duct from drivers blower motor housing, remove duct from heater unit.

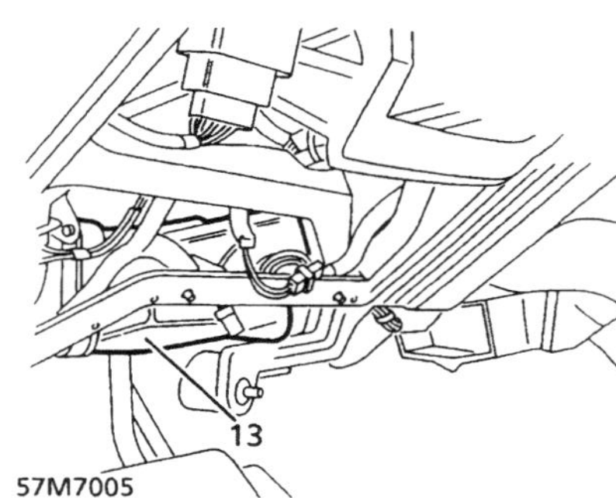

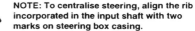

57M7005

14. Remove 2 bolts securing column to bulkhead.

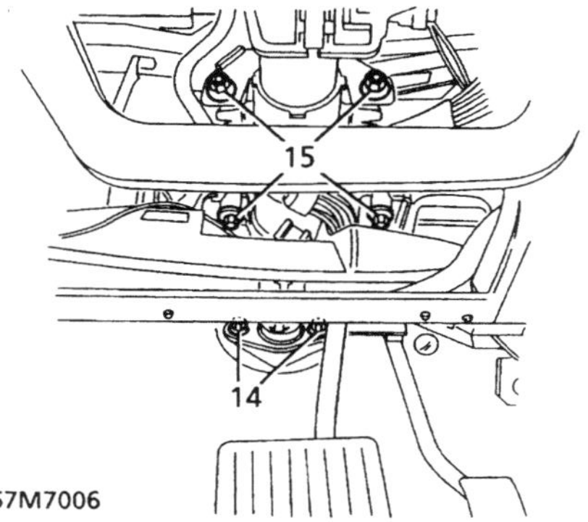

57M7006

15. Remove 2 bolts and 2 nuts securing column to pedal box.
16. Remove steering column assembly.

Refit

17. Position steering column assembly and engage to pedal box studs.

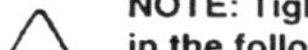

NOTE: Tighten the steering column fixings in the following sequence.

18. Fit bolts securing steering column to bulkhead. Tighten to ***25 Nm. (18 lbf.ft)***
19. Fit nuts securing steering column to pedal box. Tighten to ***25 Nm. (18 lbf.ft)***
20. Fit bolts securing steering column to pedal box. Tighten to ***25 Nm. (18 lbf.ft)***
21. Fit blower motor duct.
22. Connect column multiplugs. Secure ignition lock illumination bulb in holder, position bulb harness in clip.
23. Secure column harness clip to column bracket.
24. Connect SRS multiplug and secure SRS harness to column harness with clips.
25. Connect wiper switch stalk to multiplug, and secure stalk to column with Torx fixings.
26. Fit steering column nacelle. ***See this section.***
27. Position closing panel. Connect footwell lamp. Align and secure closing panel with scrivet fasteners.
28. Fit intermediate steering shaft. ***See this section.***
29. Connect battery terminals, positive before negative. Fit battery cover.

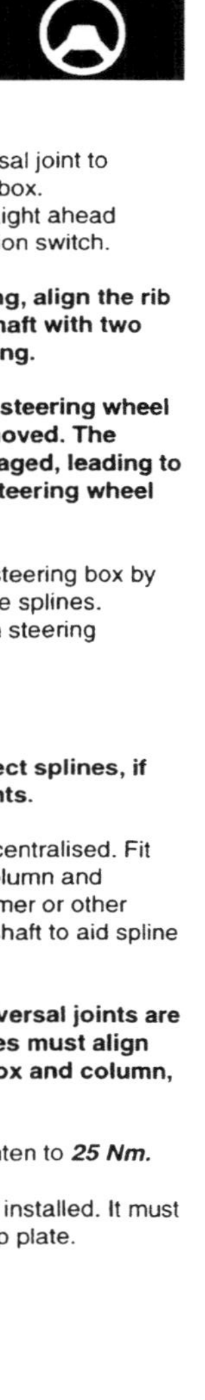

STEERING COLUMN INTERMEDIATE SHAFT

Service repair no - 57.40.22

WARNING: The intermediate shaft has a red indicator clip fitted which must be inspected at service, and after the vehicle has been subjected to an impact. If the clip is not present, or is not fully seated against the clamp plate, a new assembly must be fitted

Remove

1. Remove bolt securing intermediate shaft universal joint to steering column.

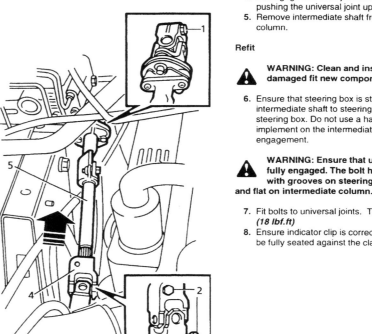

57M7014

2. Remove 2 bolts securing universal joint to intermediate shaft and steering box.
3. Set front road wheels to the straight ahead position. Remove key from ignition switch.

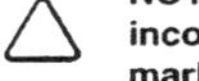

NOTE: To centralise steering, align the rib incorporated in the input shaft with two marks on steering box casing.

WARNING: Do not turn the steering wheel with intermediate shaft removed. The rotary coupler may be damaged, leading to possible malfunction of SRS and steering wheel mounted switches.

4. Disengage universal joint from steering box by pushing the universal joint up the splines.
5. Remove intermediate shaft from steering column.

Refit

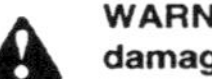

WARNING: Clean and inspect splines, if damaged fit new components.

6. Ensure that steering box is still centralised. Fit intermediate shaft to steering column and steering box. Do not use a hammer or other implement on the intermediate shaft to aid spline engagement.

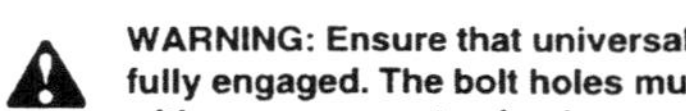

WARNING: Ensure that universal joints are fully engaged. The bolt holes must align with grooves on steering box and column, and flat on intermediate column.

7. Fit bolts to universal joints. Tighten to ***25 Nm. (18 lbf.ft)***
8. Ensure indicator clip is correctly installed. It must be fully seated against the clamp plate.

DRAG LINK

Service repair no - 57.15.17

Remove

1. Raise the vehicle.

WARNING: Support on safety stands.

2. Remove nut and bolt securing steering damper to drag link. Release damper.

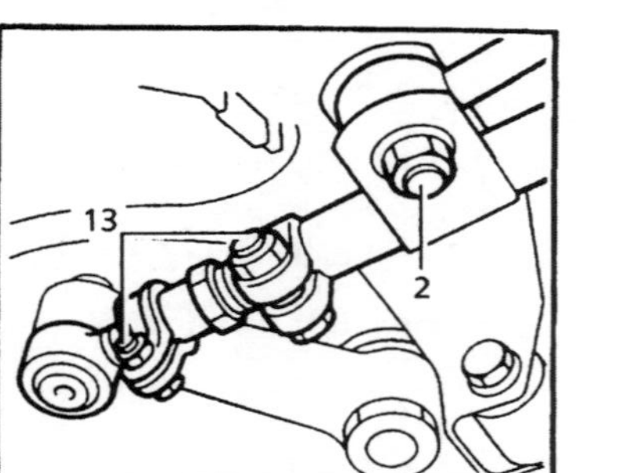
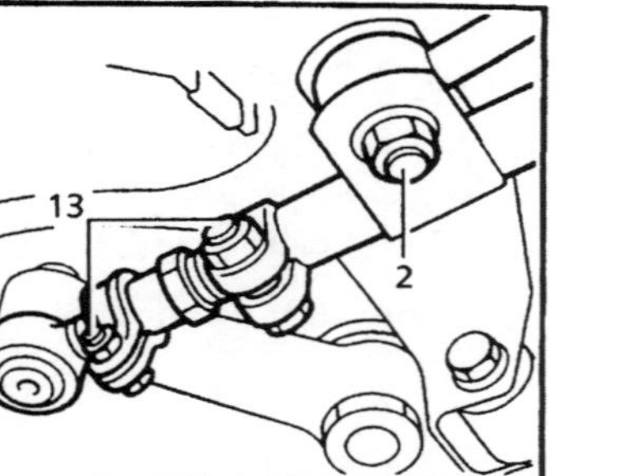
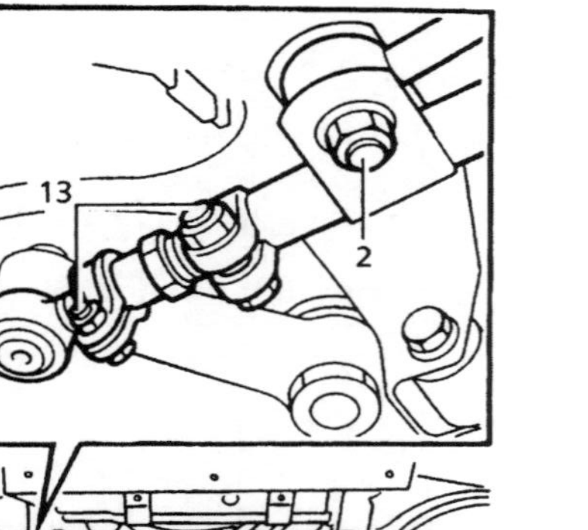
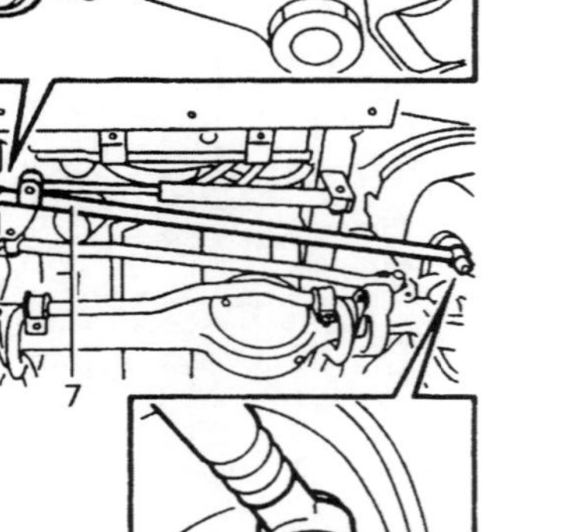

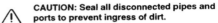

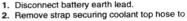

57M7015

3. **RHD** Remove right hand front road wheel.
4. **LHD** Remove left hand front road wheel.
5. Remove nut securing drag link to drop arm.
6. Remove nut securing drag link to swivel hub.
7. Break taper joints using LRT-57-018. Remove drag link.

Disassemble

8. Slacken nut and bolt securing ball joint clamp. Unscrew ball joint. Remove clamp.
9. Slacken nut and bolt securing adjuster clamp. Unscrew adjuster. Remove clamp.

Assemble

10. Loosely fit adjuster clamp and adjuster.
11. Loosely fit ball joint clamp and ball joint.
12. Adjust drag link to nominal length of 1170 mm. ± 10mm.
13. Orientate clamps as shown by illustration.
14. Secure clamps with nuts and bolts. Tighten to ***8mm, 22 Nm. (16 lbf.ft), 10mm, 47 Nm. (35 lbf.ft)***

Refit

15. Use steering box centralising feature to centralise box. Fit drag link.
16. Secure drag link to drop arm and swivel hubs with nuts. Tighten to ***80 Nm. (59 lbf.ft)***
17. Align damper to drag link. Secure with nut and bolt, tighten to:-
    Up to 97 MY - ***125 Nm (92 lbf.ft)***
    97 MY on - ***80 Nm (59 lbf.ft)***
18. Remove safety stands. Lower vehicle.
19. Check front wheel alignment. ***See Adjustment.***

STEERING DAMPER

Service repair no - 57.55.21

Remove

1. Raise the vehicle.

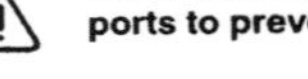

WARNING: Support on safety stands.

2. Remove damper fixings at both ends.

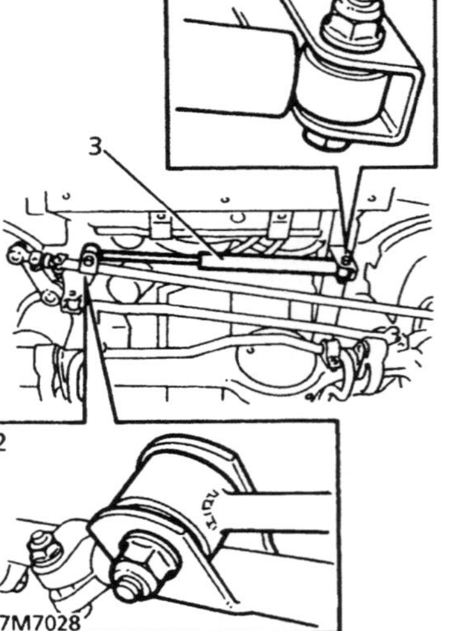

3. Remove damper.

Refit

4. Fit damper to chassis. Fit, but do not tighten nut and bolt.
5. Fit damper to drag link, fit nut and bolt, tighten to:-
   Up to 97 MY - ***125 Nm (92 lbf.ft)***
   97 MY on - ***80 Nm (59 lbf.ft)***
6. Tighten damper to chassis fixing. Tighten to ***125Nm. (92 lbf.ft)***
7. Remove safety stands. Lower vehicle.

PUMP FEED HOSE

Service repair no - 57.15.20

Remove

CAUTION: Seal all disconnected pipes and ports to prevent ingress of dirt.

1. Disconnect battery earth lead.
2. Remove strap securing coolant top hose to engine lifting bracket.
3. Release feed hose clips. Remove hose.

Refit

4. Reverse removal procedure.
5. Bleed power steering. ***See this section.***

STEERING BOX FEED HOSE

Service repair no - 57.15.21

Remove

1. Disconnect battery earth lead.
2. Raise front of vehicle.

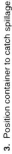

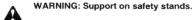

WARNING: Support on safety stands.

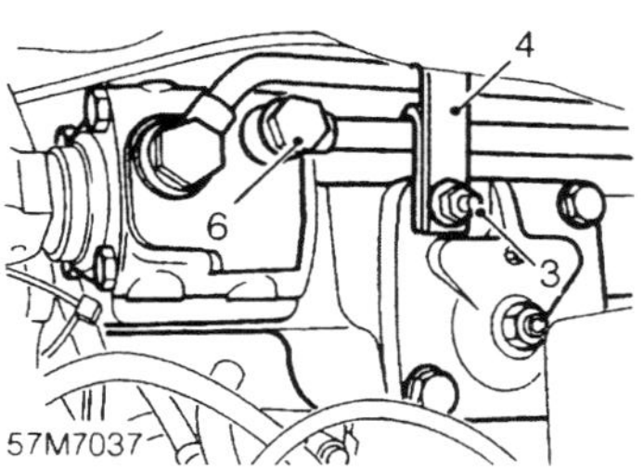

57M7037

3. Remove nut securing PAS hose brackets to steering box.
4. Release 2 hose brackets from steering box.
5. Position cloth to catch spillage.
6. Remove banjo bolt securing feed hose to steering box. Remove and discard sealing washers.

CAUTION: Plug the connections.

7. Position container to catch spillage.

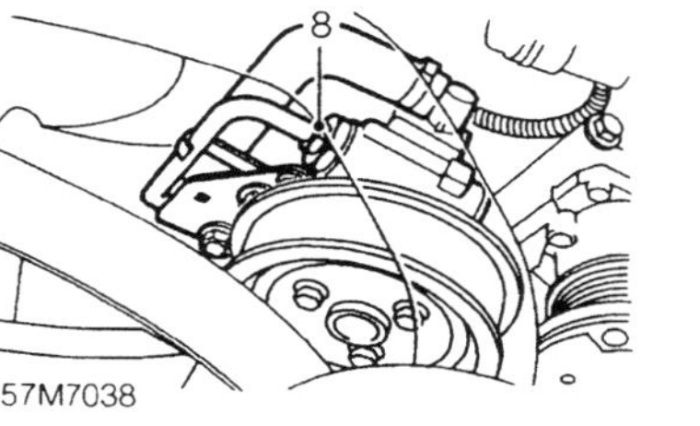

57M7038

8. **V8 up to 99MY:** Loosen union and disconnect feed hose from PAS pump.

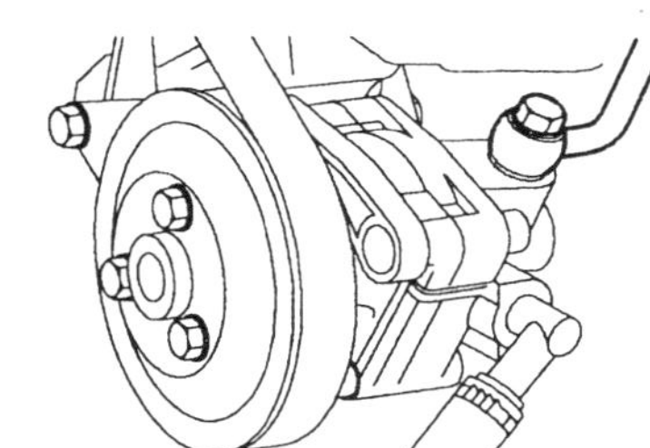

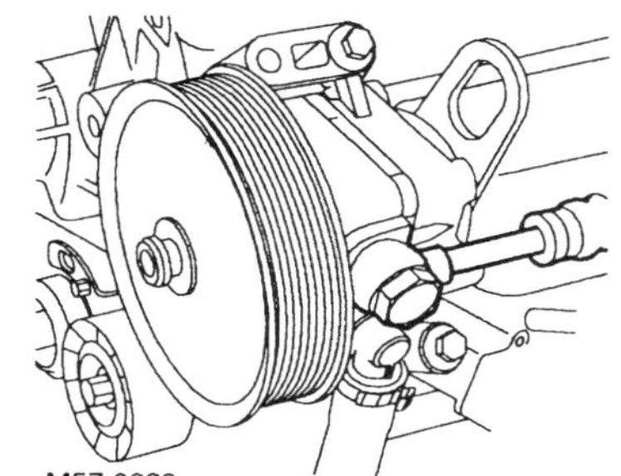
M57 0839

V8 from 99MY and diesel: Remove banjo bolt securing feed hose to pump. Remove and discard sealing washers.

CAUTION: Plug the connections.

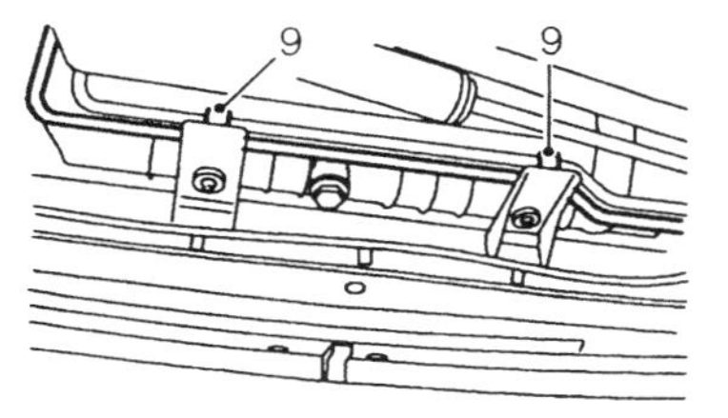

57M7039

9. Release PAS pipe from 2 radiator lower bracket clips.
10. Remove pump feed hose.

Refit

11. Position feed hose to vehicle.
12. Remove plugs from hose and PAS pump.
13. Clean hose and PAS pump union.
14. **V8 up to 99MY:** Connect feed hose union to PAS pump and tighten to ***16 Nm (12 lbf.ft).*** **V8 from 99MY and diesel:** Connect feed hose to pump using new sealing washers. Tighten banjo bolt to ***25 Nm (18 lbf.ft)*** (V8 models) or ***30 Nm (22 lbf.ft)*** (diesel models).
15. Remove plugs from hose and steering box.
16. Clean hose and steering box union.
17. Position PAS hose brackets to steering box and secure with nut.
18. Fit banjo bolt and new washers to feed hose and fit to steering box. Tighten banjo bolt to ***30 Nm. (22 lbf.ft)***
19. Position feed hose and secure to radiator lower bracket clips.
20. Bleed steering system. ***See this section.***
21. Remove stand(s) and lower vehicle.

STEERING BOX RETURN HOSE

Service repair no - 57.15.22

Remove

1. Disconnect battery earth lead.
2. Raise front of vehicle.

WARNING: Support on safety stands.

3. Position container to catch spillage.

57M7040

4. Remove 2 bolts securing PAS fluid reservoir to radiator bracket.
5. Remove clip securing return hose to PAS fluid reservoir and disconnect return hose.

CAUTION: Plug the connections.

6. Position cloth to catch spillage.

57M7041

7. Remove banjo bolt securing pump return hose to steering box and discard 2 washers.

CAUTION: Plug the connections.

8. Remove nut securing PAS hose brackets to steering box.
9. Release PAS hose brackets from stud.

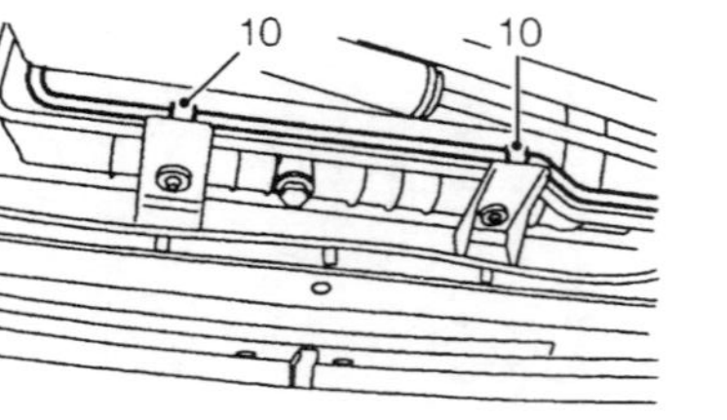

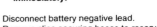

57M7042

10. Release PAS pipe from 2 radiator lower bracket clips.
11. Remove pump return hose.

Refit

12. Position return hose to vehicle.
13. Remove plugs from hose and PAS fluid reservoir.
14. Clean hose and PAS pump union.
15. Connect return hose union to PAS fluid reservoir and secure with clip.
16. Remove plugs from hose and steering box.
17. Clean hose and steering box union.
18. Position PAS hose brackets to steering box and secure with nut.
19. Fit banjo bolt and NEW washers to return hose and fit to steering box. Tighten banjo bolt to ***50 Nm. (37 lbf.ft)***
20. Position return hose and secure to radiator lower bracket clips.
21. Bleed steering system. ***See this section.***
22. Remove stand(s) and lower vehicle.

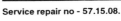

COLUMN NACELLE

Service repair no - 57.40.29

Remove

1. Remove ignition key.
2. Remove instrument binnacle. ***See INSTRUMENTS, Repair.***
3. Release steering column tilt lever, fully extend and tilt column down.
4. Remove 2 screws securing upper column nacelle.
5. Release upper column nacelle from side fillet clips and remove upper nacelle.
6. Remove 4 screws securing lower nacelle, disengage from side fillet clips and remove nacelle.

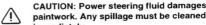

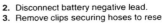

57M7008

7. Collect side fillets.

Refit

8. Position upper and lower nacelles, loosely fit screws.
9. Position side fillets, engage clips.
10. Tighten nacelle screws.
11. Fit instrument binnacle. ***See INSTRUMENTS, Repair.***
12. Return steering column to original position.
13. Fit ignition key.

OIL RESERVOIR

Service repair no - 57.15.08.

Remove

1. Place tray to catch fluid.

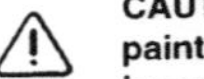

CAUTION: Power steering fluid damages paintwork. Any spillage must be cleaned immediately.

2. Disconnect battery negative lead.
3. Remove clips securing hoses to reservoir. Release hoses.
4. Slacken clamp screw securing reservoir. Remove reservoir.

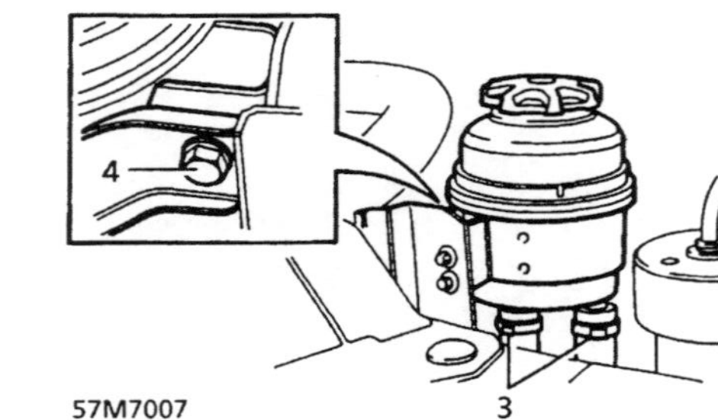

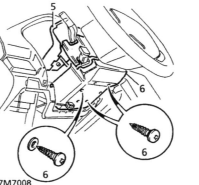

57M7007

Refit

5. Position reservoir. Tighten clamp screw.
6. Connect hoses to reservoir. Secure with new clips.
7. Fill reservoir. ***See LUBRICANTS, FLUIDS AND CAPACITIES, Information.***
8. Reconnect battery negative lead.
9. Bleed power steering. ***See this section.***

POWER STEERING SYSTEM - BLEED

Service repair no - 57.15.02

1. Fill reservoir to upper mark on dipstick. ***See LUBRICANTS, FLUIDS AND CAPACITIES, Information.***
2. Turn steering wheel 45°in both directions to open valves inside steering box.
3. Top up steering reservoir fluid level.

CAUTION: Do not run engine with less than minimum fluid level in reservoir. Top up as necessary during bleed procedure.

4. Start engine. Allow to idle.
5. Turn steering wheel back and forth to open valves inside steering box.

WARNING: Fluid is under high pressure, open bleed screw with caution.

6. With engine running, carefully open bleed screw until fluid starts to flow. Tighten bleed screw to ***4 Nm. (3 lbf.ft)***
7. Switch off engine. Top up reservoir.

STEERING BOX

Service repair no - 57.30.01

Remove

1. Disconnect battery negative lead.
2. Raise the vehicle.

WARNING: Support on safety stands.

3. Remove washer reservoir RHD only. ***See WIPERS AND WASHERS, Repair.***
4. Remove nut connecting drag link to drop arm. Separate drag link from drop arm with LRT-57-018.

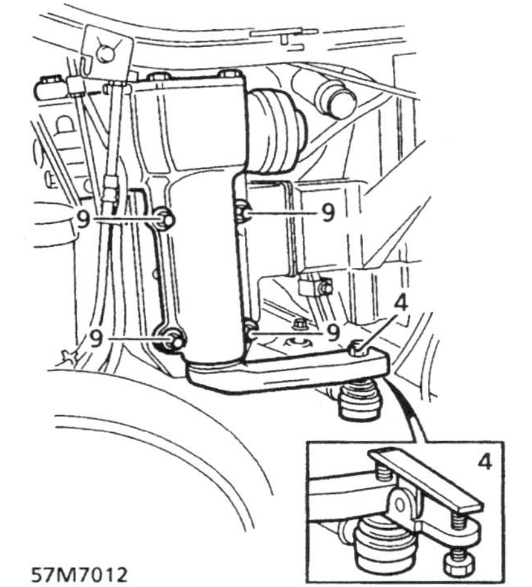

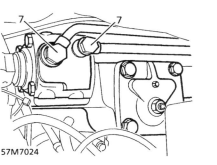

57M7012

CAUTION: To prevent damage to rotary coupler, remove key from ignition switch. Engage steering lock.

5. Remove bolts securing steering column lower universal joint to steering box.

57M7033

6. Slide universal joint up column to clear box pinion. Release steering column.
7. Disconnect power steering pipes from steering box. Collect sealing washers and discard.

57M7024

8. Plug pipes and connections.
9. Remove 4 nuts and bolts securing steering box. Remove steering box.

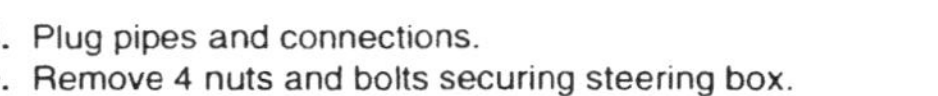

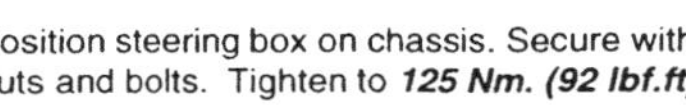

Refit

10. Position steering box on chassis. Secure with nuts and bolts. Tighten to ***125 Nm. (92 lbf.ft)***
11. Remove plugs from pipes and connections.
12. Using new sealing washers, connect fluid pipes, tighten banjo bolts to:
    M16 - ***50 Nm. (37 lbf.ft)***
    M14 - ***30 Nm. (22 lbf.ft)***
13. Ensure steering box is centralized and steering wheel is in straight ahead position.
14. Engage steering column universal joint with steering box pinion. Secure with bolts. Tighten to ***25 Nm. (18 lbf.ft)***

WARNING: Ensure universal joint is fully engaged with pinion and lower securing bolt interlocks with groove in pinion.

15. Position drag link on drop arm. Secure with nut. Tighten to ***80 Nm. (59 lbf.ft)***
16. Fit washer reservoir. ***See WIPERS AND WASHERS, Repair.***
17. Remove safety stands. Lower vehicle.
18. Reconnect battery negative lead.
19. Fill power steering reservoir. ***See LUBRICANTS, FLUIDS AND CAPACITIES, Information.***
20. Bleed power steering. ***See this section.***

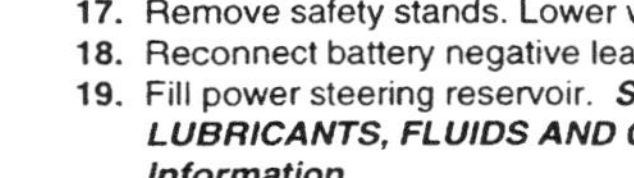

POWER STEERING PUMP - V8 - UP TO 99MY

Service repair no - 57.20.14

Remove

⚠ **CAUTION: Seal all disconnected pipes and ports to prevent ingress of dirt.**

1. Remove alternator drive belt. ***See ELECTRICAL, Repair.***
2. Remove 3 bolts securing pump pulley. Remove pulley.

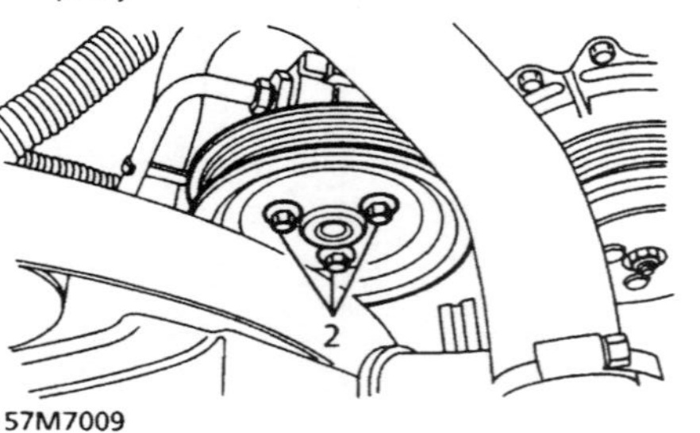

57M7009

3. Position container to catch fluid.
4. Release clip securing return hose to pump. Release hose.
5. Disconnect high pressure pipe union from pump.
6. Remove 4 bolts securing pump and compressor mounting bracket to engine.

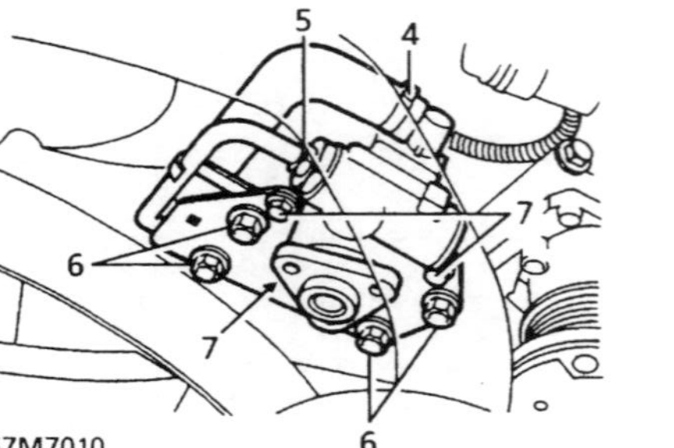

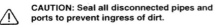

57M7010

7. Remove 3 bolts securing mounting plate to pump. Remove plate.
8. Remove pump assembly.
9. Remove 2 screws securing engine lifting bracket to pump.

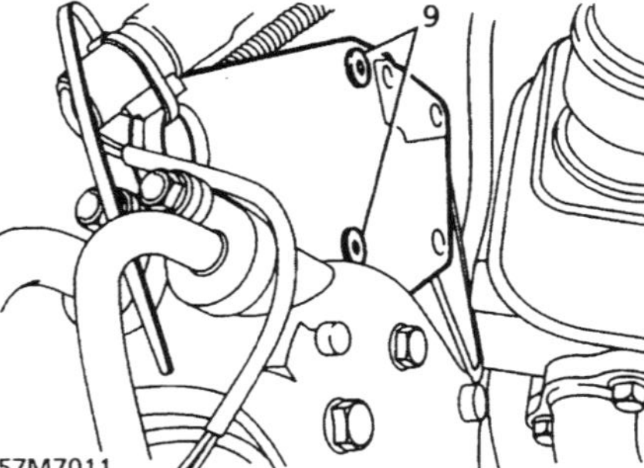

57M7011

Refit

10. Ensure mating faces are clean.
11. Position lifting bracket to pump. Secure with screws. Tighten to ***18 Nm. (13 lbf.ft)***
12. Position mounting plate to pump. Loosely fit bolts.
13. Align pump assembly and compressor mounting bracket to engine. Secure with bolts. Tighten to ***40 Nm (30 lbf.ft)***
14. Tighten pump to mounting bolts to ***18 Nm. (13 lbf.ft)***
15. Connect high pressure pipe to pump. Tighten to ***16 Nm. (12 lbf.ft)***
16. Position return hose to pump. Secure with clip.
17. Position pulley to pump. Secure with bolts. Tighten to ***25 Nm. (18 lbf.ft)***
18. Secure coolant hose to lifting bracket.
19. Fit drive belt. ***See ELECTRICAL, Repair.***
20. Reconnect battery negative lead.
21. Bleed power steering system. ***See this section.***

POWER STEERING PUMP - V8 - FROM 99MY

Service repair no - 57.20.14

Remove

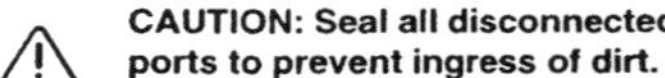

⚠ **CAUTION: Seal all disconnected pipes and ports to prevent ingress of dirt.**

1. Remove alternator drive belt. ***See ELECTRICAL, Repair.***
2. Position suitable container below vehicle to catch oil spillage.

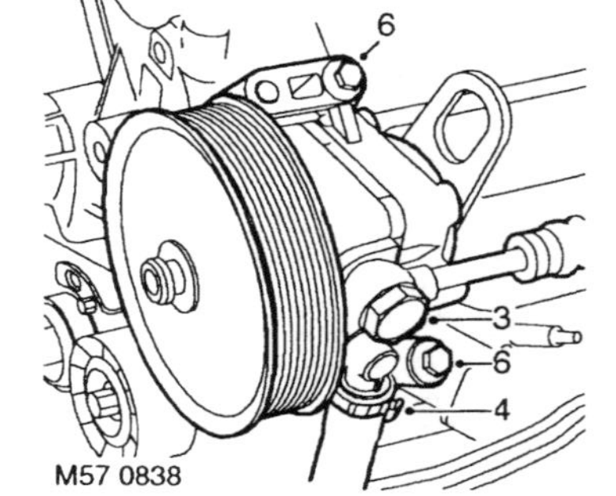

M57 0838

3. Remove banjo bolt securing high pressure pipe to pump. Remove and discard sealing washers.
4. Remove and discard clip securing feed hose to pump and disconnect hose.
5. Plug open connections on pump, high pressure pipe and feed hose.
6. Remove 2 bolts securing pump to mounting bracket and remove pump.

Refit

7. Clean pump and mounting bracket mating faces, dowel and dowel holes.
8. Fit pump to mounting bracket and tighten bolts to ***25 Nm (18 lbf.ft).***
9. Connect feed hose to pump and secure with new clip.
10. Clean high pressure pipe and banjo bolt.
11. Connect high pressure pipe to pump using new sealing washers. Tighten banjo bolt to ***25 Nm (18 lbf.ft).***
12. Fit alternator drive belt. ***See ELECTRICAL, Repair.***
13. Bleed power steering system. ***See this section.***

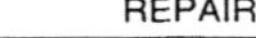

POWER STEERING PUMP - DIESEL

Service repair no - 57.20.15

Remove

1. Raise vehicle on four post lift.
2. Disconnect battery negative lead.
3. Raise lift.
4. Slacken 3 bolts securing pulley to steering pump. Do not remove bolts.

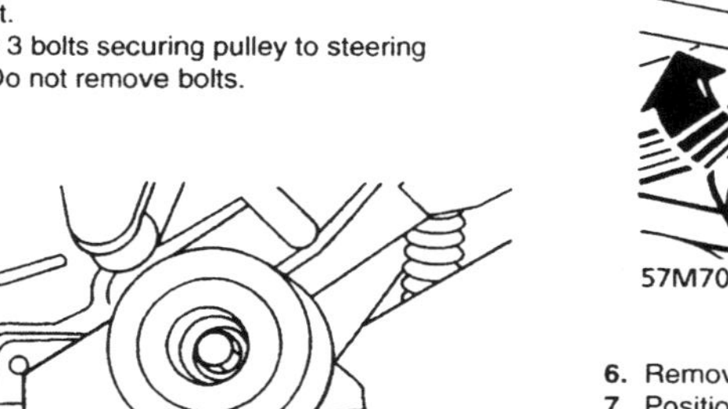
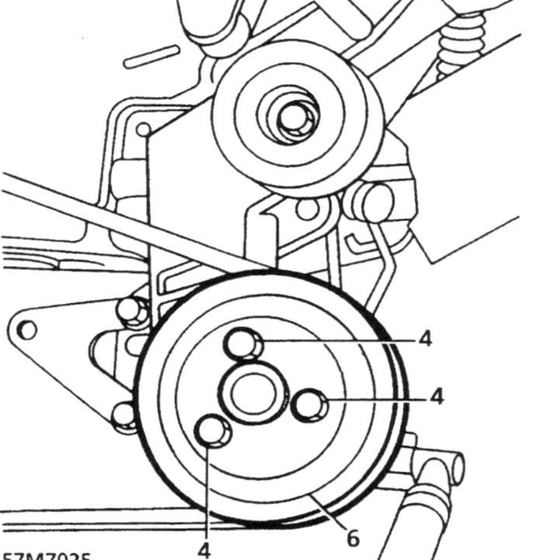

57M7025

5. Release alternator belt tension using a suitable lever beneath tensioner damper as shown. Release drive belt from steering pump pulley.

57M7034

6. Remove pulley bolts. Collect pulley.
7. Position container beneath power steering pump to catch spillage.
8. Remove 4 bolts securing steering pump. Release pump from bracket.

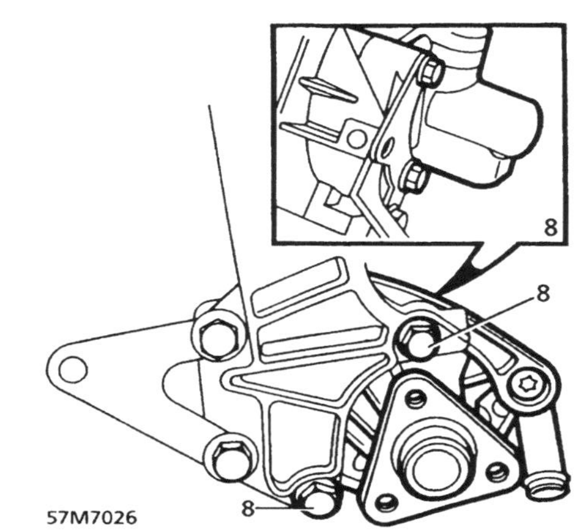

57M7026

9. Disconnect low pressure hose from pump.
10. Remove banjo bolt securing high pressure pipe to pump. Discard sealing washers.

57M7027

11. Remove steering pump. Plug all hoses and connections.

Refit

12. Remove plugs from hoses and connections.
13. Using new sealing washers, secure high pressure pipe to steering pump with banjo bolt. Tighten to ***30 Nm. (22 lbf.ft)***
14. Connect low pressure hose to pump. Secure with new clip.
15. Position steering pump on bracket. Secure with bolts.
16. Position pulley on steering pump. Fit bolts, finger tight.
17. Lever tensioner pulley to slack position. Engage belt over power steering pump pulley.
18. Tighten steering pump pulley bolts.
19. Lower lift.
20. Reconnect battery negative lead.
21. Fill power steering reservoir. ***See LUBRICANTS, FLUIDS AND CAPACITIES, Information.***
22. Bleed steering system. ***See this section.***

STEERING WHEEL

Service repair no - 57.60.01

Remove

1. Remove steering wheel pad. ***See this section.***
2. **Vehicles with SRS:** Remove drivers air bag module. ***See SUPPLEMENTARY RESTRAINT SYSTEM, Repair.***
3. Disconnect steering wheel switch multiplug.
4. Release harnesses from clip.

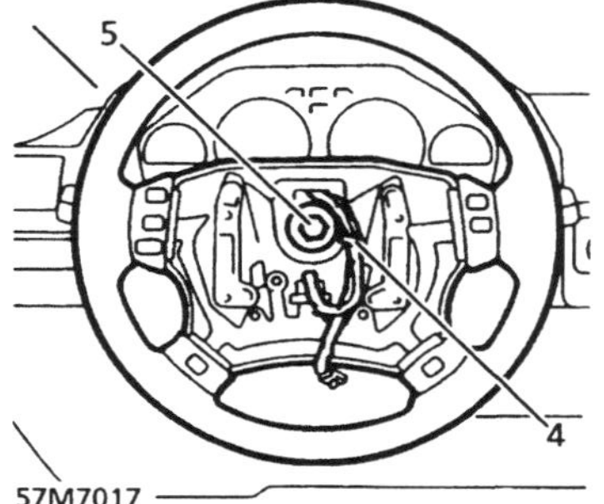

57M7017

5. Remove bolt securing steering wheel to column.
6. Remove steering wheel.

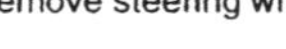
CAUTION: Ensure that air bag module and steering wheel switch harnesses are released during steering wheel removal.

Disassemble

7. Remove 2 screws securing multiplug to horn unit.

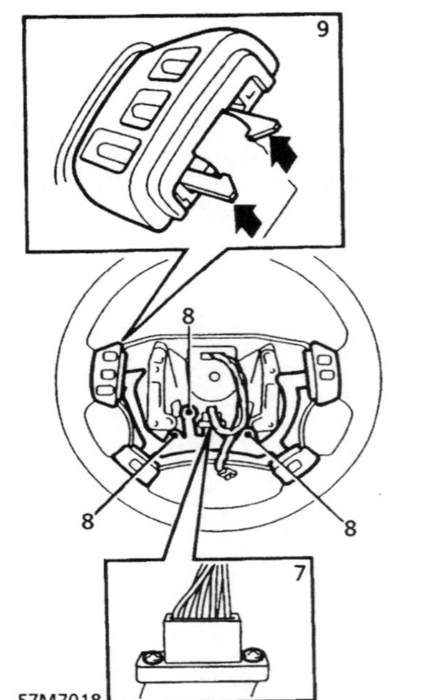

57M7018

8. Remove 3 screws securing printed circuit to horn unit.

WARNING: Take great care when removing the 3 screws securing the printed circuit to horn unit. The screws are non replacable and other fixings must not be used. If the screws are damaged during removal, the steering wheel must be renewed.

9. Lift 2 clips securing each switch pack. Remove switch packs and printed circuit assembly.

Assemble

10. Position switch pack assembly. Engage switches to steering wheel.

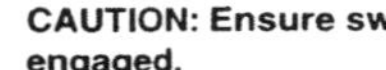

CAUTION: Ensure switches are correctly engaged.

11. Secure multiplug and printed circuit with screws.

Refit

12. Route harnesses through steering wheel aperture.
13. Position steering wheel. Secure with bolt. Tighten to ***33 Nm. (24 lbf.ft)***
14. Connect steering wheel switch multiplug.
15. Secure harnesses in clip.
16. Fit steering wheel pad. ***See this section.***
17. **Vehicles with SRS:** Fit drivers air bag module. ***See SUPPLEMENTARY RESTRAINT SYSTEM, Repair.***

STEERING WHEEL PAD

Service repair no - 57.60.03

NOTE: For vehicles fitted with supplementary restraint system (SRS). *See SUPPLEMENTARY RESTRAINT SYSTEM, Repair.*

Remove

1. Position steering wheel for access to all fixings.
2. Unscrew 4 bolts securing pad to steering wheel.

57M7019

NOTE: Bolts remain captive in steering wheel.

3. Remove steering wheel pad.

Refit

4. Position pad to steering wheel. Secure with bolts. Tighten to ***8 Nm. (6 lbf.ft)***

TRACK ROD

Service repair no - 57.55.09

Remove

1. Raise the vehicle.

WARNING: Support on safety stands.

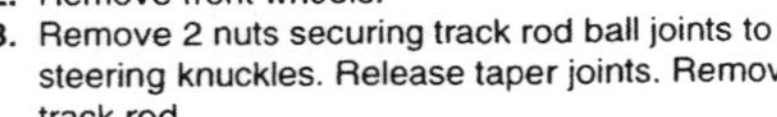

2. Remove front wheels.
3. Remove 2 nuts securing track rod ball joints to steering knuckles. Release taper joints. Remove track rod.

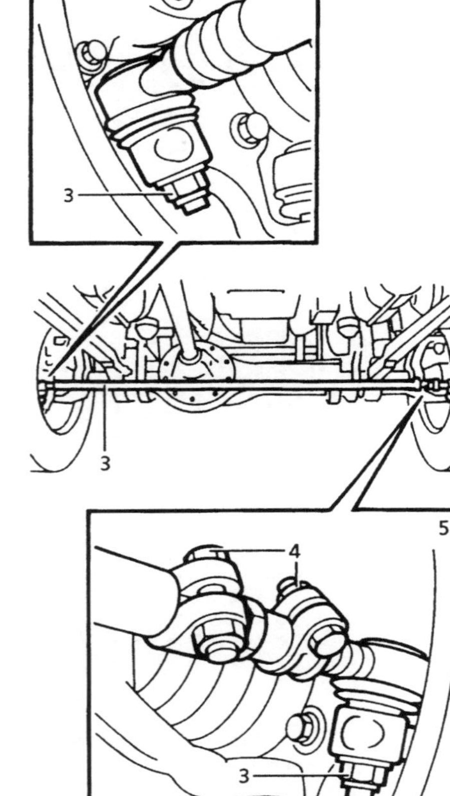
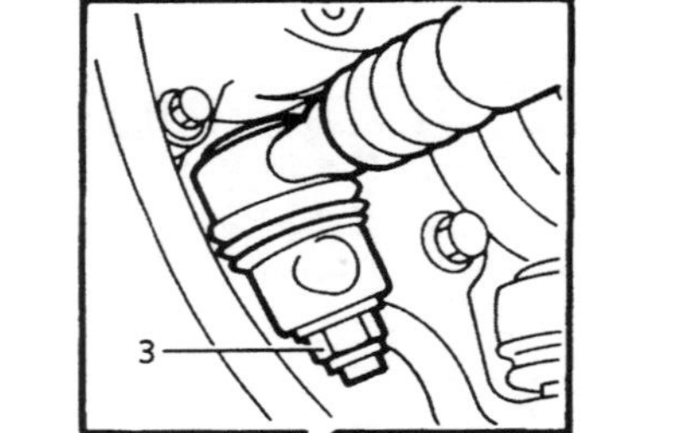
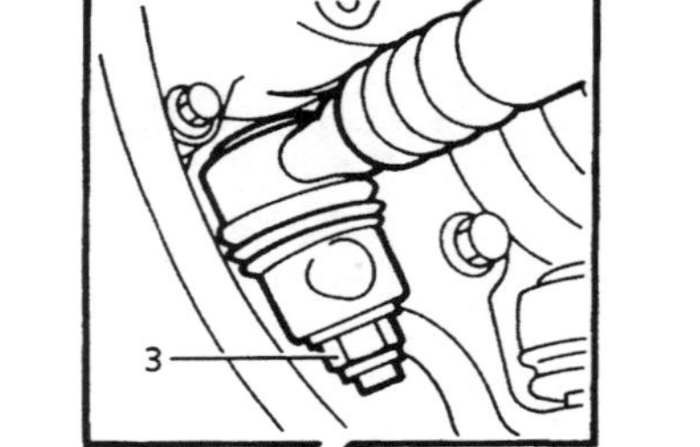

57M7016

Disassemble

4. Slacken nuts and bolts clamping ball joints and adjuster.
5. Remove ball joints, adjuster and clamps.

Assemble

6. Position ball joints, adjuster and clamps on track rod.
7. Screw adjuster and ball joints in to full extent of threads.
8. Using adjuster, set track rod to nominal length of 1340mm ± 10mm.
9. Secure clamps with nuts and bolts.

Refit

10. Position track rod on steering knuckles. Secure with nuts. Tighten to ***80 Nm. (59 lbf.ft)***
11. Fit front wheels. Tighten to ***108 Nm. (80 lbf.ft)***
12. Remove safety stands. Lower vehicle.
13. Set front wheel alignment. ***See Adjustment.***

CONTENTS

Page

ELECTRONIC AIR SUSPENSION

DESCRIPTION AND OPERATION

FAULT DIAGNOSIS

REPAIR

60 - FRONT SUSPENSION

CONTENTS

ELECTRONIC AIR SUSPENSION - EAS

Description

The Range Rover concept of air supension is already well established, the system fitted to the New Range Rover is broadly similar. Progressive development has resulted in added features to improve the control and operation of the system.
Air springs provide a soft and comfortable feel to the ride of the vehicle. The use of a microprocessor to control the system exploits the advantages of air suspension.
The system provides a near constant ride frequency under all load conditions resulting in:

- Improved ride quality
- Consistency of ride quality
- Constant ride height
- Improved headlamp levelling

The system provides five ride height settings plus self levelling. Each setting is automatically maintained at the correct height by the system logic with the minimum of driver involvement. Vehicle height is sensed by four rotary potentiometer type height sensors. Height information from each sensor signals the electronic control unit (ECU) to adjust each air spring by switching the solenoid valves to hold, add or release air.

The five height settings are as follows:

Standard: Profile

Low profile: 25 mm (1 in.) below standard.

Access: 65 mm (2.6 in.) below standard. Crawl: It is possible to drive at the access ride height at speeds less than 32 km/h (20 mph), where headroom is restricted.

High profile: 40 mm (1.6 in.) above standard.

Extended profile: 70 mm (2.75 in.) above standard. This setting is not manually selectable.

Self levelling

On a coil sprung vehicle the effect of adding weight is for the vehicle to lean either from front to back or side to side unless the increased weight is evenly spread. With air suspension, the system detects this body lean and automatically compensates for it. The vehicle will self level to the lowest corner height for 20 seconds each time the driver exits vehicle and closes the doors.
The system will check vehicle height every 6 hours and make minor corrections, not exceeding 8 mm, (0.31 in) as necessary.
When unloading through the tailgate the system will self level to compensate for the decreased load after door closure.

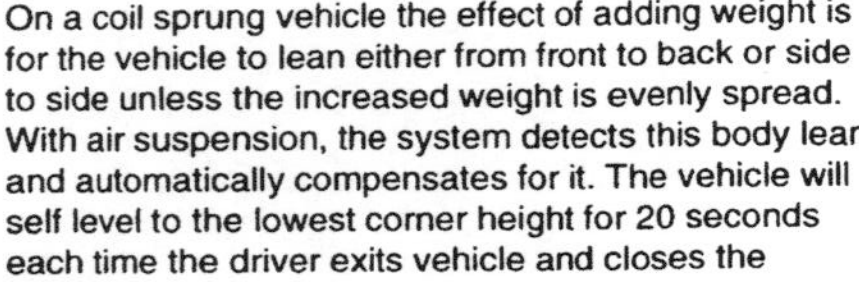

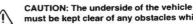

NOTE: If the vehicle is parked on uneven ground or with a wheel or wheels on the kerb, self levelling will lower the vehicle to the lowest spring height.

CAUTION: The underside of the vehicle must be kept clear of any obstacles while the vehicle is parked, as self levelling may result in a reduced trim height.

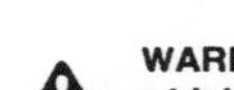

WARNING: Before commencing work which requires access to the underside or wheel arches of the vehicle, the suspension must be allowed to relevel. Relevelling is achieved by opening and closing of any of the side doors, while all other doors and tail gate remain closed, and the ignition off.

EAS must be set in 'high-lock' using TestBook, during any work which does not require chassis to axle displacement. This will hold the suspension in extended profile position, until reset by TestBook.

LOCATION OF COMPONENTS

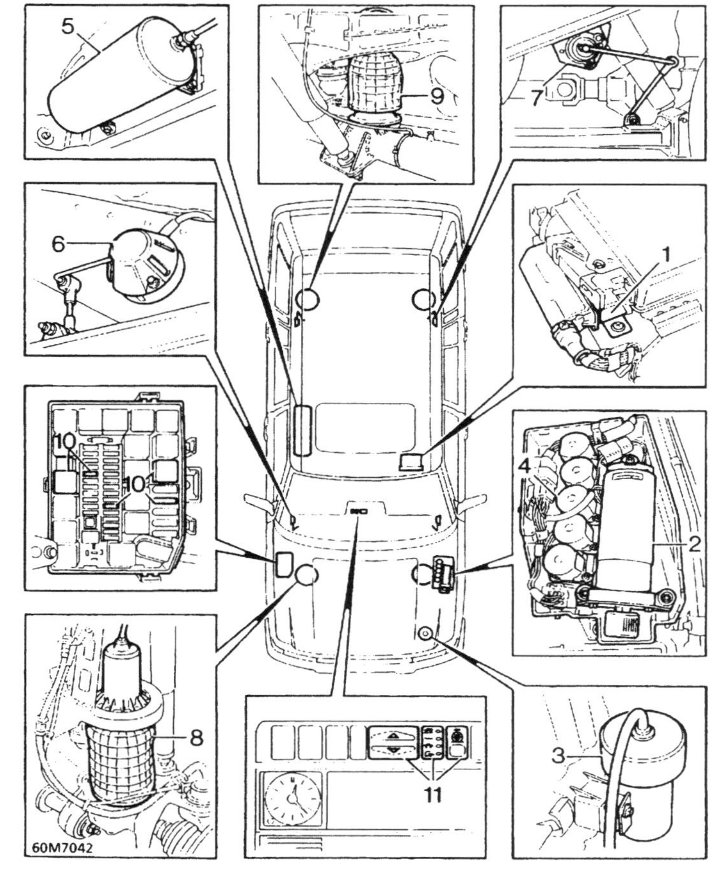

Key to location of components

1. Electrical control unit
2. Compressor
3. Air dryer
4. Valve block
5. Reservoir
6. Height sensors front
7. Height sensors rear
8. Front air spring
9. Rear air spring
10. Relays, fuses
11. Driver controls

DESCRIPTION OF COMPONENTS

Electrical Control Unit - ECU

The ECU is located underneath the front left hand seat. The ECU maintains the requested vehicle ride height by adjusting the volume in each air spring. It is connected to the cable assembly by a 35 way connector. To ensure safe operation the ECU has extensive on board diagnostic and safety features. The ECU must be replaced in case of failure.

Air compressor

NOTE: The air compressor and valve block are contained in the under bonnet unit mounted on the left hand inner wing.

The air compressor provides system pressure. A thermal switch is incorporated which cuts out compressor operation at 120°C. An air filter is fitted to the compressor head. The filter is renewed every 40,000 kms (24,000 miles), or every 30,000 miles in NAS markets.

Air dryer

The air dryer is connected into the air line between the compressor and reservoir. It is mounted on the engine air cleaner box. The dryer removes moisture from pressurised air entering the system. All air exhausted from the system passes through the dryer in the opposite direction. The air dryer is regenerative in that exhaust air absorbs moisture in the dryer and expels it to atmosphere.

The air dryer is non-servicable, designed to last the life of the vehicle. However, if any water is found in the system, the air dryer must be replaced.

CAUTION: If the air dryer is removed from the vehicle the ports must be plugged to prevent moisture ingress.

Valve block

The valve block controls the direction of air flow. Air flow to and from the air springs is controlled by seven solenoid operated valves, one for each spring plus an inlet, exhaust and outlet. In response to signals from the ECU, the valves allow high pressure air to flow in or out of the air springs according to the need to increase or decrease pressure. A diaphragm valve operated by the solenoid outlet valve ensures that all exhausted air passes through the air dryer.

Mounted on the valve block is a pressure switch which senses air pressure and signals the ECU to operate the compressor when required.The compressor will operate when the pressure falls between 7.2 and 8.0 bar (104 and 116 lbf/in^2). It will cut out at a rising pressure of between 9.5 and 10.5 bar (138 and 152 lbf/in^2).

The valve block contains the following serviceable components: solenoid coils 1 to 6, drive pack and pressure switch.
The valve block must only be dismantled after the correct diagnosis procedure.

Reservoir

The 10 litre reservoir is mounted on the right hand side of the chassis. One connection acts as air inlet and outlet for the rest of the system. The reservoir stores compressed air between set pressure levels. The reservoir drain plug requires removing to check for moisture in the system every 40,000 kms. (24,000 miles), or every 30,000 miles in NAS markets.

Height sensors

Four potentiometer type height sensors signal vehicle height information to the ECU. The potentiometers are mounted on the chassis and activated by links to the front radius arms and rear trailing links. A height sensor must be replaced in case of failure, and the vehicle recalibrated using TestBook.

Air springs - front and rear

The air springs consist of the following components:

1. Top plate
2. Rolling rubber diaphragm
3. Piston

Front and rear air springs are of similar constuction but are NOT interchangeable. The diaphragm is not repairable, if failure occurs the complete air spring must be replaced

Driver controls

Mounted in the centre of the dashboard, the driver controls consist of an UP/DOWN switch, an INHIBIT switch and a height setting indicator. For full description. ***See this section.***

Relays, fuses

Located in the under bonnet fuse/relay box are 2 relays, plus 10, 20 and 30 amp fuses.

DRIVER CONTROLS

The driver controls are located in the centre of the fascia. The controls consist of:

1. The HEIGHT CONTROL is a press and release type rocker switch which is used to select the required ride height. The vehicle will not respond until switch is released. All movements selected by operation of this switch are indicated by the ride height indicator lights located next to the switch.
2. The INHIBIT switch is a mechanically latching switch. When selected it modifies the automatic height changes of the system, for further details. ***See Electrical Trouble Shooting Manual.*** Selection of 'inhibit' is indicated by illumination of the switch tell-tale lamp, which is also bulb tested with the ride height indicator.
3. High indicator light.
4. Standard indicator light.
5. Low indicator light.
6. Access indicator light.
7. Instrument pack warning light.

Indicator lights

When the ignition key is turned to position 2 all four indicator lights, the air suspension warning light and the inhibit switch will be illuminated continuously. When the engine is started, the lights will remain illuminated for 2 seconds, after which the current ride height will be indicated. Two indicators will be illuminated if the vehicle is between ride heights, with the selected height flashing. When the new height is achieved the indicator will be illuminated constantly and the previous height indicator extinguished. The inhibit switch indicator is illuminated while it is activated. Both switches are illuminated with sidelights switched on. Additional driver information is given by the message centre in the instrument pack. For details of the messages. ***See this section.***

Air suspension warning lamp

This amber lamp is located in the instrument pack. The lamp will be constantly illuminated when driving at high ride height and will flash when vehicle is at extended height. The lamp will also illumunate if a fault within the system is detected. A bulb check is provided when the ignition switch is turned to position 2 and for 2 seconds after vehicle start.

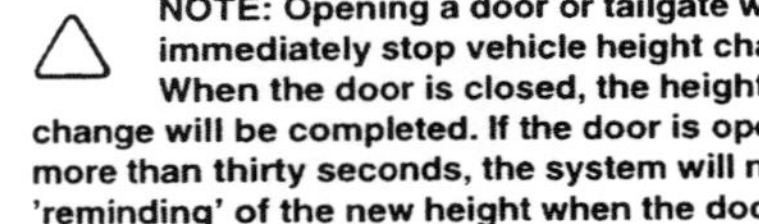

HEIGHT SETTINGS

Standard ride height

With the Inhibit switch off (unlatched), at speeds below 80 km/h (50 mph) the standaid ride height indicator will be illuminated.

Standard vehicle ride height is maintained under all load conditions. This also maintains headlamp levelling.

Low ride height

Low ride height is automatically selected when the vehicle speed exceeds 80 km/h (50 mph) for at least 30 seconds with the inhibit switch off. Low ride height indicator lamp will flash during height change and standard ride height indicator will extinguish when low ride height is attained.

Standard ride height is automatically selected when the vehicle speed drops below 56 km/h (35 mph) for at least 30 seconds with the inhibit switch off.

The driver can select low ride height at any speed. With the vehicle at low ride height, depressing the inhibit switch (latched) will result in the vehicle maintaining low ride height regardless of speed.

The height control switch can be used to change between low and standard ride heights regardless of speed.

Access mode

This position eases access to and from the vehicle. With the vehicle stationary, doors and tailgate closed, park brake applied, foot brake released and gearshift in 'Park' on automatic vehicles, press and release the down switch. The vehicle will descend to access mode. While the vehicle is descending, the access indicator will flash. When access mode is attained, the indicator will remain constantly illuminated, and standard ride height lamp will be extinguished.

Access mode can be selected up to 40 seconds before stopping vehicle. On stopping, applying the handbrake, releasing the foot brake and selecting 'Park' on automatic vehicles, the vehicle will lower to access mode.

It is possible to select access up to 40 seconds after switching engine off.

△ **NOTE: Opening a door or tailgate will immediately stop vehicle height change. When the door is closed, the height change will be completed. If the door is open for more than thirty seconds, the system will need 'reminding' of the new height when the door is closed.**

Driving the vehicle will result in vehicle rising automatically to standard ride height. Alternatively standard ride height can be achieved by closing all doors, starting engine and pressing the up switch. The standard indicator will flash during the change. When standard ride height is attained the indicator will remain constantly illuminated and access indicator will be extinguished.

Crawl mode

In areas where height is restricted, the vehicle may be driven in access mode. To achieve this, ensure the inhibit switch is unlatched and select access mode. When access height is achieved, press the inhibit switch, the lamp will be illumunated. The message centre in the instrument binnacle will beep three times and display EAS MANUAL. The vehicle may now be driven at speeds up to 32 km/h (20 mph).

If the vehicle is accelerated to 16 km/h (10 mph) the message centre will beep three times and display SLOW 20 MPH (32 KM/H) MAX.

If speed exceeds 40 km/h (25 mph) the vehicle will rise to low profile, with low warning flashing. On slowing to 32 km/h (20 mph) the vehicle will lower to access mode with access warning illuminated.

When speed falls below 8 km/h (5 mph) the message centre will beep three times and display EAS MANUAL.

To cancel crawl mode, release the inhibit switch or depress the up switch.

High ride height

This position is used to improve approach and departure angles and when wading. When at standard ride height, pressing the up switch will select high ride height provided the road speed is below 56 km/h (35 mph). The high ride height indicator will flash during the height change. When the change is complete the indicator will remain constantly illuminated, and standard ride height indicator will be extinguished. The indicator in the instrument pack will also be illuminated. If speed exceeds 56 km/h (35 mph), the vehicle will return to standard profile.

Extended ride height

This position is achieved if chassis is grounded leaving wheel or wheels unsupported. Initial ECU reaction is to lower (deflate) affected springs. After a timed period the ECU detects no height change, it therefore reinflates springs to extended profile in an attempt to regain traction. The position will be held for 10 minutes, after which time the vehicle will automatically return to standard ride height.

Pressing the down switch will lower vehicle 20 mm to high profile.

If vehicle speed exceeds 56 km/h (35 mph) the vehicle will immediately lower to standard ride height. This speed could be achieved, for example, by wheelspin.

VEHICLE TRANSPORTATION

New vehicles are transported from the factory with the EAS system electronically 'frozen' in access mode. When road speed exceeds 40 km/h (25 mph), the vehicle will rise to low ride height. It will return to access mode if speed falls below 38.4 km/h (24 mph). This condition is cancelled at pre-delivery inspection, by entering the appropriate command via TestBook.

Vehicle transportation/recovery

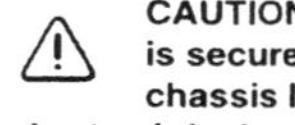

CAUTION: When an air suspension vehicle is secured to a transporter using the chassis lashing eyes, there is a possibility due to air leakage, self levelling or operation of ride height controls that the tension of the securing straps will be lost. To prevent this the ride height should be set to access mode before securing to transporter.

If the engine cannot be run and the vehicle is not in access mode, the vehicle can be transported, but it must be secured to the transporter by the roadwheels, not the chassis.

ELECTRICAL TROUBLESHOOTING

For electrical details of the air suspension circuit. ***See Electrical Trouble Shooting Manual.***

SYSTEM OPERATION

Numbers refer to pneumatic circuit diagram

Air is drawn through the inlet filter (1) to the compressor (2), where it is compressed to 10 ±0,5 bar (145 ±7.25 lbf/in²).

Compressed air passes to the air dryer (3) where moisture is removed as it flows through the dryer dessicant. The dessicant in the lower portion of the dryer becomes wet.

Dried air passes through a non-return valve NRV1 to the reservoir (4).

The 3 non-return valves (6) ensure correct air flow. They also prevent loss of spring pressure if total loss of reservoir pressure occurs.

The pressure switch (5) maintains system pressure between set limits by switching on and off the compressor via an ECU controlled relay.

For air to be admitted to an air spring (10), the inlet valve (7) must be energised together with the relevant air spring solenoid valve (9).

For air to be exhausted from an air spring, the exhaust valve (8) must be energised together with the relevant air spring solenoid valve.

The solenoid diaphragm valve (12) ensures that all air exhausted to atmosphere passses through the dryer. Exhausted air passes vertically downwards through the dryer. This action purges moisture from the dessicant and regenerates the air dryer.

Air is finally exhausted through the system air operated diaphragm valve (13) and to atmosphere through a silencer (14) mounted below the valve block.

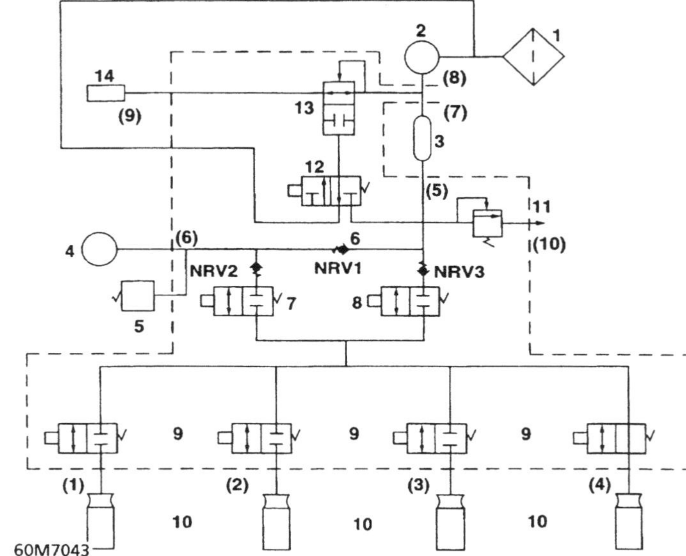

FRONT SUSPENSION

Description

The front suspension design on the New Range Rover allows maximum wheel travel and axle articulation, providing good ground clearance without loss of traction or directional stability.

Near constant ride frequency under all load conditions is achieved by utilizing advancements in suspension geometry complemented to control and operation of the air suspension system. ***See this section.***

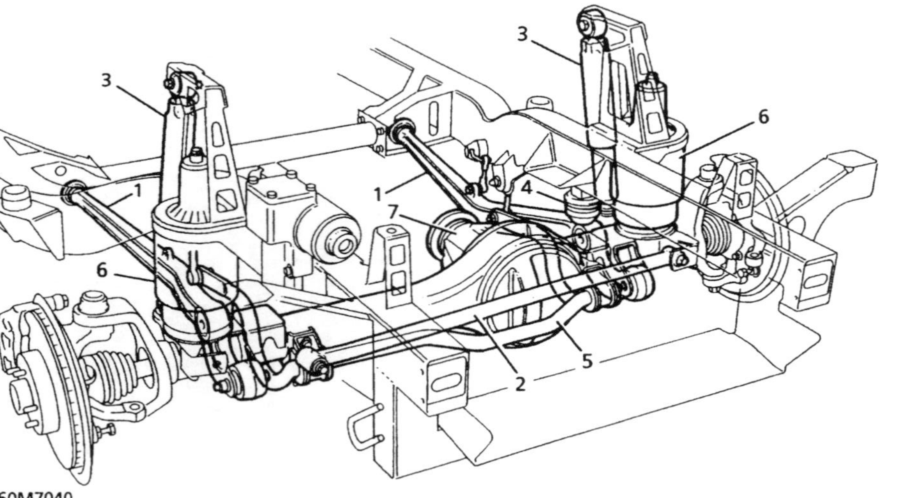

Front axle suspension

1. Radius arms
2. Panhard rod
3. Shock absorbers
4. Bump stops
5. Anti-roll bar
6. Air springs
7. Front axle

Long front radius arms (1) are fitted to the front axle (7) and provide maximum axle articulation which is vital for off road performance. The radius arm, comprising a forged steel link with twin front mountings using ferrule rubber bushes, is secured to fabricated mounting brackets welded to the front axle. Flexible rubber bushes are used on a stem end joint to secure the rear of the radius arm to a mounting on the chassis cross member as shown in 60M7040. The vehicle height sensors are also linked to the front radius arms; for full details of the height settings. ***See this section.***

A panhard rod (2), which ensures that the axle remains centrally located, is fitted transversely and also uses ferrule rubber bush mountings at both axle and chassis locations. An anti-roll bar (5) is fitted to the front axle to control body roll and directional stability. Two rubber bearing bushes, with retaining straps, secure the anti-roll bar to the front axle, while ball jointed links, suspended from the chassis, support the rear of the anti-roll bar.

Conventional telescopic shock absorbers (3), used to control body movement, are secured to fabricated towers which are welded to the chassis. The upper fixing uses a single retaining bolt passing through a flexible rubber bush. The lower fixing of the shock absorber comprises of a stem type mounting with two flexible rubber bushes and support washers secured to an axle mounting by a single retaining nut. Cellular foam bump stops (4) are fitted under the chassis adjacent to the air springs (6) and prevent possible damage that could occur should there be excessive axle to chassis movement. Should there be a loss of air pressure in the air springs the vehicle can still be driven safely at a speed not exeeding 35 mph (56kph) with the bump stops resting on the axle, although this will result in a hard ride. The loss of air pressure should be investigated as soon as possible. The bump stops are 'progressive' and will reform from a compressed state when the load is released.

Notes

FRONT SUSPENSION FAULTS

This section covers possible mechanical, fuse and relay faults that could occur in the front suspension system, including air suspension components.

Visual checks of components within the system and relevant fuses and relays should be carried out before undertaking detailed fault diagnosis procedures, which are covered on **TestBook** .

Symptom - Hard Ride.

POSSIBLE CAUSE	REMEDY
1. Seized or inoperable front shock absorber/s.	1. Renew shock absorber. ***See Repair.***
2. Loss of air pressure in the air system resulting in the chassis bump stops resting on the front and rear axles.	2. Check air system components for faults and air harness for leaks etc. ***See Repair.*** Rectify or renew components where necessary.
3. Contaminated or fouled suspension components with off road debris.	3. Remove/clean off debris and check for damage. Renew components where necessary.
4. Incorrect ride height calibration.	4. Re-calibrate air suspension system. Refer to **TestBook** .

Symptom - Vehicle Suspension Permanently In 'Standard Height' Mode.

POSSIBLE CAUSE	REMEDY
1. Height sensor/s inoperative due to loose or disconnected multi-plug.	1. Reconnect multi-plug.
2. Height sensor linkage disconnected or damaged.	2. Reconnect or renew sensor linkage.
3. Faulty height sensor/s.	3. Renew height sensor/s. ***See Repair.***
4. Leaking air supply to air spring/s.	4. Check air harness connections and pipes for damage or scoring.
5. Faulty/leaking air spring diaphragm.	5. Renew air spring assembly. ***See Repair.***
6. Faulty ABS speed sensor in ECU.	6. Refer to **TestBook** .
7. Faulty pressure switch.	7. Refer to **TestBook** .

Symptom - Excessive Body Roll At Front Of Vehicle.

POSSIBLE CAUSE	REMEDY
1. Anti-roll bar damaged or broken.	1. Renew anti-roll bar. ***See Repair.***
2. Worn anti-roll bar axle mounting rubbers.	2. Renew mounting rubbers. ***See Repair.***
3. Worn or broken anti-roll bar link ball joints.	3. Renew link asembly. ***See Repair.***
4. Loose anti-roll bar chassis and axle fixings.	4. Check and tighten all relevant fixings.
5. Worn or leaking shock absorber/s.	5. Renew shock absorber/s. ***See Repair.***
6. Worn radius arm axle mounting bushes.	6. Renew radius arm bushes. ***See Repair.***
7. Loose radius arm fixings.	7. Check and tighten all relevant fixings.
8. Worn radius arm chassis mounting bushes.	8. Renew radius arm bushes. ***See Repair.***
9. Deflated air spring.	9. Check air system components for faults and air harness for leaks etc. ***See Repair.*** Rectify or renew components where necessary.
10. Faulty valve block.	10. Refer to **TestBook** .
11. Damaged or broken chassis or axle mounting brackets.	11. Vehicle should be recovered and not driven.
12. Failed or loose body mountings giving excessive body movement to chassis.	12. Tighten fixings or renew rubber body mountings if failed.

Symptom - Suspension Knock.

POSSIBLE CAUSE	REMEDY
1. Loose or worn suspension component mountings and fixings.	1. Check, tighten or renew relevant components and fixings.
2. Missing bump stop/s.	2. Fit new bump stop/s. ***See Repair.***

Symptom - Air Suspension System Faulty Or Inoperative.

POSSIBLE CAUSE	REMEDY
1. Blown air suspension system fuse.	1. Check and renew fuse F44.
2. Blown fuse covering dashboard 'height control' or 'inhibit' switch.	2. Check and renew fuse F17.
3. Faulty 'height control' switch; could result in vehicle height remaining at last setting until ignition switched off.	3. Refer to **TestBook** to confirm fault and renew 'height control' switch. ***See ELECTRICAL, Repair.***
4. Faulty 'inhibit' switch; could result in vehicle not operating automatically between standard and low modes.	4. Refer to **TestBook** to confirm fault and renew 'inhibit' switch. ***See ELECTRICAL, Repair.***
5. Compressor inoperative; no air pressure due to loose or disconnected multi-plug.	5. Check and reconnect compressor multi-plug.
6. Blown compressor maxi fuse.	6. Check and renew maxi fuse 2.
7. Faulty compressor relay, resulting in compressor running continuously.	7. Renew relay RL20.
8. Loss of air pressure in the air system.	8. Check air system components for faults and air harness for leaks. ***See Repair.***
9. Faulty delay relay. If the delay relay fails with a closed circuit the system will be powered, resulting in a flat battery.	9. Renew relay AMR3284.

Symptom - Vehicle Leaning Side To Side Or Front To Rear With Air Suspension System Operative.

POSSIBLE CAUSE	REMEDY
1. Faulty height sensor.	1. Refer to **TestBook** to locate faulty height sensor. Renew height sensor and re-calibrate air suspension system. Refer to **TestBook** .
2. Incorrect height sensor calibration.	2. Re-calibrate air suspension system. Refer to **TestBook** .

NOTE: Critical warning messages relating to the air suspension system are displayed on the message centre, should a fault occur.

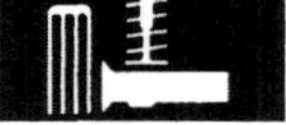

UNDERBODY WAX

CAUTION: Ensure all under body wax is removed from mating surfaces of fixings before fitting.

DEPRESSURISE SYSTEM

Service repair no - 60.50.38

Equipment required: TestBook

Depressurise

WARNING: Air suspension is pressurised up to 10 bar (150 lbf/in²). Dirt or grease must not enter the system. Wear hand, ear and eye safety standard protection when servicing system.

1. Connect **TestBook** and follow instructions to depressurise complete system.

CAUTION: Depressurising system will lower body on to bump stops.

2. Ensure system is completely depressurised: Check that all air springs are deflated, and vehicle has dropped evenly on to the bump stops. If a spring, or springs, remains inflated possibly due to a stuck solenoid valve, it will be necessary to disconnect the pressurised pipe at that air spring.

WARNING: Wear hand, ear and eye safety standard protection. For extra protection wrap a clean cloth around pipe to be disconnected. Note that vehicle will lower to bump stop when pipe is disconnected.

3. Disconnect air pipe. ***See this section.***

Repressurise

4. Run engine to repressurise system.

SYSTEM CALIBRATION

Equipment required: TestBook

NOTE: This procedure must be carried out when a new ECU or height sensor has been fitted.

Calibration will also be required if any part affecting damper relationship to body is changed i.e. damper mounts, axles, chassis unit and body panels. The vehicle can be calibrated laden or unladen, but Gross Vehicle Weight must not be exceeded. Tyres must all be the same size and at the correct pressures.

IMPORTANT: The floor used for calibration must be level and smooth in all directions to enable procedure to be carried out successfully.

AIR SPRINGS/HEIGHT SENSORS - INSPECT

Visually check air springs for cuts, abrasions and stone damage to alloy end plates. Check security of retention clips. Check height sensors for damage to housing, operating links and cable assembly.

AIR HARNESS INSPECT

Check air harness (pipes) for damage and security over its full length around vehicle.

LEAK TEST PROCEDURE

Service repair no - 60.50.35

If an air leak is suspected the use of a proprietary leak detection spray is recommended. This procedure should also be used where pneumatic components have been disturbed.

The spray used must have a corrosion inhibitor, and must not cause damage to paintwork, plastics, metals and plastic pipes.

Recommended leak detection spray is GOTEC LDS. This is available under part number STC1090.

1. Ensure system is fully pressurised.
2. Clean around area of suspected leak.
3. Using manufacturer's instructions, spray around all component joints and air springs, working systematically until source of leak is found.
4. If a component eg: air spring, air drier is leaking, rectify by fitting a new component.
5. If an air pipe connection is leaking cut 5 mm (0.2 in) off end of pipe. Fit new collet. ***See this section.***
6. Reinflate system, carry out leak test.

SUSPENSION COMPONENTS

CAUTION: It is essential to note that repairs to other suspension and transmission components are affected by air suspension.

The air suspension must be DEPRESSURISED before attempting to remove the following components:

Radius arms, Front axle

Rear axle, Trailing arms

WARNING: Before inflation, the air spring must be restricted by suspension and the shock absorbers fitted. Unrestricted movement of a pressurised air spring will result in failure of the assembly, causing component and possible personal injury.

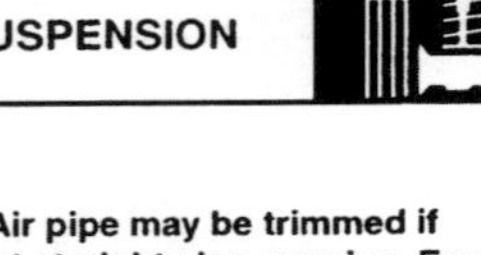

DISCONNECT AND CONNECT AIR PIPES

Remove

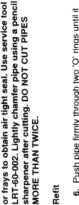

WARNING: Air suspension is pressurised up to 10 bar (150 lbf/in²). Dirt or grease must not enter the system. Wear hand, ear and eye safety standard protection when servicing system.

1. Depressurise complete system. ***See this section.***

CAUTION: Air pipes may be damaged if not disconnected correctly, resulting in possible leaks.

2. Clean air pipe connection with stiff brush and soapy water. Peel back rubber boot.

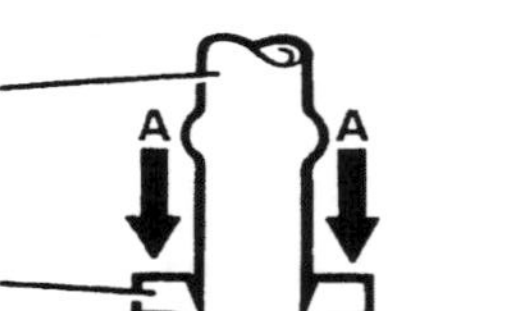

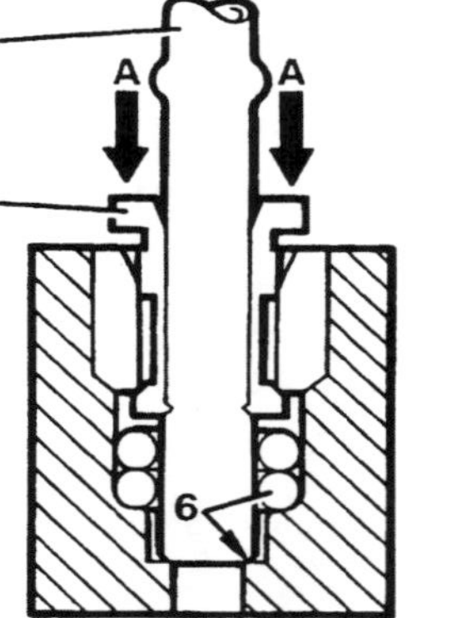

3. Apply equal downward pressure on collet flange at 'A' as shown.
4. Pull air pipe firmly out through centre of collet.
5. Inspect disconnected end of air pipe for damage and scores. Rectify as necessary.

NOTE: Air pipe may be trimmed if sufficient straight pipe remains. Ensure pipe end is cut square, without distortion or frays to obtain air tight seal. Use service tool LRT-60-002. Lightly chamfer pipe using a pencil sharpener after cutting. DO NOT CUT PIPES MORE THAN TWICE.

Refit

6. Push pipe firmly through two 'O' rings until it contacts base of housing as shown. Gently pull pipe to ensure connection. The collet will retain some movement while depressurised. Refit rubber boot.
7. Pressurise system. ***See this section.***
8. Leak test connection. ***See this section.***

AIR PIPE CONNECTION COLLET AND 'O' RINGS

Remove

WARNING: Air suspension is pressurised up to 10 bar (150 lbf/in²). Dirt or grease must not enter the system. Wear hand, ear and eye safety standard protection when servicing system.

1. Clean area with stiff brush and soapy water.
2. Depressurise system. ***See this section.***

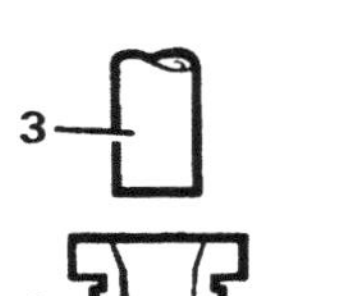
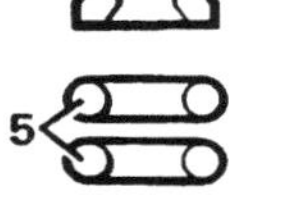
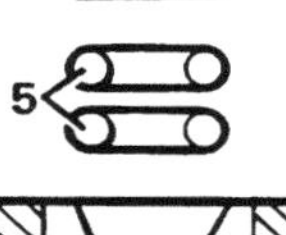

RR3593M

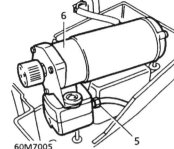

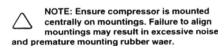

3. Disconnect air pipe. ***See this section.***
4. Remove collet.
5. Carefully pry out two 'O' rings, using a smooth plastic hook, eg: a crochet hook.

CAUTION: Avoid scratching inside wall of housing, creating possible leak path.

Refit

6. Lightly grease new 'O' rings.
7. Fit 'O' rings into recess. Use a crochet hook to avoid damage to 'O' rings and housing.
8. Locate collet legs into housing, push fully home.
9. Inspect end of air pipe for damage and scores rectify by trimming.

NOTE: Air pipe may be trimmed if sufficient straight pipe remains. Ensure pipe end is cut square, without distortion or frays to obtain air tight seal. Use service tool LRT-60-002. Lightly chamfer pipe using a pencil sharpener after cutting. DO NOT CUT PIPES MORE THAN TWICE.

10. Connect air pipe. ***See this section.***
11. Pressurise system. ***See this section.***
12. Leak test connection. ***See this section.***

AIR COMPRESSOR

Service repair no - 60.50.10

Remove

WARNING: The air suspension is pressurised to 10 bar (150 lbf/in²) . Dirt or grease must not enter the system. Wear hand, ear and eye safety standard protection when servicing system.

1. Depressurise system. ***See this section.***

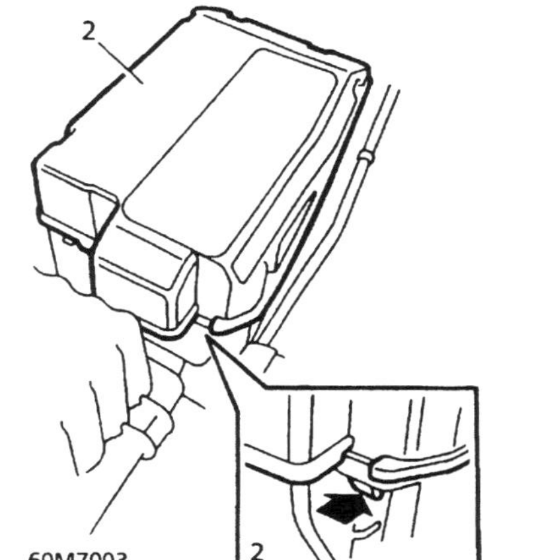

60M7003

2. Remove cover from air supply unit.
3. Release compressor multiplug from casing and disconnect plug.

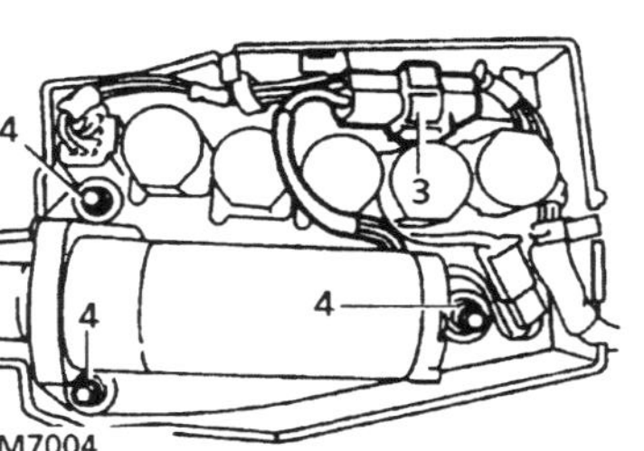

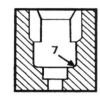

60M7004

4. Remove 3 nuts and dished washers securing compressor. Note orientation of dished washers.
5. Remove compressor outlet pipe, seal exposed ends.

60M7005

6. Remove compressor.

Refit

7. Remove seals from air hose and compressor. Connect air hose to compressor and tighten union nut to ***7 Nm. (5 lbf.ft)***
8. Fit compressor ensuring correct orientation of dished washers. Tighten fixings to ***2 Nm. (1.5 lbf.ft)***

NOTE: Ensure compressor is mounted centrally on mountings. Failure to align mountings may result in excessive noise and premature mounting rubber waer.

9. Connect compressor multiplug, secure to casing.
10. Leak test connection. ***See this section.***
11. Fit cover to air supply unit.

AIR RESERVOIR

Service repair no - 60.50.03

WARNING: Air suspension is pressurised to 10 bar (150 lbf/in²). Dirt or grease must not enter the system. Wear hand, ear and eye safety standard protection when servicing system.

Remove

1. Depressurise system. ***See this section.***
2. Raise the vehicle.

WARNING: Support on safety stands.

3. Clean air connection.

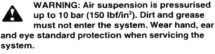

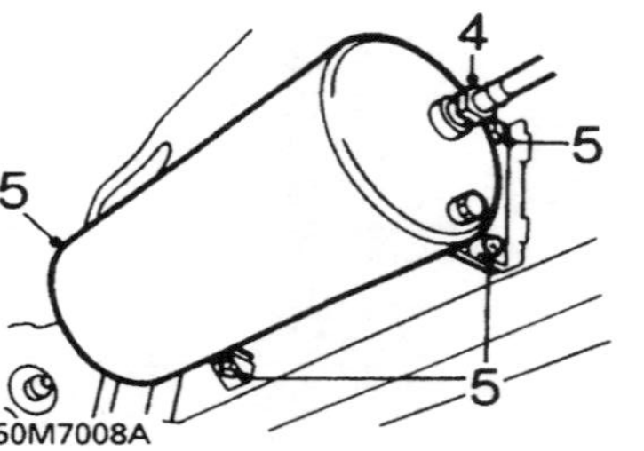

4. Release air pipe from reservoir, seal hose and reservoir.
5. Remove 3 bolts securing reservoir. Remove reservoir.

Refit

6. Fit reservoir, tighten bolts to ***25 Nm. (18 lbf.ft)***
7. Remove seals from air pipe and reservoir.
8. Connect air hose to reservoir.
9. Leak test reservoir. ***See this section.***
10. Fit rubber boot to connection.
11. Remove safety stands. Lower vehicle.

AIR SPRING

Service repair no - 60.21.01

Remove

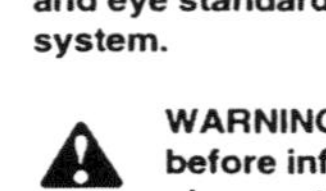

WARNING: Air suspension is pressurised up to 10 bar (150 lbf/in²). Dirt and grease must not enter the system. Wear hand, ear and eye standard protection when servicing the system.

WARNING: Shock absorbers must be fitted before inflating air springs. Failure to observe this warning could cause air spring damage. DO NOT ATTEMPT TO DISMANTLE AIR SPRINGS.

1. Raise the vehicle.

WARNING: Support on safety stands.

2. Remove wheel arch liner. ***See CHASSIS AND BODY, Repair.***
3. Support chassis under front cross member.
4. Depressurise system. ***See this section.***
5. Clean area, disconnect hose from air spring. Seal hose and spring.
6. Remove clips securing air spring.

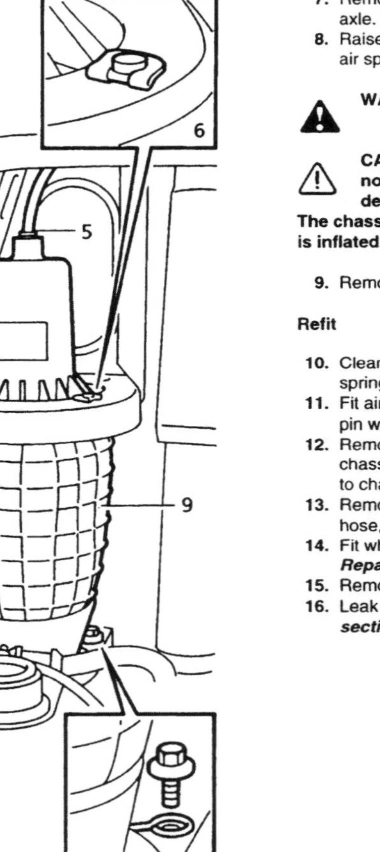

60M7035

7. Remove bolt securing air spring retaining pin to axle. Remove pin.
8. Raise chassis on jack for clearance to remove air spring.

WARNING: Support on safety stands.

CAUTION: When refitting the air spring, do not allow the vehicle to rest on the deflated air spring. The chassis must be supported until the air spring is inflated.

9. Remove air spring.

Refit

10. Clean mating faces of axles chassis and air spring.
11. Fit air spring to axle,fit retaining pin and secure pin with bolt.
12. Remove support from under chassis, lower chassis onto air spring. Fit clips to secure spring to chassis.
13. Remove seals from spring and air pipe. Clean hose, connect to spring.
14. Fit wheel arch liner. ***See CHASSIS AND BODY, Repair.***
15. Remove safety stands. Lower vehicle.
16. Leak test air spring and connector. ***See this section.***

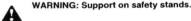

ANTI-ROLL BAR AND BUSHES

Service repair no - 60.10.01 - Anti-roll bar
Service repair no - 60.10.05 - Bushes

Remove

1. Raise the vehicle.

WARNING: Support on safety stands.

2. Remove nuts securing links to anti-roll bar.

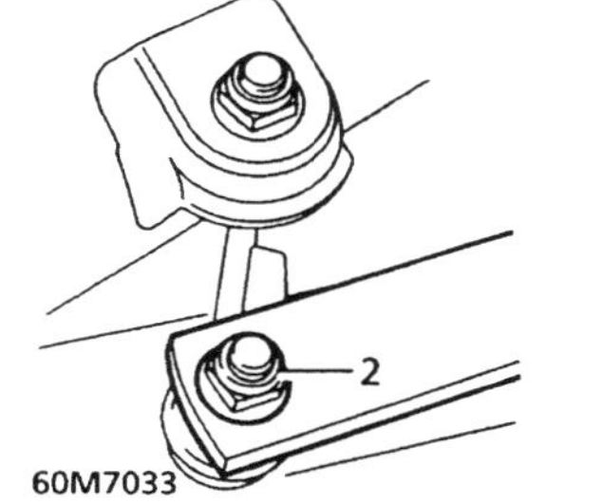

60M7033

3. Remove screws securing rubber bush clamps. Remove clamps.

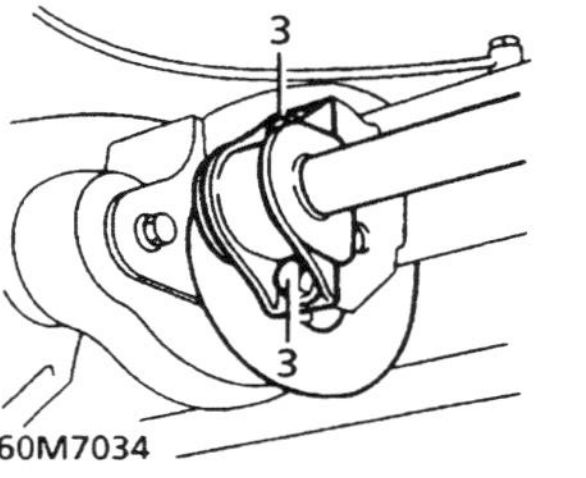

60M7034

4. Release anti-roll bar from links.
5. Remove anti-roll bar.
6. Remove bushes.

Refit

7. Fit and align anti-roll bar.
8. Connect links to anti-roll bar.
9. Fit, do not tighten, link retaining nuts.
10. Clean anti-roll bar bush location.
11. Apply suitable lubricant to bushes
12. Fit bushes and clamps.
13. Fit clamp screws. Tighten to ***to 125 Nm. (92 lbf.ft)***
14. Tighten link nuts to ***125 Nm. (92 lbf.ft)***
15. Remove safety stands. Lower vehicle.

BUMP STOP

Service repair no - 60.30.10

Remove

1. Raise the vehicle.

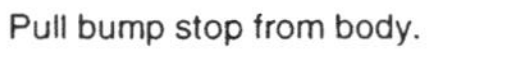
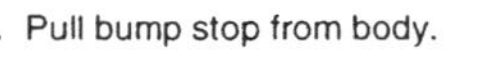

WARNING: Support on safety stands.

2. Pull bump stop from body.

60M7016

Refit

3. Fit bump stop.
4. Remove safety stands. Lower vehicle.

COMPRESSOR INLET FILTER

Service repair no - 60.50.12

Remove

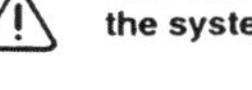

CAUTION: Dirt or grease must not enter the system.

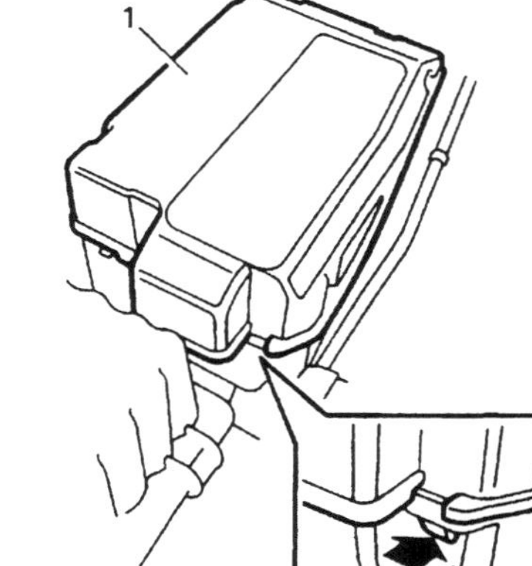

60M7015

1. Remove cover from air supply unit.
2. Remove inlet filter from compressor.

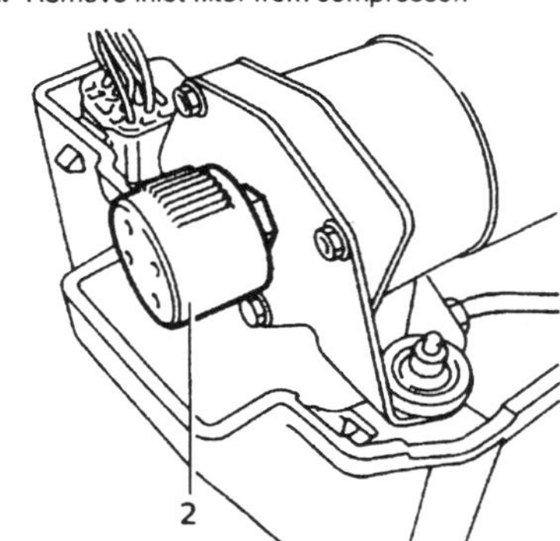

60M7006

Refit

3. Apply Loctite 572 to filter threads.
4. Fit filter Tighten to ***1.0 Nm. (0.74 lbf.ft).*** Refit cover.

DELAY TIMER UNIT

Service repair no - 60.50.46

Remove

1. Raise LH front seat cushion to full extent to improve access to timer unit.

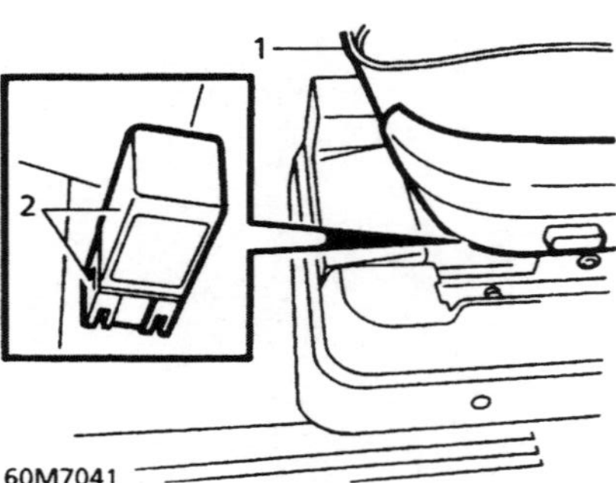

60M7041

2. Remove timer unit from terminal block.

Refit

3. Reverse removal procedure.

AIR DRIER

Service repair no - 60.50.09

Remove

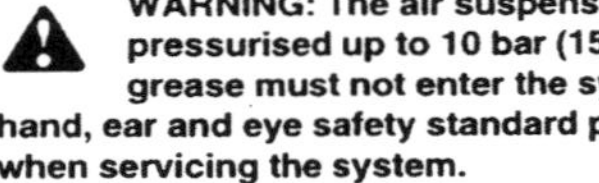

WARNING: The air suspension is pressurised up to 10 bar (150 psi). Dirt or grease must not enter the system. Wear hand, ear and eye safety standard protection when servicing the system.

1. Disconnect 2 pipes from air drier.
2. Seal pipes. Seal drier to prevent moisture ingress.
3. Remove air drier fixing, remove drier.

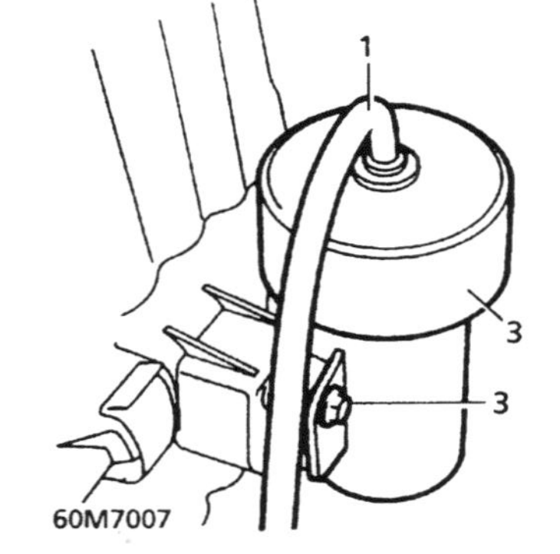

60M7007

Refit

4. Fit drier, tighten fixing to ***12 Nm (9 lbf.ft)***.
5. Remove seals, clean end of pipes.
6. Connect hoses to drier.
7. Leak test connections. ***See this section.***

ELECTRONIC CONTROL UNIT (ECU)

Service repair no - 60.50.04

Remove

1. Move front left hand seat fully rearwards.
2. Disconnect battery negative lead.

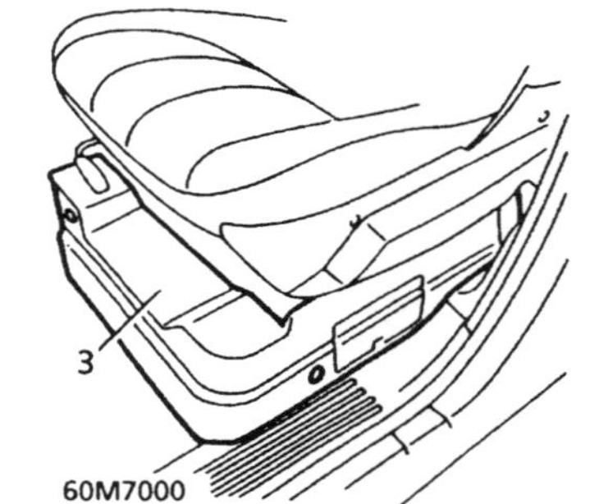

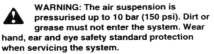

60M7000

3. Remove 3 trim fixings, remove trim from seat base.

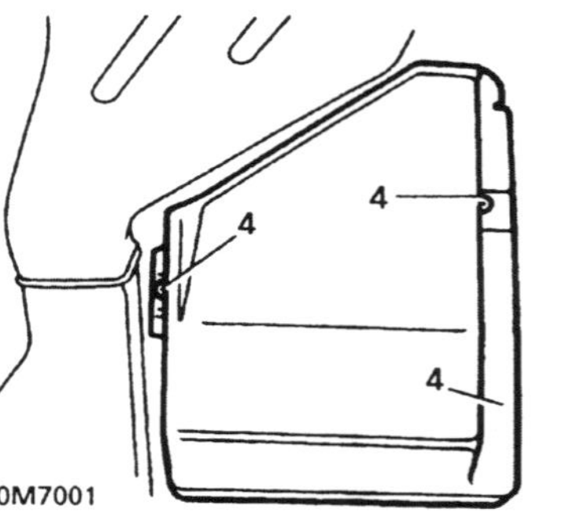

60M7001

4. Remove 2 screws from ECU cover (automatic only), remove cover.

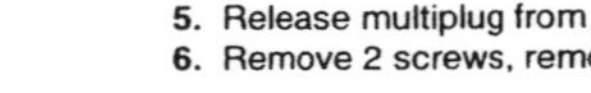

60M7002

5. Release multiplug from ECU.
6. Remove 2 screws, remove ECU.

Refit

7. Reverse removal procedure.

HEIGHT SENSOR

Service repair no - 60.36.01

Remove

1. Raise the vehicle.

WARNING: Support on safety stands.

2. Remove scrivet from rear lower edge of front wheel arch liner. Lift liner for access to height sensor multiplug.

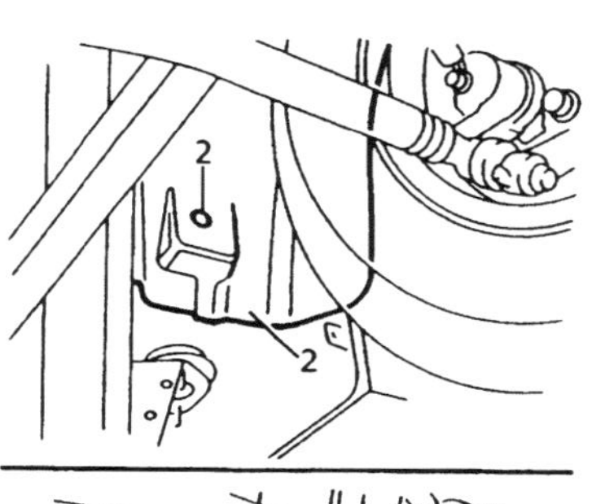

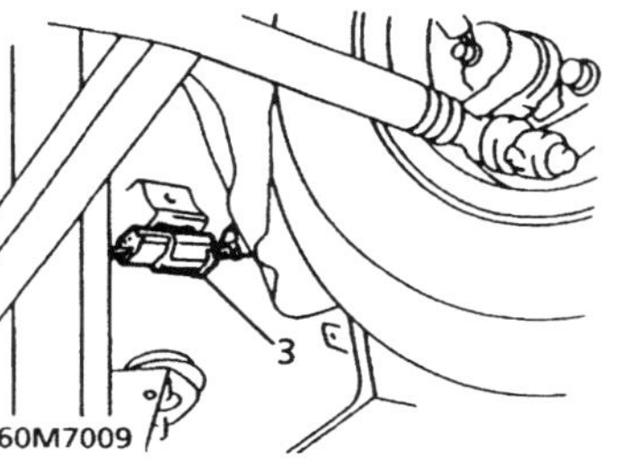

60M7009

3. Disconnect multiplug.
4. Release sensor link from radius arm.

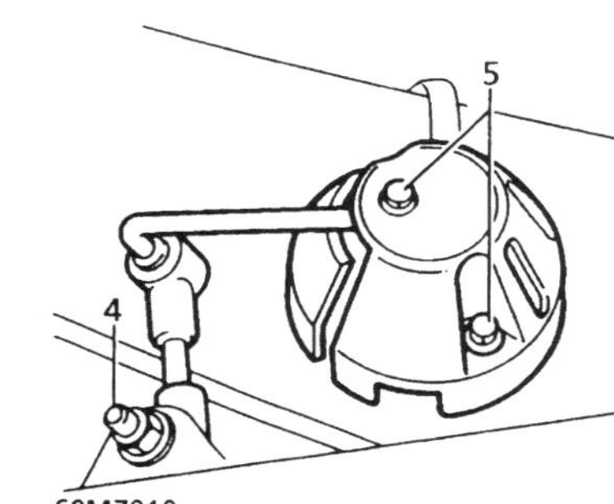

60M7010

5. Remove 2 bolts and remove sensor and sensor cover.
6. Remove cover from sensor.

Refit

7. Fit cover to sensor.
8. Fit sensor, tighten bolts to ***12 Nm. (9 lbf.ft)***

CAUTION: Ensure bolts pass through cover and sensor.

9. Fit sensor link to radius arm. Tighten to ***8 Nm. (6 lbf.ft)***
10. Reverse removal procedure.
11. Recalibrate system if a new sensor has been fitted ***See this section.***

HEIGHT SENSOR - 97 MY ON

Service repair no - 60.36.01

Remove

WARNING: Ensure air suspension is made safe before commencing work. Chassis may otherwise lower onto axle bump stops during repair.

1. Raise front of chassis and position LRT-60-003 between bump stop and axle.
2. Lower chassis onto LRT-60-003.
3. Raise front of vehicle.

WARNING: Support on safety stands.

60M7052

4. Remove 2 bolts securing heat shield to height sensor.
5. Remove heat shield.

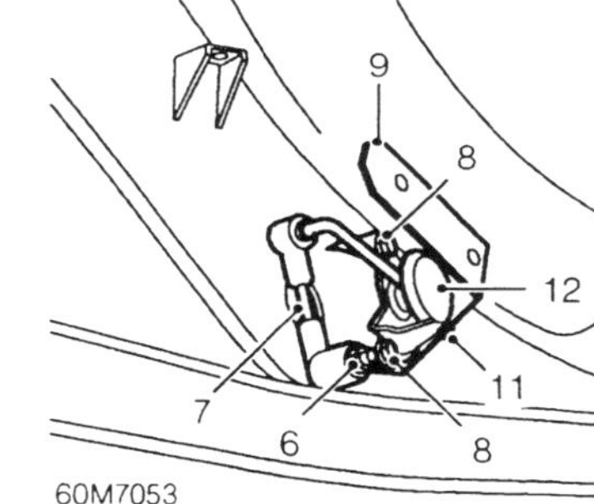

60M7053

6. Remove nut securing height sensor lever arm to radius arm.
7. Release sensor lever arm from radius arm.
8. Remove 2 bolts securing height sensor to chassis.
9. Collect heat shield mounting bracket and 2 washers.
10. Position height sensor cover to gain access to height sensor multiplug.
11. Disconnect multiplug and remove height sensor assembly.
12. Remove cover from height sensor.

Refit

13. Fit cover to height sensor.
14. Fit bolts and washers to height sensor assembly.
15. Position height sensor to chassis and connect multiplug.
16. Position heat shield bracket, fit height sensor assembly and tighten bolts to ***6 Nm. (4 lbf.ft)***.
17. Engage sensor lever arm to radius arm, fit nut and tighten to ***8 Nm (6 lbf.ft)***.
18. Position heat shield to bracket, fit bolts and tighten to ***6 Nm (4 lbf.ft)***.
19. Remove stand(s) and lower vehicle.
20. Raise chassis and remove LRT-60-003.
21. Lower chassis.
22. Recalibrate system using TestBook if a new sensor has been fitted.

DRIVE SHAFT AND HUB ASSEMBLY

Service repair no - 60.25.01

Remove

NOTE: This procedure gives removal instructions for the drive shaft and oil seal, plus the hub, bearing and drive flange assembly.

1. Remove centre cap from front wheel, release stake from drive shaft nut. Slacken nut.

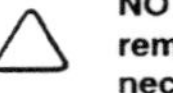

NOTE: If the hub and drive shaft are to be removed as an assembly, it is not necessary to slacken the drive shaft nut.

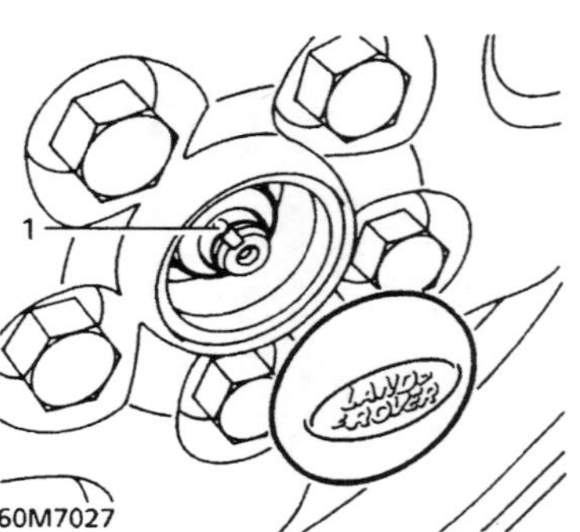

60M7027

2. Raise the vehicle.

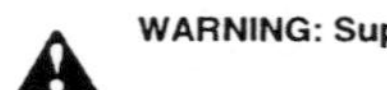

WARNING: Support on safety stands.

3. Remove brake disc shield. ***See BRAKES, Repair.***
4. Release ABS sensor harness from brackets on hub and axle.
5. Release sensor from hub.
6. Remove sensor bush.

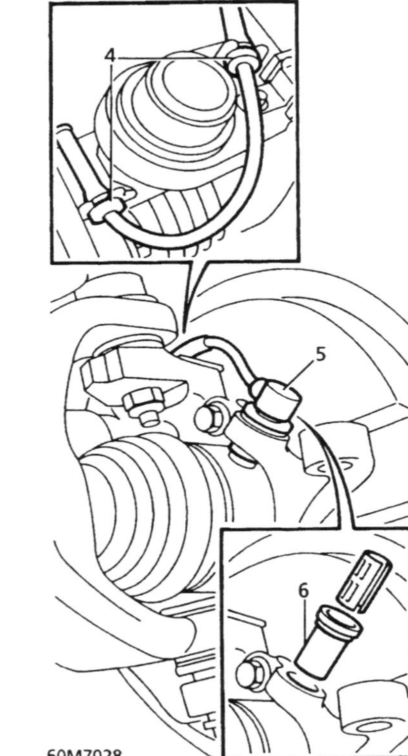

60M7028

7. Remove 4 bolts securing hub to carrier.

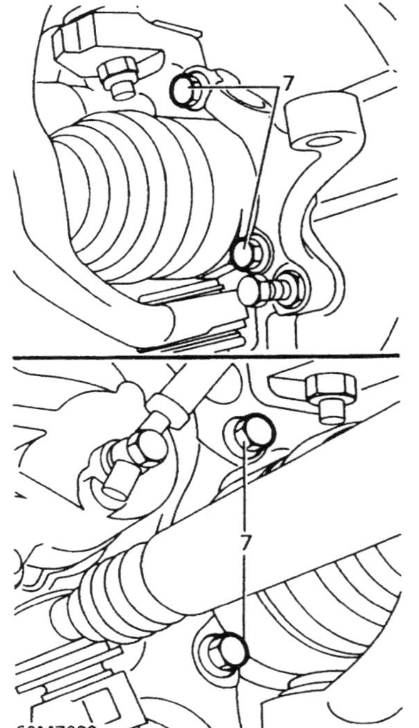

60M7029

8. Release hub from carrier. Remove hub and drive shaft assembly.
9. Remove drive shaft nut. Remove shaft assembly from hub.

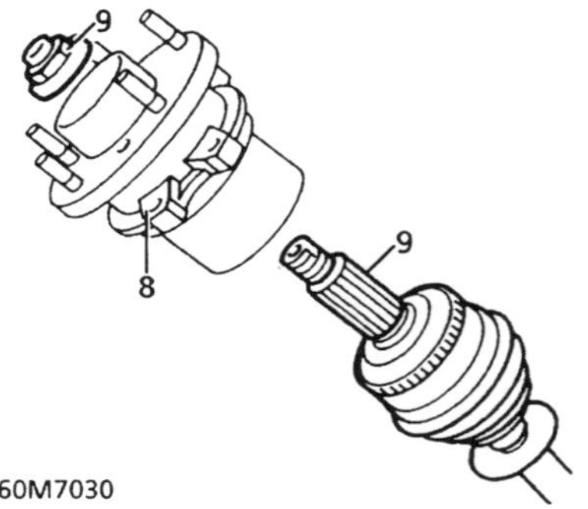
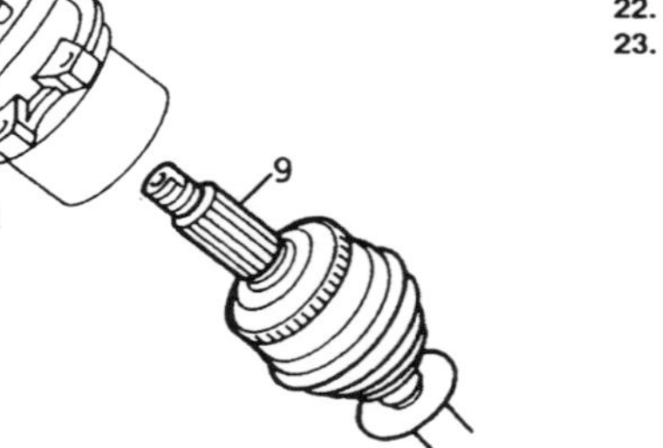

60M7030

10. Remove drive shaft seal from axle casing.

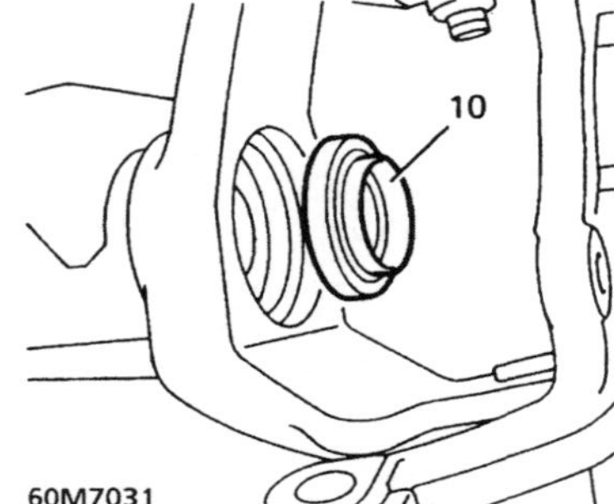

60M7031

Refit

11. Clean ABS sensor and location. Clean drive shaft and its seal location. Clean hub bearing carrier and its location in hub.
12. Lubricate oil seal lip and its running surface on drive shaft.
13. Fit oil seal to axle case, using service tool LRT-51-012.
14. Fit drive shaft to hub. Fit stake nut, do not tighten.
15. Fit hub and drive shaft assembly. Fit bolts. Tighten to ***135 Nm (100lbf.ft)***
16. Lightly grease ABS sensor and bush, using the correct silicone grease. ***See LUBRICANTS, FLUIDS AND CAPACITIES, Information.***
17. Fit ABS sensor bush.
18. Fit ABS sensor fully into bush, secure lead to brackets.
19. Fit brake disc shield. ***See BRAKES, Repair.***
20. Tighten drive shaft nut to ***260 Nm. (192 lbf.ft)***
21. Stake the nut.
22. Fit road wheel centre.
23. Remove safety stands. Lower vehicle.

ANTI-ROLL BAR LINK

Service repair no - 60.10.02

Remove

1. Raise the vehicle.

WARNING: Support on safety stands.

2. Remove nuts securing link to chassis and anti-roll bar.

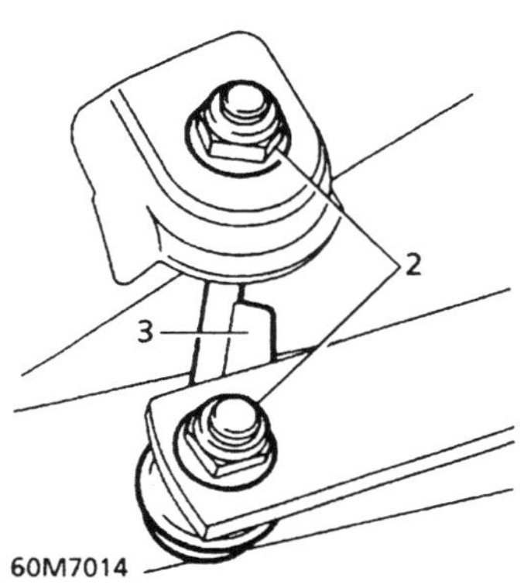

60M7014

3. Remove link.

Refit

4. Fit link to anti-roll bar and chassis.
5. Fit securing nuts. Tighten to ***125 Nm. (92 lbf.ft)***
6. Remove safety stands. Lower vehicle.

PANHARD ROD AND BUSHES

Service repair no - 60.10.10. Panhard rod
Service repair no - 60.10.07. Bushes

Remove

1. Raise the vehicle.

WARNING: Support on safety stands.

2. Remove nut and bolt securing panhard rod to chassis.

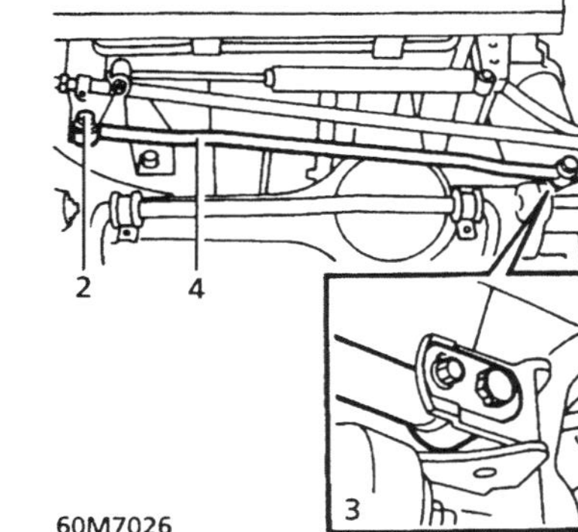

60M7026

3. Remove locking plate screw, locking plate and bolt securing panhard rod to axle.
4. Remove panhard rod.
5. Press out bushes from rod.

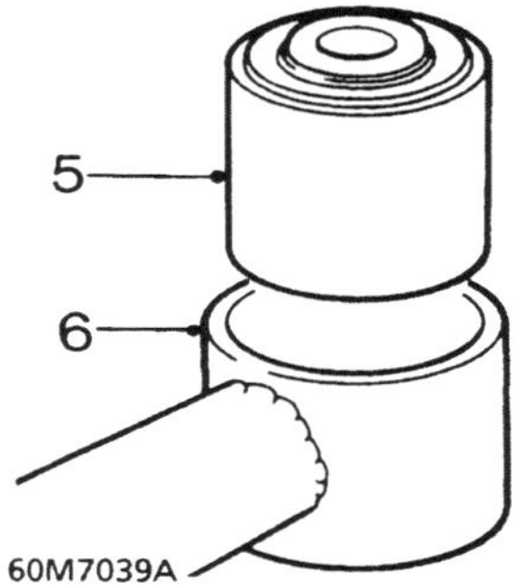

5
6
60M7039A

Refit

6. Clean bush mating faces in rod.
7. Fit replacement bushes centrally in rod.

CAUTION: When pressing in the new bushes ensure that pressure is applied to ONLY the outer edge of the bush, NOT to the rubber inner.

8. Fit panhard rod to axle and chassis.
9. Fit securing nut and bolt. Tighten to ***200Nm. (148 lbf.ft)***
10. Fit securing bolt. Tighten to ***200 Nm. (148 lbf.ft)***
11. Fit locking plate and secure with screw. Tighten screw Tighten to ***20Nm (15 lbf.ft)***
12. Remove safety stands. Lower vehicle.

RADIUS ARM AND BUSHES

Service repair no - 60.10.16

Remove

1. Depressurise air suspension. ***See this section.***
2. Remove anti-roll bar. ***See this section.***
3. Remove front road wheel.
4. Remove nut, disconnect track rod from swivel hub. Move rod aside.
5. Remove nut, disconnect height sensor link from radius arm.
6. Support axle on a jack.
7. Remove nuts and bolts securing radius arm to axle.

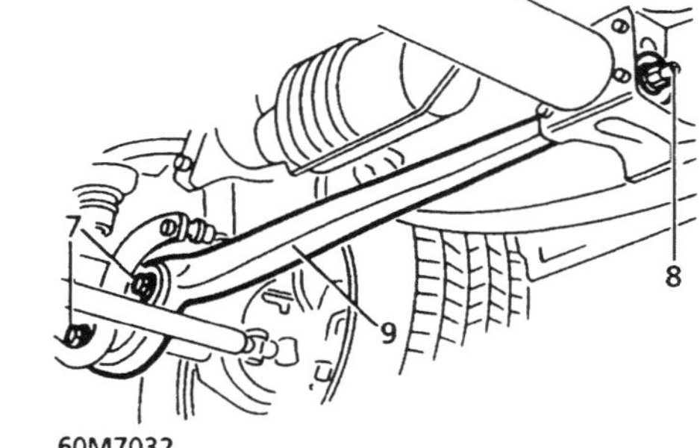

60M7032

8. Remove nut securing radius arm to chassis bracket.
9. Remove radius arm.
10. Press bushes from radius arm using LRT-60-004.

60M7024

Refit

11. Clean radius arm, lubricate bushes and their mating faces.
12. Fit rubber bushes using LRT-60-004.

60M7025

13. Fit radius arm and tighten chassis fixings to ***160 Nm. (118 lbf.ft)***
14. Tighten fixings to axle to ***125 Nm. (92 lbf.ft)***
15. Fit anti-roll bar, connect height sensor link and track rod.
16. Remove safety stands. Lower vehicle.
17. Repressurise air suspension.

SHOCK ABSORBER

Service repair no - 60.30.02

Remove

WARNING: Unrestricted movement of a pressurised air spring will result in failure of the assembly, causing component damage and possible personal injury. It is possible to remove the shock absorber without depressurising air springs, BUT the distance between the axle and chassis must be held as if the shock absorber was still fitted. This is achieved by supporting the vehicle on safety stands, with a jack under the axle.

1. Raise the vehicle.

WARNING: Support on safety stands.

2. Support axle on jack.
3. Remove front road wheel.

WARNING: Do not lower axle when shock absorber is removed. This may result in air spring damage.

4. Remove lower shock absorber retaining nut.

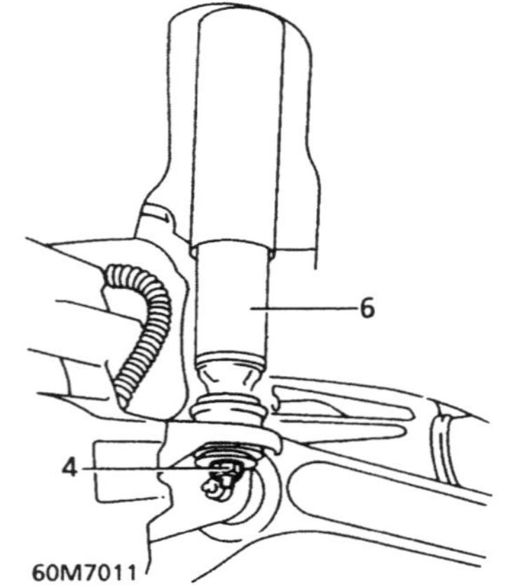
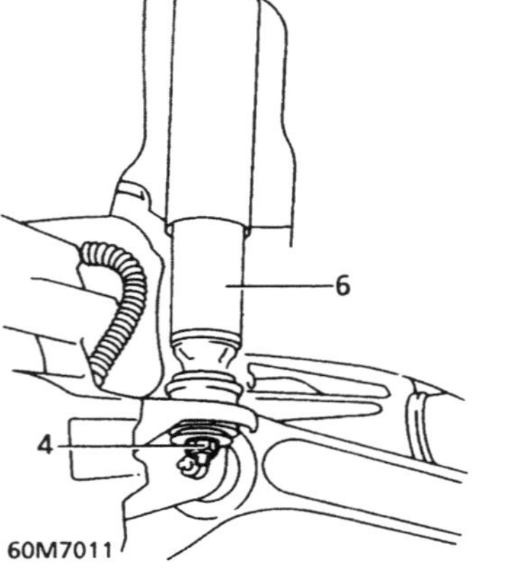

60M7011

5. Remove upper shock absorber retaining bolt.

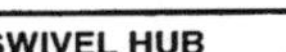

60M7012

6. Remove shock absorber.

Refit

7. Fit shock absorber.
8. Fit upper and lower fixings. Ensure lower mounting rubbers are fitted as shown.

60M7013A

9. Tighten upper retaining bolt to ***125 Nm. (92 lbf.ft)***
10. Tighten lower retaining nut to ***45 Nm. (33 lbf.ft)***
11. Refit front road wheel, tighten nuts to ***108 Nm. (80 lbf.ft)*** .
12. Remove jack.
13. Remove safety stands. Lower vehicle.

SWIVEL HUB

Service repair no - 60.15.19

Remove

1. Remove front hub and drive shaft assembly. ***See this section.***
2. Remove 2 nuts securing track rod and drag link to swivel hub.
3. Break taper joints, move track rod and drag link aside.
4. Remove 2 nuts securing joints to swivel hub.
5. Break taper joints using LRT-54-009 and remove swivel hub. If joint pin turns in taper, use a 6mm Allen key to restrain.

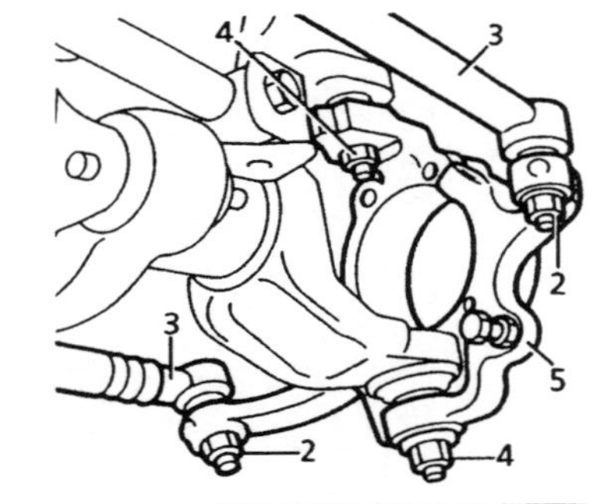
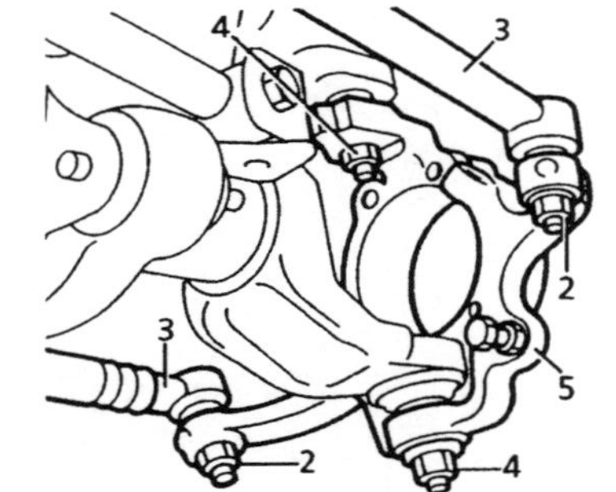

60M0509

6. Remove taper collet from swivel hub.

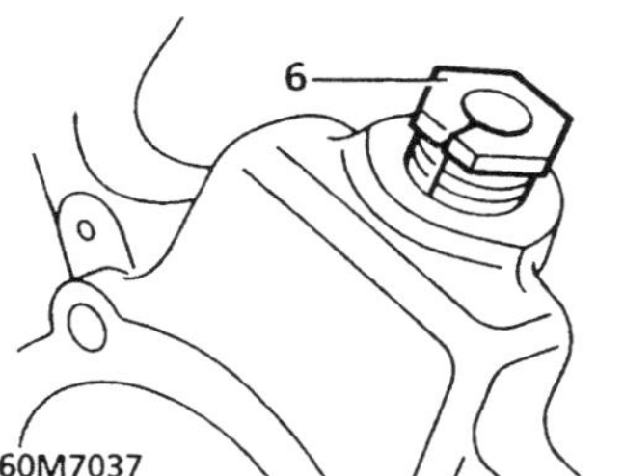

60M7037

Refit

7. Clean taper registers in swivel hub and collet.
8. Fit taper collet into swivel, until a 4 mm (0.16 in) gap exists between the shoulder of the collet and the swivel.
9. Fit swivel hub to axle. Fit upper joint nut. Holding joint with Allen key, tighten nut to ***110 Nm. (81 lbf.ft).***
10. Clean seal register in axle case.
11. Turn clamp screw of LRT-54-006/1 fully anti-clockwise. Ensure that clamp toggle rotates freely. Locate tool into axle casing with 'TOP' mark upwards.

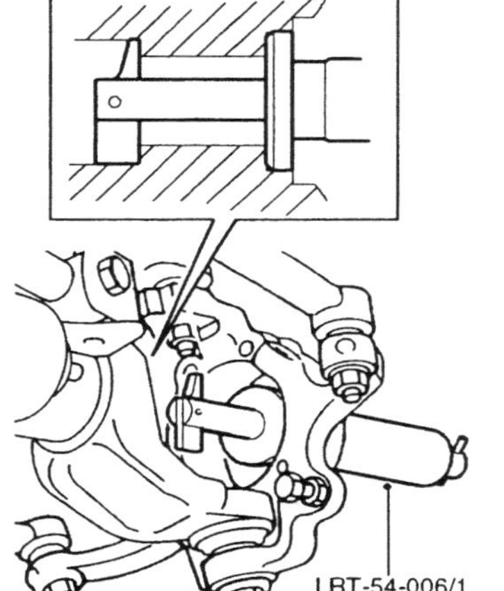

60M0511

12. Ensure tool is located correctly in seal register, tighten clamp screw. Using a copper mallet, tap end of clamp screw to ensure correct seating. Tighten clamp screw if necessary.
13. Fit and tighten lower swivel joint nut until the taper is seated in the collet, but the collet can still turn. Adjust the height of the hub using taper collet until LRT-54-006/2 is a sliding fit in hub.

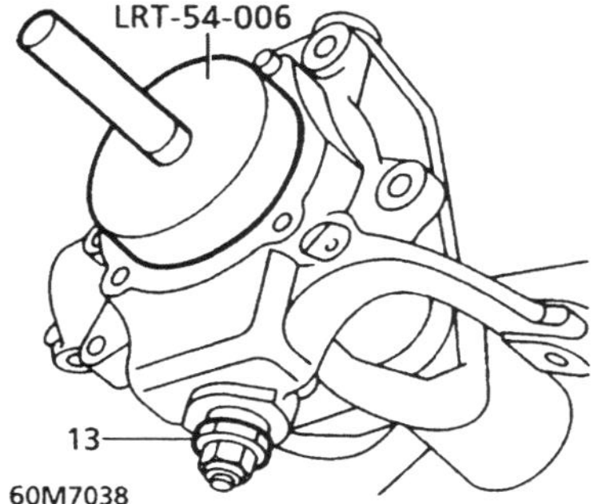

60M7038

14. Remove LRT-54-006/2. Tighten collet 1.25 turns to allow for further seating into taper when tightening lower swivel joint nut.
15. Tighten lower swivel joint nut. Tighten to ***135 Nm. (100 lbf.ft).***
16. Check adjustment of swivel hub using LRT-54-006/2.
17. If swivel hub is out of adjustment, loosen lower swivel joint nut, break taper. Reseat taper into collet, turn collet as required. If swivel hub is high, tighten collet, if it is low, loosen collet. Retorque lower swivel nut. Recheck adjustment using tool LRT-54-006/2.
18. Loosen clamp screw, remove LRT-54-006/1 from axle casing.
19. Clean drag link and track rod end mating faces, connect to swivel hub.
20. Tighten track rod and drag link nuts to ***80 Nm. (59 lbf.ft)***
21. Fit front hub and drive shaft assembly. ***See this section.***

SWIVEL HUB - CHECK/ADJUST

Service repair no - 60.15.13

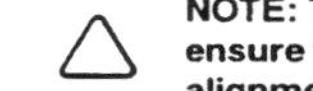

NOTE: This procedure must be followed to ensure the axle assembly is in correct alignment with the swivel hub. Incorrect adjustment may result in oil seal failure. The check is carried out with drive shaft assembly and oil seal removed.

1. Clean seal register in axle case.
2. Turn clamp screw of LRT-54-006/1 fully anti-clockwise. Locate tool into axle casing with 'TOP' mark upwards.

LRT-54-006/1

60M0511

NOTE: Ensure that clamp toggle rotates freely.

3. Ensure tool is correctly located in seal register, tighten clamp. Using a copper mallet, tap end of clamp screw to ensure correct seating. Tighten clamp screw if necessary.
4. Insert LRT-54-006/2 to check height of hub. Adjustment is correct if the tool is a sliding fit in hub.

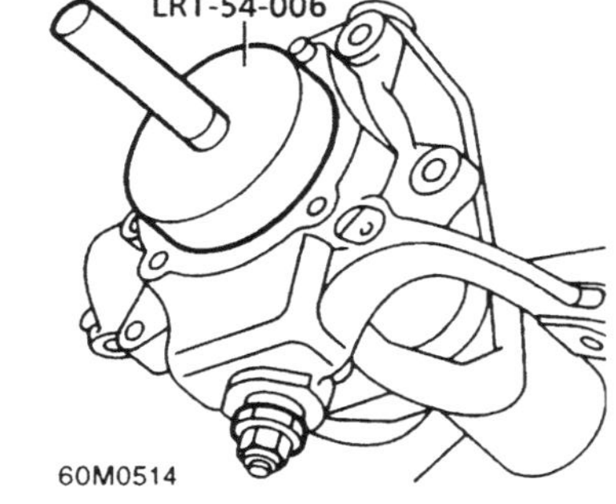

60M0514

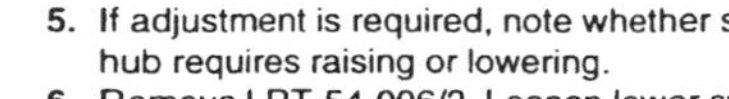

5. If adjustment is required, note whether swivel hub requires raising or lowering.
6. Remove LRT-54-006/2. Loosen lower swivel joint nut, break taper.
7. Reseat taper into collet, tighten lower swivel joint nut until the taper is seated in the collet, but the collet can still turn.
8. Turn collet as required. If swivel hub is high, tighten collet, if it is low, loosen collet. Note that the thread on the collet is very fine.
9. Tighten lower swivel joint nut. Tighten to ***135 Nm. (100 lbf.ft).***
10. Recheck adjustment using tool LRT-54-006/2. Repeat procedure if necessary.
11. Loosen clamp screw, remove LRT-54-006/1 from axle casing.
12. Fit hub and drive shaft assembly. ***See this section.***

BALL JOINT - UPPER

Service repair no - 60.15.02

CAUTION: Each ball joint can be replaced up to three times before the axle yoke bore becomes oversize. before commencing work, clean surrounding area of joint to be renewed and check for yellow paint marks. If any more than 2 marks are found, axle case must be renewed.

Remove

1. Remove swivel hub. ***See this section.***
2. Fit adaptor LRT-54-008/4 to base tool and secure with screw.
3. Fit base tool to upper joint.
4. Fit adaptor LRT-54-008/5.
5. Press upper joint from axle.

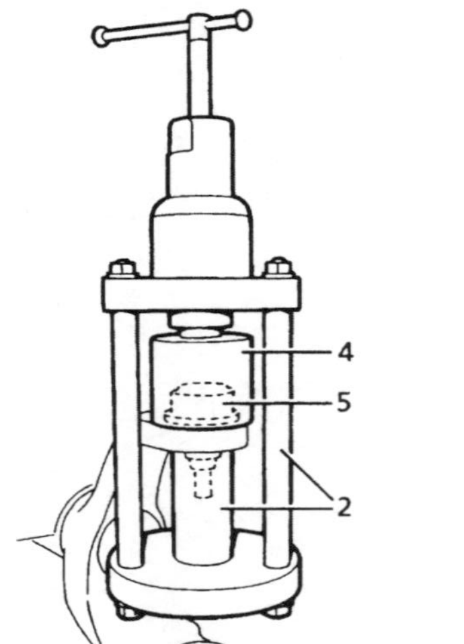

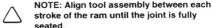

60M7045

NOTE: When ram leadscrew reaches end of stroke, retract leadscrew, screw ram into base tool and repeat operation until joint is free from axle yoke.

6. Remove screw and collect adaptor from base tool.

Refit

7. Clean joint location and surrounding area of axle yoke.
8. Make a 12mm wide yellow paint stripe on axle yoke, adjacent to joint location.
9. Fit adaptor LRT-54-008/8 to base tool and secure with screw.
10. Position joint to axle yoke.
11. Fit LRT-54-008/7 to base tool and position base tool assembly over joint and axle.

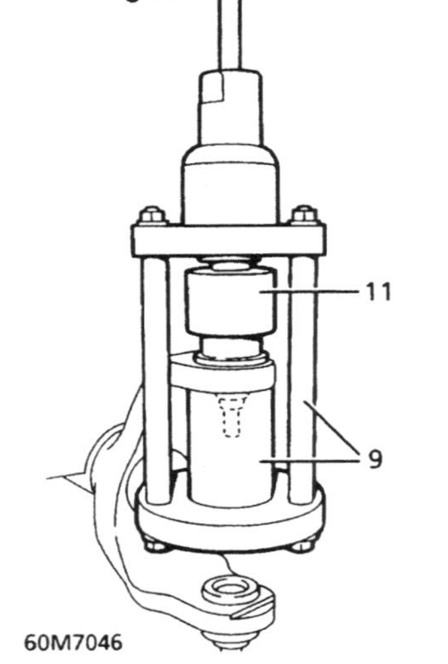
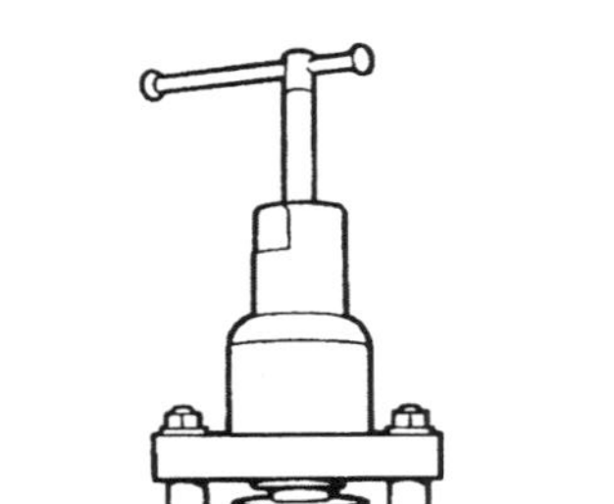

60M7046

12. Align tool assembly and press joint into axle.

NOTE: Align tool assembly between each stroke of the ram until the joint is fully seated.

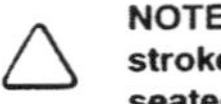

CAUTION: Damage to joint boot will result if tool is not correctly aligned during fitment.

13. Remove base tool assembly.
14. Fit swivel hub. ***See this section.***

BALL JOINT - LOWER

Service repair no - 60.15.03

CAUTION: Each ball joint can be replaced up to three times before the axle yoke bore becomes oversize. before commencing work, clean surrounding area of joint to be renewed and check for yellow paint marks. If more than 2 marks are found, axle case must be renewed.

Remove

1. Remove swivel hub, ***See this section.***
2. Fit adaptor LRT-54-008/10 to base tool and secure with screw.
3. Fit adaptor LRT-54-008/11 to underside of lower joint.
4. With assistance, fit base tool assembly onto joint.
5. Press lower joint from axle.

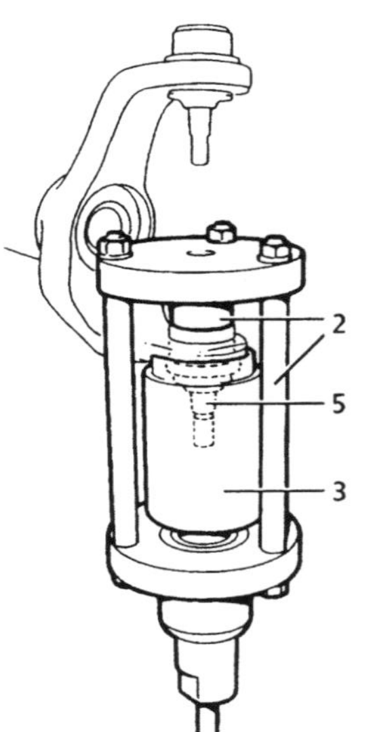

60M7047

NOTE: When ram leadscrew reaches end of stroke, retract leadscrew, screw ram into base tool and repeat operation until joint is free from axle yoke.

6. Remove screw and collect adaptor from base tool.

Refit

7. Clean joint location and surrounding area of axle yoke.
8. Make a 12mm wide yellow paint stripe on axle yoke, adjacent to joint location.
9. Fit adaptor LRT-54-008/13 to base tool and secure with screw.
10. Position base tool assembly to axle yoke.
11. Fit lower joint to adaptor LRT-54-008/14

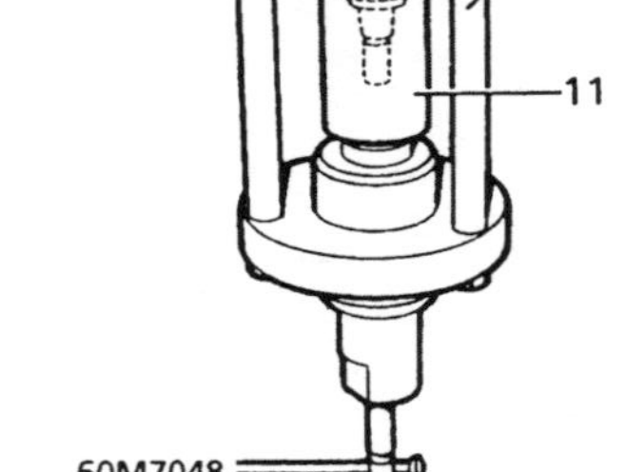
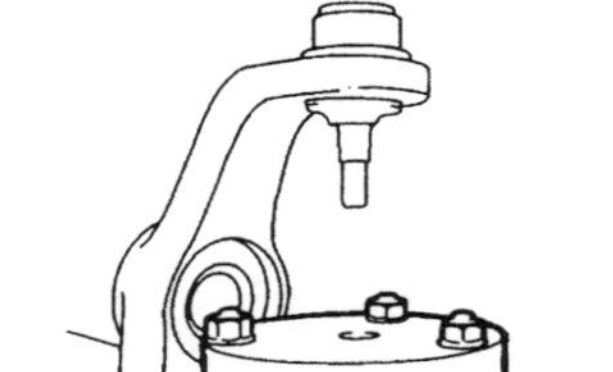

60M7048

12. Fit adaptor and joint assembly onto base tool.
13. Align tool assembly and press joint into axle.

NOTE: Align tool assembly between each stroke of the ram until the joint is fully seated.

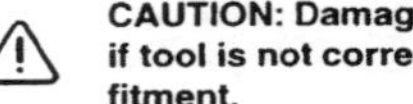

CAUTION: Damage to joint boot will result if tool is not correctly aligned during fitment.

14. Remove base tool assembly.
15. Fit swivel hub. ***See this section.***

SOLENOID VALVE BLOCK AND DRIVE PACK

Service repair no - 60.50.07 - Pressure switch
Service repair no - 60.50.42 - Solenoid valve drive pack
Service repair no - 60.50.11 - Valve block
Service repair no - 60.50.44 - Air supply unit

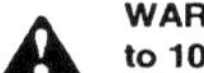

WARNING: The system is pressurised up to 10 bar. Dirt or grease must not enter the system. Wear hand, ear and eye safety standard protection when servicing system.

Remove

Petrol Vehicles Only:

1. Disconnect vacuum dump hose from 'T' piece on cruise control actuator.
2. Remove 2 screws securing actuator bracket to air supply unit. Move actuator aside.

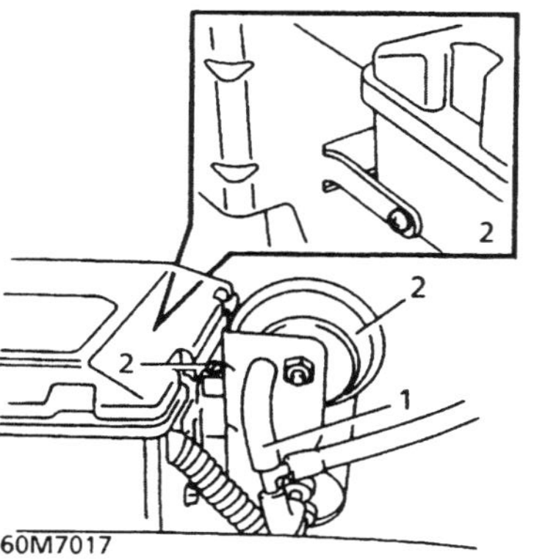

60M7017

All Models:

3. Depressurise system. ***See this section.***
4. Remove air compressor. ***See this section.***
5. Disconnect all air pipes. Remove exhaust silencer from valve block.

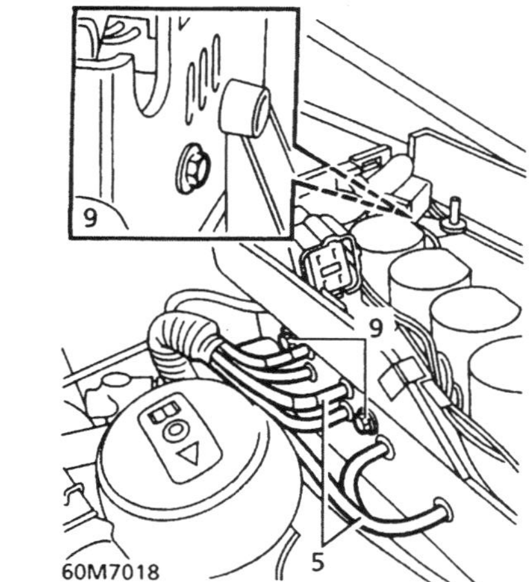

60M7018

6. Seal exposed air hoses and valve block.
7. Release harness from 2 clips inside air supply unit. Disconnect multiplug from valve block, move harness aside.
8. Release valve block multiplug and clips from unit.
9. Remove 3 screws, remove valve block from unit.

Pressure Switch

10. Disconnect pressure switch multiplug.

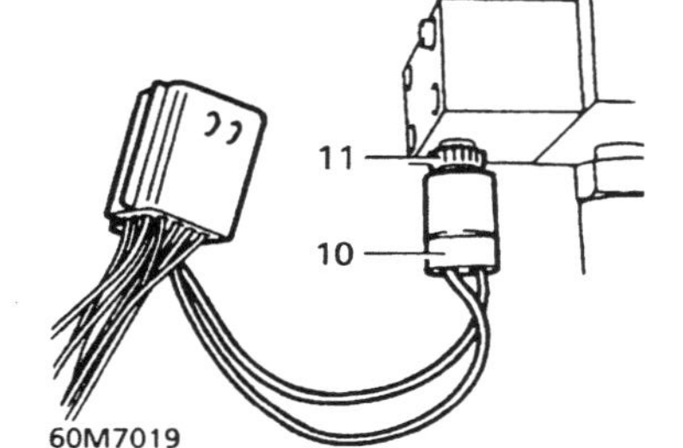

60M7019

11. Remove pressure switch.
12. Seal switch and valve block.

Drive Pack

13. Remove 4 screws securing drive pack to valve block.

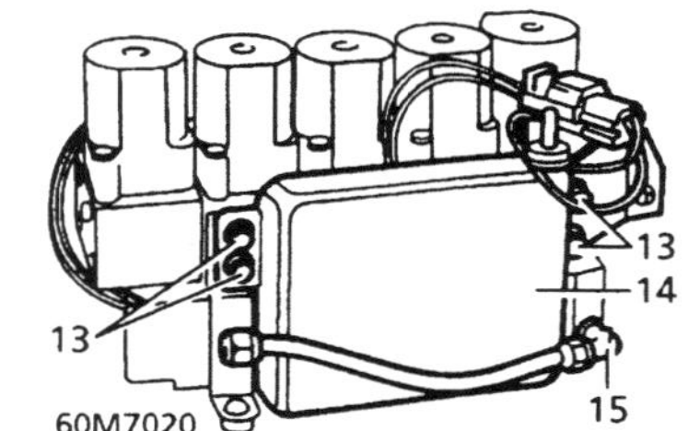

60M7020

14. Disconnect 2 drive pack multiplugs, remove drive pack.

Valve Block

15. Remove compressor hose from valve block.
16. Seal exposed hose and valve block.
17. Remove rear support bracket from multiplug.

Air Supply Unit

18. Remove 4 bolts securing air supply unit, remove unit.

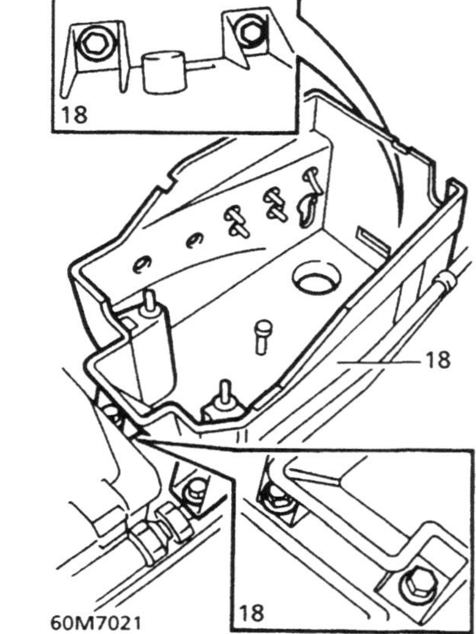

60M7021

Refit

19. Fit air supply unit, fit and tighten bolts.
20. Remove seals from compressor hose and valve block. Clean end of hose, fit hose to valve block and tighten union nut.
21. Position drive pack to valve block, connect multiplugs.
22. Align drive pack to valve block. Fit support brackets, fit and tighten Allen screws.
23. Remove seals from pressure switch and valve block.
24. Clean pressure switch, apply LOCTITE 572 to thread of switch. Fit switch to valve block. Tighten to ***23 Nm. (17 lbf.ft)***
25. Connect pressure switch leeds to multiplug.
26. Fit valve block and drive pack assembly to air supply unit. Secure with bolts.

27. Secure valve block multiplug to case, fit harness clip.
28. Remove all seals from valve block and pipes. Clean pipe ends, connect pipes to valve block.
29. Fit exhaust silencer to valve block with new O ring.

CAUTION: New exhaust silencers are supplied with a protective sleeve, which must be removed and discarded prior to fitting the silencer.

30. Reposition harness to valve block and unit, ensuring valve block multiplug passes under compressor multiplug. Connect multiplugs, secure harness to clips.
31. Fit compressor. ***See this section.***

Petrol Models Only:

32. Reposition cruise control actuator. Fit and tighten screws.
33. Connect servo vacuum dump hose to 'T' piece.

All models:

34. Leak test connections. ***See this section.***

SOLENOID COIL

Service repair no - 60.50.48

NOTE: Solenoid 'A', which has blue fly-leads, is not serviceable.

Remove

1. Remove valve block assembly. ***See this section.***
2. Identify solenoid coil to be removed.
3. Disconnect solenoid coil multiplug.
4. Clean area around solenoid coil and valve block.

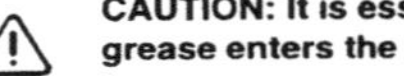

CAUTION: It is essential that no dirt or grease enters the system.

5. Remove 2 screws securing coil to valve block.
6. Release coil from valve block. Collect and discard 'O' ring seal.

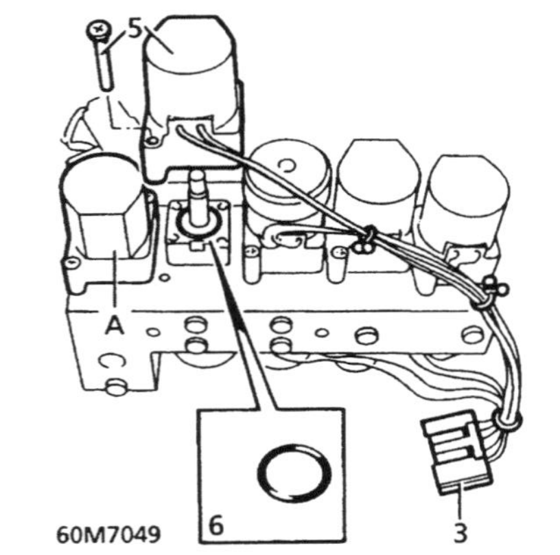

60M7049

7. Remove face protector from connector.

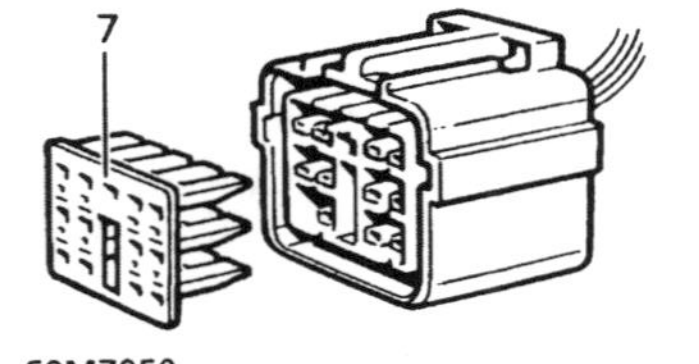

60M7050

8. Identify correct wires at multiplug.
9. Use the wires to push the terminals forward.
10. Using a suitable sharp tool, gently lift the locking tags.

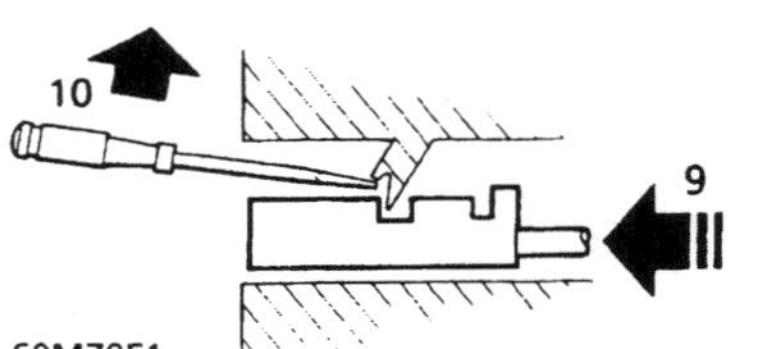

60M7051

11. With the tags held, gently pull rearwards on the wires until the terminals are extracted.

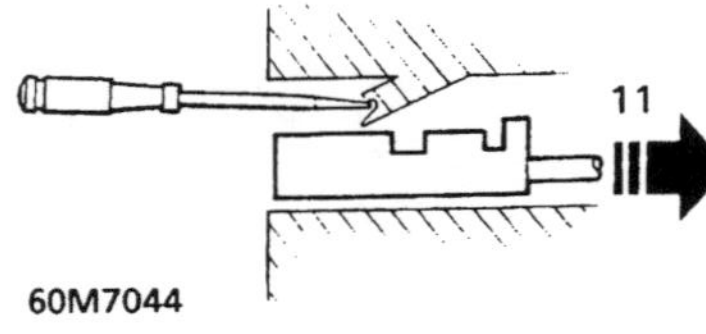

60M7044

12. Release harness clips as necessary.
13. Remove solenoid coil.

Refit

14. Fit new 'O' ring to valve block and position valve.
15. Coat threads of screws with Loctite 242. Tighten to ***1.3 Nm (1 lbf.ft)***
16. Fully engage pins into correct connector locations.
17. Secure harness ties as necessary.

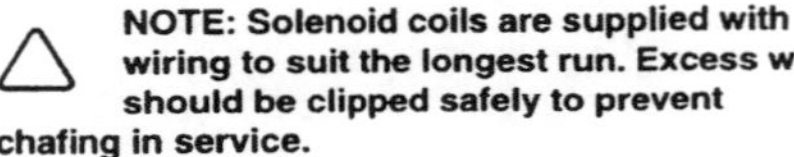

NOTE: Solenoid coils are supplied with wiring to suit the longest run. Excess wire should be clipped safely to prevent chafing in service.

18. Fit valve block assembly. ***See this section.***

CONTENTS

Page

ELECTRONIC AIR SUSPENSION

DESCRIPTION AND OPERATION

FAULT DIAGNOSIS

REPAIR

REAR SUSPENSION

Description

The rear suspension design locates the rear axle with two lightweight composite radius arms (1) and a panhard rod (2). The system allows maximum axle articulation and wheel travel while maintaining roll stiffness, directional stability and vehicle refinement. The composite radius arm is mounted to the chassis through a ferrule rubber bush and to the axle using a 'sealed for life' isolation rubber.

The vehicle height sensors are also linked to the radius arms; for full details of the height settings. ***See FRONT SUSPENSION, Description and operation.*** The panhard rod is mounted to the chassis through ferrule rubber bushes as shown in 64M7005.

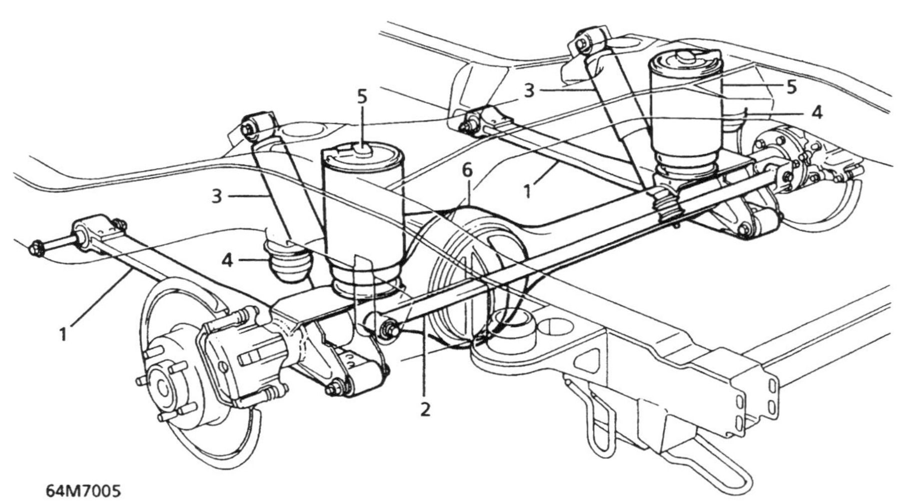

Rear axle suspension

1. Radius arms
2. Panhard rod
3. Shock absorbers
4. Bump stops
5. Air springs
6. Rear axle

Conventional telescopic shock absorbers (3) used to control body movement, are secured to the chassis cross frame and a fabricated lower mounting, welded to the axle, that also supports the radius arms. The upper fixing comprises a single bolt passing through a ferrule rubber bush. The lower fixing of the shock absorber comprises of a stem type mount with two rubber bushes and support washers, secured to the axle mounting with a single retaining nut.

Celular foam bump stops (4) are fitted under the chassis adjacent to the air springs and prevent any possible damage that could occur should there be excessive axle to chassis movement. Should there be a loss of air pressure in the air springs (5) the vehicle can still be driven safely, at a speed not exceeding 35mph (56kph), with the bump stops resting on the axle, although this will result in a hard ride. The loss of air pressure should be investigated as soon as possible. 'Progressive' bump stops are used and will reform from a compressed state when the load is released.

REAR SUSPENSION FAULTS

This section covers possible mechanical, fuse and relay faults that could occur in the rear suspension system, including air suspension components. Visual checks of components within the system and relevant fuses and relays should be carried out before undertaking detailed fault diagnosis procedures, which are covered on **TestBook** .

1. Symptom - Hard Ride.

POSSIBLE CAUSE	REMEDY
1. Seized or inoperable rear shock absorber/s.	1. Renew shock absorber/s. ***See Repair.***
2. Loss of air pressure in the air system resulting in the chassis bump stops resting on the front rear axle.	2. Check air system components for faults and air harness for leaks etc. ***See FRONT SUSPENSION, Repair.*** Rectify or renew components where necessary.
3. Contaminated or fouled suspension components with off road debris.	3. Remove/clean off debris and check for damage. Renew components where necessary.
4. Incorrect ride height calibration.	4. Re-calibrate air suspension system. Refer to **TestBook** .

2. Symptom - Vehicle Suspension Permanently In 'Standard Height' Mode.

POSSIBLE CAUSE	REMEDY
1. Height sensor/s inoperative due to loose or disconnected multi-plug.	1. Reconnect multi-plug.
2. Height sensor linkage disconnected or damaged.	2. Reconnect or renew sensor linkage.
3. Faulty height sensor/s.	3. Renew height sensor/s. ***See Repair.***
4. Leaking air supply to air spring assembly.	4. Check air harness connections and pipes for damage or scoring.
5. Faulty/leaking air spring diaphragm.	5. Renew air spring assembly. ***See Repair.***
6. Faulty ABS speed sensor in ECU.	6. Refer to **TestBook** .
7. Faulty pressure switch.	7. Refer to **TestBook** .

3. Symptom - Excessive body roll at rear of vehicle.

POSSIBLE CAUSE	REMEDY
1. Worn or leaking shock absorber/s.	1. Renew shock absorber/s. ***See Repair.***
2. Worn radius arm bushes at chassis mounting.	2. Renew radius arm bushes. ***See Repair.***
3. Loose radius arm fixings.	3. Check and tighten all relevant fixings.
4. Deflated air spring.	4. Check air system components for faults and air harness for leaks etc. ***See FRONT SUSPENSION, Repair.*** Rectify or renew components where necessary.
5. Faulty valve block.	5. Refer to **TestBook** .
6. Damaged or broken chassis and/or axle mounting brackets.	6. Vehicle should be recovered and not driven.
7. Failed or loose body mountings giving excessive body movement to chassis.	7. Tighten fixings or renew rubber body mountings if failed.

4. Symptom - Suspension Knock.

POSSIBLE CAUSE	REMEDY
1. Loose or worn suspension component mountings and fixings.	1. Check, tighten or renew relevant components and fixings.

5. Symptom - Air System Faulty Or Inoperative.

POSSIBLE CAUSE	REMEDY
1. Blown air suspension system fuse.	1. Check and renew fuse F44.
2. Blown fuse covering dashboard 'height control' or 'inhibit' switch.	2. Check and renew fuse F17.
3. Faulty 'height control' switch; could result in vehicle height remaining at last setting until ignition switched off.	3. Refer to **TestBook** to confirm fault and renew 'height control' switch. ***See ELECTRICAL, Repair.***
4. Faulty 'inhibit' switch; could result in vehicle height not operating automatically between standard and low.	4. Refer to **TestBook** to confirm fault and renew 'inhibit' switch. ***See ELECTRICAL, Repair.***
5. Compressor inoperative; no air pressure due to loose or disconnected multi-plug.	5. Check and reconnect compressor multi-plug.
6. Blown compressor maxi fuse.	6. Check and renew maxi fuse 2.
7. Faulty compressor relay, resulting in compressor running continuously.	7. Renew relay RL20.
8. Loss of air pressure in the air system.	8. Check air system components for faults and air harness for leaks etc. ***See FRONT SUSPENSION, Repair.***
9. Height sensor linkage damaged or linkage mount on composite radius arm damaged.	9. Renew height sensor. Refer to Height sensor. ***See Repair.*** or Refer to Trailing arm. ***See Repair.***
10. Faulty delay relay. If the delay relay fails with a closed circuit the system will be powered, resulting in a flat battery.	10. Renew relay AMR3284.

6. Symptom - Vehicle Leaning Side To Side Or Front To Rear With Air Suspension Operative.

POSSIBLE CAUSE	REMEDY
1. Faulty height sensor.	1. Refer to **TestBook** to locate faulty height sensor. Renew height sensor and re-calibrate air suspension system. Refer to **TestBook** .
2. Incorrect height sensor calibration.	2. Re-calibrate air suspension system. Refer to **TestBook** .
3. Deflated rear air spring.	3. Check air system components for faults and air harness for leaks etc. ***See FRONT SUSPENSION, Repair.*** Rectify or renew components where necessary

NOTE: Critical warning messages relating to the air suspension system are displayed on the message centre, should a fault occur.

CHASSIS FIXINGS

CAUTION: Ensure all under body wax is removed from mating surfaces of fixings before fitting.

AIR SPRING - REAR

Service repair no - 64.21.01

Remove

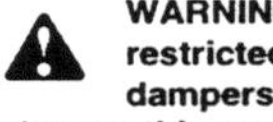

WARNING: Air suspension is pressurised up to 10 bar (150 psi). Dirt or grease must not enter the system. Wear hand, eye and ear standard protection when servicing system.

WARNING: The air spring must be restricted by suspension loading, with dampers fitted before inflation. Failure to observe this warning could result in air spring damage, resulting in component failure or personal injury. DO NOT ATTEMPT TO DISMANTLE AIR SPRING.

1. Remove wheel arch liner. ***See CHASSIS AND BODY, Repair.***
2. Support chassis under rear cross member. Depressurise suspension. ***See FRONT SUSPENSION, Repair.***
3. Using a suitable hooked tool, remove clip securing air spring to chassis.

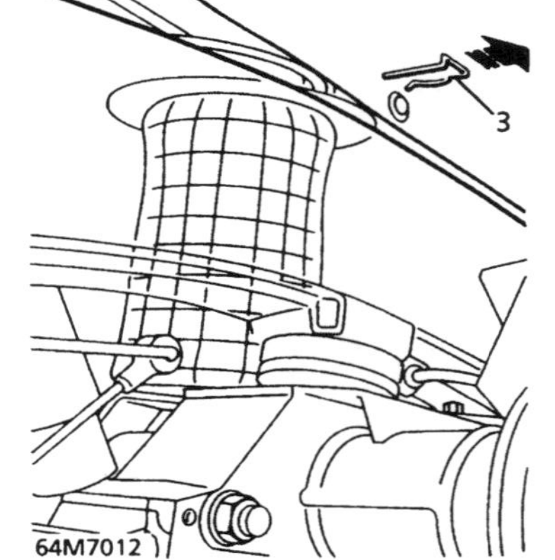

NOTE: Access to clip is under wheel arch between body and chassis.

4. Remove clip securing air spring to axle.

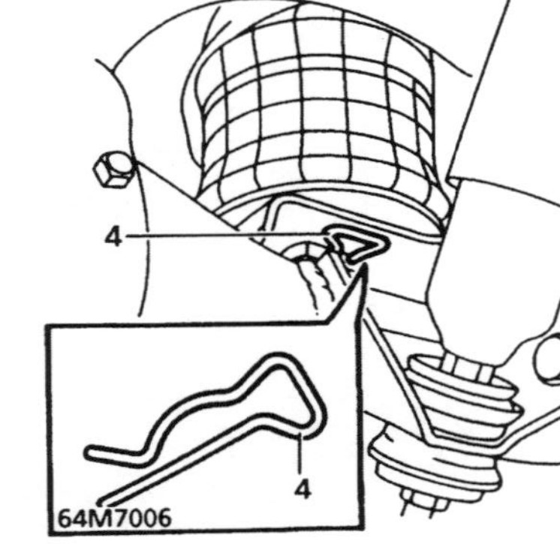

5. Raise chassis for clearance to remove spring. Resupport chassis.
6. Release air spring from chassis and axle for access to air pipe connection, clean connection and disconnect pipe.

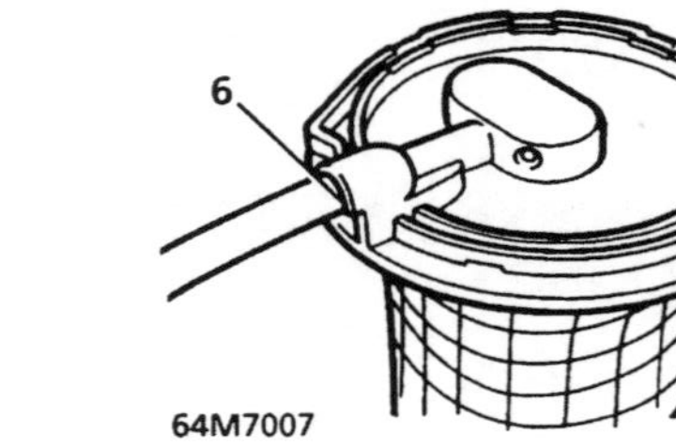

7. Seal pipe and air spring. Remove spring.

CAUTION: When refitting the air spring, DO NOT allow the vehicle to rest on the deflated air spring.
The chassis must be supported until the air spring is inflated.

Refit

8. Clean mating faces of axle, chassis and air spring.
9. Fit air spring, remove seal from spring and air pipe. Connect pipe to spring.
10. Align spring to chassis, with assistance fit securing clip.

CAUTION: Ensure air hose is correctly routed.

11. Remove support from chassis, lower spring onto axle and refit support.
12. Fit clip to secure spring to axle.
13. Carry out leak test. ***See FRONT SUSPENSION, Repair.***

BUMP STOP

Service repair no - 64.30.15

Remove

1. Raise the vehicle.

WARNING: Support on safety stands.

2. Remove bump stop from body.

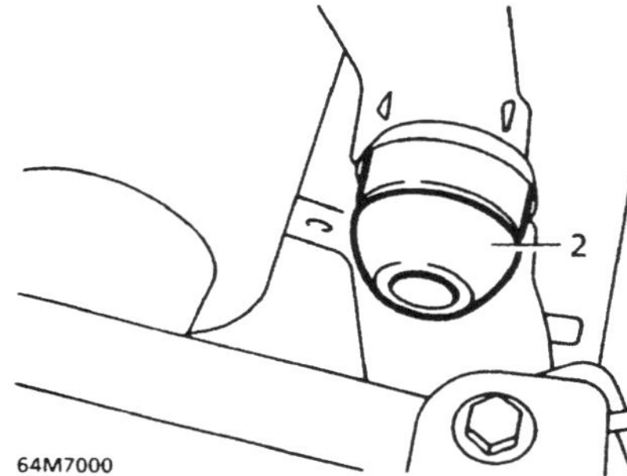

Refit

3. Fit bump stop.
4. Remove safety stands. Lower vehicle.

HEIGHT SENSOR - REAR

Service repair no - 64.36.01

Remove

1. Raise the vehicle.

WARNING: Support on safety stands.

2. Release height sensor multiplug from bracket on body. Disconnect multiplug from body harness.

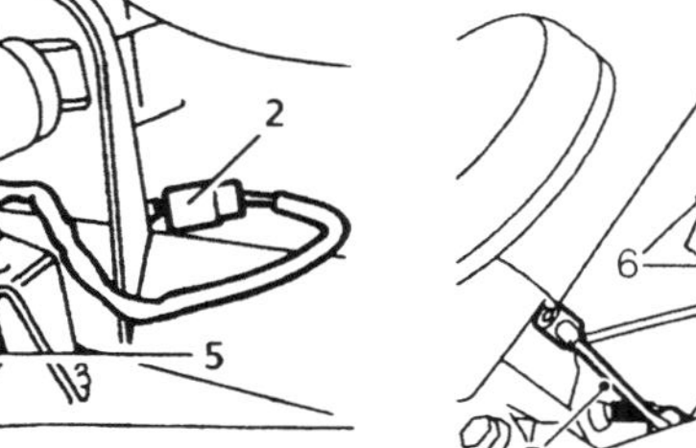

3. Disconnect height sensor link from trailing link.

CAUTION: Ensure that rubber mounting does not become damaged.

4. Remove 2 bolts securing height sensor to chassis.
5. Remove height sensor.

Refit

6. Fit height sensor to chassis, fit bolts. Tighten to ***12 Nm. (9 lbf.ft)***
7. Connect height sensor link to trailing link.
8. Connect height sensor multiplug to body harness. Secure multiplug to bracket on body. Ensure that cable is correctly routed around brackets.
9. Remove safety stands. Lower vehicle.
10. Recalibrate system if a new sensor has been fitted. ***See FRONT SUSPENSION, Repair.***

HEIGHT SENSOR - REAR - 97 MY ON

Service repair no - 64.36.01

Remove

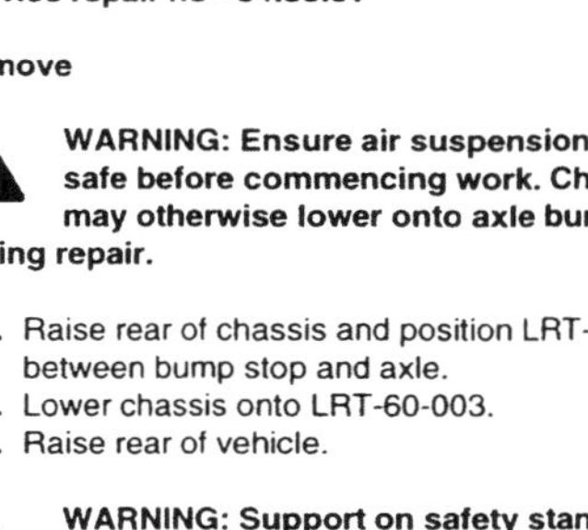

WARNING: Ensure air suspension is made safe before commencing work. Chassis may otherwise lower onto axle bump stops during repair.

1. Raise rear of chassis and position LRT-60-003 between bump stop and axle.
2. Lower chassis onto LRT-60-003.
3. Raise rear of vehicle.

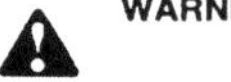

WARNING: Support on safety stands.

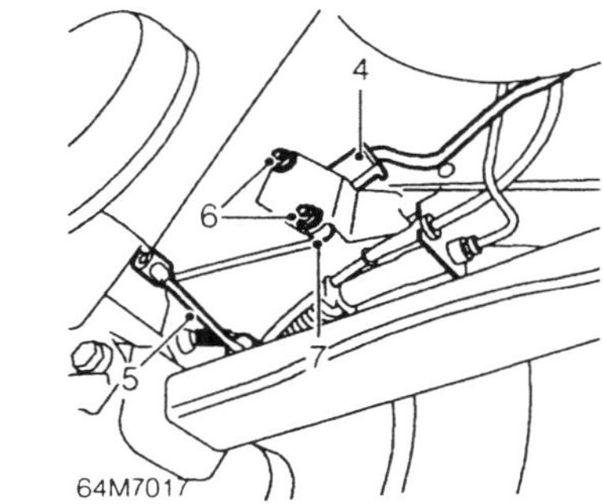

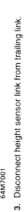

4. Disconnect multiplug from height sensor.
5. Disconnect height sensor lever arm from trailing arm.
6. Remove 2 nuts securing height sensor to chassis.
7. Remove height sensor.

Refit

8. Position height sensor to chassis.
9. Fit nuts and tighten to ***6 Nm. (4 lbf.ft)***
10. Connect height sensor lever arm to trailing arm.
11. Connect multiplug to height sensor.
12. Remove stand(s) and lower vehicle.
13. Raise chassis and remove LRT-60-003.
14. Lower chassis.
15. Recalibrate system using TestBook if a new sensor has been fitted.

DRIVE SHAFT AND HUB ASSEMBLY

Service repair no - 64.15.01

Remove

⚠ **NOTE: This procedure gives removal instructions for the drive shaft and oil seal, plus the hub, bearing and drive flange assembly.**

⚠ **NOTE: If the hub and drive shaft are to be removed as an assembly, it is not necessary to slacken the drive shaft nut.**

1. Remove centre cap from front wheel, release stake from drive shaft nut. Slacken nut.
2. Remove brake disc shield. ***See BRAKES, Repair.***
3. Remove 2 bolts, remove backplate strap from hub.

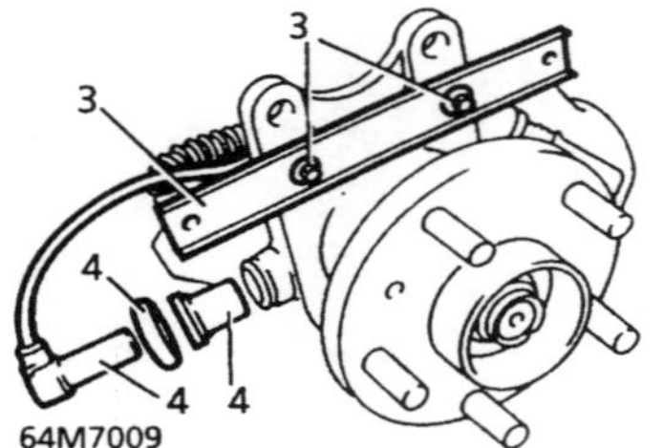

64M7009

4. Release ABS sensor from hub, remove sensor seal and bush.
5. Remove 6 bolts, remove hub and half shaft assembly from axle.

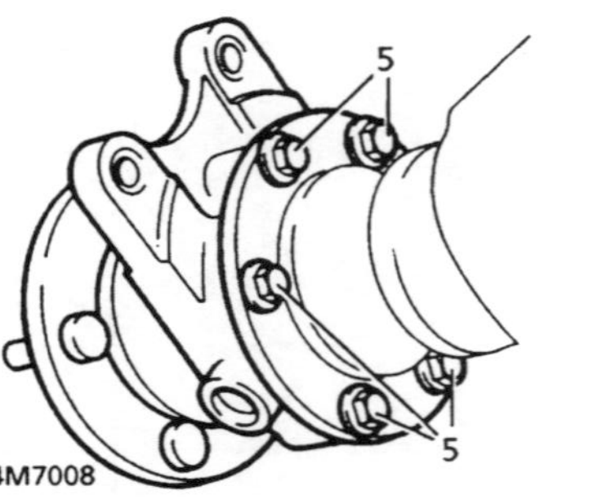

64M7008

6. Secure hub and half shaft assembly in vice. Remove drive shaft nut and remove hub from shaft.

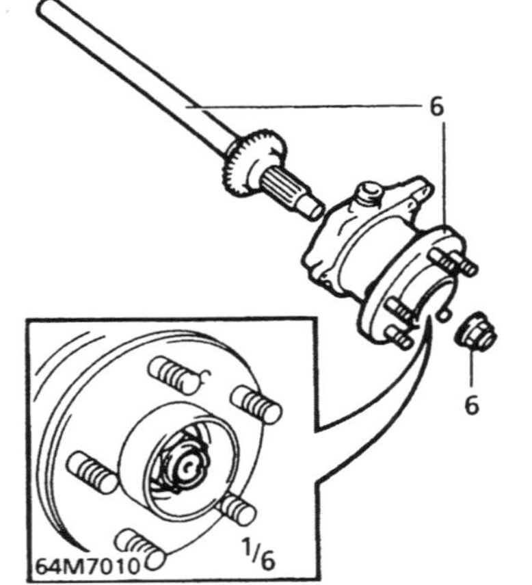

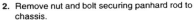

64M7010

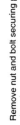

7. Remove seal from axle casing.

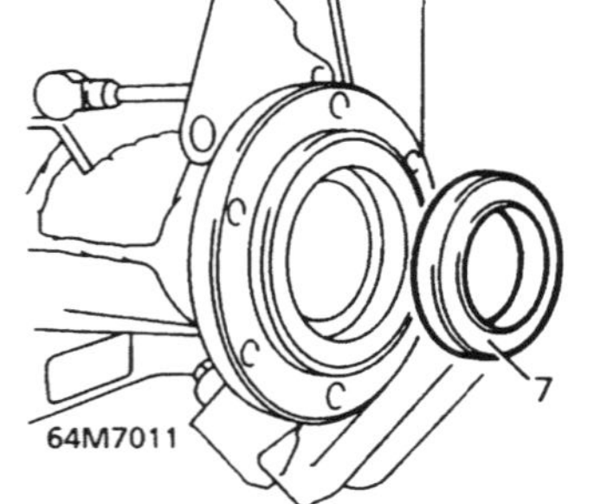

64M7011

Refit

8. Clean splines and seal mating faces.
9. Lubricate lip of oil seal, fit to axle case.
10. Fit hub to half shaft and fit nut, finger tight.
11. Remove shaft and hub assembly from vice.
12. Fit hub to axle case, fit bolts. Tighten to ***65 Nm. (48 lbf.ft)***
13. Clean ABS sensor, bush and mating face.
14. Fit a new ABS sensor bush. Fit sensor to location in hub.
15. Fit brake disc shield. ***See BRAKES, Repair.***
16. Remove safety stands. Lower vehicle.
17. Tighten drive shaft nut to ***260 Nm. (192 lbf.ft)***
18. Stake the nut.
19. Fit road wheel centre.

PANHARD ROD AND BUSHES

Service repair no - 64.35.50 - Panhard rod
Service repair no - 64.35.51 - Bushes

Remove

1. Raise the vehicle.

⚠ **WARNING: Support on safety stands.**

2. Remove nut and bolt securing panhard rod to chassis.

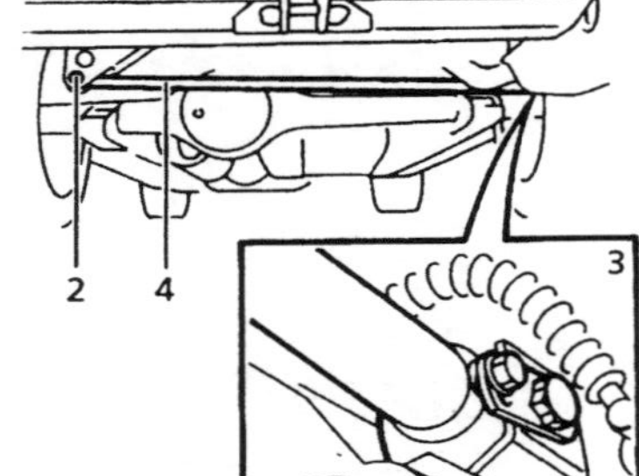

64M7003

3. Remove locking plate screw, locking plate and bolt securing panhard rod to axle.
4. Remove panhard rod.
5. Press out bushes from panhard rod. Ensure that pressure is applied to the outer edge of bush, not rubber inner.

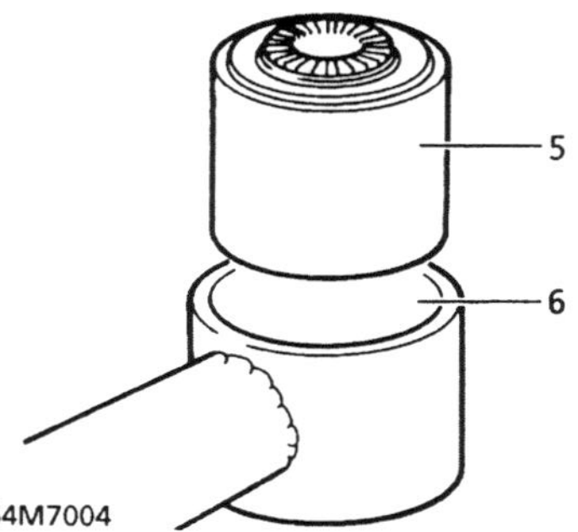

64M7004

Refit

6. Clean mating faces of bushes in rod.
7. Press in new bushes.

CAUTION: Ensure that pressure is applied to the outer edge of bush, not rubber inner.

8. Fit panhard rod. Tighten nut and bolt to ***200 Nm. (148 lbf.ft)***
9. Tighten bolt to ***200 Nm. (148 lbf.ft)***
10. Fit locking plate and screw. Tighten screw to ***20 Nm. (15 lbf.ft)***
11. Remove safety stands. Lower vehicle.

SHOCK ABSORBER

Service repair no - 64.30.02

Remove

WARNING: Unrestricted movement of pressurised air spring will result in failure of the assembly, causing component damage and possible personal injury. It is possible to remove the shock absorber without depressurising air springs, BUT the distance between axle and chassis must be held as if damper assembly is fitted. This is achieved by supporting vehicle on safety stands with a jack under the axle.

1. Raise the vehicle.

WARNING: Support on safety stands.

2. Support axle on jack.
3. Remove road wheel.

WARNING: Do not lower axle when shock absorber is removed. This may result air spring failure.

4. Remove bolt securing shock absorber to chassis.

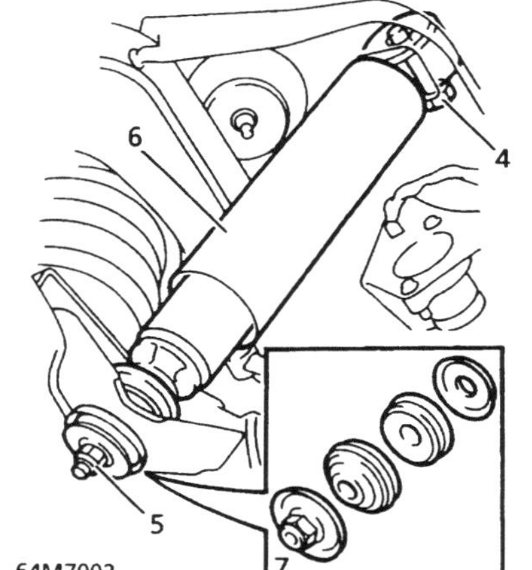

64M7002

5. Remove shock absorber lower fixing.
6. Remove shock absorber.

Refit

7. Fit shock absorber, ensure lower mounting rubbers are fitted as shown.
8. Tighten top mounting bolt to ***125 Nm. (92 lbf.ft)***
9. Tighten lower mounting nut to ***45 Nm. (33 lbf.ft)***
10. Fit road wheel. Tighten to ***108 Nm. (80 lbf.ft)***
11. Remove jack.
12. Remove safety stands. Lower vehicle.

TRAILING ARM AND BUSHES

Service repair no - 64.35.46 - Trailing arm
Service repair no - 64.35.48 - Bushes

Remove

1. Raise vehicle on four post lift.
2. Depressurise air suspension. ***See FRONT SUSPENSION, Repair.***
3. Raise rear of vehicle to give enough clearance for shock absorber to be disconnected.
4. Remove nut securing shock absorber to axle. Release shock absorber, collect mounting rubbers.

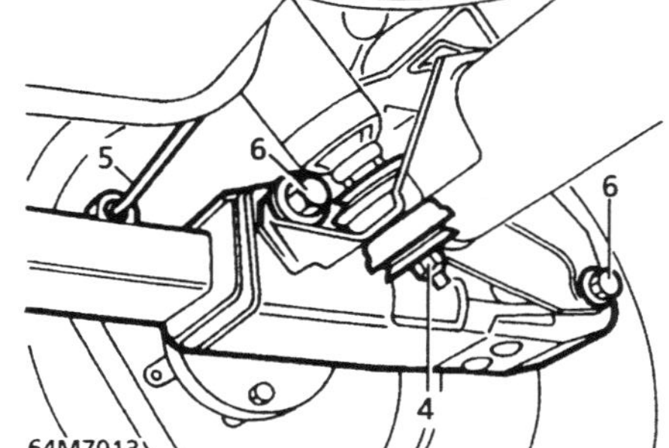

64M7013

5. Release height sensor link from trailing arm.

CAUTION: Ensure that rubber mounting does not become damaged.

6. Remove 2 nuts and bolts securing trailing arm to axle.
7. Remove nut and bolt securing trailing arm to chassis.
8. Remove trailing arm.

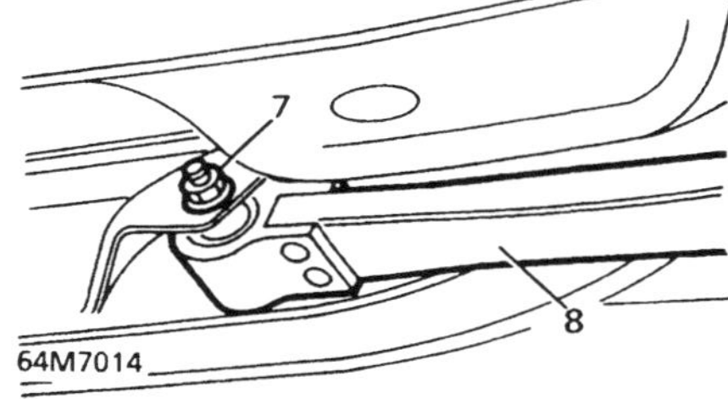

64M7014

Do not carry out further dismantling if component is removed for access only.

9. Using LRT-64-001, press bush from trailing arm.

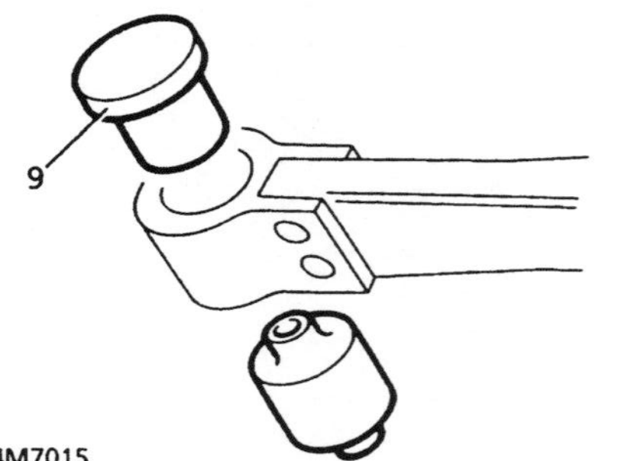

64M7015

10. Using LRT-64-001, press new bush into trailing arm.

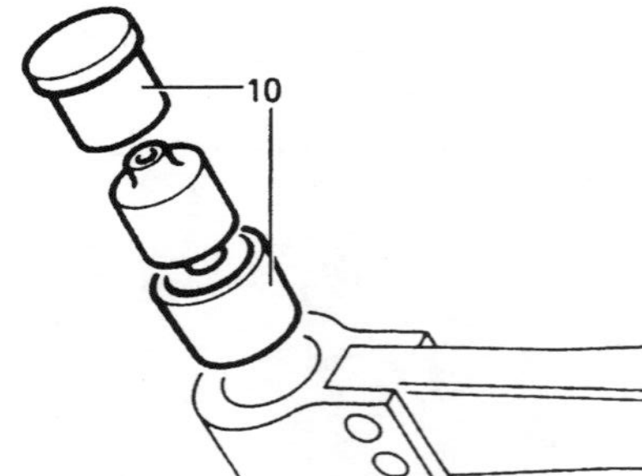

64M7016

CAUTION: LRT-64-001 must be used to compress the bush as it is pressed into the arm. Damage to bush will result if correct tool is not used.

Refit

11. Position trailing arm to vehicle and align to chassis. Fit bolt but do not tighten at this stage.
12. Secure trailing arm to axle with nuts and bolts.
    M16 with 8.8 strength grade - Tighten to ***160 Nm. (118 lbf.ft),***
    M16 with 10.9 strength grade - Tighten to ***240 Nm. (177 lbf.ft),***
    M12 - Tighten to ***125 Nm. (92 lbf.ft)***
13. Engage height sensor link into trailing arm location.
14. Position upper mounting rubber. Engage shock absorber to axle.
15. Position lower mounting rubber and washer. Secure shock absorber to axle with nut. Tighten to ***45 Nm. (33 lbf.ft)***

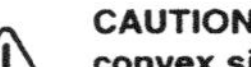

CAUTION: Washer must be fitted with convex side towards rubber.

16. Remove safety stands. Lower vehicle.
17. Tighten bolt securing trailing arm to chassis. Tighten to ***160 Nm. (118 lbf.ft)***
18. Lower ramp.

Notes

70 - BRAKES

CONTENTS

LOCATION OF COMPONENTS - ABS UP TO 99MY

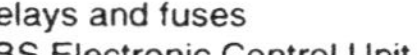

1. Relays and fuses
2. ABS Electronic Control Unit (ECU)
3. Brake booster/ABS modulator unit
4. Front and rear sensors/exciter rings
5. Pressure Conscious Reducing Valve (PCRV)
6. ABS power unit

LOCATION OF COMPONENTS - ABS FROM 99MY

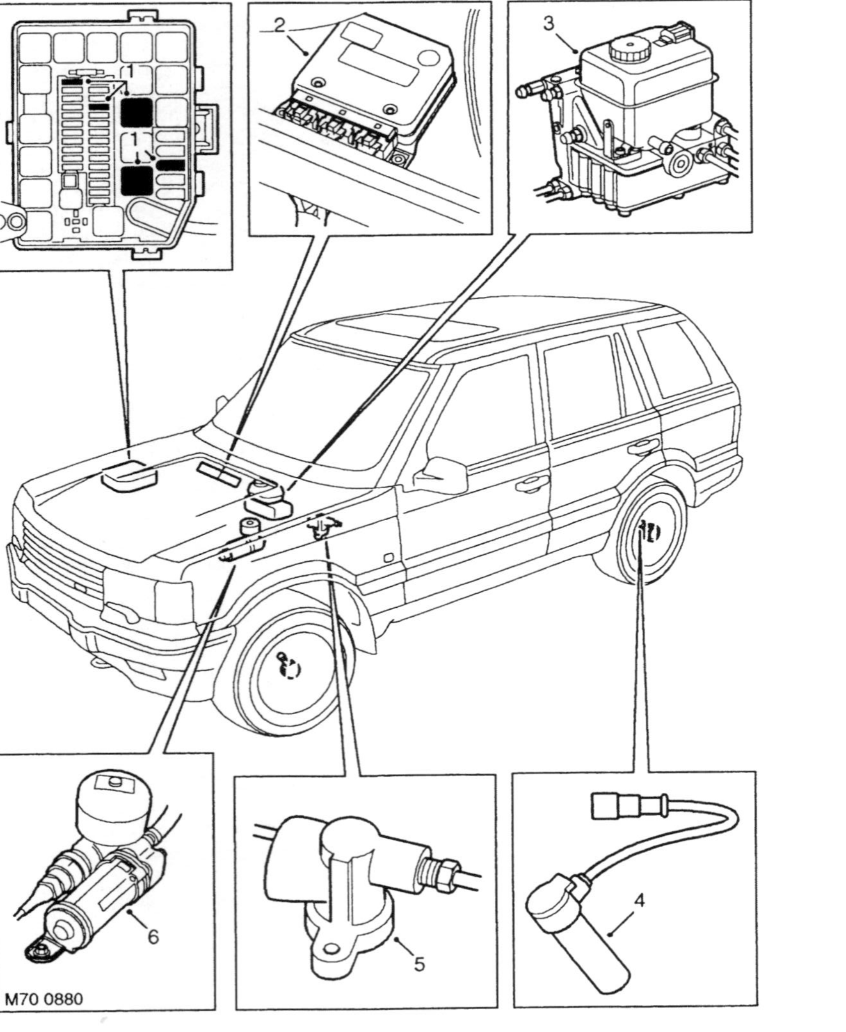

1. Relays and fuses
2. ABS Electronic Control Unit (ECU)
3. Brake booster/ABS modulator unit
4. Front and rear sensors/exciter rings
5. Pressure Conscious Reducing Valve (PCRV)
6. ABS power unit

This page is intentionally left blank

ABS CONTROL SCHEMATIC

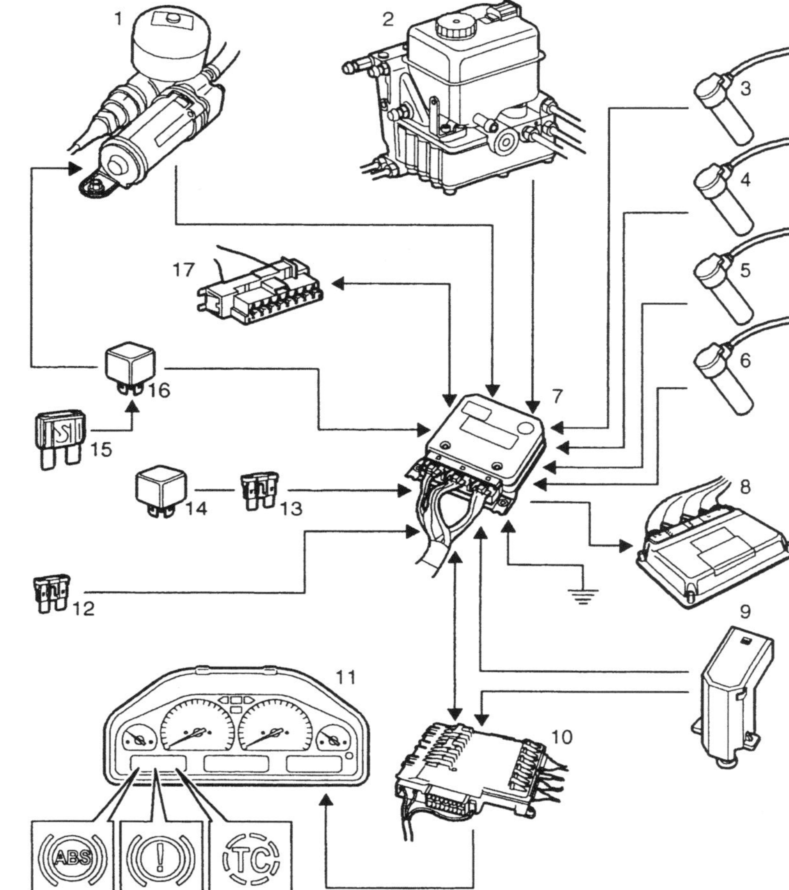

M70 0878

1. ABS power unit
2. Brake booster/ABS modulator unit
3. Front left speed sensor
4. Front right speed sensor
5. Rear left speed sensor
6. Rear right speed sensor
7. ABS ECU (From 99MY shown)
8. Engine Control Module (V8 only)
9. Brake pedal switch
10. Body electrical Control Module (BeCM)
11. Instrument pack
12. Fuse - Battery supply
13. Fuse - Ignition supply
14. Ignition relay
15. Maxi fuse - ABS power unit relay supply
16. ABS power unit relay
17. Diagnostic socket

ANTI-LOCK BRAKE SYSTEM - DESCRIPTION

Anti-lock Braking System (ABS)

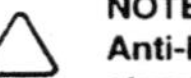

NOTE: On vehicles up to 99MY, the Anti-lock Brake System (ABS) is a standard feature, with Electronic Traction Control (ETC) optional. On vehicles from 99MY the ABS and ETC is standard on all models.

The brake system is hydraulically power assisted with an integrated, electronically controlled four channel ABS system.
The use of a power assisted brake system means that, during brake application, additional hydraulic energy is provided by the hydraulic power unit.
This hydraulic power unit consists of an electrically driven pump and an accumulator which stores hydraulic energy in readiness for brake application. A pressure switch controls hydraulic pump operation to maintain fluid pressure in the accumulator.

Fluid pressure is distributed from the brake booster/ABS modulator unit to each of the four brake calipers. Foot pedal pressure is assisted by pressure created in the master cylinder and direct pressure from the power valve. The combination of the master cylinder and the power valve allows the driver to vary braking force by varying force applied to the brake pedal.

The hydraulic system comprises two completely independent circuits, with a vertical i.e. front/rear split. The combined POWER and HYDROSTATIC CIRCUIT supplies the front calipers. The POWER CIRCUIT supplies the rear calipers.

The purpose of ABS is to prevent the vehicle wheels locking during brake application, maintaining vehicle steerability and stability. This allows the vehicle to be steered while the brakes are applied, even under emergency conditions, and to avoid obstacles where there is sufficient space to redirect the vehicle.

The ABS system on vehicles up to 99MY uses a 'C' series ABS ECU which includes an optional two wheel electronic traction control feature. The ECU has a single connector and is located on the bulkhead behind the glovebox.

On vehicles from 99MY a 'D' series ABS ECU is used. The 'D' series ECU features four wheel electronic traction control which is a standard feature on all models. The ECU has three connectors and is located in the same position as the 'C' series ECU.

The ABS ECU receives wheel speed information from four wheel speed sensors. The ECU monitors the deceleration of each wheel during braking and, in the event of one or more wheels being outside the expected values, controls via the hydraulic system the braking force available to that wheel.

When the wheel speed has returned to within the expected limits, the ECU restores the hydraulic pressure to the wheel. The ABS system allows optimal stopping distances to be achieved and prevents the wheels from locking.

The system is active after the ignition is switched to position II and has completed a bulb check. ABS and ETC warning lamps in the instrument pack warn of system operation and failure. Normal (non-ABS) braking remains available in the event of an ABS system failure.

When the ABS system operates, the driver will experience an audible noise from the ABS modulator and vibration transmitted through the brake pedal.

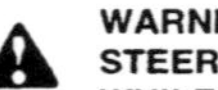

WARNING: ABS IS AN AID TO RETAINING STEERING CONTROL AND STABILITY WHILE BRAKING.

- **ABS CANNOT DEFY THE NATURAL LAWS OF PHYSICS ACTING ON THE VEHICLE.**
- **ABS WILL NOT PREVENT ACCIDENTS RESULTING FROM EXCESSIVE CORNERING SPEEDS, FOLLOWING ANOTHER VEHICLE TOO CLOSELY OR AQUAPLANING, I.E. WHERE A LAYER OF WATER PREVENTS ADEQUATE CONTACT BETWEEN TYRE AND ROAD SURFACE.**
- **THE ADDITIONAL CONTROL PROVIDED BY ABS MUST NEVER BE EXPLOITED IN A DANGEROUS OR RECKLESS MANNER WHICH COULD JEOPARDISE THE SAFETY OF DRIVER OR OTHER ROAD USERS.**

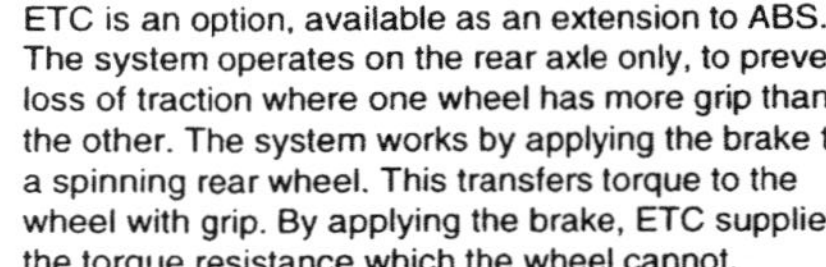

Electronic Traction Control (ETC) - Up to 99MY

ETC is an option, available as an extension to ABS. The system operates on the rear axle only, to prevent loss of traction where one wheel has more grip than the other. The system works by applying the brake to a spinning rear wheel. This transfers torque to the wheel with grip. By applying the brake, ETC supplies the torque resistance which the wheel cannot.

An example of when the system would operate is where one side of the vehicle is on ice, with the other side on tarmac. ETC will control the spinning rear wheel.

If both wheels spin the system does not operate, as braking one wheel will not aid traction.

The system switches itself out at 50 km/h (30 mph). A vehicle travelling above this speed will not need ETC.

ETC system operation is smooth and continuous and will not affect the comfort of the vehicle.

ETC is inhibited when the brakes are applied. When the ETC feature is operating the 'TC' warning lamp in the instrument pack will illuminate for a minimum of two seconds, a single audible warning will sound and on earlier vehicles 'TRACTION' will be displayed in the message centre.

Electronic Traction Control (ETC) - From 99MY

ETC is standard on all models from 99MY onwards. ETC operates in conjunction with the ABS system to give improved traction for all wheels where one wheel has more grip than the other. The system operates by applying the brake to a spinning wheel. This transfers torque to the remaining wheels with grip. By applying the brake, ETC supplies the torque resistance which the wheel cannot.

An example of when the system would operate is where one side of the vehicle is on ice, with the other side on tarmac. The ABS ECU monitors the speed of the each wheel. If any wheels are rotating faster than the others, brake pressure is applied to that wheel, slowing it down to match the other wheel speeds.

If all wheels spin at the same speed the system does not operate, as braking one wheel will not aid traction.

The system switches itself out at 100 km/h (62.5 mph). A vehicle travelling above this speed will not need ETC.

ETC system operation is smooth and continuous and will not affect the comfort of the vehicle. No driver intervention is required.

ETC is inhibited when the brakes are applied. When the ETC feature is operating the 'TC' warning lamp in the instrument pack will illuminate for a minimum of two seconds and a single audible warning will sound.

Hydraulic Circuit Diagram
Brake booster/ABS modulator unit - up to 99MY

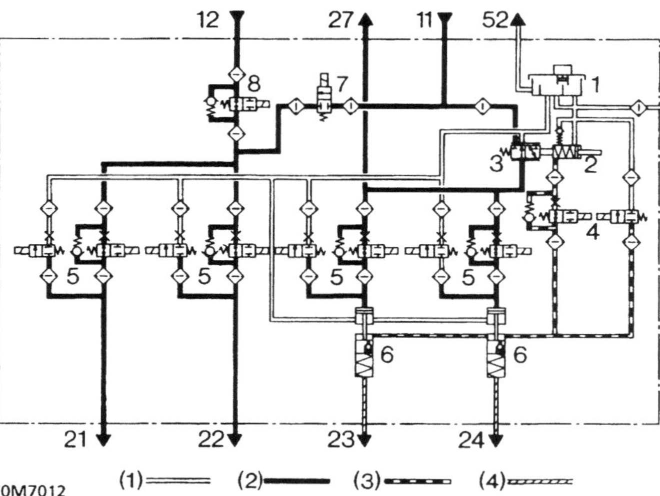

(1) Fluid feed/return
(2) Power circuit
(3) Hydrostatic (master cylinder) circuit
(4) Combined hydrostatic/power circuit

Brake booster/ABS modulator unit components

1. Fluid reservoir
2. Master cylinder
3. Power valve
4. Isolating valve
5. ABS solenoid control valves
6. Servo cylinders

ETC option

7. ETC inlet solenoid valve - normally closed
8. ETC isolating solenoid valve - normally open

Brake booster/ABS modulator unit port identification

11. High pressure supply from hydraulic pump
12. Supply from PCRV
21. Supply to left hand rear caliper
22. Supply to right hand rear caliper
23. Supply to left hand front caliper
24. Supply to right hand front caliper
27. Supply to PCRV
51. Low pressure supply to hydraulic pump
52. Supply to clutch master cylinder (manual vehicles)

Hydraulic Circuit Diagram
Brake booster/ABS modulator unit - from 99MY

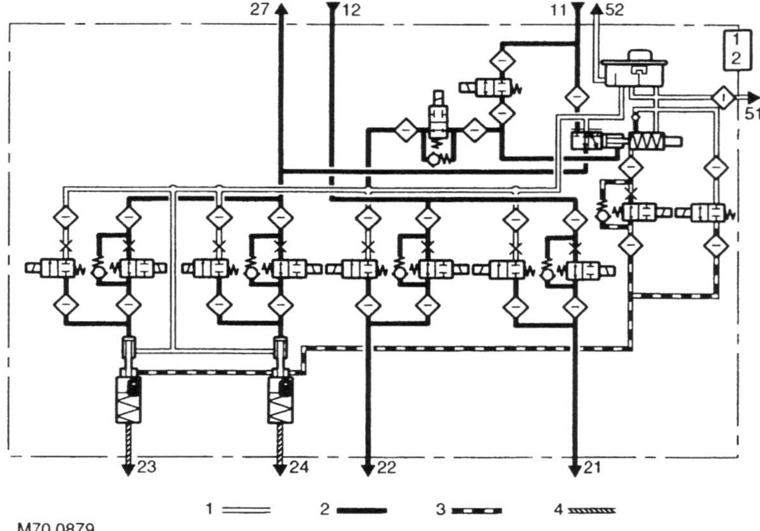

(1) Fluid feed/return
(2) Power circuit
(3) Hydrostatic (master cylinder) circuit
(4) Combined hydrostatic/power circuit

Brake booster/ABS modulator unit components

1. Fluid reservoir
2. Master cylinder
3. Power valve
4. Isolating valve
5. ABS solenoid control valves
6. Servo cylinders
7. ETC inlet solenoid valve - normally closed
8. ETC isolating solenoid valve - normally open

Brake booster/ABS modulator unit port identification

11. High pressure supply from hydraulic pump
12. Supply from PCRV
21. Supply to left hand rear caliper
22. Supply to right hand rear caliper
23. Supply to left hand front caliper
24. Supply to right hand front caliper
27. Supply to PCRV
51. Low pressure supply to hydraulic pump
52. Supply to clutch master cylinder (manual vehicles)

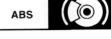

Hydraulic components

Numbers refer to location of components illustrations

Brake booster/ABS modulator unit

Mounted in the same position as a conventional brake master cylinder/servo unit, the brake booster/ABS modulator contains the following components: fluid reservoir, power valve, master cylinder, isolating valve, ABS control valves and servo cylinders. It also contains the ETC solenoid control valves

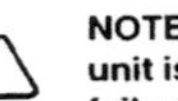

NOTE: The brake booster/ABS modulator unit is not a serviceable item, if internal failure occurs a new unit must be fitted. The fluid reservoir and its seals may be changed in the event of damage.

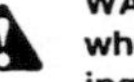

WARNING: Extreme care must be taken when changing reservoir seals to avoid ingress of debris.

Fluid reservoir - 1.

Mounted on top of the unit, the plastic reservoir is subdivided internally to provide separate capacity for brake fluid used in the hydrostatic and power circuits. A central tube incorporates a filter. A built in fluid level warning switch and a finer filter for the power circuit fluid are also incorporated. The fluid level warning switch is closed when there is sufficient fluid in reservoir.

On manual vehicles, the reservoir also supplies fluid to the clutch system.

Master cylinder - 2.

Operation the of master cylinder displaces a volume of brake fluid into the servo cylinders and increases fluid pressure. Piston movement inside the master cylinder will also activate the power valve.

Power valve - 3.

The power valve is an extension of the master cylinder, it controls fluid pressure in the power circuit in direct proportion to pressure in the master cylinder. The power valve is of spool valve design.

Isolating valve - 4.

The isolating valve consists of two solenoid valves controlling fluid inlet and outlet. Their function is to disconnect the master cylinder from the servo cylinders and to connect the servo cylinders to the reservoir return during ABS function.

ABS solenoid control valves, 8 off - 5.

Each pair, comprising inlet and outlet solenoid valves, control ABS braking to each wheel. In response to signals from the ECU, the valves decrease, hold or increase brake pressure according to the need to retain wheel rotation and obtain optimum braking. The solenoid valves are designed to respond rapidly to ECU signals.

Servo cylinders, 2 off - 6.

Servo cylinders have five functions:

1. To provide combined energy from both hydrostatic and power circuit to brake calipers.
2. To provide 'brake feel' at the brake pedal.
3. To provide hydrostatic (master cylinder) braking through the servo cylinders to calipers in the event of no power circuit pressure to servo cylinders.
4. To provide braking from the power circuit and from hydrostatic fluid remaining in servo cylinder, in event of no hydrostatic circuit pressure from master cylinder.
5. To provide ABS control to the front calipers in response to pressure modulations in the power circuit.

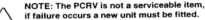

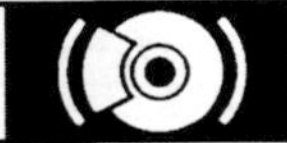

ETC control valves - up to 99MY - 7 & 8

The ETC control valves are optional on vehicles up to 99MY. The ETC inlet solenoid valve (7) is normally closed and the ETC isolating solenoid valve (8) is normally open when ETC operation is not required.

When ETC operation is required, the inlet solenoid valve opens allowing fluid from the power circuit to flow to the rear ABS solenoid control valves. Simultaneously, the ETC isolating solenoid valve closes, isolating the connection to the PCRV. The ABS ECU energises the applicable ABS solenoid valve to pressurise the applicable rear wheel brake.

ETC control valves - from 99MY - 7 & 8

The ETC control valves are standard on vehicles from 99MY. The ETC inlet solenoid valve (7) is normally closed and the ETC isolating solenoid valve (8) is normally open when ETC operation is not required.

When ETC operation is required, the inlet solenoid valve opens allowing fluid from the power circuit to flow to the power valve. The power valve is actuated by the pressure and opens to allow fluid from the power circuit to flow directly to the front ABS solenoid control valves and to the rear solenoid control valves via the PCRV. The ETC isolating solenoid valve closes isolating the return flow from each ABS solenoid control valve. The ABS ECU energises the applicable ABS solenoid valve(s) to pressurise the applicable front and/or rear wheel brake.

ABS power unit

The ABS power unit consists of an electrically driven pump, a pressure switch and an accumulator.

The pressure switch incorporates three electro-mechanical switches: one for the pump, another, at a different pressure setting, to illuminate the pressure warning lamp. The latter switch plus a third switch inform the ECU of low pressure and that ABS function should cease while pressure remains low.
The pump also incorporates a non-return valve and a pressure relief valve to protect the system.

NOTE: The pump and pressure switch are not serviceable, if failure occurs a new unit must be fitted.

The diaphragm type accumulator is fitted to the power unit. The accumulator is precharged with nitrogen at up to 80 bar. Its function is to store hydraulic energy ready for the next brake application.

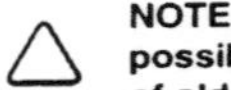

NOTE: Accumulator replacement is possible if failure occurs. Correct disposal of old accumulators is essential. ***See Repair.***

Pressure Conscious Reducing Valve (PCRV)

The PCRV is located adjacent to the brake booster/ABS modulator unit. It is connected between the power valve and ABS solenoid valves for the rear axle. Its function is to limit brake pressure to rear axle.

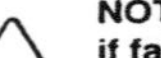

NOTE: The PCRV is not a serviceable item, if failure occurs a new unit must be fitted.

Brake calipers - front and rear

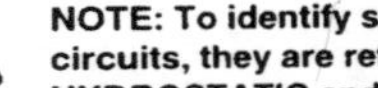

NOTE: To identify separate hydraulic circuits, they are referred to as HYDROSTATIC and POWER circuits.

Power circuit - Consists of rear calipers and servo cylinders, supplied by direct hydraulic power from the power valve.

Hydrostatic circuit - Consists of servo cylinders supplied by master cylinder pressure. The front calipers are supplied with direct hydraulic energy from the servo cylinders, comprising a combination of master cylinder pressure and direct hydraulic power.

ABS Electronic Control Unit - ECU

ABS/ETC operation is controlled by the ECU. The ECU is attached to a bracket which in turn is attached to the bulkhead. A closing plate beneath the passenger side fascia provides access to the ECU.

The ECU is connected to the ABS harness by a 35 pin connector on up to 99MY vehicles and by 9, 15 and 18 pin connectors on vehicles from 99MY.

When system faults are detected by the ECU, warning lamps in the instrument pack can be illuminated for ABS, ETC and braking system faults. Certain faults are also displayed in the instrument pack message centre. Refer to Operation - Warning lamps for lamp and message centre operation.

The ABS ECU generates a digital road speed signal from the average speed of the four wheels. The ABS ECU passes the road speed signal to the BeCM. The BeCM outputs the road speed signal to the following interfaces:

- Engine Control Module (ECM)
- Cruise control ECU (V8 only)
- Instrument pack
- Air Temperature Control (ATC) ECU
- In-Car Entertainment (ICE)
- Electronic Air Suspension (EAS) ECU
- Electronic Automatic Transmission (EAT) ECU.

The ABS ECU also outputs a rough road signal to the ECM on V8 engine vehicles only. The digital rough road signal is generated from the difference in rotational speed of each wheel.

The ECU is a non-serviceable item, it must be replaced if failure occurs.

This page is intentionally left blank

ABS ECU connector pin details - up to 99MY

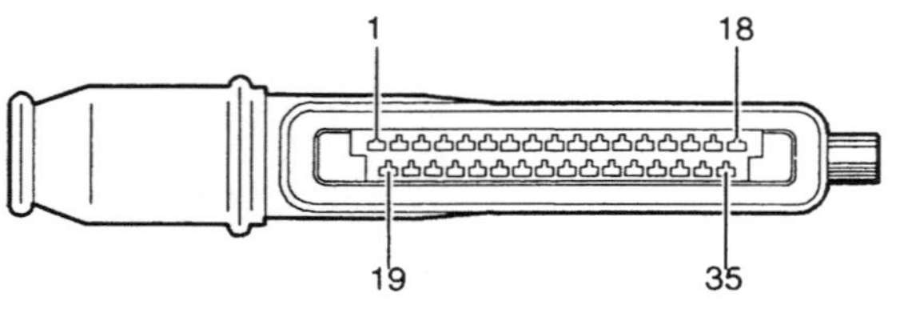

M70 0881

ABS ECU connector face view

35 pin connector No.C116

Pin No.	Description	Input/Output
1	ABS valve relay (battery supply)	Input
2	Brake booster/ABS modulator - ETC normally open valve	Output
3	BeCM - ETC information lamp	Output
4	Brake booster/ABS modulator - Rear right inlet valve	Output
5	Brake booster/ABS modulator - Rear right outlet valve	Output
6	Brake booster/ABS modulator - Front right inlet valve	Output
7	Brake booster/ABS modulator - Front right outlet valve	Output
8	ABS valve relay coil	Output
9	Ignition supply	Input
10	Brake switch 2 (normally closed)	Input
11	Brake booster/ABS modulator - Isolating inlet valve	Output
12	Brake booster/ABS modulator - Isolating outlet valve	Output
13	Diagnostic socket - K line	Input
14	Diagnostic socket - L line	Input
15	Front left wheel speed sensor	Input
16	Rear right wheel speed sensor	Input

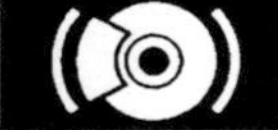

ABS ECU connector pin details - Up to 99MY (Continued)

Pin No.	Description	Input/Output
17	Front right wheel speed sensor	Input
18	Rear left wheel speed sensor	Input
19	Not used	-
20	Brake booster/ABS modulator - ETC normally closed valve	Output
21	Brake booster/ABS modulator - Rear left inlet valve	Output
22	Brake booster/ABS modulator - Rear left outlet valve	Output
23	Brake booster/ABS modulator - Front left inlet valve	Output
24	Brake booster/ABS modulator - Front left outlet valve	Output
25	Brake switch 1 (normally open)	Input
26	BeCM - ABS warning lamp	Output
27	Earth	Input
28	BeCM - Road speed signal	Output
29	ECM - Rough road signal	Output
30	ABS pump low pressure warning switch 1	Output
31	ABS pump low pressure warning switch 2	Input/Output
32	Front left wheel speed sensor	Input
33	Rear right wheel speed sensor	Input
34	Front right wheel speed sensor	Input
35	Rear left wheel speed sensor	Input

ABS ECU connector pin details - From 99MY

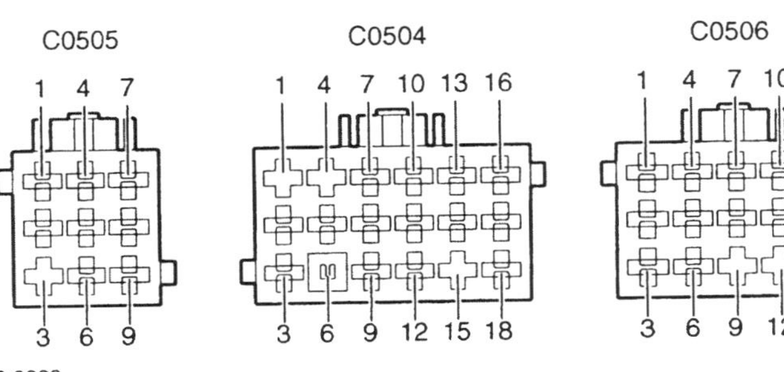

ABS ECU connector face view

18 pin connector No. C504
9 pin connector No. C505
15 pin connector No. C506

Pin No.	Description	Input/Output
C504		
1	Battery supply	Input
2	Ignition supply	Input
3	BeCM - Road speed signal	Input
4	ECM - Rough road signal (V8 only)	Output
5	Diagnostic socket - K line	Input
6	Not used	-
7	Brake pedal switch 1 (normally closed)	Input
8	ABS pump monitor	Input
9	ABS pump relay override	Input
10	ABS pump low pressure switch 2	Input
11	ABS pump low pressure switch 3	Input
12	ABS ECU earth	Input
C505		
1	Front left wheel speed sensor	Input
2	Front left wheel speed sensor	Input
3	Right rear wheel speed sensor	Input

ABS ECU connector pin details - From 99MY - (Continued)

Pin No.	Description	Input/Output
4	Front right wheel speed sensor	Input
5	Front right wheel speed sensor	Input
6	Right rear wheel speed sensor	Input
7	Rear left wheel speed sensor	Input
8	Rear left wheel speed sensor	Input
9	Not used	-
C506		
1	Front left ABS solenoid control valve	Output
2	Front left ABS solenoid control valve	Output
3	Reference earth	Input
4	Front right ABS solenoid control valve	Output
5	Front right ABS solenoid control valve	Output
6	Not used	-
7	Rear left ABS solenoid control valve	Output
8	Rear left ABS solenoid control valve	Output
9	Not used	-
10	Rear right ABS solenoid control valve	Output
11	Rear right ABS solenoid control valve	Output
12	ETC Normally open solenoid control valve	Output
13	Isolating valve	Output
14	Isolating valve	Output
15	ETC Normally closed solenoid control valve	Output
13	Not used	-
14	Brake pedal switch 2 (normally open)	Input
15	Not used	-
16	Not used	-
17	ETC warning lamp	Output
18	ABS warning lamp	Output

Relays and fuses - Up to 99MY

The ABS electrical system has two relays and three fuses, located in the engine compartment fusebox.

- Relay 2 (yellow) - ABS valve relay.
- Relay 15 (green) - Ignition relay - ABS power.
- Relay 17 (black) - ABS pump relay. Note that this relay is unique to the ABS system.
- Fuse Maxi 3 (40 Amp) - ABS pump relay.
- Fuse 24 (5 Amp) - ABS ECU - Ignition supply.
- Fuse 27 (30 Amp) - ABS ECU - Battery supply.

Relays and fuses - From 99MY

The ABS electrical system has two relays and three fuses, located in the engine compartment fusebox.

- Relay 15 (green) - Ignition relay - ABS power.
- Relay 17 (black) - ABS pump relay. Note that this relay is unique to the ABS system.
- Fuse Maxi 3 (40 Amp) - ABS pump relay.
- Fuse 24 (5 Amp) - ABS ECU - Ignition supply.
- Fuse 38 (30 Amp) - ABS ECU - Battery supply.

Sensors, exciter rings - 4 off

A sensor is mounted at each wheel, sensing a 60 tooth exciter ring. When the vehicle is in motion the inductive sensors send signals to the ECU.

The front exciter ring is fitted adjacent to the constant velocity joint in each front hub. The rear exciter ring is inside the axle adjacent to the wheel bearing assembly.

NOTE: Road speed information from the ECU is transmitted to the Body electrical Control Module (BeCM) to drive the speedometer and all systems requiring speed information, except the transfer box ECU.

Brake calipers

Lucas Colette type calipers are used all round. The front disc brake calipers each house two pistons, hydraulic pressure is supplied by a combination of power and hydrostatic circuit. The rear disc brake calipers each house one piston, hydraulic pressure is supplied by the power circuit via a Pressure Conscious Reducing Valve (PCRV).

The operation of both front and rear calipers is in principle the same. The Colette type caliper consists of two main components, a carrier and a hydraulic body assembly. The carrier is bolted to the hub assembly. The hydraulic body slides on two greased guide pins housed in the carrier. The guide pins are sealed by the dust covers to avoid unequal sliding loads caused by dirt or corrosion.

When the footbrake is applied hydraulic pressure pushes the piston and, with it, the inboard pad on to the disc. The hydraulic body reacts and slides on the guide pins to bring the outboard pad into contact with the disc. The clamping force on both sides of the disc is then equal.

When hydraulic pressure is released, the piston seal retracts the piston a small amount. This allows the moving parts to relax sufficiently for the brake pads to remain in close proximity to the disc ready for the next brake application.

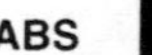

Brake caliper assembly

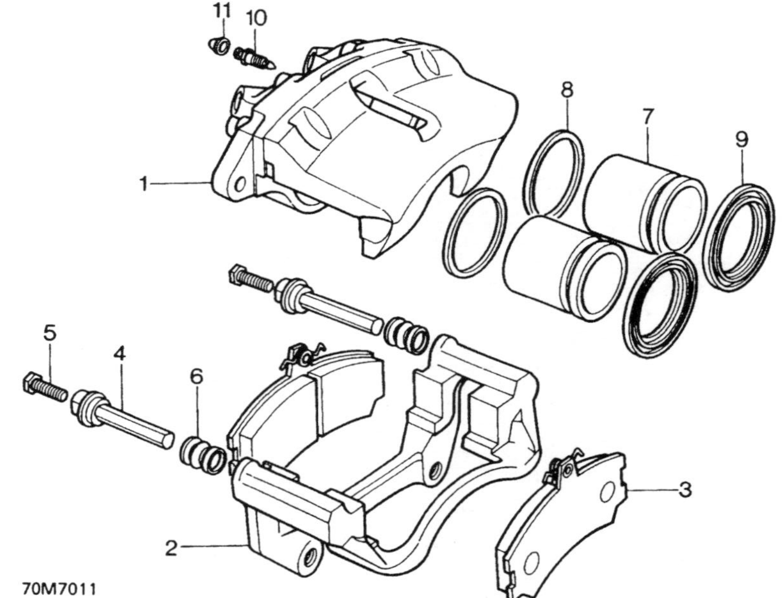

1. Hydraulic body
2. Carrier
3. Brake pad
4. Guide pin
5. Guide pin bolt
6. Guide pin boot
7. Piston
8. Fluid seal
9. Dust cover
10. Bleedscrew
11. Dustcap

The hand operated parking brake acts on a brake drum at the rear of the transfer gearbox and is completely independent of the hydraulic circuits.

NOTE: Illustration shows a front, two piston, caliper. Rear calipers are of similar construction with a single piston.

Brake pipe layout - Left hand drive

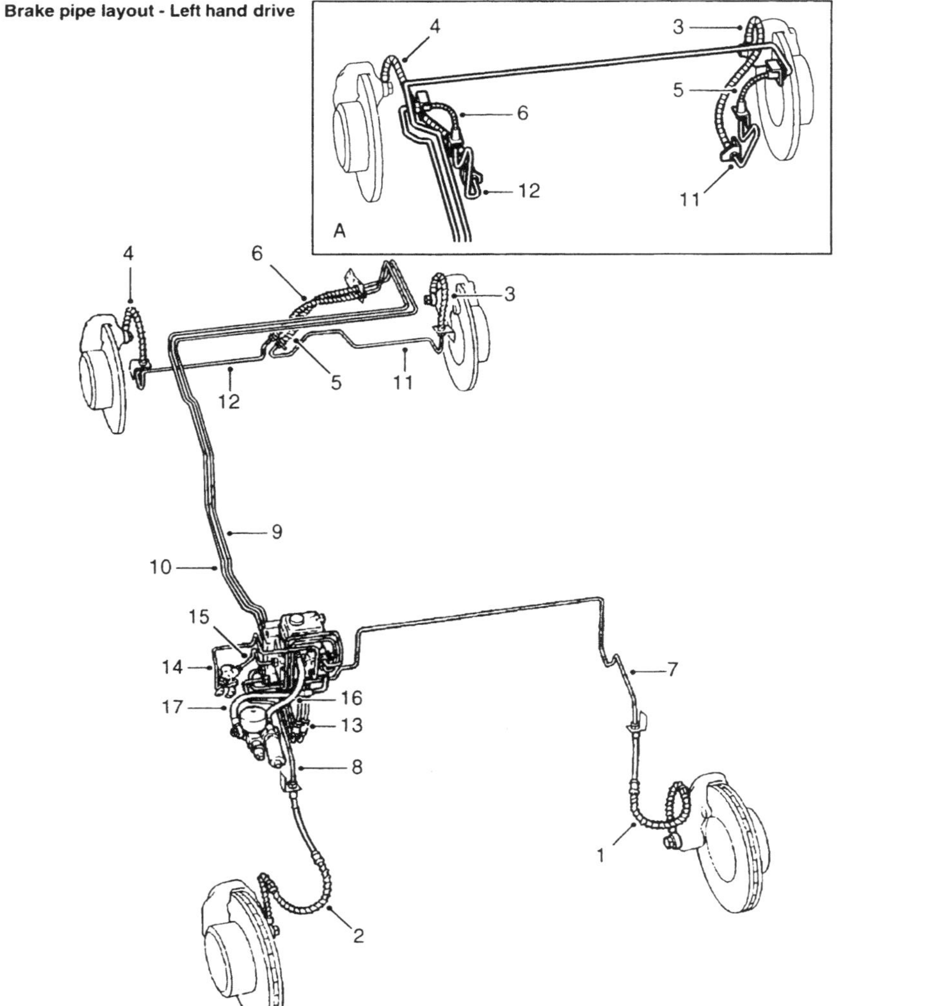

M70 0893

INSET A = VEHICLES FROM 97MY

FLEXIBLE HOSES

1. Front left hand
2. Front right hand
3. Rear left hand
4. Rear right hand
5. Rear left hand intermediate
6. Rear right hand intermediate

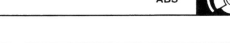

Brake pipe layout - Right hand drive

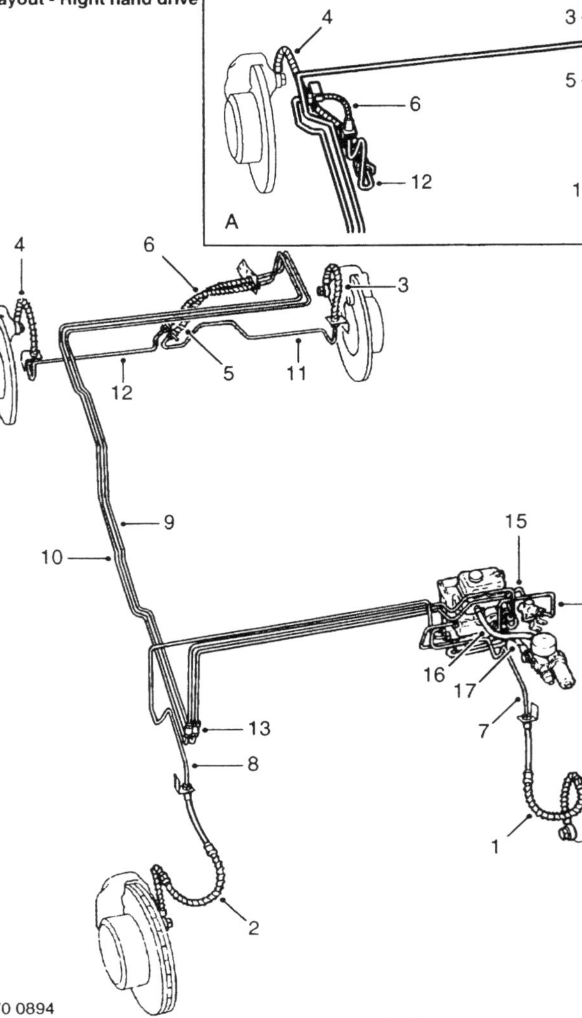

M70 0894

PIPES

7. Feed to front left hand
8. Feed to front right hand
9. Feed to rear left hand intermediate hose
10. Feed to rear right hand intermediate hose
11. Feed to rear left hand flexible hose
12. Feed to rear right hand flexible hose
13. Two way connectors
14. From PCRV
15. To PCRV

Power unit hoses

16. Fluid feed to pump
17. Pressure fluid from pump

ANTI-LOCK BRAKE SYSTEM - OPERATION

Warning lights

Brake fluid pressure/level and parking brake warning lamp - (red)

The warning lamp situated in instrument binnacle indicates insufficient pressure in system and/or low fluid level and/or park brake applied. The warning lamp will illuminate, for 3 seconds when ignition is switched ON as part of initial bulb check, and continuously when parking brake is applied.
If the pressure in hydraulic system is lower than the cut-in pressure for the warning lamp, the lamp will illuminate. When the lamp is on hydraulic pump will be heard running.

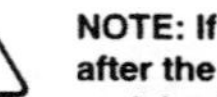

NOTE: If the lamp remains illuminated after the bulb check AND releasing the park brake, DO NOT drive the vehicle until the lamp extinguishes.

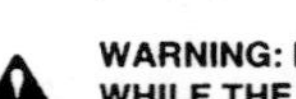

WARNING: IF THE LAMP ILLUMINATES WHILE THE VEHICLE IS IN MOTION, INVESTIGATE FAULT IMMEDIATELY. BRAKING WILL BE AVAILABLE AFTER LOSS OF PRESSURE, BUT GREATER FORCE AND TRAVEL WILL BE REQUIRED AT THE PEDAL TO SLOW THE VEHICLE.

ABS warning lamp - (yellow)

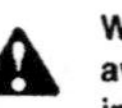

WARNING: Power assisted braking is not available if ignition is switched off. An increase in effort at brake pedal will be required to apply brakes.

The ABS warning lamp situated in instrument binnacle indicates a failure in ABS system.

The warning lamp will illuminate for 1 second when ignition is switched ON, it will briefly extinguish and will illuminate again. This indicates that the system self monitoring check was successful, and system performs correctly.

If it does not extinguish and illuminate again a system fault has occurred.

The warning lamp will extinguish when vehicle speed exceeds 7 km/h (5 mph).

If lamp remains on or subsequently illuminates with ignition ON a fault in ABS system is indicated. The self monitoring procedure is repeated frequently while ignition is ON. If a fault is detected during self monitoring, the lamp will illuminate indicating that one or more wheels are not under ABS control.

WARNING: Reduced ABS control is possible with ABS warning lamp illuminated depending on severity and type of fault. If both ABS and brake failure warning lamps are illuminated, loss of system pressure or hydraulic pump failure is indicated.
STOP VEHICLE AND IMMEDIATELY INVESTIGATE THE FAULT.

Traction control warning lamp - (amber)

The Traction Control warning lamp situated in instrument pack informs the driver that traction control is active. The warning lamp will illuminate when the ignition is switched ON, and the ABS and ETC systems have completed their self checks, the 'TC' lamp will illuminate for 3 seconds. This indicates that the ETC system is operative, and also performs the bulb check.

When traction control is active the lamp will illuminate for a minimum of 2 seconds, a single audible chime will sound and the message centre will display 'TRACTION'. The message and lamp will be extinguished when ETC has stopped working.

On later models, the 'TRACTION' message is not displayed in the message centre. The driver is informed of ETC operation by the 'TC' warning lamp and the single audible chime.

If a fault disables TC, the TC lamp will illuminate and the message 'TRACTION FAILURE' will be displayed. A single audible chime will sound on the first occurence of the message.

If the system is over used and there is a risk of components overheating, the system will shut itself down. The TC lamp will flash for 10 seconds minimum, a single audible chime will sound and the message 'TRACTION OVERHEAT' will be displayed. Traction control will be available after components have cooled down.

NOTE: Traction control only operates below 50 km/h (30 mph) on models up to 99MY and below 100 km/h (62.5 mph) on models from 99MY.

Warning lamp functionality

System Condition	ABS Warning Lamp - Amber	ETC Lamp - Amber	Brake Warning Lamp - Red
Bulb check with no faults in ECU memory and system pressurised.	Lamp ON for 1 second, then goes OFF for 0.5 second, then ON until vehicle speed exceeds 4.3 mph (7 km/h).	Lamp OFF for 1 second, ON for 3 seconds, then goes OFF.	Lamp ON for 3 seconds, then goes OFF providing handbrake is off and fluid level is correct.
Ignition ON, system being pressurised.	Lamp ON until 110 bar (1595 lbf.in^2) pressure in system. Lamp will stay ON until vehicle speed exceeds 4.3 mph (7 km/h).	Lamp ON until 110 bar (1595 lbf.in^2) pressure in system.	Lamp ON until 110 bar (1595 lbf.in^2) pressure in system.
Bulb check with fault stored in ECU memory, but no current fault present.	Lamp ON until vehicle speed exceeds 4.3 mph (7 km/h).	Lamp OFF for 1 second, then ON for 3 seconds, then goes OFF.	ON for 3 seconds, then goes OFF providing handbrake is off and fluid level is correct.
Bulb check with fault present and stored in ECU memory.	Lamp stays ON until ignition is turned off.	Lamp ON for 3 seconds, then goes OFF.	Lamp ON for 3 seconds, then goes OFF providing handbrake is off and fluid level is correct.
ABS fault condition detected by ECU.	Lamp stays ON, 'ABS FAULT' displayed in instrument pack message centre.	Lamp stays OFF.	Lamp stays OFF.
ABS fault/ETC fault condition detected by ECU.	Lamp stays ON, 'ABS FAULT' displayed in instrument pack message centre.	Lamp stays ON, 'TRACTION FAILURE' displayed in instrument pack message centre.	Lamp ON, only if ABS pump/pressure switch fault is detected by ECU.
ABS system active.	Lamp stays OFF.	Lamp stays OFF.	Lamp stays OFF.
ETC system active.	Lamp stays OFF.	Lamp is ON for a minimum of 2 seconds.	Lamp stays OFF.
ETC system fault detected by ECU.	Lamp stays OFF.	Lamp stays ON.	Lamp stays OFF.
Diagnostic operation	Lamp stays ON.	Lamp stays ON.	Lamp stays ON.

Diagnostics

While the ignition is in position II, the ABS ECU monitors the system for faults. Diagnostic information and system function monitoring can be accessed by connecting TestBook to the vehicle diagnostic connector in the passenger footwell, near the centre console.

After detecting a fault, the ABS ECU will select a suitable default strategy which will retain, if possible, some operational ABS capability. If ABS is not active, conventional braking will be remain available. Fault codes are stored in the ECU's memory for current and historic faults. The stored fault codes can be accessed, read and then cleared when the fault is rectified.

Driving the vehicle

WARNING: On surfaces which are soft and deep, for example deep powdery snow, sand or gravel, braking distance may be greater than with non ABS braking. In these conditions wheel lock and the build up of snow or gravel under wheels may be an aid to shorter stopping distance. However it is still an advantage to maintain the stability and manoeuvrability available with ABS control.

1. Switch on ignition, system will automatically carry out self test function. This will be felt as a slight movement in brake pedal and a short, rapid series of clicks indicating that solenoid valves have been checked.
2. Observe warning lights, check parking brake/fluid warning light extinguishes after initial bulb check or when parking brake is released, indicating that power assistance is available. Note time taken to pressurise system is up to 40 seconds.
3. Start vehicle and drive away, at 7 km/h (5 mph) the ABS warning light must be extinguished. *See this section.*
4. In road conditions where surface friction is sufficient to slow or stop the vehicle without wheel lock, ABS does not operate.
5. In an emergency braking situation, if one or more wheels begin to slow rapidly in relation to vehicle speed, ABS will detect wheel locking tendency and will regulate brake pressure to maintain wheel rotation.
6. ABS operation will be felt as a vibration through pedal, at same time solenoid cycling will be heard.

NOTE: Constant pressure on foot pedal whilst ABS is operating is more effective than cadence braking. Do not pump brake pedal, this may reduce ABS efficiency and increase stopping distance.

7. Downward travel of pedal will also feel hard at point at which ABS operates. Little further pedal travel is possible at this point, BUT, force on the pedal can be varied to influence braking force while ABS retains control.

Brake application with partial failure

WARNING: IF A FAULT DEVELOPS IN THE BRAKE SYSTEM IT IS ESSENTIAL THAT IT IS INVESTIGATED IMMEDIATELY.

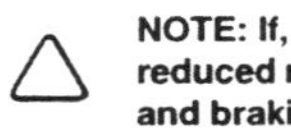

NOTE: If, during braking, a drastically reduced resistance is detected at pedal and braking effectiveness is very much reduced, failure of the non-powered (master cylinder) portion of system is indicated. When this occurs DO NOT PUMP BRAKE PEDAL. Push the pedal through free movement to obtain braking effort from the power circuit. It is essential that brake pedal travel is not obstructed by items such as extra footwell mats.

8. When power assistance is not available, ABS braking is not operative. Both warning lights are illuminated. Braking effort is available from master cylinder only. This results in longer pedal travel and greater pedal effort required to decelerate vehicle.

WARNING: FOOT PRESSURE ON THE PEDAL, USING MASTER CYLINDER ONLY, WILL NOT ACHIEVE THE SAME DEGREE OF BRAKING AS IS AVAILABLE FROM POWER ASSISTANCE.

9. If master cylinder fails, i.e. there is insufficient fluid in master cylinder to create pressure, braking to all four wheels is retained and ABS remains operative. The red warning light will be illuminated if cause of the master cylinder failure is a fluid leak and level in fluid reservoir is low enough to actuate fluid level switch.

WARNING: LONGER PEDAL TRAVEL IS REQUIRED, BUT POWER ASSISTED BRAKING IS AVAILABLE AT REDUCED EFFICIENCY.

10. If brake failure occurs due to a fractured brake pipe between a servo cylinder and a wheel, there may be no pressure in the master cylinder. The fluid warning light will illuminate when level in fluid reservoir is low enough to actuate fluid level switch. Master cylinder and power valve will operate as for master cylinder failure, BUT, fluid from power circuit will push all moving parts in servo cylinder associated with failure to limit of travel. No pressurised fluid passes to the front brake caliper served by the affected servo cylinder, but pistons in rear calipers will be supplied with direct pressure from power valve. The front caliper served by the other servo cylinder retain braking as fluid from master cylinder is retained in servo cylinder not associated with the leakage.

WARNING: BRAKE PEDAL TRAVEL WILL BE GREATER AND EXTRA PEDAL EFFORT WILL BE REQUIRED, ACCOMPANIED BY THE VEHICLE PULLING TO ONE SIDE.

PARKING BRAKE - ADJUST

Service repair no - 70.45.09

Adjust

Shoes

1. Raise vehicle on four post lift.
2. Ensure brake lever is released. Raise lift.
3. Raise one rear wheel clear of lift.
4. Tighten brake shoe adjusting bolt to ***25 Nm. (18 lbf.ft).*** Ensure brake drum is locked.

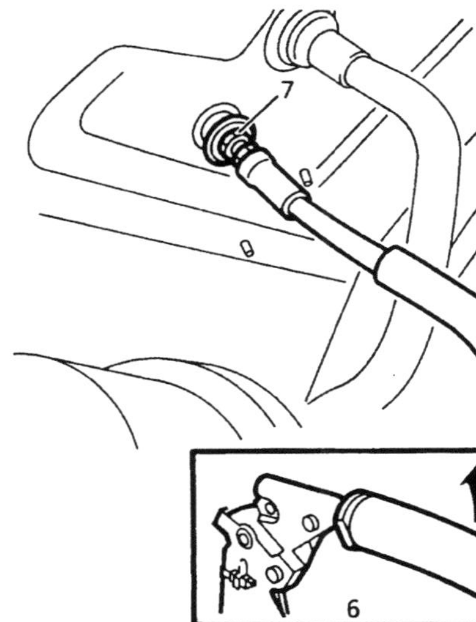

70M7015

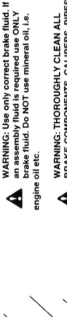

5. Back off adjusting bolt by 1.5 turns. Check brake drum is free to rotate.

Cable

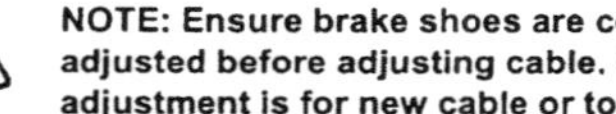

NOTE: Ensure brake shoes are correctly adjusted before adjusting cable. Cable adjustment is for new cable or to compensate for cable stretch. Cable adjustment must not be used to take up brake shoe wear.

6. Parking brake should be fully operational on the third notch of ratchet with a pull of 15 kg. (30 lbs) on end of the brake lever.
7. To achieve this, release brake lever. From under vehicle, adjust length of outer cable.

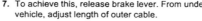

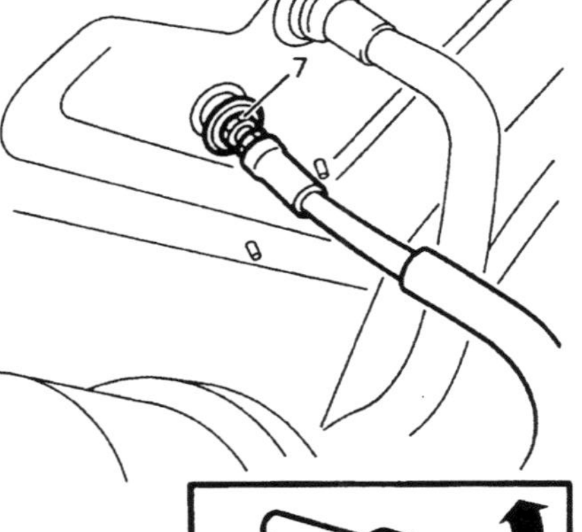

70M7016

8. Lower vehicle.

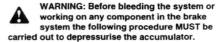

GENERAL SERVICE INFORMATION

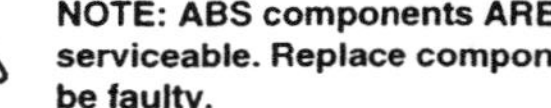

NOTE: ABS components ARE NOT serviceable. Replace components found to be faulty.

Brake fluid precautions

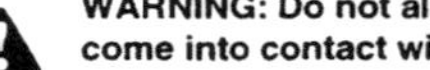

WARNING: Do not allow brake fluid to come into contact with eyes or skin.

CAUTION: Brake fluid can damage paintwork, if spilled wash off immediately with plenty of clean water.

WARNING: Use only correct brake fluid. If an assembly fluid is required use ONLY brake fluid. Do NOT use mineral oil, i.e. engine oil etc.

WARNING: THOROUGHLY CLEAN ALL BRAKE COMPONENTS, CALIPERS, PIPES AND FITTINGS BEFORE COMMENCING WORK ON BRAKE SYSTEM. FAILURE TO DO SO COULD CAUSE FOREIGN MATTER TO ENTER SYSTEM AND DAMAGE SEALS AND PISTONS, WHICH WILL SERIOUSLY IMPAIR BRAKE SYSTEM EFFICIENCY.

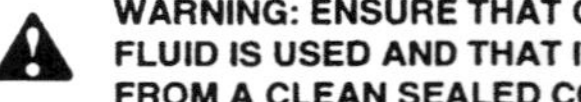

WARNING: ENSURE THAT ONLY NEW FLUID IS USED AND THAT IT IS TAKEN FROM A CLEAN SEALED CONTAINER.

DO NOT USE BRAKE FLUID PREVIOUSLY BLED FROM SYSTEM.

DO NOT USE OLD OR STORED BRAKE FLUID.

Brake system must be drained and flushed at recommended service intervals.

DO NOT flush brake system with any fluid other than recommended brake fluid.

DEPRESSURISE SYSTEM - Fluid pressure of 190 bar is produced by hydraulic pump. It is essential that the system is depressurised where instructed. ***See this section.***

FLUID LEVEL CHECK/TOP UP

1. Park vehicle on level ground.
2. Turn ignition ON, to activate hydraulic pump. If pump does not operate depress brake pedal several times until pump operates.
3. When pump stops, check level is between 'MIN' and 'MAX' marks.

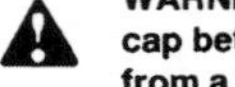

WARNING: Clean reservoir body and filler cap before removing cap. Use only fluid from a sealed container.

4. If level is below 'MIN' mark top up fluid level to 'MAX' mark on reservoir, using correct fluid. ***See LUBRICANTS, FLUIDS AND CAPACITIES, Information.***

DO NOT OVER FILL RESERVOIR

DEPRESSURISE SYSTEM

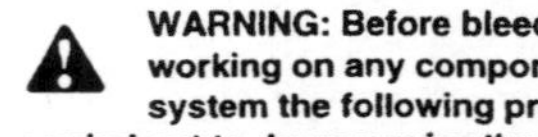

WARNING: Before bleeding the system or working on any component in the brake system the following procedure MUST be carried out to depressurise the accumulator.

1. Switch off ignition.
2. Operate the brake pedal 30 times. Pedal travel will increase slightly and reduced resistance will be felt as pressure decreases.
3. Wait for 60 seconds, press the brake pedal four more times. This procedure will ensure that all pressure is evacuated from the system.

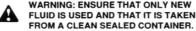

BRAKE SYSTEM BLEED

Service repair no - 70.25.02

Equipment: Bleed tube and a clean bottle containing a small amount of clean brake fluid.

CAUTION: Thoroughly clean all bleed screws, filler cap and connections using only clean brake fluid. DO NOT USE MINERAL OIL I.E. ENGINE OIL ETC. MAINTAIN CLEANLINESS THROUGHOUT.

NOTE: Do not allow reservoir fluid level to fall below 'MIN' level during bleeding. Regularly check level and keep topped up to 'MAX' level.

WARNING: Do not use previously used brake fluid. Ensure only new fluid is used, taken from a clean sealed container. Carefully dispose of unwanted fluid in a sealed container, marked USED BRAKE FLUID.

1. Depressurise system. ***See this section.***

NOTE: Ensure ignition remains OFF until instruction 13.

2. Fill fluid reservoir with specified fluid to 'MAX' level.
3. Bleed master cylinder as follows: Open bleed screw on booster, when fluid appears, close bleed screw.

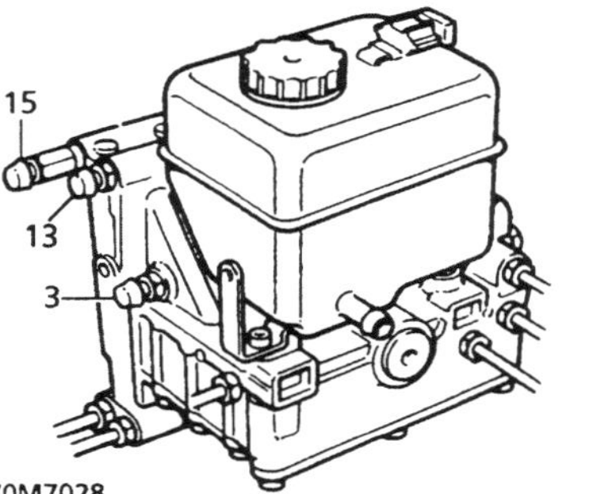

70M7028

4. Fit tube to bleed screw.
5. Open bleed screw, depress pedal slowly and progressively.
6. Close bleed screw. Release brake pedal.
7. Repeat instructions 5. and 6. until fluid is clear of air bubbles.
8. Open bleed screw, fully depress pedal, close bleed screw.
9. Bleed front calipers, driver's side caliper first, as follows: Open bleed screw, depress brake pedal slowly and progressively, Close bleed screw at bottom of each stroke, release pedal.

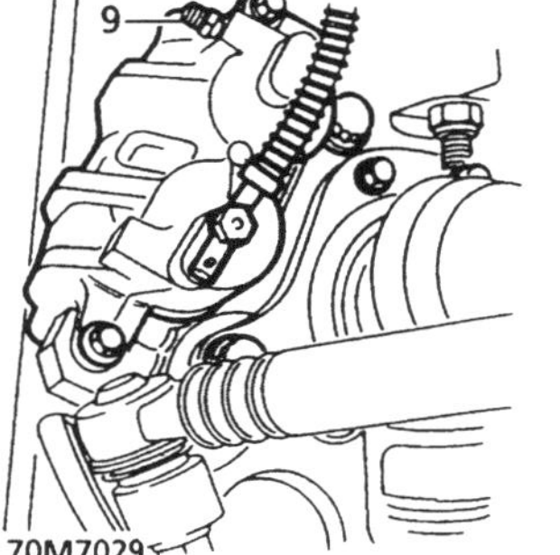

70M7029

10. Repeat instruction 9. until fluid is clear of air bubbles.
11. Open bleed screw again. Fully depress brake pedal, close bleed screw.
12. Repeat instructions 9. to 11. for passenger side caliper.
13. Bleed two booster bleed screws, starting at the front bleed screw, as follows: Open bleed screw, depress brake pedal, switch ignition on.
14. Allow fluid to flow until clear of air bubbles. Switch ignition off, close bleed screw, release pedal.
15. Repeat instructions 13. and 14. for the rear booster bleed screw.

16. Bleed each rear caliper, driver's side caliper first, as follows: Open bleed screw, depress brake pedal slowly and progressively.

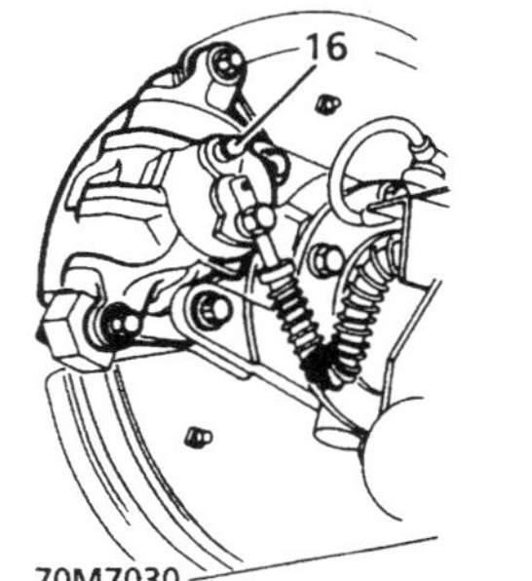

70M7030

17. Switch on ignition for 4 seconds. Switch off ignition for 4 seconds. Repeat until fluid is clear of air bubbles.
18. Switch off ignition, close bleed screw, release pedal.
19. Switch on ignition, wait for ABS pump to stop running. Press brake pedal down firmly and fully release it five times.
20. With ignition on, repeat front caliper bleed instructions 9. to 12. Use only the lower two thirds of pedal travel when bleeding.
21. Repeat instruction 19.
22. Check/top up reservoir fluid level, ***See this section.***

NOTE: If ABS pump makes a ticking noise when running during this procedure, repeat instructions 13. to 19. When the bleed procedure has been successfully completed, the ABS pump will not make any ticking noises.

ACCUMULATOR

Service repair no - 70.65.21

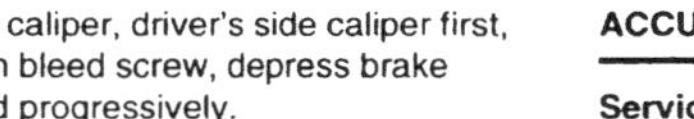

WARNING: The accumulator is precharged with nitrogen at a pressure of up to 80 bar (1160 lbf/in²). Handle with extreme caution. DO NOT puncture or burn if disposal is necessary.

Remove

1. Disconnect battery negative lead.
2. Depressurise system. ***See this section.***
3. Position cloth beneath accumulator to catch any fluid spillage.
4. Remove accumulator. Discard 'O' ring.

70M7031

Disposal

WARNING: It is essential that safety goggles are worn when carrying out this procedure.

5. Secure accumulator firmly in a suitable vice.
6. Drill 5mm hole in top of accumulator to depressurise nitrogen chamber.
7. Dispose of accumulator in an approved manner

Refit

8. Using a new 'O' ring, fit accumulator to pump.
9. Reconnect battery negative lead.
10. Bleed braking system. ***See this section.***

ACCUMULATOR PRECHARGE - CHECK

The diaphragm type accumulator is precharged with nitrogen at 80 bar (1160 lbf/in²), its function is to store hydraulic energy. Over a period of years, a normal loss of precharge will occur. This procedure will indicate the extent to which precharge pressure has fallen.

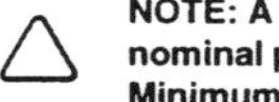

NOTE: A new accumulator at 20°C has a nominal pressure of 80 bar (1160 lbf/in²). Minimum acceptable pressure is 50 bar (725 lbf/in²).

1. Depressurise braking system. ***See this section.***
2. Remove 3 nuts securing pump/motor assembly to valance. Raise assembly from mounting to allow clearance for pressure test adaptor.
3. Remove banjo bolt securing high pressure hose to pump. Collect sealing washers.

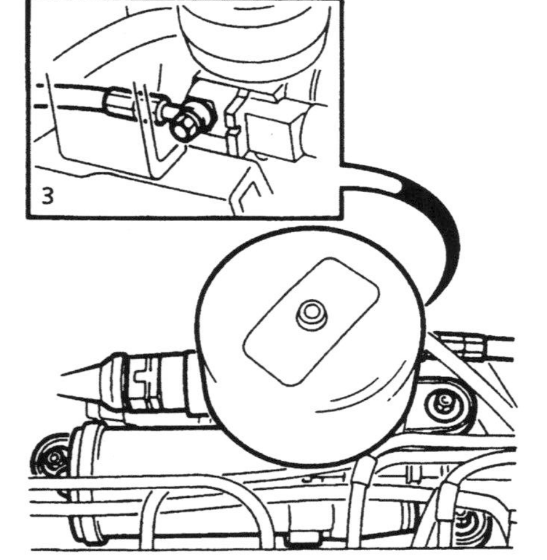

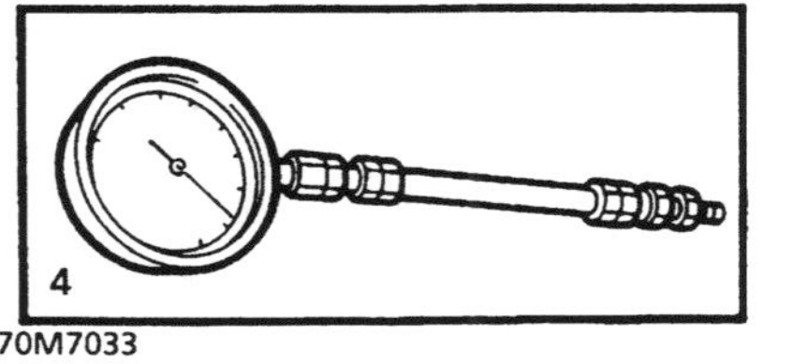

70M7033

4. Connect pressure gauge to pump using LRT-70-003 through high pressure hose union.

NOTE: Use original sealing washers.

5. Switch ignition on. Observe pressure gauge.
6. Pressure will rapidly rise to the accumulator precharge value, point X, at which point rate of increase will reduce as pressure rises to system pressure of approx. 170 bar - see graph 'A'.

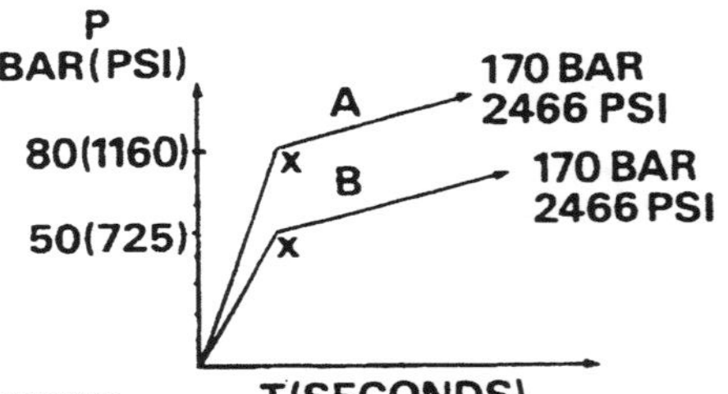

70M7035

7. With a new accumulator, point 'X' will occur at 80 bar.
8. Renew accumulator if point 'X' occurs below 50 bar.
9. Depressurise system. Remove test equipment.
10. Using new sealing washers, position high pressure hose to pump. Secure with banjo bolt. Tighten to ***24 Nm. (18 lbf.ft)***
11. Align pump/motor assembly to mounting. Secure with nuts. Tighten to ***8 Nm. (6 lbf.ft)***
12. Bleed brake system. ***See this section.***

HYDRAULIC BOOSTER UNIT

Service repair no - 70.65.20

Remove

1. Disconnect battery negative lead.
2. Depressurise braking system. ***See this section.***
3. **RHD Vehicles Only:** Release coolant expansion tank from clips and bracket. Position tank aside for access to booster pipe connections.
4. **LHD Diesel Vehicles Only:** Remove 2 bolts securing fuel filter assembly to chassis turret. Move filter aside.

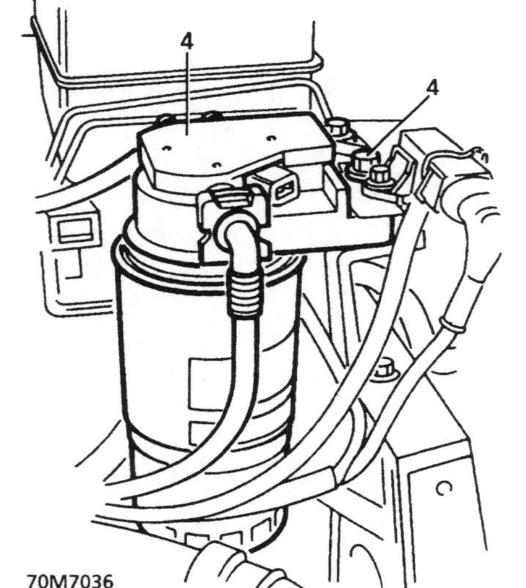

70M7036

5. Position cloth under booster to collect fluid spillage.
6. Release clip from fluid reservoir hose at pump. Disconnect hose.
7. Allow fluid to drain into suitable container. Discard fluid. Plug hose and pump.
8. Disconnect hose from reservoir. Plug hose and reservoir.

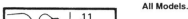

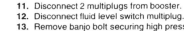

70M7037

Manual Vehicles only.

9. Reposition container beneath clutch master cylinder feed hose.
10. Disconnect clutch hose from reservoir. Allow fluid to drain. Plug hose and reservoir.

All Models.

11. Disconnect 2 multiplugs from booster.
12. Disconnect fluid level switch multiplug.
13. Remove banjo bolt securing high pressure hose to pump. Discard sealing washers. Plug hose and pump.
14. Unscrew pipe unions from booster. Plug pipes and booster.
15. Remove closing panel. ***See CHASSIS AND BODY, Repair.*** Remove stop light switch. ***See this section.***
16. Release booster push rod from brake pedal.

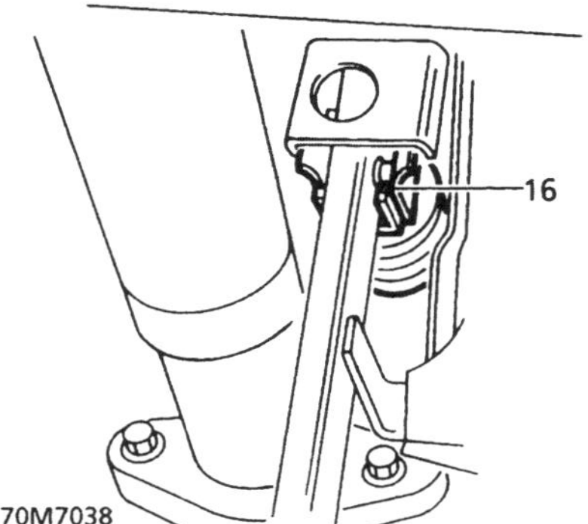

70M7038

17. Remove 2 bolts securing booster assembly to pedal box. Remove booster.

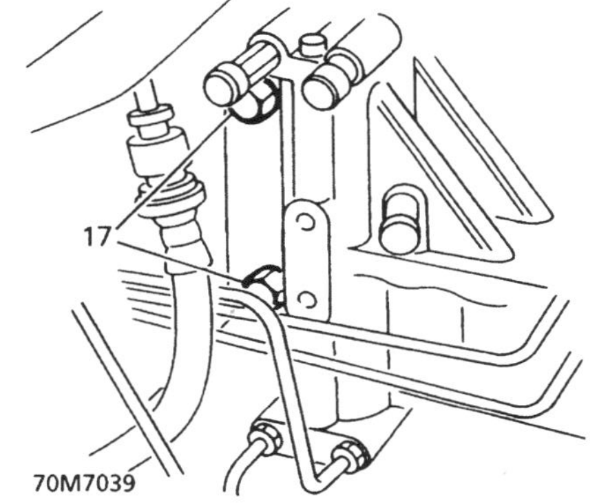

70M7039

18. Remove banjo bolt securing high pressure hose to booster. Discard sealing washers. Plug hose and booster.

70M7040

Refit

19. Remove plugs from high pressure hose and booster.
20. Position high pressure hose to booster. Secure with banjo bolt and new sealing washers. Tighten to ***24 Nm. (18 lbf.ft)***
21. Position booster to pedal box. Ensure push rod engages with pedal. Secure booster with bolts. Tighten to ***45 Nm. (33 lbf.ft)***
22. Remove plugs from brake pipes and booster. Align pipes to booster. Secure union nuts. Tighten to ***14 Nm. (10 lbf.ft)***
23. Remove plugs from high pressure hose and pump.
24. Position high pressure hose to pump. Secure with banjo bolt and new sealing washers. Tighten to ***24 Nm. (18 lbf.ft)***
25. Connect fluid level switch multiplug.
26. Connect 2 multiplugs to booster.
27. **Manual Vehicles only.** Remove plugs from clutch fluid hose and reservoir. Connect hose. Secure with clip.
28. Remove plugs from reservoir, brake fluid hose and pump.
29. Position hose to reservoir and pump. Secure with new clips.
30. Remove cloth from under booster.
31. **LHD Diesel Vehicles Only:** Align fuel filter to chassis turret. Secure with 2 bolts.
32. **RHD Vehicles Only:** Engage coolant expansion tank beneath bracket. Engage with clips.
33. Reconnect battery negative lead.
34. Bleed braking system. ***See this section.***
35. Fit Fascia closing panel. ***See CHASSIS AND BODY, Repair.***

FRONT CALIPER

Service repair no - 70.55.02

Remove

1. Remove brake pads. ***See this section.***
2. Using an approved hose clamp, clamp flexible hose at caliper.
3. Remove banjo bolt securing flexible hose to caliper. Discard sealing washers.

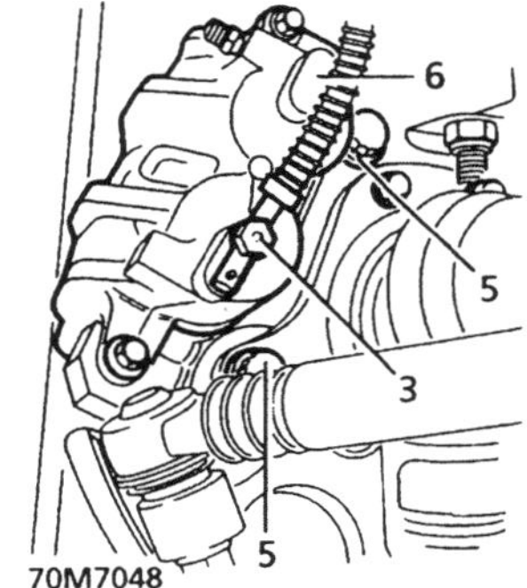

70M7048

4. Plug caliper and hose to prevent ingress of dirt.
5. Remove 2 bolts securing caliper.
6. Remove caliper.

Refit

7. Clean exposed parts of caliper pistons with brake fluid.
8. Fit caliper to hub and secure with bolts. Tighten to ***165 Nm. (122 lbf.ft)***
9. Remove plugs from caliper and hose.
10. Using new sealing washers, position hose to caliper. Secure with banjo bolt. Tighten to ***32Nm. (24 lbf.ft)***
11. Remove hose clamp.
12. Refit brake pads. ***See this section.***
13. Bleed both front brake calipers. ***See this section.***
14. Remove safety stands. Lower vehicle.
15. Press brake pedal firmly several times to seat brake pads.

REAR CALIPER

Service repair no - 70.55.03

Remove

1. Remove brake pads. ***See this section.***
2. Using an approved hose clamp, clamp flexible hose at caliper.
3. Remove banjo bolt securing flexible hose to caliper. Discard sealing washers.

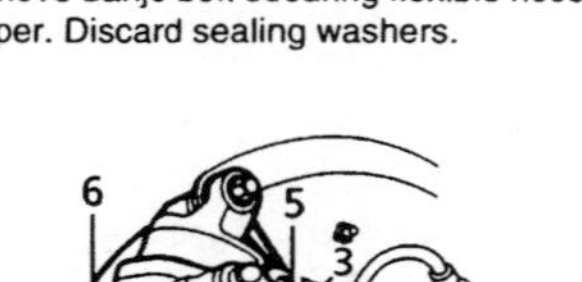
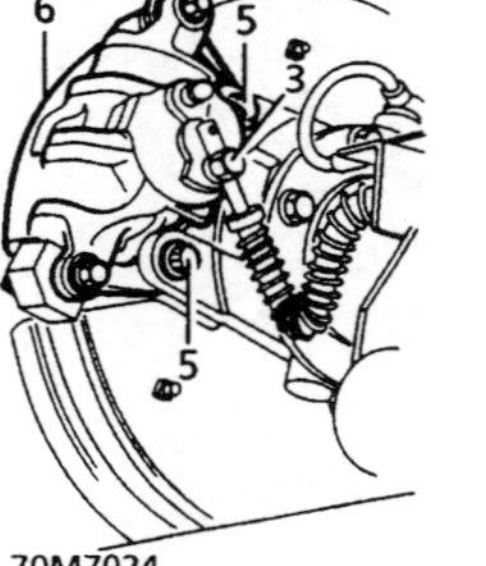

70M7024

4. Plug caliper and hose to prevent ingress of dirt.
5. Remove 2 bolts securing caliper.
6. Remove caliper.

Refit

7. Clean exposed parts of caliper piston with brake fluid.
8. Fit caliper to hub and secure with bolts. Tighten to ***100Nm. (74 lbf.ft)***
9. Remove plugs from caliper and hose.
10. Using new sealing washers, position hose to caliper and secure with banjo bolt. Tighten to ***32Nm. (24 lbf.ft)***
11. Remove hose clamp.
12. Refit brake pads. ***See this section.***
13. Bleed both rear brake calipers. ***See this section.***
14. Remove safety stands. Lower vehicle.
15. Press brake pedal firmly several times to seat brake pads.

ELECTRONIC CONTROL UNIT (ECU)

Service repair no - 70.25.34

Remove

1. Remove 3 scrivet fasteners securing the passenger side fascia closing panel. Release panel for access to ABS ECU.

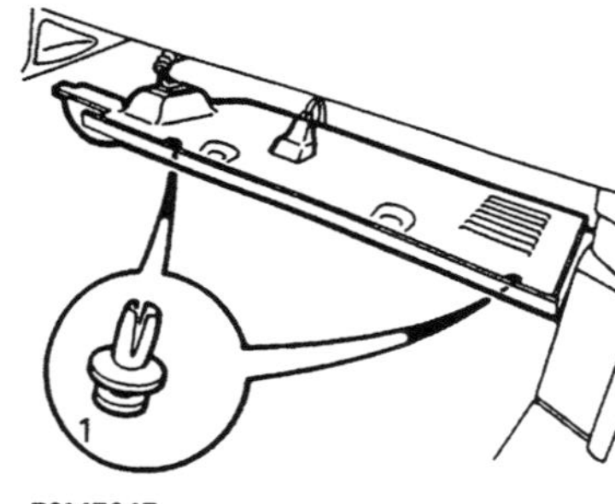

70M7047

2. Disconnect ECU multiplug.

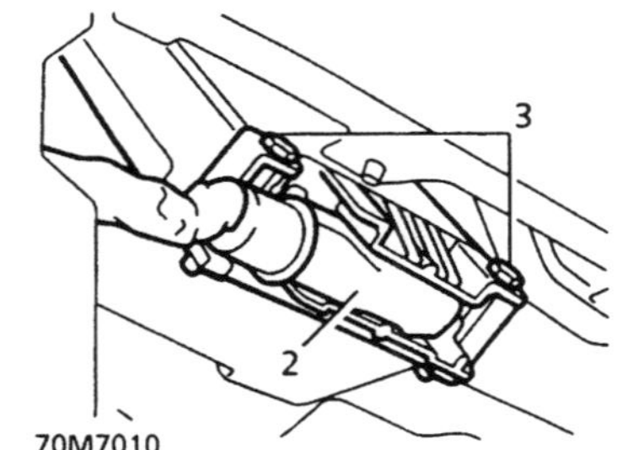

70M7010

3. Remove 2 bolts securing ECU to bracket.
4. Remove ECU.

Refit

5. Locate ECU to bracket, fit securing bolts. Tighten to ***6 Nm. (4 lbf.ft)***
6. Connect multiplug to ECU. Position closing panel, secure with scrivet fasteners.

BRAKE DISC AND SHIELD - FRONT

Service repair no - 70.10.12 - Front disc
Service repair no - 70.10.18 - Disc shield

Remove

1. Remove front brake pads. ***See this section.***
2. Remove 2 bolts securing caliper.

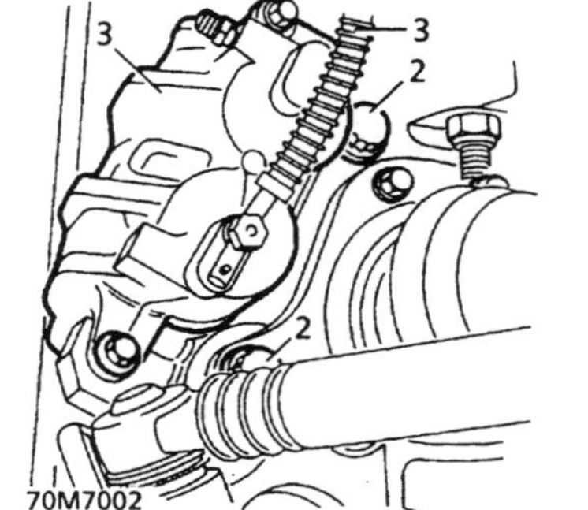

70M7002

3. Tie caliper aside, ensuring brake hose is not stressed.
4. Remove screw securing disc, remove disc.

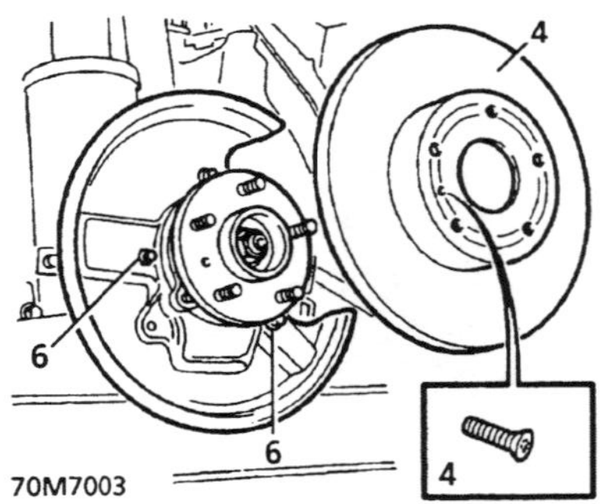

70M7003

5. Using a wire brush, remove corrosion from mating faces. Clean with a suitable solvent.
6. Remove 3 bolts, remove disc shield.

Refit

7. Fit disc shield, secure with bolts. Tighten to ***8 Nm. (6 lbf.ft)***
8. Fit brake disc, secure with screw. Tighten to ***25 Nm. (18 lbf.ft)***
9. Untie brake caliper.
10. Fit brake caliper, secure with bolts. Tighten to ***165 Nm. (122 lbf.ft)***
11. Fit front brake pads. ***See this section.***

BRAKE DISC AND SHIELD - REAR

Service repair no - 70.10.34 - Rear disc
Service repair no - 70.10.19 - Disc shield

Remove

1. Remove rear brake pads. ***See this section.***
2. Remove 2 bolts securing caliper.

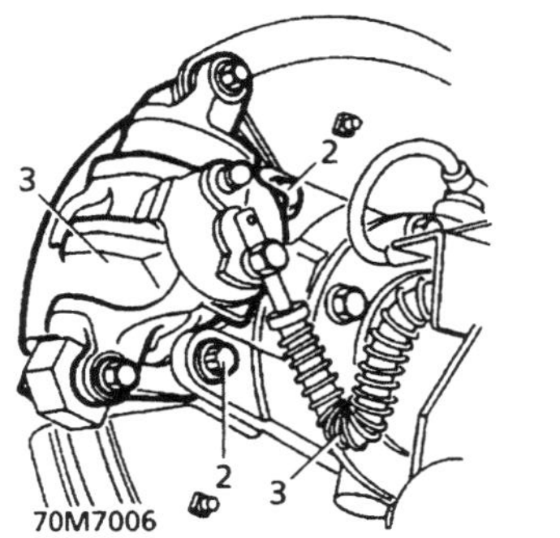

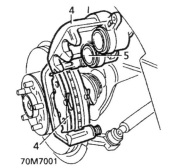

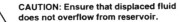

70M7006

3. Tie caliper aside, ensuring brake hose is not stressed.
4. Remove screw securing disc, remove disc.

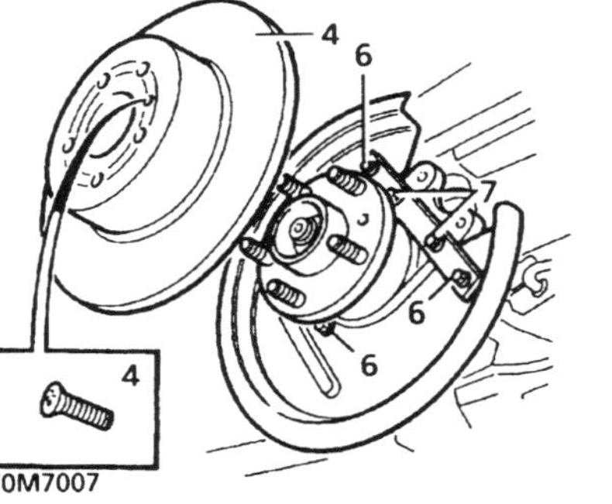

70M7007

5. Using a wire brush, remove corrosion from disc mating faces before cleaning with a suitable solvent.
6. Remove 3 bolts, remove disc shield.
7. Remove 2 bolts, remove shield strap.

Refit

8. Fit shield strap, secure with bolts. Tighten to ***8 Nm. (6 lbf.ft)***
9. Fit disc shield, fit securing bolts. Tighten to ***8 Nm. (6 lbf.ft)***
10. Fit brake disc, secure with screw. Tighten to ***25 Nm. (18 lbf.ft)***
11. Untie brake caliper.
12. Fit brake caliper, fit bolts. Tighten to ***100 Nm. (74 lbf.ft)***
13. Fit rear brake pads. ***See this section.***

BRAKE PADS - FRONT

Service repair no - 70.40.02

Service tool:
LRT-70-500 - Piston clamp

Remove

1. Raise the vehicle.

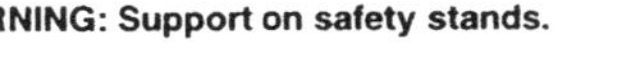

WARNING: Support on safety stands.

2. Remove front road wheels.
3. Remove bolt from lower guide pin of each caliper.

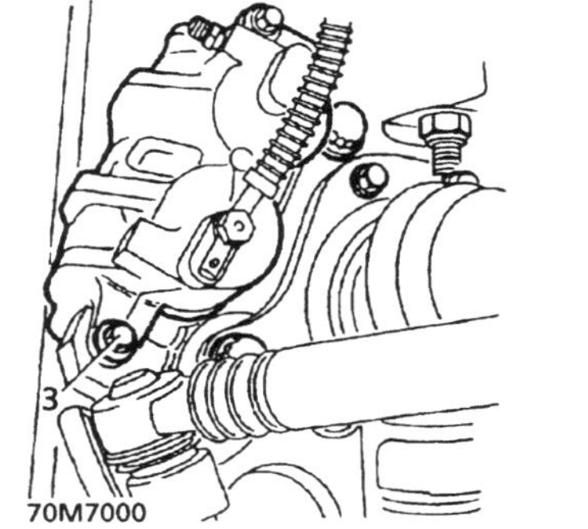
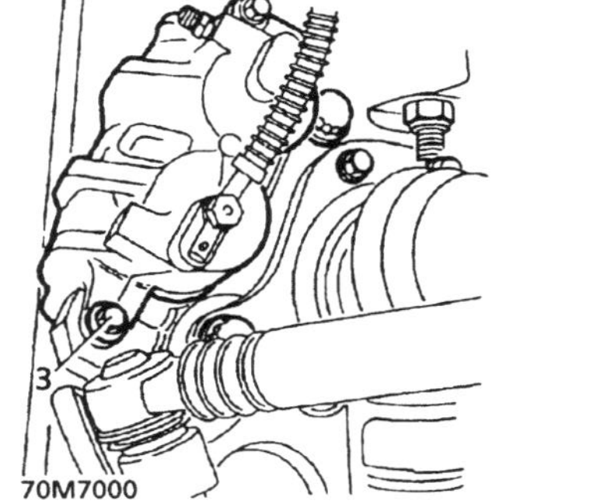

70M7000

CAUTION: Guide pin uses a special, flange headed bolt. DO NOT use any other type of bolt.

4. Swivel caliper upwards, remove brake pads.

70M7001

5. Using piston clamp, LRT-70-500, press caliper pistons fully into bores.

CAUTION: Ensure that displaced fluid does not overflow from reservoir.

6. Clean faces of pistons and pad locations in caliper.
7. Check condition of guide pin boots, replace if perished or split.

Refit

8. Fit brake pads with chamfer towards leading edge of disc (towards rear of vehicle). Swivel caliper downwards into position.
9. Fit new guide pin bolt. Tighten to ***30 Nm. (22 lbf.ft)***
10. Apply brake pedal several times to locate pads.
11. Check fluid reservoir level, top-up if necessary using correct grade of fluid. ***See LUBRICANTS, FLUIDS AND CAPACITIES, Information.***
12. Fit road wheels. Tighten nuts to ***108 Nm (80 lbf.ft).***
13. Remove safety stands. Lower vehicle.

BRAKE PADS - REAR

Service repair no - 70.40.03

Service tool:
LRT-70-500 - Piston clamp

Remove

1. Raise the vehicle.

WARNING: Support on safety stands.

2. Remove rear road wheels.
3. Remove bolt from lower guide pin of each caliper.

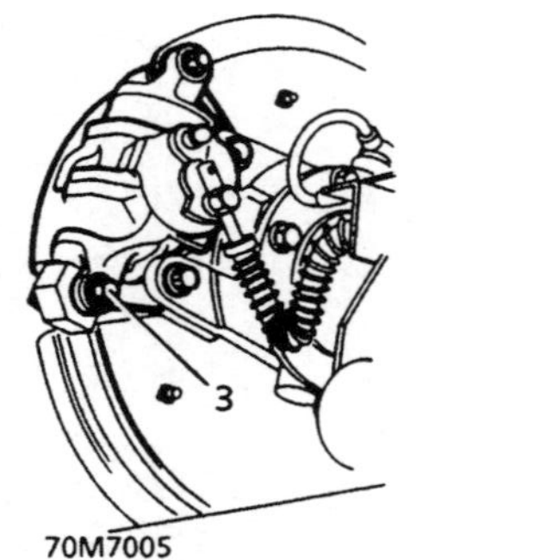

70M7005

4. Swivel caliper upwards, remove brake pads.

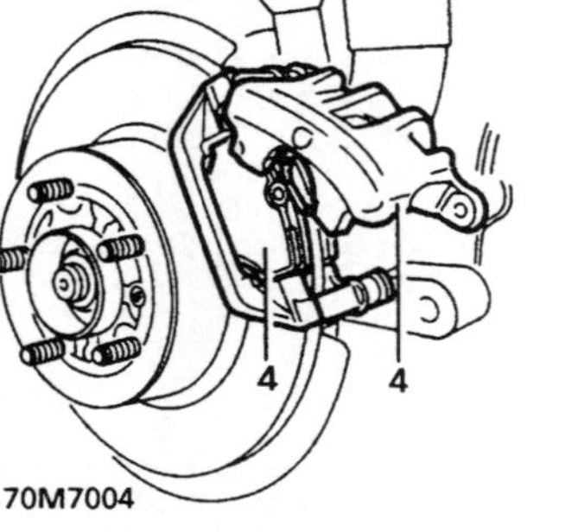

70M7004

5. Using piston clamp, LRT-70-500, press caliper piston fully into bore.

CAUTION: Ensure that displaced fluid does not overflow from reservoir.

6. Clean faces of piston and pad locations in caliper.
7. Check condition of guide pin boots, replace if perished or split.

Refit

8. Fit brake pads with chamfer towards leading edge of disc (towards rear of vehicle). Swivel calipers downwards into position.
9. Fit new guide pin bolts, tighten to ***30 Nm. (22 lbf.ft).***
10. Apply brake pedal several times to locate pads.
11. Check fluid reservoir level. Top-up if necessary using correct grade of fluid. ***See LUBRICANTS, FLUIDS AND CAPACITIES, Information.***
12. Refit road wheels. Tighten nuts to ***108 Nm. (80 lbf.ft).***
13. Remove safety stands. Lower vehicle.

PARKING BRAKE CABLE

Service repair no - 70.35.25

Remove

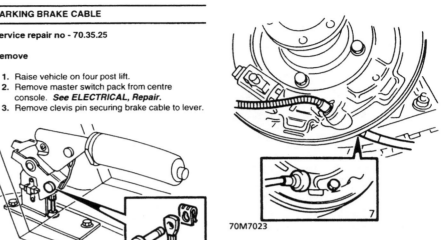

1. Raise vehicle on four post lift.
2. Remove master switch pack from centre console. ***See ELECTRICAL, Repair.***
3. Remove clevis pin securing brake cable to lever.

70M7022

4. Raise lift.
5. From under vehicle pull cable through grommet in floor. Refit grommet to floor.
6. Remove brake shoes. ***See this section.***
7. Release cable from backplate.

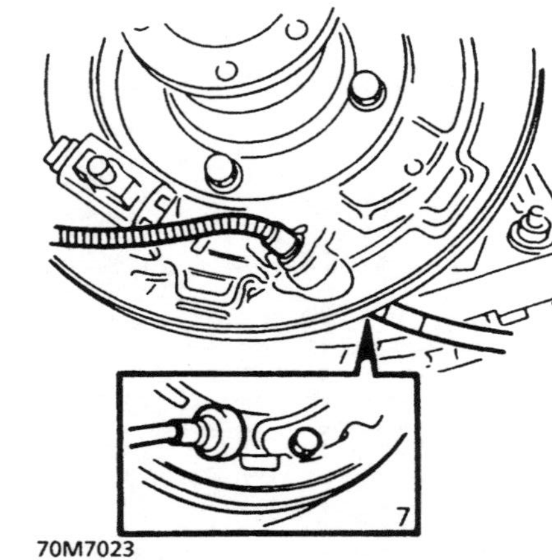

70M7023

Refit

8. Fit cable to backplate.
9. Fit brake shoes and drum. ***See this section.***
10. Feed brake cable through grommet into vehicle.
11. From inside vehicle, align cable to handbrake lever. Secure with clevis pin and clip.
12. Fit master switch pack. ***See ELECTRICAL, Repair.***
13. Adjust parking brake. ***See Adjustment.***

PARK BRAKE LEVER

Service repair no - 70.45.01

Remove

1. Raise vehicle on four post lift.
2. Disconnect battery negative lead.
3. Remove centre console. ***See CHASSIS AND BODY, Repair.***
4. Disconnect 2 Lucars from parking brake warning switch.

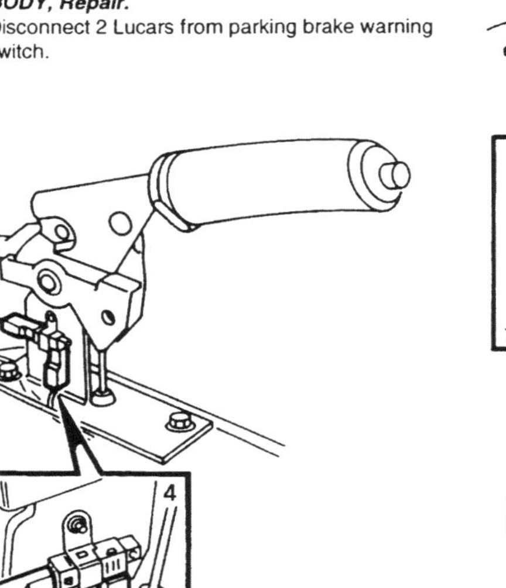

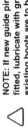

5. Raise lift.
6. Pull brake cable through grommet in base of lever.
7. Remove 2 bolts securing lever. Remove lever.

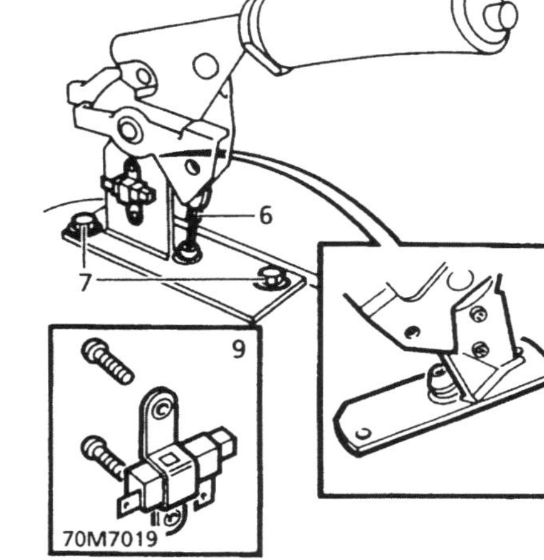

8. Remove grommet from lever.
9. Remove 2 screws securing warning switch. Remove switch.

Refit

10. Reverse removal procedure.
11. Adjust parking brake. ***See Adjustment.***

CALIPER GUIDE PIN BOOTS

Service repair no - 70.55.32

Remove

1. Remove brake pads. ***See this section.***
2. Remove remaining bolts securing caliper body to carrier.
3. Release caliper body from carrier. Tie aside. Do not strain hydraulic hose.
4. Remove 2 guide pins. Collect boot from each guide pin.

Check

5. Clean guide pins, bores and boots.
6. Inspect guide pins and bores. Renew guide pins if scored or excessively corroded.
7. Inspect boots for splits. Replace as necessary.

Refit

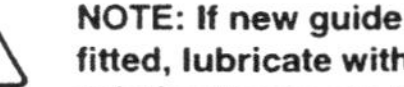

NOTE: If new guide pin boots are to be fitted, lubricate with grease supplied. If existing boots are to be re-used, lubricate with Kluber Syntheso 'GLK 1' grease.

8. Fit guide pins and boots. Ensure boots locate correctly.
9. Untie caliper body, position to carrier. Fit upper guide pin bolt. Tighten to ***30 Nm. (22 lbf.ft)***
10. Fit brake pads. ***See this section.***

PARKING BRAKE DRUM AND SHOES

Service repair no - 70.45.17 - Brake Drum
Service repair no - 70.45.18 - Brake Shoes

WARNING: Do not use an air line to remove dust from brake assembly. Dust from brake linings can be a serious health risk if inhaled.

Remove

1. Raise vehicle on four post lift.
2. Release hand brake. Raise lift.
3. Remove 4 bolts securing rear propshaft guard. Remove guard.

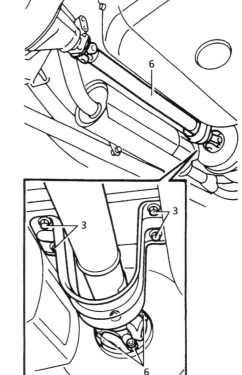

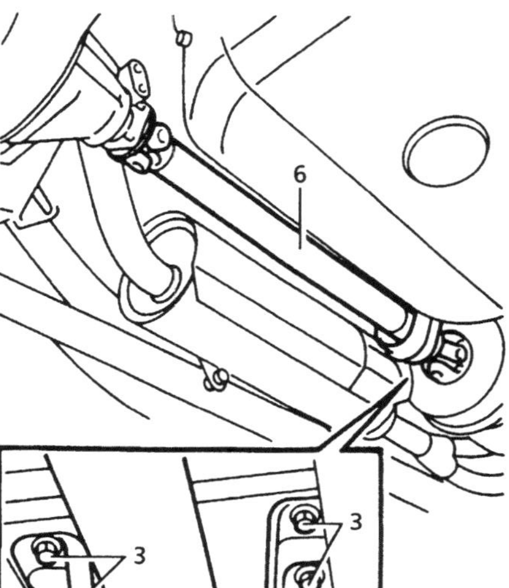

4. Mark propeller shaft flange and brake drum to aid re-assembly.
5. Raise one rear wheel to allow rotation of propeller shaft.
6. Remove 4 nuts securing shaft to drum. Release shaft. Tie aside.
7. Remove screw securing drum to drive flange. Remove drum.
8. Remove 2 washers, springs and pins retaining brake shoes to backplate.
9. Remove brake shoe. Collect pull off springs and abutment plate. Release remaining shoe from brake cable.
10. Remove adjuster plungers.
11. Remove 'C' clip securing cable lever to shoe. Remove flat washer, lever, 2 bellville washers and pivot pin.
12. Clean components with aerosol brake cleaner. Allow to dry. Examine components for wear. Replace as necessary.

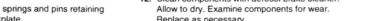

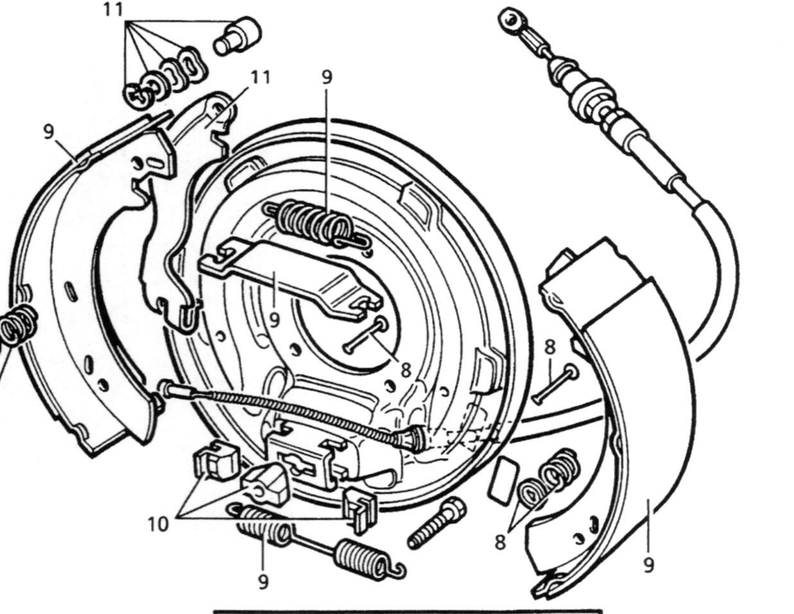
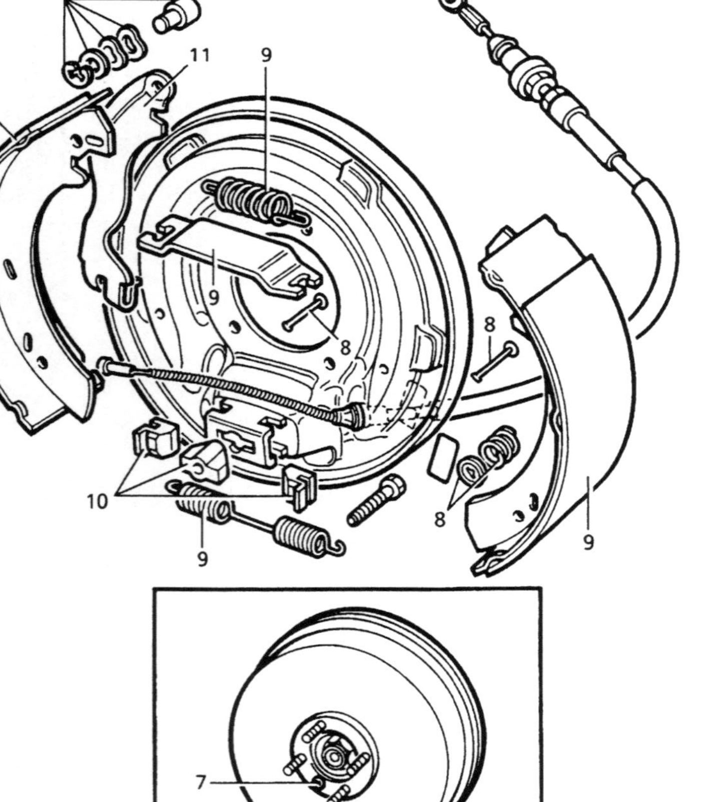

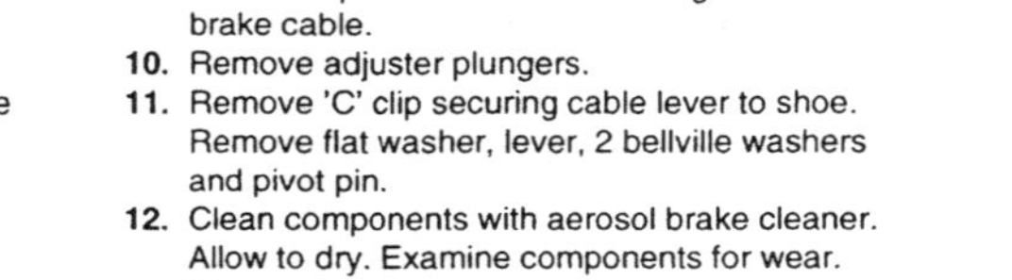

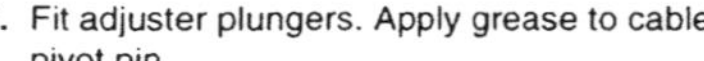

70M7014

Refit

13. Fit adjuster plungers. Apply grease to cable lever pivot pin.
14. Fit pivot pin to shoe.
15. Fit 2 bellville washers, cable lever and flat washer. Secure with 'C' clip.
16. Fit shoe to brake cable, align to backplate and adjuster. Secure shoe to back plate with pin, spring and washer.
17. Fit abutment plate to shoe.
18. Fit pull off springs with remaining shoe. Secure shoe to backplate with pin, spring and washer.
19. Fit brake drum. Secure with screw.
20. Position propeller shaft to brake drum. Align marks. Secure with bolts. Tighten to ***48 Nm. (35 lbf.ft)***
21. Fit rear propeller shaft guard. Secure with bolts.
22. Adjust park brake. ***See Adjustment.***
23. Remove support from under rear wheel. Lower lift.

PRESSURE CONSCIOUS REDUCING VALVE (PCRV)

Service repair no - 70.25.21

Remove

1. Depressurise braking system. ***See this section.***
2. **RHD Vehicles Only:** Release coolant reservoir from clips and bracket. Place reservoir aside for access to PCRV.

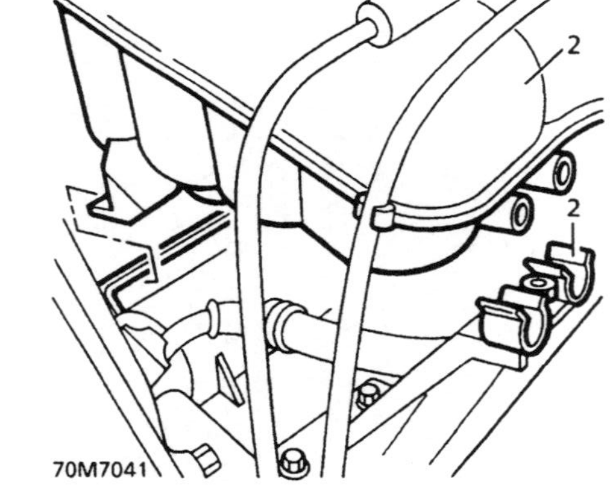

70M7041

3. Position cloth beneath PCRV to catch fluid spillage.
4. Disconnect pipes from PCRV.

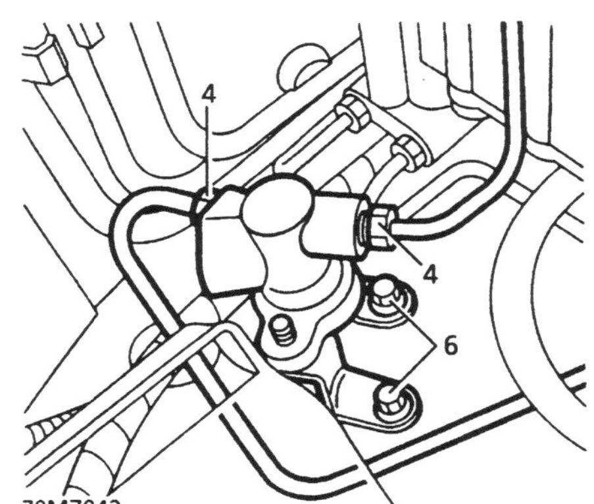

70M7042

5. Plug pipes and connections.
6. Remove 2 bolts securing PCRV to valance. Remove PCRV.

Refit

7. Position PCRV to valance. Secure with bolts. Tighten to ***8 Nm. (6 lbf.ft)***
8. Remove plugs from PCRV and pipes.
9. Connect pipes to PCRV. Tighten unions to ***14 Nm. (10lbf.ft)***
10. **RHD Vehicles Only:** Engage coolant reservoir beneath bracket. Secure to clips.
11. Bleed brake system. ***See this section.***

PUMP AND MOTOR

Service repair no - 70.65.02

Remove

CAUTION: Whenever pump/motor assembly is replaced, the ABS relay must also be replaced - See Description and Operation - Location Of Components - ABS Illustration.

1. Disconnect battery negative lead.
2. Remove accumulator. ***See this section.***
3. Position cloth to catch fluid spillage.
4. Release clip securing reservoir hose to pump.
5. Disconnect reservoir hose. Plugs hose and connection.
6. Remove banjo bolt securing high pressure hose to pump. Collect sealing washers and discard. Plug hose and connection.

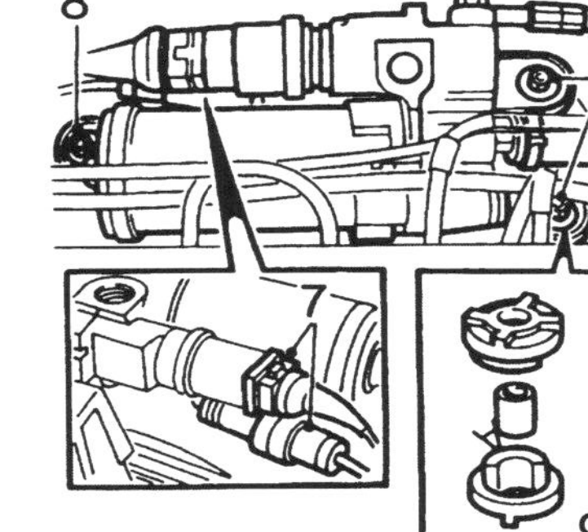

70M7034A

7. Disconnect multiplugs from motor and pressure switch.
8. Remove 3 nuts securing pump/motor assembly to valance. Remove assembly.
9. Collect rubber mountings and inserts from pump brackets.
10. Remove and discard ABS pump relay.

Refit

11. Fit rubbers and inserts to pump mountings.
12. Position pump/motor assembly to valance. Secure with nuts. Tighten to ***8 Nm. (6 lbf.ft)***
13. Connect motor and pressure switch multiplugs.
14. Remove plugs from high pressure hose and pump.
15. Position high pressure hose to pump, ensuring correct location of the banjo timing peg into the slot. Secure with banjo bolt and new sealing washers. Tighten to ***24 Nm. (18 lbf.ft)***
16. Remove plugs from reservoir hose and pump. Connect hose. Secure with clip.
17. Fit accumulator. ***See this section.***
18. Fit replacement ABS pump relay.
19. Reconnect battery negative lead.

RESERVOIR AND SEALS

Service repair no - 70.65.22

Remove

1. Disconnect fluid level switch multiplug. Remove fluid filler cap.

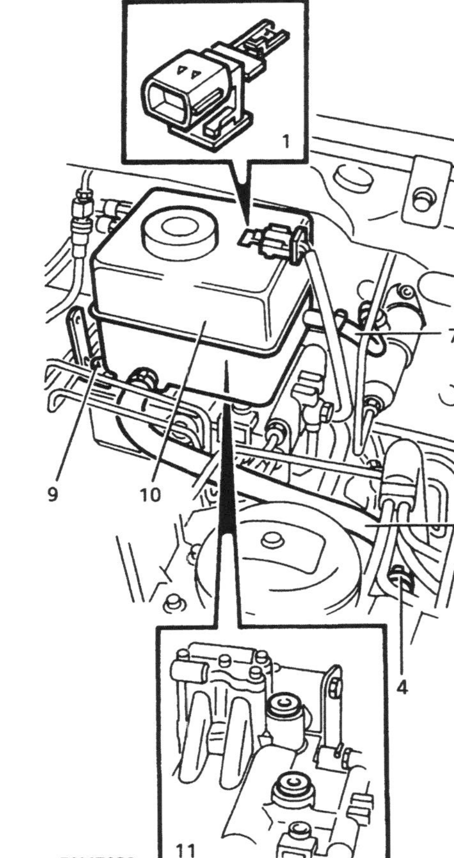

70M7032

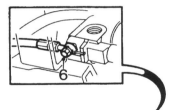

2. Position container to collect fluid.
3. Position cloth beneath pump to catch spillage.
4. Release clip securing reservoir hose to pump.
5. Release reservoir hose from pump. Drain reservoir into container.

Manual Vehicles only.

6. Reposition container beneath clutch reservoir hose.
7. Disconnect clutch master cylinder hose. Drain fluid into container.

All Vehicles.

8. Plug pipes and connections.
9. Remove bolt. Collect reservoir securing bracket.
10. Remove reservoir from 2 seals.
11. Remove reservoir seals from booster unit.

CAUTION: Do not allow seal debris to enter booster ports.

12. Plug reservoir and booster ports.
13. Release 2 clips securing fluid level switch to reservoir. Remove switch.

Refit

14. Fit fluid level switch to reservoir.
15. Remove plugs from booster ports and reservoir.
16. Lubricate new reservoir seals with clean brake fluid. Fit to booster ports.
17. Position reservoir. Engage fully into seals.
18. Position reservoir bracket. Secure with bolt. Tighten to ***10 Nm. (7 lbf.ft)***

Manual Vehicles only.

19. Remove plug from clutch master cylinder hose. Connect hose to reservoir. Secure with clip.

All Vehicles.

20. Remove plug from reservoir hose and pump. Connect hose to pump. Secure with clip.
21. Connect fluid level switch multiplug.
22. Fill reservoir. ***See LUBRICANTS, FLUIDS AND CAPACITIES, Information.***
23. Bleed brake system. ***See this section.***

Manual Vehicles only.

24. Bleed clutch system. ***See CLUTCH, Repair.***

ABS SENSORS - FRONT

Service repair no - 70.65.30

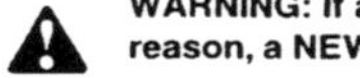

WARNING: If a sensor is removed for any reason, a NEW sensor bush must be fitted.

Remove

1. Raise the vehicle.

WARNING: Support on safety stands.

2. Remove road wheel.
3. Release sensor harness multiplug from clip. Disconnect multiplug.

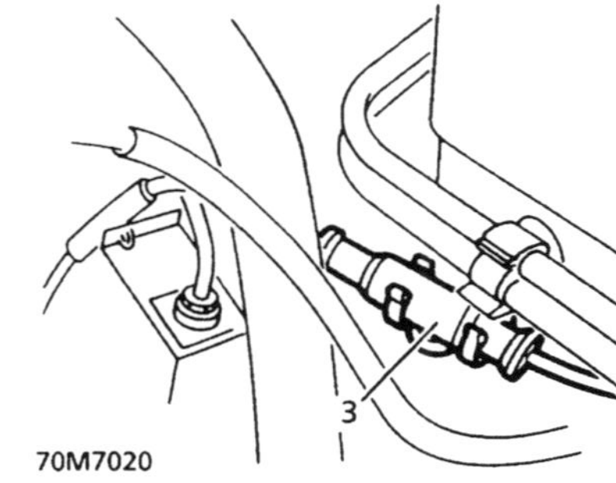

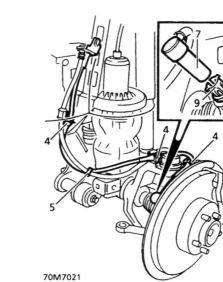

70M7020

4. Release sensor harness from 3 brackets.

70M7021

5. Release sensor harness from brake hose clip.
6. Clean area around sensor to prevent ingress of dirt.
7. Using a suitable lever, prise sensor from bush.
8. Remove sensor/harness assembly.
9. Remove sensor bush.
10. Clean sensor location.

Refit

11. Lubricate new sensor bush with silicone grease. ***See LUBRICANTS, FLUIDS AND CAPACITIES, Information.***
12. Fit sensor bush.
13. Lubricate sensor with silicone grease.
14. Push sensor fully into bush until it contacts reluctor ring. Correct sensor position will be gained when vehicle is driven.
15. Engage sensor harness to brackets and brake hose clip.
16. Connect multiplug. Secure plug in clip.
17. Fit road wheel, tighten nuts to ***108 Nm (80 lbf.ft).***
18. Remove safety stands. Lower vehicle.
19. Clear ECU error code using **TestBook** .
20. Carry out short road test to ensure that ABS warning light remains extinguished.

ABS SENSORS - REAR

Service repair no - 70.65.33

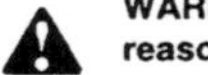

WARNING: If a sensor is removed for any reason, a NEW sensor bush must be fitted.

Remove

1. Raise the vehicle.

WARNING: Support on safety stands.

2. Remove road wheel.
3. Release sensor harness multiplug from clip. Disconnect multiplug.

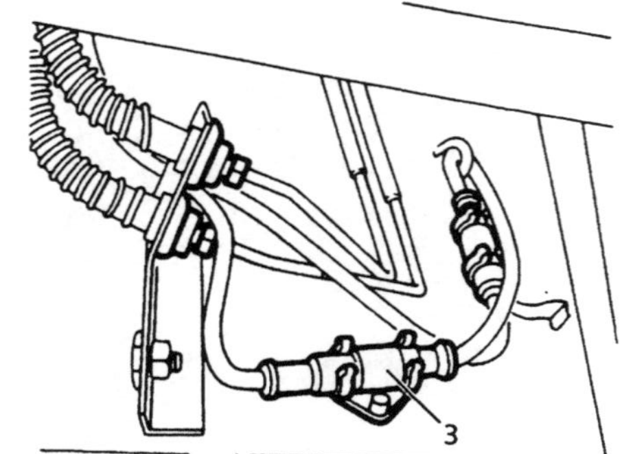

70M7044

4. Release sensor harness grommets from bracket. Withdraw sensor harness.
5. Remove 2 bolts securing sensor harness guard to axle. Release 2 harness clips from brake pipe.

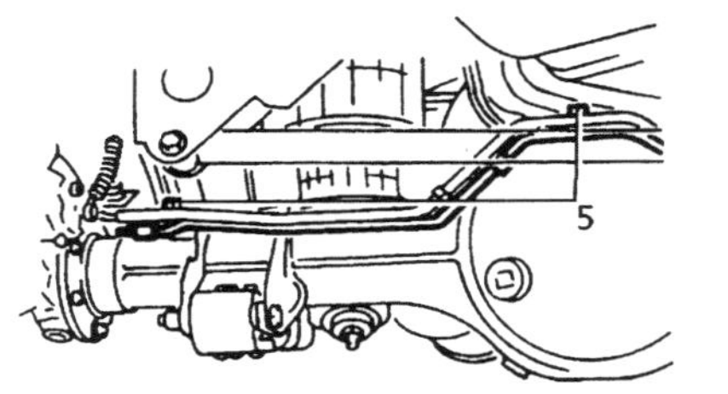

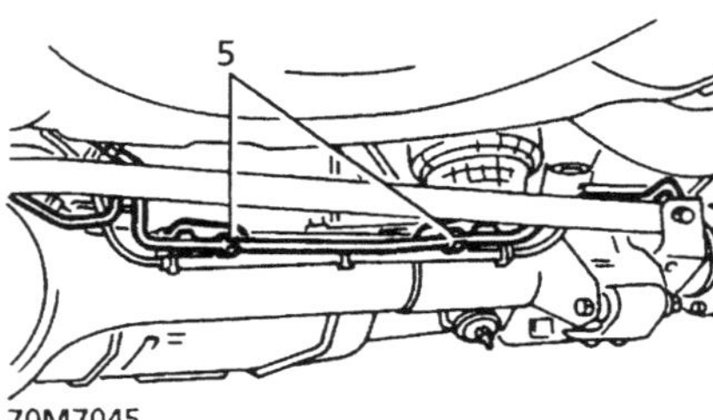

70M7045

6. Clean area around sensor to prevent ingress of dirt.
7. Using a suitable lever, prise sensor from bush.

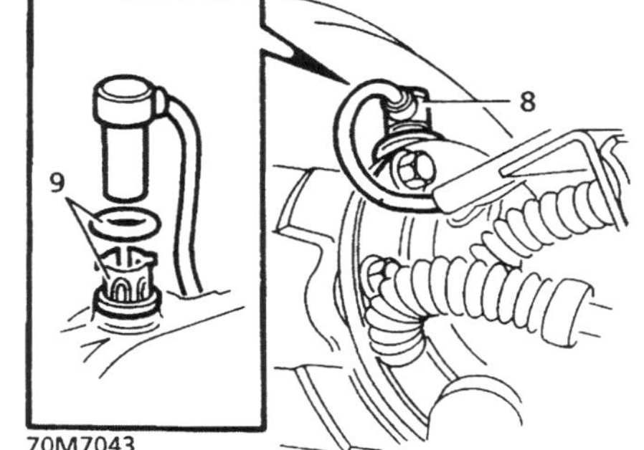

70M7043

8. Remove sensor/harness assembly.
9. Remove seal and bush.
10. Clean sensor location.

Refit

11. Lubricate new sensor bush with silicone grease. ***See LUBRICANTS, FLUIDS AND CAPACITIES, Information.***
12. Fit sensor bush and seal.
13. Lubricate sensor with silicone grease.
14. Push sensor fully into bush until it contacts reluctor ring. Correct sensor position will be gained when vehicle is driven.
15. Position sensor harness guard. Secure with bolts.
16. Engage sensor harness guard clips to brake pipe.
17. Thread sensor harness through grommets. Engage grommets in bracket.
18. Connect multiplug. Secure in clip.
19. Fit road wheel, tighten nuts to ***108 Nm (80 lbf.ft).***
20. Remove safety stands. Lower vehicle.
21. Clear ECU error code using **TestBook** .
22. Carry out short road test to ensure that ABS warning light remains extinguished.

STOP LIGHT SWITCH - UP TO 99MY

Service repair no - 70.35.42

Remove

1. Remove driver side fascia closing panel. ***See CHASSIS AND BODY, Repair.***
2. Remove 3 scrivet fasteners securing lower closing panel. Release panel for access to blower motor ducting.

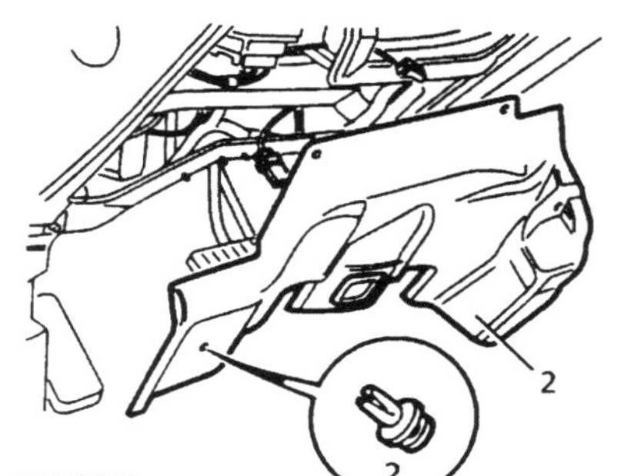

70M7046

3. Release ducting from blower motor housing and heater. Remove blower motor ducting.
4. Release multiplug from stop light switch.

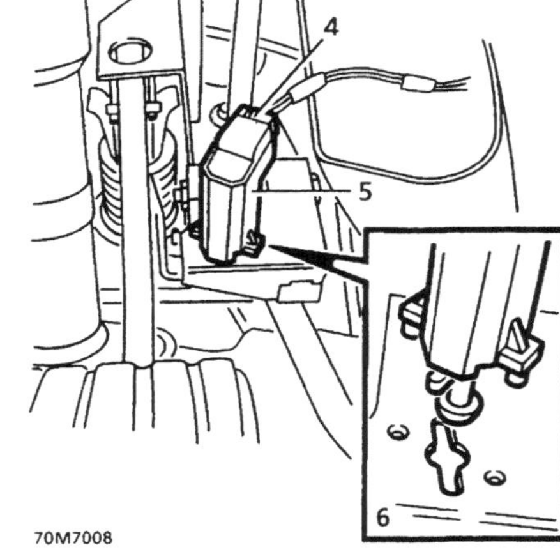

70M7008

5. Remove stop light switch from pedal bracket.

Refit

6. Engage switch fully into pedal bracket location.
7. Connect multiplug.

NOTE: The stop light switch is factory set and requires no adjustment in service.

8. Position blower ducting, fit to heater and blower motor housing locations.
9. Position lower closing panel and secure with scrivet fasteners.
10. Fit driver side fascia closing panel. ***See CHASSIS AND BODY, Repair.***

STOP LIGHT SWITCH - FROM 99MY

Service repair no - 70.35.42

1. Remove closing panel from fascia. ***See CHASSIS AND BODY, Repair.***

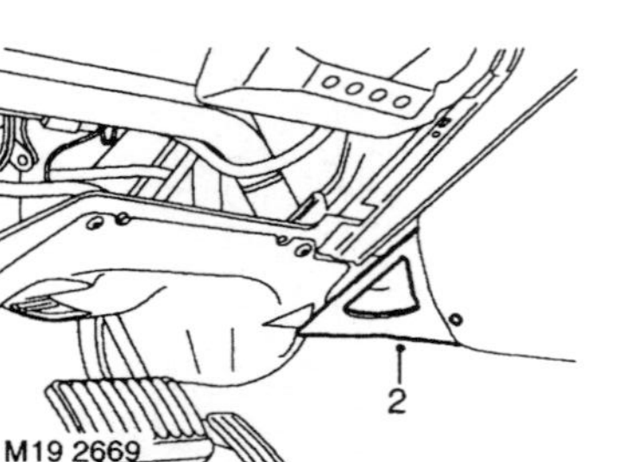

2. Remove screw and remove heater outlet duct.
3. Remove 4 scrivets and remove access panel from fascia.
4. Release and remove heater air duct for access to stop light switch.

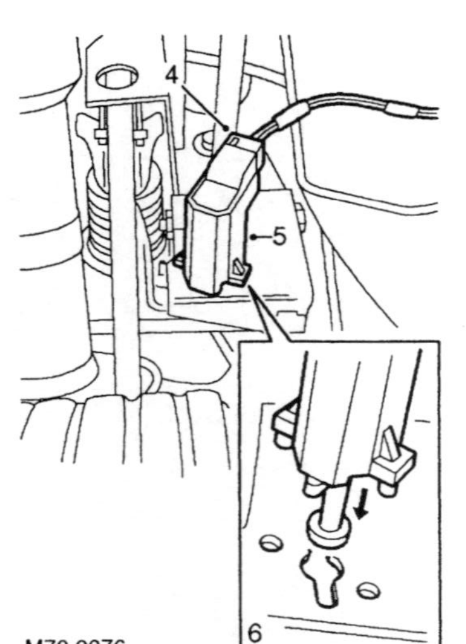

5. Disconnect multiplug from stop light switch.
6. Remove stop light switch from pedal bracket.

Refit

7. Ensure new stop light switch plunger is fully extended for initial setting.
8. Fit stop light switch to pedal bracket and connect multiplug.
9. Fit heater air duct.
10. Fit access panel and secure with scrivets.
11. Fit heater outlet duct and secure with screw.
12. Fit closing panel to fascia. ***See CHASSIS AND BODY, Repair.***

Notes

75 - SUPPLEMENTARY RESTRAINT SYSTEM

CONTENTS

SYSTEM DESCRIPTION

The supplementary restraint system (SRS) provides enhanced passive protection for the driver and front passenger in the event of a serious collision. The protection afforded is above that which would normally be provided using standard restraint systems (seat belts). The system is regarded as passive in the respect that it operates automatically without pre-conditional interactions by the vehicle occupants.

The distributed SRS system consists of the following components:

- SRS diagnostic and control unit (DCU)
- Front crash sensors (distributed systems only)
- Driver airbag module
- Passenger airbag module
- Side airbag modules (2 off - driver and front passenger) - from 99MY onwards
- Seat belt pre-tensioners (2 off - driver and front passenger) - from 99MY onwards
- Rotary coupler
- SRS warning lamps

Interconnecting wiring for the system is contained in distinctive yellow sleeving and integrated into the vehicle harness.

An ISO 9141 K-line (bi-directional) serial communication link connects the SRS DCU to the vehicle's diagnostic socket.

SYSTEM COMPONENTS LOCATION

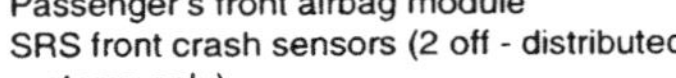

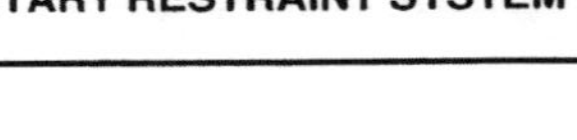

1. Passenger's front airbag module
2. SRS front crash sensors (2 off - distributed systems only)
3. SRS warning lamp
4. Rotary coupler
5. Driver's front airbag module
6. Seatbelt pre-tensioner (from 99MY only)
7. SRS diagnostic control unit (DCU)
8. Side airbag - 1 x front passenger & 1 x driver mounted in outboard side of squab seat frame (from 99MY only)
9. Diagnostic connector
10. SRS harness

SYSTEM SCHEMATIC

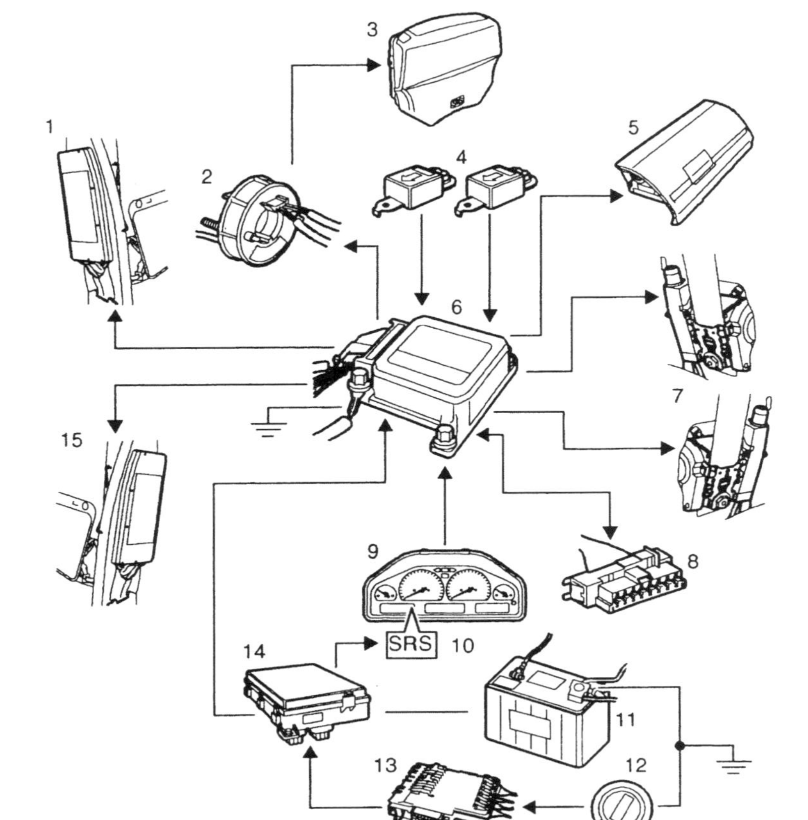

1. Side airbag (RH) - (from 99MY)
2. Rotary coupler
3. Driver's front airbag module
4. Front crash sensors - (distributed systems only)
5. Passenger's front airbag module
6. SRS DCU
7. Seat belt pre-tensioners - (from 99MY)
8. Diagnostic socket
9. Instrument Pack
10. SRS warning lamp
11. Battery
12. Ignition switch
13. BeCM (Body electrical Control Module)
14. Engine compartment fusebox
15. Side airbag (LH) - (from 99MY)

SYSTEM COMPONENTS DESCRIPTION

SRS Diagnostic and Control Unit (DCU)

The SRS DCU controls the operation of the supplementary restraint systems by using collision detection sensors to determine the incidence of a crash event. There are two basic types of system utilised:

- Single point sensed SRS system
- Distributed SRS system

Both systems utilise the same basic DCU, but the distributed system also features additional front crash sensors mounted external to the DCU. The type of system configuration used is dependent on the relative market requirements.

The DCU is fitted to the centre console bracket underneath the console storage bin and mounted to the bracket by three Torx bolts. The unit is connected to ground via a dedicated earth eyelet located under the centre console next to the DCU and attached to the mounting bracket by a Torx bolt.

A yellow 50-pin connector provides the SRS DCU connection with the vehicle harness on models from 99MY onwards.

The DCU can sense crash events to the vehicle, monitored via internal accelerometers. The acceleration data is electronically processed by an internal microprocessor controller to determine the severity of the crash condition. The DCU is able to use the input data to distinguish between a severe crash situation and a minor impact or rough road conditions and so prevent spurious deployment.

An electromechanical safing sensor is incorporated into the DCU which is a normally open switch, but closes at a preset deceleration limit. Electronic switches for each of the squibs are activated if the severity of the crash condition exceeds a pre-determined trigger value.

CAUTION: It is important that the DCU is correctly mounted and is fitted in the designated location and orientation.

MAIN SENSOR
The main sensor is a deceleration detection device which is contained in the DCU. The sensor consists of a spring and weight system which is attached to strain guages in a Wheatsone bridge circuit. The 'balance' nodes of the bridge circuit is connected to an integrated circuit that can instantly detect a change in the monitored resistance.

In the event of a collision, the spring and weight move causing a corresponding change in the resistance of the related strain gauge. If the change in strain guage resistance is greater than a preset value, it corresponds to a crash condition of sufficient severity to warrant SRS component deployment. In this case, the processor provides a signal to initiate airbag and/or seatbelt pre-tensioner deployment. Deployment will only be carried out if a confirmation signal that a crash condition is occurring is received by the SRS DCU. Crash condition confirmation is achieved by simultaneous actuation of the safing sensor and/or one or more of the front crash sensors in the case of a distributed system.

SAFING SENSOR
This sensor is also contained within the DCU and is included in the DCU internal circuitry to prevent unintentional detonation of SRS components. The safing sensor is connected in series with the main sensor and operates at comparitively lower rates of deceleration. When the safing sensor closes in conjunction with the main sensor exceeding the trigger value, the electronic switches are activated, allowing electrical current to be supplied to the driver and passenger airbag squibs.

The side airbag modules are controlled by electronic switching and the safing sensor acts as an arming sensor for the seatbelt pre-tensioners.

SINGLE POINT SENSED SYSTEM
This system relies on the DCU's internal deceleration sensor and safing sensor to provide the control inputs required to confirm activation conditions for SRS component deployment.

DISTRIBUTED SRS SYSTEM
The DCU used for the distributed SRS system is identical to the single point system, with the exception that two external front crash sensors provide additional inputs to the unit for determining and confirming a crash condition in conjunction with the DCU's internal accelerometer.

DCU monitoring

When the ignition switch is turned to position 'II', the DCU monitors the readiness of the SRS components during the power-up phase and continues monitoring during the complete ignition cycle. The DCU monitors the status of the following components:

- Accelerometers
- Safing sensor
- Microprocessor
- Front airbags
- Side airbags (from 99MY)
- Seatbelt pre-tensioners (from 99MY)
- Front crash sensors (distributed systems only)
- SRS warning lamps

If a system or component fault is detected, the SRS lamps are illuminated.

Power supply and back-up

The ignition power feed provides a positive voltage supply to the SRS DCU and the SRS warning lamps via a dedicated system fuse located in the engine compartment fusebox. In the event of power supply failure, check the condition of the fuse and the connection between the Main and Fascia harnesses located on the lower right hand side 'A' post.

The DCU incorporates capacitors which store enough electrical charge to ensure the system will continue to function for a short period of time in the event that the normal power supply is disconnected during a collision. If the power supply is disconnected, the capacitors store enough charge to enable operation of the triggering device and firing circuitry.

SRS DCU pin-outs (from 99MY)

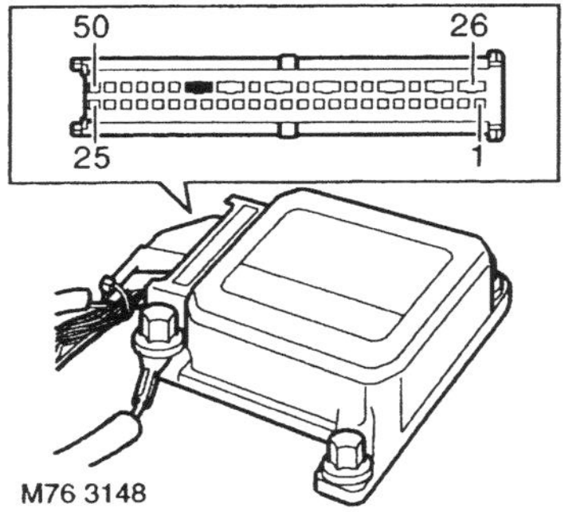

M76 3148

1. LH seatbelt pre-tensioner +ve supply
2. LH seatbelt pre-tensioner -ve supply
3. RH seatbelt pre-tensioner -ve supply
4. RH seatbelt pre-tensioner +ve supply
5. Ignition switched DCU power supply input
6. DCU ground connection
7. SRS warning lamp one
8. Spare
9. Diagnostic connector K-line
10. Driver's airbag module +ve supply
11. Driver's airbag module -ve supply
12. Spare
13. Passenger's airbag module +ve supply
14. Passenger's airbag module -ve supply
15. Front crash sensor - Right +ve supply (distributed systems only)
16. LH side airbag +ve supply
17. LH side airbag -ve supply
18. RH side airbag +ve supply
19. RH side airbag -ve supply
20. Spare
21. Spare
22. Spare
23. Spare
24. Front crash sensor - RH -ve supply (distributed systems only)
25. Front crash sensor - LH -ve supply (distributed systems only)
26. Shorting bar for LH seatbelt pre-tensioner
27. Shorting bar for LH seatbelt pre-tensioner
28. Shorting bar for RH seatbelt pre-tensioner
29. Shorting bar for RH seatbelt pre-tensioner
30. Spare
31. Shorting bar for SRS warning lamp one
32. Shorting bar for SRS warning lamp one
33. SRS warning lamp two
34. Spare
35. Shorting bar for driver's airbag
36. Shorting bar for driver's airbag
37. Front crash sensor - LH +ve supply (distributed systems only)
38. Shorting bar for passenger airbag
39. Shorting bar for passenger airbag
40. Spare
41. Shorting bar for LH side airbag
42. Shorting bar for LH side airbag
43. Shorting bar for RH side airbag
44. Shorting bar for RH side airbag
45. Spare
46. Spare
47. Spare
48. Spare
49. Spare
50. Spare

WARNING: Never use multimeters or other general test equipment on SRS components or connectors.

Front Crash Sensors (distributed systems only)

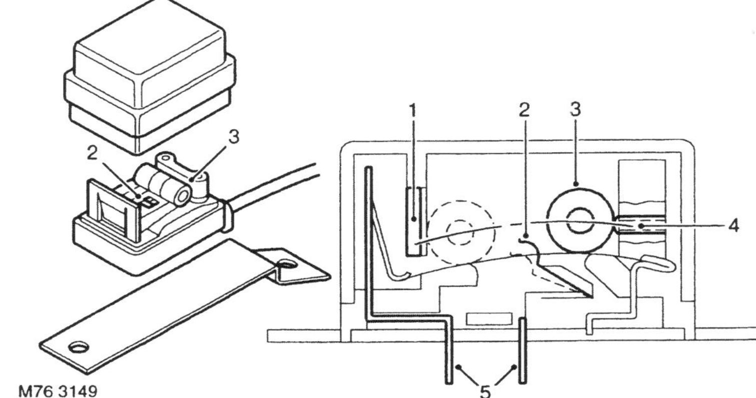

M76 3149

1. Roller stop
2. Contact spring
3. Weight roller
4. Stop screw in "off" position
5. Electrical connection

The front crash sensors are located behind each headlamp in the engine compartment. The sensors are provided in a yellow, plastic encapsulated housing with an integral mounting bracket for attaching the units to the vehicle body. A yellow 3-pin connector connects each impact sensor to the main harness and an additional 4-way orange connector interfaces between the main harness and the fascia harness and is located on the lower left hand 'A' post. In the event of a crash sensor fault being detected by the diagnostics system, the connection between the fascia and main harnesses should be checked.

The sensors must be fitted in the correct orientation; an arrow is moulded into the upper surface of the housing to indicate the end of the sensor which must face the front of the vehicle. Each sensor is attached to the vehicle body by two Torx bolts. It is important to ensure the crash sensors are mounted correctly.

The internal components of the crash sensor consist of a weighted roller with a spring contact around it. Under deceleration, the roller unwinds the spring until a contact is made to provide a short circuit input to the DCU. This signal indicates that a rapid deceleration has been detected such as that which would be experienced during a frontal collision.

Driver and passenger front airbag modules

The driver's front airbag module is located in the steering wheel and the passenger front airbag is located above the glovebox, within the fascia directly in front of the passenger seat. Both driver and passenger front airbags are activated by a control signal from the SRS DCU in the event of a frontal collision. The modules house a folded nylon fabric bag, the gas generant capsules and an igniter squib.

When a severe frontal impact is detected by the DCU, electronic switches are closed causing a small electrical current to be applied to the igniter squib. The igniter is activated to produce heat and cause the gas pellets to generate nitrogen gas which quickly inflates the nylon bag.

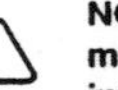

NOTE: Driver and passenger front airbag modules must be replaced at 10 year intervals.

DRIVER'S AIRBAG MODULE

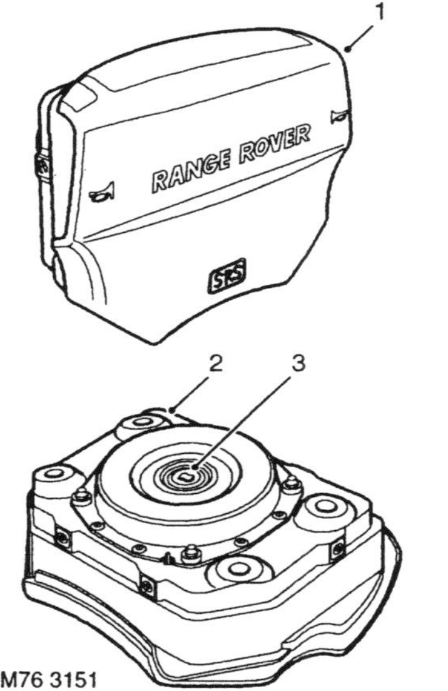

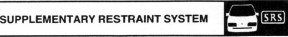

M76 3151

1. Polyurethane cover
2. Housing
3. Electrical connector

The driver's airbag module is attached to the steering wheel by four captive bolts. Electrical connection to the SRS DCU is provided via the rotary coupler.

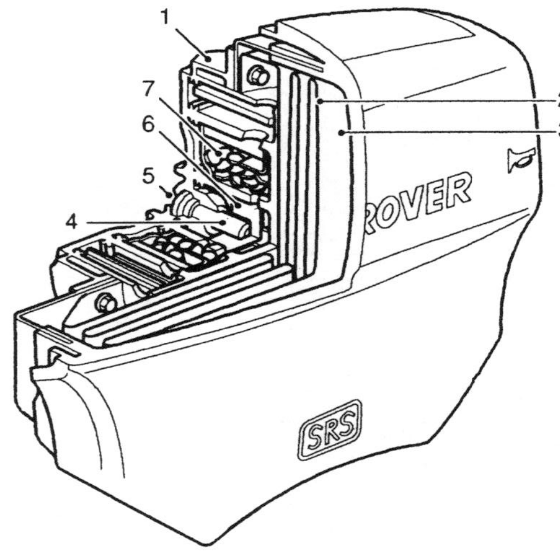

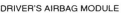

M76 3152

1. Housing
2. Nylon airbag
3. Steering wheel pad
4. Squib
5. Electical connector
6. Igniter charge
7. Sodium Azide pellets

When a deployment signal has been received at the airbag module, the squib initiates combustion of the igniter charge. The igniter charge burns rapidly and produces sufficient heat to cause the gas generant pellets to burn and so produce a large quantity of nitrogen gas which is routed to the folded nylon airbag. The force of the inflating airbag causes the steering wheel polyurethane centre pad to split at deliberately weakened break points, and expands to form a protective cushion between the driver and the steering wheel/ windscreen.

The fully inflated airbag has a capacity of 4.5 litres. Once the airbag is fully inflated, vents in the airbag prevent further pressure build-up, so that progressive deceleration is provided as the driver contacts the cushion.

PASSENGER FRONT AIRBAG MODULE

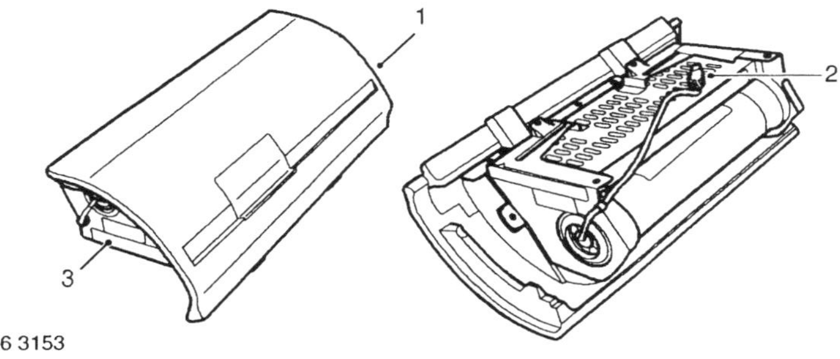

M76 3153

1. Trim panel
2. Electrical connector
3. Housing

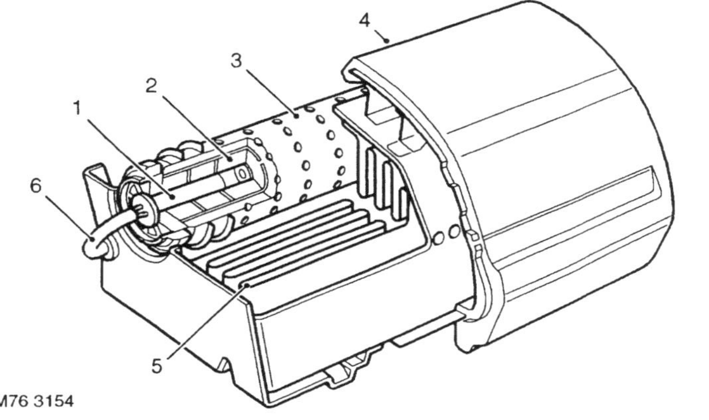

M76 3154

1. Squib
2. Gas generant (Sodium Azide)
3. Filters
4. Trim cover
5. Nylon airbag
6. Electrical connector

The front passenger airbag module is mounted to the fascia by way of four bolts. A link lead connects the module to the fascia harness, with a red multiplug connector located on the bracket behind the glove box.

When an activation signal is received by the passenger airbag squib, the activated igniter produces heat causing the gas pellets to generate nitrogen gas which fills the airbag. The force of the inflating airbag breaks the specially weakened break lines in the polyurethane cover. Once free of the module, the nylon bag inflates to its full extent to provide a protective cushion between the front seat passenger and the fascia / windscreen.

When the bag is fully inflated, vents in the airbag prevent further pressure build-up so that progressive deceleration is provided as the occupant contacts the cushion.

Side airbag modules

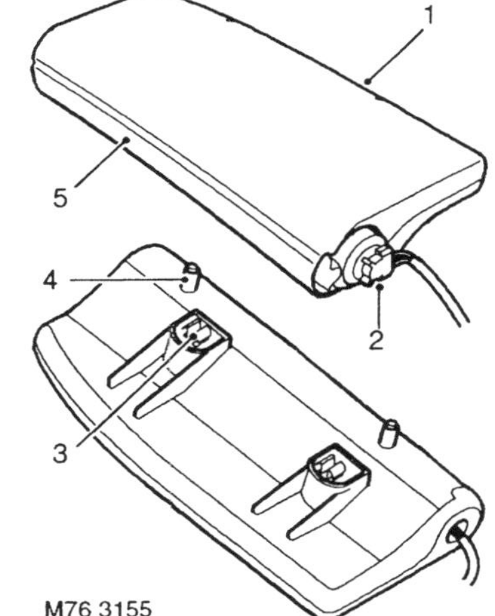

M76 3155

1. Module front edge (airbag emergence point)
2. Electrical connector (non-removable)
3. Location lugs
4. Fixing studs
5. Module hinge

The driver and passenger side airbags are mounted to the squab seat frame. The modules are handed (i.e. a right hand module must be fitted to a RH seat and a left hand module must be fitted to a LH seat). The side airbags are activated by a control signal from the SRS DCU in the event of a side impact or a front angled impact of sufficient severity to cause both front and side airbag deployment.

The side airbag module is a moulded plastic case which houses a folded nylon fabric bag, the gas generant capsules and an igniter squib. The rear of the side airbag module features two studs which are used for mounting the module to the seat frame and are secured in position by two nylock nuts. The back of the module also has moulded plastic location lugs, which are offset to ensure that only the correct handed module is fitted to the relevant seat.

WARNING: If the location lugs on the back of the module casing are damaged or missing, the module should not be used. Dispose of using the controlled procedures detailed in this manual.

WARNING: If a new side airbag module shows any sign of damage, DO NOT USE.

The side airbag modules have a flying lead which terminates in a yellow 2-pin connector. The connector connects to the DCU via the main harness and is located beneath the seat cushion.

CAUTION: Do not try to remove the connector at the module end, it is a permanent connection.

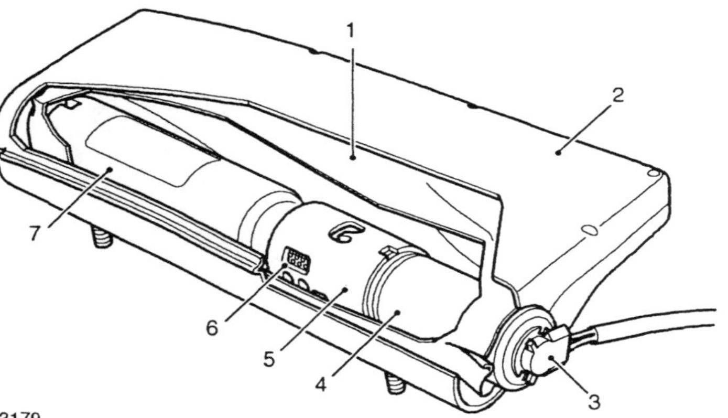

M76 3179

1. Folded nylon bag
2. Case
3. Electrical connector
4. Nitrocellulose chamber (containing squib)
5. Mixing chamber
6. Filter / gas release port
7. Nitrogen / argon chamber

When a severe side impact is detected by the DCU, electronic switches are closed causing a small electrical current to be supplied to the igniter squib in the airbag on the side of the vehicle affected by the impact. The activated igniter charge produces heat causing the 3g of nitrocellulose to ignite and generate nitrogen gas. The pressure of the expanding gas from the nitrocellulose chamber punctures the port of the nitrogen/argon gas chamber. The gas released from the nitrogen/argon chamber is then mixed with the gas from the nitrocellulose chamber in the central mixing chamber. The resulting nitrogen gas escapes from holes in the mixing chamber to rapidly fill the nylon bag. The force of the inflating bag, forces the module casing to split open and deploy the airbag through the seat seam at the piping line.

The module is mounted at the outboard side bolster seam of the seat squab, and the expanding airbag initiates a seam thread failure in a designed and controlled manner. Once free of the module housing and seat cover, the nylon bag inflates to its full extent, pushing the seat occupant away from the side of the vehicle suffering the impact. When the bag is fully inflated, vents in the airbag prevent further pressure build-up and when the gas generation is exhausted, the airbag begins to deflate. The side airbag has a capacity of 12 litres.

NOTE: Side airbag modules must be replaced at 15 year intervals.

NOTE: The front doors contain side impact beams to help reduce intrusion of the impact object and give additional protection to the front seat occupants.

Seatbelt pre-tensioners

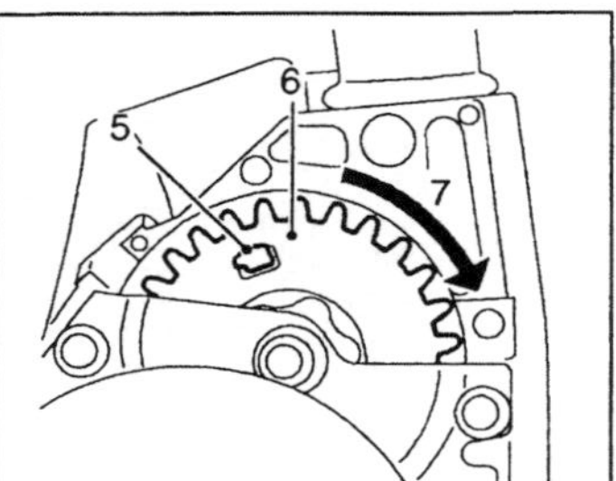

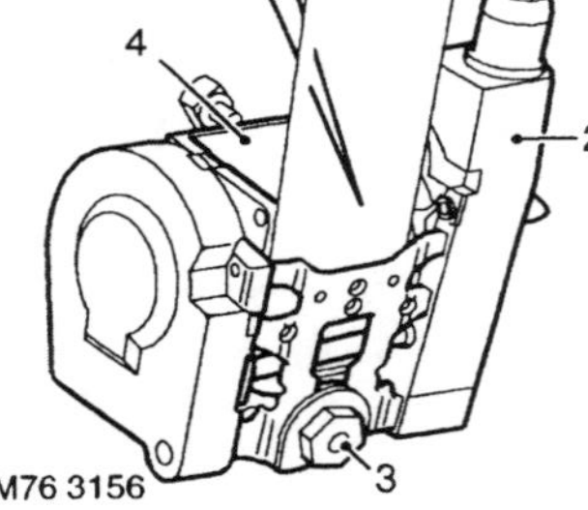

M76 3156

1. Exhaust port
2. Propellant tube
3. Inertia reel fixing bolt
4. Reel
5. Pinion locking tab
6. Pinion
7. Direction of rotation

During a frontal collision, the seat belt pre-tensioners tighten the front seat belts to ensure the occupants are securely held in their seats. The pre-tensioner units are located with the seat belt inertia reel assembly located at the bottom of the 'B' post.

The seatbelt pre-tensioners are activated by a control signal from the SRS DCU in the event of a frontal collision. The two pre-tensioners are handed, but are otherwise identical. Each of the pre-tensioner units is fitted with an igniter and a propellant generator which acts on a rotor which is attached to the seatbelt inertia reel.

When a severe frontal impact is detected by the DCU, electronic switches are closed causing a small electrical current to be applied to the igniter squib. The igniter is activated to produce heat and cause the gas capsules to generate a propellant which forces a piston up the cylinder. The piston draws a rack and pinion mechanism which pulls back the seatbelt inertia reel to hold the occupant securely in the seat in a position suitable for airbag deployment. When the rotor reaches the extent of its travel, excess propellant is ejected to atmosphere via a port in the top of the propellant tube.

WARNING: Once the pre-tensioner has been operated, it cannot be reset. The pinion locking pin will have been broken and the gas generant will be exhausted. The unit must be replaced.

Each pre-tensioner unit has a flying lead which terminates in a yellow 2-pin connector that connects to the DCU through the main harness. The pre-tensioner to main harness connector is located below the lower 'B' post finisher.

Rotary coupler

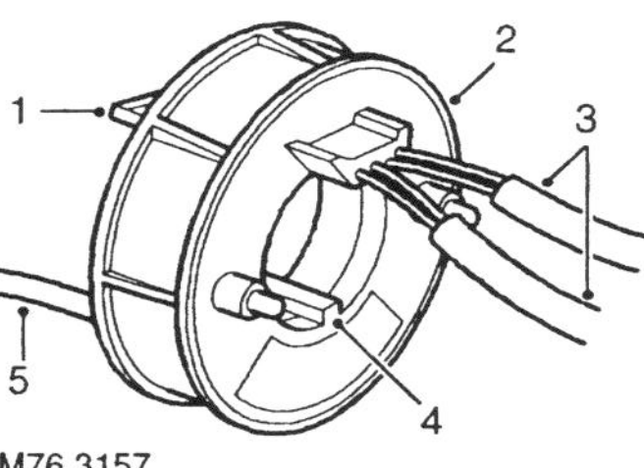

M76 3157

1. Securing clips
2. Outer housing
3. Electrical fly leads (to driver airbag module and steering wheel switches)
4. Alignment key
5. Electrical flylead (to SRS and main harness)

The rotary coupler is installed on the steering column, behind the steering wheel to provide the electrical interface between the fixed wiring harness and the moveable driver airbag module. In addition to the wiring for the driver airbag, the rotary coupler also provides the wiring for other electrical functions built into the steering wheel area, these may include:

- ICE system control switches
- Cruise control system switches
- Horn switches

A rotating link harness is encapsulated into a plastic cassette comprising outer and inner housings with integral connectors. The cassette contains a flat ribbon type flexible cable with seven wires (not all the wires are utilised on all vehicle derivatives). The rear of the rotary coupler features two clips which align to mating holes within the steering column die cast bracket. The inner housing can turn a maximum of 4.2 revolutions in relation to the outer housing.

The rotary coupler connects the fascia harness to the driver's airbag module via a 2-way red connector located below the steering column cowl.

OPERATION

All system operations become active when the ignition switch is turned to position 'II' and remains operational when the ignition switch is in the CRANK position. When the ignition switch is turned on, the SRS warning lamp illuminates for approximately 5 seconds then turns off, this indicates that the system is functional.

Front impacts

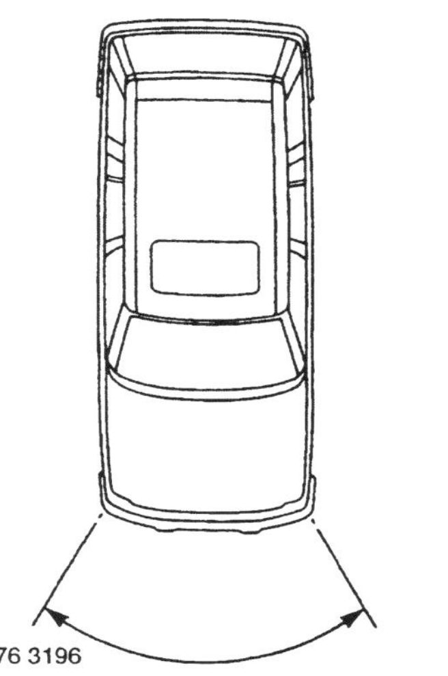
M76 3196

The front airbags and the seatbelt pre-tensioners are deployed in the event of a frontal impact of sufficient severity which exceeds the impact trigger threshold.

When the accelerometer and safing sensor in the SRS diagnostic control unit senses the impact, the diagnostic control unit triggers the front airbag modules by firing an igniter. This in turn ignites tablets of sodium azide which generate a large amount of Nitrogen gas causing airbag inflation. For vehicles fitted with a distributed sensing system, an activation signal is also provided to the DCU from one or both of the front crash sensors.

The DCU simultaneously triggers the seatbelt pre-tensioner operation. This is achieved by activating a propellant which acts on the seatbelt inertia reel causing an increase in the tension of the seatbelt to restrain the occupant in a safe and secure position during airbag deployment. The seatbelt pre-tensioners are armed by the safing sensor which have a faster deployment time than the front airbags, so that the occupant is held in the restrained position before the airbag is fully inflated.

The diagnostic control unit (DCU) is able to distinguish between rough road conditions and a frontal collision. If the DCU's main sensor (or front crash sensors for distributed systems) detects a frontal collision of sufficient severity and it is confirmed by the safing sensor, the DCU sends a fire signal to the airbag module and seatbelt pre-tensioner initiators.

The front airbags offer additional protection to the front seat occupants. The front airbags are fully inflated, then as the occupant moves into the airbag it immediately discharges the gas from vent holes to provide progressive deceleration and reduce the risk of injuries.

WARNING: All the SRS system components, including the wiring harness, MUST be renewed after the airbags and seatbelt pre-tensioners have been deployed.

Side impacts

The driver and passenger side airbags are deployed in the event of a side impact of sufficient severity which exceeds the side impact trigger threshold. When the SRS diagnostic control unit senses the impact, the diagnostic control unit activates the seat airbag module on the side of the vehicle suffering the impact. A current from the DCU triggers the module to ignite pellets of nitrocellulose which generate a large amount of Nitrogen gas, causing airbag inflation. The inflating airbag bursts out of the seat cover at the outboard piping and pushes the seat occupant away from the impact force.

When fully deployed, the side airbags offer additional protection to the front seat occupants in the event of a collision acting on the side of the vehicle. Either the driver's side airbag circuit or the passenger's side airbag circuit is activated depending on the side of the vehicle suffering the impact. After the airbag has fully inflated, the airbag progressively deflates the gas from vent holes to reduce the risk of injuries.

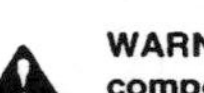

WARNING: All the SRS system components, including the wiring harness, MUST be renewed after the side airbags have been deployed.

Front angled impacts

The deployment of airbags and pre-tensioners that occur when a vehicle is involved in a front angled collision is dependent on the speed and angle of the impact. Four possible conditions could apply:

- Impact is below the threshold value for front and side triggers - no response, none of the airbags or seatbelt pre-tensioners are activated.
- The speed of the impact is in excess of the front impact trigger threshold - the driver's airbag, passenger's airbag and seatbelt pre-tensioners are activated.
- The speed of the impact is in excess of the side impact trigger threshold - the driver's side airbag circuit is activated in a driver's side impact and the passenger side airbag circuit is activated in a passenger's side impact.
- Both the front and side impact trigger thresholds are exceeded - the driver's front airbag, passenger's front airbag and seatbelt pre-tensioners are activated, and the side airbag circuit on the side of the vehicle suffering the impact is activated.

Rear impact and roll over

The SRS system does not specifically detect rear impact and roll over conditions, but if as a consequence of the crash situation the system front or side trigger thresholds are exceeded, the relevant airbags and pre-tensioners are deployed.

SRS warning lamps and system diagnostics

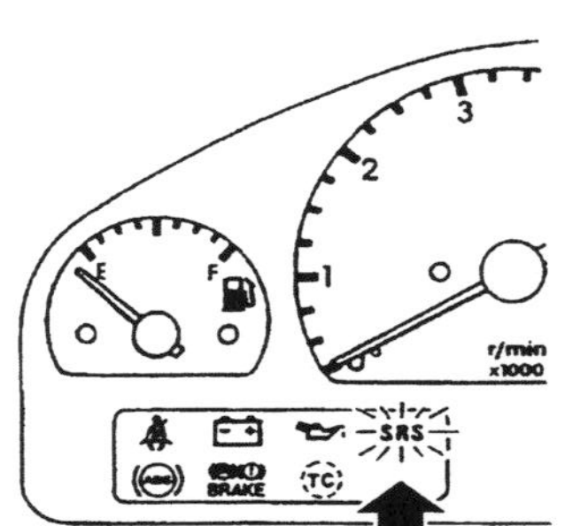

M76 3197

The SRS warning lamp is located in the instrument pack and has two bulbs behind the SRS warning lamp window. If either of the bulbs fail, the DCU will illuminate the other bulb permanently to indicate that a system fault is present (i.e. warning lamp bulb failure).

The SRS warning lamp illuminates after the ignition switch has been turned to position 'II' in order to provide a lamp check. After about 5 seconds, the warning lamp will go out for the remainder of the ignition cycle, providing the SRS system integrity is maintained. The system checks the condition of the SRS DCU, crash sensors and the SRS harnesses.

If one of the following faults are experienced when the ignition switch is turned to position 'II', the SRS warning lamp will illuminate and remain on for the duration of the ignition cycle:

- DCU connector not engaged or faulty
- Harness fault
- Earth connection fault
- Fuse open circuit

If a system fault is detected whilst driving, the warning lamp illuminates, to indicate that there is a fault with the SRS system. With the warning lamp on, the SRS system may not operate in the event of a collision.

While the ignition is on, the diagnostic function of the SRS DCU monitors the SRS system for faults. If a fault is detected, the DCU stores a related fault code in non-volatile memory and switches the earth output to illuminate the SRS warning lamp. A maximum of five faults can be stored in memory along with the timing information associated with each fault. The fault memory is accessible through the use of testbook and the K-line communications bus.

With a supply voltage range fault the warning lamp is illuminated, once the correct system voltage returns within range the lamp will extinguish. The warning lamp will remain lit for a minimum of 5 seconds. With all other faults including intermittent faults, the warning lamp is illuminated for the remainder of the drive cycle. The SRS warning lamp will not illuminate on the next ignition cycle unless the fault re-occurs, but the fault code remains stored in memory.

For a permanent fault, the SRS lamp will stay on after the initial warning lamp test and latch on for every ignition cycle until the cause of the fault has been resolved. In addition, the diagnostic system will record an 'AIR BAG FAULT'.

After detecting a fault, the system may retain some operational capability:

- If a fault is detected in a SRS circuit, only that particular circuit is disabled; the other airbag and pre-tensioner circuits remain operational and will still be deployed in the event of a collision.
- If an internal DCU or power supply fault is detected, the complete system will be disabled.
- If a fault exists in the SRS warning lamp circuit, the lamp will not illuminate during the lamp check at ignition on, but provided there are no other faults, the system will remain fully operational.

Additional information that can be accessed using 'Testbook' via the diagnostics socket include:

- SRS DCU code number
- Evolution number of the hardware, software and diagnostic protocol
- Status of the crashed lock mode
- Vehicle identification number (VIN) data

The SRS DCU logs the fault in internal memory, this can be accessed using **TestBook** via the diagnostic socket located on the passenger side fascia closing panel.

GENERAL PRECAUTIONS

The SRS system contains components which could be potentially hazardous to the service engineer if not serviced and handled correctly. The following guidelines are intended to alert the service engineer to potential sources of danger and emphasise the importance of ensuring the integrity of SRS components fitted to the vehicle.

It should be noted that these precautions are not restricted to operations performed when servicing the SRS system, the same care should be exercised when working on ancillary systems and components located in the vicinity of the SRS components; these include but are not limited to:

- Steering system - (steering wheel airbag)
- Body and trim components - (passenger airbag, seatbelt pre-tensioners and SRS DCU).
- Seats - (side airbags)
- Electrical system components - (SRS harnesses etc.)

WARNING: Do not use rear facing child seats in the front passenger seat when a vehicle is fitted with a front passenger airbag.

WARNING: Always follow the Safety Guidelines and correct procedures for working on SRS components.

WARNING: The front airbag modules contain Sodium Azide which is poisonous and extremely flammable. Contact with water, acid or heavy metals may produce harmful or explosive compounds. Do not dismantle, incinerate or bring into contact with electricity.

CAUTION: Do not expose an airbag module or seatbelt pre-tensioner to heat exceeding 85°C (185°F).

NOTE: Front airbag modules should be replaced every ten years; side airbag modules should be replaced every fifteen years.

Making the system safe

Before working on, or in the vicinity of SRS components, ensure the system is rendered safe by performing the following procedures:

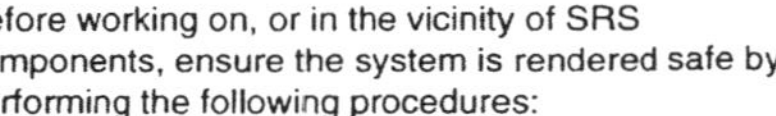

- Remove the ignition key from the ignition switch.

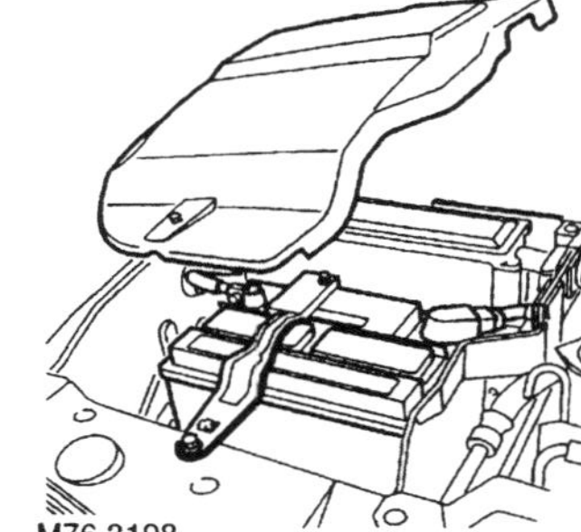

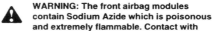

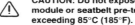

M76 3198

- Disconnect both battery leads, earth lead first.
- Wait 10 minutes for the SRS DCU back-up power circuit to discharge.

The SRS system uses energy reserve capacitors to keep the system active in the event of electrical supply failure under crash conditions. It is necessary to allow the capacitor sufficient time to discharge (10 minutes) in order to avoid the risk of accidental deployment.

WARNING: Always remove the ignition key from the ignition switch, disconnect the vehicle battery and wait 10 minutes before commencing work on the SRS system.

CAUTION: Always disconnect both battery leads before beginning work on the SRS system. Disconnect the negative battery cable first. Never reverse connect the vehicle battery and always ensure the correct polarity when connecting test equipment.

CAUTION: Always disconnect the vehicle battery before carrying out any electric welding on a vehicle fitted with an SRS system.

Installation

WARNING: Always follow the safety guidelines and correct procedures for working on SRS components. Persons working on SRS systems must be fully trained and have been issued with copies of the Safety / Manufacturing guidelines.

In order to assure system integrity, it is essential that the SRS system is regularly checked and maintained so that it is ready for effective operation in the event of a collision. Carefully inspect SRS components before installation. Do not install a part that shows signs of being dropped or improperly handled, such as dents, cracks or deformation.

CAUTION: Ensure SRS components are not contaminated with oil, grease, detergent or water.

CAUTION: It is essential that SRS components are fitted using the recommended torques, and always use new fixings when replacing SRS parts. Special bolts are necessary for installing the airbag module, do not use other bolts.

CAUTION: Never attempt to repair an SRS component. Do not try to dismantle an airbag module, there are no serviceable parts. Once an airbag or pre-tensioner has been deployed, it cannot be repaired or re-used.

CAUTION: Do not install used SRS components from another vehicle. When repairing an SRS system, only use genuine new parts.

CAUTION: Ensure the SRS DCU and front crash sensors (if fitted) are installed correctly. There must not be any gap between the component and the bracket to which it is mounted. An incorrectly mounted unit could cause the system to malfunction.

WARNING: When removing, testing or installing an airbag module, do not lean directly over it.

SRS component testing precautions

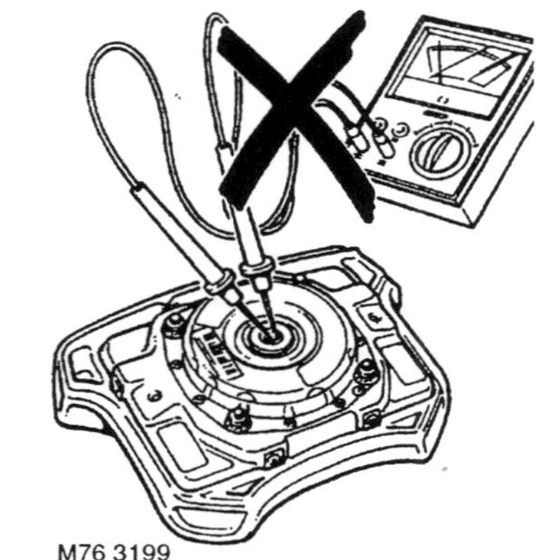

M76 3199

WARNING: Never use multimeters or other general purpose test equipment to check SRS components or connectors. System faults should be diagnosed through the use of recommended test equipment only.

WARNING: Never apply electrical power to an SRS component unless instructed to do so as part of an approved test procedure.

CAUTION: Prior to commencing any test procedure on the vehicle, ensure that only test equipment approved for the purpose is being utilised and that it is in good working order. Ensure any harness or connectors are in good condition and any warning lamps are fully functional.

Handling and storage

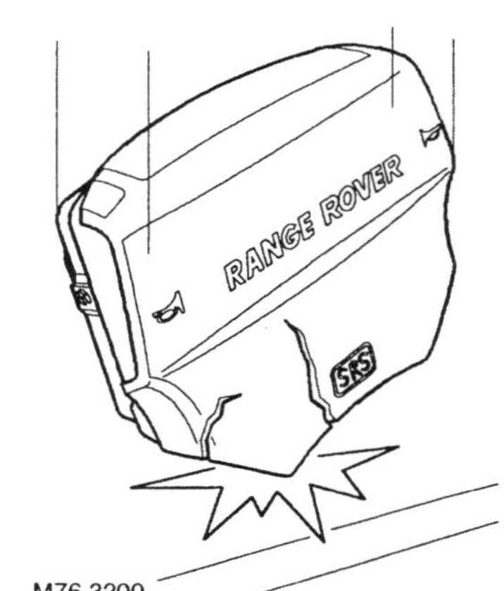

M76 3200

WARNING: The SRS components are sensitive and potentially hazardous if not handled correctly; always comply with the following handling precautions:

- Never drop an SRS component. The airbag diagnostic control unit is a particularly shock sensitive device and must be handled with extreme care. Airbag modules and seatbelt pre-tensioner units could deploy if subjected to a strong shock.
- Never wrap your arms around an airbag module. If it has to be carried, hold it by the cover with the cover uppermost and the base away from your body.
- Never transport airbag modules or seatbelt pre-tensioners in the cabin of a vehicle. Always use the luggage compartment of the vehicle for carrying airbag modules and seatbelt pre-tensioner units.
- Never attach anything to the airbag cover or allow anything to rest on top of the airbag module.
- Always keep components cool, dry and free from contamination.

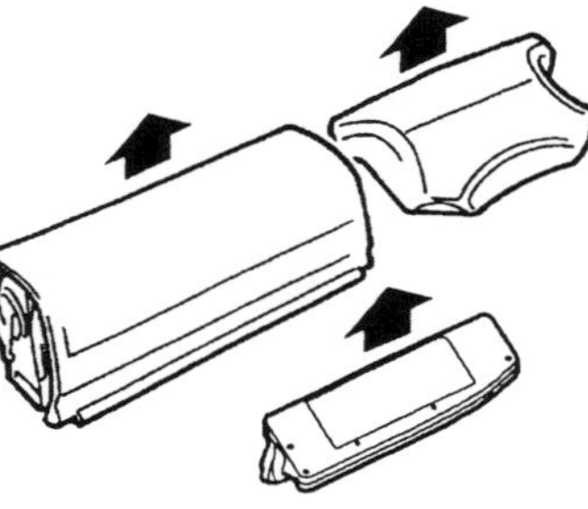

M76 3158

WARNING: Always store airbag modules with the cover face up. If the airbag module is stored face down, accidental deployment could propel the unit with enough force to cause serious injury.

WARNING: Airbag modules and seatbelt pre-tensioners are classed as explosive devices. For overnight and longer term storage, they must be stored in a secure steel cabinet which has been approved as suitable for the purpose and has been registered by the local authority.

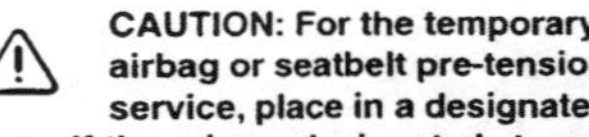

CAUTION: For the temporary storage of an airbag or seatbelt pre-tensioner during service, place in a designated storage area. If there is no designated storage area available, store in the luggage compartment of the vehicle and inform the workshop supervisor.

CAUTION: Improper handling or storage can internally damage the airbag module, making it inoperative. If you suspect the airbag module has been damaged, install a new unit and refer to the Deployment/Disposal Procedures for disposal of the damaged airbag.

SRS Harnesses and Connectors

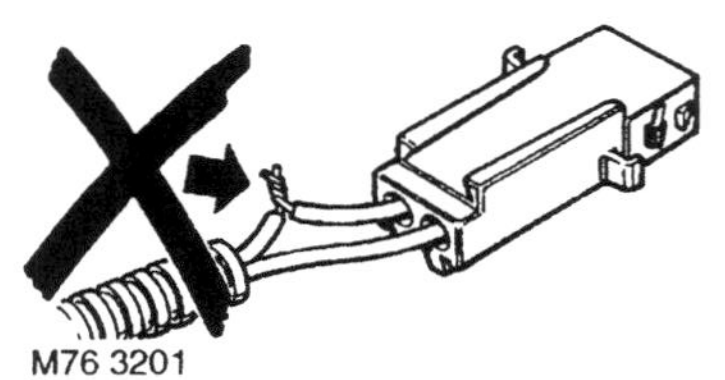

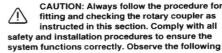

M76 3201

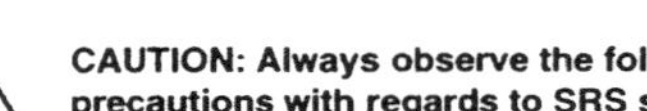

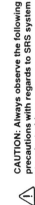

CAUTION: Always observe the following precautions with regards to SRS system electrical wiring:

- **Never attempt to modify, splice or repair SRS wiring.**
- **Never install electronic equipment (such as a mobile telephone, two-way radio or in-car entertainment system) in such a way that it could generate electrical interference in the airbag harness. Seek specialist advice when installing such equipment.**

NOTE: SRS system wiring can be identified by a special yellow outer sleeve protecting the wires (black with yellow stripe protective coverings are sometimes used).

CAUTION: Always use specified earth fixings tightened to the correct torque. Poor earthing can cause intermittent problems that are difficult to diagnose.

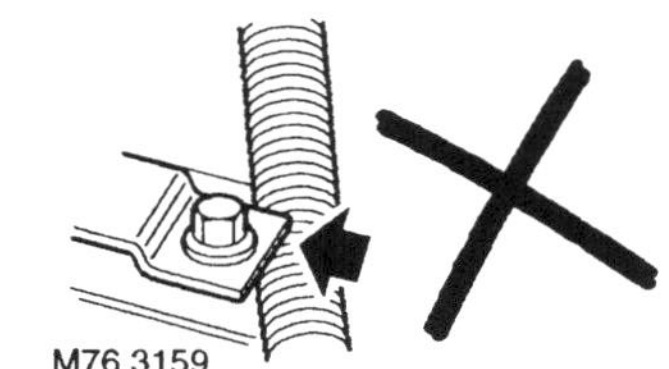

M76 3159

CAUTION: Always ensure airbag wiring is routed correctly. Be careful to avoid trapping or pinching the airbag wiring. Look for possible points of chafing.

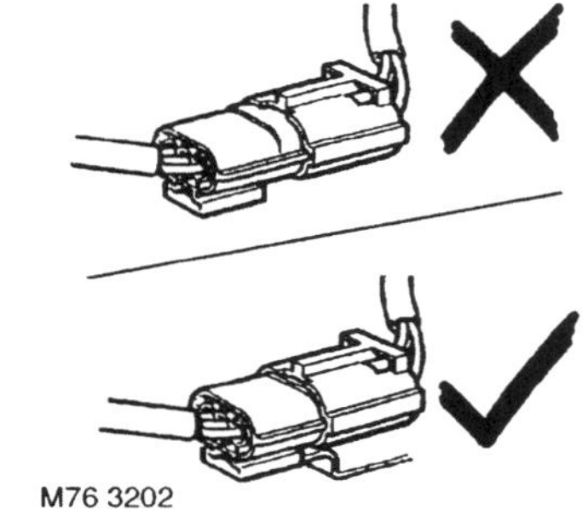

M76 3202

CAUTION: Ensure all airbag harness connectors are mated correctly and securely fastened. Do not leave the connectors hanging loose or allow SRS components to hang from their harnesses.

CRASH SENSOR INSPECTION - DISTRIBUTED SRS SYSTEM ONLY

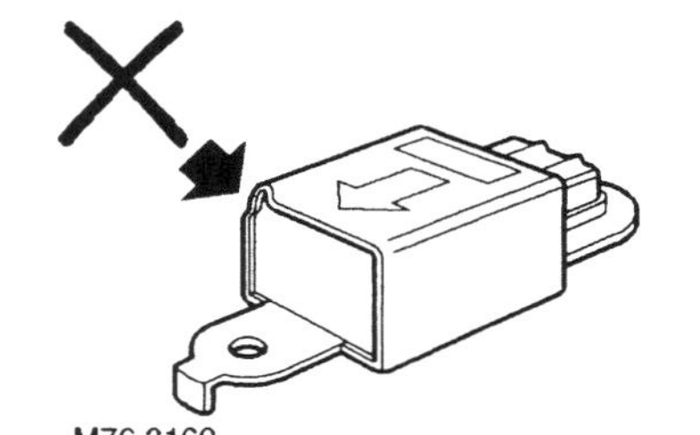

M76 3160

1. After any degree of front body damage, inspect both front crash sensors. Replace a sensor if there are any signs of dents, cracks or deformation.

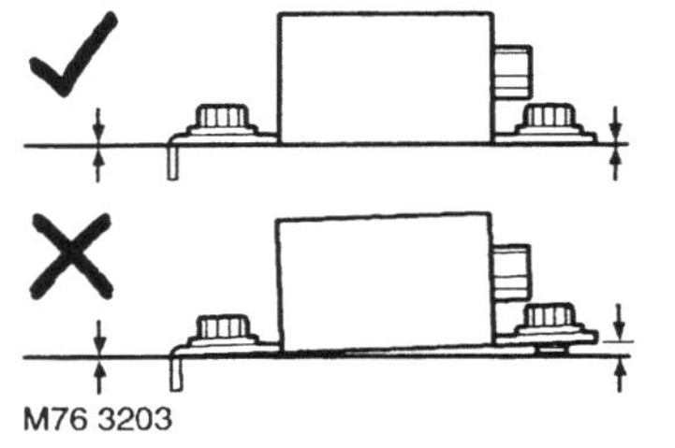

M76 3203

2. Ensure the sensors are installed correctly. An arrow is moulded into the upper case of the sensor indicating the front, the sensor must be installed with the arrow pointing towards the front of the vehicle. There must be no gap between the sensor and body of the vehicle. Use the fixing screws supplied with the sensor and tighten to the correct torque. Tighten front sensor fixing before rear sensor fixing.

CAUTION: Take extra care when painting or carrying out bodywork repairs in the vicinity of the sensors. Avoid direct exposure of the sensors or harness to heat guns, welding or spraying equipment.

ROTARY COUPLER PRECAUTIONS

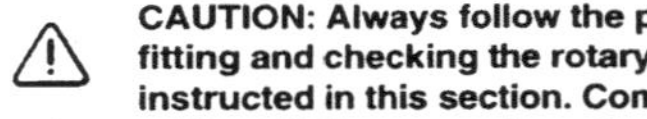

CAUTION: Always follow the procedure for fitting and checking the rotary coupler as instructed in this section. Comply with all safety and installation procedures to ensure the system functions correctly. Observe the following precautions:

- **Do not install a rotary coupler if it is suspected to be defective.**
- **Do not attempt to service, modify or repair a rotary coupler.**
- **Do not cut, splice or modify the wires attached to a yellow SRS connector and lead.**
- **Do not unlock and rotate the rotary coupler when it is removed from the vehicle.**
- **Do not turn the road wheels when the rotary coupler is removed from the vehicle.**
- **Always ensure the rotary coupler connectors are mated correctly and securely fastened.**
- **Always ensure the power is off and the battery disconnected before attempting to do any work involving the rotary coupler.**
- **Always ensure the rotary coupler is removed and installed in its centred position and with the front road wheels in the straight ahead position - refer to the SRS repair section for the correct removal and installation procedure.**
- **If a new rotary coupler is being installed, ensure the locking tab holding the coupler's rotational position is not broken; units with a broken locking tab should not be used.**

WARNING LABELS

Warning symbols are displayed at various positions in the vehicle (in a suitable prominent position such as bonnet locking platform, centre fascia, sunvisor or etched onto the driver and passenger side glass), the front seats have a warning tag sewed to the beading of the seat trim to indicate the presence of the side airbag modules. SRS components have additional warnings displayed on them to indicate that particular care is needed when handling them. These include airbag modules, DCU, seat belts and rotary coupler.

The following warnings are included:

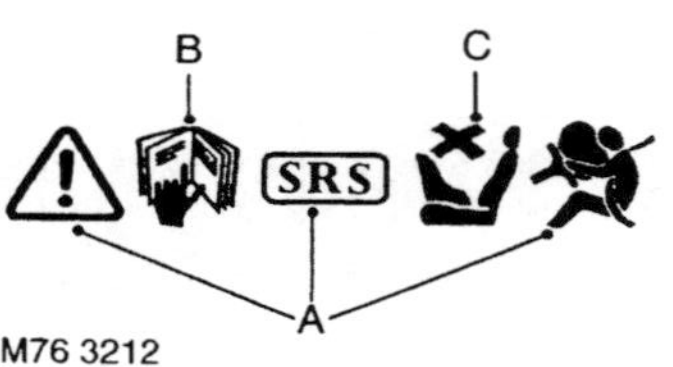

M76 3212

A - The need for caution when working in close proximity to SRS components.

B - Refer to the publication where the procedures, instructions and advice can be found (usually Workshop Manual or Owner's Handbook) for working on the SRS system.

C - Do not use rear facing child seats in the front passenger seat if the vehicle is fitted with a passenger airbag.

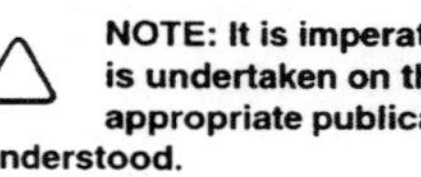

NOTE: It is imperative that before any work is undertaken on the SRS system that the appropriate publication is read and understood.

NOTE: The following list indicates possible locations and content for warning labels. Exact positions and content may vary dependent on model year, legislation and market trends.

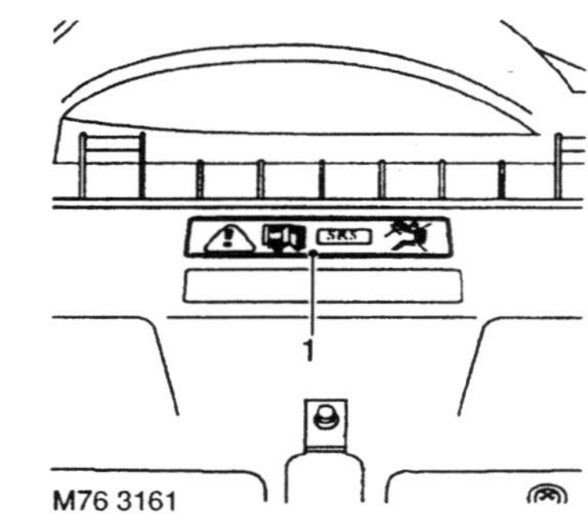

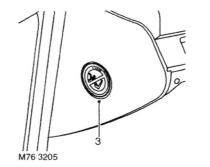

M76 3161

1. Bonnet locking platform. Refer to Owner's Handbook for information on the SRS system.

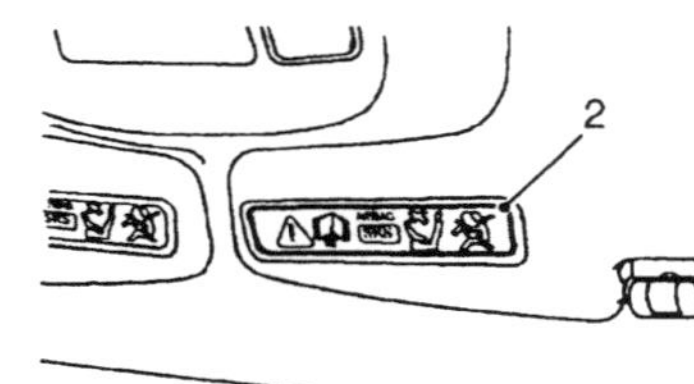

M76 3204

2. Driver's and passenger's sun visor. Refer to Owner's Handbook for information on the SRS system.

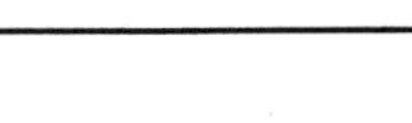

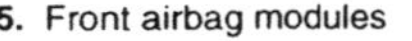

M76 3205

3. End of fascia, passenger's side (not all markets). Do not use rear facing child seat in passenger seat of vehicles fitted with passenger airbag.

4. Rotary coupler

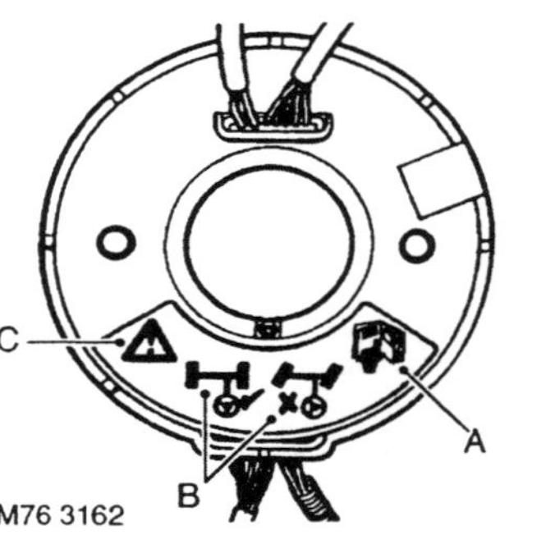

M76 3162

A - Refer to the Workshop Manual for detailed instructions.

B - Ensure the wheels are in the straight ahead position before removal and refitting.

C - The need for caution when working in close proximity to SRS components.

5. Front airbag modules

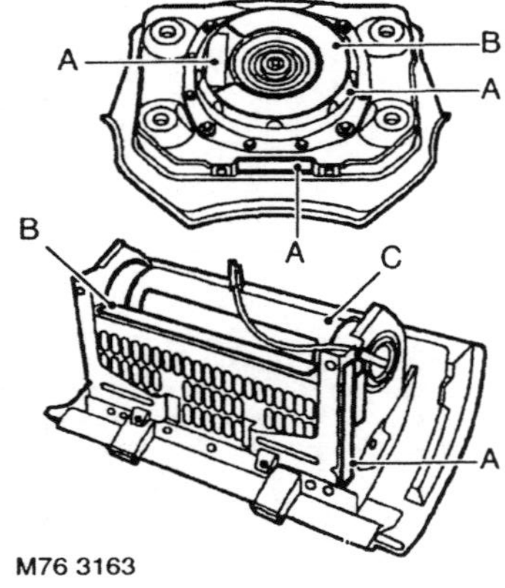

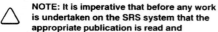

M76 3163

A - Land Rover bar codes. The code number(s) must be recorded if the airbag module is to be replaced.

B - Warning, the use of gas generators is permitted only for occupant restraint systems in vehicles fitted with airbags. Not repairable. Handling is permitted only by authorized personnel. Do not use any live electrical test equipment. Do not open, remove or install in another vehicle. Risk of malfunction and personal injury. Upon deployment, an airbag unit which is not properly mounted may become a dangerous projectile. Refer to Repair Manual for further instructions.

C - Danger Poison. Keep out of reach of children. Contains sodium azide and sodium nitrate. Contents are poisonous and extremely flammable. Contact with acid or heavy metals may produce toxic gases.

6. Side Airbag Modules

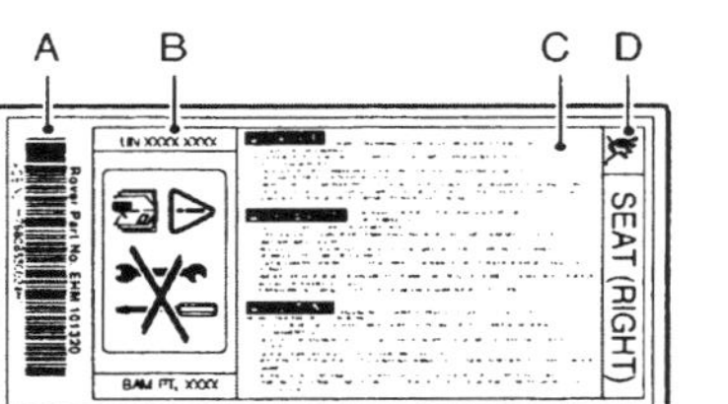

M76 3164

A - Land Rover bar code. The code number must be recorded if the airbag module is to be replaced.

B - Exercise caution; refer to the Workshop Manual for detailed instructions; do not attempt to repair or prise open module case.

C - **DANGER** contains high pressure gas and flammable material. To prevent personal injury:

- Do not repair, dismantle, incinerate or bring into contact with electricity (such as voltmeters)
- Do not store in a place where temperature reaches 93°C (200°F) or more
- Do not install into another vehicle
- Do not install any foreign objects between airbag and its cover or within module
- Follow the installation procedure in the repair manual when installing seat cover
- Service or dispose of as directed in the repair manual

D - Seat identification (right or left hand side seat).

7. 'B' Post label

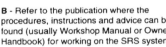

M76 3166

WARNING: Never let a child's head rest near side airbag. Inflating airbag can cause serious or fatal injury.

WARNING: Always use safety belts and child restraints. *See owner's manual.*

8. Seat labels

M76 3216

Indicate that the seat is fitted with a side airbag and caution should be exercised when removing seat cover or performing repair operations to seat assembly.

CAUTION: The seat covers are specially manufactured to facilitate side airbag deployment:

- **DO NOT replace seat covers with other than approved specification covers.**
- **DO NOT put additional covers or other non-approved seat accessories over the seat, they could impair operation.**
- **DO NOT hang jackets or other garments or materials over the seats.**
- **To clean the seat covers, follow the recommendations outlined in the Owner's Manual.**
- **DO NOT allow the seat covers to become saturated with water or other liquids.**
- **DO NOT puncture the seat covering.**

9. Seatbelt pre-tensioner

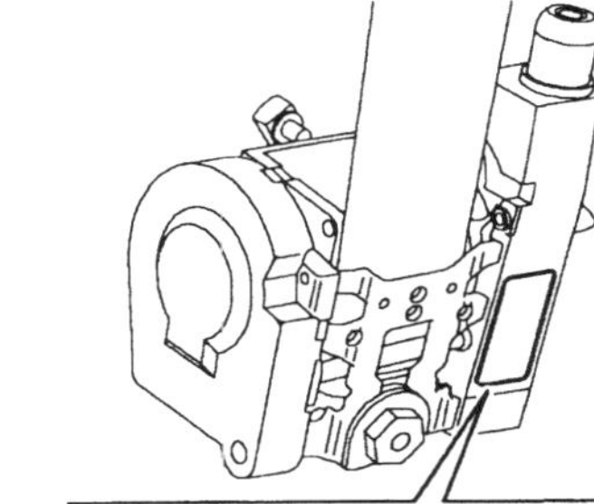

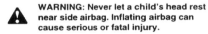

M76 3167

A - Exercise caution

B - Refer to the publication where the procedures, instructions and advice can be found (usually Workshop Manual or Owner's Handbook) for working on the SRS system.

C - Do not attempt to repair or disassemble unit.

VEHICLE RECOVERY

Towing - airbag not deployed

Normal towing procedures are unlikely to cause an airbag to deploy. However, as a precaution, switch the ignition off and then disconnect both battery leads. Disconnect the negative '-' lead first.

Towing - airbag deployed

Once the driver's airbag has been deployed the vehicle must have a front suspended tow. However, as a precaution, switch the ignition off and then disconnect both battery leads. Disconnect the negative '-' lead first.

SRS COMPONENT DEPLOYMENT

If a vehicle is to be scrapped and contains an undeployed airbag module, the module must be manually deployed. Always observe the following precautions:

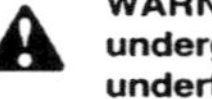

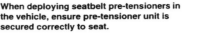

WARNING: Only personnel who have undergone the appropriate training should undertake deployment of airbag and pre-tensioner modules.

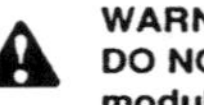

WARNING: A deployed airbag is very hot, DO NOT return to a deployed airbag module until at least 30 minutes have elapsed since deployment.

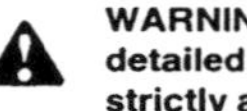

WARNING: Deployment procedures detailed in this service manual should be strictly adhered to. Compliance with the following precautions MUST be ensured:

- **Only use deployment equipment approved for the intended purpose.**
- **Before commencing deployment procedure, ensure the deployment tool functions properly by performing the self test procedure detailed in this section.**
- **Deployment of airbag / pre-tensioner modules should be performed in a well ventilated area which has been designated for the purpose.**
- **Ensure airbag / pre-tensioner modules are not damaged or ruptured before attempting to deploy.**
- **Notify the relevant authorities of intention to deploy airbag and pre-tensioner units.**
- **When deploying airbag pre-tensioner units, ensure that all personnel are at least 15 metres away from the deployment zone.**
- **Ensure deployment tool is connected correctly, in compliance with the instructions detailed in this manual. In particular, ensure deployment tool is NOT connected to battery supply before connecting to airbag module connector.**

- **When deploying seatbelt pre-tensioners in the vehicle, ensure pre-tensioner unit is secured correctly to seat.**
- **When removing deployed airbag modules and pre-tensioner units, wear protective clothing. Use gloves and seal deployed units in a plastic bag.**
- **Following deployment of any component of the SRS system within the vehicle, all SRS components must be replaced. DO NOT re-use or salvage any parts of the SRS system.**
- **Do not lean over airbag module when connecting deployment equipment.**

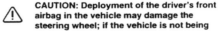

WARNING: If a vehicle is to be scrapped, undeployed airbag modules and pre-tensioner units must be manually deployed in the vehicle; before deployment, ensure the airbag module is secure within its correct mounting position.

CAUTION: Deployment of the driver's front airbag in the vehicle may damage the steering wheel; if the vehicle is not being scrapped, deploy the module outside of the vehicle.

CAUTION: Deployment of the side airbags will rupture the seat covers; if the vehicle is not being scrapped, deploy the module outside of the vehicle.

Airbag module and seatbelt pre-tensioner deployment procedure

Before deployment is started, the deployment tool self test should be carried out.

Deployment tool SMD 4082/1 self test procedure

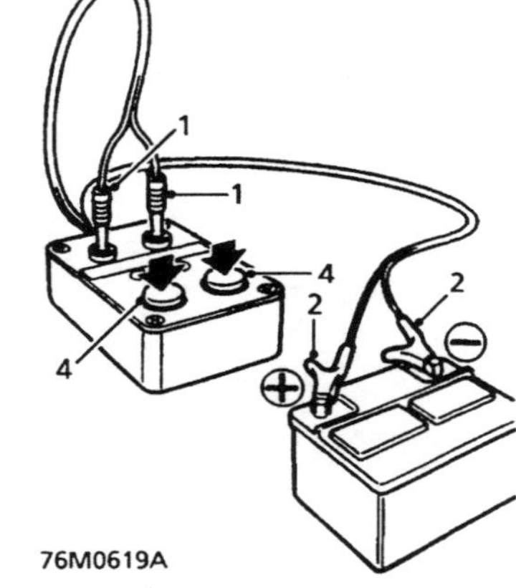

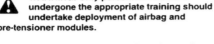

76M0619A

1. Insert blue and yellow connectors of tool lead into corresponding sockets on face of tool.
2. Connect crocodile clips of second tool lead to battery, red to positive and black to negative.
3. Red "READY" light should illuminate.
4. Press and hold both operating buttons.
5. Green "DEFECTIVE" light should illuminate.
6. Release both operating buttons.
7. Red "READY" light should illuminate.
8. Disconnect tool from battery.
9. Disconnect blue and yellow connectors from tool face sockets.
10. Self test is now complete.

Deployment with module fitted to vehicle

These guidelines are written to aid authorised personnel to carry out the safe disposal of airbag modules and seatbelt pre-tensioner units when fitted to the vehicle.

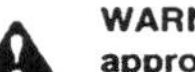

WARNING: Only use the Land Rover approved deployment equipment. Deploy airbag modules and seatbelt pre-tensioner units in a well ventilated, designated area. Ensure airbag module or seatbelt pre-tensioner unit is not damaged or ruptured before deploying.

Driver's airbag module

1. Carry out deployment tool self test.
2. Remove driver's side fascia closing panel. ***See CHASSIS AND BODY, Repair.***

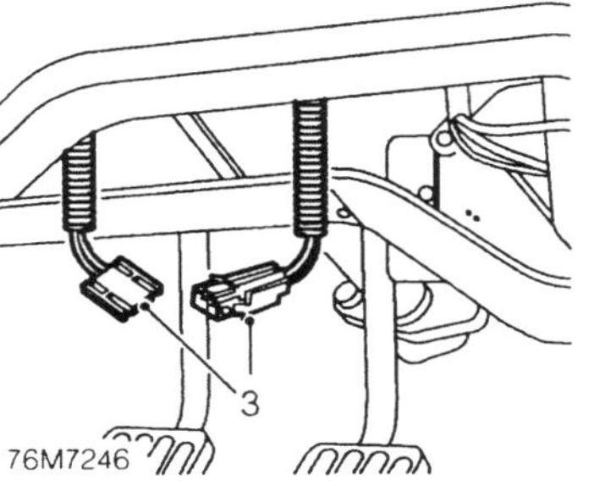

3. Release airbag multiplug from fascia and disconnect multiplug.

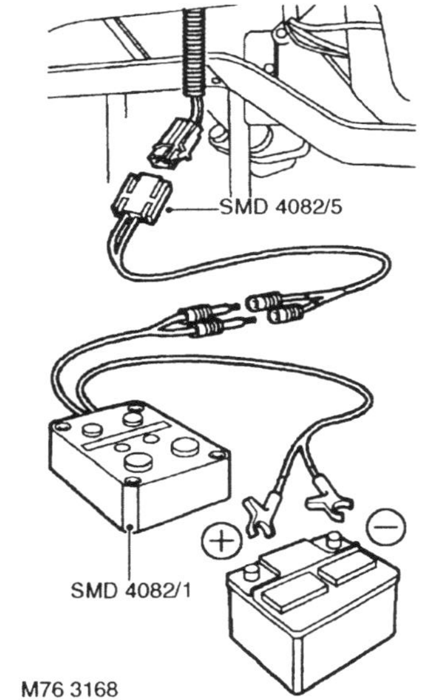

WARNING: Ensure tool SMD 4082/1 is not connected to battery.

4. Connect flylead SMD 4082/5 to airbag connector.
5. Connect flylead SMD 4082/5 to tool SMD 4082/1.

WARNING: Ensure airbag module is secure within steering wheel.

6. Connect tool SMD 4082/1 to battery.

WARNING: Ensure all personnel are standing at least 15 metres away from vehicle.

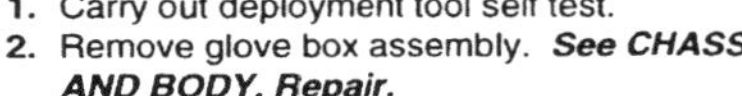

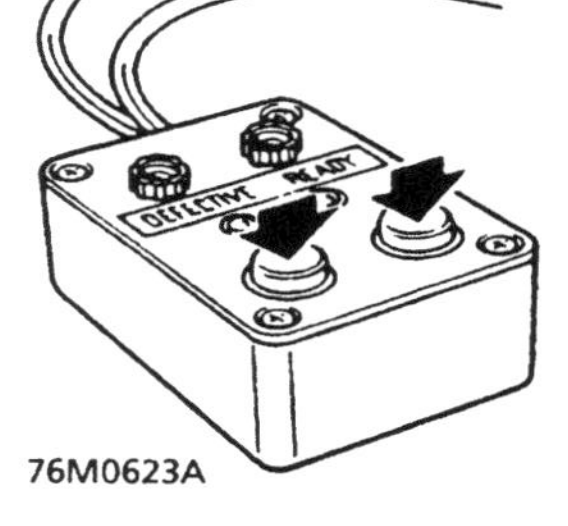

7. Press both operating buttons to deploy airbag module.
8. DO NOT return to airbag module for 30 minutes.
9. Using gloves and face mask, remove airbag module from steering wheel, place airbag module in plastic bag and seal bag ***See Repair.***
10. Transport deployed airbag module to designated area for incineration.

NOTE: DO NOT transport airbag module in the vehicle passenger compartment.

11. Scrap all remaining parts of SRS system. DO NOT re-use or salvage any parts of the SRS system, including steering wheel and steering column.

Passenger's airbag module

1. Carry out deployment tool self test.
2. Remove glove box assembly. ***See CHASSIS AND BODY, Repair.***

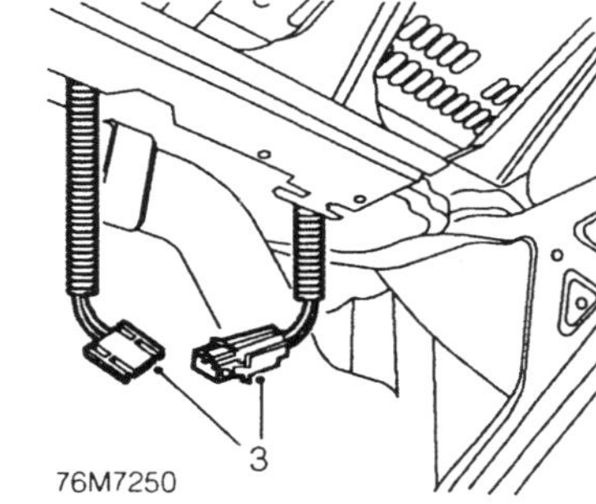

3. Release airbag connector from fascia and disconnect multiplug.

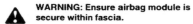

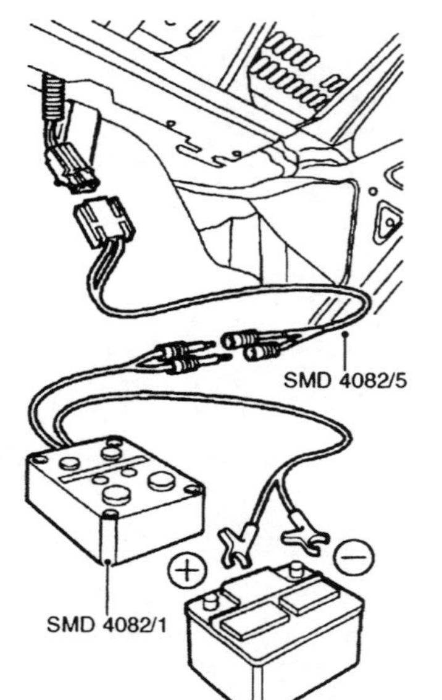

M76 3169

WARNING: Ensure tool SMD 4082/1 is not connected to battery.

4. Connect flylead SMD 4082/5 to harness connector.
5. Connect flylead SMD 4082/5 to tool SMD 4082/1.

WARNING: Ensure airbag module is secure within fascia.

6. Connect tool SMD 4082/1 to battery.

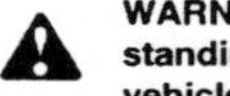
WARNING: Ensure all personnel are standing at least 15 metres away from vehicle.

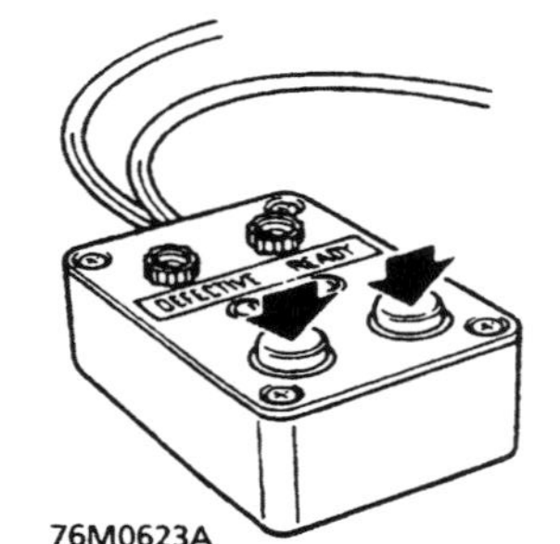
76M0623A

7. Press both operating buttons to deploy airbag module.
8. DO NOT return to airbag module for 30 minutes.
9. Using gloves and face mask, remove airbag module from fascia. Place airbag module in plastic bag and seal bag. *See Repair.*
10. Transport deployed airbag module to designated area for incineration.

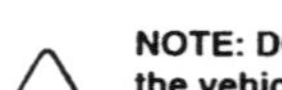
NOTE: DO NOT transport airbag module in the vehicle passenger compartment.

11. Scrap all remaining parts of SRS system. DO NOT re-use or salvage any parts of the SRS system.

Side airbag modules

1. Carry out deployment tool self test.
2. Remove seat valance ***See SEATS, Repair.***

M76 3170

3. Release side airbag connector from beneath seat cushion and disconnect multiplug.

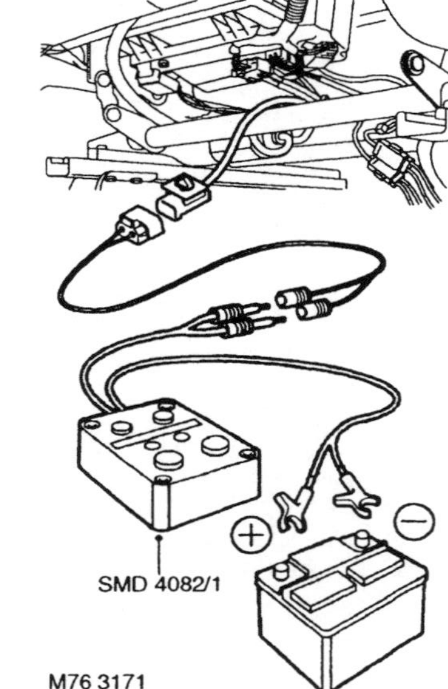

M76 3171

WARNING: Ensure tool SMD 4082/1 is not connected to battery.

4. Connect deployment tool flylead to seat harness connector.
5. Connect deployment tool flylead to deployment tool SMD 4082/1.
6. Connect deployment tool SMD 4082/1 to battery.

WARNING: Ensure all personnel are standing at least 15 metres away from vehicle.

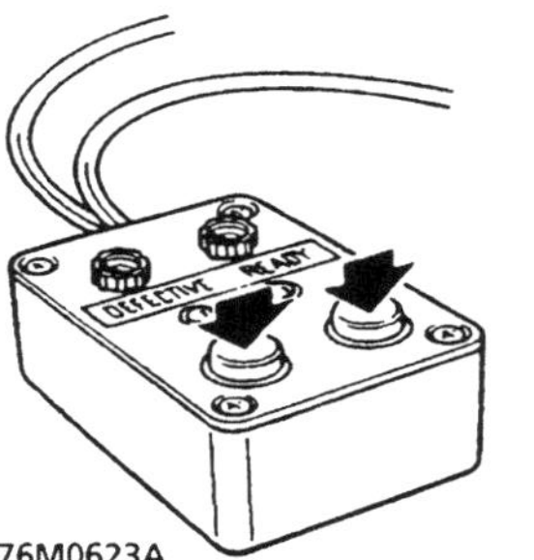
76M0623A

7. Press both operating buttons to deploy airbag module.
8. DO NOT return to airbag module for 30 minutes.
9. Using gloves and face mask, remove airbag module from seat. Place airbag module in plastic bag and seal bag. ***See Repair.***
10. Transport deployed airbag module to designated area for incineration.

NOTE: DO NOT transport airbag module in the vehicle passenger compartment.

11. Scrap all remaining parts of SRS system. DO NOT re-use or salvage any parts of the SRS system.

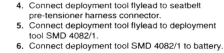

Seatbelt pre-tensioners

1. Carry out deployment tool self test.
2. Remove lower 'B' post finisher. ***See CHASSIS AND BODY, Repair.***

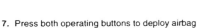

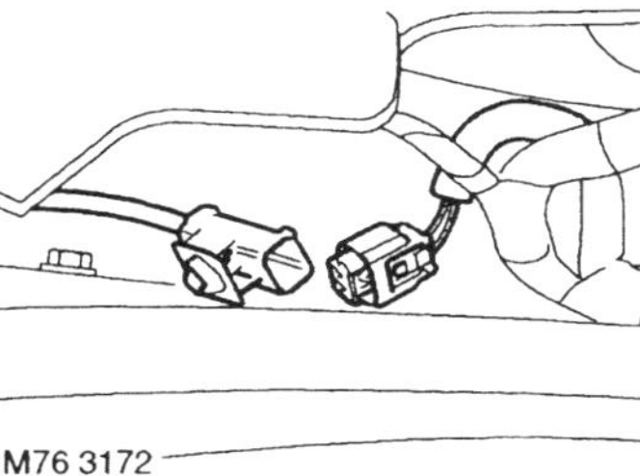
M76 3172

3. Release pre-tensioner connector from 'B' post mounting and disconnect multiplug.

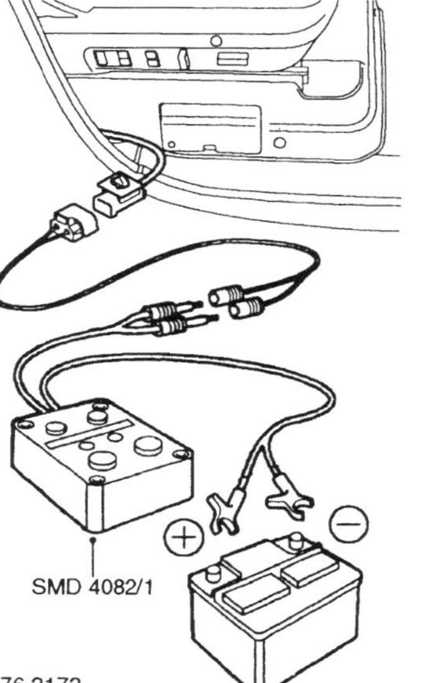

M76 3173

WARNING: Ensure tool SMD 4082/1 is not connected to battery.

4. Connect deployment tool flylead to seatbelt pre-tensioner harness connector.
5. Connect deployment tool flylead to deployment tool SMD 4082/1.
6. Connect deployment tool SMD 4082/1 to battery.

WARNING: Ensure all personnel are standing at least 15 metres away from vehicle.

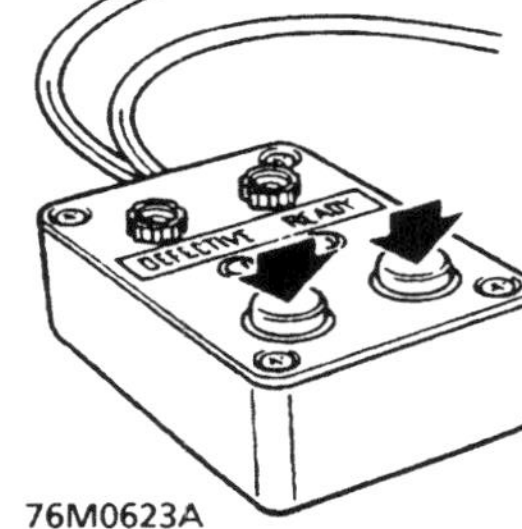
76M0623A

7. Press both operating buttons to deploy airbag module.
8. DO NOT return to seatbelt pre-tensioner module for 30 minutes.
9. Using gloves and face mask, remove seatbelt pre-tensioner unit from vehicle. Place seatbelt pre-tensioner unit in plastic bag and seal bag. ***See Repair.***
10. Transport deployed seatbelt pre-tensioner unit to designated area for incineration.

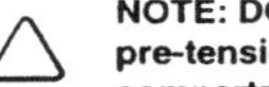

NOTE: DO NOT transport seatbelt pre-tensioner unit in the vehicle passenger compartment.

11. Scrap all remaining parts of SRS system. DO NOT re-use or salvage any parts of the SRS system.

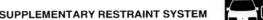

SRS system component replacement policy

Following the deployment of the airbags and/or seatbelt pre-tensioners, the following components must be replaced:

- SRS wiring harness,
- Front impact sensors (NAS - distributed system only),
- Rotary coupler,
- Driver's airbag module,
- Passenger's airbag module,
- Front seat side airbag modules,
- Seatbelt pre-tensioners,
- SRS diagnostic control unit,
- Complete steering wheel assembly including associated switches.

STEERING COLUMN PRECAUTIONS

Dimensions 'A' AND 'B' on steering column must be within tolerance.

Dimension 'A': 3.5 mm ± 1.0 mm (0.14 in. ± 0.04 in.)
Dimension 'B': 75.5 mm ± 1.0 mm (2.97 in. ± 0.04 in.)

If dimension 'A' is incorrect replace steering column.

If dimension 'B' is incorrect replace steering column, and pedal box.

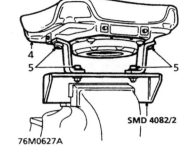

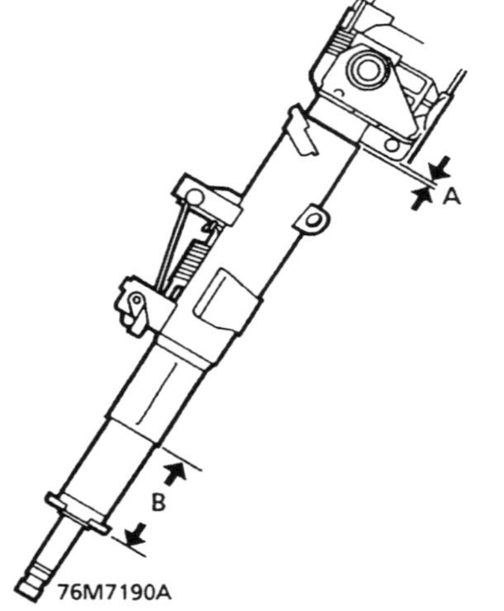

Deployment with module removed from vehicle

These guidelines are written to aid authorised personnel to carry out the safe disposal of airbag modules when they are removed from the vehicle.

WARNING: Only use Land Rover approved deployment equipment. Deploy airbag modules in a well ventilated, designated area.

Driver's airbag module

1. Carry out deployment tool self test.
2. Remove airbag module from steering wheel. ***See Repair.***

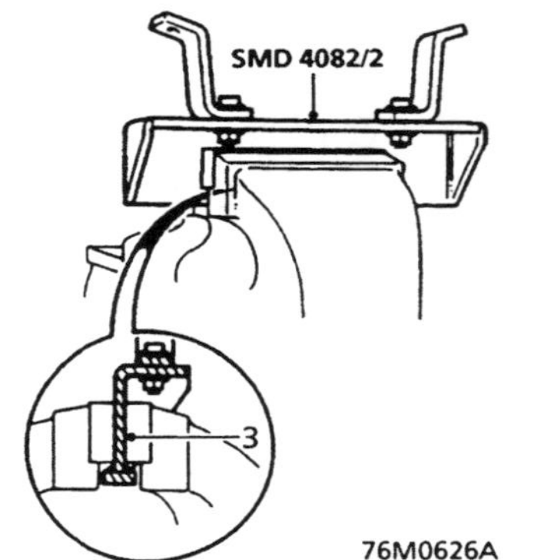

3. Position tool SMD 4082/2 in vice, ensuring that vice jaws grip tool above bottom flange to prevent possibility of tool being forced upwards from vice. Tighten vice.

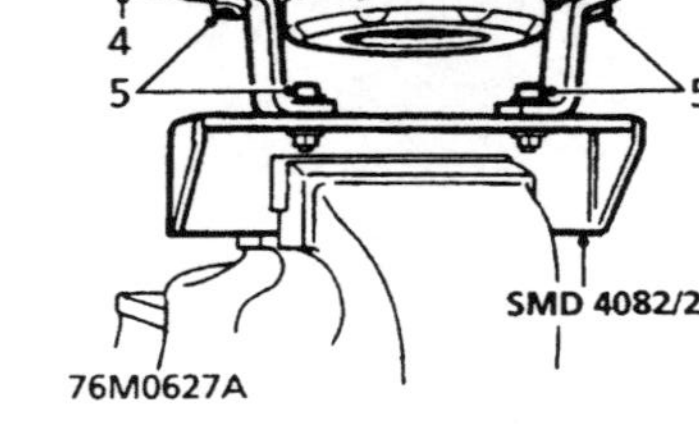

4. Secure airbag module to tool SMD 4082/2. Ensure module is correctly secured using both fixings.
5. Ensure airbag module mounting brackets are secure.

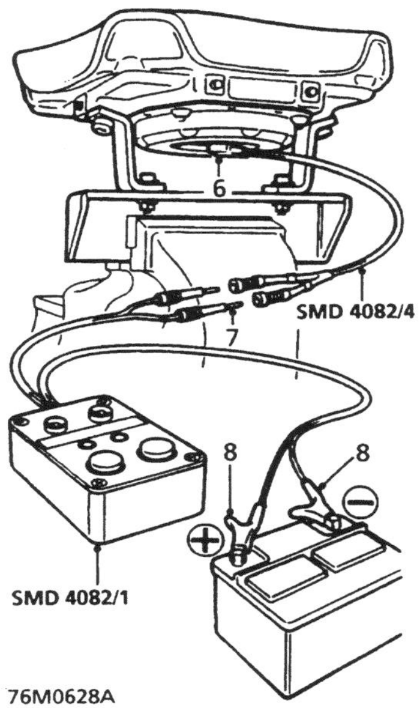

SMD 4082/4

SMD 4082/1

76M0628A

WARNING: Ensure tool SMD 4082/1 is not connected to battery.

6. Connect flylead SMD 4082/4 to airbag module.
7. Connect flylead SMD 4082/4 to tool SMD 4082/1.

WARNING: Do not lean over module whilst connecting.

8. Connect tool SMD 4082/1 to battery.

WARNING: Ensure all personnel are standing at least 15 metres away from module.

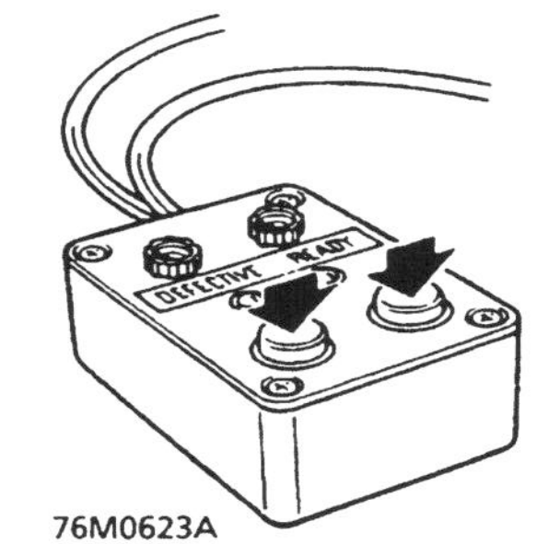

76M0623A

9. Press both operating buttons to deploy airbag module.
10. DO NOT return to airbag module for 30 minutes.
11. Using gloves and face mask, remove airbag module from tool SMD 4082/2, place airbag module in plastic bag and seal bag.
12. Wipe down tool SMD 4082/2 with damp cloth.
13. Transport deployed airbag module to designated area for incineration.

NOTE: DO NOT transport airbag module in the vehicle passenger compartment.

Passenger's airbag module

1. Carry out deployment tool self test.
2. Remove airbag module from fascia. ***See Repair.***

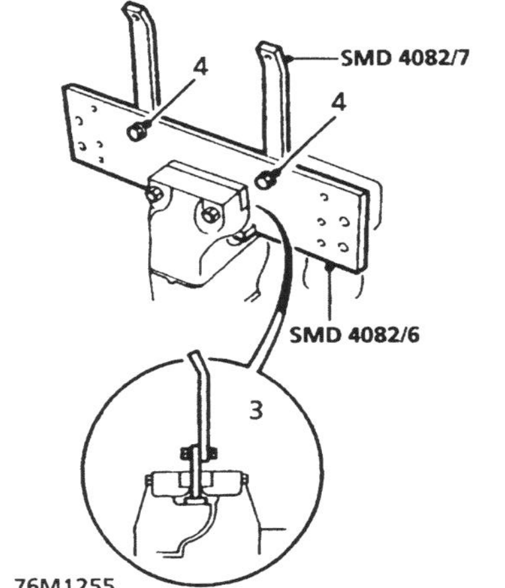

76M1255

3. Position tool SMD 4082/6 in vice, ensuring that vice jaws grip tool above bottom flange to prevent possibility of tool being forced upwards from vice. Tighten vice.
4. Position brackets SMD 4082/7 to tool; lightly tighten bolts.

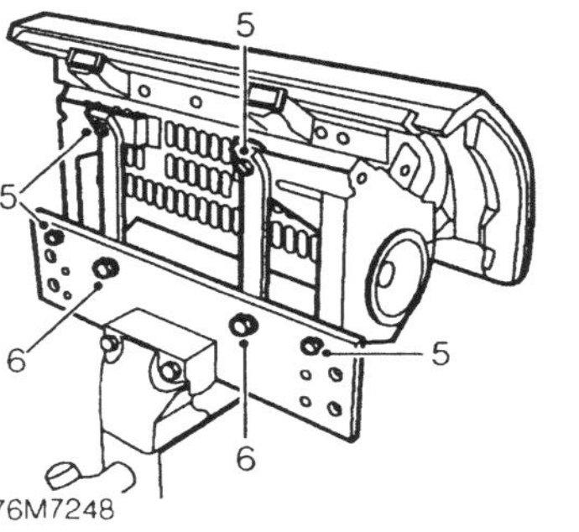

76M7248

5. Secure airbag module to tool SMD 4082/6. Ensure module is correctly secured using all fixings.

6. Ensure airbag module mounting brackets are secure.

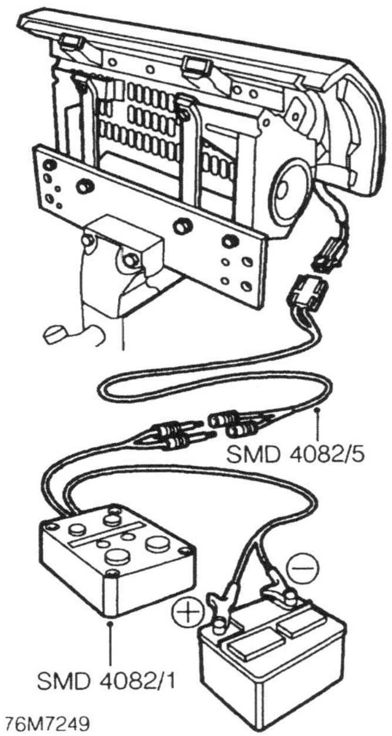

SMD 4082/5

SMD 4082/1

76M7249

WARNING: Ensure tool SMD 4082/1 is not connected to battery.

7. Connect flylead SMD 4082/5 to airbag module.
8. Connect flylead SMD 4082/5 to tool SMD 4082/1.

WARNING: Do not lean over module whilst connecting.

9. Connect tool SMD 4082/1 to battery.

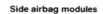

WARNING: Ensure all personnel are standing at least 15 metres away from module.

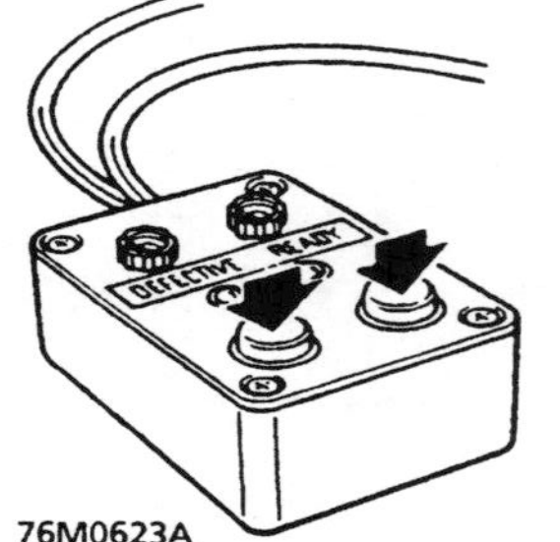

76M0623A

10. Press both operating buttons to deploy airbag module.
11. DO NOT return to airbag module for 30 minutes.
12. Using gloves and face mask, remove airbag module from tool, place airbag module in plastic bag and seal bag.
13. Wipe down tool SMD 4082/6 with a damp cloth.
14. Transport deployed airbag module to designated area for incineration

NOTE: DO NOT transport airbag module in the vehicle passenger compartment.

Side airbag modules

1. Carry out deployment tool self test.
2. Remove side airbag module from seat. ***See Repair.***

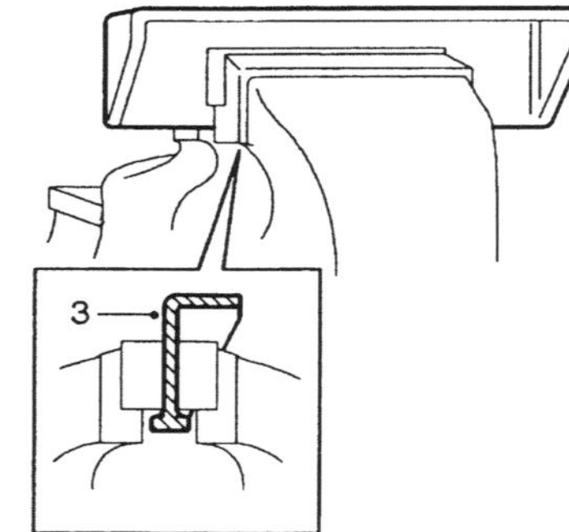

M76 3176

3. Position tool SMD 4082/2 in vice, ensuring that vice jaws grip tool above bottom flange to prevent possibility of tool being forced upwards from vice. Tighten vice.

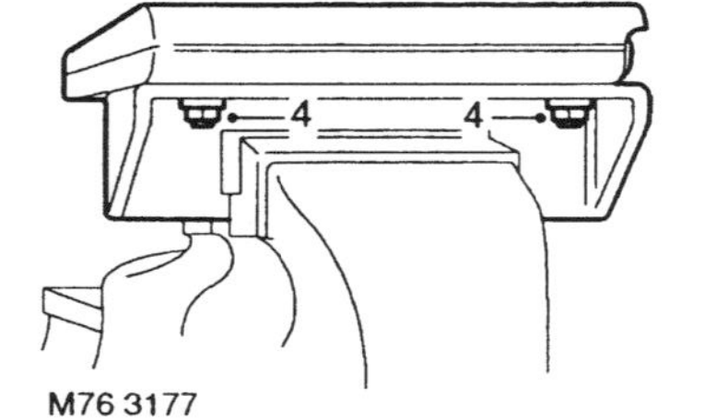

M76 3177

4. Secure airbag module to tool SMD 4082/2. Ensure side airbag module is correctly secured using all fixings.

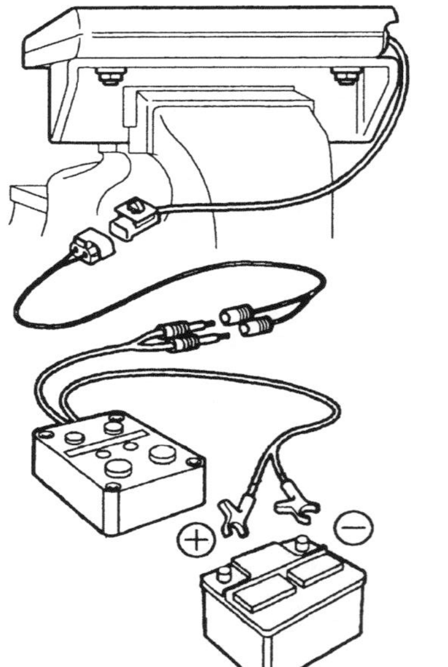

M76 3178

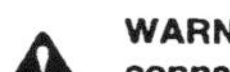

WARNING: Ensure tool SMD 4082/1 is not connected to battery.

5. Connect deployment tool flylead to side airbag module connector.
6. Connect deployment tool flylead to deployment tool SMD 4082/1.

WARNING: Do not lean over module whilst connecting.

7. Connect deployment tool SMD 4082/1 to battery.

WARNING: Ensure all personnel are standing at least 15 metres away from module.

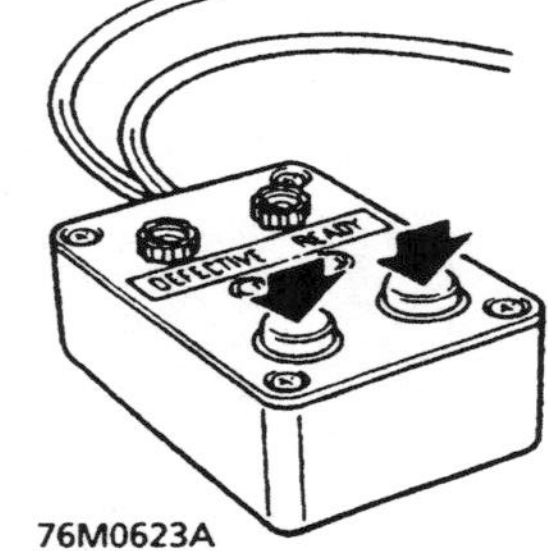
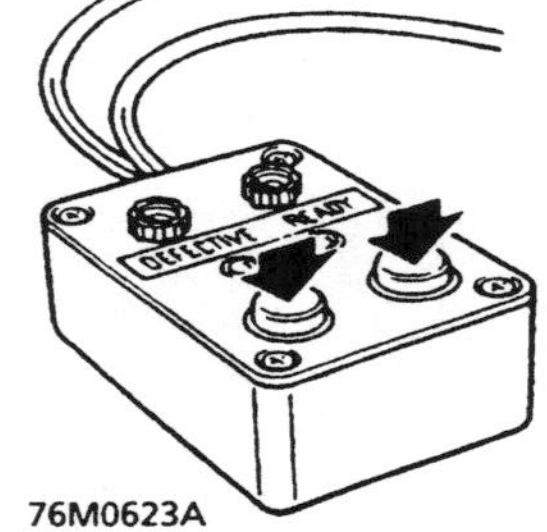

76M0623A

8. Press both operating buttons to deploy airbag module.
9. DO NOT return to airbag module for 30 minutes.
10. Using gloves and face mask, remove airbag module from tool, place airbag module in plastic bag and seal bag.
11. Wipe down tool SMD 4082/2 with a damp cloth.
12. Transport deployed airbag module to designated area for incineration

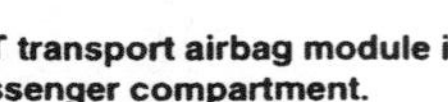

NOTE: DO NOT transport airbag module in the vehicle passenger compartment.

Notes

AIRBAG MODULE - PASSENGER SIDE

Service repair no - 76.73.69

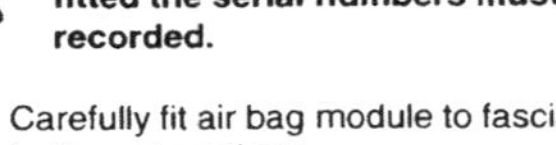

WARNING: All the airbag system components, including the wiring harness, MUST be renewed after the airbags have deployed.

Remove

1. Disconnect both battery terminals, disconnect negative lead first.
2. Remove glove box assembly. ***See CHASSIS AND BODY, Repair.***
3. Remove veneered panel from passenger side of fascia. ***See CHASSIS AND BODY, Repair.***

76M7029

4. Release and disconnect air bag module multiplug.
5. Remove 4 bolts and washers (E-10 Torx Bit) securing air bag module to fascia frame.

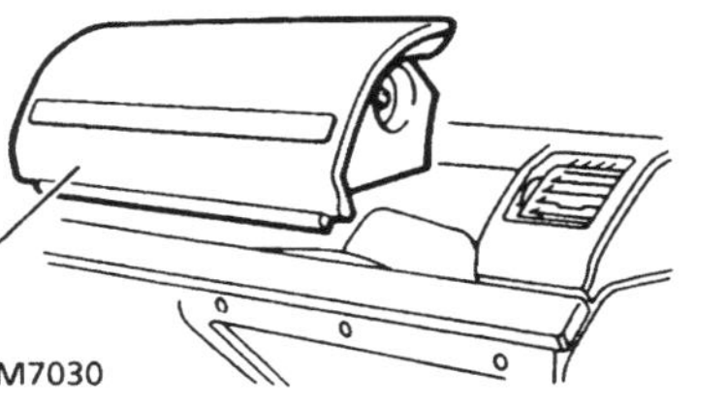

76M7030

6. Carefully release and remove air bag module.

CAUTION: Store the airbag module correctly. *See this section.*

Refit

NOTE: If a new airbag module is being fitted the serial numbers must be recorded.

7. Carefully fit air bag module to fascia. Fit Torx bolts, and washers.
8. Tighten bolts to ***9 Nm. (7 lbf.ft)***
9. Connect air bag module multiplug and secure to location.
10. Fit glove box assembly. ***See CHASSIS AND BODY, Repair.***
11. Connect battery terminals, fit battery cover and secure with turnbuckles.
12. Check Supplementary Restraint System using **TestBook** .

SRS DCU

Service repair no - 76.73.72

Remove

WARNING: Always disconnect negative lead from battery first. Disconnection of positive lead with negative lead connected risks short circuit and severe sparking through accidental grounding of spanner. Personal injury could result.

1. Disconnect both battery terminals.
2. Remove centre console. ***See CHASSIS AND BODY, Repair.***
3. Lift rear of sound deadener pad from transmission tunnel.

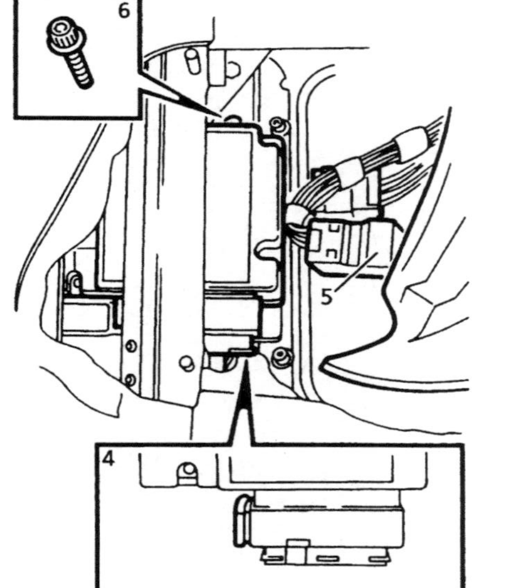

4. Disconnect SRS DCU multiplug.
5. Release 2 multiplugs from bracket.
6. Remove 2 bolts securing DCU to bracket. Remove DCU.

Refit

7. Reverse removal procedure.

SRS HARNESS - SINGLE POINT SENSED SYSTEM

Service repair no - 76.73.73

The SRS harness is incorporated into the fascia harness. ***See ELECTRICAL, Repair.***

SRS HARNESS - DISTRIBUTED SYSTEM

Service repair no - 76.73.73

Remove

1. Raise the vehicle.

WARNING: Support on safety stands.

2. Remove battery. ***See ELECTRICAL, Repair.***
3. Remove centre console. ***See CHASSIS AND BODY, Repair.***
4. Remove passenger air bag module. ***See this section.***
5. Remove radio. ***See ELECTRICAL, Repair.***
6. Remove instrument pack binnacle. ***See INSTRUMENTS, Repair.***
7. Remove 5 screws securing switch pack to fascia.

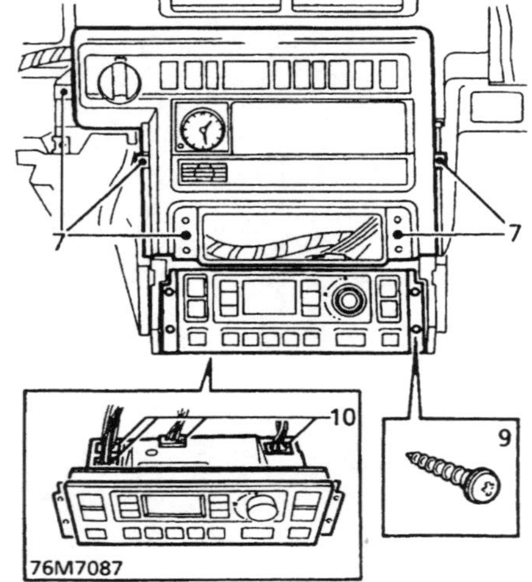

8. Disconnect switches, clock and temperature sensor. Remove switch pack.
9. Remove 4 screws securing heater control panel.
10. Disconnect multiplugs. Remove control panel.
11. Release door aperture seal adjacent to A post lower trim panels.
12. **Driver's side - LHD automatic vehicles only:** Remove 3 bolts securing foot rest. Remove foot rest.

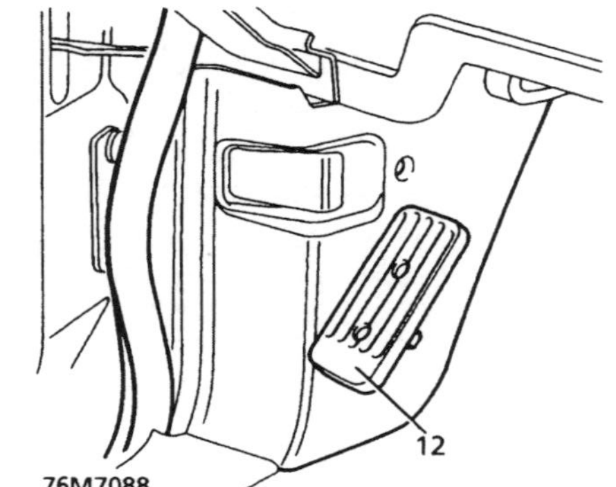

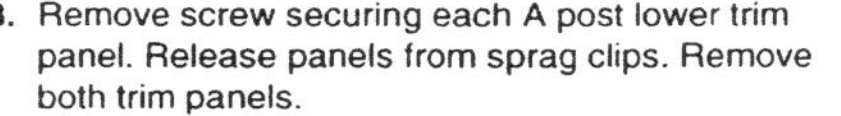

13. Remove screw securing each A post lower trim panel. Release panels from sprag clips. Remove both trim panels.

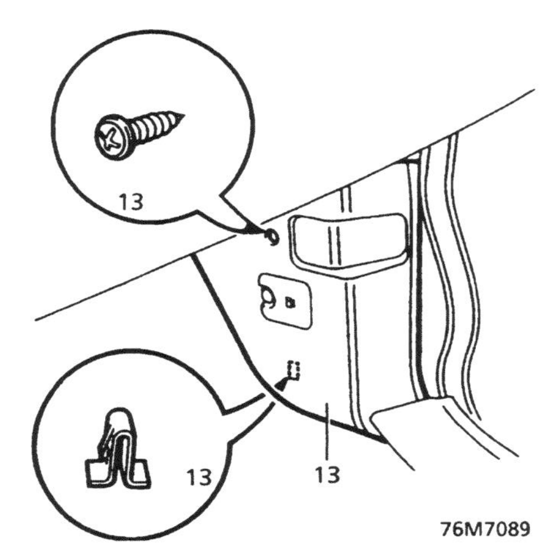

76M7089

14. Remove 4 scrivet fasteners securing driver's side lower closing panel.

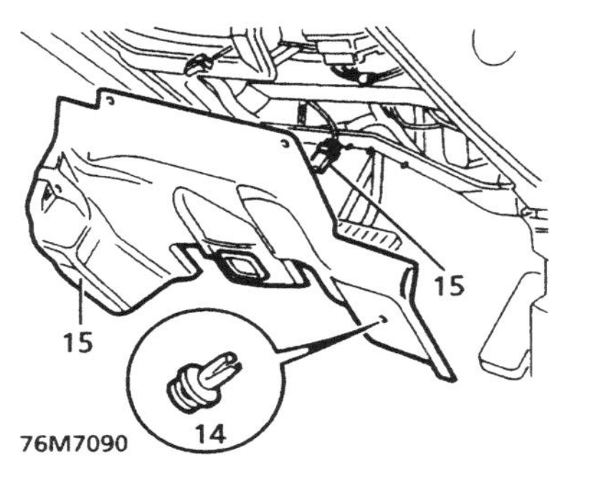

76M7090

15. Disconnect footwell lamp multiplug. Remove closing panel.
16. Disconnect SRS harness from main harness. Release multiplug from clip.

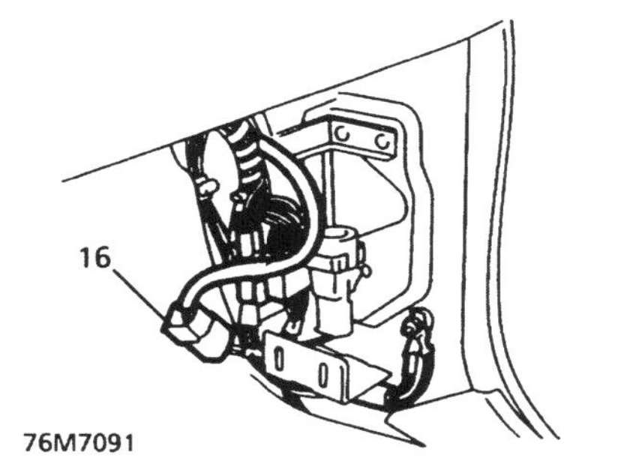

76M7091

17. Remove sound deadener pad from transmission tunnel.

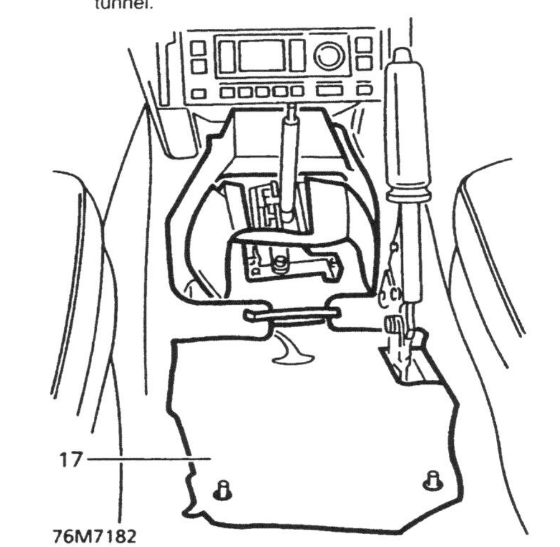

76M7182

18. Disconnect multiplug from SRS DCU. Release 3 harness clips.
19. Remove both front wheel arch liners. *See* ***CHASSIS AND BODY, Repair.***

20. Remove 2 trim studs securing air cleaner baffle beneath LH wheel arch. Remove baffle.

76M7092

21. Disconnect both SRS crash sensor multiplugs.

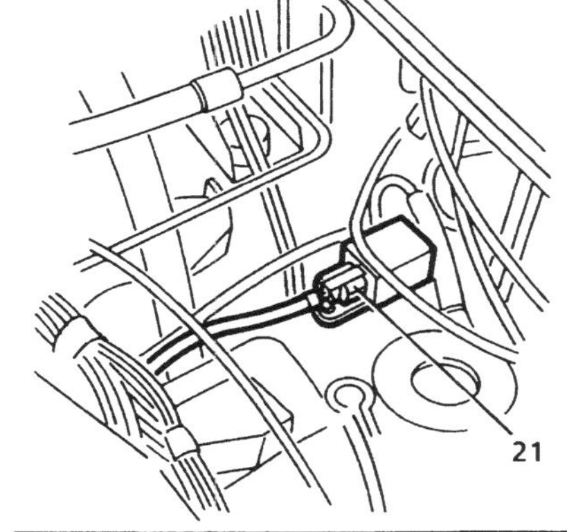

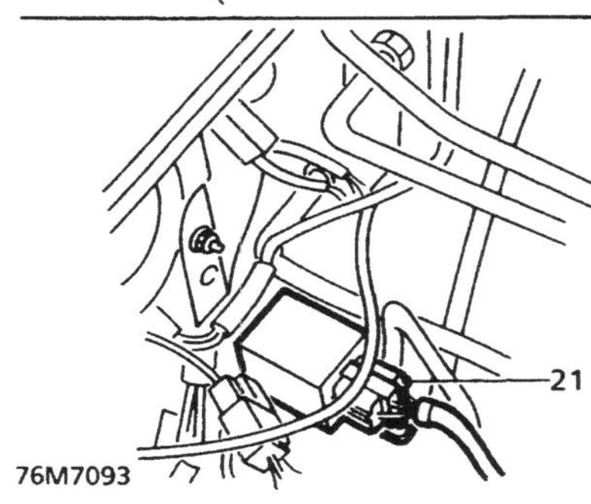

76M7093

22. Remove 4 bolts securing battery tray.

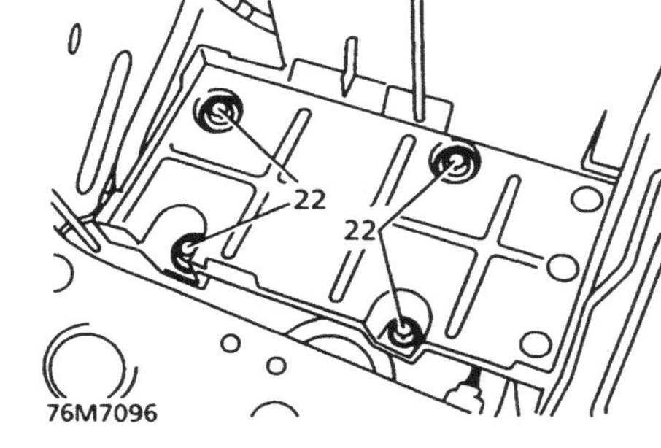

76M7096

23. Remove 2 bolts securing air cleaner to valance.

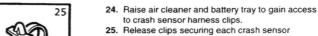

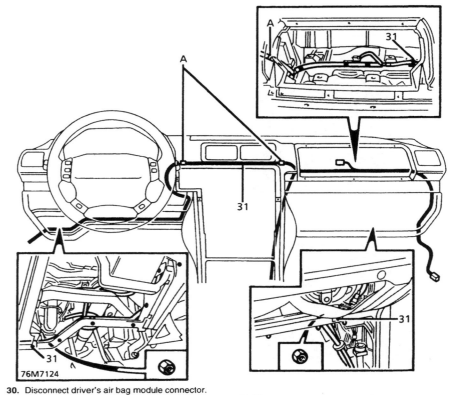

24. Raise air cleaner and battery tray to gain access to crash sensor harness clips.
25. Release clips securing each crash sensor harness to valance.
26. Release harness grommets. Feed both harnesses through valance into wheel arches.
27. Release 3 clips securing each crash sensor harness to underside of wheel arches.
28. Release harness bulkhead grommets. Feed harnesses through bulkhead into passenger compartment.
29. Disconnect SRS multiplug from instrument pack.

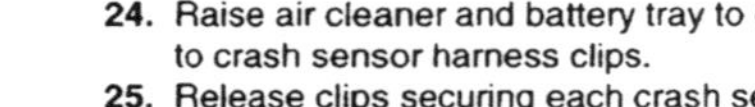

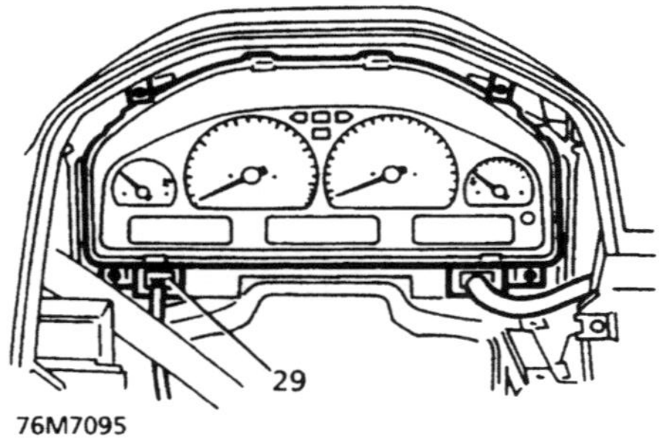
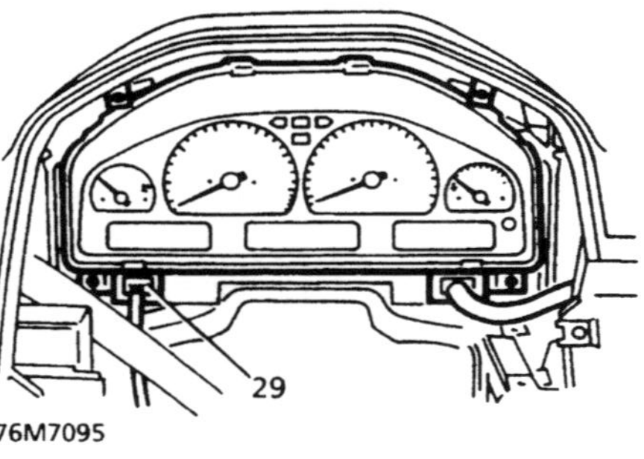
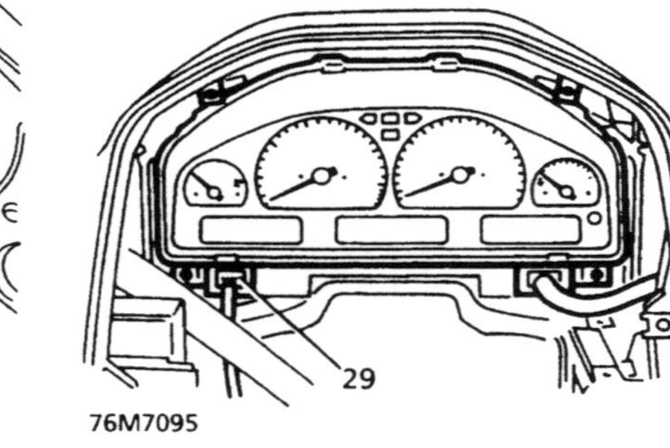
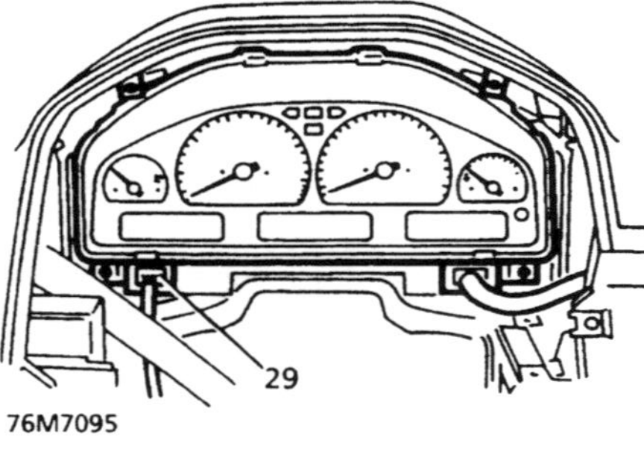

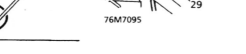

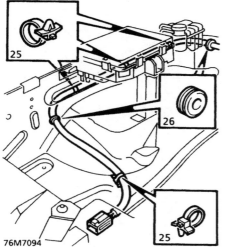

30. Disconnect driver's air bag module connector. Release connector and harness from clips.
31. Release 13 clips securing SRS harness to fascia frame.

NOTE: Due to restricted access, two outer clips 'A' securing harness above heater unit may have to be cut. Ensure that location holes are clear. Collect loose ends of clips.

32. Release 3 clips securing fascia harness trunking to passenger side fascia frame.
33. Remove nut securing lower end of each blower assembly to fascia frame.
34. Route crash sensor ends of harness into passenger air bag module space.
35. Feed SRS DCU connector into passenger air bag module space.
36. Remove harness.

Refit

37. Position harness in passenger air bag module space. Feed SRS DCU connector between heater and fascia frame.
38. Route harness along transmission tunnel. Secure harness clips.
39. Connect multiplug to DCU.
40. Fit sound deadener pad to transmission tunnel.
41. Route crash sensor ends of harness correctly around fascia frame and behind blower assemblies.
42. Secure harness clips to fascia frame.
43. Position fascia harness trunking. Secure with clips.
44. Secure blower assemblies to fascia frame with nuts.
45. Connect drivers air bag module, secure multiplug and harness to trunking.
46. Connect SRS multiplug to instrument pack.

47. Route SRS crash sensor harnesses through bulkhead into wheel arches, locate harness grommets.
48. Secure harness clips beneath wheel arches.
49. Route harnesses through valances into engine bay. Locate harness grommets.
50. Raise battery tray and air cleaner for access. Route crash sensor harnesses. Secure harness clips.
51. Connect multiplugs to crash sensors.
52. Secure battery tray and air cleaner with bolts.
53. Connect SRS harness multiplug to main harness. Secure multiplug to bracket.
54. Fit air cleaner baffle beneath LH wheel arch. Secure with trim studs.
55. Fit wheel arch liners. ***See CHASSIS AND BODY, Repair.***
56. Position driver's side lower closing panel. Connect footwell lamp multiplug.
57. Align closing panel. Secure with scrivet fasteners.
58. Position 'A' post lower trim panels. Engage sprag clips. Secure with screws.
59. Re-fit door aperture seals.
60. **LHD automatic vehicles only:** Position foot rest. Secure with bolts.
61. Position heater controls. Connect multiplugs. Secure to fascia with screws.
62. Position fascia switch pack. Connect multiplugs. Secure to fascia with screws.
63. Fit instrument pack binnacle. ***See INSTRUMENTS, Repair.***
64. Fit radio. ***See ELECTRICAL, Repair.***
65. Fit passenger air bag module. ***See this section.***
66. Fit centre console. ***See CHASSIS AND BODY, Repair.***
67. Fit battery. ***See ELECTRICAL, Repair.***
68. Remove safety stands. Lower vehicle.

SRS CRASH SENSOR

Service repair no - 76.73.70

Remove

WARNING: Always disconnect negative lead from battery first. Disconnection of positive lead with negative lead connected risks short circuit and severe sparking through accidental grounding of spanner. Personal injury could result.

1. Disconnect both battery terminals.
2. Disconnect sensor multiplug.
3. Remove 2 bolts securing sensor to valance. Remove sensor.

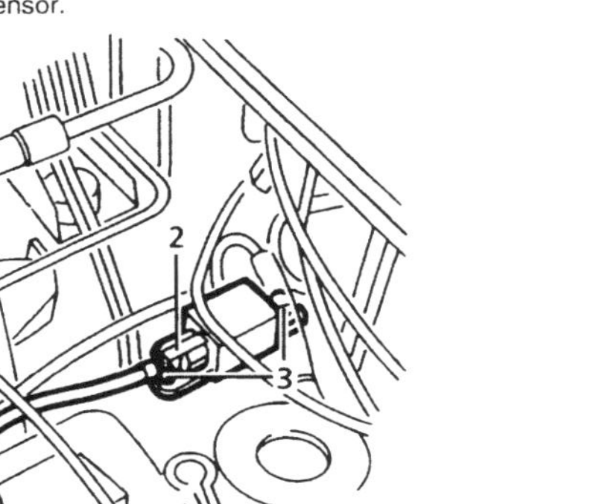

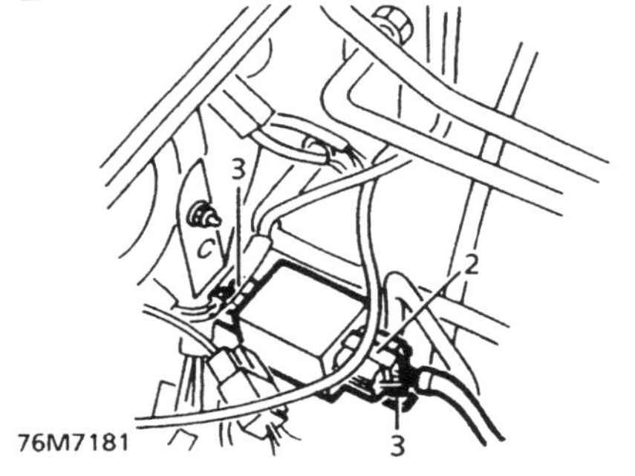

76M7181

Refit

4. Reverse removal procedure.

AIRBAG MODULE - DRIVER SIDE

Service repair no - 76.73.71

Remove

1. Disconnect both battery terminals, negative lead first.
2. Disconnect Supplementary Restraint System (SRS) 'shorting link'.

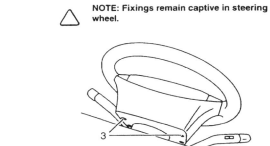

76M2708

3. Unscrew 4 bolts (TX 30 Torx bit) securing module to steering wheel.

NOTE: Fixings remain captive in steering wheel.

76M2709

NOTE: Rotate steering wheel for access to all fixings.

4. Release module from steering wheel, disconnect multiplug.
5. Remove module.

CAUTION: Store the airbag module correctly. *See Description and operation.*

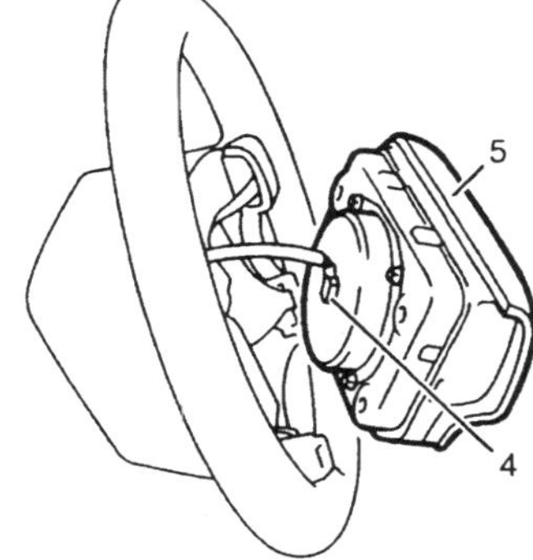

76M2710

Refit

NOTE: If a new airbag module is being fitted, the serial numbers must be recorded.

6. Position module and connect multiplug.
7. Tighten bolts to ***9 Nm. (7 lbf.ft)***
8. Connect SRS 'shorting link'and secure connector to location.
9. Connect battery terminals, positive before negative. Fit and secure battery cover.
10. Check SRS using **TestBook** .

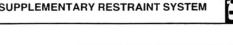

PRE-TENSIONER - SEAT BELT - FRONT - from 99MY

Service repair no - 76.73.75

Remove

WARNING: See SRS safety precautions before commencement of repair. See SUPPLEMENTARY RESTRAINT SYSTEM, Precautions.

1. Remove 'B' post lower finisher. ***See CHASSIS AND BODY, Repair.***

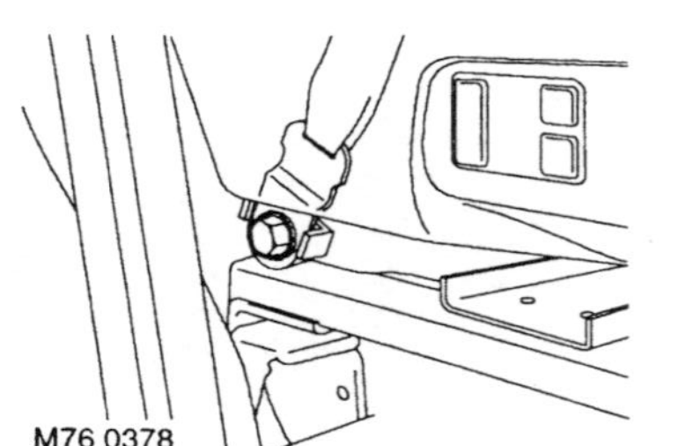
M76 0378

2. Remove bolt securing seat belt to seat and release belt from seat.

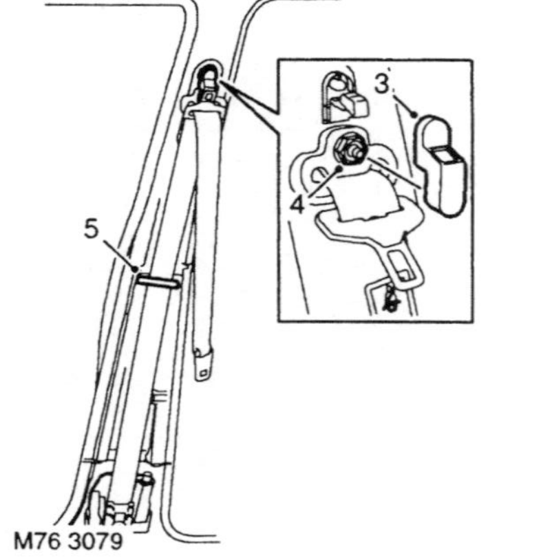

M76 3079

3. Remove cover from upper mounting.
4. Remove nut from upper mounting.
5. Release seat belt guide from 'B' post.

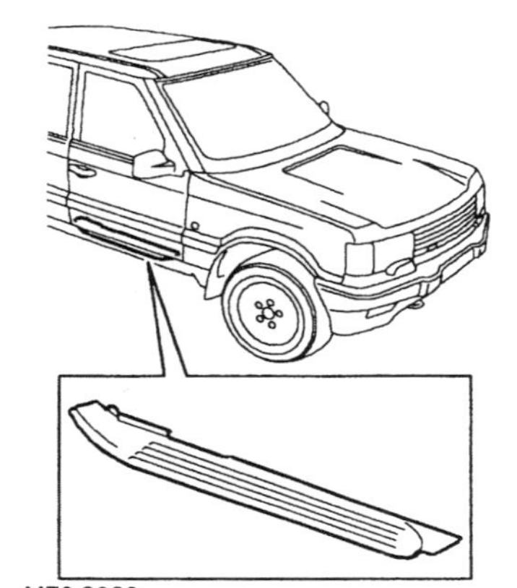
M76 3080

6. Remove front carpet retainer.

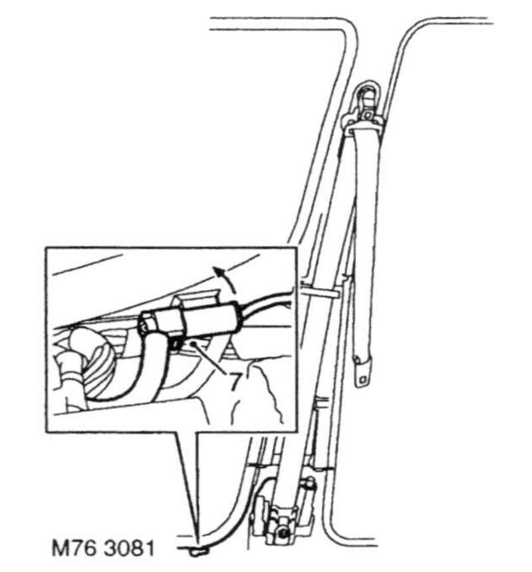

M76 3081

7. Release pre-tensioner multiplug from inner sill and disconnect multiplug.

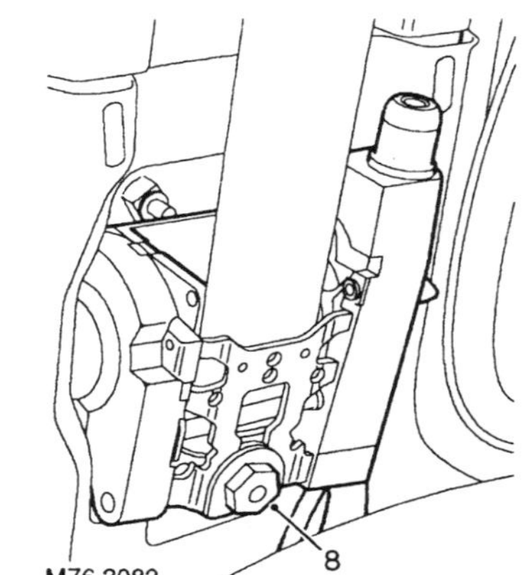

M76 3082

8. Remove bolt securing belt reel to 'B' post. Remove reel.

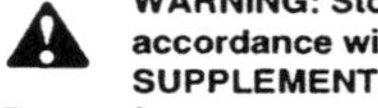

WARNING: Store pre-tensioner in accordance with storage procedures. See SUPPLEMENTARY RESTRAINT SYSTEM, Precautions.

Refit

9. Fit reel, fit bolt and tighten to ***32 Nm (24 lbf.ft).***
10. Connect pre-tensioner multiplug and secure to inner sill.
11. Fit front carpet retainer.
12. Extend belt and secure belt guide to 'B' post.
13. Locate belt to upper mounting, fit nut and tighten to ***22 Nm (16 lbf.ft).***
14. Fit cover to upper mounting.
15. Position belt to seat mounting, fit bolt and tighten to ***32 Nm (24 lbf.ft).***
16. Fit 'B' post lower finisher ***See CHASSIS AND BODY, Repair.***
17. Connect battery, earth lead last.
18. Check SRS using **TestBook.**

AIRBAG - SIDE IMPACT - from 99MY

Service repair no - 76.74.31 - Driver's side
Service repair no - 76.74.32 - Passenger's side

Remove

WARNING: See SRS safety precautions before commencement of repair. See SUPPLEMENTARY RESTRAINT SYSTEM, Precautions.

1. Remove squab cover and squab foam as an assembly. ***See SEATS, Repair.***

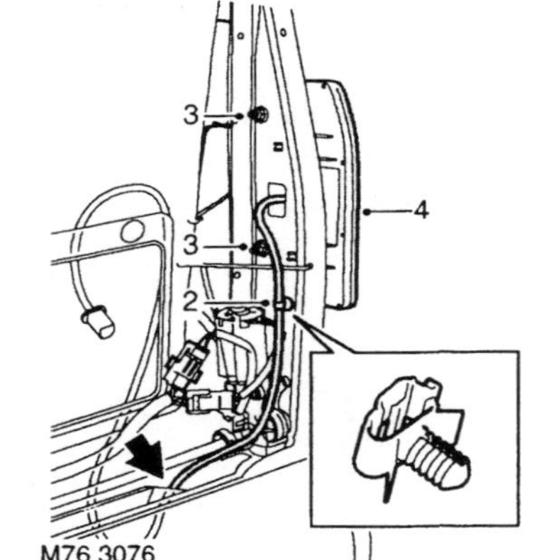

M76 3076

2. Release airbag harness from clip.
3. Remove 2 nuts securing airbag.
4. Release and remove airbag.

WARNING: Store airbag module in accordance with storage procedures. See SUPPLEMENTARY RESTRAINT SYSTEM, Precautions.

Refit

NOTE: If airbag is replaced, bar code of new airbag must be recorded in vehicle handbook.

5. Fit airbag and secure with nuts. Tighten to ***5.5 Nm (4 lbf.ft).***
6. Route harness through slotted hole in seat frame and secure to clip.
7. Fit squab cover ***See SEATS, Repair.***

Notes

CONTENTS

76 - CHASSIS AND BODY

CONTENTS

76 - CHASSIS AND BODY

CONTENTS

SUNROOF

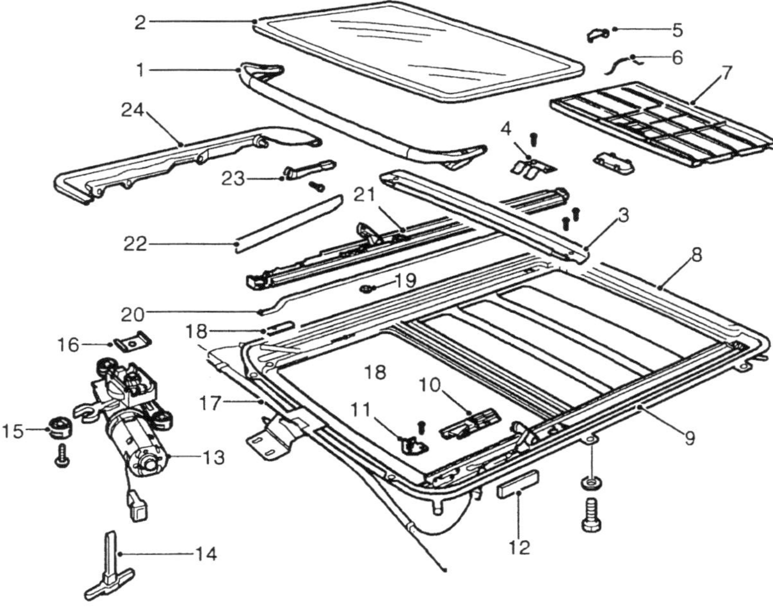

76M2793

1. Wind deflector
2. Sunroof panel
3. Drain channel
4. Rear stop spring
5. Slide block
6. Spring
7. Sunshade
8. Frame
9. Guide assembly LH
10. Locator
11. Lifter block
12. Anti-rattle pad
13. Sunroof motor
14. Special key
15. Spacer
16. Insert
17. Cable assemblies
18. Wind deflector gasket
19. Guide gasket
20. Seal
21. Guide assembly RH
22. Cover
23. Lever
24. Sunroof panel attachment frame

DESCRIPTION

The sunroof is electrically operated through a rocker switch located on the centre console. An electric motor, attached to the sunroof frame, drives the glass sunroof panel to the tilt or open positions. The glass panel is operated by two cables which are driven by the motor.

The sunroof frame is bolted to eight mounting points on the roof panel. The frame is constructed from pressed steel and supports all of the sunroof components. A bracket at the front of the frame provides an attachment point for the sunroof motor. The motor is supported on the frame with three spacers and secured with three self tapping screws.

A guide is fitted to each side of the sunroof frame. Each guide has an attachment at its forward end for the sunroof panel. The rear of the panel is attached to each guide on levers which operate the tilt function. The forward attachments and the levers slide in the guide to allow the panel to move in the desired position. Each lever has a peg located in a curved slot in the guide.

The sunroof motor has a worm drive which drives a gear in a cast housing attached to the end of the motor. The gear has a small pinion gear attached to the outer part of its spindle. The pinion engages with the spiral cables to form a rack and pinion drive. Rotation of the motor turns the pinion which in turn drives the cables in the required direction.

The two cables are attached either side of the pinion. One end of each cable is attached to the guide. The opposite end is clamped in its position on the pinion by a riveted bracket. The cables run in metal tubes to the guides. As the sunroof panel is closed, the cables are pulled through the metal tubes. The displaced cable is guided into plastic tubes which protect the cable and prevent the cable snagging. The cables are made from rigid spring steel and therefore can push as well as pull the sunroof along the guides.

A sunshade is also located in the guides. When the sunroof panel is closed or tilted, the sunshade can be retracted or pulled forward to cover the sunroof panel. When the sunroof panel is opened, two brackets on the sunshade engage with the panel as it is retracted. The sunshade is then pulled back by the retracting panel. When the panel is closed, the sunshade remains retracted until pulled manually to its closed position.

Drain hoses are connected to the front and rear corners of the frame. The drain hoses are located inside the 'A' and 'D' post pillars to allow water which has collected in the frame to escape. A one way valve is fitted to the end of each drain hose to prevent the ingress of dirt and moisture.

OPERATION

The sunroof can be operated with the ignition switch in position I or II. The sunroof can also be operated for up to 45 seconds after the ignition is switched off provided the driver's door is not opened. When the driver's door is opened, a further 45 second period commences. During the 45 second period the one touch function is inoperative.

If a failure of the sunroof motor occurs for whatever reason, the sunroof can be closed manually. Removal of the interior courtesy lamp allows the fitment of a special key into a slot in the motor drive. The sunroof can then be manually driven to the closed position.

The motor contains a microswitch and a Hall effect sensor. Two gears, driven by the motor at one end of the pinion drive spindle, trip the microswitch every thirteen revolutions of the spindle. When the microswitch is tripped, an open circuit signal is sensed by the Body electrical Control Module (BeCM). The signal from the microswitch, combined with signals received from the Hall effect sensor, are used by the BeCM to calculate the exact position of the sunroof. The Hall effect sensor is also responsible for the operation of the anti-trap function.

Tilt Operation

With the sunroof panel closed, pushing the lower part of the rocker switch operates the sunroof motor to 'tilt' the rear of the sunroof upwards. The motor operates for as long as the switch is operated until the glass is tilted to its full extent. If the switch is released before the full tilt position is reached, the sunroof panel stops at the chosen position.

When the tilt function is requested, the cables pull the guide forward, forcing the peg on each lever to move in the slot which raises the sunroof panel to the tilt position.

With the sunroof panel in the tilted position, pushing the upper part of the rocker switch, operates the sunroof motor to lower the sunroof panel. The motor operates to lower the panel for as long as the switch is operated until the panel is fully lowered. If the switch is released before the fully lowered position is reached, the sunroof panel stops at the chosen position.

Open (slide) Operation

With the sunroof panel closed, pushing the upper part of the rocker switch operates the sunroof motor to lower the sunroof panel and retract it backwards. If the switch is held, the motor operates until the switch is released or the panel reaches its fully open position. If the switch is pushed momentarily (less than 0.5 seconds), the panel will retract automatically to a half open position. A second short push on the switch will automatically retract the panel fully. When the panel retracts, a wind deflector automatically raises at the front of the sunroof aperture which serves to reduce wind noise.

When the open function is requested, the cables pull the guide in a rearward direction, forcing the peg on the lever to move in the slot which lowers the rear of the sunroof panel below the roof. As the panel begins to move, the forward panel attachments slide down a ramp in the guide, lowering the forward end of the panel below the roof.

With the sunroof panel half or fully open, pushing the lower part of the switch operates the motor to close the sunroof panel. If the switch is held, the panel closes until the switch is released or the panel reaches its fully closed position. If the switch is pushed momentarily (less than 0.5 seconds), the panel will close automatically until it reaches the half open position. A second short push on the switch will automatically close the panel fully.

The sunroof has an 'anti-trap' function which prevents the sunroof panel from closing if an obstruction is sensed. When an obstruction is sensed, the motor will automatically retract the panel to the half or fully open position. A message 'SUNROOF BLOCKED' is displayed on the message centre in the instrument pack. When the obstruction is removed, the panel can be closed by the normal method.

Battery Disconnection

If the battery has been disconnected, the one touch and anti-trap function will become inoperative. These functions can be reset by fully opening and closing, then fully tilting and closing the sunroof panel in one continuous operation. An audible warning will sound and 'SUNROOF NOT SET' will be displayed on the message centre in the instrument pack when the sunroof is being operated.

When the above procedure has been successfully completed, an audible warning will sound and 'SUNROOF SET' will be displayed on the message centre.

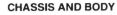

Notes

FRONT DOOR

Service repair no - 76.28.07

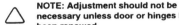

NOTE: Adjustment should not be necessary unless door or hinges have been renewed.

Alignment of door to aperture.

1. Gain access to 'A' post hinge bolts by removing relevant wheel arch liner. ***See Repair.***
2. Slacken 2 bolts securing striker to 'B/C' post.
3. Slacken 6 bolts securing door hinges to 'A' post.
4. With assistance, adjust door position in aperture. Tighten hinge bolts to ***30 Nm. (22 lbf.ft)***

Profile adjustment, door skin/frame to adjacent body panels.

5. Slacken 4 bolts securing hinges to door.
6. With assistance adjust inboard/outboard position of door. Tighten hinge bolts to ***30 Nm. (22 lbf.ft)***

CAUTION: Ensure that leading edge of door is flush with adjacent panels or wind noise will result.

7. When alignment of door is correct, adjust height and inboard/outboard position of striker. Tighten striker bolts. Check for correct door latching.
8. Slacken bolts and readjust striker position as necessary. Tighten striker bolts to ***22 Nm. (16 lbf.ft)***
9. Fit wheel arch liner. ***See Repair.***

REAR DOOR

Service repair no - 76.28.08

NOTE: Adjustment should not be necessary unless door or hinges have been renewed.

1. Open door and slacken 2 bolts securing striker to 'D' post.
2. Open front door and slacken 6 bolts securing rear door hinges to 'B/C' post.
3. With assistance, adjust door position in aperture and tighten hinge bolts to ***25 Nm. (18 lbf.ft)***
4. To adjust profile of door skin and frame relative to adjacent body panels, slacken 4 bolts securing hingess to door.
5. With assistance adjust inboard/outboard position of door. Tighten hinge bolts to ***25 Nm. (18 lbf.ft)***

CAUTION: Ensure that leading edge of door is flush with adjacent panels or wind noise will result.

6. When alignment of door is correct, adjust height and inboard/outboard position of striker. Tighten striker bolts and check for correct door latching.
7. Slacken bolts and readjust striker position as necessary. Tighten striker bolts to ***22 Nm (16 lbf.ft).***

SUNROOF - PANEL

Service repair no - 76.82.04

Adjust

1. Slide back sunshade.
2. Tilt sunroof panel.
3. Remove mechanism covers. ***See Repair.***
4. Close sunroof panel.

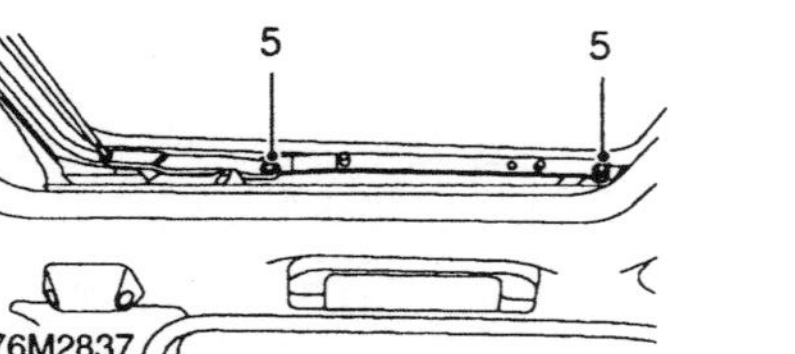

76M2837

5. Slacken 4 Torx screws, securing mechanism to sunroof panel.
6. Align sunroof panel to aperture in roof.
7. Position leading edge of sunroof panel so that it is flush or not more than 0.5 mm lower than roof outer surface.
8. Position trailing edge of sunroof panel so that it is flush or not more than 0.5 mm higher than roof outer surface.
9. Hold in position and torque tighten Torx screws to ***6 Nm (4.5 lbf.ft).***
10. Tilt sunroof panel.
11. Fit mechanism covers.
12. Close sunroof panel.

BONNET

Service repair no - 76.16.01

Remove

1. Open bonnet.
2. Mark hinge outlines on bonnet.
3. Remove 2 hinge bolts from each side.

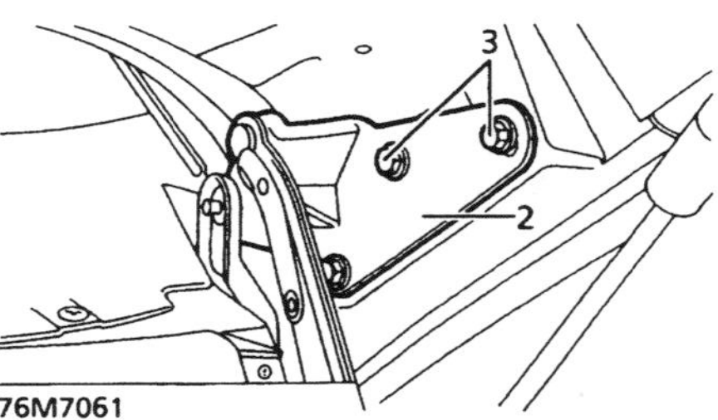

76M7061

4. Disconnect washer tube at T piece on bonnet, release tube from clip.

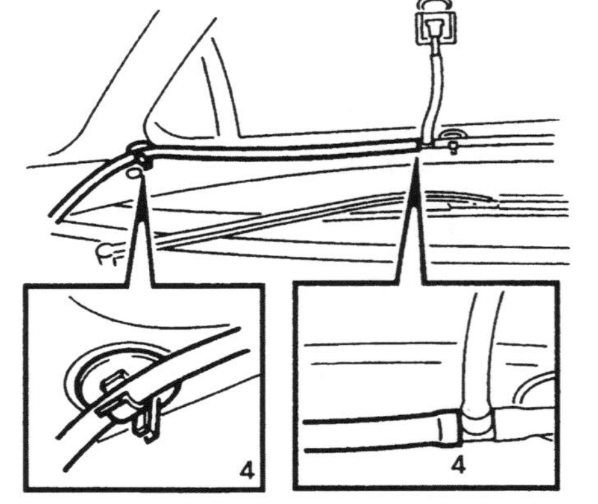

76M7062

5. With assistance, release bonnet support struts at lower ends.
6. With assistance, remove 2 remaining hinge bolts and remove bonnet.

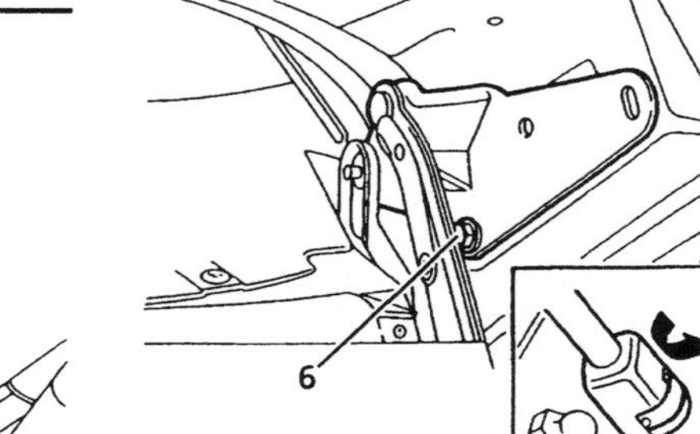

76M7063

Refit

7. With assistance, fit bonnet. Fit, but do not tighten bolts.
8. With assistance, connect bonnet support struts.
9. Connect washer tube, secure to clip.
10. Close bonnet, check alignment.
11. Open bonnet, tighten hinge bolts.
12. Close bonnet.

BONNET LOCK PIN

Service repair no - 76.16.24

Remove

1. Remove bolts securing lock pin to bonnet.
2. Remove pin.

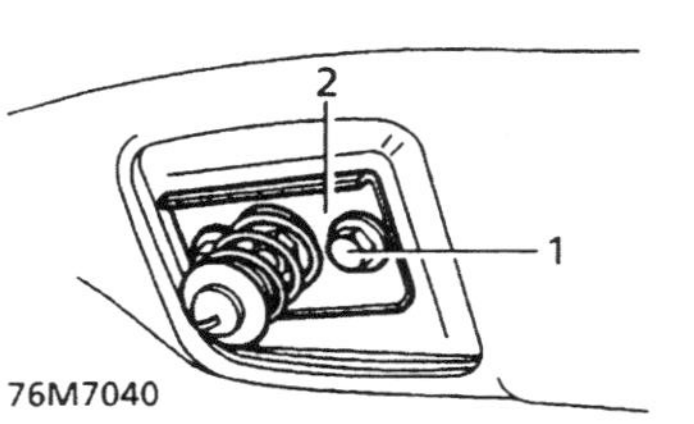

76M7040

Refit

3. Position lock pin to bonnet.
4. Fit bolts but do not tighten.
5. Close and open bonnet to align pin.
6. Secure pin with bolts.
7. Lubricate pin.

BONNET LOCK - LEFT HAND

Service repair no - 76.16.21

Remove

1. Remove bolts securing bonnet lock.

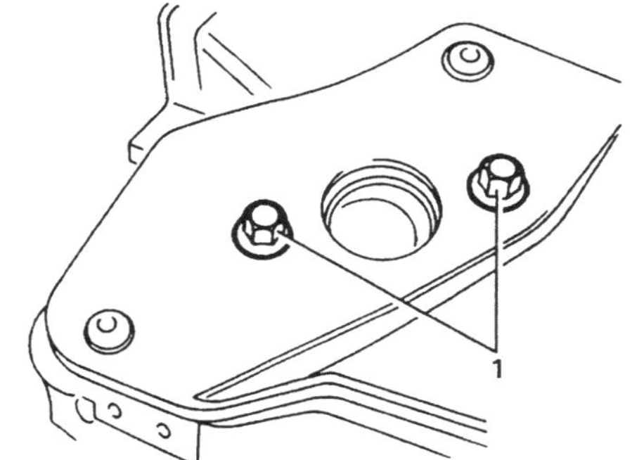

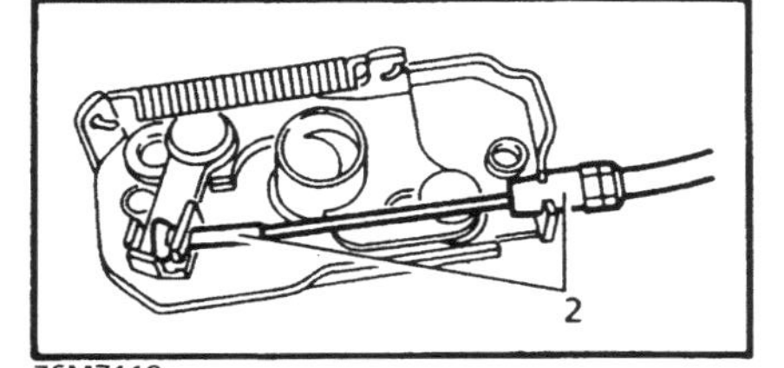

76M7118

2. Release outer and inner cables from lock.
3. Remove lock.

Refit

4. Reverse removal procedure.

BONNET LOCK - RIGHT HAND

Service repair no - 76.16.25

Remove

1. Release 3 turnbuckles securing battery cover. Remove cover

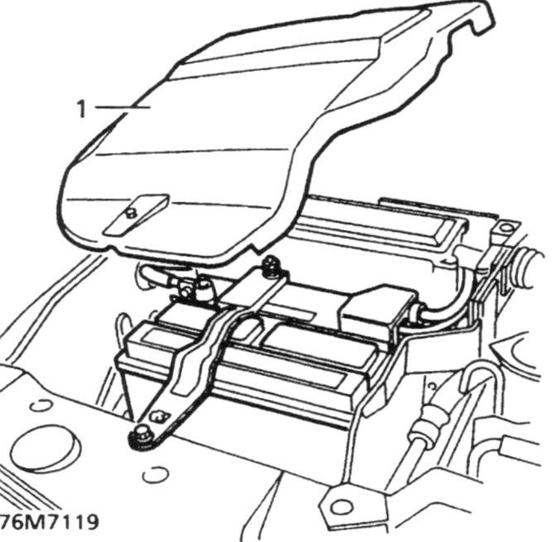

76M7119

2. Remove 2 bolts securing bonnet lock to platform.

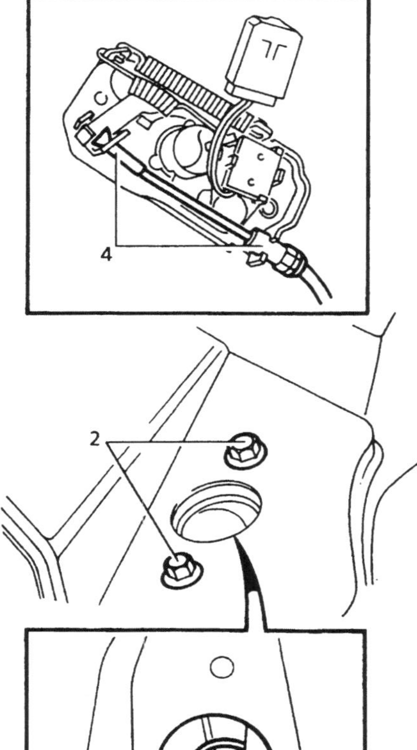

76M7120

3. Manoeuvre lock and disconnect alarm switch multiplug.
4. Release inner and outer cables from lock.
5. Remove lock.

Refit

6. Reverse removal procedure.

BONNET SAFETY CATCH

Service repair no - 76.16.34

Remove

1. Remove bolts securing safety catch to bonnet.
2. Remove safety catch.

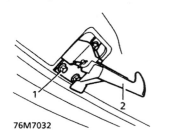

76M7032

Refit

3. Position catch to bonnet.
4. Fit bolts, do not tighten.
5. Close and open bonnet to align catch.
6. Secure catch with bolts.

BONNET STRUT

Service repair no - 76.16.14

Remove

1. Support bonnet in open position.
2. Release clip securing strut lower ball joint.

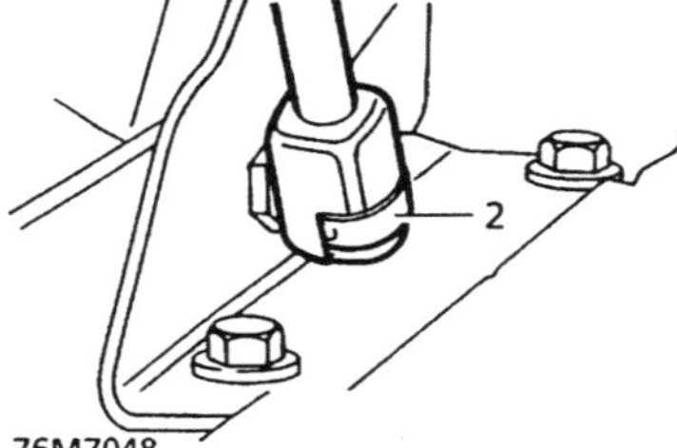

76M7048

3. Remove screws securing strut bracket to bonnet.
4. Remove strut and bracket.

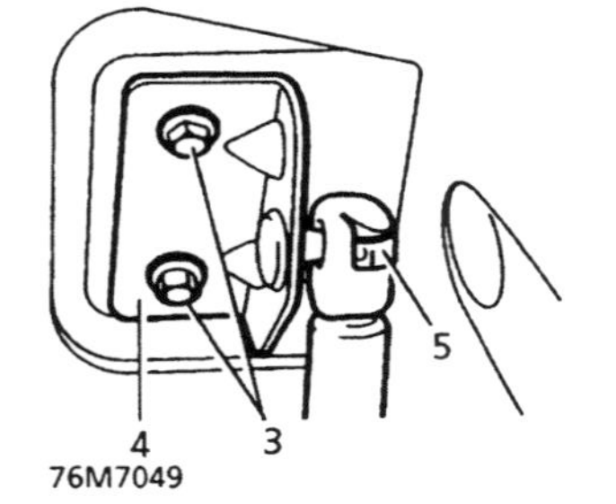

76M7049

5. Remove strut from bracket.

Refit

6. Fit strut to bonnet bracket, fit to bonnet.
7. Secure strut to lower ball joint.
8. Fit bracket screws. Remove support, close bonnet.

CENTRE CONSOLE

Service repair no - 76.25.01

Remove

1. Remove electric window switch pack. ***See ELECTRICAL, Repair.***
2. Disconnect rear footwell lamp multiplug.
3. Remove base in console bin.

76M7020A

4. Remove nuts securing rear of console to floor studs.
5. Move both front seats fully rearward.
6. Remove 2 screws securing each side panel to centre console. Release sprag clips from fascia switch pack by firmly pulling rearwards. Remove side panels.

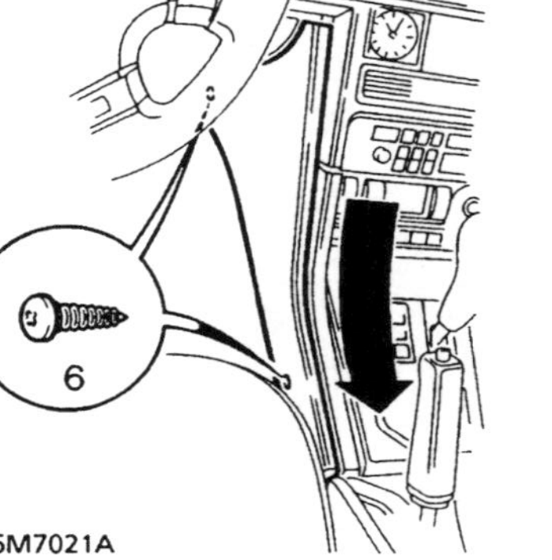

76M7021A

7. Remove screw at rear of gear lever applique. Raise rear end of applique to disengage 2 spring clips at forward end.

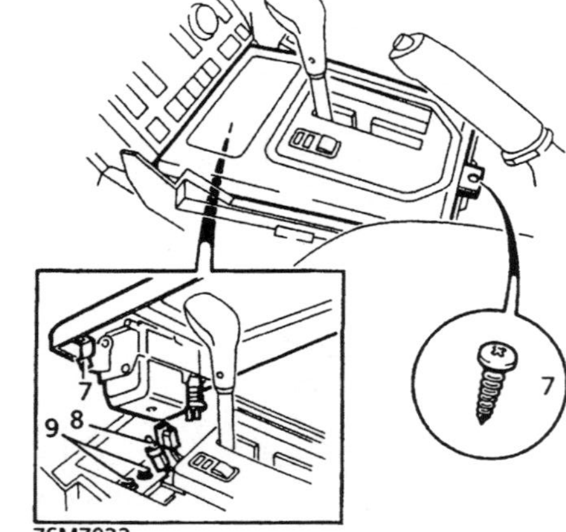

76M7022

8. Disconnect cigar lighter multiplug, release cigar lighter bulb. Remove gear lever applique.
9. **Manual gearbox models:** Remove gear knob. Remove 2 bolts securing front of console to floor.
10. **Automatic gearbox models:** Remove 2 screws securing selector lever.
11. Remove selector lever.

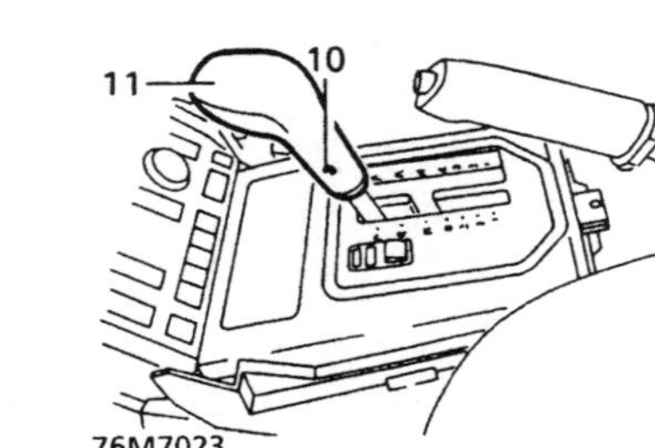

76M7023

12. Remove 3 screws securing selector graphics plate.
13. Raise selector graphics plate, disconnect multiplug.

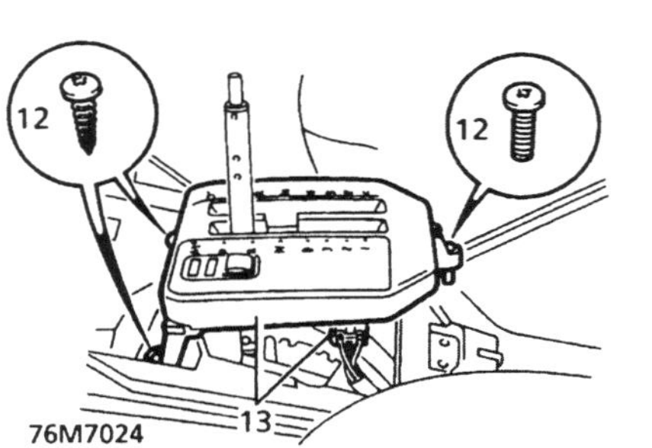

76M7024

14. Remove selector graphics plate.
15. **All models:**
Remove clip securing park brake lever clevis pin, remove clevis pin. Raise park brake lever to vertical position.

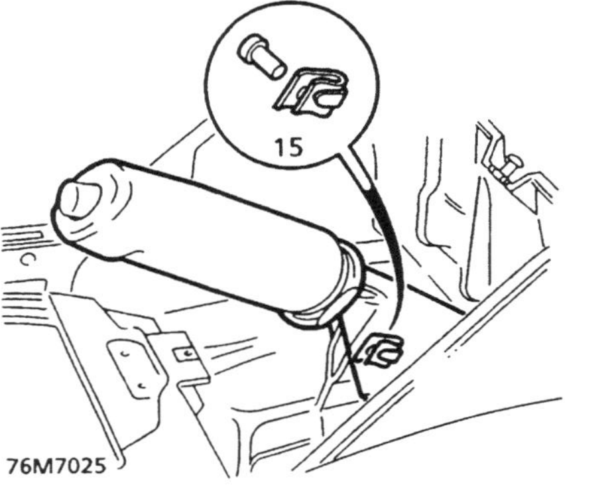

76M7025

16. Raise rear of console to disengage rear vent ducts. Remove centre console.

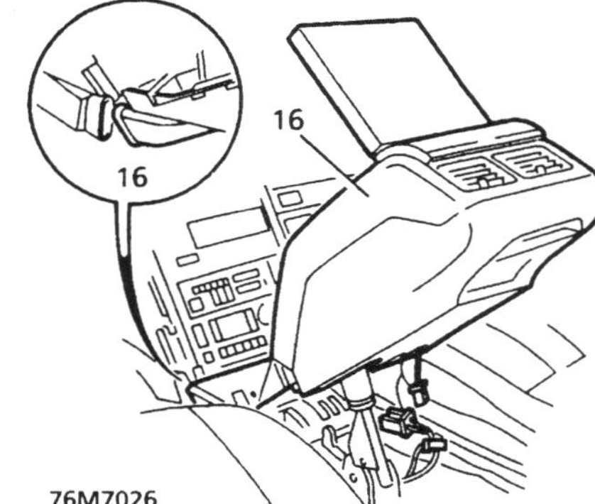

76M7026

Refit

17. Fit centre console, ensuring that ducts to rear fresh air vents are correctly engaged.
18. Fit nuts securing centre console to floor.
19. Automatic - position graphics plate over selector lever, connect multiplug.
20. Align graphics plate to console, secure with screws.
21. Fit selector lever, secure with screws.
22. Manual - secure front of centre console to floor with bolts.
23. Fit gear knob.
24. Lower park brake lever, fit clevis pin and secure pin with clip.
25. Position gear/selector lever applique, connect cigar lighter multiplug and insert illumination bulb in holder.
26. Engage applique clips to console. Secure applique with screw.
27. Position console side panels. Firmly push forward to engage sprag clips into fascia switch pack. Fit and tighten screws.
28. Return front seats to original positions.
29. Fit base to console bin, tighten with screws.
30. Connect rear footwell lamp multiplug.
31. Fit electric window switch pack. ***See ELECTRICAL, Repair.***

CHASSIS CROSS MEMBER

Service repair no - 76.10.92

Remove

1. Release fixings and remove battery cover.
2. Disconnect battery earth lead.
3. Raise vehicle on 4 post ramp.
4. Support gearbox on a suitable jack.

M76 3193

5. Remove 4 nuts and 2 bolts securing gearbox mounting to crossmember and discard nuts.
6. Remove gearbox snubber bar.

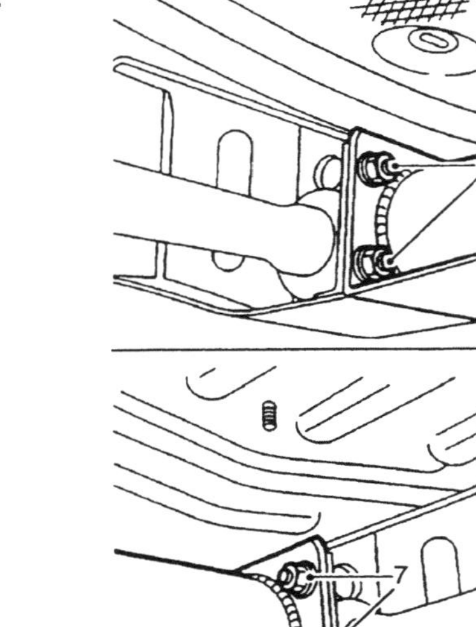

M76 3194

7. Remove 3 of 4 nuts and bolts securing each side of crossmember to chassis.
8. With assistance, remove 2 remaining nuts and bolts securing crossmember and remove crossmember.

Refit

9. With assistance, fit crossmember and tighten nuts and bolts to ***45 Nm (33 lbf.ft).***
10. Fit gearbox snubber bar and tighten bolts to ***45 Nm (33 lbf.ft).***
11. Fit new nuts securing gearbox mounting to crossmember and tighten to ***45 Nm (33 lbf.ft).***
12. Remove support from gearbox.
13. Lower vehicle.
14. Connect battery earth lead.
15. Fit battery cover and secure with fixings.

ENGINE ACOUSTIC COVER

Service repair no - 76.11.06

Remove

1. Raise front of vehicle.

WARNING: Support on safety stands.

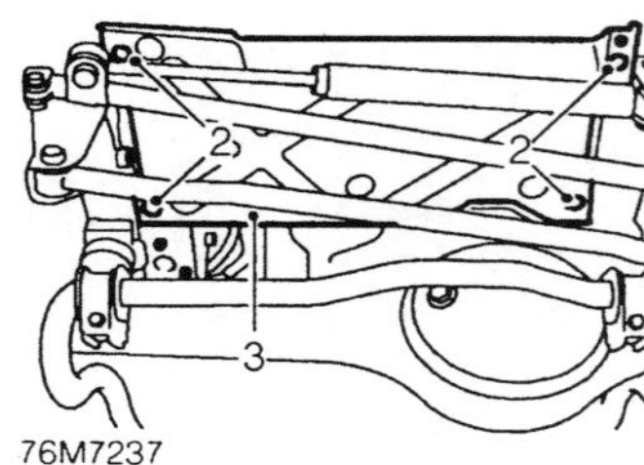

76M7237

2. Release 4 threaded fasteners securing engine acoustic cover to chassis brackets.
3. Release acoustic cover from brackets and manoeuvre past steering gear.

Refit

4. Fit acoustic cover to brackets and secure with threaded fasteners.

GEARBOX LOWER ACOUSTIC COVER

Service repair no - 76.11.13

Remove

1. Raise front of vehicle.

WARNING: Support on safety stands.

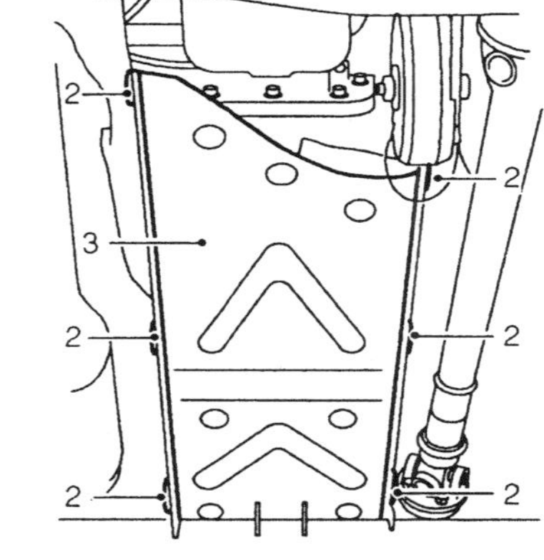

76M7238

2. Release 6 threaded fasteners securing lower acoustic cover to side acoustic covers.
3. Remove lower acoustic cover.

Refit

4. Fit acoustic cover to side acoustic covers.
5. Tighten threaded fasteners securing lower cover to side covers.
6. Remove stand(s) and lower vehicle.

GEARBOX ACOUSTIC COVER - RH

Service repair no - 76.11.14

Remove

1. Raise front of vehicle.

WARNING: Support on safety stands.

2. Remove gearbox lower acoustic cover. ***See this section.***

76M7240

3. Remove bolt securing RH acoustic cover to crossmember.
4. Remove bolt securing RH acoustic cover to chassis member.
5. Remove gearbox RH acoustic cover.

Refit

6. Fit acoustic cover to chassis and secure with bolts.
7. Fit gearbox lower acoustic cover. ***See this section.***

GEARBOX ACOUSTIC COVER - LH

Service repair no - 76.11.15

Remove

1. Raise front of vehicle.

WARNING: Support on safety stands.

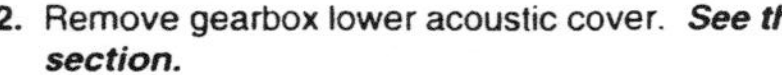

2. Remove gearbox lower acoustic cover. ***See this section.***

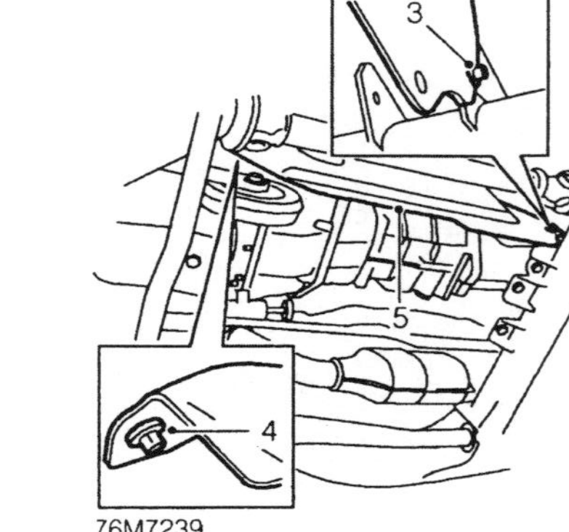

76M7239

3. Remove bolt securing LH acoustic cover to crossmember.
4. Remove bolt securing LH acoustic cover to chassis member.
5. Remove gearbox LH acoustic cover.

Refit

6. Fit acoustic cover to chassis and secure with bolts.
7. Fit gearbox lower acoustic cover. ***See this section.***

FRONT BUMPER VALANCE

Service repair no - 76.22.72

Remove

1. Raise the vehicle.

WARNING: Support on safety stands.

2. Remove battery cover for access to RH fog lamp.

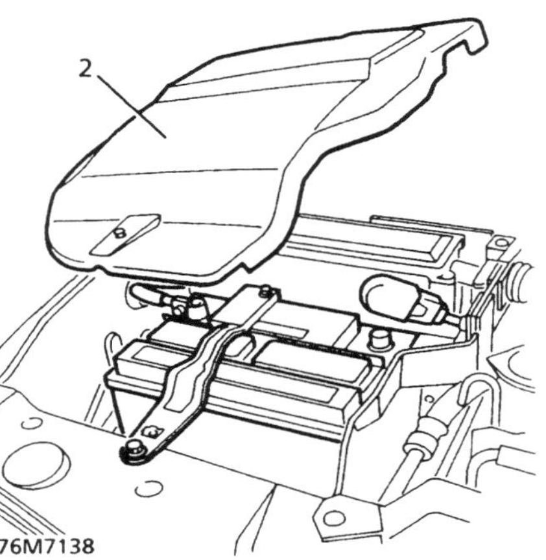

76M7138

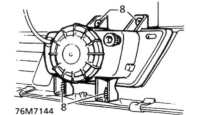

3. Disconnect fog lamp multiplugs and breather hoses.

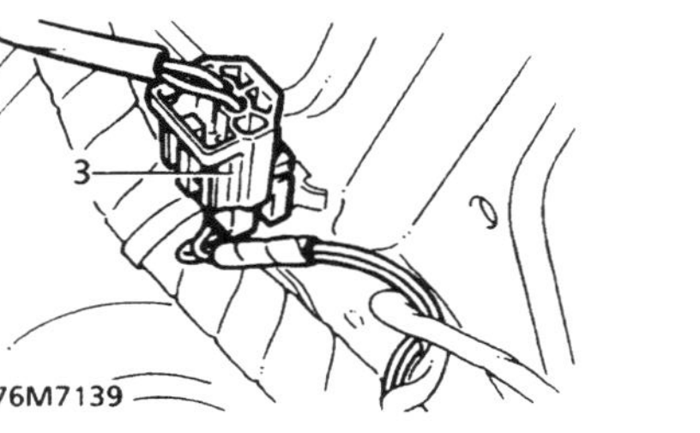

76M7139

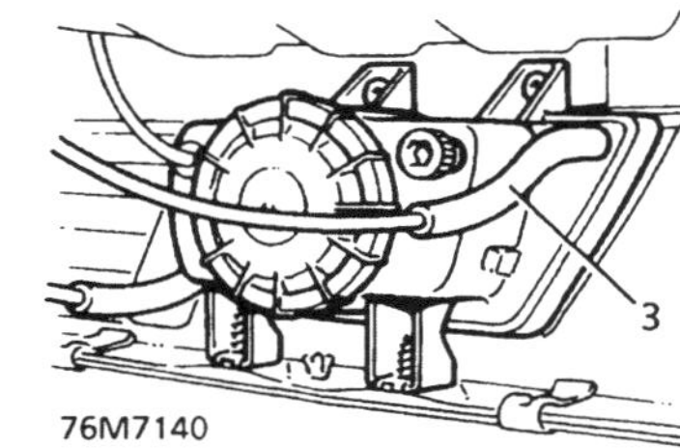

76M7140

4. Release 2 clips securing bumper ends to mounting brackets.

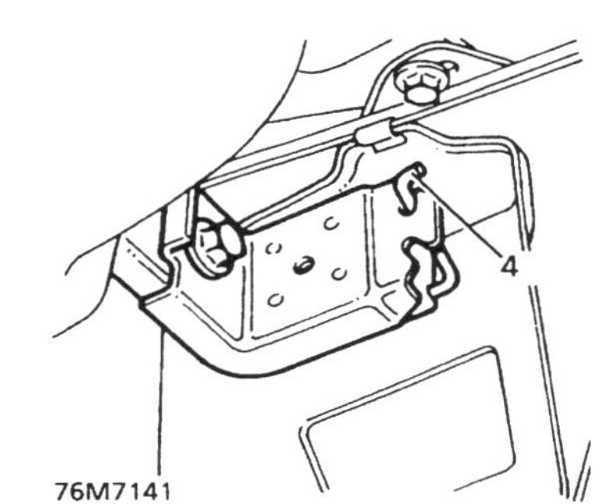

76M7141

CAUTION: Loosen bolts securing bumper end mounting brackets to chassis frame to avoid damage to sealing rubber during bumper remove and refit.

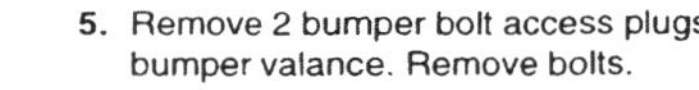

5. Remove 2 bumper bolt access plugs from bumper valance. Remove bolts.

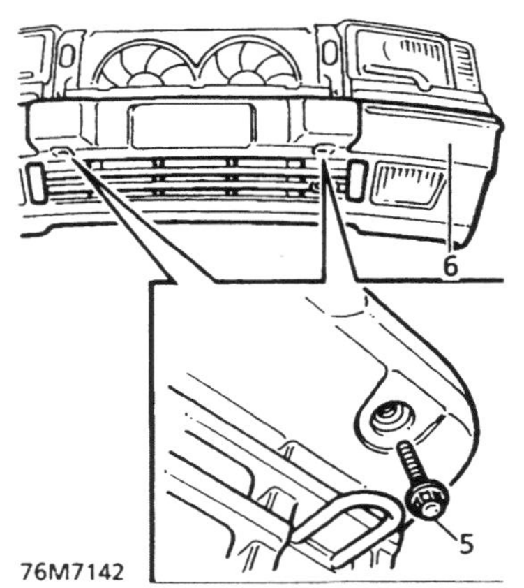

76M7142

6. With assistance remove bumper assembly. ***Do not carry out further dismantling if component is removed for access only.***
7. Remove 8 studs and 6 clips securing extensions spoiler. Remove extension.

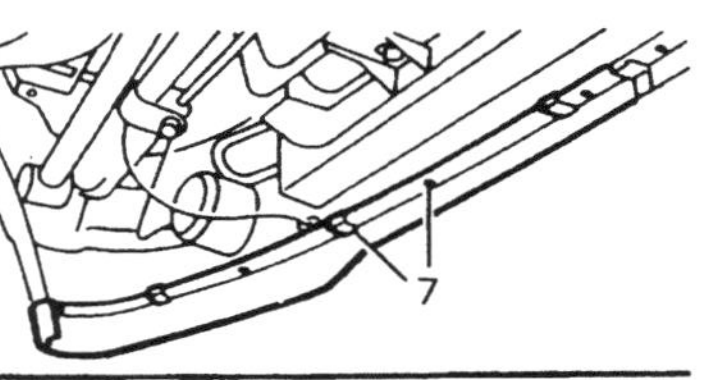

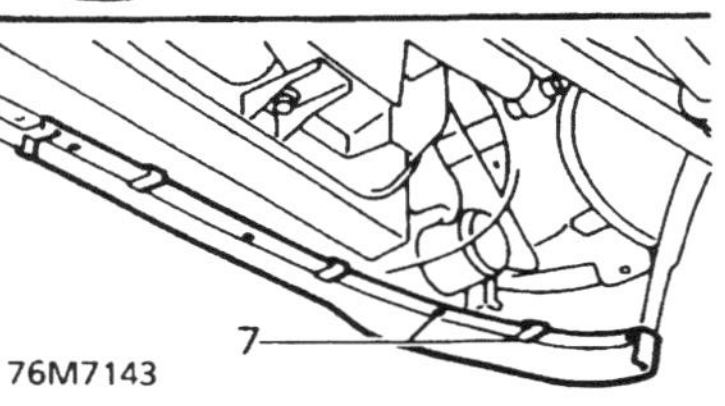

76M7143

8. Remove 8 screws securing fog lamps. Remove lamps.

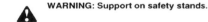

76M7144

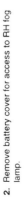

9. Remove 8 bolts securing bumper end brackets to bumper. Remove brackets.

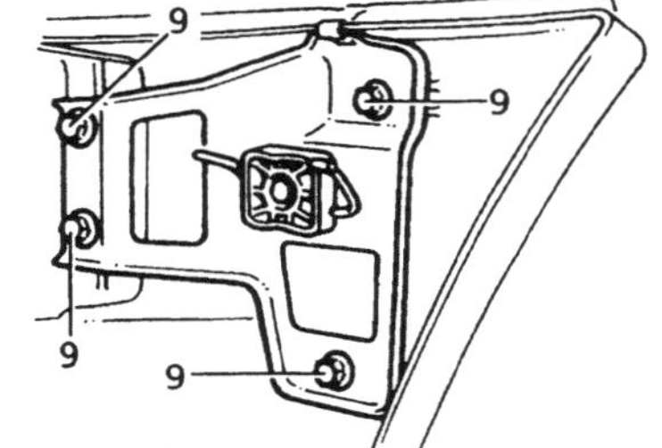

76M7145

WARNING: If front bumper is damaged due to impact, the impact cans must be inspected. There must be no visible deformation. The overall length must be 188.25 mm æ 0.5 mm. Replace the impact cans if necessary.

Refit

10. Fit end brackets and secure with bolts. Fit fog lamps and secure with screws.
11. Fit extension and secure with clips and studs.
12. With assistance fit bumper assembly, tighten bolts to ***70Nm. (52 lbf.ft)***
13. Fit bolt access plugs.
14. Align end brackets, tighten bolts and secure bumper end clips.
15. Connect fog lamp multiplugs and breather hoses, fit battery cover.
16. Remove safety stands. Lower vehicle.

EXTENSION SPOILER FRONT BUMPER

Service repair no - 76.22.78

Remove

1. Raise the vehicle.

WARNING: Support on safety stands.

2. Remove 8 studs and 6 clips securing spoiler to front bumper.
3. Remove spoiler halves.

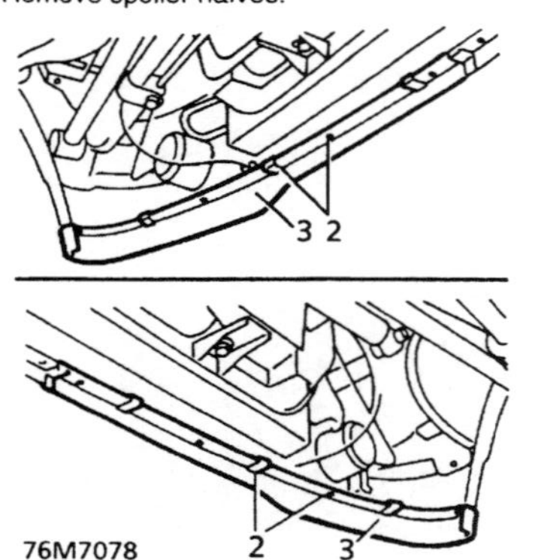

76M7078

Refit

4. Fit spoiler halves to bumper. Secure with clips and studs.
5. Remove safety stands. Lower vehicle.

REAR BUMPER VALANCE

Service repair no - 76.22.74

Remove

1. Raise the vehicle.

WARNING: Support on safety stands.

2. Remove rear road wheels.
3. Remove 3 screws securing each mud flap. Remove mud flaps.
4. Remove 2 screws securing each wheel arch liner extension panel to rear bumper/chassis.
5. Remove 2 wheel arch liner extension panels.
6. Release 2 clips securing bumper ends to mounting brackets.

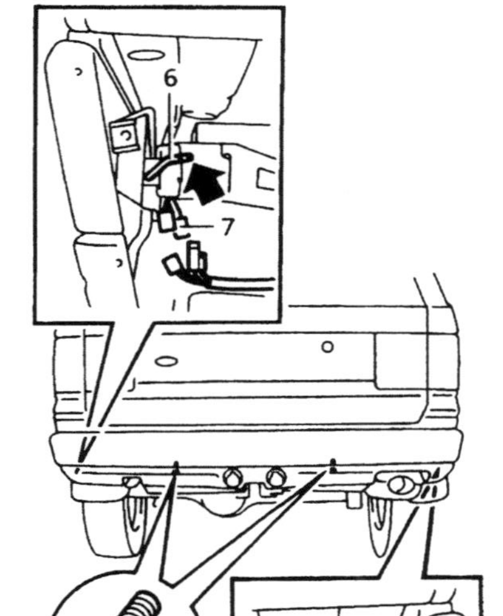

76M7102

7. Disconnect 3 towing harness multiplugs.
8. Remove 2 mounting bolt covers.
9. Remove 2 bolts securing bumper to chassis.
10. With assistance, release bumper ends from brackets. Remove bumper.

Refit

11. With assistance, position bumper. Engage nylon end supports to brackets.
12. If necessary, slacken bolts securing end support brackets. Align bumper to body. Tighten to ***29 Nm. (22 lbf.ft)***
13. Fit bumper mounting bolts. Tighten to ***70 Nm. (52 lbf.ft)***
14. Fit bolt covers.
15. Secure bumper end clips.
16. Connect towing harness multiplugs.
17. Position wheel arch liner extensions. Secure with screws.
18. Position mud flaps. Secure with screws.
19. Fit road wheels. Tighten to ***108 Nm. (80 lbf.ft)***
20. Remove safety stands. Lower vehicle.

FASCIA ASSEMBLY

Service repair no - 76.46.23/99

WARNING: The fascia assembly houses the heater distribution unit, blower assemblies and air conditioning evaporator. Assistance is essential during removal and refit procedures.

CAUTION: When removed from the vehicle, the fascia should be placed on a soft covered work surface, supported on suitable wooden blocks.

Remove

1. **Vehicles with SRS only:** Remove battery. ***See ELECTRICAL, Repair.***
2. **Vehicles without SRS:** Disconnect battery negative lead.
3. Drain cooling system. ***See COOLING SYSTEM, Repair.***
4. Loosen hose clips, disconnect hoses from heater pipes.

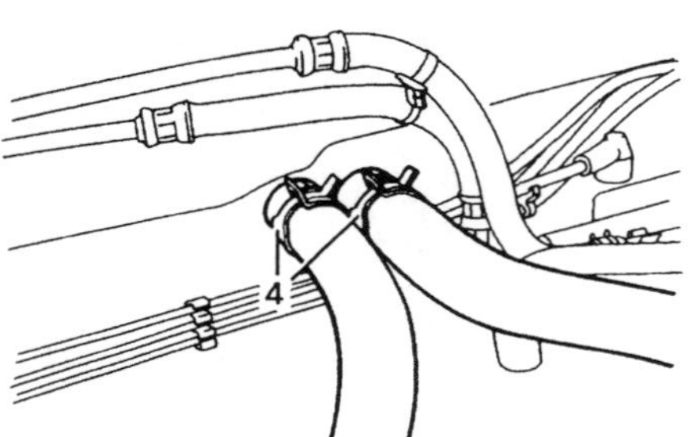

76M7161

5. Remove centre console. ***See this section.***
6. Remove steering column. ***See STEERING, Repair.***
7. Remove wiper motor and linkage. ***See WIPERS AND WASHERS, Repair.***
8. Disconnect passenger side heated front screen multiplug. Release multiplug from clip.

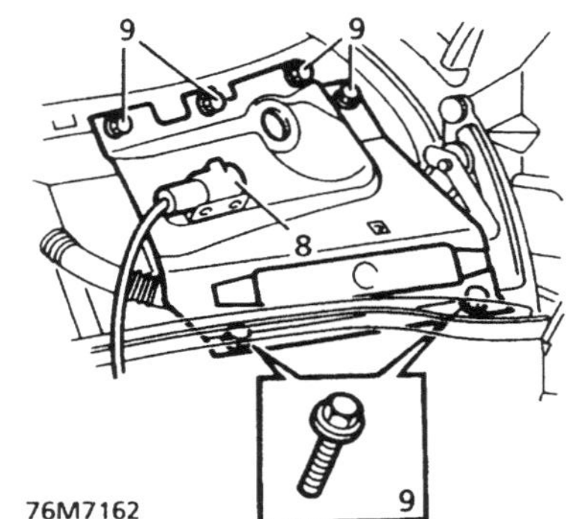

76M7162

9. Remove 6 bolts, remove remaining scuttle side panel.
10. Remove heater intake pollen filters.
11. Remove 8 screws securing each pollen filter housing. Remove both housings.

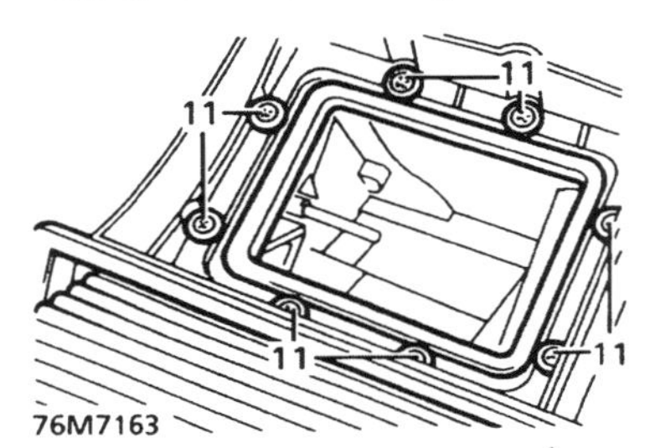

76M7163

12. Remove radio. ***See ELECTRICAL, Repair.***
13. Release door aperture seal adjacent to 'A' post lower trim panels.

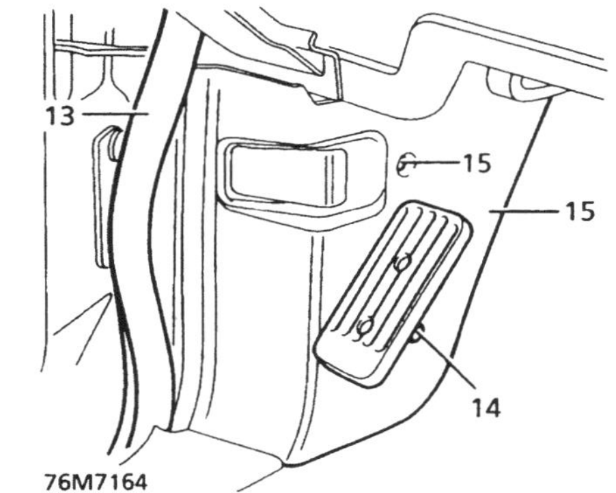

76M7164

14. **Driver's side - LHD automatic vehicles only:** Remove 3 bolts securing foot rest through 'A' post lower trim, remove foot rest.
15. Remove screw securing each 'A' post lower trim panel, release from single sprag clip, remove both trim panels.

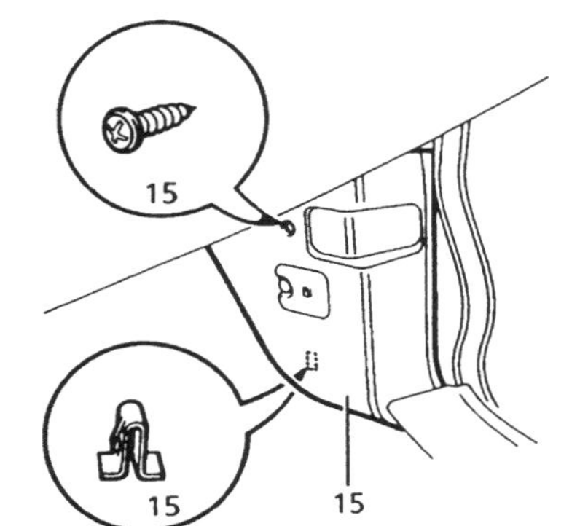

76M7165

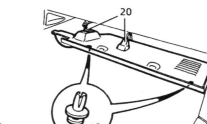

16. Remove fuse cover from driver's seat base trim.

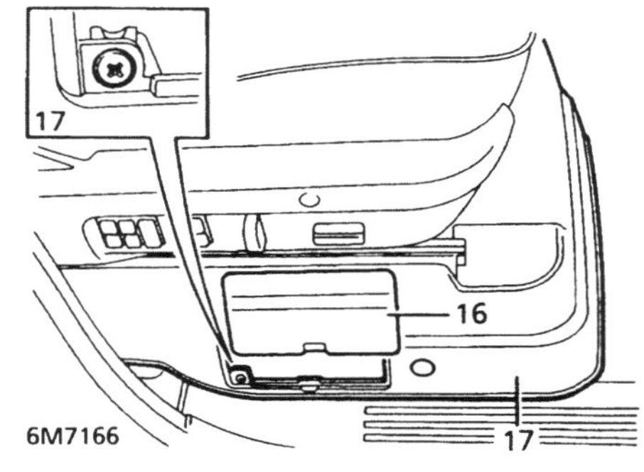

6M7166

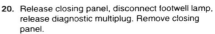

17. Remove screw and 2 trim studs, remove seat base trim.

76M7167

18. Release 4 sprag clips, remove driver's side carpet retainer.

19. Remove 2 scrivet fasteners securing lower closing panel to passenger side of fascia.

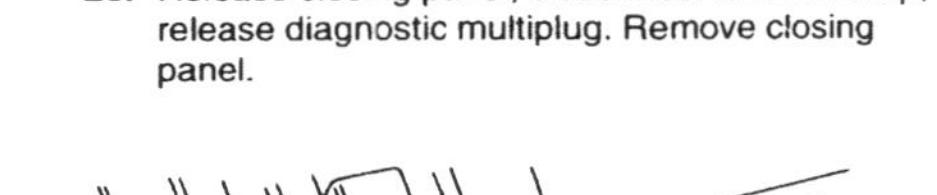

76M7168

20. Release closing panel, disconnect footwell lamp, release diagnostic multiplug. Remove closing panel.

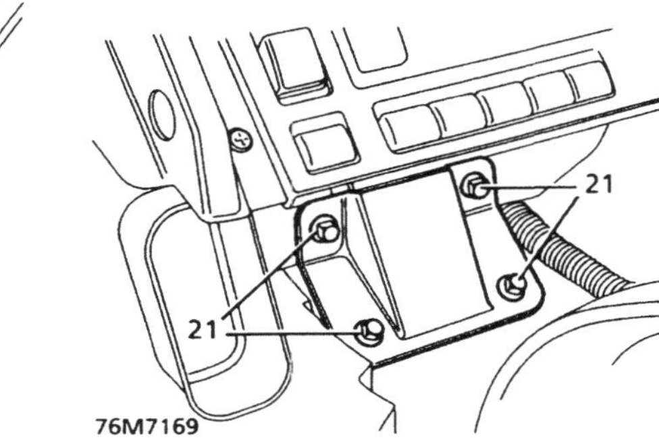

76M7169

21. Remove 4 bolts, remove fascia centre bracket.

22. Disconnect 4 multiplugs from Body Electrical Control Module (BeCM)

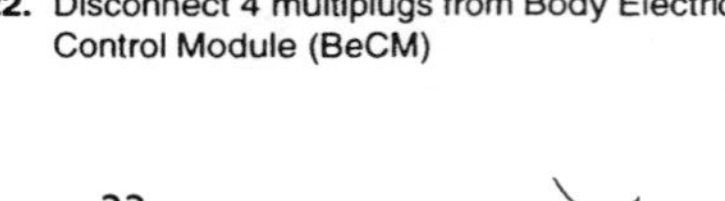

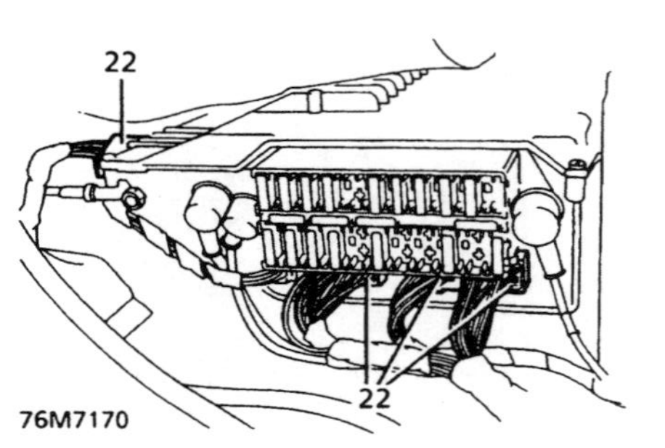

76M7170

23. Remove captive nut, remove earth wires from stud at base of driver's side 'A' post.

76M7171

24. Disconnect multiplugs at base of each 'A' post.

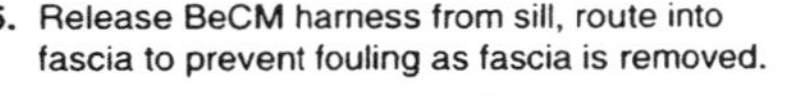

25. Release BeCM harness from sill, route into fascia to prevent fouling as fascia is removed.

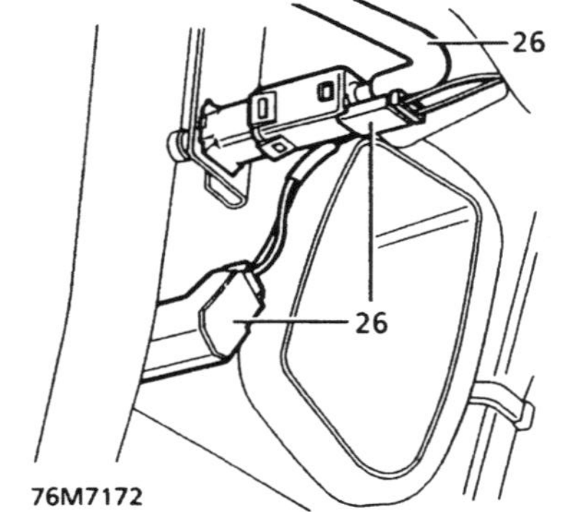

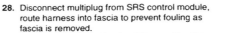

76M7172

26. Disconnect multiplugs and release vacuum hose from brake and clutch switches.
27. **Models with SRS only:** Disconnect SRS multiplug from main harness.

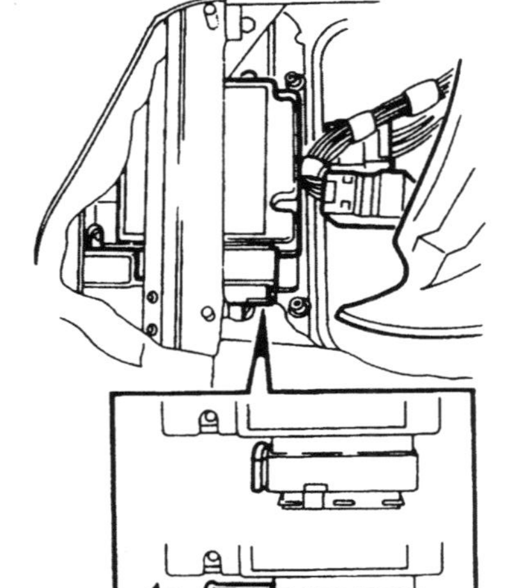

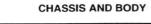

76M7173

28. Disconnect multiplug from SRS control module, route harness into fascia to prevent fouling as fascia is removed.
29. Remove both front wheel arch liners. ***See this section.***

76M7174

30. Remove 2 scrivet fasteners securing air cleaner baffle beneath LH wheel arch. Remove baffle.

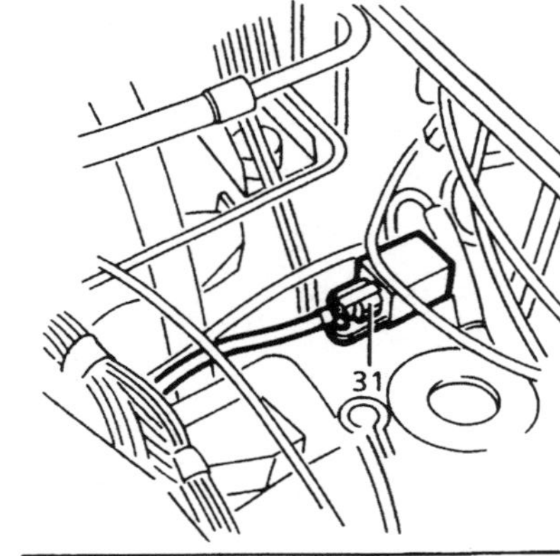

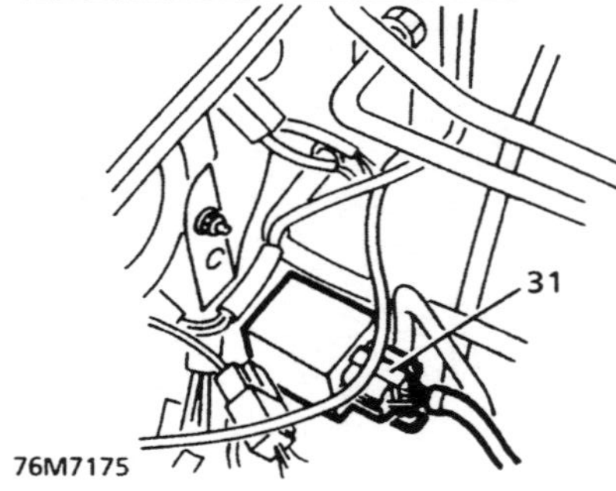

76M7175

31. Disconnect both SRS crash sensor multiplugs.

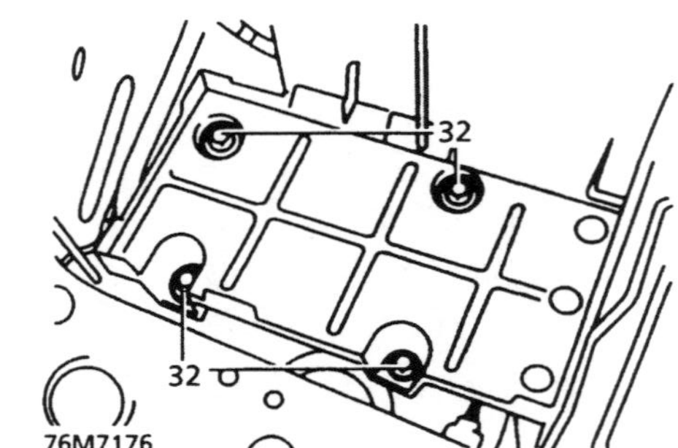

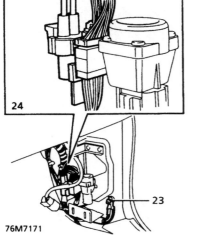

76M7176

32. Remove 4 bolts securing battery tray and 2 bolts securing air cleaner to valance.

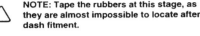

33. Raise air cleaner and battery tray for access to crash sensor harness clips.

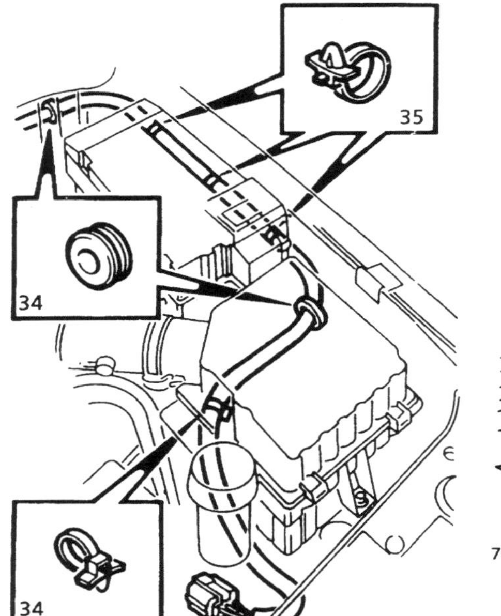

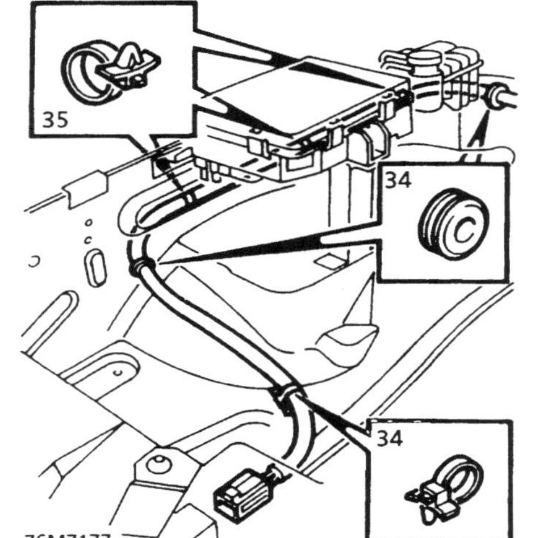

76M7177

34. Release clips securing each crash sensor harness to valance. Release harness grommets and feed both harnesses through valance into wheel arches.
35. Release 3 clips securing each crash sensor harness to underside of wheel arches.
36. Release harness grommets, feed harnesses through bulkhead and route into fascia to prevent fouling as fascia is removed.
37. **Vehicles with air conditioning only:** Discharge air conditioning system. ***See AIR CONDITIONING, Adjustment.***

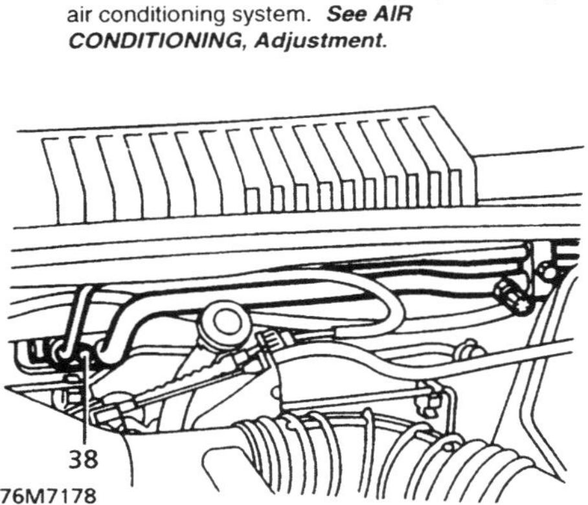

76M7178

38. Remove bolt securing pipe clamp to Thermostatic Expansion Valve (TXV).
39. Release pipes from TXV and remove 'O' rings. Seal pipes and ports of TXV.

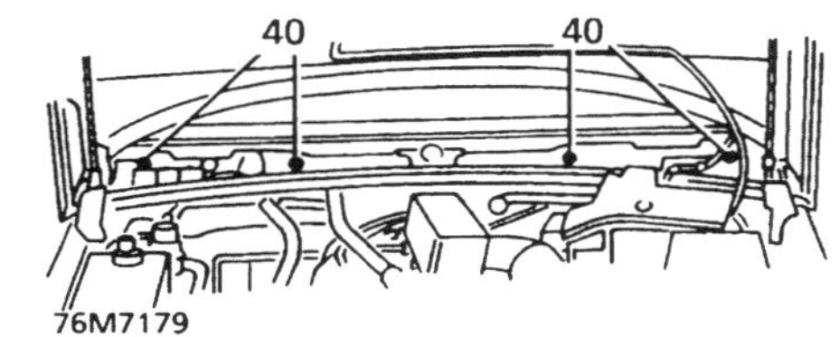

76M7179

40. **All models:** Remove 4 tube bolts securing fascia to scuttle panel.

41. Remove nuts and washers securing fascia to base of 'A' posts.

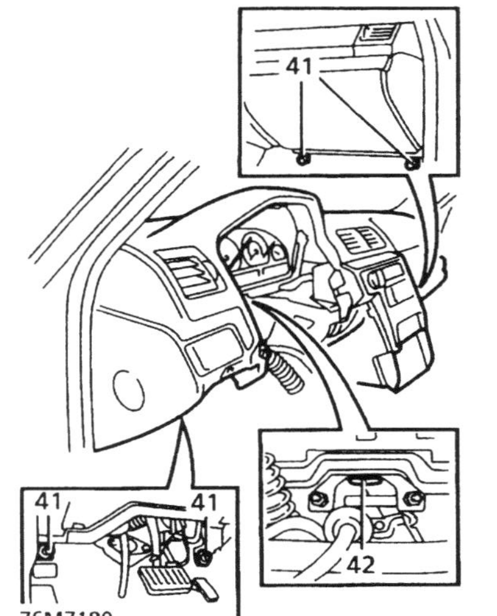

76M7180

42. Remove bolt securing fascia to pedal box.
43. Using assistance, carefully manoeuvre the fascia through the driver's door aperture. Place fascia on a soft covered work surface, supported on suitable wooden blocks.
44. Remove rubber seals from air intake ducts.
45. Collect rear heater duct connecting tubes.

Refit

46. Fit intake seals to blower motor ducts. Tape rubbers inside blower ducts to aid fitment.

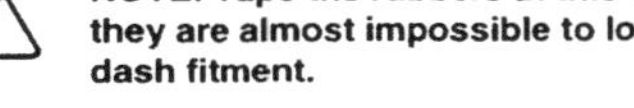

NOTE: Tape the rubbers at this stage, as they are almost impossible to locate after dash fitment.

47. Fit guide pins LRT-76-001 to outer fascia studs.
48. With assistance, manoeuvre fascia into position through driver's front door aperture. Locate guide pins.

NOTE: Assistance from a third person may be necessary when guiding heater pipes through bulkead.

49. Loosely fit 1 tube bolt, fascia to scuttle.
50. Fit bolt securing fascia to pedal box. Tighten to ***25 Nm. (18 lbf.ft)***
51. Fit nuts and washers at base of A posts. Tighten to ***25 Nm. (18 lbf.ft)***
52. Remove guide pins.
53. Fit remaining tube bolts. Tighten to ***25 Nm. (18 lbf.ft)***
54. Fit rear heater duct connecting pipes.
55. Remove tape from intake seals.
56. Engage lips of sealing rubbers around scuttle apertures.
57. Fit pollen filter housings, tighten bolts.
58. Fit scuttle side panel to passenger side of vehicle, tighten bolts.
59. Connect heated screen multiplug, fit to side panel clip.
60. Connect hoses to heater pipes. Tighten clips.
61. **Air conditioning vehicles:** Remove seals from air conditioning pipes and TXV ports.
62. Lubricate new O rings with clean compressor oil, fit to pipes.
63. Locate pipes in TXV ports, position clamp and fit clamp bolt.
64. Engage evaporator drain tubes over pipes in transmission tunnel.
65. **Vehicles with SRS only:** Route SRS crash sensor harnesses through bulkhead into wheel arches, locate harness grommets.
66. Secure harness clips beneath wheel arches, route harnesses through valances into engine bay, locate harness grommets.

67. Raise battery tray and air cleaner for access. Route crash sensor harnesses, secure harness clips, connect multiplugs to crash sensors.
68. Tighten battery tray and air cleaner bolts.
69. Connect multiplug to SRS control module.
70. Connect SRS harness multiplug to main harness.
71. Fit air cleaner baffle beneath LH wheel arch, secure with scrivet fasteners.
72. Fit wheel arch liners. ***See this section.***
73. **All models:**Route harness along sill, connect multiplugs to BeCM.
74. Connect multiplugs at base of 'A' posts and secure plugs to brackets.
75. Fit earth wires to stud, tighten captive nut.
76. Connect vacuum hose and multiplugs to brake and clutch pedal switches.
77. Position closing panel beneath passenger side of fascia. Secure dianostic plug, connect footwell lamp. Align closing panel, secure with scrivet fasteners.
78. Fit carpet retainer, engage sprag clips.
79. Fit seat base trim panel, secure trim studs, tighten screw.
80. Fit fuse cover to seat base trim.
81. Fit both 'A' post lower trim panels, secure sprag clips. Engage door aperture seals.
82. **LHD automatic vehicles only:** Fit foot rest, secure with bolts.
83. Fit radio. ***See ELECTRICAL, Repair.***
84. Fit wiper motor and linkage. ***See WIPERS AND WASHERS, Repair.***
85. Fit steering column. ***See STEERING, Repair.***
86. Fit centre console. ***See this section.***
87. Refill cooling system. ***See COOLING SYSTEM, Repair.***
88. **Vehicles with SRS only:** Fit battery. ***See ELECTRICAL, Repair.***
89. Reconnect battery negative lead.
90. Evacuate and recharge air conditioning. ***See AIR CONDITIONING, Adjustment.***

FASCIA ASSEMBLY - VEHICLES WITH SINGLE POINT SENSED SRS

Service repair no - 76.46.23/99

WARNING: Refer to SRS safety precautions before commencing repair.

WARNING: The fascia assembly houses the heater distribution unit, blower assemblies and air conditioning evaporator and is therefore heavy. Assistance is essential during removal and refit procedures.

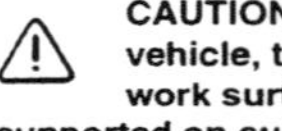

CAUTION: When removed from the vehicle, the fascia should be placed on a work surface with a soft covering and supported on suitable wooden blocks.

Remove

1. Remove key from starter switch and wait 10 minutes for SRS back up power circuit to discharge.
2. Disconnect both battery terminals, earth lead first.
3. Drain cooling system. ***See COOLING SYSTEM, Repair.***

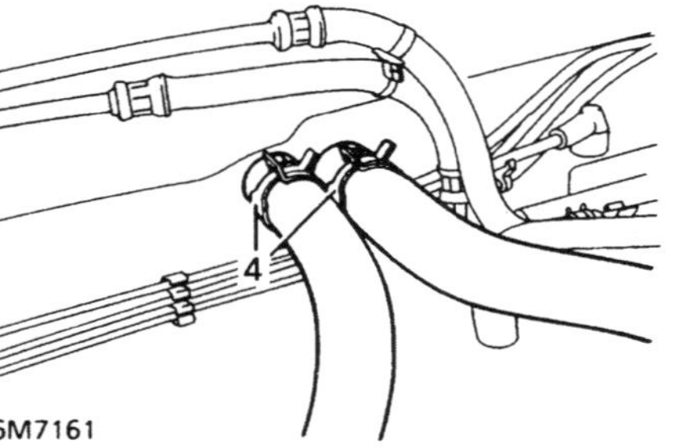

76M7161

4. Release 2 clips securing heater hoses to heater matrix and disconnect hoses.
5. Cap both heater matrix pipes to prevent coolant spillage inside vehicle during fascia removal.
6. Recover refrigerant from air conditioning system. ***See AIR CONDITIONING, Adjustment.***

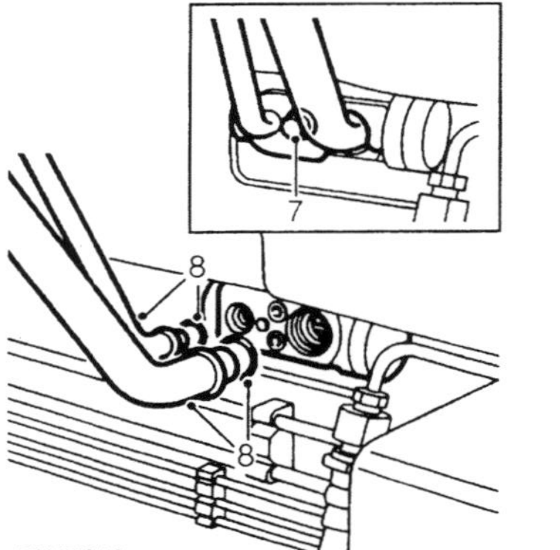

76M7216

7. Remove bolt securing pipe clamp to thermostatic expansion valve (TXV) and release pipes.
8. Remove and discard 'O' ring seals from air conditioning pipes.
9. Immediately cap both air conditioning pipes and TXV ports to prevent moisture entering the air conditioning system.
10. Remove wiper motor and linkage. ***See WIPERS AND WASHERS, Repair.***

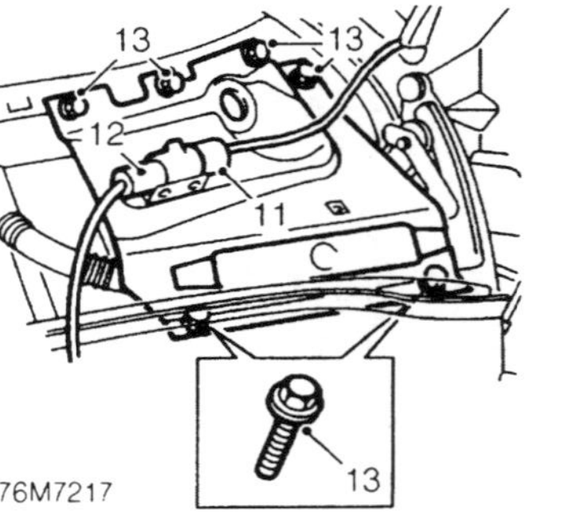

76M7217

11. Disconnect passenger side heated screen multiplug.
12. Release heated screen multiplug from scuttle side panel and position aside.
13. Remove 6 bolts securing scuttle side panel to scuttle and remove panel.

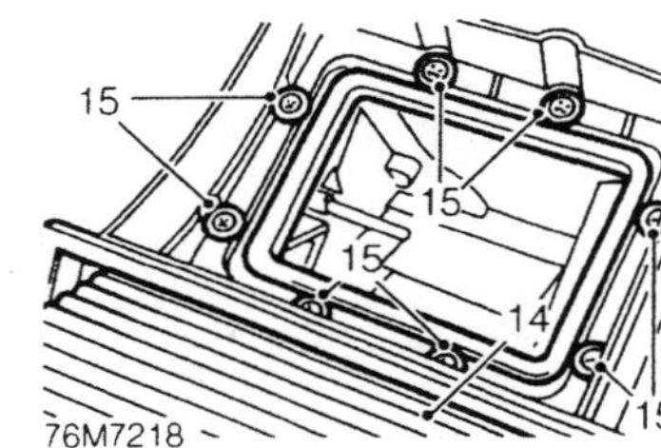

76M7218

14. Remove pollen filter from both heater intake housings.
15. Remove 8 screws securing each heater intake housing to scuttle and remove intake housings. Release sealing rubbers from scuttle panel aperture.
16. Remove centre console. ***See this section.***

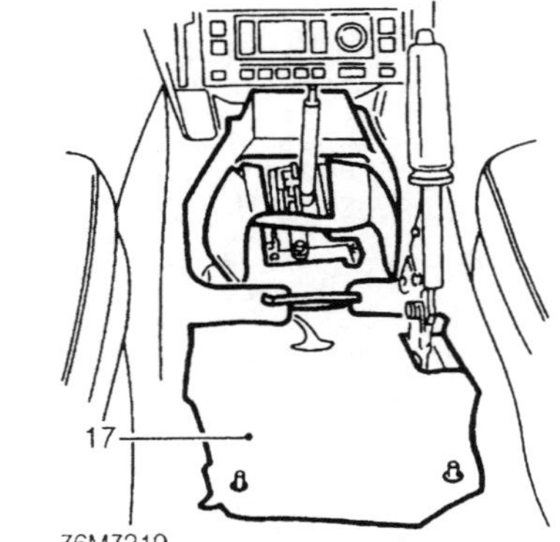

76M7219

17. Remove transmission tunnel insulation pad.

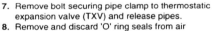

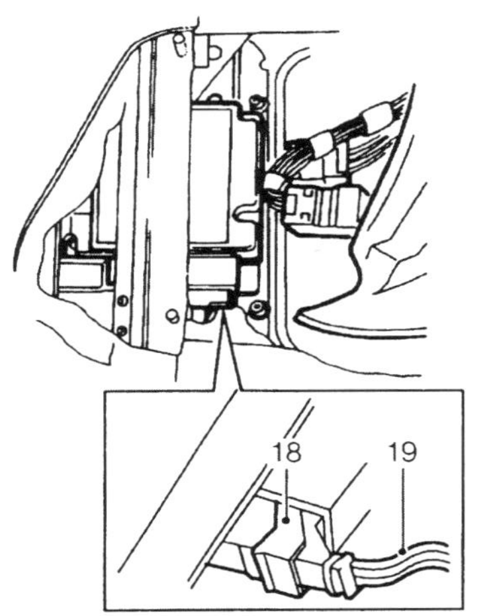

76M7220

18. Release latching mechanism and disconnect multiplug from airbag diagnostic and control unit (DCU).
19. Release SRS harness from transmission tunnel and position to fascia to avoid snagging.

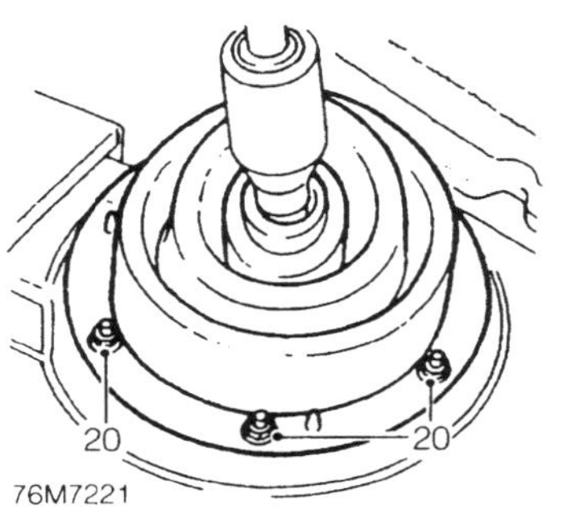

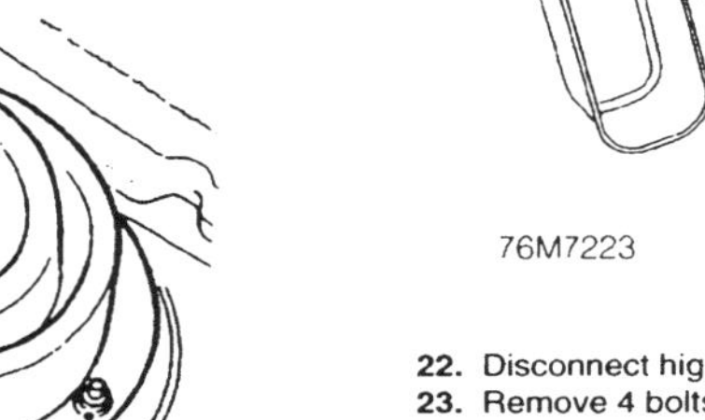

76M7221

20. Remove 6 nuts securing gear lever gaiter ring to transmission tunnel and release gaiter.

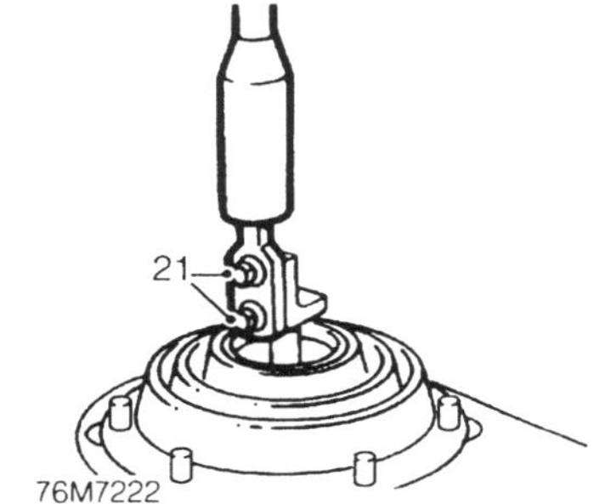

76M7222

21. Remove 2 bolts securing gear lever to gearbox remote and remove gear lever.

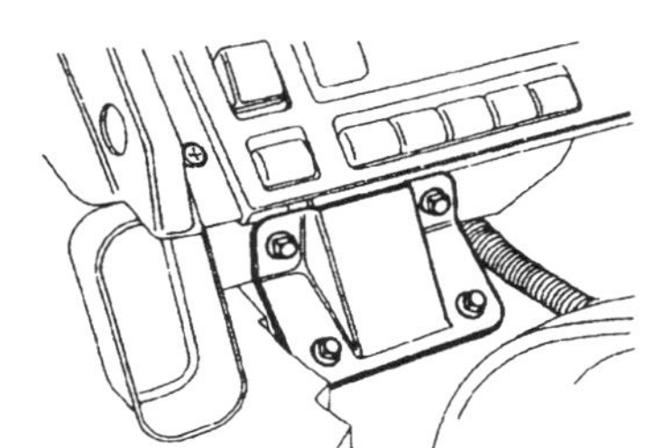

76M7223

22. Disconnect high/low switch multiplug.
23. Remove 4 bolts securing fascia centre bracket to fascia and transmission tunnel.
24. Remove fascia centre bracket.
25. Remove radio. ***See ELECTRICAL, Repair.***
26. Remove steering column. ***See STEERING, Repair.***

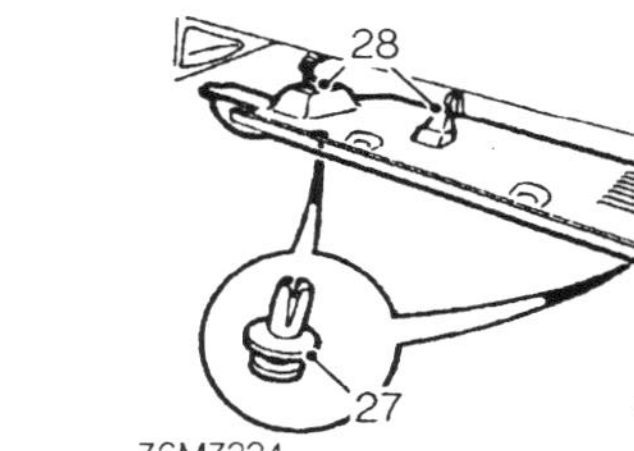

76M7224

27. Remove 3 scrivets securing lower fascia closing panel to passenger's side of fascia.
28. Release closing panel and release diagnostic connector from panel.

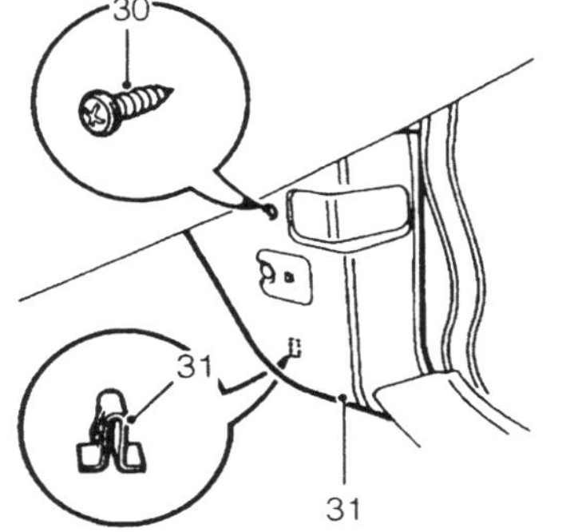

76M7225

29. Release door aperture seal adjacent to 'A' post lower trim panels.
30. Remove screw securing each 'A' post lower trim panel to 'A' post.
31. Release 'A' post lower trim panels from sprag clip and remove panels.

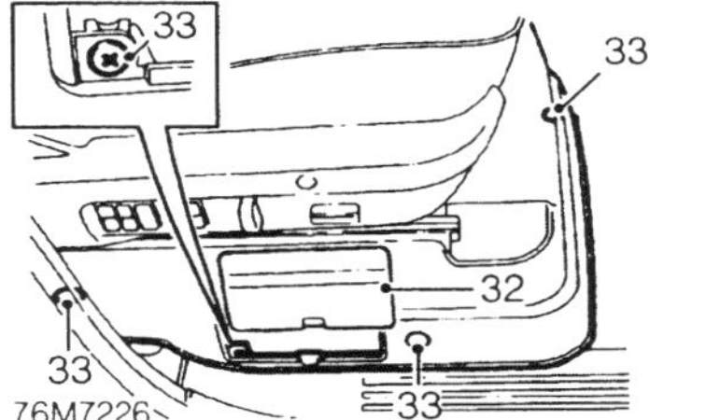

76M7226

32. Remove fuse box cover from driver's seat base trim.

33. Remove screw and 3 trim studs securing seat base trim to body and remove seat base trim.

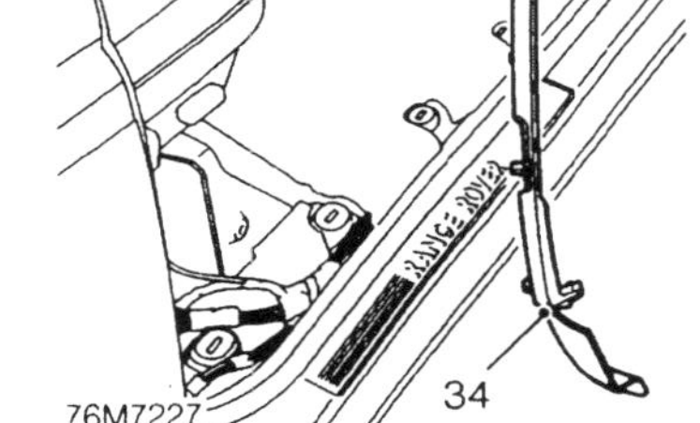

76M7227

34. Release 4 sprag clips securing driver's side carpet retainer to body and remove carpet retainer.

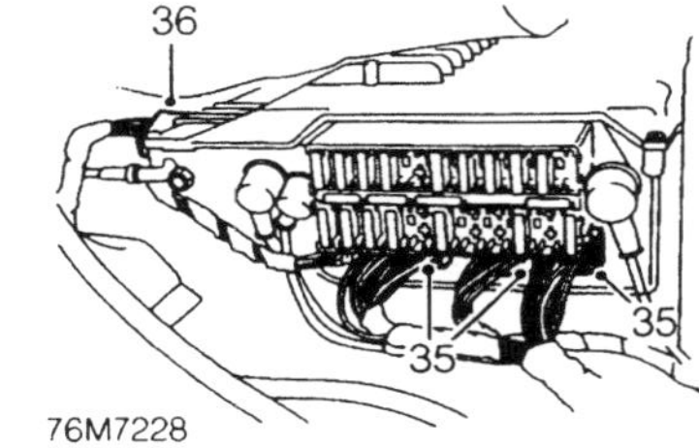

76M7228

35. Disconnect 3 multiplugs from Body Electrical Control Module (BeCM).
36. Position carpet aside and disconnect multiplug from rear of BeCM.

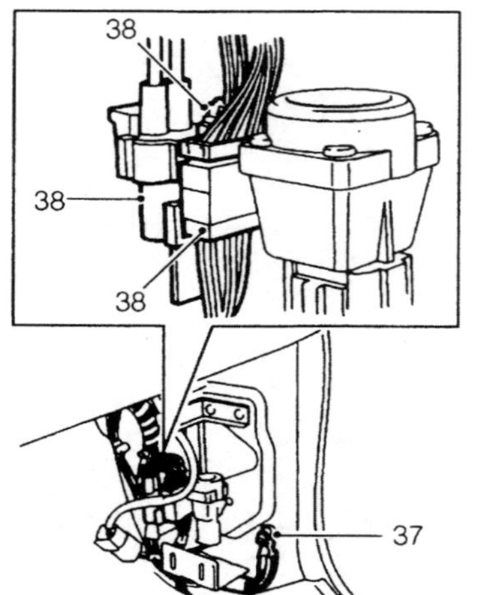

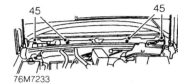

76M7229

37. Remove captive nut securing earth wires to driver's side lower 'A' post and release 3 additional earth wires.
38. Disconnect 3 multiplugs at base of driver's side 'A' post.
39. Release harness from driver's side carpet and position to fascia to avoid snagging.

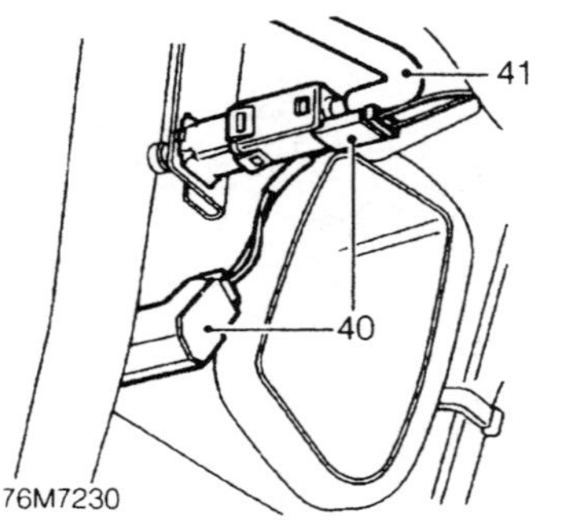

76M7230

40. Disconnect multiplugs from clutch and 2 brake pedal switches.
41. Disconnect vacuum hose from clutch and brake pedal switches.

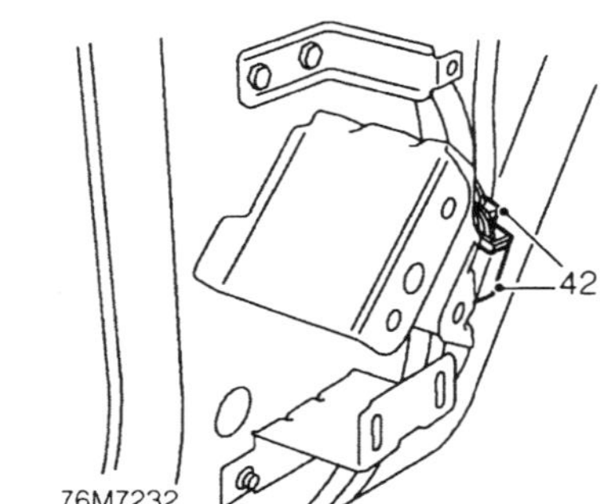

76M7232

42. Disconnect 2 multiplugs at base of passenger's side 'A' post.

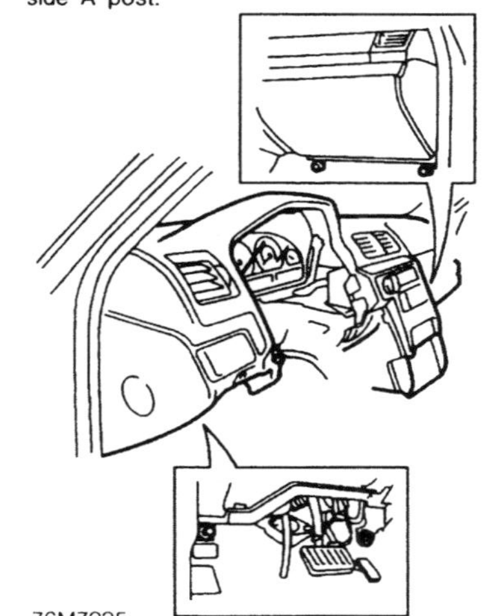
76M7235

43. Remove 2 nuts securing fascia to 'A' post and transmission tunnel bracket, passenger's side
44. Remove 2 nuts securing fascia to 'A' post and transmission tunnel bracket, driver's side.

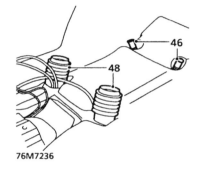

45 45
76M7233

45. Remove 4 tube bolts securing fascia assembly to scuttle panel.

46 48
76M7236

46. Disconnect 2 evaporator drain hoses from evaporator.
47. Using assistance, carefully manoeuvre fascia assembly through the driver's door aperture. Position the fascia on a work surface with a soft covering and support on suitable wooden blocks.
48. Collect 2 ducts connecting rear heating pipes to fascia assembly.

Refit

49. Tape intake duct seals inside blower duct to aid fitment.
50. Fit guide pins LRT-76-001 to outer fascia studs.
51. With assistance, manoeuvre fascia assembly through driver's door aperture and locate guide pins to scuttle panel.

NOTE: Assistance from a third person may be required to guide heater pipes through bulkhead.

52. Fit one tube bolt securing fascia to scuttle panel but do not tighten.
53. Fit nuts securing fascia to lower 'A' posts and tighten to ***25 Nm. (18 lbf.ft)***
54. Fit nuts securing fascia to transmission tunnel brackets and tighten to ***25 Nm. (18 lbf.ft)***
55. Remove LRT-76-001.
56. Fit remaining tube bolts securing fascia to scuttle panel and tighten to ***25 Nm. (18 lbf.ft)***
57. Fit fascia centre bracket, fit bolts and tighten to ***25 Nm. (18 lbf.ft)***
58. Connect evaporator drain hoses to evaporator.
59. Fit ducts connecting rear heating pipes to fascia assembly.
60. Fit gearlever to gearbox remote, fit bolts and tighten to ***25 Nm. (18 lbf.ft)***
61. Fit gear lever gaiter and ring to transmission tunnel and secure with nuts.
62. Connect high/low switch multiplug.
63. Position SRS harness to transmission tunnel.
64. Connect multiplug to airbag DCU. Ensure connector latching mechanism is correctly engaged.
65. Fit transmission tunnel insulation pad to transmission tunnel and position multiplugs through pad.
66. Fit radio. ***See ELECTRICAL, Repair.***
67. Connect multiplugs at base of passenger's side 'A' post.
68. Fit passenger's side 'A' post lower trim panel and secure with screw.
69. Engage door aperture seal to door aperture.
70. Position fascia lower closing panel and engage diagnostic connector to panel.
71. Position closing panel to fascia and secure with scrivets.
72. Connect vacuum hose to clutch and brake pedal switches.
73. Connect multiplugs to clutch and brake pedal switches.

74. Position harness to driver's side carpet.
75. Connect multiplugs to BeCM.
76. Connect multiplugs at base to driver's side 'A' post.
77. Position earth wires to 'A' post stud, fit and secure captive nut.
78. Fit driver's side carpet retainer and engage to clips.
79. Fit seat base trim and secure with trim studs and screw.
80. Fit seat base fuse box cover.
81. Fit driver's side lower 'A' post trim and secure with screw.
82. Fit steering column. ***See STEERING, Repair.***
83. Fit radio. ***See ELECTRICAL, Repair.***
84. Fit centre console. ***See this section.***
85. Remove tape from heater intake ducts.
86. Engage heater intake seals to scuttle apertures.
87. Fit heater intake housings and secure with screws.
88. Fit pollen filters to intake housings.
89. Fit wiper motor and linkage. ***See WIPERS AND WASHERS, Repair.***
90. Fit scuttle side panel to scuttle and secure with bolts.
91. Connect heated screen multiplug and engage multiplug to scuttle side panel bracket.
92. Remove caps from heater matrix pipes.
93. Engage heater matrix grommet to bulkhead aperture.
94. Connect heater hoses to heater matrix and secure with clips.
95. Remove caps from air conditioning pipes and TXV.
96. Lubricate NEW 'O' ring seals with clean compressor oil and fit to air conditioning pipes.
97. Connect air conditioning pipes to TXV, position clamp and fit bolt.
98. Tighten clamp bolt to ***6 Nm. (4 lbf.ft)***
99. Charge air conditioning system. ***See AIR CONDITIONING, Adjustment.***
100. Fill coolant system. ***See COOLING SYSTEM, Repair.***
101. Connect both battery terminals, earth lead last.

PANELS - VENEERED - FASCIA

Service repair no - 76.46.24

Remove

1. **Drivers side:** Remove fascia closing panel. ***See this section.***

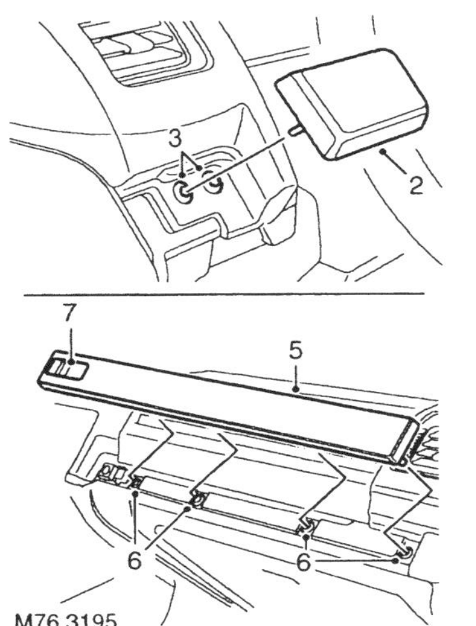

M76 3195

2. With suitable protection against fascia, carefully lever veneered panel away from fascia to release 2 fixing studs.
3. Remove fixing stud inserts.
4. **Passenger side:** Open glove box.
5. With suitable protection against fascia, carefully lever veneered panel away from fascia to release 4 fixings studs.
6. Remove fixing stud inserts.
7. Remove glove box lock bezel from veneered panel.

Refit

8. **Passenger side:** Fit glove box lock bezel.
9. Fit fixing stud inserts to fascia.
10. Fit veneered panel to fascia.
11. Close glove box.
12. **Drivers side:** Fit fixing stud inserts to fascia.
13. Fit veneered panel to fascia.
14. **Drivers side:** Fit fascia closing panel. ***See this section.***

PANEL - FASCIA CLOSING

Service repair no - 76.46.28

Remove

1. Release steering column adjustment lock, raise and extend column for access to panel upper screws.

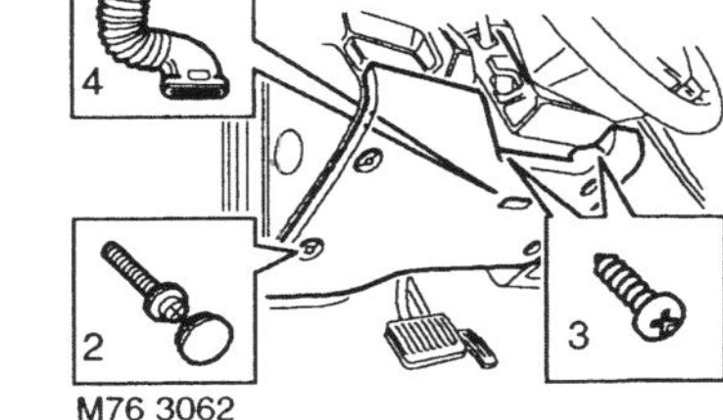

M76 3062

2. Remove 4 screw covers from fascia closing panel and remove screws.
3. Remove 2 screws securing top of closing panel.
4. Disconnect air tube and remove closing panel.

Refit

5. Position closing panel and connect air tube.
6. Fit closing panel to fascia and secure with screws.
7. Fit screw covers and reposition steering column.

FRONT DOOR ASSEMBLY

Service repair no - 76.28.01/99

Remove

1. Release door harness protective sleeve from 'A' post.
2. Disconnect door harness multiplugs.

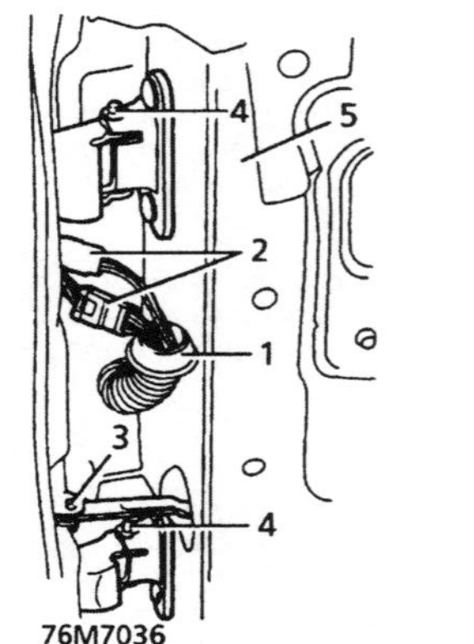

76M7036

3. Remove door check strap retaining pin.

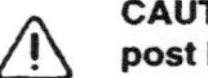

CAUTION: Apply protective tape to 'A' post before drifting out retaining pin.

4. Remove door hinge pin retaining clips.
5. With assistance, remove door assembly.

Refit

6. With assistance, position door on hinges. Fit retaining clips.
7. Align door check strap. Fit retaining pin.
8. Remove protective tape from 'A' post.
9. Connect harness multiplugs. Secure protective sleeve to 'A' post.
10. If necessary adjust door. ***See Adjustment.***

GLASS - FRONT DOOR

Service repair no - 76.31.01

Remove

1. Remove front door outer waist seal. ***See this section.***
2. Remove front door plastic sheet. ***See this section.***
3. Turn ignition ON.
4. Lower glass approximately 120mm (5 in.) Remove rear regulator arm retaining clip.

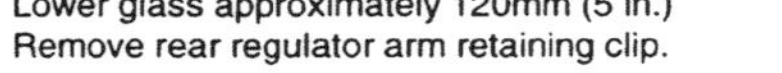

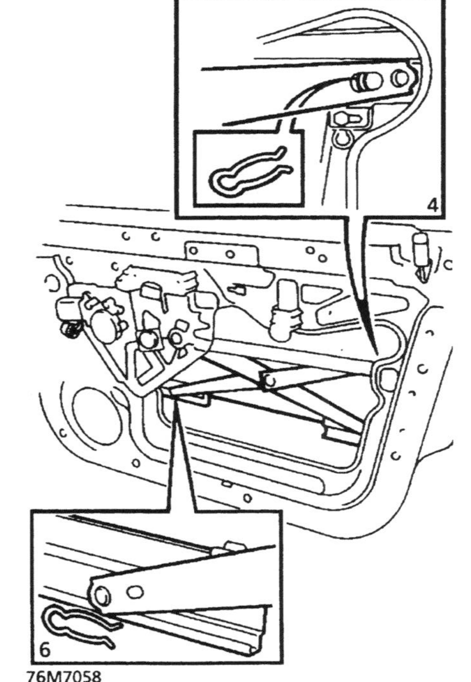

76M7058

5. Lower glass to align forward clip with the regulator plate lower retaining rivet. Turn ignition OFF.

6. Remove front lower fixing clip.
7. Remove nut securing bracket to vertical slide.
8. Release bracket from slide.

CAUTION: Chock glass with wooden block, or retain with tape, to prevent glass dropping when regulator arms are released.

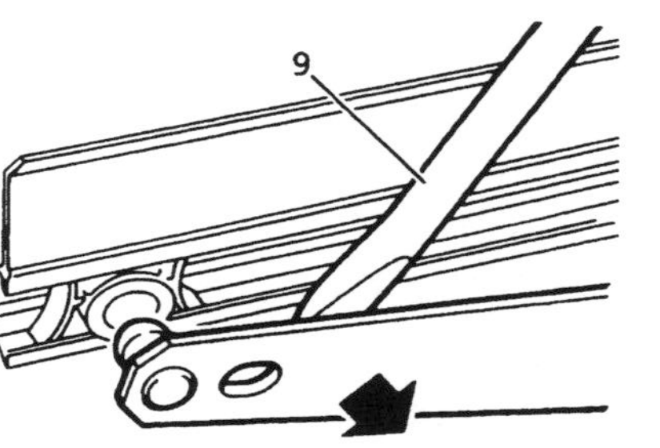

76M7059

9. Using a suitable lever, release 2 regulator arms from glass lower fixings.
10. Support weight of glass. Remove wooden chock or tape.

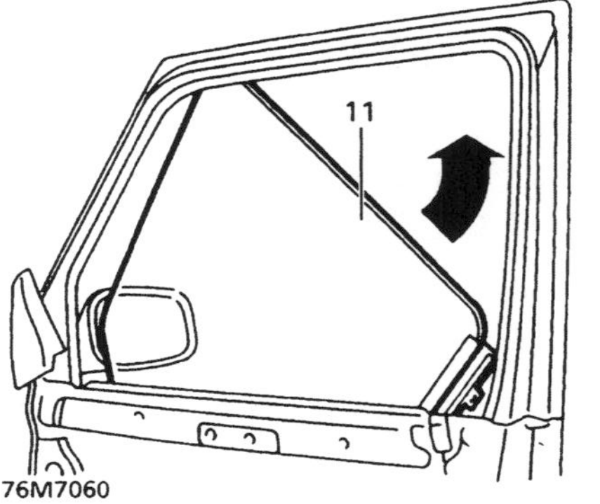

76M7060

11. Rotate glass anti-clockwise to release from runners.
12. Remove front door glass.

Refit

13. Refit front door glass.
14. Rotate glass anti-clockwise, fit to runners.
15. Secure glass fixings to regulator arms.
16. Position glass bracket to vertical runner, fit retaining nut.
17. Fit clip securing regulator arm to glass runner.
18. Turn ignition ON.
19. Raise door glass approximately 120mm (5 in.) Fit rear glass retaining clip.
20. Raise door glass.
21. Turn ignition OFF.
22. Fit front door plastic sheet. ***See this section.***
23. Fit front door outer waist seal. ***See this section.***

GLASS REGULATOR - FRONT DOOR

Service repair no - 76.31.45

Remove

1. Remove front door glass. ***See this section.***
2. Disconnect window lift motor harness connector.
3. Remove rivet securing regulator runner to door panel.

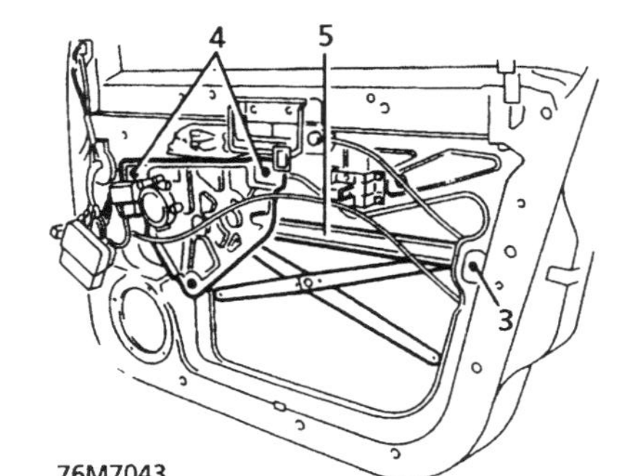

76M7043

4. Remove 3 rivets.
5. Remove regulator assembly.

Refit

6. Reverse removal procedure.

LATCH - FRONT DOOR

Service repair no - 76.37.12

Remove

1. Remove front door trim casing. ***See this section.***
2. Release rear of plastic sheet.
3. Release retaining clip, private lock to latch operating rod, at latch end.

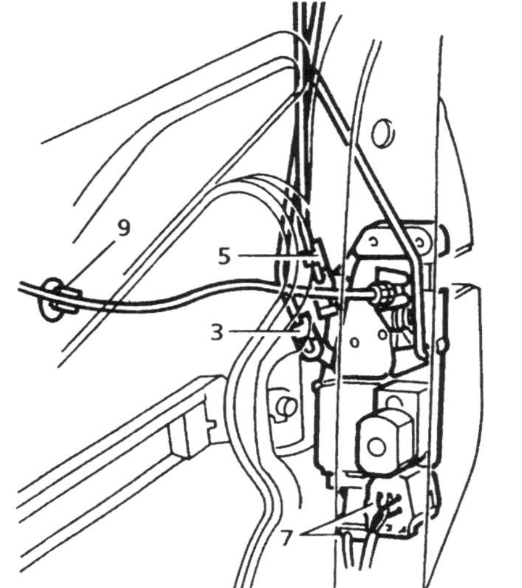

76M7015

4. Release control rod from latch.
5. Release retaining clip, outside handle to latch operating rod, at latch end.
6. Release control rod from latch.
7. Disconnect 2 latch motor multiplugs.
8. Remove door sill button from operating rod.
9. Release remote handle to latch operating cable from clip.
10. Remove 3 screws securing latch.
11. Release latch from door.
12. Remove sill button operating rod from latch.

76M7016A

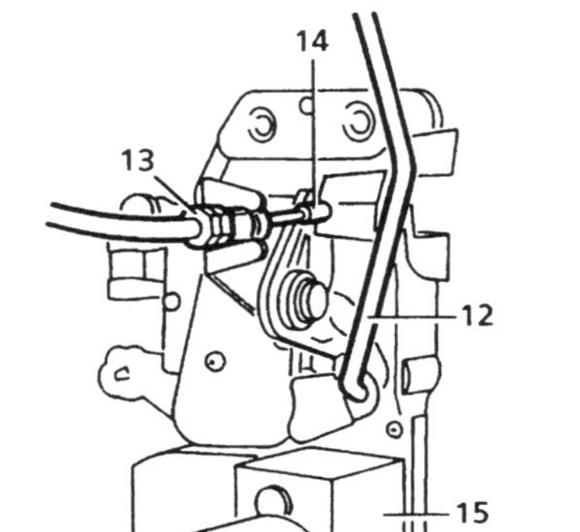

76M7017

13. Release outer operating cable from latch abutment.
14. Release inner cable from latch.
15. Remove latch from door.

Refit

16. Fit latch.
17. Fit inner operating cable to latch.
18. Fit outer operating cable to latch abutment.
19. Fit sill button operating rod to latch.
20. Align latch to door, tighten 3 screws.
21. Secure remote handle cable to door panel clip.
22. Fit sill button to operating rod.
23. Reconnect 2 latch motor multiplugs.
24. Fit outside handle operating rod to latch.
25. Fit retaining clip.
26. Fit private lock operating rod to latch.
27. Fit retaining clip.
28. Secure plastic sheet.
29. Fit front door trim casing. ***See this section.***

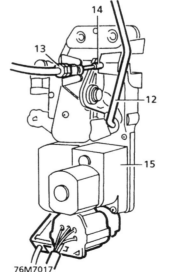

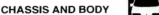

REMOTE CONTROL - FRONT DOOR

Service repair no - 76.37.31

Remove

1. Remove front door trim casing. ***See this section.***
2. Release top rear corner of plastic sheet.
3. Pull remote handle out. Release inner cable from remote handle.

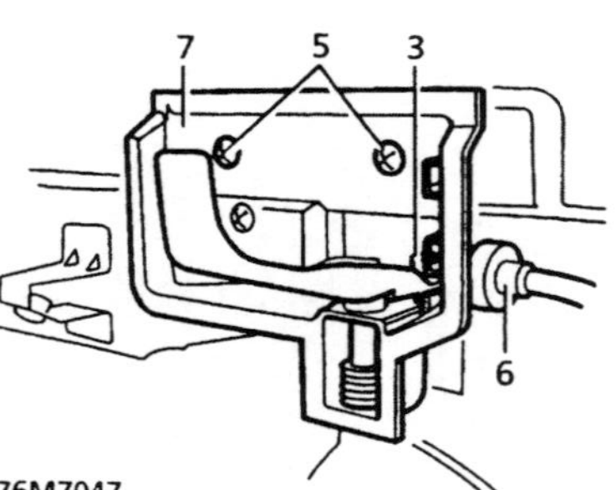

76M7047

4. Release remote handle.
5. Remove 2 screws securing remote handle.
6. Remove outer cable from housing.
7. Remove remote by sliding rearwards.

Refit

8. Reverse removal procedure.

OUTER WAIST SEAL - FRONT DOOR

Service repair no - 76.31.53

Remove

1. Remove screw securing rear edge of outer waist seal.
2. Remove outer waist seal.

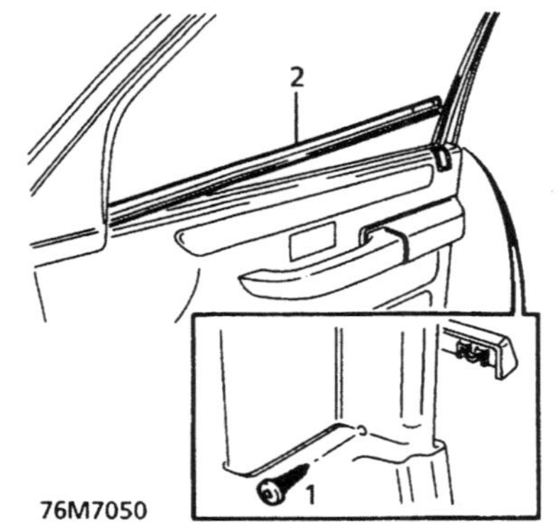

76M7050

Refit

3. Reverse removal procedure.

OUTSIDE HANDLE - FRONT DOOR

Service repair no - 76.58.07

Remove

1. Remove front door trim casing. ***See this section.***
2. Release rear half of plastic sheet.
3. Remove retaining clip, private lock to latch operating rod, at latch end.

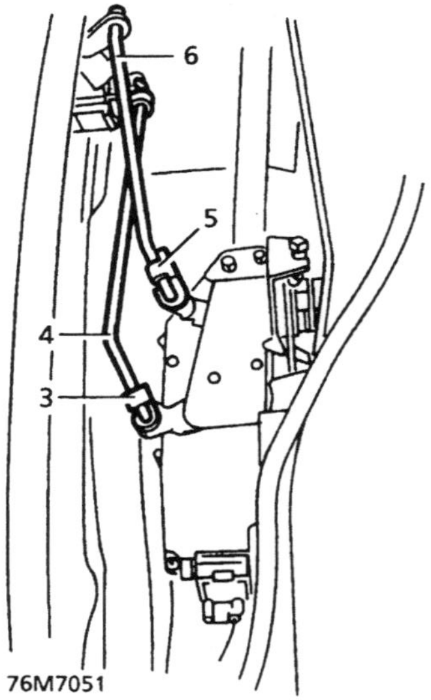

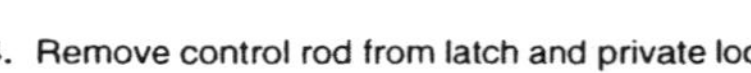

76M7051

4. Remove control rod from latch and private lock.
5. Remove retaining clip, outside handle to latch operating rod, at latch end.
6. Remove control rod from latch and outside handle.
7. Remove bolt securing rear of outside handle.

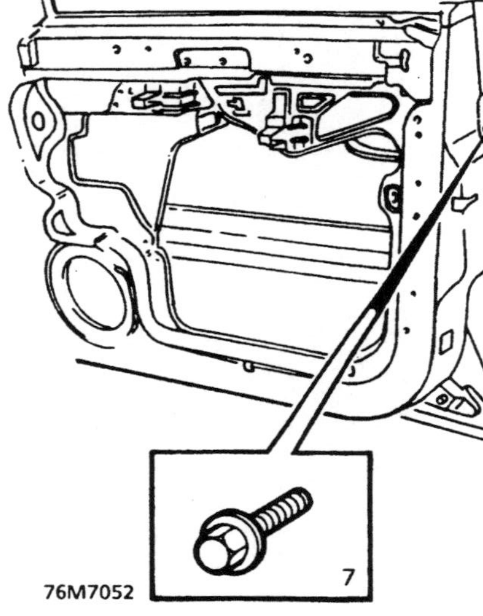

76M7052

8. Slide outside handle forwards. Pull handle out, release rear of handle from door.

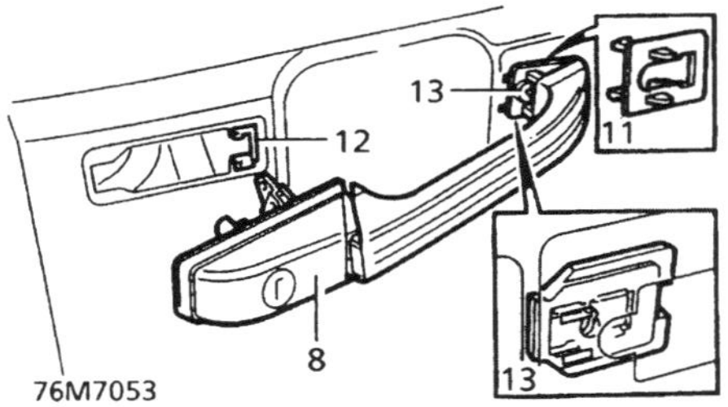

9. Remove handle from front fixing by pivotting rear end of handle out.
10. Remove gasket from handle.
11. Remove rubber locking plate from door.
12. Remove plastic locking plate from door.
13. Remove screw securing mounting plate to door, remove plate.

Refit

14. Clean handle and door mating faces.
15. Reverse removal procedure.

PLASTIC SHEET - FRONT DOOR

Service repair no - 76.34.26

Remove

1. Remove front door trim casing. ***See this section.***
2. Remove 2 screws securing door outstation ECU.

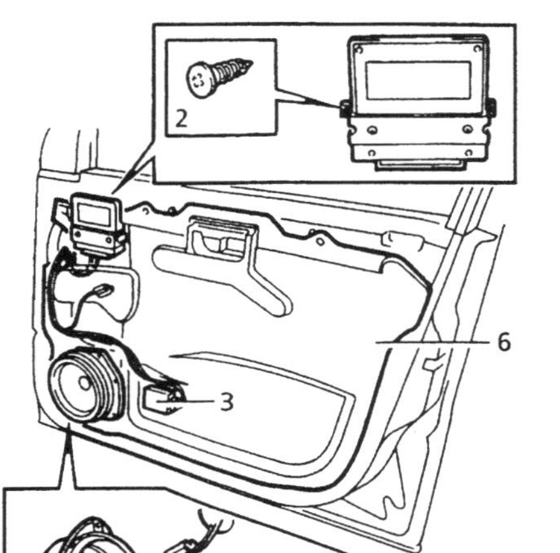

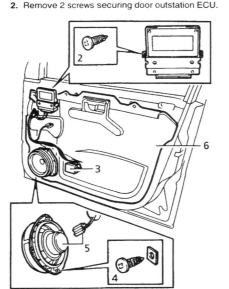

76M7042

3. Remove 2 screws securing speaker amplifier.
4. Remove 4 screws securing front door speaker.
5. Release speaker, disconnect multiplug.
6. Remove plastic sheet.

Refit

7. Reverse removal procedure.

PRIVATE LOCK - FRONT DOOR

Service repair no - 76.37.39

Remove

1. Remove outside handle. ***See this section.***
2. Fit door lock key.
3. Remove screw securing lock.
4. Remove cam and washer from lock.
5. Remove cam lock and stop from lock.
6. Remove cam return spring. Remove lock from outside handle.

Refit

7. Apply grease to lock barrel.
8. Fit lock to outside handle.
9. Fit cam return spring, cam stop, cam lock, washer and cam.
10. Fit screw securing lock to outside handle.
11. Remove door lock key.
12. Refit front door outside handle. ***See this section.***

TRIM CASING - FRONT DOOR

Service repair no - 76.34.01

Remove

1. Release cheater panel.

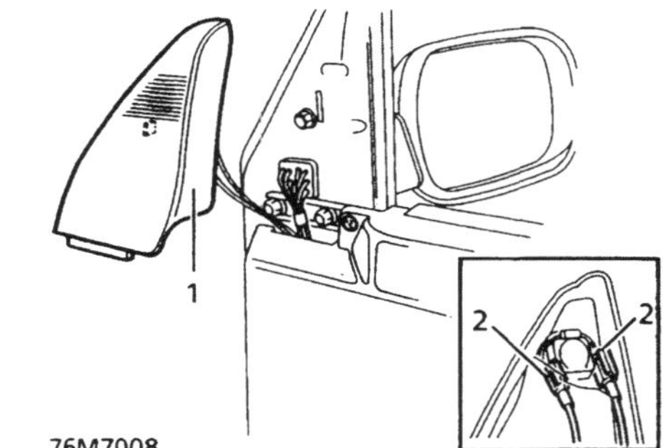

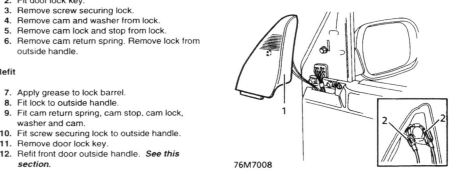

76M7008

2. Disconnect 2 tweeter speaker connectors, remove cheater panel.
3. Remove screw securing remote handle escutcheon, remove escutcheon.

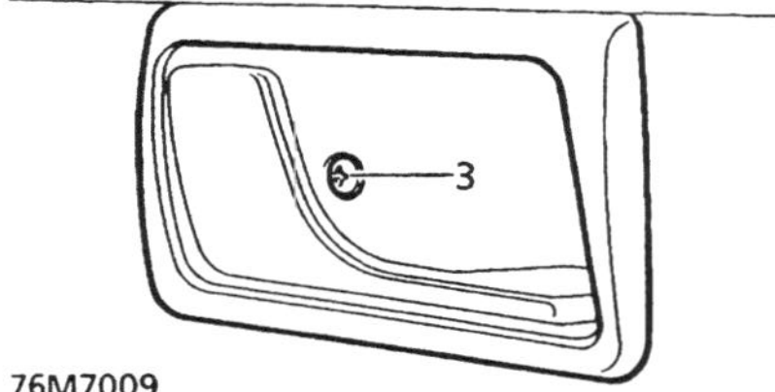

76M7009

4. Remove 3 screws securing trim casing.
5. Release 12 clips retaining trim casing.

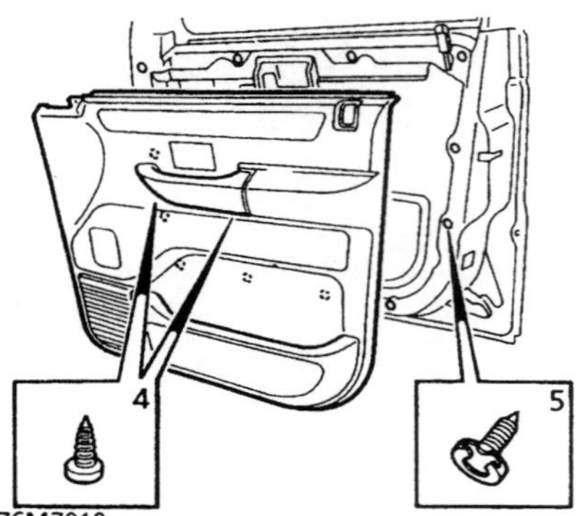

76M7010

6. Disconnect speaker connector.

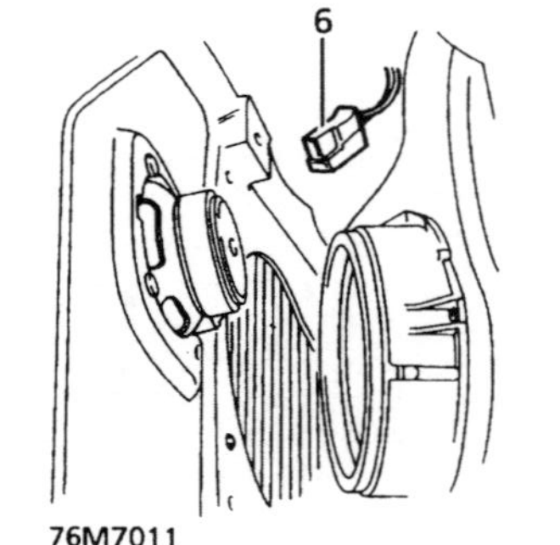

76M7011

7. Remove door trim casing.

Disassemble

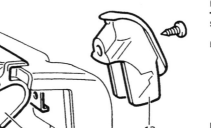

8. Remove 12 trim casing retaining clips.
9. Remove 4 screws, remove speaker.

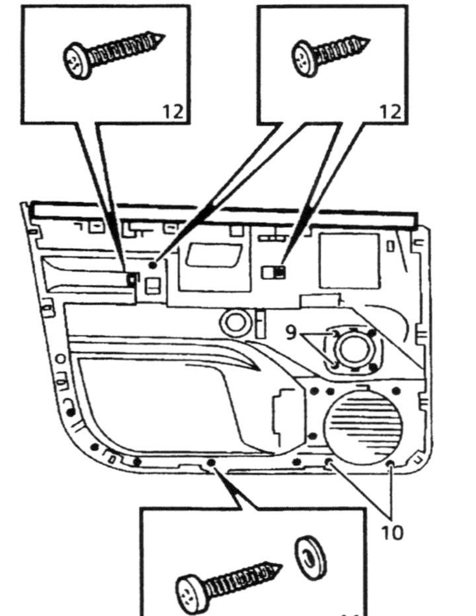

76M7013

10. Remove 4 screws, remove speaker grille.
11. Remove 7 screws, remove trim casing pocket.
12. Remove 3 screws, remove arm rest.
13. Remove retaining clamp and sill button escutcheon.

76M7014

14. Remove door trim casing waist seal.

Assemble

15. Fit door trim casing waist seal.
16. Fit sill button escutcheon, position retaining clamp, tighten screw.
17. Fit arm rest to trim casing, tighten 3 screws.
18. Fit trim casing pocket, tighten 7 screws.
19. Fit speaker grille to trim casing, tighten 4 screws.
20. Fit speaker to trim, tighten 4 screws.
21. Fit 12 retaining clips.

Refit

22. Connect trim casing speaker connector.
23. Fit trim casing, locating 12 retaining clips.
24. Fit 3 screws securing trim casing.
25. Fit remote handle escutcheon, tighten screw.
26. Position cheater panel, connect 2 tweeter speaker connectors.
27. Secure cheater panel.

INSERT CAPPING - FRONT DOOR

Service repair no - 76.34.32

Remove

1. Fit protection to door trim casing.
2. Position a blunt flat blade between trim casing and insert upper edge.
3. Gently raise blade to remove insert.
4. Remove retaining clips from insert.

Refit

5. Fit insert to door casing. Secure with clips.
6. Remove protection from door casing.

REAR DOOR ASSEMBLY

Service repair no - 76.28.02/99

Remove

1. Release door harness protective sleeve from 'B/C' post.
2. Disconnect door harness multiplugs.
3. Remove check strap retaining pin.

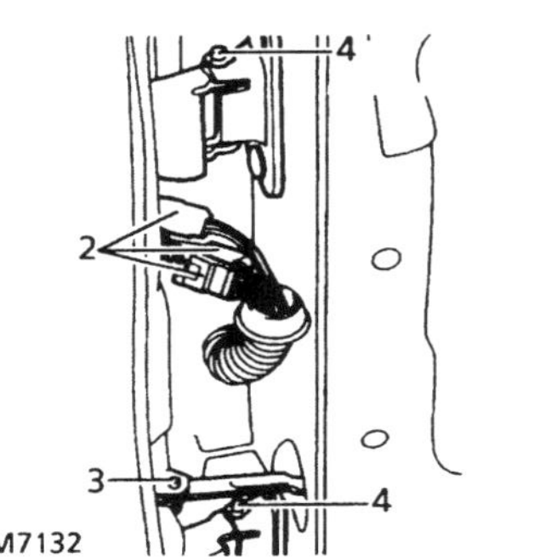

76M7132

CAUTION: Apply protective tape to 'B/C' post before drifting out pin.

4. Remove hinge pin retaining clips.
5. With assistance, remove door assembly.

Refit

6. With assistance fit door to hinges.
7. Fit hinge retaining clips.
8. Align check strap and fit retaining pin.
9. Remove protective tape.
10. Connect harness multiplugs, secure protective sleeve to 'B/C' post.
11. If necessary adjust door. ***See Adjustment.***

GLASS - REAR DOOR

Service repair no - 76.31.02

Remove

1. Remove outer waist seal. ***See this section.***
2. Remove door trim casing. ***See this section.***
3. Remove speaker and plastic sheet. ***See this section.***
4. Remove window motor and control panel assembly. ***See ELECTRICAL, Repair.***
5. Remove glass rear channel. ***See this section.***
6. Remove wedges or tape from glass.
7. Release glass from channel. Raise to remove glass from door.

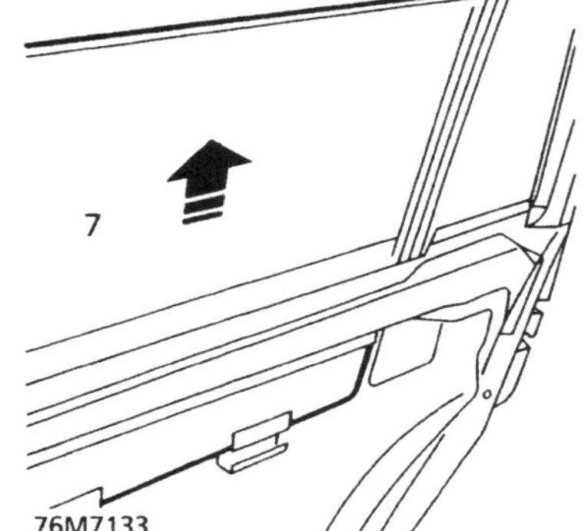

76M7133

Refit

8. Fit glass to door and align to frame.
9. Wedge or use tape to hold glass in door.
10. Fit glass rear channel. ***See this section.***
11. Fit window motor and control panel. ***See ELECTRICAL, Repair.***
12. Fit speaker and plastic sheet. ***See this section.***
13. Fit trim casing. ***See this section.***
14. Fit outer waist seal. ***See this section.***

PLASTIC SHEET - REAR DOOR

Service repair no - 76.34.28

Remove

1. Remove rear door trim casing. ***See this section.***
2. Remove speaker. ***See ELECTRICAL, Repair.***
3. Remove 2 screws securing amplifier to door.
4. Remove plastic sheet.

Refit

5. Reverse removal procedure.

OUTSIDE HANDLE - REAR DOOR

Service repair no - 76.58.02

Remove

1. Remove rear door trim casing. ***See this section.***
2. Remove bolt securing handle.

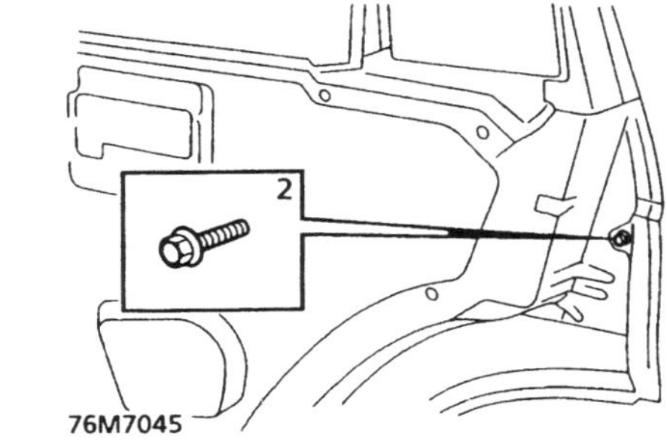

76M7045

3. Remove outside handle.

NOTE: Operate and pull handle outward, pivotting at forward mounting point.

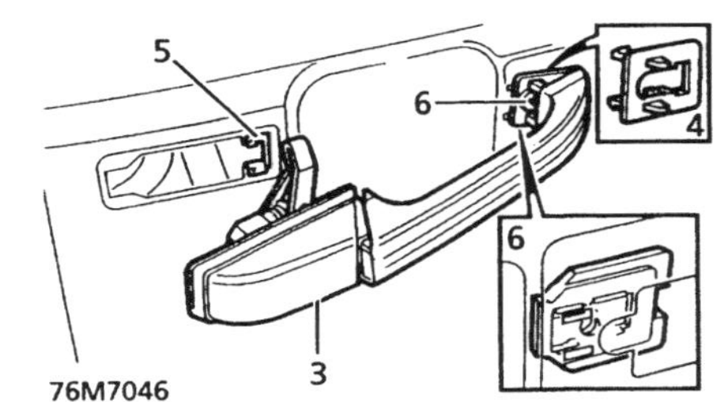

76M7046

4. Remove gasket.
5. Remove locking plates.
6. Remove screw securing mounting plate, remove plate.

Refit

7. Clean handle face on door.
8. Fit handle mounting plate, tighten screw.
9. Fit locking plates.
10. Fit gasket to handle, position handle, secure with screw.
11. Refit door trim casing. ***See this section.***

LATCH - REAR DOOR

Service repair no - 76.37.13/70

Remove

1. Remove window lift motor/control unit assembly. ***See ELECTRICAL, Repair.***
2. Release door lock remote control cable from clip on window lift panel.
3. Remove 2 studs securing latch to window lift panel.

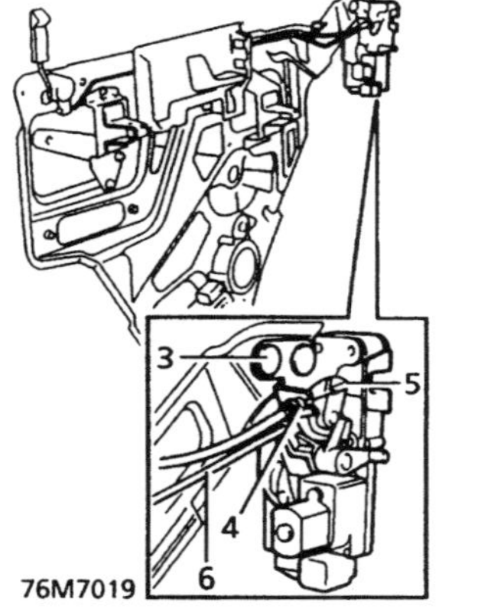

76M7019

4. Disconnect outer cable from abutment bracket.
5. Release remote cable from latch.
6. Release sill button link rod from latch. Remove latch.

Refit

7. Lubricate new latch.
8. Fit latch to sill button link rod.
9. Fit remote control cable to latch.
10. Fit latch to window lift panel, secure with 2 retaining studs.
11. Refit window lift motor/control unit assembly. ***See ELECTRICAL, Repair.***

FIXED QUARTER LIGHT - REAR DOOR

Service repair no - 76.31.31

Remove

1. Remove outer waist seal. ***See this section.***
2. Remove door trim casing. ***See this section.***
3. From inside release seal from frame. Remove seal and glass assembly outwards.
4. Remove seal from glass.

76M7031

Refit

5. Clean glass, seal and frame.
6. Fit seal to glass. Fit assembly to door frame. If necessary use a draw string to locate rubber.

NOTE: The opening light seal fits over the fixed glass seal.

7. Fit door trim casing. ***See this section.***
8. Fit outer waist seal. ***See this section.***

REMOTE CONTROL - REAR DOOR

Service repair no - 76.37.32

Remove

1. Remove rear door trim casing. ***See this section.***
2. Release plastic sheet to clear remote.
3. Remove foam pad from under window lift switch multiplug.
4. Disconnect switch multiplug.

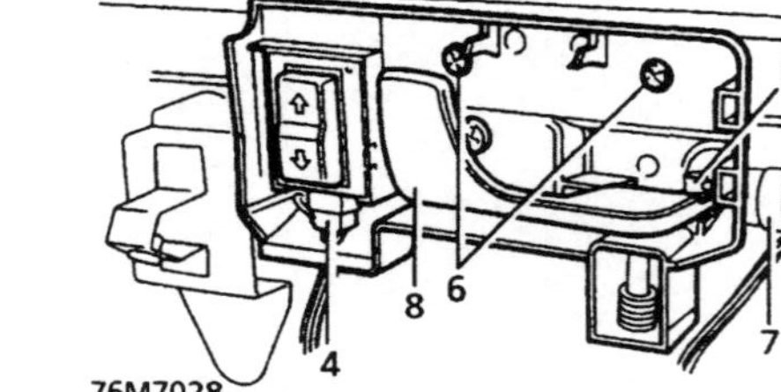

76M7028

5. Release inner cable from remote lever.
6. Remove 2 screws securing remote to window lift control panel.
7. Release remote outer cable from remote housing.
8. Remove remote control.

Refit

9. Reverse removal procedure.

GLASS CHANNEL - REAR DOOR

Service repair no - 76.31.17

Remove

1. Remove window lift motor/control panel assembly. ***See ELECTRICAL, Repair.***
2. Remove 2 bolts securing channel to door and remove channel.

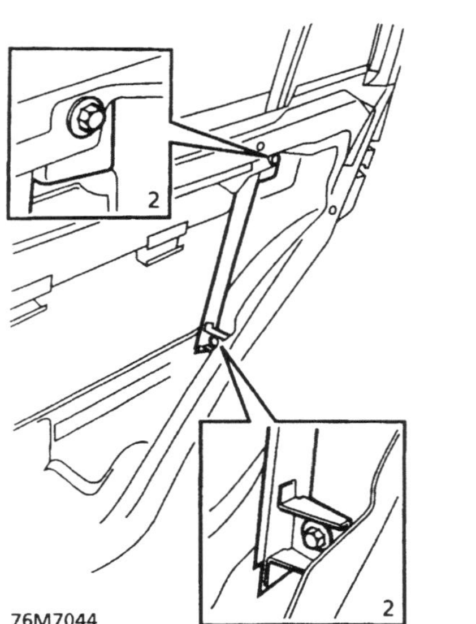

76M7044

Refit

3. Fit channel to door, secure with 2 bolts.
4. Refit window lift motor/control panel assembly. ***See ELECTRICAL, Repair.***

SEAL - REAR DOOR

Service repair no - 76.40.02

Remove

1. Open rear door.
2. Remove rear door carpet retainer.
3. Remove rear door aperture seal.

Refit

4. Fit rear door aperture seal.
5. Refit rear door carpet retainer.
6. Close rear door.

TRIM CASING - REAR DOOR

Service repair no - 76.34.04

Remove

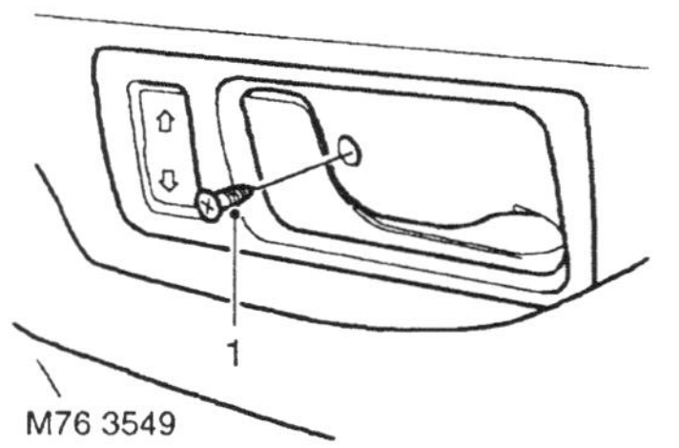

M76 3549

1. Remove screw securing remote handle escutcheon and remove escutcheon.

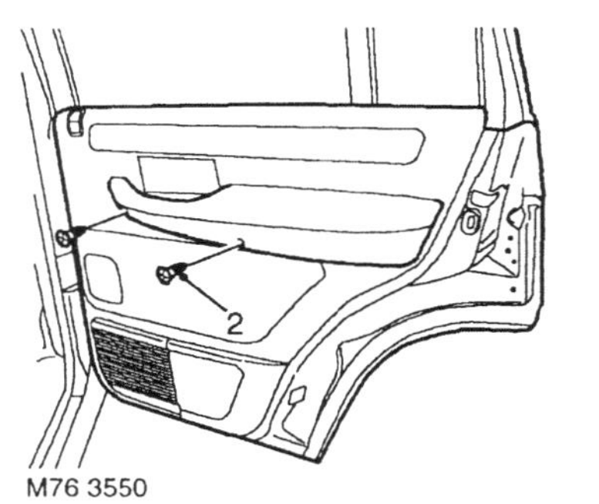

M76 3550

2. Remove 2 screws securing trim casing to door.

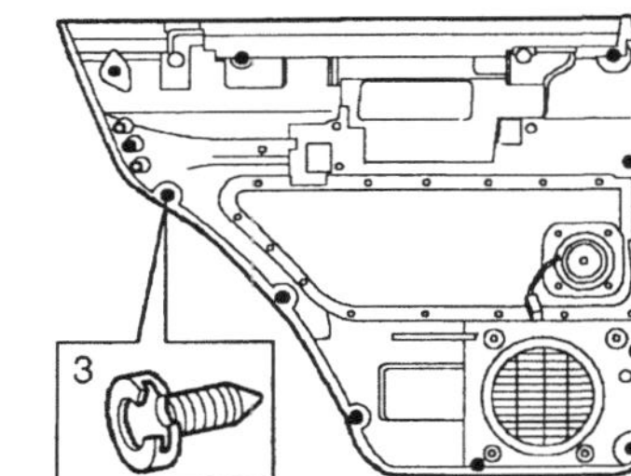

M76 3551

3. Release 11 door trim casing retaining studs.

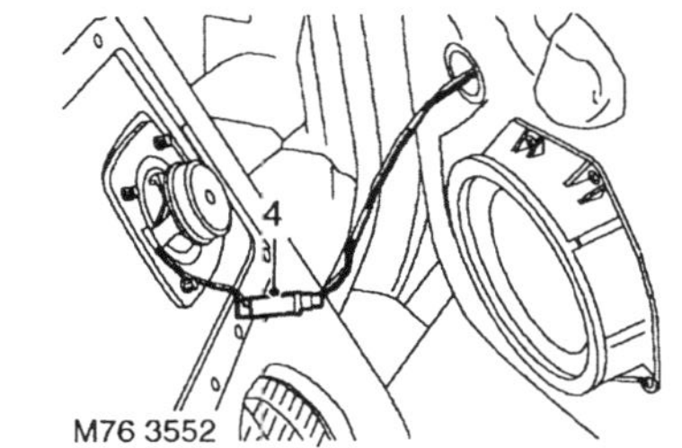

M76 3552

4. Disconnect rear door speaker and remove door trim.

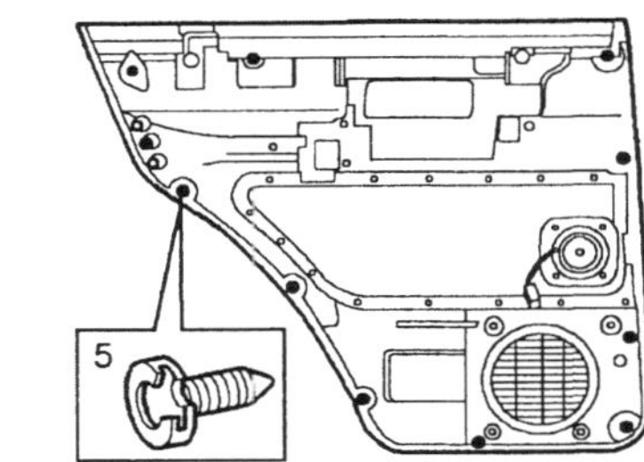

M76 3553

5. Remove 11 trim casing retaining studs from trim casing.

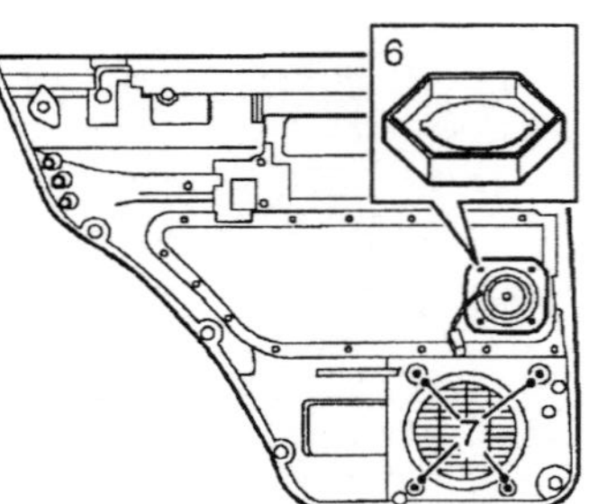

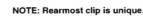

M76 3554

6. Remove 4 speed nuts securing speaker to trim casing and remove speaker.
7. Remove 4 Torx bolts securing speaker grille to trim casing and remove grille.

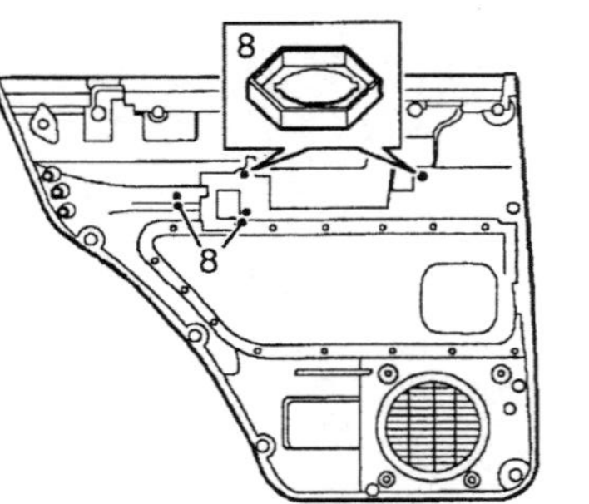

M76 3556

8. Remove 4 speed nuts securing arm rest to trim casing and remove arm rest.

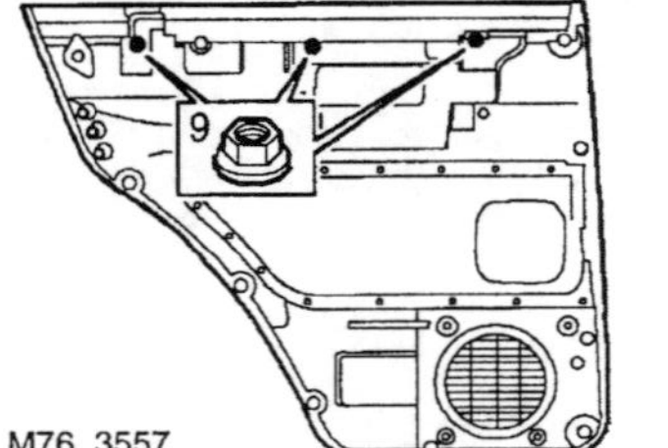

M76 3557

9. Remove 3 nuts securing door trim finisher to door trim and remove finisher.

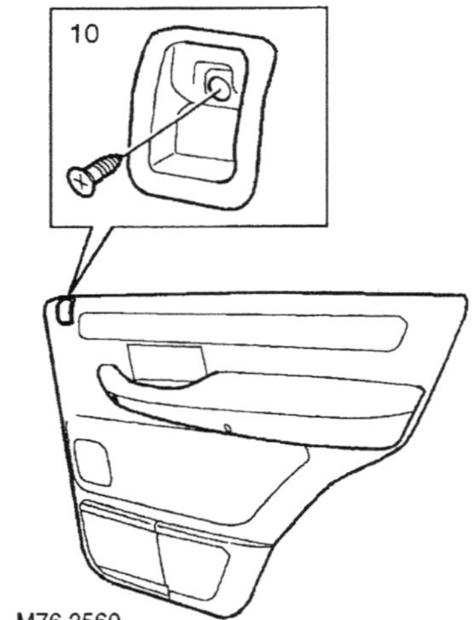

M76 3560

10. Remove screw securing door lock button escutcheon to door trim and remove escutcheon.

Refit

11. Fit door lock button escutcheon to door trim and secure with screw.
12. Fit door trim finisher to door trim and secure with nuts.
13. Fit arm rest to door trim and secure with speed nuts.
14. Fit speaker grille to door trim and secure with Torx bolts.
15. Fit speaker to trim casing and secure with speed nuts.
16. Fit trim casing retaining studs.
17. Position door trim to rear door and connect multiplug to speaker.
18. Fit door trim to rear door and secure with screws and retaining studs.
19. Fit door handle escutcheon to door and secure with screw.

OUTER WAIST SEAL - REAR DOOR

Service repair no - 76.31.54

Remove

1. Remove screw securing seal finisher to forward edge of door.
2. Release seal finisher from clip at rear edge of door.
3. Remove seal and finisher assembly.
4. Remove screw and securing clip.

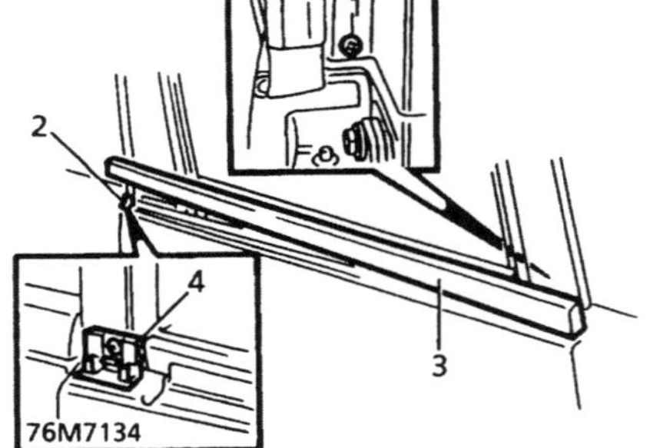

Refit

5. Fit clip to door, secure with screw.
6. Fit seal and finisher assembly to door. Align at forward edge, secure with screw.

RUBBING STRIPS & DOOR FINISHERS

Remove

CAUTION: When removing exterior trim, NEVER lever directly against body panels. Use an approved trim fork. Protect body panel with suitable material, such as fabric covered hardboard.

Rubbing Strip - Front Fender

1. Remove relevant wheel arch liner. ***See this section.***
2. Remove nut securing forward edge of rubbing strip.
3. Remove rubbing strip from single clip.

Rubbing Strip - Rear Quarter Panel

4. Release 5 clips securing rubbing strip. Remove strip.

NOTE: Rearmost clip is unique.

Rubbing Strips - Front & Rear Doors

5. Remove nut securing rear of rubbing strip.
6. **Front Door Rubbing Strip:** Release 5 clips securing rubbing strip.
7. **Rear Door Rubbing Strip:** Release 3 clips securing rubbing strip.
8. Remove rubbing strips.

Lower Door Finishers

9. Remove screw securing rear of fininsher.
10. **Front Door Finisher:** Release 5 clips securing rubbing strip.
11. **Rear Door Finisher:** Release 3 clips securing rubbing strip.
12. Remove finishers.

Refit

13. Reverse removal procedure.

GLOVE BOX AND LID

Service repair no - 76.52.03 - Glove Box
Service repair no - 76.52.02 - Glove Box Lid
Service repair no - 76.52.13 - Glove Box Lid - Align

Remove

1. Remove centre screw from 2 scrivet fasteners. Release closing panel for access to glove box hinge fixings. Collect outer parts of fasteners from closing panel.

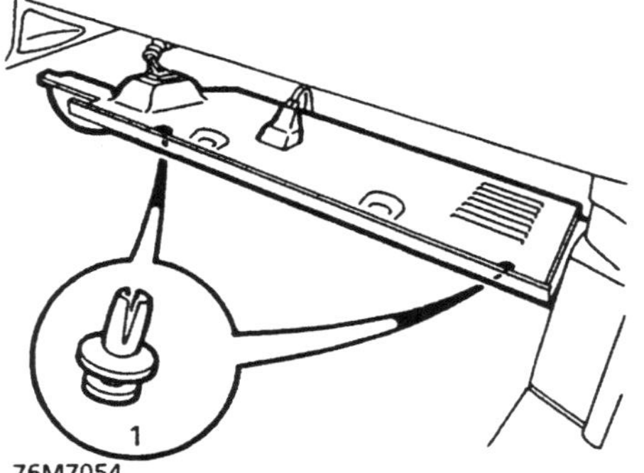

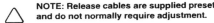

76M7054

2. Remove 2 bolts securing glove box hinges to fascia frame.
3. Open glove box lid, remove 5 screws securing glove box. Release glove box from fascia.

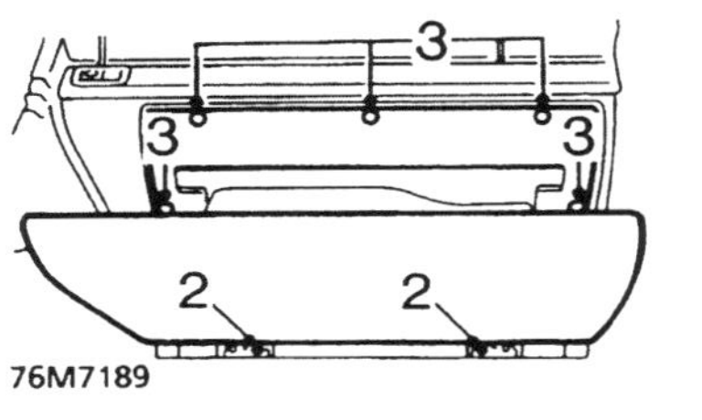

76M7189

4. Disconnect glove box lamp multiplug.
5. Disconnect cable latch, remove glove box assembly.

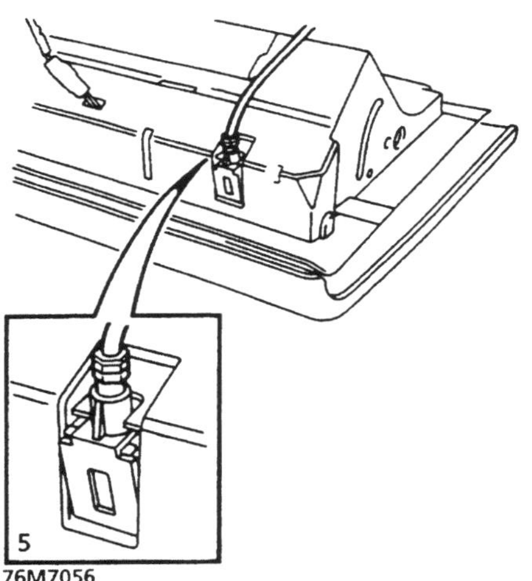

76M7056

Glove Box Lid

6. Remove split pin, disengage gas strut from lid.

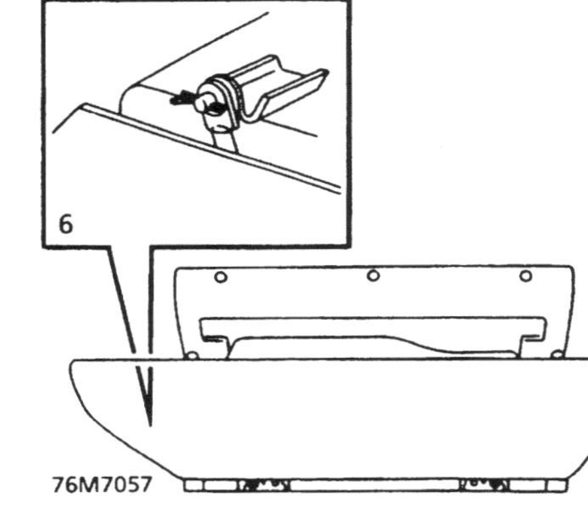

76M7057

7. Remove 2 bolts and square nuts, remove lid from glove box.

Refit Glove Box Lid

8. Position lid to glove box and secure with bolts and square nuts.
9. Engage gas strut, secure with split pin.

Refit Glove Box Assembly

10. Position glove box assembly, connect lamp multiplug. Secure cable latch.
11. Open glove box lid, align assembly to fascia. Secure with screws.
12. Fit bolts securing hinges to fascia frame, do no tighten.
13. Check alignment and latching of glove box lid, adjusting hinges as necessary using central adjusting screws.
14. Tighten screws, hinges to fascia.
15. Close glove box lid.
16. Position closing panel. Secure with scrivet fasteners.

GLOVE BOX RELEASE CABLE

Service repair no - 76.52.14

NOTE: Release cables are supplied preset and do not normally require adjustment.

Remove

1. Open glove box. Remove 5 screws securing glove box liner to fascia.

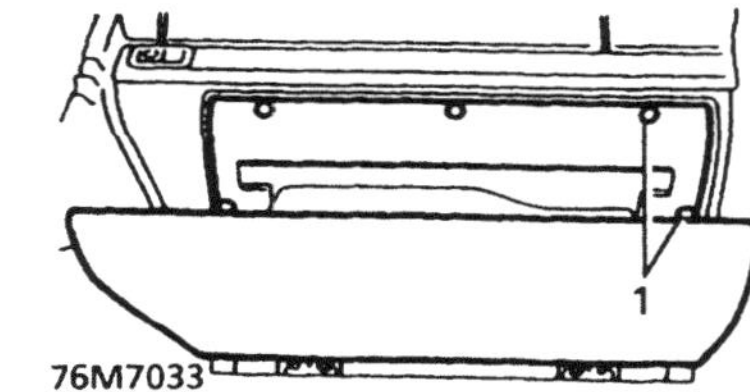

76M7033

2. Lower glove box liner. Release 2 clips to disengage cable latch from location.

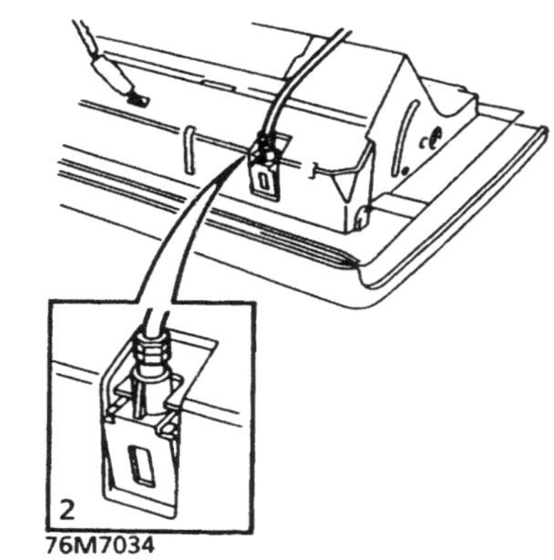

76M7034

3. Remove finisher from lock.

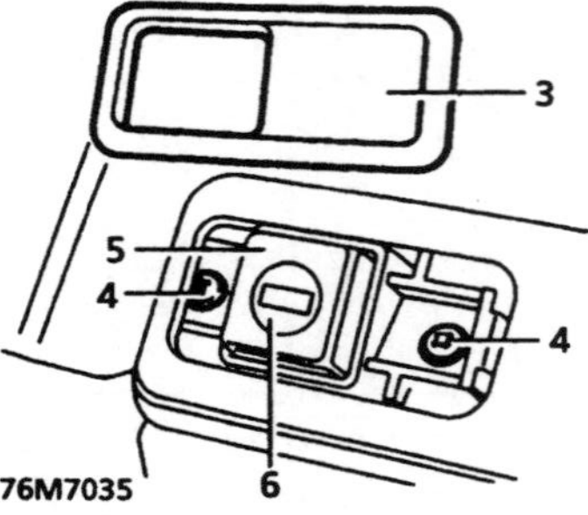

76M7035

4. Remove 2 screws securing lock and withdraw cable assembly from fascia.
5. Pry cover from lock button.
6. Insert key into lock, turn key through 45 degrees, remove barrel.

Refit

7. Insert barrel, turn to engage in button.
8. Remove key, fit cover to lock button.
9. Route release cable assembly into fascia. Engage cable latch to glove box.
10. Align glove box liner to fascia, tighten screws.
11. Close glove box lid.
12. Position glove box lock to fascia, check operation of latch.
13. If adjustment is necessary, release lock from fascia, loosen cable lock nut, adjust outer cable length. Tighten cable lock nut.
14. Reposition lock to fascia. Recheck operation of latch before securing lock with screws.
15. Fit finisher to lock.

GRAB HANDLE

Service repair no - 76.58.30

Remove

1. Pull down grab handle.
2. Remove 2 grab handle retaining screw access covers.
3. Remove 2 screws, remove grab handle.

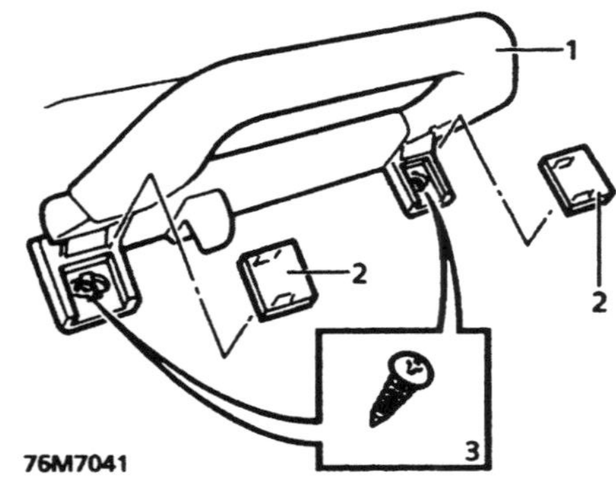

76M7041

Refit

4. Position grab handle, fit 2 retaining screws.
5. Fit 2 retaining screw access covers.
6. Release grab handle.

FRONT GRILLE

Service repair no - 76.55.03

Remove

1. Remove 6 screws securing grille.
2. Remove front grille.

1
2
1
76M7038

Refit

3. Reverse removal procedure.

EXTERIOR MIRROR

Service repair no - 76.10.52

Remove

1. Release cheater panel, disconnect 2 tweeter speaker connectors. Remove cheater panel.
2. Disconnect mirror multiplug.
3. Remove 3 screws, remove mirror.

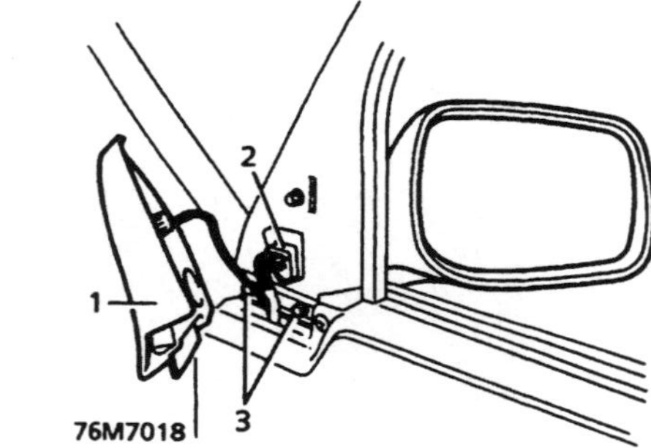

76M7018

Refit

4. Fit mirror, tighten 3 retaining screws.
5. Connect mirror multiplug.
6. Position cheater panel, connect 2 tweeter speaker connectors, secure panel to door.

INTERIOR MIRROR

Service repair no - 76.10.51

Remove

1. Remove cover.
2. If fitted, disconnect multiplug.
3. Remove mirror from windscreen location by pulling sharply downwards.

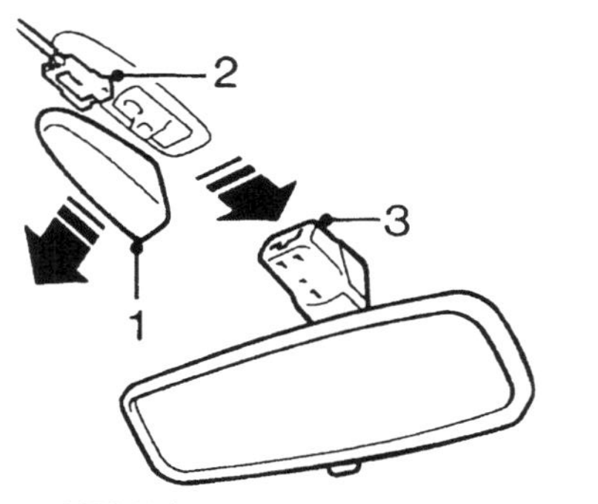

76M7039 A

Refit

4. Reverse removal procedure.

INTERIOR MIRROR - ELECTRONIC DIP - FROM 2000MY

Service repair no - 76.10.53

Remove

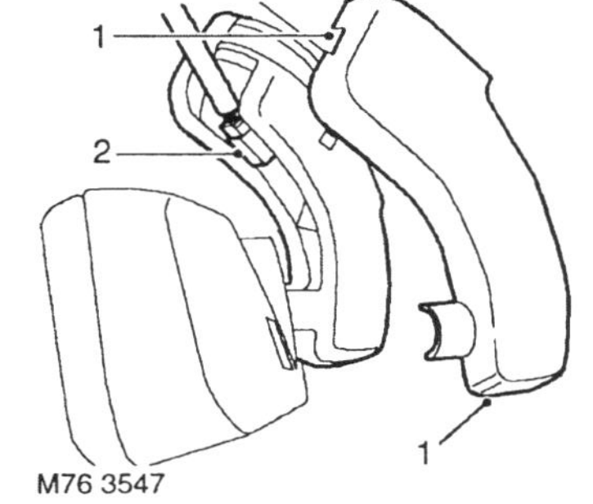

M76 3547

1. Release 2 clips securing interior mirror cover to interior mirror and remove cover.
2. Disconnect multiplug from interior mirror.

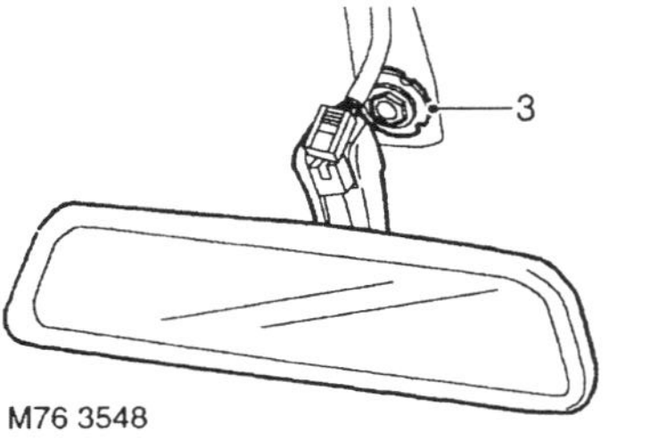

M76 3548

3. Rotate interior mirror to release from bracket and remove mirror.

Refit

4. Position mirror to bracket and rotate to secure.
5. Connect multiplug to interior mirror.
6. Fit interior mirror cover to interior mirror and secure clips.

PARCEL TRAY SUPPORT

Service repair no - 76.67.11

Remove

1. Release 2 squab catches and fold rear seats forward.

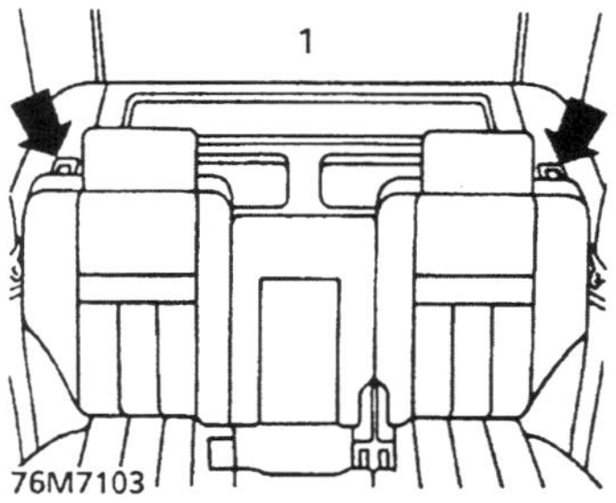

76M7103

2. Remove parcel tray.
3. Remove 3 studs securing parcel tray support. Remove support.

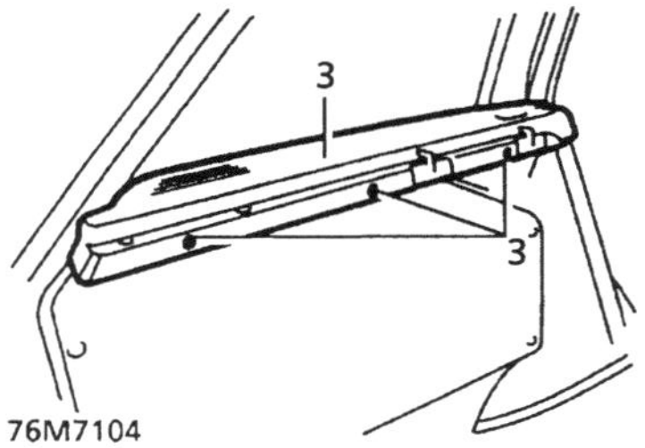

76M7104

Refit

4. Reverse removal procedure.

PARCEL TRAY SUPPORT - FROM 2000MY

Service repair no - 76.67.11

Remove

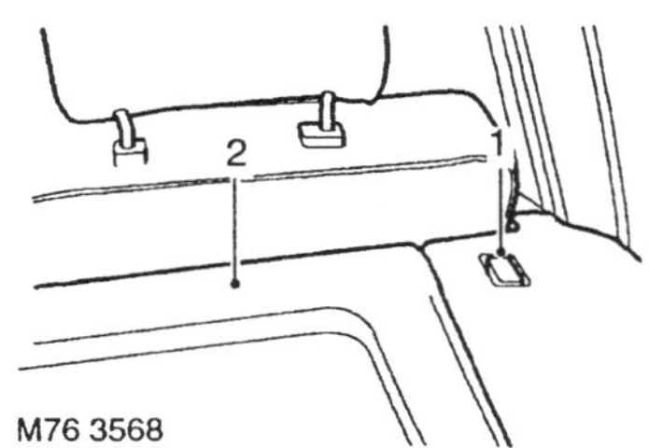

M76 3568

1. Release 2 squab catches and fold rear seats forward.
2. Remove parcel tray.

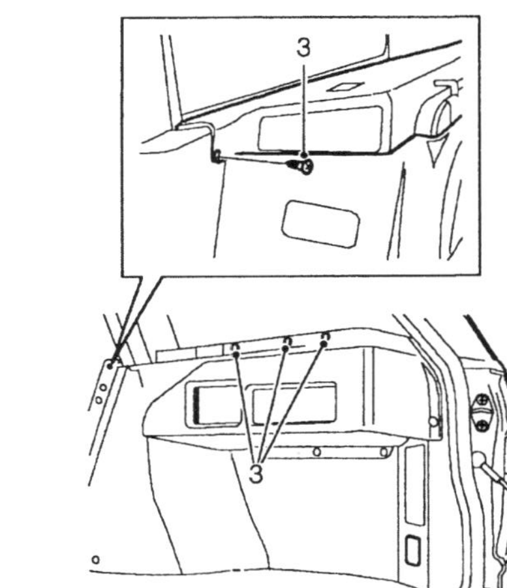

M76 3569

3. Remove 3 studs and 1 screw securing parcel tray support.

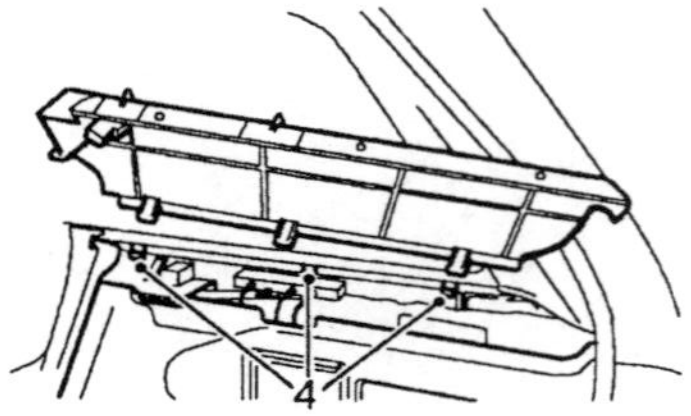

M76 3570

4. Release support tray from 3 clips and remove tray.

Refit

5. Position support tray and secure clips.
6. Secure support tray to trim with studs and screw.
7. Fit parcel tray.
8. Reposition seats and secure catches.

PARCEL TRAY SUPPORT TRIM

Service repair no - 76.67.12 - RH
Service repair no - 76.67.09 - LH

Remove

1. Remove parcel tray support. ***See this section.***
2. Remove 'D' post lower trim.
3. Release tailgate aperture seal from support trim flange.
4. Remove 3 trim studs.

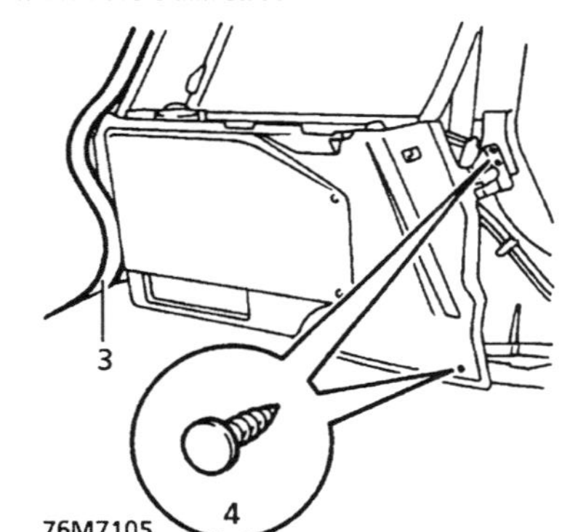

76M7105

LH Trim Only

5. Remove CD autochanger. ***See ELECTRICAL, Repair.***
6. Remove 2 nuts and 2 bolts securing sub-woofer assembly.

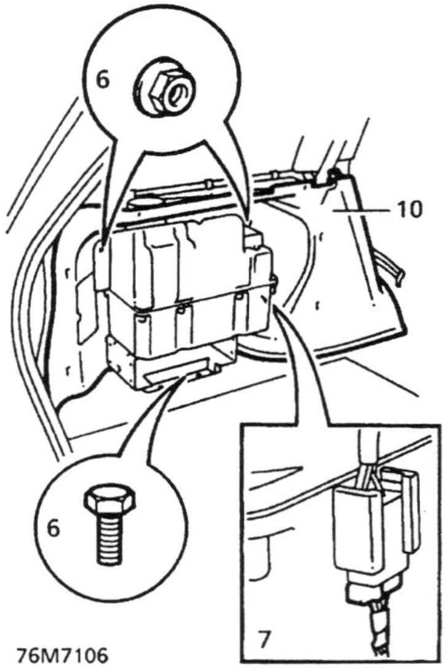

76M7106

7. Disconnect multiplug from sub-woofer.

Both Trim Panels

8. Release 2 sprag clips securing support trim to body.
9. Remove support trim panel.
10. **LH Trim Only:** Separate sub-woofer from trim panel.

Refit

11. Reverse removal procedure.

PARCEL TRAY SUPPORT TRIM - WITH NAVIGATION

Service repair no - 76.67.12

Remove

1. Remove parcel tray support. ***See this section.***
2. Remove satellite navigation computer. ***See ELECTRICAL, Repair.***

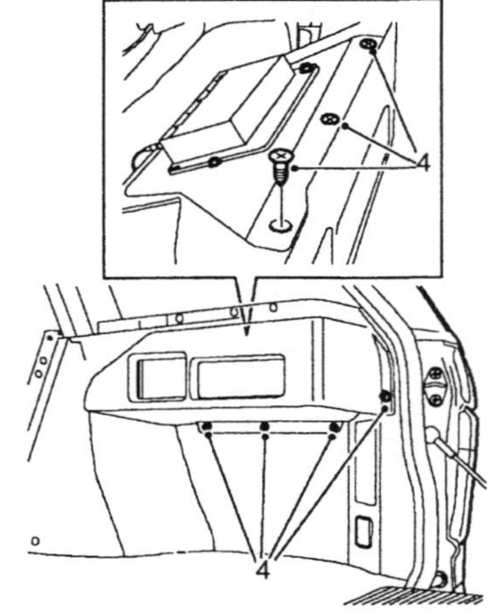

M76 3563

3. Remove 3 screws and 4 scrivets securing satellite navigation computer trim to parcel tray support trim and remove trim.

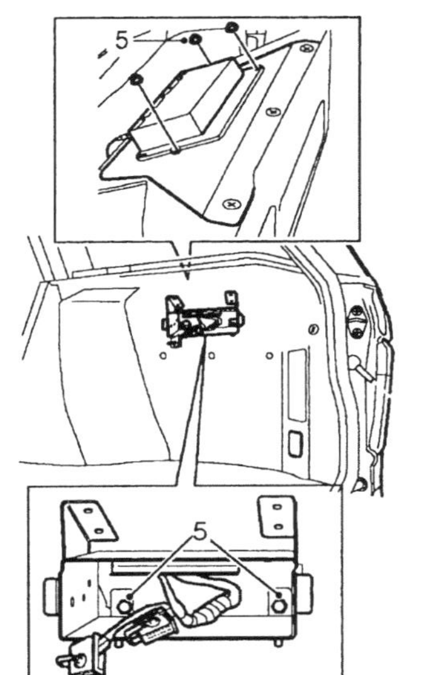

M76 3564

4. Remove 5 nuts securing satellite navigation computer bracket to support trim and remove bracket.

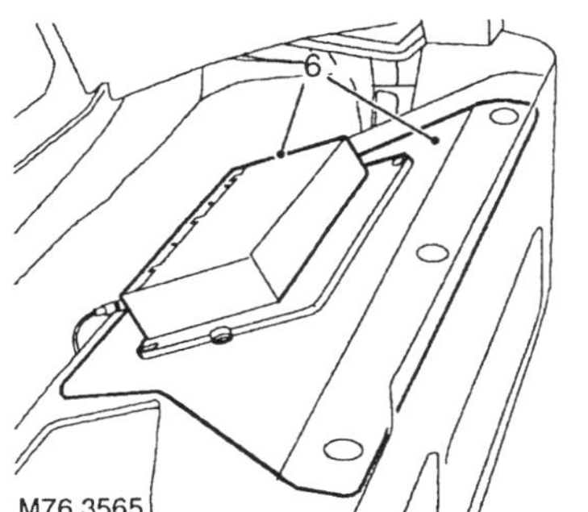

M76 3565

5. Position GPS receiver aside and remove mounting plate.
6. Remove power socket. ***See this section.***

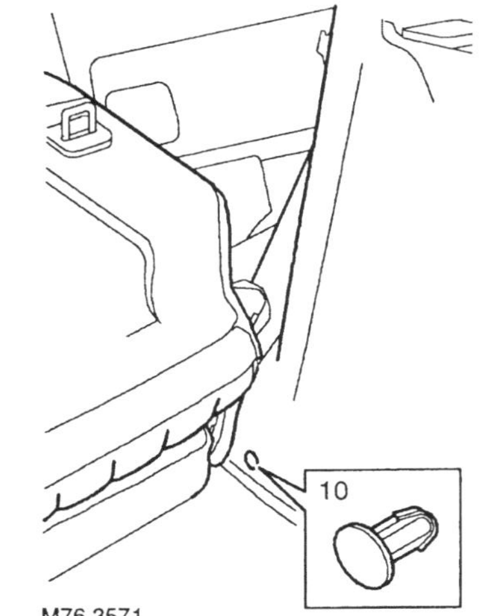

M76 3571

7. Remove trim clip securing support trim to body.

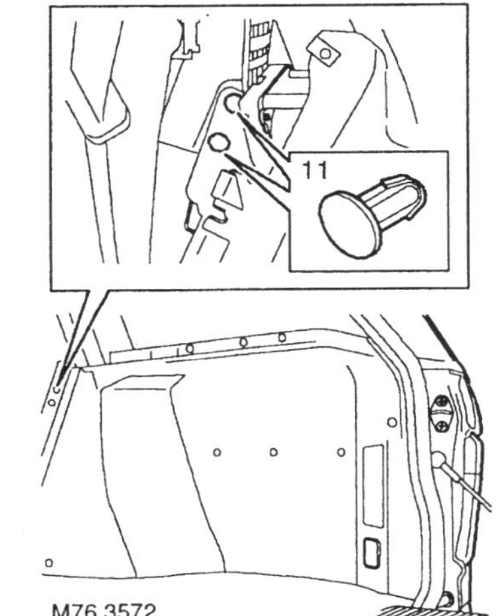

M76 3572

8. Move support trim forward and release 2 clips securing trim bracket to body.

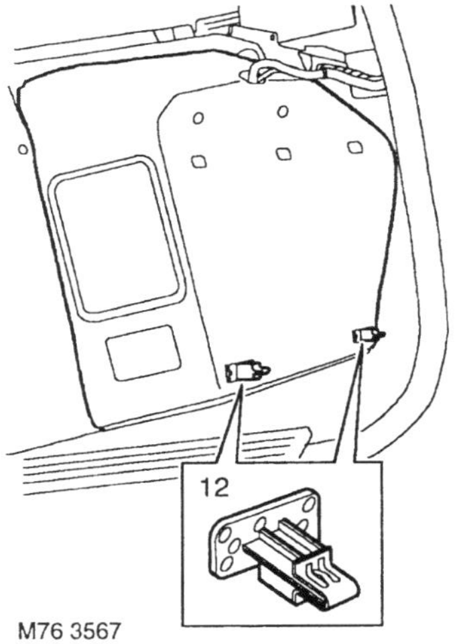

M76 3567

9. Release 2 clips securing trim to body and remove trim.

Refit

10. Position trim panel to body and secure clips.
11. Fit mounting bracket to body with trim clips.
12. Feed satellite navigation and power socket wires through correct holes, Push trim into place and secure with trim clip.
13. Position mounting bracket behind trim and feed mounted threads through holes in trim.
14. Position power socket bracket, feed wires through bracket and connect socket.
15. Fit socket to bracket and secure clip and screw.
16. Position mounting plate to top of trim and position GPS receiver to mounting plate.
17. Fit satellite navigation computer bracket to trim and secure with nuts.
18. Fit satellite navigation trim cover and secure with screws and trim clips.
19. Fit satellite navigation computer. ***See ELECTRICAL, Repair.***
20. Fit parcel tray support. ***See this section.***

A,B,D and E POST TRIMS

Remove

1. Remove aperture seal from appropriate area.
2. Remove retaining screws ('A' post lower trims)
3. Remove seat belt top mounting ('B' and 'D' post upper trims)
4. Release retaining clips, remove finisher.

Refit

5. Position finisher, secure with retaining clips and screws.
6. Fit seat belt top mounting. Tighten to ***25 Nm. (18lbf. ft)***
7. Secure aperture seal.

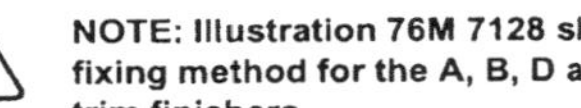

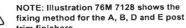

NOTE: Illustration 76M 7128 shows the fixing method for the A, B, D and E post trim finishers.

1. A post upper
2. A post lower left hand
3. A post lower right hand
4. B post upper
5. B post lower
6. D post upper
7. D post lower
8. E post

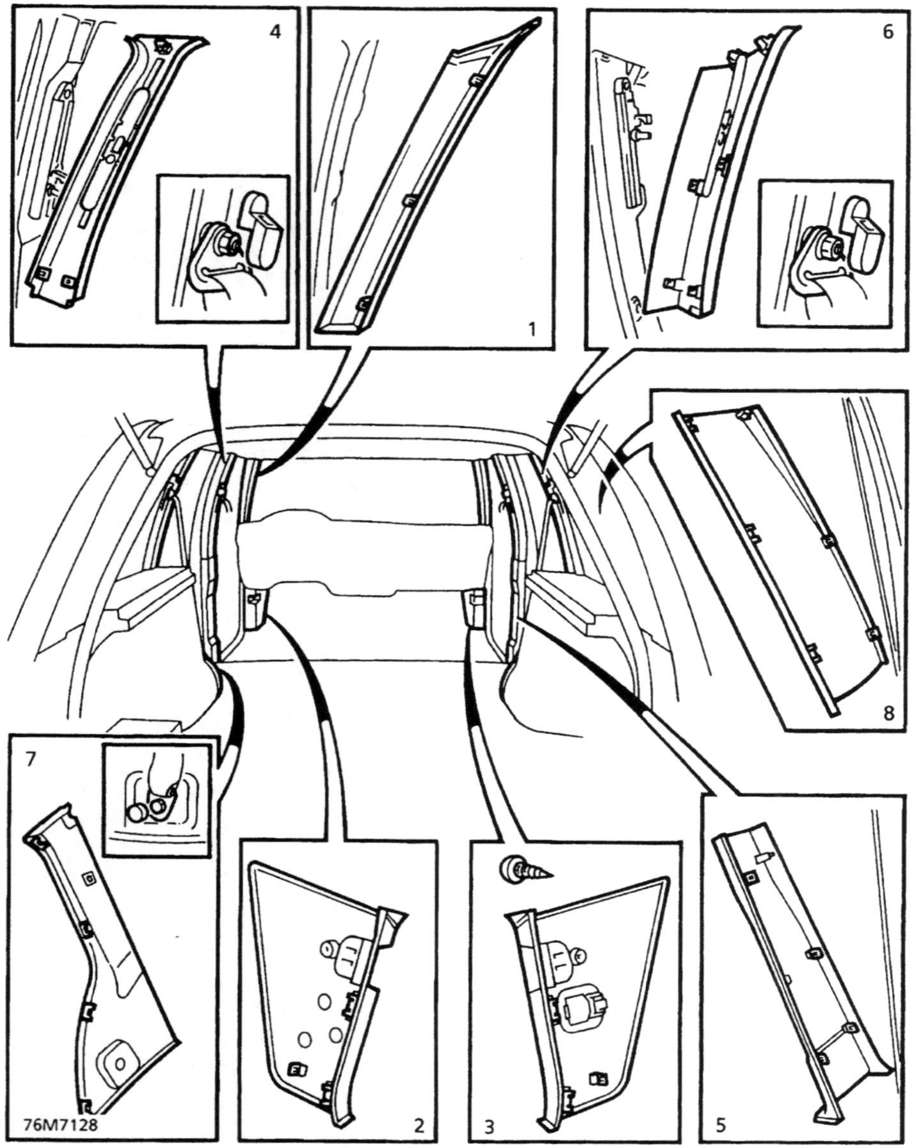

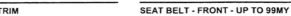

76M7128

'E' POST - EXTERIOR TRIM

Service repair no - 76.43.

Remove

1. Open upper tailgate.
2. Remove 3 screws securing trim to 'E' post.

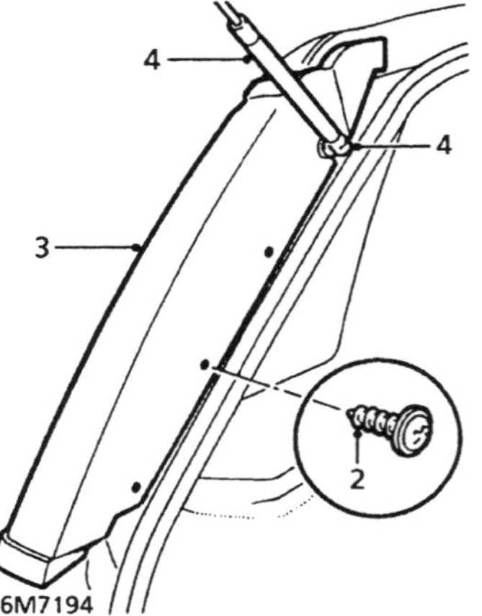

3. Remove trim.

Refit

4. Position trim to 'E' post, engage slot beneath special washer on tailgate strut ball joint and engage channel to rear edge of quarter glass.
5. Secure trim with screws.
6. Close tailgate.

SEAT BELT - FRONT - UP TO 99MY

Service repair no - 76.73.13

Remove

1. Remove lower 'B' post finisher.

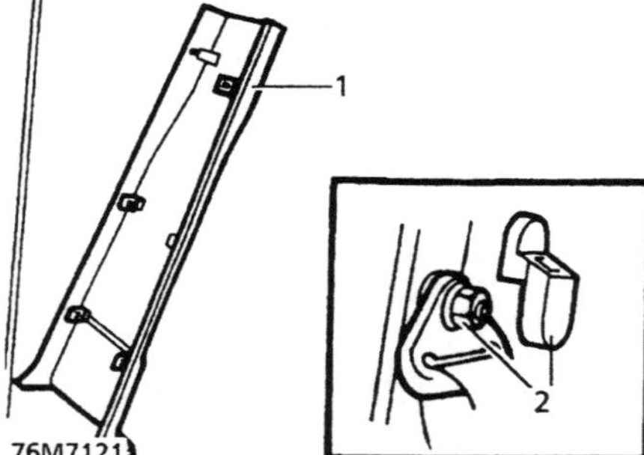
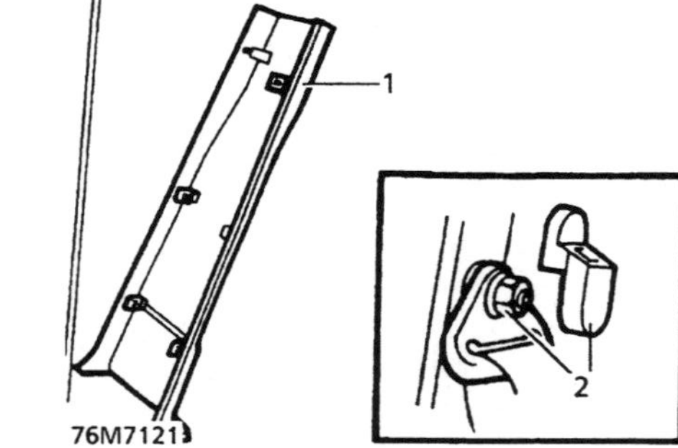

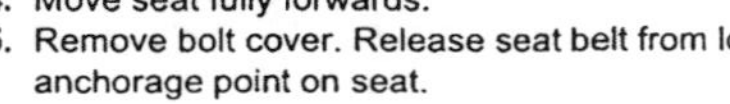

2. Remove cover and nut securing seat belt to upper anchorage point.
3. Release seat belt guide from 'B' post.
4. Move seat fully forwards.
5. Remove bolt cover. Release seat belt from lower anchorage point on seat.

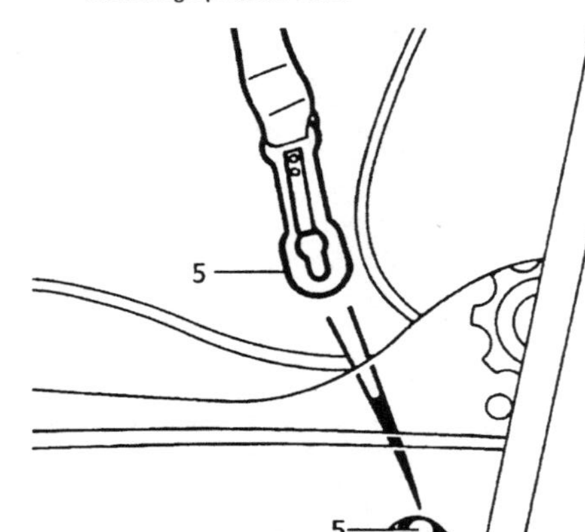

6. Remove bolt securing belt reel to 'B' post, remove belt reel.

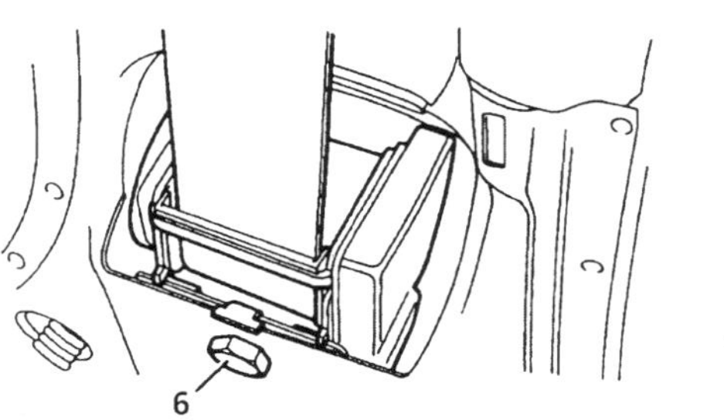

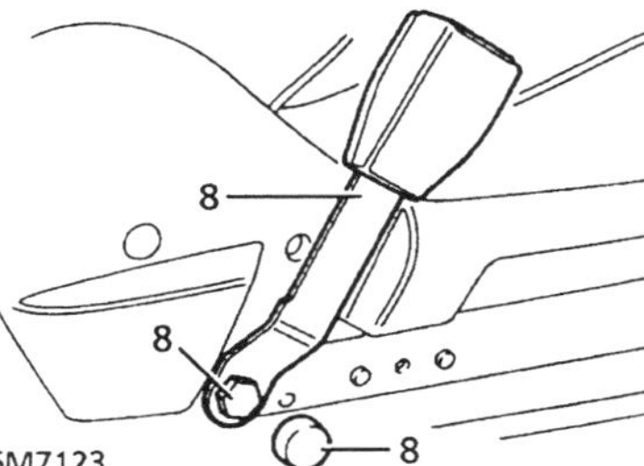

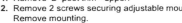

76M7123

7. Move seat fully rearwards.
8. Remove cover from seat belt stalk fixing. Remove bolt. Collect stalk.

Refit

9. Position seat belt stalk. Secure with retaining bolt. Tighten to ***35 Nm. (26 lbf.ft).*** Fit bolt cover.
10. Fit seat belt reel to 'B' post. Secure with retaining bolt. Tighten to ***35 Nm. (26 lbf.ft)***
11. Move seat fully forwards.
12. Secure seat belt to lower anchorage point. Fit bolt cover.

WARNING: Ensure that belt is correctly located before fitting bolt cover.

13. Align belt to upper anchorage point. Secure with nut. Tighten to ***25 Nm. (18 lbf.ft).*** Fit cover.
14. Secure seat belt guide to 'B' post.
15. Refit lower 'B' post finisher.

FRONT SEAT BELT ADJUSTABLE MOUNTING

Service repair no - 76.73.26

Remove

1. Remove 'B' post trim upper.
2. Remove 2 screws securing adjustable mounting. Remove mounting.

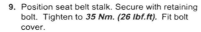

2
2
76M7098

Refit

3. Position adjustable mounting. Secure with screws. Tighten to ***25 Nm. (18 lbf.ft)***
4. Fit 'B' post trim upper.

SEAT BELT ADJUSTABLE MOUNTING - 'D' POST

Service repair no - 76.73.36

Remove

1. Remove 'D' post trim - upper.
2. Remove 2 screws securing adjustable mounting. Remove mounting.

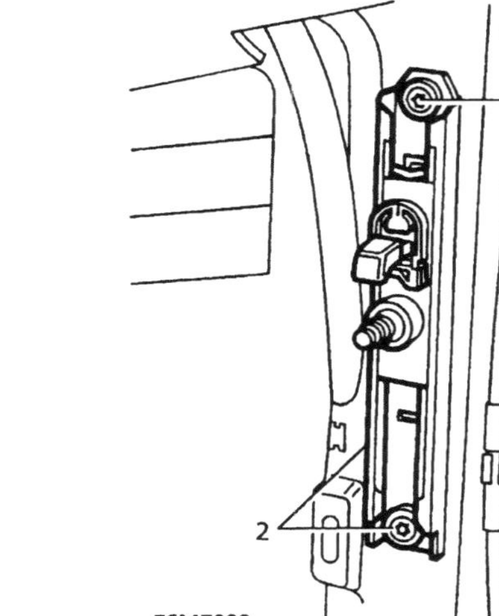

76M7099

Refit

3. Position adjustable mounting. Secure with screws. Tighten to ***25 Nm. (18 lbf.ft)***
4. Refit 'D' post trim - upper.

REAR SEAT BELT - CENTRE

Service repair no - 76.73.20

Remove

1. Remove right hand rear seat. ***See SEATS, Repair.***
2. Remove 3 screws securing squab hinge cover. Remove cover.

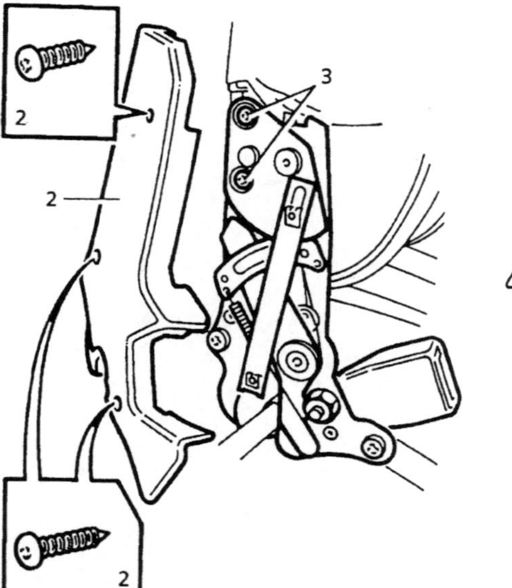

76M7114

3. Remove 2 bolts securing squab to cushion assembly.
4. Remove squab from cushion assembly.
5. Remove bolt and wave washer securing stalk to squab hinge. Remove stalk. Collect plain washer.
6. Release beaded edge of cushion cover from seat pan flange. Remove cushion cover/foam assembly.

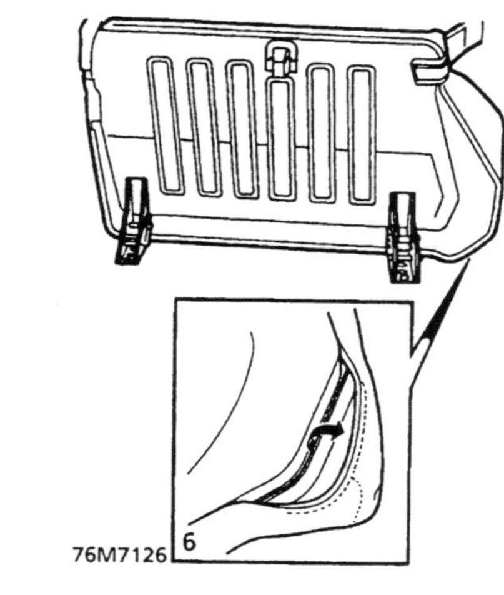
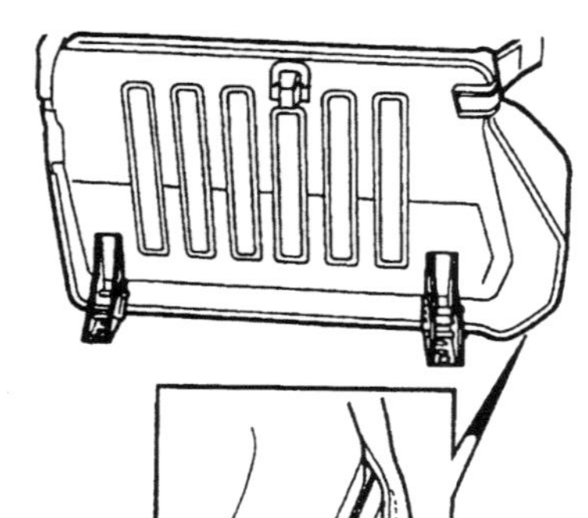

76M7126

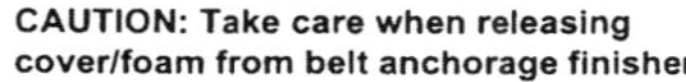

CAUTION: Take care when releasing cover/foam from belt anchorage finisher.

7. Remove 3 screws securing anchorage cover to seat pan. Remove cover in 2 pieces.

76M7115

8. Remove bolt securing seat belt to seat pan. Remove belt, collect spacer.

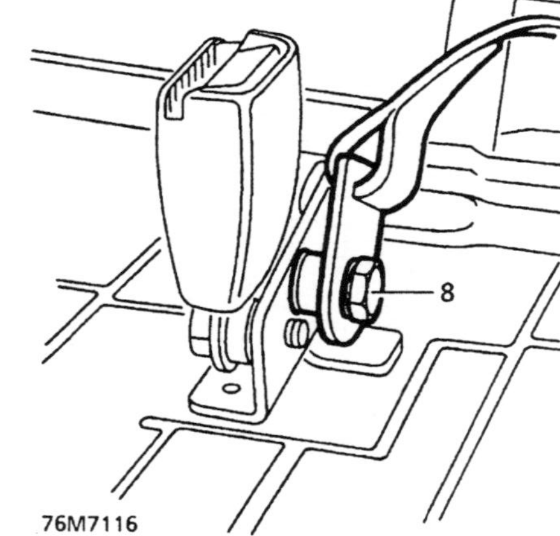

76M7116

Refit

9. Fit seat belt to seat pan. Secure with bolt and spacer. Tighten to ***35 Nm. (26 lbf.ft)***
10. Fit seat belt anchorage cover. Secure with screws.
11. Fit cushion assembly to seat pan. Secure beaded edge of cover to seat pan flange.
12. Fit stalk to squab hinge. Secure with bolt. Tighten to ***35 Nm. (26 lbf.ft)***
13. Position seat squab to cushion assembly. Secure with bolts. Tighten to ***45 Nm. (33 lbf.ft)***
14. Refit squab hinge cover. Secure with screws.
15. Refit rear seat assembly. ***See SEATS, Repair.***

REAR SEAT BELT - LEFT HAND

Service repair no - 76.73.23

Remove

1. Remove parcel shelf support trim. ***See this section.***
2. Remove 'D' post lower trim. ***See this section.***
3. Remove cover and nut securing seat belt to upper anchorage point.
4. Remove bolt securing seat belt reel.

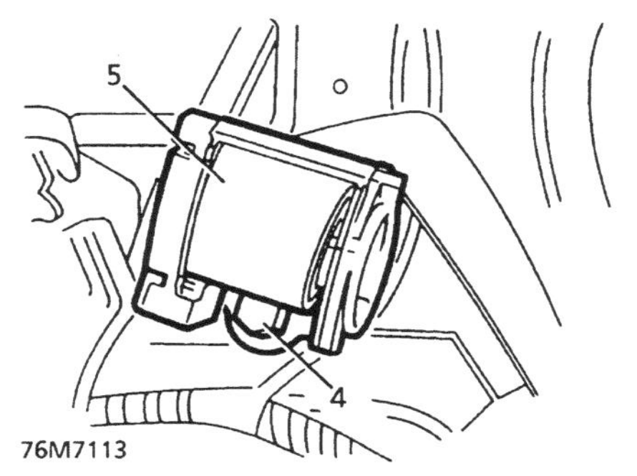

76M7113

5. Remove seat belt reel.
6. Remove left hand rear seat. ***See SEATS, Repair.***
7. Remove 3 screws securing squab hinge cover. Remove cover.

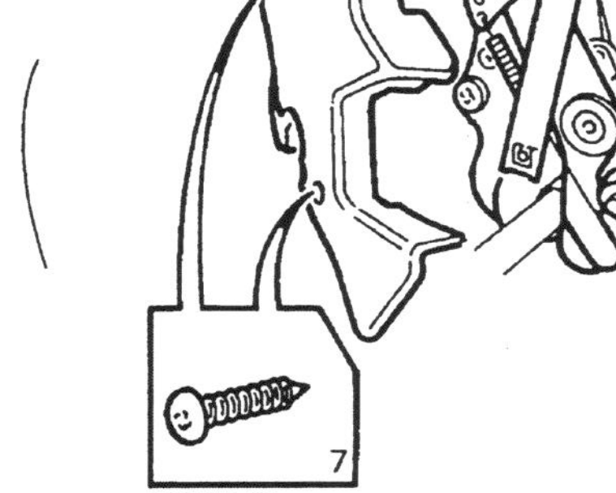

76M7112

8. Remove 2 bolts securing squab to cushion assembly.
9. Remove squab from cushion assembly.
10. Remove bolt and wave washer securing stalk to squab hinge.
11. Remove stalk. Collect plain washer.

Refit

12. Fit stalk to squab hinge. Secure with bolt. Tighten to ***35 Nm. (26 lbf.ft)***
13. Position seat squab to cushion assembly. Secure with bolts. Tighten to ***45 Nm. (33 lbf.ft)***
14. Refit squab hinge cover. Secure with screws.
15. Refit rear seat assembly. ***See SEATS, Repair.***
16. Position belt to upper anchorage point. Secure with nut. Tighten to ***25 Nm. (18 lbf.ft).*** Fit cover.
17. Position seat belt reel. Secure with bolt. Tighten to ***35 Nm. (26 lbf.ft)***
18. Fit 'D' post lower trim. ***See this section.***
19. Fit parcel shelf support trim. ***See this section.***

REAR SEAT BELT - RIGHT HAND

Service repair no - 76.73.24

Remove

1. Remove parcel shelf support trim. ***See this section.***
2. Remove 'D' post lower trim.
3. Remove cover and nut securing seat belt to upper anchorage point.
4. Remove bolt securing seat belt reel.

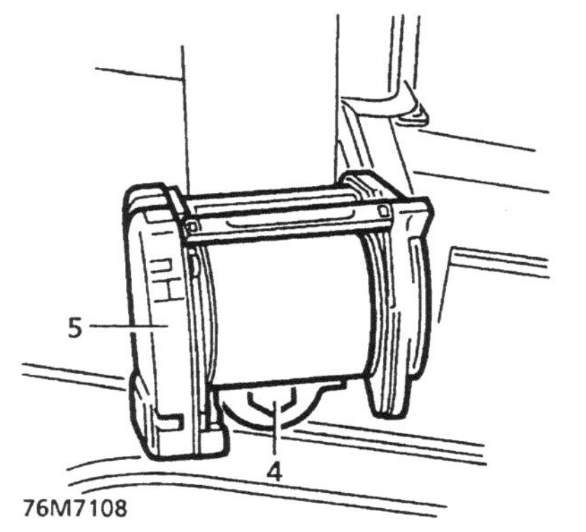

76M7108

5. Remove seat belt reel.
6. Remove right hand rear seat. ***See SEATS, Repair.***
7. Remove 3 screws securing squab hinge cover. Remove cover.

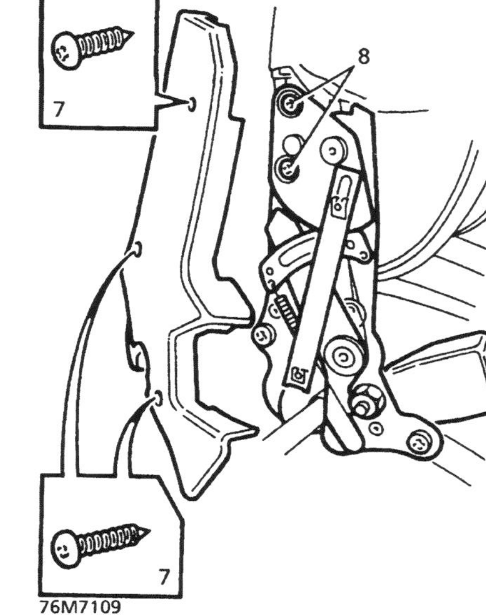

76M7109

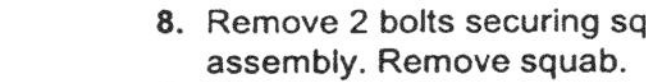

8. Remove 2 bolts securing squab to cushion assembly. Remove squab.
9. Release beaded edge of cushion cover from seat pan flange. Remove cushion cover/foam assembly.

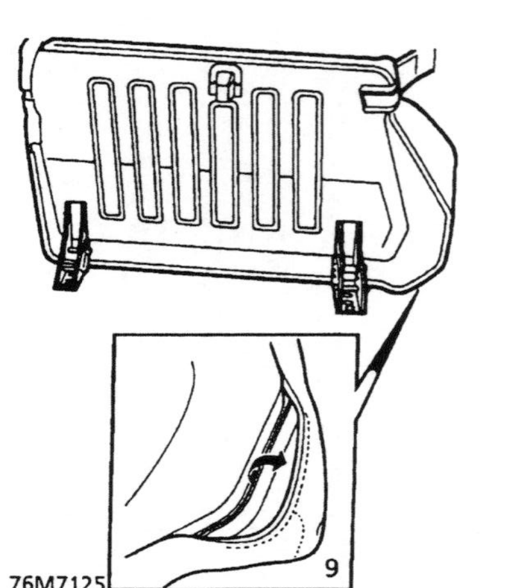

76M7125

> ⚠ **CAUTION: Take care when releasing cover/foam from belt anchorage finisher.**

10. Remove 3 screws securing anchorage cover to seat pan. Remove cover in 2 pieces.

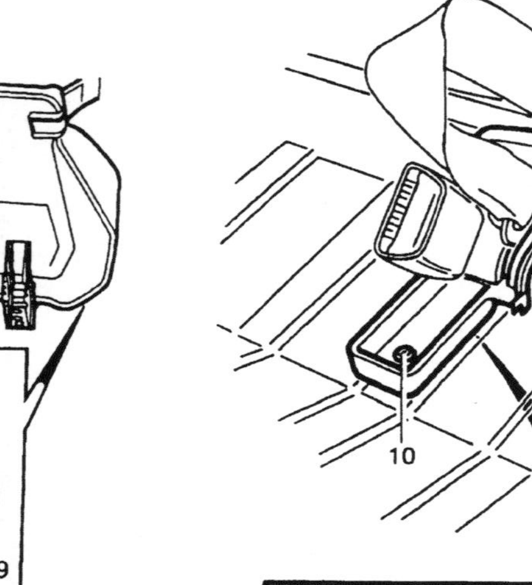
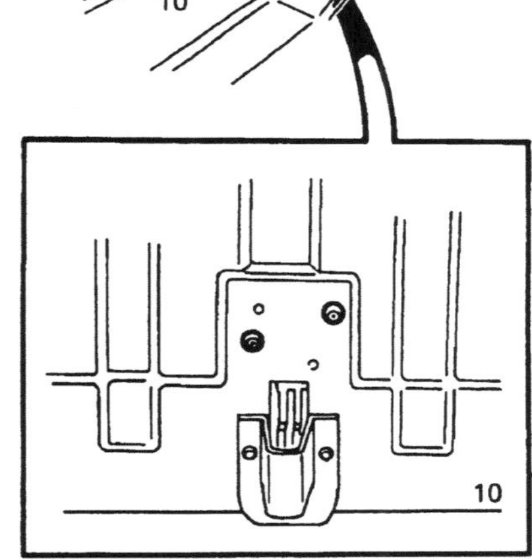

76M7110

11. Remove bolt securing stalk to seat pan. Remove stalk. Collect 2 spacers and wave washer.

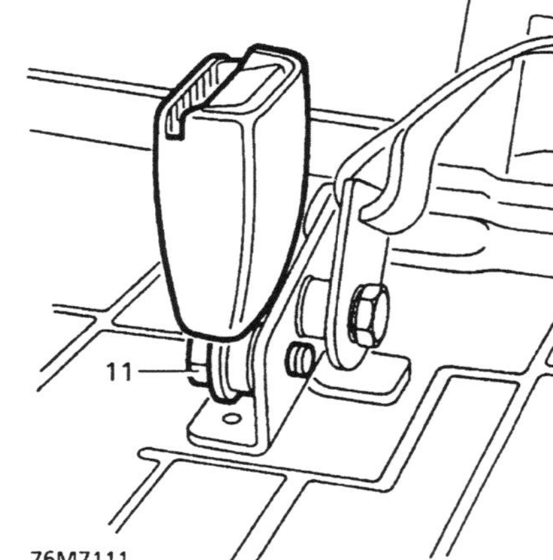

76M7111

Refit

12. Fit stalk to seat pan. Secure with bolt, spacers and wave washer. Tighten to ***35 Nm. (26 lbf.ft)***
13. Fit seat belt anchorage cover. Secure with screws.
14. Fit cushion assembly to seat pan. Secure beaded edge of cover to seat pan flange.
15. Fit stalk to squab hinge. Secure with bolt. Tighten to ***35 Nm. (26 lbf.ft)***
16. Position seat squab to cushion assembly. Secure with bolts. Tighten to ***45 Nm. (33 lbf.ft)***
17. Refit squab hinge cover. Secure with screws.
18. Refit rear seat assembly. ***See SEATS, Repair.***
19. Position belt to upper anchorage point. Secure with nut. Tighten to ***25 Nm. (18 lbf.ft).*** Fit cover.
20. Position seat belt reel. Secure with bolt. Tighten to ***35 Nm. (26 lbf.ft)***
21. Fit 'D' post lower trim.
22. Fit parcel shelf support trim. ***See this section.***

SLIDING ROOF - ELECTRIC

Service repair no - 76.82.44

Remove

1. Remove headlining. ***See this section.***
2. Disconnect motor multiplug.
3. Disconnect sliding roof drain tubes.
4. Remove 8 bolts securing sliding roof.
5. With assistance, remove 2 remaining bolts. Remove sliding roof.
6. Remove seal from sliding roof.

Refit

7. Ensure mating faces are clean.
8. Fit new seal to sliding roof.
9. With assistance, position sliding roof. Fit 2 bolts.
10. Fit remaining bolts.
11. Connect drain tubes. Secure with clips.
12. Connect motor multiplug.
13. Refit headlining. ***See this section.***

76M7027

HEADLINING - SLIDING ROOF

Service repair no - 76.64.15

Remove

1. Remove upper trims from 'A','B','D' & 'E' posts. ***See this section.***

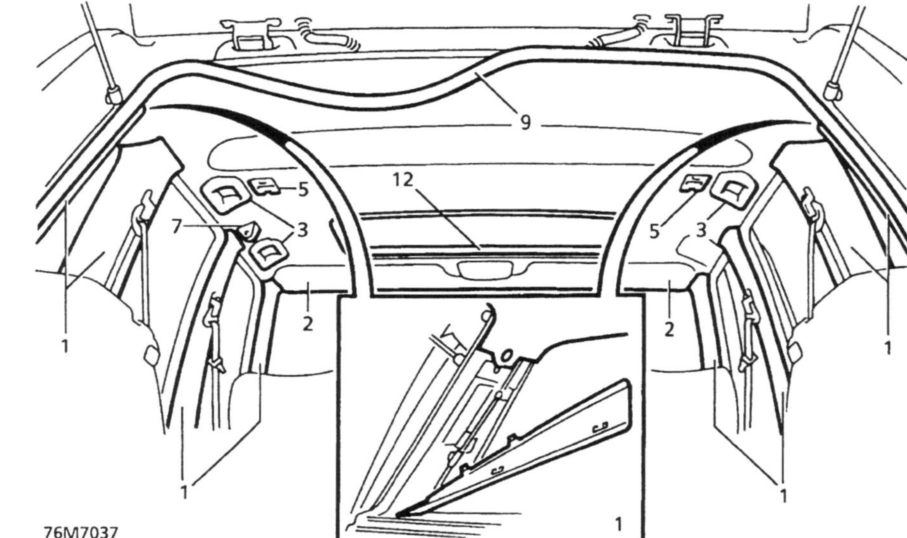

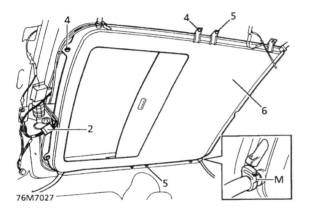

76M7037

2. Remove both sun visors. ***See this section.***
3. Remove grab handles. ***See this section.***
4. Remove parcel tray support trim. ***See this section.***
5. Remove interior lamps. ***See ELECTRICAL, Repair.***
6. Remove front courtesy lamp. ***See ELECTRICAL, Repair.***
7. Remove ultrasonic sensor. ***See ELECTRICAL, Repair.***
8. Fold down rear seat squabs. Recline front seat squabs.
9. Release aperture sealing rubbers at tops of doors and tailgate.
10. Release sun visor clip retaining screw cover plugs.
11. Remove sun visor retaining clip screws. Remove clips.
12. Remove sun roof aperture finisher.
13. Remove 2 headlining grab handle blanks.
14. Remove 2 studs securing rear of headlining.
15. With assistance remove headlining.

Refit

16. Reverse removal procedure.

SUNROOF DRAIN TUBE - FRONT

Service repair no - 76.82.21

Remove

1. Remove headlining. ***See this section.***
2. Remove wheel arch liner. ***See this section.***
3. Release drain tube from sunroof.

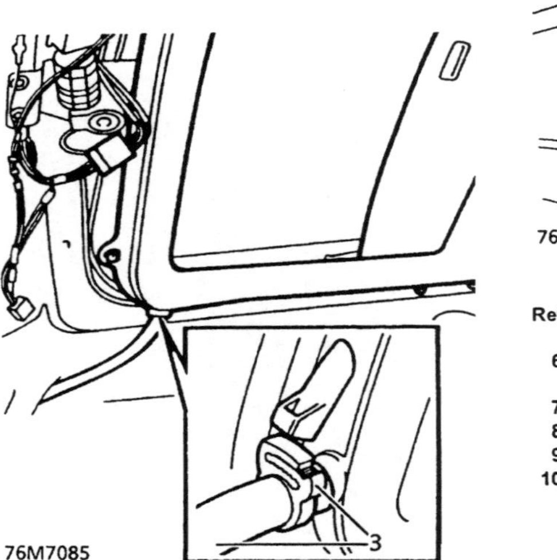

76M7085

4. Release drain tube grommet from body behind wheel arch liner.
5. Tie draw string to one end of drain tube and pull tube from 'A' post.

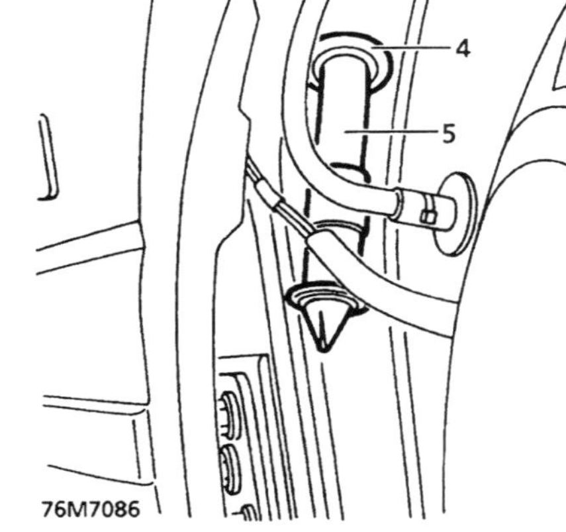

76M7086

Refit

6. Tie draw string to new drain tube and pull through 'A' post.
7. Fit grommet to drain tube, secure to body.
8. Secure drain tube to sunroof.
9. Fit headlining. ***See this section.***
10. Refit wheel arch liner. ***See this section.***

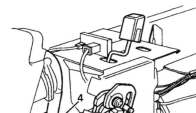

SUNROOF DRAIN TUBE - REAR

Service repair no - 76.82.22

Remove

1. Remove headlining. ***See this section.***

NOTE: Ensure that parcel shelf support panel is removed from side of drain tube to be removed.

2. Release clip from drain tube.

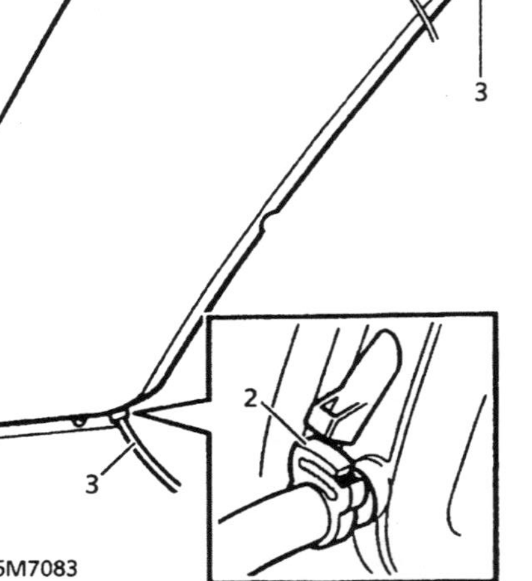
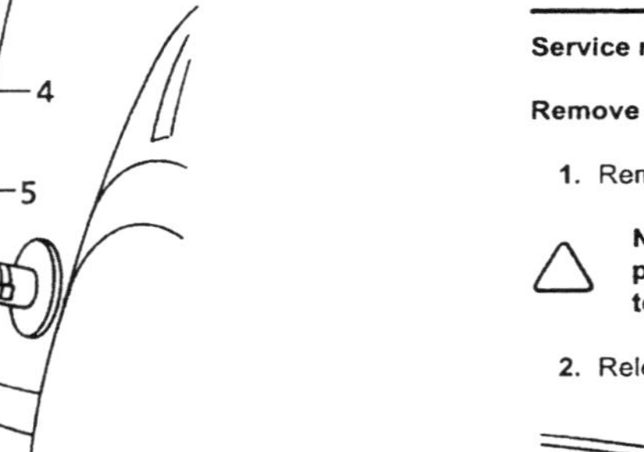
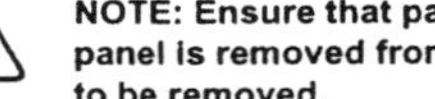
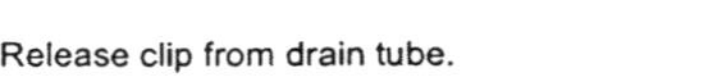

76M7083

3. Disconnect drain tube from sunroof.
4. Remove drain tube from wheel arch grommet.

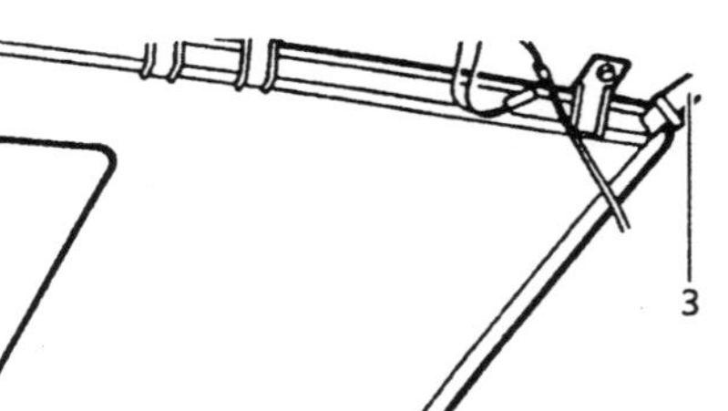

76M7084

Refit

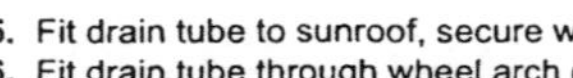
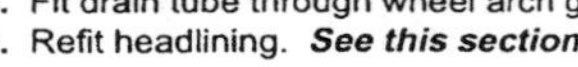

5. Fit drain tube to sunroof, secure with clip.
6. Fit drain tube through wheel arch grommet.
7. Refit headlining. ***See this section.***

SUNROOF - WIND DEFLECTOR

Service repair no - 76.82.31

Remove

1. Open sunroof panel.

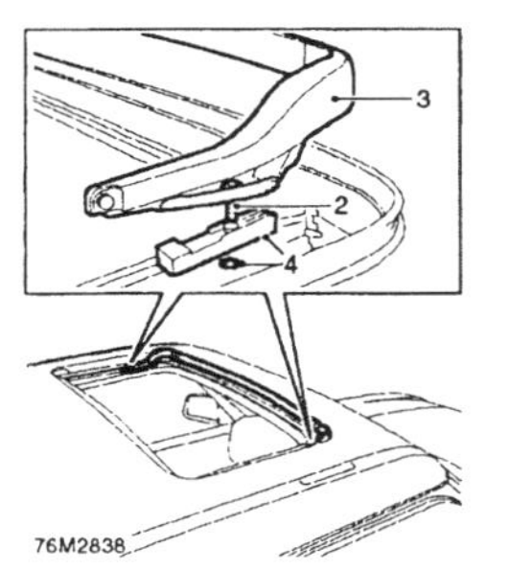

2. Remove 2 Torx screws securing wind deflector to sunroof frame.
3. Remove wind deflector assembly.
4. Collect 2 spacer blocks and 2 nylon washers from sunroof frame.

Refit

5. Position nylon washers and spacer blocks to sunroof frame.
6. Align wind deflector assembly and secure with Torx screws. Torque tighten Torx screws to ***2 Nm (1.5 lbf.ft).***
7. Close sunroof panel.

SUNROOF - PANEL

Service repair no - 76.82.05

Remove

1. Remove wind deflector. ***See this section.***
2. Tilt the sunroof panel.

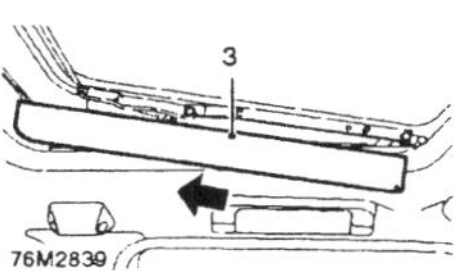

3. Remove 2 mechanism covers by sliding rearward.

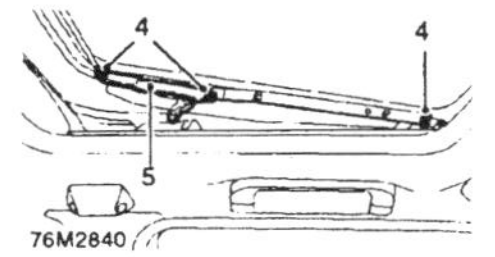

4. Remove 4 Torx screws and 2 'C' clips, connecting mechanism to sunroof panel.
5. Collect 2 slide brackets.
6. Release sunroof panel from locating pins.
7. Remove sunroof panel.

Refit

8. Lightly grease mechanism.
9. Position sunroof panel to locating pins.
10. Fit slide brackets.
11. Fit 'C' clips and Torx screws, do not tighten at this stage.
12. Adjust sunroof panel. ***See Adjustment.***
13. Fit wind deflector. ***See this section.***

SUNROOF - SUNSHADE

Service repair no - 76.82.03

Remove

1. Remove sunroof panel. ***See this section.***
2. Remove wind deflector. ***See this section.***
3. Remove front map/courtesy lamp. ***See ELECTRICAL, Repair.***
4. Wind mechanism (manually) in a clockwise direction to open position using sunroof key.

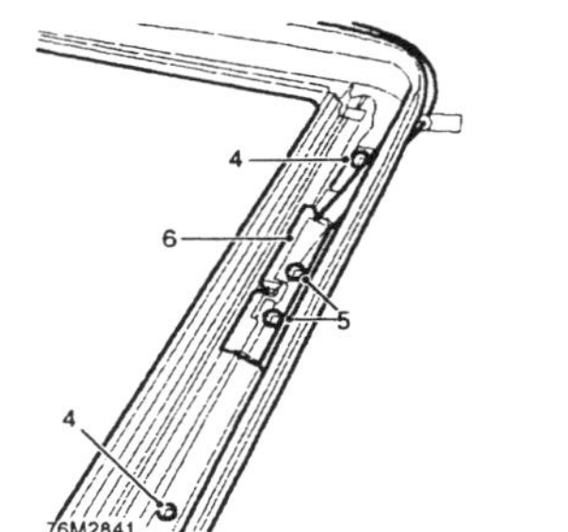

5. Remove 2 screws securing RH guide assembly.
6. Remove 2 screws securing RH drive cable locator.
7. Remove the drive cable locator.
8. Move LH guide assembly aside.
9. Remove sunshade.
10. Collect 4 slide clips.

Refit

11. Position sunshade to LH guide assembly and insert clips.
12. Position RH guide assembly to sunshade and insert clips.
13. Secure RH guide assembly with screws and torque tighten front screws to ***3 Nm (2.2 lbf.ft)*** and rear screws to ***1.5 Nm (1.1 lbf.ft).***
14. Position drive cable locator and secure with screws and torque tighten screws to ***3 Nm (2.2 lbf.ft).***
15. Fit wind deflector. ***See this section.***
16. Wind mechanism in an anti-clockwise direction to closed position using sunroof key.
17. Fit front map/courtesy lamp. ***See ELECTRICAL, Repair.***
18. Fit sunroof panel. ***See this section.***

SUNROOF - MOTOR

Service repair no - 76.82.53

Remove

1. Close sunroof panel.
2. Remove front map/courtesy lamp. ***See ELECTRICAL, Repair.***

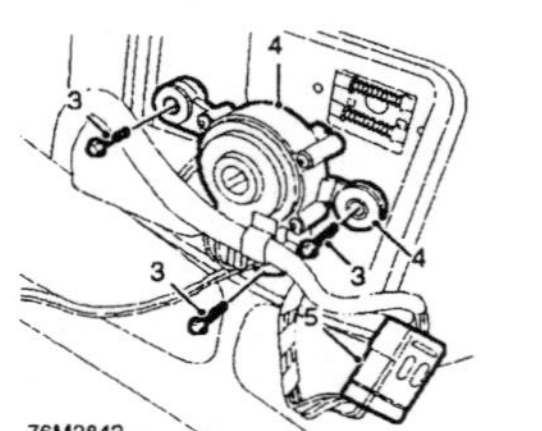

76M2842

3. Remove 3 screws securing sunroof motor to mounting bracket.
4. Remove motor and collect spacers.
5. Remove sunroof motor multiplug from mounting clip and disconnect multiplug.

Refit

6. If position of sunroof motor is not known, synchronise motor to closed position before fitment as follows:
Connect motor to motor multiplug. With ignition in position I or II, operate sunroof switch to open position. Press and hold sunroof switch to closed position until motor stops.
7. Connect motor multiplug and secure to mounting clip.
8. Fit spacers to motor.
9. Position motor to mounting bracket and secure with screws. Torque tighten screws to ***2 Nm (1.5 lbf.ft).***
10. Fit front map/courtesy lamp. ***See ELECTRICAL, Repair.***

SUNROOF - CABLE

Service repair no - 76.82.14

Remove

1. Remove sunroof panel. ***See this section.***
2. Remove sunroof motor. ***See this section.***

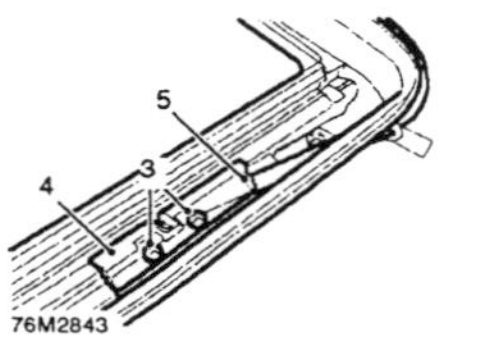

76M2843

3. Remove 2 screws securing the cable locator.
4. Remove cable locator.
5. Remove cable from slide.
6. Withdraw cable from tube.

Refit

7. Grease cable.
8. Feed cable into tube and locate into slide.
9. Position locator and secure with screws. Torque tighten screws to ***3 Nm (2.2 lbf.ft).***
10. Fit the sunroof motor. ***See this section.***
11. Fit the sunroof panel. ***See this section.***

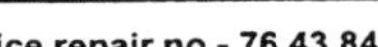

SUN VISOR

Service repair no - 76.10.47

Remove

1. Release visor from clip.
2. Remove 3 visor retaining screws.

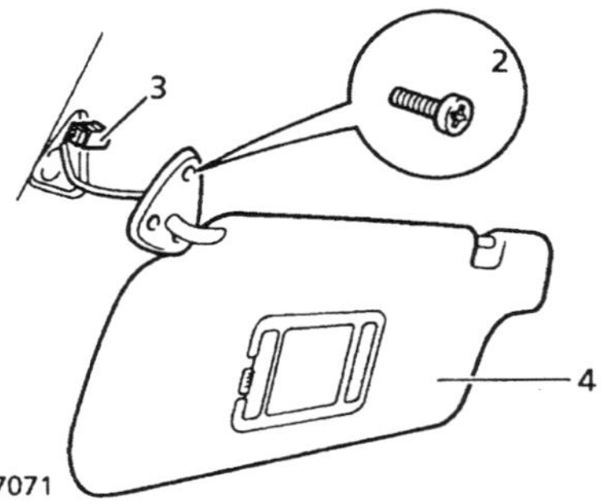

76M7071

3. Disconnect visor lamp multiplug.
4. Remove visor.
5. Remove clip if required. Carefully lever plastic tag down.

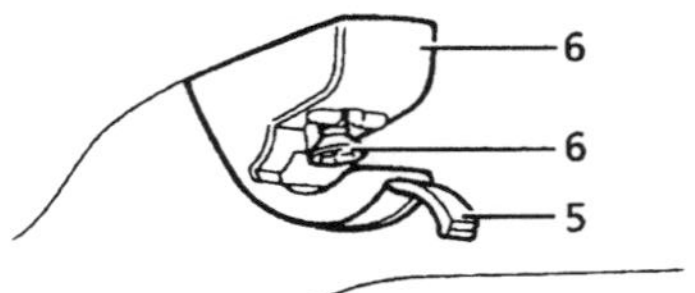

76M7072

6. Remove screw, remove clip.

Refit

7. Reverse removal procedure.

SILL FINISHER

Service repair no - 76.43.84

Remove

1. Remove 3 screws securing front tread plate.
2. Remove 2 screws securing rear tread plate.
3. Remove trim stud securing rear of sill finisher.
4. Release 8 clips securing finisher to sill.
5. Remove sill finisher.

Refit

6. Renew clips as necessary.
7. Reverse removal procedure.

TAILGATE - UPPER

Service repair no - 76.28.29

Remove

1. Remove both 'E' post finishers.
2. Remove 2 trim fixing studs. Release headlining from 'E' posts.

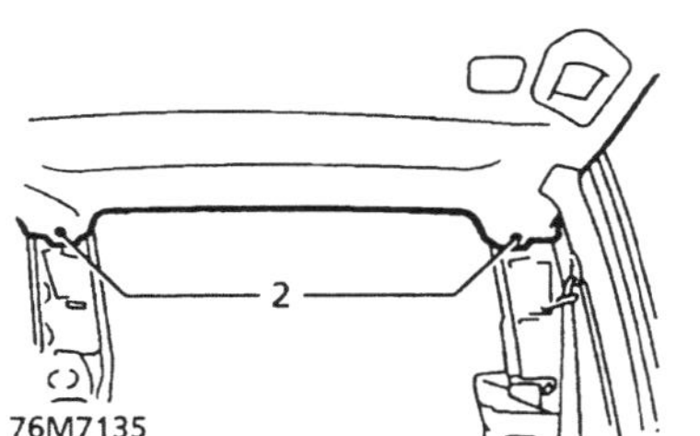

76M7135

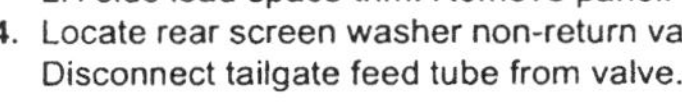

3. Release 4 turn buckles securing access panel to LH side load space trim. Remove panel.
4. Locate rear screen washer non-return valve. Disconnect tailgate feed tube from valve.

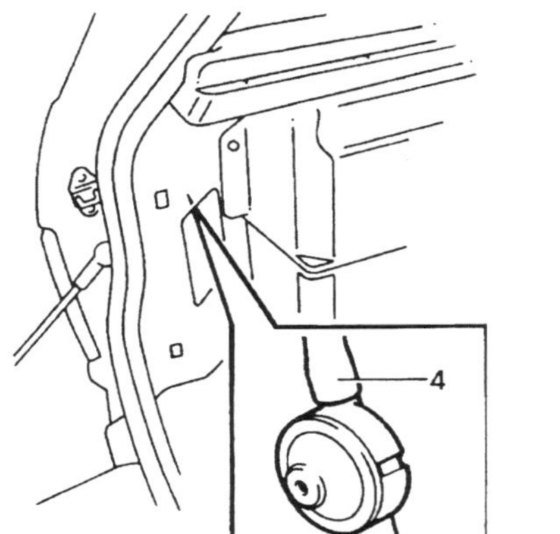
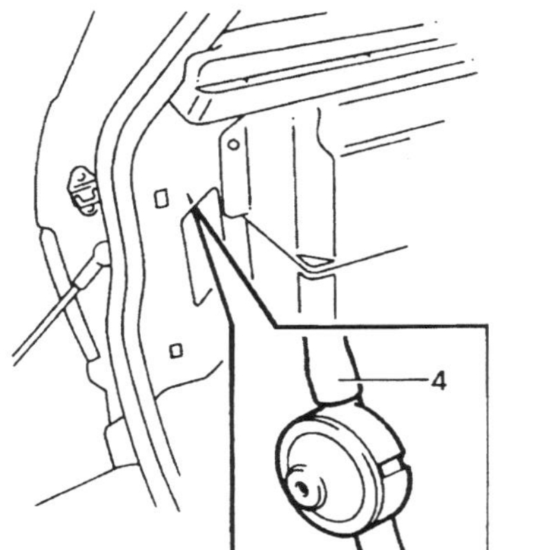

76M7136

5. Attach draw string to tube to aid re-assembly.
6. Release tailgate harness protective sleeve from roof panel.

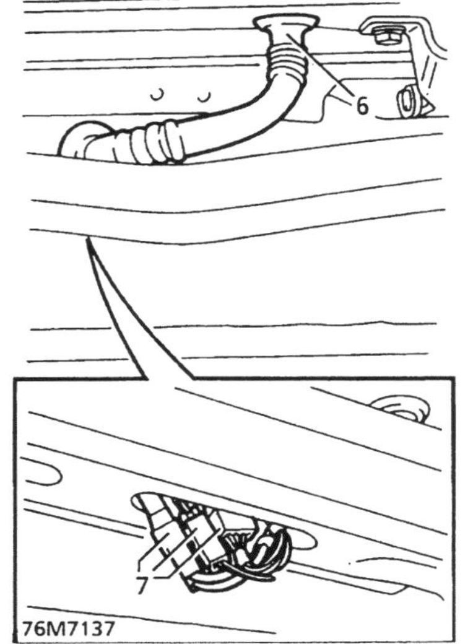

76M7137

7. Disconnect 3 tailgate harness multiplugs from body harness. Pull plugs out through hole in roof panel.
8. Pull screen washer tube out through hole in roof panel. Disconnect draw string.
9. Mark outline of hinge on tailgate to aid re-assembly.
10. Apply protective tape to roof panel before releasing tailgate.
11. With assistance, disconnect gas struts from tailgate.
12. With assistance, remove 4 bolts securing hinges to tailgate. Remove tailgate.

Refit

13. With assistance, position tailgate to hinges. Align marks. Secure with bolts. Tighten to ***25 Nm. (18 lbf.ft)***
14. With assistance, connect gas struts to tailgate.
15. Remove protective tape from roof panel.
16. Attach draw string to washer tube. Pull tube along roof into position at 'E' post. Remove draw string.
17. Connect tube to non-return valve.
18. Feed 3 tailgate harness multiplugs through roof panel. Connect to body harness.
19. Secure tailgate harness protective sleeve to roof panel.
20. Reposition headlining at 'E' posts. Secure with studs.
21. Fit load space access panel. Secure with turn buckles.
22. Fit both 'E' post finishers.

Adjust

23. Check alignment of lower tailgate. ***See this section.***
24. Align tailgate to aperture by adjusting position of hinges on tailgate or body.
25. Align tailgate to adjacent body panels by adjusting position of hinges on body.

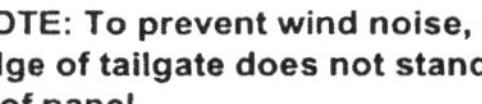

NOTE: To prevent wind noise, ensure top edge of tailgate does not stand proud of roof panel.

TAILGATE - LOWER

Service repair no - 76.28.30

Remove

1. Remove parcel tray support trim from RH side of luggage area. ***See this section.***
2. Disconnect tailgate harness multiplug from body harness. Release grommet from lower of 'E' post. Pull harness from body.

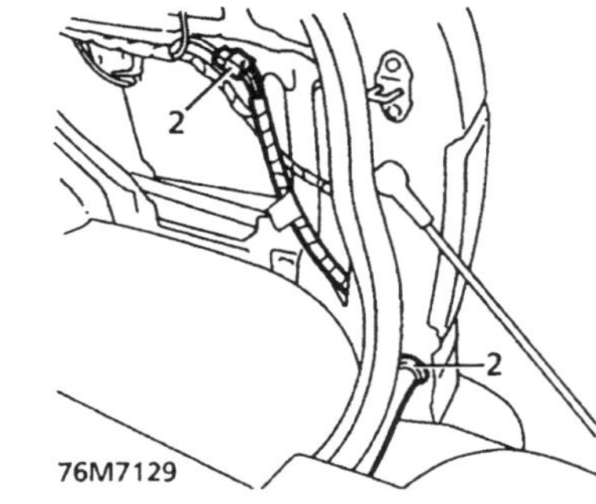

76M7129

3. Fit protection under tailgate.
4. Mark outline of hinges to body to aid reassembly.
5. Remove bolt securing each check strap to body. Collect spacer and fibre sealing washer.

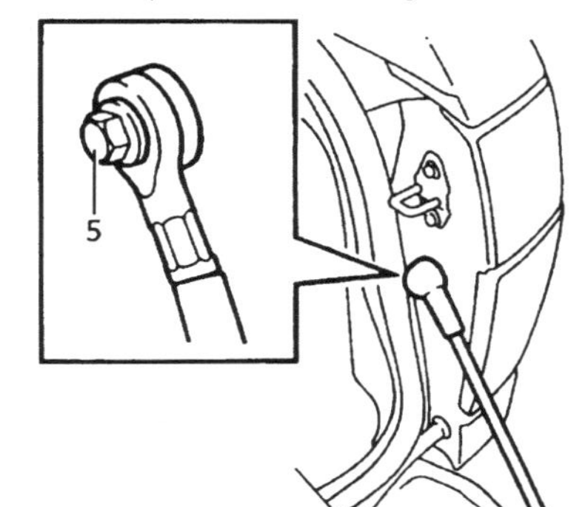

76M7130

6. With assistance, remove bolts securing tailgate hinges to body. Remove tailgate complete with hinges.

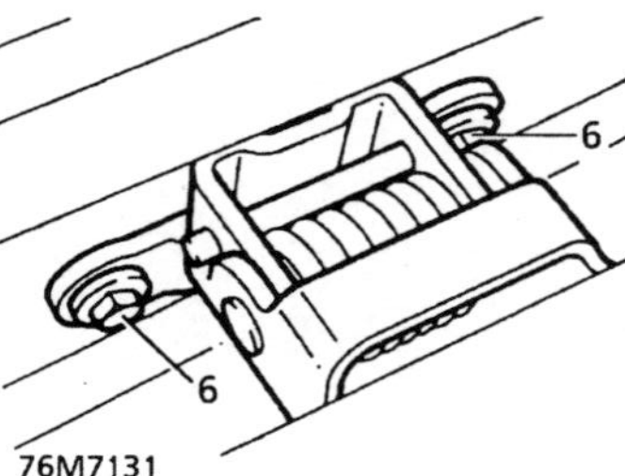

76M7131

Refit

7. With assistance, position tailgate to body. Secure with bolts. Tighten to ***25 Nm. (18 lbf.ft)***
8. Position support stays with spacer and sealing washer next to body. Tighten to ***22 Nm. (16 lbf.ft)***
9. Remove protection.
10. Feed tailgate harness into 'E' post. Connect multiplug to body harness.
11. Fit harness grommet to 'E' post.
12. Fit parcel tray support trim. ***See this section.***

Adjust

13. Align tailgate to aperture by adjusting position of hinges on tailgate or body.
14. Align tailgate to adjacent body panels by adjusting position of hinge to tailgate.
15. When tailgate alignment is correct, adjust height and inboard/outboard position of each striker. Tighten striker bolts. Check for correct latching.
16. Slacken bolts, re-adjust striker positions as necessary. Tighten to ***8 Nm. (6 lbf.ft)***

TAILGATE STRIKER

Service repair no - 76.37.26

Remove

1. Remove 2 bolts securing striker. Remove striker.

76M7000

Refit

2. Position striker. Secure with bolts
3. Close tailgate. Check alignment.
4. If necessary, open tailgate, slacken bolts, realign striker. Re-tighten bolts.

TAILGATE LATCH

Service repair no - 76.37.17

Remove

1. Release studs securing tailgate board. Remove board.

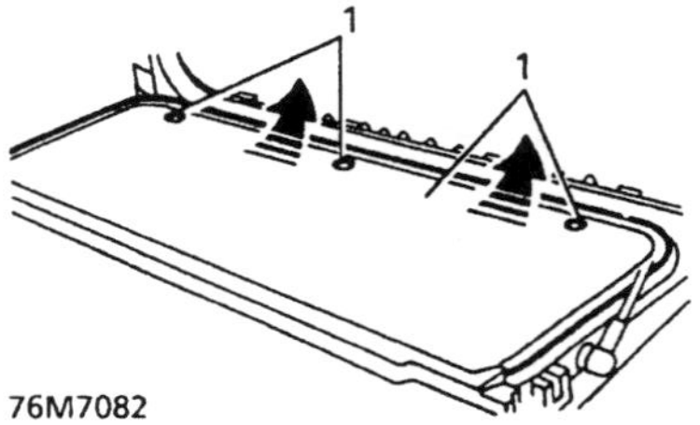

76M7082

2. Release clips securing operating rods to tailgate centre latch. Release rods.

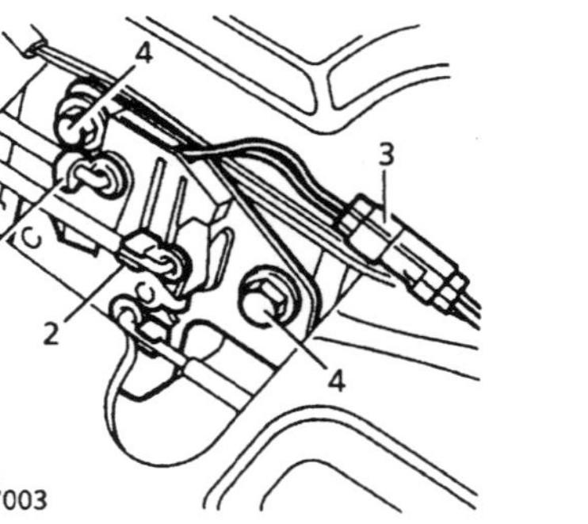

76M7003

3. Disconnect latch multiplug.
4. Remove 2 bolts securing latch to tailgate. Remove latch.

Refit

5. Reverse removal procedure.

TAILGATE LATCH - OUTER

Service repair no - 76.37.73

Remove

1. Release studs securing tailgate board. Remove board.

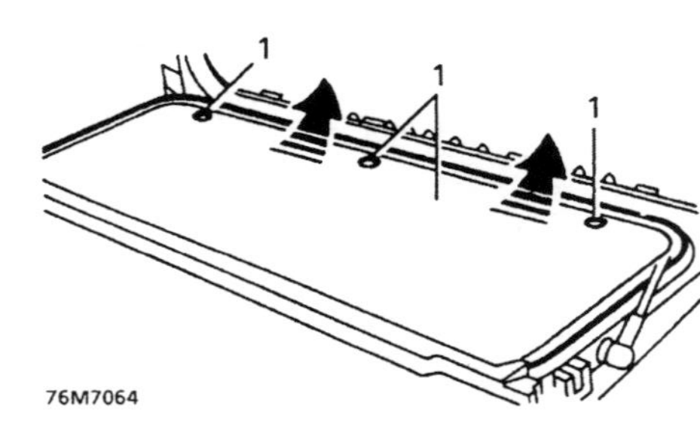

76M7064

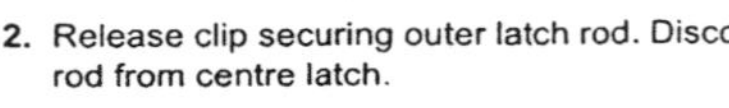

2. Release clip securing outer latch rod. Disconnect rod from centre latch.

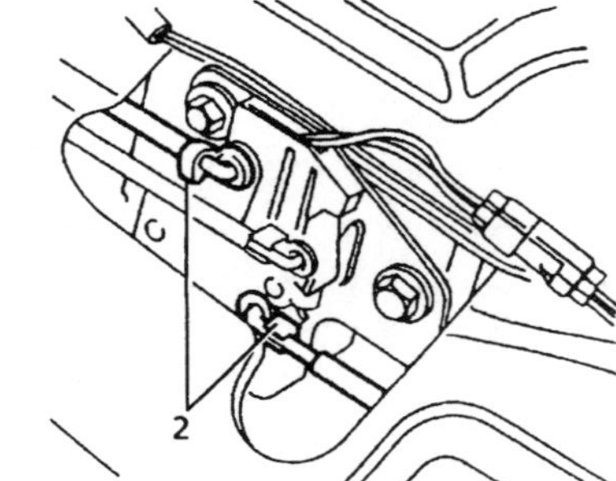

76M7065

3. Remove 2 bolts securing outer latch to tailgate. Remove latch and rod.

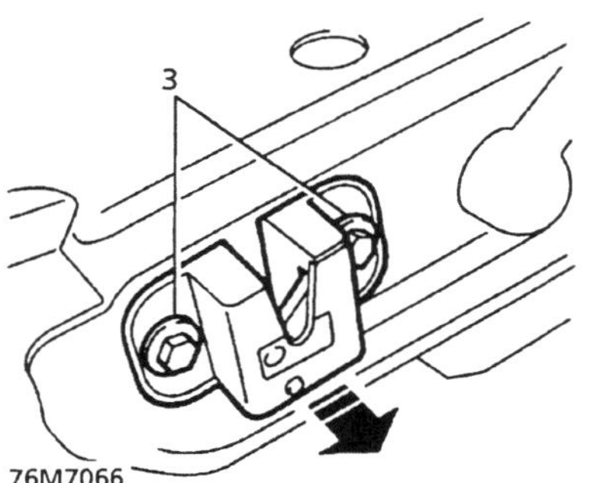

4. Rotate release rod 90° to remove from outer latch.

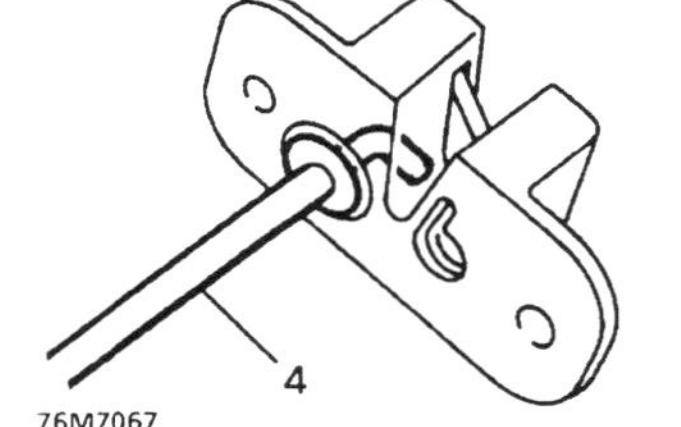

Refit

5. Reverse removal procedure.

UPPER TAILGATE - INTERIOR TRIM

Service repair no - 76.34.13

Remove

Lower trim assembly

1. Release load space lamp from trim panel, disconnect 2 Lucar terminals and remove lamp.
2. Remove 6 screws securing trim panel to side trims and tailgate.

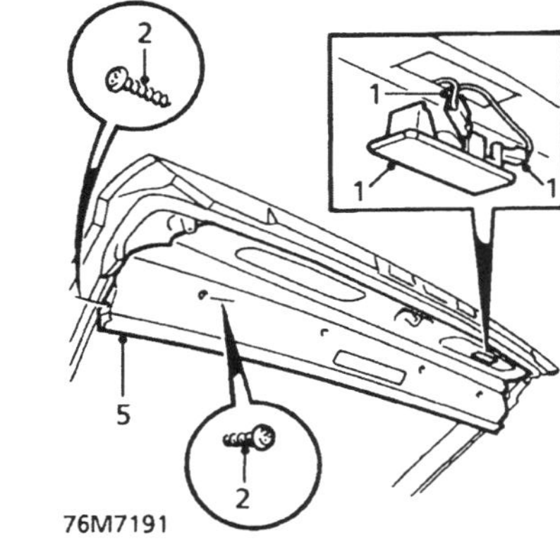

3. Release 4 studs securing trim panel to tailgate.
4. Disconnect high level stop lamp multiplug, if fitted.
5. Remove lower trim assembly.

Upper trim

6. Remove 6 screws securing trim panel to tailgate.

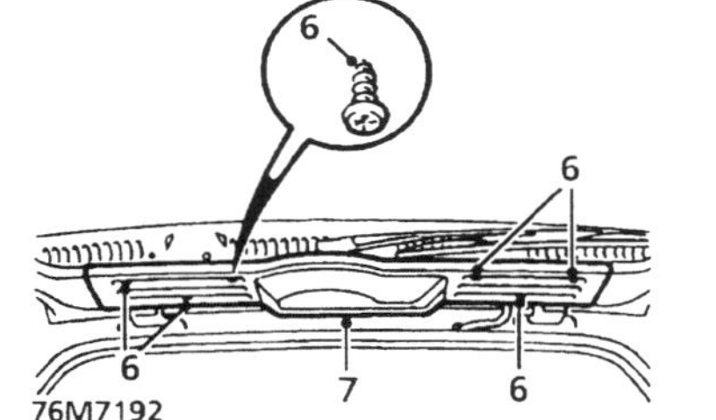

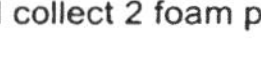

7. Remove trim panel and collect 2 foam pads.

Side trims

8. Release 3 studs securing each side trim.

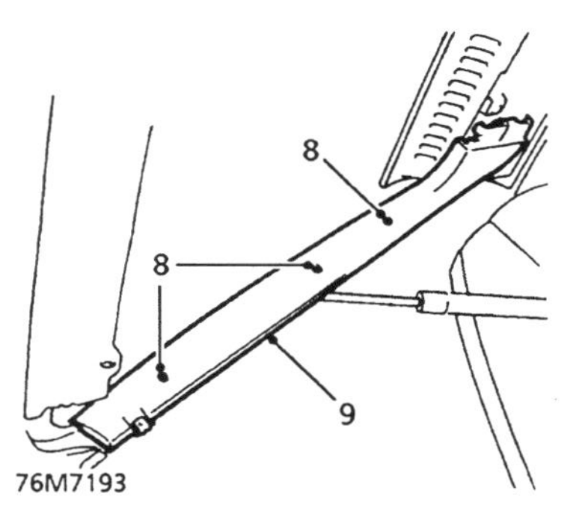

9. Remove 2 side trims.

Refit

10. Reverse removal procedure.

TAILGATE STRUT

Service repair no - 76.40.33

Remove

1. Secure tailgate in open position using suitable support.
2. Release clips securing strut to ball joints. Remove strut.

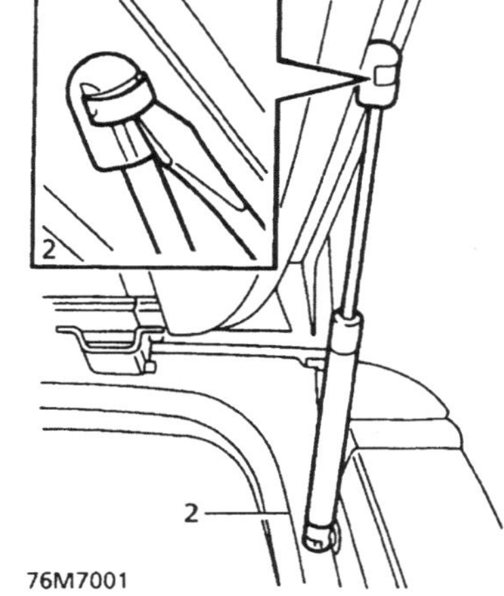

Refit

3. Reverse removal procedure.

WHEEL ARCH LINER - FRONT

Service repair no - 76.10.48

Remove

1. Raise the vehicle.

WARNING: Support on safety stands.

2. Remove relevant road wheel.
3. Remove 3 screws securing mud flap. Remove mud flap.
4. Remove 8 studs securing wheel arch liner.

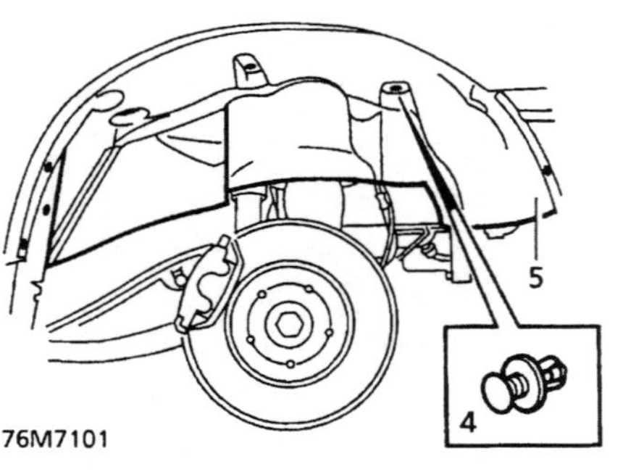

76M7101

Refit

5. Position liner and secure with trim studs.
6. Fit mud flap and secure with screws.
7. Refit road wheel. Secure with nuts. Tighten to ***108 Nm. (80 lbf.ft)***
8. Remove safety stands. Lower vehicle.

WHEEL ARCH LINER - REAR

Service repair no - 76.10.49

Remove

1. Raise the vehicle.

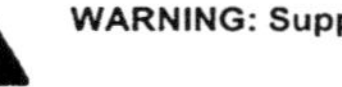

WARNING: Support on safety stands.

2. Remove relevant road wheel.
3. Remove screws from wheel arch liner fixings. Remove fixings.

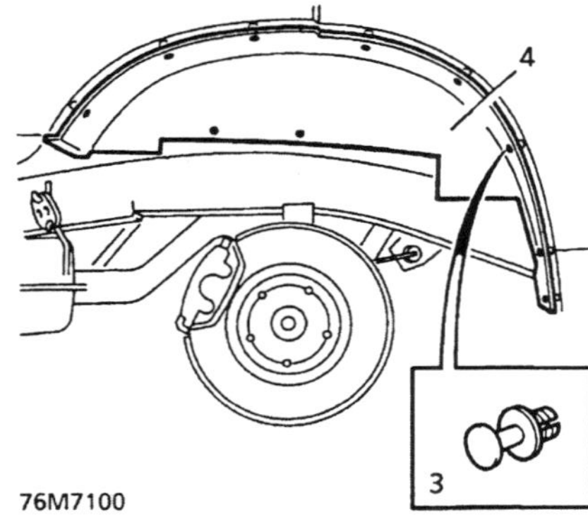

76M7100

4. Remove liner.

Refit

5. Position liner. Fit liner fixings. Secure with screws.
6. Refit road wheel. Secure with nuts. Tighten to ***108 Nm. (80 lbf.ft)***
7. Remove safety stands. Lower vehicle.

WINDSCREEN

Service repair no - 76.81.01

NOTE: The following equipment is required:

masking tape;
sharp knife;
reciprocating blade, powered cutting knife*, or cutting wire and handles;
suction lifters;
windscreen repair kit;
sealer applicator gun.

* A reciprocating blade cutting tool, such as 'FEIN Special Cutter', is recommended for this operation. A flat blade, with an effective length of at least 25mm and a 'U' shaped blade of at least 30mm is required.

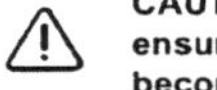

CAUTION: Extreme care is necessary to ensure that paintwork and trim does not become damaged during the removal process.
Particular care should be taken when using cutting wire and handles to avoid damage to seal along leading edge of fascia.

WARNING: Wear protective gloves when handling glass, solvents and primers.

Remove

1. Remove interior mirror. ***See this section.***
2. Remove plenum panels. ***See HEATING AND VENTILATION, Repair.***

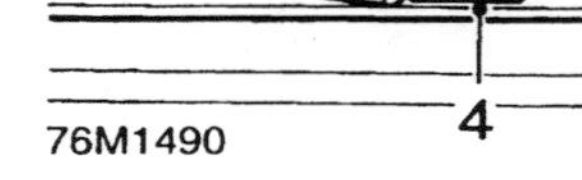

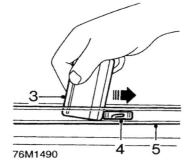

76M1490

3. Insert a thin plastic strip, such as a credit card, between windscreen upper finisher and roof panel.
4. Disengage 8 clips securing upper finisher by sliding clips towards left hand side of vehicle.
5. Remove upper screen finisher.

76M1491

6. If fitted, disconnect heating element multiplugs. Disconnect heating element earth wire. Tape heater connections onto windscreen to prevent fouling during removal procedure.
7. Mask around windscreen aperture to protect paintwork.
8. Fit protective cover over fascia and bonnet.

Removal Using Reciprocating Blade Tool

9. Cut through P.U. adhesive along sides of screen using flat blade.
10. Using a 'U' shaped blade, cut through adhesive bead along upper and lower edges of screen.

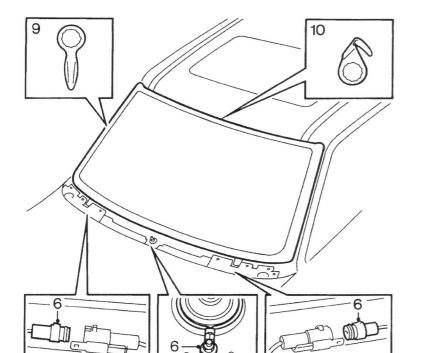

CAUTION: Access to adhesive around lower screen supports is restricted. Manoeuvre blade to cut as much sealant from around screen supports as possible.

11. Attach suction lifters to glass. With assistance, cut through remaining sealant around screen supports using a sharp knife.
12. With assistance, remove windscreen glass.

Removal Using Cutting Wire and Handles.

13. Remove both 'A' post finishers. ***See this section.***
14. Remove both sun visors. ***See this section.***
15. Remove map/courtesy lamp assembly. ***See ELECTRICAL, Repair.***

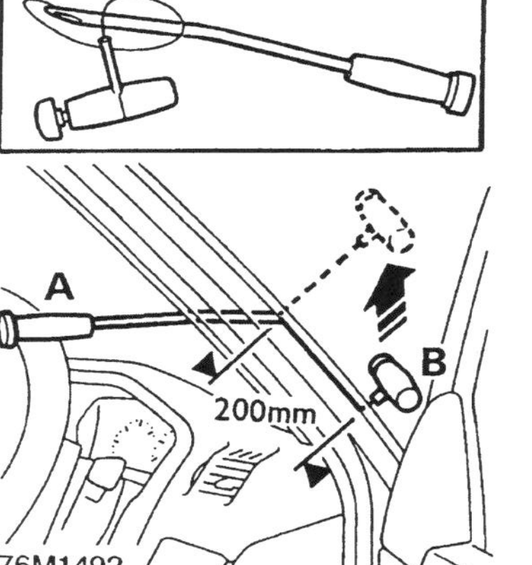
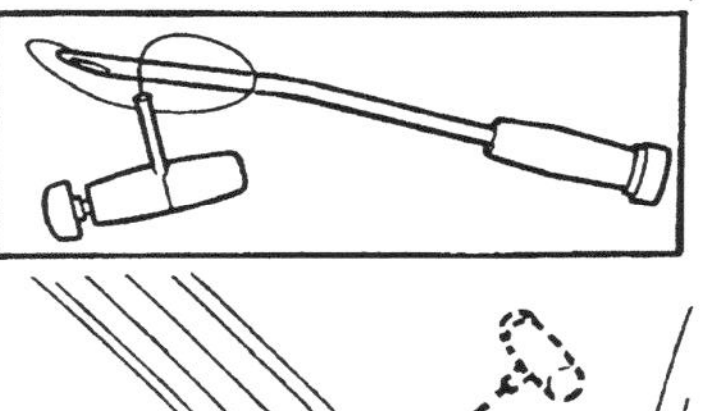
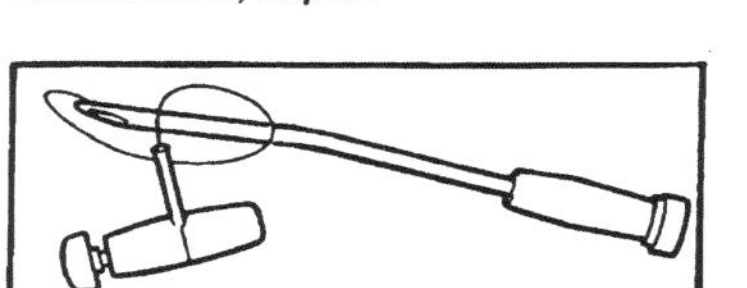
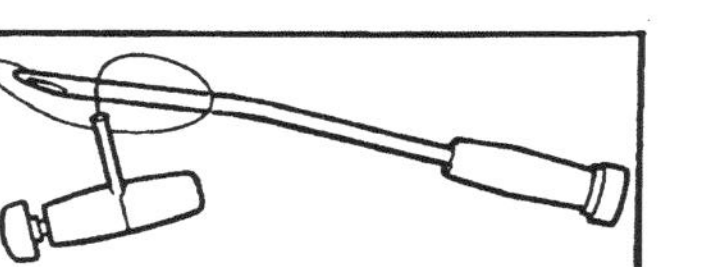
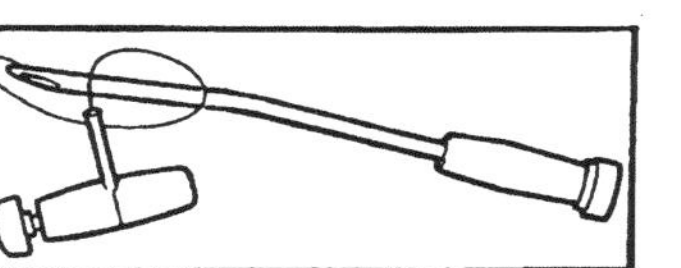
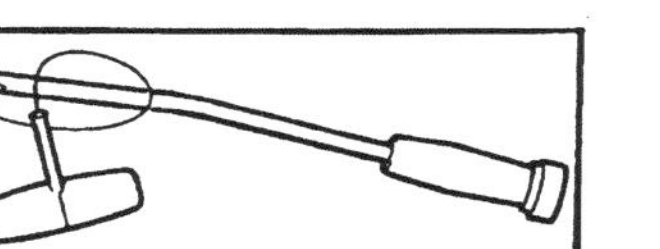
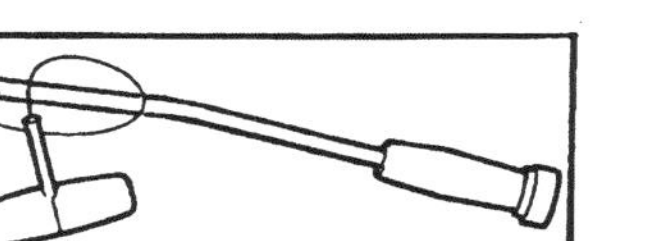
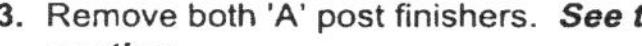

76M1492

16. Mask along leading edge of headlining.
17. Using a sharp knife, cut through P.U. sealer at side of screen, towards lower corner.
18. Insert cutting wire through knife cut and fit handles, as shown, with approximately 200 mm (8 in) of wire between handles.
19. With assistance, wedge tube of handle 'A' between glass and body, ahead of the cutting position, and carefully cut the sealer using a continuous pull on handle 'B' from the outside. Cut side and top edges first. Attach suction lifters and restrain glass as last of sealant is cut.

NOTE: When cutting along lower edge, manoeuvre wire between glass edge and screen supports to reduce strain on wire.

20. Attach suction lifters to glass. With assistance, remove windscreen.

Refit

21. carefully cut old sealer from body flange to obtain a smooth surface, approximately 2 mm (1/16 in) thick.

CAUTION: Do not cut down to painted surface.

22. Inspect supports, renew if damaged.
23. Position screen on felt covered surface.
24. If original screen is to be refitted, cut old sealer from glass to obtain a smooth surface, approximately 2 mm (1/16 in) thick.

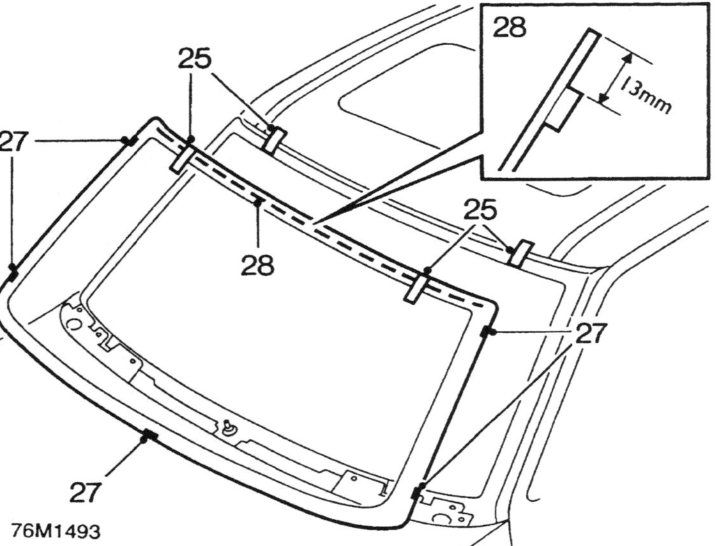

76M1493

⚠ **CAUTION: Do not cut down to surface of glass.**

25. Position and centralise new windscreen to body. Apply tape reference marks to aid final fitment. Remove screen and position to work surface.
26. Apply cleaning solvent to sealing surface of glass and body flange.

⚠ **CAUTION: Do not touch cleaned or primed areas with fingers.**

27. Position 5 screen spacer blocks on inside edge of glass, over cut-out marks in obscuration band.
28. If necessary, peel off backing strip and stick foam glazing dam along inside surface of glass, approximately 13 mm (1/2 in) from top edge.
29. Shake primer tins for at least 30 seconds. Apply body primer to sealing surface of body flange using supplied applicator.
30. Apply glass primer to sealing surface of glass.

CAUTION: Use a separate applicator for each primer.

31. Remove lid from sealer cartridge, remove crystals, pierce membrane and fit pre-cut nozzle. Fit cartridge to applicator gun.

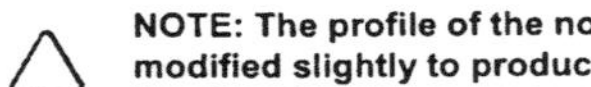
NOTE: The profile of the nozzle must be modified slightly to produce the required bead section.

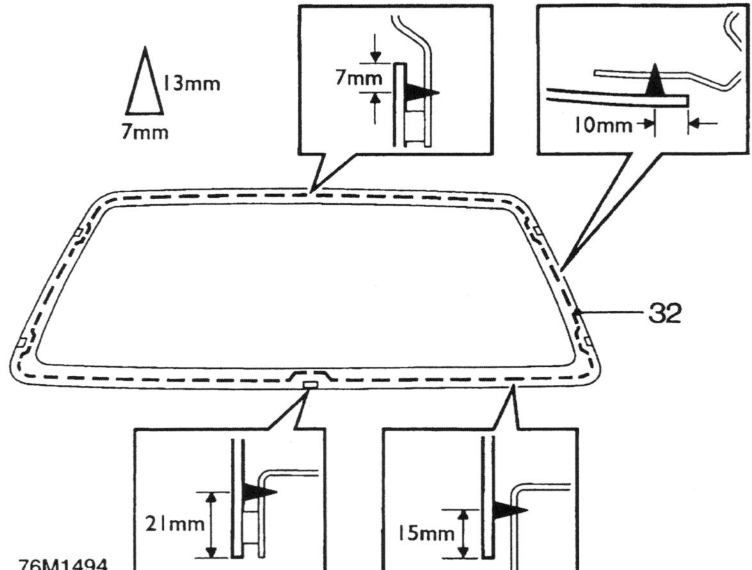

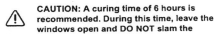

76M1494

32. Apply a continuous bead of sealer to windscreen as shown.
33. Fit suction lifters to glass.
34. With assistance, position glass centrally, using previously made tape markings and lower onto supports. Seat glass to spacer blocks.

⚠ **CAUTION: Do not apply heavy pressure to the sides of the screen. Lightly press screen from centre outwards until edges are to required gap. Pushing screen edges into position can bend screen and lead to cracking in service.**

35. Remove protection from fascia and bonnet.
36. Remove masking tape.
37. If fitted, connect heating element multiplugs and earth wire.
38. Remove clips from upper screen finisher.
39. Fit clips to body studs. Position upper screen finisher and engage to clips.
40. Fit plenum panels. ***See HEATING AND VENTILATION, Repair.***
41. Fit interior mirror. ***See this section.***

If Cutting Wire and Handles Used

42. Remove masking from leading edge of headlining.
43. Fit map/courtesy lamp assembly. ***See ELECTRICAL, Repair.***
44. Fit sun visors. ***See this section.***
45. Fit 'A' post finishers. ***See this section.***

CAUTION: A curing time of 6 hours is recommended. During this time, leave the windows open and DO NOT slam the doors.

WINDSCREEN LOWER FINISHER

Service repair no - 76.43.41

Remove

1. Remove both windscreen side finishers. ***See this section.***
2. Remove both windscreen wiper arms. ***See WIPERS AND WASHERS, Repair.***
3. Release 10 clips securing windscreen lower finisher.

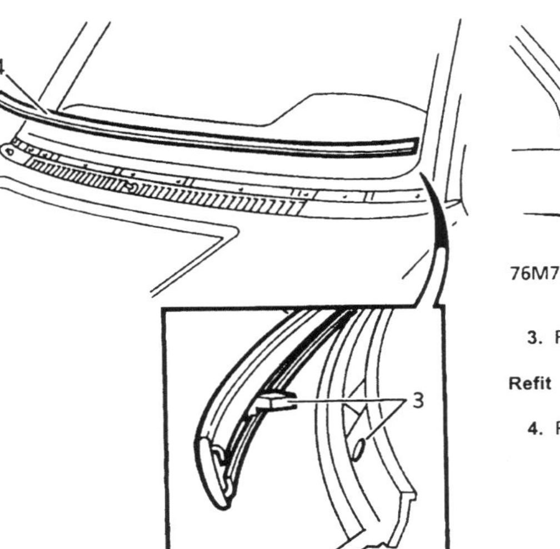

76M7117

4. Remove windscreen lower finisher.

Refit

5. Reverse removal procedure.

WINDSCREEN SIDE FINISHER

Service repair no - 76.43.39

Remove

1. Lift side finisher seal to reveal fixings.
2. Remove 4 screws securing side finisher.

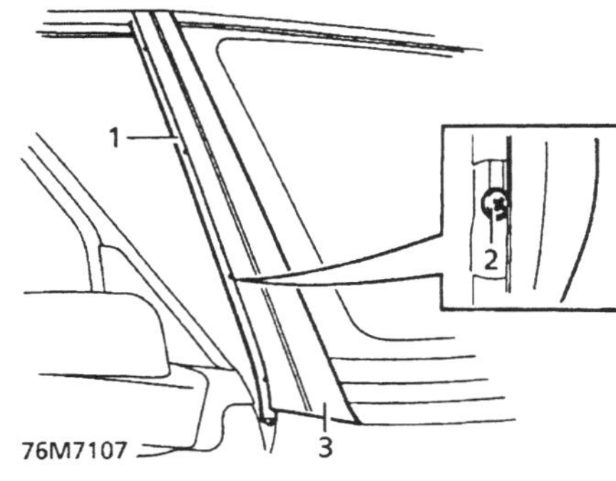

76M7107

3. Remove side finisher.

Refit

4. Position side finisher. Secure side with screws.

BACKLIGHT GLASS

Service repair no - 76.81.10

NOTE: The following equipment is required:

masking tape.
Sharp knife.
Cutting wire and handles, or a reciprocating blade, powered cutting knife*.
Suction lifters.
Windscreen repair kit.
Sealer applicator gun.

*A reciprocating blade cutting tool, such as 'FEIN Special Cutter' is recommended for this operation. A flat blade, with an effective length of at least 25mm and a 'U' shaped blade of at least 30mm are required.

WARNING: Wear protective gloves when handling glass, solvents and primers.

Remove

1. Remove interior trim from tailgate, ***See this section.***
2. Release backlight lower finisher from 7 clips.
3. Remove backlight lower finisher.

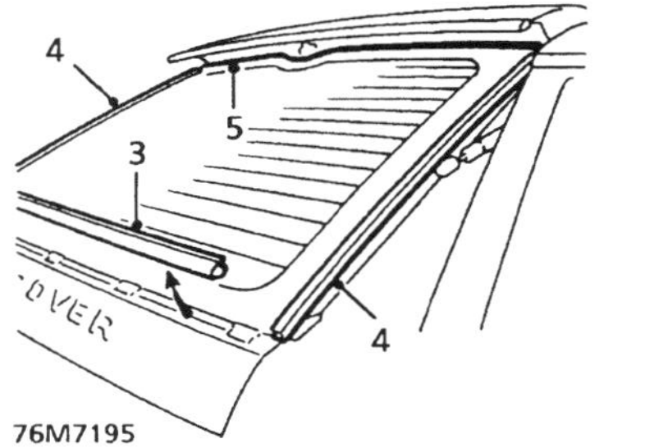

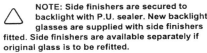

76M7195

4. Remove backlight side finishers.

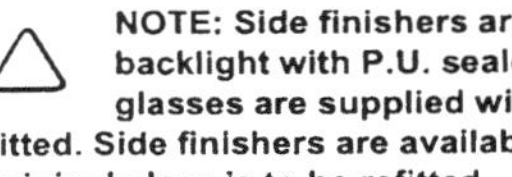

NOTE: Side finishers are secured to backlight with P.U. sealer. New backlight glasses are supplied with side finishers fitted. Side finishers are available separately if original glass is to be refitted.

5. Remove rubber finisher from upper edge of backlight glass.
6. Protect tailgate panel with masking tape.
7. Disconnect two Lucar terminals from screen heater element.

Removal Using Reciprocating Blade Tool

8. Cut through P.U. adhesive along sides of screen using flat blade.

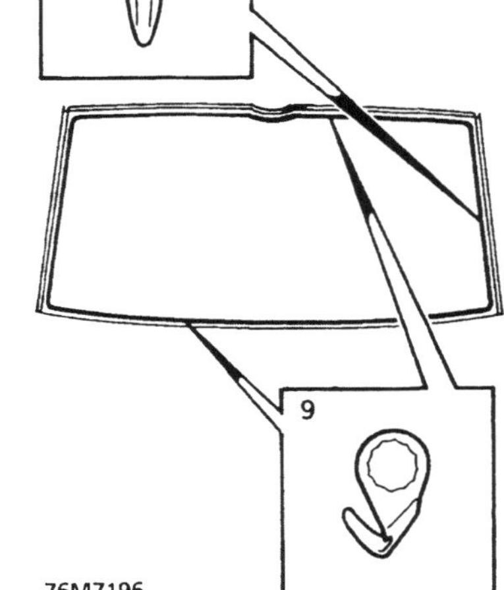

76M7196

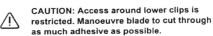

9. Using a 'U' shaped blade, cut through adhesive bead along upper and lower edges of glass.

CAUTION: Access around lower clips is restricted. Manoeuvre blade to cut through as much adhesive as possible.

10. Attach suction lifters to glass. With assistance, cut through remaining sealant around lower clips.
11. With assistance, remove backlight glass.

Removal Using Cutting Wire Handles

12. Using a sharp knife, cut through P.U. sealer at side of backlight.
13. Insert cutting wire through knife cut and fit handles, as shown, with approximately 200mm of wire between handles.

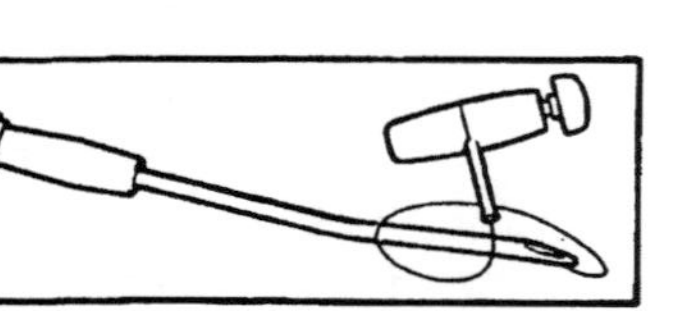

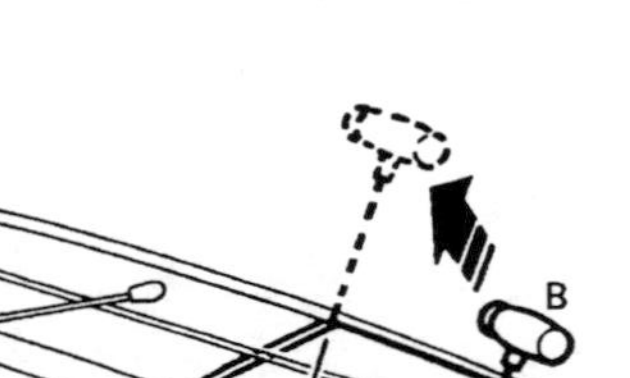

76M7197

14. With assistance, wedge tube of handle 'A' between glass and body, ahead of the cutting position, and carefully cut the sealer using a continuous pull on handle 'B' from the outside. Cut side and top edges first. Attach suction lifters and restrain glass as last of sealant is cut.

NOTE: When cutting along lower edge, manoeuvre wire between glass edge and finisher clips to reduce strain on wire.

15. With assistance, remove backlight glass.

Refit

16. Carefully cut old sealer from body flange to obtain a smooth surface, approximately 2mm thick.

CAUTION: Do not cut down to painted surface.

17. Renew broken finisher clips as necessary. Position finisher clips centrally on tailgate studs.

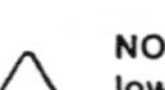
NOTE: Clips control height and seating of lower glass edge.

18. Position and centralize new backlight to tailgate. Apply tape reference mark to aid final fitment.

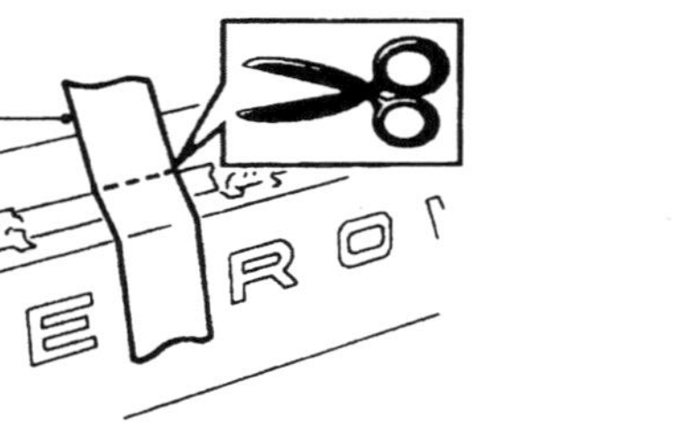

76M7207

19. Position new backlight on felt covered surface.
20. Fit and centralize rubber finisher to top of glass.

NOTE: Finisher controls seating depth of glass top edge.

21. Apply cleaning solvent to sealing surface of glass and body flange.

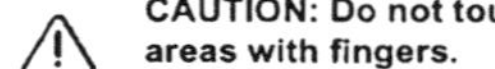
CAUTION: Do not touch cleaned or primed areas with fingers.

22. Shake primer tins for at least 30 seconds. Apply body primer to sealing surface of body flange using supplied applicator.
23. Apply glass primer to sealing surface of glass.

CAUTION: Use a separate applicator for each primer.

24. Remove lid from sealer cartridge, remove crystals, pierce membrane and fit pre-cut nozzle. Fit cartridge to applicator gun.

NOTE: The profile of the nozzle must be modified slightly to produce the required bead section.

25. Apply a continuous bead of sealer to backlight as shown.

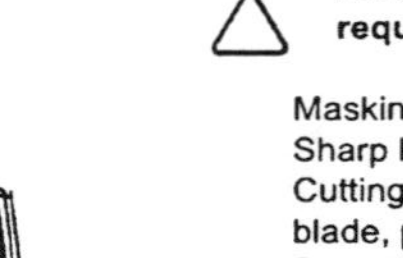

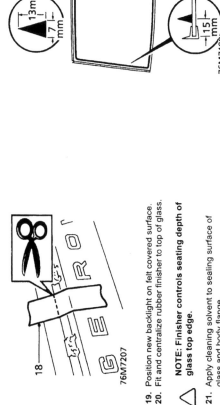

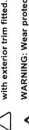

76M7198

26. **Original glass:** Apply 3mm bead of sealer to channels of side finishers and fit to backlight.
27. Fit suction lifters to glass.
28. With assistance, fit glass and centralize to previously made tape markings. Set glass to correct depth.
29. Connect screen heater.
30. Remove reference and protective tapes.
31. Position lower finisher and secure to clips.
32. Fit interior trim to tailgate, ***See this section.***

CAUTION: A curing time of 6 hours is recommended. During this time, leave the windows open and DO NOT slam the doors.

REAR QUARTER LIGHT

Service repair no - 76.81.20

NOTE: The following equipment is required:

Masking tape.
Sharp knife.
Cutting wire and handles, or a reciprocating blade, powered cutting knife*.
Suction Lifters.
Windscreen repair kit.
Sealer applicator gun.

*A reciprocating blade cutting tool, such as 'FEIN Special Cutter' is recommended for this operation. A flat blade, with an effective length of at least 25mm and a 'U' shaped blade of at least 30mm is required.

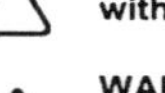
NOTE: New rear quarter glass is supplied with exterior trim fitted.

WARNING: Wear protective gloves when handling glass, solvents and primers.

Remove

1. Remove parcel tray support, ***See this section.***
2. Remove both 'E' post trims, ***See this section.***
3. Remove relevant 'B' post upper trim, ***See this section.***
4. Remove relevant side interior lamp assembly, ***See ELECTRICAL, Repair.***
5. Remove relevant grab handle, ***See this section.***
6. Remove relevant exterior 'E' post finisher, ***See this section.***

7. Remove 2 trim studs securing headlining to 'E' posts.

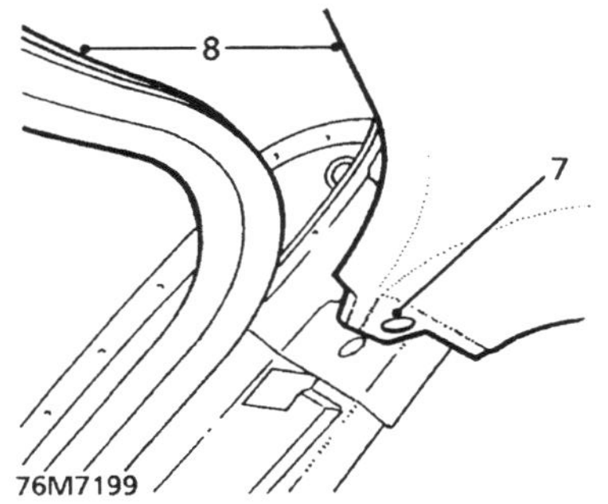

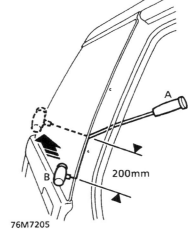

76M7199

8. Release headlining from tailgate seal. Lower headlining as necessary during glass removal to provide access to sealant along top edge of glass.
9. Disconnect aerial amplifier plugs.

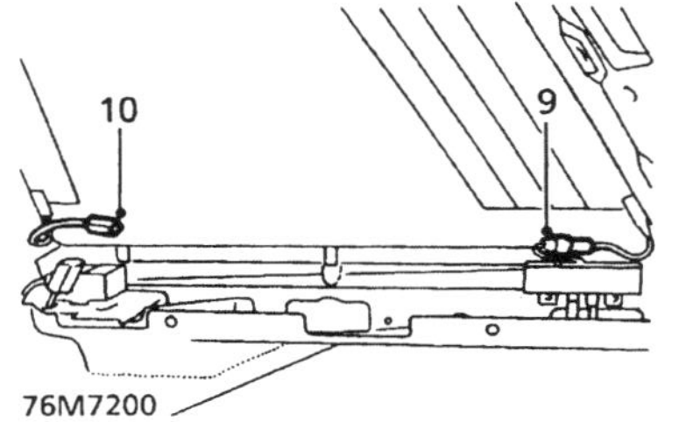

76M7200

10. **R.H. glass only:**Disconnect alarm receiver plug.
11. Protect surrounding area of body using masking tape.

Removal Using Reciprocating Blade Tool

12. Lift flip seal to reveal trim fixings.

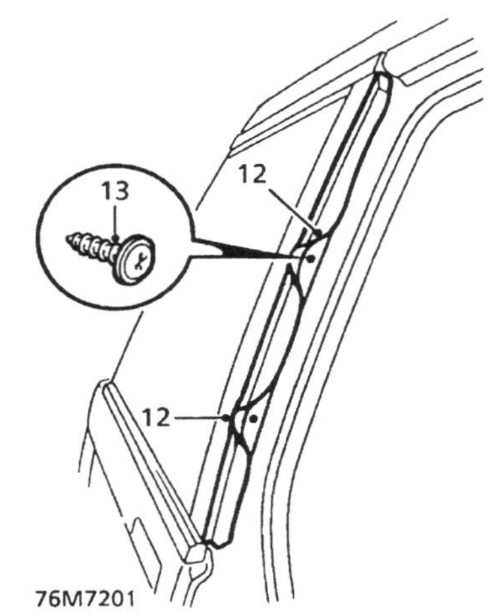

76M7201

13. Remove 2 screws securing exterior trim to 'D' post.
14. Cut through P.U. adhesive from inside of glass along lower and side edges.

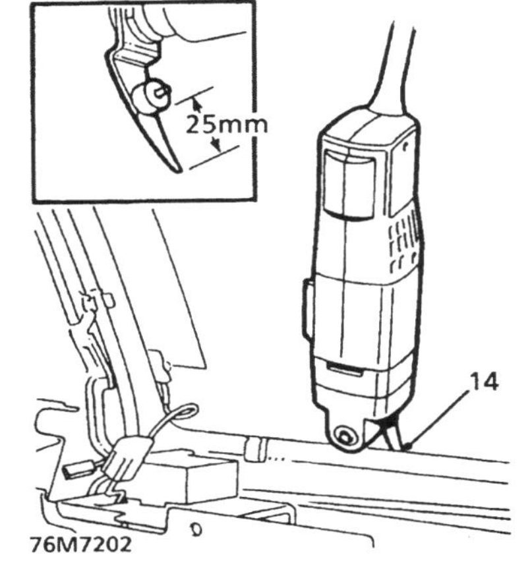

76M7202

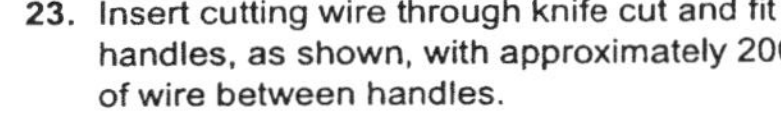

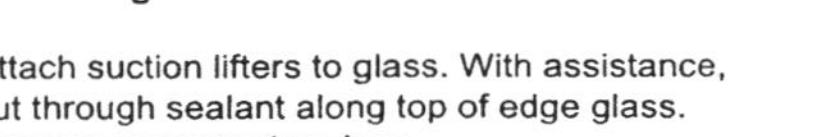

CAUTION: Manoeuvre knife blade around 3 parcel tray support clips. Ensure aerial amplifier and alarm receiver plugs do not become damaged.

15. Attach suction lifters to glass. With assistance, cut through sealant along top of edge glass.
16. Remove rear quarter glass.

Removal Using Cutting Wire Handles

17. Protect surrounding area of body using masking tape.
18. Lift flip seal to reveal trim fixings.
19. Remove 2 screws securing exterior trim to 'D' post.

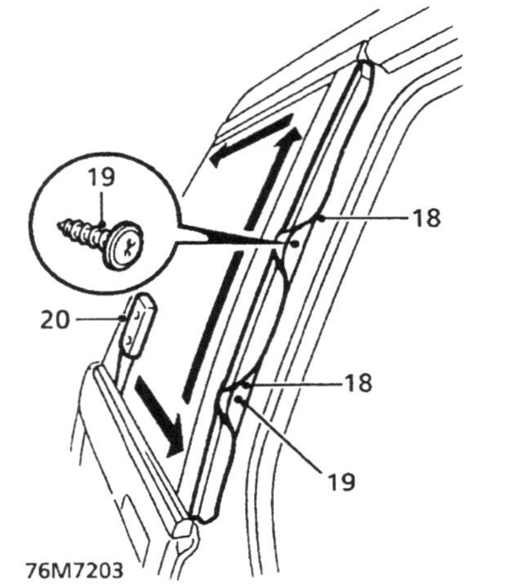

76M7203

20. Carefully cut through adhesive bead between glass and trim using a sharp knife.

NOTE: A reciprocating blade cutting tool, such as 'FEIN Special Cutter' will ease the removal of the trim. Use a cranked blade with an effective length of not more than 22mm.

21. Remove and discard quarter light trim.

NOTE: Rear quarter lights are supplied with finisher fitted. Finisher is not available separately.

22. Using a sharp knife, cut through P.U. sealer at forward edge of quarter glass.

23. Insert cutting wire through knife cut and fit handles, as shown, with approximately 200mm of wire between handles.

76M7205

24. With assistance, wedge tube of handles 'A' between glass and body, ahead of the cutting position, and carefully cut the sealer using a continuous pull on handle 'B' from the outside. Cut side and top edges first. Attach suction lifters as last sealant is cut.

NOTE: When cutting along lower edge, manoeuvre wire between glass edge and parcel tray support clips to reduce strain on wire.

CAUTION: Ensure aerial amplifier and alarm receiver plugs do not become damaged.

25. Remove rear quarter glass.

Refit

26. Carefully cut old sealer from body flange to obtain a smooth surface, approximately 2mm thick.

CAUTION: Do not cut down to painted surface.

27. Position new quarter glass on felt covered surface.
28. Apply cleaning solvent to sealing surface of glass and body flange.

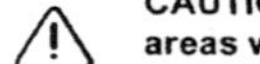

CAUTION: Do not touch cleaned or primed areas with fingers.

29. Stick 4 self adhesive spacers on the inside edge of glass at corners.
30. Shake primer tins for at least 30 seconds. Apply body primer to sealing surface of body flange using supplied applicator.
31. Apply glass primer to sealing surface of glass.

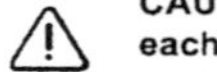

CAUTION: Use a separate applicator for each primer.

32. Remove lid from sealer cartridge, remove crystals, pierce membrane and fit pre-cut nozzle. Fit cartridge to applicator gun.

NOTE: The profile of the nozzle must be modified slightly to produce the required bead section.

33. Apply a continuous bead of sealer to rear quarter glass as shown.

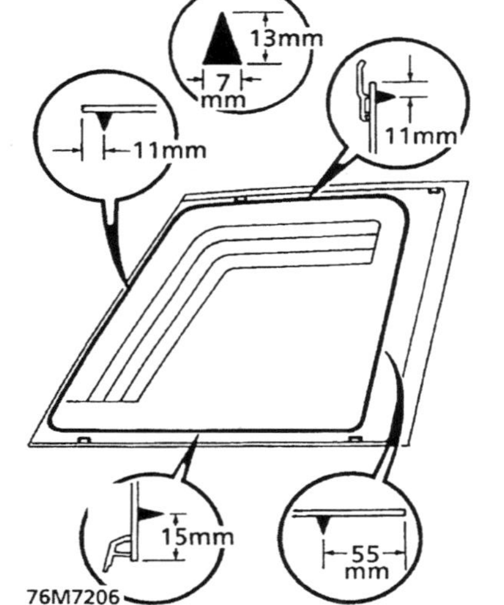

34. Fit suction lifters to glass.
35. With assistance, fit glass and align to body. Seat glass to spacer rubbers.
36. Remove protective tape.
37. Secure exterior trim to 'D' post with screws.
38. Connect aerial amplifier plug.
39. **R.H. glass only:** Connect alarm receiver plug.
40. Position headlining and engage beneath tailgate flip seal.
41. Secure headlining to 'E' posts with trim studs.
42. Fit exterior 'E' post finisher. *See this section.*
43. Fit grab handle. *See this section.*
44. Fit side interior lamp assembly. *See ELECTRICAL, Repair.*
45. Fit 'B' post upper trim. *See this section.*
46. Fit 'E' post trims. *See this section.*
47. Fit parcel tray support. *See this section.*

CAUTION: A curing time of 6 hours is recommended. During this time, leave the windows open and DO NOT slam the doors.

77 - PANEL REPAIRS

CONTENTS

Page

77 - PANEL REPAIRS

CONTENTS

BODY REPAIRS

Body shells are of welded construction and bolted to the chassis frame. Front and rear sections of the shell are designed as 'energy absorbing' zones. This means they are designed to deform progressively when subjected to impact in order to minimise the likelihood of injury to vehicle occupants.

It is essential that design dimensions and strength are restored in accident rectification. It is important that neither structural weakness nor excessive local stiffness are introduced into the vehicle during body or chassis repair.

Repairs usually involve a combination of operations ranging from straightening procedures to renewal of either individual panels or panel assemblies. The repairer will determine the repair method and this decision will take into account a balance of economics between labour and material costs and the availability of repair facilities in both equipment and skills. It may also involve considerations of vehicles down-time, replacement vehicle availability and repair turn-around time.

It is expected that a repairer will select the best and most economic repair method possible, making use of the facilities available. The instructions given are intended to assist a skilled body repairer by expanding approved procedures for panel replacement with the objective of restoring the vehicle to a safe running condition and effecting a repair which is visually acceptable and which, even to the experienced eye, does not advertise the fact that it has been damaged.

This does not necessarily mean that the repaired vehicle will be identical in all respects with original factory build. Repair facilities cannot always duplicate methods of construction used during production.

Operations covered in this Manual do not include reference to testing the vehicle after repair. It is essential that work is inspected and suspension geometry checked after completion and if necessary a road test of the vehicle is carried out, particularly where safety related items are concerned.

Where major units have been disconnected or removed, it is necessary to ensure that fluid levels are checked and topped up when necessary. It is also necessary to ensure that the repaired vehicle is in a roadworthy condition in respect of tyre pressures, lights, washer fluid etc.

Body repairs often involve the removal of mechanical and electrical units as well as associated wiring. **See BODY and SRS sections.**

Taking into consideration the differences in body styles, steering and suspension systems as well as engine and suspension layouts, the location of the following components as applicable to a particular vehicle is critical:

- Front suspension upper damper mountings.
- Front suspension or sub frame mountings.
- Engine mounting on RH and LH chassis longitudinals.
- Rear suspension upper damper mountings.
- Rear suspension mountings or lower pivots.
- Steering rack mountings.

Additional points which can be used to check alignment and assembly are:

- Inner holes in crossmember - side - main floor.
- Holes in valance front assembly.
- Body to chassis mounting holes.
- Holes in rear floor.
- Holes in rear lower panels or extension rear floor.
- Fuel tank mountings.

Apertures for windscreen, backlight, bonnet and doors can be checked by offering up an undamaged component as a gauge and also by measuring known dimensions. **See BODY DIMENSIONS section.**

Straightening

Whenever possible, structural members should be cold straightened under tension. Do not attempt to straighten with a single pull, but rework the damaged area using a series of pulls, releasing tension between each stage and using the opportunity to check alignment.

Body jig

Unless damage is limited to cosmetic panels, all repair work to body members must be carried out on a body jig, to ensure that impact damage has not spread into more remote parts of the body structure. Mounting on a jig will also ensure that the straightening and panel replacement procedures do not cause further distortion. If original dimensions cannot be satisfactorily restored by these methods, damaged structural members should be replaced. Damaged areas should be cut away using a high speed saw, NOT an oxy-acetylene torch.

As a rule, body dimensions are symmetrical about the centre line. A good initial check for distortion is therefore to measure diagonally and to investigate apparent differences in dimensions.

Inspection

Every accident produces individual differences in damage. Each repair is influenced by the extent of the damage and by the facilities and equipment available for its rectification.

Most accident damage can be visually inspected and the approximate extent of the damage assessed. Sometimes deformation will extend beyond the area of direct damage, and the severity of this must be accurately established so that steps may be taken to restore critical body components to their original dimensions.

An initial check of critical dimensions can be carried out by means of drop checks or (preferably) trammels. Gauges are available which will check accurately for body twist. Where repairs necessitate renewal of a critical body component it is recommended that a body jig is used.

ELECTRONIC CONTROL UNITS

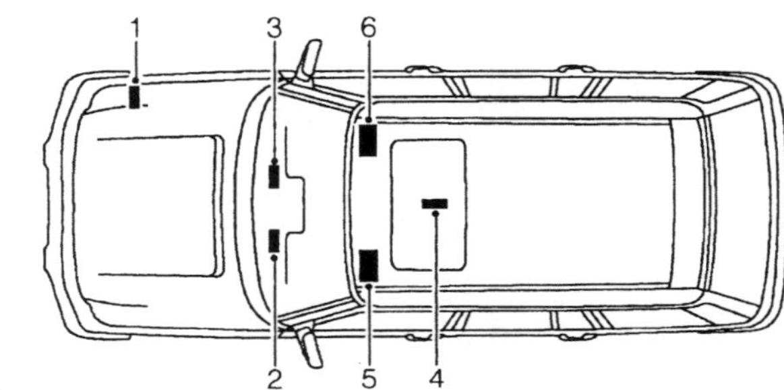

1. Engine control module (ECM) (at RH of engine bay)
2. ABS ECU (behind access plate at LH of fascia)
3. Cruise control ECU (behind fascia closing panel)
4. Diagnostic control unit (on centre tunnel)
5. Electronic suspension ECU (beneath LH front seat)
6. Body electrical control module (BeCM) (beneath RH front seat)

The electronic control units fitted to Range Rover vehicles make it advisable to follow suitable precautions prior to carrying out welding repair operations. All electronic control units must be diconnected before any welding operations take place. Harsh conditions of heat and vibration may be generated during these operations which could cause damage to the units. **See ELECTRICAL PRECAUTIONS section.**

In particular, it is essential to follow the appropriate precautions when disconnecting or removing the SRS diagnostic unit. **See SUPPLEMENTARY RESTRAINT SYSTEM, Precautions section.**

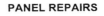

Notes

CHASSIS DIMENSIONS

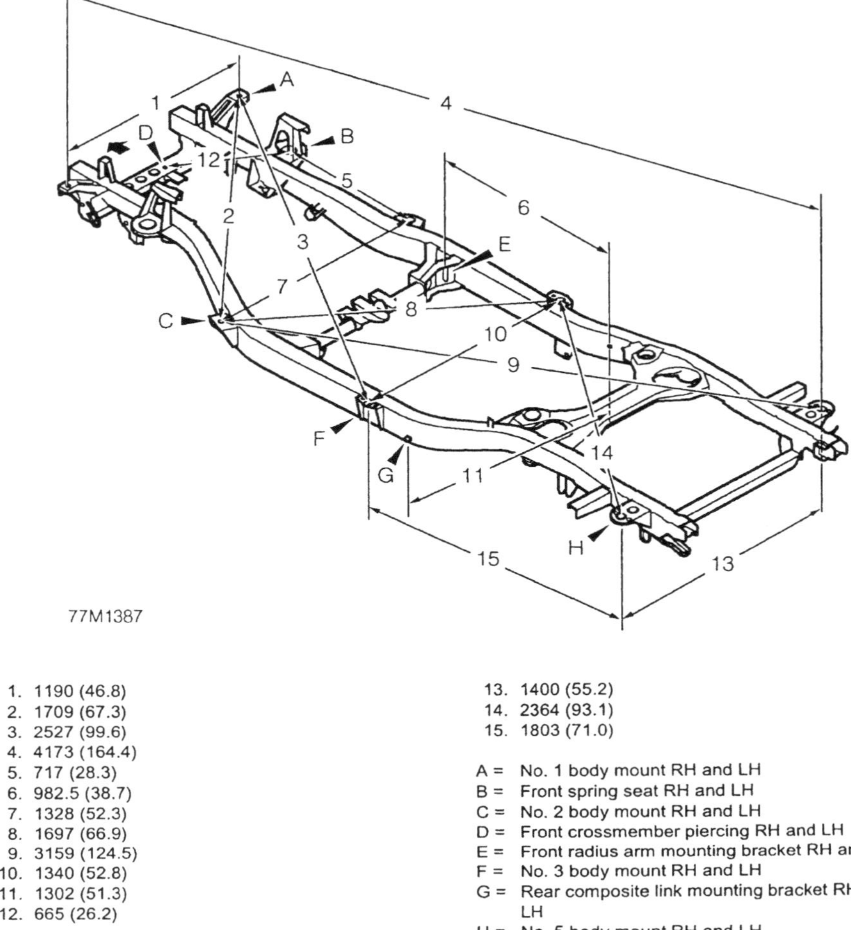

77M1387

1. 1190 (46.8)
2. 1709 (67.3)
3. 2527 (99.6)
4. 4173 (164.4)
5. 717 (28.3)
6. 982.5 (38.7)
7. 1328 (52.3)
8. 1697 (66.9)
9. 3159 (124.5)
10. 1340 (52.8)
11. 1302 (51.3)
12. 665 (26.2)
13. 1400 (55.2)
14. 2364 (93.1)
15. 1803 (71.0)

A = No. 1 body mount RH and LH
B = Front spring seat RH and LH
C = No. 2 body mount RH and LH
D = Front crossmember piercing RH and LH
E = Front radius arm mounting bracket RH and LH
F = No. 3 body mount RH and LH
G = Rear composite link mounting bracket RH and LH
H = No. 5 body mount RH and LH

Dimensions shown outside brackets are metric measurements (millimetres) and those inside brackets are imperial measurements (inches).

Where holes are used as a point of measurement the dimensions shown are always taken from the hole centre.

Chassis body mounting holes (front end)

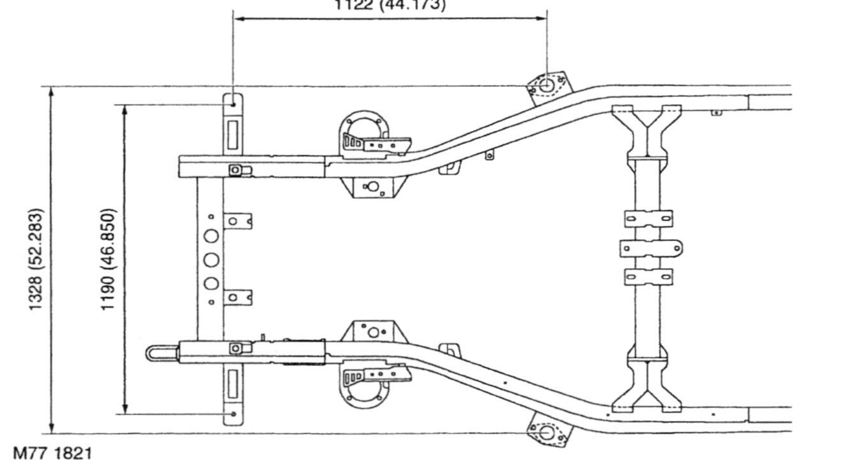
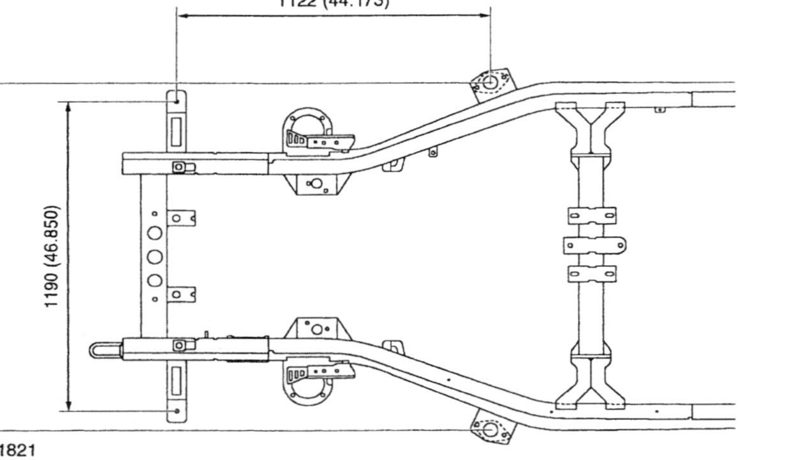

M77 1821

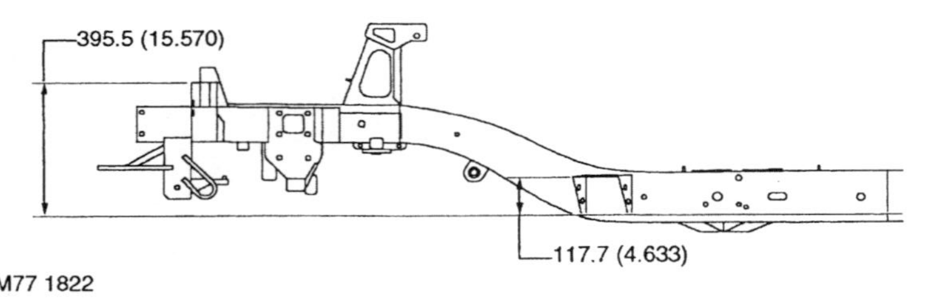

M77 1822

Chassis body mounting holes (rear end)

M77 1823

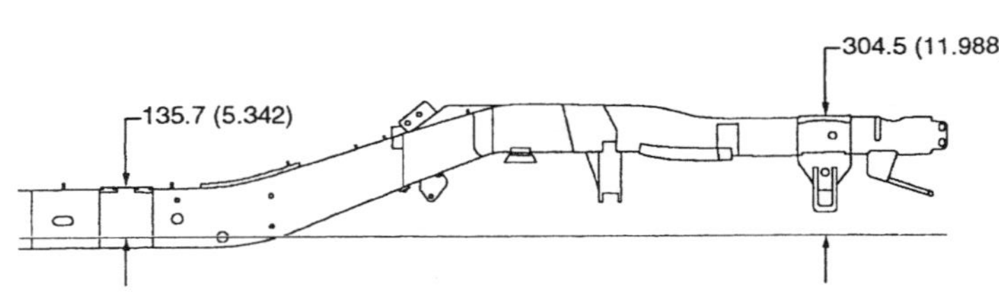

M77 1824

Additional Chassis dimensions (front end)

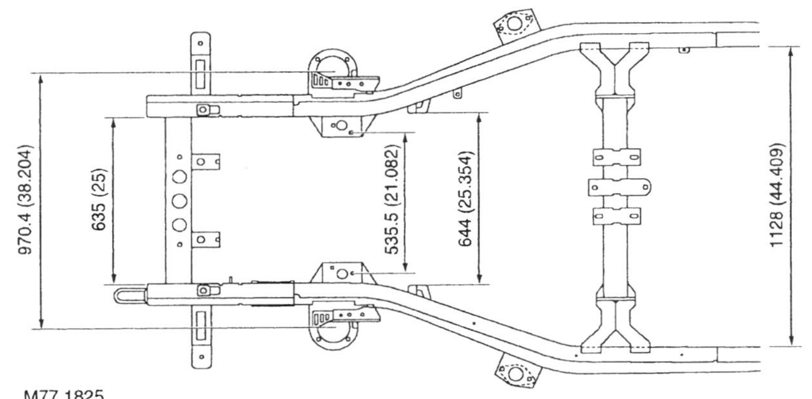

M77 1825

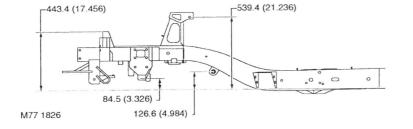

443.4 (17.456)
539.4 (21.236)
84.5 (3.326)
126.6 (4.984)

M77 1826

Additional Chassis dimensions (rear end)

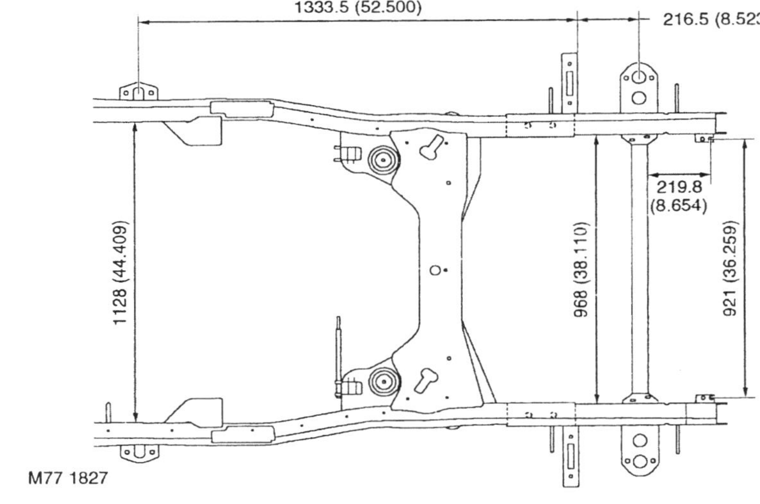

M77 1827

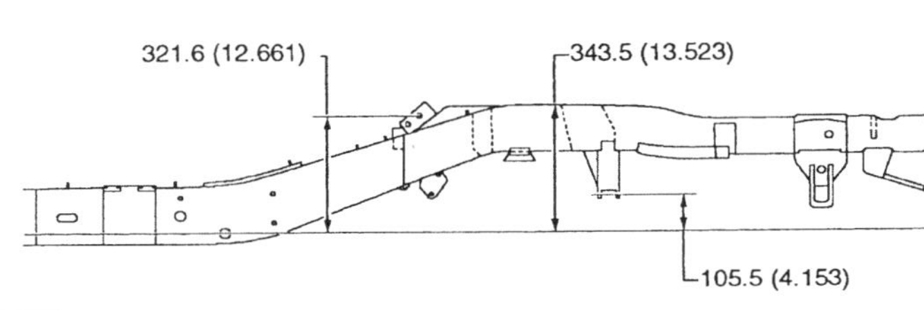

M77 1828

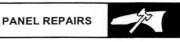

Body dimensions

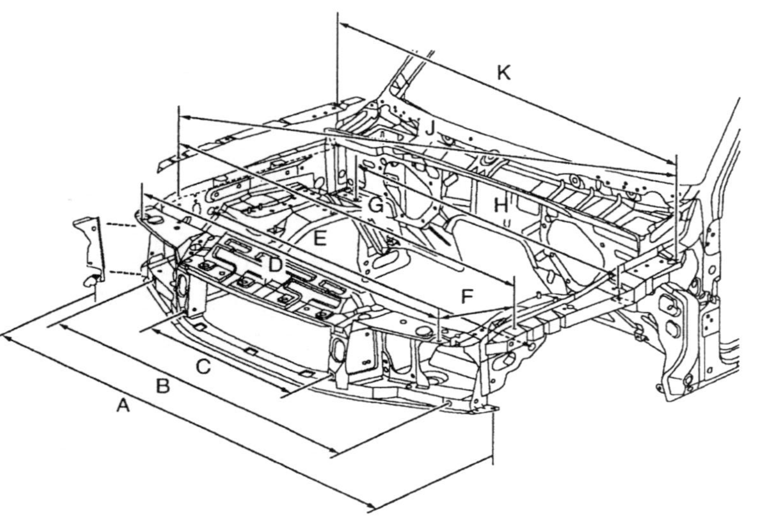

M77 1746

ITEM	FROM	TO	DIMENSION
A	Wing, lower fixing hole - RH	Wing, lower fixing hole - LH	1712 (67.4)
B	Crossmember tooling hole - RH	Crossmember tooling hole - LH	1484.6 (58.45)
C	Grille location slot - RH	Grille location slot - LH	730 (28.74)
D	Headlamp fixing hole - RH	Headlamp fixing hole - LH	1468 (57.79)
E	Valance tooling hole - RH	Valance tooling hole - LH	1628.8 (64.12)
F	Headlamp fixing hole	Wing, front fixing hole	259.5 (10.22)
G	Wing, front fixing hole - RH	Wing, front fixing hole - LH	1668 (65.67)
H	Wheel arch tooling hole - RH	Wheel arch tooling hole - LH	1315 (51.77)
J	Wing, front fixing hole - RH	Wing, rear fixing hole - LH	1845.6 (72.66)
K	Wing, rear fixing hole - RH	Wing, rear fixing hole - LH	1696.1 (66.77)

Dimensions shown outside brackets are metric measurements (millimetres) and those inside brackets are imperial measurements (inches).

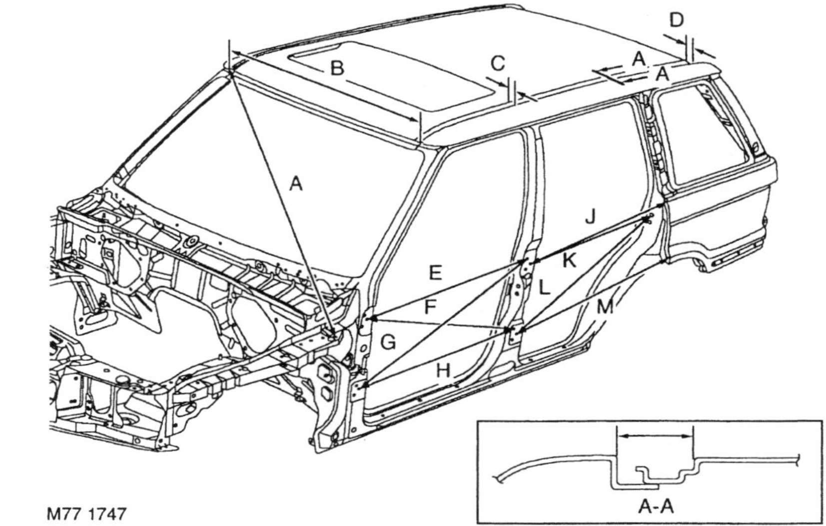

M77 1747

ITEM	FROM	TO	DIMENSION
A	Body side, top front corner point - RH	Wing, rear fixing hole - LH	1758 (69.21)
B	Body side, top front corner point - RH	Body side, top front corner point - LH	1196 (47.09)
C	Roof, top break line	Body side, top break line	36.2 (1.42)
D	Roof, top break line	Body side, top break line	36.2 (1.42)
E	Top hinge fixing - rear hole - front door	Top hinge fixing - top hole - rear door	1061.1 (41.77)
F	Top hinge fixing - rear hole - front door	Bottom hinge fixing - top hole - rear door	1085.4 (42.73)
G	Bottom hinge fixing - rear hole - front door	Top hinge fixing - top hole - rear door	1140.9 (44.92)
H	Bottom hinge fixing - rear hole - front door	Bottom hinge fixing - top hole - rear door	1045.2 (41.15)
J	Top hinge fixing - middle hole - rear door	Body side rear - corner point	973 (38.31)
K	Top hinge fixing - middle hole - rear door	Striker - top fixing hole - rear door	932.8 (36.72)
L	Bottom hinge fixing - rear hole - rear door	Striker - top fixing hole - rear door	1040.4 (40.96)
M	Bottom hinge fixing - rear hole - rear door	Body side rear - corner point	1024.7 (40.34)

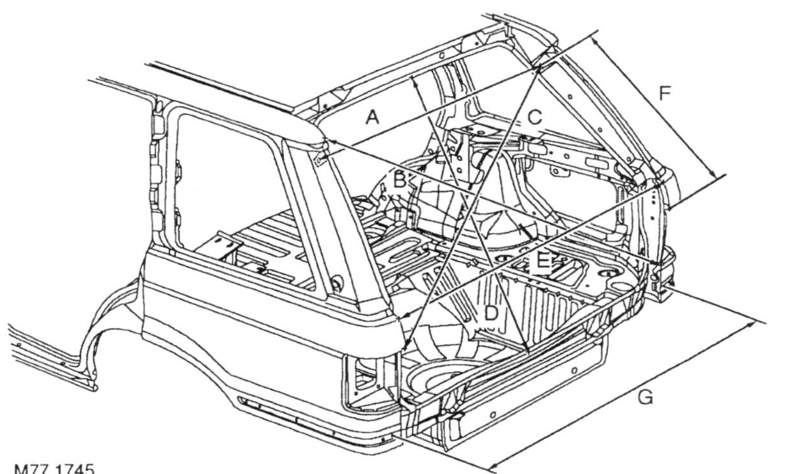

M77 1745

ITEM	FROM	TO	DIMENSION
A	Gas strut spigot fixing hole - RH	Gas strut spigot fixing hole - LH	1175.4 (46.27)
B	Body side rear, lower intersection point - RH	Body side rear, upper intersection point - LH	1620.8 (63.81)
C	Gas strut spigot fixing hole - RH	Body side rear, middle intersection point - LH	1483.2 (58.39)
D	Roof channel break line (centre line of car)	Crossmember rear, top break line (centre line of car)	1109.3 (43.67)
E	Body side rear, middle intersection point - RH	Body side rear, middle intersection point - LH	1415.6 (55.73)
F	Gas strut spigot fixing hole	Body side rear, middle intersection point	727.2 (28.63)
G	Body side rear, trim fixing hole - RH	Body side rear, trim fixing hole - LH	727.2 (28.63)

M77 1748

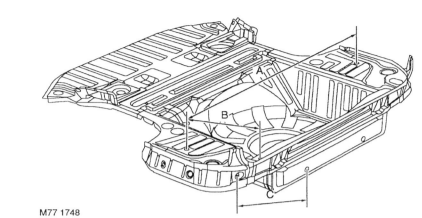

ITEM	FROM	TO	DIMENSION
A	Load floor side - top tooling hole - RH	Load floor side - top tooling hole - LH	1360 (53.54)
B	Load floor side - top tooling hole	Crossmember rear tooling hole	377 (14.84)
C	Load floor side - bottom tooling hole	Lower panel - tooling hole	474.8 (18.69)

Notes

APPROVED MATERIALS

MATERIAL	MANUFACTURER
SEALERS	3M: Bodygard (08158, 08159) Weld Thru' Sealer (08625) Drip-Chek Clear (08401) Drip-Chek Heavy (08531) Flexseal Polyurethane Seam Sealer (08684, 08689, 08694) Polyurethane Sealer (sachet) (08703, 08783, 08788) Super Seam Sealer (08537) Sprayable Sealer (08800, 08823) Bolted Panel Sealer (08572) Body Caulking (08568) Windscreen Sealer (08509) Gurit-Essex: Betafill Clinch and Brushable Sealer (Black) (10215) Betafill Clinch and Brushable Sealer (Grey) (10211) Betafill Clinch and Brushable Sealer (White) (10220) Clinch Joint and Underbody Coating (Grey) (10101) Clinch Joint and Underbody Coating (Beige) (10707) Kent Industries: Leak-Chek Clear Putty (10075) PPG: Polyurethane Seam Sealer (6500) Polyurethane Seam Sealer (92) Terostat Preformed Strip (V11) Terolan Light Seam Sealer Teroson: Terolan Special Brushable Seam Sealer Terostat 1K PU Seam Sealer (SE20) Terostat Sprayable Seam Sealer (9320) Unipart: Promatch Sealing Compound (UBS605, UBS606, UBS607) Promatch Bolted Panel Sealer (UBS111) Wurth: Sealing Compound (890100, 890101, 890102, 890103, 890104, 890105, 890106) Astrolan Engine Bay Wax & Cosmetic Wax (DA3241/DA3243) Weld Thru' Coating (05913)

Approved materials (continued)

MATERIAL	MANUFACTURER
ADHESIVES	3M: Automotive Structural Adhesive (08120) Aerosol Auto Adhesive (Trim) (08080) Spray 80 Adhesive (08090) Ciba-Geigy: Structural Two-Part Epoxy (XB5106/XB5107)
UNDERBODY COATINGS	3M: Spray Schutz (08877) Body Schutz (08861) Stone Chip Coating (Textured) (08868, 08878, 08879) Stone Chip Coating (Smooth) (08158, 08160, 08886) Croda: Crodapol Brushable Underbody Sealer (PV75) Underbody Wax (PW61) Dinol: Tectacote Underbody Wax (205) Teroson: Terotex Underseal CP02 (9320) Unipart: Promatch Underbody Schutz (UBS410) Promatch Underbody Wax (PW61)
WAX COATINGS	3M: Inner Cavity Wax (Transparent) (08909, 08919, 08929) Inner Cavity Wax (Amber) (08901, 08911, 08921) Dinol: Engine Bay & Cosmetic Wax/Lacquer (PW197) Cavity Wax (PW57) Engine Bay Cosmetic Wax/Lacquer (4010) Unipart: Promatch Cavity Wax (UBS508)

Approved materials (continued)

MATERIAL	MANUFACTURER
WELD-THROUGH PRIMERS	3M: Zinc Spray (09113) ICI: Zinc Rich Primer (P-565 634)
GENERAL MATERIALS	3M: Flexible Parts Repair Material (05900) Cleaner and Wax Remover (1 litre) (08984) Waterproof Cloth Tape (Y387/YS3998) Teroson: Sprayable Aerosol, Water Shedder Repair Unipart: Waterproof Tape (GWS121) Urethane Butyl Tape (BHM605)

MATERIALS APPLICATIONS

Joint Types:

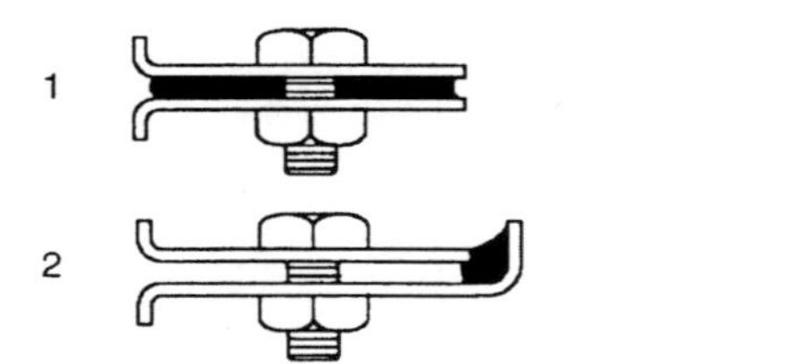

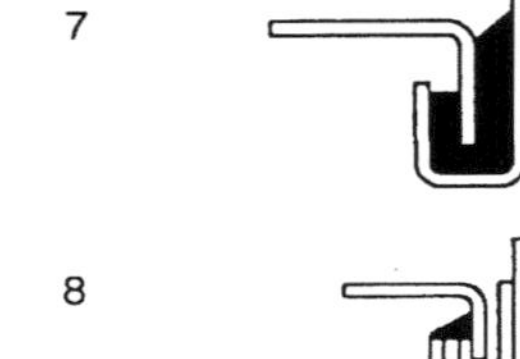

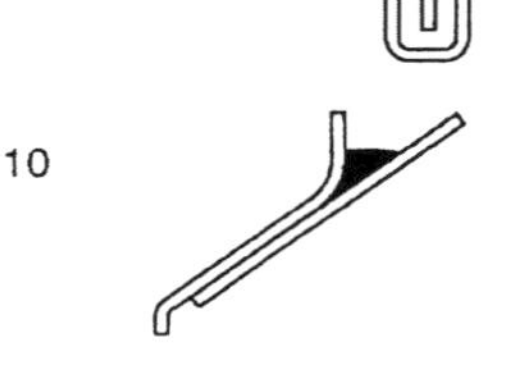

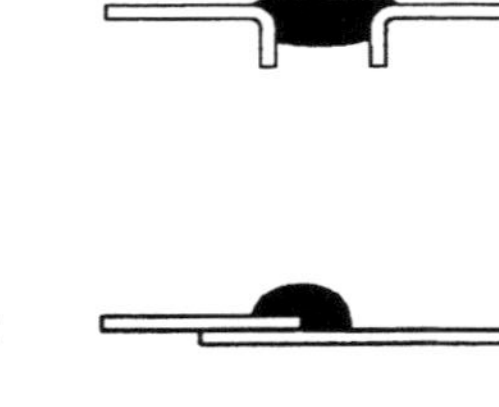

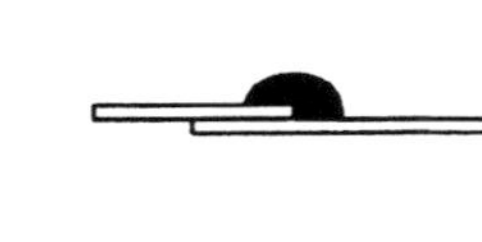

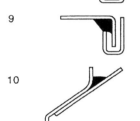

77M1584

1. Between bolted panels
2. Between bolted panel edges
3. Between spot welded panels
4. Between spot welded panel edges
5. Between bonded panels
6. Between bonded panel edges
7. Clinch joints (type a)
8. Clinch joints (type b)
9. Clinch joints (type c)
10. Gaps between panels (type a)
11. Gaps between panels (type b)
12. Lap joint

Materials applications (continued)

MANUFACTURER	MATERIAL/JOINT TYPE
ICI P565 634 3M 09113	Zinc rich primer. Between bolted and spot welded panels, clinch joints (type a). Brush or spray application.
Teroson Terostat V11	Preformed strip. Between bolted panels. Hand application.
Kent Industries 10075 3M 08401 3M 08572 3M 08684 3M 08689 3M 08694 3M 08703 3M 08783 3M 08788 PPG Polyurethane 6500 Teroson 92 Terolan Light Terostat 1K PU Terostat 9320 Unipart UBS 605/6/7 Wurth 890100/1/2/3/4/5/6	Seam sealer. Between bolted panel edges. Applicator gun/by hand.
Ciba-Geigy XBS106/7 3M 08120	Structural adhesive. Between spot welded and bonded panels, clinch joints (type a). Applicator gun, caulking gun.
3M 08625	Seam sealer. Between spot welded panels. Applicator gun.
Kent Industries 10075 3M 08401 3M 08684 PPG 6500 Teroson 92 Terolan Light Terostat 9320 Terostat 1K PU Unipart UBS605/6/7 Wurth 890100/1/2/3/4/5/6	Seam sealer light. Between spot welded panel edges. Hand applicator gun.

Materials applications (continued)

MANUFACTURER	MATERIAL/JOINT TYPE
Ciba-Geigy XBS106/7 3M 08120	Structural adhesive. Between bonded panels. Caulking gun.
PPG 6500 Teroson 92 Terostat 9320 Unipart UBS605/6/7 Wurth 890100/1/2/3/4/5/6	Semi-structural adhesive/anti-flutter material. Between bonded panels. Caulking gun.
Kent Industries 10075 3M 08401 3M 08694 PPG 6500 Teroson 92 Teroson Light Teroson 9320 Terostat 1K PU Unipart UBS605/6/7 Wurth 890100/1/2/3/4/5/6	Seam sealer light. Between bonded panel edges. Hand applicator gun.
Gurit-Essex 10211 Gurit-Essex 10215 Gurit-Essex 10220 3M 08531 3M 08537 3M 08703 3M 08783 3M 08788	Seam sealer. Clinch joints (type b). Caulking gun.

Materials applications (continued)

MANUFACTURER	MATERIAL/JOINT TYPE
Kent Industries 10075 3M 08401 3M 08531 Teroson Terolan Light	Seam sealer light. Clinch joints (type c). Caulking gun, hand applicator gun.
Kent Industries 10075 3M 08401 3M 08684 3M 08689 3M 08694 PPG 6500 Teroson 92 Terolan Light Terostat 1K PU Unipart UBS605/6/7 Wurth 890100/1/2/3/4/5/6	Seam sealer light. Gaps between panels (type a). Hand applicator gun.
Kent Industries 10075 Kent Industries Putty 3M 08401 3M 08531 3M 08568 3M 08684 3M 08689 3M 08694 PPG 6500 Teroson 92 Terolan Light Terostat 9320 Terostat 1K PU Unipart UBS605/6/7 Wurth 890100/1/2/3/4/5/6 Gurit-Essex 10101 Gurit-Essex 10707 3M 08537	Seam sealer heavy. Gaps between panels (type b). Hand applicator gun, applicator tube or caulking gun.
Gurit-Essex 10211 Gurit-Essex 10215 Gurit-Essex 10220 Teroson Brushable Sealer	Brushable sealer. Lap joints (e.g. floor pans). Brush.
Croda PW57 3M Cavity Waxes Unipart UBS508	Cavity wax. Box members, sills. Injection equipment.

Materials applications (continued)

MANUFACTURER	MATERIAL/JOINT TYPE
Croda PV75 3M 08861 3M 08877 Teroson Terotex Underseal Unipart UBS410	Underbody sealing coat. Underbody. Schutz gun, aerosol.
Croda PW61 Dinol 205 Unipart PW61	Underbody wax coat. Underbody. Spray gun or brush.
Astors 3241/3 Croda PW197 Dinol 4010	Engine bay cosmetic wax/lacquer. Spray gun or brush.
3M Stone Chip Coatings	Anti-chip coating. Sill panels. Schutz gun.
3M 05900 Plastic Parts Repair Material	Two-pack material. Repair of plastic parts. Spreader or palette knife.
3M 08509	Dry glazed windscreen sealer. Applicator gun.
Unipart BHM605	Urethane butyl sealer for direct glazing. Caulking gun.
3M YS3998 3M Y387 Unipart GS121	Waterproof tape for sealing apertures. Hand application.
Evode Evo-Stik 3M 08030 3M 08034 3M 08080 3M 08090	Trim fixing adhesive. Brush or aerosol.
3M 08984	Adhesive cleaner/wax remover. Hand application with cloth.

APPLICATION EQUIPMENT

SATA Schutz Gun Model UBE

Specifications:
Air consumption .... 200 litres/min. (7 ft^3/min.) @ 45 psi
Weight 660grams (23.3oz)
Manufactured and supplied by:
Sata Gmbh
Minden Industrial Ltd.
16 Greyfriars Road
Moreton Hall
Bury St. Edmunds
Suffolk IP32 7DX
Tel. (01284) 760791

The Sata Schutz Gun is approved for the re-treatment of vehicle underbody areas with protective coatings as supplied in 1-litre (1.76pt.), purpose-designed, 'one-way' containers. The screw thread fitting (female on the gun) will fit most Schutz-type packs.

Full operating details are supplied with the equipment.

NOTE: Always clean gun after use with the appropriate solvent.

Sata HKD1 Wax Injection Equipment
The Sata HKD1 is approved by Rover for use in all cavity wax re-treatment operations. The equipment comprises a high quality forged gun with 1-litre capacity pressure feed container, a flexible nylon lance, 1100 mm (43.3 in) straight steel lance and hooked wand lance. A quick-change coupling is a standard fitting to enable lances to be easily interchanged. The lances each have their own spray pattern characteristics to suit the type of box section to be treated.

The Sata HKD1 is covered by a 12 month warranty. All replacement parts and service are obtainable from the suppliers.

Cooper Pegler Falcon Junior Pneumatic (Airless)
Manufacturer and supplier:
Cooper Pegler & Co. Ltd.
Burgess Hill
Sussex RH15 9LA
Tel. 04 446 42526

Intended primarily for applying transit wax, the Falcon Junior pneumatic sprayer has a 5-litre (1 gal.) container with integral hand pump. This high quality unit provides a simple and effective means of wax spraying without the need for compressed air or additional services.

A selection of nozzles, lances and hoses together with a trigger valve assembly incorporating a filter enable the sprayer to be used in a variety of applications. These include general maintenance, wax injection and paint application. All parts are fully replaceable and include a wide range of nozzle configurations.

The Falcon Junior is fitted with Viton seals and is guaranteed for 12 months.

3M Application Equipment
Manufacturer:
3M UK PLC
Automotive Trades Group
3M House
PO Box 1
Market Place
Bracknell
Berks. RG12 1JU
Tel. (01344) 858611

All 3M equipment is available from local trade factors or 3M refinishing factors.

3M Caulking Gun 08002
A lightweight, robust metal skeleton gun designed to accommodate 325 mm (12.8 in) cartridge for dispensing sealants etc. This gun facilitates rapid cartridge loading and features a quick-release lever for accurate material ejection and cut-off control.

3M Pneumatic Cartridge Gun 08012
An air line fed gun for application of 3M cartridge products. Excellent ease of application for a smooth sealant bead, and incorporates a regulator valve for additional control.

Other 3m applicator equipment available:

3M Pneumatic Applicator Guns
Air line fed gun for application of 3M sachet sealers (Part No. 08006 for 200 ml [6 fl oz] and 310 ml [9 fl oz] sachets, and Part No. 08007 for all size sachets including 600 ml [18 fl oz]).

3M Applicator Gun 08190
For application of 3M Structural Adhesive 08120.

3M Inner Cavity Wax Applicator Gun
Features 750 mm (29.6 in) flexible tube and using 1-litre (1.76 pt) canisters, this approved equipment is available from all 3M refinishing factors.

Other 3m applicator equipment available:

Heavy Duty Manual Gun.

MATERIALS GUIDE

3M Automotive Structural Adhesive 08120
a two-part epoxy structural adhesive, with 'automix' twin-cartridge dispenser. For door skin and for bonding panel stiffeners. Supplied as twin pack for use in small trigger gun (No. 08190).

3M Bolted Panel Sealer 08572
Preformed strip 20 mm (0.8 in) wide x 2 mm (0.08 in) thick supplied in 4.6 metre (81.2 in) reels. Permanently flexible with good adhesion, for sealing wing to body joints and other bolted or riveted panels.

3M Body Caulking 08568
Thumb-applied sealing compound supplied in 60-packs of preformed strips 300mm (11.8in) long x 6mm (0.24in) wide. For sealing large openings and fissures. Non-hardening, does not dry out or crack, can be overpainted immediately.

3M Drip-Chek Sealer Heavy 08531

For use on vertical fissures and seams up to 3mm (0.12in.) wide for a firm but flexible seal which will not harden or shrink. Self-levelling, will not sag on vertical surfaces. May be worked with a tool or smoothed with a wet finger.

Supplied in 150 ml (4.5 fl oz) tubes.

3M Drip-Chek Sealer Clear 08401
An easily flowing sealer similar to Drip-Chek Heavy but of clear consistency. Ideal for an almost invisible spot weal over finished paintwork. Can be overpainted or even mixed with paint colour to form a self-coloured sealant.

Supplied in 150 ml (4.5 fl oz) tubes.

3M Super Seam Sealer 08537
A brushable sealer designed to simulate original factory-applied sealer on all overlap joints such as floor pans, wheel arches, boot and load space seams and fuel filler cap surrounds. Resistant to oil, petrol and water. Should be brushed on in **ONE** direction only for best results.

WARNING: Must be stored under conditions applicable to highly flammable materials.

3M Flexseal 08684, 08689 AND 08694
A high solid, non-shrinking, polyurethane body sealer for use in either a hand gun or pneumatic applicator gun. Excellent adhesion and sealing properties. Resistant to oil, petrol and water. Supplied in 310 ml (9 fl oz) cartridges and in a choice of black, white or grey.

3M Polyurethane Sachet Sealer 08703, 08783, 08788
Similar to Flexseal polyurethane but available in collapsible foil sachets in 310 ml (9 fl oz) and 600 ml (18 fl oz) sizes with a choice of three colours: black, grey or white.

3M Windscreen Sealer 08509
Non-hardening sealant for dry-glazed, weatherstrip-type windscreens. Applied with applicator gun.

Supplied in 310 ml (9 fl oz) cartridges.

3M Spray Schutz 08877, Body Schutz 08861
Flexible, rubberised, fast-drying coating which dries to a black textured finish.

Spray Schutz supplied in 600 ml (18 fl oz) aerosols. Spray Schutz and Body Schutz also supplied in 1-litre (1.76 pt) cartridges to fit Schutz Gun.

3M Flexible Parts Repair Material 05900
A fast-curing, two-part system for repairing minor damage to plastic bumpers, spoilers, valances etc. Dries in 30 mins.

Supplied as two-pack 320 ml (10 fl oz) kit.

3M Weld Thru' SEALER 08625
For anti-corrosion protection between spot welded panels. Brush application.

Supplied in 1-litre (1.76 pt) canisters.

3M Bodygard
Rubber-based, stone chip protective coating for panels. Fast drying, low bake compatible and may be overpainted. Varying textures obtainable depending on type of finish required. Available in black (1-litre [1.76 pt] pack 08858, aerosol 08158) or grey (1-litre [1.76 pt] pack 08859, aerosol 08159).

3M Inner Cavity Wax
For protective coating on inner panels. Excellent anti-corrosion properties. Available in transparent or amber consistencies, and 1-litre (1.76 pt) canister or 500 ml (0.88 pt) aerosol packs.

3M Zinc Spray 09113
Anti-corrosive coating for spot welding applications on joints and seams. Supplied in 500 ml (0.88 pt) aerosol packs.

3M Waterproof Cloth Tape YS3998
Black waterproof tape for sealing door apertures and body box section access holes. Long-lasting, moisture-resistant adhesive will withstand immersion in water.

Supplied in 50-metre (164.2 ft) rolls in a variety of widths.

3M Adhesive Cleaner and Wax Remover 08984
For surface preparation before application of most types of adhesive, coating and sealant, also for removal of tar, silicone polish, wax, grease and oil. Non-staining. May also be used for cleaning adhesive remnants from sander disc backing pads.

Supplied in 1-litre (1.76 pt) canisters.

CORROSION PROTECTION

Factory Treatments
The New Range Rover is treated with the following anti-corrosion materials in production:

- A PVC-based underbody sealer material which is sprayed onto the underfloor, wheel arches and undersill areas.
- An application of cavity wax which is sprayed into enclosed cavities, box sections and lower inner door panels.
- A final coating of underbody wax to cover the complete underfloor including components but excluding brake discs.
- A coat of protective lacquer or wax applied to the engine bay area.

In addition to the above measures, all steel parts are zinc-coated both sides, and front wings, door and tailgate skins are manufactured from aluminium.

The information given on the following pages is intended as a guide and shows the areas to be treated with cavity wax, as well as the access holes used during manufacture. **See GENERAL INFORMATION DATA, Sealing and corrosion protection section.**

Underbody Wax
A coat of underbody wax is applied to the entire underbody inboard of the sill vertical flanges, and covers all moving and flexible components EXCEPT for wheels and tyres, brakes and exhaust. The wax is applied over paints and underbody sealers.

The underbody wax must be reinstated following all repairs affecting floor panels.

CAUTION: Old underbody wax must be completely removed from a zone extending at least 200 mm (7.9 in) beyond the area where new underbody sealer is to be applied.

Underbody Sealer
Underfloor areas and outer sill panels are treated with a Plastisol PVC underbody sealer. This material is not suitable for re-treatment.

When repairing areas of underbody sealer, strip the factory-applied material back to a suitable break point, ensuring that a clean metal surface is exposed and that the edge of the existing material adheres soundly to the panel.

Blanking plugs and grommets in the floor pan (except those used for wax injection) MUST be fitted before underbody sealer application. Heat-fusible plugs which have been disturbed should either be refitted with the aid of a hot air blower or replaced with rubber grommets.

NOTE: Application of new underbody sealer must be carried out between primer and surfacer paint operations. Areas where seam sealer is used should be re-treated as necessary before application of underbody sealer.

CAUTION: Ensure that suspension units, wheels, tyres, power unit, driveshafts, exhaust and brakes (including all mounting points) are shielded prior to application of fresh underbody sealer.

Engine Bay Wax
Reinstate protective engine bay wax disturbed during repairs using the approved material.

Stone Chip Resistant Paint/Primer
Re-treat all areas protected with factory-applied anti-chip primer with suitable approved material in repair.

Inspections during Maintenance Servicing
It is a requirement of the Land Rover Corrosion Warranty that the vehicle body is checked for corrosion by an authorised Land Rover dealer at least once a year, to ensure that the factory-applied protection remains effective.

Service Job Sheets include the following operations to check bodywork for corrosion:

- With the vehicle on a lift, carry out visual check of underbody sealer for damage.
- With the vehicle lowered, inspect exterior paintwork for damage and body panels for corrosion.

NOTE: Wash the vehicle and ensure that it is free from deposits prior to inspection. It is part of the owner's responsibility to ensure that the vehicle is kept free of accumulations of mud which could accelerate the onset of corrosion. The Dealer MUST wash the vehicle prior to inspection of bodywork if the customer has offered it in a dirty condition, and pay special attention to areas where access is difficult.

NOTE: The checks described above are intended to be visual only. It is not intended that the operator should remove trim panels, finishers, rubbing strips or sound deadening materials when checking the vehicle for corrosion and paint damage.

With the vehicle on a lift, and using an inspection or spot lamp, visually check for the following:

- Corrosion damage and damaged paintwork, condition of underbody sealer on front and rear lower panels, sills and wheel arches.
- Damage to underbody sealer on main floor and chassis members. Corrosion in areas adjacent to suspension mountings and fuel tank fixings.

NOTE: The presence of small blisters in PVC underbody sealer is acceptable, providing they do not expose bare metal.

Special attention must be paid to signs of damage caused to panels or corrosion material by incorrect jack positioning.

It is essential to follow the correct jacking and lifting procedures. **See GENERAL INFORMATION DATA, Information section.**

With the vehicle lowered, visually check for evidence of damage and corrosion on all painted areas, in particular the following:

- Front edge of bonnet.
- Visible flanges in engine compartment and boot.
- Lower body and door panels.

Where bodywork damage or evidence of corrosion is found during inspection, rectify this as soon as is practicable, both to minimise the extent of the damage and to ensure the long term effectiveness of the factory-applied corrosion protection treatment. Where the cost of rectification work is the owner's responsibility, the Dealer must advise the owner and endorse the relevant documentation accordingly.

Where corrosion has become evident and is emanating from beneath a removable component (e.g. trim panel, window glass, seat etc.), remove the component as required to permit effective rectification.

Underbody Protection Repairs
When body repairs are carried out, always ensure that full sealing and corrosion protection treatments are restored. This applies both to the damaged area, and also to areas where protection has been indirectly impaired as a result of accident damage or repair operations.

Prior to straightening out or panel beating, remove all corrosion protection material in the damaged area. This applies in particular to panels coated with wax, PVC underbody sealer, sound deadening pads etc.

WARNING: DO NOT use oxy-acetylene gas equipment to remove corrosion prevention materials. Large amounts of fumes and gases are liberated by these materials when they burn.

Equipment for the removal of tough anti-corrosion sealers offers varying degrees of speed and effectiveness. The compressed air-operated scraper (NOT an air chisel) offers a relatively quiet mechanical method of removal using an extremely rapid reciprocating action. During use, direct the operating end of the tool along the work surface.

The most common method is by the use of a hot air blower with integral scraper.

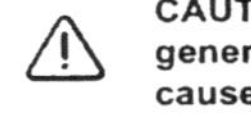

CAUTION: High temperatures can be generated with this equipment which may cause fumes. Always exercise care in its use.

Another tool, and one of the most efficient methods, is the rapid-cutting 'hot knife'. This tool uses a wide blade and is quick and versatile, able to be used easily in profiled sections where access is otherwise awkward.

Use the following procedure when repairing underbody coatings:

1. Remove existing underbody coatings.
2. After panel repair, clean the affected area with a solvent wipe, and treat bare metal with an etch phosphate material.
3. Re-prime the affected area. **DO NOT under any circumstances apply underbody sealer directly to bare metal surfaces.**
4. Replace all heat-fusible plugs which have been disturbed. Use rubber grommets of equivalent size if plugs are not available, but ensure that they are embedded in sealer.
5. Mask off all mounting faces from which mechanical components, hoses and pipe clips, have been removed. Underbody sealer must be applied **before** such components are refitted.
6. Brush sealer into all exposed seams.
7. Spray the affected area with an approved service underbody sealer.
8. Remove masking from component mating faces, and touch-in where necessary. Allow adequate drying time before applying underbody wax.

Underbody Wax
After refitting mechanical components, including hoses, pipes and small fixtures, mask off the brake discs and apply a coat of approved underbody wax.

NOTE: Where repairs include the application of finish paint coats in the areas requiring underbody wax, paint operations must be carried out BEFORE wax application.

Underbonnet Wax
Where repairs have involved replacement of engine bay panels, treat the entire engine compartment including all components, clips and small fixtures with an approved underbonnet lacquer or wax.

Proprietary Anti-Corrosion Treatments
The application of proprietary anti-corrosion treatments in addition to the factory-applied treatment could invalidate the Corrosion Warranty and should be discouraged. This does not apply to approved, compatible, preservative waxes which may be applied on top of existing coatings.

Fitting Approved Accessories
When fitting accessories it is important that the vehicle's corrosion protection is not affected, either by breaking the protective coating or by introducing a moisture trap.

DO NOT screw self-tapping screws directly into the body panel but fit plastic inserts first. Protect the edges of holes drilled into panels, chassis members and other body parts with a suitable zinc rich or acid etch primer, followed by a protective wax coating brushed onto the surrounding area.

DO NOT affix unpainted metal surfaces of any accessory directly to the vehicle bodywork unless they are suitably protected. Where metal faces are bolted together always interpose a suitable interface material such as weldable zinc rich primer, extruded strip or zinc tape.

Cavity Wax Injection
Box sections treated with cavity wax are shown in this section. Repairs affecting these areas must include re-treatment with an approved cavity wax, using the access points illustrated. In addition, all interior surfaces which have been disturbed during repairs must be wax injected whether they have been treated in production or not. This includes all box members, cavities, door interiors etc. It is permissible to drill extra holes for access where necessary, provided these are not positioned in load-bearing members. Ensure that such holes are treated with a suitable zinc rich primer, brushed with wax and then sealed with a rubber grommet.

Prior to wax injection, ensure that the cavity to be treated is free from any contamination or foreign matter. Where necessary, clear out any debris using a compressed air supply.

Carry out wax injection after final paint operations. During application, ensure that the wax covers all flange and seam areas and that it is applied to all repaired areas of both new and existing panels.

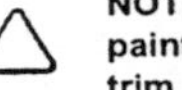

NOTE: Apply cavity wax AFTER the final paint process and BEFORE refitting of any trim components.

It should also be noted that new panel assemblies and body shells are supplied without wax injection treatment which must be carried out after repairs.

Effective cavity wax protection is vital. Always observe the following points:

- Complete all finish paint operations before wax application.
- Clean body panel areas and blow-clean cavities if necessary, before treatment.
- Maintain a temperature of 18°C (64°F) during application and drying.
- Check the spray pattern of injection equipment.
- Mask off all areas not to be wax coated and which could be contaminated by wax overspray.
- Remove body fixings, such as seat belt retractors, if contamination is at all likely.
- Move door glasses to fully closed position before treating door interiors.
- Treat body areas normally covered by trim before refitting items.
- Check that body and door drain holes are clear after the protective wax has dried.
- Keep all equipment clean, especially wax injection nozzles.

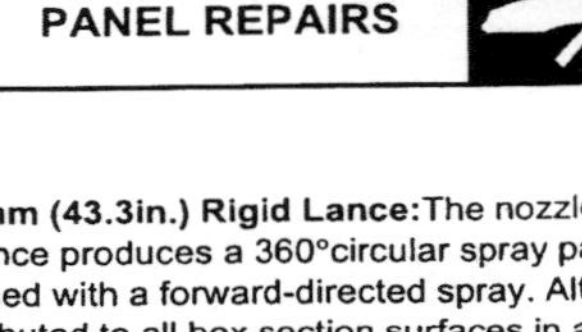

Application Equipment and Techniques

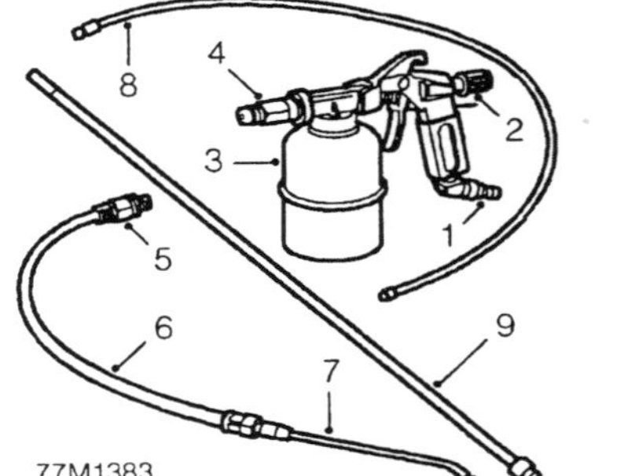

1. Air inlet
2. Flow control (spray pattern adjustment)
3. Pressure cup (1 litre [1.7 pt] capacity). Maximum pressure 140 psi (9.7 bar, 9.8 kg/cm^2).
4. Gun connector
5. Lance nipple connection
6. Flexible lance
7. Rigid directional hook wand (forward cone spray pattern)
8. Flexible nylon 1100mm (43.3in.) lance with 360°spray pattern
9. Rigid 1100mm (43.3in.) lance with 360°spray pattern

When re-treating wax-injected areas which have been disturbed during repairs, it is necessary to use a compressed air spray gun with integral pressure cup and a selection of interchangeable lances.

The following points must be observed during use, according to the attachments fitted:

- Use the rigid or flexible lance attachments with 360°spray dispersal when treating enclosed areas, to ensure maximum coverage.
- Where openings are restricted, use the hook nozzle to provide a more directional spray (e.g. inside narrow or short box sections).
- Spray exposed underbody surfaces directly from the gun less lance attachment and without disconnecting the fluid coupling.

1100 mm (43.3in.) Rigid Lance: The nozzle on the rigid lance produces a 360°circular spray pattern combined with a forward-directed spray. Although wax is distributed to all box section surfaces in a single stroke, effective and complete coverage is best achieved in long, straight structures and box section cavities by spraying on both outbound and return strokes of the lance.

The rigid lance also provides the positional accuracy required in shaped sections, by allowing visual assessment.

CAUTION: Do not force the lance into access holes when using this attachment.

1100 mm (43.3in.) Flexible Nylon Lance: This lance is similar in pattern to the rigid version, but provides the additional penetration needed for curved sections or in places where access is difficult. Its main limitation is a lack of positional accuracy inside box sections.

Carry out spraying on the outward stroke of the lance. Withdraw the lance slowly to ensure sufficient coverage. **DO NOT withdraw the lance too quickly.**

Keep the nylon tube of the lance away from the edges of the access hole to eliminate abrasion and extend the life of the tube. Take care to ensure that spraying ceases just before the nozzle emerges from the access hole. To assist this process, apply RED paint to the final 30mm (1.2in.) of the nozzle.

Hook Nozzle on Flexible Lance: The rigid hook produces a highly atomised, forward-directed, fully conical spray pattern having long range and good dispersion characteristics. This combination has good directional capabilities for the treatment of short, narrow sections and may also be used for direct spraying of inner wheel arches etc.

Position the flat area at the end of the lance at 180°to the nozzle spray direction. This will help to guide the spray more accurately when it is concealed in a box section or access hole.

For general spraying move the nozzle in an arc from side to side, to ensure full coverage.

NOTE: Keep all wax injection/application equipment clean. Use white spirit for this purpose immediately after wax injection operations.

Precautions during Body Repairs and Handling

Take care when handling the vehicle in the workshop. PVC underbody sealers, seam sealers, underbody wax and body panels may be damaged if the vehicle is carelessly lifted.

Always follow the correct lifting, jacking and towing procedures as shown in **GENERAL INFORMATION DATA, Information section**, paying particular attention to the following points:

- Locate trolley jack pads properly before lifting and lower the jack fully before withdrawal.
- Use only the approved hoisting points when overhead hoisting is required.
- Locate the lifting heads of wheel-free lifts correctly, with rubber or similar material placed between lifting head and underbodv.

Steam Cleaning and Dewaxing
Due to the high temperatures generated by steam cleaning equipment, there is a risk that certain trim items could be damaged and some adhesives and corrosion prevention materials softened or liquified.

Adjust the equipment so that the nozzle temperature does not exceed 90°C (194°F). Take care not to allow the steam jet to dwell on one area, and keep the nozzle at least 300mm (11.8in.) from panel surfaces.

Do NOT remove wax or lacquer from underbody or underbonnet areas during repairs. Should it be necessary to steam clean these areas, apply a new coating of wax or underbody protection as soon as possible.

CAVITY WAX

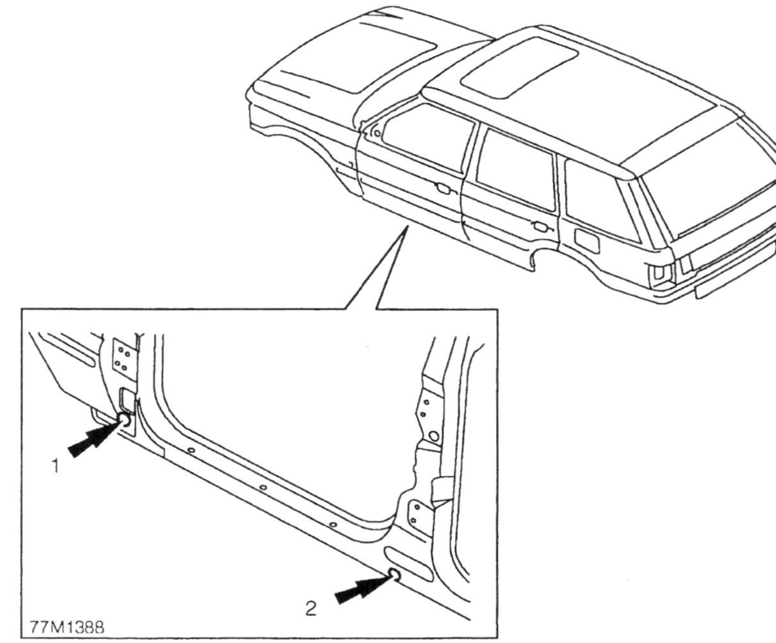

1. Injection hole at lower 'A' post.
2. Injection hole at lower 'BC' post.

All areas symmetrically opposite to those shown are also treated.

See GENERAL INFORMATION DATA, Information section.

SEALANTS AND ADHESIVES

Structural Adhesive

Metal-to-metal adhesive is applied to critical joint areas during factory assembly. The material used is a high-temperature, heat cured, nitrile phenolic which serves both to bond two metal surfaces and also to seal the joint against ingress of dust, water, petrol and fumes. This material is not suited for service use, and should be substituted in repair using a suitable medium strength adhesive.

When separating a joint treated with metal-to-metal adhesive, to avoid distortion it is recommended that the joint be gently heated until the bond weakens sufficiently to permit panel separation.

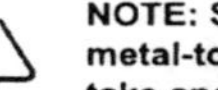

NOTE: Spot welding through metal-to-metal adhesive is feasible, but take special care to adjust the transformer setting to ensure a reliable weld. DO NOT carry out MIG welding on a joint area which has been treated with metal-to-metal adhesive until all traces of adhesive have been removed.

Seam Sealers

A heat cured, PVC Plastisol sealer is applied to joint areas during factory assembly. This material is not suitable for service use.

Carry out seam sealing after the application of primer and before the surfacer and final paint coats. Ensure that surfaces are first cleaned of all grease and oil. Apply the sealer material to the joint as a bead, either by hand or using an applicator gun. Brush sealer well into the joint and wipe smooth using a cloth soaked with solvent such as Shell SBP3. This will ensure an acceptable cosmetic finish.

Apply sealer to ALL accessible joints following repair work. Be aware that damage to a vehicle can often result in deflection to those areas of the body which are remote from the impact. The sealers in these areas can therefore be disturbed by subsequent straightening and repair operations. Check joints in the vicinity of the area undergoing repair for evidence of cracked sealer, clean them out as required and re-treat them with fresh sealer using the following procedure:

- Clean the affected joint or seam and re-treat any exposed metal areas with a suitable etch phosphate primer.
- Treat affected area with an acid-etch primer.
- Apply appropriate seam sealer as necessary.
- Apply appropriate colour coat (and underbody sealer as applicable).

Where joints are inaccessible following the reassembly or fitment of components, ensure that a paste-type sealer is applied to such joints. Certain seams also become inaccessible after the completion of panel repairs. In such instances the paint process should be carried out and sealers applied before final assembly.

Provided access is adequate, apply the sealer to both sides of the repair joint. Where access is limited to one side only (e.g. box sections), inject the affected box member with cavity wax.

CAUTION: ALWAYS deploy an extractor unit to remove toxic fumes when using oxy-acetylene equipment to remove panels treated with wax and sealers.

Sealing Water Leaks

Sealing charts in this section show those areas of the bodyshell most likely to be affected by accident damage and water leaks, and which could therefore require re-treatment in repair. They do not show those joint areas which only apply to factory assembly operations and which are unlikely to be disturbed in service (e.g. centre tunnel), or where the damage would be so severe that the entire bodyshell would normally be written off.

When water leakage occurs, always adopt a logical approach to the problem using a combination of skill, experience and intuition. Do not attempt to reach a conclusion based only on visual evidence, such as assuming that a leak emanates from the windscreen because the footwell is wet. It will often be found that the source of the leak is elsewhere. The correct procedure will increase the chance of locating a leak, however obscure it may seem.

Tools and Equipment

The following tools and equipment are recommended for detection and rectification of water leaks:

1. Garden sprayer (hand-operated).
2. Wet/dry vacuum cleaner.
3. Dry absorbent cloths.
4. Battery torch.
5. Small mirror.
6. Weatherstrip locating tool.
7. Trim panel remover.
8. Small wooden or plastic wedges.
9. Dry compressed air supply.
10. Hot air blower.
11. Sealer applicators.
12. Ultrasonic leak detector.

During leak detection, the vehicle should be considered in three basic sections:

- The front interior space,
- The rear passenger space (where applicable), and
- The rear loadspace or boot.

Testing

From the information supplied by the customer it should be possible for the bodyshop operator to locate the starting point from which the leak may be detected. After the area of the leak has been identified, find the actual point of entry into the vehicle. A simple and effective means initially is an ordinary garden spray with provision for pressure and jet adjustment. This will allow water to be directed in a jet or turned into a fine spray. Use a mirror and a battery-powered torch (NOT a mains voltage inspection lamp) to see into dark corners.

The sequence of testing is particularly important. Start at the lowest point and work slowly upwards, to avoid testing in one area while masking the leak in another. For example, if testing started at the level of the windscreen, any water cascading into the plenum chamber could leak through a bulkhead grommet and into the footwells. Even at this point it could still be wrongly assumed that the windscreen seal was at fault.

Another important part of identifying a water leak is by visual examination of door aperture seals, grommets and weatherstrips for damage, deterioration or misalignment, together with the fit of the door itself against the seals.

Sealing
When the point of the leak has been detected, proceed to rectify it using the following procedure:

1. Renew all door aperture seals and weatherstrips which have suffered damage, misalignment or deterioration.
2. Check all body seals to ensure that they are correctly located on their mounting flanges/faces using a locating tool if necessary.
3. Dry out body seams to be treated using compressed air and/or a hot air blower as necessary.
4. Apply sealant on the outside of the joint wherever possible to ensure the exclusion of water.
5. When rectifying leaks between a screen glass and its weatherstrip (or in the case of direct glazing, between the glass and bodywork), avoid removing the glass if possible. Apply the approved material either at the glass to weatherstrip or glass to body.

SEALING CHARTS

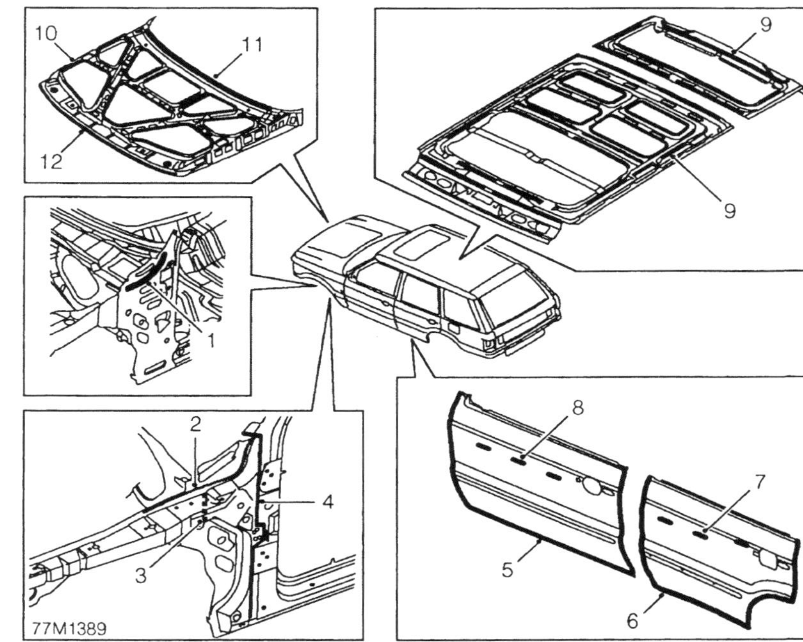

1. Structural adhesive
2. Structural adhesive
3. Structural adhesive
4. Structural adhesive
5. Structural adhesive, seam sealer
6. Structural adhesive, seam sealer
7. Semi-structural adhesive/anti-flutter material
8. Semi-structural adhesive/anti-flutter material
9. Semi-structural adhesive/anti-flutter material
10. Semi-structural adhesive/anti-flutter material
11. Structural adhesive
12. Structural adhesive

All areas symmetrically opposite to those shown are also treated.

see **GENERAL INFORMATION DATA, Information section.**

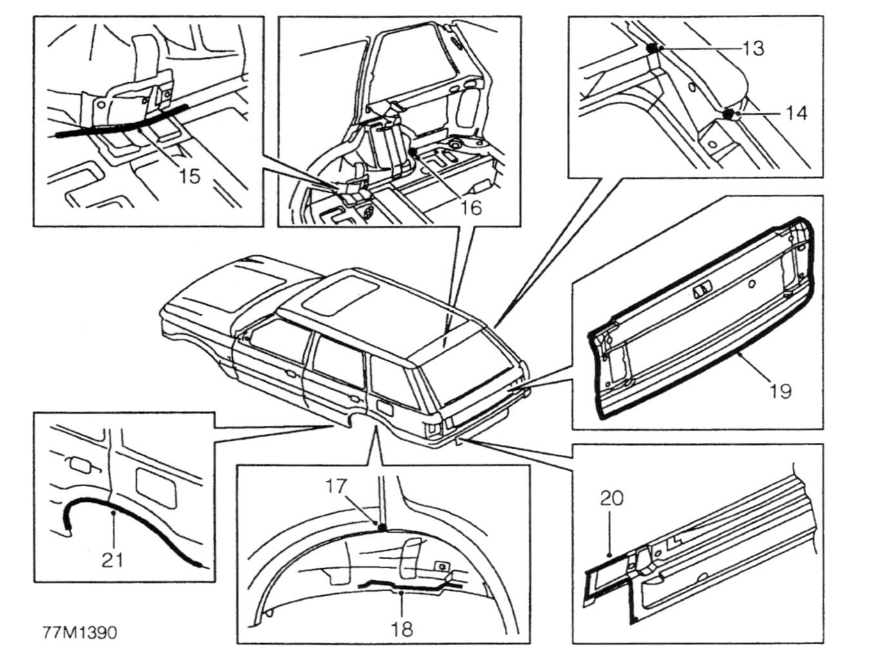

77M1390

13. Putty
14. Putty
15. Structural adhesive
16. Putty, seam sealer heavy
17. Putty, seam sealer heavy
18. Structural adhesive
19. Structural adhesive
20. Structural adhesive
21. Structural adhesive

All areas symmetrically opposite to those shown are also treated.

See GENERAL INFORMATION DATA, Information section.

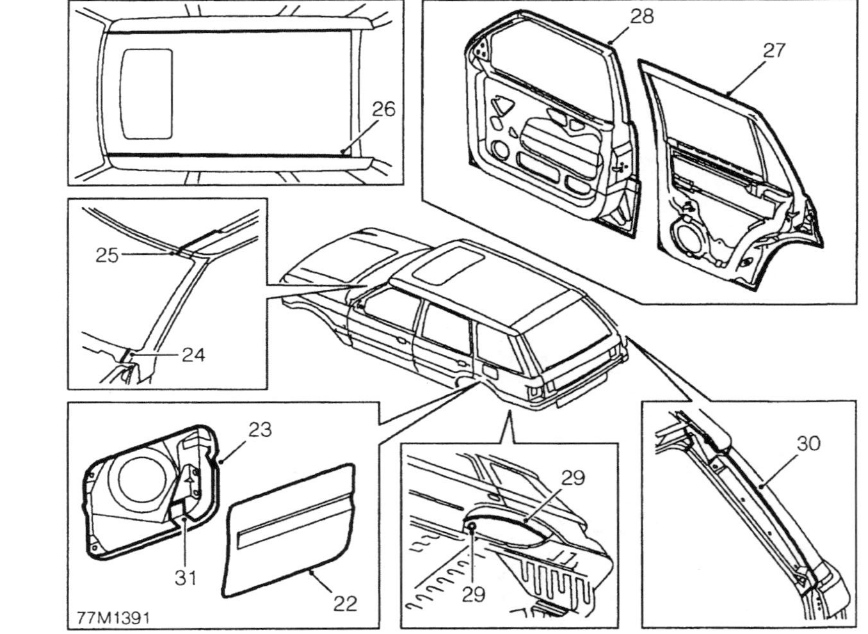

77M1391

22. Structural adhesive
23. Semi-structural adhesive/anti-flutter material
24. Seam sealer light
25. Seam sealer light, structural adhesive
26. Seam sealer light
27. Seam sealer
28. Seam sealer
29. Seam sealer heavy
30. Seam sealer light
31. Seam sealer light

All areas symmetrically opposite to those shown are also treated.

See GENERAL INFORMATION DATA, Information section.

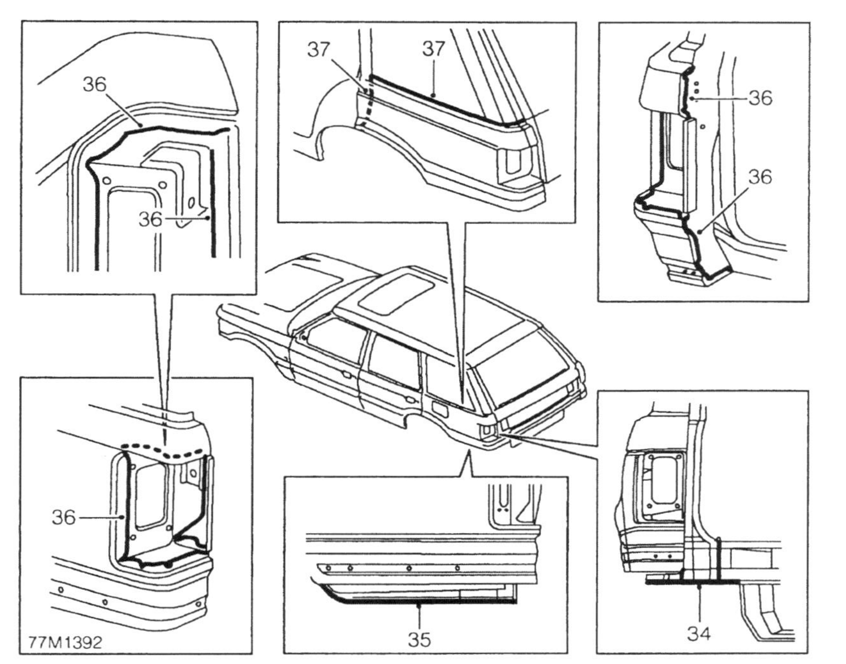

34. Seam sealer light
35. Seam sealer light
36. Seam sealer light
37. Seam sealer light

All areas symmetrically opposite to those shown are also treated.

See GENERAL INFORMATION DATA, Information section.

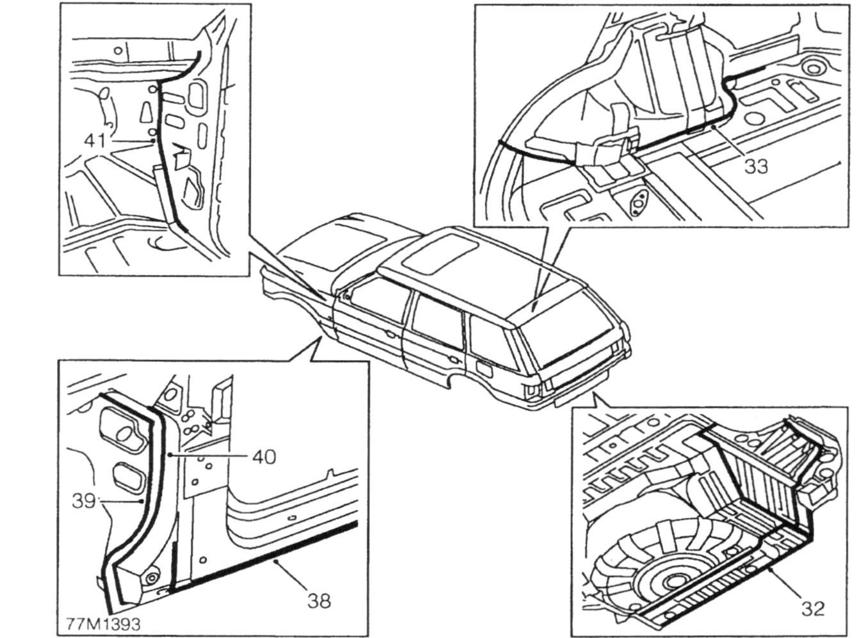

32. Brushable sealer
33. Seam sealer light
38. Seam sealer light
39. Seam sealer light
40. Seam sealer light
41. Seam sealer light

All areas symmetrically opposite to those shown are also treated.

See GENERAL INFORMATION DATA, Information section.

Notes

SERVICE CONDITION OF PANELS

Bodyshell Assembly

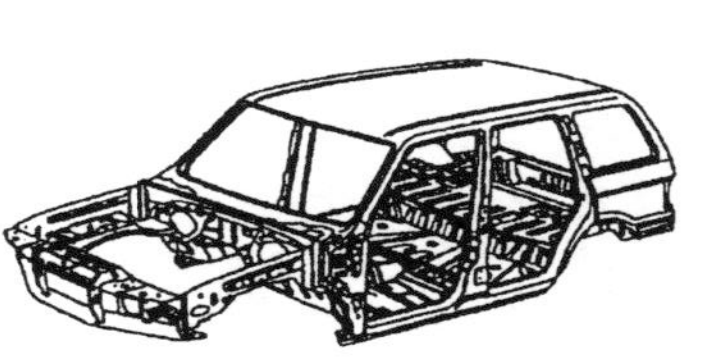

77M1453

Bodyshells, which are also supplied with sunroof aperture (not shown), are serviced less front wings, bonnet, door assemblies and upper/lower tailgates.

Headlamp and Grille Panel

77M1454

Headlamp/grille panels are serviced as a complete assembly including a bolt-on bonnet lock platform.

Front Wing

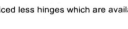

77M1455

Front wings are serviced as separate bolt-on aluminium panels.

Bonnet

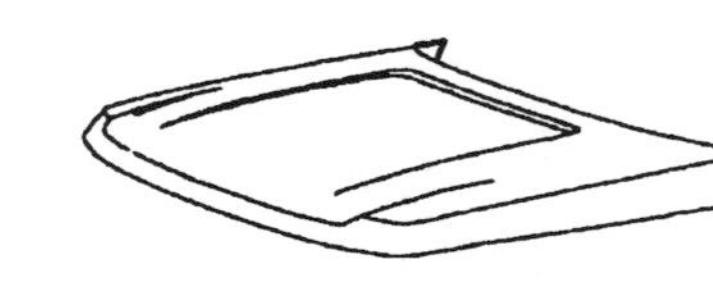

77M1456

Bonnets are serviced less hinges which are available separately.

Valance and Wheel arch

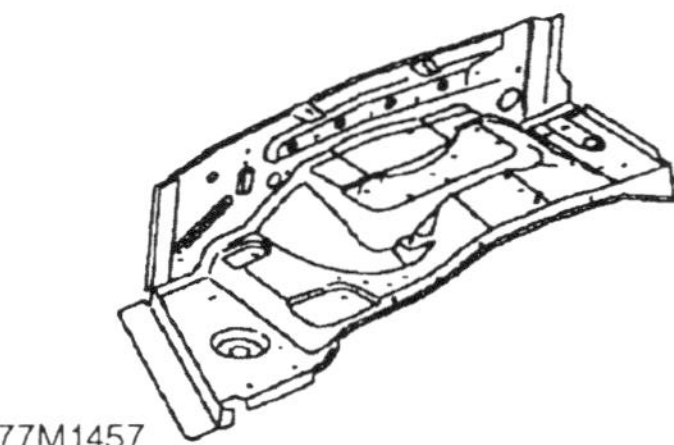

77M1457

Valance and wheel arch panels are serviced as a separate part and are fitted to the bulkhead.

Front Side member

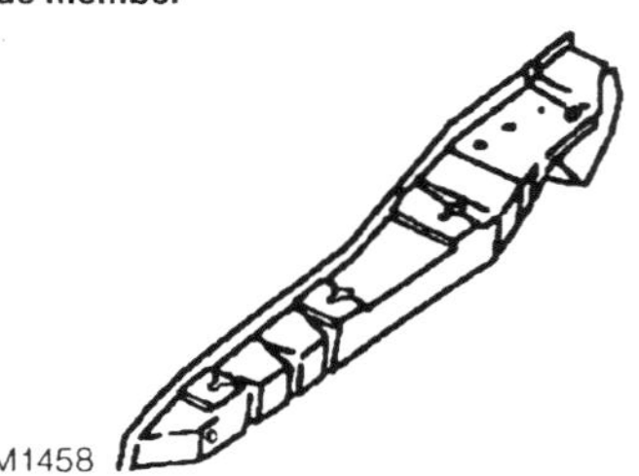

77M1458

Front side members are fitted to the 'A' post and valance/wheel arch.

'A' Post Lower

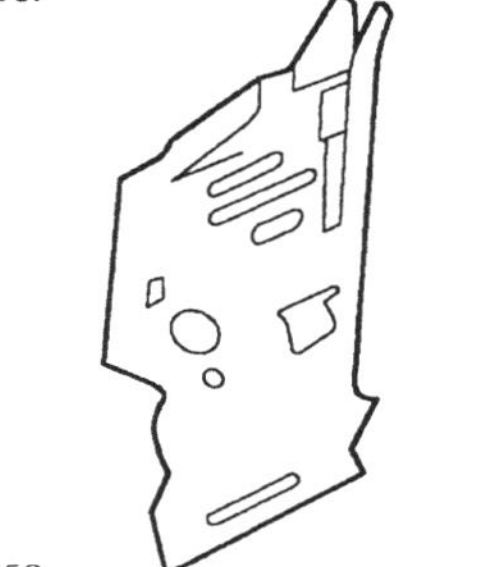

77M1459

The 'A' post lower is fitted to the bulkhead, inner sill and 'A' post reinforcement.

'A' Post Panels

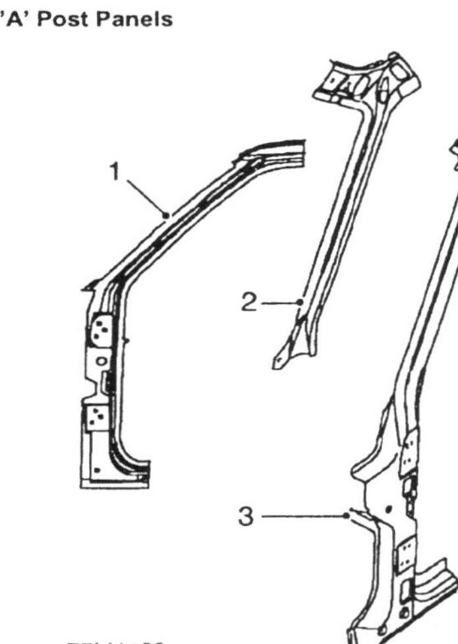

77M1460

'A' posts are serviced as separate 'A' post repair panel (1), upper 'A' post (2) and 'A' post reinforcement (3).

'BC' Post Panels

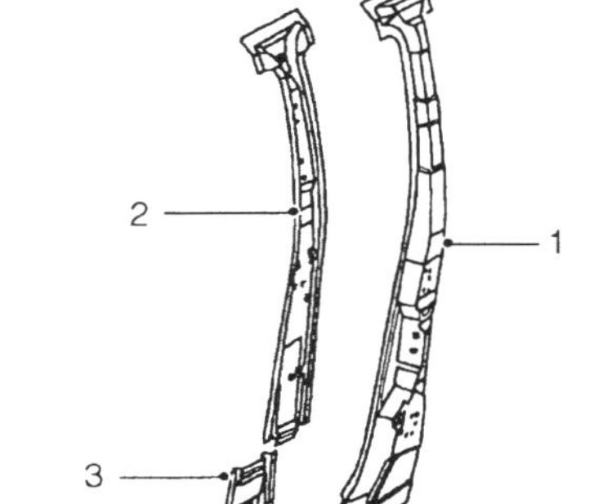

77M1461

'BC' posts are serviced as separate 'BC' post reinforcement (1) and inner 'BC' post panels (2, 3).

Door Assemblies and Outer Door Panels

77M1462

Door assemblies comprise an aluminium outer panel fitted to a steel frame.

'BC' Post Repair Panel

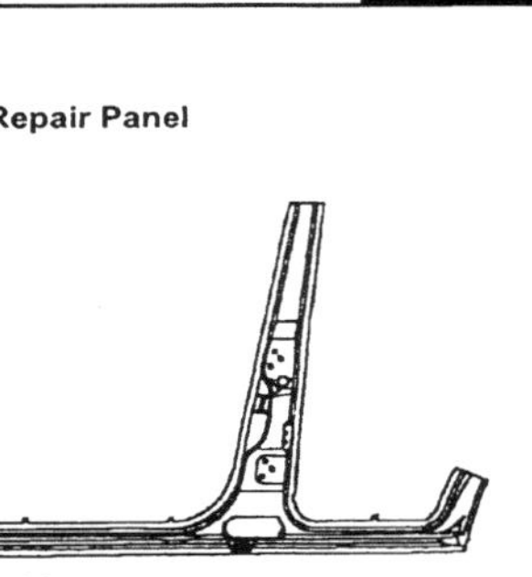

77M1463

'BC' posts are serviced as a complete panel including the sill.

Roof Assembly

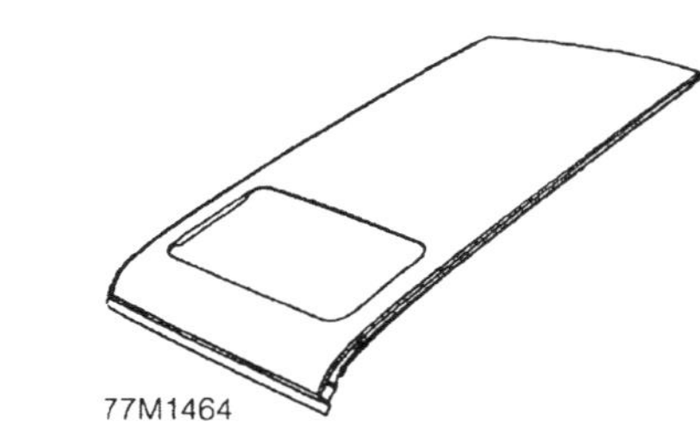

77M1464

Roof assemblies are serviced complete with inner frames. Roof assemblies less sun roof aperture are also available.

Outer Rear Quarter Panel

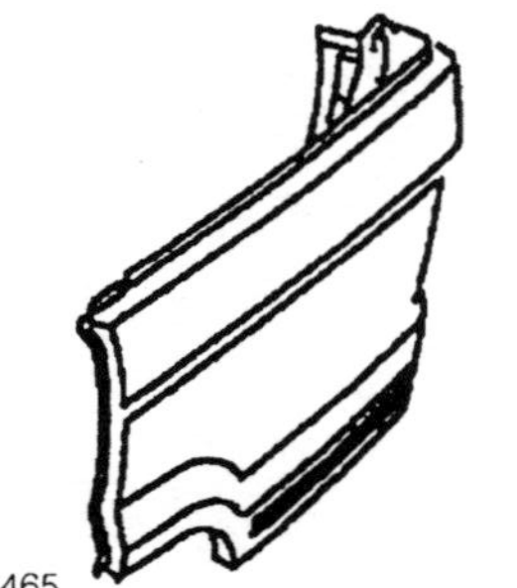

77M1465

Outer rear quarters are serviced as a separate panel.

Lower Panel

77M1466

Lower panels are serviced as an assembly including the tailgate lock reinforcement.

Upper Tailgate Assembly

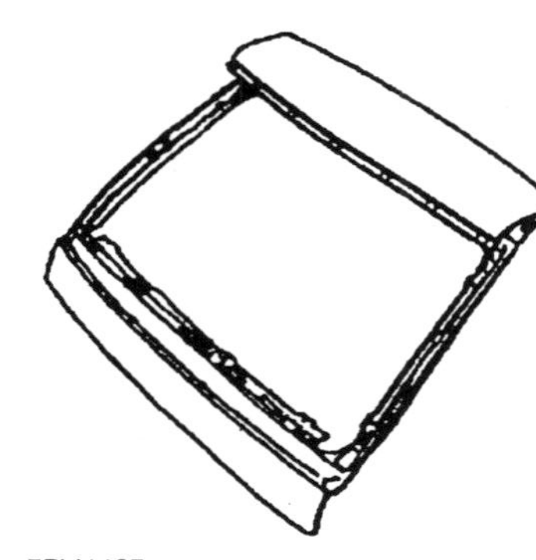

77M1467

Upper tailgates are serviced less hinges, which are available separately.

Lower Tailgate Assembly

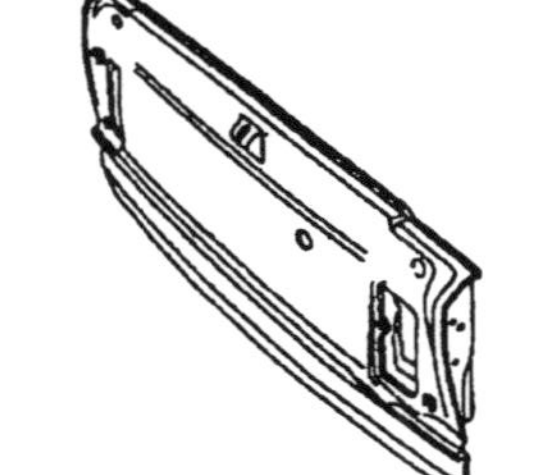

77M1468

Lower tailgate assemblies comprise an aluminium outer panel fitted to a steel frame and are serviced less hinges, which are available separately. Lower tailgate outer panels are also serviced as separate items.

Inner Rear Quarter Panel

77M1469

Inner rear quarters are serviced as an assembly with associated reinforcements and brackets.

Rear Crossmember Panel

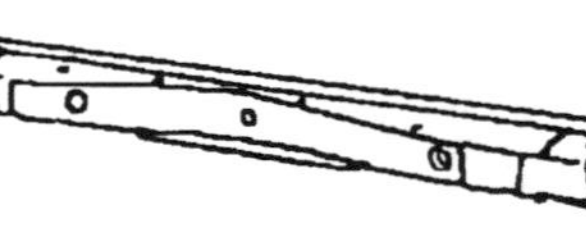

77M1470

The rear crossmember is serviced as a separate panel.

Load Floor Side

77M1471

Load floor sides are serviced as a separate panel.

Rear Crossmember Extension

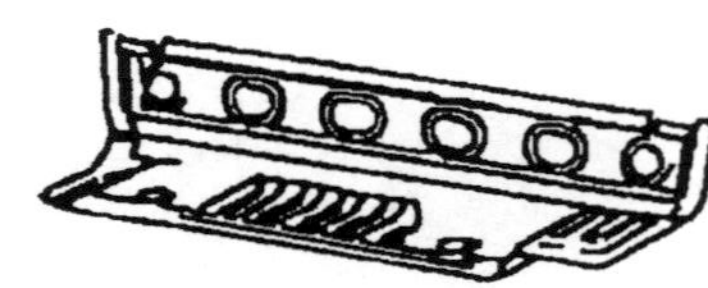

77M1472

The rear crossmember extension is serviced separately.

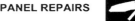

Rear Quarter Repair Panel

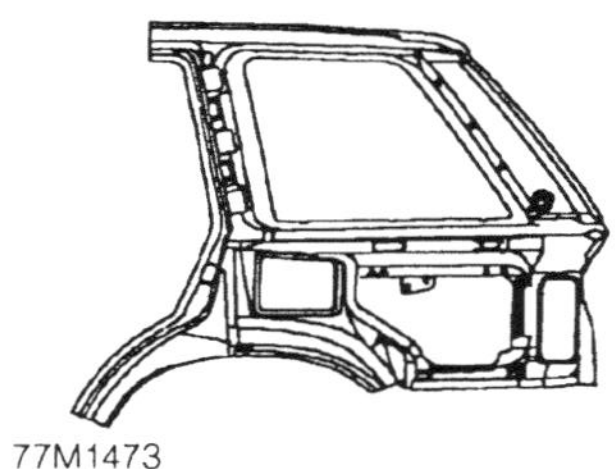

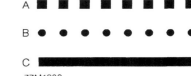

77M1473

The rear quarter which is fitted between the outer panel and inner quarter is serviced as a separate repair panel.

Spare Wheel Closing Panel

77M1474

The spare wheel closing panel is serviced separately and fits at the upper front of the spare wheel well.

GENERAL WELDING PRECAUTIONS

For ease of reference the diagrams on the following pages show only the type of weld used in repair where this varies from that used in production.

When carrying out welding operations the following criteria must be observed:

- Where resistance spot welds have been used in production, these must be reproduced with new spot welds in replacement where possible. All such reproduction spot welds must be spaced 30mm (1.2in.) apart.
- When spot welding, it is recommended that test coupons of the same metal gauges and materials are produced to carry out peel tests to ensure that welding equipment being used can produce a satisfactory joint. Plug welds must be used if a satisfactory spot weld cannot be produced.
- The electrode arms on hand-held spot welding guns must not exceed 300mm (11.81in.)in length.
- Single-sided spot welding is not acceptable.
- Brazing and gas welding are not acceptable EXCEPT where they have been specified in production.
- Where 3 metal thicknesses or more are to be welded together it is imperative to use MIG plug welds to ensure joint strength.
- MIG plug welds must be used in repair joints where there is no access for a resistance spot welder. To replace each production spot weld an 8 mm (0.31 in) hole must be drilled and/or punched, and a MIG weld then made in its place. The number of plug welds must match exactly the number of spot welds which have been removed.
- Where holes are left in an existing panel after removal of the spot welds, a single MIG plug weld will be made in each hole as appropriate.
- The replacement welds in the welding diagrams are denoted by the following symbols:

77M1386

A. Single thickness plug welds

B. Multiple thickness plug welds

C. MIG seam weld

Seat Belt Anchorages
Seat belt anchorages are safety critical. When making repairs in these areas it is essential to follow design specifications. Note that High Strength Low Alloy (HSLA) steel may be used for seat belt anchorages.

Where possible, the original production assembly should be used, complete with its seat belt anchorages, or the cut line should be so arranged that the original seatbelt anchorage is not disturbed.

All welds within 250mm (9.9in.) of seat belt anchorages must be carefully checked for weld quality, including spacing of spot welds.

WARNING: Body parts incorporating seat belt anchorages MUST be renewed completely if damaged beyond repair, as the welds in these areas are safety critical and cannot be disturbed.

PANEL REPLACEMENT PROCEDURE

General
This information is designed to explain the basic panel removal and replacement method. This standard method may vary slightly from one vehicle to another. The main criterion in removal and replacement of body panels is that Land Rover's original standard is maintained as far as possible.

Remove Panel

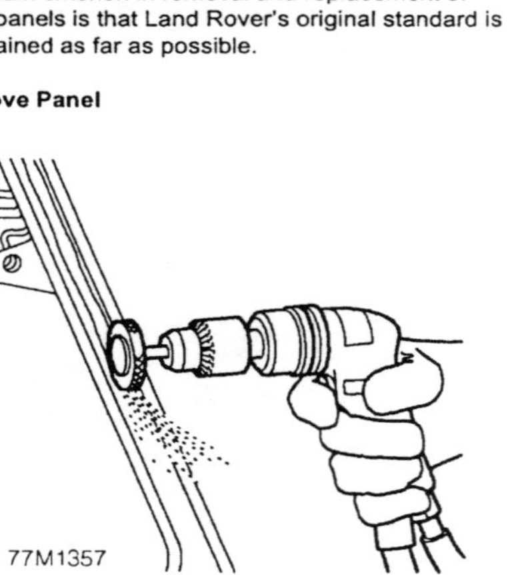
77M1357

1. Expose resistance spot welds. For those spot welds which are not obviously visible, use a rotary drum sander or wire brush fitted to an air drill, or alternatively a hand held wire brush.

NOTE: In wheel arch areas it may be necessary to soften underbody coating using a hot air gun, prior to exposing spot welds.

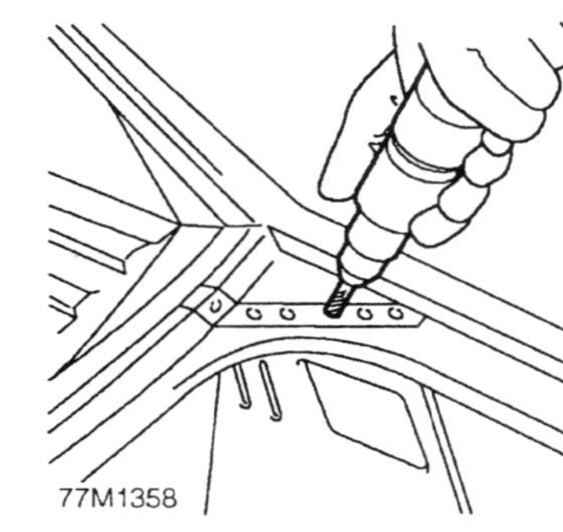
77M1358

2. Cut out welds using a cobalt drill.

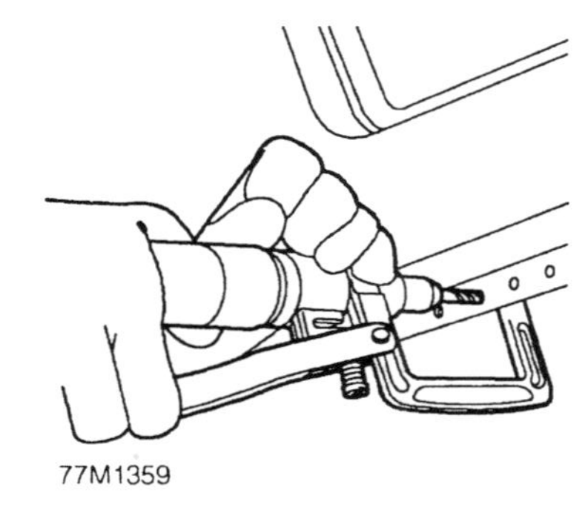
77M1359

3. Alternatively use a clamp-type spot weld remover.

77M1360

4. Cut away the bulk of the panel as necessary using an air saw.

NOTE: On certain panel joints MIG welds and braze should be removed using a sander where possible, before cutting out the panel bulk.

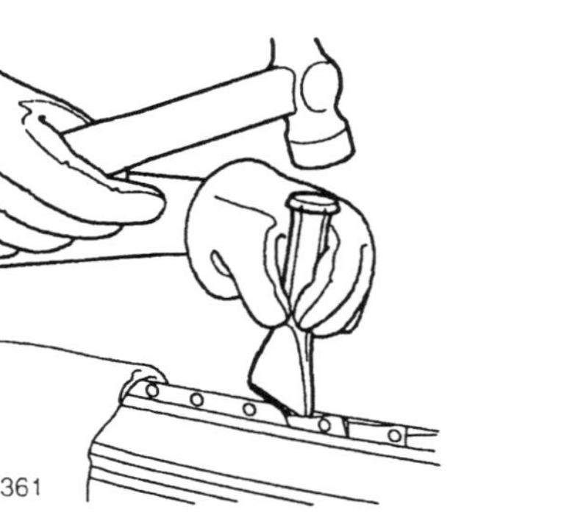
77M1361

5. Separate spot welded joints and remove panel remnants using hammer, bolster chisel and pincers.

Prepare Old Surfaces

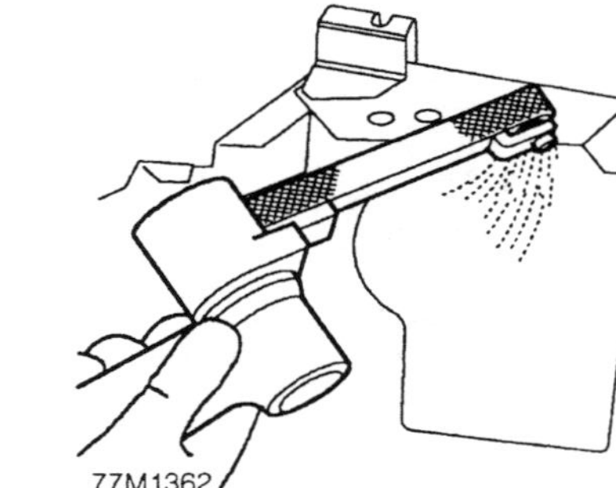
77M1362

6. Clean all panel joint edges to a bright smooth finish, using a belt-type sander.

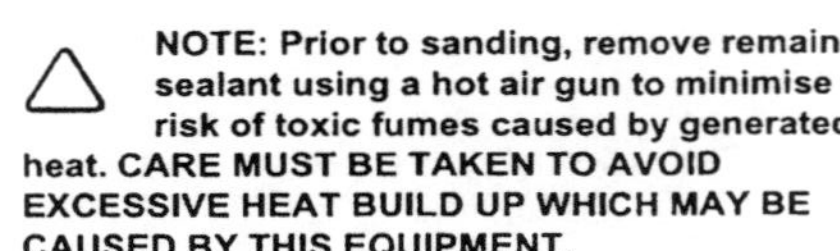
NOTE: Prior to sanding, remove remaining sealant using a hot air gun to minimise the risk of toxic fumes caused by generated heat. CARE MUST BE TAKEN TO AVOID EXCESSIVE HEAT BUILD UP WHICH MAY BE CAUSED BY THIS EQUIPMENT.

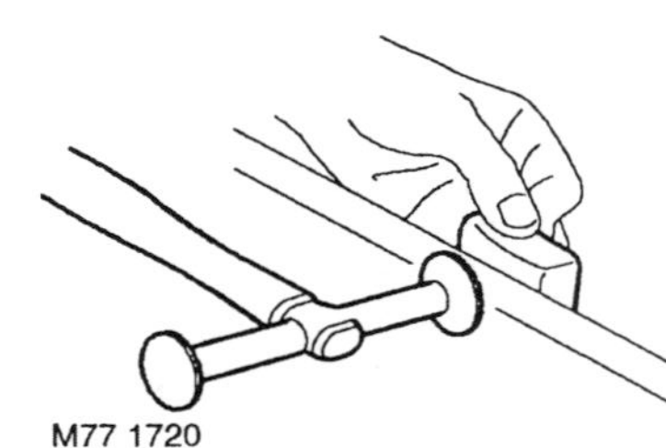
M77 1720

7. Straighten existing joint edges using shaping block and hammer.

Prepare New Surfaces

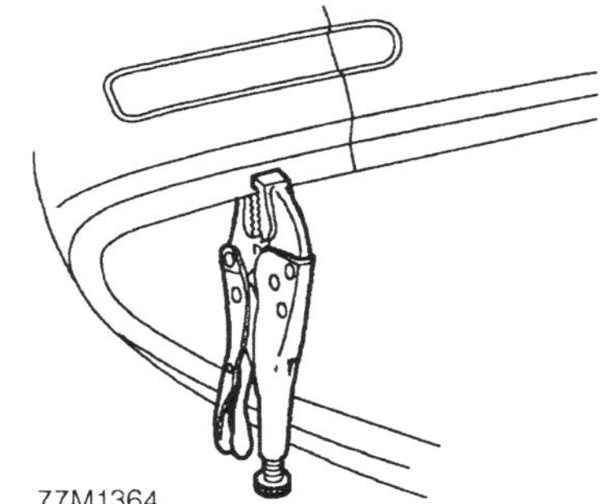
77M1364

8. Mark out bulk of new panel and trim to size, leaving approximately 50mm (1.9in.) overlap with existing panel. Offer up new panel/section, align with associated panels (e.g. new rear quarter aligned with door and tailgate). Clamp into position.

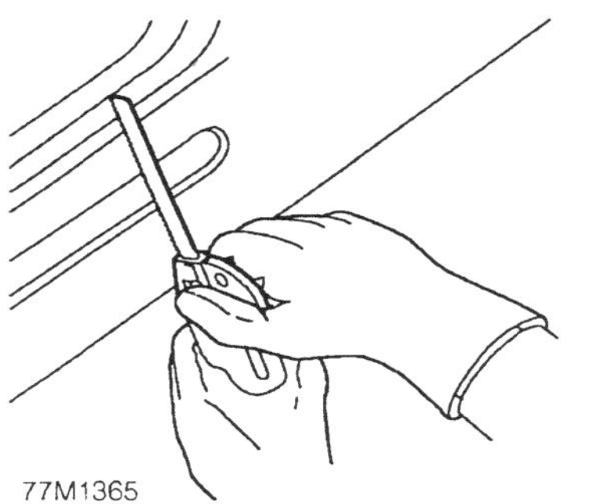
77M1365

9. Cut new and existing panels as necessary to form butt, joggle or brace joint as required. Remove all clamps and metal remnants.

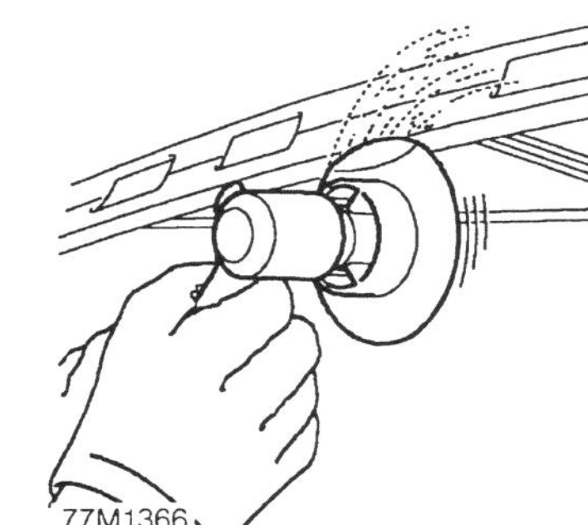
77M1366

10. Prepare new panel joint edges for welding by sanding to a bright finish. This must include inner as well as outer faces.

77M1367

11. Apply suitable weld-through primer to panel joint surfaces to be welded, using brush or aerosol can.

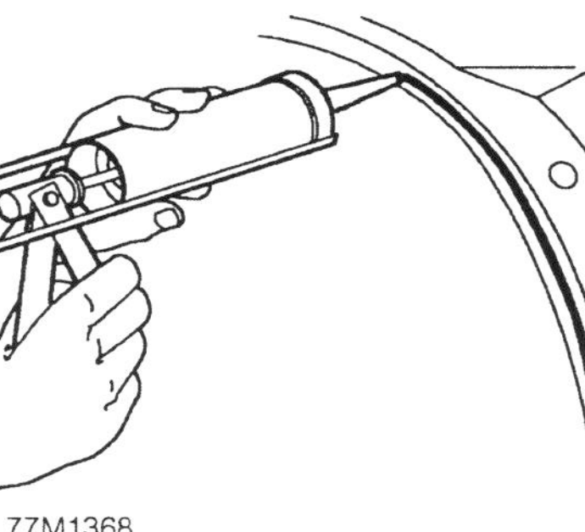
77M1368

12. Apply adhesive sealant to panel joint surfaces. **See GENERAL SPECIFICATION DATA, Information section.**

Offer Up and Align

Offer up new panel and align with associated panels. Clamp into position using welding clamps or Mole grips. Where a joggle or brace joint is being adopted, make a set in the original panel joint edge or insert a brace behind the joint.

NOTE: In cases where access for welding clamps is difficult, it may be necessary to use tack welds.

Welding

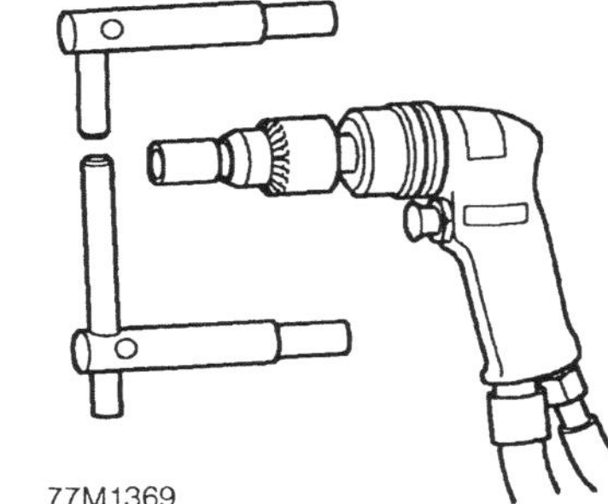
77M1369

13. Select arms for resistance spot welding and shape electrode tips using a tip trimmer. Tips should be dressed so the diameter is equal to twice the thickness of the metal to be welded plus 3mm (0.12in.).

NOTE: To maintain efficiency, the tips will require regular cleaning and dressing.

CAUTION: Use electrode arms not exceeding 300mm (11.8in.) in length.

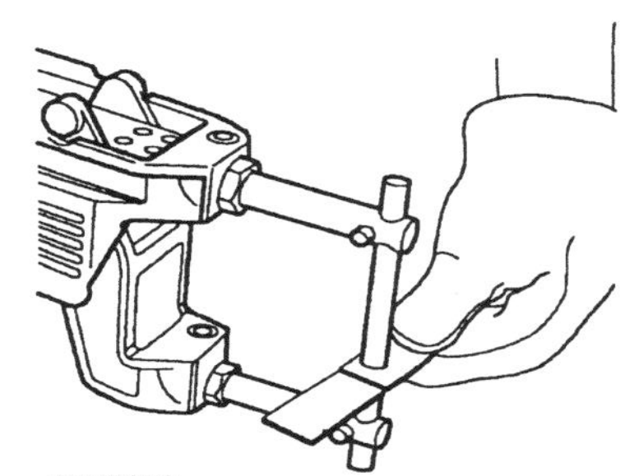
77M1370

14. Fit resistance spot welding arms and test equipment for satisfactory operation, using test coupons. Where monitoring equipment is not available, verify weld strength by checking that metal around the weld puddle pulls apart under tension during pulling.

77M1371

15. Use a resistance spot welder where access permits. Try to ensure weld quality by using a weld monitor where possible.

77M1372

16. MIG tack weld butt joints and re-check alignment and panel contours where necessary. Ensure that a gap is maintained to minimise welding distortion, by inserting a hacksaw blade as an approximate guide.

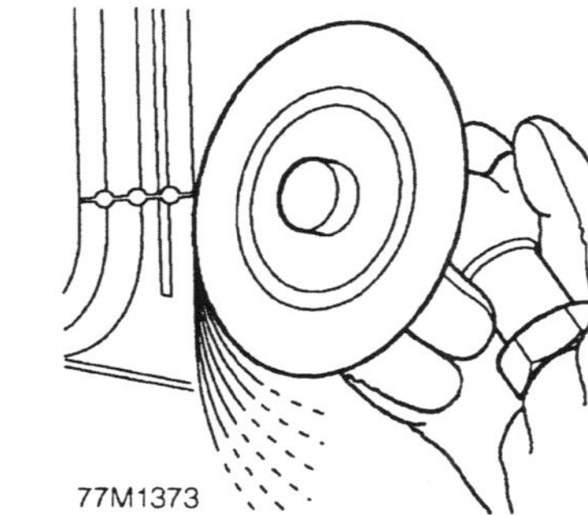

77M1373

17. Dress MIG tack welds using a sander with 36 grit disc, or a belt-type sander where access is limited.

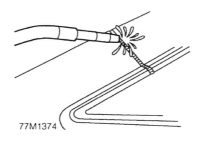

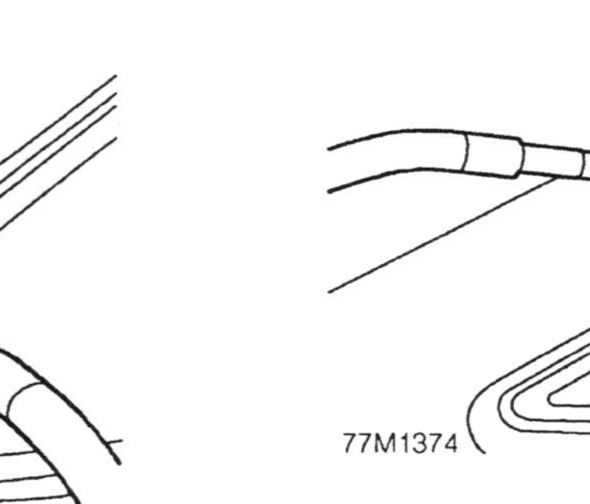

77M1374

18. MIG seam weld butt joints.

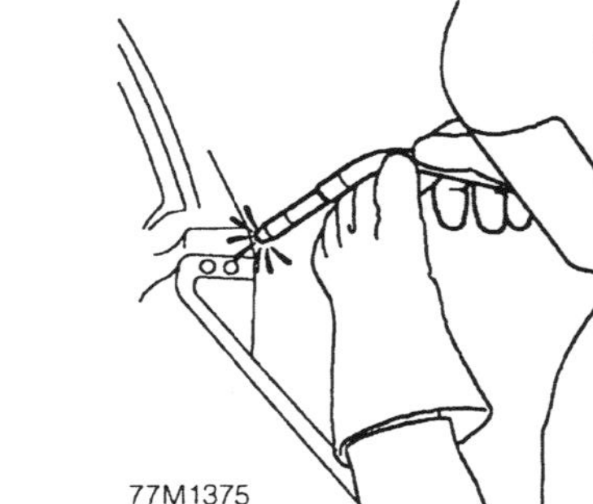

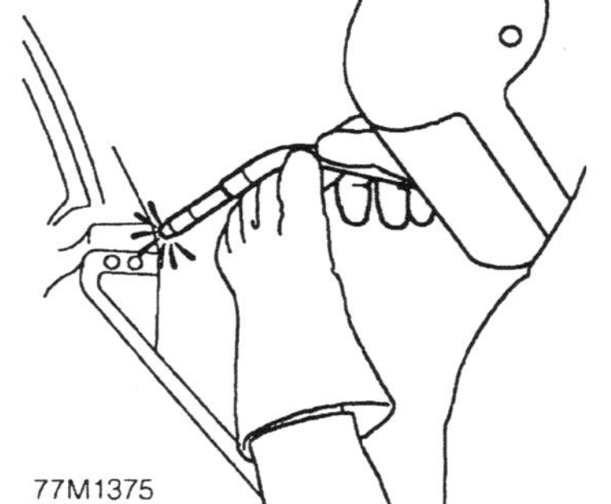

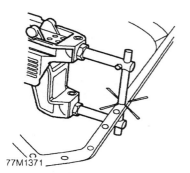

77M1375

19. Always use MIG plug welds where excessive metal thickness or lack of access make resistance spot welding impractical. Make plug welds either by using holes left by the spot weld cutter, or through holes punched or drilled for the purpose.

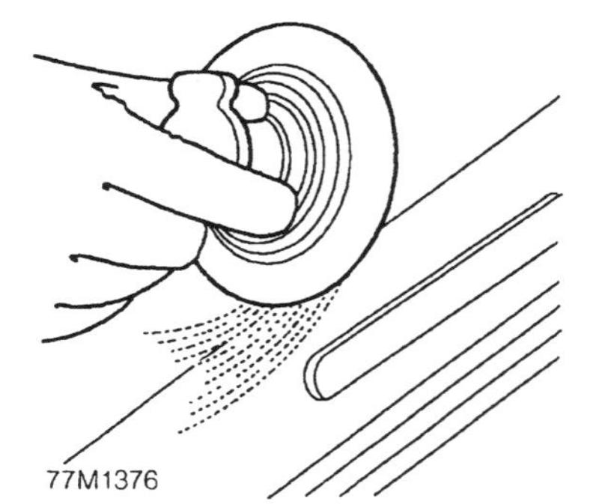

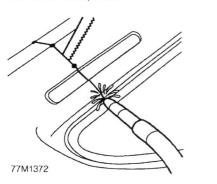

77M1376

20. Dress all welds using a sander with 36 grit disc, or a belt-type sander and/or wire brush. When dressing welds ensure an area as small as possible is removed to protect the zinc coating.

NOTE: Brazing operations, if required, must be carried out at this point.

Body Trim

The following panel repair operations itemise body trim components which must be removed for access during each repair. **See Repairs section.**

Because of the unpredictable nature of accident damage, the items listed make no allowance for any difficulties which may be found in removal and only apply to an undamaged vehicle. No allowance is made for any difficulties which may be found during panel removal. Damaged body trim items must be renewed as necessary following body repairs.

Notes

VALANCE AND WHEEL ARCH

Remove

1. Disconnect both battery leads, negative lead first.
2. Raise front of vehicle.

WARNING: Support on safety stands.

3. Disconnect all ECUs.
4. Disconnect airbags and sensor system.
5. Remove airbag modules. ***See SUPPLEMENTARY RESTRAINT SYSTEM, Repair.***
6. Disconnect alternator.
7. Remove front bumper valance. ***See CHASSIS AND BODY, Repair.***
8. Remove extension spoiler front bumper. ***See CHASSIS AND BODY, Repair.***
9. Remove front grille. ***See CHASSIS AND BODY, Repair.***
10. Remove headlamp. ***See Workshop Manual - ELECTRICAL.***
11. Remove bonnet. ***See CHASSIS AND BODY, Repair.***
12. Remove bonnet strut. ***See CHASSIS AND BODY, Repair.***
13. Remove bonnet lock RH or LH. ***See CHASSIS AND BODY, Repair.***
14. Remove wheel arch liner - front. ***See CHASSIS AND BODY, Repair.***
15. Remove front door assembly. ***See CHASSIS AND BODY, Repair.***
16. Remove 'A' post trim. ***See CHASSIS AND BODY, Repair.***
17. Remove fascia. ***See CHASSIS AND BODY, Repair.***
18. Remove front wing.
19. Remove engine. ***See Workshop Manual - ENGINE.***
20. Remove gearbox. ***See Workshop Manual - GEARBOX.***

Refit

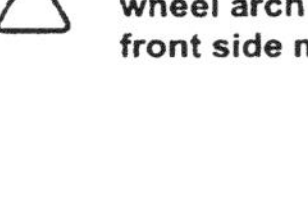

NOTE: In this operation the valance and wheel arch is fitted in combination with a front side member.

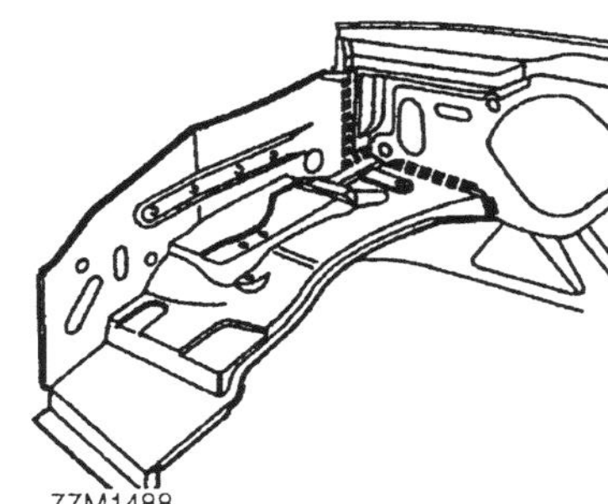

21. Prepare and clean panel joint faces. Punch or drill holes in new valance and wheel arch for plug welding as shown.
22. Reverse removal procedure.
23. Remove stands and lower vehicle.

FRONT SIDE MEMBER

Remove

1. Disconnect both battery leads, negative lead first.
2. Raise front of vehicle.

WARNING: Support on safety stands.

3. Disconnect all ECUs.
4. Disconnect airbags and sensor system.
5. Remove airbag module. ***See SUPPLEMENTARY RESTRAINT SYSTEM, Repair.***
6. Disconnect alternator.
7. Remove front bumper valance. ***See CHASSIS AND BODY, Repair.***
8. Remove extension spoiler front bumper. ***See CHASSIS AND BODY, Repair.***
9. Remove front grille. ***See CHASSIS AND BODY, Repair.***
10. Remove headlamp. ***See Workshop Manual - ELECTRICAL***
11. Remove bonnet. ***See CHASSIS AND BODY, Repair.***
12. Remove bonnet strut. ***See CHASSIS AND BODY, Repair.***
13. Remove bonnet lock RH or LH. ***See CHASSIS AND BODY, Repair.***
14. Remove wheel arch liner - Front. ***See CHASSIS AND BODY, Repair.***
15. Remove front door assembly. ***See CHASSIS AND BODY, Repair.***
16. Remove 'A' post trim. ***See CHASSIS AND BODY, Repair.***
17. Remove front wing.

Refit

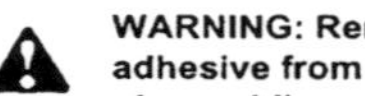

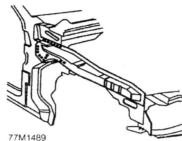

77M1489

18. Prepare and clean panel joint faces. Punch or drill holes in new front side member for plug welding as shown.

WARNING: Remove ALL traces of adhesive from valance upper edge before plug welding.

19. Reverse removal procedure.
20. Remove stands and lower vehicle.

UPPER 'A' POST PANEL AND REPAIR PANEL

Remove

1. Disconnect both battery leads, negative lead first.
2. Raise front of vehicle.

WARNING: Support on safety stands.

3. Disconnect all ECUs.
4. Disconnect airbags and sensor system.
5. Remove both airbag modules. ***See SUPPLEMENTARY RESTRAINT SYSTEM, Repair. See SUPPLEMENTARY RESTRAINT SYSTEM, Repair.***
6. Disconnect alternator.
7. Remove front bumper valance. ***See CHASSIS AND BODY, Repair.***
8. Remove extension spoiler front bumper. ***See CHASSIS AND BODY, Repair.***
9. Remove front grille. ***See CHASSIS AND BODY, Repair.***
10. Remove windscreen. ***See CHASSIS AND BODY, Repair.***
11. Remove headlamp. ***See Workshop Manual - ELECTRICAL.***
12. Remove bonnet. ***See CHASSIS AND BODY, Repair.***
13. Remove wheel arch liner - front. ***See CHASSIS AND BODY, Repair.***
14. Remove front door assembly. ***See CHASSIS AND BODY, Repair.***
15. Remove 'A' post trim. ***See CHASSIS AND BODY, Repair.***
16. Remove fascia assembly. ***See CHASSIS AND BODY, Repair.***
17. Remove front wing.

Refit

NOTE: In this operation, the 'A' post panel and repair panel are replaced in combination with the lower 'A' post and reinforcement. It is also necessary to remove the front side member for access.

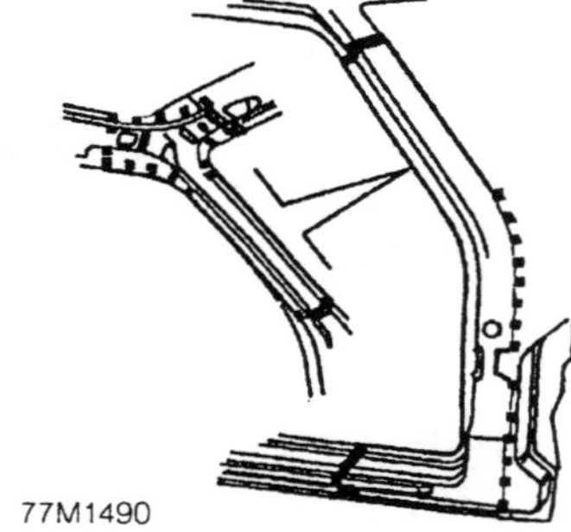

77M1490

18. Prepare and clean panel joint faces. Punch or drill holes in new panels for plug welding as shown.

WARNING: Remove ALL traces of adhesive from outer face of 'A' post reinforcement before plug welding.

Cut upper 'A' post and repair panel to form seam welded joints with existing panels.

19. Reverse removal procedure.
20. Remove stands and lower vehicle.

LOWER 'A' POST AND REINFORCEMENT

Remove

1. Disconnect both battery leads, negative lead first.
2. Raise front of vehicle.

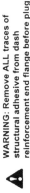

WARNING: Support on safety stands.

3. Disconnect all ECUs.
4. Disconnect airbags and sensor system.
5. Remove both airbag modules. ***See SUPPLEMENTARY RESTRAINT SYSTEM, Repair. See SUPPLEMENTARY RESTRAINT SYSTEM, Repair.***
6. Disconnect alternator.
7. Remove front bumper valance. ***See CHASSIS AND BODY, Repair.***
8. Remove extension spoiler front bumper. ***See CHASSIS AND BODY, Repair.***
9. Remove front grille. ***See CHASSIS AND BODY, Repair.***
10. Remove windscreen. ***See CHASSIS AND BODY, Repair.***
11. Remove headlamp. ***See Workshop Manual - ELECTRICAL.***
12. Remove bonnet. ***See CHASSIS AND BODY, Repair.***
13. Remove wheel arch liner - front. ***See CHASSIS AND BODY, Repair.***
14. Remove front door assembly. ***See CHASSIS AND BODY, Repair.***
15. Remove 'A' post trim. ***See CHASSIS AND BODY, Repair.***
16. Remove fascia assembly. ***See CHASSIS AND BODY, Repair.***
17. Remove front wing.

Refit

NOTE: In this operation, the lower 'A' post and reinforcement are replaced in combination with the upper 'A' post and repair panel. It is also necessary to remove the front side member for access.

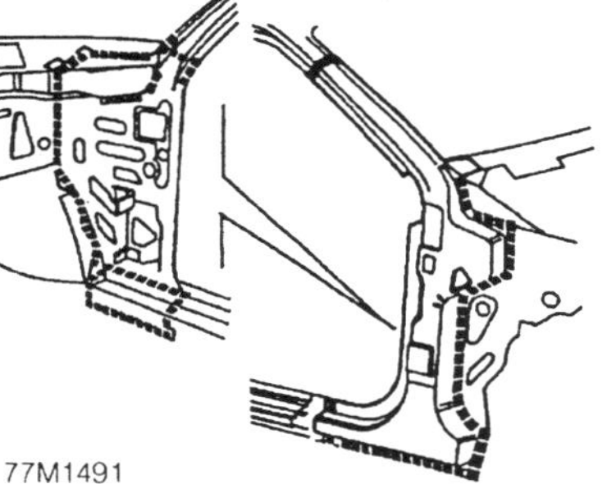

77M1491

18. Prepare and clean panel joint faces. Punch or drill holes in new panels for plug welding as shown.

WARNING: Remove ALL traces of structural adhesive from dash reinforcement end flange before plug welding.

Cut 'A' post reinforcement to form a seam welded butt joint with existing panel.

19. Reverse removal procedure.
20. Remove stands and lower vehicle.

'BC' POST REPAIR PANEL

Remove

1. Disconnect both battery leads, negative lead first.
2. Raise side of vehicle.

WARNING: Support on safety stands.

3. Disconnect all ECUs.
4. Disconnect airbags and sensor system.
5. Remove both airbag modules. ***See SUPPLEMENTARY RESTRAINT SYSTEM, Repair. See SUPPLEMENTARY RESTRAINT SYSTEM, Repair.***
6. Disconnect alternator.
7. Remove front seat. ***See CHASSIS AND BODY, Repair.***
8. Remove seat belt - front. ***See CHASSIS AND BODY, Repair.***
9. Remove front seat belt adjustable mounting. ***See CHASSIS AND BODY, Repair.***
10. Remove 'BC' post trim. ***See CHASSIS AND BODY, Repair.***
11. Remove rear door assembly. ***See CHASSIS AND BODY, Repair.***

Refit

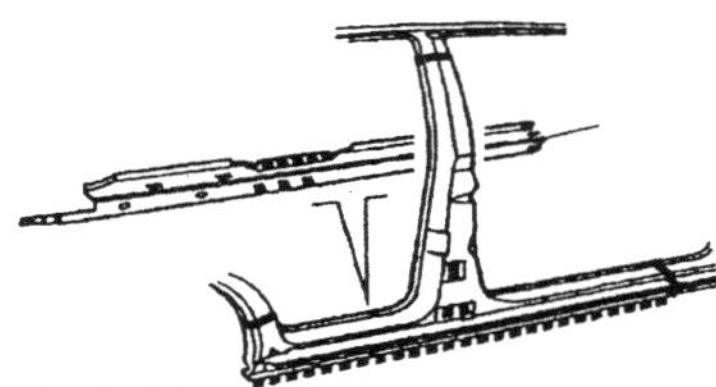

77M1492

12. Prepare and clean panel joint faces. Punch or drill holes in new 'BC' post repair panel for plug welding as shown. Cut panel to form seam welded butt joints with existing panel.
13. Reverse removal procedure.
14. Remove stands and lower vehicle.

'BC' POST REINFORCEMENT

Remove

1. Disconnect both battery leads, negative lead first.
2. Raise side of vehicle.

WARNING: Support on safety stands.

3. Disconnect all ECUs.
4. Disconnect airbags and sensor system.
5. Disconnect alternator.
6. Remove front seat. ***See CHASSIS AND BODY, Repair.***
7. Remove seat belt - front. ***See CHASSIS AND BODY, Repair.***
8. Remove front seat belt adjustable mounting. ***See CHASSIS AND BODY, Repair.***
9. Remove 'BC' post trim. ***See CHASSIS AND BODY, Repair.***
10. Remove rear door assembly. ***See CHASSIS AND BODY, Repair.***

Refit

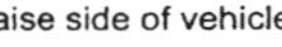

NOTE: In this operation, the 'BC' post reinforcement and 'BC' post repair panel are replaced in combination.

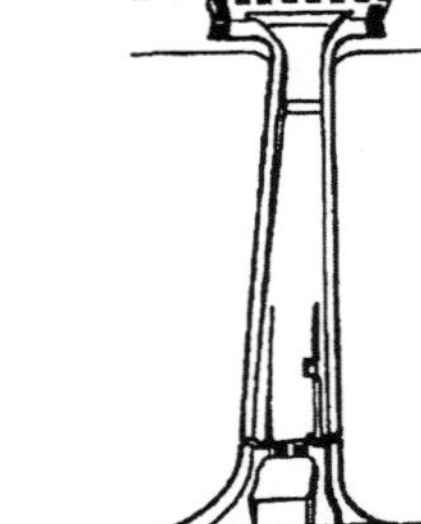

77M1493

11. Prepare and clean panel joint faces. Punch or drill holes in new panel for plug welding as shown. Cut new panel to form seam welded butt joint with existing panel.
12. Reverse removal procedure.
13. Remove stands and lower vehicle.

'BC' POST INNER PANELS

Remove

1. Disconnect both battery leads, negative lead first.
2. Raise side of vehicle.

WARNING: Support on safety stands.

3. Disconnect all ECUs.
4. Disconnect airbags and sensor system.
5. Disconnect alternator.
6. Remove front seat. ***See CHASSIS AND BODY, Repair.***
7. Remove seat belt - front. ***See CHASSIS AND BODY, Repair.***
8. Remove front seat belt adjustable mounting. ***See CHASSIS AND BODY, Repair.***
9. Remove 'BC' post trim. ***See CHASSIS AND BODY, Repair.***
10. Remove rear door assembly. ***See CHASSIS AND BODY, Repair.***

Refit

NOTE: In this operation, the inner panels are replaced in combination with a 'BC' post reinforcement and repair panel.

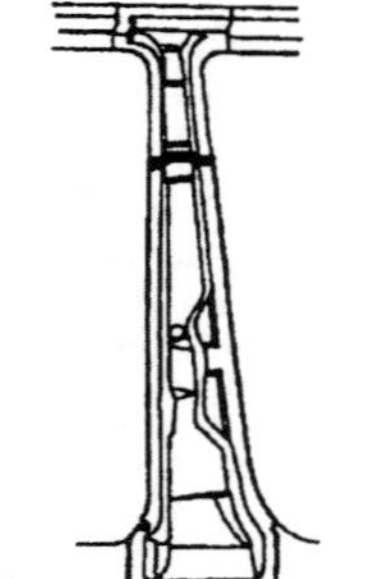

77M1494

11. Prepare and clean panel joint faces. Punch or drill holes in new 'BC' post inner panels for plug welding as shown.
12. Reverse removal procedure.
13. Remove stands and lower vehicle.

ROOF ASSEMBLY

Remove

1. Disconnect both battery leads, negative lead first.
2. Disconnect all ECUs.
3. Disconnect airbags and sensor system.
4. Disconnect alternator.
5. Remove headlining - sliding roof. ***See CHASSIS AND BODY, Repair.***
6. Remove sliding roof - electric. ***See CHASSIS AND BODY, Repair.***
7. Remove windscreen. ***See CHASSIS AND BODY, Repair.***
8. Remove front door assembly. ***See CHASSIS AND BODY, Repair.***
9. Remove rear door assembly. ***See CHASSIS AND BODY, Repair.***
10. Remove tailgate - upper. ***See CHASSIS AND BODY, Repair.***
11. Remove seat belt - front. ***See CHASSIS AND BODY, Repair.***
12. Remove front seat belt adjustable mounting. ***See CHASSIS AND BODY, Repair.***
13. Remove 'A', 'BC', 'D' and 'E' post trims. ***See CHASSIS AND BODY, Repair.***
14. Remove sunroof drain tube - front. ***See CHASSIS AND BODY, Repair.***
15. Remove sunroof drain tube - rear. ***See CHASSIS AND BODY, Repair.***

Refit

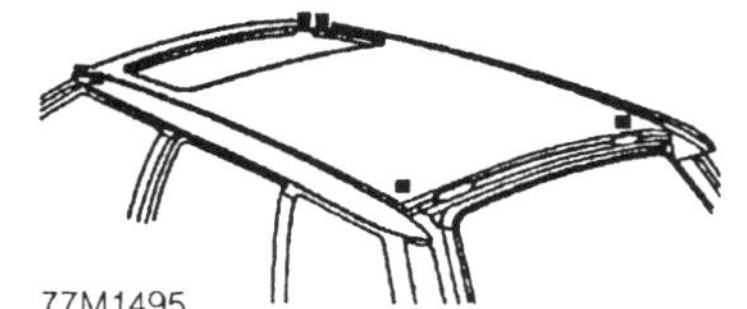

77M1495

16. Prepare and clean panel joint faces. Punch or drill holes in new roof assembly for plug welding as shown.

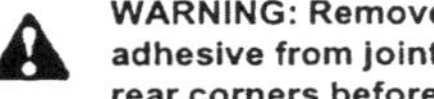

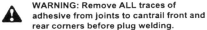

WARNING: Remove ALL traces of adhesive from joints to cantrail front and rear corners before plug welding.

17. Reverse removal procedure.

OUTER REAR QUARTER PANEL

Remove

1. Disconnect both battery leads, negative lead first.
2. Raise rear of vehicle.

WARNING: Support on safety stands.

3. Disconnect all ECUs.
4. Disconnect airbags and sensor system.
5. Disconnect alternator.
6. Remove tailgate - lower. ***See CHASSIS AND BODY, Repair.***
7. Remove parcel tray support. ***See CHASSIS AND BODY, Repair.***
8. Remove parcel tray support trim. ***See CHASSIS AND BODY, Repair.***
9. Remove 'E' post - exterior trim. ***See CHASSIS AND BODY, Repair.***
10. Remove 'D' and 'E' post trims. ***See CHASSIS AND BODY, Repair.***
11. Remove wheel arch liner - rear. ***See CHASSIS AND BODY, Repair.***
12. Remove rear quarter light. ***See CHASSIS AND BODY, Repair.***
13. Remove quarter panel rubbing strips. ***See CHASSIS AND BODY, Repair.***
14. Remove rear bumper valance. ***See CHASSIS AND BODY, Repair.***
15. Remove rear seat belt - left hand or right hand. ***See CHASSIS AND BODY, Repair. See CHASSIS AND BODY, Repair.***
16. Remove sunroof drain tube - rear. ***See CHASSIS AND BODY, Repair.***

Refit

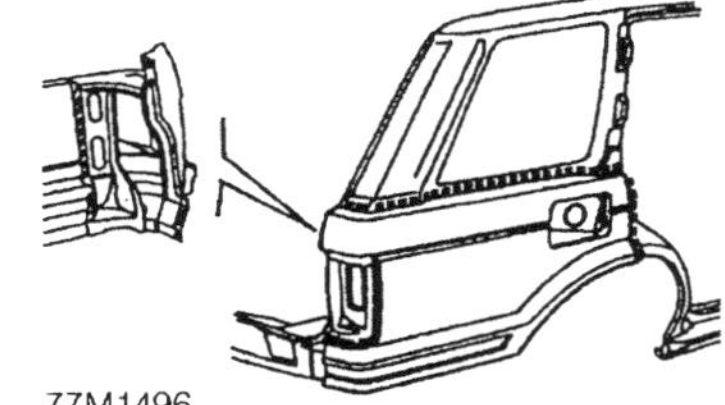

77M1496

17. Prepare and clean panel joint faces. Punch or drill holes in new panel for plug welding as shown. Apply structural adhesive at joint to outer wheel arch. ***See Corrosion protection.***

WARNING: Remove ALL traces of adhesive from joint to lower panel before plug welding.

18. Reverse removal procedure.
19. Remove stands and lower vehicle.

INNER REAR QUARTER PANEL

Remove

1. Disconnect both battery leads, negative lead first.
2. Raise rear of vehicle.

WARNING: Support on safety stands.

3. Disconnect all ECUs.
4. Disconnect airbags and sensor system.
5. Disconnect alternator.
6. Remove tailgate - lower. ***See CHASSIS AND BODY, Repair.***
7. Remove tailgate - upper. ***See CHASSIS AND BODY, Repair.***
8. Remove parcel tray support and trim. ***See CHASSIS AND BODY, Repair.***
9. Remove 'E' post - exterior trim. ***See CHASSIS AND BODY, Repair.***
10. Remove 'D' and 'E' post trims. ***See CHASSIS AND BODY, Repair.***
11. Remove DSP amplifier. ***See ELECTRICAL, Repair.***
12. Remove wheel arch liner - rear. ***See CHASSIS AND BODY, Repair.***
13. Remove rear quarterlight. ***See CHASSIS AND BODY, Repair.***
14. Remove appropriate rubbing strip. ***See CHASSIS AND BODY, Repair.***
15. Remove rear bumper valance. ***See CHASSIS AND BODY, Repair.***
16. Remove rear seat belt - left hand or right hand. ***See CHASSIS AND BODY, Repair. See CHASSIS AND BODY, Repair.***
17. Remove sunroof drain tube - rear. ***See CHASSIS AND BODY, Repair.***

Refit

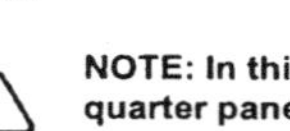

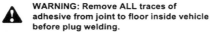

NOTE: In this operation, the inner rear quarter panel, outer quarter and rear quarter repair panel are replaced in combination .

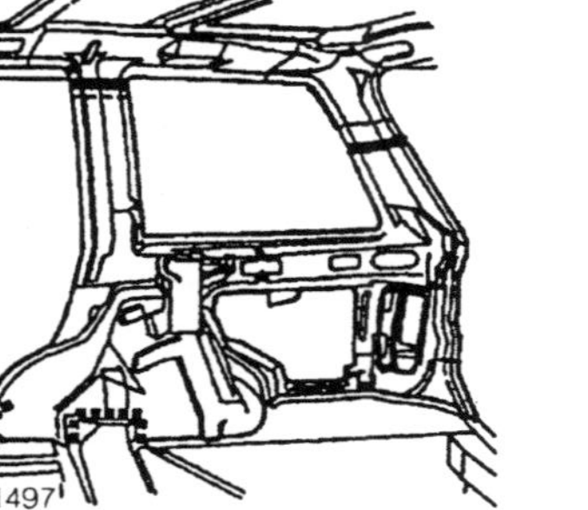

77M1497

18. Prepare and clean panel joint faces. Apply structural adhesive at joint to floor at lower edge of wheel arch. ***See Corrosion protection.***

Plug weld at joints to floor using holes left by spot weld cutter. Cut inner rear quarter to form seam welded butt joints with existing panel.

WARNING: Remove ALL traces of adhesive from joint to floor inside vehicle before plug welding.

19. Reverse removal procedure.
20. Remove stands and lower vehicle.

REAR QUARTER REPAIR PANEL

Remove

1. Disconnect both battery leads, negative lead first.
2. Raise rear of vehicle.

WARNING: Support on safety stands.

3. Disconnect all ECUs.
4. Disconnect airbags and sensor system.
5. Disconnect alternator.
6. Remove tailgate - lower. ***See CHASSIS AND BODY, Repair.***
7. Remove tailgate - upper. ***See CHASSIS AND BODY, Repair.***
8. Remove parcel tray support and trim. ***See CHASSIS AND BODY, Repair.***
9. Remove 'E' post - exterior trim. ***See CHASSIS AND BODY, Repair.***
10. Remove 'D' and 'E' post trims. ***See CHASSIS AND BODY, Repair.***
11. Remove wheel arch liner - rear. ***See CHASSIS AND BODY, Repair.***
12. Remove rear quarterlight. ***See CHASSIS AND BODY, Repair.***
13. Remove rear quarter rubbing strip. ***See CHASSIS AND BODY, Repair.***
14. Remove rear bumper valance. ***See CHASSIS AND BODY, Repair.***
15. Remove rear seat belt - left hand or right hand. ***See CHASSIS AND BODY, Repair.***
16. Remove sunroof drain tube - rear. ***See CHASSIS AND BODY, Repair.***

Refit

NOTE: In this operation, the rear quarter repair panel, outer quarter and rear quarter repair panel are replaced in combination.

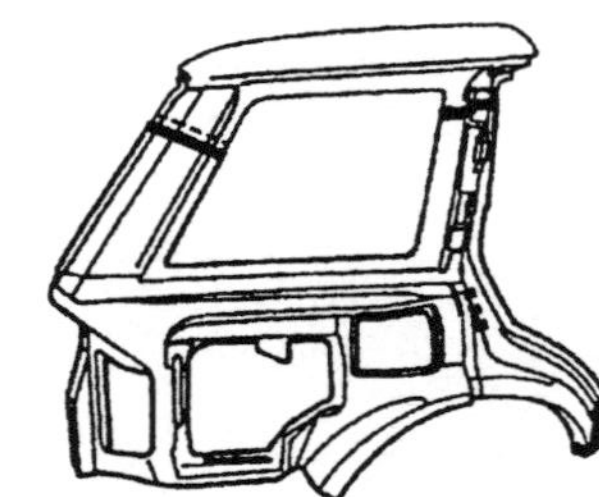

77M1498

17. Cut new rear quarter repair panel to form MIG welded butt joints with existing panels.

CAUTION: Do NOT cut into the inner quarter during this operation.

18. Reverse removal procedure.
19. Remove stands and lower vehicle.

LOAD FLOOR SIDE

Remove

1. Disconnect both battery leads, negative lead first.
2. Raise rear of vehicle.

WARNING: Support on safety stands.

3. Disconnect all ECUs.
4. Disconnect airbags and sensor system.
5. Disconnect alternator.
6. Remove tailgate - lower. ***See CHASSIS AND BODY, Repair.***
7. Remove rear bumper valance. ***See CHASSIS AND BODY, Repair.***

Refit

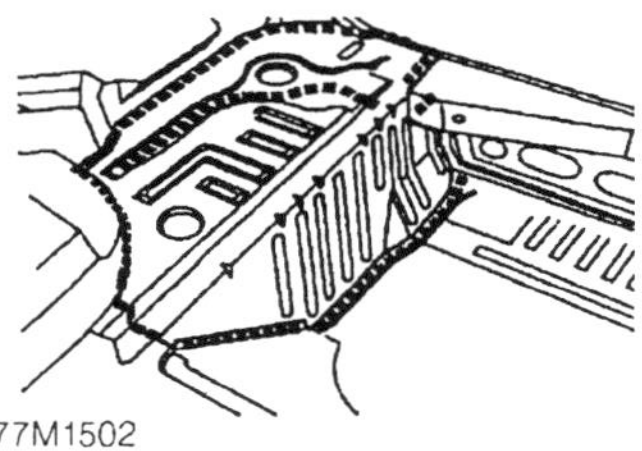

77M1502

8. Prepare and clean panel mating faces. Punch or drill holes in new rear floor panel for plug welding as shown. Plug weld also to spare wheel well edges using holes left by spot weld cutter.
9. Reverse removal procedure.
10. Remove stands and lower vehicle.

REAR CROSSMEMBER PANEL

Remove

1. Disconnect both battery leads, negative lead first.
2. Raise rear of vehicle.

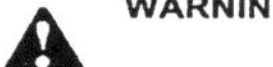

WARNING: Support on safety stands.

3. Disconnect all ECUs.
4. Disconnect airbags and sensor system.
5. Disconnect alternator.
6. Remove tailgate - lower. ***See CHASSIS AND BODY, Repair.***
7. Remove rear bumper valance. ***See CHASSIS AND BODY, Repair.***

Refit

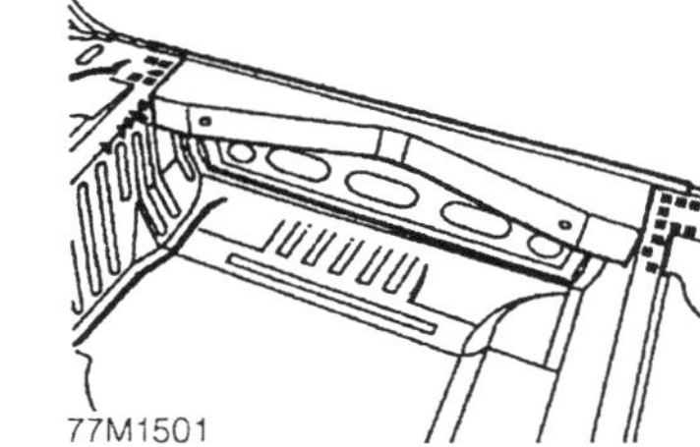

77M1501

8. Prepare and clean panel joint faces. Punch or drill holes in new rear crossmember panel for plug welding as shown.
9. Reverse removal procedure.
10. Remove stands and lower vehicle.

REAR FLOOR EXTENSION PANEL

Remove

1. Disconnect both battery leads, negative lead first.
2. Raise rear of vehicle.

WARNING: Support on safety stands.

3. Disconnect all ECUs.
4. Disconnect airbags and sensor system.
5. Disconnect alternator.
6. Remove tailgate - lower. ***See CHASSIS AND BODY, Repair.***
7. Remove rear bumper valance. ***See CHASSIS AND BODY, Repair.***

Refit

77M1500

8. Prepare and clean panel joint faces. Punch or drill holes in new rear crossmember extension panel for plug welding as shown.
9. Reverse removal procedure.
10. Remove stands and lower vehicle.

SPARE WHEEL CLOSING PANEL

Remove

1. Disconnect both battery leads, negative lead first.
2. Disconnect all ECUs.
3. Disconnect airbags and sensor system.
4. Disconnect alternator.
5. Remove rear seat belt - left hand. ***See CHASSIS AND BODY, Repair.***
6. Remove rear seat belt - right hand. ***See CHASSIS AND BODY, Repair.***
7. Remove rear seatbelt - centre. ***See CHASSIS AND BODY, Repair.***

Refit

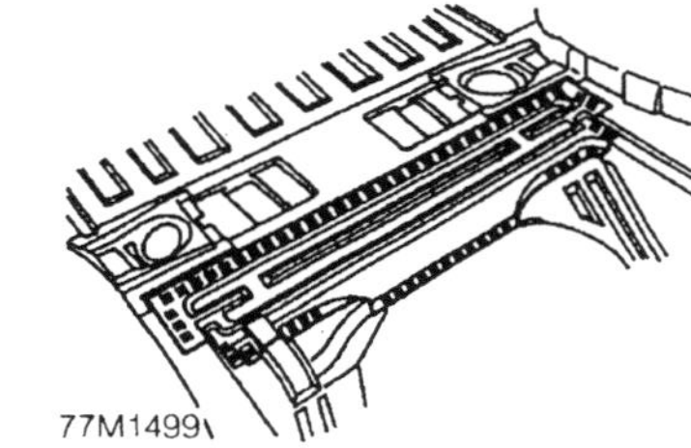

77M1499

8. Prepare and clean panel joint faces. Punch or drill holes in new spare wheel closing panel for plug welding as shown.
9. Reverse removal procedure.

LOWER PANEL

Remove

1. Disconnect both battery leads, negative lead first.
2. Disconnect all ECUs.
3. Disconnect airbags and sensor system.
4. Disconnect alternator.
5. Remove tailgate - lower. ***See CHASSIS AND BODY, Repair.***
6. Remove tailgate striker. ***See CHASSIS AND BODY, Repair.***
7. Remove rear bumper valance. ***See CHASSIS AND BODY, Repair.***

Refit

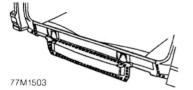

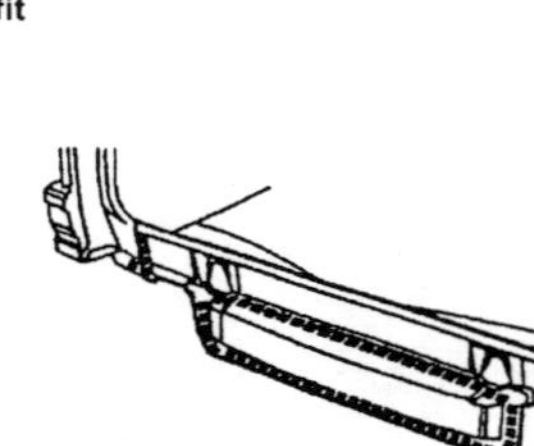
77M1503

8. Prepare and clean panel joint faces. Punch or drill holes in new lower panel for plug welding as shown.

WARNING: remove ALL traces of adhesive from joints to quarter panels before plug welding.

9. Reverse removal procedure.

PAINT PROCEDURES

Replacement Panels

Service panels are supplied with a cathodic primer coating as part of the panel protection, and in compliance with the vehicle's Corrosion Warranty where applicable. **DO NOT remove this primer before paint refinishing. In the event of localised surface damage or imperfections, ensure that the minimum of primer is removed during rectification work for effective repair.**

Rectify damage by panel beating or straightening. To remove corrosion or paint runs on outer surfaces, abrade primer coat in the affected area as necessary using the following procedure:

1. Clean the panel using a solvent wipe.
2. Treat exposed areas of metal with an etch phosphate process.
3. Re-treat the affected area using either a separate acid-etch primer and two-pack surfacer, or an integrated etch primer/filler.

Bolted Panels

Before fitting bolt-on panels, ensure that all mating and adjacent surfaces on the vehicle and replacement panel are free from damage and distortion. Rectify if necessary as described in this section, and apply preformed strip sealer where specified.

Welded Panels

1. Remove primer from the immediate vicinity of new and existing panel flanges, cleaning to bright metal finish.
2. On joints to be spot welded, apply weld-through zinc rich primer to joint faces of both flanges. Make spot welds while primer is still wet or according to the manufacturer's instructions.
3. Dress accessible weld seams.
4. Clean panel using solvent wipe.
5. Treat bare metal with an etch phosphate process.
6. Re-treat repaired areas.

NOTE: It is not satisfactory to use weld-through, zinc rich primers in conjunction with arc or MIG welding.

Sectioned Panels

When replacing part or sectioned panels, the basic procedure is the same as for welded panels described above, with the following variations:

1. Remove primer from both new and existing joint faces, cleaning to a bright metal finish.
2. Where an overlap joint with the existing panel is to be spot welded, apply weld-through, zinc rich primer to both joint faces and spot weld while the primer is still wet or according to the manufacturer's instructions.
3. MIG weld butt joints where applicable.
4. Clean the panel with a solvent wipe.
5. Treat bare metal areas using an etch phosphate process.
6. Re-prime affected areas as necessary as for rectifying transit damage. **See this section.**
7. Treat the inner faces of lap or butt joints with a suitable cavity wax. **See Sealing and corrosion protection.**

Clinch Panels (eg Door skins etc.)

1. Abrade primer on new and existing panel joint faces, and clean using a solvent wipe.
2. Apply metal-to-metal adhesive where applicable.
3. Where joints are to be spot welded, apply suitable weld-through, zinc rich primer to weld areas.
4. Where joints are to be MIG, arc or gas welded, apply zinc rich primer in adjacent areas **but leave the welded area untreated**.
5. To retain the panel whilst clinching the flanges, tack spot weld or plug weld as appropriate.
6. Clean the panel with a solvent wipe.
7. Treat bare metal areas with a suitable etch phosphate process.
8. Re-prime affected areas as necessary as for rectifying transit damage. **See this section.**

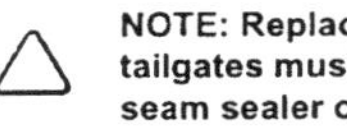

NOTE: Replacement doors, bonnets and tailgates must be treated with a suitable seam sealer on clinched seams, following the primer coat.

Paint Refinishing

1. Seal all accessible exterior and interior seams with an approved seam sealer. Certain joints such as sill lower flange seams must be left unsealed.
2. Apply a suitable anti-chip primer where specified.
3. Apply a two-pack paint refinishing system.
4. Repair any damage to underbody sealers either at this stage or before paint operations.

Paint Repairs

Before carrying out paintwork repairs, the vehicle must be thoroughly cleaned using either a steam cleaner or high-pressure washer.

Wash locally repaired areas using a mild water-mixable detergent and wipe them clean with solvent, immediately prior to paint application.

Abrade damaged paintwork where bare metal has been exposed until the metal is clean and extends beyond the area of immediate damage. Treat the bare metal with an etch phosphate to remove all traces of rust and provide a key for new paint coats. Re-treat the affected area using either a separate acid-etch primer and two-pack surfacer or an integrated etch primer/filler, and follow with a two-pack paint system. Those surfaces not receiving paint must be treated with a cavity wax following paint operations.

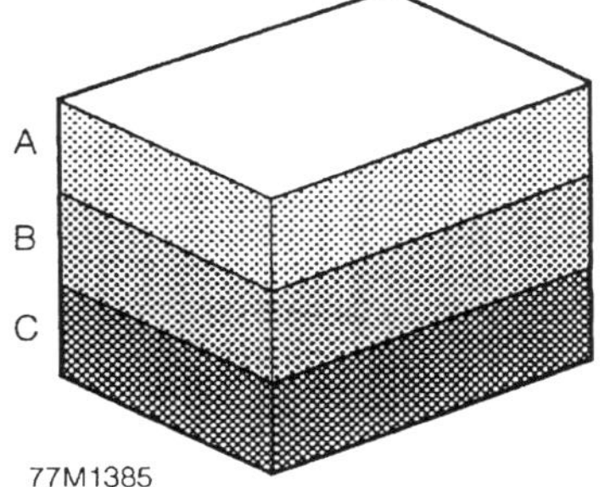

A. Two-pack top coat

B. Two-pack primer filler and etch primer

C. Etch phosphate

Notes

78 - SEATS

CONTENTS

BLADDER - LUMBAR SUPPORT - FRONT SEAT - up to 99MY

Service repair no - 78.60.01

Remove

1. Remove front seat. ***See this section.***
2. Remove headrest.
3. Remove headrest retainers by turning through 90°to release.

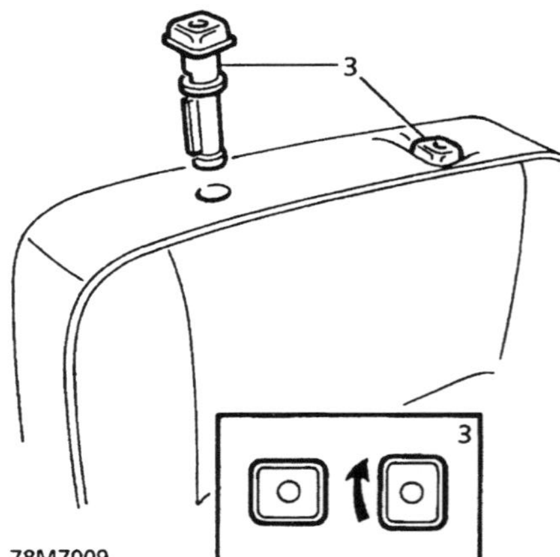

78M7009

4. Remove 2 plugs from seat valance retaining screws. Remove 3 screws. Remove valance.

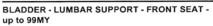

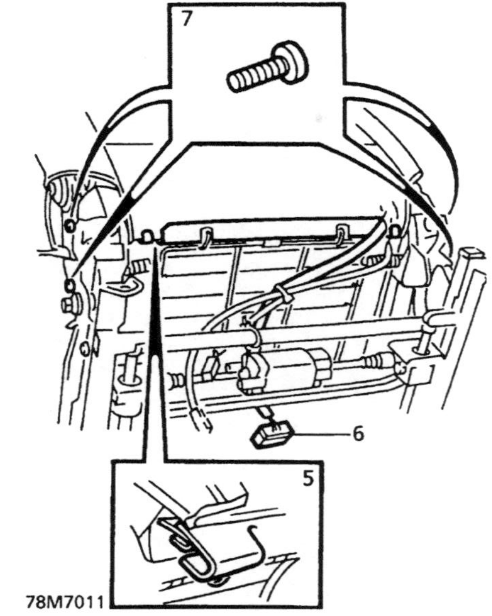

78M7010

5. Remove 2 clips securing squab cover retainer to cushion frame. Release retainer.
6. Disconnect headrest and recline multiplug from connection under cushion.

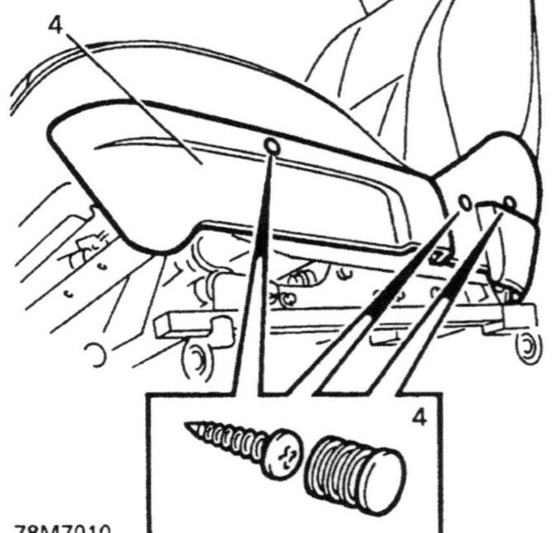

78M7011

7. Remove 4 bolts securing squab to seat. Remove squab.

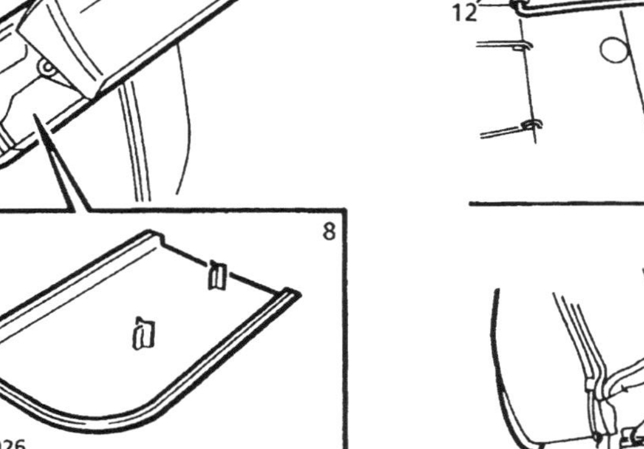

78M7026

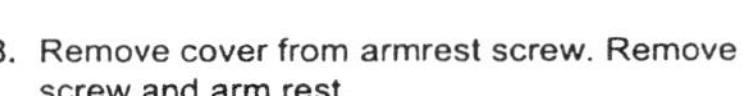

8. Remove cover from armrest screw. Remove screw and arm rest.
9. Remove 2 clips securing squab cover retainer to squab frame. Release retainer.

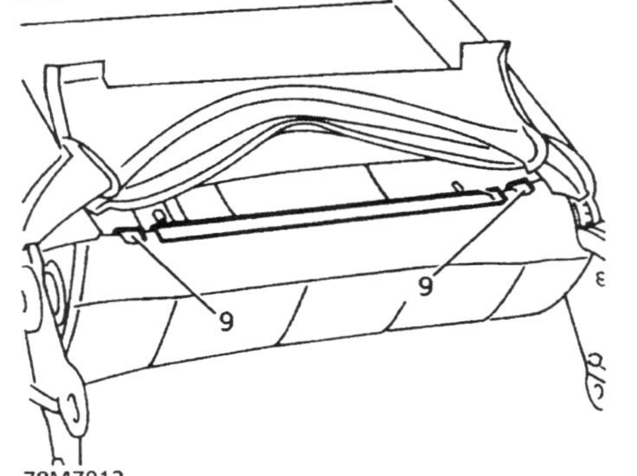

78M7012

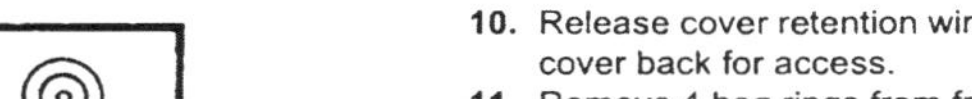

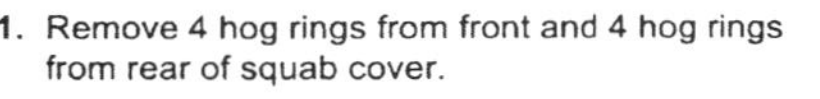

10. Release cover retention wires from frame. Roll cover back for access.
11. Remove 4 hog rings from front and 4 hog rings from rear of squab cover.

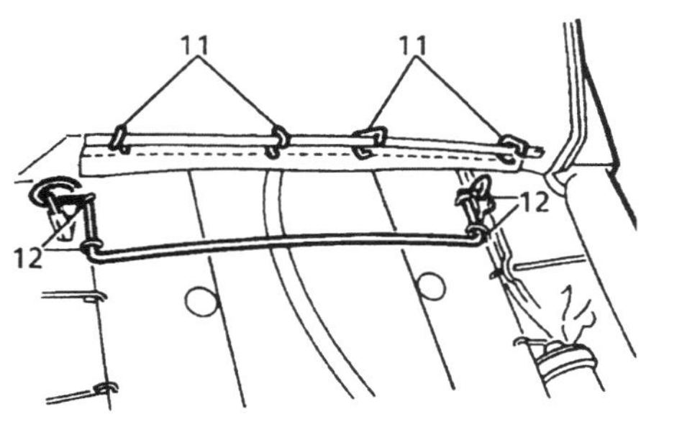

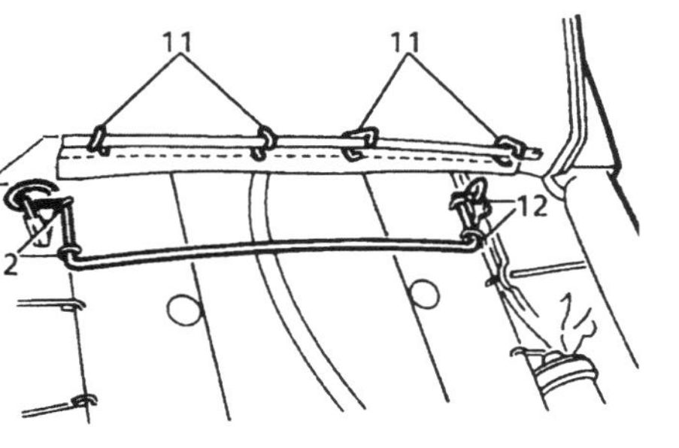

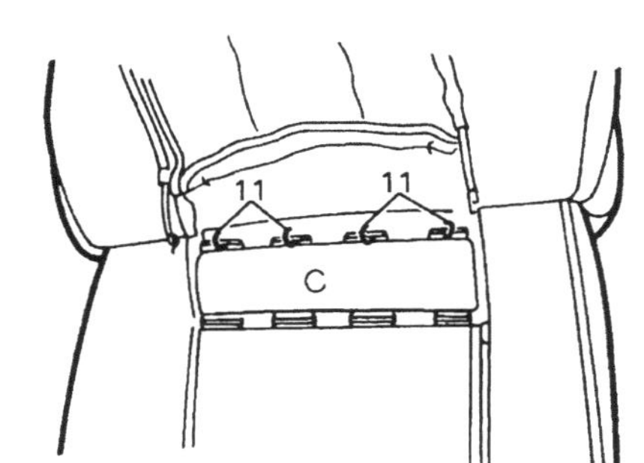

78M7025

12. Roll cover back further. Remove 4 hog rings securing front of cover.
13. Disconnect remaining ends of retention wires.
14. Remove cover from frame.

78M7013

15. Remove foam.
16. Disconnect lumbar motor multiplug.

78M7014

17. Release 10 clips securing lumbar pump and bladder to frame. Remove pump and bladder.
18. Remove clips from pump and bladder.
19. Note position of 4 hog rings securing squab cover retention wire to front of bladder frame. Remove hog rings.

Refit

20. Reverse removal procedure.

BLADDER - LUMBAR SUPPORT - FRONT SEAT - from 99MY

Service repair no - 78.60.01

Remove

1. Remove squab cover and squab foam as an assembly. ***See this section.***

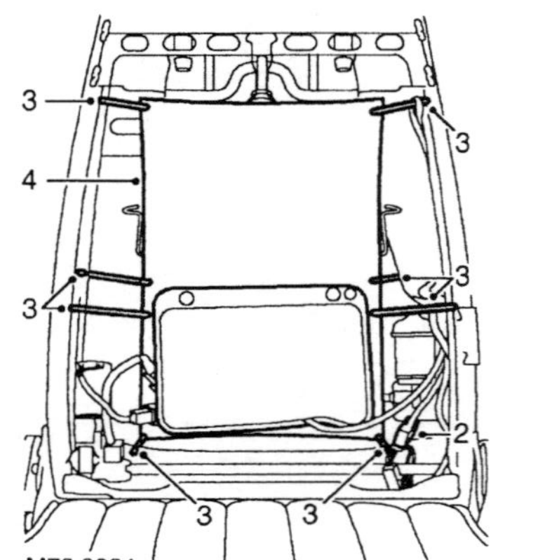

M78 0394

2. Disconnect lumbar pump multiplug.
3. Release 8 clips securing squab diaphragm and bladder assembly to squab frame.
4. Remove diaphragm and bladder assembly. **Do not carry out further dismantling if component is removed for access only.**

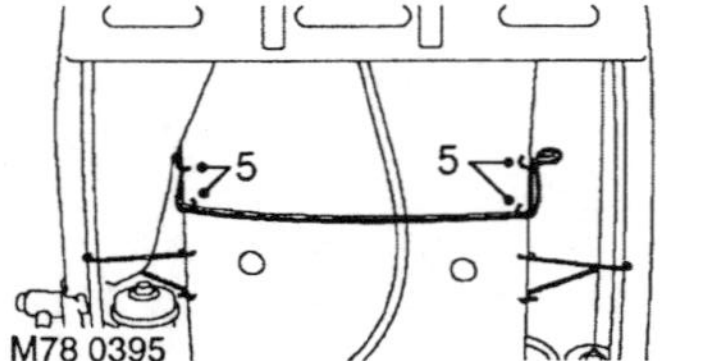

M78 0395

5. Noting position of retention wire and hog rings securing wire to diaphragm, remove hog rings and retention wire.

Refit

6. Position retention wire to diaphragm and secure with hog rings.

WARNING: Position and security of retention wire is critical for effective airbag performance.

7. Position diaphragm assembly and secure clips.
8. Connect lumbar pump multiplug.
9. Fit squab cover. ***See this section.***

DRIVE CABLE - HEADREST - up to 99MY

Remove

1. Remove squab heating element. ***See this section.***
2. Remove 2 clips securing drive cable to motor and headrest saddle.
3. Remove cable.

Refit

4. Fit cable to motor and saddle. Secure with clips.

NOTE: Cable run is under the squab cover retention wire upper anchor rod.

5. Fit squab heating element. ***See this section.***

78M7046

DRIVE CABLE - HEADREST - from 99MY

Service repair no - 78.70.50

Remove

1. Remove squab cover and squab foam as an assembly. ***See this section.***

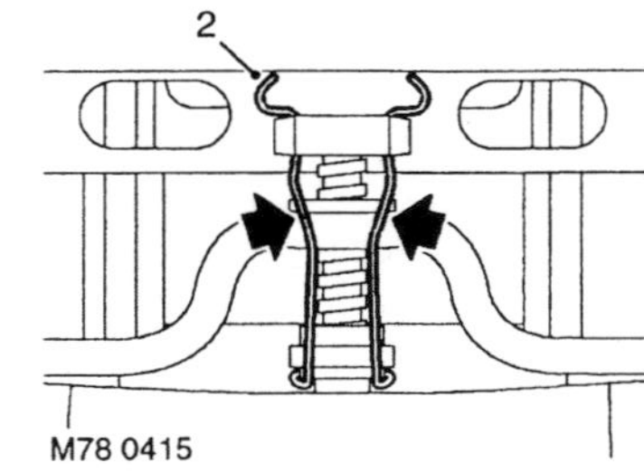

M78 0415

2. Remove clip securing cable to headrest saddle.

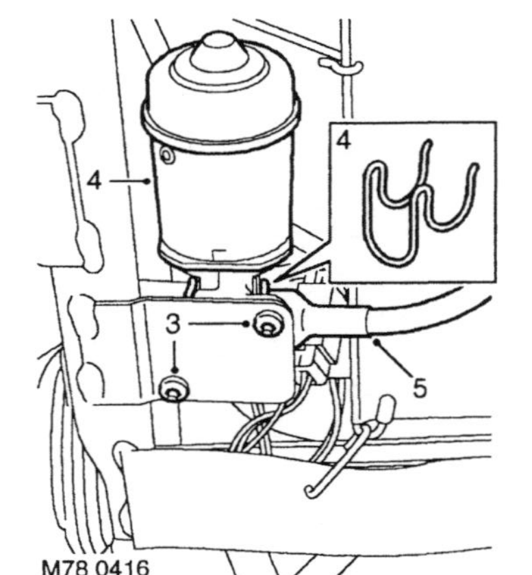

M78 0416

3. Remove 2 Torx screws securing motor.
4. Release motor and remove drive cable retaining clip.
5. Remove drive cable.

Refit

6. Locate drive cable to motor and secure with clip.
7. Align motor to frame and fit Torx screws.
8. Locate cable to headrest saddle and fit clip.

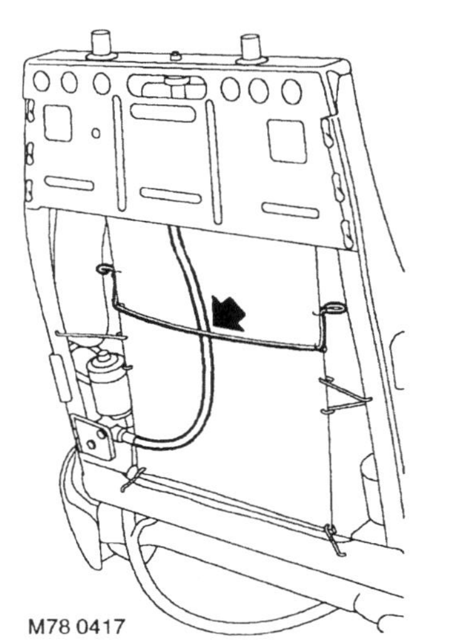

M78 0417

△ **NOTE: Cable run is under squab cover shock cord retention wire.**

9. Fit squab cover. ***See this section.***

FRONT SEAT - up to 99MY

Service repair no - 78.10.44/99

Remove

1. **LH Seat Only:** Remove 4 studs securing cover at base of seat.

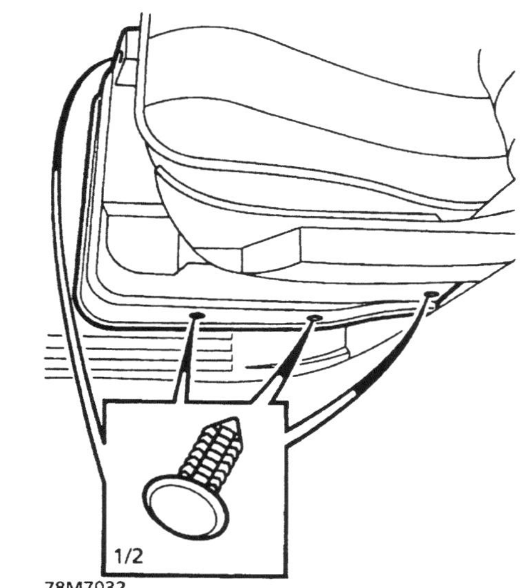

78M7032

2. **RH Seat Only:** Remove 3 studs from cover at base of seat.
3. Remove fuse cover for access to retaining screw. Remove screw.

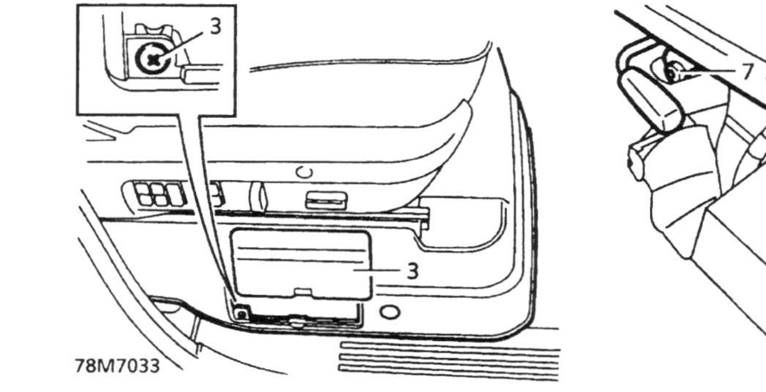

78M7033

4. Remove seat base cover.
5. Remove bolt cover from seat belt lower anchorage point.

78M7034

6. Unclip seat belt from lower anchorage point.
7. Remove 4 bolts securing seat.

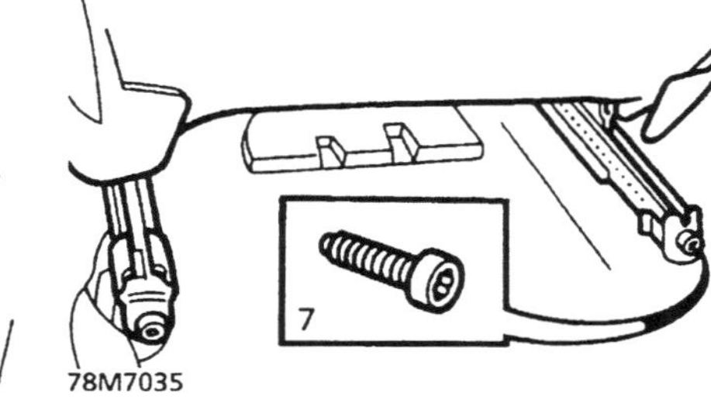

78M7035

8. Raise seat for access. Disconnect multiplugs.

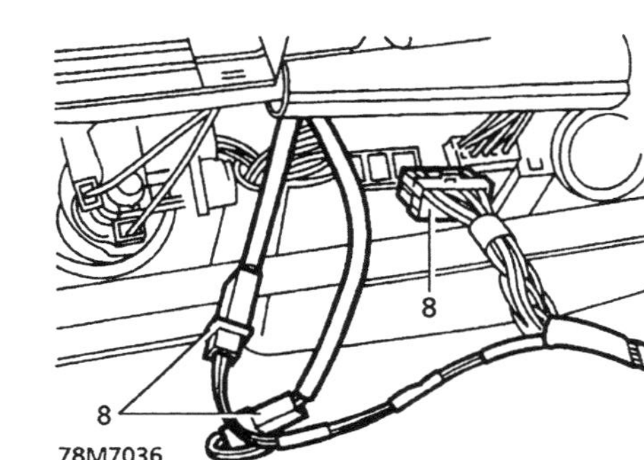

78M7036

9. Remove seat.

Refit

10. Reverse removal procedure.
11. Tighten seat fixings to ***29 Nm (21 lbf.ft)***

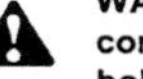

WARNING: Ensure that seat belt locates correctly over mounting bolt before fitting bolt cover.

FRONT SEAT - from 99MY

Service repair no - 78.10.43/99

Remove

WARNING: See SRS safety precautions before commencement of repair. See SUPPLEMENTARY RESTRAINT SYSTEM, Precautions.

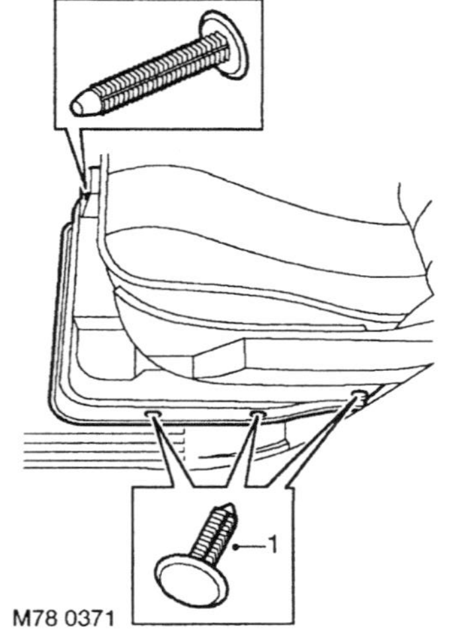

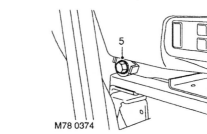

M78 0371

1. **LH seat:** Remove 4 fixings securing seat base finisher. Remove finisher.

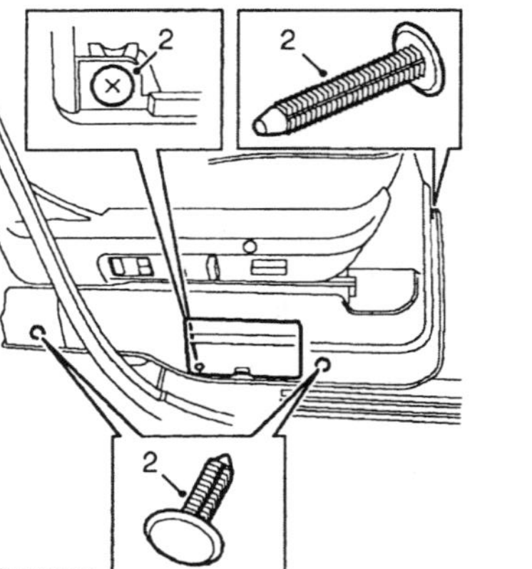

M78 0372

2. **RH seat:** Remove fuse cover from seat base finisher. Remove 3 fixings and 1 screw securing finisher. Remove finisher.

M78 0373

3. Remove 3 fixings securing rear outer base finisher to seat mounting bracket. Remove finisher.
4. Remove 4 fixings securing rear inner seat base finisher to seat mounting bracket. Remove finisher.

M78 0374

5. Remove bolt securing seat belt to seat. Release seat belt from seat.

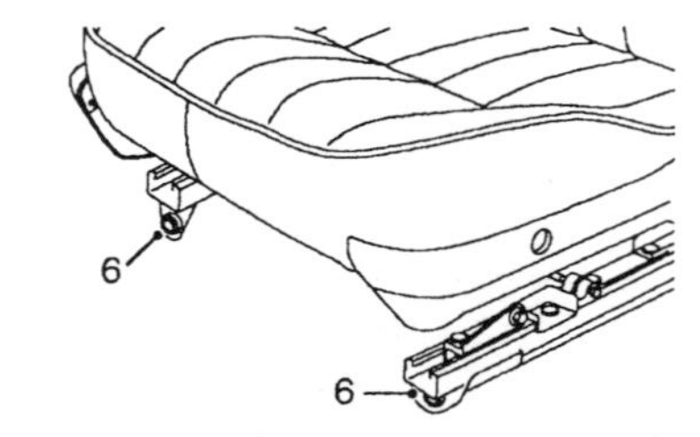

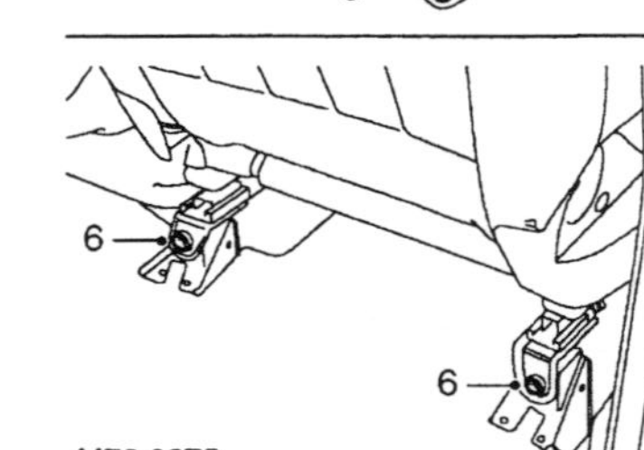

M78 0375

6. Remove 4 Torx bolts securing seat to seat mounting brackets.
7. Release seat from mountings for access to seat base.

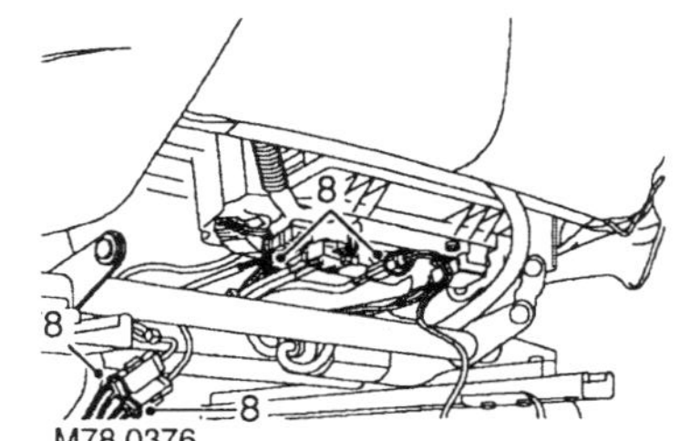

8. Disconnect 4 multiplugs underneath seat and remove seat from vehicle.

Refit

9. Fit seat to vehicle, connect multiplugs, align seat to mountings and tighten torx bolts to ***29 Nm (21 lbf.ft).***
10. Position seat belt to seat and tighten bolt to ***32 Nm (23 lbf.ft).*** Fit bolt cover.
11. Fit both rear seat base finishers and secure with fixings.
12. **LH seat:** Fit seat base finisher and secure with fixings.
13. **RH seat:** Fit screw securing finisher and fit fuse box cover.
14. Connect battery, earth lead last.

COVER - CUSHION - FRONT SEAT - from 99MY

Service repair no - 78.30.01/81

Remove

1. Remove front seat. ***See this section.***

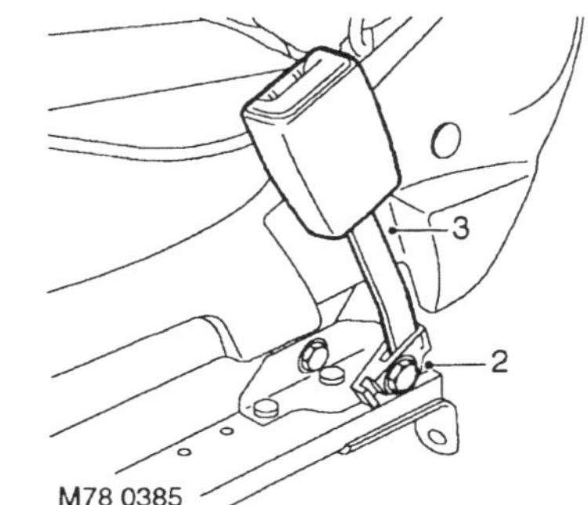

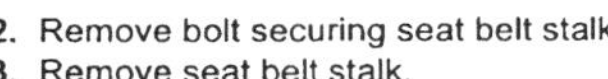

2. Remove bolt securing seat belt stalk.
3. Remove seat belt stalk.

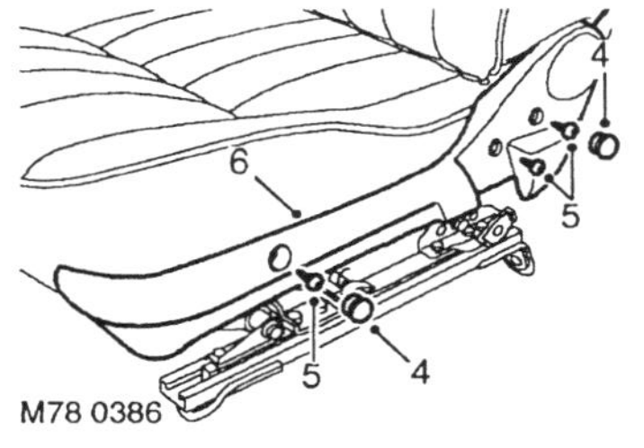

4. Remove 2 screw covers.
5. Remove 3 screws securing inner side finisher.
6. Remove side finisher.

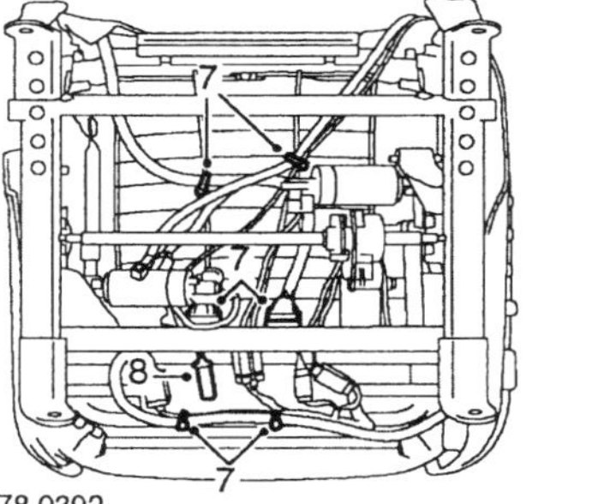

7. Remove cable ties securing harnesses to seat base and disconnect multiplugs from outstation.
8. Release airbag harness 2 way connector from bracket.

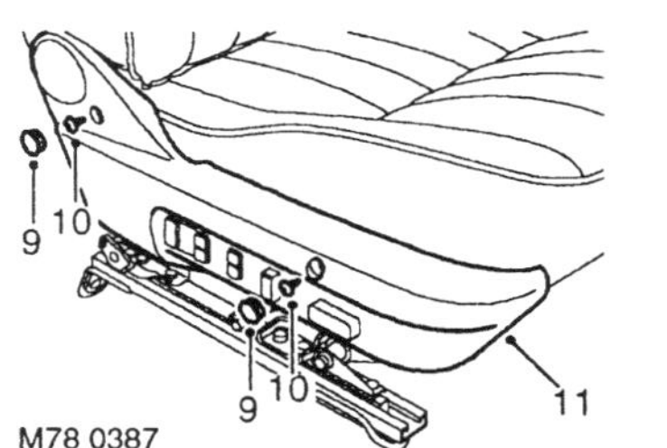

9. Remove 2 screw covers.
10. Remove 2 screws securing outer side finisher.
11. Release switch harness and remove side finisher.

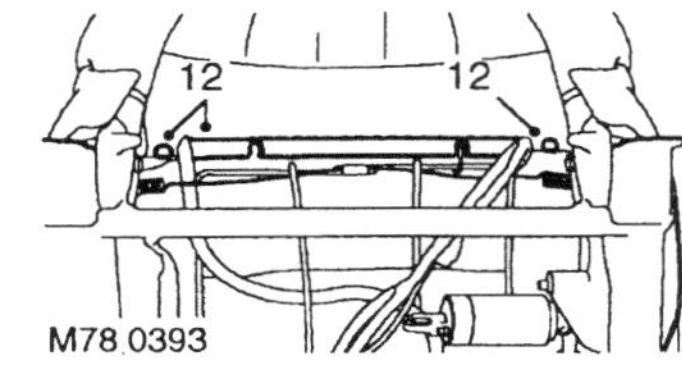

12. Remove 2 clips securing squab cover to cushion frame and release squab cover retainer.

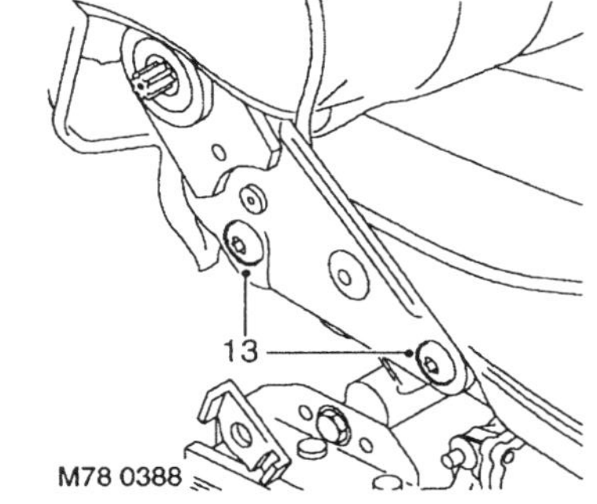

13. Remove 4 Torx screws securing squab assembly to cushion assembly.
14. Remove cushion assembly from squab assembly.

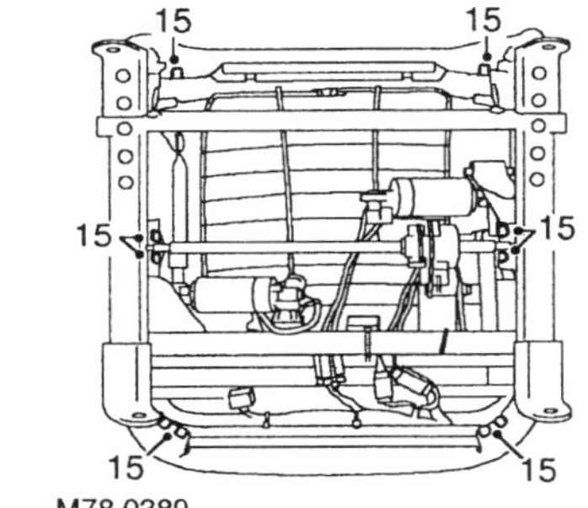

15. Remove 10 clips securing cushion cover to frame.

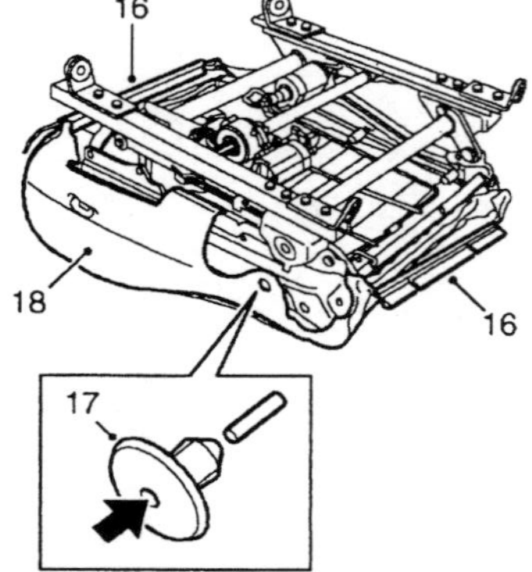

M78 0390

16. Release 2 retainers securing cover to frame.
17. Remove 2 studs securing cover to frame.
18. Remove cover and foam assembly from frame. **Do not carry out further dismantling if cover and foam is removed for access only.**

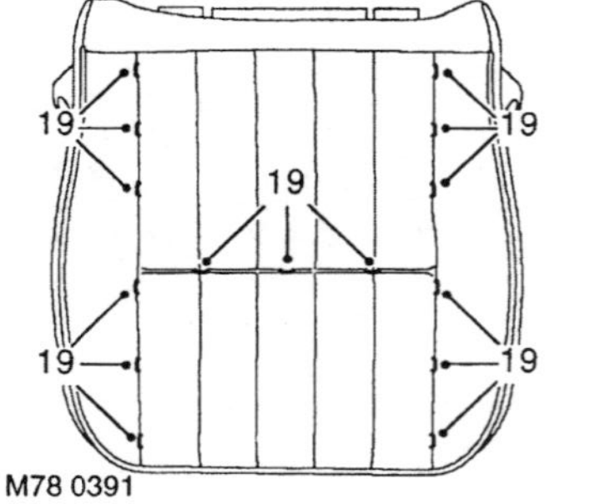

M78 0391

19. Remove 15 hog rings securing cover to foam. Remove cover.
20. Remove retention wires from pockets in cover.
21. Remove side finisher retaining wire from cushion cover retainer.

Refit

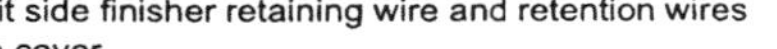

22. Fit side finisher retaining wire and retention wires to cover.
23. Position cover to foam align retention wires and fit hog rings.
24. Fit cover and foam assembly to frame.
25. Fit studs securing cover and secure retainers.
26. Fit clips securing cover.
27. Using assistance, position cushion assembly to squab assembly.
28. Fit Torx screws securing cushion assembly to squab assembly and tighten to ***30 Nm (22 lbf. ft).***
29. Secure squab retainer and fit clips.
30. Position outer side finisher and feed harness through, locate finisher and fit screws and covers. Connect multiplugs to outstation.
31. Fit outer side finisher, fit screws and screw covers.
32. Secure airbag harness connector to bracket.
33. Align harnesses and secure with cable ties.
34. Position seat belt stalk, fit bolt and tighten to ***35 Nm (26 lbf.ft).***
35. Fit seat. ***See this section.***

COVER - SQUAB - FRONT SEAT - from 99MY

Service repair no - 78.90.08/81

Remove

WARNING: The squab cover is constructed specifically for use on a seat with a side airbag fitted and must not in any way be repaired. Covers designed to be used in conjunction with side airbags can be identified by an 'AIRBAG' label sewn into the cover seam adjacent to the airbag location and an 'AIRBAG PASS' label with date of manufacture, sewn inside the cover.

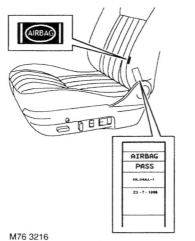

M76 3216

WARNING: For effective airbag performance, when fitting the cover, ensure retention wires, shock cords and hog rings are correctly located and secure.

1. Remove front seat. ***See this section.***

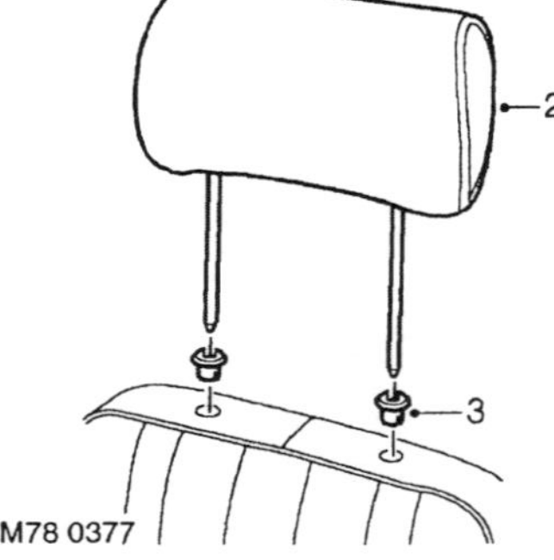

M78 0377

2. Remove headrest.
3. *Power headrest:* Remove 2 finisher caps. *Manual headrest:* Turn retainers through 90° and remove retainers.

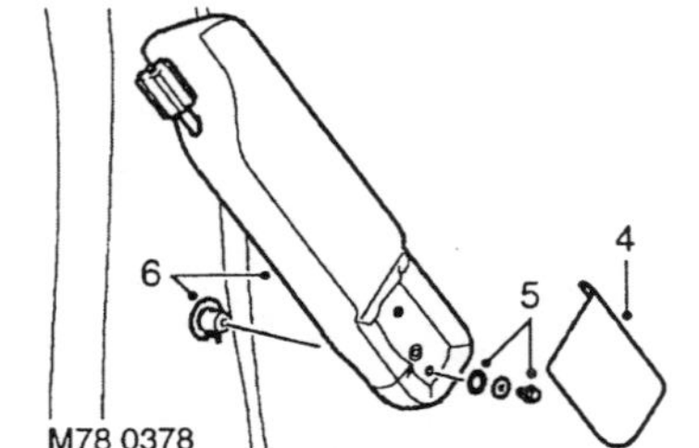

M78 0378

4. Remove armrest retaining screw cover.
5. Remove screw securing armrest, collect anti-rattle washer.
6. Remove armrest and escutcheon.

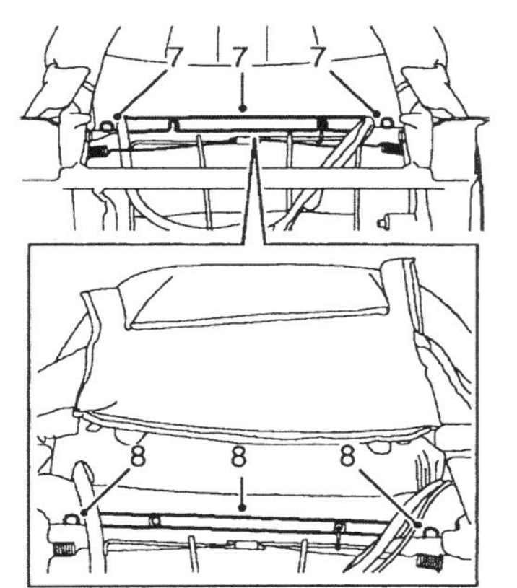

M78 0379

7. Remove 2 clips and release retainer securing rear section of cover to frame.
8. Remove 2 clips and release retainer securing front section of cover to frame.

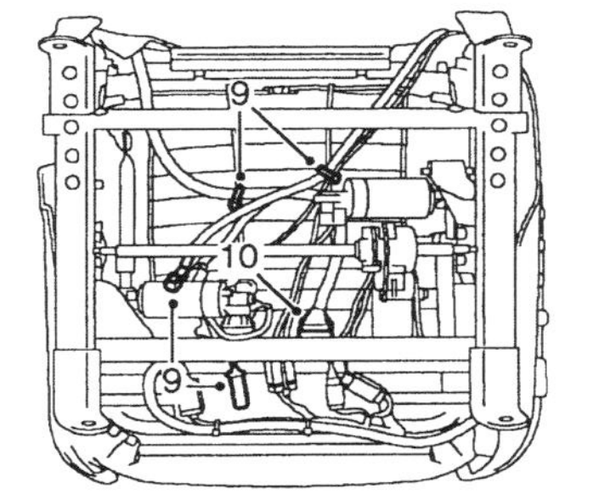

M78 0380

9. Remove cable ties securing harnesses to cushion spring. Release heating element harness and SRS harness 2 way connector.
10. *Seats with memory function:* Disconnect multiplug from seat outstation.

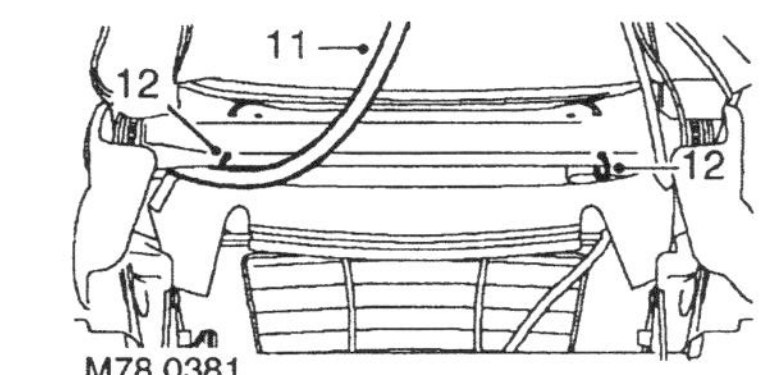

M78 0381

11. Release harness from opening in squab cover.
12. Release shock cords from frame.

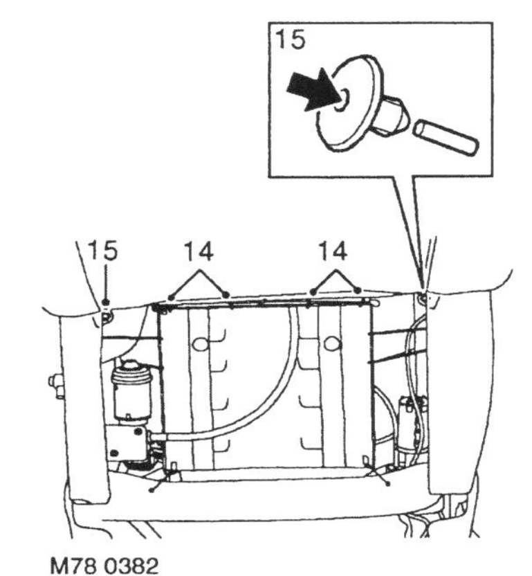

M78 0382

13. Raise squab cover.
14. Remove 4 hog rings securing rear of cover for map pocket.
15. Remove 2 studs securing map pocket strap.

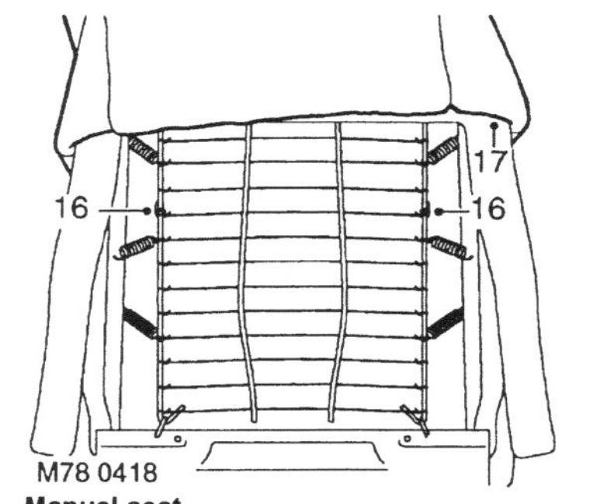

M78 0418
Manual seat

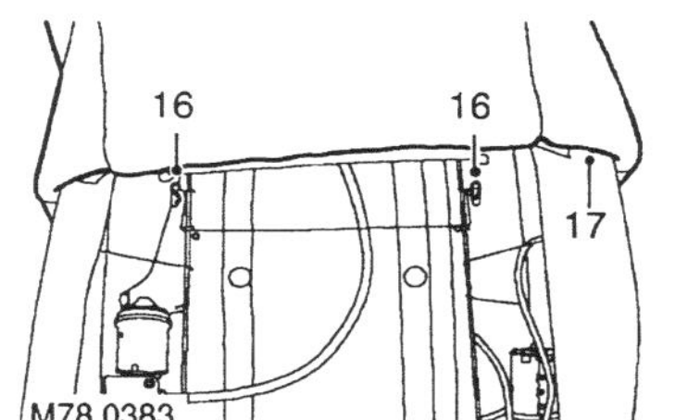

M78 0383

Electric seat

16. Release shock cords from retention wire.
17. Release and remove cover and foam assembly. **Do not carry out further dismantling if cover and foam is removed for access only.**

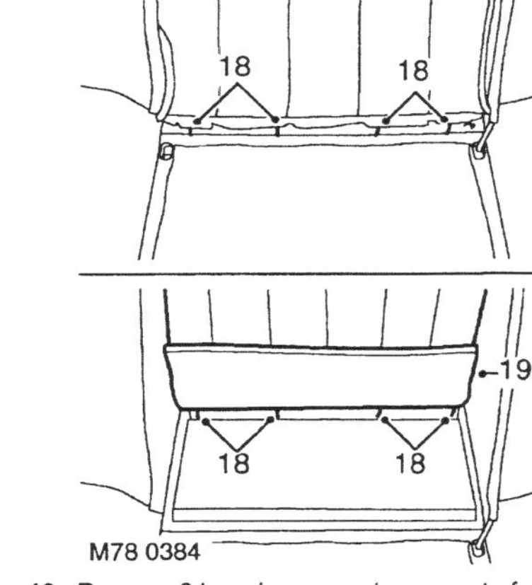

M78 0384

18. Remove 8 hog rings securing cover to foam.
19. Remove cover from foam.
20. Remove 3 retention wires and 2 shock cords from cover.

Refit

21. Fit retention wires and shock cords to cover.
22. Fit cover to foam, align retainers and fit hog rings.
23. Fit cover and foam assembly to frame.
24. Connect and secure shock cords to cross wire.
25. Align map pocket strap and fit studs.
26. Fit hog rings securing rear of cover for map pocket.
27. Lower cover.
28. Secure shock cords to frame.
29. Pass harness through cover and connect multiplug.
30. Align seat heating element harness and secure harnesses with cable ties.
31. Secure SRS multiplug to bracket.
32. Secure front section cover retainer to frame and fit clips.
33. Secure rear section cover retainer to frame and fit clips.
34. Fit armrest escutcheon.
35. Fit armrest and position anti-rattle washer. Fit and tighten bolt.
36. Fit headrest retainers and headrest.
37. Fit seat. ***See this section.***

HEATING ELEMENT - CUSHION - FRONT SEAT - up to 99MY

Service repair no - 78.30.24

Remove

1. Remove front seat. ***See this section.***
2. Remove 2 plugs from seat valance retaining screws. Remove 3 screws. Remove valance.

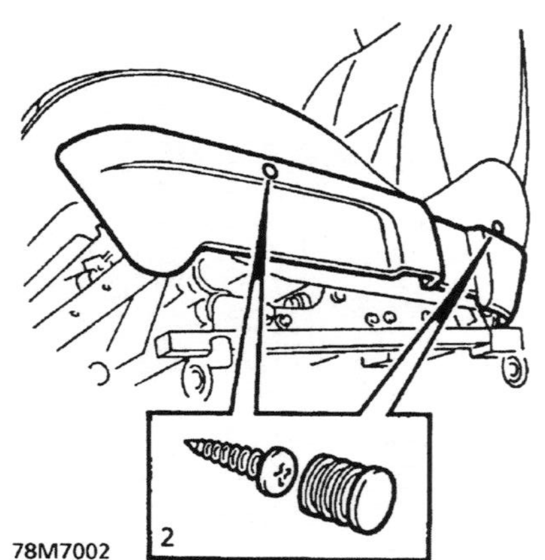

78M7002

3. Remove 2 clips securing squab cover retainer to cushion frame. Release retainer.

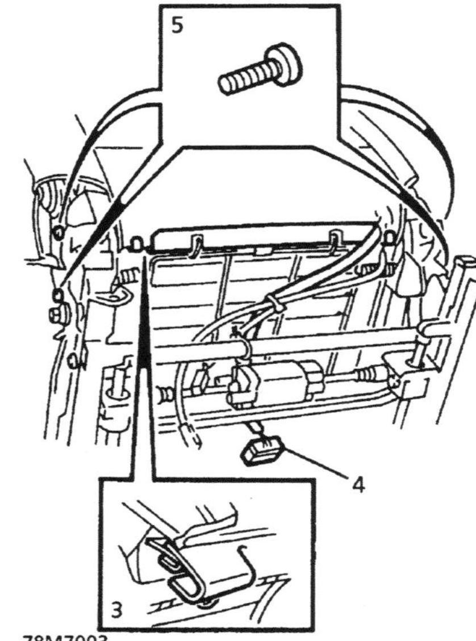

78M7003

4. Disconnect headrest/recline multiplug from connection under cushion.
5. Remove 4 bolts securing squab to seat. Remove squab.
6. Remove 4 screws securing seat slides to cushion frame. Remove slides.
7. Remove 8 clips securing cushion cover to frame.

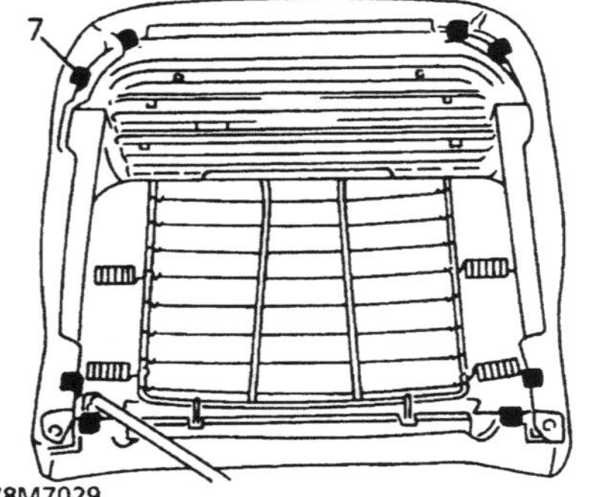

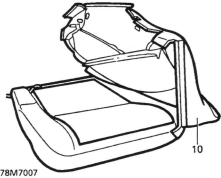

78M7029

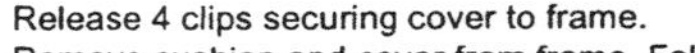

8. Release 4 clips securing cover to frame.
9. Remove cushion and cover from frame. Fold back cover.
10. Remove 13 hog rings securing cover to cushion. Remove cover.

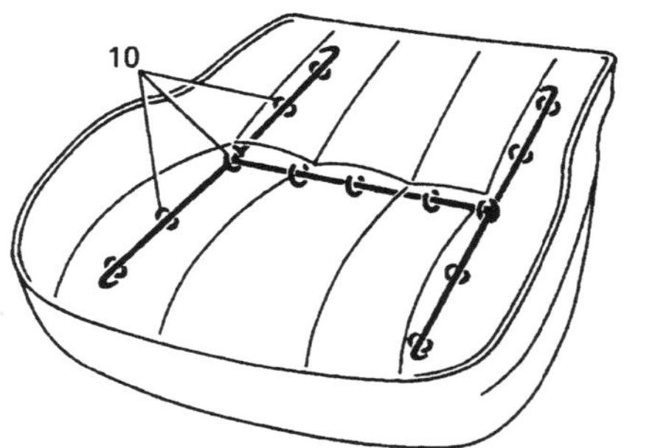

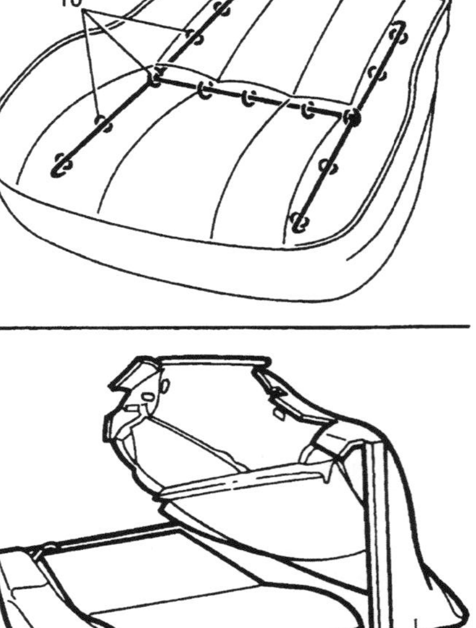

78M7007

NOTE: Heating element is part of cushion.

Refit

11. Position cover on cushion. Fit hog rings.
12. Position cushion assembly to frame. Secure with clips and retainers.
13. Fit seat slides to cushion frame. Secure with screws. Tighten to ***30 Nm. (22 lbf.ft)***
14. Fit cushion to seat. Secure with bolts.
15. Connect headrest/recline multiplug.
16. Connect squab cover retainer to cushion frame. Position cover trim. Secure with clips.
17. Fit valance to cushion. Secure with screws. Fit screw covers.
18. Fit front seat. ***See this section.***

HEATING ELEMENT - CUSHION - FRONT SEAT - from 99MY

Service repair no - 78.30.24

Remove

1. Remove cushion cover. ***See this section.***

△ **NOTE: Heating element is integral with cushion foam.**

Refit

2. Fit cushion cover. ***See this section.***

HEATING ELEMENT SQUAB FRONT SEAT

Service repair no - 78.90.36

Remove

1. Remove front seat. ***See this section.***
2. Remove headrest.

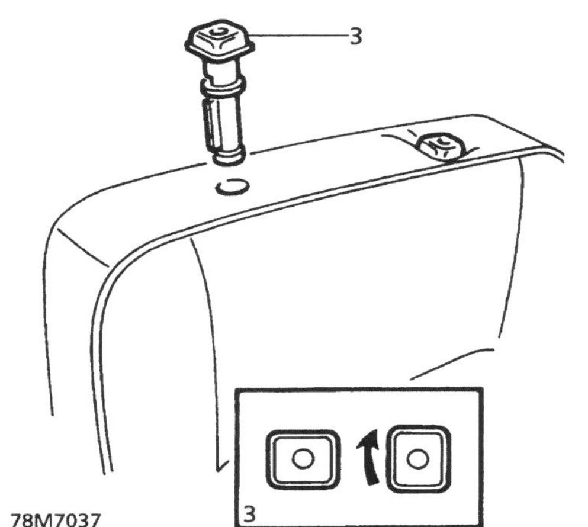

78M7037

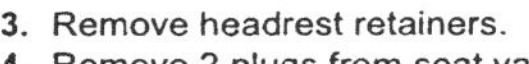

3. Remove headrest retainers.
4. Remove 2 plugs from seat valance retaining screws. Remove 3 screws. Remove valance.

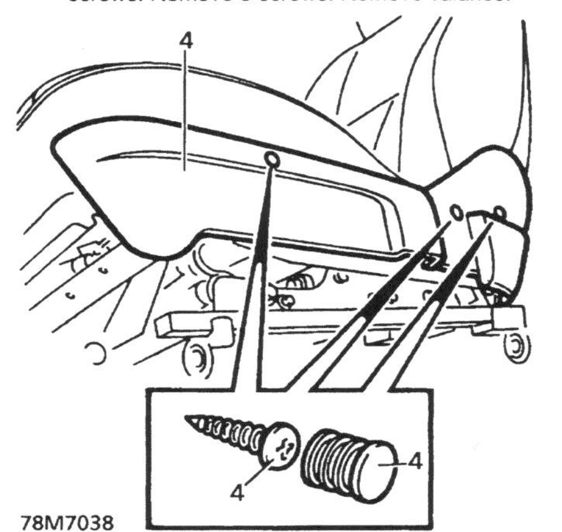

78M7038

5. Remove 2 clips securing squab cover retainer to cushion frame. Release retainer.

78M7039

6. Disconnect headrest and recline multiplug from connection under cushion.
7. Remove 4 bolts securing squab to seat. Remove squab.

8. Remove cover from armrest screw. Remove screw and armrest.

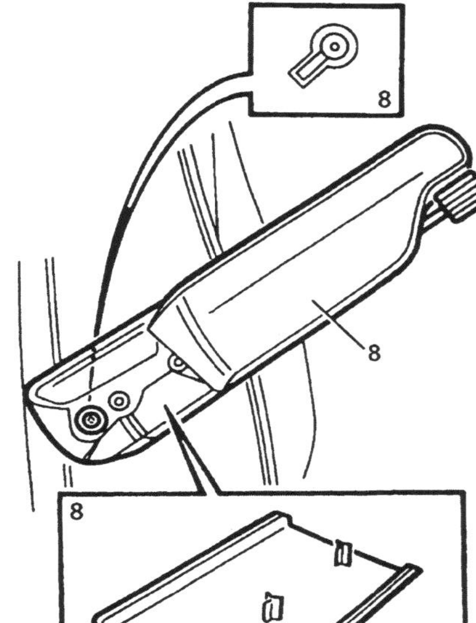

78M7040

9. Remove 2 clips securing squab cover retainer to squab frame. Release retainer.

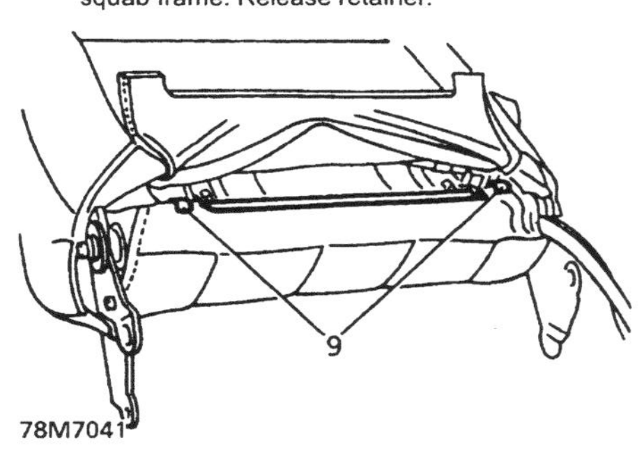

78M7041

10. Release cover retention wires from frame. Roll cover back for access.
11. Remove 4 Hog rings from front and 4 Hog rings from rear of squab cover.
12. Roll cover back further. Remove 4 Hog rings securing front of cover.

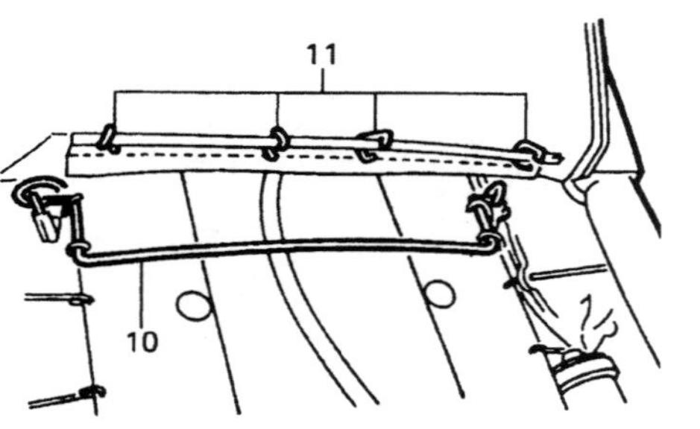
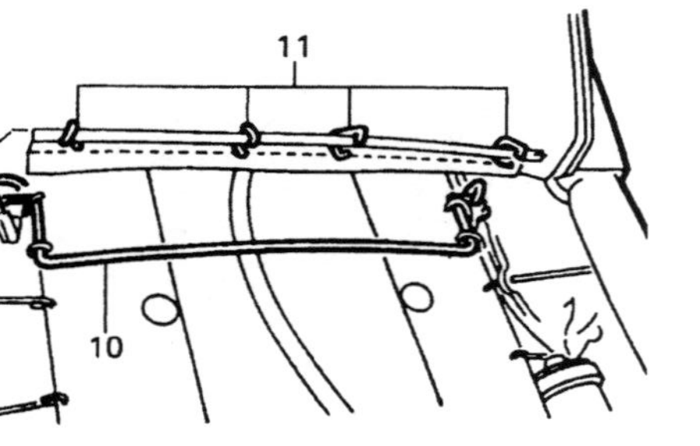

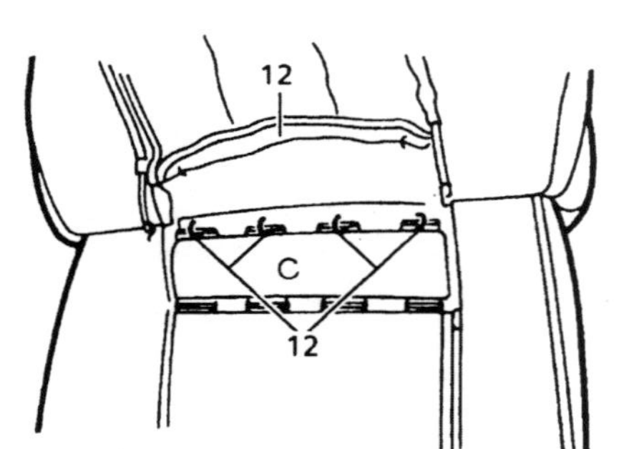

78M7042

13. Disconnect remaining ends of retention wires.

14. Remove cover from frame.

78M7043

15. Remove foam.

NOTE: Heating element is integral with foam.

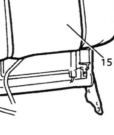

78M7044

Refit

16. Reverse removal procedure.

LATCH REAR SQUAB

Service repair no - 78.80.16.

Remove

1. Lower rear seat squab.
2. Remove parcel tray and trim support panels. ***See CHASSIS AND BODY, Repair.***
3. Disconnect squab release rod from latch.
4. Remove 2 screws securing latch. Remove latch.

Refit

5. Reverse removal procedure.
6. Tighten latch securing screws to ***14 Nm. (10 lbf.ft)***

MOTOR FORWARD/REARWARD

Service repair no - 78.70.25

Remove

1. Remove front seat. ***See this section.***
2. Remove 2 plugs from seat inner valance retaining screws. Remove 2 screws.

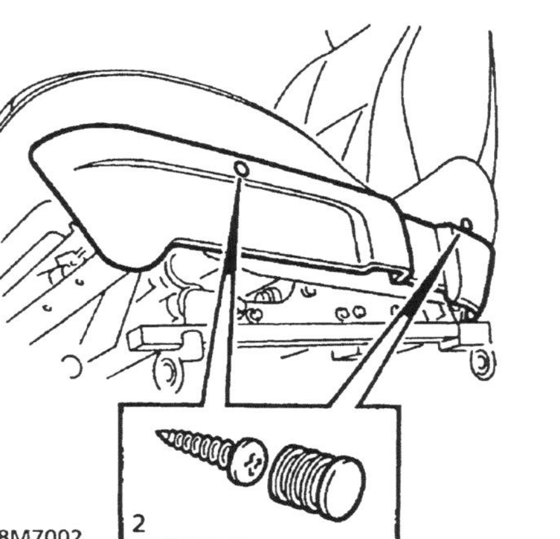

78M7002

3. Remove inner valance.
4. Disconnect multiplug from forward/rear motor.

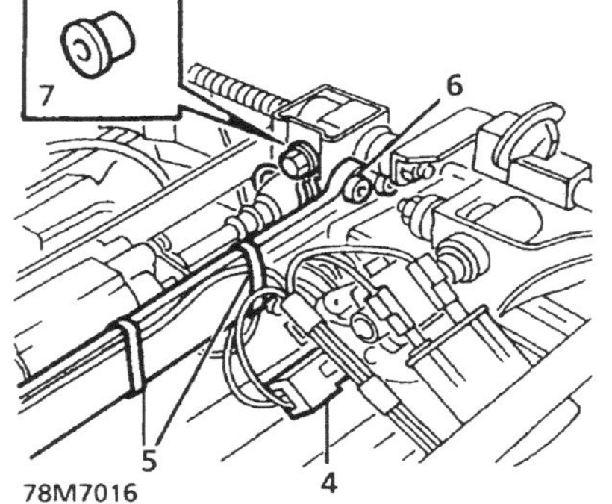

78M7016

5. Release multiplug from bracket. Remove strap securing motor harness to motor mounting bracket.
6. Remove 2 screws securing motor mounting bracket to gearbox bracket.
7. Remove bolt and shouldered spacer securing gearbox to mounting bracket.
8. Remove rear nut securing forward/rear slide bracket to cross tubes.

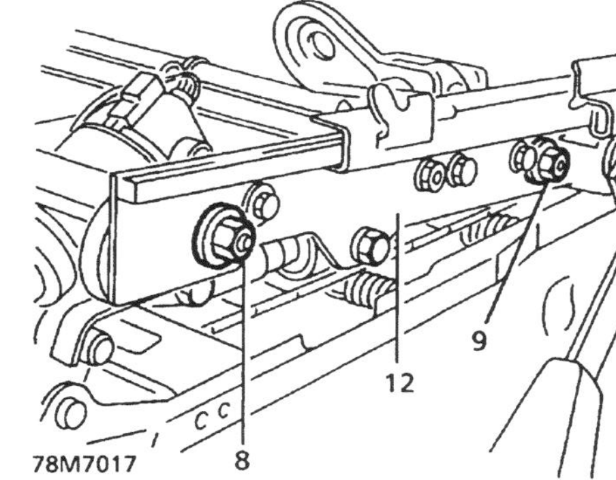

78M7017

9. Slacken front nut securing forward/rear slide bracket to cross tubes.
10. Remove spring clip securing drive cable cover to gearbox.

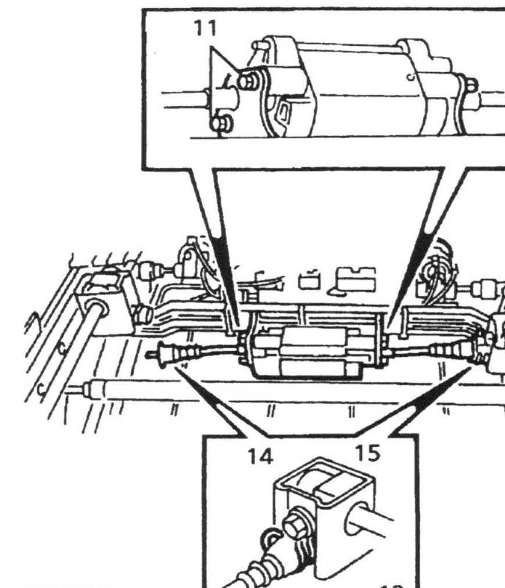

78M7018

11. Remove 4 screws securing motor to mounting bracket.
12. Release forward/rear slide bracket from rear cross tube.
13. Raise slide bracket. Disconnect drive cable from gearbox.
14. Remove drive cable from motor. Remove motor from mounting bracket.
15. Remove second drive cable from gearbox.

Refit

16. Reverse removal procedure.

MOTOR - HEADREST - FRONT SEAT - up to 99MY

Service repair no - 78.70.31

Remove

1. Remove front seat. ***See this section.***

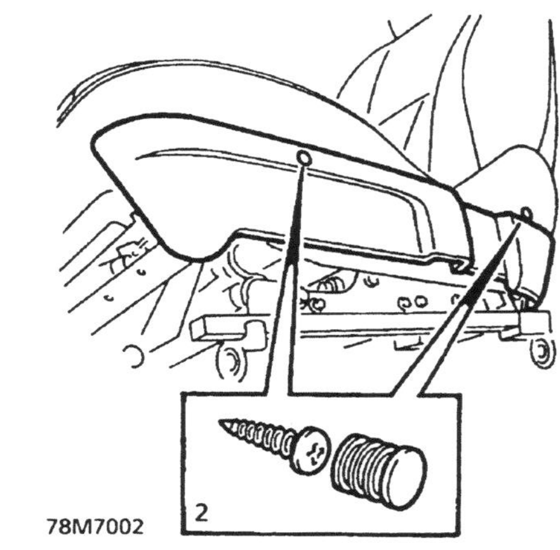

78M7002

2. Remove 2 plugs from seat inner valance retaining screws. Remove 2 screws. Remove valance.
3. Remove 2 clips securing squab cover retainer to cushion frame. Release retainer.

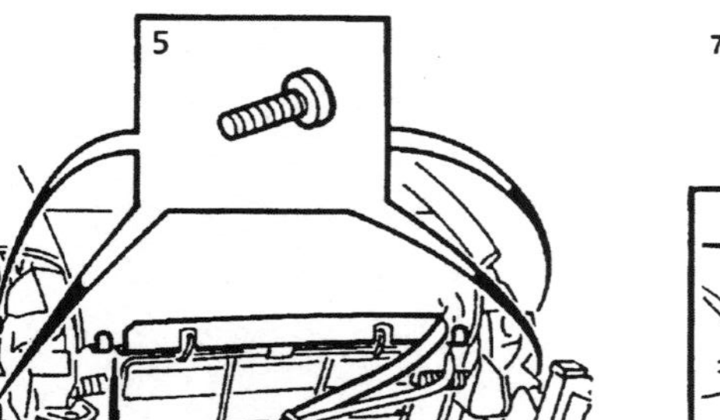

78M7003

4. Disconnect headrest and recline multiplug from connection under cushion.
5. Remove 4 bolts securing squab to seat. Remove squab.
6. Remove 2 squab cover clips. Release squab retainer from squab frame.

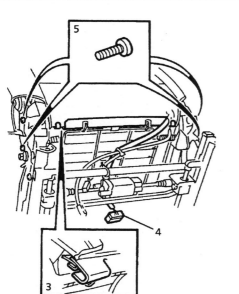

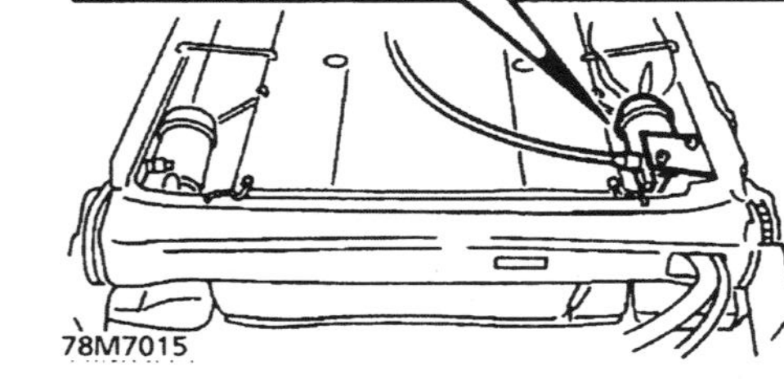

78M7004

7. Release cover retention wires from frame. Roll cover back for access

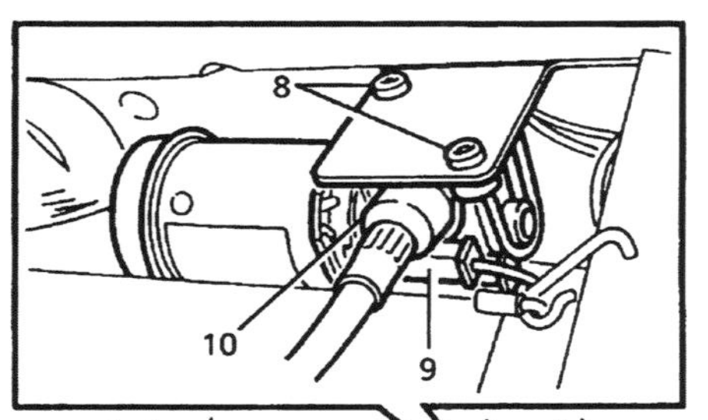

78M7015

8. Remove 2 bolts securing motor to frame. Release motor.
9. Note fitted position of wires. Disconnect 2 Lucars from motor.
10. Remove cable retaining clip. Remove motor from cable.

Refit

11. Reverse removal procedure.

MOTOR - HEADREST - FRONT SEAT - from 99MY

Service repair no - 78.70.31

Remove

1. Remove front seat. ***See this section.***

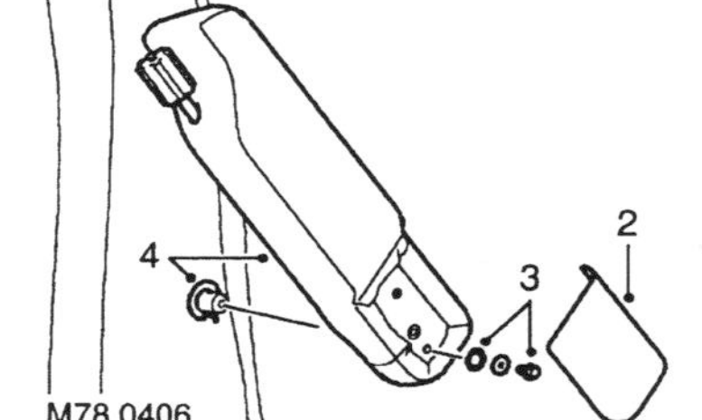

M78 0406

2. Remove armrest retaining screw cover.
3. Remove screw securing armrest, collect anti-rattle washer.
4. Remove armrest and escutcheon.

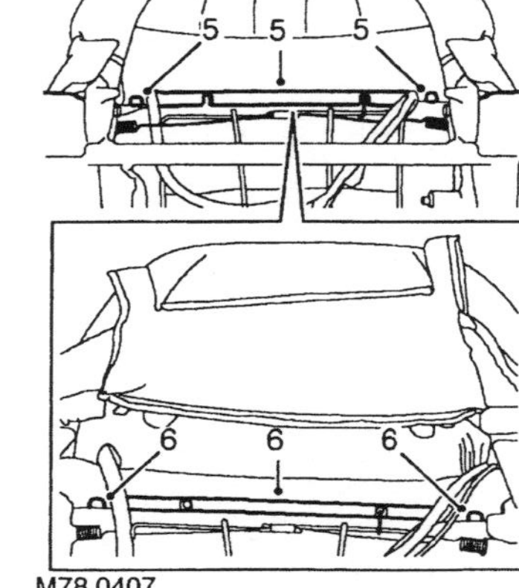

M78 0407

5. Remove 2 clips and release retainer securing rear section of cover to frame.
6. Remove 2 clips and release retainer securing front section of cover to frame.

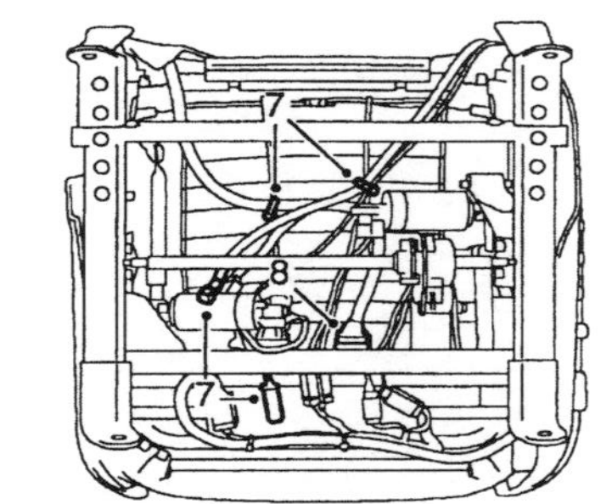

M78 0408

7. Remove cable ties securing harnesses to cushion spring. Release heating element harness and SRS harness 2 way connector.
8. Disconnect multiplug from control unit.
9. Release harness from squab cover.
10. Raise squab cover for access.

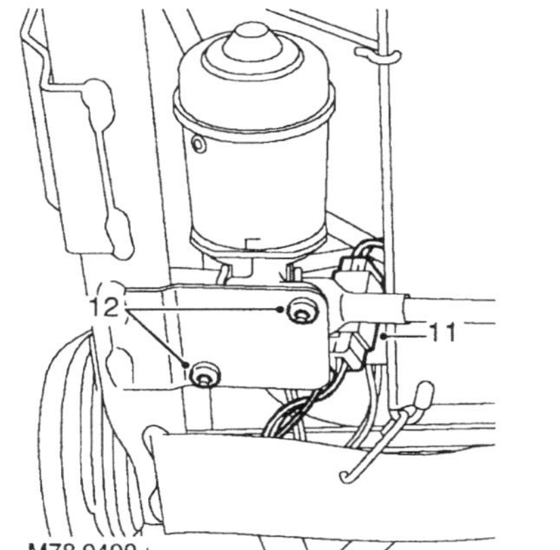

M78 0409

11. Disconnect motor multiplug.
12. Remove 2 Torx screws securing motor.

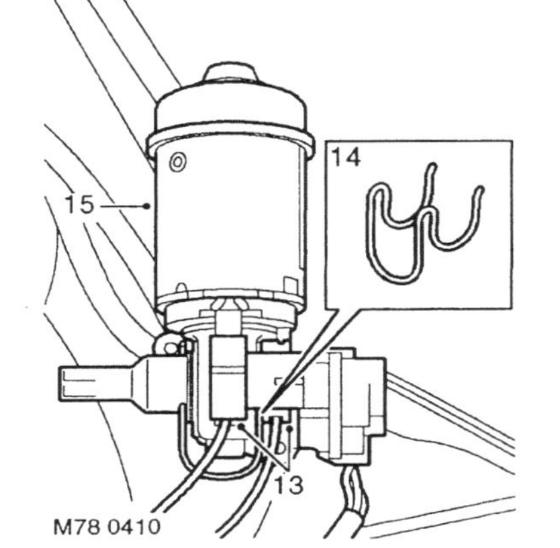

M78 0410

13. Release motor and noting fitted positions, disconnect 2 Lucars from motor.
14. Remove drive cable retaining clip.
15. Remove motor.

Refit

16. Fit motor, locate drive cable and secure with clip.
17. Connect Lucars, align motor to frame and fit Torx screws.
18. Lower squab cover.
19. Pass harness through squab cover and connect multiplug.
20. Align seat heating element harness and secure harnesses with cable ties.
21. Secure SRS connector to bracket.
22. Secure front section cover retainer to frame and fit clips.
23. Secure rear section cover retainer to frame and fit clips.
24. Fit armrest escutcheon.
25. Fit armrest and position anti-rattle washer. Fit and tighten bolt.
26. Fit seat. ***See this section.***

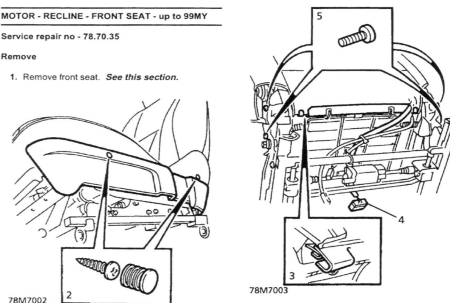

MOTOR - RECLINE - FRONT SEAT - up to 99MY

Service repair no - 78.70.35

Remove

1. Remove front seat. ***See this section.***

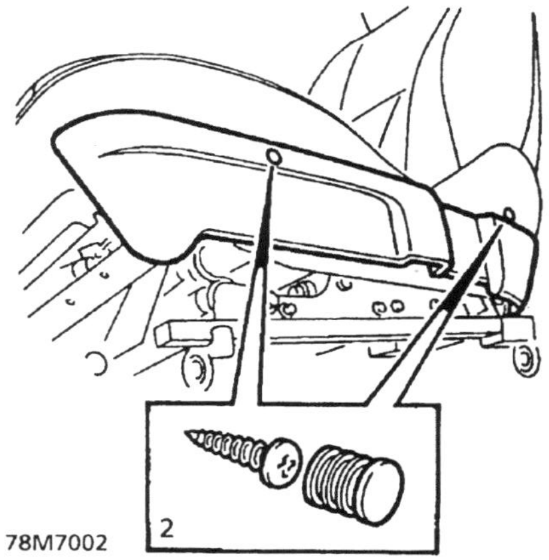

2
78M7002

2. Remove 2 plugs from seat inner valance retaining screws. Remove 2 screws. Remove valance.
3. Remove 2 clips securing squab cover retainer to cushion frame. Release retainer.

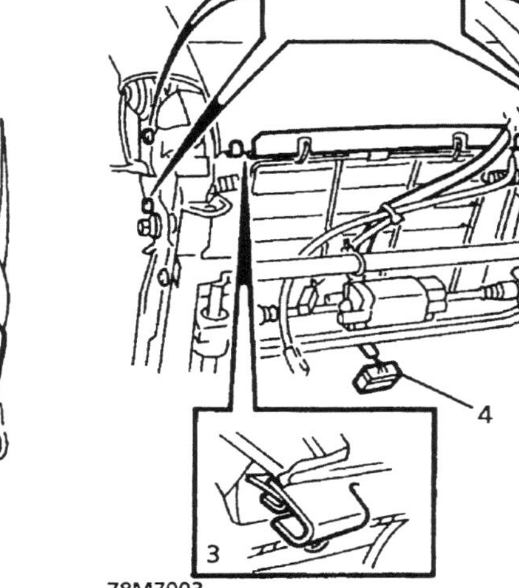

78M7003

4. Disconnect headrest/recline multiplug from connection under cushion.
5. Remove 4 bolts securing squab to seat. Remove squab.
6. Remove 2 squab cover clips. Release squab retainer from squab frame.

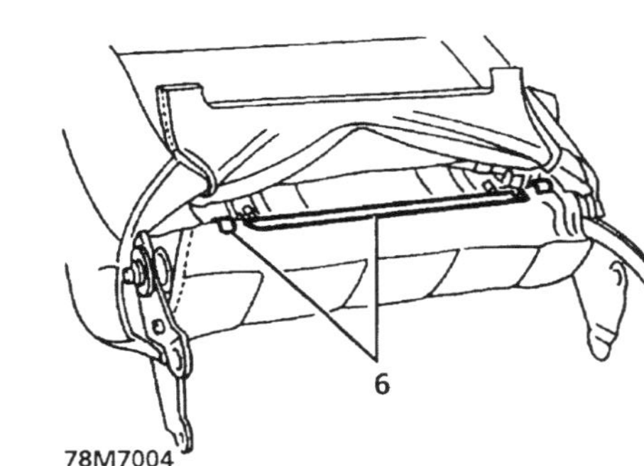

78M7004

7. Release cover retention wires from frame. Roll cover back for access.
8. Disconnect recline motor multiplug from seat harness.
9. Remove 2 bolts securing motor to frame. Remove motor.

Refit

10. Reverse removal procedure.

MOTOR - RECLINE - FRONT SEAT - from 99MY

Service repair no - 78.70.35

Remove

1. Remove front seat. ***See this section.***

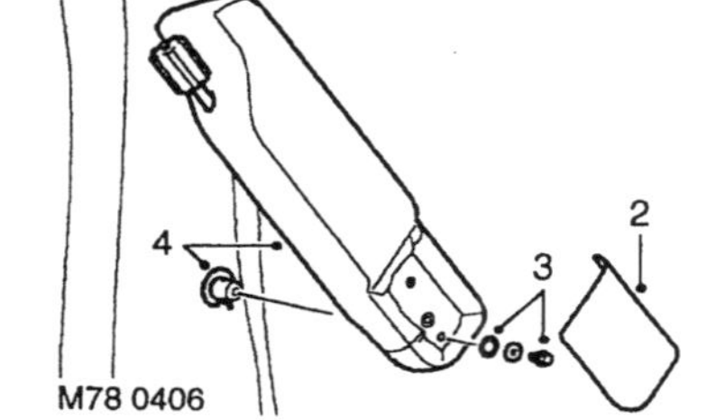

M78 0406

2. Remove armrest retaining screw cover.
3. Remove screw securing armrest, collect anti-rattle washer.
4. Remove armrest and escutcheon.

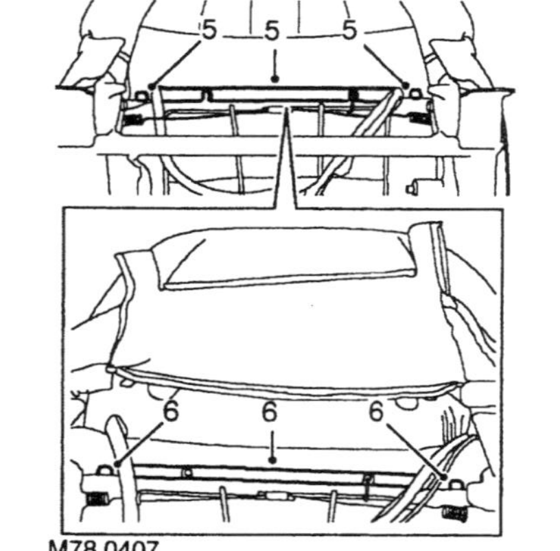

M78 0407

5. Remove 2 clips and release retainer securing rear section of cover to frame.
6. Remove 2 clips and release retainer securing front section of cover to frame.

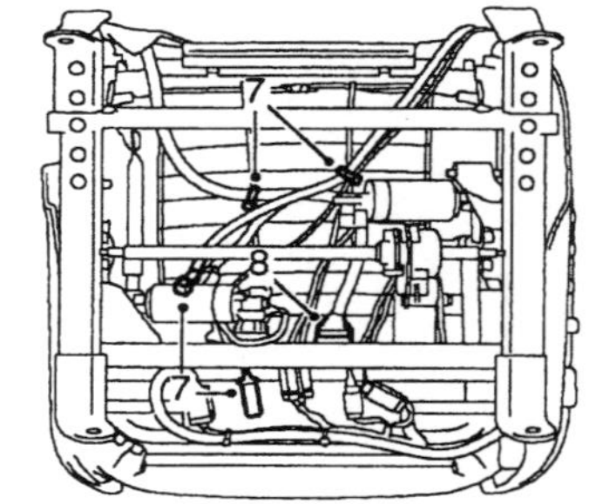

M78 0408

7. Remove cable ties securing harnesses to cushion spring. Release heating element harness and SRS harness 2 way connector.
8. Disconnect multiplug from control unit.
9. Release harness from squab cover.

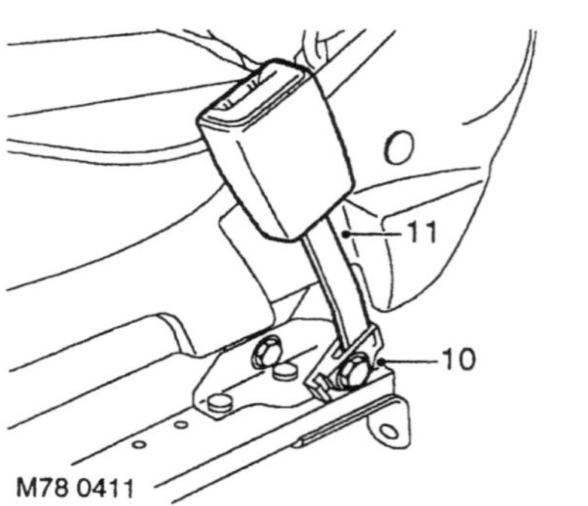

M78 0411

10. Remove bolt securing seat belt stalk.
11. Remove seat belt stalk.

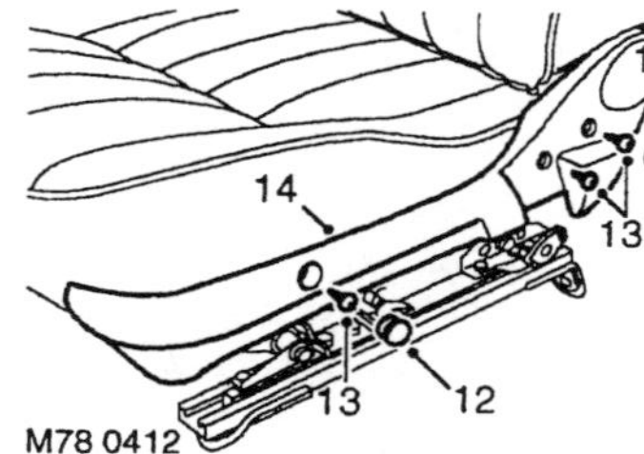

M78 0412

12. Remove 2 screw covers.
13. Remove 3 screws securing inner side finisher.
14. Remove side finisher.

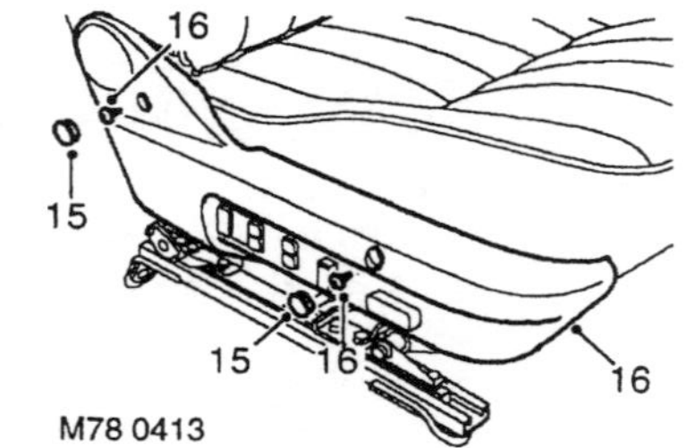

M78 0413

15. Remove 2 screw covers.
16. Remove 2 screws securing outer side finisher. Release side finisher and move aside for access.
17. Raise squab cover for access.

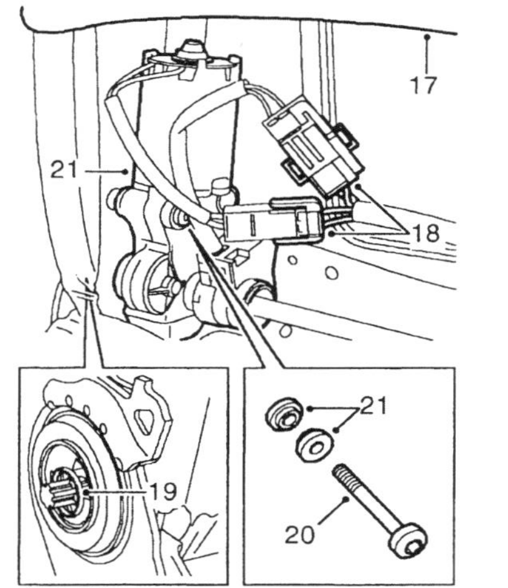

M78 0414

18. Disconnect 2 multiplugs from motor.
19. Remove clip securing drive shaft and withdraw drive shaft from motor.
20. Remove Torx screw securing motor.
21. Remove motor and collect 2 rubber washers.

Refit

22. Fit rubber washers, position motor and fit Torx screw.
23. Locate drive shaft and fit clip.
24. Connect multiplug.
25. Lower squab cover.
26. Pass harness through cover and connect multiplug.
27. Align seat heating element harness and secure harnesses with cable ties.
28. Secure SRS connector to bracket.
29. Secure front section cover retainer to frame and fit clips.
30. Secure rear section cover retainer to frame and fit clips.
31. Fit armrest escutcheon.
32. Fit armrest and position anti-rattle washer. Fit and tighten bolt.
33. Position outer side finisher and fit screws and covers.
34. Fit inner side finisher, fit screws and screw covers.
35. Position seat belt stalk, fit bolt and tighten to ***35 Nm (26 lbf.ft).***
36. Fit seat. ***See this section.***

SEAT POWER RELAY

Service repair no - 78.70.47

NOTE: 2 power relays are fitted to electrically operated seats without position memory function.

Remove

1. If possible, raise seat cushion to full extent to improve access to relays.
2. Remove relay from connector block.

Refit

3. Reverse removal procedure.

MOTOR - RISE AND FALL - FRONT SEAT - up to 99MY

Service repair no - 78.70.27

Remove

1. Remove front seat. ***See this section.***
2. Note fitted position of wires. Disconnect 2 Lucars from motor.

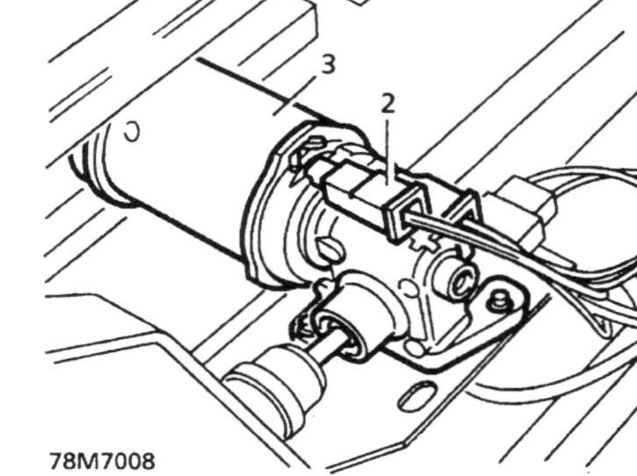

78M7008

3. Remove 2 screws securing motor to mounting bracket. Remove motor.

Refit

4. Reverse removal procedure.

MOTOR - RISE AND FALL - FRONT SEAT - from 99MY

Service repair no - 78.70.27

Remove

1. Remove front seat. ***See this section.***

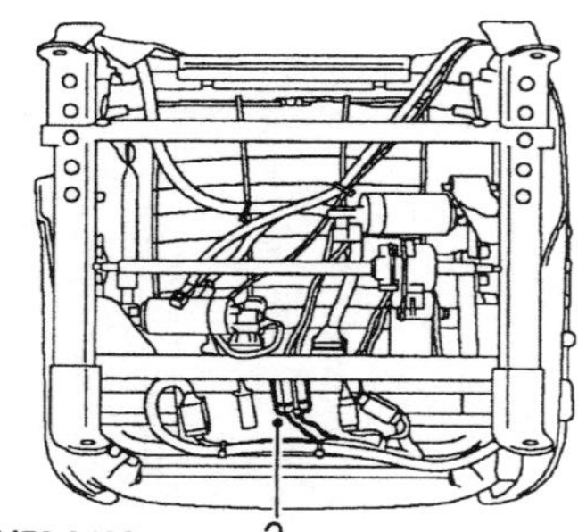

M78 0402

2. Disconnect and release multiplug from bracket.

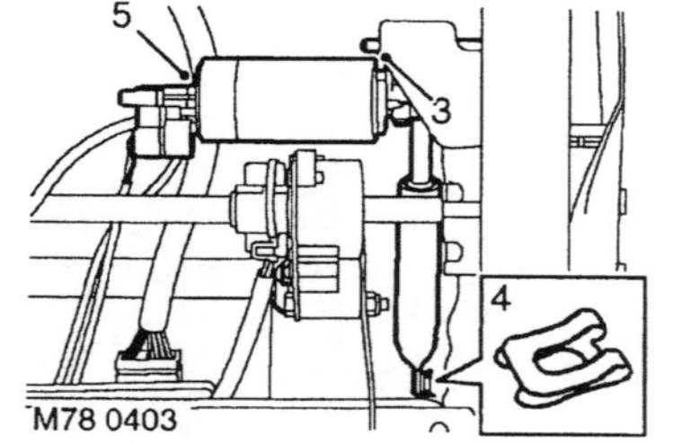

M78 0403

3. Remove roll pin securing motor.
4. Remove spring clip securing operating rod to lever.
5. Release and remove motor assembly.

Refit

6. Clean lever pivot and smear with grease.
7. Position motor assembly and locate operating rod to lever. Fit new spring clip.
8. Align motor and fit new roll pin.
9. Connect multiplug and secure to bracket.
10. Fit seat. ***See this section.***

REAR SEATS

Service repair no - 78.10.47/99

Remove

1. Remove screws securing seat bolt covers. Remove covers.

78M7019

2. Remove 2 front retaining bolts.
3. Release seat and fold forward.

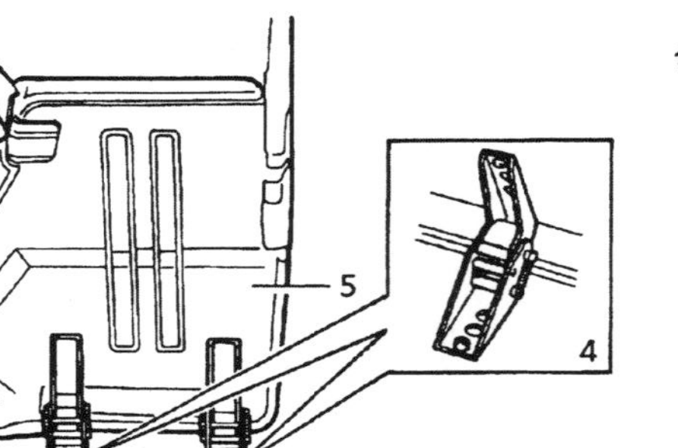

78M7020

4. Remove 2 rear retaining bolts.
5. Remove seat.

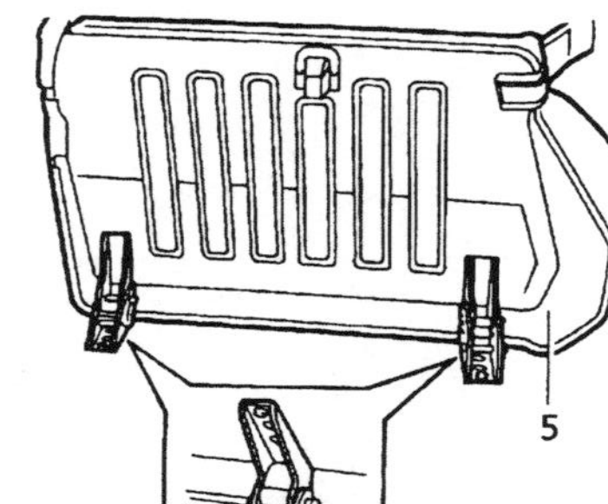

78M7021

Refit

6. Position seat.
7. Fit front bolts. Do not tighten.
8. Fit rear bolts. Tighten to ***29 Nm. (22 lbf.ft)***
9. Tighten front bolts. Tighten to ***29 Nm. (22 lbf.ft)***
10. Fit bolt covers. Secure with screws.

SEAT OUTSTATION - up to 99MY

Service repair no - 78.70.01

NOTE: Seat outstation is used on electrically operated seats with position memory function.

Remove

1. Remove seat. ***See this section.***
2. Remove 2 bolts securing front of seat frame to cushion pan.

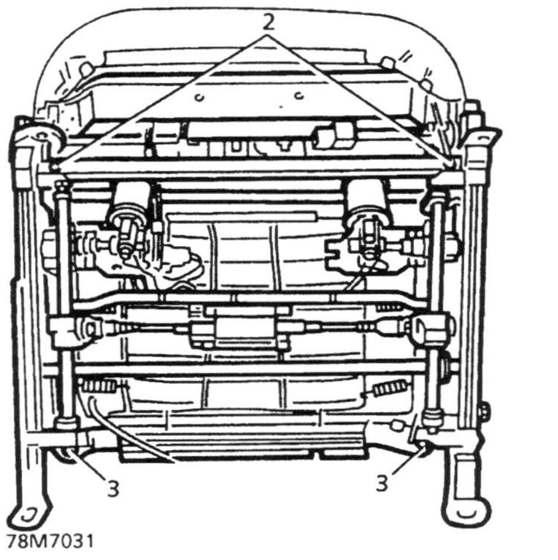

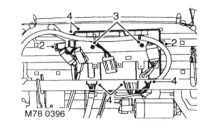

78M7031

3. Slacken 2 bolts securing rear of seat frame.
4. Disconnect 4 multiplugs.

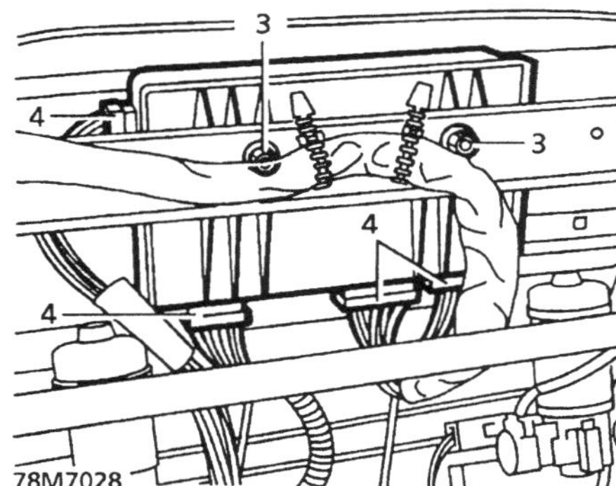

78M7028

5. Remove 2 nuts securing outstation to frame.
6. Lift front of seat frame away from cushion pad to provide clearance for outstation removal. Remove outstation.

Refit

7. Reverse removal procedure.
8. Tighten bolts securing cushion pan to frame to ***29 Nm. (21 lbf.ft)***

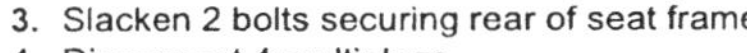

SEAT OUTSTATION - from 99MY

Service repair no - 78.70.01

NOTE: Seat outstation is used on electrically operated seats with memory function.

1. Remove front seat. ***See this section.***

M78 0396

2. Remove 2 screws securing seat outstation mounting bracket to cushion frame.
3. Remove 2 nuts securing outstation to mounting bracket.
4. Release outstation from mounting bracket and disconnect 4 multiplugs.
5. Remove outstation.

Refit

6. Position outstation, connect multiplugs and locate on mounting bracket. Fit and tighten nuts.
7. Align outstation mounting bracket to cushion frame and fit screws.
8. Fit seat. ***See this section.***

MOTOR - TILT - FRONT SEAT - from 99MY

Service repair no - 78.70.29

Remove

1. Remove front seat. ***See this section.***

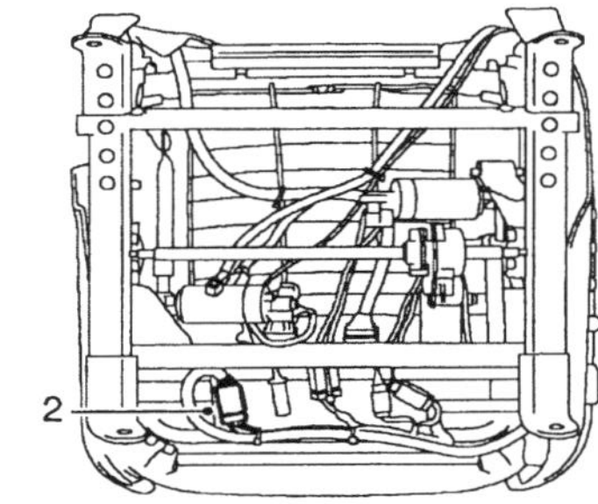

M78 0404

2. Disconnect and release multiplug from bracket.

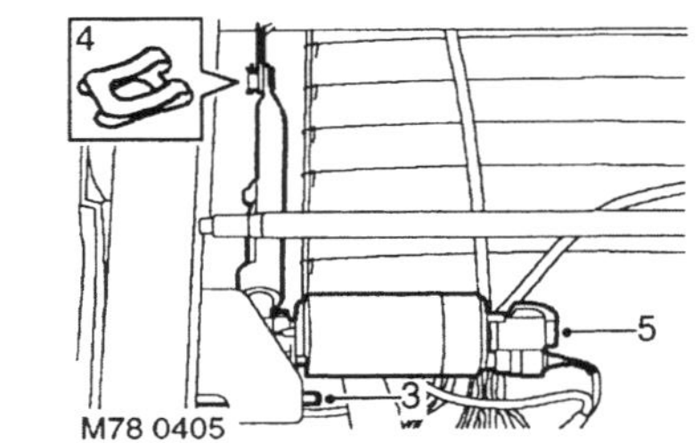

M78 0405

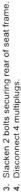

3. Remove roll pin securing motor.
4. Remove spring clip securing operating rod to lever.
5. Release and remove motor assembly.

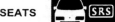

Refit

6. Clean lever pivot and smear with grease.
7. Position motor assembly and locate operating rod to lever. Fit new spring clip.
8. Align motor and fit new roll pin.
9. Connect multiplug and secure to bracket.
10. Fit seat. ***See this section.***

LATCH REAR SEAT

Service repair no - 78.80.12

Remove

1. Fold adjacent seat forward.
2. Remove 3 screws securing latch cover. Remove cover.

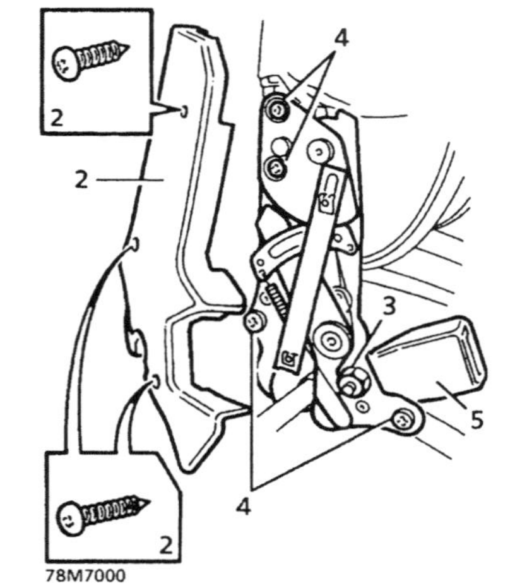

78M7000

3. Slacken seat belt stalk bolt.
4. Remove 4 screws securing latch to seat assembly. Remove latch.

NOTE: Fold top of latch forward to release.

5. Remove bolt securing seat belt stalk. Remove stalk.

Refit

6. Hold latch in vice. Position seat belt stalk. Secure with bolt. Tighten to ***35 Nm. (26 lbf.ft)***
7. Position latch. Align to cushion and squab.
8. Secure with screws. Tighten to ***30 Nm. (22 lbf.ft)***
9. Fit latch cover. Secure with screws.
10. Return seat to original position.

Remove

1. Remove 2 screw plugs from seat valance.

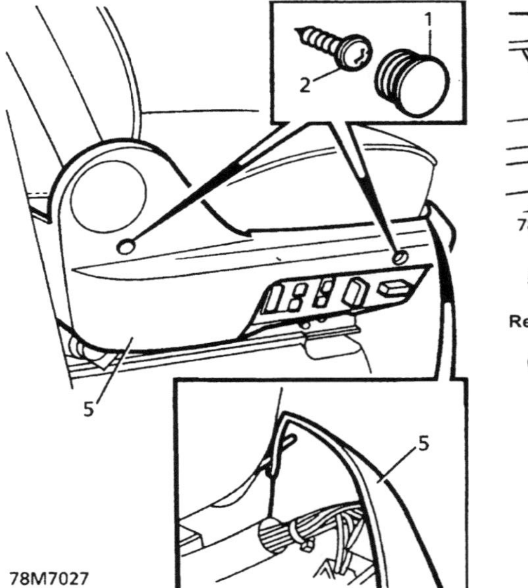

78M7027

2. Remove 2 screws securing valance.
3. Release stud securing harness to seat frame.
4. Disconnect harness from seat ECU.

SWITCH - FRONT SEAT CONTROL

Service repair no - 78.70.89

4
4
78M7030

5. Remove valance/switch assembly.

Refit

6. Reverse removal procedure.

80 - HEATING AND VENTILATION

CONTENTS

Heating and ventilation components

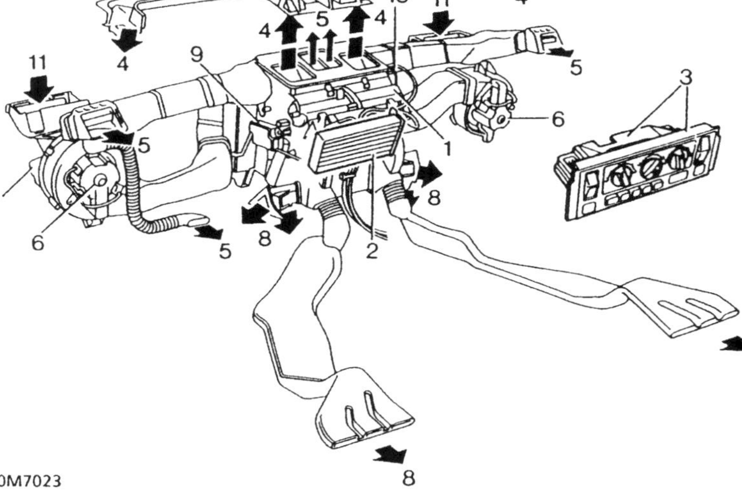

80M7023

1. Heater unit
2. Heater matrix
3. Heater ECU
4. Air to windscreen and front side window vents
5. Air to fascia centre vents, side vents and lap vent (driver only)
6. Blower
7. Fresh/Recirculated air servo
8. Air to front and rear footwells
9. LH temperature servo
10. Distribution servo
11. Fresh air inlet and pollen filter

DESCRIPTION

The heating and ventilation system controls the vehicle's interior heating and air distribution.

The heating and ventilation system consists of two air inlet housings, a heater unit, distribution ducts and a Heater ECU. Fresh or recirculated air flows into the heater unit, from the air inlet housings, assisted by an electric blower in each housing and/or ram effect. In the heater unit the temperature of the air is controlled by servo operated flaps. Additional servo operated flaps then direct the air to front heater and rear vents via moulded distribution ducts. Operation of the flap servos and the blowers is controlled by the Heater ECU.

Air inlet housings

LH and RH air inlet housings supply fresh or recirculated air to the air inlets on each side of the heater unit. Fresh air is drawn through the grille at the base of the windscreen and into the plenum, from where it passes through pollen filters into the air inlet housings. Recirculated air is drawn from the vehicle interior through grilles in the air inlet housings. Servo operated flaps in the air inlet housings control the selection of fresh or recirculated air. Each air inlet housing also incorporates a blower consisting of an open hub, centrifugal fan powered by an electric motor.

Heater unit

The heater unit consists of a housing containing a heater matrix which is connected to the engine cooling system. As water is circulated continuously through the heater matrix, the selection of hot or cold air is controlled by servo operated LH and RH blend flaps directing the air through or around the heater matrix. The LH and RH blend flaps operate independently to allow different temperatures to be set for the LH and RH air vents. The servo operated distribution flaps control the flow of air from the heater unit to the outlet vents. Air distribution is common to both sides of the vehicle interior.

The two temperature servos and the distribution servo each incorporate a feedback potentiometer which provides the Heater ECU with a flap position signal to enable accurate control of air temperature and distribution.

Distribution ducts

Molded ducts are installed for the distribution of air to the face level vents and the front and rear footwell vents. A corrugated duct directs air to the driver's lap vent. Distribution ducts for the windscreen and side window vents are integrated into the fascia.

Vent assemblies in the fascia allow occupants to control the flow and direction of face level air. Each vent assembly incorporates a thumbwheel to regulate the flow and moveable vanes to control direction. The thumbwheel of the outboard vent assembly on the driver's side also controls the flow of air from the driver's lap vent.

Heater ECU

The Heater ECU comprises an integrated ECU and control panel, and is mounted in the centre console below the in-car entertainment unit. To control the heating and ventilation system, the ECU outputs signals to the flap servos and blowers in response to selections made on the rotary switches and momentary push switches installed on the control panel. In addition to the heating and ventilation system, the Heater ECU also controls the rear screen heater and, where fitted, the windscreen heaters and the seat heaters. Each push switch on the control panel has a LED to indicate the selections made.

After installation of a new Heater ECU, it must be initialised using TestBook to ensure correct operation of the heating and ventilation system.

Heater ECU control panel

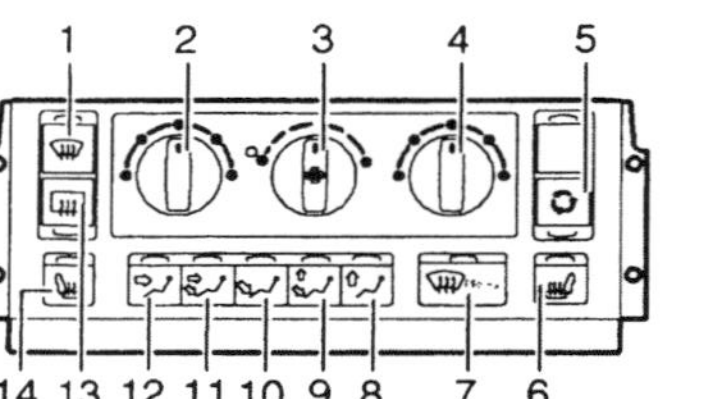

M82 0570

1. Windscreen heater switch
2. LH temperature switch
3. Blower switch
4. RH temperature switch
5. Fresh/ Recirculated air switch
6. RH front seat heater switch
7. Demist mode switch
8. Windscreen/ Side window distribution switch
9. Windscreen/ Side window and footwells distribution switch
10. Footwells distribution switch
11. Face and footwells distribution switch
12. Face distribution switch
13. Rear screen heater switch
14. LH front seat heater switch

Windscreen heater switch

Push switch that operates the windscreen heaters. A timed function that automatically goes off after approximately 4 minutes, or immediately if the switch is pressed again. The switch LED is illuminated while the heater is active.

LH temperature switch

Rotary switch that controls the temperature of the air to the LH side of the vehicle interior:

- Driver's side temperature control is dominant over passenger's. The temperature set by the passenger is restricted to a tolerance band of 6 °C (11 °F) above or below that set by the driver.
- The control is overridden when demist programme switch is selected.

Blower switch

Rotary switch that simultaneously controls the speed of both blowers:

- Clockwise rotation progressively increases blower speed. Anti-clockwise rotation progressively decreases blower speed.
- The control is overridden when demist programme is selected.

RH temperature switch

Rotary switch that controls the temperature of the air to the RH side of the vehicle interior. Operates the same as the LH temperature switch.

Fresh/ Recirculated air switch

Push switch that simultaneously controls selection of fresh or recirculated air in both air inlet housings:

- Demist programme overrides recirculated air selection.
- First press of switch selects recirculated air. Switch LED illuminated while recirculated air selected.
- A second press of the switch restores fresh air selection. Switch LED extinguished while fresh air selected.

RH front seat heater switch

Push switch that controls the RH front seat heaters. Operation is independent of the heating and ventilation system. The heaters remain active until the switch is pressed again. The switch LED is illuminated while the heaters are on.

Demist mode (PROG) switch

Push switch for initiating automatic demist mode:

- Air inlets set to fresh air.
- Blower speeds set to optimum.
- LH and RH temperatures set to maximum.
- Distribution set to windscreen and side windows only.
- Rear screen heater selected on and rear screen heater switch LED illuminated.
- Windscreen heaters selected on and windscreen heater switch LED illuminated.

Windscreen/ Side window distribution switch

Push switch that sets air distribution to windscreen and front side window vents.

Windscreen/ Side window and footwells distribution switch

Push switch that sets air distribution to windscreen, front side windows and footwell vents.

Footwell distribution switch

Push switch that sets air distribution to the footwell vents.

Face and footwell distribution switch

Push switch that sets air distribution to the face level, driver's lap and footwell vents.

Face distribution switch

Push switch that sets air distribution to the face level and driver's lap vents.

LH front seat heater switch

Push switch that controls the LH front seat heaters. Operation is independent of the heating and ventilation system. The heaters remain active until the switch is pressed again. The switch LED is illuminated while the heaters are on.

Rear screen heater switch

Push switch that operates the rear screen heater. A timed function that automatically goes off after approximately 15 minutes, or immediately if the switch is pressed again. The switch LED is illuminated while the heater is active.

The exterior mirror heaters are activated for approximately 10 minutes when either the windscreen or rear screen heaters are activated. There is no active indicator or independent control for the exterior mirror heaters.

Heater ECU connectors

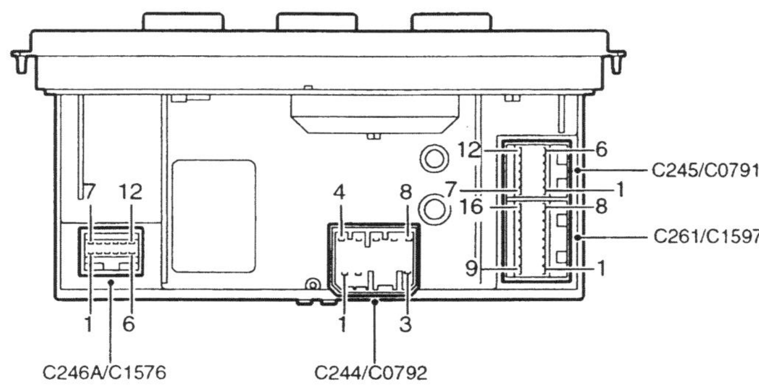

M80 0351

Heater ECU connector pin details

Connector/ Pin No.	Description	Input/Output
C244 (up to 99MY) C0792 (from 99MY)		
1	Auxiliary power supply	Input
2	Battery power supply	Input
3	Ignition power supply	Input
4	Earth	-
5	Windscreen heaters	Output
6	Instrument/ Switch illumination	Input
7 and 8	Not used	-

Connector/ Pin No.	Description	Input/Output
C245 (up to 99MY) C0766 (from 99MY)		
1	RH blower control	Output
2	RH blower safety	Output
3	RH blower voltage feedback	Input
4	LH blower control	Output
5	LH blower safety	Output
6	LH blower voltage feedback	Input
7 and 8	Not used	-
9	RH fresh/ recirculated air servo (+/-)	Input/Output
10	RH fresh/ recirculated air servo (+/-)	Input/Output
11	LH fresh/ recirculated air servo (+/-)	Input/Output
12	LH fresh/ recirculated air servo (+/-)	Input/Output
C246A (up to 99MY) C1596 (from 99MY)		
1	Not used	Input
2	Diagnostics K line	Input/Output
3	Diagnostics L line	Input/Output
4	Engine running (alternator charging)	Input
5 to 8	Not used	-
9	Rear screen heater request	Output
10	Not used	-
11	LH seat heater request	Output
12	RH seat heater request	Output

Connector/ Pin No.	Description	Input/Output
C261 (up to 99MY) C1597 (from 99MY)		
1	RH temperature servo feedback reference voltage (-)	Input
2	Distribution servo feedback reference voltage (-)	Input
3	Not used	
4	Distribution servo feedback reference voltage (+)	Output
5	RH temperature servo feedback reference voltage (+)	Output
6	Distribution servo voltage (+/-)	Input/Output
7	RH temperature servo feedback	Input
8	LH temperature servo feedback	Input
9	RH temperature servo voltage (+/-)	Input/Output
10	RH temperature servo voltage (+/-)	Input/Output
11	LH temperature servo voltage (+/-)	Input/Output
12	LH temperature servo voltage (+/-)	Input/Output
13	LH temperature servo feedback reference voltage (-)	Output
14	LH temperature servo feedback reference voltage (+)	Output
15	Distribution servo feedback	Input
16	Distribution servo voltage (+/-)	Input/Output

OPERATION

Heating and ventilation control diagram

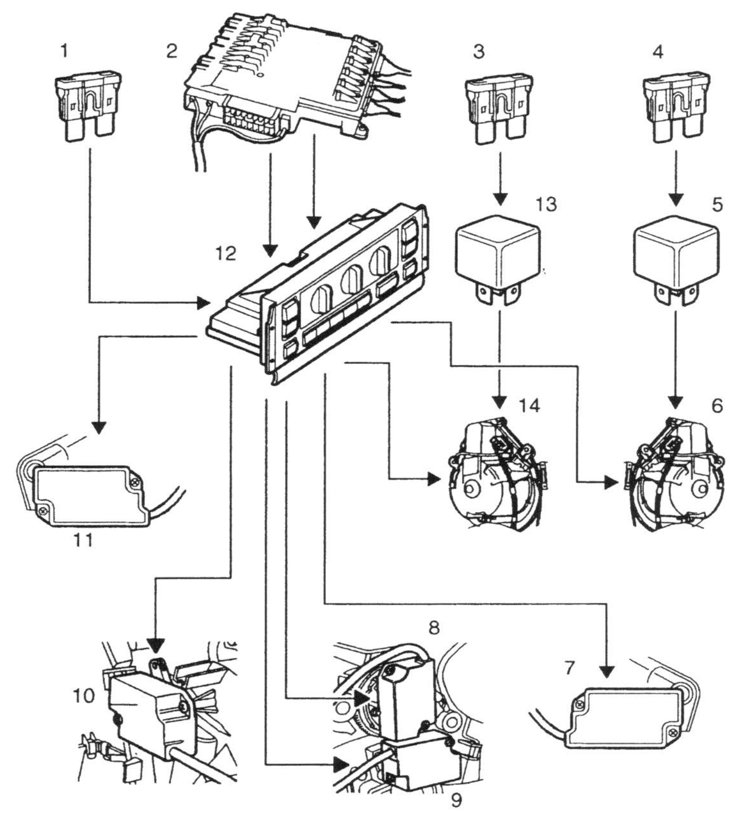

M82 0571

1. Fuse 42 (battery power)
2. BeCM
3. Fuse 34 (battery power)
4. Fuse 43 (battery power)
5. Relay 6 (auxiliary 1)
6. RH blower
7. RH fresh/ recirculated air servo
8. RH temperature servo
9. Distribution servo
10. LH temperature servo
11. LH fresh/ recirculated air servo
12. Heater ECU
13. Relay 7 (auxiliary 2)
14. LH blower

The Heater ECU operates the heating and ventilation system to produce the conditions selected on the control panel. The system operates when the ignition switch is in position II. For operation of the automatic demist function, the engine must be running. Power for system operation is supplied from the engine compartment fuse box. The BeCM supplies the Heater ECU with auxiliary power and an engine running signal.

Fresh/ Recirculated air selection

When the fresh/ recirculated air switch is pressed, the switch LED illuminates and the Heater ECU supplies battery voltage to the fresh/ recirculated air servos to drive the flaps in the air inlet housings to the recirculated air position. A second press of the switch extinguishes the LED and the Heater ECU reverses the polarity of the supply to the fresh/ recirculated air servos, which then drive the flaps to the fresh air position.

Blower control

Battery voltage is supplied to the positive side of the blower motors via the auxiliary relays. Blower speed is controlled by the blower rotary switch, which regulates the voltage of blower control signals from the Heater ECU to the negative side of the blower motors. At the off position, the blower control signals are equal to battery voltage. Turning the blower rotary switch clockwise progressively reduces the voltage of the blower control signals, and increases blower speed, until the signals are earthed and the blowers are at maximum speed. When the demist mode is active, the Heater ECU overrides the rotary switch and operates the blowers at maximum speed.

For diagnostic purposes, the Heater ECU monitors the blower motor's positive and negative voltages via the blower voltage feedback and blower safety inputs respectively.

Temperature control

When one of the temperature control switches is turned the Heater ECU supplies battery voltage to the related temperature servo to drive the flaps in the heater unit to the applicable position. To change the direction of drive, the Heater ECU reverses the polarity of the supply.

Distribution

When one of the distribution switches is pressed, the switch LED illuminates and the Heater ECU supplies battery voltage to the distribution servo to drive the flaps in the heater unit to the applicable position. To change the direction of drive, the Heater ECU reverses the polarity of the supply.

Demist mode

When the PROG switch is pressed, the Heater ECU overrides the manual selections and operates the heating and ventilation system in the automatic demist mode. A second press of the PROG switch returns the system to the previous manual settings. While the automatic demist mode is engaged, the windscreen and rear screen heaters can be operated to reset their timer start point without effecting the demist programme.

Self tuning

Periodically, the Heater ECU performs a self tuning routine of the temperature and distribution servos, to accommodate bedding in of the flaps and their control mechanisms. During the routine, operation of the blowers is inhibited and the servos are driven through their full range to re-calibrate their flap positions. The routine is invoked at the beginning of the 1st, 10th, 20th, 50th, 100th, 500th and every subsequent 500th start up. The routine should also be invoked, using TestBook, after replacement of a temperature or distribution servo.

Diagnostics

The Heater ECU continuously monitors the servo and blower circuits for continuity and short circuits. The feedback signals of the temperature and distribution servos are also checked for plausibility at each end of the servo travel range. If a fault is detected a related fault code is stored in memory and can be retrieved using TestBook.

Notes

HEATING AND VENTILATION FAULTS

This section covers mechanical, fuse and possible flap servo motor faults that could occur in the heating and ventilation system.

Visual checks of components within the system and relevant fuses should be carried out before undertaking detailed fault diagnosis procedures on **TestBook.**

Symptom - Heater Emits Cold Air Only, Driver Or Passenger Sides.

POSSIBLE CAUSE	REMEDY
1. Engine running cold.	1. ***See COOLING SYSTEM, Fault diagnosis.***
2. Heater pipes or hoses blocked.	2. Clear or renew heater pipes and hoses.
3. LH or RH temperature vent flaps in closed position due to inoperative servo motor.	3. Renew servo motor.
4. Blown heating and ventilation system fuse.	4. Check and renew fuses 8 or 17.

Symptom - Heater Emits Hot Air Only, Driver Or Passenger Sides.

POSSIBLE CAUSE	REMEDY
1. LH or RH temperature vent flaps in open position due to inoperative servo motor.	1. Renew servo motor.
2. Blown heating and ventilation system fuse.	2. Check and renew fuses 8 or 17.

Symptom - Heater Emits Hot or Cold Air To Demist Only.

POSSIBLE CAUSE	REMEDY
1. Heater distribution vent flap locked in 'demist' position due to inoperative servo motor.	1. Renew servo motor.
2. Blown heating and ventilation system fuse.	2. Check and renew fuses 8 or 17.

Symptom - Heater Emits Hot or Cold Air To Footwell Only.

POSSIBLE CAUSE	REMEDY
1. Heater distribution vent flap locked in 'footwell' position due to inoperative servo motor.	1. Renew servo motor.
2. Blown heating and ventilation system fuse.	2. Check and renew fuses 8 or 17.

Symptom - Heater emits hot or cold air to fascia vents only.

POSSIBLE CAUSE	REMEDY
1. Heater distribution vent flap locked in 'fascia' position due to inoperative servo motor.	1. Renew servo motor.
2. Blown heating and ventilation system fuse.	2. Check and renew fuses 8 or 17.

Symptom - Heater Emits Hot or Cold Air To Fascia and Footwell Vents Only.

POSSIBLE CAUSE	REMEDY
1. Heater distribution vent flap locked in 'fascia/footwell' position due to inoperative servo motor.	1. Renew servo motor.
2. Blown heating and ventilation system fuse.	2. Check and renew fuses 8 or 17.

Symptom - Heater Emits Recirculate Air Only.

POSSIBLE CAUSE	REMEDY
1. Air inlet housing vent flap locked in closed 'recirculate' position due to inoperative servo motor.	1. Renew servo motor.
2. Blown heating and ventilation system fuse.	2. Check and renew fuses 8 or 17.

Symptom - Heater Emits Ambient Air Only

POSSIBLE CAUSE	REMEDY
1. Air inlet housing vent flap locked in 'open' position due to inoperative servo motor.	1. Renew servo motor.
2. Blown heating and ventilation system fuse.	2. Check and renew fuses 8 or 17.

Symptom - No Boosted Air Supply To Heater Distribution Unit.

POSSIBLE CAUSE	REMEDY
1. Blower motor(s) inoperative.	1. Renew blower motor(s).
2. Blown motor fuse.	2. Check and renew fuses 42 or 43.
3. Loose electrical connections.	3. Check and tighten all relevant connections.

Symptom - Individual Heating and Ventilation Function/s Inoperative When Switch Control/s Are Used.

POSSIBLE CAUSE	REMEDY
1. Switch function faulty.	1. Renew switch control panel.
2. Switch control panel ECU faulty.	2. Check and renew fuse 8 or fit new control panel.

Symptom - Heating and Ventilation System Inoperative.

POSSIBLE CAUSE	REMEDY
1. Blown heating and ventilation system fuse.	1. Check and renew fuses 8 or 17.
2. Switch control panel ECU faulty.	2. Check and renew fuse 8 or fit new control panel.

Symptom - Poor Air Supply From Distribution Unit To Demist, Fascia or Footwell Vents.

POSSIBLE CAUSE	REMEDY
1. Air distribution ducting leaking at joints or defective.	1. Repair sealing joints or renew ducting.
2. Check through 1.1-12.1.	2. Refer to 1.1 through to 12.1.

NOTE: Should any fault occur in the heating and ventilation system on vehicles fitted with air conditioning a 'book' and '!' symbol will be displayed on the switch control panel.

FACE LEVEL VENTS

Service repair no - 80.15.04 - RH
Service repair no - 80.15.05 - LH
Service repair no - 80.15.63 - Centre

Remove

Centre Vent

CAUTION: Use of the following method may cause damage to the vanes of the vent. It is not advisable to remove the vent unless it is to be renewed.

1. Carefully insert a 5mm Allen key, or similar hooked tool, through vent as shown.

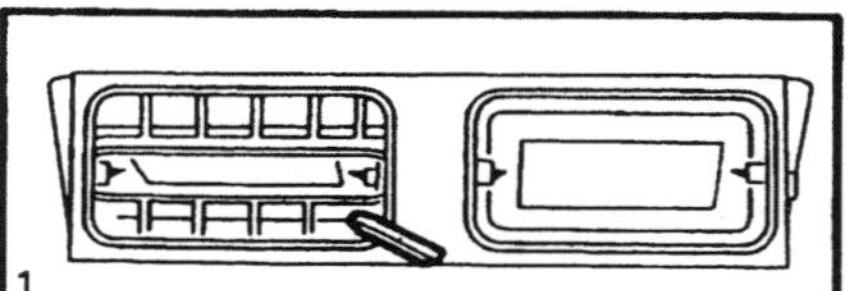

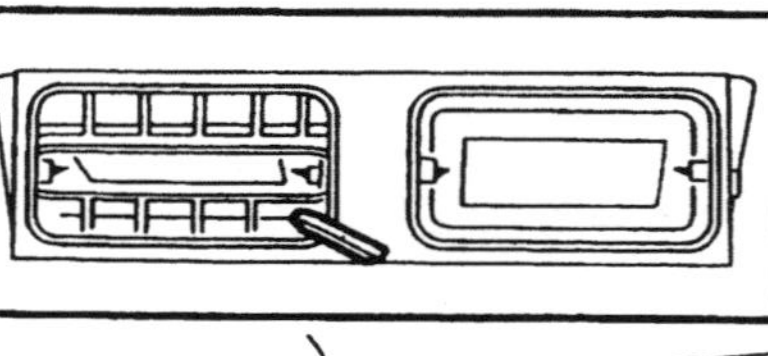

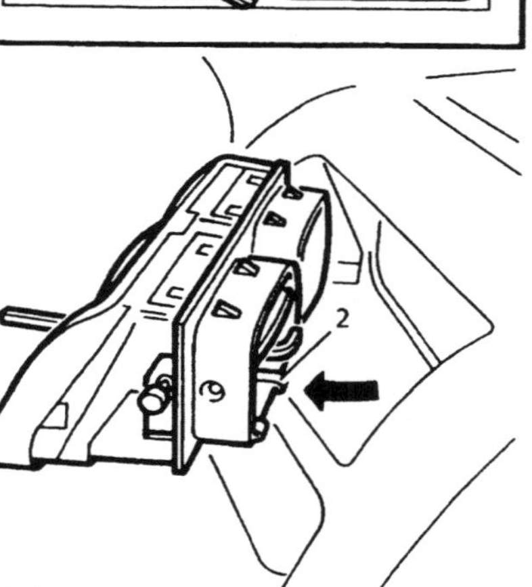

80M7008

2. Withdraw central face level vent from fascia.

Side Vents

3. **Passenger side.** Open glove box. Remove 5 screws securing glove box liner to fascia and lower glove box for access to rear of vent.

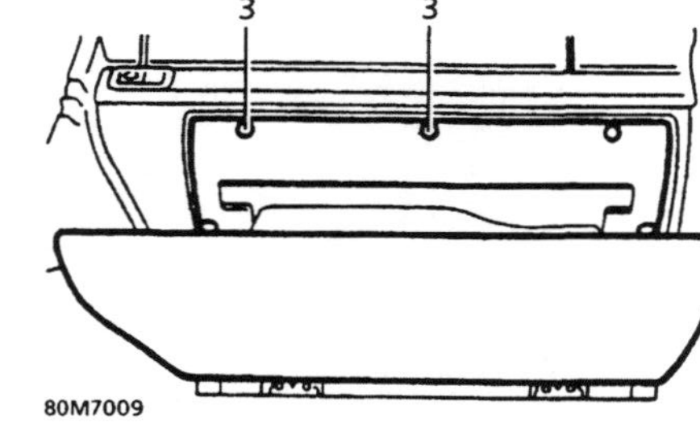

80M7009

4. **Drivers side.** Remove fascia closing panel for access to rear of vent. ***See CHASSIS AND BODY, Repair.***
5. **Drivers side.** Remove lap vent elbow and tube.
6. Remove clip securing vent to fascia. Release vent from fascia. Remove vent.

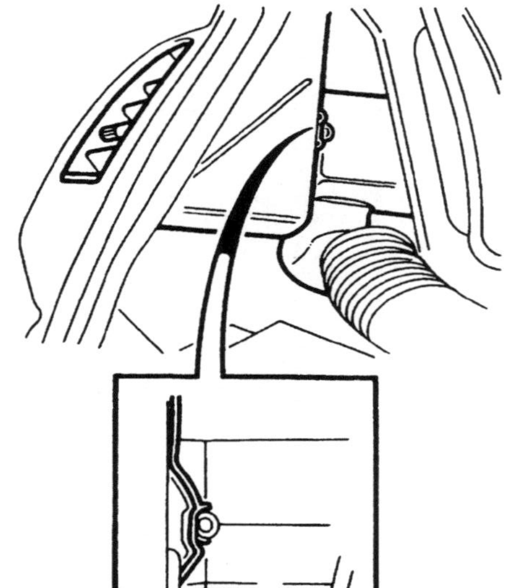

80M7010

Refit

7. Reverse removal procedure.

HEATER UNIT

Service repair no - 80.20.01 - Heater Only
Service repair no - 80.20.01/20 - With Air Conditioning

Remove

1. Remove fascia. ***See CHASSIS AND BODY, Repair.***
2. With fascia supported on 50mm deep wooden blocks, remove screws securing face level vent ducts to either side of fascia.
3. Slide inserts in face level vent ducts away from heater unit.
4. Remove passenger side blower duct.
5. Remove 4 screws securing heater control panel to fascia. Release panel.
6. Disconnect 4 multiplugs. Remove heater control panel.
7. Remove 5 screws securing fascia switch pack. Release switch pack for access to forward heater mounting bolts.

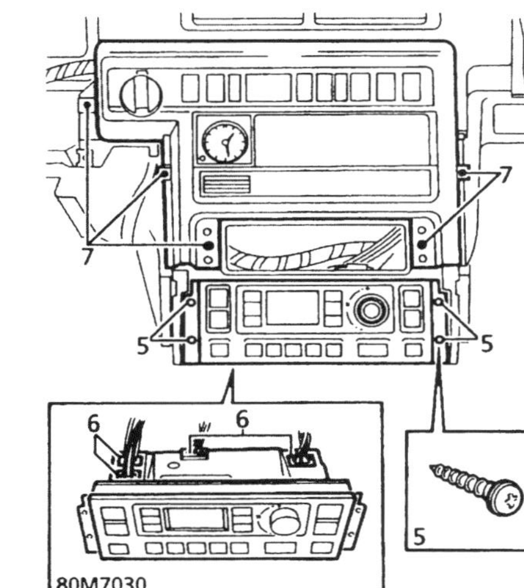

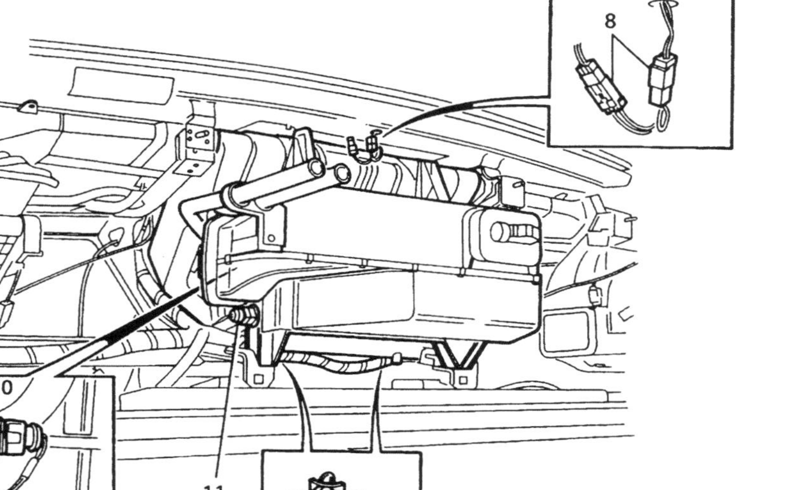

8. Disconnect solar sensor and alarm LED multiplugs. Push fly-leads into fascia ducting.
9. Release clip securing harness to fascia ducting. Position solar sensor/LED harness aside.
10. Release clip securing water temperature sensor to heater matrix inlet pipe. Position sensor aside.
11. Disconnect evaporator sensor multiplug.
12. Release 2 clips securing fascia harness to base of heater unit.
13. Remove 4 bolts securing heater unit to fascia frame.

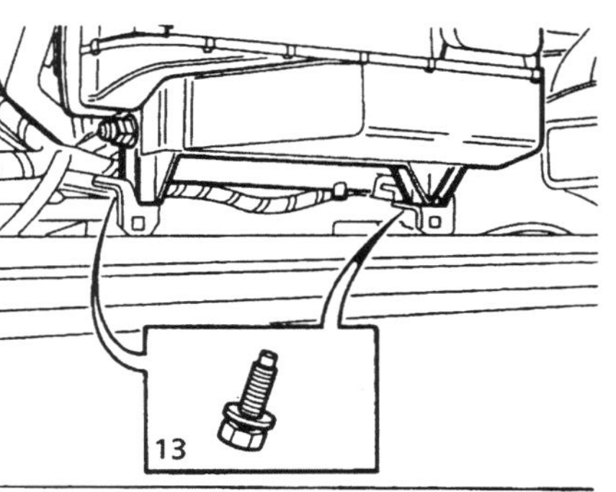

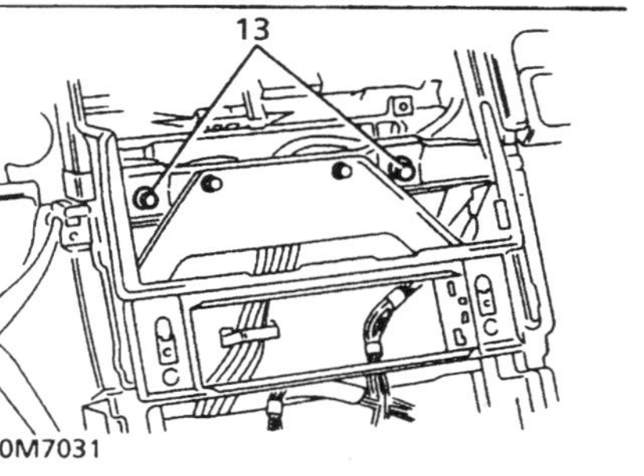

14. With assistance to hold harness away from heater, remove heater unit from fascia.

Refit

15. Reverse removal procedure.

HEATING AND AIR CONDITIONING SERVOS

Service repair no - 80.20.03 - Distribution
Service repair no - 80.20.04/20 - Blend - air conditioned vehicles
Service repair no - 80.20.10 - Recirculation

Remove

1. **Vehicles with heater only.** Blend servos can be replaced with fascia in position. ***See this section.***
2. Remove fascia assembly. ***See CHASSIS AND BODY, Repair.***

Recirculation Flap Servos.

3. Disconnect multiplug. Release from recirculation flap housing.

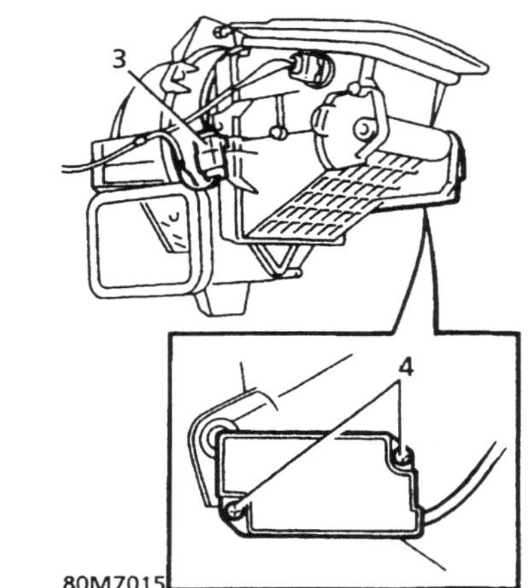

4. Remove 2 screws securing servo to recirculation flap housing. Remove servo.

Blend and Distribution Servos.

5. Remove heater unit. ***See this section.***
6. Remove 2 screws securing rear vent ducting. Remove ducting from relevant side of heater.

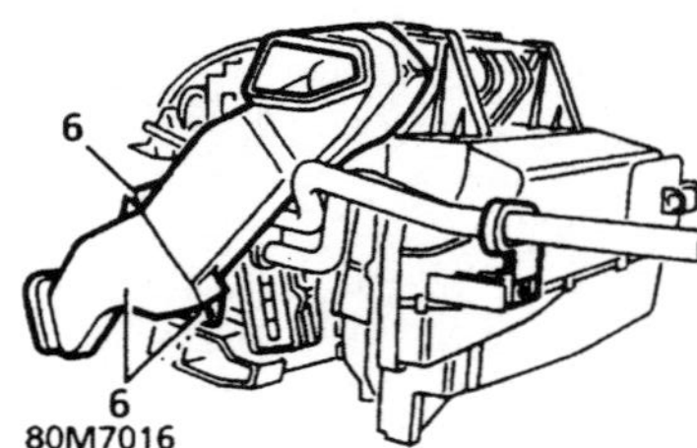

80M7016

7. Identify relevant pins in servo harness connector. Release 2 locking tags on rear of connector.

80M7017

8. Release relevant pins from connector by inserting thin probe into front face as shown.

9. Remove 2 harness clamps.

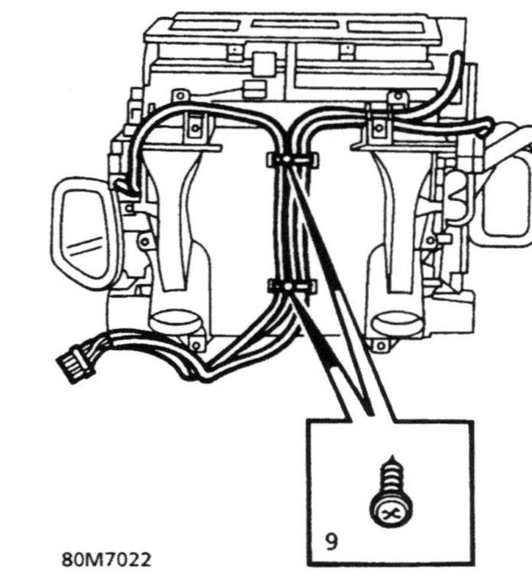

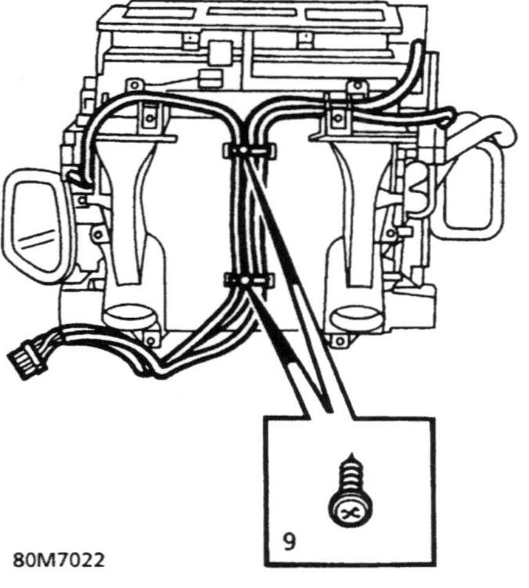
80M7022

10. Remove 2 screws securing servo to heater casing. Remove servo.

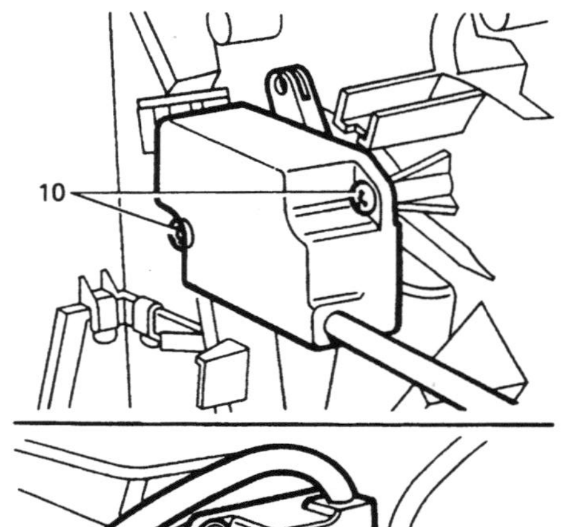
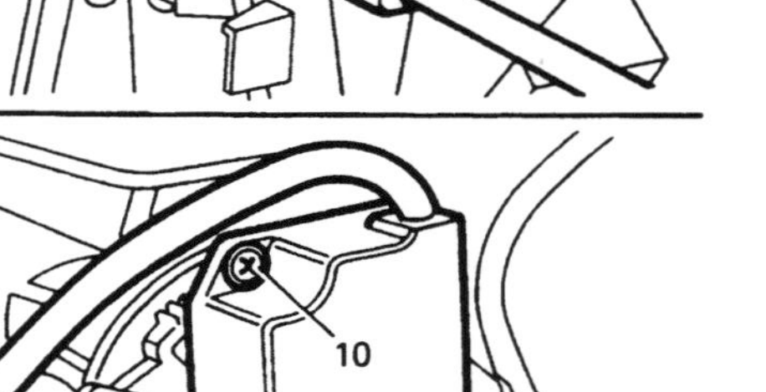

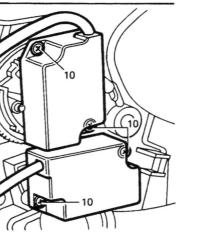

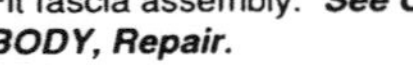
80M7018

Refit

Blend and Distribution Servos.

11. Reverse removal procedure.

Recirculation Flap Servos.

12. Hold flap in 'fresh air' position.
13. Position servo. Engage drive gear with flap gear.
14. Secure servo with screws. Connect multiplug. Secure plug to casing.
15. Fit fascia assembly. ***See CHASSIS AND BODY, Repair.***

HEATER MATRIX

Service repair no - 80.20.29

Remove

1. Remove heater unit. ***See this section.***
2. Remove 2 screws securing duct to RH side of heater. Remove duct.

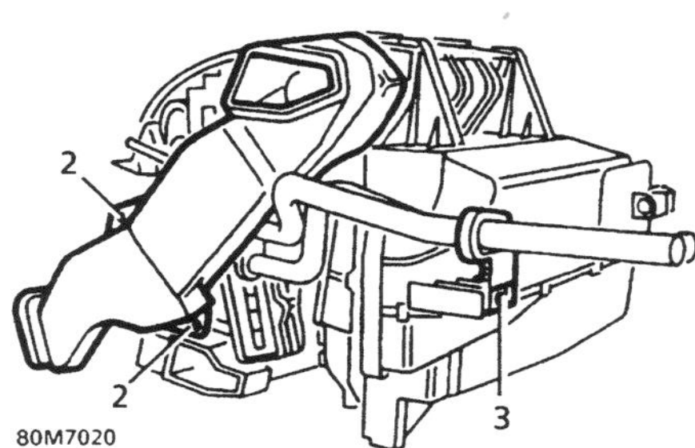

80M7020

3. Remove screw securing heater pipe bracket.
4. Remove 2 screws securing RH servo to heater casing. Remove servo.
5. Release 2 clips securing matrix to heater. Remove matrix and pipe assembly.

NOTE: Matrix has provision for 2 screws in the event that the retaining clips break.

6. Remove 2 screws securing pipes to matrix. Remove pipe assembly.
7. Remove and discard 'O' rings from pipe assembly.

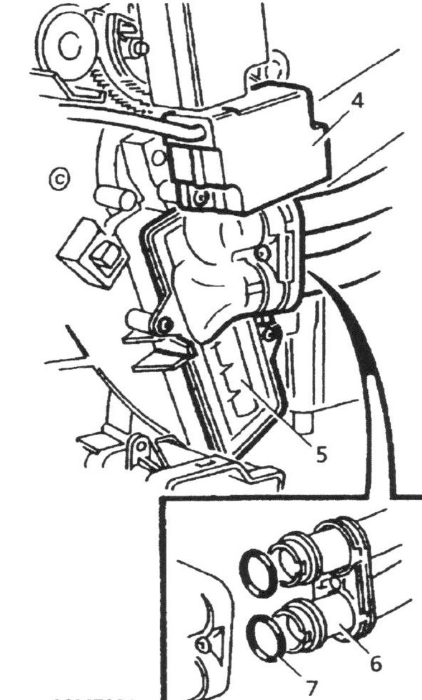

80M7021

Refit

8. Lubricate new 'O' rings with anti freeze. Fit to pipes.
9. Reverse removal procedure.

BLOWER MOTOR

Service repair no - 80.20.15

Remove

1. Remove glove box assembly. ***See CHASSIS AND BODY, Repair.***
2. Release 2 clips securing fascia harness trunking to fascia frame.

2

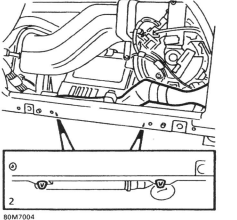

80M7004

3. Remove centre screws from 4 scrivet fasteners securing drivers side lower closing panel.

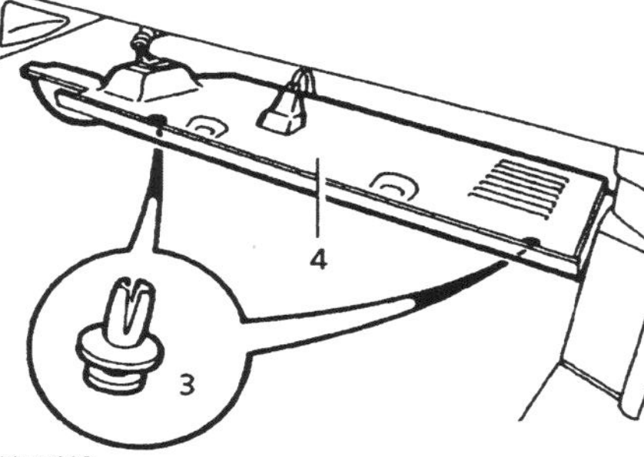

80M7005

4. Release panel for access to harness clip. Collect outer parts of fasteners from closing panel.
5. Remove upper fascia closing panel. ***See CHASSIS AND BODY, Repair.***
6. Release clip securing harness trunking to fascia frame.

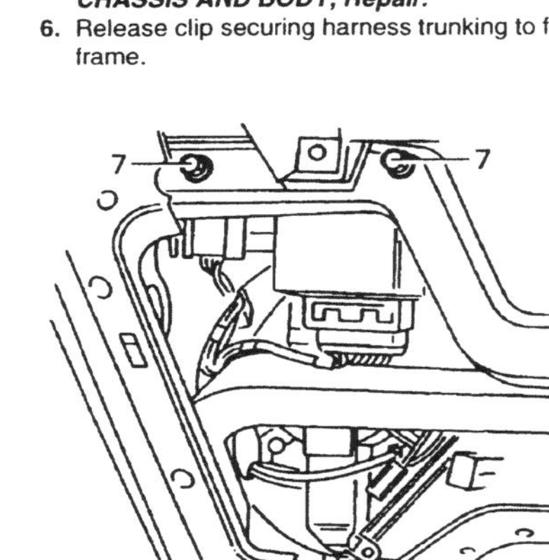

80M7006

7. Remove 2 bolts securing cruise control ECU bracket to fascia frame. Place bracket aside.
8. Release SRS harness connector from bracket. Position harness aside.
9. Disconnect Lucar connector and multiplug from blower motor.

80M7007

10. Remove 4 screws securing blower motor to casing.
11. Remove motor and fan assembly. Do not stress fascia harness.

Refit

12. Reverse removal procedure.

BLEND FLAP SERVOS - HEATER ONLY

Service repair no - 80.20.04

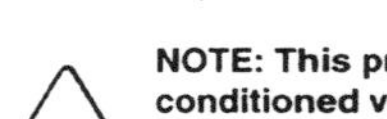

NOTE: This procedure applies to non air conditioned vehicles. For air conditioned vehicles. *See this section.*

Remove

1. Open glove box. Remove 5 screws securing glove box liner to fascia.

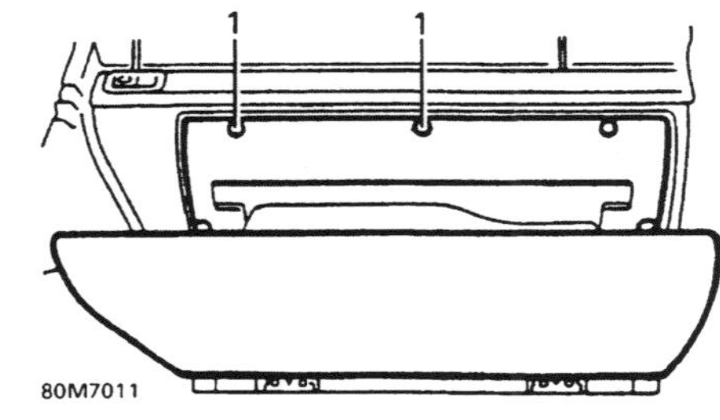

80M7011

2. Release glove box liner. Disconnect lamp multiplug.
3. Release cable from glove box latch.

4. Lower glove box liner from fascia gaining access to servo.
5. **Drivers Side.** Remove fascia closing panel. ***See CHASSIS AND BODY, Repair.***
6. Remove radio. ***See ELECTRICAL, Repair.***
7. Remove heater control panel. ***See this section.***
8. Release fascia switch pack. Position aside. ***See ELECTRICAL, Repair.***
9. Remove 4 bolts securing fascia centre support plate to transmission tunnel and fascia.
10. Remove 2 harness clamps.

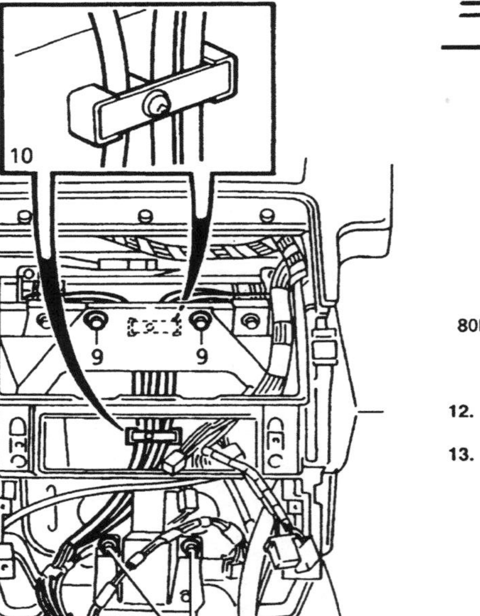

80M7012

11. Identify relevant pins in servo harness connector. Release 2 locking tags on rear of connector.

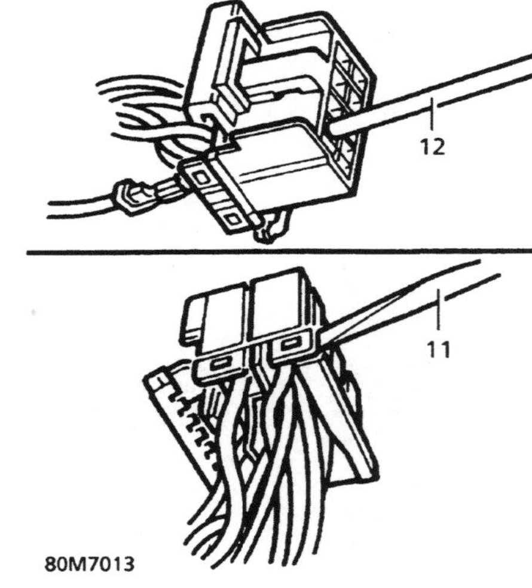

80M7013

12. Release relevant pins from connector by inserting thin probe into front face as shown.
13. Remove 2 screws securing servo to heater casing. Remove servo.

13

13

80M7014

Refit

14. Reverse removal procedure.

HEATER AND AIR CONDITIONING CONTROLS

Service repair no - 80.10.02

Remove

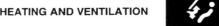

1. Move front seats to rearmost positions.
2. Remove 2 screws securing each side panel to centre console. Release sprag clips from fascia switch pack. Remove side panels.

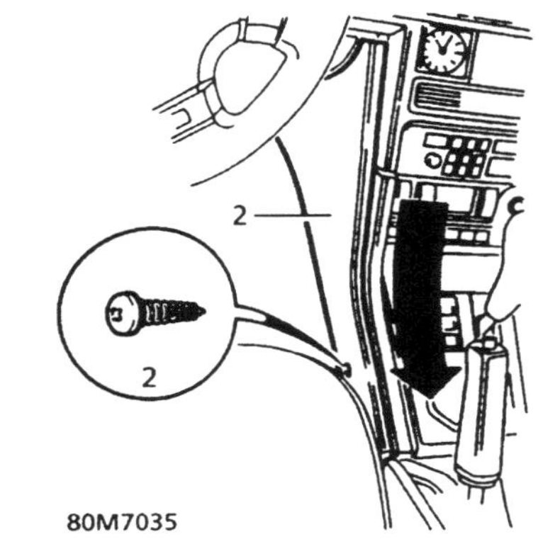

80M7035

3. Remove 4 screws securing control panel to fascia. Release panel.

4
4
3

80M7028

4. Disconnect multiplugs. Remove control panel.

Refit

5. Reverse removal procedure.

PLENUM AIR INTAKE PANELS

Service repair no - 80.15.62

Remove

1. Remove windscreen lower finisher. ***See CHASSIS AND BODY, Repair.***
2. Remove 3 screws securing each outer plenum panel.
3. Remove RH plenum panel.
4. Raise LH plenum panel. Disconnect bonnet harness multiplug.
5. Release harness sleeve from panel. Remove LH plenum panel.
6. Remove 8 screws securing centre plenum panel. Remove panel

Refit

7. Reverse removal procedure.

POLLEN FILTER

Service repair no - 80.15.42

Remove

1. Remove 2 screws securing each pollen filter cover.

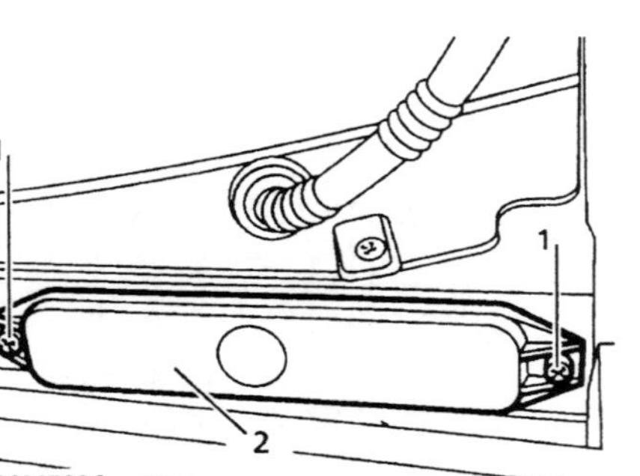

80M7036

2. Remove pollen filter covers.
3. Remove pollen filters.

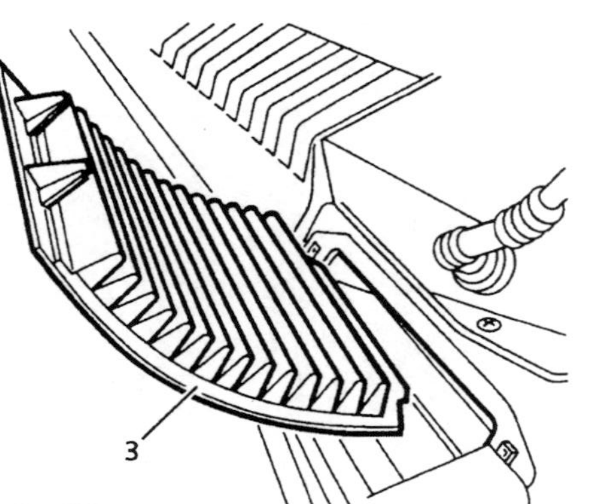

80M7037

Refit

4. Reverse removal procedure.

PIPE - HEATER - FEED

Service repair no - 80.25.07

Remove

1. Remove heater return pipe. ***See this section.***

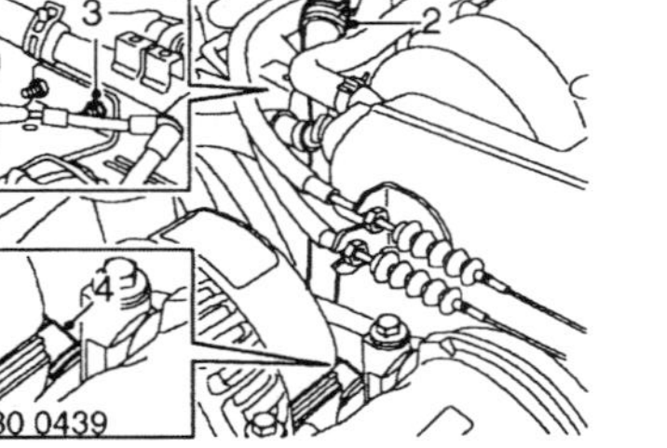

M80 0439

2. Release clip securing heater feed hose to heater feed pipe and disconnect hose from pipe.
3. Remove nut securing heater feed pipe to plenum chamber.
4. Press quick release connector and release heater feed pipe from plenum chamber.
5. Remove and discard 'O' ring from pipe.

Refit

6. Fit new 'O' ring to heater feed pipe and lubricate with castor oil.
7. Secure heater feed pipe to plenum chamber.
8. Fit and tighten nut securing heater feed pipe to plenum chamber.
9. Connect heater feed hose to heater feed pipe and secure with clip.
10. Fit heater return pipe. ***See this section.***

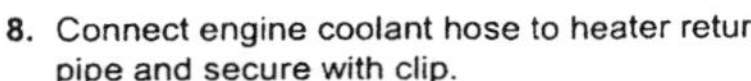

PIPE - HEATER - RETURN

Service repair no - 80.25.12

Remove

1. Drain engine coolant. ***See COOLING SYSTEM, Adjustment.***

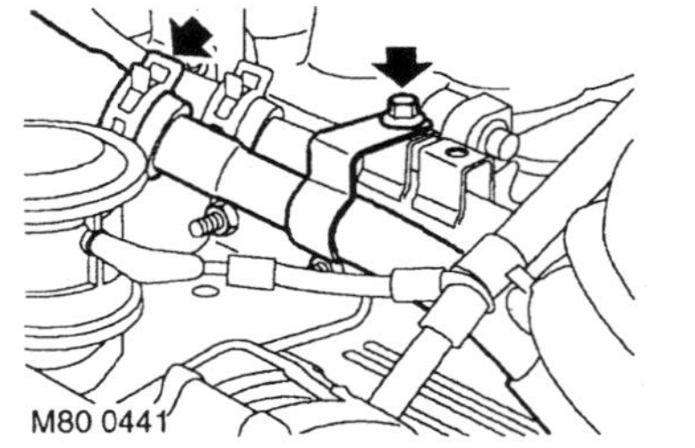
M80 0441

2. Release clip securing heater return hose to heater return pipe and disconnect hose from pipe.
3. Remove bolt securing heater return pipe to heater feed pipe.

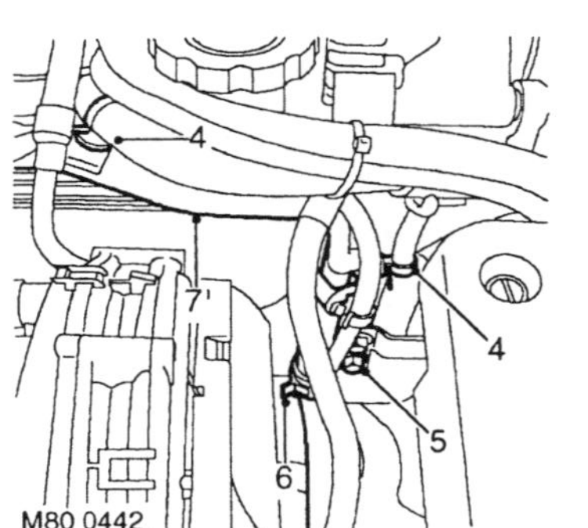

M80 0442

4. Release clips securing engine harness and vacuum pipe to heater return pipe.
5. Remove bolt securing heater return pipe to cylinder head.
6. Release clip securing engine coolant hose to heater return pipe.
7. Release engine coolant hose from heater returr pipe and collect pipe.

Refit

8. Connect engine coolant hose to heater return pipe and secure with clip.
9. Position heater return pipe to cylinder block and secure with bolt.
10. Secure engine harness and vacuum pipe to heater return pipe and secure with clips.
11. Fit and tighten bolt securing heater return pipe to heater feed pipe.
12. Connect heater return hose to heater return pipe and secure with clip.
13. Refill engine coolant. ***See COOLING SYSTEM, Adjustment.***

CONTENTS

Page

Refrigerant system components - V8 system shown

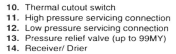

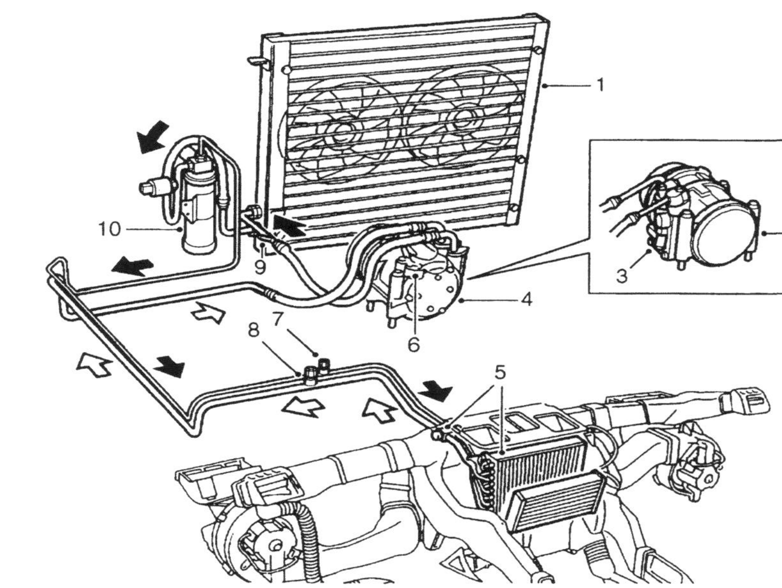

5. Condenser
6. Compressor (from 99MY)
7. Pressure relief valve
8. Compressor (up to 99MY)
9. Evaporator unit and expansion valve
10. Thermal cutout switch
11. High pressure servicing connection
12. Low pressure servicing connection
13. Pressure relief valve (up to 99MY)
14. Receiver/ Drier

Control system components

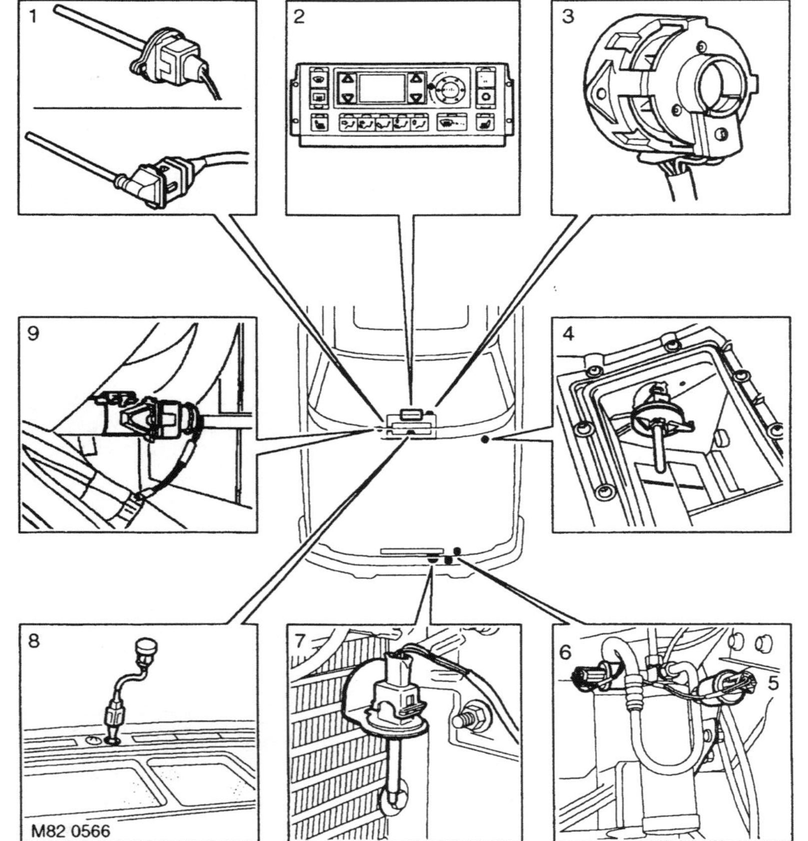

M82 0566

15. Evaporator temperature sensor
16. ATC ECU
17. In-car temperature sensor
18. Ambient air temperature sensor (up to VIN 381430)
19. Single pressure switch
20. Dual pressure switch
21. Ambient air temperature sensor (from VIN 381431)
22. Sunlight sensor
23. Heater coolant temperature sensor

Heating and distribution components

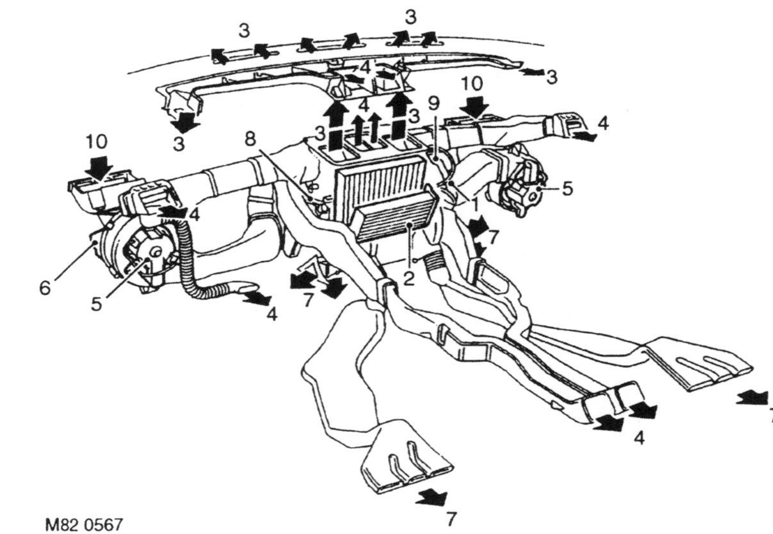

M82 0567

24. Heater unit
25. Heater matrix
26. Air to windscreen and front side window vents
27. Air to fascia centre vents, side vents, lap vent (driver only) and rear face vents
28. Blower
29. Fresh/ Recirculated air servo
30. Air to front and rear footwells
31. LH temperature servo
32. Distribution servo
33. Fresh air inlet and pollen filter

DESCRIPTION

The air conditioning system controls the temperature, distribution and volume of air supplied to the vehicle interior. The system is electronically controlled and features automatic and manual modes of operation, with separate temperature control of the LH and RH air outlets. The automatic modes provide optimum control of the system. The manual modes allow individual functions of automatic operation to be overridden to accommodate personal preferences.

The air conditioning system consists of a refrigerant system and a control system. It also uses the same air inlet housings and heater unit, and similar distribution ducts, as the Heating and Ventilation system. ***See HEATING AND VENTILATION, Description and operation.***

Refrigerant system

The refrigerant system comprises four major units:

- A compressor.
- A condenser.
- A receiver/ drier.
- An evaporator and thermostatic expansion valve.

The four units are interconnected by preformed aluminium and flexible refrigerant pipes routed around the perimeter of the engine compartment. A pressure relief valve is incorporated to protect the refrigerant system from unacceptably high pressure:

- On vehicles up to 99MY, the pressure relief valve is incorporated in the refrigerant pipe between the compressor and the condenser.
- On vehicles from 99MY, the pressure relief valve is incorporated into the refrigerant outlet of the compressor.

Compressor

The compressor, a pump specially designed to raise the pressure of the refrigerant, is mounted on the front of the engine. The compressor is driven via an electro-magnetic clutch by a single pulley drive belt that also serves the other engine ancillaries. Operation of the clutch is controlled by the ATC ECU. On vehicles up to 99MY, the compressor incorporates a thermal cutout switch in the electrical connection to the clutch.

The compressor draws vaporized refrigerant from the evaporator. It is compressed with a resulting rise in temperature and passed on to the condenser as a hot, high pressure vapour.

Condenser

The condenser is mounted directly in front of the radiator. It consists of a refrigerant coil mounted in a series of thin cooling fins to provide the maximum heat transfer. Air flow across the condenser is induced by vehicle movement and assisted by two electric fans attached to the frame of the condenser. The refrigerant high pressure vapour enters the condenser inlet midway on the LH side. As the vapour passes through the condenser coils the air flow, assisted by the two fans, carries the latent heat away from the condenser. This induces a change of state resulting in the refrigerant condensing into a high pressure warm liquid. From the condenser, the refrigerant continues to the receiver/ drier.

Receiver/ Drier

This component acts as a reservoir and is used to hold extra refrigerant until it is needed by the evaporator. The drier within the receiver unit contains a filter and dessicant (drying material) which absorb moisture and prevent dessicant dust from being carried with the refrigerant into the system.

Evaporator and thermostatic expansion valve

High pressure liquid refrigerant is delivered to the thermostatic expansion valve which is the controlling device for the air conditioning system circuit. A severe pressure drop occurs across the valve and as the refrigerant flows through the evaporator it picks up heat from the ambient air, boils and vaporizes. As this change of state occurs, a large amount of latent heat is absorbed. The evaporator is therefore cooled and as a result heat is extracted from the air flowing across the evaporator. The refrigerant leaves the evaporator, on its way to the compressor, as a low pressure gas.

Control system

The control system operates the refrigerant system and the control flaps in the heater unit to control the temperature and distribution of air in the vehicle interior. It also outputs signals to the fresh/ recirculated air servos and the blowers to control the volume and source of inlet air. The control system consists of:
An Air Temperature Control (ATC) ECU.
An in-car temperature sensor.
An ambient air temperature sensor.
An evaporator temperature sensor.
A heater coolant temperature sensor.
A sunlight sensor.
A dual pressure switch.
A single pressure switch.

ATC ECU

The ATC ECU comprises an integrated ECU and control panel, and is mounted in the centre console below the in-car entertainment unit. The control panel contains switches for system control inputs and a Liquid Crystal Display (LCD) to provide system status information. Inputs from the sensors and the control panel switches are processed by the ECU, which then outputs the appropriate control signals.

In addition to the air conditioning system, the ATC ECU also controls the rear screen heater and, where fitted, the windscreen heaters and the front seat heaters. Each push switch on the control panel has a LED to indicate the selections made.

After installation of a new ATC ECU, it must be initialised using TestBook to ensure correct operation of the air conditioning system.

ATC ECU control panel

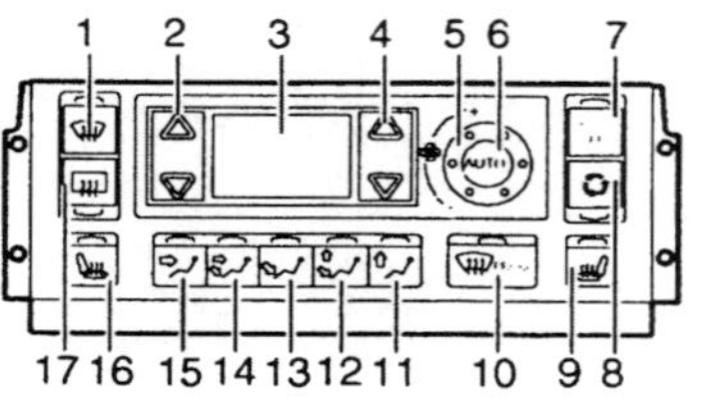

M82 0568

1. Windscreen heater switch
2. LH temperature switch
3. LCD
4. RH temperature switch
5. Blower switch
6. Automatic mode switch
7. Compressor (economy) switch
8. Fresh/ Recirculated air switch
9. RH front seat heater switch
10. Demist mode switch
11. Windscreen/ Side window distribution switch
12. Windscreen/ Side window and footwells distribution switch
13. Footwells distribution switch
14. Face and footwells distribution switch
15. Face distribution switch
16. LH front seat heater switch
17. Rear screen heater switch

Windscreen heater switch. Push switch for control of the windscreen heaters. A timed function that automatically goes off after approximately 4 minutes, or immediately if the switch is pressed again. The switch LED is illuminated while the heaters are active.

LH temperature switch. Rocker switch that sets air temperature target for the LH side of the vehicle interior:

- Temperature is increased by pressing the upper part of the switch and decreased by pressing the lower part of the switch.
- A short press of the switch gives a 1 °C (2 °F) change of the air temperature target and a long press gives a scrolling movement of the air temperature target.
- HI or LO is displayed when the system reaches an extreme of the temperature range.

Passenger side temperature cannot be set outside the tolerance of 6 °C (11 °F) above or below the temperature set on the driver's side.

LCD. Display that shows the following:

- Blower speed when set manually (fan symbol and dashed line). The longer the dashed line, the faster the blower speed.
- Automatic (climate control) mode activated (AUTO legend).
- Fault detected (handbook symbol).
- LH and RH air temperature targets in °C (°F).
- Low external air temperature warning (snowflake symbol). Comes on if the ambient air temperature is approximately 3 °C (37.5 °F) or less, to warn of the possibility of road ice.
- Programmed demist function activated (demist symbol + PROG legend).
- Exterior air temperature in °C (°F) (EXT legend and temperature value). Permanently displayed while the system is on.

The temperature indications on the display can be shown in either °C or °F. To switch between the two scales, simultaneously press and hold the two outermost air distribution switches (face and windscreen/side windows demist) for approximately 4 seconds.

LCD symbols

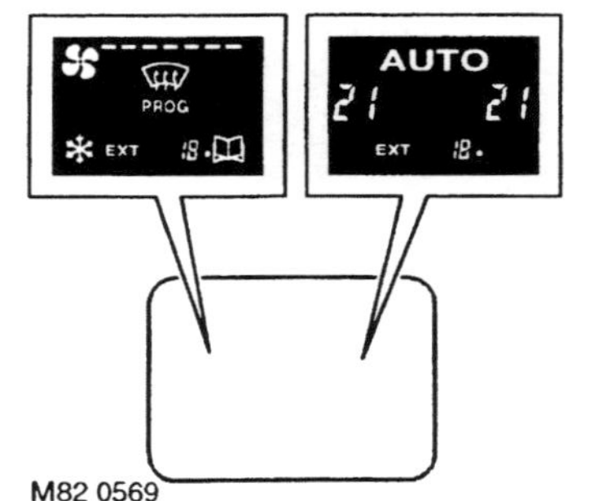

M82 0569

RH temperature switch. Rocker switch that sets air temperature target for the RH side of the vehicle interior. Operates the same as the LH temperature switch.

Blower switch. Rotary switch with no positive stop for manual control of blower speeds. Rotation through 180 degrees covers complete speed range:

- Clockwise rotation increases speed of blowers.
- Anti-clockwise rotation decreases speed of blowers.

RH front seat heater switch. Push switch that operates the RH front seat heater. Operation is independent from the air conditioning system. The heater remains active until the switch is pressed again. The switch LED is illuminated while the heater is active.

Automatic mode (AUTO) switch. Push switch that controls the on/ off selection of the automatic mode. With the switch depressed the refrigerant system, inlet air source, blower speed, air temperature and air distribution are automatically controlled. When AUTO is on:

- The AUTO symbol is displayed.
- The exterior air temperature is displayed.
- The display of the blower speed and the distribution mode ceases.
- The ATC ECU selects fresh air and engages the compressor. If the system automatically switches to recirculated air or disengages the compressor, the related LED will not illuminate.
- The selected air distribution LED will not illuminate.

If an alternative distribution mode is manually selected, the system operates in a semi-automatic mode and:

- The AUTO symbol extinguishes.
- The appropriate distribution LED illuminates.
- The ATC ECU varies the remaining functions to attempt to achieve/ maintain the target air temperatures.
- A second press of the illuminated distribution switch returns the distribution to automatic control.

If an alternative blower speed is selected the system will also function in a semi-automatic mode and:

- The blower speed is displayed.
- The ATC ECU varies the remaining functions to attempt to achieve/ maintain the target air temperatures.

If the target temperatures are changed:

- The ATC ECU remains in the automatic mode.
- The new temperature is displayed.

If the target temperatures are changed to either HI or LO:

- The ATC ECU sets the blend flaps to full hot or full cold, as applicable.
- The AUTO symbol on the LCD extinguishes.
- The distribution mode is adjusted to the most appropriate setting.
- The blower speeds increase to maximum.
- The inlet air source and compressor are selected as appropriate.

Air conditioning on/off (A/C OFF) switch. Push switch that operates the clutch of the refrigerant system compressor.

- The switch LED illuminates to confirm that the compressor is off (i.e. clutch is disengaged).
- The inlet air source defaults to fresh air.
- The ATC ECU operates the remaining functions to attempt to achieve/ maintain the target air temperatures. If the ATC ECU is unable to achieve/ maintain the target air temperatures, the switch LED flashes for 10 seconds to advise the driver that the compressor needs to be switched on.
- A second press of the A/C OFF switch returns the compressor to automatic control and extinguishes the LED.

Fresh/ Recirculated air switch. Push switch for manual selection of recirculated air.

- The switch LED illuminates when recirculated air is selected.
- The system defaults to compressor on.
- A second press of the fresh/ recirculated air switch returns the system to automatic control and extinguishes the LED.

Demist mode (PROG) switch. Push switch that operates the automatic demist function:

- The PROG switch LED illuminates when demist is selected.
- The demist symbol and external air temperature are displayed.
- The inlet air source is set to fresh air.
- The blowers are set to the optimum speed.
- The LH and RH target air temperatures are set to maximum.
- Distribution is set to windscreen/ side windows and the related switch LED illuminates.
- The rear screen heater comes on for a timed cycle or, if already on, restarts the timed cycle, and the switch LED illuminates.
- The windscreen heaters come on for a timed cycle or, if already on, restart the timed cycle, and the switch LED illuminates.
- While in the demist mode, the windscreen and rear screen heaters can be operated to reset the timers.
- A second press of the PROG switch cancels the demist mode. All functions return to their previous settings.

Windscreen/ Side window distribution switch. Push switch for manual control of air distribution to direct air through the windscreen and front side windows vents.

Windscreen/ Side window and footwell distribution switch. Push switch for manual control of air distribution to direct air through the windscreen, front side windows and footwell vents.

Footwell distribution switch. Push switch for manual control of air distribution to direct air through the footwell vents.

Face and footwell distribution switch. Push switch for manual control of air distribution to direct air through the face level and footwell vents.

Face distribution switch. Push switch for manual control of air distribution to direct air through the face level and driver's lap vents.

LH front seat heater switch. Push switch that operates the LH front seat heater. Operation is independent from the air conditioning system. The heater remains active until the switch is pressed again. The switch LED is illuminated while the heater is active.

Rear screen heater switch. Push switch for control of the rear screen heater. A timed function that automatically goes off after approximately 15 minutes, or immediately if the switch is pressed again. The switch LED is illuminated while the heater is active.

The exterior mirror heaters are activated for approximately 10 minutes when either the windscreen or rear screen heaters are activated. There is no active indicator or independent control for the exterior mirror heaters.

ATC ECU connectors

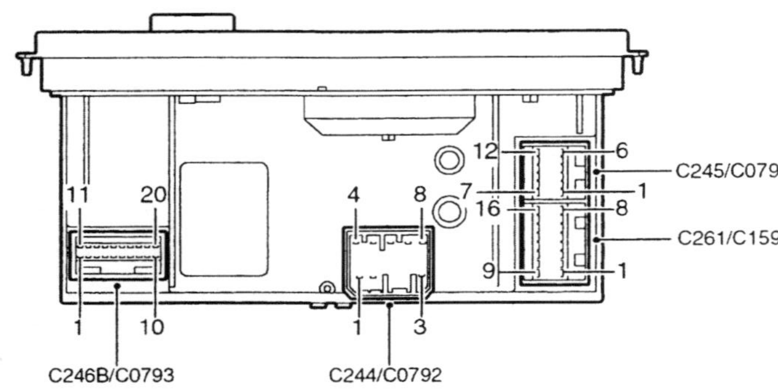

M82 0576

ATC ECU connector pin details

Connector/ Pin No.	Description	Input/Output
C244 (up to 99MY) C0792 (from 99MY)		
1	Auxiliary power supply	Input
2	Battery power supply	Input
3	Ignition power supply	Input
4	Earth	-
5	Windscreen heaters	Output
6	Instrument/ Switch illumination	Input
7	A/C compressor clutch	Output
8	Condenser fans	Output
C245 (up to 99MY) C0791 (from 99MY)		
1	RH blower control	Output
2	RH blower safety	Output
3	RH blower voltage feedback	Input
4	LH blower control	Output
5	LH blower safety	Output
6	LH blower voltage feedback	Input
7	Ambient air temperature sensor (-)	Input
8	Ambient air temperature sensor (+)	Output
9	RH fresh/ recirculated air servo (+/-)	Input/Output
10	RH fresh/ recirculated air servo (+/-)	Input/Output
11	LH fresh/ recirculated air servo (+/-)	Input/Output
12	LH fresh/ recirculated air servo (+/-)	Input/Output

Connector/ Pin No.	Description	Input/Output
C246B (up to 99MY) C0793 (from 99MY)		
1	Not used	-
2	Heater coolant temperature sensor	Input
3	Not used	-
4	Sunlight sensor	Input
5	Road speed	Input
6	Diagnostics K line	Input/Output
7	Diagnostics L line	Input/Output
8	Engine running (alternator charging)	Input
9	In-car temperature sensor, thermistor supply	Output
10	Sensor earth (evaporator temperature, heater coolant temperature and sunlight sensors)	Input
11	LCD dimming	Input
12	Evaporator temperature sensor	Input
13	A/C request	Output
14	A/C grant	Input
15	In-car temperature sensor, aspirator earth	Input
16	In-car temperature sensor, aspirator supply	Output
17	Rear screen heater request	Output
18	In-car temperature temperature sensor, thermistor earth	Input
19	RH seat heater request	Output
20	LH seat heater request	Output

Connector/ Pin No.	Description	Input/Output
C261 (up to 99MY) C1597 (from 99MY)		
1	RH temperature servo feedback reference voltage (-)	Input
2	Distribution servo feedback reference voltage (-)	Input
3	Not used	-
4	Distribution servo feedback reference voltage (+)	Output
5	RH temperature servo feedback reference voltage (+)	Output
6	Distribution servo voltage (+/-)	Input/Output
7	RH temperature servo feedback	Input
8	LH temperature servo feedback	Input
9	RH temperature servo voltage (+/-)	Input/Output
10	RH temperature servo voltage (+/-)	Input/Output
11	LH temperature servo voltage (+/-)	Input/Output
12	LH temperature servo voltage (+/-)	Input/Output
13	LH temperature servo feedback reference voltage (-)	Input
14	LH temperature servo feedback reference voltage (+)	Output
15	Distribution servo feedback	Input
16	Distribution servo voltage (+/-)	Input/Output

In-car temperature sensor

The in-car temperature sensor provides the ATC ECU with an input of interior air temperature. The sensor is integrated into the inlet of an electric fan, which is installed behind a grille in the centre of the fascia, immediately below the clock. The fan runs continuously, while the A/C system is on, to draw air through the grille and across the sensor.

Ambient air temperature sensor

The ambient temperature sensor provides the ATC ECU with an input of external air temperature. Up to VIN 381430, the sensor is installed in the LH air inlet housing. From VIN 381431, the sensor is installed in a bracket attached to the LH chassis rail, behind the front bumper and immediately in front of the condenser.

Evaporator temperature sensor

The evaporator temperature sensor provides the ATC ECU with an input of the evaporator air outlet temperature. The sensor is installed in the RH side of the heater unit casing and protrudes into the airflow leaving the the evaporator. The ATC ECU uses the input to prevent the formation of ice on the evaporator.

Heater coolant temperature sensor

The heater coolant temperature sensor provides the ATC ECU with an input related to the temperature of the coolant entering the heater matrix. The sensor is attached to the outside of the coolant inlet pipe, next to the heater matrix.

Sunlight sensor

The sunlight sensor is installed in the centre of the windscreen demist vents in the fascia and provides the ATC ECU with an input of light intensity. The ATC ECU uses the input to measure the solar heating load on the vehicle.

Dual pressure switch

The dual pressure switch protects the refrigerant system from extremes of pressure and controls the operating speed of the condenser fans. The dual pressure switch is installed in the top of the receiver/ drier and senses receiver/ drier outlet pressure.

If the minimum or maximum refrigerant pressure limit is exceeded, switch contacts open to disconnect the power supply line between the ATC ECU and the compressor clutch. The minimum pressure limit protects the compressor, by preventing operation of the system unless there is a minimum refrigerant pressure (and thus refrigerant and lubricating oil) in the system. The maximum pressure limit keeps the refrigerant system within a safe operating pressure.

A separate set of switch contacts control the operating speed of the condenser fans. Depending on the refrigerant pressure, the switch contacts:

- Close to energise the condenser fan relays and run the condenser fans in parallel (fast speed).
- Open to de-energise the condenser fan relays and run the condenser fans in series (slow speed).

Single pressure switch

The single pressure switch controls the on/ off switching of the condenser fans while the air conditioning is on. The single pressure switch is installed in the refrigerant line between the condenser and the receiver/ drier. Depending on the refrigerant pressure, the switch contacts:

- Close to energise the condenser fan control relay and run the condenser fans.
- Open to de-energise the condenser fan control relay and stop the condenser fans.

Distribution ducts

The distribution ducts are the same as those on non A/C vehicles except for two additional ducts which supply air to rear passenger face vents. The additional ducts are installed in the centre console, and connect the ducts supplying the outboard face level vents in the fascia to a dual vent assembly at the rear of the centre console cubby box.

Pressure switch nominal operating pressures

Switch	Description	Opening pressure, bar (lbf.in²)	Closing pressure, bar (lbf.in²)
Dual pressure switch:			
	Compressor clutch:		
	Minimum limit	1.2 (17), pressure decreasing	2.4 (35), pressure increasing
	Maximum limit	30 (435), pressure increasing	21 (305), pressure decreasing
	Condenser fans speed	17 (247), pressure decreasing	21 (305), pressure increasing
Single pressure switch:			
	Condenser fans control	13 (189), pressure decreasing	17 (247), pressure increasing

OPERATION

A/C control diagram

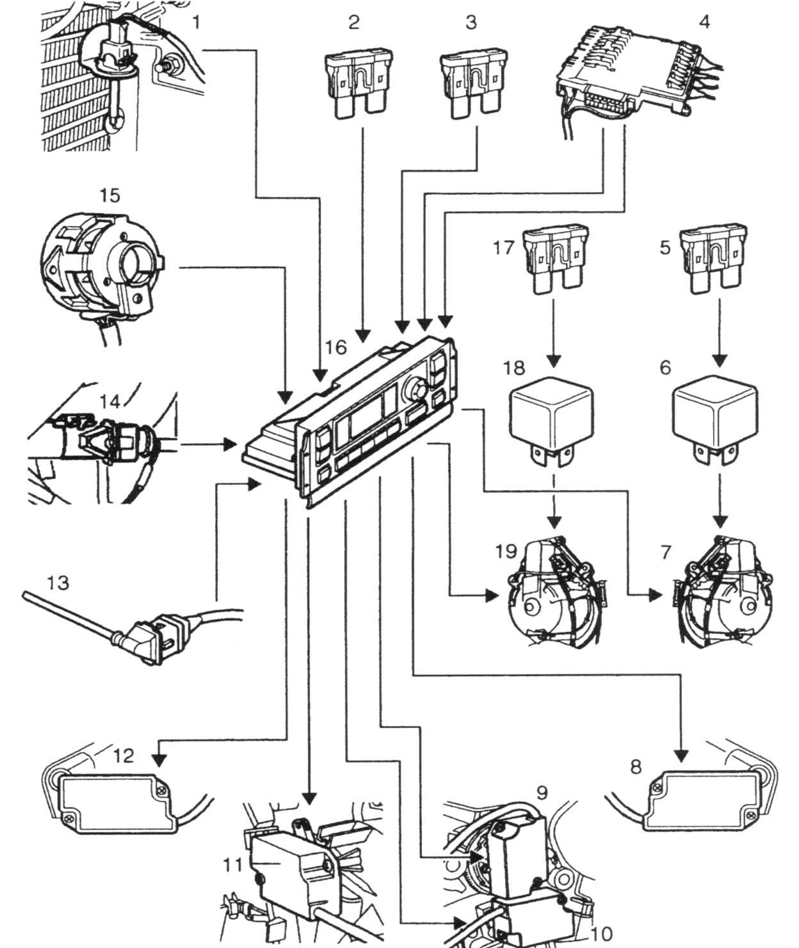

M82 0572

Key to A/C control diagram

1. Ambient air temperature sensor
2. Fuse 37 (ignition power)
3. Fuse 42 (battery power)
4. BeCM
5. Fuse 43 (battery power)
6. Relay 6 (auxiliary relay 1)
7. RH blower
8. RH fresh/ recirculated air servo
9. RH temperature servo
10. Distribution servo
11. LH temperature servo
12. LH fresh/ recirculated air servo
13. Evaporator temperature sensor
14. Heater coolant temperature sensor
15. In-car temperature sensor
16. ATC ECU
17. Fuse 34 (battery power)
18. Relay 7 (auxiliary 2)
19. LH blower

The air conditioning system only operates while the engine is running. Ignition and battery power feeds for the ATC ECU are supplied from fuses in the engine compartment fuse box. The BeCM supplies the ATC ECU with auxiliary power, an engine running signal and a road speed input.

Fresh/ Recirculated air selection

The ATC ECU supplies battery voltage to the fresh/ recirculated air servos to set the position the flaps in the air inlet housings. To change the direction of drive, the ATC ECU reverses the polarity of the supply. When the system is in the automatic mode, the inlet air source is determined by ambient air temperature and vehicle speed. The inlet air source can be manually latched to recirculated air using the fresh/ recirculated air switch.

Blower control

Battery voltage is supplied to the positive side of the blower motors via the auxiliary relays. Blower speed is controlled by regulating the voltage of blower control signals from the ATC ECU to the negative side of the blower motors. When the blower control signals are equal to battery voltage, the blowers are stopped. Reducing the voltage of the blower control signals increases blower speed until, when the signals are earthed, the blowers are at maximum speed.

When the system is in the automatic mode, the ATC ECU regulates the blower control signals to run the blowers at a speed derived from the ambient air temperature, solar heating load, vehicle speed and distribution setting (if manually selected). When the blower speed is set manually, the blower control signals are regulated by the blower switch.

For diagnostic purposes, the ATC ECU monitors the blower motor's positive and negative voltages via the blower voltage feedback and blower safety inputs respectively.

Temperature control

The ATC ECU supplies battery voltage to the temperature servos to set the position the blend flaps in the heater unit. To change the direction of drive, the ATC ECU reverses the polarity of the supply. The ATC ECU determines the required position of the blend flaps from the ambient air temperature, the target temperatures and the fresh/ recirculated air selection.

Distribution

The ATC ECU supplies battery voltage to the distribution servo to set the position the distribution flaps in the heater unit. To change the direction of drive, the ATC ECU reverses the polarity of the supply. When the system is in the automatic mode, the ATC ECU determines the required position of the distribution flaps from the ambient air temperature and the solar heating load. The distribution can be set manually using the five distribution switches.

Demist mode

When the PROG switch is pressed, the ATC ECU overrides the automatic and manual selections and operates the heating and ventilation system in the demist mode. A second press of the PROG switch returns the system to the previous settings. While the automatic demist mode is engaged, the windscreen and rear screen heaters can be operated to reset their timer start point without effecting the demist programme.

Cold start up

If the heater coolant temperature and ambient air temperature are relatively low when the air conditioning is switched on, the ATC ECU delays operation of the blowers to avoid blowing cold air into the vehicle. As the heater coolant temperature increases, so the ATC ECU progressively increases the speed of the blowers to heat up the vehicle interior to the target air temperatures. As the in-car temperature approaches the target temperatures, blower speed decreases.

Hot start up

If the ambient temperature is relatively high when the air conditioning is switched on, the ATC ECU initially runs the blowers at slow speed and sets the inlet air source to fresh air in order to purge the stagnant air from the system. After approximately 60 seconds the ATC ECU then switches the inlet air source to recirculated air and progressively increases the speed of the blowers to cool down the vehicle interior. As the in-car temperature approaches the target temperatures, blower speed decreases.

Ambient temperature damping

When the ambient temperature increases, the ATC ECU imposes a rate of change limit of 0.5 °C (1 °F) /minute. When the ambient temperature is decreasing, the ATC ECU accepts an unlimited rate of change.

Ambient temperature input strategy (from VIN 381431)

The ATC ECU incorporates a software strategy to overcome the effect of radiant heat from the engine and cooling systems on the ambient temperature sensor:

- At vehicle speeds of 15 mph (24 km/h) and above, the input is considered valid and changes are accepted. The value of the input is stored in memory and constantly updated while the vehicle speed is above 15 mph (24 km/h).
- At vehicle speeds below 15 mph (24 km/h), changes of input are considered suspect and changes are ignored. In place of the actual input, the ATC ECU uses the value stored in memory.
- When the ignition is switched on, if the ATC ECU detects warm heater coolant, it uses the ambient temperature stored in memory. If the ATC ECU detects cold coolant, it uses the input from the ambient temperature sensor.

Compressor control diagram

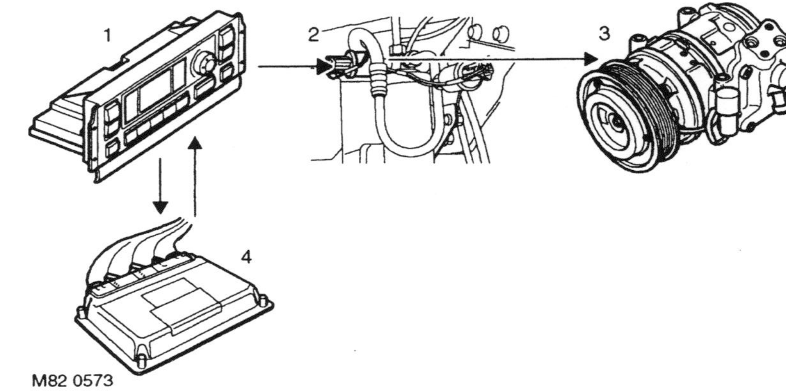

1. ATC ECU
2. Dual pressure switch
3. Compressor
4. ECM

Compressor control

To engage the compressor clutch, the ATC ECU first outputs an A/C request signal to the Engine Control Module (ECM). If the ECM agrees that the compressor can be engaged, it responds with an A/C grant signal to the ATC ECU. The ATC ECU then energises the compressor clutch via the dual pressure switch. Automatic compressor operation is then governed by the input from the evaporator temperature sensor. If the temperature of the air leaving the evaporator decreases to the point where ice may form and restrict the air flow, the ATC ECU de-energises the compressor clutch until the temperature of the air leaving the evaporator increases again.

The ATC ECU also de-energises the compressor clutch if the A/C OFF switch is pressed, or if the ECM withdraws the A/C grant signal (e.g. because of engine overheat or high load conditions).

Condenser fans control diagram - slow speed

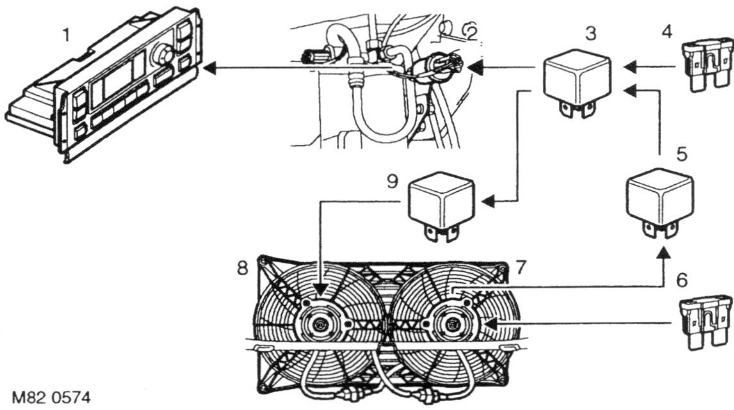

M82 0574

1. ATC ECU
2. Single pressure switch
3. Relay 18 (condenser fans control)
4. Fuse 37 (ignition power)
5. Relay 13 (LH condenser fan)
6. Fuse 31 (battery power)
7. LH condenser fan
8. RH condenser fan
9. Relay 14 (RH condenser fan)

Condenser fans control

The need to run the condenser fans, and the speed at which they operate, is dependent on the pressure in the refrigerant system, which in turn is dependent on the amount of heat being extracted from the vehicle interior and the ambient conditions.

When the ATC ECU energises the compressor clutch, it simultaneously earths the line from the coil of the condenser fans control relay. If refrigerant pressure is sufficient to require operation of the condenser fans, the contacts in the single pressure switch are closed, and the condenser fans control relay energises. At refrigerant pressures that require the condenser fans to run at slow speed, the energised condenser fans control relay connects the condenser fans in series, via the LH and RH condenser fan relays, and the fans run at slow speed.

If the refrigerant pressure increases to the upper limit for slow speed operation of the condenser fans, the fan speed contacts in the dual pressure switch close and connect an earth to the coils of the LH and RH condenser fan relays. The two condenser fan relays then energise and connect the two condenser fans to separate power supplies (i.e. in parallel) and the condenser fans run at fast speed. If the refrigerant pressure decreases to the lower limit for fast speed operation, the fan speed contacts in the dual pressure switch open, de-energise the condenser fan relays and the condenser fans return to slow speed.

Condenser fans control diagram - fast speed

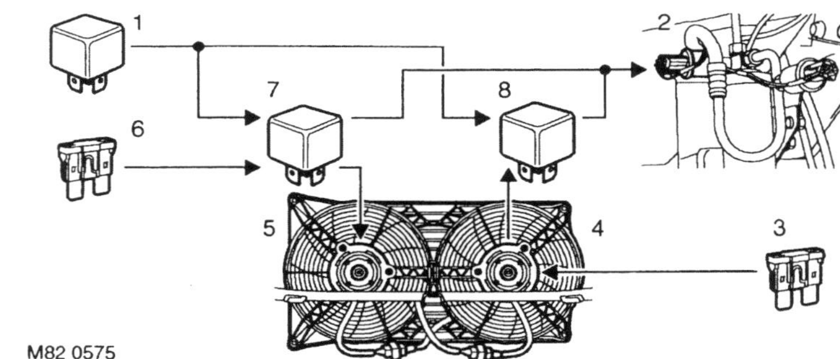

M82 0575

1. Relay 15 (ignition)
2. Dual pressure switch
3. Fuse 31 (battery power)
4. LH condenser fan
5. RH condenser fan
6. Fuse 36 (battery power)
7. Relay 14 (RH condenser fan)
8. Relay 13 (LH condenser fan)

Self tuning

Periodically, the ATC ECU performs a self tuning routine of the temperature and distribution servos, to accommodate bedding in of the flaps and their control mechanisms. During the routine, operation of the blowers is inhibited and the servos are driven through their full range to re-calibrate their flap positions. The routine is invoked at the beginning of the 1st, 10th, 20th, 50th, 100th, 500th and every subsequent 500th start up. The routine should also be invoked, using TestBook, after replacement of a temperature or distribution servo.

Diagnostics

The ATC ECU continuously monitors the sensor, servo and blower circuits for continuity and short circuits. The feedback signals of the temperature and distribution servos are also checked for plausibility at each end of the servo travel range. If a fault is detected the ATC ECU shows the handbook symbol on the LCD and stores a related fault code in memory. The fault codes can be retrieved using TestBook.

Notes

AIR CONDITIONING FAULTS

This section covers mechanical and possible fuse faults that could occur in the air conditioning system. Visual checks of components within the system and relevant fuses should be carried out before undertaking detailed fault diagnosis procedures on **TestBook** .

For details of possible faults to vent flap servo motors that are common to heating, ventilation and air conditioning systems. ***See HEATING AND VENTILATION, Fault diagnosis.***

Symptom - Condenser Fan Motor Inoperative or Slow Running.

POSSIBLE CAUSE	REMEDY
1. Blown fuse.	1. Check and renew fuse 34.
2. Loose electrical connections.	2. Check and tighten all relevant connections.
3. Worn internal motor components.	3. Renew fan motor.

Symptom - Condenser Fan Motor and/or Condenser Vibration.

POSSIBLE CAUSE	REMEDY
1. Fan motor and/or blades out of alignment.	1. Check for visual damage.
2. Fan motor/s out of balance.	2. Balance fan motors.
3. Build up of debris on fan blades.	3. Clean blades with a suitable non-inflamable cleaner.
4. Excessive wear of fan motor bearings.	4. Renew condenser fan and motor assembly.
5. Condenser unit not mounted securely.	5. Secure as necessary.

Symptom - Compressor Clutch Inoperative

POSSIBLE CAUSE	REMEDY
1. Blown air conditioning system fuse.	1. Check and renew fuse 8 or 17.
2. Loose electrical connections.	2. Check and tighten all electrical connections.
3. Defective electrical or mechanical components.	3. Renew compressor.
4. Refrigerant circuit problem.	4. Check and rectify.

Symptom - Compressor Clutch Noisy

POSSIBLE CAUSE	REMEDY
1. Loose drive belt.	1. Check drive belt tensioner or renew drive belt.
2. Compressor not mounted securely.	2. Secure as necessary.
3. Bearing in clutch pulley not pressed in.	3. Renew compressor.
4. Clutch will not spin freely.	4. Renew compressor.
5. Oil on clutch face.	5. Check compressor seals for leaks; if apparent, renew compressor.
6. Slipping clutch.	6. Renew compressor.
7. Compressor pump siezing.	7. Renew compressor.
8. Icing.	8. Check for suction line frosting. Renew expansion valve or receiver/drier, if necessary.

Symptom - Blower Motors Inoperative or Slow Running.

POSSIBLE CAUSE	REMEDY
1. Blown fuse.	1. Check and renew fuse 42 or 43.
2. Loose electrical connections.	2. Check and tighten all relevant connections.
3. Worn internal motor components.	3. Renew blower motor/s.

Symptom - Blower Motor vibration

POSSIBLE CAUSE	REMEDY
1. Blower motor/fan out of alignment.	1. Check for visual damage.
2. Blower motor/s out of balance.	2. Balance or renew motor/fan assembly.
3. Excessive wear of motor bearings.	3. Renew motor/fan assembly.
4. Blower motor not mounted securely.	4. Secure as necessary.

Symptom - Air conditioning system inoperative

POSSIBLE CAUSE	REMEDY
1. Blown air conditioning system fuse.	1. Check and renew fuses 8 or 17.
2. Switch control panel/ ECU faulty.	2. Check and renew fuse 8 or fit new switch control panel.

REFRIGERANT SYSTEM FAULTS

For any refrigeration system to function efficiently all components must be in good working order. The system cooling cycle and the relationship between air discharge temperature and ambient temperature and the pressures at the compressor can help in determining the correct operation of the system. The length of any cooling cycle is determined by such factors as ambient temperature and humidity, thermostat setting, compressor speed and air leakage into the cooled area, etc. With these factors constant, any sudden increase in the length of the cooling cycle would be indicative of abnormal operation of the air conditioning system.

The low and high side pressures at the compressor will vary with changing ambient temperature, humidity, in-car temperature and altitude.

Where the efficiency of the refrigerant system is suspect, carry out a system performance test. ***See Adjustment.*** The following components should be checked before operating the system:

- Drive belt tension.
- Compressor clutch operation.
- Blower motor operation.
- Condenser unit fins. Build up of dirt will cause poor cooling and higher operating temperatures.
- Air filter elements. A blocked filter will restrict cooling of the evaporator and it is, therefore, important to renew both filters at the recommended service schedule.

The following conditions should be checked after operating the system for several minutes:

- All high pressure lines should be hot to the touch.
- All low pressure lines should be cool to the touch.
- Inlet and outlet temperatures at the receiver/drier should be at the same temperature (warm). Any noticeable temperature difference would indicate a blocked receiver/drier.
- Heavy frost on the expansion valve inlet would indicate a defective valve or moisture in the system.

Symptom - High Head Pressure

POSSIBLE CAUSE	REMEDY
1. Overcharge of refrigerant.	1. Discharge, evacuate and recharge system.
2. Air in system.	2. Discharge system, fit new receiver/drier, evacuate and recharge system.
3. Condensor air passage blocked with dirt etc.	3. Clean condenser of debris.
4. Condenser fan motor/s defective.	4. Renew motor/s.
5. Loose compressor drive belt.	5. Check drive belt tensioner or renew drive belt.
6. Siezed compressor.	6. Renew compressor.

Symptom - Low Head Pressure

POSSIBLE CAUSE	REMEDY
1. Undercharge of refrigerant.	1. Evacuate and recharge system.
2. Leaking compressor valves.	2. Renew compressor.
3. Defective compressor.	3. Renew compressor.

Symptoms - High Suction Pressure

POSSIBLE CAUSE	REMEDY
1. Loose drive belt.	1. Check drive belt tensioner or renew drive belt.
2. Refrigerant flooding through evaporator into suction line; evident by ice on suction line.	2. Renew expansion valve.
3. Expansion valve stuck open.	3. Renew expansion valve.
4. Leaking compressor valves.	4. Renew compressor.
5. Receiver/drier blocked; evident by temperature difference between input and output lines.	5. Fit new receiver/drier, evacuate and recharge system.

Symptoms - Low Suction Pressure

POSSIBLE CAUSE	REMEDY
1. Expansion valve sticking or closed.	1. Clean or if renew if necessary.
2. Moisture freezing in expansion valve orifice. Valve outlet tube will frost while inlet tube will have little or no frost.	2. Fit new receiver/drier, evacuate and recharge system.
3. Debris restricting external air intake grille.	3. Clean air intake grille.
4. Blocked air inlet housing filters.	4. Renew air filters.
5. Defective blower motor/s, blown fuse/s or loose electrical connections.	5. Check and renew fuses 42 or 43, tighten all relevant wiring connections or renew blower motor/s.

Symptom - Noisy Expansion Valve (Steady hissing)

POSSIBLE CAUSE	REMEDY
1. Low refrigerant charge.	1. Test system for leaks; renew components as required.

Symptom - Insufficient Cooling

POSSIBLE CAUSE	REMEDY
1. Expansion valve not operating efficiently.	1. Renew expansion valve.
2. Low refrigerant charge.	2. Test system for leaks. Evacuate system and renew components as required. Recharge system.
3. Compressor not pumping.	3. Renew compressor.

GENERAL PRECAUTIONS

The refrigerant used in the air conditioning system is HFC (Hydrofluorocarbon) R134a.

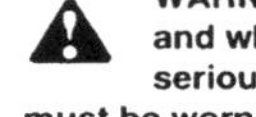

WARNING: R134a is a hazardous liquid and when handled incorrectly can cause serious injury. Suitable protective clothing must be worn when carrying out servicing operations on the air conditioning system.

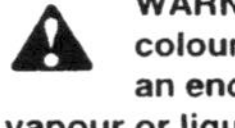

WARNING: R134a is odourless and colourless. Do not handle or discharge in an enclosed area, or in any area where the vapour or liquid can come in contact with naked flame or hot metal. R134a is not flammable but can form a highly toxic gas.

WARNING: Do not smoke or weld in areas where R134a is in use. Inhalation of concentrations of the vapour can cause dizziness, disorientation. uncoordination, narcosis, nausea or vomiting.

WARNING: Do not allow fluids other than R134a or compressor lubricant to enter the air conditioning system. Spontaneous combustion may occur.

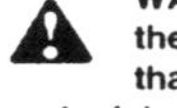

WARNING: R134a splashed on any part of the body will cause immediate freezing of that area. Also refrigerant cylinders and replenishment trolleys when discharging will freeze skin to them if contact is made.

WARNING: The refrigerant used in an air conditioning system must be reclaimed in accordance with the recommendations given with a Refrigerant Recovery Recycling Recharging Station.

NOTE: Suitable protective clothing comprises: Wrap around safety glasses or helmet, heatproof gloves, rubber apron or waterproof overalls and rubber boots.

REMEDIAL ACTIONS

1. If liquid R134a strikes the eye, do not rub it. Gently run large quantities of eyewash over the eye to raise the temperature. If eyewash is not available cool, clean water may be used. Cover eye with clean pad and seek immediate medical attention.
2. If liquid R134a is splashed on the skin run large quantities of water over the area as soon as possible to raise the temperature. Carry out the same actions if skin comes into contact with discharging cylinders. Wrap affected parts in blankets or similar material and seek immediate medical attention.
3. If suspected of being overcome by inhalation of R134a vapour seek fresh air. If unconscious remove to fresh air. Apply artificial respiration and/or oxygen and seek immediate medical attention.

NOTE: Due to its low evaporating temperature of -30°C, R134a should be handled with care.

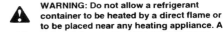

WARNING: Do not allow a refrigerant container to be heated by a direct flame or to be placed near any heating appliance. A refrigerant container must not be heated above 50°C.

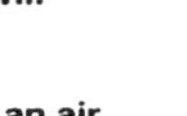

WARNING: Do not leave a container of refrigerant without its cap fitted. Do not transport a container of refrigerant that is unrestrained, especially in the boot of a car.

SERVICING PRECAUTIONS

Care must be taken when handling refrigeration system components. Units must not be lifted by their hoses, pipes or capillary lines. Hoses and lines must not be subjected to any twist or stress. Ensure that hoses are positioned in their correct run before fully tightening the couplings, and ensure that all clips and supports are used. Torque wrenches of the correct type must be used when tightening refrigerant connections to the stated value. An additional spanner must be used to hold the union to prevent twisting of the pipe.
Before connecting any hose or pipe ensure that refrigerant oil is applied to the seat of the new '0' ring but not to the threads.
Check the oil trap for the amount of oil lost.
All protective plugs on components must be left in place until immediately prior to connection.
The receiver/drier contains desiccant which absorbs moisture. It must be positively sealed at all times.

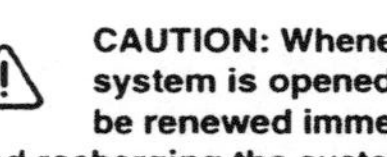

CAUTION: Whenever the refrigerant system is opened, the receiver/drier must be renewed immediately before evacuating and recharging the system.

Use alcohol and a clean cloth to clean dirty connections.
Ensure that all new parts fitted are marked for use with **R134a.**

Refrigerant oil

Use the approved refrigerant lubricating oil:
V8 models up to 99MY: Sanden SP10
V8 models from 99MY and diesel models: Nippon Denso ND-OIL 8

CAUTION: Do not use any other type of refrigerant oil.

Refrigerant oil easily absorbs water and must not be stored for long periods. Do not pour unused oil back into the container.
When renewing system components, add the following quantities of refrigerant oil:

Condenser .... 40 cm^3
Evaporator .... 80 cm^3
Pipe or hose .... 20 cm^3
Receiver/drier .... 20 cm^3

A new compressor is sealed and pressurised with Nitrogen gas, slowly release the sealing cap, gas pressure should be heard to release as the seal is broken.

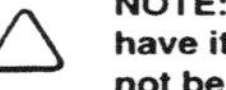

NOTE: A new compressor should always have its sealing caps in place and must not be removed until immediately prior to fitting

Fitting a new compressor

A new compressor is supplied with an oil fill (Xcm^3) of:
V8 up to 99MY .... 150 cm^3
V8 from 99MY .... 180 cm^3
Diesel .... 140 cm^3
A calculated quantity of oil must be drained from a new compressor before fitting.
To calculate the quanity of oil to be drained:

1. Remove sealing plugs from the OLD compressor.
2. Invert compressor and gravity drain oil into measuring cylinder. Rotating the compressor clutch plate will assist complete draining.
3. Note the quantity of oil drained (Ycm^3).
4. Calculate the quantity (Qcm^3) of oil to be drained from the NEW compressor using the following formula:

$$Xcm^3 - (Ycm^3 + 20cm^3) = Qcm^3$$

Rapid refrigerant discharge

When the air conditioning system is involved in accident damage and the circuit is punctured, the refrigerant is discharged rapidly. The rapid discharge of refrigerant will also result in the loss of most of the oil from the system. The compressor must be removed and all the remaining oil in the compressor drained and refilled as follows:

1. Gravity drain all the oil, assist by rotating the clutch plate (not the pulley).
2. Refill the compressor with the following amount of new refrigerant oil:
   V8 up to 99MY .... 100 cm^3
   V8 from 99MY .... 130 cm^3
   Diesel .... 90 cm^3
3. Plug the inlet and outlet ports.

Servicing Equipment

The following equipment is required for full servicing of the air conditioning system.

Recovery, recycling and charging station
Leak detector
Thermometer +20°C to -60°C
Safety goggles and gloves

REFRIGERANT RECOVERY, RECYCLING AND RECHARGING

Service repair no - 82.30.02

Refrigerant recovery

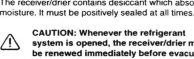

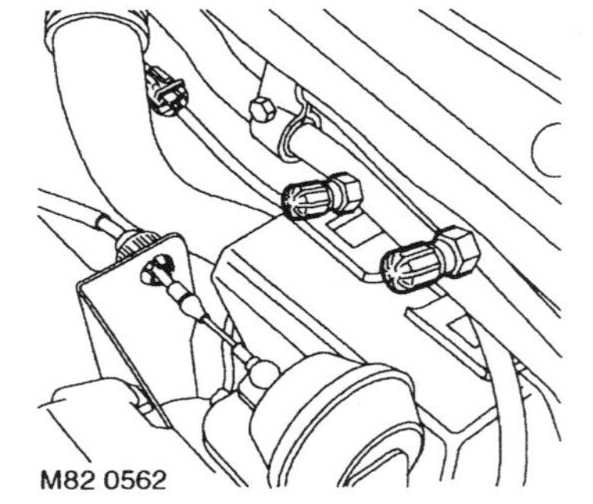

M82 0562

1. Remove dust caps from high and low pressure connectors.
2. Connect high and low pressure hoses to appropriate connections.
3. Open valves on connectors.
4. Turn valves on refrigerant station to correct positions.

NOTE: Operate the refrigerant station in accordance with the manufacturers instructions.

5. Turn Process switch to correct position.
6. Turn Main switch to 'ON'.
7. Allow station to recover refrigerant from system.

WARNING: Refrigerant must always be recycled before re-use to ensure that the purity of the refrigerant is high enough for safe use in the air-conditioning system. Recycling should always be carried out with equipment which is design certified by Underwriter Laboratory Inc. for compliance with SAE J1991. Other equipment may not recycle refrigerant to the required level of purity. A 134a Refrigerant Recovery Recharging Station must not be used with any other type of refrigerant. Refrigerant R134a from domestic and commercial sources must not be used in motor vehicle air conditioning systems.

8. Close valves on refrigerant station.
9. Turn Main switch to 'OFF'.
10. Close valves on connectors.
11. Disconnect connectors high and low pressure hoses from connectors.
12. Fit dust caps to connectors.
13. Open tap at rear of station to drain refrigerant oil.
14. Measure and record quantity of refrigerant oil recovered from system.
15. Close tap at rear of station.

Evacuation

WARNING: Servicing must be carried out by personnel familiar with both the vehicle system and the charging and testing equipment. All operations must be carried out in a well ventilated area away from open flame and heat sources

1. Remove dust caps from high and low pressure connectors.
2. Connect high and low pressure hoses to appropriate connections.
3. Open valves on connectors.
4. Turn valves on refrigerant station to correct positions.
5. Turn Process switch to correct position.
6. Turn Main switch to 'ON'.
7. Allow station to evacuate system.

Recharging

1. Close valves on refrigerant station.
2. Close valve on oil charger.
3. Disconnect yellow hose from refrigerant station.
4. Remove lid from oil charger.
5. Pour correct quantity of refrigerant oil into oil charger.
6. Fit lid to oil charger.
7. Connect yellow hose to refrigerant station.
8. Open valve on oil charger.
9. Move pointer on refrigerant gauge to mark position of refrigerant drop.
10. Slowly open correct valve on refrigerant station and allow vacuum to pull refrigerant into system.
11. Close valve on refrigerant station when correct amount of refrigerant has been drawn into air conditioning system.
12. Turn Main switch to 'OFF'.
13. Close valves on connectors.
14. Disconnect high and low pressure hoses from connectors.
15. Fit dust caps to connectors.

LEAK TEST SYSTEM

The following instructions refer to an electronic type Refrigerant Leak Detector for use with R134a, which is the safest and most sensitive.

CAUTION: When a major repair has been carried out, a leak test should be carried out using an inert gas (see below).

1. Place the vehicle in a well ventilated area but free from draughts, as leakage from the system could be dissipated without detection.
2. Follow the instructions issued by the manufacturer of the particular leak detector being used.
3. Commence searching for leaks by passing the detector probe around all joints and components, refrigerant gas is heavier than air.
4. Insert the probe into an air outlet of the evaporator or into the evaporator drain tube. Switch the air conditioning blower on and off at intervals of ten seconds. Any leaking refrigerant will be gathered in by the blower and detected.
5. Insert the probe between the magnetic clutch and compressor to check the shaft seal for leaks.
6. Check all service valve connections, valve plate, head and base plate joints and back seal plate.
7. Check the condenser for leaks at the pipe unions.
8. If any leaks are found, the system must be discharged before rectification.
9. Rectify any leaks and recheck for leaks during evacuation prior to charging.

Leak test using inert gas

Use Nitrogen or Helium gas.

1. Connect gas line to recharging station.
2. Pressurise system to 3 bar.
3. Carry out leak test as above.

AIR CONDITIONING SYSTEM - PERFORMANCE TEST

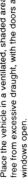

WARNING: R134a is hazardous. ***See this section.***

Carry out this test with bonnet and doors or windows open, air conditioning switched on, temperature control set to cold and blower at maximum speed. Set the air supply control to supply fresh air.

1. Close low pressure valve on refrigerant station.
2. Close high pressure valve on refrigerant station.
3. Connect a Refrigerant Station to the high and low pressure servicing connections.
4. Insert dry bulb thermometer into cold air outlet and position dry and wet bulb thermometer close to outside air inlet.
   Do not spill water from the wet thermometer (psychrometer).
5. Start engine and run it at 1500 rev/min for 10 minutes with air conditioning switched on.
6. Read both pressure gauges and thermometers. Check readings against table below with humidity between 60% and 80%. If readings are incorrect. ***See Fault diagnosis.***
7. Switch off air conditioning, stop engine, disconnect test equipment.

Performance range

Intake temperature	Outlet temperature	Low pressure	High pressure
20 - 24°C	4 - 10°C	18 - 28 lbf/in^2 1.2 - 1.9 bar	213 - 299 lbf/in^2 14.7 - 20.6 bar
25 - 29°C	9 - 19°C	27 - 37 lbf/in^2 1.9 - 2.6 bar	256 - 341 lbf/in^2 17.6 - 23.5 bar
30 - 35°C	20 - 27°C	33 - 47 lbf/in^2 2.3 - 3.2 bar	299 - 384 lbf/in^2 20.6 - 26.5 bar

Table 1

Ambient Temperature		Compound Gauge Readings		High Pressure Gauge Readings	
°C	°F	bar	lbf/in^2	bar	lbf/in^2
16	60	1,03-1,4	15-20	6,9-10,3	100-150
26,7	80	1,4-1,72	20-25	9,6-13,1	140-190
38	100	1,72-2,1	25-30	12,4-15,5	180-225
43,5	110	2,1-2,4	30-35	14,8-17,2	215-250

SYSTEM TEST

1. Place the vehicle in a ventilated, shaded area free from excessive draught, with the doors and windows open.
2. Check that the surface of the condenser is not restricted with dirt, leaves, flies, etc. Do not neglect to check the surface between the condenser and the radiator. Clean as necessary.
3. Switch on the ignition and the air conditioner air flow control. Check that the blower is operating efficiently at low, medium and high speeds. Switch off the blower and the ignition.
4. Check that the evaporator condensate drain tubes are open and clear.
5. Check the tension of the compressor driving belt, and adjust if necessary.
6. Inspect all connections for the presence of refrigerant oil. If oil is evident, check for leaks, and repair as necessary.

NOTE: The compressor oil is soluble in Refrigerant R134a and is deposited when the refrigerant evaporates from a leak.

7. Start the engine.
8. Set the temperature controls to cold and switch the air conditioner blower control on and off several times, checking that the magnetic clutch on the compressor engages and releases each time.
9. With the temperature control at maximum cooling and the blower control at high speed, warm up the engine and fast idle at 1000 rev/min.
10. Repeat at 1800 rev/min.
11. Gradually increase the engine speed.
12. Check for frosting on the service valves.
13. Check the high pressure hoses and connections by hand for varying temperature. Low temperature indicates a restriction or blockage at that point.
14. Switch off the air conditioning blower and stop the engine.
15. If the air conditioning equipment is still not satisfactory, carry out a pressure test as previously described in this section.

PRECAUTIONS IN HANDLING REFRIGERANT LINES

WARNING: Wear eye and hand protection when disconnecting components containing refrigerant. Plug all exposed connections immediately.

1. When disconnecting any hose or pipe connection the system must be discharged of all pressure. Proceed cautiously, regardless of gauge readings. Open connections slowly, keeping hands and face well clear, so that no injury occurs if there is liquid in the line. If pressure is noticed, allow it to bleed off slowly.
2. Lines, flexible end connections and components must be capped immediately they are opened to prevent the entrance of moisture and dirt.
3. Any dirt or grease on fittings must be wiped off with a clean alcohol dampened cloth. Do not use chlorinated solvents such as trichloroethylene. If dirt, grease or moisture cannot be removed from inside the hoses, they must be replaced with new hoses.
4. All replacement components and flexible end connections must be sealed, and only opened immediately prior to making the connection.
5. Ensure the components are at room temperature before uncapping, to prevent condensation of moisture from the air that enters.
6. Components must not remain uncapped for longer than fifteen minutes. In the event of delay, the caps must be fitted.
7. Receiver/driers must never be left uncapped as they contain Silica Gel crystals which will absorb moisture from the atmosphere. A receiver/ drier left uncapped must not be used, fit a new unit.
8. The compressor shaft must not be rotated until the system is entirely assembled and contains a charge of refrigerant.
9. A new compressor contains an initial charge of refrigerant oil. The compressor also contains a holding charge of gas when received which should be retained by leaving the seals in place until the pipes are re-connected.

10. The receiver/drier should be the last component connected to the system to ensure optimum dehydration and maximum moisture protection of the system.
11. All precautions must be taken to prevent damage to fittings and connections. Slight damage could cause a leak with the high pressures used in the system.
12. Always use two wrenches of the correct size, one on each fitting when releasing and tightening refrigeration unions.
13. Joints and 'O' rings should be coated with refrigeration oil to aid correct seating. Fittings which are not lubricated with refrigerant oil are almost certain to leak.
14. All lines must be free of kinks. The efficiency of the system is reduced by a single kink or restriction.
15. Flexible hoses should not be bent to a radius less than 90mm radius.
16. Flexible hoses should not be within 100mm of the exhaust manifold.
17. Completed assemblies must be checked for refrigeration lines touching metal panels. Any direct contact of lines and panels transmits noise and must be eliminated.

PERIODIC MAINTENANCE

Routine servicing, apart from visual checks, is not necessary. The visual inspections are as follows:

Condenser
With a water hose or air line, clean the fins of the condenser to remove flies, leaves, etc. Check the pipe connections for signs of oil leakage.

Compressor
Check pipe connections for signs of oil leakage. Check flexible hoses for swelling. Examine the compressor belt for tightness and condition.

Evaporator
Examine the refrigeration connections at the unit. If the system should develop a fault, or if erratic operation is noticed. ***See Fault diagnosis.***

COMPRESSOR DRIVE BELT - DIESEL

Service repair no - 82.20.01

Adjust

1. Disconnect battery negative lead.
2. Raise the vehicle.

WARNING: Support on safety stands.

3. Remove cover from tensioner pulley. Slacken pulley bolt.

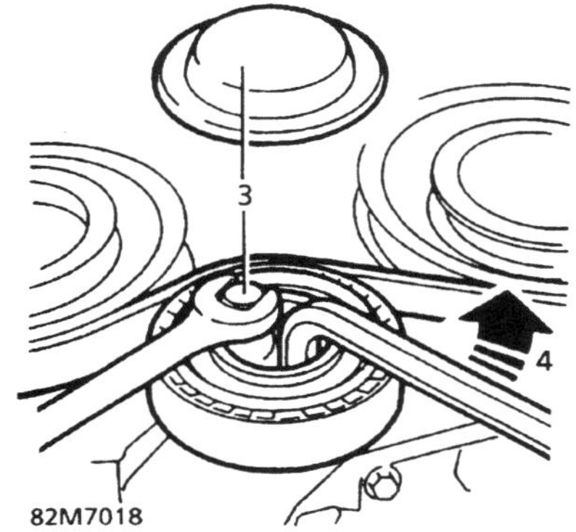

82M7018

4. Rotate tensioner pulley anti-clockwise. Apply following tension:
   New belt = 8 Nm. (6 lbf.ft)
   Existing belt = 6 Nm. (4 lbf.ft)
5. Tighten pulley bolt whilst applying correct load.
6. Fit cover to tensioner pulley.
7. Remove safety stands. Lower vehicle.
8. Reconnect battery negative lead.

INTERIOR TEMPERATURE SENSOR

Service repair no - 82.20.93

Remove

1. Remove instrument pack binnacle. ***See INSTRUMENTS, Repair.***
2. Move front seats fully rearward.
3. Remove screw securing each side panel to centre console.

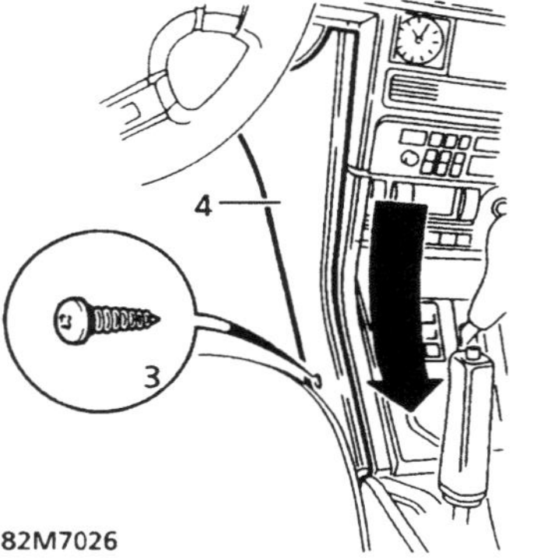

82M7026

4. Release sprag clip by firmly pulling panel rearwards. Remove side panels.
5. Remove radio applique.

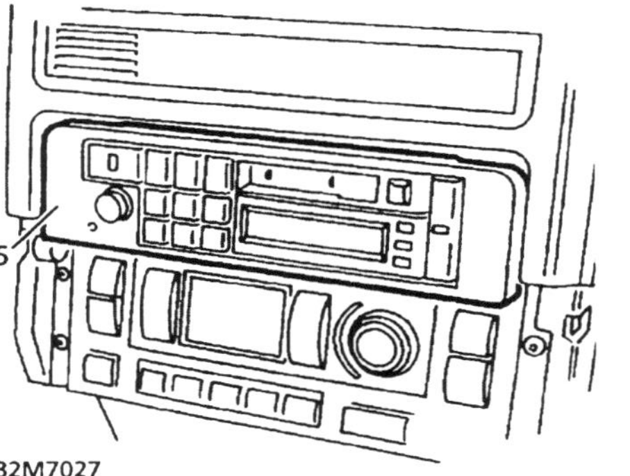

82M7027

6. Remove 5 screws securing switch pack.

82M7028

7. Release switch pack from fascia. Sensor is located behind grille of switch panel.
8. Disconnect multiplug from interior temperature sensor.
9. Remove 2 screws securing interior temperature sensor. Remove sensor.

82M7029

Refit

10. Reverse removal procedure.

AMBIENT TEMPERATURE SENSOR - UP TO VIN 381430

Service repair no - 82.20.91

Remove

1. Remove plenum air intake panels. ***See HEATING AND VENTILATION, Repair.***
2. **LHD only:** Remove plastic cover, nut and washers from LH wiper spindle.

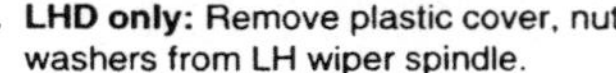

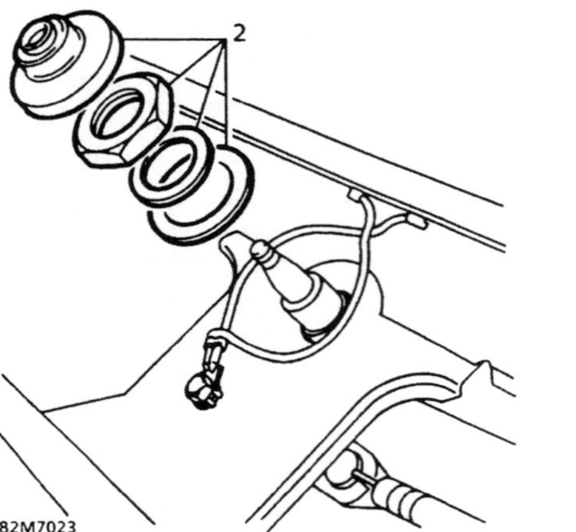

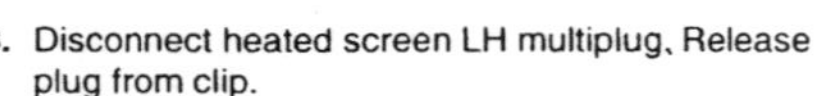

3. Disconnect heated screen LH multiplug, Release plug from clip.

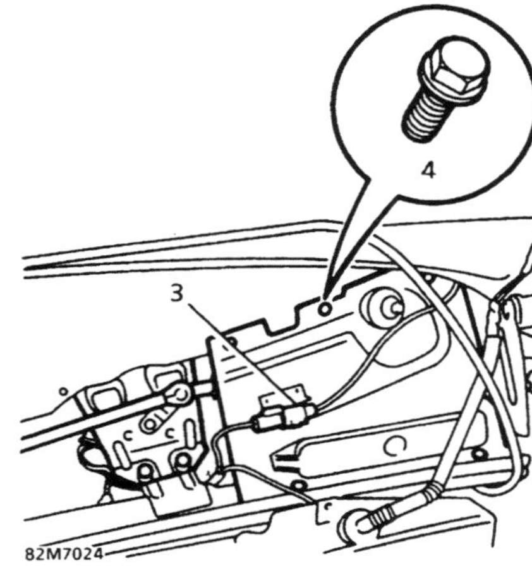

4. Remove 6 bolts securing LH scuttle side panel. Remove panel.
5. Remove pollen filter.

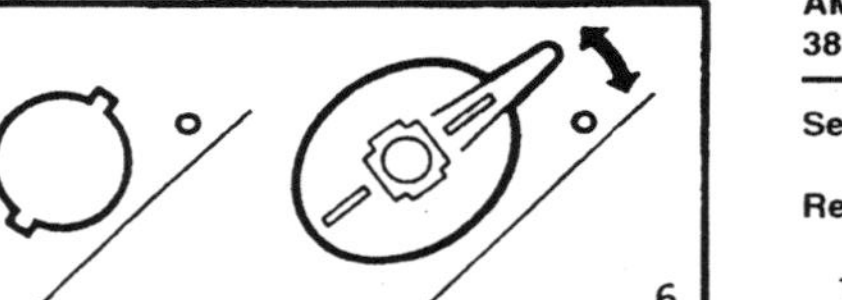

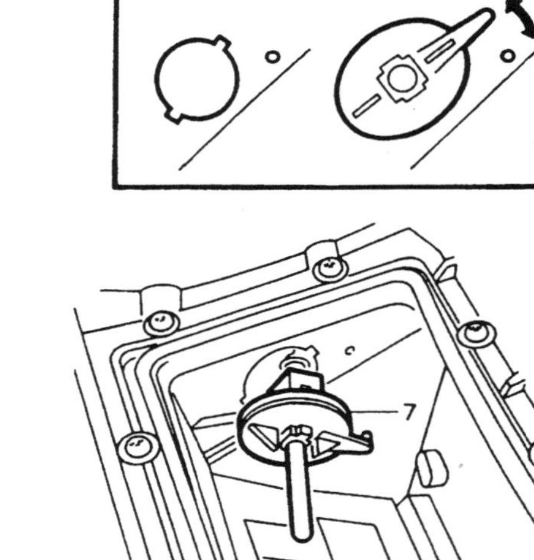

6. Turn sensor anti-clockwise. Release from recirculation flap housing.
7. Remove sensor from multiplug.

Refit

8. Reverse removal procedure.

> **NOTE: *LHD only:* Tighten nut on LH wiper spindle to *11 Nm. (8 lbf.ft)***

AMBIENT TEMPERATURE SENSOR - FROM VIN 381431

Service repair no - 82.20.91

Remove

1. Remove front bumper valance. ***See CHASSIS AND BODY, Repair.***

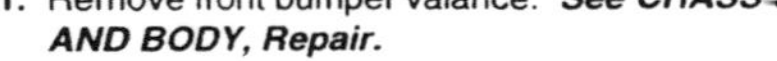

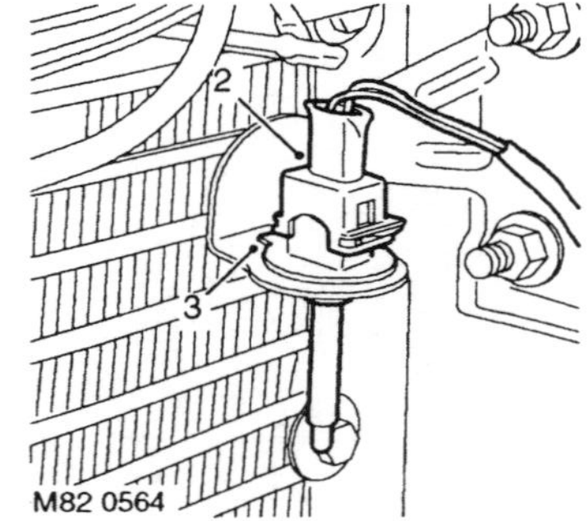

2. Disconnect multiplug from sensor.
3. Release sensor locating lug from hole in sensor mounting bracket, rotate and remove sensor.

Refit

4. Fit sensor to mounting bracket, ensuring that locating lug is fully engaged.
5. Connect multiplug to sensor.
6. Fit front bumper valance. ***See CHASSIS AND BODY, Repair.***

HEATER TEMPERATURE SENSOR

Service repair no - 82.20.94

Remove

1. **RHD vehicles.** Remove fascia closing panel to gain access to sensor. ***See CHASSIS AND BODY, Repair.***
2. **LHD vehicles.** Open glove box. Remove 5 screws securing glove box liner to fascia.
3. Release glove box liner. Disconnect lamp multiplug.

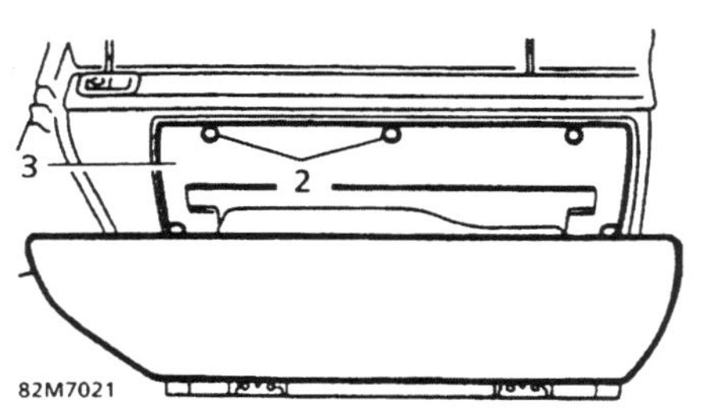

82M7021

4. Release cable from glove box latch.
5. Lower glove box liner from fascia to gain access to sensor.
6. **All vehicles.** Disconnect sensor multiplug.
7. Release clip. Remove sensor from heater feed pipe.

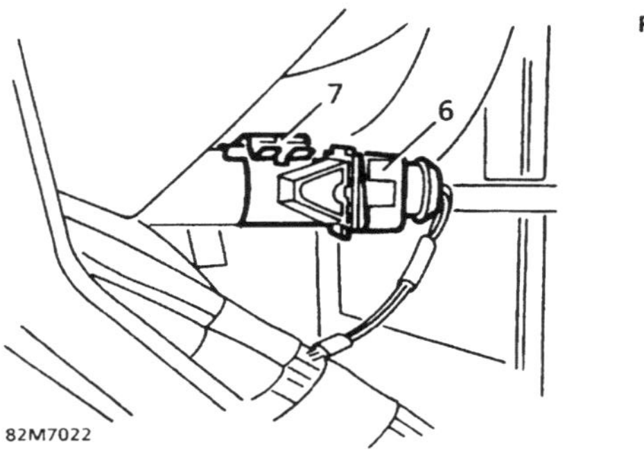

82M7022

Refit

8. Reverse removal procedure.

COMPRESSOR DRIVE BELT - DIESEL

Service repair no - 82.10.02

Remove

1. Disconnect battery negative lead.
2. Raise the vehicle.

 **WARNING: Support on safety stands.**

3. Remove cover from tensioner pulley. Slacken pulley bolt.
4. Remove belt.

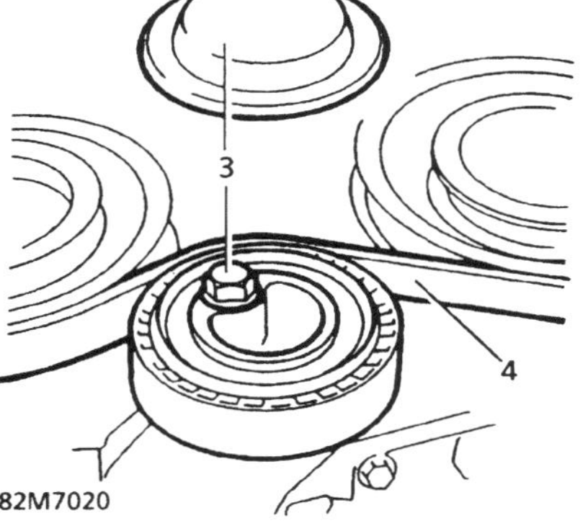

82M7020

Refit

5. Fit belt around crankshaft, compressor and tensioner pulleys.
6. Adjust belt tension. ***See Adjustment.***
7. Remove safety stands. Lower vehicle.
8. Reconnect battery negative lead.

EVAPORATOR TEMPERATURE SENSOR

Service repair no - 82.20.95

Remove

1. **RHD vehicles.** Remove fascia closing panel to gain access to sensor. ***See CHASSIS AND BODY, Repair.***
2. **LHD vehicles.** Open glove box. Remove 5 screws securing glove box liner to fascia.

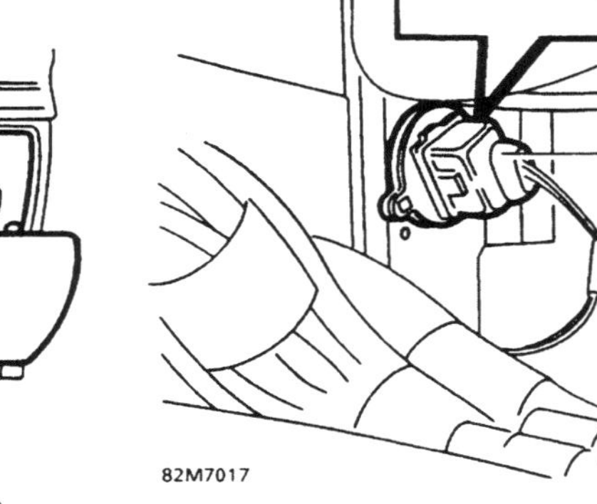

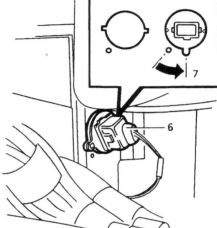

82M7016

3. Release glove box liner. Disconnect lamp multiplug.
4. Release cable from glove box latch.
5. Lower glove box liner from fascia to gain access to sensor.
6. **All vehicles.** Disconnect sensor multiplug.
7. Turn sensor anti-clockwise, remove from evaporator casing.

82M7017

Refit

8. Reverse removal procedure.

CONDENSER - V8

Service repair no - 82.15.07

Remove

1. Disconnect battery negative lead.
2. Remove front grille. ***See CHASSIS AND BODY, Repair.***
3. Remove front bumper. ***See CHASSIS AND BODY, Repair.***
4. Discharge air conditioning system. ***See Adjustment.***
5. Remove 4 bolts securing bonnet platform.

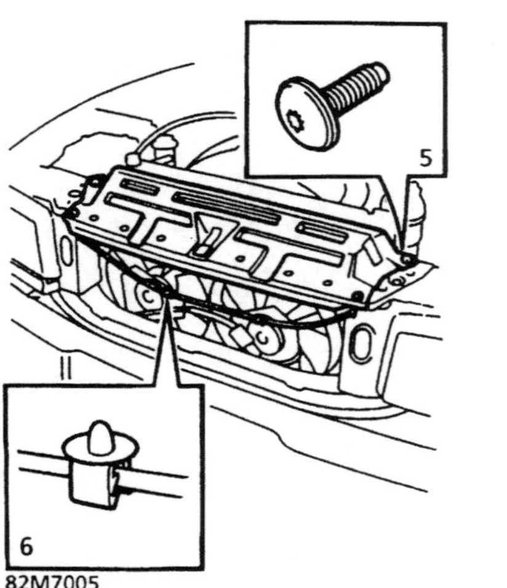

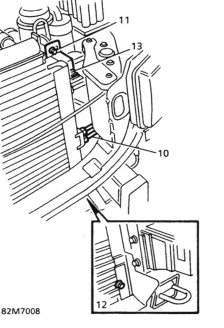

82M7005

6. Release clips securing bonnet release cable. Remove bonnet platform.
7. Disconnect 2 multiplugs from condenser cooling fans.

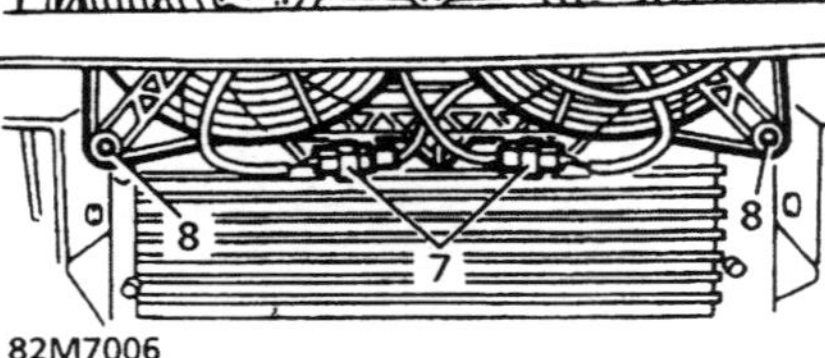

82M7006

8. Remove 4 bolts securing fans to condenser. Remove fans.
9. Remove studs securing oil cooler LH air deflector to body. Remove deflector.

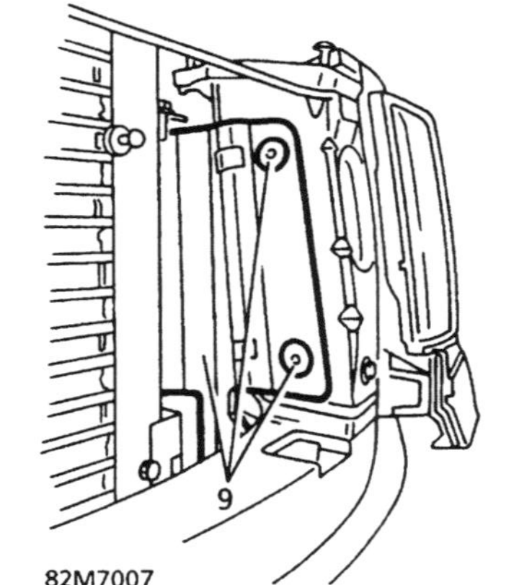

82M7007

10. Disconnect 2 pipes from condenser. Remove 'O' rings and discard. Plug pipes and connections.

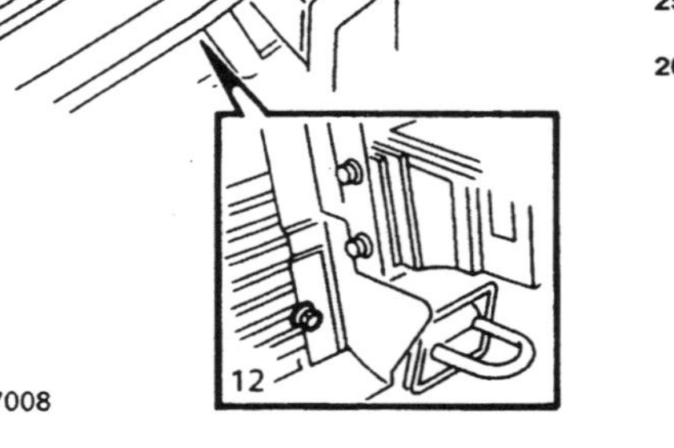

82M7008

11. Remove 2 bolts securing condenser upper mounting brackets to radiator mounting.
12. Remove 2 lower securing bolts. Remove condenser.
13. Remove 2 bolts securing mounting brackets to condenser. Remove brackets.

Refit

14. Fit mounting brackets to condenser. Secure with bolts.
15. Position condenser. Secure with bolts.
16. Remove plugs from pipes and condenser.
17. Lubricate new 'O' rings with compressor oil. Fit to connections.
18. Connect pipes to condenser. Tighten to ***15 Nm. (11 lbf.ft)***
19. Position LH air deflector. Secure with studs.
20. Position cooling fans. Secure with bolts. Connect multiplugs.
21. Position bonnet platform. Secure bonnet release cable with strap.
22. Secure bonnet platform with bolts.
23. Refit front bumper. ***See CHASSIS AND BODY, Repair.***
24. Refit front grille. ***See CHASSIS AND BODY, Repair.***
25. Evacuate and recharge air conditioning system. ***See Adjustment.***
26. Reconnect battery negative lead.

CONDENSER - DIESEL

Service repair no - 82.15.07

Remove

1. Disconnect battery negative lead.
2. Discharge air conditioning system. ***See Adjustment.***
3. Remove intercooler. ***See FUEL SYSTEM, Repair.***
4. Remove 2 studs securing LH deflector panel. Remove panel.

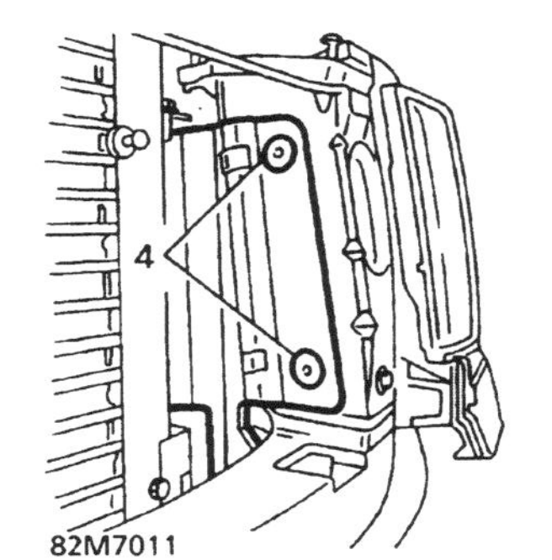

82M7011

5. Release 2 bolts securing condenser to radiator bracket.

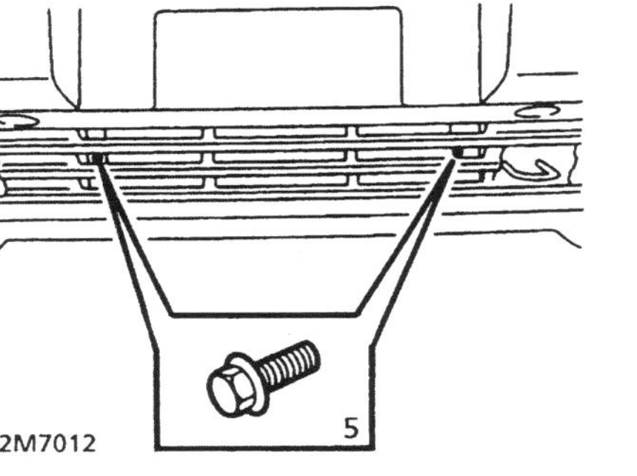

82M7012

NOTE: Gain access to bolts through bumper grille. Leave bolts positioned in condenser to aid assembly.

6. Remove 2 nuts securing air conditioning pipe clips to condenser fans.

82M7013

7. Disconnect 2 pipes from condenser. Remove 'O' rings and discard.
8. Plug pipe connections.
9. Raise condenser for access. Disconnect 2 condenser fan multiplugs.

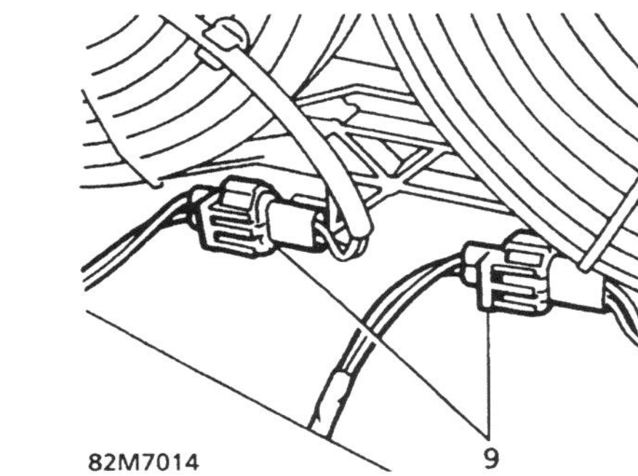

82M7014

10. Remove condenser assembly.

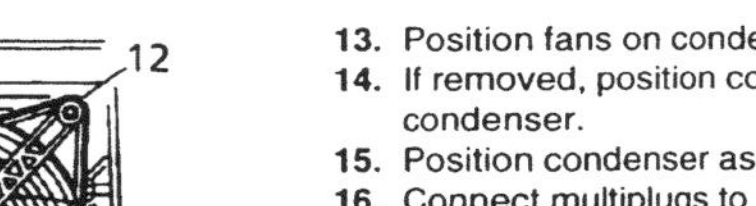

82M7015

NOTE:
Do not carry out further dismantling if component is removed for access only.

11. Remove condenser securing bolts from locations.
12. Remove 4 bolts securing fans to condenser. Remove fans.

Refit

13. Position fans on condenser. Secure with bolts.
14. If removed, position condenser securing bolts in condenser.
15. Position condenser assembly.
16. Connect multiplugs to fans.
17. Remove plugs from condenser and pipes.
18. Ensure mating faces are clean.
19. Lubricate new 'O' rings with compressor oil. Fit to pipes.
20. Connect pipes to condenser.
21. Align pipe clips to condenser fan studs. Secure with nuts.
22. Secure condenser to radiator bracket with bolts.
23. Position deflector panel. Secure with studs.
24. Fit intercooler. ***See FUEL SYSTEM, Repair.***
25. Evacuate and recharge air conditioning system. ***See Adjustment.***
26. Reconnect battery negative lead.

COMPRESSOR - V8 - UP TO 99MY

Service repair no - 82.10.20

Remove

1. Disconnect battery negative lead.
2. Discharge air conditioning system. ***See Adjustment.***
3. Remove drive belt tension. Release belt from compressor. ***See ELECTRICAL, Repair.***

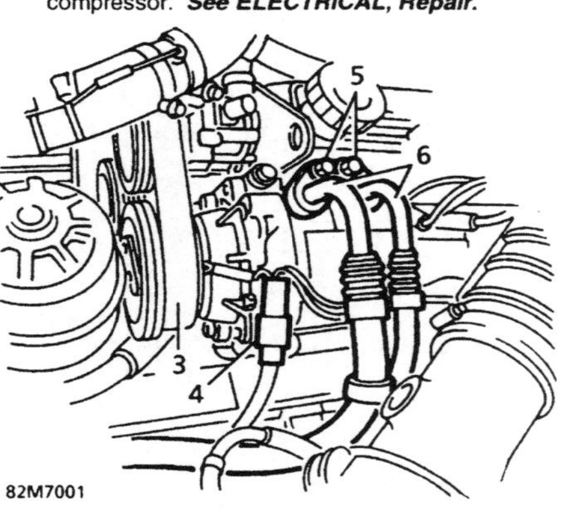

82M7001

4. Disconnect compressor multiplug.
5. Remove 2 bolts securing pipes to compressor.
6. Release pipes from compressor. Discard 'O' rings. Plug pipes and connections.
7. Remove 3 bolts securing compressor to mounting bracket. Remove compressor.

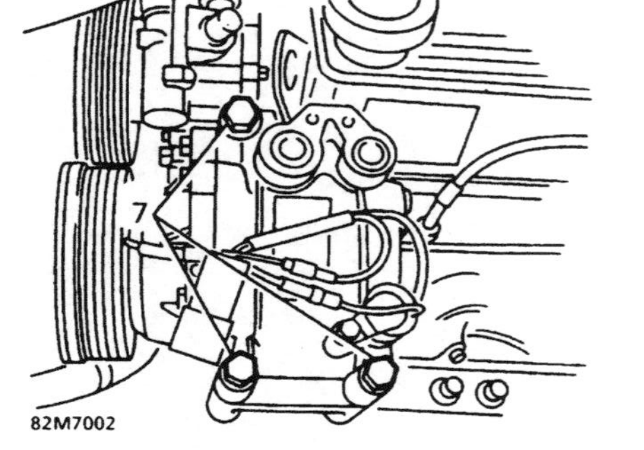

82M7002

Refit

8. Position compressor on mounting bracket. Secure with bolts.
9. Remove plugs from pipes and connections.
10. Lubricate new 'O' rings with compressor oil. Fit to connections.
11. Align pipes to compressor. Tighten bolts to ***23 Nm (17 lbf.ft).***
12. Connect compressor multiplug.
13. Engage drive belt over compressor pulley.
14. Evacuate and recharge air conditioning system. ***See Adjustment.***
15. Reconnect battery negative lead.

COMPRESSOR - V8 - FROM 99MY

Service repair no - 82.10.20

Remove

1. Depressurise A/C system. ***See Adjustment.***
2. Remove auxiliary drive belt. ***See ELECTRICAL, Repair.***

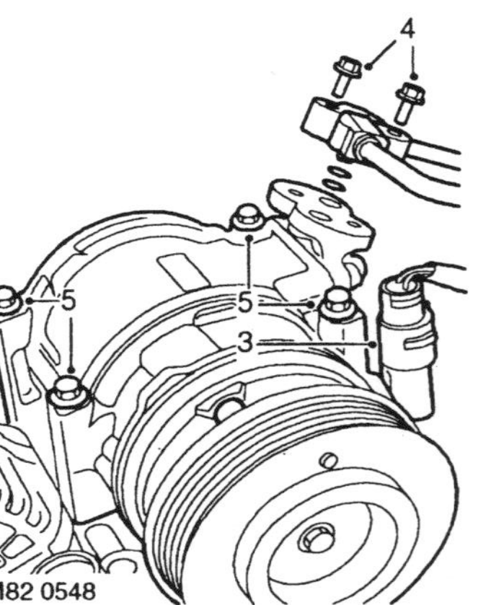

M82 0548

3. Disconnect multiplug from compressor.
4. Remove 2 bolts securing A/C pipes to compressor and discard 'O' rings.

CAUTION: Immediately cap all air conditioning pipes to prevent ingress of dirt and moisture into the system.

5. Remove 4 bolts securing compressor to mounting bracket and remove compressor.

Refit

6. Clean compressor dowels and dowel holes.
7. Position compressor to mounting bracket and tighten bolts to ***25 Nm (16 lbf.ft).***
8. Remove caps from compressor and pipe connections.
9. Clean compressor and pipe connections.
10. Lubricate new 'O' rings with refrigerant oil and fit to compressor.
11. Position A/C pipes to compressor and tighten bolts to ***9 Nm (7 lbf.ft).***
12. Connect multiplug to compressor.
13. Fit auxiliary drive belt. ***See ELECTRICAL, Repair.***
14. Recharge A/C system. ***See Adjustment.***

COMPRESSOR - DIESEL

Service repair no - 82.10.20

Remove

1. Raise vehicle on four post lift.
2. Disconnect battery negative lead.
3. Raise lift.
4. Discharge air conditioning system. ***See Adjustment.***
5. Remove drive belt. ***See this section.***
6. Disconnect compressor multiplug.
7. Remove 2 bolts securing high and low pressure pipes.
8. Release pipes from compressor. Discard 'O' rings. Plug pipes and connections
9. Remove 4 bolts securing compressor to mounting bracket. Remove compressor.

NOTE: On RHD vehicles, bolts cannot be removed completely.

Refit

10. Position compressor on bracket ring dowels. Secure with bolts.
11. Remove plugs from pipes and compressor.
12. Lubricate new 'O' rings with compressor oil. Fit to connections.
13. Connect pipes to compressor. Secure with bolts. Tighten to ***23 Nm. (17 lbf.ft)***
14. Connect compressor multiplug.
15. Fit drive belt. ***See this section.***
16. Evacuate and recharge air conditioning system. ***See Adjustment.***
17. Lower lift.
18. Reconnect battery negative lead.

EVAPORATOR

Service repair no - 82.25.20

Remove

1. Remove heater. ***See HEATING AND VENTILATION, Repair.***
2. Remove screw inside centre vent duct.

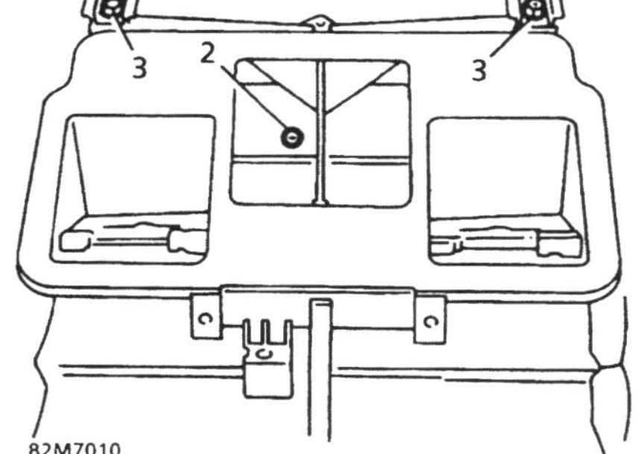

3. Remove 2 bolts securing evaporator to heater unit.
4. Remove evaporator from heater unit.

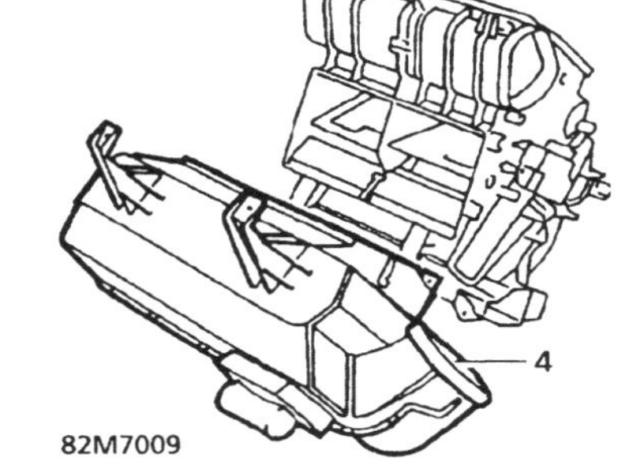

Refit

5. Reverse removal procedure.

CONDENSER FAN

Service repair no - 82.15.01

Remove

1. Disconnect battery negative lead.
2. Raise the vehicle.

WARNING: Support on safety stands.

3. Remove front grille. ***See CHASSIS AND BODY, Repair.***
4. Remove front bumper. ***See CHASSIS AND BODY, Repair.***
5. Disconnect 2 multiplugs from condenser cooling fans.

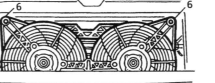

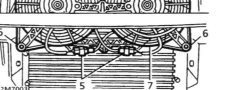

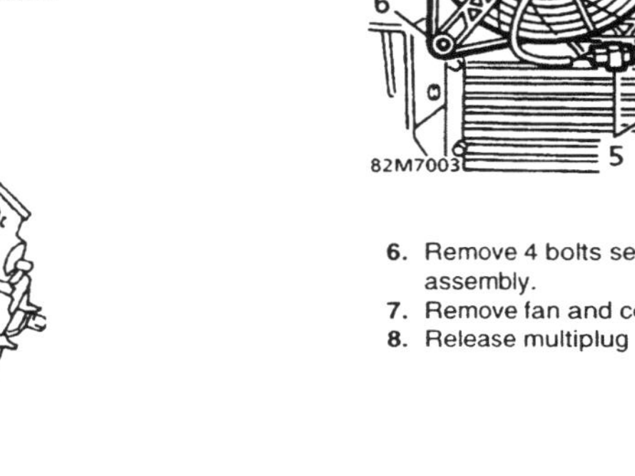

6. Remove 4 bolts securing condenser fan assembly.
7. Remove fan and cowl assembly.
8. Release multiplug holder from fan cowl.

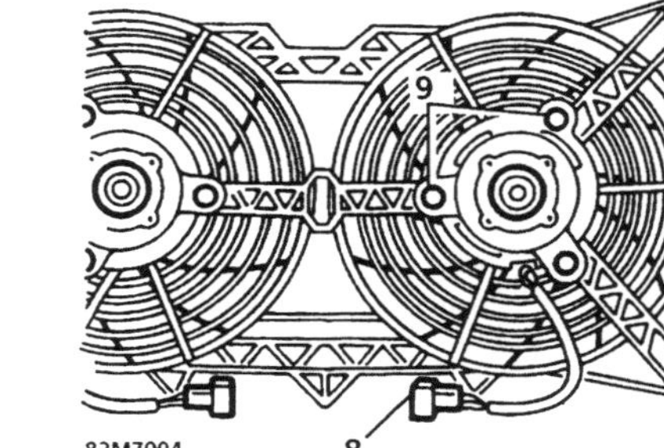

9. Remove 3 nuts securing motor to cowl. Remove motor.

Refit

10. Reverse removal procedure.

THERMOSTATIC EXPANSION VALVE (TXV) - V8 UP TO 99MY AND DIESEL FROM 95MY

Service repair no - 82.25.01

Remove

1. Disconnect battery negative lead.
2. Depressurise air conditioning system. ***See Adjustment.***
3. Remove clamp securing air conditioning pipes to bulkhead.

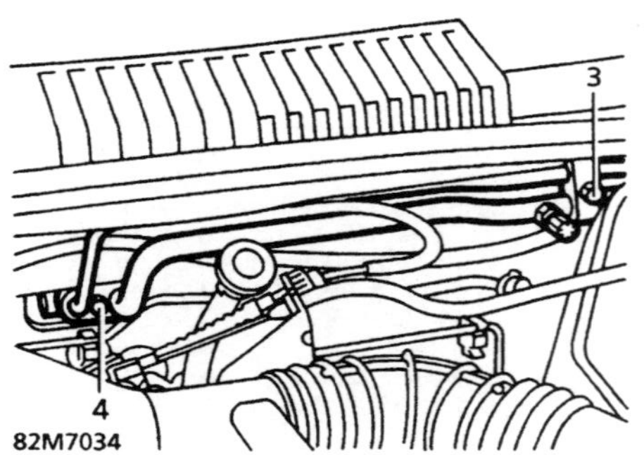

82M7034

4. Remove bolt securing pipe clamp to TXV. Position clamp aside.
5. Release pipes from TXV. Position aside. Discard 'O' rings. Plug pipes and connections.
6. Remove 2 bolts securing TXV to evaporator.
7. Remove TXV.
8. Remove 'O' rings and discard. Plug evaporator and TXV ports.

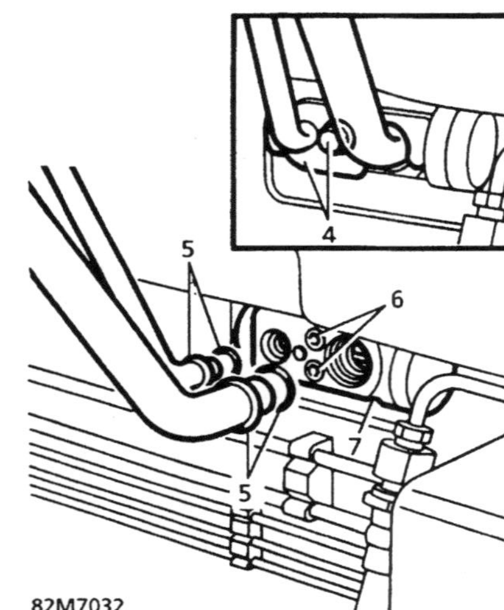

82M7032

Refit

9. Remove plugs.
10. Ensure all mating faces are clean.
11. Lubricate new 'O' rings with compressor oil. Fit to pipes.
12. Position TXV to evaporator pipes.
13. Ensure TXV is fully engaged to evaporator pipes. Secure with bolts.
14. Engage pipes to TXV. Secure pipe clamp with bolt.
15. Secure air conditioning pipes to bulkhead with clamp.
16. Evacuate and recharge air conditioning system. ***See this section.***
17. Reconnect battery negative lead.

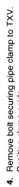

VALVE - THERMOSTATIC EXPANSION (TXV) - V8 FROM 99MY

Service repair no - 82.25.01

Remove

1. Depressurise A/C system. ***See Adjustment.***
2. Remove IAC valve. ***See FUEL SYSTEM, Repair.***

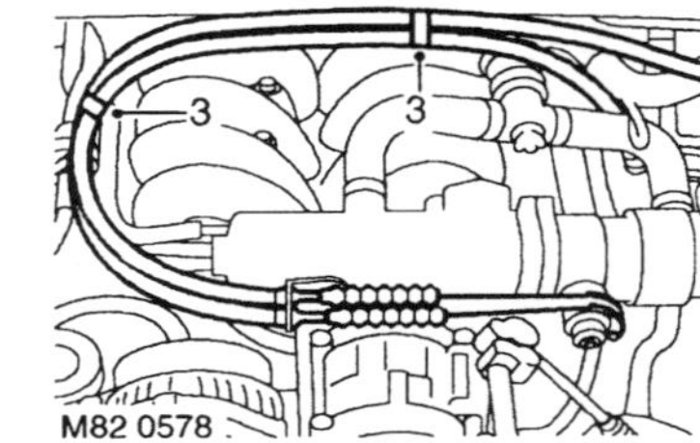

M82 0578

3. Release throttle and cruise control cables from clips on manifold chamber and position cables aside.

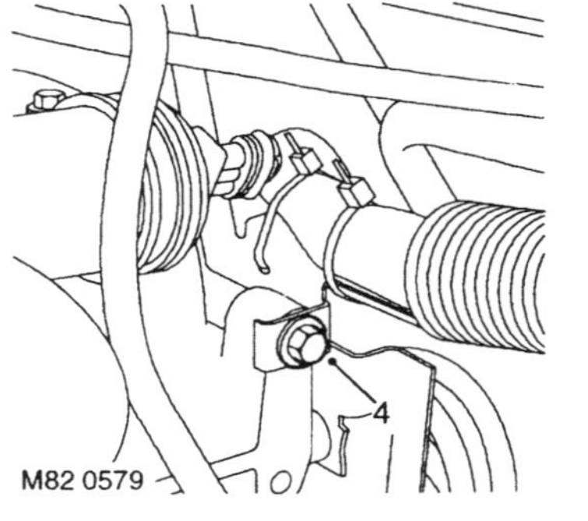

M82 0579

4. Remove bolt securing engine harness mounting bracket to manifold chamber.

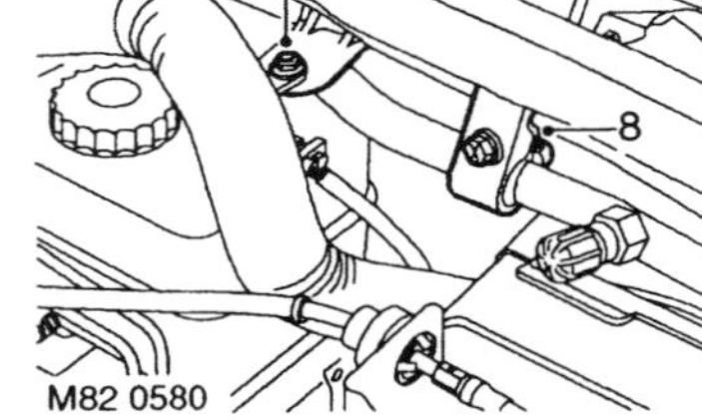

M82 0580

5. Remove nut securing engine harness to bracket on bulkhead and release harness.
6. Remove clamp securing A/C pipes to bulkhead.

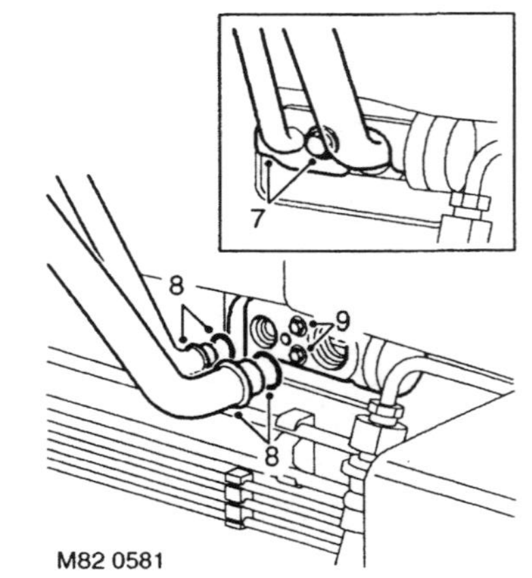

M82 0581

7. Remove bolt securing A/C pipe clamp to TXV and position clamp aside.
8. Release A/C pipes from TXV, discard 'O' rings and position pipes aside.

CAUTION: Immediately cap all air conditioning pipes to prevent ingress of dirt and moisture into the system.

9. Remove 2 bolts securing TXV to evaporator pipes and remove TXV.
10. Remove and discard 'O' rings from evaporator pipes.

CAUTION: Immediately cap all air conditioning pipes to prevent ingress of dirt and moisture into the system.

Refit

11. Ensure mating faces of TXV and pipes are clean.
12. Lubricate new 'O' rings with compressor oil and fit rings to pipes.
13. Fit TXV to evaporator pipes, ensuring that TXV is fully engaged to pipes.
14. Fit and tighten bolts securing TXV to evaporator pipes.
15. Fit A/C pipes to TXV, position pipe clamp and secure with bolt.
16. Secure A/C pipes to bulkhead with clamp.
17. Fit engine harness to bracket on bulkhead and secure with nut.
18. Align engine harness mounting bracket to manifold chamber and secure with bolt.
19. Fit throttle and cruise control cables to clips.
20. Fit IAC valve. ***See FUEL SYSTEM, Repair.***
21. Recharge A/C system. ***See Adjustment.***

SOLAR SENSOR

Service repair no - 82.20.92

Remove

1. Prise solar sensor from central screen demist vent.
2. Disconnect sensor from multiplug. Remove sensor.

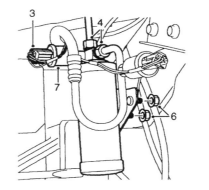

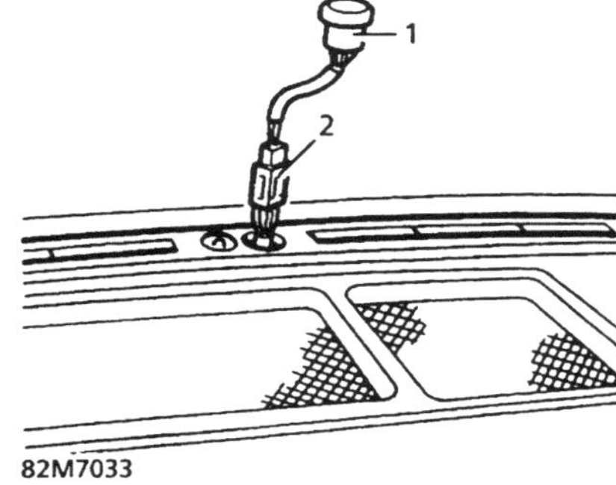

82M7033

Refit

3. Reverse removal procedure.

RECEIVER/DRIER - FROM 99MY

Service repair no - 82.17.03

Remove

1. Remove front bumper valance. ***See CHASSIS AND BODY, Repair.***
2. Depressurise A/C system. ***See Adjustment.***

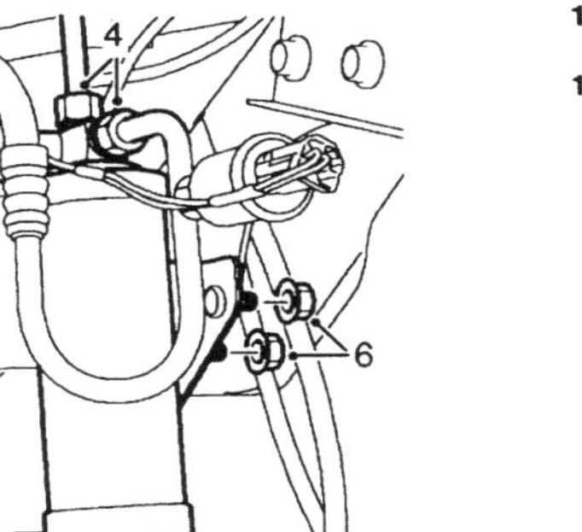

M82 0563

3. Disconnect multiplug from dual pressure switch.
4. Loosen 2 unions and release pipes from receiver drier.
5. Remove and discard 'O' rings from pipes.

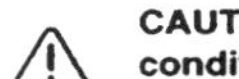

CAUTION: Immediately cap all air conditioning pipes to prevent ingress of dirt and moisture into the system.

6. Remove 2 nuts securing receiver drier to bracket and remove receiver drier.
7. Remove dual pressure switch from receiver drier and discard 'O' ring.

CAUTION: Plug the connections.

Refit

8. Clean mating faces of pipes, receiver drier and dual pressure switch.
9. Lubricate new 'O' rings with compressor oil.
10. Fit 'O' rings to pipes and dual pressure switch.
11. Fit and tighten dual pressure switch to receiver drier.
12. Fit receiver drier to bracket and secure with nuts.
13. Fit pipes to receiver drier and tighten unions to ***18 Nm (13 lbf.ft).***
14. Connect multiplug to dual pressure switch.
15. Evacuate and recharge A/C system. ***See Adjustment.***
16. Fit front bumper valance. ***See CHASSIS AND BODY, Repair.***

84 - WIPERS AND WASHERS

CONTENTS

Page

WIPER AND WASHER SYSTEM

The illustration below locates and identifies the main components in the wiper and washer system, which is operated by a multi-switch (1) on the RH side of the steering column. All functions of the system are described in the following pages.

84M7012

1. Multi-switch
2. Wiper motor, windscreen
3. Wiper arm/blade
4. Washer reservoir
5. Filler cap tube, washer reservoir
6. Windscreen washer pump
7. Non return valve
8. Washer jets
9. Rear screen washer pump
10. Non return valve
11. Wiper motor, rear screen
12. Wiper arm/blade
13. Washer jet
14. Wiper motor, headlamp
15. Wiper arm/blade
16. Washer pump, headlamp
17. Non return valve
18. Washer jet
19. Low screen wash sensor

Description

A chassis mounted washer reservoir (4), with low screen wash sensor (19) and extended filler cap tube (5), is fitted and supplies both front and rear washers using integral pump motors (6) and (9). When headlamp wash/wipe is installed a separate pump (16) is used in the system, including a non return valve (17) for each side.

Two bonnet mounted windscreen washer jets (8), using a single non return valve (7) are linked to the system by rubber tubing and plastic connectors. Reinforced plastic tubing, supplying the front and rear screen washers, is taped in with the electrical harness routed along the inside wings of the engine compartment to facilitate production. A similar arrangement is used to route the rear washer tubing from the vehicle 'A' post to the non return valve (10).

The windscreen wiper motor (2) is located in the plenum chamber on the driver's side and uses a conventional linkage arrangement to operate the wiper arms and blades (3). The rear wiper motor (11) is secured to the screen frame and drives a single wiper arm/blade (12) that parks horizontally behind a finisher panel, which also hides the washer jet (13). When fitted, the headlamp wiper motor (14) is installed in the lower rear of the headlamp unit and drives a wiper arm/blade assembly, which includes twin washer jets (18), see 84M7013.

WINDSCREEN WIPER AND WASHER OPERATION

The windscreen wipers and washers can only function with the starter switch turned to positions 1 or 2.

Raise or lower the multi-switch lever to operate the windscreen wipers only, from position O for each function, see 84M7013.

Single wipe

Raise the lever to position 1.
The wipers will continue to wipe for as long as the lever is held in this position.

Intermittent wipe

Lower the lever to position 2.
To vary the delay between wipes rotate the thumb wheel to the right to increase the delay; to the left to decrease the delay.

Continuous wipe, slow speed

Lower the lever to position 3.

Continuous wipe, fast speed

Lower the lever to position 4.

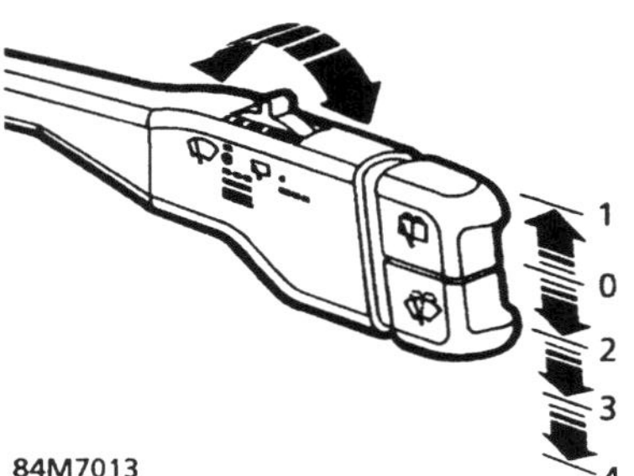

84M7013

NOTE: **Functions 1 to 4 will also operate when the lever is pulled rearwards. However, in this position the rear screen intermittent wipe will also function.**

Windscreen wash/wipe

Press and hold the lower button (5) at the end of the lever, see 84M7014.
The washers and wipers will operate for as long as the button is pressed. When the button is released the washers stop, but the wipers will continue for a further three full wipes before parking.

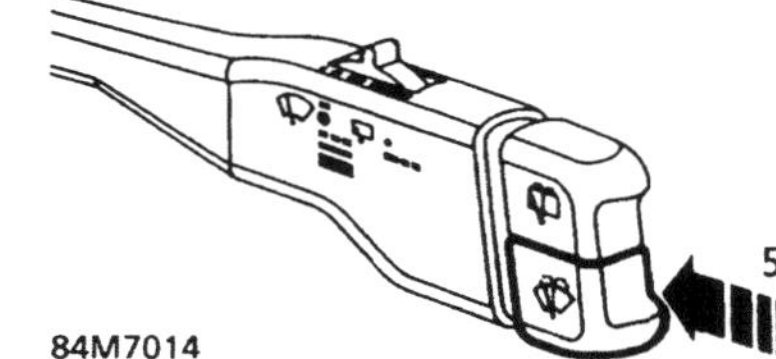

84M7014

A momentary press of the button will initiate a programmed wash/wipe cycle.After a short period the washers will stop and the wipers continue for a further three full wipes before parking. Moving the lever to any other front wipe position during the programmed wash/wipe will cancel the remainder of the programmed cycle.

If the fluid level in the washer reservoir is low, the programmed wash/wipe will only operate for as long as the button is pressed; there will be no timed wash or additional three wipes.

REAR SCREEN WIPER AND WASHER OPERATION

Intermittent wipe

Pull the multi-switch lever back to engage rear screen intermittent wipe, see 84M7015.
All functions of the windscreen wipers are also available in this position.

If the front wipers are operating in intermittent mode the rear wiper will function on every second operation of the front wipers.

84M7015

Rear screen wash/wipe

Press and hold the upper button (6) at the end of the lever, see 84M7016. The washer and wiper will operate for as long as the button is pressed. When the button is released the washer will stop, but the wiper will continue for a further three wipes before parking.

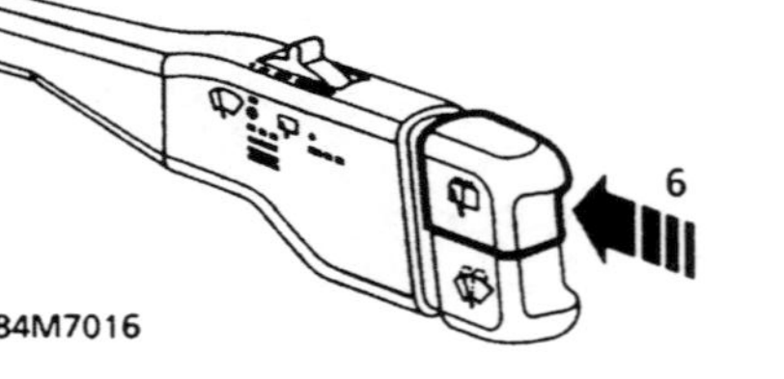

84M7016

A momentary press of the button will initiate a programmed wash/wipe cycle. After a short period, the washer will stop and the wiper will complete a further three wipes before parking. Moving the lever to any other rear wipe position during the programmed wash/wipe will cancel the remainder of the programmed cycle.

If the fluid level in the washer reservoir is low, the programmed wash/wipe will only operate for as long as the button is pressed; there will be no timed wash or additional three wipes.

The rear wash/wipe will not operate if the tailgate is open.

The rear wiper will operate automatically when reverse gear is selected, if the windscreen wipers are functioning in any mode.

HEADLIGHT WASH/WIPE

Headlight wash/wipe is controlled via a timer unit which is activated by the windscreen washer system, only when the headlamps are switched on.

Headlight wash/wipe functions on the first operation of the windscreen wash/wipe and thereafter at every other wash/wipe.

If the fluid level in the washer reservoir is low the headlight wash/wipe will not function at all.

WASHER RESERVOIR LOW SCREEN WASH LEVEL

The message centre will display 'LOW SCREEN WASH LEVEL' whenever the front or rear wash/wipe systems are used and the screen wash level is low. The message is also activated whenever the starter switch is turned to, or from position 2.

WIPER AND WASHER SYSTEM FAULTS

This section covers mechanical, fuse, and possible relay faults that could occur in the wiper and washer system. Visual checks of components within the system and relevant fuses should be carried out before undertaking detailed fault diagnosis procedures, which are covered on **TestBook** .

1. Symptom - Front Wiper System Inoperative.

POSSIBLE CAUSE	REMEDY
1. Blown wiper system fuse.	1. Check and replace fuse 25.
2. Loose wiper system electrical connections	2. Secure relevant connections.
3. Faulty relay.	3. Renew relay RL-1.
4. Faulty wiper motor.	4. Renew wiper motor.
5. Faulty multi-switch.	5. Refer to **TestBook** to confirm fault and renew multi-switch.

2. Symptom - Front Wipers Inoperative.

POSSIBLE CAUSE	REMEDY
1. Loose wiper motor electrical connections.	1. Check and secure all relevant connections.
2. Disengaged or loose wiper motor linkage.	2. Check, tighten, or renew linkage fixings.
3. Faulty wiper motor.	3. Renew wiper motor.

3. Symptom - Front Wipers Not Operating In Slow Or Fast Modes.

POSSIBLE CAUSE	REMEDY
1. Faulty relay.	1. Renew relay RL-8.

4. Symptoms - Windscreen Washer Jets - Inoperative Or Functioning Erratically.

POSSIBLE CAUSE	REMEDY
1. Empty washer reservoir.	1. Refill washer reservoir.
2. Washer jet/s blocked.	2. Clear obstruction with a needle or strand of wire.
3. Loose or disconnected washer tubes/connectors.	3. Check and secure all relevant connections.
4. Faulty non return valve.	4. Renew non return valve.
5. Screen wash flow restricted or blocked in washer tubes.	5. Check for kinks in washer tubes or that retaining clips are not over tightened.
6. Loose or disconnected washer pump multi-plug.	6. Reconnect multi-plug.
7. Faulty washer pump.	7. Renew washer pump.

5. Symptom - Rear Wiper Motor - Inoperative.

POSSIBLE CAUSE	REMEDY
1. Blown wiper motor fuse.	1. Check and renew fuse 15.
2. Loose or disconnected wiper motor plug lead.	2. Reconnect plug lead.
3. Faulty wiper motor.	3. Renew wiper motor.
4. Faulty multi-switch.	4. Refer to **TestBook** to confirm fault and renew multi-switch.

6. Symptom - Rear Wiper Arm/Blade Inoperative.

POSSIBLE CAUSE	REMEDY
1. Loose or disconnected wiper motor plug lead.	1. Reconnect plug lead.
2. Loose wiper arm fixing.	2. Secure fixing.

7. Symptom - Rear Screen Washer Jet - Inoperative or Functioning Erratically.

POSSIBLE CAUSE	REMEDY
1. Empty washer reservoir.	1. Refill washer reservoir.
2. Washer jet blocked.	2. Clear obstruction with a needle or strand of wire.
3. Loose or disconnected washer tubes/connectors.	3. Check and secure all relevant connections.
4. Faulty non return valve.	4. Renew non return valve.
5. Loose or disconnected washer pump multi-plug.	5. Reconnect multi-plug.
6. Screen wash flow restricted or blocked in washer tubes.	6. Check for kinks in washer tubes or that retaining clips are not over tightened.
7. Faulty or inoperative washer pump.	7. Renew washer pump.

8. Symptom - Headlight Wiper System Inoperative.

POSSIBLE CAUSE	REMEDY
1. Screen wash level in reservoir low or empty.	1. Refill washer reservoir.
2. Blown headlight wiper system fuse.	2. Check and renew fuse 38.
3. Loose or disconnected wiper motor multi-plug.	3. Reconnect multi-plug.
4. Faulty wiper motor relay.	4. Renew relay RL-11.
5. Faulty wiper motor.	5. Renew wiper motor.
6. Faulty multi-switch.	6. Refer to **TestBook** to confirm fault and renew multi-switch.

9. Symptom - Headlight Wiper Arm/Blade Inoperative.

POSSIBLE CAUSE	REMEDY
1. Loose or disconnected wiper motor multi-plug.	1. Reconnect multi-plug.
2. Loose wiper arm fixing.	2. Secure fixing

10. Symptom - Headlight Washer Jets - Inoperative Or Functioning Erratically.

POSSIBLE CAUSE	REMEDY
1. Empty washer reservoir.	1. Refill washer reservoir.
2. Washer jet/s blocked.	2. Clear obstruction with a needle or strand of wire.
3. Loose or disconnected washer tubes/connectors.	3. Check and secure all relevant connections.
4. Faulty non return valve.	4. Renew non return valve.
5. Screen wash flow restricted or blocked in washer tubes.	5. Check for kinks in washer tubes or that retaining clips are not over tightened.
6. Loose or disconnected headlight washer pump multi-plug.	6. Reconnect multi-plug.
7. Faulty or inoperative washer pump.	7. Renew washer pump.

11. Symptom - 'Low Screen Wash Level' - Shown On Message Centre.

POSSIBLE CAUSE	REMEDY
1. Screen wash level low in reservoir.	1. Refill washer reservoir.
2. Low level sensor plug loose or disconnected.	2. Reconnect sensor plug.
3. Faulty low level sensor.	3. Renew sensor.

HEADLAMP WIPER BLADE, ARM & WASHER JET

Service repair no - 84.25.06 - Blade
Service repair no - 84.25.02 - Arm

Blade

1. Lift wiper arm away from headlamp.
2. Remove wiper blade.

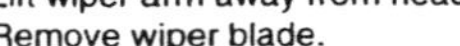

84M7020

Arm and Washer jet Assembly

3. Lift cover. Remove nut securing arm to spindle.

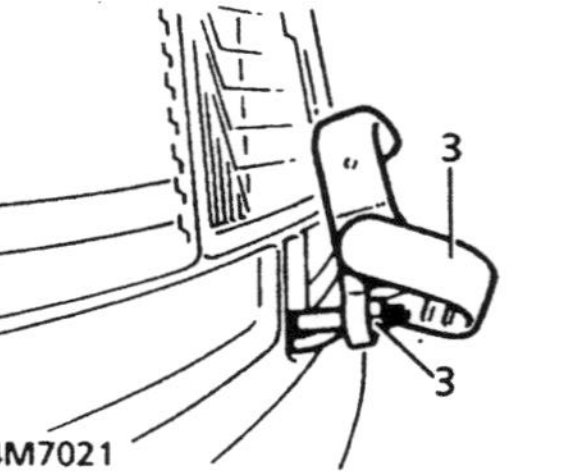

84M7021

4. Disconnect hose from washer jet.
5. Remove wiper arm/jet assembly from spindle.

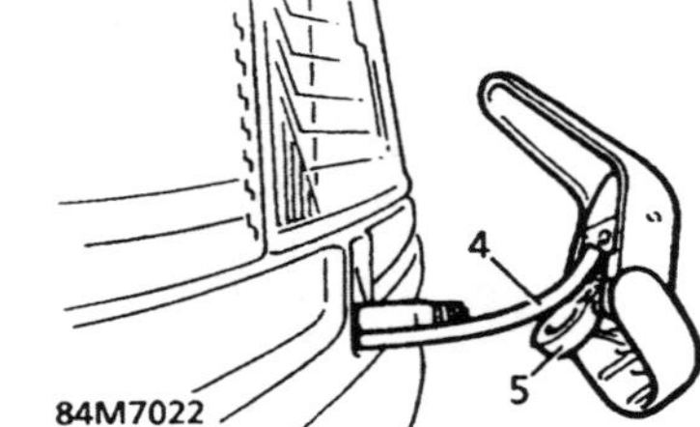

84M7022

Refit

6. Connect washer tube to jet.
7. Ensure wiper arm is in 'park' position.
8. Position wiper arm to spindle. Set wiper arm horizontal.
9. Secure wiper arm with nut. Tighten to ***10 Nm. (7 lbf.ft)***. Secure cover.

Blade

10. Clip blade into wiper arm.

HEADLAMP WIPER MOTOR

Service repair no - 84.25.12

Remove

1. Remove relevant wiper blade. ***See this section.***
2. Remove relevant headlamp assembly. ***See ELECTRICAL, Repair.***
3. Release wiper motor multiplug from bracket.

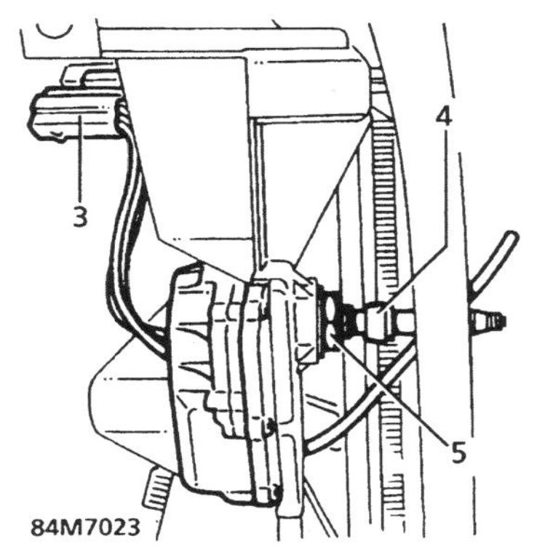

84M7023

4. Remove spindle seal.
5. Remove nut and flat washer securing motor to headlamp.
6. Remove wiper motor.

Refit

7. Reverse removal procedure.
8. Tighten motor securing nut to ***10 Nm. (7 lbf.ft).***

WIPER MOTOR AND LINKAGE

Service repair no - 84.15.11

Remove

1. Remove air intake plenum. ***See HEATING AND VENTILATION, Repair.***
2. Remove covers from wiper spindles.
3. Remove nuts and flat washers securing wiper spindle housings.

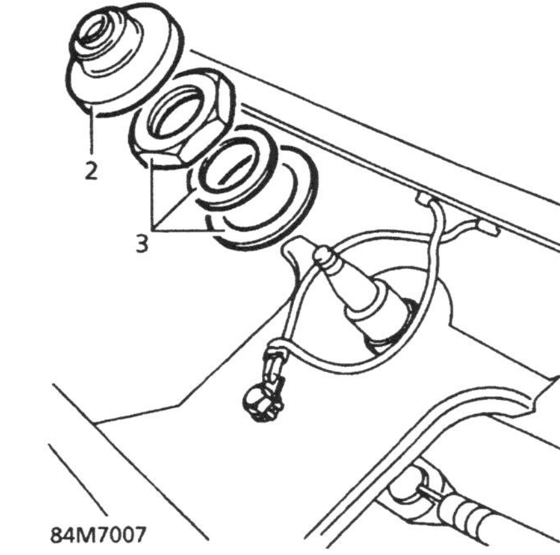

84M7007

4. Disconnect screen heater multiplug. Release multiplug clip from scuttle side panel on driver's side of vehicle.
5. Remove 6 bolts securing scuttle side panel. Remove panel.

5

84M7008

6. Disconnect multiplug from wiper motor.

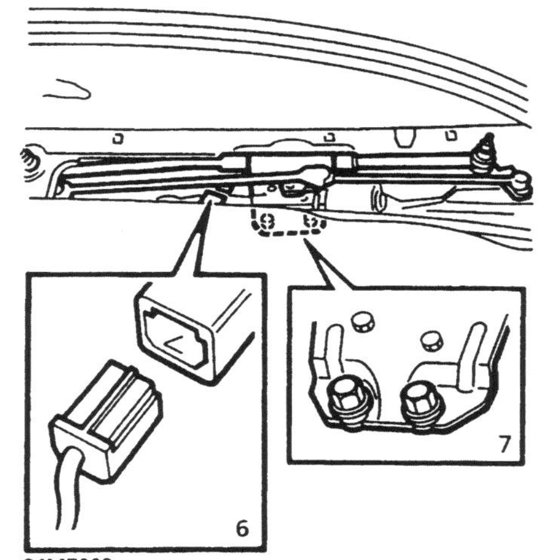

84M7009

7. Remove 2 bolts securing wiper motor to scuttle. Remove wiper motor/linkage assembly.

Refit

8. Position wiper motor/linkage assembly. Fit bolts loosely securing motor to scuttle panel.
9. Position scuttle side panel. Secure with bolts.
10. Connect screen heater multiplug. Secure multiplug clip to scuttle panel.
11. Secure wiper spindle housings to scuttle with nuts and flat washers. Tighten to ***11 Nm. (8 lbf.ft)***
12. Tighten motor securing bolts to ***7 Nm. (5 lbf.ft)***
13. Connect multiplug to wiper motor.
14. Fit covers over wiper spindles.
15. Fit air intake plenum. ***See HEATING AND VENTILATION, Repair.***

REAR WIPER ARM

Service repair no - 84.35.01 - Wiper Arm
Service repair no - 84.35.02 - Wiper Blade

Remove

1. Remove wiper arm nut cover. Remove nut.

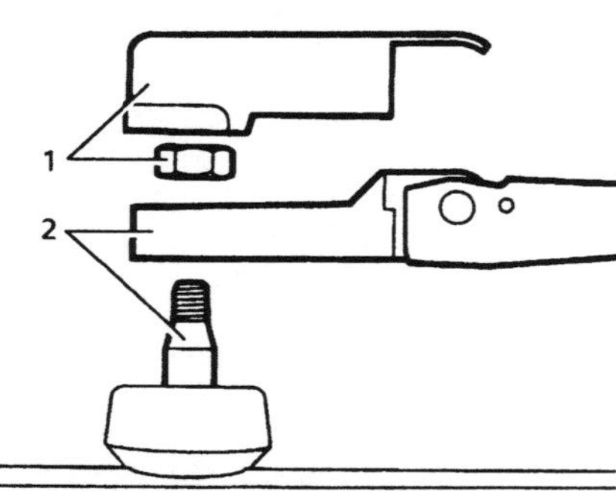

84M7000

2. Remove wiper arm from motor spindle.

Wiper Blade

3. Release clip. Remove blade from arm

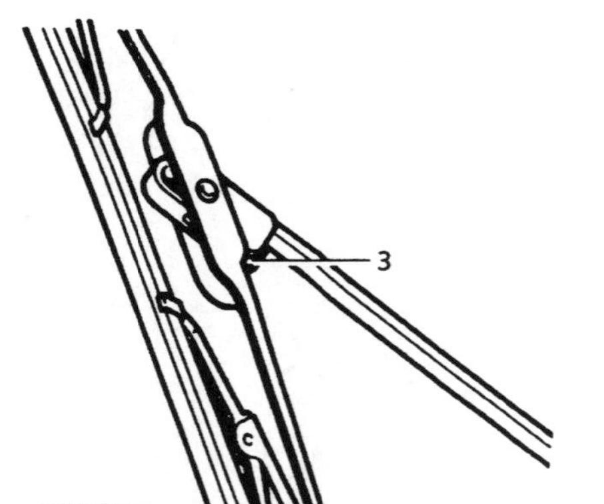

84M7001

Refit

4. Fit wiper blade to arm.
5. Position arm to motor spindle. Secure with nut. Tighten to ***17 Nm. (12 lbf.ft)***
6. Fit nut cover.

REAR WIPER MOTOR

Service repair no - 84.35.12

Remove

1. Remove wiper arm nut cover. Remove nut.

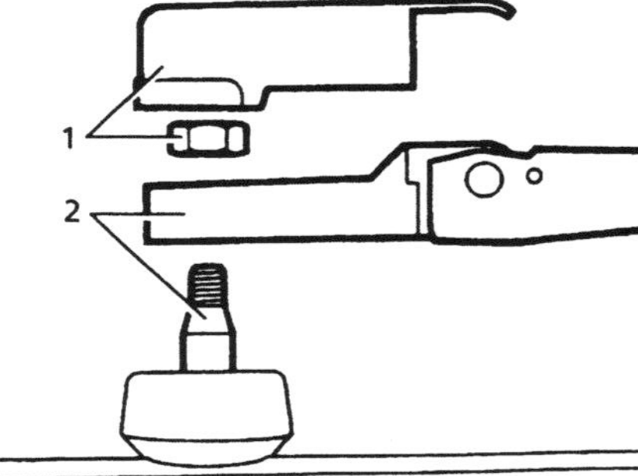

84M7002

2. Remove wiper arm from motor spindle.
3. Remove motor spindle cover, retaining nut and seal.

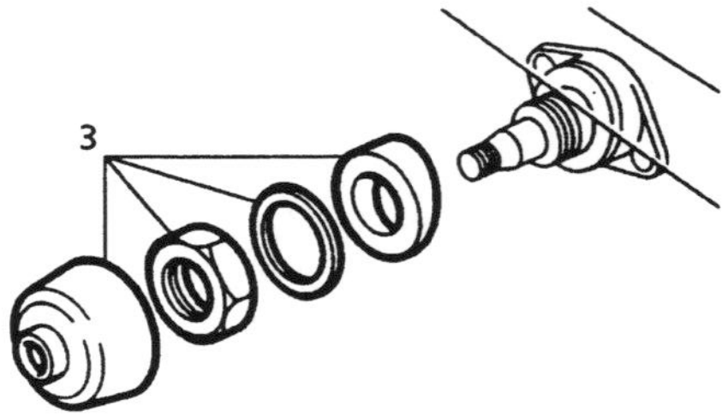

84M7003

4. Open tailgate.
5. Remove 6 screws securing wiper motor cover.

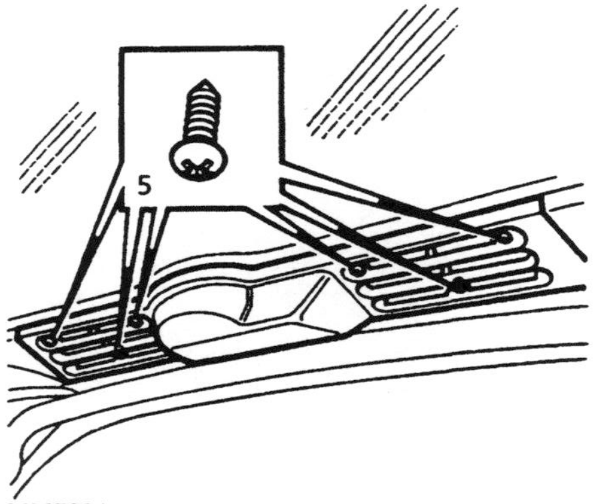

84M7004

6. Disconnect motor multiplug.

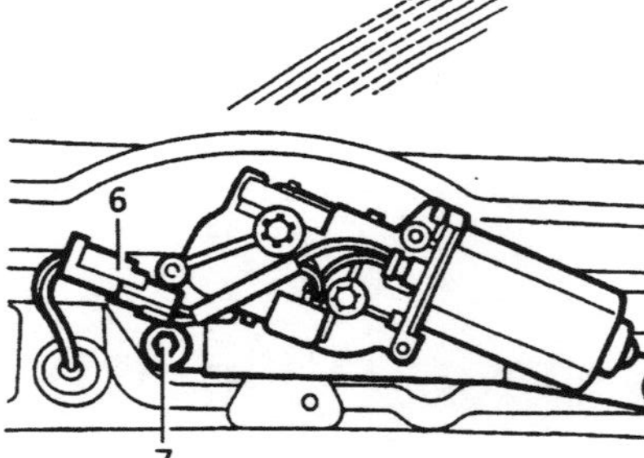

84M7005

7. Remove 2 bolts securing motor. Remove motor.
8. Remove 4 bolts securing mounting plate to motor.
9. Release multiplug holder. Remove mounting plate.
10. Remove sealing rubber from motor spindle.

84M7006

Refit

11. Fit sealing rubber to motor spindle.
12. Fit mounting plate. Secure with bolts.
13. Connect multiplug holder to mounting plate.
14. Position motor. Secure with bolts. Tighten to ***7 Nm. (5 lbf.ft)***
15. Connect multiplug.
16. Position motor cover. Secure with screws.
17. Close tailgate.
18. Fit motor spindle seal. Fit retaining nut. Tighten to ***4 Nm. (3 lbf.ft).*** Fit cover.
19. Position wiper arm. Secure with retaining nut. Tighten to ***17 Nm. (12 lbf.ft).*** Fit cover.

WASHER JET - FRONT

Service repair no - 84.10.08

Remove

1. Disconnect washer tube elbow from base of jet.

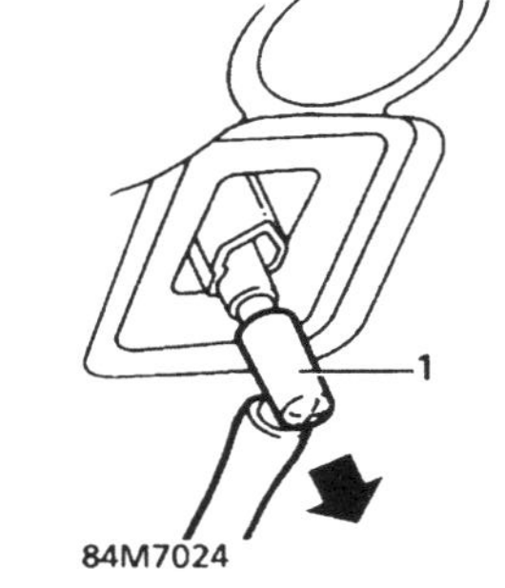

84M7024

2. Remove jet from retainer.

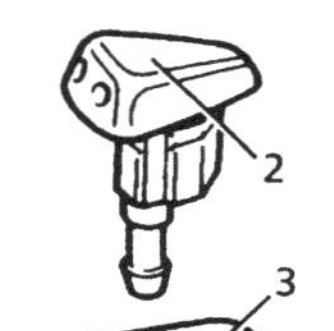

84M7025

3. Remove retainer.

Refit

4. Reverse removal procedure.

WASHER JET - REAR

Service repair no - 84.30.09

Remove

1. Prise washer jet from tailgate.

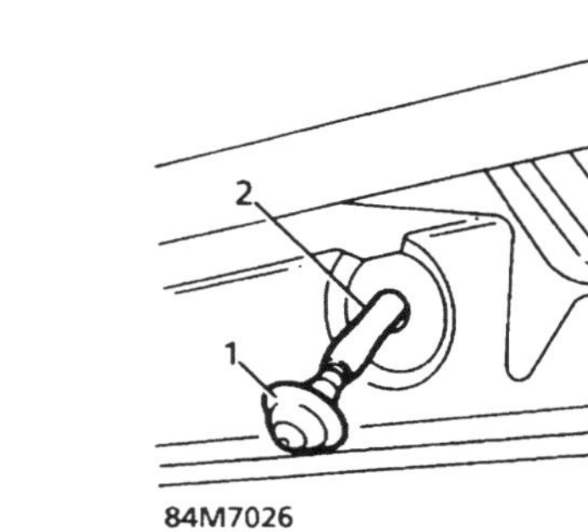

84M7026

CAUTION: Do not use a metal lever, or painted surface may be damaged.

2. Remove washer jet from tube.

Refit

3. Reverse removal procedure.

WASHER PUMP

Service repair no - 84.10.21

Remove

1. Raise the vehicle.

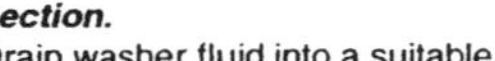

WARNING: Support on safety stands.

2. Release washer reservoir for access. ***See this section.***
3. Drain washer fluid into a suitable container.
4. Disconnect pump multiplug and hose.
5. Remove pump from reservoir. Collect seal and discard.

Refit

6. Fit seal and pump to reservior.
7. Connect multiplug and hose.
8. Refit washer reservoir. ***See this section.***
9. Remove safety stands. Lower vehicle.

WASHER RESERVOIR

Service repair no - 84.10.01

Remove

1. Raise the vehicle.

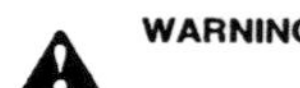

WARNING: Support on safety stands.

2. Remove RH wheel arch liner. ***See CHASSIS AND BODY, Repair.***
3. Remove bolt and screw securing filler neck to chassis and radiator bracket.

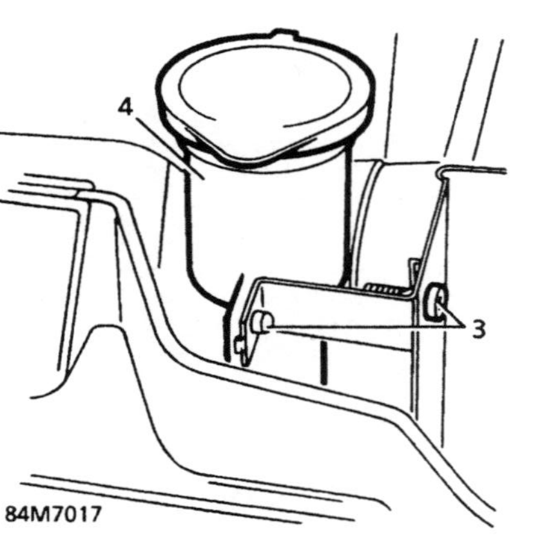

84M7017

4. Remove filler neck.
5. Remove 2 bolts securing reservoir to chassis.

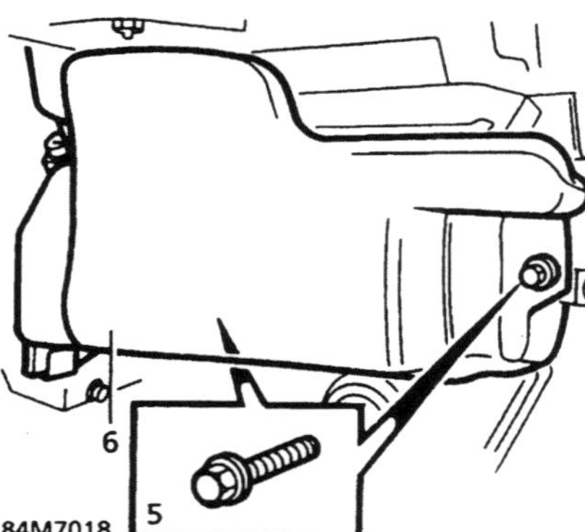

84M7018

6. Release reservoir from mounting for access to washer pumps.
7. Disconnect multiplugs and hoses from 3 washer pumps.

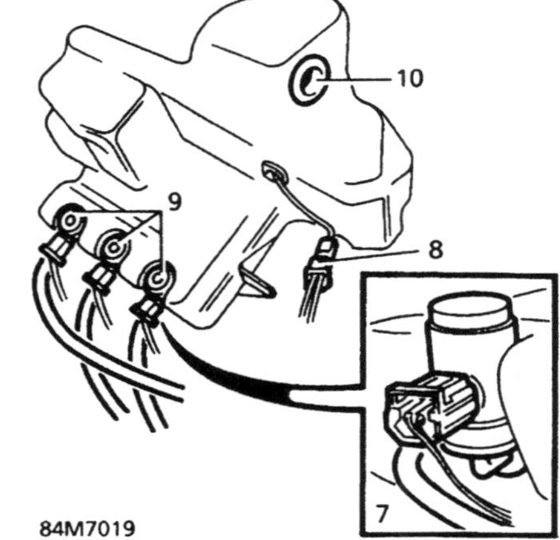

84M7019

8. Disconnect fluid level indicator multiplug.
9. Remove washer pumps and seals from reservoir.
10. Remove filler neck seal.

Refit

11. Reverse removal procedure.

FRONT WIPER ARM

Service repair no - 84.15.01 - Pair
Service repair no - 84.15.02 - Each

Remove

1. Remove cover from wiper arm nut.

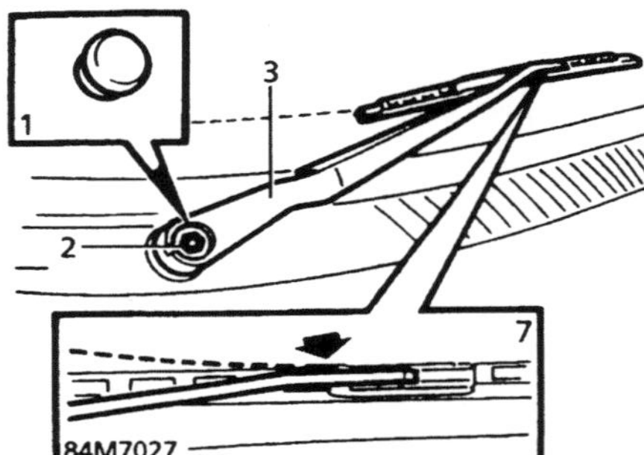

84M7027

2. Remove nut securing wiper arm to spindle.
3. Remove wiper arm/blade assembly.
4. If necessary, release clip and remove blade from wiper arm.

Refit

5. If necessary, fit blade to wiper arm.
6. Ensure motor is in "park" position.
7. Position wiper arm/blade assembly. Ensure tip of wiper arm is level with top edge of screen obscuration band.
8. Secure wiper arm with nut. Tighten to ***19 Nm. (14 lbf.ft)***
9. Lift wiper arm slightly. Remove pin.
10. Fit cover to wiper arm nut.
11. Operate wipers on wet screen to ensure correct setting.

FRONT WIPER BLADE

Service repair no - 84.15.05 - Pair
Service repair no - 84.15.06 - Each

Remove

1. Raise wiper arm.
2. Release clip securing blade to wiper arm.

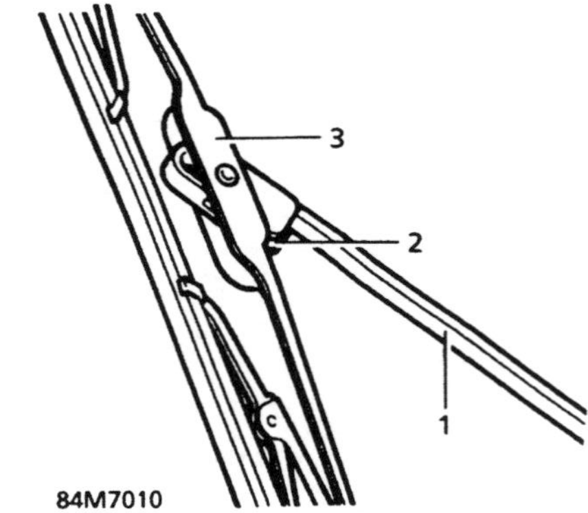

84M7010

3. Remove wiper blade.

Refit

4. Position blade. Push into arm until clip engages in slot.
5. Lower wiper arm.

WIPER STALK

Service repair no - 84.15.34

Remove

1. Remove steering column nacelle. ***See STEERING, Repair.***
2. Remove 2 screws securing wiper stalk to steering column.
3. Release stalk for access to multiplug.

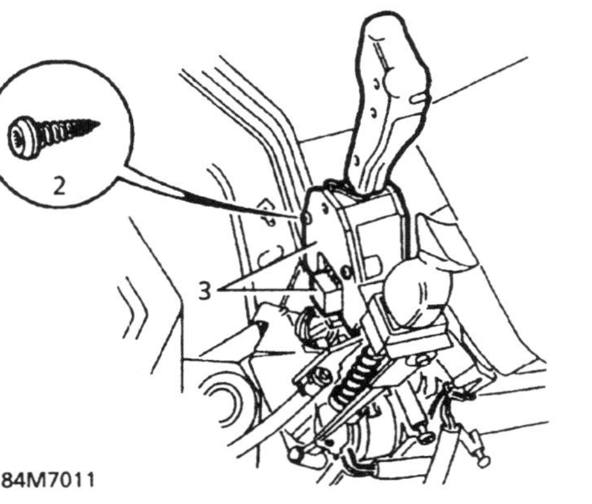

84M7011

4. Disconnect multiplug. Remove wiper stalk.

Refit

5. Reverse removal procedure.

CONTENTS

86 - ELECTRICAL

CONTENTS

This page is intentionally left blank

LOCATION OF BeCM COMPONENTS

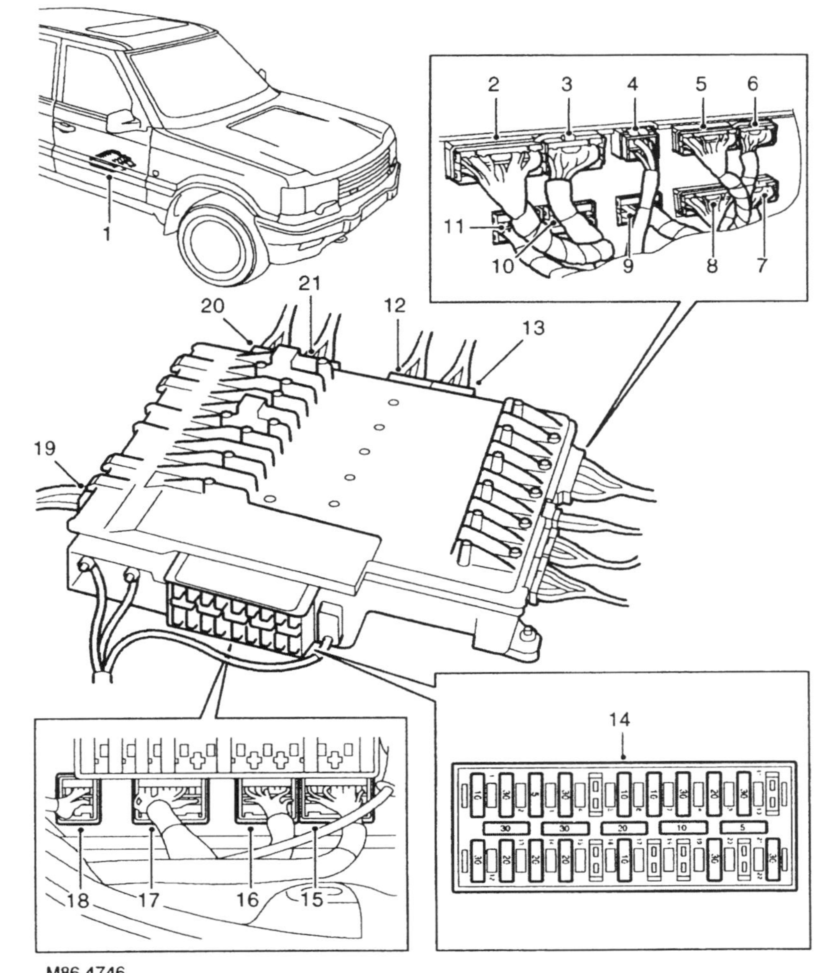

M86 4746

1. Body electrical Control Module (BeCM)
2. Connector C325 (C1283) - 18 pin grey
3. Connector C323 (C1284) - 12 pin grey
4. Connector C324 (C1292) - 4 pin natural
5. Connector C120 (C1281) - 14 pin yellow
6. Connector C113 (C1282) - 10 pin yellow
7. Connector C626 (C1287) - 20 pin black
8. Connector C362 (C1286) - 16 pin black
9. Connector C326 (C1285) - 20 pin blue
10. Connector C114 (C1289) - 20 pin green
11. Connector C112 (C1288) - 16 pin green

From 99MY connector numbers and colour differences shown in brackets

12. Connector C625 (C1290) - 12 pin white
13. Connector C361 (C1291) - 18 pin white
14. BeCM Fusebox
15. Connector C255 (C1279) - 20 pin white
16. Connector C256 (C1280) - 16 pin white
17. Connector C257 (C1278) - 20 pin yellow
18. Connector C907 (C1277) - 8 pin blue (black)
19. Connector C258 (C1276) - 10 pin white
20. Connector C912 (C0877) - 12 pin green
21. Connector C624 (C1293) - 4 pin natural

BeCM CONTROL SCHEMATIC

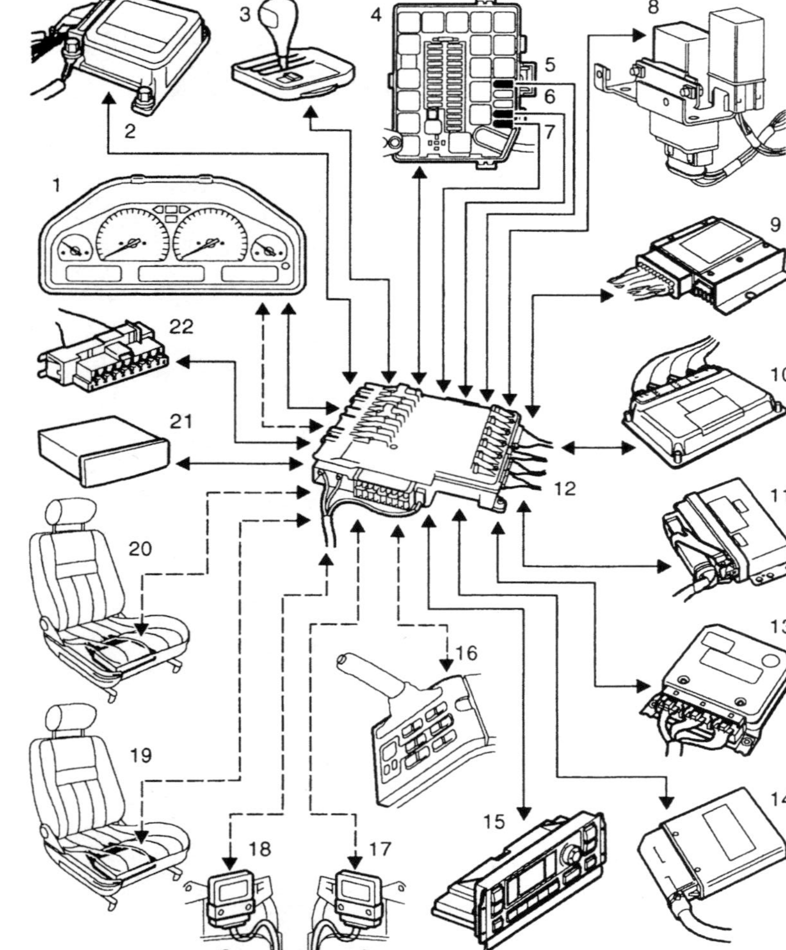

A. Serial data bus
B. Direct link

1. Instrument pack
2. SRS Diagnostic Control Unit (DCU)
3. Selector lever display panel (Automatic transmission vehicles only)
4. Engine compartment fusebox
5. Maxi fuse 1 - Power supply
6. Maxi fuse 4 - Power supply
7. Maxi fuse 5 - Power supply
8. Cruise control ECU
9. Transfer box ECU
10. Engine Control Module (ECM)
11. Electronic Automatic Transmission (EAT) ECU
12. ABS ECU (99MY shown)
13. Electronic Air Suspension (EAS) ECU
14. HEVAC ECU
15. Centre console switch pack
16. RH door outstation
17. LH door outstation
18. RH seat outstation
19. LH seat outstation
20. BeCM
21. ICE unit
22. Diagnostic socket

BODY ELECTRICAL CONTROL MODULE (BeCM) - DESCRIPTION

General

The Body electrical Control Module (BeCM) is located below the front RH seat and is secured to the floor pan with two nuts and a screw.

The BeCM controls, monitors and provides power supplies to many of the vehicle electrical functions. The BeCM interfaces with other Electronic Control Units (ECU's) via hardwired connections or via a digital serial data bus as follows:

- SRS DCU
- ABS ECU
- HEVAC ECU
- Cruise control ECU
- Engine Control Module
- EAS ECU
- Transfer box ECU
- EAT ECU
- Instrument pack

The BeCM also communicates with several outstations via a digital serial data bus. The data bus allows the BeCM to 'talk' to the outstations by passing electrical information through the same wires. Each data bus comprises five wires as follows:

- Feed wire   Battery voltage supply
- Earth wire   Vehicle earth
- Clock wire   Reference signal
- Signal wire   Transmits digital signals
- Direction wire   Identifies direction of signal

The data bus reduces the number of wires required to perform the various electrical functions. Each wire in the data bus is duplicated to increase the reliability of the connections.

The BeCM has two modes of operation; activation mode or sleep mode. A number of inputs to the BeCM will change the state of the BeCM from sleep to activation mode. Sleep mode is required to avoid excessive drain on the vehicle battery when the vehicle is not being used.

Sleep mode is entered when certain timers have 'timed out' (i.e. courtesy lights go off) and all activation inputs have been inactive for more than two minutes. If the vehicle is unlocked in sleep mode, the current used by the BeCM is 30 mA. If the vehicle alarm is armed in sleep mode, the current used by the BeCM increases to 40 mA.

When an activation input is sensed and the BeCM 'wakes up', the current used by the BeCM increases to approximately 1 Amp.

The BeCM is connected to the other ECU's and the electrical functions it controls by nineteen connectors. Tables containing a description of the connector pins and the functions they serve are detailed later in this section.

The BeCM has its own integral fusebox containing 22 fuses. The fuses are accessible via an access panel located on the side of the front RH seat trim panel. Each fuse protects one or more electrical functions controlled by the BeCM.

The function and rating of each fuse is shown in the following table. The outstations each receive two feeds from the battery to supply feeds for window and locking operations and seat functions from different fuses.

Fuse	Rating	Function
1	10A	Instrument pack, Clock, Radio, Centre console switch pack
2	30A	RH rear window, LH/RH seat heater
3	5A	EAT ECU - Battery supply
4	30A	Transfer box ECU - Battery supply
5	-	Spare
6	10A	Rear view mirror dip, Spare 1 ignition, Sun visor illumination. Up to 99MY: EAT ECU Ignition supply, Transfer box ECU ignition supply
7	10A	Up to 99MY: Airbag. From 99MY: EAT ECU Ignition supply, Transfer box ECU ignition supply
8	30A	Car phone, radio, front cigar lighter, HEVAC. Up to 99MY: Aerial amplifier
9	20A	LH/RH front ICE amplifier, LH/RH door Battery 2
10	30A	RH seat Battery 1, RH seat battery 2, RH seat lumbar, Rear cushion battery 1, Fore/aft adjustment battery 1, Front cushion battery 2, backrest battery 2, headrest battery 2
11	-	Spare (When spare fuse of at least 5 Amps is inserted, transfer box moves to neutral position)
12	30A	Heated rear window, LH rear window
13	20A	Shift interlock solenoid, Sunroof Up to 99MY: Key inhibit solenoid
14	30A	LH/RH rear central door locking, Fuel flap release, trailer battery supply
15	20A	LH/RH rear ICE amplifiers, Courtesy/Load space lamps, ICE subwoofer, RH rear courtesy lamp, RF remote receiver, Tail door central door locking, Rear wiper
16	30A	Spare
17	10A	Brake switch feed Up to 99MY: HEVAC ignition signal, Air suspension switches
18	30A	6th outstation battery supply (not fitted)
19	-	Spare
20	30A	LH seat battery 1, LH seat battery 2, LH seat lumbar, Rear cushion battery 1, Fore/aft adjustment battery 1, Backrest battery 2, Front cushion battery 2, Headrest battery 2
21	-	Spare
22	30A	LH door battery 1 (front window only), RH door battery 2 (front window only)

The following text gives a brief overview of BeCM functionality and interfaces with other electrical components.

Engine Management

On all models, the BeCM receives an engine speed signal from the EDC ECM or the ECM. This signal is passed to the instrument pack for tachometer operation and is also passed to the EAS ECU and the EAT ECU.

Electronic Diesel Control (EDC)

The BeCM inputs a remobilisation code signal to the EDC ECM when the vehicle is in an unarmed state.

On 95 MY vehicles the BeCM transmits a single remobilisation code to the EDC ECM. When the BeCM is satisfied that the vehicle is in an unarmed state, engine cranking is permitted. There is no MIL warning lamp illumination to confirm that the code has been accepted.

On 96MY onwards Diesel vehicles, as on 95MY vehicles, the EDC ECM does not respond to confirm that the remobilisation signal from the BeCM has been accepted. When the vehicle is in an unarmed condition, the BeCM continually transmits the engine remobilisation code at 144 ms intervals from the ignition being turned on. The code originates from the EDC ECM with each ECM having a different code. If a new EDC ECM or BeCM is fitted, TestBook must be used to input the code to the BeCM before the ignition is turned on.

Engine Control Module (GEMS up to 99MY)

When the vehicle is in an unarmed condition, the BeCM will transmit and engine remobilisation code 48 ms after the ignition is turned on until the BeCM receives an acknowledgement that the ECM has received the correct code.

The ECM confirms receipt of the correct code by signalling the BeCM to illuminate the check engine warning lamp and allow engine cranking when requested. The ECM also enables the engine fuelling system on receipt of the correct code from the BeCM.

The code sent from the BeCM is unique to the vehicle and the same code is transmitted each time the ignition is turned on. If the BeCM is replaced the new BeCM will automatically generate the same code. If the GEMS ECM is replaced, TestBook must be used to input the code to the new ECM.

Engine Control Module (Bosch M5.2.1 from 99MY)

The remobilisation strategy is the same as that described for 96MY Diesel vehicles. The BeCM repeatedly transmits the remobilisation code to the ECM at intervals of 144 ms. The code originates from the ECM with each ECM having a different code. If a new ECM or BeCM is fitted, TestBook must be used to input the code to the BeCM before the ignition is turned on.

Security

Locking

There are six modes of vehicle locking used on the vehicle: sill locking, slam locking, key CDL locking, remote CDL locking, key superlocking and remote superlocking. The BeCM controls all locking and alarm functions.

Sill locking

Sill locking is achieved by depressing either of the front door sill buttons when both front doors are closed. All doors and the tail door will CDL lock, but immobilisation and the alarm system will not enable. Sill locking operates independent of key-in and ignition state.

On vehicles from 96.5MY an accidental sill locking feature was introduced to prevent accidental sill locking of the doors. If the sill button on either of the front doors is depressed within 0.5 seconds of that door being closed, all doors will unlock.

If the ignition is on and the inertia switch is tripped, all doors, including the tail door, will unlock. Further re-locking is prevented until one of the front doors is opened with the key removed from the ignition.

Slam locking

Slam locking is only available on vehicles up to 96.5MY. Slam locking is performed by depressing either of the front door sill buttons with the door open and then closing the door. All the doors and the tail door will CDL lock and the alarm will be armed in perimetric mode with cranking disabled and immobilisation activated. If the vehicle is slam locked with the key in the ignition or the ignition on, all doors will immediately unlock when the door is closed.

Key CDL locking

A single turn of the key in the driver's door lock towards the rear of the vehicle will cause all the doors including the tail door to CDL lock. The alarm system will enter perimetric mode with cranking disabled and immobilisation active.

Remote CDL locking

A single press of the lock button on the remote handset will cause all the doors including the tail door to CDL lock. The alarm system will enter perimetric mode with cranking disabled and immobilisation active.

Key superlocking

A double turn of the key within two seconds in the driver's door lock towards the rear of the vehicle will cause all the doors including the tail door to superlock providing that they and the bonnet are closed. The alarm system will enter perimetric mode with cranking disabled and immobilisation active.

Remote superlocking

A double press of the lock button within two seconds on the remote handset will cause all the doors including the tail door to superlock providing that they and the bonnet are closed. The alarm system will have crank disable and immobilisation active and if all windows and sunroof are closed the volumetric and perimetric systems will be activated. If any of the windows or the sunroof are open, then only the perimetric system will be activated. Remote superlocking is prevented if the key is in the ignition.

Lazy Locking

The lazy locking procedure will close all open windows and the sunroof when locking the vehicle. Lazy locking is initiated by holding the key turned to the lock position or holding the locking button on the remote handset pressed for more than one second. The windows close simultaneously, followed by the sunroof after the last window has closed.

In some markets, the key must be held in the lock position or the remote handset lock button held depressed until all windows and the sunroof are closed. If the button is released prematurely, the windows and sunroof will stop and a mislock will sound.

Mislock

A mislock is indicated by two short 'beeps' from the alarm sounder or by three short flashes of the courtesy lamps depending on the market programmed. In some markets there is no audible or visual mislock warning. The mislock warning will not operate if the ignition is in position I or II.

The message centre in the instrument pack will display the cause of the mislock, i.e. 'RHF DOOR OPEN'. The message will be cancelled when the cause of the mislock has been rectified.

Auto Relock

When a valid unlock request is received from the remote handset and all windows are closed, the ultrasonic sensor is activated for a period of 60 seconds or until movement is detected or:
- a door is opened or closed
- the tail door is opened
- the key is inserted in the ignition
- the ignition is turned to position I
- the vehicle is re-locked with the key or the remote handset.

If, after 60 seconds, none of the above has occurred, the vehicle will relock to its previous locked condition.

Resynchronisation

On vehicles up to 97MY, resynchronisation is achieved by locking or unlocking the driver's door using the vehicle key with 30 seconds of locking, superlocking or unlocking using the remote handset. The BeCM monitors the condition of the driver's door CDL switch to initiate the resynchronisation.

On vehicles from 97MY, friendly resynchronisation was introduced on vehicles with passive immobilisation. A remote handset that is not synchronised to the BeCM will automatically be resynchronised when the key is inserted in the ignition without using the vehicle key or Emergency Key Access (EKA) procedure.

The resynchronisation uses a pick-up coil in the remote handset and a passive coil located around the ignition barrel. The passive coil provides a signal for the remote handset to transmit an unlock signal to remobilise the vehicle.

Emergency Key Access (EKA)

If the vehicle is locked using the remote handset and loss or failure of the handset occurs, the vehicle can be unlocked and the alarm disarmed by entering a four digit code using the key in the driver's door lock. The code is either a unique code for the vehicle and can be found on the security information card or a default value obtainable from the factory.

EKA procedure - Vehicles up to 96MY

1. Unlock driver's door with the key.
2. Open the door and the alarm sounder will sound twice. If the key is inserted in the ignition at this point and an attempt is made to start the engine, the engine will not crank and the message centre will display 'ENGINE DISABLED PRESS REMOTE OR USE KEY CODE'.
3. Close the driver's door and ensure that all doors, tail door and bonnet are closed.
4. Turn the key to the lock position.

NOTE: The code cannot be entered if the message centre displays 'KEY CODE LOCKOUT'.

5. Enter the code as follows. At each turn of the key to the lock or unlock position, the side lamps warning lamp in the instrument pack will flash to indicate that the key turn has been recognised.
6. Enter the first digit. If the first digit is 2, turn and release the key two times in the unlock direction.
7. Enter the second digit. If the second digit is five, turn and release the key five times in the lock direction.
8. Enter the third digit. If the third digit is four, turn and release the key four times in the unlock direction.
9. Enter the fourth digit. If the fourth digit is two, turn and release the key two times in the lock direction.
10. Turn the key to the unlock direction and, provided that the code has been entered correctly, all the doors and the tail door will be unlocked and the alarm will be partially disarmed.

When the EKA code has been entered, the security LED will continue to flash in deterrent mode to show that the alarm is partially disarmed and will be triggered if the bonnet is opened.

If the EKA code is entered incorrectly, on the final unlock turn of the key, a mislock will sound and the remaining doors and the tail door will remain locked and the alarm partially armed. If five incorrect attempts are made to enter the code, the BeCM enters a ten minute 'lockout' period. Further attempts to enter the code will cause a mislock to sound each time the key is turned. During the lockout period, the message centre displays 'KEY CODE LOCKOUT'.

If either of the front doors are opened while entering the code, a mislock will sound and the door will need to be closed and key locked and the code re-entered from the beginning. This will not count as an incorrect entry.

With the vehicle in EKA mode, if the remote handset unlock button is pressed all doors will be unlocked and the alarm disarmed. The lock button will not operate while entering the EKA code.

EKA procedure - Vehicles from 96MY

If the vehicle is locked using the remote handset and loss or failure of the handset occurs, the vehicle can be unlocked and the alarm disarmed by entering a four digit code using the key in the driver's door lock as described in the EKA procedure for vehicles up to 96MY with the following exceptions:

1. If the vehicle had not been locked with the remote handset, then in step 4, the key must be turned four times to the lock position.
2. The number of incorrect attempts is reduced to three and the lockout period increased to thirty minutes.

Lazy Seats

The lazy seat function is only available on vehicles with memory seats. Holding the unlock button on the remote handset for longer than 1.5 seconds will cause automatic movement of the driver's seat, door mirrors and instrument panel illumination to a predetermined position. The lazy seat operation is as programmed in one of the two memory seat configurations corresponding to the initiating remote handset.

The vehicle must be in a superlocked condition with volumetric sensors active and the alarm armed. Once the lazy seat function is operating the remote handset unlock button can be released. Opening any door or locking the vehicle will stop the seats and mirrors moving.

Security LED

The security LED operates in two modes; confirmation of lock status and theft deterrent.

In the confirmation mode, the LED will flash rapidly for ten seconds to show that the lock request is successful. After the ten second period the LED will flash at the slower deterrent mode rate. If a panel is left open or the vehicle has been slam locked, the LED will remain unlit.

If a lock request is made and one or more panels remain open, when the panels are closed, the LED will flash rapidly for ten seconds to confirm lock status and will then change to a slower flash in deterrent mode.

Alarm Audible and Visual Warnings

Audible warnings

Audible warnings can be generated from a klaxon, battery backed up sounder (BBUS - from 96MY) or the vehicle horns. Some markets do not have any audible alarm warnings. If a klaxon or BBUS is used the output will be pulsed and synchronised with the visual warning. If the vehicle horns are used the output will be continuous.

Mislock warnings are always generated from either the klaxon or the BBUS.

Visual warnings

External visual warnings are dependant on the selected market, but are generated from either the hazard warning indicators, side and tail lamps or head and tail lamps.

If the hazard warning lamps are operating when a visual warning using the hazard warning lamps is required, the visual warning will be cancelled. If the side or headlamps are on when a visual warning using the side or headlamps is required, the lamps will flash off instead of on.

Battery Backed-Up Sounder (BBUS) - certain vehicles from 96MY

The BBUS was introduced into some markets from 96MY onwards and since the drive requirements are different from the klaxon, the BBUS is market programmable.

The BBUS has its own internal power supply. If the vehicle battery or the BBUS is disconnected, the BBUS will be triggered and will sound for approximately 4.5 minutes.

To disconnect the BBUS, the ignition should be turned on and then off. The BBUS connector must be disconnected within 17 seconds of the ignition being turned off or the BBUS will be triggered. When the BBUS is sounding it can be cancelled by unlocking the vehicle with the key or the remote handset only if it is connected to the vehicle harness.

Ultrasonic Sensor

The ultrasonic sensor is located adjacent to the left hand 'B/C' post on the interior headlining and is used to detect movement within the vehicle when the volumetric function of the alarm system is active.

Self check

Each time the ignition is switched off, the BeCM initiates the ultrasonic sensor to perform a self check procedure to ensure correct operation. When the ignition is switched off the sensor is activated for a period of 60 seconds or until the driver's door has been opened and closed or the vehicle has been locked using the key or the remote handset.

During the self check, the sensor expects to detect the driver leaving the vehicle. If the sensor detects no movement but a driver's door open and close sequence has occurred, the BeCM logs this as a sensor failure. If five consecutive failures are logged, the BeCM will log a sensor failure and 'ALARM FAULT' will be displayed on the message centre when an attempt to superlock the vehicle is made or the ignition key is inserted in the ignition switch.

When a valid self check sequence occurs, the BeCM will set the log counter back to zero. If no movement is detected during a self check and a driver's door open and close sequence has not occurred, the BeCM will not count this as a failure or a valid self check.

Nuisance triggering

When a valid superlock request is received and all windows are closed and set, the BeCM will wait 5 seconds before activating the ultrasonic sensor to allow the air in the vehicle to settle. After the 5 second period, the BeCM monitors, via the sensor, for movement within the vehicle.

If movement is detected in this 10 second period the alarm will be triggered and superlocking will be prevented. If no movement is detected, the vehicle will superlock and volumetric sensing will be active to monitor the vehicle interior.

Perimetric Alarm

The doors, tail door and bonnet are all monitored by the BeCM. Microswitches within the door latch mechanisms, and a plunger type switch for the bonnet, signal the BeCM if the panel is opened. If the alarm is armed, the BeCM will trigger the alarm sounder and visual indications if a panel is opened.

Immobilisation

Refer to 'Engine Management' earlier in this description and operation for immobilisation information.

Passive immobilisation

On petrol and Diesel vehicles from 96MY, a market programmable passive immobilisation feature was introduced. The feature automatically immobilises the vehicle when the ignition is turned off even if the vehicle is not locked.

When the key is removed from the ignition and the driver's door opened, the BeCM will immobilise the engine after a 30 second period. If the ignition is turned off or the key is removed from the ignition and the driver's door is not opened, the BeCM will immobilise the ignition after a 10 minute period.

Unlocking the vehicle with the remote handset or using the EKA procedure, if the key is not inserted in the ignition within 30 seconds, the BeCM will change to the immobilised condition. Inserting the key in the ignition causes the passive coil around the ignition switch to be energised. The passive coil remains energised until a valid code from the remote handset is received or the BeCM goes into sleep mode.

Remote handset

The remote handset locking signals are encoded via a rolling code algorithm. The BeCM has a capture range of 100 codes after the previously received value. The remote handset can be operated up to 100 times, out of range of the vehicle before synchronisation with the BeCM is lost. The code sequence is stored in the BeCM RAM and resynchronisation will be required if the battery is disconnected for a length of time.

If the remote handset code moves outside the BeCM capture range, resynchronisation can be achieved by locking or unlocking the driver's door using the vehicle key within 30 seconds of locking, superlocking or unlocking using the remote handset. The BeCM monitors the condition of the driver's door CDL switch to initiate the resynchronisation.

If the vehicle has EKA and the alarm system is not active the above procedure can be used to resynchronise the remote handset. The EKA code procedure must be used to resynchronise the remote handset if the alarm system is active.

On vehicles from 97MY onwards, the passive immobilisation feature will reprogramme the code using the passive coil and the remote handset when the key is inserted into the ignition switch.

Decoding of the remote handset signal is performed by the BeCM not the RF receiver. The BeCM uses a code taken from a 14 digit lockset bar code, programmed into the BeCM at the factory. The BeCM compares this code with that transmitted by the remote handset to ensure that the correct code for the vehicle is being transmitted. Once programmed the code cannot be changed. If a new lockset is required, then the BeCM must be replaced to match the lockset bar code.

RF Receiver

The RF receiver is located under the RH rear parcel shelf. The receiver is not unique to each vehicle, although several different receivers are used to cover differing operating frequencies and market legislation. The RF receiver frequency to be used can be found on a label on the remote handset.

Power Windows and Sunroof

The front windows are controlled by the BeCM via outstations in each front door and the centre console switch outstation. When a centre console switch is operated for front window operation, the centre console outstation inputs information to the BeCM, which then outputs the appropriate command signals, via the serial data bus, to operate the front windows as required. The rear windows and sunroof are controlled directly by the BeCM which responds to operation of the applicable rear window or sunroof switches.

The front windows and sunroof have 'one touch' and 'inch' modes of operation. The sunroof and the front and rear window systems have an 'anti-trap' function to prevent injury to driver or passengers.

Windows Initialisation

Initialisation of the windows enables the one shot function on the front windows and the anti-trap function on all windows after battery disconnection. Initialisation is achieved by holding the applicable window switch in the down position until the window stalls. Then hold the switch in the up position and when the window is fully closed hold the switch in the up position for a further 1 second. An audible chime will sound and the message centre will display a message to confirm that the applicable window has been set.

Sunroof Initialisation

Initialisation of the sunroof enables the one shot and anti-trap functions after battery disconnection. Initialisation is achieved by holding the sunroof slide slide switch in the open position until the sunroof stalls. Then hold the sunroof slide switch in the closed position until the sunroof stalls at fully closed. Repeat the operation for the tilt open and close functions. When the sunroof is successfully initialised, the message centre will display a 'SUNROOF SET' message.

Front Windows and Sunroof 'One-Touch' Function

Operation of the front window switches or the sunroof slide switch for less than 0.4 seconds in either direction, will start the selected aperture to move in the one-touch mode of operation. The aperture will move in the selected direction until the motor stalls or, if the aperture is closing, a trap is detected. The aperture can be stopped at any point by operating the applicable switch in the opposite direction. The one-touch function is market programmable. Note that the sunroof tilt function only operates in the inch mode of operation.

Front and Rear Windows and Sunroof 'Inch Mode' Function

Operation of any aperture switch for more than 0.4 seconds will cause that aperture to move in inch mode of operation. The aperture will move in the selected direction until the motor stalls or the switch is released or, if the aperture is closing, a trap is detected. The aperture can be stopped in any position by releasing the applicable switch.

Windows and Sunroof Anti-Trap Function

The anti-trap function is capable of detecting a trap situation over the full range of the aperture opening. When the BeCM detects a trap situation when the aperture is closing:

- the rear window will open approximately 200 mm (7.8 in) or until the motor stalls
- the front windows will open fully to the motor stall position
- the sunroof will open fully to the motor stall position in the tilt and slide operation.

Anti-trap is sensed by two Hall effect sensors located within each window and sunroof motor. The sensors output pulses to the BeCM at a frequency of 62.5 Hz. When a trap condition occurs, the frequency of the pulses is reduced and sensed by the BeCM, which immediately backs off the affected aperture.

Anti-trap override

In extreme temperature conditions the window mechanism may become partly frozen causing the window anti-trap function to operate. Anti-trap can be overridden by operating the window switch in the up position within 10 seconds of the window having detected the trap situation and backing off. The window up function will only operate in inch mode and the anti-trap override will only continue for along as the switch is depressed.

Anti-trap override is displayed in the message centre by an 'ANTI TRAP OFF' message and the applicable window denoted. Three audible warning chimes will sound and will be repeated continuously while the window is operated with anti-trap override active. Anti-trap override is only available from the window control switches in the centre console.

Main Lighting System

The main lighting system is operated by a latching rotary switch located on the fascia. Movement of the switch to the side/parking lamps or headlamps position completes an earth path to the BeCM. When the switch is in the side lamp position, the earth path is completed on one of two pins to the BeCM.

When the switch is moved to the headlamp position, the earth path is completed on both pins. The BeCM interprets the earth path as request for side or headlamps and provides power outputs to the applicable circuits to operate the lamps as requested.

The BeCM outputs are driven by Field Effect Transistors (FET). The FET's detect the continuity of the lighting circuits. In the event of a bulb failure or a short or open circuit, the break in continuity in that circuit is sensed by the BeCM which then generates a 'BULB FAILURE' message in the message centre specifying the bulb which has failed.

When an FET detects a break in continuity, the output from the BeCM to the affected circuit is deactivated. When the fault is corrected, the lighting switch must be switched off and then on again to reinstate the output. On certain circuits, the output will be reinstated by the BeCM automatically.

The number plate lamp circuit is internally linked inside the BeCM to the glove box lamp circuit. If a number plate circuit failure occurs, it is advisable to check the glove box circuit at the same time.

To maximise battery voltage during engine cranking, most BeCM controlled functions are inhibited. During cranking, only the side lamps will remain on irrespective of lighting systems active at the time of cranking.

Parking Lamps

The parking lamps are located in the tail lamps and the headlamps. On NAS vehicles the front parking lamps are located in the front direction indicator lamp assemblies.

The parking lamps are operated by moving the lighting switch to the side lamp position with the key out of the ignition switch. The parking lamps are activated by the BeCM and operate according to the position of the direction indicator switch as follows:

A. If the indicator switch is in the central position, all side and tail lamps will be on
B. If the indicator switch is in the left hand position, only the front left side and tail lamps will be on
C. If the indicator switch is in the right hand position, only the front right side and tail lamps will be on.

When the parking lamps are on, the interior switch and instrument illumination remains off to minimise battery drain.

When the parking lamps are selected on and the key is inserted in the ignition the BeCM changes the parking lamp switch position functionality to side lamps.

If the parking lamps are operative and the driver's door is opened, the BeCM generates a 'PARK LIGHTS', 'LEFT PARK LIGHT' or 'RIGHT PARK LIGHT' message in the message centre to inform the driver that the parking lamps are on.

On vehicles from 96MY, the message centre displays the applicable message as detailed above, but also informs the driver via a triple audible chime that the parking lamps are on.

Side Lamps

The side lamps are operated by moving the lighting switch to the side lamp position with the key in the ignition switch. The parking lamps are activated by the BeCM which illuminates filament bulbs located in the headlamps, tail lamp assemblies and number plate lamps.

On NAS vehicles, the front side lamps are integral with the front direction indicator lamp assemblies.

A 'lights on' warning lamp is located in the instrument pack and is illuminated to inform the driver that side lamps or headlamps are on.

When the side lamps are selected on, the BeCM also activates the illumination for the instrument pack, fascia switches, ICE, HEVAC, centre console switches and gear selector. The level of the interior illumination is controlled by the panel dimmer control located on the direction indicator column stalk.

If the key is removed from the ignition the BeCM changes the lamps functionality to that detailed in 'parking lamps'.

Dipped Beam Headlamps

The dipped headlamps are operated by moving the lighting switch, past the parking/side lamp position, to the second headlamp position. The headlamps operate regardless of the ignition switch position. When dipped headlamps are selected, the BeCM supplies power to illuminate halogen bulbs in the headlamps and bulbs in the tail lamp assemblies.

On NAS vehicles the side lamps in the front direction indicators remain illuminated.

Interior switch and instrument illumination is activated by the BeCM as detailed in side lamps above. The 'lights on' warning lamp in the instrument pack is also illuminated to inform the driver that the headlamps are on.

If the headlamps are operative and the driver's door is opened and the key removed from the ignition, the BeCM generates a 'LIGHTS ON' message in the message centre to inform the driver that the headlamps are on.

On vehicles from 96MY, the message centre displays the applicable message as detailed above, but also informs the driver via a triple audible chime that the headlamps lamps are on.

Daylight Running Lamps

Daylight running lamps are a legislative requirement in some markets. With the engine running at an engine speed above 500 rpm, the BeCM will activate the daylight running lamps regardless of the position of the lighting switch. The daylight running feature has no effect on other vehicle lighting systems.

When daylight running lamps are on, but the lighting switch is off, the BeCM does not activate the interior fascia illumination.

Main Beam and Headlamp Flash

There are two main beam outputs to each headlamp unit. One output operates a main beam only halogen bulb located in the driving lamp on the inner side of the headlamp unit. A second output operates a dip/main beam halogen bulb located in the outer side of the headlamp unit.

The headlamp main beam and flash function is operated by pulling the direction indicator stalk backwards. Two non-latching momentary switches operate the main beam and flash function, with each switch providing a momentary earth path to the BeCM when operated. A short pull backwards operates the flash switch and a further pull operates the main beam switch. When the main beam and flash function is active, a warning lamp in the instrument pack is illuminated.

When the stalk is pulled to operate the flash switch, the BeCM will activate the main beam and driving lamp outputs for as long as the switch is held. When the switch is released, the switch contact closes and the BeCM deactivates the main beam and driving lamp outputs. If the dip beam headlamps and the front fog lamps are operative, the BeCM will only activate the main beam. With any other combinations of lamps the BeCM will operate both the main beam and driving lamp outputs.

When the stalk is pulled to operate the main beam switch, the BeCM will activate the main beam and driving lamp outputs and de-activate the dip beam headlamp output. When the stalk is pulled a second time, the second operation of the main beam switch signals the BeCM to de-activate the main beam and driving lamp outputs and re-instate the dip beam headlamp output.

Headlamp Delay

The BeCM has a headlamp delay function to illuminate the driveway after leaving the vehicle. The headlamp will operate on dip or main beam depending on the selected position on the column stalk switch.

The headlamp delay is operated by turning off the ignition and removing the key with the headlamps on. When the lighting switch is turned to the off position quickly, with a dwell of less than 1 second in the parking/side lamp position, a 25 second headlamp delay period will be activated by the BeCM.

The delay, when active, can be cancelled at any time by inserting the key in the ignition, moving the lighting switch to the parking/side lamp position or the headlamp position.

Direction Indicators and Hazard Warning Lamps

The direction indicators and the hazard warning lamp switches, when operated, each complete an earth path to the BeCM. The BeCM interprets the earth path completion as a request for indicator operation and provides power outputs to either left or right hand direction indicators or the hazard warning lamps.

The BeCM outputs are driven by Field Effect Transistors (FET). The FET's detect the continuity of the indicator lamp circuits (except the side repeater lamps). In the event of a bulb failure or a short or open circuit, the break,in continuity in that circuit is sensed by the BeCM.

The BeCM will operate the applicable, or both in the case of hazard warning lamps, instrument pack direction indicator warning lamps at double speed. The BeCM also generates a 'FRONT or REAR INDICATOR FAILURE' message in the message centre. This message is displayed alternately with a 'BULB FAILURE' message.

Direction Indicators

The direction indicators are operated from the direction indicator stalk located on the left hand side of the steering column. Pushing the stalk downwards activates the left hand direction indicators and pushing the stalk upwards operates the right hand direction indicators. The direction indicators operate only with the ignition in position II.

Two direction indicator warning lamps are located in the instrument pack. When the direction indicators are selected, the applicable left or right warning lamp flashes and the instrument pack emits an audible 'tick' in time with the pulsed operation of the lamps. The direction indicators and the audible 'tick' operate at a frequency of 1.3 Hz.

Hazard Warning Lamps

The hazard warning lamps are operated from a latching pushbutton switch located on the fascia and can be activated at all times irrespective of the ignition switch state. The switch has a tell-tale lamp to inform the driver that the hazard warning lamps are operational. The direction indicator warning lamps in the instrument pack both flash together and the instrument pack emits an audible 'tick' in time with the pulsed operation of the lamps. In the event of the inertia switch being tripped, the BeCM will automatically activate the hazard warning lamps.

Fog, Brake and Reversing Lamps

The fog, brake and reverse lamps are controlled by switches which, when operated, complete an earth path to the BeCM. The BeCM interprets the earth path completion as a request for fog, brake or reverse lamp operation and provides power outputs to the applicable circuits to operate the lamps as requested.

The BeCM outputs are driven by Field Effect Transistors (FET). The FET's detect the continuity of the applicable circuit. In the event of a bulb failure, with the exception of the high mounted brake lamp, the break in continuity is sensed by the BeCM which generates the applicable 'BULB FAILURE' message in the message centre specifying the bulb or circuit which has failed.

Fog Lamps

Front fog lamps

The front fog lamps are operated from a non-latching switch on the fascia. The switch has a tell-tale lamp to indicate that front fog lamps are active. When the switch is operated it completes a momentary earth path to the BeCM. The BeCM interprets the earth as a request for front fog lamp operation and provides power outputs to the LH and RH front fog lamps. If the ignition is off or the side lamps or headlamps are off, the request will not be granted and the tell-tale lamp will not be illuminated.

With the ignition in position II and the side lamps or headlamps are switched on, the BeCM will grant the request and provide power to the fog lamps and the tell-tale lamp. A second operation of the switch will signal the BeCM to terminate fog lamp operation.

Also if the ignition or the side lamps or headlamps are switched off, the output to the fog lamps is removed. The fog lamps will be inactive when the ignition and the side lamps or headlamps are next switched on.

On NAS vehicles, the front fog lamps will only operate with the ignition in position II and headlamps switched on. They will not operate with only the side lamps on.

Rear fog lamps

The rear fog lamps are operated from a non-latching switch on the fascia. The switch has a tell-tale lamp to indicate that the rear fog lamps are active. The rear fog lamps operate in the same way as described for the front fog lamps, with the exception that the rear fog lamps will not operate unless the front fog lamps are on. Switching off the front fog lamps will also extinguish the rear fog lamps.

Brake Lamps

The brake lamps are operated from a plunger type microswitch which is activated by the brake pedal. The switch is a self adjusting microswitch with two interlinked contacts, one normally open and the normally closed.

When the brake pedal is depressed, the normally open contacts close, supplying a 12 V signal to the BeCM, cruise control ECU and the ABS ECU. Simultaneously, the normally closed contacts open, interrupting a 12 V supply to the ABS ECU.

The BeCM interprets the 12 V supply from the switch as a request for brake lamp operation and provides power outputs to the brake lamp circuits. When the brake pedal is released the 12 V supply to the BeCM is terminated and the BeCM deactivates the power output to the brake lamp circuits.

Reversing Lamps

Manual transmission

The reverse lamps are operated by a plunger type microswitch which is activated by a mechanical linkage within the gearbox. When reverse gear is selected with the ignition in position II, the microswitch plunger is depressed completing an earth path to the BeCM.

The BeCM interprets the earth path as a request for reverse lamp operation and provides power outputs to the LH and RH reverse lamp circuits. When reverse gear is deselected, the earth path to the BeCM is terminated and the BeCM deactivates the power output to the reverse lamp circuits.

Automatic transmission

The reverse lamps are operated by a signal generated from the gearbox selector position switch located on the side of the gearbox. The BeCM determines the gear position from three microswitches (X, Y, Z) in the selector position switch.

When the BeCM sees the correct output from the position switch and the ignition is in position II, it activates the power outputs to the reverse lamp circuits. When reverse gear is deselected, the signal from the position switch changes and the BeCM deactivates the power output to the reverse lamp circuits. ***See AUTOMATIC GEARBOX, Description and operation.***

Trailer Lamps

The BeCM is programmed to accomodate additional lighting loads when a trailer is being towed. The trailer lamps have the same functionality as described previously for rear fog lamps, reversing lamps, parking/side lamps, direction indicators and hazard warning lamps.

If the trailer lamps are of too high a Wattage, the BeCM may interpret the loads as a short circuit to ground and deactivate the power outputs to the trailer and vehicle lighting circuits.

Wash Wipe System

Washer Fluid Level

The washer fluid reservoir has three motors for front, rear and headlamp washer operation. The reservoir is located in the right hand side of the engine compartment below the battery. Each motor is operated by the BeCM.

A level switch, operated by a float, is located in the washer fluid reservoir. When the washer fluid is at a sufficient level, the switch is closed and an earth path to the BeCM is complete. When the washer fluid falls to a level to open the switch, the BeCM monitors the switch condition.

If the switch is open for longer than 5 seconds, the BeCM generates a 'LOW SCREEN WASH' message in the message centre and disables the headlamp wash/wipe function to preserve fluid. The message is removed when the BecM senses that the switch is closed and the ignition is off.

Front Wipers

Two front wipers are operated by a linkage assembly and an electric motor located under the plenum grill below the windscreen. The linkage and motor are handed for left and right hand drive vehicles.

The front wiper motor has two speeds of operation; slow and fast. The dc motor contains two permanent magnets, three brushes and a park switch. The park switch signals the BeCM that the wipers are in the park position. When the wiper motor operates the park switch closes, creating an earth path to the BeCM. When the wipers reach the park position the park switch opens, breaking the earth path to the BeCM. The BeCM will then stop the wipers at this position if requested.

If the park switch fails, the BeCM cannot monitor the wiper position on the screen. To protect the motor from damage, the BeCM will allow wiper operation but will stop the wiper motor at a random position when the wiper switch is moved to the off position.

The BeCM controls all front wiper functions, with the wiper motor being supplied power via relays 1 and 8 in the engine compartment fusebox. The front wipers and washers will only operate with the ignition in position I or II. If the ignition is moved to position 0 (off) when the wipers are operating, the wipers will continue to operate until they reach the park position.

To maximise battery voltage during engine cranking, most BeCM controlled functions are inhibited. During cranking, the BeCM will suspend wiper operation until cranking has finished and then reinstate wiper operation.

All front wiper functions are controlled from a stalk switch located on the right hand side of the steering column. The front wiper functions, with the exception of the programmed wash wipe function, are operated by a combination of three switches. The following table details the switch combinations for each function.

Function	Switch 1	Switch 2	Switch 3
Flick wipe	Closed	Open	Open
Off	Open	Open	Open
Intermittent	Open	Closed	Open
Slow	Open	Closed	Closed
Fast	Open	Open	Closed

Flick wipe

The flick wipe function is operated by pushing the stalk vertically upwards and releasing to perform one cycle of the front wipers. Holding the stalk in this position will operate the wipers for as long as the switch is held.

When the three switches are in a combination for flick wipe operation, the BeCM output to relay 1 is earthed, energising the relay coil. With the relay energised, a feed from fuse 25 in the engine compartment fusebox is supplied, via the contacts of relay 8, to the slow speed brushes in the wiper motor. When the wiper motor moves from the park position, the contacts of the park switch open.

When the switch is released, the BeCM continues to energise the coil of relay 1 to allow the wipers to move to the park position. When the motor reaches the park position, the park switch closes completing an earth path to the BeCM. The BeCM senses the completed earth path and removes the earth for the relay 1 coil, replacing it with a 12 V output. The relay 1 coil is de-energised and the relay contacts open, removing the feed to the motor and stopping the wipers.

Intermittent wipe

The intermittent function is operated by pushing the switch one position vertically downwards to the first position. The intermittent delay can be adjusted by rotating the thumb wheel on the top of the stalk to the left or right to reduce or increase the delay period.

When the three switches are in a combination for intermittent operation, the BeCM output to relay 1 is earthed, energising the relay coil. With the relay energised, a feed from fuse 25 in the engine compartment fusebox is supplied, via the contacts of relay 8, to the slow speed brushes in the wiper motor. When the wiper motor moves from the park position, the contacts of the park switch open.

When the wiper motor reaches the park position, the park switch closes completing an earth path to the BeCM. The BeCM senses the completed earth path and removes the earth for the relay 1 coil, replacing it with a 12 V output. The relay 1 coil is de-energised and the relay contacts open, removing the feed to the motor and stopping the wipers.

The BeCM then initiates a delay by passing a voltage to the delay potentiometer and measuring the resistance through the potentiometer. The resistances sensed by the BeCM and the associated delays are listed in the following table.

Delay (Seconds)	Resistance (Ohms)
2	1.9K
4	4.7K
8	9.2K
16	17.4K
32	53K

When the delay has elapsed, the BeCM will operate the wipers for one more cycle and then reinstate the delay period. This will continue until the intermittent function is deselected.

When the intermittent function is switched off, if the wipers are midway through a cycle, the BeCM continues to energise the coil of relay 1 to allow the wipers to move to the park position. When the motor reaches the park position, the park switch closes completing an earth path to the BeCM. The BeCM senses the completed earth path and removes the earth for the relay 1 coil, replacing it with a 12 V output. The relay 1 coil is de-energised and the relay contacts open, removing the feed to the motor and stopping the wipers. If the wipers are not operating when the intermittent function is deselected, then no further wiper operation will take place.

Slow speed

The slow wipe function is operated by pushing the stalk two positions vertically downwards.

When the three switches are in a combination for slow wipe operation, the BeCM output to relay 1 is earthed, energising the relay coil. With the relay energised, a feed from fuse 25 in the engine compartment fusebox is supplied, via the contacts of relay 8, to the slow speed brushes in the wiper motor. When the wiper motor moves from the park position, the contacts of the park switch open.

When the switch moved to the off position, the BeCM continues to energise the coil of relay 1 to allow the wipers to move to the park position. When the motor reaches the park position, the park switch closes completing an earth path to the BeCM. The BeCM senses the completed earth path and removes the earth for the relay 1 coil, replacing it with a 12 V output. The relay 1 coil is de-energised and the relay contacts open, removing the feed to the motor and stopping the wipers.

Fast speed

The fast wipe function is operated by pushing the stalk three positions vertically downwards.

When the three switches are in a combination for fast wipe operation, the BeCM output to relays 1 and 8 are earthed, energising the relay coils. With the relay energised, a feed from fuse 25 in the engine compartment fusebox is supplied, via the contacts of relay 8, to the fast speed brushes in the wiper motor. When the wiper motor moves from the park position, the contacts of the park switch open.

When the switch moved to the off position, the BeCM continues to energise the coils of relays 1 and 8 to allow the wipers to move to the park position. When the motor reaches the park position, the park switch closes completing an earth path to the BeCM. The BeCM senses the completed earth path and removes the earths for the coils of relays 1 and 8, replacing them with a 12 V output. The relay 1 coil is de-energised and the relay contacts open, removing the feed to the motor and stopping the wipers.

Programmed wash/wipe

Programmed wash/wipe is selected by pressing the lower button on the end of the wiper stalk. The washer will continue to operate for as long as the button is pressed.

When the switch is pressed an earth path is completed to the BeCM. The BeCM interprets the earth path as a request for programmed wash/wipe and provides a 12 V output to the windscreen washer pump. The output is supplied for 1.5 seconds or for as long as the switch is held.

The BeCM changes the output to relay 1 to an earth 0.5 seconds after the switch is pressed, energising the relay coil. With the relay energised, a feed from fuse 25 in the engine compartment fusebox is supplied, via the contacts of relay 8, to the slow speed brushes in the wiper motor. When the wiper motor moves from the park position, the contacts of the park switch open.

The BeCM operates the wipers for three complete cycles and then continues to energise the coil of relay 1 to allow the wipers to move to the park position. When the motor reaches the park position, the park switch closes completing an earth path to the BeCM.

The BeCM senses the completed earth path and removes the earth for the relay 1 coil, replacing it with a 12 V output. The relay 1 coil is de-energised and the relay contacts open, removing the feed to the motor and stopping the wipers.

If the BeCM receives a washer fluid low signal in the form of a completed earth path through the fluid level sensor, programmed wash/wipe is restricted to only operate the washer pump and the wipers for as long as the switch is held.

Speed dependant wipers (From 99MY)

Vehicles from 99MY can have a programmed speed dependant wiper function. When this function is active the following changes over normal wiper operation will occur when the vehicle speed is reduced to 2 mph (3.2 km/h) or less with a front wiper function active.

If the wipers are operating at fast speed, they will change to slow speed when the vehicle stops.

If the wipers are operating at slow speed, they will change to intermittent operation with a fixed delay of 2 seconds. The delay is irrespective of delay potentiometer position.

If the wipers are operating on intermittent operation, they will continue to operate intermittently, but the selected delay time will be doubled.

When the vehicle speed increases to 3 mph (4.8 km/h) or more, the wipers will operate one complete cycle and continue as previously selected. When the vehicle is stationary, if the wiper switch is moved the selected function will operate normally.

Headlamp Wash/Wipe

When the headlamps are switched on and the programmed wash/wipe switch is pressed, the headlamp wash/wipe will operate on the first and every alternate operation of the wash/wipe switch. The headlamp wash/wipe motor will operate for two seconds, irrespective of how long the switch is depressed. If the screen wash fluid level is low the headlamp wash/wipe function is disabled by the BeCM.

When the BeCM detects the correct conditions for headlamp wash wipe operation, a 12 V output to relay 11 in the engine compartment fusebox is earthed, energising the relay coil and closing the relay contacts. A feed from fuse 38 in the engine compartment fusebox passes through the relay contacts and powers the LH and RH headlamp wiper motors and the headlamp washer pump motor.

After two seconds, the BeCM removes the earth path for the relay 11 coil, replacing it with a 12 V output. The relay 11 coil is de-energised and the relay contacts open, removing the feed to the headlamp motors and washer pump. The headlamp wiper motors continue to operate on a feed from fuse 38, until the RH motor park switch connects the feed to earth, stopping the motors and the washer pump.

Rear Wipers

A single rear wiper is operated direct from a motor located in the tail door. The rear wiper and washer will only operate with the ignition in position I or II. If the ignition is moved to position 0 (off) when the wiper is operating, the wiper will continue to operate until it reaches the park position.

All rear wiper functions are controlled from a stalk switch located on the right hand side of the steering column.

Intermittent wipe

When the rear wiper switch is moved to the on position, the BeCM detects a completed earth path through the switch. The BeCM then provides a 12 V output direct to the rear wiper motor. The motor will operate for two complete cycles until the BeCM senses a second operation of the motor park switch.

When the motor is operating, the park switch is closed completing an earth path to the BeCM. When the motor reaches the park position, the switch opens removing the earth path and signals the BeCM that the wiper is in the park position. The BeCM then connects the output to the rear wiper motor to earth, stopping the motor.

The functionality of the rear wiper is dependant on the selected front wiper function.

If no front wiper function is selected, the BeCM then initiates a delay by passing a voltage to the delay potentiometer and measuring the resistance through the potentiometer. The delay is twice that of the front intermittent delay. The resistances sensed by the BeCM and the associated delays are listed in the following table.

Delay (Seconds)	Resistance (Ohms)
4	1.9K
8	4.7K
16	9.2K
32	17.4K
64	53K

The BeCM will provide a 12 V output to the motor until the park switch opens. The BeCM initiates the delay by passing a voltage to the delay potentiometer and measuring the resistance through the potentiometer. The resistance is sensed by the BeCM which initiates the appropriate delay period before supplying the output to the motor for the next wiper operation.

If the front wiper is selected in the intermittent mode, the BeCM will provide a 12 V output to the rear wiper motor at the same time as it provides the earth path for relay 1 to operate the front wipers. This synchronises the front and rear wiper cycles at the same time. The rear wiper operates on every alternate operation of the front wipers until the front or rear wiper functions are deselected.

If the front wipers are operating in the slow or fast mode, the rear wiper will operate intermittently as detailed above.

Reverse gear wipe

If reverse gear is selected with a front wiper function active, the BeCM will operate the rear wiper as detailed in the following table.

Front Wiper	Rear Wiper
Intermittent	Intermittent
Slow	Continuous
Fast	Continuous

The BeCM controls the reverse wipe operation when an input from a gearbox reverse switch is sensed. The intermittent operation is as detailed previously. When reverse gear is deselected, the BeCM operates the rear wiper motor until one full cycle is complete.

Programmed wash/wipe

Programmed wash/wipe is selected by pressing the upper button on the end of the wiper stalk. The washer will continue to operate for as long as the switch is pressed.

When the switch is pressed an earth path is completed to the BeCM. The BeCM interprets the earth path as a request for programmed wash/wipe and provides a 12 V output to the rear screen washer pump. The output is supplied for 1.5 seconds or for as long as the switch is held.

The BeCM provides a 12 V output to the rear wiper motor 0.5 seconds after the pump starts. The BeCM operates the wiper motor for three complete cycles until it senses that the park switch is open and removes the 12 V output to the motor, stopping the wiper in the park position.

If the BeCM receives a washer fluid low signal in the form of a completed earth path through the fluid level sensor, programmed wash/wipe is restricted to only operate the washer and the wiper for as long as the switch is held.

Power Seats

The power seats are only available on the driver and passenger front seats. The seats can be operated when either front door is open and/or the ignition is in position I or II. The power seats are each operated by axis and lumbar control switches located on the side of each seat trim panel.

The seat heater function is controlled by switches on the HEVAC ECU control panel. Each switch when pressed, completes an earth path which is sensed by the BeCM as a seat heater request and activates the appropriate seat heater. The seat heaters only operate with the ignition in position II and the engine running.

The electric seat operation is controlled by the BeCM via the seat outstations. The BeCM receives input information from the outstations for the selected functions. It then outputs the appropriate command signals, via the serial data bus, to the applicable outstation, which then operates the selected function.

Power Mirrors

The power mirrors operate with the ignition in position I or II. The mirrors are operated by a multifunction direction switch and a separate switch to select the left or right hand mirror. Both switches are located on the centre console switch panel.

When the mirror selection switch is in the left or right hand mirror position, the switch provides an earth path which the BeCM interprets as left or right hand mirror.

When the direction switch is operated, an appropriate signal is sent from the centre console switch outstation, via the serial data bus, to the BeCM. The BeCM interprets the signal and outputs the appropriate signal, via the serial data bus, to the applicable door outstation to activate the output and operate the mirror in the required direction. The direction of each motor is changed by reversing the polarity of the outputs from the door outstation.

When the ignition is in position II and the engine is running, the door mirrors will operate constantly or when mirror movement is requested.

The door mirrors have a reverse dip function. When the ignition is in position II and reverse gear is selected, the BeCM senses the earth path completed by the reverse gear switch, and outputs the appropriate signals to the applicable door outstation to operate the motors to drive the applicable mirror to its preset reverse position.

Rear View Mirror

On vehicles fitted with an automatic photochromic rear view mirror, the BeCM provides a 12 V output to the mirror. The mirror automatically adjusts the brightness of the reflected light.

When reverse gear is selected, the BeCM senses the earth path completed by the reverse gear switch and outputs a signal of less then 1.0 V to the rear view mirror. When the mirror receives the low output, it restores the mirror to normal brightness to aid reversing.

Instrument Pack

The BeCM communicates with the instrument pack via a digital serial data bus. The use of the serial data bus greatly reduces the number of wires which would normally be required between the instrument pack and the BeCM. All the wires in the data bus are duplicated to increase the reliability of the connections.

The speed signal, sounder, tachometer signal and the power supply each have their own dedicated lines. All other communications are directed via the data bus.

Electronic Air Suspension (EAS)

The BeCM communicates with the EAS ECU via hardwired connections. The BeCM provides outputs to the EAS ECU for road speed, engine speed, park/handbrake status and door open signals.

The BeCM receives inputs from the EAS ECU for warning lamp control and message centre displays. ***See FRONT SUSPENSION, Description and operation.***

Transfer Box ECU

The BeCM communicates with the transfer box ECU via hardwired connections. The BeCM receives signal information from the transfer box ECU with regard to the range selected via three status lines. The BeCM processes this information and illuminates warning lamps and/or generates messages for the instrument pack message centre as applicable.

The messages generated vary between manual and automatic transmission vehicles. ***See TRANSFER BOX, Description and operation.***

Supplementary Restraint System DCU

The BeCM communicates with the SRS DCU via hardwired connections. The BeCM provides a secondary ignition feed output to the engine compartment fusebox. When the ignition switch is in position II, the BeCM provides an output which generates an ignition supply to the SRS DCU from the engine compartment fusebox. ***See SUPPLEMENTARY RESTRAINT SYSTEM, Description and operation.***

Cruise Control ECU

The BeCM communicates with the cruise control ECU via hardwired connections. The BeCM provides a 12 V square wave speed signal input to the cruise control ECU. The speed signal is derived from the ABS ECU.

The BeCM also supplies a power input to the cruise control ECU for actuator power. This is supplied via the normally closed brake switch located in series between the BeCM and the ECU. When the switch is closed the BeCM provides a 12 V supply for actuator power.

When the brake pedal is depressed the switch opens, pulling the supply low and removing the power supply. The ECU responds by cancelling cruise control and opens a dump valve releasing all air stored in the vacuum system. ***See FUEL SYSTEM, CRUISE CONTROL, Description and operation.***

Heating, Ventilation and Air Conditioning (HEVAC) ECU

The BeCM communicates with the HEVAC ECU via hardwired connections. The BeCM provides a 12 V square wave speed signal input to the HEVAC ECU. The speed signal is derived from the ABS ECU and is used to control the fan speed.

The BeCM also outputs an alternator signal to inform the HEVAC ECU that the engine is running and air conditioning can be operated. Two further outputs are transmitted to the HEVAC ECU for ignition positions I and II.

The BeCM also receives a Heated Rear Window (HRW) request signal from the HEVAC ECU in the form of a momentary completion of an earth path when either the manual HRW switch is depressed or the programmed demist switch is depressed. When the BeCM receives the request, it energises an internal relay and supplies a 12 V supply to the HRW element via fuse 12.

LH and RH seat heater request signals are also generated by the HEVAC ECU in the form of a momentary completion of an earth path when the applicable switch is depressed. The BeCM outputs a 12 V supply to the requested seat heater element, provided that the ignition is in position II and the engine is running. ***See HEATING AND VENTILATION, Description and operation.***

Anti-Lock Braking System ECU

The BeCM communicates with the ABS ECU via hardwired connections. The BeCM receives inputs from the ABS ECU for ETC/ABS warning lamp illumination and message centre displays to the instrument pack.

Inputs are also passed from the ABS pressure switch in the form of completed earth paths for ABS warning lamp operation.

The ABS ECU generates a road speed signal which is passed to the BeCM. The BeCM uses the road speed signal and also passes it to other ECU's to control various vehicle functions. ***See BRAKES, Description and operation.***

Electronic Automatic Transmission ECU

The BeCM is connected via hardwired connections to the EAT ECU. The BeCM receives inputs from the gearbox position switch and generates outputs to the selector lever cover illumination for gear position LED illumination. Outputs are also provided to the instrument pack message centre for gear positions.

The BeCM outputs an engine speed signal to the EAT ECU and also transfers diagnostic information from the ECU to the diagnostic socket. ***See AUTOMATIC GEARBOX, Description and operation.***

Engine Running Detection

The BeCM has two methods of detecting that the engine is running; tachometer pulse monitoring and alternator charge input.

The tachometer pulse monitoring is used for safety related functions i.e. memory seat one-touch inhibition. The engine rpm thresholds for the tachometer pulse monitoring is as follows:

Petrol 180 rpm ± 10%
Diesel 240 rpm ± 10%.

The alternator charge input is used for load control of electrical functions. If certain functions are operating simultaneously, i.e. both rear windows operating and seat heaters active, the BeCM will determine which function has priority and temporarily deactivate one function.

Key Inhibit Solenoid (NAS/JAPAN Only)

NAS and Japanese automatic transmission vehicles have a key inhibit function which prevents removal of the ignition key if the automatic transmission selector lever is not in the PARK position.

The key inhibit function is controlled by the BeCM. The BeCM de-energises a key inhibit solenoid located in the ignition switch assembly when a park signal is passed to the BeCM from the PARK switch located in the H-gate.

On vehicles up to 97.5MY, the key inhibit solenoid is not de-energised until the BeCM receives a PARK signal from the park switch and the ignition is moved to position 0 (off).

On vehicles from 97.5MY, the key inhibit solenoid is de-energised via the park switch, irrespective of the ignition switch position. This overcomes key removal problems if a rapid key removal is attempted.

BeCM pin-Out Information

The following tables show the BeCM inputs and outputs for the nineteen associated connectors.

C112 (up to 99MY)
C1288 (from 99MY)

Pin No.	Description	Input/Output
1	Not used	-
2	Parking brake on	Output
3	Side/Tail door open	Output
4	Gearbox oil temperature (automatic models)	Input
5	Security code	Output
6 and 7	Not used	-
8	Ignition switch position I	Output
9	Engine speed	Input
10	ABS warning lamp and message	Input
11	Brake pressure (brakes on)	Input
12	Not used	-
13	Road speed	Output
14	Catalytic converter overheat (Japanese V8 models) or glowplug warning lamp (diesel models)	Input
15	Not used	-
16	Fuel level (V8 models)	Output

C113 (up to 99MY)
C1282 (from 99MY)

Pin No.	Description	Input/Output
1	RH headlamp main beam (dual element bulb)	Output
2	Starter motor on	Output
3	RH headlamp dipped beam	Output
4	RH front direction indicator lamp	Output
5	RH headlamp main beam (auxiliary bulb)	Output
6	Headlamp wash/wipe	Output
7	Front wipers fast speed	Output
8	Front wipers slow speed	Output
9	RH front side lamp	Output
10	RH front fog lamp	Output

C114 (up to 99MY)
C1289 (from 99MY)

Pin No.	Description	Input/Output
1	Low screen wash fluid level	Input
2	Inertia switch tripped	Input
3	Front wiper park switch	Input
4	Not used	-
5	Engine warning lamp	Input
6	Not used	-
7	Low engine oil pressure	Input
8	Air suspension wade warning lamp	Input
9	Air suspension messages 1	Input
10	Fuel level	Input
11	Road speed	Input
12	ETC messages and warning lamp	Input
13	Not used	-
14	Bonnet open	Input
15	Alternator charge	Input
16	Low brake fluid level	Input
17	Not used	-
18	Air suspension messages 2	Input
19	Engine coolant temperature	Input
20	Engine speed	Output

C120 (up to 99MY)
C1281 (from 99MY)

Pin No.	Description	Input/Output
1	Ignition power supply (SRS DCU)	Output
2	Alarm sounder	Output
3	LH front fog lamp	Output
4	Rear screen washer pump	Output
5	LH front side lamp	Output
6	RH (direction indicator) side repeater lamp	Output
7	Horn	Output
8	LH headlamp main beam (auxiliary bulb)	Output
9	Ignition switch position II	Output
10	LH headlamp main beam (dual element bulb)	Output
11	LH headlamp dipped beam	Output
12	LH front direction indicator lamp	Output
13	Windscreen washer pump	Output
14	LH (direction indicator) side repeater lamp	Output

C255 (up to 99MY)
C1279 (from 99MY)

Connector/ Pin No.	Description	Input/Output
1	Rear fog lamps on/off	Input
2	Not used	-
3	Key in ignition switch	Input
4	Clutch pedal depressed (manual models)	Input
5	Not used	-
6	RH front seat heater on/off	Input
7	Hazard warning lamp telltale	Output
8	Diagnostic K line	Input/Output
9	Alternator charging (engine running)	Input
10	Road speed (to ATC ECU)	Output
11	Rear screen heater on/off	Input
12	Immobiliser passive coil supply	Output
13	Hazard warning on/off	Input
14	Cruise control on/off	Input
15	LH front seat heater on/off	Input
16	Not used	-
17	Diagnostic L line	Input/Output
18	Power to cruise control ECU, switch telltale and inverter/converter	Output
19	Not used	-
20	Road speed (to cruise control ECU)	Output

C256 (up to 99MY)
C1280 (from 99MY)

Pin No.	Description	Input/Output
1	Instrument pack serial data bus (direction)	Output
2	Instrument pack serial data bus (clock)	Output
3	Instrument pack serial data bus (data, duplicate)	Output
4	Instrument dimming supply	Input
5	Instrument pack serial data bus (earth, duplicate)	Output
6	Rear fog lamp switch telltale	Output
7	Security LED	Output
8	Engine speed (to instrument pack)	Output
9	Instrument pack serial data bus (direction, duplicate)	Output
10	Instrument pack serial data bus (clock, duplicate)	Output
11	Instrument pack serial data bus (data)	Output
12	Instrument dimming supply	Input
13	Ignition switch position I	Input
14	Instrument pack serial data bus (earth)	Output
15	Instrument pack audible warning	Output
16	Road speed (to instrument pack)	Output

C257 (up to 99MY)
C1278 (from 99MY)

Pin No.	Description	Input/Output
1	Rear screen washer on/off	Input
2	RH direction indicators on/off	Input
3	Headlamp dipped beam on/off	Input
4	Windscreen washer on/off	Input
5	Front wipers switch input 2	Input
6	Ignition switch position III	Input
7	LH direction indicators on/off	Input
8	Headlamp flash	Input
9	Side lamps on/off	Input
10	Front fog lamp switch telltale	Input
11	Wiper time delay	Input
12	Headlamps main beam on/off	Input
13	Rear wiper on/off	Input
14	Front fog lamps on/off	Input
15	Front wipers switch input 3	Input
16	Front wipers switch input 1	Input
17	Horn on/off	Input
18	Fuel filler flap release on/off	Input
19 and 20	Not used	-

C258 (up to 99MY)
C1276 (from 99MY)

Pin No.	Description	Input/Output
1	Cruise control pump supply	Output
2	Illumination (clock, fascia switches, ATC ECU, instrument pack and radio cassette player)	Output
3	Illumination (front footwell lamps and ignition switch)	Output
4	Brakes on/off	Input
5	Illumination (glovebox lamp)	Output
6	Auxiliary power supply (ATC ECU and radio cassette player)	Output
7	Battery power supply (clock, radio cassette player and instrument pack)	Output
8	Ignition switch position II	Input
9	Ignition power supply (brakes, PAS, air suspension switches and ATC ECU)	Output
10	Ignition key inhibit - up to 97.5MY	Output

C323 (up to 99MY)
C1284 (from 99MY)

Pin No.	Description	Input/Output
1	Ignition power supply (rear view mirror dip)	Output
2	Battery power supply (RH front door outstation)	Output
3	Trailer LH tail lamp	Output
4	Battery power supply (RH rear ICE amplifier)	Output
5	RH rear window down	Output
6	RH rear door marker (puddle) lamp	Output
7	Fuel filler flap release	Output
8	RH rear window anti-trap supply	Output
9	Sunroof anti-trap supply	Output
10	RH rear window up	Output
11	RH rear window switch illumination	Output
12	Battery power supply (RH front door outstation (window))	Output

C324 (up to 99MY)
C1292 (from 99MY)

Pin No.	Description	Input/Output
1	Sunroof backwards	Output
2	Rear screen heater	Output
3	Sunroof forwards	Output
4	Ignition power supply (sun visor)	Output

C325 (up to 99MY)
C1283 (from 99MY)

Pin No.	Description	Input/Output
1	LH rear fog lamp	Output
2	LH reverse lamp	Output
3	RH rear fog lamp and trailer fog lamp	Output
4	RH rear direction indicator lamp	Output
5	Auxiliary power supply (aerial amplifier)	Output
6	RH rear door superlocking	Output
7	Rear screen wiper motor	Output
8	RH rear door locking	Output
9	RH reverse lamp	Output
10	RH tail lamp and trailer RH tail lamp	Output
11	RH rear, front and loadspace courtesy lamps	Output
12	RH brake lamp and trailer brake lamps	Output
13	Centre High Mounted Stop Lamp (CHMSL)	Output
14	Trailer LH direction indicator lamp	Output
15	Trailer RH direction indicator lamp	Output
16	Number plate lamps	Output
17	Battery power supply (front, RH rear and loadspace courtesy lamps, tail gate central locking, alarm RF receiver)	Output
18	RH rear door unlocking	Output

C326 (up to 99MY)
C1285 (from 99MY)

Pin No.	Description	Input/Output
1	Rear wiper park	Input
2	Front courtesy lamp switch	Input
3	Tail door open	Input
4	Sunroof anti-trap 1	Input
5	RH rear window anti-trap 1	Input
6	Radio cassette remote on/off	Input
7	RH front window anti-trap 1	Input
8	RH rear window down	Input
9	RH front door serial data bus (clock)	Output
10	RH front door serial data bus (direction)	Output
11	Sunroof closed	Input
12	RH door mirror position	Input
13	RH rear door open	Input
14	Sunroof anti-trap 2	Input
15	RH rear window anti-trap 2	Input
16	RH front window anti-trap 2	Input
17	RH rear window up	Input
18	Not used	-
19	RH front door serial data bus (data)	Output
20	Reverse selected	Output

C361 (up to 99MY)
C1291 (from 99MY)

Pin No.	Description	Input/Output
1	Auxiliary power supply (telephone)	Output
2	LH rear window up	Output
3	LH rear door marker (puddle) lamp	Output
4	Battery power supply (trailer)	Output
5	Trailer reverse lamps	Output
6	Battery power supply (LH rear courtesy lamp, LH loadspace lamp, sub-woofer amplifier and LH rear ICE amplifier)	Output
7	Battery power supply (LH front door outstation, window)	Output
8	Battery power supply (LH front door outstation)	Output
9	LH rear courtesy lamp	Output
10	LH rear window down	Output
11	Not used	-
12	LH tail lamp	Output
13	LH rear door unlocking	Output
14	LH rear direction indicator lamp	Output
15	LH rear door superlocking	Output
16	Illumination (LH rear window switch)	Output
17	LH brake lamp	Output
18	LH rear door locking	Output

C362 (up to 99MY)
C1286 (from 99MY)

Pin No.	Description	Input/Output
1	LH front door serial data bus (data)	Output
2	LH rear window anti-trap 2	Input
3	LH front window anti-trap 2	Input
4	LH rear door open	Input
5	LH rear window anti-trap 1	Input
6	Movement detected (by volumetric sensor)	Input
7	LH rear window down	Input
8	LH door mirror position	Input
9	LH front door serial data bus (direction)	Output
10	LH front door serial data bus (clock)	Output
11	LH front window anti-trap 1	Input
12 and 13	Not used	-
14	LH rear window up	Input
15	Volumetric sensor power supply	Output
16	LH rear window anti-trap power supply	Output

C624 (up to 99MY)
C1293 (from 99MY)

Pin No.	Description	Input/Output
1 and 2	Not used	-
3	Battery power supply (transfer box ECU)	Output
4	Not used	-

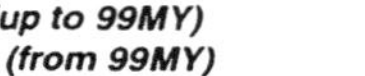

C625 (up to 99MY)
C1290 (from 99MY)

Pin No.	Description	Input/Output
1	Ignition power supply (transfer box ECU)	Output
2	Ignition power supply (gear selector lever (automatic models))	Output
3	Ignition power supply (EAT ECU (automatic models))	Output
4	Transfer box neutral tow link	Output
5	Auxiliary power supply (cigar lighter)	Output
6	Shift interlock solenoid (automatic models)	Output
7	Battery power supply (EAT ECU (automatic models)	Output
8	Battery power supply (centre console switch pack)	Output
9 and 10	Not used	-
11	Interior illumination (centre console switch pack, cigar lighter and gear selector lever (automatic models))	Output
12	Rear footwell lamps	Output

C626 (up to 99MY)
C1287 (from 99MY)

Pin No.	Description	Input/Output
1	EAT ECU diagnostic L line (automatic models)	Input/Output
2	Centre console serial data bus (direction)	Output
3	Transfer box high range	Input
4	Transfer box neutral	Input
5	Shift mode status 2 (automatic models)	Input
6	Transfer box over temperature	Input
7	Transfer box low range	Input
8	Gear position switch X signal (automatic models)	Input
9	Gear position switch Y signal (automatic models)	Input
10	Not used	-
11	Engine speed (to EAT ECU (automatic models))	Output
12	EAT ECU diagnostic K line (automatic models)	Input/Output
13	Centre console serial data bus (clock)	Output
14	Centre console serial data bus (data)	Output
15	Not used	-
16	Shift mode status 1 (automatic models)	Input
17	Handbrake on/off	Input
18	Gear position switch Z signal (automatic models)	-
19	Seat belt latched/unlatched	Input
20	Clutch pedal depressed (manual diesel models); ECM (automatic diesel models); gear selector lever park/neutral (NAS V8 models)	Output

C907 (up to 99MY)
C1277 (from 99MY)

Pin No.	Description	Input/Output
1	RH front seat serial data bus (clock)	Output
2	LH front seat serial data bus (direction)	Output
3	LH front seat serial data bus (data)	Output
4	LH front seat position	Input
5	RH front seat serial data bus (direction)	Output
6	RH front seat serial data bus (data)	Output
7	LH front seat serial data bus (clock)	Output
8	RH front seat position	Input

C912 (up to 99MY)
C0877 (from 99MY)

Pin No.	Description	Input/Output
1	RH front seat heater	Output
2	LH front seat heater	Output
3	RH front seat enable	Output
4	LH front seat earth	Input
5	RH front seat lumbar support	Output
6	LH front seat lumbar support	Output
7	LH front seat battery power supply 2	Output
8	LH front seat battery power supply 1	Output
9	LH front seat enable	Output
10	RH front seat earth	Input
11	RH front seat power supply 1	Output
12	RH front seat power supply 2	Output

Notes

ALTERNATOR DRIVE BELT - V8 - UP TO 99MY

Service repair no - 86.10.03

Remove

1. Disconnect battery negative lead.
2. Release 2 clips securing fan cowl. Remove cowl.

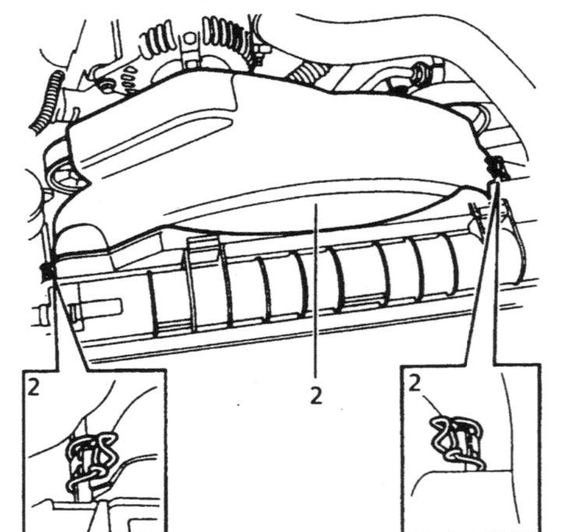

3. Rotate tensioner to release tension from alternator drive belt.

4. Remove drive belt.

Refit

5. Reverse removal procedure.

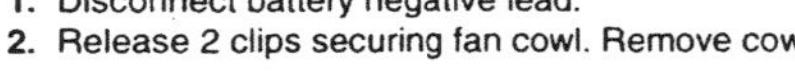

ALTERNATOR DRIVE BELT - V8 - FROM 99MY

Service repair no - 86.10.03

Remove

1. Remove cooling fan. ***See COOLING SYSTEM, Repair.***

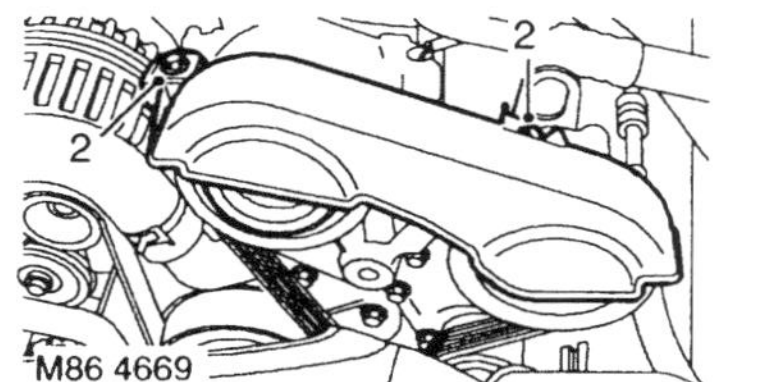

2. Remove 2 bolts securing auxiliary drive belt cover, remove cover and collect spacers.

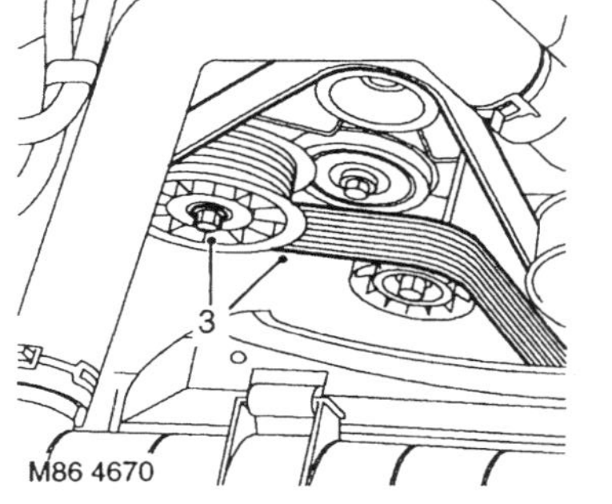

3. Release drive belt tensioner using a 15 mm ring spanner and remove belt from pulleys.

Refit

4. Clean drive belt pulley grooves and ensure grooves are not damaged.
5. Fit new drive belt around pulleys, ensure belt is correctly aligned in pulley grooves.
6. With assistance, hold tensioner fully clockwise and fit drive belt around remaining pulley.
7. Fit auxiliary drive belt cover and spacers and secure with bolts.
8. Fit cooling fan. ***See COOLING SYSTEM, Repair.***

ALTERNATOR DRIVE BELT - DIESEL

Service repair no - 86.10.03

Remove

1. Disconnect battery negative lead.
2. Remove air conditioning compressor drive belt, ***See AIR CONDITIONING, Repair.***
3. Remove 3 bolts securing upper fan cowl. Remove fan cowl.

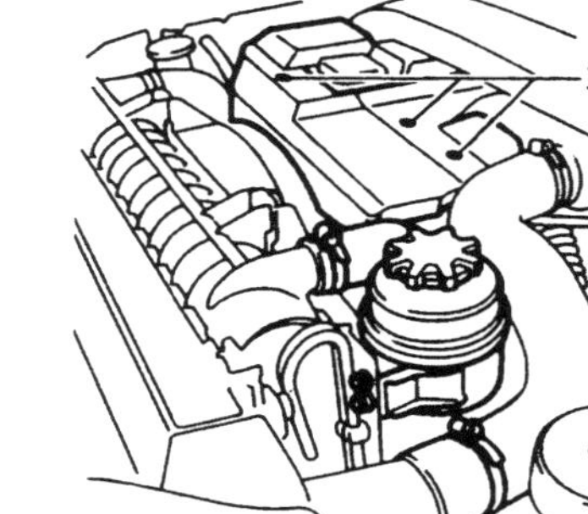

4. Release belt tension using a suitable lever beneath tensioner damper as shown.

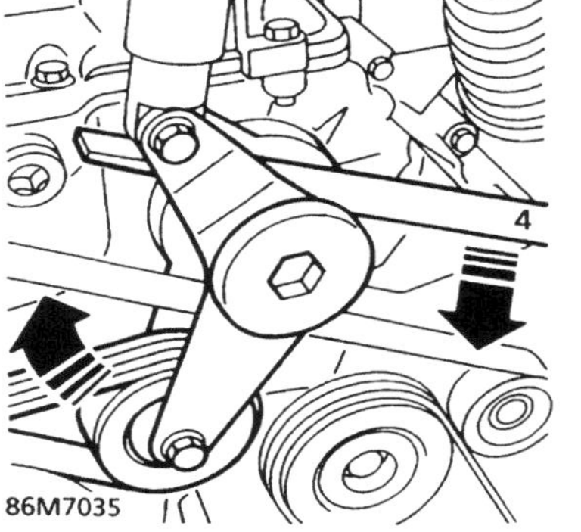

5. Release belt from pulleys. Withdraw belt from between cooling fan and cowl.

Refit

6. Ensure belt surfaces of pulleys are clean.
7. Thread belt between cooling fan and cowl.
8. Route belt around pulleys as shown.

9. Finally, lever tensioner to slack position. Engage belt over alternator pulley.
10. Position upper fan cowl. Secure with bolts.
11. Fit air conditioning compressor drive belt. ***See AIR CONDITIONING, Repair.*** Reconnect battery negative lead.

ALTERNATOR - V8 - UP TO 99MY

Service repair no - 86.10.02

Remove

1. Disconnect battery negative lead.
2. Remove alternator drive belt. ***See this section.***
3. Remove 2 bolts securing alternator to mounting bracket.

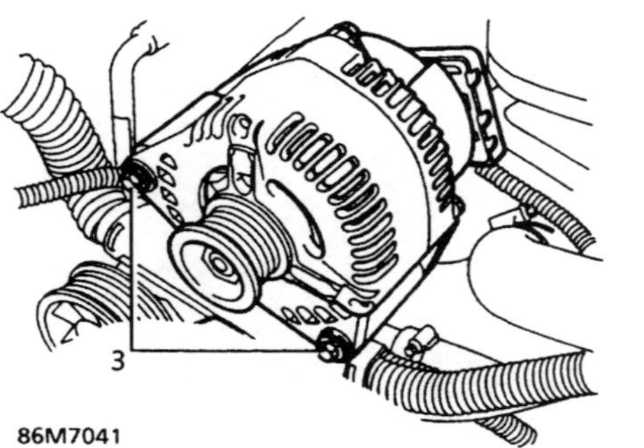

86M7041

4. Release alternator from mounting bracket to gain access to terminal cover.
5. Remove terminal cover.
6. Remove 2 nuts securing leads to alternator terminals. Remove leads.

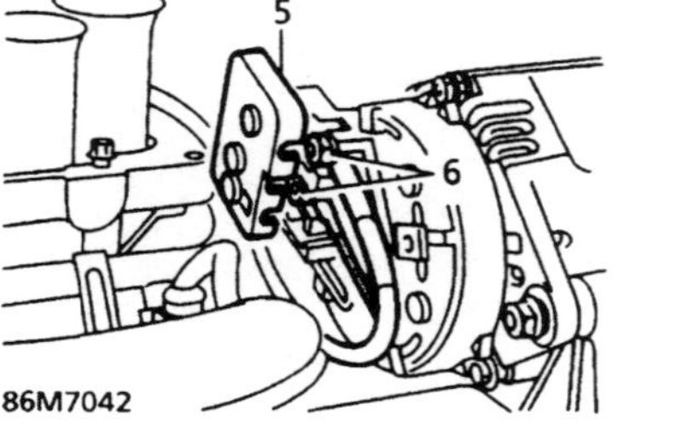

86M7042

7. Remove alternator.
Do not carry out further dismantling if component is removed for access only.
8. Restrain shaft using an Allen key. Remove pulley nut. Remove pulley.

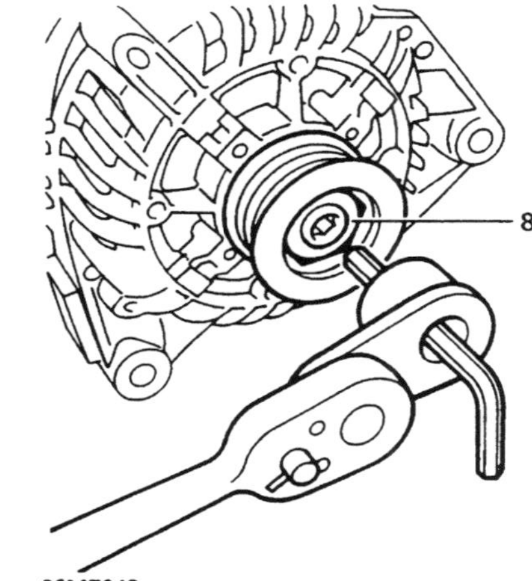

86M7043

9. Ensure shaft and pulley are clean.
10. Position pulley. Secure with nut. Tighten to ***40 Nm. (30 lbf.ft)***

Refit

11. Position alternator.
12. Fit 2 leads to alternator. Secure with nuts. Fit terminal cover.
13. Align alternator to mounting bracket. Secure with bolts. Tighten to ***25 Nm. (18 lbf.ft)***
14. Fit alternator drive belt. ***See this section.***
15. Reconnect battery negative lead.

ALTERNATOR - V8 - FROM 99MY

Service repair no - 86.10.02

Remove

1. Remove alternator drive belt. ***See this section.***

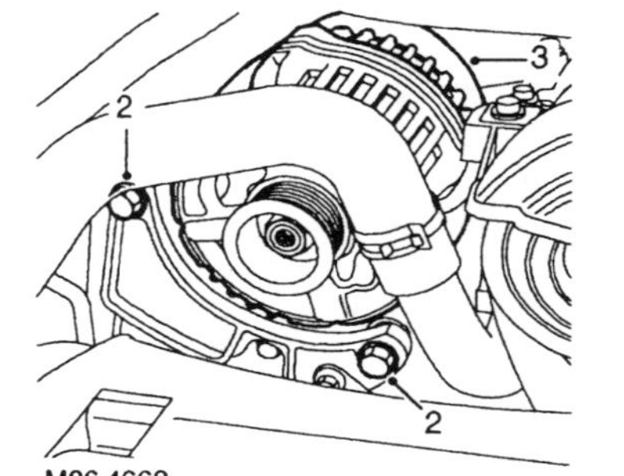

M86 4668

2. Remove 2 bolts securing alternator to mounting bracket.
3. Release alternator from mounting bracket.

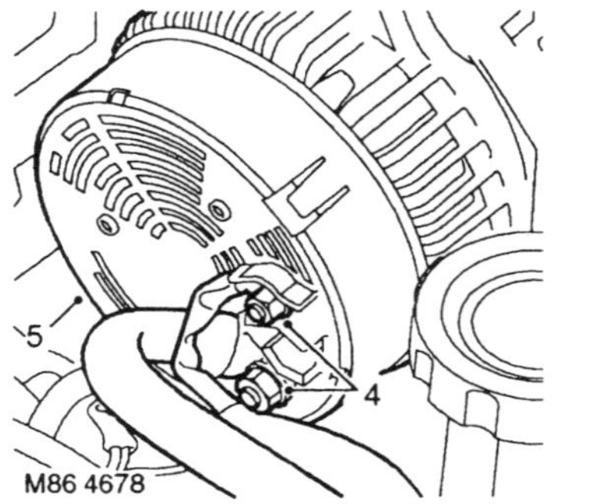

M86 4678

4. Remove nuts securing alternator cables, and release cables.
5. Remove alternator from mounting bracket.

Refit

6. Position alternator to mounting bracket.
7. Connect alternator cables, fit nuts and tighten B+ nut to ***18 Nm (13 lbf.ft)*** max. D+ nut to ***5 Nm (3.5 lbf.ft)*** max. B+ and D+ are marked on the rear of the alternator, adjacent to each cable connection.
8. Locate alternator in mounting bracket.
9. Fit bolts and tighten to ***45 Nm (33 lbf.ft).***
10. Fit alternator drive belt. ***See this section.***

ALTERNATOR - DIESEL

Service repair no - 86.10.02

Remove

1. Disconnect battery negative lead.
2. Remove alternator drive belt.
3. Release harness from terminal cover.
4. Release cover from alternator terminals.
5. Disconnect leads from alternator terminals.

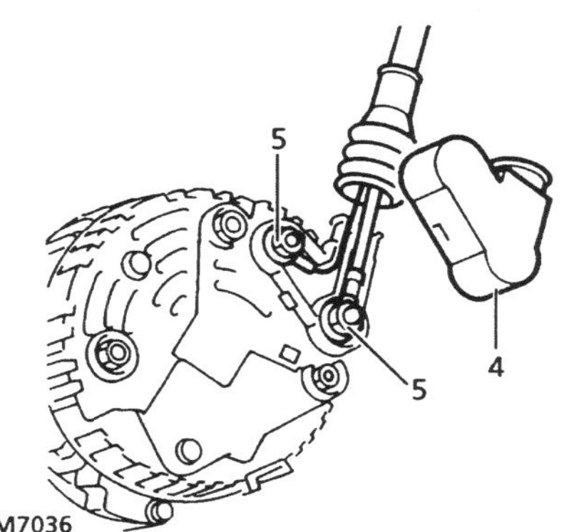

86M7036

6. Remove 2 bolts securing alternator to bracket.

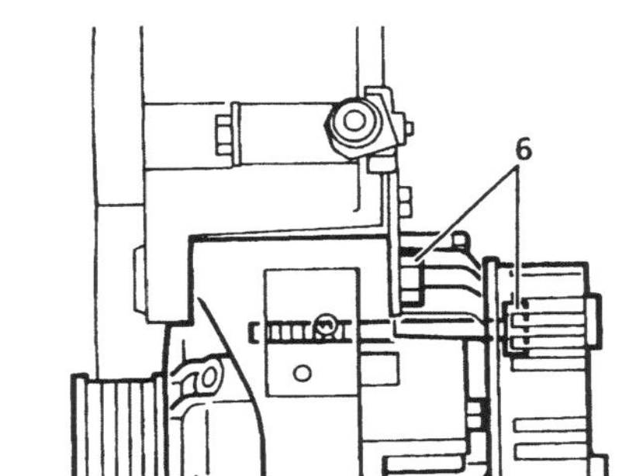

86M7037

7. Manoeuvre alternator clear of pipework. Remove alternator.
   Do not carry out further dismantling if component is removed for access only.
8. Restrain shaft using an Allen key. Remove pulley nut. Remove pulley.

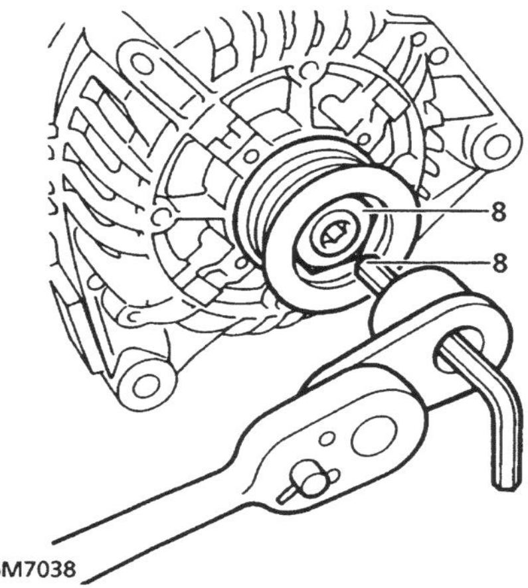

86M7038

9. Clean shaft and pulley.
10. Position pulley. Secure with nut. Tighten to ***50 Nm. (37 lbf.ft)***

Refit

11. Position alternator to bracket. Secure with bolts.
12. Connect leads to alternator terminals. Secure with nuts.
13. Secure terminal cover. Engage harness sheath.
14. Fit and tension alternator drive belt.
15. Reconnect battery negative lead.

DRIVE BELT TENSIONER - V8

Service repair no - 86.10.06

Remove

1. Disconnect battery negative lead.
2. Remove radiator cooling fan cowl.

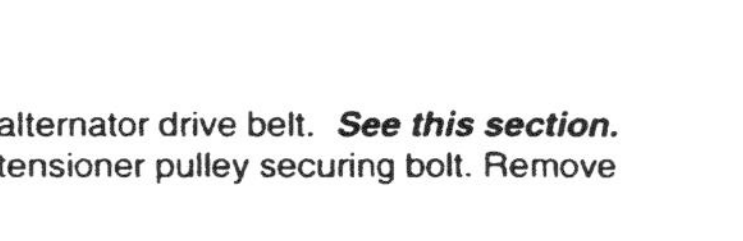

86M7026

3. Remove alternator drive belt. ***See this section.***
4. Remove tensioner pulley securing bolt. Remove pulley.

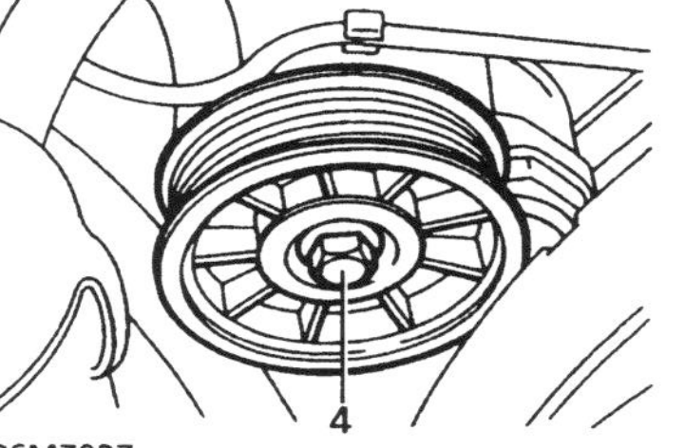

86M7027

5. Remove tensioner securing bolt. Remove tensioner.

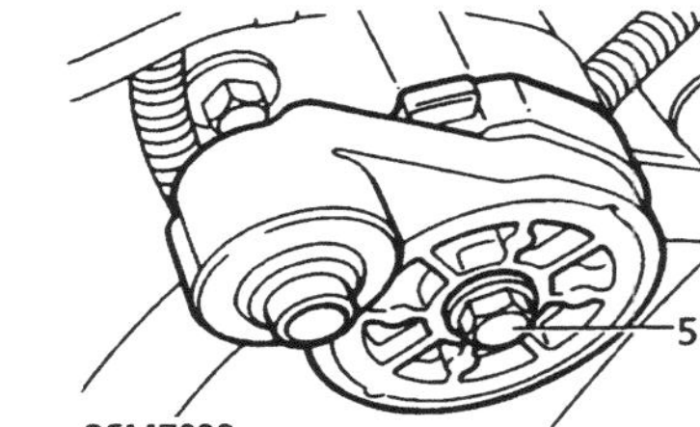

86M7028

Refit

6. Ensure mating faces are clean.
7. Fit tensioner.

CAUTION: Ensure tensioner dowel is correctly located.

8. Fit tensioner securing bolt. Tighten to ***39 Nm. (29 lbf.ft)***
9. Fit tensioner pulley. Secure with bolt. Tighten to ***50 Nm. (37 lbf.ft)***

CAUTION: Fit special washer with raised face towards pulley.

10. Fit alternator drive belt. ***See this section.***
11. Fit radiator cooling fan cowl.
12. Reconnect battery negative lead.

DRIVE BELT TENSIONER - DIESEL

Service repair no - 86.10.06

Remove

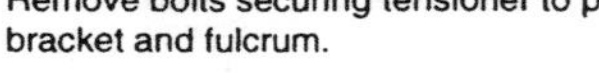

1. Disconnect battery negative lead.
2. Remove drive belt. ***See this section.***
3. Remove bolts securing tensioner to pulley bracket and fulcrum.

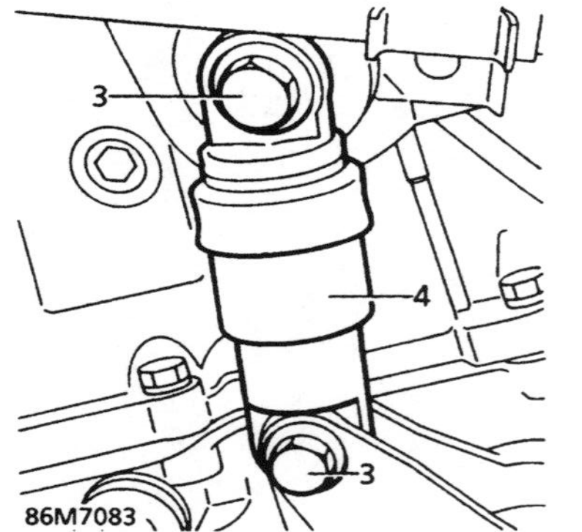

4. Remove tensioner.

CAUTION: The tensioner is an oil filled damper which must be stored vertically. An incorrectly stored damper must be bled before fitment by compressing several times.

Refit

5. Reverse removal procedure.

STARTER MOTOR - V8

Service repair no - 86.60.01

Remove

1. Disconnect battery negative lead.
2. Raise the vehicle.

WARNING: Support on safety stands.

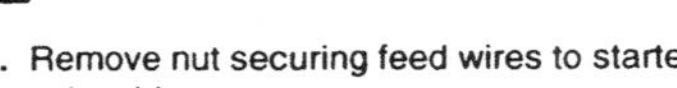

3. Remove nut securing feed wires to starter solenoid.
4. Remove 2 feed wires from solenoid terminal.
5. Release Lucar from solenoid.

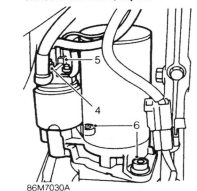

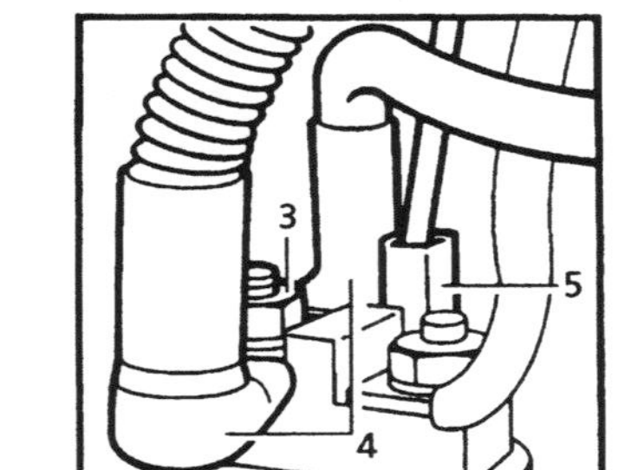

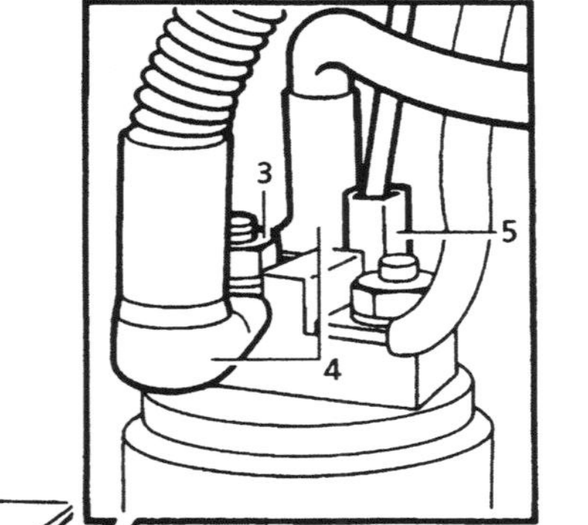
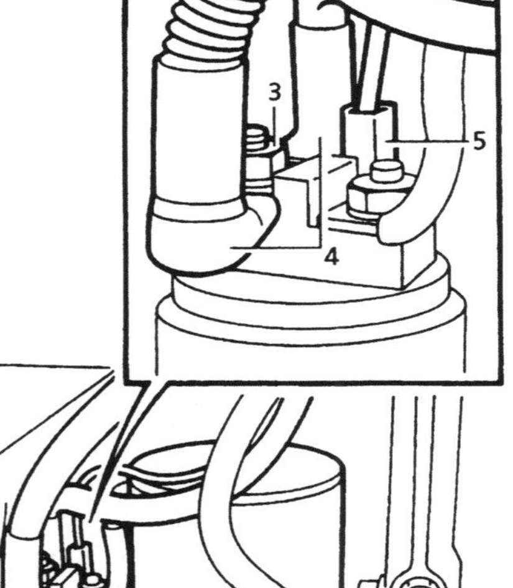
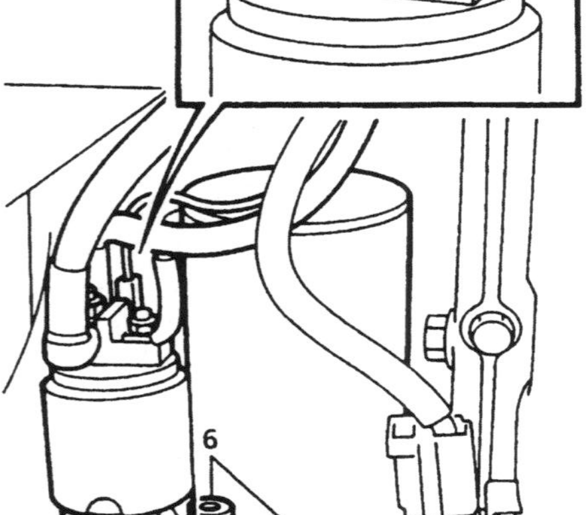

6. Remove 2 bolts securing starter motor to engine.

NOTE: Use two extensions as illustrated to gain access to the top bolt.

7. Remove starter motor.

Refit

8. Ensure mating faces are clean.
9. Fit starter motor.
10. Fit bolts. Tighten to ***45 Nm. (33 lbf.ft)***
11. Fit Lucar to starter solenoid.
12. Connect feed wires to solenoid terminal. Secure with nut.
13. Remove stands and lower vehicle.
14. Reconnect battery negative lead.

STARTER MOTOR - V8 - 97 MY ON

Service repair no - 86.60.01

Remove

1. Disconnect battery earth lead.
2. Raise front of vehicle.

WARNING: Support on safety stands.

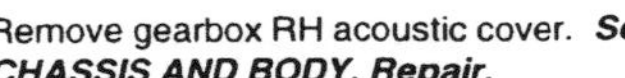

3. Remove gearbox RH acoustic cover. ***See CHASSIS AND BODY, Repair.***

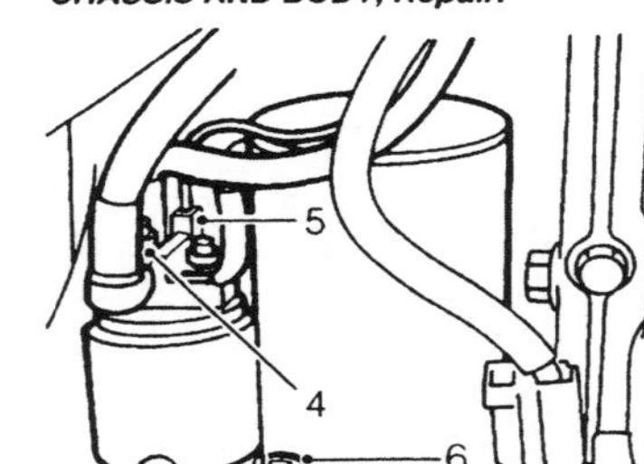

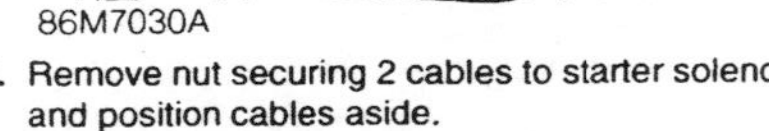

4. Remove nut securing 2 cables to starter solenoid and position cables aside.
5. Disconnect lucar from starter solenoid.
6. Remove 2 bolts securing starter motor to engine.

STARTER MOTOR - DIESEL

Service repair no - 86.60.01

Remove

1. Disconnect battery negative lead.
2. Remove nut and bolt securing dipstick tube.
3. Remove dipstick/tube assembly from sump. Collect 'O' ring and discard.
4. Remove nut and bolt securing rear support stay to inlet manifold. Remove stay.

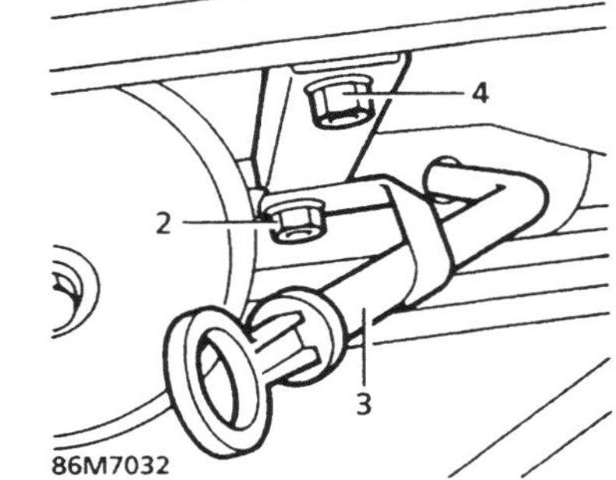

86M7032

5. Raise the vehicle.

WARNING: Support on safety stands.

6. Remove nuts securing wires to starter solenoid terminals. Disconnect wires.
7. Slacken lower bolt securing clutch fluid pipe bracket to engine.
8. With assistance remove nuts and bolts securing starter motor.
9. Move fluid pipe bracket clear, release starter motor from dowel. Remove starter motor.

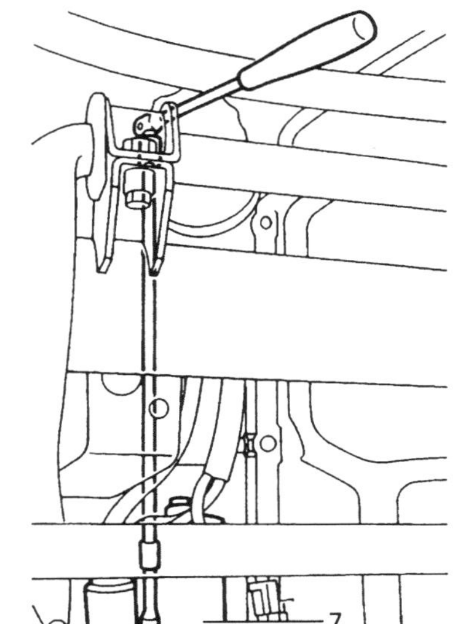

86M7031

NOTE: Use extensions as illustrated to gain access to top bolt.

7. Remove starter motor.

Refit

8. Clean mating faces of starter motor and engine.
9. Fit starter motor to engine.
10. Fit bolts securing starter motor to engine and tighten to ***45 Nm. (33 lbf.ft)***
11. Connect Lucar to starter solenoid.
12. Connect cables to starter solenoid and secure with nut.
13. Fit gearbox RH acoustic cover. ***See CHASSIS AND BODY, Repair.***
14. Remove stand(s) and lower vehicle.

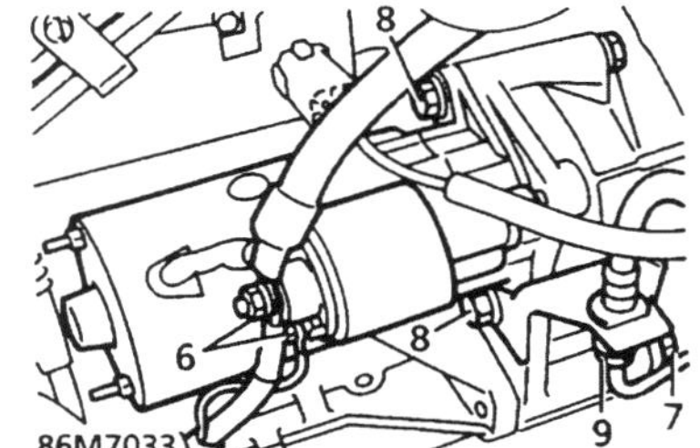

86M7033

Refit

10. Ensure mating faces are clean.
11. Position starter motor. Locate onto dowel.
12. Align fluid pipe bracket. Secure starter motor with nuts and bolts. Tighten to ***48 Nm. (35 lbf.ft).***
13. Tighten clutch fluid pipe bracket lower bolt to ***86 Nm (63 lbf.ft).***

INDICATOR STALK

Service repair no - 86.65.64

Remove

1. Remove steering column nacelle. ***See STEERING, Repair.***
2. Disconnect multiplug from stalk.

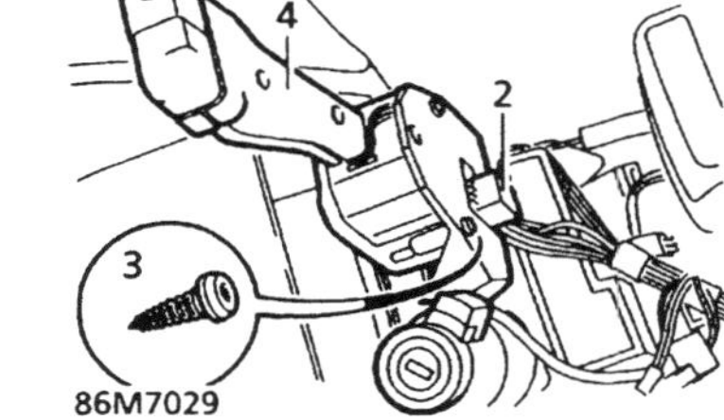

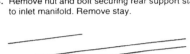

86M7029

3. Remove 2 screws securing stalk to steering column.
4. Remove indicator stalk.

Refit

5. Reverse removal procedure.

HANDBRAKE WARNING SWITCH

Service repair no - 86.65.45

Remove

1. Remove centre console. ***See CHASSIS AND BODY, Repair.***
2. Disconnect 2 Lucars from warning switch.

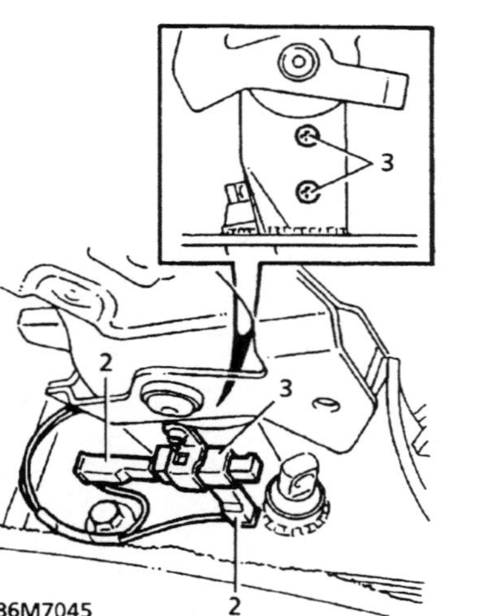

86M7045

3. Remove 2 screws securing switch. Remove switch.

Refit

4. Reverse removal procedure.

STEERING WHEEL MOUNTED SWITCHES

Service repair no - 86.50.13 - Radio Controls

Remove

1. Remove steering wheel pad. ***See STEERING, Repair.***
2. **Vehicles with SRS:** Remove drivers air bag module. ***See SUPPLEMENTARY RESTRAINT SYSTEM, Repair.***
3. Disconnect steering wheel switch multiplug.

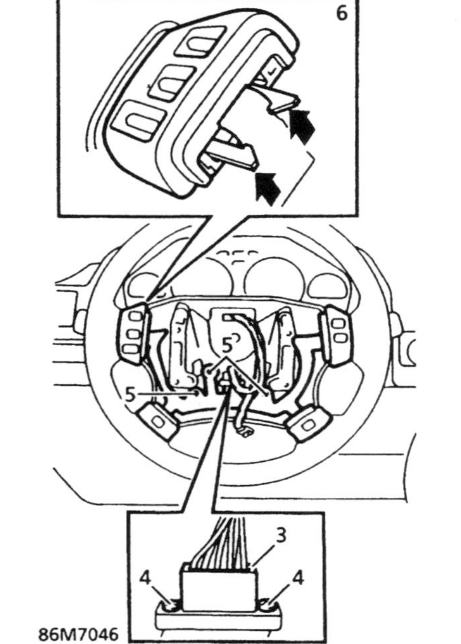

86M7046

4. Remove 2 screws securing multiplug to horn unit.
5. Remove 3 screws securing printed circuit to horn unit.

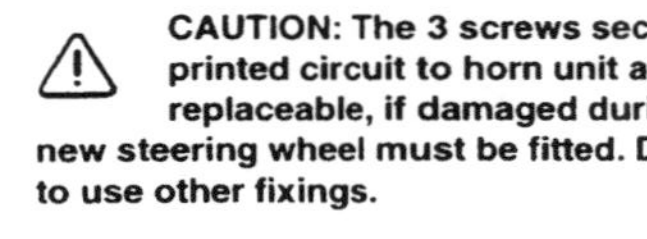

CAUTION: The 3 screws securing the printed circuit to horn unit are not replaceable, if damaged during removal a new steering wheel must be fitted. Do not attempt to use other fixings.

6. Lift 2 clips securing each switch pack. Remove switch packs and printed circuit assembly.

Refit

7. Reverse removal procedure.

ELECTRIC WINDOW SWITCH PACK

Service repair no - 86.25.08

Remove

1. Remove 2 screws securing switch pack to centre console.

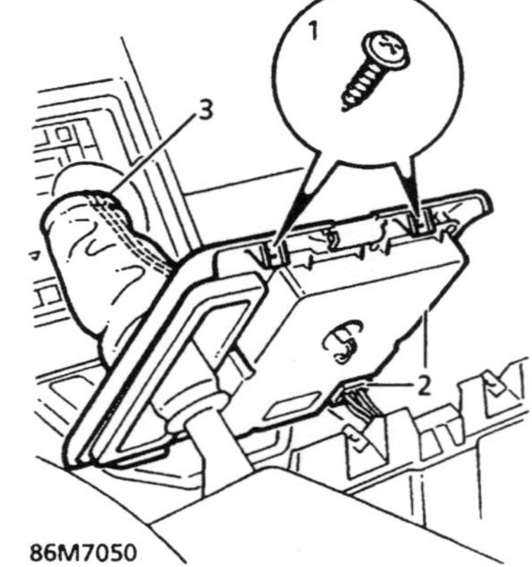

86M7050

2. Release switch pack. Disconnect multiplug.
3. Withdraw gaiter over handbrake. Remove switch pack.

Refit

4. Reverse removal procedure.

ULTRASONIC SENSOR

Service repair no - 86.55.96

Remove

1. Release ultrasonic sensor from headlining.
2. Disconnect multiplug. Remove sensor.

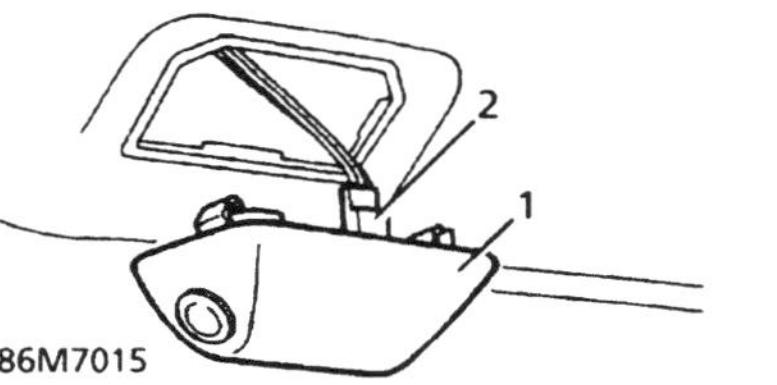

86M7015

Refit

3. Reverse removal procedure.

RECEIVER

Service repair no - 86.55.38

Remove

1. Remove RH parcel shelf support trim. *See* ***CHASSIS AND BODY, Repair.***
2. Disconnect Lucar and multiplug from receiver.
3. Remove screw. Remove receiver.

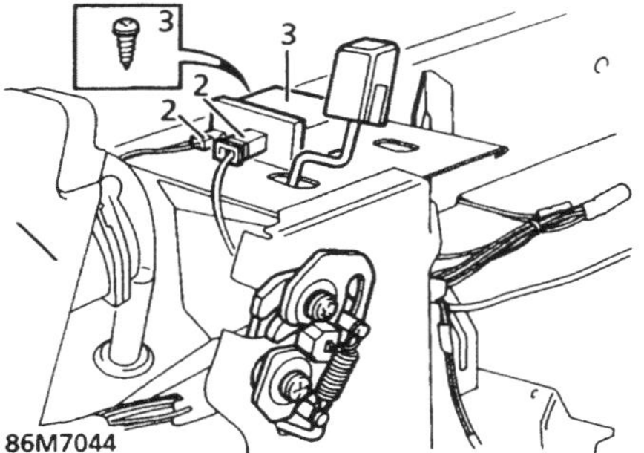

86M7044

Refit

4. Reverse removal procedure.

SWITCH TAILGATE RELEASE

Service repair no - 86.26.26

Remove

1. Release 3 studs securing tailgate board. Remove board.
2. Disconnect tailgate switch multiplug.

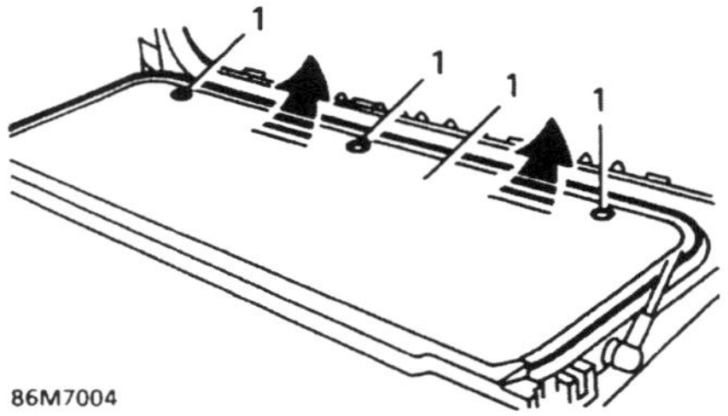

86M7004

3. Remove 2 screws securing switch to tailgate.

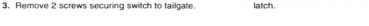

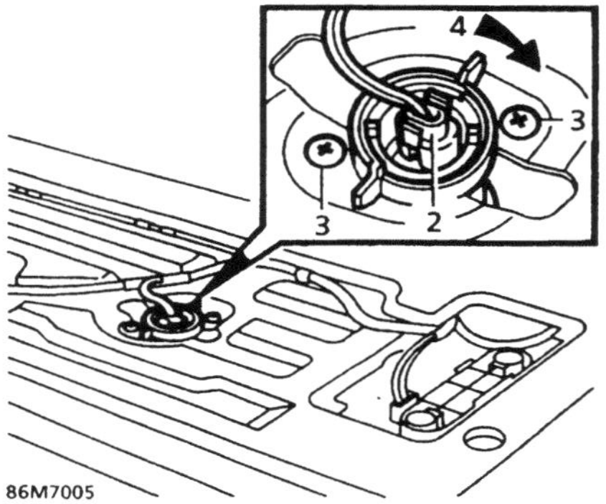

86M7005

4. Turn switch clockwise to remove.

Refit

5. Reverse removal procedure.

TAILGATE SOLENOID

Service repair no - 86.26.02

Remove

1. Release studs securing tailgate board. Remove board.

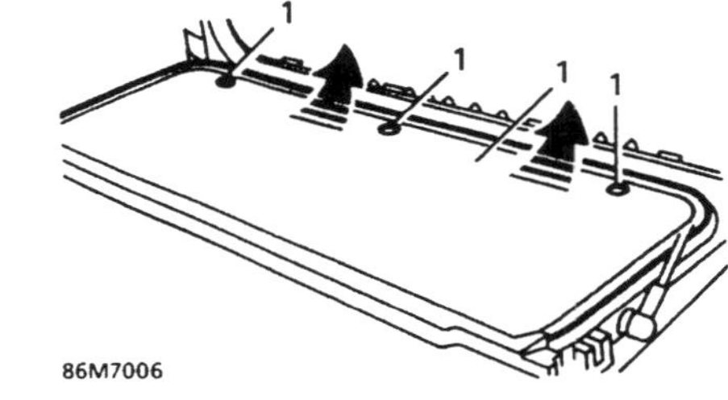

86M7006

2. Release solenoid operating rod from tailgate latch.

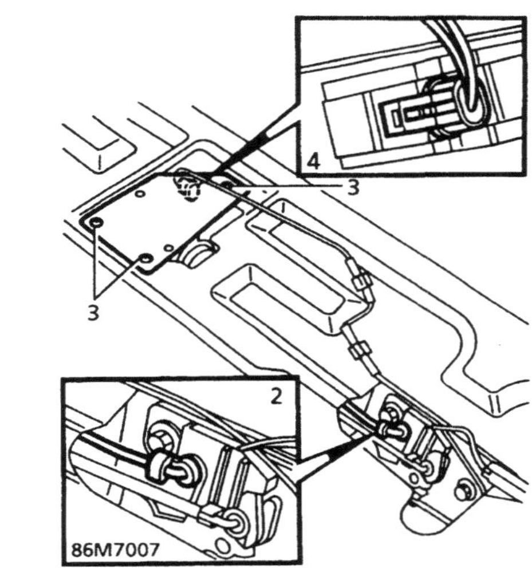

86M7007

3. Remove 3 screws securing solenoid assembly.
4. Disconnect multiplug. Remove solenoid.

86M7008

5. Remove 2 screws securing solenoid to mounting plate. Remove solenoid.
6. Release clip. Remove operating rod from solenoid.

Refit

7. Reverse removal procedure.

BODY ELECTRICAL CONTROL MODULE (BeCM)

Service repair no - 86.55.98

Remove

1. Disconnect battery negative lead.
2. Remove RH front seat for access. ***See SEATS, Repair.***
3. Remove 2 screws securing heater rear outlet duct. Remove duct.
4. Release carpet over BeCM. Position aside.
5. Remove 2 nuts and screw securing BeCM to mounting.
6. Disconnect multiplugs from BeCM.
7. Release terminal covers.
8. Disconnect 1 earth and 3 feed wires.
9. Remove BeCM.

Refit

10. Reverse removal procedure.

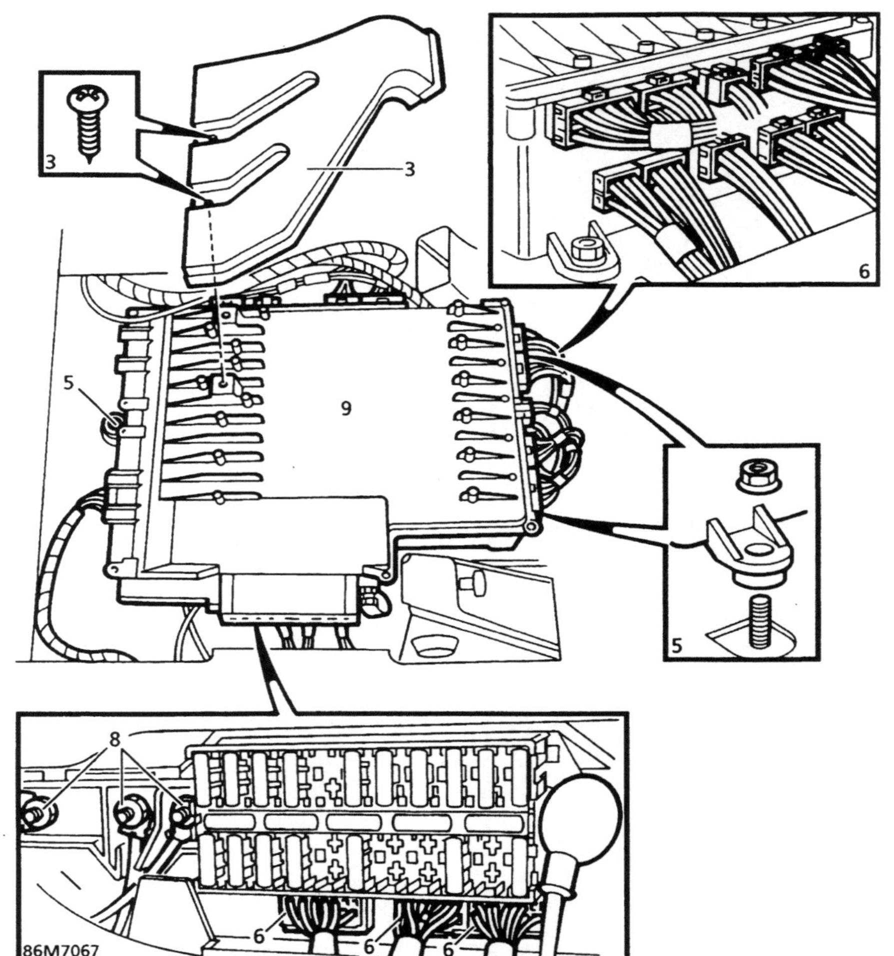

HEADLAMP

Service repair no - 86.40.09

Remove

1. Remove indicator. ***See this section.***
2. Remove front grille. ***See CHASSIS AND BODY, Repair.***
3. Release headlamp wiper arm securing nut cover.
4. Remove nut.
5. Release headlamp washer tube from wiper arm. Remove wiper arm.

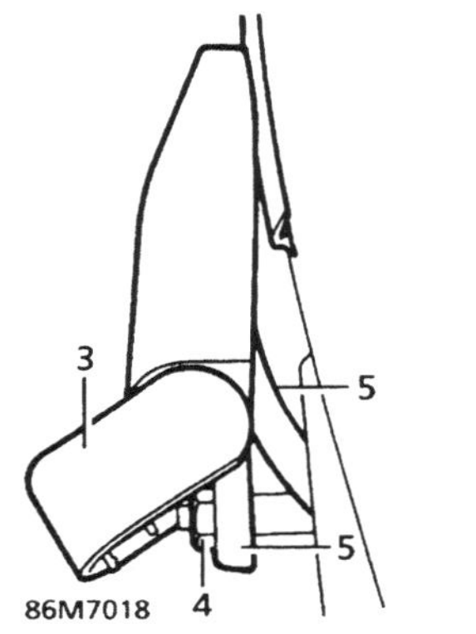

86M7018

6. Remove bolt securing headlamp housing to bonnet platform
7. Remove bolt securing housing to inner wing platform.
8. Remove 2 nuts securing housing to front panel.

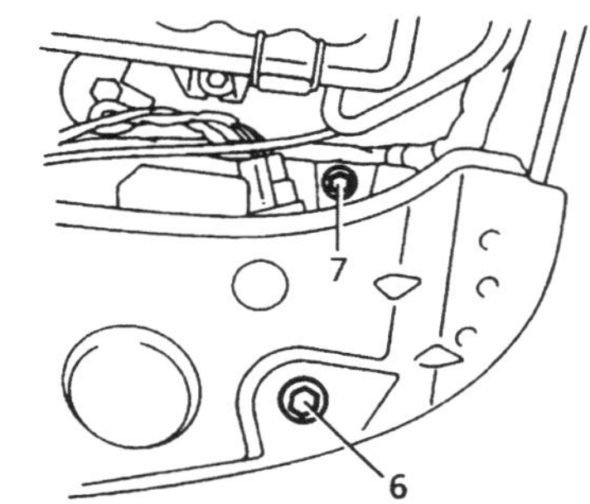

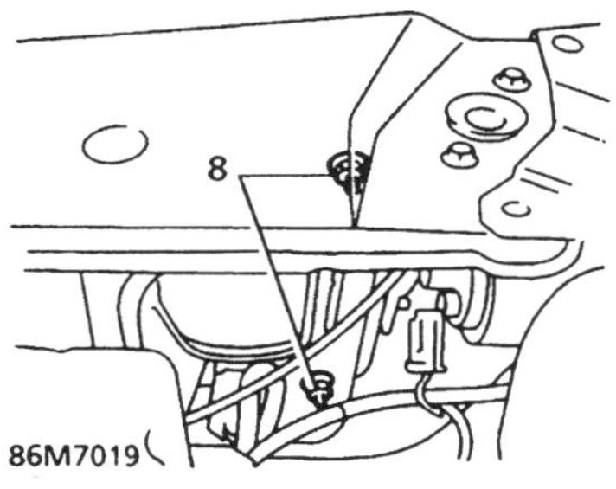

86M7019

9. Disconnect multiplugs from headlamp and wiper motor.
10. Remove headlamp housing assembly.

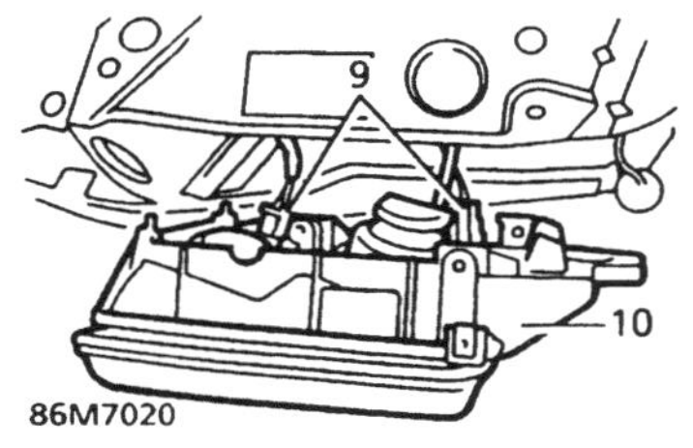

86M7020

Disassemble

11. Remove 2 screws securing trim moulding to headlamp housing. Remove trim.

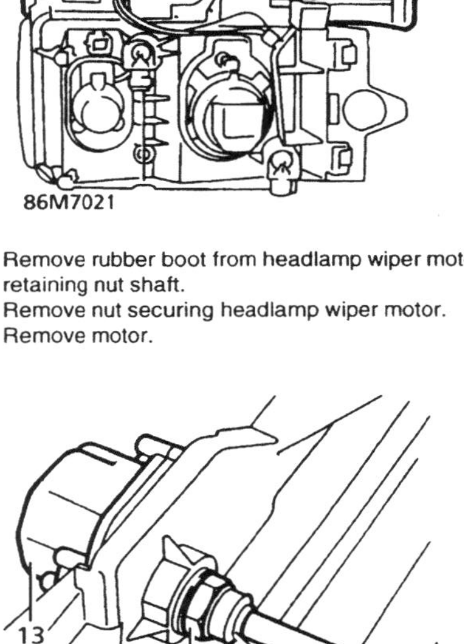

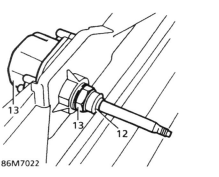

86M7021

12. Remove rubber boot from headlamp wiper motor retaining nut shaft.
13. Remove nut securing headlamp wiper motor. Remove motor.

86M7022

Assemble

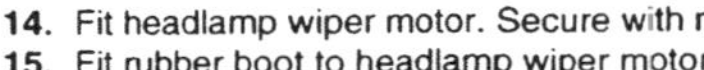

14. Fit headlamp wiper motor. Secure with nut.
15. Fit rubber boot to headlamp wiper motor retaining nut shaft.
16. Fit trim moulding to headlamp assembly. Secure with screws.

Refit

17. Position headlamp housing assembly.
18. Connect headlamp and wiper motor multiplugs.
19. Secure housing to front panel with screws.
20. Secure housing to bonnet platform with bolt.
21. Secure housing to inner wing platform with bolt.
22. Position wiper arm to drive spindle. Connect wash wipe tube.
23. Secure wiper arm with nut, tighten to ***10 Nm (7 lbf.ft).***
24. Secure headlamp wiper arm retaining nut cover.
25. Refit front grille. ***See CHASSIS AND BODY, Repair.***
26. Refit indicator. ***See this section.***

REAR FOG GUARD LAMP

Service repair no - 86.41.15

Remove

1. Release 3 studs securing tailgate board. Remove board.

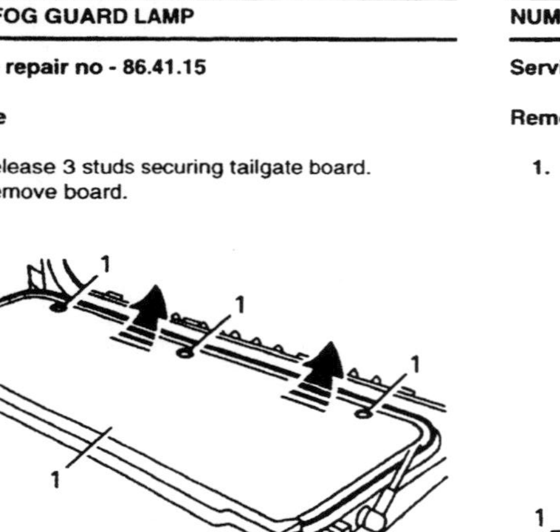

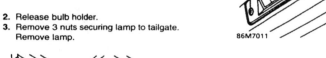

86M7002

2. Release bulb holder.
3. Remove 3 nuts securing lamp to tailgate. Remove lamp.

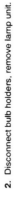

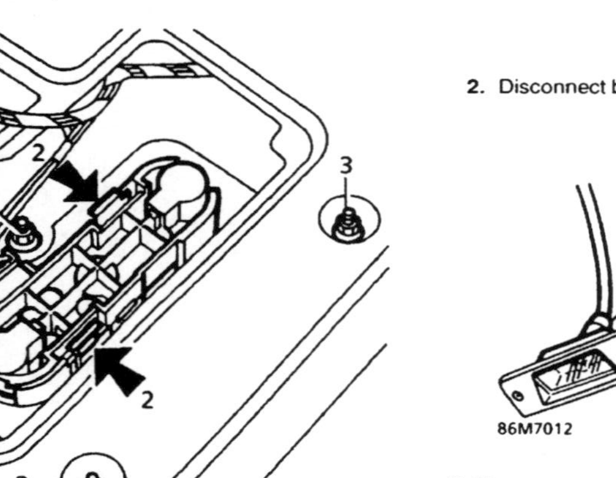

86M7003

Refit

4. Reverse removal procedure.

NUMBER PLATE LAMP

Service repair no - 86.40.86

Remove

1. Remove 4 screws securing lamps to tailgate.

86M7011

2. Disconnect bulb holders, remove lamp unit.

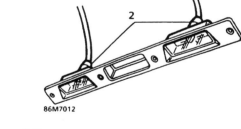

86M7012

Refit

3. Reverse removal procedure.

INTERIOR LAMP ASSEMBLY

Service repair no - 86.45.13

Remove

1. Remove lamp lens.
2. Remove 2 screws securing lamp to roof.

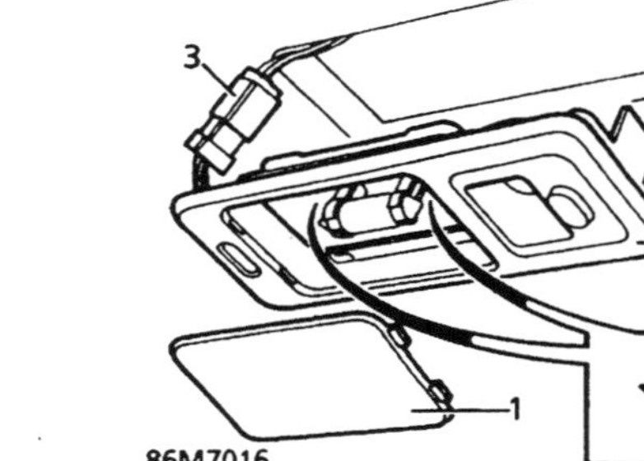

86M7016

3. Release lamp assembly. Disconnect multiplug. Remove lamp.

Refit

4. Reverse removal procedure.

LOAD SPACE LAMP

Service repair no - 86.45.16

Remove

1. Release lamp from tailgate.
2. Disconnect leads. Remove lamp.

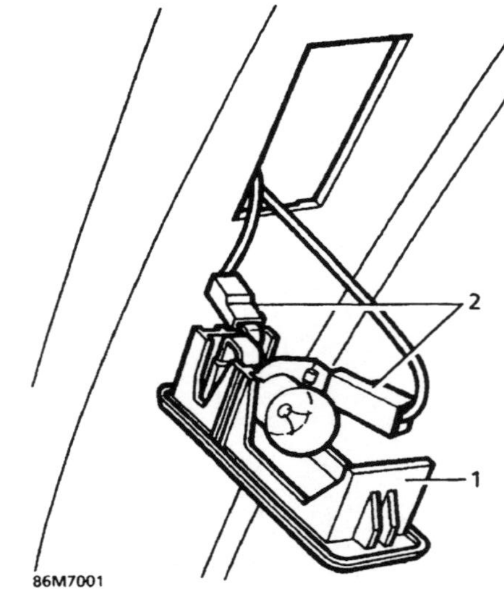

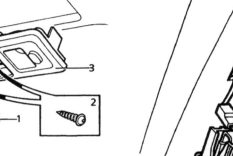

86M7001

Refit

3. Reverse removal procedure.

AERIAL AMPLIFIER

Service repair no - 86.50.29

Remove

1. Remove parcel tray support panel. ***See CHASSIS AND BODY, Repair.***
2. Disconnect 2 multiplugs from amplifier.

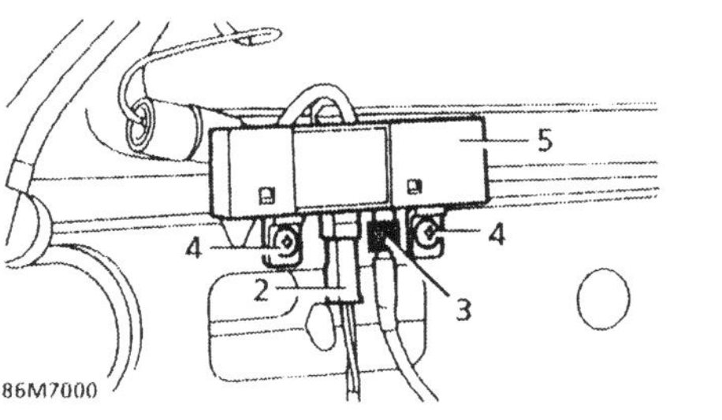

86M7000

3. Release co-axial lead from amplifier.
4. Remove 2 screws securing aerial amplifier to body.
5. Remove aerial amplifier.

Refit

6. Reverse removal procedure.

SPEAKER AMPLIFIER - FRONT

Service repair no - 86.50.92

Remove

1. Remove door trim casing. ***See CHASSIS AND BODY, Repair.***
2. Disconnect multiplug from speaker amplifier.
3. Remove 2 screws securing amplifier. Remove amplifier.

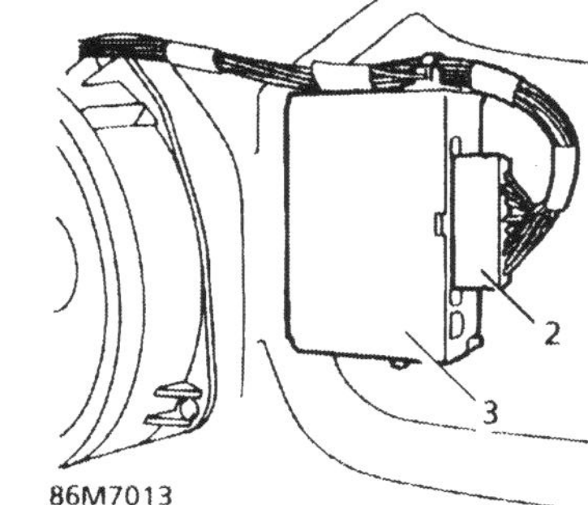

86M7013

Refit

4. Reverse removal procedure.

SPEAKER AMPLFIFIER - REAR

Service repair no - 86.50.92

Remove

1. Remove door trim casing. ***See CHASSIS AND BODY, Repair.***
2. Disconnect multiplug from speaker amplifier.
3. Remove 2 screws securing amplifier. Remove amplifier.

86M7014

Refit

4. Reverse removal procedure.

COMPACT DISC AUTOCHANGER

Remove

1. Release 4 turnbuckles securing access panel. Remove panel.

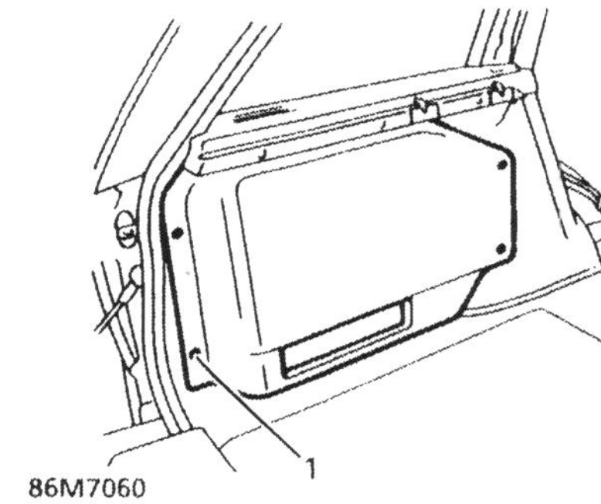
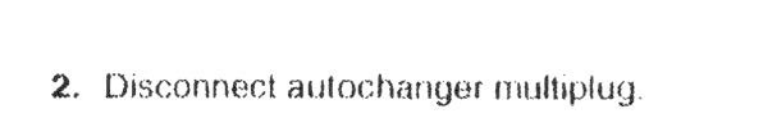

86M7060

2. Disconnect autochanger multiplug.

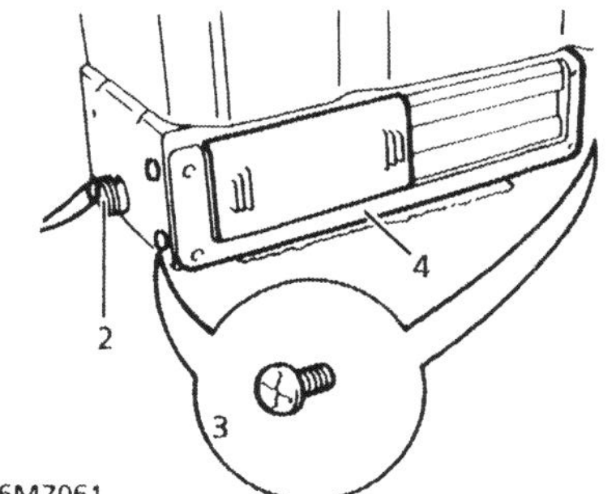

86M7061

3. Remove 4 screws securing autochanger to bracket.
4. Remove compact disc autochanger.

Refit

5. Reverse removal procedure.

SPEAKER AMPLIFIER - REAR

Service repair no - 86.50.92

Remove

1. Remove door trim casing. ***See CHASSIS AND BODY, Repair.***
2. Disconnect multiplug from speaker amplifier.
3. Remove 2 screws securing amplifier. Remove amplifier.

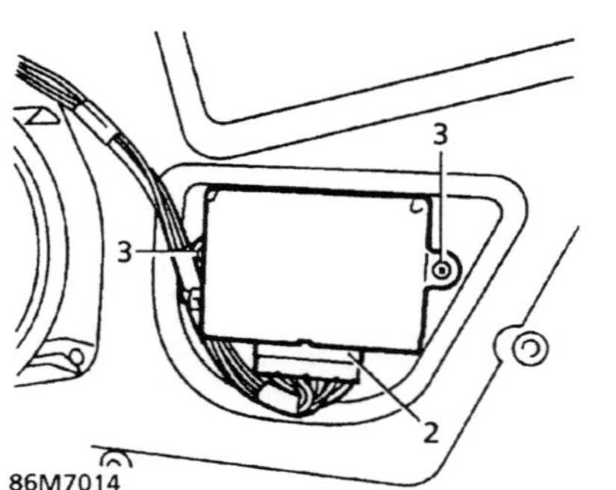

86M7014

Refit

4. Reverse removal procedure.

COMPACT DISC AUTOCHANGER

Remove

1. Release 4 turnbuckles securing access panel. Remove panel.

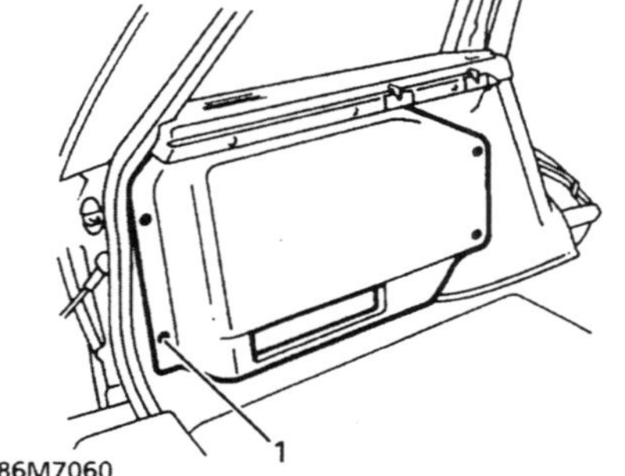

86M7060

2. Disconnect autochanger multiplug.

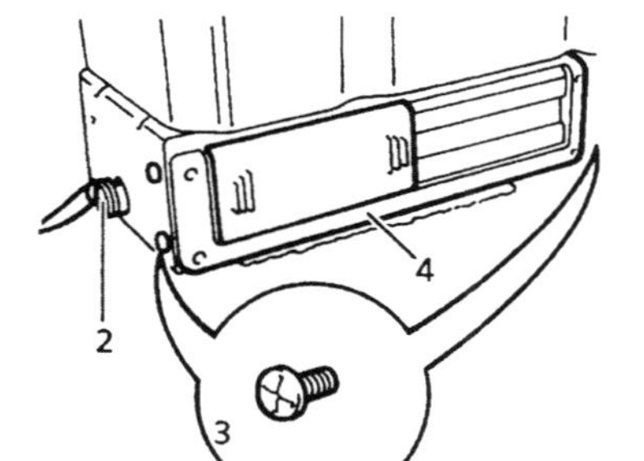

86M7061

3. Remove 4 screws securing autochanger to bracket.
4. Remove compact disc autochanger.

Refit

5. Reverse removal procedure.

SUBWOOFER UNIT

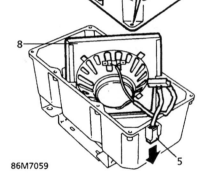

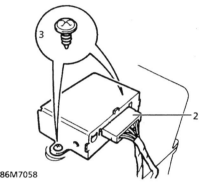

Service repair no - 86.50.51 - Assembly
Service repair no - 86.50.92 - Speaker
Service repair no - 86.50.52 - Amplifier

Remove

1. Remove subwoofer assembly. ***See CHASSIS AND BODY, Repair.***

Amplifier

2. Disconnect multiplug from amplifier.

3
2
86M7058

3. Remove 2 screws securing amplifier to subwoofer box.
4. Remove amplifier.

Speaker

5. Release multiplug from casing.

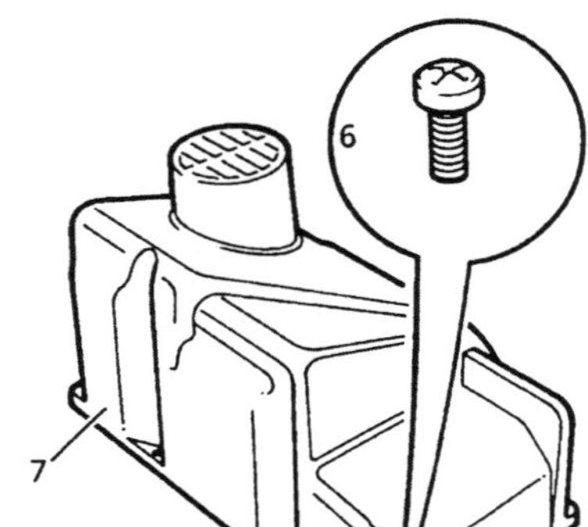

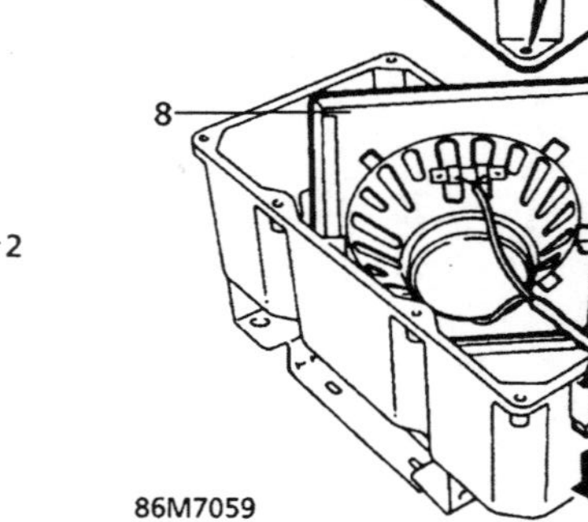

86M7059

6. Remove 8 screws securing subwoofer unit halves.
7. Remove upper half of unit.
8. Remove speaker.

Refit

9. Reverse removal procedure.
10. Check condition of all foam seals before assembly.
11. Seal speaker harness to subwoofer unit using black RTV silicone or similar sealant.

ROTARY COUPLER - STEERING WHEEL AND SRS

Service repair no - 86.65.85

WARNING: Do not turn steering wheel independently of steering box. Damage to the internal harness may occur, resulting in possible malfunction of SRS and steering wheel mounted switches.

Remove

1. Remove steering wheel. ***See STEERING, Repair.***
2. Release SRS harness from clips.

86M7064

3. Disconnect steering wheel multiplug.
4. Release 2 clips securing rotary coupler. Remove coupler.

Refit

5. Position rotary coupler. Engage clips.
6. Route SRS harness correctly. Secure to clips.

WARNING: Do not connect SRS multiplug/'shorting link' until drivers air bag module has been fitted.

7. Connect steering wheel multiplug.
8. Fit steering wheel. ***See STEERING, Repair.***

BATTERY

Service repair no - 86.15.01

NOTE: From '96 MY, vehicles maybe fitted with a back-up battery, the purpose of which is to power the anti-theft alarm if the main battery is disconnected. If the main vehicle battery is to be removed it is essential to adopt the following procedure before disconnecting the terminals in order to prevent the alarm sounding:

1. **Turn the starter switch 'on' and then 'off'.**
2. **Disconnect the battery WITHIN 17 SECONDS (if the battery is not disconnected within 17 seconds, the alarm will sound).**

Remove

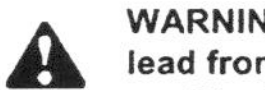

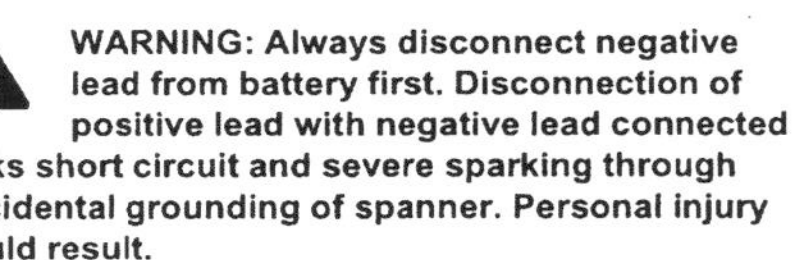

WARNING: Always disconnect negative lead from battery first. Disconnection of positive lead with negative lead connected risks short circuit and severe sparking through accidental grounding of spanner. Personal injury could result.

1. Release 3 turnbuckles securing battery cover. Remove cover.

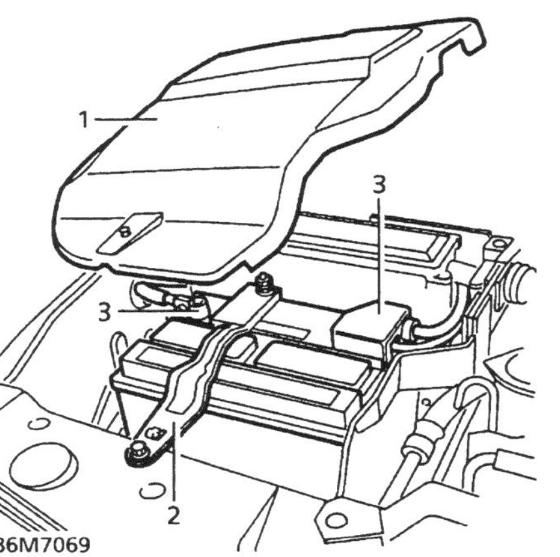

86M7069

2. Remove 2 nuts and 1 bolt securing battery clamp. Remove clamp.
3. Disconnect battery terminals. Remove battery.

Refit

NOTE: Coat battery clamps and terminals with petroleum jelly before refitting.

4. Reverse removal procedure. Reconnect battery negative lead.

BONNET SWITCH

Service repair no - 86.55.89

NOTE: Bonnet switch is integral with RH bonnet lock.

Remove

1. Remove bonnet switch/lock assembly. ***See CHASSIS AND BODY, Repair.***

Refit

2. Reverse removal procedure.

DOOR OUTSTATION

Service repair no - 86.55.99

Remove

1. Remove front door trim casing. ***See CHASSIS AND BODY, Repair.***
2. Remove 2 screws securing outstation.
3. Disconnect 3 outstation multiplugs. Remove outstation.

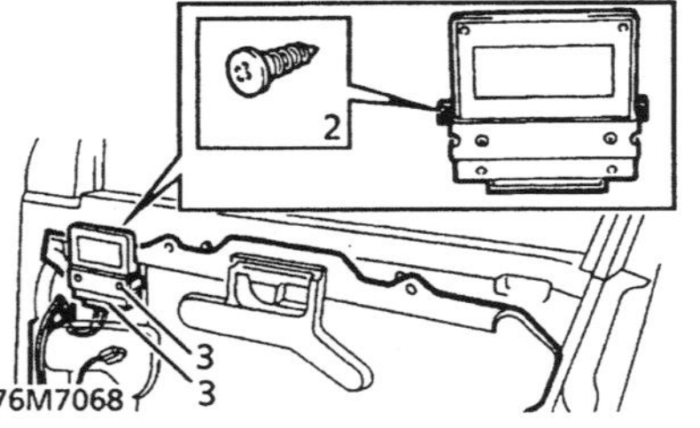

Refit

4. Reverse removal procedure.

FASCIA MOUNTED SWITCHES

Remove

1. Remove instrument pack binnacle. ***See INSTRUMENTS, Repair.***
2. Remove screw securing each side panel to centre console.

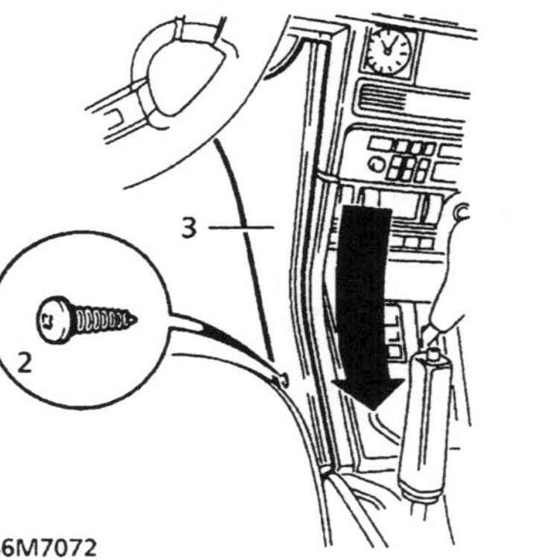

3. Disengage sprag clips from fascia switch pack. Remove side panels.
4. Remove radio applique.

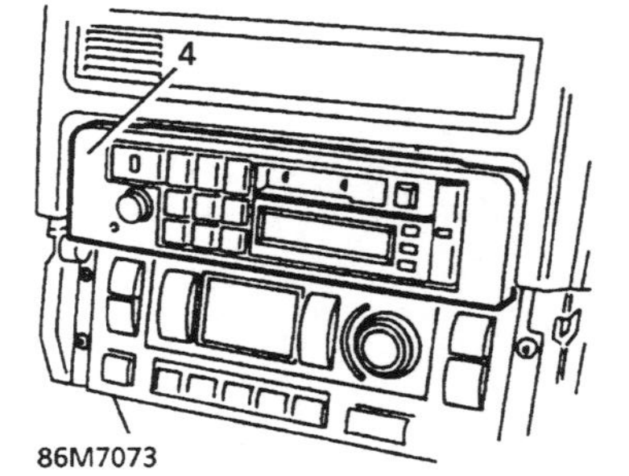

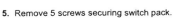

5. Remove 5 screws securing switch pack.

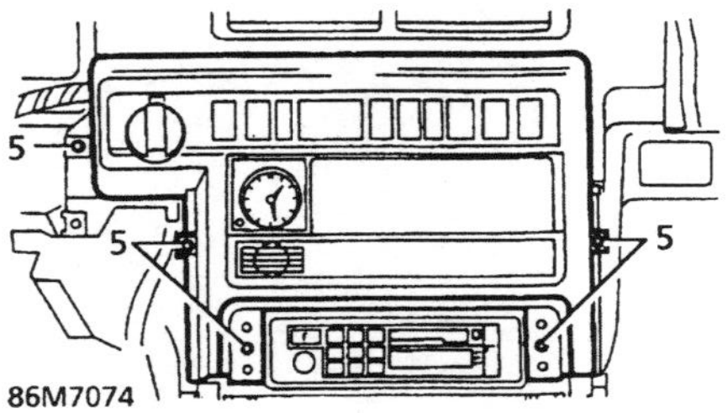

86M7074

6. Release switch pack from fascia.

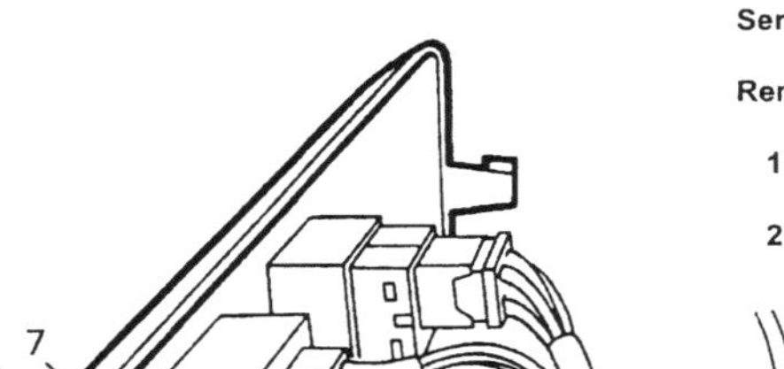

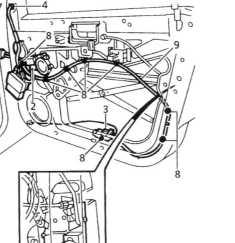

86M7075

7. Disconnect multiplug from relevant switch.
8. Release clips securing switch to switch pack. Remove switch.

Refit

9. Reverse removal procedure.

HARNESS - FRONT DOOR

Service repair no - 86.70.65

Remove

1. Remove plastic sheet. ***See CHASSIS AND BODY, Repair.***
2. Disconnect window lift motor multiplug.

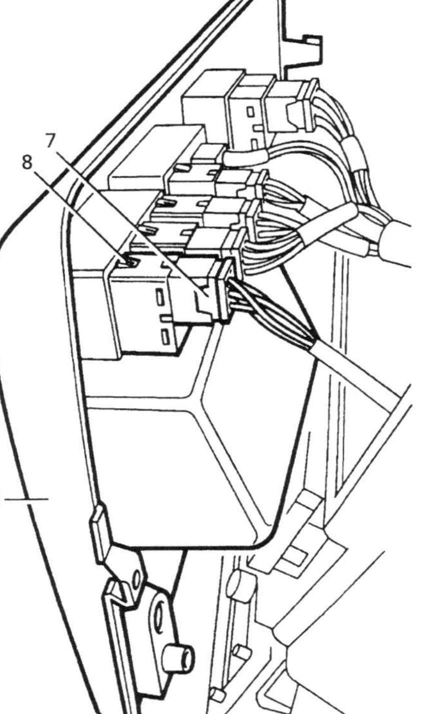
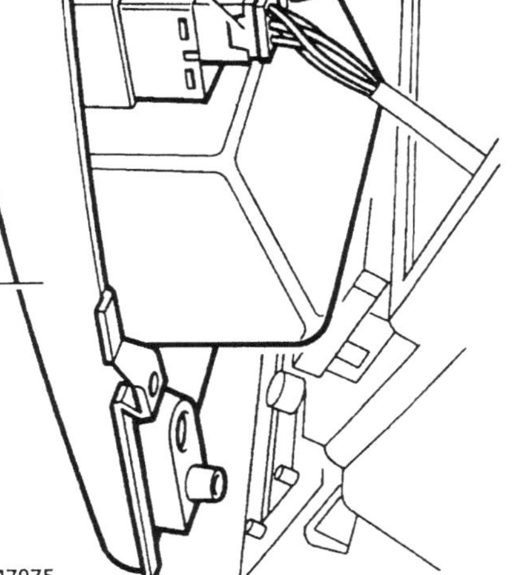

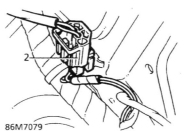

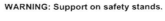

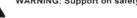

86M7071

3. Disconnect puddle lamp multiplug.
4. Disconnect door mirror multiplug.
5. Disconnect 2 door latch motor multiplugs.
6. Release door to body harness sheath at both ends.
7. Release 2 door harness connectors from body and disconnect.
8. Release 8 clips securing door harness.
9. Remove harness from door.

Refit

10. Reverse removal procedure.

FRONT FOG LAMP

Service repair no - 86.40.96

Remove

1. Raise the vehicle.

WARNING: Support on safety stands.

2. Disconnect multiplug.

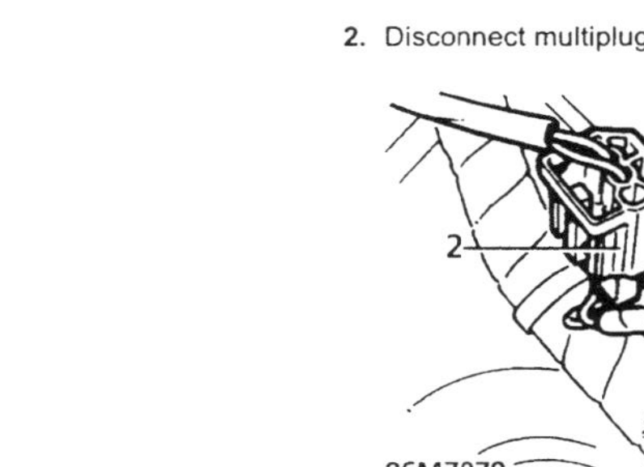

86M7079

3. Disconnect 2 breather tubes.

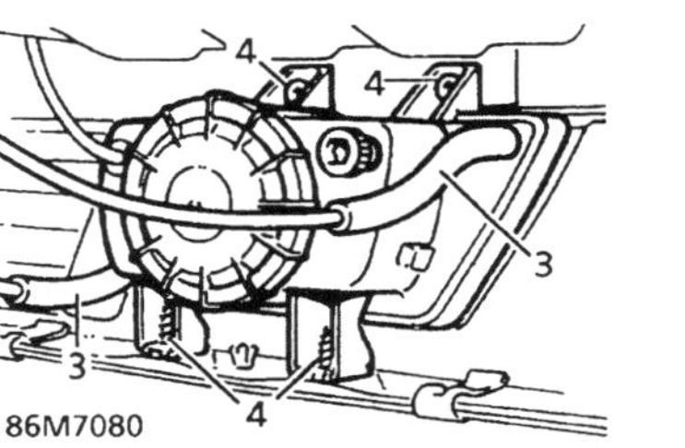

86M7080

4. Remove 4 screws securing fog lamp to bumper.
5. Remove fog lamp assembly.

Refit

6. Reverse removal procedure.

FRONT SPEAKER

Service repair no - 86.50.15

Remove

1. Remove front door trim casing. ***See CHASSIS AND BODY, Repair.***
2. Remove 4 screws securing speaker.

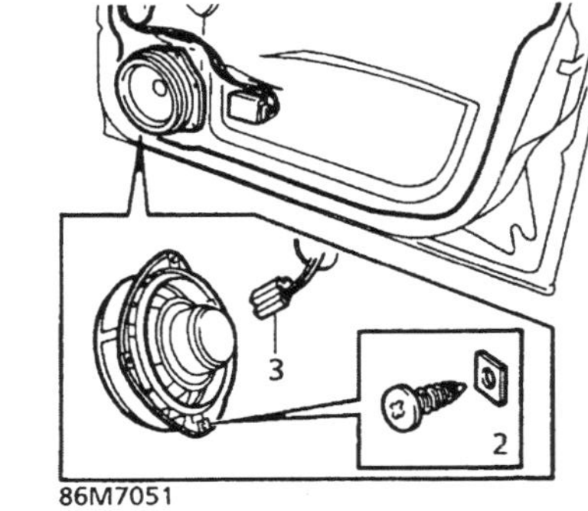

86M7051

3. Release speaker. Disconnect multiplug. Remove speaker.

Refit

4. Reverse removal procedure.

TWEETER SPEAKER - FRONT DOOR

Service repair no - 86.50.34

Remove

1. Remove cheater panel from door.
2. Rotate tweeter speaker to release from cheater.

86M7082

3. Disconnect terminals. Remove speaker.

Refit

4. Reverse removal procedure.

IGNITION SWITCH

Service repair no - 86.65.02

Remove

1. Disconnect battery negative lead.
2. Remove steering column nacelle. ***See STEERING, Repair.***
3. Remove 3 bolts securing steering tilt lever to column.

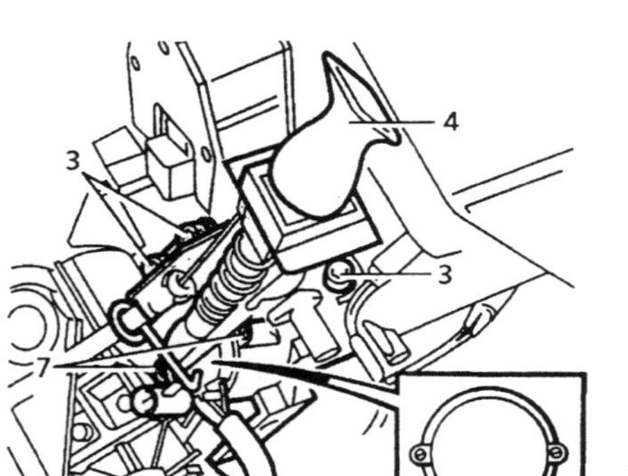

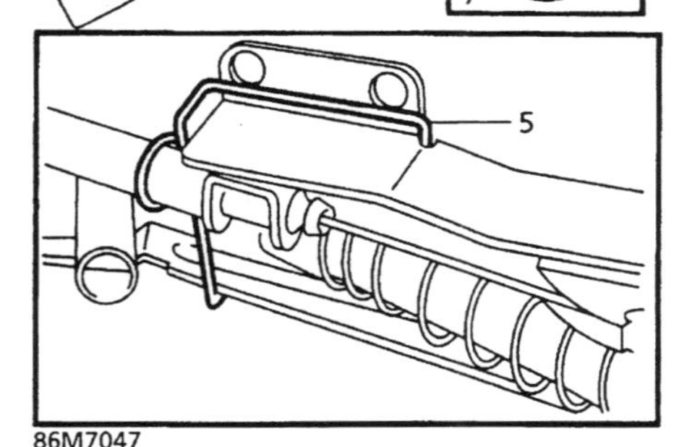

86M7047

4. Release column tilt lever assembly and plunger.
5. Collect lever return spring.
6. Collect plunger and spring if necessary.
7. Remove 2 screws securing ignition switch.

8. Release harness clip from steering column.
9. Release switch multiplug from bracket.

86M7048

10. Remove ignition switch.

Refit

11. Reverse removal procedure.

INDICATOR - FRONT

Service repair no - 86.40.42

Remove

1. **RH indicator only:** Release battery cover fixings. Remove cover.

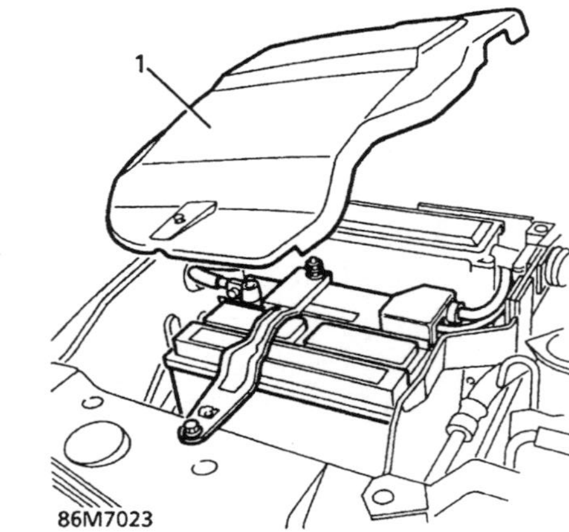

86M7023

2. Release lamp retaining clip. Disconnect multiplug.

2

86M7024

3. Remove indicator unit. Remove bulb holder.

Bulb replacement

4. Rotate bulb holder anti-clockwise. Release from lamp.

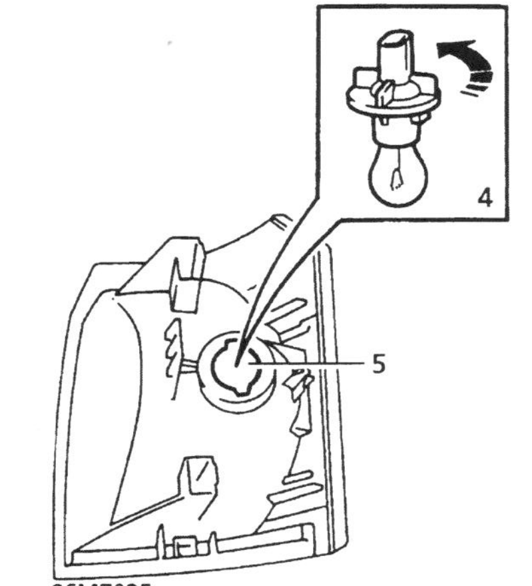

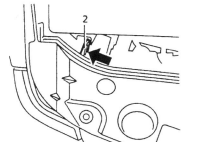

86M7025

5. Remove bulb from holder.
6. Fit bulb to holder.
7. Position bulb holder to lamp. Rotate clockwise to secure.

Refit

8. Reverse removal procedure.

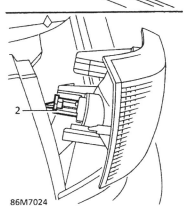

MAP/COURTESY LAMP - FRONT

Service repair no - 86.45.14

Remove

1. Release lamp unit from headlining.
2. Disconnect lamp multiplug.
3. Remove lamp unit.

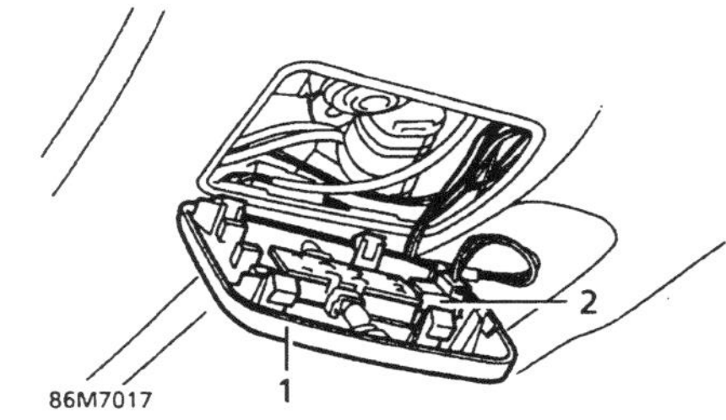

86M7017

Refit

4. Reverse removal procedure.

MOTOR AND CONTROL UNIT - FRONT DOOR

Service repair no - 86.25.01

Remove

1. Remove front door glass. ***See CHASSIS AND BODY, Repair.***
2. Disconnect window lift motor harness connector.
3. Remove rivet securing regulator runner to door panel.
4. Remove 3 rivets securing regulator to door. Remove regulator assembly.
5. Remove 3 screws securing window lift motor. Remove motor.

Refit

6. Fit window lift motor to regulator, secure with 3 screws.
7. Fit regulator assembly. Secure with rivets.
8. Align regulator runner to door panel. Secure with rivet.
9. Reconnect window lift motor harness connector.
10. Refit front door glass. ***See CHASSIS AND BODY, Repair.***

WINDOW MOTOR CONTROL PANEL - REAR DOOR

Service repair no - 86.25.02

Remove

1. Remove rear door plastic sheet. ***See CHASSIS AND BODY, Repair.***
2. Position window to gain access control arm fixings.

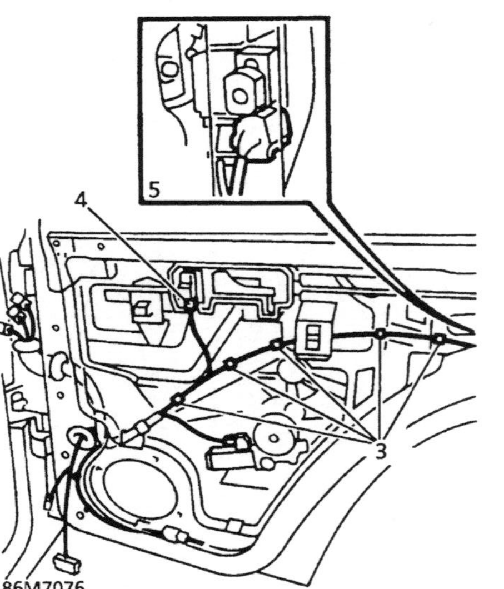

86M7076

3. Release 5 harness clips from window lift cover panel.
4. Disconnect harness multiplug from window lift motor.
5. Disconnect multiplug from window lift switch.
6. Disconnect multiplug from latch solenoid.
7. Remove 3 screws securing door latch.

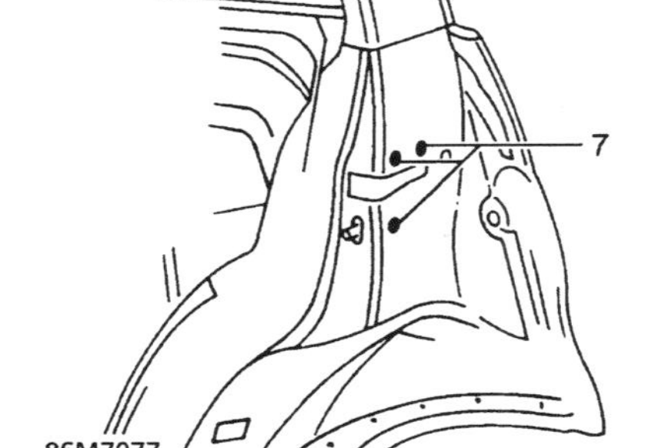

86M7077

8. Secure glass with wedge or tape.
9. Remove 2 spring clips securing glass channel slides to control arms.

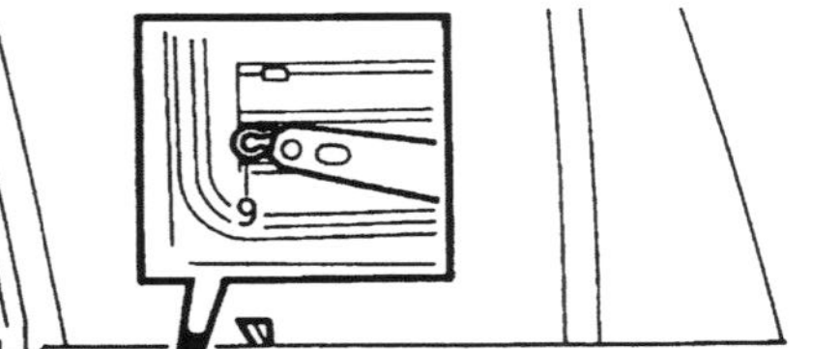
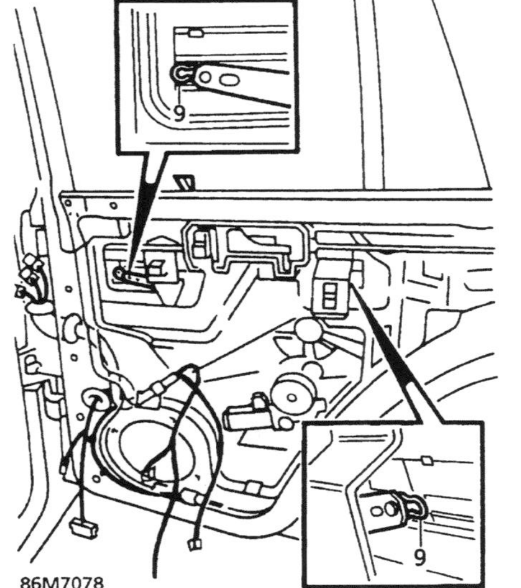

86M7078

10. Release control arms.
11. Remove 4 bolts securing window lift panel.
12. Remove panel.

Disassemble

13. Release door latch remote cable from panel clip.
14. Remove 2 screws securing door latch remote. Release remote.
15. Release sill locking button rod from 2 clips.
16. Remove sill button bellcrank securing screw.
17. Remove 2 studs securing door latch.
18. Position latch remote and sill button assembly aside.
19. Remove 3 plastic clips and 2 plastic nuts from panel.

Assemble

20. Fit 3 plastic clips and 2 plastic nuts to panel.
21. Position latch remote and sill button assembly.
22. Align sill button bellcrank. Secure with screw.
23. Secure sill button link to panel clips.
24. Position door latch remote. Secure with screws.
25. Secure door latch remote cable to panel clip.
26. Align latch. Secure with studs.

Refit

27. Apply grease to channels and control arms. ***See LUBRICANTS, FLUIDS AND CAPACITIES, Information.***
28. Reverse removal procedure.

RADIO

Service repair no - 86.50.03

Remove

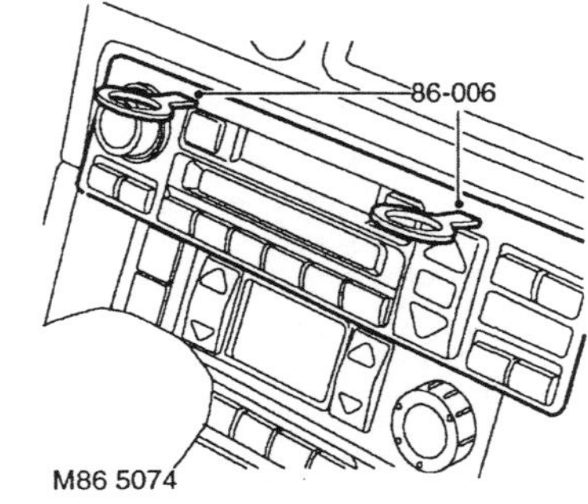

M86 5074

1. Using tool 86-006 release radio from centre console.

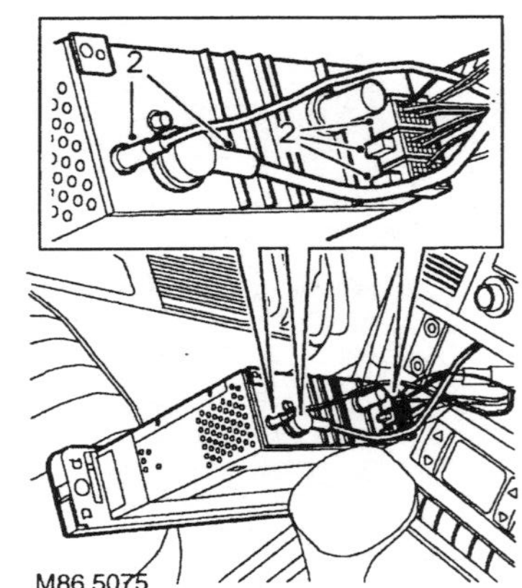

M86 5075

2. Disconnect 3 multiplugs and 2 aerial connections from radio and remove radio.

Refit

3. Position radio to centre console and connect 3 multiplugs and 2 aerial connections.

4. Fit radio to centre console and secure clips.
5. Enter security code and check radio for correct operation.

HARNESS - REAR DOOR

Service repair no - 86.25.21

Remove

1. Remove rear door plastic sheet. ***See CHASSIS AND BODY, Repair.***
2. Release window lift switch from location and disconnect multiplug.
3. Disconnect multiplugs from door lock, puddle lamp and window lift motor.

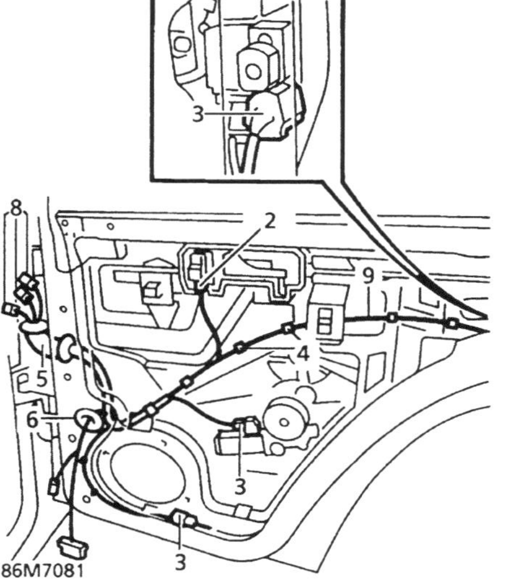

86M7081

4. Release 8 clips securing harness to window lift panel and inner door skin.
5. Release harness protection sheath from door and 'B/C' post.
6. Release grommet and feed amplifier/speaker harness into door.
7. Remove harness from door.
8. Release harness from 'B/C' post to access 3 multiplugs. Disconnect multiplugs.
9. Remove rear door harness.

Refit

10. Reverse removal procedure.

SPEAKER - REAR DOOR

Service repair no - 86.50.12

Remove

1. Remove rear door trim casing. ***See CHASSIS AND BODY, Repair.***
2. Remove 4 screws securing rear door speaker.

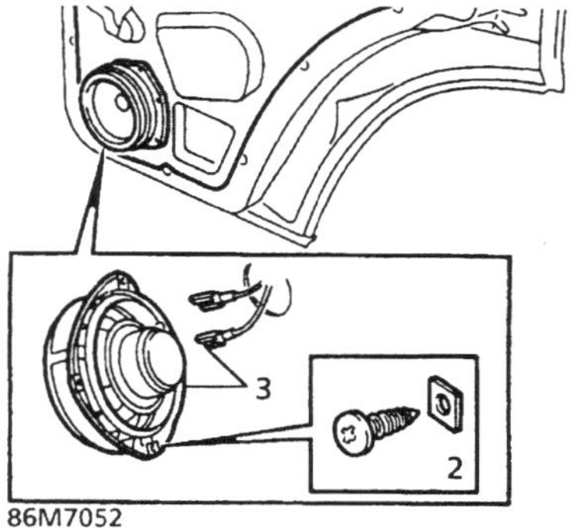

86M7052

3. Release speaker. Disconnect terminals. Remove speaker.

Refit

4. Reverse removal procedure.

REAR WINDOW - DOOR SWITCH

Service repair no - 86.25.10

Remove

1. Remove screw securing handle escutcheon to rear door trim casing. Remove escutcheon.

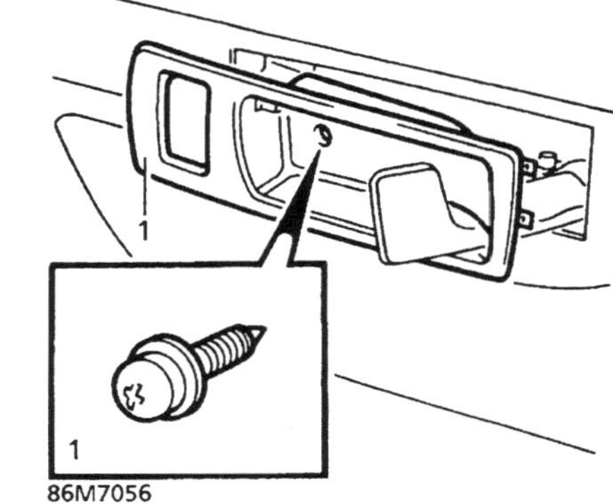

86M7056

2. Release switch from location. Disconnect multiplug.

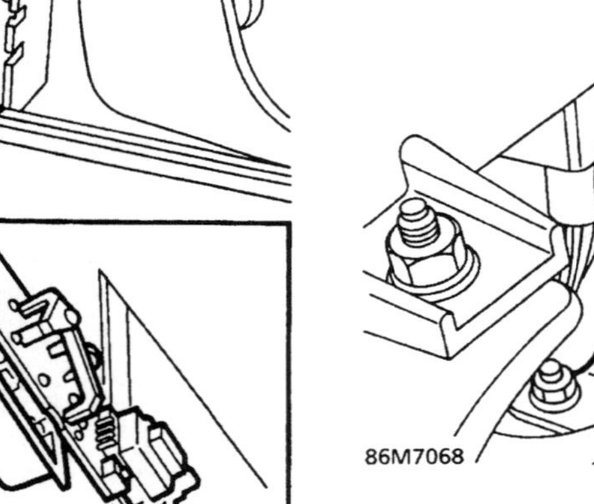

86M7057

CAUTION: Do not allow multiplug to drop behind trim casing.

Refit

3. Reverse removal procedure.

SOUNDER - ANTI-THEFT

Service repair no - 86.55.87

Remove

1. Remove nut securing sounder to bracket.

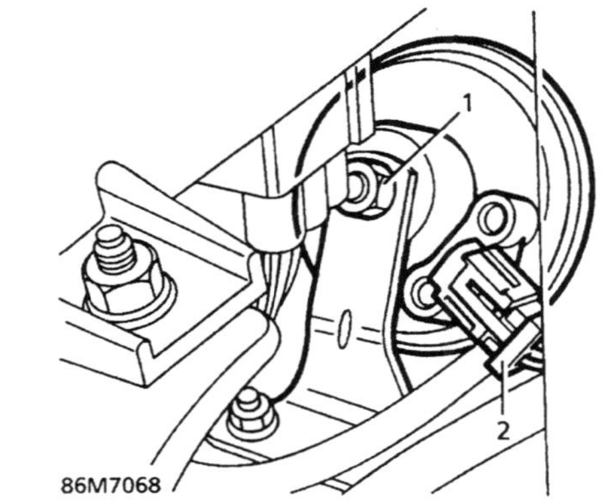

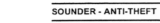

86M7068

2. Disconnect sounder multiplug.

Refit

3. Reverse removal procedure.

HIGH LEVEL STOP LAMP

Service repair no - 86.41.32

NOTE: An access panel is provided in the upper tailgate trim panel to allow bulb replacement.

Remove

1. Remove lower trim panel assembly from upper tailgate.
2. Remove rubber finisher from panel assembly.
3. Release 6 lugs securing halves of trim panel assembly.
4. Separate finisher halves.
5. Remove 4 screws securing stop lamp assembly to upper trim half.
6. Remove stop lamp assembly.

Refit

7. Position stop lamp assembly and secure with screws.
8. Fit rubber finisher to upper trim half.
9. Fit trim halves together and engage lugs.
10. Fit lower trim panel assembly to upper tailgate.

TAIL LAMP

Service repair no - 86.40.70

Remove

1. Release 2 studs securing rear speaker resonator cover. Release cover.

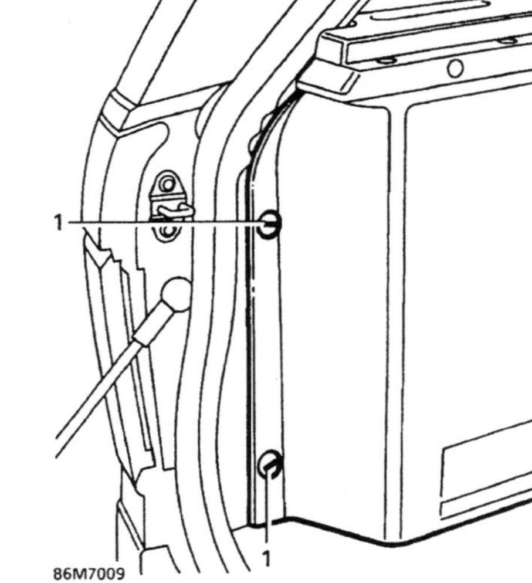

86M7009

2. Remove tail lamp access cover.

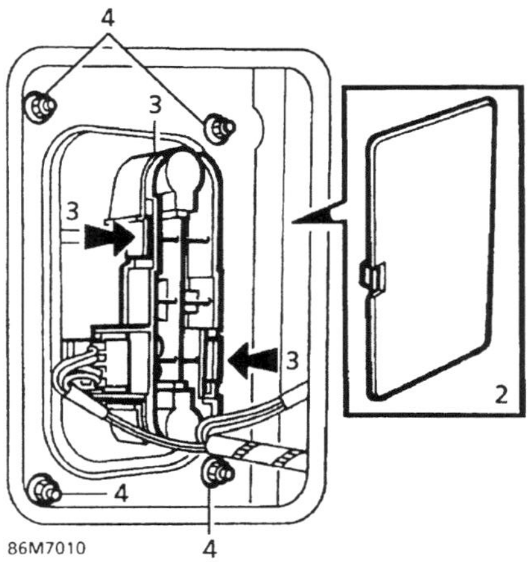

86M7010

3. Release bulb holder from lamp.
4. Remove 4 nuts. Remove tail lamp.

Refit

5. Reverse removal procedure.

WINDOW MOTOR - FRONT

Service repair no - 86.25.04

Remove

1. Remove front door glass. ***See CHASSIS AND BODY, Repair.***
2. Disconnect multiplug from window lift motor.
3. Remove lower regulator plate retaining bolt.
4. Remove bolt securing regulator runner to door panel.
5. Slacken 2 upper regulator plate retaining bolts.
6. Slide regulator assembly rearwards. Release from upper retaining bolts.
7. Remove regulator assembly.
8. Remove 3 screws securing window lift motor.
9. Remove window lift motor from regulator.

Refit

10. Fit window lift motor to regulator. Secure with screws.
11. Fit regulator assembly.
12. Position regulator plate to upper retaining bolts. Slide regulator forwards. Tighten bolts.
13. Secure regulator runner to door panel with bolt.

NOTE: Position runner midway in its slot.

14. Fit lower regulator plate retaining bolt.
15. Reconnect window lift motor multiplug.
16. Refit front door glass. ***See CHASSIS AND BODY, Repair.***

WINDOW MOTOR - REAR DOOR

Service repair no - 86.25.09

Remove

1. Remove rear window motor control panel. ***See this section.***
2. Remove 3 screws securing motor to control panel. Remove motor.

Refit

3. Ensure window lift control gear and motor support are clean. Grease moving parts.
4. Reverse removal procedure.

FASCIA HARNESS - VEHICLES WITH SINGLE POINT SENSED SRS

Service repair no - 86.70.10

Remove

1. Remove fascia assembly. ***See CHASSIS AND BODY, Repair.***
2. Remove passenger airbag module. ***See SUPPLEMENTARY RESTRAINT SYSTEM, Repair.***

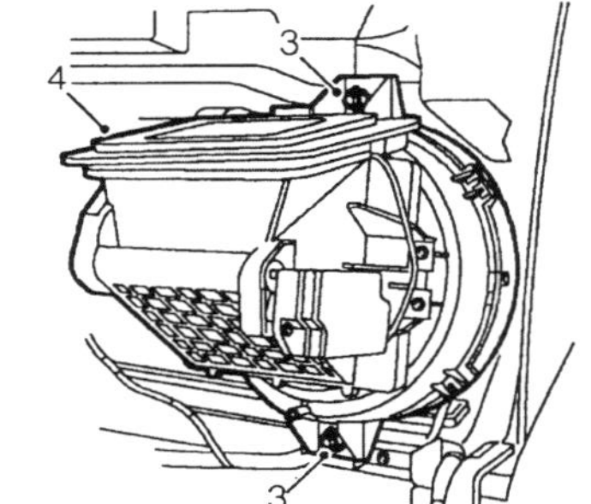

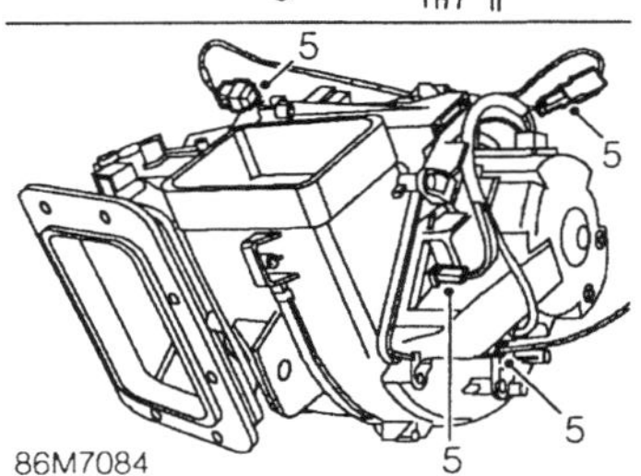

86M7084

3. Remove 2 nuts securing passenger side heater blower unit to fascia.
4. Release blower unit from fascia and heater duct.
5. Disconnect 3 multiplugs and 1 Lucar from blower unit.
6. Remove passenger blower unit.

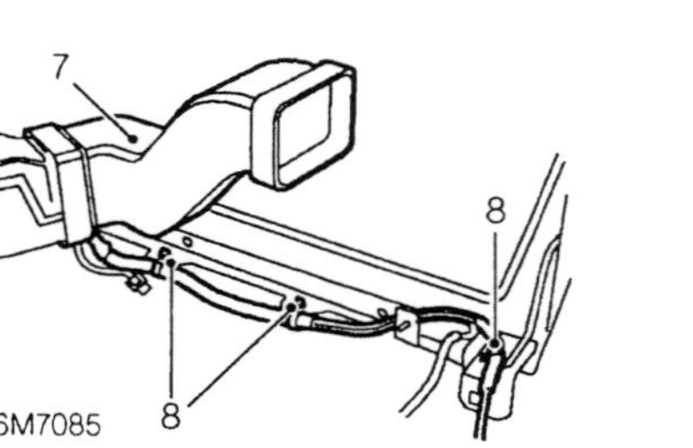

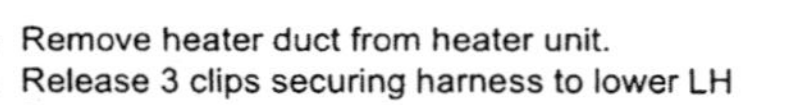

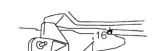

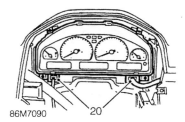

7. Remove heater duct from heater unit.
8. Release 3 clips securing harness to lower LH fascia.

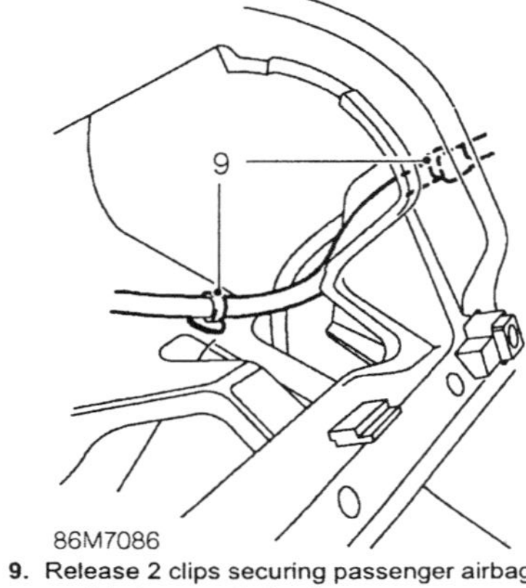

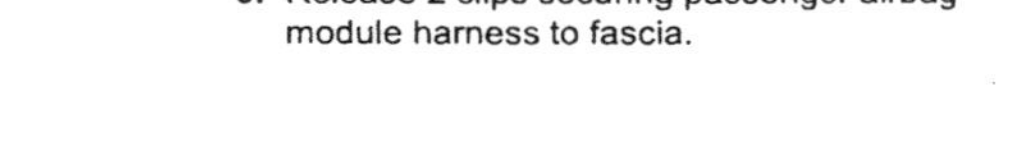

9. Release 2 clips securing passenger airbag module harness to fascia.

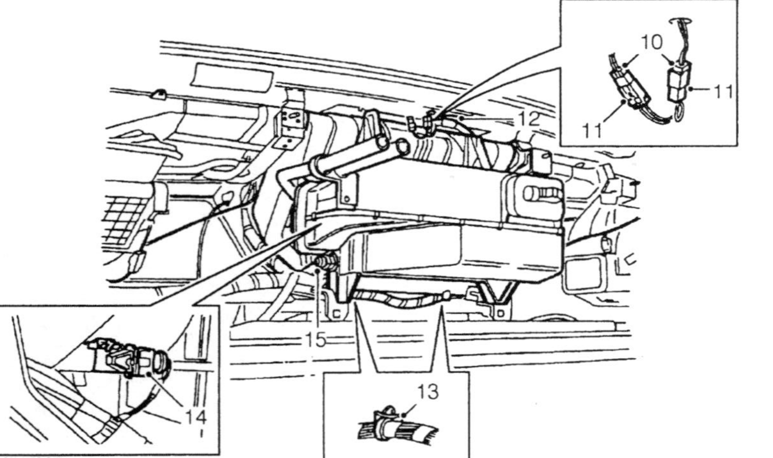

10. Release sunlight sensor and alarm warning lamp harness from fascia panel.
11. Disconnect 2 multiplugs from sunlight sensor and alarm warning lamp.
12. Release clip securing harness to fascia.
13. Release 2 clips securing harness to evaporator.
14. Disconnect multiplug from evaporator sensor.
15. Disconnect multiplug from heater matrix pipe sensor.

16. Remove 2 nuts securing driver side heater blower to fascia.
17. Position blower and disconnect 2 multiplugs and 1 Lucar from unit.
18. Remove blower unit.

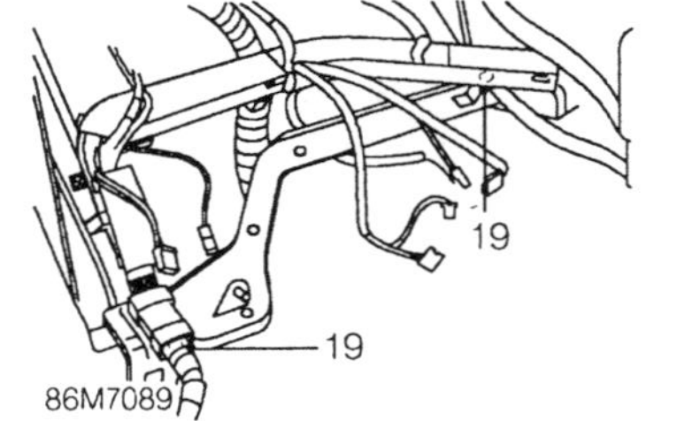

19. Release 2 clips securing harness duct to lower RH fascia.

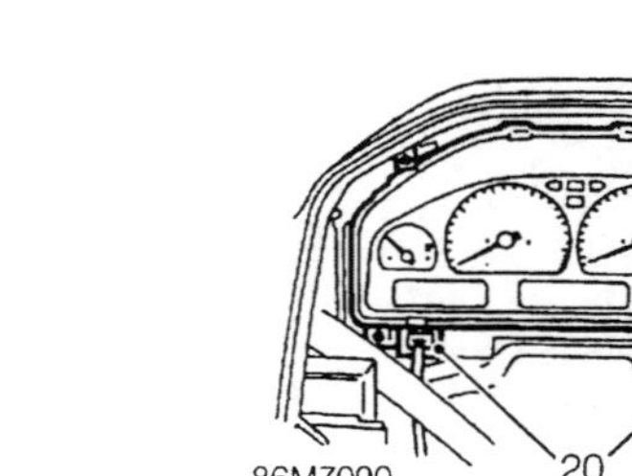

20. Disconnect 2 multiplugs from instrument pack.

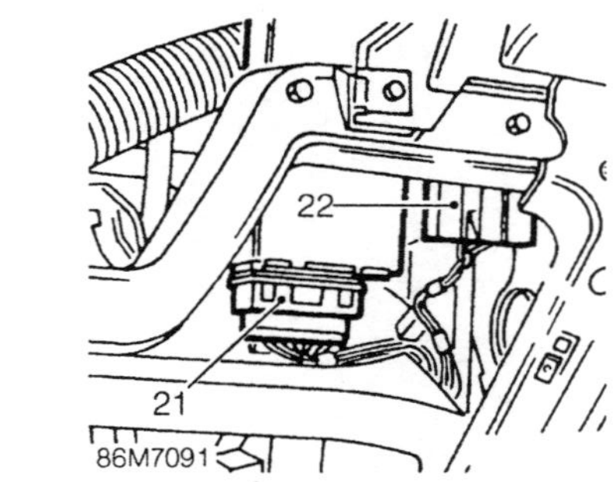

21. Disconnect multiplug from cruise control ECU.
22. Release cruise control relay from fascia bracket and remove relay.

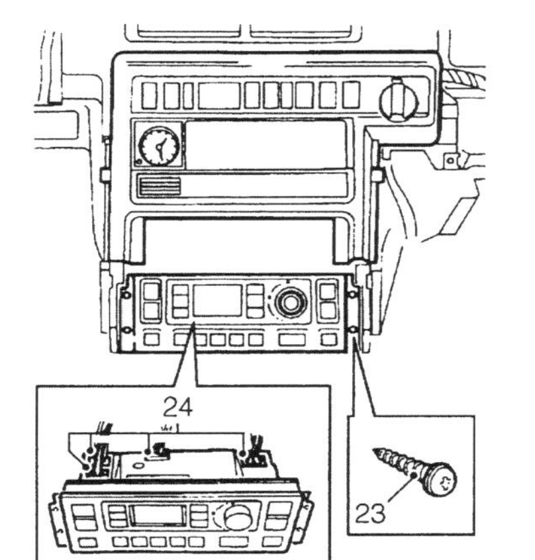

86M7092

23. Remove 4 screws securing heater control unit to fascia.
24. Position heater control unit and disconnect 4 multiplugs from unit.
25. Remove heater control unit.

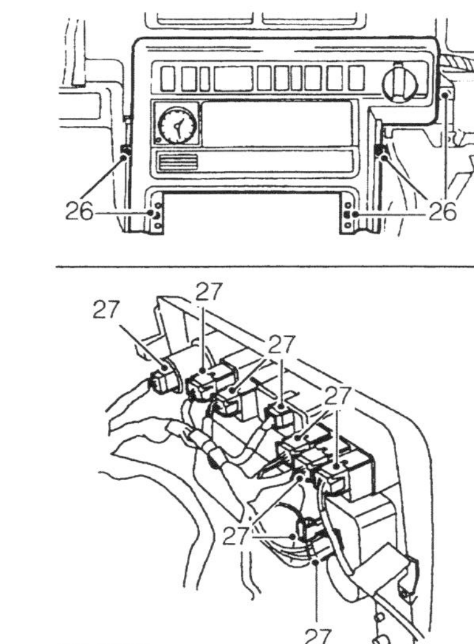

86M7093

26. Remove 5 screws securing fascia switch pack to fascia.
27. Position fascia switch pack and disconnect 7 multiplugs and 2 Lucars from rear of switch pack. Do not disconnect multiplug from high/low switch.
28. Remove fascia switch pack.

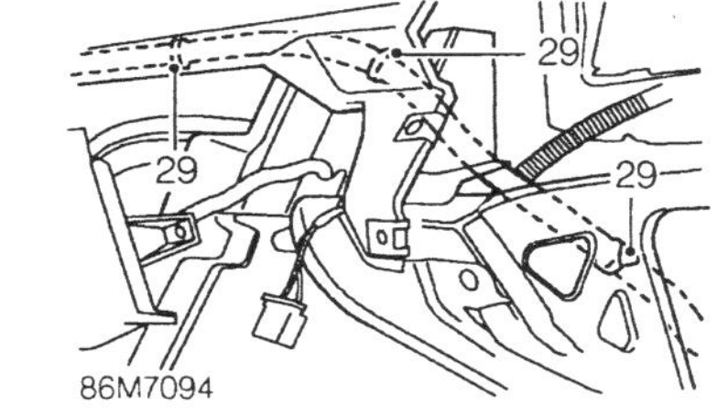

86M7094

29. Release 3 clips securing harness to fascia.
30. Remove fascia harness.

Refit

31. Position fascia harness to fascia.
32. Position harness to fascia and secure with clips.
33. Position fascia switch pack and connect multiplugs and Lucars.
34. Align switch pack to fascia and secure with screws.
35. Position heater control unit and connect multiplugs.
36. Align heater controls to fascia and secure with screws.
37. Fit cruise control relay to harness and secure to fascia bracket.
38. Connect cruise control ECU multiplug.
39. Connect multiplugs to instrument pack.
40. Position harness duct and secure with clips.
41. Position driver side blower unit and connect multiplugs and Lucar.
42. Align blower unit to fascia and secure with nuts.
43. Connect multiplug to heater matrix pipe sensor.
44. Connect multiplug to evaporator sensor.
45. Position harness to evaporator and secure with clips.
46. Position harness to sunlight sensor and connect multiplugs.
47. Secure harness to fascia with clip.
48. Position sunlight sensor multiplug inside fascia.
49. Position passenger airbag harness to fascia and secure with clips.
50. Position harness to LH lower fascia and secure with clips.
51. Fit heater duct to heater.
52. Position passenger's side heater blower and connect multiplugs and Lucar.
53. Fit blower unit to heater duct and fascia and secure with nuts.
54. Fit passenger airbag module. ***See SUPPLEMENTARY RESTRAINT SYSTEM, Repair.***
55. Fit fascia assembly. ***See CHASSIS AND BODY, Repair.***

HORN - FROM 99MY

Service repair no - 86.30.10

Remove

1. Release fixings and remove battery cover.
2. Disconnect battery earth lead.
3. **RH horn:** Remove battery positive lead and remove battery.
4. **RH horn:** Remove 2 screws securing harness clamp to carrier and release harnesses from carrier.
5. **RH horn:** Remove 4 bolts securing battery carrier to body and remove carrier.

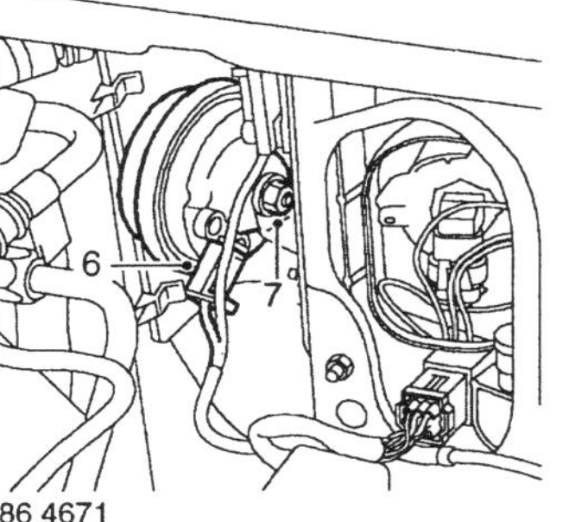

M86 4671

6. Release multiplug from horn.
7. Remove nut securing horn to bracket and remove horn.

Refit

8. Fit new horn to bracket and tighten nut to ***13 Nm (10 lbf.ft).***
9. Connect multiplug to horn.
10. **RH horn:** Fit battery carrier and secure with bolts.
11. **RH horn:** Position harnesses and secure clamp with screws.
12. **RH horn:** Fit battery and connect positive lead.
13. Connect battery earth lead.
14. Fit battery cover and secure with fixings.

AUXILIARY POWER SOCKET - FROM 2000MY

Service repair no - 86.65.62

Remove

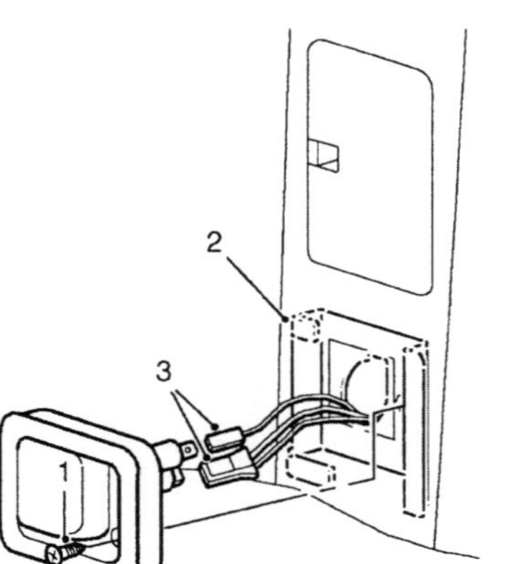

M86 5073

1. Remove screw securing power socket to mounting bracket.
2. Release clip securing power socket to power socket bracket and remove bracket.
3. Disconnect 1 multiplug and 1 lucar from power socket and remove socket.

Refit

4. Position socket and bracket and connect lucar and multiplug.
5. Secure socket to mounting bracket with clip and screw.

HARNESS - ENGINE - V8 - FROM 99MY

Service repair no - 86.70.17

Remove

1. Remove alternator drive belt. ***See this section.***
2. Remove ignition coils. ***See ENGINE MANAGEMENT SYSTEM, Repair.***
3. Remove ignition ECM. ***See ENGINE MANAGEMENT SYSTEM, Repair.***

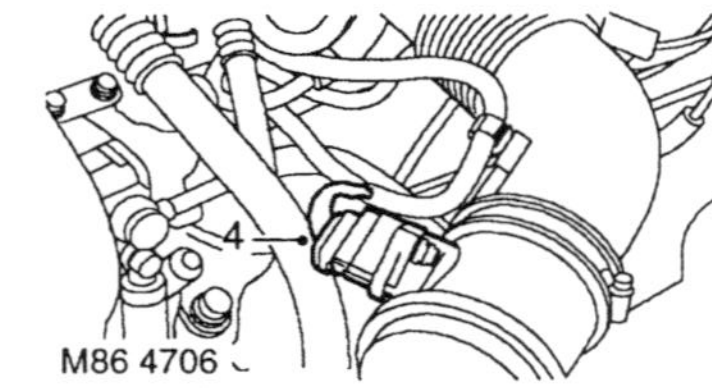

M86 4706

4. Disconnect MAF sensor multiplug.

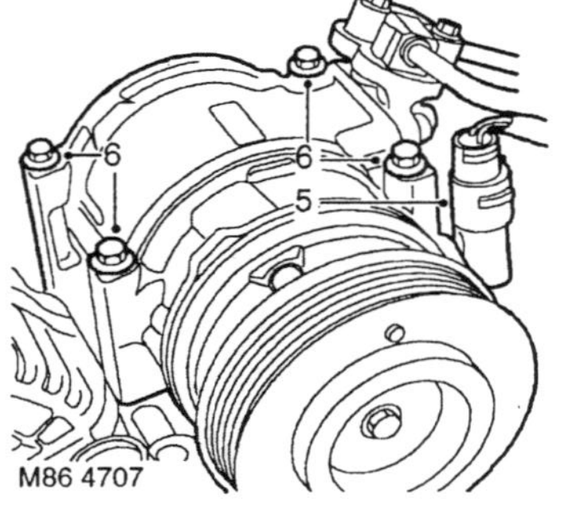

M86 4707

5. Disconnect A/C compressor multiplug.
6. Remove 4 bolts securing A/C compressor, release compressor and tie aside.

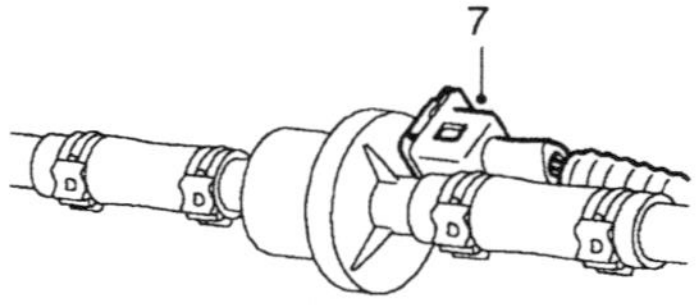

M86 4708

7. Disconnect multiplug from purge valve.

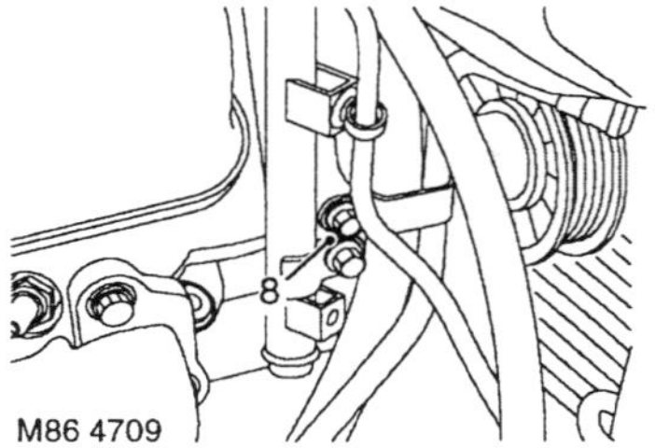

M86 4709

8. Remove bolt securing engine oil cooler return pipe to alternator mounting bracket.

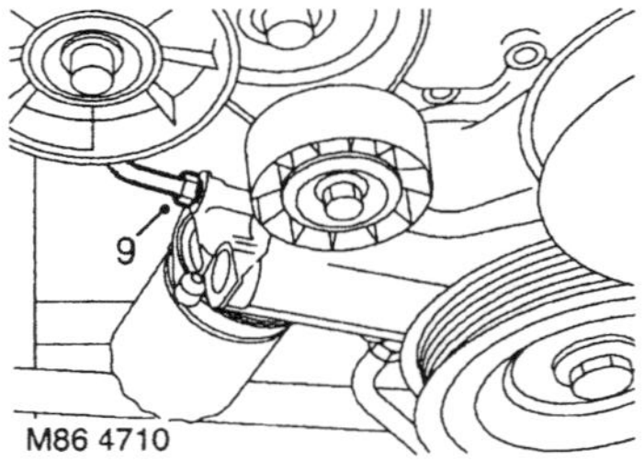

M86 4710

9. Loosen engine oil cooler return pipe union from oil pump.
10. Release return pipe, remove and discard 'O' ring.

CAUTION: Plug the connections.

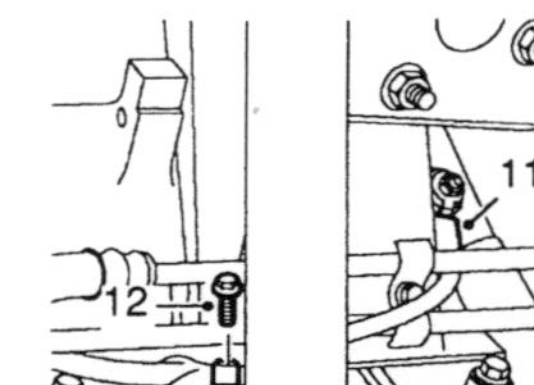
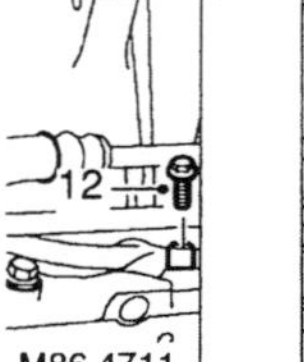
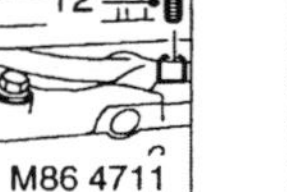
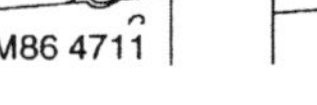

M86 4711

11. Disconnect multiplug from LH KS.
12. Remove bolt securing harness 'P' clip to cylinder block.

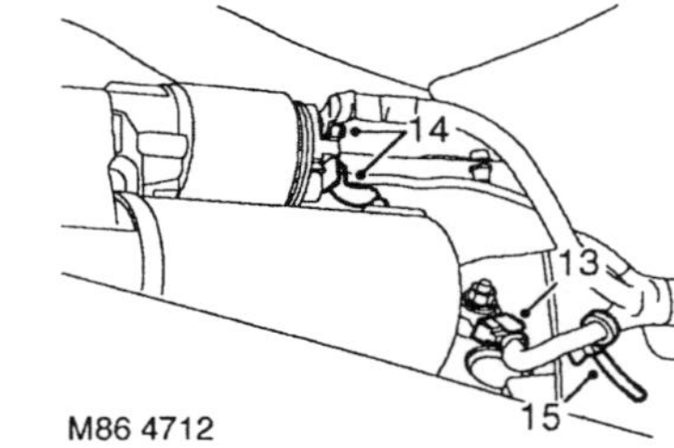

M86 4712

13. Disconnect multiplug from RH KS.
14. Remove nut securing battery lead to starter solenoid, release lead and disconnect Lucar from solenoid.
15. Release clip securing harness to engine RH mounting bracket.

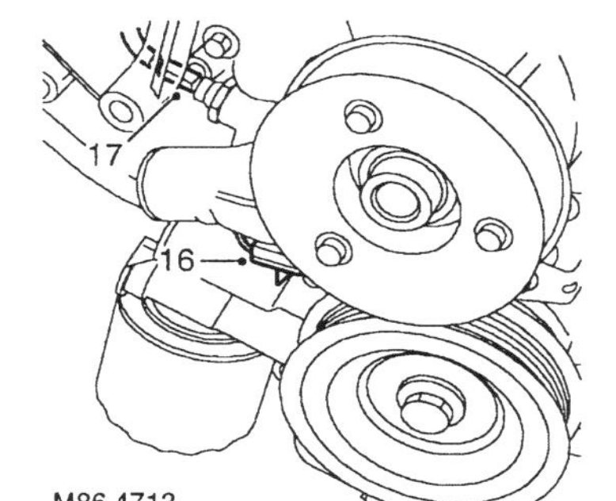

M86 4713

16. Disconnect multiplug from CMP sensor.
17. Disconnect Lucar from oil pressure switch.

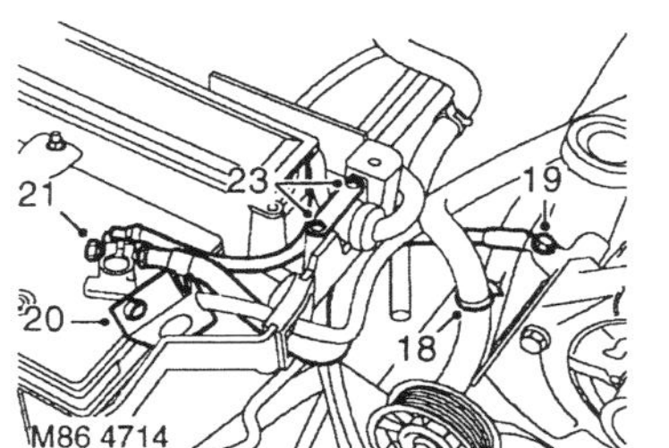

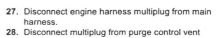

M86 4714

18. Release clip securing harness to coolant rail.
19. Remove bolt securing engine earth lead and position lead aside.
20. Release cover from battery positive terminal.
21. Remove nut securing positive lead to battery terminal, release fuse box feed lead, and disconnect positive lead from battery terminal.
22. Release positive lead from battery carrier.
23. Remove 2 screws and remove harness clamp from battery carrier.

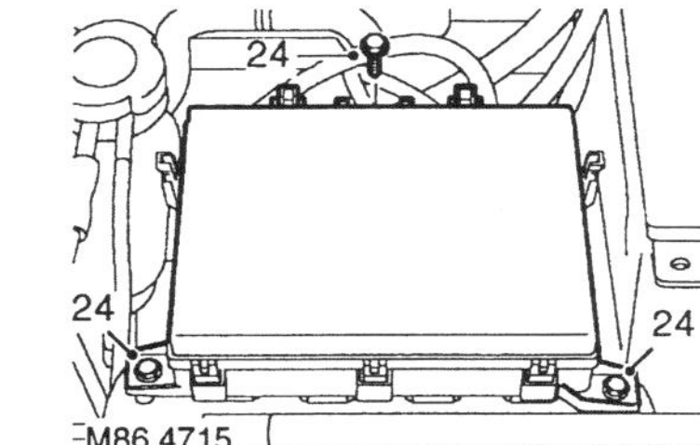

M86 4715

24. Remove 3 bolts securing under bonnet fuse box.

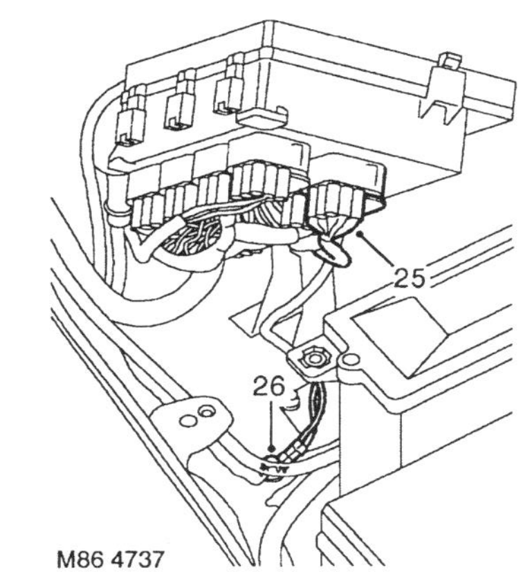

M86 4737

25. Disconnect engine harness multiplug from fuse box.
26. Remove nut and disconnect 2 earth leads from RH wing valance.

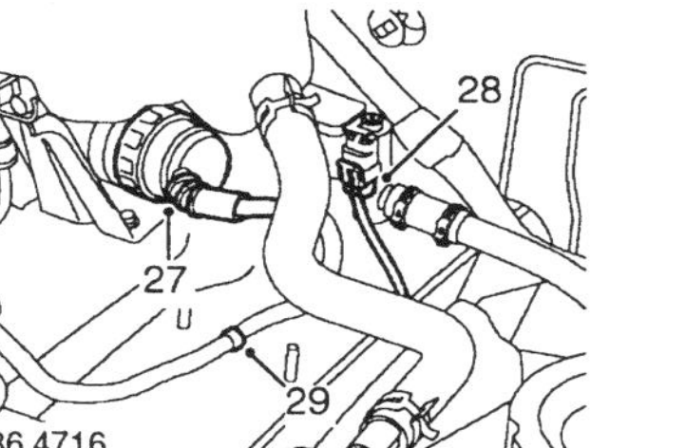
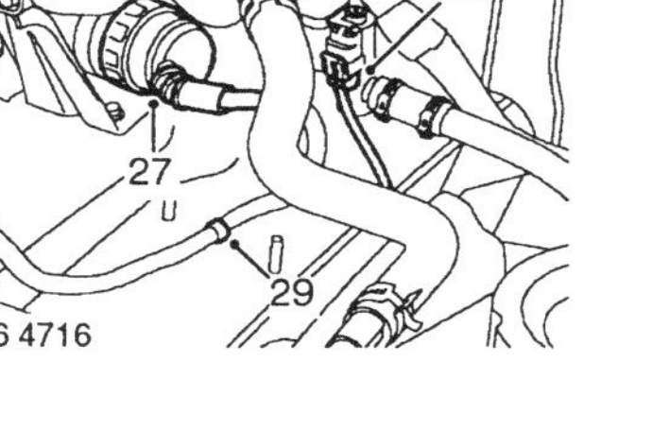

M86 4716

27. Disconnect engine harness multiplug from main harness.
28. Disconnect multiplug from purge control vent valve.
29. Release clip securing harness to RH wing valance.

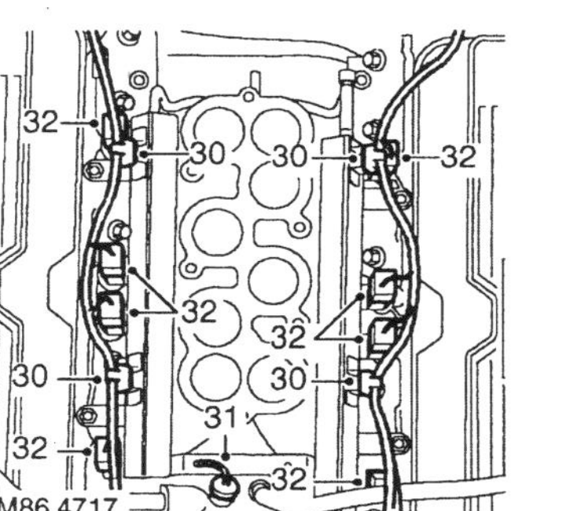

M86 4717

30. Release harness clips from fuel rail and heater coolant pipe.
31. Disconnect multiplug from ECT sensor.
32. Disconnect multiplugs from fuel injectors.

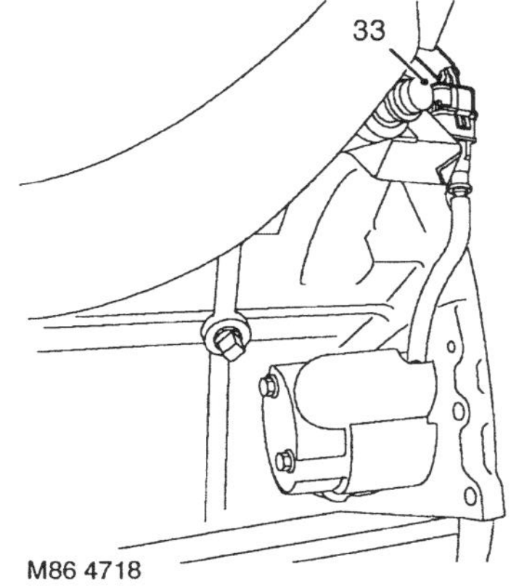

M86 4718

33. Disconnect multiplug from CKP sensor.

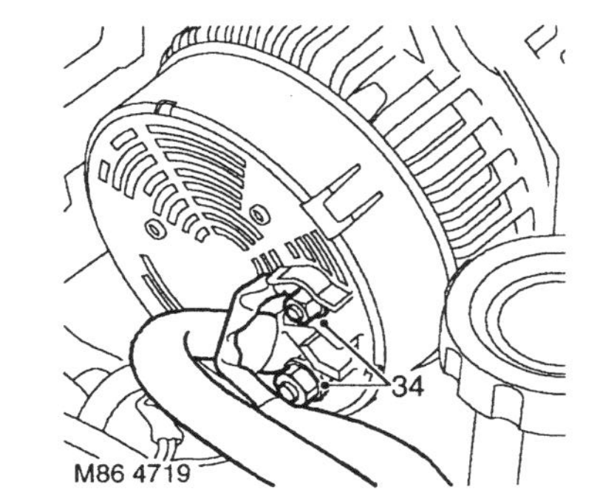

M86 4719

34. Remove 2 nuts securing engine harness to alternator.

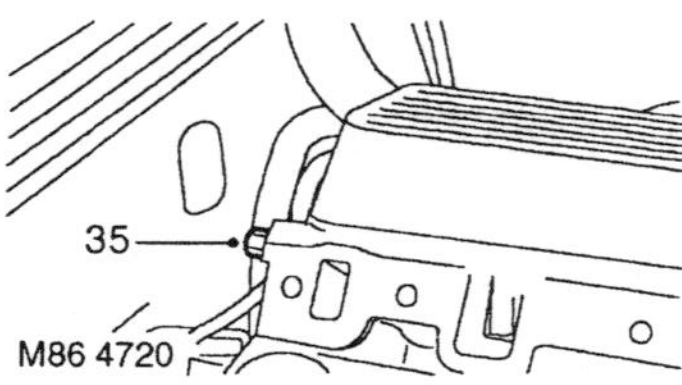

M86 4720

35. Remove bolt securing engine harness 'P' clip to rear of LH cylinder head.

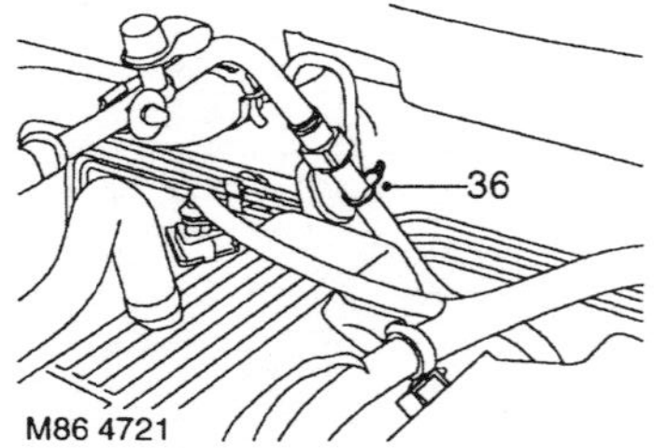

M86 4721

36. Remove cable tie securing purge pipe to engine rear lifting eye.
37. **Models with automatic gearbox:** Remove window switch pack. ***See this section.***
38. **Models with manual gearbox:** Remove centre console. ***See CHASSIS AND BODY, Repair.***

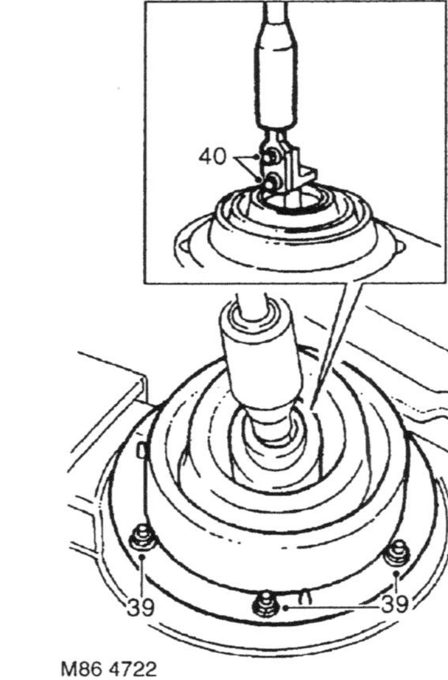

M86 4722

39. **Models with manual gearbox:** Remove 6 nuts securing gear lever gaiter ring and remove gaiter ring and gaiter.
40. **Models with manual gearbox:** Remove 2 bolts securing gear lever and remove lever.

M86 4723

41. With handbrake released, remove clip and clevis pin securing handbrake cable to handbrake.
42. Remove chassis crossmember. ***See CHASSIS AND BODY, Repair.***

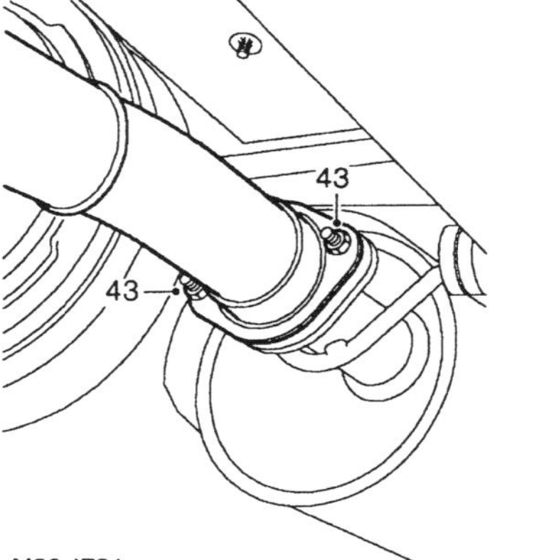

M86 4724

43. Remove 2 nuts securing pipe clamp and release exhaust front pipe from intermediate pipe.

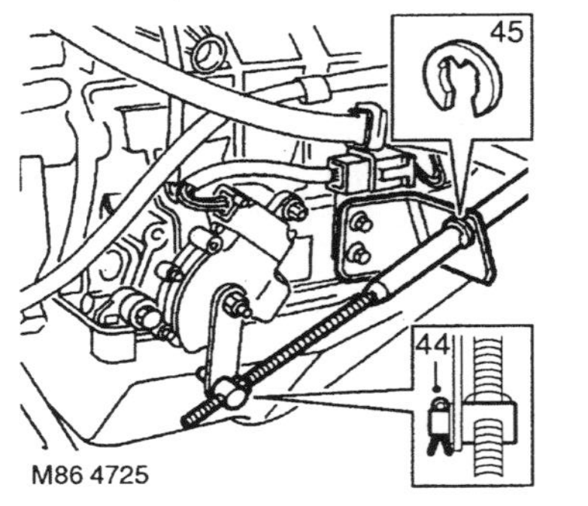

M86 4725

44. **Models with automatic gearbox:** Remove split pin from gear selector trunnion and release trunnion from lever.
45. **Models with automatic gearbox:** Remove 'C' clip and release gear selector cable from abutment bracket.

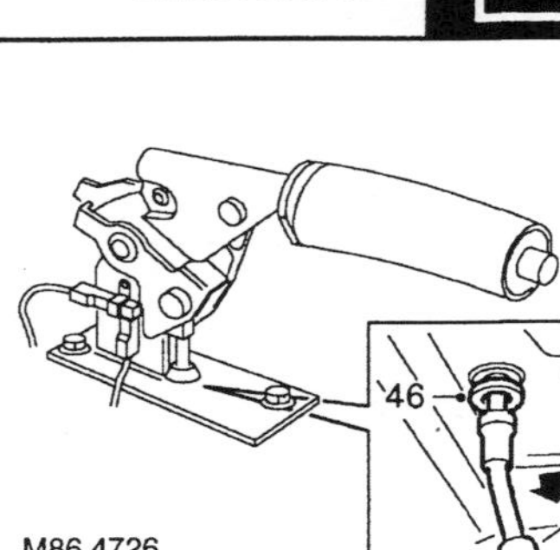

M86 4726

46. Release handbrake cable and grommet from tunnel.
47. Carefully lower transmission on jack sufficiently only for access to engine harness.

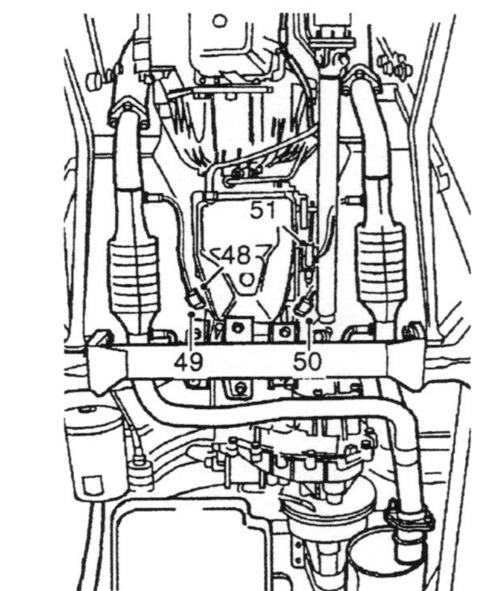

M86 4727

48. Release RH front HO2S multiplug from bracket and disconnect from engine harness.
49. Disconnect engine harness from RH rear HO2S multiplug.
50. Disconnect engine harness from LH rear HO2S multiplug.
51. Release LH front HO2S multiplug from bracket and disconnect from engine harness.

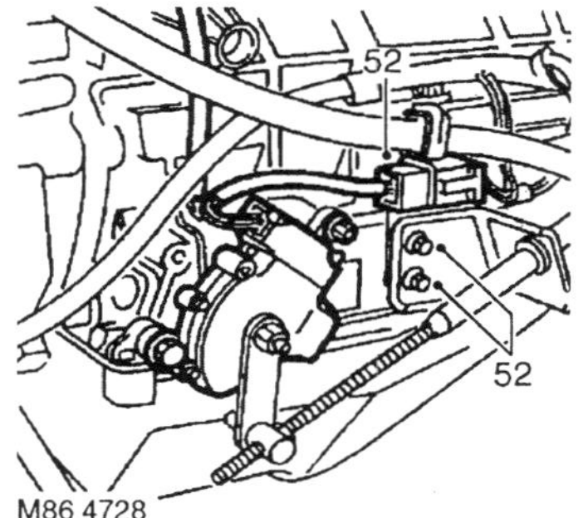

M86 4728

52. **Models with automatic gearbox:** Remove 2 bolts securing gear selector position switch multiplug and selector cable abutment brackets to gearbox.
53. Release engine harness from support bracket.
54. Release engine harness from above gearbox and from behind LH cylinder head.
55. Remove engine harness.

Refit

56. Position engine harness behind LH cylinder head and over gearbox.
57. Secure engine harness to support bracket.
58. **Models with automatic gearbox:** Position gear selector position switch multiplug and selector cable abutment brackets to gearbox and secure with bolts.
59. Connect engine harness to LH front oxygen sensor multiplug and fit multiplug to support bracket.
60. Connect engine harness to LH rear oxygen sensor multiplug.
61. Connect engine harness to RH rear oxygen sensor multiplug.
62. Connect RH front oxygen sensor multiplug to engine harness and secure multiplug to bracket.
63. Carefully raise transmission on jack.
64. Fit handbrake cable grommet to transmission tunnel.
65. **Models with automatic gearbox:** Fit gear selector cable to abutment bracket and secure with 'C' clip.
66. **Models with automatic gearbox:** Fit selector cable trunnion to lever and secure with split pin.
67. **Models with automatic gearbox:** Adjust gear selector cable. ***See AUTOMATIC GEARBOX, Adjustment.***
68. Clean exhaust front and intermediate pipe mating faces.
69. Align intermediate pipe to front pipe and tighten clamp nuts to ***25 Nm (18 lbf.ft)***
70. Fit chassis crossmember. ***See CHASSIS AND BODY, Repair.***
71. Connect handbrake cable to lever, fit clevis pin and secure pin with clip.
72. **Models with manual gearbox:** Position gear lever and tighten bolts to ***25 Nm (18 lbf.ft)***
73. **Models with manual gearbox:** Fit gear lever gaiter and gaiter ring and secure with nuts.
74. **Models with manual gearbox:** Fit centre console. ***See CHASSIS AND BODY, Repair.***
75. **Models with automatic gearbox:** Fit window switch pack. ***See this section.***
76. Fit bolt to secure harness 'P' clip to LH cylinder head.
77. Connect harness to alternator and tighten B + terminal nut to ***18 Nm (13 lbf.ft)*** max and D + terminal nut to ***5 Nm (3.5 lbf.ft)*** max. B+ and D+ are marked on the rear of the alternator, adjacent to each cable connection.
78. Connect multiplug to CKP sensor.
79. Connect multiplugs to fuel injectors and ECT sensor.
80. Fit harness clips to fuel rail and heater coolant pipe.
81. Connect multiplug to purge vent valve.
82. Connect engine harness multiplug to main harness.

83. Connect earth leads to stud on RH wing valance and tighten nut to ***10 Nm (7 lbf.ft).***
84. Connect engine harness multiplug to fuse box.
85. Secure harness clip to RH wing valance.
86. Fit bolts to secure fuse box.
87. Fit harness clamp to battery carrier and secure with screws.
88. Fit battery positive lead to battery carrier and connect cable to battery terminal. Connect fuse box positive feed to terminal clamp bolt and secure with nut. Fit terminal cover.
89. Fit engine earth lead to alternator bracket and tighten bolt to ***18 Nm (13 lbf.ft).***
90. Secure harness to coolant rail.
91. Connect Lucar to oil pressure switch.
92. Connect multiplug to CMP sensor.
93. Connect battery lead to starter solenoid and tighten nut to ***18 Nm (13 lbf.ft).***
94. Connect Lucar to starter solenoid.
95. Connect multiplug to RH KS and secure harness clip to engine RH mounting bracket.
96. Connect multiplug to LH KS, align harness 'P' clip to cylinder block and tighten bolt to ***18 Nm (13 lbf.ft).***
97. Ensure engine oil cooler return pipe union is clean, fit new 'O' ring, connect pipe to pump and tighten union to ***30 Nm (22 lbf.ft).***
98. Align engine oil cooler return pipe to alternator mounting bracket and secure with bolt.
99. Connect multiplug to purge valve.
100. Ensure compressor and mating face is clean. Fit compressor to mounting bracket and tighten bolts to ***25 Nm (18 lbf.ft).***
101. Connect multiplug to compressor.
102. Connect multiplug to MAF sensor.
103. Fit ignition ECM. ***See ENGINE MANAGEMENT SYSTEM, Repair.***
104. Fit ignition coils. ***See ENGINE MANAGEMENT SYSTEM, Repair.***
105. Fit alternator drive belt. ***See this section.***

HARNESS - GEARBOX - FROM 99MY

Service repair no - 86.70.20

Remove

1. Remove centre console. ***See CHASSIS AND BODY, Repair.***

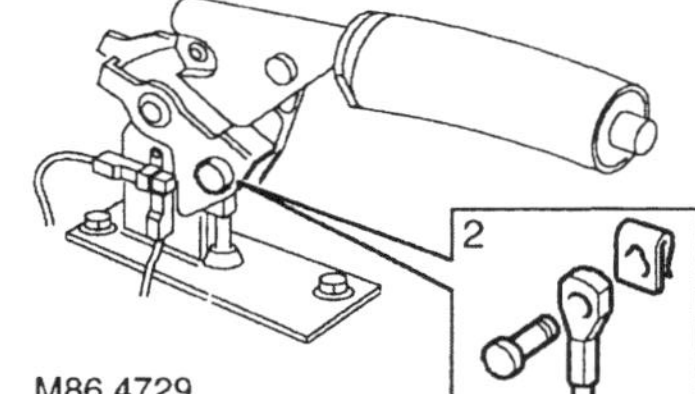

M86 4729

2. With handbrake released, remove clip and clevis pin securing handbrake cable to handbrake.

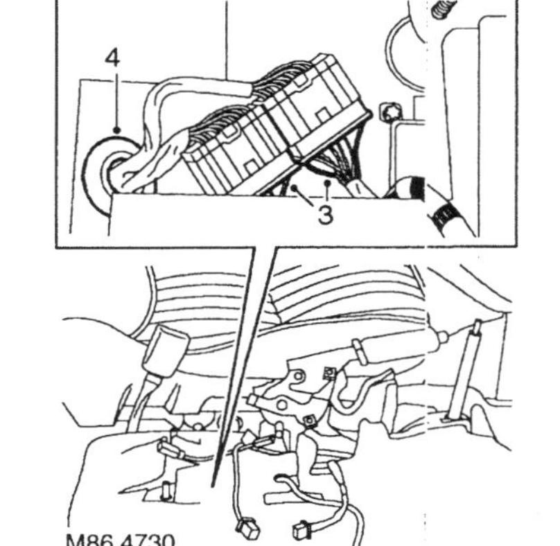

M86 4730

3. Disconnect 2 gearbox harness multiplugs from main harness.
4. Release harness grommet and push multiplugs through tunnel.
5. Remove chassis crossmember. ***See CHASSIS AND BODY, Repair.***

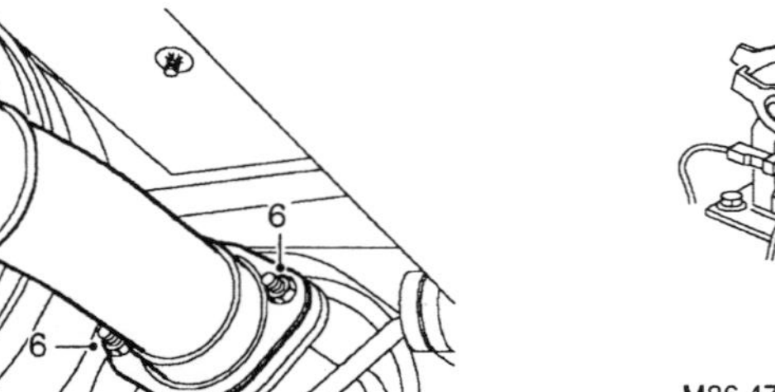

M86 4731

6. Remove 2 nuts securing pipe clamp and release exhaust front pipe from intermediate pipe.

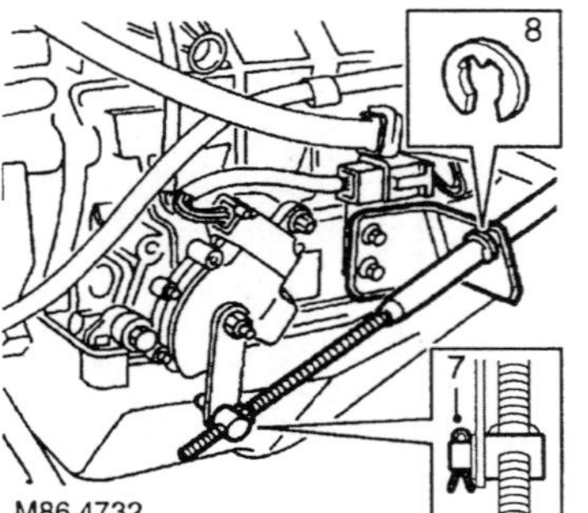

M86 4732

7. **Models with automatic gearbox:** Remove split pin from gear selector trunnion and release trunnion from lever.
8. **Models with automatic gearbox:** Remove 'C' clip and release gear selector cable from abutment bracket.

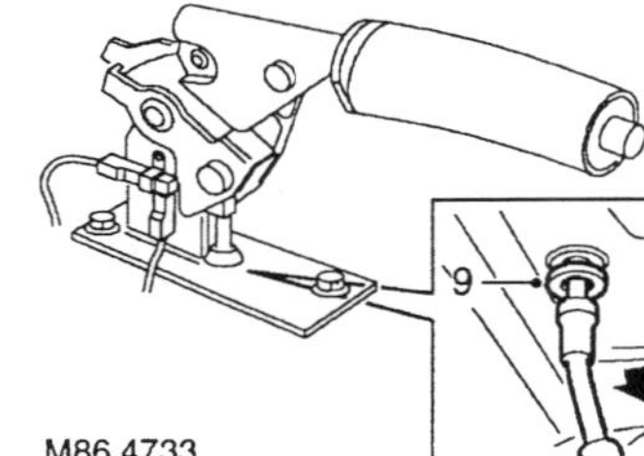

M86 4733

9. Release handbrake cable and grommet from tunnel.
10. Carefully lower transmission on jack sufficiently only for access to gearbox harness.

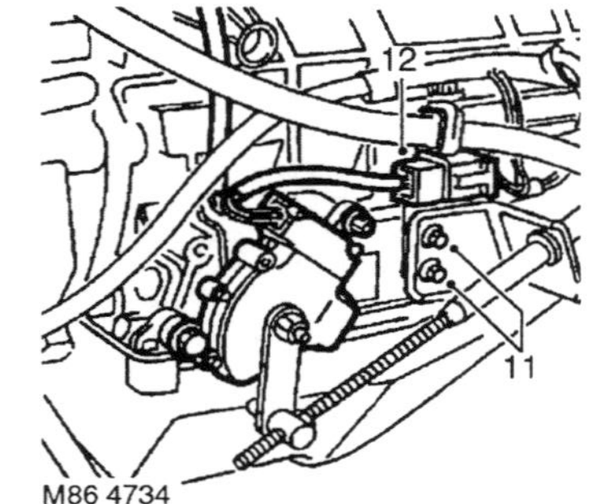

M86 4734

11. Remove 2 bolts securing gear selector position switch multiplug and selector cable abutment brackets to gearbox.
12. **Models with automatic gearbox:** Disconnect gearbox harness from selector position switch and position switch multiplug from support bracket.

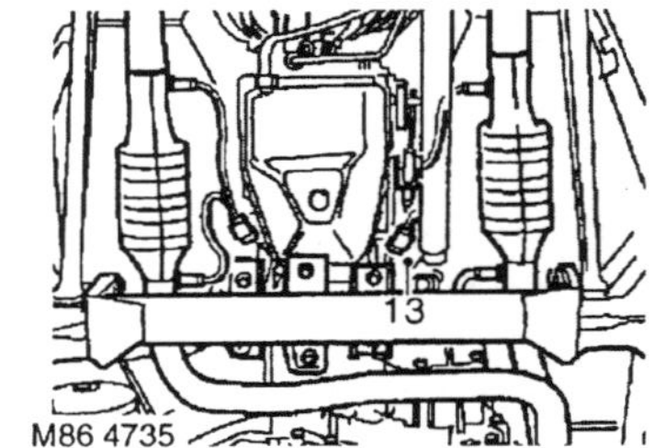
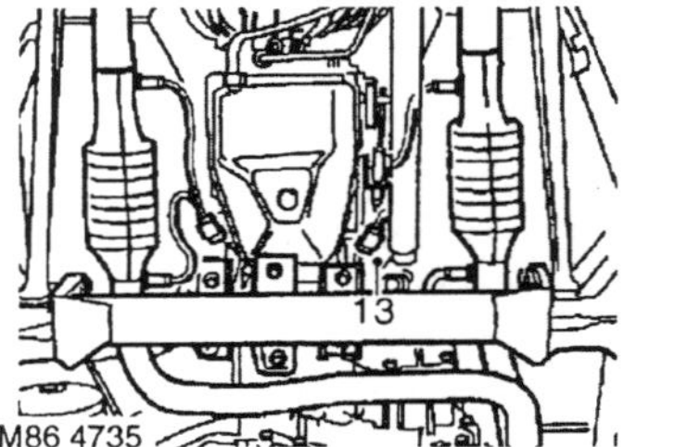

M86 4735

13. Release LH rear HO2S multiplug from support bracket.

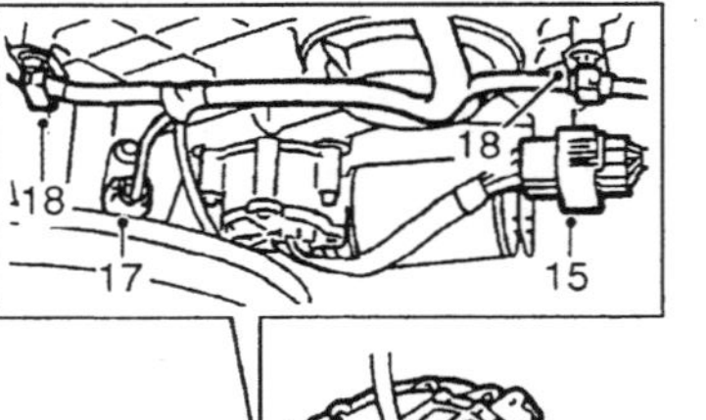

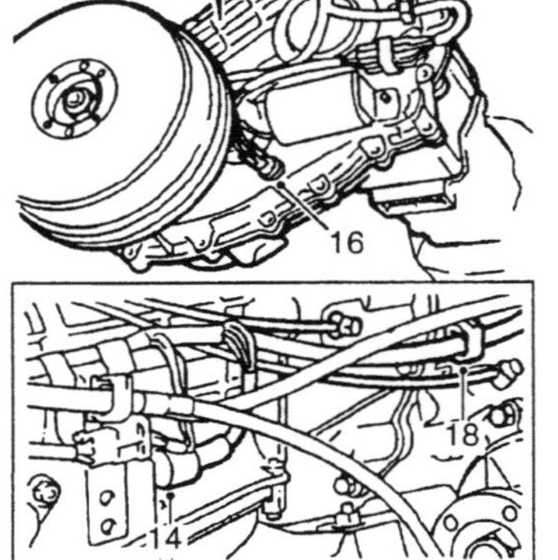

M86 4736

14. Disconnect gearbox speed sensor multiplug.
15. Disconnect multiplug from transfer box High/Low motor.
16. Disconnect 2 Lucars from transfer box oil temperature sensor.
17. Disconnect multiplug from output shaft speed sensor.
18. Open 3 harness support clips.
19. Remove gearbox harness from vehicle.

Refit

20. Position harness on top of gearbox.
21. Connect multiplug to output shaft speed sensor.
22. Connect 2 Lucars to transfer box temperature sensor.
23. Connect multiplug to transfer box High/ Low motor.
24. Fit and secure harness to support clips.
25. Fit LH rear oxygen sensor multiplug to support bracket.
26. Connect multiplug to gearbox speed sensor.
27. **Models with automatic gearbox:** Fit selector position switch multiplug to support bracket and connect gearbox harness to selector position switch multiplug.
28. Align multiplug bracket and selector cable abutment bracket to gear box and secure with bolts.
29. Raise gearbox on jack.
30. Push to locate handbrake cable grommet in transmission tunnel.
31. **Models with automatic gearbox**: Fit gear selector cable to abutment bracket and secure with 'C' clip.
32. **Models with automatic gearbox:** Fit selector cable trunnion to lever and secure with split pin.
33. **Models with automatic gearbox:** Adjust gear selector cable. ***See AUTOMATIC GEARBOX, Adjustment.***
34. Clean exhaust front and intermediate pipe mating faces.
35. Align intermediate pipe to front pipe and tighten clamp nuts to ***25 Nm (18 lbf.ft).***
36. Fit chassis crossmember. ***See CHASSIS AND BODY, Repair.***
37. Feed harness multiplug through tunnel. and connect multiplugs to main harness.
38. Fit harness multiplug to tunnel.
39. Connect handbrake cable to lever, fit clevis pin and secure pin with clip.
40. Fit centre console. ***See CHASSIS AND BODY, Repair.***

87 - NAVIGATION SYSTEM

CONTENTS

NAVIGATION SYSTEM COMPONENT LAYOUT

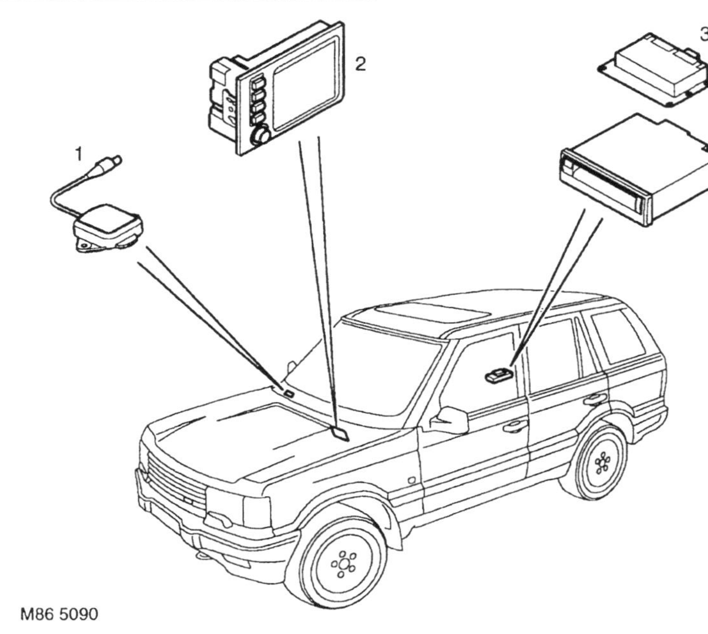

1. GPS antenna
2. Navigation display unit
3. GPS receiver
4. Navigation computer

NAVIGATION SYSTEM CONTROL DIAGRAM

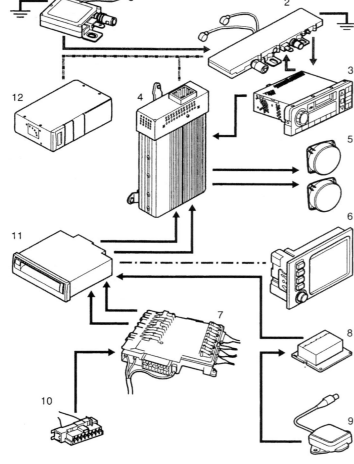

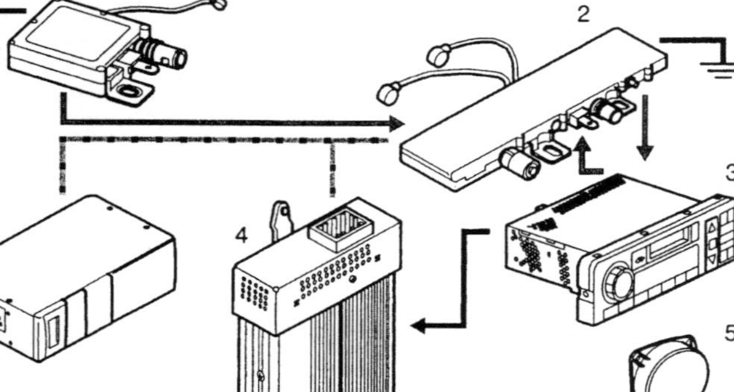

A=Hardwired connections; B=K Bus; F=RF Transmission; K=I Bus

1. Antenna Amplifier LH
2. Antenna Amplifier RH
3. Headunit
4. DSP Amplifier
5. Speakers
6. Navigation display unit
7. BeCM
8. GPS receiver
9. GPS antenna
10. Diagnostic socket
11. Navigation computer
12. CD Autochanger

DESCRIPTION

General

Each navigation system provides computer generated audible and visual route guidance information to enable the driver to reach a desired destination. The system allows the driver to choose the desired route using minor or major roads or motorways and the quickest or shortest route. Directions to hospitals, museums, monuments and hotels are also available. The computer uses map information stored on a CD-ROM to determine the best route for the journey and provide the driver with details of directions and approaching junctions.

The current position of the vehicle is determined using a Global Positioning System (GPS). The GPS uses satellites which orbit the earth every 12 hours at a height of 12500 miles (20000 km) and transmit radio signals to provide information about the satellite position i.e. latitude, longitude, altitude, almanac data and time.

The almanac data is the current status of the 24 satellites which orbit the earth. The computer determines which satellites are 'visible' to the system and their current position and relationship to each other. Using this information the computer can account for positional deviations of the satellites and compensate to enhance the accuracy of the navigation system. The navigation system requires the almanac data from at least four different satellites to calculate a three dimensional 'fix' on its location. As the vehicle moves the computer continually up dates this information so that at all times the computer knows the precise location of the vehicle.

The direction of the vehicle is determined by the navigation computer using a solid state gyro sensor located inside the computer. The gyro sensor supplies angular acceleration data for the vehicle to the navigation computer. The computer uses this information to determine the direction of travel of the vehicle.

NAVIGATION SYSTEM COMPONENTS

The following components make up the navigation system:

- Navigation computer
- GPS receiver
- GPS antenna
- Navigation display unit

Navigation Computer

The navigation computer is located in the right hand side of the luggage compartment, attached to a bracket. The computer is the main component in the navigation system and receives inputs from the BeCM and the GPS receiver. The navigation computer contains a solid state piezo gyro which measures the motion of the vehicle around its vertical axis. The gyro operates on the principle known as the Coriolis force. The Coriolis force is the force that appears to accelerate a body moving away from its rotational axis against the direction of rotation of the axis. Refer to Operation in this section for detailed operation.

Using the inputs from the BeCM, the GPS receiver and the gyro sensor, the computer can determine the vehicle's current position, direction and speed.

The navigation computer also houses the CD-ROM drive. The drive is used to read map data from country specific CD's and also to load updated software into the computer. A button, located adjacent to the CD slot, is provided to eject the CD from the unit. If ignition is on, one press of the button will eject the CD. If the ignition is off, two presses are required, one to wake up the system and the second to eject the CD.

The D&C unit is connected with a 12-way MQL connector and a 6 way AMP connector.

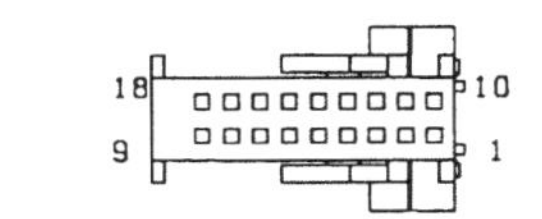

18 way MQL - Blue

Pin No.	Description	Input/Output
1	+12V Permanent feed	Input
2	Not used	-
3	K-bus	Input/Output
4	Not used	-
5	Green Video + sync 50Ω to LCD display	Output
6	Blue video 50Ω to LCD display	Output
7	Red video 50Ω to LCD display	Output
8	Green video 75Ω output to video module	Output
9	Navigation audio +	Output
10	Ground	Input
11	Not used	-
12	Ground for LCD display	Output
13	Not used	-
14	Video ground for 50Ω output	Output
15	Not used	-
16	Video ground for 50Ω output	Output
17	Not used	-
18	Navigation audio -	Output

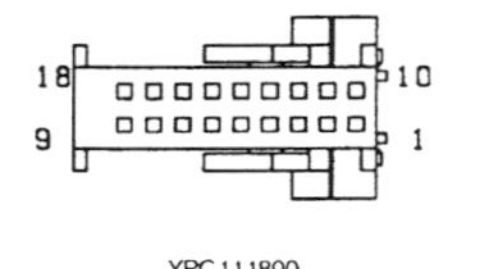

18 way MQL

Pin No.	Description	Input/Output
1	Reversing light signal	Input
2	Navigation audio -	Output
3	+12V Auxiliary feed	Input
4	Navigation audio +	Output
5	RS232 data transmit	Output
6	RS232 data receive	Input
7	Not used	-
8	Serial data link to GPS receiver	Output
9	Serial data link from GPS receiver	Input
10	Left road speed signal	Input
11	Not used	-
12	Not used	-
13	Test output (MUTE)	Output
14	Ground for RS232 data transmit	Output
15	Ground for RS232 data receive	Input
16	Pulse per second from GPS receiver	Input
17	Serial data link to GPS receiver - inverted	Output
18	Serial data link from GPS receiver - inverted	Input

Global Positioning System (GPS) Receiver

The GPS receiver is located in the right hand side of the luggage compartment underneath the parcel tray support panel. The GPS receiver receives information from between 1 and 8 satellites at any one time. This information is received from the GPS antenna. The GPS receiver fulfills the following functions:

- Calculation of position (i.e. Latitude, longitude and height), direction and speed.
- Collection and storage of almanac data.
- Real-time clock.

The GPS receiver communicates with the navigation computer via a serial link. The GPS receiver transmits position and time information to the navigation computer via its serial link. The navigation computer can also extract configuration and status information from the GPS receiver via this link.

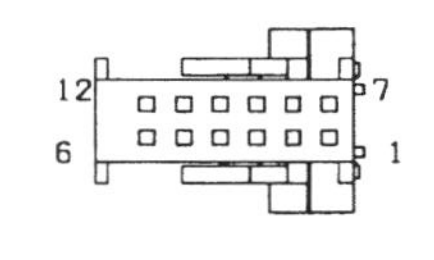

YPC111790

C959 - 12 way MQL - Black

Pin No.	Description	Input/Output
1	Ground	Input
2	RS422 from navigation computer	Input
3	RS422 from navigation computer - inverted	Input
4	RS422 to navigation computer - inverted	Output
5	RS422 to navigation computer	Output
6	Pulse per second to navigation computer	Output
7	+12V Accessory feed	Input
8	+12V Permanent	-
9	Not used	-
10	Not used	-
11	Not used	-
12	Not used	-

GPS Antenna

The GPS antenna is located underneath the air intake plenum. The antenna is connected to the GPS receiver via a single co-axial cable and passes signals received from the GPS satellites to the receiver for processing.

It is possible for the antenna to lose the signals from the satellites in hilly or tree lined areas, built up areas with tall buildings, multi-storey car parks, garages, tunnels, bridges and during heavy rain/thunderstorms. When the signal is lost, the navigation computer will continue to give guidance using memory mapped data from the CD map until the signal is restored.

Connector Details

SMB Connector 1

Pin 1 - RF signal from GPS antenna

Screen - RF ground

Display and Control Unit

The display and control unit is an integrated display and control unit, which allows the user to operate all the functions of the navigation system.

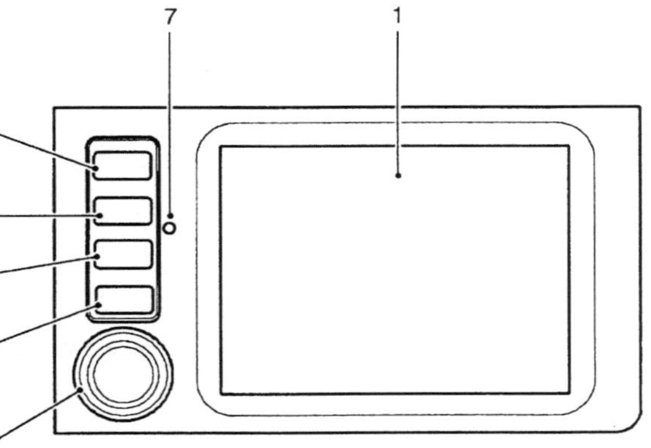

M86 5094

1. Liquid Crystal Display (LCD)
2. Mute button
3. RE-RTE (Re-Route) button
4. Menu button
5. Repeat button
6. Navigation rotary controller
7. Photosensor

The display unit is located in the centre of the fascia. The unit comprises of a 127 mm (5 in) colour Liquid Crystal Display (LCD) screen and controls to operate the navigation functions. The display unit comprises four control switches, one rotary press menu control and one status LED. A photosensor is used to control the brightness of the screen in day and night time conditions.

The D&C unit is connected with a 12-way MQL connector and a 6 way AMP connector.

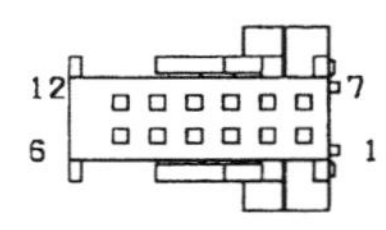

YPC111790

C815 - 12 way MQL - White

Pin No.	Description	Input/Output
1	Red Video 50Ω from Nav Computer	Input
2	Video ground from Nav Computer	Input
3	Green Video & Sync 50Ω from Nav Computer	Input
4	Video ground from video module II	Input
5	Blue Video from video module II	Input
6	Video ground from video module II	Input
7	LCD Ground from video module II	Input
8	Not used	-
9	Not used	-
10	Not used	-
11	Not used	-
12	Not used	-

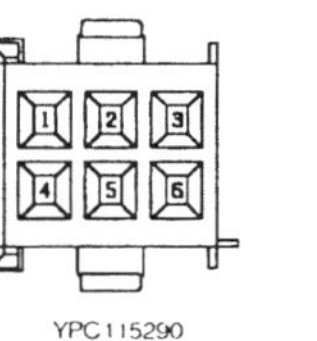

YPC115290

6 way AMP - Black

Pin No.	Description	Input/Output
1	PWM variable illumination signal	Input
2	Ground	Input
3	K-bus	Input/Output
4	+12V Permanent feed	Input
5	+12V Accessory feed	Input
6	Display Frame Rate (60Hz/50Hz) changeover signal	Input

OPERATION

Display and Control Unit

Rotary Menu Controller

Turning the rotary menu controller one step counter-clockwise sends a message to the navigation computer. If the highlighted cursor is not at the top of the list, then the navigation computer should respond by moving the cursor up one position. If the cursor is at the top of the list then there should be no action. If the cursor is on a horizontal list the cursor should move one step left.

Turning the rotary menu controller one step clockwise sends a message to the navigation computer. If the highlighted cursor is not at the bottom of the list, then the navigation computer should respond by moving the cursor down one position. If the cursor is at the bottom of the list then there should be no action. If the cursor is on a horizontal list the cursor should move one step right.

Pressing and releasing the rotary menu controller sends a message to the navigation computer. The navigation computer should select the currently highlighted menu item or icon and change the display appropriately. If the LCD screen is switched off, pressing and releasing the rotary menu controller will switch the screen on.

Mute Key

Pressing and releasing the mute key causes the mute status LED to be 'lit'. By having the mute function enabled (LED on), this causes any audio instructions given by the navigation system to be disabled. If the mute function is already enabled (LED on), pressing and releasing the mute key will cause it to be disabled.

Repeat Key

Pressing and releasing the repeat key causes the last audio instruction given by the navigation system to be repeated through the vehicle speakers.

Re-Rte Key

Pressing and releasing the Re-Rte key, in road navigation during guidance, causes the deviation menu to overlay onto the screen, and the user is then able to select a deviation distance between 0 and 6 miles. The system then calculates a new route once the rotary menu controller has been pushed to accept the deviation distance.

Menu key

Pressing and releasing the Menu key causes the main menu screen to be displayed on the LCD. Pressing and releasing the menu key while the screen is off sends a message to the navigation computer. The navigation computer should respond by turning the LCD screen on and presenting the main menu.

Navigation Computer - Gyro Sensor

The piezo gyro sensor measures the motion of the vehicle around its vertical axis using the Coriolis force. The Coriolis force is a force which accelerates a foreign body moving away from the rotational axis against the direction of rotation of that axis.

In operation, a mass inside the sensor is excited to a point where it begins to vibrate, similar to the principle of a tuning fork. The vibrations travel perpendicular to the rotational axis and cause continuous potential charge of the mass in relation to the rotational axis. The forces can be measured easily and are converted into a yaw rate to calculate direction.

Peizo Gyro Sensor

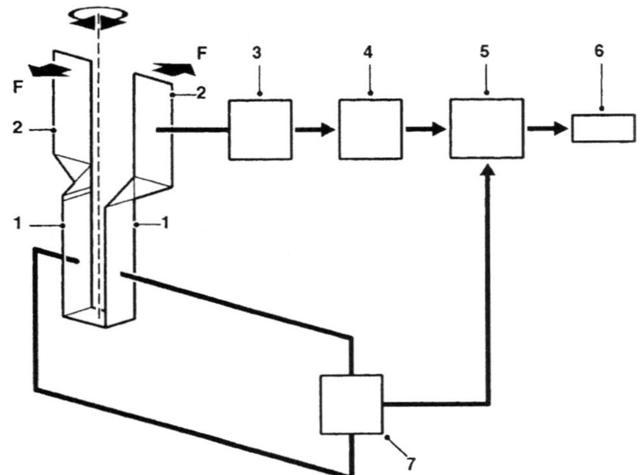

M86 5095

1. Driver elements
2. Retaining element
3. Amplifier
4. Phase detector
5. Frequency filter
6. Navigation computer
7. Driver stage

The sensor is supplied with a current from a driver. The driver is used to induce vibrations in the driver elements and retaining elements. As the vehicle turns a corner, i.e.; a left hand bend, the rotational motion is detected by the retaining elements, caused by the Coriolis force, and a small electrical voltage is produced.

The voltage is passed to an amplifier and the amplified signal is then passed to a phase detector. The phase detector establishes the direction of rotation and passes a signal to a frequency filter. Because the gyro sensor is subject to vibrations produced by means other than cornering, the frequency filter analyses the signals and removes signals not produced by cornering forces. The filtered signal is passed from the frequency filter to the navigation computer which uses it to calculate direction of travel.

Software Loading

The system is capable of having operating software loaded via the CD-ROM drive. This allows for different languages to be loaded and also allows systems to be updated when new software/features are available. The Navigation computer is delivered pre-loaded with operating software, 2 default languages and the Off Road navigation software. The 2 pre-loaded languages are:-

- UK English (Female)
- German (Male)

Software loading can be achieved at any time by inserting Software CD into the CD-ROM drive. The navigation computer compares of the version of software on the CD with that currently loaded. If the software version on CD is a later version it automatically starts to load the software. The status of software loading is displayed on the display and control unit's screen. On completion of software loading, the CD is automatically ejected. The user is prompted to remove the CD and confirm. The computer then resets and restarts with the new software.

Language loading is also achieved by inserting the software CD (as this also contains all the navigation languages). By selecting a language to load, then selecting a language to delete in its place the replacement language is loaded with a status screen to accompany it. On completion of language loading, the CD is automatically ejected from the navigation computer. The computer then resets and restarts with the new language loaded. This needs to be selected from the settings menu.

Diagnostics Mode

The navigation system may be put into a on-board diagnostics mode (service mode) by selecting the 'settings' menu from the main menu then pushing and holding the menu key for about 10 seconds. The service mode has four main functions:

1. To check that components are fitted and to determine their hardware/software levels.
2. To perform a quick 'health check' of the major input signals to the system.
3. To check for correct operation of the Display and Control unit keys.
4. To check the status of the GPS reception.

Selecting the On-Board Monitor item from the service mode menu causes the version info to be displayed. The screen displays the software and hardware level of the display and control unit together with the diagnostics and bus index. The supplier of the unit is also displayed as a number code defined by BMW. The system queries the display and control unit before displaying the information on the screen. If the unit responds with Software Hardware levels this implies that the component is connecting to at least Power, Ground and K-bus.

Display and Control Key Check

Selecting 'Key Function ' from the display and control units 'Functions' menu displays three pieces of information:

1. Key - This item displays a value indicating whether any keys are pressed and if so which one. With no key pressed the value 'FF' should be displayed. If any other value is shown then it may indicate that a key is sticking. The sticking key can be determined by one of the following codes:

- 01 Mute key
- 02 Re-Rte key
- 03 Menu key
- 04 Repeat key
- 05 Rotary-turn push
- FE Multiple key presses
- FF No key pressed

2. OBM Increment Sensor - This value should decrease if the rotary menu selector is turned clockwise and increase if the rotary menu selector is turned anticlockwise.
3. Radio Increment Sensor - This value will not register on the 2000MY Range-Rover system.

If there is no user action on the display and control unit for 3 seconds, the system stops updating the values, and the 'Functions' item becomes active.

Selecting '<Return' returns the system to the Service Mode menu.

Brightness

Selecting 'Brightness' from the display produces a pop-up menu with a selecting 'Slider'. This allows the user to alter the brightness setting on the display by moving the slider up and down with the rotary menu controller. Pushing the rotary menu controller accepts the new value.

Selecting '<Return' returns the system to the Service Mode menu.

Navigation Computer Version Information

Selecting the Navigation/ Graphic Element item from the service mode menu causes the Version information of the Navigation computer to be displayed. The screen displays the software and hardware level of the navigation computer together with the diagnostics and bus index. The supplier of the unit is also displayed as a number code defined by BMW.

Selecting '<Return' returns the system to the service mode menu.

GPS Version Information

Selecting the GPS item from the service mode menu causes the GPS Version info to be displayed.

Selecting '<Return' returns the system to the service mode menu. Selecting 'Functions' shows the pop up menu.

The status of the GPS system can be checked as follows:
From the Service mode menu select GPS. Selecting 'Function' brings up a menu. On selecting 'GPS Status' the system displays the status screen.

When the GPS system is exposed to satellites for the first time it can take up to 15 minutes to determine the position of the vehicle.

The Receiver status ('Rec Stat') and Position source ('Pos Src') may be used to check that the GPS system is functioning correctly. Receiver status displays one of the following:

COMERR
There is a communication error between the GPS receiver and the navigation computer.

SEARCH
The system is tracking a number of satellites. If this is displayed it may simply be that there is a failure in the GPS system. First check that the GPS antenna's view of the sky is not blocked in any way. Check harness connections between the GPS Receiver and the GPS antenna.

TRACK
The system is tracking a number of satellites. The number displayed in the Pos Src indicates how many satellites the GPS system can see. This indicates that the system is all connected correctly but does not have enough information to determine the position of the vehicle. Check that there is nothing obstructing the GPS antenna's view of the sky - e.g. a metallic object on the right hand side plenum area. It may take several minutes for the GPS system to aquire enough satellites to determine the vehicle position (POS).

POS
The system has a current position fix. This indicates that the GPS system is functioning normally. The Pos Src indicates the type of position fix (2D or 3D) and the number of satellites that are available.

The screen shows the current position in Latitude and Longitude, the approximate height of the vehicle and the GPS time and date. The GPS time and date is always displayed in Greenwich meantime (GMT).

The ground speed and heading can be checked when the vehicle is in motion - The indicated ground speed should be the actual vehicle speed in m/s and the heading should be the actual direction of the vehicle.

GPS Tracking Information

Selecting the 'GPS Tracking Information' from the GPS functions menu displays the satellite being tracked on each channel together with a signal level. The screen also displays the number of satellites that are currently visible and the Almanac status.

Sensor Input 'Health Check'

Selecting the 'Sensor Check' item from the service mode menu causes the sensor check screen to be displayed. The sensor check screen is used to provide a quick visual check that all the input sensors are working. Some of the tests below involve driving the vehicle for short distances. Before starting these tests ensure that an appropriate location, away from public roads and obstructions, is chosen. The system-input sensors can be tested as follows:

1. Wheel speed sensors - When the car is stationary the values in the wheel sensor boxes should both be zero. The car should be driven for a short distance. Whilst driving, a number should be displayed in the left wheel sensor box. The value in the box should be proportional to the speed of the vehicle - i.e. the value will increase as the speed increases. As the speed becomes more constant, just the left box should display a value - this indicates the speed signal from the front left ABS sensor (buffered and averaged through the vehicle BeCM).
2. Gyro - The navigation computer has an inbuilt Gyro, which is used to determine changes in direction of the vehicle. With the vehicle driving forward in a straight line the direction arrow should be pointing to the top of the screen. The Gyro value beside the direction icon should remain fairly constant. The vehicle should then be made to make a turn first to the right and then to the left. When the vehicle turns to the right, the direction icon should turn clockwise and the Gyro value should increase. The size of the angle through which the direction icon turns depends on the tightness of the turn. When the vehicle turns to the left, the direction icon should turn counter-clockwise and the Gyro value should decrease.
3. Direction sensor - The direction sensor is used to determine whether the vehicle is travelling forwards or backwards. When the vehicle is in any forward gear, and in neutral or in park in the case of an automatic transmission, the vehicle display should show 'Forwards'. With the vehicle in reverse the display should change to 'Backwards'.
4. **GPS System**- The sensor check screen displays the number of satellites being received and the status of the GPS system. The different states are listed below.
   GPS Error
   There is a communication error between the GPS receiver and the Navigation computer.
   Satellite Search
   The system is searching for satellites. If this is displayed it may imply that there is a failure in the GPS system. First check that the GPS antenna's view of the sky is not blocked in any way. Check harness connections between the GPS Receiver and the GPS antenna.
   Satellite Contact
   The system is tracking a number of satellites. This indicates that the system is all connected correctly but does not have enough information to determine the position of the vehicle. Check that there is nothing obstructing GPS antenna's view of the sky - e.g. a metallic object covering the right-hand side plenum area. It may take several minutes for the GPS system to acquire enough satellites to determine the vehicle position (Position known).
   Position Known
   The system has a current position fix. This indicates that the GPS system is functioning normally.

Selecting '<Return' returns the system to the service mode menu.

Service Diagnostics

No serial diagnostic link is provided with the 2000 MY Range Rover navigation system, so TestBook cannot interact with the system. However, a TestBook diagnostic is available, comprising a series of prompt screens to complement the on-board diagnostics feature.

OFF ROAD NAVIGATION

Off road navigation builds on the technology of road navigation to replace the hand held GPS location devices, and to some degree, the use of paper maps.

Off Road Navigation Route Structure

The off road navigation route comprises a series of waypoints which are followed sequentially. Direct point to point guidance is given to the first waypoint in the route. When the vehicle arrives at the first waypoint guidance is given to the second waypoint in the route. This process continues for subsequent waypoints until the final waypoint (destination) is reached.

The routes are stored in the non-volatile memory of the navigation computer in the same way as the address book is currently stored.

Level Zero System

The level zero off road navigation system operates normally in 'road navigation mode' with conventional road data maps. The system functions in 'data guidance mode' giving direct point to point directions and in 'map guidance mode' giving a visual map representation of the route and terrain information. The user can select between the guidance screens. The vehicle position and proposed route is shown on the map display and is updated in real time.

Arrival at a waypoint or destination is governed by the waypoint acceptance radius, which tells you when you are within a certain radius of a waypoint. This is set by the user from a list of available options. When the vehicle arrives at the waypoint or destination an audio message is given. If the route is being followed then the system provides guidance to the next waypoint of that route.

At the start of guidance, but after the guidance screen has been updated, an audio message is given to confirm the type of guidance requested and to give the bearing of the waypoint or destination. As the vehicle approaches the waypoint or destination an audible warning is given to indicate that the waypoint is ahead.

The language used by off road navigation is the same as that selected for road navigation.

Off Road Navigation Features

Routes

- 20 routes may be stored
- Titles may be placed against routes (20 characters)
- 35 waypoints programmable per route
- Waypoints of one route to be followed sequentially
- Routes may be copied and pasted as a new route
- The user may review and edit routes
- Routes may be followed both forwards and in a reverse direction
- Enter route and waypoints into the system prior to commencing a journey
- Create a route by entering current location as waypoint

Waypoints

- The user may place titles against waypoints (10 characters)
- The user may copy and paste waypoints
- The user may review and edit waypoints
- The user may skip waypoints in route
- Notification of reaching waypoint (destination) both audible and visual

General

- The user may select between imperial and metric measurements
- The user may select between data guidance mode and map guidance mode
- The user may change the scale of the map
- Input and direction to a one off destination that is not part of a route
- Read and display vector (road maps) map information from a CD-ROM.

Off Road Guidance Screens

The system has three screens to provide step by step off road guidance to the user.

- Full data guidance screen
- Map guidance screen

The guidance screens give the user the information required for direct point to point direction to the selected destination (guidance mode). The same guidance screens are also available even when guidance is not being given (compass mode). All the destination and guidance information is not shown on the guidance screens when in compass mode. When the system is in compass mode with no guidance being given the route title is 'COMPASS MODE'.

Full Guidance Screen

When guidance is being given the full data guidance screen shows the following information:

- Current latitude and longitude
- Destination (waypoint) latitude and longitude
- Destination (waypoint) title and reference number
- Direct point to point distance to the destination (waypoint)
- Altitude
- Arrow to the destination (waypoint)
- Compass
- Bearing
- Heading
- GPS reception icon
- GMT (All vehicles except NAS)

When guidance is not being given (compass mode) the full guidance screen shows the following information:

- Current latitude and longitude
- Altitude
- Compass
- Heading
- GPS reception icon
- GMT (All vehicles except NAS)

Map Guidance Screen

When guidance is being given (guidance mode) the map guidance screen shows the following information:

- Current latitude and longitude
- Destination (waypoint) title and reference number
- Direct point to point distance to destination (waypoint)
- Arrow to destination
- Compass
- Bearing
- GPS reception icon
- Visual representation of the map stored on the CD ROM database

When guidance is not being given (compass mode) the map guidance will show the following information:

- Current latitude and longitude
- Compass
- GPS reception icon
- Visual representation of the map stored on the CD ROM database

Off Road Map Guidance Display Menu

For the map guidance display the menu options are:

Map/Data Display

This changes the guidance display from map display to data display, if the guidance display is in map. If the guidance display is in data display this will change it back.

Map Scale

Changes the scale of the map shown on the map guidance display. To change the map scale use the rotary menu controller to bring up the menu, and from the menu select scale. The scale can then be changed between 100 metres and 100 kilometres (125 yards and 50 miles).

Routes List

The route list menu option displays a list of all the routes, with route titles, available to the system. The routes are sorted alphabetically and the default cursor position is the first route in the list. If guidance is being given for a route, then the route text shown in the route list is gold in colour and the default cursor position will be the current route.

Go To

This option allows the user to be given guidance to a selected individual destination. An audible conformation is given once guidance has been selected. The user inputs the destination with the text input screen and map input screen. The text input screen is used to input the destination title and may be used to input the destination co-ordinates.

End Guidance

The end guidance menu option allows the user to end the guidance information that is currently being given. End guidance will end all types of guidance specified. The guidance screens no longer give guidance information and all audio instructions are halted.

Settings

The settings menu option allows the user to change the off road navigation settings. The following settings are available:

- The guidance screen can be set to either full information or reduced information.
- The acceptance radius for notification of arrival at waypoint can be set to between 50 metres and 500 metres (50 yards and 550 yards). The waypoint acceptance radius is used for all destinations within off road navigation.

Help

The Off Road Navigation Help menu option gives the user basic 'on line' help. The 'on line' help is given in the user selected language. The user selects the required help topic from the help index. The help list comprises of:

- Routes
- Review Route
- Delete Route
- Copy Route
- Paste as New
- New Route
- Waypoints
- Insert Waypoint
- Insert Current Position
- Copy Waypoint
- Paste Waypoint
- Delete Waypoint
- Edit Waypoint
- Go To
- Timing
- Backtrack.

Guidance Screen Functionality

The information shown on the guidance screens functions as follows:

Waypoint Reference Number

The waypoint reference number is shown on the selected guidance screen only when guidance to a waypoint is being followed. If a route is not being followed but guidance is being given to a single waypoint selected from a route, then the waypoint reference number is shown. If a route is not being followed but guidance is being given to a 'one off' destination that is not part of a route, then the waypoint reference number will not be shown. A single space is placed between the decimal point separator after the route reference number and before the waypoint reference number.

Waypoint (destination) Title

The waypoint title is shown on the selected guidance screen only when guidance to a waypoint is being followed and indicates the current waypoint for which the guidance is being given. If a route is not being followed but guidance is being given to a single waypoint selected from a route, then the waypoint title is shown. If a route is not being followed but guidance is being given to a 'one off' destination that is not part of a route, then the destination title is shown.

Destination (waypoint) Co-ordinates

The destination co-ordinates are shown on the full guidance screen when guidance is being given and indicates the current destination (waypoint) for which the guidance is being given. The destination co-ordinates are shown in the format selected within the settings menu option.

Bearing

The bearing is the direction from the current vehicle position and the heading to the destination (waypoint). The bearing is displayed on the selected guidance screen to the nearest whole degree starting at 0 degrees and is updated every 2 seconds +/- 0.1 seconds. The bearing is updated at the same time as the heading.

Destination Arrow

The destination arrow forms part of the guidance icon shown on the selected guidance screen and indicates to the user the direction from the current vehicle position and heading to the destination (waypoint). The arrow changes colour to indicate the mode of the guidance. The destination arrow has an accuracy of 15 degrees starting at 0 degrees. The destination arrow is updated as required when dictated by an 'event' and at the same time as the bearing and heading. The destination arrow is placed underneath the compass arrow.

Compass

The compass arrow forms part of the guidance icon shown on the selected guidance screen and indicates to the user the direction of North as selected from the settings menu option. The compass arrow has an accuracy of 15 degrees starting with 0 degrees. The compass arrow is updated as required when dictated by an 'event' and at the same time as the destination arrow. The compass arrow is placed on top of the destination arrow.

Heading Up Icon

The heading up icon forms part of the guidance icon shown on the selected guidance screen and indicates to the user the direction the destination arrow should point to achieve the minimum distance from the vehicle position to the destination (waypoint). The heading up icon has an accuracy of 15 degrees starting at 0 degrees. The heading up icon is updated as required when dictated by an 'event' and at the same time as the destination arrow.

Heading

The heading gives the user the direction in which the vehicle is pointing. The heading is displayed on the full guidance screen to the nearest whole degree starting at 0 degrees and is updated as required when dictated by an 'event'. The heading is updated at the same time as the bearing.

GMT 24 hour

The GMT 24-hour clock time is shown on the full guidance screen and is taken directly from the GPS data and cannot be adjusted by the user.

Altitude

The accuracy of the altitude is 50 metres or 150 feet depending on the system settings. The altitude is displayed on the full guidance screen even if the latest altitude data is not available. If valid altitude data is not available, the last known altitude is displayed. The altitude is updated as required when dictated by an 'event'. The altitude is updated at the same time as the bearing and heading.

Current Car Position Icon

The current car position is the same as is used for road navigation. The Current Car Position icon has an accuracy of 15 degrees starting with 0 degrees. The Current Car Position icon is updated as required when dictated by an 'event'.

Current Co-ordinates

The current co-ordinates are shown on the selected guidance screen. The current co-ordinates are the coordinates of the current vehicle position in the format selected in the settings menu option. The resolution of the co-ordinates is to be such that the least significant displayed digit remains as close as possible to the calculated vehicle position. The current co-ordinates are updated at the same time as the heading and bearing.

Distance to the Destination

The distance to the destination is shown on the selected guidance screen. The distance to the destination is the direct point to point distance from the current vehicle position to the destination (waypoint) in the selected system settings. The distance to destination is updated as required when dictated by an 'event'. The distance to destination is updated at the same time as the heading and bearing.

Arrival at Destination (waypoint)

When a waypoint is achieved and the guidance screen is updated to direct the user to the next waypoint of the route, the following items are updated for the new waypoint:

- Waypoint reference number
- Waypoint title
- Destination arrow
- Destination co-ordinates
- Distance to destination
- Bearing to destination.

If the waypoint is the final waypoint of the route or the destination is not part of a route, the existing guidance data remains active.

Map

When the map guidance screen is selected a background map is shown. The map is stored on the CD-ROM. The map scale cannot be changed as it is fixed by the map image stored on the CD-ROM. The following information is displayed on the map:

- Map scale
- The current vehicle position (icon as road navigation)
- Guidance start position
- Route waypoints
- Lines joining route waypoints and start position
- Terrain information
- Points of interest.

If a route is not being followed, the lines that join the waypoints, the current position, the guidance start position and the destination position, are double pixel in width with black for the completed part of the guidance and red for the not achieved part of the guidance.

Map Display Layering

The information that constitutes the map display has the displayed information layered as specified below, starting at the bottom layer and working its way to the top layer:

Vector map (if available)
Lines joining waypoints and current car position icon
Waypoint icons
Current car position icon
Cursor (cross Hairs)
Scale indicator

Heading Up

The heading up icon remains at the top (0 degrees) position of the guidance icon. The guidance arrow indicates the the destination bearing and the compass arrow indicates the position of North. The heading up icon indicates to the user the direction the destination arrow should point to achieve the minimum distance from the current vehicle position to the destination (waypoint).

Timing Algorithm

Timing calculation is carried out when the ignition is on. The 'distance covered' is that given by the vehicle speed signal only. The 'time to' shown on the timing screen is updated every 30 seconds +/- 5 seconds. Timing calculations, for both waypoint and route, commences as soon as the 'distance covered' is greater than 100 metres. All times used in the calculations are to the nearest second and all distances covered are to the nearest 10 metres.

The 'time to' for the next waypoint in the route shown on the timing screen is recalculated as the current waypoint is achieved. For timing calculations the 'average speed' remains valid from the current waypoint to the next waypoint in the route and the 'distance to waypoint' is reset to that distance to the next waypoint in the route.

If the average speed is below 1 metre per second, then the time to the waypoint and time to complete route is not calculated and the previous data remains displayed on the timing screen. If the average speed is below 1 metre per second for more than 2 minutes, then the average speed calculations are reset but the previous data remains displayed on the timing screen. Therefore when the vehicle's speed is again above 1 metre per second the average speed calculations begin again as if guidance had just been selected. When the timing calculations are reset all existing data is lost and calculations begin again as if guidance had just been selected.

Co-ordinates

Latitude and Longitude

Latitude and longitude denotes a position as up to 90 degrees for North and South of the equator (up to the poles, which are 90 degrees North and 90 degrees South; the equator is 0 degrees) for latitude and up to 180 degrees East and West of the prime meridian, which is 0 degrees longitude. The prime meridian passes through Greenwich, England. Each degree of latitude and longitude can be divided into 60 minutes (60'). Each minute of latitude and longitude can be divided into 60 seconds (60"). It is also possible to express each minute as decimals. Therefore it will be possible to display latitude and longitude in two formats:

1. DD˚MM.MM
2. DD˚MM'SS"

Where D represents the degrees, M represents the minutes and S represents the seconds.

Within the co-ordinate entry and edit text screens the following sections of the co-ordinates are entered or edited in blocks.

For DD˚MM.MM

1. DD Degrees North
2. MM Minutes North
3. MM Decimal Minutes North
4. DD Degrees East
5. MM Minutes East
6. MM Decimal Minutes East

For DD˚MM'SS"

1. DD Degrees North
2. MM Minutes North
3. SS Seconds North
4. DD Degrees East
5. MM Minutes East
6. SS Seconds East

NAVIGATION COMPUTER

Service repair no - 86.53.01

Remove

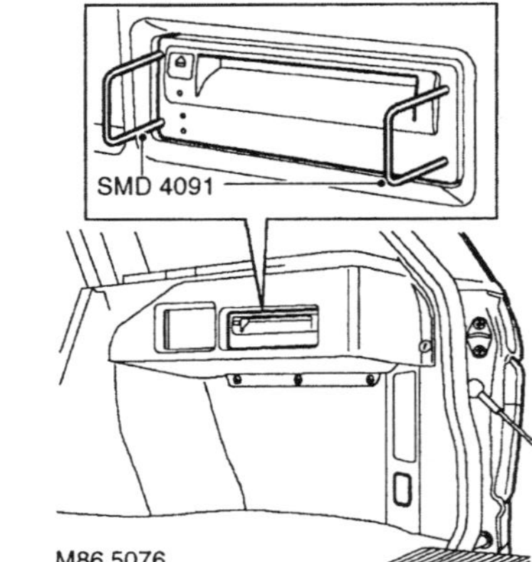

M86 5076

1. Using tool SMD 4091 release clips securing navigation computer to bracket and pull computer forward.

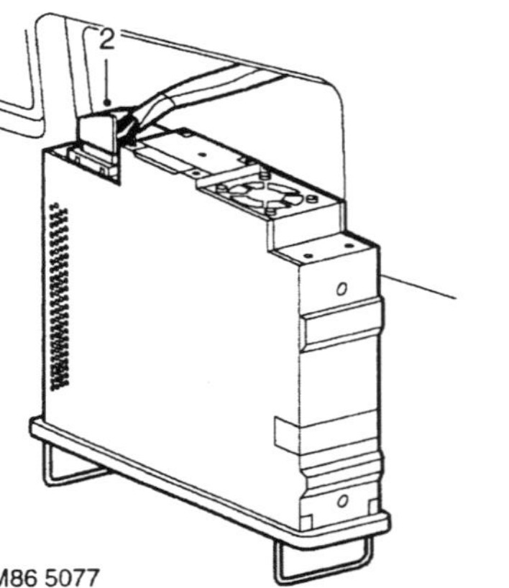

M86 5077

2. Disconnect 2 multiplugs from navigation computer and remove computer.

Refit

3. Connect multiplugs to navigation computer.
4. Fit computer to bracket and secure clips.

GLOBAL POSITIONING SYSTEM (GPS) RECEIVER

Service repair no - 86.53.04

Remove

1. Remove RH parcel tray support. ***See CHASSIS AND BODY, Repair.***

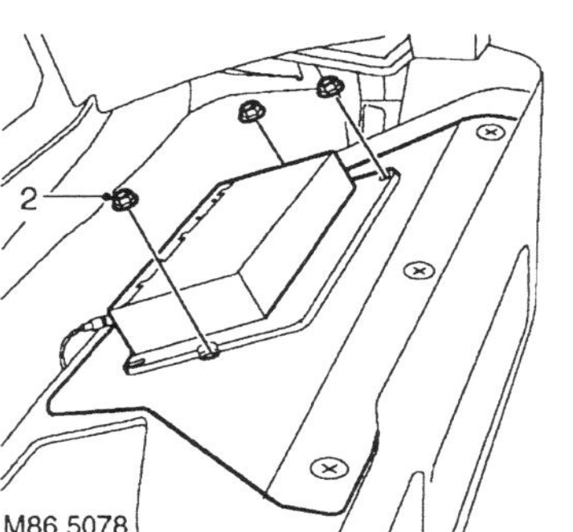

M86 5078

2. Remove 3 nuts securing GPS receiver to mounting plate.

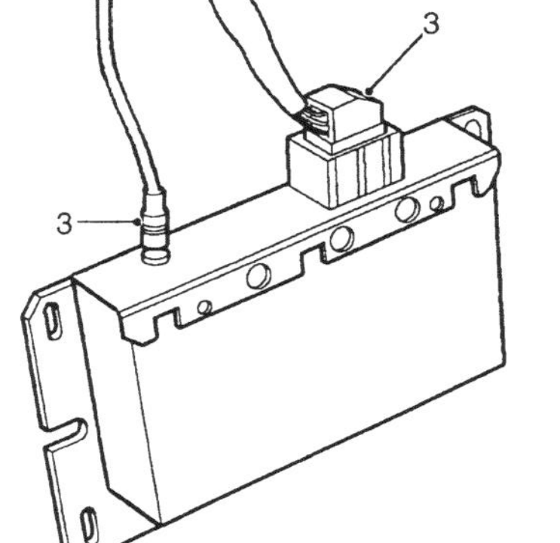

M86 5079

3. Disconnect 1 multiplug and 1 aerial connector from GPS receiver and remove receiver.

Refit

4. Position GPS receiver and connect multiplug and aerial connector.
5. Secure GPS receiver to mounting plate with nuts.
6. Fit RH parcel tray support. ***See CHASSIS AND BODY, Repair.***

AERIAL - GLOBAL POSITIONING SYSTEM (GPS)

Service repair no - 86.53.05

Remove

1. Disconnect battery earth lead.
2. Open bonnet and cover lower RH 'A' post to wing with tape, to prevent clips falling into cavity.

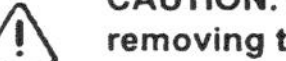

CAUTION: Always protect paintwork when removing trim finishers.

3. Remove RH windscreen wiper arm. ***See WIPERS AND WASHERS, Repair.***

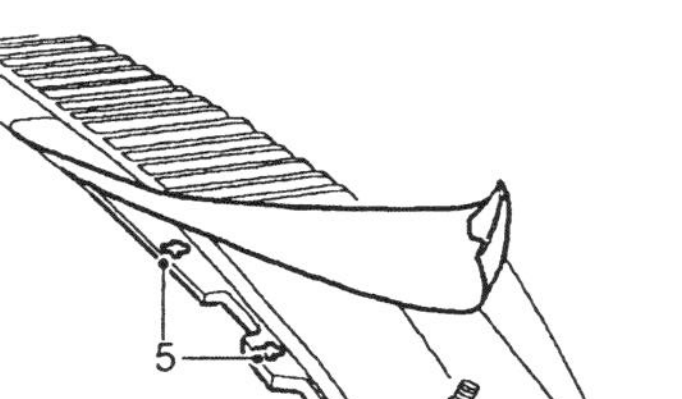

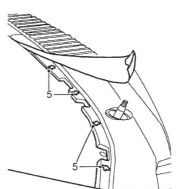

M86 5081

4. With care release RH edge of lower windscreen finisher from 'A' post finisher.
5. Carefully release 4 clips securing lower windscreen finisher to RH side of windscreen.

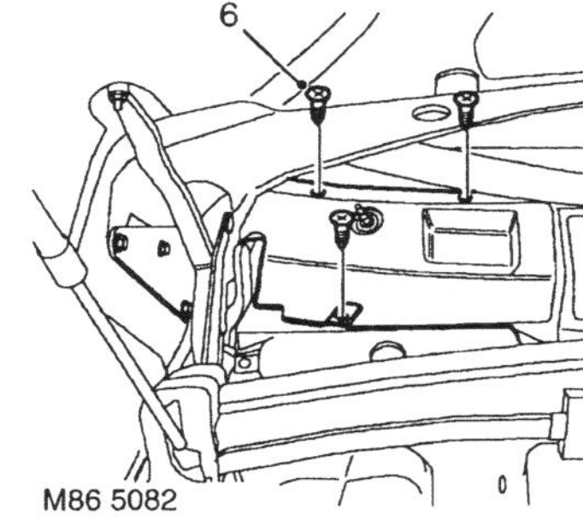

M86 5082

6. Remove 3 screws from RH plenum cover.

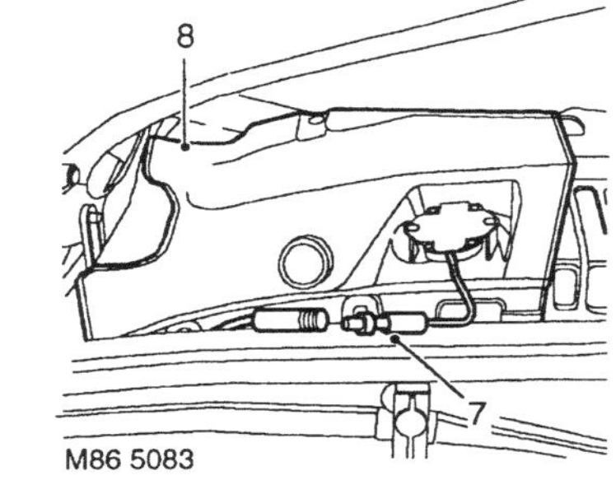

M86 5083

7. Lift RH plenum cover to gain access to GPS aerial, disconnect lead from waterproof sleeve.

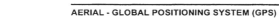

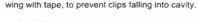

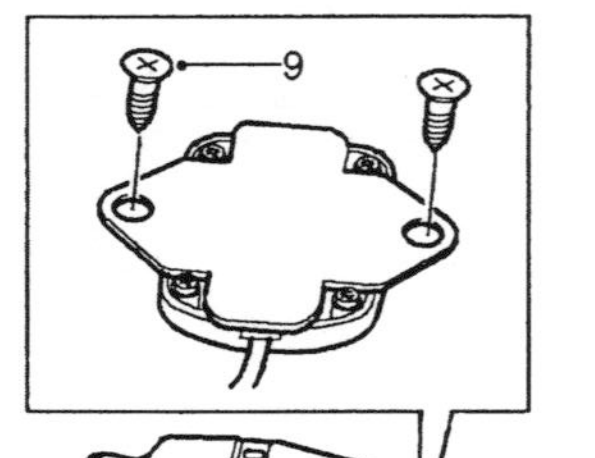

M86 5084

8. Remove plenum cover from vehicle.
9. Remove 2 screws securing GPS aerial to plenum cover and separate.

Refit

10. Fit GPS aerial to plenum cover and secure with screws.
11. Connect GPS aerial lead and cover with waterproof sleeve.
12. Fit plenum cover to vehicle and tighten screws.
13. Raise lower edge of RH 'A' post finisher, align lower windscreen finisher and fit clips.
14. Fit wiper arm assembly. ***See WIPERS AND WASHERS, Repair.***
15. Remove tape from RH wing.
16. Connect battery earth lead.

DISPLAY UNIT - NAVIGATION SYSTEM

Service repair no - 86.53.20

Remove

1. Remove radio. ***See ELECTRICAL, Repair.***
2. Remove instrument binnacle. ***See INSTRUMENTS, Repair.***
3. Move both front seats to the fully rearward position.

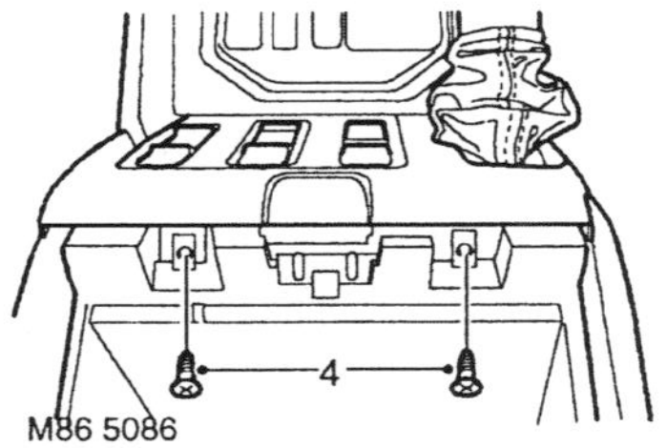

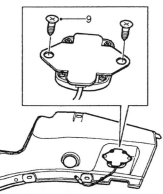

M86 5086

4. Remove 2 screws securing electric window switch pack to centre console and position switch pack aside.

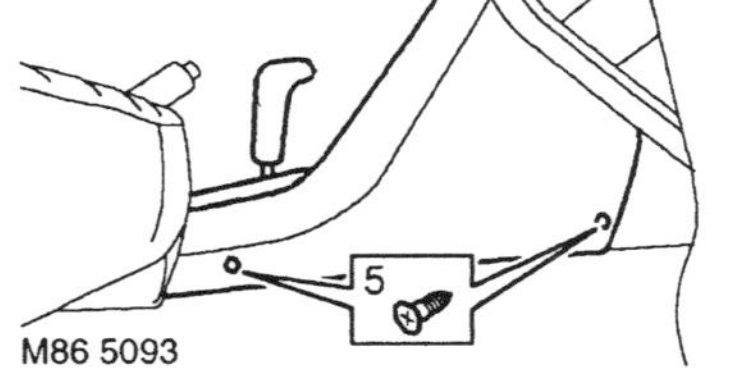

M86 5093

5. Remove 2 screws securing each side panel to centre console. Release sprag clips from fascia switch pack by firmly pulling rearwards. Remove side panels.

M86 5087

6. Remove 5 screws securing switch pack to centre console.

M86 5088

7. Move switch pack forward, disconnect 1 lucar and 11 multiplugs from switch pack and remove switch pack.

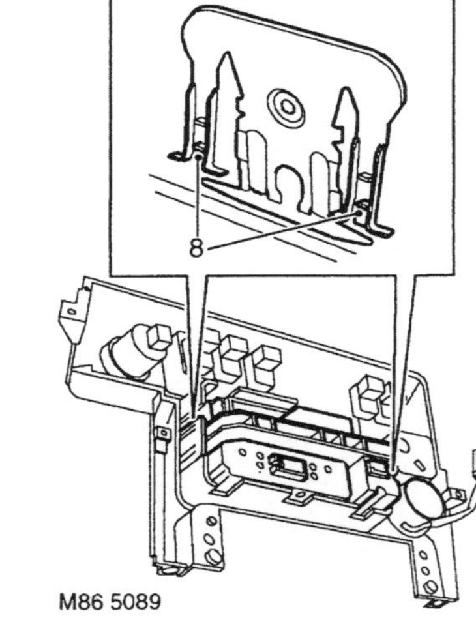

M86 5089

8. Release 4 clips securing satellite navigation display unit to switch pack and remove display unit.

Refit

9. Fit satellite navigation display unit to switch pack and secure clips.
10. Position switch pack to centre console and connect lucar and multiplugs.
11. Fit switch pack to centre console and secure with screws.
12. Fit side panels to centre console and secure clips and screws.
13. Fit electric window switch pack to centre console and secure with screws.
14. Fit instrument binnacle. ***See INSTRUMENTS, Repair.***
15. Fit radio. ***See ELECTRICAL, Repair.***

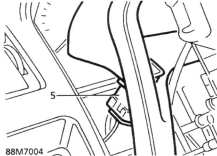

88 - INSTRUMENTS

CONTENTS

INSTRUMENT BINNACLE

Service repair no - 88.20.02

Remove

1. Remove covers from screws securing fascia closing panel.
2. Remove 4 screws, release fascia closing panel.
3. Disconnect drivers lap vent duct. Remove fascia closing panel.

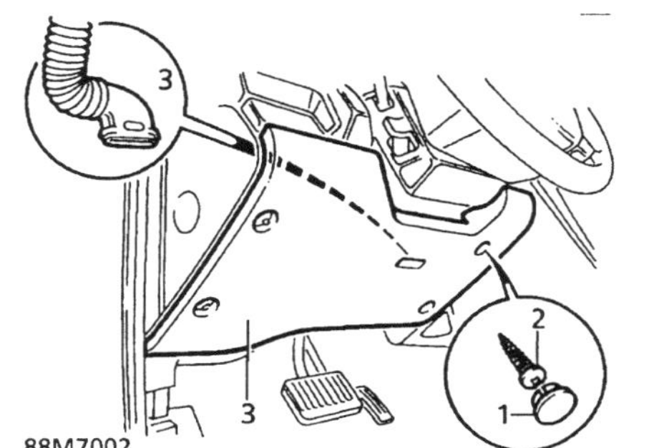

88M7002

4. Remove 4 screws securing instrument binnacle to fascia.

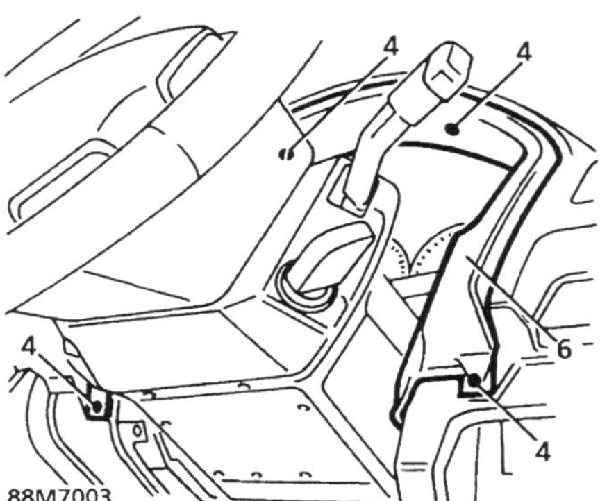

88M7003

5. Release binnacle from fascia. Disconnect fuel filler flap release switch multiplug.
6. Remove binnacle.

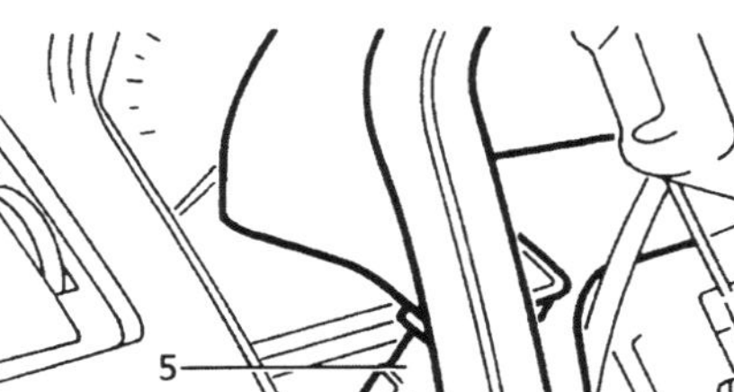

88M7004

Refit

7. Position binnacle.
8. Connect multiplug to fuel filler flap release switch. Align to fascia.
9. Fit screws securing instrument binnacle to fascia.
10. Position fascia closing panel. Connect drivers lap vent.
11. Align closing panel. Secure with screws.
12. Fit screw covers.

CLOCK

Service repair no - 88.15.07

Remove

1. Remove instrument pack binnacle. ***See this section.***
2. Move both front seats to the fully rearward position.
3. Remove screws securing each side panel to centre console, release sprag clips from fascia switch pack. Remove side panels.

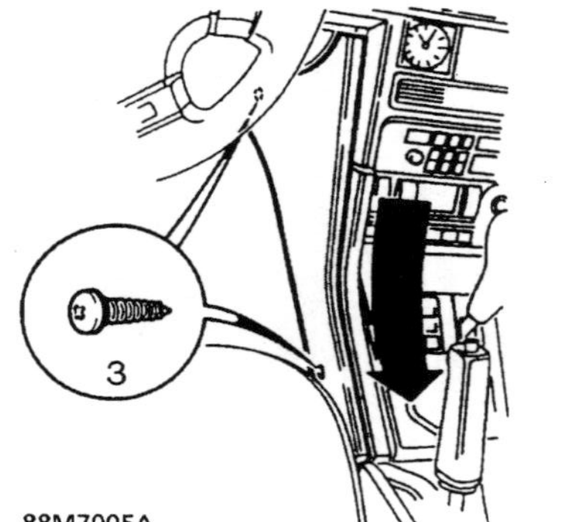

88M7005A

4. Remove radio applique.

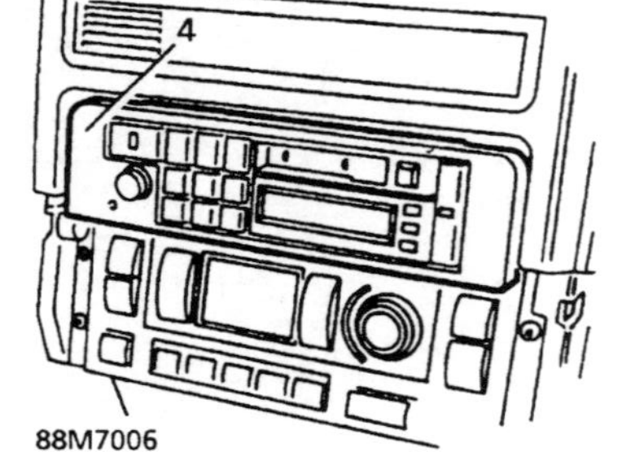

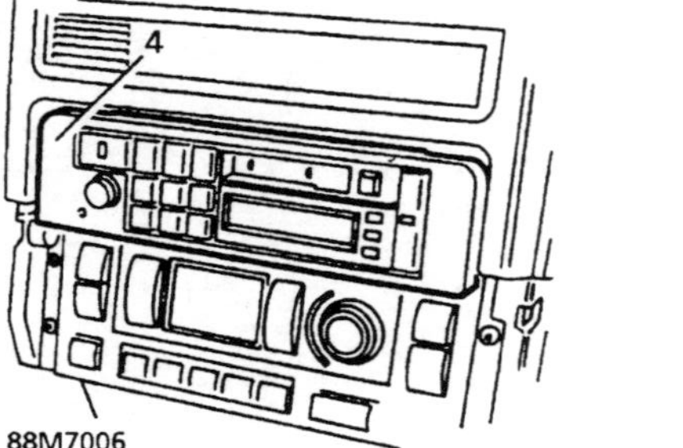

88M7006

5. Remove 5 screws securing switch pack.

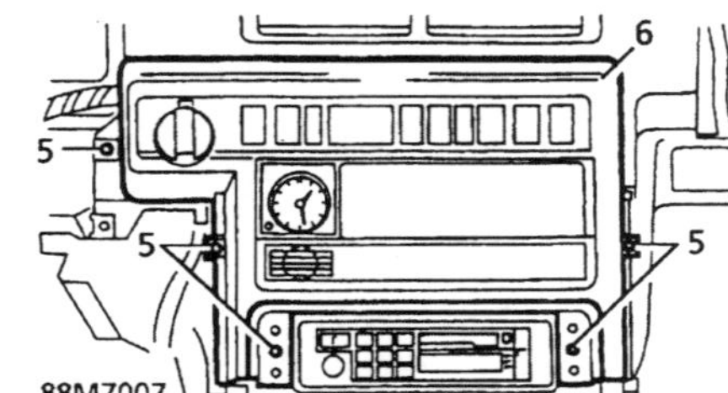

88M7007

6. Release switch pack from fascia.
7. Disconnect multiplug and Lucar connector from clock.

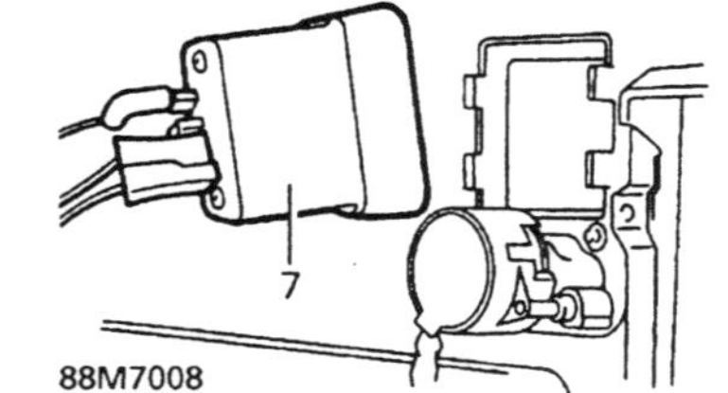

88M7008

8. Release clips. Remove clock from switch pack.

Refit

9. Reverse removal procedure.

COOLANT TEMPERATURE SENSOR - V8 - UP TO 99MY

Service repair no - 88.25.20

Remove

1. Partially drain cooling system. ***See COOLING SYSTEM, Repair.***
2. Disconnect coolant temperature sensor.
3. Position rag around sensor to catch spillage.
4. Remove sensor.

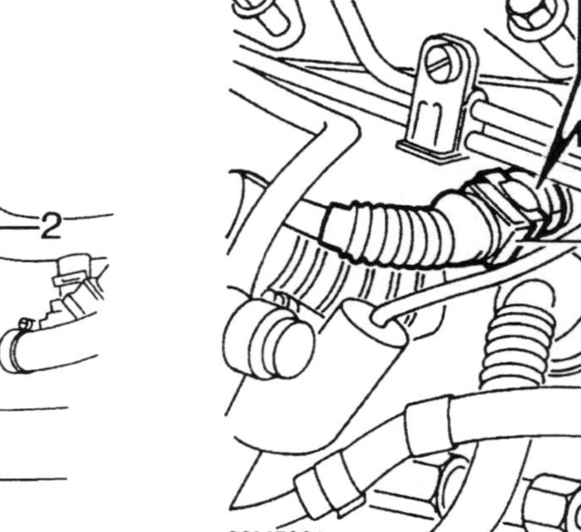

88M7010

Refit

5. Ensure sensor seat in manifold is clean.
6. Coat sensor threads with Loctite 577.
7. Fit sensor. Tighten to ***10 Nm. (7 lbf.ft)***
8. Connect sensor.
9. Refill cooling system. ***See COOLING SYSTEM, Repair.***
10. Run engine to normal operating temperature. Check for leaks around sensor.

COOLANT TEMPERATURE SENSOR - DIESEL

Service repair no - 88.25.20

Remove

1. Partially drain cooling system. ***See COOLING SYSTEM, Repair.***
2. Disconnect coolant temperature sensor multiplug.

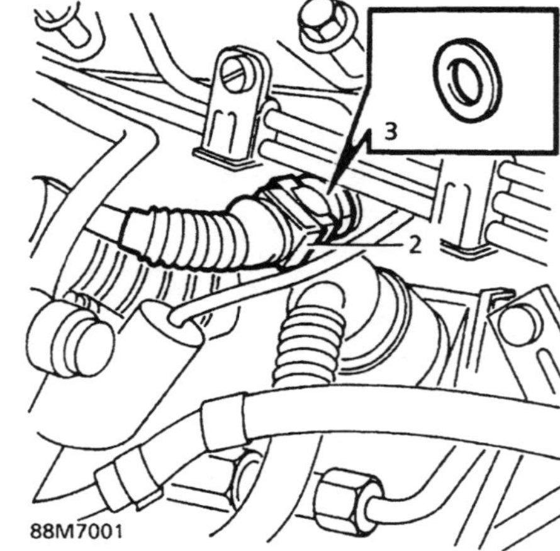

88M7001

3. Remove sensor using a deep 19mm socket with sufficient clearance for connector. Collect sealing washer and discard.

Refit

4. Ensure sensor seat in cylinder head is clean.
5. Using a new sealing washer, fit sensor. Tighten to ***20 Nm. (15 lbf.ft)***
6. Connect multiplug to sensor.
7. Refill cooling system. ***See COOLING SYSTEM, Repair.***
8. Run engine to normal operating temperature. Check for leaks around sensor.

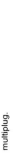

INSTRUMENT PACK

Service repair no - 88.20.01

CAUTION: If vehicle has SRS fitted, both battery terminals must be disconnected (negative lead first) prior to removing instrument pack.

1. Adjust steering column to fully extended/lowered position.
2. Remove instrument pack binnacle. ***See this section.***
3. Disconnect instrument pack multiplugs.

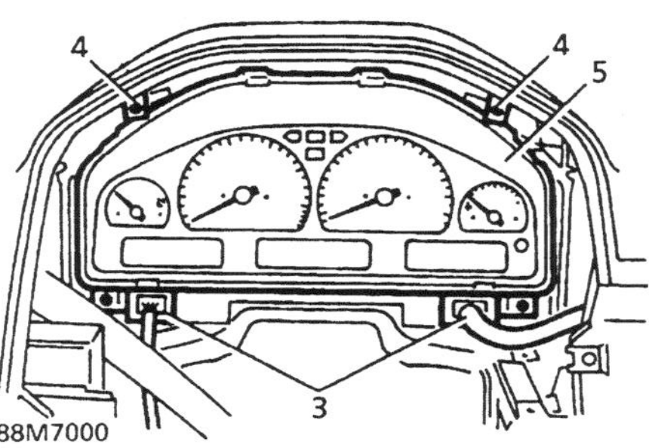

88M7000

4. Remove 4 screws securing instrument pack to fascia.
5. Remove instrument pack.

Refit

6. Reverse removal procedure.

FUEL TANK SENDER UNIT

Service repair no - 88.25.32

Remove

1. Remove fuel tank. ***See FUEL SYSTEM, Repair.***

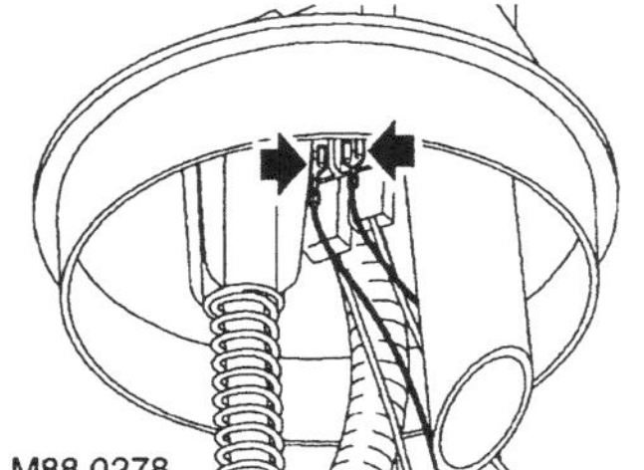
M88 0278

2. Disconnect 2 sender unit lucars. (1large 1 small)difficult to disconnect.

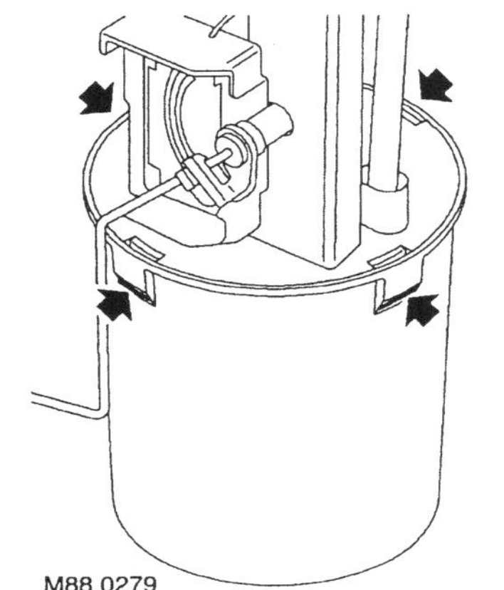
M88 0279

3. Carefully release 4 clips around fuel pump housing, lower housing disengage pump from mounting.

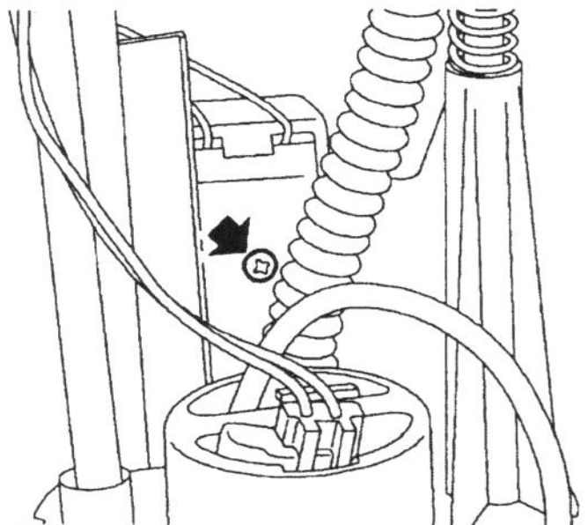

M88 0280

4. Carefully pivot the pump assembly, enabling access past fuel pipe to pozidrive screw retaining sender unit.
5. Remove 1 pozidrive screw from sender unit and move sender aside.

Refit

6. Fit sender unit to mounting on fuel pump assembly,locate and tighten pozidrive screw
7. Align fuel pump with lugs inside fuel pump housing.
8. Align housing male and female connectors with main body, carefully push fully home.
9. Fit sender unit lucar connections
10. Fit Fuel Tank ***See FUEL SYSTEM, Repair.***

FUEL TANK SENDER UNIT - ADVANCED EVAPS

Service repair no - 88.25.32

Remove

1. Remove fuel tank. ***See FUEL SYSTEM, Repair.***

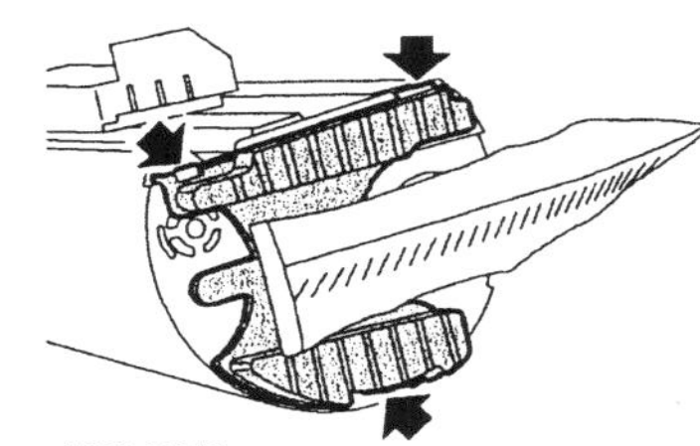
M88 0275

2. Carefully release 3 clips retaining fuel gauge tank unit rubber foot and move aside.

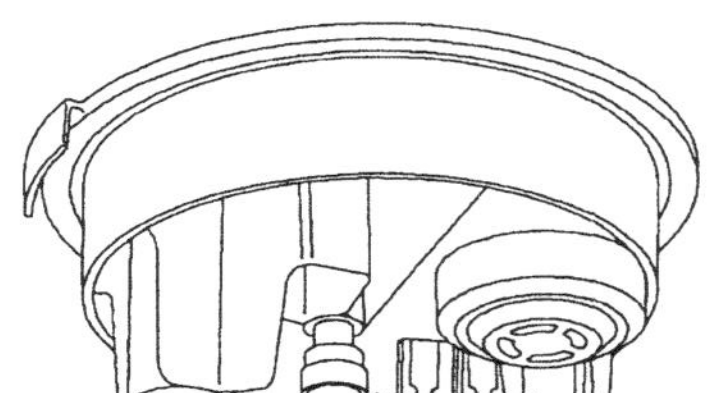
M88 0276

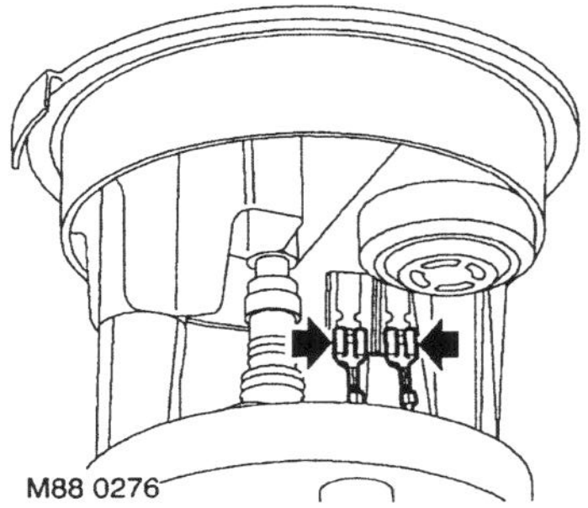

3. Release 2 lucar connections from top of fuel tank unit, difficult to remove.

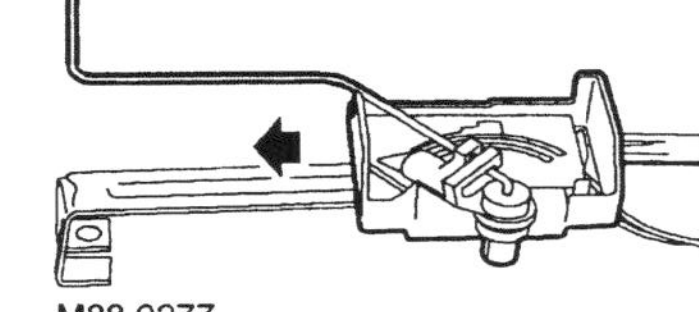
M88 0277

4. Carefully slide sender unit toward filter until bracket clears main assembly then move aside.

Refit

5. Fit sender unit bracket to slots in main assembly and press home.
6. Align clips and fit rubber foot to base of main assembly.
7. Fit sender lucar connections to top of tank unit, ensure wires pass through centre ring. Connect black sender wire to red and blue sender wire to black.
8. Fit fuel tank ***See FUEL SYSTEM, Repair.***

Notes

Distributed by Brooklands Books Ltd., PO Box 146, Cobham, Surrey KT11 1LG, England Phone: 01932 865051 Fax: 01932 868803
E-mail: sales@brooklands-books.com

Part No. LRL 0326ENG

4.0 & 4.6 LITRE V8 ENGINE

OVERHAUL MANUAL

These engines having Serial No. Prefix 42D, 46D, 47D, 48D, 49D, 50D, or 51D are fitted to the following models:

New Range Rover

Discovery - North American Specification - 1996 MY Onwards

Defender - North American Specification - 1997 MY Onwards

Defender V8i Automatic

4.0 & 4.6 LITRE V8 ENGINE OVERHAUL MANUAL

Publication Part No. LRL 0004ENG - 3rd Edition

This Overhaul Manual covers the 4.0 and 4.6 Litre V8 engines
as fitted to:

New Range Rover
Discovery (North American Spec. 1996 MY onwards)
Defender (North American Spec. 1997 MY onwards)
Defender V8i Automatic

CONTENTS

INTRODUCTION

How to use this Manual

To assist in the use of this Manual the section title is given at the top and the relevant sub-section is given at the bottom of each page.

This manual contains procedures for overhaul of the V8 engine on the bench with the gearbox, clutch, inlet manifold, exhaust manifolds, coolant pump, starter motor, alternator, and all other ancillary equipment removed. For information regarding General Information, Adjustments, removal of oil seals, engine units and ancillary equipment, consult the Repair Manual.

This manual is divided into 3 sections:
- Data, Torque & Tools
- Description and Operation and
- Overhaul

To assist filing of revised information each sub-section is numbered from page 1.

Individual items are to be overhauled in the sequence in which they appear in this manual. Items numbers in the illustrations are referred to in the text.

Overhaul operations include reference to Service tool numbers and the associated illustration depicts the tool. Where usage is not obvious the tool is shown in use. Land Rover tool numbers are quoted, for the equivalent Rover Cars tool number refer to the Service Tool section. Operations also include reference to wear limits, relevant data, and specialist information and useful assembly details.

WARNINGS, CAUTIONS and **NOTES** have the following meanings:

WARNING: Procedures which must be followed precisely to avoid the possibility of injury.

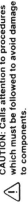

CAUTION: Calls attention to procedures which must be followed to avoid damage to components.

NOTE: Gives helpful information.

References

With the engine and gearbox assembly removed, the crankshaft pulley end of the engine is referred to as the front. References to RH and LH banks of cylinders are taken viewing from the flywheel end of the engine.

Operations covered in this Manual do not include reference to testing the vehicle after repair. It is essential that work is inspected and tested after completion and if necessary a road test of the vehicle is carried out particularly where safety related items are concerned.

Engine serial number

The engine serial number and compression ratio will be found stamped on a cast pad on the cylinder block between numbers 3 and 5 cylinders. The compression ratio is above the serial number.

Dimensions

The dimensions quoted are to design engineering specification with Service Limits where applicable.

REPAIRS AND REPLACEMENTS

When replacement parts are required it is essential that only Land Rover recommended parts are used.

Attention is particularly drawn to the following points concerning repairs and the fitting of replacement parts and accessories.

Torque wrench setting figures given in this Manual must be used. Locking devices, where specified, must be fitted. If the efficiency of a locking device is impaired during removal it must be renewed.

The terms of the vehicle warranty may be invalidated by the fitting of parts other than Land Rover recommended parts. All Land Rover recommended parts have the full backing of the vehicle warranty.

Land Rover dealers are obliged to supply only Land Rover recommended parts.

SPECIFICATION

Land Rover are constantly seeking to improve the specification, design and production of their vehicles and alterations take place accordingly. While every effort has been made to ensure the accuracy of this Manual, it should not be regarded as an infallible guide to current specifications of any particular vehicle.

This Manual does not constitute an offer for sale of any particular component or vehicle. Land Rover dealers are not agents of the Company and have no authority to bind the manufacturer by any expressed or implied undertaking or representation.

CONTENTS

Notes

DATA

Firing order	1, 8, 4, 3, 6, 5, 7, 2 Cylinders 1, 3, 5, 7 - LH side of engine Cylinders 2, 4, 6, 8 - RH side of engine	
Cylinder heads		
Maximum warp	0.05 mm	0.002 in
Reface limit	0.50 mm	0.02 in
Valve springs		
Free length	48.30 mm	1.90 in
Fitted length	40.40 mm	1.60 in
Load - valve open	736 ± 10 N	165 ± 2 lbf
Load - valve closed	339 ± 10 N	76 ± 2 lbf
Valves		
Valve stem diameter:		
Inlet	8.664 to 8.679 mm	0.341 to 0.342 in
Exhaust	8.651 to 8.666 mm	0.340 to 0.341 in
Valve head diameter:		
Inlet	39.75 to 40.00 mm	1.5 to 1.6 in
Exhaust	34.226 to 34.480 mm	1.3 to 1.4 in
Valve installed height - maximum	47.63 mm	1.9 in
Valve stem to guide clearance:		
Inlet	0.025 to 0.066 mm	0.001 to 0.002 in
Exhaust	0.038 to 0.078 mm	0.0015 to 0.003 in
Valve guides		
Valve guide installed height	15.0 mm	0.590 in
Inside diameter after reaming	8.7 mm	0.34 in
Valve seats		
Valve seat angle	46° to 46° 25'	
Valve seat width:		
Inlet	36.83 mm	1.45 in
Exhaust	31.50 mm	1.24 in
Valve seating width:		
Inlet	0.89 to 1.4 mm	0.035 to 0.055 in
Exhaust	1.32 to 1.83 mm	0.052 to 0.072 in
Valve seating face angle	45°	
Oil pump		
Inner to outer rotor clearance - maximum	0.25 mm	0.01 in
Rotors to cover plate clearance - maximum	0.1 mm	0.004 in
Drive gear wear step depth - maximum	0.15 mm	0.006 in
Oil pressure relief valve		
Spring free length	60.0 mm	2.4 in
Camshaft		
End-float	0.05 to 0.35 mm	0.002 to 0.014 in
Maximum run-out	0.05 mm	0.002 in

Piston rings

Ring to groove clearance:		
1st compression	0.05 to 0.10 mm	0.002 to 0.004 in
2nd compression	0.05 to 0.10 mm	0.002 to 0.004 in
Ring fitted gap:		
1st compression	0.3 to 0.5 mm	0.01 to 0.02 in
2nd compression	0.40 to 0.65 mm	0.016 to 0.03 in
Oil control rails	0.38 to 1.40 mm	0.014 to 0.05 in
Oil control ring width	3.00 mm	0.12 in - maximum

Pistons

Piston diameter:		
Production - Grade A	93.970 to 93.985 mm	3.700 to 3.7002 in
Production - Grade B*	93.986 to 94.0 mm	3.7003 to 3.701 in
Clearance in bore	0.02 to 0.045 mm	0.001 to 0.002 in

Gudgeon pins

Length	60.00 to 60.50 mm	2.35 to 2.4 in
Diameter	23.995 to 24.000 mm	0.94 to 0.95 in
Clearance in piston	0.006 to 0.015 mm	0.0002 to 0.0006 in

Connecting rods

Length between centres:		
4.0 litre	155.12 to 155.22 mm	6.10 to 6.11 in
4.6 litre	149.68 to 149.78 mm	5.89 to 5.91 in

Cylinder bore

Cylinder bore:		
Grade A piston fitted	94.00 to 94.015 mm	3.700 to 3.701 in
Grade B piston fitted	94.016 to 94.030 mm	3.7014 to 3.702 in
Cylinder bore maximum ovality	0.013 mm	0.0005 in

Crankshaft

Main journal diameter	63.487 to 63.500 mm	2.499 to 2.52 in
Minimum regrind diameter	62.979 to 62.992 mm	2.509 to 2.510 in
Maximum out of round	0.040 mm	0.002 in
Big-end journal diameter	55.500 to 55.513 mm	2.20 to 2.22 in
Minimum regrind diameter	54.992 to 55.005 mm	2.16 to 2.165 in
Maximum out of round	0.040 mm	0.002 in
End-float	0.10 to 0.20 mm	0.004 to 0.008 in
Maximum run-out	0.08 mm	0.003 in

Main bearings

Main bearing diametrical clearance	0.010 to 0.048 mm	0.0004 to 0.002 in
Oversizes	0.254, 0.508 mm	0.01, 0.02 in

Big-end bearings

Big-end bearing diametrical clearance	0.015 to 0.055 mm	0.0006 to 0.0021 in
Oversizes	0.254, 0.508 mm	0.01, 0.02 in
End-float on journal	0.15 to 0.36 mm	0.006 to 0.01 in

Flywheel

Flywheel minimum thickness	40.45 mm	1.6 in

Drive plate

Drive plate setting height:		
Up to engine no. 42D00593A - 4.0 litre	21.25 to 21.37 mm	0.83 to 0.84 in
Up to engine no. 46D00450A - 4.6 litre	7.69 to 7.81 mm	0.30 to 0.31 in

* Grade B piston supplied as service replacement

Notes

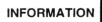

ENGINE

Crankshaft pulley bolt	270 Nm	200 lbf.ft
Camshaft gear bolt	50 Nm	37 lbf.ft
Camshaft thrust plate bolts	25 Nm	18 lbf.ft
Rocker cover bolts: +		
Stage 1	4 Nm	3 lbf.ft
Stage 2	8 Nm	6 lbf.ft
Stage 3 - re-torque to:	8 Nm	6 lbf.ft
Rocker shaft to cylinder head bolts	38 Nm	28 lbf.ft
Cylinder head bolts: +*		
Stage 1	20 Nm	15 lbf.ft
Stage 2	Then 90 degrees	
Stage 3	Further 90 degrees	
Lifting eye to cylinder head bolts	40 Nm	30 lbf.ft
Connecting rod bolts:		
Stage 1	20 Nm	15 lbf.ft
Stage 2	Further 80 degrees	
Main bearing cap bolts - Nos. 1 to 8: +		
Stage 1 - initial torque	13.5 Nm	10 lbf.ft
Stage 2 - final torque	72 Nm	53 lbf.ft
Rear main bearing cap bolts - Nos. 9 and 10: +		
Stage 1 - initial torque	13.5 Nm	10 lbf.ft
Stage 2 - final torque	92 Nm	68 lbf.ft
Main bearing cap side bolts - Nos. 11 to 20: +		
Stage 1 - initial torque	13.5 Nm	10 lbf.ft
Stage 2 - final torque	45 Nm	33 lbf.ft
Flywheel bolts	80 Nm	59 lbf.ft
Drive plate assembly bolts	45 Nm	33 lbf.ft
Drive plate hub aligner to crankshaft socket head cap screws	85 Nm	63 lbf.ft
Oil sump drain plug	45 Nm	33 lbf.ft
Oil sump nuts and bolts +	23 Nm	17 lbf.ft
Oil pump cover plate screws **	4 Nm	3 lbf.ft
Oil pump cover plate bolt **	8 Nm	6 lbf.ft
Spark plugs	20 Nm	15 lbf.ft
Timing cover/coolant pump to cylinder block bolts +	22 Nm	16 lbf.ft
Oil pick-up pipe to oil pump bolts	8 Nm	6 lbf.ft
Oil pick-up pipe nut	24 Nm	18 lbf.ft
Knock sensors to cylinder block	16 Nm	12 lbf.ft
Camshaft sensor to timing cover bolt	8 Nm	6 lbf.ft
Crankshaft position sensor bolts	6 Nm	4 lbf.ft
Oil cooler connections	15 Nm	11 lbf.ft

+ Tighten in sequence
* Lightly oil threads prior to assembly.
** Coat threads with Loctite 222 prior to assembly.

GENERAL

For bolts and nuts not otherwise specified

M5	4 Nm	3 lbf.ft
M6	6 Nm	4 lbf.ft
M8	18 Nm	13 lbf.ft
M10	35 Nm	26 lbf.ft
M12	65 Nm	48 lbf.ft
M14	80 Nm	59 lbf.ft
M16	130 Nm	96 lbf.ft
$^1/_4$ UNC/UNF	9 Nm	7 lbf.ft
5/16 UNC and UNF	25 Nm	18 lbf.ft
$^3/_8$ UNC and UNF	40 Nm	30 lbf.ft
7/16 UNC and UNF	75 Nm	55 lbf.ft
$^1/_2$ UNC and UNF	90 Nm	66 lbf.ft
$^5/_8$ UNC and UNF	135 Nm	100 lbf.ft

SERVICE TOOLS

Land Rover Number	Rover Number	Description
LRT-12-013	18G1150	Remover/replacer - gudgeon pin
LRT-12-126/1	-	Adapter - remover/replacer - gudgeon pin
LRT-12-126/2	-	Adapter - remover/replacer - gudgeon pin
LRT-12-126/3	-	Parallel sleeve - gudgeon pin
LRT-12-034	18G1519A	Valve spring compressor
LRT-12-037	RO274401	Drift - remover - valve guide
LRT-12-038	RO600959	Drift - replacer - valve guide
LRT-12-055	-	Distance piece - valve guide
LRT-12-089	-	Replacer - timing cover oil seal
LRT-12-090	-	Retainer - oil pump gears
LRT-12-091	-	Replacer - crankshaft rear oil seal
LRT-12-095	-	Protection sleeve - crankshaft rear oil seal
LRT-12-501	MS76B	Basic handle set - valve seat cutters
LRT-12-503	MS150-8.5	Adjustable valve seat pilot
LRT-12-515	RO605774A	Distance piece - valve guide
LRT-12-517	-	Adjustable valve seat cutter

Service tools must be obtained direct from the manufacturers:
V.L. Churchill,
P.O. Box No 3,
London Road,
Daventry,
Northants, NN11 4NF
England.

CONTENTS

CONTENTS

Notes

This page is intentionally left blank

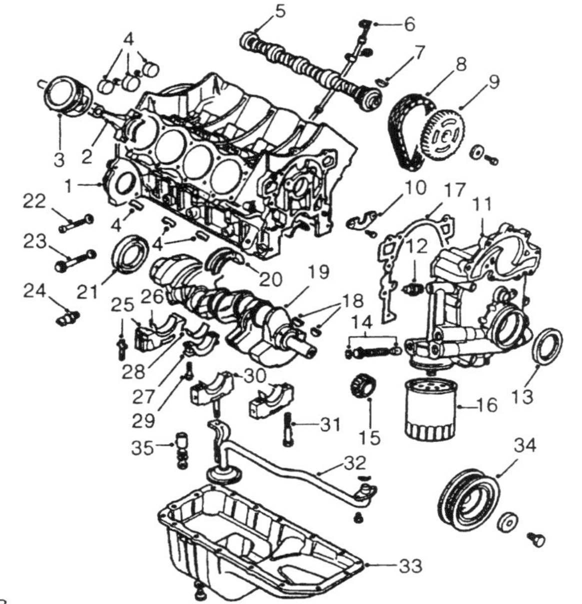

12M1374B

CYLINDER BLOCK COMPONENTS

1. Cylinder block
2. Connecting rod
3. Piston and gudgeon pin
4. Core plugs
5. Camshaft
6. Dipstick
7. Camshaft Woodruff key
8. Timing chain
9. Camshaft sprocket
10. Thrust plate
11. Timing cover and oil pump assembly *
12. Oil pressure switch
13. Timing cover oil seal
14. Oil pressure relief valve assembly
15. Crankshaft sprocket
16. Oil filter
17. Timing cover gasket
18. Woodruff keys
19. Crankshaft
20. Centre main bearing shell - upper
21. Crankshaft rear oil seal
22. Main bearing socket head cap bolt
23. Main bearing hexagonal head bolt
24. Crankshaft knock sensor
25. Rear main bearing cap and side seals
26. Rear main bearing shell
27. Big end bearing cap
28. Big end bearing shell
29. Big end bearing bolt
30. Centre and front main bearing caps
31. Main bearing cap bolt
32. Oil pick-up pipe
33. Sump
34. Crankshaft pulley
35. Oil pick-up pipe spacer, washers and nut

* New Range Rover timing cover illustrated

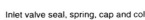

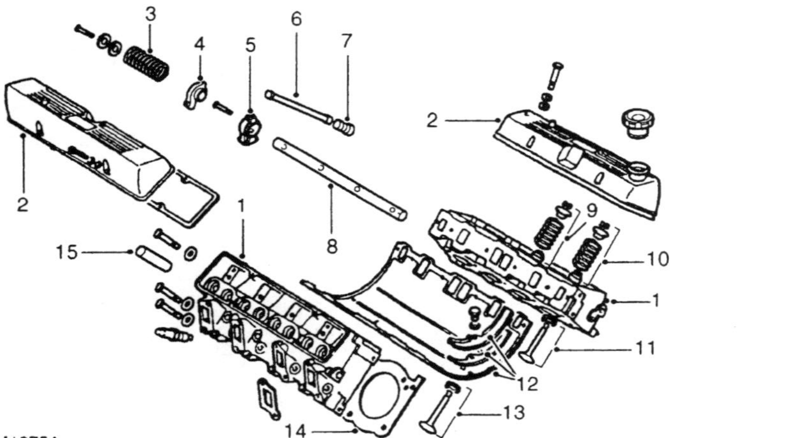

CYLINDER HEAD COMPONENTS

1. Cylinder head
2. Rocker cover
3. Rocker shaft spring
4. Rocker arm
5. Rocker shaft bracket
6. Pushrod
7. Tappet
8. Rocker shaft
9. Inlet valve seal, spring, cap and collets
10. Exhaust valve seal, spring, cap and collets
11. Exhaust valve and seat
12. Inlet manifold gasket and seals
13. Inlet valve and seat
14. Cylinder head gasket
15. Valve guide

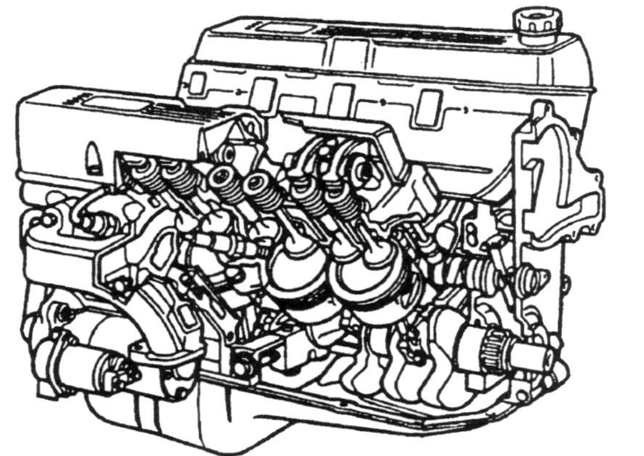

12M1384

OPERATION

The V8 engine is an eight cylinder, water cooled unit comprising cast aluminium cylinder block and cylinder heads.

The cast iron cylinder liners are shrink fitted and located on stops in the cylinder block. The banks of cylinders are at 90° to each other. The crankshaft is carried in five main bearings, end-float being controlled by the thrust faces of the upper centre main bearing shell.

The centrally located camshaft is driven by the crankshaft via a chain. The valves are operated by rockers, pushrods and hydraulic tappets. Exhaust valves used on later engines are of the 'carbon break' type which incorporate a machined undercut at the combustion chamber end of the valve. The design prevents carbon build-up on the valve stem which could lead to valves sticking. These valves are interchangeable with valves fitted to early engines.

Each of the aluminium alloy pistons has two compression rings and an oil control ring. The pistons are secured to the connecting rods by semi-floating gudgeon pins. The gudgeon pin is offset 0.5 mm (0.02 in), identified by an arrow mark on the piston crown, which must always point to the front of the engine. Plain, big-end bearing shells are fitted to each connecting rod.

12M1256A

1. Oil strainer
2. Oil pump
3. Pressure relief valve
4. Oil pressure switch
   A Oil to cooler
   B Oil from cooler

Lubrication

The full flow lubrication system uses a gear type oil pump driven from the crankshaft. The assembly is integral with the timing cover which also carries the full flow oil filter, oil pressure switch and pressure relief valve.

Oil is drawn from the pressed steel sump through a strainer and into the oil pump, excess pressure being relieved by the pressure relief valve. The oil pressure warning light switch is screwed into the timing cover and registers the oil pressure in the main oil gallery on the outflow side of the filter.

Pressurised oil passes through an oil cooler mounted in front of the radiator to the full flow oil filter. The oil then passes through internal drillings to the crankshaft where it is directed to each main bearing and to the big end bearings via numbers 1, 3 and 5 main bearings.

An internal drilling in the cylinder block directs oil to the camshaft where it passes through further internal drillings to the hydraulic tappets, camshaft journals and rocker shaft. Lubrication to the thrust side of the cylinders is either by oil grooves machined in each connecting rod big end joint face or by splash.

Hydraulic tappets

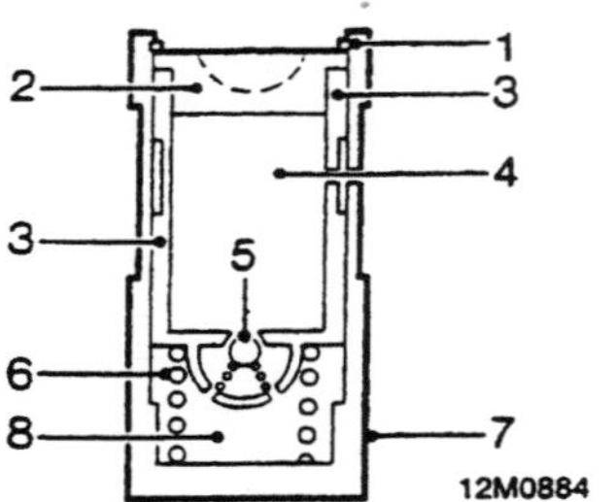

12M0884

1. Clip
2. Pushrod seat
3. Inner sleeve
4. Upper chamber
5. Non-return ball valve
6. Spring
7. Outer sleeve
8. Lower chamber

The purpose of the hydraulic tappet is to provide maintenance free and quiet operation of valves. It achieves this by utilising engine oil pressure to eliminate the mechanical clearance between the rockers and the valve stems.

During normal operation, engine oil pressure, present in the upper chamber, passes through the non-return ball valve and into the lower chamber.

When the cam begins to lift the outer sleeve, the resistance of the valve spring, felt through the push rod and seat, causes the tappet inner sleeve to move downwards inside the outer sleeve. This downward movement of the inner sleeve closes the ball valve and increases the pressure in the lower chamber sufficiently to ensure that the push rod opens the valve fully.

As the tappet moves off the peak of the cam, the ball valve opens to equalise the pressure in both chambers which ensures the valve closes when the tappet is on the back of the cam.

ROCKER SHAFTS

Rocker shafts - remove

12M0890A

1. *LH rocker shaft only:* Remove screw securing dipstick tube to rocker cover.

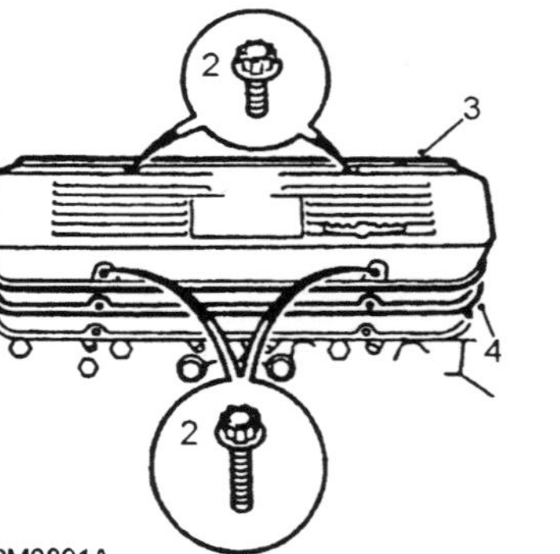

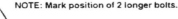

12M0891A

2. Remove 4 bolts securing rocker cover to cylinder head.

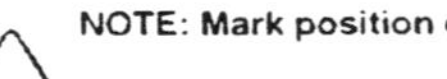

NOTE: **Mark position of 2 longer bolts.**

3. Remove rocker cover.
4. Remove and discard gasket from rocker cover.

5. Mark each rocker shaft in relation to original cylinder head.

CAUTION: Incorrect fitment of rocker shafts will lead to an oil feed restriction.

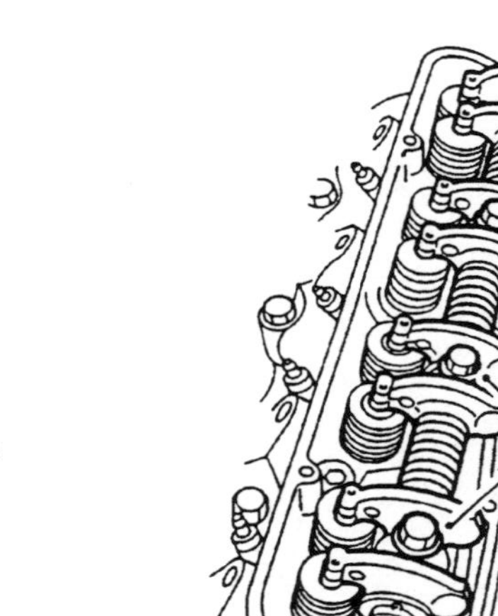

12M0892

6. Progressively slacken and remove 4 bolts securing rocker shaft assembly to cylinder head.
7. Remove rocker shaft assembly.
8. Remove pushrods and store in fitted order.

Rocker shafts - dismantling

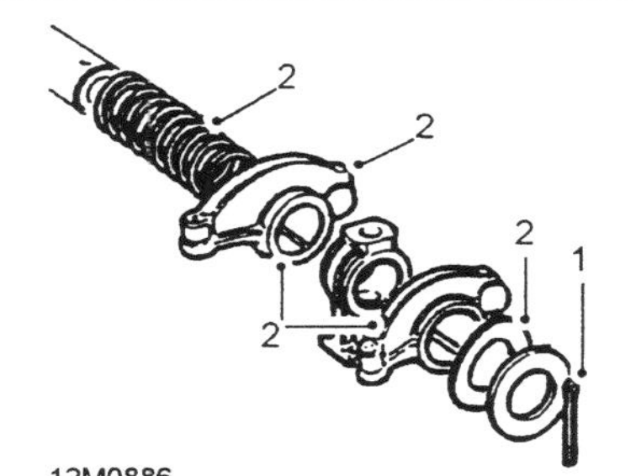

12M0886

1. Remove and discard split pin from one end of rocker shaft.
2. Remove plain washer, wave washer, rocker arms, brackets and springs.

Inspecting components

1. Thoroughly clean components.
2. Inspect each component for wear, in particular rocker arms and shafts. Discard weak or broken springs.
3. Inspect pushrod seats in rocker arms.
4. Check pushrods for straightness and inspect ball ends for damage, replace as necessary.

Rocker shafts - assembling

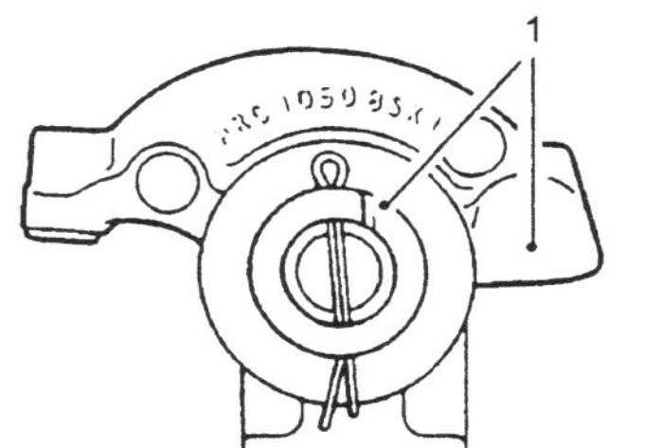

12M0887

1. Assemble rocker shafts with identification groove at one o'clock position with push rod end of rocker arm to the right.

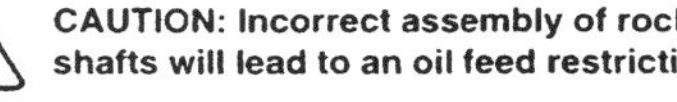

CAUTION: Incorrect assembly of rocker shafts will lead to an oil feed restriction.

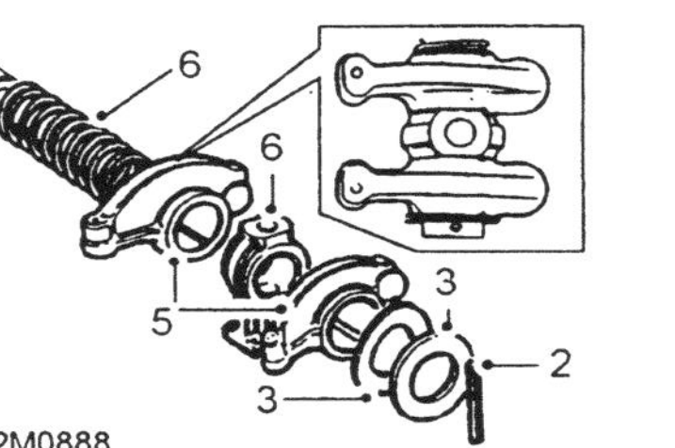

12M0888

2. Fit new split pin to one end of rocker shaft.
3. Fit plain washer and wave washer.
4. Lubricate rocker arm bushes with engine oil.
5. Fit rocker arms with offsets as illustrated.
6. Assemble rocker arms, brackets and springs to rocker shaft.
7. Compress springs, fit wave washer, plain washer and secure with new split pin.

Rocker shafts - refit

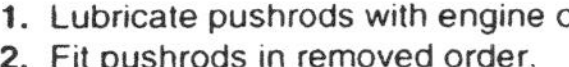

1. Lubricate pushrods with engine oil.
2. Fit pushrods in removed order.

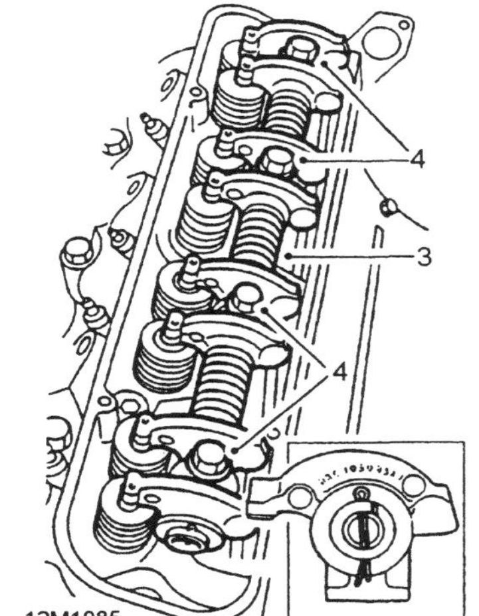

12M1085

3. Fit each rocker shaft assembly, ensuring identification groove is uppermost and towards front of engine on RH side and towards rear of engine on LH side.

CAUTION: Incorrect fitment of rocker shafts will lead to an oil feed restriction.

4. Fit bolts and starting at centre brackets, tighten to 38 Nm (28 lbf.ft).

5. Clean gasket surface in rocker cover.

NOTE: Gaskets fitted to early engines were manufactured from cork whilst those fitted to later engines are manufactured from rubber. The later type gaskets should be fitted as replacements to all engines. Cork gaskets were retained by an adhesive whereas rubber gaskets do not need an adhesive. If cork gaskets were originally fitted. remove all traces of adhesive using Bostik Cleaner 6001 or equivalent.

6. Fit new gasket, dry to rocker cover.
7. Fit rocker cover to cylinder head, fit bolts and tighten in diagonal sequence to:
   Stage 1 - 4 Nm (3 lbf.ft)
   Stage 2 - 8 Nm (6 lbf.ft)
   Stage 3 - Re-torque to 8 Nm (6 lbf.ft)

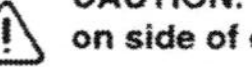

CAUTION: The 2 short bolts must be fitted on side of cover nearest centre of engine.

8. *LH rocker shaft only:* Align dipstick tube to rocker cover, fit and tighten screw.

CYLINDER HEAD

Cylinder head - remove

1. Remove rocker shaft assembly.
2. Mark heads LH and RH for reassembly.

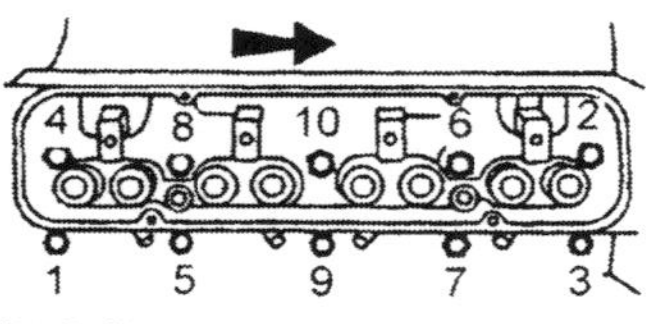

12M1249A

NOTE: RH cylinder head illustrated.

3. Using sequence shown, remove and discard 10 bolts securing cylinder head to cylinder block.
4. Release cylinder head from 2 dowels and remove cylinder head.
5. Remove and discard cylinder head gasket.
6. Repeat above procedures for remaining cylinder head.

Valves and springs - remove

1. Remove spark plugs.

3
LRT-12-034
12M0895B

2. Using valve spring compressor **LRT-12-034** or a suitable alternative, compress valve spring.
3. Compress valve spring sufficiently to release collets from valve spring cap.

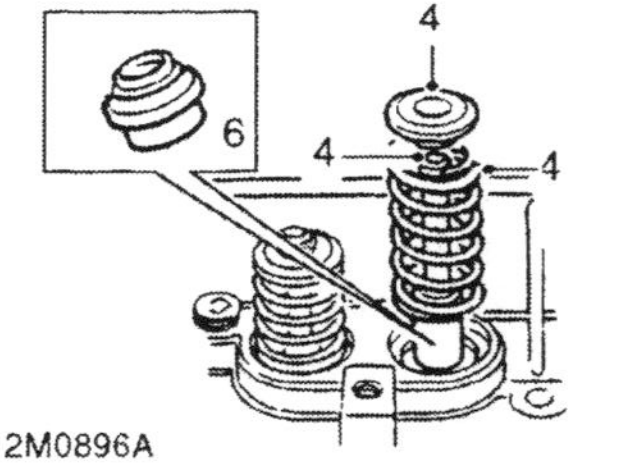

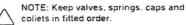

12M0896A

4. Release spring compressor and remove collets, valve, valve spring cap and valve spring.
5. Repeat above operations for remaining valves.

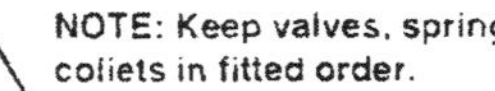

NOTE: Keep valves, springs, caps and collets in fitted order.

6. Remove and discard valve stem oil seals.

Cylinder head - inspection

1. Clean all traces of gasket material from cylinder head using a plastic scraper.
2. Check core plugs for signs of leakage and corrosion, replace as necessary. Apply Loctite 572 to threads of screwed core plugs.

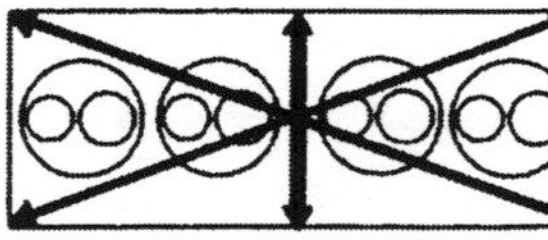

12M2902A

3. Check gasket face of each cylinder head for warping, across centre and from corner to corner.
   Maximum warp = 0.05 mm (0.002 in)

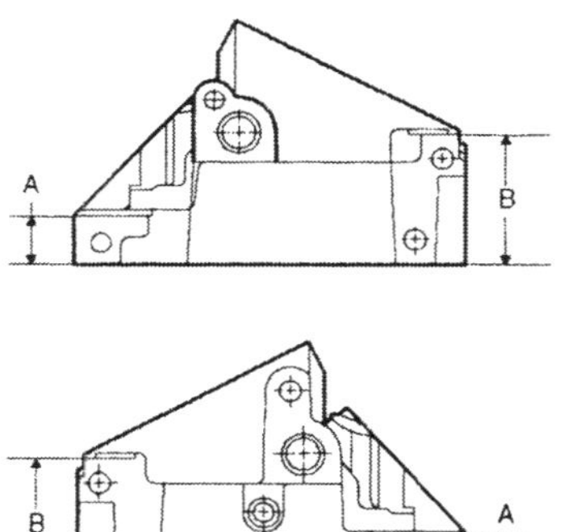

12M4236

4. Check cylinder head height at each end of cylinder head:
   A= 22.94 mm (0.903 in) - New
   B= 62.56 mm (2.463 in) - New

5. Cylinder heads may be refaced:
   Reface limit = 0.50 mm (0.02 in) from new dimension

Valves, valve springs and guides - inspection

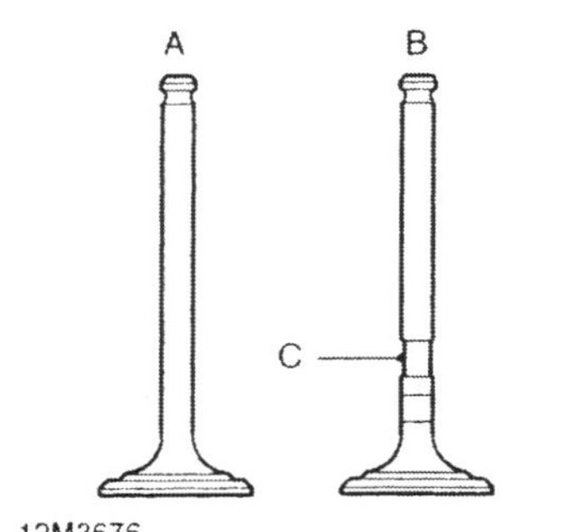

12M3676

NOTE: Two types of exhaust valve may be fitted - standard valves A in illustration or carbon break valves - B in illustration Carbon break valves may be identified by the machined profile C on the valve stem. To prevent exhaust valves sticking, standard exhaust valves should be replaced with carbon break valves during engine overhaul.

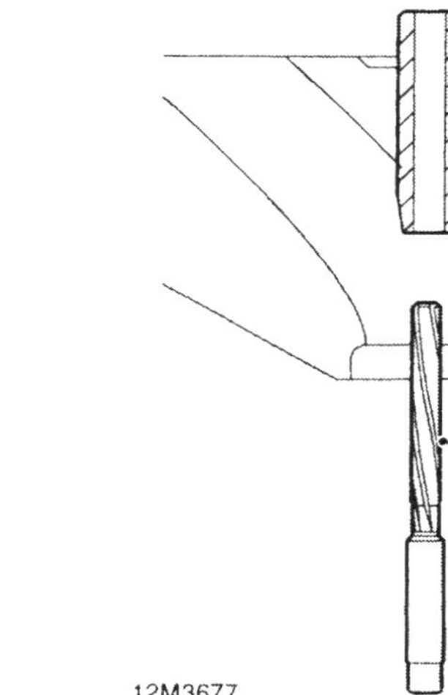

12M3677

1. Remove carbon deposits from valve guides using an 8.70 mm (0.34 in) diameter reamer inserted from combustion face side of cylinder head.
2. Clean valve springs, cotters, caps and valves. Clean inlet valve guide bores. Ensure all loose particles of carbon are removed on completion.
3. Check existing valve stem and head diameters.
4. Check valve stem to guide clearance using new valves.

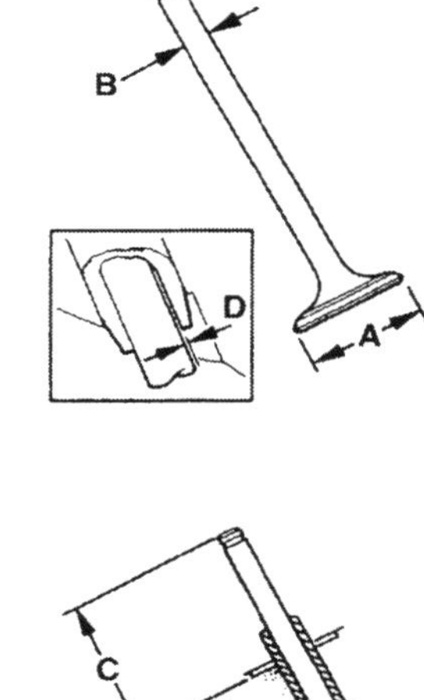

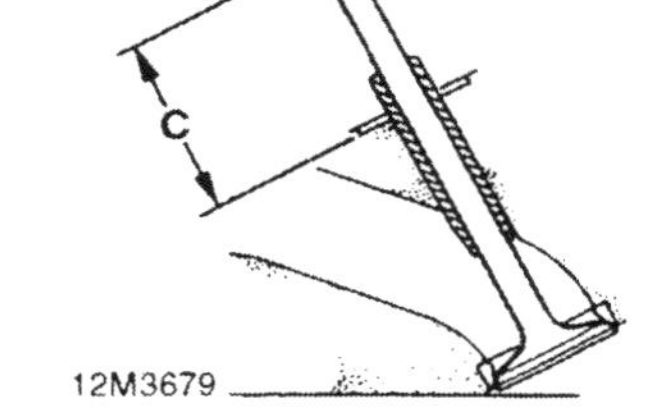

12M3679

5. Renew valves and guides as necessary. Valve head diameter **A:**
   Inlet = 39.75 to 40.00 mm (1.5 to 1.6 in)
   Exhaust = 34.226 to 34.48 mm (1.3 to 1.4 in)
   Valve stem diameter **B:**
   Inlet = 8.664 to 8.679 mm (0.341 to 0.342 in)
   Exhaust = 8.651 to 8.666 mm (0.340 to 0.341 in)
6. Check installed height of each valve.
   Valve installed height **C** = 47.63 mm (1.9 in)
7. Renew valve/valve seat insert as necessary.
8. Check valve stem to guide clearance.
   Valve stem to guide clearance **D:**
   Inlet = 0.025 to 0.066 mm (0.001 to 0.002 in)
   Exhaust = 0.038 to 0.078 mm (0.0015 to 0.003 in)

9. Check condition of valve springs:
   Free length = 48.30 mm (1.90 in)
   Fitted length = 40.40 mm (1.60 in)
   Load - valve closed = 339 ± 10 N (76 ± 2 lbf)
   Load - valve open = 736 ± 10 N (165 ± 2 lbf)

NOTE: Valve springs must be replaced as a complete set.

Valve guides - renew

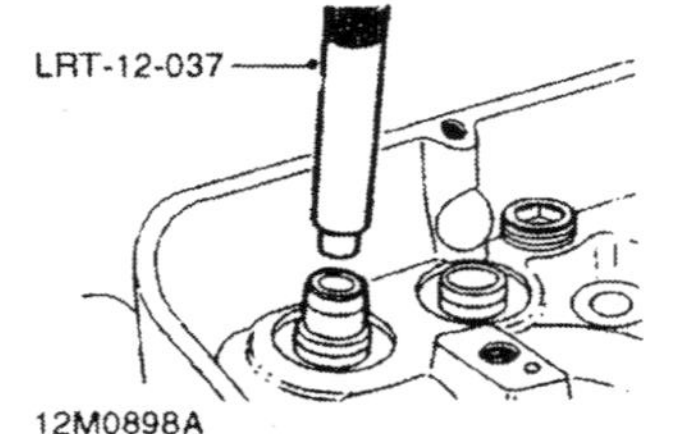

12M0898A

1. Using valve guide remover, **LRT-12-037** press valve guide out into combustion face side of cylinder head.

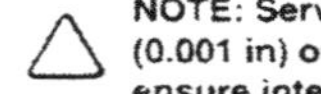

NOTE: Service valve guides are 0.025 mm (0.001 in) oversize on outside diameter to ensure interference fit.

2. Lubricate new valve guide with engine oil and place in position.

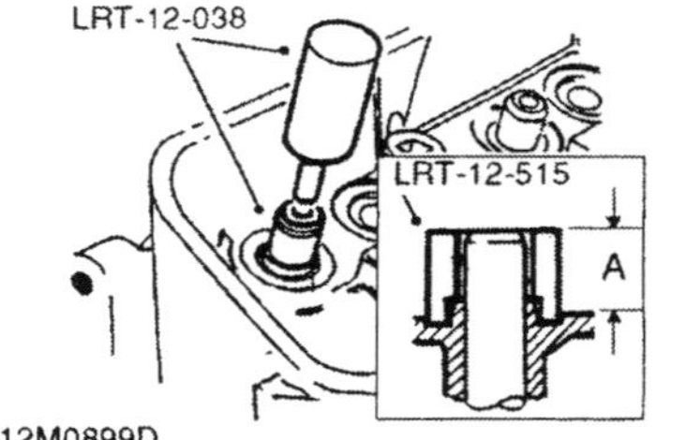

12M0899D

3. Using **LRT-12-038** partially press guide into cylinder head, remove tool.
4. Fit **LRT-12-515** over valve guide and continue to press guide into cylinder head until tool **LRT-12-038** contacts tool **LRT-12-515**; remove tool.
   Valve guide installed height **A** = 15.0 mm (0.590 in)
5. Ream valve guides to 8.70 mm (0.34 in) diameter.
6. Remove all traces of swarf on completion.

Valve seat inserts - inspection

1. Check valve seat inserts for pitting, burning and wear. Replace inserts as necessary.

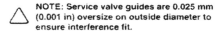

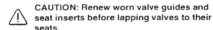

Valve seat inserts - renew

NOTE: Service valve seat inserts are available 0.025 mm (0.001 in) oversize on outside diameter to ensure interference fit.

1. Remove worn valve seats.

CAUTION: Take care not to damage counterbore in cylinder head.

12M3642

2. Heat cylinder head evenly to approximately 120° C (250° F).

WARNING: Handle hot cylinder head with care.

3. Using a suitable mandrel, press new insert fully into counterbore.
4. Allow cylinder head to air cool.

Valve seats and seat inserts - refacing

CAUTION: Renew worn valve guides and seat inserts before lapping valves to their seats.

1. Check condition of valve seats and valves that are to be re-used.
2. Remove carbon from valve seats.

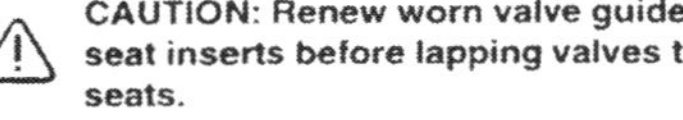

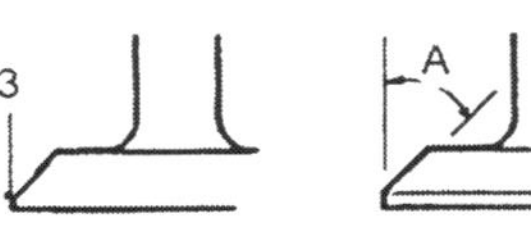

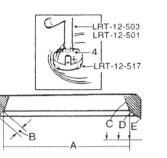

12M0901

3. Reface valves as necessary. If a valve has to be ground to a knife-edge to obtain a true seat, fit a new valve.
Valve seating face angle **A** = 45°

12M0918D

4. Cut valve seats using **LRT-12-501** with **LRT-12-503** and **LRT-12-517.**
Valve seat:
Width **A:**
Inlet = 36.83 mm (1.45 in)
Exhaust = 31.50 mm (1.24 in)

Seating width **B:**
Inlet = 0.89 to 1.4 mm (0.035 to 0.055 in)
Exhaust = 1.32 to 1.83 mm (0.052 to 0.072 in)

Angle **C**= 56° to 70°
Angle **D**= 46° to 46° 25'
Angle **E**= 20°

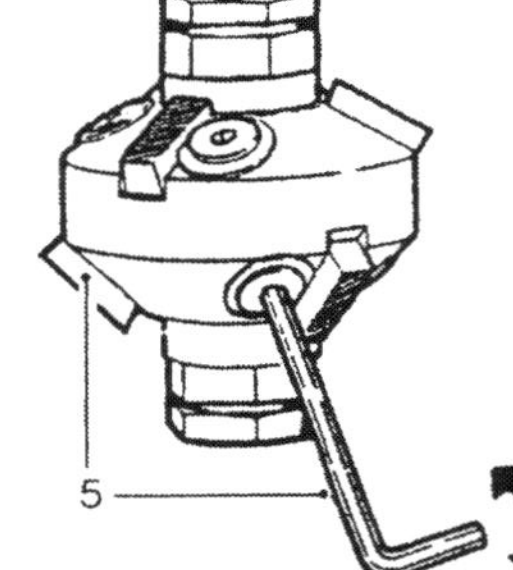

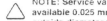

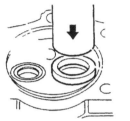

12M0902

5. Ensure cutter blades are correctly fitted to cutter head with angled end of blade downwards, facing work, as illustrated. Check that cutter blades are adjusted so that middle of blade contacts area of material to be cut. Use light pressure and remove only minimum of material necessary.
6. Remove all traces of swarf on completion.

Valves - lapping-in

1. Lap each valve to its seat using fine grinding paste.
2. Clean valve and seat.

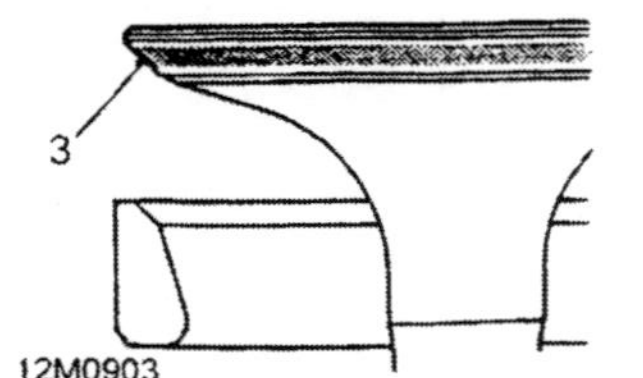

12M0903

3. Coat valve seat with a small quantity of engineer's blue, insert valve and press it into position several times without rotating. Remove valve and check for even and central seating. Seating position shown by engineer's blue should be in centre of valve face.

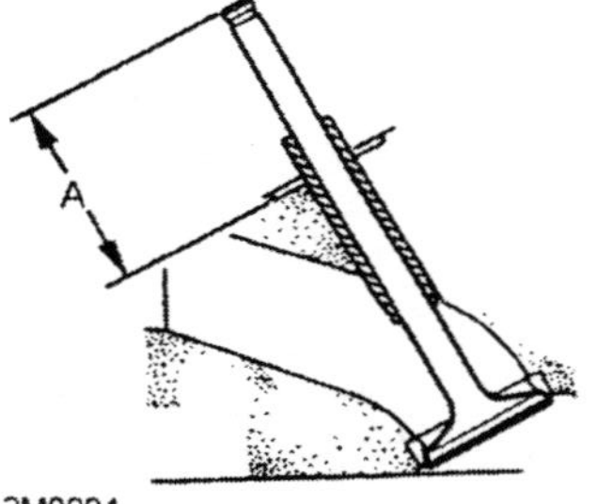

12M0904

4. Check valve installed height if valve seats have been recut or new valves or valve seat inserts have been fitted.
   Valve installed height **A**= 47.63 mm (1.9 in) - maximum
5. Thoroughly clean cylinder head, blow out oilways and coolant passages.

Valves and springs - refit

1. Fit new valve stem oil seals, lubricate valve stems, fit valves, valve springs and caps, compress valve springs using **LRT-12-034** and fit collets.
2. Using a wooden dowel and mallet, lightly tap each valve stem two or three times to seat valve cap and collets.
3. Fit spark plugs and tighten to 20 Nm (15 lbf.ft).

Cylinder head - refit

1. Clean cylinder block and cylinder head faces using suitable gasket removal spray and a plastic scraper.
2. Eensure that bolt holes in cylinder block are clean and dry.

CAUTION: Do not use metal scraper or machined surfaces may be damaged.

3

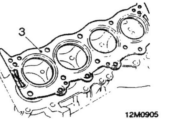

12M0905

3. Fit cylinder head gasket with the word 'TOP' uppermost.

NOTE: Gasket must be fitted dry.

4. Carefully fit cylinder head and locate on dowels.
5. Lightly oil threads of new cylinder head bolts.

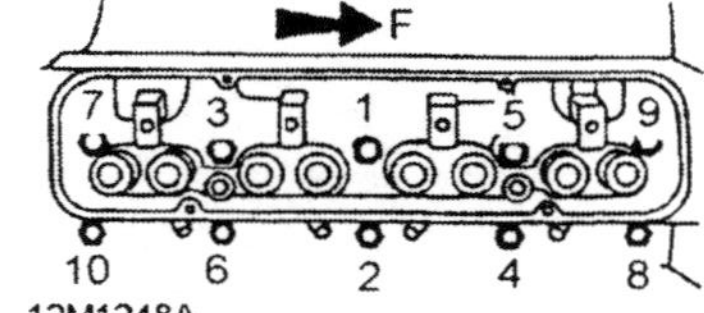

12M1248A

NOTE: RH cylinder head illustrated.

6. Fit new cylinder head bolts:
   Long bolts: 1, 3 and 5
   Short bolts: 2, 4, 6, 7, 8, 9 and 10
7. Using sequence shown, tighten cylinder head bolts to:
   Stage 1 - 20 Nm (15 lbf.ft)
   Stage 2 - 90 degrees
   Stage 3 - Further 90 degrees

CAUTION: Do not tighten bolts 180° in one operation.

8. Fit rocker shaft assembly.
9. Repeat above procedures for remaining cylinder head.

TIMING CHAIN AND GEARS

Sump - remove

1. Remove dipstick.

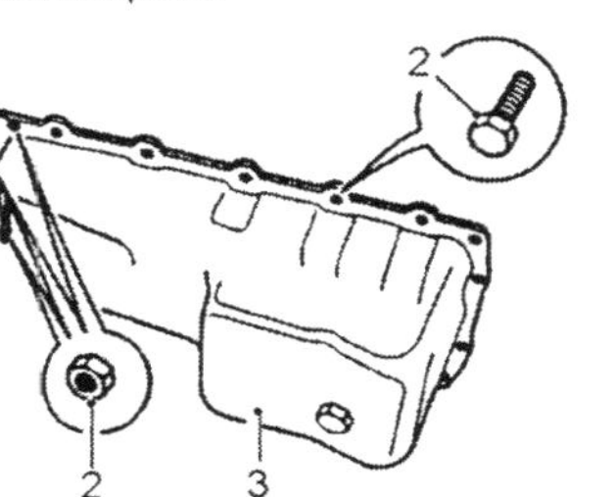

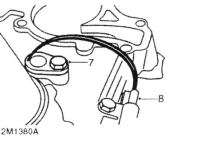

12M1377A

2. Remove 14 bolts and 3 nuts securing sump to cylinder block and timing cover.
3. Taking care not to damage sealing faces, carefully release sump from timing cover and cylinder block.
4. Remove sump.

Timing cover - remove

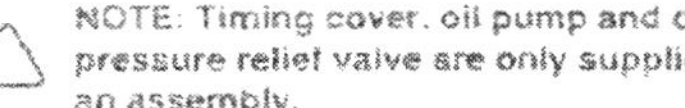

NOTE: Timing cover, oil pump and oil pressure relief valve are only supplied as an assembly.

1. Using assistance, restrain flywheel/drive plate and remove crankshaft pulley bolt; collect spacer washer - if fitted.
2. Remove crankshaft pulley.
3. Remove sump.

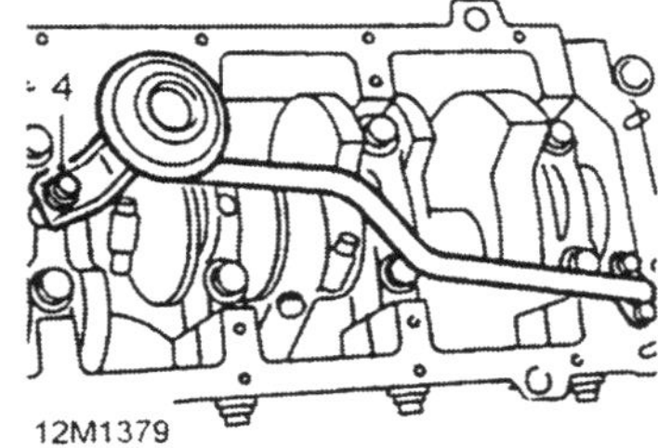

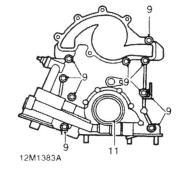

12M1379

4. Remove nut and washers securing oil pick-up pipe to stud.

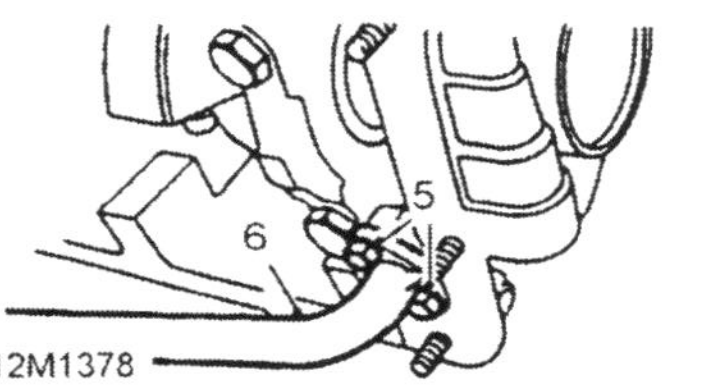

12M1378

5. Remove 2 bolts securing oil pick-up pipe to oil pump cover, withdraw pipe from cover; remove and discard 'O' ring.
6. Remove oil pick-up pipe, recover spacer from stud.

12M1380A

7. Remove bolt securing camshaft sensor to timing cover, withdraw sensor; remove and discard 'O' ring.
8. Release harness connector from mounting bracket.

12M1383A

NOTE: New Range Rover timing cover illustrated.

9. Noting their fitted position, remove 9 bolts securing timing cover to cylinder block; remove cover; collect camshaft sensor harness mounting bracket.

NOTE: Timing cover is dowel located.

CAUTION: Do not attempt to remove oil pump drive gear at this stage.

10. Remove and discard gasket.
11. Remove and discard oil seal from timing cover.

Timing gears - remove

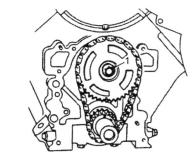

12M1396A

1. Restrain camshaft gear and remove bolt securing gear.

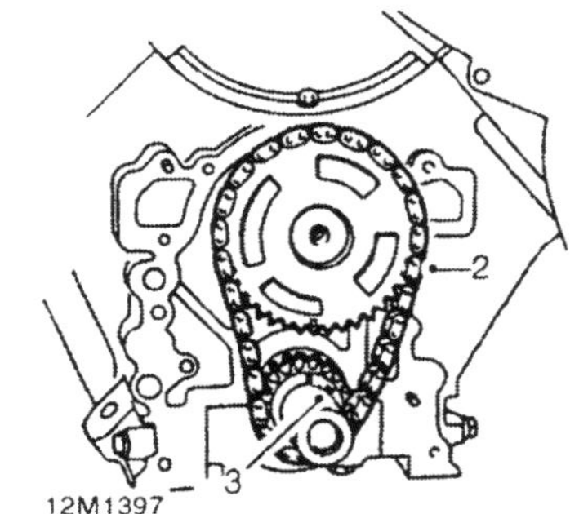

12M1397

2. Remove timing chain and gears as an assembly.
3. Collect Woodruff key from crankshaft.

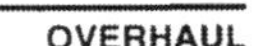

Timing chain and gears - inspection

1. Thoroughly clean all components.
2. Inspect timing chain links and pins for wear.
3. Inspect timing chain gears for wear. Replace components as necessary.

Timing gears - refit

1. Clean gear locations on camshaft and crankshaft, fit Woodruff key to crankshaft.

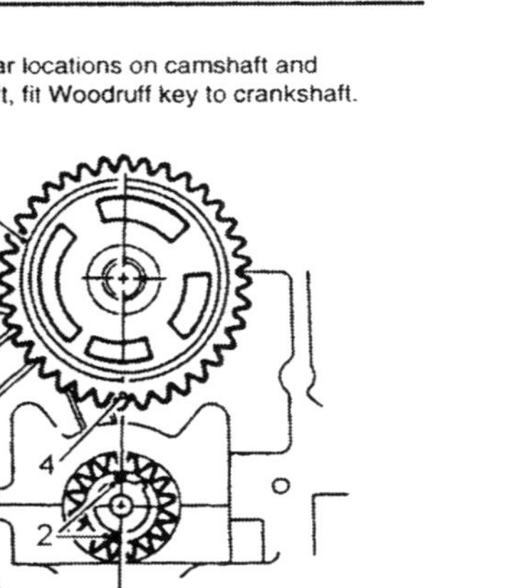
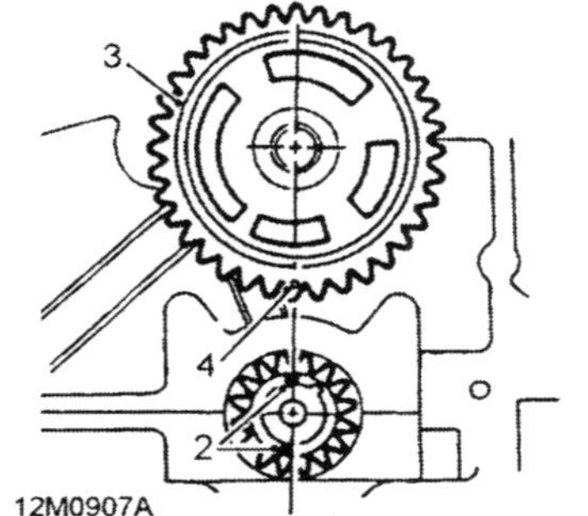

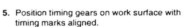

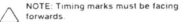

12M0907A

2. Temporarily fit crankshaft gear and if necessary, turn crankshaft to bring timing mark on gear to the twelve o'clock position, remove gear.
3. Temporarily fit camshaft gear.
4. Turn camshaft until mark on camshaft sprocket is at the six o'clock position, remove gear without moving camshaft.

6

12M0914A

5. Position timing gears on work surface with timing marks aligned.
6. Fit timing chain around gears, keeping timing marks aligned.
7. Fit gear and chain assembly.

NOTE: Timing marks must be facing forwards.

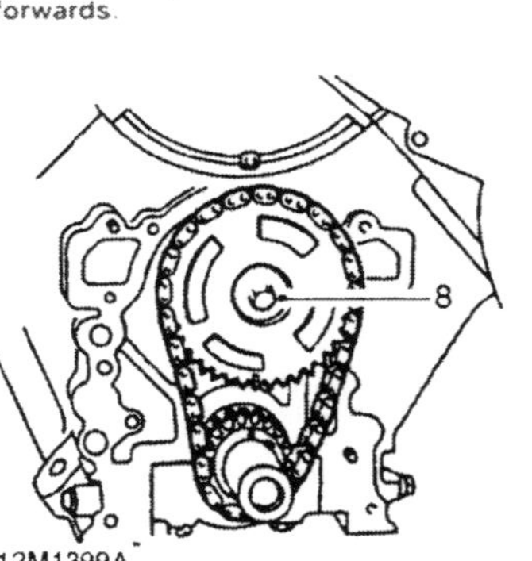

12M1399A

8. Fit camshaft gear bolt, restrain camshaft gear and tighten bolt to 50 Nm (37 lbf.ft).

Timing cover - refit

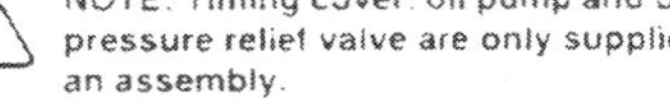

NOTE: Timing cover, oil pump and oil pressure relief valve are only supplied as an assembly.

1. Clean sealant from threads of timing cover bolts.
2. Clean all traces of gasket material from mating faces of timing cover and cylinder block.

CAUTION: Use a plastic scraper.

3. Clean oil seal location in timing cover.
4. Lubricate oil pump gears and oil seal recesses in timing cover with engine oil.
5. Apply Hylosil jointing compound to new timing cover gasket, position gasket to cylinder block.

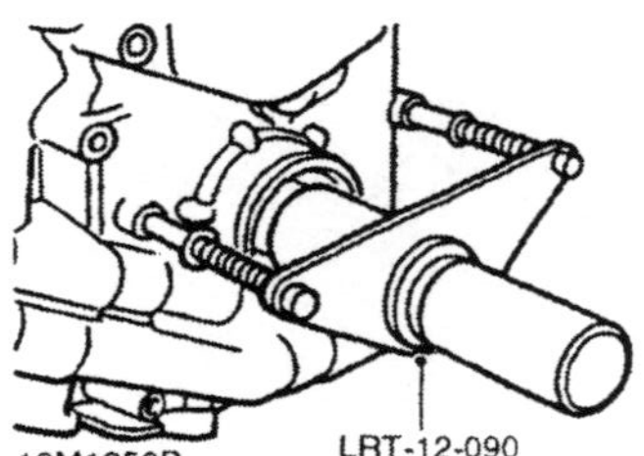

12M1253B

6. Locate tool **LRT-12-090** on timing cover and oil pump drive gear.
7. Position timing cover to cylinder block and at the same time, rotate tool **LRT-12-090** until drive gear keyway is aligned with Woodruff key.
8. Fit timing cover to cylinder block.

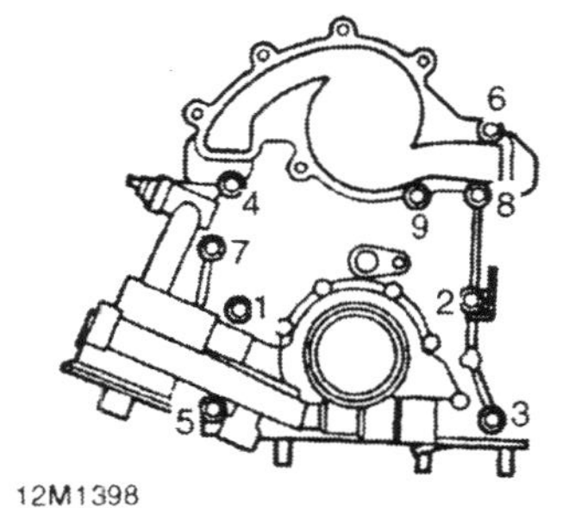

12M1398

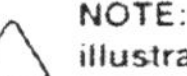
NOTE: New Range Rover timing cover illustrated.

9. Position camshaft sensor harness mounting bracket to timing cover ensuring that bracket is positioned parallel to crankshaft centre line. Fit bolts and tighten in sequence shown to 22 Nm (16 lbf.ft).

CAUTION: Do not fit coolant pump bolts at this stage.

10. Remove tool **LRT-12-090.**

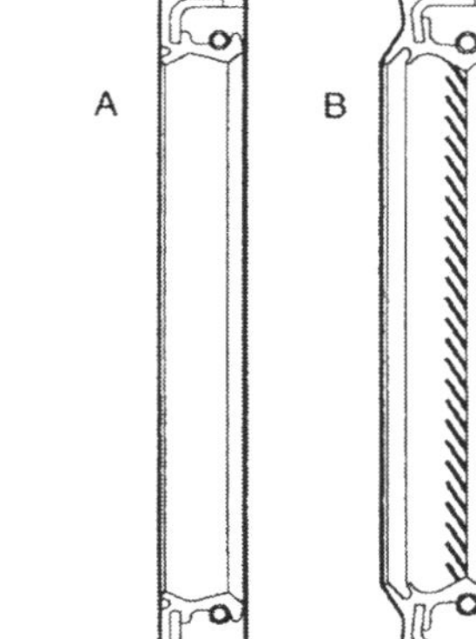

12M3678

A- Early type seal
B- Later type seal - use as replacement on all engines

11. Lubricate new timing cover oil seal with Shell Retinax LX grease ensuring that space between seal lips is filled with grease.

CAUTION: Do not use any other type of grease.

LRT-12-089
12M1254B

12. Fit timing cover oil seal using tool **LRT-12-089.**
13. Smear a new 'O' ring with engine oil and fit to oil pick-up pipe.
14. Position oil pick-up pipe spacer on number 4 main bearing cap stud.
15. Fit oil pick-up pipe ensuring that end of pipe is correctly inserted in oil pump body.
16. Fit oil pick-up pipe to oil pump body bolts and tighten to 8 Nm (6 lbf.ft).
17. Fit washers and nut securing oil pick-up pipe to stud, tighten nut to 24 Nm (18 lbf.ft).
18. Smear a new 'O' ring with engine oil and fit to camshaft sensor.
19. Insert camshaft sensor into timing cover, fit bolt and tighten to 8 Nm (6 lbf.ft).
20. Position camshaft sensor harness connector on mounting bracket.
21. Fit sump.
22. Fit crankshaft pulley, fit bolt and spacer washer - if fitted; tighten bolt to 270 Nm (200 lbf.ft).

NOTE: Crankshaft pulleys which incorporate a mud flinger can be fitted to all engines.

Sump - refit

1. Remove all traces of old sealant from mating faces of cylinder block and sump.

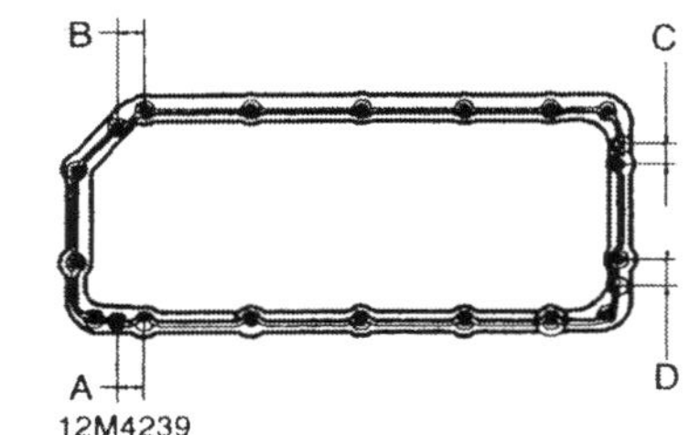

12M4239

2. Clean mating faces with suitable solvent and apply a bead of Hylosil Type 101 or 106 sealant to sump joint face as shown:
Bead width - areas A, B, C and D = 12 mm (0.5 in)
Bead width - remaining areas = 5 mm (0.20 in)
Bead length - areas A and B = 32 mm (1.23 in)
Bead length - areas C and D = 19 mm (0.75 in)

CAUTION: Do not spread sealant bead. Sump must be fitted immediately after applying sealant.

3. Fit sump, taking care not to damage sealant bead.

12M1382A

4. Fit sump bolts and nuts and working in sequence shown, tighten to 23 Nm (17 lbf.ft).
5. Fit sump drain plug and tighten to 45 Nm (33 lbf.ft).
6. Fit dipstick.

OIL PUMP AND OIL PRESSURE RELIEF VALVE

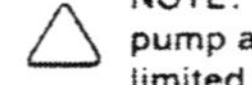

NOTE: Overhaul procedures for the oil pump and oil pressure relief valve are limited to carrying out dimensional checks. In the event of wear or damage being found, a replacement timing cover and oil pump assembly must be fitted.

Oil pump - remove

1. Remove timing cover.

CAUTION: Do not attempt to remove oil pump drive gear from inner rotor at this stage.

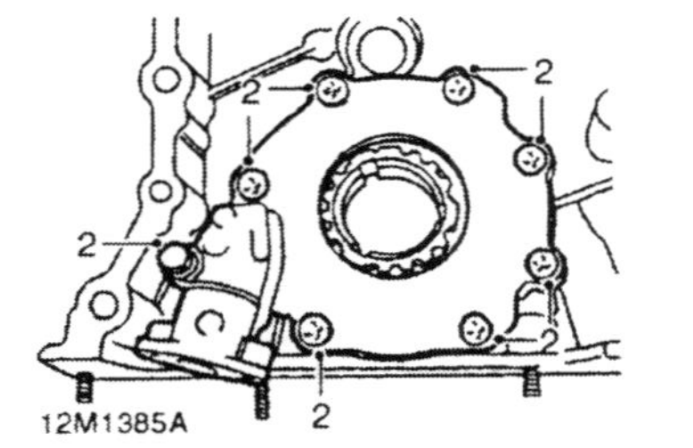

12M1385A

2. Remove 7 screws and bolt securing oil pump cover plate, remove plate.

12M1386

3. Make suitable alignment marks on inner and outer rotors, remove rotors and oil pump drive gear as an assembly.

Oil pressure relief valve - remove

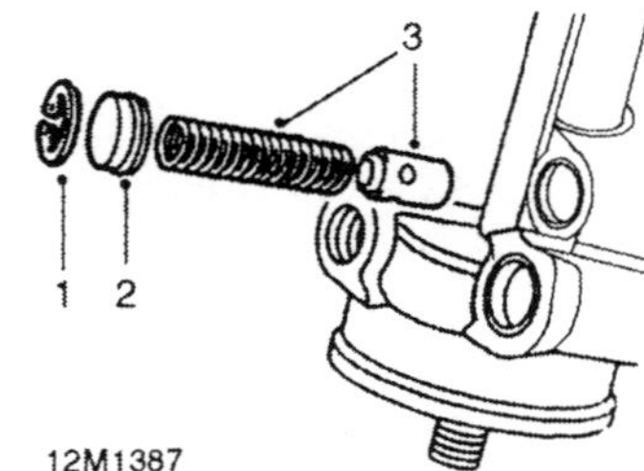

12M1387

1. Remove circlip.
2. Remove relief valve plug, remove and discard 'O' ring.
3. Remove relief valve spring and piston.

Oil pump - inspection

1. Thoroughly clean oil pump drive gear, cover plate, rotors and housing. Remove all traces of Loctite from cover plate securing screws; ensure tapped holes in timing cover are clean and free from oil.
2. Check mating surfaces of cover plate, rotors and housing for scoring.
3. Assemble rotors and oil pump drive gear in housing ensuring that reference marks are aligned.

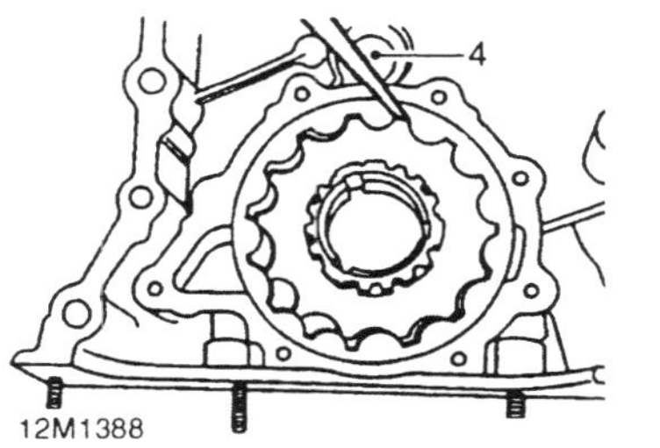

4. Using feeler gauges, check clearance between teeth of inner and outer rotors:
   Maximum clearance = 0.25 mm (0.01 in)

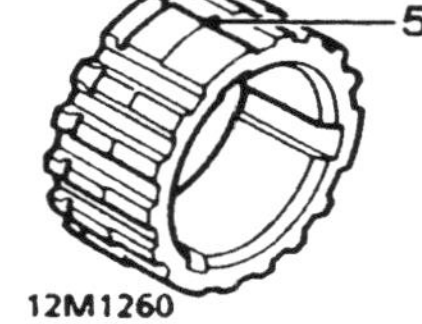

5. Remove oil pump drive gear, check depth of any wear steps on gear teeth:
   Wear step maximum depth = 0.15 in (0.006 in)

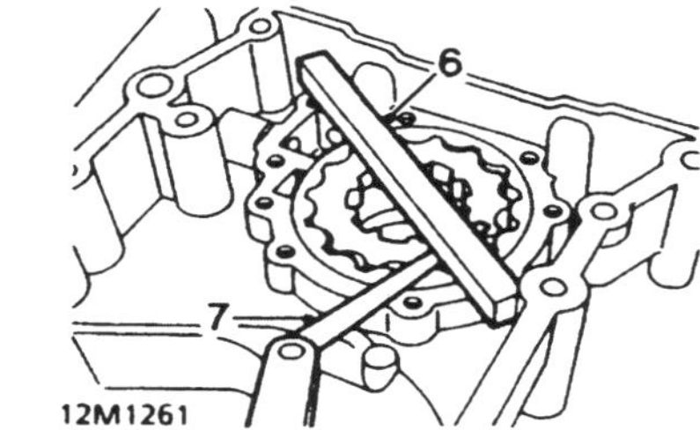

6. Place a straight edge across housing.
7. Using feeler gauges, check clearance between straight edge and rotors:
   Maximum clearance = 0.1 mm (0.004 in).

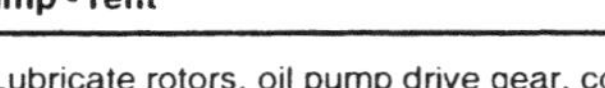

Oil pressure relief valve - inspection

1. Clean relief valve components and piston bore in timing cover.
2. Check piston and bore for scoring and that piston slides freely in bore with no perceptible side movement.
3. Check relief valve spring for damage and distortion; check spring free length:
   Spring free length = 60.0 mm (2.4 in).

Oil pump - refit

1. Lubricate rotors, oil pump drive gear, cover plate and housing with engine oil.
2. Assemble rotors and drive gear in housing ensuring that reference marks are aligned.
3. Position cover plate to housing.
4. Apply Loctite 222 to threads of cover plate screws and bolt.
5. Fit cover plate screws and bolt and tighten to:-
   Screws - 4 Nm (3 lbf.ft)
   Bolt - 8 Nm (6 lbf.ft)
6. Fit timing cover.

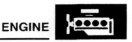

Oil pressure relief valve - refit

1. Lubricate new 'O' ring with engine oil and fit to relief valve plug.
2. Lubricate relief valve spring, piston and piston bore with engine oil.
3. Assemble piston to relief valve spring, insert piston and spring into piston bore.
4. Fit relief valve plug, depress plug and fit circlip.
5. Ensure circlip is fully seated in groove.

CAMSHAFT AND TAPPETS

Camshaft end-float - check

1. Remove rocker shaft assemblies.
2. Remove pushrods and store in their fitted order.
3. Remove timing chain and gears.

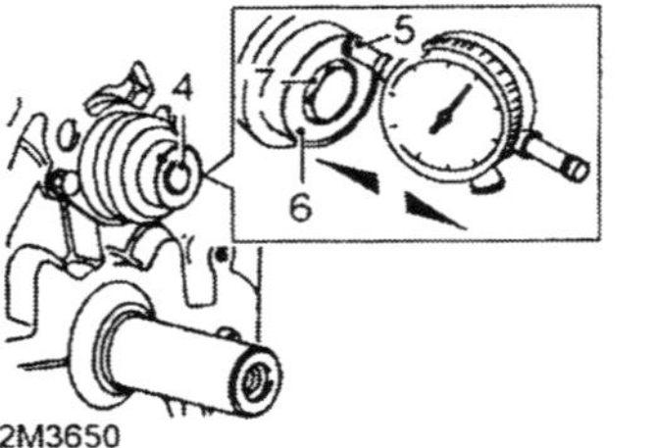

12M3650

4. Temporarily fit camshaft gear bolt.
5. Attach a suitable DTI to front of cylinder block with stylus of gauge contacting end of camshaft.
6. Push camshaft rearwards and zero gauge.
7. Using camshaft gear bolt, pull camshaft forwards and note end-float reading on gauge. End-float = 0.05 to 0.35 mm (0.002 to 0.014 in)

8. If end-float is incorrect, fit a new thrust plate and re-check. If end-float is still incorrect, a new camshaft must be fitted.

Camshaft and tappets - remove

12M0924B

1. Remove tappets and retain with their respective pushrods.

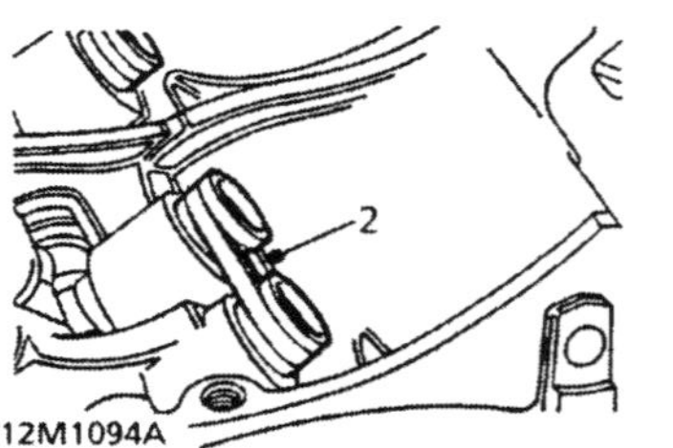

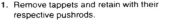

12M1094A

2. When tappets prove difficult to remove due to damaged camshaft contact area, proceed as follows. Lift tappets in pairs to the point where damaged face is about to enter tappet bore and fit rubber bands to retain tappets. Repeat until all tappets are retained clear of camshaft lobes. The tappets can then be withdrawn out the bottom of their bores when the sump and camshaft are removed.

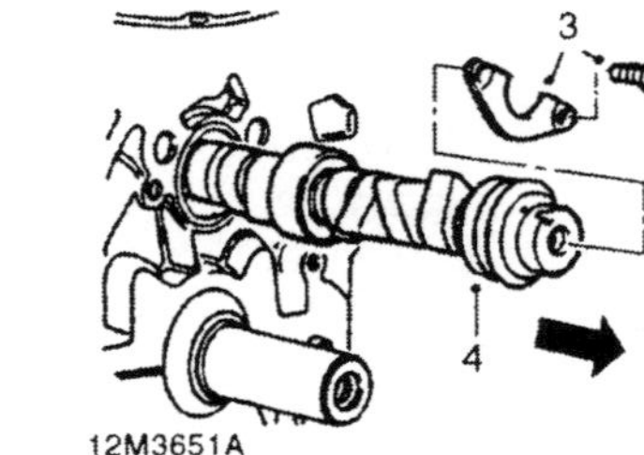

12M3651A

3. Remove 2 bolts securing camshaft thrust plate to cylinder block, remove plate.
4. Withdraw camshaft, taking care not to damage bearings in cylinder block.

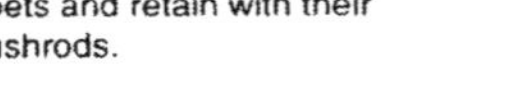

NOTE: Camshafts fitted to 4.0 litre engines are colour coded ORANGE whilst those fitted to 4.6 litre engines are colour coded RED.

Camshaft and tappets - inspection

1. Thoroughly clean all components.
2. Inspect camshaft bearing journals and lobes for signs of wear, pitting, scoring and overheating.
3. Support camshaft front and rear bearings on vee blocks, and using a DTI, measure camshaft run-out on centre bearing:
   Maximum permitted run-out = 0.05 mm (0.002 in)
4. Inspect thrust plate for wear, replace plate if wear is evident.
5. Clean and inspect tappets. Check for an even, circular wear pattern on the camshaft contact area. If contact area is pitted or a square wear pattern has developed, tappet must be renewed.
6. Inspect tappet body for excessive wear or scoring. Replace tappet if scoring or deep wear patterns extend up to oil feed area. Clean and inspect tappet bores in cylinder block.
7. Ensure that tappets rotate freely in their respective bores.
8. Inspect pushrod contact area of tappet, replace tappet if surface is rough or pitted.

Camshaft and tappets - refit

NOTE: If a replacement camshaft is to be fitted, ensure colour coding is correct. Camshafts fitted to 4.0 litre engines are colour coded ORANGE whilst those fitted to 4.6 litre engines are colour coded RED.

1. Lubricate camshaft journals with engine oil and carefully insert camshaft into cylinder block.
2. Fit camshaft thrust plate, fit bolts and tighten to 25 Nm (18 lbf.ft).

NOTE: If camshaft or thrust plate has been replaced, it will be necessary to re-check camshaft end-float.

3. Immerse tappets in engine oil. Before fitting, pump the inner sleeve of tappet several times using a pushrod to prime tappet; this will reduce tappet noise when engine is first started.
4. Lubricate tappet bores with engine oil and fit tappets in removed order.

NOTE: Some tappet noise may still be evident on initial start-up. If necessary, run the engine at 2500 rev/min for a few minutes until noise ceases.

5. Fit timing chain and gears.
6. Fit rocker shaft assemblies.

PISTONS, CONNECTING RODS, PISTON RINGS AND CYLINDER BORES

Pistons and connecting rods - remove

1. Remove cylinder head(s).
2. Remove big-end bearings.
3. Remove carbon ridge from top of each cylinder bore.
4. Suitably identify each piston to its respective cylinder bore.
5. Push connecting rod and piston assembly to top of cylinder bore and withdraw assembly.
6. Repeat above procedure for remaining pistons.

CAUTION: Big-end bearing shells must be replaced whenever they are removed.

Piston rings - remove

1. Using a suitable piston ring expander, remove and discard piston rings.
2. Remove carbon from piston ring grooves.

NOTE: Use an old broken piston ring with a squared-off end.

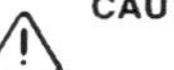

CAUTION: Do not use a wire brush.

Piston rings - inspection

1. Temporarily fit new compression rings to piston.

NOTE: If replacement pistons are to be fitted, ensure rings are correct for piston.

The 2nd compression ring marked 'TOP' must be fitted, with marking uppermost, into second groove. The 1st compression ring fits into top groove and can be fitted either way round.

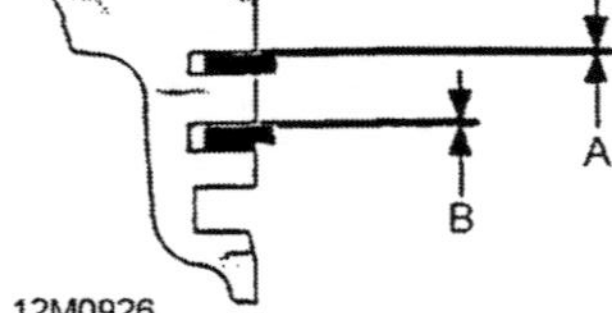

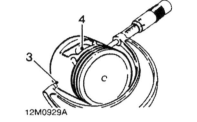

12M0926

2. Check compression ring to groove clearance:
   1st compression ring **A** = 0.05 to 0.10 mm (0.002 to 0.004 in).
   2nd compression ring **B** = 0.05 to 0.10 mm (0.002 to 0.004 in).

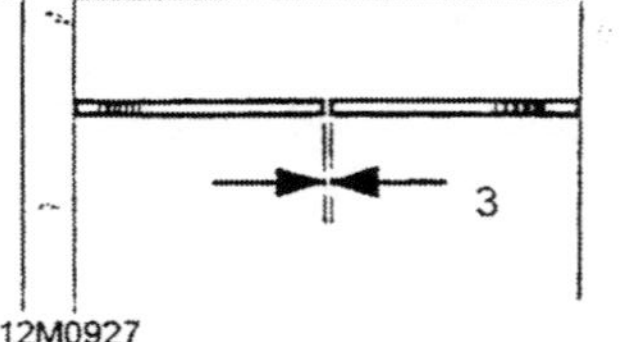

12M0927

3. Insert piston ring into its relevant cylinder bore, held square to bore with piston and check ring gaps.
   1st compression ring = 0.3 to 0.5 mm (0.01 to 0.02 in)
   2nd compression ring = 0.40 to 0.65 mm (0.016 to 0.03 in)
   Oil control ring rails = 0.38 to 1.40 mm (0.014 to 0.05 in)
4. Retain rings with their respective pistons.

Pistons- remove

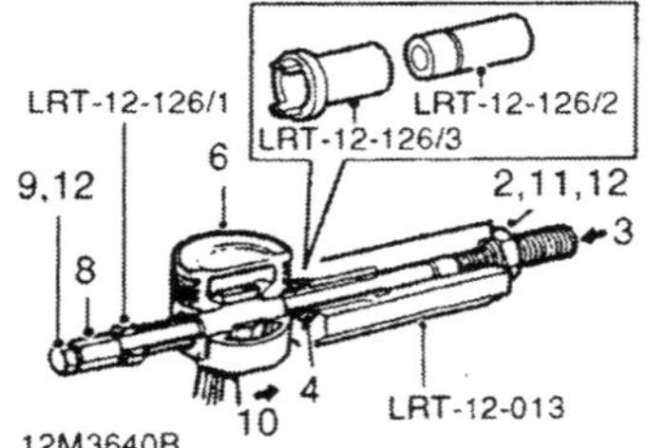

12M3640B

1. Clamp hexagon body of **LRT-12-013** in vice.
2. Screw large nut back until flush with end of centre screw.
3. Push centre screw forward until nut contacts thrust race.
4. Locate remover/replacer adapter **LRT-12-126/2** with its long spigot inside bore of hexagon body.
5. Position remover/replacer adapter **LRT-12-126/3** on **LRT-12-126/2** with cut-out facing away from body of **LRT-12-013**.
6. Locate piston and connecting rod assembly on centre screw and up to adapter **LRT-12-126/2.**
7. Position cut-out of adapter **LRT-12-126/3** to piston.

CAUTION: Ensure cut-out does not contact gudgeon pin.

8. Fit remover/replacer bush **LRT-12-126/1** on centre screw with flanged end away from gudgeon pin. Screw stop nut on to centre screw.
9. Lock the stop nut securely with lockscrew.
10. Push connecting rod to right to locate end of gudgeon pin in adapter **LRT-12-126/2.**
11. Screw large nut up to **LRT-12-013**.
12. Hold lockscrew and turn large nut until gudgeon pin is withdrawn from piston.
13. Dismantle tool and remove piston, connecting rod and gudgeon pin.

NOTE: Keep each piston and gudgeon pin with their respective connecting rod.

14. Repeat above operation for remaining pistons.

Pistons - inspection

1. Clean carbon from pistons.
2. Inspect pistons for distortion, cracks and burning.

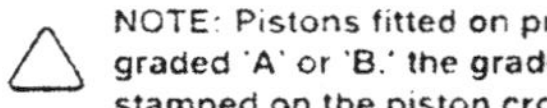

12M0929A

3. Measure and record piston diameter at 90° to gudgeon pin axis and 10 mm (0.4 in) from bottom of skirt.
4. Check gudgeon pin bore in piston for signs of wear and overheating.

NOTE: Pistons fitted on production are graded 'A' or 'B.' the grade letter is stamped on the piston crown.

Production piston diameter:
Grade **A** = 93.970 to 93.985 mm (3.700 to 3.7002 in)
Grade **B** = 93.986 to 94.00 mm (3.7003 to 3.701 in)

Grade **B** pistons are supplied as service replacements. Worn cylinder liners fitted with grade **'A'** pistons may be honed to accept grade **'B'** pistons provided that specified cylinder bore and ovality limits are maintained.

CAUTION: Ensure replacement pistons are correct for the compression ratio of the engine. The compression ratio will be found on the cylinder block above the engine serial number. Ensure that replacement connecting rods are correct length for engine being overhauled.

Connecting rod length between centres:
4.0 litre = 155.12 to 155.22 mm (6.10 to 6.11 in)
4.6 litre = 149.68 to 149.78 mm (5.89 to 5.91 in)

Gudgeon pins - inspection

NOTE: Gudgeon pins are only supplied as an assembly with replacement pistons.

1. Check gudgeon pins for signs of wear and overheating.
2. Check clearance of gudgeon pin in piston. Gudgeon pin to piston clearance = 0.006 to 0.015 mm (0.0002 to 0.0006 in).
3. Check overall dimensions of gudgeon pin. Overall length = 60.00 to 60.50 mm (2.35 to 2.4 in).
   Diameter - measured at each end and centre of pin = 23.995 to 24.00 mm (0.94 to 0.95 in).

Cylinder liner bore - inspection

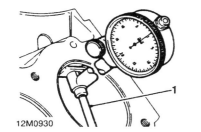

12M0930

1. Measure cylinder liner bore wear and ovality in two axis 40 to 50 mm (1.5 to 1.9 in) from top of bore.
   Cylinder liner bore:
   Grade 'A' piston fitted = 94.00 to 94.015 mm (3.700 to 3.701 in)
   Grade 'B' piston fitted = 94.016 to 94.030 mm (3.7014 to 3.702 in)
   Maximum ovality = 0.013 mm (0.0005 in)
   Cylinder liners having grade 'A' pistons fitted may be honed to accept grade 'B' pistons provided specified wear and ovality limits are maintained.

CAUTION: The temperature of piston and cylinder block must be the same to ensure accurate measurement.

2. If only new piston rings are to be fitted, break cylinder bore glazing using a fine grit, to produce a 60° cross-hatch finish. Ensure all traces of grit are removed after above operation.
3. Check alignment of connecting rods.

Pistons - refit

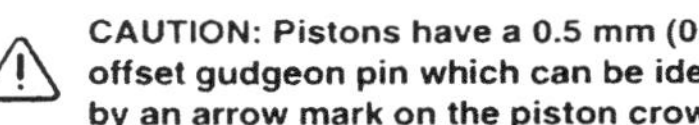

CAUTION: Pistons have a 0.5 mm (0.02 in) offset gudgeon pin which can be identified by an arrow mark on the piston crown. This arrow MUST always point to the front of the engine.

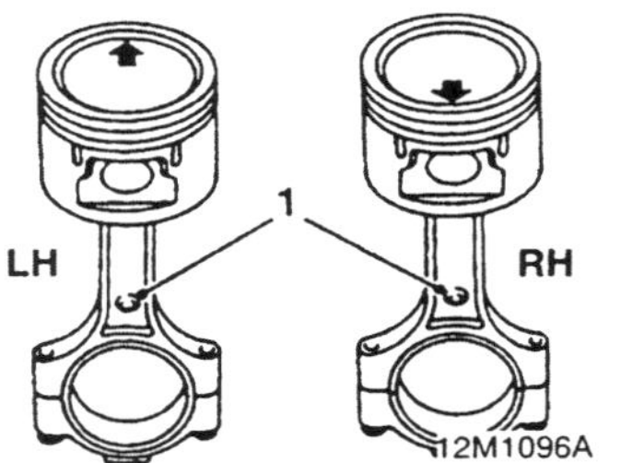

12M1096A

1. Assemble pistons to connecting rods with arrow on piston pointing towards domed shaped boss on connecting rod for RH bank of cylinders, and arrow pointing away from dome shaped boss for LH bank of cylinders.

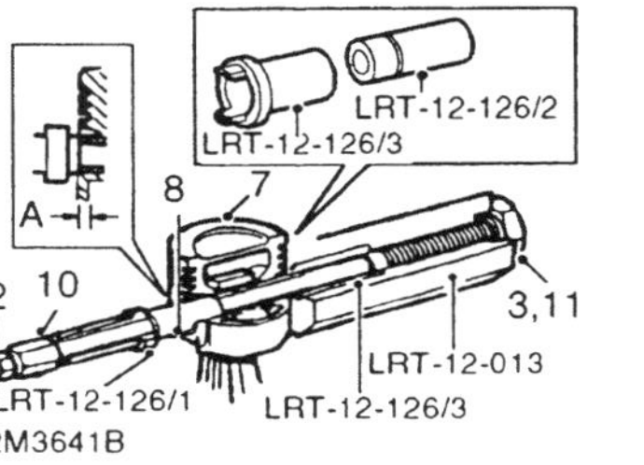

12M3641B

2. Clamp hexagon body of **LRT-12-013** in vice.
3. Slacken large nut and pull the centre screw 50.8 mm (2.0 in) out of hexagon body.
4. Locate remover/replacer adapter **LRT-12-126/2** with its long spigot inside bore of hexagon body.
5. Fit remover/replacer adapter **LRT-12-126/3** with cut-out towards piston, up to shoulder on centre screw.
6. Lubricate gudgeon pin and bores of connecting rod and piston with graphited oil.
7. Locate connecting rod and piston to centre screw with connecting rod entered on sleeve up to groove.
8. Fit gudgeon pin on to centre screw and into piston bore up to connecting rod.
9. Fit remover/replacer bush **LRT-12-126/1** with flanged end towards gudgeon pin.
10. Screw the stop nut onto centre screw and position piston against cut-out of adapter **LRT-12-126/3.**
11. Lubricate centre screw threads and thrust race with graphited oil, screw large nut up to **LRT-12-013.**
12. Lock the stop nut securely with lockscrew.
13. Set torque wrench to 16 Nm (12 lbf.ft), and using socket on large nut, pull gudgeon pin in until flange of **LRT-12-126/1** is distance **A** from face of piston.
    Distance **A** = 0.4 mm (0.016 in).

CAUTION: If torque wrench 'breaks' during above operation, fit of gudgeon pin to connecting rod is not acceptable and components must be replaced. The centre screw and thrust race must be kept well lubricated throughout operation.

14. Dismantle tool, remove piston, check no damage has occurred during pressing and piston moves freely on gudgeon pin.
15. Repeat above operations for remaining pistons.

Piston to cylinder bore clearance - checking

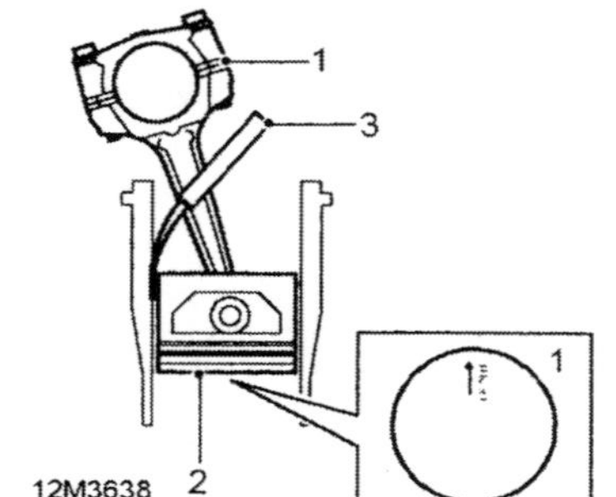

12M3638

1. Starting with number 1 piston, invert piston and with arrow on piston crown pointing towards REAR of cylinder block, insert piston in cylinder liner.
2. Position piston with bottom of skirt 30 mm (1.2 in) from top of cylinder block.
3. Using feeler gauges, measure and record clearance between piston and left hand side of cylinder - viewed from front of cylinder block: Piston to bore clearance = 0.02 to 0.045 mm (0.001 to 0.002 in)
4. Repeat above procedures for remaining pistons.

Pistons and connecting rods - refit

1. Fit oil control ring rails and expander, ensuring ends butt and do not overlap.

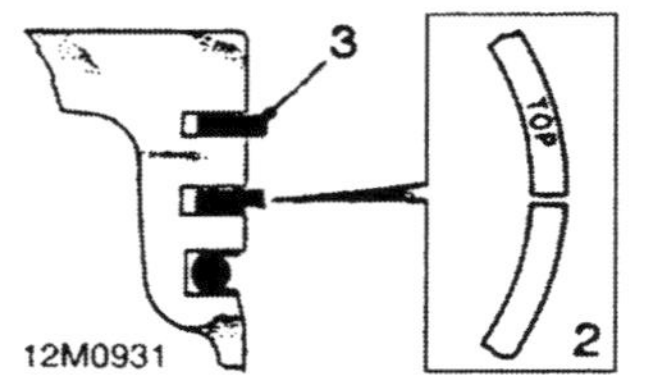
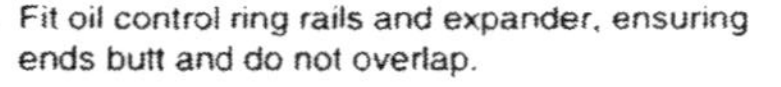

12M0931

2. Fit 2nd compression ring marked 'TOP' with marking uppermost into second groove.
3. Fit 1st compression ring into first groove either way round.

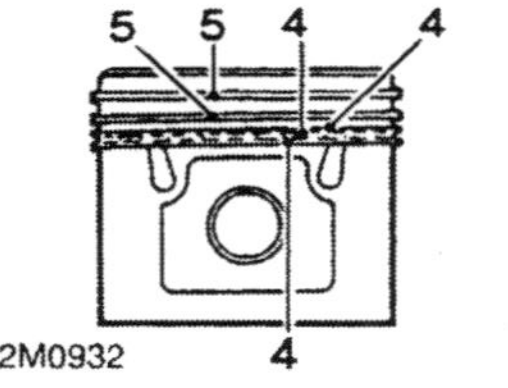

12M0932

4. Position oil control expander ring joint and ring rail gaps all at one side, between gudgeon pin and away from left hand (thrust) side of piston - viewed from front of piston. Space gaps in ring rails approximately 25 mm (1.0 in) each side of expander ring joint.
5. Position compression rings with ring gaps on opposite sides of piston between gudgeon pin and right hand side of piston - viewed from front of piston.
6. Thoroughly clean cylinder bores.
7. Lubricate piston rings and gudgeon pin with engine oil.
8. Lubricate cylinder bores with engine oil.

12M0933

9. Fit ring clamp to piston and compress piston rings.

12M0934A

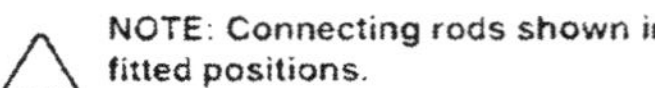

NOTE: Connecting rods shown in final fitted positions.

10. Insert connecting rod and piston assembly into respective cylinder bore ensuring domed shaped boss on connecting rod faces towards front of engine on RH bank of cylinders, and towards rear on LH bank of cylinders.
11. Fit big-end bearing caps and bearing shells.
12. Fit cylinder head(s).

FLYWHEEL AND STARTER RING GEAR

Flywheel - remove

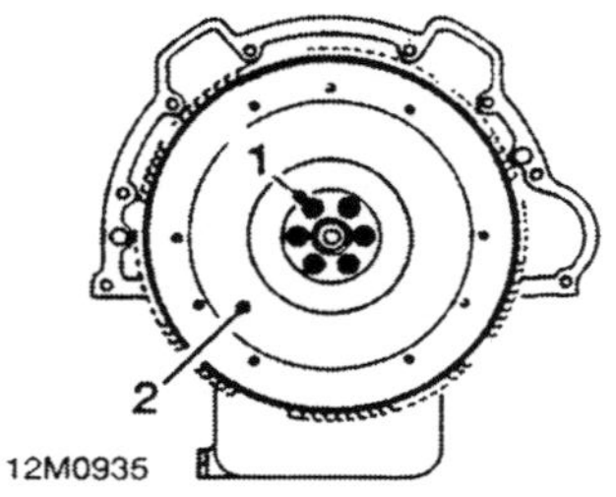

12M0935

1. Restrain crankshaft and remove 6 bolts securing flywheel.
2. Remove flywheel.

NOTE: Dowel located

Flywheel and starter ring gear - inspection

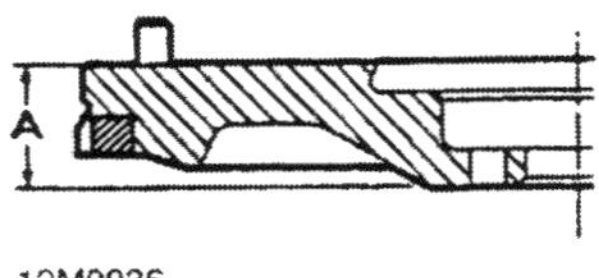

12M0936

1. Inspect flywheel face for cracks, scores and overheating. The flywheel can be refaced on the clutch face providing thickness does not go below minimum.
   Flywheel minimum thickness **A** = 40.45 mm (1.6 in)
2. Inspect starter ring gear for worn, chipped and broken teeth.

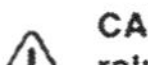

CAUTION: Do not attempt to remove reluctor ring.

3. Renew starter ring gear if necessary.

Starter ring gear - renew

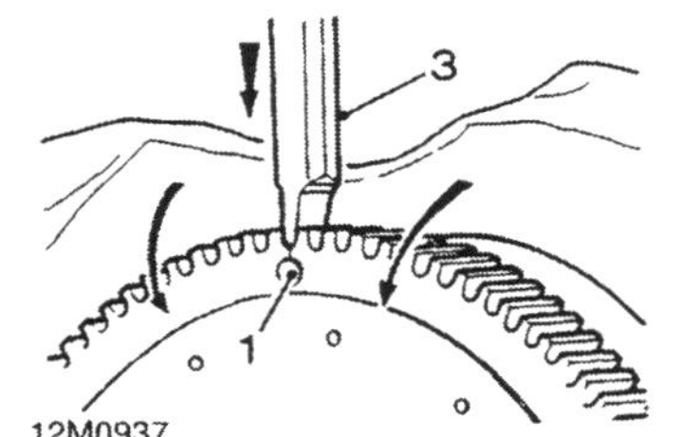

12M0937

1. Drill a 6 mm (0.250 in) diameter hole at root of 2 teeth.

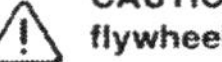

CAUTION: Do not allow drill to enter flywheel.

2. Secure flywheel in soft jawed vice.
3. Split ring gear using a cold chisel.

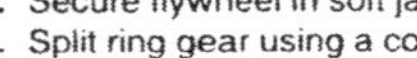
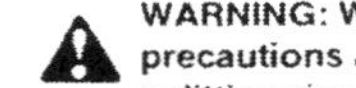

WARNING: Wear safety goggles and take precautions against flying fragments when splitting ring gear.

4. Remove flywheel from vice, remove old ring gear, and place flywheel, clutch side down, on a flat surface.

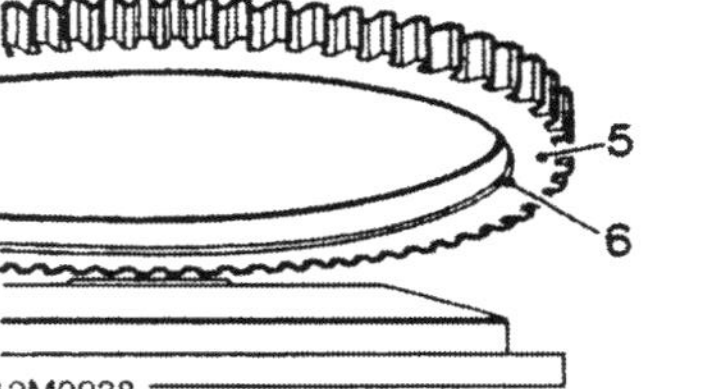

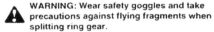

12M0938

5. Heat new ring gear uniformly to between 170° and 175° C (340° and 350° F).

CAUTION: Do not exceed this temperature.

WARNING: Take care when handling hot ring gear.

6. Locate ring gear on flywheel with chamfered inner diameter towards flywheel flange.

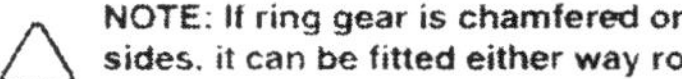

NOTE: If ring gear is chamfered on both sides, it can be fitted either way round.

7. Press ring gear on to flywheel until it butts against flywheel flange.
8. Allow flywheel to air cool.

Flywheel - refit

1. Fit flywheel and locate on 2 dowels.
2. Fit flywheel bolts.
3. Using assistance, restrain crankshaft and tighten flywheel bolts to 80 Nm (59 lbf.ft).

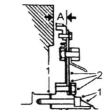

DRIVE PLATE AND RING GEAR ASSEMBLY

Drive plate and ring gear assembly - remove - Up to engine nos. 42D00593A and 46D00450A

1. Suitably identify each component to its fitted position.

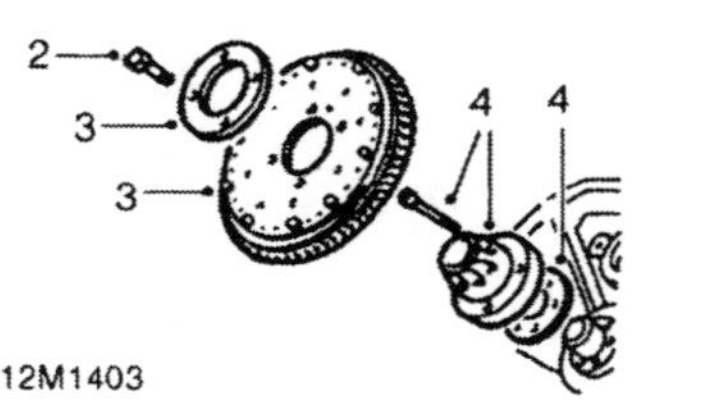

12M1403

NOTE: 4.0 litre drive plate illustrated.

2. Remove 4 bolts securing drive plate assembly.
3. Remove buttress ring and drive plate assembly.

NOTE: Drive plate assembly is dowel located.

4. Remove 6 socket head cap screws securing hub aligner to crankshaft, remove hub aligner and selective shim; retain shim.

NOTE: Dowel located.

Drive plate and ring gear assembly - remove - From engine nos. 42D00594A, 46D00451A and all engines having serial no. prefixes 47D to 51D

1. Suitably identify each component to its fitted position.

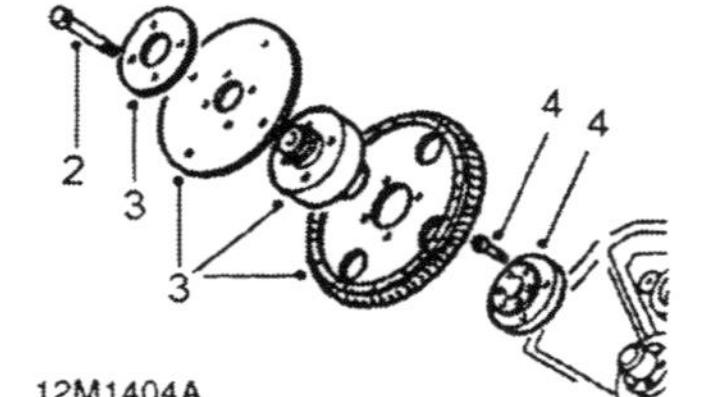

12M1404A

NOTE: 4.0 litre drive plate illustrated.

2. Remove 4 bolts securing buttress ring, drive plate, spacer and ring gear assembly to hub aligner.
3. Remove buttress ring, drive plate, spacer and ring gear assembly.

NOTE: Ring gear assembly is dowel located.

4. Remove 6 socket head cap screws securing hub aligner to crankshaft, remove hub aligner.

NOTE: Dowel located.

Drive plate and ring gear - inspection

1. Inspect drive plate for cracks and distortion.
2. Renew drive plate if necessary.
3. Inspect ring gear for worn, chipped and broken teeth.
4. Renew ring gear assembly if necessary.

Drive plate and ring gear assembly - refit - Up to engine nos. 42D00593A and 46D00450A

CAUTION: To prevent distortion to drive plate when bolted to torque converter, drive plate setting height must be checked as follows:

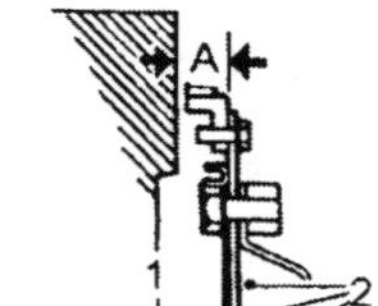

12M1402

1. Fit original selective shim and hub aligner, fit socket head cap screws and tighten to 85 Nm (63 lbf.ft).
2. Fit drive plate assembly and buttress ring ensuring that reference marks are aligned; fit bolts and tighten to 45 Nm (33 lbf.ft).

CAUTION: If a new drive plate assembly is being fitted, paint mark on plate must face towards torque converter.

3. Check the setting height **A.**
   Up to engine no. 42D00593A = 21.25 to 21.37 mm (0.83 to 0.84 in)
   Up to engine no. 46D00450A = 7.69 to 7.81 mm (0.30 to 0.31 in)
4. If setting height is not as specified, remove buttress ring, drive plate assembly, hub aligner and selective shim.

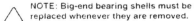

5. Measure existing shim and, if necessary, select appropriate shim to achieve setting height.
   Shims available:
   1.20 - 1.25mm (0.048 to 0.050 in)
   1.30 - 1.35mm (0.051 to 0.053 in)
   1.40 - 1.45mm (0.055 to 0.057 in)
   1.50 - 1.55mm (0.059 to 0.061 in)
   1.60 - 1.65mm (0.063 to 0.065 in)
   1.70 - 1.75mm (0.067 to 0.070 in)
   1.80 - 1.85mm (0.071 to 0.073 in)
   1.90 - 1.95mm (0.075 to 0.077 in)
   2.00 - 2.05mm (0.079 to 0.081 in)
   2.10 - 2.15mm (0.083 to 0.085 in)

6. Fit shim selected, fit hub aligner; fit socket head cap screws and tighten to 85 Nm (63 lbf.ft).
7. Fit drive plate assembly and buttress ring ensuring that reference marks are aligned or that paint mark on replacement drive plate is facing towards torque converter.
8. Fit bolts and tighten to 45 Nm (33 lbf.ft).

Drive plate and ring gear assembly - refit - From engine nos. 42D00594A, 46D00451A and all engines having serial no. prefixes 47D to 51D

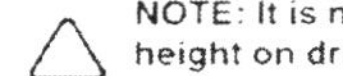

NOTE: It is not necessary to check setting height on drive plates fitted to engines from the above numbers.

1. Fit hub aligner, fit socket head cap screws and tighten to 85 Nm (63 lbf.ft).
2. Fit ring gear assembly, spacer, drive plate and buttress ring ensuring that reference marks are aligned.

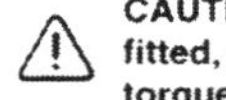

CAUTION: If a new drive plate is being fitted, paint mark must face towards torque converter, ensure holes in plate are aligned with clearance holes in ring gear.

3. Fit bolts and tighten to 45 Nm (33 lbf.ft).

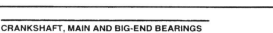

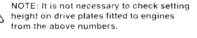

CRANKSHAFT, MAIN AND BIG-END BEARINGS

Big-end bearings - remove

1. Remove sump.

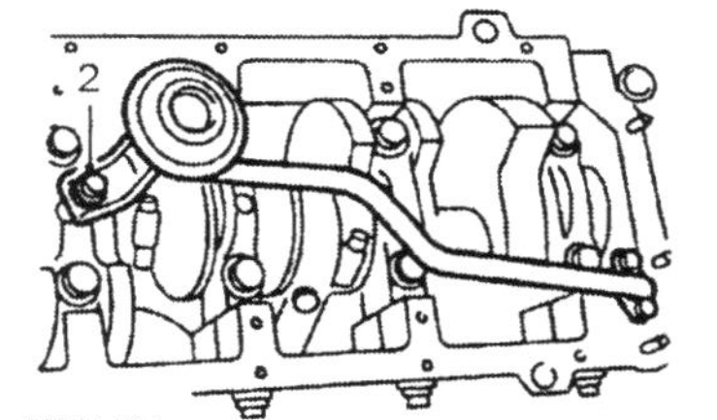

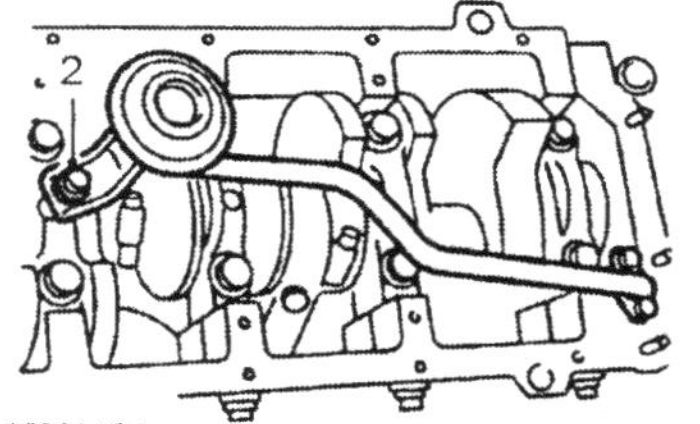

12M1404

2. Remove nut and washers securing oil pick-up pipe to stud.

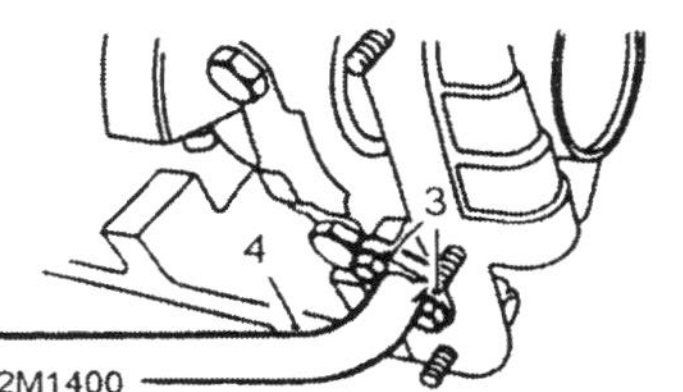

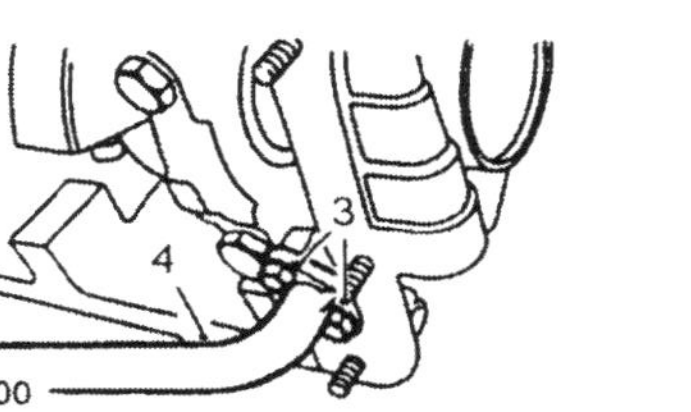

12M1400

3. Remove 2 bolts securing oil pick-up pipe to oil pump cover, withdraw pipe from cover; remove and discard 'O' ring.
4. Remove oil pick-up pipe, recover spacer from stud.
5. Suitably identify bearing caps to their respective connecting rods.

12M0945B

6. Remove 2 bolts securing each bearing cap.
7. Remove bearing cap and bearing shell.

NOTE: Keep bearing caps and bolts in their fitted order.

8. Push each piston up its respective bore and remove shells from connecting rods.

NOTE: Big-end bearing shells must be replaced whenever they are removed.

Big-end bearings - refit

1. Fit bearing shells to each connecting rod.

NOTE: Big-end bearings are available in 0.254 mm (0.01 in) and 0.508 mm (0.02 in) oversizes.

2. Lubricate bearing shells and crankshaft journals with engine oil.
3. Pull connecting rods on to crankshaft journals.
4. Fit bearing shells to each big-end bearing cap.

NOTE: If crankshaft has been reground, ensure appropriate oversize bearing shells are fitted.

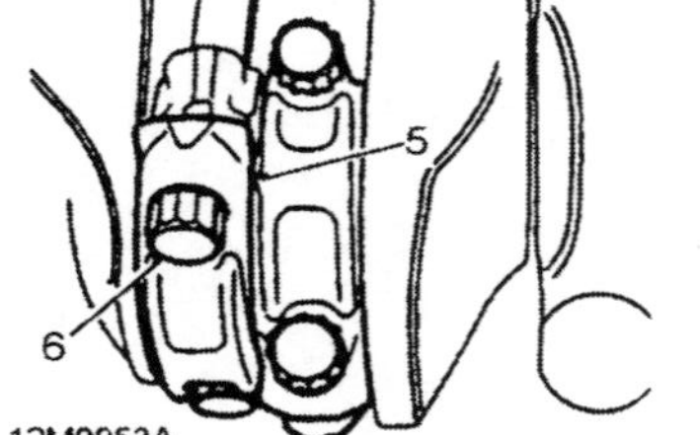

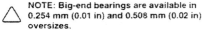

12M0953A

5. Lubricate bearing shells and fit bearing caps ensuring reference marks on connecting rods and bearing caps are aligned.

NOTE: Rib on edge of bearing cap must face towards front of engine on RH bank of cylinders and towards rear on LH bank of cylinders.

6. Fit bearing cap bolts and tighten to 20 Nm (15 lbf.ft) then a further 80 degrees.
7. Check connecting rods move freely sideways on crankshaft. Tightness indicates insufficient bearing clearance or misaligned connecting rod.

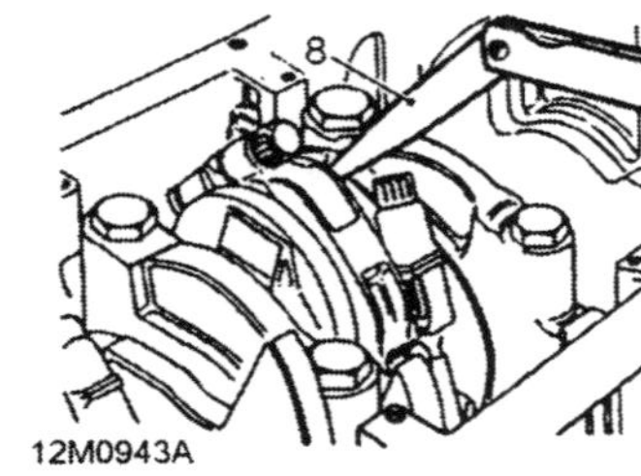
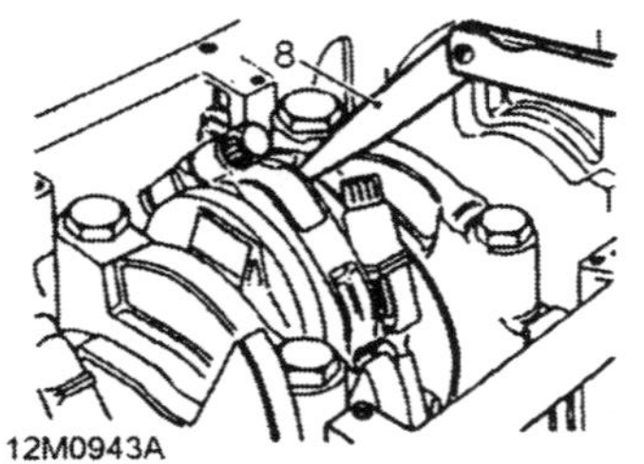

12M0943A

8. Check clearance between connecting rods on each crankshaft journal.
   Connecting rod clearance = 0.15 to 0.36 mm (0.006 to 0.014 in).
9. Clean oil strainer and oil pick-up pipe.
10. Smear a new 'O' ring with engine oil and fit to oil pick-up pipe.
11. Position oil pick-up pipe spacer on number 4 main bearing cap stud.
12. Fit oil pick-up pipe ensuring that end of pipe is correctly inserted in oil pump body.
13. Fit oil pick-up pipe to oil pump body bolts and tighten to 8 Nm (6 lbf.ft).
14. Fit washers and nut securing oil pick-up pipe to stud; tighten nut to 24 Nm (18 lbf.ft).
15. Fit sump.

Crankshaft - remove

1. Remove flywheel or drive plate and ring gear assembly.
2. Remove timing cover.
3. Remove timing gears.
4. Remove big-end bearings.

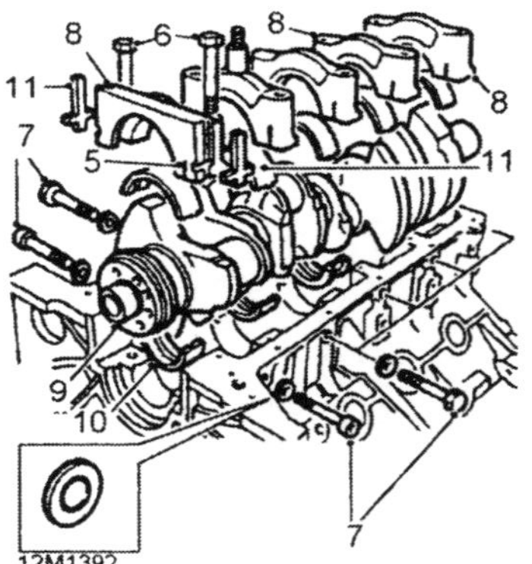

12M1392

5. Make suitable reference marks between each main bearing cap and cylinder block.
6. Starting at centre main bearing and working outwards, progressively slacken then remove 10 main bearing cap bolts.

CAUTION: Keep bolts in their fitted order.

7. Starting at centre main bearing and working outwards, progressively slacken then remove 5 LH side hexagonal head bolts and 4 RH side hexagonal head bolts and one socket head cap bolt; remove and discard Dowty washers.
8. Remove 5 main bearing caps, remove and discard bearing shells.

NOTE: Number 4 main bearing cap is drilled to accommodate oil pick-up pipe stud.

9. Lift out crankshaft; remove and discard rear oil seal.
10. Remove and discard 5 bearing shells from cylinder block.

CAUTION: Main bearing shells must be replaced whenever they are removed.

11. Remove and discard side seals from rear main bearing cap.
12. Remove all traces of sealant from bearing cap and cylinder block.
13. Remove Woodruff key from crankshaft.

Knock sensor - remove

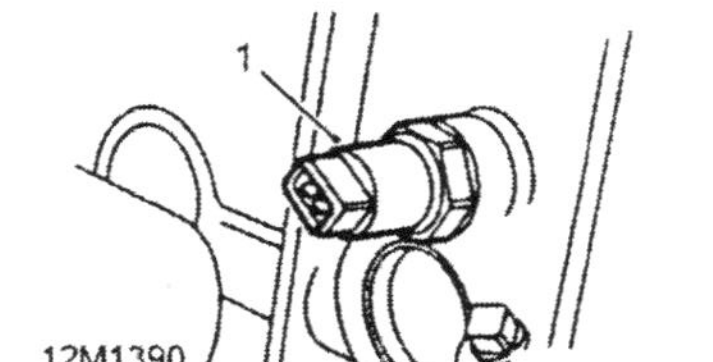

1. Remove knock sensor from cylinder block.

Crankshaft position sensor - remove

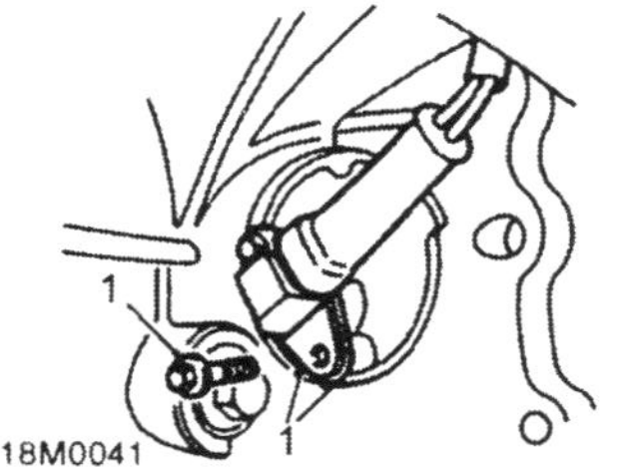

1. Remove 2 bolts securing crankshaft position sensor to gearbox adaptor plate, remove sensor; collect spacer - if fitted.

Crankshaft - inspection

1. Clean crankshaft and blow out oil passages.

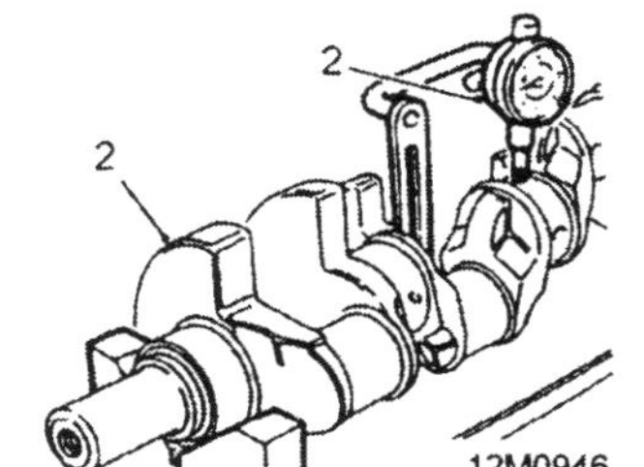

2. Support crankshaft front and rear bearing journals on vee blocks, and using a DTI, measure run-out on centre main bearing.
   Maximum permitted run-out = 0.08 mm (0.003 in).
   If run-out exceeds permitted maximum, crankshaft is unsuitable for regrinding and should be replaced.

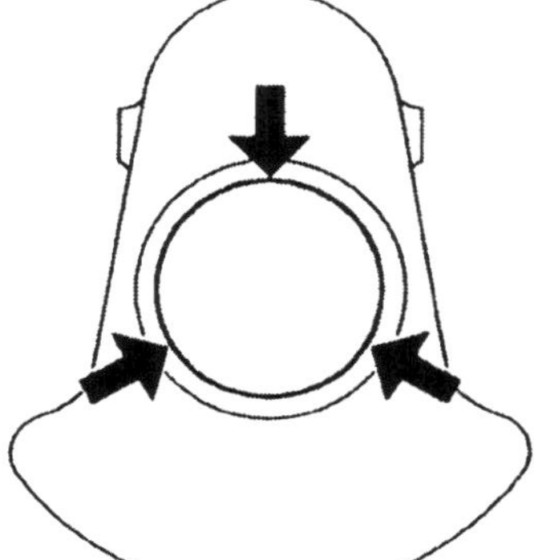

3. Measure each journal for overall wear and ovality, take 3 measurements at 120° intervals at each end and centre of journals.
   Main bearing journal diameter = 63.487 to 63.500 mm (2.499 to 2.52 in)
   Maximum out of round = 0.040 mm (0.002 in).
   Big-end bearing journal diameter = 55.500 to 55.513 mm (2.20 to 2.22 in)
   Maximum out of round = 0.040 mm (0.002 in).
   If measurements exceed permitted maximum, regrind or fit new crankshaft.

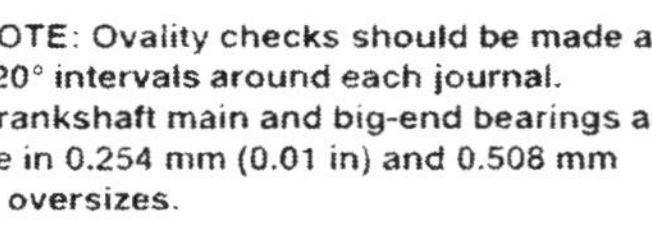

NOTE: Ovality checks should be made at 120° intervals around each journal. Crankshaft main and big-end bearings are available in 0.254 mm (0.01 in) and 0.508 mm (0.02 in) oversizes.

Crankshaft dimensions:

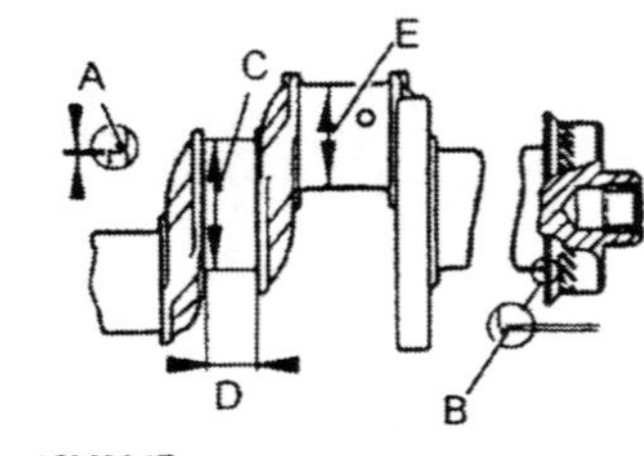

12M0947

Bearing journal radius - all journals except rear main journal **A** = 1.90 to 2.28 mm (0.075 to 0.09 in).
Rear main bearing journal radius **B** = 3.04 mm (0.12 in).

Bearing journal diameter **C**:
Standard = 63.487 to 63.500 mm (2.499 to 2.52 in).
0.254 mm (0.01 in) undersize = 63.233 to 63.246 mm (2.511 to 2.512 in).
0.508 mm (0.02 in) undersize = 62.979 to 62.992 mm (2.509 to 2.510 in).

Bearing journal width **D**:
Standard = 26.975 to 27.026 mm (1.061 to 1.064 in).

Bearing journal diameter **E**:
Standard = 55.500 to 55.513 mm (2.20 to 2.22 in).
0.254 mm (0.01 in) undersize = 55.246 to 55.259 mm (2.17 to 2.18 in).
0.508 mm (0.02 in) undersize = 54.992 to 55.005 mm (2.16 to 2.165 in).

CAUTION: if crankshaft is to be replaced, ensure replacement is correct for engine being overhauled. Crankshafts are not interchangeable between 4.0 and 4.6 litre engines.

1. Check crankshaft spigot bearing for wear, renew if necessary.

Crankshaft spigot bearing - renew

1. Carefully extract old spigot bearing.
2. Clean bearing recess in crankshaft.

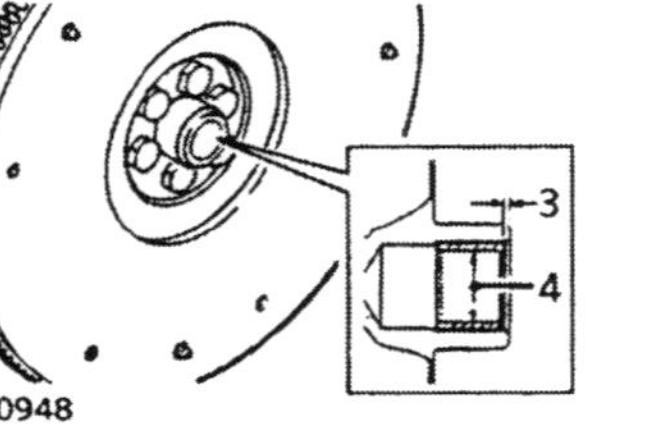

12M0948

3. Fit new bearing flush with, or to a maximum of 1.6 mm (0.06 in) below end face of crankshaft.
4. Ream bearing to correct inside diameter. Spigot bearing inside diameter = 19.177 + 0.025 - 0.000 mm (0.75 + 0.001 - 0.000 in).
5. Remove all traces of swarf.

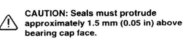

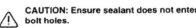

Crankshaft - refit

1. Clean main bearing caps, bearing shell recesses and mating surfaces of cylinder block.

CAUTION: Ensure bolt holes in cylinder block and main bearing caps are clean and dry.

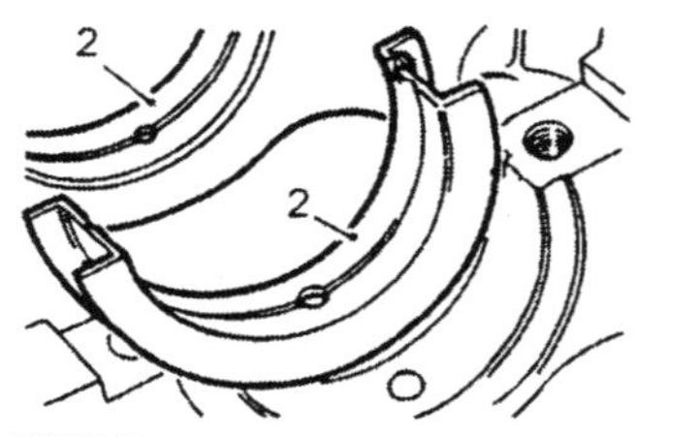

12M0949

2. Fit new upper main bearing shells, with oil holes and grooves, in cylinder block, ensuring flanged shell is fitted in centre position.

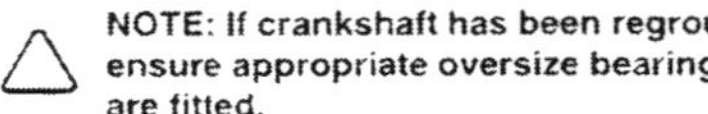
NOTE: If crankshaft has been reground ensure appropriate oversize bearing shells are fitted.

3. Lubricate main bearing shells with engine oil and position crankshaft in cylinder block.
4. Fit new main bearing shells to bearing caps.
5. Lubricate main bearing shells with engine oil.
6. Fit numbers 1 to 4 main bearing caps ensuring that reference marks made during dismantling are aligned, fit and tighten main bearing cap bolts to 5 Nm (4 lbf.ft).

NOTE: Do not fit side bolts at this stage.

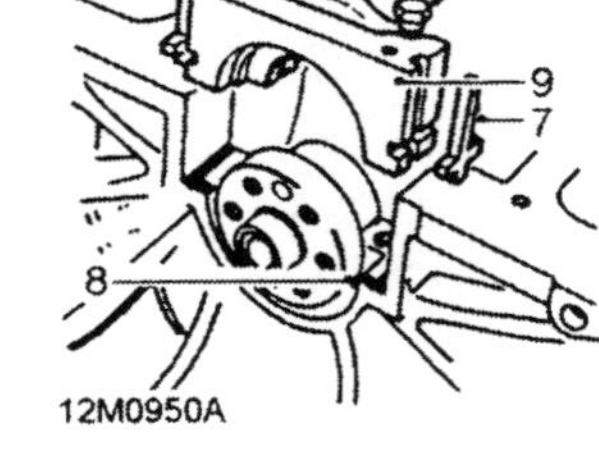

12M0950A

7. Fit side seals to rear main bearing cap.

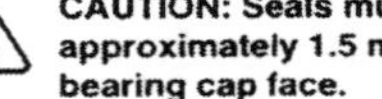
CAUTION: Seals must protrude approximately 1.5 mm (0.05 in) above bearing cap face.

8. Apply a 3 mm (0.12 in) wide bead of Hylomar PL32 jointing compound to bearing cap rear mating face on cylinder block.

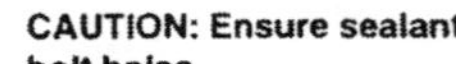
CAUTION: Ensure sealant does not enter bolt holes.

9. Lubricate rear main bearing shell and side seals with engine oil, carefully fit rear main bearing cap assembly; fit and tighten main bearing cap bolts to 5 Nm (4 lbf.ft).

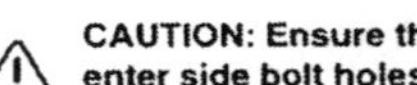
CAUTION: Ensure that engine oil does not enter side bolt holes in bearing cap.

10. Smear new Dowty washers with engine oil and fit to main bearing cap side bolts.
11. Fit and tighten RH then LH side bolts to 5 Nm (4 lbf.ft) ensuring that socket head cap bolt is fitted to rear main bearing cap on RH side of cylinder block adjacent to starter motor aperture.

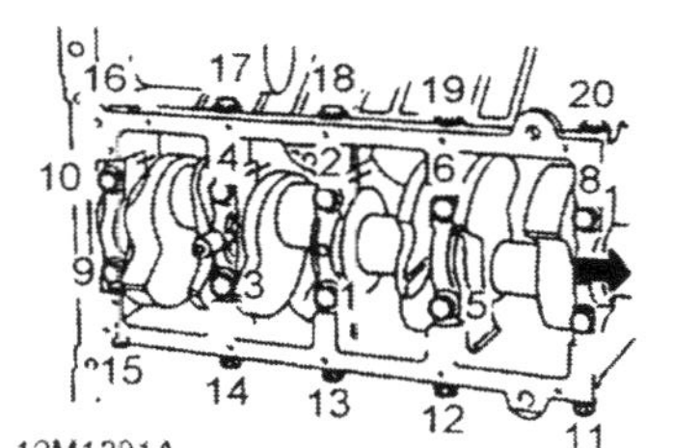

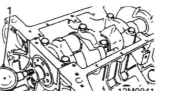

12M1391A

12. Using sequence shown, tighten bolts to:
    Stage 1 - Initial torque
    Main bearing cap bolts - 13.5 Nm (10 lbf.ft)
    Main bearing cap side bolts - 13.5 Nm (10 lbf.ft)
    Stage 2 - Final torque
    Main bearing cap bolts numbers 1 to 8 - 72 Nm (53 lbf.ft)
    Main bearing cap bolts numbers 9 and 10 - 92 Nm (68 lbf.ft)
    Main bearing cap side bolts 11 to 20 - 45 Nm (33 lbf.ft)
13. Trim off excess material from rear main bearing cap side seals.
14. Clean seal location and running surface on crankshaft.
15. Clean seal protector **LRT-12-095** and lubricate with engine oil.
16. Lubricate oil seal lip with engine oil.

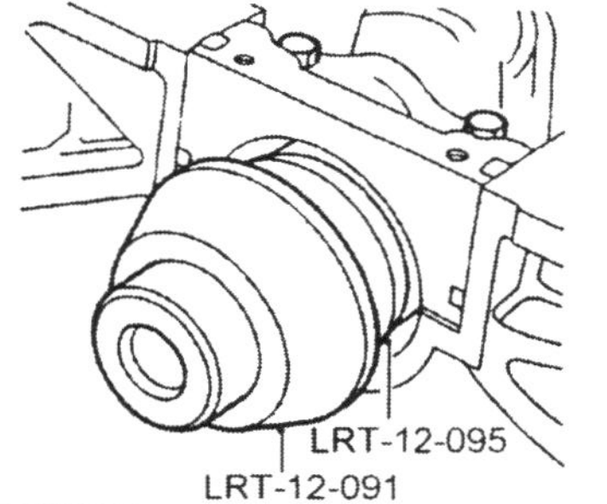

12M1255A

17. Position seal protector **LRT-12-095** to crankshaft.
18. Fit seal using tool **LRT-12-091**.
19. Fit Woodruff key to crankshaft.
20. Check crankshaft end-float.

NOTE: If 0.508 mm (0.02 in) oversize main **bearings have been fitted, it may be necessary to machine thrust faces of crankshaft centre** main bearing location to **achieve correct end-float. Ensure an equal amount of material is removed from each thrust face.**

21. Fit big-end bearings.
22. Fit timing cover and gears.
23. Fit flywheel or drive plate and ring gear assembly.
24. Fit sump.

Crankshaft end - float - check

12M0941

1. Set-up DTI to measure end float.
2. Move crankshaft forwards and zero gauge.
3. Move crankshaft rearwards, record end-float reading obtained.
   Crankshaft end-float = 0.10 to 0.20 mm (0.004 to 0.008 in).
4. Remove DTI.

NOTE: **Crankshaft end-float is controlled by thrust faces on upper half of centre main bearing shell. If crankshaft has been reground and 0.508 mm (0.02 in) oversize main bearing shells are to be fitted, it may be necessary to machine thrust faces of crankshaft centre main bearing journal to achieve correct end-float. Ensure an equal amount of material is removed from each thrust face.**

Knock sensor - refit

1. Clean threads of knock sensor and mating threads in cylinder block.
2. Fit knock sensor and tighten to 16 Nm (12 lbf.ft).

CAUTION: Do not apply any type of sealant to threads.

Crankshaft position sensor - refit

1. Position crankshaft position sensor and spacer - if fitted to gearbox adaptor plate, fit bolts and tighten to 6 Nm (4 lbf.ft).

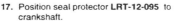

Distributed by Brooklands Books Ltd., PO Box 146, Cobham,
Surrey KT11 1LG, England Phone: 01932 865051 Fax: 01932 868803
E-mail: sales@brooklands-books.com

Part Nos. LRL 0004

R380 Manual Gearbox Overhaul Manual

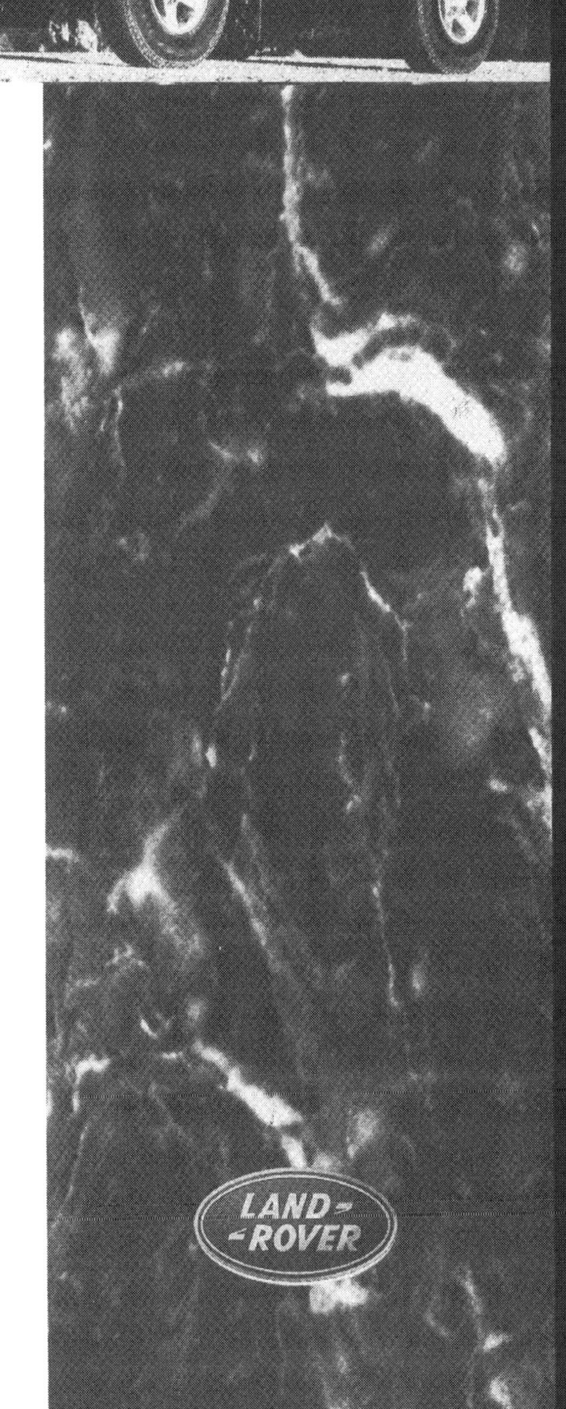

LRL 0003

R380 Manual Gearbox Overhaul Manual

LRL 0003 ENG (3rd Edition)

R380 GEARBOX

OVERHAUL MANUAL

This Overhaul Manual contains information applicable to the following models:

New Range Rover
Range Rover Classic 1995 Models on
Discovery 1995 Models on
Defender 1995 Models on
Discovery 2

Publication Part No.LRL 0003ENG - 3rd Edition

CONTENTS

Page

INTRODUCTION

How to use this manual

To assist in the use of this manual the section title is given at the top and the relevant sub - section is given at the bottom of each page.

This manual contains procedures for overhaul of the R380 gearbox on the bench with the clutch and, if applicable, the transfer box removed. For all other information regarding Adjustments, Removal of oil seals, clutch, transfer box and gearbox unit, consult the appropriate Repair Manual for the model concerned.

This manual is divided into 5 sections, Data, Torque Settings, Service Tools, Description and finally, Overhaul.To assist filing of revised information each sub - section is numbered from page 1.

The individual overhaul items are to be followed in the sequence in which they appear. Items numbered in the illustrations are referred to in the text.

Overhaul operations include reference to Service Tool numbers and the associated illustration depicts the tool in use. Operations also include reference to wear limits, relevant data, torque figures, and specialist information and useful assembly details.

WARNINGS, CAUTIONS and **NOTES** have the following meanings:

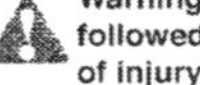

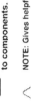

Warning: Procedures which must be followed precisely to avoid the possibility of injury.

CAUTION: Calls attention to procedures which must be followed to avoid damage to components.

NOTE: Gives helpful information

References

Operations covered in this manual do not include reference to testing the vehicle after repair. It is essential that work is inspected and tested after completion and if necessary, a road test of the vehicle is carried out, particularly where safety related items are concerned.

Dimensions

The dimensions quoted are to design engineering specification with Service Limits where applicable.

REPAIRS AND REPLACEMENTS

When replacement parts are required it is essential that only Land Rover recommended parts are used.

Attention is particularly drawn to the following points concerning repairs and the fitting of replacement parts and accessories.

Safety features embodied in the car may be impaired if other than Land Rover recommended parts are fitted. In certain territories, legislation prohibits the fitting of parts not to the manufacturer's specification.

Torque wrench setting figures given in this Manual must be used. Locking devices, where specified, must be fitted. If the efficiency of a locking device is impaired during removal it must be renewed.

The Terms of the vehicle Warranty may be invalidated by the fitting of other than Land Rover recommended parts. All Land Rover recommended parts have the full backing of the vehicle Warranty.

Land Rover Dealers are obliged to supply only recommended parts.

SPECIFICATION

Land Rover are constantly seeking to improve the specification, design and production of their vehicles and alterations take place accordingly. While every effort has been made to ensure the accuracy of this Manual, it should not be regarded as an infallible guide to current specifications of any particular component or vehicle.

This Manual does not constitute an offer for sale of any particular component or vehicle. Land Rover Dealers are not agents of Land Rover and have no authority to bind the manufacturer by any expressed or implied undertaking or representation.

GEARBOX IDENTIFICATION

The procedures given in this manual cover overhaul of the R380 gearbox fitted to a range of vehicles and as such, certain differences exist between gearboxes, particularly in respect of the extension housings, gear change housings and transfer box selector housings. It is important therefore that before starting work, the gearbox to be overhauled is correctly identified. Identification can be made by noting the gearbox serial number prefix stamped on the RH side of the gearbox casing and referring to the following table which lists four types of gearbox, A, B, C and D together with their appropriate serial number prefixes.

NOTE: The gearbox types listed are only intended as an aid to identification and do not relate to gearbox part numbers or a particular vehicle.

Overhaul operations in this manual list the applicable gearbox type referred to and it is important that the relevant operation is followed.

Type A gearbox prefixes: - 50A; 51A; 56A; 58A; 60A; 61A; 66A; 68A; 70A; 74A

Type B gearbox prefixes: - 53A; 55A; 63A; 67A; 69A; 73A

Type C gearbox prefix: - 18A

Type D gearbox prefixes: - 64A; 65A

CONTENTS

Page

CONTENTS

Page

GENERAL DATA

	NEW	SERVICE LIMIT
Baulk ring clearances	0.5 mm (0.02 in)	0.5 mm (0.02 in)
1st gear end float	0.05 - 0.20 mm (0.002 - 0.008 in)	0.327 mm (0.012 in)
2nd gear end float	0.04 - 0.21 mm (0.0016 - 0.008 in)	0.337 mm (0.013 in)
3rd gear end float	0.11 - 0.21 mm (0.004 - 0.008 in)	0.337 mm (0.013 in)
Adjust 5th - reverse hub - shim to:-	0.005 - 0.055 mm (0.0002 - 0.002 in)	0.055 mm (0.002 in)
Reverse gear idler shaft clearance	0.04 - 0.38 mm (0.0016 - 0.015 in)	0.38 mm (0.015 in)
Output shaft end float Early gearboxes:-	0.01 - 0.06 mm (0.0004 - 0.0024in)	0.06 mm (0.0024 in)
Later gearboxes having letter K added to gearbox serial number:-	0.00 - 0.05 mm (0.00 - 0.002 in)	0.05 mm (0.002 in)
Layshaft end float Early gearboxes:-	0.01 - 0.06 mm (0.0004 - 0.0024 in)	0.06 mm (0.0024 in)
Later gearboxes having letter K added to gearbox serial number:-	0.0 - 0.05 mm (0.0 - 0.002 in)	0.05 mm (0.002 in)

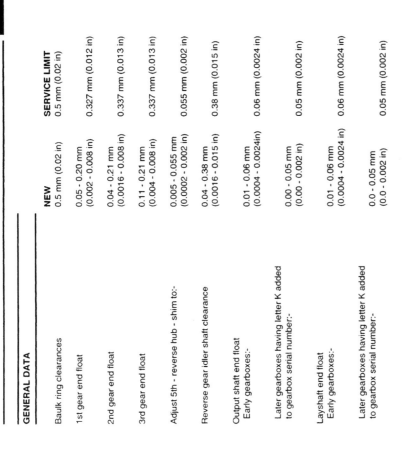

This page is intentionally left blank

TORQUE WRENCH SETTINGS

Oil pump to extension case	6 Nm (4.5 lbf.ft)
Attachment plate to gearcase	8 Nm (6 lbf.ft)
Attachment plate to remote housing	8 Nm (6 lbf.ft)
Splash shield bolts	8 Nm (6 lbf.ft)
Bottom cover to clutch housing	8 Nm (6 lbf.ft)
Breather baffle	8 Nm (6 lbf.ft)
Clip to clutch release lever	8 Nm (6 lbf.ft)
Cover to gear change housing*	8 Nm (6 lbf.ft)
Interlock spool retainer to gear case	8 Nm (6 lbf.ft)
Torsion spring locknut - adjusting screw	8 Nm (6 lbf.ft)
Screw - gear lever retention	8 Nm (6 lbf.ft)
Breather	15 Nm (11 lbf.ft)
Gear lever cap retainer bolt	15 Nm (11 lbf.ft)
Reverse inhibitor shaft	16 Nm (12 lbf.ft)
Reverse light switch	24 Nm (17 lbf.ft)
Transfer box to remote housing bolts	25 Nm (18 lbf.ft)
Bias adjustment plate bolts*	25 Nm (18 lbf.ft)
Selector quadrant setscrew*	25 Nm (18 lbf.ft)
Gear change lever yoke setscrew*	25 Nm (18 lbf.ft)
Bridge plates to gear change housing*	25 Nm (18 lbf.ft)
Extension case to gear case*	25 Nm (18 lbf.ft)
Front cover to gear case*	25 Nm (18 lbf.ft)
Gear change housing to extension case	25 Nm (18 lbf.ft)
Gear lever housing to remote housing	25 Nm (18 lbf.ft)
Guide - clutch release sleeve to clutch housing	25 Nm (18 lbf.ft)
Mounting bracket	25 Nm (18 lbf.ft)
Pivot clutch lever to clutch housing	25 Nm (18 lbf.ft)
Pivot plate to clutch housing	25 Nm (18 lbf.ft)
Plug - detent ball and spring*	25 Nm (18 lbf.ft)
Plunger housing to gear change housing	25 Nm (18 lbf.ft)
Remote selector housing to extension case	25 Nm (18 lbf.ft)
Slave cylinder to clutch housing	25 Nm (18 lbf.ft)
Upper gear lever assembly to lower gear lever	25 Nm (18 lbf.ft)
Yoke to selector shaft	25 Nm (18 lbf.ft)
Oil filler/level plug	30 Nm (22 lbf.ft)
Oil drain plug	50 Nm (37 lbf.ft)
Clutch housing to gearbox	72 Nm (53 lbf.ft)
Output flange bolt	90 Nm (66 lbf.ft)
5th gear layshaft stake nut	220 Nm (162 lbf.ft)
Remote housing blanking plug*	30 Nm (22 lbf.ft)
Selector shaft trunnion setscrew*	25 Nm (18 lbf.ft)
Transfer box gaiter support plate bolts	15 Nm (11 lbf.ft)
Gate plate bolts	15 Nm (11 lbf.ft)

* Apply Loctite 290 to threads

This page is intentionally left blank

SERVICE TOOLS

Note: When the use of specific tools is specified, only these tools should be used to prevent the possibility of personal injury and damage to components

Land Rover Number	Description
LRT-37-001/2	Adaptor for output shaft oil seal collar and bearing track remover
LRT-37-004	Adaptor for input shaft pilot bearing track remover
LRT-37-009	Puller, bearing and oil seal collar remover
LRT-37-010	Adaptor for output shaft oil seal collar and bearing track
LRT-37-014	Output shaft rear oil seal replacer
LRT-37-015	Output shaft rear support bearing track and oil seal collar replacer.
LRT-37-021	Adaptor for output shaft rear support bearing track and oil seal collar replacer.
LRT-37-022	Adaptor for layshaft bearings
LRT-37-023	Layshaft holding tool
LRT-37-043	Adaptor for input shaft bearing
LRT-37-043/2	Adaptor
LRT-37-044	Adaptor for layshaft bearings
LRT-51-003	Flange holder
LRT-99-002	Hand press
LRT-99-004	Impulse extractor

This page is intentionally left blank

DESCRIPTION

The R380 5 speed all synchromesh gearbox comprises an input shaft, output shaft, layshaft and reverse idler shaft .

Gearbox casings consist of a front cover, gearcase, centre plate and extension housing, all casings are located by dowels and sealed.

Selector forks for 1st/2nd and 3rd/4th gears are located on a single selector shaft inside the main gearcase whilst the selector fork for fifth and reverse gear is located on the same selector shaft inside the extension housing.

The input shaft, output shaft and layshaft are supported by taper roller bearings with all gears running on caged needle roller bearings. Output shaft and layshaft bearings end float is controlled by selective thrust washers located in the centre plate.

Lubrication is by an oil pump located in the extension housing which directs oil via internal drillings in the output shaft to lubricate the components.

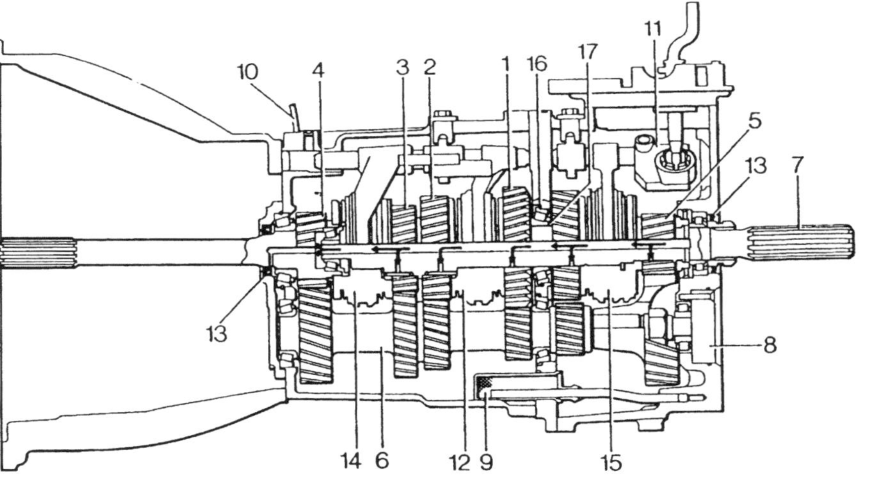

37M7132

1. Output shaft 1st gear
2. Output shaft 2nd gear
3. Output shaft 3rd gear
4. Input shaft/4th gear
5. Output shaft 5th gear
6. Layshaft
7. Output shaft
8. Oil pump
9. Oil filter
10. Breather
11. Single rail gear selector
12. 1st/2nd synchromesh
13. Oil seals
14. 3rd/4th gear synchromesh
15. 5th/reverse gear synchromesh
16. Selective spacers (output shaft and layshaft end float)
17. Selective spacer (5th gear/reverse hub)

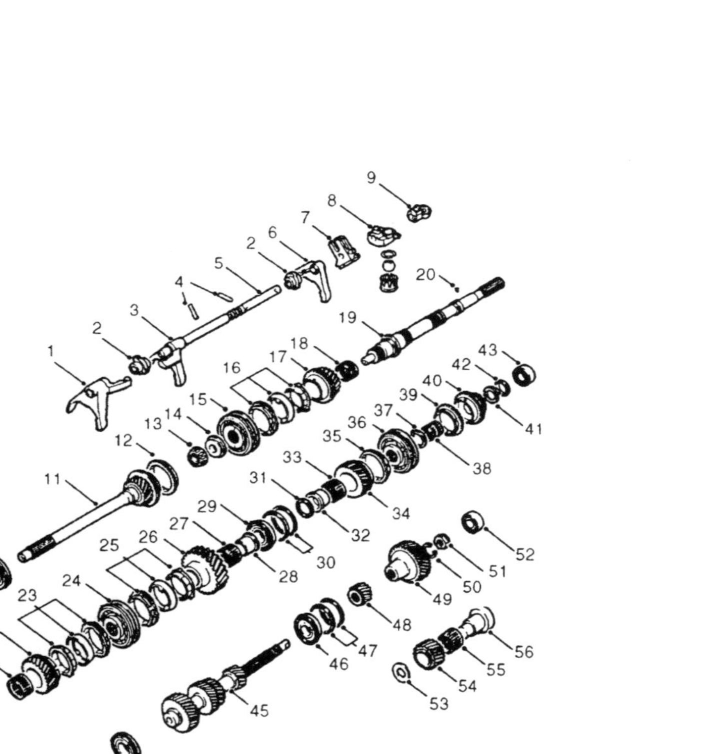

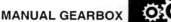

M37 1779

GEARBOX COMPONENTS - GEARS AND SHAFTS

1. 3rd/4th gear selector fork
2. Interlock spool
3. 1st/2nd gear selector fork
4. Selector shaft yoke pins
5. Selector shaft
6. Reverse/5th gear selector fork
7. Selector quadrant - Type A gearbox
8. Gear change lever yoke - Type B/D gearbox
9. Gear change lever yoke - Type C gearbox
10. Input shaft front taper bearing
11. Input shaft
12. 4th gear synchromesh ring
13. Pilot taper bearing
14. Spacer
15. 3rd/4th gear synchromesh hub and sleeve
16. 3rd gear synchromesh rings
17. 3rd gear
18. Needle roller bearings
19. Output shaft
20. Roll pin
21. Needle bearing
22. 2nd gear
23. 2nd gear synchromesh rings
24. 2nd/1st gear synchromesh hub and sleeve
25. 1st gear synchromesh rings
26. 1st gear
27. Needle roller bearing
28. Bush
29. Output shaft taper bearing
30. Selective shims
31. Selective washer
32. Bush
33. Needle roller bearing
34. Reverse gear
35. Reverse gear synchromesh ring
36. Reverse/5th gear synchromesh hub and sleeve
37. Circlip
38. Needle roller bearings
39. 5th gear synchromesh ring
40. 5th gear
41. 5th gear segments
42. 5th gear segment retaining ring
43. Output shaft rear support bearing
44. Layshaft support bearing
45. Layshaft
46. Layshaft support bearing
47. Selective shims
48. Layshaft reverse gear
49. Layshaft 5th gear
50. Split washer - later gearboxes
51. 5th gear nut
52. Layshaft rear support bearing
53. Spacer
54. Reverse idler gear
55. Needle roller bearing
56. Reverse idler shaft

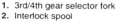

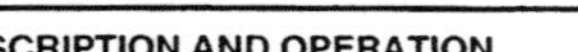

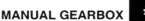

M37 1780

GEARBOX CASINGS

1. Front cover - Early gearboxes
2. Front cover - Later gearboxes
3. Input shaft oil seal
4. Oil filler/level plug
5. Oil drain plug
6. Sealing washer
7. Gearcase
8. Interlock spool retainer, bolt and 'O' ring - if fitted
9. Centre plate
10. Locating dowels
11. Selector plug, detent balls and springs
12. Splash shield and bolt
13. Extension housing - Types A and B gearbox
14. Gate plate and bolt
15. Interlock spool retainer, bolt and 'O' ring
16. Inhibitor cam spring
17. Inhibitor cam
18. Reverse inhibitor shaft
19. Output shaft oil seal collar
20. Oil seal
21. Oil pump
22. 'O' ring
23. Reverse light switch
24. Oil cooler by-pass and bolt
25. 'O' ring
26. Oil pick-up pipe
27. Oil filter
28. Oil pick-up ring
29. Oil cooler adaptor
30. Bolt
31. 'O' ring
32. Extension housing - Type C gearbox
33. Gate plate and bolt - Type C gearbox
34. Inhibitor cam end plate and bolt - Type C gearbox
35. Interlock spool retainer, bolt and 'O' ring - Type C gearbox
36. Selector shaft oil seal - Type C gearbox
37. Spacer - Type C gearbox
38. Speedometer pinion - Type C gearbox
39. Oil seal - Type C gearbox
40. Output shaft drive flange - Type C gearbox
41. 'O' ring - Type C gearbox
42. Spacer - Type C gearbox
43. Tab washer - Type C gearbox
44. Drive flange bolt - Type C gearbox
45. Drive flange propeller shaft bolt - Type C gearbox
46. Support bracket - Type C gearbox
47. Extension housing - Type D gearbox
48. Oil seal - Type D gearbox
49. Interlock spool retainer, bolt and 'O' ring - Type D gearbox

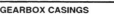

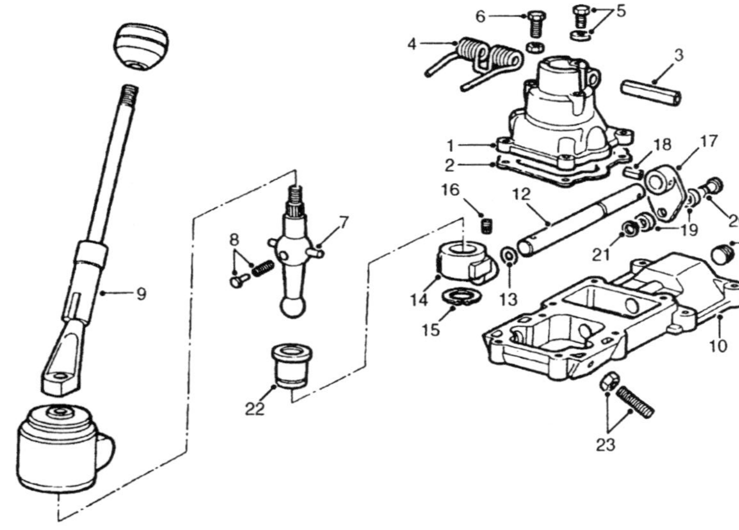

M37 1819

GEAR CHANGE HOUSING - TYPE A GEARBOX

1. Gear change housing
2. Gasket
3. Roll pin
4. Bias spring
5. Gear lever retaining bolt and washer
6. Gear change housing bolts
7. Gear lever
8. Nylon pad and spring
9. Gear lever extension
10. Remote housing
11. Blanking plug
12. Selector shaft
13. 'O' ring
14. Trunnion
15. Circlip
16. Trunnion retaining screw
17. Quadrant
18. Roll pin or setscrew
19. Rollers
20. Pin
21. Circlip
22. Ball pin seating
23. 5th gear stop screw and locknut

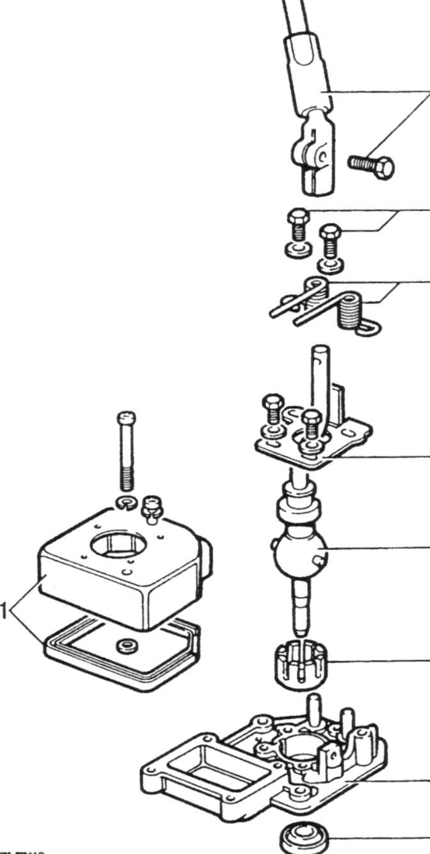

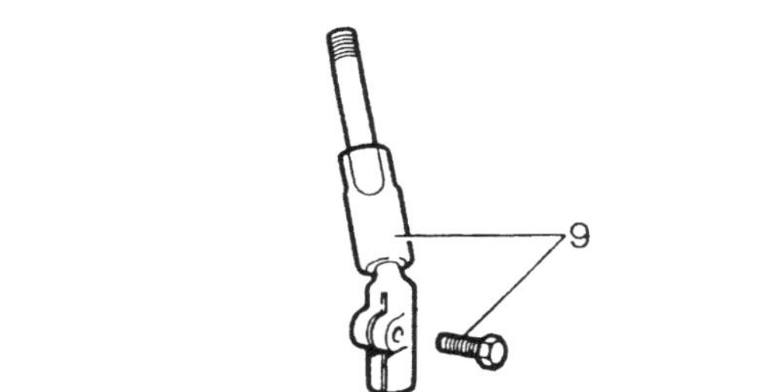

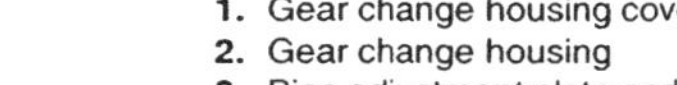

GEAR CHANGE HOUSING - TYPE B GEARBOX

1. Gear change housing cover and gasket
2. Gear change housing
3. Bias adjustment plate and bolts
4. Lower gear lever
5. Railko bush
6. Lower gear lever housing oil seal
7. Bias springs
8. Bias spring retaining bolts
9. Upper gear lever and bolt

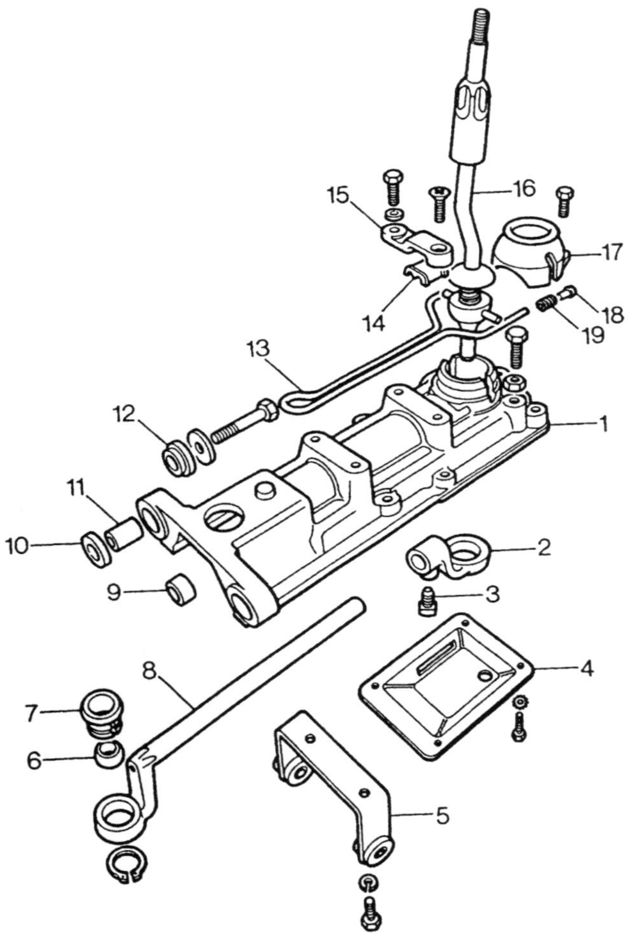

37M7117

REMOTE GEAR CHANGE HOUSING - TYPE C GEARBOX

1. Remote gear change housing
2. Selector rod yoke
3. Pinch bolt
4. Bottom cover plate
5. Remote gear change bracket
6. Ball pin
7. Ball pin seating
8. Selector rod
9. Selector rod bush
10. Spacer
11. Mounting rubbers
12. Flexible mounting
13. Bias spring
14. Bridge plate liner
15. Bias spring bridge plate
16. Gear lever
17. Gear lever cap
18. Plunger
19. Anti-rattle spring

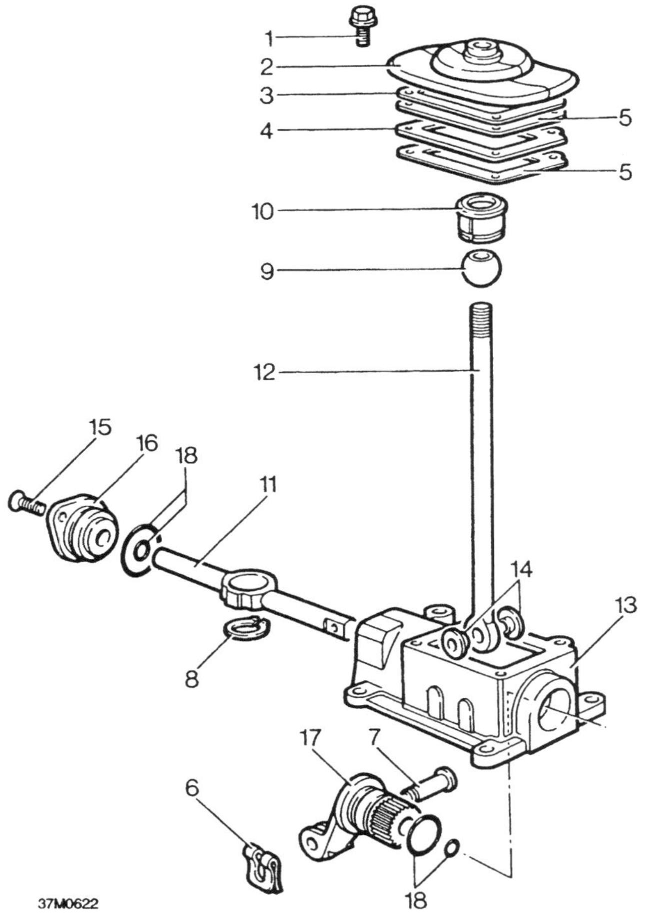

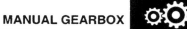

37M0622

TRANSFER BOX SELECTOR HOUSING - TYPE A GEARBOX

1. Gaiter retaining bolt
2. Gaiter
3. Gaiter support plate
4. Gasket plate
5. Gaskets
6. Spring clip
7. Clevis pin
8. Circlip retaining nylon seat
9. Gear lever ball
10. Nylon seat
11. Cross shaft
12. Gear lever
13. Selector housing
14. Bushes
15. Countersunk screws
16. End cover
17. Selector fork
18. 'O' rings

This page is intentionally left blank

MANUAL GEARBOX 

GEARBOX DISMANTLE

Clutch housing - Type A gearbox - Remove

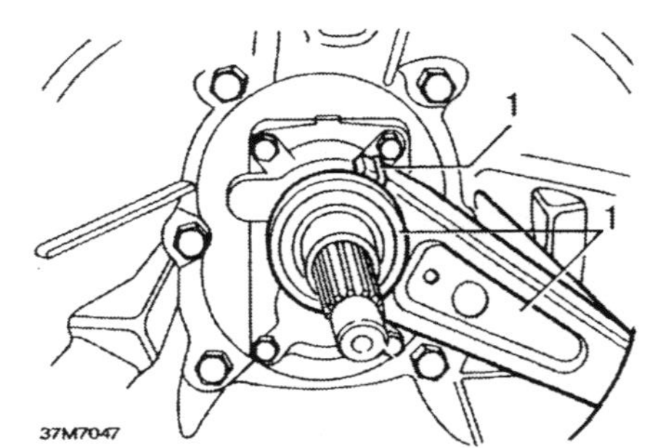

NOTE: Early type front cover illustrated.

1. *If fitted:* Remove and discard clips retaining clutch release bearing pads, remove bearing and clutch release lever, recover pads.

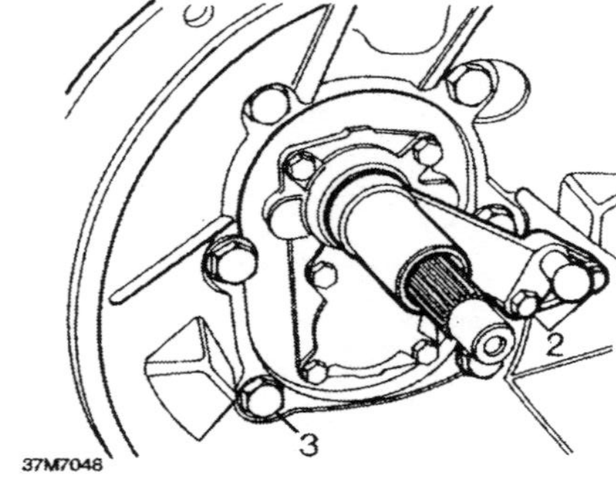

NOTE: Early type front cover illustrated.

2. Remove 2 bolts securing release lever pivot post, remove post.
3. Remove 6 bolts securing clutch housing to gearbox, remove housing.

NOTE: Dowel located.

Clutch housing - Type B gearbox - Remove

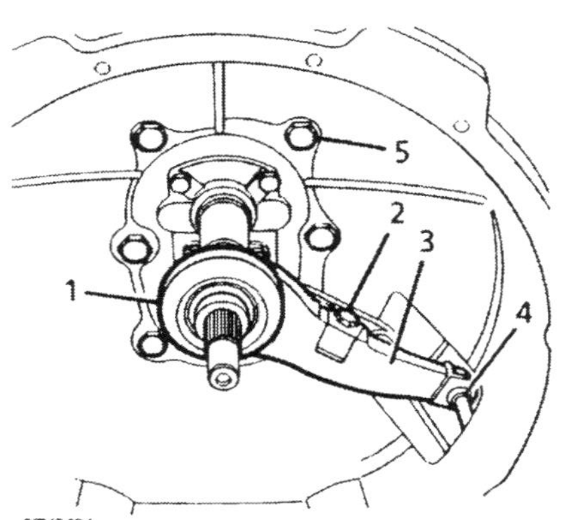

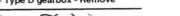

37M0494

NOTE: Early type front cover illustrated.

1. Remove clutch release bearing.
2. Remove bolt securing spring clip to clutch release lever, remove clip.
3. Remove clutch release lever.
4. Remove 'C' clip from release lever pivot post, discard clip.
5. Remove 6 bolts securing clutch housing to gearbox, remove housing.

NOTE: Dowel located.

Clutch housing Type C gearbox - Remove

37M0495

1. Pull clutch release lever off pivot post, remove lever and clutch release bearing.

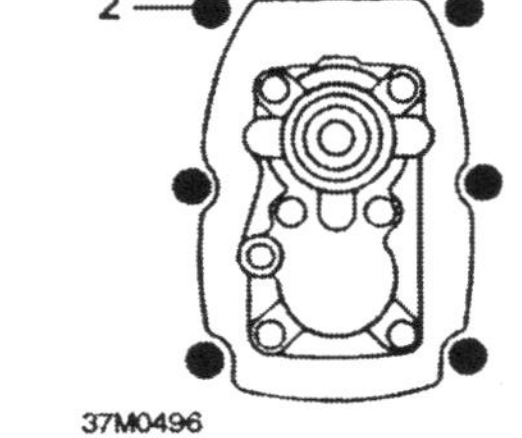

37M0496

NOTE: Early type front cover illustrated.

2. Remove 6 bolts securing clutch housing to gearbox, remove clutch housing.

NOTE: 2 longest bolts are fitted at dowel locations and have plain washers under their heads.

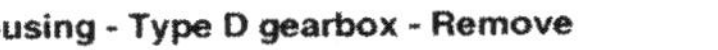

Clutch housing - Type D gearbox - Remove

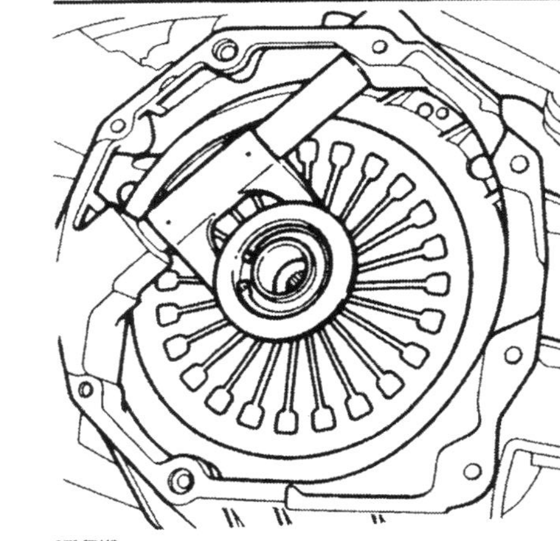
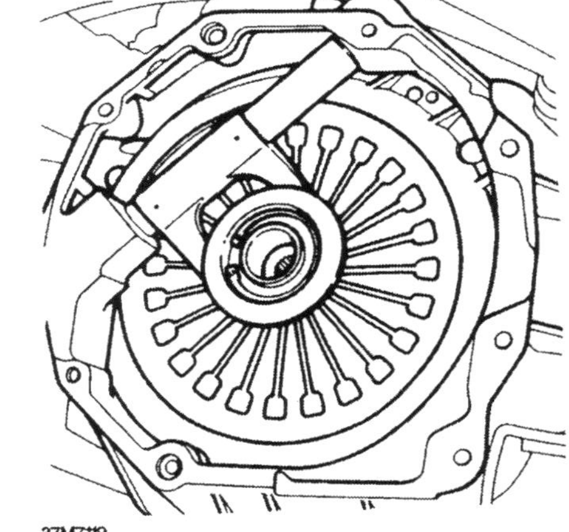

37M7119

NOTE: Type D gearboxes have a standard clutch housing adaptor which mates with both v8 and diesel engine clutch housings.The above illustration shows the gearbox removed at the clutch housing adsptor with the clutch housing adaptor (containing the clutch mechanism) still fitted to the engine.

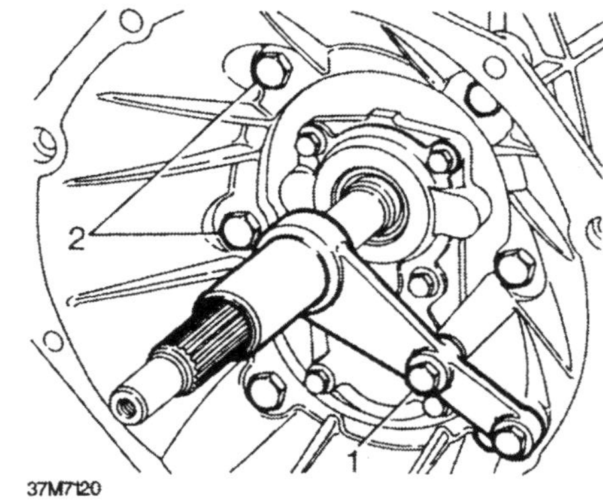

37M7120

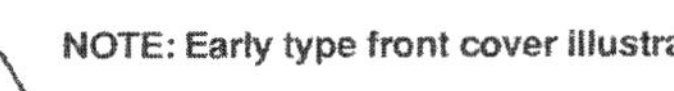

NOTE: Early type front cover illustrated.

1. Remove 2 bolts securing release lever pivot post; remove post.
2. Remove 6 bolts securing adaptor housing to gearbox; remove adaptor housing.

Gear change/selector housings - Type A gearbox - Remove

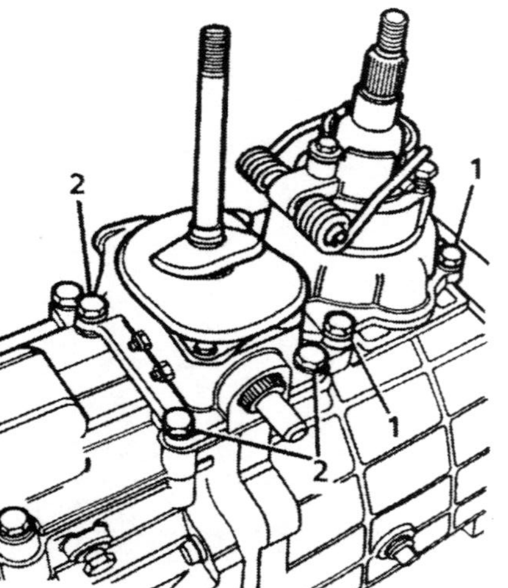

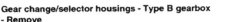

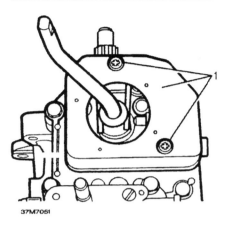

37M7049

1. Remove 4 bolts securing gear change housing, remove housing.

NOTE: Dowel located.

2. Remove 4 bolts securing transfer box selector housing, remove housing.

Remote housing - Type A gearbox - Remove

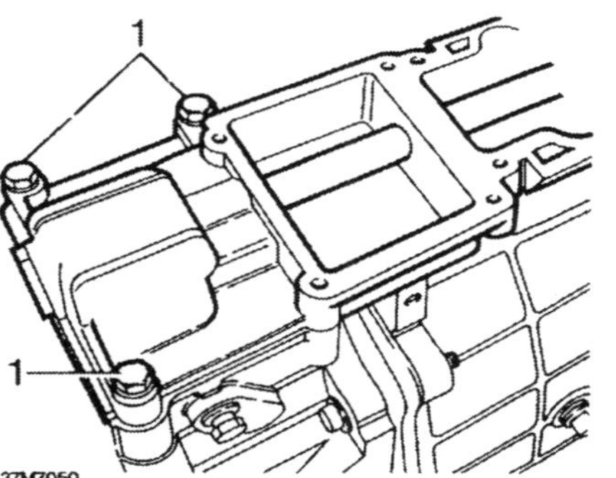

37M7050

1. Noting their fitted position, remove 3 bolts securing remote housing, remove housing.

NOTE: Dowel located.

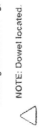

Gear change/selector housings - Type B gearbox - Remove

37M7051

1. Remove 2 Torx screws securing gear change housing cover, remove cover; recover sealing rubber.

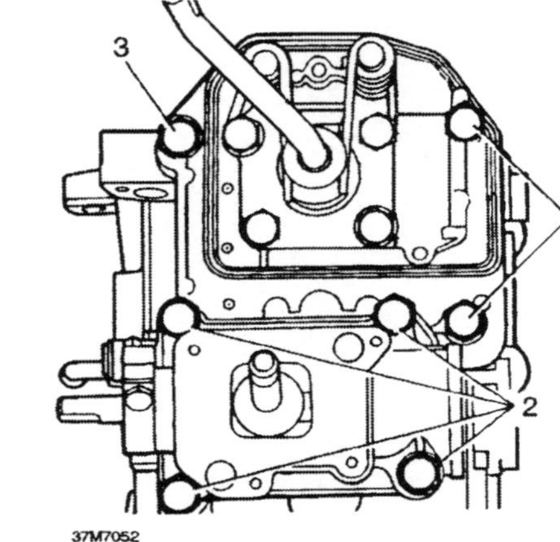

37M7052

2. Remove 4 bolts securing transfer box selector housing, remove housing.
3. Noting their fitted position, remove 3 bolts securing gear change housing, remove housing.

NOTE: Dowel located.

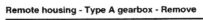

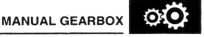

Selector quadrant - Type A gearbox - Remove

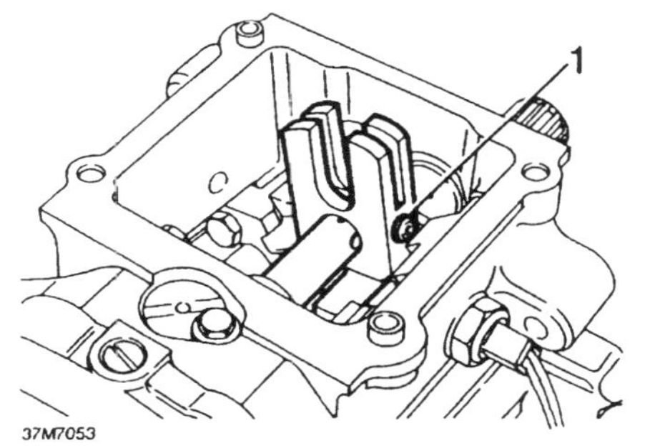

37M7053

1. Remove and discard set screw securing selector quadrant.
2. Move selector shaft forwards, remove quadrant.

Gear change lever yoke - Type B gearbox - Remove

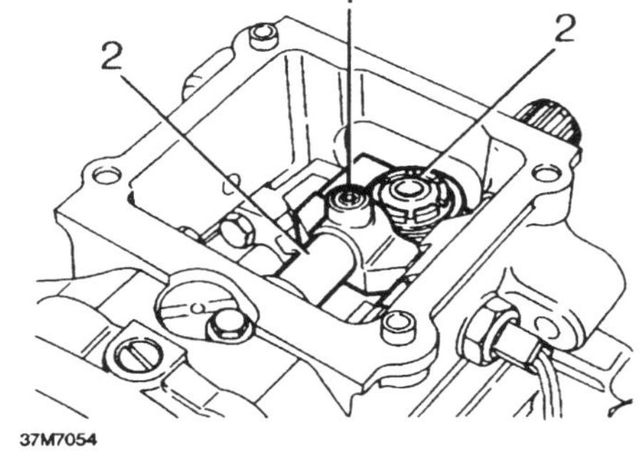

37M7054

1. Remove and discard set screw securing yoke.
2. Move selector shaft forwards, remove yoke.

Remote gear change - Type C gearbox - Remove

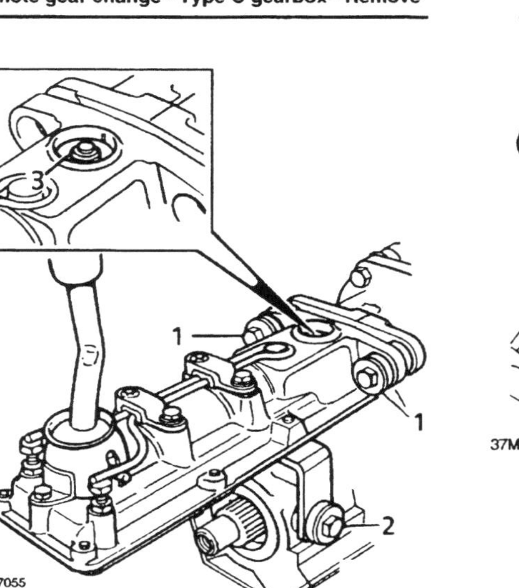

37M7055

1. Noting fitted positions of mounting rubbers and washers, remove 2 bolts securing remote gear change to extension housing, recover washers and mounting rubbers.
2. Remove 2 bolts securing remote gear change bracket to extension housing, recover washers and mounting rubbers.
3. Release remote gear change from extension housing, disconnect selector rod from selector shaft pin.

Remote gear change - Type D gearbox - Remove

37M7121

1. Remove 4 bolts securing remote gear change to extension housing; release remote gear change from extension housing.

Gear change lever yoke - Type D gearbox - Remove

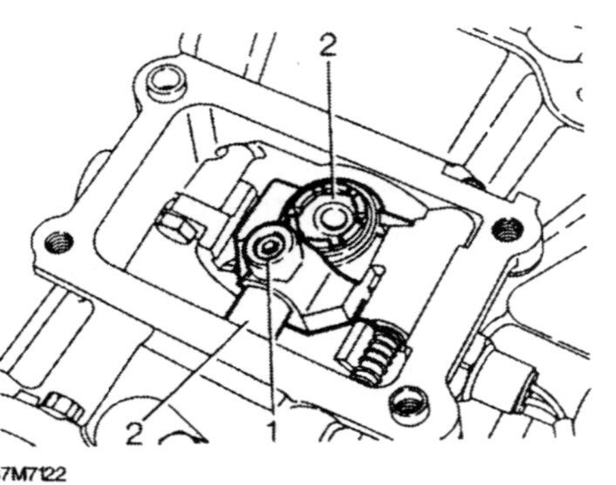

37M7122

1. Remove and discard set screw securing yoke.
2. Move selector shaft forwards, remove yoke.

Extension housing - Types A and B gearbox - Remove

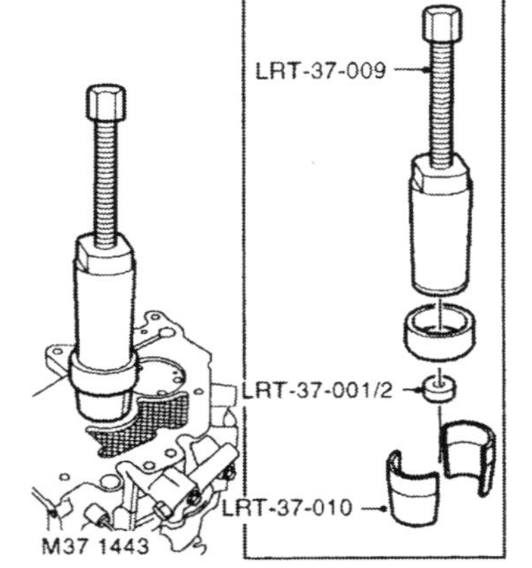

1. Using **LRT-37-009, LRT-37-010** and **LRT-37-001/2**, remove output shaft oil seal collar.

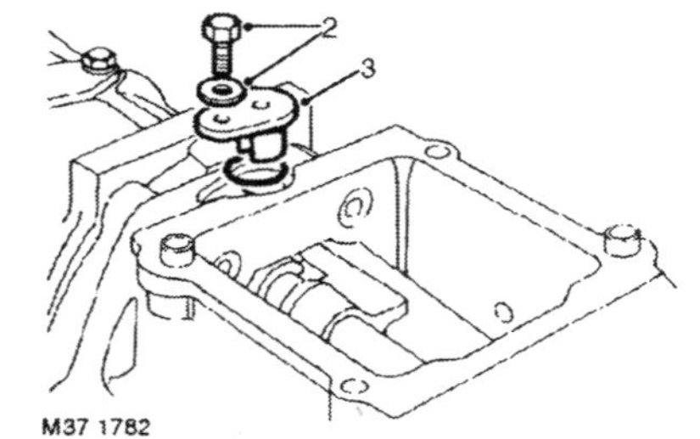

M37 1782

2. Remove bolt and washer securing interlock spool retainer.
3. Remove interlock spool retainer, remove and discard 'O' ring.

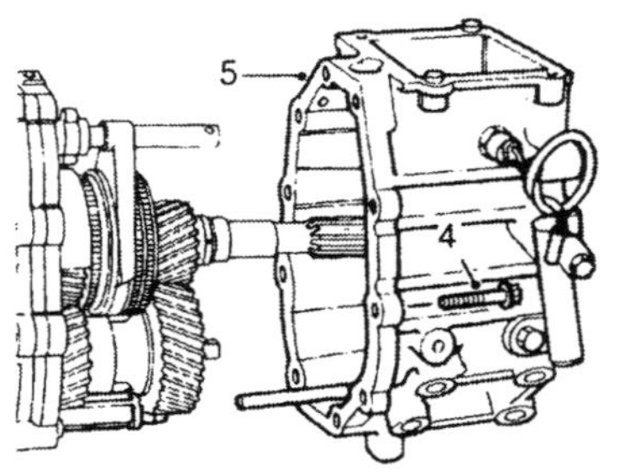

M37 1445

4. Noting fitted of 2 longest bolts, remove 10 bolts securing the extension housing.
5. Place a suitable container underneath the gearbox to catch any oil spillage and remove the extension housing.

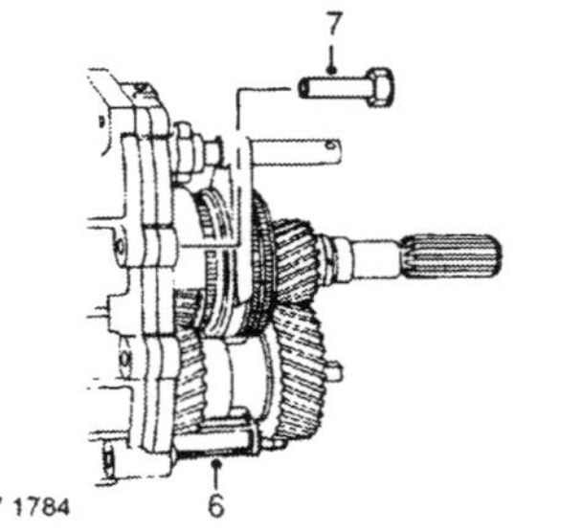

M37 1784

6. Remove oil filter.
7. Secure centre plate to gearcase with 2 off 8 x 35 mm slave bolts.

Extension housing - Type C gearbox - Remove

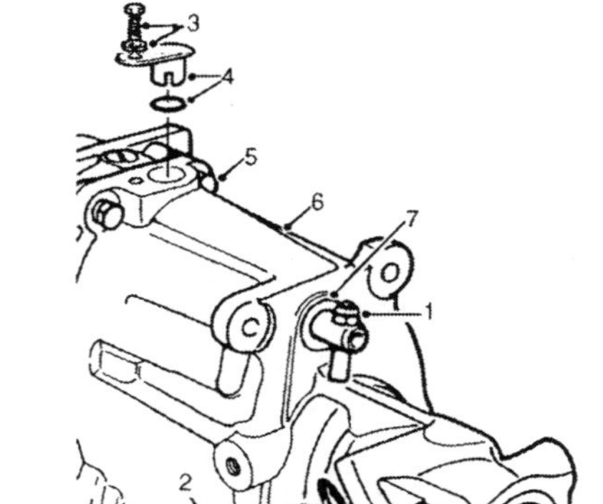

M37 1785

1. Remove and discard self-locking nut securing selector shaft pin to selector shaft; remove pin.
2. Carefully prise speedometer pinion housing and gear out of extension housing, remove and discard 'O' ring.
3. Remove bolt and washer securing interlock spool retainer.
4. Remove interlock spool retainer, remove and discard 'O' ring.
5. Noting fitted position of 2 longest bolts, remove 10 bolts securing extension housing to gearcase.
6. Place a suitable container underneath the gearbox to collect any oil spillage and remove the extension housing.

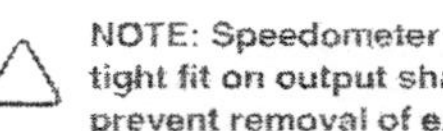
NOTE: Speedometer drive gear may be a tight fit on output shaft and this can prevent removal of extension housing. Insert suitable blocks of wood between extension housing and centre plate and carefully lever extension housing away until drive gear is released.

7. Remove and discard selector shaft oil seal.

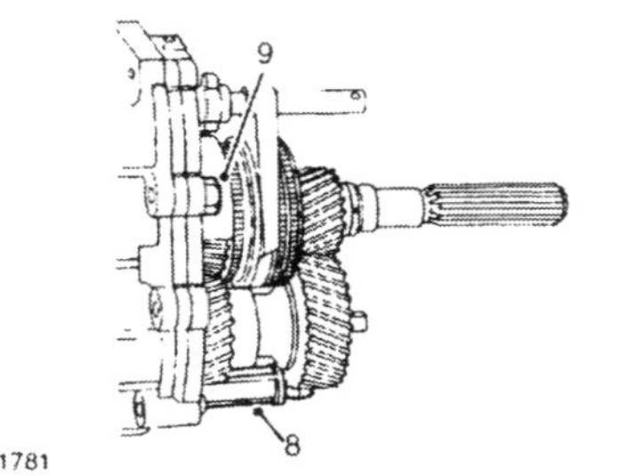

M37 1781

8. Remove oil filter.
9. Secure centre plate to gearcase with 2 off 8 x 35 mm slave bolts.

Extension housing - Type D gearbox - Remove

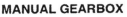

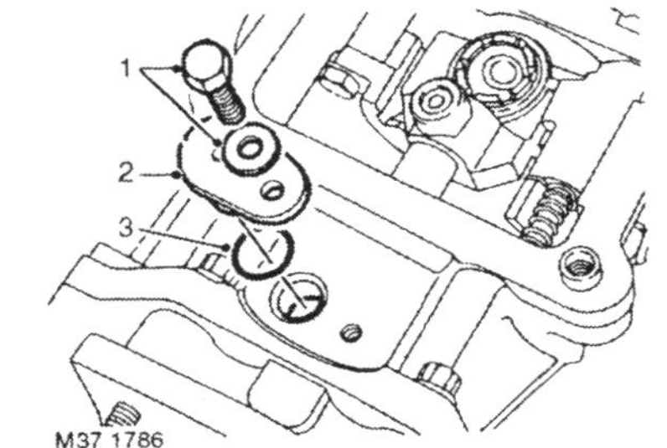

M37 1786

1. Remove bolt and washer securing interlock spool retainer.
2. Remove interlock spool retainer.
3. Remove and discard 'O' ring - if fitted.

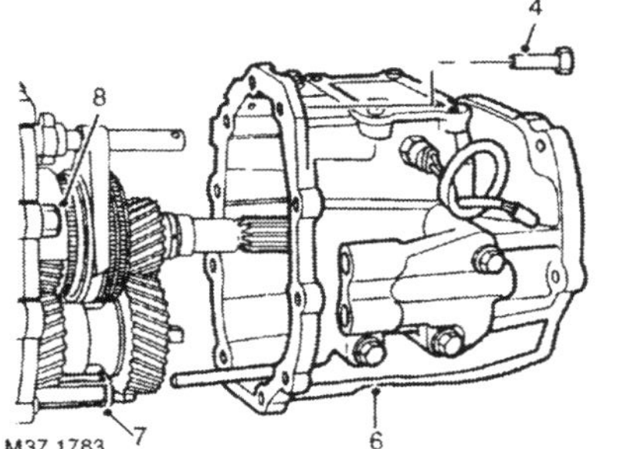

M37 1783

4. Noting fitted position of 2 longest bolts, remove 10 bolts securing extension housing to main gearcase.
5. Using a soft faced mallet, tap extension housing free from its location dowels.
6. Place a suitable container underneath the gearbox to collect any oil spillage and remove the extension housing.
7. Remove oil filter.
8. Secure centre plate to gearcase using 2 off 8 x 35 mm slave bolts.

5th and Reverse gear - Remove

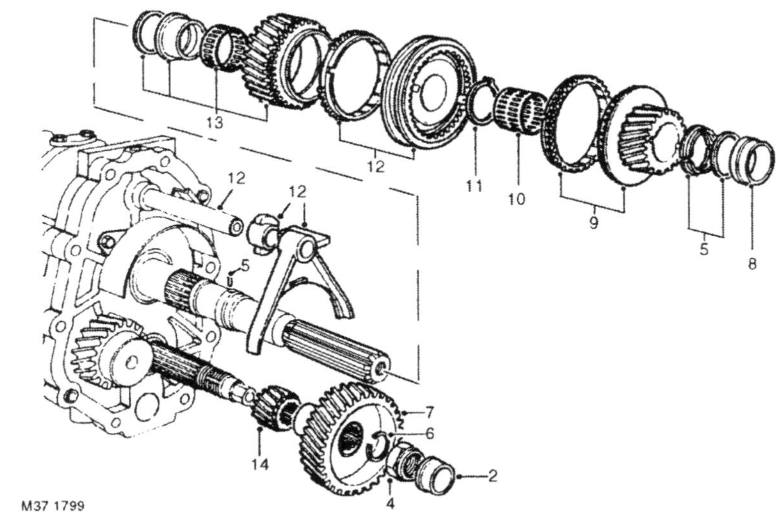

M37 1799

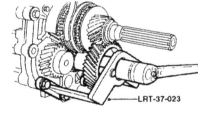

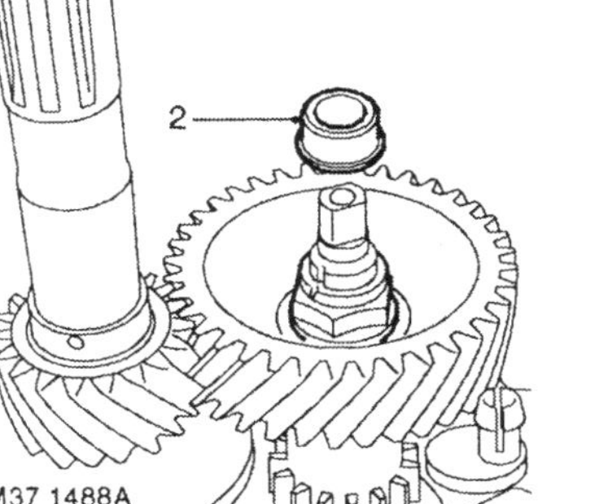

M37 1488A

1. Position gearcase as shown
2. Using a suitable two legged puller remove 5th gear layshaft support bearing track from the end of layshaft.

LRT-37-023

M37 1800

3. Remove staking from 5th laygear retaining nut, fit tool **LRT-37-023** to hold the 5th laygear.

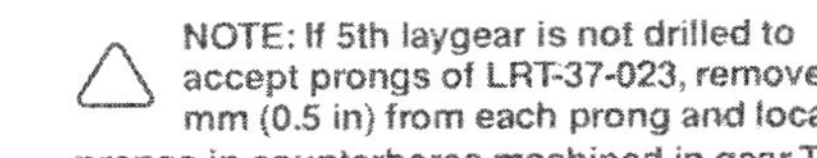

NOTE: If 5th laygear is not drilled to accept prongs of LRT-37-023, remove 13 mm (0.5 in) from each prong and locate prongs in counterbores machined in gear.The modified tool may still be used on gearboxes fitted with drilled gears.

4. Remove and discard the nut.

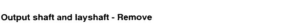

5. Remove thrust collar segments, retaining ring and segments, drift out the roll pin.
6. *Later gearboxes:* Remove split washer securing 5th laygear to shaft.
7. Remove 5th laygear.

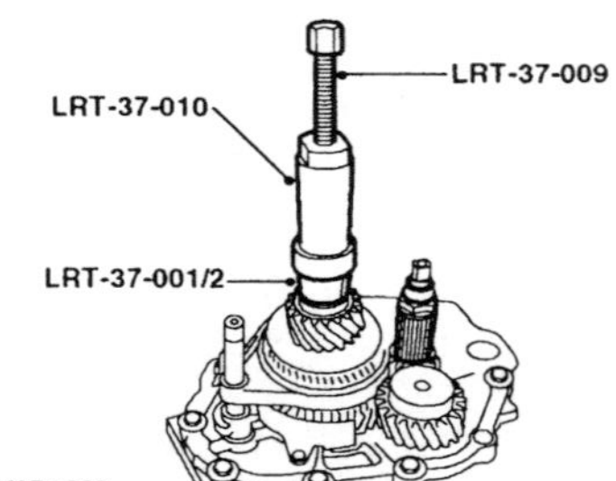

M37 1802

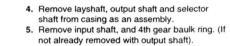

8. Remove output shaft rear support bearing track using tools **LRT-37-009, LRT-37-010** and **LRT-37-001/2**.
9. Remove output shaft 5th gear with synchromesh baulk ring.
10. Remove output shaft 5th gear split needle roller bearing.
11. Remove and discard circlip securing 5th gear synchromesh hub.

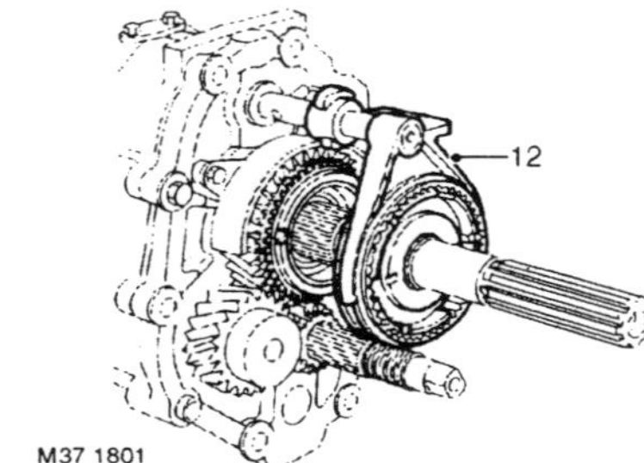

M37 1801

12. Pull selector shaft out of gearcase until selector spool can be rotated clear of fork. Remove 5th and reverse synchromesh hub assembly complete with fork and spool.
13. Remove output shaft reverse gear complete with needle roller bearing and bush noting selective spacer between reverse gear bush and centre plate bearing.
14. Remove layshaft reverse gear.

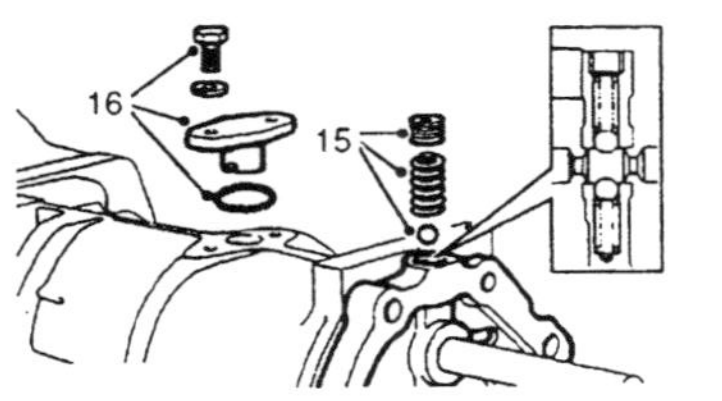

M37 1803

15. Remove centre plate Torx detent plug, spring and ball.
16. Remove 2 bolts securing spool retainer, remove retainer; remove and discard 'O' ring - if fitted.

Output shaft and layshaft - Remove

1. Remove slave bolts securing centre plate.

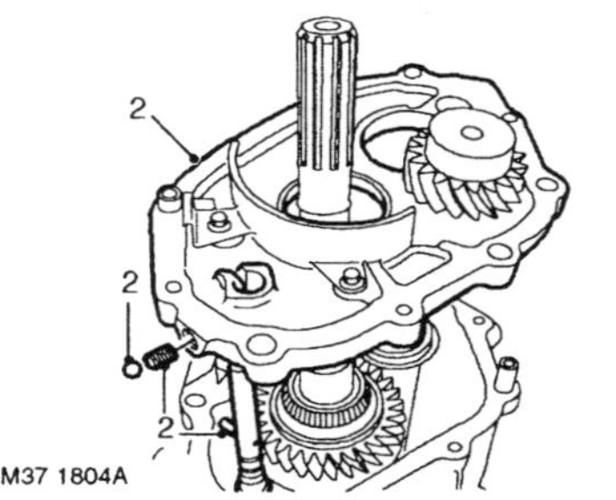

M37 1804A

2. Align selector shaft pin with slot in centre plate and using wooden blocks and hide mallet, drive off centre plate; collect lower detent ball and spring.

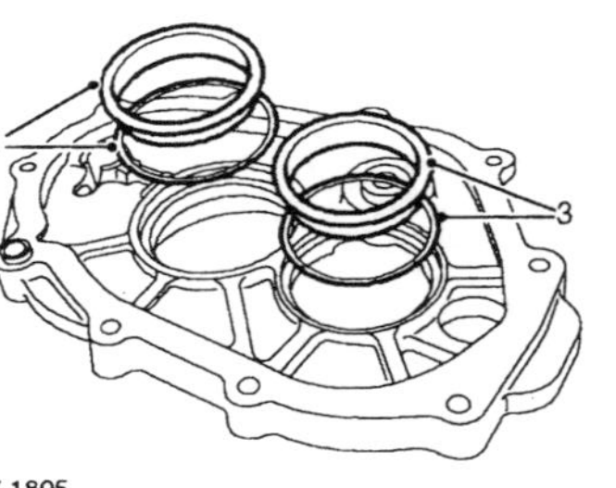

M37 1805

3. Remove bearing tracks and shims from centre plate.

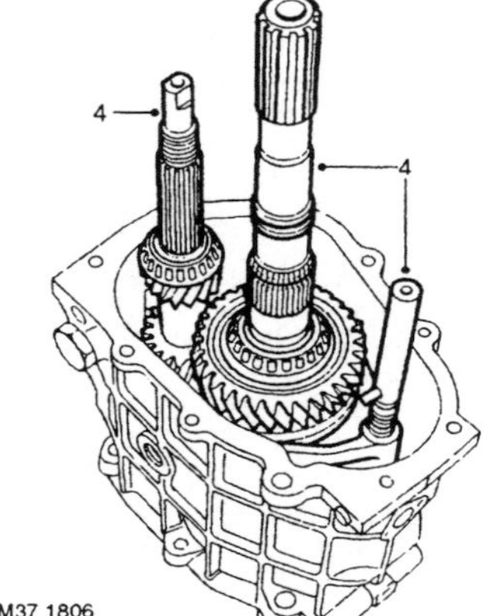

M37 1806

4. Remove layshaft, output shaft and selector shaft from casing as an assembly.
5. Remove input shaft, and 4th gear baulk ring. (If not already removed with output shaft).

Output shaft - Dismantle

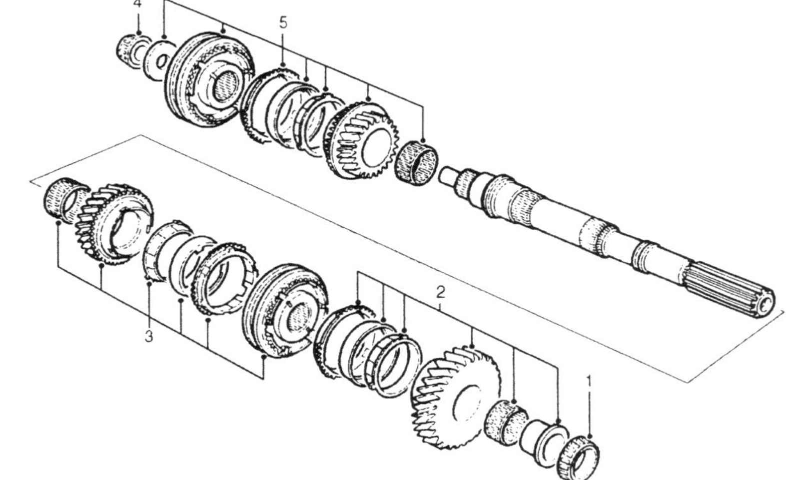

M37 1808

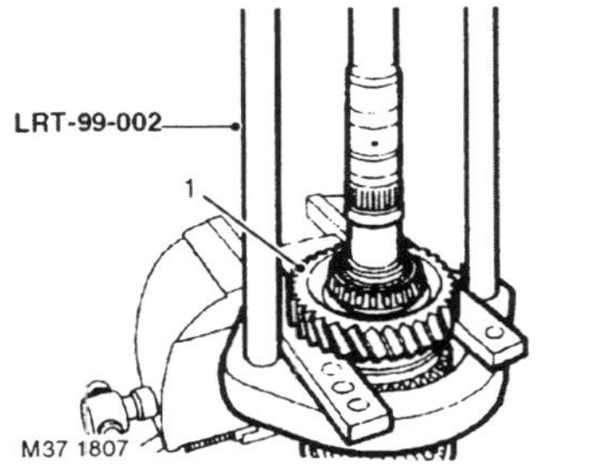

M37 1807

1. Using **LRT-99-002** and support bars under 1st gear, press output shaft support bearing from output shaft.
2. Remove 1st gear, bush, needle bearing and synchromesh baulk rings.
3. Remove 1st/2nd gear synchromesh selector hub, 2nd gear synchromesh baulk rings, second gear and needle bearing.

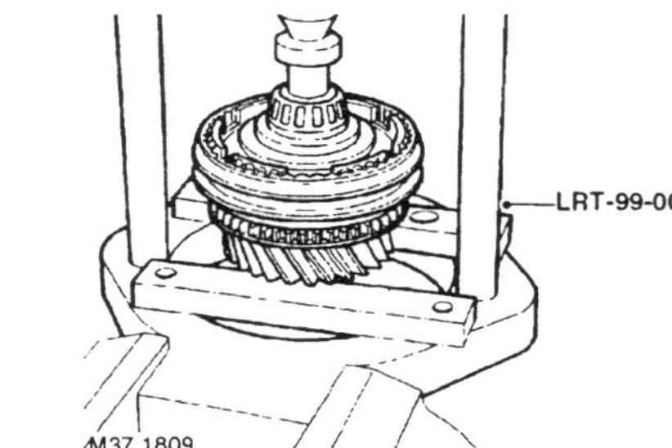

M37 1809

4. Invert output shaft and using **LRT-99-002** and support bars under 3rd gear, press off pilot bearing.
5. Remove spacer, 3rd/4th gear synchromesh selector hub, synchromesh baulk rings, 3rd gear and needle bearing.

Gearcase

Degrease and clean all components. Inspect casing for damage, cracks and stripped threads.

1. Fit oil filer/level plug.

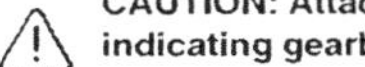

CAUTION: Attach a suitable label indicating gearbox oil is drained.

2. Fit new sealing washer to drain plug, fit plug and tighten to 50 Nm (37 lbf.ft).

Front Cover - Remove

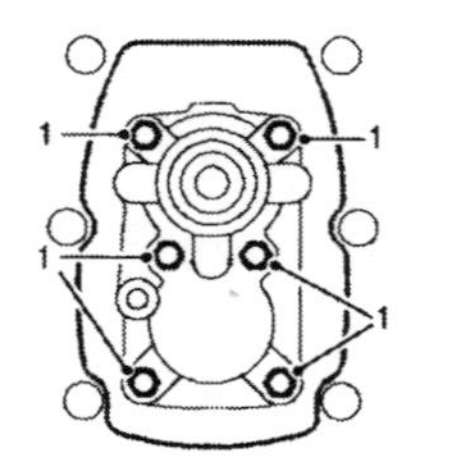

M37 1810

NOTE: Early type front cover illustrated.

1. Remove 6 bolts securing front cover to gearcase, remove cover.

Front Cover - Early Type - Dismantle

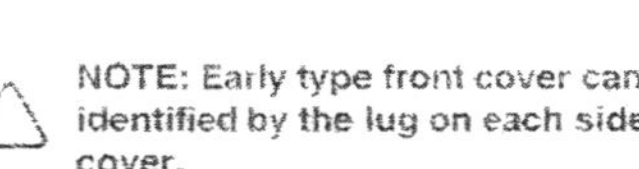

NOTE: Early type front cover can be identified by the lug on each side of the cover.

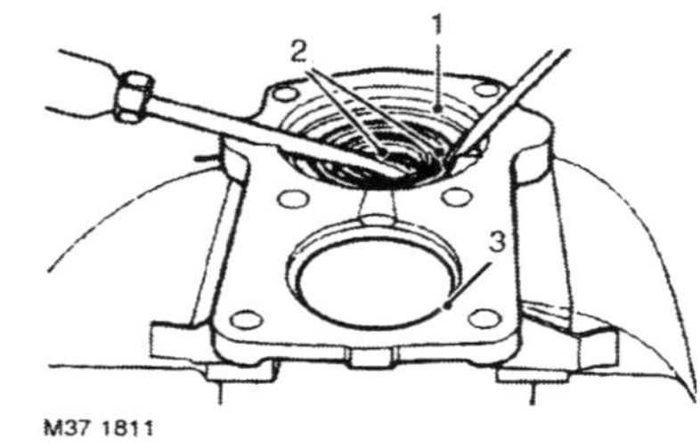

M37 1811

1. Remove input shaft bearing track from front cover. Check that spring clips are intact.
2. Remove and discard oil seal from front cover.
3. Remove layshaft bearing track from front cover.

Front cover - Later Type - Dismantle

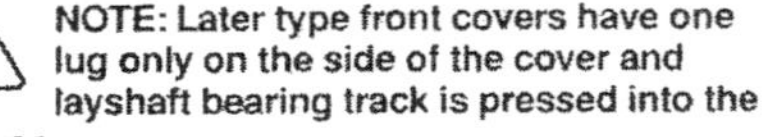

NOTE: Later type front covers have one lug only on the side of the cover and layshaft bearing track is pressed into the cover.

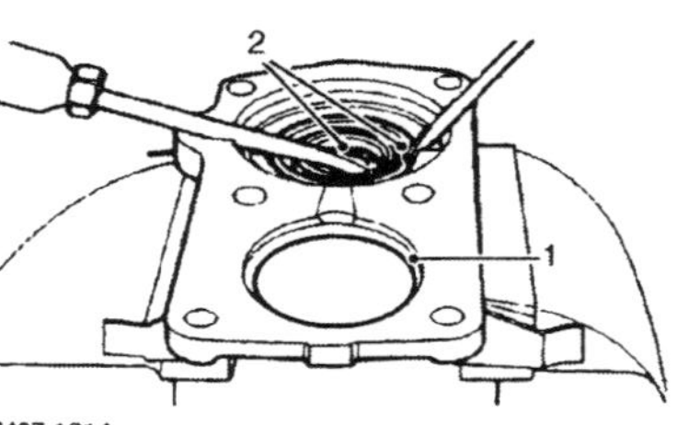

M37 1814

1. Remove layshaft bearing track from front cover.
2. Remove input shaft bearing track from front cover, remove and discard oil seal .

Centre plate - Dismantle

1. Remove bearing tracks and shims.
2. Check selector rail bore for wear.

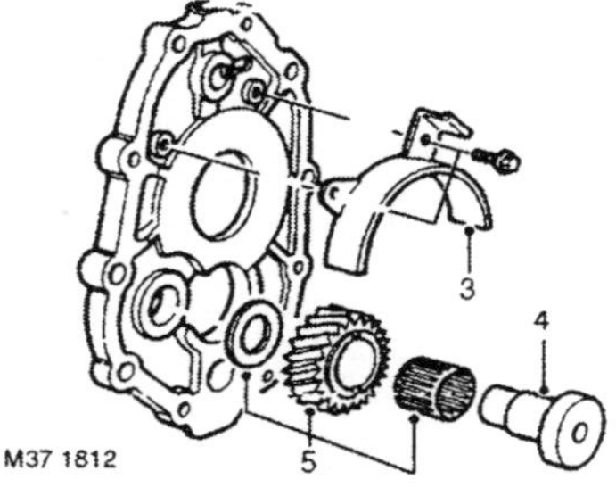

M37 1812

3. Remove 2 bolts securing splash shield.
4. Press out reverse idler gear shaft using suitable press and check shaft for wear.
5. Remove idler gear, needle bearing and spacer and check for wear and damage.
6. Check centre plate detent balls for wear and springs for distortion, replace as necessary.
7. Check that threads of detent plug are not damaged.

Extension housings - Overhaul

Types A and B gearbox

1. Examine for damage to threads and machined faces.

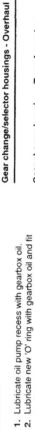

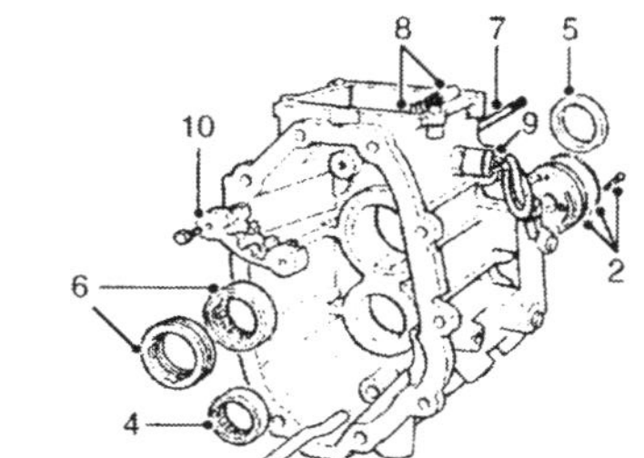

M37 1815

NOTE: Types A and B gearbox extension housing shown.

2. Remove 3 screws and remove oil pump, remove and discard 'O' ring.
3. Remove oil pick-up pipe and check for obstruction.
4. Drift out layshaft support bearing.
5. Remove and discard output shaft rear oil seal.
6. Drift out output shaft support bearing and oil pick up ring.
7. Unscrew reverse inhibitor shaft.
8. Remove reverse inhibitor cam and spring.
9. Remove reverse light switch and sealing washer, discard sealing washer.
10. Remove gate plate.
11. Check all components for wear and renew as necessary.

Type C gearbox - As for A and B Types and including the following:

12. Recover speedometer drive gear and spacer.
13. Check speedometer drive gear for wear and damage, renew if necessary.
14. Check speedometer pinion for wear and damage. Check that scrolling on shaft is clear; renew pinion and shaft if necessary.
15. Check slots in interlock spool for wear, renew interlock spool if necessary.

Type C and D gearboxes

CAUTION: The output shaft rear oil seal fitted to Type C and D extension housings is different to Types A and B. When levering out seal, take care not to damage the seal location surfaces.

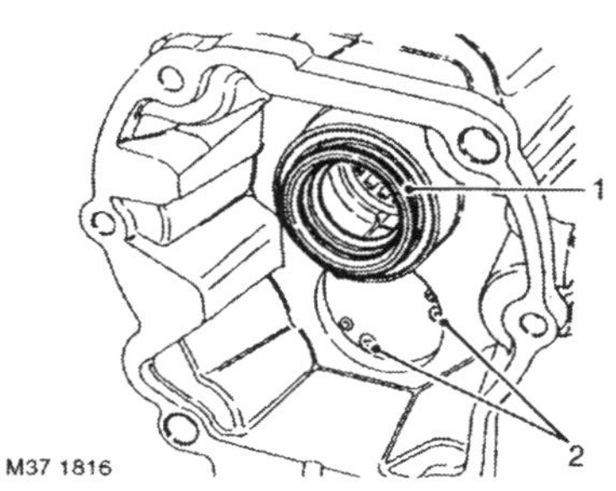

M37 1816

NOTE: Type D gearbox extension housing shown.

1. Remove and discard output shaft oil seal.
2. Remove 3 screws and remove oil pump, remove and discard 'O' ring.

Reassemble

1. Lubricate oil pump recess with gearbox oil.
2. Lubricate new 'O' ring with gearbox oil and fit to oil pump.
3. Locate oil pump into extension housing ensuring that word 'TOP' on pump is towards top of housing.
4. Align fixing screw holes and tap pump lightly at edges until it is fully in housing, fit screws and tighten to 6 Nm (4.5 lbf.ft).

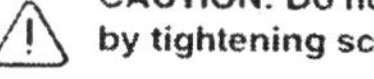
CAUTION: Do not pull pump into housing by tightening screws.

5. Fit new output shaft support bearing.

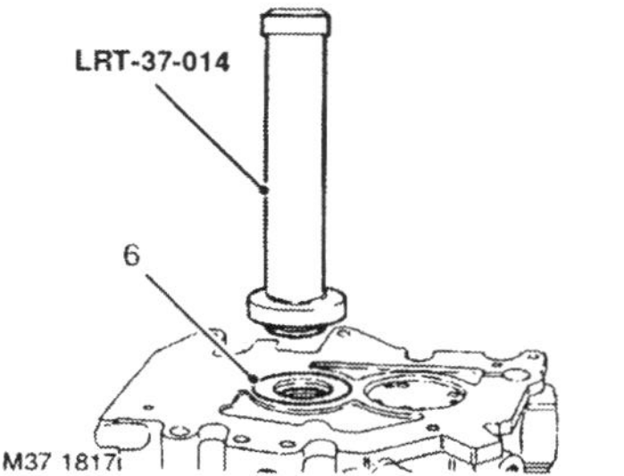

M37 1817

6. Lubricate a new output shaft rear oil seal with gearbox oil and fit seal using tool **LRT-37-014.**
7. Fit new layshaft support bearing.
8. Fit new oil pick-up ring ensuring that tag is aligned with centre of drain slot.
9. Examine gate plate and renew if worn or damaged.
10. Fit gate plate, fit bolts and tighten to 15 Nm (11 lbf.ft).
11. Fit reverse light switch and new sealing washer. Tighten to 24 Nm (17 lbf.ft).
12. Apply Loctite 290 to threads of reverse inhibitor shaft, position shaft and fit reverse inhibitor cam and spring.
13. Tighten reverse inhibitor shaft.
14. Refit oil pick-up pipe, bend uppermost.

Gear change/selector housings - Overhaul

Gear change housing - Type A gearbox

Dismantle

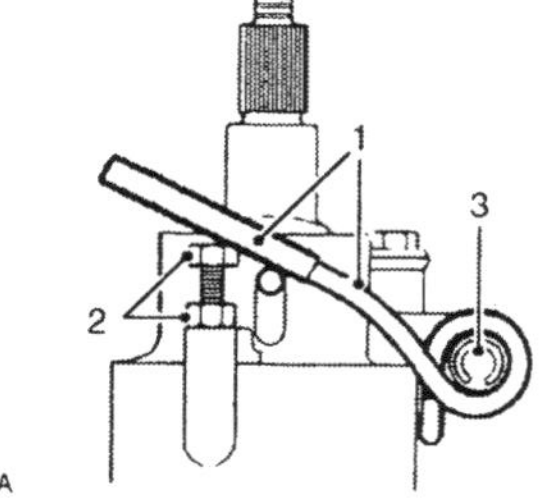

M37 1818A

1. Using a suitable piece of tubing, release both ends of bias spring from ball pins.
2. Slacken locknuts and remove bias spring adjusting screws.
3. Drift out roll pin, remove bias spring.

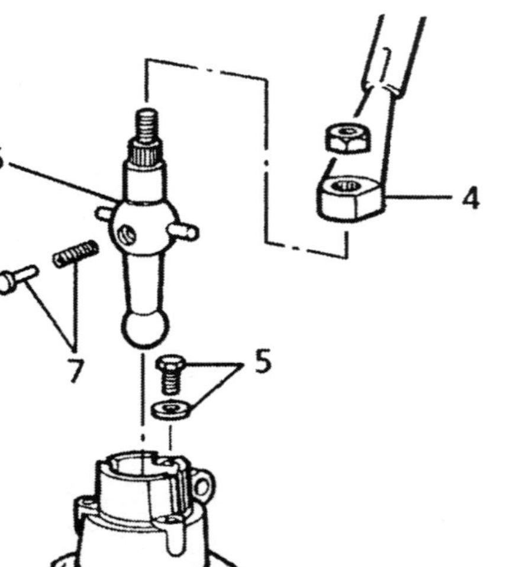

37M0535

4. Remove extension from lower gear lever.
5. Remove bolt and special washer securing lower gear lever.
6. Carefully withdraw lower gear lever from housing ensuring that spring loaded nylon pad is retained during removal.

WARNING: Personal injury may result if pad is not retained.

7. Release nylon pad, recover spring.
8. Clean all components.

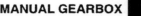

Inspection

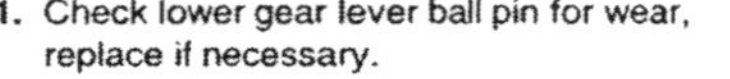

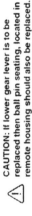

1. Check lower gear lever ball pin for wear, replace if necessary.

CAUTION: If lower gear lever is to be replaced then ball pin seating, located in remote housing should also be replaced.

2. Check nylon pad and spring for wear and damage, replace if necessary.
3. Check bias spring roll pin for damage, replace if necessary.

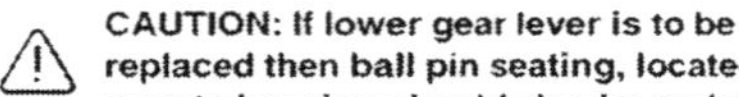

Reassemble

1. Smear ball pin with multi-purpose grease and fit spring and nylon pad.
2. Depress nylon pad against spring pressure, position lower gear lever in housing.

CAUTION: Ensure nylon pad is facing away from bias spring location.

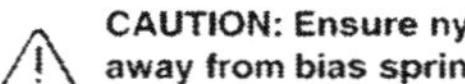

3. Fit lower gear lever retaining bolt and special washer, tighten bolt to 15 Nm (11 lbf.ft).
4. Fit extension to lower gear lever.
5. Position roll pin and bias spring to housing, fit roll pin.
6. Fit bias spring adjusting screws and locknuts.
7. Using a suitable piece of tubing locate both ends of bias spring over ball pins.

NOTE: Do not adjust bias spring at this stage.

Remote housing - Type A gearbox

Dismantle

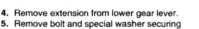

37M7072

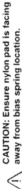

1. Remove setscrew securing trunnion to selector shaft, remove trunnion.
2. Remove and discard circlip securing ball pin seating to trunnion, remove seating.
3. Loosen locknut, remove 5th gear stop screw.

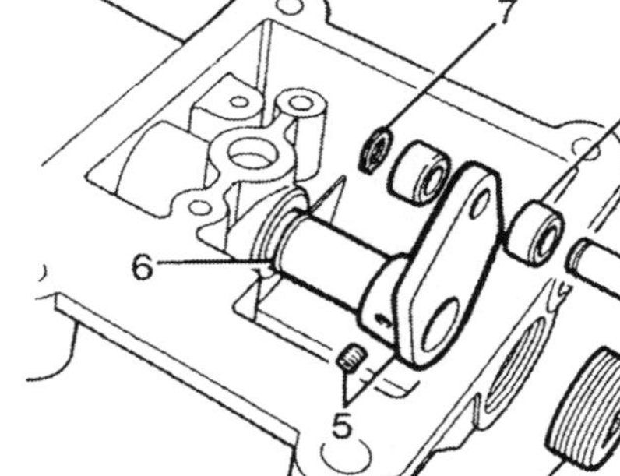

37M7073

4. Remove blanking plug from end of remote housing.
5. Remove setscrew securing quadrant to selector shaft, remove quadrant.

NOTE: Early gearboxes: Quadrant is secured by a roll pin.

6. Remove selector shaft from remote housing, remove and discard 'O' ring.
7. Remove and discard circlip retaining rollers and pin to quadrant.
8. Remove pin, recover rollers.
9. Clean all components.

Inspection

1. Check selector shaft and bore in remote housing for wear.
2. Check quadrant rollers and pin for wear.
3. Check ball pin seating for wear.
4. Replace worn components as necessary.

Reassemble

1. Lubricate selector shaft and new 'O' ring with gearbox oil.
2. Fit 'O' ring to selector shaft.
3. Fit shaft to remote housing.
4. Position rollers to quadrant, fit pin and secure with new circlip.

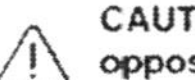

CAUTION: Ensure that head of pin is on opposite side of quadrant to selector shaft boss.

5. Fit quadrant to selector shaft.
6. Apply Loctite 290 to threads of setscrew, fit setscrew and tighten to 25 Nm (18 lbf.ft).

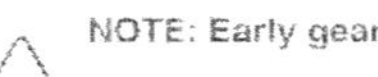

NOTE: Early gearboxes: Fit new roll pin.

7. Apply Loctite 290 to threads of blanking plug, fit plug and tighten to 30 Nm (22 lbf.ft).
8. Smear ball pin seating with multi-purpose grease.
9. Position ball pin seating in trunnion, secure with a new circlip.
10. Position trunnion on selector shaft.
11. Apply Loctite 290 to threads of setscrew, fit setscrew and tighten to 25 Nm (18 lbf.ft).
12. Fit 5th gear stop screw, fit but do not tighten locknut.

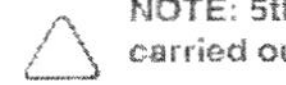

NOTE: 5th gear stop screw adjustment is carried out during gearbox reassembly.

Gear change housing - Type B gearbox

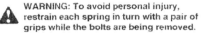

Dismantle

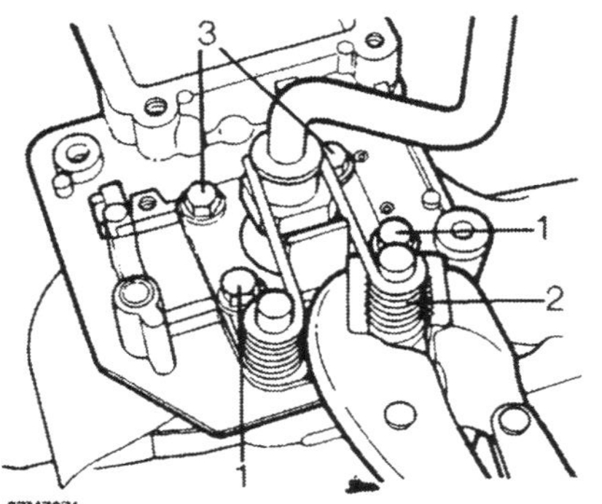

1. Remove bolts retaining bias springs.

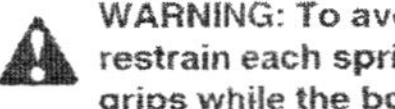

WARNING: To avoid personal injury, restrain each spring in turn with a pair of grips while the bolts are being removed.

2. Remove the two bias springs.
3. Remove 2 bolts securing bias spring adjustment plate.

M37 1820

4. Lift lower lever assembly out of gear change housing.
5. Remove and discard Railko bush.
6. Remove and discard oil seal from housing.
7. Clean all components.

Inspection

1. Check ball cross pin slots in gear change housing for wear.
2. Check ball and pins for wear.
3. Check bias springs for distortion.
4. Replace worn components as necessary.

Reassemble

1. Apply multi-purpose grease to ball and cross pins.
2. Apply multi-purpose grease to new Railko bush and fit to gear change housing.

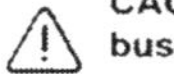

CAUTION: Ensure that the slots in each bush are aligned with slots in housing.

3. Lubricate a new oil seal with gearbox oil.
4. Fit oil seal, lip side towards housing, using a suitable mandrel.
5. Position gear lever to gear change housing ensuring ball cross pins are located in slots in housing and Railko bush.
6. Position bias spring adjustment plate to gear change housing.
7. Apply Loctite 290 to threads of 2 short bias spring adjustment plate bolts.
8. Fit bolts to secure front of bias adjustment plate and tighten to 25 Nm (18 lbf.ft).
9. Position bias spring to pillar ensuring longest end of spring is against gear lever.
10. Apply Loctite 290 to threads of 2 long bias adjustment plate bolts.
11. Restrain bias spring using a suitable pair of grips, ensure short end of bias spring is positioned on outside edge of bolt hole.

WARNING: Personal injury may result if bias spring is not retained.

12. Fit bolt and washer ensuring end of bias spring is restrained beneath washer; tighten bolt to 25 Nm (18 lbf.ft).
13. Repeat above procedures for remaining bias spring.

Remote gear change - Type C gearbox

Dismantle

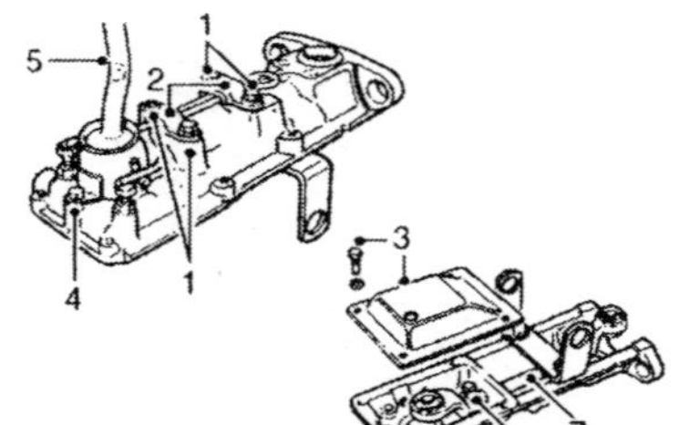

M37 1787

1. Remove 2 bolts and 2 countersunk screws securing bias spring bridge plates.
2. Remove bridge plates, bridge plate liners and bias spring.
3. Remove 4 bolts and washers securing bottom cover plate, remove plate.
4. Remove bolt securing gear lever cap, remove cap.
5. Remove gear lever, recover anti-rattle spring and plunger.
6. Remove pinch bolt securing selector rod yoke, remove yoke.
7. Withdraw selector rod from remote housing.
8. Clean all components.

Inspection

1. Check selector rod bushes in remote housing for wear.

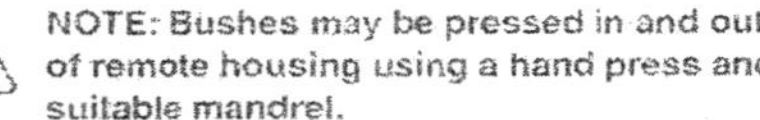

NOTE: Bushes may be pressed in and out of remote housing using a hand press and suitable mandrel.

2. Check selector rod for wear, replace if necessary.
3. Check anti-rattle spring for distortion and plunger for wear; replace if necessary.
4. Check gear lever ball pin, cross pins, bushes and selector rod yoke balls for wear and replace if necessary. If yoke balls are worn, remove and discard circlip, press ball and seating out of yoke.
5. Lubricate replacement ball and seating with multi-purpose grease and press into yoke; secure using new circlip.
6. Check bias spring for distortion, replace if necessary.
7. Check condition of mounting rubbers, replace as a set if necessary.

Reassemble

1. Lubricate selector rod and bushes with multi - purpose grease, insert rod in remote housing.
2. Lubricate gear lever ball pin and selector rod yoke balls with multi-purpose grease.
3. Fit yoke to selector rod, fit pinch bolt and tighten to 25 Nm (18 lbf.ft).
4. Assemble anti-rattle spring and plunger to gear lever.
5. Fit gear lever ensuring ball pin is located in yoke and anti-rattle spring and plunger are not displaced.
6. Fit gear lever cap, fit bolt and tighten to 15 Nm (11 lbf.ft).

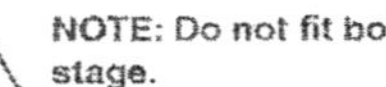

NOTE: Do not fit bottom cover plate at this stage.

7. Loosen bias spring adjustment bolt locknuts.
8. Fit bias spring, bridge plate liners and bridge plates.
9. Fit bolts and countersunk screws and tighten to 25 Nm (18 lbf.ft).

NOTE: Final adjustment of bias spring is carried out after remote gear change is fitted to gearbox.

Remote gear change - Type D gearbox

37M7126

NOTE: With the exception of the reverse light switch, the remote gear change fitted to Type D gearboxes is not a repairable item. It must be replaced if components are found to be worn.

Transfer box selector housing - Type A gearbox - Overhaul

Dismantle

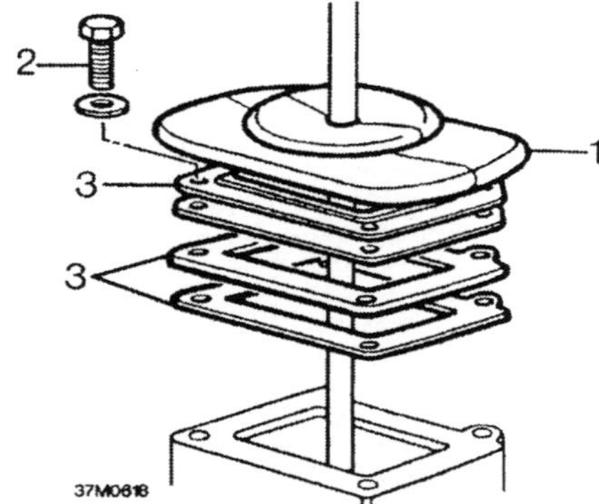

37M0618

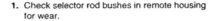

1. Slide gaiter off gear lever.
2. Remove 4 bolts securing gaiter support plate and gate plate.
3. Remove gaiter support plate and gate plate, discard gaskets.

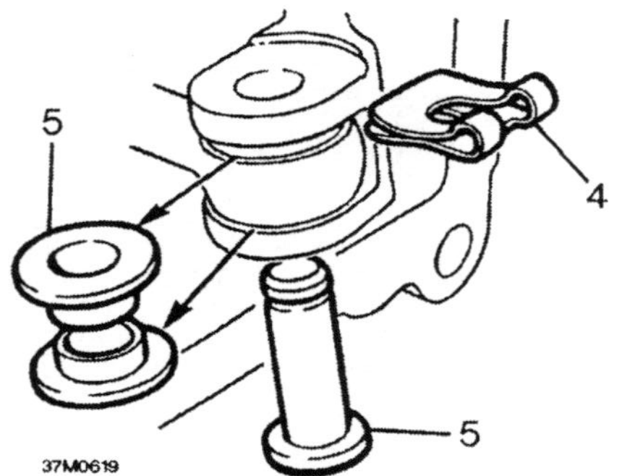

37M0619

4. Remove and discard spring clip retaining selector fork clevis pin.
5. Remove clevis pin from selector fork, remove and discard 2 bushes.

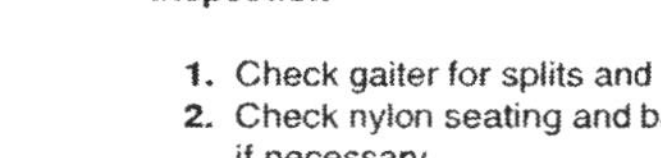

37M0620

6. Remove and discard circlip retaining nylon ball seating.
7. Remove gear lever, recover nylon seating and ball.

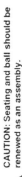

37M0544

8. Remove 2 countersunk head screws securing end cover to housing.
9. Remove end cover, remove and discard 2 'O' rings.
10. Withdraw cross shaft.
11. Remove selector fork, remove and discard 2 'O' rings.
12. Clean all components.

Inspection

1. Check gaiter for splits and damage.
2. Check nylon seating and ball for wear, replace if necessary.

CAUTION: Seating and ball should be renewed as an assembly.

3. Check selector fork and clevis pin for wear.
4. Check cross shaft and end cover for wear.
5. Replace components as necessary.

Reassemble

1. Lubricate new 'O' rings with gearbox oil and fit to selector fork, position fork in housing.
2. Lubricate cross shaft with multi-purpose grease and locate longest end of shaft in selector fork.
3. Lubricate new 'O' rings with gearbox oil and fit to end cover.
4. Position end cover on cross shaft, fit and tighten countersunk screws.
5. Assemble ball and nylon seating to gear lever ensuring that groove in seating is towards cross shaft.
6. Lubricate ball and nylon seating with multi - purpose grease and locate in cross shaft; retain with a new circlip.
7. Position new bushes to gear lever, locate in selector fork and fit clevis pin.
8. Fit new spring clip to retain clevis pin.
9. Position gate plate and gaiter support plate to housing, use new gaskets.
10. Fit retaining bolts and tighten to 15 Nm (11 lbf.ft).
11. Fit gaiter.

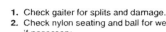

Synchromesh assemblies - Overhaul

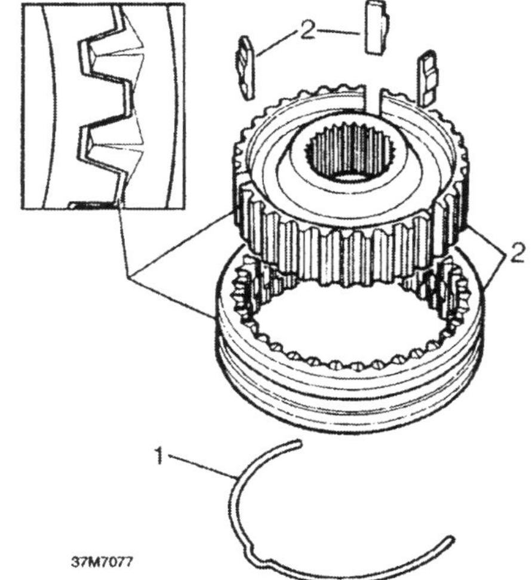

37M7077

1. Remove spring clips from both sides of assembly.
2. Remove slippers and separate the hub from the sleeve.
3. Examine all parts for damage and wear, check spring clips for tension.
4. Check no excessive radial movement exists between inner members and output shaft splines.
5. Examine inner and outer splines for wear.

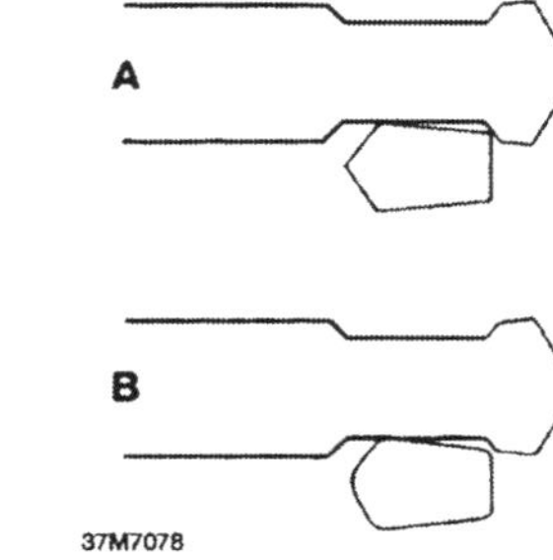

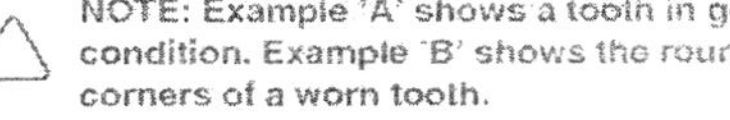

37M7078

6. Examine the dog teeth for wear and damage.

NOTE: Example 'A' shows a tooth in good condition. Example 'B' shows the rounded corners of a worn tooth.

7. Replace unit if excessively worn.

Reassemble

8. Refit inner hub to sleeve.

NOTE: Hubs and sleeves have a master spline combination and can only be assembled one way. The sleeves are further identified with a series of half moon notches which clearly identify which side of the assembly faces which gear. Ensure the slot in the hub aligns with the centre notch on the sleeve.

Assy	Hub	Sleeve	Against Gear
1st/2nd	-	1 Notch	1st
	2 gear side	-	2nd
3rd/4th	-	3 Notches	3rd
	-	-	4th
5th/Rev	-	5 Notches	5th

9. Fit slippers and secure with a spring each side of the synchromesh assembly ensuring the step on each spring locates on a different slipper.

NOTE: 5th and reverse synchromesh hubs have different springs which are coloured yellow.

Checking baulk ring clearances

M37 1821

Check clearance of all baulk rings and gears by pressing the baulk rings against the gear and measuring the gap.
Minimum clearance - 0.5 mm (0.020 in).

Input shaft - Overhaul

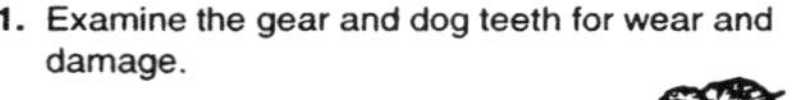

1. Examine the gear and dog teeth for wear and damage.

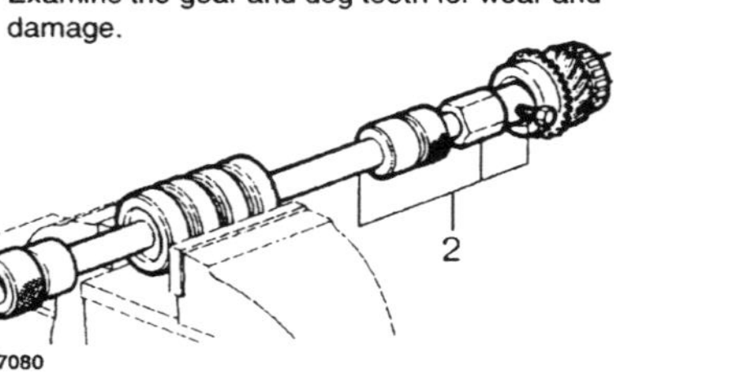

37M7080

2. Using **LRT-99-004** and **LRT-37-004** remove pilot bearing track.

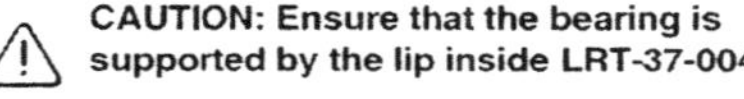

CAUTION: Ensure that the bearing is supported by the lip inside LRT-37-004.

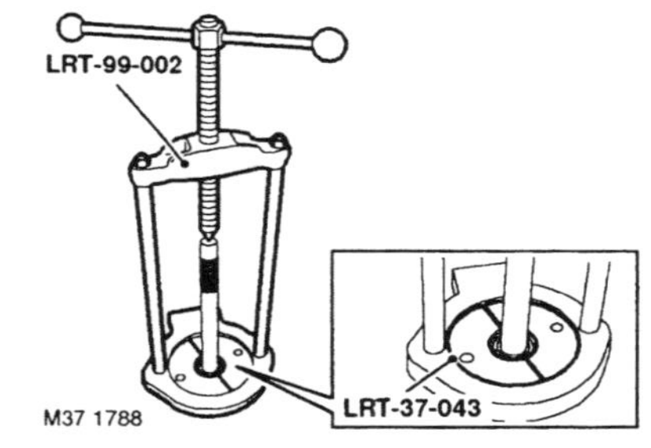

M37 1788

3. Using **LRT-37-043** and **LRT-99-002** remove taper roller bearing.

LRT-99-002

4

LRT-37-043
LRT-37-043/2

M37 1789

4. Using **LRT-99-002, LRT-37-043** and **LRT-37-043/2**, fit a new taper roller bearing.

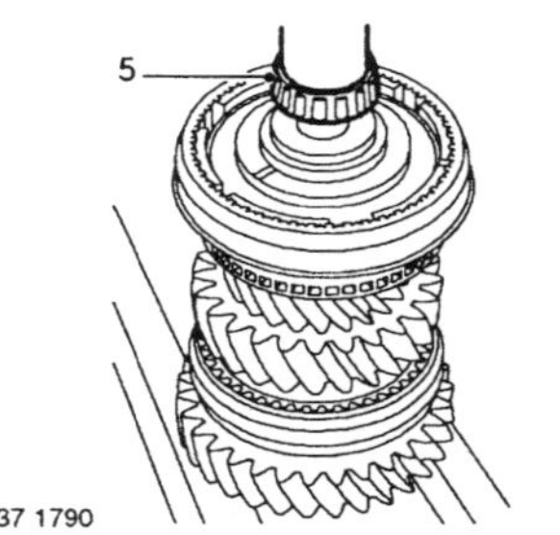

M37 1790

5. Support the shaft under **LRT-99-002** and using a suitable mandrel, fit a new taper roller bearing.

Output shaft - Inspection

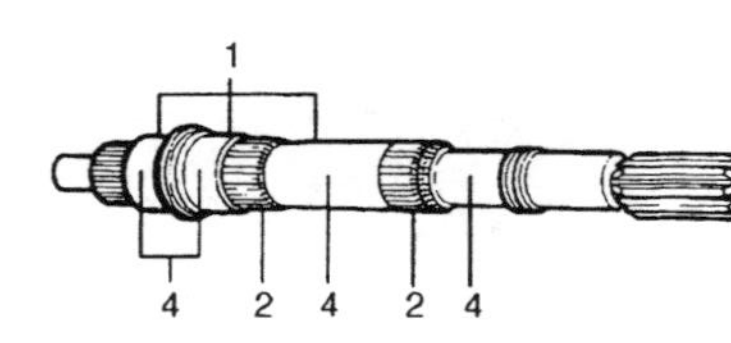

M37 1791

1. Examine bearing journals for wear and scores.
2. Examine splines for wear and damage.
3. Use an air line to check that the main oil feed from pump and feed to spigot bearing are clear.
4. Check oil feed holes to roller bearing are clear.

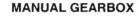

Layshaft - Overhaul

1. Using **LRT-99-002, LRT-37-022** and **LRT-37-044**, remove layshaft bearings.
2. Examine layshaft for wear and damage.

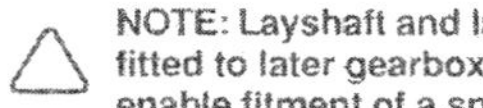

NOTE: Layshaft and layshaft 5th gear fitted to later gearboxes are machined to enable fitment of a split washer to prevent gear movement on shaft. The modified layshaft, gear and split washer may be fitted to early gearboxes as an assembly.

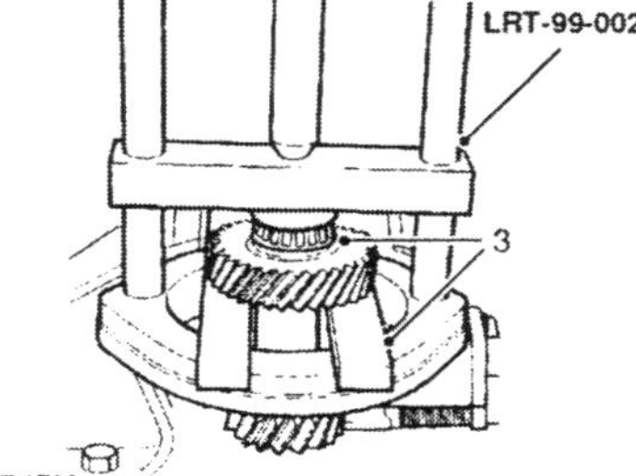

M37 1792

3. Using press **LRT-99-002** and a suitable mandrel, positioned on bearing inner race, fit new taper roller bearings.

Output shaft - Reassemble

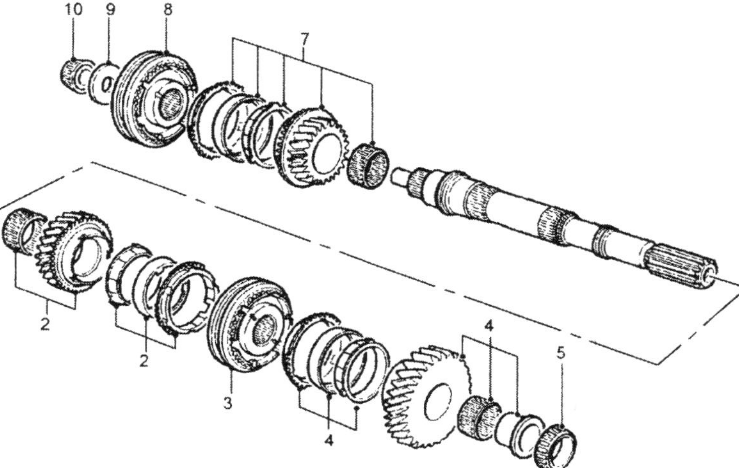

M37 1793

1. Clamp output shaft in protected vice jaws, output end upwards.
2. Fit 2nd gear needle roller bearing, 2nd gear and synchromesh baulk rings on to output shaft.

NOTE: Rotate each baulk ring to ensure they locate onto each other.

3. Assemble the 1st and 2nd synchromesh selector hub on to output shaft splines, noting the 2nd gear side marking. Ensure that baulk ring has located correctly inside hub.

NOTE: Rotate the ring slightly as the hub is lowered.

4. Fit 1st gear synchromesh baulk rings, needle roller bearing, 1st gear and bush on to output shaft ensuring baulk rings locate correctly inside selector hub.
5. Using **LRT-99-002**, and a suitable mandrel positioned on bearing inner race, press on output shaft taper roller bearing taking care not to disturb the position of the synchromesh baulk rings and gears.
6. Check 1st and 2nd gear end-float.

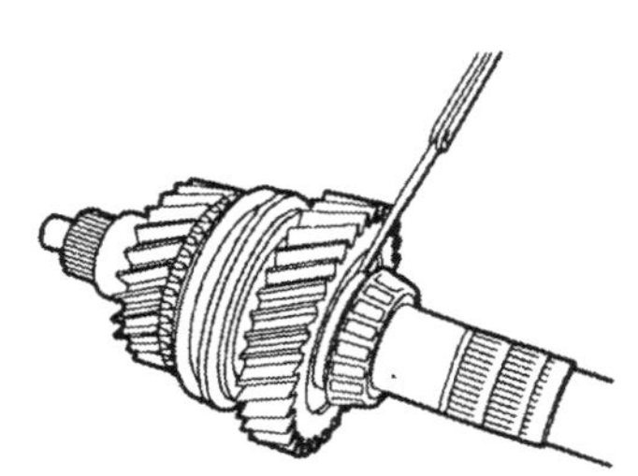

M37 1525

Checking 1st gear end-float

New: 0.05 - 0.20 mm (0.002 - 0.008 in)
Service limit: 0.327 mm (0.012 in)

M37 1526

Checking 2nd gear end-float

New: 0.04 - 0.21 mm (0.0016 - 0.008 in)
Service limit: 0.337 mm (0.013 in)

7. Invert output shaft in vice and fit 3rd gear needle roller bearing, third gear and synchromesh baulk rings.
8. Assemble 3rd/4th gear synchromesh selector hub, noting 3rd speed side markings, on to output shaft splines taking care to locate the baulk rings into recesses in the selector hub.
9. Fit spacer.

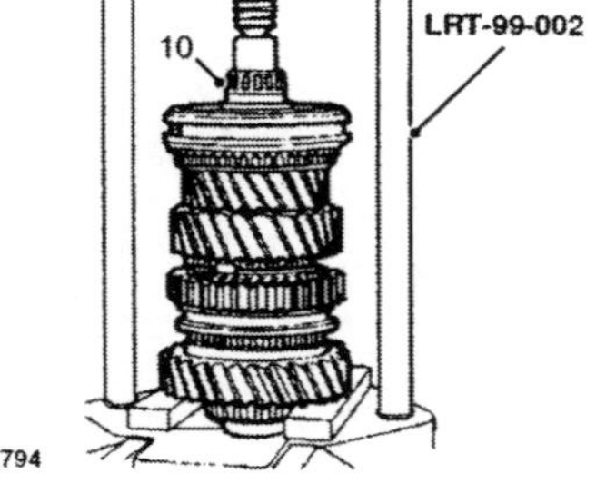

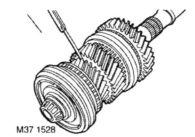

M37 1794

10. Using **LRT-99-002** and a suitable mandrel positioned on bearing inner race, press on new pilot bearing.

Check end float of 3rd gear.

M37 1528

Checking 3rd gear end-float

New: 0.11 - 0.21 mm (0.004 - 0.008 in)
Service limit: 0.337 mm (0.013 in)

Reverse idler gear and centre plate - Reassemble

1. Examine components for wear and damage.

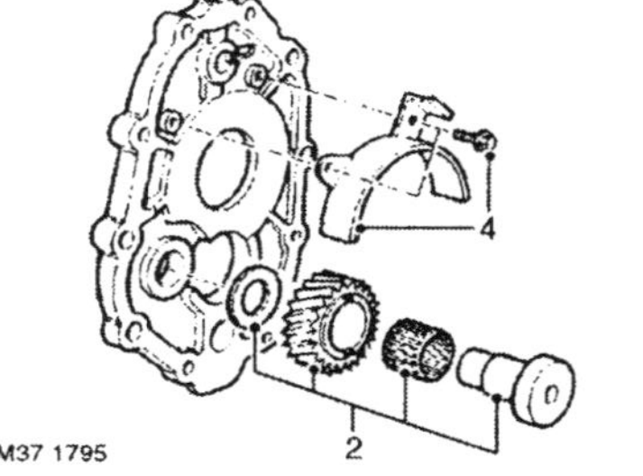

M37 1795

2. Assemble reverse idler gear needle roller bearing, idler gear, spacer and shaft and using suitable tool, press into centre plate.
3. Using feeler gauges, check clearance between reverse idler gear and shaft flange, fit a thicker or thinner spacer if necessary in order to achieve correct clearance.
New clearance:
0.04 - 0.38 mm (0.0016in - 0.015 in)
Service limit:
0.38 mm (0.015 in)

4. Fit splash shield, fit bolts and tighten to 8 Nm (6 lbf.ft).

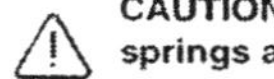

CAUTION: Do not fit detent balls or springs at this stage.

Selectors - Inspection

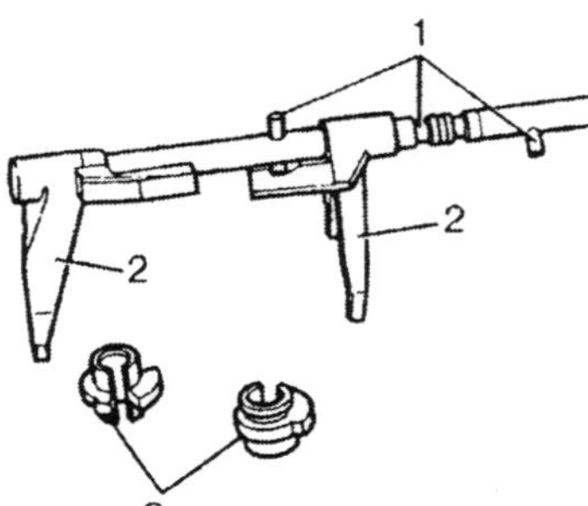

37M7088

1. Examine selector rail and pins for wear and damage.
2. Examine selector forks for wear and damage.

NOTE: The selector rail and fork is only supplied as a complete assembly.

3. Examine interlock spools for wear and damage.

Selectors - Reassemble

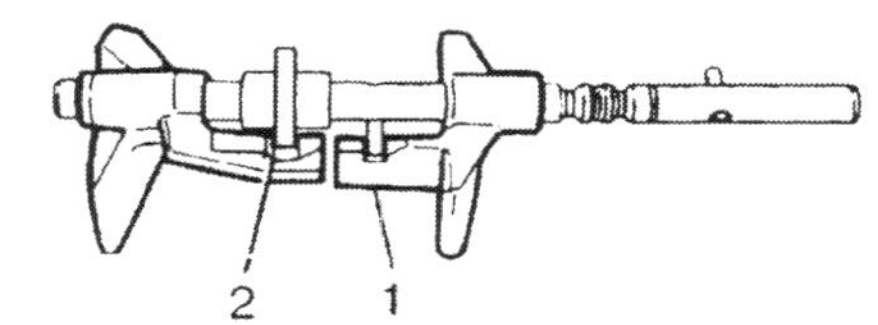

37M7091

1. Rest 1st/2nd fork and shaft assembly on bench and locate pin in jaw of fork.
2. Fit interlock spool and 3rd/4th fork and engage spool in jaw of fork.

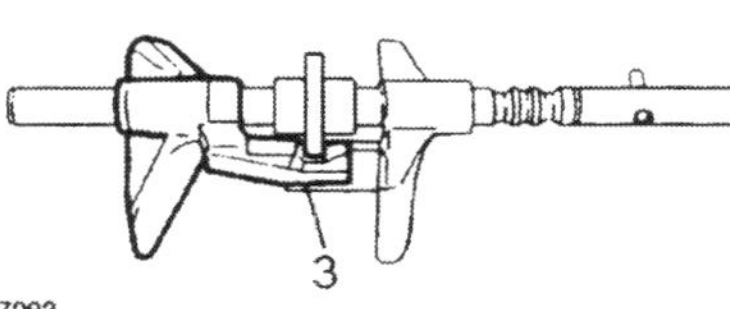

37M7092

3. Slide spool and fork towards 1st/2nd selector until slot in spool locates over pin keeping the spool engaged in 3rd/4th fork jaw.

GEARBOX REASSEMBLE

Output shaft and layshaft end float

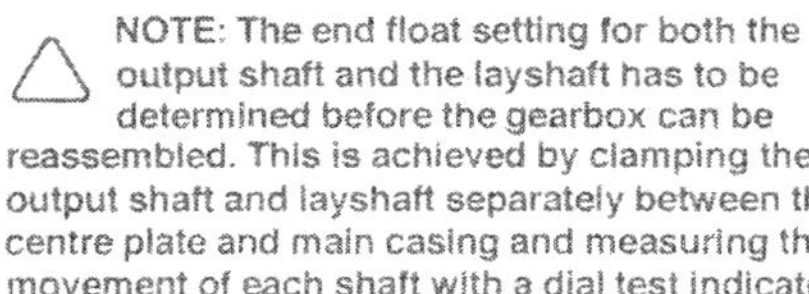

NOTE: The end float setting for both the output shaft and the layshaft has to be determined before the gearbox can be reassembled. This is achieved by clamping the output shaft and layshaft separately between the centre plate and main casing and measuring the movement of each shaft with a dial test indicator.

Shimming

1. Fit new bearing tracks to front cover.

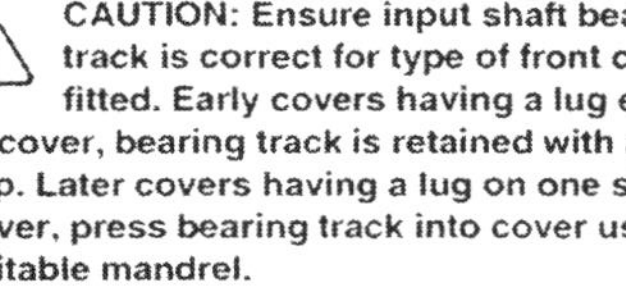

CAUTION: Ensure input shaft bearing track is correct for type of front cover fitted. Early covers having a lug each side of cover, bearing track is retained with a spring clip. Later covers having a lug on one side of cover, press bearing track into cover using a suitable mandrel.

2. Fit front cover to gearcase without oil seal.
3. Clamp gearcase in vice with front cover downwards.
4. Fit input shaft.

CAUTION: Do not fit 4th gear baulk ring.

5. Fit output shaft assembly to input shaft.
6. Fit output shaft bearing shim and track to centre plate.

8
9
7

M37 1796

7. Fit centre plate and bolt down using 8 off 8 x 35 mm slave bolts.

CAUTION: Do not fit detent ball or spring at this stage.

8. Fit large ball bearing to rear of output shaft.
9. Mount dial test indicator.
10. Rotate output shaft to settle bearings.
11. Lift output shaft and note DTI reading.

The end float setting for the output shaft and layshaft is:-
Early gearboxes without suffix K added to serial number:
New: 0.01 - 0.06 mm (0.0004 - 0.0024 in)
Service limit: 0.06 mm (0.0024 in)

Later gearboxes with suffix K added to serial number:
New: 0.00 - 0.05 mm (0.00 - 0.002 in)
Service limit: 0.05 mm (0.002 in)

Shims to make up the required clearances are placed under the respective bearing tracks in the centre plate.

12. Dismantle and substitute shims if reading incorrect.
13. Remove output shaft assembly and repeat procedure for layshaft.
14. Remove centre plate, layshaft and output shaft.
15. Remove front cover.
16. Remove input shaft bearing track from front cover, retain track with cover.

Assembling output shaft and layshaft to centre plate

1. Secure centre plate to suitable workstand.
2. Fit selected shims and bearing tracks.
3. Fit lower detent ball and spring, use a dummy bar to temporarily hold the ball in place.

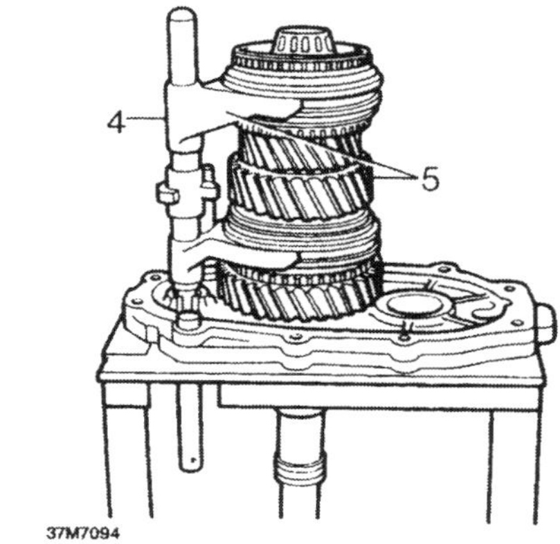

37M7094

4. Check both synchromesh units are in neutral and fit selector shaft assembly to output shaft.
5. Fit output shaft and selectors as complete unit to centre plate aligning pin with slot in plate.

CAUTION: Take care that as dummy shaft is removed, detent spring and ball are not displaced.

6. Fit 4th gear synchromesh baulk ring.

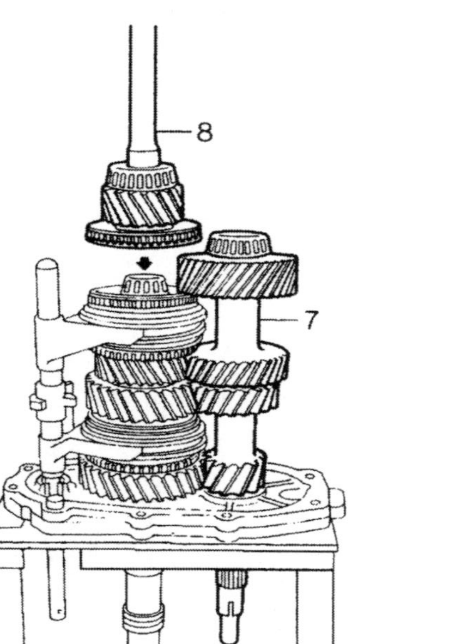

37M7095

7. Fit layshaft whilst lifting output shaft to clear layshaft rear bearing.
8. Lubricate pilot bearing with gearbox oil and fit input shaft.

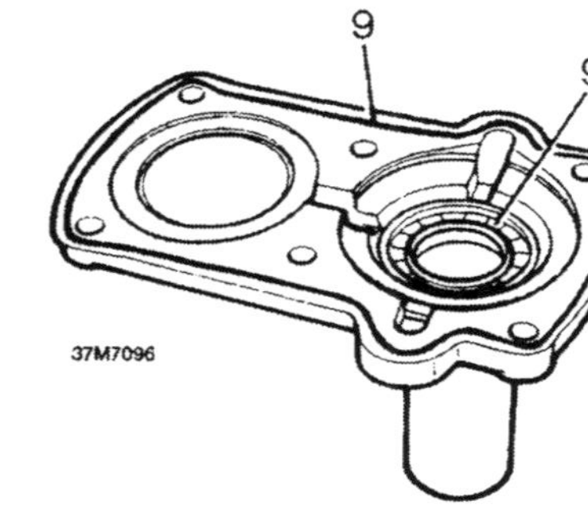

37M7096

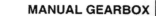

NOTE: Early type front cover illustrated.

9. Fit new oil seal to front cover. Ensure seal is fitted down to shoulder. Apply sealant, Part No. STC 3254 to front cover as shown.

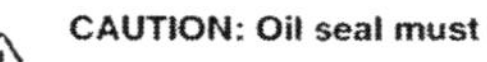

CAUTION: Oil seal must be fitted dry.

10. Fit input and layshaft bearing tracks in front cover.
11. Apply Loctite 290 to threads of front cover bolts, fit bolts and tighten by diagonal selection to 25 Nm (18 lbf.ft).
12. Apply sealant, Part No. STC 3254 to centre plate and fit main casing to centre plate.
13. Bolt casing and centre plate together using 2 off 8 x 35 slave bolts.
14. Lubricate a new 'O' ring with gearbox oil and fit to interlock spool retainer.
15. Fit interlock spool retainer, fit bolt and tighten to 8 Nm (6 lbf.ft).
16. Remove casing from stand and clamp in vice.

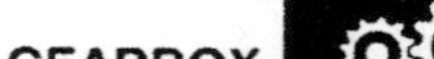

Reverse and 5th gear - Reassemble

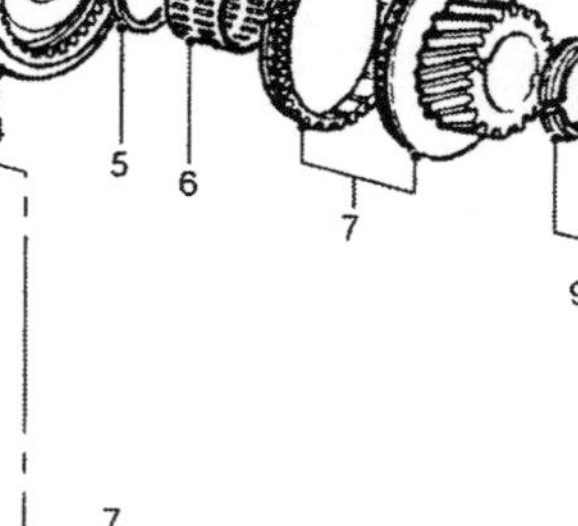

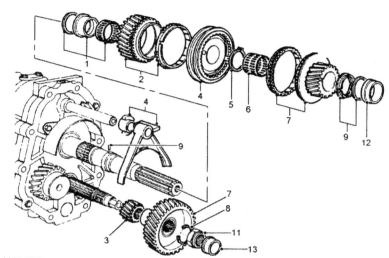

M37 1797

1. Fit output shaft reverse gear selective washer, bush and needle bearing.
2. Fit output shaft reverse gear and synchromesh baulk ring.
3. Fit layshaft reverse gear.
4. Assemble selector spool, selector fork and reverse/5th gear synchromesh hub. Fit as one assembly to output shaft splines and selector shaft.

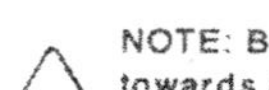

CAUTION: Ensure synchromesh baulk ring locates inside hub.

5. Fit new circlip.

NOTE: The fit of the circlip is controlled by the selective washer behind the reverse gear. Adjust to 0.005 - 0.055 mm (0.0002 - 0.002 in).

6. Fit 5th gear split needle bearing.
7. Fit 5th gear and 5th gear synchromesh baulk ring to output shaft, fit layshaft 5th gear.
8. *Later gearboxes:* Fit split washer to retain layshaft 5th gear.

NOTE: Bevelled side of washer must face towards gear.

9. Fit new output shaft thrust collar roll pin. Locate 5th gear thrust segments and retaining ring.

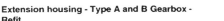

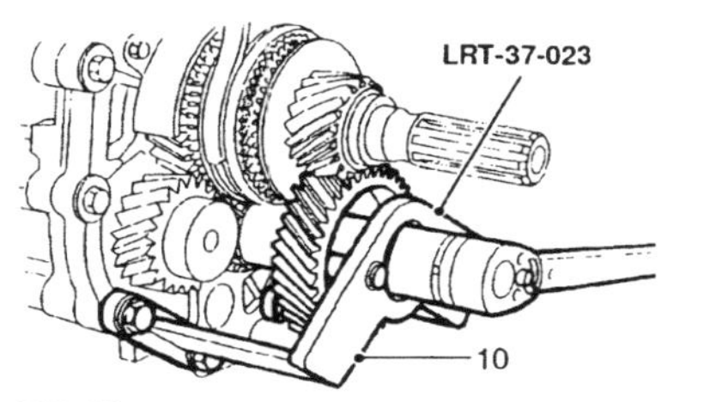

M37 1798

10. Using **LRT-37-023** to hold layshaft 5th gear, fit a new layshaft stake nut and tighten to 220 Nm (162 lbf.ft).
11. Stake layshaft 5th gear nut.

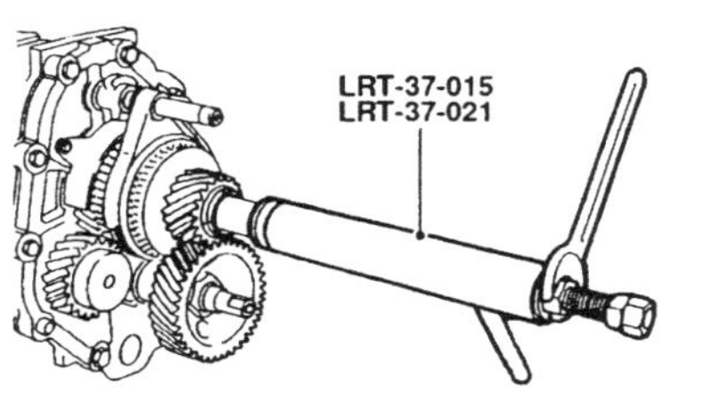

M37 1822

12. Using **LRT-37-015** and **LRT-37-021** press output shaft rear support bearing track to collar on output shaft.
13. Apply small amount of heat and fit layshaft rear support bearing.

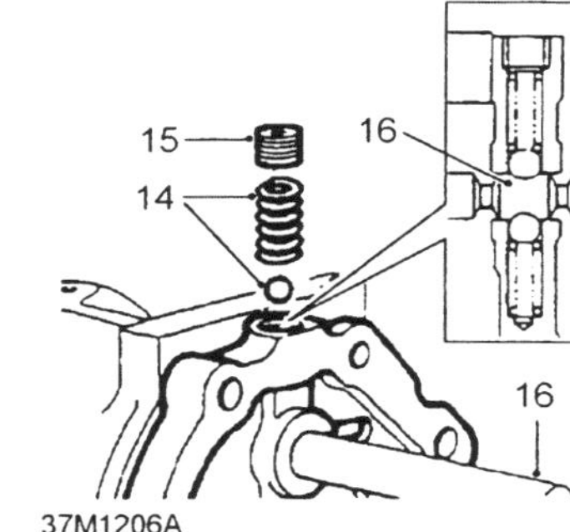

37M1206A

14. Fit centre plate detent ball and spring.
15. Apply Loctite 290 to threads of detent plug, fit plug and tighten to 25 Nm (18 lbf.ft).
16. Move selector shaft and check that detent balls can be felt to engage in detent.

Extension housing - Type A and B Gearbox - Refit

1. Remove slave bolts from centre plate.

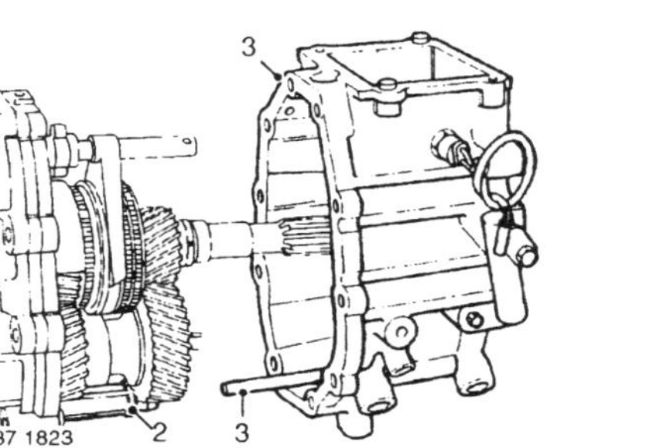

M37 1823

2. Fit oil filter.
3. Apply sealant, Part No. STC 3254 to mating surfaces and fit extension housing ensuring oil pipe locates in filter and drive locates in oil pump.

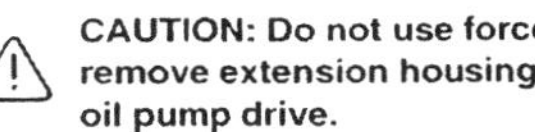

CAUTION: Do not use force, if necessary, remove extension housing and re - align oil pump drive.

4. Apply Loctite 290 to threads of extension housing securing bolts, fit bolts and tighten by diagonal selection to 25 Nm (18 lbf.ft).

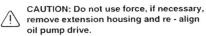

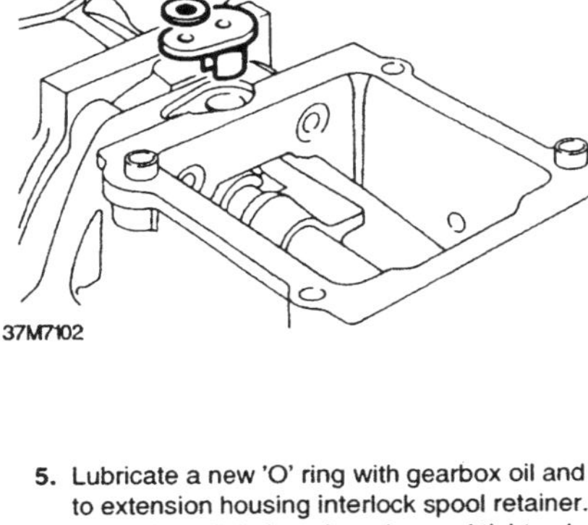

37M7102

5. Lubricate a new 'O' ring with gearbox oil and fit to extension housing interlock spool retainer. Fit retainer, fit bolt and washer and tighten bolt to 8 Nm (6 lbf.ft).

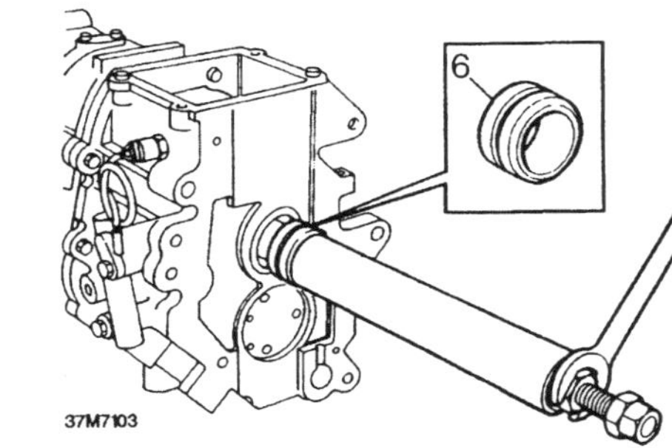

37M7103

6. Using **LRT-37-015** and **LRT-37-021** press on output shaft oil seal collar, narrow portion of collar leading.

Extension housing - Type C gearbox - Refit

1. Lubricate a new selector shaft oil seal with gearbox oil and fit seal.
2. Remove slave bolts from centre plate.
3. Fit oil filter.
4. Fit spacer
5. Position speedometer drive gear on output shaft splines.
6. Using a round nosed punch, carefully tap speedometer drive gear into position.
7. Apply sealant, Part No. STC 3254 to mating surfaces.
8. Fit extension housing ensuring oil pipe locates in filter and drive locates in oil pump.

CAUTION: Do not use force, if necessary, remove extension housing and re-align oil pump drive.

9. Apply Loctite 290 to threads of extension housing bolts, fit bolts and tighten by diagonal selection to 25 Nm (18 lbf.ft).
10. Lubricate a new 'O' ring with gearbox oil and fit to speedometer pinion housing.
11. Lubricate speedometer pinion with silicone grease.
12. Fit speedometer pinion housing ensuring teeth of pinion mesh with those of driven gear.
13. Lubricate a new 'O' ring with gearbox oil and fit to extension housing interlock spool retainer. Fit retainer, fit bolt and washer and tighten bolt to 8 Nm (6 lbf.ft).
14. Fit selector shaft pin to selector shaft, fit and tighten a new self-locking nut.

Extension housing - Type D gearbox - Refit

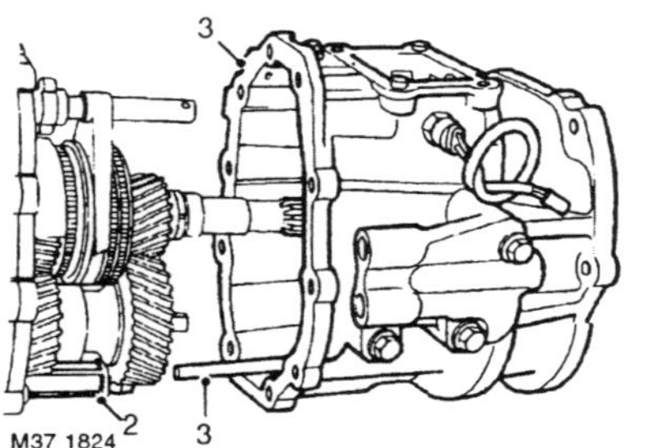

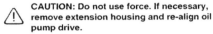

1. Remove slave bolts from centre plate.
2. Fit oil filter.
3. Apply sealant, Part No. STC 3254 to mating surfaces and fit extension housing. Ensure that oil pipe locates in filter and that drive locates in oil pump.

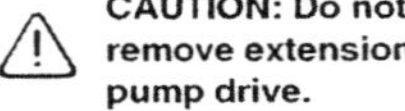

CAUTION: Do not use force. If necessary, remove extension housing and re-align oil pump drive.

4. Apply Loctite 290 to threads of extension housing retaining bolts, fit bolts and tighten by diagonal selection to 25 Nm (18 lbf.ft).

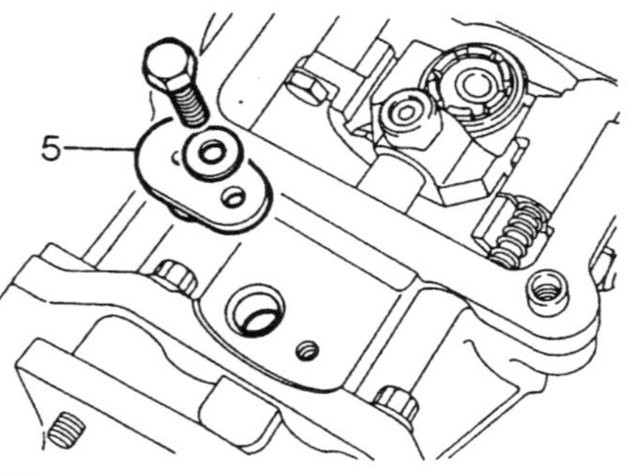

5. Lubricate a new 'O' ring with gearbox oil and fit to interlock spool retainer. Fit retainer, fit bolt and washer and tighten bolt to 8 Nm (6 lbf.ft).

Selector quadrant - Type A gearbox - Refit

37M7104

1. Position selector quadrant to selector shaft.
2. Apply Loctite 290 to threads of a new setscrew. Fit and tighten screw to 25 Nm (18 lbf.ft).

CAUTION: Ensure end of setscrew locates in hole in selector shaft.

3. Move selector shaft to neutral position.

Gear change lever yoke - Type B gearbox - Refit

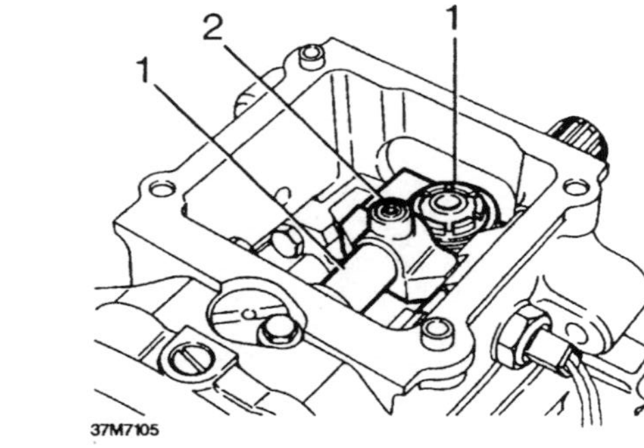

1. Position gear change lever yoke on selector shaft with ball facing towards output shaft.
2. Apply Loctite 290 to threads of a new setscrew, fit and tighten screw to 25 Nm (18 lbf.ft).

CAUTION: Ensure end of setscrew locates in hole in selector shaft.

Gear change lever yoke - Type D gearbox - Refit

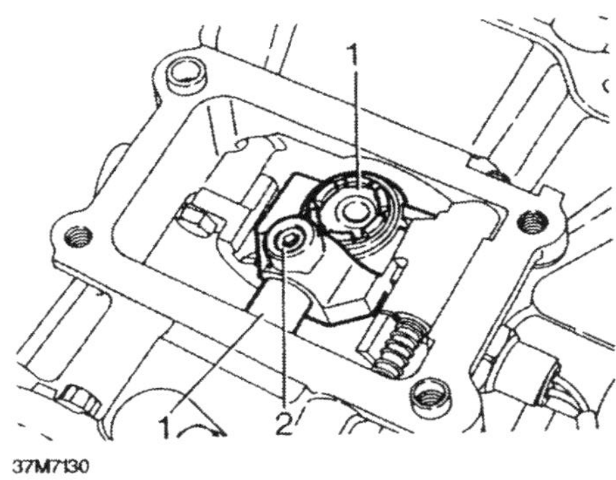

37M7130

1. Position gear lever yoke on selector shaft with ball facing towards output shaft.
2. Apply Loctite 290 to threads of a new setscrew. Fit and tighten screw to 25 Nm (18 lbf.ft).

CAUTION: Ensure end of setscrew locates in hole in selector shaft.

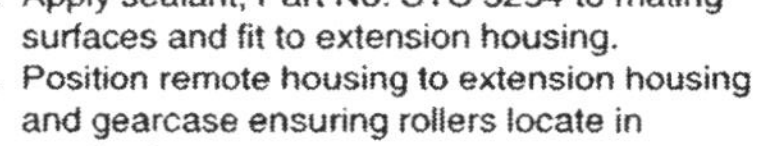

Remote housing - Type A gearbox - Refit

1. Apply sealant, Part No. STC 3254 to mating surfaces and fit to extension housing.
2. Position remote housing to extension housing and gearcase ensuring rollers locate in quadrant.

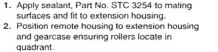

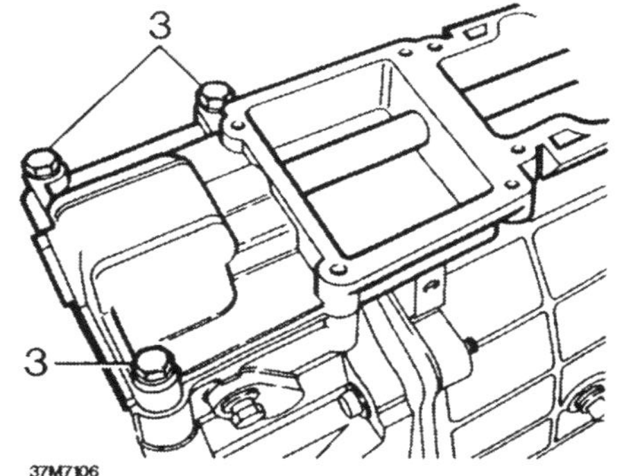

37M7106

3. Fit and lightly tighten 3 bolts in positions shown.

NOTE: Bolts are tightened when gear change housing is fitted.

Transfer box selector housing - Type A gearbox - Refit

1. Smear a new gasket with grease and fit to remote housing.
2. Position transfer box selector housing to remote housing.
3. Fit and lightly tighten 4 bolts.

NOTE: Bolts are tightened when gear change housing is fitted.

Gear change housing - Type A gearbox - Refit

1. Smear a new gasket with grease and fit to remote housing.
2. Position gear change housing to remote housing ensuring gear lever ball is correctly located.
3. Fit and lightly tighten 4 bolts.
4. Tighten remote housing, transfer box selector housing and gear change housing bolts to 25 Nm (18 lbf.ft).
5. Adjust 5th gear stop screw.

5th gear stop screw adjustment - Type A gearbox

1. Select reverse gear. While applying light pressure to gear lever towards left, turn screw clockwise until it contacts yoke.
2. Turn screw anti-clockwise until 25 mm (1.0 in) of free play is felt at knob, ensure 5th gear can be engaged.
3. Tighten locknut.
4. Check all other gears can be selected.

Transfer box selector housing - Type B gearbox - Refit

1. Smear a new gasket with grease and fit to gearcase.
2. Position transfer box selector housing to gearcase, fit 4 bolts and tighten to 25 Nm (18 lbf.ft).

Gear change housing - Type B gearbox - Refit

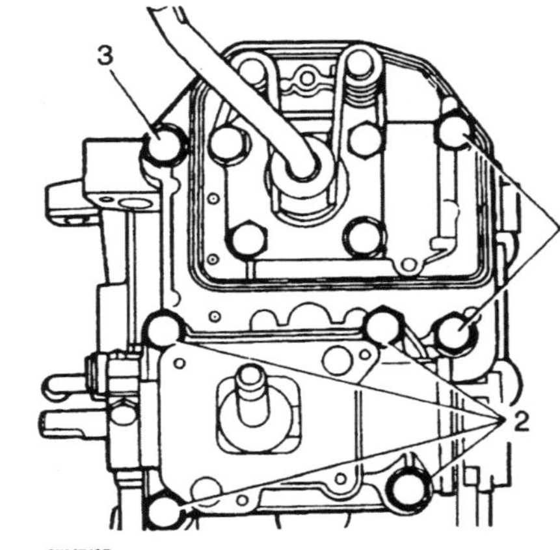

1. Apply sealant, Part No. STC 3254 to mating surfaces of extension housing.
2. Position gear change housing to extension housing ensuring that gear lever passes through centre of gear change lever yoke and engages in the gate plate.
3. Fit bolts and tighten to 25 Nm (18 lbf.ft).

Remote gear change - Type C gearbox - Refit

1. Apply lithium based grease to selector rod yoke.
2. Position remote gear change to extension housing ensuring selector shaft pin is located in selector rod yoke.
3. Fit bolts, washers and mounting rubbers securing remote gear change to extension housing; do not tighten bolts at this stage.
4. Fit bolts, washers and mounting rubbers securing bracket to extension housing.
5. Tighten all bolts to 25 Nm (18 lbf.ft).

Remote gear change - Type D gearbox - Refit

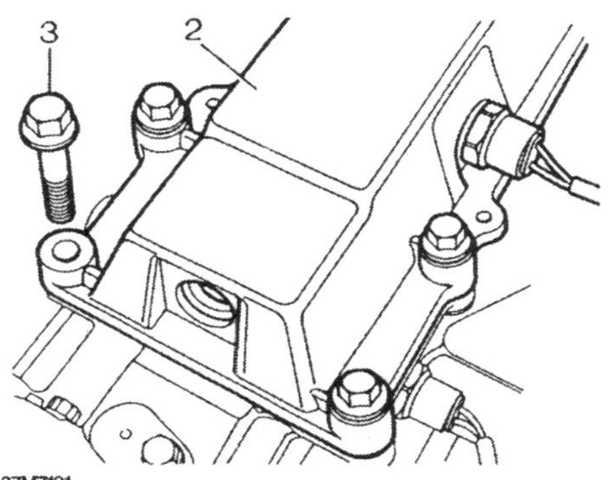

37M7131

1. Apply sealant, Part No. STC 3254 to mating surfaces of extension housing and remote gear change housing.
2. Position remote gear change housing on extension housing. Ensure that gear lever ball is correctly located.
3. Fit bolts and tighten to 25 Nm (18 lbf.ft).

Bias spring adjustment - Type A gearbox

NOTE: The purpose of this adjustment is to set both bolts so that the bias spring legs apply equal pressure on both ends of the gear lever cross pin when third or fourth gear is engaged. This will ensure that when the gear lever is in neutral, the gear change mechanism is automatically aligned for 3rd or fourth gear.

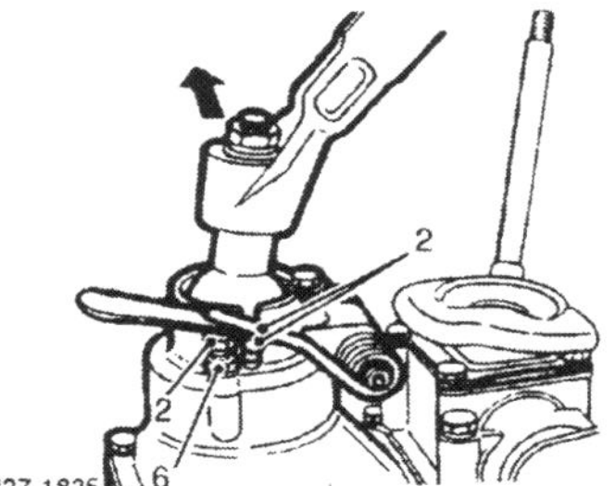

M37 1825

1. Select third or fourth gear.
2. Adjust the two adjusting screws until both legs of the spring are approximately 0.5 mm (0.02 in) clear of the cross pin in the gear lever.
3. Apply a light load to the gear lever in a left hand direction and adjust the right hand adjusting screw downward until the right hand spring leg just makes contact with the cross pin.
4. Repeat the same procedure for the left hand adjusting screw.
5. Lower both adjusting screws equal amounts until the radial play is just eliminated.
6. Tighten locknuts.
7. Return gear lever to neutral position and rock across the gate several times. The gear lever should return to the third and fourth gate.

Bias spring adjustment - Type B gearbox

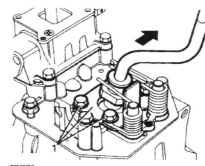

37M7109

1. Loosen bias adjustment plate bolts. Select fourth gear and move lever fully to the right.
2. Tighten bias adjustment plate bolts to 25 Nm (18 lbf.ft).
3. Check adjustment is correct by selecting third and fourth gears.

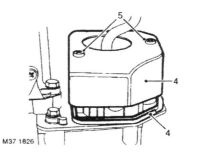

M37 1826

4. Fit sealing rubber to gear change housing, fit housing.
5. Apply Loctite 290 to threads of securing screws, fit screws and tighten to 8 Nm (6 lbf.ft)

Bias spring adjustment - Type C gearbox

NOTE: The purpose of this adjustment is to ensure that when bias spring is correctly adjusted the gear change mechanism is automatically aligned for 3rd or 4th gear selection when gear lever is in neutral.

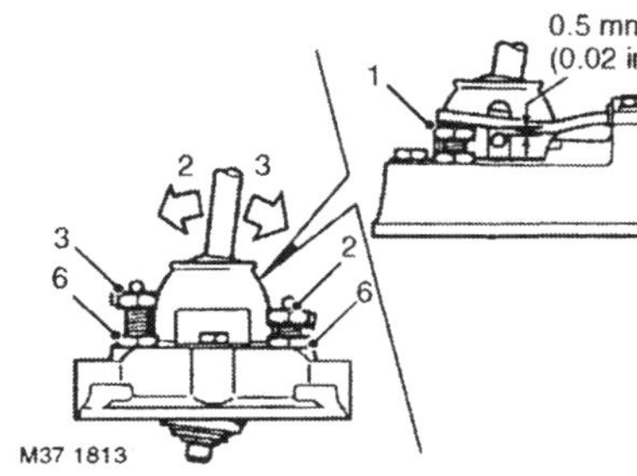

M37 1813

1. Adjust both bias spring adjustment bolts until a clearance of 0.5 mm (0.02 in) exists between both legs of bias spring and gear lever cross pin.
2. Apply a light load to move gear lever to the left and adjust right hand bolt until right hand leg of bias spring just contacts gear lever cross pin.
3. Move gear lever to the right and adjust left hand bolt.
4. Check that with gear lever moved fully to the left and right, spring legs just contact gear lever cross pin.
5. Select neutral then rock gear lever across the gate; when released, lever should return to 3rd/4th position.
6. Tighten adjusting bolt locknuts.

Clutch housing - Type A gearbox - Refit

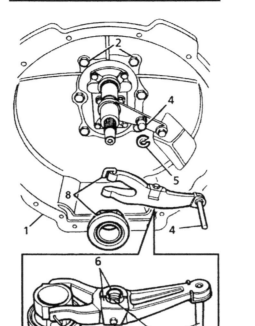

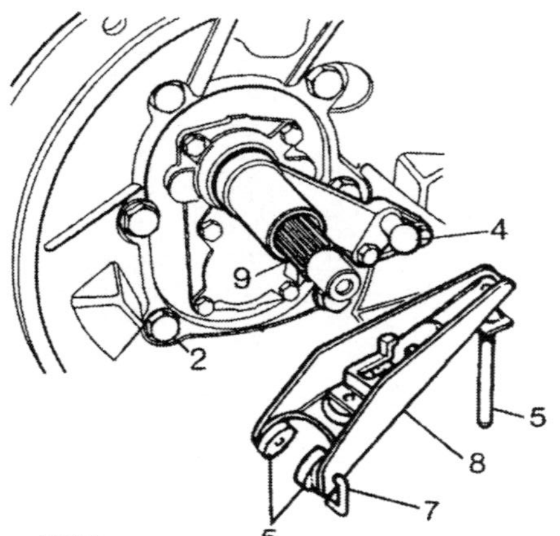

1. Position clutch housing to gearbox.
2. Fit securing bolts.

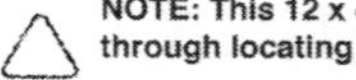

NOTE: This 12 x 45mm bolts must be fitted through locating dowels.

3. Tighten bolts by diagonal selection to 72 Nm (53 lbf.ft).
4. Fit pivot post, fit and tighten bolts.
5. Apply lithium based grease to pivot post, pads and push rod.
6. Position pads to clutch release lever, fit release bearing.
7. Fit new clips to retain pads.

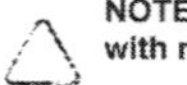

NOTE: Clips may become displaced in service with no loss of performance.

8. Fit release lever.
9. Apply lithium based grease to splines of input shaft.

Clutch housing - Type B gearbox - Refit

1. Position clutch housing to gearbox.
2. Fit securing bolts.

NOTE: This 12 x 45mm bolts must be fitted through locating dowels.

3. Tighten bolts by diagonal selection to 72 Nm (53 lbf.ft).
4. Apply lithium based grease to pivot post, release lever, socket and push rod.
5. Fit a new 'C' clip to pivot post, fit post.
6. Fit spring clip to release lever, fit but do not tighten bolt.
7. Position release lever to pivot post ensuring spring clip is located behind 'C' clip; tighten bolt.
8. Fit clutch release bearing and retain using new clips.

NOTE: Clips may become displaced in service with no loss of performance.

9. Apply lithium based grease to splines of input shaft.

Clutch housing - Type C gearbox - Refit

1. Position clutch housing to gearbox.
2. Fit securing bolts.

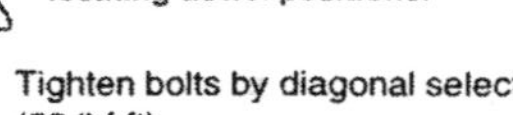

NOTE: The 2 longest bolts must be fitted at locating dowel positions.

3. Tighten bolts by diagonal selection to 72 Nm (53 lbf.ft).
4. Apply lithium based grease to pivot post.
5. Fit release lever and clutch release bearing.
6. Apply lithium based grease to splines of input shaft.

Adaptor housing - Type D gearbox - Refit

1. Position adaptor housing to gearbox.
2. Fit securing bolts.

NOTE: The 2 longest bolts must be fitted at locating dowel positions.

3. Tighten bolts by diagonal selection to 72 Nm (53 lbf.ft).
4. Apply lithium based grease to pivot post.
5. Fit pivot post, fit 2 bolts and tighten to 25 Nm (18 lbf.ft).
6. Apply lithium based grease to splines of input shaft.

BORG WARNER
44-62
TRANSFER BOX

OVERHAUL MANUAL

This transfer box is used on the following models:

New Range Rover

Published by Rover Technical Communication

Publication Part No. LRL 0090ENG

BORG WARNER 44-62 TRANSFER BOX OVERHAUL MANUAL

LRL0090 ENG

Notes

INTRODUCTION

How to use this Manual

To assist in the use of this Manual the section title is given at the top and the relevant sub-section is given at the bottom of each page.

This Manual contains procedures for overhaul of the Borg Warner transfer gearbox on the bench. For all other information regarding General Information, Adjustments, removal of transmission unit and ancillary equipment, consult the relevant section of the New Range Rover Workshop Manual.

This Manual is divided into 3 sections, Description and Operation, Overhaul and Torque & Tools. To assist filing of revised information each sub-section is numbered from page 1.

Items numbered in the illustrations are referred to in the text. Overhaul operations include reference to Service Tool numbers and the associated illustration depicts the tool. Where usage is not obvious the tool is shown in use. Operations also include reference to wear limits, relevant data, torque figures, and specialist information and useful assembly details.

WARNINGS, CAUTIONS and **NOTES** have the following meanings:

WARNING: Procedures which must be followed precisely to avoid the possibility of injury.

CAUTION: Calls attention to procedures which must be followed to avoid damage to components.

NOTE: Gives helpful information.

References

Operations covered in this Manual do not include reference to testing the vehicle after repair. It is essential that work is inspected and tested after completion and if necessary a road test of the vehicle is carried out particularly where safety related items are concerned.

Dimensions

The dimensions quoted are to design engineering specification with Service limits where applicable.

REPAIRS AND REPLACEMENTS

When replacement parts are required it is essential that only Land Rover recommended parts are used.

Attention is particularly drawn to the following points concerning repairs and the fitting of replacement parts and accessories.

Safety features and corrosion prevention treatments embodied in the vehicle may be impaired if other than Land Rover recommended parts are fitted. In certain territories, legislation prohibits the fitting of parts not to the manufacturer's specification.

Torque wrench setting figures given in this Manual must be used. Locking devices, where specified, must be fitted. If the efficiency of a locking device is impaired during removal it must be renewed.

The Terms of the vehicle Warranty may be invalidated by the fitting of other than Land Rover recommended parts. All Land Rover recommended parts have the full backing of the vehicle Warranty.

Land Rover Dealers are obliged to supply only Land Rover recommended parts.

SPECIFICATION

Land Rover are constantly seeking to improve the specification, design and production of their vehicles and alterations take place accordingly. While every effort has been made to ensure the accuracy of this Manual, it should not be regarded as an infallible guide to current specifications of any particular component or vehicle.

This Manual does not constitute an offer for sale of any particular component or vehicle. Land Rover Dealers are not agents of Land Rover and have no authority to bind the manufacturer by any expressed or implied undertaking or representation.

GEARBOX COMPONENTS

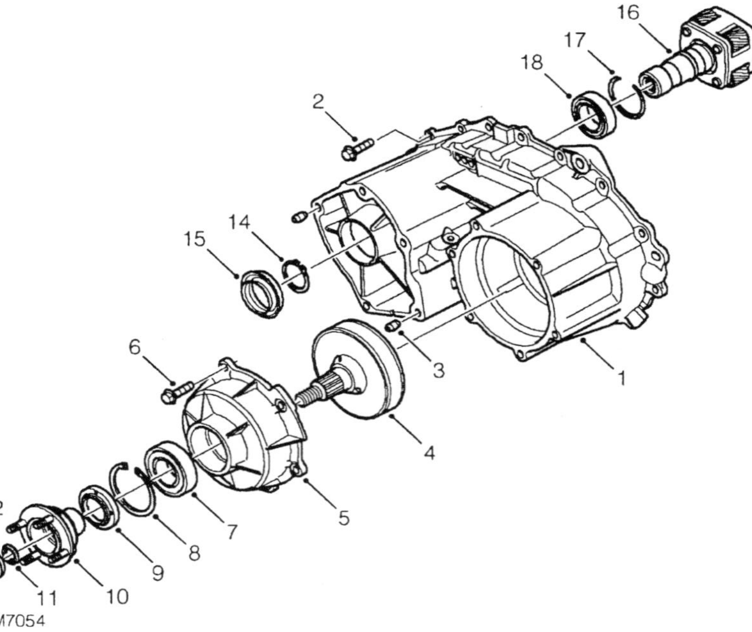

1. Front casing - transfer box
2. Bolt - front casing to rear casing
3. Dowel - transfer box to gearbox
4. Viscous coupling
5. Housing - viscous coupling
6. Bolt - viscous coupling housing to front casing
7. Bearing - front output shaft
8. Circlip - bearing retention
9. Oil seal - front output shaft
10. Drive flange - front output shaft
11. Sealing washer
12. Plain washer
13. Nut - drive flange
14. Circlip - epicyclic gear to bearing
15. Oil seal - input shaft
16. Epicyclic gear set
17. Circlip - bearing retention
18. Bearing - input shaft

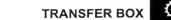

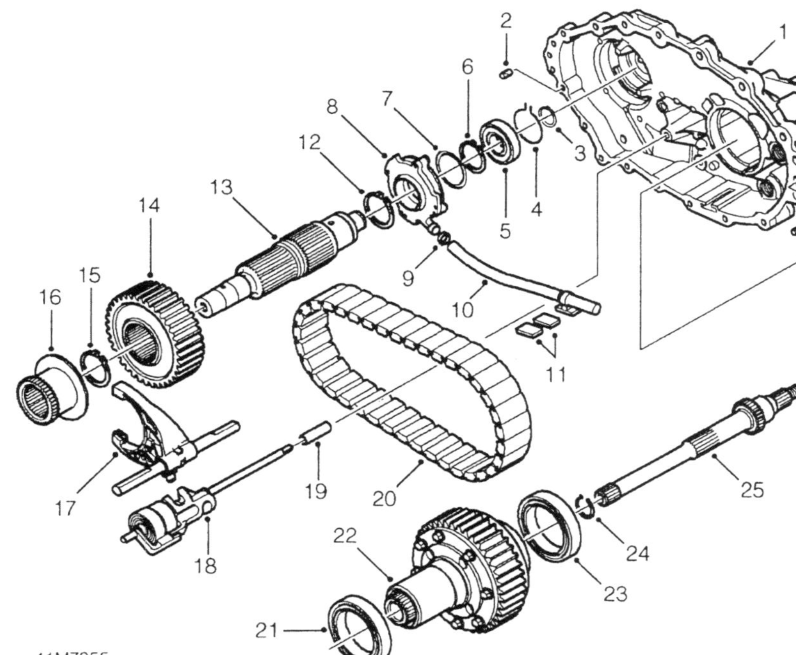

41M7055

1. Rear casing - transfer box
2. Dowel - front casing to rear casing
3. Circlip - bearing retention
4. Snap ring - bearing to rear casing
5. Bearing - intermediate shaft
6. Circlip - oil pump retention
7. Shim
8. Oil pump
9. Clip - hose to pump
10. Hose and strainer
11. Magnet
12. Circlip - gear retention
13. Intermediate shaft
14. Gear
15. Circlip - gear retention
16. Reduction hub
17. Selector fork assembly
18. Interlock spool
19. Tube spacer
20. Morse chain
21. Bearing - differential
22. Differential assembly
23. Bearing - differential
24. Circlip - gear retention
25. Rear output shaft

41M7056

1. Rear casing - transfer box
2. Plug - oil drain
3. Plug - oil fill
4. Sealing washer - temperature sensor
5. Temperature sensor
6. Parking brake assembly
7. Bolt - parking brake to rear casing
8. Bearing - rear output shaft
9. Circlip - bearing retention
10. Oil seal - rear output shaft
11. Dust shroud
12. Drive flange - rear output shaft
13. Sealing washer
14. Plain washer
15. Nut - drive flange
16. Drum - parking brake
17. Screw - drum to flange
18. Oil seal - interlock spool shaft
19. 'O' ring seal - speed sensor
20. Speed sensor
21. Bolt - speed sensor
22. Bolt - ratio control motor to rear casing
23. Ratio control motor

OPERATION

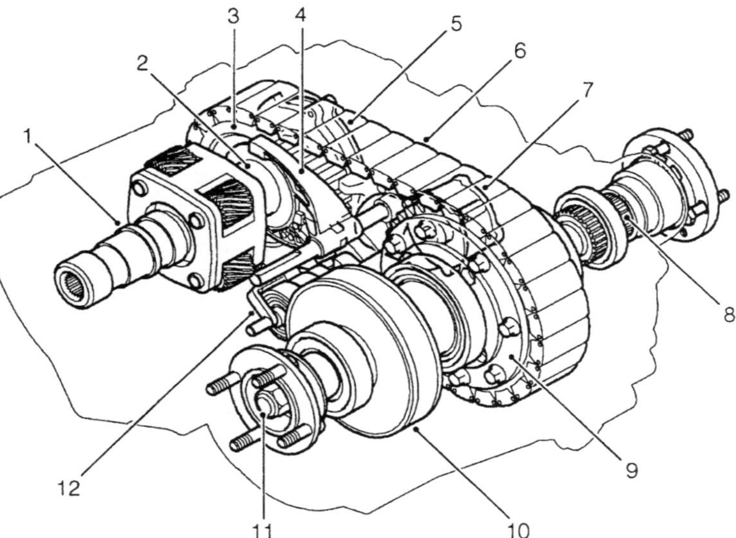

41M7057

1. Epicyclic gear set
2. Reduction hub
3. Drive gear
4. Selector fork
5. Oil pump
6. Morse chain
7. Raito control motor
8. Rear output shaft
9. Differential unit
10. Viscous coupling unit
11. Front output shaft
12. Selector spool

Introduction

The Borg Warner transfer box splits the drive from the main gearbox to the front and rear axles through the propeller shafts. Two speed ratios and a neutral position are provided by means of a single, epicyclic gear set. The two speed ratios, High and Low range, and neutral position are selected electronically by the ratio control motor.

A Morse chain transmits the drive through a gear from the intermediate shaft to the differential unit. The differential unit allows the front and rear output shafts to rotate at different speeds. A viscous coupling unit (VCU) limits the amount of slippage allowed between the front and rear output shafts and renders a conventional differential lock unnecessary.

High and Low Range

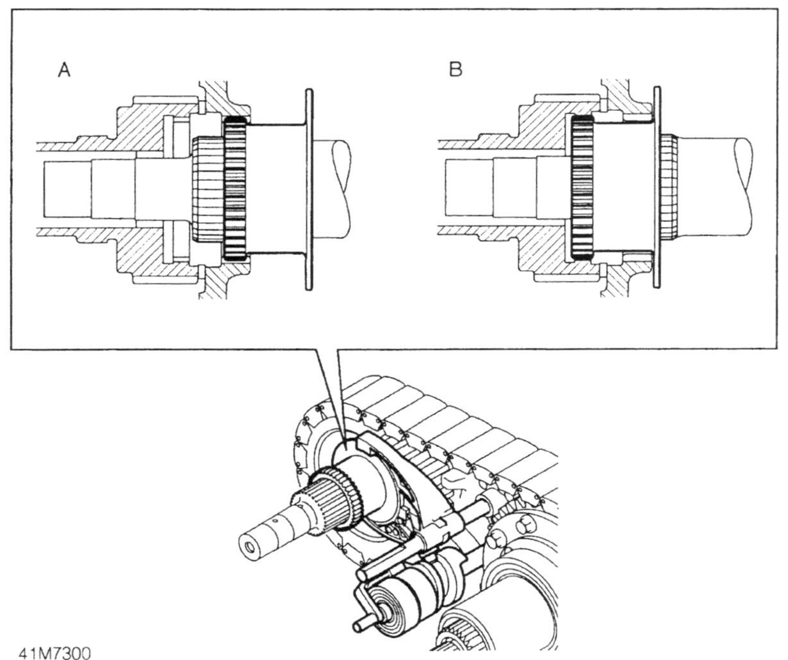

41M7300

High and Low range are selected by the driver from a dashboard mounted switch on manual vehicles and via the selector lever on automatic vehicles. Transfer neutral is selected by inserting a 5 Amp fuse in position 11 of the driver's seat fuse box. Refer to Owner's Handbook.

Drive from the main gearbox is permanently engaged to the sun gear of the epicyclic gear set. When in High range (position B) the sun gear transmits drive directly to the reduction hub. The reduction hub and intermediate shaft rotate at the same speed as the main gearbox output shaft. When in Low range (position A) the reduction hub is driven through the planet carrier. The reduction hub and intermediate shaft rotate at a lower speed than the gearbox output shaft. When in transfer neutral, the reduction hub is positioned between the sun gear and planet carrier.

Changing between ratios is achieved by the reduction hub sliding along a splined section of the intermediate shaft to engage with the required gear. The ratio change mechanism comprises the ratio control motor, reduction hub, interlock spool and selector fork.

The interlock spool consists of a shaft which locates in the front casing and protrudes through the rear casing to engage with the ratio control motor. The shaft carries an aluminium casting with a helical cam track and two springs, which are anchored at one end to the shaft and at the other to the cam track casting.

The selector fork is mounted on a second shaft located within the front and rear casings but is able to slide in the casing mountings. A cam follower on the selector fork engages with the cam track of the interlock spool. When the ratio control motor rotates the interlock spool, the cam follower of the selector fork follows the cam track of the interlock spool. This converts rotational movement of the interlock spool into linear movement of the selector fork.

The selector fork is engaged to the reduction hub. Linear movement of the selector fork is transmitted to the reduction hub, moving it between High, Low and neutral positions. In the event of the reduction hub gear failing to mesh with the epicyclic gear set, wind-up of the interlock is prevented by the interlock spool springs. The springs apply a constant torque to the cam track casting until the reduction hub engages with the epicyclic gear.

Ratio control motor

The ratio control motor drives the selector mechanism and is controlled by the transfer box electronic control unit (ECU). The ECU monitors a number of variables including the position of the ratio control motor, the speed of the vehicle, and the drive ratio selected by the driver. When a ratio change is requested, the transfer box ECU checks that conditions are favourable for the change, for example that the vehicle speed is sufficiently low to permit engagement. The ECU then drives the ratio control motor to the required position. When the conditions for a ratio change are unfavourable, the transfer box ECU communicates instructions to the driver through the Message Centre and will not attempt to change ratios until the correct conditions are met.

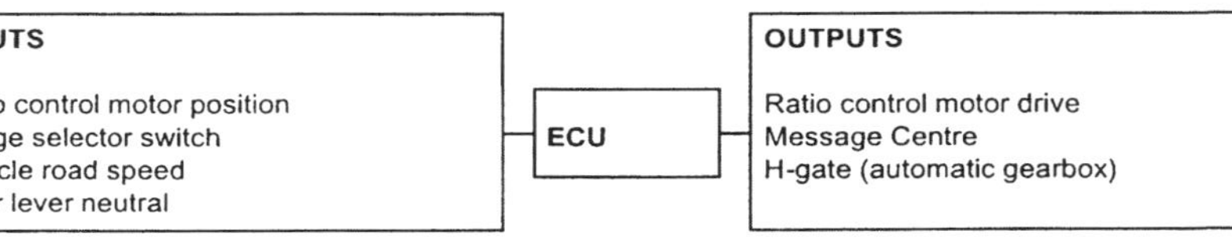

Differential unit

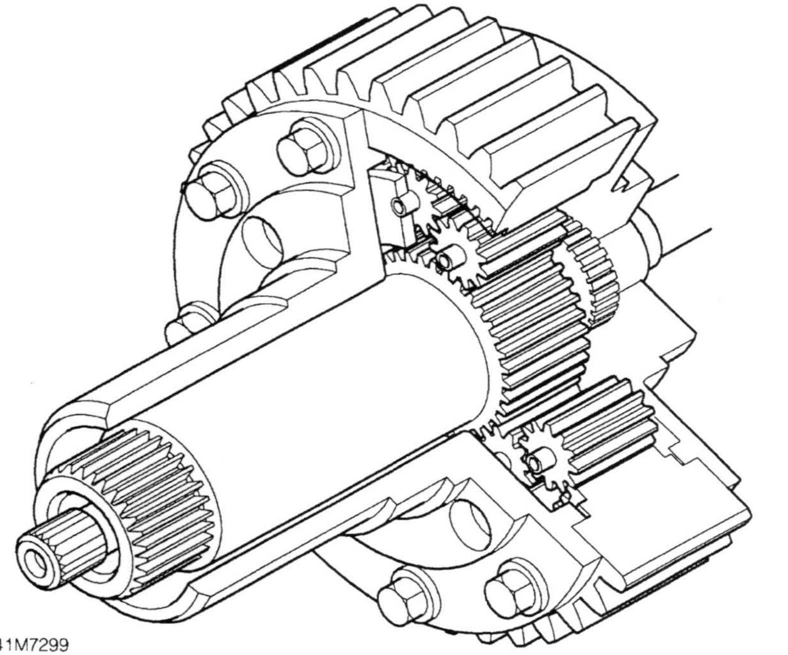

41M7299

The differential unit is driven from the intermediate shaft through a Morse chain. The outer casing of the differential unit is the differential input, while the sun gear provides the front output and the planet carrier the rear output.

The planet carrier contains three sets of gears, which mesh in pairs to maintain the correct directional relationship between front and rear differential outputs. The rear output shaft passes through the differential unit, engaging with the planet carrier and protruding through the sun gear shaft to locate to the VCU inner spline. The sun gear shaft locates to the VCU outer spline.

Viscous coupling (VCU)

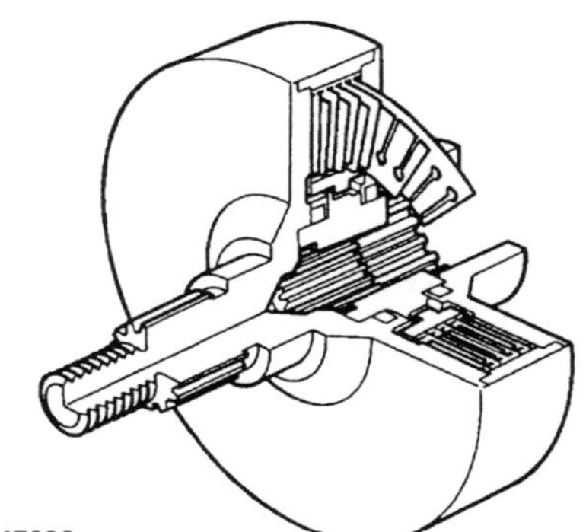

41M7020

The VCU comprises a short cylinder which contains an inner shaft with slotted discs attached to its outer surface, and a similar set of discs attached to the inner surface of the cylinder. Both sets of discs are arranged so that they interleave alternately and in close proximity to each other. The VCU is sealed, and filled with a type of silicone jelly which has the property of increasing its viscosity with rises in temperature and shear forces.

Variations in speed between the front and rear output shafts are transmitted through the VCU, with the speed differential occurring between the inner shaft and the cylinder. In normal road conditions where the speed variation between front and rear shafts is low, the difference in rotational speed between the VCU discs is also low. As a result, the shear forces acting on the silicon jelly are marginal and offer little resistance to the different rotational speeds of the output shafts.

In cases where large rotational speed differences occur between the front and rear output shafts, such as in rough terrain conditions, the speed variation between the discs is high with a subsequent increase in the shear forces acting on the viscous jelly. The resulting increase in viscosity generates sufficient shear resistance to force both sets of discs to rotate at similar speeds, reducing axle slippage and loss of traction.

Lubrication

Internal lubrication of the transfer gearbox is provided by a low pressure, plunger-type oil pump mounted on the rear of the intermediate shaft. Oil pick-up is through a strainer in the transfer box sump. From the pump, oil is supplied through the intermediate shaft to the epicyclic gear set. The differential and Morse chain are partially immersed in oil and lubricated as the components rotate. The VCU is a fully sealed unit and does not require separate lubrication.

RATIO CONTROL MOTOR

Service repair no - 41.30.03/01

Remove

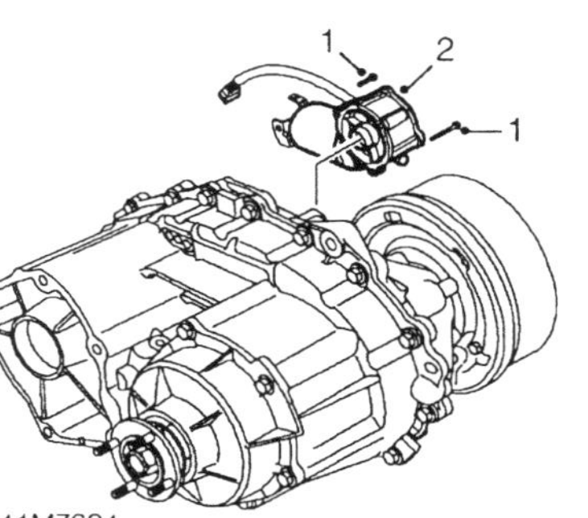

1. Remove 4 bolts securing motor to transfer box.
2. Remove motor.

Refit

1. Fit motor and engage to drive spindle.
2. Tighten bolts to 10 Nm. (7 lbf.ft).

INPUT SHAFT OIL SEAL

Service repair no - 41.20.50/01

Remove

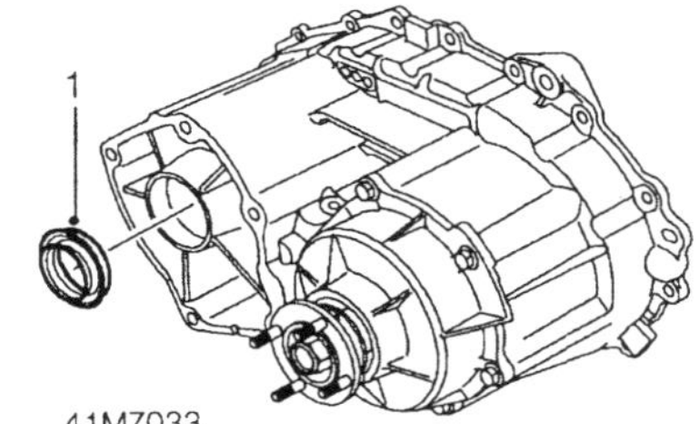

1. Using a flat bladed screwdriver free of rough edges, ease input shaft oil seal from transfer box front casing.

CAUTION: Do not mark sealing surface of front casing.

Refit

1. Clean sealing surface of front casing and running surface of input shaft. Ensure all traces of rubber are removed.

CAUTION: Do not use a metal scraper as this may damage sealing surfaces.

2. Lubricate oil seal sealing face with clean gearbox oil.

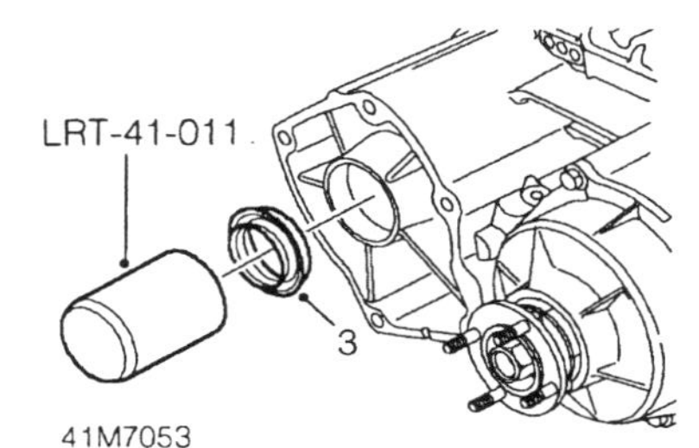

3. Position oil seal to transfer box front casing and fit oil seal using LRT-41-011.

FRONT OUTPUT SHAFT DRIVE FLANGE

Service repair no - 41.20.15/01

Remove

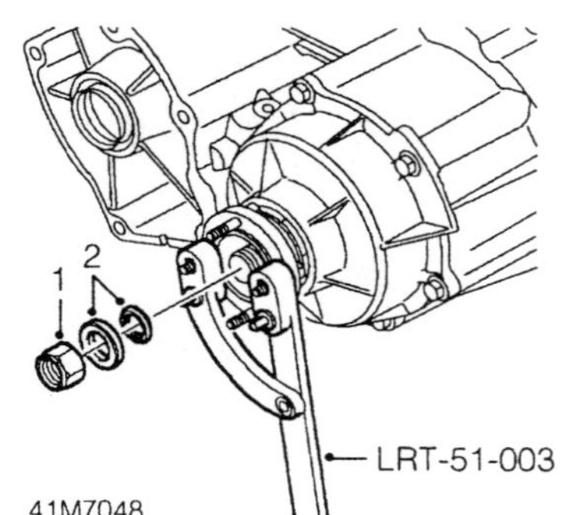

41M7048

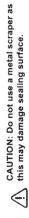

1. Using LRT-51-003 to restrain front output shaft drive flange, remove and discard nut securing drive flange to front output shaft.
2. Collect washer and seal.

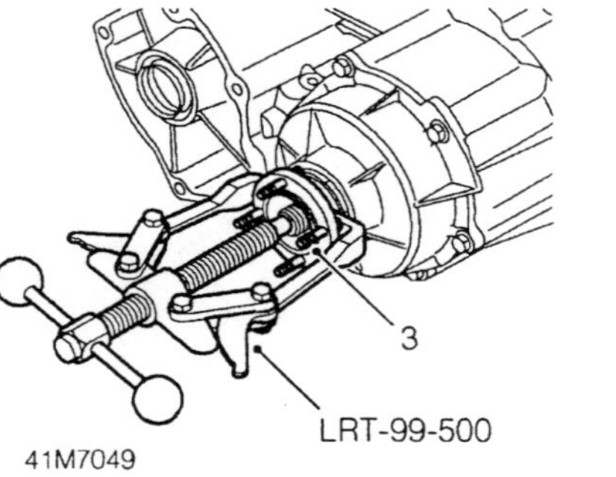

41M7049

3. Using LRT-99-500 if necessary, remove drive flange from front output shaft.

Refit

1. Clean running surface of drive flange. Ensure all traces of rubber are removed.

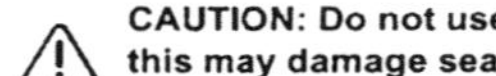
CAUTION: Do not use a metal scraper as this may damage sealing surface.

2. Fit drive flange to front output shaft.
3. Fit seal, washer and new nut to front output shaft.
4. Using LRT-51-003 to restrain drive flange, tighten nut to 220 Nm. (162 lbf.ft)

FRONT OUTPUT SHAFT OIL SEAL

Service repair no - 41.20.51/01

Remove

1. Remove front output shaft drive flange. ***See this section.***

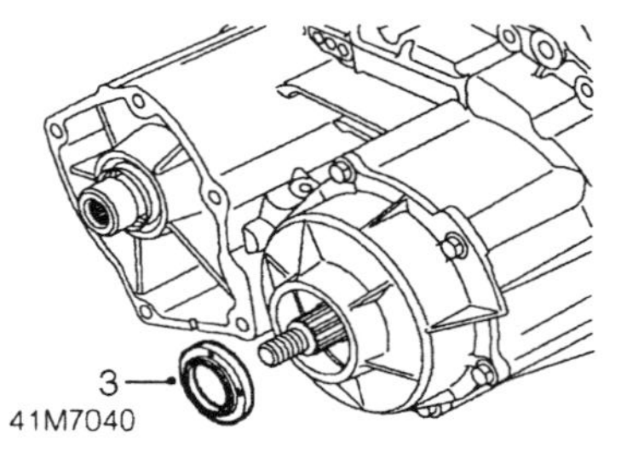

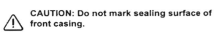

41M7040

2. Using a flat bladed screwdriver free of rough edges, ease front output shaft oil seal from front casing.

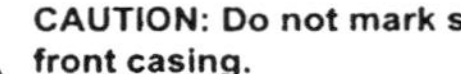
CAUTION: Do not mark sealing surface of front casing.

3. Remove oil seal.

Refit

1. Clean sealing area of front casing and running surface of front drive flange. Ensure all traces of rubber are removed.

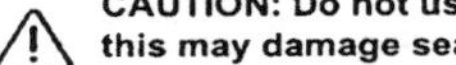
CAUTION: Do not use a metal scraper as this may damage sealing surfaces.

2. Lubricate sealing faces of new seal with clean gearbox oil.

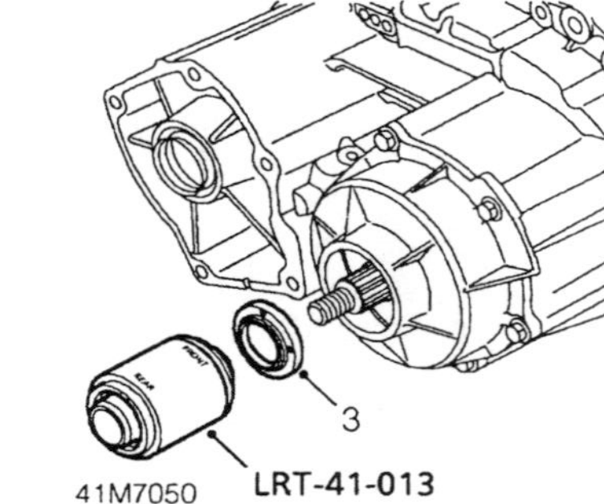

41M7050

3. Using LRT-41-013 fit front output shaft oil seal to front casing. Ensure that seal is square to casing bore.
4. Fit front output shaft drive flange. ***See this section.***

VISCOUS COUPLING UNIT (VCU)

Service repair no - 41.20.66/01

Remove

1. Remove front output shaft drive flange. ***See this section.***

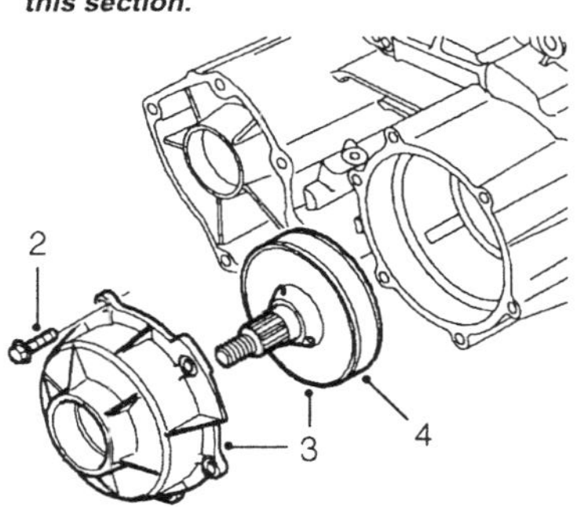

41M7039

2. Remove 6 bolts securing VCU housing to transfer box.
3. With care, break front face RTV seal and remove VCU assembly.
Do not carry out further dismantling if component is removed for access only.
4. Press out viscous coupling from housing.

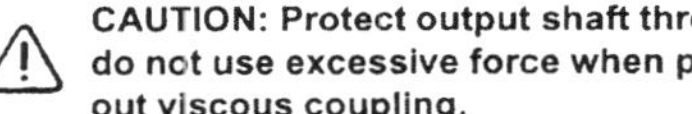
CAUTION: Protect output shaft thread and do not use excessive force when pressing out viscous coupling.

Refit

1. Clean mating surfaces of viscous coupling housing and transfer box.

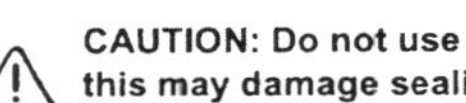
CAUTION: Do not use a metal scraper as this may damage sealing surfaces.

2. Clean bearing and VCU mating faces.
3. Press VCU into bearing.
4. Apply a continuous 2mm bead of sealant to VCU housing mating face. Path to be around inside of bolt holes.
5. Fit VCU assembly to transfer box ensuring correct alignment of bolt holes before disturbing RTV bead.
6. Fit bolts and progressively tighten to 35 Nm. (26 lbf.ft)
7. Fit front output shaft drive flange. ***See this section.***

EPICYCLIC GEAR SET

Service repair no - 41.20.68/01

Remove

1. Remove viscous coupling assembly. ***See this section.***

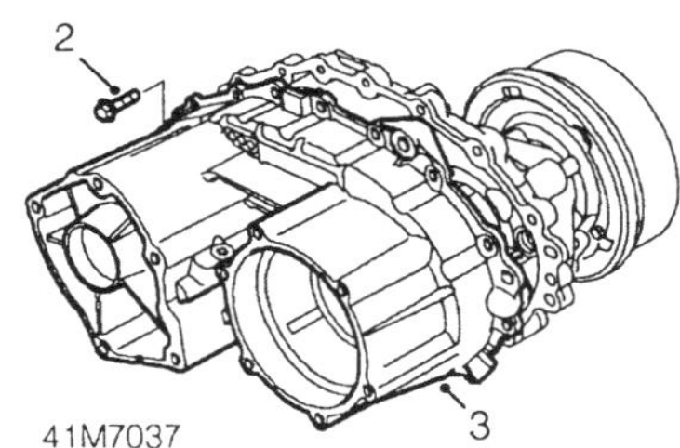

41M7037

2. Remove 17 bolts securing halves of transfer box casing.
3. Carefully break RTV seal and remove front transfer gearbox casing from rear casing.
4. Position front casing, input shaft upwards. Position block of wood under epicyclic gear set.

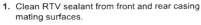

41M7038

5. Using a flat bladed screwdriver free of rough edges, ease input shaft oil seal from front casing.

CAUTION: Do not mark sealing surface of front casing.

6. Release circlip retaining epicyclic gear to front casing. Epicyclic gear set will fall onto block of wood.
7. Remove epicyclic gear set.

Refit

1. Clean RTV sealant from front and rear casing mating surfaces.

CAUTION: Do not use a metal scraper as this may damage sealing surfaces.

2. Clean bearing and input shaft mating faces.
3. Clean sealing area of front casing and running surface of input shaft. Ensure all traces of rubber are removed from sealing surfaces.

CAUTION: Do not use a metal scraper as this may damage sealing surfaces.

4. Fit epicyclic gear set to front casing.
5. Fit circlip retaining epicyclic gear set to front casing.
6. Lubricate sealing faces of seal with clean gearbox oil.

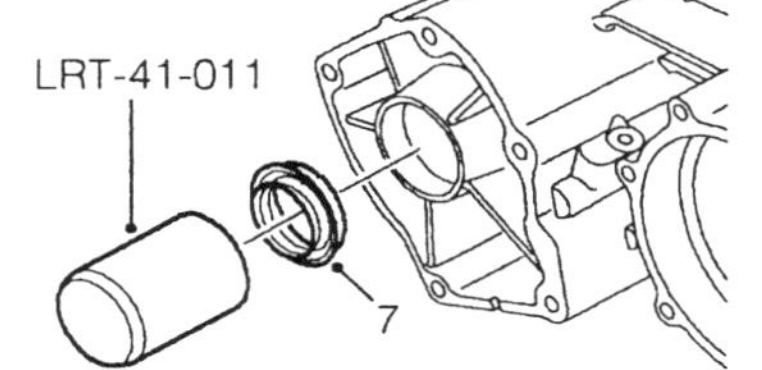

41M7052

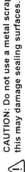

7. Using LRT-41-011 drift input shaft seal into front casing.
8. If removed, fit 2 dowels to front casing.
9. Apply a continuous 2 mm bead of RTV sealant to rear casing mating face. Path to be around inside of bolt holes.
10. Fit front casing to rear casing, ensure bolt holes are aligned before disturbing RTV sealant.
11. Fit bolts securing front casing to rear casing and progressively tighten to 35 Nm. (26 lbf.ft)
12. Check freedom of rotation of input shaft and that rear output shaft rotates.
13. Fit viscous coupling assembly. ***See this section.***

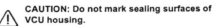

INPUT SHAFT BEARING

Service repair no - 41.20.65/01

Remove

1. Remove epicyclic gear set. ***See this section.***

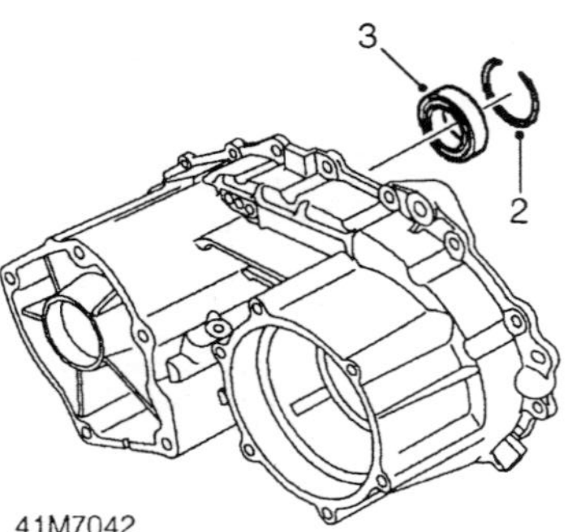

41M7042

2. Remove snap ring retaining input shaft bearing to front casing.
3. Press out input shaft bearing.

Refit

1. Clean bearing and front casing mating faces, ensure casing is free from burrs.
2. Press bearing into front casing.
3. Fit snap ring retaining bearing to front casing.
4. Fit epicyclic gear set. ***See this section.***

FRONT OUTPUT SHAFT BEARING

Service repair no - 41.20.08/01

Remove

1. Remove viscous coupling unit (VCU). ***See this section.***

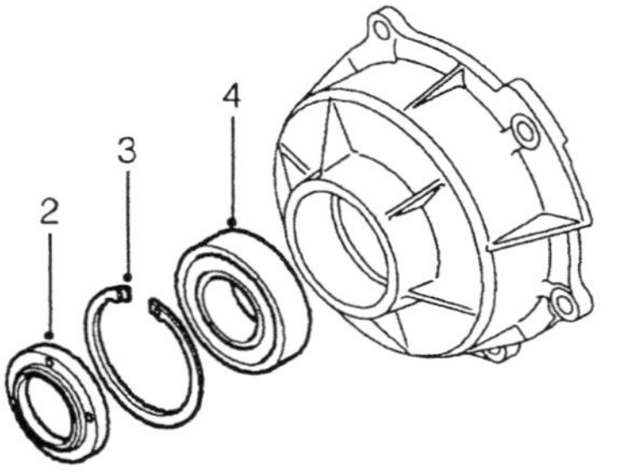

41M7022

2. Using a flat bladed screwdriver free of rough edges, ease oil seal from VCU housing.

CAUTION: Do not mark sealing surfaces of VCU housing.

3. Remove circlip retaining output shaft bearing to casing.
4. Press out bearing from VCU casing.

Refit

1. Clean bearing and VCU casing mating faces.

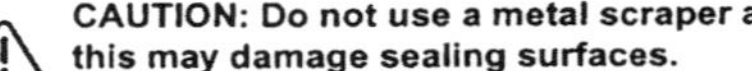

CAUTION: Do not use a metal scraper as this may damage sealing surfaces.

2. Press bearing into VCU housing and fit retaining circlip.
3. Clean sealing area of VCU housing and running surface of front output shaft drive flange. Ensure all traces of rubber are removed.

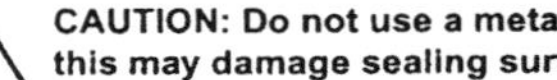

CAUTION: Do not use a metal scraper as this may damage sealing surfaces.

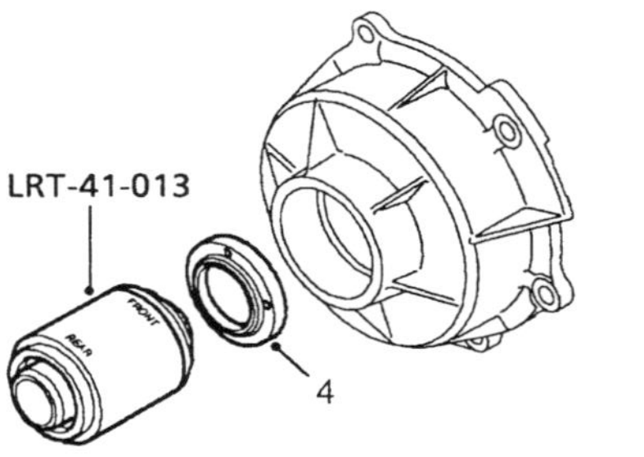

41M7051

4. Using tool LRT-41-013 , drift oil seal into VCU housing. Ensure the seal is square to housing bore.
5. Fit VCU to housing. ***See this section.***

SELECTOR FORK ASSEMBLY

Service repair no - 41.20.40/01

Remove

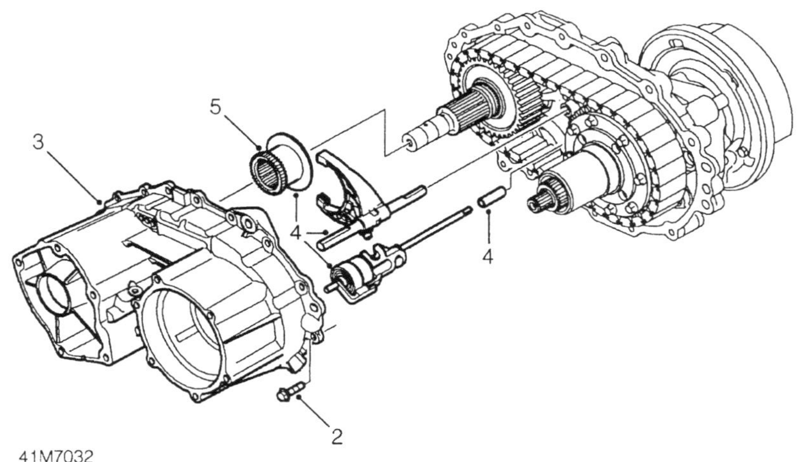

41M7032

1. Remove viscous coupling assembly. ***See this section.***
2. Remove 17 bolts securing halves of transfer box casing.
3. Carefully break RTV seal and remove front transfer box casing from rear casing.
4. Remove selector fork assembly, interlock spool shaft and reduction hub from rear casing. Collect tube spacer.
5. Remove reduction hub from selector fork assembly.

Refit

1. Clean RTV sealant from front and rear casing mating surfaces.

CAUTION: Do not use a metal scraper as this may damage sealing surfaces.

2. Fit reduction hub to selector fork assembly with hub splines towards the shorter end of shift rail.
3. Fit tube spacer to interlock spool shaft.
4. Engage selector fork cam follower to interlock spool cam track.
5. Fit reduction hub to intermediate shaft and engage interlock spool shaft and shift rail to holes in rear casing.
6. Rotate interlock spool shaft to position reduction hub and selector fork to low ratio position, nearest rear casing half. Ensure tube spacer is in position and selector fork cam follower is correctly engaged in interlock spool.
7. If removed, fit 2 dowels into front casing.
8. Apply a continuous 2 mm bead of RTV sealant to rear casing mating face. Path to be around inside of bolt holes.
9. Fit front casing to rear casing, ensure bolt holes and dowels are aligned before disturbing RTV sealant.
10. Fit bolts securing front casing to rear casing and progressively tighten to 35 Nm. (26 lbf.ft)
11. Check freedom of rotation of input shaft and that rear output shaft rotates.
12. Fit viscous coupling assembly. ***See this section.***

REDUCTION HUB

Service repair no - 41.20.70/01

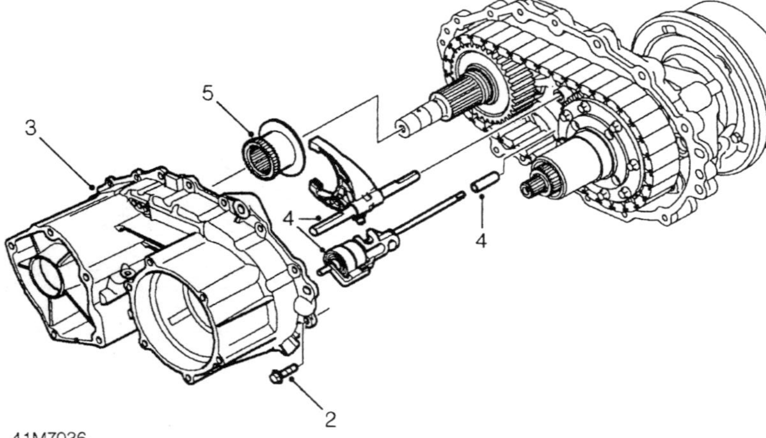

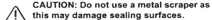

41M7036

Remove

1. Remove viscous coupling assembly. ***See this section.***
2. Remove 17 bolts securing halves of transfer gearbox casing.
3. Carefully break RTV seal and remove front transfer box casing from rear casing.
4. Remove selector fork assembly, interlock spool shaft and reduction hub from rear casing. Collect tube spacer.
5. Remove reduction hub from selector fork.

Refit

1. Clean RTV sealant from front and rear casing mating surfaces.

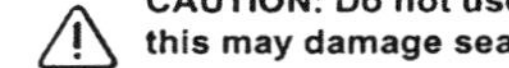
CAUTION: Do not use a metal scraper as this may damage sealing surfaces.

2. Fit reduction hub to selector fork with hub splines towards the shorter end of shift rail.
3. Fit tube spacer to interlock spool shaft.
4. Engage selector fork cam follower to interlock spool cam track.
5. Fit reduction hub to intermediate shaft and engage interlock spool shaft and shift rail to holes in rear casing.
6. Rotate interlock spool shaft to position reduction hub and selector fork to low ratio position, nearest rear casing half. Ensure tube spacer is in position and selector fork cam follower is correctly engaged to interlock spool.
7. If removed, fit 2 dowels to front casing.
8. Apply a continuous 2 mm bead of RTV sealant to rear casing mating face. Path to be around inside of bolt holes.
9. Fit front casing to rear casing, ensure bolt holes and dowels are aligned before disturbing RTV sealant.
10. Fit bolts securing front casing to rear casing and progressively tighten to 35 Nm. (26 lbf.ft)
11. Check freedom of rotation of input shaft and that rear output shaft rotates.
12. Fit viscous coupling assembly. ***See this section.***

INTERLOCK SPOOL

Service repair no - 41.20.74/01

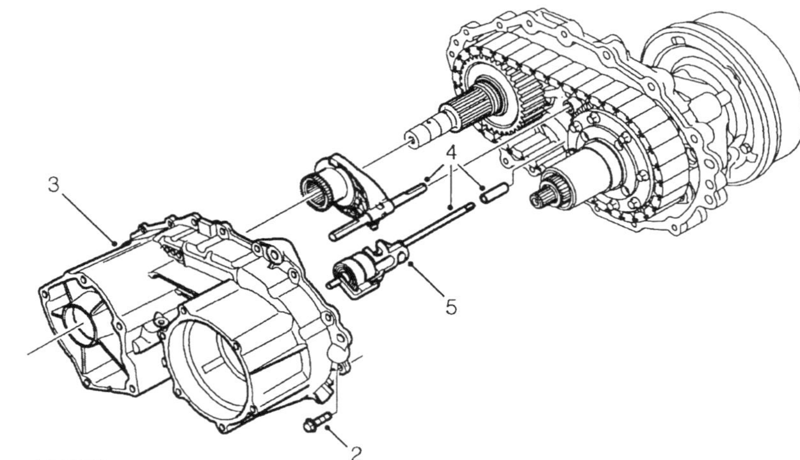

41M7035

Remove

1. Remove viscous coupling assembly. ***See this section.***
2. Remove 17 bolts securing halves of transfer box casing.
3. Carefully break RTV seal and remove front transfer box casing from rear casing.
4. Remove selector fork assembly, interlock spool shaft and reduction hub from rear casing. Collect tube spacer.
5. Collect interlock spool.

Refit

1. Clean RTV sealant from front and rear casing mating surfaces.

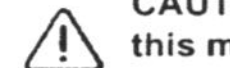

CAUTION: Do not use a metal scraper as this may damage sealing surfaces.

2. Fit tube spacer to interlock spool shaft.
3. Engage selector fork cam follower to interlock spool cam track.
4. Fit reduction hub to intermediate shaft and engage interlock spool shaft and shift rail to holes in rear casing.
5. Rotate interlock spool shaft to position reduction hub and selector fork to low ratio position, nearest rear casing half. Ensure tube spacer is in position and selector fork cam follower is correctly engaged in interlock spool.
6. If removed, fit 2 dowels into front casing.
7. Apply a continuous 2 mm bead of RTV sealant to rear casing mating face. Path to be around inside of bolt holes.
8. Fit front casing to rear casing, ensure bolt holes and dowels are aligned before disturbing RTV sealant.
9. Fit bolts securing front casing to rear casing and progressively tighten to 35 Nm. (26 lbf.ft)
10. Check freedom of rotation of input shaft and that rear output shaft rotates.
11. Fit viscous coupling assembly. ***See this section.***

REAR OUTPUT SHAFT DRIVE FLANGE

Service repair no - 41.20.14/01

Remove

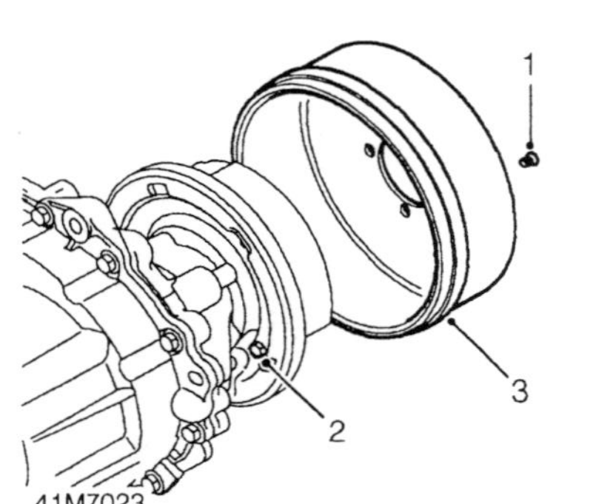

1. Remove screw securing brake drum to flange.
2. Loosen park brake drum adjusting screw.
3. Remove brake drum.

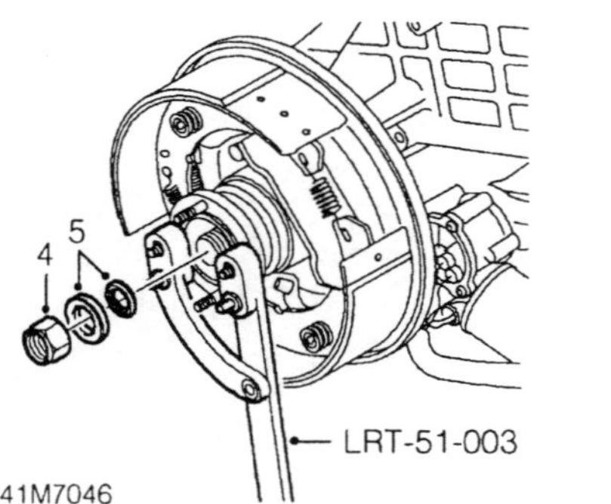

4. Using LRT-51-003 to restrain drive flange, remove nut securing drive flange to rear output shaft.
5. Collect washer and seal.

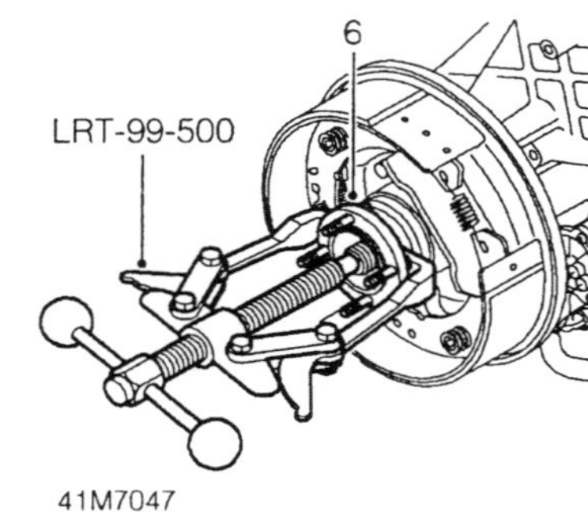

6. Using LRT-99-500 if necessary, remove flange from output shaft.

Refit

1. Clean running surface of drive flange. Ensure all traces of rubber are removed.

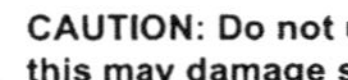
CAUTION: Do not use a metal scraper as this may damage sealing surface.

2. Fit drive flange to rear output shaft.
3. Fit seal, washer and new nut to rear output shaft.
4. Using LRT-51-003 to restrain drive flange, tighten nut to 220 Nm. (162 lbf.ft)
5. Fit brake drum to drive flange and secure with screw.
6. Adjust park brake drum screw. ***See New Range Rover Workshop Manual.***

REAR OUTPUT SHAFT OIL SEAL

Service repair no - 41.20.54/01

Remove

1. Remove rear output shaft drive flange. ***See this section.***

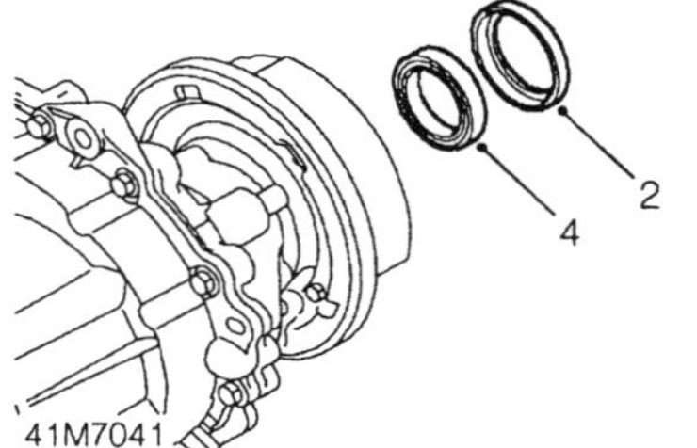

2. Remove dust shroud from transfer box rear casing.
3. Using a flat bladed screwdriver free of rough edges, ease oil seal from rear casing.

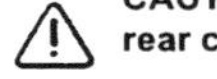
CAUTION: Do not mark sealing surface on rear casing.

4. Remove rear output shaft oil seal.

Refit

1. Clean sealing area of rear casing and running surface of drive flange. Ensure all traces of rubber are removed.

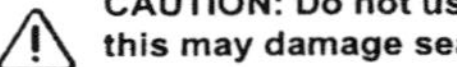
CAUTION: Do not use a metal scraper as this may damage sealing surfaces.

2. Lubricate sealing surfaces of seal with clean gearbox oil.

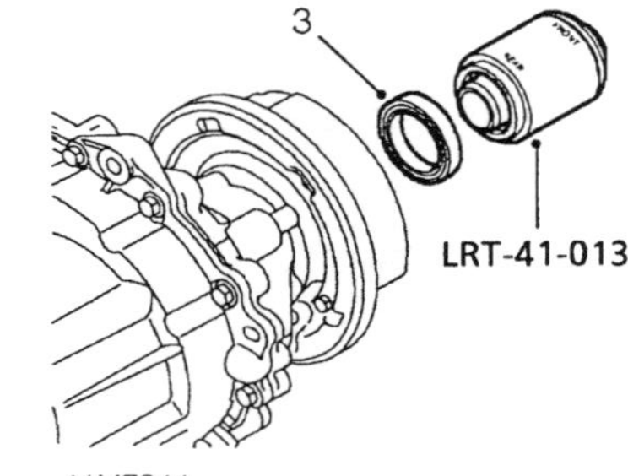

3. Using LRT-41-013 fit oil seal to transfer box rear casing.
4. Fit dust shroud to transfer box rear casing.
5. Fit rear output shaft drive flange. ***See this section.***

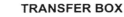

DRIVE CHAIN

Service repair no - 41.20.67/01

Remove

1. Remove rear output shaft drive flange. ***See this section.***
2. Remove interlock spool. ***See this section.***

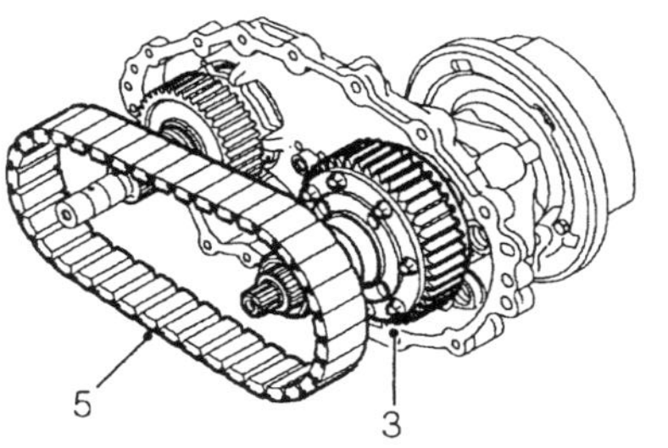

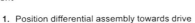

41M7031

3. Release differential assembly from rear casing until differential rear bearing is clear of casing.

NOTE: Ensure rear output drive shaft moves with differential.

4. Tilt differential assembly towards drive sprocket, take care not to bruise casing.
5. Remove drive chain from gears.
6. Position differential assembly to rest in rear casing.

Refit

1. Position differential assembly towards drive gear and fit drive chain to both gears.
2. Engage chain to gears and align differential rear bearing to rear casing.
3. Engage differential rear bearing to rear casing and output shaft to output shaft bearing.
4. Fit interlock spool. ***See this section.***
5. Fit rear output shaft drive flange. ***See this section.***

DIFFERENTIAL UNIT

Service repair no - 41.20.13/01

Remove

1. Remove drive chain. ***See this section.***

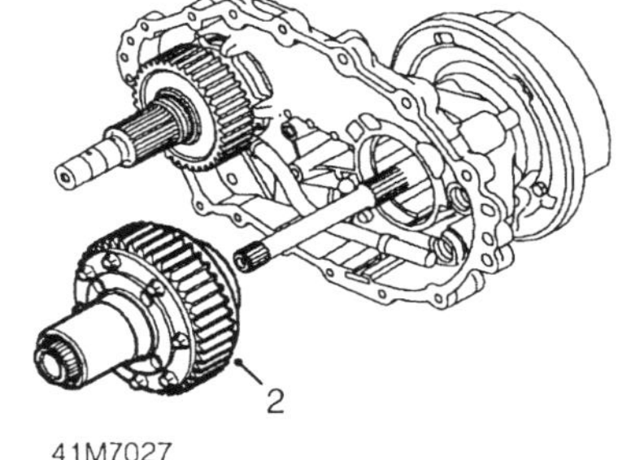

41M7027

2. Remove differential unit from rear output shaft.

Refit

1. Fit differential unit to rear output shaft.
2. Fit drive chain. ***See this section.***

DIFFERENTIAL BEARINGS

Service repair no - 41.20.17/01

Remove

1. Remove differential unit from transfer box. ***See this section.***

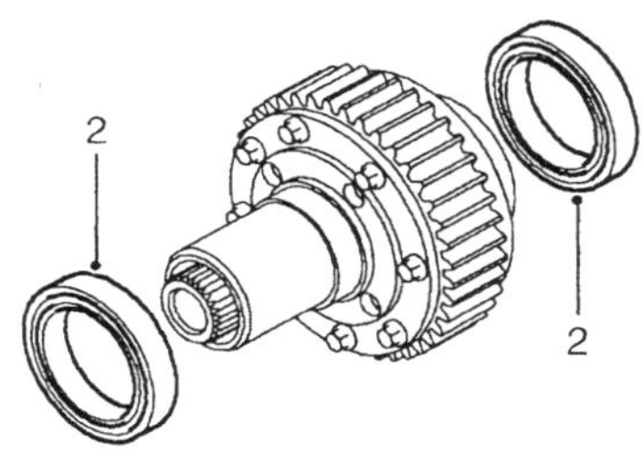

41M7021

2. Using a suitable puller, remove 2 bearings from differential unit.

Refit

1. Ensure bearing and differential mating faces are clean.
2. Press bearings onto differential unit.
3. Fit differential unit to transfer box. ***See this section.***

REAR OUTPUT SHAFT

Service repair no - 41.20.18/01

Remove

1. Remove differential unit. ***See this section.***

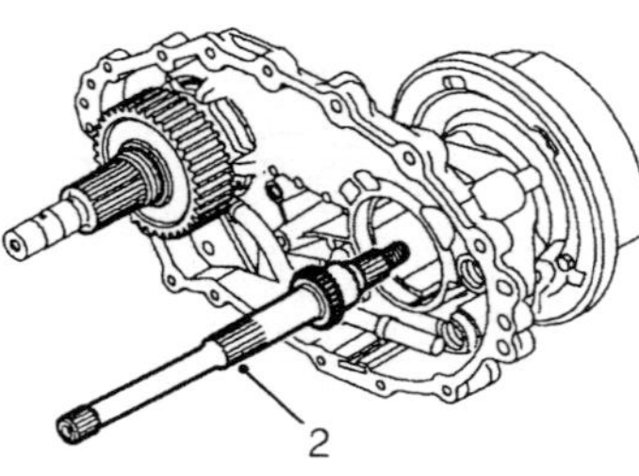

41M7024

2. Remove rear output shaft from rear casing.

Refit

1. Fit rear output shaft to rear casing.
2. Fit differential unit. ***See this section.***

REAR OUTPUT SHAFT BEARING

Service repair no - 41.20.19/01

Remove

1. Remove rear output shaft. ***See this section.***

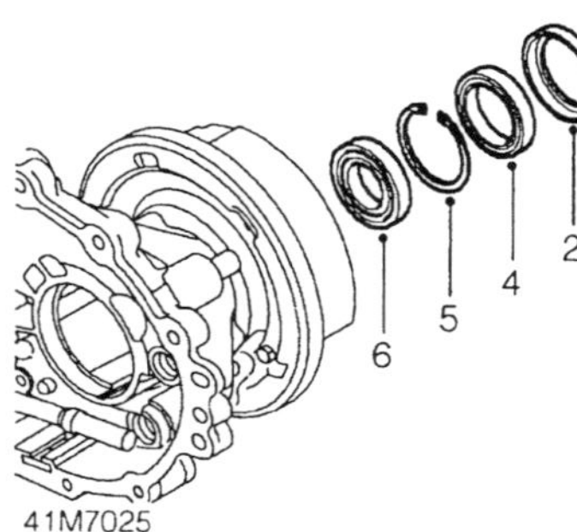

41M7025

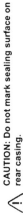

2. Remove dust shroud from transfer box rear casing.
3. Using a flat bladed screwdriver free of rough edges, ease oil seal from rear casing.

 **CAUTION: Do not mark sealing surface on rear casing.**

4. Remove rear output shaft oil seal.
5. Remove circlip retaining rear output shaft bearing to rear casing.
6. Press out rear output shaft bearing from rear casing.

Refit

1. Clean bearing and rear casing mating surfaces.
2. Press bearing into rear casing.
3. Fit circlip retaining bearing in rear casing.
4. Clean sealing area of rear casing and running surface of drive flange. Ensure all traces of rubber are removed.

CAUTION: Do not use a metal scraper as this may damage sealing surfaces.

5. Lubricate sealing surfaces of seal with clean gearbox oil.

LRT-41-013

41M7043

6. Using LRT-41-013, fit oil seal to transfer gearbox rear casing.
7. Fit dust shroud to transfer box rear casing.
8. Fit rear output shaft. ***See this section.***

INTERMEDIATE SHAFT DRIVE GEAR

Service repair no - 41.20.22/01

Remove

1. Remove drive chain. ***See this section.***

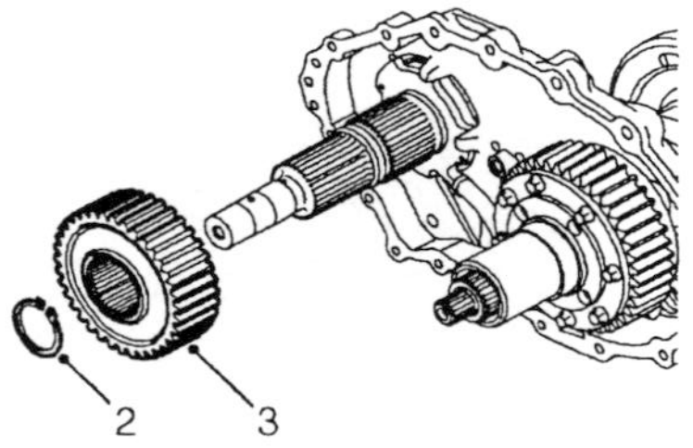

41M7029

2. Remove circlip securing drive gear to intermediate shaft.
3. Remove drive gear from intermediate shaft.

Refit

1. Ensure drive gear and intermediate shaft are clean and free from burrs.
2. Fit drive gear to intermediate shaft.
3. Fit circlip retaining drive gear to intermediate shaft.
4. Fit drive chain. ***See this section.***

INTERMEDIATE SHAFT REAR BEARING

Service repair no - 41.20.21/01

Remove

1. Remove intermediate shaft drive gear. ***See this section.***

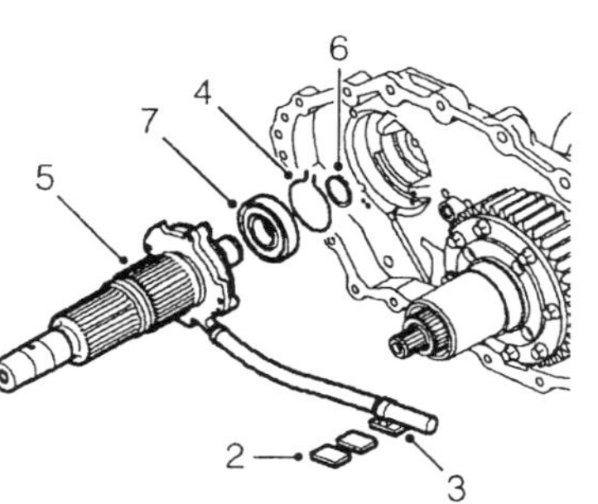

41M7028

2. Remove 2 magnets from rear casing.
3. Release oil strainer clip from rear casing.
4. Expand snap ring retaining intermediate shaft rear bearing to rear casing.
5. Remove intermediate shaft, oil pump and strainer assembly from rear casing.
6. Remove circlip retaining intermediate shaft bearing to intermediate shaft.
7. Using a suitable puller, remove bearing from rear of intermediate shaft.

Refit

1. Ensure bearing and intermediate shaft mating surfaces are clean and free of burrs.
2. Press bearing onto intermediate shaft.
3. Fit circlip retaining bearing to intermediate shaft.
4. Expand snap ring in rear housing and fit intermediate shaft assembly to rear casing.
5. Ensure snap ring is correctly located to rear bearing.
6. Fit filter hose clip to rear casing.
7. Fit magnets to rear casing.
8. Fit intermediate shaft drive gear. ***See this section.***

OIL PUMP

Service repair no - 41.20.30/01

Remove

1. Remove intermediate shaft rear bearing. ***See this section.***

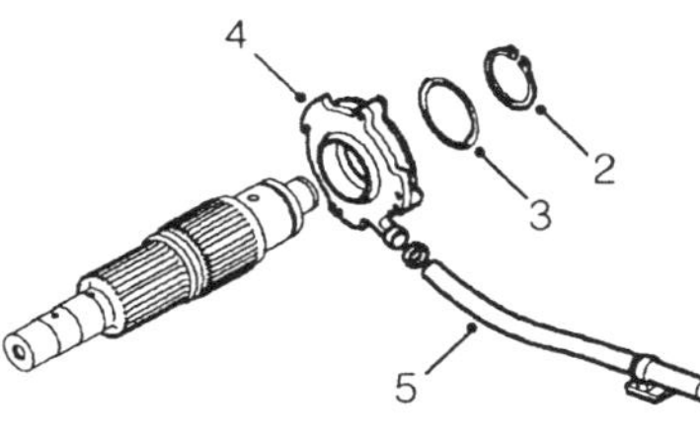

41M7030

2. Remove circlip retaining oil pump to intermediate shaft.
3. Remove washer from intermediate shaft.
4. Remove oil pump and hose assembly from intermediate shaft.
5. Release clip and remove hose from oil pump.

Refit

1. Fit hose to oil pump and secure with clip.
2. Fit oil pump to intermediate shaft.
3. Fit washer and circlip securing pump to intermediate shaft.
4. Fit intermediate shaft rear bearing. ***See this section.***

INTERMEDIATE SHAFT

Service repair no - 41.20.20/01

Remove

1. Remove oil pump. ***See this section.***

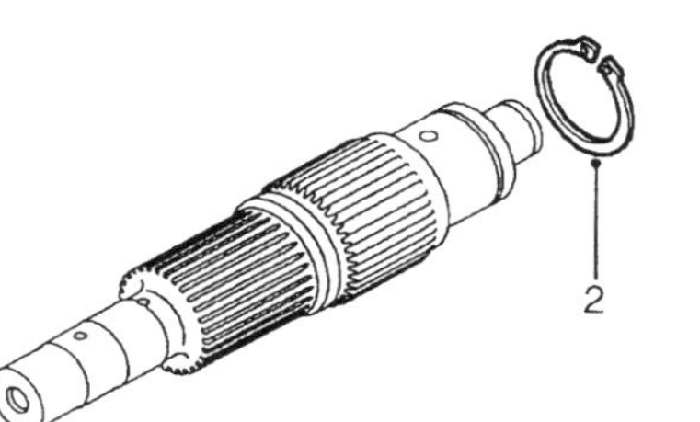

41M7026

2. Remove circlip from intermediate shaft.

Refit

1. Fit circlip to intermediate shaft.
2. Fit oil pump. ***See this section.***

TORQUE SETTINGS

Output shaft drive flange nut	220 Nm. (162 lbf.ft)
Front gearcase to rear gearcase bolts	35 Nm. (26 lbf.ft)
VCU housing to gearcase bolts	35 Nm. (26 lbf.ft)
Speed sensor	30 Nm. (22 lbf.ft)
Drain/Refill plugs	25 Nm. (18 lbf.ft)
Temperature sensor	15 Nm. (11 lbf.ft)
Ratio control motor to gearcase bolts	10 Nm. (7 lbf.ft)
Breather hose	10 Nm. (7 lbf.ft)

TOOL NUMBERS

LRT 41 011	Input shaft oil seal replacer
LRT 41 013	Output shaft oil seal replacer
LRT 51 003	Drive flange restraining tool
LRT 99 500	Drive flange puller

LAND ROVER OFFICIAL FACTORY PUBLICATIONS

Land Rover Series 1 Workshop Manual	4291
Land Rover Series 1 1948-53 Parts Catalogue	4051
Land Rover Series 1 1954-58 Parts Catalogue	4107
Land Rover Series 1 Instruction Manual	4277
Land Rover Series 1 and II Diesel Instruction Manual	4343
Land Rover Series II and IIA Workshop Manual	AKM8159
Land Rover Series II and Early IIA Bonneted Control Parts Catalogue	605957
Land Rover Series IIA Bonneted Control Parts Catalogue	RTC9840CC
Land Rover Series IIA, III and 109 V8 Optional Equipment Parts Catalogue	RTC9842CE
Land Rover Series IIA/IIB Instruction Manual	LSM64IM
Land Rover Series 2A and 3 88 Parts Catalogue Supplement (USA Spec)	606494
Land Rover Series III Workshop Manual	AKM3648
Land Rover Series III Workshop Manual V8 Supplement (edn. 2)	AKM8022
Land Rover Series III 88, 109 and 109 V8 Parts Catalogue	RTC9841CE
Land Rover Series III Owners Manual 1971-1978	607324B
Land Rover Series III Owners Manual 1979-1985	AKM8155
Military Land Rover (Lightweight) Series III Parts Catalogue	61278
Military Land Rover Series III (L.W.B.) User Handbook	608179
Military Land Rover (Lightweight) Series III User Manual	608180
Land Rover 90/110 and Defender Workshop Manual 1983-1992	SLR621ENWM
Land Rover Defender Workshop Manual 1993-1995	LDAWMEN93
Land Rover Defender 300 Tdi and Supplements Workshop Manual 1996-1998	LRL0097ENGBB
Land Rover Defender Td5 Workshop Manual and Supplements 1999-2006	LRL0410BB
Land Rover Defender Electrical Manual Td5 1999-06 and 300Tdi 2002-2006	LRD5EHBB
Land Rover 110 Parts Catalogue 1983-1986	RTC9863CE
Land Rover Defender Parts Catalogue 1987-2006	STC9021CC
Land Rover 90 • 110 Handbook 1983-1990 MY	LSM0054
Land Rover Defender 90 • 110 • 130 Handbook 1991 MY - Feb. 1994	LHAHBEN93
Land Rover Defender 90 • 110 • 130 Handbook Mar. 1994 - 1998 MY	LRL0087ENG/2
Military Land Rover 90/110 All Variants (Excluding APV and SAS) User Manual	2320-D-122-201
Military Land Rover 90 and 110 2.5 Diesel Engine Versions User Handbook	SLR989WDHB
Military Land Rover Defender XD - Wolf Workshop Manual - 2320D128 -	302 522 523 524
Military Land Rover Defender XD - Wolf Parts Catalogue	2320D128711
Discovery Workshop Manual 1990-1994 (petrol 3.5, 3.9, Mpi and diesel 200 Tdi)	SJR900ENWM
Discovery Workshop Manual 1995-1998 (petrol 2.0 Mpi, 3.9, 4.0 V8 and diesel 300 Tdi)	LRL0079BB
Discovery Series II Workshop Manual 1999-2003 (petrol 4.0 V8 and diesel Td5 2.5)	VDR100090/6
Discovery Parts Catalogue 1989-1998 (2.0 Mpi, 3.5, 3.9 V8 and 200 Tdi and 300 Tdi)	RTC9947CF
Discovery Parts Catalogue 1999-2003 (petrol 4.0 V8 and diesel Td5 2.5)	STC9049CA
Discovery Owners Handbook 1990-1991 (petrol 3.5 V8 and diesel 200 Tdi)	SJR820ENHB90
Discovery Series II Handbook 1999-2004 MY (petrol 4.0 V8 and Td5 diesel)	LRL0459BB
Freelander Workshop Manual 1998-2000 (petrol 1.8 and diesel 2.0)	LRL0144
Freelander Workshop Manual 2001-2003 ON (petrol 1.8L, 2.5L and diesel Td4 2.0)	LRL0350ENG/4
Land Rover 101 1 Tonne Forward Control Workshop Manual	RTC9120
Land Rover 101 1 Tonne Forward Control Parts Catalogue	608294B
Land Rover 101 1 Tonne Forward Control User Manual	608239
Range Rover Workshop Manual 1970-1985 (petrol 3.5)	AKM3630
Range Rover Workshop Manual 1986-1989 (petrol 3.5 and diesel 2.4 Turbo VM)	SRR660ENWM & LSM180WS4/2
Range Rover Workshop Manual 1990-1994 (petrol 3.9, 4.2 and diesel 2.5 Turbo VM, 200 Tdi)	LHAWMENA02
Range Rover Workshop Manual 1995-2001 (petrol 4.0, 4.6 and BMW 2.5 diesel)	LRL0326ENGBB
Range Rover Workshop Manual 2002-2005 (BMW petrol 4.4 and BMW 3.0 diesel)	LRL0477
Range Rover Electrical Manual 2002-2005 UK version (petrol 4.4 and 3.0 diesel)	RR02KEMBB
Range Rover Electrical Manual 2002-2005 USA version (BMW petrol 4.4)	RR02AEMBB
Range Rover Parts Catalogue 1970-1985 (petrol 3.5)	RTC9846CH
Range Rover Parts Catalogue 1986-1991 (petrol 3.5, 3.9 and diesel 2.4 and 2.5 Turbo VM)	RTC9908CB
Range Rover Parts Catalogue 1992-1994 MY and 95 MY Classic (petrol 3.9, 4.2 and diesel 2.5 Turbo VM, 200 Tdi and 300 Tdi)	RTC9961CB
Range Rover Parts Catalogue 1995-2001 MY (petrol 4.0, 4.6 and BMW 2.5 diesel)	RTC9970CE
Range Rover Owners Handbook 1970-1980 (petrol 3.5)	606917
Range Rover Owners Handbook 1981-1982 (petrol 3.5)	AKM8139
Range Rover Owners Handbook 1983-1985 (petrol 3.5)	LSM0001HB
Range Rover Owners Handbook 1986-1987 (petrol 3.5 and diesel 2.4 Turbo VM)	LSM129HB

Engine Overhaul Manuals for Land Rover and Range Rover

300 Tdi Engine, R380 Manual Gearbox and LT230T Transfer Gearbox Overhaul Manuals	LRL003, 070 & 081
Petrol Engine V8 3.5, 3.9, 4.0, 4.2 and 4.6 Overhaul Manuals	LRL004 & 164
Land Rover/Range Rover Driving Techniques	LR369
Working in the Wild - Manual for Africa	SMR684MI
Winching in Safety - Complete guide to winching Land Rovers and Range Rovers	SMR699MI

Workshop Manual Owners Edition

Land Rover 2 / 2A / 3 Owners Workshop Manual 1959-1983
Land Rover 90, 110 and Defender Workshop Manual Owners Edition 1983-1995
Land Rover Discovery Workshop Manual Owners Edition 1990-1998

Range Rover Parts Catalogue

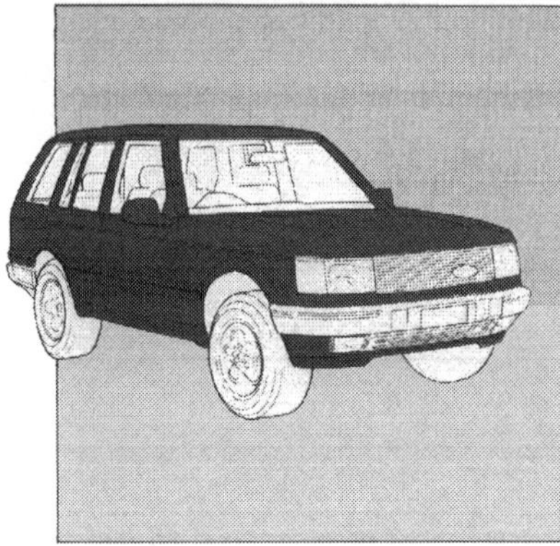

Covering:
4.0 & 4.6 Petrol Engines
BMW 2.5 Diesel Engines

Part No RTC9970CE

Range Rover Parts Catalogue 1995-2001

Complete listing including part numbers, descriptions and drawings to help keep your 4x4 on the road. Covers vehicles 1995 to end of the 2001 model year with 4.0 & 4.6 Litre V8 petrol plus the diesel BMW 2.5 litre.
With 784 pages. RTC9970CE. Soft Bound.

REF: RR01PH ISBN: 9781855206168

Brooklands Books Ltd., PO Box 146, Cobham,
Surrey KT11 1LG, England Phone: (44) 1932 865051
E-mail: sales@brooklands-books.com www.brooklandsbooks.com

ISBN: 9781855207462 Part No. LRL0326ENG BB Ref: RR95WH 5T0/2063

Printed in Great Britain
by Amazon